lonely planet

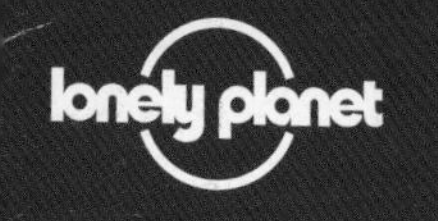

southeast asia
on a shoestring

China Williams, Greg Bloom, Celeste Brash, Muhammad Cohen, Dan Eldridge, Josh Krist, Mat Oakley, Nick Ray, Chris Rowthorn, Adam Skolnick, Iain Stewart, Ryan Ver Berkmoes, Richard Waters

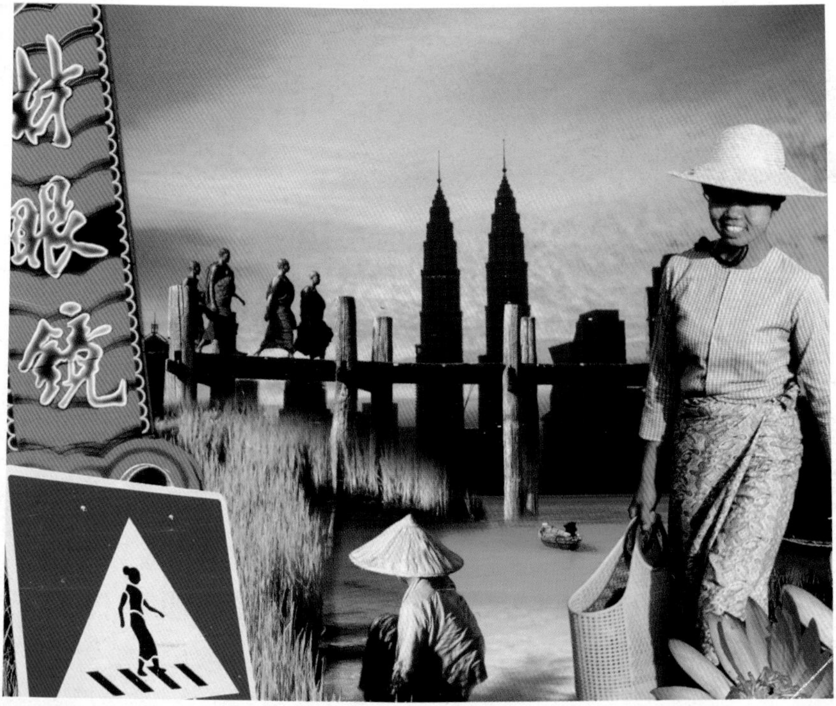

Responsible Travel

In Southeast Asia, tourism is both a blessing and a curse. It fosters family businesses, and promotes cultural and environmental conservation. Even the ruins of Angkor in Cambodia benefit from the tourist economy, which provides an incentive to conserve the temples rather than dismantling them for collectors.

But tourism also puts pressure on the host country's hospitality and resources. Whether clueless or callous, irresponsible tourism can adversely affect the local culture. Popular destinations rarely have the capability to properly dispose of the waste produced by visitors. And then there are the one-on-one confrontations that occur due to cultural ignorance and economic disparity.

To ensure that your trip is a gift, not a burden, remember to mind your manners, to be kind to the local environment and to be a conscientious consumer.

- **Ask before you click** Learn to say 'May I take your picture?' in the language of every country you visit.
- **Shop locally** Spend your money at family businesses and in local shops.
- **Be money wise** Know how much things should cost; don't expect something for nothing, but also don't allow hustlers to take advantage of you.
- **Learn the language** Take a course before leaving home or sign up for classes in the country.
- **Protect the environment** Don't touch or step on coral, and don't collect pieces as souvenirs. Don't litter or toss those cigarette butts on the beach. Don't buy souvenirs or eat meals produced from endangered species or flora.
- **Respect the local culture** Dress modestly and treat religious centres like delicate treasures.
- **Be informed** Learn about the country's history and current events, and about ways to help communities maintain their dignity.

INTERNET RESOURCES

- **www.coralreefalliance.org** Coral-friendly guidelines for divers and news about global reef health.
- **www.ecologyasia.com** Profile of the region's flora, fauna and eco-organisations.
- **www.humantrafficking.org** Country-specific information on human trafficking.
- **www.oxfam.org** Oxfam International programmes combating social and economic issues.
- **www.seasite.niu.edu** Interactive resource for information on Southeast Asian languages and culture.

Contents

The Authors

CHINA WILLIAMS
Coordinating Author

Southeast Asia is an odoriferous place to find out you're pregnant, but after a decade of companionship with the region, China was glad that her son-to-be had a connection to this place. China's name propelled her to this continent, and the kinship of the climate with that of her hometown in South Carolina (US) sealed the deal. China has studied (and forgotten) philosophy in college, taught English in Thailand, matured into a liberal in San Francisco and written numerous Lonely Planet titles on Southeast Asia. Now she lives in Takoma Park, Maryland (US), with her son, Felix, and husband, Matt.

GREG BLOOM
Philippines

Manila's gritty charms take a while to grow on you, and so it was for Greg. But grow on him they did, and as he enters his fourth year living in the Philippines he claims – with a straight face – to love living in Manila. When not writing about his country of residence (and favourite travel destination), Greg might be found snouting around the former Soviet Union for Lonely Planet or running around Asia's ultimate Frisbee fields with the Philippine national team.

CELESTE BRASH
Malaysia

After attending Chiang Mai University in Thailand for a semester, Celeste made her first foray into Malaysia and quickly fell in love with the country's food, ease of travel and cultural treats. She's visited several times since on long-haul trips through Southeast Asia. For this book she introduced her husband and two kids to the Malay peninsula, where they played with giant insects, tried every variation of *roti canai* (Indian-style flaky flat bread) and discovered the joys of leeches. When not desensitising her taste buds with *sambal* (relish), she lives with her family in Tahiti.

MUHAMMAD COHEN
Indonesia

Native New Yorker Muhammad Cohen first travelled to Southeast Asia in 1992, returning as a backpacking reporter in 1994, and moving to Hong Kong a year later. Once a diplomat in Tanzania, Muhammad first stopped in Indonesia to visit a neighbour from his time in Dar es Salaam. He's been going back for over a dozen years, picking up the language and a taste for *ikan bakar lalapan* (grilled fish with aromatic leaves and *sambal*). Muhammad is also the author of *Hong Kong on Air*, a novel about the 1997 handover.

DAN ELDRIDGE
Thailand

Dan began his journalism career at the age of 17, when a pen-pal relationship with the editor of a punk-rock magazine led to a music-reviewing gig. After graduating from university and bulking up his CV with an impressive range of odd jobs (dishwasher, taxi driver, telemarketer), he launched *Young Pioneers*, an independent travel magazine. His first visit to Thailand happened during the SARS epidemic, when airfares to Asia reached (understandably) historic lows. Like Andy Warhol and Christina Aguilera, Dan hails from Pittsburgh, although he's currently based in Philadelphia.

JOSH KRIST — Vietnam

Josh has backpacked around Thailand, Vietnam and Egypt; spent a month on a sailing boat in the Caribbean; lived in a kibbutz in the north of Israel; and worked as a cook at a hostel in Jerusalem. He's also lived and worked in Paris and Kyoto. He loves to swap crazy stories, eat good food, drink pastis, bask in warm weather and scuba dive – Vietnam suits him just fine.

MAT OAKLEY — Singapore

Mat was born in the kind of English town David Brent would have lived in had Slough not existed. After stints living in Laos, Thailand, Australia and Fiji, he has spent the last three years in Singapore with his wife and a couple of badly behaved Fijian cats (who are banned from entering New Zealand for being undemocratic). The author of the Lonely Planet *Singapore* city guide, Mat was happy to be forced back onto the streets to find more excuses to stuff his face during the research for this book.

NICK RAY — Cambodia

Nick comes from Watford, the sort of town that makes you want to travel. He has been cavorting around Southeast Asia for a more than a decade now, first as a traveller, later leading people astray as a tour leader, and more recently as a location scout. Nick lives in Phnom Penh and has written several editions of the *Cambodia* guidebook, as well as coauthoring *Vietnam* and *Cycling Vietnam, Laos & Cambodia*. He has covered almost every corner of Southeast Asia, and includes Angkor, Bagan, Hoi An, Luang Prabang and the Gili islands in his top 10.

CHRIS ROWTHORN — Brunei Darussalam & Malaysia

Chris was born in England and raised in the US, but has lived in Kyoto, Japan, since 1992. After working as a regional correspondent for the *Japan Times*, he joined Lonely Planet in 1996 and has written books about Japan, Malaysia, the Philippines and Australia. He's a keen hiker, diver and snorkeller, and considers Borneo to be the greatest adventure-travel destination in Southeast Asia. When he's not on the road, he conducts private tours of Japan.

ADAM SKOLNICK — Indonesia

Adam Skolnick was diagnosed with travel obsession while working as an environmental activist in the mid-'90s. As a result he has travelled to nearly 40 countries (Indonesia's his favourite) on six continents: he's been lost in the Amazon, scaled Kilimanjaro, backpacked through Mexico and Central America, toured baseball stadiums in Cuba, meditated with Hindu priests in Bali and Buddhist monks in Myanmar, and hiked through the rainforest with devout Muslim farmers in Sumatra. As a freelance journalist he writes about travel, culture, health and the environment, and between adventures he writes movies.

IAIN STEWART

Indonesia

Iain first travelled through Indonesia in 1992, journeying from Sumatra to Timor by Pelni ferries and too many bemo (three-wheeled pick-up trucks). He's returned several times since to dive the reefs of Pulau Bunaken and the Gilis, haggle over handicrafts in Sumba and coauthor Lonely Planet's *Indonesia* and *Bali & Lombok* guides. On this trip Iain discovered that Jakarta just might be the best night out in Asia, and that even 40 year olds can learn to surf (well, stand up on a board). Iain's written numerous guidebooks, mainly devoted to Ibiza and Central America.

RYAN VER BERKMOES

East Timor

Years of travel across the Indonesian archipelago in no way prepared Ryan for East Timor. The mix of Asian and European cultures is like that of no where else, and the country's beauty gave him a major pain in the jaw from all the dropping. More importantly, despite his experience as an international journalist, which taught him to never take headlines at face value, Ryan was amazed at how the reality of the country never matched the pervasive reports of doom. Within the myriad challenges are a multitude of rewards for the traveller ready for adventure.

RICHARD WATERS

Laos

Richard's first of taste of travel was as a 21 year old, driving around Central America in an old jalopy; it took him through Guatemala's civil war and gave him his first taste of wanderlust. He's been travelling across Southeast Asia, Europe, the US and North Africa ever since. His first visit to Laos in '99 brought the Hmong guerrillas to his attention, and in 2002 he was among the first to creep into the Special Zone in search of their story. He lives with his son and girlfriend in Brighton, England.

CONTRIBUTING AUTHOR

Dr Trish Batchelor is a general practitioner and travel medicine specialist who works at the CIWEC Clinic in Kathmandu, Nepal, as well as being a Medical Advisor to the Travel Doctor New Zealand clinics. Trish teaches travel medicine through the University of Otago, and is interested in underwater and high-altitude medicine, and in the impact of tourism on host countries. She wrote the Health chapter.

LONELY PLANET AUTHORS

Why is our travel information the best in the world? It's simple: our authors are independent, dedicated travellers. They don't research using just the internet or phone, and they don't take freebies in exchange for positive coverage. They travel widely, to all the popular spots and off the beaten track. They personally visit thousands of hotels, restaurants, cafés, bars, galleries, palaces, museums and more – and they take pride in getting all the details right, and telling it how it is. Think you can do it? Find out how at lonelyplanet.com.

Destination Southeast Asia

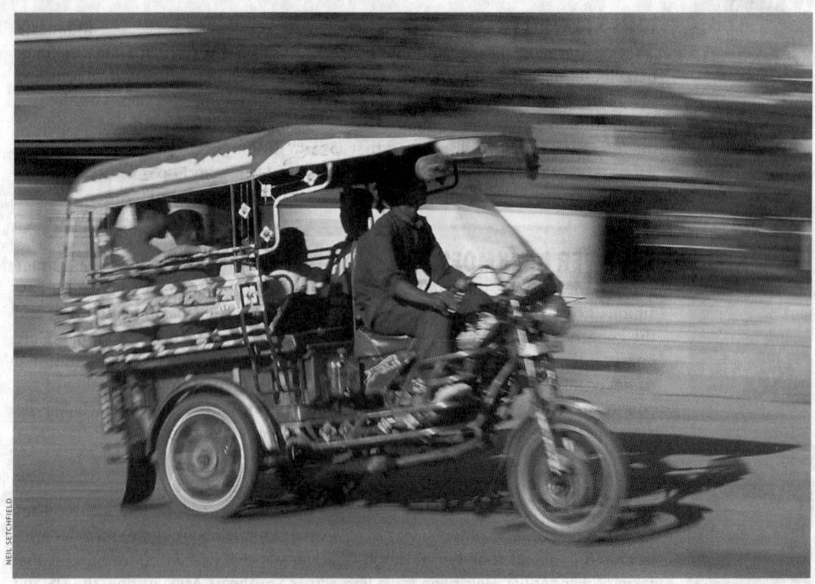

NEIL SETCHFIELD

Grab a túk-túk and rush headlong into Southeast Asian life in Vientiane (p351), Laos

Southeast Asia sticks to you. The tropical climate is so humid that the air becomes something akin to goo. The red dust of Cambodia steals through the open bus windows and settles into the fibres of your clothes. The joss sticks lit for the household shrines in Thailand impart a sweet perfume to the thick air. The pungent stench of a durian orchard in Sumatra follows you for days. And without noticing, you'll begin to shuffle between shady patches, as the locals do, rather than marching through the sun.

This is a spiritual place infused with the gods of past and present: the ancient spirits of the land and the family, the deities of Buddhism and the rules of Islam. In a parched corner of Cambodia is Angkor, one of the world's greatest monuments to heaven on earth. The Angkor temple trail extends into Thailand, but sacred spaces are everywhere, from the sagging ruins of other bygone kingdoms to the slumbering volcanoes of the island nations.

It is on the sublime coastlines where most travellers will find an earthly paradise: the coral-protected bays of the Malay peninsula, Indonesia's bulwark of beaches, and the languorous Vietnamese coastline. Each spit of sand has its own personality – from rave scene to stargazing retreat – and there's a constant flow of travellers looking for their own idyll.

Strangely though, the journey can be more moving than the destination. Beyond the bus window, the rolling landscape is fed by the monsoon rains, which impart the kind of fertility that occurs only in the absence of winter. But the soothing agricultural rhythms of Southeast Asia – where a season of hard work is rewarded with bounty and rest – are morphing into an urban tempo. Farmers are becoming factory workers, roads are replacing ditches and shopping malls are shoving out open-air markets. Your visit is well timed to catch a region in flux as an old way of life belatedly yields to the 21st century.

HIGHLIGHTS

BEST ARCHITECTURAL WONDERS

Temples of Angkor (Cambodia) ■ world-famous Hindu-Buddhist temples built by the great Khmer kingdom (p90)

Bagan (Myanmar) ■ a deserted city of ancient temples rippling into the distance like an artificial mountain range (p562)

Borobudur (Indonesia) ■ a stunning stupa (religious monument, often containing Buddha relics) ringed by mist and mountains (p197)

Petronas Towers (Malaysia) ■ one of the world's tallest skyscrapers, displaying delicate Islamic designs (p428)

Luang Prabang (Laos) ■ a blushing beauty with temples coloured in emerald and gold (p368)

BEST BEACHES & DIVE SPOTS

Bali (Indonesia) ■ synonymous with sun and fun, from the brassy beach scene at Kuta to the castaway cult of Amed (p209)

Ko Phi Phi (Thailand) ■ humpbacked limestone mountains jutting out of a sea of sapphire (p797)

Palawan (Philippines) ■ a remote island where you can sea kayak through isolated lagoons and dive WWII wrecks (p636)

Pulau Perhentian (Malaysia) ■ lounge all day on the beach and never get hassled – except by the changing tide (p466)

Gili Islands (Indonesia) ■ a trio of jungle-island pearls, each differing in personality (p276)

COREY WISE

Admire the shapely silhouettes of Myanmar's ancient temples as the sun sets over Bagan (p562)

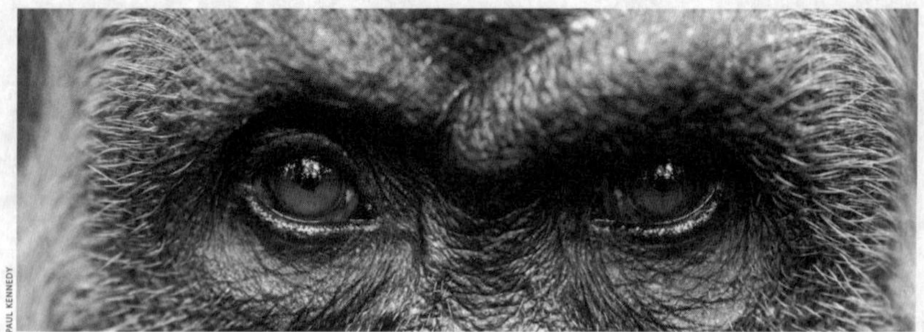
PAUL KENNEDY

Eyeball the orang-utans in Taman Nasional Gunung Leuser (p263), Indonesia

BEST WILD PLACES

Gunung Bromo (Indonesia) ▪ an active volcano and supernatural moonscape that's best viewed at sunrise (p207)

Bukit Lawang (Indonesia) ▪ have a staring contest with semiwild orang-utans at a jungle rehabilitation centre (p262)

Muang Sing (Laos) ▪ a sleepy market town with a model ecotrekking programme through the Nam Ha National Protected Area (p387)

Komodo (Indonesia) ▪ a desolate island where the world's biggest lizards prove that dragons aren't just myths (p287)

Bario and the Kelabit Highlands (Malaysia) ▪ take in the fresh air and jungle wonders at this verdant place (p507)

BEST CULINARY CAPITALS

Penang (Malaysia) ▪ eat your way around the world with Indian curries, Chinese dim sum and Malay desserts (p444)

Chiang Mai (Thailand) ▪ tame the Thai chilli at a cooking course in Thailand's boho city (p727)

Singapore ▪ gulp and savour Singapore's multiethnic cheap eats (p665)

Hoi An (Vietnam) ▪ an antique city of lacquered wooden shopfronts and hands-on cooking courses (p862)

Phnom Penh (Cambodia) ▪ dine for a cause at the city's various vocational-training restaurants (p74)

STEPHANE VICTOR

Forget the diet – nibble, gobble and munch your way through Southeast Asia's delectable cuisines (p34)

OLIVER STREWE

Discover your inner tightrope walker on the bridges of the Cordillera region (p606), Philippines

BEST PLACES TO WANDER

Cameron Highlands (Malaysia) ■ a mellow highland base for an expedition through knotted jungle (p439)

Mekong Delta (Vietnam) ■ Vietnam at half speed, with floating markets and bike-friendly countryside (p896)

Preah Vihear Province (Cambodia) ■ forgotten temple ruins on the old Angkor trail, where modern machines travel as slowly as the ox carts of yore (p102)

Cordillera region (Philippines) ■ a vast bowl-shaped valley with ancient rice terraces and long meditative walks (p606)

East Timor ■ a rarely trodden spot with a twist on East-meets-West (p128)

BEST WATER JOURNEYS

Halong Bay (Vietnam) ■ sail amid torpedo-shaped limestone mountains aboard an old-fashioned junk (p842)

Ko Tao (Thailand) ■ catch the overnight ferry from Surat Thani and be rocked to sleep by the ocean (p771)

Taman Negara (Malaysia) ■ settle into your cramped wooden seat as the longtail boat sails deep into this ancient jungle (p472)

Bangar (Brunei) ■ whiz into the jungle aboard the speedboats that link Bandar Seri Begawan and this small town on the Sungai Temburong (p50)

Batang Rejang (Malaysia) ■ a mighty and muddy 'highway' of Sarawak that leads to indigenous villages and traditional longhouses (p499)

RICHARD I'ANSON

Float into paradise amid the gorgeous islands of Halong Bay (p842), Vietnam

ITINERARIES

TAKING THE BEACH CURE

From **Bangkok** (p688), bus south to a string of beach-bumming islands in the Gulf of Thailand: resorty **Ko Samui** (p772), hammock-friendly **Ko Pha-Ngan** (p777) or dive-crazy **Ko Tao** (p771). All of these islands are reached from the mainland town of **Surat Thani** (p769). High step across the peninsula to the Andaman beaches: upscale **Phuket** (p791), magnificent **Ko Phi Phi** (p797), rock-climbing haven **Krabi** (p798) and navel-gazing retreat **Ko Lanta** (p801). Need more sand to yourself? Plant yourself on the underdeveloped beaches of **Ko Tarutao National Marine Park** (p802).

Jump the Thailand–Malaysia border by boat from **Satun** (p803) and head to the wide beaches of family-friendly **Pulau Langkawi** (p453). Next continue by boat to **Georgetown** (p444), an old spice-era port city on Pulau Penang. Take a bus from **Butterworth** (p444) to **Kota Bharu** (p468), the

HOW LONG?
1-2 months

WHEN TO GO?
Malaysia, Indonesia, & Thailand: roughly May-Oct

Philippines: Oct-May

BUDGET?
US$25-30 per day

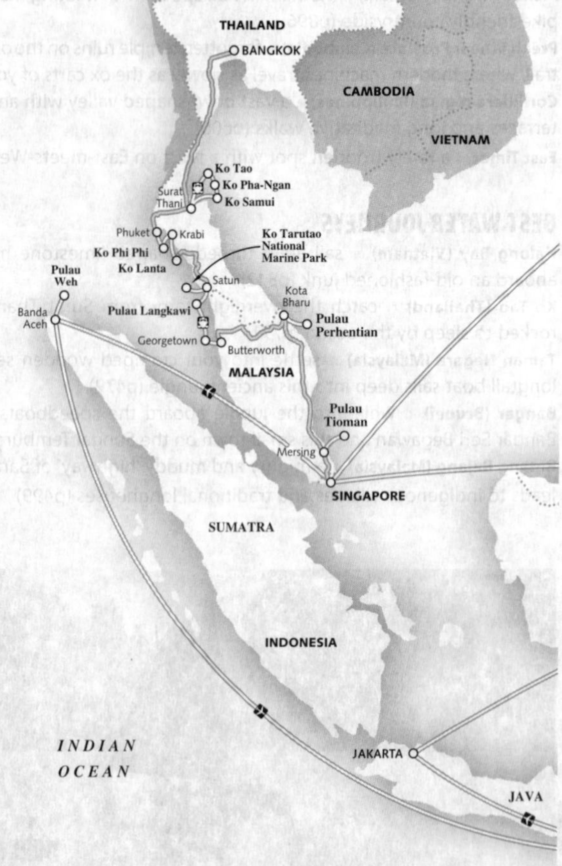

jumping-off point for the jungle islands of **Pulau Perhentian** (p466). Then chase the coastline south to **Mersing** (p457) and the villagelike beaches of **Pulau Tioman** (p457) before returning to civilization in **Singapore** (p655).

Fly across the Strait of Melaka to **Banda Aceh** (p263) for the brief boat ride to the underwater canyons and coral of **Pulau Weh** (p265) – it's how Thailand's beaches were 20 years ago. Hop on a flight to the sun-worship temple that is **Bali** (p209), and learn how to surf, dance and be trouble free.

Check out the uninterrupted R and R on **Lombok** (p270), then ferry to the deservedly celebrated **Gili Islands** (p276) for translucent water and Technicolor reefs, or to **Sumbawa** (p285) for surfable swells and a dramatic deserted coastline. Fly from **Jakarta** (p166) to **Manado** (p321) on Sulawesi to access the **Togean Islands** (p320), where you can dive beneath the ocean's rippling skin into the heart of pristine coral canyons.

The trip between Singapore and **Manila** (p592) in the Philippines might seem like a long haul, but the island of **Palawan** (p636) is a self-contained paradise hardly marred by modernity. Explore hidden coves, paddle through limestone caves and dive for WWII-era wrecks.

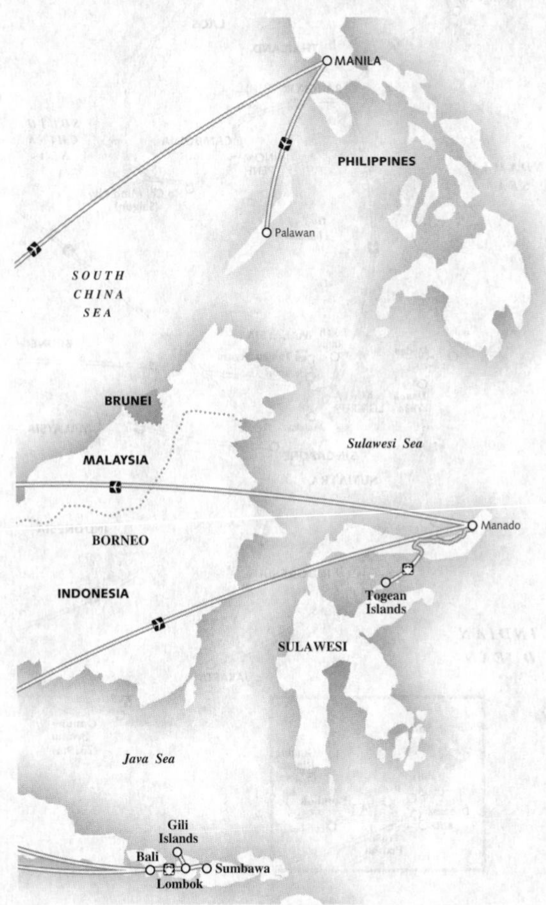

Become a beach connoisseur: first nibbling on the busy beaches of Thailand and Malaysia, then chewing on the known and unknown islands of Indonesia and the Philippines. Don't forget to pay proper homage to Bali.

THE REGIONAL RUNDOWN

Start in shopaholic **Bangkok** (p688), then fly to **Siem Reap** (p81) to see Angkor's magnificent temples. Bus to Cambodia's once genteel capital, **Phnom Penh** (p65), and on to capitalist-crazy **Ho Chi Minh City** (Saigon; p881). Work your way north to the leafy boulevards of **Hanoi** (p823), and then be air-lifted out of Vietnam's intensity to laid-back **Luang Prabang** (p368), Laos' World Heritage–listed city of temples and river scenery. Hop over to Thailand's cool enclave of **Chiang Mai** (p688), then

HOW LONG?
3-6 months

WHEN TO GO?
High season: Dec-Feb (Philippines & mainland Southeast Asia), May-Sep (Indonesia & East Timor)

Low season: May-Oct (Philippines & mainland Southeast Asia), Nov-Feb (Indonesia & East Timor)

BUDGET?
US$20-30 per day

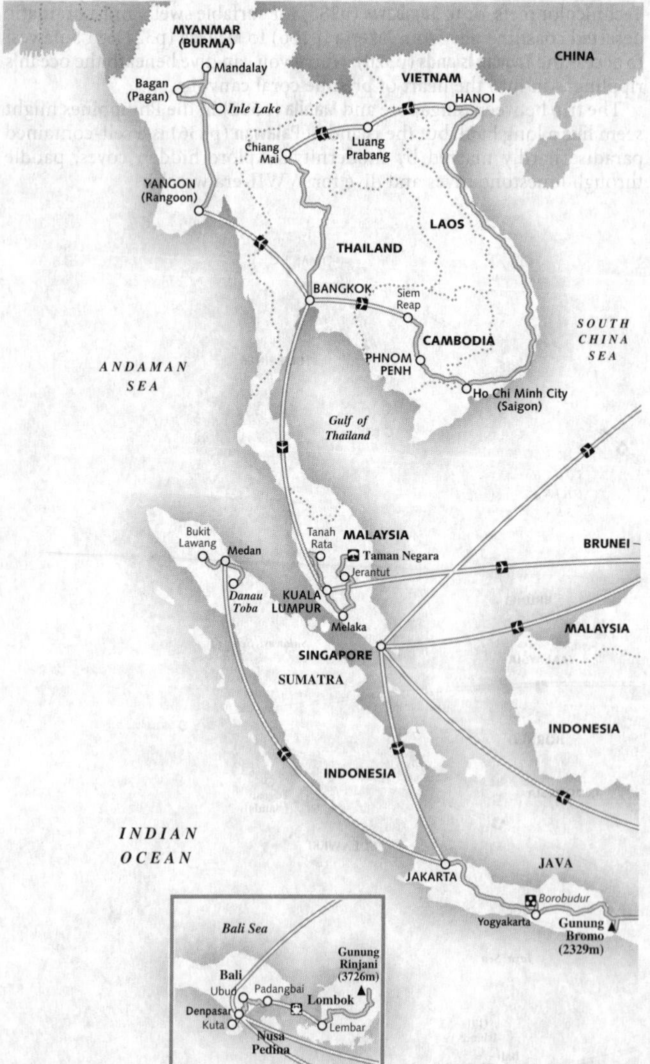

return to Bangkok and head on to **Yangon** (Rangoon; p528), located in the cloistered country of Myanmar (Burma). Stops along the Burma trail include the ruins of **Bagan** (Pagan; p562); **Inle Lake** (p547), with its floating gardens and island monasteries; and the ancient capital of **Mandalay** (p552).

From Bangkok fly to multiethnic **Kuala Lumpur** (p422), and bus to the tranquil hill station of **Tanah Rata** (p439) in the Cameron Highlands. Bus south to the historic port town of **Melaka** (p434), and on to **Jerantut**

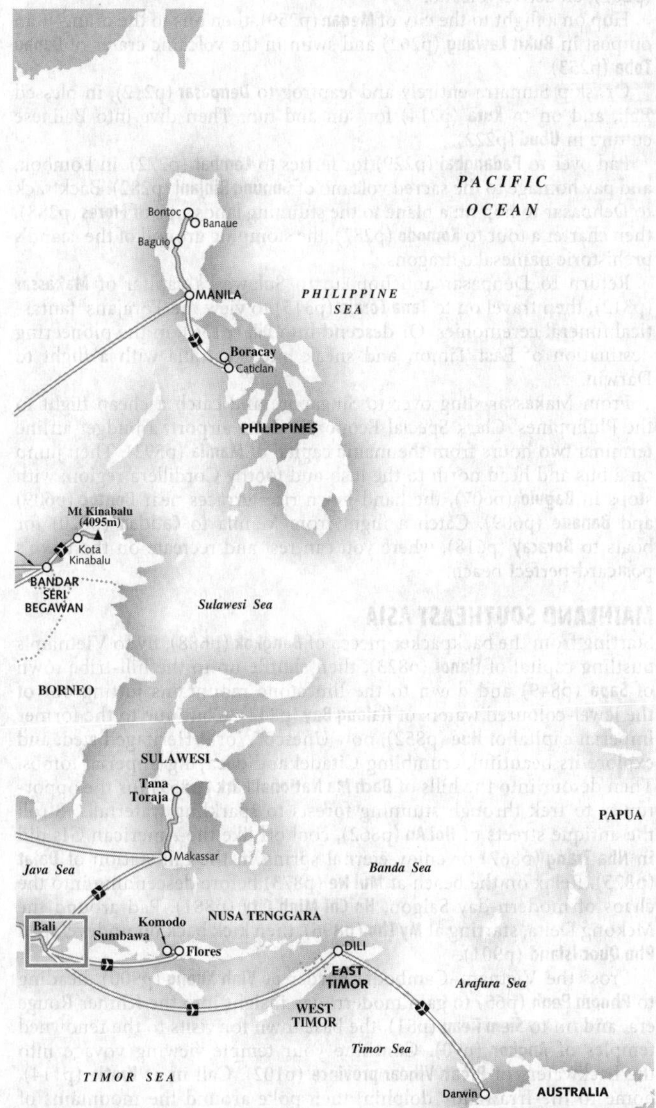

Think visiting the whole region is out of the question? Thanks to the budget airlines, you can country-hop in a matter of hours. Now enjoy the Southeast Asian buffet.

(p471), where longtail boats dive into the rainforests of **Taman Negara** (p472). Return to Kuala Lumpur and fly to Borneo through **Bandar Seri Begawan** (p44), the capital of Brunei. On the Malaysian side of Borneo is **Kota Kinabalu** (p477) and towering **Mt Kinabalu** (p484), where you can almost tickle the clouds.

Travel to sophisticated **Singapore** (p655) before touching down in the mayhem of **Jakarta** (p166). Soak up Javanese culture in **Yogyakarta** (p190) and witness the giant stupa of **Borobudur** (p197), then bus to **Gunung Bromo** (p207), an active volcano.

Hop on a flight to the city of **Medan** (p259), then bus to the orang-utan outpost in **Bukit Lawang** (p262) and swim in the volcanic crater of **Danau Toba** (p253).

Or, skip Sumatra entirely and leapfrog to **Denpasar** (p212), in blessed Bali, and on to **Kuta** (p214) for sun and fun. Then dive into Balinese culture in **Ubud** (p222).

Pad over to **Padangbai** (p229) for ferries to **Lembar** (p272), in Lombok, and pay homage to the sacred volcano of **Gunung Rinjani** (p282). Backtrack to Denpasar to hop on a plane to the stunning landscape of **Flores** (p288), then charter a tour to **Komodo** (p287), the stomping ground of the island's prehistoric namesake dragons.

Return to Denpasar and hop up to Sulawesi's capital of **Makassar** (p312), then travel on to **Tana Toraja** (p315) to view the Torajans' fantastical funeral ceremonies. Or descend into **Dili** (p136), in the pioneering destination of East Timor, and sneak into Australia with a flight to Darwin.

From Makassar sling over to Singapore and catch a cheap flight to the Philippines' Clark Special Economic Zone airport, a budget-airline terminal two hours from the manic capital of **Manila** (p592). Then jump on a bus and head north to the lush and toothy Cordillera region, with stops in **Baguio** (p607), the hand-hewn rice terraces near **Bontoc** (p609) and **Banaue** (p609). Catch a flight from Manila to **Caticlan** (p620) for boats to **Boracay** (p618), where you can rest and recreate on the town's postcard-perfect beach.

MAINLAND SOUTHEAST ASIA

HOW LONG?
2-6 months

WHEN TO GO?
High season: Dec-Feb

Low season: May-Oct

BUDGET?
US$20-25 per day

Starting from the backpacker mecca of **Bangkok** (p688), fly to Vietnam's bustling capital of **Hanoi** (p823), then shuffle up to the hill-tribe town of **Sapa** (p849) and down to the limestone mountains jutting out of the jewel-coloured waters of **Halong Bay** (p842). Continue to the former imperial capital of **Hué** (p852), now Unesco World Heritage listed, and explore its beautiful, crumbling Citadel and decaying imperial tombs. Then detour into the hills of **Bach Ma National Park** (p859) for the opportunity to trek through stunning forests to sparkling waterfalls. Stroll the antique streets of **Hoi An** (p862), cool off like the American GIs did in **Nha Trang** (p867) or enjoy eternal spring in the hill station of **Dalat** (p875). Relax on the beach at **Mui Ne** (p873) before descending into the chaos of modern-day Saigon, **Ho Chi Minh City** (p881). Pad around the Mekong Delta, starting at **My Tho** (p896), then kick back on undeveloped **Phu Quoc Island** (p901).

Cross the Vietnam–Cambodia border at **Vinh Xuong** (p900), heading to **Phnom Penh** (p65) to gain modern-day insight into the Khmer Rouge era, and on to **Siem Reap** (p81), the base town for visits to the renowned temples of **Angkor** (p90). Continue your temple-viewing voyage into the backwaters of **Preah Vihear province** (p102). Call in at **Kratie** (p114), home to the Irrawaddy dolphin, then poke around the mountains of remote **Ratanakiri province** (p116) before crossing into Laos from **Stung Treng** (p115).

Relax amidst the river islands of Laos' **Si Phan Don** (Four Thousand Islands; p400) – simply enjoy the stunning river scenery, or get active and take a trip to view rare Irrawaddy dolphins. Visit the imposing Khmer sanctuary in **Champasak** (p399) and explore the waterfalls of the **Bolaven Plateau** (p398). Save time by hopping a flight from **Pakse** (p395) to Laos' unassuming capital of **Vientiane** (p351), then board a bus to bewitching **Luang Prabang** (p368).

Travel along the Mekong River to the Laos–Thailand border crossing at **Chiang Khong** (p744) and **Huay Xai** (p389). Drop into **Chiang Rai** (p742), then hightail it to bohemian **Chiang Mai** (p727) for great food, ancient temples and a plethora of courses in cooking, language, massage and meditation. Take trekking detours in **Pai** (p737) and **Mae Hong Son** (p739), then shoot over to the ancient capital of **Sukhothai** (p722) before going waterfall-spotting in **Khao Yai National Park** (p751). Finally, take a deep breath and return to Bangkok.

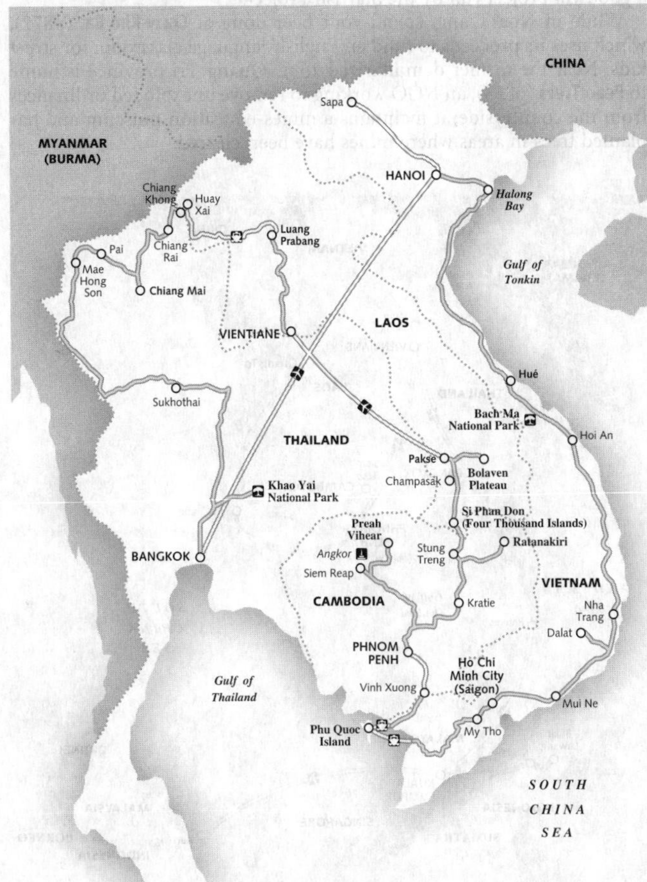

These are the celebrities of the region, enjoying lots of patronage by guidebook-toting travellers. Look for small-town detours to get off the beaten trail, and allow for lots of time on the road in Laos and Cambodia.

ECOTOURING & VOLUNTEERING

HOW LONG?
1-2 months

WHEN TO GO?
High season: Dec-Feb

Low season: May-Oct

BUDGET?
US$20-25 per day

From **Bangkok** (p688) drop south to Phuket, home to the **Phuket Gibbon Rehabilitation Centre** (p795), where volunteers and visitor donations help reintroduce captive gibbons into the wild. Head to **Kuala Lumpur** (p422) and catch a flight to Kuching in Malaysian Borneo for the **Rainforest World Music Festival** (p496), which celebrates traditional Borneo culture. Or fly to **Medan** (p259) and bump up to the jungle village of **Bukit Lawang** (p262), where red-haired orang-utans live among the trees.

If you're committed to mainland Southeast Asia, fly to **Vientiane** (p351) from Bangkok and stop by Vang Vieng, where the **Phoudindaeng Organic Farm** (p365) uses extra hands for community development. Then head north to **Luang Nam Tha** (p385) and **Muang Sing** (p387), the base camps for trekking programmes that follow ecosustainable practices.

While touring Cambodia, you can eat, drink and get a massage all in the name of charity. **Phnom Penh** (p76) and **Siem Reap** (p87) both have restaurants and bars that support good causes. Break up a sunbathing session in Sihanoukville by making a donation to **Sala Santepheap** (p106), a goodwill project run by the Starfish Project.

While in Nha Trang, spend your beer dong at **Crazy Kim Bar** (p872), which uses its proceeds to fund an English-language classroom for street kids. Near the former demilitarized zone, Quang Tri province is home to **PeaceTrees** (p853), an NGO working to remove unexploded ordinances from the countryside; it maintains a mines-education museum and has planted trees in areas where mines have been cleared.

Weave a few simple do-gooder deeds into a tour of the region: visit a wildlife rehabilitation centre, undertake a volunteering stint, or support a charitable business. These are some ideas along the trail.

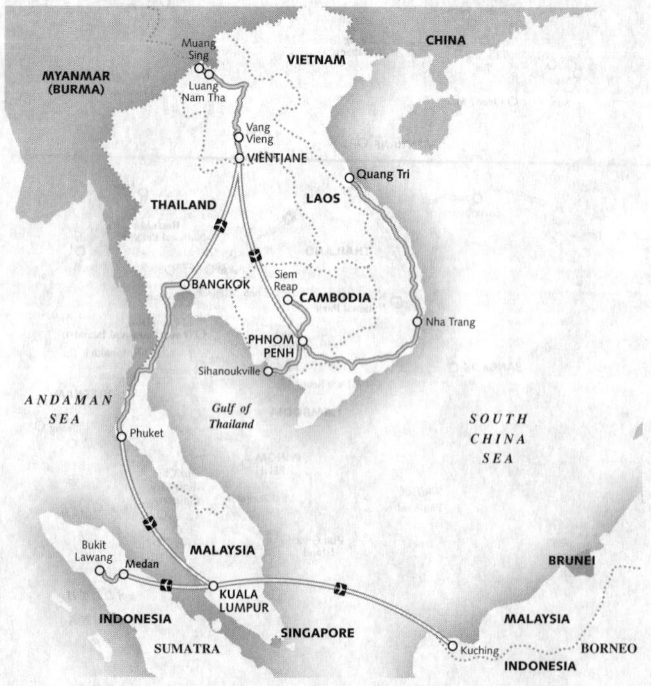

GETTING STARTED

WHEN TO GO

Southeast Asia is always hot and humid. The mainland countries (Myanmar, Laos, Cambodia, Thailand and Vietnam) tend to share similar weather patterns, enjoying a 'cool' season from roughly December to February (peak months for tourism) and a 'hot' season from March to May. The monsoons last from June to October, bringing sudden torrential downpours for an hour or two every day, which are followed just as suddenly by sunshine. In Cambodia and Laos, travel can be disrupted by flooded roads during the monsoon season, but otherwise the rains bring a predictable relief from the heat.

See p916 for more climate information.

Along the Malay peninsula, two monsoons strike: from November to February, the east coast gets all the action; from May to October, the west coast gets soaked. Alternating between the coasts will relieve the drawbacks of inclement weather. The duration of monsoon season varies from year to year.

Indonesia also gets two monsoons; the best time to visit is from May to September. The rains start in September in Sumatra and head east, arriving in East Timor around November or December. April to June is the best time to visit East Timor.

The wet and dry seasons vary within the Philippines but, by and large, January and February are dry months. Typhoons can hit both the Philippines and Vietnam between June and October.

There are, of course, regional variations within each country; these are detailed in the respective country chapters' Climate sections.

Large festivals are also factors in plotting an arrival date. Check Festivals & Events in the country chapters for upcoming events that might attract or impede a visit. Businesses tend to close during Muslim Ramadan and Chinese New Year, and everyone goes water-gun crazy during the Thai, Lao and Cambodian New Year in April.

COSTS & MONEY

Western currencies enjoy a favourable exchange rate with many of the Southeast Asian currencies. If you travel and eat like a local, your daily budget might be a positively emaciated US$20 to US$30 a day.

Even if you are strapped for cash, remember to keep prices in perspective. Compared to the average worker in Southeast Asia, your pathetic bank account is the equivalent of a robber baron's. Many of the locals have never left their hometowns, much less travelled to a foreign country. Granted, the 'walking ATM' (everyone wants a withdrawal) treatment is frustrating and offensive, but there is no quicker route to a bad time than to get paranoid about being ripped off. Be a smart shopper, but realise that even in developing countries US$1 doesn't buy everything.

For more information on local currency and exchange rates, see p920 or Money in the individual country directories.

HOW MUCH?

Bottle of beer US$1.50-3

Bottled water US$1

Bus ticket US$5-12

Food-stall meal US$1-2

Guesthouse bed US$5-12

Internet access US$1-2

Restaurant meal US$5-12

Taxi ride US$3.50-8

LIFE ON THE ROAD

Southeast Asia is loud, no doubt about it. The roosters have been crowing all night, the screaming motorcycles have been doing circles around your bed and the guttural call to prayers seems to emanate from next door.

It isn't even noon yet and the temperature has already reached boiling point. You climb off the rock-hard mattress and head down to the shared toilet at the end of the hall. The mirror is too short, the sink is too low

SOUTHEAST ASIA PLANNING CHECKLIST

Where to Start

Try the internet for inspiration and information.

Central Intelligence Agency – The World Factbook (https://www.cia.gov/library/publications/the-world-factbook/index.html) Know the basic stats by searching the CIA world factbook.

Lonely Planet (http://lonelyplanet.mytripjournal.com) Set up your trip blog.

What to Take

Here's a challenge: reduce the size of your pack to fit in an aircraft overhead locker. The reward: the less junk in your trunk, the less of a target you are for touts and con artists.

Cash and credit cards Some small US dollar bills will be useful in places where ATM access is limited. Make sure the bills are crisp and clean as some banks, especially in Indonesia, can be fickle. Take both a Visa and a MasterCard credit card in case merchants only accept one brand.

Clothes Bring lightweight, light-coloured, breathable clothes; leave the denim at home. Pack silk long johns and a fleece for cool climates, and remember your rain gear. Line your pack with a plastic bag to keep the contents dry.

Earplugs An indispensable friend for sleeping through your neighbours' drunken fight or the zealous rooster's predawn alert.

Medicine A first-aid kit and any speciality medicines from home. Most large cities have pharmacies and clinics with English-speaking staff. See p935 for advice on stocking a first-aid kit.

Odds and ends Sewing kit, candles, padlock, Swiss army knife, money belt, safety pins, toilet paper, universal sink plug, small torch (flashlight), travel adaptor.

Photocopies of important documents Definitely photocopy your passport, tickets, travellers-cheque serial numbers, and credit and ATM cards, and pack the copies separately from the originals. Leave a copy at home with a friend, just in case.

Repellent A heavy-duty number is good for sweet-tasting travellers.

Speciality gear If you plan to do serious (not occasional) camping, trekking or climbing, you should bring the equipment with you from home. Otherwise you can hire items of mediocre quality at your destination.

USB drive Allows you to store photos and files. By storing a portable web browser on the drive, you can protect your password at public machines.

What to Get There

In the large cities, you can buy every imaginable Western product, as well as medicines and the following useful products:

Mosquito coils These coils are lit and placed at your feet to discourage a mossie feast; available at markets.

Talcum Powder Does wonders for heat rash and keeps you and your clothes smelling pretty; available at markets and pharmacies.

Sarong Can be used as a towel, mosquito net, sheet, head gear and general backpacker fashion; available at markets.

Surgical masks These masks prevent the region's dust- and pollution-induced smoker's cough; available at various shops.

Tiger balm This all-purpose salve relieves headaches, soothes mosquito bites and acts as a bug repellent; available at pharmacies.

and the whole room needs to be sprayed down with bleach. Now it's time for a shower (cold water for this penny-pincher), a powdering (keeps you cool and sweet smelling) and a desperate search for clean clothes.

Today is the day you pack up and move to the next town. Arriving at the destination station, the bus is flanked by touts all thirsty for your business. You haggle the price, which is always inflated due to an informal 'I'm new in town' tax. The first guesthouse you visit has a shady yard with chickens scratching around in the dirt but the room is dank and noisy, so you thank the testy desk clerk and set off down the road. You use your budget senses to sniff out the best score in town, and in a

TOP 10 TIPS TO STAY ON A BUDGET

- Always ask the price before agreeing to any services.
- Buy souvenirs from craft villages rather than from tourist shops.
- Eat and drink at food stalls and markets.
- Go outside the tourist district to buy odds and ends.
- If travelling solo, team up with a fellow traveller to save on room costs.
- Keep a daily diary of expenses.
- Leave expensive electronics and jewellery at home, so you aren't advertising deep pockets.
- Pack light so you can walk into town from the train or bus station.
- Travel in the low season.
- Take overnight buses to save on room costs.

few hours you're camped out in the shade with a steamy bowl of noodles and a sweaty bottle of beer. Beats the wage-slave life.

The empty seat beside you is soon filled by a curious local who wants to practice his English. He asks you all the usual Southeast Asia interrogation questions: where do you come from? How old are you? Are you married? With those formalities out of the way, this stranger and you are now the dearest of friends, according to local conventions, and you might pose for a picture with him before either parting ways or joining him for a night of karaoke. Yes, Southeast Asia is loud – but it's friendly.

CONDUCT

You have an extraordinary responsibility upon arriving in Southeast Asia: you're an ambassador for your own country, as well as for the whole Western world. You can either charm the flip-flops off the locals, which is easy to do in these laid-back cultures, or you can leave behind a sour taste.

So few travellers make an effort to speak the local language or adhere to social customs that the smallest attempts are usually rewarded with genuine appreciation and kindness. Learn how to say 'thank you', 'hello' and 'delicious' in every country you visit. Remember to smile – it expresses tons of emotions.

Dress modestly, covering yourself from the shoulders to the knees; this is the number-one way to communicate genuine gratitude to your host country. But it's so hot, you might whine. What's funny about this argument is that walking in the shade is a better sun deflector than showing your belly. Women who dare to wear more will help promote a healthier image of all Western women abroad; topless sunbathing is also a no-no. For men, resist the inexplicable urge to strut around without a shirt.

In Southeast Asia, the feet are the cesspool of the body and the head is the temple. Treat the rules of proper foot etiquette like an exotic dance without a partner. Feet for the most part should stay on the ground, not on chairs, tables or bags. Showing someone the bottom of your foot expresses the same insult as flipping them your middle finger. Remove your shoes when entering a home. Don't point your feet towards sacred images or people, and follow the locals' lead in sitting in a temple or mosque.

Women aren't allowed to come into contact with monks; this means women can't sit or stand next to them on the bus, pass anything directly to them or touch their belongings. Most mosques have rules about where women can be and how they should be dressed.

WHOOPS!

China Williams

I've mastered walking and talking and even chewing gum at the same time, but walking and checking maps is another matter. With my nose in a map, I've bruised both my body and my pride. I've fallen into holes in the footpath and tripped over stray metal pipes, causing a passing motorcyclist to laugh and point.

TOP 10 WAYS TO LOOK LIKE A SOUTHEAST ASIAN VETERAN

- Never bump your head climbing into and out of local transport trucks.
- Sniff out an internet connection in the remotest town.
- Use mosquito repellent as deodorant.
- Forsake proper English grammar for local pidgin.
- Walk through a pack of stray dogs without flinching.
- Sleep through all-night karaoke parties.
- Squat bomber style on Western toilets.
- Sit down to a banana pancake breakfast and reach for the fish sauce.
- Be able to recount more than one 'I almost died' story.
- Pose for group photos with complete strangers.

For more guidance on how to avoid being a sore-thumb tourist, see p4 and the Culture in country chapters throughout this guidebook.

Some dos and don'ts to remember:

- Ask before taking someone's photograph.
- Bring a gift when visiting someone's home.
- Remove your shoes before entering a home or religious building.
- Don't engage in public displays of affection.
- Don't touch people on the head; this is considered rude in Buddhist countries.
- Don't use your left hand for eating or shaking hands; in many Asian countries, the left hand is used for toilet business.

Snapshots

CURRENT EVENTS

Southeast Asia has played a quieter role on the world stage since its tragic appearance in international headlines after the 2004 Boxing Day tsunami. But the regional news has been full of high drama.

Elections and the lack thereof were a running theme in the region. After 29 years of guerrilla war, the Indonesian province of Aceh and the central government in Jakarta forged a peace agreement that resulted in a provincial gubernatorial election in 2006, marking an unprecedented level of provincial sovereignty in the country's federalist system.

Fewer people were killed in the Philippines' most recent election than in years past, but observers note that the relative peace is hardly a sign that democracy has been released from Mafia-style attacks on opposition leaders.

Vietnam has made ceremonial gestures towards democracy by allowing 'independent' candidates (hand-picked by the Communist Party) to run for vacant National Assembly seats. The communist country continues to dismantle the curtain of isolation; in early 2007 it became the 150th country to join the World Trade Organization.

Asia Times (www.atimes.com) has informative news essays and reporting that covers the region.

Meanwhile, Thailand's military kicked out its democratically elected government in 2006 after months of street protests against the prime minister; this was followed by the dissolution of the Parliament, and hastily arranged and later aborted elections. It's been a whirlwind political year for the kingdom, which is now run by a military-appointed government. In August 2007, the Thai public voted to adopt a new constitution.

The military junta in Myanmar (Burma) has built its wall of isolation ever higher by quietly moving the national capital to a purpose-built city located some 390km away from the scrutiny of international diplomats in Yangon (Rangoon). The government is also collaborating with Russia to design a nuclear facility, and it continues to attack ethnic minorities, creating a humanitarian crisis that looks like ethnic cleansing.

The birth of East Timor as a nation in 2002 was difficult, and the ensuing years have been full of growing pains. Various factions are manoeuvring for power in the nascent democracy, leading to widespread riots in 2006 and internal population displacement. However, national elections in 2007 were more peaceful than most observers could have hoped.

In Cambodia, courts have been hammering out the details of a tribunal that will prosecute 10 surviving leaders of the Khmer Rouge. It is widely believed that the trials have been delayed in part because members of the current government had ties to the Khmer Rouge.

Outbreaks of avian influenza (bird flu) have continued to affect commercially raised flocks, and humans in close contact with infected birds throughout Southeast Asia. The World Health Organization is concerned that the virus will mutate in such a way as to be spread from one human to another, creating a pandemic. At present, experts believe that the greatest danger of a pandemic resides in Indonesia, where there is concern that the low compensation for culling an infected flock acts as a disincentive to reporting. See p937 for more information on bird flu.

The region, especially the sleepier corners, is changing fast – and the bringer of modernity is China, not the Western nations. Chinese-funded highways (see boxed text, above), and hydroelectric dams in Laos and

SOUTHEAST ASIA'S AUTOBAHN

Say goodbye to the bumpy and sweaty overland journey through Southeast Asia. Backed primarily by China and Japan, two regional highways – currently in various states of completion – will fuse interior areas of mainland Southeast Asia with the Pacific Ocean, facilitating trade with East Asia and the emergence of a modern intraregional transport system through areas that once were frontiers or were used by guerrilla armies and smugglers. The first route to be completed in this asphalt revolution is an east–west corridor that links Da Nang (Vietnam) to Savannakhet (Laos) and crosses the Mekong River to Mukdahan (Thailand). The road will eventually continue on to Mawlamyine in southern Myanmar. The north–south corridor will run from Kunming, China, through Laos and on to Bangkok, and is expected to boost expanding Chinese influence and trade in the region.

Cambodia are transforming these dusty outposts into energy producers and commercial crossroads. What will former Indochina look like with the commercial backing of China? You'll have to come back in five years to see.

HISTORY

Early Kingdoms

The mainland Southeast Asia countries owe much of their early historical happenings to the more dominant kingdoms in China and India. As early as 150 BC, China and India interacted with the scattered Southeast Asian communities for trade and tribute. Vietnam, within short reach of China, was a subject, student and reluctant offspring of its more powerful neighbour for over 1000 years. India, on the other hand, conquered through the heart, spreading Hinduism, Buddhism and later Islam across the region, and influencing art and architecture.

An easily digestible survey, *A History of South-East Asia* by DGE Hall sketches the early and not-so-distant history of Southeast Asia.

Several highly organised states emerged in the region as a result of contact with India. During the 7th to 9th centuries AD, the Srivijaya empire controlled all shipping through the Java Sea from its capital at Palembang in southeast Sumatra. The Srivijaya capital was also a religious centre for Mahayana Buddhism (Greater Vehicle Buddhism; see p38) and attracted scholars as well as merchants.

But the region's most famous fallen empire emerged in the interior of present-day Cambodia. The Khmer empire ruled the land for four centuries, consuming territory and labour to build unparalleled and enduring Hindu-Buddhist monuments to its god-kings. Eventually the Khmer empire included most of what is now Thailand, Laos and Cambodia. Its economy was based on agriculture, and a sophisticated irrigation system cultivated vast tracts of land around Tonlé Sap (Great Lake). Attacks from emerging city-states in the Thai frontier contributed to the decline of the empire and the abandonment of the Angkor capital.

TIMELINE

2800BC | 0 AD | 700 | 850 | 900 | 1025 | 1400 | 1500 | 1565 | 1600 | 1650 AD

- **Beginning Of Time:**
- **2800BC:** Ancestors of modern Southeast Asians begin to migrate south from China
- **AD 700:** Srivijaya empire emerges in present-day Malaysia and Indonesia, and later prospers from the India–China shipping trade
- **AD 802–50:** King Jayavarman consolidates the Khmer empire in present-day Cambodia and Thailand
- **1025:** Srivijaya empire is toppled by the Chola kingdom of South India
- **1511:** Melaka falls to the Portuguese
- **1565:** Spain establishes Cebu and later invades Manila

The Classical Period, Arrival of Europeans & Imperialism

As the larger powers withered, Southeast Asia entered an age of cultural definition and international influence. Regional kingdoms created distinctive works of art and literature, and joined the international sphere as important ports. The Thais, with their capital first in Sukhothai (1219) and later in Ayuthaya (1350), expanded into the realm of the dying Khmer empire and exerted control over parts of Cambodia, Laos and Myanmar. Starting around 1331, the Hindu kingdom of Majapahit united the Indonesian archipelago from Sumatra to New Guinea and dominated the age-old trade routes between India and China. The kingdom's reign continued until the advent of Islamic kingdoms and the emergence of the port town of Melaka on the Malay peninsula in 1402. Melaka's prosperity soon attracted European interest, and it fell first to the Portuguese in 1511, then the Dutch and finally the English.

Comprehensive and thoughtful, *The Emergence of Modern Southeast Asia: A New History,* by Norman Owen et al, examines colonialism and globalisation in recent times.

At first the European nations were only interested in controlling shipping in the region, usually brokering agreements and alliances with local authorities. Centred on Java and Sumatra, the Dutch monopolised European commerce with Asia for 200 years. The Spanish, French and later the English had 'civilisation' and proselytizing on their minds. Spain occupied the loosely related tribes of the Philippine archipelago. Britain steadily rolled through India, Myanmar and the Malay peninsula. The Dutch grasped Indonesia to cement a presence in the region. And France, with a foothold in Vietnam, usurped Cambodia and Laos, formerly territories of the Thai kingdom, to form Indochina.

Although its sphere of influence was diminished, Thailand was the only Southeast Asian nation to remain independent. One reason for this was that England and France agreed to leave Thailand as a 'buffer' between their two colonies. Credit is also frequently given to the Thai kings who Westernised the country and played competing European powers against each other.

Independence & the Modern Day

The 20th century and WWII signalled an end to European domination in Southeast Asia. As European power receded to its own shores during the war, the Japanese expanded their control throughout the region, invading Thailand, Malaysia and Indonesia. After the war, the power vacuums in formerly colonised countries provided leverage for a regionwide independence movement. Vietnam and Indonesia clamoured most violently for freedom, resulting in long-term wars with their respective colonial powers. For the latter half of the 20th century, Vietnam fought almost uninterrupted conflicts against foreign powers. After the French were defeated by communist nationals, Vietnam faced another enemy, the USA, which hoped to 'contain' the spread of communism within the region. Cambodia's civil war ended in one of the worst nightmares of modern times, with the ascension of the Khmer

Edward Gargan, a former draft dodger, visits the former battlefield countries some 30 years later in his book *The River's Tale: A Year on the Mekong*.

1819: Singapore is founded by British official Thomas Stamford Raffles

1862: France occupies Vietnam

1946: The Philippines wins independence

1949: Indonesia wins independence

1700 1750 1820 1860 1898 1914 1920 1930 1940 1945 1946 1948 1949

1824: Britain invades Myanmar (Burma), capturing the capital, Yangon (Rangoon)

1898: The USA annexes the Philippines in the aftermath of the Spanish-American War

1939–45: WWII; Japan occupies much of Southeast Asia

1948: Myanmar wins independence

PIRATES OF THE SOUTH CHINA SEA

Pirates still sail the high seas – and not just in children's books or movie franchises. In the shipping corridor of the Strait of Melaka, the gateway to the South China Sea, the sabres and cutlasses of yore have been replaced with machine guns but the unsavoury hijacking of booty and even vessels remains true to the old tales. Modern-day pirates, many of whom are Indonesian, use speedboats to sneak up on hulking container ships and oil tankers en route to and from Singapore or Hong Kong. Armed robbery in the South China Sea spiked after the Asian currency crisis in 1997, but 10 years of increased policing of the waters, as well as the emergence of more-legitimate economic opportunities has seen the number of piracy incidents decrease in the last few years.

Rouge. The revolutionary army evacuated the cities, separated families into labour camps and closed the country off from the rest of the world. An estimated 1.7 million people were killed by the regime during its brief four-year term (1975–79).

Many of the newly liberated countries struggled to unite a land mass that shared only a colonial legacy. Dictatorships in Myanmar, Indonesia and the Philippines thwarted the populace's hopes for representative governments and civil liberties. Civilian rioters, minority insurgents and communist guerrillas further provoked the unstable governments, and the internal chaos was usually agitated by the major superpowers: China, the Soviet Union and the USA.

Brunei has no income tax but provides free health care to its citizens.

With the thawing of the Cold War, several raging national economies in the 1990s, and the onset of the new millennium, Southeast Asia enjoyed renewed stability and vitality. Singapore has become the shining star of the region, while Thailand and Malaysia boast decades of stable governments and an affluent, educated middle class. Vietnam, Laos and Cambodia have opened themselves to foreign trade, regional cooperation and tourism. Vietnam is racing through the milestones of development with almost unprecedented speed, boosted by a new generation of young people flush with disposable income and untouched by the war with the USA. Laos and Cambodia are plodding more slowly; infrastructure is improving gradually, but feudal divisions and corruption are thwarting the proliferation of a middle class. Only Myanmar remains cloistered today. Indonesia and the Philippines rode the first wave of postcolonial development, but have since stalled with the attendant industrialized problems of unemployment and urban pollution.

Democratically elected governments continue to experience yo-yo status, but armed conflicts appeared trivial after the 2004 Boxing Day tsunami that claimed lives and livelihoods. With the help of international aid, the region proved its tenacity by almost completely rebuilding and recovering in just three years.

1954: Vietnam defeats the French, disintegrating French Indochina

1957: Independent Malaysia is founded

1965: The British leave Singapore

1975: Saigon falls to the North Vietnamese, who name it Ho Chi Minh City; the Khmer Rouge takes over Cambodia

1999: East Timor votes for independence

2004: An Indian Ocean earthquake and tsunami destroys lives and communities in four Southeast Asian countries

2006: Thailand's government is ousted by a military coup; renewed violence in East Timor after UN peacekeeping troops withdraw

2007: Vietnam joins the World Trade Organization

1954 1957 1960 1965 1970 1975 1990 1999 2002 2004 2006 2007

THE CULTURE

The most remarkable and unifying aspect of the diverse Southeast Asian societies is the importance placed on acting in a group rather than following the Western ideal of independence and self-determination. Social harmony is ensured by the concept of 'face' – that is, avoiding embarrassing yourself or others. This is translated into everyday life by not showing anger or frustration and by avoiding serious debates that could cause offence. When the bus breaks down, the passengers calmly file out into the sun and wait for the repairs without causing a scene – in this way an undercurrent of peace is brought to a chaotic situation.

Thais celebrate three New Year's festivals.

See the Culture sections in country chapters in this book for notes on each country's culture and lifestyle.

Lifestyle

The setting may vary vastly – from the hulking megacities of Bangkok and Jakarta to rural villages in Laos – but Southeast Asia moves through time with the underlying architecture of an agricultural village, no matter how big or small the town or how distant the rice fields. Families tend to stick together, pitching in to run the family noodle shop or helping Grandma do her market shopping. Because of the tropical temperature, most family life spreads out into the public space, replacing a sense of privacy with community. Babies get lots of group mothering, neighbours do lots of gossiping and possessions are often shared or pooled, depending on the affluence of the community. In addition to blood, religion binds the society and the family with daily obligations of prayers in Muslim communities or spirit offerings in Buddhist countries.

In the villages, life revolves around the harvest, a calendar set by the rains, the sun and the moon. In these old-fashioned corners, the food markets and the mosque or temple are the 'happening' parts of town.

More and more, the trappings of a modern and decidedly Western world are moving in and replacing the open-air markets and providing the new middle class with new things to consume. In the cities of Thailand, Vietnam and Malaysia, the young dare to be different to their parents by adopting the latest fashions, texting their friends and scooting around town till all hours of the night. These countries are becoming transient, with the young people leaving the villages for a job in the city. Their children may grow up separated from the rhythms of an agrarian society, feeling more comfortable in a shopping mall than a rice field. Comfortably entrenched in a middle-class world, Singaporeans often 'visit' the village, yearning to reconnect with a romantic version of the past.

One of the most diverse nations on the planet, Indonesia comprises approximately 300 ethnic groups that speak some 365 languages and dialects.

Population

Each country in Southeast Asia has a dominant ruling class, typically the national ethnicity. It is believed that many of the mainland Southeast Asian peoples are descendants of Austronesian, Tai and Mon-Khmer peoples who migrated south from China. Countries with a high percentage of homogeneity include Vietnam, Cambodia, Brunei, Thailand and Singapore. More demographically diverse countries include Myanmar, the Philippines, Indonesia and East Timor, which doesn't have a majority ethnicity.

Many of the Southeast Asian countries share varying percentages of minority groups in isolated pockets or cultural islands. Regarded as the Jews of Asia, ethnic Chinese filtered into the region as merchants and labourers, establishing distinct neighbourhoods within their host communities. Every small town has a Chinatown, typically in the business district. In places such as Malaysia and Singapore, the Chinese diaspora

TENDER TOURISM

Tourism provides much-needed income to the region but it is an economic machine that should operate with delicacy and empathy to preserve and respect the host country's culture and integrity.

Customs & Culture

Become a cultural chameleon, not just a travelling consumer. Learn, appreciate and adopt, if possible, the local ways, etiquette and values.

Tourist Economy

Independent travel empowers family-run businesses. Carry on the 'backpacker' tradition by staying in guesthouses or locally owned hotels, eating at food stalls and travelling on local transport.

Charitable Acts

The disparity between rich and poor in Southeast Asia often ignites a charitable spirit that might have been dormant in your home country. But sharing your wealth and privilege in a constructive way can be tricky. Throughout this book, we recommend organisations that are lending a helping hand to struggling communities. In many cases, all you need to give is your time, a small donation or commercial patronage.

has morphed into a distinct entity, frequently termed Straits Chinese, which has merged Chinese and Malay customs, most notably in the kitchen and in conversation. While most countries derive cultural and commercial strength from Chinese immigrants, in times of economic hardship, ethnic Chinese are frequently targets of abuse because of their prosperity; this is especially the case in Malaysia and Indonesia. Ethnic Indians from the southern provinces of Tamil Nadu have also settled along the Malay peninsula and remain a distinct group.

High up in the mountains that run through Myanmar, Laos, northern Thailand and Vietnam, a diverse mix of minority groups, collectively referred to as hill tribes, maintain prehistoric traditions and wear elaborate tribal costumes. Believed to have migrated from the Himalayas or southern China, hill-tribe communities such as the Akha, Karen and Mon, thanks to the geography, have been relatively isolated from foreign influences. They were considered a nuisance by lowland governments until hill-tribe trekking became a widespread tourist attraction. Myanmar represents the largest concentration of hill tribes. In the outer areas of Indonesia, such as Kalimantan, Papua, Sulawesi and Sumba, indigenous people practise customs that have entered the global imagination through the pages of *National Geographic*.

Hot Sour Salty Sweet: A Culinary Journey Through Southeast Asia by Jeffrey Alford samples the four pillars of the cuisine of the Mekong area.

Food

Southeast Asia's tropical climate creates a year-round bounty. Rice and fish are the primary staples in the region, and are often revered in various harvest festivals and local legends. A penchant for chillies is another Southeast Asian hallmark, with almost every cultural cuisine claiming a variation on a chilli condiment, including *sambal* in Indonesia and Malaysia, and *naam phrik* in Thailand.

Traces of Southeast Asia's cultural parents – India and China – can be detected in the individual nations' cuisines. Myanmar is the best example of this marriage; many of its Indian-inspired curries are more like stews, and some are even served over egg noodles, a Chinese invention, rather than the common staple of rice. Thai, Indonesian and Malay curries have been adapted from that of their Indian predecessor with regional flourishes, while Malaysia has incorporated roti, an Indian flat bread, into its cuisine. The Chinese donated noodle soups, which have assumed various aliases: laksa in Malaysia and Singapore, *pho* in Vietnam or *kŭaytĭaw* in Thailand. Noodle soups are the quintessential comfort food, eaten in the morning, after a night carousing or at midday when pressed for time. In most Southeast Asian countries, chopsticks are used only for this dish. Culinary imports also came from the French, who imparted a taste for crusty baguettes and thick coffees in former Indochina.

Vietnam has perfected the cuisine of its culinary professor. Where Chinese food can be bland and oily, Vietnamese dishes are light and refreshing. A quintessential Vietnamese dish is the spring rolls stuffed with shrimp, mint, basil leaves and cucumbers that are sold at roadside stands.

Thailand and Laos share many common dishes, often competing for the honour of spiciest cuisine. Green papaya salad is a mainstay of the two – the Thais like theirs with peanuts and dried shrimp; the Lao version uses fermented fish sauce and inland crab. In Laos and in neighbouring Thai provinces, the local people eat 'sticky rice' (a shorter grain than the standard fluffy white rice), which is eaten with the hands and usually rolled into balls and dipped into spicy sauces.

Eat your way through these Southeast Asian foodie blogs: Real Thai (http://realthai.blogspot.com), Phnomenon (www.phnomenon.com), Babe in the City - KL (http://babeinthecitykl.blogspot.com) and Sticky Rice (http://stickyrice.typepad.com) .

As dictated by the strictures of Islam, Muslim communities in Malaysia and Indonesia don't eat pork. Indonesians traditionally eat with their fingers – hence the rice is a little stickier than in mainland Southeast Asia. Perfecting the delicate shovelling motion is a true traveller accomplishment.

Filipino cooking is a mixture of Malay, Spanish and Chinese influences blended with typical Filipino exuberance. *Adobo*, a Spanish-inspired stew with local modifications, has come to symbolise Filipino cuisine.

In a postcolonial age, Singapore displays its position as a cosmopolitan crossroads with its development of Pacific Rim fusion cuisine.

Art

Southeast Asia's most notable artistic endeavours are religious in nature, and distinctively depict the deities of Hinduism and Buddhism.

Both an artistic and architectural wonder, the temples of Angkor in Cambodia defined much of the region's artistic interpretation of these religions. Hindu temples include elaborate sculptured murals that pay homage to the Hindu gods Brahma (represented as a four-headed, four-armed figure) and Shiva (styled either in an embrace with his consort or as an ascetic), while also recording historical events and creation myths. Many of the temples were later altered to include images of Buddha after the kingdom converted to Buddhism.

Bangkok, Singapore and Jakarta all host international film festivals that also allow local directors to showcase their cinematic creations.

Statues of Buddha reflect the individual countries' artistic interpretations of an art form governed by highly symbolic strictures. Across mainland Southeast Asia, the Buddha is depicted sitting, standing and reclining – all representations of moments in his life that act as visual parables or sermons. In Vietnam, representations of the Buddha are more reminiscent of Chinese religious art. *Naga* (mythical serpent-beings) are found decorating many temple railings in the region; they represent the life-giving power of water.

In Indonesia, Malaysia, Brunei and the Philippines, Islamic art and architecture intermingle with Hindu and animist traditions. Every town in Malaysia has a grand fortressed mosque with an Arabic minaret and Moorish tile work. Indonesia is also home to Borobudur, a Buddhist monument that complements the temples of Angkor in religious splendour.

The literary epic of the Ramayana serves as cultural fodder for traditional art, dance and shadow puppetry throughout the region. In this fantastic tale, Prince Rama (an incarnation of the Hindu god Vishnu) falls in love with beautiful Sita and wins her hand in marriage by completing the challenge of stringing a magic bow. Before the couple can live in peace, Rama is banished from his kingdom and his wife is kidnapped by Ravana. With the help of the monkey king, Hanuman, Sita is rescued, but a great battle ensues. Rama and his allies defeat Ravana and restore peace and goodness to the land.

ENVIRONMENT

The Land

Diverse and fertile, this tropical landmass spans the easternmost range of the Himalayas, which reaches through northern Myanmar, Thailand, Laos and Vietnam; the rich flood plains of the mighty Mekong River; and the scattered archipelagos of Indonesia and the Philippines, made by crashing tectonic plates and exploding volcanoes.

Singapore contains a patch of primary rainforest in its urban core.

Indonesia and the Philippines, the world's largest island chains, together contain more than 20,000 islands, some of them uninhabited. The Philippines has 11 active volcanoes; Indonesia has at least 120. While the fiery exhausts destroy homes and forests, the ashen remains of the earth's inner core creates fertile farmland.

More regulative than the seasonal temperature is the seasonal deposit of rain. When the rains come, the rivers transform from smooth mirrors to watery bulldozers sweeping towards the sea. In the rainy season, the dry deciduous forests that occupy central mainland Southeast Asia spring to life. The tropical rainforests of the Malay peninsula, Sumatra and Borneo get two monsoon seasons, and like sponges they soak up the moisture to feed their dense canopy and limblike tendrils.

Monsoon forests occur in regions with a dry season of at least three months; most trees are deciduous, shedding their leaves in an attempt to conserve water. Rainforests occur in areas where rain falls more than nine months a year.

Living as a parasite in the thick jungles, the leafless plant rafflesia sprouts what looks like a cabbage head, which opens some nine months later to reveal one of the world's largest flowers – and an unrivalled putrid scent. Other plant species include a huge variety of bamboo and orchids. One of the region's most famous exports, teak, grows in the monsoon forests of Myanmar.

Much of the landmass of Southeast Asia is covered with a thick layer of limestone, the erosion of which yields distinctive limestone towers known as karsts. Fine examples can be found in Indonesia, Malaysia, Thailand and Vietnam.

Coastal areas of Southeast Asia are famous around the world for their blonde sandy beaches and protective barriers of coral reefs. Part of the region's coastline is protected by the Gulf of Thailand, a shallow body of water taming the hulking mass of the greater ocean. But the real power of the sea can be felt in Indonesia, where the Indian Ocean hammers at the landmass, creating barrel waves and destructive walls of water. The land's primary defence against ocean invasions is the mangrove forest or dune forests, which grow along the high-tide line, and consist of palms, hibiscus, casuarinas and other tree varieties that can withstand high winds and waves.

Wildlife

Tigers, elephants, monkeys, and Sumatran and Javan rhinoceroses once reigned over the region's forests. Today, these animals are facing extinction due to habitat loss and poaching. Of the 'celebrity' species, monkeys and, to a lesser extent, elephants are the forest dwellers visitors are most likely to meet, although most encounters are in domesticated settings. Found in Sumatra and Kalimantan, the orang-utan is the only great ape species outside of Africa.

There are numerous bird species in Southeast Asia: Indonesia's Papua alone has more than 600 species; Thailand has more than 1000, making up an estimated 10% of the world's total. Parts of Southeast Asia are flyover zones for migratory species, and their arrival often heralds the approach of the monsoons. The Borneo rainforests boast a stunning array of birdlife, from the turkey-sized hornbill, represented in local mythology and art, to ground-dwelling pheasants, prized by ancient Chinese traders for their plumage. Many parts of the Indonesian jungle are so thick and remote that scientists have yet to explore and catalogue the resident flora and fauna.

Some species of tropical reptiles have successfully adapted to living in the human environment. The ubiquitous geckos have adopted human habitats as their hunting grounds; they are frequently spotted catching bugs around fluorescent lights. The shy tookay is more frequently heard than seen: in rural areas the lizard croaks its name again and again, and the number of recitations has prophetic significance to the local people. Perhaps the star of the Southeast Asian animal theatre is the Komodo dragon, the world's largest lizard, which is found only on the Indonesian island of Komodo and a few neighbouring islands. The monitor lizard, a smaller cousin of the Komodo dragon, hangs out in the cool shade of the Malaysian jungles.

National Parks

In recent years there has been a huge increase in the amount of land set aside across Southeast Asia as national parks and wildlife sanctuaries, but these protected areas are often undermined by commercial logging interests and inadequate funding for conservation enforcement.

Thailand leads the way with an astonishing 13% of land and sea under protection, one of the world's highest ratios (compare this figure with France at 4.2% and the USA at 10.5%). Indonesia and Malaysia also boast fairly extensive national park systems. Laos remains one of the most environmentally undisturbed countries in the region, in part because of its lack of development and resource extraction, and low population density.

Southeast Asia's national parks play an ever increasing role in the region's tourism industry. Some parks are relatively undisturbed with little infrastructure, but in parks such as Thailand's marine islands, development and profit outstrip environmental protection.

Environmental Issues

Environmental degradation is immediately tangible in Southeast Asia: smoke fills the air as the forests are cleared for more beach bungalows or small-scale farms; major cities are choked with smog and pollution; the waterways are clogged with plastic bags and soft-drink cans; and raw sewage is dumped into turquoise waters. Southeast Asia also faces huge challenges from its growing population and increased energy consumption; projections estimate that, at the current pace, Southeast Asia's total carbon-dioxide emissions will increase fourfold by 2030.

More shipping passes through the Strait of Melaka than the Panama Canal and Suez Canal combined.

LAND

The last half of the 20th century saw massive deforestation in Southeast Asia through logging and slash-and-burn agriculture. Indonesia, which contains 10% of the world's remaining tropical forests, is estimated to be losing up to 3 million hectares of forest per year. Forests in all of the Southeast Asian countries are disappearing at similarly alarming rates, earning the region the dubious title of a 'hot spot' for deforestation.

Habitat loss and poaching take a huge toll on Southeast Asia's biodiversity. As in other parts of the world, large mammals – including tigers, elephants and orang-utans – are the most visible and often the most critically endangered species. The number of plant species lost is probably higher, but precise figures are unavailable because science has yet to catalogue all that the forests have to offer.

WATER

Southeast Asia's coral reefs are regarded as the world's most diverse, holding more than 600 species of coral. However, increased coastal activity and global temperature changes mean scientists are concerned that the majority of the region's reefs are in danger of extinction.

The major culprits include runoff from rampant coastal development, dumping of untreated sewage, damage by fishing nets and anchors, and dynamite and cyanide fishing. Careless divers are also fingered for stepping on, and in turn destroying, coral formations. In recent years, some of the governments of Southeast Asia have made efforts to preserve their reefs by establishing marine parks and other protected zones; however, enforcement is spotty at best.

Mangrove forests along the coasts have also suffered. Countries such as the Philippines, Thailand and Cambodia have each been losing approximately 2000 sq km of mangrove forest per year. Much of this forest is being cleared for prawn farming and tourism development, but pollution also plays a role.

As the region continues to urbanize, the pressures on the environment will grow – indeed, the pace of building commercial enterprises often exceeds municipal infrastructure such as sewage treatment and garbage removal.

RELIGION

The dominant religions of Southeast Asia have absorbed many of the traditional animistic beliefs of spirits, ancestor worship and the power of the celestial planets in bringing about good fortune. Southeast Asia's spiritual connection to the realm of magic and miracles commands more respect, even among intellectual circles, than the remnants of paganism in Western Christianity: Thais erect spirit houses in front of their homes, ethnic Chinese set out daily offerings to their ancestors, and Indonesians offer prayers to the volcano spirits.

Master storyteller VS Naipaul profiles the devout of Malaysia and Indonesia in *Beyond Belief: Islamic Excursions among the Converted Peoples.*

Buddhism

The sedate smile of the Buddhist statues decorating the landscapes and temples reflects the nature of the religion in Southeast Asia. Religious devotion within the Buddhist countries is highly individualistic, omnipresent and nonaggressive, with many daily rituals rooted in the indigenous religions of ancestor worship.

Buddhism begins with the story of an Indian prince named Siddhartha Gautama in the 6th century BC, who left his life of privilege at the age of 29 on a quest to find the truth. After years of experimentation and ascetic practices, he meditated under a Bodhi Tree for 49 days, reaching final emancipation and breaking the cycle of birth, death and rebirth. He returned as Buddha, the 'Awakened One', to teach the 'middle way' between extremes. Passion, desire, love and hate are regarded as extremes in Asia, so Buddhism counsels that constant patience, detachment, and renouncing desire for worldly pleasures and expectations brings peace and liberation from suffering.

Thailand, Cambodia, Laos and Myanmar practise Theravada Buddhism (Teaching of the Elders), which travelled to the region via Sri Lanka. Vietnam adopted Mahayana (Greater Vehicle) Buddhism, which is also found in Tibet, China and Japan. One of the major theological differences between the two types of Buddhism lies in the outcome of a devout life. In Theravada, followers strive to obtain nirvana (release from the cycle of existence), which is accomplished over the course of many reincarnations, the final one of which is as a member of the monastic order. In Mahayana, a layperson can become a bodhisattva (one who has almost reached nirvana but renounces it in order to help others attain it) within a single lifetime. The artistic expressions of temple architecture and sculpture create the greatest cultural differences between the Theravada Buddhist countries; similarly, religious art and temples in Vietnam favour Chinese influences over those of its Theravada neighbours.

Islam

Islam in Southeast Asia bears much of the region's hallmark passivity, lacking the fervour that results from religious persecution. Trade played an important role in the introduction of the religion to the region, with Southeast Asians converting to Islam to join a brotherhood of spice traders and to escape the inflexible caste system of the previous Hindu empires. The mystical Sufi sect of Islam also played an important role in spreading Islamic belief through Malaysia, Indonesia, parts of the Philippines and southern Thailand.

Revealed by the Prophet Mohammed in the 7th century, and meaning 'Submission' in Arabic, Islam states the duty of every Muslim is to submit to Allah (God). This profession of faith is the first of the five pillars of Islam; the other four are to pray five times a day, give alms to the poor, fast during Ramadan and make the pilgrimage to Mecca.

A type of Sharia'a (Islamic law) is in effect in the Indonesian province of Aceh, and in some areas of Java and Sulawesi. It is also in effect in Malaysia, but it is only enforced for Muslim Malays. Traditionally, Southeast Asian Muslim women were never cloistered, but headscarves have proliferated in recent years. While the traditional Muslim cultures retain many animistic beliefs and practices, there are periodic attempts to purge Islam of its pagan past, especially in Indonesia.

More recommended reading: *What the Buddha Taught* by Walpola Rahula, and *Living Faith: Inside the Muslim World of Southeast Asia* by Steve Raymer.

Muslim independence movements affecting southern Thailand and the southern Philippines are considered to be more economic than jihadist; typically the movements are in the poorest parts of the respective countries, virtually ignored by the majority government.

Christianity

Catholicism was introduced to Vietnam by the French, to the Philippines by the Spanish and to East Timor by the Portuguese. The Philippines adeptly juggle Spanish, American and Chinese traditions in Catholic festivals; at Christmas, for example, Chinese red lanterns decorate homes, families attend midnight Mass and carollers go from house to house. Parts of Indonesia are also Christian due to the efforts of Western missionary groups.

Hinduism

Hinduism ruled the spiritual lives of Southeast Asians more than 1500 years ago, and the great Hindu empires of Angkor and Srivijaya built grand monuments to their pantheon of gods. The primary representations of the multiple faces of the one omnipresent god are Brahma, the creator; Vishnu, the preserver; and Shiva, the destroyer or reproducer. All three gods are usually shown with four arms, but Brahma has the added advantage of four heads to represent his all-seeing presence. Although Buddhism and Islam have filtered across the continent, Hinduism has managed to survive on the island of Bali. Within the last 100 years, the influx of Indian labourers to Southeast Asia has bolstered the religion's followers.

Brunei Darussalam

HIGHLIGHTS

- **Kampung Ayer** – checking out the heart and soul of the capital from the Sungai Brunei (p47)
- **Royal Regalia Museum** – finding the answer to the question of what you give the man who has everything (p46)
- **Omar Ali Saifuddien Mosque** – savouring the otherworldly appearance of this mosque as it floats over its surrounding lagoon (p46)
- **Ulu Temburong National Park** – trekking in the pristine rainforests of this national park (p51)
- **Off the beaten track** – taking a fantastic speedboat ride through *nipa*-lined waterways to Bangar (p48)

FAST FACTS

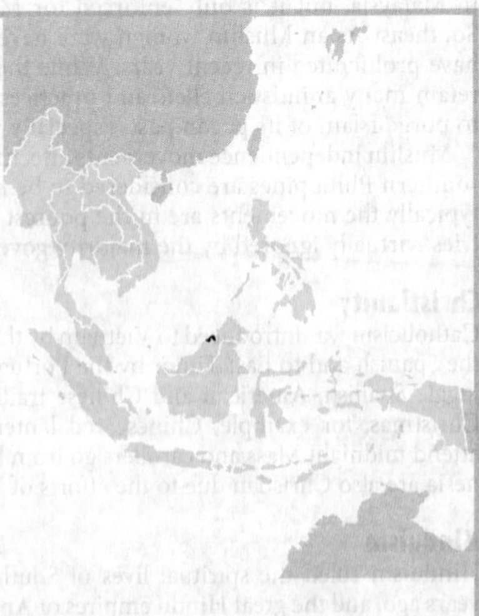

- **Budget** US$30 to US$40 a day
- **Capital** Bandar Seri Begawan (BSB)
- **Costs** cheap room B$30, cheap meal B$4, local bus ride B$1
- **Country code** ☎ 673
- **Languages** Malay, English
- **Money** US$1 = B$1.51 (Brunei dollar)
- **Phrases** *selamat pagi* (good morning), *selamat petang* (good afternoon), *selamat jalan* (goodbye), *terima kasih* (thank you)
- **Population** 375,000
- **Time** GMT + eight hours
- **Visas** not needed for citizens of the UK, Germany, New Zealand or the US; most others get a 14-day visa on arrival

TRAVEL HINT

Fill up on cheap food at night markets, but be warned that the nutritional value will often be minimal.

OVERLAND ROUTES

From Brunei you can travel west into Sarawak and east into another fraction of Sarawak and on to Sabah. Both Sabah and Sarawak are Malaysian states (Malaysian Borneo, to be exact).

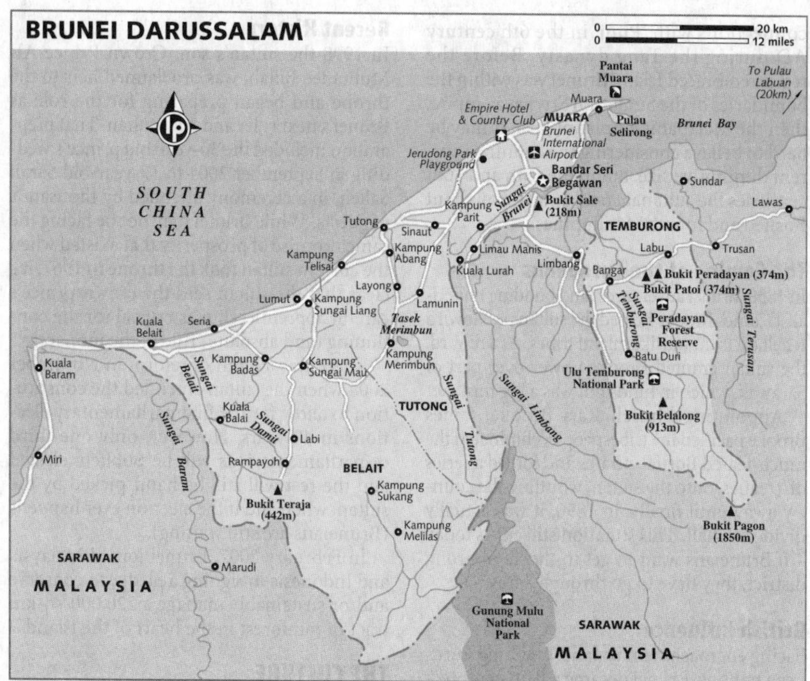

The last remnants of an empire that once included all of Borneo and the southwest Philippines, Brunei is now one of the smallest countries on earth – two tiny slivers of land lodged in the northern coast of Sarawak. This tiny country is blessed with some of the largest oil fields in Southeast Asia and, perhaps not surprisingly, one of the wealthiest rulers on earth. Thanks to these underground riches, Brunei has been able to spare most of its above-ground resources, and the country boasts some of the most intact primary rainforest in all of Borneo.

Chances are this little country will surprise you, for it is neither the mini Dubai nor the strict Muslim theocracy that most people expect. Instead, it is a rather relaxed and even charming little corner of Borneo with enough attractions to make it an interesting stop between Sabah and Sarawak. First there is the capital of Bandar Seri Begawan (BSB), with its soaring mosques and picturesque water villages. Then there is the aforementioned rainforest, which is best experienced in the fine Ulu Temburong National Park. Beyond these, there is a thrilling boat ride between the capital and Bangar, one of the highlights of Borneo.

CURRENT EVENTS

From the outside, Brunei appears to be an immensely wealthy country with few socio-economic problems: all local education and medical treatment is free, there's no income tax and the government loans cash to all prospective home buyers. But the sources of the sultanate's financial contentment – oil and natural gas – are predicted to run out in the next few decades, and when this happens it will have a profound effect on how the next generation of Bruneians live and work. The government, overseen by Sultan Sir Hassanal Bolkiah, is beginning to prepare for this by concentrating on the development of tourism and aquaculture industries, as well as investing widely abroad. How this will allow Bruneians to live in the manner to which they've become accustomed remains to be seen.

HISTORY

Early Years

The first recorded references to Brunei are in documents regarding China's trading connections with 'Puni' in the 6th century AD during the Tang dynasty. Before the region embraced Islam, Brunei was within the boundaries of the Sumatran Srivijaya empire, then the Majapahit empire of Java. It may be hard to believe considering the country's current diminutive size, but in the 15th and 16th centuries the sultanate held sway throughout Borneo and into the Philippines.

The Coming of the Europeans

In 1838, British adventurer (and budding imperialist) James Brooke helped the sultan put down a rebellion from warlike inland tribes. As a reward, the sultan granted Brooke power over part of Sarawak, which in hindsight was a big mistake.

Appointing himself Raja Brooke, James Brooke pacified the tribespeople, eliminated the much-feared Borneo pirates and forced a series of 'treaties' onto the sultan, whittling the country away until finally, in 1890, it was actually divided in half. This situation still exists today – if Bruneians want to get to the Temburong district, they have to go through Sarawak.

British Influence

Facing encroachment by land-grabbing European nations, Brunei became a British protectorate in 1888. But it got its own back when oil was discovered in 1929. The development of offshore oil fields in the 1960s allowed Brunei to flourish. In 1984 Sultan Sir Hassanal Bolkiah, the 29th of his line, led his country somewhat reluctantly into independence from Britain. He celebrated in typically grandiose style by building a US$350 million palace.

Currency Crisis & Scandals

The Asian crisis of 1997 (when Thailand's currency nose-dived after too many years of unsustainable growth, sparking similar recessions across Southeast Asia) was a wake-up call for Brunei, with the sultan's personal fortune being considerably depleted. But the greatest shock to the country was delivered by the sultan's younger brother, Prince Jefri, who around the same time apparently managed to go on a US$16 billion spending spree. This included gambling debts that totalled nearly US$25 million. He was eventually reeled in by his brother and forced to hold an auction in 2001, where many of his prized possessions, including gold-plated toilet-roll holders and a helicopter flight simulator, went under the hammer.

Recent History

In 1998 the sultan's son, Crown Prince Al-Muhtadee Billah, was proclaimed heir to the throne and began preparing for the role as Brunei's next ruler and 30th sultan. That preparation included the 30-year-old prince's wedding in September 2004 to 17-year-old Sarah Salleh, in a ceremony attended by thousands of guests. While Brunei may not be facing the same promise of prosperity that existed when the current sultan took the throne in 1967, it's clear that the sultan sees the crown prince's careful apprenticeship as crucial for the continuing (and absolute) rule of the monarchy.

There was a whiff of reform in November 2004 when the sultan amended the constitution to allow for the first parliamentary elections in 40 years. However, only one-third of parliamentarians will be publicly elected and the rest will still be hand-picked by the sultan, when and if the election ever happens (Bruneians are still waiting).

In February 2007, Brunei joined Malaysia and Indonesia in signing a pledge to conserve and/or sustainably manage a 220,000-sq-km tract of rainforest in the heart of the island.

THE CULTURE

Brunei is the most observant Islamic country in Southeast Asia. The sale of alcohol was banned in 1991, stricter dress codes were introduced and, in 1992, Melayu Islam Beraja (MIB; the national ideology that stresses Malay culture, Islam and monarchy) became a compulsory subject in schools. The country is also ruled by an Islamic monarchy. The sultan is head of the religion of the country, and holds the three key cabinet positions: prime minister, defence minister and finance minister.

However, don't expect to find some grim Southeast Asian enclave of fundamentalism. Bruneians enjoy all the material comforts of the modern age and harbour an international perspective and openness towards visitors.

Overall, Bruneian customs, beliefs and pastimes are very similar, if not identical, to

LEGAL AGE

In Brunei:

- you can begin driving at 18
- heterosexual sex is legal at 14 for males and 16 for females

MUST READ

Green Days in Brunei, by Bruce Sterling, is a classic cyberpunk short story (albeit less punkish than the work of contemporaries such as William Gibson), in which programmer Turner Choi slowly comes to grips with this multiracial society and, in the process, himself. You can read it in the collection of Sterling's stories called *Crystal Express*.

those of the Malays of western Malaysia (see p416). *Adat* (customary law) governs many local ceremonies, particularly royal ceremonies and formal state occasions.

People of Malay heritage and indigenous Kedayan, Tutong, Belait, Bisayah, Dusun and Murut peoples make up approximately 67% of the 375,000-strong population. Iban, Kelabit and other tribes contribute to around 6%, and people of Chinese heritage account for 15% of the population. Westerners, Thais, Filipinos, Indonesians, Indians and Bangladeshis – generally the population of temporary workers – make up the rest.

RELIGION

Although Brunei is a strict Muslim country, with a Ministry of Religious Affairs that fosters and promotes Islam, only 67% of the population is actually Muslim. Buddhists and Christians make up 13% and 10% of the population respectively, and 10% of people have kept their indigenous beliefs.

ARTS

Traditional arts have all but disappeared in modern Brunei. In its heyday, the sultanate was a source of brassware in the form of gongs, cannons and household vessels (such as kettles and betel containers) that were prized throughout Borneo and beyond. The lost-wax technique used to cast bronze declined with the old fortunes of the Brunei sultanate. Brunei's silversmiths were also celebrated. *Jong sarat* sarongs, using gold thread, are still prized for ceremonial occasions, and the art of weaving has survived.

ENVIRONMENT

The Land

Brunei consists of two areas, separated by the Limbang district of Sarawak, and covers a total area of just 5765 sq km. The western part of Brunei contains the main towns: BSB, the oil town of Seria (where the sultanate's billionth barrel was filled in 1991) and the commercial town of Kuala Belait. The eastern part of the country, the rural Temburong district, is much less developed. Away from the coast, Brunei is mainly jungle, with approximately 78% of the country still covered by forest.

Wildlife

Wildlife species found in Brunei are similar to those found in the rest of Borneo. Proboscis monkeys, gibbons, hornbills, deer, monitor lizards, crocodiles and the rare clouded leopard live in the rainforest.

National Parks

Brunei has several recreational parks and forest reserves, plus one national park – the superb Ulu Temburong National Park, a 500-sq-km swathe of protected primary rainforest.

TRANSPORT

GETTING THERE & AWAY

Air

Brunei's sole airport is 10km from the centre of the capital. The national airline, **Royal Brunei Airlines** (code BI; ☎ 221 2222; www.bruneiair.com), has direct flights between BSB and major Asian destinations such as Jakarta, Bangkok, Hong Kong, Kuala Lumpur and Manila, as well as flights to Kota Kinabalu in Sabah. **Malaysia Airlines** (code MH; ☎ 222 4141; www.malaysiaairlines.com), **Singapore Airlines** (code SQ; ☎ 224 4901; www.singaporeair.com) and **Thai Airways International** (THAI, code TG; ☎ 224 2991; www.thaiair.com) also fly into BSB.

Land

The main overland route to the west is between Kuala Belait in Brunei and Miri in Sarawak, which is a straightforward journey by bus or taxi; see p50 for more information.

DEPARTURE TAX

The departure tax at Brunei International Airport is B$5 for flights to Sabah and Sarawak and B$12 to west Malaysia, Singapore and all other destinations. It must be paid in Brunei dollars.

DID YOU KNOW?

Brunei has a cattle station in Australia that is larger than Brunei itself. The 5986-sq-km station in Willaroo, in the Northern Territory, supplies Brunei with beef and other meat products. The live cattle are brought direct to Brunei from Darwin and slaughtered according to halal practices.

It's also possible to travel between BSB and Limbang and Lawas in Sarawak and onward to Kota Kinabalu in Sabah, but it's an extremely time-consuming and fiddly journey. For details on this journey, see p51.

If you're heading to/from Limbang or Kota Kinabalu, we recommend going by boat (see p49).

Sea

There are boats between Brunei and Pulau Labuan in Sabah and Limbang in Sarawak. These boats operate from the Muara Ferry Terminal, 25km northeast of BSB. There's also a boat service running between BSB itself and Limbang. For details on these services, see p49.

GETTING AROUND

Boat

The only significant boat service within Brunei connects BSB with Bangar in the Temburong district (see p48).

Most short water-taxi trips cost around B$2, and you can hire your own water taxi for B$20 to B$25 per hour. To flag one down, head out to one of the many jetties jutting onto the river in and around BSB, and simply wave. The city's waterfront is filled with buzzing water taxis, even at night.

Bus

Brunei isn't a huge place, but outside BSB and off the main routes it's hard to get around without a car. The local bus system within and around BSB is very good and gets you to most places for B$1 to B$2. However, services stop at 6pm and after that you'll have to rely on expensive taxis (if you can find one).

Car

Renting a car is the easiest way to get around Brunei, and Bruneian drivers are quite sane by Southeast Asian standards. However, it's expensive (rental starts from B$70 per day) and involves a steep learning curve if you're not used to driving on the left-hand side.

Hitching

Hitching is remarkably easy in Brunei. Chances are if you stick out your thumb you'll get a ride instantly, and it's a great way to meet local people. Women travellers, however, should take extreme care and consider going by other means.

BANDAR SERI BEGAWAN

pop 81,500

Bandar Seri Begawan (usually called BSB or Bandar) is the capital of Brunei and is most notable for the absence of the mayhem that most travellers in Southeast Asia expect to greet them upon arrival. In fact, central BSB introduces itself to the traveller as a quiet, pleasant, greenery-dotted city with a low skyline that's decorated with minarets and neat arrangements of buildings. But despite the city's rather sterile atmosphere and almost total lack of nightlife, it's still an interesting place to spend a day or two.

To start with, you can visit the Royal Regalia Museum and then wander over to the nearby Omar Ali Saifuddien Mosque. Then, you can take a bus down to the Brunei Museum and check out the Islamic Art Gallery contained therein. Finally, as another brilliant Borneo sunset starts to set the sky on fire, you can hail a water taxi and cruise around the water villages.

ORIENTATION

The centre of BSB lies at the confluence of the Sungai Brunei and Sungai Kedayan, and is compact enough to explore in about an hour. Jl Sultan runs down the middle of the city and forms its main artery. It's also home to the major banks, the post office, airline offices, coffee shops and some good restaurants, as well as the fine Royal Regalia Museum. The western edge of the city is marked by the magnificent Omar Ali Saifuddien Mosque. The Brunei Museum is about 6km southeast of the city centre, on Jl Residency, overlooking the Sungai Brunei and accessible by bus or taxi. With the exception of this museum, most of the sights are in the city centre and within easy walking distance of the main hotels.

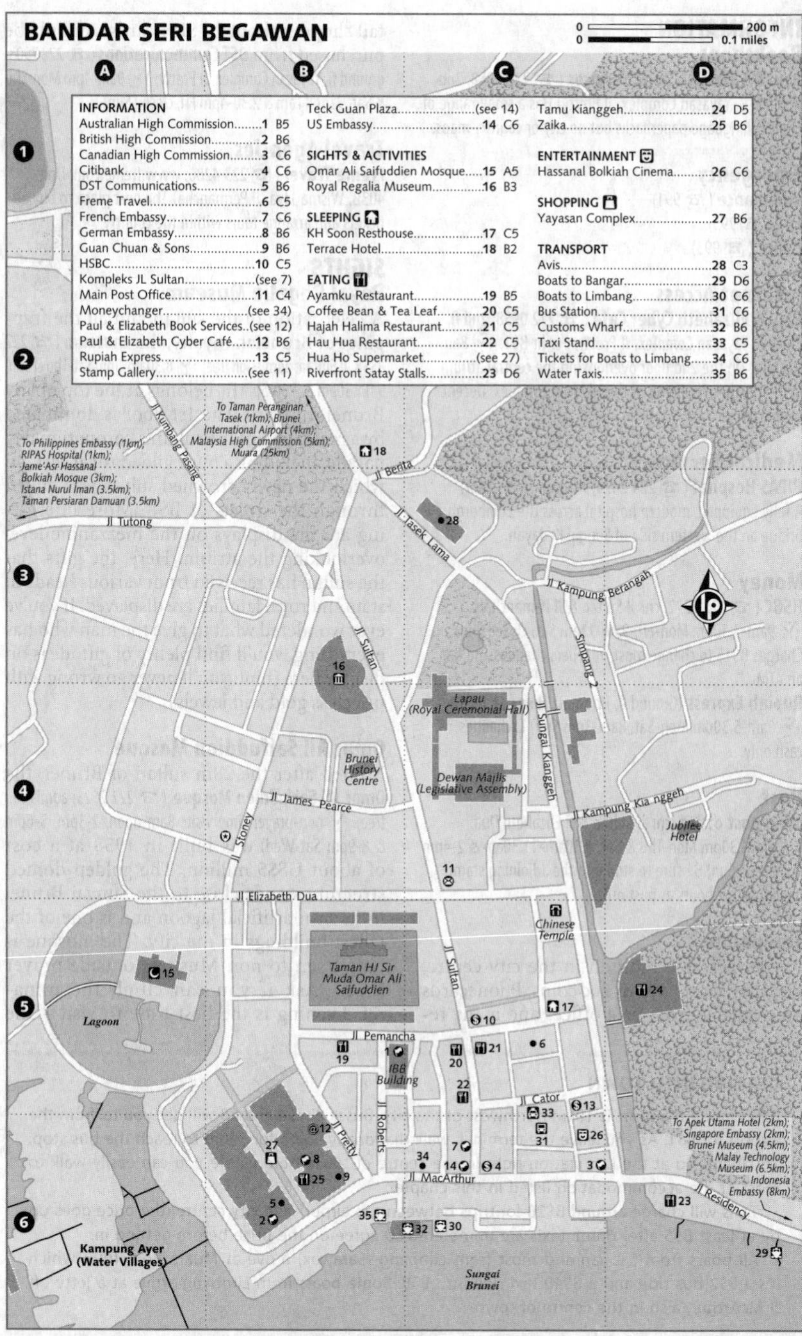
BANDAR SERI BEGAWAN
0 200 m
0 0.1 miles
A
B
C
D
1
2
3
4
5
6
INFORMATION
Australian High Commission........1 B5
British High Commission..............2 B6
Canadian High Commission.........3 C6
Citibank...4 C6
DST Communications....................5 B6
Freme Travel..................................6 C5
French Embassy.............................7 C6
German Embassy............................8 B6
Guan Chuan & Sons.......................9 B6
HSBC...10 C5
Kompleks JL Sultan...................(see 7)
Main Post Office..........................11 C4
Moneychanger.........................(see 34)
Paul & Elizabeth Book Services..(see 12)
Paul & Elizabeth Cyber Café.......12 B6
Rupiah Express.............................13 C5
Stamp Gallery..........................(see 11)
Teck Guan Plaza.......................(see 14)
US Embassy..................................14 C6
SIGHTS & ACTIVITIES
Omar Ali Saifuddien Mosque.....15 A5
Royal Regalia Museum..............16 B3
SLEEPING
KH Soon Resthouse....................17 C5
Terrace Hotel.............................18 B2
EATING
Ayamku Restaurant....................19 B5
Coffee Bean & Tea Leaf..............20 C5
Hajah Halima Restaurant............21 C5
Hau Hua Restaurant...................22 C5
Hua Ho Supermarket..............(see 27)
Riverfront Satay Stalls...............23 D6
Tamu Kianggeh...........................24 D5
Zaika..25 B6
ENTERTAINMENT
Hassanal Bolkiah Cinema............26 C6
SHOPPING
Yayasan Complex.......................27 B6
TRANSPORT
Avis..28 C3
Boats to Bangar..........................29 D6
Boats to Limbang........................30 C6
Bus Station.................................31 C6
Customs Wharf...........................32 B6
Taxi Stand..................................33 C5
Tickets for Boats to Limbang.......34 C6
Water Taxis................................35 B6
To Taman Peranginan Tasek (1km); Brunei International Airport (4km); Malaysia High Commission (5km); Muara (25km)
To Philippines Embassy (1km); RIPAS Hospital (1km); Jame'Asr Hassanal Bolkiah Mosque (3km); Istana Nurul Iman (3.5km); Taman Persiaran Damuan (3.5km)
Jl Kumbang Pasang
Jl Tutong
Jl Berita
Jl Jasek Lama
Jl Kampung Berangah
Simpang 2
Jl Sultan
Lapau (Royal Ceremonial Hall)
Dewan Majlis (Legislative Assembly)
Jl Sungai Kianggeh
Brunei History Centre
Jl James Pearce
Jl Stoney
Jl Kampung Kia nggeh
Jubilee Hotel
Jl Elizabeth Dua
Chinese Temple
Taman HJ Sir Muda Omar Ali Saifuddien
Lagoon
Jl Pemancha
IBB Building
Jl Cator
Jl Roberts
Jl Pretty
Jl MacArthur
Jl Residency
To Apek Utama Hotel (2km); Singapore Embassy (2km); Brunei Museum (4.5km); Malay Technology Museum (6.5km); Indonesia Embassy (8km)
Kampung Ayer (Water Villages)
Sungai Brunei

INFORMATION

Bookshops

Paul & Elizabeth Book Services (☎ 222 0958; 2nd fl, Block B, Yayasan Complex, Jl Pretty) Has a small range of English-language paperbacks but no city or country maps.

Emergency

Ambulance (☎ 991)
Fire (☎ 995)
Police (☎ 993)

Internet Access

Paul & Elizabeth Cyber Café (☎ 222 0958; 2nd fl, Block B, Yayasan Complex, Jl Pretty; per hr B$1; ⌚ 8am-9.30pm) On the 2nd floor overlooking the central atrium in the northern building of the Yayasan complex. Decent connections.

Medical Services

RIPAS Hospital (☎ 224 2424; Jl Tutong; ⌚ 24hr) A fully equipped, modern hospital across the Edinburgh bridge on the western side of Sungai Kedayan.

Money

HSBC (☎ 225 2222; cnr Jl Sultan & Jl Pemancha; ⌚ 9am-3.30pm Mon-Fri, 9am-11am Sat, closed Sun) Charges B$15 to change most travellers cheques and has an ATM.

Rupiah Express (Ground fl, Britannia House, 1 Jl Cator; ⌚ 8am-5.30pm Mon-Sat, 8am-3pm Sun) Exchanges cash only.

Post

Main post office (cnr Jl Sultan & Jl Elizabeth Dua; 8.30am-4.30pm Mon-Thu & Sat, 8.30am-11.30am & 2-4pm Fri, closed Sun) Be sure to stop into the adjoining stamp gallery (same hours as post office).

Telephone

Payphones are common in the city centre, and they accept 10c or 20c coins. Phonecards are available from post offices and many retail shops and hotels. SIM cards can only be purchased from **DST Communications** (☎ 223 2903; ground fl, Yayasan Complex, Jl Pretty; ⌚ 9am-4pm Mon-Thu & Sat, 9am-11am & 2.30-4pm Fri, closed Sun).

Travel Agencies

Freme Travel (☎ 223 4280; www.freme.com; Unit 403B, Wisma Jaya, Jl Permancha) The best place to buy air tickets and arrange tours within the country.

SIGHTS

Royal Regalia Museum

A celebration of the sultan and all the trappings of Bruneian royalty, this **museum** (☎ 222 8358; Jl Sultan; admission free; ⌚ 8.30am-5pm Sat-Thu & Sun, 9-11.30am & 2.30-5pm Fri) belongs at the top of any Brunei itinerary. The 1st floor is dominated by a recreation of the sultan's coronation day parade, including a huge gilded royal cart, on which the newly crowned sultan was pulled through the streets of BSB. More interesting are the displays on the mezzanine level overlooking the atrium. Here, the gifts that the sultan has received from various heads of state and royal families are displayed. If you've ever wondered what to give the man who has everything, you'll find plenty of gift ideas on display here (hint: you'll never go wrong with priceless gold and jewels).

Omar Ali Saifuddien Mosque

Named after the 28th sultan of Brunei, the **Omar Ali Saifuddien Mosque** (☎ 222 2623; admission free; ⌚ non-prayer-time visits 8am-noon, 2-3pm, 5-6pm & 8-9pm Sat-Wed) was built in 1958 at a cost of about US$5 million. The golden-domed structure stands close to the Sungai Brunei in its own artificial lagoon and is one of the tallest buildings in the city. The mosque is only open to non-Muslims outside prayer times. Ask if you can climb the minaret. Evening is the best time to visit – the

GETTING INTO TOWN

BSB's modern airport is 10km northwest of the city. Buses 23, 24 and 38 will get you to/from the airport for B$1. As you leave the terminal, walk diagonally south for 300m to reach the bus stop. You'll end up at the bus station right in the centre of town, from where you can easily walk to most of the accommodation listed in this chapter.

Taxis will charge around B$20 for trips between the airport and city centre (the price goes up by at least B$5 after 6pm); taxis are unmetered so agree on the price before getting in.

All boats from Labuan and most from Limbang (Sarawak) arrive at Muara Port, from which it's a B$2 bus ride and a B$40 taxi ride into BSB. Some boats from Limbang arrive at a jetty off Jl McArthur, also in the centre of town.

illuminated mosque appears to float like an apparition over its lagoon.

Kampung Ayer

The rustic collective of 30 stilt villages on either side of Sungai Brunei is referred to as Kampung Ayer (Water Village). It's home to a population of around 32,000, who pursue a mostly traditional way of life, albeit in prefab dwellings with plumbing, electricity and colour TV.

The best way to see the water villages is from a water taxi, which can be chartered along the waterfront for B$20 per hour (don't worry about finding one – any time a foreign tourist goes anywhere near the waterfront in BSB, a small school of taxi boats forms with eager drivers offering their services). Be sure to ask the driver to stop off at Taman Persiaran Damuan for great views of the sultan's palace.

Late afternoon or early evening is best for a tour, not only because the midday heat is unbearable, but also to enjoy the sunset over the city. If there's any wind about, you will see kites come rising out of the *kampung* (kite flying is a popular pastime in Brunei).

Brunei Museum

The **Brunei Museum** (☎ 222 3235; Jl Kota Batu; admission free; ⏲ 9.30am-5pm Sat-Thu & Sun, 9-11.30am & 2.30-4.30pm Fri) is 6km east of central BSB, sitting on a bluff overlooking the Sungai Brunei. The main building contains the excellent Islamic Art Gallery, which has some wonderful illuminated (decorated) copies of the Koran, as well as an incredible model of the Dome of the Rock executed in mother of pearl and abalone shell.

In the same building, the Oil and Gas Gallery is surprisingly interesting. It answers all your questions about how they get the stuff from under the ground to your nearest petrol pump. Finally, don't miss the Brunei Traditional Culture Gallery, also in the main building. It has good exhibits on all aspects of Bruneian culture, including a picture of two young fellows enjoying a spot of grass sledding – a sport we didn't know existed until we visited this museum.

Descend the stairs from the car park behind the museum, then turn right to reach the **Malay Technology Museum** (admission free; ⏲ 9.30am-5pm Sat-Thu & Sun, 9-11.30am & 2.30-4.30pm Fri). A pair of rooms here have interesting life-sized re-creations of stilt houses with accompanying information on traditional cultures. The rest of the large building, however, is strangely empty.

To get to the museum, take bus 39 from the bus terminal in downtown BSB.

Other Attractions

A fine example of Islamic architecture is **Jame'Asr Hassanal Bolkiah Mosque** (☎ 223 8741; Jl Hassan Bolkiah, Gadong; admission free; ⏲ 8am-noon, 2-3pm, 5-6pm & 8-9pm Sat-Wed), the largest mosque in the country. This fabulous sight is in Gadong, a few kilometres northwest of town. Equally photogenic is the **Istana Nurul Iman** (☎ 222 9988; Jl Tutong), the sultan's magnificent palace, which looks particularly impressive when illuminated at night. The Istana is open to the public only at the end of the fasting month of Ramadan and is 2.5km out of town. The best vantage points are from the river and **Taman Persiaran Damuan**, a landscaped park nearby. From BSB, take a water taxi there in the early evening and get off at the park.

Taman Peranginan Tasek is a beautiful forested area with waterfalls and trails. In the early morning or late evening, you may be lucky enough to see some proboscis monkeys. Walk or take a bus past the Terrace Hotel. After passing two sets of traffic lights, turn right and you'll see the entrance.

SLEEPING

Most of BSB's accommodation options are located in the city centre. Unlike the rest of Borneo, there are few budget options.

KH Soon Resthouse (☎ 222 2052; email khsoon_resthouse_brunei@hotmail.com; 2nd fl, 140 Jl Pemancha; s B$30-35, d B$35-39; ❄) This simple guesthouse is a decent budget choice for those seeking a central location. Rooms are spartan but huge and an extra B$5 snags you an attached bathroom. If all you need is a clean place to lay your head in BSB, this should suit.

Apek Utama Hotel (☎ 222 0808; Simpang 229, Jl Kota Batu, Kampung Pintu Malim; r from B$30; ❄) This basic hotel has acceptable rooms with fan or air-con. The management is friendly and a good source of information on travelling around Brunei. The downside is the somewhat inconvenient location: it's 3km east of town, accessed by bus 39 or by water taxi. Note that buses stop running at 6pm, so plan accordingly.

Terrace Hotel (☎ 224 3554; www.terracebrunei.com; Jl Tasek Lama; r from B$60; ❄ 🏊) Since you may only be in town for a day or two, consider spending a little more to enjoy the comforts of this excellent midrange hotel. Rooms are clean and well taken care of, and there's a great little swimming pool and wi-fi. There's also a decent restaurant on the ground floor. Deluxe rooms cost about B$10 more than standard rooms, but are well worth the price.

EATING

Hajah Halima Restaurant (☎ 223 4803; 54 Jl Sultan; meals from B$2; ⏰ breakfast, lunch & dinner) This popular and friendly Indian Muslim place has just about everything the traveller could ask for: good coffee, tea, fresh juice and roti in the morning, and great biryani and set meals for lunch and dinner, not to mention great *mee goreng* (fried noodles) and *murtabak* (*roti* stuffed with meat or vegetables). It's the best of the three similar joints on this part of Jl Sultan. There is no sign – look for the blue paint around the entrance. It's almost directly opposite the Coffee Bean & Tea Leaf.

Riverfront satay stalls (Jl Residency; ⏰ noon to early evening) This collection of satay and drink vendors right on the riverfront offer one of life's great combinations: satay and fresh coconut juice. You can get 10 sticks of chicken or beef satay here for about B$2.50. A fresh coconut will add another B$1.50. This is a great place to watch the sunset – when the colours really start working, why not jump into a waiting water taxi and enjoy the view from sea level?

Ayamku Restaurant (Jl Permancha; meals from B$3.50; ⏰ lunch & dinner) Brunei's answer to KFC, this may be the cheapest place in town to get a meal. You can get a big piece of fried chicken, some rice and a drink for about B$3. And, the chicken is surprisingly good.

Hau Hua (☎ 222 5396; 48 Jl Sultan; meals B$10; ⏰ lunch & dinner) This surprisingly good Chinese restaurant does all the standard Chinese dishes and a few lesser known ones, like broccoli with crab meat. There is an excellent drinks menu that includes daily changing specials and good fresh juices.

Coffee Bean & Tea Leaf (cnr Jl Sultan & Jl Permancha; coffee drinks from B$3; ⏰ breakfast, lunch & dinner) Travellers and expats alike are drawn like moths to the invisible waves of wi-fi and the aroma of good coffee emanating from this downtown caffeine emporium. Drop by in the afternoon and you'll run into about half of the Western tourists in BSB at any one time.

Zaika (☎ 223 1155; Block C, Yayasan Complex; meals from B$15; ⏰ lunch & dinner) This dimly lit northern Indian restaurant is the place to go for a proper sit-down meal in BSB. The kitchen does well with favourites such as kebabs, nan bread and standard curries, but its attempts at more creative dishes are sometimes less successful.

Tamu Kianggeh (Jl Sungai Kianggeh; ⏰ breakfast, lunch & dinner) Self-caterers can walk across the canal to this local produce market, where food stalls are sometimes set up.

Hua Ho Supermarket (☎ 223 1120; basement, Yayasan Complex, Jl Pretty; ⏰ 10am-10pm) Housed in the basement of the Yayasan complex, look for shrink-wrapped durian here (just don't try sneaking it into your hotel room).

ENTERTAINMENT

Hassanal Bolkiha Cinema (Jl Sungai Kianggeh; admission B$4-8) This small cinema screens a variety of Hollywood action films and Hong Kong kung fu movies. It's about the only game in town as far as 'nightlife' goes in BSB.

GETTING THERE & AWAY

Air

See p43 for airlines flying to BSB.

Boat

Boats to/from Bangar (B$6, 45 minutes, roughly one per hour departing BSB from 7am to 1pm) operate from the jetty just east of the riverfront satay stalls, along Jl Residency. Bangar is the starting point for attractions in Brunei's Temburong district. Boats generally don't depart until they have enough passengers to warrant the trip, so you might have to wait around for a while.

Even if you do nothing more than grab a quick cup of tea in Bangar and then return to BSB, we highly recommend this journey. The speedboats tear through *nipa*-lined waterways at incredible speeds and you wonder how they manage not to get lost in this watery maze.

GETTING AROUND

Boat

Water taxis are a good way of getting around if your destination is anywhere near the river. You can find them on the waterfront at the southern end of town (or, more likely, they'll find you). Fares for short trips shouldn't cost more than B$2 – don't accept higher rates (the locals certainly don't). Hourly rates should be no more than B$20 and you might be able to negotiate a rate as low as B$15 per hour.

Bus

BSB's reliable bus network operates from 6am to 6pm. The bus station is beneath the multistorey car park on Jl Cator. All trips within BSB proper cost B$1.

An express bus (B$2, 40 minutes) departs from this bus station about once an hour between 7am and 2pm for the Muara Ferry Terminal.

Car

Prices for car rental start at B$75 per day.

Avis (☎ 242 6345; nscsb@brunet.bn; Sheraton Utama Hotel, Jl Tasek Lama; compact cars per day from B$75) will send cars to the airport for those with reservations.

Taxi

Taxis are hard to find in Brunei and you should never count on being able to flag one down on the street. The only place where you can reliably find taxis is outside the bus station on Jl Caor. Otherwise, arrange a taxi through your hotel.

Taxis in BSB are all unmetered and you need to negotiate the fare with the driver. A trip across town will usually cost B$10, but rates can climb by as much as 30% after 6pm.

AROUND BANDAR SERI BEGAWAN

The serene expanses of forest around Bandar Seri Begawan, particularly those located within the protective borders of Ulu Temburong National Park, make for excellent day trips from the Bruneian capital. To the north of the city there are also some nice beaches, a massive amusement park, and a grand hotel that must be seen to be believed.

PANTAI MUARA

Pantai Muara (Muara Beach) is a popular weekend retreat located 2km from Muara town, which is 25km northeast of BSB. The white sand is clean but like many Borneo beaches it's fairly shallow and littered with flotsam and jetsam. If you want solitude, don't go on the weekend.

To get to Muara, take an express bus (B$2) from the bus station in downtown BSB. Once at Muara, bus 33 will take you from Muara town to either Pantai Muara or Pantai Serasa for B$1.

JERUDONG

The Jerudong area to the northwest of BSB has a couple of sites that make decent half-day trips out of the city, particularly for

GETTING TO MALAYSIA

To Pulau Labuan

For those heading north to Kota Kinabalu in Sabah, the easiest way is to go by boat via Pulau Labuan in Sabah. From Muara Port, 25km northeast of BSB, express boats go to Pulau Labuan (B$15, 1½ hours, six departures between 7.30am and 4.40pm). From Pulau Labuan, you can easily travel by boat onward to Kota Kinabalu. Check the ferries link on www.bruneibay.net for the latest schedules from Muara. Passengers are charged B$1 departure tax at the ferry terminal.

For info on getting to BSB from Pulau Labuan see the boxed text, p484.

To Limbang

Boats to Limbang in Sarawak (B$10, 30 minutes) make irregular morning departures from the riverfront along Jl MacArthur, but the service is highly unreliable and departures are often delayed until more passengers turn up. Buy your ticket from the moneychanger along the waterfront (Map p45). An alternative to the boat trip is to catch bus 42, 44 or 48 south to Kuala Lurah (B$1, 30 minutes, last departure 5pm) on the Brunei–Sarawak border. After crossing the **border** (🕓 6am-9pm), you can take another bus (RM5.50) or taxi (RM20) to Limbang.

Note that return boat services from Limbang are as unreliable as those in the other direction and you may have to re-enter Brunei by road; for more on the return trip see the boxed text, p508.

DID YOU KNOW?

The Empire Hotel & Country Club, on the Brunei coast, is said to have cost over US$1 billion, making it the world's most expensive hotel (to build).

those fascinated by ostentatious displays of wealth.

The **Empire Hotel & Country Club** (☎ 241 8999; www.empire.com.bn; Muara-Tutong Rd) is a prominent reminder of Prince Jefri's scandalous spending habits. The palatial Empire cost US$1.1 billion to build, and it shows – from the soaring height of the monumentally lavish atrium to the Jack Nicklaus–designed golf course. While it's true that the hotel has all the subtlety of a Las Vegas casino, it's definitely a spectacle worth seeing. And, as you wander the grounds, you can't help but wonder how they ever expect this place to pay for itself.

Jerudong Park Playground (☎ 261 1894; Jerudong; admission & unlimited rides B$15, or admission B$1 & individual rides B$3; 5pm-midnight Wed-Fri & Sun, 5pm-2am Sat) is a sprawling amusement park which the sultan built as a gift to his people. Divided into two sections, one for older kids and adults, and one for smaller children, it's now in a semi-dormant state – over half of the rides are 'closed for maintenance' (read: closed forever, or, at least until Michael Jackson comes back to stage another concert). This gives the park a rather surreal air, and you may feel like you're living out a child's fantasy of having an amusement park all to yourself (albeit with most of the rides closed). If you go on a weekend, you'll be less lonely and find a few more rides in operation.

Bus 55 travels to Jerudong (B$1) from the BSB bus terminal, passing near the amusement park. From the last stop on the route it's a 25-minute walk along the highway to the Empire Hotel. However, the service inconveniently stops running after 5.30pm. Due to the difficulty of going by bus, we recommend sharing a taxi with some other travellers (the ride costs about B$30 each way).

Some hostels and hotels in BSB can arrange group tours to Jerudong, including stops at the Empire Hotel and the Jerudong Park Playground.

KUALA BELAIT

Buses to/from Sarawak (Miri/Sibu/Kuching etc) operate from this small town near the Sarawak border. There's really no reason to stay here unless you miss your onward connection. The HSBC bank opposite the bus station has an ATM – handy for arrivals from Sarawak.

If you do find yourself in need of a place to stay, the **Sentosa Hotel** (☎ 333 4341; www.bruneisentosahotel.com; 92 Jln McKerron; s/d from B$70/88;) is an excellent midrange hotel. It's just up the street from the bus and taxi stations.

From Kuala Belait there are regular buses to Seria (B$1) and from there frequent services to BSB (B$6). There are also buses to/from Miri and other points in Sarawak.

TEMBURONG

Temburong is the eastern slice of Brunei that is surrounded by a claw of Sarawak. It's a region of lush virgin rainforest that is usually reached by a thrilling speedboat ride from BSB. You can explore Temburong on a tour from BSB (p55), or rock up in Bangar and try to organise things yourself.

Bangar

Bangar is a small town on the banks of Sungai Temburong that seems perpetually half-asleep, even though it's the administrative centre of (and gateway to) the Temburong district.

The **Temburong tourist information centre** (☎ 522 1439; 13 Kedai Rakyat Jati; 8am-noon & 1.30-4.30pm Mon-Sat, 8am-noon Sun) provides useful information and books tours. Exiting the boat wharf in Bangar, turn left and you'll find the information centre in the cinnamon-coloured block of offices just before the road bridge.

The basic **Youth Hostel** (☎ 522 1694, 522 1718; dm B$10) is part of a youth centre and sits in a fenced compound almost directly behind

GETTING TO MALAYSIA

To get to Sarawak from Kuala Belait, take an express bus (B$15, two hours) or a taxi (per car B$50 to B$80) to Miri. Immigration and customs formalities are taken care of on both sides of the Brunei–Sarawak **border** (6am-9pm). For information on crossing the border in the other direction, see the boxed text, p506.

GETTING TO MALAYSIA

Travelling from Bangar (Brunei) to Lawas or Limbang (both in Malaysia) is extremely fiddly, time consuming and expensive. There is no public transport, so private taxis are the only option; drivers congregate near the wharf, or you can ask at the **Temburong tourist information centre** (☎ 522 1439; 13 Kedai Rakyat Jati; 🕑 8am-noon & 1.30-4.30pm Mon-Sat, 8am-noon Sun). Taxis don't have meters and prices must be negotiated.

We'd recommend heading back to Bandar Seri Begawan (BSB) and crossing into Malaysia from there; in particular, those heading on to Kota Kinabalu are advised to travel to Pulau Labuan and to take a boat from there.

If you do go by road, note that border posts are open daily from 6am to 9pm.

Getting to Lawas

If you can find a taxi, the trip from Bangar to the eastern Sarawak border costs around B$30. You may be able to persuade the driver to take you all the way to Lawas, but this will cost around B$80. See p509 for details on doing the trip in the opposite direction.

There are buses from Lawas to Kota Kinabalu (RM20) at 7am and 1pm daily.

Getting to Limbang

A private taxi (if you can find one) from Bangar to the western Sarawak border costs around B$30. If you can persuade your driver to continue on to Limbang, the trip will cost around B$80. See p508 for information on doing the trip in the reverse direction.

the information centre. It offers bunk beds in clean fan-cooled rooms.

Bangar Resthouse (☎ 522 1239; Jl Batang Duri; dm B$15-30; ❄) is a government-run complex with hospitable staff and lots of six-bed rooms, each with attached bathroom, a small fridge and TV. Families or small groups might also consider renting one of the four-person chalets (B$80 per night). From the boat wharf, walk to the bridge, turn right and head 200m to the Jl Batang Duri turn-off – the resthouse is on the corner, signed 'Rumah Persinggahan Keragaan Daerah Temburong'. Bring your own towel and soap.

The first restaurant in the row of shops on your right as you walk from the boat jetty to the information centre, **RR Max Cafe** (1 Kedai Pekan Bangar; meals B$2-6; 🕑 breakfast, lunch & dinner) is a simple *kedai kopi* (coffee shop) that serves a surprisingly good plate of fried noodles and good hot or iced tea to wash it down.

Boats from BSB to Bangar (B$6, 45 minutes, roughly one per hour from 7am to 1pm) operate from the jetty just east of the riverfront satay stalls, along Jl Residency. The last boat back to BSB leaves Bangar at 3.30pm.

Ulu Temburong National Park

The **Ulu Temburong National Park** (admission B$5), with an area of 500 sq km, is surrounded by the Batu Apoi Forest Reserve, which covers most of southern Temburong. One of the many pleasures of visiting this stronghold of primary rainforest is that the only access is by longboat. The park contains an excellent canopy walkway and has simple accommodation in the form of cabins within the park (call the Temburong tourist information centre three days prior to your visit if you want to stay in the park accommodation).

Unfortunately, it's difficult and expensive to visit the park on your own. Access to the park is limited by the availability of the longboats that make the journey to the park from the jetty at Batu Duri (these are usually used by BSB-based tour operators; see p46). If you are on your own and haven't arranged a tour, the best thing to do is to arrive at the information office in Bangar before 9am and ask to join one of the day's tours.

Peradayan Forest Reserve

Fifteen kilometres southeast of Bangar and protected within the **Peradayan Forest Reserve** (admission free) are the peaks of **Bukit Patoi** and **Bukit Peradayan**, which can be reached along walking tracks (bring your own water and trail food). The climb through rainforest to Bukit Patoi (5km, one hour) has fine views and starts at the park entrance. Most walkers descend back down this trail but it's possible to continue over the summit and around to Bukit Peradayan (four hours) on a harder, less distinct path.

The Temburong tourist information centre in Bangar can arrange transport to the reserve. A private car (the only means of getting there), will cost about B$10 each way.

BRUNEI DIRECTORY

ACCOMMODATION

If you're arriving from other countries in Southeast Asia, be prepared for a shock – accommodation in Brunei is expensive. The youth hostel in BSB was closed at the time of research and there is only one truly budget place to stay. Accommodation in Bangar in the Temburong district is reasonably priced. Except for most hostels and the cheapest hotels, room prices will include an attached bathroom.

ACTIVITIES

Besides swimming at a couple of reasonable beaches to the north of BSB (see p49), the only activity of note in Brunei is walking and jungle trekking. At Ulu Temburong National Park and the nearby Peradayan Forest Reserve walkers can stride through undisturbed rainforest and up jungle-covered hills.

BOOKS

For more in-depth coverage of travel in Brunei, grab a copy of Lonely Planet's *Malaysia, Singapore & Brunei* guidebook.

History of Brunei (2002) by Graham Saunders is a thorough, up-to-date history of the sultanate from its beginnings to modern times.

Time and the River (2000) by Prince Mohamed Bolkiah describes the changes to the country as seen through the eyes of the sultan's youngest brother.

By God's Will – A Portrait of the Sultan of Brunei (1989) by Lord Chalfont takes a measured look at the sultan and his dominion.

New World Hegemony in the Malay World (2000) by Geoffrey C Gunn gives an insight into the more contemporary political issues for Brunei and the region.

BUSINESS HOURS

Usual business hours in Brunei:

Banks 9am to 3pm Monday to Friday, 9am to 11am Saturday
Government offices 7.45am-12.15pm and 1.30pm to 4.30pm Monday to Thursday and Saturday
Kedai kopi 7am to 6pm (sometimes 9pm)
Offices 8am to 5pm Monday to Friday, 8am to noon Saturday
Restaurants 11am to 9pm
Shops 10am to 9.30pm

Exceptions to the above hours are noted in individual reviews. During Ramadan, office hours are often shorter.

CLIMATE

Brunei is warm to hot year-round, with heavy (albeit variable) rainfall that peaks from September to January. See the BSB climate chart on p916.

CUSTOMS

Brunei is a strict Muslim country and does not sell alcohol. However, non-Muslims are permitted to bring in up to 12 cans of beer and two bottles of liquor for their personal consumption. You must declare any alcohol to customs upon entering Brunei or risk being charged with trafficking an illegal substance, which is an extremely serious charge.

DRIVING LICENCE

An International Driving Permit (IDP) is required to drive in Brunei.

EMBASSIES & CONSULATES

Embassies & Consulates in Brunei

For locations of the following embassies and consulates, see the BSB map (p45).

Australia (☎ 222 9435; austhicom.brunei@dfat.gov.au; 6th fl, DAR Takaful IBB Utama, Jl Pemancha)
Canada (☎ 222 0043; hicomcda@brunet.bn; 5th fl, Jl McArthur Bldg, 1 Jl McArthur)
France (☎ 222 0960; france@brunet.bn; 3rd fl, 301-306 Kompleks Jl Sultan, 51-55 Jl Sultan)
Germany (☎ 222 5547; prgerman@brunet.bn; 2nd fl, Unit 2.01, Block A, Yayasan Complex, Jl Pretty)
Malaysia (☎ 238 1095; mwbrunei@brunet.bn; 61 Simpang 336, Jl Kebangsaan)
Philippines (☎ 224 1465; bruneipe@brunet.bn; 17 Simpang 126, Km 2, Jl Tutong)
Singapore (☎ 222 7583; singa@brunet.bn; 8 Simpang 74, Jl Subok)

UK (☎ 222 2231; brithc@brunet.bn; 2nd fl, Unit 2.01, Block D, Yayasan Complex, Jl Pretty)
USA (☎ 222 0384; amembassybrunei@state.gov; 3rd fl, Teck Guan Plaza, Jl Sultan)

Brunei Embassies & Consulates Abroad

Australia (☎ 02-6285 4500; 10 Beale Cres, Deakin, ACT 2600)
Canada (☎ 613-234 5656; 395 Laurier Ave East, Ottawa ON, K1N 6R4)
France (☎ 01-53 64 67 60; 7 rue de Presbourg, Paris 75017)
Germany (☎ 030-206 07 600; Kronenstrasse 55-58, 10117 Berlin)
Japan (☎ 03-3447 7997; 5-2 Kita-Shinagawa 6-Chome, Shinagawa-ku, Tokyo 141-0001)
UK (☎ 020-7581 0521; 19 Belgrave Sq, London SW1X 8PG)
USA (☎ 202-237 1838; www.bruneiembassy.org; 3520 International Court, Washington DC 2008)

For details of visa requirements, see p55.

FESTIVALS & EVENTS

Hari Raya Aidilfitri Feasting and celebration marking the end of Ramadan (a variable date, based on the Islamic calendar). Sultan's palace is open to visitors.
National Day Parade and procession in central BSB on 23 February.
Sultan's Birthday Marked by fireworks and various processions on 15 July.

FOOD & DRINK

Food

Bruneian cookery is almost identical to Malaysian cuisine (see p513), with strong Chinese and Indian influences. There are also a few Western-style restaurants and cafés to please expats, businesspeople and tourists. One traditional Bruneian dish to look out for is *ambuyat*, which is prepared sago served in a gluey mass and eaten with chopsticks.

At markets and in food courts you can expect to pay from B$1 to B$5 for simple dishes, while a typical *kedai kopi* meal usually costs from B$4 to B$8.

Drink

Drinks are also similar to those you will find in Malaysia, with tea and coffee predominating (see p513). Unlike Malaysia, however, you won't find anything with alcohol in it.

GAY & LESBIAN TRAVELLERS

Homosexual acts are illegal in Brunei; those caught can be subject to 10 years of imprisonment and a fine of up to B$30,000. Needless to say, whatever gay scene there is in Brunei is rather discreet.

HOLIDAYS

As in Malaysia, the dates of most religious festivals are not fixed as they are based on the Islamic calendar. Fixed holidays:

New Year's Day 1 January
National Day 23 February
Anniversary of the Royal Brunei Armed Forces 31 May
Sultan's Birthday 15 July
Christmas Day 25 December

Variable holidays:

Chinese New Year January/February
Hari Moulud (Prophet's Birthday) March
Israk Mikraj July
Ramadan August/September
Nuzul Al-Quran September
Hari Raya Aidilfitri September
Anniversary of the Revelation of the Quran September/October
Hari Raya Haji November/December
Hijrah December/January

School holidays occur from mid-November to the beginning of January, and for a week at the end of March, the last two weeks of June and the second week of September.

INTERNET ACCESS

Internet cafés are becoming more common in Brunei and connections are fast. The price per hour is generally B$1. Wireless internet is also becoming common, and several hotels and coffee shops in BSB and elsewhere offer free wi-fi to their customers.

INTERNET RESOURCES

Borneo Bulletin Online (www.brunet.bn/news/bb) Website of the *Borneo Bulletin*, the most popular English-language newspaper in Brunei, with plenty of news on the sultanate.
Brunei Bay (www.bruneibay.net) Plugs programmes for Intrepid Tours and is geared to an upmarket crowd, but has detailed information, including a very useful ferry schedule.
Brunei Tourism (www.tourismbrunei.com) Official tourism website, lacking in practical details but has a BSB map and accommodation and travel agency listings.

LEGAL MATTERS

Drug trafficking in Brunei does carry a mandatory death penalty, and being a foreigner will not save you from the gallows. If you do happen to bring alcohol into this strict Islamic country without declaring it to customs and you are caught, you face severe penalties. See p52 for a summary of what visitors are permitted to bring in when it comes to the subject of alcohol.

MAPS

At some hotels in Brunei, you may be able to find a copy of *Brunei: A Kingdom of Unexpected Treasures*, a leaflet which has a BSB map and bus route info. The best map of the sultanate is probably the *Road Map and Street Index of Brunei Darussalam*, published by Shell, which can sometimes be found in local bookstores.

MONEY

The official currency is the Brunei dollar (B$), but Singapore dollars are widely used and have the same value as the Brunei dollar, meaning they are accepted at face value. Don't worry if you receive Singapore dollars as change from a Brunei dollar bill – you'll have no trouble using them anywhere in Brunei.

Banks give around 10% less for cash than travellers cheques.

Brunei uses 1c, 5c, 20c and 50c coins, and notes in denominations of B$1, B$5, B$10, B$50, B$100, B$500, B$1000 and B$10,000.

ATMs are common, and if the banks are closed you can usually find a moneychanger who can also change travellers cheques. Bargaining is reserved for taxis, water taxis and markets (not for food). Credit cards are widely accepted.

Exchange rates at the time of writing:

Country	Unit	Brunei dollars (B$)
Australia	A$1	1.28
Canada	C$1	1.47
Euro zone	€1	2.10
Japan	¥100	1.31
Malaysia	RM10	4.36
New Zealand	NZ$1	1.08
UK	£1	3.04
USA	US$1	1.51

POST

Postal services in Brunei are quite reliable. BSB's main post office has a poste restante service. Post offices are open from 8.30am to 4.30pm Monday to Thursday and Saturday, and from 8.30am to 11.30am and 2pm to 4pm Friday.

The cost of an airmail postcard to Malaysia and Singapore is B$0.20; to most other countries in Southeast Asia B$0.35; to Europe, Africa, Australia and the Pacific B$0.50; and to the Americas B$0.60.

RESPONSIBLE TRAVEL

Bruneians are scrupulous about keeping their cities and towns relatively clean, due in no small part to some rigid social standards. It's out in the fragile rainforest that visitors can play their part. Just remember the golden rule when it comes to walking or trekking: if you carry it in, carry it out. This applies to easily forgotten items such as foil, plastic wrapping and tissues. Never bury your rubbish – it may be out of sight, but it won't be out of reach of animals.

Bruneians are also quite conservative in terms of dress. Though you don't have to adopt Islamic dress code when travelling here, it is best to dress somewhat conservatively as a mark of respect to the locals. Sleeveless T-shirts and ripped jeans are inappropriate for men, and tube tops and short shorts are unacceptable for women (and save those bikini tops for empty beaches).

TELEPHONE

Brunei has no area codes. The country code is ☎ 673 and the international access code is ☎ 00. Payphones are common in the city centre, and they accept 10c or 20c coins. Phonecards are available from post offices and many retail shops and hotels. There are three types of phone cards: Hallo, JTB and Zippi. SIM cards are only available at DST Communications in BSB (see p46).

TOILETS

Toilets in Brunei are a mixture of Western-style devices and Asian-style squat toilets, with the latter predominating once you get outside BSB. Toilet paper isn't usually provided in most public bathrooms; if using a hose or a bucket of water isn't to your liking, carry your own roll of toilet paper or a packet of tissues.

TOURIST INFORMATION

Brunei's tourist infrastructure isn't well established and at this stage is a cooperative effort between government and private enterprise. At the time of writing, the only real tourist information centre was the office in

Bangar (see p50). The information centre in the capital has plenty of material to look at, and helpful staff.

TOURS

An organised tour is often the cheapest and most trouble-free way to explore the rainforest of Brunei's Temburong District. **Freme Travel** (☎ 223 4280; www.freme.com; Unit 403B, Wisma Jaya, Jl Permancha, BSB) is the best established and most reliable tour operator in the country.

TRAVELLERS WITH DISABILITIES

The streets of BSB are easier to negotiate than those of neighbouring Malaysia and most other countries of Southeast Asia. Ramps for wheelchairs and public transport that allows ready access to the mobility impaired are unfortunately still lacking. On the plus side, most hotels in the capital have lifts.

VISAS

Countries whose citizens are eligible for visa-free entry for 14 days include Belgium, Canada, Denmark, France, Indonesia, Italy and Japan. Nationals of Germany, Ireland, Malaysia, the Netherlands, New Zealand, Singapore, South Korea and the UK are among those eligible for 30-day visa-free entry. US citizens do not need a visa for visits of up to 90 days. Australians are issued on arrival with a visa valid for a 14-day stay or can apply on arrival for a 30-day multiple-entry visa (B$20), which is useful if you are traversing the country overland, say, from Miri up to Kota Kinabalu.

It's a good idea to ring your nearest Bruneian embassy or consulate (see p53) to confirm what visa options are available to you.

There are visa-granting facilities at the borders with Sabah and Sarawak, but the process is time-consuming – it's much easier if you can organise one in advance of your visit.

WOMEN TRAVELLERS

Brunei is a relatively safe country for women travelling on their own. Several women readers, however, have written to report that they were subject to catcalls, hissing and other forms of harassment, mostly from occupants of passing cars, when they were walking alone. Blond women in particular seem to come in for this kind of abuse, probably because they stick out so much in Brunei. Try to respect local customs and avoid wearing shorts above the knee and sleeveless shirts.

Cambodia

HIGHLIGHTS

- **Temples of Angkor** – encountering the mother of all temples, the world's largest religious building, the one and only Angkor Wat (p90)
- **Phnom Penh** – the tarnished 'pearl of Asia' is regaining its shine, with striking museums, a stunning riverside setting and surprisingly sharp nightlife (p65)
- **Sihanoukville** – brilliant beaches, uninhabited tropical islands, a superb selection of seafood and a happening night scene (p104)
- **Ratanakiri province** – swimming in a volcanic crater, discovering sacred burial sites in the forest and exploring the uncharted forests of Virachay National Park in Cambodia's 'Wild East' (p116)
- **Kampot and around** – slowing the pace in this relaxed riverside town with a stunning setting in the shadow of Bokor (p109)
- **Off the beaten track** – doing the Indiana Jones thing and turning temple hunter in remote Preah Vihear province, home to lost ruins and ancient Angkor highways (p102)

FAST FACTS

- **Budget** US$15 to US$20 a day
- **Capital** Phnom Penh
- **Costs** guesthouse in Siem Reap US$3 to US$10, four-hour bus ride US$3, draught beer US$0.50 to US$1
- **Country code** ☎ 855
- **Languages** Khmer, English, French, Mandarin
- **Money** US$1 = 4029r (riel)
- **Phrases** *sua s'dei* (hello), *lia suhn hao-y* (goodbye), *aw kohn* (thank you), *somh toh* (I'm sorry)
- **Population** 15 million
- **Time** GMT + seven hours
- **Visas** US$20 for one month; issued at most land borders and all airports

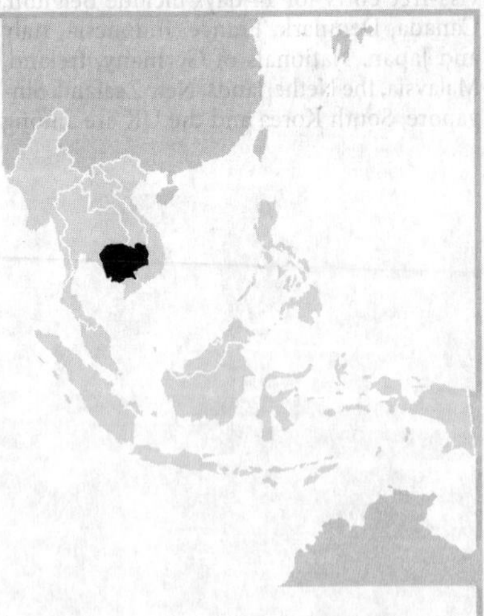

TRAVEL HINT

Do as the locals do and buy a *krama* (checked scarf). It's great for sun protection, dust protection, as a towel, as a bandage…anything is possible with the *krama* chameleon.

OVERLAND ROUTES

There are overland routes to Cambodia from Thailand and Vietnam, or break the mould and enter Cambodia in the northeast from Laos.

There's a magical aura about Cambodia that casts a spell on many who visit this charming yet confounding kingdom. Here you can ascend to the kingdom of the gods at Angkor Wat, a spectacular fusion of symbolism, symmetry and spirituality, or you can descend into the hell of Tuol Sleng, and come face to face with the Khmer Rouge and their killing machine. Welcome to the conundrum that is Cambodia, an intoxicating place with a glorious past, a tragic present and an unwritten future.

The years of fear and loathing are over. Peace has come to this beautiful yet blighted land after three decades of war, and the Cambodian people are opening their arms to the world. Tourism has taken off, but a journey here is still as much an adventure as a holiday.

Cambodia was once the heart of the mighty Khmer empire, which ruled much of what is now Laos, Thailand and Vietnam. The sacred skeleton of this empire can be seen at the fabled temples of Angkor, monuments unrivalled in scale and grandeur in Southeast Asia. But just as Angkor is more than its wat, so too is Cambodia much more than its temples. Stay on a tropical island paradise with barely a beach hut in sight. Float down the Mekong to see rare freshwater dolphins near Kratie. And explore the wild east of the country, home to minority peoples, working elephants and pristine mountain landscapes.

And what of the Cambodian people? They have struggled through years of bloodshed, poverty and political instability. Thanks to an unbreakable spirit and infectious optimism, they have prevailed with their smiles intact, and no visitor comes away from Cambodia without a measure of admiration and affection for the inhabitants of this enigmatic kingdom.

CURRENT EVENTS

The veneer of democracy is wearing thin in Cambodia. Elections come around every five years, but the Cambodian People's Party (CPP) continues to control the military, the police, the civil service and the judiciary, so there is no separation between party and state. The leadership is good at talking the talk when the donors are in town, but it walks (or swaggers) a different walk once the donors leave.

In Cambodia, corruption has been elevated to an art form. Democracy has been supplanted by kleptocracy, governance by theft, and millions of dollars have been siphoned away in recent years. An anticorruption law has been on the table for more than a decade, but international donors seem to suffer a bout of collective amnesia every time it comes around to signing the cheques.

Evictions and land grabs continue apace, with the rich getting richer and the poor getting screwed. Several communities have been kicked out of Phnom Penh and dumped unceremoniously in arid (or flooded) fields, miles from the city. Refugees within their own country, these people's fate remains uncertain.

The Khmer Rouge trial stumbles along. After several false starts, the cast of characters is in place, but there are still many powerful interests who would rather see the whole issue forgotten. Another key figure, Khmer Rouge military commander Ta Mok, passed away in 2006 before justice could be served. Cambodians deserve closure, but it is a travesty that it is coming 30 years too late.

But despite this depressing diagnosis, life is improving for many Cambodians. The economy is booming thanks to tourism and industry, and regional investors such as the Koreans can't put enough money into the country. However, the progress is often despite the government and not because of it. It is down to the ingenuity and adaptability of the long-suffering Khmer people that they continue to succeed against the odds.

HISTORY

The good, the bad and the ugly is the easiest way to sum up the history of Cambodia. Things were good in the early years, culminating in the vast Khmer empire, unrivalled in the region for three centuries. From the 13th century, the bad set in as ascendant neighbours steadily chipped away at Cambodian territory. In the 20th century it turned downright ugly, as a brutal civil war culminated in the genocidal rule of the Khmer Rouge (1975–79), from which Cambodia is still recovering.

The Early Years

From the 1st to 6th century AD, much of present-day Cambodia was part of the kingdom of Funan, whose prosperity was due in large part to its position on the great trade route between China and India. India had

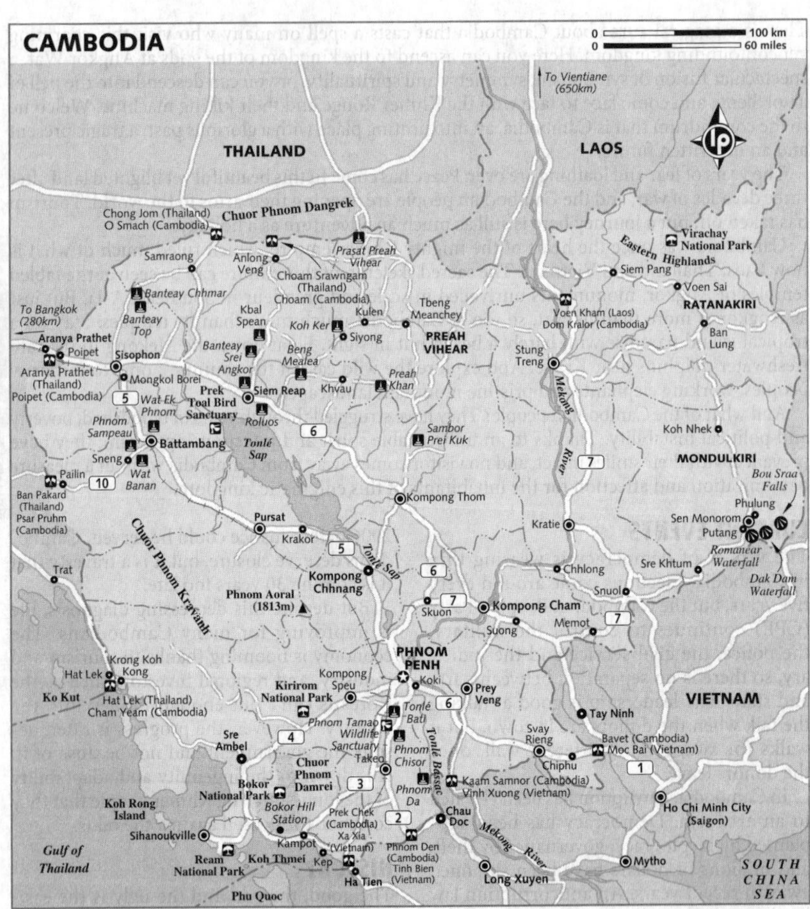

the greatest cultural impact, and its language, religion and culture were absorbed by Cambodians. A series of small kingdoms eventually unified to create the Khmer empire, the mightiest in the history of Southeast Asia.

The Rise & Fall of Angkor

The Khmer empire, renowned for its unparalleled expression in architecture and sculpture, began under Jayavarman II in 802. During his rule, a new state religion established the Khmer ruler as a *devaraja* (god-king). Vast irrigation systems facilitated intensive cultivation around the empire's capital of Angkor, allowing Khmers to maintain a densely populated, highly centralised state that controlled vast swaths of territory across the region. But overstretched outposts, overambitious construction projects and increasingly belligerent neighbours weakened the Khmer empire. When the Thais sacked Angkor in 1432, it was the final straw; the city was abandoned and the capital moved near Phnom Penh. Subsequently, Thai and Vietnamese kingdoms steadily occupied areas of Cambodia, and by the mid-19th century the kingdom was in danger of being squeezed off the map.

Enter the French

For once the French 'protectorate' really did protect Cambodia's dwindling borders, controlling the country from 1864 until independence in 1953. However, the French were more interested in Vietnam's economic potential and left Cambodia to fester. As WWII drew to a close, there were still no universities and only one secondary school!

Independence Days

A new world emerged from the war, and colonialism was a dying force despite the worst intentions of the French. Cambodia's young king Norodom Sihanouk soon began his crusade for independence, which the French reluctantly granted in 1953. For 15 years, King Sihanouk (later prince, prime minister, chief of state, king again and now his majesty the king father) dominated Cambodian politics. The late 1950s and early 1960s were Cambodia's golden years, as the economy prospered while neighbouring countries grappled with domestic insurgencies. However, Sihanouk's erratic and repressive policies alienated both the left and right; the army overthrew him in 1970 and he fled to Beijing. Under pressure from the Chinese, he threw in his lot with Cambodia's weak communist rebels, the Khmer Rouge (French for 'Red Khmer'), boosting their support dramatically.

The Coming of War

During the late 1960s, Cambodia was sucked into the Vietnam conflict. The US secretly began carpet bombing suspected communist base camps in Cambodia and, shortly after the 1970 coup, American and South Vietnamese troops invaded the country to root out Vietnamese communist forces. They failed, and only pushed Cambodia's communists and their Vietnamese allies deep into Cambodia's interior. Savage fighting soon engulfed the entire country, ending only when Phnom Penh fell to the Khmer Rouge on 17 April 1975, two weeks before the fall of Saigon.

Khmer Rouge Takeover

After taking Phnom Penh, the Khmer Rouge, under Pol Pot's leadership, implemented one of the most bloody revolutions the world has ever seen. It was 'Year Zero', money was abolished, cities abandoned and Cambodia transformed into a Maoist, peasant-dominated, agrarian cooperative.

During the next four years, hundreds of thousands of Cambodians, including the vast majority of the country's educated people, were relocated to the countryside, tortured to death or executed. Thousands of people who spoke foreign languages or wore spectacles were branded as 'parasites' and systematically killed. Hundreds of thousands more died of mistreatment, malnutrition and disease. About two million Cambodians died between 1975 and 1979 as a direct result of the policies of the Khmer Rouge.

In late 1978, Vietnam invaded and overthrew the Khmer Rouge, who fled westward to the jungles bordering Thailand. In the subsequent chaos, millions of Cambodians set off on foot to find out if family members had survived the apocalypse. The harvest was neglected and the resulting famine in 1979 and 1980 killed hundreds of thousands more. Meanwhile, the Khmer Rouge maintained a guerrilla war throughout the 1980s, armed and financed by China and Thailand (and with indirect US support), against the Vietnamese-backed government in Phnom Penh.

> **DID YOU KNOW?**
>
> The UN allowed the Khmer Rouge to occupy the Cambodian seat at the UN General Assembly until 1991, meaning the murderers represented their victims for 12 years.

A Sort of Peace

In 1991 the warring sides met in Paris and signed a peace accord, which facilitated UN-administered elections in 1993. A new constitution was drawn up and adopted, and Norodom Sihanouk once again became king. The government was a volatile coalition of Prince Norodom Ranariddh's National Front for an Independent, Neutral, Peaceful and Cooperative Cambodia (Funcinpec) and Hun Sen's CPP. Although they were co-prime ministers, the real power was wielded by Hun Sen, the erroneously named second prime minister, whom the Vietnamese had originally installed. As the bickering intensified, he overthrew First Prime Minister Ranariddh during a July 1997 coup.

The End of the Khmer Rouge

While hardly a triumph for democracy, the first parliament did witness the Khmer Rouge's eventual demise in 1998 after it was decimated by a series of mass defections.

Two decades after the tragic Khmer Rouge revolution, a historic agreement between the UN and the Cambodian government created

DID YOU KNOW?

Pol Pot, born Saloth Sar in 1925, learnt about radical Marxism in Paris before becoming a school teacher back in Cambodia. Very few people knew of him until he emerged as the public face of the Khmer Rouge revolution towards the end of 1976. Pol Pot died on 15 April 1998, after facing a Khmer Rouge show trial for his crimes. His death perhaps forever robbed the Cambodian people of the chance for truth and justice, which raises the question: did he jump or was he pushed?

the first court to bring surviving Khmer Rouge members to trial, but bureaucratic bickering at home and abroad has stalled its opening. Many Cambodians lament that it's already too late to try Pol Pot, who escaped justice when he died in 1998.

Cambodia Today

Despite the existence of the Cambodian royal family, Prime Minister Hun Sen continues to wear the metaphorical crown. He may have lost an eye in the 1975 battle of Phnom Penh but, with a poorly educated electorate and the opposition on the run or under his thumb, he has never lost sight of how to control the country.

The one thorn in the side of the CPP government is the Sam Rainsy Party, which is winning the hearts and minds of the younger generation and urban dwellers. Time is on their side as more and more of the young generation migrate to the cities. Funcinpec has imploded of late, unceremoniously booting out leader Prince Norodom Ranariddh (who went on to found an eponymous party), and teeters on the edge of electoral oblivion.

For more on the latest in Cambodia, see p57.

THE CULTURE

The National Psyche

On the surface Cambodia appears to be a nation full of shiny, happy people, but a deeper look reveals a country of contradictions. Light and dark, old and new, rich and poor, love and hate, life and death – all are visible on a journey through the kingdom, but most telling is the glorious past set against Cambodia's tragic present.

Angkor is everywhere: it's on the flag, the national beer, hotel and guesthouse signage, cigarettes – it's anything and everything. A symbol of nationhood and fierce pride, it's giving the finger to the world, stating no matter how bad things have become lately, Cambodians built Angkor and it doesn't get better than that. This explains why it's a touchstone for most Cambodians, and why the fact that Thailand occupied it for more than a century still troubles relations today. Jayavarman VII, Angkor's greatest king, is still a national hero for vanquishing the occupying Chams and taking the empire to its greatest glories. As a result, he's nearly as omnipresent as his temples.

The contrast with the hellish abyss into which Cambodia was sucked by the Khmer Rouge has left an entire people profoundly shocked. Pol Pot is still a dirty word due to the death and suffering he inflicted. Whenever you hear his name, there'll be stories of endless personal tragedy, of dead brothers, mothers and babies, from which most Cambodians have never been able to recover. Such suffering takes generations to heal. Meanwhile the country is crippled by a short-term outlook that encourages people to live for today rather than thinking about tomorrow, because a short while ago there was no tomorrow.

If Jayavarman and Angkor are loved and Pol Pot hated, the mercurial Great Heroic King Sihanouk is somewhere in the middle, the last of the god-kings, who has ultimately shown himself to be human. Many Cambodians love him as the nation's father, but to others he's the man who failed them with his association with the Khmer Rouge. In many ways, his contradictions are those of contemporary Cambodia. Understand him and what he's had to survive, and you'll understand much of Cambodia.

Lifestyle

The defining influences for many older Cambodians are the three Fs: family, faith and

MUST READ

First They Killed My Father (2001) was written by Luong Ung and covers the steady destruction of an urban Cambodian family through execution and disease during the Khmer Rouge period.

food. Family is more than the nuclear family Westerners know; it's an extended family that includes third cousins and obscure aunts. As long as there's a bloodline there's a bond. Families stick together, solve problems collectively, listen to elders' wisdom and pool resources. Whether the house is big or small, one thing's for sure – there'll be a big family inside.

Faith is another rock in the lives of many older Cambodians, and Buddhism has helped the Cambodian people rebuild their shattered lives. Most Cambodian houses contain a small shrine to pray for luck, and wats (Buddhist temple-monasteries) fill with the faithful come the twice-monthly Buddhist Day.

Food is more important to Cambodians than to most, as they have tasted what it's like to be without. Rice is a staple with every meal and many Cambodians cannot go on without their daily fix.

But to the young generation of teenagers brought up on a steady diet of MTV and steamy soaps, it's a different story. They'll defer to their parents as long as they have to, but what they really want is what teenagers everywhere want. Cambodia is a country undergoing rapid change, but for now the traditionalists are just about holding their own, although the onslaught of karaoke is proving hard to resist.

Population

The 1998 Cambodian census counted 11.8 million people, but it's believed the population now stands at nearer 15 million. With the country's 2.4% birth rate, it should be even higher, but grinding poverty and a poor health-care system have bred disease and led to a depressing infant mortality rate of 59 per 1000 live births, three times that of neighbouring Thailand. An incredible 40% of the population is under the age of 15.

Officially 96% of Cambodians are described as ethnic Khmer (ethnic Cambodians), suggesting Cambodia is the most ethnically homogeneous country in Southeast Asia. Unofficially it's another story, as there are many more Chinese and Vietnamese in Cambodia than the government ever admits, and a great deal of intermarriage. The Chinese have long played a dominant role in Cambodian commerce. While official estimates put their numbers at around 50,000, it's probably 10 times that – and more. As for the Vietnamese, many migrated under the French and later during Vietnam's 1980s occupation, and are engaged in fishing and skilled trades across the country.

Cambodia's Cham and Malay Muslims probably account for up to half a million people in the provinces around Phnom Penh. They suffered vicious persecution between 1975 and 1979, and many were exterminated.

Cambodia's diverse *chunchiet* (ethnolinguistic minorities) have traditionally isolated themselves in the country's remote mountainous regions. This suited the Cambodians, who were, the truth be told, somewhat scared of them. Today, *chunchiet* total about 70,000, with the most important groups being the Kreung in Ratanakiri and the Pnong in Mondulkiri.

RELIGION

Theravada Buddhism is the dominant religion in Cambodia and guides the lives of many Khmers. The Khmer Rouge launched an assault on all beliefs but their own, murdering most of Cambodia's monks, and destroying wats or turning them into pigsties. However, in the past decade there's been a dramatic resurgence in religious worship and Buddhism once again leads the way.

Hinduism flourished alongside Buddhism from the 1st century AD until the 14th century, and some elements of it are still incorporated into important ceremonies involving birth, marriage and death.

There is also a significant minority of Cham and Malay people who practise Islam.

ARTS

The fact that centuries-old sculptures, stylised dances and architecture still spellbind the modern visitor speaks volumes.

The Khmers' astounding architecture and sculpture reached its zenith during the Angkorian era, exemplified by Angkor Wat, the many temples of Angkor Thom and the sublime carvings of Banteay Srei. Many of the finest Khmer sculptures are on display at the sublime National Museum (p72) in Phnom Penh.

Perhaps more than any other traditional art, the royal ballet of Cambodia is a tangible link with the glories of Angkor. The *apsara* dance is unique to Cambodia, while the court dance has roots in India and Java, with

> **MUST SEE**
>
> *The Killing Fields* (1984) is a poignant Roland Joffé film about American journalist Sydney Schanberg and his Cambodian assistant during and after the civil war.

many dances enacting scenes from the Hindu epic the Ramayana, known as the Reamker in Cambodia. To see how much traditional dance has blossomed after the apocalyptic Pol Pot years, catch a traditional dance show in Phnom Penh or Siem Reap.

Like much of Southeast Asia, when it comes to contemporary culture, music rules the roost. This has spawned home-grown talent such as the prolific pop star Preap Sovath, who at the age of 35 has already recorded more than 10,000 songs! You won't need to search for his music, it'll find you – trust us.

While you'll have no clue what he's saying, Nay Krim's comedy antics will likely leave you laughing. He often graces the TVs aboard long-distance buses.

The film industry in Cambodia was given a new lease of life in 2000 with the release of *Pos Keng Kong* (The Giant Snake). A remake of a 1950s Cambodian classic, it tells of a powerful young girl born from a rural relationship between a woman and a snake king. Since its release local directors have cranked up production, with dozens of films a year.

ENVIRONMENT

The Land

Cambodia covers an area of 181,035 sq km, almost half the size of Italy or Vietnam. The country is dominated by water, and it doesn't get much bigger than the Mekong River, cutting through the country from north to south, and the Tonlé Sap (Great Lake), Southeast Asia's largest lake. There are three main mountainous regions: the Chuor Phnom Damrei (Elephant Mountains) and Chuor Phnom Kravanh (Cardamom Mountains) in the southwest, the Chuor Phnom Dangrek (Dangkrek Mountains) along the northern border with Thailand, and the Eastern Highlands in the northeast.

The average Cambodian landscape is a patchwork of cultivated rice paddies guarded by numerous sugar palms, the national tree. Elsewhere are grasslands, lush rainforests, and, at higher elevations, unlikely clumps of pines.

Wildlife

Some environmentalists believe what's left of Cambodia's dense jungle may hide a host of secrets, including biodiversity as rich as anywhere in Asia. The country's large mammals include tigers, leopards, bears, elephants, wild cows and deer, although exact numbers are unclear due to remote habitats and the impact of hunting. There are several dangerous species of snake, including the king cobra, banded krait and the Malayan pit viper.

The many bird species in the country include cormorants, cranes, kingfishers and pelicans, but these often end up in the cooking pot thanks to eagle-eyed kids with catapults. Keen birders should make the boat trip between Siem Reap and Battambang (see p89) to glimpse the Prek Toal Bird Sanctuary, which is home to rare water birds such as lesser and greater adjutants, milky storks and spot-billed pelicans.

The Mekong River is second only to the Amazon in fish biodiversity and hosts some mighty 3m-long catfish. The rare freshwater Irrawaddy dolphin also inhabits the Mekong north of Kratie.

National Parks

More than 20% of Cambodia consists of protected areas and national parks, although these are little more than lines on a map – in practice there's very little protection. Four national parks can handle visitors, although facilities at each are pretty limited: huge and unexplored Virachey, in the far

> **DID YOU KNOW?**
>
> During the rainy season (June to October), the Mekong River rises dramatically, forcing the Tonlé Sap river to flow northwest into Tonlé Sap (Great Lake). During this period, the vast lake swells from around 3000 sq km to almost 13,000 sq km, and from the air Cambodia looks like one almighty puddle. As the Mekong falls during dry season, the Tonlé Sap river reverses its flow, and the lake's floodwaters drain back into the Mekong. This unique process makes the Tonlé Sap one of the world's richest sources of freshwater fish.

northeast, spanning Ratanakiri and Stung Treng provinces; Kirirom, popular with Khmers, just off the road to Sihanoukville; Ream, a maritime park near Sihanoukville; and beautiful Bokor, a former French hill station near Kampot.

Environmental Issues

Head into the remote northwest or northeast corners of Cambodia and you will soon realise that deforestation is the biggest threat to the country's environment. Smouldering stumps seem to outnumber trees in some areas of Cambodia and the rainforest that covered almost 75% of the country in the 1960s now covers less than 30%. Environmental watchdog **Global Witness** (www.globalwitness.org) published a damning report in 2007, *Cambodia's Family Trees,* which implicated senior officials and members of the elite in plundering the country's forests.

An emerging environmental threat is the damming of the Mekong River, as the fragile Tonlé Sap biosphere could be destabilised by any significant change in river activity. The financial boom of the numerous mega-projects isn't lost on organisations such as the Asian Development Bank (ADB), which has offered to pay for much of the development. Let's hope long-term interests won't be scrapped for short-term profits.

TRANSPORT

GETTING THERE & AWAY

Air

Cambodia has regular air links with its Southeast Asian neighbours. Some airlines offer open-jaw tickets into Phnom Penh and out of Siem Reap, which can save some time and money. The following telephone numbers with ☎023 area codes are for Phnom Penh offices, while those with ☎063 codes are for Siem Reap offices.

Air Asia (code AK; ☎ 023-356011; www.airasia.com) Daily budget flights connecting Phnom Penh and Siem Reap to Kuala Lumpur and Bangkok.

Angkor Airways (code G6; ☎ 023-222056, 063-964166; www.angkorairways.com) Regular connections from Phnom Penh and Siem Reap to Taipei.

Bangkok Airways (code PG; ☎ 023-722545, 063-380191; www.bangkokair.com) Daily connections from Phnom Penh and Siem Reap to Bangkok.

China Eastern Airlines (code MU; ☎ 063-965229; www.ce-air.com) Regular flights from Siem Reap to Kunming.

China Southern Airlines (code CZ; ☎ 023-430877; www.cs-air.com) Regular flights from Phnom Penh to Guangzhou.

Dragon Air (code KA; ☎ 023-424300; www.dragonair.com) Daily flights between Phnom Penh and Hong Kong.

Jetstar Asia (code 3K; ☎ 023-220909, 063-964388; www.jetstarasia.com) Daily budget flights from Phnom Penh and Siem Reap to Singapore.

Lao Airlines (code QV; ☎ 023-216563, 063-963283; www.laoairlines.com) Regular flights from Phnom Penh and Siem Reap to both Pakse and Vientiane.

Malaysia Airlines (code MH; ☎ 023-426688, 063-964135; www.malaysiaairlines.com; hub Kuala Lumpur) Daily connections from Phnom Penh and Siem Reap to Kuala Lumpur.

PMT Air (code U4; ☎ 023-221379; www.pmtair.com) Regular flights from Siem Reap to Hanoi and Ho Chi Minh City (Saigon).

Shanghai Airlines (code FM; ☎ 023-723999; www.shanghai-air.com) Regular flights linking Phnom Penh with Shanghai.

Siem Reap Airways (code FT; ☎ 023-720022, 063-380191; www.siemreapairways.com) Regular connections from Phnom Penh and Siem Reap to Hong Kong. High season flights connect Luang Prabang and Siem Reap.

SilkAir (code MI; ☎ 023-426807; www.silkair.com) Daily flights linking Phnom Penh and Siem Reap with Singapore.

Thai Airways International (THAI, code TG; ☎ 023-214359; www.thaiair.com) Daily flights connecting Phnom Penh and Bangkok.

Vietnam Airlines (code VN; ☎ 023-363396, 063-964488; www.vietnamair.com.vn) Daily flights linking Phnom Penh and Siem Reap with both Hanoi and Ho Chi Minh City.

Land

Cambodia shares one border crossing with Laos (via Stung Treng; see p115) and five crossings with Thailand, although only Poipet (see p97) and Krong Koh Kong (see p113) are regularly used. The three other crossings are at O Smach (see p89), Choam (see p101) and Psar Pruhm (see p101).

There are three border crossings with Vietnam: via Bavet (see p79), via Kaam Samnor

> **DEPARTURE TAX**
>
> There's a hefty departure tax of US$25 on all international flights out of Phnom Penh and Siem Reap airports.

CAMBODIA

DEPARTURE TAX

The departure tax for domestic flights is US$6 from Phnom Penh and Siem Reap, and US$5 from Ban Lung.

(see p79) and via Phnom Den (see p81). However, just as we were going to press the word was out that the border at Prek Chek–Xa Xia, linking Kampot and Kep in Cambodia with Ha Tien in Vietnam, was open. Double-check this in Kampot or Kep but, if it's true, this is great news for overland travellers.

See p121 for information on issues when crossing borders, and p126 for details on Cambodian visas.

GETTING AROUND

Air

Domestic airlines have been in a state of turmoil in recent years. The most reliable carriers right now are **Angkor Airways** (code G6; ☎ in Phnom Penh 023-222056; www.angkorairways.com) and **Siem Reap Airways** (code FT; ☎ in Phnom Penh 023-720022; www.siemreapairways.com), connecting Phnom Penh and Siem Reap, and **PMT Air** (code U4; ☎ in Phnom Penh 023-221379; www.pmtair.com) connecting Ban Lung in Ratanakiri province with the capital, and Siem Reap with Sihanoukville.

Boat

The most popular boat for foreigners runs on the Tonlé Sap, connecting Phnom Penh and Siem Reap. Be warned: the 5½-hour trip can be insanely overcrowded and breakdowns aren't unknown. Less crowded and more stunning are the speedboats between Siem Reap and Battambang. Both trips can be slowed by low water in the dry season, and are overpriced given buses run the routes for a fraction of the price.

The beautiful boat trips on the Mekong, which travelled from Kompong Cham to Kratie and on to Stung Treng, are no longer an option, as sealed roads and cheap buses have put them out of business. Riding the Gulf of Thailand's swells between Sihanoukville and Krong Koh Kong is another viable route.

Bus

A proliferation of sealed roads and improved dirt tracks means buses reach further than ever before. The cities of Stung Treng and Sen Monorom are now easily reachable in a day from Phnom Penh, a feat unimaginable just a few years ago. Competition between bus companies is rife along the major routes, causing prices for comfortable air-con buses to plummet on routes to Siem Reap, Poipet, Battambang and Sihanoukville. Phnom Penh Sorya Transport has the most extensive network, which also serves smaller centres like Tonlé Bati, Takeo, Kompong Chhnang, Kompong Cham and Kratie. Hour Lean's buses are the newest and delve deeper into the northeast, covering the provinces of Kratie, Stung Treng, Ratanakiri and Mondulkiri.

Car & Motorcycle

Self-drive car hire is a bit of a masochistic option, given the state of roads, vehicles and other drivers (in no particular order). However, guesthouses and travel agencies can arrange a car and driver for anything between US$20 and US$50 a day, depending on the destination. For the sticky roads in the wet season, a 4WD plus driver is more like US$50 to US$100.

While major roads are a bit wild for motorcycles, many of Cambodia's less travelled tracks are perfect for two-wheeled exploration. However, forays on motorcycles into the remote and diabolical roads of the northwest and northeast should only be attempted by experienced riders. If you're lacking experience, it's best to hire a motorcycle and driver for those long days through seas of sand – it'll set you back about US$15 to US$20 per 24-hour period. In all cases, proceed cautiously as medical facilities are limited in Cambodia.

Phnom Penh has the best motorbikes, with daily rates ranging from US$3 for 100cc motorbikes to US$7 or more for 250cc dirt bikes. Kampot also has a good range of bikes with competitive prices. In other provincial towns, it's usually possible to find a 100c motorbike for around US$5 a day. Rental of self-drive motorcycles is currently prohibited in Siem Reap and Sihanoukville, although rules keep changing in Sihanoukville.

Local Transport

There are no local bus networks in Cambodia, save for a couple of routes to towns near Phnom Penh. Most people use motos (motorcycle taxis), *remorque-motos* (motorcycled-pulled trailers) or cyclos (pedicabs).

CYCLO

As in Vietnam and Laos, cyclos are a cheap way to get around urban areas. Being pedalled about is a slower, more relaxing way to see the sights, but for everyday journeys cyclos are fast being pushed out of business by motos.

Cyclo fares vary wildly depending on your negotiating skills, but aim to pay about the same as moto prices.

MOTO

Motos are a quick way of making short hops around towns and cities. Prices range from 1000r to 4000r, depending on the distance and the town. Most journeys are about 1000r to 2000r – expect to pay double late at night.

It's best to set the price before mounting the moto, as some drivers assume foreigners will pay more. Most also presume you know the route and this can create complications if they don't speak English – drivers will often just keep going until you tell them to turn, so be vigilant unless you want to end up in Bangkok or Ho Chi Minh City. The unofficial uniform of the moto driver is the baseball cap.

REMORQUE-KANG & REMORQUE-MOTO

The *remorque-kang* is a trailer pulled by a bicycle, a sort of reverse cyclo. In places such as Battambang and Kompong Cham, the *remorque-kang* are used in place of the cyclo. A trailer hitched to a motorcycle is called a *remorque-moto,* also often called a túk-túk à la Thailand. This is the Cambodian equivalent of a local bus in the countryside. *Remorque-motos* with covered carriages are pretty popular with tourists in Phnom Penh and Siem Reap.

Share Taxi, Pick-up & Minibus

While vast road improvements across Cambodia have boosted bus transport, the country's minibuses, pick-up trucks and share taxis are still a crucial part of the equation for those wishing to lose the crowd.

> **WARNING**
>
> Since burning flesh doesn't smell very nice and takes a long time to heal, get in the habit of climbing off the moto to your left, stepping clear of the scorching exhaust pipe. The exhaust burn is one of the most common traveller ailments in Cambodia.

Pick-ups continue to take on the worst roads in Cambodia. Squeeze in the air-con cab or, if you feel like a tan and a mouthful of dust, sit on the back. They leave when seriously full. Much quicker are share taxis, which run on the same routes during the dry season. It is quite possible to buy spare seats to make the journey more comfortable. Arrange pick-ups and share taxis independently, as it's cheaper than going through a guesthouse. Haggle patiently to ensure fair prices. There are almost no metered taxis in Cambodia, save for a couple in the capital.

Minibuses usually travel sealed roads and are the cheapest and most cramped of transport options. While they offer little in savings, they tend to leave more regularly than other options.

Train

As Cambodia's roads improve, so its railways continue their descent into oblivion. There are currently no passenger services operating in Cambodia, but it is just about still possible to pay your way on to a cargo train. However, this is only for serious train spotters, as these are some of the slowest trains in the world.

A lack of maintenance since before the civil war means tracks are more crooked than a Cambodian politician. Trains can't travel at more than 20km/h, so the 274km Battambang trip takes 15 hours. Optimists might say this offers more time to take in the countryside – a lot more time.

It's possible to sit on the roof of Cambodian trains, a novelty that many travellers enjoy.

PHNOM PENH

☎ 023 / pop 1.5 million

Oh Phnom Penh. It's exotic, it's chaotic, it's beguiling, it's distressing, it's compulsive, it's repulsive. Every day brings a different experience, some a shock to the senses, others that bring a smile, some that confound all logic, others that wrench the emotions. Many cities are captivating, but Phnom Penh is unique in its capacity to both charm and chill to the bone. Relax on the riverfront beneath swaying palms and take in saffron-clad monks wandering the streets, or dig up the crimes of the past in Tuol Sleng

PHNOM PENH
0 800 m
0 0.5 miles
A B C D E F
1 2 3 4
Mekong River
To Heng Lay (1km); Hang Neak (1.5km); Kompong Cham (120km); Siem Reap (317km)
To Kompong Chhnang (91km); Battambang (293km)
To Apsara Arts Association (1km)
Chrouy Changvar Bridge (Japanese Friendship Bridge)
Tonlé Sap Rd
Tonlé Sap
Boeng Kak
See Central Phnom Penh Map (p70)
Wat Phnom
Sisowath Quay
Phnom Penh
Monivong Blvd
Psar Thmei (Central Market)
National Museum
Royal Palace
Silver Pagoda
Charlesde Gaulle Blvd
Russian Confederation Blvd
Kampuchea Krom Blvd
Jawaharlal Nehru (Sivutha Blvd)
Mao Tse Toung Blvd
To NH 3 (1.5km); NH 4 (1.5km); Phnom Penh International Airport (3km); Kirirom National Park (110km); Kampot (148km); Sihanoukville (230km)
Ph 598
Ph 528
Ph 355
Ph 339
Ph 337
Ph 335
Ph 617
Ph 273
Ph 283
Ph 281
Ph 70
Ph72
Ph74
Ph 75
Ph 80
Ph 74
Ph 566
Ph 317
Ph 315
Ph 313
Ph 592
Ph 528
Ph 285
Ph 291
Ph 289
Ph 287
Ph 566
Ph 614
Ph 608
Ph 86
Ph 102
Ph 106
Ph 108
Ph 110
Ph 118
Ph 136
Ph 144
Ph 148
Ph 112
Ph 118
Ph 122
Ph 134
Ph 137
Ph 53
Ph 63
Ph 172
Ph 166
Ph 107
Ph 178
Ph 184
Ph 200
Ph 208
Ph 211
Ph 156
Ph 132
Ph 259
Ph 257
Ph 253
Ph 180
Ph 186
Ph 182
Ph 213
Ph 182

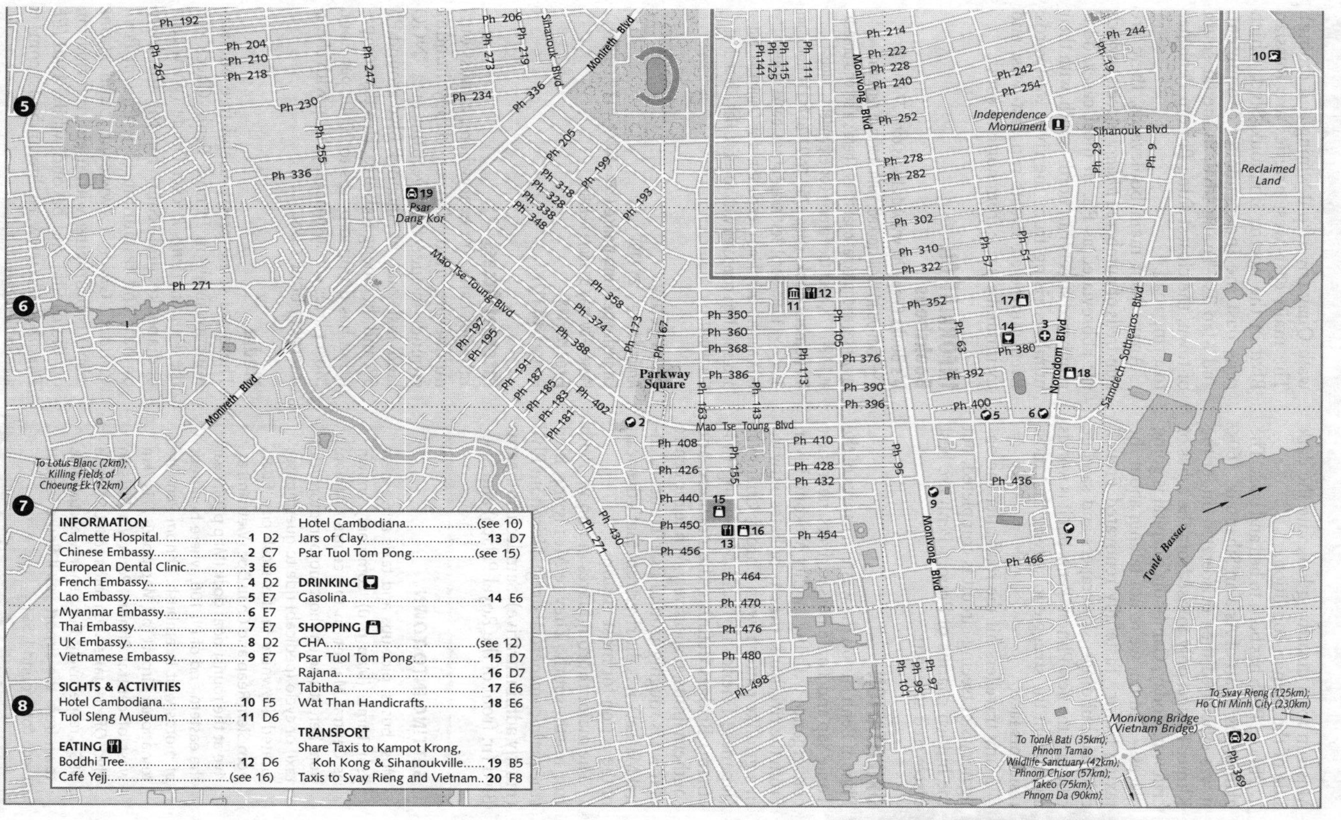
INFORMATION
Calmette Hospital 1 D2
Chinese Embassy 2 C7
European Dental Clinic 3 E6
French Embassy 4 D2
Lao Embassy 5 E7
Myanmar Embassy 6 E7
Thai Embassy 7 E7
UK Embassy 8 D2
Vietnamese Embassy 9 E7
SIGHTS & ACTIVITIES
Hotel Cambodiana 10 F5
Tuol Sleng Museum 11 D6
EATING
Boddhi Tree 12 D6
Café Yejj (see 16)
Hotel Cambodiana (see 10)
Jars of Clay 13 D7
Psar Tuol Tom Pong (see 15)
DRINKING
Gasolina 14 E6
SHOPPING
CHA (see 12)
Psar Tuol Tom Pong 15 D7
Rajana 16 D7
Tabitha 17 E6
Wat Than Handicrafts 18 E6
TRANSPORT
Share Taxis to Kampot Krong, Koh Kong & Sihanoukville 19 B5
Taxis to Svay Rieng and Vietnam 20 F8
To Lotus Blanc (2km); Killing Fields of Choeung Ek (12km)
To Tonlé Bati (35km); Phnom Tamao Wildlife Sanctuary (42km); Phnom Chisor (57km); Takeo (75km); Phnom Da (90km)
To Svay Rieng (125km); Ho Chi Minh City (230km)
Monivong Bridge (Vietnam Bridge)
Tonlé Bassac
Reclaimed Land
Independence Monument
Parkway Square
Psar Dang Kor
Monivong Blvd
Norodom Blvd
Sihanouk Blvd
Mao Tse Toung Blvd
Monireth Blvd
Samdech Sothearos Blvd

Museum for a disturbing look into the dark side of the human condition.

Phnom Penh has been to hell and back. The glamorous 'pearl of Asia' in Sihanouk's '60s, it was evacuated then eviscerated under the Khmer Rouge, only to rise from the ashes of civil war. Today, Cambodia's capital is going places – and no, we're not talking about the taxing traffic. Tastefully renovated French colonial buildings, skyscrapers and satellite cities are the new Phnom Penh, but it is worlds away from the struggle to survive that most residents face.

Many travellers hit the road after the obligatory sightseeing circuit is completed, but the hidden charms of Phnom Penh are best discovered at leisure.

ORIENTATION

Phnom Penh sits on the western shores of the Tonlé Sap and Tonlé Bassac rivers, near their convergence with the mighty Mekong River. From the riverbank, the city radiates outward in a gridlike pattern, with Chrouy Changvar (Japanese Friendship) and Monivong (Vietnam) Bridges defining the northern and southern limits, respectively. While the centre of town is roughly around Psar Thmei (Central Market), it is the riverfront that's the heart of the action for most visitors.

The major thoroughfares in Phnom Penh run north–south. They're Monivong Blvd (the main commercial drag), Norodom Blvd (mostly administrative), Samdech Sothearos Blvd (in front of the Royal Palace) and Sisowath Quay (riverfront wining and dining). The main east–west arteries are Russian Blvd in the north; Sihanouk Blvd, which runs past the Independence Monument; and Mao Tse Toung Blvd, in the far south of town, the closest thing Phnom Penh has to a ring road.

Apart from main boulevards, there are hundreds of numbered *phlauv* (streets), which are abbreviated as Ph. In most cases, odd-numbered streets run north–south, with their numbers rising from the river westwards. Even-numbered streets run east–west and their numbers rise from north to south.

GETTING INTO TOWN

Most buses, pick-ups and taxis arrive near Psar Thmei (Map p70), commonly known as Central Market, in the centre of town; from here it's just a short moto (motorcycle taxi) or cyclo (pedicab) ride to guesthouses located anywhere in this small city. Boats from Siem Reap and Chau Doc (Vietnam) arrive at the tourist boat dock (Map p70), near the eastern end of Ph 106, where hundreds of motos wait in ambush. Phnom Penh International Airport (off Map pp66–7) is 7km west of central Phnom Penh via Russian Blvd. Official taxis and motos cost US$7 and US$2, respectively, but a short walk towards town from the airport you'll find a regular moto for around US$1.

INFORMATION

Bookshops

D's Books (Map p70; www.ds-books.com; 77 Ph 240; 9am-9pm) Well stocked, with stacks of regional favourites and international titles. There's a second branch at 12 Ph 178, near the Foreign Correspondents' Club.

Monument Books (Map p70; ☎ 217617; 111 Norodom Blvd; 10am-9pm) Best range of new books in town, with almost everything ever published on Cambodia, but prices are high compared with Bangkok. Has a branch at the airport.

Emergency

Ambulance (☎ 119)

English-speaking police (☎ 366841, 012 999999) Passers-by may be more helpful.

Fire (☎ 118)

Police (☎ 117)

Internet Access

Internet cafés are everywhere, almost outnumbering moto drivers. Happy hunting grounds include the riverfront area, 'NGO land' just south of Sihanouk Blvd around Ph 57, and the Boeng Kak area. Healthy competition has dropped prices to 2000r per hour. Most places can also hook you up with cheap internet phone calls.

Media

There are some pretty useful free publications available in Phnom Penh. Check out the *Phnom Penh Pocket Guide* (www.cambodiapocketguide.com) for the lowdown on bars and restaurants. The *Phnom Penh Visitors' Guide* (www.canbypublications.com) is brimming with useful information on the capital and beyond, while *AsiaLIFE Phnom Penh* (www.asialifecambodia.com) is a reliable read.

Medical Services

Calmette Hospital (Map pp66-7; ☎ 426948; 3 Monivong Blvd; 24hr) The daddy among the local hospitals.

European Dental Clinic (Map pp66-7; ☎ 211363, 012 854408; 160A Norodom Blvd; 8am-noon & 2-7pm Mon-Sat) The place to get your teeth checked out.

SOS International Medical Centre (Map p70; ☎ 216911; www.internationalsos.com; 161 Ph 51; 8am-5.30pm Mon-Fri & 8am-noon Sat, emergencies 24hr) One of the town's most expensive medical establishments.

Tropical & Travellers Medical Clinic (Map p70; ☎ 336802; www.travellersmedicalclinic.com; 88 Ph 108; 8am-8pm) English-run clinic with reasonable prices.

Money

While several banks offer free credit-card advances, the most convenient and often cheapest places to cash travellers cheques are at exchange kiosks along Sisowath Quay. Some guesthouses and travel agents can also change travellers cheques outside banking hours. Several major banks now have credit-card-compatible ATMs; there are also some ATMs at the airport.

ANZ Royal Bank (Map p70; ☎ 726900; 265 Sisowath Quay) Also has ATMs galore, including at supermarkets and petrol stations.

Canadia Bank (Map p70; ☎ 215286; 265 Ph 110) Free cash advances on MasterCard and Visa, plus a 24-hour Visa- and MasterCard-compatible ATM.

Foreign Trade Bank (Map p70; ☎ 723466; 3 Ph 114) At 1%, this has the lowest commission in town on US-dollar travellers cheques.

SBC Bank (Map p70; ☎ 990688; 315 Sisowath Quay; 8am-8pm) Convenient hours and location, plus it represents Western Union.

Post

Main post office (Map p70; Ph 13; 7am-7pm) In a grand old building, this has increasingly reliable postal services along with expensive express mail.

Telephone

The cheapest local and domestic calls in Phnom Penh are found at private kerbside stalls. Local calls start from 300r a minute. There are now cheap international calls available through mobile providers, so expect the kiosks to start offering overseas calls soon.

There are public phone boxes operated by Camintel and the Ministry of Post & Telecommunications (MPTC) around town. Nearby will be a local shop that sells phonecards for pricey international calls – expect to shell out US$2 per minute.

Many internet cafés offer ridiculously low-cost international calls via the internet, starting from 300r per minute.

STREET NUMBERS

The complete lack of effective house numbering in Phnom Penh makes addresses hard to track down. It's not uncommon to find a row of houses numbered, say, 13A, 34, 7, 26 – makes sense, doesn't it? Worse, several different houses might use the same number in the same street.

Try to get a cross-reference for an address, such as 'close to the intersection of Phlauv (Ph) 107 and Ph 182'.

Tourist Information

Due to lack of funding, forget about useful government-issued tourist information in Phnom Penh. Guesthouses and travellers who seem to know where they're going are your prime sources of knowledge – oh, and this guidebook isn't too bad either!

Travel Agencies

Reliable travel agencies include the following places:

Hanuman Tourism (Map p70; ☎ 218396; www.hanumantourism.com; 12 Ph 310)

Neak Krorhorm Travel & Tours (Map p70; ☎ 219496; 128 Ph 108)

PTM Travel & Tours (Map p70; ☎ 364768; 200 Monivong Blvd)

DANGERS & ANNOYANCES

Phnom Penh is by no means as dangerous as many guesthouses make it out to be – after all, if you head into town, you won't be eating or drinking at their restaurant! However, it's still important to keep your wits about you. At night it's unwise to travel alone or carry a bag as it could attract the wrong kind of attention. Should you be unlucky enough to be a victim of robbery, stay calm and keep your hands up, as going for your pockets is as good as going for a weapon in the assailant's mind.

When riding a motorcycle don't ignore the No Left Turn signs, as traffic police are

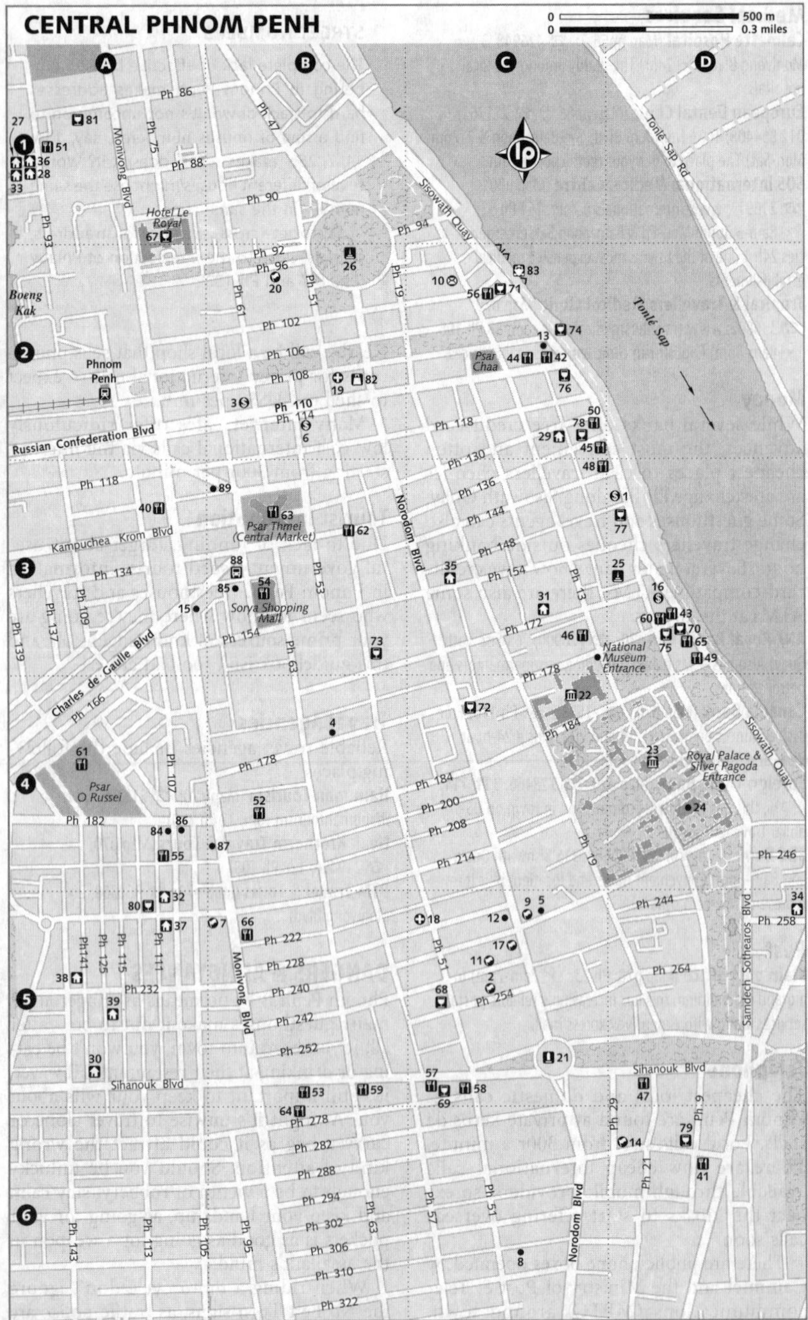
CENTRAL PHNOM PENH
0 500 m
0 0.3 miles
Tonlé Sap
Sisowath Quay
Tonlé Sap Rd
Monivong Blvd
Norodom Blvd
Russian Confederation Blvd
Kampuchea Krom Blvd
Charles de Gaulle Blvd
Sihanouk Blvd
Samdech Sothearos Blvd
Hotel Le Royal
Boeng Kak
Phnom Penh
Psar Chaa
Psar Thmei (Central Market)
Sorya Shopping Mall
Psar O Russei
National Museum Entrance
Royal Palace & Silver Pagoda Entrance

INFORMATION
- ANZ Royal Bank...1 D3
- Australian Embassy...2 C5
- Canadia Bank...3 B2
- Canadian Embassy...(see 2)
- Cooperation Committee for Cambodia...4 B4
- D's Books...(see 70)
- D's Books...5 C5
- Foreign Trade Bank...6 B2
- German Embassy...7 B5
- Hanuman Tourism...8 C6
- Indonesian Embassy...9 C5
- Main Post Office...10 C2
- Malaysian Embassy...11 C5
- Monument Books...12 C5
- Neak Krorhorm Travel & Tours..13 C2
- Philippines Embassy...14 D6
- PTM Travel & Tours...15 A3
- SBC Bank...16 D3
- Singaporean Embassy...17 C5
- SOS International Medical Centre...18 C5
- Tropical & Travellers Medical Clinic...19 B2
- US Embassy...20 B2

SIGHTS & ACTIVITIES
- Independence Monument...21 C5
- National Museum...22 C4
- Royal Palace...23 D4
- Seeing Hands Massage...(see 10)
- Silver Pagoda...24 D4
- Wat Ounalom...25 D3
- Wat Phnom...26 B2

SLEEPING
- Bright Lotus Guesthouse...(see 75)
- Capitol Guesthouse...(see 84)
- Floating Island...27 A1
- Grand View Guesthouse...28 A1
- Hotel Indochine...(see 1)
- Indochine 2...29 C2
- King Guesthouse...30 A5
- Last Home...31 C3
- Narin II Guesthouse...32 A5
- Number 9 Guesthouse...33 A1
- Okay Guesthouse...34 D5
- Royal Guesthouse...35 C3
- Simon's II Guesthouse...36 A1
- Spring Guesthouse...37 A5
- Sunday Guesthouse...38 A5
- Tat Guesthouse...39 A5

EATING
- Bayon Market...40 A3
- Boat Noodle Restaurant...41 D6
- Café 151...42 C2
- Cantina...43 D3
- Chi Cha...44 C2
- Chiang Mai Riverside...45 C2
- Friends...46 C3
- Frizz Restaurant...(see 16)
- Happy Herb's Pizza...(see 43)
- Java Café & Gallery...47 D5
- Kandal House...48 D3
- Khmer Borane Restaurant...49 D3
- Kiwi Bakery...50 C2
- Lazy Gecko Café...51 A1
- Le Café du Centre...52 B4
- Le Rit's...(see 8)
- Lucky Supermarket...53 B5
- Lucky Supermarket...54 B3
- Mama's Restaurant...55 A4
- Monsoon...56 C2
- Mount Everest...57 C5
- Nature & Sea...58 C5
- Nike's Pizza House...59 B5
- Pho Fortune...60 D3
- Psar O Russei...61 A4
- Psar Ta Pang...62 B3
- Psar Thmei (Central Market)...63 B3
- Romdeng...64 B6
- Sa Em Restaurant...65 D3
- Wah Kee Restaurant...66 B5

DRINKING
- California 2 Guesthouse...(see 16)
- Elephant Bar...67 A1
- Elsewhere Bar...68 C5
- Equinox...69 C5
- Foreign Correspondents' Club..70 D3
- Green Vespa...71 C2
- Gym Bar...72 C4
- Heart of Darkness...73 B3
- Pontoon Lounge...74 C2
- Rising Sun...75 D3
- Riverhouse Lounge...76 C2
- Riverside Bar & Bistro...77 D3
- Salt Lounge...78 C2
- Talkin To A Stranger...79 D6
- Teukei Bar...80 A5
- Zeppelin Café...81 A1

SHOPPING
- NCDP Handicrafts...82 B2

TRANSPORT
- Boats to Siem Reap & Chau Doc...83 C2
- Capitol Tour...84 A4
- GST...85 B3
- Japan Rentals...86 A4
- Lucky! Lucky!...87 B4
- Neak Krorhorm...(see 13)
- New! New!...(see 87)
- Phnom Penh Sorya Transport (PPST)...88 B3
- Share Taxis, Pick-ups & Minibuses...89 B3

only too willing to help you part with your cash. They may demand US$20, but if you're patient and smile, a dollar should see you on your way.

Begging is a problem in Phnom Penh. Check out p125 for advice on how to help the less fortunate.

SIGHTS

The sights in Phnom Penh highlight the contradictions of Cambodia. The stunning legacy of god-kings exhibited at the National Museum is in stark contrast to the horrific legacy of killers displayed at Tuol Sleng, and the grandeur of the Royal Palace is a world away from the ghoulishness of Choeung Ek. All around the city you will witness both splendour and sorrow.

After exploring the dark depths of the city's markets (such as Psar Thmei and Psar Tuol Tom Pong), head to the thriving riverfront and enjoy a sunset stroll.

Royal Palace & Silver Pagoda

With its classic Khmer roofs and ornate gilding, the **Royal Palace** (Map p70; Samdech Sothearos Blvd; admission US$3, camera/video US$2/5; 7.30-11am & 2.30-5pm) dominates the diminutive local skyline. Hidden away behind protective walls and beneath the shadows of striking ceremonial buildings, it's an oasis of calm, with lush gardens and leafy havens. As it's the official residence of King Sihamoni, parts of the massive compound are closed to the public.

Within the compound is the extravagant **Silver Pagoda**, the floor of which is covered with five tons of gleaming silver. You can sneak a peek at some of the 5000 tiles near the entrance – most are covered to protect them. Rivalling the floor, an extraordinary Baccarat-crystal Buddha sits atop an impressive gilded pedestal. Adding to the lavish mix is a life-sized solid-gold Buddha, which weighs 90kg and is adorned with 2086 diamonds, the largest weighing in at 25 carats.

Photography is not permitted inside the pagoda itself, so the camera prices are a little ambitious; buy some postcards instead.

Visitors are not permitted into the grounds with bare shoulders or skimpy shorts.

National Museum

A millennium's worth of masterful Khmer artwork, including the world's finest collection of Angkor-era sculpture, spills out from open-air galleries into the inviting inner courtyard of the **National Museum** (Map p70; Ph 13; admission US$3, camera/video US$1/3; 8am-5pm).

One of the most celebrated works is the statue of Jayavarman VII (r 1181–1219), his head bowed slightly in a meditative pose. The oldest artefacts are examples of pottery and bronze from the Funan and Chenla empires (4th–9th centuries AD).

English- and French-speaking guides are available for a bit of context, and there's also a useful exhibition booklet, *The New Guide to the National Museum,* available at the front desk.

Tuol Sleng Museum

While walking down the corridors of the **Tuol Sleng Museum** (Map pp66-7; Ph 113; admission US$2; 8am-5.30pm), with their checked tile floors and cream walls, it's not hard to imagine the site's simple origins as the Tuol Svay Prey High School. However, delving into former classrooms shatters any illusion of normalcy. A single rusty bed and a disturbingly gruesome black-and-white photo are all that adorn some rooms, but they stand as testament to the unthinkable horrors that happened here.

In 1975 Pol Pot's security forces turned the school into Security Prison 21 (S-21), the largest centre of detention and torture in the country. Almost everyone held here was later executed at the Killing Fields of Choeung Ek (below). Detainees who died during torture were buried in mass graves inside the prison grounds. During the first part of 1977, S-21 claimed a terrifying average of 100 victims per day.

Tuol Sleng demonstrates the darkest side of the human spirit that lurks within us all. It is not for the squeamish, but a visit here is instrumental in understanding Cambodia's past and present.

Try to catch the documentary film running daily at 10am and 3pm. Visit the **Documentation Center of Cambodia** (www.dccam.com) for more on the crimes of the Khmer Rouge.

READING UP

For a greater insight into the methodical machine of death that was Tuol Sleng, pick up *Voices from S-21* by David Chandler, a chilling yet incisive description of life in the prison pieced together from accounts from the torturers and the tortured.

DID YOU KNOW?

In 2005 the government privatised the Killing Fields of Choeung Ek, and was paid an undisclosed sum by a Japanese company who'll manage the site and charge admission fees. This has enraged relatives of victims, who feel the government is trading their murdered loved ones for profit.

Killing Fields of Choeung Ek

Rising above the 129 mass graves in the **Killing Fields** (off Map pp66-7; admission US$2; 7am-5.30pm) is a blinding white stupa (religious monument, often containing Buddha relics) that serves as a memorial to the approximately 17,000 men, women and children who were executed here by the Khmer Rouge between mid-1975 and December 1978. Encased inside the stupa are almost 9000 human skulls found during excavations here in 1980. Many of these skulls still bear witness to the fact that they were bludgeoned to death for the sake of saving precious bullets.

Hearing the sounds of joyful children playing at a nearby school while spotting human bone and clothing poking from the churned ground reinforces the contradictions of Cambodia today.

The Killing Fields of Choeung Ek are 14km southwest of central Phnom Penh, clearly signposted from Monireth Blvd. Return moto rides are about US$4, or it's a pleasant bicycle ride once beyond the city limits.

Wat Phnom

Occupying the city's highest point – don't get too excited, it's just a 27m-high, tree-covered bump – **Wat Phnom** (Map p70; admission

US$1; 🕒 6am-6pm) is a quiet, shady and incense-infused respite. According to legend, the first pagoda on this site was erected in 1373 to house four Buddha statues deposited here by the waters of the Mekong. These were discovered by a woman named Penh, hence the name Phnom Penh, literally 'Hill of Penh'. As well as the temple, you'll find droves of Khmers praying for luck and a few amputees looking for some sympathy and riel.

Independence Monument

Soaring over the city's largest roundabout is the grand **Independence Monument** (Map p70; cnr Norodom & Sihanouk Blvds), built in 1958. It's now also a memorial to Cambodia's war dead.

Wat Ounalom

The headquarters of the Cambodian Buddhist patriarchate, **Wat Ounalom** (Map p70; Samdech Sothearos Blvd; 🕒 6am-6pm) is the country's pre-eminent centre of Buddhist education and the focal point of the Buddhist faith in Phnom Penh.

There's not much to see, but a stroll through the complex, much of which was heavily damaged during Pol Pot's regime, will let you soak up the peaceful ambience.

ACTIVITIES

Massages

'You want massage?' While it's tempting and innocent sounding, most of the massages involve truly wandering hands – yes, most are of the naughty variety. For a real, rewarding rub, visit the highly skilled blind masseurs of **Seeing Hands Massage** (Map p70; Ph 13; per hr US$4; 🕒 7am-9pm), opposite the main post office. Besides being a fabulous way to relax after a long journey, having a massage also helps blind Cambodians stay self-sufficient. It's busy, so drop in to make an appointment for later.

Swimming

Dying for a dip? Don't take the plunge into Boeng Kak, no matter what you've been smoking. Several upmarket hotels offer the chance to escape the heat of the day by a pool. The pool at **Hotel Cambodiana** (Map pp66-7; 313 Sisowath Quayd; 🕒 7am-9pm) is the most atmospheric, with sun chairs and views of the Mekong river – but prepare to part with US$6 during the week or US$8 on the weekend.

TOURS

Most of the leading guesthouses organise city tours, including the sights listed earlier, for around US$5 per person. Note that prices mentioned don't include entrance fees. While these tours may seem cheap and handy, sights such as the Killing Fields of Choeung Ek and Tuol Sleng Museum should not be rushed and are best visited independently.

FESTIVALS & EVENTS

The Chinese New Year (p121) and most national holidays (see p123) are celebrated with vigour in Phnom Penh. Festivals focused primarily in the capital city:

Royal Ploughing Ceremony This ritual agricultural festival takes place in early May in front of the National Museum. The noses of the royal oxen are said to predict the success of the upcoming harvest.

Bon Om Tuk (Water Festival) Hundreds of thousands of Cambodians flock to the riverfront in late October or November to watch some 350 boats compete in races on the Tonlé Sap river. The population of Phnom Penh doubles during this time.

SLEEPING

There's no real Khao San Rd area in Phnom Penh, although the Boeng Kak lakefront and the Psar O Russei area have emerged as the most popular backpacker haunts. Boeng Kak's wooden guesthouses are perched over water on stilts, a sort of Ko Pha-Ngan without the Gulf of Thailand, while the less atmospheric backstreets south of Psar O Russei house hotel-like guesthouses with a few more creature comforts.

Boeng Kak Area

Despite some solid structures going up in recent years, this rickety area is still slated for redevelopment some time in the future. 'Tis a shame, as the guesthouses here have a unique ambience, with wooden chill-out areas stretching over the water. They also offer very basic rooms at extremely cheap prices – though bugs are thrown in for free. Valuables should be kept in lockers, as most rooms aren't very secure.

> **WARNING**
>
> During large celebrations in Phnom Penh, women should watch out for the overeager attention of young groups of males.

CAMBODIA

Number 9 Guesthouse (Map p70; ☎ 012 766225; Ph 93; s US$2-4, tw US$5-8; ❄) The original lakefront guesthouse is still a popular place thanks to its blooming plants and billowing hammocks. There are more than 50 rooms, but be selective as some are shabby. Lively drinking scene by night.

Grand View Guesthouse (Map p70; ☎ 430766; Ph 93; r US$3-8; ❄) This is a tall skinny hotel à la Ho Chi Minh City with rooms that are a cut above the competition. Sleep in comfort at night and snag a spot in someone else's hammock by day.

Floating Island (Map p70; ☎ 012 551227; floating island_pp@yahoo.com; 11 Ph 93; r US$3-9; ❄) Head upstairs for a breeze or save some dollars downstairs in the darker rooms. This is a good drinking spot thanks to a double-decker area with sunset views.

Simon's II Guesthouse (Map p70; ☎ 012 608892; Ph 93; r US$10-15; ❄) This wedding-cake-like villa is home to the smartest rooms in the area, including satellite TV and hot-water showers.

Psar O Russei Area

Tat Guesthouse (Map p70; ☎ 012 921211; 52 Ph 125; r US$2-10; ❄) The friendly family here ensures Tat Guesthouse is a home away from home. Cheapies involve shared showers, but a hot shower and cable TV for US$6 is hard to beat. The rooftop restaurant is above the dust.

Narin II Guesthouse (Map p70; ☎ 986131; 20 Ph 111; r US$4-15; ❄ 💻) Almost a hotel, this big pad has some affordable budget rooms, as well as cheap quads for US$15.

our pick Sunday Guesthouse (Map p70; ☎ 211623; 97 Ph 141; r US$5-15; ❄) Rooms – but not prices – have been upgraded here, making this a fine deal. The friendly English-speaking (sometimes English-accented) staff can help with travel arrangements.

Spring Guesthouse (Map p70; ☎ 222155; 34 Ph 111; r US$6-12; ❄) An unfortunate typo on the business card says 'bland new building', but it's interior comfort that matters and this place has bright, spotless rooms complete with cable TV.

Other possibilities:

Capitol Guesthouse (Map p70; ☎ 724104; capitol@online.com.kh; 14 Ph 182; r US$4-10; ❄) The oldest guesthouse in town has several annexes with good value rooms, and a bustling café on the corner of Ph 182.

King Guesthouse (Map p70; ☎ 220512; 74 Ph 141; r US$3-25; ❄ 💻) The range of rooms is as wide as the King's (Elvis, not Sihanouk!) girth, and there is a huge restaurant and travel centre downstairs.

Other Areas

Okay Guesthouse (Map p70; ☎ 012 920556; Ph 258; r US$2-15; ❄) Okay is more than OK thanks to a popular restaurant, appealing garden, great rooms and the best backpacker vibe beyond Boeng Kak.

our pick Royal Guesthouse (Map p70; ☎ 218026; 91 Ph 154; r US$6-12; ❄) An old favourite with a new look, Royal Guesthouse has recently been renovated by its owners. Good value comfort and sparkling bathrooms in a central location.

Last Home (Map p70; ☎ 012 831702; 21 Ph 172; r US$6-20; ❄) Recently relocated to a spiffing new building behind Wat Ounalom, the Last Home has a loyal following among regular visitors. Extras include cable TV and newish bathrooms.

Hotel Indochine (Map p70; ☎ 724239; indochine htl@camnet.com.kh; 251 Sisowath Quay; r US$10-20; ❄) Location, location, location – this is the original riverfront hotel. Fork out for the fancier rooms looking over the river, as the cheapies are showing their age. For bigger comfort but a smaller view, try Indochine 2 (☎ 211525; 28 Ph 130; room US$15 to US$20), located a couple of blocks away.

Bright Lotus Guesthouse (Map p70; ☎ 990446; 22 Ph 178; r US$12-18; ❄) Occupying a super corner with a top view of the National Museum, Royal Palace and, if you have a neck like Mr Fantastic, the riverfront, this guesthouse is one place where it is worth climbing the stairs.

One area that is worth seeking out for those wanting a modicum more comfort is the so-called golden mile, a strip of hotels on Ph 278 that all feature 'Golden' in their name. There is little to choose between them, as all offer air-con, cable TV, fridge, hot water and free laundry for US$13/15 a single/double.

EATING

Some travellers get in the habit of hunkering down on the guesthouse balcony, encouraged by proprietors talking up the dangers of Phnom Penh – don't do it. Phnom Penh is home to fantastic flavours. Make for the markets and dip into cheap Cambodian chow or delve into the city's impressive range of cosmopolitan eateries.

Unless stated otherwise, restaurants are open for breakfast, lunch and dinner.

Khmer

After dark, the Khmer eateries scattered across town illuminate their beaconlike Angkor Beer signs, drawing in locals for fine fare and generous jugs of draught beer. Don't be shy – the food is great and the atmosphere lively. A typical meal will cost just 4000r to 6000r, and a jug of beer is only 8000r. *Soup chnnang dei* (cook-your-own soup) is a big thing with Cambodians and a great idea for group dining.

Sa Em Restaurant (Map p70; 379 Sisowath Quay; mains US$1-3) Cheap and cheerful is the best way to sum up this place, where you can enjoy the riverfront setting without the riverfront prices. It serves simple Khmer specials beneath its leafy canopy.

our pick **Khmer Borane Restaurant** (Map p70; 389 Sisowath Quay; mains US$1.50-3) For the traditional taste of Cambodia, come to Khmer Borane, located on the riverfront near the Royal Palace. Delightful Khmer dishes such as fish in palm sugar, pomelo salad or *lok lak* (stir-fried beef) proves that Khmer cuisine can keep up with that of its better-known neighbours.

Frizz Restaurant (Map p70; ☎ 220953; 335 Sisowath Quay; mains US$2-5) Ignore the German-sounding name, as this place serves up wonderfully aromatic Khmer cuisine. It also operates cooking classes for those wanting to learn its secrets.

The best markets for dining are **Psar Thmei** (Map p70; breakfast & lunch), **Psar Tuol Tom Pong** (Map pp66-7; cnr Ph 440 & Ph 163; breakfast & lunch) and **Psar O Russei** (Map p70; breakfast & lunch), which is handy given these are also great shopping venues. Most dishes cost a reasonable 2000r to 4000r. There are also several areas around the city with open-air food stalls during the early evening – try **Psar Ta Pang** (Map p70; cnr Ph 51 & Ph 136; dinner) for excellent *bobor* (rice porridge) and tasty desserts.

For a sanitised version of the street stall experience, head to the upper levels of Sorya Shopping Mall, where there is an excellent food court with about 30 stalls selling a range of Khmer and Asian food. Continue into the dome to a mini food court with spectacular views over Psar Thmei.

Swanky Khmer restaurants line NH6 on the east side of the Chruoy Changvar Bridge and offer a unique and authentic dining experience for less money than likely at first glance. Try **Hang Neak** (off Map pp66-7; ☎ 369661; NH6; mains US$3-10; dinner) or **Heng Lay** (off Map pp66-7; ☎ 430888; NH6; mains US$3-10; dinner), which both host local Charlie Chaplin–esque comedians and karaoke stars.

Other Asian

Wah Kee Restaurant (Map p70; 296 Monivong Blvd; mains US$1-10; dinner) If the midnight munchies come a calling, this all-night diner is the place to be. Cheap noodle dishes start at just US$1, sizzling spicy beef hot plates are delicious, and there is plenty of fresh seafood in tanks.

Chiang Mai Riverside (Map p70; 227 Sisowath Quay; mains US$2-5) Easily overlooked along the ever glitzier riverfront strip, this place has delicious and inexpensive Thai food, including fish cakes, spicy *laap* (a Lao dish of chopped meat or fish with a ton of herbs and spices) and creative curries.

Mount Everest (Map p70; ☎ 213821; 98 Sihanouk Blvd; curries US$2-4) This is one of the oldest curry houses in town, with a menu that includes popular Indian and Nepalese dishes.

Monsoon (Map p70; 17 Ph 104; curries US$3-5) OK, so it is also a sophisticated wine bar and happens to be in the middle of a 'lively' bar strip, but do not be deceived – this is home to some of the best Pakistani curries this side of Lahore.

Or try these:

Boat Noodle Restaurant (Map p70; Ph 294; mains 3000-12,000r) Consistently popular thanks to bargain Thai food and a sprinkling of Khmer dishes for good measure.

Chi Cha (Map p70; ☎ 336065; 27 Ph 110; set meals from US$2) Cheap Bangladeshi curry house turning out a savoury subcontinent selection, including bargain *thalis* (traditional 'all-you-can-eat' meals).

Pho Fortune (Map p70; ☎ 012 871753; 11 Ph 178; mains from US$1-4) Serves good *pho,* the rice-noodle soup that drives Vietnam forward.

International

our pick **Boddhi Tree** (Map pp66-7; 50 Ph 113; dishes US$1-4) This lush garden is the perfect antidote to the horrors of neighbouring Tuol Sleng Museum. Asian dishes, sandwiches, salads, tapas and desserts are available here, all freshly prepared and packed full of flavour.

Kandal House (Map p70; 239 Sisowath Quay; mains US$2-4) The menu at this tiny restaurant on the riverfront includes some delicious homemade pastas, salads and soups, plus a smattering of Asian favourites. Chilled Anchor draught is available in pints.

Cantina (Map p70; 347 Sisowath Quay; mains US$2-4; dinner) Right next door to Happy Herb's, this is the place for *tostadas* (fried tortillas), fajitas and other Mexican favourites. It's also a lively bar, thanks to local legend and owner Hurley Scroggins.

Java Café & Gallery (Map p70; ☎ 987420; 56 Sihanouk Blvd; mains US$2.50-5) Interesting art exhibitions, wi-fi internet access, a large airy terrace – and that's even before we get to the menu. Wholesome and filling sandwiches and wraps are a speciality, plus global coffees.

Happy Herb's Pizza (Map p70; ☎ 362349; 345 Sisowath Quay; pizzas US$3-6) No, it doesn't mean extra toppings for free, it means pizza à la ganja. Ask for extra happy and they won't be able to wipe the smile off your face for a week. Nonhappy pizzas are also good.

Jars of Clay (Map pp66-7; 39 Ph 155; 🕑 Tue-Sat) As the thermometer hits 40°C, and you feel like you will melt in Psar Tuol Tom Pong, make for this little café. Frappuccinos, milk shakes and speciality coffees will cool things off, plus there are light bites.

Some other eateries to scratch that international itch:

Mama's Restaurant (Map p70; Ph 111; mains 2000-6000r) This is one of the cheapest international eateries in town, with a menu that ranges from shepherd's pie to French food and even African specials.

nature & sea (Map p70; Ph 51; mains 9000-20,000r) Breezy rooftop spot with wholemeal savoury crepes, salads, and fantastic fish and chips – and not forgetting divine fruit shakes.

Nike's Pizza House (Map p70; 160 Ph 63; pizzas US$3-6) Reliable pizzas. Try the 'pineapple porn moan' pizza – silly spelling or pure pleasure?

Self-Catering

Inexpensive restaurants actually offer more savings than self-catering, but for midday snacks or treats from home, supermarkets are perfect. Baguettes are widely available for around 500r and the open-air markets have heaps of fresh fruit and vegetables.

Lucky Supermarket (Map p70; 160 Sihanouk Blvd; 🕑 8am-9pm) Home to a serious range of

DINING FOR A CAUSE

These fantastic eateries have been established as funding initiatives for worthy causes and as training centres for young staff.

Café 151 (Map p70; www.theglobalchild.com; 151 Sisowath Quay; drinks US$1-2) A hole in the wall offering coffee and shakes, with 100% of profits going to help street children.

Café Yejj (Map pp66-7; 170 Ph 450; www.yejj.com; mains US$2-4) An air-conditioned bolt hole, this bistro-style café specialises in tasty pastas and healthy salads. Or forget the healthy and have a frappuccino and a chocolate brownie. It promotes fair trade and responsible employment.

Friends (Map p70; ☎ 426748; www.friends-international.org; 215 Ph 13; dishes US$1-5; ☎ lunch & dinner) With a prime location near the National Museum, this restaurant has a lively little menu of light bites and innovative specials. The shakes are exquisite, as are the raspberry and mango daiquiris. Friends gives former street children a helping hand into the hospitality industry.

Lazy Gecko Café (Map p70; ☎ 012 1912935; 23B Ph 93; mains US$1.50-4.50) Boasting 'homemade hummus just like when Mum was dating that chap from Cyprus', this little eatery serves international dishes and supports a local orphanage. Thursday is quiz night, while Saturdays involves an orphanage visit that includes dinner and a performance by the children.

Le Café du Centre (Map p70; ☎ 992432; French Cultural Centre Ph 184; mains US$1.50-4.50) This Friends-run restaurant comes in the form of a leafy hideaway in a lush garden courtyard. It serves sandwiches and crepes, plus a good selection of ice creams.

Le Rit's (Map p70; ☎ 213160; 14 Ph 310; breakfast from US$3, set lunch or dinner US$5) The three-course lunch and dinners in the well-groomed garden here are a relaxing experience. The main menu is Thai style, and the food comes with a French flourish. Proceeds assist disadvantaged women re-enter the workplace.

Lotus Blanc (Map p70; ☎ 995660; Stung Mean Chey; US$3-6; 🕑 12-2pm Mon-Fri) Fifteen minutes from the city centre, this restaurant acts as a vocational-training centre for youths found scouring the city dump for a meagre living. Run by French NGO Pour un Sourire d'Enfant (For the Smile of a Child), it serves classy Western and Khmer cuisine.

Romdeng (Map p70; ☎ 092 219565; 21 Ph 278; mains US$4-6.50; 🕑 Mon-Sat) Also under the Friends umbrella, elegant Romdeng specialises in traditional food from the provinces and offers a staggering choice of traditional Khmer fare.

goodies from near and far. There's another in **Sorya Shopping Mall** (Map p70; 8am-9pm).

Bayon Market (Map p70; 133 Monivong Blvd; 7am-8pm) A smaller shop with a surprisingly big range of stock, from local favourites to Gatorade to McVitie's biscuits.

Kiwi Bakery (Map p70; ☎ 215784; 199 Sisowath Quay; 7am-11pm) Located on the riverfront strip, this is one of the best Cambodian-owned bakeries in town, with cakes from several continents.

Another trick is to call at the bakeries of five-star hotels such as **Hotel Cambodiana** (Map pp66-7; 313 Sisowath Quay; 7am-7pm) after 6pm, when all cakes are half price.

DRINKING

Should it survive the developer's wrecking ball, the lakeside is a great place for a sunset drink. Lazing in a hammock and watching the sun burn red is a must. However, there is a whole lot more to Phnom Penh nightlife, including some tempting happy hours – drinks are often half price.

For the ins and outs on the drinking and entertainment scene, check the Friday edition of the *Cambodia Daily*, or the latest issues of *AsiaLIFE Phnom Penh* or the *Bayon Pearnik*.

Bars

Elephant Bar (Map p70; Ph 92; 2pm-midnight) The signature bar of the Raffles-owned Hotel Le Royal, this is a sophisticated spot that offers two-for-one happy hours between 4pm and 8pm. Play pool, and tuck into the free chips and salsa. Enjoy two original Singapore slings for just US$7 or so.

Foreign Correspondents' Club (FCC; Map p70; ☎ 724014; 363 Sisowath Quay; mains US$5-15; 7am-midnight) Most people pass through this Phnom Penh institution at some time during their time in Phnom Penh. Occupying a grand old building with striking views over the Tonlé Sap river and the National Museum, this is a good place to hit for happy hour between 5pm and 7pm, when drinks are half price. There is also food from the four corners of the globe.

Green Vespa (Map p70; www.greenvespa.com; 95 Sisowath Quay; 6am-late) The friendly face of Phnom Penh, this bar draws a crowd thanks to a huge drinks selection, top pub grub, cracking music and alluring promotions. Voted bar of the year in 2006 by readers of the *Phnom Penh Pocket Guide*.

Zeppelin Café (Map p70; 49 Ph 86; 4pm-late) Who says vinyl is dead? It lives on here in Phnom Penh, thanks to the owner of this old-skool rock bar, who mans the turntables every night. Fun.

Talkin to a Stranger (Map p70; ☎ 012 798530; 21B Ph 294; 5pm-late Tue-Sun) One of the best-loved bars in Phnom Penh thanks to the convivial hosts, killer cocktails and an original menu. Regular events include quiz nights and live music.

Elsewhere Bar (Map p70; ☎ 211348; 175 Ph 51; 10am-late Wed-Mon) Why go Elsewhere? Ambient vibes, lush garden setting, great drinks menu and a beckoning swimming pool, that's why! Order an amnesia cocktail and forget your worries. Happy hour from 5pm to 8pm.

Gasolina (Map pp66-7; ☎ 012 373009; 56-58 Ph 57; 6pm-late Tue-Sun) Filled with the sensual sounds of South America, this Latin bar is housed in a spacious villa with a huge garden. Salsa lessons every Tuesday, Wednesday and Thursday nights.

Gym Bar (Map p70; 42 Ph 178; 11am-late) This is the number-one sports bar in town – you won't see a better selection of big screens in this part of the world. Cold beer, pub grub and a rowdy crowd for the big games.

Salt Lounge (Map p70; 217 Ph 136; 6pm-late) Sleek, modern and minimalist, this cool cocktail bar is a great place to while away the night. A gay-friendly that welcomes everyone.

Riverhouse Lounge (Map p70; cnr Ph 110 & Sisowath Quay; 4pm-late) The closest thing to a club on the riverfront, this lounge bar has DJs or live music most nights. It's chic and cool, but look out for promotions to keep it cheap.

Heart of Darkness (Map p70; 26 Ph 51; 8pm-late) The Heart of Business these days, this is more a nightclub than a bar but remains a place to see and be seen. Be very wary of large gangs of rich young Khmers here… some are children of the elite and rely on their bodyguards to do their dirty work.

Other admired establishments with liquid menus:

California 2 Guesthouse (Map p70; 317 Sisowath Quay; 7am-10pm) Biker bar with the cheapest beer on the riverfront.

Pontoon Lounge (Map p70; Tonlé Sap river, Ph 108; 11.30am-late) Floating on the river, this cool bar is where the beautiful people come. Happy hour from 5pm to 8pm.

Rising Sun (Map p70; 20 Ph 178; 7am-late) English pub meets backpacker bar.

teukei bar (Map p70; Ph 111; 7pm-late Mon-Sat) Linger beneath Chinese lanterns and chill to ambient sounds and classic reggae cuts. Close to the Psar O Russei guesthouses.

There is quite a 'girlie bar' scene in Phnom Penh, with dozens of places dotted about town. They are pretty welcoming to guys and girls, although 'I love you long time' should be taken with a pinch of salt. Ph 104 and Ph 51 are popular haunts if you want to join the circus.

Live Music

Equinox Bar (Map p70; ☎ 012 586139; 3A Ph 278; 10am-late) Acoustic jam sessions are held every Thursday and Saturday night in this cool little bar. Happy hour from 5pm to 8pm.

Riverside Bar & Bistro (Map p70; ☎ 213898; 273 Sisowath Quay; 7am-1am) A mainstay of the riverfront scene, this place often has bands jamming away in the back room. Pricey drinks are offset by free wi-fi.

ENTERTAINMENT

If you want to catch a glimpse of Cambodia's graceful classical dance, watch students train at the **Apsara Arts Association** (off Map pp66-7; 71 Ph 598; 7.30-10.30am & 2-5pm Mon-Sat). Remember, this is a school of learning, not a tourist attraction, so keep noise levels and flash photography to a minimum. Dance performances are held at Apsara every Saturday at 7pm (admission US$5); classical dance and folk dance alternate.

SHOPPING

The one item you'll be glad you purchased here is the mighty *krama*, a versatile checked cotton scarf worn by Cambodians on their heads, around their necks or around their midriffs, just perfect for blocking both sun and dust. Wearing them is an affirmation of identity for many Cambodians.

Other popular items include antiques, silver, jewellery, gems, woodcarvings, papier-mâché masks, stone copies of ancient Khmer art, brass figurines, oil paintings, silk, sarongs and branded clothing from local factories.

Several stores sell lovely wares to support local organisations striving to improve the lives of Cambodia's disabled community or disenfranchised women. Shop for the cause at the following places:

CHA (Map p70; 40 Ph 113; 8am-6pm) This well-stocked boutique and workshop sells fine handmade clothing, scarves, toys, bags and photo albums.

NCDP Handicrafts (Map p70; 3 Norodom Blvd; 8am-6pm) Exquisite silk scarves, throws, bags and cushions. Other items include *krama*, shirts, purses, notebooks and greeting cards.

Rajana (Map pp66-7; 170 Ph 450; 10am-6pm) Beautiful selection of cards, some quirky metalware, quality jewellery, bamboo crafts and a range of Cambodian condiments.

Tabitha (Map pp66-7; cnr Ph 360 & Ph 51; 7am-6pm) This place sells premium silk, and has a fantastic collection of bags, tableware, bedroom decorations and children's toys.

Wat Than Handicrafts (Map pp66-7; Norodom Blvd; 7.30am-noon, 1.30-5pm) Set inside Wat Than, this place has a similar selection to NCDP Handicrafts.

Bargains, and bargaining sessions, await in Phnom Penh's lively markets – put on your haggling hat and enter the fray. Most markets are open between 6.30am and 5.30pm.

Psar Tuol Tom Pong (Map pp66-7; cnr Ph 440 & Ph 163), nicknamed the Russian Market (not to be confused with Psar O Russei), is packed to the rafters with genuine, and not so genuine, Columbia, Gap and other branded clothing. There's also beautiful Cambodian silk, handicrafts and pirated DVDs, CDs and software.

GETTING THERE & AWAY

Air

See p63 for international flights to Phnom Penh.

The Phnom Penh–Siem Reap route is well serviced by **Angkor Airways** (code G6; ☎ 222056; www.angkorairways.com) and **Siem Reap Airways** (code FT; ☎ 720022; www.siemreapairways.com), with up to six flights a day (one way/return from US$65/110). Seats are usually available without much advance notice.

PMT Air (code U4; ☎ 221379; www.pmtair.com) serves Ratanakiri several times a week from Phnom Penh (one way/return US$100/180). However, this service is often suspended, despite high prices supposedly guaranteeing departure.

Boat

Several companies take turns offering popular daily fast boats up the Tonlé Sap to Siem Reap (US$18 to US$25, five to six hours), leaving the boat dock on Sisowath Quay at

CAMBODIA

GETTING TO VIETNAM

To Vinh Xuong

The bus-boat combination via Kaam Samnor (Cambodia) and Vinh Xuong (Vietnam) is the most scenic way to travel between Cambodia and Vietnam, although be aware it links Phnom Penh to Chau Doc in the Mekong Delta, not Ho Chi Minh City. The border crossing is open from 7am to 5pm.

Capitol Tour (Map p70; ☎ 217627; 14 Ph 182) charges just US$6 for the trip, which includes a bus from Phnom Penh to Neak Luong on the Mekong River and a boat from there to Chau Doc (six to seven hours).

For the adventurous or independent, it can be done for a similar price by first catching a bus from Psar Thmei (Central Market) in Phnom Penh to Neak Luong (4500r), then taking a speedboat from there to the border at Kaam Samnor (10,000r), then a moto between the borders (4000r), and finally a minibus from Vinh Xuong to Chau Doc (US$1).

See p900 for information on doing the trip in the opposite direction.

To Moc Bai

The run from Phnom Penh to Ho Chi Minh City via the border Bavet (Cambodia) and Moc Bai (Vietnam) is pretty smooth these days, taking between five and six hours. Many of the cheap guesthouses in Phnom Penh used to run bargain buses on this route, but the resulting cut-throat competition saw them kill each other off. There are now several bus companies running direct international services every day (US$9 to US$12, six hours), including **Phnom Penh Sorya Transport** (PPST; Map p70; ☎ 210359), whose buses leave from Psar Thmei, **Mai Linh** (☎ 211888; 391 Sihanouk Blvd) and **Mekong Express** (☎ 427518; 87 Sisowath Quay). The border is open from 7am to 5pm.

See p893 for details on travelling from Vietnam to Cambodia.

7am. Tickets can be arranged through guesthouses or near the dock itself. The boats can be packed like sardines, so it's best to sit on the roof and marinate in plenty of sunscreen. Given the fact that buses to Siem Reap start at US$4, the boat is a very expensive option. See p64 for other rewarding, and less expensive, Cambodian boat journeys.

Bus

Super-duper sealed sections of road now connect Phnom Penh with Siem Reap, Battambang and Sihanoukville, making for bountiful bus services. Most currently leave from company offices, which are spread throughout town. The government is slowly but surely developing out-of-town bus stations, so the points of departure may change in time.

Competition ensures that prices are low, although there are a few premium services for those who want a little more comfort, a little less karaoke.

Phnom Penh Sorya Transport (PPST; Map p70; ☎ 210359; Psar Thmei) is the longest-running company, and serves Battambang (16,000r, five hours), Kampot (12,000r, three hours), Kompong Cham (10,000r, two hours), Kompong Chhnang (6000r, two hours), Kratie (21,000r, six hours), Neak Luong (4500r, two hours), Poipet (26,000r, eight hours), Siem Reap (16,000r, six hours), Sihanoukville (15,000r, four hours) and Takeo (5500r, two hours).

The following are a few more of the many companies:

Capitol Tour (Map p70; ☎ 217627; 14 Ph 182) Serves Battambang, Bangkok, Ho Chi Minh City, Poipet, Siem Reap and Sihanoukville.
GST (Map p70; ☎ 012 895550; Psar Thmei) Buses to Battambang, Bangkok, Poipet, Siem Reap and Sihanoukville.
Hour Lean (Map p70; ☎ 012 939905; 97 Sisowath Quay) Buses to Battambang, Kampot, Kompong Cham, Kratie, Poipet, Sen Monorom, Siem Reap, Sihanoukville, Stung Treng and Takeo.
Mekong Express (Map p70; ☎ 427518; 87 Sisowath Quay) Serves Ho Chi Minh City, Siem Reap and Sihanoukville.
Neak Krorhorm (Map p70; ☎ 219496; 127 Ph 108) Serves Battambang, Poipet, Siem Reap and Sisophon.

For more details on any of these services, see the individual city entries throughout the chapter.

Car & Motorcycle

Guesthouses and travel agencies can arrange a car and driver from US$20 a day, depending on the destination. Motorcycles are a liberating way to see places of interest near Phnom Penh. See right for rental details.

Share Taxi, Pick-up & Minibus

With cheap, comfortable and fast buses, and blissful sealed roads heading off in every direction from town, Phnom Penh's share taxis, pick-ups and minibuses offer few advantages besides flexible departure times.

Share taxis to Kampot, Krong Koh Kong and Sihanoukville leave from Psar Dang Kor (Map pp66–7), while share taxis, pick-ups and minibuses for most other places leave from near Psar Thmei (Map pp66–7). Vehicles for Svay Rieng and Vietnam leave from Chbah Ampeau taxi park (Map pp66–7).

Train

There are currently no passenger services operating in Cambodia. However, some train-spotter types have negotiated their way on to cargo trains. While more costly, uncomfortable and lengthy than the bus, it's the last chance to experience a rooftop ride in this region.

GETTING AROUND

Bicycle

Japan Rentals (Map p70; Ph 107; per day US$1) is the perfect place to pick up some pedals.

Cyclo

Cyclos are still common, but have lost a lot of business to motos. Costs are generally 1000r to 2000r for a short trip, 3000r and up for longer rides, but the guys who hang outside tourist hot spots will pick a number, any number!

Moto

Motos are generally recognisable by the baseball caps that are worn by many drivers. In areas frequented by foreigners, moto drivers generally speak English and sometimes a little French, making them useful guides as well (US$6 to US$10 per day, depending on the destinations). Elsewhere in town it can be difficult because eager Khmer-speaking drivers will adamantly nod that they know the destination when they clearly have no clue. If you don't want to end up in the 'burbs, pay attention and give directions if necessary.

Most short trips are 1000r to 2000r and about double that at night. Longer trips will cost more – it's about 3000r from the National Museum to Psar Tuol Tom Pong. While Khmers don't usually negotiate a price in advance, it's a good idea for foreigners to do so to prevent opportunist overcharging.

Motorcycle

The best of the numerous places to hire motorcycles are **Lucky! Lucky!** (Map p70; ☎ 212788; 413 Monivong Blvd; 🕑 7am-6pm) and nearby **New! New!** (Map p70; ☎ 012 855488; 417 Monivong Blvd; 🕑 7am-6pm). A 100cc Honda costs US$4 per day or around US$20 per week, and 250cc dirt bikes cost US$7/40 per day/week.

Motorcycle theft is a problem and if the bike goes bye-bye you'll be liable – use a hefty padlock.

Taxi

Phnom Penh has no metered taxis of the sort found in Thailand or Vietnam. **Bailey's Taxis** (☎ 012 890000) and **Taxi Vantha** (☎ 012-855000) offer taxis 24 hours a day, but have a limited number of cars. The airport run costs US$5 and elsewhere taxis charge about US$1 per kilometre.

AROUND PHNOM PENH

TONLÉ BATI

Tonlé Bati (admission incl drink US$3; 🕑 7am-6pm) is home to two Angkorian-era temples and a popular lakeside picnic area. Set among flowers and wavering palms, **Ta Prohm** and its bas-reliefs depicting stories of birth, infidelity and murder is much more evocative than the diminutive **Yeay Peau**. Ta Prohm was built by King Jayavarman VII (r 1181–1219) on the site of a 6th-century Khmer shrine.

It's 2km off National Highway (NH) 2, 33km south of Phnom Penh. Grab an hourly **PPPT** (Map p70; ☎ in Phnom Penh 023-210359; Psar Thmei) bus to Takeo and it'll drop you at the turn-off (3000r, one hour).

PHNOM TAMAO WILDLIFE SANCTUARY

The **Phnom Tamao Wildlife Sanctuary** (admission US$2; 🕑 7am-6pm) for rescued animals is home to gibbons, sun bears, elephants, tigers and deer, and has a massive bird enclosure. The animals were all taken from poachers or abusive masters, and are housed here to keep them safe and to take part in a sustainable breeding programme. All the money raised goes back into protecting Cambodia's frequently preyed-upon wildlife.

To get here, you will require your own wheels or a moto. A moto should cost around US$8. The sanctuary is located about 45km south of Phnom Penh; take NH2 for about 39km then turn right at the sign. From here, head straight down the sandy track lined with local beggars.

PHNOM CHISOR

Some spectacular views of the surrounding countryside are on offer from the summit of Phnom Chisor, although the landscape screams Gobi Desert during the dry season. An 11th-century laterite-and-brick **temple** (admission US$2; 7am-6pm), with carved sandstone lintels, guards the hilltop's eastern face. From atop the temple's southern stairs, the sacred pool of **Tonlé Om** is visible in the distance.

It's a 2000r pick-up ride from Tonlé Bati to the Phnom Chisor turn-off on NH2, 57km south of Phnom Penh. From there, a return trip to Phnom Chisor's base by moto is about 8000r. Flag down a bus back to Phnom Penh (4000r, 1½ hours, hourly).

TAKEO & PHNOM DA

☎ 032 / pop 44,000

Poking its head from hilltop foliage and looking over endless rice paddies is the small laterite temple of **Phnom Da** (admission US$2; 6am-6pm), in an area that once was part of the pre-Angkorian Chenla civilisation's remarkable capital. In the dry season access is by boat along an ancient canal dating from the pre-Angkorian people. During the wet season the surrounding land sinks beneath the waters and Phnom Da is only accessible by speedboat (US$20 to charter) from Takeo, an unremarkable provincial capital 75km south of Phnom Penh. En route, speedboats access Angkor Borei, where there's a small **Chenla Museum** (admission US$1; 7am-6pm).

Boeung Takeo Guesthouse (☎ 931306; Ph 3; r US$5-10;) boasts a lakefront location, large rooms and clean conditions – just the spot for a night's kip. Rooms with a view are no harder on the pocket.

GETTING TO VIETNAM

The Phnom Den–Tinh Bien crossing, linking Takeo province with An Giang province, sits 60km southeast of Takeo town, but has little traffic as it is quite remote. Share taxis make the run to the border from Takeo and cost about 4000r per person. You must have a valid Cambodian or Vietnamese visa before making this crossing.

See p901 for information on doing the trip in the opposite direction.

Standing on stilts and overlooking the canal to Angkor Borei, **Restaurant Stung Takeo** (Ph 9; meals 3000-6000r; breakfast, lunch & dinner) is a popular Khmer diner. It's the place to fill up before journeying to Phnom Da.

Local buses link Takeo to Phnom Penh (5500r, two hours, hourly) between 6am and 4pm. To reach Kampot take a *remorque-moto* to Angkor Tasaom on NH3 before nabbing a share taxi heading south.

KIRIROM NATIONAL PARK

Set amid elevated pine forests, **Kirirom National Park** (admission $5; 7am-6pm) offers some small waterfalls and decent walking trails. Hook up with a **ranger** (about US$5) for a two-hour hike up to **Phnom Dat Chivit** (End of the World Mountain), where an abrupt cliff face offers an unbroken view of the western mountain ranges. Near the national park is the **Chambok community-based ecotourism site** (☎ 023-214409; www.geocities.com/chambokcbet; admission US$3); proceeds from its educational walks are pumped back into the community. There is a pretty waterfall, a visitor centre and a restaurant here.

Kirirom is 112km southwest of Phnom Penh. It's not easy to access by public transport – Sihanoukville buses can let you off at the Kirirom turn-off, but you'll have to find a moto for the remaining 25km west. The easiest option is to hire a motorcycle or charter a taxi with others. A large sign marks the turn-off, about 85km south of Phnom Penh.

SIEM REAP

☎ 063 / pop 158,000

Siem Reap is the life-support system for the temples of Angkor, the eighth wonder of the

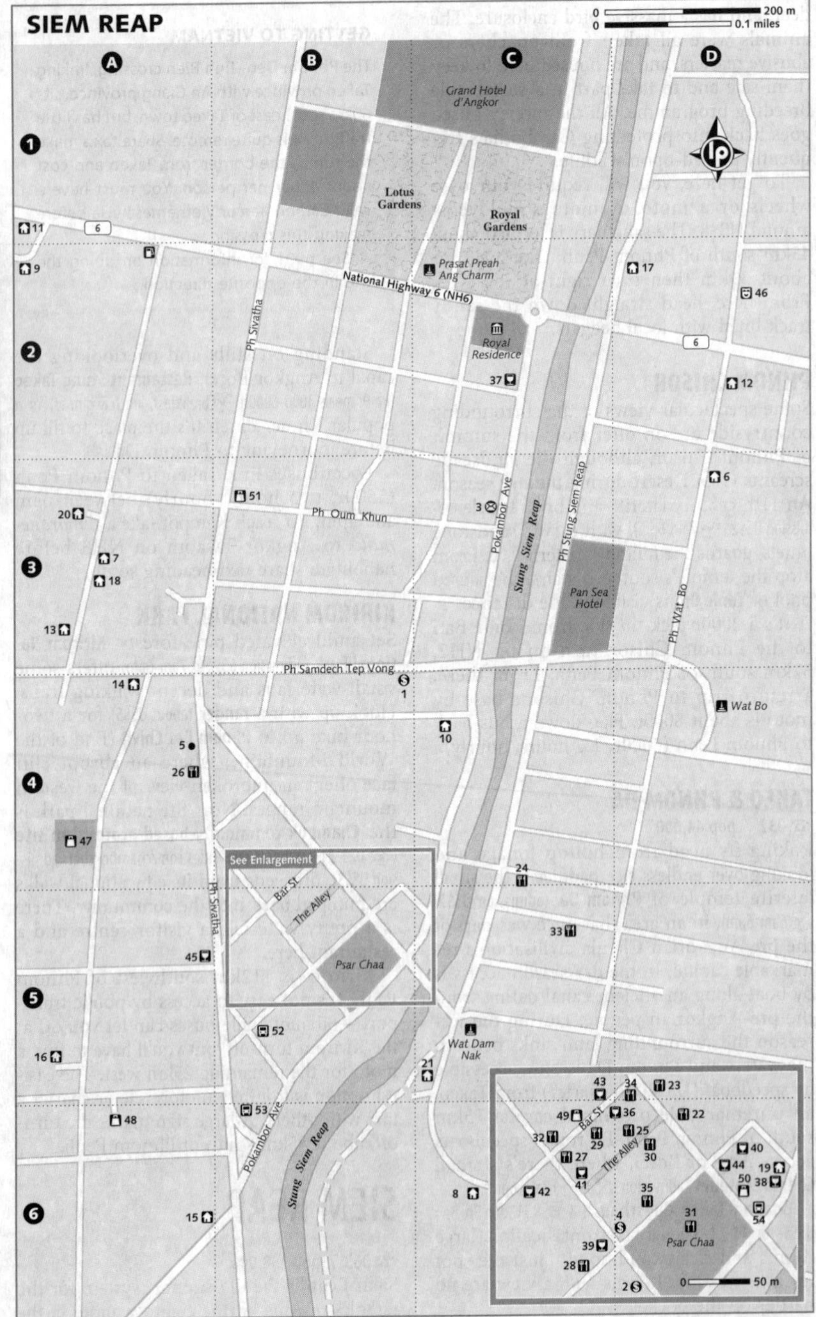
SIEM REAP
0 200 m
0 0.1 miles
Grand Hotel d'Angkor
Lotus Gardens
Royal Gardens
Prasat Preah Ang Charm
National Highway 6 (NH6)
Royal Residence
Ph Sivatha
Ph Oum Khun
Pokambor Ave
Stung Siem Reap
Ph Stung Siem Reap
Pan Sea Hotel
Ph Wat Bo
Ph Samdech Tep Vong
Wat Bo
See Enlargement
Bar St
The Alley
Psar Chaa
Wat Dam Nak
0 50 m

INFORMATION		
ANZ Royal Bank	1	B4
Canadia Bank	2	D6
Main Post Office	3	C3
Union Commercial Bank	4	D6
SIGHTS & ACTIVITIES		
Artisans d'Angkor	(see 48)	
Le Tigre de Papier Cooking School	(see 36)	
Seeing Hands Massage	5	A4
SLEEPING		
Angkor Thom Hotel	6	D3
Baca Villa	7	A3
Green Village Palace	8	C6
Hello Guesthouse	9	A2
Ivy Guesthouse 2	10	C4
Jasmine Lodge	11	A1
Mahogany Guesthouse	12	D2
Mommy's Guesthouse	13	A3
Naga Guesthouse	14	A4
Popular Guesthouse	15	A6
Prince Mekong Villa	(see 9)	
Red Lodge	16	A5
Rosy Guesthouse	17	D2
Sala Bai Hotel & Restaurant School	18	A3
Shadow of Angkor Guesthouse	19	D6
Smiley Guesthouse	20	A3
Wat's Up Guesthouse	21	C5
EATING		
Angkor Market	(see 51)	
Angkor Palm	22	D6
Blue Pumpkin	23	D5
Butterflies Garden Restaurant	24	C4
Cambodian BBQ	25	D6
Dead Fish Tower	26	A4
In Touch	27	C6
Joe-to-Go	28	C6
Kama Sutra	29	C6
Khmer Kitchen Restaurant	30	D6
Psar Chaa	31	D6
Red Piano	32	C6
Sala Bai Hotel & Restaurant School	(see 18)	
Singing Tree Café	33	C5
Soup Dragon	34	D5
Taj Mahal	35	D6
DRINKING		
Angkor What?	36	C6
FCC Angkor	37	C2
Funky Munky	38	D6
Ivy Bar	39	C6
Laundry Bar	40	D6
Linga Bar	41	C6
Molly Malone's	42	C6
Temple Club	43	C5
Warehouse	44	D6
X Bar	45	A5
ENTERTAINMENT		
Bayon II Restaurant	46	D2
SHOPPING		
Angkor Night Market	47	A4
Artisans d'Angkor	48	A6
Psar Chaa	(see 31)	
Rajana	49	C6
Rehab Craft	50	D6
Shenga	(see 47)	
Tabitha Cambodia	51	B3
TRANSPORT		
Capitol Tour	52	B5
GST	53	B6
Neak Krohorm	54	D6

world. In a state of slumber until a few years ago, it has woken up with a jolt and is now one of the regional hot spots for wining and dining, shopping and schmoozing.

Angkor is a place to be savoured, not rushed, and Siem Reap is the perfect place from which to plan your adventures. At its heart, it remains a charming town with rural qualities. Old French shophouses, shady tree-lined boulevards and a gentle winding river are remnants of the past, while five-star hotels, air-conditioned buses and international restaurants are pointers to the future. The gold rush continues unabated, and without careful management it could become Siem Reapolinos, the not so Costa del Culture of Southeast Asia. One way or the other, the world has finally woken up to Angkor and this little town is set for big, big changes.

ORIENTATION

Straddling Stung Siem Reap's narrow waters, Siem Reap spreads outwards from Psar Chaa, which is the epicentre of ingestion, with tasty eats and liquid treats. It's still a small town and easy to navigate, with budget accommodation spread throughout. NH6 runs east–west and cuts the town in two. Street numbering is wholly haphazard, so take care when hunting down specific addresses.

INFORMATION

Bookshops

Some of the cheapest books on Angkor are hawked by local kids and amputees around temples – buying one is a decent way of assisting the disadvantaged.

Emergency

Ambulance (☎ 119)
Fire (☎ 118)
Police (☎ 117)
Tourist Police (Map pp92-3; ☎ 012 402424; 24hr) Located at the main Angkor ticket office.

Internet Access

Internet access is everywhere, with the highest concentrations of internet cafés found on Ph Sivatha and around Psar Chaa. Charges range from 2000r to 4000r per hour. Some restaurants offer free wi-fi, including the Blue Pumpkin (p86).

Medical Services

Naga Medical Centre (Map pp92-3; ☎ 964500; 593 NH6; 24hr) One of the better private clinics in Siem Reap.

Royal Angkor International Hospital (Map pp92-3; ☎ 761888; www.royalangkorhospital.com; NH6 West; 24hr) A new international facility, affiliated with the Bangkok Hospital Medical Centre.

GETTING INTO TOWN

Travellers coming independently by road will usually be dropped near Psar Leu (Map pp92–3) in the east of town and from here it's just a short ride by moto (motorcycle taxi; 2000r to 4000r) into town. If you're arriving with bus services sold by guesthouses, the bus will head straight to a partner guesthouse.

Most travellers arriving by boat aren't surprised by hordes of motos waiting at Phnom Krom dock (off Map pp92–3), 11km from town, but they are taken aback by the sight of their name on a board being furiously waved by a driver – guesthouses in Phnom Penh pass on or sell names to guesthouses in Siem Reap! If you follow the sign and stay at that guesthouse, then the lift is free; if you choose to stay elsewhere expect to pay the driver about US$1.

Most guesthouses have a free airport pick-up service; otherwise the 7km ride to town costs US$1 by moto or US$5 for a taxi.

Media

To keep on top of the constant changes in Siem Reap, pick up a free copy of *Siem Reap Angkor Visitors Guide*, published quarterly. For more on the bar and restaurant scene, pick up the *Siem Reap Pocket Guide*, also free.

Money

ANZ Royal Bank (Map p82; ☎ in Phnom Penh 023-726900; Ph Samdech Tep Vong) Free credit-card advances and can change travellers cheques in most major currencies. International ATMs all over town.

Canadia Bank (Map p82; ☎ 964808; Psar Chaa) Provides free credit-card cash advances and changes travellers cheques in most major currencies at a 2% commission. International ATM.

Union Commercial Bank (Map p82; ☎ 964703; Psar Chaa) Charges 2% commission for travellers cheques and offers free Visa advances.

Post

Main post office (Map p82; Pokambor Ave; 🕑 7am-5pm) Improving services, but it's still advisable to ensure the postcards are franked.

Telephone

The cheapest international calls are via the internet, although the connection is not always that clear. Unblemished but more expensive international calls can be made at numerous private booths advertising telephone services, which also offer inexpensive local calls starting from 300r per minute.

DID YOU KNOW?

The name Siem Reap actually means 'Siamese Defeated' – hardly the most tactful name for a major city near Thailand!

Tourist Information

Unbelievably, there's still no helpful tourist office for independent travellers in Siem Reap. Guesthouses and fellow travellers are the best sources of general information.

DANGERS & ANNOYANCES

Siem Reap is a pretty safe city, even at night. However, if you rent a bike don't keep your bag in the basket, as it will be easy pickings for a drive-by snatch.

There are many commission scams run by guesthouses, the worst involving those arriving by bus from Bangkok; see p89 for more information.

Begging is prevalent in Siem Reap – have a read of p125 for advice on how to help the less fortunate.

SIGHTS & ACTIVITIES

Temples, schmemples. There is more to Siem Reap than the Temples of Angkor – but not a lot.

Forming part of the Cambodian Land Mind Relief Fund (CLMMRF), the **Cambodia Landmine Museum** (off Map pp92-3; ☎ 012 598951; admission free, donations accepted; 🕑 7am-6pm) showcases a large collection of mines and artillery with a fascinating documentary on their destructive capabilities. Check out the garden where visitors are challenged to find hidden (deactivated!) mines. It recently moved and is located more than 20km from town on the road to Banteay Srei.

Yee-haa! The **Happy Ranch** (Map pp92-3; ☎ 012 920002; www.thehappyranch.com; horse rides US$15-80; 🕑 6am-6pm) offers you the chance to explore Siem Reap on horseback, taking in surrounding villages and secluded temple spots.

Artisans d'Angkor (☎ 963330; Angkor Silk Farm ⏰ 8am-5pm; Chantiers Ecoles Map p82; ⏰ 7.30am-6.30pm), a centre of arts and crafts, has two workshops that are open to visitors. The Chantiers Ecoles branch is the centre of traditional carving and masonry, while the Angkor Silk Farm showcases the entire silk-making process, from mulberry trees and silk worms to spinning and weaving.

Massages & Spas

With all that traipsing around temples, exhausted limbs and muscles are an inevitability. Thankfully Siem Reap has tapped into the lucrative market of rejuvenation and is bursting with spas and treatment centres. All the upmarket hotels have swish spas, but there are affordable massages elsewhere.

The massages at **Seeing Hands Massage** (Map p82; ☎ 012 836487; 324 Ph Sivatha; massage US$4; ⏰ 7am-9pm) are performed by the blind, with part of the profits going to help the sight-impaired of Siem Reap.

Krousar Thmey (Map pp92-3; Krousar Thmey Tonlé Sap Exhibition Centre; massage US$6) is a well-known NGO that offers massages by professionally trained blind masseurs in the school behind the exhibition centre.

You can also visit one of the many massage places near Psar Chaa for a cheap but effective rubdown.

Swimming

It's hot work clambering about the temples and there is no better way to wind down than with a dip in a swimming pool. You can pay by the day at most hotels for use of the swimming pool and/or gym, or head to **Aqua** (Map pp92-3; www.aquacambodia.com; Ph 7 Makara; swimming US$2) where there is a large pool and a lively little late-night bar.

COURSES

Learn the secrets of Cambodian cooking with **Le Tigre de Papier Cooking School** (Map p82; ☎ 760930; letigredepapier@hotmail.com; Bar St; courses US$12). It starts at 10am daily and includes a visit to the market. Proceeds go to supporting Sala Bai Hotel & Restaurant School (right, p87).

SLEEPING

There are now more guesthouses and hotels in Siem Reap than temples around Angkor – and that's a lot. While accommodation is spread throughout town, four areas hold the bulk of quality choices: Psar Chaa, Ph Sivatha, NH6 west, and the east bank of the river.

Psar Chaa Area

Popular Guesthouse (Map p82; ☎ 963578; chom@camnet.com.kh; r US$5-14; ❄ 💻) Popular by name, popular by nature, this expanding guesthouse has a huge selection of well-tended rooms and a rooftop restaurant with great food.

Ivy Guesthouse 2 (Map p82; ☎ 012 380516; r US$6-8) A homely guesthouse with a cool chill-out area with hammocks and TV, the Ivy shows a little more decorative flair than most in this price range.

our pick Shadow of Angkor Guesthouse (Map p82; ☎ 964774; 353 Pokambor Ave; shadowofangkor@hotmail.com; r US$6-20; ❄) Probably the best-located guesthouse in town, Shadow of Angkor occupies a grand old French-era building overlooking the river. Invest in the arty air-con rooms if the budget allows.

Red Lodge (Map p82; ☎ 012 707048; www.redlodgeangkor.com; r incl breakfast US$8-12; ❄ 💻) Hidden in a maze of backstreets, Red Lodge has bright and spacious rooms. Prices include free fruit, toast, tea and coffee, plus free bike rentals, so it's a steal.

Phlauv Sivatha Area

Naga Guesthouse (Map p82; ☎ 963439; r US$3-10; ❄) We first bunked here back in 1995 and it still remains true to its roots, a real crash pad. Rooms with shared bathroom are just US$3 and there's a pool table if you're after some cue action.

our pick Garden Village (Map pp92-3; ☎ 012 217373; www.gardenvillage-angkor.com; dm US$1, r US$3-12; ❄ 💻) With probably the cheapest beds in town, here you can choose from eight-bed dorms or US$3 cubicles with shared bathrooms. The bargains don't stop there, with US$0.50 beer at the rooftop bar. Nice.

Baca Villa (Map p82; ☎ 965328; www.baca-villa.com; r US$7-10; ❄ 💻) This small but smart guesthouse offers a warm welcome to all. Fan rooms include hot water, plus there is a lively little bar-restaurant out front.

Sala Bai Hotel & Restaurant School (Map p82; ☎ 963329; www.salabai.com; r US$10-25; ❄) Enjoy the intimate surrounds of this training-school hotel, where the sweet staff are ever helpful. Decorative touches include silk wall hangings, woven throw pillows and wicker wardrobes.

A couple of other friendly, family-run options:

Mommy's Guesthouse (Map p82; ☎ 012 941755; r US$4-15; ❄) This modern villa includes large rooms with air-con, as well as cheaper pads with cold showers.

Smiley Guesthouse (Map p82; ☎ 012 852955; r US$6-15; ❄) One of the first guesthouses to undergo a hotel-tastic make-over, this place has more than 70 rooms.

CAMBODIA

NH6 West

Jasmine Lodge (Map p82; ☎ 760697; www.jasminelodge.com; NH6 west; r US$2-15; ❄ 💻) A friendly and fun little guesthouse, the Jasmine has cheapies with shared bathroom and a range of smarter options. The elevated bar-restaurant includes a pool table.

Earthwalkers (Map pp92-3; ☎ 760107; www.earthwalkers.no; dm US$4, s/d from US$9/12, all incl breakfast; ❄ 💻 🏊) This is the closest thing Siem Reap has to a full-blown backpacker hostel. Rooms are superclean and even dorm beds include a hearty breakfast.

our pick **Damnak Chan** (Moon Inn; Map pp92-3; ☎ 760334; damnakchan@yahoo.com; r US$13-23; ❄ 💻 🏊) This tranquil spot is a haven from the bustle of NH6 and includes a smart new pool. Rooms are smart, service is speedy and breakfast is an extra US$2.

More? You want more? Try these:

Hello Guesthouse (Map p82; ☎ 012 920556; r US$4-15; ❄) Linked to Okay Guesthouse (p74) in Phnom Penh, this place has cracking-value rooms. The restaurant has handy Khmer phrases to learn written all over its walls.

Prince Mekong Villa (Map pp92-3; ☎ 012 437972; www.princemekong.com; s/tw incl breakfast from US$4/6) Satisfied guests buzz about the range of services provided here: good travel info, and free laundry, breakfast and bicycles.

East Bank of the River

Mahogany Guesthouse (Map p82; ☎ 760909; proeun@online.com.kh; Ph Wat Bo; r US$5-15; ❄ 💻) There's still some mahogany in long-running Mahogany Guesthouse. The old house has cheap rooms, while a newer block has rooms with whistles and bells. Good upcountry travel information available.

Angkor Thom Hotel (SR Map p82; ☎ 964862; r US$13-15; ❄ 💻) This is a cut above the guesthouse competition; rooms have satellite TV, fridge and hot water, plus Angkor photos line the corridors.

Green Village Palace (SR Map p82; ☎ 760623; www.greenvillagepalace.com; Ph Wat Dam Nak; r US$15-25; ❄ 🏊) If you feel like bending the budget for a little treat, this hotel has smart rooms with silk trim, plus a small swimming pool *and* a gym.

Other options among dozens:

Rosy Guesthouse (Map p82; ☎ 965059; r US$7-15; ❄) Reasonably priced rooms, and it's not far to the bustling bar downstairs.

Wat's Up Guesthouse (SR Map p82; ☎ 012 675881; r US$8-15; ❄ 💻) A smart place with a memorable name.

EATING

Yeah, yeah, all the guesthouses have extensive menus of Khmer classics and comfort food, but hit the town to experience the dynamic dining scene that is Siem Reap. The gastronomic extravaganza of Khmer and international flavours won't break the bank and you can keep on rolling for a night on the town. Unless stated otherwise, restaurants are open for breakfast, lunch and dinner.

Soup Dragon (Map p82; ☎ 964933; Bar St; meals US$1-7) Hit the ground floor for classic Asian breakfasts such as *pho* for less than US$1 – just the recipe for traipsing around the temples. Upstairs is a smarter restaurant with a huge menu of Asian and international dishes.

our pick **Blue Pumpkin** (Map p82; ☎ 963574; mains US$1.50-5) Downstairs it looks like any old café, albeit one with a wondrous selection of cakes, breads and homemade ice cream. Upstairs is a white world of minimalist expression with beds to lounge on and free wi-fi. Light bites, great sandwiches and shakes.

our pick **Khmer Kitchen Restaurant** (Map p82; ☎ 964154; The Alley; mains US$2-3; 🕑 lunch & dinner) Can't get no culinary satisfaction? Mick Jagger was here for the delectable Khmer and Thai dishes, including a sublime pumpkin and coconut soup. This restaurant has been so successful it's now doubled in size (there's another entrance from Psar Chaa); the best seats are at the candlelit tables spilling out into the atmospheric alley.

Dead Fish Tower (Map p82; Ph Sivatha; dishes US$2-5) Floor dining, comfy cushions and tree-trunk tables is the way to go here. The Thai teasers on the menu are extensive, and it promises 'be sure we don't serve dog, cat, rat or worm' – so bad luck if these are your delicacies of choice.

Kama Sutra (Map p82; ☎ 012 1824474; Bar St; mains US$2.50-7) Enjoy it in 80 different positions… ahem, that's Indian food and seating arrangements we're talking about here. This slick and stylish Indian restaurant offers authentic curries and isn't as expensive as it looks.

Red Piano (Map p82; ☎ 963240; Bar St; mains US$3-5) A restored colonial gem, Red Piano has a big balcony for watching the action unfold on Bar St below. The menu has a great selection of Asian and international food, and former patron Angelina Jolie even has a cocktail named in her honour.

Angkor Palm (Map p82; ☎ 761436; mains US$3-6) Voted Siem Reap's restaurant of the year in 2006 in the *Siem Reap Pocket Guide* awards, Angkor Palm has legendary *amoc* (baked fish in banana leaf) that even Khmers go crazy for. Cooking classes are available from 10am .

In Touch (Map p82; ☎ 963240; Bar St; mains US$3-6) Just across the road from the Red Piano and every bit as alluring, In Touch has some spectacular lighting. The flavours are mainly Thai and there is often live music.

Cambodian BBQ (Map p82; ☎ 965407; The Alley; mains US$7-9; dinner) The Alley is now wall-to-wall restaurants, but this place offers a twist on the traditional *phnom pleung* (hill of fire) grills, serving up crocodile, snake, ostrich and kangaroo, plus free noodles and vegetables.

Other spots include the following:

Angkor Market (Map p82; Ph Sivatha) The best supermarket in town has an excellent supply of international goodies for those heading upcountry.

Taj Mahal (Map p82; curries US$2-5) Well-established Indian restaurant. Liberal portions will slake the most serious of curry cravings.

When it comes to the cheapest Cambodian eats, Psar Chaa (Map p82) has plenty of dishes on display and many more cooked to order. It's a lively and atmospheric place for a local meal at local-ish prices. By night, there are lots of street strips turning out bargain meals: try the strip at the end of Bar St, opposite Molly Malone's. Alternatively, ask a moto driver for recommendations of the best hole-in-the-walls, as these guys know the rub.

DRINKING

Siem Reap rocks. It used to be as dead as the ancient kings of Angkor, but dozens of bars have opened up in recent years. The Psar Chaa area is a good hunting ground, with one street even earning the moniker Bar St – dive in, crawl out!

Angkor What? (Map p82; Bar St; 6pm-late) This is the original Siem Reap bar, and it's still going strong. The 5pm to 8pm happy hour – with bargain buckets of Mekong whiskey, Coke and Red Bull, and cheap pitchers of Anchor – lubes things up for later when everyone's bouncing along to indie anthems.

Temple Club (Map p82; Bar St; 10am-late) The only worshipping going on at this temple is 'all hail the ale'. There is a free traditional dance show upstairs from 7.30pm, then things start rocking downstairs from 9pm. Good food and loud tunes seem to draw a crowd.

DINING (OR DRINKING) FOR A CAUSE

These are some fabulous restaurants that support worthy causes or assist in the training of Cambodia's future hospitality gurus.

Joe-To-Go (Map p82; ☎ 092 532640; www.theglobalchild.org; drinks US$0.50-2; 5am-3pm) Gourmet coffee is the main draw here – it's a good wake-up option before sunrise at the temples. Proceeds support education for street children.

Singing Tree Café (Map p82; ☎ 965210; www.singingtreecafe.com; mains US$1.50-3; closed Mon) This garden café serves scrumptious muffins, coffee with a kick and health food. It doubles as a community centre, yoga studio and gallery, and commits a percentage of profits to wildlife conservation and helping street children.

Butterflies Garden Restaurant (Map p82; ☎ 761211; www.butterfliesofangkor.com; mains US$3-6; 9am-10pm) Set in a blooming garden that provides a backdrop for more than 1000 butterflies, this is dining with a difference. The menu includes Khmer flavours with an international touch and some indulgent desserts. The restaurant supports good causes, including Cambodian Living Arts, dedicated to reviving Cambodian performing arts..

Sala Bai Hotel & Restaurant School (Map p82; ☎ 963329; www.salabai.com; set lunch US$5; 12-2pm Mon-Fri Nov-June) This school trains young Khmers in hospitality services and serves a menu of Western and Cambodian cuisine.

Les Jardins des Delices (Map pp92-3; ☎ 963673; Paul Dubrule Hotel & Tourism School, NH6; set lunch US$7; lunch only) Enjoy Sofitel standards at a snip with a three-course meal of Asian and Western food prepared by students training in the culinary arts.

Warehouse (Map p82; ⌚ 10.30am-3am) Top tunes, drinks aplenty and a lively crowd ensures this is one of the better bars in town. All-nighters have been known to occur if the crowd is on form.

Laundry Bar (Map p82; Psar Chaa; ⌚ 6pm-late) Put on your cleanest undies for a trip to the Laundry, a lavishly decorated nightspot with a dance floor. It gets busy on weekends or when guest DJs crank up the sound system.

Funky Munky (Map p82; ☎ 012 1824553; www.funkymunkycambodia.com; ⌚ noon-late) This great little bar turns out more than 20 different burgers, including the slightly scary 'cardiac arrest'. Crash the quiz night, held every Thursday, where proceeds go to a variety of worthy causes.

Molly Malone's (Map p82; Bar St; ⌚ 7.30am-late) An authentic Irish pub, this is the place to come if you are missing the Emerald Isle. There's Powers Whisky, Guinness and steaming stews, and the soundtrack, inevitably, includes the Pogues and U2.

Linga Bar (Map p82; The Alley; ⌚ 5pm-late) This chic gay bar is attracting all comers thanks to a cracking cocktail list and some big beats, which draw a dancing crowd later into the night.

FCC Angkor (Map p82; Pokambor Ave; ⌚ 7am-midnight) The place to pretend you are in old Indochina, FCC is set in a beautiful building with a reflective pool and lazy lounge chairs. Half-price happy hour runs from 5pm to 7pm.

Other places to imbibe:

Ivy Bar (Map p82; ⌚ 6am-late) A great little bar with excellent food and a friendly crowd.

X Bar (Map p82; Ph Sivatha; ⌚ 4pm-late) Currently *the* late-night spot in town, drawing revellers for the witching hour when other places are closing up.

ENTERTAINMENT

Several restaurants and hotels offer cultural performances during the evening and for many this is the only chance to witness classical Cambodian dance. Unfortunately the shows are either expensive or hardly authentic.

Bayon II Restaurant (Map p82; just north of NH6) A cheaper choice, it offers a decent dance performance and a buffet dinner for US$11.

SHOPPING

Siem Reap is a shop-till-you-drop kind of place, be it **Psar Chaa** (Map p82; ⌚ 6am-9pm), lesser-known markets, souvenir shops or the endless temple shenanigans. Buying at the temples is a great way to help the local economy, as many vendors are descended from the original Angkor inhabitants. The **Angkor Night Market** (Map p82; ⌚ 4pm-midnight) is a good one-stop shop for everything and is just off the main Sivatha strip.

Another way to let your shopping dollars do well is to visit shops that support Cambodia's disabled and disenfranchised:

Artisans d'Angkor (Map p82; ☎ 380354) High-quality reproduction carvings and exquisite silks are available. Impoverished youngsters are trained in the arts of their ancestors.

Rajana (Map p82; ☎ 964744; Bar St) Sells quirky wooden and metalware objects, well-designed silver jewellery and handmade cards. Rajana promotes fair trade and employment opportunities for Cambodians.

Rehab Craft (Map p82; ☎ 380335) This shop opposite Psar Chaa specialises in quality silk products such as wallets, handbags and the like. Profits train and sustain the disabled community.

Shenga (☎ 012 260015; www.shenga.net; Angkor Night Market) Housed in the lively little night market, this is a fair-trade boutique with sexy lingerie.

Tabitha Cambodia (Map p82; ☎ 760650; Ph Sivatha) Home to a beautiful range of silk scarves, cushion covers and throws, this shop puts its proceeds towards projects such as house building and well drilling.

GETTING THERE & AWAY

Air

For the lowdown on international destinations from Siem Reap, see p63.

There are up to six flights a day by **Angkor Airways** (code G6; ☎ 964166; www.angkorairways.com) and **Siem Reap Airways** (code FT; ☎ 380191; www.siemreapairways.com) between Siem Reap and Phnom Penh. Flights start at US$65/100 one way/return, and tickets are usually available without much advance notice.

PMT Air (code U4; ☎ in Phnom Penh 023-221379; www.pmtair.com) connects Siem Reap with Sihanoukville (one way/return US$80/120) several times a week, a popular option to link temples and beach.

CONSPIRACY THEORY

Why is the road between Siem Reap and the Thailand border at Poipet still in notoriously bad shape when it should be a major priority for trade and tourism? Well, it's rumoured that an unnamed airline is paying an unstated commission to an unnamed political party to indefinitely stall this road's upgrade!

BANGKOK TO SIEM REAP: THE SCAM BUS

While direct Bangkok–Siem Reap bus tickets are cheap and sound convenient, they're anything but. Since the bus operators make their real money from Siem Reap guesthouses paying them commission for bringing guests, their goal is to make the journey as long and uncomfortable as humanly possible. Why? Well, if they dropped you off at an average guesthouse at 4pm, you will probably search out better accommodation. However if you arrive battered, exhausted and in the dark, you're more likely to succumb to pressure and just collapse at their chosen guesthouse.

Some companies are actually secretly using the painful Psar Pruhm–Ban Pakard border (p101) instead of the much faster (though still painfully bumpy) Poipet–Aranya Prathet crossing (p97)! Others also try to 'help' you with your visa, resulting in you being overcharged.

Make travel the adventure it was always supposed to be – catch a bus to the border and go it alone from there.

Boat

Daily express boats service Phnom Penh (US$18 to US$25, five to six hours), but are overpriced given it's just as fast by road and only US$4. Guesthouses usually include transport to the dock at Phnom Krom, 11km south of town, with the boat tickets; otherwise expect to pay motos about US$1. Aim for the roof and don't forget to apply the war paint (ie sunscreen).

Express boats to Battambang (US$15, three to eight hours) pass near Prek Toal Bird Sanctuary on arguably Cambodia's most scenic stretch of water. Low water in the dry season means only smaller speedboats make the run, but they often fall prey to sticky mud, making for seemingly endless journeys. Try to ensure the boat driver keeps to a sensible speed, as big waves have proved a major problem for local communities over the years. Hovercrafts are rumoured to be in the pipeline.

GETTING TO THAILAND

Foreigners can cross from O Smach in northern Cambodia to Chong Jom in Thailand, although few pass through this way. First arrange a taxi from Siem Reap to Samroang (four hours, US$30 for the taxi) and continue from there to O Smach by moto (US$5), taking up to two hours. Once on the Thai side, it gets much easier with several minibuses and săwngthăew (small pick-up trucks with two benches in the back) each day from Chong Jom to Surin.

See p753 for information on doing the trip in the reverse direction.

Bus

The road to Phnom Penh is now glorious tarmac, making for smooth journeys, whereas the road west to Sisophon and Poipet is still one hell of a bumpy ride. Bridges are being built, which suggests there might actually be a decent road during the lifetime of this book. Competition ensures low and consistent pricing among the various bus companies. Buses arrive and depart from the taxi park (Map pp92–3), east of town near NH6.

Neak Krorhorm (Map p82; ☎ 964924) offers the most destinations, with buses to Phnom Penh (US$3.50, five to six hours), Battambang (US$4, four to five hours), Poipet (US$4, four to five hours) and Bangkok (US$10, 10 to 14 hours). Its office is opposite Psar Chaa.

Other companies with Siem Reap offices:

Capitol Tour (Map p82; ☎ 963883) Buses to Phnom Penh, Poipet and Bangkok; its office is off Ph Sivatha.

GST (Map p82; ☎ 012 888981; Ph Sivatha) Buses to Phnom Penh.

PPST (☎ 016 222588) Services to Phnom Penh, Kompong Cham and Poipet; its office is in the Psar Chaa area.

Share Taxi, Pick-up & Moto

For details on travelling to Anlong Veng, see p102. The best way to travel to Preah Vihar province is by moto; see p102 for more info.

GETTING AROUND

For all the juicy details on how best to explore the temples of Angkor, see p91.

Navigating Siem Reap on foot is pretty straightforward, as it's a relatively small place. If you need to cross town quickly, a moto will cost 1000r to 2000r, and double that at night. *Remorque-motos* start at US$1.

Motorbike hire is prohibited in Siem Reap.

TEMPLES OF ANGKOR

Prepare for divine inspiration! The temples of Angkor, capital of Cambodia's ancient Khmer empire, are the perfect fusion of creative ambition and spiritual devotion. Between the 9th and 13th centuries the Cambodian *devaraja* strove to better the temples of their ancestors in size, scale and symmetry, culminating in the world's largest religious building, Angkor Wat. The hundreds of temples surviving today are but the sacred skeleton of the vast political, religious and social centre of an empire that stretched from Myanmar (Burma) to Vietnam, a city that boasted a population of one million at a time when London was a little town of 50,000 inhabitants. The houses, public buildings and palaces were constructed of wood – now long decayed – because the right to dwell in structures of stone was reserved for the gods.

Angkor is the heart and soul of the Kingdom of Cambodia, a source of inspiration and national pride to all Khmers as they struggle to rebuild their lives after the years of terror and trauma. Today, the temples are a point of pilgrimage for all Cambodians and no traveller will want to miss their extravagant beauty when passing through the region.

The 'lost city' of Angkor became the centre of intense European popular and scholarly interest after the publication in the 1860s of *Le Tour du Monde,* an account by the French naturalist Henri Mouhot of his voyages. A group of talented and dedicated archaeologists and philologists, mostly French, soon undertook a comprehensive programme of research. Under the aegis of École Française d'Extrême-Orient (EFEO), they made an arduous effort – begun in 1908 and interrupted in the early 1970s by war – to clear away the jungle vegetation that was breaking apart the monuments, and to rebuild the damaged structures, restoring them to something approaching their original grandeur.

The three most magnificent temples at Angkor are the enigmatic Bayon, in the fortified ancient city of Angkor Thom, with its eerie faces staring down; romantic Ta Prohm, parts of which are slowly being digested by nature; and the immense Angkor Wat, the mother of all temples, which sends a tingle down your spine on the first encounter. Take your time and spend five days, even a week, as all these monuments are well worth several visits each and there are dozens of less celebrated but no less rewarding temples to dig around in the area – not literally, mind you, that's best left to the archaeologists!

ANGKOR WAT

Soaring skywards and surrounded by a moat that would make its European castle counterparts blush, Angkor Wat is one of the most inspired and spectacular monuments ever conceived by the human mind.

Some researchers believe a walk from its outer causeway to its inner confines is a symbolic trip back to the first age of the universe's creation. Others point out it also replicates the spatial universe in miniature; the Hindu's mythical Mt Meru represented by the massive central tower, with its surrounding smaller peaks (lesser towers) surrounded in turn by continents (lower courtyards) and oceans (moat). The seven-headed *naga* (mythical serpent-beings) along the causeway become a symbolic rainbow bridge for man to reach the abode of the gods.

Enough of the metaphors, you say. What do you really need to know? Well, it's the largest religious building in the world and it'll blow your socks off! Not wearing socks? Strap up those sandals, as they're in for a wild ride…

It was built by Suryavarman II (r 1112–52) to honour Vishnu, his patron deity, and to be his funerary temple. The central temple consists of three elaborate levels, each of which encloses a square surrounded by intricately interlinked galleries. Rising 31m above the 3rd level and 55m above the ground is the central tower, which gives the whole ensemble its sublime unity.

Surrounding the central temple complex is an 800m-long series of extraordinarily exquisite bas-reliefs. The most celebrated scene, the **Churning of the Ocean of Milk**, is located along the southern section of the east gallery. This brilliantly executed carving depicts 88 *asura* (demons) on the left and 92 *deva* (gods) with crested helmets on the right, churning up the sea to extract the elixir of immortality.

Spend a few hours in awe of this unique place. Many tourists come for sunrise before heading back to town for breakfast. Explore the vast corridors from 7am when Angkor Wat is cool and quiet.

EXPLORING THE TEMPLES

INFORMATION

The official **Angkor ticket office** (Map pp92-3; 1-day/3-day/1-week passes US$20/40/60; 5am-5.30pm) is a large checkpoint on the road to Angkor. All passes require a photo and the authorities now insist on taking the shots. Expect queues. Lose the pass and you'll be fined US$30 if spotted in a temple. The temple complex is open from 5am to 6.30pm, unless there is a special show on at one of the temples.

Try to be patient with the hordes of children selling food, drinks and souvenirs, as they're pretty young and are only doing what their families have asked them to do to survive – you'll find their ice-cold bottled water is heavenly in the heat, although the merits of their bamboo flutes and wooden crossbows aren't immediately so clear.

ITINERARIES

One Day

Hit Ta Prohm for sunrise and a look at this dramatic wrestling match with nature. Continue to Angkor Wat while it is still quite early and the crowds are light. After lunch enter the ancient city walls of Angkor Thom and check out its incredible terraces and temples, including the enigmatic faces of the Bayon. Biggest mistake – trying to see too much.

Three Days

Start with some of the smaller temples and build up to the big hitters. Visit the early Roluos group on the first day for some chronological consistency and try the stars of the grand circuit, including Preah Khan, Preah Neak Pean, Ta Som and sunset at Pre Rup. Day two might include Ta Prohm and the temples on the small circuit, plus the distant but stunning Banteay Srei. Then the climax: Angkor Wat at dawn and the immense city of Angkor Thom in the afternoon.

One Week

Angkor is your oyster – relax, enjoy and explore at will. Make sure you visit Beng Mealea, Kbal Spean and Koh Ker (p103).

EATING

Food stalls are found at most of the more popular temples such as Banteay Srei, Preah Khan and Ta Prohm. Angkor Wat even has full-blown cafés and restaurants. It's a great way to fit more into your day and it's also nice to relax in the popular temples without the masses of package tourists – they usually eat lunch in town. Rest assured, you'll never go hungry around Angkor.

GETTING THERE & AROUND

The most popular way to explore has traditionally been to hook up with a moto driver for about US$6 to US$8 per day, or a little more if you're including remote temples. Some know a lot about the temples and can act as de facto guides. An enjoyable alternative for incurable romantics is to opt for the *remorque-moto* (motorcycle-pulled trailer) – just perfect for two. Prices range from US$10 to US$15 per day depending on the destinations.

Bicycles have been picking up in popularity and can be rented from guesthouses and shops around town for about US$2 per day. Check out the White Bicycles project supported by some guesthouses, where the money goes to help community development. Cycling is a rewarding way to explore nearby temples, provided you glug water at every opportunity; there is a 'big circuit' and a 'little circuit' marked on Map pp92–3. Or ditch the bike and go back to basics by heading out on foot. There are obviously limitations to what you can see due to the distances involved, but exploring Angkor Thom's walls on foot or walking to and from Angkor Wat are both feasible.

Those with an aversion to exercise and the elements can opt for a car and driver. Most guesthouses can organise one for just US$20 to US$25 per day.

Finally there are unconventional options. Elephant rides are possible from Angkor Thom's south gate to Bayon (US$10) during the day and make for some memorable photos. Elephants also climb Phnom Bakheng in the evening (US$15), but this can't be much fun for the poor creatures. Or aim high and take the massive hot air balloon (US$11 per person). It's on a fixed line, so only offers a view from a distance, but it's the best aerial shot available unless you have the budget for a helicopter ride (US$75 for eight minutes).

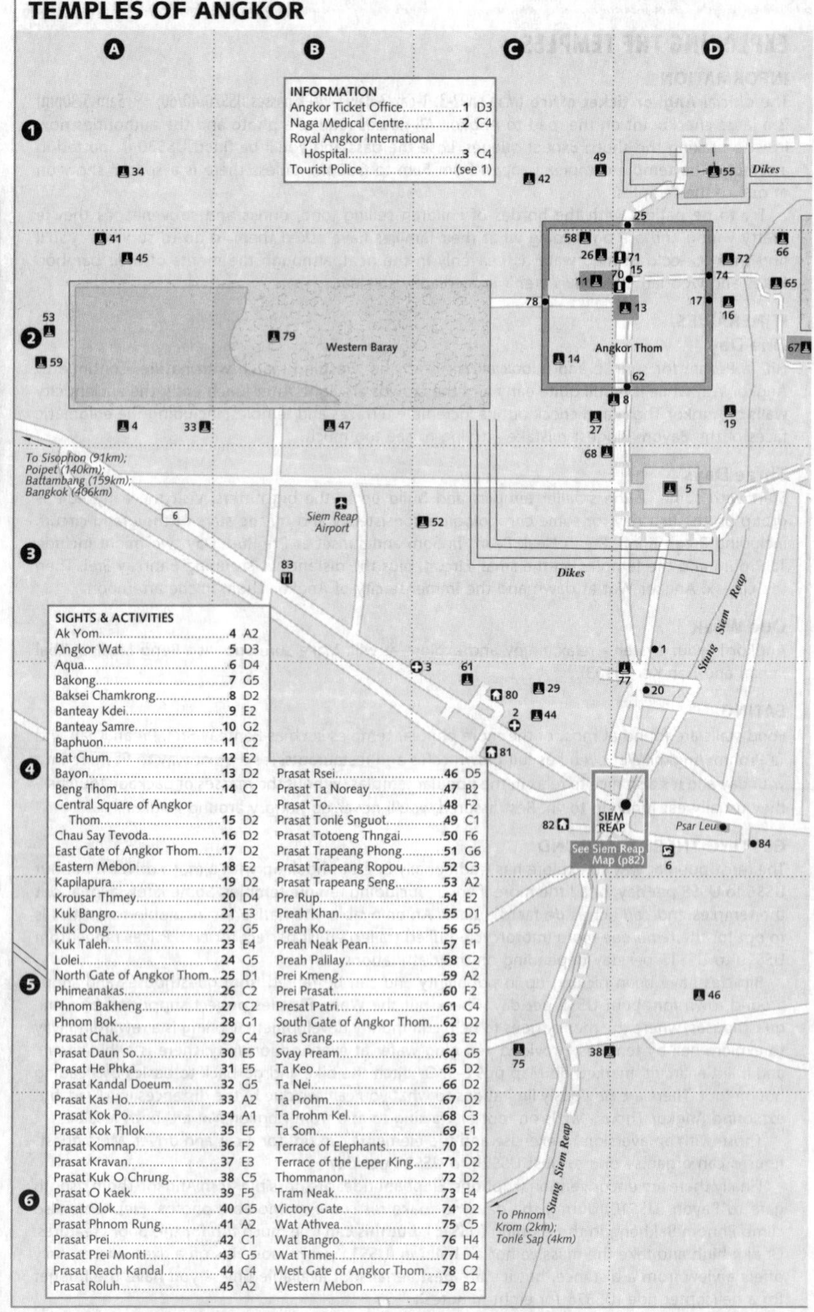
TEMPLES OF ANGKOR
INFORMATION
Angkor Ticket Office....1 D3
Naga Medical Centre....2 C4
Royal Angkor International Hospital....3 C4
Tourist Police....(see 1)
SIGHTS & ACTIVITIES
Ak Yom....4 A2
Angkor Wat....5 D3
Aqua....6 D4
Bakong....7 G5
Baksei Chamkrong....8 D2
Banteay Kdei....9 E2
Banteay Samre....10 G2
Baphuon....11 C2
Bat Chum....12 E2
Bayon....13 D2
Beng Thom....14 C2
Central Square of Angkor Thom....15 D2
Chau Say Tevoda....16 D2
East Gate of Angkor Thom....17 D2
Eastern Mebon....18 E2
Kapilapura....19 D2
Krousar Thmey....20 D4
Kuk Bangro....21 E3
Kuk Dong....22 G5
Kuk Taleh....23 E4
Lolei....24 G5
North Gate of Angkor Thom....25 D1
Phimeanakas....26 C2
Phnom Bakheng....27 C2
Phnom Bok....28 G1
Prasat Chak....29 C4
Prasat Daun So....30 E5
Prasat He Phka....31 E5
Prasat Kandal Doeum....32 G5
Prasat Kas Ho....33 A2
Prasat Kok Po....34 A1
Prasat Kok Thlok....35 E5
Prasat Komnap....36 F2
Prasat Kravan....37 E3
Prasat Kuk O Chrung....38 C5
Prasat O Kaek....39 F5
Prasat Olok....40 G5
Prasat Phnom Rung....41 A2
Prasat Prei....42 C1
Prasat Prei Monti....43 G5
Prasat Reach Kandal....44 C4
Prasat Roluh....45 A2
Prasat Rsei....46 D5
Prasat Ta Noreay....47 B2
Prasat To....48 F2
Prasat Tonlé Snguot....49 C1
Prasat Totoeng Thngai....50 F6
Prasat Trapeang Phong....51 G6
Prasat Trapeang Ropou....52 C3
Prasat Trapeang Seng....53 A2
Pre Rup....54 E2
Preah Khan....55 D1
Preah Ko....56 G5
Preah Neak Pean....57 E1
Preah Palilay....58 C2
Prei Kmeng....59 A2
Prei Prasat....60 F2
Presat Patri....61 C4
South Gate of Angkor Thom....62 D2
Sras Srang....63 E2
Svay Pream....64 G5
Ta Keo....65 D2
Ta Nei....66 D2
Ta Prohm....67 D2
Ta Prohm Kel....68 C3
Ta Som....69 E1
Terrace of Elephants....70 D2
Terrace of the Leper King....71 D2
Thommanon....72 D2
Tram Neak....73 E4
Victory Gate....74 D2
Wat Athvea....75 C5
Wat Bangro....76 H4
Wat Thmei....77 D4
West Gate of Angkor Thom....78 C2
Western Mebon....79 B2
Western Baray
Angkor Thom
Dikes
Siem Reap Airport
To Sisophon (91km); Poipet (140km); Battambang (159km); Bangkok (406km)
SIEM REAP
Psar Leu
See Siem Reap Map (p82)
Stung Siem Reap
To Phnom Krom (2km); Tonlé Sap (4km)

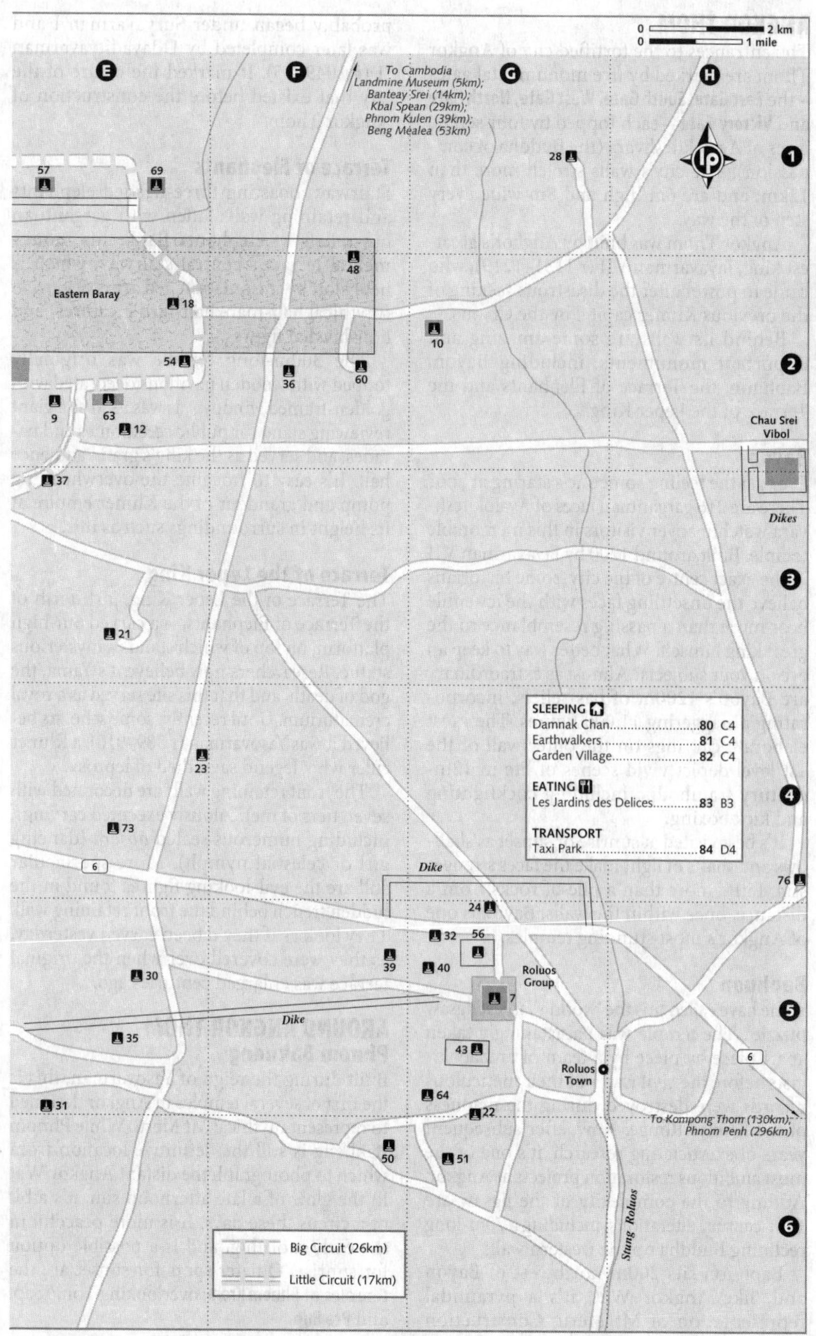

0 2 km
0 1 mile
E
F
G
H
To Cambodia Landmine Museum (5km); Banteay Srei (14km); Kbal Spean (29km); Phnom Kulen (39km); Beng Mealea (53km)
1
2
3
4
5
6
57
69
28
48
Eastern Baray
18
10
54
36
60
9
63
12
Chau Srei Vibol
37
Dikes
21
23
73
6
Dike
76
24
32
56
39
40
Roluos Group
30
7
Dike
35
43
6
Roluos Town
31
64
22
To Kompong Thom (130km); Phnom Penh (296km)
50
51
Stung Roluos
Big Circuit (26km)
Little Circuit (17km)
SLEEPING
Damnak Chan....80 C4
Earthwalkers....81 C4
Garden Village....82 C4
EATING
Les Jardins des Delices....83 B3
TRANSPORT
Taxi Park....84 D4
CAMBODIA

ANGKOR THOM

The entrances to the fortified city of Angkor Thom are marked by five monumental gates – the **East Gate**, **South Gate**, **West Gate**, **North Gate** and **Victory Gate** – each topped by four serene faces of Avalokiteshvara (the Buddha of compassion). The city's walls stretch more than 12km, and are 6m high and 8m wide every step of the way.

Angkor Thom was built by Angkor's greatest king, Jayavarman VII (r 1181–1219), who came to power after the disastrous sacking of the previous Khmer capital by the Chams.

Behind its walls are some amazing and important monuments, including Bayon, Baphuon, the Terrace of Elephants and the Terrace of the Leper King.

Bayon

Ever get the feeling someone's staring at you? There are 216 gargantuan faces of Avalokiteshvara watching over visitors in this memorable temple. Built around 1200 by Jayavarman VII in the exact centre of the city, some historians believe the unsettling faces with the icy smile bear more than a passing resemblance to the great king himself. What better way to keep an eye on your subjects? Almost as extraordinary are Bayon's 1200m of bas-reliefs, incorporating a staggering 11,000 figures. The most elaborate carvings on the outer wall of the 1st level depict vivid scenes of life in 12th-century Cambodia, including cockfighting and kick boxing.

It's best visited at sunrise or sunset as shadows and shafts of light make the faces stranger still. Little more than a pile of rocks from a distance, once within the walls, Bayon is one of Angkor's most stunning temples.

Baphuon

Some have called this the 'world's largest jigsaw puzzle'. The temple was painstakingly taken apart piece by piece by a team of archaeologists before the civil war, but their meticulous records were destroyed during the madness of the Khmer Rouge. Now, after subsequent years of excruciating research, it's one of the most ambitious restoration projects at Angkor. Adding to the complexity of the jigsaw are 16th-century alterations, including a 70m-long reclining Buddha on the western wall.

Baphuon sits 200m northwest of Bayon and, like Angkor Wat, it's a pyramidal representation of Mt Meru. Construction probably began under Suryavarman I and was later completed by Udayadityavarman II (r 1049–65). It marked the centre of the city that existed before the construction of Angkor Thom.

Terrace of Elephants

Stairways boasting three-headed elephants and retaining walls laden with gargantuan bas-reliefs of elephants flank this monumental terrace's central stairway, which is held aloft by the outstretched arms of *garuda* (mythical half-man, half-bird creatures) and lion-headed figures.

The 300m-long terrace was originally topped with wooden pavilions decorated with golden-framed windows. It was used as a giant reviewing stand for public ceremonies and parades, and served as the king's grand audience hall. It's easy to imagine the overwhelming pomp and grandeur of the Khmer empire at its height in surroundings such as this.

Terrace of the Leper King

The Terrace of the Leper King, just north of the Terrace of Elephants, is a carved 6m-high platform, on top of which stands a mysterious statue. Researchers now believe it's Yama, the god of death, and that this site served as a royal crematorium. Until recently, some scholars believed it was Yasovarman (r 889–910), a Khmer ruler who, legend says, died of leprosy.

The front retaining walls are decorated with seven tiers of meticulously executed carvings, including numerous seated *apsara* (dancing girl or celestial nymph). More spectacular still are the evil-looking figures found in the hidden trench behind the front retaining wall. They look as if they'd been carved yesterday, as they were covered over when the original terrace was enlarged centuries ago.

AROUND ANGKOR THOM

Phnom Bakheng

Built during the reign of Yasovarman, this is the first of several temples in Angkor designed to represent mythical Mt Meru. While Phnom Bakheng is still the definitive location from which to photograph the distant Angkor Wat in the glow of a late afternoon sun, it's a bit of a circus these days. It is more peaceful in the early morning, and is a possible option for sunrise. Quieter spots for sunset are the temples of **Phnom Krom**, overlooking Tonlé Sap, and **Pre Rup**.

DID YOU KNOW?

Much of Thai culture has its links to the Cambodian artisans, dancers, scholars and fighters whom the Thais made off with after they sacked Angkor in 1432. Have a peek at the bas-reliefs at Bayon and you'll see something that looks much like the 'Thai' kick boxing of today. The history of Angkor remains a seriously sensitive topic between the two cultures, fuelling a centuries-old rivalry.

Ta Keo

Built by Jayavarman V (r 968–1001), this massive pyramid rises more than 50m but, as it was never completed, it's missing the elaborate carvings seen at other temples. Inscriptions suggest it was struck by lightning during construction and abandoned. Others have suggested the death of the king or the extremely hard sandstone may explain its unfinished state. Those suffering from vertigo should stick to the eastern stairway.

Ta Prohm

One of the most popular of Angkor's many wonders, Ta Prohm looks like it fell straight out of a film set from *Indiana Jones;* in fact, Ta Prohm was used as a set for shooting both *Tomb Raider* and *Two Brothers*. This 12th-century Mahayana Buddhist temple is one of the Angkorian era's largest edifices and has been left much as it looked when the first French explorers set eyes on it more than a century ago. While other major monuments of Angkor have been preserved with a massive programme to clear away the all-devouring jungle, this temple has been abandoned to riotous nature – and it is quite a riot in some places.

Inside, the temple is a maze of narrow corridors and crumbling stonework, areas of which are roped off as the chances of collapse are serious. There are plenty of incredible photo opportunities inside, as the tentacle-like roots of mature trees slowly strangle the stonework. According to inscriptions it took an incredible 80,000 people to maintain the building!

There is a poetic cycle to this venerable ruin, with humans first conquering nature to create, and nature once again conquering humans to destroy.

Preah Khan

Preah Khan (Sacred Sword) once housed more than 1000 teachers and may have been a Buddhist university. It's one of Angkor's largest complexes, a maze of vaulted corridors, fine carvings and lichen-clad stonework. Its floor plan resembles that of Ta Prohm, but it is in a superior state of preservation. The temple is shaped in a cruciform. It's southern corridor is a wonderfully atmospheric jumble of vines and stones, while near the eastern entrance there is a curious two-storey structure that would look more at home in Greece than Cambodia. Preah Khan is a genuine fusion temple, the eastern entrance dedicated to Mahayana Buddhism, with equal sized doors, and the other cardinal directions dedicated to Shiva, Vishnu and Brahma, with successively smaller doors, emphasising the unequal nature of Hinduism.

Preah Neak Pean

Like the ultimate ornamental pond at some Balinese resort, Preah Neak Pean comprises a central tower set in a square pool and four smaller pools laid out symmetrically around the centre, each with an interesting subterranean carved fountain. The temple was originally set in a massive *baray* (reservoir) called Jayatataka that fed Preah Khan.

Ta Som

This tiny temple is easy to overlook with so many other temptations to choose from, but the eastern gate here has been absolutely overwhelmed by an ancient tree that has sent its intrusive roots on a destructive mission into every nook and cranny. Unlike Ta Prohm, you won't have to wait in line for a photograph.

ROLUOS GROUP

Southeast of Angkor Wat, Roluos (then called Hariharalaya) served as the capital of Indravarman I (r 877–89). While the temples here can't compete with the major monuments, they are among the earliest large, stone temples built by the Khmer and mark the beginning of classical art; it's worth visiting them early on for a chronological insight into the evolution of Khmer architectural ingenuity.

Bakong, the grandest of Angkor's earlier temples, was also created by Indravarman. Dedicated to Shiva, the complex consists of a five-tiered sandstone central pyramid, flanked by eight towers of brick and sandstone.

Preah Ko is a direct link to the earlier brick structures of the pre-Angkorian Chenla period, with six brick *prasat* (towers) decorated with carved sandstone and plaster reliefs. It was erected by Indravarman I in the late 9th century.

OTHER TEMPLES

The following temples are beyond the central area of Angkor, but both Banteay Srei and Kbal Spean can be combined together with Angkor if you toss a few dollars more your moto driver's way (US$10 to US$15 for the day). For a fistful of dollars (US$15 for the day), it's possible to add Beng Mealea to the list. A standard Angkor pass is only good for entry into Banteay Srei and Kbal Spean.

Banteay Srei

Banteay Srei is considered by many to be the jewel in Angkor's artistic crown. At first sight, some visitors are disappointed by its size, but once within its walls it's impossible not to be impressed by the elaborate carvings that adorn the doorways and walls. The carvings are roped off these days.

The site is located about 32km north of Siem Reap, and late afternoon or early morning (before the tour buses arrive) is a fine time to visit, as the sun's rays bring out the best in the pink sandstone.

Kbal Spean

The River of a Thousand Lingas, Kbal Spean is home to the most intricate riverbed carvings in the Angkor area and was only 'rediscovered' in 1969. Sadly, its remote location has led to some looting in recent years. Beneath the carvings there is a small waterfall, which is best visited from June to December as the river dries up during the dry season. The site is about 15km north of Banteay Srei and a 30-minute scenic jungle trek from the parking area.

READING UP

The definitive guidebook to Angkor was long *A Guide to the Angkor Monuments* by Maurice Glaize, first published in the 1940s. It's hard to find, but you can download it free at www.theangkorguide.com. Among the modern titles, *Angkor: An Introduction to the Temples* by Dawn Rooney is the most popular. Complete with illustrations and photographs, it's a useful companion around Angkor. Another popular title is *Angkor: Heart of an Asian Empire* by Bruno Dagens, with the emphasis more on the discovery and restoration of Angkor; it's lavishly illustrated and dripping with interesting asides.

DID YOU KNOW?

Banteay Srei means 'Citadel of the Women'; it is said that it must have been built by women because the elaborate carvings are too fine for the hand of a man.

Beng Mealea

The *Titanic* of temples, **Beng Mealea** (admission US$5) is a huge, truly abandoned temple, sunk in the jungle, that makes Ta Prohm look like they just forgot to mow the lawn. Built by Suryavarman II, the man who gave the world Angkor Wat, Beng Mealea has a layout that is remarkably similar to that of its more famous sibling, although this is hard to imagine given the mess it is today. Much of the jungle has been cleared in recent years, but the site still has a magical atmosphere. It's about 70km northeast of Siem Reap on surfaced roads and it can take as little as one hour to get here.

As well the US$5 admission charge there are additional charges for cars and motorbikes – agree on who is paying these in advance.

Phnom Kulen

One of the most sacred places in Cambodia, this famous **mountain** (admission US$20) was the birthplace of the Khmer empire; Jayavarman II proclaimed independence from Java here in 802. At the mountain's summit (487m) is an ancient reclining Buddha, carved into a massive boulder, and an active monastery, though visitors usually prefer the large waterfall and the impressive carvings found on the riverbed nearby.

It costs a whopping US$20 on top of the US$15 you'll have to fork out for the moto here – quite frankly, it's not worth it compared with Angkor. Head instead to Kbal Spean which is included in the Angkor pass. Still interested? It's about 60km from Siem Reap and getting here takes about three hours.

NORTHWESTERN CAMBODIA

Nowhere else in Cambodia, perhaps even in Southeast Asia, is there a region with such an intoxicating mix of history and adventure. Battle Preah Vihear province's jungle paths to sit alone atop immense temple complexes, cruise the kingdom's most scenic water route to Battambang, an elegant French colonial town, or wade into the region's recent and painful past as the home of the Khmer Rouge.

POIPET

☎ 054 / pop 45,000

Viva Poipet! Long the cesspool of Cambodia, Poipet is reinventing itself as the Las Vegas of Cambodia, home to more than half-a-dozen major casino resorts. It's the first place in the kingdom many visitors encounter, thanks to the nearby Thailand border crossing at Aranya Prathet. Scams abound in this Wild West town, so don't stick around.

Canadia Bank (☎ 967107; NH5) is not far from the border post and will change travellers cheques.

If you are unlucky enough to get stuck here, **Ngy Heng Hotel** (☎ 967101; NH5; r US$5-10; ❄) is a reliable option that isn't fully occupied by casino employees. The clean rooms include hot water and satellite TV.

There are many transport scams, so negotiate hard. The local authorities insist foreigners use tourist transport, which effectively means inflated prices. A free shuttle takes you to the 'Tourist Lounge', which is the bus terminal for Phnom Penh, Siem Reap and Battambang. Share taxis are fixed at a cheeky US$50 to Siem Reap, but greedy touts sometimes demand US$60 or more; official buses to Siem Reap are about US$10. The best strategy is to ignore all offers of help and consider going as far as Sisophon first before arranging the onward journey to Siem Reap or Battambang. To dodge the dodgy types, check out Cambodia Overland on **Tales of Asia** (www.talesofasia.com) for all the nitty-gritty.

The roads east from Poipet will shock those arriving from Thailand. Times stated are for the dry season – it can take much, much longer in the wet season. A pick-up is a slower, slightly cheaper and much dirtier option.

SISOPHON

☎ 054 / pop 111,700

Most people who've been here never even know it – for them, Sisophon (known as Svay, or 'Mango' to locals) is just a dusty stop between Poipet and Siem Reap. However, for those in the know, it's the perfect base for a day trip to the huge temple complex of Banteay Chhmar. It's also the jumping-off point for those heading to Phnom Penh by road via the French colonial town of Battambang.

Cheap guesthouses line the road to Siem Reap. The best of the bunch is **Sara Torn Guesthouse** (NH6 east; s/tw with shared bathroom 100/150B), which has an inviting veranda. Rooms are spacious, but very, very basic.

Neak Meas Hotel (☎ 012 555349; r US$12-20; ❄) is the largest hotel in town – and it's still expanding. Consider bringing earplugs as the karaoke bar and nightclub kick in every night. A great all-rounder, but the restaurant is not so hot.

For cheap eats, head to the friendly food stalls lining the taxi park. One of the better eateries in town is **Phkay Proek Restaurant** (NH5; mains US$1.50-4; 🕑 breakfast, lunch & dinner), next door to the Phnom Svay Hotel. Thai dishes feature heavily, plus plenty of Cambodia's most wanted.

After some negotiating, a share taxi seat should cost 60B to Battambang (one hour) and about 150B to Siem Reap (two to three hours). For more comfort, pay double and have the front seat to yourself. Locals pay about 60B for transport to Poipet (one hour).

BANTEAY CHHMAR

Vast and remote, the vestiges of **Banteay Chhmar** (admission US$5; 🕑 6am-6pm) linger in the jungle and are a playground for the adventurous. Wander around rubble strewn with carvings and climb into the shadows of dark corridors.

GETTING TO THAILAND

When leaving Cambodia walk across the border at Poipet and take a túk-túk (80B) or motorcycle taxi (60B) to Aranya Prathet, from where there are two daily trains (70B, six hours) and regular air-con buses (1st/2nd class 220/180B, four hours, hourly) to Bangkok. The border is open from 7am to 8pm.

See p709 for information on doing the trip in reverse.

What's left of the massive structure houses some brilliant bas-reliefs, including the famous 32-armed Avalokiteshvaras adorning the rear outer gallery. Sadly, only two remain, as six were smuggled into Thailand after a brazen act of looting in 1998. The front outer gallery houses a sublime series of bas-reliefs depicting sea battles between the Khmer and Cham empires.

Set among rice fields, **Banteay Top** (Fortress of the Army) is almost 14km southeast of Banteay Chhmar. Although it's only a little 'un, there's something special about its atmosphere. One damaged tower appears partially rebuilt and looks decidedly precarious, a bony finger pointing skyward.

NH69 from Sisophon to Banteay Chhmar (two to three hours) ranges from tolerable to bad depending on the season. Arrange a return moto trip in Sisophon (US$10 or so) or take a pick-up to Thmar Puok (outside/inside 4000/6000r) and arrange a moto from there (US$5).

BATTAMBANG

☎ 053 / pop 158,100

Battambang is an elegant riverside town, home to the best-preserved French-period architecture in the country. The stunning boat trip from Siem Reap lures travellers here, but it's the remarkably chilled atmosphere that keeps them lingering; you'd never guess it's the kingdom's second-largest city. Battambang is also the ideal base for exploring nearby temples and villages that offer a real slice of rural Cambodia.

Orientation

Battambang is fairly compact and easily negotiable on foot. Most of the restaurants, shops and hotels are on the west bank of the Stung Sangker, within a few blocks of Psar Nat (Meeting Market), which marks the town centre.

Information

Numerous Interphone shops south of Psar Nat on the riverfront offer cheapish international phone calls. There are lots of internet places along the riverfront and around the market.

Battambang Referral Hospital Limited services and little English is spoken; it's opposite the boat dock.

Canadia Bank (☎ 952267) Offers free Visa and MasterCard cash advances and can change most major currencies or travellers cheques. Also has an international ATM. It's opposite Psar Nat.

Main post office (Ph 1) Not worth the risk – wait until Phnom Penh or Siem Reap.

Tourist office Eagerly dishes out info on local sights, though there's little in the way of hand-outs. It's near the governor's residence.

Union Commercial Bank (Ph 1) Offers free Visa cash advances.

Sights

Although it's the pace, not the sights, that seems to keep people here, there are a few things to brighten up the day. Lazing on the riverbank, in true French fashion, are a series of charming **French shophouses**. Slightly south, the **Battambang Museum** (Ph 1; admission US$1; 8-11am & 2-5pm Mon-Fri) houses an attractive but limited collection of fine-carved lintels.

Phare Ponleu Selpak (☎ 952424; www.phareps.org) stages lively circus shows and dances at its arts centre for disadvantaged children. Give it a call or look out for its posters for schedules. It's located outside town.

Battambang's surrounding countryside is laced with contrasting histories: ancient and recent, brilliant and bloody. An excursion can't be recommended enough.

Courses

Take a lesson at **Smokin' Pot** (☎ 012 821400). First you'll be taught the finer points of purchasing at the open market before delving into the art of Khmer and Thai…*cooking!* What were you thinking? Lesson, lunch and a morning of fun for just US$7.

Sleeping

Chhaya Hotel (☎ 952170; chhaya.best@yahoo.com; 118 Ph 3; r US$4-12;) The popular Chhaya has a huge number of clean and comfortable rooms. Free shuttles to the boat dock and switched-on local guides ensure it remains a traveller favourite.

Park Hotel (☎ 953773; r with shared bathroom US$3, r with private bathroom US$5-12;) The location is not the best in town, but the rooms are seriously good value. Rooms with bathroom include satellite TV and other little touches.

Royal Hotel (☎ 016 912034; royalasiahotelbb@yahoo.com; r US$4-20;) Rooms come in every shape and size here; opt for just using the fan in one of the air-con rooms for a real deal. Check out the rooftop restaurant for views over Battambang.

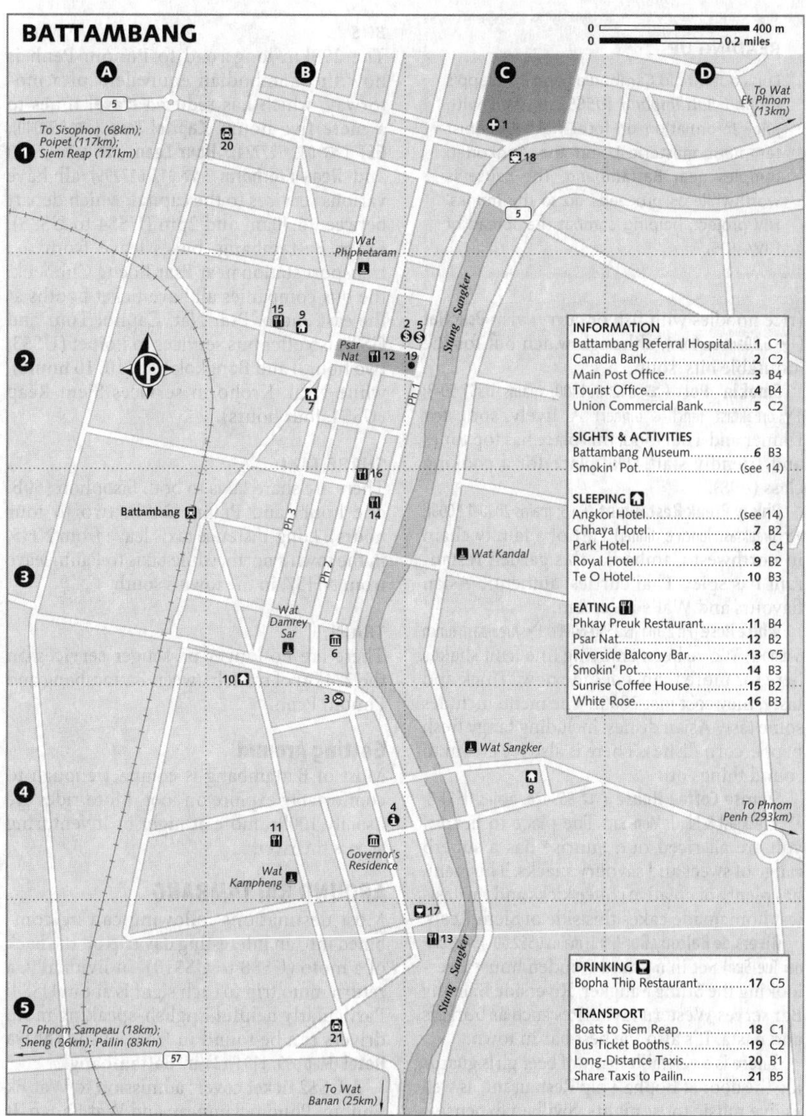

Te O Hotel (☎ 952288; Ph 3; s/d US$11/13) One of the oldest hotels in town, this is still a favourite with the NGO crowd. The rooms are clean and well finished, and include satellite TV and fridge.

Angkor Hotel (☎ 952310, Ph 1; r US$11-13; ❄) It boasts a great location on the riverfront, but is an ugly duckling compared to the fine old buildings nearby. All rooms are the same, with TV and fridge, but hot water is extra. Ask for a river view.

Eating & Drinking

Battambang has a good blend of restaurants with the option of Khmer classics or some international enticements. For truly cheap Khmer treats like *bobor* and *nam ben choc*

READING UP

Look out for old Cambodia hand Ray Zepp's *Around Battambang* (US$5), packed with juicy information on local wats (Buddhist temple-monasteries) and the Angkorian temples near Battambang. The cause is worthwhile as proceeds go to the monks' HIV project, helping combat the spread of HIV/AIDS.

(rice noodles with fish or curry) visit **Psar Nat** (6.30am-5.30pm), although watch out for the 'unusable bits' soup.

Smokin' Pot (☎ 012 821400; mains US$1.50-3; breakfast, lunch & dinner) A lively spot for Khmer and Thai food, this place has top tunes and friendly staff. *The* place for a cooking class (p98).

Phkay Preuk Restaurant (Ph 3; mains 2000-12,000r; breakfast, lunch & dinner) Part of a family chain in northwest Cambodia, this garden restaurant has spicy Thai curries, authentic Asian flavours and Walls ice cream.

White Rose (Ph 2; mains 2500-6000r; breakfast, lunch & dinner) We've been enjoying fine fruit shakes here for more than a decade now. Thick and tasty, they cost just 2000r. The menu includes some tasty Asian dishes, including tangy fresh peppercorn dishes. There is also ice cream to round things off.

Sunrise Coffee House (☎ 953426; mains US$1-3; breakfast & lunch Mon-Sat) The place to head if you are all riced out, Sunrise has a superb range of sweet and savoury snacks. The menu has plenty of creative coffee kicks and the tastiest homemade cakes this side of Siem Reap.

Riverside Balcony Bar (Ph 1; mains US$2.50-4; dinner Tue-Sun) Set in a grand wooden house overlooking the Stung Sangker, Riverside Balcony Bar serves Western favourites such as burgers and pasta. It's also the best bar in town.

There is a veritable army of beer girls guarding the door at Bopha Thip Restaurant, as well as live music most nights. Swill an expensive beer and try out your *rom vong* (Cambodia circle dancing) moves with the locals.

Getting There & Away

BOAT

For the inside story on the speedboats to Siem Reap (US$15, three to eight hours), see p89. The dock is in the north of town, not far from the hospital.

BUS

The 293km-long road to Phnom Penh is now the Cambodian equivalent of a motorway, which has reduced travel times to a mere five hours. **Capitol Tour** (☎ 953040), **GST** (☎ 012 727774), **Hour Lean** (☎ 012 307252) and **Neak Krorhorm** (☎ 012 627299) all have various services to the capital, which depart between 6.30am and 2pm (US$4 to US$5). From Battambang, buses leave from the transport station near Psar Boeng Chhoeuk; the bus companies all have ticket booths at the east end of Psar Nat. Capitol Tour and GST also offer bus services to Poipet (US$3, two hours) and Bangkok (US$10, 10 hours), while Neak Krohorm services Siem Reap (US$4, four hours).

SHARE TAXI

There are share taxis to both Sisophon (60B, one hour) and Pailin (200B, two to four hours). Long-distance taxis leave from NH5, in the town's north, while taxis to Pailin leave from NH57, in the town's south.

TRAIN

There are no longer passenger services on the 274km of track between Battambang and Phnom Penh.

Getting Around

Most of Battambang is compact enough to comfortably explore on foot. Moto rides are usually 1000r, more at night or if venturing across the river.

AROUND BATTAMBANG

Most destinations following can be combined into an interesting day trip on the back of a moto (US$8 to US$10). Individually, a return moto trip to each sight is about US$4. Particularly helpful English-speaking moto drivers can be found in front of the **Chhaya Hotel** (Map p99; 118 Ph 3) in Battambang.

A US$2 ticket covers admission to Wat Ek Phnom, Phnom Sampeau and Wat Banan. It can be bought at any of the three sights, all of which are open during daylight hours.

WARNING

Pailin is one of the most heavily mined areas in Cambodia so be doubly careful to avoid straying from the path.

GETTING TO THAILAND

Leaving Cambodia, take a share taxi (100B, one hour) or moto (100B) from Pailin to the border at Psar Pruhm. From Ban Pakard on the Thai side of the border, there are regular minibuses to Chanthaburi (100B, 1½ hours). From there you'll have no problem hopping on a bus to Bangkok. The border crossing is open from 7am to 5pm.

See p765 for information on doing the trip in the reverse direction.

Wat Ek Phnom

The Angkorian-era temple of Ek Phnom is not in the league of Angkor Wat, but it is a beautiful ride out here. The shady road hugs the river, passing old wooden houses and snippets of real life before arriving at the temple, 13km north of Battambang. Try to visit in the early morning or late afternoon light.

Phnom Sampeau

Phnom Sampeau is a striking hill, 18km from town. With its limestone cavities and memories of genocide, it is a sad juxtaposition of beauty and brutality. The eerie caves were used as slaughter chambers by the Khmer Rouge and still contain the skeletal remains of its victims. Climb further and you'll see two massive guns used by the Vietnamese during the war. Finally, at the summit there's a stunning view over the countryside and a small wat with a golden **stupa**. A massive 38m-high and 112.5m-long Buddha montage is being hewn into the outcrop's base. Local children make excellent guides for a couple of thousand riel.

Wat Banan

Locals claim Wat Banan was the inspiration for Angkor Wat, but its teeny-tiny five towers suggest they're hopelessly optimistic. Still, it's in impressive shape for its age, and its hillside location makes it the most striking and peaceful temple in the area. There are 359 stairs to climb but good views lie in wait. The temple is 25km south of Battambang.

On the way back to town ask the driver to test drive Battambang's infamous **bamboo train**. Basically it's a little platform on wheels, powered by a portable motor, but it sure flies – great fun until you meet something coming the other way!

PAILIN

☎ 053 / pop 17,800

Pailin has an attractive location amid the foothills of Chuor Phnom Kravanh (Cardamom Mountains), but the town itself lacks major attractions unless you know a bit about gemstones. Pailin has long been a haven for retired Khmer Rouge leaders, so it will be interesting to see the local reaction here if or when the trial moves forwards. Not that many foreigners make it here, although some have unwittingly passed through on the bus from Bangkok to Siem Reap (see p89).

There are some really rough-and-ready guesthouses here, but **Guesthouse Ponleu Pich Pailin** (r 100B) is just about bearable with its basic rooms. It's opposite Psar Pailin.

Hang Meas Pailin Hotel (☎ 012 787546; NH57; r US$11-50; ❄) is the leading hotel in town, with smart rooms that include satellite TV, fridge and hot shower. There's a decent restaurant here with regular live music.

Share taxis to Battambang (200B, two to four hours) regularly ply the bumpy but bearable road.

ANLONG VENG

☎ 065

The dusty and isolated town of Anlong Veng was long the stronghold of the Khmer Rouge, and many ex-revolutionaries still live here. Anlong Veng finally succumbed to government forces in 1998 and the government has since encouraged both development and an influx of moderate migrants from other parts of the kingdom.

Attractions include military commander **Ta Mok's House** (admission US$2; 🕑 7am-5pm), **Pol Pot's**

GETTING TO THAILAND

The Choam–Choam Srawngam border crossing with Thailand is just a few kilometres north of Anlong Veng. Catch a moto (US$2) and hop off en route to see the decapitated statue of Khmer Rouge soldiers carved into a boulder. On the other side, transport is not so frequent. Catch a taxi to Si Saket, the closest town. For details about getting from the major Cambodian cities to Choam see p102.

See p755 for information on doing the trip in the reverse direction.

cremation site and other remarkably dull places catapulted to 'mildly interesting' by their connection with mass murderers. More interesting are the majestic views from the **Chuor Phnom Dangrek** looming over town. Anlong Veng is also the western gateway to Prasat Preah Vihear.

For accommodation, **Bot Uddom Guest House** (☎ 012 779495; r US$5-15; ❄) overlooks a pretty lake. Rooms are very clean and there are some comfortable common areas.

Anlong Veng is 142km north of Siem Reap. Share taxis (20,000r, three to five hours) and pick-ups (15,000/8000r inside/outside) regularly ride the roller-coaster dust express (NH67) to Siem Reap. It costs about US$2 for a seat to the border at Choam.

PREAH VIHEAR PROVINCE

Home to hard-core journeys and rich rewards, this is the province for adventure addicts and those who long for personal encounters with forgotten Khmer temples in the forests of Cambodia. Preah Vihear is one of the poorest provinces in the country and the infrastructure is the kingdom's worst, but while sandy ox cart trails and tortuous roads ensure long, painful, dirty journeys, they also guarantee solitude at the temples.

As roads slowly get better, the number of visitors will increase, so say a prayer for your backside now and hit the road. The most gratifying trip is one that links Siem Reap and Kompong Thom (the best jumping-off points) via Koh Ker, Preah Khan and Prasat Preah Vihear temple complexes. Throw in some ancient Angkor bridges such as Spean Ta Ong, and you have a mission worthy of Indiana Jones.

Thanks to seas of sand that swallow Suzukis, it's a challenge for highly experienced motorbike riders, so it's definitely not for gung-ho beginners. Find a good moto driver (about US$15 per day plus petrol) or get a group together and rent a sturdy 4WD with a driver. Carry a hammock and mosquito net, and don't even think about it during the wet season.

> **WARNING**
>
> Preah Vihear province is one of Cambodia's most heavily mined provinces and most were laid in the past decade. Do not, under any circumstances, stray from well-trodden paths anywhere in the province, including remote temple sites. Those with their own transport should only travel on roads or trails that locals use regularly.

Tbeng Meanchey

☎ 064 / pop 24,400

The only thing going for this small and nondescript town is its proximity to the glorious temple of Prasat Preah Vihear, 115km to the north. Locals refer to the town as Preah Vihear, a fact that confounds many a foreigner.

There are cheap cells at **27 May Guesthouse** (r 5000-15,000r), but what do you expect for US$1.25? It can get noisy here, as it's near the market and taxi park.

The best all-rounder in town is the **Prum Tep Guesthouse** (☎ 012 964645; r US$5-10; ❄), which has spacious, comfortable rooms with satellite TV. Bathrooms include Western-style toilets and it's the only place with air-con, if it's working.

The **Mlop Dong Restaurant** (4000-8000r; 🕑 breakfast, lunch & dinner) is a lively local restaurant that does a roaring local trade from breakfast through to close. By night, it's the closest thing to a bar in town. It's opposite the taxi park.

Share taxis (20,000r) travel the 155km along sometimes good, often bad, NH64 to Kompong Thom daily.

Prasat Preah Vihear

Occupying the most breathtaking location of all Angkorian temples, **Prasat Preah Vihear** (admission US$5) is perched atop a mountain escarpment on the border with Thailand, with enormous views across the plains of northern Cambodia, 550m below. It was built during the reign of Suryavarman I (c 1002–49) and embellished by successive monarchs, resulting in an impressive series of sanctuaries rising to the cliff's summit. The upper level is the best preserved and hosts some exquisitely carved lintels.

You'll see some incredibly clean tourists from Thailand, thanks to a major motorway that Thailand built to the temple's front door – try not to drool or cry when you see it. Just remember, your filth is your passport and you can smile knowing that you've undertaken a modern-day pilgrimage that's easily the equal of any undertaken at the height of the Khmer empire. The temple only became accessible in recent years after the Khmer Rouge, who gained control in the early 1990s, finally surrendered in 1998.

Sleep at the rudimentary **Raksaleap Guest House** (092 224838; r US$5), located below the escarpment in Kor Muy Village, or better still, hitch a hammock on the cliff by the temple.

A long day trip here from Anlong Veng by moto (US$15) is feasible; the 103km trip takes about three hours each way on decent dirt roads. Sporadic pick-ups leave Anlong Veng for nearby Sa Em (10,000r, two hours), from where motos can get you to the escarpment's base (US$3, 40 minutes). The road to Tbeng Meanchey is a nightmare after the rainy season, but usually gets graded some time during the dry season. The 115km journey can take anything from two to five hours. Pick-ups and share taxis leave from the taxi station at around 9am daily (outside/inside US$2.50/5, entire front cabin US$10) or hire a moto (US$15 per day plus petrol).

The road up the escarpment is stupidly steep, with 35-degree slopes in areas, meaning you'll either have to hike up in the heat for 1½ hours or hire a moto (US$5 return).

Preah Khan

Covering almost 5 sq km, Preah Khan is the largest temple enclosure constructed during the Angkorian period – quite a feat when you consider the competition. Thanks to its back-of-beyond location, it's astonishingly quiet and peaceful. **Prasat Preah Stung** is perhaps the most memorable of the many temples here, with four enigmatic Bayon-style faces. The dramatic *garudas* and delicate elephant carvings clinging to the crumbling remains of **Prasat Damrei**, a few kilometres east, are also worth a peek. Although looters and time have taken their toll at Preah Khan, there's enough rising from the sea of rubble to imagine the complex's former splendour.

The best bet is to stay with one of the friendly families in 'downtown' **Ta Seng**, the village 4km away. Expect to pay about 10,000r per person with a basic meal. It's also possible to sling a hammock in the temple, but there is no food or drink available (although there are lots of mossies for company).

Preah Khan is a gruelling five-hour trip from Kompong Thom or Tbeng Meanchey. An amazing, exhaustive and rewarding alternative is to approach along the ancient Angkor highway from Beng Mealea, which is 70km northeast of Siem Reap (the trip takes about six hours). You'll cross several splendid Angkor bridges, like the remarkable 77m-long **Spean Ta Ong**, just west of Khvau. Even if you have your own bike, it's still best to hire a knowledgeable moto driver (US$15 per day plus petrol) to help navigate the countless jungle trails on these three routes.

Koh Ker

Home to almost 30 ancient structures, including **Prasat Thom**, an immense seven-tier pyramid, **Koh Ker** (admission US$10; 6am-6pm) was briefly the capital of the Khmer empire under king Jayavarman IV (r 928–42). Walking past the shattered lion guarding **Prasat Krahom** (Red Temple), you'll soon see the Mayan-like pyramid climbing skyward. The views and breeze at its summit are well worth the steep 40m climb. Much of the jungle that once cloaked Prasat Krahom has recently been cleared, killing some of the romance but opening up the scale of the complex.

For richer or poorer – richer in the case of the Cambodian businessmen, poorer in the case of the average backpacker – Koh Ker represents the future of Preah Vihear's remote temple complexes, with a new toll road, admission charges and an increasing number of visitors. That said, most tourists still don't make it this far and the future crowds have yet to materialise. Get here now.

To overnight here, sling a hammock near the temples, stay with friendly villagers in Koh Ker (prices are negotiable, but 10,000r is probably fair, plus extra if food is available), or make for the **Kohké Guesthouse** (s US$3) in the village of Siyong, 9km southeast.

Koh Ker is now only two to three hours from Siem Reap via Beng Mealea. The 292km return trip should be about US$15 to US$20 by moto, or about US$65 by car. It's just two hours from Tbeng Meanchey, and a moto is about US$10 to US$15 for the day.

KOMPONG THOM

☎ 062 / pop 74,600

Kompong Thom is a perfect springboard for adventure seekers wishing to see the pre-Angkorian temples of Sambor Prei Kuk or the remarkable remote temples of Preah Vihear province. Surrounding this otherwise dull and dusty town are endless rice paddies, dirt tracks and glimpses into Cambodia's traditional rural life, something those sticking to the capital and Angkor miss.

All rooms at cheap and central **Arunras Guesthouse** (☎ 012 865935; NH6; s US$3-8, tw US$4-8; ❄) come with TV and bathroom, but not all rooms have windows. There's an excellent restaurant (mains 3000r to 6000r; open breakfast, lunch and dinner) downstairs, always packed with itinerants digging into local favourites. Try the deep-fried honeycomb if possible.

The tallest building in Kompong Thom, **Arunras Hotel** (☎ 961294; NH6; s US$3-7, tw US$6-12; ❄) is also home to the first lift in town. The smart rooms all include satellite TV, fridge and bathroom. The big restaurant has the same menu as the guesthouse, but with fancier décor.

The numerous buses running along NH6 between Phnom Penh and Siem Reap often drop off or pick up passengers here. A seat to Phnom Penh (2½ hours) or Siem Reap (2½ hours) is about 10,000r.

SAMBOR PREI KUK

This **complex** (admission US$3; 🕑 6am-6pm) has the most impressive group of pre-Angkorian temples found anywhere in Cambodia. Formerly a 7th-century Chenla capital called Isanapura, it's now dotted with ancient vestiges and US bomb craters. The best-preserved structure is **Prasat Yeay Peau**, with a solitary tree strangling its east gate like a boa enveloping its prey. Donning elegantly coiffured ringlets, several lion statues guard the complex's largest remaining structure, **Prasat Tao**. The smaller **Prasat Sambor** is notable for the seven linga (phallic symbols) surrounding it. There's a special serenity here in the forest, and it's a great prelude to the more famous capital of Angkor.

Take NH6 north of Kompong Thom, veer right after 5km on NH64 and 11km north is a massive sign. Turn right on a delightful dirt road and it's another 14km; all up, it's about 30km. A return moto trip costs about US$5.

SOUTH COAST

The south coast of Cambodia is an alluring mix of clear blue water, castaway islands, rousing colonial towns and jungle-clad mountains. The coastal cities are developing fast, but there is still a great expanse of Cambodia less travelled, and adventurers will find the region just as rewarding as the sun seekers looking for sand will. Taking in these attractions can be done in as little as a week, making a loop between Phnom Penh and Sihanoukville. With more time you could find yourself alone on one of the many pristine beaches dotting the coast's undeveloped tropical islands. Forget finding *The Beach* in Thailand, it was discovered a long time ago, but it just might exist here.

SIHANOUKVILLE

☎ 034 / pop 77,000

Angkor blows your mind, the Killing Fields squeezes your soul and the back roads of the north bust your butt, so it's hardly surprising that travellers have fallen for Sihanoukville's silicon sands and unspoiled tropical islands. Sihanoukville is the perfect Cambodian cure-all, and a visit brings bliss and relaxation by day, drinking and decadence by night.

The airport has now reopened and the town is taking off. Sadly, this has provoked messy land disputes in the local community, but gladly it means a happening selection of guesthouses, restaurants and bars awaits.

Orientation

Sihanoukville is spread out across a sprawling headland, with its underwhelming city centre squarely in the middle. To the west is Victory Beach and Weather Station Hill, which constitute the traditional backpackers' hang-out, and to the south is the budding backpacker haven nicknamed Serendipity Beach, which merges with upmarket Ochheuteal Beach to the south.

Information

Things are evolving quickly here, so get the lowdown in the *Sihanoukville Visitor's Guide*, a pocket-sized listings magazine available at local guesthouses and bars.

> **GETTING INTO TOWN**
>
> Most buses and share taxis from Phnom Penh, Kampot and Krong Koh Kong stop in the town centre, and from there it's just a moto ride (3000r to 5000r) to the most popular guesthouses on Weather Station Hill above Victory Beach, or down at Serendipity Beach. Those coming by ferry from Krong Koh Kong will be greeted by motos galore at the ferry port (2km north of town) and charged 3000r to 8000r.

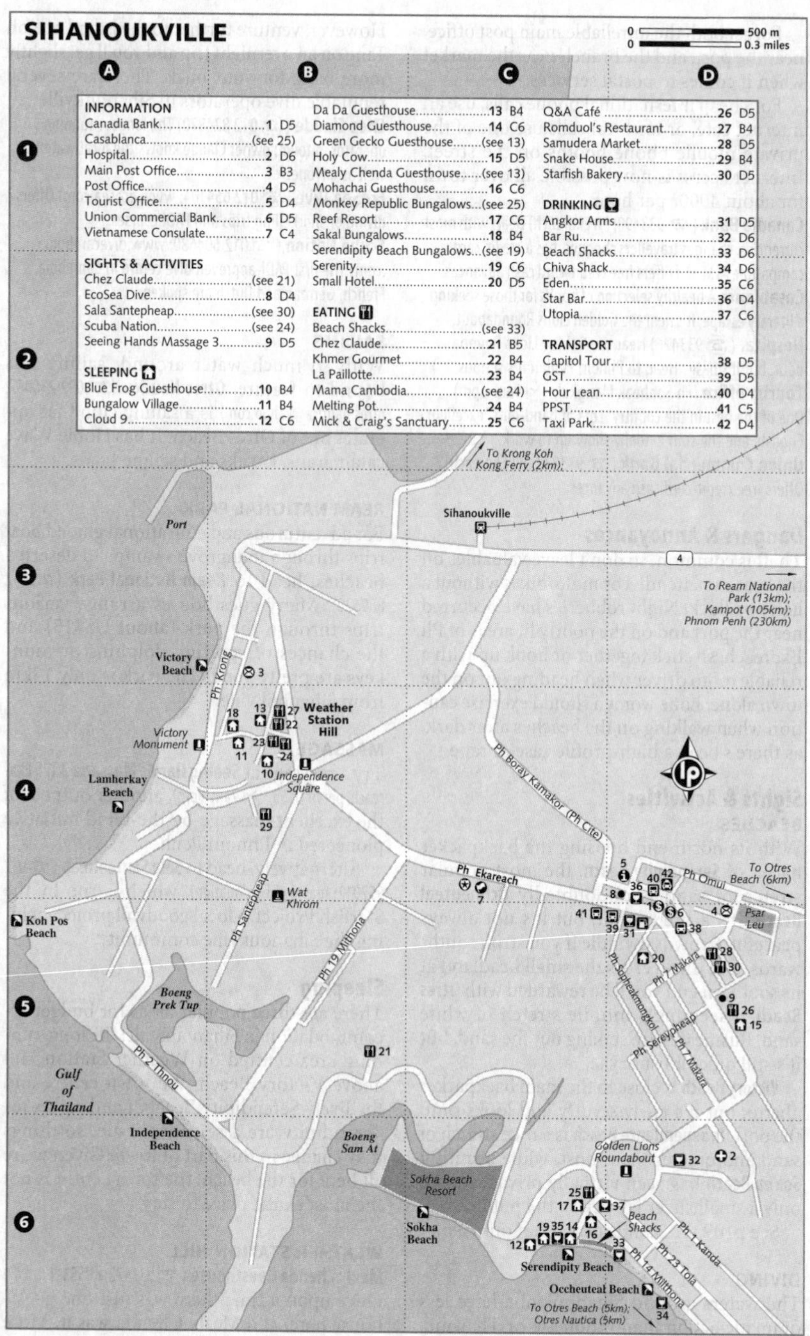
SIHANOUKVILLE
0 500 m
0 0.3 miles
A
B
C
D
1
2
3
4
5
6
INFORMATION
Canadia Bank....1 D5
Casablanca....(see 25)
Hospital....2 D6
Main Post Office....3 B3
Post Office....4 D5
Tourist Office....5 D4
Union Commercial Bank....6 D5
Vietnamese Consulate....7 C4
SIGHTS & ACTIVITIES
Chez Claude....(see 21)
EcoSea Dive....8 D4
Sala Santepheap....(see 30)
Scuba Nation....(see 24)
Seeing Hands Massage 3....9 D5
SLEEPING
Blue Frog Guesthouse....10 B4
Bungalow Village....11 B4
Cloud 9....12 C6
Da Da Guesthouse....13 B4
Diamond Guesthouse....14 C6
Green Gecko Guesthouse....(see 13)
Holy Cow....15 D5
Mealy Chenda Guesthouse....(see 13)
Mohachai Guesthouse....16 C6
Monkey Republic Bungalows....(see 25)
Reef Resort....17 C6
Sakal Bungalows....18 B4
Serendipity Beach Bungalows....(see 19)
Serenity....19 C6
Small Hotel....20 D5
EATING
Beach Shacks....(see 33)
Chez Claude....21 B5
Khmer Gourmet....22 B4
La Paillotte....23 B4
Mama Cambodia....(see 24)
Melting Pot....24 B4
Mick & Craig's Sanctuary....25 C6
Q&A Café....26 D5
Romduol's Restaurant....27 B4
Samudera Market....28 D5
Snake House....29 B4
Starfish Bakery....30 D5
DRINKING
Angkor Arms....31 D5
Bar Ru....32 D6
Beach Shacks....33 D6
Chiva Shack....34 D6
Eden....35 C6
Star Bar....36 D4
Utopia....37 C6
TRANSPORT
Capitol Tour....38 D5
GST....39 D5
Hour Lean....40 D4
PPST....41 C5
Taxi Park....42 D4
To Krong Koh Kong Ferry (2km)
Sihanoukville
Port
4
To Ream National Park (13km); Kampot (105km); Phnom Penh (230km)
Victory Beach
Ph Krong
Weather Station Hill
Victory Monument
Independence Square
Lamherkay Beach
Ph Boray Kamakor (Ph Cite)
Ph Ekareach
Ph Omui
To Otres Beach (6km)
Psar Leu
Wat Khrom
Ph Santepheap
Koh Pos Beach
Ph 19 Mithona
Ph Sopheakmongkol
Ph 7 Makara
Ph Sereypheap
Boeng Prek Tup
Ph 2 Thnou
Gulf of Thailand
Independence Beach
Boeng Sam At
Sokha Beach Resort
Sokha Beach
Golden Lions Roundabout
Beach Shacks
Serendipity Beach
Ph 1 Kanda
Ph 23 Tola
Ph 14 Mithona
Occheuteal Beach
To Otres Beach (5km); Otres Nautica (5km)

CAMBODIA

Forget both the unreliable main post office, near the port, and the branch near the market when it comes to postal services.

For cheap international phone calls, use an internet café, or for local calls use one of the private mobile phone booths on the street. Internet access is now possible all over town for about 4000r per hour.

Canadia Bank (☎ 933490; Ph Ekareach) Deals with most currencies, changes travellers cheques, has a credit-card-compatible ATM and offers free credit-card cash advances.

Casablanca A healthy selection of books for those seeking a literary escape; it's near the Golden Lions Roundabout.

Hospital (☎ 933426) Near the Golden Lions Roundabout, but it's basic. Head to Phnom Penh if it's serious.

Tourist office (Ph Sopheak Mongkul; 9am-6pm) One of the best in the country. Lots of hand-outs, excellent English, and the staff actually show up to work.

Union Commercial Bank (☎ 933833; Ph Ekareach) Offers free credit-card cash advances.

Dangers & Annoyances

Theft is common, so don't leave valuables on the beach unattended or motorbikes without a hefty padlock. Night robberies have occurred near the port and on the poorly lit areas of Ph Ekareach, so stick together or hook up with a reliable moto driver when heading out on the town alone. Lone women should exercise caution when walking on the beaches after dark, as there's been a high-profile case of rape.

Sights & Activities

BEACHES

With its north end housing the backpacker haven of **Serendipity Beach**, the most popular stretch of sand is undoubtedly **Ochheuteal Beach**. It's a pretty spot, but it's not always peaceful. Crowds dwindle if you stroll southwards, and if you cross the small headland at its southern end you'll be rewarded with **Otres Beach**, a seemingly infinite stretch of white sand. Businesses are staking out the sand, but it's still quiet most days.

Victory Beach is close to the main backpacker ghetto, but it's fairly scruffy and looks onto the port. **Independence Beach** is a nice stretch of sand and quieter than most, while beautiful **Sokha Beach** has been virtually privatised and only a small sliver is open to the public.

See p109 for islands near Sihanoukville.

DIVING

The waters around Sihanoukville have less dramatic action than Indonesia or Thailand. However, venture further to the island of Koh Tang on an overnight trip and you'll get slightly more bang for your buck. There are several reputable dive operators in Sihanoukville:

Chez Claude (☎ 012 824870) The longest-running operator in town; owner Claude knows the local waters as well as anyone.

EcoSea Dive (☎ 012 654104; www.ecosea.com) Offers diving or snorkelling trips and PADI courses.

Scuba Nation (☎ 012 604680; www.divecambodia.com) The first PADI-approved dive centre in Cambodia. French, German and Dutch are spoken.

SAILING

With so much water around, sailing was bound to feature. **Otres Nautica** (☎ 092 230065; otres.nautica@yahoo.com) is a sailing club that operates out of Otres Beach. It has Hobie Wave catamarans, kayaks and sailing boats.

REAM NATIONAL PARK

For adventurous and educational guided boat trips through mangrove swamps to deserted beaches, head to **Ream National Park** (☎ 012 889620). Many guesthouses arrange various trips through the park (about US$15) and the chances of spotting dolphins or monkeys are pretty good. The park is only 13km from Sihanoukville.

MASSAGE

Try a massage at **Seeing Hands Massage 3** (Ph Ekareach; per hr US$3; 7am-9pm), another outpost of the excellent massage-by-the-blind initiative pioneered in Phnom Penh.

Alternatively, head to **Sala Santepheap** (☎ 012 952011; massage by donation), which is run by the Starfish Project, a local goodwill project helping the Sihanoukville community.

Sleeping

There are three popular areas for budget accommodation in Sihanoukville: the long-running area centred on Weather Station Hill above Victory Beach, the town centre and the lively Serendipity Beach. Land rights for Serendipity are a sensitive issue, so things may change in this part of town. Given we're all here for the beach, the town centre is not the most exotic place to stay.

WEATHER STATION HILL

Mealy Chenda Guesthouse (☎ 933472; r US$3-17;) Once upon a time there was just one guesthouse here, and Mealy Chenda was it. More a hotel these days, it still has a friendly family vibe thanks to the caring owners. Cheap rooms are under the restaurant-bar, while the top-dollar rooms include a sunset view. Wholesome food.

Bungalow Village (☎ 933875; bungalows US$4-10) Exactly what it sounds like, this is a hamlet of bungalows spread across the hillside. It's nearer the beach than most, and the garden gives this place more charm than many cheapies.

Sakal Bungalows (☎ 012 806155; r US$5-13;) The atmospheric bungalows blend into the lush garden at this likeable little place, plus there is a shiny new wing with air-con. A very chilled-out spot with a busy bar.

Blue Frog Guesthouse (☎ 012 838004; www.bluefroghotel.com; r US$8-12;) This wooden house is more sophisticated than it looks, with all the rooms crammed with goodies such as TV, fridge and, wait for it, DVD player.

Other good options among many:

Green Gecko Guest House (☎ 012 560944; r US$2-12;) A friendly hotel with caring customer service; the rooms are clean and well maintained.

Da Da Guesthouse (☎ 012 879527; r US$5-10;) One of the longer-running places on the hill; the friendly family offers a good selection of rooms.

SERENDIPITY BEACH

Mohachai Guesthouse (☎ 933586; r US$5-15) Located just a short stroll up the hill from the beach, there are nearly 40 rooms here. Tiled floors and attached bathrooms are about as flash as it gets, but good travel tips are available.

Serendipity Beach Bungalows (☎ 016 513599; r US$5-30) Snuggling into the hillside with fantastic views, the bungalows here are like honeymoon hideaways. Each bungalow has a sea-view terrace.

Serenity (☎ 011 696009; edenserendipity@yahoo.com; r US$6-30) A hideaway at the end of Serendipity, Serenity has adopted its name wholeheartedly and is a sanctuary of calm and tranquillity. The upmarket bungalows are seriously sweet and the views are superb. The cheapies include private bathrooms and a slice of the beachfront action.

Monkey Republic Bungalows (☎ 012 490290; monkeyrepubliccambodia@yahoo.co.uk; r US$7) The epitome of what all seaside accommodation should be: cool, friendly, laid-back, and with plenty of banana trees. Bungalows are simple, but the lofty chill-out zone with swinging hammocks is a smooth touch.

Reef Resort (☎ 012 315338; reefresort-cambodia@nni.com; r US$30;) A short stroll from the beach, this new resort has smart rooms complete with TV, fridge and well-appointed bathrooms. There is also an inviting pool and a popular bar-restaurant.

Other worthy spots:

Diamond Guest House (☎ 016 948929; r US$7-10;) Tucked behind Serendipity Beach, this family-run guesthouse is quiet, safe and very relaxed.

Cloud 9 (☎ 012 479365; bungalows US$12-17) An attractive little resort with bungalows draped down the hillside to the sea. Includes a bar near the water.

TOWN CENTRE

Holy Cow (☎ 012 478510; Ekareach St; r US$3-8) Holy cow indeed – this is a cool place for the downtown area. Set back from the main strip, the wooden house has cosy rooms, and doubles as a popular restaurant-bar.

Small Hotel (☎ 012 716385; r US$7-15) Popular with expats escaping for the weekend, this small hotel has a big personality thanks to the Swedish owners. Spotless rooms, Swedish food and slick service.

Eating

There are plenty of places to eat all over Sihanoukville, many with a lively mix of Khmer and Western dishes. Most of the aforementioned guesthouses and hotels have restaurants, including Mealy Chenda (opposite), which draws a mixed crowd of backpackers and locals. Unless stated otherwise, all restaurants listed here are open for breakfast, lunch and dinner.

WEATHER STATION HILL

Khmer Gourmet (☎ 012 1799450; snacks 2000-4000r) No, it's not an upmarket Khmer restaurant; instead, it's the home of fresh pies, cakes and sweet treats. The *pièce de résistance* is the coffee machine, complete with authentic sound effects.

Romduol's Restaurant (mains 3000-8000r) Don't be fooled by the simple setting, as the menu is a whole lot more sophisticated and meals are a real deal.

Melting Pot (☎ 012 913714; mains 4000-16,000r) The eclectic menu here includes fresh *pain au chocolat* for breakfast, and French, Indian and even South American food for lunch and dinner. Indian specials include *dhal amritsari* (lentils with fruit) and *murg makhani* (succulent chicken in rich butter gravy).

CAMBODIA

Mama Cambodia (☎ 012 221468; mains US$2-3) 'Mama' is a Khmer lady with a serious flair for cooking. Unlike the bizarre beauty queens laminated into her menus, her traditional Khmer meals are authentic and tasty.

Snake House (☎ 012 673805; mains US$2-5) If you have a phobia about snakes, avoid this place. Serpents slither around glass-topped tables while you eat, plus there's a python to your left, a cobra to your right. Memorable indeed.

La Paillote (☎ 012 633247; mains US$5-14; ⏰ lunch & dinner) This fine-dining restaurant is a little out of place in the backpacker haven of Sihanoukville, but is set in a delightful garden courtyard. Treat yourself to a selection of international dishes, most with a French accent.

SERENDIPITY BEACH

Mick & Craig's Sanctuary (☎ 012 727740; mains US$2-7) Come hungry, as this long-running restaurant specialises in hearty portions of home-cooked food. The menu includes vegetarian options, as well as a serious selection of proper pub grub and popular Khmer dishes. It's open late as it's also a bar.

Chez Claude (☎ 012 824870; mains US$3-12) One of the best restaurants on the south coast, Chez Claude is perched on a hill above Independence and Sokha Beaches. The menu includes Franco-Khmer fish dishes, as well as clams, scallops or whatever else the fisherfolk bring in. Drop by for a sunset beer to experience the immense views.

The sublime stretch of sand that links Serendipity to Ochheuteal is now home to dozens of beach shacks turning out freshly barbecued seafood. It's hard to recommend one above the other, as they all have comfy satellite chairs, low tables with candles, enthusiastic sellers, and meals priced from US$2 to US$4. Wander up and down and take your pick.

TOWN CENTRE

Starfish Bakery (☎ 012 952011; meals US$1-3; ⏰ breakfast & lunch) The place to come for choice cakes, super shakes and light bites, this leafy garden café is tucked down a little side street off Ph 7 Makara. It's for a good cause, as the Starfish Project supports local disadvantaged Cambodians.

Café Q & A (☎ 012 342720; 95 Ph Ekareach; mains US$2-3) This is a library, secondhand bookstore and restaurant rolled into one. Tuck into the Western fare and a book simultaneously.

Self-caterers should check out **Samudera Market** (Ph 7 Makara; ⏰ 7am-8pm), near Starfish Bakery, which has the best stock of international foods, including cheese, meats and chocolate.

Drinking

The sands of Serendipity are a happening night spot, while Weather Station Hill and the town centre boast many venues knocking out locally brewed Angkor at just US$0.50 a glass, the cheapest draught in Cambodia. The hill is getting a bit 'girlie' of late, as a new crowd moves in, but there are still plenty of backpacker bars.

Eden (Serendipity Beach; ⏰ 24hr) Koh Pha-Ngan comes to Cambodia, with candlelit tables by night and revellers washed up on the beach. The Eden gang love an excuse for a party, but it's pretty loud for anyone planning on taking a room nearby.

Utopia (Serendipity Beach; ⏰ 24hr) Home to the 24-hour party people, this great garden bar rocks on through the night and offers free accommodation for those who just can't drag themselves away.

Bar Ru (☎ 012 388860; Golden Lions Roundabout; ⏰ 8am-late) Knock back the drinks at this unpretentious bar and take part in its charity crab races or quiz nights. Money raised goes to community organisations based in Sihanoukville. It also offers beach bungalows on Koh Ru.

Angkor Arms (☎ 933847; Ph Ekareach; ⏰ 9am-late) The original 'Snookyville' pub, this place spills out on to the street and is a friendly spot for a beer. Pool, darts and big sporting occasions on a big screen.

Star Bar (☎ 012 377398; Ph Sopheakmongkol) Remember the rickety staircase before you have one too many. This is one of the latest spots in town, and the owners now operate bungalows on rising Otres Beach.

Heading south from Serendipity to Occheuteal, there are numerous beach shacks that also rock on until the early hours. They change names quicker than most of us change underwear, so it's hard to single any out. That said, **Chiva Shack** (☎ 012 360911; Occheutal Beach; ⏰ 24hr) has made a name for itself with full-moon parties, fire throwers, happy pizzas and some delicious cocktails right on the beach. There's also free accommodation if you crash out.

Getting There & Away

AIR

Sihanoukville Airport is open for business once more and there are regular flights to and from Siem Reap (one way US$80) with **PMT Air** (code U4; ☎ in Phnom Penh 023-221379; www.pmtair.com).

BOAT

See p113 for fast-boat services between Sihanoukville and Krong Koh Kong.

BUS

Many companies operate buses between Sihanoukville and Phnom Penh (14,000r, four hours), including Capitol Tour, GST, Hour Lean, Mekong Express and PPST. All have offices in town. PPST and several guesthouses run minibuses to Krong Koh Kong (US$13, six hours).

MOTORCYCLE

NH4 to Phnom Penh is busy, boring and dangerous, so riding isn't recommended. However, renting motorcycles is banned in Sihanoukville, so Phnom Penh or Kampot are now the only options to kick start a two-wheeled adventure.

SHARE TAXI

Cramped taxis head to Phnom Penh (15,000r, three hours) and Kampot (12,000r, two hours) from the new taxi park in the town centre. Buses are the better option to the capital.

TRAIN

Sadly, passenger trains no longer service Sihanoukville.

Getting Around

Bicycles are a pleasant and environmentally friendly way to get around, and some guesthouses offer rentals for US$1 to US$2 per day.

With moto drivers having a well-earned reputation for overcharging, it's important to negotiate in advance. From the town centre to Victory or Serendipity Beaches expect to pay about 3000r, while a trip between these beaches is around 5000r. Costs almost double at night.

Motorbike rentals are currently forbidden in Sihanoukville. However, the situation is on and off again, so here's the rub if it's permitted: numerous guesthouses and restaurants rent 100cc motos for US$3 per day, and **GST** (☎ 933826; Ph Ekareach) rents out larger 250cc trail bikes for US$7 per day, just the medicine for Bokor National Park.

Around Sihanoukville

There are numerous islands off the coast, but the scene is low-key compared with honky-tonk Thailand. **Bamboo Island** (Koh Russei) and **Koh Ru** both have basic accommodation, with boat trips out there encompassing stops for snorkelling along the way. It's not quite Mama Linh's of Nha Trang fame, but fun all the same.

Bamboo Island is surrounded by clear waters, and the **bungalows** (r with shared bathroom US$8-10) are sweet, with breezy terraces. There is also a large restaurant. A boat out here costs US$8 return.

Koh Ru has beach **bungalows** (US$10) plus its own restaurant and bar. It's more secluded than Bamboo Island and costs US$10 for a return boat trip.

KAMPOT

☎ 033 / pop 37,400

There is something about this little charmer that encourages visitors to linger. It might be the lovely riverside setting or the ageing French buildings, it could be the great little guesthouses and burgeoning bar scene. Whatever the magic ingredient, this is the perfect base to explore nearby caves and tackle the challenge that is Bokor National Park.

Information

There's a basic tourist office, but little info is to be had. There are a couple of internet places near the central roundabout charging 6000r per hour.

Canadia Bank (☎ 932392) Offers free credit-card cash advances, and changes most currencies and travellers cheques.

Hospital (☎ 016 877689) Get yourself back to Phnom Penh sharpish! This hospital is very basic.

Kepler's Books (☎ 016 618906) The best used-book shop in town.

DID YOU KNOW?

In the years before civil war took its toll, no self-respecting French restaurant in Paris would be without Kampot pepper on the table.

CAMBODIA

Sights & Activities

Remember, this is not a town where you come and do, but a place to come and feel. Sit on the riverbank and watch the sun set beneath the mountains or take in some of the town's fine **French architecture**.

About 10km east are the bat-filled caves of **Phnom Chhnork** (admission free), one containing a remarkably preserved 7th-century brick temple. Also outside of town are the **Tuk Chhouu Falls** (admission US$1; dawn-dusk), which are really no more than a series of not-so-rapid rapids. They're 8km west of town and are filled with bathing locals on weekends.

Sleeping

Guesthouses have been mushrooming in the past couple of years. The following are just a few standouts.

Long Villa Guesthouse (☎ 012 210820; r US$3-10) The friendly family here promises 'what you see is what you get', and it has been treating travellers well for a few years now. Rooms are good value and travel information is available. It's near Psar Leu.

Bodhi Villa (☎ 012 419140; bodhivilla@mac.com; Tuk Chhouu Rd; r US$3-10) Laid-back and friendly, this happy hideaway is tucked behind a flourishing garden on the banks of the river. The location provides a good base for the water sports on offer, including water-skiing and boat cruising.

Blissful Guesthouse (☎ 012 513024; blissfulguesthouse@yahoo.com; r US$4-5) This is a fine place to unwind and relax. The large rooms are simple but have a few thoughtful trimmings, while a lush garden, great chill-out area and popular bar-restaurant make this a great guesthouse.

Utopia (r US$8-10) Spot the enormous birdhouse surrounded by an emerald forest and you have found Utopia, where you can while away the day on floating pontoons. It even offers free spots to crash (sofas, cushions, hammocks) for those who flake out after too much partying. It's off Tuk Chhouu Rd.

Other reliable options:

Kampot River View Guesthouse (☎ 012 821570; r US$4-6) Right on the river's edge, this is a breezy place with some rooms overlooking the water.

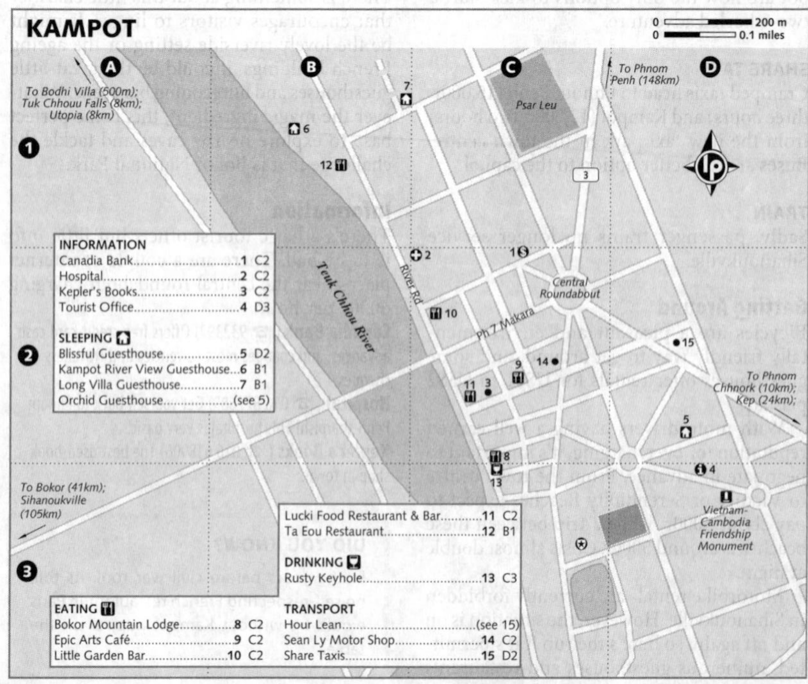

Orchid Guest House (☎ 932634; orchidguesthousekampot@yahoo.com; r US$4-15; ❄) A lovely lodging set in a manicured garden full of, you guessed it, orchids.

Eating & Drinking

There is something for everyone in Kampot these days, with recipes from as far afield as Mexico and Sri Lanka. There are now more bars than guesthouses along the riverfront, but many are quiet most nights.

Epic Arts Cafe (☎ 012 350824; www.epicarts.org.uk; snacks 3000-10,000r; ⏲ breakfast & lunch) This tiny little café offers divine cakes, tasty shakes and plenty of light bites. The staff are hearing impaired, and all proceeds go to support Epic Arts, which uses performance to promote expression among the disabled community.

Ta Eou Restaurant (☎ 932422; River Rd; mains 4000-12,000r; ⏲ breakfast, lunch & dinner) Sit over the water contemplating the challenge of Bokor, as the blood-red sun drops over the mountain. Seafood is sublime here, including fresh crab laden with tasty green peppercorns.

Little Garden Bar (☎ 012 256901; www.littlegardenbar.com; ⏲ 7am-late) The garden may be little but the hearts are big. As well as serving up fine international food (mains cost from 4000r to 28,000r), lively cocktails and the odd glass of vino, the team here supports and launches community-based projects.

Rusty Keyhole (☎ 012 679607; mains 5000-20,000r; ⏲ breakfast, lunch & dinner) With tables spilling on to the street, the Keyhole is the most welcoming bar in town – unless you happen to be a missionary. Happy hours run from 5pm to 7pm and there is hearty fare at any time.

Lucki Food Restaurant & Bar (☎ 012 806105; mains US$2.50-4; ⏲ breakfast, lunch & dinner) The interior may be no frills, but the menu promises plenty of thrills, with authentic Sri Lankan and Indian dishes served up with a free drink or snack.

Bokor Mountain Lodge (☎ 932314; www.bokorlodge.com; mains US$4-9.50; ⏲ breakfast, lunch & dinner) The oldest bar-restaurant in town has been through many incarnations, and currently offers an international menu that includes hearty steaks and pies. There's a pool table for some action with the beers.

Getting There & Away

Share taxis leave from the old Total station in the southeast of town and ply NH3 to Phnom Penh (14,000r, two hours) and Sihanoukville (12,000r, two hours).

A more comfortable, slower, but equally cheap option to the capital are the buses of **Hour Lean** (☎ 012 939917), which take four hours. For details on getting to Bokor or Kep, see the respective entries following.

Getting Around

Sean Ly Motor Shop (☎ 012 944687) rents small motorbikes from US$3 per day and big bikes from US$4, plus cars/minibuses/pick-ups for US$20/25/30. A moto to explore the caves and even Kep for the day starts from US$6.

BOKOR NATIONAL PARK

One of Cambodia's most alluring protected areas, **Bokor National Park** (admission US$5) clings to the southern tip of the Chuor Phnom Damrei. You can stay in the park all day, but entry is only from 6am to noon. Besides a refreshingly cool climate, the park has secluded **waterfalls**, commanding ocean views, the abandoned and eerie **Bokor hill station** (elevation 1080m), and exceedingly elusive animals including tigers and elephants. Unfortunately, illegal logging in the 1990s cost the park its shot at World Heritage status.

At great financial and human expense (many indentured labourers perished in the process), the French forged a road into the area in the first quarter of the 20th century. A small community was created, and the grand colonial hotel, known as the **Bokor Palace**, was inaugurated in 1925. The hill station was twice abandoned: first in the late 1940s when the Vietnamese and Khmer Issarak (Free Khmer) forces overran it while fighting for independence against the French, and again in 1970 when it was left to the invading Khmer Rouge. It now has a genuine ghost-town feel, especially when thick mists envelop the skeletons of the original structures. However, the old hill station looks set for another rebirth, as private company Sokha Hotels is planning to build a casino-resort on the site of the old Bokor Palace.

The picturesque two-tiered drop of **Popokvil Falls**, a peaceful three-hour walk from the hill station, is best seen in the wet season as it's disappointingly drippy at other times. While in the jungle, remember to stick to well-worn paths and keep an ear out for tigers.

It is possible to spend the night at the **ranger station** (per bunk US$5), which has basic bunk beds. Pack warm clothing, a torch (electricity goes off at about 9pm) and some food as supplies are limited.

The access road is 7km west of Kampot and from there it's a scenically stunning, but bruisingly bumpy, 25km up to the plateau's first ruin, the **Black Palace**. It's about a two-hour drive from Kampot, making for a perfect day trip. The road is too tough for first-time bikers; hiring a 250cc dirt bike and driver for the trip will cost about US$12. Less painful and much cheaper are the day trips arranged by guesthouses in Kampot (see p110), which cost US$6 and include pick-up transport, lunch and an English-speaking guide.

KEP

☎ 036 / pop 11,500

Kep is the comeback kid. Ravaged by the civil war and pillaged during the famine of 1979–80, it remained a ghost town until very recently. Founded by the French elite in 1908, the town is once again thriving and the seaside is as peaceful as ever, with lapping seas and swaying palms.

There aren't many beachside places to stay, but there are some great budget bungalows with sublime ocean views lining the forested hillside above the coast. The beach itself is a touch scrappy, as it was never a natural sandy bay. Before the war, white sand was shipped in from Sihanoukville to keep up appearances!

Better beaches are found off the coast on islands such as **Koh Tonsay** (Rabbit Island), which now has a couple of basic guesthouses. A boat for the day can be arranged from the seafood sellers as you enter town for about US$15, depending on numbers. Guesthouses can also help arrange boats if you're tired of haggling.

Sleeping & Eating

Kep Seaside Guesthouse (☎ 012 684241; r US$5-7) One of the few budget places by the sea, Kep Seaside Guesthouse has good-value big, breezy rooms. Try Room 10, which has a big balcony and a grandstand view. Shady hammocks line the rocky shore.

Le Bout du Monde (☎ 012 242166; r US$5-15) The original hilltop guesthouse, this wooden longhouse has basic rooms with smart trim, plus some bungalows. The restaurant is well regarded (mains US$2 to US$5).

Vanna Bungalow (☎ 012 755038; r US$6-20) Just below Bout du Monde, this place is set in verdant gardens and offers attractive bungalows at affordable prices.

Veranda Guesthouse (☎ 012 888619; www.veranda-resort.com; bungalows US$20-60) A maze of individual bungalows connected by wooden boardwalks, this stunning resort has an alluring mix of modern luxury and a natural setting. Sit back and soak up the views from your private veranda, complete with hammock. The restaurant specialises in Western fare (mains US$1 to US$4).

Away from the accommodation options, dining is easy, as there are numerous bamboo shacks along the coast offering fresh seafood, although be sure to agree to a price in advance and make sure the crab is fresh.

Getting There & Away

Kep is just 24km from Kampot, so it's easiest to take a moto (about US$4 return) or share taxi from there. The Cambodian–Vietnamese border at Prek Chek–Xa Xia had just opened at the time of going to press, suggesting Kep will see a lot more traffic in the next few years.

KRONG KOH KONG

☎ 035 / pop 33,100

Krong Koh Kong is a frontier town of smugglers, gamblers and prostitutes, which acts as a functional stop on the southern overland trail between Thailand and Cambodia. Most people zoom through before getting to know that it is a laid-back town full of friendly locals.

You can while away time on the beaches outside town or head to **Ta Tai Waterfall**, a wide, shallow set of falls spilling over a 4m limestone shelf, about 20km from town. Casinos dominate the border line, and are popular with gambling Thais.

Information

Baht, US dollars and riel are all accepted here, despite what scammers at the border might say. The nearest banks that can deal with credit cards or travellers cheques are in Sihanoukville or Thailand. Internet access is readily available around town. Check out **Koh Kong, Cambodia** (http://kohkong.sihanoukville-cambodia.com) for some more background information.

Sleeping & Eating

Otto's (☎ 963163; Ph 8; r with shared/private bathroom 100/150B) Set in a traditional wooden house near the boat dock, Otto's has basic rooms with mossie nets. Travel information is on tap here, plus there's a popular Western restaurant (mains 60B to 200B; open breakfast, lunch and dinner), which serves a hearty bratwurst.

Phou Mint Koh Kong Hotel (☎ 936221; Ph 1; r US$5-15; ❄) Lately overshadowed by the towering Koh Kong City Hotel, the Phou Mint is still top value for its riverside location. It has huge sparkling rooms with fans and satellite TVs.

With a garden setting and Thai menu bursting with vegetarian options and fresh seafood, **Baan Peakmai** (cnr Ph 3 & Ph 6; mains 50-150B; 🕑 breakfast, lunch & dinner) is the best Thai restaurant in town. For your first or last taste of Khmer cuisine, slide into **Samras Angkor Restaurant** (mains 50-150B; 🕑 breakfast, lunch & dinner).

Drinking

Sunset Lounge (☎ 012 1724909; 🕑 24hr) Sip drinks over the water at this striking bar that creeps all the way out into the river. The views are undeniably stunning and this is the best place to come for frank and funny travel advice.

Getting There & Away

Daily buses to Phnom Penh or Sihanoukville both depart around 9am and charge a cheeky 500B; share taxis charge about 300B for a berth. Both destinations take about six hours to reach, but journey times will drop once the four bridges come on line.

Fast boats leave daily for Sihanoukville (US$15, four hours, 8am). Coming the other way, boats depart Sihanoukville at noon. These boats were designed for rivers, so it can get rough during high winds, particularly in the wet summer season.

> **GETTING TO THAILAND**
>
> Leaving Cambodia, take a moto (motorcycle taxi; 80B per person) or share taxi (200B for the whole car) from Krong Koh Kong over the big bridge to the border at Hat Lek. Walk across the border to where there are minibuses (100B, one hour, every 30 minutes) to Trat for connections to Bangkok or Koh Chang. The border post is open daily from 7am to 5pm.
>
> See p765 for information on doing the trip in the opposite direction.

Getting Around

Chartering a moto for a whole day of sightseeing, taking in the waterfalls, beaches and town, should cost about US$10 to US$15. Guesthouses can usually organise a bicycle for rent (US$2 to US$3 per day).

Chartered boats can take you to the islands, and cost between US$30 and US$40 depending on the size of the boat and how long you want to hang out.

NORTHEASTERN CAMBODIA

The northeast is one of the wildest regions in Cambodia. The provinces of Mondulkiri and Ratanakiri are home to some of Cambodia's most beautiful landscapes, as well as tigers, leopards and elephants. You can plod through the jungle to secret waterfalls on elephant back, and to glimpse the rare Irrawaddy dolphins in the Mekong River. Or you can live the wild life in the northeast, as the area is home to ethnic minority groups known as Khmer Loeu (Upper Khmer) or *chunchiet*. Different dialects, different lifestyles and different looks – these people are a world away from their lowland neighbours. It's not for everyone, which also means it's far from the madding crowds of Siem Reap.

There are no longer regular fast boat services on this stretch of the Mekong, as new roads and cheap buses have picked off all the punters.

KOMPONG CHAM

☎ 042 / pop 51,200

Sitting on the shores of the Mekong, Kompong Cham was an important trading post during the French period, and the legacy lives on in bruised but beautiful buildings around the town. It's a good stopover, but otherwise there's little reason to linger.

Information

ABC Computer (11 Ph Ang Duong) Internet access.

Cambodia Asia Bank (☎ 942149) Near the transport stop, this bank offers an international ATM.

Canadia Bank (☎ 941361; Preah Monivong Blvd) Near the market, Canadia Bank changes cash and travellers cheques in most currencies and offers free Visa and MasterCard advances.

CAMBODIA

Sights & Activities

Wat Nokor (admission US$2) is an 11th-century Mahayana Buddhist shrine of sandstone and laterite set slap-bang in the centre of an active and slightly kitsch Theravada wat. A peaceful atmosphere pervades the place, which rests about 1km from town, just off the road to Phnom Penh. Equally tranquil is a bike ride or walk on the nearby rural island of **Koh Paen**, which is connected to town in the dry season by an elaborate bamboo bridge.

Sleeping

One street near the market boasts guesthouses advertising rooms at 5000r, although most rooms are cells and most 'guests' seem to pay by the hour, so it could get oh, ohh, ohhh! so noisy.

Bophea Guesthouse (☎ 012 796803; Vithei Pasteur; r US$2-3) One of the original guesthouses in town, the more 'expensive' rooms include a bathroom. Bicycles are the best way to explore town, and they're available for rent here (4000r per day).

Phnom Brak Trochak Cheth Guest House (☎ 941507; s/d US$4/5) Ten points if you can say this name after a few beers. This guesthouse has been upgraded by its new owners and now has smart rooms, although they're cooled by fan only.

Mekong Hotel (☎ 941536; Ph Preah Bat Sihanouk; r US$5-20; ❄) In a prime riverfront location, this is the best all-rounder in town. All rooms come with TV, while 10 bucks brings the bonus of air-con, hot water and a Mekong view. Consider an ultimate Frisbee game in the huge corridors.

Eating & Drinking

For cheap eats, hit the stop-and-dip food stalls in the market. *Tukalok* (fruit shake) stalls near the police station also offer a selection of snacks.

Two Dragons Restaurant (Ph Ang Duong; mains 4000-8000r; 🕑 breakfast, lunch & dinner) Incredibly popular with Khmers, this restaurant has exotic dishes and an ever changing specials menu.

Lazy Mekong Daze (Ph Preah Bat Sihanouk; Riverfront; mains US$1.50-3; 🕑 breakfast, lunch & dinner) Run by a British-Khmer couple, this bolt hole is a great place to unwind with Mekong views and tasty food.

Mekong Crossing (Vithei Pasteur; meals US$2-4; 🕑 lunch & dinner) Wholesome Western grub, Khmer classics and a (un?)healthy drinks list make this a popular place. The owner knows Cham like the back of his hand.

In the early evening locals gather on the waterfront outside the Mekong Hotel, where a number of stalls sell cheap beers.

Getting There & Away

For Phnom Penh, there are buses (10,000r, three hours), and share taxis (10,000r, two hours). PPST, Hour Lean and GST all have regular services, leaving from the respective bus company's office.

Hour Lean buses to Kratie (three to four hours, 17,000r) depart from near the roundabout in Kompong Cham.

Travellers motorbiking to Kratie should consider following the western bank of the Mekong to the Stung Trang district, crossing the river and continuing northward through Chhlong for a really pretty ride.

KRATIE

☎ 072 / pop 89,400

The best place in Cambodia to glimpse the region's remaining freshwater Irrawaddy dolphins, Kratie (Kra-*cheh*) wraps around the east bank of the river and sits under the most dramatic of skies. Thanks to the marine life, its striking riverside setting and well-preserved French and Khmer architecture, the town is becoming a hot stop on the overland route to Laos or Ratanakiri Province.

Information

Telephone calls can be made at kiosks around the market and internet is available at the You Hong Guest House. Western Union money transfers are available at **Acleda Bank** (☎ 971707).

Sights & Activities

Just 15km north of town at Kampi, the endangered **Irrawaddy dolphins** often breach the Mekong's silent surface for a breath of fresh air. It costs US$2 to visit the site, plus about US$3 per person for a boat, depending on the number of passengers. Return trips by moto should cost about US$3 or so. Alternatively, it's an enjoyable 60-minute bicycle ride to Kampi. Take in a dramatic sunset over the Mekong from **Phnom Sombok** on the way back to town.

Opposite town in the middle of the Mekong is an idyllic slice of rural Cambodia on the island of **Koh Trong**.

Sleeping & Eating

The best budget sleeping and eating options are found in the vicinity of the market.

Star Guesthouse (☎ 971663; Ph Preah Sihanouk; r US$2-5) A budget favourite where the rooms are cheap, travel information is on tap and the friendly staff speak good English. The restaurant turns out good grub (meals cost from US$1 to US$3).

You Hong Guesthouse (☎ 012 957003; 91 Ph 8; r US$2-5) This is another good spot for weary travellers to rest their head, with rooms that are clean and kempt. The restaurant has a serious veggie selection, including tofu mushroom burgers and tofu curries (meal prices range from US$1 to US$3).

Santhepheap Hotel (☎ 971537; r US$5-20; ❄) The reliable Santhepheap offers smart, comfortable accommodation, with the front-facing rooms providing a good view of the riverfront action.

Red Sun Falling (Ph Preah Suramarit; mains US$1-3) The larger-than-life owner of Red Sun Falling has created a relaxing retreat with fine furnishings, good music and a small bookshop. The menu includes some Asian greatest hits and some home comfort food, including excellent homemade brownies. By night, it doubles as Kratie's leading bar.

Cheap dining can be had during the evening, when food stalls set up shop overlooking the Mekong. This area doubles as a superb spot for a sunset drink.

Getting There & Away

The 348km road south to Phnom Penh is now entirely surfaced, cutting journey times dramatically. **PPST** (☎ 012 523400) and **Hour Lean** (☎ 012 535387) each run one bus a day to the capital (18,000r, six hours) at 7.30am. More frequent and faster, though less comfortable, are the share taxis (departing from Taxi Park) to the capital (25,000r, five hours).

Hour Lean also serves Stung Treng (14,000r, two hours), leaving at around 1pm and heading along the recently surfaced NH7. You can also take a share taxi (US$7.50) to Stung Treng.

For Mondulkiri take a share taxi to Snuol (8000r, 1¼ hours) and hop on Hour Lean's noon bus to Sen Monorom (17,000r, 2½ hours).

STUNG TRENG

☎ 074 / pop 27,700

Stung Treng is back on the map thanks to the popular Cambodia–Laos border crossing just 50-odd klicks north. It's no longer the ends of the earth, but the downside is that the new road connections mean many travellers are only passing through on their way to more exciting Ratanakiri and Kratie.

There are no banks, but Riverside Restaurant & Guesthouse can cash travellers cheques. If you're coming from Laos, US dollars are accepted everywhere. There are several internet places around the market.

Whether just off the boat, bus or bumpy moto, the shady riverfront rooftop at **Riverside Restaurant & Guesthouse** (☎ 012 439454; mains 3500-10,000r; 🕑 breakfast, lunch & dinner) is the place to enjoy fine food and cool drinks. The menu includes Khmer, Thai and Chinese specials to go with the odd international dish. Rooms here

GETTING TO LAOS

The beautiful river border (open from 7am to 5pm) between Stung Treng Province in Cambodia and Champasak province in Laos has been open to foreigners since late 2000 and is growing in popularity as an adventurous and cheap way to combine northeastern Cambodia and southern Laos. Have you got your Lao visa (see p411)? OK, read on…

In theory, if you're armed with a Lao or Cambodian visa, there should be no extra charges at the border, but in reality expect border officials on both sides to ask for more money (up to US$5) in 'stamp fees'.

Take a minibus from Stung Treng to the border at Dom Kralor (US$10, two hours). Transport at Voen Kham on the Lao side is very hit and miss for those arriving from Cambodia, but easy when leaving Laos. It's probably going to be necessary to take a motorcycle taxi or túk-túk to Nakasong, where there are good public transport connections to points north, including Don Khong island.

See p402 for information on doing the trip in the opposite direction.

are only US$3 and include private bathroom, plus reliable travel information is available.

Cheap food stalls can be found on the riverfront and around the market.

An early-morning Hour Lean bus leaves at 7am for Kratie (22,000r, 3½ hours) and Phnom Penh (42,000r, 10 hours) along NH7. Crowded share taxis travel south to Kratie (30,000r) and east to Ban Lung (30,000r, 4½ hours) along a rough but gradually improving road. There is also a minibus to Ban Lung (US$8, four hours) at 7.30am; book your seat the night before and the bus will pick you up from your hotel. Times given here are for the dry season; count on longer during the wet season. All transport leaves from the transport stop, near the Riverside Restaurant & Guesthouse.

RATANAKIRI PROVINCE

Up-and-coming Ratanakiri is making a name for itself as a diverse region of outstanding natural beauty that provides a remote home for a mosaic of minority peoples (including the Jarai, Tompoun and Kreung) with their own languages, traditions and customs. Adrenaline-rush activities are plentiful. Swim in clear volcanic lakes, shower under waterfalls, glimpse an elephant or trek in the vast Virachey National Park – it's all here.

The roads through the province look like a papaya shake during the wet season, so the ideal time to explore is from December to February. Prepare to do battle with the red dust of Ratanakiri, which will leave you with a fake tan and orange hair.

Ban Lung

☎ 075 / pop 17,000

Cloaked in dust in the dry season, mired in mud in the wet season, Ban Lung isn't the best introduction to Ratanakiri, but it is a functional base for some romps around the region. Check out the kingdom's best swimming pool, lurking in the nearby volcanic crater of Yeak Laom, or take the plunge under a quiet waterfall to cleanse your skin and soothe your soul.

INFORMATION

There are no banks, but travellers cheques can be exchanged for a stiff commission at some guesthouses. Internet access is possible at some guesthouses, but prices are high and connection speeds woefully slow.

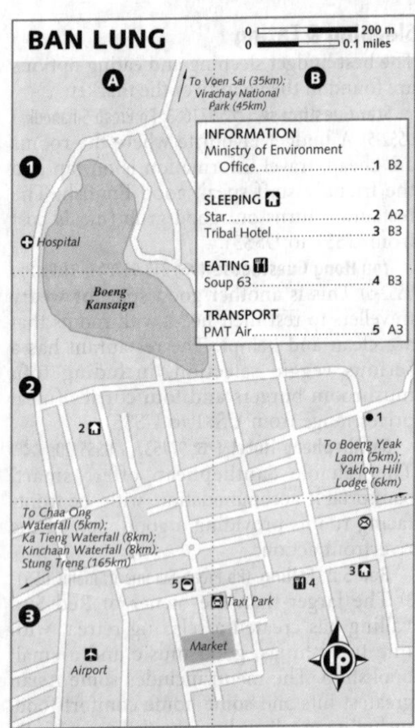

SIGHTS & ACTIVITIES

Boeng Yeak Laom

Through a clearing in a dark green forest is the bright blue water of this cracking **crater lake** (admission US$1), a mere 5km east of town. Get the swimming togs on and make a splash. There's a small **visitors centre** (admission free) on the west shore run by **Yeak Loam Community Based Eco-Tourism** (☎ 012 981226; yeak_laom@camintel.com). The centre offers community walks with English-speaking guides (US$3 to US$7 per person depending on numbers), which are an interesting insight into the life of the Tompuon minority.

A moto here will cost about US$1, or US$2 if they stick around to drive you back.

Waterfalls

For a power shower, head to **Chaa Ong Waterfall** (admission 2000r), which is set in a scenic rocky jungle gorge, allowing you to clamber straight under the falls. **Ka Tieng Waterfall** (admission free) is perhaps the most fun, as there are some vines on the far side that are strong enough to swing on for some Tarzan action. Another beautiful waterfall in the neighbourhood is **Kinchaan Waterfall** (admission 2000r).

These three waterfalls are located separately about 5km to 8km west of town. Although they're signposted en route to Stung Treng, hook up with a local as they're difficult to find.

Trekking

With many local minority villages and attractive areas situated around Ban Lung, trekking has really started to take off here. Figure on US$15 to US$25 a day for a good guide, plus more for transport, food and accommodation along the way. You'll need a group to make it affordable. Star Hotel and Yaklom Hill Lodge are the best places to make arrangements for treks, but make sure you get what you sign up for. See right for trekking options in Virachey National Park, as well as treks run by the Ministry of the Environment.

Ask around town about arranging **elephant treks** (per hour from US$10), although Mondulkiri is the better choice for a date with Dumbo.

SLEEPING & EATING

Star Hotel (☎ 012 958322; r US$5-10; ❄) This large villa has spacious rooms, but it's more about the friendly service. The effusive Mr Leng runs a tight ship and ensures guests are wanting for nothing. The restaurant is one of the best in town, particularly for the *phnom pleung*.

Lakeside Chheng Lok Hotel (☎ 390063; lakeside-chhenglokhotel@yahoo.com; r US$5-20; ❄) Pristine rooms in the main building and gorgeous brick bungalows by Boeng Kansaign out the back make this address one of the most appealing in Ratanakiri.

Tribal Hotel (☎ 974074; tribalhotel@camintel.com; r US$5-25; ❄) This huge compound of watlike buildings houses a wide range of options. Cheap budget rooms include bathroom but, if you want the world according to CNN, you should splash out on the more expensive rooms in the main building.

Yaklom Hill Lodge (☎ 012 644240; www.yaklom.com; s/d/tr incl breakfast US$10/13/16) This option promotes itself as Ratanakiri's ecolodge, and its gorgeous garden is dotted with wooden bungalows that have been decorated with tribal touches. There's no electricity during the day, but the fan and lights work at night. The restaurant at this place serves tasty Thai and Khmer food. It's about 6km east of town.

Star Hotel, Tribal Hotel and Yaklom Hotel all offer tasty fare at their respective restaurants. **Soup 63** (mains 5000-8000r; 🕑 breakfast, lunch & dinner) is popular with locals for *sait ko ang Ratanakiri* (Ratanakiri grilled beef). Although not on the menu, great tofu and veg meals are also available.

GETTING THERE & AWAY

PMT Air (code U4; ☎ 974098; www.pmtair.com) offers erratic connections between Ban Lung and Phnom Penh (one way/return US$100/200). The high price is meant to 'guarantee' three departures a week, but cancellations are common.

For details of costs to Stung Treng and continuing south overland, see opposite and p115. For more on the hard-core ride south to Mondulkiri, see p119.

GETTING AROUND

Most guesthouses rent motorbikes (from US$8 to US$10 per day), as well as pick-ups (US$35) and jeeps (US$50), which both include a driver. A moto for the day ranges from US$7 to US$10, depending on your destinations.

AROUND RATANAKIRI PROVINCE

Located 35km northwest of Ban Lung on the Tonlé Sap, **Voen Sai** is a kaleidoscope of a community that includes Chinese, Lao and Kreung villagers. Across the river is an old **Chinese settlement** dating back to the 19th century that's a slice of Sichuan, and further downstream are several **Lao** and **chunchiet villages**, some with traditional cemeteries complete with effigies of the dead.

Virachey National Park (www.bpamp.org.kh) is the largest protected area in Cambodia, stretching east to Vietnam, north to Laos and west to Stung Treng. The park has not been fully explored, but is probably home to a number of larger mammals, including elephants, leopards and tigers. Many guesthouses offer 'treks' in the park, but this usually means an expensive walk in denuded forest near the park, as it's at least a day's walk just to reach the park boundary.

For some serious trekking, contact the **Ministry of Environment office** (☎ 075-974176; virachey@camintel.com) in Ban Lung. Treks on offer include a four-day adventure that heads off into the forest, over the Ho Chi Minh Trail and down the river in kayaks, and the seven-day **Phnom Veal Thom Wilderness Trek**, a challenging affair over mountains and through forests.

MONDULKIRI PROVINCE

A world away from lowland Cambodia, Mondulkiri is the Wild East of Cambodia, home to the hardy Pnong people and their noble elephants. Climatically and culturally, it's also another world, which comes as a real relief after the heat of the plains. The landscape of the province is a seductive mix of pine clumps, grassy hills and windswept valleys that fade beguilingly into jade green forests and hidden waterfalls. Wild animals are more numerous in Mondulkiri than elsewhere, including bears and tigers, although chances of seeing these are about as good as winning the lottery.

Green grass or brown brush, messy mud or the dreaded dust, the contrasts between the wet and dry season are stark – take your pick.

Sen Monorom

☎ 073 / pop 7900

Mondulkiri means 'Meeting of the Hills', and sitting in the spot where this occurs is sleepy Sen Monorom, an overgrown village of exiles from distant parts of Cambodia, drawn here to start afresh.

The town is set at more than 800m, so when the winds billow it's notably cooler than the rest of Cambodia. It's the perfect base to explore the province and is a popular stop for domestic tourists.

INFORMATION

There are no banks, so carry US dollars or riel. Everything from food to transport is slightly more expensive here than the rest of the country. Phone calls are possible from mobiles around town and sporadic internet access is available at **Arun Reah II Hill Lodge & Restaurant** (per hr US$4). The local tourist office is more helpful than most, plus Long Vibol, who runs a guesthouse, is loaded with useful information and can arrange English-speaking guides.

SIGHTS & ACTIVITIES

About 3km northwest of town are **Monorom Falls**, the closest thing to a public swimming pool for Sen Monorom. More enticing falls are found slightly further afield; see opposite for details.

Elephant day treks in nearby Pnong villages such as Putang and Phulung can be arranged by guesthouses or the local tourist office for around US$30 per elephant (two passengers), including moto transport. Bring a comfy pillow to sit on or you'll be waddling like a duck for days. It's possible to negotiate an overnight trek from US$60 per person.

SLEEPING & EATING

Sen Monorom has erratic electricity, so a torch is useful for late-night toilet trips. With chilly evening temperatures, hot water is a welcome touch.

Sovankiri Guesthouse (☎ 012 821931; s/tw US$3/5) Just a stroll from the ambitiously named 'airport', this is where the Hour Lean buses from Phnom Penh alight. The wood-trim singles are large and include a bathroom for a top deal.

Arun Reah II Hill Lodge & Restaurant (☎ 012 999191; r US$5-10; 💻) This place pulls in the punters, as it has a strategic setting on the road into town. Big views of rolling hills, attractive bungalows with bathroom and TV, plus extras such as free bicycles, cheap motorbike hire and internet access ensure its popularity.

Long Vibol Guesthouse (☎ 012 944647; r US$5-15) Set amid a flourishing garden, this place buzzes with a lively mix of international and Khmer guests, all ably managed by English-speaking staff who are helpful and knowledgeable about the area. The more expensive rooms include a welcome hot shower. Good restaurant too.

Pech Kiri Guest House (☎ 012 932102; r US$5-15) Aim for the newer spacious bungalows, as the older rooms are smaller and less airy. The garden is a peaceful retreat and the restaurant turns out decent Khmer and European dishes.

Nature Lodge Café (☎ 012 230272; Mains US$1-3; 🕑 breakfast, lunch & dinner) Boasting an atmosphere as chilled as the hilltop air, this unique café occupies a picturesque setting. Offering an eclectic menu ranging from Israeli salad to pad thai (fried noodles, bean sprouts, peanuts, eggs, chillies and often prawns), it also has a herbal sauna for weary travel bones.

DRINKING

Middle of Somewhere Bar (☎ 012 1613833; 🕑 3pm-late) Fairy lights twinkling at the back door will lure you into the yard with a delightful beer garden. The only bar in town, it serves cheap beer.

GETTING THERE & AWAY

Amazingly, there is a scheduled bus linking Sen Monorom with Phnom Penh (32,000r, eight hours), leaving at 7am. From Phnom Penh, share taxis depart from the southwest corner of Psar Thmei (70,000r, nine hours). If you want to return to Phnom Penh by share taxi, guesthouses in Sen Monorom can arrange for a morning pick-up. There is a 7am bus from Sen Monorom to Stung Treng (50,000r, eight to nine hours), via Kratie and with a changeover at Snuol. Get your ticket the night before as it fills up fast. It leaves from opposite the Pech Kiri Guest House. Pick-ups also service Snuol (outside/inside 15,000/20,000r, three hours).

An adventurous and extremely arduous path connects Sen Monorom with Ban Lung in Ratanakiri Province – hard-core bikers should see Long Vibol Guesthouse for advice. Leaving Sen Monorom, the road has been sealed to Koh Nhek (two hours). From there on, it's an old-skool mess and takes at least five more hours to Ban Lung in Ratanakiri.

GETTING AROUND

Guesthouses rent out 100cc motorbikes for US$5 to US$10 per day. If you want a 250cc bike, you'll have to rent it in Phnom Penh (p80). Jeeps costs US$40 to US$50 a day, depending on the season and how far you want to go.

Around Sen Monorom

The real joy of the Mondulkiri Province is exploring by motorbike or on foot at your own pace, following small paths to hidden tribal villages or waterfalls spilling out of the jungle. Popular waterfalls include the low and wide **Romanear Waterfall**, 18km southeast of Sen Monorom, and the single-drop **Dak Dam Waterfall**, 25km to the city's east. Both are very difficult to find without a guide.

Bou Sraa Falls, a 35m-high double drop into a jungle gorge, is one of the largest and most famous waterfalls in Cambodia. No longer the bastard son of the devil himself, the road to the falls is now in reasonable shape, with new bridges across the major rivers. Hire a moto driver for the day or charter a Russian jeep (US$60) with a group.

CAMBODIA DIRECTORY

ACCOMMODATION

There are budget guesthouses in popular destinations throughout Cambodia, costing around US$3 to US$5 for a room. In many rural parts of Cambodia, the standard rate for the cheapest hotels is US$5, usually with attached bathroom and satellite TV, although there may be a few places starting at 10,000r that make more by the hour as brothels than they do by the night – don't count on much sleep!

All rooms quoted in this chapter have attached bathrooms unless stated otherwise.

ACTIVITIES

Tourism in Cambodia is still in its infancy, with few activities on offer. Snorkelling and diving are popular in Sihanoukville, and boat trips on rivers and around coastal areas can usually be arranged with locals keen to make some money. Improving roads are drawing an increasing number of cyclists, while the few remaining roller-coaster roads are paradise for experienced dirt bikers. Elephant rides and rewarding trekking are both possible in the wilds of Ratanakiri and Mondulkiri provinces.

BOOKS

For the full story on travelling in Cambodia, pick up Lonely Planet's *Cambodia*.

There's also a great selection of books on Cambodia in the better bookshops located in Phnom Penh and Siem Reap, but prices are relatively high. Markets and disabled street sellers pawn cheap copies of most titles, but we know you wouldn't dream of buying a photocopied Lonely Planet guide. Be warned, if this is a photocopy, it may self-destruct in five seconds.

The best introduction to the history of Cambodia is David P Chandler's *A History of Cambodia,* which covers the ups and downs of the Khmers over two millennia. Also by Chandler is *Brother Number One,* the menacing biography of Pol Pot. However, Philip Short's biography *Pol Pot: The History of a Nightmare* is more detailed and a riveting read.

When the War was Over by Elizabeth Becker is an insight into life in the last days

CAMBODIA

of Pol Pot's regime and its aftermath by one of the few journalists to visit Democratic Kampuchea back in 1978.

In *The Gate*, François Bizot recounts being kidnapped by the Khmer Rouge and interrogated by Comrade Duch, the head of Tuol Sleng prison; he is believed to be the only foreigner to have survived capture. Later he was holed up in the French embassy in April 1975 and became the negotiator between the foreigners inside and the Khmer Rouge outside.

Jon Swain's *River of Time* is as much about a personal hell as Cambodia's descent into hell, but it takes us back to an old Indochina and includes the real story behind the film *The Killing Fields*, in which Swain was played by Julian Sands.

The classic travel literature option is Norman Lewis' *A Dragon Apparent* (1951), an account of his 1950 foray into an Indochina that was soon to disappear.

To Asia With Love: A Connoisseur's Guide to Cambodia, Laos, Thailand and Vietnam (2004), an anthology edited by Kim Fay, is a delightful introduction to Cambodia and the Mekong Region for those looking for some inspiration and adventure. A new *To Cambodia with Love* will be out by the time you read this.

See p96 for books on Angkor.

BUSINESS HOURS

Most Cambodians get up very early and it's not unusual to see people out exercising at 5.30am when you're heading home – ahem, sorry, getting up – at that time. Government offices (closed Sundays) theoretically open at 7.30am, break for a siesta from 11.30am to 2pm and end the day at 5pm. However, it's a safe bet that few people will be around early in the morning or after 4pm, as their real income is earned elsewhere.

Businesses and shops open from around 8am to 6pm Monday to Saturday, and most are open on Sunday too.

Banking hours vary slightly, but you can reckon on core weekday hours of 8.30am to 3pm. Most are also usually open Saturday mornings.

Local restaurants are generally open from about 6.30am until 9pm and international restaurants until a little later. In this chapter, we consider 7am to 10am breakfast, noon to 3pm lunch and 5pm to 9pm dinner.

Any exceptions to these hours are listed in individual reviews.

CLIMATE

The climate of Cambodia is governed by two seasons, which set the rhythm of rural life. The cooler, dry season occurs from around November to May, with temperatures increasing from February; from June to October, there are strong winds, high humidity and heavy rains. Even during the wet season, it rarely rains in the morning – most precipitation falls in the afternoon and, even then, only sporadically. See the climate charts on p916 for more information.

CUSTOMS

A 'reasonable amount' of duty-free items is allowed into the country. Travellers arriving by air might bear in mind that alcohol and cigarettes are on sale at well below duty-free prices on the streets of Phnom Penh – a branded box of 200 cigarettes costs just US$8! International spirits start as low as US$7 a litre.

DANGERS & ANNOYANCES

As memories of war grow ever more distant, Cambodia has become a much safer country in which to travel. However, remember the golden rule – stick to marked paths in remote areas! Check on the latest situation before making a trip off the beaten track, particularly if travelling by motorcycle.

HOW TO AVOID A BAD TRIP

Watch out for *yama* (known as *yaba* in Thailand), which ominously shares its name with the Hindu god of death. Known as ice or crystal meth back home, it's not the usual diet pills but instead homemade meta-amphetamines often laced with toxic substances, such as mercury and lithium. It's more addictive than users would like to admit, provoking powerful hallucinations, sleep deprivation and psychosis.

Also be very careful about buying 'cocaine' in Cambodia. Most of what is sold as coke is actually pure heroin and far stronger than any smack found on the streets back home. Bang this up your nose and you're in serious trouble – several backpackers die each year.

The *Cambodia Daily* (www.cambodia daily.com) and *Phnom Penh Post* (www .phnompenhpost.com) are good sources for breaking news on Cambodia – check their websites before travelling here.

Border Crossings

Cambodian immigration officers at the country's land-border crossings have a bad reputation for petty extortion. Travellers are occasionally asked for an 'immigration fee', particularly at the Lao crossing. Overcharging on the Thai borders is common, usually between 1000B (Thai baht) and 1300B for the US$20 (less than 800B) visa. Some trave are even forced to change US dollars into riel at a poor rate in Poipet. Hold your breath, stand your ground, don't start a fight and remember that not all Cambodians are as mercenary as the boys in blue.

Mines, Mortars & Bombs

Never, ever touch any rockets, artillery shells, mortars, mines, bombs or other war material; Cambodia is one of the most heavily mined countries in the world with an estimated four to six million of these 'enemies within' littering the countryside. A gentle reminder: *do not* stray from well-marked paths under any circumstances, as even stepping from the roadside in some areas could have horrific consequences.

De-mining organisations are working throughout the country to clear these arbitrary assassins but, even with their dedicated work, the most common way a landmine is discovered is by a man, woman or child losing a limb.

Theft & Street Crime

Given the number of guns in Cambodia, there's less armed theft than one might expect. Still, hold-ups and motorcycle theft are a potential danger in Phnom Penh and Sihanoukville. See p69, p84 and p106 for more info. There's no need to be paranoid, just cautious. Walking or riding alone late at night is not ideal, certainly not in rural areas.

Pickpocketing isn't a huge problem in Cambodia, but it does happen in crowded markets. Bag snatching is a possibility here, particularly in popular parts of Phnom Penh.

EMBASSIES & CONSULATES

Embassies & Consulates in Cambodia

The following embassies are found in Phnom Penh:

Australia (Map p70; ☎ 213470; 11 Ph 254)
Canada (Map p70; ☎ 213470; 11 Ph 254)
China (Map pp66-7; ☎ 720920; 256 Mao Tse Toung Blvd)
France (Map pp66-7; ☎ 430020; 1 Monivong Blvd)
Germany (Map p70; ☎ 216381; 76-78 Ph 214)
Indonesia (Map p70; ☎ 216148; 90 Norodom Blvd)
Laos (Map pp66-7; ☎ 982632; 15-17 Mao Tse Toung Blvd)
Malaysia (Map p70; ☎ 216177; 5 Ph 242)
Myanmar (Map pp66-7; ☎ 223761; 181 Norodom Blvd)
Philippines (Map p70; ☎ 222303; 33 Ph 294)
Singapore (Map p70; ☎ 221875; 92 Norodom Blvd)
Thailand (Map pp66-7; ☎ 726306; 196 Norodom Blvd)
UK (Map pp66-7; ☎ 427124; 29 Ph 75)
USA (Map p70; ☎ 728000; 1 Ph 96)
Vietnam (Map pp66-7; ☎ 362531; 436 Monivong Blvd)

There's also a handy **Vietnamese consulate** (Map p105; Ph Ekareach) in Sihanoukville, which turns out the fastest Vietnamese visas in Southeast Asia (one month US$35).

Cambodian Embassies & Consulates Abroad

Australia (☎ 02-6273 1259; 5 Canterbury Cres, Deakin, ACT 2600)
France (☎ 01 45 03 47 20; 4 rue Adolphe Yvon, 75116 Paris)
Germany (☎ 030-48 63 79 01; Arnold Zweing Strasse, 1013189 Berlin)
Japan (☎ 03-5412 8521; 8-6-9 Akasaka, Minato-ku, Tokyo 1070052)
UK (☎ 020-8451 7850; 64 Brondesbury Park, London NW6 7AT)
USA (☎ 202-726 7742; 4500 16th St NW, Washington, DC, 20011)

For information on visas, see p126.

FESTIVALS & EVENTS

The festivals of Cambodia take place according to the lunar calendar, so the dates vary from year to year.

Chinese New Year The big Chinese community goes wild for the new year in late January or early to mid-February, with dragon dances filling many of Phnom Penh's streets. As it's also Tet, the Vietnamese live it up too.

CAMBODIA

Chaul Chnam Held in mid-April, this is a three-day celebration of Khmer New Year, with Khmers worshipping in wats to wash away their sins, and plastering each other with water and talc.

Visakha Puja Celebrated collectively as Buddha's birth, enlightenment and *parinibbana* (passing in nirvana), this festival's activities are centred on wats. The festival falls on the eighth day of the fourth moon (that's May or June to you and me) and is best observed at Angkor Wat, where there are candlelit processions of monks.

P'chum Ben This festival falls between mid-September and early October, and is a kind of All Souls' Day, when respects are paid to the dead through offerings made at wats.

Bon Om Tuk This festival is held in early November to celebrate the epic victory of Jayavarman VII over the Chams in 1177 and the reversal of the Tonlé Sap river. This is one of the most important festivals in the Khmer calendar and a wonderful, if hectic, time to be in Phnom Penh.

FOOD & DRINK

Food

It is definitely no secret that Cambodia's neighbouring countries, Thailand and Vietnam, are home to some of the finest food in the world, so it should come as no surprise to discover that Khmer cuisine is also rather special. *Amok* (baked fish with coconut and lemongrass in banana leaf) is sublime and *kyteow* (a rice-noodle soup packed with a punch), otherwise known as Cambodia in a bowl, will keep you going throughout the day.

Rice and *prahoc* – a fermented fish paste that your nose will soon recognise at a hundred paces – form the backbone of Khmer cuisine. Built around these are flavours that give the cuisine its kick: secret roots, pungent herbs and aromatic tubers. Together they give salads, snacks, soups and stews an aroma and taste that smacks of Cambodia.

Cambodian meals almost always include *samlor* (soup). *Samlor machou banle* is a popular hot and sour fish soup with pineapple and a splash of spices. Other popular soups include *samlor chapek* (ginger-flavoured pork soup), *samlor machou bawng kawng* (prawn soup similar to the popular Thai *tôm yam*) and *samlor ktis* (fish soup with coconut and pineapple).

Most fish eaten in Cambodia is freshwater, and *trey aing* (grilled fish) is a Cambodian speciality (*aing* means 'grilled' and can be applied to many dishes). Fish is traditionally eaten as pieces wrapped in lettuce or spinach leaves and dipped into a fish sauce known as *tuk trey,* similar to Vietnam's *nuoc mam* but with ground peanuts added.

TRAVEL YOUR TASTEBUDS

You're going to encounter food that's unusual, strange, maybe even immoral, or just plain weird. The fiercely omnivorous Cambodians find nothing strange in eating insects, algae, offal or fish bladders. They'll dine on a duck embryo, brew up some brains or snack on some spiders. They'll peel live frogs to grill on a barbecue or down the wine of a cobra to increase their virility.

To the Khmers, there's nothing 'strange' about anything that will sustain the body. They'll try anything once, even a burger.

For obvious reasons, please avoid eating endangered species.

WE DARE YOU! THE TOP FIVE

Try these Cambodian treats:

- crickets
- duck embryo
- durian
- *prahoc* (fermented fish paste)
- tarantulas

Drink

Don't drink tap water. Guzzle locally produced drinking water (500r per litre), which is available everywhere. Ice is made from treated water in local factories, so relax and enjoy it. Don't be surprised if waitresses try to put it in your beer or wine.

Soft drinks and coffee are found everywhere and a free pot of Chinese-style tea will usually appear as soon as you sit down in local restaurants.

Excellent fruit smoothies, known locally as *tukalok,* are omnipresent in Cambodia. Look out for stalls with fruit and a blender. If you don't want heaps of sugar and condensed milk, even an egg, keep an eye on the preparatory stages.

The most popular beer is the local Angkor, but Anchor, Beer Lao, Tiger, San Miguel, Stella Artois, Carlsberg and Heineken also grace many a menu. Cans sell for around US$1 to US$1.50, and local draughts are similarly priced.

In Phnom Penh, foreign wines and spirits are sold at bargain prices. 'Muscle wines', something like Red Bull meets absinthe, with names such as Commando Bear Beverage and Brace of Loma, are popular with Khmers. They contain enough unknown substances to contravene the Geneva Chemical Weapons Convention and should only be approached with extreme caution.

GAY & LESBIAN TRAVELLERS

While Cambodian culture is tolerant of homosexuality, the scene is certainly nothing like that of neighbouring Thailand. Phnom Penh and Siem Reap have the best of the action. As with heterosexual couples, passionate public displays of affection are considered a basic no-no, so it's prudent not to flaunt your sexuality. That said, same sexes often hold hands in Cambodian society, so it's unlikely to raise eyebrows.

Utopia (www.utopia-asia.com) features gay travel information and contacts, including detailed sections on the legality of homosexuality in Cambodia and some local gay terminology.

HOLIDAYS

Banks, government ministries and embassies close down for public holidays, so plan ahead during these times. Holidays usually roll over if they fall on a weekend, and some people take a day or two extra during major festivals. See p121 for longer holidays that move with the lunar calendar.

International New Year's Day 1 January
Victory over the Genocide 7 January
International Women's Day 8 March
International Workers' Day 1 May
HM the King's Birthday 13 to 15 May
International Children's Day 1 June
Former Queen's Birthday 18 June
Constitution Day 24 September
Paris Peace Accords 23 October
King Father's Birthday 31 October
Independence Day 9 November
International Human Rights Day 10 December

INSURANCE

Do not visit Cambodia without medical insurance. Anyone who has a serious injury or illness while in Cambodia may require emergency evacuation to Bangkok. With an insurance policy costing no more than the equivalent of a bottle of beer a day, this evacuation is free. Without an insurance policy, it will cost between US$10,000 and US$20,000 – somewhat more than the average traveller's budget!

INTERNET ACCESS

Internet access has spread throughout much of Cambodia. Charges range from 2000r per hour in major cities to US$4 an hour in the smaller provincial capitals.

INTERNET RESOURCES

Angkor.com (http://angkor.com) When it comes to links, this site has them, spreading its cybertentacles into all sorts of interesting areas.

Cambodia Tales (http://andybrouwer.co.uk) A great gateway to all things Cambodian, it includes comprehensive links to other sites and regular Cambodian travel articles.

Lonely Planet (www.lonelyplanet.com) Summaries on travelling to Cambodia, the Thorn Tree bulletin board and travel news.

Tales of Asia (www.talesofasia.com) Up-to-the-minute road conditions, including Poipet to Siem Reap, and other overland Cambodian travel information.

LEGAL MATTERS

Narcotics, including marijuana, are not legal in Cambodia and police are beginning to take a harder line – the days of free bowls in guesthouses are long gone. However, marijuana is traditionally used in some Khmer food, so its presence will linger on. If you're a smoker, be discreet as police may soon turn the busting of foreigners into a lucrative sideline.

Moral grounds alone should be enough to deter foreigners from seeking underage sexual partners in Cambodia but, sadly, in some cases it's not. Paedophilia is a serious crime and now many Western countries have also enacted much-needed legislation to make offences committed overseas punishable at home. See also p125.

MAPS

Unless you're looking to head into the wilds on the back of a dirt bike, you won't require additional maps to those in this guidebook. If you need one, the best all-rounder for Cambodia is Gecko's *Cambodia Road Map* at 1:750,000 scale, which has lots of detail and accurate place names. Another popular foldout map is Nelles' *Cambodia, Laos and Vietnam Map* at 1:1,500,000, although the detail is limited.

MEDIA

Magazines & Newspapers

The *Cambodia Daily* (www.cambodiadaily.com) is a popular English-language newspaper, while the *Phnom Penh Post* (www.phnompenhpost.com) offers in-depth analysis every two weeks. Local travel magazines include the informative *AsiaLIFE Phnom Penh* (www.asialifecambodia.com) and the mildly amusing *Bayon Pearnik* (www.bayonpearnik.com), both free.

Radio & TV

The BBC (100MHz FM) has broadcasts in Khmer and English in the capital.

Many guesthouses and hotels in Cambodia have satellite TV, offering access to BBC World, CNN, Star Sports, HBO and more.

MONEY

Cambodia's currency is the riel, abbreviated here by a lower-case r written after the sum. The riel comes in notes with the following values: 50r, 100r, 200r, 500r, 1000r, 2000r, 5000r, 10,000r, 20,000r, 50,000r and 100,000r.

Throughout this chapter, each establishment's prices are in the currency quoted to the average punter. This is usually in US dollars or riel, but in the west of the country it is sometimes in Thai baht. While this may seem inconsistent, this is the way it is done throughout Cambodia and the sooner you get used to thinking comparatively in riel, dollars or baht, the easier travelling will be.

Currency exchange rates at the time this book went to press:

Country	Unit	Riel (r)
Australia	A$1	3396
Canada	C$1	3912
Euro zone	€1	5590
Japan	¥100	3497
Laos	10,000 kip	4185
New Zealand	NZ$1	2875
Thailand	10B	1259
UK	UK£1	8089
USA	US$1	4029
Vietnam	10,000d	2483

ATMs

There are now credit-card-compatible ATMs (Visa and MasterCard only) in most major cities, including Phnom Penh, Siem Reap, Sihanoukville, Battambang and Kompong Cham. Machines dispense US dollars. Stay alert when using them late at night.

Bargaining

Bargaining is the rule when shopping in markets, when hiring vehicles and sometimes when taking a room. Siem Reap and Angkor aside, the Khmers are not ruthless hagglers and a smile goes a long way.

See opposite for appropriate bargaining etiquette.

Cash

There are no banks at Cambodian land-border crossings, so arrive with some US dollars in hand. US dollars are accepted everywhere so there's no compelling need to change money, although riel is useful to pay for motos and such. Hardened travellers may argue that spending dollars makes things slightly more expensive, but you'll soon pick up plenty of riel in change along the way. Exchanging dollars is best done at markets, as there are no queues and no paperwork. Those with cash in another major currency can change it in major centres.

Credit Cards

Cash advances on credit cards are now available in Phnom Penh, Siem Reap, Sihanoukville, Kampot, Battambang and Kompong Cham. Canadia Bank offers the best service, with free MasterCard and Visa cash advances. Credit cards are accepted at some hotels, restaurants, shops, airlines and travel agents.

Travellers Cheques

Like credit cards, travellers cheques aren't much use when venturing beyond the main tourist centres. Most banks charge a commission of 2% to cash travellers cheque, and dish out US dollars rather than riel. Some hotels and travel agents will also cash travellers cheques after banking hours.

PHOTOGRAPHY & VIDEO

Many internet cafés in Phnom Penh, Siem Reap, Battambang and Sihanoukville will burn CDs from digital images using card readers or USB connections. The price is about US$2.50 if you need a CD or US$1.50 if you don't. Digital memory is widely available in Cambodia and pretty cheap.

Film and processing are cheap in Cambodia. A roll of 36 exposures costs about US$2.

Processing charges are around US$4 for 36 standard prints. Cheap slide film is widely available in Phnom Penh and Siem Reap, but elsewhere it's hard to find.

POST

Don't send mail from provinces; stick with Phnom Penh's main post office and make sure postcards and letters are franked before they vanish from your sight. Postcards cost 1500r to 2100r – cross your fingers and hope your mail arrives in two or three weeks.

Phnom Penh's main post office has a poste restante service. Although it now checks identification, don't have anything valuable sent there. It costs 200r per item received.

RESPONSIBLE TRAVEL

Cambodia continues to experience unprecedented growth in tourism and this inevitably brings the bad along with the good. Your goal is a simple one: minimise the negatives and maximise the positives.

If you witness suspicious behaviour of tourists with Cambodian children, it's your duty to report it. Child exploitation and sexual abuse is now rightly taken very seriously here. Report any suspicions to **ChildSafe** (☎ 012 296609; www.childsafe-cambodia.org). When booking into a hotel or jumping on transport, look out for the ChildSafe logo; each establishment or driver who earns this logo supports the end to child-sex tourism and has undergone child-protection training.

When bargaining for goods in a market or for a ride on a moto, remember the aim is not to get the lowest possible price, but one that's acceptable to both you and the seller. Coming on too strong or arguing over a few hundred riel does nothing to foster Cambodians' positive feelings towards travellers. Be thankful there's room for discussion in Cambodia, so try not to abuse it.

On the topic of money, Cambodia is an extremely poor country and begging is prevalent in Phnom Penh and Siem Reap. Try not to become numb to the pleas as there's no social security network and no government support. Amputees may also find themselves stigmatised by mainstream society and unable to make ends meet any other way. If you do give – which is viewed positively by Buddhists – keep the denominations small, so expectations don't grow too big. Many amputees now sell books on the street and buying from them may encourage others to become more self-sufficient. Please don't give money to children as they rarely get to keep the money and it only fuels the problem – giving them some food is preferable. A great option in Phnom Penh and Siem Reap is to shop or eat in establishments whose profits benefit street children, disabled people and disenfranchised women – check out the restaurants listed on p76 and p87, and the shops on p78 and p88 for more details.

Looting from Cambodia's ancient temples has been a huge problem over the past couple of decades. Don't contribute to this cultural rape by buying old stone carvings. Classy reproductions are available in Phnom Penh and Siem Reap, complete with export certificates. For more on the issue of trafficking in antiquities, check out **Heritage Watch** (www.heritagewatch.org) or pick up a copy of its quarterly *Touchstone* magazine.

On a similar note, pick up a copy of the *Stay Another Day Cambodia* (www.stay-another-day.org), which has a list of sustainable-tourism initiatives.

Finally, don't forget what the Cambodians have been through in the protracted years of war, genocide and famine. Support local Cambodian-owned businesses; if anyone deserves to profit from the new-found interest in this wonderful country, it's surely the long-suffering Khmers.

STUDYING

Organised courses are few and far between in Cambodia. Sadly, the only Khmer language courses on offer are strictly aimed at Phnom Penh's expat community. However, travellers can indulge in Khmer cooking lessons in Phnom Penh (p75), Siem Reap (p85) and Battambang (p98).

TELEPHONE

Brightly numbered private mobile phone booths found on every town's kerbs offer cheap local calls for about 300r a minute. Mobile numbers start with ☎ 011, ☎ 012, ☎ 015, ☎ 016, ☎ 092 and ☎ 099. The cheapest international calls are via the internet and cost 300r to 2000r a minute. Although the price is great, the lengthy delay can be infuriating. Hello? Hello? More expensive international calls can be made from public phonecard booths, which are found in major cities. However, prices are dropping, particularly if you use the MFone network. Roaming charges are high in Cambodia; consider buying a local sim card if you are here for a full month.

The cheapest fax services are also via the internet and cost around US$1 to US$2 per page for most destinations.

TOILETS

Although the occasional squat toilet turns up now and then, particularly in the most budget of budget guesthouses, toilets are usually of the sit-down variety. In remote regions you'll find that hygiene conditions deteriorate somewhat.

The issue of what to do with used toilet paper is a cause for concern. Generally, if there's a wastepaper basket next to the toilet, that is where the toilet paper goes, as many sewage systems cannot handle toilet paper. Toilet paper is seldom provided, so keep a stash with you at all times.

Should nature call in rural areas, don't let modesty drive you into the bushes: there may be landmines not far from the road or track. Stay on the roadside and do the deed, or grin and bear it until the next town.

TOURIST INFORMATION

Official tourist information in Phnom Penh and Siem Reap is pretty limited. In the provinces it's a different story, with more and more towns ambitiously opening somewhat helpful tourist offices. While the staff have little in the way of brochures or hand-outs, they'll do their best to tell you about local places of interest and may even drag the director out of a nearby karaoke bar to answer your questions. Guesthouses and free local magazines are generally more useful than tourist offices.

Cambodia has no official tourist offices abroad and it's unlikely that Cambodian embassies will be of much assistance in planning a trip, besides issuing a visa.

TOURS

Despite every English-speaking moto driver in the country claiming to be a tour guide, there are actually few organised tours on offer in Cambodia. The most abundant are city tours of Phnom Penh and its surrounds, promoted by numerous guesthouses. Guesthouses in Sihanoukville promote boat tours to nearby tropical islands, as do some places in Kep. Organised day trips to Bokor National Park are a popular option in Kampot. In the northeast, guesthouses in Mondulkiri offer elephant treks and village homestay trips, while in Ratanakiri it is possible to visit vast Virachey National Park. Even Siem Reap is at last getting in on the act, with some guesthouses offering trips to the remote temples of Preah Vihear province.

TRAVELLERS WITH DISABILITIES

Uneven pavements, potholed roads and, in Angkor, stairs as steep as ladders ensure that Cambodia isn't an easy country in which to travel for most people with mobility impairments. Few buildings have been designed with disabled people in mind, and transport in the provinces is usually very overcrowded, although taxi hire from point to point is at least an affordable option.

On the positive side, Cambodians are usually very helpful towards all foreigners, and it's cheap to hire someone to accompany you.

VISAS

Most nationalities receive a one-month visa on arrival at land borders (except for the Phnom Den–Tinh Bien Vietnam crossing),

DOMESTIC TELEPHONE CODES

Banteay Meanchey	☎ 054
Battambang	☎ 053
Kampot	☎ 033
Kandal	☎ 024
Kep	☎ 036
Kompong Cham	☎ 042
Kompong Chhnang	☎ 026
Kompong Speu	☎ 025
Kompong Thom	☎ 062
Kratie	☎ 072
Koh Kong	☎ 035
Mondulkiri	☎ 073
Oddar Meanchey	☎ 065
Phnom Penh	☎ 023
Preah Vihear	☎ 064
Prey Veng	☎ 043
Pursat	☎ 052
Ratanakiri	☎ 075
Siem Reap	☎ 063
Sihanoukville	☎ 034
Stung Treng	☎ 074
Svay Rieng	☎ 044
Takeo	☎ 032

and Phnom Penh and Siem Reap airports. The visa costs US$20 and one passport-sized photo is required. It is also possible to arrange a visa through Cambodian embassies overseas or an online visa (US$25) through the **Ministry of Foreign Affairs** (http://evisa.mfaic.gov.kh/). Arranging a visa ahead of time can help prevent potential overcharging at some land crossings. Anyone planning an extended stay should get a one-month business visa for US$25.

Visa extensions are granted in Phnom Penh; visit the shiny immigration office opposite Phnom Penh International Airport to arrange one. Tourist visas can be extended only once for one month, whereas business visas can be extended ad infinitum. Officially, an extension for one month costs US$30, three months US$60, six months US$100 and one year US$150. However, the police will keep your passport for about 25 days. Strangely enough there's an express, next-day service at inflated prices: one month US$39 (for both tourist and business visas), three months US$80 (business visas only) and so on. You'll need one passport photo for the extension. Overstayers are charged US$5 per day at the point of exit.

VOLUNTEERING

Cambodia hosts a huge number of NGOs, but most recruit skilled volunteers from home, so opportunities are few and far between. The best way to find out who is working in Cambodia is to hit the **Cooperation Committee for Cambodia** (CCC; ☎ in Phnom Penh 023-426009; 35 Ph 178, Phnom Penh). This organisation has a handy list of all NGOs, both Cambodian and international.

Grass-roots organisations are particularly appreciative of volunteers. Try the following places:

Lazy Gecko Café (Map p70; ☎ 023-012 1912935; 23B Ph 93) Based in Phnom Penh, it supports Jeannie's Orphanage; see p76 .

Starfish Project (Map p105; ☎ 012 952011) Down in Sihanoukville this place helps to raise funds for local projects, and it encourages volunteers; see (p108).

Also check out these websites:

Volunteer Abroad (www.volunteerabroad.com) Has 53 programmes in Cambodia.

Volunteer in Cambodia (www.volunteerincambodia.org) Organises voluntary teaching posts.

WOMEN TRAVELLERS

Women will generally find Cambodia a hassle-free place to travel, although some guys in the guesthouse industry may try their luck occasionally. If you're planning a trip off the beaten track it would be best to find a travel companion.

Khmer women dress fairly conservatively, and it's best to follow suit, particularly when visiting wats. In general, long-sleeved shirts and long trousers or skirts are preferred. In a skirt and hitting the town on a moto? Do as the Khmer women do and sit side-saddle.

Tampons and sanitary napkins are available in major cities and provincial capitals.

WORKING

Job opportunities are limited in Cambodia, partly as Cambodians need the jobs more than foreigners and partly as the foreigners who work here are usually professionals recruited overseas. The easiest option is teaching English in Phnom Penh, as experience isn't a prerequisite at the smaller schools. Pay ranges from about US$5 to US$6 per hour (for the inexperienced) to about US$15 to US$20 per hour for those with a TEFL certificate teaching at the better schools. Places to look for work include the classifieds sections of local English-language newspapers.

East Timor

HIGHLIGHTS

- **Diving Dili** – some of the world's best shore diving can be found right near the scruffy capital (p139)
- **Atauro Island** – East Timor in a microcosm, with funky lodgings on untouched beaches plus perfect reefs offshore (p141)
- **Hatubuilico and Mt Ramelau** – coffee plantations and misty valleys give way to sweeping views that are best reached via predawn climbs (p144)
- **Baucau** – the Old Town reeks of Portuguese colonial charm, while a perfect beach lies below (p142)
- **Jaco Island** – a sacred spot with pristine white-sand beauty, and settlements unchanged for centuries (p143)
- **Off the beaten track** – roads that barely merit the name penetrate the lush interior and the unvisited south coast; try the road from Bobonaro to Zumalai (p144)

FAST FACTS

- **Budget** US$20 to US$50 a day
- **Capital** Dili
- **Costs** guesthouse room US$10, 1.5L bottle of water US$0.50, beer US$2.50, noodle dish from a local eatery US$1 to US$2, shore dive US$40
- **Country code** ☎ 670
- **Languages** Tetun, Portuguese, Indonesian, English
- **Money** US$ (US dollar)
- **Phrases (Tetun)** *olá* (hello), *adeus* (goodbye), *obrigadu/a* (m/f) (thank you), *kolisensa* (excuse me)
- **Time** GMT + nine hours
- **Visas** US$30 on arrival

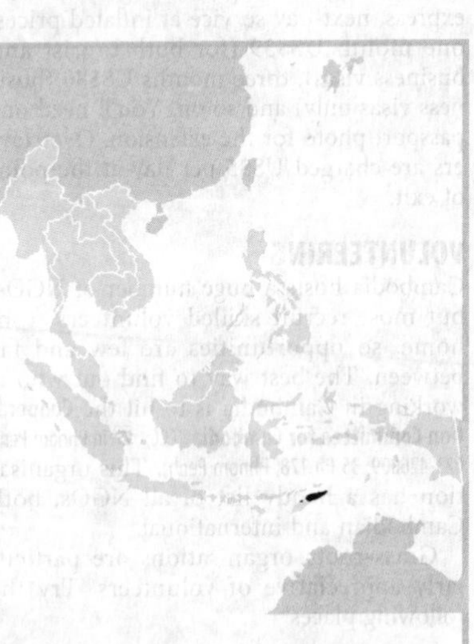

TRAVEL HINTS

East Timor is a timeless place, so ditch your watch. Transport departure times are vague notions and journey times – due to weather, goats in the road, wash-outs etc – are highly variable. Go with the flow and you'll be relaxed even when the restaurant preparing your meal seems to be growing the plant.

OVERLAND ROUTES

Overland travel is possible between East Timor and Indonesian West Timor, but give yourself plenty of time.

Nothing is easy about East Timor (Timor-Leste in the locally preferred Portuguese) and that's both its blessing and its curse.

Independence hasn't been simple; years spent under Portuguese and Indonesian thumbs have been burdened by tragedy, and recent history shows why you can't just declare yourself a new country (as happened in 2002) and expect things to be hunky-dory.

Travellers will experience some of the challenges the Timorese contend with on a daily basis, and that may be the best reason to visit. The tourism infrastructure is barely developed, yet there's just enough for the adventurous to experience this beautiful place without undue travail. The diving is magnificent, the countryside superb and the people genuinely welcoming. And just as the locals have found ways to get by, you will too – which only makes your journey more rewarding.

Sure the roads are crap and getting from one place to another can take forever, but the flip side is that you'll rarely be following in others' footsteps. You can get into the unique cultural rhythm that combines European and Asian beats. There's a nod and a wave from everyone you meet. Soon you'll realise that what's easiest about East Timor is its charm.

CURRENT EVENTS

East Timor stays in the news for all the wrong reasons: political turmoil, unrest, catastrophe. Although problems abound, people outside the country are left with an overly dire picture. Yes there were bad riots in 2006, yes there are tens of thousands of refugees living in camps in and around the capital, and yes Dili and much of the rest of the country is scarred by rounds of destruction that began when the Indonesians pillaged the place on their way out in 1999.

But what news reports don't show is that East Timor is a place where people are surprisingly relaxed, where they go about the business of getting on with life, and where threats to visitors are relatively few.

The significance of the elections held in 2007 cannot be stated strongly enough. A mere five years after independence, the Timorese turned out in droves to elect a president and parliament in polls that were remarkably trouble free.

That East Timor has accomplished so much in such little time is extraordinary. In 2002 it was still effectively a one-party nation under Fretilin, which had led the struggle for independence during the entire Indonesian occupation. After the UN backed away from propping up the government in 2005, it was natural that divisions would occur. Fretilin splintered and old animosities played out. Prime Minister Mari Alkatiri sacked one third of the army in March 2006, and in the ensuing months of rioting more than 150,000 people fled their homes. Relative peace only returned after public demonstrations forced Alkatiri to quit, and forces from the UN, Australia and others returned to the country.

Given the turmoil, many predicted that the 2007 elections would be a disaster. Yet a funny thing happened on the way to the riot: things went off pretty smoothly, mostly due to the determination of the average Timorese. The Fretilin monopoly was replaced by 14 political parties, representing a broad spectrum of politics.

After two rounds of elections, José Ramos-Horta was chosen as president by 70% of the voters in May 2007. One month later, the parliamentary elections resulted in no party having a clear majority. Fretilin had the most votes but only received 29% of the overall vote; Xanana Gusmão's Council of National Resistance of Timor (CNRT) got 24% of the vote, and the rest was split between other parties. Eventually, Gusmão was able to form a coalition with the other parties and was named prime minister, which infuriated Fretilin. In an all-too-familiar spectacle, Fretilin supporters rioted, causing damage in Dili and across the nation; tens of thousands joined the 100,000-plus people already living in camps.

As long as the party politics trump unified action, it will be very difficult for the government to confront the long list of problems that bedevil East Timor, including education, food, roads and more. With the UN and other international forces anxious to leave, it will be up to the Timorese to start building a viable future.

HISTORY

Portuguese Settle In

Little is known of Timor before AD 1500, although Chinese and Javanese traders visited the island from at least the 13th century, and possibly as early as the 7th century. These

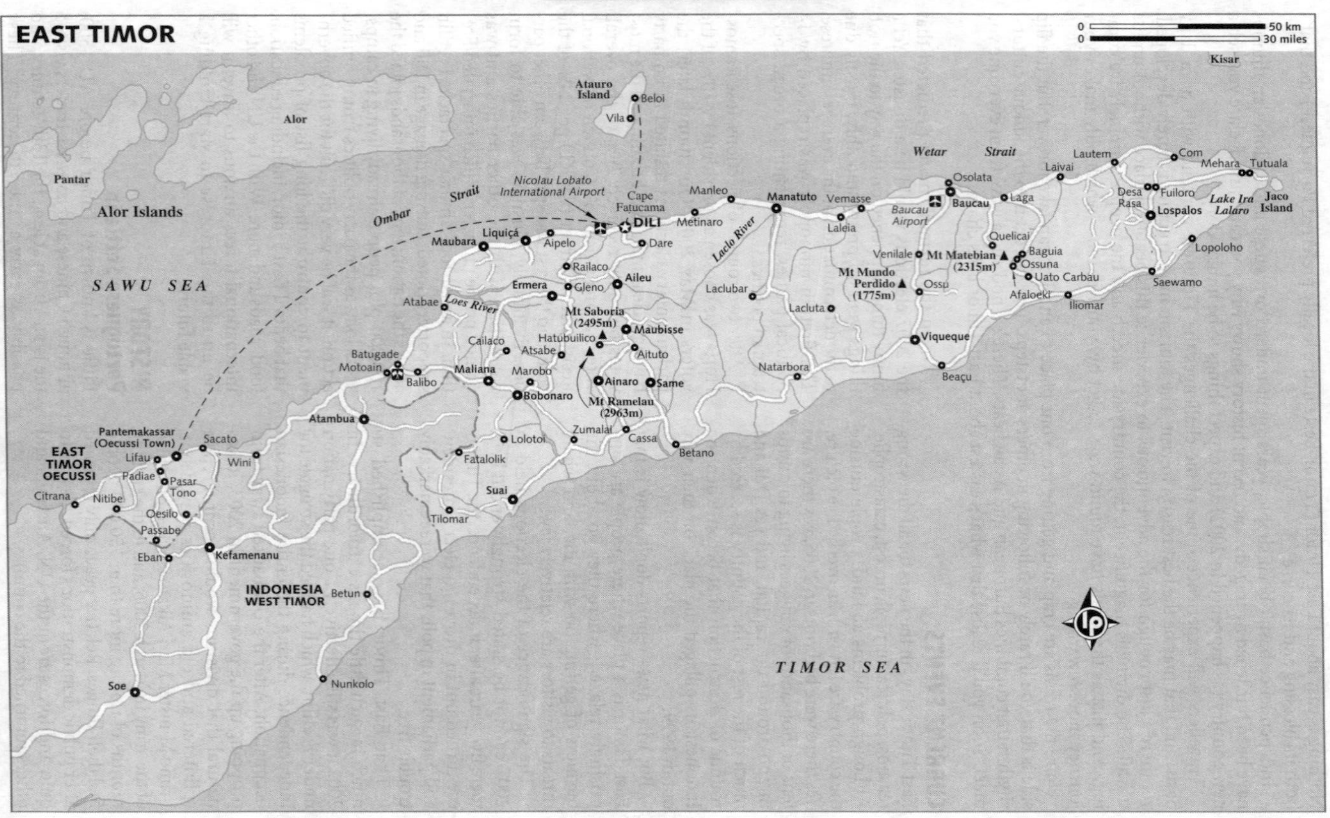

EAST TIMOR
0 50 km
0 30 miles
Kisar
Atauro Island
Beloi
Vila
Alor
Pantar
Alor Islands
Ombar Strait
Wetar Strait
SAWU SEA
TIMOR SEA
Nicolau Lobato International Airport
Cape Fatucama
DILI
Manleo
Metinaro
Manatuto
Vemasse
Laleia
Baucau Airport
Baucau
Osolata
Laga
Laivai
Lautem
Com
Mehara
Tutuala
Desa Rasa
Fuiloro
Lospalos
Lake Ira Lalaro
Jaco Island
Lopoloho
Saewamo
Quelicai
Baguia
Ossuna
Uato Carbau
Afaloeki
Iliomar
Venilale
Mt Matebian (2315m)
Mt Mundo Perdido (1775m)
Ossu
Viqueque
Beaçu
Laclo River
Laclubar
Lacluta
Natarbora
Maubara
Liquiçá
Aipelo
Dare
Railaco
Aileu
Ermera
Gleno
Atabae
Loes River
Mt Saboria (2495m)
Maubisse
Hatubuilico
Aituto
Cailaco
Atsabe
Batugade
Motoain
Balibo
Maliana
Marobo
Bobonaro
Ainaro
Same
Mt Ramelau (2963m)
Atambua
Zumalai
Cassa
Lolotoi
Betano
Fatalolik
Suai
Tilomar
Pantemakassar (Oecussi Town)
Sacato
EAST TIMOR OECUSSI
Lifau
Wini
Padiae
Pasar Tono
Citrana
Nitibe
Oesilo
Passabe
Kefamenanu
Eban
INDONESIA WEST TIMOR
Betun
Soe
Nunkolo

traders searched the coastal settlements for aromatic sandalwood, which was valued for its use in making furniture and incense, and beeswax, used for making candles. Portuguese traders arrived between 1509 and 1511, but it wasn't until 1556 that a handful of Dominican friars established the first Portuguese settlement at Lifau – in the present-day Oecussi enclave – and set about converting the Timorese to Catholicism.

In 1642, Francisco Fernandes led a Portuguese military expedition to weaken the power of the Timor kings. Comprised primarily of Topasses, the 'black Portuguese' mestizos (people of mixed parentage) from neighbouring Flores, his small army of musketeers settled in Timor, extending Portuguese influence into the interior.

To counter the Portuguese, the Dutch established a base at Kupang in western Timor in 1653. The Portuguese appointed an administrator to Lifau in 1656, but the Topasses went on to become a law unto themselves, driving out the Portuguese governor in 1705.

By 1749 the Topasses controlled central Timor and marched on Kupang, but the Dutch won the ensuing battle, expanding their control of western Timor in the process. On the Portuguese side, after more attacks from the Topasses in Lifau, the colonial base was moved east to Dili in 1769.

The 1859 Treaty of Lisbon divided Timor, giving Portugal the eastern half, together with the north coast pocket of Oecussi; this was formalised in 1904. Portuguese Timor was a sleepy and neglected outpost ruled through a traditional system of *liurai* (local chiefs). Control outside Dili was limited and it wasn't until the 20th century that the Portuguese intervened in the interior.

World War Two

In 1941, Australia sent a small commando force into Portuguese Timor to counter the Japanese, deliberately breaching the colony's neutral status. Although the military initiative angered neutral Portugal and dragged Portuguese Timor into the Pacific War, it slowed the Japanese expansion. Australia's success was largely due to the support it received from the locals, for whom the cost was phenomenal. In 1942 the Portuguese handed control to the Japanese whose soldiers razed whole villages, seized food supplies and killed Timorese in areas where the Australians were operating. By the end of the war, between 40,000 and 60,000 Timorese had died.

Portuguese Pull Out; Indonesia Invades

After WWII the colony reverted to Portuguese rule until, following the coup in Portugal on 25 April 1974, Lisbon set about discarding its

CAST OF CHARACTERS

Three men are important to East Timor's future.

Mari Alkatiri is the leader of Fretilin, and is uncompromising in his response to what he sees as the desertion of Fretilin by other party members who've joined the many new political parties. After being ousted as prime minister following the 2006 riots, he has staunchly defended Fretilin's role in the country; in 2007 he led protests after Fretilin won 29% of the vote but was unable to form a government. A descendent of an old Muslim trading family, Alkatiri is a bit of an anomaly in a staunchly Catholic country.

Xanana Gusmão is East Timor's most charismatic leader. The first president of the country, he earned the enmity of many of his old Fretilin brethren by breaking with the party after independence. In the 2007 parliamentary elections, he led the Council of National Resistance of Timor (CNRT) party, which favours a pragmatic approach to relations with neighbours such as Australia and Indonesia. Gusmão was a leader of guerrilla forces from 1978 until 1992, when he was captured and imprisoned in Jakarta. A close ally of Ramos-Horta, Gusmão formed a coalition government and was named prime minister after the troubled 2007 parliamentary elections. His wife is Australian-born Kirsty Sword Gusmão, who runs the prominent charity the Alola Foundation.

José Ramos-Horta is the charismatic Nobel Prize winner who spent 20 years in exile during the Indonesian occupation. He took over as prime minister after Alkatiri was forced from office in 2006. Elected president in 2007 with a huge margin, he has disassociated himself from any political party. Single and known for his courtly ways, Ramos-Horta has said that all the nation's women are his first ladies.

colonial empire. Within a few weeks political parties had been formed in East Timor, and the Timorese Democratic Union (UDT) attempted to seize power in August 1975. A brief civil war saw its rival Fretilin (previously known as the Timorese Social Democrats) come out on top, declaring the independent existence of the Democratic Republic of East Timor on 28 November. But on 7 December the Indonesians launched their attack on Dili.

Indonesia opposed the formation of an independent East Timor, and the leftist Fretilin raised the spectre of Communism. The full-scale invasion of the former colony came one day after Henry Kissinger and Gerald Ford departed Jakarta, having tacitly given their assent. (Indeed, the Americans urged the Indonesians to conduct a swift campaign so that the world wouldn't see them using weapons provided by the USA.) Australia also sided with Indonesia, leaving the Timorese to face Indonesia alone.

By 1976 there were 35,000 Indonesian troops in East Timor. Falintil, the military wing of Fretilin, fought a guerrilla war with marked success in the first few years, but weakened considerably thereafter. The cost of the brutal takeover to the East Timorese was huge; it's estimated that at least 100,000 died in the hostilities, and ensuing disease and famine.

By 1989, Indonesia had things firmly under control and opened East Timor to tourism. Then, on 12 November 1991 Indonesian troops fired on protesters gathered at the Santa Cruz Cemetery in Dili to commemorate the killing of an independence activist. With the event captured on film and aired around the world, the embarrassed Indonesian government admitted to 19 killings, although it's estimated that over 200 died in the massacre.

While Indonesia introduced a civilian administration, the military remained in control. Aided by secret police and civilian Timorese militia to crush dissent, reports of arrest, torture and murder were numerous.

Independence

Timorese hopes for independence remained high, but Indonesia showed no signs of making concessions until the fall of the Soeharto regime. Shortly after taking office in May 1998, Soeharto's successor, President Habibie, unexpectedly announced a referendum for East Timorese autonomy, much to the horror of the military. On 30 August 1999, East Timor voted overwhelmingly (78.5%) for independence from, rather than autonomy within, Indonesia. Though the Indonesian government promised to respect the results of the UN-sponsored vote, military-backed Timorese militias massacred, burnt and looted the country.

International condemnation led to UN troops bringing peace to East Timor beginning in September 1999. Half a million people had been displaced, and telecommunications, power installations, bridges, government buildings, shops and houses were destroyed. Today these scars are everywhere.

The UN set up a temporary administration during the transition to independence, and aid and foreign workers flooded into the country. As well as physically rebuilding the country, East Timor has had to create a civil service, police, judiciary, education, health system and so on, with staff recruited and trained from scratch.

The UN handed over government to East Timor on 20 May 2002. Falintil leader Xanana Gusmão was president of the new nation, and the longtime leader of Fretilin Mari Alkatiri, who ran the organisation from exile in Mozambique, was prime minister.

Birth Pangs

In December 2002, Dili was wracked by riots as years of poverty and frustration proved too much for the nascent democracy. The economy was in a shambles and people were ready for things to start improving – and fast. But without any viable industry or employment potential, East Timor was reliant almost entirely on foreign aid.

Only a small UN contingent remained in East Timor by mid-2005. As the number of outsiders shrank, the challenges of creating a new nation virtually from scratch became all too apparent. Government factions squabbled while the enormous needs of the people festered. By 2006 it was clear that too much had been expected too soon.

The Future

East Timor will continue to rely on foreign money as it struggles to establish a viable economy.

Gas and oil deposits in the Timor Sea have the greatest potential to help East Timor's

EAST TIMOR

economy to develop without the assistance of foreign aid. Proud of its image as a benefactor of East Timor, Australia was anything but in negotiations with the tiny country over revenues from the oil fields; through outright bullying, the Howard government tried to keep payments to East Timor negligible, despite the fact that it is one of the world's poorest countries. Only perseverance on the part of the Timorese won them an agreement that will provide US$4 billion in the next few years and much more thereafter.

High in the hills above Dili is another resource: coffee. Some 50,000 people work to produce the country's sought-after arabica beans, noted for their cocoa and vanilla character. Shade-grown and mostly organic (because few farmers can afford fertilizers and pesticides), Timorese coffee is prized by companies such as Starbucks, and production is increasing.

East Timor's tourism industry has great potential, although there needs to be a perception of stability for numbers to grow beyond the 1500 people who visit each year.

THE CULTURE

The National Psyche

East Timor's identity is firmly rooted in its survival of extreme hardship and foreign occupation. As a consequence of the long and difficult struggle for independence, the people of East Timor are profoundly politically aware – not to mention proud and loyal. While there is great respect for elders and church and community leaders, there lurks a residual suspicion surrounding foreign occupiers, most recently in the form of the UN. In a country where Catholicism cloaks animistic beliefs and practices, religious beliefs also greatly inform the national consciousness.

Lifestyle

Most East Timorese lead a subsistence lifestyle: what is farmed (or caught) is eaten. Traditional gender roles are firmly in place, with men doing much of the physical work, and women tending to family needs. Large families are common and infant mortality is high. The infrastructure in East Timor is limited: the majority of the population does not have access to money, electricity or clean water. With a high birth rate (35% of the population is under 15) and limited agricultural output, it's thought that 20% of the Timorese are living on the edge of malnutrition at any time.

The average family income is US$800 a year, much less in the countryside. Here you find people living much as they have for centuries, housed in thatched huts without even the barest of modern improvements such as corrugated metal or plastic sheeting. Since independence, a slew of NGOs and aid projects have tried to improve living conditions and raise agricultural production so that people will have something to sell in markets.

A small percentage of people – mostly in Dili – have jobs that provide income for consumer goods. Motorised vehicles remain rare; on weekends, buses are packed with people travelling to the family events that form the backbone of Timorese life.

Of the scores of people living in refugee camps, many are there simply because the promise of daily food and water trumps their hardscrabble existence at home.

> **MUST READ**
>
> *Shakedown: Australia's Grab for Timor Oil* by Paul Cleary details the hard-nosed efforts by the Howard government to force East Timor to sign away oil and gas rights in the Timor Sea to Australia for a song.

Population

East Timor has at least a dozen indigenous groups, the largest of which is formed by the Tetun (about 25%), who live around Suai, Dili and Viqueque, as well as in West Timor. The next largest group (around 10%) is the Mambai, who live in the mountains of Maubisse, Ainaro and Same.

Other groups each account for 5% or less of the population. The Kemak live in the Ermera and Bobonaro districts around Maliana; the Bunak also live in Bobonaro, and their territory extends into West Timor and the Suai area. The Fataluku people are famous for their high-peaked houses in the area around Lospalos. More groups are scattered amongst the interior mountains.

East Timor is a young country with a booming birth rate. Life expectancy for East Timorese males is about 64 years (compared to Australia's 78); it's somewhat more for females.

RELIGION

It's estimated that about 90% of East Timor's population is Catholic (underpinned by animist beliefs); as in Poland, the church was the rallying point of dissent during the years of occupation. The remainder of the population is Protestant, Muslim and Buddhist.

Indigenous religions revolve around an earth mother, from whom all humans are born and shall return after death, and her male counterpart, the god of the sky or sun. These are accompanied by a complex web of spirits from ancestors and nature. The *matan d'ok* (medicine man) is the village mediator with the spirits; he can divine the future and cure illness. Many people believe in various forms of black magic and it's not uncommon for people to wish evil spells upon their rivals.

ARTS

Despite 24 years of imposed Indonesian culture, East Timor has its own music and dance, architecture and textiles.

Music & Dance

Almost all Timorese celebrations involve singing and dancing. Known as *tebe* or *tebedai*, Timorese traditional music has changed little since pre-occupation times; it is performed on ceremonial occasions. The second generation of music is *koremetan*, which is strongly influenced by country-and-western music and Portuguese folk music; guitars are the instrument of choice. You may also hear contemporary East Timorese rock, which has many similarities to cover bands of the Philippines.

Architecture

The traditional houses of East Timor vary from the large conical thatched Bunak houses known as *deuhoto*, still widely used in the west, to the unique Fataluku houses in the east. The tall, elongated Fataluku houses have stilts supporting a main living room and are topped by a high, tapering thatch roof. Although uncommon, you can still see a few of these national icons on the road to Tutuala.

Textiles

Women use simple back-strap looms to weave East Timor's magnificent fabrics, known as *tais*. The relatively small looms result in pieces of limited size, which are commonly used as shawls, baby slings or scarfs, or stitched together as clothing. Various regions have their own distinct styles, designs and dye colours. *Tais* make excellent souvenirs (see p140).

ENVIRONMENT

The Land

Covering an area of 15,007 sq km, East Timor consists of the eastern half of the island of Timor, as well as Atauro and Jaco Islands, and the enclave of Oecussi on the north coast, 70km to the west and surrounded by Indonesian West Timor.

Once part of the Australian continental shelf, Timor fully emerged from the ocean only some four million years ago, and is therefore composed mainly of marine sediment, principally limestone. Rugged mountains, a product of the collision with the Banda Trench to the north, run the length of the country, the highest of which is Mt Ramelau (2963m).

Wildlife

East Timor is squarely in the area known as Wallacea, a kind of crossover zone between Asian and Australian plants and animals, and one of the most biologically distinctive areas on earth.

East Timor's coral reefs are home to a highly diverse range of marine life. Marine mammals include dolphins, whales and dugongs (a captivating manatee relative), while manta rays and whale sharks are found along the north coast.

More than 240 species of birds have been recorded in the skies over Timor. The Lautem district at the eastern end of the island is noted for its abundance and diversity of bird species, which include honeyeaters, yellow-crested cockatoos and flowerpeckers.

The number of mammals and reptiles in the wild are limited.

Environmental Issues

Human impact has had severe effects on East Timor's environment. Deforestation is a major concern, with around two-thirds of the country's forests destroyed. Slash and burn agricultural practices combined with Timor's climate continue to threaten the natural habitat. As yet, few areas are formally protected as national parks although parts of the mostly untouched and mangrove-heavy south coast are in line for preservation.

TRANSPORT

GETTING THERE & AWAY

There are no boat services to East Timor from other countries.

Air

Dili's Nicolau Lobato International Airport (code DIL) is not an impressive entry to the country. Dirty toilets, busted light bulbs and just plain dirt are its hallmarks. There are only two airline routes to the rest of the world: to Darwin in Australia's Northern Territory and Denpasar in Bali.

Air North (code TL; ☎ in Australia 1800 627 474; www.airnorth.com.au) flies twice daily between Darwin and Dili (return fares from a shocking US$500, 1½ hours).

Merpati (code MZ; ☎ 332 1880; www.merpati.co.id) flies almost daily between Denpasar (Bali) and Dili (return fares from an almost shocking US$300, two hours).

Generally, most people will fly via Bali, not only because it makes a delightful stopover but also because airfares to Bali from much of the world are more competitive than those to Darwin.

Land

See p141 for information on leaving East Timor by land.

GETTING AROUND

Bicycle

New bikes can be purchased in Dili for around US$200. Road conditions away from the north coast can be brutal, which may appeal to mountain bikers.

Boat

Ferry transport is available between Dili and Atauro Island (p142), and Dili and the Oecussi enclave (p146) on the new German-built ferry *Nakroma*. It features three classes of service: economy, business and VIP. The seats in all the classes are the same, but those in VIP are in a small and unpleasant room. In practice business class tickets are for foreigners and economy tickets are for locals, but people freely mix across the ship. Secure space on the small top deck to avoid the many passengers who find eruptive discomfort in even the calmest of seas.

DEPARTURE TAX

There's a departure tax of US$10 when leaving Dili's airport.

Bus

Cramped *mikrolet* (small minibuses) operate at least daily between most towns, and generally depart early in the morning. Outlying villages are serviced less frequently by *angguna* (tray trucks where passengers, including the odd buffalo or goat, all pile into the back). Ask locally for departure points. Large but still crowded buses run frequently on important routes such as Dili–Baucau.

Car & Motorcycle

Driving in East Timor is optimistically termed an adventure. Except for streets in Dili and the main road running along the north coast, most roads are deeply potholed and rutted. You'll be lucky to average 30km/h, and even then you'll need to be on the lookout for children, goats, dogs etc. Bridges and entire segments of road flood or wash away during the rainy season. Check conditions with the **UN** (☎ 331 2210 ext 5454, 723 0635).

Conventional cars can handle Dili and the road along the north coast east to Com and west to Batugade, as well as the road inland to Maubisse. Otherwise you will need a 4WD; bring along extra supplies, especially water, in case you get stranded.

Rentlo (☎ 723 5089; www.rentlocarhire.com; Avenida dos Martires de Patria, Comoro, Dili) is the main source of rental vehicles; it's 3km from the airport on the main road. A compact car costs from US$40 per day, a small 4WD from US$70. Rentals include 100km free per day. Limited liability coverage is available from $15 per day (with a whopping US$6000 deductible); it's probably useful given the toll the roads take on cars.

Motorcycles are quite handy in East Timor, breezing over bumps at a respectable pace. **East Timor Backpackers** (☎ 723 8121; Avenida Almirante Americo Tomas, Dili) charges US$15 to US$25 per day.

Alternatively you could make arrangements with a driver so that you can enjoy the scenery while he tackles the potholes (and uses his local knowledge). Ask around and expect to negotiate; prices start from US$40 per day.

The myriad of hazards make driving at night foolish.

Petrol (gasoline) in Portuguese is *besin,* diesel fuel is *solar;* expect to pay around US$1 per litre.

Hitching

It's not uncommon for locals walking 5km or so into town to ask for a ride. A traveller doing the same would be expected to pay a small sum – usually the price of a *mikrolet* ride. However, hitchhiking is never entirely safe, so it's not recommended.

DILI

pop 130,000

Scruffy and chaotic, Dili is not one of Asia's great capitals. But look past the burnt-out buildings and refugee camps and you'll find a place with a quiet charm. Dignified colonial buildings await restoration, and frangipani trees drop flowers on streets trodden as often by goats and chickens as by people. The waterfront is serene and a short walk brings you to golden beaches with good snorkelling. You may not wish to linger, but Dili is where you'll find all of East Timor's services, as well as the supplies you need to explore the country. Its delightful nightspots are good places to discover the welcoming local vibe.

ORIENTATION

Dili sprawls along the waterfront from the airport to the Jesus statue at the eastern end of the bay. The central area is reasonably compact, stretching back a few parallel blocks from the waterfront.

> **GETTING INTO TOWN**
>
> The standard taxi fare from Nicolau Lobato International Airport, 6km west of town, is US$5 – steep given that fares around town are US$1 or US$2. Alternatively, you could walk the few hundred metres past the refugee camp out to the main road and hail a *mikrolet* (small minibus) for around US$0.25.

Accommodation and restaurant options are spread across town; there's no travellers' hub as such.

INFORMATION

As yet there's no tourist office. Check out the internet resources listed on p148 for tourist information.

Emergency

Ambulance (☎ 723 3212)
Fire (☎ 723 0686)
Police (☎ 112, 723 0686)
UN Police (☎ 723 0365)

Internet Access

Global Net (Rua Jacinto de Candido; per hr US$6; 8am-9pm) Download photos and burn CDs here.

Internet Cafe (cnr Rua Presidente Nicolau Lobato & Rua Belarmino Lobo; per hr US$6; 8.30am-8.30pm) Across from ANZ Bank; the orchid collection is more interesting than the name.

Medical Services

Medical services in East Timor are limited; serious cases may require evacuation to Darwin. Your embassy may have information on a number of options available among the local NGOs and UN.

Australian embassy (☎ 332 2111; www.easttimor.embassy.gov.au; Avenida dos Mártires da Pátria) You can make an appointment with a physician here.

Dili Nacional Hospital (☎ 331 1008; Rua Cicade Viana do Castelo) A cadre of Western volunteers assists locals at this busy place just east of Estrada de Bidau.

Foho Osan Mean Farmacia (☎ 725 6978; Rua Quinze de Outubro; 8am-9pm Mon-Sat, 8am-1pm Sun) Offers simple consultations and a full range of pharmaceuticals.

Money

Banks are generally open between 9am and 3.30pm Monday to Friday.

ANZ (☎ 332 4800; www.anz.com/timorleste; cnr Rua Presidente Nicolau Lobato & Rua Belarmino Lobo) The ATM dispenses US dollars but often runs dry on weekends.

Western Union (☎ 332 1586; Rua José Maria Marques) Transfers funds internationally.

Post & Telephone

The following places share a building east of the Palacio de Govierno.

Post office (Rua Presidente Nicolau Lobato; 8am-5pm Mon-Fri)

Timor Telecom (☎ 332 2245; www.timortelecom.tp; Rua Presidente Nicolau Lobato; 8am-6pm Mon-Sat)

EAST TIMOR

You can make international and local calls, access the internet and purchase SIM cards here.

DANGERS & ANNOYANCES

Dili is no Potemkin village, as the many burnt-out buildings and refugee camps attest. But the reality is actually not as bad as first impressions suggest. See p147 for general information on safety. Take care at night, avoid demonstrations and steer clear of areas south of the airport road, which are known for rock throwing.

SIGHTS

Waterfront

Dili's lively waterfront is lined with tangible references to East Timor's present and past. Groups of men pass hours playing cards or talking politics beneath the banyan trees. Faded Portuguese-style buildings – once the preserve of colonial officials – line the pockmarked esplanade, interspersed with businesses, burnt-out buildings and refugee camps.

The **Palacio de Govierno** (Government Palace) dominates the centre of town. East of here are **fruit and fish markets** with prices that weaken as the smells strengthen. Opposite the wharf, the Indonesian-installed **Integration Monument** represents an angst-ridden Timorese breaking the chains of colonialism. Further west, the seaside **Motael Church** is one of East Timor's oldest institutions. The **Farol lighthouse** beams just beyond.

Cape Fatucama & the Jesus Statue

The coast road crosses a small river at the east end of town before ending where the 27m-tall **Jesus statue** beckons from the tip of Cape Fatucama (about 7km). The series of serene **beaches** here seems a world away from the chaos of Dili just across the water.

From the top of the statue, the turquoise bays backed by green-covered mountains are stunning. As you climb the well-marked path up to Jesus, look for a little path after the last of 14 grottos. It leads down to an often deserted beach, known as **Jesus Backside beach**, where there's decent snorkelling.

There's a sprinkling of popular beachfront bars and restaurants on the cape.

A taxi to the statue from town should cost US$2.

Xanana Reading Room

Part museum, part library, part cultural centre, the **Xanana Reading Room** (☎ 332 2831; Rua Belarmino Lobo; admission free; 🕑 9am-5pm Mon-Fri, 9am-3pm Sat) is a must visit. The foyer displays photos and information dedicated to President Xanana Gusmão, while various fan-cooled rooms hold a decent selection of titles. Make time to watch a video about East Timor from the reading room's comprehensive collection. There's a small selection of books – the best in Dili – to trade (US$1) or buy.

Resistance Museum

The 24-year struggle against the Indonesians is commemorated in the impressive new **Resistance Museum** (Rua Formosa; admission US$1; 🕑 9.30am-5.30pm Tue-Sat, 1.30-5.30pm Sun) There's a good timeline in English, plus photos and exhibits of the gear used by Falintil while they hid in the hills (satellite phones are the tools of the modern revolution). The catalogue (US$10) is impressive.

Arte Moris

Set in the vast remains of an Indonesian-era museum, **Arte Moris** (☎ 723 3507; Rua dos Martires da Patria, Comoro; admission free; 🕑 9am-6pm Mon-Sat) encompasses everything weird and wonderful about Dili. Art students live here while they train in a variety of media; some of the best results grace a funky sculpture garden or are on display in a gallery. Although at times whimsical, many of the works address the ongoing tragedy of life in East Timor. Many local artists are in residence, including Bibi Bulak, an inventive acting troupe that performs on stage and screen.

Travelling west from town, the compound is over the Comoro bridge, just before the airport.

Santa Cruz Cemetery

On 12 November 1991, Indonesian soldiers fired on a peaceful memorial procession at the Santa Cruz Cemetery. More than 200 civilians died, many of them after they were rounded up and trucked away by the military.

TRAVEL COURTESY

Smile and say *Bele?* (OK?) before taking someone's photo. You'll usually be rewarded with a *Bele!* and a smile.

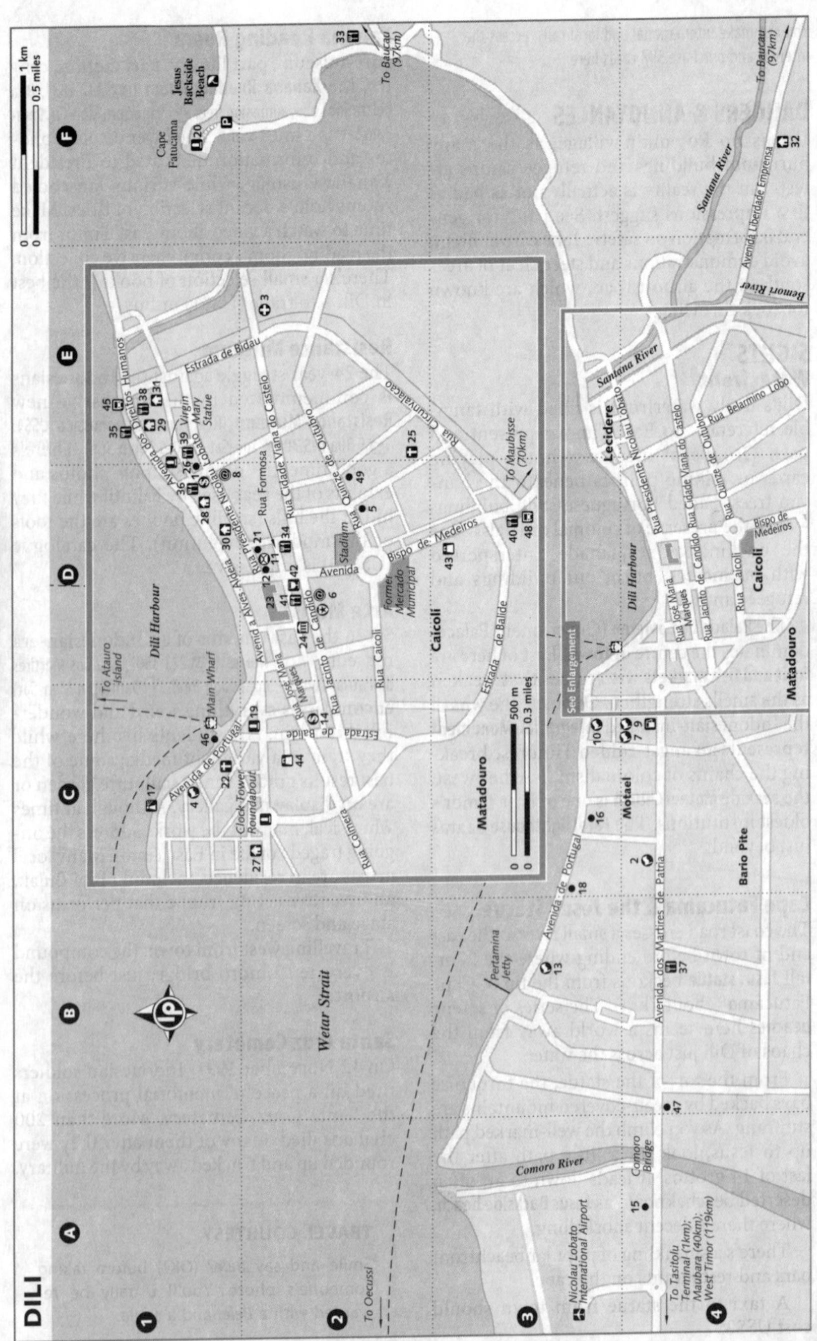
DILI
Wetar Strait
Dili Harbour
To Oecussi
To Atauro Island
Main Wharf
Cape Fatucama
Jesus Backside Beach
To Baucau (97km)
Avenida de Portugal
Avenida dos Direitos Humanos
Avenida a Alves Aldeia
Rua Presidente Nicolau Lobato
Rua Formosa
Rua Cidade Viana do Castelo
Rua Quinze de Outubro
Rua José Maria Marques
Rua Jacinto de Candido
Rua Caicoli
Estrada de Balide
Estrada de Bidau
Rua Circunvalacao
Avenida Bispo de Medeiros
Rua Colmeira
Clock Tower Roundabout
Virgin Mary Statue
Stadium
Former Mercado Municipal
Caicoli
Matadouro
To Maubisse (70km)
See Enlargement
Pertamina Jetty
Motael
Bario Pite
Lecidere
Santana River
Bemori River
Avenida Liberdade Empresa
Rua Belarmino Lobo
Avenida dos Martires de Patria
Comoro River
Comoro Bridge
Nicolau Lobato International Airport
To Tasitolu Terminal (1km); Maubara (40km); West Timor (119km)
0 1 km
0 0.5 miles
0 500 m
0 0.3 miles

One of the people killed was Kamal Bamadhaj, a New Zealand citizen and the subject of the film *Punitive Damage*; two of the many people the soldiers beat up turned out to be American journalists. The bloody attack was filmed by British journalist Max Stahl, whose footage features in the documentary *In Cold Blood*. The massacre at the Santa Cruz Cemetery is cited as a turning point in the independence struggle. The Xanana Reading Room has films about the event available for viewing.

ACTIVITIES

The reef fringing the entire north coast of East Timor provides spectacular **diving** and **snorkelling** opportunities. Many sites, including the legendary K41 east of town, are easily accessed by walking in from the beach, with dramatic drop-offs just 10m offshore in parts. The two main dive operators are located in Dili and arrange trips throughout the country and Atauro. Both offer trips for snorkellers.

Free Flow (☎ 723 4614; www.freeflowdiving.com; Avenida de Portugal) offers guided shore dives for US$40 per dive, including transport. Many trips include delicious lunches. There's also a full range of PADI courses from US$300.

Dive Timor Lorosae (☎ 723 7092; www.divetimor.com; Avenida de Portugal) offers day-trip diving around Atauro, including two dives from US$125 per person (minimum four people). Shore dives around Dili (including two dives) cost from US$75. PADI courses cost from US$300.

SLEEPING

Beds in Dili are no bargain: the influx of UN and NGO types has jacked up rates. Should things settle down, the rates listed below may decrease by 25% or more.

East Timor Backpackers (☎ 723 8121; Avenida Almirante Americo Tomas; dm US$10;) Dili's one hostel has 11 beds in three small rooms. Out the back there's a delightful café-bar called the Smokehouse, which is often a real travellers' scene. Up front there's a cheap-and-cheerful Indian restaurant.

Vila Harmonia (☎ 723 8265; vilaharmonia@hotmail.com; Avenida Liberdade Emprensa 418, Becora; r per person US$10) About 3km from town, this reliable old-timer has been here for over a decade. The 10 basic rooms, with bathrooms attached, form an 'L' around the garden. You're free to use the kitchen.

Rocella (☎ 723 7993; Rua Presidente Nicolau Lobato 18; r US$20-25;) There's a bit of a Kuta-guesthouse feel at this eight-room compound. Satellite TV and sprightly décor add life to the diminutive rooms.

Venture Hotel (☎ 331 3276; venture_hotel@hotmail.com; Rua Filomena de Camera, Lecidere; r US$23-33;) Lots of plants, a vibrant bar and an alluring pool help overcome architecture that's familiar to anyone who's worked in a remote mining camp. The Spartan rooms don't have TVs, and the cheapest share bathrooms (but you can clean up at the occasional foam parties).

Hotel Turismo (☎ 331 0555; hotelturismo_04@yahoo.com; Avenida dos Direitos Humanos, Lecidere; r US$25-65;) Step back in time at this genteel veteran of

EAST TIMOR

INFORMATION
- ANZ 1 D1
- Australian Embassy 2 C4
- Dili Nacional Hospital 3 E2
- European Commission 4 C1
- Foho Osan Mean Farmacia 5 D2
- Global Net 6 D2
- Indonesian Embassy 7 C4
- Internet Cafe 8 D1
- Ireland Embassy 9 C4
- New Zealand Embassy 10 C3
- Post Office 11 D2
- Timor Telecom 12 D2
- US Embassy 13 B3
- Western Union 14 C2

SIGHTS & ACTIVITIES
- Arte Moris 15 A4
- Dive Timor Lorosae 16 C3
- Eco Discovery (see 37)
- Farol Lighthouse 17 C1
- Free Flow 18 C3
- Fruit & Fish Market (see 35)
- Harmonia Eco Tours (see 21)
- Integration Monument 19 C2
- Jesus Statue 20 F1
- MegaTours 21 D2
- Motael Church 22 C1
- Palacio de Govierno 23 D2
- Resistence Museum 24 D2
- Santa Cruz Cemetery 25 E2
- Xanana Reading Room 26 D1

SLEEPING
- East Timor Backpackers 27 C2
- Hotel Dili 28 D1
- Hotel Turismo 29 E1
- Rocella 30 D1
- Venture Hotel 31 E1
- Vila Harmonia 32 F4

EATING
- Castaway Bar (see 16)
- Caz Bar 33 F2
- Depot Mie Bakso 34 D2
- Fruit & Fish Market 35 E1
- Kebab Club 36 D1
- Landmark 37 B4
- Lita 38 E1
- One More Bar 39 E1
- Taibessi Market 40 D3
- Terrace Cafe 41 D2

DRINKING
- AAJ Bar 42 D2

SHOPPING
- Alola Foundation 43 D3
- Tais Mercado 44 C2

TRANSPORT
- Bidau Terminal 45 E1
- East Timor Backpackers (see 27)
- Nakroma Ferry Office 46 C1
- Rentlo 47 B4
- Taibessi Terminal 48 D3
- Timor Tour & Travel 49 D2

the 1970s. The rooms are a bit faded, but you won't notice on the balconies of the best ones, from where you can enjoy views of Atauro Island, the sound of the surf and the smells of the fish vendors.

Hotel Dili (☎ 331 3958; reservation@hoteldili.com; Avenida dos Direitos Humanos; r US$25-100;) A rambling place with disparate buildings served by great staff, this is the best choice for business travellers to Dili. The cheapest rooms share bathrooms; all rooms have high-speed (by local standards) internet and satellite TV.

EATING & DRINKING

There are numerous pleasant restaurant-bars aimed at foreigners all along the waterfront, especially east towards the Jesus statue. You'll find cheap and cheerful storefront joints wherever there are shops.

Depot Mie Bakso (Rua Formosa; meals from US$1.25) Popularity translates into quick turnover and very fresh food at this open-air pavilion. Fried chicken, beef *rendang* (spicy coconut curry) and silky potato cakes are usually among the offerings.

Kebab Club (☎ 726 3642; Rua Belarmino Lobo; mains US$3-6) Darn authentic Turkish fare, including velvety hummus, is on offer at this restaurant where the charm of the owners manages to outshine the tasty fare.

Terrace Cafe (☎ 725 9100; Rua Formosa; meals from US$4) Join students and government workers on the breezy terrace of this popular place. Food is served up Padang-style: choose your fare from the fresh offerings behind the counter. The avocado-chocolate shake is fresh, frothy and oddly addictive.

Caz Bar (☎ 723 3961; Area Branca; dishes US$4-8) Settle back in your chair, set right on the beach, at this popular place that tops the line-up of beachside joints east from town. Breakfast and sunset are popular times here. Watch for full-moon parties.

One More Bar (Rua Governador Filomena da Camara, Lecidere; mains US$4-9) One More Bar has a fine second-storey position on the waterfront, behind the Virgin Mary statue. Fresh seafood is the highlight of a menu of pizza, burgers and Asian stir-fries. There's darts and a pool table, as well as live music some nights.

Castaway Bar (☎ 723 5449; Avenida de Portugal; mains US$4-12) A very popular second-storey joint overlooking the western waterfront, Castaway Bar packs in crowds enjoying typical pizza-sandwich-Asian fare while taking in the cool breezes and plotting ways to foil the diabolical pool table.

AAJ Bar (☎ 732 4066; Avenida Bispo de Medeiros; noon-4am) A legendary second-floor dive where locals and expats alike cram the close quarters for hot music, bad karaoke and conflict over rugby.

Dili's many markets include a large market at Taibessi, just south of the centre, and a smaller fruit and fish market on the waterfront near the Hotel Tourismo. Look for tropical fruits, sweet potatoes and betel nuts. Vendors selling cold bottled water and beer (wipe the tops) can be found everywhere. There are also several supermarkets that sell everything from Tim Tams to bug repellent to fishing tackle; these include **Lita** (Avenida dos Direitos Humanos, Lecidere), whose goods include the little plastic couple for the top of your wedding cake. **Landmark** (☎ 723 1313; Avenida dos Martires de Patria, Comoro) is a large complex of shops on the airport road.

SHOPPING

Tais Mercado (Rua Sebastiao da Costa) A *tais* is a piece of East Timorese woven cloth (see p134), and each region possesses its own distinct style; this market has *tais* that are from all over the country. Quality varies greatly.

Alola Foundation (www.alolafoundation.org; Avenida Bispo de Medeiros) The shop of the revered local charity has *tais* and other crafts from around the country. Quality is high and prices are low.

GETTING THERE & AWAY

Air

See p135 for details of getting in and out of Dili by air.

Boat

The **Nakroma ferry office** (☎ 728 09638; Avenida de Portugal; 9am-5pm) is in the large building at the port. Buy your tickets in advance. Ferries for Oecussi (economy/business class US$4/14, 12 hours) leave at around 5pm Monday and Thursday. The Atauro service (business class $5, two hours) runs Saturdays. See p135 for more details.

Bus

Dili's bus terminals (really little more than shabby shelters) are served by taxis and *mikrolet*. Buses run most often in the morning.

GETTING TO INDONESIA

The four-hour bus ride from Dili to the border town of Batugade costs US$5. You have to walk 200m across the border to Motoain in West Timor, from where a *mikrolet* (small minibus) costs less than US$2 to Atambua. Buses from Atambua to Kupang cost about US$5 and take eight hours. Buses from Dili stop running by mid-afternoon, so don't get caught at the border as there's no place to stay. You'll need an Indonesian visa before crossing the border into West Timor (see p150).

Much easier is the through bus service between Dili and Kupang offered by **Timor Tour & Travel** (Dili ☎ 333 1014; Rua Quinze de Outubro 17; Kupang ☎ 0380-881 543; Jl Timor Raya 8). There's a daily service, which costs US$18 and takes 12 hours in an air-conditioned minibus; book in advance.

See p297 for information on crossing the border from the opposite direction.

Tasitolu Terminal, west of the airport, is the hub for destinations to the west of the country. Travelling to the east (Baucau, Lospalos, Viqueque etc), buses go from the simple Bidau Terminal, on the waterfront near the Hotel Turismo. The Taibessi Terminal, at the huge Taibessi market, is the stop for transport to Maubisse and beyond.

GETTING AROUND

Bus

Mikrolet, buzz about on designated routes during daylight hours (US$0.25). They stop frequently over relatively short distances, often making a taxi a more efficient option.

Car

See p135 for car-hire options. However, Dili's compact and you'll be able to reach most places on foot or by taxi.

Taxi

There are loads of clapped-out unmetered taxis beeping their way around Dili. Almost anywhere around town costs a standard US$1, rising to US$2 for a longer journey. A major problem is that taxis here stopped operating at night after the 2006 riots; until this changes, going out at night means setting up rides or sticking close to your lodgings.

ATAURO ISLAND

Its lush mountain interior hemmed by uninterrupted beach and coral reef, the alluring island getaway of Atauro is visible from Dili but seems a world away. This is pure escapism: you're free to do a lot or a little, with excellent walking trails and snorkelling opportunities (off the pier at Beloi and in front of Tua Koin), and seemingly endless beaches to prop on and watch passing outriggers.

Atauro's isolation made it a natural prison, and it's been used by both the Portuguese and Indonesian governments as a place of exile.

The community today comprises around 8000 people, mostly subsistence fishers and farmers, living in a few villages spread across the island. The main centres are along the east coast: Makili (a carving centre), Vila (with leafy lanes and a few colonial vestiges) and Beloi (where the public ferry docks), with Macadade in the mountains.

The Dili dive shops (p139) arrange underwater tours; you can arrange for snorkelling trips with local fishing boats from US$15. Ask the locals about the many hiking possibilities.

SLEEPING

Atauro has two sleeping options that almost perfectly fit the clichés of the remote beach escape. At either place you must book in advance as food on the island is so limited that arrangements will have to be made so you can eat (meals cost from US$4). Polite expats from Dili ask what they can bring from the supermarkets before heading over.

Tua Kóin Eco-Village (☎ 723 6085; www.atauroisland.com; r per person Sun-Thu US$13, Fri & Sat US$15) Eight simple thatched-roof cabins are located in this shady compound on the beach north of Vila. Operated by Atauro's NGO Roman Luan, the ecovillage runs on solar power, recycles grey water and has a great beachfront setting. The website is a fantastic source of local info.

Nemas (☎ 723 6084; r per person US$15) Just north of the ferry dock in Beloi, Nemas is run by an Australian named Barry. There are four sun-drenched thatched cabins right on the beach; the one Barry calls his writer's cabin has mesmerizing views from an upper level.

GETTING THERE & AROUND

The island of Atauro is 30km directly north of Dili. The **Nakroma ferry** (☎ 728 09638; Avenida de Portugal, Dili) departs from Dili every Saturday at 9am and returns at 4pm, taking two hours each way. Fares in 'business class (meaning those charged to foreigners) are US$5 each way.

A fishing boat also makes the run from Vila to Dili (US$10, three hours) several days a week depending on tides. Check details with Tua Kóin Eco-Village or Nemas.

Only Vila and Beloi are linked by road, which is served by constantly shuttling trucks. Flag any down; the cost is about US$2. If arriving by ferry, scramble aboard the first one you see before it fills up with chickens, kids and bags of rice.

If you are doing a day trip on the *Nakroma*, you'll have time to ride between the two villages, do a little exploring, including the seaside market at Beloi, and possibly have a prearranged lunch at Tua Kóin or Nemas.

EAST OF DILI

Finding beaches around every bend is one of the treats in store as you head along the north coast east of Dili. Some of the best diving in the country is found right off the shore along here.

A long bridge spans the Laclo River at **Manatuto**, 64km east of Dili, which has its own Jesus statue overlooking town. The road continues another 19km to **Laleia**, which has a twin-towered pastel-pink church. **Vemasse** is a further 9km and is noted for the fortress-like Portuguese construction on the hillside overlooking the town.

BAUCAU

The atmospheric Old Town streets of Baucau, East Timor's second city, zigzag downhill dominated by the ruins of the impressive **mercado municipal** (municipal market), built during the Portuguese era. The **town market** operates in the block next to the *mercado municipal*, with pyramid-shaped piles of potatoes, neat bunches of greens and mounds of maize forming a colourful patchwork on the pavement. Just below town, turn off the main road and follow the lush ravine 5km down to the beach at **Osolata**. Called Pantai Wataboo, it's a series of white sand coves fringed by palms and hemmed by turquoise water.

The characterless Kota Baru (New Town) sprang up during the Indonesian era and overlooks the Old Town. On the road linking the two, **Timor Telecom** (☎ 413 0017; 9am-5pm) has slow internet access (US$2 per hour) and offers currency exchange services.

Sleeping & Eating

Hotel Loro-Sae (Old Town; r with shared mandi per person US$10) This unlovely five-room place has basic accommodation with shared *mandi* (large concrete basin from which you scoop water to rinse your body and flush the squat toilet). It's located above street level, upstairs from a very nice café.

Baucau Beach Bungalows (☎ 731 9127; Osolata; r per person US$15) Choose between rooms in old houses and thatched bungalows at this little slice of paradise down by the beach. Meals can be arranged for US$6 and are sourced from the fishing boats across the road.

Pousada de Baucau (☎ 724 1111; Rua de Catedral, Old Town; r from US$55) One of East Timor's nicest hotels, this vision in pink overlooking the Old Town combines old colonial buildings with a newer wing of 10 rooms. The restaurant has good Portuguese food (meals from US$5) and the service is delightful.

Restaurante Amalia (☎ 726 3610; Old Town; dishes US$4-6) This charmer with a wide terrace is in an old Portuguese officers' quarters near the market. Garlic is a featured ingredient in many of the spicy dishes, and there's wine by the glass.

Getting There & Away

Numerous buses per day drive the 123km between Dili and Baucau (US$2, three hours). Buses also run to Viqueque (US$2, two hours) and Lospalos (US$3, 3½ hours). Ask to be dropped off in the Old Town.

SOUTH OF BAUCAU

From Baucau you can head over rugged roads deep into the lush hills where Fretilin members hid during the Indonesian occupation. The area remains a stronghold for the party.

Some 28km south, the charming hill village of **Venilale** is nestled between Mt Matebian (2315m) in the east and Mt Mundo Perdido (Lost World; 1775m) in the west. Another

EAST TIMOR

16km brings you to the misty village of **Ossu**. Some 9km south of here look for a sign on the left for the **Timor Village Hotel** (☎ 728 5611; r per person US$20), a spotless seven-room place set on a lush hillside near a surging river and waterfall. You can arrange hiking guides here.

Viqueque, 63km from Baucau, is the centre for the identically named surrounding district, which is lined with sinuous rice terraces. The market is the centre of town. On the road leading in you'll see a series of guesthouses, including **Motel Borala** (☎ 726 7866; r per person US$9), which has seven rooms with private bathrooms, as well as electricity for a few hours at night. Shops and cafés are nearby.

Buses and *mikrolet* make runs daily between Viqueque and Baucau (US$2, two hours) and on to Dili.

If you have the nerve to tackle the roads, you can continue to the coast, where the stunning beach at **Beaçu** is slowly swallowing the Portuguese-built customs building. From here it's possible to continue east along the coast road in the dry season; plan on six or more hours to Lospalos.

EAST OF BAUCAU

About 20km east of Baucau is the coastal village of **Laga**, surrounded by virescent rice paddies. From here a road wends south through the mountains to the hill town of **Baguia**, set in the shadow of **Mt Matebian** (2315m). Topped with a statue of Christ and known as 'Mountain of the Souls', this holy place attracts thousands of pilgrims annually for All Souls Day (2 November) to honour deceased friends and family. Ask at the church in Baguia for trekking info.

At least three *mikrolet* per day run between Baucau and Baguia (US$2, 2½ hours) via Laga.

Com

You hit the end of the road when you reach the austere fishing village of Com, 80km from Baucau via Lautem. If any place in East Timor is likely to develop as a travellers' scene, it's here. There's excellent snorkelling and a good, long beach (although it's beaten by the one at the 171km marker to the west).

Several bare-bones guesthouses have emerged near the shore and your arrival will set off a frenzy of pitches. Look at a few before deciding; expect to pay about US$10 per person.

A few levels up in quality, the shell-studded **Com Beach Resort** (☎ 728 3311; r US$20-80; ❄) has basic rooms that share a bathroom block, as well as pricier ones with bathrooms (value goes down as you pay more); book ahead. Snorkelling gear is available. The resort's Ocean View Restaurant (dishes US$4 to US$10) has a menu that includes a whole roast pig for US$100 – only eight hours' notice is needed for the unlucky victim to be selected and cooked.

Tutuala & Jaco Island

Views of the shimmering waters of Lake Ira Lalaroe and the occasional stilted Fataluku house are just some of the highlights of the rugged 50km-long road from Lautem to Tutuala. The road ends on a bluff in Tutuala village, where there's sweeping views out to sea and an old Portuguese *pousada* (traditional Portuguese lodging) where you might be able to rent a vintage room for US$5 per person.

And the fun has only begun, for a steep 8km track runs down to **Pantai Walu**, a stunning white-sand beach. Just offshore is Jaco Island, the ultimate beach experience; it's mostly a ring of alluring sand that seems to have been constantly sifted and bleached. The island is also a place with sacred meaning to the Timorese. You can't spend the night there, but you can usually catch a ride over with a fisherman for US$5. The trip takes all of two minutes.

Back on Pantai Walu, the fishing folk often serve up grilled fish with garlic (US$5) and you might be able to get a bed in a thatched hut for about the same. Then again you might not, and since food is not guaranteed here or up in Tutuala you'd best bring your own provisions and camping gear.

You can get a daily *mikrolet* to/from Lospalos (US$1, three hours), or you can charter one from Com for about US$15.

Lospalos

Lospalos, home to the Fataluku language group of people, is a workaday town about 28km south of Lautem. It's mostly of interest for its market and smattering of shops. The six rooms at **27@** (r with shared bathroom per person US$8) are spotless; it's set in a shady compound near the old market. Good meals (from US$3) are available. The name derives from the day in August 1999 when the owner's husband was among scores of locals murdered by the retreating Indonesians.

Buses and *mikrolet* run at several times daily between Lospalos and Baucau (US$3, 3½ hours). Ask to be dropped off near the centre or old market, not in the new market far out of town.

WEST OF DILI

The western part of East Timor is quiet and often arid. Long black-sand beaches, rarely trodden, line the smooth main road that follows the jagged coast to the border town of Batugade. Inland a circuitous road in much worse shape than the one on the coast tracks though coffee plantations and desertlike stretches via Ermera.

There are numerous places all the way to the border to don a mask and wade out to reefs that are a kaleidoscope of colours and teeming with marine life.

Liquiçá, 35km west of Dili, warrants a wander for its fine Portuguese architecture and bustling market. You'll recognise **Maubara**, 40km from Dili, by the fort walls and cannons pointing out to sea. The sandy ocean floor slopes away here to a coral bed that attracts its fair share of colourful fish. Some 3km west, look for a sign marked Maubara-Fatubessi and follow a steep track up to a **retreat** (r per person US$17) run by Carmelite nuns. The 20 immaculate rooms enjoy sweeping views, and food is available for an extra charge (meals from US$3).

A steady stream of *mikrolet* depart Dili daily stopping at both villages. A very few go as far as the skimpy border town of **Batugade** (111km from Dili); see p141 for further details. Some *mikrolet* turn inland, travelling 14km to the misty mountain town of **Balibo**. In the main square is Australia Flag House, a restored community centre with a memorial commemorating five Australian-based journalists murdered by invading Indonesian soldiers in 1975.

Twenty-six kilometres further inland on the edge of a fertile flood plain, **Maliana** has some simple guesthouses. Another 25km east a rough track leads 1km off the main road to the mist-covered old colonial centre of **Bobonaro**, which awaits rediscovery by travellers. Near here a 'road' that sullies the very concept runs 40km down to **Zumalai**. Although rugged in the extreme – plan on three hours or more – it passes through verdant landscape and ancient villages of thatched huts that have changed little in eons. If you stop you'll be surrounded by shrieking children; everyone you pass waves, including the goats.

SOUTH OF DILI

The thatched roofs of round houses fleck the sides of soaring mountains south of Dili, while coffee beans fleck the trees lining the road. After climbing 28km out of Dili you'll be treated to cool views of the north coast and Atauro Island beyond. Nestled in a crest is the cloud-caressing mountain town of Maubisse, while the countryside peaks further south, reaching its highest point at Mt Ramelau (2963m), a popular spot for climbs. Those with time should continue to the black sands along the south coast.

MAUBISSE

Dew-soaked Maubisse, 70km south of Dili and 1400m up, is a classic mountain town that will have you regretting those shorts. Get a bed at the classic **Pousada de Maubisse** (☎ 724 9567; r per person Mon-Thu US$17, Fri & Sat US$51, Sun US$20) which overlooks the region from a knoll. Its fading grace and gorgeous grounds make for great value weekdays; the restaurant offers Portuguese-inspired dishes (US$8 to US$10). You could also stay with the faithful at Maubisse's elaborate **church** (r incl all meals per person US$15). Simple stalls sell food across from the market.

Buses depart from Dili for Maubisse (US$2, three hours) each morning.

HATUBUILICO & MT RAMELAU

Wild roses grow by the road and mountain streams trickle through the precious teeny town of Hatubuilico, located at the base of Mt Ramelau. Stay at the five-room **Pousada Alecrim Namrau** (☎ 724 9567; Rua Gruta Ramelau Hun 1; r per person US$10) where meals can be arranged for US$2. The uniquely decorated guesthouse is run by the village chief, who can arrange a guide (US$5) to get you up the mountain – and up at 3am in time to reach the peak for sunrise.

Hiking from the village to the Virgin Mary statue at the top of Mt Ramelau takes around three hours; with a 4WD you can drive 2.5km to a meadow from where it's two hours to

EAST TIMOR

the top. The trail leads steadily up, with an open-air 'church' on a plateau at the 2700m mark. From the peak, mountaintops ripple out to the coast, which is visible to both the south and the north. Sunrise will give you chills, both down your spine and up your arms (temperatures average 5°C).

From Maubisse, the Hatubuilico turn-off is at the 81km post; you'll reach the village after 18km. From Maubisse, *angguna* travel to Hatubuilico on market days: Wednesday and Saturday. The price depends on the number of passengers, but the trip should cost around US$2 and take three hours.

SAME & BETANO

Same (Sar-may), 43km south of Maubisse, is at the centre of the region's hard-working coffee plantations. The rugged road here clings to hillsides dotted with banana and orange trees, and cleaved by waterfalls. Same is a sizable town, with a bustling daily market. It's a good base for exploring the remote south coast.

The niftiest place in the south, **Hotel & Restaurant Same** (Rua Na Raran; s/d US$25/35) has 12 clean rooms with big beds and private toilets. The little compound has a decent restaurant (meals US$4) and a small grocery.

The road continues down to the black-sand beach at Betano on the coast. From here you can journey over narrow tracks east in dry season through crocodile-infested mangroves to Viqueque (six or more hours).

Mikrolet run frequently between Maubisse and Same (US$1, one hour), and between Same and Betano (US$1, one hour).

SUAI

The south coast's main town, Suai sprawls 5km inland and is a confusing collection of villages. The main one, Debos, is dominated by an enormous unfinished **cathedral**, the scene of a mass slaughter by the Indonesians in 1999. If the ghosts don't bother you, the nuns offer the usual pristine but humble **accommodation** (per person US$10). Avoid overpriced and run-down Eastern Dragon, which charges ridiculous rates to air-con-seeking NGO and UN types. Traverse the mangroves to see the moody black-sand beaches at the ocean.

Mikrolet run between Suai and Maubisse (around US$2, at least four hours), via Ainaro (with its colourful church) or Same.

OECUSSI

Welcome to Oecussi, a serene slice of East Timor that's surrounded on three sides by Indonesian West Timor and a series of jagged mountain ranges, and fronted by the sea. A cocktail of wild beauty, isolation, deliciously slow pace and incredibly warm population, Oecussi oozes serenity.

But Oecussi does have a past. When Dominican missionaries settled here in 1556, it became the first Portuguese colony in Timor before being abandoned in favour of Dili in 1769. It was annexed by Indonesia without resistance in 1976, but it didn't escape the violence following the independence referendum in '99; houses and businesses were burned, and members of local resistance groups were shot in cold blood.

Pantemakassar, aka Oecussi town, is a sweet conglomeration of thatched and rusted tin-roofed houses cradled by groves of banana and coconut palms. Its wide dirt roads are scattered with far more goats, cows and pedestrians than cars, it's backed by red-clay coastal mountains, and there are almost no street lights, allowing the black night sky to reveal endless galaxies. There's good **snorkelling** (think schools of giant trevally and resident reef sharks) along the sheer coral drop-off about 20m offshore.

The old Portuguese fort **Fatusuba** slowly decays atop the hill 1.5km south of town. **Lifau**, located 5km west of Pantemakassar, is the site of the original Portuguese settlement; there is a monument to the first landing, and the lovely beach attracts local families for Sunday picnics. The best beach begins 2km east of town on **Pantai Mahata**, which ends at a stunning red-rock headland.

Pasar Tono, 12km south of Pantemakassar, has a colourful produce **market** that attracts villagers in traditional garb to the luscious shade of giant banyan trees along the Tono River.

Lodging is bare-bones basic. The cleanest digs are at **Rao Homestay** (r US$10) a block south of the sports complex. **Lily Homestay** (Jl Integrasi; r US$10) has the best kitchen (think tasty and filling chicken, beef or fish dinners; meals US$5), and a guesthouse with shared *mandi*. Decent internet and international phone services are available at **Timor Telecom** (Rua Francisco Mousino), east of the traffic circle. Change rupiah into US dollars at Fernando's General Store, directly opposite the sports complex.

The **Nakroma ferry** (☎ 724 0388; Avenida de Portugal, Dili; ⏲ 9am-5pm) travels from Dili to Oecussi (economy/business class US$4/US$14, 12 hours) twice a week, departing the capital on Monday and Thursday nights. The return departure is around 5.30pm the following evening. In Pantemakassar the office is opposite the vaguely functional dock near the Integration Monument. See p135 for more details.

It's possible to travel overland from Indonesian West Timor to Oecussi, but crossing back requires an Indonesian visa, only available in Dili, so a night ferry is likely in your future.

EAST TIMOR DIRECTORY

ACCOMMODATION

Simple accommodation in East Timor costs between US$5 and US$10 for the night, variously charged per person or per room. The majority of places have a bed in a small room with a concrete floor; prices rise to US$30 for air-con or private bathrooms, although outside of Dili these niceties are uncommon.

A large number of the hotels Dili's hotels were built to accommodate the influx of UN and aid workers post-1999. These places are the most likely to have air-con, sit-down loos and in-room power sockets (220V, 50Hz; there's no standard socket, so bring adaptors for Indonesian, US and Australian plugs). Should the expat/UN/NGO population ever contract, hotel prices will as well. Note that few of these places rank as posh – many were assembled from old shipping containers.

Outside Dili, guesthouses are the most common form of accommodation throughout the country, providing a basic room with shared *mandi* (a large concrete basin from which you scoop water to rinse your body and flush the squat toilet). Convents attached to churches often have cheap and spotless rooms. Most places provide meals; there's almost always free coffee and bread in the morning, as well as cooked meals on request. In rural areas, running water and power may only be available from 6pm to midnight, if at all, and hot water is a rarity.

In remote areas where there is little or no commercial accommodation, locals usually open their homes to travellers; etiquette would encourage payment (around US$10).

There are no formal camping options in East Timor, though it's not unknown for travellers to pitch a tent in isolated areas, such as Tutuala beach. In Dili, **Mega Tours** (☎ 723 5199; timormegatours@netscape.net; Rua Presidente Nicolau Lobato, Dili) rents camping equipment for US$5 per person.

ACTIVITIES

Diving the incredible coast and exploring the remote interior are two major reasons to visit East Timor.

Though there are few companies offering packaged activities in East Timor, there are loads of opportunities for adventurers with time and their own equipment. The island's interior has networks of limestone caves, and untrafficked roads and tracks are crying out for hardy cyclists. You can purchase a new Chinese-made mountain bike from several places in Dili for about US$200.

Diving

Experts guess that only about 10% of East Timor's dive sites have been properly charted; there's a vast amount of incredible diving to explore. The coral reef that rims most of the island provides plenty of stellar opportunities and it's been called a 'shore-diving paradise'. Both soft and hard corals play home to a vivid variety of reef fish, and pelagic marine life cruises around spectacular drop-offs just metres offshore. Most sites are on the north coast – with a number in or near Dili – and around Atauro Island. Conditions are best during the dry season (March to September), when visibility is at around 20m to 30m. There are dive companies in Dili offering guided trips, courses and gear hire; see p139. To get some sample views, check out **Reefscenes.net** (www.reefscenes.net) and **Underwater East Timor** (www.uwet.net).

Hiking

There are fabulous hiking opportunities passing through traditional villages and traversing a variety of terrains. Many happy hikers can claim to have seen the south and north coasts of the country from its highest peak, Mt Ramelau. For hikes here or to places such as the sacred peak of Mt Matebian, you can make arrangements through the Dili-based tour companies; see p150.

For real adventure hike in the steamy interior of Atauro Island or pretty much anywhere else in the country, especially the thinly populated south coast.

BOOKS

Books are hard to come by. Bring many.

Timor-Leste Land of Discovery is a very impressive coffee-table book filled with gorgeous images of the land and people. It's widely available in Dili.

A Not-so-Distant Horror: Mass Violence in East Timor by Joseph Nevins covers the bloody recent history of East Timor and shows how the US, Australia et al allowed the Indonesian government to slaughter thousands from 1975 to 1999.

The Redundancy of Courage by Timothy Mo is a gripping novel whose fictional country's struggle against occupation is a deliberately thinly veiled account of East Timor's actual struggle. This novel was shortlisted for the Booker Prize in 1991.

A Woman of Independence by Kirsty Sword Gusmão is the autobiographical account of how this Australian teacher came to be East Timor's first lady in 2002.

BUSINESS HOURS

Few places outside Dili keep strict business hours.

Offices 8am to noon and 1pm to 5pm Monday to Friday
Restaurants 10am to 9pm
Shops 9am to 6pm Monday to Friday, 9am to noon Saturday

Exceptions are noted in individual reviews.

CLIMATE

East Timor has two seasons: wet (December to April) and dry (May to November). In the dry season the north coast sees little rain (although climate change is altering this); the cooler central mountains and south coast have an occasional shower. When the rains come, they cause floods and landslides, cutting off access to roads.

Day temperatures are around 30°C to 35°C (85°F to 95°F) year-round in the lowland areas, dropping to the low 20s overnight. In the mountain areas, warm-to-hot daytime temperatures drop to a chillier 15°C (60°F) at night, less at altitude. At the end of the dry season in parts of the north coast the mercury hovers over 35°C. See p916 for climate charts.

A good time to visit is after the wet season, from late April to July.

CUSTOMS

The usual rules (1L of alcohol, 200 cigarettes) apply to arrivals in East Timor.

DANGERS & ANNOYANCES

Malaria and dengue are common and are real concerns for those staying in East Timor; take precautions (see p939 and p938). Consider all tap water and ice as highly suspect (bottled water is widely available) and do as the locals do: wipe off any water from the tops of beverage cans before drinking. Antibiotics and other pharmaceuticals are easily bought in Dili but are hard to find elsewhere.

The main risks associated with East Timor besides political upheaval are those universal concerns of road safety and petty crime.

The driving in East Timor is generally passive and traffic is far from dense; however, vehicles and roads are generally in poor condition, and are made more hazardous by wandering livestock. Sudden wash-outs of roads is just one reason why driving after nightfall outside Dili is foolish.

Theft most frequently occurs from cars, with mobile phones a prime target. Wandering alone on the beach at night is never a good idea, and women travelling solo should take particular care (see p923), but generally the crime rate is not high.

Given the regular bouts of political instability in East Timor, check the current situation before you visit (although government travel advisories are usually cautious in the extreme). Outside of mass unrest, political violence is not aimed at non-Timorese. If you see stone throwing or other provocations, vamoose.

DRIVING LICENCE

Your home-country driving licence or permit is acceptable in East Timor.

EMBASSIES & CONSULATES

Embassies & Consulates in East Timor

A number of countries have embassies in Dili. Citizens of Canada and the UK should contact their embassies in Indonesia (see p336).

Australia (☎ 332 2111; www.easttimor.embassy.gov.au; Avenida dos Mártires de Pátria)
European Commission (☎ 332 5171; ectimor@arafura.net.au; Rua Santo António de Motael 8, Farol)
Indonesia (☎ 331 7107; kukridil@hotmail.com; cnr Rua Marinha & Rua Governador Cesar, Farol)
Ireland (☎ 332 4880; charles.lathrop@dfe.ie; Rua Alferes Duartre Arbiro 12, Farol)
New Zealand (☎ 331 0087; kiwidili@gmail.com; Rua Alferes Duarte Arbiro, Farol)
USA (☎ 332 4684; consdili@state.gov; Avenida de Portugal, Farol)

East Timorese Embassies & Consulates Abroad

There's only a handful of East Timorese diplomatic offices overseas.
Australia (☎ 02-6260 8800; tl_emb.canberra@bigpond.com; 25 Blaxland Cres, Griffith, Canberra, ACT 2603)
European Union (☎ 280 0096; jo_amorim@yahoo.com; Ave de Cortenbergh 12; 1040 Brussels, Belgium)
Indonesia (☎ 021 390 2978; tljkt@yahoo.com; 11th fl, Surya Bldg, Jl MH Thamrin Kav 9, Jakarta 10350)
USA (☎ 202 965 1515; embtlus@earthlink.net; 3415 Massachusetts Ave, NW Washington, DC, 20007)

FESTIVALS & EVENTS

As a staunchly Catholic country, Christian holidays are celebrated with gusto; see right for dates. During any of the major holidays there will be a church celebration. Easter is particularly colourful, with parades and vigils.

FOOD & DRINK

Food

The food is not what you'll remember most about your visit to East Timor. For many locals, meat added to the staple rice-and-veg dish is a treat. That said, coastal communities do good barbecued fish, flipped straight from the sea to the grill.

The years of Indonesian and Portuguese rule have flavoured the country's palate, with Indonesian-style fried-noodle dishes and signature Portuguese items such as *bacalhau* (cod) available at many restaurants. In Dili, numerous places serve the usual melange of pizza, sandwiches and pasta plus Thai and Indian treats. You can join locals at modest places and eat well for under US$5.

Outside of Dili and Baucau, choices dwindle. You'll usually find a couple of simple places near the town market serving variations of chicken and beef.

Drink

Coffee is a speciality in East Timor: it's strong, black and full-bodied – and available everywhere. Bottled drinking water is readily available. Favourite beers include Indonesia's Bintang and Singapore's Tiger. Away from Dili, beverages may not be cold. That milky liquid for sale from stalls is *sopi*, a home-brewed palm wine that tastes of fermenting palm fruit, which is exactly what it is. Think of it more as punch (it has one) than wine.

GAY & LESBIAN TRAVELLERS

There's no organised network for gay men and lesbians in East Timor, but it's unlikely that there'll be any overt discrimination.

HOLIDAYS

East Timor has a large list of holidays. Many special days of commemoration are declared each year – sometimes on the morning of what becomes a holiday. Particularly Timorese holidays include Independence Restoration Day, which commemorates the day in 2002 when sovereignty was transferred from the UN; Popular Consultation Day, which celebrates the start of independence in 1999; and National Youth Day, which commemorates the Santa Cruz Cemetery massacre (see p137).

East Timor also celebrates Idul Adha (the Muslim day of sacrifice) and Idul Fitri (the end of Ramadan), but dates vary each year.

New Year's Day 1 January
Good Friday March/April
Labour Day 1 May
Independence Restoration Day 20 May
Corpus Christi Day May/June
Popular Consultation Day 30 August
All Saints' Day 1 November
All Souls' Day 2 November
National Youth Day 12 November
Proclamation of Independence Day 28 November
National Heroes' Day 7 December
Immaculate Conception 8 December
Christmas Day 25 December

INTERNET ACCESS

There are plenty of internet cafés in Dili, with access averaging US$6 per hour. Other than in Baucau, access is unheard of elsewhere.

INTERNET RESOURCES

East Timor Tourism News (www.easttimortourismassociationnews.blogspot.com) Has updated tourism news from the Tourism Association of East Timor.

LANGUAGE? WHICH LANGUAGE?

Babel only had a little on East Timor. Portuguese and Tetun are East Timor's official languages, with Tetun and 15 other Timorese languages acknowledged by the constitution as national languages of great importance to the country's heritage. It's estimated that only 25% of the population speaks Portuguese, while at least 80% speaks Tetun. Most young adults also speak Bahasa Indonesia – the imposed official language from 1975 to 1999. Due to the huge UN presence in recent years, English is marginally understood, particularly in Dili. English is also taught in schools.

Any attempts made by travellers to speak Tetun are greatly appreciated. Lonely Planet's *East Timor Phrasebook* is a handy introduction. The resources at the Linguistic Institute website at the **National University** (www.asianlang.mq.edu.au/INL/) include bilingual guides for myriad languages, and entertaining commentary on the nation's convoluted language situation.

East Timor Action Network (www.etan.org) The website of this US-based organisation has a vast and compelling array of web links, and loads of information and articles.
Lonely Planet (www.lonelyplanet.com) Has information on travel in East Timor; check out the Thorn Tree forum.
Turismo de Timor-Leste (www.turismotimorleste.com) Official Department of Tourism site.
United Nations Integrated Mission in Timor-Leste (www.unmit.org) This site has news and official information.
Xanana Republic Gazette (www.xananarepublic.blogspot.com) This Dili-based blog is both entertaining and informative. It has links to the ever changing line-up of local blogs, some of which are excellent.

LEGAL MATTERS

If you are the victim of serious crime go to the nearest police station and notify your embassy. The Timorese police force is only one of a passel of groups providing security in the country. If arrested, you have the right to a phone call and legal representation, which your embassy can help to locate.

Possession and trafficking of illicit drugs carry stiff penalties.

MAPS

The Timorese government's tourism department distributes a free *Timor-Leste* country map (1:750,000), which you'll find around Dili. Otherwise, accurate and up-to-date maps are a business opportunity for someone.

MEDIA

Newspapers

The *Timor Post* and the *Suara Timor Lorosae* are among the daily local newspapers; they're mainly in Indonesian but with some news in Tetun. The *Guide Post* is aimed at English-speaking expats in Dili, and has useful service listings and maps. Don't expect to find any other newspapers or magazines in English.

Radio & TV

Radio is the most important branch of the media, with the national broadcaster Radio de Timor Leste (RTL) and a host of community stations. The Catholic Church's Radio Timor Kmanek (RTK) is popular. You can pick up Australian programming from the ABC in Dili on 106.5FM; the BBC is on 105.9FM.

The national public TV station is Televisao de Timor Leste (TVTL), which broadcasts for a few hours each evening. Its news programme ignores no political speech. Shows featuring local concerts have the same uneven charms as videos of your cousin's recital. Many Dili hotels have satellite TV with all the expected international channels.

MONEY

The US dollar is the official currency of East Timor. Locally minted centavos coins also circulate, which are of equal value to US cents. Make sure you arrive with some US dollars.

You'll need to make all financial transactions in Dili, where ATMs dispense US dollars and banks change travellers cheques. A few establishments in Dili accept credit cards, though there's often a hefty 5% surcharge attached.

The following are the exchange rates at the time of press:

Country	Unit	US dollars (US$)
Australia	A$1	0.84
Canada	C$1	0.97
Euro zone	€1	1.39
Indonesia	10,000Rp	1.07
Japan	¥100	0.87
New Zealand	NZ$1	0.71
UK	£1	2.01

POST

Dili's **post office** (Rua Presidente Nicolau Lobato; 8am-5pm Mon-Fri) doesn't have poste restante. The mail service is pretty reliable.

RESPONSIBLE TRAVEL

East Timor is not yet developed for tourism; visitors need to be mindful of the significant impact their behaviour can have on the environment and the population. The majority of East Timorese are highly religious so will appreciate travellers dressing conservatively and eschewing public displays of affection.

Formal protection for geographic areas and species is relatively new, limited, low profile and underresourced. You need to be mindful of the impact you have on the environment – there are no signs, rangers or information centres to remind you to 'do the right thing'.

TELEPHONE

If you're phoning an East Timor number from overseas, the international country code is ☎ 670. When making an international call from East Timor, the access code is ☎ 0011. There are no area codes in East Timor, and few land-line numbers outside Dili. Land-line numbers begin with 3 or 4; mobile numbers start with 7. You can make local and international calls from any Timor Telecom office.

A mobile phone is useful in East Timor. You can purchase a SIM card from **Timor Telecom** (www.timortelecom.tp) for US$20, which includes US$10 of credit. In Dili you will besieged by street vendors offering cards with additional credit in many amounts. You'll soon need them as the monopoly on phone service allows Timor Telecom to charge up to US$2 a minute for international calls.

TOURIST INFORMATION

East Timor doesn't have a tourist office. However, the expat community is especially generous with information. Drop by any of the popular bars, restaurants or dive shops and soon you'll be hooked into all sorts of info. Language differences aside, locals are also very happy to help.

TOURS

A tour can allow you to visit places not easily accessible by public transport, and a guide can bridge the language barrier. The following agencies are based in Dili.

Eco Discovery (☎ 332 2454; www.ecodiscovery-easttimor.com; Landmark Plaza, Avenida dos Martires de Patria, Dili) Manny Napoleaõ's knowledge of East Timor is encyclopedic. Custom tours plunge deep.

Harmonia Eco Tours (☎ 728 5611; www.timorvillagehotels.com; Rua Presidente Nicolau Lobato, Dili) Next to the Central Hotel and affiliated with the Timor Village Hotel, south of Ossu, Harmonia Eco Tours has multiday trips to the east and south starting from US$100 per person per day.

Mega Tours (☎ 723 5199; timormegatours@netscape.net; Rua Presidente Nicolau Lobato, Dili) Two-day trips to Mt Ramelau are popular; they cost US$280 for up to four people. Custom trips to places such as Jaco Island cost from US$150 per day for up to four people.

TRAVELLERS WITH DISABILITIES

There are no provisions for travellers with disabilities in East Timor. Potholed pavements makes wheelchair travel difficult.

VISAS

An entry visa (for up to 30 days) is granted to valid-passport holders for US$30 on arrival in East Timor. To avoid hassles if plans change, always ask for a 30-day visa. Visas can be extended for US$30 per month if the applicant has a valid reason to do so.

Many travellers visit East Timor to renew their Indonesian visas. An Indonesian visa takes three to five working days to process. A 30-day Indonesian tourist visa costs US$45 from a consulate. A single-entry seven-day transit visa costs US$20 and a double-entry version costs US$40 (the latter is useful for land trips to Oecussi as you'll need a visa both to get there via Indonesia as well as leave).

VOLUNTEERING

Major volunteer organisations include **Australian Volunteers International** (www.australianvolunteers.com) and **UN Volunteers** (www.unv.org). There are scores more groups working in the country; visit the Links page at **East Timor Action Network** (www.etan.org) for a voluminous listing.

WOMEN TRAVELLERS

Women travellers need to be aware of personal security issues, particularly in Dili, as assault do occur. Do not walk or take taxis after dark, unless you're in a group.

Women travellers will attract less attention by wearing knee-length (or longer) clothes, and may want to cover their shoulders. Bikinis are tolerated in only a few locations, such as the popular beaches in Dili.

Indonesia

HIGHLIGHTS

- **Bali** – believing the hype, for Bali has it all: dynamic clubbing, stellar surf and exquisite Hindu culture (p209)
- **Gunung Bromo** – experiencing the supernatural beauty of East Java's vast cone-studded caldera at sunrise (p207)
- **Central Java** – ascending the ancient Buddhist stupa of Borobudur (p197), before trawling the batik markets of bustling Yogyakarta (p196)
- **Orang-utans** – paying primate-to-primate respects to the 'man of the jungle', unique to Borneo (p309) and Sumatra (p262)
- **Togean Islands** – diving the pristine walls and coral canyons beneath seas of dimpled glass in remote Central Sulawesi (p320)
- **Off the beaten track** – hiking along raging rivers and scaling exposed ridges to reach interior Papua's remote tribal villages in the Baliem Valley (p331)

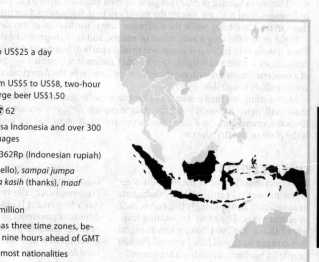

FAST FACTS

- **Budget** US$15 to US$25 a day
- **Capital** Jakarta
- **Costs** cheap room US$5 to US$8, two-hour bus ride US$2, large beer US$1.50
- **Country code** ☎ 62
- **Languages** Bahasa Indonesia and over 300 indigenous languages
- **Money** US$1 = 9362Rp (Indonesian rupiah)
- **Phrases** *salam* (hello), *sampai jumpa* (goodbye), *terima kasih* (thanks), *maaf* (sorry)
- **Population** 255 million
- **Time** Indonesia has three time zones, between seven and nine hours ahead of GMT
- **Visas** 30 days for most nationalities

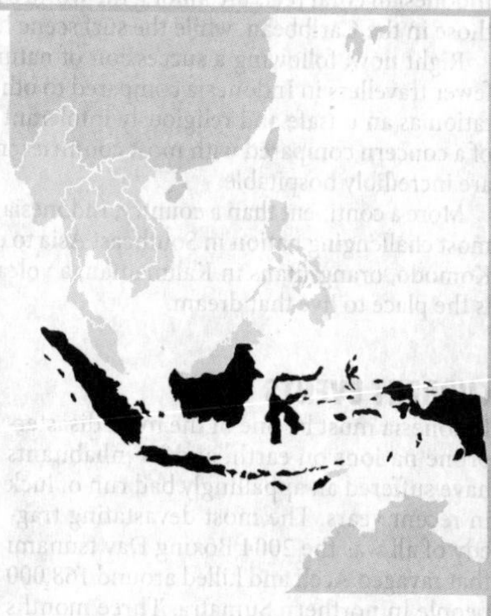

TRAVEL HINTS

Kaki lima (mobile food stalls) offer the cheapest grub. And learn some local lingo – Bahasa Indonesia is easy to pick up.

OVERLAND ROUTES

The Entikong border links Kalimantan with Sarawak (Malaysia) and West and East Timor connect at Motoain.

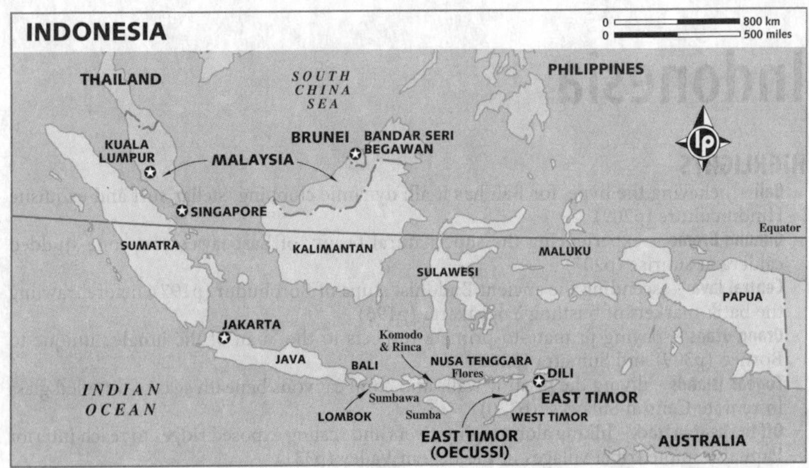

Bestriding the equator and bridging the Indian and Pacific Oceans, Indonesia is a vast, dazzling tropical archipelago of over 13,000 islands that stretches between Malaysia and Australia. The nation's natural diversity is simply staggering, taking in snowcapped peaks in Papua, sandalwood forests in Sumba, primary jungle in Borneo and shimmering rice paddies in Bali and Java. Indonesian coral reefs are among the world's richest, harbouring four times more species than those in the Caribbean, while the surf scene here is world class by any definition.

Right now, following a succession of natural and human-provoked disasters, there are far fewer travellers in Indonesia compared to other parts of Southeast Asia. But the nation's reputation as an unsafe and religiously intolerant nation is unjustified – personal safety is far less of a concern compared with most countries in Europe or the Americas, and most Indonesians are incredibly hospitable.

More a continent than a country, Indonesia is the largest, most culturally diverse and perhaps most challenging nation in Southeast Asia to explore. So if you've come in search of dragons in Komodo, orang-utans in Kalimantan, a volcano to climb or just the perfect beach, Indonesia is the place to live that dream.

CURRENT EVENTS

Indonesia must be one of the most disaster-prone nations on earth, and its inhabitants have suffered an appallingly bad run of luck in recent years. The most devastating tragedy of all was the 2004 Boxing Day tsunami that ravaged Aceh and killed around 168,000 people in northern Sumatra. Three months later Pulau Nias suffered an earthquake. Then in 2006, another quake rocked Yogyakarta, killing 6800 people (and damaging the Prambanan temples), and Java's main beach resort of Pangandaran was engulfed by another tsunami. Combine this with a series of ferry sinkings and aeroplane crashes that exposed the decrepit state of Indonesia's transport network and it doesn't paint a pretty picture.

Politically, however, Indonesia has benefited from a period of stability and economic progress. Peace talks between Acehnese Free Aceh Movement (GAM) rebels and the Indonesian government led to a suspension of hostilities and peaceful elections for the governorship in December 2006. Conflicts rumble on in parts of the nation (particularly in central Sulawesi and Papua), however, and a proposed 'decency' law (see p339) has inflamed religious tensions. But all in all Indonesia has enjoyed a period of relative calm under President Susilo Bambang Yudhoyono, and with the next election set for 2009 things look good for another peaceful handover of power, proof the nation's embryonic democracy is beginning to mature steadily.

HISTORY

Beginnings

Until the last few years it was widely believed that the first humanoids (*Homo erectus*) lived in Central Java around 500,000 years ago, having reached Indonesia across land bridges from Africa, before either dying off or being wiped out by the arrival of *Homo sapiens*.

But the discovery in 2003 of the remains of a tiny islander, dubbed the 'hobbit' (see boxed text, p289), seems to indicate that *Homo erectus* survived much longer than was previously thought, and that previously accepted timelines of Indonesia's evolutionary history need to be re-examined (though many scientists continue to challenge the hobbit theory).

Most Indonesians are descendents of Malay people who began migrating around 4000 BC from Cambodia, Vietnam and southern China. They steadily developed small kingdoms and by 700 BC these settlers had developed skilful rice-farming techniques.

Hinduism & Buddhism

The growing prosperity of these early kingdoms soon caught the attention of Indian and Chinese merchants, and along with silks and spices came the dawn of Hinduism and Buddhism in Indonesia.

These religions quickly gained a foothold in the archipelago and soon became central to the great kingdoms of the 1st millennium AD. The Buddhist Srivijaya empire held sway over the Malay Peninsula and southern Sumatra, extracting wealth from its dominion over the strategic Straits of Melaka, while the Hindu Mataram and Buddhist Sailendra kingdoms dominated Central Java, raising their grandiose monuments, Borobudur and Prambanan, over the fertile farmland that brought them their prosperity.

Indeed, when Mataram slipped into mysterious decline around the 10th century AD, it was fast replaced with an even more powerful Hindu kingdom. Founded in 1294, the Majapahit empire made extensive territorial gains under its ruler, Hayam Wuruk, and prime minister, Gajah Mada, and while claims that they controlled much of Sulawesi, Sumatra and Borneo now seem fanciful, most of Java, Madura and Bali certainly fell within their realm.

But things would soon change. Despite the Majapahit empire's massive power and influence, greater fault lines were opening up across Indonesia, and Hinduism's golden age was swiftly drawing to a close.

DID YOU KNOW?

- The name 'Indonesia' is derived from *Indus* (Latin for 'India') and *nesos* (Greek for 'island').
- Indonesia has 129 active volcanoes.
- The Indonesian coastline is 54,716km long.
- Maluku (population 2 million) has over 130 languages.

Rise of Islam

With the arrival of Islam came the power, the reason and the will to oppose the hegemony of the Majapahits, and satellite kingdoms soon took up arms against the Hindu kings. In the 15th century the Majapahits fled to Bali, where Hindu culture continues to flourish, leaving Java to the increasingly powerful Islamic sultanates. Meanwhile, the influential trading kingdoms of Melaka (on the Malay Peninsula) and Makassar (in southern Sulawesi) were also embracing Islam, sowing the seeds that would later make modern Indonesia the most populous Muslim nation on earth.

European Expansion

Melaka fell to the Portuguese in 1511 and European eyes were soon settling on the archipelago's riches, prompting two centuries of unrest as the Portuguese, Spanish, Dutch and British wrestled for control. By 1700 the Dutch held most of the trump cards, with the Dutch East India Company (VOC) controlling the region's lucrative spice trade and becoming the world's first multinational company (see p154). Following the VOC's bankruptcy, however, the British governed Java under Sir Stamford Raffles (see p180) between 1811 and 1816, only to relinquish control again to the Dutch after the end of the Napoleonic wars, who then held control of Indonesia until its independence 129 years later.

It was not, however, a trouble-free tenancy and the Dutch had to face numerous rebellions: Javan Prince Diponegoro's five-year guerrilla war was finally put down in 1830, costing the lives of 8000 Dutch troops.

DUTCH EAST INDIA COMPANY (VOC)

Dominating Asian trade routes for two centuries, the Dutch East India Company (VOC) was the world's first multinational corporation, monopolising the spice trade from Asia to Europe. Set up in 1602, it primarily traded pepper, nutmeg, cinnamon and sugar, and its profitability and clout was such that it minted its own currency.

By the late 17th century the VOC had established a city, Batavia, as its capital in the region, had 50,000 employees and owned over 150 merchant ships and 40 warships. It also had a private army of 10,000 soldiers, outposts from Japan to southern Africa, and was the first company to pay stock dividends (which averaged an annual 18% over 200 years).

But this trading behemoth struggled in the 18th century, ultimately collapsing in 1800, being unable to compete financially with the Caribbean and Latin America, which became more productive sugar-production centres.

Road to Independence

By the beginning of the 20th century, the Dutch had brought most of the archipelago under their control, but the revolutionary tradition of Diponegoro was never truly quashed, bubbling beneath the surface of Dutch rule and finding a voice in the young Soekarno. The debate was sidelined as the Japanese swept through Indonesia during WWII, but with their departure came the opportunity for Soekarno to declare Indonesian independence, which he did from his Jakarta home on 17 August 1945.

The Dutch, however, were unwilling to relinquish their hold over Indonesia and – supported by the British, who had entered Indonesia to accept the Japanese surrender – moved quickly to reassert their authority over the country. Resistance was stiff and for four bitter years the Indonesian resistance fought a guerrilla war. But American and UN opposition to the reimposition of colonialism and the mounting casualty toll eventually forced the Dutch to pack it in, and the Indonesian flag – the *sang merah putih* (red and white) – was finally hoisted over Jakarta's Istana Merdeka (Freedom Palace) on 27 December 1949.

Depression, Disunity & Dictatorship

Unity in war quickly became division in peace, as religious fundamentalists and nationalist separatists challenged the fledgling central government. But after almost a decade of political impasse and economic depression, Soekarno made his move, declaring Guided Democracy (a euphemism for dictatorship) with army backing and leading Indonesia into nearly four decades of authoritarian rule.

Despite moves towards the one-party state, Indonesia's three-million-strong Communist Party (Partai Komunis Indonesia; PKI) was the biggest in the world by 1965 and Soekarno had long realised the importance of winning its backing. But as the PKI's influence in government grew, so did tensions with the armed forces. Things came to a head on the night of 30 September 1965, when elements of the palace guard launched an attempted coup. Quickly put down by General Soeharto, the coup was blamed – perhaps unfairly – on the PKI and became the pretext for an army-led purge that left as many as 500,000 communist sympathisers dead. Strong evidence later emerged that both the US (implacably opposed to communism) and the UK (seeking to protect its interests in Malaysia) aided and abetted Soeharto's purge by drawing up hit lists of communist agitators. By 1968 Soeharto had ousted Soekarno and was installed as president.

Soeharto brought unity through repression, annexing Irian Jaya (Papua) in 1969, and reacting to insurgency with an iron fist. In 1975, Portuguese Timor was invaded, leading to tens of thousands of deaths, and separatist ambitions in Aceh and Papua were also met with a ferocious military response. But despite endemic corruption, the 1980s and 1990s were Indonesia's boom years, with meteoric economic growth and a starburst of opulent building ventures transforming the face of the capital.

Soeharto's Fall

As Asia's economy went into freefall during the closing years of the 1990s, Soeharto's house of cards began to tumble. Indonesia went bankrupt overnight and the country found an obvious scapegoat in the cronyism and corruption endemic in the dictator's regime. Protests erupted across Indonesia in 1998 and the May riots in Jakarta left thousands, many of them Chinese, dead. After three decades of dictatorial rule, Soeharto resigned on 21 May 1998.

Passions cooled when Vice President BJ Habibie took power on a reform ticket, but ambitious promises were slow to materialise, and in November of the same year riots again rocked many Indonesian cities. Promises of forthcoming elections succeeded in closing the floodgates, but separatist groups took advantage of the weakened central government and violence erupted in Maluku, Irian Jaya, East Timor and Aceh. East Timor won its independence after a referendum in August 1999, but only after Indonesian-backed militias had destroyed its infrastructure and left thousands dead.

Democracy & Reform

Against this unsettled backdrop, the June 1999 legislative elections passed surprisingly smoothly, leaving Megawati Soekarnoputri (Soekarno's daughter) and her reformist Indonesian Democratic Party for Struggle (PDI-P) as the largest party with 33% of the vote. But months later the separate presidential election was narrowly won by Abdurrahman Wahid (Gus Dur), whose efforts to undo corruption met with stiff resistance. Megawati was eventually sworn in as president in 2001, but her term proved a disappointment for many Indonesians, as corrupt infrastructures were left in place, the military's power remained intact and poverty levels remained high. Nevertheless Indonesia gained from a period of economic stability and healthy growth, though much of this was at the expense of the environment through vast logging and mining concessions.

Megawati lost the 2004 presidential elections to Susilo Bambang Yudhoyono (or 'SBY'), an ex-army officer who served in East Timor but who also has a master's degree in business management from Wester University in the United States. Dubbed the 'thinking general', his successes have included cracking down on Islamic militants, pumping more money into education and health, and introducing basic social security payments. SBY's term has been rocked by a series of disasters, beginning with the 2004 tsunami and continuing through 2006 and 2007 with an alarming number of transport disasters as planes fell from the sky and ferries went down with hundreds of casualties.

Economically, Indonesia has remained relatively healthy, however, with growth averaging around 5% to 6% a year. SBY has a reputation as a prudent leader, cutting the nation's huge fuel subsidies in 2005 (which forced very unpopular fuel price rises) and even paying back an International Monetary Fund (IMF) loan four years early. A decade after the fall of Soeharto, the consensus is that Indonesia is establishing itself as a workable democracy, but a nation confronted with myriad development issues. Corruption, the destruction of the environment, poverty, fundamentalism and taxation reform are just a selection of some of these huge challenges.

THE CULTURE

The National Psyche

Soekarno, often referred to as the founder of Indonesia, must have pondered long and hard when faced with the task of welding together a nation from tens of millions of Javanese (with millennia of elaborate cultural traditions), longhouse-dwelling tribal Dayaks, Sumabanese animists and the Saudi-devout Muslims of Aceh. His solution, founded on five principles of nationhood known as the Pancasila, maintained that loyalty to the state should supersede ethnic and religious divisions, and this philosophy remains crucial to understanding what makes Indonesia tick today.

Alongside commitments to democracy and humanity, the Pancasila also enshrined the principle that all citizens must have an official state religion and that it should be 'based in the belief in one and only God'. This has meant that Indonesia's many practitioners of indigenous religions, particularly remote tribal communities, have been pressurised to adopt a state-sanctioned religion – usually Islam or Christianity. The Balinese also had to tweak their belief system, so that a supreme deity could emerge from a pantheon of gods, and Hinduism could be declared an officially recognised faith.

In recent years Indonesia's unique syncretic Islamic culture, which borrowed heavily from Hindu and animist traditions, has become much more conservative and orthodox, due to increased influence and contact with the wider Islamic world. Geopolitical factors (such as the wars in Iraq and Afghanistan) and the arrival of Saudi-sponsored mullahs have also helped radicalise many, creating tensions with those Indonesians who practise other faiths. Yusman Roy, an imam who quotes from the Quran in Bahasa Indonesia (not Arabic), has been jailed for doing so, and a proposed 'decency' law (see p339) threatens to outlaw the wearing of swimsuits on the beach (as well as Papuan penis-gourd wearers).

The old Javanese saying *'bhinneka tunggal ika'* (they are many; they are one) is said to be Indonesia's national dictum, but with a population of over 250 million, 742 languages and 17,000 islands it's not surprising that many from the outer islands resent Java, where power is centralised. Separatist groups in Aceh, Papua and East Timor fought guerrilla wars against Jakarta for decades, with East Timor gaining independence in 2001. Indonesia is loosely bound together by a single flag and single language (Bahasa Indonesia) but in some ways can be compared to the EU – a richly diverse confederacy of peoples.

Lifestyle

The world's most populous Muslim nation is no hard-line Islamic state. Indonesians have traditionally practised a very loose-fitting, relaxed form of Islam and though there's no desire to imitate the West, most see no conflict in catching a Hollywood movie in an American-style shopping mall after prayers at the mosque. The country is becoming more cosmopolitan, as internet usage soars and chat rooms proliferate, and Indonesian hip-hop, indie, ska and reggae acts emerge. Millions of Indonesians now work overseas – mainly in the Gulf, Hong Kong and Malaysia – bringing back extraneous influences to their villages when they return. A boom in low-cost air travel has enabled a generation of Indonesians to travel internally and overseas conveniently and cheaply for the first time, while personal mobility is much easier today – it's possible to buy a motorbike on hire purchase with as little as a 500,000Rp deposit.

But not everyone has the cash or time for overseas jaunts and there remains a yawning gulf between the haves and the have-nots. Indonesia is much poorer than many of its Asian neighbours, with almost 50% surviving on US$2 a day, and in many rural areas opportunities are few and far between. Underemployment is a serious issue and educational standards, despite recent improvements and extra governmental cash, are way behind countries like Malaysia or Thailand, restricting overseas investment.

Population

Indonesia's population is the fourth-biggest in the world, with over 255 million people. Over half this number live on the island of Java, one of the most crowded places on earth with a population density of 940 people per square kilometre. But while Java (and Bali and Lombok) teem with people, large parts of the archipelago are very sparsely populated, particularly Papua (under 10 per square kilometre) and Kalimantan.

Birth rates have fallen considerably in recent years (from an average of 3.4 children per woman in 1987 to 2.4 today) thanks to successful family planning campaigns and increasing prosperity levels.

The majority of Indonesia's hundred or so ethnic groups are made up of the Javanese (42%) and their neighbours from West Java, the Sundanese (15%). Other large groups include the Madurese (3.3%), coastal Malays (3.4%) and Batak (3%).

RELIGION

If Indonesia has a soundtrack, it is the muezzin's call to prayer. Wake up to it once and it won't come as a surprise that Indonesia is the largest Islamic nation on earth, with over 220 million Muslims (88% of the total population).

But while Islam has a near-monopoly on religious life, many of the country's most impressive historical monuments, such as the temples of Borobudur and Prambanan, hark back to when Hindu and Buddhist kingdoms dominated Java. These religions maintain important communities, with Hinduism (2% of the population) continuing to flourish in Bali while Buddhists (1%) are scattered through the country. Christians make up nearly 9% of the nation, forming the majority in Papua, several islands of Nusa Tenggara and Maluku, and in parts of Sumatra. But animist traditions survive below the surface in many rural areas.

Although nominally a secular state, religious organisations (the conservative Nahdlatul Ulama has over 40 million members) still wield considerable clout in the corridors of power.

ARTS

Dance

Indonesia has a rich heritage of traditional dances. In Yogyakarta there's the Ramayana ballet, a spectacular dance drama; Lombok has a mask dance called the *kayak sando* and war dances; Malaku's *lenso* is a handkerchief dance; while Bali has a multitude of elaborate dances including the *barong, kecak, topeng, legong* and *baris.*

Literature

Pramoedya Ananta Toer, a Javanese author, is perhaps Indonesia's best-known novelist. His famous quartet of historical realist novels set in the colonial era comprises *This Earth of Mankind, Child of All Nations, Footsteps* and *House of Glass.*

Mochtar Lubis is another well-known Indonesian writer. His most famous novel, *Twilight in Djakarta,* is a scathing attack on corruption and the plight of the poor in Jakarta in the 1950s.

Ayu Utami's *Saman* ushered in a new era of modern Indonesian writing dubbed *sastra wangi* ('fragrant literature') with her taboo-breaking tale of sex, politics and religion. *The Invisible Palace* by José Manuel Tesoro recounts the murder of a journalist in Yogyakarta, plotting the intersections of hierarchy, Islam, animism and corruption in government and Javanese culture.

Music

There's much more to the Indonesian music scene than the saccharine sweet pop and *dangdut* (Indonesian dance music with strong Arabic and Hindi influences) that dominates most airwaves. Alongside a vibrant punk scene (see p158), led by bands such as Bali's Superman is Dead and Yoyya's Blackboots, there's social invective from hip-hoppers Homicide and Iwa K, while House and techno DJs like Romy (see boxed text, below) play to thousands in Jakartan clubs and around Asia.

The best-known traditional Indonesian music is *gamelan:* both Java and Bali have orchestras composed mainly of percussion instruments including drums, gongs and *angklung* (shake-drums), along with flutes and xylophones.

Theatre

Javanese *wayang* (puppet) plays have their origins in the Hindu epics, the Ramayana and the Mahabharata. There are different forms of *wayang*: *wayang kulit* uses leather shadow puppets, while *wayang golek* uses wooden puppets.

CLUB INDONESIA

Forget Bangkok (or even New York), Jakarta's clubbing scene has to be one of the world's most decadent. Centred in the Kota district, home to five vast temples of trance, one club here (Stadium, capacity 4000; p175) opens on Thursday and doesn't shut till Monday morning. Clubbers get mashed-up for hours, some losing days in dark-as-sin techno clubs, where the spirit of Acid House is definitely still alive and kicking.

One of those responsible for developing the scene was DJ Romy, who spent three years in London in the early 1990s, where he collected vinyl and began DJ-ing, later returning to Java to get the party started.

By 1993 Indonesians began organising warehouse parties in Jakarta and Bali, and by 1994 the first pirate stations devoted to dance music began broadcasting. Today the scene is massive, with all genres – electro, minimal, techno, tribal, progressive and House – represented.

Many young Indonesians do not drink alcohol and, perhaps consequently, ecstasy is a big part of Indonesia's club scene. It became the drug of choice for Indonesia's wealthy elite in the mid-1990s, and its popularity now transcends all social classes.

Indonesia is not only a dance-drug consumer nation but also – as Dedi Permana, a senior police commissioner, acknowledged – 'the world's biggest ecstasy producer'. One illegal factory busted in November 2005 in Serang, Banten had a production capacity of one million ecstasy pills per week.

For more on Indonesian club culture consult www.indodj.com. For the risks associated with recreational drug use in Indonesia, see p915.

INDO PUNK

Just as British bands like the Stones raided the USA for their blues-influenced tunes in the '60s, Indonesian groups have absorbed American and British musical movements, added an indigenous dimension and created a vibrant new scene. Indonesian hip-hop, reggae and metal are all healthy, but today's teenagers have really identified with punk and new wave, and bands like the Ramones are massive in Indonesia, their T-shirts, stickers and garage-band style all pervasive.

Superman is Dead are one of the biggest acts, their raw social commentary and antiestablishment stance selling tens of thousands of legitimate CDs and perhaps millions of pirated copies. Their name refers to the fall of Soeharto, and SiD fills stadiums with fans who know every word of every song, the venue a maelstrom of slam-dancing mosh pits, crowdsurfing and pogoing kids. Drummer Jerinx is a superstar in Indonesia.

ENVIRONMENT

Indonesia has lost more tropical forest than anywhere else in the world bar Brazil in the last few decades. That said, some incredible national parks and pristine landscapes remain virtually untouched, mainly in remote areas away from the main centres of population.

For more information on Indonesia's environment, visit the **Indonesian Forum for the Environment** (WALHI; www.eng.walhi.or.id).

The Land

At 1.92 million sq km, Indonesia is an island colossus, incorporating 10% of the world's forest cover and 11,508 uninhabited islands (6000 more have human populations). From the low-lying coastal areas, the country rises through no fewer than 129 active volcanoes – more than any country in the world – to the snow-covered summit of Puncak Jaya (4884m), in Papua. Despite the incredible diversity of its landscapes, it is worth remembering that Indonesia is predominantly water; Indonesians refer to the country as Tanah Air Kita (literally 'Our Earth and Water'). The main islands are Kalimantan (Indonesian Borneo; 539,460 sq km), Sumatra (473,606 sq km), Papua (Indonesian New Guinea; 421,981 sq km), Sulawesi (202,000 sq km) and Java (132,107 sq km).

Wildlife

In his classic study *The Malay Archipelago*, British naturalist Alfred Russel Wallace divided Indonesia into two zones. To the west of the so-called Wallace Line (which runs between Kalimantan and Sulawesi and south through the straits between Bali and Lombok) flora and fauna resemble those of the rest of Asia, while the species and environments to the east become increasingly like those of Australia. Scientists have since fine-tuned Wallace's findings, but while western Indonesia is known for its (increasingly rare) orang-utan, rhinos, tigers and spectacular *Rafflesia* flowers, eastern Indonesia boasts the Komodo dragon and marsupials including Papuan tree kangaroos.

National Parks

There are officially 50 *taman nasional* (national parks) in Indonesia. Most are in remote areas, and only have basic visitor facilities, but they are remarkable in their ecological diversity and wildlife. Some of the finest include Tanjung Puting in Kalimantan (p309) for proboscis monkeys and wetland birds, and Komodo with its dragons and astonishing coral reefs.

Environmental Issues

Start with the pressures of poverty, chuck in the impact of unchecked greed and corruption and finish off with a desperate paucity of resources and it's not surprising that Indonesia's recent environmental record is so woeful. Environmental education has started very late in Indonesia, and already much of the nation's natural resources have been, and continue to be, ravaged and inadequately protected – in 2004 a law was passed allowing mining in protected areas.

Illegal logging remains commonplace despite a 2001 law banning the export of timber, and deforestation rates are some of the worst on the planet. An area the size of Switzerland goes up in a (mega) puff of smoke every year, as slash 'n' burn farming and forest fires choke neighbouring countries in acrid smoke. In 1998 the Indonesian environment minister, Juwono Sudarsono, likened Kalimantan to

DO YOUR BIT

- Refill your water bottle from the large water dispensers provided in some hotels and restaurants.
- Refuse plastic bags from shopkeepers.
- Show locals that you're getting rid off litter responsibly.
- Trekkers should take all disposable waste away with them.
- Souvenirs made from animals, such as tortoiseshell trinkets and framed butterflies, coral jewellery and sea shells, should be left well alone.
- Dive responsibly; see p912.

the American Wild West because of governmental inaction tackling illegal logging and forest fires. Forest loss often triggers floods and landslides, washing away topsoil and devastating farmland.

A booming urban population is also contributing to Indonesia's pollution crisis. Only a fraction of Jakarta's population is connected to a sewer system, leading to epidemics of water-borne diseases like typhoid. Chronic air pollution caused by an explosion in vehicle numbers (particularly motorbikes, which are not fitted with catalytic converters) affects all city dwellers, which the World Bank estimates costs Jakarta US$400 million a year. Respiratory health issues, directly linked to air quality, are the sixth leading cause of death in Indonesia (after accidents, diarrhoea, cardiovascular disease, tuberculosis and measles).

Industrialisation is unregulated, WALHI estimating that 2.2 million tonnes of toxic water are dumped into the rivers of West Java each year. Coastal pollution is worsening – as much as 86% of Indonesia's reef area is thought to be at medium or high risk of destruction.

Government initiatives are frequently drawn up to deal with the issues, but are rarely enforced. However, in the last few years, three ex-governors of provinces in Sumatra and East Kalimantan have been given prison sentences for granting illegal logging concessions (Aceh's Abdullah Puteh getting 10 years).

But while many Indonesians continue to live on the breadline, the environment is likely to remain a secondary concern.

TRANSPORT

GETTING THERE & AWAY

Air

Jakarta and Denpasar in Bali are the two main hubs, but there are also useful international connections to Medan, Palembang and Padang in Sumatra; Solo, Bandung and Surabaya in Java; Manado (Sulawesi), Balikpapan (Kalimantan) and Mataram (Lombok).

The following are some major international airlines; phone numbers beginning with ☎021 are Jakarta numbers, while phone numbers beginning with ☎0361 are for Bali.

Air Asia (code AK; ☎0804 133 3333; www.airasia.com) The region's biggest budget, web-based airline.

Air New Zealand (code NZ; ☎0361-756170; www.airnewzealand.com)

INDONESIAN SUPERLATIVES

Biggest archipelago Covering an area of 1.92 million sq km, Indonesia's 17,508 islands make up the world's largest archipelago.

Biggest lizard The Komodo dragon *(Varanus komodoensis)* is the biggest lizard in the world. The largest authenticated specimen was a gift from the Sultan of Bima to a US scientist and measured 3.1m.

Largest flower The world's biggest flower, *Rafflesia arnoldi,* often blooms in the thick Sumatran forests near Bukittinggi between August and November.

Longest snake The reticulated python, native to Indonesia, is the world's longest snake. A specimen killed in Sulawesi in 1912 measured 9.85m.

Most diverse Kalimantan is one of the most biologically diverse places on earth, with twice as many plant species as the whole of Africa.

Most populous Java has the largest population of any island in the world, with an estimated 140 million inhabitants.

DEPARTURE TAX

Airport tax for international departures is 100,000Rp and for domestic flights the tax varies with the airport, from 10,000Rp to 25,000Rp.

Cathay Pacific (code CX; ☎ 021-515 1747, 0361-753942; www.cathaypacific.com)
Continental Airlines (code CO; ☎ 021-3193 4417, 0361-768358; www.continental.com)
Eva Air (code BR; ☎ 0361-759773; www.evaair.com.tw)
Garuda (code GA; ☎ 0361-751011, ext 5228; www.garuda-indonesia.com)
Malaysia Airlines (code MH; ☎ 021-522 9685, 0361-764995; www.malaysiaairlines.com)
Qantas (code QF; ☎ 021-230 0655, 0361-288511; www.qantas.com)
Singapore Airlines (code SQ; ☎ 021-5790 3747, 0361-768388; www.singaporeairlines.com)
Thai Airways International (THAI, code TG; ☎ 021-230 2552, 0361-288511; www.thaiairways.com)

MALAYSIA

Kuala Lumpur has good connections with Jakarta and Denpasar. Air Asia often has the best prices (from US$40 one way) and also serves other cities in Indonesia including Bandung, Solo and Palembang; or try Malaysia Airlines. Batavia Air operates the short hop between Pontianak and Kuching in Borneo. Garuda Indonesia has several alternative routes including KL to Surabaya.

SINGAPORE

Apart from the numerous links to/from Jakarta and Denpasar, SilkAir flies to Solo, Palembang, Medan, Surabaya, Mataram, Balikpapan and Manado. Garuda links Singapore with Manado, Medan and Surabaya.

OTHER DESTINATIONS

All other Southeast Asian capitals are easily reached from Jakarta or Denpasar. Merpati offers a link between Dili and Denpasar.

Sea

MALAYSIA

Most sea connections are between Malaysia and Sumatra. The comfortable, high-speed ferries between Penang (Malaysia) and Belawan (near Medan, Sumatra) are one of the most popular ways to reach Indonesia. There are also ferry connections between Dumai (Sumatra) and Melaka (Malaysia); Pulau Bintan (Sumatra) and Johor Bahru (Malaysia); and Pulau Batam (Sumatra) and Kuala Tungkal (Malaysia).

For east-coast Kalimantan, fast ferries connect Tarakan and Tawau (Malaysia), and speedboats depart frequently from Tarakan to Nunukan and from Nunukan to Tawau; see p304 for full details.

PAPUA NEW GUINEA

Boats leave daily (weather permitting) from Hamadi port near Jayapura to Vanimo in Papua New Guinea; charters are also possible (350,000Rp per person). A visa is required if travelling into Indonesia.

SINGAPORE

Ferries link Singapore with Pulau Batam (S$18) and Pulau Bintan (S$25), both in Sumatra.

GETTING AROUND

Air

About a dozen airlines fly internally within Indonesia, some flying to just a handful of destinations on ancient prop planes; others, including Air Asia, use modern Boeing and Airbus aircraft.

Many Indonesian airlines have a history of operating with poor safety standards, and maintenance levels are not what they should be. The airlines with the best reputations are Air Asia, Merpati, TransNusa and the national carrier Garuda (though this airline has had accidents in the last few years). Adam Air has a particularly poor safety record and had several of its aircraft grounded by the government in 2006 after a series of accidents.

Flight prices have fallen on the most popular routes in recent years. As many carriers now operate on low-cost airline price schemes, it really pays to book early – a ticket from Jakarta to Denpasar can be as little as 349,000Rp including all taxes.

Note that many of the smaller Indonesian airlines' websites don't function for weeks on end, so be prepared to have to purchase tickets on arrival for many routes. Delays and cancellations are very common, particularly in remote areas, so build plenty of flexibility into your travel plans.

For contact details of the main domestic airlines see p176 and p211.

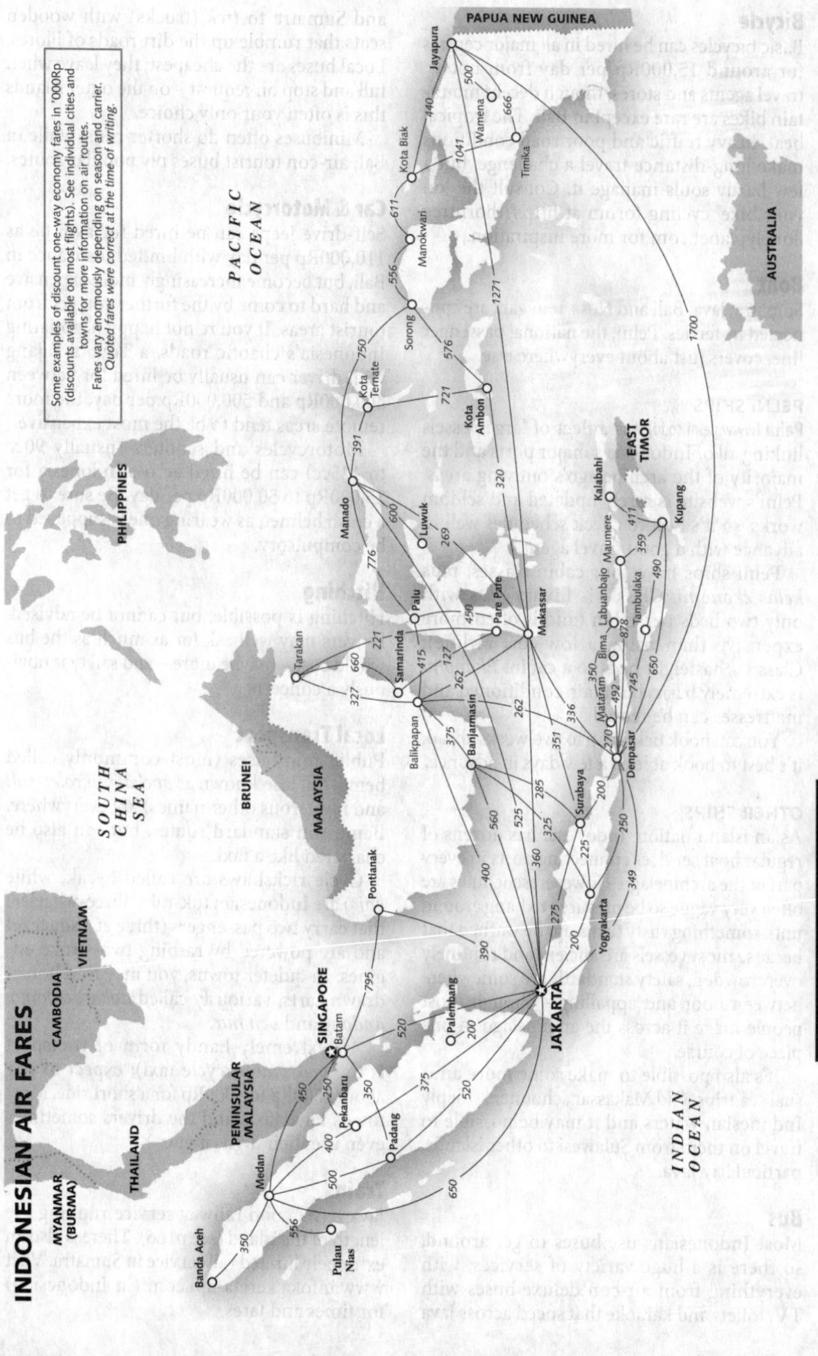

INDONESIAN AIR FARES
Some examples of discount one-way economy fares in '000Rp (discounts available on most flights). See individual cities and towns for more information on air routes. Fares vary enormously depending on season and carrier. Quoted fares were correct at the time of writing.
MYANMAR (BURMA)
THAILAND
CAMBODIA
VIETNAM
PENINSULAR MALAYSIA
SINGAPORE
SOUTH CHINA SEA
MALAYSIA
BRUNEI
PHILIPPINES
PACIFIC OCEAN
INDIAN OCEAN
PAPUA NEW GUINEA
EAST TIMOR
AUSTRALIA
Banda Aceh
Medan
Pulau Nias
Padang
Pekanbaru
Batam
Palembang
Pontianak
JAKARTA
Yogyakarta
Surabaya
Banjarmasin
Balikpapan
Samarinda
Tarakan
Palu
Pare Pare
Makassar
Manado
Luwuk
Kota Ternate
Kota Ambon
Sorong
Manokwari
Kota Biak
Jayapura
Wamena
Timika
Denpasar
Mataram
Bima
Labuanbajo
Tambulaka
Maumere
Kalabahi
Kupang

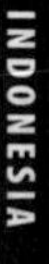

Bicycle

Basic bicycles can be hired in all major centres for around 15,000Rp per day from hotels, travel agents and stores; though decent mountain bikes are rare except in Bali. The tropical heat, heavy traffic and poor road conditions make long-distance travel a challenge, but a few hardy souls manage it. Consult the 'on your bike' cycling forum at http://thorntree.lonelyplanet.com for more inspiration.

Boat

Sumatra, Java, Bali and Nusa Tenggara are connected by ferries. Pelni, the national passenger line, covers just about everywhere else.

PELNI SHIPS

Pelni (www.pelni.co.id) has a fleet of large vessels linking all of Indonesia's major ports and the majority of the archipelago's outlying areas. Pelni's website is rarely updated and seldom works, so it's best to check schedules well in advance with a good travel agent.

Pelni ships have four cabin classes, plus *kelas ekonomi*. Class I is luxury-plus with only two beds per cabin (and is often more expensive than using a low-cost airline); Class IV has eight beds to a cabin. *Ekonomi* is extremely basic, but is air-conditioned and mattresses can be rented.

You can book tickets up to two weeks ahead; it's best to book at least a few days in advance.

OTHER SHIPS

As an island nation, Indonesia has dozens of regular boat services connecting ports in every part of the archipelago. However, schedules are often very vague so be prepared to hang around until something rusty turns up. Be warned that because most vessels are ancient and routinely overcrowded, safety standards are somewhere between poor and appalling – though most people make it across the archipelago in one piece of course.

It's also possible to make some more unusual sea trips. Old Makassar schooners still ply Indonesian waters and it may be possible to travel on them from Sulawesi to other islands, particularly Java.

Bus

Most Indonesians use buses to get around, so there is a huge variety of services, with everything from air-con deluxe buses with TV, toilets and karaoke that speed across Java and Sumatra to *trek* (trucks) with wooden seats that rumble up the dirt roads of Flores. Local buses are the cheapest; they leave when full and stop on request – on the outer islands this is often your only choice.

Minibuses often do shorter runs, while in Bali air-con tourist buses ply popular routes.

Car & Motorcycle

Self-drive jeeps can be hired for as little as 110,000Rp per day with limited insurance in Bali, but become increasingly more expensive and hard to come by the further you get from tourist areas. If you're not happy negotiating Indonesia's chaotic roads, a Toyota Kijang with driver can usually be hired for between 300,000Rp and 500,000Rp per day; the more remote areas tend to be the most expensive.

Motorcycles and scooters (usually 90cc to 125cc) can be hired across Indonesia for 25,000Rp to 50,000Rp per day. Be sure to get a crash helmet, as wearing one is supposed to be compulsory.

Hitching

Hitching is possible, but cannot be advised. Drivers may well ask for as much as the bus would cost – maybe more – and safety is obviously a concern.

Local Transport

Public minibuses (most commonly called bemo, but also known as *opelet, mikrolet, colt* and numerous other names) are everywhere. Bemo run standard routes, but can also be chartered like a taxi.

Cycle rickshaws are called becak, while *bajaj* are Indonesian túk-túks: three-wheelers that carry two passengers (three at a squeeze) and are powered by rasping two-stroke engines. In quieter towns, you may find horse-drawn carts, variously called *dokar, cidomo, andong* and *ben hur*.

An extremely handy form of transport is the *ojek* (motorcycle taxi); expect to pay about 2500Rp to 5000Rp for a short ride. Most towns have taxis and the drivers sometimes even use their *argo* (meters).

Train

Java has a good railway service running the length of the island (see p166). There is also an extremely limited rail service in Sumatra. Visit www.infoka.kereta-api.com (in Indonesian) for times and fares.

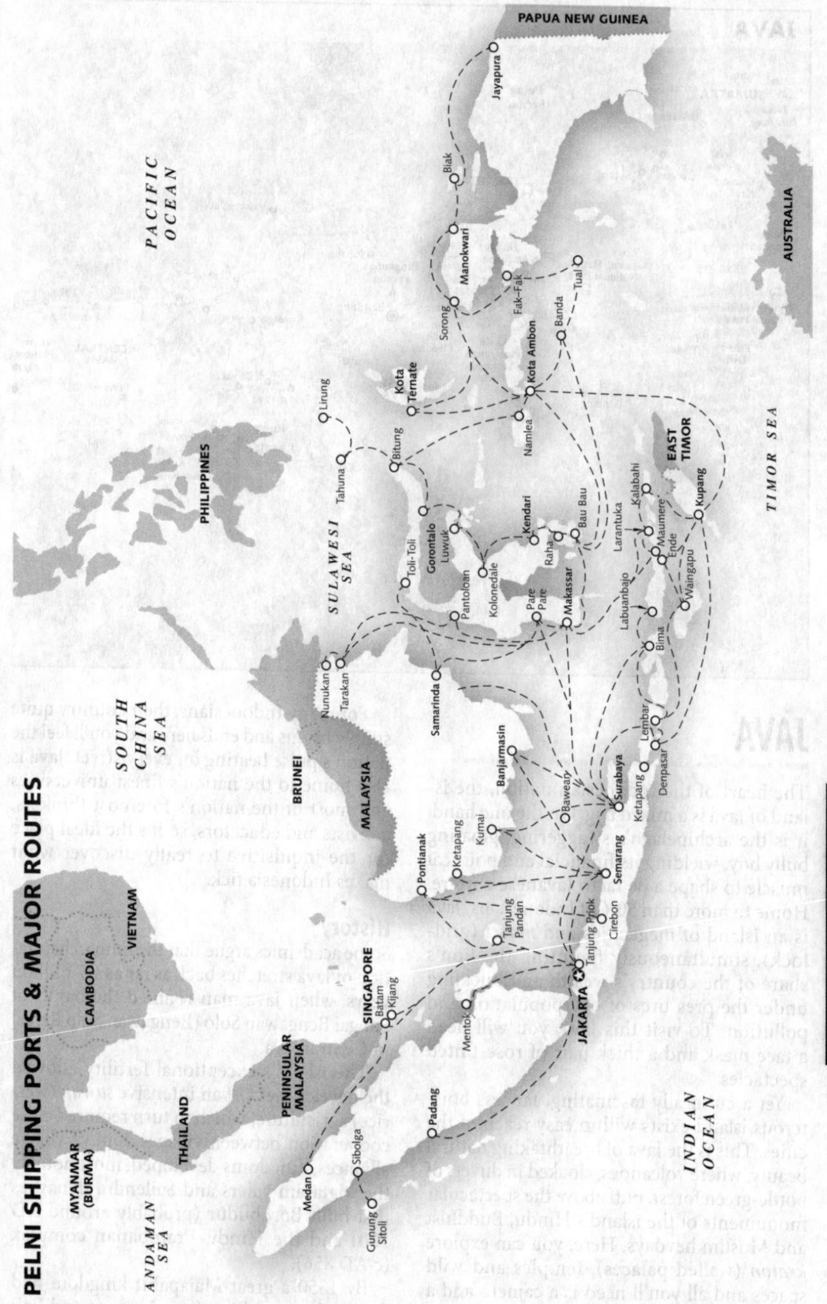
PELNI SHIPPING PORTS & MAJOR ROUTES
MYANMAR (BURMA)
THAILAND
CAMBODIA
VIETNAM
PENINSULAR MALAYSIA
SINGAPORE
MALAYSIA
BRUNEI
PHILIPPINES
PAPUA NEW GUINEA
AUSTRALIA
EAST TIMOR
ANDAMAN SEA
SOUTH CHINA SEA
SULAWESI SEA
PACIFIC OCEAN
INDIAN OCEAN
TIMOR SEA
Medan
Sibolga
Gunung Sitoli
Padang
Batam
Kijang
Mentok
JAKARTA
Tanjung Priok
Cirebon
Tanjung Pandan
Pontianak
Ketapang
Kumai
Semarang
Baweam
Surabaya
Banjarmasin
Ketapang
Denpasar
Lembar
Samarinda
Nunukan
Tarakan
Bima
Labuanbajo
Waingapu
Ende
Maumere
Larantuka
Kalabahi
Kupang
Pantoloan
Toli-Toli
Pare Pare
Makassar
Kolonedale
Luwuk
Gorontalo
Raha
Kendari
Bau Bau
Tahuna
Bitung
Lirung
Kota Ternate
Namlea
Kota Ambon
Banda
Tual
Fak-Fak
Sorong
Manokwari
Biak
Jayapura

INDONESIA

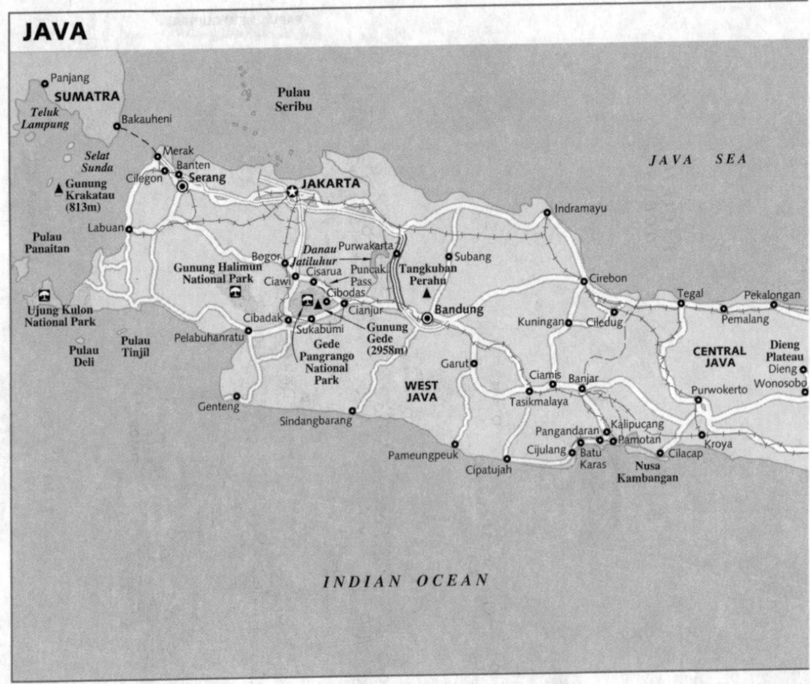

JAVA

The heart of the Indonesian nation, the island of Java is a mixed bag. On the one hand, it is the archipelago's swaggering, gloating bully boy, wielding its financial and political muscle to shape a de facto Javanese empire. Home to more than 50% of Indonesians, Java is an island of megacities and *macet* (gridlock), simultaneously flaunting the lion's share of the country's wealth and buckling under the pressures of overpopulation and pollution. To visit this Java, you will need a face mask and a thick pair of rose-tinted spectacles.

Yet a culturally fascinating, far less boisterous island exists within easy reach of the cities. This is the Java of breathtaking natural beauty, where volcanoes, cloaked in duvets of bottle-green forest, puff above the spectacular monuments of the island's Hindu, Buddhist and Muslim heydays. Here, you can explore *kraton* (walled palaces), temples and wild spaces and all you'll need is a camera and a sense of adventure.

For many Indonesians, their country quite simply begins and ends here and you'll feel the nation's pulse beating on every street. Java is also home to the nation's finest universities and most of the nation's foremost thinkers, activists and educators, so it's the ideal place for the inquisitive to really discover what makes Indonesia tick.

History

Some academics argue that the human habitation of Java stretches back as far as 1.7 million years, when Java man roamed the banks of Sungai Bengawan Solo (Bengawan Solo River) in Central Java.

The island's exceptional fertility allowed the development of an intensive *sawah* (wet-rice) agriculture, which in turn required close cooperation between villages. Out of village alliances, kingdoms developed, most notably the Mataram rulers and Sailendra dynasties that built Borobudur (probably around AD 780) and the Hindu Prambanan complex (c AD 856).

By 1350 a great Majapahit kingdom had emerged, controlling Java, Madura and Bali

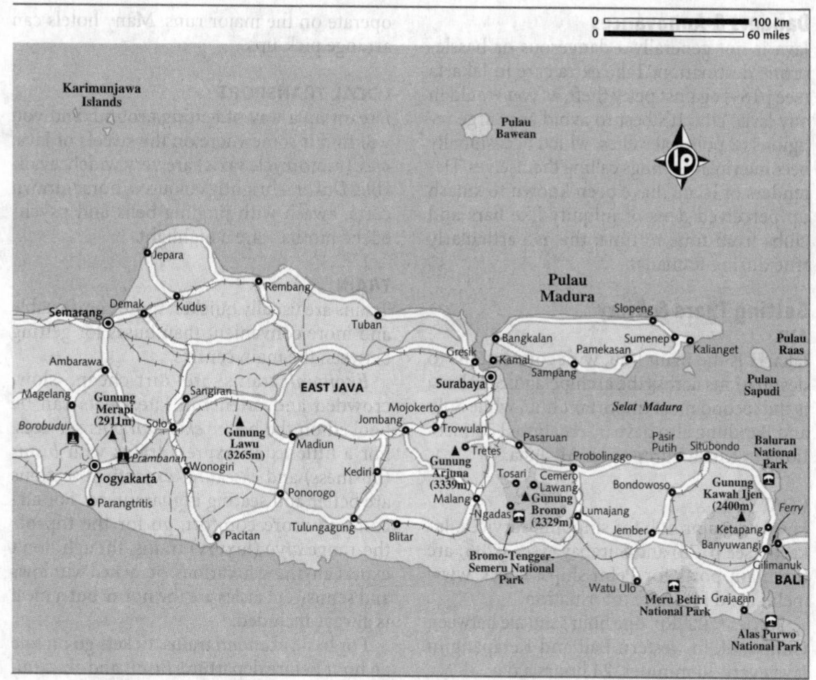

under the leader Hayam Wuruk. By the 15th and 16th centuries, Islamic principalities were emerging, the greatest centred in Mataram, and holding sway over central and eastern Java. Intense regional rivalries hindered Javanese efforts to confront the invading Dutch, and most of the island had fallen to the colonists by the end of the 18th century – although principalities in Solo and Yogyakarta survived until the foundation of the Indonesian republic.

After independence, Java became the centre of the new Indonesia. And that has led to resentment; to a large extent the rebellions of the Sumatrans, Minahasans and Ambonese in the 1950s and 1960s were reactions to Javanese domination of the new country. Furthermore, the abortive communist coup of 1965 started in Jakarta, and some of its most dramatic and disastrous events took place in Java as thousands of communist sympathisers were massacred. During Soeharto's rule, Java benefited as it became the most industrialised part of the nation, its businesses dominating the economy and concentrating wealth in the island (although this remained largely in the hands of a privileged few who had close links to the president).

Java continues to be the powerhouse of Indonesia, receiving the lion's share of foreign investment. Bali excepted, it's the most cosmopolitan corner of the nation. Each major city has glitzy malls that rival anything in the West, full of latte-sipping students and nightclubs where DJs spin cutting-edge electronica to designer-clad dancers.

But across the tracks in the poor backstreets another Java exists, where radical Islam thrives and youths taught in *madrassah* (Islamic schools) vent their fury at Western imperialism in Iraq and Afghanistan. Some have taken it far further than street protests, exporting a twisted vision of jihad to fight Christians in Sulawesi and bomb Bali and Jakarta. These extremists don't enjoy widespread support in Java, and opposition to their terrorist agenda has strengthened in the last few years, as many of their intended targets have killed many more Indonesians than Westerners.

Dangers & Annoyances

Java is not generally a dangerous or hassle-prone destination. Take extra care in Jakarta (see p169) against petty theft, as you would in any large city. It's best to avoid any large religious or political rallies, which occasionally become violent. Thugs calling themselves 'Defenders of Islam' have been known to smash up perceived dens of iniquity like bars and clubs from time to time; this is particularly true during Ramadan.

Getting There & Away

AIR

Jakarta is the main hub, with connections to destinations across the archipelago. Surabaya is the second most important hub, while Solo and Bandung also have international connections to Kuala Lumpur on Air Asia.

BOAT

Java is a major hub for shipping services. Jakarta (see p176) and Surabaya (see p206) are the main ports for Pelni ships; check www.pelni.co.id for more information.

Ferries (7000Rp, one hour) shuttle between Gilimanuk in western Bali and Ketapang in Java every 30 minutes, 24 hours a day.

Between Merak in Java and Bakauheni at the southern tip of Sumatra, ferries (13,000Rp, two hours) operate every 30 minutes, 24 hours a day.

Getting Around

AIR

As more budget airlines open their doors, flying around Java is becoming an increasingly attractive proposition. Jakarta and Surabaya are Java's main airports, but Yogyajarkta, Solo, Bandung and Semarang are also serviced by flights.

BUS

Bus travel is often slow and nerve-racking; night buses are a little faster. Trains are usually better for the long hauls, but bus departures are usually more frequent.

Public buses, 'cooled' by a flow of sooty air from an open window, are very frequent but they also stop for passengers every five minutes. Better air-con buses also run the major routes and are well worth paying the extra 25% or so they cost.

Small minibuses run the shortest routes. *Travel* (door-to-door air-con minibuses) also operate on the major runs. Many hotels can arrange pick-ups.

LOCAL TRANSPORT

Dream up a way of getting around, and you will find it somewhere on the streets of Java; *ojek* (motorcycle taxis) are very widely available. *Dokar* – brightly coloured, horse-drawn carts, awash with jingling bells and psychedelic motifs – are a highlight.

TRAIN

Trains are usually quicker, more comfortable and more convenient than buses for getting between the main centres.

Ekonomi trains are dirt-cheap, slow, crowded and often run late. Seats can be booked on the better *ekonomi plus* services. For a little extra, express trains with *bisnis* (business) and *eksekutif* (executive) sections are better and seating is guaranteed. For air-con and more comfort, go for the top-of-the-range *argo* (luxury) trains, though don't expect anything luxurious – cracked windows and semiswept aisles are the norm, but a meal is always included.

For basic *ekonomi* trains, tickets go on sale an hour before departure. *Bisnis* and *eksekutif* trains can be booked weeks ahead, and the main stations have efficient, computerised booking offices for *eksekutif* trains.

Try to book at least a day in advance, or several days beforehand for travel on public holidays and long weekends.

For details of times and prices, check out www.infoka.kereta-api.com.

JAKARTA

☎ 021 / pop 8.9 million

America can keep its big apple; Indonesia's capital was never going to be an easy fruit to swallow. Dubbed the 'Big Durian', Jakarta is a chaotic landscape of freeways, skyscrapers, slums and traffic jams built on a plain that floods (often to biblical proportions) every wet season (see boxed text, opposite). A vast waiting lounge for those queuing up for their share of Indonesia's financial stir-fry, this is a fast-paced city of function rather than form; somewhere for the rich to forge political alliances and for the rest to escape a humdrum life hunched over a rice paddy. Tourists, as a result, are at a premium.

But just like the big fruit itself, Jakarta rewards those who are prepared to hold

WATERWORLD

In February 2007 Jakarta experienced the worst floods in living memory as around 60% of the city was left under water, and in parts of Cawang, East Jakarta, levels reached 6m. Around 450,000 people were displaced from their homes and 85 lost their lives. Entire slum areas built along river banks were washed away.

The reasons for the annual deluge are complex, but what's certain is that environmental malpractices and unchecked construction are key factors. Much of Greater Jakarta (population around 14 million) has been built over a floodplain – the city is crossed by 13 rivers – and designated green belt. Of the 218 lakes in the Jakarta area present in 1990, only a quarter remained by 2007; many filled in and built over by apartment complexes and shopping malls. The city authorities reckon Jakarta should have two million absorption wells, yet it actually has less than 19,000.

A masterplan for a flood-prevention network of drainage canals and sluice gates that was drawn up during the Dutch era (when the city's population was a million or so) is still only half-built, and will take decades to complete.

So if you're visiting Jakarta in the wet season, pack your raincoat and rubber boots.

their noses and dig in. Pull back the concrete curtain and Indonesia's capital contains elements from the four corners of the archipelago – Batak taxi drivers, musicians from Maluku, religious radicals from Solo and gangsters from Flores – with all the cultural traits and culinary treats that a nation of 250 million has to offer. From the steamy streets of Chinatown, through the swanky expat suburbs, to the city's decadent nightclubs, Jakarta is unique, stuffed with all the excesses, contradictions and wonders of Indonesian life.

Lacking a coherent centre, Jakarta is a tough city to explore. The old city around Kota offers a clutch of museums and sights, however, as does the area around Freedom Sq, which is capped with Soekarno's suspiciously phallic national monument. But sometimes it is best just to accept Jakarta for what it is, and explore the restaurants, bars, clubs and shopping malls that the city does best.

Orientation

Metropolitan Jakarta sprawls 28km from the docks to the southern suburbs. Soekarno's national monument (Monas) in Lapangan Merdeka (Freedom Sq) is an excellent central landmark. North of the monument is the older part of Jakarta, which includes Chinatown, the former Dutch area of Kota and the old port of Sunda Kelapa. Tanjung Priok, the main harbour, is several kilometres further east. The sprawling modern suburbs of Jakarta are south of the monument.

Jl Thamrin is the main north–south street of the new city and has Jakarta's big hotels and banks. A couple of blocks east along Jl Kebon Sirih Raya is Jl Jaksa, the cheap accommodation centre of Jakarta.

Information

BOOKSHOPS

Periplus (Map p168; ☎ 718 7070; Level 3, Plaza Senayan, Jl Asia Afrika; 🕑 9am-7pm) Has a wide range of English-language titles, including Lonely Planet guidebooks and Periplus maps.

QB World Books (Map p168; ☎ 718 0818; Jl Kemang Raya 17) Sells English-language literature and magazines.

CULTURAL CENTRES

Australian Cultural Centre (Map p168; ☎ 2550 5555; Australian Embassy, Jl Rasuna Said Kav C15-16)

British Council (Map p168; ☎ 252 4115; www.britishcouncil.org/indonesia.htm; S Widjojo Centre, Jl Sudirman 71)

GETTING INTO TOWN

Soekarno-Hatta International Airport is 35km northwest of the city. It's about an hour away via a toll road (up to two hours during rush hour).

There's a Damri bus service (15,000Rp) every 30 minutes from 3am to 7pm between the airport and Gambir train station.

Alternatively, a metered taxi costs about 130,000Rp, including the airport service charge and toll-road charges. These should be organised through the official booths in the arrival terminal; avoid the freelance drivers outside for safety reasons.

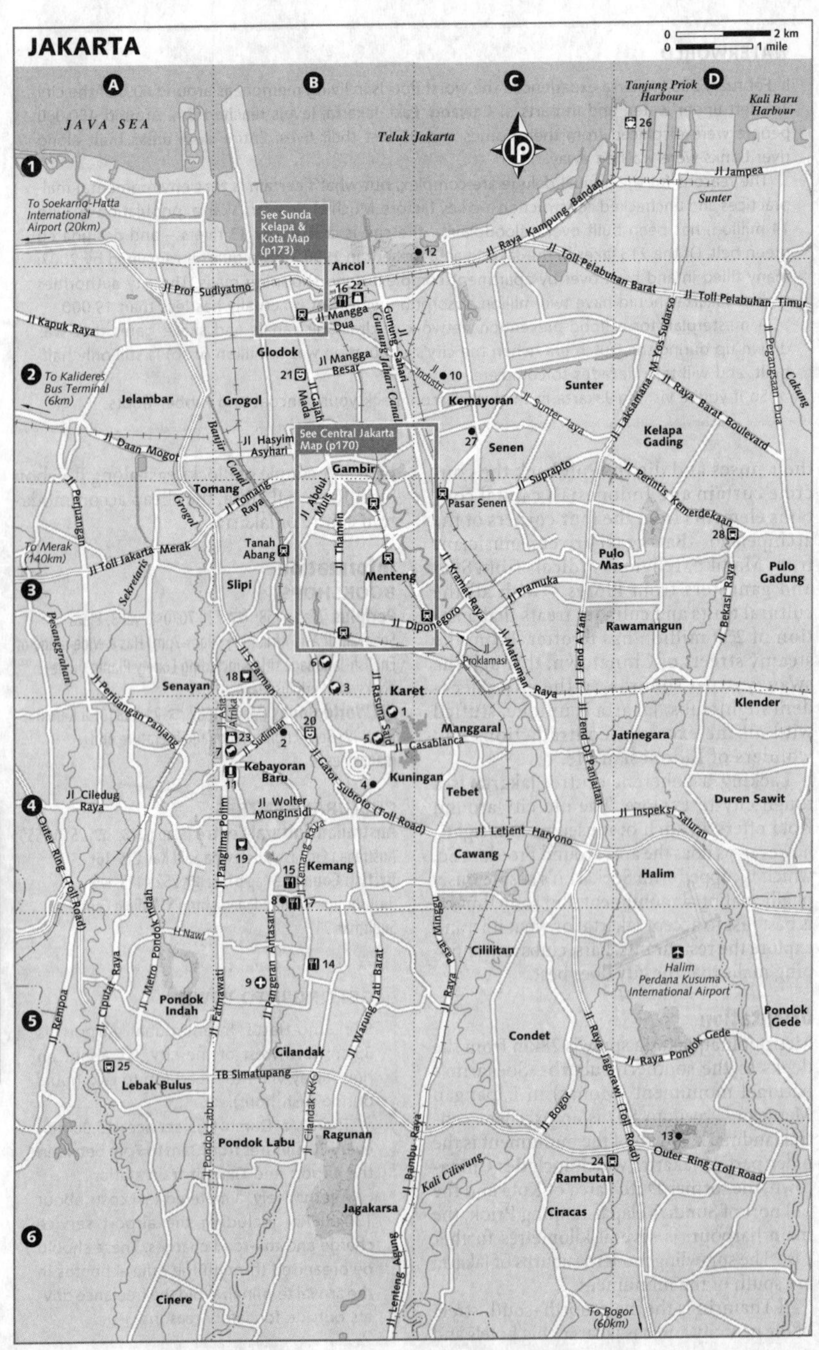

JAKARTA
JAVA SEA
Teluk Jakarta
Tanjung Priok Harbour
Kali Baru Harbour
To Soekarno-Hatta International Airport (20km)
See Sunda Kelapa & Kota Map (p173)
See Central Jakarta Map (p170)
To Kalideres Bus Terminal (6km)
To Merak (140km)
To Bogor (60km)
Ancol
Glodok
Jelambar
Grogol
Kemayoran
Sunter
Kelapa Gading
Senen
Gambir
Tomang
Tanah Abang
Slipi
Menteng
Pasar Senen
Pulo Mas
Pulo Gadung
Rawamangun
Senayan
Karet
Manggaral
Jatinegara
Klender
Kebayoran Baru
Kuningan
Tebet
Duren Sawit
Cawang
Halim
Kemang
Cililitan
Halim Perdana Kusuma International Airport
Pondok Indah
Condet
Pondok Gede
Cilandak
Lebak Bulus
Pondok Labu
Ragunan
Rambutan
Ciracas
Jagakarsa
Cinere
INDONESIA

Erasmus Huis (Map p168; ☎ 524 1069; www.erasmushuis.or.id; Jl Rasuna Said Kav S-3) This Dutch centre has classical music and jazz performances and screens films.

EMERGENCY

Fire (☎ 113)
Police (☎ 110)
Medical help (☎ 118, 119)
Tourist police (Map p172; ☎ 566000; Jl Wahid Hasyim)

INTERNET ACCESS

Access typically costs 5000Rp to 10,000Rp per hour in Jakarta.

Virtual Net (Map p172; Jl Jaksa 33; 8am-10pm)

INFORMATION	
Australian Cultural Centre	(see 1)
Australian Embassy	1 B4
British Council	2 B4
Canadian Embassy	3 B3
Dutch Embassy	(see 4)
Erasmus Huis	4 B4
Malaysian Embassy	5 B4
New Zealand Embassy	6 B3
Papua New Guinean Embassy	7 B4
Periplus	(see 23)
QB World Books	8 B4
Singaporean Embassy	(see 4)
SOS Medika	9 B5
SIGHTS & ACTIVITIES	
Jakarta Fair Grounds	10 C2
Pizza Man Statue	11 B4
Purna Bhakti Pertiwi Museum	(see 13)
Taman Impian Jaya Ancol	12 C1
Taman Mini Indonesia Indah	13 D6
EATING	
Izzi Pizza	14 B5
Kemang Food Festival	15 B4
Pasar Pagi	16 B2
Place	17 B4
DRINKING	
Bugils	18 B3
My Bar	19 B4
Top Gun	(see 19)
ENTERTAINMENT	
Embassy	(see 18)
Retro	20 B4
Stadium	21 B2
SHOPPING	
Pasar Pagi Mangga Dua	22 B2
Pasar Seni	(see 12)
Plaza Senayan	23 B4
TRANSPORT	
Kampung Rambutan Bus Terminal	24 C6
Lebak Bulus Bus Terminal	25 A5
Pelni Passenger Terminal	26 D1
Pelni Ticket Office	27 C2
Pulo Gadung Bus Terminal	28 D3

INTERNET RESOURCES

Jakarta.go.id (www.jakarta.go.id) The Jakarta City Government's website.
Jakweb.com (www.jakweb.com) Has a useful diary of cultural events.
Living in Indonesia (www.expat.or.id) Includes a comprehensive guide to Jakarta.

MEDIA

The daily *Jakarta Post* (www.thejakartapost.com; 5000Rp) newspaper offers good balanced coverage of the city's news stories. The glossy *Jakarta Kini* (www.jakartajavakini.com; 20,000Rp) has features, reviews and entertainment listings, while *The Beat* deals mainly with bars and clubs.

MEDICAL SERVICES

SOS Medika (Map p168; ☎ 750 6001; Jl Puri Sakti 10, Kemang; 24hr)

MONEY

Hundreds of banks and ATMs are spread across town, including the following:

Bank Mandiri (Map p172; Jl Wahid Hasyim)
BII (Map p170; Plaza Indonesia, Jl Thamrin) Also has an ATM.
BNI (Map p172; Jl Kebon Sirih Raya)

POST

Main post office (Map p170; Jl Gedung Kesenian 1; 8am-7pm Mon-Fri, to 1pm Sat)

TELEPHONE

Wartel Bhumi Bhakti (Map p172; Jl Wahid Hasyim; 10am-10pm)

TOURIST INFORMATION

Jakarta Visitor Information (Map p172; ☎ 315 4094; www.jakarta.go.id; Jakarta Theatre Bldg, Jl Wahid Hasyim 9; 9am-5pm Mon-Fri, to 2pm Sat) Offers plenty of leaflets and an excellent colour map that shows the city's busway routes. There's also a desk at the airport. Both branches have English-speaking staff.

TRAVEL AGENCIES

24-Hour Tickets (Map p172; ☎ 3192 3173; Jl Haji Agus Salim 57A)
Robertur (Map p172; ☎ 314 2926; Jl Jaksa 20B)

Dangers & Annoyances

Considering its size and the scale of poverty here, Jakarta is generally a safe city and security incidents are extremely rare. That said, you should be careful late at night in Glodok

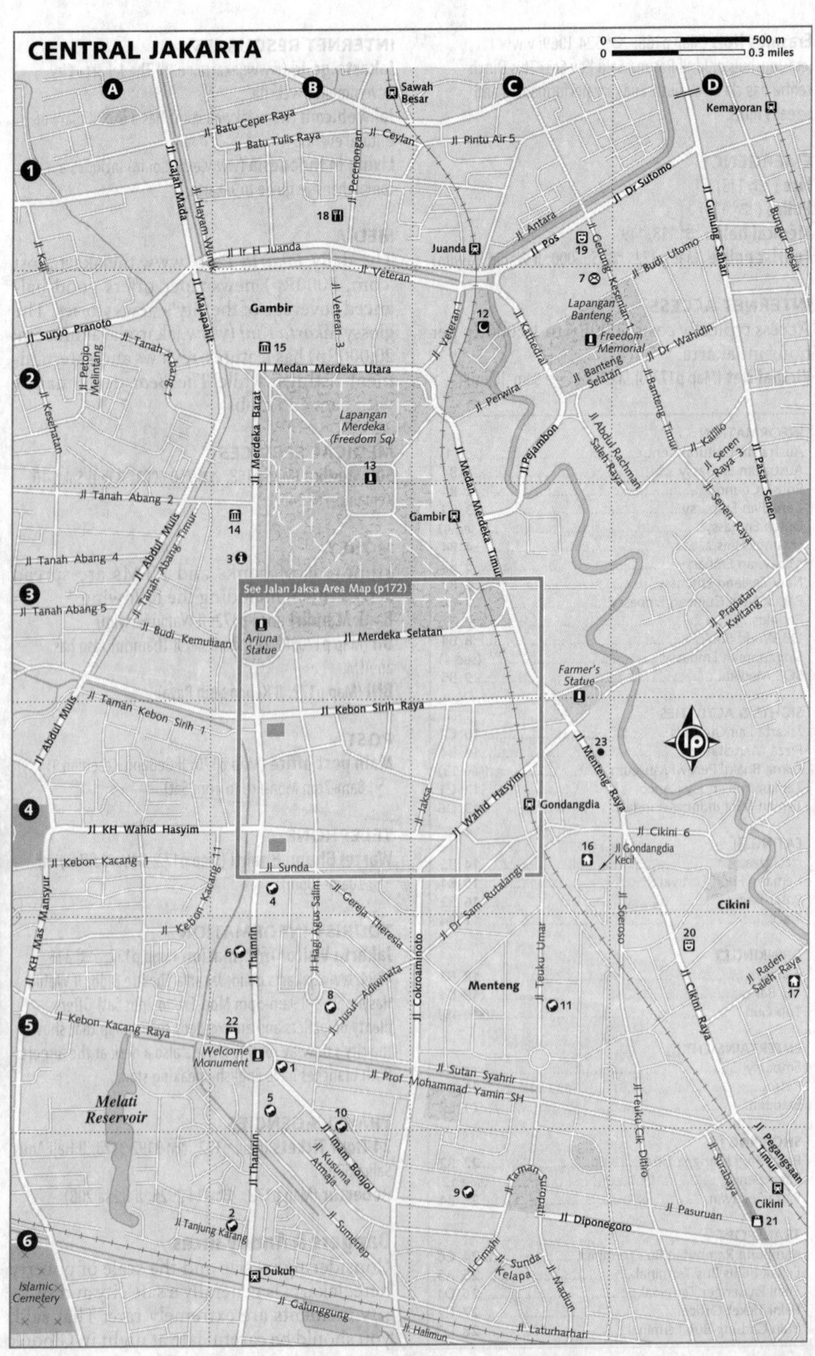
CENTRAL JAKARTA
0 500 m
0 0.3 miles
A
B
C
D
1
2
3
4
5
6
Sawah Besar
Kemayoran
Jl Batu Ceper Raya
Jl Batu Tulis Raya
Jl Pecenongan
Jl Ceylan
Jl Pintu Air 5
Jl Gajah Mada
Jl Hayam Wuruk
Jl Dr Sutomo
Jl Gunung Sahari
Jl Bungur Besar
18
Jl Antara
Jl Pos
Jl Gedung Kesenian 1
19
Jl Kaji
Jl Ir H Juanda
Juanda
Jl Budi Utomo
Jl Veteran
7
Jl Majapahit
Gambir
Jl Veteran 3
Jl Veteran 1
12
Lapangan Banteng
Jl Suryo Pranoto
Jl Tanah Abang 1
15
Jl Kathedral
Freedom Memorial
Jl Dr Wahidin
Jl Petojo Melintang
Jl Medan Merdeka Utara
Jl Banteng Selatan
Jl Kesehatan
Jl Perwira
Lapangan Merdeka (Freedom Sq)
Jl Banteng Timur
Jl Pejambon
Jl Abdul Rachman Saleh Raya
Jl Kalilio
Jl Senen Raya 3
Jl Pasar Senen
Jl Merdeka Barat
Jl Medan Merdeka Timur
13
Jl Tanah Abang 2
Gambir
Jl Senen Raya
14
Jl Abdul Muis
Jl Tanah Abang Timur
Jl Tanah Abang 4
3
See Jalan Jaksa Area Map (p172)
Jl Tanah Abang 5
Jl Prapatan
Jl Kwitang
Jl Budi Kemuliaan
Arjuna Statue
Jl Merdeka Selatan
Farmer's Statue
Jl Taman Kebon Sirih 1
Jl Kebon Sirih Raya
Jl Abdul Muis
23
Jl Menteng Raya
Jl Jaksa
Jl Wahid Hasyim
Gondangdia
Jl KH Wahid Hasyim
Jl Cikini 6
16
Jl Gondangdia Kecil
Jl Kebon Kacang 1
Jl Sunda
Jl Kebon Kacang 11
4
Jl Haji Agus Salim
Jl Gereja Theresia
Jl Dr Sam Rutalangi
Jl Teuku Umar
Jl Soeroso
Cikini
Jl KH Mas Mansyur
6
Jl Thamrin
Jl Cokroaminoto
20
Jl Jusuf Adiwinata
Menteng
Jl Raden Saleh Raya
17
8
11
Jl Cikini Raya
Jl Kebon Kacang Raya
22
Welcome Monument
1
Jl Sutan Syahrir
Jl Prof Mohammad Yamin SH
Melati Reservoir
5
10
Jl Teuku Cik Ditiro
Jl Pegangsaan Timur
Jl Imam Bonjol
Jl Kusuma Atmaja
Jl Surabaya
Jl Thamrin
Jl Taman Suropati
9
Cikini
Jl Pasuruan
Jl Diponegoro
21
2
Jl Tanjung Karang
Jl Sumenep
Jl Cimahi
Jl Sunda Kelapa
Jl Madiun
Dukuh
Islamic Cemetery
Jl Galunggung
Jl Halimun
Jl Laturharhari

INFORMATION	
BII Bank	(see 22)
British Embassy	1 B5
Brunei Embassy	2 B6
Directorate General of Tourism	3 B3
French Embassy	4 B4
German Embassy	5 B5
Japanese Embassy	6 B5
Main Post Office	7 C2
Myanmar Embassy	8 B5
Philippines Embassy	9 C6
Thai Embassy	10 B5
Vietnamese Embassy	11 C5
SIGHTS & ACTIVITIES	
Mesjid Istiqlal	12 C2
National History Museum	(see 13)
National Monument (Monas)	13 B2
National Museum	14 B3
Presidental Palace	15 B2
SLEEPING	
Gondia International Guesthouse	16 C4
Yannie International Guesthouse	17 D5
EATING	
Night Warung	18 B1
ENTERTAINMENT	
Gedung Kesenian Jakarta	19 C1
Taman Ismail Marzuki (TIM)	20 D5
SHOPPING	
Flea Market	21 D6
Plaza Indonesia	22 B5
TRANSPORT	
Menara Buana Surya	23 C4

and Kota, and only use reputable taxi companies (p178) – muggings do occasionally occur. Keep your eyes open on buses and trains, which are a favourite haunt of pickpockets. It's wise to steer clear of political and religious demonstrations, which may draw anti-Western militants.

Dengue fever outbreaks occur in the wet season, so come armed with mosquito repellent. See p938 for more on dengue fever.

Sights & Activities

KOTA

Jakarta's crumbling historic heart is Kota, home to the remnants of the Dutch capital of Batavia. **Taman Fatahillah** (Map p173), the old town square, features cracked cobblestones and lonely postcard vendors as well as some fine colonial buildings and some ho-hum museums. From Jl Jaksa take the train (2000Rp) to Kota station from Gondangdia station; or, by bus, a northbound Koridor 1 service from the Sarinah busway on Jl Thamrin.

By far the finest way to relive the colonial experience is to take a drink in the magnificent Café Batavia (p175) and then explore Kota's quirkier sights on foot. The old Portuguese cannon **Si Jagur** (Mr Fertility; Map p173; Taman Fatahillah) was believed to be a cure for barrenness because of its suggestive clenched fist, and women sat astride it in the hope of bearing children.

Nearby, **Gereja Sion** (Map p173; Jl Pangeran Jayakarta 1; dawn-dusk) is the oldest remaining church in Jakarta. It was built in 1695 for the 'black Portuguese' brought to Batavia as slaves and given their freedom if they joined the Dutch Reformed Church.

More fine Dutch architecture lines the grotty Kali Besar canal, including the **Toko Merah** (Map p173; Jl Kali Besar Barat), formerly the home of Governor General van Imhoff. Further north, the last remaining Dutch drawbridge, the **Chicken Market Bridge** (Map p173), spans the canal.

The area's museums and their dusty exhibits are decidedly disappointing. Check out the **Wayang Museum** (Map p173; ☎ 692 9560; Jl Pintu Besar Utara 27; admission 2000Rp; 9am-1.30pm Tue-Fri & Sun, to 12.30pm Sat) for its shadow puppet performances (Sundays at 10am). At the **Jakarta History Museum** (Map p173; ☎ 692 9101; Taman Fatahillah 2; admission 2000Rp; 9am-1.30pm Tue-Fri & Sun, to 12.30pm Sat), there's little but colonial bric-a-brac; the fine old (1710) City Hall building, which houses the museum, is the real star.

To the south of Kota, **Glodok** (Map p173) is a run-down Chinese district of traditional markets and infamous nightclubs that suffered very badly in the 1998 riots. These days most Jakartans favour air-conditioned shopping malls, but a stroll through Glodok's steamy, scruffy lanes past spitting street kitchens will provide plenty of colour for the day's blog entry. Avoid dark side streets at night in this zone.

SUNDA KELAPA

Among the hubbub, floating debris and oil slicks, the old Dutch **port** (Map p173; admission 1000Rp) is still used by magnificent Buginese *pinisi* (fishing boats), their cargo unloaded by teams of porters walking along wobbly gangplanks. It's a 1km walk from Taman Fatahillah, or take one of the area's unique push-bike taxis known as *ojek sepeda* (2500Rp).

Close by are the early-morning **Pasar Ikan** (Fish Market; Map p173; Jl Pasar Ikan; 6am-2pm) and

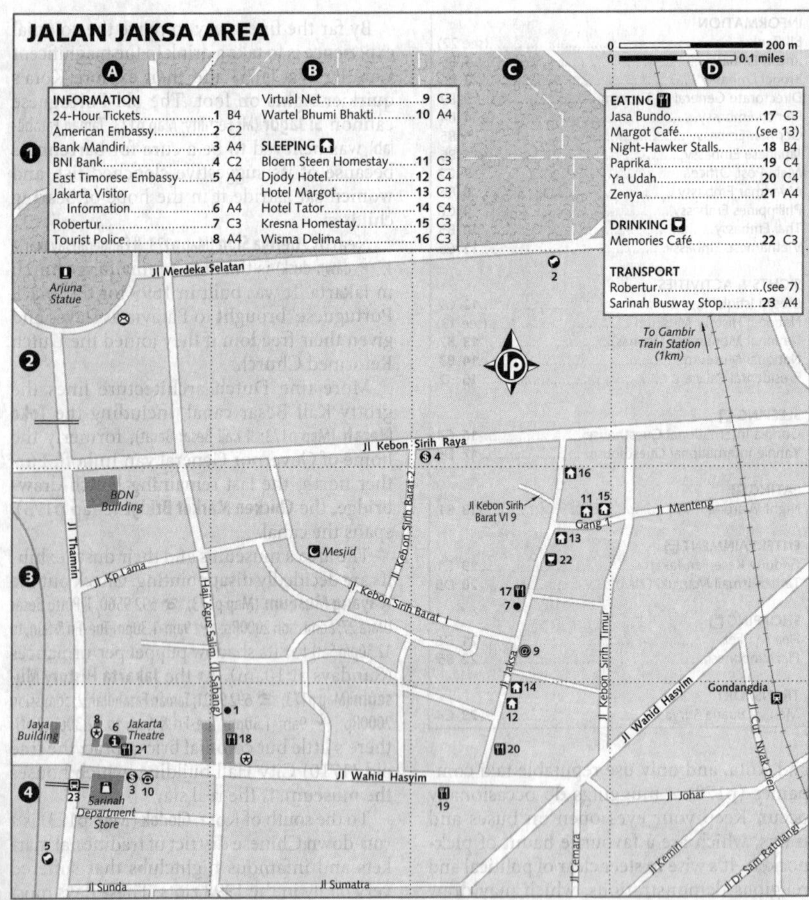

Museum Bahari (Maritime Museum; Map p173; ☎ 669 3409; Jl Pasar Ikan 1; admission 2000Rp; 9am-1.30pm Sun-Fri, to 12.30pm Sat), located in one of the old Dutch East India Company warehouses (1645), which exhibits some fine photographs, and sailing boats from across Indonesia.

LAPANGAN MERDEKA

Soekarno attempted to tame Jakarta by giving it a central space, **Lapangan Merdeka** (Freedom Sq; Map p170), and topping it with a gigantic monument to his machismo, the **National Monument** (Monas; Map p170; ☎ 384 0451; admission 6000Rp; 8.30am-5pm Mon-Fri, to 7pm Sat & Sun). The towering, 132m-high column, capped with a gilded flame, has been ungraciously dubbed 'Soekarno's last erection'; whiz up the shaft for a shot of the city. The **National History Museum** (Map p170; 8.30am-5pm Mon-Fri, 8.30am-7pm Sat & Sun), in the base, tells the story of Indonesia's independence struggle in 48 dramatic, overstated dioramas. Admission is included in the Monas entry fee.

Many of Soekarno's triumphalist monuments have acquired derogatory nicknames over the years: the guy at Kebayoran roundabout holding the flaming dish is now **'Pizza Man'** (Map p168).

INDONESIAN NATIONAL MUSEUM

A 15-minute walk from Jl Jaksa, the **National Museum** (Map p170; ☎ 386 8171; Jl Merdeka Barat 12; admission 750Rp; 8.30am-2.30pm Tue-Thu & Sun, to 11.30am Fri, to 1.30pm Sat) is something of an oddity in

Jakarta, being a museum that is genuinely worth visiting. There are excellent displays of Han ceramics and ancient Hindu statuary, magnificent *kris* (traditional dagger) handles studded with rubies, and a huge relief map on which you can pick out all those volcanoes you plan to climb. The museum is also known as Gedung Gajah (Elephant House) on account of the bronze elephant outside, donated by the king of Thailand in 1871.

The **Indonesian Heritage Society** (☎ 572 5870) conducts free tours of the museum in English every Tuesday and Thursday at 9.30am.

TAMAN MINI INDONESIA INDAH

A vast theme park built to celebrate the nation, **Taman Mini Indonesia Indah** (Map p168; ☎ 545 4545; www.jakweb.com/tmii; TMII Pintu 1; admission 6000Rp; ⌚ 8am-5pm) includes traditional houses from (most) Indonesian provinces set around a lagoon (boats are available to hire), an IMAX theatre and a bird park. There's also an assortment of museums, including an insect house full of alarming-looking specimens, and, best of all, the air-conditioned **Purna Bhakti Pertiwi Museum** (⌚ 8am-5pm), which houses the stupendously opulent (and downright gaudy) gifts given to Soeharto, including a 5m ship carved entirely from jade.

To get here take the Koridor 7 bus from Kampung Melayu to Kampung Rambutan bus station and then hop on a T15 metro-mini; it's about an hour from central Jakarta.

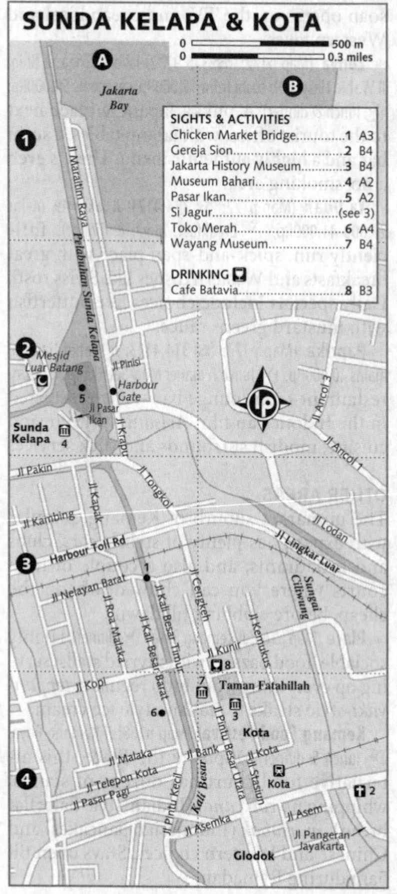

OTHER ATTRACTIONS

Taman Impian Jaya Ancol (Map p168; ☎ 640 6777; www.ancol.co.id; admission 10,000Rp; ⌚ 10am-10pm) is a huge waterfront amusement complex with an oceanarium, art market and an Indonesian-style Disneyland (entrance an additional 70,000Rp). To get there, take a 64 or 65 bus (1500Rp) from Kota station.

To the north of Lapangan Merdeka you can stroll past the gleaming white **Presidential Palace** (Map p170; Jl Medan Merdeka Utara) – beware of the jumpy armed guards. To the northeast is the vast **Mesjid Istiqlal** (Map p170; Jl Veteran 1; ⌚ dawn-dusk), one of the grandest mosques in Southeast Asia.

Festivals & Events

Java Jazz Festival (www.javajazzfestival.com) If you are here in March, keep an eye out for this festival.

Jakarta Anniversary On 22 June. Marks the establishment of the city by Gunungjati back in 1527, and is celebrated with fireworks and the Jakarta Fair. The latter is held at the Jakarta Fair Grounds (Map p168), northeast of the city centre in Kemayoran, from late June until mid-July.

Jl Jaksa Street Fair Features Betawi dance, theatre and music, as well as popular modern performances. It is held for one week in August.

Independence Day Held on 17 August. The parades in Jakarta are the biggest in the country.

Sleeping

JL JAKSA AREA

Jakarta's budget hotel enclave is no Khao San Rd, but there are plenty of cheap beds (and beers) on offer. There's a cosmopolitan atmosphere, as the area is also a popular place for Jakarta's young intelligentsia and artistic types to socialise. Jaksa is a short stroll from the main drag, Jl Thamrin, and also close to Gambir train station.

Wisma Delima (Map p172; ☎ 3190 4157; Jl Jaksa 5; dm/s/d with shared mandi 20,000/40,000/50,000Rp) Ancient family-run place with cell-like rooms (with mossie nets and fans) but extremely cheap and it's not dodgy – just read the rules above reception.

Bloem Steen Homestay (Map p172; ☎ 3192 5389; Gang I 173; s/d with shared mandi 25,000/40,000Rp) On a quiet lane, this place has ubersparse rooms with ancient mattresses (but clean sheets). There's a tiny garden out front.

Kresna Homestay (Map p172; ☎ 3192 5403; Gang I 175; d with shared/private mandi 40,000/50,000Rp) Dark, brooding and a little tumbledown, Kresna is barely big enough to swing a durian in, never mind a cat. Still it's secure and benefits from a quiet location, and the owners are helpful.

Djody Hotel (Map p172; ☎ 390 5976; Jl Jaska 27; r 55,000-135,000Rp; ❄) Get past the Jaksa minimalist (read bare and striplight-lit) lobby and this place has equally plain but clean, tiled rooms that are fair value. There's a safety-deposit box at reception.

Hotel Tator (Map p172; ☎ 3192 3941; Jl Jaksa 37; r 75,000-120,000Rp; ❄) Cleanliness standards are high here, where the 21 plain, orderly rooms come with bleach-fresh aromas and there's a front patio where you can munch your breakfast.

Hotel Margot (Map p172; ☎ 391 3830; Jl Jaksa 15; r 170,000Rp; ❄) Just off the main drag, this hotel's 34 rooms are not as grand as the imposing entrance would suggest, but they do all come with hot-water bathrooms, wardrobes and reliable air-conditioning. Those upstairs are slightly bigger.

CIKINI AREA

The Cikini area is east of Jl Jaksa, and has a few good, but pricier, guesthouses. Both offer an inclusive breakfast.

Yannie International Guesthouse (Map p170; ☎ 314 0012; Jl Raden Saleh Raya 35; s/d 125,000/140,000Rp; ❄) Cut from similar cloth as the Gondia International Guesthouse, Yanni has well-kept rooms with hot-water bathrooms. There is no sign, just a 'Y' out front.

Gondia International Guesthouse (Map p170; ☎ 390 9221; www.geocities.com/gondia_hotel; Jl Gondangdia Kecil 22; d from 160,000Rp; ❄) Pleasantly old-fashioned suburban place with cosy, neat rooms that have hot-water bathrooms, phones and reading lights. There's a small garden area here too.

Eating

JL JAKSA AREA

Jl Jaksa's fine for no-nonsense, inexpensive Indonesian and Western grub, though many local dishes are toned down a notch to suit tourist tastes. For something more authentic, head to the night-hawker stalls grouped around the southern end of Jl Hagi Agus Salim (also known as Jl Sabang), which is famous for its street food (including satay).

Jasa Bundo (Map p172; ☎ 390 5607; Jl Jaksa 20A; mains 12,000Rp; 🕑 breakfast, lunch & dinner) Agreeable, inexpensive *masakan Padang* (Padang restaurant) where all the usual Sumatran favourites are present, correct and piled up on the counter.

Margot Café (Map p172; ☎ 391 3830; Jl Jaksa 15; mains 15,000Rp; 🕑 breakfast, lunch & dinner) Classic Jaksa hang-out with bamboo walls, wood floors, soap operas on the TV, and cheap local and Western faves.

Zenya (Map p172; ☎ 315 9232; Jakarta Theatre Bldg, Jl Wahid Hasyim 9; sushi from 15,000Rp, set meals 50,000Rp; 🕑 lunch & dinner) A pukka Japanese place next to the tourist office, with tatami tables, a sushi bar and a highly authentic menu. There's even a no-smoking area.

Ya Udah (Map p172; ☎ 314 4121; Jl Jaksa 49; mains 20,000-41,000Rp; 🕑 breakfast, lunch & dinner). Efficiently run, spick-and-span place with great breakfasts and Western dishes like Swiss rosti. Daily specials include choices like butterfish with mustard greens sauce.

Paprika (Map p172; ☎ 314 4113; Jl Wahid Hasyim; mains 40,000Rp; 🕑 lunch & dinner Mon-Sat) Hip, classy restaurant-cum-lounge bar – it even starred in the Indonesian film *Arisan!* – with fusion cuisine, modish surrounds and slick service.

OTHER AREAS

The upmarket suburb of Kemang, popular with expats, has plenty of stylish bars, clubs and restaurants, and also a couple of food courts where you can chow down on the cheap, before clubbing till dawn.

Place (Map p168; Jl Kemang Raya; 🕑 dinner) Highly sociable 'food bazaar' with myriad stalls, serving up everything from Indo regulars, *teppanyaki*-style steaks to Italian-style ice cream.

Kemang Food Festival (Map p168; Jl Kemang Raya; 🕑 lunch & dinner) Opposite the Place, this alternative food court has dozens of stands, whipping up *roti canai* (Indian-style flaky flat bread), *martabak* (Indonesian pancakes) and Chinese and Western choices. Stays open till 5am during Ramadan.

Pasar Pagi (Map p168; Jl Mangga Dua; ⏲ dinner) Another wonderful food bazaar, this one is located next to the Mangga Dua mall. Half of the stalls serve up Indonesian and halal cuisine, the other foodie zone concentrates on Asian food. It's a great place to pick 'n' mix dishes and socialise with locals, and is open until midnight.

Izzi Pizza (Map p168; ☎ 719 2020; Jl Kemang Raya 93A; mains 30,000Rp; ⏲ lunch & dinner) Peddling the kind of pizza that could get Mamma upping sticks and reaching for her passport, getting hooked on Izzi Pizza is, quite literally, easy peasy.

Street food can be picked up at the **night warung** (Map p170; Jl Pecenongan), about 1km north of the National Monument.

Drinking

Jakarta nights are (or can be if you have the stamina and funds) some of the most hedonistic in Asia. From expat pubs to gorgeous lounge bars with cocktail lists set at (near) London or New York prices, and far more beautiful people, Jakarta has it all. The bar zone on Jl Falatehan near Blok M (6km southwest of Jl Jaksa) is a good all-round bet, with everything from European-style pubs where you can shoot pool and sip wine to raucous bar-clubs with heaving dance floors.

Subscribe to the nightlife newsletter at www.bartele.com for the insider's view.

Bugils (Map p168; ☎ 574 7650; www.bugils.com; Taman Ria Senayan, Jl Jenderal Gatot Subroto; ⏲ 11am-late) Jakarta's prime expat watering hole, a friendly, sociable, pub-style place in the *Cheers* mould that's ideal for a pint and a game of pool. The Dutch owner and author, Bartele (see p335), is a mine of information about his adopted city.

our pick **Cafe Batavia** (Map p173; ☎ 691 5531; Jl Pintu Besar Utara 14; ⏲ 24hr) This refined bar-restaurant, dating from 1805, is a Kota landmark. Revel in the quintessential colonial surrounds – teak floors, giant baroque mirrors, Deco sofas and a sweeping bar with cow-hide detailing – as you sip your cocktail (from 57,000Rp) or beer (from 27,000Rp). Mains are available from 50,000Rp. Bizarrely, the place is often achingly empty, making it a wonderfully relaxing escape from the hectic pace of life outside.

Memories Café (Map p172; ☎ 392 8839; Jl Jaksa 17; ⏲ 24hr) A backpacking institution, with street-side bar stools and a very social vibe. There's also a small bookstore, internet access and (so so) tucker (mains 20,000Rp).

My Bar (Map p168; ☎ 720 4731; Jl Falatehan 1-16, Blok M, Kebayoran Baru; ⏲ 6pm-late) This place must be Jakarta's self-appointed decency brigade's worst nightmare: an East-meets-West maelstrom of local office and bar girls, leering Western guys and pounding Euro dance and *dangdut* music. It's not quite as sleazy as it sounds. There are about a dozen other places on the Falatehan strip.

Top Gun (Map p168; ☎ 720 4731; Jl Falatehan 1-11, Blok M, Kebayoran Baru; ⏲ 5pm-late) Rivalling My Bar, this large bar-club is a bit more tacky but does showcase live bands most nights at 10pm.

Clubbing

Jakarta has a quite extraordinary clubbing scene, with several trance venues centred in Glodok and Kota catering to thousands (see boxed text, p157). In the south of the city the scene revolves around a richer crowd, with less hands-in-the-air action, and plenty of lounge and funky House music. Most places don't get going until 11pm, and rarely close before 4am. All of the following spots have cover charges of 30,000Rp to 60,000Rp, depending on the night.

Embassy (Map p168; ☎ 574 2047; Taman Ria, East Bldg 704, Senayan) Upmarket club where Jakarta's rich and beautiful gather to groove.

Retro (Map p168; ☎ 5296 2828; Jl Gatot Subroto Kav 2-3) In the Crown Plaza Hotel, this slick number with spectacular sound and visuals draws a young, hip and largely clean-cut crowd at the weekends.

Stadium (Map p168; ☎ 626 3323; www.stadiumjakarta.com; Jl Hayum Waruk 111 FF-JJ) Jakarta's – Asia's? – most hardcore clubbing experience, with a capacity of 4000, which opens on a Thursday and doesn't close until Monday morning. It's darker than a bat cave inside, with an atmosphere that's somewhere between spiritual and apocalyptic. Expect fearsome trance and tribal sounds. DJs including Sasha and Steve Lawler have manned the decks, but the local turntablists are talented and know how to move the crowd. Be warned that alcohol is not the drug of choice here, access is via two tiny lifts, and care should be taken outside as this is not Jakarta's safest area.

Entertainment

Check the entertainment pages of the *Jakarta Post, Djakarta!* or *Jakarta Kini* for the latest listings.

Taman Ismail Marzuki (TIM; Map p170; ☎ 3193 7325; tamanismailmarzuki@yahoo.com; Jl Cikini Raya 73) Not far from Jl Jaksa, Jakarta's premier cultural centre stages everything from Balinese dance to poetry readings. Prices start at 30,000Rp.

Gedung Kesenian Jakarta (Map p170; ☎ 380 8283; Jl Gedung Kesenian 1) Hosts traditional dance and drama, as well as European classical music.

The various cultural centres, particularly Erasmus Huis (p169), also hold regular events. For Javan puppet shows, check out the Wayang Museum (p171).

Shopping

Given the climate, it not surprising that Jakartans love their air-conditioned malls – there are over a hundred in the metropolitan area. Electronic goods are particularly good value.

Plaza Indonesia (Map p170; Jl Thamrin; ⏰ 9am-9pm) Upmarket mall with dozens of designer stores.

Pasar Pagi Mangga Dua (Map p168; Jl Mangga Dua; ⏰ 9am-7pm) Very cheap clothes, accessories and shoes and has a great food court (see p175). Across the road is the Mangga Dua Mall for computers and electronics.

Plaza Senayan (Map p168; Jl Asia Afrika; ⏰ 9am-9pm) One of Jakarta's glossiest malls, with a fine bookstore and a Body Shop.

For arts and crafts, also check out **Pasar Seni** (Art Market; Map p168; Jl Raya Kampung Bandan; ⏰ 10am-10pm), at Taman Impian Jaya Ancol (p173), and Jakarta's famous **flea market** (Map p170; Jl Surabaya; ⏰ 9am-6pm).

Getting There & Away

Jakarta is the main travel hub for Indonesia, with flights and ships to destinations all over the archipelago. Buses depart for cities across Java, and Bali and Sumatra, while trains are an excellent way to get across Java.

AIR

Soekarno-Hatta International Airport is 35km northwest of the city; see boxed text, p167 for transport options.

Domestic airlines serving Jakarta include the following:

Adam Air (code KI; ☎ 550 7505, 690 9999; www.adamair.co.id)

Air Asia (code AK; ☎ 0804 133 3333; www.airasia.com)

Garuda (code GA; ☎ 0807 142 7832; www.garuda-indonesia.com)

Lion Air (code JT; ☎ 632 6039; www.lionair.co.id)

Merpati Nusantara Airlines (code MZ; ☎ 654 8888; www.merpati.co.id)

For typical prices see Map p161.

For international flights, check Air Asia or the travel agencies on Jl Jaksa. See p159 for international airlines serving Jakarta.

BOAT

The **Pelni ticket office** (Map p168; ☎ 421 2893; www.pelni.co.id; Jl Angkasa 18; ⏰ 8am-4pm Mon-Fri, to Sat) is 13km northeast of the city centre in Kemayoran. Tickets (plus commission) can be bought through Pelni agents including **Menara Buana Surya** (Map p170; ☎ 314 2464; Jl Menteng Raya 29), in the Tedja Buana building, 500m east of Jl Jaksa. Routes and sample fares can be found on the boat transport map (p163).

Pelni ships all arrive at and depart from Pelabuhan Satu (Dock 1) at Tanjung Priok (Map p168), 13km northeast of the city centre. Koridor 10 Transjakarta buses should start serving the terminal by the time you read this or you can take bus 10 from Jl Agus Salim, located 300m west of Jl Jaksa (allow at least an hour). The bus terminal is at the old Tanjung Priok train station, from where it is a 1km walk to the dock, or 4000Rp by *ojek*. A taxi to/from Jl Jaksa will cost around 50,000Rp.

BUS

So many buses leave Jakarta's bus stations that you can usually just front up at the station and join the chaos, though it pays to book ahead. Travel agencies on Jl Jaksa sell tickets and usually include transport to the terminal, which saves a lot of hassle, though they'll charge a commission for this. Jakarta has four main bus stations, all well out of the city centre. There are buses that will take you to each station from the city centre; see the following text and the boxed text, p178.

Kalideres (off Map p168; ☎ 541 4996) is 15km northwest of the city centre and has frequent buses to destinations west of Jakarta, such as Merak (14,000Rp, three hours). Take a Koridor 3 Transjakarta bus to get here.

Kampung Rambutan (Map p168; ☎ 840 0062) is 18km south of the city and primarily handles buses to destinations south and southeast of Jakarta, such as Bogor (from 9000Rp, 45 minutes) and Cianjur (17,000Rp, 2½ hours). Koridor 7 Transjakarta buses serve this terminal.

Pulo Gadung (Map p168; ☎ 489 3742), 12km east of the centre, serves central and eastern Java, Sumatra and Bali. Most buses to Sumatra leave between 10am and 3pm, including Palembang (from 140,000Rp, 12 hours) and Bukittinggi (from 190,000Rp, 20 to 36 hours). Heading east you'll find direct buses to Bandung via the Cipularang toll road (from 40,000Rp, three hours), Yogyakarta (from 90,000Rp, 12 hours) and even Denpasar (300,000Rp, 26 hours). Koridor 4 or 2 Transjakarta buses will get you to this terminal.

Lebak Bulu (Map p168) is 16km southwest of the city and also handles some deluxe buses to Yogyakarta, Surabaya and Bali. Most departures are in the late afternoon or evening.

MINIBUS

Door-to-door *travel* minibuses are not a good way to leave Jakarta, as it can take hours to pick up or drop off passengers in the traffic jams. Jl Jaksa travel agencies, like **Robertur** (Map p172; ☎ 314 2926; Jl Jaksa 20B; 24hr), can book direct minibuses to Bandung (70,000Rp, three hours), Pangandaran (160,000Rp, 10 hours) and Yogyakarta (195,000Rp, 12 hours).

TRAIN

Jakarta's four main train stations are quite central, making the trains the easiest way out of the city. The most convenient and important is **Gambir** (☎ 386 2361), on the eastern side of Lapangan Merdeka, a 15-minute walk from Jl Jaksa. Gambir handles express trains to Bogor, Bandung, Yogyakarta, Solo, Semarang and Surabaya. Some Gambir trains also stop at **Kota** (☎ 692 9083), the train station in the old city area in the north. **Pasar Senen** (☎ 421 0164), to the east, has mostly *ekonomi* trains to eastern destinations. **Tanah Abang** (☎ 314 9872) has trains west to Merak.

Smaller, but useful if you are staying in Jl Jaksa, is Gondangdia, 500m east of most of the area's guesthouses. From here, there are trains to Bogor and Kota.

For long hauls, the express trains (*bisnis* and *eksekutif*) are far preferable to the *ekonomi* trains and can be booked in advance at the air-con booking offices at the northern end of Gambir train station.

From Gambir, taxis cost a minimum of 18,000Rp from the taxi booking desk. A cheaper alternative is to go out the front to the main road and hail down a *bajaj*, which will cost 10,000Rp to Jl Jaksa after bargaining.

For train times and prices, visit www.info ka.kereta-api.com. Note that some trains have a 10,000Rp surplus for weekend travel.

Bandung

Nine *Parahyangan* trains depart Gambir daily for Bandung (*bisnis/eksekutif* 45,000/65,000Rp, three hours) and there are also seven *Argo Gede* trains (*eksekutif* 75,000Rp, 2¾ hours).

Bogor

Ekonomi trains to Bogor (3500Rp, 1½ hours) leave Gambir and Gondangdia every 20 minutes or so from 5am to 7pm. Much better express trains leave Gambir hourly from 6.30am to 6pm (*bisnis* 10,000Rp, one hour).

Surabaya

Express trains include the *Bima* (*eksekutif* 190,000Rp, 14½ hours), departing Gambir at 5pm, and the luxurious *Argo Bromo Anggrek* (*eksekutif* 200,000Rp, 10 hours), which departs from Gambir at 9.30am and 9.30pm. The *Gumarang* also travels between Gambir and Surabaya (*bisnis/eksekutif* 120,000/220,000Rp, 11½ hours), leaving at 5.50pm.

The cheapest train service taking the north-coast route is the *ekonomi Kertajaya* (52,000Rp, 15½ hours), which leaves Pasar Senen at 4.45pm.

Yogyakarta & Solo

Luxurious trains include the *Argo Lawu* (210,000Rp, eight hours), departing from Gambir at 8pm, and the *Argo Dwipangga* (180,000Rp, nine hours), departing at 8am. These trains cost the same to either destination; for Solo add an extra hour.

Cheaper services to Yogyakarta are the *Fajar Utama Yogya* (*bisnis* 100,000Rp, 8½ hours), departing from Pasar Senen at 6.20am, and the *Senja Utama Yogya* (*bisnis* 100,000Rp, 9¾ hours), departing Pasar Senen at 7.30pm. The *Senja Utama Solo* goes to Solo (*bisnis* 100,000Rp, 10 hours) from Pasar Senen at 8.25pm and also stops in Yogyakarta.

Getting Around

BUS

For details of Jakarta's excellent new Transjakarta busway network, see the boxed text, p178. Otherwise, standard buses cost 2000Rp, *patas* (express) buses cost 2000Rp to 2500Rp. *Mikrolet* and other minibuses also operate in some areas (1000Rp to 2500Rp).

JAKARTA ON THE MOVE

Jakarta's bus system has been revolutionised in recent years and the city now has a network of clean air-conditioned buses called Transjakarta that run on designated busways (lanes that are closed to all other traffic). Journey times have been slashed, and they now represent by far the quickest way to get around the city.

Most busways have been constructed in the centre of existing highways, and stations have been positioned (roughly) at kilometre intervals. Access is via elevated walkways and each station has a shelter. At the time of research, seven busway lines (called *koridor*) were up and running, with a total of 15 due to be operational by 2010, forming a network extending from Tanjung Priok south to Kampung Rambutan.

Tickets cost 3500Rp, payable before you board, which covers you to any destination in the network (regardless of how many *koridor* you use). Buses (5am-10pm) are well maintained and not too crowded as conductors (usually) ensure that maximum passenger numbers are not exceeded.

The busway system has been a great success, but as most middle- and upper-class Jakartans remain as addicted as ever to their cars, the city's famous *macet* (traffic jams) look set to continue for a good few years yet. Efforts to reduce congestion have failed miserably (one initiative that ruled that all rush-hour vehicles using toll roads must have a minimum of three passengers only succeeded in creating an army of riders-for-hire, nicknamed *joki*). But as things stand, busway users can snigger as they speed past kilometres of traffic-snarled cars.

Work began on a monorail system in 2004, and though financial problems mean that it probably won't be completed for a few years yet, some infrastructure is in place. Eventually, two lines (a total of 27km) should connect the main business districts with Kampung Melayu in the south. Plans for an underground metro exist too, and some preparatory work actually started on the project in 2005, but it's currently dead in the water due to a lack of funds.

LOCAL TRANSPORT

A short ride on a *bajaj* costs about 8000Rp, but they are not allowed along main roads, including Jl Thamrin.

TAXI

Metered taxis cost 5000Rp for the first kilometre and 250Rp for each subsequent 100m. Make sure the *argo* (meter) is used.

Bluebird cabs (☎ 794 1234; www.bluebirdgroup.com) can be booked ahead and have the best reputation; do *not* risk travelling with the less reputable firms.

Typical taxi fares from Jl Thamrin: to Kota (20,000Rp) or Blok M (30,000Rp). Any toll road charges are extra and are paid by the passengers.

INDONESIA

BOGOR

☎ 0251 / pop 801,000

Known throughout Java as *kota hujan* (city of rain), Bogor became a home from home for Sir Stamford Raffles (see p180) during the British interregnum, a respite for those mad dogs and Englishmen that preferred *not* to go out in the midday sun. These days, this once quiet town is practically becoming a suburb of Jakarta, with the traffic and hubbub to match. But while Bogor itself clogs up with bemo and mopeds, the real oasis remains untouched. Planted at the very hub of the city, with *macet* to north, south, east and west, the town's world-class botanical gardens remain – in the words of one upstanding British visitor – 'a jolly fine day out'.

Information

There are *wartel* (telecommunications stalls) across town, and Bogor has plenty of banks, many with ATMs.

Bank Central Asia (BCA; Jl Ir H Juanda 28) Has an ATM and changes money.

Post office (Jl Ir H Juanda; 8am-5pm Mon-Fri, to noon Sat)

Tourist office (☎ 081 111 0347; Jl Ir H Juanda 10; 8am-4pm) Tours of the region can also be organised here.

Wartel Paledang (Jl Paledang; per hr 8000Rp; 8am-9pm) Offers internet, and phone services at fair rates.

Sights

A veritable 'green lung' in the heart of the city, Bogor's botanical gardens, the **Kebun Raya** (☎ 322187; www.bogor.indo.net.id/kri; Jl Otto Iskandardinata; admission 5500Rp; 8am-5pm) are simply outstanding. British governor Sir Stamford

Raffles first laid out a garden, but this was later expanded by Dutch botanists, including Johannes Teysmann, who planted and developed the garden over a 50-year period in the 19th century. Today the garden is an important research centre, and scientists based here are investigating new medical and agricultural uses for its many rare specimens. President Bush even dropped by here in 2006 when his scheduled trip to Jakarta was diverted to Bogor.

Things can get hectic on Sundays, but during the week this is one of West Java's true oases (apart from the odd mosquito – bring some repellent). Highlights include the incredible collections of palms, the bizarre pandan trees with their 'spider leg' roots and the orchid house (2000Rp extra). There's a fine, if pricey, café-restaurant in the grounds (Café de daunen, p180).

The **Istana Bogor** (Presidential Palace), built by the Dutch and much favoured by Soekarno (Soeharto ignored it), stands beside the gardens, and deer graze on its lawns. Visits are by organised tour only; the tourist office may be able to squeeze you into one.

Near the garden entrance, the **Zoological Museum** (Jl Otto Iskandardinata; admission 1000Rp; 8am-4pm Sat-Thu, to noon Fri) has a curious collection of mouldy stuffed animals, including a skeleton of a blue whale, 30cm stick insects and a pooch-sized Flores rat.

If you are interested in seeing a Javanese craftsman at work, Pak Dase makes quality

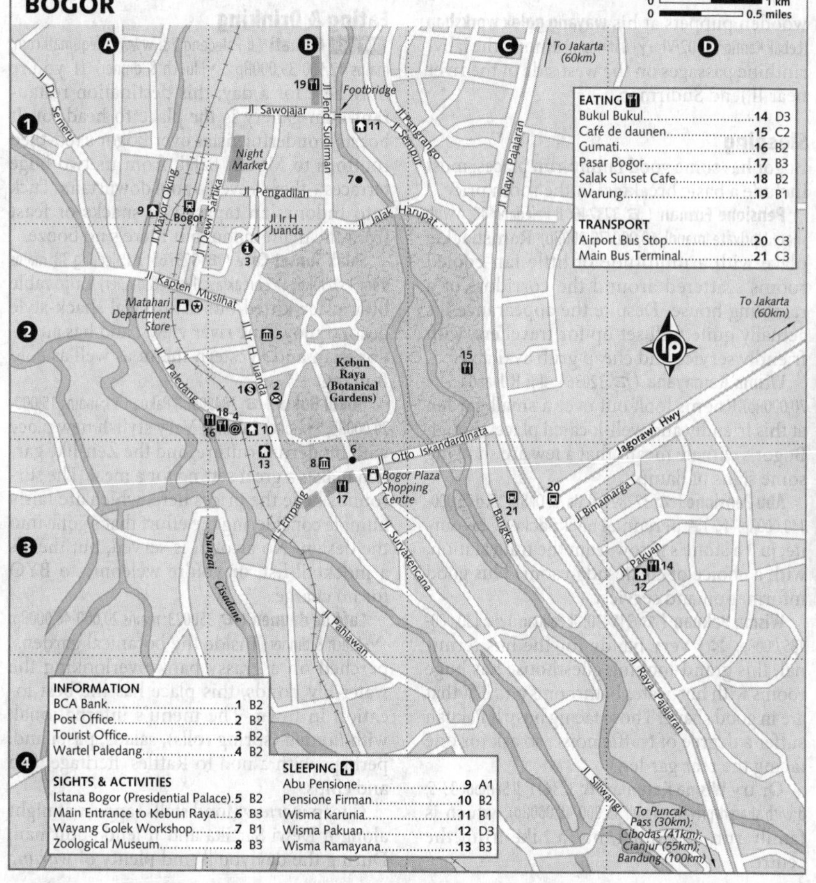

RAFFLES

British botanist, antislavery campaigner and founder of Singapore, Sir Thomas Stamford Raffles had a deep love of Java. Born on a ship off the coast of Jamaica, he learnt Malay while working in Penang and became governor of Java in 1811, when he founded the Bogor gardens during the British interim.

An enlightened governor, he opposed the opium trade, banned slavery in Java and introduced a degree of self-government. Raffles organised many expeditions across Indonesia, rediscovering Borobudur, and, during another trip, encountered the world's largest flower, *Rafflesia,* which takes his name. Later he wrote the well-received *History of Java.*

After three of his four children died in a six-month period in 1821–22, Raffles concentrated on his love of natural sciences, becoming the first president of the Zoological Society of London, and founding London zoo. Raffles' progressive ideals were in stark contrast to his family background (his father was a slave trader), and when he died at 45 his local parish vicar refused to grant a church burial because of his antislavery principles.

Dozens of educational establishments bear his name today including the Raffles Museum of Biodiversity Research in Singapore.

wooden puppets at his **wayang golek workshop** (Lebak Kantion RT 02/VI; 8am-6pm) among the labyrinthine passages on the west side of the river near Jl Jend Sudirman.

Sleeping

Bogor has some good family-run places; most include a basic breakfast in the room price.

Pensione Firman (323246; Jl Paledang 48; r with shared/private mandi 60,000/70,000Rp) Ramshackle place with a multitude of little fan-cooled rooms scattered around the corridors of a rambling house. Despite the appearance it's actually quite well set up for travellers, with friendly service and cheap grub available.

Wisma Ramayana (320364; Jl Ir H Juanda 54; r 70,000Rp) Rooms look out over a small garden at this friendly and well-located place, though Bogor's climate means that a few are showing some signs of damp.

Abu Pensione (322893; Jl Mayor Oking 15; d 75,000-140,000Rp;) A perennial backpackers' favourite, just a stone's throw from the train station, with a choice of clean, tidy rooms plus good information and service.

Wisma Pakuan (319430; Jl Pakuan 12; r 130,000-185,000Rp;) Very handy for the bus terminal, this grand-looking guesthouse has huge rooms with hot-water bathrooms and TV that are in good shape. Those facing busy Jl Pakuan suffer a degree of traffic noise, so ask for one facing the rear garden.

Or try **Wisma Karunia** (323411; Jl Sempur 33-5; d with shared/private mandi 35,000/45,000Rp), which is family run and quiet, but a hike from the centre.

Eating & Drinking

our pick **Gumati** (Jl Paledang 28; www.cafegumati.com; mains 12,500-39,000Rp; lunch & dinner) If you're only here for a day, this destination restaurant-cum-gallery is *the* place to head for. It boasts wonderful vistas over Bogor's red-tiled rooftops to Mount Salak from its two huge terraces – there's even a pool downstairs. Tuck into Indonesian tapas-style snacks or feast from the main menu, but there's no booze.

Salak Sunset Café (329765; Jl Paledang 38; mains from 15,000Rp; breakfast, lunch & dinner) Enjoyable little place kitted out in tropical shack-style décor. Enjoys fine river views, and has an Indonesian and Western menu as well as cold Bintang.

Bukul Bukul (384905; Jl Pakuan 14; mains 15,000-20,000Rp; lunch & dinner) Very stylish new place with modern furniture, and the Zen-like garden makes a great setting for a meal. The surrounds belie the prices here, which are fairly humble considering the effort that's gone into the design. No alcohol is served, but there's a mocktail list, or you're welcome to BYO for no charge.

Café de daunen (350023; mains 20,000-46,000Rp; lunch & dinner) Inside the botanical gardens, perched on a grassy bank overlooking the water-lily ponds, this place has the best location in town. The menu's international, with *lumpia* (spring rolls), salads, pasta and, perhaps with a nod to Raffles' heritage, fish and chips.

Cheap *warung* (food stalls) appear at night along Jl Dewi Sartika and Jl Jend Sudirman. During the day you'll find plenty of *warung* and good fruit at Pasar Bogor, the market close to the main Kebun Raya gates.

Getting There & Away

BUS

Buses to Jakarta depart every 15 minutes from the main bus terminal on Jl Raya Pajajaran (normal/air-con 9000/12,000Rp, 45 minutes) to the Kampung Rambutan station via the toll road. Some services also go directly to Jakarta's Pulo Gadung bus station and Tanjung Priok harbour.

There are buses to Bandung (26,000/38,000Rp, 3½ hours) via Cianjur (12,000/18,000Rp, two hours) every 20 minutes. On weekends, buses are not allowed to go via the scenic Puncak Pass (below) and have to travel via Sukabumi (add an extra hour to your journey time, and 5000Rp). **Rama Travel** (☎ 653672) offers air-con, door-to-door minibuses to Bandung (60,000Rp, 3½ hours) and Yogyakarta (140,000Rp, 11 hours), and will collect you from your hotel.

Damri buses head direct to Jakarta's Soekarno-Hatta airport (30,000Rp, 1½ hours) hourly from 4am to 6pm. They leave from Jl Bimamarga 1, near the end of the Jagorawi Hwy toll road.

TRAIN

Trains are the best way to reach the Jl Jaksa area of Jakarta. Frequent *ekonomi* trains leave for Gambir or Gondangdia stations roughly every 20 minutes until 7pm (3500Rp, 1½ hours). Better *Pakuan* express services to Gambir (10,000Rp, one hour) leave less frequently until 6pm.

Getting Around

Angkot (2000Rp) make slow circuits of the gardens, taking in most central locations en route.

CIBODAS & CIANJUR

☎ 0263 / pop Cibodas 18,000, Cianjur 151,000

Leaving Bogor you pass through the **Puncak Pass**, a once-lovely highland area destroyed by a rampant resort sprawl of motels, weekend homes and factory-shopping outlets. But continuing east of here you'll travel through some of Java's finest highland scenery: a bewitching landscape of plunging valleys, tea plantations and cool, misty mornings.

Cibodas, 4km off the main road, is home to the stunning **Kebun Raya Botanical Gardens** (☎ 512233; admission 4000Rp; 8am-5pm), an incredible collection of over 5000 plants and trees from over 1000 species set in impossibly lush grounds of alpine forest, waterfalls and grasslands. First established in 1830 by botanist Teysmann, the Dutch tried to cultivate quinine here (its bark is used in malaria medication), though the climate proved better in East Java. Cibodas' gardens were listed by Unesco as a World Heritage Reserve in 1977. Highlights include the cacti greenhouse, eucalyptus forests, some vertiginous Japanese bamboo and the prolific birdlife, including rare sightings of the Javan hawk eagle.

From April to October, you can also climb **Gunung Gede**, a spectacular 2958m volcanic peak with a huge crater; from its summit it's possible to see the Indian Ocean and Java Sea on clear days. The Perlindungan Hutan & Konservasi Alam (PHKA; Directorate General of Forest Protection & Nature Conservation) office, opposite the entrance to the gardens in Cibodas, issues permits (issued one day in advance, 5000Rp). It's six hours to the summit so start early (usually around 2am). PHKA guides can be hired for 250,000Rp for the hike, or speak to Freddy at Freddy's Homestay (see below).

Continuing east it's 19km to the market town of Cianjur, an important, if sprawling, rice-growing centre that makes a good base to explore the intriguing sights of the region. These include the lush hillsides and processing plants of the **Gedeh tea plantation** (admission free; 8am-4pm Mon-Sat), 15km northwest of town, and **Jangari**, a 'floating village' on a large lake with a substantial fish-farming community and a wonderful fish restaurant 18km northeast of town. Cianjur has several banks (with ATMs) on main drag Jl Cokroaminoto, and internet cafés are grouped together on Jl Siti Jenab.

Sleeping & Eating

Accommodation tends to be expensive close to the Puncak Pass as the area is popular with wealthy weekending Jakartans. The Cianjur homestay programme (see p182) is an excellent and very affordable way to interact with local people.

Freddy's Homestay (☎ 515473; Jl Raya Cibodas, Cibodas; s/d with shared mandi 35,000/70,000Rp) The English- and Dutch-speaking owner at this rustic homestay is an excellent source of information about the region and its hiking, and his

CIANJUR HOMESTAY PROGRAMME

Set up by Yudi Sujana, a Javanese teacher who lived for years in New Zealand, the **Cianjur Homestay Programme** (☎ 081 7085 6691; westjava2002@yahoo.com) is a superb initiative that is very well set up to enable travellers to experience life in a nontouristy town in Java, and do some voluntary work. Yudi and his team all speak fluent English, so it's a wonderful opportunity to get to understand Sundanese and Indonesian culture. Guests can help English-language teachers in local schools, visit the town's plastic-recycling plant or join workers planting or harvesting rice. Hiking trips and tours of all the region's sights can be arranged at backpacking prices. Guests pay US$10 per person per day, which includes family accommodation and three meals; it's best to book a place a few days in advance. Airport pick-ups and drop-offs can also be arranged at very moderate rates, allowing you to bypass Jakarta completely.

wife prepares lunchboxes. Located down a narrow alleyway 500m before the gardens, the rooms here are modest but acceptable.

Cianjur's speciality is *lontong* (sticky rice with tofu in a delicious sweet coconut sauce); there are several *warung* on Jl Dewisartika that specialise in this dish.

Getting There & Away

On weekdays buses leave Jakarta's Kampung Rambutan every 30 minutes to Cipanas (normal/air-con 15,000/21,000Rp, two hours) and Cianjur (17,000/25,000Rp, 2½ hours). At weekends (when traffic is terrible around Puncuk Pass) buses are routed via Sukabumi (add an extra hour to your journey time, and 5000Rp). Buses to/from Bandung (11,000/16,000Rp, 1¾ hours) leave every half-hour.

There are buses to Bogor from Cianjur (12,000/18,000Rp, two hours) and the highway by Cipanas every 20 minutes; *colt* ply the route on Sundays.

INDONESIA

BANDUNG

☎ 022 / pop 2.7 million

Big, burly Bandung comes like a rush of blood to the head after the verdant mountains around Cibodas. Once dubbed the 'Paris of Java', today there's little left to admire in a city centre that's prone to Jakarta-style congestion. But if you rummage through the concrete sprawl, odd pockets of interest remain, including some Dutch Art Deco monuments, the quirky fibreglass statues of Jeans St and some stylish cafés popular with the thousands of students that call this city home. At an altitude of 750m, Bandung's climate is also far less oppressive than the capital's, and with a new toll road cutting driving times, it's even become a bit of a weekend retreat.

Orientation

The main drag, Jl Asia Afrika, runs through the heart of city centre past the *alun alun* (main public square). Most budget accommodation is dotted around the train station, while Jl Braga has a strip of cafés, bars and restaurants.

Information

Adventist Hospital (☎ 203 4386; Jl Cihampelas 161) A missionary hospital with English-speaking staff.

Bandung Tourist Information Centre (☎ 420 6644; Jl Asia Afrika; 9am-5pm Mon-Sat, to 2pm Sun) Run by the ever-helpful Ajid Suriana, this office is currently in the foyer of the central mosque, but should move to an adjacent office in the *alun alun*. There's also a desk at the train station.

Bank Mandiri (Jl Merdeka) Has an ATM and exchanges travellers cheques and cash.

Main post office (cnr Jl Banceuy & Jl Asia Afrika; 8am-7pm Mon-Sat) Opposite the *alun alun*.

Wartel (Jl Kebonjati; 8am-9pm) International calls can be made here.

X-net (Jl Lengkong Kecil 38; per hr 5000Rp; 8am-10pm)

Sights & Activities

CITY CENTRE

The **Museum Konperensi** (Conference Museum) in the **Gedung Merdeka** (Freedom Bldg; ☎ 423 8031; Jl Asia Afrika 65; admission free; 9am-3pm Mon-Fri) is dedicated to Bandung's 1955 Asia-Africa conference, attended by Soekarno, Ho Chi Minh, Nasser, Nehru and other leaders from the developing world.

NORTH BANDUNG

Bandung's **Institute of Technology** (ITB; Jl Ganeca) is one of the most important universities in Indonesia, with a reputation for activism – students here published corruption

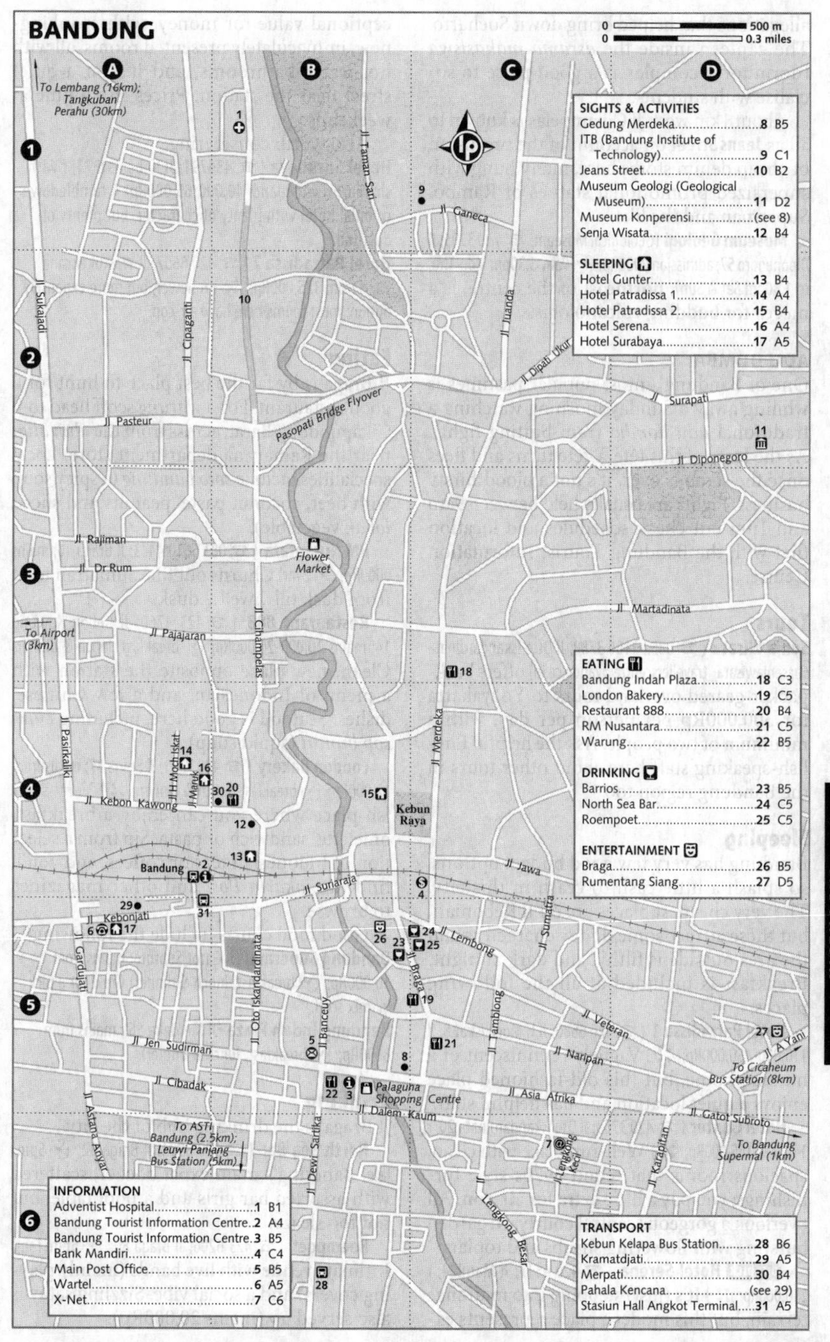
BANDUNG
0 500 m
0 0.3 miles
A
B
C
D
1
2
3
4
5
6
To Lembang (16km); Tangkuban Perahu (30km)
SIGHTS & ACTIVITIES
Gedung Merdeka....8 B5
ITB (Bandung Institute of Technology)....9 C1
Jeans Street....10 B2
Museum Geologi (Geological Museum)....11 D2
Museum Konperensi....(see 8)
Senja Wisata....12 B4
SLEEPING
Hotel Gunter....13 B4
Hotel Patradissa 1....14 A4
Hotel Patradissa 2....15 B4
Hotel Serena....16 A4
Hotel Surabaya....17 A5
Jl Taman Sari
Jl Ganeca
Jl Sukajadi
Jl Cipaganti
Jl Juanda
Jl Dipati Ukur
Jl Surapati
Pasopati Bridge Flyover
Jl Pasteur
Jl Diponegoro
Jl Rajiman
Jl Dr Rum
Flower Market
Jl Martadinata
To Airport (3km)
Jl Pajajaran
Jl Champelas
EATING
Bandung Indah Plaza....18 C3
London Bakery....19 C5
Restaurant 888....20 B4
RM Nusantara....21 C5
Warung....22 B5
DRINKING
Barrios....23 B5
North Sea Bar....24 C5
Roempoet....25 C5
ENTERTAINMENT
Braga....26 B5
Rumentang Siang....27 D5
Jl Pasirkaliki
Jl H Moch Iskat
Jl Maruk
Jl Merdeka
Jl Kebon Kawong
Kebun Raya
Bandung
Jl Jawa
Jl Suniaraja
Jl Kebonjati
Jl Lembong
Jl Sumatra
Jl Braga
Jl Garduiati
Jl Oto Iskandardinata
Jl Tamblong
Jl Veteran
Jl Jen Sudirman
Jl Banceuy
Jl Naripan
Jl A Yani
To Cicaheum Bus Station (8km)
Jl Cibadak
Palaguna Shopping Centre
Jl Asia Afrika
Jl Dalem Kaum
Jl Gatot Subroto
To Bandung Supermal (1km)
Jl Astana Anyar
To ASTI Bandung (2.5km); Leuwi Panjang Bus Station (5km)
Jl Dewi Sartika
Jl Lengkong Kecil
Jl Karapitan
Jl Lengkong Besar
INFORMATION
Adventist Hospital....1 B1
Bandung Tourist Information Centre....2 A4
Bandung Tourist Information Centre....3 B5
Bank Mandiri....4 C4
Main Post Office....5 B5
Wartel....6 A5
X-Net....7 C6
TRANSPORT
Kebun Kelapa Bus Station....28 B6
Kramatdjati....29 A5
Merpati....30 B4
Pahala Kencana....(see 29)
Stasiun Hall Angkot Terminal....31 A5
INDONESIA

allegations that helped bring down Soeharto. The canteen inside the *asrama mahasiswa* (dormitory) complex is a good place to socialise with students.

About 1km west, Jl Cihampelas is known to all as **Jeans Street** on account of the profusion of cheap denim stores here, many hung with supersized promotional statues of Rambo, Superman and the like.

Museum Geologi (Geological Museum; ☎ 720 3205; Jl Diponegoro 57; admission 2000Rp; 🕑 9am-3.30pm Mon-Thu, to 1.30pm Sat & Sun), northeast of the centre, is a mecca for budding vulcanologists.

ADU DOMBA

One of Bandung's most popular pastimes is whiling away a Sunday morning watching a traditional *adu domba* (ram-butting fight). As the loser of this tête-à-tête turns and flees once the scrap is over, it's not a bloodthirsty business. Fights are usually held between 9am and 1pm but check schedules and location first with the Bandung Tourist Information Centre.

Tours

Senja Wisata (☎ 0852 2106 3788; Jl Otto Iskandardinata 6a; senjawisata_travellerscentre@yahoo.co.id) offers backpacker-geared overland tours to Yogyakarta for 300,000Rp per person per day, with a minimum of two people. Ask the helpful English-speaking staff here about other tours in the Bandung region too.

Sleeping

Bandung has very few good budget options, so splash a little cash to crash in this city. The very cheapest places are on Jl Kebonjati, but these attract some dodgy characters and the area outside is filthy, and dark at night. Breakfast is included at all the following places.

Hotel Patradissa 1 (☎ 420 6680; Jl H Moch Iskat 8; d 110,000-180,000Rp; ❄) Vaguely reminiscent of a nursing home, but this old-fashioned place enjoys a quiet location and has helpful staff.

Hotel Gunter (☎ 420 3763; Jl Oto Iskandardinata 20; r 140,000-165,000Rp; ❄) Well-run place with clean, spacious rooms that retain 1970s-style furnishings; you pay a little extra for air-con. All overlook a gorgeous central courtyard garden bursting with flowering shrubs and topiary.

our pick **Hotel Serena** (☎ 420 4317; Jl Maruk 4; r 210,000Rp; ❄) It's (just) stepping into midrange terrain, but this modern place represents exceptional value for money, with spanking-new, immaculately presented rooms, all with hot-water bathrooms, and it's on a quiet street near the station. Prices rise a little at weekends.

Also worth considering:

Hotel Surabaya (☎ 436791; Jl Kebonjati 71; r with shared/private mandi 40,000/65,000Rp) A tumbledown colonial hotel with plenty of character, but plenty of dust too.

Hotel Patradissa 2 (☎ 420 6657; Jl Wastukencana 7a; d from 125,000Rp; ❄) A newer, but more expensive option; most rooms here have air-con.

Eating

Jl Braga is by far the best place to hunt for a good restaurant. For a *warung* scoff head to Jl Cikapundung Barat, across from the *alun alun* near the Ramayana department store. Local specialities include *soto bandung* (a spicy soup with beef, coconut paste, peanuts and sliced *lobak* vegetable).

RM Nusantara (☎ 081 5610 4443; Jl Braga 10; mains 9000Rp; 🕑 24hr) Churns out fine Sumatran food from dusk till…well…dusk.

Restaurant 888 (☎ 423 4760; Jl Kebon Kawung 14; mains 10,000-26,000Rp; 🕑 breakfast, lunch & dinner) Clean, new place opposite the station with a menu of Indonesian, and a few Chinese, dishes. Seafood is good here, including *cumi sop buntut* (squid soup).

London Bakery (☎ 420 7351; Jl Braga 37; meals from 12,000Rp; 🕑 breakfast, lunch & dinner; ❄) Very stylish place where you can enjoy a breakfast, omelette, sandwich or pasta. Sip from a selection of Indonesian teas or coffees, and you'll find the *Jakarta Post* and other magazines to browse.

Good food courts include the following:

Bandung Supermal (Jl Gatot Subroto; mains from 10,000Rp; 🕑 breakfast, lunch & dinner) Great for a pick 'n' mix scoff.

Bandung Indah Plaza (Jl Merdeka 56l; mains from 8000Rp; 🕑 breakfast, lunch & dinner)

Drinking

Jl Braga is the drinking hub of the city.

North Sea Bar (☎ 420 8904; Jl Braga 82; 🕑 5pm-late) Bandung's main expat boozer, scattered with assorted bar girls and a pool table, but not too sleazy.

Roempoet (☎ 423 6206; Jl Braga 80; 🕑 5pm-1am) Intimate venue with live bands (mainly playing covers) and a social vibe. Sizzling satay is also served up (mains 20,000Rp).

Barrios (Braga City Walk Mall 48; 11am-2am) This is a hip lounge bar with *Wallpaper** magazine-influenced décor, 25 brands of bottled beer and live music at weekends.

Clubbing

Braga (423 3292; Jl Suriaraja 7-9; 7pm-3am) An unpretentious club where House music and Indonesian dance rule the dance floor. There's a small cover charge of around 30,000Rp.

Entertainment

Bandung is a capital of Sundanese culture, particularly performing arts. Performance times are haphazard; check with the tourist information centre for the latest schedules.

Rumentang Siang (423 3562; Jl Baranangsiang 1; performances from 5000Rp) Bandung's principal arts centre hosts *wayang golek* performances, Jaipongan (West Javanese dance), *sandiwara* (traditional Javanese theatre) and *ketoprak* (folk theatre).

ASTI-Bandung (731 4982; Jl Buah Batu 212; performances from 5000Rp) South of the centre, ASTI is a school for traditional arts: Sundanese music, dance and *pencak silat* (self-defence).

Getting There & Away

AIR

Air Asia (080 4133 3333; www.airasia.com) offers a direct daily link with Kuala Lumpur. **Merpati** (426 0253; www.merpati.co.id; Jl Kebon Kawong 16) has flights to cities including Surabaya, Denpasar and Tarakan. **Garuda** (420 9468; www.garuda-indonesia.com) is in the Grand Hotel Preanger.

BUS

The **Leuwi Panjang bus station** (522 0768), 5km south of the city centre on Jl Soekarno-Hatta, has half-hourly buses west to Cianjur (normal/air-con 11,000/16,000Rp, 1¾ hours) and Bogor (26,000/38,000Rp, 3½ hours), and, via the toll road, to Jakarta's Kampung Rambutan station (40,000Rp, three hours). Buses to Bogor are not allowed to take the scenic Puncak Pass route on weekends.

Buses leave from the Cicaheum station, 8km east of town, for destinations to the east, including hourly buses to Pangandaran (48,000Rp, six hours) until 1pm, and Yogyakarta (normal/air-con 70,000/92,000Rp, 10 hours).

Sari Harum (607 7065) provides air-con *travel* minibuses to Pangandaran (70,000Rp, five hours); phone to arrange a pick-up from your hotel.

For luxury buses to long-distance destinations including Yogyakarta, **Kramatdjati** (420 0858; Jl Kebonjati 96) and **Pahala Kencana** (423 2911; Jl Kebonjati 90) are two upmarket agencies.

TRAIN

Between them the *Parahyangan* and *Argo Gede* (*bisnis* 40,000Rp to 50,000Rp, *eksekutif* 60,000Rp to 75,000Rp; three hours) offer hourly trains to Jakarta's Gambir train station between 4am and 7pm.

The *eksekutif Argo Wilis* leaves Bandung at 7am for Surabaya (165,000Rp, 12½ hours). It calls at Yogyakarta and Solo en route. For train time and fare information, visit www.infoka.kereta-api.com.

Getting Around

Bandung's airport is 4km northwest of the city centre; it costs about 30,000Rp to get there by taxi. Regular *angkot* (2500Rp) link the airport and the centre of town.

Angkot (2000Rp to 3000Rp) to most places, such as Jl Cihampelas and Tangkuban Perahu, leave from the south side of the train station (Stasiun Hall). Abdul Muis terminal, at the Kebun Kelapa bus station, has *angkot* to Cicaheum and Luewi Panjang bus stations. Big Damri city buses 9 and 11 (2000Rp) run from west to east down Jl Asia Afrika to Cicaheum.

TANGKUBAN PERAHU AREA

Thirty kilometres north of Bandung, Tangkuban Perahu (literally 'Overturned Boat') is a huge active volcanic crater. Legend tells of a god challenged to build a huge boat during a single night. His opponent, on seeing that he would probably complete this impossible task, brought the sun up early and the boat builder turned his nearly completed boat over in a fit of anger.

The huge **Kawah Ratu** (Queen Crater) at the top is impressive, but as cars can also drive right up here, it's a weekend tourist trap with the usual parade of touts offering eggs to cook in the crater's scalding surface. A park entrance fee of 20,000Rp is payable on arrival. For safety, check the volcano's activity status first with the tourist information centre in Bandung.

You can escape the crowds by walking (anticlockwise) around the main crater and along the ridge between the two craters, but parts of it are steep and slippery. Safer and more interesting is the walk to **Kawah Domas**, an active volcanic area of steaming vents and bubbling pools about 1km down from the car park. From here you can follow the trail back to the main road (ask for directions) and flag down a *colt* back to Bandung, or continue to the **Sari Ater Hot Springs Resort** (☎ 0260-471700; admission 10,000Rp, pools extra 20,000Rp; 24hr) at **Ciater**, 8km northeast of Tangkuban Perahu. Guides at Tangkuban Perahu will also offer to lead you to Ciater through the jungle.

To get here, take a Subang-bound *colt* (10,000Rp, 45 minutes) from Bandung's minibus terminal (Stasiun Hall) to the park entrance. Then take a minibus (8000Rp per person if full) to the crater; you may have to charter one or walk the 4.5km to the top on weekdays.

PANGANDARAN

☎ 0265

Java's principal beach resort, famous for its sweeping beaches and rolling surf, was struck by a tsunami in July 2006, claiming over 600 lives and laying waste to the shoreline. Pangandaran has picked itself remarkably quickly, and is back in business, though some sea-front structures at its southern end still bear gaping holes and will have to be pulled down.

Few Javanese visit (except in peak holiday periods), but with near-empty beaches, easy access to a national park, bags of budget hotels and great surf, Pangandaran is a great place to break your journey across Java.

Information

A once-only tourist tax (3000Rp) is charged when entering Pangandaran – keep your ticket safe. Note that at the time of research, none of the local ATMs were accepting Visa/Plus cards; the nearest Visa-friendly ATMs are in Sukaraja and Sidareja.

BNI ATM (Jl Bulak Laut) Opposite the Relax Restaurant, the ATM accepts MasterCard/Cirrus cards only.

BRI bank (Jl Kidang Pananjung; 8am-2.30pm Mon-Fri) Changes money and travellers checks for so-so rates; its ATM takes MasterCard/Cirrus cards.

CV Sawargi (☎ 639180; Jl Kidang Pananjung 123; per hr 18,000Rp; 9am-11pm) Internet access and local tours.

Magic Mushroom Books (Jl Pasanggrahan; 8.30am-8pm) Books can be bought here and money changed.

Main post office (Jl Kidang Pananjung; 7.30am-3pm Mon-Thu, to 1.30pm Sat) On the main street.

PT Lotus Wisata (☎ 639635; lotus_wisata@yahoo.com; Jl Bulak Laut; 6am-midnight) Helpful travel agency with excellent transport information.

Telkom office (Jl Kidang Pananjung; 6am-midnight)

Sights & Activities

The **Taman Nasional Pangandaran** (Pangandaran National Park; ☎ 081 2149 0153; admission 2500Rp; dawn-dusk), which fringes the southern end of town, is a stretch of untouched forest populated by barking deer, hornbills and Javan gibbons, and with some spectacular white-sand beaches. The **Boundary Trail** offers the best walk through the park, skirting the jungle. Other trails are very vague, so it's best to ask a ranger (50,000Rp) to accompany you. You can also take a guided walk with a tour company.

Surf lessons (per half-day incl board hire 100,000Rp) are offered at the northern end of the beach; just look out for the 'Surf here' banner spread between the palm trees. Pangandaran is a good place to learn, and local instructors have 'soft' boards ideal for beginners.

Pangandaran can have big seas, and drownings do occur – swimmers take care!

Tours

The top trip is to the Green Canyon (see p189), which costs around 70,000Rp (minimum four people). Guided walks through the national park (50,000Rp, five hours, minimum four people) are also offered. Contact **CV Sawargi** (☎ 639180; mponxz@yahoo.com; Jl Kidang Pananjung 123).

Sleeping

As Pangandaran has close to 100 hotels you should have no bother finding a bed, except during Christmas and Lebaran (the end of Ramadan) when half of Java seems to head here, and prices skyrocket.

The northern end of Jl Pamugaran, on the west beach, is the best place to start looking. All places include breakfast unless stated.

Hotel Melati Nugraha (☎ 639225; Jl Pasanggrahan 3; r 35,000Rp) New place with a row of clean if bare rooms facing a grassy plot. Atmospheric? Not really, but it is great value.

our pick **Mini Tiga Homestay** (☎ 639436; katmaja95@yahoo.fr; s/d 50,000/65,000Rp) Very well-run, French-owned place with clean, bright rooms, well-scrubbed *mandi* (large concrete basin from which you scoop water to rinse your body and flush the squat toilet) and communal

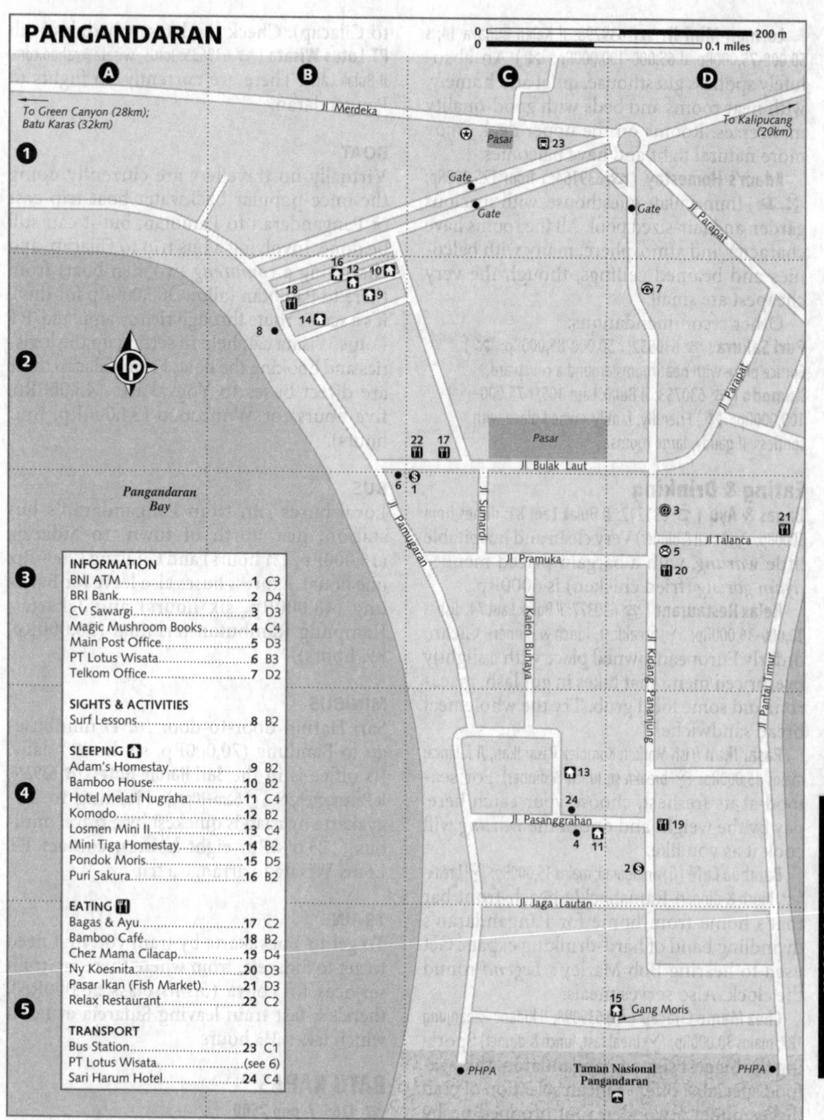

areas decorated with artwork. Guests can slurp free tea and coffee all day long too.

Pondok Moris (☎ 639490; Gang Moris 3; s/d 50,000/75,000Rp) Within easy striking distance of the national park, this quirky six-roomed place has clean if slightly dark digs, each with a little porch and a *mandi*, all set off a little lane bursting with greenery. Pack your ear plugs though, there's a mosque on your doorstep.

Bamboo House (☎ 639419; r 50,000-85,000Rp;) First impressions aren't great here but once you get past the shabby lobby you'll see the rooms are in decent nick and good value, though the air-con options are a tad uninspiring décorwise.

INDONESIA

Losmen Mini II (☎ 639298; Jl Kalen Buhaya 14; s 50,000-75,000Rp, d 65,000-100,000Rp; ❄) An absolutely spotless guesthouse, quiet and homely, with neat rooms and beds with good-quality mattresses. Rooms on the upper deck enjoy more natural light and have balconies.

Adam's Homestay (☎ 639164; r from 125,000Rp; ❄) Immaculate guesthouse, with spacious garden and fair-sized pool. All the rooms have character and atmosphere, many with balconies and beamed ceilings, though the very cheapest are small.

Other recommendations:

Puri Sakura (☎ 630552; r 50,000-85,000Rp; ❄) Spruce place with neat rooms around a courtyard.

Komodo (☎ 630753; Jl Bulak Laut 105; r 75,000-100,000Rp; ❄) Friendly, family-owned place with spotless, if gaudy, large rooms.

Eating & Drinking

Bagas & Ayu (☎ 631712; Jl Bulak Laut 81; dishes from 5000Rp; 🕑 lunch & dinner) Very clean and hospitable little *warung*, with a bargain-priced menu – *ayam goreng* (fried chicken) is 6000Rp.

Relax Restaurant (☎ 630377; Jl Bulak Laut 74; dishes 10,000-36,000Rp; 🕑 breakfast, lunch & dinner) Clean, orderly European-owned place with a slightly overpriced menu that takes in goulash, macaroni and some local grub. Try the wholemeal bread sandwiches.

Pasar Ikan (Fish Market; Komplek Pasar Ikan, Jl Talanca; mains 15,000Rp; 🕑 breakfast, lunch & dinner) For seafood at its freshest, choose your catch here, pay by the weight and one of the *warung* will cook it as you like.

Bamboo Café (Jl Pamugaran; mains 15,000Rp; 🕑 breakfast, lunch & dinner) Ramshackle beach-front bar that's home from home for Pangandaran's dwindling band of hard-drinking expats. Get used to hearing Bob Marley's *Legend* round the clock. Also serves meals.

Chez Mama Cilacap (☎ 639098; Jl Kidang Pananjung 187; mains 30,000Rp; 🕑 breakfast, lunch & dinner) Sporting the biggest sign in Pangandaran, this seafood specialist offers a mean selection of crab dishes under a wooden roof propped up by palm trees.

Also try **NY Koesnita** (☎ 630028; Jl Kidang Pananjung; mains 15,000Rp; 🕑 breakfast, lunch & dinner) for authentic Sundanese and Padang dishes.

Getting There & Away

With tourist numbers down in Pangandaran, many transport options have ceased (including the regular ferry and boat connections to Cilacap). Check the latest schedules with **PT Lotus Wisata** (☎ 639635; lotus_wisata@yahoo.com; Jl Bulak Laut). There are currently no flights to Pangandaran.

BOAT

Virtually no travellers are currently doing the once-popular backwater boat trip east of Pangandaran to Pamotan, but it can still be done. Involving a bus trip to Cilacap, and chartering a *compreng* (wooden boat) from there to Pamotan (allow 300,000Rp for this), it's a scenic route through rich swampland. PT Lotus Wisata can help in setting up the logistics and booking the boat. From Cilacap there are direct buses to Yogyakarta (46,000Rp, five hours) or Wonosobo (34,000Rp, four hours).

BUS

Local buses run from Pangandaran's bus station, just north of town, to Sidareja (15,000Rp, 1¾ hours) and Cijulang (9000Rp, one hour). Express buses also leave for Bandung (48,000Rp, six hours) and Jakarta's Kampung Rambutan terminal (88,000Rp, 8½ hours).

MINIBUS

Sari Harum door-to-door *travel* minibuses go to Bandung (70,000Rp, six hours) daily. Its office is in the **Sari Harum Hotel** (☎ 639276; Jl Pasanggrahan; 🕑 6am-10pm). Heading to Yogyakarta by road is quickest by a *travel* minibus (125,000Rp, eight hours); contact PT Lotus Wisata to arrange a trip.

TRAIN

To get to Yogyakarta by train you first need to get to Sidareja, from where there are train services to Yogya (*bisnis* class 50,000Rp); there's a fast train leaving Sidareja at noon which takes 3½ hours.

BATU KARAS

☎ 0265 / pop 2500

The one-lane fishing village of **Batu Karas** (admission 1500Rp), 32km from Pangandaran, is the perfect antidote to Java's teeming cities, with great swells and a slightly scruffy but very relaxed charm. Alongside the two fine beaches and a scattering of *warung*, there's a lot of surf talk. The locally run surf co-op here charges 80,000Rp per person per day for lessons, board hire is extra.

INDONESIA

Most of Batu Karas dodged the 2006 tsunami that hit Java's south coast, though some places in the northern part of town suffered some damage.

Sleeping & Eating

Reef Hotel (☎ 0813 2034 0193; d 75,000-200,000Rp) This attractive place, right by one of the main surf breaks, was affected by the tsunami, but it's up and running again (apart from the pool). Rooms are large, and filling Indonesian and Western food is served (meals from 15,000Rp).

Java Cove (☎ 633683; www.javacovehotel.com; economy r 80,000Rp, luxury 290,000-450,000Rp; ❄) An old concrete monster of a hotel that's been superbly renovated by its new Australian owners into something very special indeed. The gorgeous decked, beach-facing garden with its hip bar area looks as if it'd be far too flash for a backpacker's budget, but there are clean, plain economy rooms on the ground floor.

Other places to stay:

Alana's (Jl Legokpari; d with shared mandi 30,000Rp) Basic bamboo shacks.

Teratai (☎ 633681; r 80,000-120,000Rp) Welcoming family-owned place with accommodation scattered around a large grassy plot.

Kang Ayi Restaurant (☎ 633676; Jl Legokpari; mains 10,000Rp; ⏰ breakfast, lunch & dinner) The best of three *warung* near Java Cove hotel, serving fresh fish, Indonesian faves and some Western food including omelettes.

Getting There & Away

There are no buses to Batu Karas. To get here from Pangandaran take a bus to Cijulang (9000Rp, one hour) then a 3km ride in an *ojek* (4000Rp) over the bamboo bridge (toll 1000Rp).

AROUND BATU KARAS

About 6km inland from Batu Karas, pleasure boats run upriver to the **Green Canyon**, a lush river valley where you can swim in surging emerald currents and take a natural power shower under the streams that tumble into the gorge (don't look up!). Boats cost 70,000Rp, and run between 7.30am and 4pm. Day trips can be organised from Pangandaran (see p186) but it's easy enough to get here on a hired motorbike, as the route to the canyon is very well signposted.

WONOSOBO

☎ 0286 / pop 103,000

Wonosobo is the main gateway to the Dieng Plateau and has some reasonable budget accommodation; otherwise it's a forgettable agricultural centre.

The **BNI bank** (Jl A Yani) has an ATM and exchange facilities. There's also internet access at **Bina** (Jl Veteran 36, per hr 5000Rp; ⏰ 24hr), and a centrally located **tourist office** (☎ 321194; Jl Kartini 3; ⏰ 8am-3pm Mon-Fri).

Just south of the bus station, **Wisma Duta Homestay** (☎ 321674; Jl Rumah Sakit 3; r with shared/private mandi 50,000-250,000Rp) has very simple but tidy budget rooms and some swanky upmarket options.

Hotel Sri Kencono (☎ 321522; Jl A Yani 81; d from 50,000Rp; ❄) is a good bet, with everything from no-frills fan rooms with shared *mandi* to air-con doubles with hot-water bathrooms (220,000Rp).

Popular with travellers, **Dieng Restaurant** (☎ 21266; Jl Mayjend Bambang; mains from 20,000Rp; ⏰ 7am-9.30pm) has Indonesian, Chinese and Western grub served up buffet style. Tours of the plateau can be arranged too.

Wonosobo's bus station is 3km out of town on the Magelang road. From Yogyakarta, take a bus to Magelang (10,000Rp, one hour) and then another bus to Wonosobo (15,000Rp, two hours). **Rahayu Travel** (☎ 321217; Jl A Yani 95) has door-to-door minibuses to Yogyakarta (38,000Rp, three hours). Hotels can arrange pick-ups.

Frequent buses to Dieng (8000Rp, one hour) leave from Dieng terminal, 500m west of the town centre, throughout the day.

DIENG PLATEAU

☎ 0286

A startling contrast from the heat and fecundity of the lowlands, the plateau of Dieng (Abode of Gods) is another world: a windswept volcanic landscape of swirling clouds, green hills, mist and damp punctuated with ancient ruins.

Information

The small tourist info office near Losmen Bu Djono has extremely sporadic opening times.

BRI bank (⏰ 8am-2pm Mon-Fri) Near Hotel Gunung Mas, changes US dollars (cash) at poor rates.

Kios Telephone Dian (⏰ 8am-6pm) A *wartel* just before the Hotel Gunung Mas.

Sights & Activities

It costs 12,000Rp to visit the plateau and the main temples (Telaga Warna is an extra 7000Rp) and there's a small **ticket office** (8am-5.30pm) in the village which has a basic map of Dieng region.

On the swampy plain in front of Dieng village are the five Hindu temples of the **Arjuna Complex** that are thought to be the oldest in Java, dating back to AD 680. Though historically important, they are small, squat and visually not that impressive. **Candi Gatutkaca**, a temple to the south, has a small site **museum** (admission included in entrance ticket; 8am-4pm) containing statues and sculpture from the temples.

The plateau's natural attractions and remote allure are the main reasons to visit. From the village, you can do a two-hour loop walk that takes in the turquoise lake of **Telaga Warna** and **Kawah Sikidang**, a volcanic crater with steaming vents and frantically bubbling mud pools. You can see all the main sights, including the temples, on foot in a morning or afternoon, though to really explore the plateau and its crater lakes, allow a couple of days.

The walk to **Sembungan** village (2300m) to see the sunrise is heavily touted by the guesthouses, though having to pay to get up at 3.30am is a dubious privilege (particularly on cloudy mornings). All the guesthouses can arrange **guides** (per person 40,000Rp) and hire out warm clothing.

Sleeping & Eating

Arctic-cold *mandi* are the norm unless stated.

Hotel Asri (☎ 642034; r with shared mandi 30,000-40,000Rp) As cheap as chips, but very basic. It's 200m south of the bus stop for Wonosobo.

Losmen Bu Djono (☎ 642046; Jl Raya, Km 27; r 30,000-40,000Rp, with hot water 70,000-80,000Rp) Friendly place with good info if slightly shabby digs, though there is reliable hot water and a café that sells Bintang.

Dieng Plateau Homestay (Jl Raya, Km 27; r 50,000Rp) Rooms here are clean enough and there's food available.

Hotel Gunung Mas (☎ 592417; Jl Raya, Km 27.5; r 80,000, with hot water 100,000Rp) The most 'upmarket' hotel in town, but it's overpriced considering the sparse rooms.

Getting There & Away

Frequent buses (8000Rp, one hour) run between Dieng and Wonosobo throughout the day.

YOGYAKARTA

☎ 0274 / pop 669,000

A hotbed of Javanese intellectual and political thought, and boasting an incredibly rich artistic and cultural heritage, Yogya is one of the nation's most enjoyable and cosmopolitan cities. Architecturally, much of its historic core remains intact – despite some damage inflicted by the 2006 earthquake – and though traffic woes and pollution levels are worsening, it remains a highly rewarding destination for travellers.

Still headed by its sultan, whose *kraton* remains the focus of traditional life, modern Yogya is as much a city of batik, *gamelan* and ritual, as *macet*, chic cafés and internet junkies. It's also a terrific place to shop, with bargains galore at perhaps Java's premier market, and dozens of stores selling everything from antique textiles to tie-dyed sarongs.

With the puffing summit of volcanic Gunung Merapi on one flank, the ancient ruins of Borobudur on the other and the crashing waves of the Indian Ocean to the south, Yogyakarta is a vital pit stop on any Indonesian itinerary.

Orientation

Jl Malioboro is the main drag, running south from the train station to become Jl A Yani at its southern end (where you'll find the *kraton*). It's lined with stores, and you'll find the main budget accommodation enclave of Sosrowijayan just off it. A second hotel and restaurant district lies to the south around Jl Prawirotaman.

Information

BOOKSHOPS

Lucky Boomerang (Map p193; ☎ 895006; Gang 1-67; 8am-9pm) Stocks Periplus maps, guidebooks, fiction and souvenirs.

Rama Bookshop (Map p193; ☎ 0818 0274 7533; off Jl Sosrowijayan; 9am-7pm) Stocks a small selection of fiction.

GETTING INTO TOWN

Prepaid taxis from a booth at the airport to Yogya, 10km away, cost 35,000Rp. From the main road, only 200m from the terminal, you can get a *colt* into the centre (3000Rp).

INDONESIA

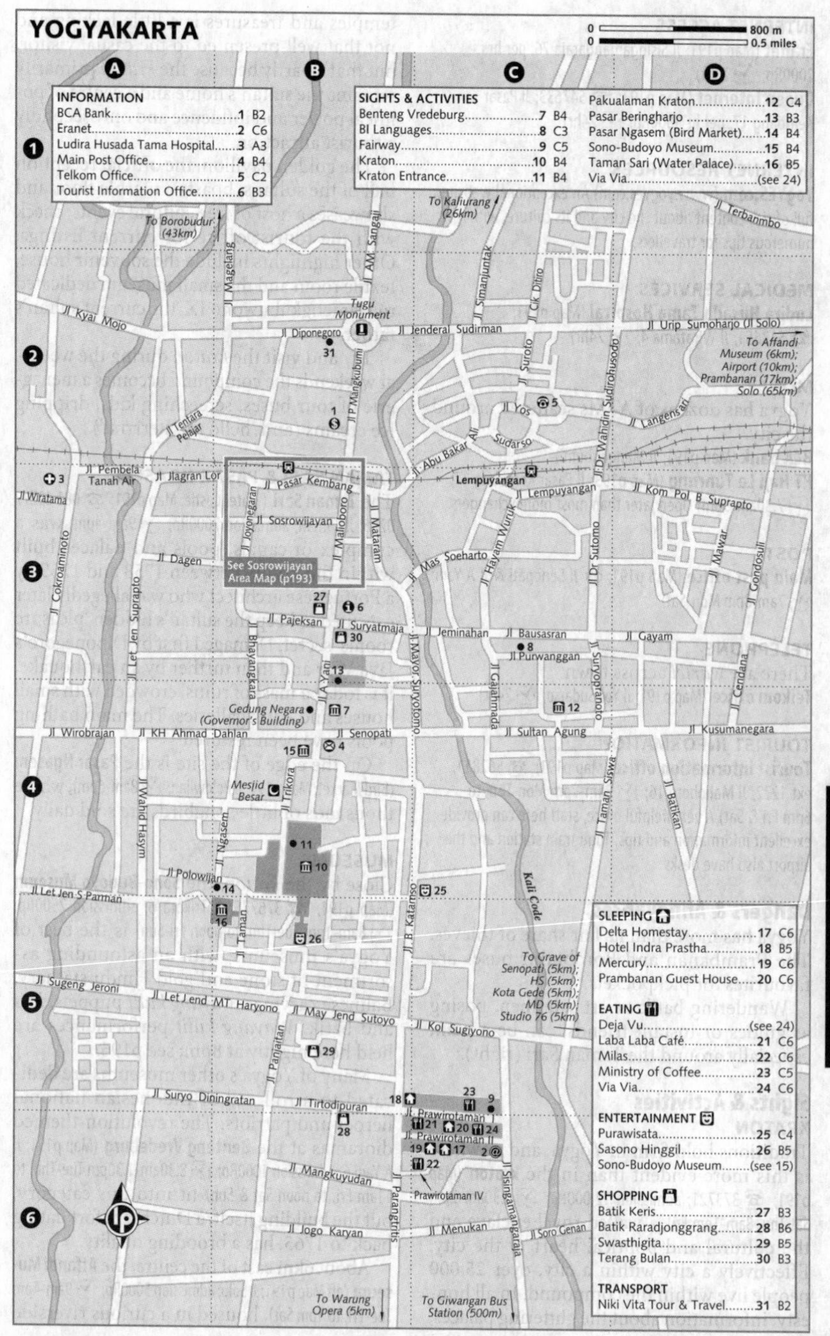
YOGYAKARTA
INFORMATION
BCA Bank.....1 B2
Eranet.....2 C6
Ludira Husada Tama Hospital.....3 A3
Main Post Office.....4 B4
Telkom Office.....5 C2
Tourist Information Office.....6 B3
SIGHTS & ACTIVITIES
Benteng Vredeburg.....7 B4
BI Languages.....8 C3
Fairway.....9 C5
Kraton.....10 B4
Kraton Entrance.....11 B4
Pakualaman Kraton.....12 C4
Pasar Beringharjo.....13 B3
Pasar Ngasem (Bird Market).....14 B4
Sono-Budoyo Museum.....15 B4
Taman Sari (Water Palace).....16 B5
Via Via.....(see 24)
SLEEPING
Delta Homestay.....17 C6
Hotel Indra Prastha.....18 B5
Mercury.....19 C6
Prambanan Guest House.....20 C6
EATING
Deja Vu.....(see 24)
Laba Laba Café.....21 C6
Milas.....22 C6
Ministry of Coffee.....23 C5
Via Via.....24 C6
ENTERTAINMENT
Purawisata.....25 C4
Sasono Hinggil.....26 B5
Sono-Budoyo Museum.....(see 15)
SHOPPING
Batik Keris.....27 B3
Batik Raradjonggrang.....28 B6
Swasthigita.....29 B5
Terang Bulan.....30 B3
TRANSPORT
Niki Vita Tour & Travel.....31 B2
To Borobudur (43km)
To Kaliurang (26km)
Tugu Monument
To Affandi Museum (6km); Airport (10km); Prambanan (17km); Solo (65km)
Lempuyangan
See Sosrowijayan Area Map (p193)
Gedung Negara (Governor's Building)
Mesjid Besar
Kali Code
To Grave of Senopati (5km); HS (5km); Kota Gede (5km); MD (5km); Studio 76 (5km)
Prawirotaman IV
To Warung Opera (5km)
To Giwangan Bus Station (500m)
Jl Kyai Mojo
Jl Diponegoro
Jl Jenderal Sudirman
Jl Urip Sumoharjo (Jl Solo)
Jl Terbanmbo
Jl Magelang
Jl AM Sangaji
Jl P Mangkubumi
Jl Simanjuntak
Jl Cik Ditiro
Jl Suroto
Jl Dr Wahidin Sudirohusodo
Jl Yos Sudarso
Jl Langensari
Jl Tentara Pelajar
Jl Abu Bakar Ali
Jl Pembela Tanah Air
Jl Jlagran Lor
Jl Pasar Kembang
Jl Wiratama
Jl Sosrowijayan
Jl Joyonegaran
Jl Malioboro
Jl Mataram
Jl Lempuyangan
Jl Kom Pol B Suprapto
Jl Dagen
Jl Mas Soeharto
Jl Hayam Wuruk
Jl Dr Sutomo
Jl Mawar
Jl Gondosuli
Jl Cokroaminoto
Jl Let Jen Suprapto
Jl Pajeksan
Jl Suryatmaja
Jl Jeminahan
Jl Bausasran
Jl Gayam
Jl Purwanggan
Jl Bhayangkara
Jl A Yani
Jl Mayor Suryotomo
Jl Gajahmada
Jl Suryopranoto
Jl Cendana
Jl Wirobrajan
Jl KH Ahmad Dahlan
Jl Senopati
Jl Sultan Agung
Jl Kusumanegara
Jl Trikora
Jl Wahid Hasym
Jl Ngasem
Jl Taman Siswa
Jl Batikan
Jl Polowijan
Jl Let Jen S Parman
Jl Taman
Jl B Katamso
Jl Sugeng Jeroni
Jl Let Jend MT Haryono
Jl May Jend Sutoyo
Jl Kol Sugiyono
Jl Panjaitan
Jl Suryo Diningratan
Jl Tirtodipuran
Jl Prawirotaman I
Jl Prawirotaman II
Jl Mangkuyudan
Jl Parangtritis
Jl Sisingamangaraja
Jl Jogo Karyan
Jl Menukan
Jl Soro Genan
0 800 m
0 0.5 miles

INTERNET ACCESS

Eranet (Map p191; Jl Sisingamangaraja 76; per hr 2000Rp; 🕒 24hr)
Queen Internet (Map p193; ☎ 547633; Jl Pasar Kembang 17; per hr 5000Rp; 🕒 24hr)

INTERNET RESOURCES

YogYES.com (www.yogyes.com) An exceptional website, full of rich content about the city and its culture, with numerous tips for travellers.

MEDICAL SERVICES

Ludira Husada Tama Hospital (Map p191; ☎ 513651; Jl Wiratama 4; 🕒 24hr)

MONEY

Yogya has dozens of ATMs scattered around the city.
BCA bank (Map p191; Jl Mangkubumi)
PT Haji La Tunrung (Map p193; Jl Pasar Kembang 17; 🕒 7.30am-9pm) Open later than most moneychangers.

POST

Main post office (Map p191; cnr Jl Senopati & Jl A Yani; 🕒 7am-8pm Mon-Sat)

TELEPHONE

There are *wartel* across town.
Telkom office (Map p191; Jl Yos Sudarso; 🕒 24hr)

TOURIST INFORMATION

Tourist information office (Map p191; ☎ 562811, ext 1222; Jl Malioboro 16; 🕒 8am-7pm Mon-Thu, to 6pm Fri & Sat) A very helpful office, staff here can provide excellent information and tips. Tugu train station and the airport also have desks.

Dangers & Annoyances

Yogya has more than its fair share of thieves. The Prambanan and Borobudur buses are favourites for pickpockets.

Wandering batik or art salesmen, posing as guides or instant friends, can be a pain, especially around the Taman Sari (right).

Sights & Activities

KRATON

Traditions hold firm in Yogya, and nowhere is this more evident than in the **kraton** (Map p191; ☎ 373721; admission 12,000Rp; 🕒 8.30am-2pm Sat-Thu, 8am-1pm Fri), a walled royal enclave and the cultural and political heart of the city. Effectively a city within a city, over 25,000 people live within the compound. In all honesty, information about the glittering palaces, temples and treasures is a little lacking and not that well presented to the casual visitor, but that's partly because the *kraton* primarily remains the sultan's home and a centre of political power and influence and only secondly a tourist attraction.

The golden pavilion, the official reception hall of the sultans, boasts a marble floor and showcases a host of free cultural events; check with the tourist office for current listings. Other highlights include the souvenir house, textile room and the small museum dedicated to Hamengkubuwono IX, the current sultan's father.

Try and visit the *kraton* during the week – at weekends the compound becomes a menagerie of tour buses, screeching kids, dripping ice creams (and 'hello missterrrrs!').

TAMAN SARI & PASAR NGASEM

The **Taman Sari** (Water Castle; Map p191; ☎ 081 80277 0296; Jl Taman; admission 7000Rp; 🕒 9am-4pm) was a complex of canals, pools and palaces built within the *kraton* between 1758 and 1765 by a Portuguese architect who was allegedly later executed to keep the sultan's hidden 'pleasure rooms' secret. Damaged first by Diponegoro's Java War and then further by an earthquake, it is today a mass of ruins, crowded with small houses and batik galleries. The main bathing pools have been restored.

On the edge of the site is the **Pasar Ngasem** (Bird Market; Map p191; Jl Polowijan; 🕒 8am-6pm), where thousands of little songbirds are sold daily.

MUSEUMS

Close by the *kraton*, the **Sono-Budoyo Museum** (Map p191; ☎ 376775; Jl Trikora 6; admission 7500Rp; 🕒 8am-1pm Tue-Thu, to noon Fri-Sun) is the best of Yogya's museums, with an astounding assortment of stone and gold Hindu statuary, Balinese carvings, *wayang kulit* puppets, *kris* and batik. *Wayang kulit* performances are held here nightly at 8pm; see p196.

Many of Yogya's other museums are dedicated to a roll call of Indonesian national heroes and patriots. The revolution-themed dioramas at the **Benteng Vredeburg** (Map p191; Jl A Yani 6; admission 1000Rp; 🕒 8.30am-1.30pm Tue-Thu, to 11am Fri, to noon Sat & Sun) fit into this category, but the building itself, a Dutch-era fort dating back to 1765, has a brooding quality.

About 6km east of the centre, the **Affandi Museum** (off Map p191; Jl Solo; admission 5000Rp; 🕒 9am-4pm Tue-Fri, to 1pm Sat), housed in a curious riverside tree house, exhibits the impressionist works of Affandi, Indonesia's best-known artist.

OTHER ATTRACTIONS

The smaller **Pakualaman Kraton** (Map p191; Jl Sultan Agung; admission 2000Rp; 9.30am-1.30pm Tue, Thu & Sun) has a small museum, a *pendopo* (open-sided pavilion), which can hold a full *gamelan* orchestra, and a curious colonial house.

Yogya's superb main market, **Pasar Beringharjo** (Map p191; Jl A Yani; 7.30am-5pm), is a wonderful place to spend an hour or two. Buzzing with life, here you can shop for cheap batik, clothes, bags and sandals. On the upper floors there's a spice market and an area devoted to curios and antiques.

The main street of **Kota Gede** (off Map p191), 5km southeast of Yogya, is a silverwork centre with plenty of silver jewellery on offer. The sacred **grave of Senopati**, the first king of Mataram, can also be seen here.

MASSAGE

For a traditional Javanese massage with oils, **Fairway** (Map p191; ☎ 970810; Jl Prawirotaman 17; massages per hr from 40,000Rp) is recommended.

Courses

BI Languages (Map p191; ☎ 588192; www.puribahasa.net; Jl Purwanggan 15) A professional language school offering Bahasa Indonesia classes (US$7 per hour for one-on-one tuition). Family homestays can be arranged, starting at 450,000Rp per week.

Studio 76 (off Map p191; ☎ 714 7676; Jl Purbayan, Kota Gede) Recommended for its full-day silversmith courses (200,000Rp per person including lunch and 10g of silver to play around with).

Via Via (Map p191; ☎ 386557; www.viaviacafe.com; Jl Prawirotaman I 30) Has excellent half-day cooking (75,000Rp), batik- and silver jewellery-making (both 70,000Rp) courses.

Sleeping

Yogya has dozens of good guesthouses and hotels. Sosrowijayan is the main budget zone, while the Prawirotaman area, 2km south of the *kraton*, also has some cheap places as well as midrange options. All provide a small breakfast unless stated.

SOSROWIJAYAN AREA

Situated within a short walk of the train station, Sosrowijayan is a fascinating traditional

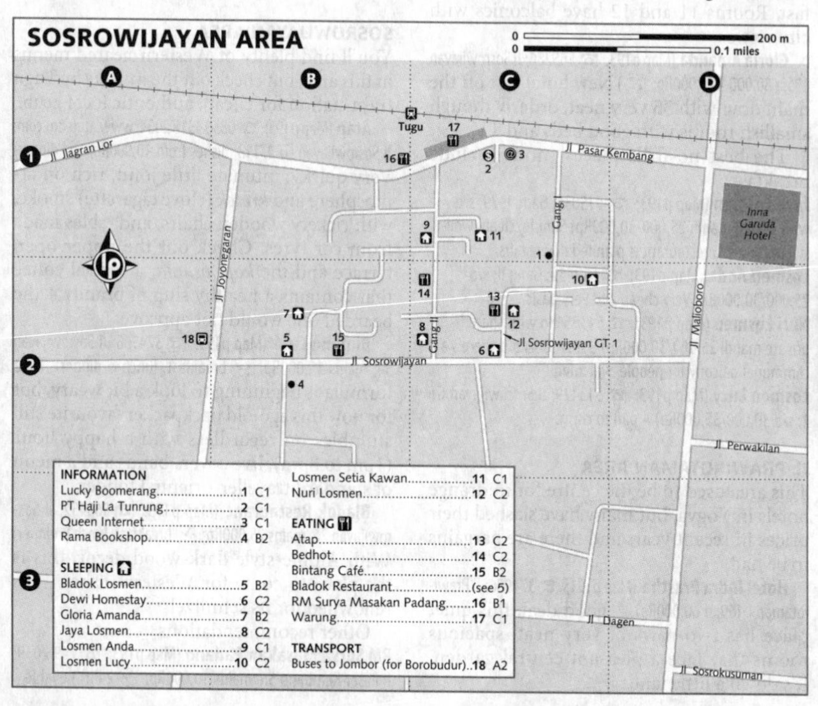

INDONESIA

neighbourhood of narrow *gang* (alleyways), lined with backpacker-geared accommodation, eateries, laundries and the like.

Dewi Homestay (Map p193; ☎ 516014; dewihomestay@hotmail.com; s/d 45,000/50,000Rp) Highly atmospheric converted house, replete with mosaic-tiled hallways and a leafy front garden. The rooms, though many have four-poster beds, are a tad dark.

our pick Losmen Setia Kawan (Map p193; ☎ 512452; www.bedhots.com; Gang II 58; s 50,000-80,000, d 60,000-100,000Rp;) The first choice for travellers in this area, this very well-run and kept place has atmosphere in abundance, with lovely old floor tiles, magazines to read and free tea and coffee. Prepare yourself for walls covered in hippy-dippy Roger Dean–style psychedelic murals, though. You should book ahead.

Bladok Losmen & Restaurant (Map p193; ☎ 560452; Jl Sosrowijayan 76; s/d from 70,000/80,000Rp;) Elegant, classy little hotel of real character and charm with three floors of immaculate rooms, all with hand-carved wooden beds, fan and bathroom. Pot plants adorn every corridor and there's a heat-busting pool, but no breakfast. Rooms 11 and 12 have balconies with city views.

Gloria Amanda (Map p193; ☎ 565286; Jl Sosrowijayan 195; r 80,000-175,000Rp;) New hotel just off the main drag with 35 very neat, orderly though smallish rooms with good beds and TV.

The best no-frills places (none include breakfast):

Jaya Losmen (Map p193; ☎ 515035; Gang II 79; s/d with shared mandi 25,000/30,000Rp) Simple, clean, well-swept rooms; a restaurant is planned downstairs.

Losmen Anda (Map p193; ☎ 512452; Gang II; s/d 25,000/30,000Rp) Very cheap and very basic.

Nuri Losmen (Map p193; ☎ 543654; d with shared/private mandi 25,000/30,000Rp) Bare rooms but there's a communal balcony for people-watching.

Losmen Lucy (Map p193; ☎ 513429; Jl Sosrowijayan GT 1; s/d 30,000/35,000Rp) A pad to crash.

JL PRAWIROTAMAN AREA

This area used to be the centre for midrange hotels in Yogya, but many have slashed their prices in recent years and there are bargains to be had.

Hotel Indra Prastha (Map p191; ☎ 374086; Jl Prawirotaman I 169; d 60,000Rp) A good deal, this quiet place has two rows of very neat, spacious rooms that face a pleasant central garden. It's down a little lane.

Mercury (Map p191; ☎ 370846; Jl Prawirotaman II 595; s/d 60,000/80,000Rp) Bizarre-looking place with an ostentatious *kraton*-style reception hall where you can swan around like a sultan at breakfast time, though you'll have to retire at night to a plain, almost featureless bedroom.

our pick Delta Homestay (Map p191; ☎ 372064; Jl Prawirotaman II 597A; d with shared/private mandi from 75,000/90,000Rp;) The lovely pool area is this place's trump card, but rooms are very decent too, if small, with stylish wooden beds and the odd artistic touch; all but the cheapest have hot water.

Prambanan Guest House (Map p191; ☎ 376167; Jl Prawirotaman I No 14; r 80,000-140,000Rp;) Set off the road, this deservedly popular place has fine rooms, with *ikat*-style bedspreads (cloth in which a pattern is produced by dyeing individual threads before the weaving process), that look out over a peaceful garden and pool. Staff are switched on here and can organise transport and tours.

Eating & Drinking

Try to taste some of the local specialities; see opposite.

SOSROWIJAYAN AREA

You'll find plenty of Western-geared menus in this area, but check out the *warung* by Tugu train station for cheap, authentic local grub.

Atap (Map p193; ☎ 0856 4318 2004; www.atap.8m.com; Jl Sosrowijayan GT 1/113; dishes from 10,000Rp; dinner) Very quirky, intimate little joint, rich on atmosphere and *kretek* (clove cigarette) smoke, with rickety wooden chairs, and tables made from car tyres. Check out the upper open terrace and the *kopi osama*, a special coffee that contains a healthy slug of brandy – the bearded one would not approve.

Bintang Café (Map p193; ☎ 374566; Jl Sosrowijayan 54; mains 15,000Rp; breakfast, lunch & dinner) The formula is beginning to look a bit weary, but for now this age-old backpacker favourite still stumbles on regardless with a happy hour (1pm to 8pm), live covers bands and a menu of standard traveller-oriented fodder.

Bladok Restaurant (Map p193; ☎ 560452; Jl Sosrowijayan 76; mains 25,000Rp; breakfast, lunch & dinner) With Alpine-style dark-wood décor, this is the place to come for Western dishes – it's renowned for its schnitzel.

Other recommendations:

RM Surya Masakan Padang (Map p193; ☎ 749 2039; Jl Pasar Kembang 55; mains 10,000Rp; 24hr) Reliable

INDONESIA

chilli-rich Padang food in authentic (read net curtains and tiled floors) surrounds.

Bedhot (Map p193; ☎ 512452; Gang II; mains 18,000-27,000Rp; ⏲ breakfast, lunch & dinner) Reliable, if overpriced, backpacker eats in clichéd backpacker surrounds, complete with swirling psychedelic murals.

JL PRAWIROTAMAN AREA

our pick Via Via (Map p191; ☎ 386557; www.viaviacafe.com; Jl Prawirotaman I 30; mains 12,000-25,000Rp; ⏲ breakfast, lunch & dinner) This happening place gets everything right. The modernist concrete building, with an open-air upper area and greenery to screen you from the road, is superb and the (all) female staff are efficient, friendly and helpful. Plenty of thought has gone into the menu: feast on well-presented and executed local dishes, Western treats and daily specials. There are always vegetarian selections and wine by the glass. You'll also find magazines to browse and information boards. Via Via offers a number of trips and courses too, see p193.

Milas (Map p191; ☎ 742 3399; Jl Prawirotaman IV 127; meals 20,000Rp; ⏲ lunch & dinner) Down a quiet side road, this project centre for street youth has a vegetarian restaurant set in a spacious garden and a menu of healthy snacks, sandwiches, salads and organic coffee.

Ministry of Coffee (Map p191; ☎ 747 3828; www.ministryofcoffee.com; Jl Prawirotaman I 15A; mains 25,000Rp; ⏲ breakfast, lunch & dinner) Occupies a striking modern structure, with a library (with English-language books and periodicals) upstairs and a café below. It's a great place for a Java hit (espresso and cappuccino are available) but the food (mainly sandwiches, and cakes) is only so-so.

Other recommendations:

Deja Vu (Map p191; ☎ 782 2844; Jl Prawirotaman 28; mains from 15,000Rp; ⏲ breakfast, lunch & dinner) Stylish place ideal for a sandwich or a *nasi goreng*. Daily specials are on the blackboard.

Laba Laba Café (Map p191; ☎ 374921; Jl Prawirotaman I 2; mains 20,000Rp; ⏲ lunch & dinner) Bar-eatery with cheapish Western and local nosh. Not a gar bar, but popular with gays.

OTHER AREAS

Warung Opera (off Map p191; ☎ 718 1977; Jl Parangtritis, Km 6.3; dishes 5500-13,000Rp; ⏲ dinner) On the road to the beach, about 5km south of Prawirotaman, Warung Opera is a wonderfully flamboyant-looking restaurant scattered with antique furniture and chandeliers but with an extremely moderately priced, creative menu of Indonesian dishes and Yogya specialities. Donny, your host, can also read your fortune from the residue of your *kopi java*.

Entertainment

Dance, *wayang* or *gamelan* are performed most mornings at the *kraton* (admission free). Check with the tourist office for current listings.

DANCE

Most dance performances are based on the Ramayana. The spectacular Ramayana ballet held in the open air at Prambanan in the dry season (see p197) is the one to catch if you can.

Purawisata (Map p191; ☎ 380644; Jl B Katamso; tickets 100,000Rp, with dinner 175,000Rp) Stages the Ramayana daily at 8pm.

PUPPET PERFORMANCES

Wayang kulit performances can be seen at several places around Yogya every night of the week.

Sasono Hinggil (Map p191; tickets 20,000Rp) Marathon all-night performances are held every second Saturday from 9pm to 5am in the *alun*

YOGYA SPECIALITIES

Yogya has a rich culinary tradition and many dishes are unique to the region. To try many of these you'll have to head into the market areas, where some stallholders have been churning out a particular speciality for decades. *Gudeg* is young jackfruit served in a spicy coconut sauce, served with a little tempeh (or chicken), egg, and sweetened with palm sugar. Look out too for *nasi brongkos,* a dark bean and tofu stew served with small chunks of meat, rice and *krupuk* (prawn crackers).

Yogya-style espresso is *kopi jos,* a cup of potent coarsely ground Java coffee that's dunked with a few pieces of glowing charcoal – try it at the stalls around Tugu train station. *Teh poci* (traditional tea served with unprocessed sugar in a clay pot) is best sampled from the *warung* in front of the Pakualaman Kraton.

alun selatan (south main square) of the *kraton*. Bring a pillow.

Sono-Budoyo Museum (Map p191; ☎ 376775; Jl Trikora 6; tickets 3000Rp) Near the *kraton,* the museum has performances nightly from 8pm to 10pm.

Wayang golek plays are also performed frequently; check listings at the tourist information office.

Shopping

Yogya is a great place to shop for crafts and artefacts; try the Beringharjo market first for bargains, or the Prawirotaman area which has several fine antique stores.

Jl Malioboro is one great, long, throbbing bazaar of souvenir shops and stalls selling cheap cotton clothes, leatherwork, batik bags, *topeng* masks and *wayang golek* puppets.

BATIK

Have a good look around first before you buy, as quality is very variable. Batik in the markets, especially Pasar Beringharjo, is cheaper than in the shops, but toughen up your bargaining skills first. The best quality is *batik tulis* (hand-drawn batik), which has incredibly intricate detailing, with the designs created by using wax to 'resist' the multiple dying processes. It's much less bother to use a *cap* (metal stamp) to form patterns, and most of the textiles you'll be offered are made using this method. *Batik cap* is much duller on the reverse side.

Good fixed-price places to try:

Batik Keris (Map p191; ☎ 557893; Jl Malioboro 21; 🕐 9am-9pm)

Terang Bulan (Map p191; ☎ 588522; Jl A Yani 108; 🕐 9am-8pm)

Most of the batik workshops and several large showrooms are along Jl Tirtodipuran, south of the *kraton*. These places cater to tour groups so prices are very high. **Batik Raradjonggrang** (Map p191; ☎ 375209; Jl Tirtodipuran 6A; 🕐 8am-7pm) gives free guided tours of its factory.

LEATHERWORK

Yogya's leatherwork can be excellent value for money; shops and stalls on Jl Malioboro are the best places to look.

Swasthigita (Map p191; ☎ 378346; Ngadinegaran MJ 3/122; 🕐 9am-4pm) Just north of Jl Tirtodipuran, this is a large *wayang kulit* puppet manufacturer.

SILVERWORK

Head to the silver village of Kota Gede for the best prices and to see the silversmiths at work – or even make your own (see p193). In Yogya, Jl Kemesan and Jl Mondorakan have some good buys.

HS (Jl Mandarokan I, Kota Gede) Has a good selection of jewellery, but bargain hard.

MD (☎ 375063; Jl Pesegah KG 8/44, Kota Gede) Down a small alley; good discounts can be negotiated here.

Getting There & Away

AIR

Garuda (☎ 0807 142 7842; www.garuda-indonesia.com) has twice-daily flights to Jakarta (from 252,000Rp), a daily flight to Denpasar (308,000Rp) and flights to Balikpapan and Kuala Lumpur.

Lion Air and its subsidiary **Wings Air** (☎ 555028; www.lionair.co.id) operate daily flights to Jakarta (149,000Rp to 246,000Rp), Denpasar (199,000Rp) and Surabaya (from 110,000Rp).

Mandala (☎ 520602; www.mandalaair.com) has daily flights, including to Jakarta (188,000Rp), Balikpapan and Banjarmasin (both 325,000Rp).

BUS

Yogyakarta's **Giwangan bus station** (☎ 410015; Jl Imogiri) is 5km southeast of the city centre, on the ring road.

Economy/air-con bus services include Semarang (19,000/27,000Rp, 3½ hours), Bandung (70,000/92,000Rp, 10 hours), Surabaya (62,000/80,000Rp, eight hours), Probolinggo (68,000/90,000Rp, nine hours), Solo (12,000/18,000Rp, two hours), and Denpasar (from 170,000Rp, 16 hours). Services to Jakarta (12 hours) cost from 90,000Rp depending on the quality of the bus.

Buses also operate regularly to towns in the immediate area, including Borobudur (11,000Rp, 1½ hours) and Kaliurang (6000Rp, one hour).

If you're travelling long distance, tickets for the luxury buses can be bought at the bus station but it's far less hassle to check fares and departures with the ticket agencies along Jl Sosrowijayan and Jl Prawirotaman. These agencies can also arrange pick-up from your hotel.

Local bus 4 leaves from Jl Malioboro (2000Rp) for Giwangan.

MINIBUS

Door-to-door *travel* service all major cities from Yogyakarta, including Surabaya (110,000Rp, eight hours), Jakarta (195,000Rp, 12 hours), Denpasar (200,000Rp, 15 hours), Gunung Bromo (150,000Rp, 10 hours) and Pangandaran (125,000Rp, eight hours). Most *travel* will pick you up from your hotel. Hotels and travel agencies can arrange tickets for the minibuses, or you can book directly through **Niki Vita Tour & Travel** (Map p191; ☎ 561884; Jl Diponegoro 25).

TRAIN

Yogya's main **Tugu station** (☎ 512870) is conveniently central, although some *ekonomi* trains run to/from the Lempuyangan station 1km further east.

For journeys to Jakarta, the smart *Argo Lawu* (210,000Rp, eight hours) and decent but slower *Taksaka* (160,000Rp, nine hours) are both scheduled to leave at 9am. *Argo Dwipanggaa* (180,000Rp, nine hours) departs at 9pm.

For Solo, the best option is the *Prameks* (*bisnis* 7000Rp, one hour) departing from Tugu at 6.50am, 9.45am, 1pm, 4.10pm and 6.52pm.

To Surabaya, *Sancaka* leaves at 7.30am and 4pm (*bisnis* 70,000Rp, 5½ hours), while for Bandung the *Lodaya* (*eksekutif*/*bisnis* 155,000/90,000Rp, eight hours) leaves at 10.05am and again at 9.20pm, or the *Argo Wilis* (155,000Rp, six hours) leaves at 12.15pm.

For details of all times and prices, visit www.infoka.kereta-api.com.

Getting Around

BUS

Bis kota (city buses) operate on set routes around the city for a flat 2000Rp fare.

LOCAL TRANSPORT

Bicycles (12,000Rp per day) and motorcycles (25,000Rp) can be hired from travel agents and hotels. Furious bargaining is required with local becak drivers – count on 5000Rp for a short trip.

TAXI

Metered taxis are readily available in Yogyakarta at 4500Rp for the first kilometre and 2500Rp for subsequent kilometres; try **JAS Taxi** (☎ 373737).

PRAMBANAN

The grandest and most evocative Hindu temple complex in Java, **Prambanan** (☎ 0274-496435; admission US$10; 6am-6pm, last admission 5.15pm) features some 50 temple sites. Many of these were damaged by the large earthquake that struck the region in 2006, and the main temples were off limits at the time of research, though the authorities hope to reopen (most) of the site by the time you read this. Nevertheless, the temples still look stunning from a distance, and Prambanan is definitely still worth a visit. The main temples face Prambanan village on the highway, while others are scattered across the surrounding fields. Prambanan is 17km east of Yogya on the Solo road.

The **Shiva temple** is the largest and most lavish, towering 47 dizzy metres above the valley and decorated with an entire pantheon of carved deities. The statue of Shiva stands in the central chamber and statues of the goddess Durga, Shiva's elephant-headed son Ganesh and Agastya the teacher stand in the other chapels of the upper part of the temple. The Shiva temple is flanked by the **Vishnu** and **Brahma temples**, the latter carrying further scenes from the Ramayana. In the small central temple, opposite the Shiva temple, stands a statue of the bull Nandi, Shiva's mount.

Built in the 9th century AD, the complex at Prambanan was mysteriously abandoned soon after its completion. Many of the temples had collapsed by the 19th century and only in 1937 was any form of reconstruction attempted.

The spectacular **Ramayana ballets** performed here have been suspended in the aftermath of the earthquake. If they've resumed they are well worth attending, with a cast of hundreds performing in front of a floodlit Shiva temple; check with the Yogya tourist information office.

From Yogya, take a bus (3500Rp, 30 minutes) from Giwangan bus station; Solo-bound buses also stop here. A motorbike or bicycle is a good way to explore all the temples in the area via the back roads; Via Via (p195) organises good half-day trips for 100,000Rp per person including guide/motorbike chauffer.

BOROBUDUR

☎ 0293

Ranking with Bagan and Angkor Wat as one of the great Southeast Asian monuments, **Borobudur** (☎ 788266; www.borobudurpark.com;

admission 99,000Rp; ⌚ 6am-5.30pm) is a stunning and poignant epitaph to Java's Buddhist heyday.

The temple, 42km northwest of Yogya, consists of six square bases topped by three circular ones, and it was constructed at roughly the same time as Prambanan in the early part of the 9th century AD. With the decline of Buddhism, Borobudur was abandoned, covered in volcanic ash by an eruption in 1006, and only rediscovered in 1814 when Raffles governed Java.

Nearly 1500 narrative relief panels on the terraces illustrate Buddhist teachings and tales, while 432 Buddha images sit in chambers on the terraces. On the upper circular terraces there are latticed stupas, which contain 72 more Buddha images.

Borobudur is best witnessed at sunrise, when morning mist hangs over the lush surrounding valley and distant hills. By 7am, the hordes have arrived: it's a very popular school trip for students, so expect requests for pictures from giggling teenagers.

Unfortunately the two site **museums** (entrance included in ticket price) have little information in English, but check out the 16m wooden outrigger, a replica of a boat depicted in one of Borobudur's panels. This boat was sailed to Africa in 2003, a voyage retracing Javanese trading links, the original spice trade, with the continent over a thousand years ago. Around 750m southeast of the main monument, a new **monastery** is being constructed by Indonesian Buddhists.

The **Mendut Temple** (admission free), 3.5km east of Borobudur, has a magnificent 3m-high statue of Buddha seated with two disciples. It has been suggested that this image was originally intended to top Borobudur but proved impossible to raise to the summit. Your tour bus from Yogya will stop here if you ask, otherwise a bemo is 1500Rp.

Knowledgeable guides for Borobudur can be hired (50,000Rp) at the ticket office.

Sleeping & Eating

There are plenty of cheap *warung* around the site's exit.

Lotus II (☎ 788845; Jl Balaputradewa 54; r 110,000Rp) Offers spacious, stylish rooms with quality beds and mosquito nets, plus great rice-paddy views from the balcony.

Also recommended:

Pondok Tingal Hostel (☎ 788245; Jl Badrawati; dm 15,000Rp, r from 80,000Rp; ✖) Ultracheap dorms, good rooms, a restaurant and a leafy garden; 1km east of the site.

Hotel Bhumisambhara (☎ 788205; Jl Badrawati; r 50,000-60,000Rp) Quiet and homely, on the eastern side of the temple complex.

Lotus Guest House (☎ 788281; Jl Medang Kamulan 2; s/d 65,000/85,000Rp) Old-timer that's seen better days, but run by friendly folk.

Getting There & Away

Most travellers get to Borobudur on a tour, which costs around 50,000Rp per person and includes door-to-door pick-up/drop off at about 4am/noon; all the Yogya hotels can book this for you. To do the trip yourself, direct buses leave Yogya's Giwangan terminal (11,000Rp, 1½ hours). Or from the Sosrowijayan area, flag down a northbound bus 5 on the corner of Jl Sosrowijayan and Jl Joyonegaran, which will take you to Jombor (2000Rp, 20 minutes), where you can get a Borobudur bus (7000Rp, 50 minutes). The last bus back from Borobudur leaves around 6pm.

KALIURANG & GUNUNG MERAPI

☎ 0274

On the flanks of Gunung Merapi, Kaliurang is a pleasant mountain resort, with crisp air and some spectacular views of one of Java's most boisterous volcanoes. It is 26km north of Yogya.

Gunung Merapi (Mountain of Fire) is Indonesia's most active volcano and has been in a near-constant state of eruption for hundreds of years. People living on its conical flanks are regularly killed by pyroclastic flows, and in 2006 28,000 villagers had to be evacuated after intense seismic activity. It's extremely unlikely anyone will be allowed anywhere near its summit in the near future, though you get a spectacular view from the viewing point of Kali Aden.

In Kaliurang, the owner of **Vogels Hostel** (☎ 895208; Jl Astamulya 76; dm 12,000Rp, r 30,000-100,000Rp), Christian Awuy, has been conducting tours of Merapi for two decades, and while little at the hotel has changed in that time it remains Kaliurang's best budget option, with excellent info and filling grub. Otherwise **Christian Hostel** (r 40,000Rp) is very spartan, while **Hotel Satriafi** (☎ 895128; Jl Kesehatan 193; r from 80,000Rp) is a bit more comfortable.

Buses to Kaliurang (6000Rp, one hour) run regularly from Yogya's Gilwangan terminal. To get to Kali Aden yourself, get off at the

Kalurang Hill Resort, then catch one of the waiting *ojek* (8000Rp) from there for a view of the action, lava and gas. Tour agencies in Yogya can also arrange Merapi-viewing trips, which are best at night.

SOLO

☎ 0271 / pop 560,000

Perhaps the least Westernised city in Java, Solo (also known as Sala and Surakarta) has long rivalled Yogyakarta as a centre of Javanese culture and identity. Briefly rising to prominence as the capital of the Mataram empire, Solo is known today for its *wayang*, dance and music, *kraton*, crumbling back alleys and a thriving arts scene, minus the tourist hordes of Yogyakarta.

Solo's culture is undeniably rich, and it makes a fascinating place to visit, but it also has a reputation throughout Indonesia as being a base for radicals and political firebrands. Terrible riots engulfed the city in 1998, when Chinese-owned businesses were torched, and anti-Western protests are not uncommon. Many Jemaah Islamiya (JI) members attend the city's Pesantren Ngruki *madrassah*. That said, most citizens are extremely hospitable and welcome visitors, but it's best to bear in mind that this is a conservative city, with a volatile temperament.

Orientation

Solo's main street is Jl Slamet Riyadi, running east–west through the centre of the city, with most budget accommodation conveniently clustered just off it around Jl Yos Sudarso and Jl Ahmad Dahlan. The oldest part of Solo is east of here around the Kraton Surakarta and Pasar Klewer.

Solo's train station is about 2km north of the city centre, the main Tirtonadi bus terminal about 1.5km north again.

Information

BCA bank (cnr Jl Dr Rajiman & Jl Gatot Subroto) Has ATM and currency-exchange facilities.

BumiNet (Jl Ahmad Dahlan 39; per hr 4000Rp; 🕑 11am-2am) Huge place with dozens of internet-wired PCs.

Main post office (Jl Jen Sudirman; 🕑 8am-6pm Mon-Fri, to noon Sat)

Rumah Sakit Panti Kosala (Jl Slamet Riyadi; 🕑 24hr) Hospital with English-speaking doctors.

Telkom office (Jl Mayor Kusmanto; 🕑 7am-8pm) Also has internet access.

Tourist office (☎ 711435; Jl Slamet Riyadi 275; 🕑 8am-4pm Mon-Sat) The helpfulness of this office very much depends on who you speak to (ask for Patrick Orlando). Can provide listings of cultural events, but also drop by the Istana Griya guesthouse for a brilliant map and information.

Sights & Activities

The once-mighty **Kraton Surakarta** (☎ 656432; admission 8000Rp; 🕑 9am-2pm Tue-Thu, to 2pm Sat & Sun) dates back to 1745, when it was first opened as Susuhunan of Mataram, Pakubuwono II's royal home. Unfortunately much of its splendour was lost in a 1985 fire, which gutted much of the place including the *pendopo*, and most of the compound is off limits to visitors. Nevertheless, some fine silver and bronze Hindu-Javanese figures remain alongside dusty Javanese weapons, parasols and what must qualify as a near-definitive horse carriage collection. Presentation could be so much better, however, and labelling is poor or nonexistent. The distinctive pagodalike tower, Panggung Songgo Buwono, built in 1782, is original and is used for meditation.

Children's **dance practice** can be seen here on Sunday from 10am to noon and adult practice from 1pm to 3pm.

Istana Mangkunegaran (☎ 644946; Jl Ronggowarsito; admission 10,000Rp; 🕑 8.30am-4pm Mon-Sat, to 1pm Sun) is a rival palace founded in 1757 by a dissident prince, Raden Mas Said. The weathered main structure itself, built in Javanese-European style with an extended front canopy, is in urgent need of restoration, but the museum rooms at the rear have some fascinating curios, including a diminutive gold genital cover, a tremendous mask collection and wonderfully gaudy dining room complete with lashings of gild and a mirrored ceiling. One of Java's finest *gamelan* orchestras is based here.

Guided tours (a 12,000Rp donation is acceptable) are much less hurried and more informative than at Kraton Surakarta. Try to time your visit to coincide with **dance practice** (10am to 12.30pm Wednesday and Sunday) or Javanese singing (10am to noon Tuesday).

Solo's markets are always worth a browse, especially **Pasar Klewer** (Jl Secoyudan; 🕑 8am-6pm), the multistorey batik market, and **Pasar Triwindu** (Jl Diponegoro; 🕑 8am-5pm), the flea market, which always turns up something of interest.

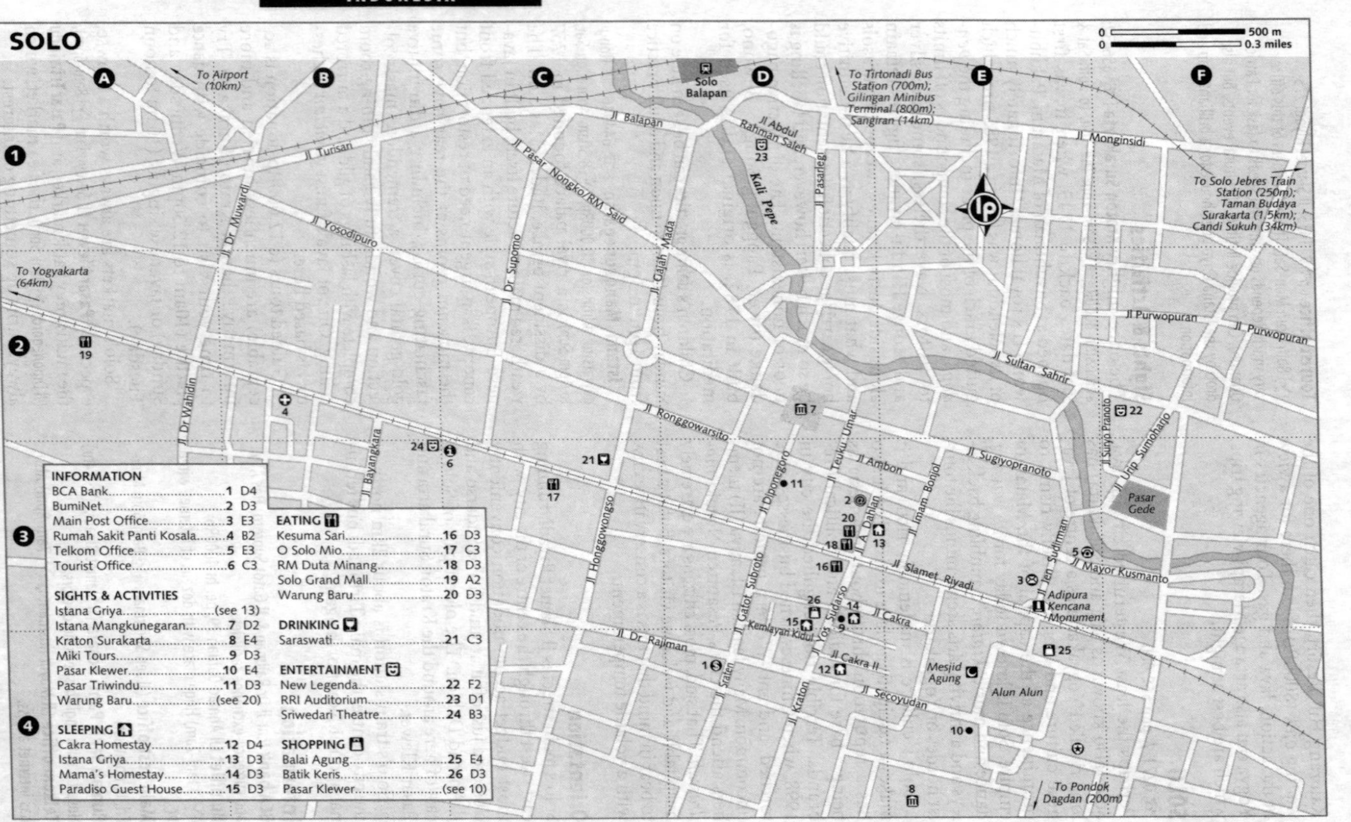
SOLO
0 500 m
0 0.3 miles
A
B
C
D
E
F
1
2
3
4
INFORMATION
BCA Bank 1 D4
BumiNet 2 D3
Main Post Office 3 E3
Rumah Sakit Panti Kosala 4 B2
Telkom Office 5 E3
Tourist Office 6 C3
SIGHTS & ACTIVITIES
Istana Griya (see 13)
Istana Mangkunegaran 7 D2
Kraton Surakarta 8 E4
Miki Tours 9 D3
Pasar Klewer 10 E4
Pasar Triwindu 11 D3
Warung Baru (see 20)
SLEEPING
Cakra Homestay 12 D4
Istana Griya 13 D3
Mama's Homestay 14 D3
Paradiso Guest House 15 D3
EATING
Kesuma Sari 16 D3
O Solo Mio 17 C3
RM Duta Minang 18 D3
Solo Grand Mall 19 A2
Warung Baru 20 D3
DRINKING
Saraswati 21 C3
ENTERTAINMENT
New Legenda 22 F2
RRI Auditorium 23 D1
Sriwedari Theatre 24 B3
SHOPPING
Balai Agung 25 E4
Batik Keris 26 D3
Pasar Klewer (see 10)
To Airport (10km)
To Yogyakarta (64km)
To Tirtonadi Bus Station (700m); Gilingan Minibus Terminal (800m); Sangiran (14km)
To Solo Jebres Train Station (250m); Taman Budaya Surakarta (1.5km); Candi Sukuh (34km)
To Pondok Dagdan (200m)
Solo Balapan
Kali Pepe
Pasar Gede
Alun Alun
Mesjid Agung
Adipura Kencana Monument
Jl Turisan
Jl Balapan
Jl Abdul Rahman Saleh
Jl Pasar Nongko/RM Said
Jl Gajah Mada
Jl Monginsidi
Jl Pasadeg
Jl Sultan Sahrir
Jl Purwopuran
Jl Urip Sumoharjo
Jl Suryo Pranoto
Jl Mayor Kusmanto
Jl Jen Sudirman
Jl Sugiyopranoto
Jl Imam Bonjol
Jl Slamet Riyadi
Jl Ambon
Jl Teuku Umar
Jl A Dahlan
Jl Cakra
Jl Cakra II
Jl Yos Sudarso
Jl Kemlayan Kidul
Jl Secoyudan
Jl Kraton
Jl Diponegoro
Jl Gatot Subroto
Jl Slaten
Jl Dr Rajiman
Jl Ronggowarsito
Jl Honggowongso
Jl Dr Supomo
Jl Yosodipuro
Jl Bayangkara
Jl Dr Muwardi
Jl Dr Wahidin

Festivals & Events

The **Solo dance festival** is held in late April. There are traditional and modern Javanese dance performances, and film screenings.

Courses

Solo is renowned as a centre for traditional Javanese religion and mysticism, but few travellers now come here to participate; speak to the tourist office about schools offering meditation classes. Batik courses (one day, 70,000Rp) are also popular; contact the restaurant **Warung Baru** (☎ 656369; Jl Ahmad Dahlan 23) for further information.

Tours

Several places, including the hotel **Istana Griya** (☎ 632667; istanagriya@yahoo.com; Jl Ahmad Dahlan 22), **Miki Tours** (☎ 653278; Jl Yos Sudarso 17) and **Warung Baru** (☎ 656369; Jl Ahmad Dahlan 23), organise excellent trips around Solo by bicycle (around 70,000Rp) or motorbike (100,000Rp to 150,000Rp) to the sights of the region, including tea plantations, batik workshops and *gamelan* factories. Trips beyond the city to Candi Sukuh (120,000Rp) and Gunung Merapi can also be arranged.

Sleeping

Solo has some great budget hotels.

Paradiso Guest House (☎ 652960; Kemlayan Kidul 1; d incl breakfast 37,000-66,000Rp) Occupying a superb, ornate whitewashed city mansion, this inexpensive, quiet, likable place has corridors strewn with pot plants and artistic touches including Venetian mirrors. The rooms are well kept and airy.

our pick **Istana Griya** (☎ 632667; istanagriya@yahoo.com; Jl Ahmad Dahlan 22; r 50,000-200,000Rp; ❄) Extremely well-run place where every effort is directed at making the traveller at home and highly informed about the city. Rudi, the switched-on owner, understands his backpacking clientele well, organises superb tours and ensures the wide selection of rooms are all absolutely spotless. Guests can socialise in the little terrace, and slurp on free tea and coffee, and everyone's provided with a map dotted with good restaurant and sightseeing recommendations.

Cakra Homestay (☎ 634743; Jl Cakra II/15; d with shared/private mandi from 60,000/75,000Rp; ❄ 🏊) Tucked away down an anonymous backstreet, this enigmatic and historic hotel scores top marks for its architecture, tranquil location and lovely pool area. If only a little more love and affection was devoted to the plain, if clean, rooms it really would be a gem.

Also recommended:

Pondok Dagdan (☎ 669324; Jl Carangan Baluarti 42; s/d with shared mandi 25,000/35,000Rp) Simple bamboo rooms in a quiet garden south of the centre.

Mama's Homestay (☎ 662466; Jl Cakra 33; s/d with shared mandi 35,000/45,000Rp) The hospitable family here rents out three bare rooms in their home.

Eating

Solo's street food is varied and can be wonderful. Roaming *kaki lima* (mobile food stall) hawkers pack the streets at night advertising their wares by screeching, striking buffalo bells or clattering cutlery. Certain areas are synonymous with specific dishes: to try *nasi gudeg* (young jackfruit served with sweet coconut sauce, rice and chicken) head to the lanes around Pasar Triwindu. For Solo-style satay the stalls on the south side of Jl Slamet Riyadi where it meets Jl Yos Sudarso excel.

Kesuma Sari (☎ 656406; Jl Slamet Riyadi 111; mains 7000Rp; 🕑 lunch & dinner) Very popular, inexpensive place that offers a fair attempt at Indo-style Western dishes including steaks and chicken Maryland.

Warung Baru (☎ 656369; Jl Ahmad Dahlan 23; mains 12,000Rp; 🕑 breakfast, lunch & dinner) Solo's original travellers' scoff stop has fallen on hard times as fewer folk traverse Java, but it still bakes good bread even if the cooking's pretty average. Tours can be organised here.

O Solo Mio (☎ 727264; Jl Slamet Riyadi 253; mains 35,000Rp; 🕑 lunch & dinner) If you can't be bothered climbing Gunung Merapi, you can instead eat a pizza here that has been cooked on a slab of stone from the mountain. The décor oozes Mediterranean pizzazz and there's a little yard out back for alfresco dining.

Other recommendations:

Solo Grand Mall (Jl Slamet Riyadi; dishes from 8000Rp 🕑 breakfast, lunch & dinner) About 2km west of the centre, this mall has an inexpensive, diverse food court.

RM Duta Minang (☎ 648440; Jl Slamet Riyadi 66; meals 9000Rp; 🕑 24hr) Serving up Padang's finest around the clock.

Drinking

A pub crawl is not on the agenda here. Solo's few bars are attached to expensive hotels.

Saraswati (Novotel, Jl Slamet Riyadi 272; 🕑 6pm-late) This smart hotel bar attracts a hip crowd, including a gay contingent at weekends.

Clubbing

This isn't Ibiza – club action is limited.

New Legenda (Jl Suryo Pranoto; admission 25,000Rp; 8pm-late Fri & Sat) Crepuscular club where the dance floor bounces to modern *dangdut* dance beats. There's a modest cover charge of around 30,000Rp.

Entertainment

Solo is an excellent place to see traditional Javanese performing arts; the tourist office has a full schedule of events.

Sriwedari Theatre (Jl Slamet Riyadi; tickets 3000Rp) Located at the back of Sriwedari Amusement Park, this theatre has a long-running *wayang orang* (dance-drama enacted by masked performers, recounting scenes from the Ramayana) troupe. Performances are staged nightly, Mondays to Saturdays, from 8pm to 10pm.

RRI auditorium (☎ 641178; Jl Abdul Rahman Saleh 51; tickets from 6000Rp) The radio auditorium hosts an erratic but eclectic schedule of cultural performances.

Taman Budaya Surakarta (TBS; ☎ 635414; Jl Ir Sutami 57) In the east of the city, this culture centre holds all-night *wayang kulit* and some Western plays.

Istana Mangkunegaran and Kraton Surakarta also have traditional Javanese dance practice (see p199).

Shopping

Balai Agung (8am-4pm) On the northern side of the *alun alun*, you can see high-quality *wayang kulit* puppets being made here, and *gamelan* sets are for sale.

Solo is a major batik centre. You can see the batik process on one of Warung Baru's batik tours (see p201).

Other recommendations:

Batik Keris (☎ 643292; Jl Yos Sudarso 62; 9am-7pm) Expensive, but top quality and fixed prices.

Pasar Klewer (Jl Secoyudan; 8am-6pm) Market stuffed with cheap batik.

Getting There & Away

AIR

Air Asia (code AK; ☎ 080 4133 3333; www.airasia.com) connects Solo with Kuala Lumpur daily from 110,000Rp. **SilkAir** (code MI; ☎ 724604/5; www.silkair.com) flies Tuesday, Thursday and Saturday to Singapore for US$350 return. **Garuda** (code GA; ☎ 630082; www.garuda-indonesia.com) has four daily flights to Jakarta.

BUS & MINIBUS

The Tirtonadi bus station is 2.5km north of the city centre. Frequent buses go to Prambanan (9000Rp, 1½ hours) and Yogyakarta (normal/air-con 12,000/18,000Rp, two hours), and numerous buses go to Surabaya (56,000/72,000Rp, six hours). Agents at the bus station sell tickets for the longer express routes (eg Jakarta from 130,000Rp; Denpasar from 150,000Rp).

Across the road from here, the Gilingan minibus terminal has air-con services to almost all the same destinations, with prices usually about 10% to 20% higher.

Homestays and travel agencies also sell tickets for *travel;* a door-to-door service to Bromo (Ngadisiri) costs 150,000Rp.

TRAIN

Solo is on the main Jakarta–Yogyakarta–Surabaya train line. **Solo Balapan** (☎ 714039) is the main station, but some local trains depart from Solo Jebres, further east.

The quickest and most convenient way to get to Yogyakarta is on the *Prameks* (*bisnis* 7000Rp, one hour), which departs from Balapan five times daily at 5.45am, 8.36am, 11.35am, 2.26pm and 5.55pm. All these trains start in Jebres 15 minutes earlier.

Express trains to Jakarta include the *Argo Lawu* (*eksekutif* 210,000Rp, 8½ hours, once daily at 8.10am), which is the most luxurious day train; the *Senja Utama* (*bisnis* 100,000Rp, 10 hours, once a day at 6pm); and the *eksekutif Bima* (from 200,000Rp, nine hours, once daily at 9pm).

The *Lodaya* (*bisnis/eksekutif* 100,000/150,000Rp, nine hours) departs for Bandung at 8pm and the *Sancaka* (*bisnis/eksekutif* 60,000/85,000Rp, five hours) swings through Balapan at 8.14am and 4.58pm on its way from Yogyakarta to Surabaya.

For further information on all times and prices, visit www.infoka.kereta-api.com.

Getting Around

A metered taxi from the airport, 10km northwest of the city centre, costs 55,000Rp, or take a bus via Kartasura. An *ojek* or becak from the train or bus station into the city centre costs around 5000Rp, a taxi about 15,000Rp. Minibus 06 costs 2000Rp to Jl Slamet Riyadi.

After dark many taxis refuse to use their meters and want a minimum of 10,000Rp for short trips. Bicycles and motorcycles (motorcycle/bicycle per day 50,000/15,000Rp) can be hired from homestays.

AROUND SOLO

Sangiran

Prehistoric 'Java Man' fossils were discovered at Sangiran, 16km north of Solo, where a small **museum** (admission 10,000Rp; 9am-4pm Tue-Sun) has fossil exhibits of *Homo erectus*, mammoth bones and hippo teeth. To get there take a Purwodadi bus to Kalijambe (3000Rp) and it's a 4km walk from there (by *ojek* 6000Rp).

Candi Sukuh

This fascinating, remote temple complex on the slopes of Gunung Lawu (3265m), some 36km east of Solo, is well worth a visit. Dating from the 15th century, Sukuh was one of the last temples to be built in Java by Hindus, who were on the run from Muslims and forced to isolated mountain regions (and Bali). From the site, there are sweeping views across terraced fields.

The main pyramid resembles an Incan or Mayan monument, with steep sides and a central staircase; at its base are flat-backed turtles that may have been sacrificial altars. It's clear a fertility cult built up around the temple, as there are all manner of erotic carvings, including a *yoni-lingga* (vagina-phallus) representation and a figure clasping his erect penis.

Take a bus to Karangpandan (5000Rp, 40 minutes), then a Kemuning minibus to the turn-off for Candi Sukuh (3000Rp, 20 minutes). On market days the bus goes right to the temple; otherwise it's a steep 2km uphill walk; or grab an *ojek* from the turn-off for about 6000Rp.

SURABAYA

☎ 031 / pop 2.4 million

The smog-prone capital of East Java is first and foremost a business city. It's not a cosmopolitan place, and is a hard city to get to like (especially when you've spent 10 minutes trying to cross one of the five-lane highways that tear through its city centre). But though Surabaya's sheer size seems intimidating at first, it does have the odd curious attraction, including a remarkable *Arabian Nights*–style bazaar district and a vibrant Chinatown. But a night is enough for most travellers, if that.

Orientation

There's no natural centre to this sprawling city but Jl Permuda, which runs west from Gubeng train station, is something of a main drag, with two shopping malls plus several hotels and banks.

Around 5km north of here is the Chinatown district and the Arab quarter of Qubah.

Information

Jl Pemuda has several banks with ATMs, including a BNI branch. The Tunjungan Plaza is also ATM-rich.

Abacommnet (LG fl, Tunjungan Plaza, Jl Tunjungan; per hr 10,000Rp; 8am-9pm) Has broadband connections and doubles as a *wartel*.

Main post office (Jl Kebon Rojo; 8am-7.30pm Mon-Sat) North of the centre.

Rumah Sakit Darmo (☎ 567 6253; Jl Raya Darmo 90) Hospital with English- and Dutch-speaking doctors. It's west of the centre.

Tourist Information Centre (☎ 534 0444; www.sparklingsurabaya.com; Jl Pemuda; 9am-5pm Mon-Sat) There are helpful staff at this office, and good colour maps are proffered.

Sights

Surabaya may have a grand history, but she wears it lightly, for little substantial remains. The **Qubah** – the city's labyrinthine Arab quarter, centred upon the imposing **Mesjid Ampel** (Jl Ampel Suci) – is fascinating, however, and begs exploration. The mosque itself marks the burial place of Sunan Ampel, one of the *wali songo* (holy man) who brought Islam to Java; pilgrims chant and present rose-petal offerings at his grave behind the mosque. The warren of surrounding lanes are reminiscent of a Damascene souk, with stalls selling perfumes, sarongs, prayer beads, *peci*

GETTING INTO TOWN

Taxis from Juanda Airport (15km away) operate on a coupon system and cost 55,000Rp to the city centre. Damri airport buses (5000Rp) drop off in the city centre and at Purabaya bus station.

Official taxis from the Gubeng train station should cost 10,000Rp to 15,000Rp for journeys of 2km to 3km. It's easy to get a freelance taxi in the parking area outside, but to be safe call **Bluebird** (☎ 372 1234) or **Silver cabs** (☎ 560 0055) for a ride.

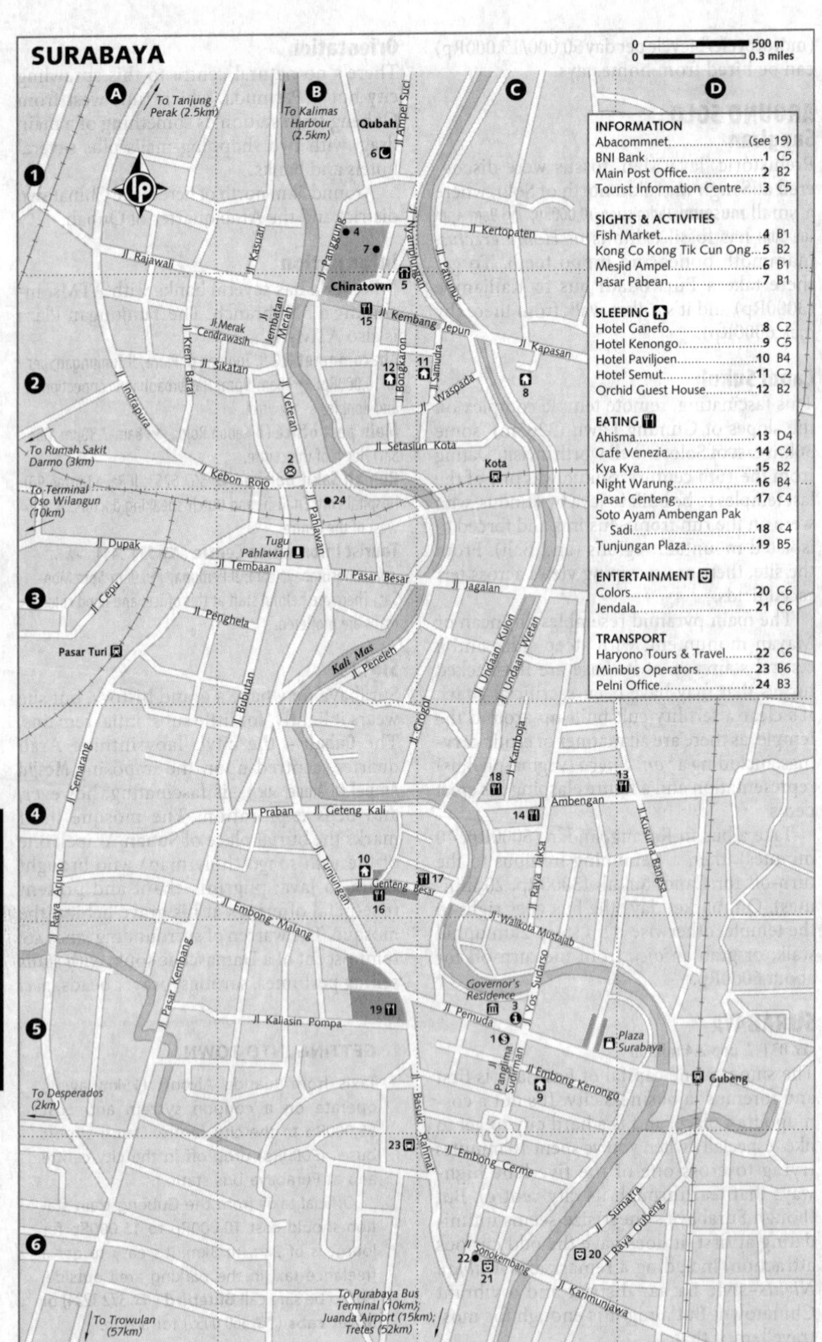
SURABAYA
0 500 m
0 0.3 miles
A
B
C
D
1
2
3
4
5
6
INFORMATION
Abacommnet........................(see 19)
BNI Bank.........................1 C5
Main Post Office.................2 B2
Tourist Information Centre.......3 C5
SIGHTS & ACTIVITIES
Fish Market......................4 B1
Kong Co Kong Tik Cun Ong.........5 B2
Mesjid Ampel.....................6 B1
Pasar Pabean.....................7 B1
SLEEPING
Hotel Ganefo.....................8 C2
Hotel Kenongo....................9 C5
Hotel Paviljoen..................10 B4
Hotel Semut......................11 C2
Orchid Guest House...............12 B2
EATING
Ahisma...........................13 D4
Cafe Venezia.....................14 C4
Kya Kya..........................15 B2
Night Warung.....................16 B4
Pasar Genteng....................17 C4
Soto Ayam Ambengan Pak Sadi.....18 C4
Tunjungan Plaza..................19 B5
ENTERTAINMENT
Colors...........................20 C6
Jendala..........................21 C6
TRANSPORT
Haryono Tours & Travel...........22 C6
Minibus Operators................23 B6
Pelni Office.....................24 B3
To Tanjung Perak (2.5km)
To Kalimas Harbour (2.5km)
Qubah
Jl Ampel Suci
Jl Kertopaten
Jl Nyamplungan
Jl Pattiunus
Jl Rajawali
Jl Kasuari
Jl Panggung
Chinatown
Jl Kembang Jepun
Jl Kapasan
Jl Merak Cendrawasih
Jl Jembatan Merah
Jl Krem Barat
Jl Sikatan
Jl Bongkaron
Jl Samudra
Jl Waspada
Jl Indrapura
Jl Veteran
To Rumah Sakit Darmo (3km)
Jl Setasiun Kota
Kota
Jl Kebon Rojo
To Terminal Oso Wilangun (10km)
Jl Pahlawan
Jl Dupak
Tugu Pahlawan
Jl Tembaan
Jl Pasar Besar
Jl Jagalan
Jl Cepu
Jl Penghela
Pasar Turi
Kali Mas
Jl Peneleh
Jl Undaan Kulon
Jl Undaan Wetan
Jl Bubutan
Jl Grogol
Jl Kamboja
Jl Semarang
Jl Praban
Jl Geteng Kali
Jl Ambengan
Jl Kusuma Bangsa
Jl Tunjungan
Jl Genteng Besar
Jl Raya Jaksa
Jl Embong Malang
Jl Walikota Mustajab
Jl Raya Arjuno
Jl Pasar Kembang
Governor's Residence
Jl Yos Sudarso
Jl Pemuda
Jl Kaliasin Pompa
Plaza Surabaya
Jl Panglima Sudirman
Jl Embong Kenongo
Gubeng
To Desperados (2km)
Jl Basuki Rahmat
Jl Embong Cerme
Jl Sumatra
Jl Raya Gubeng
Jl Sonokembang
Jl Karimunjawa
To Purabaya Bus Terminal (10km); Juanda Airport (15km); Tretes (52km)
To Trowulan (57km)

(black Muslim felt hats) and other religious paraphernalia.

Chinatown, just south of here, bursts into life at night when Jl Kembang Jepun becomes a huge street kitchen known as Kya Kya (see below). Much of the food here is sourced from the nearby **Pasar Pabean** (Jl Panggung; 8am-6pm) and the nearby **fish market** (pasar ikan; Jl Panggung; from 8pm). Close by too is the 300-year-old Chinese temple **Kong Co Kong Tik Cun Ong** (Jl Dukuh; admission by donation; dawn-dusk).

Elsewhere in the city, plenty of **Makassar schooners** can be seen at the Kalimas wharf north of town.

Sleeping

Some of the very cheapest, and roughest, hotels can be found near Kota train station. It's best to spend a little extra. All the following prices include breakfast.

Hotel Ganefo (☎ 371 1169; Jl Kapasan 169-171; d with shared/private mandi 70,000/105,000Rp;) Boasts a dramatic Chinese-style veranda, a panelled lobby and two classes of accommodation: bare, cell-like but clean rooms in the main house or functional, if bland air-con, doubles in the modern extension. Pity the poor caged monkeys at the rear.

Hotel Paviljoen (☎ 534 3449; Jl Genteng Besar 94; r 77,000-126,000Rp;) This beautiful, if flaky, colonial mansion has clean, spartan rooms each with gorgeous shutters and a little porch. Breakfast is *roti* and tea or coffee.

Orchid Guest House (☎ 355 0211; orchidguesthousesby@yahoo.com; Jl Bongkaran 49; d 150,000Rp;) Good new hotel near the Kya Kya, run by an ever-helpful English-speaking team who can help with travel and city info. The rooms' wallpaper is a tad garish, but all have top-quality mattresses, colour TV, air-con and spotless bathrooms with hot water. There's a little café here too.

Other recommendations:

Hotel Semut (☎ 353 1770; Jl Samudra 9; s/d from 127,000/145,000Rp;) A bizarre chintz-rich time warp of a hotel.

Hotel Kenongo (☎ 534 1359; Jl Embong Kenongo 12; s/d from 180,000/190,000Rp;) Benefits from a quiet central location and the rooms are light and airy.

Eating

There's a strip of night *warung* on Jl Genteng Besar and along the nearby riverbank on Jl Genteng Kali.

Kya Kya (Jl Kembang Jepun; mains from 9000Rp; dinner) A pedestrianised strip lined with dozens of street stalls, flaming woks and steaming cauldrons on Chinatown's main drag. Highly enjoyable and sociable; feast on local faves like *pangsit mie* (egg noodle and wonton soup) and fresh seafood.

Tunjungan Plaza (5th fl, Jl Tunjungan; mains from 12,000Rp; breakfast, lunch & dinner) Offers a mind-boggling array of squeaky-clean eateries, each specialising in a cuisine: Malay-style chicken, *roti*, noodles and all the usual Indonesian dishes.

Ahisma (☎ 535 0466; Jl Kusuma Bangsa 80; mains from 25,000Rp; lunch & dinner) Escape the madness of the city at this peaceful, elegant vegetarian restaurant run by a hospitable Indo-Chinese family. Choose from salads, soups, rice and noodle dishes, and save some room for the vegan ice cream. The small veggie deli here stocks *krupuk* (prawn crackers), cookies and other treats.

Cafe Venezia (☎ 534 3335; Jl Ambengan 16; mains 40,000Rp; lunch & dinner) Set in swanky colonial surrounds, this pricey restaurant raids Europe, Japan, Korea, and even Indonesia, for inspiration.

Also recommended:

Pasar Genteng (Jl Genteng Besar; mains 6000Rp; breakfast, lunch & dinner) Come here for Indonesian street food par excellence; try the *soto madura* (beef broth).

Soto Ayam Ambengan Pak Sadi (☎ 532 3998; Jl Ambengan 3A; mains 20,000Rp; lunch & dinner) Renowned for its chicken, but also serves a few Madurese specialities.

Drinking

There's very, very little drinking culture in Surabaya, with the soulless hotel bars the only (overpriced) option.

Desperados (☎ 566 1550; Shangri La Hotel, Jl Mayjend Sungkono 120; 6pm-1.30am Sun-Thu, to 2.30am Fri & Sat) Swish hotel bar west of the centre with live music and Tex-Mex food; try the margaritas. There's a cover charge of around 40,000Rp.

Clubbing

Colors (☎ 503 0562; www.colorspub.com; Jl Sumatra 81; 7pm-3am) This place can be a riot, with a young, hip clientele largin' it to propulsive DJ-driven dance mixes, and some live bands. The outrageous fashionista door staff set the tone here.

Entertainment

Jendala (☎ 531 4073; Jl Sonokembang 4-6) A varied programme of so-called culturetainment (sometimes dance, sometimes live music, sometimes theatre), plus food.

Getting There & Away

AIR

Surabaya's Juanda airport has a few international departures and is an important hub for domestic flights.

The following airlines all operate flights out of Surabaya.

Adam Air (code KI; ☎ 505 5999; www.flyadamair.com) Daily flights to Jakarta (from 142,000Rp).

Air Asia (code AK; ☎ 531 0303; www.airasia.com) Two daily flights to Kuala Lumpur (from 425,000Rp) via Jakarta.

Garuda (code GA; ☎ 080 7142 7832; www.garuda-indonesia.com) Over a dozen daily flights to Jakarta (from 221,000Rp) and four daily to Denpasar (from 187,000Rp).

Lion Air (code JT; ☎ 535 3500; www.lionair.co.id) Low cost carrier with six daily flights to Jakarta, and also daily to Kupang (from 378,000Rp), Pulau Batam and Balikpapan.

Merpati (code MZ; ☎ 568 8111; www.merpati.co.id) Flights to Denpasar, Makassar and Kuala Lumpur (US$178).

TransNusa (☎ 546 7505; www.transnusa.co.id)

Haryono Tours & Travel (☎ 532 5800; Jl Panglima Sudirman; 8am-4.30pm Mon-Fri, to 1pm Sat) can book tickets for all airlines.

BOAT

Surabaya is an important port and **Pelni** (☎ 355 9950; www.pelni.co.id; Jl Pahlawan 112) ships serve destinations including Pontianak (197,000Rp, 40 hours), Makassar and Banjarmasin. Boats depart from Tanjung Perak harbour; to get there take bus P1 from Tunjungan Plaza.

Ferries to Kamal on Pulau Madura (5000Rp, 30 minutes) also leave every half-hour from Tanjung Perak.

BUS & MINIBUS

Most buses operate from Surabaya's main Purabaya bus terminal in Bungurasih, 10km south of the city centre. Buses along the north coast and to Semarang depart from the Terminal Oso Wilangun, 10km west of the city.

Services from Purabaya include Yogyakarta (normal/air-con 62,000/80,000Rp, eight hours), Banyuwangi (38,000/58,000Rp, six hours), Solo (56,000/72,000Rp, six hours), Probolinggo (17,000/26,000Rp, two hours), Jakarta (230,000Rp, 18 hours), and Sumanep on Pulau Madura (44,000Rp, 4½ hours).

Luxury long-haul buses also depart from Purabaya. Most are night buses leaving in the late afternoon/early evening. Bookings can be made at the terminal, or travel agencies in the centre of town sell tickets with a mark-up.

Door-to-door *travel* operate to Denpasar (165,000Rp, 10 hours), Solo (95,000Rp, six hours) and Yogyakarta (110,000Rp, eight hours). Hotels can make bookings and there are minibus operators on Jl Basuki Rahmat.

TRAIN

Trains from Jakarta, taking the fast northern route via Semarang, arrive at the Pasar Turi train station. Trains taking the southern route via Yogyakarta, and trains from Banyuwangi and Malang, arrive at Gubeng and most carry on to Kota. **Gubeng** (☎ 503 3115) is central and sells tickets for all trains.

Most fast Jakarta trains leave from **Pasar Turi** (☎ 534 5014), such as the *Gumarang* (*bisnis/eksekutif* 120,000/220,000Rp, 11½ hours), which leaves at 5.20pm. Coming the other way, it leaves Gambir in Jakarta at 5.50pm.

From Gubeng, the slower *Bima* (*eksekutif* 200,000Rp, 14½ hours) departs at 5pm for Jakarta, via Yogyakarta, and the *bisnis Mutiara Selatan* (90,000Rp, 13 hours) departs at 4.05pm for Bandung.

The *Sancaka* is the best day train for Yogyakarta, leaving Gubeng at 7.30am and 3.10pm for Solo (4½ hours) and Yogyakarta (5½ hours). It costs 45,000/70,000Rp in *bisnis/eksekutif* to either destination.

Apart from services to the main cities, trains leave Gubeng for Malang (4000Rp, two hours) every two hours. Heading east towards Bromo and Bali the *Mutiara Timur* goes at 9.02am via Probolinggo (two hours) to Banyuwangi (seven hours); tickets to both destinations are the same (*bisnis/eksekutif* 40,000/55,000Rp).

Getting Around

Surabaya has plenty of air-con metered taxis; **Bluebird** (☎ 372 1234) and **Silver** (☎ 560 0055) are the most reliable companies.

Bemo are labelled A, B, C etc and charge 2000Rp.

AROUND SURABAYA

Scattered around **Trowulan**, 60km southwest of Surabaya on the Solo road, are the ruins of the capital of the ancient Majapahit empire, Java's last great Hindu kingdom. One kilometre from the main Surabaya–Solo Hwy, the **Trowulan Museum** (admission 2000Rp; 7am-3.30pm Tue-Sun) houses superb examples of Majapahit sculpture and pottery from throughout East Java. Reconstructed temples are scattered over a large area, some within walking distance, though you need to hire a becak to see them all.

The hill resort of **Tretes**, 55km south of Surabaya, is a cool break if you have to kill time in Surabaya, with walks around town and trekking to **Gunung Welirang**.

PPLH Environmental Education Centre (0321-618752; pplh@indo.net.id; dm/bungalows 15,000/150,000Rp), in a stunning setting near Trawas, a few kilometres northwest of Tretes, is the perfect place to unwind. It mainly caters to groups, but its trekking packages and herbal-medicine and ecology courses are open to individuals. There's fine accommodation and a humble but excellent organic restaurant. Take a bus to Pandaan, then a Trawas bemo (ask for PPLH) and then take an *ojek*.

PULAU MADURA

Only half an hour from Surabaya by ferry, but soon to be connected by Indonesia's largest bridge, the rugged, poor island of Madura is famed for its colourful **bull races**. Called *kerapan sapi*, these kick off in late August and September and climax with the finals held at Pamekasan. The bulls are harnessed in pairs, two teams compete at a time and they're raced along a 120m course in a special stadium – the bulls can do nine seconds over 100m. Bull races for tourists are sometimes staged at the Bangkalan Stadium, and race practice is held throughout the year in Bangkalan, Pamekasan and Sumenep, but dates are not fixed. Contact the **Surabaya Tourist Information Centre** (031-534 0444; www.sparklingsurabaya.com; Jl Pemuda; 9am-5pm Mon-Sat) for race details.

Pamekasan, the capital of Madura, comes alive in the bull-racing season, but is quiet the rest of the year. **Sumenep**, 53km northeast of Pamekasan, is a more refined, royal town and the most interesting on Madura. It has a **tourist office** (0328-667148; Jl Sutomo 5; 7am-3pm Tue-Sat), banks with ATMs, and a few internet cafés. You can see Sumenep's 18th-century mosque, and the **kraton** (admission 1000Rp; 7am-5pm) with its water palace and interesting museum. **Asta Tinggi**, the royal cemetery, is only about 3km from the town centre.

In Pamekasan, **Hotel Ramayana** (0324-324575; Jl Niaga 55; r 45,000-85,000Rp;) has bright, airy accommodation; the more expensive rooms have air-con.

In Sumenep, **Hotel Wijaya I** (0328-662433; Jl Trunojoyo 45-47; r 30,000-70,000Rp;) is a long-running place with a range of rooms. It's popular with travellers.

The 5km Suramadu bridge linking Surabaya and Kamal on Madura is scheduled to open in late 2008. Until that time ferries (5000Rp) run from Tanjung Perak, Surabaya to Kamal. Buses and *colt* head from Kamal to all other towns, including Bangkalan. Buses from Surabaya's Purabaya terminal run direct to Sumenep (44,000Rp, 4½ hours).

GUNUNG BROMO

0335

Gunung Bromo's extraordinary volcanic landscape is East Java's biggest attraction, and the perfect escape from all the island's teeming cities. The smoking cone of Bromo is just one of three peaks to emerge from a vast caldera, the Tengger Massif (which stretches 10km across), its steep walls plunging down to a vast, flat sea of lava and sand. This desolate landscape has a distinctly end-of-the-world feeling, particularly at sunrise.

An even larger cone – Java's largest mountain, the fume-belching Gunung Semeru (3676m) – oversees Bromo's supernatural beauty, and the entire volcanic wonderland forms the Bromo-Tengger-Semeru National Park.

Bromo is an easy side trip from the main backpacking highway that runs between Bali and Yogyakarta, or it's about three hours from Surabaya. The usual jumping-off point is the town of Probolinggo, served by trains and buses from Surabaya and Banyuwangi.

Information

However you approach Bromo, a 25,000Rp park fee is payable at one of the many PHKA checkpoints.

The **PHKA post** (541038; 8am-4pm Mon-Fri) in Cemoro Lawang is opposite Hotel Bromo Permai and has information about Bromo.

Sights & Activities

The best vantage point over this bewitching landscape is from the viewpoint known as Gunung Penanjakan (2770m). All the hotels, and several freelance guides, can put together

INDONESIA

4WD trips (around 240,000Rp for four people and warm jackets), leaving around 4am to catch the sunrise from Penanjakan. It's usually well worth the early start, as the views of Bromo, the Tengger crater and towards smoking Gunung Semeru are spellbinding – this is where those postcard shots are taken. You'll then be driven back down the lip of the caldera and across the crater bed to the squat grey cone of Gunung Bromo itself, allowing you to gaze into the steaming guts of this small but highly active volcano.

Alternatively, it's a straightforward hike (around an hour) from Cemoro Lawang to Bromo. Take the wide track downhill from the village and follow the white stone markers that lead the way to Bromo. In the pitch-black the route can be a little indistinct, but remember that Bromo is on the left, accessed by 253 steps (the neighbouring peak is Batok).

The beautiful Hindu temple at the foot of Bromo and Bator is a relatively recent addition to the moonscape, but it's only open for religious ceremonies.

Though Probolinggo is the usual approach, Bromo can also be reached via **Tosari** from the northwest and **Ngadas** from the southwest.

Festivals & Events

The **Kesada festival** is staged annually by the local Hindu community, when offerings are made to appease Bromo. The date changes each year – check with the **Surabaya Tourist Information Centre** (☎ 031-534 0444; www.sparklingsurabaya.com; Jl Pemuda; ⌚ 9am-5pm Mon-Sat).

Sleeping & Eating

CEMORO LAWANG

At the lip of the Tengger crater and right at the start of the walk to Bromo, Cemoro Lawang is the most popular place to stay.

our pick **Cafe Lava Hostel** (☎ 541020; d with shared mandi 55,000, with private mandi from 100,000Rp) Spilling down a hillside, this backpacker-geared hostel is the most popular place to stay in town. The miniscule economy rooms were being renovated at the time of research to offer more comfort, while the larger digs are very pleasant rustic affairs, many with lovely views from their verandas. The café here is also the most popular place to eat in the village, and serves filling Indonesian and Western grub (meals from 12,000Rp), and cool Bintang, though it is periodically cursed by plagues of flies of near-biblical proportions.

Cemara Indah Hotel (☎ 541019; r with shared/private mandi from 60,000/160,000Rp; ✖) On the crater's edge with sublime views over Bromo, but the basic rooms are seriously spartan.

Lava View Lodge (☎ 541009; r from 160,000Rp) Right on the lip of the crater, this hotel's location is unmatched. Efficiently run by a friendly team, the cabin-style rooms are homely and the hot water is reliable. Prices rise 20% between June and October. There's a large café-restaurant here (meals from 17,000Rp), but few diners, unless a tour group rolls in.

NGADISARI

Another 3km back towards Probolinggo is the tiny village of Ngadisari.

Yoschi's Guest House (☎ 541018; yoschi_bromo@telkom.net; d with shared/private mandi 75,000/150,000Rp) Well-run place with Alpine-style kitsch décor, a garden area, a restaurant (meals from 11,000Rp) and helpful staff. Offers small, neat rooms and daily tours to the volcano (240,000Rp for four).

PROBOLINGGO

On the highway between Surabaya and Banyuwangi, this is the jumping-off point for Gunung Bromo. Most travellers only see the bus or train station, but the town has hotels if you get stuck.

Hotel Bromo Permai (☎ 422256; Jl Panglima Sudirman 237; r from 65,000Rp; ✖) Popular travellers' hotel, with comfy rooms and an English-speaking owner. It's on the main road close to the centre of town.

Hotel Paramita (☎ 421535; Jl Siaman 7; r 80,000-150,000Rp; ✖) New place with plain, spotless rooms around a landscaped garden.

Getting There & Away

Probolinggo's bus station is 5km west of town on the road to Bromo; catch a yellow *angkot* from the main street or the train station for 2000Rp.

Some of the ticket desks here try to overcharge travellers, so shop around before you purchase a ticket. Normal/air-con buses include Surabaya (17,000/26,000Rp, two hours), Banyuwangi (27,000/40,000Rp, five hours), Yogyakarta (52,000/77,000Rp, eight hours) and Denpasar (85,000/120,000Rp, nine hours).

Colt from the terminal go to Cemoro Lawang (12,000Rp, two hours) via Ngadisari until around 5.30pm. Some late-afternoon buses ask for more to go to Cemoro

Lawang, when fewer passengers travel beyond Ngadisari.

Probolinggo's train station is 2km north of the centre. The *Mutiara Timur* travels to Banyuwangi (*bisnis/eksekutif* 40,000/55,000Rp, five hours) at 11.16pm, and on the return trip heads to Surabaya (*bisnis/eksekutif* 40,000/55,000Rp, two hours) at 13.44pm. The *Tawang Alun* leaves at 16.49 (*ekonomi* 19,000Rp) for Banyuwangi, returning to Surabaya at 11.15.

Travel agencies in Solo and Yogyakarta book *travel* to Bromo.

BALI

Bali is a brand unto itself, an island that has long outgrown its cramped spot on the map to become the very epitome of the tropical paradise. Like a stack of picture postcards, the images are straight from the drawer marked 'Southeast Asian clichés': a technicolour fanfare of golden beaches, ultramarine seas, emerald palm tops and boot-polish suntans. Boasting world-class surf, some of Asia's most chic restaurants and euphoric nightlife, it's hardly surprising that Bali is Indonesia's premier-league tourist destination.

Flip the postcard over, however, and Bali's unique Hindu culture with its devotion to art, dance, religious rituals and elaborate ceremonies remains as enduring and impressive as ever. Much of the Kuta area may be wall-to-wall bars and boutiques, but once you leave this strip the island's volcanic interior beckons with its dazzling crater lakes, white-water rapids, temples and highland markets. And wherever you go, it's impossible not to be seduced by the grace and warmth of the Balinese people, who maintain such great pride in their island and care of its unique traditions. So whether you're here for the waves, the sculpture, the hangovers, or the culture, Bali is the little isle with everything.

History

Bali's first prehistoric tourists strolled out of the spume and onto the island's western beaches around 3000 BC. Perhaps distracted by primitive beach life, however, they got off to a relaxed start and it was only in the 9th century that an organised society began to develop around the cultivation of rice.

Hinduism followed hot on the heels of wider cultural development and as Islam swept through neighbouring Java in the following centuries, the kings and courtiers of the embattled Hindu Majapahit kingdom began crossing the straits into Bali, making their final exodus in 1478. The priest Nirartha brought many of the complexities of the Balinese Hindu religion to the island, and established superb offshore temples, including Rambut Siwi, Tanah Lot and Ulu Watu.

In the 19th century the Dutch began to form alliances with local princes in northern Bali. A dispute over the ransacking of wrecked ships was the pretext for the 1906 Dutch invasion of the south, which climaxed in a suicidal *puputan* (fight to the death). The Denpasar nobility burnt their own palaces, dressed in their finest jewellery and, waving golden *kris*, marched straight into the Dutch guns. The rajas of Tabanan, Karangasem, Gianyar and Klungkung soon capitulated, and Bali became part of the Dutch East Indies.

In later years Balinese culture was actually encouraged by many Dutch officials. International interest was aroused and the first Western tourists arrived.

After WWII the struggle for national independence was fierce in Bali. Independence was declared on 17 August 1945 (still celebrated as Independence Day), but power wasn't officially handed over until 27 December 1949, when the Dutch finally gave up the fight. The island languished economically in the early years of Indonesian sovereignty, but Bali's greatest national resource, beauty, was subsequently marketed to great effect. In the years that followed the island's promotion, the tourist industry brought with it all the good (growing prosperity) and bad (massive overdevelopment) of the modern age. It also dragged Bali into the international limelight, making it a target for investors and terrorists alike.

In October 2002 two simultaneous bomb explosions ripped through Kuta, killing 202 people and decimating Bali's tourist industry overnight. Three years later, just as the island was regaining confidence, the bombers struck again. But despite these atrocities, Bali's allure is unique: traditional 'bucket-and-spade' family tourism has dipped but the island is increasingly becoming a mecca for a hip globetrotting tribe of designers, clubbers and gay Asians.

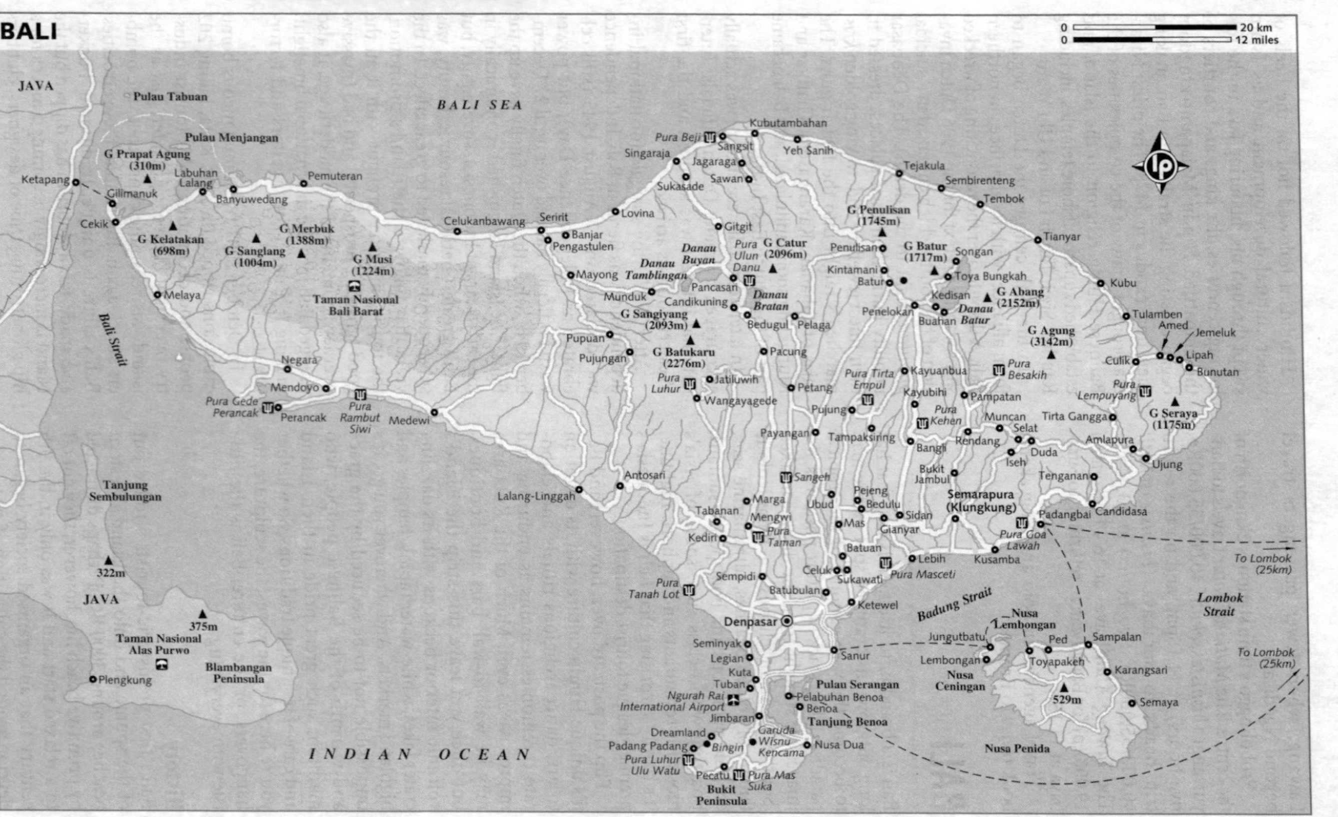
BALI
0 20 km
0 12 miles
JAVA
Pulau Tabuan
BALI SEA
Pulau Menjangan
G Prapat Agung (310m)
Ketapang
Labuhan Lalang
Gilimanuk
Cekik
Banyuwedang
Pemuteran
G Kelatakan (698m)
G Sanglang (1004m)
G Merbuk (1388m)
G Musi (1224m)
Taman Nasional Bali Barat
Melaya
Bali Strait
Negara
Mendoyo
Pura Gede Perancak
Perancak
Pura Rambut Siwi
Medewi
Celukanbawang
Seririt
Banjar
Pengastulen
Lovina
Singaraja
Pura Beji
Sangsit
Kubutambahan
Yeh Sanih
Jagaraga
Sawan
Sukasade
Gitgit
Mayong
Danau Tamblingan
Danau Buyan
Munduk
Pancasari
Pura Ulun Danu
G Catur (2096m)
Candikuning
Danau Bratan
Bedugul
Pelaga
G Sangiyang (2093m)
G Batukaru (2276m)
Pupuan
Pujungan
Pura Luhur
Jatiluwih
Wangayagede
Pacung
Petang
Antosari
Lalang-Linggah
Tejakula
Sembirenteng
Tembok
G Penulisan (1745m)
Penulisan
Kintamani
Batur
G Batur (1717m)
Songan
Toya Bungkah
Kedisan
Penelokan
Buahan
Danau Batur
G Abang (2152m)
Tianyar
Kubu
Tulamben
Amed
Jemeluk
Lipah
Bunutan
Culik
G Agung (3142m)
Pura Besakih
Pura Lempuyang
G Seraya (1175m)
Kayuanbua
Pura Tirta Empul
Kayubihi
Pampatan
Pura Kehen
Pujung
Tirta Gangga
Muncan
Selat
Rendang
Payangan
Tampaksiring
Bangli
Amlapura
Duda
Iseh
Ujung
Bukit Jambul
Tenganan
Sangeh
Pejeng
Bedulu
Marga
Ubud
Semarapura (Klungkung)
Candidasa
Padangbai
Tabanan
Mengwi
Mas
Sidan
Gianyar
Pura Taman
Kediri
Pura Goa Lawah
Batuan
Lebih
Kusamba
Celuk
Sukawati
Pura Masceti
Sempidi
Pura Tanah Lot
Batubulan
Ketewel
To Lombok (25km)
Lombok Strait
Badung Strait
Nusa Lembongan
Denpasar
Jungutbatu
Ped
Sampalan
Seminyak
Sanur
Lembongan
Toyapakeh
Legian
Nusa Ceningan
Karangsari
Kuta
Tuban
Pulau Serangan
Ngurah Rai International Airport
Pelabuhan Benoa
Benoa
529m
Semaya
To Lombok (25km)
Jimbaran
Tanjung Benoa
Dreamland
Garuda Wisnu Kencana
Padang Padang
Bingin
Nusa Dua
Nusa Penida
Pura Luhur Ulu Watu
Pecatu
Pura Mas Suka
Bukit Peninsula
INDIAN OCEAN
Tanjung Sembulungan
322m
JAVA
375m
Taman Nasional Alas Purwo
Plengkung
Blambangan Peninsula

Dangers & Annoyances

Persistent hawkers are the bane of most visitors to Bali. The best way to deal with them is to ignore them from the first instance.

Take a little extra care in the Kuta area. Pickpockets sometimes target drunk revellers stumbling home after a night out and you may be offered drugs and solicited by sex workers of every gender. Drug-users and dealers are dealt with very strictly in Indonesia – you could face years in jail for having a joint, and entrapment by police is a possibility. Bali's famed *oong* (magic mushrooms) contain psilocybin, a powerful hallucinogen that can have unpredictable effects.

Travellers have been stung badly by card-game cons and dodgy holiday 'timeshare' deals. Some have been tricked into paying large amounts for unnecessary repairs to rental cars and motorcycles. Gigolos, 'guides' and friendly locals have persuaded visitors to hand over money to help pay for education expenses and life-saving operations. Moneychangers are adept at switching notes at the last minute – a healthy scepticism is your best defence if you're offered a great rate.

The beaches of Kuta, Legian and Seminyak are subject to heavy surf and strong currents – swim between the flags.

Getting There & Away

AIR

The internal Indonesian flight market is now extremely competitive, with new airlines starting (and folding) each year. Prices have tumbled on many routes, particularly if you book up early. Unfortunately many of the airlines' websites do not function well, if at all, so you may be faced with having to pitch up and grab the first available flight, or using a good travel agent.

Merpati offers the most comprehensive network of flights in Indonesia, covering virtually the entire archipelago. For sample one-way fares see Map p161).

Ngurah Rai airport (code DPS; ☎ 0361-751011), a few kilometres south of Kuta, is a major international hub and well connected globally. See p159 for international airlines servicing Bali.

Domestic airline offices (located at Ngurah Rai airport unless specified otherwise):

Adam Air (code KI; ☎ 0361-761104; www.adamair.com)
Air Asia (code AK; ☎ 080 4133 3333; www.airasia.com)
Batavia Air (code 7P; ☎ 0361-254955; www.batavia-air.co.id)
Garuda (code GA; in Denpasar ☎ 080 7142 7832, Ngurah Rai airport 0361-751011, ext 5228; www.garuda-indonesia.com)
Lion Air (code JT; ☎ 0361-236666; www.lionair.co.id)
Mandala (in Denpasar ☎ 0361-222751, Ngurah Rai airport 0361-759761; www.mandalaair.com)
Merpati (code MZ; in Denpasar ☎ 080 0101 2345, Ngurah Rai airport 0361-235358; www.merpati.co.id)
Pelita Air (code PAS; ☎ 0361-762248; www.pelita-air.com)
TransNusa (☎ 0361-754421; www.transnusa.co.id)

BOAT

Ferries (7000Rp, one hour) travel between Gilimanuk in western Bali and Ketapang (Java) every 30 minutes, 24 hours a day.

Ferries (21,000Rp, 4½ to 5½ hours) run between Padangbai and Lombok every two hours, 24 hours a day.

The **Gili Shop** (Map p215; ☎ 0361-753241; www.gili-paradise.com; Poppies 1-12, Kuta) operates a pricey fast charter boat between Bali and Lombok (690,000Rp, two hours) from Beroa harbour. By the time you read this, the shop should also be running trips from Kuta to Gili Trawangan on the *Mahi Mahi* (550,000Rp).

Three Pelni boats stop at Pelabuhan Benoa, linking Bali with most major Indonesian destinations. In Kuta, the **Pelni office** (☎ 0361-763963; www.pelni.co.id; Jl Raya Kuta 288; 🕑 8am-noon & 1-4pm Mon-Thu, 8-11.30am Fri, 8am-1pm Sat) has the latest schedules.

BUS

Many buses travel daily between the Ubung terminal in Denpasar and major cities in Java; most travel overnight. Fares from Denpasar: Surabaya (150,000Rp, 12 hours), Yogyakarta (170,000Rp, 16 hours) and Jakarta (300,000Rp, 26 hours).

Perama (☎ 0361-751551; www.peramatour.com; Jl Legian 39, Kuta) runs daily bus-boat services between all tourist destinations and Mataram/Senggigi/Gilis in Lombok (100,000Rp to 300,000Rp).

Getting Around

BICYCLE

You can hire bicycles in tourist centres for 15,000Rp per day; most have gears.

BEMO & BUS

Most of Bali's public transport is provided by minibuses called bemo; the main hub is in Denpasar, (see p214).

You can flag down a bemo pretty much anywhere along its route, but Bali's bemo are notorious for overcharging tourists.

You can also charter a whole vehicle for a trip (negotiate the price beforehand), or by the day (for around 375,000Rp depending on the distance). The price should include driver and petrol.

Several shuttle bus companies link Kuta-Legian with the other main tourist centres. **Perama** (Map p215; ☎ 0361-751551; www.peramatour.com; Jl Legian 39, Kuta) is highly recommended. Book a ticket at least one day before you want to travel.

CAR & MOTORCYCLE

Virtually every hotel and many businesses in Bali can offer you a hire car or motorbike. This should involve you signing a written contract with the owner, agreeing to an excess in case of damage, and includes limited insurance. Obviously check the vehicle first for signs of damage. Make sure you obtain an International Driving Permit (IDP) before you leave home – there are steep fines for unlicensed driving, and travel insurance may be invalidated.

Four-seater Suzuki Jimnys cost around 110,000Rp a day, larger Toyota Kijangs around 150,000Rp. Alternatively, **Avis** (☎ 0361-282635; www.avis.com; Ngurah Rai airport) offers cars from US$35 per day, including full insurance.

Motorcycles cost about 30,000Rp per day, including limited insurance. If you don't have an IDP, ask the renter to take you to the relevant police station in Denpasar, where you can buy a temporary SIM Turis licence (200,000Rp).

TAXI

Prepaid taxis from the airport cost 40,000Rp to Kuta or 175,000Rp to Ubud. Otherwise, walk across the airport car park to the main road, from where bemo go to Denpasar's Tegal terminal via Kuta (2000Rp).

Taxis cost 5000Rp for the first kilometre and then 2000Rp for each subsequent kilometre. **Bluebird** (☎ 0361-701111), in Kuta and Denpasar, is reliable.

DENPASAR

☎ 0361 / pop 412,000

Denpasar is a typical provincial Indonesian city – a grey place that's heavy on the concrete, choked by traffic and cursed by relentless heat. It holds near-zero interest for the visitor, but if Bali is your only stop in the country, you may just be tempted to see what an Indonesian city entails, warts and all. Otherwise there's no real reason to linger – bar a museum and a temple.

Orientation

The main street of Denpasar starts as Jl Gajah Mada in the west, becomes Jl Surapati in the centre, then Jl Hayam Wuruk and finally Jl Raya Sanur in the east. The airport is south of the city.

Information

There are banks with ATM and exchange facilities across town, including several on Jl Gajah Mada.

Post office (Jl Raya Puputan; ⌚ 8.30am-5pm Mon-Fri, to noon Sat) Way out in the Renon district.

Prima Medika (☎ 236225; www.primamedika.com; Jl Pulau Serangan No 9X; ⌚ 24hr) Private hospital with English-speaking staff.

Target Tours (☎ 240967; Jl Diponegoro 75; ⌚ 8.30am-4.30pm Mon-Fri, to noon Sat) For plane tickets.

Tourist office (☎ 223602; Jl Surapati 7; ⌚ 7.30am-3.30pm Mon-Thu, 8am-1pm Fri) Deals with Denpasar municipality, including Sanur; has copies of the useful Bali-wide *Calendar of Events*.

Warung@internet (Jl Nakula 33; per hr 6000Rp; ⌚ 9am-5am)

Sights & Activities

The **Museum Negeri Propinsi Bali** (☎ 222680; Puputan Sq; admission 2000Rp, camera 1000Rp; ⌚ 8am-3pm Sun-Thu, to 12.30pm Fri) showcases Balinese crafts and is worth an hour or two. Alongside the fine hand-spun textiles are some incredibly intricate drawings of the Ramayana, and startling *barong* costumes used for Balinese dance.

Next to the museum is **Pura Jagatnatha** (Puputan Sq; ⌚ dawn-dusk), the state temple with a striking tiered central monument. Opposite here is **Puputan Square**, with its heroic **Catur Mukha statue**. Despite the statue's rather macabre role commemorating the suicidal stand against the Dutch in 1906, it is a popular local meeting place.

Downtown Denpasar rotates around Bali's biggest market, **Pasar Badung** (Jl Gajah Mada; ⌚ 7am-7pm). There are a few handicrafts here, but it's best used as a place to get a grip on the hubbub of day-to-day Denpasar and fire off a few colourful snaps.

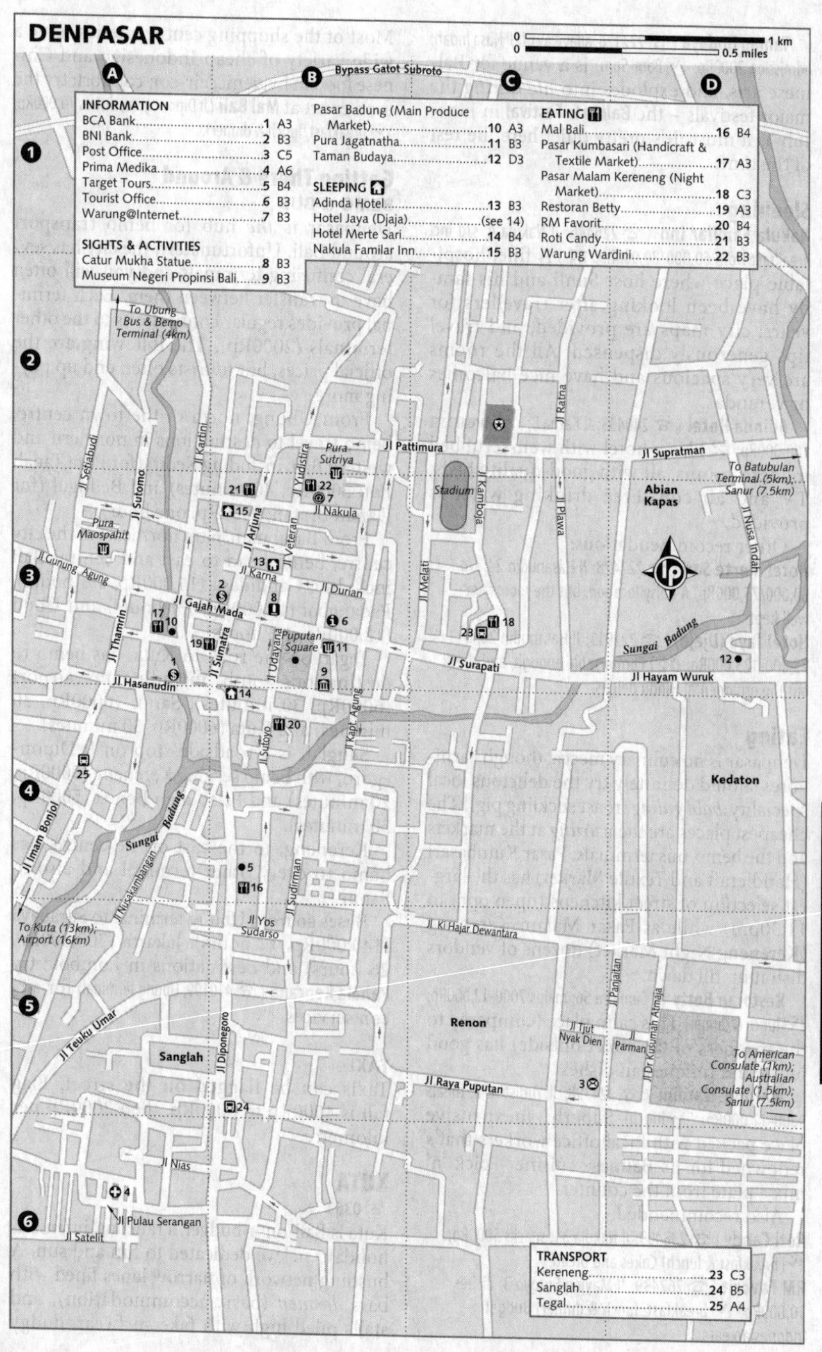
DENPASAR
0 1 km
0 0.5 miles
INFORMATION
BCA Bank.....1 A3
BNI Bank.....2 B3
Post Office.....3 C5
Prima Medika.....4 A6
Target Tours.....5 B4
Tourist Office.....6 B3
Warung@Internet.....7 B3
SIGHTS & ACTIVITIES
Catur Mukha Statue.....8 B3
Museum Negeri Propinsi Bali.....9 B3
Pasar Badung (Main Produce Market).....10 A3
Pura Jagatnatha.....11 B3
Taman Budaya.....12 D3
SLEEPING
Adinda Hotel.....13 B3
Hotel Jaya (Djaja).....(see 14)
Hotel Merte Sari.....14 B4
Nakula Familar Inn.....15 B3
EATING
Mal Bali.....16 B4
Pasar Kumbasari (Handicraft & Textile Market).....17 A3
Pasar Malam Kereneng (Night Market).....18 C3
Restoran Betty.....19 A3
RM Favorit.....20 B4
Roti Candy.....21 B3
Warung Wardini.....22 B3
TRANSPORT
Kereneng.....23 C3
Sanglah.....24 B5
Tegal.....25 A4
Bypass Gatot Subroto
To Ubung Bus & Bemo Terminal (4km)
To Batubulan Terminal (5km); Sanur (7.5km)
To Kuta (13km); Airport (16km)
To American Consulate (1km); Australian Consulate (1.5km); Sanur (7.5km)
Jl Pattimura
Jl Supratman
Jl Ratna
Jl Kamboja
Jl Plawa
Jl Melati
Jl Nusa Indah
Stadium
Abian Kapas
Pura Sutriya
Pura Maospahit
Jl Setiabudi
Jl Sutomo
Jl Kartini
Jl Yudistira
Jl Nakula
Jl Arjuna
Jl Veteran
Jl Karna
Jl Durian
Jl Gunung Agung
Jl Gajah Mada
Jl Thamrin
Jl Sumatra
Jl Udayana
Puputan Square
Jl Hasanudin
Jl Surapati
Jl Hayam Wuruk
Sungai Badung
Jl Kapt Agung
Jl Sutoyo
Jl Imam Bonjol
Jl Nusakambangan
Jl Sudirman
Jl Yos Sudarso
Kedaton
Jl Ki Hajar Dewantara
Jl Panjaitan
Jl Dr Kusumah Atmaja
Jl Tjut Nyak Dien
Parman
Renon
Jl Raya Puputan
Jl Teuku Umar
Sanglah
Jl Diponegoro
Jl Nias
Jl Pulau Serangan
Jl Satelit
INDONESIA

Taman Budaya (☎ 227176; alleyway off Jl Nusa Indah; admission 2000Rp; 🕑 8am-5pm) is a venue for Balinese arts, and explodes into life during the major festivals – the **Bali Arts Festival** in June-July is a must. It's pretty quiet here the rest of the time.

Sleeping

Nakula Familar Inn (☎ 226446; Jl Nakula 4; s/d incl breakfast from 60,000/80,000Rp; ❄) A fine, hospitable place where host Sunli and his family have been looking after travellers for years: city maps are provided, and travel tips generously dispensed. All the rooms are very spacious and have nice balconies or verandas.

Adinda Hotel (☎ 240435; Jl Karna 8; r incl breakfast 160,000Rp; ❄) New hotel with well-scrubbed modern rooms, all with good-quality beds, TV and air-con. Free drinking water is provided.

Other recommendations:

Hotel Merte Sari (☎ 222428; Jl Hasanudin 24; s/d 60,000/75,000Rp) A noisy location, but the rooms are well kept.

Hotel Jaya (Djaja) (☎ 222911; Jl Hasanudin 26; d 75,000-125,000Rp; ❄) Comfortable enough, and check out the ornamental Hindu deities.

Eating

Denpasar is no culinary mecca, though carnivores should definitely try the delicious local speciality, *babi guling* (roast suckling pig). The cheapest places are the *warung* at the markets and the bemo/bus terminals: Pasar Kumbasari (Handicraft and Textile Market) has the largest selection of street kitchens (open 6pm to 11.30pm) while at Pasar Malam Kereneng (Kereneng Night Market) dozens of vendors dish it up till dawn.

Restoran Betty (Jl Sumatra 56; mains 7000-12,000Rp; 🕑 lunch & dinner) This calm place (compared to the madness of the street outside) has good juices and Indonesian dishes.

Warung Wardini (☎ 224398; Jl Yudistira 2; meals 8000-11,000Rp; 🕑 lunch) Superb, inexpensive place packed with local office workers that's renowned for its Balinese cuisine – pick 'n' mix a plate from the counter.

Also recommended:

Roti Candy (☎ 238409; Jl Nakula 31; snacks 5000Rp; 🕑 breakfast & lunch) Cakes and bread.

RM Favorit (☎ 262439; Jl Mayjen Sutoyo 3; dishes 10,000Rp; 🕑 breakfast, lunch & dinner) Budget Indonesian eats.

Most of the shopping centre eateries serve a wide variety of cheap Indonesian and Chinese food in hygienic, air-con comfort; try the food court at **Mal Bali** (Jl Diponegoro; dishes 10,000Rp; 🕑 breakfast, lunch & dinner).

Getting There & Around

BEMO & BUS

Denpasar is *the* hub for bemo transport around Bali. Unfortunately, the city has several confusing terminals and you will often have to transfer between them. Each terminal provides regular connections to the other terminals (2000Rp). The following are the official prices, but tourists often end up paying more.

From Ubung, north of the town centre, bemo travel to destinations in northern and western Bali, including Kediri (for Pura Tanah Lot; 5000Rp, 40 minutes) and Bedugul (for Danau Bratan; 9000Rp, one hour).

From Batubulan, 6km northeast of the city centre, bemo head to east and central Bali including Candidasa (14,000Rp, 1½ hours), Padangbai (17,000Rp, 1¾ hours) and Ubud (12,000Rp, 1½ hours).

Tegal, on the road to Kuta, has bemo to destinations south, including the airport (6000Rp, 30 minutes), Sanur (6000Rp, 30 minutes) and Kuta (6000Rp, 30 minutes).

Sanglah is a roadside stop on Jl Diponegoro, with bemo serving Kereneng (3000Rp, 20 minutes) and Pelabuhan Benoa (5000Rp, 30 minutes).

Kereneng, to the east of the centre, has bemo to every other terminal and also to Sanur.

Buses go from Ubung terminal to Surabaya (140,000Rp, 12 hours), Jakarta (300,000Rp, 26 hours) and destinations in Lombok; try **Pahala Kencana** (☎ 410199; Ubung terminal) for air-con services.

TAXI

Taxis can be flagged on the street. Flag fall is 4000Rp to 5000Rp, then 2000Rp per kilometre.

KUTA

☎ 0361

Kuta is Bali-on-a-budget, a raucous, infamous holiday enclave dedicated to fun and sun. A bustling network of narrow lanes lined with bars, *losmen* (basic accommodation), and stalls piled high with fake surfwear, dodgy

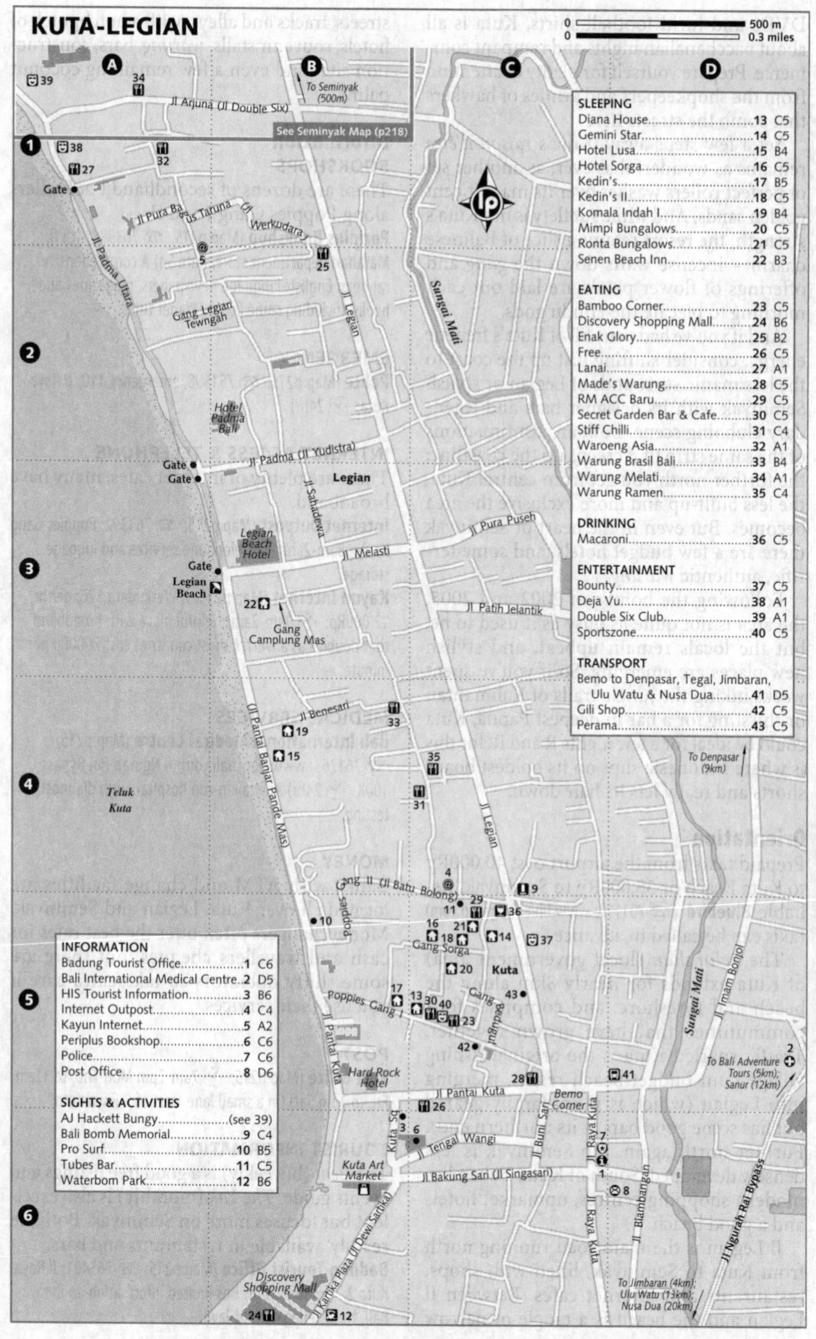
KUTA-LEGIAN
0 500 m
0 0.3 miles
To Seminyak (500m)
See Seminyak Map (p218)
Jl Arjuna (Jl Double Six)
Gate
Jl Pura Bagus Taruna (Jl Werkudara)
Jl Padma Utara
Gang Legian Tewngah
Sungai Mati
Jl Legian
Hotel Padma Bali
Jl Padma (Jl Yudistra)
Legian
Jl Sahadewa
Jl Pura Puseh
Legian Beach Hotel
Jl Melasti
Legian Beach
Jl Patih Jelantik
Gang Camplung Mas
Jl Benesari
Jl Pantai Banjar Pande Mas
Teluk Kuta
To Denpasar (9km)
Gang II (Jl Batu Bolong)
Poppies II
Gang Sorga
Kuta
Poppies Gang I
Gang Bedugul
Jl Pantai Kuta
Hard Rock Hotel
Bemo Corner
Kuta Sq
Jl Tengal Wangi
Jl Buni Sari
Jl Raya Kuta
Jl Bakung Sari (Jl Singasari)
Kuta Art Market
Jl Blambangan
Jl Imam Bonjol
Jl Ngurah Rai Bypass
To Bali Adventure Tours (5km); Sanur (12km)
Jl Kartika Plaza (Jl Dewi Sartika)
Discovery Shopping Mall
To Jimbaran (4km); Ulu Watu (13km); Nusa Dua (20km)
SLEEPING
Diana House 13 C5
Gemini Star 14 C5
Hotel Lusa 15 B4
Hotel Sorga 16 C5
Kedin's 17 B5
Kedin's II 18 C5
Komala Indah I 19 B4
Mimpi Bungalows 20 C5
Ronta Bungalows 21 C5
Senen Beach Inn 22 B3
EATING
Bamboo Corner 23 C5
Discovery Shopping Mall 24 B6
Enak Glory 25 B2
Free 26 C5
Lanai 27 A1
Made's Warung 28 C5
RM ACC Baru 29 C5
Secret Garden Bar & Cafe 30 C5
Stiff Chilli 31 C4
Waroeng Asia 32 A1
Warung Brasil Bali 33 B4
Warung Melati 34 A1
Warung Ramen 35 C4
DRINKING
Macaroni 36 C5
ENTERTAINMENT
Bounty 37 C5
Deja Vu 38 A1
Double Six Club 39 A1
Sportszone 40 C5
TRANSPORT
Bemo to Denpasar, Tegal, Jimbaran, Ulu Watu & Nusa Dua 41 D5
Gili Shop 42 C5
Perama 43 C5
INFORMATION
Badung Tourist Office 1 C6
Bali International Medical Centre 2 D5
HIS Tourist Information 3 B6
Internet Outpost 4 C4
Kayun Internet 5 A2
Periplus Bookshop 6 C6
Police 7 C6
Post Office 8 D6
SIGHTS & ACTIVITIES
AJ Hackett Bungy (see 39)
Bali Bomb Memorial 9 C4
Pro Surf 10 B5
Tubes Bar 11 C5
Waterbom Park 12 B6
INDONESIA

DVDs and lurid football shirts, Kuta is all about bacchanalian nights and rampant commerce. Prepare yourself for plenty of attention from the shopkeepers and armies of hawkers that comb the streets here.

Yet a few steps away, Kuta's *raison d'être* remains as wonderful as ever, as another set of perfect rollers washes over its magnificent golden sands. And while subtlety is not Kuta's strength, the resort retains a slice of Balinese charm – incense wafts down the *gang* and offerings of flower petals are laid out each morning to placate the Hindu gods.

And if you've had your fill of Kuta's frenetic energy, consider shifting just up the coast to the less manic surrounds of Legian or stylish Seminyak with its designer bars and legendary clubbing scene. Both are continuations of the same strip that creeps up the coastline; the further north you get from central Kuta, the less built-up and more exclusive the area becomes. But even in the heart of Seminyak there are a few budget hotels, and some terrific, authentic *warung*.

Following the bombs of 2002 and 2005, the area is not quite as busy as it used to be, but the locals remain upbeat, and stylish new places are emerging. So if you've spent weeks hiking the jungle trails of Kalimantan or thirsting for a bar in deepest Papua, Kuta could be ideal for a few nights R and R, for this is where Indonesia slips on its boldest board shorts and really lets its hair down.

Orientation

Prepaid taxis from the airport cost 40,000Rp to Kuta Beach or 55,000Rp to Seminyak. Reliable **Bluebird** (☎ 701111; www.bluebirdgroup.com) taxis can be called in advance.

The *kelurahan* (local government area) of Kuta extends for nearly 8km along the beach and foreshore, and comprises four communities that have grown together. Traffic-snarled Kuta is the original fishing village-cum-budget-beach resort, merging into Legian (which is more family-geared but has some good bars at its northern end). Further north again, hip Seminyak is less densely developed. South of Kuta, Tuban has modern shopping centres, upmarket hotels and a good beach.

Jl Legian is the main road running north from Kuta to Seminyak, lined with shops, restaurants and internet cafés. Between Jl Legian and the beach is a tangle of narrow streets, tracks and alleys, with a hotchpotch of hotels, souvenir stalls, *warung*, bars, construction sites and even a few remaining coconut palms.

Information

BOOKSHOPS

There are dozens of secondhand booksellers along Poppies Gang I and II.

Periplus Bookshop (Map p215; ☎ 763988; 4th fl, Matahari department store, Kuta Sq) A comprehensive range of English-language newspapers, magazines and books, including some Lonely Planet titles.

EMERGENCY

Police (Map p215; ☎ 751598, emergency 110; Jl Raya Kuta; 24hr)

INTERNET ACCESS & TELEPHONE

There are plenty of internet cafés, many have broadband.

Internet Outpost (Map p215; ☎ 763392; Poppies Gang II; 8am-2am) Has telephone services and luggage storage.

Kayun Internet (Map p215; Jl Werkudara 526; per hr 12,000Rp; 9am-2am) Helpful place with broadband that doubles as a *wartel;* most countries cost 7000Rp per minute.

MEDICAL SERVICES

Bali International Medical Centre (Map p215; ☎ 761263; www.bimcbali.com; Jl Ngurah Rai Bypass 100X; 24hr) Australian-run hospital, with diagnostic testing.

MONEY

Banks with ATM and change facilities are located all over Kuta, Legian and Seminyak. Moneychangers often offer the best rates for cash and travellers cheques, but there are some shifty operators so take extra care if you use their services.

POST

Post office (Map p215; 7am-2pm Mon-Thu, to 11am Fri, to 1pm Sat) On a small lane, east of Jl Raya Kuta.

TOURIST INFORMATION

The *Beat* (biweekly) is a good free listings and events guide; *The Yak* (monthly) is also excellent but focuses more on Seminyak. Both are readily available in restaurants and bars.

Badung Tourist Office (Map p215; ☎ 765401; Jl Raya Kuta 2; 8am-5pm) Has limited information on Kuta, Bali, Nusa Tenggara and Java.

TRAVEL AGENCIES

Most so-called 'tourist information centres' are actually travel agencies selling organised tours, bus tickets and airline tickets.

HIS Tourist Information (Map p215; ☎ 758377; Kuta Sq Block C-17)

Sights & Activities

Kuta's biggest thrills roll in 24/7 and the resort town is a mighty fine place to catch a wave. Plenty of freelance beach-based surf instructors, some of whom are excellent, offer tuition for about 120,000Rp a half-day including board rental. Otherwise, surf schools are far more pricey. **Pro Surf** (Map p215; ☎ 081 2367 5141; www.prosurfschool.com; Grand Istana Rama Hotel, Jl Pantai Kuta) offers half-day lessons from US$35. **Tubes Bar** (Map p215; ☎ 753510; Poppies Gang II) was being rebuilt at the time of research but when it reopens it should reclaim its mantle as Kuta's premier surf info spot.

Those after some more mild-mannered waves should head for **Waterbom Park** (Map p215; ☎ 755676; www.waterbom.com; Jl Kartika Plaza; admission US$18.50; 9am-5pm), where you'll find slides and pools galore.

From Kuta you can go sailing, diving, fishing, horse riding or white-water rafting anywhere in the southern part of Bali, and still be back in time for dinner. For information and bookings, try **Bali Adventure Tours** (off Map p215; ☎ 721480; www.baliadventuretours.com; Adventure House, Jl Ngurah Rai). Bungy freaks can get airborne at **AJ Hackett Bungy** (Map p215; ☎ 731144; www.aj-hackett.com/bali; Double Six Club, Jl Arjuna; noon-8pm), where a leap from its 45m tower costs 600,000Rp.

It certainly isn't a tourist attraction, but you will be hard-pressed to walk down Jl Legian without noticing the **Bali Bomb Memorial** (Map p215; cnr Jl Legian & Poppies Gang II). It is a simple and sombre monument, listing the names of those killed by the 2002 blast.

Sleeping

Kuta is the budget accommodation capital of Indonesia, with hundreds of cheapies on and around Poppies Gang I and II. Most places chuck in a simple breakfast.

With so much competition, there are some great deals: simple, clean rooms start at 40,000Rp, but spend around 80,000Rp to 100,000Rp and a swimming pool can be yours for the splashing.

KUTA

Many cheap places are along the tiny alleys and lanes between Jl Legian and Jl Pantai Kuta, only a short walk from the beach, shops, bars and restaurants.

Ronta Bungalows (Map p215; ☎ 754246; s/d 40,000/60,000Rp) A solid choice, this simple place consists of two blocks of 10 rooms that face a well-maintained garden.

Komala Indah I (Map p215; ☎ 751422; Jl Benesari; s/d from 40,000/60,000Rp;) Not the prettiest kid on the block but the rooms here are spacious and good value, set around a sprawling grassy plot.

our pick **Kedin's** (Map p215; ☎ 756711; Poppies Gang I; s/d from 70,000/90,000Rp;) Eschew the uninviting lobby area and you'll find a welcome quiet retreat that's been recently renovated to something approaching backpacking boutique chic. The spacious rooms are stylishly kitted out and boast modern design details, and most have balconies. Outside, the garden and pool area, complete with hip sun loungers, is an ideal base for chillin' away the day if you've a hangover to nurse, well away from the madness that is Kuta.

Kedin's II (Map p215; ☎ 763554; Gang Sorga; s/d from 70,000/90,000Rp;) Like its brother, get past reception and this is a fine place, with 16 large rooms, each with a huge balcony or veranda, and there's an attractive, leafy pool area too.

Hotel Sorga (Map p215; ☎ 751897; sorga@idola.net.id; Gang Sorga; s 75,000-145,000Rp, d 115,000-175,000Rp;) Efficient place with excellent service and a shop, laundry and internet facilities. The Sorga's accommodation is understated and very well presented, all rooms with stylish chairs, wardrobes and bathtubs.

Gemini Star (Map p215; ☎ 750558; Gang Ronta; s/d from 80,000/95,000Rp;) Previously a no-frills cheapie, this place has had a serious makeover but still offers great value. The rooms, all with balconies, are huge and come with hot-water bathrooms.

Senen Beach Inn (Map p215; ☎ 755470; Gang Camplung Mas 25; r from 85,000Rp;) Simple, tranquil family-owned place just off Legian beach where the rooms with outdoor bathrooms are set around a small garden; there's a café too.

Other recommendations:

Diana House (Map p215; ☎ 751605; Poppies Gang I; s/d 40,000/50,000Rp) Family owned and humble.

Mimpi Bungalows (Map p215; ☎ 751848; kumimpi@yahoo.co.sg; Gang Sorga; s/d

INDONESIA

100,000/150,000Rp;) Peaceful cottages in a shady garden. Good but slightly overpriced; ask for a discount.

Hotel Lusa (Map p215; 753714; www.hotellusa.net; Jl Benesari; s/d from 100,000/120,000Rp;) Midranger with some good economy options and a lovely pool, café and leafy grounds.

SEMINYAK

Considering all the nightlife here, there's a dearth of cheap places to crash.

Losmen Inada (Map p218; 732269; putuinada@hotmail.com; Gang Bima; s/d 60,000/70,000Rp) A great little 12-room guesthouse tucked away on a quiet lane with friendly owners. The pleasant tiled rooms all have wardrobes and verandas and cold-water bathrooms.

Galaxy Hotel (Map p218; 730328; www.galaxyhotelbali.com; Jl Dhyana Pura; d 175,000Rp;) Set at pole position on the main party strip, and offers large discounts for longer stays. Good value, but pack those earplugs.

Eating

There's an incredible selection of restaurants in the Kuta area, from no-nonsense noodle bars to seriously swanky eateries in Seminyak.

For a quick feed, local style, check out the street kitchens at the **Seminyak night market** (Map p218; cnr Jl Oberoi & Jl Raya Seminyak; 6-11pm) or the *warung* in the back streets near the main post office.

Don't neglect the eateries on the 2nd floor of the **Discovery Shopping Mall** (Map p215; Jl Kartika Plaza; mains from 10,000Rp; lunch & dinner), which offer authentic, inexpensive Balinese cooking in hygienic, air-conditioned surrounds.

KUTA

Warung Brasil Bali (Map p215; 752692; Jl Benesari; dishes from 8000Rp; breakfast, lunch & dinner) Brazilian-themed place with cooking from the motherland, including *feijoada* (a stew of beans with various beef and pork products), plus the usual Western and Indonesian dishes at cheap prices. Surf movies are shown upstairs.

Free (Map p215; 751330; Jl Pantai Kuta 39A; mains 8000-15,000Rp; breakfast, lunch & dinner) Right on the main drag, this place has bargain-priced Indo (try the stir-fried veggies) and Western grub and arctic-cool large Bintang for 14,500Rp.

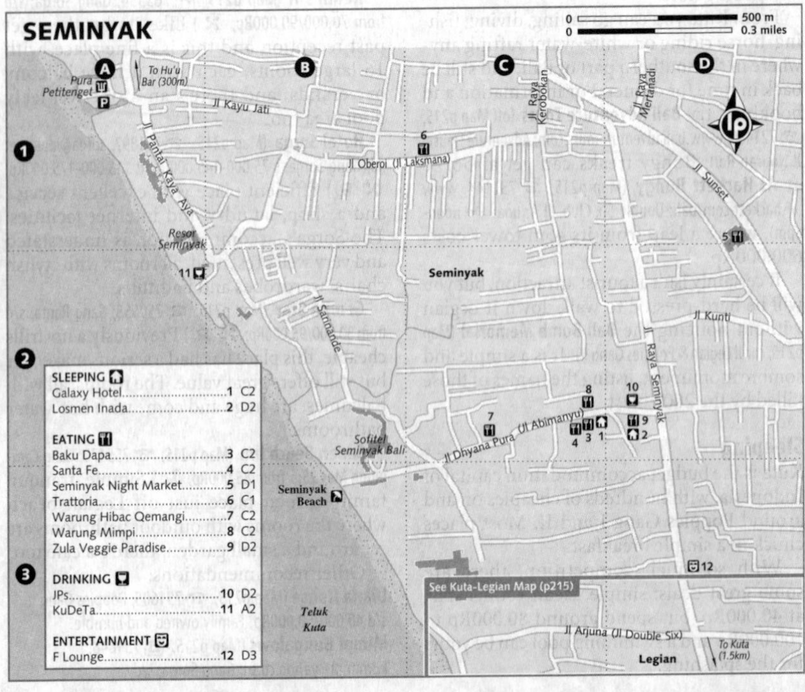

Stiff Chilli (Map p215; ☎ 745486; Jl Benesari; dishes from 16,000Rp; ⏰ lunch & dinner) Great little Italian with hip orange concrete banquette seating and fine pizza, pasta and paninis.

Wayung Ramen (Map p215; dishes 17,000-25,000Rp; ⏰ dinner) What's this, authentic Japanese cooking, including plenty of *ramen* (noodle) dishes and *gyoza* (dumplings) at backpackers prices? Better believe it.

Made's Warung (Map p215; ☎ 755297; Jl Pantai Kuta; mains from 22,000Rp; ⏰ breakfast, lunch & dinner) Perennially, and justifiably, popular Balinese restaurant with an East meets West menu taking in everything from Balinese fish curries to gourmet burgers.

Also recommended:

Bamboo Corner (Map p215; Poppies Gang I; dishes from 8000Rp; ⏰ breakfast, lunch & dinner) Breakfasts, backpacker staples and great people-watching.

RM ACC Baru (Map p215; mains from 8000Rp; ⏰ lunch & dinner) Pure Padang. It's in the Poppies Gang II area.

Secret Garden Bar & Cafe (Map p215; ☎ 757720; Poppies Gang I; mains 20,000Rp; ⏰ breakfast, lunch & dinner) Sociable, down-to-earth place ideal for filling tucker, ice-cold beer and a chinwag.

LEGIAN

Legian's best-located eateries are right on the beach, just south of where Jl Arjuna (Jl Double Six) meets the sand.

Warung Melati (Map p215; ☎ 081 2390 6506; Jl Arjuna; most dishes 6000Rp; ⏰ lunch & dinner) Hospitable little place with pavement tables serving delicious, fresh Indonesian food. You pay by the dish, about three is enough for a good feed.

Waroeng Asia (Map p215; ☎ 742 0202; Jl Arjuna 23; dishes from 13,000Rp; ⏰ breakfast, lunch & dinner) Simple yet atmospheric little place cranking out Thai food at very fair prices.

Enak Glory (Map p215; ☎ 751091; Jl Legian 445; mains from 20,000Rp; ⏰ lunch & dinner) Venerable fish restaurant, cooking up an *ikan bakar* (grilled fish) in more ways than you can cast a fly line at.

Lanai (Map p215; ☎ 753367; Jl Pantai; meals from 26,000Rp; ⏰ breakfast, lunch & dinner) A spectacular beachside location, where you could spend all day watching the wave riders from the upper deck. The menu has a bit of everything, with breakfasts, good burgers and pasta.

SEMINYAK

Surprisingly, Seminyak has a good choice of inexpensive places alongside some of Asia's most remarkable restaurants.

Warung Hibac Qemangi (Map p218; ☎ 738870; Jl Dhyana Pura 103N; meals 14,000Rp; ⏰ lunch & dinner) Enjoyable little place, with pavement seating, friendly staff and excellent Indonesian food.

our pick **Trattoria** (Map p218; ☎ 081 7972 6065; Jl Oberoi; mains from 24,000Rp; ⏰ lunch & dinner) Unquestionably the finest Italian in Bali, owned and run by Italians, who are here every night to ensure quality standards do not drop. The open-sided dining room is delightful and the menu is terrific, including pasta (from 25,000Rp), pizza (from 24,000Rp) and beef and tuna *carpaccio* (from 29,000Rp). Many unusual regional Italian and vegetarian choices are offered as daily specials, prepared from imported ingredients. And best of all, prices are fairly wallet-friendly, if you stay off the vino. Book ahead.

Zula Veggie Paradise (Map p218; ☎ 732723; Jl Dhyana Pura 5; dishes from 28,000Rp; ⏰ breakfast, lunch & dinner; ⊠) Veggie stronghold with an extensive, if slightly pricey, choice of dishes, including falafel, salads and Mediterranean platters. Wash it down with a boost juice or tonic drink.

Other recommendations:

Baku Dapa (Map p218; ☎ 731148; Jl Dhyana Pura 11A; meals 12,000Rp; ⏰ 24hr) Great *warung*-style grub around the clock.

Warung Mimpi (Map p218; ☎ 732738; Jl Dhyana Pura 29; meals 17,000Rp; ⏰ lunch & dinner) Modest, friendly place, serving authentic Indonesian food and cold Bintang at fair prices.

Santa Fe (Map p218; ☎ 731147; Jl Dhyana Pura 11; dishes 30,000Rp; ⏰ breakfast, lunch & dinner) Popular bar-restaurant that knocks out Tex-Mex eats.

Drinking

Kuta still has its share of cheap boozers but the scene is changing slowly as more hip places open. Most restaurants on Poppies Gang I and II double as lively bars and run happy hours from 6pm to 9pm.

Northern Legian and Seminyak have a very different, but equally lively scene concentrated on Jl Dhyana Pura, which has dozens of lounge bars, gay and straight, and small clubs.

KuDeTa (Map p218; ☎ 736969; www.kudeta.net; Jl Oberoi; ⏰ 8am-2am) An astonishing beachfront place, the design straight out of *Wallpaper** magazine, with a gorgeous bar area, an Asian-fusion restaurant and reclined seating where you can gaze out at the spotlit waves and sea spray. Of course it's not cheap, but you have to see this place, and beer prices are not that outrageous.

Maccaroni (Map p215; ☎ 754662; Jl Legian 52; www.maccaroniclub.com; 🕑 9am-2am) Simply stunning concrete-and-steel creation with a suspended DJ box and plenty of greenery to soften the urban nature of the bar-restaurant's design. There's a fine Italian menu (a set pasta lunch is 39,000Rp), two-for-one cocktails (after 11pm), live music, and free wi-fi.

Hu'u Bar (off Map p218; ☎ 736443; www.huubali.com; Jl Oberoi; 🕑 4pm-2am) Another striking venue, with modish seating, a pool and DJs spinning deep House mixes – though the inland location can't touch KuDeTa. Home from home for Seminyak's cocktail-quaffing classes.

JPs (Map p218; ☎ 736288; Jl Dhyana Pura; 🕑 10-3am) For more humble surrounds there's this pub-cum-*warung* with live music most nights, great staff and free wi-fi.

Clubbing

Bounty (Map p215; ☎ 752529; New Bounty Mall, Jl Legian; 🕑 24hr) Topping the decks of a giant prefab galleon, with fully rigged masts, this club is Kuta's most famous nightclub, with a mix of Aussie tourists, backpackers and a sprinkling of working girls. Musically, expect everything from bumpin' R & B to grunge classics.

Deja Vu (Map p215; ☎ 737639; Jl Arjuna 7; 🕑 6pm-4am) This stylish, hip bar-club is consistently a top night out, drawing an international crowd and plenty of Balinese scenesters. It mutates into a club after about 11pm, primarily playing progressive House. It sometimes charges 30,000Rp entry on busy nights.

F Lounge (Map p218; ☎ 730562; Jl Raya Seminyak 66; 🕑 6pm-5am) Bar-meets-club with one of the best sound systems on the island that draws respected international DJs to Bali. It's not too pretentious and not too expensive either, but can be quiet except on weekend nights.

Double Six Club (Map p215; ☎ 733067; www.doublesixclub.com; Jl Arjuna; 🕑 11pm-6am) Bali's premier club boasts a terrific beachfront location, elegant décor, a swimming pool and a good quota of Asia's beautiful crowd. Some legendary turntablists have played here including Tiesto.

Entertainment

Numerous bar-restaurants around Poppies Gang II show Hollywood and surf movies.

Large hotels and restaurants present tourist-version Balinese dances, but Ubud is a much better (and cheaper) place to see these; see p227.

Sportszone (Map p215; ☎ 736654; Poppies Gang 1; 🕑 24hr) For live cricket, basketball, tennis, and every code of football from Australia, Europe and the USA, this is the number-one bar in Kuta.

Shopping

Jl Legian is the place for fashion, with all the global surf brands represented, as well as local names such as Surfer Girl and Dreamland. The northern end of Jl Legian has the best boutiques, most of which are owned by local designers.

Poppies 1 and 2, and the 'art markets' on Jl Melasti and at the beach end of Jl Bakung Sari are loaded with stalls selling fake sports gear, pirated DVDs and CDs, beachwear and cheapo sunglasses – bargain hard.

Getting There & Away

AIR

Planes from Ngurah Rai airport, located near Kuta, serve destinations across Indonesia and the world. See the domestic airline listings on above, and international listings on p159. for more information

BOAT

Pelni ferries link nearby Pelabuhan Benoa with destinations throughout Indonesia (see p211).

BUS & BEMO

Public bemo travel regularly between Kuta and the Tegal terminal in Denpasar (6000Rp, 30 minutes). The main bemo stop in Kuta is situated on Jl Raya Kuta (Map p215), just east of Bemo Corner. Bemo head south from here to Jimbaran and Ulu Watu, but for anywhere else in Bali you'll have to go via Denpasar.

For bus tickets to Java, Lombok and Sumbawa it's most convenient to book via a travel agency; there are dozens in Kuta and Legian. Make sure the transfer to Ubung terminal in Denpasar (the bus departure point) is included.

Tourist shuttle buses travel between the Kuta area and all points of interest in Bali and Lombok. **Perama** (Map p215; ☎ 751551; www.peramatour.com; Jl Legian 39) is the best-known operator with daily services. Sample prices from Kuta are Ubud (30,000Rp, one hour), Lovina (100,000Rp, 3¼ hours), Padangbai (40,000Rp, 1¾ hours) and the Gilis (240,000Rp, nine hours).

CAR & MOTORCYCLE

Car- and motorcycle-hire places offer some of the most competitive prices in the world. To charter a vehicle, just walk up Jl Legian and listen for the offers of 'Transport? Transport?' Expect to pay 110,000Rp per day for a Suzuki Jimny, or 30,000Rp for a 90cc scooter. See p212 for advice about vehicle rental in Indonesia.

Getting Around

Bemo do a loop from Bemo Corner along Jl Pantai Kuta, Jl Melasti and Jl Legian and back to Bemo Corner (about 3000Rp). Bemo are infrequent in the afternoon and nonexistent in the evening.

Bicycles can be hired for around 15,000Rp per day from guesthouses and stores.

BUKIT PENINSULA

The southern peninsula, a limestone plateau often simply known as Bukit (Hill), is dry and sparsely populated, although it does have pockets of tourism development.

Just south of the airport, **Jimbaran Bay** is a superb crescent of white sand and blue sea, with a colourful fishing fleet, a fish market and a few luxury hotels. Seafood *warung* here offer a blissful setting for a sunset meal, right by the shoreline.

The western side of the peninsula holds some of Bali's best surf spots. The fabled cove known as **Dreamland** is perhaps the most exquisite of these, and has some very chilled little cafés popular with surfers and in-the-know travellers. Further south lies a chain of legendary surf beaches that includes **Padang Padang**, the left-handers **Bingin** and **Impossibles** and finally **Ulu Watu**. Simple, surfer-geared *losmen* and *warung* are scattered around the headlands of these beaches.

At the southwestern tip of the peninsula, **Pura Luhur Ulu Watu** (admission 3000Rp; 🕑 8am-7pm) is a stunningly sited Hindu temple that clings to sheer cliffs, high above the crashing waves below. Enchanting **kecak dances** (admission 40,000Rp) are held here every night from 6pm to 7pm. Just before the temple car park, a sign points to **Pantai Suluban**, which is yet another famous surf break.

Inland is a deserted carbuncle of a complex, the snappily titled **Garuda Wisnu Kencana Cultural Park** (☎ 0361-703603; admission 15,000Rp; 🕑 8am-10pm), which features near-empty malls and restaurants all topped by a monstrous 66m half-finished statue of a *garuda* (mythical half-man, half-bird creature).

Tanjung Benoa

☎ 0361

The peninsula of Tanjung Benoa extends about 4km north from the exclusive **Nusa Dua** resort enclave to the fishing village of **Benoa**. Jl Pratama runs the length of the peninsula, lined by a strip of midrange hotels and restaurants and holiday villas. On the beaches, water-sports centres offer diving, snorkelling, parasailing, jet skiing and water-skiing.

Near the top of Jl Pratama, a few places offer reasonably affordable accommodation, including **Pondok Agung Homestay** (☎ 771143; roland@eksadata.com; Jl Pratama; d from 130,000Rp; ❄), which has Balinese character and a lovely garden. There are plenty of excellent seafood restaurants nearby, although all are on the pricey side.

Bemo run from Tegal terminal in Denpasar, via Kuta, to Nusa Dua (one hour, 9000Rp) where you'll have to change bemo to go north up to Benoa (3000Rp, 15 minutes).

SANUR

☎ 0361

Sanur (nicknamed 'Snore' by some) is Kuta in a cardigan, offering a gentler, more effete and rather more middle-aged take on the tried-and-tested holiday cocktail of sand, sea and sundowners. Resort hotels are the norm here, but the Sanur does have a few decent budget digs.

The once-slimline beach has recently been beefed up with tons of imported sand and now ranks among Bali's best, with a lovely traffic-free promenade lined with genteel bars and restaurants.

Sleeping

Rooms tend to be a little more upmarket in Sanur, as do the prices.

Watering Hole I (☎ 288289; wateringhole_sanur bali@yahoo.com; Jl Hang Tuah 37; r 80,000-120,000Rp; ❄) At the rear of an ugly bar-restaurant, this place has 25 good-value rooms with big double beds and attractive wood furniture around a garden area.

Kaya Manis (☎ 289410; Jl Pantai Sindhu; s/d 85,000/150,000Rp; ❄) Behind this smart restaurant are five gorgeous rooms, all spotless and with stylish furnishings, that face a little garden.

Flashback's (☎ 281682; www.flashbacks-chb.com; Jl Danau Tamblingan 106; s/d from 110,000/160,000Rp;) Very hospitable and cheerful Australian-owned place with a choice of rooms, from near-economy to boutique-hotel chic. There's a tiny saltwater pool, shady garden, guests' kitchen area and a fine café out front.

Other recommendations:

Ida Homestay (☎ 288598; Jl Danau Toba Gang I 4; s/d 80,000/100,000Rp) With a quiet garden setting.

Yulia 2 Homestay (☎ 287495; Jl Danau Tamblingan; s/d 95,000/110,000Rp) Eccentric place awash with hunting-lodge kitsch. Tidy rooms and a bar-café.

Eating & Drinking

Sanur isn't exactly known for its punk-rock scene; smooth jazz bars are more the thing here. For cheap eats check out the food carts at the southern end of Jl Danau Tamblingan, and the Pasar Sindhu (Night Market) at the beach end of Jl Segara Ayu.

Warung Mama Putu (☎ 282025; Jl Kesuma Sari; mains 13,000Rp; breakfast, lunch & dinner) One of a number of cheap eateries on this strip of beach; try the seafood.

Kalimantan (☎ 289291; Jl Pantai Sindhu 11; mains from 18,000Rp; breakfast, lunch & dinner) Run by an amiable American who's been here for years, Kalimantan scores strongly for Western and Mexican grub (seasoned with Bill's home-grown peppers).

Getting There & Away

The bemo stops are at the southern end of Sanur on Jl Mertasari, and at the northern end outside the entrance to Grand Bali Beach Hotel. Blue bemo go to Denpasar's Tegal terminal (6000Rp, 30 minutes); green bemo go to Kereneng terminal (6000Rp, 30 minutes).

Perama (☎ 285592; Jl Hang Tuah 39; www.perama.co.id) is at Warung Pojok, at the northern end of town. It runs buses to Kuta and the airport (15,000Rp, 30 minutes), Ubud (20,000Rp, 45 minutes), Lovina (from 85,000Rp, three hours) and Padangbai (40,000Rp, 1½ hours).

UBUD

☎ 0361 / pop 8000

Once upon a time, there wasn't a whole lot to do in Ubud but dabble in the arts, and wander whimsically through the bottle-green paddy fields past the farm ducks (a local speciality). Now the beating heart of a thriving cultural scene, Ubud is an overgrown village where Bali's Hindu heritage is at its most vivid and there's a temple on (virtually) every street corner.

In recent years Ubud has developed at breakneck speed to satisfy the large numbers of visitors eager to experience the 'real' Bali and in some ways has become a victim of its own success. An orgy of construction has seen the village expand way beyond its previous boundaries, and buzzing bemo compete with the quacking ducks in the decibel stakes. But away from the town centre there are still plenty of peaceful corners, and the shopping, and programme of dance and music performances are exceptional. So for anyone with a degree of curiosity about the island's unique culture, Ubud is still a must.

Orientation

About 25km north of Denpasar, Ubud now encompasses its neighbours: Campuan, Penestanan, Padangtegal, Peliatan and Pengosekan. The centre of town is the crossroads near the market and the Ubud palace.

Information

Banks with ATMs and moneychangers are profuse in Ubud. Internet cafés, charging about 250Rp per minute, are scattered across town.

BOOKSHOPS

Ganesha Books (Map p223; ☎ 970320; www.ganeshabooksbali.com; Jl Raya Ubud 73; 9am-6pm) New and secondhand titles, including many books about Indonesian culture and society.

Periplus (Map p225; ☎ 975178; Monkey Forest Rd; 9am-9pm) Books, magazines, maps and some Lonely Planet titles.

INTERNET ACCESS

Bali 3000 (Map p223; ☎ 978538; Jl Raya Ubud; per hr 15,000Rp; 8am-11pm) Fast connections and serves good sandwiches, coffees and juices.

LIBRARIES

Pondok Pekak Library (Map p225; ☎ 976194; 9am-5pm Mon-Sat, 1-5pm Sun) Has a good children's section and a café, but there's a 40,000Rp joining fee.

MEDICAL SERVICES

Mua Farma (Map p225; ☎ 974674; Monkey Forest Rd; 8am-9pm) A centrally located pharmacy.

Ubud Clinic (Map p223; ☎ 974911; Jl Raya Compuan 36; 24hr) Offers round-the-clock medical services.

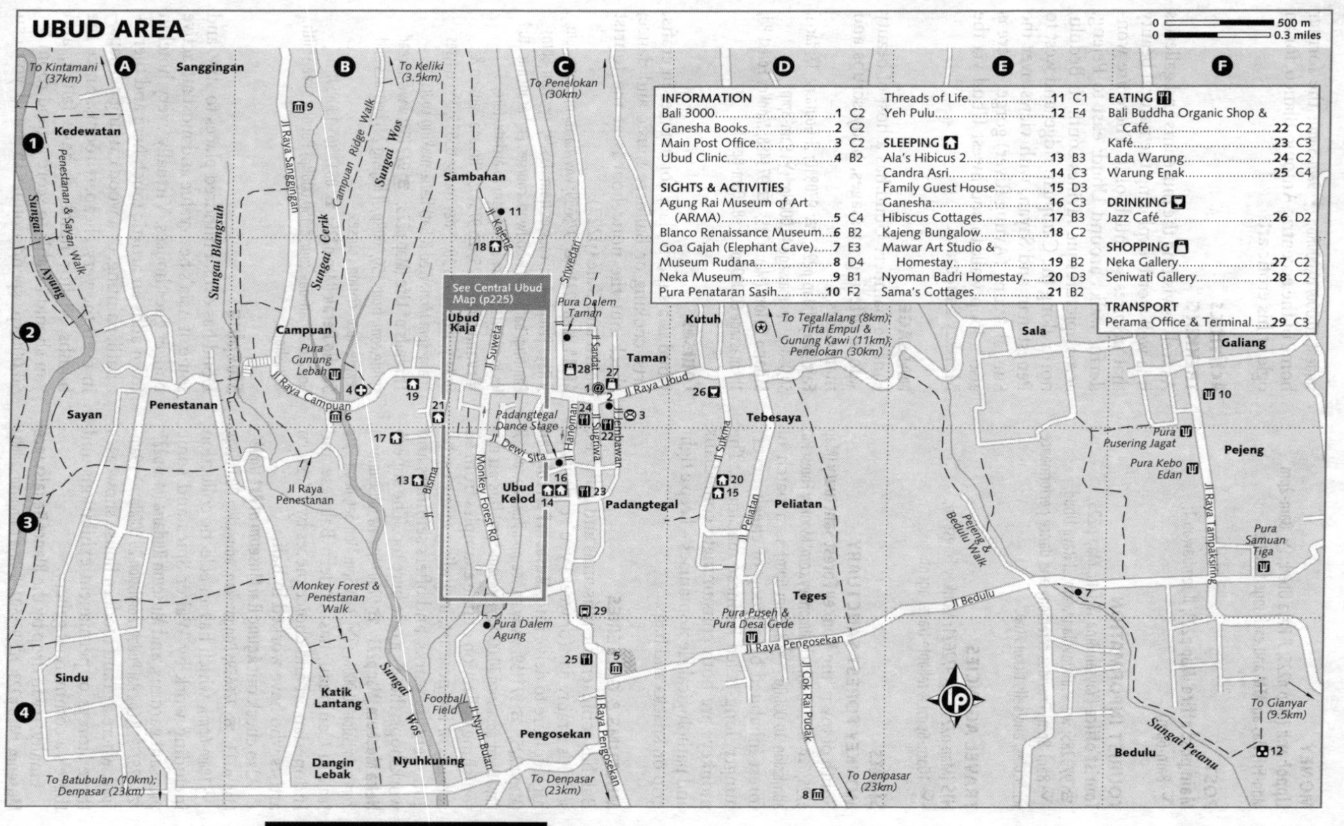
UBUD AREA
0 500 m
0 0.3 miles
INFORMATION
Bali 3000 1 C2
Ganesha Books 2 C2
Main Post Office 3 C2
Ubud Clinic 4 B2
SIGHTS & ACTIVITIES
Agung Rai Museum of Art (ARMA) 5 C4
Blanco Renaissance Museum 6 B2
Goa Gajah (Elephant Cave) 7 E3
Museum Rudana 8 D4
Neka Museum 9 B1
Pura Penataran Sasih 10 F2
Threads of Life 11 C1
Yeh Pulu 12 F4
SLEEPING
Ala's Hibicus 2 13 B3
Candra Asri 14 C3
Family Guest House 15 D3
Ganesha 16 C3
Hibiscus Cottages 17 B3
Kajeng Bungalow 18 C2
Mawar Art Studio & Homestay 19 B2
Nyoman Badri Homestay 20 D3
Sama's Cottages 21 B2
EATING
Bali Buddha Organic Shop & Café 22 C2
Kafé 23 C3
Lada Warung 24 C2
Warung Enak 25 C4
DRINKING
Jazz Café 26 D2
SHOPPING
Neka Gallery 27 C2
Seniwati Gallery 28 C2
TRANSPORT
Perama Office & Terminal 29 C3
See Central Ubud Map (p225)
To Kintamani (37km)
To Keliki (3.5km)
To Penelokan (30km)
To Tegallalang (8km); Tirta Empul & Gunung Kawi (11km); Penelokan (30km)
To Gianyar (9.5km)
To Denpasar (23km)
To Denpasar (23km)
To Batubulan (10km); Denpasar (23km)
Sanggingan
Kedewatan
Sambahan
Campuan
Ubud Kaja
Kutuh
Taman
Sala
Galiang
Sayan
Penestanan
Tebesaya
Pejeng
Ubud Kelod
Padangtegal
Peliatan
Teges
Sindu
Katik Lantang
Dangin Lebak
Nyuhkuning
Pengosekan
Bedulu
Sungai Ayung
Sungai Blangsuh
Sungai Cerik
Sungai Wos
Sungai Petanu
Penestanan & Sayan Walk
Campuan Ridge Walk
Monkey Forest & Penestanan Walk
Pejeng & Bedulu Walk
Jl Raya Sanggingan
Jl Raya Campuan
Jl Raya Penestanan
Jl Kajeng
Jl Sriwedari
Jl Suweta
Jl Sandat
Jl Raya Ubud
Jl Hanoman
Jl Sugriwa
Jl Jembawan
Jl Dewi Sita
Jl Bisma
Monkey Forest Rd
Jl Sukma
Jl Peliatan
Jl Bedulu
Jl Raya Pengosekan
Jl Cok Rai Pudak
Jl Nyuh Bulan
Jl Raya Tampaksiring
Pura Gunung Lebah
Pura Dalem Taman
Padangtegal Dance Stage
Pura Dalem Agung
Football Field
Pura Puseh & Pura Desa Gede
Pura Pusering Jagat
Pura Kebo Edan
Pura Samuan Tiga

MONEY

Lippobank (Map p225; Jl Raya Ubud; ⌚ 8am-2pm Mon-Fri) Has an ATM and exchange facilities.

POST

Main post office (Map p223; Jl Jembawan 1; ⌚ 8am-6pm)

TOURIST INFORMATION

Tourist office (Yaysan Bina Wisata; Map p225; ☎ 973285; www.ubudvillage.com; Jl Raya Ubud; ⌚ 8am-8pm) Provides ceremony and dance performance schedules, and sells tickets too.

TRAVEL AGENCIES

HIS (Map p225; ☎ 972621; Monkey Forest Rd; ⌚ 10am-6pm) A reliable travel agent.

Sights

MONKEY FOREST SANCTUARY

South of town, the **Monkey Forest Sanctuary** (Map p225; ☎ 971304; www.balimonkey.com; Monkey Forest Rd; admission 10,000Rp; ⌚ 8.30am-6pm) is a patch of forest inhabited by a troop of cheeky, ever-hungry, long-tailed Balinese macaques. The monkeys are both consummate comedians and pathological kleptomaniacs – keep a tight grip on snacks and bags.

MUSEUMS & GALLERIES

Bali has some terrific museums and galleries, so if it's a rainy day (or week) you've plenty of high culture to delve into. **Museum Puri Lukisan** (Map p225; ☎ 971159; www.museumpurilukisan.com; Jl Raya Ubud; admission 20,000Rp; ⌚ 9am-5pm) has an astonishing collection of fine examples from all schools of Balinese art, including many early-20th-century works, and offers seminars and workshops; there's a café here too. The superb **Neka Museum** (Map p223; ☎ 975074; www.museumneka.com; admission 20,000Rp; ⌚ 9am-5pm Mon-Sat, noon-5pm Sun), in Campuan, has modern Balinese and Indonesian art and choice pieces by Western artists who have worked in Bali.

Also check out **Agung Rai Museum of Art** (ARMA; Map p223; ☎ 976659; Pengosekan; admission 20,000Rp; ⌚ 10am-6pm), which has an eclectic collection including work by Walter Spies and some pleasant gardens, and **Museum Rudana** (Map p223; ☎ 975779; Jl Cok Rai Pudak; admission 20,000Rp; ⌚ 9am-5pm), where a grand modern house showcases three storeys of permanent exhibitions and there's a commercial gallery.

Finally, try to drop by the **Blanco Renaissance Museum** (Map p223; ☎ 975502; Jl Raya Campuan; adult/student 20,000/10,000Rp; ⌚ 9am-5pm), the former home of the eccentric Antonio Blanco, for an ogle at his erotic art.

INDONESIA

Activities

TREKKING

As well as visiting the museums and galleries it is well worth exploring the natural beauty that inspires so much of it. There are wonderful walks around Ubud: east to Pejeng, across picturesque ravines south to Bedulu; north along the Campuan ridge; and west to Penestanan and Sayan, with views over the Sungai Ayung (Ayung River) gorge. There is also a loop walk to southwest Ubud via the Monkey Sanctuary.

MASSAGE

Fancy a pamper? Ubud has a host of beauty salons offering massages, body scrubs and manicures.

Fair Way (Map p225; ☎ 970810; Jl Goutama 17; facial 50,000Rp, 1hr massage 40,000Rp; ⌚ 9am-8pm)

Milano Salon (Map p225; ☎ 973488; Monkey Forest Rd; 1hr massage 60,000Rp; ⌚ 8.30am-8pm)

Courses

Ubud is a superb place for courses in crafts, arts, cooking or Balinese music and dance; check out the noticeboards at the tourist board and Kafé (p227).

ARMA (Map p223; ☎ 976659; www.armamuseum.com; Jl Raya Pengosekan; courses from US$24; ⌚ 9am-6pm) Painting, batik and woodwork courses, and academic studies in everything from Hinduism to architecture.

Nirvana (Map p225; ☎ 975415; Nirvana Pension & Gallery, Jl Goutama 10; 1-day course US$35; ⌚ classes 10am-3pm Mon, Wed & Sat) Batik-making courses.

Threads of Life (Map p223; ☎ 972187; www.threadsoflife.com; from 150,000Rp; Jl Kajeng 24) Lectures and textile-appreciation courses.

Studio Perak (Map p225; ☎ 0812 365 1809; Jl Goutama; half-day course 150,000Rp) Popular silversmith workshops.

Sleeping

Ubud has over a hundred places to stay, and some of Asia's best-value and most attractive budget guesthouses. Virtually every hotel in town adds an artistic touch here and there – a batik painting, or a wood carving perhaps – in even the very cheapest rooms. Since the bombs, visitor numbers have fallen, and you should be able to score a good room for 50,000Rp; spend double that and you can

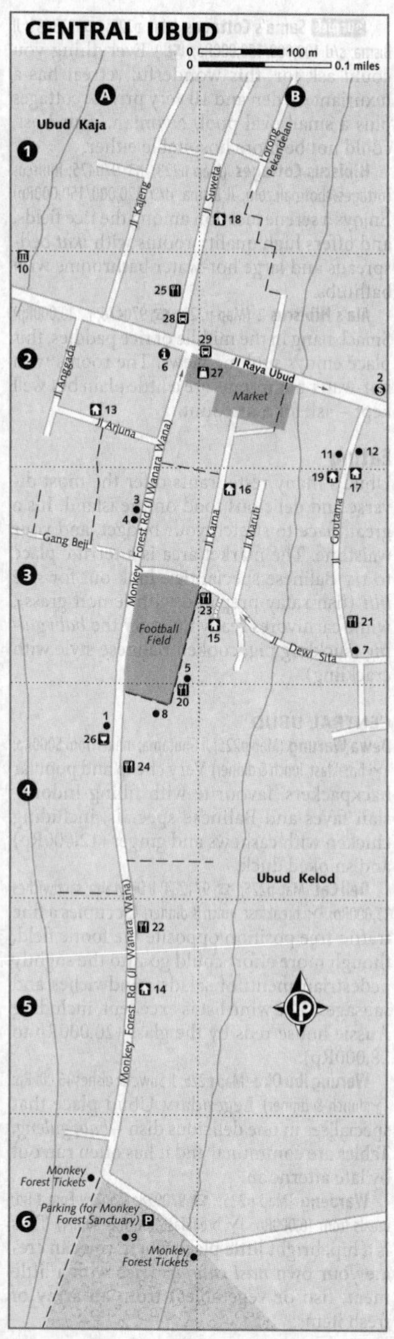

expect real comfort. Virtually everywhere throws in a basic breakfast.

CENTRAL UBUD

Jungut Inn (Map p225; ☎ 978237; Jl Arjuna; s/d 35,000/45,000Rp) If price is a real issue, look no further than this family-run place, with three spartan but clean rooms. There are more ultracheap options on this road.

Shana Bungalows (Map p225; ☎ 970545; Jl Goutama 7; s/d 50,000/60,000Rp) Old-timer that's ageing fast, but still has a little charm.

Wena (p225; ☎ 975416; Jl Goutama; r with cold/hot water 50,000/70,000Rp) Four inexpensive, large tiled rooms with bedside reading lights, large bathrooms and verandas at the rear of a family compound.

Suci Inn (Map p225; ☎ 975304; Jl Suweta; s/d 55,000/70,000Rp) This place is attractive, centrally located and popular; it's worth booking ahead for a bed here.

INFORMATION
HIS......1 A4
Lippobank......2 B2
Mua Farma......3 A3
Periplus......4 A3
Pondok Pekak Library......5 A3
Tourist Office (Yaysan Bina Wisata)......6 A2

SIGHTS & ACTIVITIES
Fair Way......7 B3
Milano Salon......8 A4
Monkey Forest Sanctuary......9 A6
Museum Puri Lukisan......10 A2
Nirvana......11 B2
Studio Perak......12 B2

SLEEPING
Jungut Inn......13 A2
Kubu Saren......14 A5
Masih Bungalow......15 B3
Sania's House......16 B3
Shana Bungalows......17 B3
Suci Inn......18 B1
Wena......19 B3

EATING
Deli Cat......20 A4
Dewa Warung......21 B3
Three Monkeys......22 A5
Tutmak......23 B3
Waroeng......24 A4
Warung Ibu Oka......25 A2

DRINKING
Putra Bar......26 A4

SHOPPING
Pasar Seni (Art Market)......27 B2

TRANSPORT
Bemo Stop......28 A2
Bemo Stop......29 B2

INDONESIA

Masih Bungalow (Map p225; ☎ 975062; Jl Dewi Sita; r 70,000Rp) Up some steps off Dewi Seta, this family-run place offers attractive, spacious rooms with balconies and hot-water bathrooms. There's a little garden area with a shade-providing, fruit-rich rambutan tree.

Kubu Saren (Map p225; ☎ 975704; Monkey Forest Rd; s/d 70,000/85,000Rp) Poke your nose into this tidy outfit and you'll be hard-pressed not to catch someone sweeping or polishing. There are eight spacious rooms.

Sania's House (Map p225; ☎ 975535; sania_house@yahoo.com; Jl Karna 7; r 80,000Rp, with hot water from 100,000Rp;) Giving the hanging gardens of Babylon a run for their money, this very well-run place has a choice of excellent accommodation, with more on the way. The more pricey rooms here have gorgeous hand-carved wooden furniture and sprung mattresses, and some even have four-poster beds.

EAST OF THE CENTRE

Nyoman Badri Homestay (Map p223; ☎ 977047; Jl Sukma; s/d 50,000/60,000Rp) No frills or spills, just a warm welcome and plain, clean if smallish rooms with high ceilings and en-suite bathrooms.

Ganesha (Map p223; ☎ 970517; Jl Hanoman 43; d from 60,000Rp) This guesthouse, down a quiet *gang*, has sweeping aspects over rice fields and large, comfortable rooms with great balconies and bathtubs.

Candra Asri (Map p223; ☎ 970517; Jl Hanoman 43; d from 60,000Rp;) Well-swept, spacious rooms with bamboo furniture and verandas, some with fine rice-paddy views.

Family Guest House (Map p223; ☎ 974054; Jl Sukma; d 88,000-250,000Rp;) Spilling down a river valley, this well-run place has a leafy garden and excellent rooms with homely touches and solid wooden furniture, the most expensive with four-poster beds. There's a book exchange here.

NORTH OF THE CENTRE

Kajeng Bungalow (Map p223; ☎ 975018; Jl Kajeng 29; s/d from 70,000/80,000Rp;) Ignore the dingy entrance, and soak up the scenery: a dramatic, plunging riverside setting and attractive rooms, some with great views.

WEST OF THE CENTRE

Mawar Art Studio & Homestay (Map p223; ☎ 975086; Jl Raya Ubud; s/d 100,000/150,000Rp) Airy light rooms with good views.

our pick **Sama's Cottages** (Map p223; ☎ 973481; Jl Bisma; s/d 100,000/150,000Rp;) Everything you could ask for, this wonderful retreat has a luxuriant garden and 10 very private cottages plus a small oval pool. Nyoman, your host, could not be more hospitable either.

Hibiscus Cottages (Map p223; ☎ 970475; hibiscus cottages@hotmail.com; Jl Bisma; d/tr 120,000/150,000Rp) Enjoys a serene location among the rice fields, and offers high quality rooms with *ikat* bedspreads and large hot-water bathrooms with bathtubs.

Ala's Hibiscus 2 (Map p223; ☎ 970476; r 120,000Rp) Smack bang in the middle of rice paddies, this place enjoys sublime views. The rooms with hot-water bathrooms are a little plain but well kept – ask for a discount.

Eating

Ubud's many restaurants offer the most diverse and delicious food on the island. It's a great place to stretch your budget, and your waistline. The market area is a terrific place to try Balinese specialities: look out for *sate lilit* (fish satay prepared with lemon grass), while carnivores really must try the *babi guling* (suckling pig, cooked Balinese style with crackling).

CENTRAL UBUD

Dewa Warung (Map p225; Jl Goutama; mains from 5000Rp; breakfast, lunch & dinner) Very cheap and popular backpackers' favourite with filling Indonesian faves and Balinese specials, including chicken with cashews and ginger (12,000Rp) and smoked duck.

Deli Cat (Map p225; ☎ 971284; Jl Dewi Sita; sandwiches 15,000Rp; breakfast, lunch & dinner) Occupies a fine traffic-free position opposite the footie field, though more effort could go into the slightly pedestrian menu of salads, sandwiches and sausages. The wine list is excellent, including Aussie house reds by the glass (20,000Rp to 28,000Rp).

Warung Ibu Oka (Map p225; Jl Suweta; dishes 15,000Rp; lunch & dinner) Legendary Ubud place that specialises in one delicious dish – *babi guleng*. Tables are communal and it has often run out by late afternoon.

Waroeng (Map p225; ☎ 970928; Monkey Forest Rd; meals from 16,000Rp; breakfast, lunch & dinner) This is a hip, bright little place where you can create your own *nasi campur* (rice with a little meat, fish or vegetables) from an array of fresh items.

Tutmak (Map p225; ☎ 975754; Jl Dewi Sita; mains 19,000-48,000Rp; ⏰ breakfast, lunch & dinner) With a double aspect overlooking the football pitch and busy Jl Dewi Sita, this enjoyable, if pricey, café-restaurant has low tables and a menu of Western dishes, sandwiches, juices and the like.

Three Monkeys (Map p225; ☎ 974830; Monkey Forest Rd; mains from 24,000Rp; ⏰ lunch & dinner) Fine restaurant with tables evocatively set right by rice fields, making a wonderfully peaceful setting for a memorable meal. By day there are sandwiches and salads, at night feast on Indonesian classics, pasta and steaks.

EAST & SOUTH OF THE CENTRE

Lada Warung (Map p223; ☎ 972822; Jl Hanoman; meals 8000-15,000Rp; ⏰ breakfast, lunch & dinner) Tiny, very clean and orderly modern *warung* with chunky wooden tables and very inexpensive and fresh local food – a *nasi goreng komplit* (*nasi goreng* with extra trimmings) is 10,000Rp.

Bali Buddha Organic Shop & Café (Map p223; ☎ 976324; Jl Jembawan 1; dishes 12,000-36,000Rp; ⏰ breakfast, lunch & dinner) Veggie temple to all things wholemeal and organic, with art exhibitions and a store downstairs selling healthy snacks and fruit and veg.

Kafé (Map p223; ☎ 970992; Jl Hanoman 446; www.balispirit.com; dishes 16,000-38,000Rp; ⏰ breakfast, lunch & dinner) Boho hang-out with a healthy eating menu (try the spiced pumpkin soup), tonic drinks and juices (like lime and mint slush), and there are magazines to browse and a great noticeboard.

Warung Enak (Map p223; ☎ 972911; Jl Raya Pengosekan; www.warungenakbali.com; dishes from 18,000Rp, mains 38,000-55,000Rp; ⏰ lunch & dinner) About 3km from central Ubud, this two-storey temple to kitsch – a riot of wacky lighting, mirrors and ornaments and mismatched furniture – has rice-paddy views from the breezy upper level. The creatively assembled modern Indonesian menu has plenty of veggie options.

Drinking

No-one comes to Ubud for wild nightlife, but these days a few bars offer after-dinner diversion.

Jazz Café (Map p223; ☎ 976594; Jl Sukma 2; ⏰ 5-11.30pm) A mellow, middle-aged expat haunt with live jazz bands (except Sunday and Monday) from 8pm. Food is pricey at 50,000Rp a main, though substantial.

Putra Bar (Map p225; ☎ 975570; Monkey Forest Rd; ⏰ 4pm-1am) The only real nightspot in town hosts live reggae, ska and indie bands, and films.

Entertainment

Try to see at least one of the Balinese dances performed in or near Ubud every night. The tourist office has the latest schedules, and sells tickets (50,000Rp).

Shopping

Pasar Seni (Art Market; Map p225; cnr Jl Raya Ubud & Monkey Forest Rd; ⏰ 8am-8pm) The two-storey market sells a wide range of clothing, sarongs and souvenirs of variable quality at very negotiable prices, as do many small shops along Monkey Forest Rd.

Paintings are sold at many commercial galleries and museums: **Neka Gallery** (Map p223; ☎ 975034; Jl Raya Ubud; ⏰ 9am-5pm) is one of the largest, while **Seniwati Gallery** (Map p223; ☎ 975485; www.seniwatigallery.com; Jl Sriwedari 2B; ⏰ 9am-5pm) showcases female artists.

For less expensive artworks, look in individual artists' studios on Jl Hanoman and in the village of Penestanan.

Getting There & Around

Public bemo stop at two convenient points in the centre of town. Orange bemo travel between Ubud and Gianyar (7000Rp, 30 minutes), which has bus and bemo connections to most of eastern Bali. Brown bemo go to/from Batubulan terminal (12,000Rp, 1½ hours), with connections to the other Denpasar terminals (another 2000Rp).

Perama (Map p223; ☎ 973316; Jl Hanoman) has a terminal that is inconveniently located south of town in Padangtegal. Sample prices: Sanur (20,000Rp, one hour); Kuta and the airport (30,000Rp, one hour); Padangbai (40,000Rp, 1¼ hours) and Lovina (from 85,000Rp, 2½ hours).

Car- and motorcycle-hire prices are as cheap as anywhere in Bali. Bicycles cost about 12,000Rp per day.

AROUND UBUD

Two kilometres east of the centre, the cavern of **Goa Gajah** (Elephant Cave; Map p223; admission 4100Rp; ⏰ 8am-6pm) was discovered in the 1920s and is believed to have been a Buddhist hermitage. Nearby is **Yeh Pulu** (Map p223; admission 4100Rp; ⏰ 8am-6pm), a complex of rock

INDONESIA

carvings with carved bas-relief. A couple of kilometres north in Pejeng, **Pura Penataran Sasih** (Map p223; admission by donation; 9am-6pm) houses a bronze drum said to be 2000 years old. A legend tells of it falling to earth as the Moon of Pejeng.

In Tampaksiring, 11km northeast of Ubud on the road to Gianyur, **Gunung Kawi** (admission 4100Rp; 8am-5pm) is an astonishing group of stone *candi* (shrines) cut into cliffs on either side of the fecund, plunging Pakrisan River valley. The shrines are thought to have been carved as monuments to an 11th-century royal family headed by King Udayana, though this theory is open to conjecture. Whatever their origin, Gunung Kawi is certainly one of Bali's most impressive sights. Access is signposted from Tampaksiring, via a 10-minute descent down a steep, slippery staircase.

A few kilometres north of Tampaksiring, in the shadow of the Soekarno-era presidential palace, is the holy spring and temple of **Tirta Empul** (admission 4100Rp; 9am-6pm). An inscription dates the spring from AD 926. There are fine carvings and *garuda* on the courtyard buildings. Both sites can be reached by bemo (3000Rp, 30 minutes) from Ubud.

PURA BESAKIH

This is Bali's 'mother temple'. With a photogenic location, 1000m up the flanks of Gunung Agung, **Pura Besakih** (☎ 0361-222387; admission 7500Rp, camera charge 1000Rp; dawn-dusk) is actually a complex of 35 separate, but related, religious structures, which only narrowly escaped destruction during the devastating eruption of Gunung Agung in 1963. Although the architecture is a bit of a disappointment and the inner courtyards are largely closed to visitors, the temple bursts into life during its colourful festivals – particularly during **Odalan**, the temple's anniversary, which falls in the 10th month of the Balinese calendar (usually April). Unfortunately you'll encounter an army of guides offering their 'services'; haggle hard and agree on a price first if you hire one.

Most trips to Pura Besakih require a change in Semarapura, about one hour away. Ask the driver to drop you at the temple, rather than the village, which is about 1km south. As transport options evaporate around 3pm, getting here with your own wheels is far more convenient.

GUNUNG AGUNG

Often obscured beneath a thick duvet of mist, Gunung Agung is a relatively infrequent feature of Bali's skyline. When the clouds part, however, Bali's highest and most revered mountain is an imposing sight and is visible from much of southern and eastern Bali.

Gunung Agung is a relatively moody volcano. A 700m-wide crater marks the mountain's summit and in 1963, Gunung Agung shrank by 126m after a devastating eruption. It now stands 3142m above sea level.

A hike to the summit is best attempted in the dry season (April to September) – the route may be treacherously slippery at other times. There are several possible approaches. From the village of Besakih (about 1km south of the temple complex) it's a very demanding climb: allow at least six hours going up and four hours coming down. Start at midnight to reach the summit for sunrise, before it's enveloped in cloud. You'll need a guide; inquire at the information office at the Pura Besakih car park or contact a guide through **Pondok Wisata Puri Agung** (☎ 0361-23037). Guides ask 350,000Rp per person (minimum two people),with discounts for larger groups.

A shorter route is from **Pura Pasar Agung** (Agung Market Temple), at around 1500m on the southern slopes of the mountain, which can be reached by a sealed road north from **Selat**. From the temple you can climb to the top in three or four hours, but it's also a demanding trek. Report to the police station at Selat before you start, and take a guide; they'll charge about 300,000Rp, plus the cost of food and transport. The closest accommodation is **Pondok Wisata Puri Agung** (☎ 0361-23037; s/d 80,000/100,000Rp), on the road between Selat and Duda.

Agung hikes can also be organised in the village of Tirta Gangga, home to several trekking operations and guides.

SEMARAPURA (KLUNGKUNG)

☎ 0366 / pop 28,000

Once the centre of an important Balinese kingdom, Semarapura (also known as Klungkung) is the capital of Klungkung regency. Formerly the seat of the Dewa Agung dynasty, the **Semara Pura Complex** (admission 5000Rp; 7am-6pm) has now largely crumbled away, but history and architecture buffs will enjoy a wander past the **Kertha Gosa** (Hall of Justice) and **Bale Kambang** (Floating Pavilion).

Frequent bemo and minibuses from Denpasar (Batubulan terminal) pass through Semarapura (11,000Rp, one hour) on the way to Padangbai and Amlapura.

NUSA LEMBONGAN

☎ 0366

Nusa Lembongan is one of three islands (along with Nusa Penida and Nusa Ceningan) that together comprise the Nusa Penida archipelago. Nusa Lembongan, with its scuba diving, surf breaks, white-sand beaches and hotels, is the biggest tourist drawcard and remains a pleasant escape from the hubbub of Bali's south coast resorts. Jungutbatu Beach is the most convenient base.

Information

Bank BPD will accept cash and travellers cheques, as will many hotels. Pondok Baruna has internet access.

Activities

World Diving (☎ 081 2390 0686; www.world-diving.com; Pondok Baruna, Jungutbatu) is a PADI school offering courses (open-water is US$350) and dive trips (from US$60 for two dives including all gear) on the exceptional reefs around Lembongan, and beyond.

The dry season is surfing season in Nusa Lembongan, with winds bringing in the waves from the southeast. The Shipwreck, Lacerations and Playground surf breaks are off the island's west coast, near the little settlement of Jungutbatu.

Sleeping & Eating

Most of the cheap accommodation is in Jungutbatu, a strip of working beach on the northwest coast.

Agung's Lembongan Lodge (☎ 24483; r 60,000-175,000Rp) Well-priced, simple but clean rooms and smarter, attractive thatched cottages. The restaurant has ocean views, a pool table and a much nicer atmosphere than most other places. It's 1km north of the dock.

Linda Bungalows (☎ 24495; r 75,000-100,000Rp) On a great section of the beach, this is a very well presented and maintained place with 12 clean cold-water rooms, one offers an ocean view. It's just north of Agung's.

Pondok Baruna (☎ 081 2390 0686; www.world-diving.com; r 75,000-100,000Rp) A popular place with friendly staff, the seven smallish tiled rooms here are pleasant and their porches face the ocean. Great food is served (dishes 10,000Rp to 12,000Rp). Just north of the dock.

Getting There & Away

Public boats (60,000Rp, 1½ hours) leave at 7.45am and other times of the day from the northern end of Sanur Beach. Or book up with Perama (which is more reliable), whose boat leaves at 8.30am (70,000Rp, 1½ hours).

PADANGBAI

☎ 0363

Padangbai is the main port for ferries to Lombok, but it's a pleasant enough place in its own right. Lying at the bottom of a wooded headland, this classic cove has a sandy beach lined with fishing boats and plenty of decent hostels, restaurants and a couple of dive schools.

Information

Made Homestay (☎ 41441; Jl Silayukti; per hr 10,000Rp; 🕘 9am-9pm) has internet access and a *wartel*. There are ATMs in nearby Candi Desa.

Activities

There's excellent diving around the east coast of Bali. **Water Worxx Dive Center** (☎ 41220; www.waterworxbali.com; Jl Silayukti) offers two dives at the blue lagoon for US$40, while **Absolute Scuba** (☎ 081 7474 5536; www.absolutescubabali.com; Jl Silayukti) charges US$55 for diving the *Tulamben* wreck.

The good folk at Topi Inn (p230) offer myriad workshops and fun activities from *ikat*-weaving and *batik*-painting (US$12 to US$15) to coconut tree-climbing!

Sleeping

Hotels fill up quickly, and some increase their prices in August, but otherwise you should have no bother finding a bed. Most places are on Jl Silayukti, the beachfront road.

Kerti Beach Inn (☎ 41391; kertibeachinn@yahoo.com; Jl Silayukti 9; s/d from 40,000/50,000Rp; 💻) Justifiably popular, Kerti's has pleasant *lumbung*-style (rice barn) bungalows all with ceiling fans and cold-water bathrooms. Catch the sunrise or, failing that, the Lombok ferries from its 1st-floor terrace eatery.

Made Homestay (☎ 41441; mades_padangbai@hotmail.com; Jl Silayukti; s/d 40,000/60,000Rp; 💻) A good budget choice, the large plain rooms here have high ceilings and bathrooms with Western

INDONESIA

toilets; those on the upper level enjoy partial sea views.

Kembar Inn (☎ 41364; Jl Segara 6; r 50,000-150,000Rp; ❄) Clean, neat little homestay in the village with six good rooms.

Padangbai Billabong (☎ 081 2360 7946; Jl Silayukti 14; cottage with fan 60,000Rp, r with air-con 150,000Rp; ❄) Choose from comfortable, if smallish, rooms with elaborately carved wooden doors, verandas and big bathrooms or go native in one of the rice barn–style two-storey cottages at the rear.

Topi Inn (☎ 41424; www.topiinn.nl; Jl Silayukti 99; d 90,000Rp; 💻) Highly sociable and atmospheric Dutch-owned place with a huge café with magazines and books to browse. Five attractive, well-presented rooms and a vast attic area that's sometimes used as an accommodation overspill. Numerous craft and cultural workshops can be organised here.

Eating & Drinking

Puri Rai (☎ 41187; Jl Silayukti 7X; mains 16,000-30,000Rp; 🕑 breakfast, lunch & dinner) Smart seafront place with an eclectic menu that takes in jaffles and a number of veggie selections, seafood and Indonesian dishes. There's espresso coffee, Bali-brewed Storm beer, and cocktails which are best savoured in the bar upstairs.

Ozone (☎ 41780; Jl Segara 8; mains from 17,000Rp; 🕑 breakfast, lunch & dinner) The nearest thing Padangbai has to a bar, this place has walls covered in travellers' scrawls, filling Western and local food and occasionally some live music.

Padang Bai (Jl Silayukti; fish 20,000Rp; 🕑 lunch & dinner) Simple *warung* where owner Dana serves up wicked fresh fish and squid cooked in your choice of either garlic, chilli, or onion-and-chilli sauce.

Getting There & Away

From the car park in front of the port, bemo go to Amlapura (11,000Rp, 45 minutes), via Candidasa (5000Rp, 20 minutes) and Denpasar (17,000Rp, 1¾ hours). Tourists are commonly overcharged.

Perama (☎ 41419; www.peramatour.com; Jl Pelabuhan), just inland from the main jetty, runs shuttle buses to Kuta and the airport (40,000Rp, 1¾ hours), Ubud (30,000Rp, one hour) and Lovina (100,000Rp, 3½ hours).

Public ferries between Padangbai and Lembar (Lombok) run every two hours, 24 hours a day (21,000Rp, 4½ to 5½ hours).

CANDIDASA

☎ 0363

Candidasa is not natural backpacking terrain, catering mainly to midrange tourists, but there are several decent budget options here as well. The resort's beach was washed out to sea years ago when developers blew up the offshore reef to make cement, but a pleasant sandy sliver survives on Candi's eastern fringes.

Orientation & Information

Candidasa is a one-street (Jl Raya Candidasa) town, cut in half by a pleasant lagoon. The area east of the lagoon tends to be a little quieter.

Internet cafés, travel agencies and ATMs are dotted along the main drag.

Sights & Activities

Right next to the lagoon, **Gedong Gandhi Ashram** (☎ 41108; www.ashramgandhi.com) is an ashram that was established in 1976, after the founder was inspired by the teachings and principles of Mahatma Gandhi. It's looking a little run-down these days, but provides a home for disadvantaged children, a kindergarten for local families, library, yoga sessions (6.30am daily) and offers free acupuncture (Mondays, Wednesdays and Fridays from 1pm to 4pm). Volunteers who want to teach English or help out are provided with free accommodation.

There's reasonable **snorkelling** offshorep; Seaside Cottages has masks and fins for rent (20,000Rp).

Sleeping

The quietest area to stay is about 1.5km east of the centre, down a shady lane known as Jl Pantai Indah. Here you'll find a slimline beach, and you're well away from traffic.

Temple Cafe & Seaside Cottages (☎ 41629; www.bali-seafront-bungalows.com; Jl Raya Candidasa; s/d from 35,000/50,000Rp; ❄) There are no fewer than six classes of room at this well-run, centrally located place that meanders right down to the sea (where you'll find some sun loungers). All are kept very neat and tidy, and there's a great café here too (see opposite).

Puri Oka Cottages (☎ 41092; puri_oka@hotmail.com; Jl Pantai Indah; r 80,000-170,000Rp; ❄ 🏊) Pass through a banana grove east of town, and this place has a beachfront plot, and homely rooms, all with bedside lights and en-suite bathrooms.

Sekar Orchid (☎ 41086; www.sekar-orchid.com; Jl Pantai Indah 26; bungalow with fan from 150,000Rp) It's not for the fiscally challenged but this place, located beachside east of the lagoon, is worth every rupiah. The Dharmawaty family used to live in Germany, and keep an efficient and immaculate ship, with gorgeous cottages decorated with local artefacts, and all the hot-water bathrooms have tubs.

Other recommendations:

Genggong (☎ 41105; Jl Pantai Indah; s/d with fan 55,000/65,000Rp, air-con bungalows 130,000Rp;) Serviceable rooms right on the beach.

Ari Homestay (☎ 081 7970 7339; Jl Raya Candidasa; d from 65,000Rp) On the traffic-blighted main drag, but run by some amiable Aussies.

Ida's Homestay (☎ 41096; jsidas1@aol.com; Jl Raya Candidasa; d from 130,000Rp) Quirky but comfy wooden bungalows in a shady setting west of the lagoon.

Eating & Drinking

There are dozens of eateries in Candidasa along the main drag. For a cheap scoff check the evening food stalls at the western end of town near the Perama office.

our pick **Temple Cafe** (☎ 41629; Jl Raya Candidasa; mains 24,000-34,000Rp; breakfast, lunch & dinner) Despite the roadside location, this is a friendly, relaxed place for a *lassi* (an Indian yogurt-based drink), cappuccino or a cocktail, with newspapers and books to read. Tuck into the generous Western mains, or British home-comfort snacks such as toast with Marmite.

Iguana Café (☎ 41973; Jl Raya Candidasa; mains from 26,000Rp; breakfast, lunch & dinner) Offers a good spread of local and seafood dishes and there's live music some nights.

Legend Rock Café (Jl Raya Candidasa; set meals 32,000Rp; breakfast, lunch & dinner) Your best bet for a (not so) wild night out; clap along with the grannies to a covers band (Wednesday and Saturday nights). Happy hour is 7pm to 8pm, when Bintangs are 11,500Rp. Also offers Western and local grub.

Getting There & Away

Candidasa is on the main road between Amlapura and Denpasar – there's no terminal, so hail bemo anywhere along the main road (buses probably won't stop).

Perama (☎ 41114; www.peramatour.com; Jl Raya Candidasa) is at the western end of the strip, near Ari Homestay. It runs tourist shuttle buses to Sanur (30,000Rp, 1¾ hours), Kuta (30,000Rp, two hours), Ubud (30,000Rp, one hour), Lovina (80,000Rp, three hours) and Padangbai (10,000Rp, 20 minutes).

AMLAPURA

☎ 0363

Amlapura isn't worth making a diversion for, but there are worse places to stop if you are already making the trip through eastern Bali. Twenty-first-century hustle and bustle dominates the streets today, but you can catch a glimpse of the fast-fading 'good old days' at the former palace of the Raja of Karangasem, the **Puri Agung Karangasem** (Jl Sultan Agung; admission 3000Rp; 8am-6pm).

Villa Amlapura (☎ 23246; Jl Gajah Mada; r 65,000-130,000Rp), around the corner from the palace, is a friendly place if you're not in a rush to get back on the road.

Amlapura's bus/bemo terminal has regular connections to/from Denpasar (Batubulan terminal; 15,000Rp, two hours) and around the north coast to Singaraja (28,000Rp, 3¼ hours).

TIRTA GANGGA

☎ 0363

The village under the volcano, Tirta Gangga (Water of the Ganges) sits in the shadow of Gunung Agung and in the midst of some of Bali's most beautiful scenery. Passed in a gear change and a slow right-hand turn, it's small, isolated and quiet and remains a blissfully serene stopover on the slow road through Bali.

Sights & Activities

The old **Taman Tirta Gangga** (www.tirtagangga.com; admission 3000Rp; 7am-6pm) water palace has ornamental ponds and swimming pools – a dip is an extra 6000Rp. A typhoon destroyed its auditorium and felled numerous trees in March 2007, but the palace remains open to visitors.

The surrounding countryside has sublime rice-field vistas and good **trekking** possibilities through stunning evergreen landscapes. Popular destinations include the temple of Pura Lempuyang (five hours return from Ngis, a village 5km northeast of Tirta Gangga and the Buddhist villages of Bukit Kusambi (six hours return from Tirta Gangga). Hikes to Agung can also be organised here: Nioman Budiasa at Genta Bali Warung asks US$45 (minimum two people) for this trip.

Sleeping & Eating

For the cheapest eats head to the *warung* near the palace gate.

Dhangin Taman Inn (☎ 22059; r 40,000-80,000Rp) Venerable, ramshackle warren of a place with bizarre colour schemes and décor mismatched enough to send a feng shui freak gaga. On the plus side the family running the place could not be more friendly, the grub is good (dishes 7000Rp to 12,000Rp), and prices are low.

Rijasa (☎ 21873; d 70,000Rp) A row of good, solid cottages that are spacious and clean and have fine views from their elevated porches. There's a cheap *warung* and a store out front.

Good Karma (☎ 22445; s/d 90,000/100,000Rp) Directly facing shimmering rice paddies, these four rustic cottages (two doubles and two twins) are clean, homely and peaceful. The attractive roadside restaurant serves delicious food (dishes 10,000Rp to 18,000Rp), including fish satay, BBQ dishes and many vegetarian options.

Puri Sawah (☎ 21847; r 100,000, bungalows 200,000Rp) A little out of town, up a steep access road, this place enjoys sweeping views and has spacious, comfy rooms and huge bungalows. There's a lush garden and a good café with Indonesian and Western food (mains 16,000Rp to 23,000Rp).

Genta Bali Warung (☎ 22436; mains from 12,000Rp; breakfast, lunch & dinner) Quirky traveller-geared roadside café with a menu of 'spaggetty' (13,000Rp), curries and local dishes.

Getting There & Away

Regular bemo and minibuses pass through Tirta Gangga on routes north of Amlapura (2000Rp to Amlapura); just flag them down.

Perama tourist buses also pass through to Kuta (40,000Rp, 2½ hours); try your hotel for tickets and times.

AMED & THE FAR EAST COAST

☎ 0363

The coast east of Amed is one of Bali's largely forgotten stretches of seaside. Developers are starting to gatecrash the party, but the island's wild east is a far cry from the concrete jungle of the south coast.

Most of the development is spread along the coastal road, around the bays of Jemeluk, Bunutan and Lipah. Facilities are improving, with several hotels and stores offering telephone, internet and money-changing services.

Euro-Dive (☎ 23469; www.eurodivebali.com), in Amed, is a professional scuba outfit offering courses and dive packages (from US$45).

Sleeping & Eating

Amed Cafe (☎ 23473; www.amedcafe.com; d from 80,000Rp;) Located a little further east than Three Brothers, Amed Cafe is a very well-run operation with several classes of attractive accommodation, including budget rooms and *lumbung*-style cottages. Diving and snorkelling trips can be arranged here, and there's also a restaurant (dishes 7000Rp to 22,000Rp) and internet café over the road.

Three Brothers (☎ 23472; r 90,000-130,000Rp) This long-running place about a kilometre east of Amed has a superb beachfront plot and neat, clean tiled bungalows with fine sea views. The café here serves up good local food, including specials like *sate ikan* (fish satay).

Aiona Health Garden (☎ 0813 3816 1730; r from 170,000) This spot has well-constructed bungalows, as well as a veggie restaurant with local and Indonesian meals (from 20,000Rp) and invigorating juices in a gorgeous, fragrant herb garden setting. It is 2km east of Bunutan.

Eka Purnama (☎ 0868 1212 1685; www.eka-purnama.com; s/d 190,000/230,000Rp) With oceanic views from its well-constructed wooden bungalows and twin-decked restaurant, this is an inspirational place to stay for vista junkies. There's also a family house that sleeps six (perfect if you can get a backpacking tribe together), and mountain bikes and snorkelling gear for hire. It's just before Aas, about 11km from Amed.

Other good places around the coast:

Galang Kangin Bungalows (☎ 23480; Jemeluk; s/d from 65,000/85,000Rp) Simple, clean rooms with expansive sea views and cold-water bathrooms.

Waeni (☎ 23515; madesani@hotmail.com; s/d 80,000/95,000Rp) Rustic cottages in a wonderful cliff-top location overlooking Bunutan.

Getting There & Around

Regular bemo between Singaraja (22,000Rp, three hours) and Amlapura (6000Rp, 40 minutes) go through Culik, the turn-off for Amed. Infrequent bemo then link Culik with the resort villages. If you arrive or leave late you may have to charter an *ojek* (around 2000Rp per kilometre).

TULAMBEN

☎ 0363

First impressions of Tulamben, a featureless sprawl strung out along the coastal road, are hardly inspiring. But don a mask and fins and an aquatic extravaganza is revealed, for offshore is the coral-encrusted wreck of the US cargo ship *Liberty* – probably the most popular dive site in Bali. Even snorkellers can enjoy the wreck (located 50m east of Puri Madhu Bungalows), and other fine dive sites are nearby. Reputable dive operations include **Tauch Terminal** (☎ 0361-774504; www.tauch-terminal.com) and **Ocean Sun** (☎ 54699; www.ocean-sun.com), based at Puri Wirata (below); two dives typically cost US$45 including all gear and a guide.

Sleeping & Eating

Most hotels have a restaurant, a dive shop and a variety of rooms.

Puri Madha Bungalows (☎ 22921; r from 70,000Rp) Right opposite the wreck, and sitting on a black pebble beach, this place has good fan-cooled economy rooms (numbers 1 and 2 have direct sea views) and pricey air-con bungalows. There's a dive shop on site and plenty of bubble-blowing banter in the little café.

Puri Wirata (☎ 54699; s/d incl breakfast 80,000/100,000Rp) Excellent new place with spotless modern rooms, all with sleek hot-water bathrooms. It's right on the main road, but a huge bacon 'n' egg breakfast is included.

Rumah Makan Sandya (☎ 22915; mains 20,000Rp; lunch & dinner) Also on the main road, this no-nonsense eatery serves up decent grub and travel information from its breezy garden setting.

Getting There & Away

Buses and minibuses pass through Tulamben en route between Amlapura (8000Rp, one hour) and Singaraja (18,000Rp, 2½ hours) but they become less frequent after 3pm.

SINGARAJA

☎ 0362 / pop 144,000

Disney fans may be amused to know that Singaraja translates as 'Lion King', but the big city of northern Bali offers little more than a handful of Dutch colonial buildings and an increasingly weathered, olde-worlde waterfront.

If you are sick, it is also worth knowing that the city is home to the biggest hospital in northern Bali, **RSUP Umum** (☎ 26277; Jl Ngurah Rai; 24hr).

It's best to stay at Lovina, about 10km to the west, which has far better options than Singaraja. Food stalls congregate around the **main market** (cnr Jl Durian & Jl Sawo; 8am-7pm).

Singaraja has three bemo/bus terminals. From the main Sukasada terminal, about 3km south of town, minibuses go to Denpasar (Ubung terminal; 22,000Rp, 2½ hours) via Bedugul (8000Rp, one hour) about every 30 minutes from 6am to 4pm.

Banyuasri terminal, on the western side of town, has minibuses for Gilimanuk (16,000Rp, two hours), Lovina (4000Rp, 25 minutes) and express buses to Surabaya (200,000Rp, 11 hours) and Jakarta (350,000Rp, 24 hours) in Java.

The Penarukan terminal, 2km east of town, has bemo to Yeh Sanih (5000Rp, 40 minutes) and Amlapura (28,000Rp, 3½ hours) via the coastal road.

AROUND SINGARAJA

Yeh Sanih

Freshwater springs at the spot, 14km east of Singaraja, are channelled into clean **swimming pools** (admission 2000Rp; 8am-6pm), set in pleasant gardens. There is frequent public transport from Singaraja.

Gitgit

About 11km south of Singaraja, there is a well-signposted path that goes 800m west from the main road to the touristy waterfall, **Air Terjun Gitgit** (admission 3300Rp; 8am-5pm). About 2km further up the hill, **Gitgit Multi-Tier Waterfall** (admission 5000Rp; 8am-5pm) is less spectacular, but it's a nicer walk. You can have a refreshing dip at both falls.

Minibuses between Singaraja and Denpasar will stop at Gitgit.

LOVINA

☎ 0362

Lovina is the north coast's beach-bum magnet, an attractive necklace of villages and black-sand beaches catering to budget travellers drawn by the calm seas, family-owned guesthouses and laid-back ambience. There's no great party scene here, but there are a few bars and some atmospheric restaurants – the resort mainly attracts couples searching for a relaxed tropical vibe rather than an all-night rave.

Lovina is still struggling to pick itself up after the tourist lulls that followed the Bali bombings, and big discounts are now on offer (except in July and August). Building a bypass and a few speed bumps would be one way to kick start a recovery: one of the banes of getting around Lovina is having to compete with the thundering traffic that rips along the north coast highway.

Information

Kalibukbuk is the focus of the Lovina area, with plenty of moneychangers and *wartel.*

BCA ATM (cnr Jl Bina Ria & Jl Raya Lovina; 24hr)

Police station (☎ 41010; Jl Raya Lovina)

Spice Cyber (☎ 41305; Jl Bina Ria; per min 300Rp; 8am-midnight;) Modern PCs but no broadband.

Activities

Divers should head to **Spice Dive** (☎ 41509; www.balispicedive.com; Jl Bina Ria, Kalibukbuk; 2 dives from US$45), which also has an office on the beach, 500m west of Jl Bina Ria. The island Pulau Menjangan, situated off Bali's northwestern tip, is home to reef sharks and prolific sea life, and has the best diving on the north coast.

Lovina's touts constantly hype **dolphin-watching trips** (40,000Rp), which leave daily at 6am.

Courses

Balinese cooking courses are offered by **Adjani** (☎ 081 2385 6802; per person from 150,000Rp), 1.5km west of Kalibukbuk.

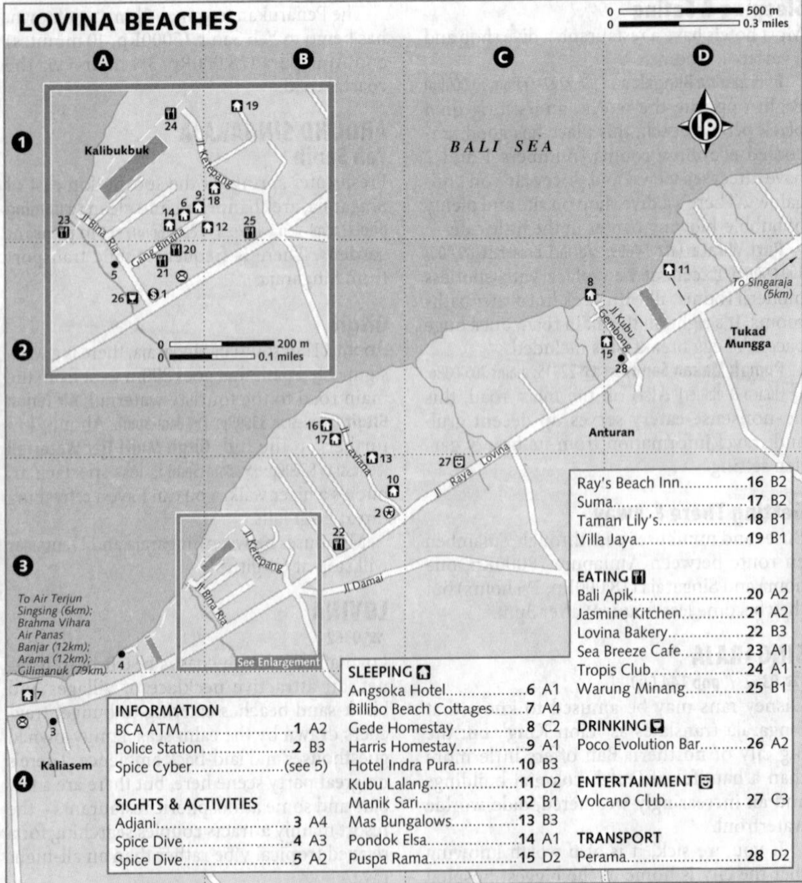

Sleeping

Most of Lovina's cheap accommodation is clustered on side roads to the beach. In high season listed prices can increase by 25% or so; in quiet periods discounts are likely. Most places include breakfast.

KALIBUKBUK

A little over 10km from Singaraja, this is the 'centre' of Lovina, with the biggest concentration of hotels, restaurants…and touts.

Harris Homestay (☎ 41152; Gang Binaria; s/d from 40,000/50,000Rp) This venerable place in a quiet location is run by a friendly soul. It has some of the cheapest beds in town.

Angsoka Hotel (☎ 41841; www.angsoka.com; Gang Binaria; d from 60,000Rp;) This large hotel complex is not the prettiest kid in town, but there's a plethora of options, including a pretty row of fine-value cold-water cottages (80,000Rp), and the pool area is very peaceful.

Taman Lily's (☎ 41307; Jl Ketepang; s/d 60,000/75,000Rp) The chintzy pink décor is a little unsettling, but this family-run place is as immaculate as Barbie's summerhouse and there's a nice garden for lounging in.

Pondok Elsa (Gang Binaria; d from 65,000Rp;) A fabulously baroque exterior, though the seven tidy rooms here are far less extrovert, but good value nonetheless.

Manik Sari (☎ 41089; Gang Binaria; d from 70,000Rp;) Good-value, spacious cottages scattered around what must be Lovina's most elaborately manicured garden, complete with concrete Hindu gods.

Villa Jaya (☎ 700 1238; Jl Ketepang; d with fan/air-con 100,000/150,000Rp;) A great deal, this newish hotel enjoys a quiet location a short stroll from the beach. All the tiled rooms are immaculate, with quality mattresses, bedside reading lights and balconies. It's run by a friendly family that also offers cooking courses.

OUTSIDE KALIBUKBUK

The little fishing village of Anturan is a bit scruffy, but there's a good community buzz, plenty of hostels and a regular stream of backpackers. Otherwise, most other places are located down dirt trails that run off the highway.

Puspa Rama (☎ 42070; agungdayu@yahoo.com; Jl Kubu Gembong, Anturan; s/d 60,000/70,000Rp) Six fan-cooled bungalows with lampshades and pictures on the walls, located in a leafy garden plot.

Gede Homestay (☎ 41526; gedehomesat@yahoo.com; Jl Kubu Gembong, Anturan; d with cold-/hot-water bathroom 60,000/80,000Rp;) A hospitable, family-run place that's been switched on to travellers' needs for years; the rooms are spacious and there's a great seafront café where you can watch the fishermen come and go. Ask the owner nicely and he'll also give you a free ride into Kalibukbuk.

our pick **Kubu Lalang** (☎ 42207; s/d from 90,000/130,000Rp) Down a lonely track through the rice paddies, this tranquil and exceptionally well-run place has a choice of beautiful rice barn–style cottages. Most have verandas with day beds and some have wonderful open-air pebble bathrooms with tubs. There's a seafront restaurant and the staff could not be more helpful. It's east of Anturan.

Suma (☎ 41566; www.sumahotel.com; Jl Laviana; r from 100,000Rp;) The frilly décor in the rooms is a bit overelaborate, but the whole place is immaculately kept, with pebble-dash detailing, a well-tended garden, large pool and café. It's between Anturan and Kalibukbuk.

Billibo Beach Cottages (☎ 41355; Jl Raya Lovina; r with fan/air-con 100,000/200,000Rp;) Right on the beach, and close to a snorkelling spot, these spacious bungalows represent decent value; all have balconies and bamboo furniture. It's west of Kalibukbuk.

Other recommendations between Anturan and Kalibukbuk:

Ray's Beach Inn (☎ 41088; Jl Laviana; s/d 35,000/45,000Rp) Grungy, but well cheap.

Hotel Indra Pura (☎ 41560; Jl Laviana; r 60,000Rp) Decent budget rooms facing a central garden.

Mas Bungalows (☎ 41773; mas_bali@hotmail.com; Jl Laviana; d from 80,000Rp;) Smallish, clean rooms, some with air-con.

Eating & Drinking

Most hotels in Lovina serve food, and there are food carts, *warung*, cafés and quite classy restaurants – Kalibukbuk has the best choices. There's a cluster of bars at the top end of Jl Bina Ria, all of which have happy hours.

Bali Apik (☎ 41050; Gang Binaria; mains from 15,000Rp; lunch & dinner) A blueprint backpackers café, where you can get a facial (yes, really) while you savour a Bintang and wait for the house special, two-person *rijsttaffel* (Indonesian feast; 70,000Rp).

Tropis Club (☎ 42090; Jl Ketepang; dishes 16,000-32,000Rp; breakfast, lunch & dinner) Large new place just off the beach with a wood-fired pizza oven. Films are shown here most nights.

Sea Breeze Cafe (☎ 41138; Jl Bina Ria; mains 20,000-36,000Rp; ⏰ lunch & dinner) This place enjoys the best location in Lovina, with beachside tables offering sweeping views along the coast to the rugged western hills. The extensive menu is a little pricey, but has Western food including cauliflower cheese and pasta, Indonesian staples, jolly fine cakes and a full cocktail list (30,000Rp to 45,000Rp).

our pick Jasmine Kitchen (☎ 41565; Gang Binaria; mains 20,000-40,000Rp; ⏰ breakfast, lunch & dinner) This stylish pan-Asian restaurant on two levels tries a lot harder than most in Kalibukbuk, and arguably serves the best food in town. Lounge on an axe-head cushion and treat yourself to a Malay-style Penang curry or Thai noodles. Definitely leave room for dessert (which include homemade ice cream) and an espresso.

Other recommendations:

Warung Minang (☎ 081 2393 0792; Jl Raya Lovina; dishes 6000-8000Rp; ⏰ lunch & dinner) A modern take on a Padang restaurant.

Poco Evolution Bar (☎ 41535; Jl Bina Ria; ⏰ 11am-1am) Probably the most popular of several bars on this strip; covers bands perform here most nights. Also serves travellers' fare (dishes 12,000-18,000Rp).

Lovina Bakery (☎ 42235; Jl Raya Lovina; sandwiches 22,000Rp; ⏰ breakfast, lunch & dinner) Upmarket deli that sells baguettes, German bread, cheese, cured meats and wines.

Clubbing

Volcano Club (☎ 41222; Jl Raya Lovina; ⏰ 9pm-late) Sculpted out of cement, like a volcano set from *The Flintstones,* this is Lovina's only nightspot. You'll probably have the dance floor to yourself unless it's high season.

Getting There & Around

From southern Bali, by public transport, you will need a connection in Singaraja, from where there are also air-con buses to Java (see p233 for details). Regular bemo go from Singaraja's Banyuasri terminal to Kalibukbuk (4000Rp, 25 minutes).

Perama (☎ 41161; www.peramatour.com; Jl Raya Lovina) links Lovina with Kuta and the airport (70,000Rp, 3¼ hours), Ubud (70,000Rp, 2½ hours) and other destinations including Padangbai (100,000Rp, 3½ hours) and even the Gilis in Lombok (300,000Rp, 12 hours), but a minimum number of passengers is required.

Lovina is an excellent base from which to explore northern and central Bali; rates and hire prices for cars and motorcycles are quite reasonable. For an excellent, experienced driver call **Made Wijana** (☎ 0813 3856 3027), who knows northern Bali very well and can organise excursions all over the island at fair rates. Bicycles can be hired for about 12,000Rp per day.

AROUND LOVINA

About 5km west of Kalibukbuk, a sign points to **Air Terjun Singsing** (Daybreak Waterfall), where you can have a refreshing swim. The falls are sometimes just a trickle in the dry season.

About 10km from Kalibukbuk, near the village of Banjar, a side road leads for 4km to **Brahma Vihara Arama**, a Buddhist monastery. It's a handsome structure with views down the valley and across to the sea. Not far from the monastery, the **Air Panas Banjar** (Hot Springs; admission 4100Rp; ⏰ 8am-6pm) feed several pools where you can soak in the soothing sulphurous water, surrounded by lush tropical gardens.

GUNUNG BATUR AREA

☎ 0366

Volcanic Gunung Batur (1717m) is a major tourist magnet, offering treks to the summit (see opposite) and spectacular views of Danau Batur (Lake Batur), at the bottom of a huge caldera. Touts and tourist coaches detract from the experience around the rim of the vast crater, but the crater lake and cone of Batur are well worth exploring. Entry to the area costs 4000Rp per person.

GETTING THERE & AROUND

Regular buses go to Kintamani from Denpasar (Batubulan terminal) via Ubud and Payangan (21,000Rp, 2½ hours); some continue to Singaraja. Bemo regularly shuttle back and forth around the crater rim, between Penelokan and Kintamani (2000Rp). Public bemo from Penelokan to the lakeside villages go mostly in the morning (5000Rp to Toya Bungkah, 30 minutes).

Perama shuttles run to Kintamani in busy periods; check with their **Kuta office** (☎ 0361-751551; www.peramatour.com; Jl Legian 39).

Around the Crater Rim

From the south, **Penelokan** is the first place you'll come to on the rim of the caldera. There's a brilliant view if it's clear, but be prepared for wet, cold and cloudy conditions, and aggressive souvenir selling. Big restaurants do buffet lunches for tour groups – small restaurants and *warung* are better value.

Further northwest, the villages of **Batur** and **Kintamani** virtually run together. Batur's **Pura Ulun Danu** (admission 3000Rp; dawn-dusk) is an important temple, while Kintamani is famed for its colourful **market**. Continue to **Penulisan**, where Bali's highest temple (at 1745m), **Pura Puncak Penulisan** (admission 3000Rp; dawn-dusk), has a great view to the north coast.

Around Danau Batur

KEDISAN

Kedisan is a quiet village at the bottom of the road down from Penelokan. There are fewer guides touting treks here than in nearby Toya Bungkah.

A stone's throw from the lake, **Hotel Surya** (☎ 51139; r with cold-/hot-water bathroom from 60,000/80,000Rp) has a choice of tidy, tiled rooms, some with great views across the water. The restaurant serves good local food and the management can advise about hiring a local guide.

Hotel Astra Dana (☎ 52091; s/d 50,000-80,000Rp) is a little cheaper but it's looking a bit worse for wear.

TOYA BUNGKAH

From Kedisan an undulating paved road weaves through fields of lava to Toya Bungkah, the usual jumping off point for an ascent of Gunung Batur. The village itself is a scruffy assembly of rusty tin-roofed homes and the locals have a reputation for being gruff and direct.

Activities

There are several sets of hot springs in Toya Bungkah, the most formal – and expensive – of which is the **Natural Hot Spring Swimming Pool** (☎ 51204; admission US$5; 7am-8pm) in the middle of the village.

The most popular trek is from Toya Bungkah to the top of Gunung Batur for sunrise – a magnificent sight requiring a 4am start from the village. The **Association of Mount Batur Trekking Guides** (HPPGB; ☎ 52362; volcanotrekk@hotmail.com) operates a local monopoly and an extremely complicated system of charges that works out at about 180,000Rp for one to four people to hike Batur; breakfast is extra. Its office is opposite Arlina's. Those attempting to trek Batur alone can expect hassle and intimidation from this association.

Sleeping & Eating

Most of the hotels listed here have restaurants, all with similar menus and prices.

Under the Volcano III (☎ 081 3386 0081; r 60,000Rp) Right by the shore, this place has the best location in town and six quiet rooms with textile wall hangings and bathtubs. If it's full try the two other nearby inns in the Volcano empire, all run by the same cheery family.

Arlina's (☎ 51165; r 60,000-100,000Rp) These semi-detached cottages facing a central garden were about to be renovated at the time of research, hopefully to a slightly less dour design. The restaurant here serves up mean grilled *mujair* (lake fish; 20,000Rp) and less impressive Western food.

Lakeside Cottages (☎ 51249; www.lakesidebali.com; r incl breakfast US$8-36;) With a perfect water's edge location, this attractive hotel has some simple tiled economy rooms with cold-water bathrooms. The breakfast is American style, and if you book via the net, you get a discount.

Volcano Breeze Cafe (☎ 51824; mains 15,000Rp; breakfast, lunch & dinner) Close to the lake, this rustic travellers-style café modestly describes itself as 'the fantastic grill house', though 'decent local grub but be prepared for a long wait' might be more apt.

DANAU BRATAN AREA

☎ 0368

This area of pretty lakes is in the crater of an old, long-extinct volcano. The main village is **Candikuning**, which has a bemo stop, a good local market with an incredible array of spices (including nutmeg and vanilla pods) and nuts. The graceful **Pura Ulun Danau Bratan** (☎ 21191; admission 3300Rp; 7am-6pm) lakeside temple is very close by, and boat rental, water-skiing and parasailing are available by the lake shore. The **Kebun Raya Eya Karya Bali** (☎ 21273; admission 3500Rp; 7am-6pm) botanical gardens, near Candikuning, are a pleasant spot for an afternoon's loafing and have a world-renowned wild-orchid section.

Southwest of Danau Bratan is **Gunung Batukaru**, with the remote **Pura Luhur** (admission 3000Rp; dawn-dusk) perched on its slopes. The road east to **Pacung** has wonderful panoramas.

Interesting trips by road or on foot can be made to the west around **Danau Buyan** and **Danau Tamblingan**.

Further west, **Munduk** is a pretty, spread-out village perched high on a ridge with good hiking in the vicinity. Budget beds are in short supply here, the best option being **Made Homestay** (☎ 081 2387 4833; r 70,000Rp), which has jaw-dropping views over the valley, and sometimes offers yoga classes.

Sleeping & Eating

The best budget accommodation is along the road to the botanical gardens.

Pondok Permata Firdous (☎ 21531; Jl Kebun Raya; d 60,000Rp) A functional spot on the gardens' doorstep with bright bedspreads and scrubbed bathrooms.

Pondok Wisata Dahlia Indah (☎ 21233; r 70,000Rp, with hot water from 90,000Rp) In Candikuning, along a lane near the road to the botanical gardens, this old favourite has two rows of good, if plain, budget rooms that face a pretty garden.

Strawberry Hill (Bukit Stroberi; ☎ 21265; meals from 13,000Rp; lunch & dinner) About a kilometre south of Candikuning, this restaurant is a dead ringer for an English pub, complete with dart board and fireplace.

Food stalls at Candikuning market offer cheap eats (mains 7000Rp), and there are food carts further north at the car park overlooking the lake.

Getting There & Away

Plenty of bemo, minibuses and buses travel between Denpasar's Ubung terminal (14,000Rp, 1¾ hours) and Singaraja's Sukasada terminal (7000Rp, one hour), and stop anywhere along the main road between Bedugul and Pancasari. Some of the **Perama** (☎ 0361-751551; www.peramatour.com) Ubud–Lovina services also stop here.

Public transport to the areas southwest and west of Danau Bratan is very scant.

SOUTHWEST BALI

From Denpasar's Ubung terminal, buses and bemo go west to Gilimanuk, via Tabanan and Negara. From this western road, turn north to **Mengwi**, where there's the impressive **Pura Taman Ayun** (admission 3000Rp; 8am-5pm) water palace and temple. About 10km further north is the monkey forest and temple of **Sangeh** (admission 3000Rp; 8am-5pm) – watch out, as the monkeys will snatch anything they can. South of the main road, **Pura Tanah Lot** (admission 3300Rp; dawn-dusk) is a reconstructed temple and a major tourist trap, especially at sunset.

The turn-off to the legendary **Medewi** surfing point is well marked on the main road. **Mai Malu** (☎ 43897; s/d 70,000/85,000Rp), near the highway, is one of the best budget options with clean fan-cooled rooms and huge portions of Western and local food; other alternatives are close by.

The beautiful temple of **Pura Rambut Siwi** (admission 3000Rp; 8am-5pm) is just south of the main road, high on a cliff top overlooking the sea. It's definitely worth a stop.

WEST BALI

Negara

Bullock races are held in nearby Perancak between July and September/October each year; check schedules with the **Taman Wisata Perancak** (☎ 0365-42173). Otherwise, Negara is a quiet, untouristy town; the banks here change money and most have ATMs. Try **Hotel Wira Pada** (☎ 0365-41161; Jl Ngurah Rai 107; d from 90,000Rp;) if you need a bed. Many buses and bemo stop here.

Taman Nasional Bali Barat

This substantial national park has prolific bird life, with many of Bali's 300 species represented, including the famous *jalak putih* (Bali starling), and encompasses offshore waters that include some of Bali's most pristine coral reefs.

The **park headquarters** (☎ 0365-41021; admission 10,000Rp; 7am-4pm) is at the junction at Cekik. You can arrange a guide here for trekking in the southern part of the park.

There's a visitors' centre at **Labuhan Lalang**, in the northwest, where you can get a guide, arrange short treks and snorkel on the reef close to shore. Labuhan Lalang is also the access point for **Pulau Menjangan**, a very popular diving and snorkelling site. A boat to Menjangan costs about 300,000Rp for a four-hour trip. Hire snorkelling gear from the *warung* here (about 40,000Rp per four hours).

Trips can also be organised in Lovina through Spice Dive (see p234).

Gilimanuk

Gilimanuk is the terminus for the ferries to/from Java (7000Rp, one hour), which run every half-hour throughout the day and night. You'll find a bank (with poor exchange rates), post office, a *wartel* and a handful of gloomy hotels here.

There are frequent buses between Gilimanuk and Denpasar (Ubung terminal; 25,000Rp, three hours), or along the north coast to Singaraja (16,000Rp, two hours).

SUMATRA

Lush, enormous and intriguing, Sumatra stretches for 2000km across the equator. Happily, there is a payoff for every pothole along the Trans-Sumatran Hwy: volcanic peaks rise around tranquil crater lakes, orang-utans swing through pristine rainforests, and long white beaches offer world-class surf breaks above the surface, and stunning coral reefs below.

Besides natural beauty, the world's sixth-largest island boasts a wealth of resources, particularly oil, gas and timber. These earn Indonesia the bulk of its badly needed export dollars, even as their extraction devastates habitats. Little of the cash has trickled back to Sumatra in the form of improved infrastructure, like badly needed sewers and roads, heightening resentment of the political centre in Java.

When mother nature is this majestic and bountiful, there is usually a flip side, and Sumatra has seen more than its share of her fury. The 2007 earthquake in the mountains of West Sumatra, near Bukittinggi, was just the latest in a string of bloody headlines since the 2004 tsunami, so it's no shock that most tourists steer clear of unpredictable Sumatra. That's their loss. Rugged travellers will find mind-bending beauty throughout this gorgeous, warm yet unforgiving island that's nearly four times the size of Java, but with less than a quarter of the population. At times you'll feel like a lone explorer rediscovering a magical landscape, and you will be rewarded with tranquillity, low prices and the gratitude of locals who are glad someone out there hasn't forgotten them.

History

Mounds of stone tools and shells unearthed near Medan prove that hunter-gatherers were living along the Straits of Melaka 13,000 years ago. But Sumatra had little contact with the outside world until the emergence of the kingdom of Srivijaya at the end of the 7th century. At its 11th-century peak, it controlled a great slab of Southeast Asia covering most of Sumatra, the Malay Peninsula, southern Thailand and Cambodia. Srivijayan influence collapsed after it was conquered by the south Indian king Ravendra Choladewa in 1025, and for the next 200 years the void was partly filled by Srivijaya's main regional rival, the Jambi-based kingdom of Malayu.

After Malayu was defeated by a Javanese expedition in 1278, the focus of power moved north to a cluster of Islamic sultanates on the east coast of present-day Aceh. The sultanates had begun life as ports servicing trade through the Straits of Melaka, but many of the traders were Muslims from India, and Islam quickly gained its first foothold in the Indonesian archipelago. These traders also provided the island with its modern name, 'Sumatra', derived from Samudra, or 'ocean' in Sanskrit.

After the Portuguese occupied Melaka in 1511 and began harassing Samudra and its neighbours, Aceh took over as the main power. Based close to modern Banda Aceh, it carried the fight to the Portuguese and won substantial territory, covering much of northern Sumatra and the Malay Peninsula. Acehnese power peaked with the reign of Sultan Iskandar Muda at the beginning of the 17th century.

The Dutch came next and kicked off their Sumatran campaign with the capture of Palembang in 1825, working their way north before running into trouble against Aceh. The Acehnese turned back the first Dutch attack in 1873, but succumbed two years later. The Dutch were booted out of Aceh in 1942, immediately before the Japanese WWII occupation, and did not attempt to return during their brief effort to reclaim their empire after the war.

Sumatra supplied several key figures to Indonesia's independence struggle, including future vice-president Mohammed Hatta and the first prime minister, Sutan Syahrir. It also provided some problems. First up were the staunchly Muslim Acehnese, who rebelled against being lumped together with the Christian Bataks in the newly created province of North Sumatra and declared an independent Islamic republic in 1953. Aceh didn't return to the fold until 1961, when it was given special provincial status.

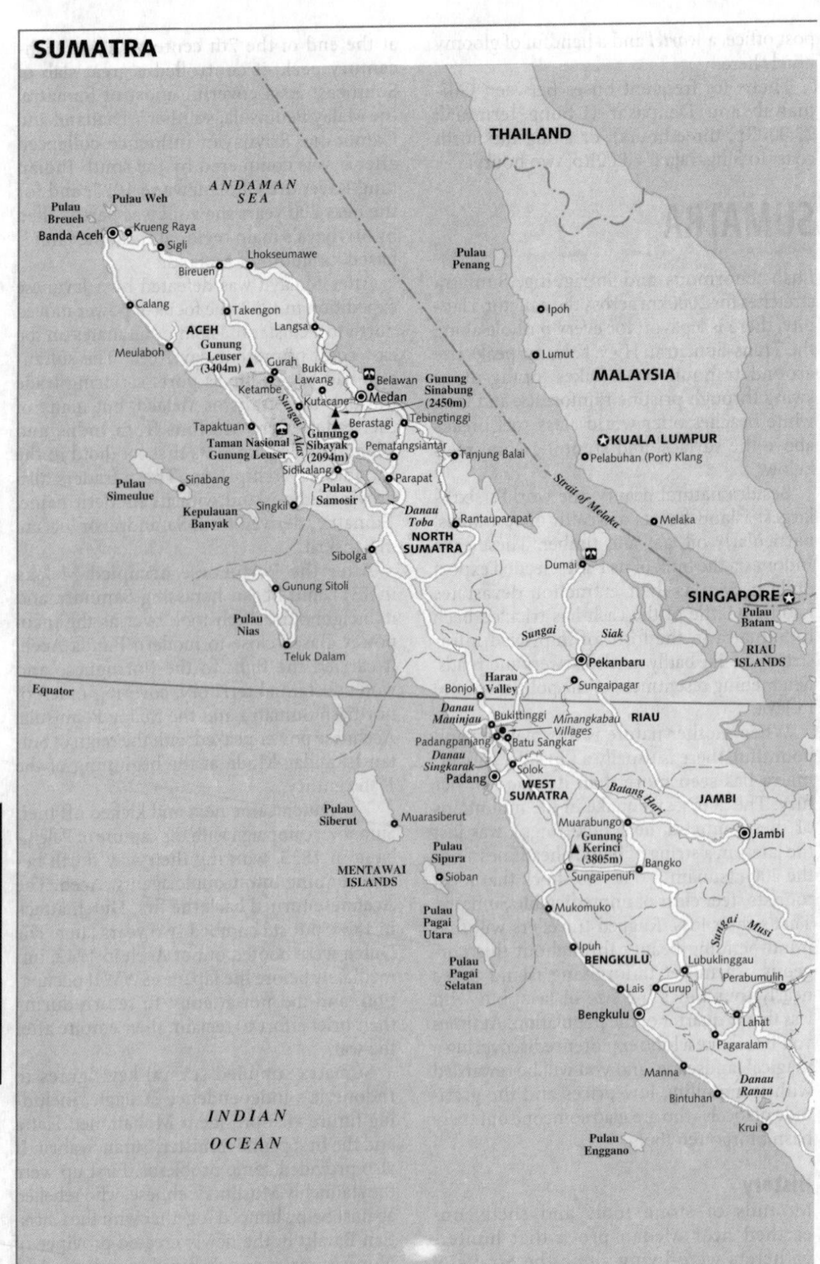
SUMATRA
THAILAND
ANDAMAN SEA
Pulau Weh
Pulau Breueh
Banda Aceh
Krueng Raya
Sigli
Lhokseumawe
Bireuen
Calang
Takengon
ACEH
Langsa
Meulaboh
Gunung Leuser (3404m)
Gurah
Bukit Lawang
Ketambe
Belawan
Medan
Gunung Sinabung (2450m)
Kutacane
Sungai Alas
Berastagi
Tebingtinggi
Tapaktuan
Gunung Sibayak (2094m)
Taman Nasional Gunung Leuser
Pematangsiantar
Tanjung Balai
Sidikalang
Sinabang
Pulau Simeulue
Pulau Samosir
Parapat
Danau Toba
Singkil
Kepulauan Banyak
Rantauparapat
NORTH SUMATRA
Sibolga
Gunung Sitoli
Pulau Nias
Teluk Dalam
Pulau Penang
Ipoh
Lumut
MALAYSIA
KUALA LUMPUR
Pelabuhan (Port) Klang
Strait of Melaka
Melaka
Dumai
SINGAPORE
Pulau Batam
RIAU ISLANDS
Sungai Siak
Pekanbaru
Sungaipagar
Equator
Bonjol
Harau Valley
Danau Maninjau
Bukittinggi
Minangkabau Villages
RIAU
Padangpanjang
Batu Sangkar
Danau Singkarak
Solok
Padang
WEST SUMATRA
Batang Hari
JAMBI
Pulau Siberut
Muarasiberut
Muarabungo
Jambi
Gunung Kerinci (3805m)
Pulau Sipura
Sioban
MENTAWAI ISLANDS
Bangko
Sungaipenuh
Pulau Pagai Utara
Mukomuko
Sungai Musi
Ipuh
BENGKULU
Lubuklinggau
Pulau Pagai Selatan
Perabumulih
Lais
Curup
Bengkulu
Lahat
Pagaralam
Manna
Danau Ranau
Bintuhan
INDIAN OCEAN
Krui
Pulau Enggano

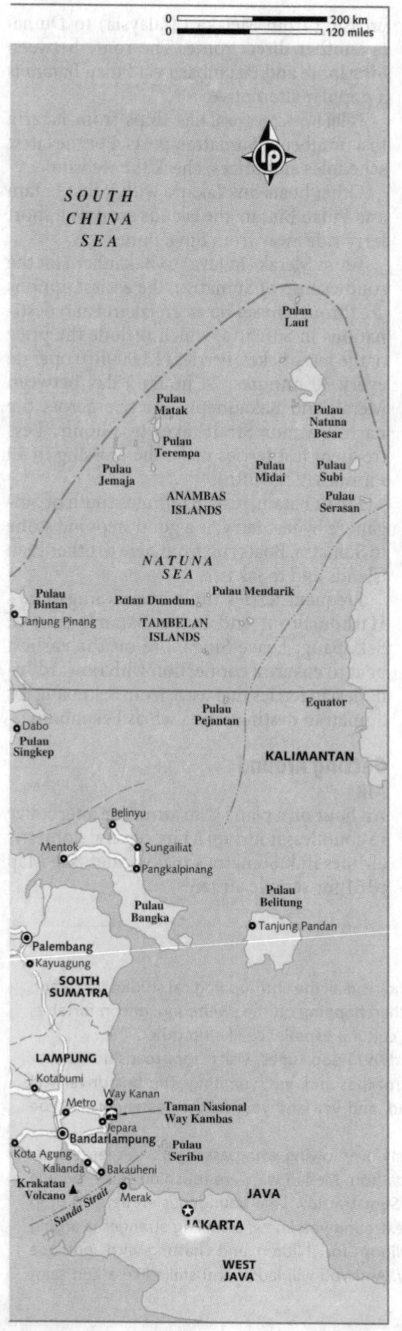

The Sumatran rebellion of 1958–61 posed a greater threat, when the rebels declared their rival Revolutionary Government of the Republic of Indonesia (PRRI) in Bukittinggi on 15 February 1958. The central government showed no interest in negotiations, however, and by mid-1958 Jakarta had regained control of all the major towns. The guerrilla war continued for another three years.

Since the 1970s, Aceh has re-emerged as a trouble spot in the archipelago, with continued calls for greater autonomy and secession from the Indonesian republic. In 1989 the Free Aceh Movement (GAM) began a low-level uprising against the government, and the Indonesian armed forces were sent in to 'monitor' the situation.

In 1998 the Indonesian press revealed years of army atrocities in Aceh, prompting armed forces chief General Wiranto to visit the area to apologise. In July 1999, however, an army massacre took place, killing a religious leader and Free Aceh Movement supporters at Lhokseumawe. Another shooting, this time of 40 people, occurred in a crowd at Krueng Geukueh. Over one million people rallied for independence in Banda Aceh on 8 November 1999.

In 2002 an internationally brokered peace deal was signed by both sides, but sporadic violence continued. In May 2003, 30,000 Indonesian troops returned to the province and attacked rebel strongholds. With rampant corruption, a broken economy and an extremely fragile social structure, peace appeared elusive.

The Boxing Day 2004 quake and tsunami brought a ray of hope, even as aftershocks continued to terrorise the local population. Both sides concentrated on providing emergency relief, and thousands of foreign aid workers flooded the region, acting as unofficial observers. Helsinki-brokered talks led to an agreement in August 2005 under which thousands of Indonesian security forces were withdrawn from the province and GAM gave up hundreds of weapons. The three-decade war appears to have come to an end, as this peace deal has held so far. However, a mysterious spring 2007 grenade attack against GAM government headquarters in Banda suggest tensions persist and that this latest bloody chapter in Sumatran history may not be over yet.

WARNING

An Aceh peace deal spurred by the common suffering brought by the tsunami appeared to have taken hold in late 2005, but a 2007 grenade attack on the new government headquarters suggest tensions persist. Check media reports and with your embassy before heading into what was a conflict zone for the better part of three decades.

Getting There & Away

The international airports at Medan, Padang and Pekanbaru are visa-free (for more on visas, see p341), as are the seaports of Sekupang (Pulau Batam), Belawan (Medan), Dumai, Padang and Sibolga.

AIR

Medan is Sumatra's major international airport and has the widest choice of destinations. Malaysian Airlines flies the 40-minute hop from Medan to Penang and to Kuala Lumpur. SilkAir and China Airlines both fly between Singapore and Medan as well.

Garuda, Merpati, Sriwijaya, Adam Air, Mandala and Batavia have services linking Jakarta and Sumatran destinations including Padang, Medan, Pekanbaru, Pulau Batam and Palembang.

BOAT

The express ferries between Penang in Malaysia and Medan's Belawan port are the quickest and easiest way to enter Sumatra by water. The crossing from Melaka (Malaysia) to Dumai is another direct route. The route between Singapore and Pekanbaru via Pulau Batam is a popular alternative.

Pelni (www.pelni.com) has ships from Jakarta to a number of Sumatran ports. For the latest schedules and prices, check the website.

Other boats link Jakarta with Pulau Batam and Pulau Bintan: the islands are only a short ferry ride away from Singapore.

From Merak (in Java) to Bakauheni (at the southern tip of Sumatra), the easiest options are through buses between Jakarta and destinations in Sumatra, which include the price of the ferry ticket. Ferries (13,000Rp) operate every 30 minutes, 24 hours a day between Merak and Bakauheni. The trip across the narrow Sunda Strait takes two hours. Less frequent fast ferries make the crossing in 40 minutes (22,500Rp).

Pulau Batam, just 45 minutes south of Singapore by fast ferry, is a good stepping stone to Sumatra. Boats run from here to other Riau islands and to Jakarta.

Frequent ferries run between Singapore's HarbourFront and Pulau Batam's port of Sekupang. Leave Singapore on the earliest boat to ensure a connection with onward Indonesian ferries that leave from Sekupang for Sumatran destinations such as Pekanbaru.

Getting Around

AIR

An hour on a plane is an attractive alternative to countless hours on a bus. Several domestic airlines link Sumatra's major cities; see Map p161 for sample air fares.

CHICKENBUS ENLIGHTENMENT

Hike all the peaks, visit all the ethnic minorities, and read all the anthropological studies you want, but nothing gets you closer to the real Sumatra than hopping on the sweltering, uncomfortable, yet somehow exhilarating economy buses. It's a cultural experience like no other.

There will be chain-smoking, deafeningly loud Indo-pop tunes, visits from roadside troubadours, rampant breast-feeding, hitchhiking cockroaches and, yes, vomiting. The bus driver will stop at random to pray, eat and perhaps get laid, and you and your fellow passengers will be at his mercy.

The aisles are packed with cargo and absolutely overflowing with passengers – at least three to a seat. At one point on our ride to Danau Toba from Medan we were touching seven people at once. At home we'd be disgusted. But in the Sumatra slow lane boundaries erode, you drop your hang-ups and begin to go with the flow. Next thing you know, a smiling stranger is urging you to share some exotic fruit, you're buying lollipops for children, and chatting with someone who speaks broken English and loves Green Day. And you will laugh and smile like a Zen saint drunk on life.

BUS

If you stick to the Trans-Sumatran Hwy and other major roads, the big air-con buses can make travel fairly comfortable – which is fortunate since you'll spend a lot of time on the road in Sumatra. The best ones have reclining seats, toilets and video but run at night to avoid the traffic, so you miss out on the scenery. The non-air-con buses are sweaty, cramped, but unforgettable. Numerous bus companies cover the main routes, and prices vary greatly, depending on the comfort level. Buy tickets direct from the bus company. Agents usually charge 10% more.

Travel on the back roads is a different story. Progress can be grindingly slow and utterly exhausting (see opposite).

TRAIN

Sumatra has a very limited rail network. The only useful service runs from Bandarlampung in the south to Palembang.

BANDARLAMPUNG

☎ 0721 / pop 857,400

Bandarlampung – Sumatra's fourth-largest city and an amalgam of the old coastal town of Telukbetung and Tanjungkarang further inland – is only worth visiting to experience the Krakatau volcano or Taman Nasional Way Kambas. Most visitors come on package tours arranged in Jakarta, but local guides and tour agencies can set you up nicely for less.

When Krakatau erupted in 1883, the tremors generated a 30m-high wave that devastated Telukbetung and claimed 36,000 lives. The **Krakatau Monument** is a huge steel buoy washed up on a hillside overlooking Telukbetung. Everything below this point was a wasteland.

Information

Banks and ATMs can be found all over town.

BCA bank (Jl Raden Intan 98) The branch on Jl Kartini offers the best exchange rates.

Central post office (Jl Kotaraja)

Squid Net (Jl Raden Intan 88A; per hr 5000Rp; 10am-8pm) Internet access.

Tours

Several travel agents on Jl Monginsidi offer tours to Taman Nasional Way Kambas. They can also arrange tours to Krakatau via a bus to Kalianda, followed by a boat ride to Krakatau. You may be able to get a cheaper deal from the port (see p244).

Sleeping

Budget options in Bandarlampung are seriously limited.

Hotel Gading (☎ 255512; Jl Kartini 72; d from 66,500Rp;) Cheap and dingy.

Kurnia Perdana Hotel (☎ 262030; Jl Raden Intan 114; d from 130,000Rp;) This is a clean, charmless option.

Hotel Purnama (☎ 261448; Jl Raden Intan 77; d from 180,000Rp;) This is the best value in town, with large, comfortable rooms.

Getting There & Away

AIR

Arie Tour & Travel (☎ 474675; Jl Monginsidi 143) is a helpful travel agency that sells Adam Air and Sriwijaya flights to Medan and Jakarta.

BUS

Rajabasa bus terminal is one of Sumatra's busiest, with a constant flow of departures 24 hours a day. Most people heading north go to Bukittinggi, a long haul that costs from 160,000Rp economy (up to 28 hours) to 300,000Rp for the best air-con services (22 hours). The trip south to Jakarta (eight to 10 hours) costs 100,000Rp to 130,000Rp for air-con, which includes the ferry between Bakauheni and Merak. Buses leave daily from the Bandarlampung train station at 9am and 9pm. Chartered minibuses to Jakarta cost 170,000Rp.

TAXI

Share taxis are a pleasant alternative to buses. Reputable **Taxi 4848** (☎ 255388; Jl Suprapto 26) runs to Jakarta (140,000Rp) and Bandung (220,000Rp). Other companies go from Bandarlampung to Bakauheni (20,000Rp) and Palembang (100,000Rp).

TRAIN

The train station, at the north end of Jl Raden Intant in the heart of Tanjungkarang, is where you'll find Sumatra's only convenient rail service. Two trains a day run between Bandarlampung and Palembang, at 9am and 9pm (economy/business 28,000/85,000Rp, 10 hours).

Getting Around

Taxis charge 80,000 to 90,000Rp for the 22km ride from the airport to town. Take the green *opelet* from the town center to the Rajabasa bus terminal for 2000Rp.

KRAKATAU

Krakatau's beauty masks a mean streak of apocalyptic proportions. When it combusted in 1883, the boom was heard as far away as Perth (Australia). Tens of thousands were killed by either the resulting 30m-high tsunami or the molten lava that flowed across 40km of ocean to incinerate coastal villages. The monster mountain spewed an 80km-high ash plume that turned day into night over the Sunda Strait and altered the world's climate for years. The earth kept rumbling under the remains of Krakatau. In 1927 it erupted again and this time it created an evil mini-me, the Child of Krakatau (Anak Krakatau). And it grumbles still, so make sure to seek the latest advice on seismic activity.

Most travellers head to Krakatau from Carita in West Java, but the island group actually belongs to Sumatra. Tours operate from Bandarlampung and Kalianda (see below).

TAMAN NASIONAL WAY KAMBAS

The Taman Nasional Way Kambas (Way Kambas National Park), a 130,000-hectare stretch of steamy lowland rainforest and mangrove coastline, is home to dozens of tigers, some 200 elephants and an estimated 20 rare red Sumatran rhinoceroses. With Sumatra's heavily logged, lowland rainforests on the verge of extinction, a visit here is one of the only ways to explore this stunning wild ecosystem. But get here soon because national parks in Sumatra lack the protection of those elsewhere in the world, and poaching, illegal logging and development pressure continue to threaten what's left. Simple tourist facilities include lodges, wooden pole houses, an observation centre and riverboat rides. The park and the Way Kambas elephant training centre, Pusat Latihan Gajah, are about two hours by road east of Bandarlampung, where travel agencies offer a variety of wildlife-spotting trips (these are separate to the Krakatau volcano tours). Or DIY and hire an *ojek* from Rajabasalama, the closest town to the national park, to Way Kanan (45,000Rp, 20 minutes), where you can hire a guide (50,000Rp to 100,000Rp) and arrange transport.

KALIANDA

☎ 0727

The small coastal port of Kalianda is the best place to arrange boat trips to Krakatau. Survey the seaworthiness of your boat and check for life jackets and a two-way radio. Kalianda is 30km north of the Bakauheni ferry terminal. Organised tours to Krakatau cost about $90 a person, but you may have to charter a whole boat from Canti, a fishing village outside of Kalianda, if visitor numbers are low. That will cost you 500,000Rp to 900,000Rp for up to 15 people.

Hotel Beringin (d from 50,000Rp) has comfortable rooms, Dutch villa charm and can organise tours to Krakatau.

There are buses that go to Kalianda from Bandarlampung (8000Rp, one hour) and Bakauheni (10,000Rp, one hour), but they drop you off at the highway turn-off. From there, grab an *opelet* into town (2000Rp).

BAKAUHENI

Bakauheni is the departure point for ferries to Merak, Java. Fast ferries run every 30 minutes from 7am to 5pm and cost 22,500Rp; the crossing takes 40 minutes. A slow ferry runs every 30 minutes, 24 hours a day and costs 13,000Rp for the two-hour trip.

Frequent buses depart from outside Bakauheni's terminal building and travel the 90km trip to Bandarlampung (economy/air-con 8000Rp/15,000Rp, one to two hours). If you're planning to stay the night in Bandarlampung, pay 30,000Rp for a private taxi, which will take you to the hotel of your choice.

PADANG

☎ 0751 / pop 899,400

Most backpackers fly into Padang only to catch the first bus out to Bukittinggi. Big mistake. Sumatra's largest west-coast city has never been more appealing. Gorgeous Minangkabau roofs soar from modern public buildings, blending the present and the past. The leafy south end is dominated by a narrow, brackish river harbour crowded with colourful fishing boats, as well as lux Bugis schooners, and modern yachts bound for the famed Mentawai surf. Old Dutch and Chinese buildings are scattered along its frontage road, and across a lovely antiquated bridge strung with lanterns is a palm-fringed hillside that is the antithesis of urban. The coastline south of town is magnificent too, and the city beach is edged by a popular promenade, which is where you'll want to be when the sun drops. Then you'll stroll to dinner and enjoy one of your best meals in Indo. Oh yes, Padang is worth your while.

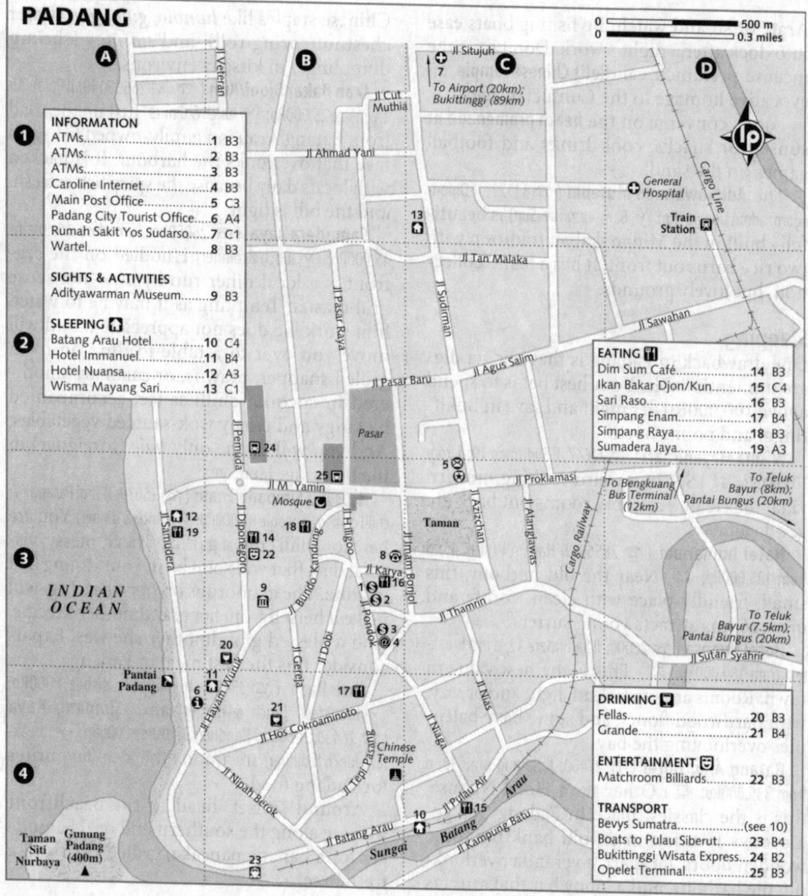

Orientation

Padang is an easy puzzle. The busy main street, Jl M Yamin, runs inland from the coast road to the junction with Jl Azizchan. Several hotels and the bus station are on Jl Pemuda, which runs north–south through the western side of town, while the techno-funky *opelet* terminal and central market are on the northern side of Jl M Yamin.

But getting out of Padang takes a bit of time. The Teluk Bayur port is 8km east of the centre, the shiny new airport is located 20km to the north, and the Bengkuang bus terminal is inconveniently located in Aie Pacah, about 12km from town. There are a few options for getting into Padang (see p247), and some Mentawai-bound boats leave from the old port on Batang Arau (see p248).

Information

Padang has branches of all the major Indonesian banks. There are ATMs all over town, and a string on Jl Pondok.

Caroline Internet (☎ 35135; Jl Pondok; per hr 5000Rp; 9am-9.45pm) Solid connection.

Main post office (Jl Azizchan 7)

Padang City Tourist Office (☎ 34186; Jl Hayam Wuruk 51; 🕑 7.30am-2.30pm Mon-Fri, to 1pm Sat) There are some useful town and regional maps here.

Rumah Sakit Yos Sudarso (☎ 33230; Jl Situjuh 1) Privately owned health clinic.

Wartel (Jl Imam Bonjol 15H; 🕑 24hr)

Sights & Activities

Stroll among antiquated Dutch and Chinese warehouses in the **old quarter** along Jl Batang

Arau, or sit and watch the fishing boats ease into dock after a night's work. Don't miss the incense-perfumed, candlelit **Chinese Temple**, an evocative homage to the Confucian age.

Locals converge on the **beach promenade** at sunset for snacks, cool drinks and football games on the sand.

The **Adityawarman Museum** (☎ 31523; Jl Diponegoro; admission 800Rp; 8am-4pm Tue-Sun) is beautifully built in the Minangkabau tradition with two rice barns out front. It has a bland collection, but lovely grounds.

Sleeping

One drawback in Padang is that budget digs are unmentionable. Your best bet is to spend above 100,000Rp per night and save in Bukittinggi and points north.

Wisma Mayang Sari (☎ 22647; Jl Sudirman 19; d from 103,000Rp;) Set in a weird-looking modern villa, the clean, economy rooms out back are good value.

Hotel Immanuel (☎ 28560; Jl Hayam Wuruk 43; d from 125,000Rp;) Near the old harbour, this small, friendly place with clean, comfy and quiet rooms attracts young surfers.

Hotel Nuansa (☎ 26000; Jl Samudera 12; d incl breakfast from 180,000Rp;) This is the best value in town. Rooms are superclean, light and breezy, with hardwood floors, and some have balconies overlooking the bay.

Batang Arau Hotel (☎ 27400; Jl Batang Arau 33; d from 335,000Rp;) Other than Hotel Nuansa, this is the classiest place in Padang. It's got a groovy location in an old bank building, wooden floors, local art, a veranda overlooking the harbour, and a lobby bar that attracts every surfboat captain in town. Come as a group of three and the price won't sting so much – a triple costs the same as a double.

Eating

The city is famous as the home of *nasi Padang* (Padang food), the spicy Minangkabau cooking that's found throughout Indonesia, and is served quicker than fast food. You simply sit down, and immediately the waiter will bring over a dozen bowls of various curries and vegetable dishes. You pay only for what you eat. But you can eat Padang food anywhere in Indonesia, and this city has choice joints serving dim sum, grilled fish and chilli crab joints that are not to be missed.

Dim Sum Café (☎ 841653; Jl Diponegoro 19; servings 10,000Rp; lunch & dinner) Come taste Indo-Chinese staples like *lumpia, gulangan* (water chestnut spring roll), and *sio may* (shrimp dumplings) in kitschy environs.

Ikan Bakar Djoni/Kun (☎ 081 2660 3149; Jl Pulau Air 1A; mains 25,000Rp; lunch & dinner) Just up the road from Batang Arau is a family-owned fish-grill fave that overlooks the harbour. It is packed with locals daily because the spicy fish is fresh, and the bill is light.

Samudera Jaya (☎ 26050; Jl Samudera 16; mains 45,000Rp; lunch & dinner) Huddled on the seafront is a local diner run by a no-nonsense grill master. Tempting as it may be to watch him work, he does not appreciate it and will move you over to a table to dine on fresh grilled snapper, prawns, or calamari smothered in coconut chilli sauce, accompanied by tangy and crispy wok-sautéed vegetables. And you will be the only *bule* (foreigner) in the building. Hell, yes!

our pick **Simpang Enam** (☎ 25030; Jl Tepi Pasang 67; chilli crab for 2 people 81,000Rp; lunch & dinner) You are here for chilli crab, a garlicky, fiery, messy, visceral dish that will soon be in your dining hall of fame. The glamorous owner-chef, Ing, will make it herself from her grandmother's recipe. And a blessed grandmother she was. Expats consider this the best meal in Padang.

Sari Raso (☎ 33498; Jl Karya 3; dishes 8000Rp; breakfast, lunch & dinner) and **Simpang Raya** (☎ 26430; Jl Bundo Kandung 3; dishes 8000Rp; breakfast, lunch & dinner) are among the local favourites for Padang food.

Around sunset, head to the beachfront *warung* along the southern end of Jl Samudera for a banana pancake, grilled corn and a fresh breeze.

Drinking

Grande (☎ 39431; Jl Hos Cokroaminoto 68; 5pm-5am) Hip, young, upwardly mobile Padangians flock here for late-night karaoke, pool, drinks and snacks.

Fellas (Jl Hayam Wuruk 47; noon-5am) Another hipster joint. This one has hookah pipes, a tasty kitchen, and a bar stocked with good liquor.

Entertainment

Matchroom Billiards (☎ 21919; Jl Diponegoro; 11am-2am) This place has everything you could want in a pool hall: it's dark (even in the daytime), smoky, and there are swarms of hipster sharks hovering over three storeys of perfect blue-felt tables to a pulsing soundtrack. It has everything, that is, except booze, thanks to the devout Muslim national-billiards champion owner.

Getting There & Away

AIR

Domestic and international prices fluctuate greatly out of Padang's Bandara Internasional Minangkabau Airport, but there are some very competitive rates to Jakarta, which make flying a far more attractive option than catching the long-distance bus.

SilkAir (code MI; ☎ 38120; www.silkair.com) flies to Singapore twice a week. **Merpati** (code MZ; ☎ 444831; www.merpati.co.id) flies three times a week to Pulau Batam, a short ferry ride from Singapore. **Garuda** (code GA; ☎ 30737; www.garuda-indonesia.com) and **Mandala** (☎ 333100; www.mandalaair.com) fly to Jakarta twice daily, **Lion Air** (code JT; ☎ 446100; www.lionair.co.id) makes the run three times a day, and **Adam Air** (code KI; ☎ 840999; www.flyadamair.com) has daily flights. Mandala and **Batavia** (code 7P; ☎ 446600; www.batavia-air.co.id) serve Medan daily.

BOAT

Pelni ships call at Padang's Teluk Bayur port once a month on their way west, and again on the way to Jakarta, Surabaya and beyond. The **Pelni office** (☎ 61624) is at the port, but you can buy tickets from agents around town.

Boats to Pulau Siberut leave from the harbour on Sungai Batang Arau, just south of Padang's city centre.

BUS

Every north–south bus comes through Padang. Popular routes include Bukittinggi (12,000Rp, two hours) and Jakarta (air-con/superexecutive 140,000/250,000Rp, 30 hours). Heading north there are regular departures to Parapat (for Danau Toba; 100,000/180,000Rp, 17 hours) and Medan (120,000/200,000Rp, 21 hours).

Bukittinggi Wisata Express (☎ 812644; Jl Pemuda 4) offers bus tickets to Medan, Bukittinggi, Dumai (economy/air-con 70,000/100,000Rp, 12 hours) and beyond.

Getting Around

Airport taxis charge between 60,000Rp and 90,000Rp for the ride into town. The budget alternative is to take one of the two white Damri buses (15,000Rp) that do a loop through Padang. Tell the conductor which street you're headed for and he'll direct you to the right bus.

Numerous *opelet* and *mikrolet* operate around town out of the Pasar Raya terminal off Jl M Yamin. The standard fare is 2000Rp.

MENTAWAI ISLANDS

☎ 0751

Surfing put the Mentawais on the tourism radar, and dozens of wave-hunting liveaboards run from Padang harbour year-round. But more and more ecotourists are braving the rugged ocean crossing and muddy malarial jungle of this remote archipelago, 85km to 135km west of Padang, to trek, glimpse traditional tribal culture and spot endemic primates. Many consider it the highlight of their trip through Southeast Asia.

The largest island, Siberut, is home to the majority of the ethnic Mentawai population – known for their tattoos and filed teeth – while sparsely populated Sipora, Pagai Utara and Pagai Selatan are seldom visited. Get here fast, though, because the tourism boom, government-sponsored housing and *transmigrasi* (transmigration) employment projects, and continued logging are no doubt changing the culture, environment and daily life on the Mentawais.

Tours

Tour operators in Bukittinggi will tell you it's cheaper to book a Mentawai tour through them. This is a falsehood. Ten-day tours out of Bukittinggi cost up to US$300, plus all your cash will land in the grip of Sumatran tour guides, rather than the local people. The economic, and culturally responsible, choice is to take a public boat to Siberut and seek out a Mentawai guide. You pay less and directly benefit the community you've come to experience. Remember, more cash in hand means less poaching and illegal logging on the ground, which will help preserve the Mentawais long after you leave.

Trips can also be organised in Padang; check with **Padang City Tourist Office** (☎ 0751-34186; Jl Hayam Wuruk 51; 🕑 7.30am-2.30pm Mon-Fri, to 1pm Sat). On the islands, be ready for rain, bland food (bring hot sauce) and malaria.

For information on surf trips to the Mentawais and other islands, check www.sumatransurfariis.com, www.surfingmentawai.com and www.wavepark.com.

Getting There & Away

Boats leave from Padang's Batang Arau harbour to Siberut every Monday, Wednesday and Thursday (from 85,000Rp, 12 hours). The return trip leaves for Padang on Tuesday, Thursday, Friday and Saturday. Make sure you spend the extra 15,000Rp for a cabin.

Asimi (☎ 23321) runs to Siberut town and Sikabaluan, both on the island of Siberut, on Monday; to Sikabaluan and Siberut town on Wednesday; and to Sioban and Tuapejat, both on the island of Sipora, on Friday. **Simeulue** (☎ 39312; Jl Arau 7) boats, on the small lane behind Jl Batang Arau, leave for Sioban on Tuesday and Tuapejat on Saturday.

Tickets can be purchased from **Bevys Sumatra** (☎ 0751-34878; Jl Batang Arau 33, Padang), a reliable travel and ticketing agency based in the Batang Arau Hotel.

BUKITTINGGI

☎ 0752 / pop 102,500

A well-maintained road snakes from Padang, between rice paddies, over raging rivers, past waterfalls and onto the jungled shoulders of Mt Merapi, which is where you'll find the cool, quiet market town of Bukittinggi, the first stop for many travellers in West Sumatra. With dozens of budget digs and accessible adventure at your fingertips, Bukittinggi is a great base for volcano treks, crater-lake canoe trips and 4WD tours of the nearby Sianok Canyon, and it's an easy place to lose track of time. Perched at 930m above sea level, the town is laced with footpaths, alleyways and staircases, and blessed with views of three volcanoes: Merapi, Singgalang and the distant Sago. Tourism is down to a trickle here, but if the clinging clouds part at sunset, exposing the volcanic triad's naked tips to the orange sun, you will quickly see why it was once a mandatory stop on the Southeast Asia trail. At the time of research an earthquake measuring 6.7 on the Richter scale shook the town (literally) to its moorings, cracking walls and crumbling a section of the lively Pasar Atas market. But repairs began immediately and should be complete when you visit.

Orientation

This is an outstanding walking town, with a compact town centre. A landmark clock tower (Jam Gadang) stands at the southern (top) end of the main street, Jl Ahmad Yani, near the Pasar Atas (market). Walk downhill along Jl Ahmad Yani to reach a cluster of cheap hotels and restaurants. The bus station, south of town, is accessible by public transport.

Information

Banks with ATMs and moneychangers are clustered along Jl Ahmad Yani. International calls can be made from dozens of *wartel*. There are dozens of travel agents in town, most on Jl Ahmad Yani.

Boom Net (☎ 33728; Jl Pemuda 15) Very reliable. It even managed to open the day after the earthquake.

Main post office (Jl Sudirman 75)

Rumah Sakit Sayang Bayi (☎ 627099; Jl Dr A Rivai 15; 24hr) Medical services.

Tourist office (Jl Muka Jam Gadang 2; 8am-3pm Mon-Fri, to noon Sat) Across from the clock tower, this little office distributes city maps and brochures.

Sights & Activities

Taman Panorama (Panorama Park; Jl Panorama; admission 2000Rp; 8am-8pm), on the southern edge of town, overlooks Sianok Canyon, which is especially thrilling at sunset when fruit bats put on an aerial show. Cool locals will casually suggest that you visit the **Gua Jepang** (Japanese Caves) with them. Don't be confused, this isn't just friendship, payment is expected. The caves are actually a labyrinth of combat tunnels constructed by the Japanese using Indonesian slave labour during WWII.

Pasar Atas (btwn Jl Minangkabau & Jl M Yamin) is almost always sprawling, colourful and alive, bursting with fruit and vegetables and handicrafts. It's open daily, but on Wednesday and Saturday villagers descend from the surrounding area and the number of stalls – and the energetic buzz – magically multiplies. Unfortunately, the market was hit hard by the 2007 quake. An entire wing collapsed and another section caught fire, claiming 13 lives. At the time of research the market was in clean-up mode.

Tours

Beware the guide gauntlet. Tourism is down, which makes you the mark for every unemployed guide in town, whether you are at your hotel, café or just wandering aimlessly down the street. But don't grumble or cower, take your time, make conversation, and you'll book a great deal with a guide who you like and trust. Popular tour destinations include architectural excursions to traditional Minangkabau villages, overnight volcano treks, and

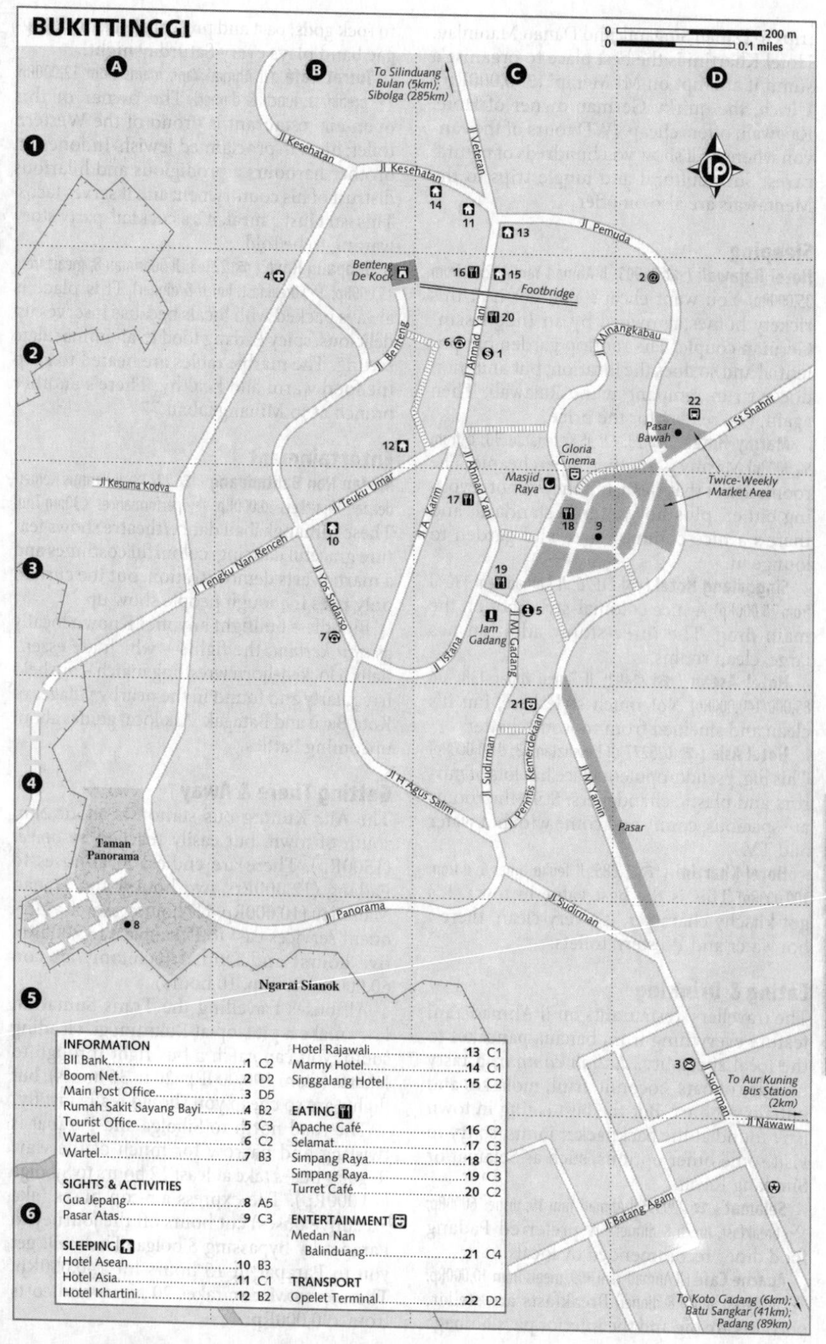
BUKITTINGGI
0 200 m
0 0.1 miles
A
B
C
D
1
2
3
4
5
6
To Silinduang Bulan (5km); Sibolga (285km)
Jl Kesehatan
Jl Veteran
Jl Pemuda
Benteng De Kock
Footbridge
Jl Benteng
Jl Ahmad Yani
Jl Minangkabau
Jl St Shahrir
Pasar Bawah
Gloria Cinema
Masjid Raya
Twice-Weekly Market Area
Jl Kesuma Kodva
Jl Teuku Umar
Jl A Karim
Jl Tengku Nan Renceh
Jl Yos Sudarso
Jl Istana
Jam Gadang
Jl MJ Gadang
Jl H Agus Salim
Jl Sudirman
Jl Perintis Kemerdekaan
Jl M Yamin
Pasar
Taman Panorama
Jl Panorama
Ngarai Sianok
To Aur Kuning Bus Station (2km)
Jl Nawawi
Jl Batang Agam
To Koto Gadang (6km); Batu Sangkar (41km); Padang (89km)
INFORMATION
BII Bank 1 C2
Boom Net 2 D2
Main Post Office 3 D5
Rumah Sakit Sayang Bayi 4 B2
Tourist Office 5 C3
Wartel 6 C2
Wartel 7 B3
SIGHTS & ACTIVITIES
Gua Jepang 8 A5
Pasar Atas 9 C3
SLEEPING
Hotel Asean 10 B3
Hotel Asia 11 C1
Hotel Khartini 12 B2
Hotel Rajawali 13 C1
Marmy Hotel 14 C1
Singgalang Hotel 15 C2
EATING
Apache Café 16 C2
Selamat 17 C3
Simpang Raya 18 C3
Simpang Raya 19 C3
Turret Café 20 C2
ENTERTAINMENT
Medan Nan Balinduang 21 C4
TRANSPORT
Opelet Terminal 22 D2

trips to Danau Singarak and Danau Maninjau. Hotel Khartini is the best place to organise a summit attempt on Mt Merapi (350,000Rp). Ulrich, the quirky German owner of Hotel Rajawali, offers cheap 4WD tours of the canyon where he'll show you hundreds of natural caves. Surf, cultural and jungle trips to the Mentawais are also on offer.

Sleeping

Hotel Rajawali (☎ 31905; Jl Ahmad Yani 152; d from 35,000Rp) You want cheap? You got it at this rickety homestay owned by an Indonesian-German couple. The rooftop garden has potential and so does the location, but ambition doesn't run rampant at the Rajawali. Then again, you're here for the price.

Marmy Hotel (☎ 23342; Jl Kesehatan 30; d from 50,000Rp) Marmy is another supercheapie. The rooms aren't that clean, but they're not revolting either, plus hot water is standard, and there's a nice common area and garden to lounge in.

Singgalang Hotel (☎ 21576; Jl Ahmad Yani 130; d from 75,000Rp) A nice colonial-style spot on the main drag. The three-storey addition has large, clean rooms.

Hotel Asean (☎ 21492; Jl Teuku Umar 13B; s/d 85,000/140,000Rp) Not much style here, but it's clean and shielded from mosque chatter.

Hotel Asia (☎ 625277; Jl Kesehatan 38; d 90,000Rp) This big, pseudo-opulent place has lots of mirrors and plastic chandeliers. Still, the rooms are spacious, comfy and come with hot water and TV.

Hotel Khartini (☎ 22885; Jl Teuku Umar 6; d from 100,000Rp) This is the best value in town. It's got kitschy character, it's very clean, there's hot water and Western toilets.

Eating & Drinking

The travellers' restaurants on Jl Ahmad Yani feature everything from banana pancakes to the local speciality, *dadiah campur*, a tasty mixture of oats, coconut, fruit, molasses and buffalo yoghurt. But the best eating in town isn't found at the backpacker joints, so try to visit some other options, such as Selamat or Simpang Raya.

Selamat (☎ 22959; Jl Ahmad Yani 19; dishes 6000Rp; 🕑 breakfast, lunch & dinner) A preferred Padang food diner recommended by locals.

Apache Café (Jl Ahmad Yani 109; meals from 10,000Rp; 🕑 breakfast, lunch & dinner) Breakfasts are stellar, portions are big and the interior pays homage to rock gods, past and present. A live rock/reggae band plays every Saturday night.

Turret Café (Jl Ahmad Yani; mains from 12,000Rp; 🕑 breakfast, lunch & dinner) The owner of this open-air restaurant is proud of the Western toilet; his self-proclaimed Jewish-Indonesian brother harbours a prodigious and hilarious distrust of his countrymen; and it serves tacos. This isn't just a meal, it's a cocktail-party story waiting to be told.

Simpang Raya (☎ 22163; Jl Sudriman 8; meals from 15,000Rp; 🕑 breakfast, lunch & dinner) This place is always packed with locals because it serves up delicious, spicy Padang food in an immaculate setting. The marble tables are heated to keep the food warm and healthy. There's another branch at Jo Minangkabau 77.

Entertainment

Medan Nan Balituduang (☎ 22438; Jl Perintis Kemerdekaan 19; tickets 40,000Rp; 🕑 performances 8.30pm Thu) These Minangkabau dance/theatre shows feature graceful dancing, colourful costumes and a martial-arts demonstration, but the curtain only rises if enough people show up.

Bloodless bullfight anyone? Known locally as *adu kerbau*, the fights – which are essentially a locked-horn wrestling match – are held irregularly and found in the nearby villages of Kota Baru and Batagak. Ask local guides about upcoming battles.

Getting There & Away

The Aur Kuning bus station is about 2km south of town, but easily reached by *opelet* (1500Rp). There are endless local buses to Padang (12,000Rp, two hours) and Danau Maninjau (10,000Rp, 1½ hours), as well as frequent services east to Pekanbaru (35,000Rp, five hours) and Dumai (economy/air-con 60,000/90,000Rp, 10 hours).

All buses travelling the Trans-Sumatran Hwy make a pit stop at Bukittinggi. Heading south, you can catch a bus right through to Jakarta (from 190,000Rp, 20 to 36 hours), but flights are so cheap you should really just fly.

The road north to Sibolga and Parapat is twisting and narrow for much of the way. Regular buses take at least 12 hours to Sibolga (70,000Rp). The express air-con buses (aka executive buses) cut hours off the journey to Parapat by bypassing Sibolga. They will get you to Parapat in 15 hours for 140,000Rp. The trip to Medan takes 20 hours and costs from 190,000Rp.

If you're arriving in Bukittinggi from the north (Parapat) or east (Pekanbaru), get off the bus near the town centre to save the hassle of an *opelet* ride back from the bus station.

Getting Around

Opelet around Bukittinggi cost 1500Rp. A *bendi* (two-person horse-drawn cart) costs from 5000Rp depending on the distance. Motorcycles are a good way to explore the district and can be hired from travel agencies on Jl Ahmad Yani or coffee shops for around 65,000Rp a day (no insurance, no petrol).

AROUND BUKITTINGGI

Handcrafted silver is the pride of **Koto Gadang**, a village 5km from Bukittinggi that can be reached by *opelet* from Aur Kuning bus station (4000Rp). Local craftsmen display their wares in antiquated Dutch colonial homes. You can walk here through the Sianok Canyon too. Go through Panorama Park, take the back exit down a series of overgrown steps, and the path through the forest is on the left off the first sharp bend. Of course, it's a route worked by local guides – only the truly determined will manage to avoid them.

Grab lunch in the bustling small town of **Batu Sangkar**, 41km southeast of Bukittinggi, in the heart of traditional Minangkabau country. Five kilometres north, the **Rumah Gadang Payarugung**, in the village of Silinduang Bulan, is a scaled-down replica of the original palace, which belonged to rulers of the former Minangkabau kingdom.

Or just cruise the countryside by rented motorbike or *ojek* and glimpse rice terraces that climb the base of a looming and jagged mountain range. In the villages you'll find traditional wooden Minangkabau houses with soaring, buffalo-horned roofs.

DANAU MANINJAU

☎ 0752

Maninjau, 38km west of Bukittinggi, is one of Sumatra's most spectacularly peaceful crater lakes. The unforgettable final descent includes 44 hairpin turns that offer stunning views over the shimmering sky blue lake (17km long, 8km wide), and the 600m crater walls. Maninjau is well set up for travellers, and should be considered an alternative to Bukittinggi as a place to stay. With early morning swims, morning canoe sessions and quiet afternoons in the shade watching clouds wisp down the mountainsides, this is the kind of place where time evaporates slowly and sweetly.

Orientation & Information

The main village (and bus stop) is also called Maninjau. It has post and Telkom offices and a BRI bank that changes US dollars. But most people stay near Bayur, 3km north. Tell the conductor where you want to stay and he'll drop you there.

Indowisata Travel (☎ 61418) At Café Bagoes; sells bus and boat tickets.

PT Kesuna Tour & Travel (☎ 61422) Arranges air travel and minibus tickets to Padang; it's in the main village of Maninjau.

Activities

This is an outstanding swimming lake. Though it's 480m deep in some places, the water is warmer than Danau Toba, and, outside of town, the water becomes pure as liquid crystal. Some guesthouses rent dugout canoes or truck inner tubes to float upon.

When relaxation becomes too much, many visitors tackle the 70km sealed road that circles the lake. It's about six hours by mountain bike or 2½ hours by moped.

There's a strenuous two-hour trek to Sakura Hill and the stunning lookout of **Puncak Lawang**. Catch a Bukittinggi-bound bus to Matur and climb 5km to the viewpoint; from there descend to the lake on foot.

Sleeping

Lakeside bungalows with eateries are strung out north of Maninjau, towards Bayur village, 3km away. Look for the roadside signs and follow the path through the rice paddies.

Lili's (Jl Lubuk Basung; d from 25,000Rp) Close to the village, Lili's sports basic cheap bungalows, just a cut above camping. But it does have some stilted rooms set among the trees – sleepwalking is not recommended!

Batu C (d 25,000Rp) Next door to Lili's is another basic joint with a collection of beach huts that have a certain ramshackle romance to them, if the bathrooms don't scare you away.

Arlen (d 100,000Rp) This secluded spot has eight bungalows with front porches that are great for lounging and provide spectacular views of the lake and jungle-covered island. Bathrooms are clean, the garden blooms, and hammocks beckon.

Hotel Tan Dirih (☎ 61263; Jl Air Angat; d from 120,000Rp) Stylish, friendly and comfortable, the family-run Hotel Tan Dirih sets the local mod-con standard with ironed towels, hot water, TV and a waterside veranda for sunset drinks.

Eating

Rumah Makan Bundo (☎ 61625; Jl Rasuna Said 10; dishes 8000Rp; breakfast, lunch & dinner) Padang food fans should head to this local favourite, offering a welcome reprieve for those sick of soulless backpacker grub.

Café Bagoes (☎ 61418; Jl Rasuna Said 6; dishes from 10,000Rp; breakfast, lunch & dinner) Right by the bus stop, Bagoes is a backpacker oasis with the usual hybrid Western-Indo culinary line-up, atmospheric dark wood décor, movies on demand, chessboards aplenty, and ephemeral internet access.

Monica Café (☎ 61879; Jl Rasuna Said 4; dishes from 10,000Rp; breakfast, lunch & dinner) Next door is Bagoes' competition, with pop-star posters, a small black-light bar, a comfy roadside terrace and videos on demand.

Waterfront Zalino (☎ 61740; mains 10,000-18,000Rp; lunch & dinner) Aspiring to a higher degree of class and service than the rest, this is the place for fresh grilled fish.

Getting There & Around

There are hourly buses between Maninjau and Bukittinggi (10,000Rp, 1½ hours). To reach Padang without backtracking all the way to Bukittinggi, take an *opelet* to Lubuk Basung (5000Rp, 20 minutes) and a bus to Padang (7000Rp, three hours). Hotels and cafés rent mountain bikes for 30,000Rp a day, mopeds for 65,000Rp (including petrol) and canoes for 10,000Rp.

Buses travel throughout the day between Maninjau and Bayur. Just stand by the road and flag one down.

SIBOLGA

☎ 0631 / pop 80,500

Before the Easter 2005 quake hit Pulau Nias and tourism ground to a halt, Sibolga was the gateway for a steady stream of surfers headed to the island. Surf traffic is down now, which has thinned out the usual army of ill-mannered, scheming port-town touts. Still, watch your wallet and know that when it comes to 'free advice', a little healthy scepticism is a good thing.

The **BNI bank** (Jl Katamso) changes money and has an ATM. Get your cash here, because options on Pulau Nias are limited. **Hotel Pasar Baru** (☎ 22167; cnr Jl Imam Bonjol & Jl Raja Junjungan; d 50,000-150,000Rp) is the only budget spot worth your time. It's relatively clean and has a decent Chinese restaurant. A string of Padang diners and coffee shops can be found opposite the harbour.

Merpati (www.merpati.co.id) has four flights a week to Medan.

Two ferries leave every evening from Sibolga's Jl Horas port for the overnight trip to Gunung Sitoli (economy/cabin 65,000/165,000Rp, 10 hours), and boats run to Teluk Dalam on Tuesday, Thursday, and Saturday (economy/cabin 65,000/140,000Rp, 10 hours). You can also take the daily fast ferry (160,000Rp, four hours) and cut your travel time in half. Twice-monthly Pelni ships sail from Sibolga to Padang (from 64,000Rp, 24 hours) and Jakarta (from 168,000Rp, two days). All ferries charge an additional cargo fee for surfboards (100,000Rp per board bag).

Trans-Sumatran Hwy express buses bypass Sibolga, but slow public buses run to Bukittinggi (70,000Rp, 12 hours), Padang (72,000Rp, 14 hours), Medan (70,000Rp, 11 hours), and Parapat (60,000Rp, six hours). Faster minibuses also run regularly to and from Medan (75,000Rp, nine hours).

PULAU NIAS

The waves deserve their legendary status, and the traditional hill villages, such as **Tundrumbaho** and famous **Bawomataluo**, captivate even casual cultural tourists and ethno-architectural buffs. But, and there is a sizable one, Pulau Nias was hit twice by major natural disasters within three months, the tsunami and then the 2005 earthquake, which left the main town, Gunung Sitoli, in ruins, thousands homeless, and has put the population on edge. The government hasn't exactly been forthcoming with resources either, which has further embittered the jaded residents and hindered reconstruction. Be advised, you are not here for laid-back island living.

On Pantai Sorake – a surf beach located in the horseshoe bay of Teluk Lagundri, decimated by the tsunami – a string of *losmen* are open for business. From south to north you can find Morris Losmen and Eddy's Losmen, both just a few minutes' walk from the famous right break – best between June and

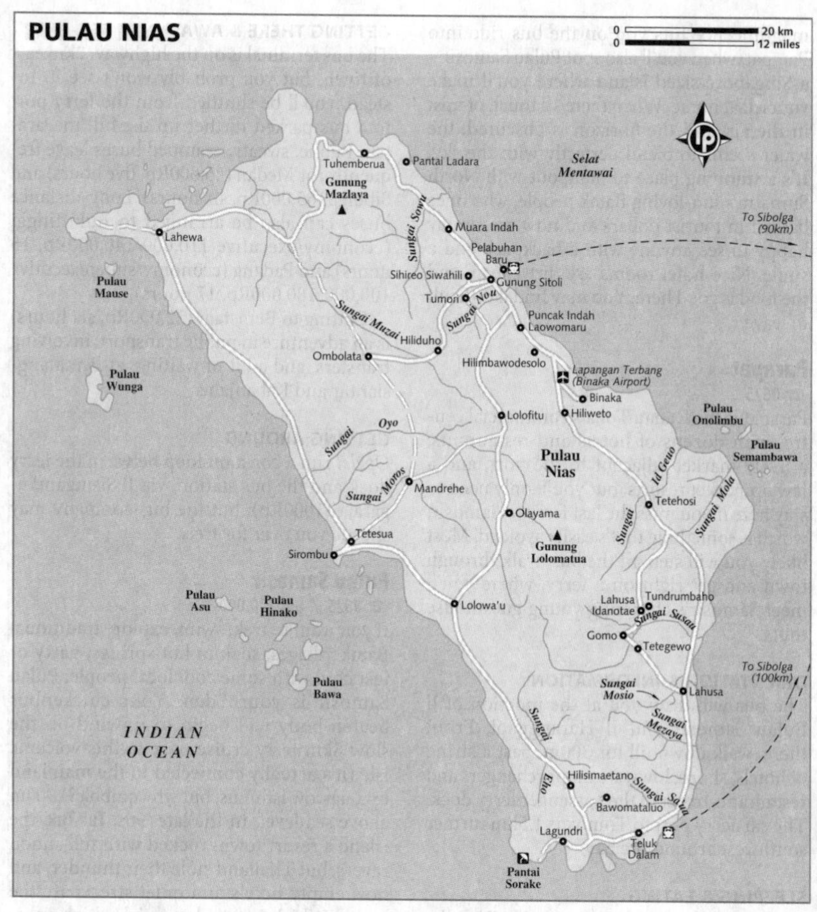

October. Lisa's, Lili's and Peeruba Losmen are on a nice patch of sand at the other end. The going rate is between 50,000Rp and 75,000Rp per night, but you are expected to eat at your *losmen* too. And that'll cost you. A plate of chicken or fish can fetch 50,000Rp. If you do not eat where you sleep, you will hear about it. Most surfers come prepared, but you can rent gear at Key Hole Losmen, in front of the keyhole in the reef, through which you'll paddle.

If you want or need to stay in Gunung Sitoli because of transport connections, try **Wisma Soliga** (☎ 21815; d from 150,000Rp), 4km south of town, accessible by *opelet* (2000Rp) or becak (10,000Rp) from the bus terminal. The airport is 14km (and 50,000Rp) away. There are numerous restaurants to choose from on the main drag, which is also where you'll find **BNI bank** (Jl Imam Bonjol).

Merpati (code MZ; ☎ 061-455 1888; www.merpati.co.id) flies four times a week from Medan (550,000Rp) to Binaka airport, just southeast of Gunung Sitoli. Three daily ferries to Sibolga operate from Gunung Sitoli, and three vessels per week sail from Teluk Dalam; see opposite) for more details.

DANAU TOBA

There's no denying the beauty of Danau Toba. This 1707-sq-km, 450m-deep lake, set in the collapsed caldera of an extinct volcano, is surrounded by mountains ribboned with waterfalls and terraced with rice fields. Its pale blue magnificence hits you on the bus ride into Parapat, when you'll also spot Pulau Samosir – a Singapore-sized island where you'll make yourself at home. When there's a touch of mist in the air, and the horizon is obscured, the water seems to blend perfectly with the sky. It's a stunning place to hang out with North Sumatra's fun-loving Batak people, who once bathed in tourist dollars and now are simply happy to see anyone with a backpack and a smile. Nice hotel rooms are dirt-cheap, and the food is good here. You may find it difficult to leave.

Parapat

☎ 0625

Parapat is the Danau Toba's commercial centre, with dozens of hotels and restaurants, a lively market adjacent to the port, and a few upmarket resorts, but you'll only need to stay here if you miss the last ferry to Samosir, which is something that's easily avoided. Most likely you will step off the bus, walk through town and get right on a ferry, where you'll meet Samosir's charming young guesthouse touts.

ORIENTATION & INFORMATION

The bus will drop you at the junction of Jl Pulau Samosir and Jl Haranggaol. From there, walk downhill for 300m, past a string of hotels, shops, low-rate moneychangers and restaurants to get to the passenger ferry dock. The car-ferry port to Tomok is 1.5km further southwest around the bay.

SLEEPING & EATING

Charlie's Guesthouse (☎ 41277; d 30,000Rp) Right by the ferry dock and market, Charlie's is cheap, and run by a local musical luminary who jams with guests deep into the night.

Mars Family Hotel (☎ 41459; Jl Kebudayaan 1; d from 80,000Rp) This place is quieter, and a touch cleaner, with a range of rooms. The lake-front rooms are the most appealing, and the most expensive.

Blue Monday Coffee Shop (Jl SM Raja; mains from 15,000; ⏰ breakfast, lunch & dinner) Run by a pop-song crooning tour guide, named Mr Diamond, who serves up tasty Indonesian fare and good coffee.

Hong Kong (☎ 41395; Jl Haranggaol 9; mains from 20,000Rp; ⏰ lunch & dinner) This sparkling Chinese place next to the Tobali Inn is the best bet for a central snack.

GETTING THERE & AWAY

The bus terminal is on the highway, 2km east of town, but you probably won't see it. Instead, you'll be shuttled from the ferry port to a bus parked further up the hill in Parapat. Public, sweaty, cramped buses leave frequently for Medan (25,000Rp, five hours) and Sibolga (65,000Rp, six hours). Long-distance buses can also be arranged to Bukittinggi (economy/executive 110,000/140,000Rp, 15 hours) and Padang (economy/superexecutive 100,000/180,000Rp, 17 hours).

Getting to Berastagi (22,000Rp, six hours) is an adventure in public transport, involving transfers, and a bit of waiting, at Pematangsiantar and Kabanjahe.

GETTING AROUND

Opelet run a constant loop between the ferry dock and the bus station, via Jl Sisingamangaraja (1000Rp), but the bus company may shuttle you over for free.

Pulau Samosir

☎ 0625 / pop120,000

If you want to trek, swim, explore traditional Batak villages, soak in hot springs, party or just chill with some cool local people, Pulau Samosir is your Eden. Your chickenbus beaten body will begin to unwind on the slow 8km ferry cruise over to this volcanic isle (it's actually connected to the mainland by a narrow isthmus, but why quibble?) 900m above sea level. In the late '90s, **Tuk Tuk**, the island's resort town, rocked with full-moon ravers, but Thailand stole their thunder, and now empty hotels and quiet streets are the norm. Which means low prices, high value and tranquillity.

INFORMATION

There are no useful banks or ATMs on the island. Exchange rates aren't great, so change money well before you get to Tuk Tuk, and preferably before you get to Parapat.

Gokhon Library (☎ 451241; Tuk Tuk) has a good book selection, rents motorbikes (65,000Rp per day), and has reliable, but slow, internet service (20,000Rp per hour). Just up the road, the Wicked Laugh has DVD rentals, a wider book selection and live football matches on satellite TV. For international calls hit **Samosir Cottages** (☎ 41050; Tuk Tuk).

The police post is near the Carolina Hotel, in Tuk Tuk; the post office is in Ambarita.

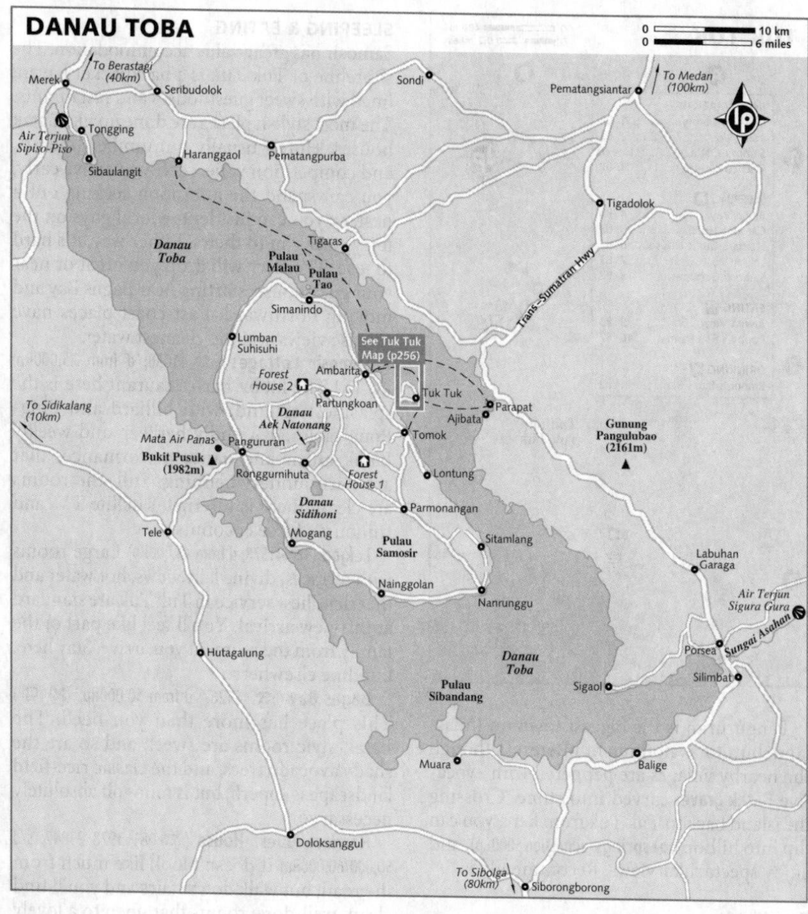

SIGHTS & ACTIVITIES

Tomok

Tomok, 5km south of Tuk Tuk, is the main village on the east coast of Samosir and the souvenir-stall capital of the island. Tucked away among them, 500m up a path from the road, is the ancient **Tomb of King Sidabutar** (admission 5000Rp; dawn-dusk), one of the last pre-Christian animist kings. The grave's hand-carved details are intriguing, but the grounds need some love.

Ambarita

A couple of kilometres north of the Tuk Tuk Peninsula, Ambarita has a group of **stone chairs** (admission 2000Rp; 8am-6pm) where important matters were discussed among village elders, and wrongdoers were tried – then apparently led to a further group of stone furnishings where they were beheaded.

Simanindo & Pangururan

The gorgeous old king's house at Simanindo, a sterling sample of Batak architecture 17km north of Tuk Tuk, has been turned into a **museum** (admission 5000Rp; 10am-4pm). The adjoining replica of a traditional village stages a **Batak dance** (tickets 30,000Rp; shows 10.30am & 11.45am Mon-Sat, 11.45am Sun), as long as at least five tourists show up.

Crave privacy? From the nearby jetty, you can charter a boat (50,000Rp) to **Pulau Tao**, aka Honeymoon Island, where a small restaurant is occasionally open to serve guests.

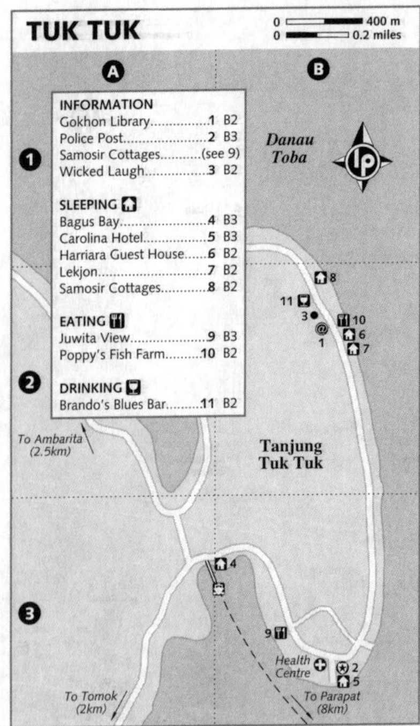

Pangururan is the biggest town on the island, but it has nothing of interest, although the nearby villages are peppered with evocative **Batak graves** carved into stone. Crossing the island back to Tuk Tuk from here, you can dip into hilltop **hot springs** (admission 5000Rp), and enjoy spectacular views. Recommended.

Trekking

If relaxation bores you, then try this two-day trek. The jungle is long gone, but the paths are challenging and interesting as they wind past coffee and clove plantations. Grab a map in Tuk Tuk because paths are not well marked.

The popular Ambarita to Pangururan trek starts opposite the bank in Ambarita. Continue along walking straight at the escarpment and take the path to the right of the graveyard. The climb to the top is hard and steep, taking about 2½ hours, more in the wet season when it becomes slippery and a bit hazardous. The path then leads to the village of **Partungkoan (Dolok)**, where you can stay at Jenny's Guesthouse or John's Losmen. From Partungkoan, it takes about five hours to walk to Pangururan via **Danau Sidihoni**.

SLEEPING & EATING

Samosir has great-value accommodation. The shoreline of Tuk Tuk is a backpacker haven, lined with sweet guesthouses and restaurants. The most stylish places are done up like Batak houses. Hotels usually outnumber tourists, and competition is fierce. If you arrive early, you can spend the afternoon seeking out a nest, or you can just let the local guys on the ferry steer you to theirs. Either way, it's hard to lose. The ferry will drop you off at or near your guesthouse, starting near Bagus Bay and moving northward. East-coast places have sunrise views and the cleanest water.

Samosir Cottages (☎ 41050; d from 25,000Rp;) The lobby-bar-restaurant here is the splashiest around, with billiard and Ping-Pong tables, a friendly barkeep and weekly Batak music and dance performances that are fairly underwhelming. Still, the rooms are clean, there is internet, satellite TV, and rumours of free coconuts.

Lekjon (☎ 41578; d from 45,000Rp) Large rooms with terraces, divine lake views, hot water and the friendliest service in Tuk Tuk are standard at this new arrival. You'll feel like part of the family from the moment you arrive. Stay here, but dine elsewhere.

Bagus Bay (☎ 451287; d from 50,000Rp;) This place has more than you need. The Batak-style rooms are sweet, and so are the shady avocado trees, and the classic rice-field landscape is superb, but is minigolf absolutely necessary?

Harriara Guest House (☎ 081 3978 23842; s/d 50,000/60,000Rp) It doesn't look like much from the road, but walk downstairs and you'll find clean, well-done rooms that open to a lovely garden and lawn area and a sweet slice of lake front. A great choice!

Carolina Hotel (☎ 451520; d from 80,000Rp;) Medan money comes calling here because the grounds are lovely, the rooms posh, the setting secluded. Spend extra for hot water and lake-front views.

Juwita View (☎ 451217; dishes 12,000Rp; ☎ breakfast, lunch & dinner) Here's a big statement: Juwita just might serve the best *gado gado* (fresh salad with prawn crackers, boiled egg and peanut sauce) in Indonesia. It also makes a mean chicken curry and sweet and sour fish. It's a bit out of the way, on the hillside above the Carolina Hotel, but it's worth the trek, and not just for the food. The easterly views from the patio towards Tomok are spectacular.

Poppy's Fish Farm (☎ 451291; fish dinners 50,000Rp; ⏲ breakfast, lunch & dinner) Poppy's has the best home cooking in Tuk Tuk. Breakfast pancakes are fluffy and packed with fresh fruit, and the farm-raised tiliapia will be netted mere hours before it's cleaned, spiced, butterflied and grilled to perfection. It's near Harriara Guest House.

DRINKING

The locals you'll meet on the ferry talk a big game about the crazy nights ahead, and if you're up for it, you will definitely meet a handful of night owls to revel with. But truthfully, Tuk Tuk is nobody's idea of a party town. However, if you do stay out late, you will almost certainly greet the wee hours at **Brando's Blues Bar** (☎ 451084; beers 16,000Rp; ⏲ 9pm-2am) because that's where nights wind down in Tuk Tuk.

ENTERTAINMENT

Hotels host rotating Batak dance performances almost every night. Check around. If you're lucky you may even get invited to a house party or Batak wedding.

GETTING THERE & AWAY

Boat

Ferries between Parapat and Tuk Tuk (7000Rp, 30 minutes) operate roughly every hour or two. The last one to Tuk Tuk leaves at 7.30pm and the last one back to Parapat leaves Tuk Tuk at about 5.30pm. Tell them where you want to get off on Samosir and you'll be dropped off nearby. When leaving for Parapat, just stand out on your hotel jetty anytime from 8am and flag a ferry down.

There are also car ferries to Tomok from Ajibata, just south of Parapat.

Bus

From Tuk Tuk you can catch a ferry to Parapat, and from there you can travel by bus (see p254 for details on bus travel to/from Danau Toba). There are daily buses from Pangururan to Berastagi (30,000Rp, four hours) via Sidikalang.

GETTING AROUND

Tuk Tuk sprawls a bit, but can be handled on foot or by pedal (bicycles hire for about 25,000Rp a day). Circumnavigators should rent a motorbike with a full tank of petrol for 65,000Rp. It takes about nine hours to get around the island, so start early. You will need to fill up along the way.

Regular minibuses run between Tomok and Ambarita (2000Rp), and on to Simanindo (3000Rp) and Pangururan (10,000Rp). Services dry up after 3pm.

BERASTAGI

☎ 0628

Come for the volcanoes, stay for the Giant Cabbage? Um, no. There is a sculpture of the world's most underrated leafy green on Berastagi's main drag, but you're here to bag peaks: Gunung Sinabung and Gunung Sibayak. They can each be done in a day and both offer sublime views of the gorgeously cultivated and thankfully cool Karo Highlands.

Information

BNI bank (Jl Veteran 22) Has an ATM.
Post office (Jl Veteran) Near the war memorial.
Telkom office (Jl Veteran; ⏲ 24hr) Also near the memorial, for international calls and internet service.
Trans Tour & Travel Agency (☎ 91122; Jl Veteran 119) Run by Losmen Sibayak (p258). Sells plane and ferry tickets from Medan, as well as local mountain and jungle trips.

Sights & Activities

Gunung Sibayak (2094m) offers summit views straight out of a tourist brochure, especially during the June–August dry season. Try to avoid weekends, when Medan day-trippers are out in force. If you're with a friend, you could probably do without a guide, but don't hike alone. Guides charge around 150,000Rp for the day. You'll need good walking shoes, warm clothes, food and drink.

The easiest route starts northwest of town, 10 minutes' walk past the Sibayak Multinational Guesthouse. Take the left track beside the entrance hut (2000Rp). From here it's 7km, and three hours, to the top.

Alternatively, you can catch a local bus (2000Rp) to Semangat Gunung at the base of the volcano, from where it's a two-hour climb to the top; there are steps part of the way, but the trail is narrow and in worse condition than the one from Berastagi.

The endurance option is to trek through the jungle from the **Air Terjun Panorama**, the waterfall on the Medan road, 5km north of Berastagi. This five-hour walk demands a local guide.

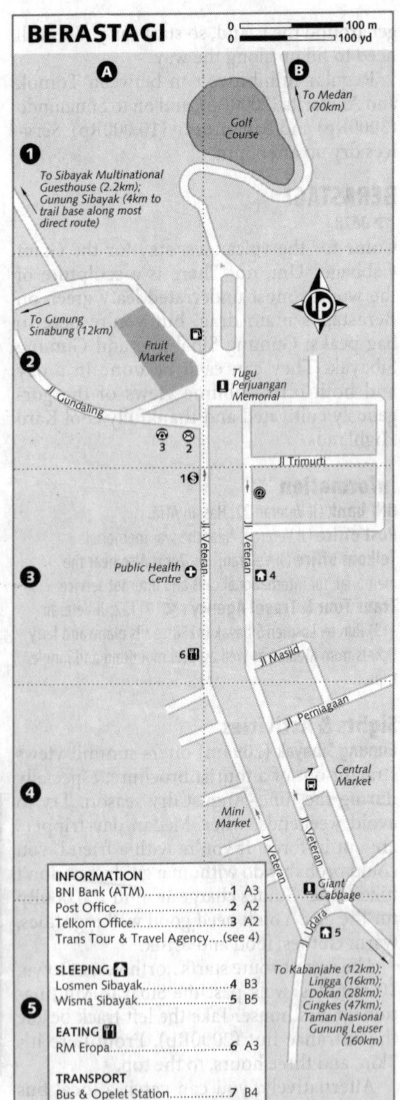

On the way down, stop and soak in the **hot springs** (admission 3000Rp), a short ride from Semangat Gunung on the road back to Berastagi.

Gunung Sinabung (2450m) is Sibayak's taller, better-looking (meaning the views), and far more difficult sister. It takes around 10 hours for the return trip, and should be tackled with a guide. Solo hikers have perished here. Sinabung is shy, often hiding behind thick cloudbanks that obscure views.

Berastagi also has plenty of guides offering treks along the well-trodden trails through **Taman Nasional Gunung Leuser** (Gunung Laeusur National Park), particularly to Bukit Lawang (three days) or Kutacane (six days).

Anthro-architecture hounds will dig the traditional villages of **Lingga**, **Dokan** and **Cingkes**.

Sleeping

Losmen Sibayak (☎ 91122; Jl Veteran 119; d from 60,000Rp) Great budget choice, with clean rooms, a chilled-out atmosphere and an all-purpose, in-house travel agency.

Wisma Sibayak (☎ 91104; Jl Udara 1; d from 100,000Rp) A popular choice, the tidy, spacious rooms here have great views, but street noise filters in. The affable staff here enables your trekking fantasies.

Sibayak Multinational Guesthouse (☎ 91031; Jl Pendidikan 93; d from 100,000Rp) An oasis of calm, unless you're here on weekends when jovial (and loud) Medan families take over. But the rooms are nice, with piping hot showers, great views and a garden for lounging and sun soaking. Catch a Kama *opelet* (1500Rp) from the monument.

Eating

The Karo Highlands are North Sumatra's breadbasket. Produce of all shapes, sizes, scents and colours pass through the local market. Passionfruit is particularly great here, and so is the *marquisa bandung*, a large, sweet, yellow-skinned fruit. The purple-hued *marquisa asam manis* is blended into a mean juice. Food stalls twinkle along Jl Veteran at night. Most of the hotels serve local and Western food, but also consider:

RM Eropa (☎ 91365; Jl Veteran 48G; dishes 12,000Rp; lunch & dinner) It has feta and sausage in the window, sizzling woks inside, and serves excellent Chinese and European fare.

Getting There & Away

Frequent buses to Medan (8000Rp, 2½ hours) go from Berastagi's central market. *Opelet* leave here every few minutes for Kabanjahe (2500Rp, 20 minutes). Getting to Parapat by public bus (22,000Rp, six hours) involves transfers, and a bit of patience, at Kabanjahe and Pematangsiantar.

MEDAN

☎ 061 / pop 1,763,900

Medan, Indonesia's third-largest city and a former Dutch tobacco town, can provoke contrasting reactions: repulsion at the toxic tangle of traffic, poverty and pollution, or enjoyment of the mayhem of a decaying city hopelessly striving to rejuvenate through the construction of shopping malls for the affluent. Don't worry, there are no wrong answers when it comes to Medan, there is just honest visceral response. But whichever way your gut leads you, whether you stay one night or five, there is no denying that Medan, which translates as 'battlefield', is a great place to get logistically organised and prepared for the next great adventure.

Orientation

A taxi ride from the airport to the nearby centre should cost 25,000Rp. From the southern bus terminal, the giant Amplas, it's a 6.5km bemo ride (5000Rp) into town.

Backpackers typically head to Jl Sisingamangaraja (SM Raja), where cheapies huddle in the shadows of the impressive Grand Mosque.

Parallel to SM Raja, to the west across the railroad tracks, runs Jl Katamso, which changes names further north to Jl Pemuda, then Jl Ahmed Yani and Jl Soekarno-Hatta. This is where you'll find many restaurants, the Chinese Night Market, major banks, travel agents and some colonial relics.

Information

EMERGENCY

Police (☎ 110)

INTERNET ACCESS

Hokki Bear Internet (☎ 735 6202; Yuki Plaza, SM Raja; per hr 4000Rp; ⏰ 10am-9.30pm Mon-Thu, 9.30am-midnight Fri-Sun)

MEDICAL SERVICES

Rumah Sakit Gleneagles (☎ 456 6368; Jl Listrik 6) English-speaking doctors.

MONEY

ATMs are everywhere, with a string on Jl Pemuda.

BCA (cnr Jl Diponegoro & Jl H Zainal Arifin) Exchanges money.

Citibank (Jl Imam Bonjol 23; ⏰ 8.30am-3pm) Has a 24hr ATM.

POST

Main post office (Jl Bukit Barisan 1) Fax, photocopy and parcel services set in an expansive Dutch colonial building.

TELEPHONE

Wartel Maymoon (Jl SM Raja 31-45) One of countless *wartel* in Medan.

TOURIST INFORMATION

North Sumatran Tourist Office (☎ 452 8436; Jl Ahmad Yani 107; ⏰ 7.30am-4pm Mon-Thu, to 3pm Fri) Centrally located, here you will get free maps, and adequate information from the quasi-friendly, almost-English-speaking staff.

TRAVEL AGENCIES

Boraspati Express (☎ 452 6802 Jl Dazam Raya 77) Phenomenal deals on air fares throughout Indonesia, and the owner, a surfer and motorcycle buff, has in-depth knowledge of North Sumatra, Pulau Nias and Aceh, and speaks flawless English. It's near Ibung Raya.

Sights & Activities

The **Istana Maimoon** (Maimoon Palace; Jl Katamso 66; admission by donation; ⏰ 8am-5.30pm) was built by the sultan of Deli in 1888. The family still occupies one wing, but it's falling down around them. The black-domed **Mesjid Raya** (Grand Mosque; cnr Jl Mesjid Raya & Jl SM Raja; admission by donation; ⏰ 9am-5pm, except prayer times) is breathtaking, especially when pilgrims stream in for Friday prayers. It was commissioned by the sultan in 1906 and built in the Moroccan style with Italian marble and Chinese stained glass.

Fans of Southeast Asian mall culture, latte globalisation or air-conditioned movie theatres on hot days should make their way to the bustling **Sun Plaza**, where current cinema, a bowling alley, an oft-defunct ice rink, decent shopping and Starbucks await.

Sleeping

Most hotels are on SM Raja, with a sprinkling of *losmen* around the Mesjid Raya (prepare for the 4am sermon/wake-up call). More bad news: the cheap joints in Medan are disgusting. On the plus side, they are near the Yuki Plaza (a low-budget Sun Plaza), which has ATMs, phone and internet services – and even a bowling alley and billiard tables. More good news: splurge for a midranger and you will get a damn-good deal.

Hotel Zakia (☎ 732 2413; Jl Sipiso-Piso 10-12; d from 40,000Rp) If you like past-their-prime, dirt-bag hotels crawling with unemployed tour guides

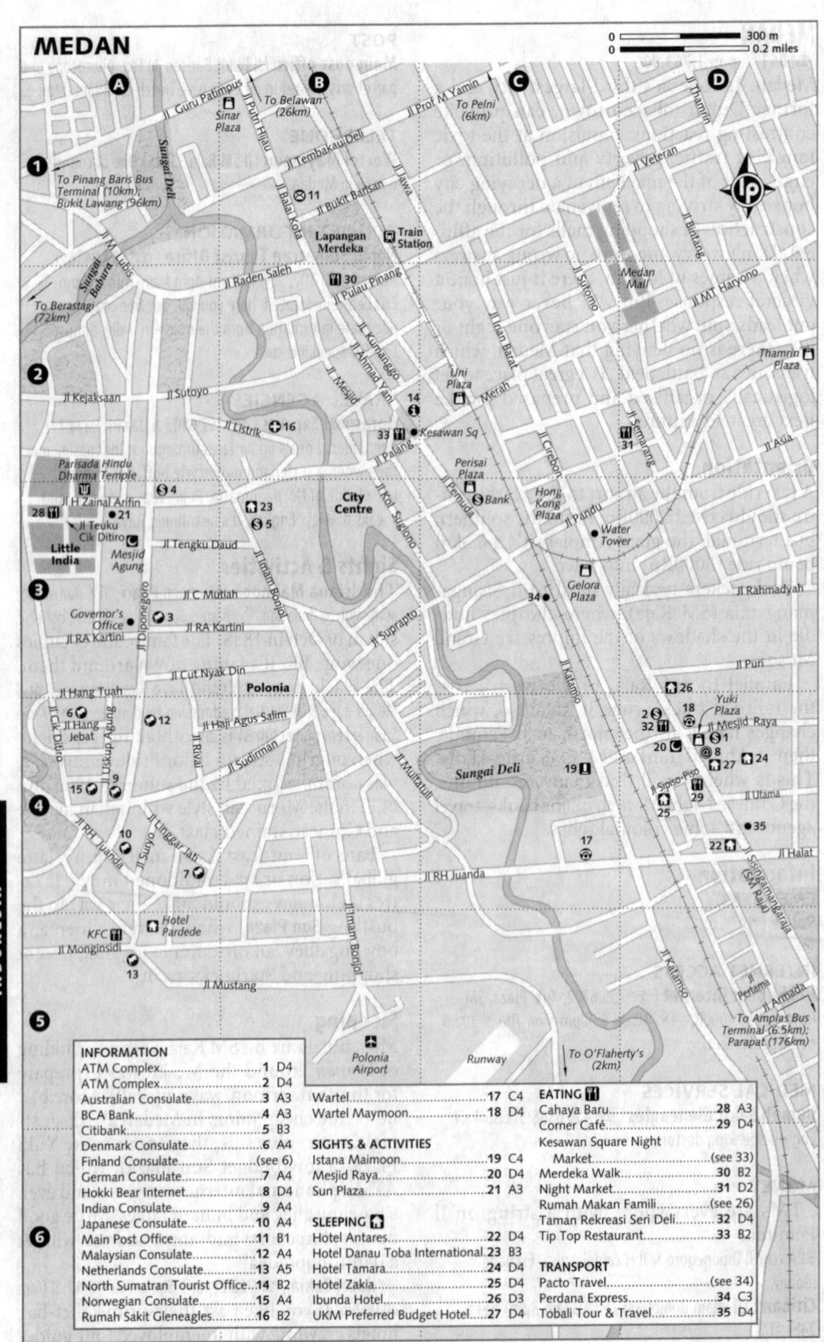

MEDAN
0 300 m
0 0.2 miles
A
B
C
D
1
2
3
4
5
6
Jl Guru Patimpus
Sinar Plaza
To Belawan (26km)
Jl Putri Hijau
Jl Prof M Yamin
To Pelni (6km)
Jl Thamrin
Sungai Deli
Jl Tembakau Deli
To Pinang Baris Bus Terminal (10km); Bukit Lawang (96km)
Jl Veteran
Jl Jawa
Jl Balai Kota
Jl Bukit Barisan
Jl Bintang
Lapangan Merdeka
Train Station
Jl M Lubis
Sungai Babura
Jl Sutomo
Medan Mall
Jl Raden Saleh
Jl Pulau Pinang
Jl MT Haryono
To Berastagi (72km)
Jl Kumanggo
Jl Ahmad Yani
Jl Mesjid
Jl Inan Barat
Thamrin Plaza
Uni Plaza
Merah
Jl Kejaksaan
Jl Sutoyo
Jl Listrik
Kesawan Sq
Jl Semarang
Jl Asia
Parisada Hindu Dharma Temple
Jl Palang
Perisai Plaza
Jl Cirebon
Jl Pemuda
Bank
Hong Kong Plaza
Jl H Zainal Arifin
Jl Teuku Cik Ditiro
City Centre
Jl Kol Sugiono
Jl Pandu
Water Tower
Little India
Mesjid Agung
Jl Tengku Daud
Gelora Plaza
Jl C Mutiah
Jl Rahmadyah
Governor's Office
Jl RA Kartini
Jl Diponegoro
Jl Imam Bonjol
Jl Suprapto
Jl Cut Nyak Din
Jl Puri
Jl Hang Tuah
Polonia
Jl Katamso
Jl Cik Ditiro
Jl Hang Jebat
Jl Uskup Agung
Jl Haji Agus Salim
Yuki Plaza
Jl Mesjid Raya
Jl Rivai
Jl Sudirman
Jl Multatuli
Sungai Deli
Jl Sipiso-Piso
Jl Utama
Jl RH Juanda
Jl Suryo
Jl Linggar Jati
Jl Halat
Jl Sisingamangaraja (SM Raja)
Hotel Pardede
KFC
Jl Monginsidi
Jl Imam Bonjol
Jl Mustang
Jl Katamso
Jl Pertama
Jl Armada
To Amplas Bus Terminal (6.5km); Parapat (176km)
Polonia Airport
Runway
To O'Flaherty's (2km)
INFORMATION
ATM Complex 1 D4
ATM Complex 2 D4
Australian Consulate 3 A3
BCA Bank 4 A3
Citibank 5 B3
Denmark Consulate 6 A4
Finland Consulate (see 6)
German Consulate 7 A4
Hokki Bear Internet 8 D4
Indian Consulate 9 A4
Japanese Consulate 10 A4
Main Post Office 11 B1
Malaysian Consulate 12 A4
Netherlands Consulate 13 A5
North Sumatran Tourist Office 14 B2
Norwegian Consulate 15 A4
Rumah Sakit Gleneagles 16 B2
Wartel 17 C4
Wartel Maymoon 18 D4
SIGHTS & ACTIVITIES
Istana Maimoon 19 C4
Mesjid Raya 20 D4
Sun Plaza 21 A3
SLEEPING
Hotel Antares 22 D4
Hotel Danau Toba International 23 B3
Hotel Tamara 24 D4
Hotel Zakia 25 D4
Ibunda Hotel 26 D3
UKM Preferred Budget Hotel 27 D4
EATING
Cahaya Baru 28 A3
Corner Café 29 D4
Kesawan Square Night Market (see 33)
Merdeka Walk 30 B2
Night Market 31 D2
Rumah Makan Famili (see 26)
Taman Rekreasi Seri Deli 32 D4
Tip Top Restaurant 33 B2
TRANSPORT
Pacto Travel (see 34)
Perdana Express 34 C3
Tobali Tour & Travel 35 D4

and accented by a midnight curfew imposed by people who aren't your parents, then you'll love it here!

Hotel Tamara (☎ 732 2484; d from 50,000Rp) Down the lane from UKM; it's not as nice, but it is quieter.

UKM Preferred Budget Hotel (☎ 736 7208; Jl SM Raja 53; d from 85,000Rp; ❄) The former Hotel Deli Raya is the best budget choice in town. That isn't necessarily an endorsement.

Hotel Antares (☎ 732 4000; Jl SM Raja 84; d from 100,000Rp) This is the best deal in town. It's plush, modern and affordable.

Ibunda Hotel (☎ 734 5555; Jl SM Raja 31; d from 150,000Rp; ❄) The popular Rumah Makan Famili restaurant is downstairs, and upstairs are comfortable air-conditioned rooms with a view.

Hotel Danau Toba International (☎ 415 7000; Jl Imam Bonjol 17; d from 270,000Rp) This ageing miniresort, close to the airport, is popular among expat corporate and nongovernmental organisation (NGO) types. It's got all the mod cons – cable TV, swimming pool, gym, prostitutes (you can't miss them) – and it's near Sun Plaza, an Indian Hindu Temple (and tasty Indian food), and not too far from Merdeka Walk and the Kesawan Sq night market. Ask for a room on the top floor, where city views are staggering.

Eating & Drinking

Taman Rekreasi Seri Deli (dishes from 5000Rp; 🕑 breakfast, lunch & dinner) Opposite the Mesjid Raya; this is where you'll find Malay street food on the cheap. Try Masaka Minang, the cart right next to the Corner Café. It's considered the best *warung* in Medan.

Rumah Makan Famili (☎ 736 8787; Jl SM Raja 31; dishes from 8000Rp; 🕑 breakfast, lunch & dinner) Below the Ibunda Hotel, this cheap and spotless Padang food haunt is popular with local businessmen. Its speciality is beef *rendang* with duck egg, or would you rather the beef heart simmered in coconut milk?

Corner Café (☎ 734 4485; Jl Sipiso-Piso; dishes 8000Rp; 🕑 breakfast, lunch & dinner) Owned by an expat Indo couple, and nestled in the shadow of Mesjid Raya, this is a great lunch spot, with cheap, ice-cold beers. Try the chicken schnitzel sandwich (20,000Rp). It's monstrous, delicious, a work of art, and should be considered for the sandwich hall of fame.

Cahaya Baru (☎ 453 0962; Jl Teuku Cik Ditiro 12; dishes from 12,000Rp; 🕑 lunch & dinner) Run by a South Indian family, near the Hindu Temple, this is one of the best kitchens in town. The smoky, peppery, tender chicken tikka is addictive. It even has wi-fi.

Tip Top Restaurant (☎ 453 2042; Jl Ahmad Yani 92; dishes from 15,000Rp; 🕑 breakfast, lunch & dinner) The first restaurant in town, this fraying-at-the-edges relic hasn't redecorated since the Dutch old days. The real attraction isn't the food, it's the original 1940s black-and-white photos on the wall that tell the story of colonial Medan.

Merdeka Walk (dishes 15,000-25,000Rp) This modern promenade is a collection of cafés serving pan-Asian food and offering outdoor seating to young, upwardly mobile Medanites.

O'Flaherty's (Jl Kom Udara Adi Sucipto 8 U-V; 🕑 lunch & dinner) The beating heart of the expat ghetto, this lively Irish pub is south of the airport. Join the international set for a Guinness or three, and make sure not to spend your 25,000Rp cab fare on one last round.

Chinese food, anyone? After dark, Jl Ahmad Yani is closed off north of Jl Palang Merah, and the excellent, greasy **Kesawan Square night market** (dishes from 10,000Rp; 🕑 7pm-1am) springs to life. There's karaoke, noodles, every kind of meat you could imagine…and some that you'd rather not. If only the beer was colder. Also good for Chinese food after midnight is the other **night market** (Jl Semarang), east of the railway line off Jl Pandu.

Getting There & Away

AIR

There are daily international flights to Singapore, Kuala Lumpur and Penang. For details see p242. Airlines with international connections include **Air Asia** (code AK; ☎ 080 4133 3333; www.airasia.com) and **SilkAir** (code MI; ☎ 453 7744; www.silkair.com).

For domestic routes, **Garuda** (code GA; ☎ 455 6777; www.garuda-indonesia.com) flies daily to Jakarta and Banda Aceh; **Mandala** (☎ 414 3430; www.mandalaair.com) connects Medan with Jakarta and Padang; **Batavia** (code 7P; ☎ 453 7620; www.batavia-air.co.id) flies to Jakarta, Padang, and Pulau Batam; **Sriwijaya** (code SJY; ☎ 455 2111) serves Pekanbaru and Pulau Batam; **Merpati** (code MZ; ☎ 455 1888; www.merpati.co.id) flies to Sibolga and Pekanbaru.

BOAT

See p262 for information on high-speed ferries to Pulau Penang in Malaysia.

INDONESIA

GETTING TO MALAYSIA

Malaysia-bound travellers can make the hop from Medan's Belawan port to Georgetown in Pulau Penang by ferry. Two high-speed ferries, *Behagia Ekspres* and **Perdana Express** (☎ 456 6222; Jl Katamso 35C) leave daily at 10am and 11am respectively. **Pacto Travel** (☎ 451 0081; Jl Katamso 35G) handles tickets for the *Bahagia Ekspres*.

Both companies charge RM95 (about 250,000Rp for the trip, plus 26,000Rp extra for the port tax and the bus from Medan to Belawan). Book tickets the day before to confirm your departure time as schedules have been known to fluctuate. Malaysian tourist visas are issued gratis upon arrival in Georgetown.

See p451 for information on doing the trip in the opposite direction.

Pelni boats leave Tuesdays for Jakarta. Perdana Express sells tickets. The main **Pelni office** (☎ 662 2526; www.pelni.com; Jl Krakatau 17A) is 8km north of the centre.

BUS

There are two main bus stations. Buses south to Parapat (25,000Rp, five hours), Bukittinggi (190,000Rp, 20 hours) and beyond leave from the **Amplas bus terminal** (Jl SM Raja), 6.5km south of downtown. Almost any *opelet* heading south on Jl SM Raja will get you to Amplas.

Buses to the north leave from **Pinang Baris bus terminal** (Jl Gatot Subroto), 10km west of the city centre. Get there by taxi (around 25,000Rp) or by *opelet* down Jl Gatot Subroto. There are public buses to both Bukit Lawang (10,000Rp, four hours) and Berastagi (8000Rp, 2½ hours) every half-hour between 5.30am and 5pm. Buses to Banda Aceh (110,000Rp, 12 hours) leave from 8am to 11pm.

Tobali Tour & Travel (☎ 732 4472; Jl SM Raja 79C) also runs a 'tourist' minibus to Parapat (80,000Rp).

Getting Around

Is it wrong to hate taxi drivers who hate using meters? This is the question you'll mutter as Medan cabbies do their best to gouge you. Don't let them get away with it. Becak drivers fetch about 5000Rp for most destinations in town, and *opelets* are omnipresent. The White line hits Kesawan Sq, Merdeka Walk and the train station; Yellows will take you to Little India and Sun Plaza. They cost 2500Rp per ride.

BUKIT LAWANG

☎ 061 / pop 3000

Bukit Lawang, a jungle village put on the map by the Bohorok Orang-Utan Viewing Centre, has endured tragedy, and risen from the ashes. In November 2003 a flash flood decimated the town and killed 280 people. Everyone who lives here was deeply affected, but slowly the people of this incredible river town, enclosed on all sides by jungle, have rebuilt it, and they welcome tourists like old friends. With great deals and spectacular scenery, this is a sweet place to be. It's also an ideal base for jungle treks into Taman Nasional Gunung Leuser, where you will see wild and semiwild orang-utans (see boxed text, opposite).

Orientation & Information

The nearby village of Gotong Royong, 2km east of the river, is the new town centre, with *wartel* and shops, but no banks or post office. Near the radio tower, Valentine Tour and Travel changes money, cashes travellers cheques and organises bus, ferry and plane tickets. The nearest clinic and police station are 15km away in the town of Bohorok. The bus station is 1km east of the riverside tourist district. Minibuses may go a bit further to the small square at the end of the road, where a rickety hanging bridge crosses the river to the hotels. At the square, the **PHKA permit office** (tickets 20,000Rp; 🕑 7am-3pm) sells tickets for the orang-utan feeding centre.

Sights & Activities

BOHOROK ORANG-UTAN VIEWING CENTRE

Twice a day (8.30am and 3pm), visitors can watch rangers feed nearly a dozen semiwild orang-utan who are being rehabilitated from captivity or sudden habitat displacement due to logging. The bland fare of bananas and milk encourages the apes to forage on their own. So far, 200 have been successfully re-released into the jungle, mating with communities of wild apes. From the PHKA permit office in town, it's a 30-minute walk up the east bank and a canoe river crossing before a steep path leads to the feeding site.

To learn more about these animals, check out these websites: www.orangutans-sos.org and www.sumatranorangutan.com.

THOSE INCREDIBLE REDHEADS

Orang-utans, the world's largest arboreal mammal, once owned Southeast Asia's rainforests. They swung through the canopy by day, foraging for kilos of fruit, shoots, leaves and nuts that they ground with their forceful jaws, and they'd nest in a new tree every night. Wired with primordial family planning – females birth an average of just three babies (one every six years) – and blessed with relatively long life (they can live 40 years), they were destined to thrive as long as the forests did, and that's the problem.

Rampant deforestation has confined our distant cousins to the last swaths of healthy rainforest in Sumatra and Borneo, and even those remnants are in jeopardy thanks to illegal logging and slash-and-burn agriculture. Rehabilitation centres in Sumatra and Kalimantan are now overcrowded with semiwild primates, but if you see an orang-utan (Malay for 'person of the forest') in the wild, her expressive face will burn into your brain, and shine in your memory forever.

TREKKING

Trekking in Taman Nasional Gunung Leuser is an absolute must. Guides are mandatory in the national park and prices are fixed. It's 150,000Rp for a three-hour guided trek, 250,000Rp fetches a full day, and 450,000Rp is good for two days and one night in the bush, including basic meals, guide fees, camping gear and park permits. That's the popular choice, because a night out increases your chances of spotting wild orang-utan. Most people count a Bukit Lawang trek among their favourite Sumatra memories. Remember, not all guides are sensitive to the environment. Check your guide's licence, talk to the park rangers and ask other travellers before signing up.

RAFTING

Ecolodge Bukit Lawang Cottages (☎ 081 2607 9983) organises white-water rafting on the Wampu River for US$40 a day. River tubing is possible from your guesthouse. Ask around. It'll cost US$5.

Sleeping & Eating

Most *losmen* that survived the flood are on the west bank, across the footbridge. Or haul your bum (and your backpack) uphill for 15 minutes to jungle hideaways with excellent views, closer to the feeding centre.

Garden Inn (d from 25,000Rp) This place has basic rooms and great views away from the devastation downriver. There are cold beers, tacos and pancakes at the nearby Indra Valley Café.

Nora's Homestay (d from 30,000Rp) It isn't riverfront, but the bamboo huts are set above ponds, near the rice fields, next to a gurgling stream. Ask the bus driver to drop you off 3km before the river.

Jungle Inn (d from 50,000Rp) Just across the river from the park entrance, this place lives up to its name. One room overlooks a waterfall, another incorporates the rock face into the interior design and has a shower that spouts from a living fern. Indulgence is easy here. The Honeymoon Suite (150,000Rp) comes with two balconies, cosy hammocks for two and panoramic jungle views.

Ecolodge Bukit Lawang Cottages (☎ 081 2607 9983; ecolodge.blc@indo.net.id; d from 125,000Rp) This downriver resort really is green. There's an organic garden, a medicinal plant botanical garden, and it recycles. The rooms are a bit upmarket, set back in the forest, and the guides who hang out here are trustworthy. Top-level Orang-Utan Suites come with open-roofed jungle bathrooms.

Well-established pizza place **Tony's Restaurant** (pizza 18,000Rp; ⏲ breakfast, lunch & dinner) has moved to the bus station. It may look closed, but it isn't. Along the river towards the park there's a string of open-air cafés serving fruit salad, *nasi goreng* and delicious views.

Getting There & Away

Direct buses (10,000Rp, four hours) and public minibuses (15,000Rp, 3½ hours) to Medan's Pinang Baris bus station go at least every half-hour between 5.30am and 5pm. Be warned: everything's big in this jungle, especially the potholes.

BANDA ACEH

☎ 0651 / pop 268,900

The provincial capital of Aceh endured a fate of biblical proportions. Banda was sucker punched twice on the same day by mama nature. The quake that produced the 2004 Boxing Day tsunami (p264) toppled all buildings

INDONESIA

BOXING DAY TSUNAMI – THE DAY THE SEA ERUPTED

On the morning of Sunday, 26 December 2004, a magnitude 9 underwater earthquake – the world's most powerful in 40 years – triggered a devastating tsunami that killed more than 220,000 people.

In Banda Aceh, ships came to rest kilometres into the city zone, palm forests were levelled, once-lush rice paddies became stagnant puddles of black water, and the stench of death lingered for months.

Like the catastrophe itself, the global aid effort was unprecedented. Australia, Germany, Japan, Spain, the US and other countries sent troops, and global tsunami-aid pledges eventually topped US$5 billion.

Of course, recovery from such incomprehensible loss of loved ones and property takes a lifetime, but the devout Acehnese, led by former rebel leaders who are suddenly legit government officials, are steadily rebuilding, and looking forward to an optimistic future.

more than three storeys tall, and the ensuing tidal wave obliterated middle-class coastal enclaves. In Banda alone, 61,000 were killed. But within a year the rubble was removed, the dead were buried, and the GAM rebel separatists disarmed peacefully. Reconstruction is moving at a snail's pace, but the city is bustling once again, and there is a new army in town – international aid workers who are helping jump-start the economy with their work and their wallets.

For all it's headline-grabbing horror, today's Banda Aceh is a fairly laid-back place. It's devoutly Muslim, yes, but women are modern and educated, and people often use official prayer times (when the city virtually shuts down) simply to visit friends rather than to log mosque hours. Still, fundamentalism persists. Adultery and extramarital sex are punishable by the cane here (see Paging Nathanial Hawthorne, opposite). Plus, a recent grenade strike against GAM civic leaders has brought back memories of a 30-year war. Check the local news before you travel here.

Orientation & Information

Thanks to bulging NGO expense accounts, airport taxis charge 60,000Rp to 70,000Rp for the 16km ride into town. Tell them you're a tourist and you may score a discount. There are plenty of ATMs around town.

BCA bank (Jl Panglima Polem 38-40)
BII bank (Jl Panglima Polem)
Jambo Internet (☎ 31270; cnr Jl Panglima Polem & Jl Nyak Arief; ⏰ 9am-11pm)
Post office (Jl Kuta Alam 33) A short walk from the city centre; has internet facilities.
Telkom wartel (Jl Nyak Arief 92) For international calls.

Sights & Activities

With its brilliant white walls and liquorice black domes, the **Mesjid Raya Baiturrahman** (Jl Mohammed Jam; admission by donation; ⏰ 7-11am & 1.30-4pm) somehow survived the tsunami intact, which, despite the rampant loss of life, has been interpreted by fundamentalists as evidence of a merciful God.

The **Museum Negeri Banda Aceh** (Jl Alauddin Mahmudsyah 12; admission 800Rp; ⏰ 8.30am-4pm Tue-Thu, to noon Fri & Sat) is the site of the Rumah Aceh, a traditional stilt home built without nails.

Sleeping

Most of the hotels were destroyed in the disaster and haven't reopened. Those that have are usually packed with aid workers. Expect high rates but not high standards.

Hotel Prapat (☎ 22159; Jl A Yani 19; d from 100,000Rp; ❄) Next to the Medan, this is a touch cheaper and a bit rougher, but it has Western toilets and clean sheets.

Hotel Medan (☎ 21501; Jl A Yani 15; d from 175,000Rp; ❄) There was a freight ship parked here for a while, but it's gone now, and the flooded rooms have been nicely renovated.

Eating

Rumah Makan Asia (☎ 23236; Jl Cut Meutia; dishes from 9000Rp; ⏰ breakfast, lunch & dinner) Aceh's answer to Padang food. Try the spicy baked fish.

Warung Ibu Pocut (Jl Nyak Adam Kamil IV 41-VII; dishes from 12,000Rp; ⏰ lunch & dinner) Set in an open-sided stilt house, this *warung* offers great local fare with a fresh breeze.

Tropicana (Jl SM Raja; mains from 15,000Rp; ⏰ lunch & dinner) One of two seafood restaurants that double as NGO magnets. You'll see the SUVs out front.

There's also a lively night food market, known as the **Pasar Malam Rek** (cnr Jl Ahmad Yani & Jl Khairil Anwar).

Getting There & Away

Adam Air (code KI; www.flyadamair.com) and Garuda fly daily to and from Medan, connecting to Jakarta and beyond. To get a current rundown on prices, schedules, and to book flights call **BP Travel** (☎ 32325; Jl Panglima Polem 75).

From **Terminal Bus Seutui** (Jl Teuku Umar), Kurnia runs 11 air-con buses to Medan, leaving between 8am and 8pm (110,000Rp, 12 hours).

Getting Around

Taxis to the Uleh-leh port (for Pulau Weh) cost 100,000Rp. The same trip via *opelet* (aka *labi-labi*) is only 5000Rp from the main **opelet terminal** (Jl Diponegoro). Motorised becak charge 5000Rp to 10,000Rp for most destinations.

PULAU WEH

☎ 0652 / pop 125,000

It's hard to believe that before WWII Pulau Weh, which means 'away from' in Acehnese, was a more important port than Singapore. Today it is a languid, mountainous isle with a muddy road, sleepy fishing villages, beckoning coconut-palm coves and spectacular diving – with walls, canyons, pinnacles and pelagic fish aplenty. And it dodged the tsunami, much to the delight of backpackers and divers, but also aid workers and Banda urbanites who come here to decompress and remember that, while tragic, life can be a beautiful gift.

Orientation & Information

You'll stop through the main town of Sabang, a laid-back little port, on the way to sun, sand and sea. You probably won't overnight here, but you'll find necessities on Jl Perdagangan, the lively main drag.

BRI bank (Jl Perdagangan) Changes money at terrible rates and has a MasterCard-only ATM.

Lumbalumba Dive Centre (☎ 081 168 2787; www.lumbalumba.com; Jl Pantai Gapang; per hr 20,000Rp) Has the most reliable internet in town.

Post office (Jl Perdagangan 66)

Rumah Sakit Umum (☎ 21310; Jl Teuku Umar) Offers medical facilities near Pantai Kasih.

Telkom office (Jl Perdagangan 68; 24hr) Next door to the post office.

Sights & Activities

The castaway vibe saturates **Iboih Beach**, which attracts backpackers to pretty bungalows set on the sand and forested slopes above turquoise waters. Just offshore (15,000Rp return by charter boat) lies the tiny, densely forested **Pulau Rubiah**, surrounded by epic coral reefs known as the **Sea Garden**.

Around the headland from Iboih is the more social **Gapang Beach**. It's terrific for swimming, with frequent turtle sightings. Rates and visitors double on weekends. **Pantai Kasih** (Lover's Beach), about a 2km walk from town, is a palm-fringed crescent of white sand.

There are two dive operators on the island. At Iboih you'll find **Rubiah Tirta Divers** (☎ 331119; www.rubiahdivers.com), which charges US$54 for two tanks. In Gapang, the Dutch-run **Lumbalumba Dive Centre** (☎ 081 168 2787; www.lumbalumba.com; Jl Pantai Gapang) charges €45 for two tanks and offers an array of PADI courses. Snorkelling gear can be hired anywhere for 15,000Rp per day.

Sleeping & Eating

In Iboih, a walking path leads to groups of palm-thatch bungalows, set on the shore or overlooking the water. Rooms start at 30,000Rp. Arina, Fatimah, Oong's and Yulia's bungalows are popular. Communal meals of *ikan bakar* are served by most *losmen* for

INDONESIA

PAGING NATHANIAL HAWTHORNE

The Scarlet Letter is alive and well in Sumatra, especially in Aceh, where Sharia'a law is observed, and Padang, a growing fundamentalist hotbed. Adultery (read: any sex out of wedlock) is dealt with harshly. In Padang, young adults in committed relationships must surreptitiously book hotel rooms to have sex. If management doesn't approve, he (it's always a he) will call the cops, who will arrest the lovers and plaster the woman's picture on the front page the next morning.

That's nothing. Sex out of wedlock is punishable by the cane in Aceh, for men and women. Recently, an Italian aid worker and his Acehnese girlfriend were caught in Banda, and caned in front of the mosque by a masked cleric in black robes who quoted scripture before each lashing as thousands of people watched in person, and on television!

15,000Rp. Arina restaurant makes lasagne and a tasty prawn curry.

At the slightly more upmarket Gapang, your choices range from basic huts on the sand to pseudoresorts. At the end of the beach, the basic, recently completed **No-name Bungalows** (bungalows from 20,000Rp) is only bare footsteps from the waves. **Ramadilla** (cabins 50,000Rp) is a collection of cabins on a hillside, with a longhouse that commands a sultan's view of the Indian Ocean. If you're flush, try **Laguna Resort** (d 175,000Rp), which has a great seaside restaurant (open breakfast, lunch and dinner), and spacious sea-view chalets.

Getting There & Away

Fast ferries to Pulau Weh (60,000Rp, two hours) leave at 9.30am and 4pm from Uleh-leh, 15km northwest of Banda. A slow ferry leaves at 2pm (40,000Rp, three hours). In the other direction the slow ferry leaves at 8am, and the fast ferry at 8.30am and 4pm. Get to the port an hour before departure to buy tickets.

Getting Around

From the port there are regular bemo to Sabang (10,000Rp, 15 minutes), and Iboih and Gapang (50,000Rp, 45 minutes). *Labi labi* run from Jl Perdagangan in Sabang to Gapang and Iboih (30,000Rp, 45 minutes).

PEKANBARU

☎ 0761 / pop 705,500

This once-sleepy river port on Sungai Siak (Siak River) is further evidence that the discovery of oil (by US engineers c WWII) is a big deal. Today Pekanbaru is a modern city, Indonesia's helter-skelter oil capital, and a business destination for multinational executives. It's also a convenient overnight stop between Singapore and Bukittinggi if you take the ferry.

Orientation & Information

Airport taxis charge 60,000Rp for the 10km trip into town. Most banks and hotels are on Jl Sudirman. The new bus station is 7km west of town.

BCA bank (Jl Sudirman 448)

Micronet (☎ 21219; Jl M Yamin; per hr 5000Rp; ⏰ 9am to 11pm) Internet service.

Riau Provincial Tourist Office (☎ 858441; Jl Gadah Mada 200; ⏰ 8am-4pm Mon-Thu, to 11am Fri)

Santa Maria Hospital (☎ 22213; Jl Ahmed Yani)

Tigobalai (☎ 28559; Jl Sam Ratulangi 62G) Reliable travel agency.

Sleeping & Eating

Poppie's Homestay (☎ 45762; Jl Cempedak III 11A; d 50,000Rp) Bunk at this budget fave located in a converted family home nestled in a residential neighbourhood. Friendly locals will point you in the right direction. It organises bus trips.

Shorea Hotel (☎ 48239; Jl Taskurun 100; d from 120,000Rp; ❄) Clean, modern rooms in a quiet location off the main strip.

If this is your first night in Indo, take an evening food-stall crawl on Jl Sudirman, at the junction with Jl Imam Bonjol. Or bypass culinary immersion to munch burgers, cakes, pastries and ice cream in scrubbed-fresh environs at **Vanhollano Bakery** (Jl Sudirman 153; meals 15,000Rp; ⏰ breakfast, lunch & dinner).

Getting There & Away

Simpang Tiga Airport is a visa-free entry point and has five flights to Jakarta each day. The flights are handled by **Batavia** (code 7P; ☎ 856031; www.batavia-air.co.id), **Lion Air** (code JT; ☎ 40670; www.lionair.co.id); **Adam Air** (code KI; www.flyadamair.com), **Sriwijaya** (code SJY; ☎ 859800) and **Garuda** (code GA; ☎ 29115; www.garuda-indonesia.com). **Merpati** (code MZ; www.merpati.co.id) and Sriwijaya fly to Medan.

Frequent buses go to Bukittinggi (economy/air-con 35,000/70,000Rp, five hours) from the uncharacteristically reserved, organised and modern Terminal Akap.

Booths at the north end of Jl Sudirman sell speedboat tickets to Pulau Batam (200,000Rp, six hours; 8am). There are also three boats a week to Melaka, Malaysia (200,000Rp, eight hours; 9am). Considering the time involved and the prevalence of affordable air fare, flying is the better choice.

DUMAI

☎ 0765 / pop 154,400

Like most of Pekanbaru's oil, travellers come and go through the industrial port of Dumai. But only to use its visa-free port for ferry trips to Melaka, Malaysia. There are two ATMs near the river end of Jl Sudirman.

If you get stuck here, stay at the tolerable **Hotel Tasia Ratu** (☎ 31307; Jl St Syarif Kasim 65; d from 150,000Rp).

There is a rash of buses to Pekanbaru (40,000Rp, five hours), Bukittinggi (economy/air-con 60,000/90,000Rp, 10 hours), and Padang (economy/air-con 70,000/100,000Rp, 12 hours).

GETTING TO MALAYSIA

High-speed ferries depart Dumai for Melaka at 8am, 10.30am and 1pm (160,000Rp, two hours). Tickets are available at the port; check in and pay your 3500Rp port tax two hours before departure. There are also three Melaka-bound boats each week that leave from Pekanbaru (200,000Rp, eight hours).

Malaysian visas are free and are issued upon arrival.

See p438 for information on doing the journey in the opposite direction.

Melaka-bound ferries leave at 8am, 10.30am and 1pm (160,000Rp, two hours) daily. Ferries travel daily to Pulau Batam, as well (195,000Rp, six hours). You must check in at the port two hours before departure. Port tax is 3500Rp. Two Pelni ships sail from Dumai to Pulau Bintan, then on to Jakarta.

PULAU BATAM

☎0778 / pop 311,800

It's not a good bet that you've chosen to overnight here. Of course, if multinational industrial plant sweatshops, bizarro retirement homes, low-end golf courses and sweaty, doughy business executives getting loose in girlie bars turns you on, then you'll have a blast. More than likely you just missed your ferry, and need a place to crash.

Orientation & Information

Travellers usually arrive at the Sekupang port by boat from Singapore, and rush to the domestic terminal next door for Sumatran connections. Arrive with cash for immigration proceedings, or you'll need to catch a cab to Nagoya.

Nagoya, in the north, is the island's largest town, a cluster of hotels, necessities and diversions. Jl Imam Bonjol is the main drag, where you will find ATMs and internet cafés. The **Batam Tourist Promotion Board** (☎322871) has a small office outside the international terminal at Sekupang; hours are erratic.

Sleeping & Eating

Most budget hotels on Pulau Batam double as brothels.

Hotel City View (☎429022; Block V, 35; d 98,000Rp; ❄) If you're stuck here for a night, this will work.

Dozens of tempting outdoor food stalls gather on Pujasera Nagoya across the canal.

Getting There & Away

AIR

Garuda (code GA; ☎458620; www.garuda-indonesia.com), **Merpati** (code MZ; ☎424000; www.merpati.co.id), **Mandala** (☎432278; www.mandalaair.com) and **Air Asia** (code AK; ☎080 4133 3333; www.airasia.com) fly daily to/from Jakarta. Merpati destinations also include Medan, Padang, Palembang, Jambi, Pekanbaru and Pontianak, Kalimantan. Most of the Nagoya hotels have travel agencies.

GETTING TO MALAYSIA & SINGAPORE

To Malaysia

From Batam Centre ferry terminal there are (almost) hourly departures to Johor Bahru in Malaysia (160,000Rp) from 8am to 5pm. Numerous taxis and public minibuses make the run between Sekupang port, Nagoya and the Batam Centre ferry terminal. For more information on tickets and schedules call **Batam Centre** (☎334704). Malaysiisas are available upon arrival in Johor Bahru.

From Pulau Bintan, there are five boats a day to Johor Bahru (140,000Rp, two hours).

See p456 for details of crossing from Malaysia to Indonesia.

To Singapore

Flying from Indonesian cities to Pulau Batam in the Riau Islands is far cheaper than catching a plane directly to Singapore, which is only a short ferry ride away. From Pulau Batam's airport, take a 50,000Rp taxi to the Sekupang ferry terminal. From here, 45-minute fast ferries (S$18) leave every half-hour between 6am and 8pm for Singapore's HarbourFront terminal, where visas are issued, on arrival, for many nationalities.

There are also frequent boats from Pulau Bintan to Singapore's Tanah Merah terminal (S$25) between 7am and 6.30pm.

For details on crossing in the reverse direction, see p654.

BOAT

The main reason travellers come here from Singapore is for its connections to Pekanbaru on the Sumatran mainland. Boats leave from the domestic wharf next to the international terminal. For Pekanbaru (190,000Rp, six hours), two boats leave Sekupang around 7.30am, so you'll need to catch the first ferry from Singapore to make it. Change money in Singapore to save time here.

There are also two morning boats from Sekupang to Dumai (195,000Rp, six hours).

From Sekupang there is one morning boat to Kuala Tungkal (231,000Rp), on the Jambi coast in Malaysia, and there are three boats weekly to Palembang (305,000Rp, eight hours). Pelni ships pass through Pulau Batam every four days, on their way to Belawan or Jakarta.

There are also boats to Singapore and Johor Bahru in Malaysia; see p267 for details.

If you're stuck in Nagoya, **Dumai Express** (☎ 427758; Komplek Lucky Plaza) sells ferry tickets.

To get to Pulau Bintan, take a taxi (65,000Rp) to the Telaga Punggur ferry dock, 30km southeast of Nagoya. Frequent boats leave for Tanjung Pinang (35,000Rp, 45 minutes) from 8.15am to 5.15pm.

Getting Around

A local *ojek* ride is around 5000Rp. A taxi from Sekupang to Nagoya costs 50,000Rp.

PULAU BINTAN

Pulau Bintan is Pulau Batam's polar opposite, with the charming old harbour town of Tanjung Pinang (a visa-free entry/exit point), interesting Muslim ruins on nearby Pulau Penyengat, a population of ethnic Hakka people and Indo-Malays, and a string of quiet beaches with several small islands sprinkled off the east coast.

GETTING THERE & AWAY

While Pulau Batam is the main link to Sumatra proper, Tanjung Pinang is the jumping-off point to the remote islands of the Riau Islands. It also has links to Singapore and Malaysia. Most services leave from the main pier at the southern end of Jl Merdeka. See p267 for more information on boats to Singapore and to Johor Bahru in Malaysia.

Regular speedboats leave from the main pier for Telaga Punggur on Pulau Batam (35,000Rp, 45 minutes) from 7.45am to 4.45pm daily.

There are daily ferry services to Pekanbaru (300,000Rp, two days), and Dumai (275,000Rp, two days).

Pelni (☎ 21513; Jl Ketapang 8, Tanjung Pinang) sails to Jakarta (195,000Rp, 28 hours) twice weekly from the southern port of Kijang. You can organise a trip and book with agents on Jl Merdeka.

GETTING AROUND

The bus terminal is 7km out of Tanjung Pinang. There are no regular public buses to Pantai Trikora, but you can probably flag one down on the highway and ask the driver to stop in Trikora (20,000Rp), or charter a taxi (100,000Rp). *Opelet* will shuttle you around Tanjung Pinang, most destinations cost

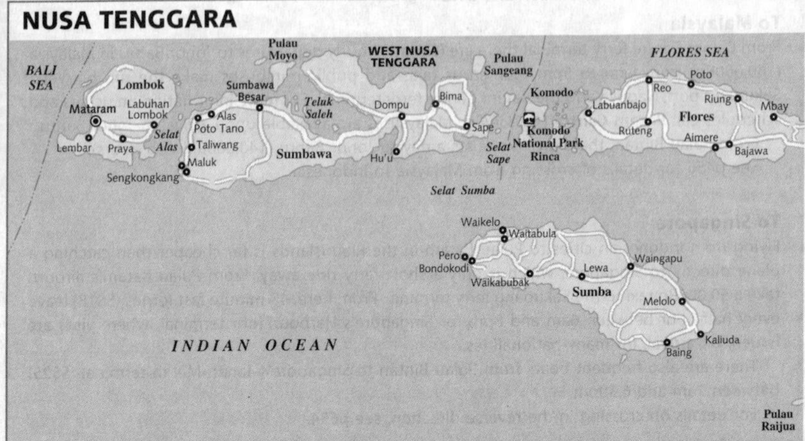

2000Rp, but negotiate before you climb aboard. Tanjung Pinang is also crawling with *ojek*.

Tanjung Pinang

☎0771 / pop 130,700

Tanjung Pinang has a busy harbour, great shopping, decent Indo-Chinese food and a smattering of traditional stilted villages on the outskirts.

INFORMATION

There are several ATMs on Jl Merdeka; bank branches are on Jl Teuku Umar.

BNI bank (Jl Teuku Umar)

Hospital (☎25310; Jl Atos Ausri; 24hr)

Post office (Jl Merdeka)

Tanjung Pinang Tourism Office (☎21284; Jl Merdeka 5; 7.30am-5pm) Has English-speaking staff and maps.

SIGHTS & ACTIVITIES

The old stilted part of town around **Jl Plantar II** is worth a wander. Turn left at the colourful **fruit market** at the northern end of Jl Merdeka.

Senggarang is a fascinating village just across the harbour from Tanjung Pinang, where the **Chinese temple** is held together by the roots of a huge banyan tree. Five hundred metres further on lies the 100-year-old **Vihara Darma Sasana** temple complex.

Boats to Senggarang (10,000Rp) leave from the end of Jl Pejantan II.

SLEEPING & EATING

Bong's Homestay (☎22605; Lorong Bintan II 20; d 30,000Rp) Backpackers have been landing here since your parents were hippies. The family speaks great English and is a wealth of information.

Hotel Surya (☎21811; Jl Bintan 49; s/d 45,000/80,000Rp) Value varies here, from dank concrete boxes to sunny, freshly painted, naturally lit rooms.

Outdoor restaurants and coffee shops line the front of the volleyball stadium.

Pulau Penyengat

This tiny island, a 15-minute *pompong* (diesel-powered wooden boat) ride (4000Rp) from the main pier, was once the capital of the Riau rajas. Explore the ruins of an old palace, visit stilted Malay villages and glimpse the sulphur-tinted Sultan Riau mosque, with its many minarets. Dress appropriately to gain access.

Pantai Trikora & Teluk Bakau

The best beaches on Pulau Bintan, with good snorkelling and attractive offshore islands, are on the east coast at **Pantai Trikora**. Beach huts are just a cut above camping. At low tide the beach becomes a dull mud flat.

South of Teluk Bakau village, try **Shady Shack** (bungalows 150,000Rp), or **Gurindam Resort** (☎26234; bungalows 150,000Rp), an overwater bungalow complex.

NUSA TENGGARA

Everything that's great about Indonesia – jaw-dropping mountains, thundering rivers, stunning beaches, ethnic and religious diversity, and exotic wildlife – can be found

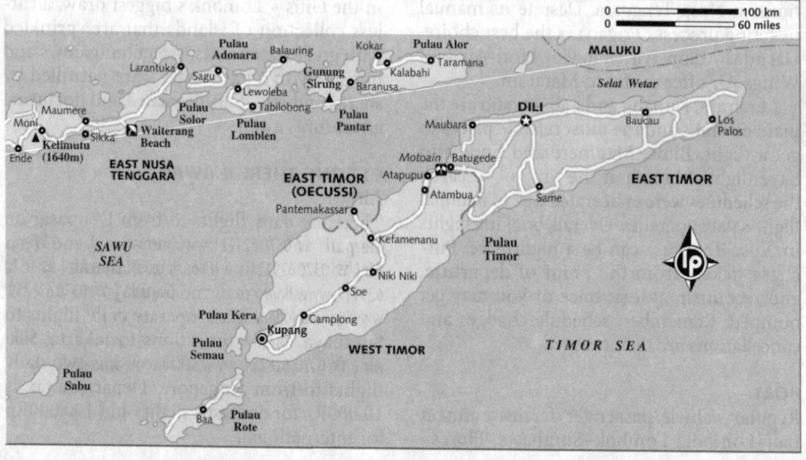

along this arc of islands that stretches towards Australia. If you get bored here it's because you missed the nightly parties on sugar-white Gili island beaches, bypassed some of the best diving in the world, thumbed your nose at lush volcanoes waiting to be climbed, missed the Komodo dragons patrolling a parched, jagged landscape, or turned down the twists and turns of a Flores road trip. In other words, it's your own fault.

The one drawback is that transportation between the islands can be unpredictable and maddening. Ferry, bus and flight departures are often less frequent than cancellations as you wander further east. But patience and intrepidness net rewards that will make your camera sing and your friends jealous.

Getting There & Away

Denpasar, Bali, is the main international gateway for Nusa Tenggara: you can go by ferry or plane across to Lombok, or fly to one of the other islands and work your way back.

Mataram, in Lombok, does have an international airport with SilkAir flights to Singapore. Merpati also flies twice weekly from Kupang, in West Timor, to Darwin, Australia.

Getting Around

The easiest and most popular way to explore Nusa Tenggara is to fly from Bali to Labuanbajo (Flores) or Kupang (West Timor) and island-hop from there.

AIR

Merpati, IAT and Trigana cover most destinations in Nusa Tenggara. Despite its manual ticketing process, Trigana is the best choice. Garuda, Adam Air, Batavia, Lion Air and Wings Air offer routes to Mataram.

Mataram, Kupang and Labuanbajo are the main air hubs and the most reliable places to get a flight. Bima, Maumere and Ende also have flights, though at the time of research the schedules were eviscerated due to national flight-safety upgrades. Overall, booking flights in Nusa Tenggara can be a nightmare. Purchase tickets from the point of departure, and reconfirm at least once or you may get bumped. Remember, schedule changes and cancellations are the norm.

BOAT

Regular vehicle/passenger ferries connect Bali–Lombok, Lombok–Sumbawa, Flores–Sumbawa, and Flores–Sumba. Perama makes the run from Lombok to Flores and back, taking in Komodo and Rinca. There are also dive liveaboards that run a similar route, but offer adventure beneath the surface.

Pelni (www.pelni.com) has regular connections throughout Nusa Tenggara. Check the website for details.

BUS

Air-con coaches run across Lombok, Sumbawa, and from Kupang to Dili in Timor, but elsewhere small, slow minibuses are the only option. They constantly stop for passengers and drive around town for hours until full. A 100km ride can take up to four hours.

CAR & MOTORCYCLE

A motorcycle is an ideal way to explore Nusa Tenggara, but hiring one is not always easy outside Lombok. You can rent one in Bali or Lombok, and portage across by ferry. Bring an extra gas can, and don't underestimate the sinuous, rutted roads. For groups, cars with driver/guides are a great option, and cost about US$40 a day.

LOMBOK

Lombok is an easy hop from Bali, and is the most popular spot in Nusa Tenggara. It has a spectacular, mostly deserted coastline with palm coves, Balinese Hindu temples, looming cliffs and epic surf. The majestic and sacred Gunung Rinjani rises from its centre – a challenging climb with rewards of seas and sunrise panoramas. And dive sites in the Gilis – Lombok's biggest draw, a carless collection of islands that are sprinkled with great restaurants, sweet bungalows and infused with a party vibe – are patrolled by sharks and rays. Sun-drenched and nocturnal adventures await.

GETTING THERE & AWAY

Air

There are daily flights to/from Denpasar on **Merpati** (☎ 0370 621111; www.merpati.co.id) and **Wings Air** (☎ 0370 629111; www.lionair.co.id). **Lion Air** (☎ 0370 629111; www.lionair.co.id) and **Garuda** (☎ 0370 638259; www.garuda-indonesia.com) operate daily flights to Surabaya with connections to Jakarta. **SilkAir** (☎ 0370 628254; www.silkair.com) has two daily flights to/from Singapore. Departure tax is 10,000Rp for domestic flights and 100,000Rp for international.

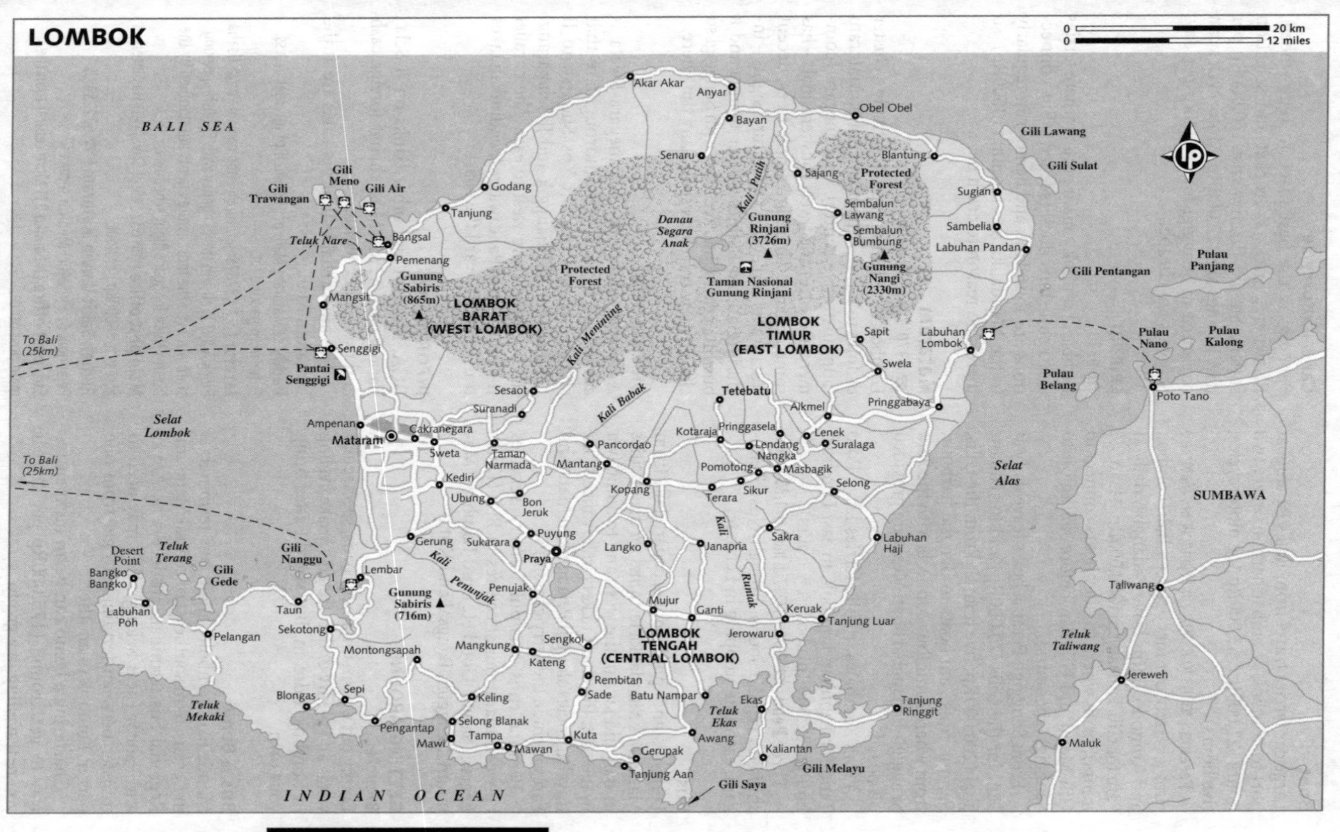
LOMBOK
0 20 km
0 12 miles
BALI SEA
Akar Akar
Anyar
Bayan
Obel Obel
Gili Lawang
Gili Sulat
Senaru
Blantung
Sajang
Protected Forest
Gili Meno
Gili Trawangan
Gili Air
Godang
Tanjung
Kali Putih
Danau Segara Anak
Gunung Rinjani (3726m)
Sembalun Lawang
Sembalun Bumbung
Sugian
Sambelia
Labuhan Pandan
Teluk Nare
Bangsal
Pemenang
Gunung Sabiris (865m)
Protected Forest
Taman Nasional Gunung Rinjani
Gunung Nangi (2330m)
Gili Pentangan
Pulau Panjang
Mangsit
LOMBOK BARAT (WEST LOMBOK)
Kali Meninting
LOMBOK TIMUR (EAST LOMBOK)
Sapit
Labuhan Lombok
Pulau Nano
Pulau Kalong
To Bali (25km)
Senggigi
Pantai Senggigi
Swela
Pulau Belang
Poto Tano
Sesaot
Tetebatu
Kali Babak
Suranadi
Alkmel
Pringgabaya
Selat Lombok
Ampenan
Mataram
Cakranegara
Sweta
Taman Narmada
Pancordao
Kotaraja
Pringgasela
Lendang Nangka
Lenek
Suralaga
To Bali (25km)
Mantang
Pomotong
Masbagik
Selat Alas
Kediri
Kopang
Sikur
Terara
Selong
SUMBAWA
Ubung
Bon Jeruk
Kali Runtak
Sakra
Gerung
Sukarara
Puyung
Langko
Janapria
Labuhan Haji
Desert Point
Teluk Terang
Gili Nanggu
Gili Gede
Kali Penunjak
Praya
Bangko Bangko
Lembar
Penujak
Taliwang
Gunung Sabiris (716m)
Labuhan Poh
Taun
Mujur
Ganti
Keruak
Tanjung Luar
Sekotong
Pelangan
Sengkol
LOMBOK TENGAH (CENTRAL LOMBOK)
Jerowaru
Teluk Taliwang
Montongsapah
Mangkung
Kateng
Rembitan
Jereweh
Blongas
Sepi
Keling
Sade
Batu Nampar
Teluk Ekas
Ekas
Tanjung Ringgit
Teluk Mekaki
Pengantap
Selong Blanak
Tampa
Mawi
Mawan
Kuta
Awang
Gerupak
Kaliantan
Maluk
Tanjung Aan
Gili Melayu
Gili Saya
INDIAN OCEAN

Boat

Large car ferries travel from Bali's Padangbai port to Lombok's Lembar harbour every two hours (21,000Rp, 65,000Rp for motorcycles; five hours).

Perama (☎ 0370-635928; Jl Pejanggik 66, Mataram) runs a variety of tours between Bali, Lombok and Komodo. Ships leave Padangbai daily at 9am for Gili Trawangan (200,000Rp, 4½ to 5½ hours), from where smaller boats connect to Gili Meno and Gili Air, before sailing on to Senggigi (six hours).

From Senggigi, Perama boats leave daily at 9am for the Gilis (70,000Rp) and for Padangbai (200,000Rp, five hours). From the Gilis, Perama runs 7am boats to Bangsal harbour, from where a minibus connects with the 9am Senggigi–Padangbai boat. Meals are provided on board.

From Sumbawa, public ferries leave Poto Tano for Labuhan Lombok, in east Lombok, hourly (12,500Rp, about 1½ hours).

Three **Pelni** (☎ 0370-637212; Jl Industri 1, Mataram) ships do regular loops through Nusa Tenggara, each one stopping in Lembar.

Bus

Long-distance public buses depart daily from Mataram's Mandalika terminal for major cities in Bali and Java in the west, and to Sumbawa in the east. Purchase tickets in advance from travel agencies along Jl Pejanggik in Mataram. Fares include the ferry crossings.

Perama runs bus/public-ferry services between main tourist centres in Bali (Kuta-Legian, Sanur, Ubud etc) and Lombok (Mataram, Senggigi, Bangsal and Kuta).

GETTING AROUND

Bicycle

Empty but well-maintained roads, spectacular vistas and plenty of flat stretches make cycling in Lombok a dream. But you'd better bring your own.

Bus & Bemo

Mandalika, Lombok's main bus terminal, is in Bertais, 6km southeast of central Mataram. Regional bus terminals are in Praya, Anyar and Pancor (near Selong). You may need to transfer between terminals to get from one part of Lombok to another.

Chartering a bemo can be an inexpensive way to get around (175,000Rp per day) if you're travelling in a group.

Car & Motorcycle

Senggigi is the best place to rent wheels. Elsewhere, prices skyrocket and selection suffers. Suzuki Jimmys cost 150,000Rp per day, Kijangs are 225,000Rp. Motorcycles can be rented in Senggigi for 60,000Rp per day. Scooters are cheaper.

Lembar

☎ 0370

Lembar, Lombok's main port, is where ferries and Pelni ships dock (see left). Bus connections are abundant, and bemos run regularly to the Mandalika bus terminal (3500Rp), so there's no reason to crash here.

Mataram

☎ 0370 / pop 323,400

Lombok's sprawling capital, actually a cluster of four towns – Ampenan (port), Mataram (administrative centre), Cakranegara (commercial centre) and Sweta (bus terminal) – has some charms. There are ample trees, decent restaurants and even a few cultural sights – including an old Balinese water temple and a bustling central market – but with Senggigi so close by few travellers spend any time here.

ORIENTATION

Ampenan-Mataram-Cakranegara-Sweta is connected by one busy thoroughfare that changes names from Jl Yos Sudarso to Jl Langko then Jl Pejanggik and Jl Selaparang. It's one-way, from west to east. The parallel Jl Panca Usaha/Pancawarga/Pendidikan takes traffic back toward the coast.

INFORMATION

BCA, Mandiri and other banks on Jl Selaparang have ATMs. Most change foreign cash and travellers cheques.

The most reliable internet cafés are at the Mataram Mall.

Deddy's (Mataram Mall; per hr 6000Rp) Internet access. Enter from parking lot.

Jatatur (☎ 632878; jatatur@yahoo.com; Jl Panca Usaha Block A 12) Well-run travel agency with English-speaking staff, but even the most astute agents are stumped by the bizarro Nusa Tenggara flight schedules.

Main post office (☎ 632645; Jl Sriwijaya) Has internet access for 6000Rp per hour.

Rumah Sakit Umum Mataram (☎ 622254; Jl Pejanggik 6; 24hr) Medical services.

Sub post office (Jl Langko 21) More central than the main post office.

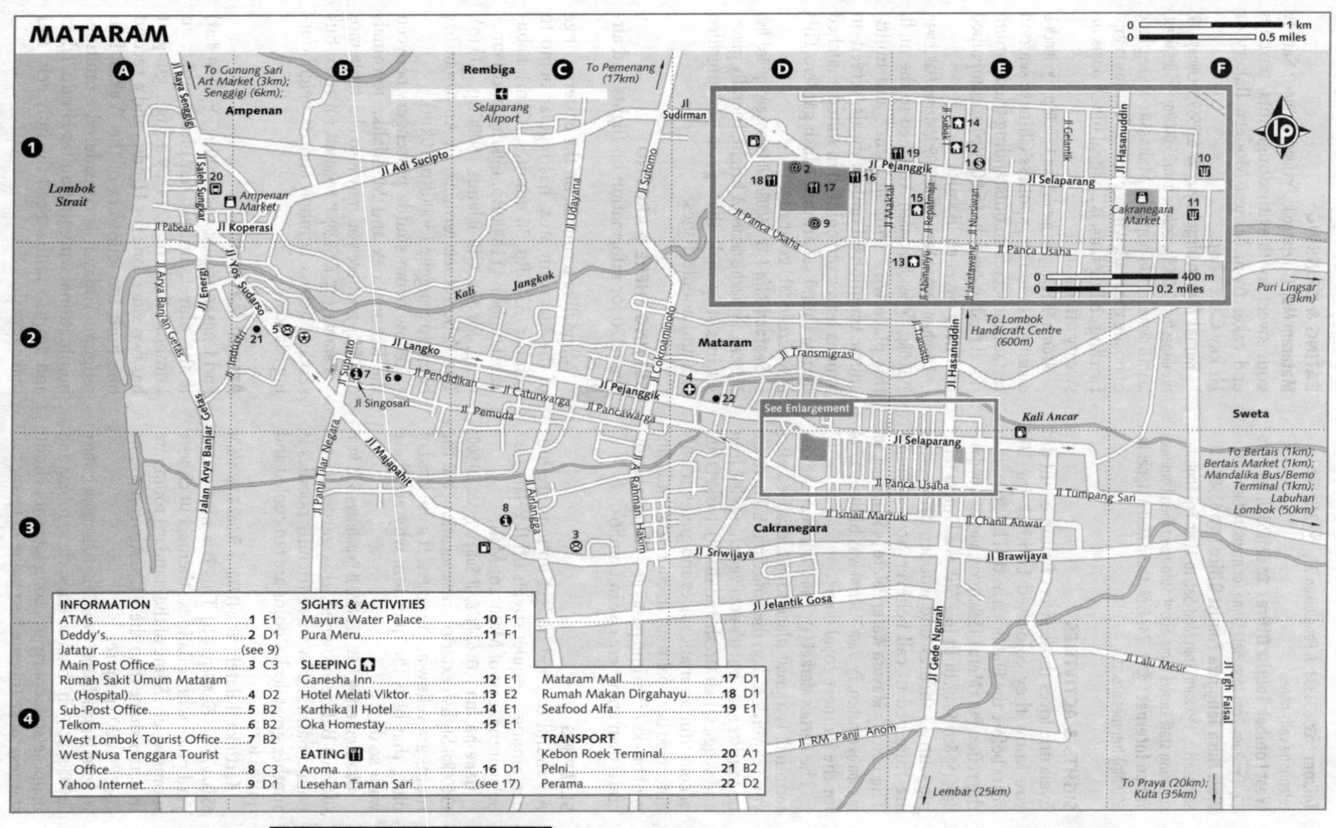
MATARAM
0 1 km
0 0.5 miles
0 400 m
0 0.2 miles
Lombok Strait
Ampenan
Rembiga
Selaparang Airport
Mataram
Cakranegara
Sweta
To Gunung Sari Art Market (3km); Senggigi (6km);
To Pemenang (17km)
Puri Lingsar (3km)
To Lombok Handicraft Centre (600m)
To Bertais (1km); Bertais Market (1km); Mandalika Bus/Bemo Terminal (1km); Labuhan Lombok (50km)
Lembar (25km)
To Praya (20km); Kuta (35km)
Ampenan Market
Cakranegara Market
Kali Jangkok
Kali Ancar
See Enlargement
Jl Raya Senggigi
Jl Saleh Sungkar
Jl Pabean
Jl Koperasi
Jl Adi Sucipto
Jl Sudirman
Jl Sutomo
Jl Udayana
Jl Arya Banjar Getas
Jalan Arya Banjar Getas
Jl Energi
Jl Yos Sudarso
Jl Industri
Jl Langko
Jl Suprato
Jl Singosari
Jl Pendidikan
Jl Caturwarga
Jl Pemuda
Jl Pejanggik
Jl Pancawarga
Jl Cokroaminoto
Jl Transmigrasi
Jl Transisto
Jl Hasanuddin
Jl Panji Tilar Negara
Jl Majapahit
Jl Airlangga
Jl A Rahman Hakim
Jl Selaparang
Jl Panca Usaha
Jl Ismail Marzuki
Jl Chanil Anwar
Jl Tumpang Sari
Jl Sriwijaya
Jl Brawijaya
Jl Jelantik Gosa
Jl Gede Ngurah
Jl Lalu Mesir
Jl Tgh Faisal
Jl RM Panji Anom
Jl Subak I
Jl Gelantik
Jl Maktal
Jl Repatmaja
Jl Nursiwan
Jl Abimanyu
Jl Jakatawang
INFORMATION
ATMs 1 E1
Deddy's 2 D1
Jatatur (see 9)
Main Post Office 3 C3
Rumah Sakit Umum Mataram (Hospital) 4 D2
Sub-Post Office 5 B2
Telkom 6 B2
West Lombok Tourist Office 7 B2
West Nusa Tenggara Tourist Office 8 C3
Yahoo Internet 9 D1
SIGHTS & ACTIVITIES
Mayura Water Palace 10 F1
Pura Meru 11 F1
SLEEPING
Ganesha Inn 12 E1
Hotel Melati Viktor 13 E2
Karthika II Hotel 14 E1
Oka Homestay 15 E1
EATING
Aroma 16 D1
Lesehan Taman Sari (see 17)
Mataram Mall 17 D1
Rumah Makan Dirgahayu 18 D1
Seafood Alfa 19 E1
TRANSPORT
Kebon Roek Terminal 20 A1
Pelni 21 B2
Perama 22 D2

INDONESIA

Telkom (☎ 633333; Jl Pendidikan 23; 24hr) Make telephone calls here.
West Lombok Tourist Office (☎ 621658; Jl Suprapto 20; 8am-2pm Mon-Sat) Come for maps, not insight.
West Nusa Tenggara Tourist Office (☎ 635874; Jl Singosari 2; 8am-3pm Mon-Sat, to 11am Fri) English-speaking staff knows more about Sumbawa than Lombok.
Yahoo Internet (☎ 627474; Mataram Mall A11; per hr 6000Rp) Internet access.

SIGHTS & ACTIVITIES

Everyone loves those sweet Balinese, but did you know they colonised Lombok for 100 years before the Dutch arrived? The proof is in the relics. **Pura Meru** (Jl Selaparang; admission by donation; 8am-5pm), built in 1720, is a Hindu temple with 33 shrines, and wooden drums that are thumped to call believers to ceremony. The nearby **Mayura Water Palace** (Jl Selaparang; admission by donation; 7am-7.30pm) was built in 1744 for the Balinese royal court.

The **Bertais Market** (7am-5pm), near the bus terminal, is a great place to get localised after you've overdosed on the *bule* circuit. There are no tourists here, but it's got everything else: fruit and veggies, fish (fresh and dried), baskets full of colourful, aromatic spices and grains, freshly butchered beef, palm sugar, enormous and pungent bricks of shrimp paste, and cheaper handicrafts than anywhere else in Lombok.

SLEEPING

A handful of good budget options are hidden among the quiet streets off Jl Pejanggik/Selaparang, east of Mataram Mall.

Ganesha Inn (☎ 624878; Jl Subak 1; s/d 30,000/40,000Rp) Stylish exterior, nice location, but the rooms are yellow at the edges. It's the kind of place that begs the question, why are these walls so dirty?

Oka Homestay (☎ 622406; Jl Repatmaya 5; d from 40,000Rp) Balinese-owned, this garden compound patrolled by three friendly poodles is another great deal. Rooms are fan cooled and quite clean.

Karthika II Hotel (☎ 641776; Jl Subak I 16; s/d/tr 65,000/70,000/80,000Rp;) This is a nice courtyard place with a Balinese theme, but choose rooms wisely. Some of the standard rooms are in better shape than the VIPs. Air-con rooms cost 20,000Rp more.

Hotel Melati Viktor (☎ 633830; Jl Abimanyu 1; d from 80,000Rp;) The high ceilings, clean rooms and Balinese-style courtyard, complete with Hindu statues, make this the best value in town.

EATING & DRINKING

Mataram Mall (Jl Pejanggik; lunch & dinner) Satisfy your sweet tooth with doughnuts, pastries and cakes from Mirasa Modern Bakery or Hokky Cake Shop.

Rumah Makan Dirgahayu (☎ 637559; Jl Cilinaya 19; rice dishes from 7,000Rp, seafood from 25,000Rp; breakfast, lunch & dinner) This popular Makassar-style place opposite the mall, with gurgling fountains and twirling ceiling fans, is an ideal lunch oasis on sweaty afternoons.

Aroma (Jl Pejanggik; meals from 15,000Rp; lunch & dinner) This modern, spotless Chinese seafood restaurant serves an outstanding fried *gurami* (local freshwater fish; 35,000Rp) accompanied by a fiery sweet chilli sauce.

Lesehan Taman Sari (☎ 629909; Mataram Mall; meals 25,000Rp; lunch & dinner) Attached to the mall, this place wins with ambience and multicourse traditional Lombok meals, served on banana leaves and enjoyed in stilted, thatched *beruga* (huts) set around a lush garden. This is where locals go at night.

Seafood Alfa (☎ 660088; Jl Pejanggik; grilled fish 30,000Rp; lunch & dinner) A bright, friendly place, set in a strip mall, that specialises in grilled fish and noodle dishes.

GETTING THERE & AROUND

See p270 for information on flights and airlines.

Mandalika terminal, on the eastern fringe of the Mataram area, has regular bemo to Lembar (3500Rp, 30 minutes, 22km), Labuhan Lombok (11,000Rp, 69km), and Pemenang, for the Gili islands (6000Rp, 31km). The Kebon Roek terminal in Ampenan has bemo to Senggigi (3000Rp, 10km).

Yellow bemo shuttle passengers between the Kebon Roek and Mandalika terminals (1500Rp), where you may also charter bemo.

Perama (☎ 635928; Jl Pejanggik 66) runs bus services across Lombok and its neighbouring islands.

Around Mataram

Puri Lingsar (admission by donation; dawn-dusk) is the oldest, holiest temple complex in Lombok. Built in 1714 by King Agung, it has two sides, one for Hindus and a second one built for followers of the Wektu Telu religion. Today it is considered a multidenominational wing that unites Hindu, Islam and animist faiths. Feed the holy eels, and make a wish.

The **Gunung Sari Art Market** (Jl Gunung Sari; ⌚ 9am-5pm), 3km west of Mataram, is a collection of a dozen art shops, each with much better deals on masks, bowls, baskets and other local handicrafts than you'll find in Senggigi.

Senggigi

☎ 0370

You can spend a lifetime of travel in search of the perfect beach, and it would be hard to top those around Senggigi, Lombok's original tourist town. Think: a series of sweeping bays with white-sand beaches, coconut palms, cliff and mountain backdrops, and blood-red views of Bali's Gunung Agung at sunset. There are sweet, inexpensive guesthouses, a few luxury hotels and dozens of restaurants and bars. Senggigi has everything, except tourists. Well, it's not completely empty, but it's desolate enough (except during July and August) to feel a bit strange. Still, the sheer beauty of the place is worth a night or two.

ORIENTATION & INFORMATION

Senggigi spans nearly 10km of coast. Hotels, shops, banks and restaurants are clustered along a central strip starting 6km north of Ampenan.

Police station (☎ 110) Also next to the Pasar Seni.

Senggigi Medical Clinic (☎ 673210) Based at the Senggigi Beach Hotel.

Super Star Net Café (☎ 693620; Senggigi Plaza B1/05; per hr 18,000Rp) High-speed internet access.

Telkom Near the Pasar Seni (Art Market).

SIGHTS & ACTIVITIES

Pura Batu Bolong (admission 5000Rp; ⌚ dawn-dusk) is a small Balinese-Hindu temple set on a rocky volcanic outcrop that spills into the sea, 2km south of central Senggigi. The detailed pagodas are oriented towards Gunung Agung, Bali's holiest mountain. You'll need to wear a sash to enter the temple.

Another must is to rent a motorbike and cruise the coast. You'll skirt fishing villages, palm groves and discover wide, deserted beaches. It's a soul-stirring, breathtaking drive.

There's decent **snorkelling** off the rocky point that bisects Senggigi's sheltered bay in front of Windy Cottages; many hotels and restaurants in central Senggigi hire out mask-snorkel-fin sets for 25,000Rp per day.

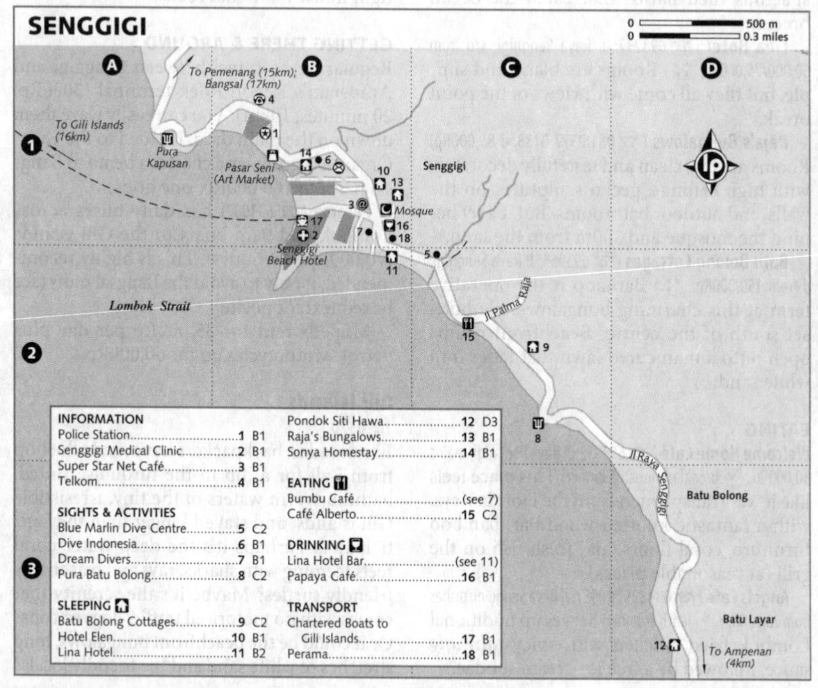

INDONESIA

There are dive centres on the main drag in Senggigi – **Dream Divers** (☎ 693738, 692047; www.dreamdivers.com), **Dive Indonesia** (☎ 642289; www.diveindonesiaonline.com) and **Blue Marlin Dive Centre** (☎ 692003; www.dive-indo.com) – but the sites are in the Gilis, so divers should base themselves there (see opposite).

SLEEPING

Pondok Siti Hawa (☎ 693414; Jl Raya Senggigi; d 40,000Rp) This isn't a homestay, it's a novelty act, starring an eccentric European expat and his family, a captive monkey, and ramshackle bamboo cottages set on one of the most beautiful beaches in Senggigi.

Sonya Homestay (☎ 0813 3989 9878; Jl Raya Senggigi; d from 40,000Rp) A shady family-run enclave of six rooms with nice patios and bright-pink bedspreads. Nathan, the owner, offers free driving tours of Mataram and the surrounding area. He'll even shuttle you to Bangsal harbour for a song.

Hotel Elen (☎ 693077; Jl Raya Senggigi; d from 55,000Rp; ❄) Elen is the current backpackers choice. Rooms are basic, but those facing the waterfall-fountain and koi pond come with spacious tiled patios that catch the ocean breeze.

Lina Hotel (☎ 693237; Jl Raya Senggigi; s/d from 60,000/75,000Rp; ❄) Rooms are bland and simple, but they all come with views of the point break.

Raja's Bungalows (☎ 081 2377 0138; d 85,000Rp) Rooms are big, clean and tastefully decorated, with high ceilings, gecko sculptures on the walls, and outdoor bathrooms. But it's set behind the mosque and 300m from the sand.

Batu Bolong Cottages (☎ 693065; Jl Raya Senggigi; d from 150,000Rp; ❄) Bamboo is the operative term at this charming bungalow-style hotel set south of the centre. Beachfront rooms open onto a manicured lawn that fades into white sand.

EATING

Welcome Home Café (☎ 693833; Jl Raya Senggigi; mains 30,000Rp; 🕑 breakfast, lunch & dinner) This place feels like it was transplanted from the Florida Keys, with a fantastic knotted-wood bar, bamboo furniture, coral floors, and fresh fish on the grill (at reasonable prices).

Angels Café (☎ 081 33974 0957; Jl Raya Senggigi; dishes from 20,000Rp; 🕑 lunch & dinner) Serves up traditional Lombok fried chicken with spicy *taliwang* sauce, followed by a free ice-cream sundae.

Café Alberto (☎ 693039; mains from 30,000Rp; 🕑 lunch & dinner) Eat beachfront at this popular Italian café on the sand.

Square (☎ 693688; Senggigi Sq; mains 35,000Rp; 🕑 lunch & dinner) Uberhip design, with lounge seating, a blue-lit, open dining room and veranda sea-views. Try the wok-tossed calamari with baby bok choy.

Bumbu Café (Jl Raya Senggigi; mains 35,000Rp; 🕑 breakfast, lunch & dinner) Popular choice for tasty pan-Asian fare. The owner says, 'We always full!' It's no coincidence.

DRINKING

Senggigi nightlife is fairly low-key. Weekends can pick up when an influx of Mataram 20-somethings hit the strip.

Lina Hotel Bar (☎ 693237; Jl Raya Senggigi; Ankor small/large 10,000/13,000Rp) There's no better place for a sundowner than Lina's seafront deck. Happy hour starts at 4pm and ends an hour after dusk.

Papaya Café (☎ 693136; Jl Raya Senggigi) The décor is slick, with exposed stone walls, rattan furniture and evocative Asmat art from Papua; there's a nice selection of liquor; and it has a tight house band that rocks.

GETTING THERE & AROUND

Regular bemo travel between Senggigi and Ampenan's Kebon Roek terminal (3000Rp, 20 minutes, 10km). You can easily wave them down on the main drag. Headed to the Gilis? Organise a group and charter a bemo to Bangsal harbour (60,000Rp, one hour).

Perama (☎ 693007) has daily buses across Lombok and 9am boats to the Gili islands (70,000Rp, 1½ hours). This is highly recommended, if only to avoid the Bangsal touts (see boxed text, opposite).

Mopeds rent for 35,000Rp per day plus petrol. Motorcycles go for 60,000Rp.

Gili Islands

☎ 0370

For decades, backpackers have made the hop from Bali for a dip in the turquoise-tinted, bathtub-warm waters of the tiny, irresistible Gili islands, and stayed longer than they anticipated. Perhaps it's the deep-water coral reefs teeming with sharks, rays and reasonably friendly turtles? Maybe it's the serenity that comes with no motorised traffic, dogs or cops? Or it could be the beachfront bungalows, long stretches of white sand and the friendly locals?

Each of these jungled pearls, located just off the northwestern tip of Lombok, have their own unique character, but they have one thing in common: they are all hard to leave.

Family-friendly Gili Air is the closest to the mainland, with plenty of homestays dotted among the palm trees. Mellow Gili Meno, the middle island, is small, quiet, a bit pricier, but a wonderful chilled-out retreat.

Gili Trawangan (population 800), the furthest out, has been tagged as the 'party island'. And it's true that you will be invited to purchase dope and magic mushrooms somewhere between six and 6000 times. But that's not the whole story. Trawangan is growing up, with stylish accommodation, a fun expat community and outstanding dining.

INFORMATION

There are no banks or ATMs on the Gilis, and though each island has shops and hotels that will change money and arrange cash advances from credit and debit cards, rates are low and commissions are high. Bring ample rupiah with you – enough for a few extra days, at least. There is mobile phone coverage, and all islands have a *wartel*. Air and Trawangan are wired for internet. Most places charge about 400Rp per minute.

Ozzy's Shop, on Gili Air next door to Abdi Fantastik, has phone and slow-motion internet services. Meno's internet access is near the harbour, and Trawangan is sprinkled with dozens of internet cafés. **Perama** (Map p280; ☎ 638514) has a small office on Gili Trawangan, just north of the jetty, and even smaller outlets on Air, close to the Gili Indah Hotel, and on Meno, at the Kintiki Meno Bungalows.

DANGERS & ANNOYANCES

Don't try to swim between the islands. The currents are strong, and people have died.

When the wind gusts, watch out for jellyfish, which sting and leave a memorable rash.

There are no police on the Gilis, so report any theft to the island *kepala desa* (village head) or Trawangan's Satgas community council. They'll help resolve issues, and recover stolen items privately, and with a minimum of embarrassment. Remember that magic mushrooms and other drugs are illegal, even if they are widely sold.

Cases of sexual harassment and assault have been reported on the Gilis. This is extremely rare, but single women should walk in pairs to the quieter, darker ends of the islands.

You'll experience the most common nuisance if, like most people, you travel to the Gilis from Bangsal harbour (see boxed text, below). Suffice it to say, these touts are adept at raising blood pressure, and you should sooner ignore than trust them.

SIGHTS & ACTIVITIES

Walking and cycling are the best land sports. Bikes can be hired for 25,000Rp per day. On Trawangan, time your circumnavigation (2½ hours on foot) with the sunset, and watch it from the hill on the southwest corner where you'll have a tremendous view of Gunung Angung.

Gili Meno's 2500-sq-metre **Taman Burung Bird Park** (☎ 642231; admission 60,000Rp; 🕒 9am-5pm) is home to 300 exotic birds from Asia and Australia, three demure kangaroos and a Komodo dragon. Birds are liberated from their cages three hours a day, to fly around an expansive atrium covered in netting.

Land diversions pale in comparison to the ocean variety. Trawangan has a fast right break that can be surfed year-round and at times swells overhead. It's just south of the Villa Ombok. **Karma Kayak** (☎ 081 8055 93710; tours

BANGSAL GAUNTLET

When you arrive at Bangsal (the principal departure point for the Gili islands) by bus, bemo or taxi, you will be dropped off at the Bangsal terminal, nearly a kilometre from the harbour. From which point irrepressible touts hustling a dishonest buck will harass you nonstop. It's not fun. Just ignore them and do not buy a ticket from them or from anyone else on the road. There is but one official Bangsal harbour ticket office, it is on the beach, not on the dirt road, and arranges all local boat transport – shuttle, public and chartered – to the Gilis. Buy a ticket anywhere else and you're taking a hit. You could also avoid Bangsal altogether by booking a speedboat transfer from Senggigi via one of the dive schools, or by travelling with Perama from Bali, Mataram, Kuta, Lombok or Senggigi (the best choice).

INDONESIA

225,000Rp), a new kayaking school on the northern end of Gili T, offers full-day kayaking trips around the Gilis. Snorkelling is fun and the fish are plentiful on all the beach reefs. Gear can be hired for 20,000Rp to 25,000Rp per day.

Diving is the big draw. The shops are highly professional, with new and well-maintained gear, and they all charge a uniform US$35 for one dive and US$30 for subsequent tanks. Five dives can get you 10% off, and a wide array of dive courses – from Open Water to Advanced – can be arranged as well.

On Trawangan, try **Manta Dive** (☎ 643649; www.manta-dive.com), **Blue Marlin** (☎ 632424; www.diveindo.com), **Dive Indonesia** (☎ 642289; www.diveindonesiaonline.com), **Big Bubble** (☎ 625020; www.bigbubblediving.com) and **Dream Divers** (☎ 634496; www.dreamdivers.com). On Gili Air, try **Blue Marlin** (☎ 634387) or **Dream Divers** (☎ 634547). On Gili Meno seek out **Blue Marlin** (☎ 639979) yet again.

Dynamite fishing and overfishing have been eliminated, thanks to the local ecotrust. As a result, fish numbers are up, but the reefs are still recovering from devastating El Nino–related warm-water bleaching. Those expecting a colourful, diverse reef system above 20m will be disappointed. Deep reefs are still reasonably healthy, however, and seeing sharks, rays and turtles up close will help take your mind off the wounded reefs.

SLEEPING & EATING

The vibe on easy-going rural Gili Air falls somewhere between sedate Meno and social Trawangan. Air and Meno only get crowded during the high season (July, August and around Christmas) when hotels double or triple their prices. Tap water on all the islands is brackish.

Gili Air

Hotels and restaurants are scattered along the southern and eastern coasts, which have the best swimming beaches. The hotels have dining rooms, but there are a few dedicated restaurants. Walking around the island takes about 90 minutes.

Nusa Tiga Bungalows (bungalows from 40,000Rp) A humble collection of bamboo bungalows nestled within an inland coconut grove.

Lucky's (bungalows 45,000Rp) Basic, cheap, and run by a friendly family in a serene locale on the south coast.

Lombok Indah (d 80,000Rp) A rare option on the north coast, this comfortable English-run place has bamboo bungalows and views of both sunrise and sunset.

Kira Kira Cottages (☎ 641021; s/d from 80,000/100,000Rp) Also a bit inland, there are some stylish thatched cottages here with ceiling fans, hammocks, garden views, and a fresh-water shower!

Sunrise Cottages & Restaurant (☎ 642370; s/d from 100,000/150,000Rp) This rustic place offers two-storey *lumbung*-style bungalows on the main east-coast strip. There's a safe for valuables and a fine seaside restaurant.

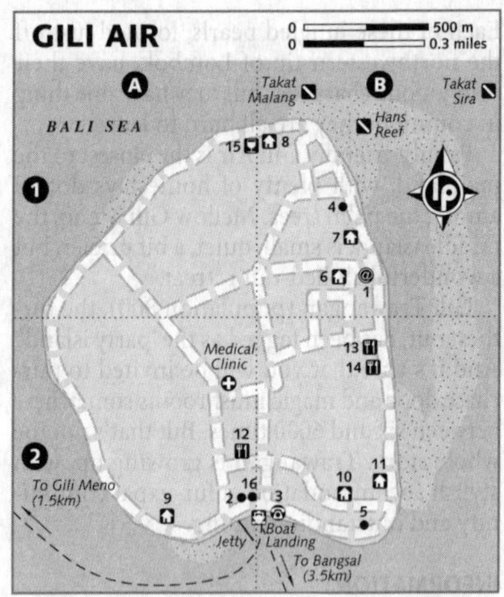

INFORMATION	
Ozzy's Shop	1 B1
Perama	2 A2
Wartel	3 B2
SIGHTS & ACTIVITIES	
Blue Marlin	4 B1
Dream Divers	5 B2
SLEEPING	
Coconut Cottages	6 B1
Kira Kira Cottages	7 B1
Lombok Indah	8 B1
Lucky's	9 A2
Nusa Tiga Bungalows	10 B2
Sunrise Cottages & Restaurant	11 B2
EATING	
Gecko Café	12 A2
Munchies	13 B2
Sasak Warung	14 B2
DRINKING	
Legend Pub	15 A1
TRANSPORT	
Koperasi/Public Boat Office	16 A2

Coconut Cottages (☎ 635365; www.coconuts-giliair.com; d 185,000Rp) Set back from the beach on the east coast, this Indo-Scottish-owned place has intricately detailed bungalows scattered around a well-loved garden. The restaurant is highly recommended.

Munchies (dishes from 7500Rp; ⏲ lunch & dinner) Nice curries, fish and skyscraper sandwiches. It's located about halfway down the east coast.

Gecko Café (☎ 641014; dishes from 10,000Rp; ⏲ lunch & dinner) The vibe and the food are consistently good here. The Wednesday night dinners (from 35,000Rp), featuring a take on mum's roast beef and apple crumble, provide comfort food for homesick dive masters. It's inland, north of the boat landing.

Sasak Warung (mains from 12,000Rp; ⏲ breakfast, lunch & dinner) Eat well, beneath beautiful shell lanterns, by the sea.

Gili Meno

Mellow Meno –the setting for your *Robinson Crusoe* fantasy – is a bit pricey and attracts a more 'mature' crowd. Electricity is ephemeral, so if the fan stops twirling, make sure you have a mosquito net. All guesthouses serve food.

Tao Kombo (☎ 081 2372 2174; huts from 60,000Rp) Known more for its bar, this place has decent Italian and Indonesian food, and more expensive bungalows have open-sky bathrooms and safety boxes.

Good Heart (☎ 081 3395 56976; bungalows from 80,000Rp) Opposite a narrow stretch of sand that faces Trawangan, these superb newish bungalows with coconut-wood roofs, freshwater(!) bathrooms and good eating are an excellent choice.

Amber House (d 100,000Rp) Cheap is done right at this northerly Zen-tinged garden compound with a glimpse of the sea. Bungalows sparkle, and the restaurant steams cappuccinos and bakes fresh muffins.

Biru Meno (r from 120,000Rp) Tranquillity is yours at this seaside spot south of the main strip. The best rooms have huge windows and native coral walls.

Malia's Child (☎ 622007; d from 200,000Rp) Attractive and clean bamboo-thatched bungalows set on a sweet stretch of beach near the boat landing.

Villa Nautilus (☎ 642143; pizza 40,000Rp; ⏲ breakfast, lunch & dinner) Order the wood-fired pizza, please. It's near Malia's Child.

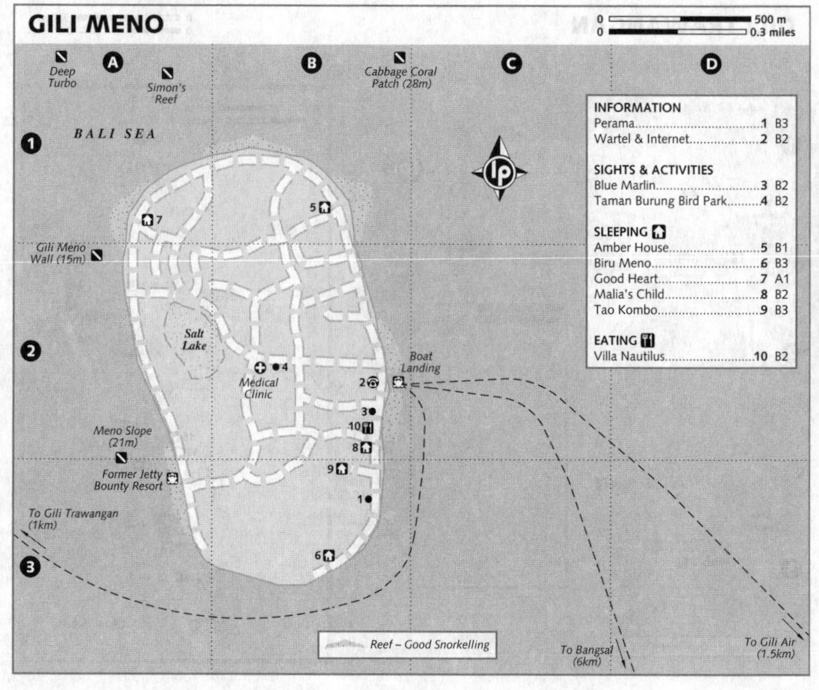

INDONESIA

Gili Trawangan

Social but not trashy, relaxed but not boring, all natural, yet updated with technology (internet, DVD pavilions and top-range soundsystems), and sprinkled with great restaurants and bars that would satisfy any devout cosmopolitan, Gili T is the road-weary backpacker's fantasy incarnate.

Dive resorts offer accommodation, as well. The bungalows tend to be a bit upmarket, and each of the seven dive centres has its own vibe and personality.

Aldi Homestay (☎ 081 33954 1102; s/d 30,000/35,000Rp) A village bargain. Some rooms are nicer than others. Look for the ripped-off logo of the German supermarket chain Aldi, which is also the name of the owner's son.

Pondok Lita (☎ 648607; s/d 40,000/50,000Rp) Popular family-run place in the village that has spacious courtyard rooms with a library and in-house laundry service.

Sandy Beach Cottage (☎ 625020; d from 50,000Rp) One of several village homestays, inland from the coastal road, catering to budgeters, this is a shady hideaway, close to the action. Could be cleaner.

Edy Homestay (d incl breakfast from 60,000Rp) The best of the village cheapies. These are very clean and come with ceiling fans and a big breakfast.

Warna Homestay (☎ 623859; d from 80,000Rp) Arguably the best value on the island, Warna has five sweet tropical-flower garden bungalows mere steps from the sea.

Balenta (☎ 081 805 203464; d from 90,000Rp) Next to the upmarket Good Heart is one of Gili T's better value places. It's opposite a great stretch of beach and the rooms are big and immaculate.

Quiet Water (☎ 081 2375 0687; d from 100,000) A plush, affordable village choice with queen beds, soft linens, air-con, hot water and in-room DVD players.

Blue Beach Cottages (☎ 623538; cottages from 200,000Rp;) Native thatch meets mod-minimalist at this locally owned collection of sea-view cottages on the north end of the strip. There are outdoor bathrooms, queen beds, wide decks and glass doors. Can bungalows look any smoother? Long-term and low-season discounts are available if you negotiate.

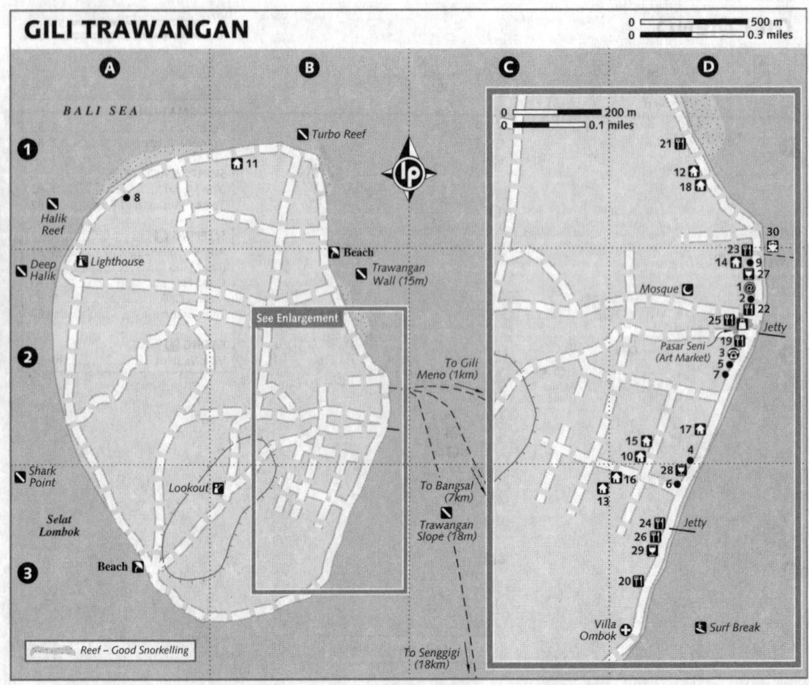

Manta Dive (☎ 643649; www.manta-dive.com; d 250,000Rp;) This laid-back English-run dive centre introduced the mod-bungalow motif to Gili T, and theirs remain some of the most stylish. It's a fun place to be after the afternoon dive when beers flow.

Big Bubble (☎ 625020; www.bigbubblediving.com; d from 250,000Rp;) More native wood, thatched modernism can be found in a row of beautiful rooms behind the dive school. These have hammocks on the front terrace.

Blue Marlin (☎ 632424; www.diveindo.com; d from US$30) The air-con rooms are nice, but not US$30 nice. It does have an excellent fresh-fish grill served on tablecloths by candlelight, and on Monday nights revellers descend for a techno dance party.

Anna's (dishes from 8,000Rp; 24hr) Backpackers rejoice: opposite the harbour is a tasty, high-turnover local *warung* serving *nasi campur* for 10,000Rp. It's the cheapest meal in town, and it's damn good.

Rumah Makan Kikinovi (nasi campur 12,000Rp; breakfast, lunch & dinner) This local *warung* has cheap, satisfying meals. It's north of the art market.

Beach House (☎ 642352; dishes from 17,000Rp, lunch & dinner) It isn't cheap, but with plush seaside digs, the best fresh fish and salad bar selection on the island and a solid jazz soundtrack, it's worth the splurge. The grilled calamari (17,000Rp) is an absolute steal.

Ryoshi (☎ 639463; dishes from 17,000Rp; lunch & dinner) Next to TiR Na Nog Irish pub, this sushi bar is a delectable Bali import. The melt-in-your-mouth tuna *carpaccio* is life altering.

Café Wayan (dishes from 20,000Rp; breakfast, lunch & dinner) The third instalment of a Balinese-owned chain (others are in Senggigi and Ubud) serves all your Indonesian faves and terrific fresh-baked breads and pastries. Try the garlic prawns. Outstanding! It's located at the northern end of the strip.

Kayangan (dishes from 20,000Rp; lunch & dinner) Across from Ryoshi is a cheap and cheerful expat fave known for its tasty curries, satays and *gado gado*.

Coco's (sandwiches 25,000Rp; breakfast & lunch) If only there was a café like this in every town. The women of Marlin Dive and TiR na Nog have made a major contribution to the dining scene with mouth-watering bacon-and-egg baguettes for breakfast and roast turkey or meatball sandwiches at lunch. The brownies and smoothies are incredible too. It's north of the art market.

Karma Kayak (☎ 081 805 593710; meals 35,000Rp; lunch & dinner) This new kayak school on the quiet north end of the island doubles as a Spanish tapas bar. It was brand-new at the time of research and generating significant buzz.

Juku (grilled fish from 35,000Rp; lunch & dinner) Among expats, this is known as the most affordable and the best-value fish grill on the island. The barracuda with ginger glaze is exceptional. You'll find it at the northern end of the strip.

DRINKING

The official party nights in Gili Trawangan are on Monday, Wednesday and Friday – although given the amount of contraband on offer and the scattering of stylish bars to investigate, each and every night can be a party here.

Rudy's Pub (8am-4am Fri, to 11pm Sat-Tue) Rudy's has as much to do with Gili T's party-hard reputation as all other bars combined. Mostly due to its debauched Friday-night parties and a preponderance of drinks and dishes involving a certain fungus.

INFORMATION

Lightening	1 D2
Perama	2 D2
Wartel	3 D2

SIGHTS & ACTIVITIES

Big Bubble	4 D2
Blue Marlin	5 D2
Dive Indonesia	6 D3
Dream Divers	7 D2
Karma Kayak	8 A1
Manta Dive	9 D2

SLEEPING

Aldi Homestay	10 D2
Balenta	11 B1
Big Bubble	(see 4)
Blue Beach Cottages	12 D1
Blue Marlin	(see 5)
Edy Homestay	13 C3
Manta Dive	14 D2
Pondok Lita	15 D2
Quiet Water	16 D3
Sandy Beach Cottage	17 D2
Warna Homestay	18 D1

EATING

Anna's	19 D2
Beach House	20 D3
Blue Marlin	(see 5)
Café Wayan	21 D1
Coco's	22 D2
Juku	23 D2
Karma Kayak	(see 8)
Kayangan	24 D3
Rumah Makan Kikinovi	25 D2
Ryoshi	26 D3

DRINKING

Ocean Dua	27 D2
Rudy's Pub	28 D3
TiR Na Nog	29 D3

TRANSPORT

Boat Landing & Koperasi	30 D1

INDONESIA

TiR na Nog (☎ 639463; drinks from 15,000Rp; ⏰ 8am-4am Wed, to midnight Thu-Tue) Known simply as 'The Irish Pub', it has a barnlike, sports-bar interior with big screens; private, thatched DVD lounges that guests can use free (its film selection is huge); and a brilliant outdoor bar with live DJs that draw the biggest crowds in town. Jameson is cheap, and Wednesday is its blow-out night.

Ocean Dua (drinks from 13,000Rp; ⏰ till the last guy leaves) With football on the telly, fun-loving bartenders, a good crowd, and no discernable closing time. It's the kind of place Charles Bukowski would have loved.

Legend Pub (Gili Air; ⏰ 10am-11.30pm Thu-Tue, party 10pm-2am Wed) The Wednesday-night reggae party bumps till the wee hours during high season.

GETTING THERE & AROUND

Perama (☎ in Senggigi 0370-693007, on Gili Trawangan 638514) operates a fleet of tourist shuttles to the Gilis – a popular option since it spares you the Bangsal menace (see boxed text, p277). Boats leave Senggigi for the Gilis at 9am (70,000Rp, 1½ hours). Perama also sells bus tickets from the Gilis to other points in Lombok and beyond.

Another way to dodge Bangsal is to book passage from Kuta to Gili Trawangan on the *Mahi Mahi* (550,000Rp) through the **Gili Islands Shop** (☎ 0361-753241; www.gili-paradise.com) in Bali. The shop and website have objective, timely information about all the Gilis.

To get to the Gilis by public transport, the cheapest option, take or charter a bemo to Pemenang, then get a *cidomo* (horse-drawn cart; 3000Rp) to the pier at Bangsal.

Here the local cartel, the Koperasi Angkutan Laut, runs boats to the islands: 8000Rp to Air, 6800Rp to Meno and 8000Rp to Trawangan. Boats leave when full, so you have to wait until 18 people buy tickets to the same island. Arrive early because there will be more people wanting to leave in the morning than in the afternoon; it's tougher to get a crowd after midday. There are regularly scheduled tourist shuttles from each Gili back to Bangsal (25,000Rp) at 7.30am and 8.15am daily. To charter a whole boat from Bangsal to the Gilis costs 155,000Rp.

For travel between the islands, a twice-daily island-hopper loops the archipelago. It launches from Air around 8.30am, drops by Meno at 8.45am, and docks at Trawangan at 9.45am. Then it loops back. The afternoon boat leaves Air at 3pm. It costs 15,000Rp between two islands and 18,000Rp between three islands.

Short *cidomo* rides on the islands are about 7000Rp, and circumnavigation costs about 20,000Rp. But, the horses don't look like they're having fun. Rent a bike (from 25,000Rp per day) and feel good about it.

Gunung Rinjani

Lombok's highest peak, the second-highest volcano in Indonesia at 3726m, is home to a smattering of small villages on her slopes, and is of great climatic importance to Lombok. Balinese call Gunung Rinjani 'the seat of the Gods', and place it alongside Gunung Agung in spiritual lore. Lombok's Sasaks also revere it, and make biannual pilgrimages here to honour the mountain spirit. It's one hell of a climb. Reach the summit and look down on a 6km-wide caldera with a crescent-shaped cobalt lake, hot springs and smaller volcanic cones. The stunning sunrise view from the rim also takes in north Lombok, Bali's Gunung Agung and the infinite ocean drenched in an unforgettable pink hue.

SENARU

pop 1330

With sweeping views east and south, and an eternal spring climate, the picturesque mountain villages of Senaru and nearby **Batu Koq** are the best bases for Rinjani climbs. Be sure to make the 30-minute walk to the spectacular **Air Terjun Sendang Gila** (admission 2500Rp; ⏰ dawn-dusk) waterfalls, and visit the traditional village, **Dusun Senaru** (admission by donation).

Many *losmen* along the main road have basic rooms with breakfast. **Bukit Senaru Cottages** (d from 40,000Rp), located just before Dusun Senaru, has four bungalows with garden verandas. Reputable **Pondok Indah** (d 100,000Rp), the first place you'll pass from Bayan, has sublime views and a good restaurant.

To reach Senaru, get to Anyar and catch a local bemo from there (4000Rp). They leave every 20 minutes until 4.30pm.

SEMBALUN LAWANG & SEMBALUN BUMBUNG

High on the eastern side of the mountain is the remote and beautiful Sembalun valley, another Rinjani launch pad.

TREKKING GUNUNG RINJANI

Agencies in Mataram and Senggigi arrange all-inclusive treks, but you can make your own, cheaper, arrangements in Senaru, Sembulan Lawang or even Sapit. Seek out the **Rinjani Trek Centre** (☎ 081 7575 7399; www.rinjani_directory.com) in Senaru. Partially funded by the New Zealand government, the centres have great maps and rotate local guides and porters for trekking tours. June to August are the best months to go. During the wet season (November to April), tracks can be slippery and very dangerous, and the view is often obscured by clouds. Trekkers were attacked and robbed on the mountain in 2000 and 2005 by armed robbers. Bandit activity is rare, but it's worth asking about.

The most common trek is to climb from Senaru to Pos III (2300m) on the first day (about five hours of steep walking), camp there and climb to Pelawangan I, on the crater rim (2600m), for sunrise the next morning (about two hours). From the rim, you descend into the crater and walk around to the **hot springs** (two hours) on a very exposed track. The hot springs, revered by locals for their healing properties, are a good place to relax and camp for the second night, before returning all the way to Senaru the next day.

For summit seekers, guides and porters are mandatory. Continue east from the hot springs, and camp at Pelawangan II (about 2900m). From there a track branches off to the summit. It's a heroic climb (three or four hours) over loose footing to the top (3726m). Start at 3am so you can see the sunrise on the summit. Return to Pelawangan II (two or three hours), and go east to Sembalun Lawang (five or six hours) to complete a traverse of the mountain.

You can trek from Senaru to the hot springs and back without a guide – the trail is fairly well defined. For summit attempts, it's perilous to hike without one. Guide and porter rates are standard and firm. Choose from four-day, all-inclusive tours (1,250,000Rp) or design an independent itinerary, and make your own food, water and transportation arrangements. Guides can be hired for 100,000Rp per day, and porters cost 80,000Rp.

Tent, sleeping bag and stove can be hired in Senaru through the **Rinjani Trek Centre** (☎ 081 7575 7399). Bring several layers of clothing, solid footwear, rain gear, extra water (do not depend on your guide for your water supply, or you may suffer), and a torch (flashlight). Buy food in Mataram or Senggigi, where it's cheaper and the selection is wider.

Hardy Kruger (☎ 081 7575 0585; www.rinjanilombok.com) offers 'deluxe trips' up the mountain, with transport to/from Mataram, equipment rental, ample food and toilet tents (three days, US$150).

In Sembalun Lawang, **Maria Guest House** (d 50,000Rp) has simple accommodation.

Take a bus from Mandalika bus terminal in Mataram to Aikmal (8000Rp) and transfer to a Sembalun Lawang–bound coach (9000Rp). Lawang and Bumbung are connected via hourly bemo.

SAPIT

Tiny Sapit, on Rinjani's southeastern slopes, boasts a huge panorama towards Sumbawa.

Hati Suci Homestay (☎ 036-722197; s/d 45,000/85,000Rp) has excellent bungalows in a fragrant garden.

Bemo go to Sapit from the Sembalun valley to the north and from Pringgabaya to the south (6000Rp).

TETEBATU

Situated on the low southern slopes of Gunung Rinjani, the village of Tetebatu (elevation 400m) is a lovely rural retreat where tobacco and rice fields unfurl into the distance in all directions. A shady 4km-long path from the main road, near the mosque, leads to a **Monkey Forest** (admission free) peppered with black monkeys and ringing with the sound of waterfalls. Balding backpackers take note: the **Air Terjun Jukut** (admission 1500Rp) waterfall, a steep 2km-long walk from the car park at the end of the road, is said to spur hair growth. Guides are recommended for both trips.

Cenderwasih Cottages (cottages 65,000Rp) has four gorgeous *lumbung* cottages with bamboo walls and a dining room with commanding views.

Losmen Hakiki (r from 60,000Rp) is another *lumbung* property situated beautifully over rice fields, with a dynamite restaurant serving Indo and Sasak cuisine.

Kuta

☎ 0370

They may share a name, but Lombok's Kuta is no tourist ghetto like the Bali version. It's languid, empty and stunningly gorgeous, with white-sand bays that lick chiselled cliffs and rugged hills, and world-class surf. There are some charming hotels in Kuta, but otherwise the coastline is undeveloped and the stomping ground of seaweed collectors, fishermen and water buffalo. You may hear whispers of impending five-star development, but thus far all attempts have fizzled, and the only real action Kuta sees is during the August high season and the *nyale* (seaworm) fishing festival in February or March. Otherwise, you'll have the place almost all to yourself.

INFORMATION

Several places change money, including the Kuta Indah Hotel and **Segara Anak Cottages** (☎ 654846; segarecottages@hotmail.com), which is also a postal agency. There is a small *wartel* in town and several places have internet access including **Kuta Corner Internet Café** (per hr 8000Rp).

ACTIVITIES

For surfing, stellar 'lefts' and 'rights' break on the reefs off Kuta and east of Tanjung Aan. Boatmen will take you out for around 70,000Rp. Seven kilometres east of Kuta is the fishing village of **Gerupak**, where there's a series of reef breaks, both close to the shore and further out, but they require a boat, at a negotiable 200,000Rp per day. Mawi also offers regular swells.

For surfing tips, forecasts, repairs and board rentals (35,000Rp per day), visit **Kimen Surf** (☎ 655064).

SLEEPING & EATING

While tourism numbers are down, standards can slip, so look around and bargain hard. Most places have their own restaurants; room rates usually include breakfast

Anda Cottages (☎ 654836; s/d 50,000/60,000Rp; 💻) For the buck, these cottages next door to Rinjani Bungalows might work, but inspect carefully as standards vary.

G'day Inn (s/d 50,000/60,000Rp) A little inland, this popular family-run place was recently renovated, the rooms are clean and the kitchen makes your mouth water.

Melon Homestay (☎ 081 736 7892; apt 60,000Rp) Tired of that beach-bungalow feeling? This place has two sweet apartments with lounges, kitchens and sea views from the balcony.

Segara Anak Cottages (☎ 654846; d from 60,000Rp; 💻) These basic huts are showing their age, but newer concrete bungalows are decent value. It's on the beach, the café has cable TV and internet access, and this is also where you'll find the local Perama office.

Mimpi Manis (☎ 081 836 9950; www.mimpimanis.com; d from 65,000Rp; ❄) If you like in-room DVD players, an ample library and tasty Indo-Western cooking, then check into one of two rooms in a house owned by an English-Balinese couple. It is 2km from the beach, but the owners will drop you off and scoop you up for free.

Rinjani Bungalows (☎ 654849; d from 95,000Rp; ❄) A nice choice at the far end of the beach. Its bamboo bungalows with hardwood furniture and *ikat* bedspreads are inviting. Air-con rooms cost 200,000Rp.

Surfer's Inn (☎ 655582; lombok_hotel@yahoo.com; d from 100,000Rp; ❄ 🏊) Six hundred metres east of the junction, this place has five classes of smart, stylish rooms with picture windows and large beds. Call ahead, because it sells out.

Astari (dishes from 8000Rp; 🕑 breakfast, lunch & dinner) Granted, its mountaintop perch, with mind-bending views of undulating surf, can make anything delicious, but the mostly veggie menu lives up to the view.

You'll find *warung* and food carts on the esplanade.

GETTING THERE & AWAY

How many bemo does it take to get to Kuta? Three. Take one from Mataram's Mandalika terminal to Praya (5000Rp), another to Sengkol (3000Rp), and a third to Kuta (2000Rp).

Or travel with **Perama** (☎ 654846; www.peramatour.com) to or from Mataram (90,000Rp, two hours) Senggigi (105,000Rp, 2½ hours), and the Gilis (185,000Rp, 3½ hours).

Labuhan Lombok

The one reason to visit this town is to catch a Sumbawa-bound ferry (see opposite).

Arrive early to avoid staying overnight. If you get mired, the only decent option is **Losmen Lima Tiga** (☎ 23316; d 55,000Rp) on the main road inland from the port.

Frequent buses and bemo travel between Labuhan Lombok and Mandalika terminal (11,000Rp, three hours).

INDONESIA

SUMBAWA

Nestled between Lombok and Flores, and separated from each by narrow straits, is Sumbawa, one of Indonesia's undiscovered treasures. Sumbawa is poor, with the most rudimentary health and education systems, and transport is uncomfortable and unpredictable. But there's so much to see. The island is larger than Bali and Lombok combined and populated by two distinct cultures (the Sumbawanese and Bimanese), each with its own language. Animist traditions still thrive in remote corners, and the topography is spectacular. Sumbawa's dry, twisted mass sprawls into the ocean in a series of jutting peninsulas. Volcanic stumps form the backbone, with dramatic and steep hills angling from the spine to the sea. Surfers drift in with the swells, but if you travel inland, you will be, literally, off the beaten path.

GETTING THERE & AWAY

Air

Bima is the one and only air hub, with direct Merpati flights to Denpasar (five times per week). You can also connect to Mataram and Maumere (although flights to east Flores are forever in flux). Departure tax is 6000Rp.

Boat

Ferries from Poto Tano depart for Lombok every hour around the clock. In the east, Sape is the departure point for daily ferries to Labuanbajo, Flores. Pelni ships bound for Lombok, Bali and Kalimantan, and those headed to Sulawesi, Papua and Timor, dock at Bima.

Bus

Night buses run in a convoy from Mataram to Bima, where they hook up with smaller shuttles to the Flores ferry at Sape.

Poto Tano & Around

Poto Tano is the Lombok-bound ferry port, but there's no reason to linger. Most travellers pass straight through to Sumbawa Besar. You can also head into town, catch a bus to Taliwang, and another 30km south to the superb surf at **Maluk**, a contemporary boom town thanks to a nearby copper mine. Backpackers and surfers flock to **Kiwi Maluk** (Jl Pasir Putih; d from 85,000Rp). Fifteen kilometres further south is another gorgeous surf beach, **Sengkongkang**, where you can find a number of beachfront *losmen*.

Ferries run regularly between Lombok and Poto Tano (see left). The through buses from Mataram to Bima include the ferry fare.

Buses also meet the ferry and go to Taliwang (5000Rp, one hour) and Sumbawa Besar (15,000Rp, two hours).

Buses run all day between Taliwang and Maluk (7000Rp, 1½ hours).

Sumbawa Besar

☎ 0371 / pop 54,300

Sumbawa Besar is the provincial principality on the western half of the island. Here *cidomo* still outnumber bemo. Aside from nearby traditional villages, the sole attraction is **Dalam Loka**, the crumbling Sultan's Palace, just off Jl Sudirman.

INFORMATION

BNI bank (Jl Kartini 10) Has an ATM and changes money.
Gaul Net Café (☎ 626110; Jl Setiabudi 14; per hr 11,000Rp) The last internet café until Ende.
Post office (Jl Garuda)
Telkom (Jl Yos Sudarso; 24hr)
Tourist office (☎ 23714; Jl Bungur 1; 7am-1pm Mon-Sat, to 11am Fri)

SLEEPING & EATING

Hotel Harapan (☎ 21629; Jl Dr Cipto 7; d 35,000Rp) The rooms, with *mandi* and Western toilets, are tiny but bearable at this family-run courtyard hotel.

Hotel Dewi (☎ 21170; Jl Hasanuddin 60; d from 50,000Rp;) Furnishings pay homage to the 1970s at this clean and basic budget spot. Air-con comes cheap if you're wilting in the Sumbawa sunlight.

Hotel Tambora (☎ 21555; Jl Kebayan; d from 51,000Rp;) Just like your nemesis in high school, this place used to be good-looking and popular, and now it just looks old, raggedy and vacant.

Ikan Bakar 99 (☎ 23065; Jl Wahidin 31; dishes from 9000Rp; breakfast, lunch & dinner) An inexpensive local haunt serving grilled fish (the house speciality) and delicious *kapitang rebus* (boiled crab).

Warung set up in front of the stadium on Jl Yos Sudarso.

GETTING THERE & AWAY

At the time of research commercial flights to and from Sumbawa Besar had ceased.

Pelni ships no longer dock in Sumbawa Besar. All traffic runs through Bima.

Morning buses to Bima leave from the **Brang Bara Terminal** (Jl Kaharuddin). Routes include Bima (60,000Rp, seven hours) via Dompu (20,000Rp, 4½ hours), and Poto Tano (15,000Rp, two hours). Deluxe, air-con buses run through between Bima and Lombok. Book them the day before at your hotel.

Pulau Moyo

Two-thirds of Pulau Moyo, 3km off Sumbawa's north coast, is a nature reserve, and its protected reefs are teeming with marine life. There are two resorts on the island: one is basic and run by the Forest Service (PHKA), the other is expensive. Hitch a ride over on a PHKA boat from Sumbawa Besar.

Hu'u

Sumbawa's south coast is a burgeoning surf mecca. The sweeping, white-sand beach of Hu'u, south of Dompu, has several attractive places to stay, from budget to midrange. This is an ideal beach retreat, even if you're not called to ride waves. The excellent **Alamanda Bungalows** (cottages from 90,000Rp) offers detached digs with ocean views.

Getting to Hu'u by public transport is an ordeal. From Dompu's Ginte bus station take a bemo to the Lepardi bus station (1000Rp), hop a bus to Rasabau (5000Rp, 1½ hours) and finally a crowded bemo to the beach (2000Rp). Most visitors come here by chartered taxi from Bima Airport (350,000Rp!).

Bima & Raba

☎ 0374 / pop 100,000

These fraternal twin cities – one is grubby but alive, the other is orderly and dull – form Sumbawa's main port and commercial hot spot. Consider it a stopover on the way through Sumbawa.

ORIENTATION & INFORMATION

Bima's airport is 17km out of town; it's 60,000Rp by taxi.

BNI bank (Jl Sultan Hasanuddin) Changes currency and has an ATM.

Tourist office (☎ 44331; Jl Soekarno-Hatta; 🕑 7am-3pm Mon-Fri, to noon Sat) About 2km east of the Raba town centre.

SLEEPING & EATING

Most hotels are in central Bima, near the market.

Hotel Lila Graha (☎ 42740; Jl Lombok 6; d from 80,000Rp; ❄) The labyrinthine passages access an array of rooms (some with phones and hot water), and a damn-good restaurant.

Hotel La'mbitu (☎ 42222; Jl Sumbawa 4; d from 80,000Rp; ❄) Bima's best, with several clean, bright and airy rooms to choose from.

Rumah Makan Mawar (☎ 42272; Jl Sulawesi 28; meals from 10,000Rp; 🕑 breakfast, lunch & dinner) Delicious and filling *nasi campur*.

Hit the *pasar* (market) for a variety of supercheap, if not nutritious, eats.

GETTING THERE & AWAY

Merpati (code MZ; ☎ 44221; www.merpati.co.id) is east of the town centre and flies five times a week to Denpasar with connections on to Mataram, Ende, Maumere, Surabaya and Jakarta.

There are currently no fast ferries to Bima. **Pelni** (☎ 42625; Jl Kesatria 2), at Bima's port, sails to Flores and Papua, or Lombok (from 263,000Rp, 24 hours), Bali (from 132,000Rp, 24 hours) and Sulawesi.

Buses to points west of Bima leave from the central bus station, just south of town. Express night bus agencies near the station sell tickets to Sumbawa Besar (60,000Rp, seven hours) and Mataram (120,000Rp, 11 hours). Most buses to Mataram leave around 7pm.

Buses to Sape (9000Rp, two hours) depart from Kumbe in Raba, a 20-minute bemo ride (1500Rp) east of Bima, but they can't be relied upon to meet the early morning ferry to Flores. Charter a bemo to Sape (about 100,000Rp, two hours) to make the 8am ferry.

Sape

☎ 0374

The only real attraction is the ferry to Labuanbajo, Flores, from Pelabuhan Sape, the small port 3km from town. There's been a history of scam artists in the area, though the downturn in Nusa Tenggara tourism has thinned out the buzzards.

The **PHKA Komodo information office** (🕑 7am-3pm) is inland from the port.

For a bed, **Losmen Mutiara** (☎ 71337; d from 30,000Rp), just outside the port entrance, is the only decent choice.

Buses go to Sape (9000Rp, two hours) from the Kumbe terminal in Bima-Raba, though you may have to charter a predawn bemo (100,000Rp, two hours) from Bima to make the 8am ferry to Flores.

Ferries to Labuanbajo (27,000Rp, eight hours) leave **Pelabuhan Sape** (☎ 71075) at 8am Wednesday to Monday, and at 3pm on Tuesday. They no longer stop at Komodo.

Ships leave for Waikelo, Sumba (32,000Rp, seven hours), on Monday at 5pm. Schedules change often, delays and cancellations are frequent. Be prepared to wait.

KOMODO & RINCA

Parched, isolated, desolate yet beautiful Komodo and Rinca rise from waters that churn with riptides and boil with whirlpools, and they are patrolled by lizard royalty, the Komodo dragon. It would be hard to create a more forbidding environment, yet a few hundred fishing families eke out a living within the Komodo National Park, the boundaries of which encompass both islands and several smaller, neighbouring isles. Thanks to its nutritious, pristine coral reefs that feed an incredible array of marine life, and those dragons you've heard so much about, the park is a World Heritage site – yours to hike, dive and explore.

Orientation & Information

The only village on Komodo is **Kampung Komodo** on the east coast, half an hour's walk from the gateway to Komodo, **Loh Liang** national park headquarters, set in a sheltered bay.

Visitors are tapped for entrance (40,000Rp) and conservation (US$15) fees upon arrival. For more information contact the **PHKA Office** (☎ 0385-41005; www.komodonationalpark.org; Jl Yos Sudarso) in Labuanbajo.

Sights & Activities

Dragons lurk year-round at the dry riverbed Banu Nggulung (below), but hunting (figuratively speaking) them on foot through primordial **Poreng Valley** feels wilder. **Gunung Ara** can be climbed (3½ hours) in an afternoon, and there's good snorkelling at **Pantai Merah** (Red Beach) and the small island of **Pulau Lasa**, near Kampung Komodo. The PHKA rents snorkels and masks for 50,000Rp. Guides (30,000Rp) are mandatory, and useful, for hikers.

Sleeping & Eating

Accommodation at Loh Liang's **PHKA camp** (d from 45,000Rp) consists of large, stilted cabins with balconies. In July/August the rooms may be full, but the PHKA will rustle up spare mattresses.

Quieter Rinca island, where wildlife is more diverse (you may even see long-tailed macaques), has a similar PHKA camp at Loh Buaya.

The camp restaurants serve simple meals and drinks.

Getting There & Away

Tours and private charters are your only way in to the islands. Expensive three- and five-day tours from Lombok to Labuanbajo abound. Most tour prime snorkelling sites and include a dragon-spotting hike on Komodo. Whether you are on a tour or organising a private charter, inspect boats carefully and make sure they have life vests and a radio. There have been shipwrecks.

Perama (☎ 0385-41289; Central Bajo Tours, Jl Yos Sudarso, Labuanbajo) boats stop at the dragon islands on their three-day trips between Labuanbajo and Lombok (deck/cabin 1,400,000/2,000,000Rp), which run every six days. They visit Komodo when sailing east and Rinca when heading west. They also stop for snorkelling and offer good food and freshwater showers.

INDONESIA

DRAGON SPOTTING

Komodo's gargantuan monitor lizards *(ora)* grow up to 3m long and can weigh in at a whopping 100kg. These prehistoric beasts feed on pigs, deer and buffalo. A blood-poisoning bite from their septic jaws dooms prey within a few days.

Banu Nggulung, a dry riverbed a half-hour walk from Loh Liang, is the most accessible place to see dragons on Komodo. It was once set up like a theatre, though the curtain has fallen on the gruesome ritual of feeding live goats to the reptiles. On Rinca, dragons will often congregate near the PHKA post when the rangers are cooking, or guides will lead hikes to their favourite lizard haunts.

Spotting dragons is not guaranteed, but a few of these royal reptiles are usually around – especially around watering holes in the June–September dry season. They rarely venture into the midday sun, so get to the islands early. A guide costs 30,000Rp per person.

Boat tours to Komodo, Rinca and other islands are easily arranged in Labuanbajo. Many hotels, various 'tourist information centres', and independent tour guides organise day and overnight trips to Komodo or Rinca (from 225,000Rp to 600,000Rp per day for up to six people). You may also charter private boats from Labuanbajo harbour and organise your own itinerary.

It takes two hours to get to Rinca, or four hours to get to Komodo. Rinca day trips make sense. Day trips to Komodo don't. Stay the night.

FLORES

Flores is the kind of gorgeous that grabs hold of you tightly. There are empty white- and black-sand beaches and bay islands; exceptional diving and snorkelling near Labuanbajo; an infinite skyline of perfectly shaped volcanoes; and a vast tapestry of hip-high, luminescent rice fields that undulate in the wind next to swaying palms in spectacular river canyons. The serpentine, potholed east–west Trans-Flores Hwy is long and slow, but never boring. It skirts waterfalls, conquers mountains, brushes by traditional villages in Bajawa, leads to the incredible multicoloured volcanic lakes of Kelimutu, and connects both coasts. The Portuguese named it 'Flowers' when they colonised Flores in the 16th century. The name stuck (so did Catholicism) because of its sheer, wild beauty.

GETTING THERE & AWAY

Air

Labuanbajo has become Flores' primary gateway because scores of tourists funnel in to see the dragons and dive the reefs of Komodo National Park. Maumere, Ende and Ruteng are also serviced by flights that are often cancelled. Purchase your ticket at an airline office at the point of departure only, and always reconfirm. Schedules change frequently.

Trigana flies daily to Denpasar from Labuanbajo. It also schedules flights from Ende to Denpasar five times weekly, and three times a week from Maumere to Denpasar, but they're often cancelled. Merpati flies from Maumere to Denpasar, Kupang and Waingapau, and from Ende to Kupang thrice weekly.

Boat

Daily ferries connect Labuanbajo with Sape, Sumbawa. From Larantuka, ferries go to Kupang (West Timor) and Pulau Solor and Pulau Alor. From Ende and Aimere, boats will take you to Waingapu on Sumba.

Pelni ships provide some useful, though rare links, including Labuanbajo–Lembar (from 140,000Rp, two days), Ende–Waingapu (from 51,000 Rp, seven hours), Maumere–Kupang (from 166,000Rp, two days), Maumere–Makassar (from 131,000Rp, two days), Labuanbajo–Makassar (from 124,000Rp, two days) and Larantuka–Kupang (from 105,000Rp, two days).

GETTING AROUND

The Trans-Flores Hwy twists and tumbles for 700 (almost always) paved, tremendously scenic kilometres from Labuanbajo to Larantuka. Luxury buses are extinct on Flores, but cheap, cramped public buses run when full, which means packed! Many tourists hire a car and driver. Trans-Flores trips run from 450,000Rp to 500,000Rp a day, including petrol. You'll need to negotiate and customise your trip, but rates don't vary that much. Ask at any hotel or travel agency in Labuanbajo or Maumere.

The flat, coastal 'Trans-Northern Hwy' now runs from Maumere to Riung.

Labuanbajo

☎ 0385 / pop 7500

Welcome to Indonesia's 'Next Big Thing' in tourism. At least it feels that way, with a steady stream of Komodo-bound package tourists and younger backpackers descending on this gorgeous ramshackle harbour. It's freckled with bay islands, blessed with surrealist sunsets, and surrounded by rugged, undeveloped coastline. Dive boats leave day and night for world-class reefs in the nearby national park, there are sweet beach bungalows on empty islands closer to shore, and there's an ever-expanding collection of restaurants with a view.

INFORMATION

The Telkom office is near the tourist office.

BNI bank (Jl Yos Sudarso) Changes money, and has an ATM.

Dinas Pariswata (☎ 41170; Jl IY Kasimo; 🕑 7am-2pm Mon-Sat, to 11am Fri) One kilometre from town on the airport road.

Dive Komodo (☎ 41354; www.divekomodo.com) One of several main-street dive shops.

Post office (Jl Yos Sudarso)

THE LITTLE PEOPLE OF FLORES

The Manggarai people of Flores have long told folk tales of child-sized, hairy people with flat foreheads who roamed the island's deep jungles during the times of their distant ancestors. Nobody paid them much attention – until September 2003, when archaeologists made a stunning find.

Digging through the limestone cave at Liang Bua, they unearthed a female skeleton that was the size of a preschooler but had the worn-down teeth and bone structure of an adult. Six more remains supported their theory that they had stumbled upon a new species of human, *Homo floresiensis,* a 1m-tall pygmy which they unkindly dubbed the lady 'hobbit'.

Lab tests brought another surprise: the pint-sized female with the nutcracker jaw, overlength arms and chimp-sized brain purportedly lived just 18,000 years ago, a blip on the scale of human evolution. Only then did *Homo sapiens* arrive and – being taller, smarter and better at the harsh survival game – push the little people off the island and into oblivion.

SIGHTS & ACTIVITIES

Diving Komodo National Park is one of the big draws to Labuanbajo. Currents are strong and unpredictable with cold up swellings and dangerous down currents thanks to the convergence of the warm Flores Sea and the cooler Selat Sumba (Sumba Strait). These conditions also nourish a rich plankton soup that attracts whales, mantas, dolphins, turtles and sharks. Factor in pristine coral and clouds of colourful fish and the diving is nothing short of exhilarating. But it isn't easy, so it's best to tune into local conditions on shallower dives before you endeavour to venture into the depths. There are several solid dive shops in Labuanbajo, each with different prices. Take your time and assess the gear before signing up for a trip. Generally, two tanks will cost you US$90.

Boats can also be chartered at reasonable rates to **Pulau Bidadari** (per person for a half-day trip 60,000Rp), where the water is crystal clear and the snorkelling is superb. Ask your hotel about charters or just walk down to the harbour and negotiate yourself.

TOURS

Labuanbajo is the main jumping-off point for tours to Komodo and Rinca; see p287 for details.

SLEEPING

Hotel Mutiara (☎ 41383; Jl Yos Sudarso; d from 60,000Rp; ❄) The wooden rooms hover above the harbour, which has a certain downmarket appeal, but the walls are thin and the rooms are grimy.

Bajo Beach Hotel (☎ 41008; Jl Yos Sudarso; s/d from 70,000/75,000Rp) In the centre of town, but set back from the main road, these clean, tiled rooms are often full. The proprietor can organise affordable tours by land and sea.

Golo Hilltop (☎ 41337; www.golohilltop.com; s/d 75,000/85,000Rp; ❄) The concrete bungalows aren't stylish, and it's a bit removed from 'downtown', but the setting – on a hillside high above the bay – is exquisite.

Gardena Bungalows & Restaurant (☎ 41258; Jl Yos Sudarso; d from 85,000Rp) A collection of basic bamboo huts on a rambling hillside overlooking a bay dotted with boats and islands all the way to the horizon. The restaurant is good. The staff is vaguely disinterested.

EATING & DRINKING

Rumah Makan Minang Indah (Jl Yos Sudarso; dishes from 8000Rp; 🕑 breakfast, lunch & dinner) A tasty Padang food joint with seafood tendencies.

Arto Moro (Jl Yos Sudarso; fried chicken & squid 10,000Rp; 🕑 breakfast, lunch & dinner) Located next to Bajo Dive Club, this funky two-storey place with warped floors and harbour views serves the best-value food in town. It's always packed with locals.

Pesona Bali (Jl Yos Sudarso; dishes from 15,000Rp; 🕑 breakfast, lunch & dinner) Faint Balinese echoes filter through this open-air dining room like the ocean breeze. The grilled whole snapper is delicious and an absolute steal at 25,000Rp.

Lounge (Jl Yos Sudarso; tapas from 20,000Rp; 🕑 breakfast, lunch & dinner) Across from Arto Moro is a sleek tapas and coffee bar with red lounges, Balinese art and (of course) amazing views. Tapas are exceptional, but servings are skimpy. And in grand coffee-house tradition, local hipsters tend the espresso machine (espresso from 18,000Rp).

Paradise Bar (Jl Yos Sudarso; 🕑 6pm-2am Fri & Sat) The staff here grill fish, and serve mixed drinks, cold beers and live music at Labuanbajo's only bar scene. If you are looking for a nightcap, and some conversation, you will almost certainly land here.

GETTING THERE & AWAY

Air

TransNusa/Trigana (code TGN; ☎ 41800; www.transnusa.co.id) flies daily to Denpasar. Purchase tickets at the airline office only, do so well in advance, and confirm your seat and departure time. In Flores, flight schedules shift with the wind.

Boat

The daily Labuanbajo–Sape ferry (27,000Rp, eight hours) usually leaves at 8am.

Pelni ships sail to Makassar (from 124,000Rp, two days) or Bima (from 59,000Rp, seven hours), Lembar (from 140,000Rp, two days) and Benoa (from 172,000Rp, two days). The **Pelni agent** (☎ 41106) is hard to find, tucked away on a side street northeast of town.

Bus

Buses leave for Ruteng (30,000Rp, four hours), Bajawa (70,000Rp, 10 hours) and even Ende (105,000Rp, 15 hours) at around 7am from the bus terminal 10km outside of town.

A car with a driver starts at 450,000Rp per day, including fuel. The driver will organise his own lodging, but you buy his meals.

Ruteng

☎ 0385 / pop 35,700

Ruteng, a highland market town, is simply a place to stretch your legs between bus trips. Compang Ruteng, 3km southwest, is a semi-traditional village, home to the local Manggarai people, and nearby Gunung Ranaka is an active volcano.

INFORMATION

BNI bank (Jl Kartini) Currency exchange, and an ATM.

Post office (Jl Dewi Sartika 6; 7am-2pm Mon-Sat)

Warnet Infokom.net (☎ 21604; Jl Pertiwi 1; per hr 5000Rp) Quick connection amid dusty environs.

SLEEPING & EATING

Losmen Agung (☎ 21080; Jl Waeces 10; d from 70,000Rp) Ditch town for this rustic rice-paddy setting with clean rooms.

Hotel Rima (☎ 22196; Jl A Yani 14; s/d 75,000/100,000Rp) A kitschy Swiss Alpine knockoff with clean, comfy rooms. Feels out of place, but still a good value.

Café Agape (Jl Bhayankari 8; mains 15,000Rp; breakfast, lunch & dinner) A coffee factory, with an attractive café that serves excellent espresso and a lovely *kwetiaw goreng* (fried flat noodles).

GETTING THERE & AWAY

Merpati (code MZ; ☎ 21197; www.merpati.co.id) flies three times a week to Kupang, but cancellations are frequent.

Buses to Labuanbajo (30,000Rp, four hours) leave every two hours, while those to Bajawa (40,000Rp, five hours) and Ende (70,000Rp, nine hours) leave around 7.30am. Take a bemo to the terminal (1000Rp), located 3.5km out of town. Tickets can be booked through hotels

Bajawa

☎ 0384

With a pleasant climate, and surrounded by forested volcanoes, Bajawa is a great base from which to explore dozens of traditional villages that are home to the Ngada people. Their fascinating architecture features *ngadhu* (carved poles supporting a conical thatched roof).

INFORMATION

BNI bank (Jl Pierre Tendean) Has an ATM.

Telkom office (☎ 21218; Jl Soekarno Hatta)

Tourist office (☎ 21554; Jl Soekarno Hatta; 8am-2pm Mon-Sat, until 11am Fri) Not much practical advice available.

SIGHTS & ACTIVITIES

Bena, 19km south of Bajawa on the flank of Gunung Inerie, is one of the most spectacular traditional villages in the area. **Nage** and **Wogo** are also interesting. Guides linger around hotels and can arrange day trips for 250,000Rp per person with transport, village entry fees and lunch.

SLEEPING & EATING

Edelweis (☎ 21345; Jl Ahmad Yani 76; d from 75,000Rp;) Nice gardens, great volcano views, very clean and owned by a friendly family who will boil water for a very welcome hot-water *mandi* in the morning. The manager, Ivan Botha, leads trips to traditional villages.

Hotel Korina (☎ 21162; Jl Ahmad Yani 81; d 75,000Rp) Across the road from the Edelweis is another tidy, family-run place with a range of rooms.

Villa Silverin (☎ 222 3865; Jl Bajawa; d from 150,000Rp) A shiny new place, on the road to Ende, with colonial panache, beckoning verandas and jaw-dropping views.

INDONESIA

Dito Restaurant (☎ 081 339 198600; Jl Ahmad Yani; mains 12,000Rp; ⏲ breakfast, lunch & dinner) Brand-new at the time of research, it's opposite the Camellia and just as good. The seafood *mie goreng* (fried noodles; 15,000Rp) are superb.

Camellia (☎ 21458; Jl Ahmad Yani 74; mains 15,000Rp; ⏲ breakfast, lunch & dinner) The dining room is too bright, but the food is delicious. Try the chicken *sate* (17,000Rp). It comes with a unique sweet, smoky pepper sauce. The guacamole rocks too.

GETTING THERE & AWAY

The Watujaji bus station is 3km south of town, but hotels arrange tickets and pick-ups. Buses to Labuanbajo (70,000Rp, 10 hours) leave around 7am. More frequent buses go to Ruteng (40,000Rp, five hours). Buses to Ende (44,000Rp, five hours) leave at 7am and noon. Buses to Riung (18,000Rp, three hours) leave at 8am and noon.

Bemo and trucks to surrounding villages depart from the Jl Basuki Rahmat terminal.

Riung

Fans of laid-back coastal mangrove villages will love Riung, but the 21 offshore islands of the **Seventeen Islands Marine Park** (nobody said governments made sense), with luscious white-sand beaches and excellent snorkelling, are the real attraction. The park entrance fee is 10,000Rp per person plus 5000Rp per boat. Day trips (250,000Rp for up to six people) are easily arranged in Riung.

Pondok SVD (d from 150,000Rp; ❄), run by missionaries, offers the best rooms in town, with nice touches like reading lights, soap, and towels. But the food is pricey.

There are a scattering of budget places on the road into town and clustered around the harbour. None stands out. **Rumah Makan Murak Muriah** (dishes from 10,000Rp; ⏲ breakfast, lunch & dinner) serves tasty local fare.

Daily buses run between Riung and Bajawa (18,000Rp, three hours), leaving Bajawa at 8am and noon. Buses from Ende (26,000Rp, two hours) go daily at 6am. Otherwise take a 1pm bus to Mbay (15,000Rp, 1½ hours) and a bemo to Riung.

Ende

☎ 0381 / pop 81,600

Muggy, dusty and crowded, this south-coast port's ultimate saving grace is its spectacular setting. The eye-catching cones of Gunung Meja and Gunung Iya loom over the city, while barrels roll in continuously from the Sawu Sea and crash over a coastline of black sand and blue stones.

Soekarno was exiled here during the 1930s, where he reinvented himself as a truly horrid playwright. Thank God that the whole national revolutionary hero-thing worked out.

INFORMATION

Bank Danamon (Jl Soekarno) Changes money and the ATM will allow you to withdraw larger amounts than some others.
Telkom office (Jl Kelimutu 5) Internet access.
Tourism office (☎ 21303; Jl Soekarno 4; ⏲ 8am-1pm Mon-Sat) Enthusiastic staff.

SIGHTS

Meander through the aromatic **waterfront market** (Jl Pasar) with the requisite fruit pyramids and an astonishing fish section including giant tuna and sharks. The adjacent **ikat market** (cnr Jl Pabean & Jl Pasar) sells hand-woven tapestries from across Flores and Sumba.

History buffs can visit Soekarno's house of exile, now **Musium Bung Karno** (Jl Perwira; admission by donation; ⏲ 7am-noon Mon-Sat); most of the original period furnishings remain. This is where he penned the epic *Frankenstein*-inspired *Doctor Satan*.

SLEEPING & EATING

Hotel Ikhlas (☎ 21695; Jl Ahmad Yani 69; s/d from 25,000/40,000Rp) High quality (from a backpacker's perspective) for a song, this is the best choice in town. Rooms are clean, service is tiptop, and the restaurant serves both Western and Indo fare (also extremely cheaply). Choose one of the garden rooms with a red tiled terrace and views of magnificent Gunung Meja peaking over the neighbours' tin roofs.

Hotel Safari (☎ 21997; Jl Ahmad Yani 65; d from 60,000Rp; ❄) Located next door to Ikhlas, this place leaves a good first impression, and there are some decent rooms, but they just aren't clean enough. You'll need to add 90,000Rp for air-con.

Restoran Istana Bambu (☎ 21921; Jl Kemakmuran 30; dishes 20,000Rp; ⏲ breakfast, lunch & dinner) Near the sea, Bambu serves top-notch Chinese seafood, as well as freshly baked bread and cakes.

GETTING THERE & AWAY

Air

TransNusa/Trigana (☎ 24222; www.transnusa.co.id) has scheduled flights from Ende to Denpasar five times a week. But during our research trip these flights were suspended indefinitely. **Merpati** (code MZ; ☎ 21355; www.merpati.co.id) flies from Ende to Kupang three times a week.

Boat

ASDP (☎ 22007) operates a Waingapu ferry (42,500Rp, six hours) every Thursday. There are also twice-weekly services to Kupang (58,000Rp, seven hours).

Pelni (☎ 21043; Jl Kathedral 2; 🕒 8am-noon & 2-4pm Mon-Sat) sails fortnightly from Ende to Waingapu (from 51,000Rp, two days), Lembar (from 140,000Rp, two days) and Benoa (from 264,000Rp, two days).

Bus

Buses to eastern Flores leave from Terminal Wolowana, 5km from town. Buses to Moni (14,000Rp, two hours) operate from 6am to 2pm. Maumere–bound coaches (37,000Rp, five hours) leave at 7am, 9am and 4pm.

Westbound buses leave from Terminal Ndao, 2km north of town, to Bajawa (44,000Rp, five hours), Ruteng (70,000Rp, nine hours) and Labuanbajo (105,000Rp, 15 hours).

Kelimutu

One of the most awesome sights in all of Indonesia, sacred Mt Kelimutu (1640m), with its trio of multihued crater lakes, will make you glad you braved the Trans-Flores Hwy. During research one was turquoise, the other dark green and the third lake was black. From the rim, colours are so dense that the lakes' water seems the thickness of paint. Minerals in the water account for the chameleonic colour scheme – although the turquoise lake never changes, the other lakes can fluctuate to yellow, orange and red.

Most visitors glimpse them at dawn, leaving nearby Moni at 4am. But afternoons are usually empty and peaceful at the top, and when the sun is high the colours sparkle. Clouds are your only obstacle, and they can drift in at anytime.

Public transport is no longer available, but you can hire an *ojek* (25,000Rp to 35,000Rp one way, 45,000Rp to 60,000Rp return) or chartered bemo (100,000Rp to 200,000Rp) from Moni. Negotiate! The park entry post, halfway up the road, charges a 2000Rp entry fee.

You can walk the 13.5km down through the forest and back to Moni in about 2½ hours. There's a short cut from just beside the entry post, which comes out by the hot springs and waterfall.

Moni

Moni is a picturesque village sprinkled with rice fields, ringed by soaring volcanic peaks, with distant sea views. It's a slow-paced, easy-going town that serves as a gateway to Kelimutu, and the cool, comfortable climate invites long walks, and a few extra days. But there are no banks and only one telephone. About 2km west of Moni is the turn-off to Kelimutu. The Monday market, held on the soccer pitch, is a major local draw and a good place to snare *ikat*.

SLEEPING & EATING

Moni has a cluster of cheapies to choose from.

Sylvester Homestay (d from 40,000Rp) A very basic, upstart homestay across from Arwanti Homestay. It's clean with tiled baths and a big bed. If you stay here you can watch the fun-loving owner weave *ikat* with her sister.

Watugana (s/d 40,000/60,000Rp) Clean, serviceable rooms, but it's across from the pool hall so noise drifts in late.

Maria Inn (d from 50,000Rp) Nice setting, back from the road. Rooms have Western toilets, 'new beds', and tiled verandas with garden and mountain views.

Sao Ria Bungalows (d from 75,000Rp) A string of bamboo bungalows – about 1.5km west of Moni, off the Kelimutu turn-off – with tremendous road appeal, and a magical panorama. Closer inspection reveals that the floors at this state-run place are warped, the garden needs work and the beds are stone. Here's another vote against government administration.

Palm Bungalows (☎ 081 339 147983; d from 80,000Rp) This is your secluded sweet spot, a ramshackle bungalow on a farmlike property off a dirt road with incredible mountain views. The dusty turquoise stream that skirts the property sings a tremendous lullaby and offers an even better wake-up call. Arnol, the manager, is also a driver and tour guide who rents motorbikes. His prices are the best in town.

Arwanti Homestay (bungalows 100,000Rp) It's a small place with two sweet, two-room bungalows set next to a gurgling brook. The roadside restaurant is inviting and road-weary travellers will be glad to have the owners arrange *ojek* shuttles to the crater.

Most homestays provide simple meals, but for variety check out the well-perched **Chenty Restaurant & Pub** (mains from 10,000Rp; ⌚ breakfast, lunch & dinner) and the cavernous **Flores Sare Inn** (mains 15,000Rp; ⌚ breakfast, lunch & dinner).

GETTING THERE & AWAY

For Ende (14,000Rp, two hours), buses start around 7am. Other buses come from Ende through to Maumere (23,000Rp, three hours) at about 9am or 10am, then later at around 7pm. Additional buses and trucks leave on Monday (market day).

Maumere

☎ 0382 / pop 49,200

Maumere lacks the looks of Ende and Labuanbajo, but it has the second-most connected airport on the island, and unless you are doubling back west by car, you'll likely do some time here. It isn't completely charmless. Beach bungalows line the coast, the recovering reefs make a decent diversion, and some of Flores' best *ikat* weavers live in traditional villages outside of town.

ORIENTATION & INFORMATION

The airport is 3km out, and a taxi there costs 10,000Rp. Bemo around town cost 2000Rp.

BNI bank (Jl Soekarno Hatta 4) Best rates in town; ATM.
Comtel (☎ 22132; Jl Bandeng 1; per hr 12,000Rp; ⌚ 9am-9pm) High-speed internet access.
Post office (Jl Pos; ⌚ 8am-2pm Mon-Sat)
Telkom office (Jl Soekarno Hatta 5)
Tourist office (☎ 21652; cnr Jl Melati & Jl Wairklau; ⌚ 8am-1pm Mon-Sat) Not a great resource.

SLEEPING & EATING

The harbour doubles as restaurant row, with a string of inexpensive seafood and Indonesian kitchens.

Hotel Wini Rai (☎ 21388; Jl Gajah Mada 50; s/d 44,000/65,000Rp; ❄) There's a wide variety of rooms here, and the budget choices are decent enough for a night or two.

Gardena Hotel (☎ 22644; Jl Patirangga 28; s/d from 70,000/100,000Rp; ❄) Touted by both guides and travellers as Maumere's top choice. It's clean and the service is great.

Hotel Maiwali (☎ 21220; Jl Raja Don Tomas 40; d from 90,000Rp) Like a bad dream, or maybe a horror movie, this seems like a nice hotel with decent rooms until the lights go off at bedtime and the roaches take over. Not good!

Rumah Makan Bunaken (☎ 081 33944 8814; mains from 10,000Rp; ⌚ breakfast, lunch & dinner) So spicy it hurts, this is another popular waterfront seafood café. Thankfully, they realise that with food this hot, cold Bintang is mandatory.

Ikan Bakar Jakarta (☎ 081 2379 5559; dishes 12,000Rp; ⌚ breakfast, lunch & dinner) Right by the port, this cheap and tasty Javanese joint serves up chilli-tinged squid, chicken and shrimp. Bring your own beer.

GETTING THERE & AWAY

Merpati (code MZ; ☎ 21342; www.merpati.co.id) flies to Denpasar, Kupang and Waingapu three times weekly. **TransNusa/Trigana** (code TGN; ☎ 23821; www.transnusa.co.id) advertises flights to Denpasar, but those flights were suspended indefinitely when we visited. Check for updates.

Pelni (☎ 21013; Jl M Sugiyo Pranoto 4) sails fortnightly to Makassar (from 131,000Rp, two days) and Kalimantan, and to Kalabahi (from 64,000Rp, two days) and Kupang (from 166,000Rp) in the other direction.

Buses and bemo travel east to Larantuka (32,000Rp, four hours), Waiara and Wodong, and depart from the Lokaria (or Timur) terminal, about 3km east of town. Westbound buses, such as those heading to Ende (37,000Rp, five hours) via Moni (23,000Rp, three hours), leave from the Ende Terminal 1.5km southwest of town.

Buses often endlessly cruise town searching for passengers. Hotels can arrange pick-up.

Around Maumere

A small army of expert artisans lays in wait in the weaving village of **Sikka**, 26km south of Maumere. Along the north coast, east of Maumere, is where you'll find the best beaches and healthiest reefs.

Waiara, 9km east of Maumere, was once considered the gateway to the Maumere 'sea gardens' before the 1992 tsunami wreaked havoc on the reefs. They are now well into recovery mode, and it's a nice spot to linger in or out of the water. **Sea World Club** (0382-21570; www.sea-world-club.com; s/d from US$15/20; ❄) is worth a splurge. It charges US$50 for two dives. To get there, catch any Talibura- or Larantuka-bound bus from Maumere (2000Rp).

The beaches of **Ahuwair** and **Waiterang**, 24km and 26km east of Maumere, ooze tranquillity. **Sunset Cottages** (bungalows 40,000Rp) has coconut wood and bamboo beachside bungalows, snorkelling trips to nearby islands, and fantastic fish dinners.

A bit further, you'll find **Ankermi** (☎ 0382-21100; s/d 30,000/35,000Rp), a mellow Swiss-Indo-owned place set back from shore, with nice food, comfy hammocks and a small dive school, and the simple **Wodong Beach Cottages** (s/d 35,000/40,000Rp). Come via a Larantuka-bound bus or bemo from Maumere's Lokaria terminal (3000Rp, 35 minutes).

Larantuka

☎ 0383

This busy little port, and former Portuguese enclave, nestles at the base of Gunung Ili Mandiri on the eastern tip of Flores, separated from the Solor and Alor archipelagos by a narrow strait. Most people come simply to hop a ferry.

The BRI bank will change money, but their 'forthcoming' ATM was still MIA.

SLEEPING & EATING

Hotel Rulies (☎ 21198; Jl Yos Sudarso 40; s/d/tr from 40,000/60,000/80,000Rp) A popular budget hotel with clean rooms, private *mandi* and saggy beds.

Hotel Fortuna II (☎ 21383; s/d 50,000/75,000Rp; air-con) The best of the three Fortunas. Rooms are spacious, and the air-con variety (from 82,000Rp) are the best in town.

Rumah Makan Nirwana (Jl Niaga; mains 14,000Rp; breakfast, lunch & dinner) It's a modest Chinese-Indo establishment, but the fish is fresh and the portions are filling.

Warung set up in the evening along Jl Niaga.

GETTING THERE & AWAY

Ferries to Kupang (50,000Rp, 13 hours) leave Monday and Wednesday at 1pm from Waibulan, 4km southwest of Larantuka (by bemo 1500Rp). They leave Kupang on Thursday and Sunday afternoons.

Wooden boats to Adonara (15,000Rp), Solor (5000Rp) and Lembata (25,000Rp, four hours) leave from the pier in the centre of town at 7.30am and noon.

Pelni ships call at Larantuka on their Labuanbajo–Papua and Kupang–Makassar trips.

Regular buses run between Maumere and Larantuka (30,000Rp, four hours). The main bus station is 5km west of town (2000Rp by bemo), but you can pick buses up in the town centre.

Solor & Alor Archipelagos

This remote, mountainous chain of volcanic islands, separated by swift, narrow straits from the eastern end of Flores, is reached by ferry from Larantuka. Lembata, in the Solor chain, is home to the traditional whaling village of Lamalera. Alor, home to head-hunters only 50 years ago, is protected by rich coral reefs that attract divers.

LEMBATA

The sleepy commercial centre of Lewoleba is overshadowed by the smoking cone, **Gunung Ili Api**. Lewoleba has no banks, but if you're stuck you can exchange money at the Flores Jaya shop opposite the post office. Stay at the central **Hotel Lewoleba** (☎ 41012; Jl Awololong 15; s/d 45,000/60,000Rp; air-con), or the long running Dutch-Indo-owned **Lile Ile homestay** (s/d 35,000/45,000Rp), with stunning volcano views.

On the south coast, **Lamalera** is an isolated whaling village, where locals hunt whales with spears, rowboats and prayer. Being a small-scale subsistence activity, the hunting is considered legal. Villagers take occasional visitors out on a hunt during the May–October whaling season. It's as harrowing as it sounds.

A daily truck bumps from the port of Lembata to Lamalera along a very poor 65km road (12,000Rp; 3½ hours). Occasional passenger ferries run between Larantuka and Lewoleba, as well. Check at the harbour.

Ferries to Kalabahi (Alor) depart from Lewoleba twice a week. They stop for the night at Balauring in eastern Lembata before continuing to Kalabahi (51,000Rp, 13 hours).

ALOR

☎ 0386 / pop 170,000

Alor, the final link in an island chain that extends east of Java, is as remote, rugged and beautiful as it gets. Thanks to impenetrable terrain, the 170,000 inhabitants are fractured into 50 tribes and 14 languages, and they were still taking heads into the 1950s. Alor is also famous for its strange, bronze *moko* drums (see boxed text, opposite), and superb diving, which can be arranged through **La Petite Kepa** (www.la-petite-kepa.com; 2 tanks US$65) on Pulau Kepa. You can also stay with La Petite Kepa on this tranquil offshore islet (from 75,000Rp), or contact **Dive Alor** (www.divealor.com) in Kupang (see p297).

Kalabahi, located on a sweeping, palm-fringed bay, is the main port. Bring ample

ALOR'S STRANGE MOKO DRUMS

Thousands of hourglass-shaped bronze drums known as *moko* have been found mysteriously buried all over Alor. They were once traded for human heads and are still highly prized in wedding dowries, sometimes indebting a family for a generation. Researchers believe the drums hail from Vietnam's ancient Dongson culture and were brought by spice traders. Locals say *moko* grew from the earth.

cash as exchange rates are criminal. The views at **Hotel Adi Dharma** (☎ 21280; Jl Martadinata 12; s/d from 57,000/77,000Rp), near the pier, make it the most popular stop.

Merpati (code MZ; ☎ 21041; www.merpati.co.id) has a dinky 12-seater that flies four times a week to Kupang. Book in advance.

The Kupang ferry (40,500Rp, 20 hours) leaves on Wednesday and Sunday at noon. Ferries to Lewoleba (51,000Rp, 14 hours) and Larantuka (42,500Rp, 16 hours) leave Thursday and Sunday at 8am. East Timor–bound folks should take the 8pm Tuesday ferry to Atapupu (22,700Rp, eight hours).

Pelni ships call fortnightly at Kalabahi and sail to Kupang, Ende, Lombok, Bali, and Makassar (Sulawesi).

WEST TIMOR

West Timor is still off the tourism radar, but with rugged countryside, empty beaches and scores of traditional villages, it's an undiscovered gem. Thanks to the recent calm nerves in historically politically tense East Timor, and the accessibility of Kupang, Nusa Tenggara's top metropolis, traffic on the inexpensive East Timor visa run is picking up. But venture further afield, where animist traditions persist alongside tribal dialects, and where *ikat*-clad, betel-nut-chewing chiefs govern beehive-shaped hut villages, and you may find that, in Timor, even Bahasa Indonesia can be a foreign tongue.

GETTING THERE & AWAY

Air

Merpati connects Kupang with Denpasar (daily), and cities throughout Nusa Tenggara (regularly). Wings Air flies the Kupang–Surabaya route daily. From there you can connect to Jakarta. A good way to explore eastern Nusa Tenggara is to fly directly from Bali to Kupang, and island-hop from there (see p297).

Boat

ASDP (☎ 0380-890420; Bolok), based in Kupang, has regular car-and-passenger ferries throughout east Nusa Tenggara. Ferries run from Kupang to Larantuka (Flores), Kalabahi (Alor), Rote and Waingapu (Sumba) via Sabu and/or Ende. From Atapupu, near Atambua in West Timor, a ferry runs once a week to/from Kalabahi. The routes are fairly constant but schedules are constantly changing; check on arrival in Kupang.

Pelni passenger ships *Awu, Dobonsolo, Sirimau, Pangarango, Tatamailau* and *Kelimutus* connect Kupang with Maumere, Ende, Kalabahi, Larantuka, Waingapu and onward destinations such as Surabaya and Makassar.

GETTING AROUND

The good main highway is surfaced all the way from Kupang to East Timor, though the buses are of the cramped, crowded, thumping-disco variety. Away from the highway, roads are improving but can be impassable in the wet season.

Kupang

☎ 0380 / pop 311,300

Kupang, the capital of Nusa Tenggara Timur (NTT), is noisy, energetic, scruffy, bustling with commerce, and a fun place to hang around for a few days. Captain Bligh did after his emasculating mutiny problem.

ORIENTATION

Kupang's El Tari airport is 15km east of town. Taxi fare into town is fixed at 50,000Rp. By public transport, turn left out of the terminal and walk 1km to the junction with the main highway. From there bemo to the city cost 2000Rp. Around town, the tricked-out, bass-booming bemo cost 1500Rp.

INFORMATION

The NTT Tourist Office is out in the sticks near the bus station – it's not worth the trip.

BNI bank (Jl Sumatera) Has fair rates and an ATM.

L'Avalon (Jl Sumatera; www.geocities.com/lavalon_edwin/) This bar-cum-tourism-information-centre has the best internet service around.

Main post office (Jl Palapa 1) Accepts poste restante mail and has internet facilities.

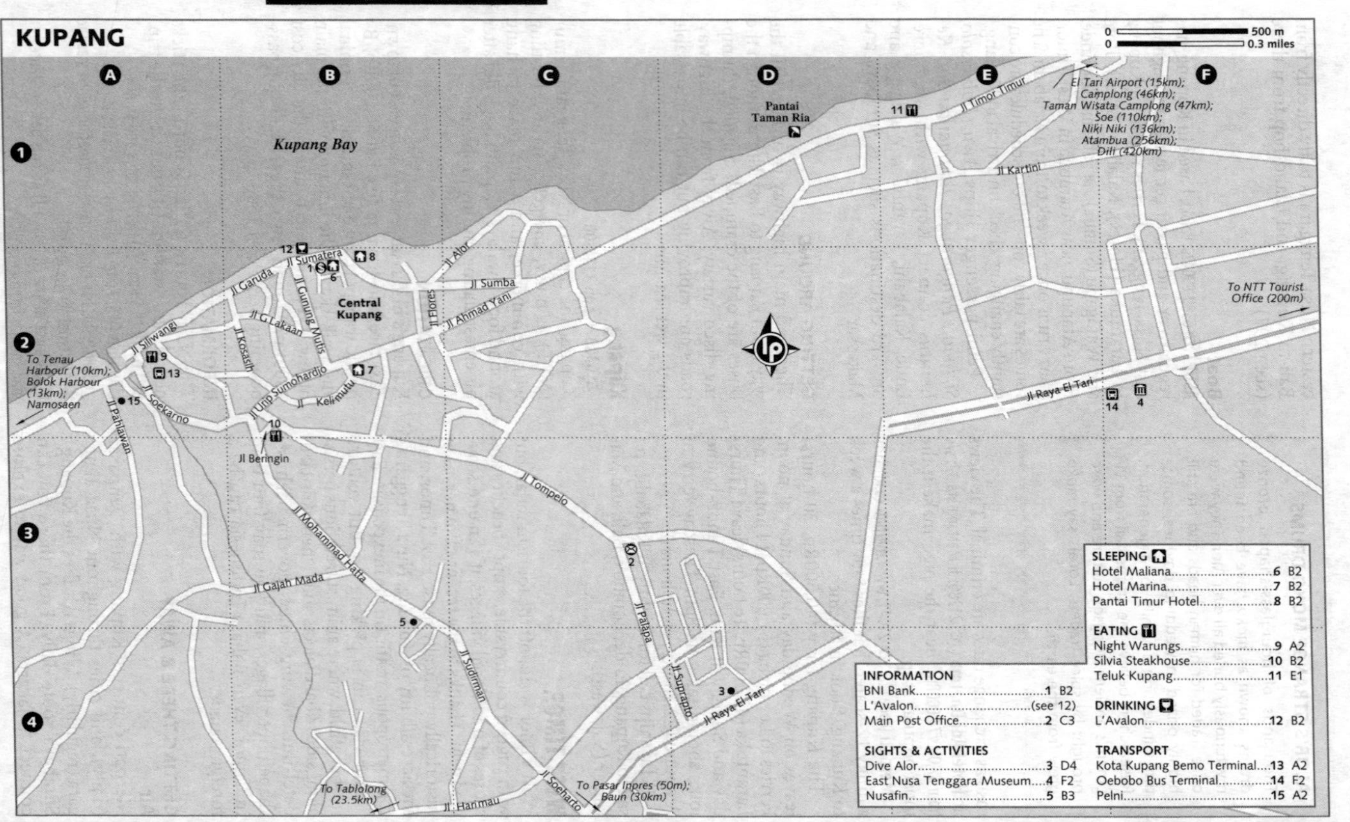
KUPANG
0 500 m
0 0.3 miles
Kupang Bay
Pantai Taman Ria
Central Kupang
El Tari Airport (15km); Camplong (46km); Taman Wisata Camplong (47km); Soe (110km); Niki Niki (136km); Atambua (256km); Dili (420km)
To NTT Tourist Office (200m)
To Tenau Harbour (10km); Bolok Harbour (13km); Namosaen
To Tablolong (23.5km)
To Pasar Inpres (50m); Baun (30km)
Jl Timor Timur
Jl Kartini
Jl Raya El Tari
Jl Sumatera
Jl Garuda
Jl Gunung Mutis
Jl Alor
Jl Sumba
Jl Flores
Jl Ahmad Yani
Jl G Lakaan
Jl Siliwangi
Jl Kosasih
Jl Urip Sumohardjo
Jl Kelimutu
Jl Soekarno
Jl Pahlawan
Jl Beringin
Jl Tompelo
Jl Mohammad Hatta
Jl Gajah Mada
Jl Palapa
Jl Suprapto
Jl Sudirman
Jl Soeharto
Jl Harimau
SLEEPING
Hotel Maliana 6 B2
Hotel Marina 7 B2
Pantai Timur Hotel 8 B2
EATING
Night Warungs 9 A2
Silvia Steakhouse 10 B2
Teluk Kupang 11 E1
DRINKING
L'Avalon 12 B2
TRANSPORT
Kota Kupang Bemo Terminal 13 A2
Oebobo Bus Terminal 14 F2
Pelni 15 A2
INFORMATION
BNI Bank 1 B2
L'Avalon (see 12)
Main Post Office 2 C3
SIGHTS & ACTIVITIES
Dive Alor 3 D4
East Nusa Tenggara Museum 4 F2
Nusafin 5 B3

SIGHTS

East Nusa Tenggara Museum (Jl Raya El Tari; admission free; 8am-3pm Mon-Sat) is worth a look for its dusty collection of crafts and artefacts. But the rambling **Pasar Inpres**, the main market, is more energizing. It's southeast of the centre.

TOURS

Many fascinating traditional villages can be visited in West Timor, but Bahasa Indonesia, let alone English, is often not spoken, so a local guide is necessary. Kupang is a decent base for dive trips around Timor and Alor. Try **Dive Alor** (821154; www.divealor.com; Jl Raya El Tari 19) or **Nusafin** (821086; Jl Sudirman 48).

SLEEPING

Hotel Marina (822566; Jl Ahmad Yani 79; d from 60,000Rp;) The economy rooms have shared bathrooms, but the air-con rooms (from 110,000Rp) are a decent deal.

Hotel Maliana (821879; Jl Sumatera 35; d 70,000Rp;) A low-rise, spotless motel, set back from the sea with helpful staff.

Pantai Timur Hotel (831651; Jl Sumatera; economy s/d 75,000/100,000Rp;) On the seafront, with good-value economy rooms, and better ones in the standard class.

EATING & DRINKING

In case you're wondering, *RW* is dog meat, a Kupang speciality that sizzles endlessly in local *warung*. We hear the best are around the Kota Kupang bemo terminal.

Teluk Kupang (833985; Jl Timor Timur; dishes from 15,000Rp; breakfast, lunch & dinner) The décor is awful, but the delicious *ikan waku* (spicy fish) is why you're here.

Silvia Steakhouse (Jl Beringin 3; steaks 30,000Rp; lunch & dinner) This almost stylish place has a frighteningly extensive Western menu, but the house speciality is steak, served with cold beer.

L'Avalon (832256; Jl Sumatera; www.geocities.com/lavalon_edwin/) The design motif at this tiny beachside bar would be considered ramshackle/tumbledown, but Edwin, the owner, is keeping it together with Band-Aids, rubber bands and personality, and it is a superb diversion.

GETTING THERE & AWAY

Air

Merpati (code MZ; 833111; www.merpati.co.id) flies daily from Kupang to Denpasar, and also serves cities throughout Nusa Tenggara. **TransNusa/Trigana** (code TGN; 822555; www.transnusa.co.id) flies to Denpasar five times a week. **Wings Air** (code 1W; 882155; www.lionair.co.id) operates flights to Surabaya. From there you can connect to Jakarta.

Boat

Pelni (821944; Jl Pahlawan 3) ships leave from Tenau, 10km southwest of Kupang, for Maumere (from 166,000Rp, two days), Kalabahi (from 72,000Rp, two days), Larantuka (from 105,000Rp, two days) and Waingapu (from 154,000Rp, two days), and many other ports, including those in Sulawesi and West Papua.

Ferries leave from Bolok, 13km southwest of Kupang. **ASDP** (890420) has ferries to Larantuka, Kalabahi and Ende. The Ende ferry continues on to Waingapu (Sumba) and another ferry runs to Kupang–Sabu–Waingapu. Most ferries sail once or twice a week.

Bus

Long-distance buses depart from Oebobo Terminal on the east side of town (take bemo 10 to get there). Departures include: Soe (25,000Rp, three hours), Niki Niki (25,000Rp, 3½ hours), Kefamenanu (36,000Rp, 5½ hours) and Atambua (52,000Rp, eight hours). Bemo to villages around Kupang go from the central Kota Kupang Terminal.

See below for information on getting to East Timor.

GETTING TO EAST TIMOR

Take a bus from Kupang to Atambua (52,000Rp, eight hours), a bemo to the Motoain border and a bus to Dili. Or book a more comfortable Kupang–Dili tourist bus (170,000Rp, 12 hours), run by **Timor Tour & Travel** (Dili 333 1014; Rua Quinze de Outubro 17; Kupang 0380-881 543; Jl Timor Raya 8). The 30-day entry visa to East Timor is US$30.

This route is also the cheapest way to renew your Indonesian visa from Nusa Tenggara; once in East Timor, you can get another 30-day visa at the Indonesian embassy. It costs a lot less than getting back to Bali and flying to Singapore or Kuala Lumpur.

See p141 for information on doing the trip in the reverse direction.

INDONESIA

Around Kupang

Head to the great **Tablolong** beaches, 27km southwest of Kupang. The small islands of **Pulau Semau** and **Pulau Kera**, just off the coast, are also interesting. Grab a local boat from Namosaen, west of the city.

Baun, a tiny village in the hills 30km southeast of Kupang, is an *ikat*-weaving hot spot with a few colonial edifices. Visit the *rumah raja,* the last raja's house, occupied by his widow.

Camplong, a mellow foothill town 46km from Kupang, is home to the **Taman Wisata Camplong**, a forest reserve that has caves and a spring-fed swimming pool.

Soe

☎ 0368

The traditional, beehive-like *lopo* (hut) villages and the indigenous Dawan people who live in them are the attraction of this modernising market town 800m above sea level. On the outskirts, ubiquitous *lopo* rise from bush reminiscent of Australia. Government has deemed the *lopo* a health hazard (they're smoky and lack much ventilation) and is in the process of replacing them with modern homes. Once received, the Dawan simply build new *lopo* behind them. It's a great system. Village tours are easily arranged in Soe.

The **tourist information centre** (☎ 21149; Jl Diponegoro) can arrange guides. **BNI** (Jl Diponegoro) and **BRI** (Jl Hatta) branches have ATMs, which is good because currency exchange rates are low.

Hotel Cahaya (☎ 21087; Jl Kartini 7; s/d 35,000/75,000Rp) is a cheap central choice.

At **Nope's Royal Homestay** (☎ 21711; Jl Merpati 8; bungalows 75,000Rp) you can bed down with royalty in a well-kept bungalow within the family compound of a former raja (the owner), who is also a well-respected tour guide and speaks perfect English.

The Haumeni bus station is 4km west of town (by bemo 2000Rp). Regular buses run from Soe to Kupang (25,000Rp, three hours), Kefamenanu (20,000Rp, 2½ hours) and Oinlasi (9000Rp, 1½ hours). Assorted bemo cover Niki Niki (8000Rp) and Kapan (5000Rp) routes.

Around Soe

Market days attract villagers from miles in every direction, who arrive wearing traditional dress and sell exquisite hand-woven *ikat*, carvings and masks. This is why you travel. The Tuesday market at **Oinlasi**, 51km from Soe, is one of the biggest and best in West Timor, and the Wednesday market at **Niki Niki**, 34km east of Soe, is a lively, more accessible, second choice.

The main attraction around Soe is **Boti**, a traditional village presided over by a self-styled raja who is something of a fundamentalist animist. Traditional dress code and hairstyle is enforced, and locals maintain strict adherence to *adat* (customary law), a devotion that has proven almost completely immune to Christian missionaries. The unique village has become an attraction, and locals are used to tourists, and even receive (gasp!) the occasional tour bus. Take a bus from Oinlasi for 2km to the Boti turn-off. Then hike the 9km rocky road to Boti. Per raja's orders, bring a guide from Soe who speaks the local dialect. You can stay overnight with the enigmatic **raja** (all-inclusive 50,000Rp).

Kefamenanu

☎ 0388 / pop 30,500

Kefamenanu (Kefa) is another cool, quiet town with a few colonial buildings, and a passionate weaving tradition. Prepare to haggle with the *ikat* cartel. They will find you. **Temkessi**, 50km northeast of Kefa, is a spectacular traditional village. The only way in is a small passage between two huge rocks. Bahasa Indonesia won't get you far, so bring a guide. Kefa is also the gateway to the poor and isolated East Timorese enclave of Oecussi. The best overnight option is **Hotel Cendana** (☎ 31168; Jl Sonbay; d with private mandi from 40,000Rp; ❄), which can help arrange a chartered *mikrolet* for the two-hour ride across the border (100,000Rp, two hours).

Atambua

☎ 0389 / pop 37,000

Atambua is the major town on the overland Dili–Kupang route, and home to some pro-Jakarta militiamen who fled now-independent East Timor with blood on their hands. In 2000, after East Timor's independence, three UN workers were murdered here by the pro-Jakarta militia, and riots broke out in 2005. Thankfully, there's no reason to stop here, as you can now make the trip to East Timor nonstop (see boxed text, p297). **Atapupu**, 25km away, is a port with a weekly ferry to Kalabahi (Alor).

If you must overnight (perhaps you want to visit the nearby villages of **Kletek**, **Kamanasa** and **Bolan** where flying foxes soar), stay at **Hotel Nusantara Dua** (☎ 21773; Jl Kasimo; d from 85,000Rp).

Timor Tour & Travel (☎ 22292; Jl Sukarno 43) arranges shuttle buses to Kupang and Dili.

SUMBA

According to local legend, humankind first made landfall on earth by climbing down a huge celestial ladder from heaven to Sumba – a dry, lowland isle made of limestone and covered in grasslands. Broken off the archipelago's southeastern arc, in the Sawu Sea, Sumba has kept to itself ever since, and although Christianity has seeped in, tribal traditions – such as *marapu*, a religious belief system that revolves around ancestral spirits, bloody sacrificial funeral rites, hand-carved tombs, divine *ikat* weaving, and the use of horses for status, wealth and to score a hot wife – remain strong and pure. Generational tribal tensions also simmer beneath the surface, and are recalled every year during western Sumba's Pasola festivals (see opposite), when mock battles between mounted warriors often descend into actual violence.

Most of the 540,000 residents live in comparatively moist and fertile West Sumba, and though some Bahasa Indonesia is spoken throughout the island, six tribal languages are more prevalent, which makes this often overlooked island even more appealing to the intrepid wanderer.

GETTING THERE & AWAY

Air

Merpati flies to Maumere and Denpasar three times a week from Waingapu, four times a week from Tambolaka in West Sumba to Maumere, and three times weekly to Denpasar. Schedules change frequently, so book flights as soon as you land here and reconfirm before departure.

Boat

Waingapu is well serviced by ASDP ferries from Ende and Aimere on Flores. Connecting ferries to/from Kupang operate via Ende, and the ship to Sabu stops at Aimere en route.

Pelni has useful services from Waingapu to Ende, and on to Laruntuka, Alor and Benoa, Bali.

Waingapu

☎ 0387 / pop 50,500

Sumba's gateway town has grown up from a dusty trading post to an urbanizing commercial centre. But just like in the old days business revolves around dyewoods, timber and the island's prized horses. You're here to explore the surrounding villages.

> **PASOLA FESTIVAL – SUMBA AT WAR**
>
> The thrilling, often gruesome mock battles between spear-hurling horsemen during Sumba's Pasola festival are a must for travellers passing through Nusa Tenggara in February and March. The high-energy pageant aims to placate the spirits and restore harmony with the spilling of blood. Happily, though, blunt spears have been used in recent decades to make the affair less lethal. The ritualistic war kicks off when a sea worm called *nyale* washes up on shore, a phenomenon that also starts the planting season. Call Waingapu or Waikabubak hotels to find out the latest schedules. The festival is generally held in the Lamboya and Kodi districts in February, and at Wanokaka and Gaura in March.

ORIENTATION & INFORMATION

Waingapu spreads from the harbour in the north, 1.5km southeast to the main market and bus station. Taxis from the airport into town, 6km away, cost 15,000Rp. There's still no internet access on Sumba.

BNI bank (Jl Ampera) Near the market, has an ATM that accepts most cards.

Post office (Jl Hasanuddin) Near the harbour.

Telkom office (Jl Tjut Nya Dien)

SLEEPING & EATING

Most hotels are in the new part of Waingapur, near the bus station. Cheap rooms are rare.

Hotel Elvin (☎ 61462; Jl Ahmad Yani 73; s/d from 55,000/66,000Rp; ❄) The air-con wing (from 140,000Rp) has been renovated and all those rooms have appealing verandas. But the budget wing is also nice enough and worth considering.

Hotel Merlin (☎ 61300; Jl Panjaitan 25; s/d from 88,000/110,000Rp; ❄) Rooms are stylish and clean, with 4th-floor views of Flores on clear days, but it's on the noisiest street in town.

Rumah Makan Restu Ibu (Jl Ir Juanda 1; dishes from 8000Rp; 🕑 breakfast, lunch & dinner) It has been around a long time, serving Indo's greatest hits.

INDONESIA

Steak House (☎ 61751; Kompek Ruko; mains to 25,000Rp; ⏰ breakfast, lunch & dinner) This tasty place has grilled T-bones, fish and chips, *nasi goreng*, cappuccino, a rather harsh 'vodka', and a lot more.

GETTING THERE & AWAY

Air

Merpati (code MZ; ☎ 61323; www.merpati.co.id; Jl Soekarno 4) flies four times a week to Maumere and three times weekly to Denpasar.

Boat

Schedules change frequently, so check at the **ASDP office** (☎ 61963; Jl Adamalik 85).

A ferry leaves Waingapu for Aimere at midnight on Monday (60,000Rp, six hours). A ship also leaves Waingapu for Ende (42,500Rp, six hours) on Friday at 7pm and returns from Ende on Friday at 9am. Ferries run to Sabu (32,000Rp, 17 hours) on Saturday at noon, arriving Sunday at 5am and continuing to Kupang. Pelni ships leave from the Dermaga dock, west of town (by bemo 2500Rp). One ship links Waingapu with Ende and Kupang. Another route stops in Ende then travels to Larantuka, Alor and Benoa (Bali).

Bus

Eastbound buses to Meolo, Rende and Baing leave from the terminal near the market. The new West Sumba terminal is 5km west of town. Buses to Waikabubak (40,000Rp, four hours) leave here at 7am, 8am, noon and 3pm. Book at the hotels or the agencies opposite the bus station.

Around Waingapu

Several traditional villages in the southeast can be visited from Waingapu by bus and bemo. The stone tombs are impressive, and the area produces some of Sumba's best *ikat*. Almost every village gatekeeper will produce a dusty visitor book to sign. Small donations are expected.

Just 3km southeast of town, **Prailiu** is a busy *ikat*-weaving centre that's worth a peek. There are also some interesting traditional thatched huts and carved concrete tombs.

Located about 7km away from unspectacular **Melolo** – accessible by bus from Waingapu (8000Rp, 1½ hours) – is **Praiyawang**, the ceremonial centre of **Rende** village, with its traditional Sumbanese compound and stone-slab tombs. The most massive belongs to a former raja. **Umabara** and **Pau**, 4km from Melolo, are other places to snap traditional Sumba architecture and tombs, and witness the weaving process. These villages are a 20-minute, 1.5km walk from the main road; the turn-off is 2km northeast of Melolo.

Some 70km from Waingapu, **Kaliuda** has Sumba's best *ikat*. Seven buses a day make the trip from Waingapu (12,500Rp, 2¾ hours).

There's epic surf at **Kalala**, about 2km from Baing, off the main road from Melolo. The well-respected namesake of **Mr David's** (www.eastsumba.com; all-inclusive US$35) has lived and surfed here for 30 years. His other resort is on blissful **Manggudu Island**, where you'll snorkel with mantas and enjoy stellar surf and fishing. Four buses a day depart Waingapu for Baing (28,000Rp, four hours), but they'll gladly drop you off at the beach.

An even more rustic and somehow more beautiful beach is at **Tarimbang**, a coco palm–draped cove south of Lewa. The reef break is superb, the snorkelling decent, and either of the two homestays will do just fine. Both charge 50,000Rp, all-inclusive. Buses run to Tarimbang from Waingapu (15,000Rp, four hours) in the morning.

Waikabubak

☎ 0387

At the greener end of Sumba, Waikabubak, a conglomeration of thatched clan houses, ancient tombs, concrete office buildings and satellite dishes, is strange but appealing. Interesting traditional villages such as **Kampung Tarung**, up a path next to Tarung Wisata Hotel, are right within the town. One of the spectacular attractions of West Sumba is the **Pasola**, the mock battle held near Waikabubak each February or March (see boxed text, p299).

The **tourist office** (☎ 21108; Jl Teratai 1; ⏰ 8am-3pm Mon-Sat, to 1pm Fri) is on the outskirts, **BNI bank** (Jl A Yani) can change money, and **BRI bank** (Jl Gajah Mada) has an ATM that accepts MasterCard and Cirrus.

SLEEPING & EATING

Hotel Pelita (☎ 21104; Jl Ahmad Yani 26; s/d from 30,000/35,000Rp) The economy rooms are severe depressants. But the renovated superior rooms (70,000Rp) are Prozac.

Hotel Artha (☎ 21112; Jl Veteran 11; s/d 30,000/60,000Rp) Golden staff that will help realise all your sightseeing desires. The decent rooms set around a tranquil garden courtyard aren't bad either.

INDONESIA

Hotel Aloha (☎ 21245; Jl Sudirman 26; d from 55,000Rp) Rooms sparkle, the food satisfies, and the staff overflows with local know-how.

Rumah Makan Fanny (☎ 21389; Jl Bhayangkara 55; dishes from 10,000Rp; breakfast, lunch & dinner) It's clean, quaint and the most popular place around. Try the *udong saos tiram* (prawns in oyster sauce).

Warung congregate opposite the mosque on the main strip.

GETTING THERE & AWAY

The airport is at Tambolaka, 42km north. Taxis there cost 100,000Rp. A bus to Waitabula and an *ojek* from there is the budget option.

The **Merpati agent** (☎ 21051; Jl Ahmad Yani 11) is above a shop. It flies four times a week to Maumere and three times weekly to Denpasar.

The bus station is central. Buses run to Waingapu (40,000Rp, four hours) throughout the day, and to Waitabula (4000Rp, one hour). Frequent bemo rattle to Anakalang, Wanokaka and Lamboya.

Around Waikabubak

Anakalang, 22km east of Waikabubak, sports some of Sumba's most captivating megalith tombs, right beside the highway. More interesting villages are south of town past the market. **Kabonduk** has Sumba's heaviest tomb. It took 2000 workers over three years to carve it. A pleasant 15-minute walk from there is the hillside village of **Matakakeri** and the original settlement in the area, **Lai Tarung**, which has more tombs and breathtaking views. A festival honouring the ancestors is held every odd year in July.

Located directly south of Waikabubak is the Wanokaka district, which is a centre for the Pasola festival (p299). **Praigoli** is a somewhat isolated, and therefore deeply traditional, village. The south coast has some blissfully desolate fishing beaches that immediately silence brain chatter. Head to **Pantai Rua**, with basic accommodation, or **Pantai Morosi**.

On the west coast, **Pero** is a charming village with a couple of decent surf breaks. If you sail due west from here, the first land you hit would be Africa. Homestay Stori is comfortable and the food is fantastic. From Waikabubak, take a bus to Waitabula and one of many bemo from there to Pero.

KALIMANTAN

Indonesia's portion of Borneo is famous for orang-utans – Malay for forest person – and Dayaks, forest people who resist modern intrusions on their traditions. Here in one of the earth's great rainforest lungs and last frontiers, visitors can still find wonders that captivated naturalist Alfred Russel Wallace and novelist Joseph Conrad.

Kalimantan's natural attractions also draw miners, loggers and oil-palm planters, legal and otherwise. Their exploitation of resources means travellers need more time, energy and money to reach unspoiled nature. But issues here come as thickly layered as the jungle: logging and mining roads are now principal paths to reach the green heart of Kalimantan. That mixed blessing also means trading pleasant and economical passenger-boat travel for more numb-bum bus rides.

Getting There & Away

AIR

Garuda (code GA; www.garuda-indonesia.com) and its Citilink subsidiary connect to international destinations via Jakarta or Surabaya from Balikpapan, Banjarmasin and Tarakan. **SilkAir** (code MI; www.silkair.net) flies daily from Balikpapan to Singapore. **Batavia Air** (code 7P; www.batavia-air.co.id) flies from Pontianak to Kuching in Sarawak and Pulau Batam near Singapore. Garuda and Batavia fly the most routes to the rest of Indonesia. Generally, Kalimantan's travel agents will offer better service, hours and prices than airline offices.

BOAT

Pelni (www.pelni.co.id) and private companies connect to Java and Sulawesi. Check with local offices for latest schedules. Fast ferries link Tarakan and Nunukan to Tawau in Sabah in Malaysia (see boxed text, p304).

BUS

Despite the long land border with Malaysia, there are only two official crossings. The Kuching–Pontianak express bus route (10 hours) crosses at Entikong in West Kalimantan (see boxed text, p310). A less-used crossing in East Kalimantan links Lumbis and Kalabakan in Sabah.

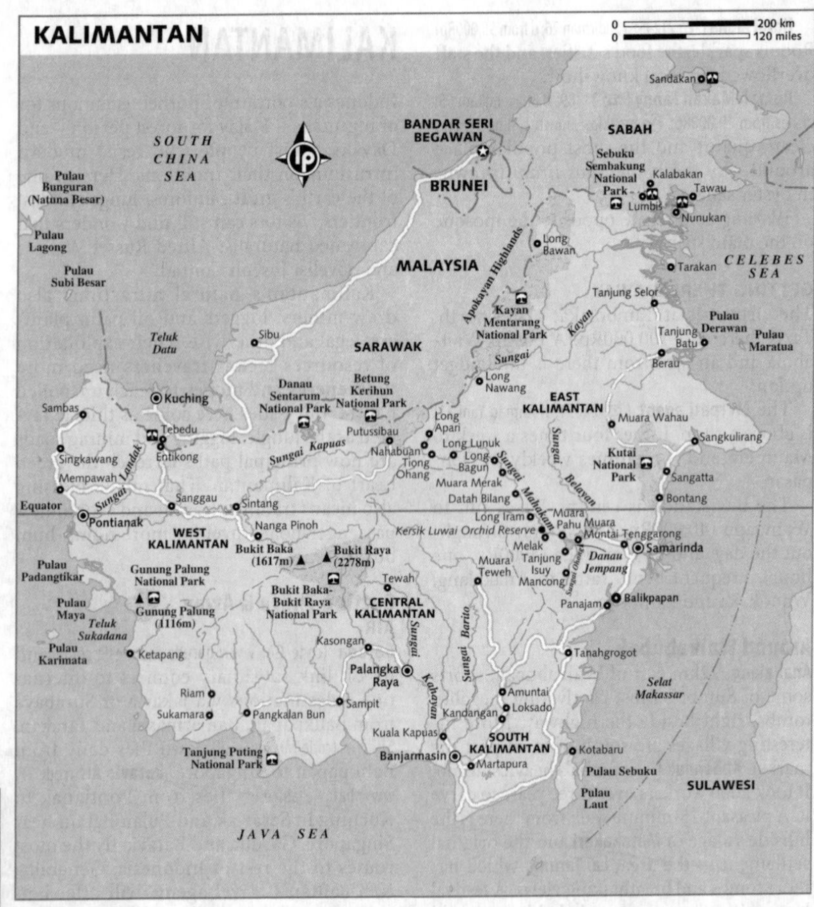

Getting Around

Roads connect nearly all major towns, though quality varies dramatically. Bus routes quickly follow road construction.

Where available, *kapal biasa* (river ferries) or *long bots* (narrow wooden boats with covered passenger cabins) are the best ways into the jungle. Expensive speedboats also ply the Barito, Kapuas, Pinoh, Kahayan and Kayan Rivers.

Kal-Star (www.kalstaronline.com) and Dirgantara Air Service (DAS) are the main air carriers within Kalimantan.

TARAKAN

☎ 0551 / pop 220,000

The usual reason to visit Tarakan is border crossing, to or from Tawau in Malaysia. Combat buffs may inspect memorials to bloody WWII battles between Australian and Japanese troops. A joint WWF-government project recently created a **mangrove forest** (Jl Gadjah Mada; admission 5000Rp; 🕒 8am-5pm) on the fringe of the town centre. From the wooden walkway, see proboscis monkeys, macaques and *ikan tempakul*, a fish exclusive to Kalimantan that crawls over mudflats on its fins.

Orientation & Information

Airport taxis are pretty pricey at 30,000Rp to 35,000Rp for the short ride (5km). Kalimantan's most accommodating *angkots* (3000Rp) stop outside the airport and harbour gates, routinely adjusting routes to suit passengers.

Find ATMs along Jl Yos Sudarso and at facing shopping centres THM Plaza and **Grand Tarakan Mall** (cnr Jl Sudirman & Jl Yos Sudarso), plus Gusher Plaza ('guess-air'), 500m west on Jl Gadjah Mada.

BNI bank (Jl Yos Sudarso) Changes currency and travellers cheques.

Haji La Tunrung Money Changer (☎ 21405; Jl Yos Sudarso 32; 7.30am-8pm) Chain throughout Kalimantan and beyond; changes cash.

Immigration office (☎ 21242; Jl Sumatra) Visa and border-crossing information.

Perta Medika Hospital (☎ 31403; Jl Mulawarman)

Tourist office (☎ 32100; 4th fl, Jl Sudirman 76; 8am-4pm Mon-Thu, to 11am Fri) Well-meaning but inept. WWF representative in the government environmental department one floor above has better information on Sebuku Sembakung and Kayan Mentarang National Parks and surrounds.

Utama Computer (☎ 33292; Jl Sudirman 155; per hr 5000Rp; 9.30am-10.30pm) Internet access.

Sleeping & Eating

Hotel Bunga Muda (☎ 21349; Jl Yos Sudarso 7; r 55,000-132,000Rp;) Located between the two harbours, Ibu Ida's establishment provides *wartel*, flight and boat bookings, plus plenty of smiles.

Hotel Bahagia (☎ 37141; Jl Gadjah Mada; r 60,000-150,000Rp;) Opposite Gusher Plaza, this place has big, bright rooms with two beds, two fans, closet, desk and chair, and shared Western or Asian bathrooms. Pricier rooms are very comfortable but not all have windows.

Hotel Sakura (☎ 22730, 0852 4657 0888; Jl Sudirman 17; s 80,000-120,000Rp, d 120,000-160,000Rp;) Small, modern, somewhat clinical digs, all with air-con and TV. Economy rooms share spotless Western bathrooms; standard rooms have private bathrooms with hot water.

Hotel Makmur (☎ 31988; r incl breakfast from 140,000Rp;) Feeling flush? Cross to Hotel Sakura's sister property with more complete furnishings.

Warung choices line Jl Seroja, north of Jl Sudirman. Food stalls in THM and Gusher serve Indonesian dishes from morning until late. More stalls bloom nightly along Jl Sudirman and environs. Try local fresh fish.

Getting There & Away

AIR

Angkasa Express (☎ 32088; Hotel Tarakan Plaza) is the local agent for Garuda and DAS, and sells tickets for all carriers. Garuda connects via Balikpapan to Jakarta, Surabaya and beyond. **Kal-Star** (☎ 51578, 25840; www.kalstaronline.com) flies twice daily except Sundays to Nunukan (230,000Rp), Berau (320,000Rp) and Samarinda. DAS flies to Malinau (250,000Rp), Long Bawan (167,000Rp), Berau and Balikpapan. **Mission Aviation Fellowship** (code MAF; ☎ 22904) has irregular service into the interior.

PULAU DERAWAN – WHERE'S PAPA?

If Ernest Hemingway came back a sensitive new-age guy, he'd go to Pulau Derawan to write. The Sangalaki archipelago off East Kalimantan is famous for diving and fishing, but you'll get hooked on local charm.

There are more than 30 islands in the archipelago, most uninhabited, visited mainly by scuba enthusiasts, turtle-egg poachers, and (successful) antipoaching patrols. Derawan is the inhabited island nearest the Borneo 'mainland'. This tear-drop-shaped oasis of 125 households can be circled on foot in less than an hour. There are no cars, and electricity only runs dusk to dawn. Shops scattered along the sandy main street offer the day's freshly arrived produce, basic supplies plus homemade sweets reflecting islanders' Bajo heritage; a few sell beer through the back door.

Losmen Danakan (☎ 081 35014 8954; r per person incl meals 75,000Rp) captures Derawan's friendly spirit. Danakan means 'family' in local sea patois, and guests will enjoy the embrace of Ibu Ridahi, Pak Kasino and their clan. Simple wooden rooms line a pier extending 50m into clear sea. Turtles paddle between the pilings, a leaping dolphin may punctuate the spectacular sunsets.

Visitors usually reach Derawan via Berau (also known as Tanjung Redep), with air and bus links to other parts of Kalimantan. A weekly ferry service (80,000Rp, four hours) leaves Berau Saturdays only if enough passengers show up, and returns Sundays. *Sepit* (speedboats) make the trip in three hours; bargaining begins at 2,000,000Rp one way. The economy alternative is a Kijang from Berau's riverfront Central Graha Hotel to Tanjung Batu (50,000Rp, 2½ hours), then a speedboat (200,000Rp, 35 minutes) or inboard (50,000Rp, 1½ hour) to Derawan. For the best deal, stick close to the Indonesian passengers leaving the Kijang.

GETTING TO MALAYSIA

A fast ferry leaves Tarakan for Tawau in Malaysia every morning, except Sunday, from Pelabuhan Malundung. Purchase a ticket (Rp180,000 including port taxes, 3½ hours), then report to the immigration counter, which collects your passport; it is returned with a departure card and 90-day visa upon arrival in Malaysia. It's also possible to cross from Tarakan via Nunukan (150,000Rp, 2½ hours; Nunukan to Tawau 75,000Rp, 1¼ hours), where the border post opens daily. For crossings in the reverse direction, see p492.

BOAT

Pelni (☎ 51169; Jl Yos Sudarso) ships steam to Makassar (250,000Rp, 24 hours), Pantaloan (110,000Rp, 10 hours), Pare Pare (221,500Rp, 22 hours), Surabaya (365,000Rp, 2½ days) and beyond from Pelabuhan Malundung at the south end of Jl Yos Sudarso. Speedboats to Tanjung Selor (70,000Rp, two hours) leave several times daily from Pelabuhan Tangkayu, opposite the post office.

SAMARINDA

☎ 0541 / pop 562,000

At the mouth of Sungai Mahakam, this trading port is the customary launch point for exploring the natural and cultural treasures of East Kalimantan's mightiest river. But Samarinda is overrated as a backpacker haven, while nearby Balikpapan is underrated.

Orientation & Information

Airport taxis cost 35,000Rp, or walk 100m down Jl Gatot Subroto to catch a route B *angkot* (3000Rp). *Angkot* (also called taxis) routes cover main streets. ATMs abound along Jl Sudirman and in shopping centres.

Acacia Travel (☎ 746744; Jl Agus Salim 21) Air tickets.

BNI (cnr Jl Panglima Batur & Jl Sebatik) Changes only US dollars (cash and traveller cheques).

Meganet (Hotel MJ, Jl Khalid 1; per hr 10,000Rp; 24hr) Internet access.

Post office (cnr Jl Awang Long & Jl Gajah Mada)

RS Bhakti Nguraha (☎ 741363; Jl Basuki Rahmat 150) For simple ailments.

Rumah Sakit Haji Darjad (☎ 732698; Jl Dahlia) Modern hospital off Jl Basuki Rahmat.

Sumangkat (Jl Agus Salim 35; per hr 6000Rp; 8am-midnight) Internet plus postal services.

Tourist office (☎ 736850; cnr Jl Awang Long & Jl Sudirman 22; 7.30am-4.30pm Mon-Thu, 8-11am Fri) Kalimantan's best government tourism office.

Sleeping & Eating

Hanyani (☎ 742653; Jl Pirus 31; r 70,000-140,000;) Large rooms in this cavernous place include *mandi* and choice of one or two beds. Fan-cooled economy rooms are marginally cleaner on the 3rd floor. Discounts are possible.

Hotel Gelora (☎ 742024; gelora@smd.mega.net.id; Jl Niaga Selatan 62; r 75,000-200,000Rp;) Overlooking Citra Niaga market and routinely overlooked by foreigners, Gelora is somewhat dark but well kept. Pricier rooms have air-con.

More choices:

Aida (☎ 742572; Jl KH Mas Tumenggung; r incl breakfast from 95,000Rp;) Variety of rooms, cleaner than its neighbours.

Hotel Hidayah I (☎ 731210, 731261; Jl KH Mas Temenggung; s 100,000-155,000Rp, d 125,000-190,000Rp, all incl breakfast;) Still popular but heading downhill; guides frequent its balcony (coffee) bar.

Sample local pride *udang galah* (giant river prawns) at seafood *warung* or Citra Niaga. Walk north from Mesra Indah Shopping Centre for a culinary *tour de* Indonesia.

Getting There & Away

AIR

Kal-Star (☎ 742110; www.kalstaronline.com) flies to Tarakan, Berau and Nunukan (796,000Rp). **DAS** (☎ 735250) serves Tarakan, Berau (500,000Rp) and Tanjung Selor (167,500Rp). Flights to Data Dawai near Long Lunak were suspended at the time of research.

BOAT

Pelni (☎ 741402; Jl Sudarso 76) routes serve Pare Pare (127,500Rp, 21 hours), Surabaya (258,000Rp, 24 hours), Toli Toli (134,000Rp, 24 hours), Tarakan (259,000Rp, 24 hours) and Nunukan (225,000Rp, 24 hours).

In addition, there's twice-weekly private service to Pare Pare (125,000Rp, 24 hours). Check with the **harbour master** (Jl Yos Sudarso 2) for details.

Mahakam river ferries *(kapal biasa)* leave at 7am from Sungai Kunjang terminal at the west end of town to Tenggarong (20,000Rp, two hours), Melak (100,000Rp, 16 hours), Long Iram (120,000Rp, 18 hours) and – sometimes – Long Bagun (350,000Rp, 36 hours).

BUS

Samarinda has multiple bus depots. Sungai Kunjang terminal serves Kota Bagun (20,000Rp, three hours), a short cut to upper Mahakam destinations, and Balikpapan (19,500Rp, two hours). Use Lempake terminal at the north end of town for Bontang (20,000Rp, three hours), Sangatta (25,000Rp, four hours) and Berau (135,000Rp, 16 hours). Buses leave as they're filled from 7am until early afternoon. Minibuses to Tenggarong (10,000Rp, one hour) depart from Harapan Baru terminal on the south bank of the Makaham, reached via *angkot* route G. Minibuses to see Sunday afternoon Dayak rituals at Pampang (7000Rp, 35 minutes) leave from Segiri terminal at the north end of Jl Pahlawan.

SUNGAI MAHAKAM

Public ferries traversing this 920km river provide economical access to Dayak tribes of East Kalimantan's interior and to jungle treks. These *kapal biasa* have dormitory-style sleeping decks upstairs. Samarinda is the usual starting point since boats originate there and independent guides frequent budget hotels. Balikpapan also has good guides; if that's your point of entry, try making arrangements there.

One usual travellers' route is to take a ferry to **Muara Muntai** (10 hours from Samarinda), stay overnight, then travel via a smaller boat to **Tanjung Isuy** on the south shore of Danau Jempang. **Louu Taman Jamrot** (Jl Indonesia Australia; r per person 60,000Rp), a longhouse, arts centre and *losmen*, stages dancing in the Kenyah, Kayan and Banuaq Dayak styles – it's touristy but worthwhile. Nearby scenic **Mancong** offers a more authentic longhouse experience; you'll need to bring your own bedding, candles and food.

The critically endangered **Irawaddy dolphin** (*orcaella bervirostris;* known locally as *pesut Mahakam*) with its rounded snout is best spotted around **Muara Pahu** (13 to 14 hours from Samarinda). **Yayasan Konservasi RASI Information Centre** (Foundation for Conservation of Rare Aquatic Species of Indonesia; ☎ 0541-206406; www.geocities.com/yayasan_konservasi_rasi) organises dolphin-spotting trips. Fewer than 80 dolphins may remain in the Mahakam.

For a more uncommon adventure, continue to **Melak** (16 hours from Samarinda), the upper Mahakam's biggest town, famous for what remains of **Kersik Luwai Orchid Reserve**, a 20-sq-km black-orchid habitat devastated by fire more than a decade ago. From there, ride a minibus to **Eheng**, with a traditional longhouse busiest on Monday nights before the festive Tuesday market. Overnight at the longhouse or in Melak at newish **Penginapan Setiawan** (☎ 0545-41437; Jl Dr Sutomo; r 50,000Rp) or neighbouring **Penginapan Blue Safir** (☎ 0545-41098; Jl Dr Sutomo; r 50,000Rp). Nearby **Mencimai** has an excellent museum detailing Banuaq Dayak traditions.

Long Iram, 409km and 18 hours from Samarinda, is where ferries terminate if the river is low. It's a pleasant 1½-hour walk or 40-minute outboard ride (60,000Rp) to Tering, three villages straddling the Mahakam where inhabitants sport elongated earlobes and traditional tattoos. Stay at **Penginapan Wahyu** (Jl Soewondo 57; r per person incl breakfast 70,000Rp).

Further upriver find Bahau, Kenyah and Punan longhouses between **Datah Bilang** and **Muara Merak. Long Bagun** (1½ days from Samarinda) is end of the line for river ferries in high water. Continue upriver by motorised canoe or trek to **Long Lunuk**, **Tiong Ohang** and **Long Apari**, the picturesque uppermost longhouse settlement on the Mahakam. From there, intrepid cross-Borneo trekkers head for West Kalimantan.

DAS flights from Samarinda to **Data Dawai**, an airstrip near Long Lunuk, were suspended at our publication time. Check with DAS for possible resumption.

Mesra Tours (☎ 0541-738787, 732772; www.mesra.com/tour) in Samarinda, **Bayu Buana Travel** (☎ 0542-422751; www.bayubuanatravel.com), **Rivertours** (☎ 0542-422269; www.borneokalimantan.com) and **TransBorneo** (☎ 0542-762671) in Balikpapan offer full-service excursions on the Mahakam and beyond. Reliable independent guides in Samarinda include **Junaid Nawawi** (junaid.nawawi@plasa.com; Hotel Pirus, Jl Pirus 30; 🕑 2-5pm), **Suryadi** (☎ 081 6459 8263), and **Rustam** (☎ 0541-735641, 081 2585 4915). Tours can be customised to fit your schedule and budget.

BALIKPAPAN

☎ 0542 / pop 450,000

An oil town gushing with some of Kalimantan's best food, nightlife and other expensive treats, Balikpapan often gets the cold shoulder from budget travellers. But sampling its charms needn't fracture finances.

Orientation & Information

Taxis from Sepinggan Airport (7km) cost 35,000Rp. Balikpapan Plaza (corner of Jl Sudirman and Jl Ahmad Yani) is the centre of town. There are plenty of banks that change currencies and have ATMs.

BNet (Budiman Hotel, Jl Ahmad Yani; per hr 6000Rp; ⌚ 9am-11pm) Internet access.

Golden Nusa Travel (☎ 417321; www.goldennusa.com; Hotel Benakutai, Jl Ahmad Yani) Sells air tickets; English is spoken.

Post office (☎ 733585; Jl Sudirman 6)

PT Agung Sedayu (☎ 420601; Jl Sudirman 28) Best source for Pelni schedules and all boat tickets. Also handles domestic flights.

Rumah Sakit Ibu Restu (Jl Ahmad Yani) Hospital, opposite Bondy's.

Sleeping

Some top budget sleeping options are near the fork of Jl Ahmad Yani and Jl Pangeran Antasari, also known as Gunung Kawi, 2km north of Balikpapan Plaza via *angkot* route 3 or 5.

Hotel Murni (☎ 738692; Jl Pangeran Antasari 2; s from 55,000Rp, d 75,000-125,000Rp; ❄) Indonesian solo travellers are mainstays of this family-run place featuring immaculate rooms on three floors. Enjoy free coffee, tea and water and the huge TV with other guests on the huger red leather sofa.

Hotel Ayu (☎ 425290; Jl Pangeran Antasari 18; r 100,000-160,000Rp; ❄) Ambience and furnishings more like a friend's place than a hotel. Climb a second flight of stairs for the cheapest fan-cooled digs.

Also consider:

Hotel Aida (☎ 731011; Jl Ahmad Yani 29; r 75,000-150,000Rp, f 200,000Rp, all incl breakfast; ❄) Student favourite with varied rooms in a maze of corridors.

Hotel Gajah Mada (☎ 734634; Jl Sudirman 328; s 95,000-235,000Rp, d 135,000-285,000Rp plus 10% tax; ❄) Next to Balikpapan Plaza; good luck beating local tourists to rooms.

Eating

Cheap *warung* abound near the water, particularly around Pasar Klandasan, 500m west of Balikpapan Plaza.

our pick **Wisma Ikan Bakar** (Jl Sudirman 16; meals 11,000-28,000Rp; ⌚ lunch & dinner) A local legend, the 'Grilled Fish Inn' is deliciously less toxic to wallets than Bondy's.

Bondy's (☎ 424438; Jl Ahmad Yani; mains from 30,000Rp; ⌚ lunch & dinner) Balikpapan institution set in a courtyard; famed for budget-busting seafood and steak.

Getting There & Away

AIR

SilkAir (code MI; ☎ 730800; www.silkair.com) flies daily to Singapore (US$291). **Merpati** (code MZ; ☎ 424452; www.merpati.co.id) flies daily to Makassar (796,000Rp). **Garuda** (code GA; ☎ 422301; www.garuda-indonesia.com) flies to Manado, Surabaya (310,000Rp), Denpasar (663,000Rp) and Tarakan (327,000Rp). **Kal-Star** (☎ 737473; www.kalstaronline.com) flies to Berau (659,000Rp). **DAS** (☎ 764362) flies three times weekly to Pontianak (965,000Rp), plus Berau and Tarakan. **Batavia** (code 7P; www.batavia-air.co.id) flies to Banjarmasin (395,000Rp), Tarakan, Jakarta, Surabaya, Yogyakarta (545,000Rp), Palu (415,000Rp) and Manado (565,000Rp). **Adam Air** (code KI; www.flyadamair.com) and **Lion Air** (code JT; www.lionair.co.id) fly to Jakarta and Surabaya. **Mandala** (www.mandalaair.com) also flies to Tarakan. **Sriwijaya Air** (code SJY; www.sriwijayaair-online.com) and **Air Asia** (code AK; www.airasia.com) serve Jakarta (from 350,000Rp).

BOAT

Pelni (☎ 424171; Jl Yos Sudarso 76) sails to Makassar (economy/1st class 122,000/377,000Rp, 36 hours), Pare Pare, Surabaya and beyond.

Dharma Lautan (☎ 422194; Kampung Baru dock) runs daily ferries to Mamuju (96,000Rp, 14 hours). **Prima Vista** (☎ 732607; Jl Sudirman 138) sells tickets for private boats to Pare Pare (120,000Rp, 20 hours), Makassar (125,000Rp, 24 hours) and Surabaya (160,000, 36 hours).

BUS

Buses to Samarinda (19,500Rp, two hours) leave from the northern Batu Ampar bus terminal. Buses to Banjarmasin (from 75,000Rp, 12 hours) leave from the terminal across the harbour. Take a route 6 *angkot* from Jl Sudirman to Jl Monginsidi and hop a speedboat (6000Rp, 10 minutes) to the other side.

BANJARMASIN

☎ **0511 / pop 800,000**

Kalimantan's largest city sprawls untidily from its riverfront roots into 21st-century suburbanization. But Banjarmasin's traditional charms still shine along its maze of waterways. This heartland of Banjar culture is also gateway to scenic trekking in Dayak villages of Pegunungan Meratus (Meratus Mountains).

Orientation & Information

Taxis cost 70,000Rp to or from the airport, located 26km from the centre of town. Alternatively, take an *angkot* from Jl Pasar Baru to Km 6 terminal, then a Martapura-bound *colt* to the branch road leading to the airport and walk (1.5km).

Find ATMs along Jl Lambung Mangkurat and outside the Istana Barito Hotel on Jl Haryono MT. The South Kalimantan Tourist Office is about 6km east of the centre; it's not worth the trip.

Adi Angkasa Travel (☎ 436 6100; fax 436 6200; Jl Hasanuddin 58) Flight bookings.

Daissy.net (☎ 336 5872; Jl Haryono MT 4; per hr 6000Rp; 24hr) This place has air-con internet; there's no smoking from 8am to 3pm.

Family Tour & Travel (☎ 326 8923; familytourtravel@yahoo.com; Jl A Yani Km 4.5) English-speaking help with flights, tours throughout Kalimantan, and car hire. It's southeast of the centre.

LippoBank (Jl Pangeran Samudera) Cashes travellers cheques.

Post office (cnr Jl Pangeran Samudera & Jl Lambung Mangkurat)

Rumah Sakit Ulin (Jl A Yani Km 2) Hospital, southeast of the centre.

Warnet Kyagi (Jl Pangeran Samudera 94-96; per hr fan/air-con 4500/5200Rp; 24hr) Internet access.

Sights & Activities

Banjarmasin's top attractions are **Pasar Kuin** and **Pasar Lokbaintan floating markets** (5-9am), as well as **canal tours** to observe residents of the

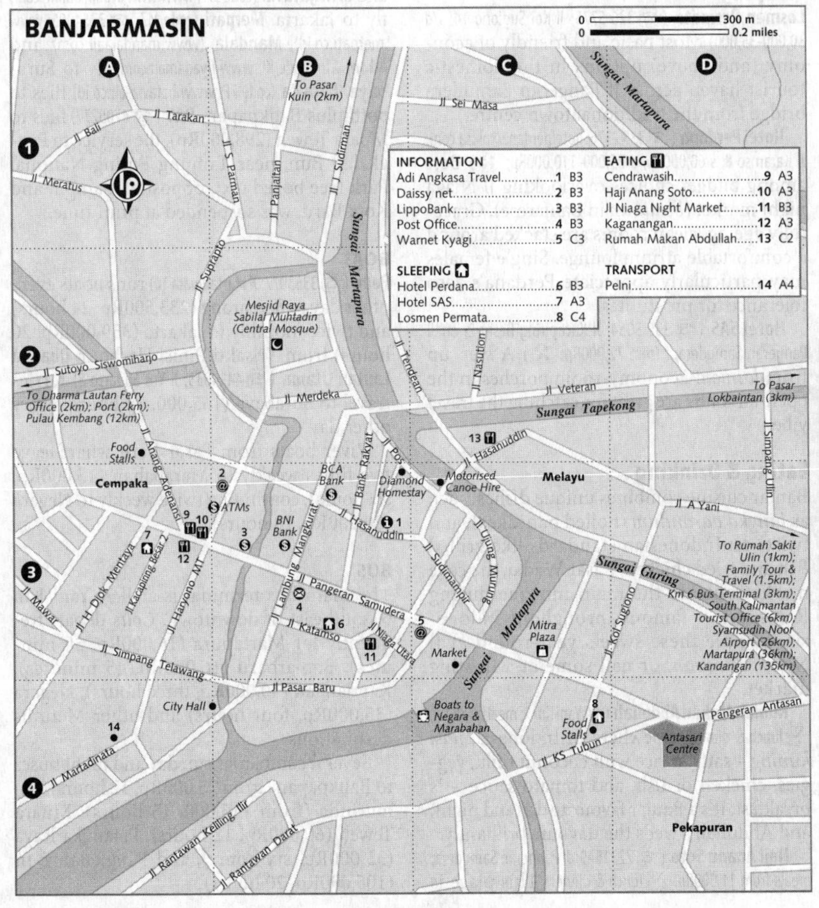

stilt homes that line the waterways washing dishes, clothing and themselves in a joyful festival of smiles, splashes and high fives.

Budget at least 25,000Rp per hour to rent a *klotok* (motorised canoe) without a guide, depending on your Bahasa Indonesia and bargaining prowess. Guided canal tours at early morning or late afternoon washing time run about two hours and start at 60,000Rp per person. Floating market tours cost around 75,000Rp and usually offer a stop at **Pulau Kembang**, home to an aggressive troop of long-tailed macaques.

Tailah (☎ 327 1685; Diamond Homestay, Jl Hasanudin 58) is an independent guide who can arrange local tours and Pegunungan Meratus treks.

Sleeping

Losmen Permata (☎ 326 5775; Jl Kol Sugiono 14; s/d 30,000-35,000) Most basic and friendly of economy (and above) options in the domestic tourist haven across Jl Pangeran Samudera bridge from the traditional town centre.

Hotel Perdana (☎ 335 2376; hotelperdana@plasa.com; Jl Katamso 8; s 60,000Rp, d 75,000-110,000Rp; ❄) Best among budget choices overlooking Jl Niaga night market (*belauran* in Banjarese). Gracefully ageing, clean rooms are stacked around a comfortable atrium lounge. Single females may particularly appreciate Perdana's zero tolerance for prostitutes.

Hotel SAS (☎ 335 3054; Jl Kacapiring Besar 2, off Jl Pangeran Samudera; r from 72,000Rp; ❄) A step up from *losmen*. Economy-room porches in the open-air lobby are great for catching the travel vibe.

Eating & Drinking

Banjar cuisine combines unique dishes, such as *bingka barandum* (boiled pancakes), and twists on Indonesian standards like grilled fish and fried chicken. Pasar Wadai, the cake market outside the main mosque during Ramadan, is famous throughout Indonesia. Sample these sweets year-round at Jl Niaga *belauran*, or nail some at a floating market.

Rumah Makan Abdullah (Jl A Yani Km 1; meals 9000Rp; 🕐 lunch & dinner) Elsewhere in Indonesia, *nasi kuning* – saffron rice with coconut milk, veggies, chicken or fish, and tomato sauce – is breakfast. It's a Banjar favourite day and night, and Abdullah's weds the flavours brilliantly.

Haji Anang Soto (☎ 7231549; Jl Pangeran Samudera; meals from 11,000Rp; 🕐 lunch & dinner) This place is renowned for its *soto banjar* (aromatic soup topped with a chicken leg or breast quarter). Ask for *lonton* (rice steamed in pandan leaves), and respect the fiery homemade *sambal* (relish).

Cendrawasih (mains from 15,000Rp; 🕐 lunch & dinner), next door to Haji Anang Soto, and **Kaganangan** (mains from 18,000Rp; 🕐 lunch & dinner), across the street, serve full Banjarese meals, best enjoyed in groups, with higher prices and free side orders of bad attitude toward foreigners. Jl Niaga is more economical and friendly for sampling local specialities.

Getting There & Away

AIR

Garuda (code GA; ☎ 3359065; www.garuda-indonesia.com) and **Sriwijaya Air** (code SJY; www.sriwijayaair-online.com) fly to Jakarta. **Merpati** (code MZ; ☎ 3264005; www.merpati.co.id), **Mandala** (www.mandalaair.com) and **Adam Air** (code KI; www.flyadamair.com) fly to Surabaya. **Batavia** (code 7P; www.batavia-air.co.id) flies to both plus Balikpapan. **DAS** (☎ 4705277) flies to Muara Teweh (298,000Rp); the service to Pangkalan Bun, near Tanjung Puting National Park (see boxed text, opposite), Sampit, and Kota Baru, was suspended at print time.

BOAT

Pelni (☎ 3353077; Jl Martadinata 10) runs boats every other day to Semarang (233,500Rp, 24 hours) and twice monthly to Jakarta (359,000Rp, 20 hours) from Trisakti Pinisi Harbour. **Dharma Lautan Utama** (☎ 4414833; Jl Yos Sudarso 8) ferries travel to Surabaya (165,000, 18 hours) every other day.

River boats from Pasar Baru wharf leave five times weekly to Marabahan (15,000Rp, six hours), continuing twice weekly to Negara (20,000Rp, 18 hours).

BUS

The main bus terminal is at Jl A Yani Km 6, southeast of downtown. *Colts* depart frequently for Martapura (16,000Rp, 30 minutes), Banjarbaru (16,000Rp, 45 minutes), Kandangan (40,000Rp, three hours), Negara (35,000Rp, four hours) and other Meratus destinations.

Several companies run day and night buses to Balikpapan (from 75,000Rp, 12 hours), Samarinda (from 115,000, 15 hours), Muara Teweh (60,000Rp, 12 hours), Palangka Raya (35,000Rp, six hours), and Pangkalan Bun (105,000Rp, 20 hours).

GO APE AT TANJUNG PUTING

Borneo has several spots for seeing orang-utans, but the best place in Kalimantan – possibly on earth – is **Tanjung Puting National Park** (☎/fax 0532-23832; Km 1.5 Jl HM Rafi'i; 🕑 7am-2pm Mon-Thu, to 11am Fri, to 1pm Sat). Once ranging across Southeast Asia, orang-utans survive only on Sumatra and Borneo, threatened by destruction of their rainforest habitat.

An oasis amid mining, logging, and oil-palm plantations, Tanjung Puting harbours gibbons, macaques, sun bears, clouded leopards, proboscis monkeys, crocodiles, hundreds of bird species, and brilliant butterflies. The park's three research camps attract orang-utans with daily hand-outs of bananas, cassava and milk. Guided jungle treks reveal more wildlife and, especially in February and March, wild orchids. Find accommodation at a pair of ecolodges or village homestays through **Friends of the National Parks Foundation** (☎ 0361-977978; www.fnpf.org).

But the best way to appreciate Tanjung Puting is staying aboard a *klotok*. These 8m wooden boats offer basic comforts for up to four adults and a put-putting motor straight out of *African Queen*. Sleep on deck, mattresses under mosquito nets, jungle sounds your lullaby and morning alarm.

Rent a *klotok* in Kumai, near Pangkalan Bun. Budget 725,000Rp daily, including boat, captain, park fees and options such as food, cook and English-speaking guide. Booking gets more difficult May to August and during Indonesian school holidays.

Getting to Kumai can be tricky. Passenger ships stop at Kumai from Surabaya and Semarang, but not from Kalimantan ports. Flights to Pangkalan Bun are difficult to find due to frequent schedule or route changes. At the time of writing there was service only from Pontianak in West Kalimantan via Ketapang, and from Semarang on Java. Once found, flights are hard to confirm without immediate cash payment or assistance from local travel agents. Bus service is available from Banjarmasin (105,000Rp, 20 hours) via Palangka Raya and Sampit, both of which may be reached by flights from Java.

For help, contact **Borneo Holidays** (☎ 0532-29673, 081 2500 0508; borneoholidays@planet-save.com) in Pangkalan Bun, **Family Tour & Travel** (☎ 0511-326 8923; familytourtravel@yahoo.com) in Banjarmasin, **Rivertours** (☎ 0542-422269; rivertours@borneokalimantan.com) in Balikpapan, **Times Tours and Travel** (☎ 0561-770259; timestravell@yahoo.com) in Pontianak, or **Nusantara Tours and Travel** (☎ 024-844 2888) in Semarang.

AROUND BANJARMASIN

For nature enthusiasts, Banjarmasin is the launch point for treks into **Pegunungan Meratus**. Travel agencies or guides in Banjarmasin such as **Tailah** (☎ 436 6100, 327 1685) can arrange treks. You should expect daily rates of 150,000Rp for an English-speaking guide, plus food, accommodation and transport costs.

To go independently, take a *colt* to Kandangan, then a pick-up (15,000Rp, 1½ hours) to Loksado, a small village that's literally the end of the road. **Amat** (☎ 081 34876 6573) assists tourists in Loksado. He can point you in the right direction for treks through breathtaking primary forest, overnighting in village homestays. Many trips end with bamboo rafting down Sungai Amandit to Muara Tanuhi and a dip in the hot-spring pool there.

Three sights near Banjarmasin can be combined into a day trip by *colt*. Banjarbaru's **museum** (☎ 0511-92453; Jl Ahmad Yani 36; admission 750Rp; 🕑 9.30am-3.00pm Tue-Sun, to 11am Fri), on the road to Martapura, features Banjar and Dayak artefacts, plus statues excavated from pre-Islamic Hindu temples. **Cempaka mines** (🕑 closed Fri), 43km south of Banjarmasin, show the dark side of diamonds. Miners labour in muddy water – often up to their necks – sifting for gold, agates and gems. Stone shops at **Martapura market** sell local finds. This Friday market also sees brightly dressed Banjar women amid a cornucopia of exotic fruit, with the town mosque's turquoise and black onion dome as backdrop.

PONTIANAK

☎ 0561 / pop 483,000

Astride the equator at the confluence of Sungai Landak and Sungai Kapuas, Pontianak is a rambling, frenetic industrial port that leads to Dayak settlements and virgin forests along the upper Kapuas, plus unspoiled South China Sea beaches to the north. A replica **longhouse** (Jl Letjen Sutoyo 4A) hosts Dayak festivities every

May. Unlike Kalimantan's usual urban sprawl, Pontianak's inner core, now centred along Jl Gajah Mada, thrives. An 18th-century gold rush attracted waves of Chinese immigrants; their ancestors and influence remain, though Pontianak's sophisticates sip coffee, not tea, at roadside cafés.

Orientation & Information

Airport taxis into town (15km) cost 60,000Rp. *Opelet* (3000Rp) routes cover downtown. Main streets have ATMs aplenty.

BNI bank (Jl Tanjungpura) Changes money.

Borneo Access (☎ 081 2576 8066; www.borneoaccess.com) Alex Afdhal, West Kalimantan Guides Association general secretary, arranges tours and is a fount of regional knowledge and enthusiasm.

Kalimantan Barat Tourist Office (☎ 742838; Jl Sutoyo 17; 8am-2pm Mon-Thu, to 11.30am Fri) Friendly Pak Iwan speaks English and has myriad travel suggestions.

Klinik Kharitas Bhakti (☎ 734373; Jl Siam 153; 24hr) Medical services.

Mitra Tour & Travel (☎ 733544; Jl Teuku Umar Komplek; per hr 4000Rp; 9.30am-midnight) Internet access, plus air bookings.

Panorama Anugrah Pratama Tour & Travel (☎ 739483; tour_panorama@yahoo.com; Jl Diponegoro 149) Air, boat and Kuching bus tickets with local delivery, plus responses to English emails.

Post office (Jl Sultan Abdur Rahman 49)

Sleeping & Eating

Meranti Guest House (☎ 731783; Jl Meranti 31A; r 50,000-130,000Rp;) On a residential street, close to downtown, Meranti has small, spotless rooms, priced according to features such as air-con and hot water.

Pontianak Raya City Hotel (☎ 732496; fax 733781; Jl Pa'kasih 44; s/d incl breakfast from 77,000/88,0000Rp plus 10% tax;) Welcoming staff and cosy rooms off a landscaped, open corridor recalling a 1960s motor inn.

GETTING TO MALAYSIA

Companies along Jl Sisingamangaraja and Jl Pahlawan offer bus service to Kuching (from 140,000Rp, 10 hours) via the border crossing at Entikong (Indonesia) and Tebedu (Malaysia). Private vehicles and hikers can also cross. The border is open 7.30am to 5pm. Malaysia grants 90-day visas to tourists at the border. For crossings in the reverse direction, see p498.

our pick **Ateng House** (☎ 732683; atenghouse@yahoo.com; Jl Gadjah Mada 201; s/d incl breakfast 79,000/89,000 plus 15% tax;) This place bills itself as a transit hotel but it's plenty comfy for longer stays. All rooms include air-con and homely extras such as bedspreads and drinking water dispensers. Above is Ateng Tour for travel assistance, and opposite Borneo's best Java at Cafe Corner.

Food and coffee stalls spring up nightly all over Pontianak, the widest selection along Jl Gajah Mada. Eat and drink until at least 10pm. For a stellar Chinese street feed, try **Sam Hak Heng** (mains 8000-14,000Rp), a stall opposite Hotel Gajahmada.

Getting There & Away

AIR

Batavia Air (code 7P; ☎ 734488; www.batavia-air.co.id) flies to Kuching (US$45), Putissibau (725,000Rp) at the head of Sungai Kapuas, Pulau Batam near Singapore (continuing to Pekanbaru), Jakarta, and Surabaya via Yogyakarta. **Kal-Star** (☎ 739090; www.kalstaronline.com) and **DAS** (☎ 736407) fly to Ketapang (320,000Rp) and Pangkalan Bun (600,000Rp). Kal-Star also serves Semarang (1,170,000Rp). **Garuda** (code GA; ☎ 734986; www.garuda-indonesia.com), **Sriwijaya** (code SJY; ☎ 768777) and **Adam Air** (code KI; ☎ 767999; www.flyadamair.com) also fly to Jakarta.

BOAT

Riverboats for the 800km journey to Putussibau are now very rare.

Pelni (☎ 748124; Jl Sultan Abdur Rahman 12) ships leave every other week for Jakarta (210,000Rp, 36 hours), Surabaya (197,000Rp, 40 hours) and Semarang (165,000Rp, 38 hours) from the harbour at Jl Pa'kasih, north of the Kartika Hotel.

Titian Kapuas (☎ 731187; Jl Usin 3) sells tickets for *Dharma Kencana* to Semarang (179,000Rp, 32 hours) and *Marisa* to Jakarta (170,000Rp, 32 hours). Daily jet-boats travel to Ketapang (90,000Rp to 135,000Rp, six hours), near Gunung Palung National Park.

BUS

Pontianak's intercity bus station is in Batu Layang, northwest of town. Take a boat across the river to Siantan bus terminal for a white bemo to Batu Layang, or a direct bemo from Jl Sisingamangaraja.

Several companies along Jl Sisingamangaraja and at the south end of town on Jl Pahlawan offer executive bus service to Kuching

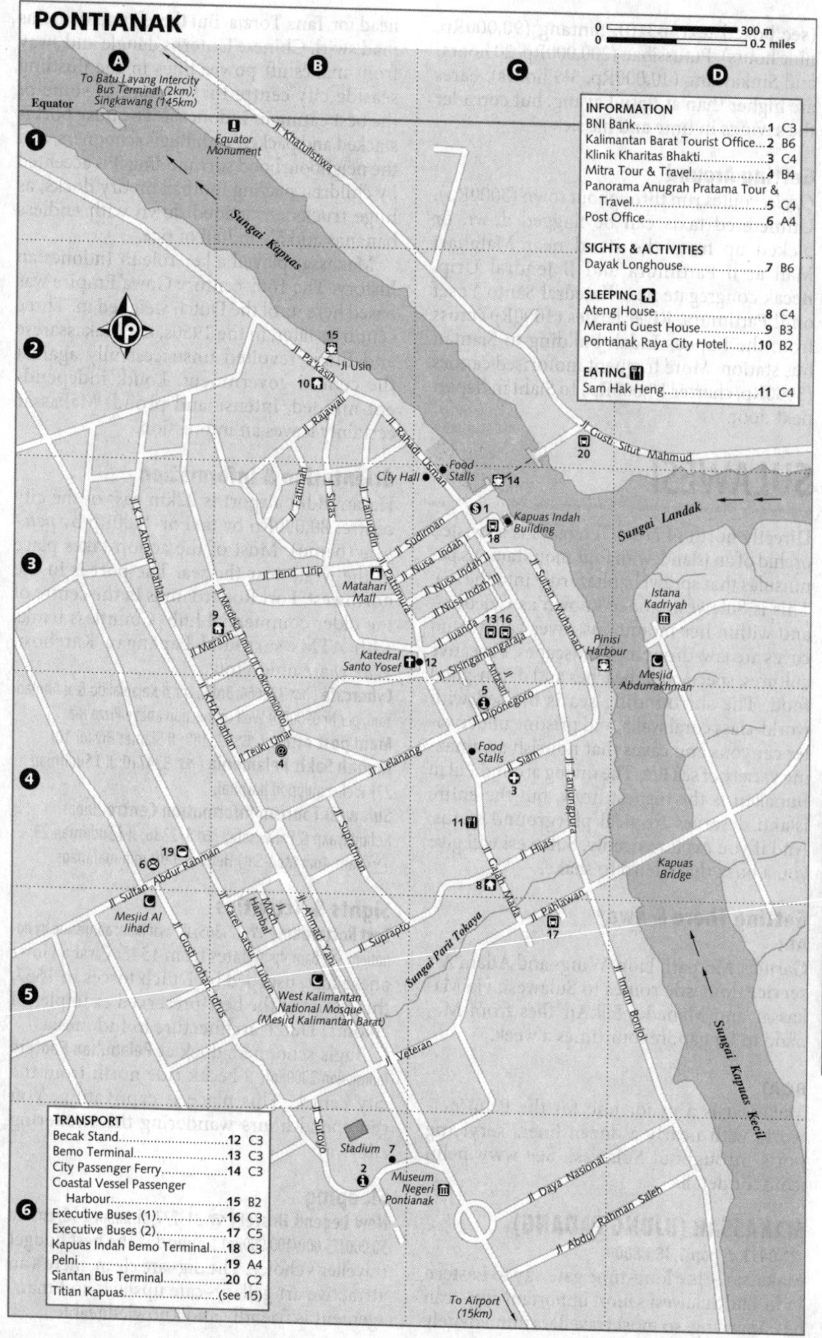
PONTIANAK
0 300 m
0 0.2 miles
INFORMATION
BNI Bank....1 C3
Kalimantan Barat Tourist Office....2 B6
Klinik Kharitas Bhakti....3 C4
Mitra Tour & Travel....4 B4
Panorama Anugrah Pratama Tour & Travel....5 C4
Post Office....6 A4
SIGHTS & ACTIVITIES
Dayak Longhouse....7 B6
SLEEPING
Ateng House....8 C4
Meranti Guest House....9 B3
Pontianak Raya City Hotel....10 B2
EATING
Sam Hak Heng....11 C4
TRANSPORT
Becak Stand....12 C3
Bemo Terminal....13 C3
City Passenger Ferry....14 C3
Coastal Vessel Passenger Harbour....15 B2
Executive Buses (1)....16 C3
Executive Buses (2)....17 C5
Kapuas Indah Bemo Terminal....18 C3
Pelni....19 A4
Siantan Bus Terminal....20 C2
Titian Kapuas....(see 15)
To Batu Layang Intercity Bus Terminal (2km); Singkawang (145km)
Equator
Equator Monument
Sungai Kapuas
Jl Khatulistiwa
Jl Pa'kasih
Jl Usin
Jl Rajawali
Jl Fatimah
Jl Sidas
Jl Zainuddin
Jl Rahadi Usman
City Hall
Food Stalls
Jl Gusti Situt Mahmud
Sungai Landak
Kapuas Indah Building
Jl Sudirman
Jl Nusa Indah I
Jl Nusa Indah II
Jl Nusa Indah III
Jl Pattimura
Jl Jend Urip
Matahari Mall
Jl KH Ahmad Dahlan
Jl Merdeka Timur (Jl Cokroaminoto)
Jl Meranti
Jl Juanda
Jl Sisingamangaraja
Jl Antasari
Katedral Santo Yosef
Jl Sultan Muhamad
Istana Kadriyah
Pinisi Harbour
Mesjid Abdurrakhman
Jl Diponegoro
Jl KHA Dahlan
Jl Teuku Umar
Jl Lelanang
Food Stalls
Jl Siam
Jl Tanjungpura
Jl Suprapman
Jl Hijas
Jl Gajah Mada
Kapuas Bridge
Jl Sultan Abdur Rahman
Mesjid Al Jihad
Jl Karel Satsui Tubun
Jl Moch Hambal
Jl Ahmad Yani
Jl Gusti Johan Idrus
Jl Suprapto
Sungai Parit Tokaya
Jl Pahlawan
Jl Imam Bonjol
West Kalimantan National Mosque (Mesjid Kalimantan Barat)
Sungai Kapuas Kecil
Jl Veteran
Jl Sutoyo
Stadium
Museum Negeri Pontianak
Jl Daya Nasional
Jl Abdul Rahman Saleh
To Airport (15km)
INDONESIA

(see boxed text, p310), Sintang (90,000Rp, nine hours), Putussibau (200,000Rp, 20 hours) and Sinkawang (40,000Rp, 3½ hours). Fares are higher than at Batu Layang, but consider the savings in time and hassle.

Getting Around

Opelet routes run throughout town (3000Rp). Unmetered taxis can be flagged down or picked up from the stand near Matahari Mall at Jl Pattimura and Jl Jendral Urip. Becak congregate near Katedral Santo Yosef on Jl Pattimura. River ferries (1000Rp) cross from the Kapuas Indah building to Siantan bus station. More frequent motorised canoes (3000Rp, charter 10,000Rp) to Siantan depart next door.

SULAWESI

Directly north of Nusa Tenggara is a twisted orchid of an island, with four mountainous peninsulas that sprawl haphazardly into the sea. This is Sulawesi – once known as Celebes – and within her mountains, river valleys and coves are jaw-dropping landscapes, evocative cultures, spectacular beaches and damn-good food. The surrounding sea is blessed with world-class coral walls, and pristine underwater canyons and caves that nourish an amazing variety of sea life. The diving around Pulau Bunaken is the biggest draw, but the entire island deserves tropical playground status. And if you explore deeply, Sulawesi will give you a buzz that's hard to shake.

Getting There & Away

AIR

Garuda, Merpati, Lion/Wings and Adam Air service domestic routes to Sulawesi, via Makassar and Manado. SilkAir flies from Manado to Singapore four times a week.

BOAT

Makassar is a major hub for the Pelni network, with nearly a dozen liners servicing ports throughout Sulawesi. See www.pelni.com for details.

MAKASSAR (UJUNG PADANG)

☎ 0411 / pop 1,380,800

Makassar – the long-time gateway to Eastern Indo, and Sulawesi's most important city – can be unnerving, so most travellers immediately head for Tana Toraja. But there's poetry in this mad swirl. Chinese lanterns dangle and sway from makeshift power lines in the bustling seaside city centre that's home to some of the best eating in Indonesia. The busy port is stacked and packed with Bugis schooners, and the neighbourhood surrounding it is accented by children playing football on dry docks, as huge trucks are loaded down with endless bananas and a windfall of rice.

Makassar played a key role in Indonesian history. The 16th-century Gowa Empire was based here until the Dutch weighed in. Three centuries later, in the 1950s, the Makassarese and Bugis revolted unsuccessfully against the central government. Loud, independent-minded, intense and proud, Makassar certainly leaves an impression.

Orientation & Information

Hasanuddin airport is 22km east of the city centre, 80,000Rp by taxi or 4000Rp by *pete-pete* (bemo). Most of the action takes place in the west, near the sea. The port is in the northwest; Fort Rotterdam is in the centre of the older commercial hub. Countless banks with ATMs surround Lapangan Karebosi. *Wartel* are ubiquitous.

Cybercafé (☎ 322664; 3rd fl, cnr Jl Kajaolalido & Jl Ahmad Yani; per hr 6900Rp) Web connection above Pizza Ria.
Main post office (☎ 323180; Jl Slamet Riyadi 10)
Rumah Sakit Pelamonia (☎ 324710; Jl J Sudirman 27) Well-equipped hospital.
Sulawesi Tourism Information Centre (Dinas Kebudayaan & Pariwisata; ☎ 872336; Jl J Sudirman 23; 8am-4pm Mon-Sat) Helpful staff, minimal maps.

Sights & Activities

Fort Rotterdam (☎ 321305; Jl Pasar Ikan; admission by donation; 8am-4pm) dates from 1545. First a Gowanese fort, usurped by Dutch forces in 1667, this is one of the best-preserved examples of colonial Dutch architecture in Indonesia.

Bugis schooners dock at **Pelabuhan Paotere** (admission 2000Rp), a becak ride north from the city centre. This place is captivating. You can spend hours wandering the sweltering alleyways.

Sleeping

New Legend Hostel (☎ 313777; Jl Jampea 5G; dm/s/d 50,000/75,000/100,000Rp) Legend is the best budget traveller's choice. The digs are clean, there's an attractive art gallery–café upstairs and management is friendly and knowledgeable.

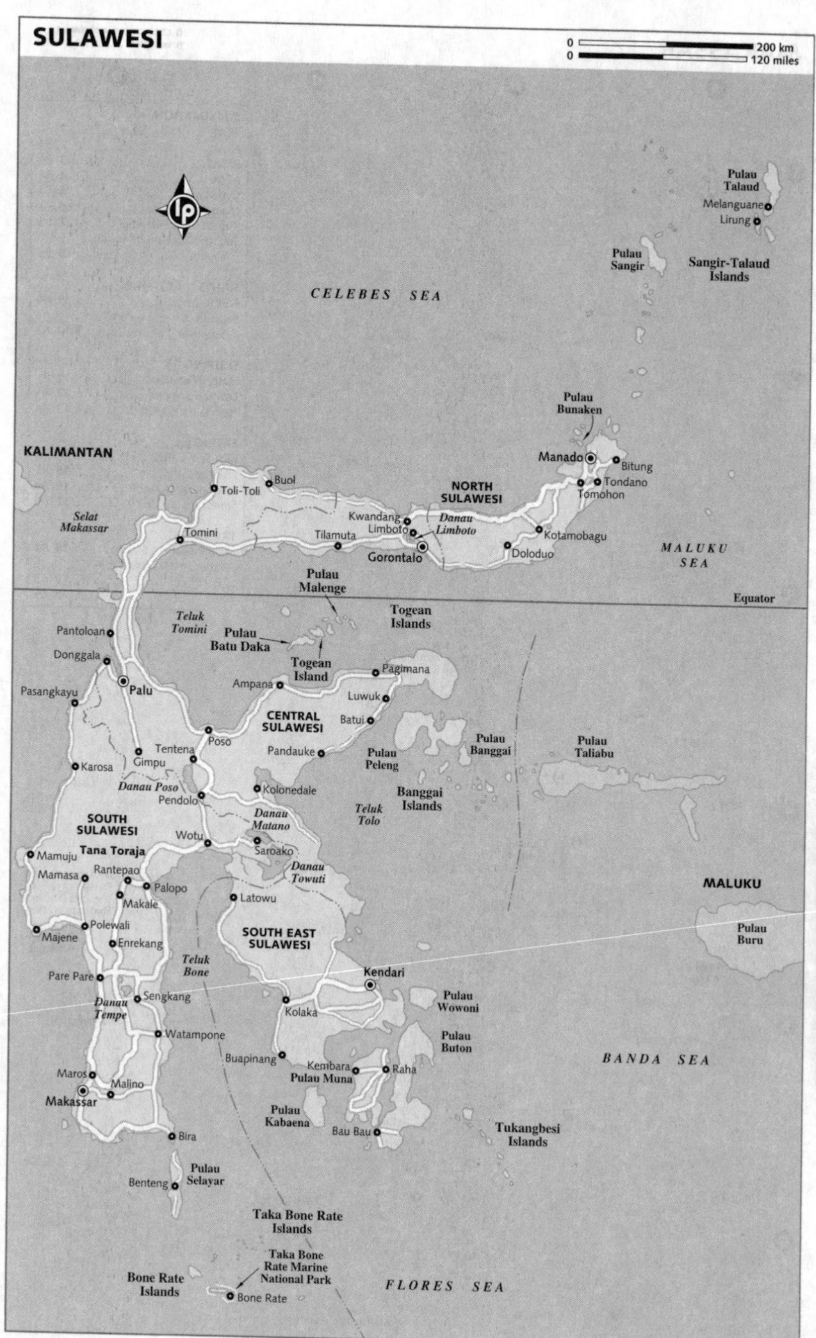
SULAWESI
0 200 km
0 120 miles
CELEBES SEA
Pulau Talaud
Melanguane
Lirung
Pulau Sangir
Sangir-Talaud Islands
Pulau Bunaken
Manado
Bitung
Tondano
Tomohon
NORTH SULAWESI
KALIMANTAN
Toli-Toli
Buol
Selat Makassar
Tomini
Kwandang
Limboto
Danau Limboto
Tilamuta
Gorontalo
Kotamobagu
Doloduo
MALUKU SEA
Pulau Malenge
Equator
Togean Islands
Teluk Tomini
Pulau Batu Daka
Pantoloan
Donggala
Togean Island
Pagimana
Ampana
Palu
Pasangkayu
Luwuk
CENTRAL SULAWESI
Batui
Poso
Tentena
Gimpu
Pandauke
Pulau Peleng
Pulau Banggai
Pulau Taliabu
Karosa
Danau Poso
Kolonedale
Pendolo
Banggai Islands
Danau Matano
Teluk Tolo
SOUTH SULAWESI
Wotu
Saroako
Mamuju
Tana Toraja
Danau Towuti
Mamasa
Rantepao
Palopo
Makale
Latowu
MALUKU
Polewali
Majene
Enrekang
SOUTH EAST SULAWESI
Pulau Buru
Teluk Bone
Pare Pare
Kendari
Sengkang
Danau Tempe
Kolaka
Pulau Wowoni
Watampone
Pulau Buton
Buapinang
BANDA SEA
Maros
Kembara
Pulau Muna
Raha
Malino
Makassar
Pulau Kabaena
Bau Bau
Tukangbesi Islands
Bira
Benteng
Pulau Selayar
Taka Bone Rate Islands
Taka Bone Rate Marine National Park
Bone Rate Islands
Bone Rate
FLORES SEA
INDONESIA

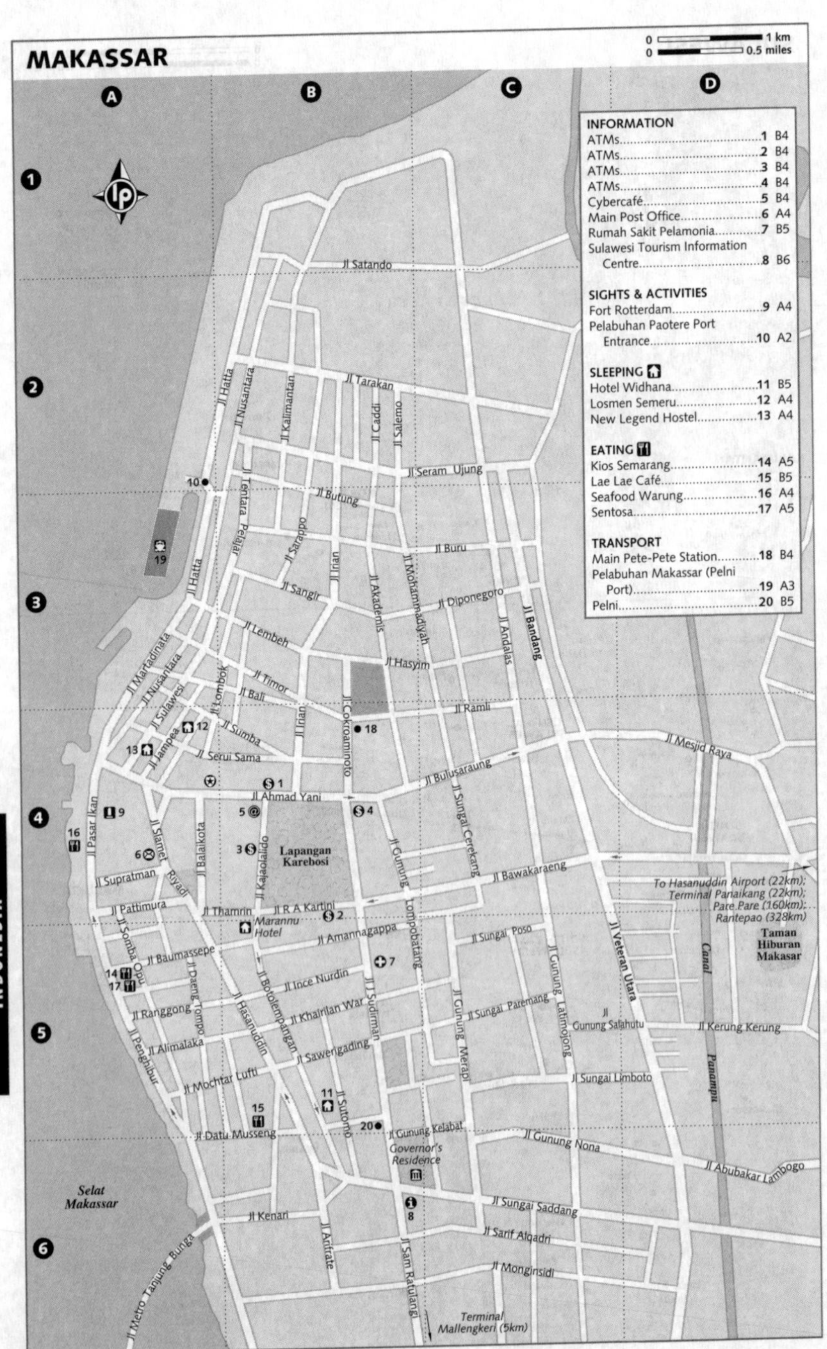
MAKASSAR
0 1 km
0 0.5 miles
A
B
C
D
1
2
3
4
5
6
INFORMATION
ATMs 1 B4
ATMs 2 B4
ATMs 3 B4
ATMs 4 B4
Cybercafé 5 B4
Main Post Office 6 A4
Rumah Sakit Pelamonia 7 B5
Sulawesi Tourism Information Centre 8 B6
SIGHTS & ACTIVITIES
Fort Rotterdam 9 A4
Pelabuhan Paotere Port Entrance 10 A2
SLEEPING
Hotel Widhana 11 B5
Losmen Semeru 12 A4
New Legend Hostel 13 A4
EATING
Kios Semarang 14 A5
Lae Lae Café 15 B5
Seafood Warung 16 A4
Sentosa 17 A5
TRANSPORT
Main Pete-Pete Station 18 B4
Pelabuhan Makassar (Pelni Port) 19 A3
Pelni 20 B5
Jl Satando
Jl Tarakan
Jl Hatta
Jl Nusantara
Jl Kalimantan
Jl Caddi
Jl Salemo
Jl Seram Ujung
Jl Butung
Jl Tentara Pelajar
Jl Sarappo
Jl Buru
Jl Irian
Jl Mohammadiyah
Jl Akademis
Jl Sangir
Jl Diponegoro
Jl Lembeh
Jl Andalas
Jl Bandang
Jl Hasyim
Jl Martadinata
Jl Timor
Jl Lombok
Jl Bali
Jl Sulawesi
Jl Ramli
Jl Sumba
Jl Jampea
Jl Cokroaminoto
Jl Mesjid Raya
Jl Serui Sama
Jl Bulusaraung
Jl Ahmad Yani
Jl Pasar Ikan
Jl Slamet Riyadi
Jl Balaikota
Jl Kajaolalido
Lapangan Karebosi
Jl Gunung Lompobatang
Jl Sungai Cerekang
Jl Bawakaraeng
Jl Supratman
To Hasanuddin Airport (22km); Terminal Panaikang (22km); Pare Pare (160km); Rantepao (328km)
Jl Pattimura
Jl Thamrin
Jl R A Kartini
Marannu Hotel
Jl Amannagappa
Jl Sungai Poso
Jl Somba Opu
Jl Baumassepe
Taman Hiburan Makasar
Canal
Jl Veteran Utara
Jl Gunung Latimojong
Jl Daeng Tompo
Jl Ince Nurdin
Jl Botolempangan
Jl Hasanuddin
Jl Ranggong
Jl Khairilan War
Jl Sudirman
Jl Gunung Merapi
Jl Sungai Paremang
Jl Gunung Salahutu
Jl Kerung Kerung
Jl Penghibur
Jl Alimalaka
Jl Sawerigading
Panampu
Jl Mochtar Lufti
Jl Sungai Limboto
Jl Sultomo
Jl Datu Musseng
Jl Gunung Kelabat
Jl Gunung Nona
Governor's Residence
Jl Abubakar Lambogo
Selat Makassar
Jl Kenari
Jl Sungai Saddang
Jl Sarif Alqadri
Jl Metro Tanjung Bunga
Jl Anfrate
Jl Sam Ratulangi
Jl Monginsidi
Terminal Mallengkeri (5km)

INDONESIA

Losmen Semeru (☎ 310410; Jl Jampea 28; d 50,000Rp; ❄) This place is shabbier and decidedly less friendly, but the rooms are clean and it's definitely a good deal.

Hotel Widhana (☎ 321393; Jl Botolempangan 53; s/d 72,000/80,000Rp; ❄) This is your cave, absent of natural light (and heat), and accented by even darker furnishings. For the price, rooms are reasonably comfy.

Eating & Drinking

Sentosa (☎ 326062; Jl Penghibur 26; wonton soup 6000Rp; ⏰ lunch & dinner) Locals flock here for endless bowls of aromatic soup. The place sells gallons of it.

Kios Semarang (Jl Penghibur; meals 15,000Rp; ⏰ lunch & dinner) At times, Makassar days can devolve into a steamy, maddening muddle. That's when you come to this local institution for fried shrimp and icy Bintang served on a shaded top-floor patio. Sip away your worries and watch windsurfers carve the bay.

Lae Lae Café (☎ 334326; Jl Datu Musseng 8; fish from 15,000Rp; ⏰ lunch & dinner) It's not exactly romantically lit, but the fish is perfectly done, and flakes off the bone. Shred the lemon basil, mix it with rice and fish, add a squeeze of lime, a dollop of spicy *sambal* and scoop it with your fingers. Utensils are for package tourists.

A line-up of makeshift seafood *warung* set up at night opposite Fort Rotterdam, serving cheap and tasty fried fish.

Getting There & Away

AIR

Makassar is well connected to airports throughout Indonesia. Flight schedules and rates fluctuate.

Merpati (code MZ; ☎ 442471; www.merpati.co.id) flies daily to Jakarta, Balikpapan, Manado and Jayapura.

Garuda (code GA; ☎ 365 4747; www.garuda-indonesia.com) has daily services to Manado, Jakarta, Balikpapan, and Denpasar. It also flies to Jayapura, Pulau Biak, and Timika.

Lion Air/Wings Air (code JT; ☎ 327038; www.lionair.co.id) flies to Manado, Gorontalo, Palu, Jakarta, Surabaya, Denpasar and Ambon.

Adam Air (code KI; ☎ 319222; www.flyadamair.com) flies to Jakarta and Surabaya.

BOAT

Pelni (☎ 331401; www.pelni.com; Jl J Sudirman 38) has connections to countless destinations across Indonesia from Makassar, one of its principal hubs. Check the website for details.

BUS

Buses heading north leave from Terminal Panaikang, aka Dayak Terminal, in the eastern suburbs, to Pare Pare (22,000Rp, three hours), Sengkang (33,000Rp, four hours) and Rantepao (normal/air-con 55,000Rp/70,000Rp, eight hours) in Tana Toraja. **Bintang Prima** (☎ 477 2888) is the new luxury bus line in town, with trips to Toraja (70,000Rp, with air-con). Get here by blue *pete-pete* from Makassar Mall (2000Rp, 30 minutes).

Southbound buses leave from Terminal Mallengkeri, 10km southeast of the centre, a 3000Rp bemo ride.

Getting Around

The main *pete-pete* station is at Makassar Mall, and the standard fare is 2000Rp. Becak drivers/hawkers can be charming and exhausting all at once. Their shortest fare is 3000Rp. Taxis are metered.

TANA TORAJA

Get ready for a dizzying cocktail of stunning serene beauty, elaborate, brutal and captivating funeral rites, exquisite traditional architecture, and a profoundly peculiar fascination with the dead. It comes garnished with a pinch of Indiana Jones intrigue, and is served by some of the warmest and toughest people you'll ever meet: the Torajans. Before Pulau Bunaken's rise to glory, Tana Toraja was Sulawesi's top attraction. During funeral season, in July and August, they still get a flow of khaki-clad package tourists, and day-trippers from cruise ships, but the rest of the year it's empty and starved for visitors, which means grateful hosts, good deals and a frontierlike appeal.

The capital, Makale, and Rantepao, the largest town and tourist magnet, are the main centres. Bemo link them to surrounding villages, where you'll find cultural hot spots tucked into spectacular countryside (see boxed text, p318).

Rantepao

☎ 0423 / pop 41,400

With a variety of budget lodging and solid public transport, Rantepao is the best base for exploring Tana Toraja. There is one unforgettable sight: **Pasar Bolu**, the market 2km northeast of town. It peaks every six days, with an overflowing livestock market. A must see for all urbanites.

INFORMATION

Bank Danamon (Jl Diponegoro) The ATM here will allow you to withdraw larger amounts than some others.

BNI bank (Jl Ahmad Yani) Changes money and has an ATM.

Post office (☎ 21014; Jl Ahmad Yani)

Rumah Sakit Elim (☎ 21258; Jl Ahmad Yani) Basic medical facilities.

Telkom office (Jl Ahmad Yani; 24hr)

Tourist office (☎ 25210; Jl Ahmad Yani 62A; 8am-2pm Mon-Sat, to noon Fri) Useful for its rudimentary trekking trail map.

Warnet Petra (Jl Andi Mappanyukki 46; per hr 10,000Rp) The only viable internet service in town.

ACTIVITIES

To truly immerse yourself in Toraja land, you've got to trek off the main roads. Good footwear is vital, and so is ample food, water, a torch (flashlight; some villages lack electricity) and rain gear. If you desire a professional trekking outfitter, contact **Indosella** (☎ 25210; www.sellatours.com; Jl Anddi Mappanyukki 111), which also organises white-water rafting trips. For a brilliant day trek, take a morning bemo to Deri, then veer off-road and traverse the incredible cascading rice fields all the way to Tikala. Farmers and villagers will help point the way, but a guide would be a wise decision for this trek. Popular multiday treks include the following:

Batumonga–Lokomata–Pangala–Baruppu–Pulu Pulu–Sapan Three days.

Bittuang–Mamasa Three days.

Pangala–Bolokan–Bittuang Two days on a well-marked trail.

Sa'dan–Sapan–Pulu Pulu–Baruppu–Pangala A gruelling three-day mountain trek.

INDONESIA

SLEEPING

Pia's Poppies Hotel (☎ 21121; Jl Pongtiku; s/d/tr 45,000/65,000/75,000Rp) A kilometre south of town, Pia's is fun and quirky, with mosaic showers, built-in stone deck furniture, and a sweet garden setting.

Hotel Pison (☎ 21344; Jl Pongtiku; s/d 50,000/75,000Rp) Next door is another clean, quiet spot, with mountain and rice-field views from tiny balconies.

Wisma Irama (☎ 21371; Jl Abdul Gani 16; economy/standard r 60,000/80,000Rp) There's an authentic Torajan rice barn in the sunny courtyard, relatively modern rooms and a nice lounge.

Wisma Surya (☎ 21312; Jl Monginsidi 36; d 75,000Rp) Cleanish and basic with a nice sitting room and inviting back porch overlooking that churning chocolate river.

Duta 88 (☎ 23477; Jl Sawerigading; d 80,000Rp) Bromeliads and ferns sprout from the grass roofs of these comfortable replica Torajan cottages, built with ample deck space. Hot water included.

EATING & DRINKING

The food here only borders on interesting. A local speciality is *pa'piong*, a mix of meat (usually pork or chicken) and leaf vegetables smoked over a low flame. Order in advance and enjoy it with black rice.

Rumah Makan Padang (☎ 21134; Jl Diponegoro 58; dishes 10,000Rp; lunch & dinner) This place is clean and friendly. Try the fried chicken, stewed greens and Padang-style baked potato.

Rimiko Restaurant (☎ 25223; Jl Andi Mappanyukki; dishes from 20,000Rp; breakfast, lunch & dinner) This is the best of a bland bunch. The avocado and shrimp salad is great, and so is the satay, while the Torajan dishes are the best around.

Riman Restoran (☎ 23626; Jl Andi Mappanyukki 113; mains 25,000Rp; breakfast, lunch & dinner) The beer's cold, but the food is so-so.

Warung sizzle along the main road.

GETTING THERE & AROUND

Bus companies are clustered in the town centre around Jl Andi Mappanyukki. For the 330km trip to Makassar (economy/air-con 55,000/70,000Rp), check **Litha** (☎ 21204) and **Bintang Prima** (☎ 21142). Even more buses head to Pare Pare (25,000Rp, five hours).

Northbound buses travel to Pendolo (80,000Rp, 10 hours), Tentena (95,000Rp, 12 hours), Poso (110,000Rp, 13 hours) and Palu (135,000Rp, 19 hours).

Kijang leave for Makale (4000Rp, 20 minutes) constantly, and will drop you at the signs for Londa, Tilanga or Lemo, to walk to the villages.

From Terminal Bolu, 2km northeast of Rantepao, frequent vehicles go east to Palopo (20,000Rp, two hours), and regular bemo and Kijang go to all the major villages, such as Lempo (near Batutumonga).

Motorbikes can be rented from hotels and tour agencies for 60,000Rp per day.

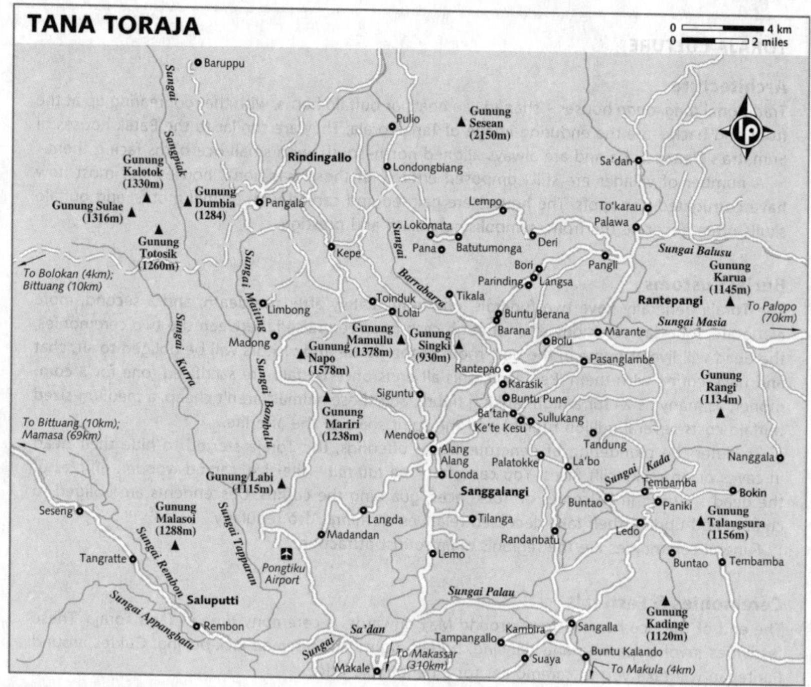

Around Rantepao

There's the beautiful: stunning panoramas, magical bamboo forests, and rice terraces, shaped by natural boulders and fed by waterfalls, that drop for 2000m. There's the strange: *tau tau* (wooden effigies) of long-lost relatives guarding graves carved out of vertical limestone rock faces or hung from the roof of deep caves. And there's the intermingling of the two: incredibly festive and colourful four-day funerals where buffalo are slaughtered and stewed, palm wine is swilled from bamboo carafes, and a spirit soars to the afterlife. All this is accessible on day trips from Rantepao. Multiday trekkers can stay overnight in private homes for a small fee and/or a carton of smokes. Guides aren't essential, but they are inexpensive (150,000Rp per day), will offer cultural insights and can escort you to local ceremonies.

SOUTH OF RANTEPAO

Karasik (1km from Rantepao) is on the outskirts of town, just off the road leading to Makale. The traditional houses were erected years ago for a funeral.

Just off the main road, southeast of Rantepao, **Ke'te Kesu** (6km) is famed for its woodcarving. On the cliff face behind the village are cave graves and some very old hanging graves – the rotting coffins are suspended from an overhang.

Located about 2km off the Rantepao–Makale road, **Londa** (6km) is an extensive burial cave, one of the most interesting in the area. Above the cave is a line-up of *tau tau* that peer down, in fresh clothes, from their cliff-side perch. Inside the dank darkness, coffins hang above dripping stalagmites. Others lie rotting on the stone floor, exposing skulls and bones. Very Indiana Jones. Hire a guide with an oil lamp from the village gate (20,000Rp).

Lemo (11km) is among the largest burial areas in Tana Toraja. The sheer rock face has dozens of balconies for *tau tau*. There would be even more *tau tau* if they weren't in such demand by unscrupulous antique dealers who deal in bad karma. A bemo from Rantepao will drop you off at the road leading up to the burial site, from where it's a 15-minute walk.

TORAJA CULTURE

Architecture

Traditional *tongkonan* houses – shaped like boats or buffalo horns, with the roof rearing up at the front and back – are the enduring image of Tana Toraja. They are similar to the Batak houses of Sumatra's Danau Toba and are always aligned north–south, with small rice barns facing them.

A number of villages are still composed entirely of these traditional houses, but most now have corrugated-iron roofs. The houses are painted and carved with animal motifs, and buffalo skulls often decorate the front, symbolising wealth and prestige.

Burial Customs

The Toraja generally have two funerals, one immediately after the death, and a second, more elaborate, four-day ceremony after enough cash has been raised. Between the two ceremonies, the dead will live at home in the best room of the house and visitors will be obliged to sit, chat and have coffee with them. Regularly. This all ends once buffalo are sacrificed (one for a commoner, as many as 24 for a high-ranking figure, and these animals aren't cheap: a medium-sized buffalo costs several million rupiah) and the spirit soars to the afterlife.

To deter the plundering of generous burial offerings, the Toraja started to hide their dead in caves or on rocky cliff faces. You can often see *tau tau* – life-size, carved wooden effigies of the dead – sitting in balconies on rock faces, guarding the coffins. Descendents are obliged to change and update their fake deceased relatives clothing. Also regularly.

Funeral ceremonies are the region's main tourist attraction.

Ceremonies & Festivals

The end of the rice harvest, from around May onwards, is ceremony time in Tana Toraja. These festivities involve feasting and dancing, buffalo fights and *sisemba* kick-boxing. Guides around Rantepao will take you to ceremonies for a negotiable price.

EAST OF RANTEPAO

Marante (6km) is a traditional village right by the road east to Palopo, near rice fields and stone and hanging graves guarded by *tau tau*. Further off the Palopo road, **Nanggala** (16km) has a grandiose traditional house with 14 rice barns. Charter a bemo from Rantepao, and they'll take you straight there, or take a public one, and walk 7km from the Palopo road.

NORTH & WEST OF RANTEPAO

This is where you'll find the finest scenery in Tana Toraja. **Batutumonga** (20km) has an ideal panoramic perch, sensational sunrise views and a few homestays. The best is **Mentirotiku** (☎ 081 142 2260; d 80,000Rp). The views are even more stunning from the summit of **Gunung Sesean**, a 2150m peak towering above the village. Most bemo stop at **Lempo**, an easy walk from Batutumonga.

There are more cave graves and beautiful scenery at **Lokomata** (26km), just a few kilometres west past Batutumonga.

The return to Rantepao is an interesting and easy trek down the slopes through tiny villages to **Pana**, with its ancient hanging graves, and baby graves in the trees. The path ends at **Tikala**, where regular bemo go to Rantepao.

The three-day, 59km trek from **Mamasa** in the west to Bittuang is popular, and there are plenty of villages en route with food and accommodation (remember to bring gifts). There's no direct transport from Rantepao to Mamasa because the roads are appalling, but you can travel to Bittuang from Mamasa by Kijang or bemo, or take a bus from Makale (80,000Rp, 10 hours) three times a week.

PENDOLO

Pendolo is a quiet village with lonely swimming beaches on the south shore of enormous **Danau Poso** in Central Sulawesi.

Mulia Poso Lake Hotel (Jl Pelabuhan; d 150,000Rp) has lovely cottages on the beach.

The daily 8am ferry from Pendolo will shuttle you across the lake to Tentena (25,000Rp, three hours). If the weather's rough, take the bus.

TENTENA

☎ 0458

This lakeside village lacks Pendolo's fine beaches, but is larger with better accommodation. There has been some sectarian violence in Tentena, and police are everywhere (see boxed text, below).

Hotel Pamona Indah (☎ 21245; Jl Yos Sudarso 25; d from 110,000Rp) is the place to stay in Tentena. The building is grand, with large columns and peach trim, the 20 rooms are spotless and comfortable and the restaurant, serving the town's famous *sugili* (giant eels), is the best in town.

Buses make the run to Poso (15,000Rp, two hours) throughout the day.

POSO

☎ 0452 / pop 50,300

Central Sulawesi's second-largest city, Poso is simply a transit point or a place to withdraw or change money before you head to the Togeans. Recent Sectarian Christian-Muslim riots and the murder of resident Balinese has scarred Poso deeply (see boxed text, below) and spurred the deployment of patrolling national *polisi* squadrons.

The city has a **BNI bank** (Jl Yos Sudarso) and a vaguely useful **tourist office** (☎ 23290; Jl Sudirman; 8am-3pm Mon-Sat, to 11am Fri).

Losmen Alugoro (☎ 21336; Jl Sumatera 20; d from 55,000Rp;) is a bit smarter than Losmen Lalanga Jaya, but only if you snag an air-con room (110,000Rp).

Losmen Lalanga Jaya (☎ 22326; Jl Yos Sudarso; d 65,000Rp) has creaky rooms with a view, and is conveniently located next to the port.

Buses leave the terminal, 800m north of the post office, for Palu (35,000Rp, six hours), Tentena (20,000Rp, two hours), Ampana (35,000Rp, five hours) and Rantepao (115,000Rp, 13 hours).

PALU

☎ 0451 / pop 307,500

Set in a rain shadow, Central Sulawesi's capital is one of the driest places in Indonesia. The main reason to visit Palu is to arrange the 100km trip to trek the remote 2290-sq-km **Taman Nasional Lore Lindu**, where you can glimpse ancient stone megaliths, and explore lowland and montane rainforest, home to 227 bird species (including 77 varieties endemic to Sulawesi). It's also the focal point of a German climate-change study that attracts a steady stream of European scientists.

Orientation & Information

Palu's airport is 7km east of town, 25,000Rp by taxi.

Balai Taman Nasional Lore Lindu office (☎ 457623; just off Jl Tanjung Manimbayan) For essential permits, maps and information.

Tourist office (☎ 455260; Jl Dewi Sartika 91; 7.15am-4pm Mon-Sat, until 11.30am Fri) Has city maps and national park tips.

Sleeping & Eating

Purnama Raya Hotel (☎ 423646; Jl Wahidin 4; s/d 30,000/40,000Rp) The brightest of Palu's subpar cheapies. The knowledgeable manager moonlights as a local guide.

Rama Garden Hotel (☎ 429500; Jl Moginsidi 81; s/d 110,000/160,000Rp;) The rooms border on plush, making this a worthy step up. The outdoor lounge is lovely.

Depot Citra (Jl Moh Yamin; mains 15,000Rp; breakfast, lunch & dinner) Friendly, hole-in-the-wall seafood joint.

Night *warung* gather in a fragrant herd along the breezy seafront, Jl Raja Moili.

Getting There & Around

Merpati (code MZ; ☎ 423341; www.merpati.co.id), **Batavia Air** (code 7P; ☎ 428888; www.batavia-air.co.id) and

INDONESIA

WARNING

Central Sulawesi is volatile and has suffered sectarian (read Christian versus Muslim) violence between young thugs since 1998. A 2001 peace deal was followed by shootings, bombings and church attacks in December 2004. Locals compare it to gang violence in the US. In April 2005 both sides agreed to another fragile peace deal. Then in late May 2005, twin explosions ripped through the morning market in the mainly Christian town of Tentena, near Poso, killing at least 20 people and wounding 40. In 2007 several Balinese Hindus were murdered. Foreigners are not considered targets, and the police presence here is tremendous, but you should watch the news and consider renting a car if you want to make the trip from Tana Toraja to Ampana or go overland from Makassar to Manado.

Lion Air (code JT; ☎ 428777; www.lionair.co.id) fly to Makassar. Merpati also flies to Luwuk. Batavia flies to Balikpapan.

Pelni (☎ 421696; Jl Kartini 96) is well connected to East Kalimantan and other Sulawesi ports. Ships dock at Pantoloan, 22km north of Palu, where there is another Pelni office.

Buses depart from Terminal Masomda for Poso (130,000Rp, six hours), Ampana (180,000Rp, 10 hours), Rantepao (170,000Rp, nine hours), Gorontalo (150,000Rp) and Manado (200,000Rp, 14 hours).

Minibuses and shared taxis to Pantoloan (for Pelni boats; 25,000Rp, 30 minutes) and Donggala (for Tanjung Karang; 15,000Rp, one hour) leave from Terminal Manonda.

DONGGALA

☎ 0457

Donggala's main attractions are the reefs at **Tanjung Karang** (Coral Peninsula), north of town. Prince John Dive Resort is the only scuba shack. Its house reef suits snorkellers and beginner divers.

Travellers buzz about this slice of white sand at **Kaluku Cottages** (bungalows all-inclusive 75,000Rp), 15km from Donggala. The nearby coral reef is ideal for snorkellers. Get here by *ojek*.

Prince John Dive Resort (☎ 71710; www.prince-john-diveresort.de; all-inclusive d from 350,000Rp) is a worthy splurge for divers, especially midweek when tranquillity reigns on the sands.

From Palu, you can catch a shared *taksi* (taxi) to Donggala for 6000Rp, and walk 30 minutes to the beach, or charter a Kijang for around 25,000Rp.

AMPANA

☎ 0464

Ampana is the gateway to the Togeans. Given bus and ferry schedules, you will likely spend a night here. Remember, the lone ATM only takes MasterCard!

Oasis Hotel (☎ 21058; Jl Kartini; dm/d 30,000/70,000Rp), run in conjunction with Kadidiri Paradise, is within sprinting distance to the ferry port, has a lovely garden and treats guests like family.

Marina Cottages (☎ 21280; cottages 77,000Rp), at Labuhan, 10 minutes east by *bendi*, has a string of wooden cottages on a pebble beach.

Ferries shove off to Gorontalo, via the Togean ports of Wakai (45,000Rp, 4½ hours), Katupat, Malenge and Dolong, on Monday, Thursday and Saturday. Two other boats share the Ampana–Wakai route. At least one boat leaves the Ampana port at 10.30am every day except Friday and Sunday. There are two departures on Monday and Wednesday and all three sail on Saturday.

Ampana is on the main road from Poso (35,000Rp, five hours by bus). A night bus from Palu goes through Ampana on the way to Luwuk (50,000Rp, six hours).

TOGEAN ISLANDS

These jungled limestone islands, with fire-streak sunsets, peaceful pink dawns, glassy seas and pure white sand are Sulawesi's true treasure. Villagers, who descend from seven ethnic groups, are warm and welcoming, and the mangroves are thick with life. There are lost lagoons and forgotten coves, and arguably the best diving in Sulawesi (which ranks it near the top worldwide). Disregard those outdated dynamite-fishing whispers, and plunge into crystal-clear, bottomless seas, to explore all three major reef systems – atoll, barrier and fringing. Colours absolutely pop. Fish are everywhere. You will extend your stay immediately upon arrival. Everyone does. Prices for lodging include meals.

GETTING AROUND

Public transport within the Togeans is snafu, but charters are easily arranged in Wakai, Bomba and Kadidiri. Kadidiri Paradise and Black Marlin shuttle their guests to/from the ferry port gratis. Otherwise you will have to pay at least 50,000Rp for a ride to Pulau Kadidiri.

Pulau Kadidiri

This island sucks stress from your bones. The beach is pure white, the sea 1000 colours of blue, there are jutting limestone karsts, and a perfectly imperfect jetty. The two eco-dive resorts both offer tasteful crash pads with varying degrees of comfort.

Kadidiri Paradise Resort (☎ 046 421 058; www.kadidiri-paradise.com; bungalows 100,000-250,000Rp) is a first-class ecodive resort that has intricately detailed bungalows with French doors and expansive verandas. There are bonfires and beach barbecues, and the fashionable matriarch, Huntje, is Central Sulawesi's answer to Martha Stewart – but with better style, and a lot more soul. The resort also has a full-service dive school run by the hilarious, iconoclastic French Swiss dive master,

Gonsag, who has been on Pualu Kadidiri for 12 years and counting. He charges US$30 per dive.

The beach bungalows at **Black Marlin Cottages** (☎ 043 583 1869; www.blackmarlindive.com; d from 100,000Rp;) lack the character of Kadidiri's, but the beach is lovely, and the dive school is solid (also US$30 per dive).

Togean Island & Around

Katupat is the main village on Togean Island, and it's a must-see. Stroll the charming streets and you'll meet warm, welcoming locals in the front yards of their stilted tin-roofed shacks. You'll also spot two-stroke coconut grinders and cows grazing on the soccer pitch, and you may contemplate following the narrow hiking trail that disappears into the nearby village.

Fadhila Cottages (cottages 95,000Rp), opposite the village on private Pagempa Island, offers new wooden cottages with superb beaches and outstanding bay views in all directions. **Bolilangga Cottages** (cottages 80,000Rp), on Bolilangga Island, is for wannabe castaways.

Pulau Malenge

Remote Pulau Malenge has great snorkelling near the village.

Malenge Indah (cottages 70,000Rp) is the choice here.

Pulau Batu Daka

BOMBA

This tiny outpost at the southeastern end of Pulau Batu Daka has nearby reefs and exquisite beaches.

Set on a spectacular beach, **Island Retreat** (www.togian-island-retreat.com; d from 125,000Rp) is run by an eccentric California refugee, and overrun by her precious animal herd. The newer, upmarket bungalows are blessed with sensational mosaic bathrooms, and the kitchen is the best in the Togean archipelago.

> **CRUSTACEANS: MASSIVE, ENDANGERED**
>
> The Togeans are one of the last remaining habitats of coconut crabs, the world's largest terrestrial arthropod. The crabs, weighing up to 5kg and as much as 90cm across, once scuttled across islands throughout the western Pacific and eastern Indian Oceans, but humans have eaten them to the verge of extinction. If you see them on the menu, go with the *nasi goreng* (fried rice). Again.

WAKAI

The Togeans' largest settlement is a departure point for ferries to Ampana and Gorontalo and for charters to Pulau Kadidiri and beyond. There are a few general stores, if you need supplies, but there's no reason to stay the night.

MANADO

☎ 0431 / pop 479,700

Once described by Alfred Russel Wallace as 'one of the prettiest [cities] in the East', Manado has become shopping-mall hell, but that doesn't mean it's unenjoyable. After all, it is relatively modern, the people are warm and charming, and it's a great base for exploring North Sulawesi.

Orientation

Mikrolet from Sam Ratulangi airport go to Paal 2 terminal, where you change to another for Pasar 45 (the central *mikrolet* terminal) or elsewhere in the city (1500Rp). Metered taxis from the airport (13km) cost around 60,000Rp.

Along Jl Sam Ratulangi, the main north-south artery, you'll find restaurants, hotels and supermarkets. The shopping-mall blitz dominates parallel Jl Tendean, closer to the sea.

Information

You're never far from a bank, ATM or *wartel* in Manado.

BCA bank (Jl Sam Ratulangi) Good conversion rates and larger credit-card advances.

Main post office (Jl Sam Ratulangi 23) There's put-put internet here for 6000Rp per hour.

North Sulawesi tourism office (☎ 851723; Jl Diponegoro 111; 8am-2pm Mon-Sat) The more useful counter is at the airport.

Rumah Sakit Umum (☎ 853191; Jl Monginsidi, Malalayang) This is a full-service hospital with decompression chamber.

Showtime (4th fl, Mega Mall, Jl Tendean; per hr 15,000Rp) Swift internet service.

Sleeping

Rex Hotel (☎ 851136; Jl Sugiono 3; economy r 30,000-65,000Rp, standard d 75,000Rp;) *Ekonomi* rooms resemble prison cells, but standard rooms are clean, comfy and great value.

RESPECT YOUR ELDERS

Think you're outgrowing your backpacker days? Tell that to Ole, a Norwegian who, at 73, standing straight as an arrow, still lives like a tramp after more than 60 years on the road. He's been to six continents, countless countries and Southeast Asia is his favourite destination. His secret is packing light. He carries two pairs each of quick-drying trousers, shirts, underwear and socks. He stuffs it all in a beat-up 30-year-old pack that he always carries himself. 'When I can no longer carry my own bag, I will stop travelling,' he says. When he does travel (at least four months a year) it's by local economy bus. 'I'm not sure my friends would like it,' he says the day after braving a 40-plus hour odyssey from Makassar through Poso to Manado. 'I enjoy the atmosphere, being with the locals. That's why I travel.'

Manado Bersehati Hotel (☎ 855022; Jl Sudirman 20; s/d from 47,000/74,000Rp; ❄) Set in a converted traditional Minahasan house, off the main road, the cleanish economy rooms here are cramped, but the huge veranda provides room to stretch.

New Angkasa (☎ 863250; Jl Sugiorno 9; s/d 50,000/75,000Rp; ❄) Excellent-value budget digs. Even the superior air-con rooms are affordable (d 85,000Rp).

Eating & Drinking

Adventurous diners migrate to the night *warung* along Jl Piere Tendean. Regional delights include *kawaok* (fried 'forest rat') and *rintek wuuk* (spicy dog meat).

Singapura Bakery (Jl Sam Ratulangi 22; pastries from 5000Rp; 🕑 breakfast, lunch & dinner) Explore an addictive array of delectable pastries at arguably Indonesia's finest bakery. Its Javanese diner (meals from 8000Rp) next door also attracts a crowd.

Famili Café (Jl Pierre Tendean; lunch 19,000Rp; 🕑 lunch & dinner) Local businesspeople flock here for the spicy grilled fish lunch specials, which include rice, greens and *sambal*.

Dabu Dabu (☎ 854511; Jl Pierre Tendean; fish 40,000Rp; 🕑 lunch & dinner) Tasty grilled fish and fresh juices served in an old converted wooden house.

The **Mega Mall** (Jl Tendean) has an extensive food court, and directly behind it is a string of oceanfront seafood *warung*. Try **Blue Terrace** (fried calamari 20,000Rp; 🕑 lunch & dinner) for icy Bintang and appetisers at sundown.

Entertainment

Studio 21 Cinema (☎ 856725; Jl Sam Ratulangi; tickets 15,000Rp) Four screens show recent Western releases.

Getting There & Away

AIR

These have useful services out of Manado:

Batavia (☎ 386 4338; www.batavia-air.co.id)
Garuda (☎ 877737; www.garuda-indonesia.com)
Lion/Wings Air (☎ 888022; www.lionair.co.id)
Merpati (☎ 842000; www.merpati.co.id)
SilkAir (☎ 863744; www.silkair.com)

International connections include SilkAir's three weekly flights to Singapore. Merpati flies to Jakarta, Gorontalo and Kota Ternate, among others. Lion flies to Luwuk, and Wings flies to Sorong, Papua.

BOAT

Pelni (☎ 33848; Jl Sam Ratulangi 7) liners call at the deep-water port of Bitung, 55km from Manado, where you'll also find the ticketing office. Ships sail once or twice a week to Makassar (from 401,000Rp, three days), Ternate (from 315,000, three days), Ambon (from 203,000Rp, two days), Sorong (from 274,000Rp, two days) and Biak (1,200,000Rp, four days).

Small, slow, uncomfortable boats from Manado sail north to Tahuna (Pulau Sangihe) and Lirung (Talaud Islands), or east to Ternate and Ambon.

BUS

From Karombasan terminal, 5km south of the city, buses go to Tomohon (4000Rp, 40 minutes) and destinations south; from Malalayang terminal they go to Gorontalo (60,000Rp, eight hours); and from Paal 2 terminal, at the eastern end of Jl Martadinata, public transport runs to Bitung (5000Rp, one hour) and the airport (2000Rp, 40 minutes).

Getting Around

There's no *mikrolet* shortage in Manado. Destinations are shown on a card in the front windscreen. There are various bus stations around town for destinations outside

Manado; get to any of them from Pasar 45. Private, inexpensive metered taxis are usually within shouting distance.

PULAU BUNAKEN

Pulau Bunaken is Sulawesi's top destination, attracting short-termers and ramblers alike to see 300 varieties of pristine coral and 3000 species of fish in Bunaken Manado Tua Marine National Park. Given Pulau Bunaken's rise to worldwide dive-mecca status, prices are a touch high and some resorts refuse nondivers, but there are still bargains hidden among the towering mangroves, crumbling cliffs and white sand.

Activities

Dive rates range from US$25 to US$35 plus US$10 for equipment hire. Check out **Living Colours** (☎ 081 2430 6401; www.livingcoloursdiving.com), **Froggies** (☎ 081 2430 1356; www.divefroggies.com), **Bunanken Village Dive Resort** (☎ 081 340 757268; www.bunakenvillage.com) and **Ocean Star** (☎ 081 340 037657; ternyt@yahoo.com).

The Bunaken park fee is 50,000Rp per day or 150,000Rp for an annual pass.

Sleeping & Eating

Pantai Liang, to the west, has a beautiful stretch of sand that doubles as Manado's de facto refuse dump when tides turn. Pantai Pangalisang, near Bunaken village, is the eco-choice. There's no beach to lie on, but it overlooks an armada of stately mangrove trees closer to Bunaken village, and the nearby reef is ideal for snorkelling. Most hotels quote rates per person for full board.

PANTAI LIANG

Panorama Cottages (☎ 081 2447 0420; 75,000Rp) Some rooms are rickety, but they're set on the cliffs with marvellous sea and volcano views. Attractive new bungalows were being completed when we visited.

Nelson's Cottages (☎ 043-185 6288; 150,000Rp) These basic huts are built into the hillside, have gorgeous turquoise bay views and are steps from the sand.

Nyiur Melambi Cottages (☎ 043-1330 9015; 150,000Rp) Next door to Nelson's with similar views, and a more modern duplex setup.

Froggies (☎ 081 2430 1356; www.divefroggies.com; from €25) This charming French-run place was the first dive resort on Pulau Bunaken, and it's almost always fully booked. You can find all the creature comforts here, including freshwater showers! But they refuse nondivers.

PANTAI PANGALISANG

Lorenso Cottages (from 100,000Rp) These rattan bungalows are situated nicely in the shadow of nearby mangrove trees, and Lorenso is known to break out the freshly caught and grilled barracuda at suppertime.

Ocean Star (☎ 081 34003 7657; 150,000Rp) A new arrival, this intimate Minahasan-run resort has just three wood-and-bamboo bungalows steps from the sea. Its affordable dive centre has brand-new gear!

Living Colours (☎ 081 2430 6401; from €25) This place has the best bungalows on Pulau Bunaken, with thick wooden floors, stylish stone bathrooms, coconut-wood beds and ample deck space. The dive center is excellent, and it shuttles guests to and from Manado for free.

Getting There & Away

Boats leave the fishing harbour in Manado daily at 3pm (25,000Rp, one hour), except Sunday. The return from Pulau Bunaken is at 8am. A charter costs at least 150,000Rp one way. If you're staying and/or diving with one of the upmarket resorts, call ahead and they'll shuttle you for free.

TOMOHON

Pleasantly cool and lush, this popular weekend escape from Manado rests at the foot of Gunung Lokon in the Minahasa Highlands.

The recently renovated bamboo bungalows at **Happy Flower Homestay** (☎ 352787; Jl Rungku Dusun 1; d 85,000Rp) have hot water. **Onong's Palace** (☎ 315 7090; d 250,000Rp) is more upmarket, with exquisite grounds and great views. Frequent *mikrolet* travel to Tomohon (4000Rp, 40 minutes) from Manado's Terminal Korombasan.

BITUNG

☎ 0438 / pop 145,900

Bitung, the chief port of Minahasa, is 55km east of Manado. The **Pelni office** (☎ 35818) is in the harbour compound.

Mikrolet depart regularly from Manado's Paal 2 terminal. They drop you at the Mapalus terminal, outside Bitung, where you catch another *mikrolet* for the short trip into town.

MALUKU (MOLUCCAS)

All alluring tropical traits can be applied to Maluku. Pristine and lonely white-sand beaches? Check. Superb snorkelling? Check. Hospitable locals, slow pace, tasty cuisine, low prices? Absolutely. Maluku's economy peaked in the 16th century, when these 'Spice Islands' were the world's sole source of cloves and nutmeg, and fabled as the place where money does grow on trees. The ensuing frantic, competitive spice grab actually sparked the bloody era of European colonisation.

These days it's protected by distance and a reputation for civil unrest, so if you land here, dust off your Bahasa Indonesia and enjoy your stint as the lone *bule* living the lucid tropical dream.

Getting There & Around

Ambon and Ternate are the regional air hubs. Both have daily connections to Jakarta via Surabaya, Makassar, Manado, and limited connections to Papua. Merpati also manages a web of regional flights with ever-shifting schedules and frequent cancellations. One-way tickets must be booked from your point of departure.

Several Pelni liners port in Maluku. Check the latest schedules at www.pelni.com. Slow ASDP ferries, wooden motorboats and Perintis cargo ships cover the more remote Maluku islands.

PULAU AMBON

Pulau Ambon is ribboned with villages, dressed in shimmering foliage, defined by two great bays, and has recovered from recent civil unrest. This is your launch pad to the Bandas.

Kota Ambon

☎ 0911 / pop 379,700

The bay and mountain backdrop are magnificent, but Maluku's trade and transport centre is a battle-scarred, dusty city that still gets politically tense around elections. Travellers don't hang around for long (see the boxed text, right).

INFORMATION

Bank Mandiri (Jl Pantai Mardika) The best conversion rates in town.

> **IS IT SAFE?**
>
> Kota Ambon, in Maluku, has been another flash point of sectarian violence, with sporadic shootings and bomb blasts. The conflict has left more than 5000 Muslims and Christians dead since 1999. The anniversary of the failed 1950 declaration of a self-styled South Maluku Republic – 25 April – is a dangerous day, when religious violence has broken out in the past. In the 2004 riots, dozens died and hundreds were injured. Although all is calm now, and has been for a few years, be sure to monitor news reports for updates.

Maluku Tourist Bureau (☎ 312300; Jl Jendral Sudirman; 🕒 8am-2pm Mon-Sat)

SLEEPING & EATING

Penginapan Beta (☎ 353463; Jl Wim Reawaru; d 90,000Rp; ❄) The reigning backpacker fave, thanks to the English-speaking owner.

Pondok Wisata Listari (☎ 355596; Jl WR Supratman 18; d from 125,000Rp; ❄) Centrally located, airy and comfortable, with English-speaking management.

For cheap eats, there are *warung* near the Batu Merah market, and on Jl Ahmad Yani.

GETTING THERE & AWAY

Lion Air/Wings Air (code JT; ☎ 342251; www.lionair.co.id) flies daily to Makassar with connections to Manado, Jakarta and beyond. **Merpati** (code MZ; ☎ 342480; www.merpati.co.id) flies Tuesday to Kota Ternate.

Pelni (☎ 342328) has an office opposite the Pattimura Memorial. Boats leave from Yos Sudarso harbour.

Smaller boats from Slamat Riyadi Harbour serve north, east and remote southeast islands in Maluku.

BANDA ISLANDS

A gathering of epic tropical gems, with deserted stretches of white sand, and crescent bays, the storied Bandas once lured greedy Chinese, Arab, Javanese and European traders with a lust for nutmeg. In the 1990s they briefly blipped onto the backpacker radar, and have now faded back into glorious anonymity. Which means you'll have the beaches and those stark undersea drop-offs draped in Technicolor coral gardens, to yourself.

INDONESIA

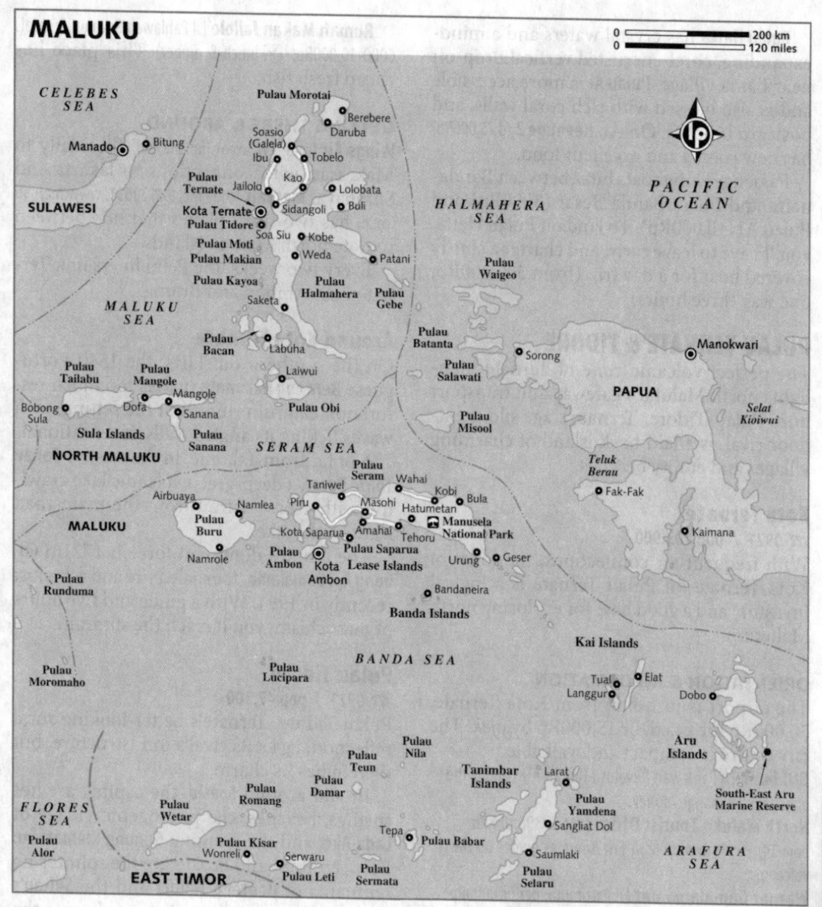

Bandaneira

☎ 0910

The main port of the Banda islands, situated on Pulau Neira, is a friendly, pleasantly sleepy town of colonial villas and blooming flowers.

Stop by the impressive **Benteng Belgica** (admission 20,000Rp; dawn-dusk), built on the hill above Bandaneira in 1611. The fort's upper reaches have incredible views of **Gunung Api**.

Hotel Maulana (☎ 21022; 2 tanks from US$90) has the Banda's only dive center. Rates are relatively expensive and equipment is 'mature'.

Think: comfortable waterfront rooms, a sweet wooden jetty, cold beer and an English-speaking owner that knows the reef. That's **Vita** (☎ 21332; d from 75,000Rp;).

At **Delfika 2** (☎ 21127; d from 75,000Rp;), two of the rooms glimpse the volcano, and the peaceful terrace has one of the best views in town.

Guesthouses serve tasty local fare.

Merpati (code MZ; ☎ 21060; www.merpati.co.id) flies to Ambon and Amahai (Seram) on Mondays. Book ahead and know that cancellations happen. Pelni ships sail from Ambon to Bandaneira. To tour the reef and explore other islands, charter a longboat at the fish market.

Other Islands

Pulau Banda Besar is the largest of the Banda islands, and the most important historical source of nutmeg. You can still visit **nutmeg groves** at the **Kelly Plantation** or explore the ruins of fort **Benteng Hollandia** (c 1624).

Pulau Hatta has crystal waters and a mind-expanding, coral-encrusted vertical drop-off near Lama village. **Pulau Ai** is more accessible and is also blessed with rich coral walls, and postcard beaches. On Ai, **Revenge 2** (d 75,000Rp) has new rooms and excellent food.

Passenger longboats buzz between Bandaneira and Pulau Banda Besar (3000Rp) and Pulau Ai (10,000Rp). To land on Pulau Hatta, you'll have to leave early, and charter a sturdy covered boat for a day trip (from 300,000Rp, one way three hours).

PULAU TERNATE & TIDORE

The perfect volcanic cone of Ternate highlights north Maluku's gateway and transport hub. Pulau Tidore, Ternate's age-old, next-door rival, is a laid-back island of charming villages and empty beaches.

Kota Ternate

☎ 0921 / pop 103,900

With frequent air connections, the town of Kota Ternate on Pulau Ternate is a logical first stop, and a good base for exploring north Maluku.

ORIENTATION & INFORMATION

The airport is just 6km from Kota Ternate; 50,000Rp for a taxi, or 15,000Rp by *ojek*. The city centre is compact and walkable.

BNI bank (Jl Pahlawan Revolusi) Has an ATM and is the only bank to change money.

North Maluku Tourist Office (☎ 27396; Jl Kamboja 14; 🕑 8am-4pm Mon-Fri) Arranges guides up the volcano.

Warnet Gamalama.net (Jl Pattimura; per hr 8000Rp) Comfortable environs, decent connection.

SIGHTS

Built in 1796, **Keraton Sultan** (Sultan's Palace; ☎ 21166; admission by donation; 🕑 6am-6pm) is 2km north of town. It has an interesting collection of colonial swords and armour, and the current Sultan's sister loves telling tales of the Ternetean royal family, a history that dates back to 1257.

SLEEPING & EATING

Taman Ria (☎ 22124; d from 75,000Rp) Pleasant rooms set in a waterfront garden south of the centre.

Hotel Sejathara (☎ 21139; Jl Salim Fabanyo 21; d from 77,000Rp) Clean and recently repainted, but the rooms are tiny.

Rumah Makan Jailolo (Jl Pahlawan Revolusi 7; meals 6000-10,000Rp; 🕑 lunch & dinner) This place has cheap fresh fish.

GETTING THERE & AROUND

Wings Air (code 1W; www.lionair.co.id) flies daily to Makassar, with connections to Jakarta and Surabaya. **Merpati** (code MZ; ☎ 21651; www.merpati.co.id) has two small planes that hop between remote north Maluku islands.

Every two weeks, the Pelni liners link Ternate with Ambon and Bitung.

Around Kota Ternate

On the southern outskirts, the 1540 Portuguese **Benteng Kalamata** proves too much restoration can ruin ruins, but the setting, with waves licking its angled walls, is sensational.

Not far from Takome, in the west, is **Danau Tolire Besar**, a deep-green volcanic lake crawling with crocs. A trail from the main road leads to the lake.

The island's dominant force is 1721m **Gunung Api Gamalama**. It exhaled fire and ash most recently in 1994. With a guide and five hours of masochism, you'll reach the summit.

Pulau Tidore

☎ 0921 / pop 47,300

Pulau Tidore, Ternate's better-looking rural reflection, lacks its rival's infrastructure, but therein lies its charm.

In and around **Soasio**, the capital, are hot springs, beaches, the photogenic village of **Lada-Ake**, and the looming **Gunung Kiematubu**. Between Rum and Soasio are the splintering remnants of **Benteng Tohula** and the **Sultan's Memorial Museum**, where you can glimpse the magical sultan's crown, if you can find the absentee curator. **Penginapan Seroja** (☎ 61456; Jl Sultan Hassanuddin; s/d 82,000/100,000Rp) is a splendid waterfront nest in Soasio.

Frequent speedboats (6000Rp) fire over from Bastiong port in Ternate.

PAPUA (IRIAN JAYA)

Papua – Indonesia's half of New Guinea, the world's second-largest island – is the living definition of wild. Its steep, layered mountains are impenetrable thanks to 400,000 sq km of thick jungle teeming with endemic species, and carved by churning chocolate rivers. Peaks are frosted with glaciers and snowfields, and slopes

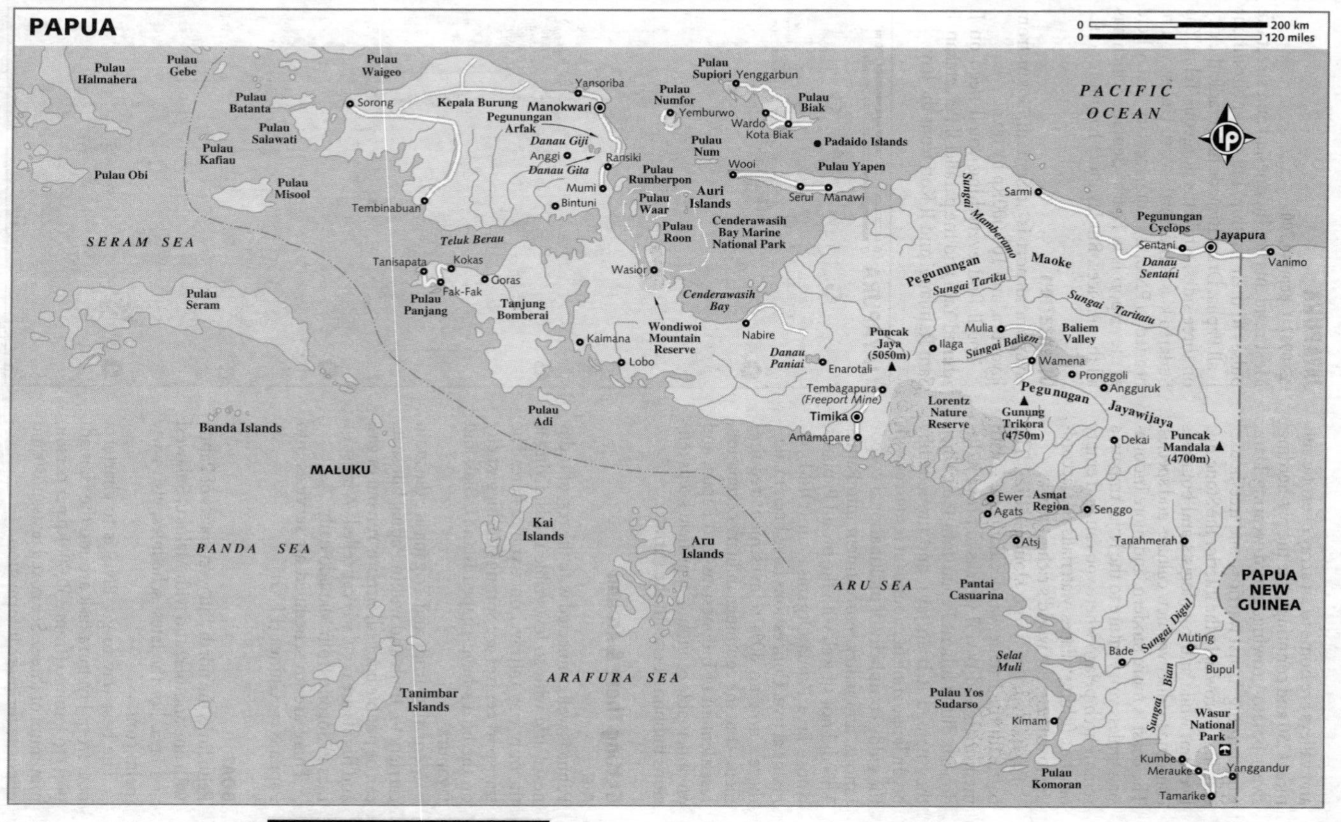
PAPUA
0 200 km
0 120 miles
Pulau Halmahera
Pulau Gebe
Pulau Waigeo
Pulau Batanta
Pulau Salawati
Pulau Kafiau
Pulau Obi
Pulau Misool
Sorong
Kepala Burung
Manokwari
Yansoriba
Pegunungan Arfak
Danau Giji
Anggi
Danau Gita
Ransiki
Mumi
Bintuni
Tembinabuan
Pulau Supiori
Yenggarbun
Pulau Numfor
Yemburwo
Wardo
Kota Biak
Pulau Biak
Padaido Islands
Pulau Num
Wooi
Pulau Yapen
Serui
Manawi
Pulau Rumberpon
Pulau Waar
Auri Islands
Pulau Roon
Cenderawasih Bay Marine National Park
PACIFIC OCEAN
SERAM SEA
Teluk Berau
Tanisapata
Kokas
Goras
Fak-Fak
Pulau Panjang
Tanjung Bomberai
Wasior
Cenderawasih Bay
Pulau Seram
Wondiwoi Mountain Reserve
Kaimana
Lobo
Nabire
Danau Paniai
Enarotali
Puncak Jaya (5050m)
Tembagapura (Freeport Mine)
Timika
Amamapare
Pulau Adi
Banda Islands
MALUKU
Sarmi
Sungai Mamberamo
Pegunungan
Sungai Tariku
Maoke
Pegunungan Cyclops
Sentani
Jayapura
Vanimo
Danau Sentani
Sungai Taritatu
Mulia
Ilaga
Sungai Baliem
Baliem Valley
Wamena
Pronggoli
Angguruk
Pegunugan
Jayawijaya
Lorentz Nature Reserve
Gunung Trikora (4750m)
Dekai
Puncak Mandala (4700m)
Ewer
Agats
Asmat Region
Senggo
Atsj
Tanahmerah
Kai Islands
Aru Islands
BANDA SEA
ARU SEA
Pantai Casuarina
PAPUA NEW GUINEA
Sungai Digul
Bade
Muting
Bupul
Selat Muli
ARAFURA SEA
Tanimbar Islands
Pulau Yos Sudarso
Sungai Bian
Kimam
Wasur National Park
Kumbe
Merauke
Yanggandur
Tamarike
Pulau Komoran

INDONESIA

and valleys are home to an array of exotic cultures (250 and counting), like the pig-herding, sweet-potato-growing, gourd-wearing Dani, woodcarving Asmat warriors, and tree-house-dwelling Korowai. In the interior the Stone Age lives on, while anthropologists and botanists continue to 'discover' new cultures and species. The coast is more modern, and more Indonesian, unless you venture to the Raja Ampats, a remote archipelago where you can find empty beaches, fishing villages, waterfalls and, according to experts, the world's richest reefs.

Papua's history is no slouch either. The battle for the Pacific was decided here – with memorials and WWII wrecks to prove it. Indonesia didn't inherit Papua until 1963, when they named it Irian Jaya, and immediately began liquidating her abundant resources with the giddy complicity of multinational corporations, and paltry reinvestment into Papua. This did not sit well with the proud Papuans, whose Free Papua Organisation (OPM) remains active. Concessions have been made – there's now an 80% reinvestment requirement – but the continued military occupation, resettlement of Indonesians into Papua, and an undeniable economic apartheid keeps tensions bubbling beneath the surface.

Getting There & Around

AIR

Papua is well connected with the rest of Indonesia, and with so few viable roads, flying is the only way to travel once you're here. The transport centres are Sorong (the biggest city on the bird's-head-shaped island), Biak and Jayapura

Merpati, Garuda and Trigana are the main carriers to, from and within Papua, but seats can be double booked, airports run out of gas, and flights are regularly cancelled. Wings Air flies to Sorong from Manado daily.

There are no scheduled air services into Papua New Guinea (PNG).

BOAT

Pelni links the north and west coasts of Papua with one another, and with Maluku, Sulawesi and Java. For the latest schedules, visit www.pelni.com.

The best way to get PNG is to charter a boat from Jayapura (ask around the Hamadi port) to Vanimo (from 350,000Rp per person, minimum of three). See boxed texts, p330 and opposite for more information.

JAYAPURA

☎ 0967 / pop 140,700

Most residents are Indonesian and street life pulses to their rhythm, but the environment is all Papua. Dramatic jade hills cradle the city on three sides, while the gorgeous Teluk Yos Sudarso kisses the north coast. Unless you're headed to PNG, it's not necessary to stay here as the airport is in nearby Sentani, which has all the services. But Jayapura has more soul.

Orientation

Jayapura airport is at Sentani, 36km from Jayapura, and 100,000Rp by taxi.

You'll find everything you'll need on Jl Ahmad Yani and the parallel Jl Percetakan. Jl Sam Ratulangi and Jl Koti front the bay.

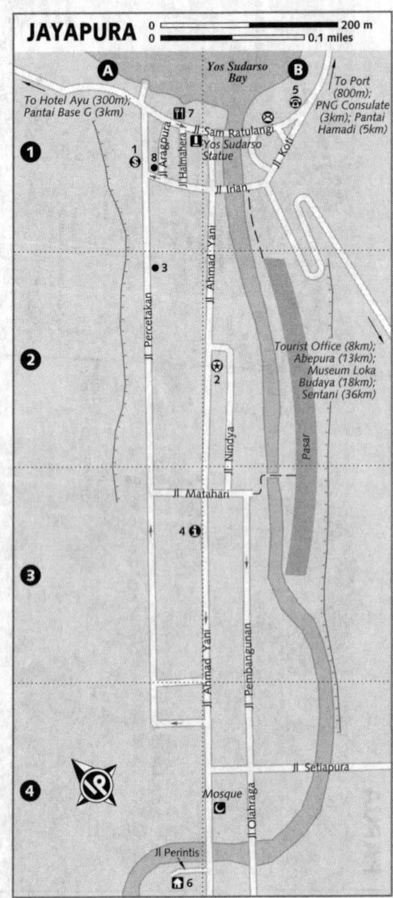

VISITOR PERMITS (SURAT JALAN)

Within 24 hours of arrival in Papua, visitors must obtain a *surat jalan*, a permission to travel, from the local police station *(polres)*. They are easiest to get in Jayapura and should be ready within one hour. Bring three passport photos, three copies of the photo page in your passport and three copies of the passport page with the Indonesian visa on it. Police will charge a flexible 'administration fee' of around 5000Rp.

List every conceivable place you might want to visit, as it might be difficult to add them later, outside the large cities. As you travel around Papua, you are supposed to have the document stamped in local police stations. It is worth keeping a few photocopies of the permit in case police or hotels ask for them.

In practice, these are only necessary if you plan on visiting the interior. In cities and within the Raja Ampats, nobody will bother you about it. But if you're going to the Baliem Valley, get your papers in order.

Information

The tourist office is about 8km from the centre; it's not worth the trip.

BII bank (Jl Percetakan 22) Changes money and has an ATM.

District police station (☎ 531027, Jl Ahmad Yani; 🕑 7am-3pm Mon-Fri) Arrange your *surat jalan* (special permit) at the 'Satuan IPP' office upstairs.

PT Kuwera Jaya (☎ 531583; Jl Ahmad Yani 39) Efficient travel agency with English-speaking staff.

Telkom office (Jl Sam Ratulangi)

Warnet Media (Jl Pencetakan; per hr 12,000Rp) Jayapura's best web connection.

Sights & Activities

On the Cenderawasih University campus is **Museum Loka Budaya** (Jl Abepura, Abepura; admission by donation; 🕑 8.30am-4pm Mon-Fri). The curator offers free tours of his incredible collection of sculptures, bark paintings, canoes, spears and shields. The small, authentic art shop is a gold mine for collectors. The museum is along the Sentani–Abepura bemo route.

Pantai Hamadi was the site of an American amphibious landing in 1944. There are rusting WWII wrecks on the beach. A famous 1944 General MacArthur photo op made **Pantai Base G**, west of the centre, famous. The beach is a 10-minute downhill walk from where the public taxis, marked 'Base G', drop you off.

INFORMATION	
BII Bank	1 A1
District Police Station	2 B2
Immigration Office	3 A2
PT Kuwera Jaya	4 A3
Telkom Office	5 B1
SLEEPING	
Hotel Kartini	6 A4
EATING	
Duta Café	(see 7)
Seafood Warung	7 A1
TRANSPORT	
Garuda	8 A1

Sleeping & Eating

Hotel Ayu (☎ 534263; Jl Tugu 11; s/d from 60,000/90,000Rp; ❄) By far the best bargain. It's nestled in an attractive, quiet neighbourhood just west of the centre. Second-floor rooms have lovely balconies.

Hotel Kartini (☎ 531557; Jl Perintis 2; s/d with outside bathroom 66,000/99,000Rp; ❄) Not especially charming, but clean enough and fairly quiet. The management is friendly and it's often full.

Seafood *warung* line the bay along Jl Sam Ratulangi. Try **Duta Café** (meals 45,000Rp; 🕑 dinner), where the Makassar-style dishes come with four types of *sambal*. Nice!

Getting There & Away

AIR

Jayapura's airport is actually located in Sentani; see p330 for flight and transport details.

BOAT

Pelni (☎ 533270; Jl Argapura 15) sails to Biak (from 144,000Rp, 24 hours), Manokwari (from 203,000Rp, two days) and Sorong (from 286,000Rp, two days) fortnightly. The port is about 800m east of the Yos Sudarso statue.

SENTANI

☎ 0967

Jayapura's airport is actually in the hamlet of Sentani (36km from Jayapura) and near the shores of magnificent **Danau Sentani**. It's quieter, cooler, more convenient, but a bit blander than Jayapura.

GETTING TO PAPUA NEW GUINEA

As far as border crossings go, this one is relatively quick and easy, once you secure a PNG visa (one-month tourist visa US$25) at the **PNG consulate** (☎ 0967-531250; Jl Raya Argapura; 🕒 8am-4pm Mon-Thu, to 2pm Fri) in Jayapura, which takes a couple of days. After that you can charter a boat between Jayapura (Hamadi) and Vamino for about 350,000Rp, with a minimum of three passengers, or you can charter a taxi to the border (250,000Rp, 2½ hours), and cross on foot. If you travel by boat, you must get stamped out, within 24 hours of your departure, at the **Immigration Office** (Jl Percetakan) opposite the Dafonsoro Hotel in Jayapura, not at the border itself, and pay a 50,000Rp 'fee'. On the PNG side, a taxi will take you to Vanimo (10kina/US$2.50).

Don't miss the soul-soothing views of Danau Sentani from **Tugu MacArthur**. This is where Douglas devised his winning strategy.

Most facilities are on Jl Kemiri Sentani Kota. **Hotel Semeru-Anaron** (☎ 591447; Jl Yabaso; d 120,000Rp; ❄) is the cheapest choice, but the rooms are tired. For another 100,000Rp you'll get hot water, cable TV, breakfast and a ride to the airport at **Hotel Ratna** (☎ 593410; Jl PLN 1; d 222,000Rp). Restaurants in town are brutal. Take an *ojek* ride to the lakeshore (20,000Rp) and eat very well at **Yougwa Restaurant** (☎ 571570; Jl Raya Danau Sentani; 🕒 lunch & dinner).

Merpati (code MZ; ☎ 533111; www.merpati.co.id) flies to Jakarta and Makassar via Biak and Timika. **Garuda** (code GA; ☎ 522222; www.garuda-indonesia.com) flies to Jakarta every day but Wednesday, and flies daily to Makassar and Denpasar. **Trigana Air Service** (code TGN; ☎ 594383; www.transnusa.co.id) runs four flights a day to and from Wamena in the Baliem Valley. Missionary airlines **AMA** (☎ 591009; Jl Misi) and **Mission Aviation Fellowship** (code MAF; ☎ 591109; Jl Misi) fly to remote airstrips within Papua's interior, and sell seats if there's room.

Getting to Sentani from Jayapura via public transport demands three different bemo, and three hours. *Ojek* are much more convenient (about 25,000Rp per hour), taxis are pricey (from 100,000Rp) but more comfortable.

PULAU BIAK

☎ 0981 / pop 41,600

Pulau Biak has an impressive line-up of WWII sights, but with the emergence of the Raja Ampats as Papua's top beach and dive destination, Biak is almost irrelevant.

Kota Biak is compact and easy to manage. Services are strung along Jl Ahmad Yani, Jl Sudriman and Jl Imam Bonjol. The Frans Kaisiepo airport is a short bemo ride away.

Don't miss **Gua Binsari** (admission 10,000Rp; 🕒 7am-5pm), a deep tunnel where thousands of Japanese soldiers lived and died after a deadly US bombing raid.

Charter boats from **Bosnik**, a famous allied WWII site, to the lovely **Padaido Islands**, where you'll find excellent snorkelling (Pulau Nusi), white sand and more rusted WWII relics (Pulau Owi).

Small, basic, yet clean, **Hotel Maju** (☎ 21841; Jl Imam Bonjol 45; s/d 65,000/85,000Rp; ❄) remains the best budget choice on Pulau Biak.

Merpati (code MZ; ☎ 21213; www.merpati.co.id) flies daily to Merauke, Jayapura and Makassar. **Garuda** (code GA; ☎ 25737; www.garuda-indonesia.com) flies daily to Jayapura, Makassar and Jakarta.

Every two weeks three **Pelni** (☎ 23255; Jl Sudirman 37) liners stop in Biak, and continue to Jayapura and Manokwari.

CENDERAWASIH BAY

Stretching from Manokwari, on the back of the bird's head, to the far eastern shore of Pulau Yapen, is the immense **Cenderawasih Bay Marine National Park** (Taman Laut Teluk Cenderawasih). Beneath the surface you'll find endangered species of giant clams, turtles and dugongs, and 130 coral varieties. On land you can trek through coastal jungle and spot 150 bird species. If it was more accessible it would be an eco-adventure jackpot, but it's just not that easy to explore. It's not impossible, however. From Manokwari you can take a three-hour shared taxi ride to Ransiki, from where you can get a boat (250,000Rp) to **Pulau Rumberpon**, where you'll find outstanding snorkelling. Or go to **Pulau Wairondi** and hang out with rare turtles. For tips, seek out the **Cenderwasih Bay Marine National Park office** (☎ 0986-222356; Jl Rendani Wosi) in Manokwari.

Manokwari

☎ 0986 / pop 56,200

The first place in Papua to be inhabited by missionaries, Manokwari is easy to navigate and well connected. Nearby there's **trekking** in the Arfak Mountains and around the Anggi Lakes. The **Cenderwasih Bay Marine National Park office** (☎ 222356; Jl Rendani Wosi) is the best place to source adventure options.

White sand and crystal water can be found 5km east of town at **Pasir Pasir Putih**. Surfers should paddle out from the black sands of **Pantai Amban**, located 3km north of Amban village and 7km north of Manokwari

Cheap sleeps include **Losmen Apose** (☎ 211369; Jl Kota Baru 4; s/d 50,000/100,000Rp; ❄), opposite the Merpati office, and **Hotel Arfak** (☎ 213079; Jl Brawijaya 8; d from 90,000Rp; ❄), set in a crumbling colonial shell.

Merpati (code MZ; ☎ 211153; www.merpati.co.id) flies four times a week to Sorong and Jayapura. **Batavia** (code 7P; ☎ 215666; www.batavia-air.co.id) flies daily to Jayapura. Four **Pelni** (☎ 215167; Jl Siliwangi 24) liners, servicing Papua's north coast, stop in Manokwari.

BALIEM VALLEY

The Baliem Valley is the most accessible gateway to tribal Papua. It's a place where *koteka* (penis gourds) are not yet out of fashion, pigs can buy love, sex or both, and the hills bloom with flowers and deep purple sweet-potato fields. Unless you land here during the August high season, when Wamena and nearby villages host a spectacular festival with pig feasts, mock wars and traditional dancing to attract the tourism buck, you will be outnumbered by Christian missionaries (a constant presence since the valley's 'discovery' in 1938) and Javanese *transmigrasi*. You may also be startled by blatant evidence of Indonesia's neocolonisation of Papua, but mostly you will marvel at the mountain views, roaring rivers, tribal villages and at the tough but sweet spirit of the warm Dani people (for more on visiting the tribal interior, see boxed text, below).

Wamena

☎ 0969 / pop 8500

The commercial centre in the Baliem Valley, Wamena is dusty and sprawling, but the air is cool, purple mountains peak through billowy white clouds, and local markets are enthralling. It's also a base from which to explore nearby tribal villages. Wamena is expensive – a consequence of having to fly everything in from Jayapura.

ORIENTATION & INFORMATION

Wamena is an easy walking town, but the becak rides are cheap and fun. The BRI and Mandiri banks have ATMs. Internet doesn't exist.

Post office (Jl Timor)

Rumah Sakit Umum (☎ 31152; Jl Trikora) Basic medical care.

Tourist office (☎ 31365; Jl Yos Sudarso 73) Look for the Indonesian flag.

SLEEPING & EATING

Hotel Syahrial Makmur (☎ 31306; Jl Gatot Subroto 45; d 100,000Rp) The cheapest place in town. The rooms aren't clean, but they're not horrible. Worth a look if your budget's tight.

Hotel Anggrek (☎ 31242; Jl Ambon 1; d 200,000Rp) Sparkling rooms, hot water, homemade jams and house-roasted coffee make this place deservedly popular. It's also almost always full, so call ahead.

Hotel Nayak (☎ 31067; Jl Gatot Subroto 63; d 220,000Rp) Just south of the airport, some of the street-front rooms here are cleaner than others. Choose wisely.

Rumah Makan Mas Budi (Jl Pattimura; dishes from 25,000Rp; ⏲ lunch & dinner) Decent Indonesian and

INDONESIA

HOW NOT TO GET YOUR SURAT JALAN

Anti-establishment types take note. To visit the tribal interior you need a *surat jalan* (special permit). So don't thumb your nose at the system, show up for your flight to Wamena, and brag to the helpful Trigana ticketing agent about how you don't have a permit and that you'll talk your way out of a jam if the 'scary' *polisi* confront you. Otherwise, you may find yourself on the back of an *ojek* in a driving rainstorm tearing along Sentani's rutted roads to the district police station outside of town in the jungle where you will bribe and beg listless clerks to type your permit on a manual typewriter so you can make a flight. Luckily these slacker clerks happen to love Tupac Shakur, and you clumsily reference hip-hop. Forty-five minutes later you will arrive back at the airport, papers in hand, drenched and 30 minutes late for the last plane of the day to Wamena. Thank God you're in Indonesia, where planes are always a minimum of 30 minutes late.

TREKKING THE BALIEM VALLEY

This is outstanding trekking country. Trails skirt and traverse rivers and sweet-potato fields, scale steep mountains, wind through remote mountain villages, and lead you to magnificent panoramas. The hiking isn't easy, but you will come across old local women carrying bulging *noken* (string bags) strapped to their forehead like saddlebags, so quit whining and enjoy the view of their wrinkled husbands working the soil dressed penis-gourd-chic. It's normally cold at night, and it often rains, so bring appropriate gear. Your guide will arrange meals, but you should bring your own water, and plenty of it

Staying in village huts is an unforgettable experience. They should cost about 50,000Rp per person per night.

In Wamena, guides greet you at the airport and can be tough to shake. But if you plan on trekking, you should hire one. They may ask for some money upfront for supplies. That's standard, so don't stress.

English-speaking guides should cost around 200,000Rp per day, and a porter around 100,000Rp.

Chinese fare, but at night they unveil an evil karaoke machine. Come for lunch.

Baliem Pilamo Hotel (Jl Trikora; meals from 25,000Rp; ⏰ lunch & dinner) The restaurant at this slightly upmarket hotel is clean and passable. Fresh fish and prawns are flown in from Sentani daily.

Wamena is officially a 'dry area', so no Bintang for you!

SHOPPING

Possible souvenirs include *noken* (string bags; (15,000Rp to 50,000Rp); *suale* (head decorations made from cassowary feathers); the inevitable *koteka* (10,000Rp to 60,000Rp), if you're that kind of man; *mikak* (necklaces made of cowrie shells, feathers and bone); and *kapak* (black- or blue-stone axe blades; upward from 50,000Rp). Prepare to bargain.

GETTING THERE & AROUND

Trigana Air Service (code TGN; ☎ 31611) flies to and from Jayapura four times a day (from Wamena 490,000Rp, from Jayapura 534,000Rp). Book ahead!

Around Wamena

Trekking is the best way to taste traditional life, and considering lodging prices in Wamena, the cost isn't prohibitive, but you can also see traditional people and customs, mummies, markets and terrific scenery during day trips from Wamena, Jiwika and Kurima.

Getting Around

From Wamena, hopelessly overcrowded *taksi* go as far south as Yetni (5000Rp, 20 minutes, 18km); as far north, on the western side of the valley, as Pyramid (10,000Rp, 45 minutes, 35km) and as far north on the eastern side as Tagime. They gather at the **'Misi' taksi terminal** (Jl Ahmad Yani).

CENTRAL & SOUTH BALIEM VALLEY

Wesaput is just across the airport, and home to the valley's only museum, the **Palimo Adat Museum** (admission by donation; ⏰ 8am-4pm Mon-Sat), with its limited collection of Dani artefacts.

Behind the museum, a swinging bridge leads to **Pugima**, a flat 4km walk on a trail that skirts charming Dani villages. At the end of Jl Yos Sudarso is **Sinatma**, where you'll find a bustling market and trails that lead to the thundering Sungai Wamena.

The road south through Baliem Valley stops a few kilometres short of **Kurima**, a village bursting with flowers, divided by the river and fed by cascading streams. This is the land of eternal spring. The walk here and around will take you through sweet-potato terraces to the best panoramas in the valley. You can rent a room in Kurima at the missionary house, but the best plan is to keep walking up the ridge to **Kilise**, where you can bed down at the **Kilise Guest House** (per person 50,000Rp, bring your own food) on clean bamboo mats in a traditional Dani grass hut with sweeping views that will simply immobilise you. Guides are a good idea for this trek, but they're not essential if you don't mind cooking. A popular three-day trek to the best southern villages is **Wamena–Kurima–Syoma–Wamena**.

INDONESIA

EAST BALIEM VALLEY

Near **Pikhe**, the northern road crosses mighty Sungai Baliem and passes **Aikima**, the resting place of a 270-year-old **Werapak Elosak mummy** (admission 5000Rp; dawn-dusk). **Jiwika** is the best base to explore the east. **Sumpaima**, 300m north of Jiwika, is home to the 280-year-old **Wimontok Mabel mummy** (admission 5000Rp; dawn-dusk), the best of its kind near Wamena.

At the turn-off to Iluwe in Jiwika, you'll find **Lauk Inn** (d 90,000Rp) the only proper accommodation outside Wamena.

In **Wosilimo**, the incredible **Gua Wikuda** (admission 5000Rp; 8am-4pm Mon-Sat) cave is 900m long and has stalagmites that are 1000 years old. Stay in a hut and fish well at **Danau Anegerak**, an hour's walk west of Wosilimo. From Wosilimo, a trekking trail continues beyond Pass Valley. A popular three-day trek will also take you from Jiwika, off the main road, to Pass Valley.

Public transport continues north to **Manda**, where there is more pretty countryside and hut-style sleeps. From Manda, trek to the Protestant, nonsmoking village of **Wolo**.

WEST BALIEM VALLEY

Pyramid is a graceful missionary village with churches, a theological college and a bustling market. You may be able to stay at **Kimbim**.

Pondok Kanopa is a pristine rainforest, in the northwest, with frequent python sightings. The jungle is also thick with OPM resisters, and a heavy military presence. It's legal to be here, but Indonesian soldiers love hassling Papuan guides (a must in the rainforest), which is why your guide will know exactly how to avoid confrontation. Edgy!

SORONG

0951 / pop 132,700

An industrial port on the beak of the bird's head, Sorong's newest industry is tourism, thanks to the nearby Raja Ampat islands' coronation as the 'it' diving destination. You won't stay long, but daily connections from Manado via **Wings Air** (043 1888 0022) make Sorong an inexpensive and accessible gateway to Papua.

The town sprawls, so taxis, *ojek*s and chartered *angkot* are the best way to visit banks, airline offices, the main port or government offices. Most hotels are on Jl Yos Sudarso. Acceptable bargain beds can be found at **Hotel Tanjung** (323782; Jl Yos Sudarso; d from 105,000Rp), next to a superb fresh-fish grill, **Lido Kuring** (322971; mains 35,000Rp; lunch & dinner). But the massive, oceanfront rooms at **Hotel Waigo** (333500; Jl Yos Sudarso; d from 200,000Rp) are the best deal in town.

RAJA AMPAT ISLANDS

Located off Papua's west coast, this cluster of 1500 lush limestone islands, protected by rich coral reefs that shelter and feed the highest fish count on earth, has divers buzzing. Some islands are huddled so close that they look like a single mountain range stacked against the sky. To move between them you cross narrow passes of deep blue water occasionally striped turquoise and green. There are 47 mapped dive sites, but the number is limitless. The original outfitter in the region is Max Ammer's **Papua Diving** (0411-401 660; www.papua-diving.com). It has two all-inclusive dive resorts in the Raja Ampats. The most affordable rooms are the stilted, overwater grass bungalows at **Kri Eco Resort** (per night €85) You can do 5 dives for €175.

If you're short on time, money or friends, these islands may remain on the horizon of your mind. It takes cash to reach these deserted beaches, sleepy lagoons, fishing villages, waterfalls and limestone peaks. You can charter a sheltered longboat from the main port in Sorong, but that will cost at least 2,000,000Rp per day, which can work for a big group, but is tough on soloists. An affordable, and far more comfortable, group alternative is to charter the **Helena** (081 148 5371; walliston@cbn.net.id; per person per day all-inclusive US$100), a beautiful wooden ship that sleeps six, with two decks. Her captain knows the Raja Ampat's hidden secrets. Guests aboard *Helena* dive with Papua Diving.

INDONESIA DIRECTORY

ACCOMMODATION

Hotel, *losmen, penginapan, wisma:* there are several words for somewhere to lay a weary head, and options to suit every budget in most Indonesian towns.

Cheap hotels are usually pretty basic and with tourist numbers down over recent years, standards tend to be lower than in many other tourist destinations. In compensation, a simple breakfast is often included. Traditional washing facilities consist of a *mandi*, a large water tank from which you scoop cool water with a dipper. Climbing into the tank is very bad form! Rooms are assumed to come with a private *mandi* in this chapter, unless otherwise specified. The air-con symbol (❄) denotes whether air-con rooms are available, otherwise rooms are assumed to come with a fan.

Accommodation prices in tourist areas peak in July and August, and also during Easter and the Christmas period, though at the budget end of the market price hikes are marginal. Elsewhere in the country, rates increase during Idul Fitri (the period following Ramadan).

Finding a room for 50,000Rp to 70,000Rp a night is possible wherever you are. In the large cities and provincial towns, expect a very plain, purely functional room for this. But along the main travelling trail, in Yogyakarta and in parts of Lombok and Sumatra, many budget places can be very attractive and decorated with artistic touches, and often come with a veranda. Bali is in a league of its own in terms of value for money, and if you can stretch to 100,000Rp a night there are some wonderful places, many with pools and stylish open-air bathrooms.

ACTIVITIES

Indonesia has world-class surfing, diving and snorkelling, trekking and rafting, and operators' prices are very competitive.

Diving & Snorkelling

Indonesian waters are some of the world's richest, its coral reefs incredibly diverse. But damage by destructive fishing practices has damaged and destroyed many once-pristine areas. Visibility can be limited during the wet season (roughly October to April).

Highlights include western Flores and Komodo, the Gili islands, Amed and Pulau Menjangan in Bali, Pulau Bunaken and the Togean Islands in Sulawesi, Pulau Weh in Sumatra, the Banda Islands in Maluku and Pulau Biak in Papua.

PADI-linked schools are by far the most common, but there are also NAUI and BSAC operators. You'll need to bring your certification card if you are already qualified. If you want to get qualified, the Gili islands, Pulau Bunaken and Labuanbajo in Flores have the best choice of dive schools.

For information on responsible diving, see p912.

All the above dive sites also offer excellent **snorkelling**, but if you're looking for a beach somewhere where you can just roll out of your bungalow in the morning, don a mask and fins and explore a wonderful reef, the Gilis and Pulau Bunaken fit the bill perfectly. Snorkelling gear costs about 20,000Rp a day to hire.

Spas & Treatments

If you fancy a pamper, Indonesia has some excellent-value options. From a humble massage on the beach (about 40,000Rp) through facials and beauty treatments (starting at 60,000Rp) in salons to luxe spa sessions (from around 100,000Rp), you'll find plenty of opportunity to indulge.

Bali leads the way, with a multitude of beauty salons and spas in all the main travellers' centres. You'll also find a fair selection of spas in Yogyakarta (Java) and Senggigi (Lombok).

Surfing

Indonesia has waves that will send most surfers weak at the knees. With waves building momentum across the expanse of the Indian Ocean, all the islands on the southern side of the Indonesian archipelago – from Sumatra to Timor – get reliable, often exceptional, and sometimes downright frightening surf. The dry season, May to September, offers the most consistent waves, but is also the busiest time of year. During the wet season, the easterly beaches of Bali such as Lebih and Nusa Dua come into their own.

If you are just starting out, courses are run in Bali (p217) and Java (p186). Surf stores in Bali and Java stock most surfing accessories, including a wide range of boards, but come fully equipped if you're planning on surfing off the beaten track.

Highlights are almost too numerous to mention, but include Pulau Nias in Sumatra, southern Lombok, Batu Karas in Java, Bukit peninsula in Bali, and Hu'u in Sumbawa.

Trekking

Despite massive potential, trekking is far less established in Indonesia than it is in, say, Thailand. Local guide services are developing where demand exists, however, and the national parks offer some wonderful terrain to explore.

In Java, organised trekking is largely confined to some spectacular volcano hikes. There's more variety in Bali, the location of the wonderful Gunung Batur region, and the region around Tirta Gangga, which offers walks on the lower slopes of Gunung Agung and through rice fields and forests. Gunung Rinjani on Lombok is one of Indonesia's most dramatic and rewarding treks (from two to five days).

The Baliem Valley in Papua is also one of Indonesia's better-known walking destinations, and Tana Toraja has plenty of fabulous trekking opportunities through Sulawesi's spectacular traditional villages.

BOOKS

Lonely Planet's *Bali & Lombok*, *Borneo* and *Indonesia* guides explore the country in more detail, while Lonely Planet's *World Food Indonesia* is the perfect guide to the nation's cuisine and *Indonesian Phrasebook* its language. Read *Healthy Travel: Asia* for the lowdown on keeping healthy during your travels.

Check out *Indonesia: Peoples and Histories* by Jean Gelman Taylor for an up-to-date history primer. *Nathaniel's Nutmeg* by Giles Milton is a fascinating account of the battle to control trade from the Spice Islands.

The Malay Archipelago by Alfred Russel Wallace is the 1869 classic of this famous naturalist's travels throughout the Indonesian archipelago.

Pramoedya Ananta Toer is perhaps Indonesia's best-known novelist. Look for the novels *This Earth of Mankind*, *Child of All Nations*, *Footsteps* and *House of Glass*.

Daniel Ziv's *Jakarta Inside Out* is a highly recommended under-the-skin portrait of the city. *Bule Gila: Tales of a Dutch Barman in Jakarta*, by Bartele Santema, manager of Bugils (p175) is light-hearted and entertaining.

BUSINESS HOURS

Government offices are *generally* open Monday to Friday from 8am to 4pm – with a break for Friday prayers from 11.30am to 1.30pm – and Saturday until noon. Go early if you want to get anything done.

Banks are open Monday to Friday, usually from 8am to 4pm. In some places banks open on Saturday until around noon. Foreign exchange hours may be more limited and some banks close their foreign exchange counter at 1pm. Moneychangers are open longer hours.

Restaurants are generally open daily from around 7am until 9pm, though many large cities have 24-jour places and late-night stalls.

Most shops are open daily between 8am and 6pm; in tourist areas, they'll often open as late as 9pm.

CLIMATE

Indonesia is hot and humid all year round, with wet and dry seasons. In coastal areas the heat is usually less oppressive, and it can get downright chilly in the high mountains at dawn.

Generally, the wet season starts later the further southeast you go. In North Sumatra, the rain begins to fall in September, but in Timor it doesn't fall until November. In January and February it rains most days. The dry season is basically from May to September. The odd islands out are those of Maluku, where the wet season is the reverse, running from May to September.

See the regional climate charts (p916).

CUSTOMS

Customs regulations allow you to bring in 1L of alcohol and 200 cigarettes (or 50 cigars).

Any material containing partial nudity may be deemed pornographic and be confiscated.

DANGERS & ANNOYANCES

If you've never been before, Indonesia might seem like one of the world's most dodgy nations: accident-prone, and cursed by natural disasters and terrorist outrages.

But while transport safety standards are poor, earthquakes are frequent and a small band of extremists have wreaked terror in Bali and Jakarta, Indonesia is actually a very safe nation for travellers, unless you're very unlucky.

Personal safety, even in the big cities, is not usually a major concern. Keep your wits about you, yes, but violent crime (and even petty theft) is very rare in Indonesia. Be mindful of your valuables and take the usual precautions and the chances of getting into trouble are tiny.

It *is* important to keep abreast of current political developments, however, and maybe give political or religious demos a wide berth. At the time of writing, areas of Central Sulawesi were of particular concern, and tensions remain in parts of Maluku, Papua and Aceh. Newspapers and the internet should keep you in touch with developments, or consult your embassy.

See also p915 for information on the risks associated with recreational drug use and p937 for an update on avian influenza (bird flu).

But most importantly, go and enjoy yourself.

DRIVING LICENCE

If you plan to drive a car or motorbike in Indonesia it's essential to have an International Driving Permit. There can be steep fines for unlicensed driving, particularly in Bali, where some policeman regularly target drivers.

EMBASSIES & CONSULATES

Consult p341 for details of visa and entry requirements.

Embassies & Consulates in Indonesia

Australia Denpasar (off Map p213; ☎ 0361-241118; Jl Hayam Wuruk 88B); Jakarta (Map p168; ☎ 021-2550 5555; Jl Rasuna Said Kav C15-16)
Brunei (Map p170; ☎ 021-3190 6080; Jl Tanjung Karang 7, Jakarta 10230)
Canada (Map p168; ☎ 021-2550 7800; 6th fl, World Trade Centre, Jl Sudirman Kav 29-31, Jakarta)
East Timor (Map p172; ☎ 021-390 2978; tljkt@yahoo.com; 11th fl, Surya Bldg, Jl Thamrin Kav 9, Jakarta 10350)
France (Map p170; ☎ 021-2355 7600; Jl Thamrin 20, Jakarta)
Germany (Map p170; ☎ 021-3985 5000; Jl Thamrin 1, Jakarta)
Japan (Map p170; ☎ 021-3192 4308; Jl Thamrin 24, Jakarta)
Malaysia (Map p168; ☎ 021-522 4947; Jl Rasuna Said Kav X/6 1, Jakarta)
Myanmar (Map p170; ☎ 021-314 0440; Jl Hagi Agus Salim 109, Jakarta)
Netherlands (Map p168; ☎ 021-524 8200; Jl Rasuna Said Kav S-3, Kuningan, Jakarta)
New Zealand (Map p168; ☎ 021-570 9460; 23rd fl, BRI II Bldg, Jl Sudirman Kav 44-46, Jakarta)
Papua New Guinea Jakarta (Map p168; ☎ 021-725 1218; 6th fl, Panin Bank Centre, Jl Sudirman 1, Jakarta); Jayapura (☎ 531250; Jl Raya Argapura; 🕑 8am-4pm Mon-Thu, to 2pm Fri)
Philippines (Map p170; ☎ 021-310 0334; Jl Imam Bonjol 6-8, Jakarta)
Singapore (Map p168; ☎ 021-520 1489; Jl Rasuna Said, Block X/4 Kav 2, Jakarta)
Thailand (Map p170; ☎ 021-390 4052; Jl Imam Bonjol 74, Jakarta)
UK (Map p170; ☎ 021-315 6264; Jl Thamrin 75, Jakarta)
USA Denpasar (off Map p213; ☎ 0361-233605; Jl Hayam Wuruk 188); Jakarta (Map p172; ☎ 021-3435 9000; Jl Medan Merdeka Selatan 4-5)
Vietnam (Map p170; ☎ 021-310 0358; Jl Teuku Umar 25, Jakarta)

Indonesian Embassies & Consulates Abroad

Countries with an Indonesian embassy:
Australia (☎ 02-6250 8600; www.kbri-canberra.org.au; 8 Darwin Ave, Yarralumla, ACT 2600)
Canada (☎ 613-724 1100; www.indonesia-ottawa.org; 55 Parkdale Ave, Ottawa, Ontario K1Y 1E5)
France (☎ 01 45 03 07 60; www.amb-indonesie.fr; 47-49 Rue Cortambert 75116, Paris)
Germany (☎ 030-478 070; www.indonesian-embassy.de; Lehrter Str 16-17, 10557 Berlin)
Japan (☎ 03-3441 4201; indonesian-embassy.or.jp; 5-2-9 Higashi Gotanda, Shinagawa-Ku, Tokyo)
Netherlands (☎ 0703-10 81 00; www.indonesia.nl; 8 Tobias Asserlaan, 2517 KC Den Haag)
New Zealand (☎ 04-475 8697; www.indonesianembassy.org.nz; 70 Glen Rd, Kelburn, Wellington)
Papua New Guinea (☎ 25 1116; 1 + 2/410 Kiro St, Sir John Guise Dr, Waigani)
UK (☎ 020-7499 7661; www.indonesianembassy.org.uk; 38 Grosvenor Sq, London W1K 2HW)
USA (☎ 202-775 5200; www.embassyofindonesia.org; 2020 Massachusetts Ave NW, Washington DC 20036)

FESTIVALS & EVENTS

Although some public holidays have a fixed date, the dates for many events vary each year depending on Muslim, Buddhist or Hindu calendars.

January/February

New Year's Day Celebrated on 1 January.
Imlek (Chinese New Year) Special food is prepared, decorations adorn stores and homes, and *barongasai* (lion dances) are performed; held in January/February.

March/April

Mohammed's Birthday Celebrated in March in 2008 and 2009; prayers are held in mosques throughout the country, and there are street parades in Solo and Yogyakarta.
Hindu New Year (Nyepi) Held in March/April; in Bali and other Hindu communities, villagers make as much noise as possible to scare away devils. Virtually all of Bali closes.
Good Friday Occurs in March or April.

April/May

Waisak (Buddha's Birthday) Mass prayers are said at the main Buddhist temples, including Borobudur.

May/June

Ascension of Christ Occurs in May/June.

INDONESIA

August

Independence Day Celebrated on 17 August with plenty of pomp and circumstance; government buildings are draped in huge red-and-white flags and banners, and there are endless marches.

September/October

Ascension of Mohammed Special prayers are held in mosques; it occurs in September in 2008 and August in 2009.

Lebaran (Idul Fitri) Celebrated in October in 2008 and September in 2009; everyone who is able to returns to their home villages for special prayers and gift giving, and it's a time for charity donations.

November/December

Idul Adha The end of the Haj is celebrated with animal sacrifices, the meat of which is given to the poor; occurs in December in 2008 and November in 2009.

Muharram (Muslim New Year) The date varies each year, but it will be celebrated in December in both 2008 and 2009.

Christmas Day Marked by gift giving and special church services in Christian areas; the celebration falls on 25 December.

The Muslim fasting month of Ramadan requires that Muslims abstain from food, drink, cigarettes and sex between sunrise and sunset. Many bars and restaurants close and it is important to avoid eating or drinking publicly in Muslim areas during this time. For the week before and after Lebaran (Idul Fitri), the festival to mark the end of the fast, transport is often fully booked and travelling becomes a nightmare – plan to stay put at this time. Ramadan, Idul Fitri and Idul Adha (Muslim day of sacrifice) move back 10 days or so every year, according to the Muslim calendar.

With such a diversity of people in the archipelago there are many other local holidays, festivals and cultural events.

The *Indonesia Calendar of Events* covers holidays and festivals throughout the archipelago; some tourist offices stock it.

FOOD & DRINK

Food

A *rumah makan* (literally 'eating house') is the cheaper equivalent of a *restoran*, but the dividing line is often hazy. The cheapest option of all is the *warung*, a makeshift or permanent food stall, but again the food may be the same as in a *rumah makan*. With any roadside food it pays to be careful about the hygiene. The *pasar* (market) is a good food source, especially the *pasar malam* (night market). Mobile *kaki lima* (food stalls) serve cheap snack foods and meals.

As with food in the rest of Southeast Asia, Indonesian cuisine is heavily based on rice. *Nasi goreng* is the national dish: it's basically fried rice, with an egg on top in *istimewa* (deluxe) versions. *Nasi campur*, rice with a little meat, fish or vegetables (whatever is available), is a *warung* favourite and is often served cold. The two other typical Indonesian dishes are *gado gado* and satay (*sate* in Bahasa Indonesia). *Gado gado* is a fresh salad with prawn crackers, boiled egg and peanut sauce. It tends to vary a lot, so if your first one isn't so special try again somewhere else. Satay are tiny kebabs served with a spicy peanut sauce.

Padang food, from the Padang region in Sumatra, is famed for its rich, chilli-heavy sauces, and is popular throughout Indonesia. It's usually delicious, though not cooked fresh – dishes are displayed for hours (days even) in the restaurant window. Padang restaurant *(masakan Padang)* food is served one of two ways. Usually a bowl of rice is plonked in front of you, followed by a whole collection of small bowls of vegetables, meat and fish. Or you approach the window display and pick a few dishes yourself. Either way you pay for what you eat (typically 8000Rp to 15,000Rp).

Drink

Bottled water and soft drinks are available everywhere, and many hotels and restaurants provide *air putih* (boiled water) for guests. The iced juice drinks can be good, but take care that the water/ice has been boiled or is bottled.

Indonesian tea is fine and coffee can be excellent; for a strong local brew ask for *kopi java* or *kopi flores*, depending where you are of course. Beer is quite superb: Bintang ('best enjoyed with friends' according to the label) is one of Asia's finest and costs 11,000Rp to 18,000Rp for a large bottle in most places. Bali Brem rice wine is really potent, and the more you drink the nicer it tastes. *Es buah*, or *es campur*, is a strange concoction of fruit salad, jelly cubes, syrup, crushed rice and condensed milk. And it tastes absolutely *enak* (delicious).

GAY & LESBIAN TRAVELLERS

Gay travellers in Indonesia will experience few problems, especially in Bali. Physical contact between same-sex couples is acceptable (Indonesian boys and girls often hold hands or link arms in public). Homosexual behaviour is not illegal – the age of consent is 16. Immigration officials may restrict entry to people who reveal HIV-positive status. Gay men in Indonesia are referred to as *homo* or *gay*; lesbians are *lesbi*.

Indonesia's transvestite/transsexual *waria* – from *wanita* (woman) and *pria* (man) – community has always had a public profile.

Indonesia's first Gay Pride celebration was staged in Surabaya in 1999.

For some background information and listings of gay-friendly bars, restaurants plus gay-scene updates and chat forums, check out www.utopia-asia.com/tipsindo.htm.

HOLIDAYS

See p336 for a list of public holidays.

INTERNET ACCESS

Internet cafés are common in most towns and tourist centres. Speeds are usually very pedestrian though, and broadband access is very rare outside Bali and the main cities. Expect to pay between 4000Rp and 12,000Rp per hour.

INTERNET RESOURCES

Antara News (www.antara.co.id/en) The official Indonesian news agency; has searchable English-language database.

CIA – The World Factbook (https://www.cia.gov) Click on the World Factbook link, and then Indonesia. Good for all the facts and figures.

Department of Foreign Affairs & Trade (www.dfat.gov.au/geo/indonesia/index.html) The up-to-date website of the Australian Government.

History of Indonesia (www.geocities.com/amemorikaze) Click on the Everything about Indonesia link for a comprehensive examination of contemporary Indonesian culture and the nation's history.

Jakarta Post (www.thejakartapost.com) The website of Indonesia's main English-language newspaper.

Living in Indonesia (www.expat.or.id) This website provides information, advice and links to the expatriate community.

Lonely Planet (www.lonelyplanet.com) Has succinct summaries to most places on earth, the Thorn Tree bulletin board, travel news and updates, and links to useful travel resources.

Some other interesting sites:

Indonesia WWW Virtual Library (http://coombs.anu.edu.au) Australian National University's links site is the ultimate portal to all things Indonesian, from human rights to shadow puppets.

Tourism Indonesia (www.tourismindonesia.com) Indonesia's official tourist information site.

Ultimate Indonesian Homepage (http://indonesia.elga.net.id) An excellent introduction to the nation and its culture.

LEGAL MATTERS

Drugs, gambling and pornography are illegal, and it is an offence to engage in paid work, or stay in the country for more than 60 days, on a tourist pass.

Despite claims of reform, corruption is still widespread. Police often stop motorists on minor or dubious traffic infringements in the hope of obtaining bribes. The best advice is to remain calm, keep your money in your pocket until it is asked for and sit through the lecture – it is unlikely more than 50,000Rp will be demanded.

In case of an accident involving serious injury or death, the best advice is to drive straight to the nearest police station as an angry mob may soon gather.

MAPS

Many locally produced maps are pretty inaccurate, Periplus produces excellent maps of most Indonesian cities and regions.

MEDIA

Newspapers & Magazines

You'll find copies of the daily *Jakarta Post* (www.jakartapost.com) available in most cities; while it's not as thorough as similar newspapers in Thailand and Malaysia it does deal with all the main stories. For in-depth reporting and analysis of political events, the bimonthly *Inside Indonesia* (www.insideindonesia.com) and weekly *Tempo* (www.tempointeractive.com) are both excellent magazines.

In Bali, European and Australian papers are sold by street hawkers; elsewhere you can find the odd one in the major bookshops.

Radio & TV

You can pick up BBC World Service, Voice of America, Radio Australia and many more stations with a short-wave radio, though reception quality varies a lot.

'DECENCY' LAW

As far as Islamic nations go, Indonesia has always had a reputation as being a pretty tolerant place. But by 2006, growing pressure from strict Muslims and the Islamic Defenders' Front (FPI) saw the drafting of a new Indonesian penal code, often dubbed the 'Decency' or 'Pornography Law', to combat declining moral standards and the introduction of Western values deemed to be corruptive.

The proposed law criminalises adulterers, cohabiting unmarried couples, public kissing and bikini-wearing tourists. Topless old ladies in islands like Sumba and Bali, and penis-gourd-wearing Papuan men could be prosecuted for wearing their traditional dress.

One of those charged with drafting the law was Yahya Zaini, a politician who was head of the Golkar party's Spiritual and Religious Affairs committee, with direct responsibility for moral issues. Unfortunately for him, a video was circulated on the internet showing the married politician naked in bed with a raunchy young *dangdut* (Indonesian dance music with strong Arabic and Hindi influences) singer called Maria Eva. He later resigned.

Despite the resultant furore, the bill looks set to be enacted, albeit with some of its more controversial clauses toned down. Christian leaders, former president Megawati Soekarnoputri and her party, the tourism industry, artists, cultural activists and human rights groups continue to oppose the law.

Many hotel rooms have TVs – a box is almost standard in midrange places. Thanks to satellite broadcasting, most major sporting events can be seen (often on ESPN) and you'll have no problem seeing English Premier League football games; Australian and American sports are far less popular.

MONEY

The unit of currency in Indonesia is the rupiah (Rp). Coins of 50, 100, 200 and 500 rupiah are in circulation in both the old silver-coloured coins and the newer bronze-coloured coins. Both 1000Rp and 25Rp coins exist but are very rarely seen. Notes come in 1000, 5000, 10,000, 20,000 50,000 and 100,000 rupiah denominations.

ATMs

ATMs are becoming very numerous in Indonesia – indeed, it's possible to travel through most of the nation with just a card or two without ever setting foot inside a bank. But ATMs fail much more frequently (sometimes due to poor satellite connections) here than in the developed world, and some only dispense pitifully small amounts (500,000Rp) in one transaction. Others will only accept one of Visa/Plus or MasterCard/Cirrus.

It's wise to take a few travellers cheques along with you – American Express are the best, and note that many minor brands are not accepted – and a cash stash of US dollars for emergencies.

Bargaining & Tipping

Bargaining is generally required in markets and for transport (particularly taxis) in places where prices are not fixed. Tipping is not a normal practice in Indonesia but is often expected for special service.

Credit Cards

MasterCard and Visa are by far the most widely accepted plastic cards.

Don't expect to pay for a meal in a *warung* with plastic; generally it's only top-end places that accept credit cards.

Getting a cash advance on your card is a particularly useful way to obtain a large chunk of money in one transaction, though it's often only the major bank branches in larger towns that will give you this facility in Indonesia; you should expect a charge of around 15,000Rp to 30,000Rp for the privilege.

Exchanging Money

After years of turmoil the rupiah has been relatively stable for several years; check out the latest rates on www.xe.com.

US dollars are the most widely accepted foreign currency and have the best exchange rates, euros are second best.

Moneychangers are open longer hours and change money (cash or cheques) much faster than the banks. Be careful in Kuta, Bali, where moneychangers are notorious for short-changing.

The following were the exchange rates at the time of press:

Country	Unit	Rupiah (Rp)
Australia	A$1	7893
Canada	C$1	9088
Euro zone	€1	12,994
Japan	¥100	8127
Malaysia	RM1	2695
New Zealand	NZ$1	6683
Singapore	S$1	6183
Thailand	10B	2932
UK	UK£1	18,806
USA	US$1	9362

POST

The postal service in Indonesia is generally good and the poste-restante service at *kantor pos* (post offices) is reasonably efficient in the main tourist centres. Expected mail always seems to arrive, eventually.

RESPONSIBLE TRAVEL

You have to haggle in Indonesia, but it's important to do so respectfully, and learn when to draw the line. It's very bad form to shout or lose your temper. Remember that a few extra rupiah may make a great deal of difference to the other party.

Indonesia is a conservative, largely Muslim country and while bikinis and Speedos are tolerated in the beach resorts of Bali, try to respect local clothing traditions wherever possible. This is particularly true if you are near a mosque.

Couples should avoid canoodling or kissing in public.

A little Bahasa Indonesia, which is very easy to pick up, will get you a long way. Not only will you delight the locals, but it'll save you cash when it comes to dealing with stall owners, hoteliers and becak drivers.

STUDYING

Many cultural and language courses are available, particularly in the main tourist areas. Bali takes the lead, offering a little something to just about everyone. Ubud is Bali's culinary capital and there are courses to teach the inquisitive gastronome a thing or two. Look for advertisements at your hotel, enquire at local restaurants and bars, ask fellow travellers and hotel staff, and check out the tourist newspapers and magazines.

Culture junkies and art addicts are also looked after with a host of courses in Ubud teaching silversmithing, woodcarving, batik, Balinese music and dance and more (see p224 for more information). Short batik courses are popular in Yogyakarta (see p193) and in Solo (p201).

Yogyakarta is probably the most popular place for Bahasa Indonesia courses; see p193 for details.

TELEPHONE

International calls (and faxes) are usually cheapest from the state-run Telkom offices found in every town. Privately run *wartel* offer the same services. You can also call home using phonecards (*kartu chip*) for similar rates to a *wartel*.

It's cheaper to ring on weekends and public holidays, when a 25% to 50% discount applies, or on weekdays from 9pm to 6am for Asia and Oceania, or midnight to 7am for North America, Europe and Africa.

Indonesia has an extensive and reliable mobile network. SIM cards (around 25,000Rp) are very widely available in Indonesia, allowing you to use your phone for cheap local calls. International texts (and even international calls) can also be very reasonable depending on the supplier. SimPATI is the market leader. You may have to get your phone's SIM unlocked before using it in Indonesia.

It's also possible to use your own phone and home provider's SIM card in Indonesia, but international roaming rates can be extortionate – check before you leave.

The country code for Indonesia is ☎ 62; the international access code is usually ☎ 001, but it varies from *wartel* to *wartel*.

TIME

Indonesia has three time zones. Western Indonesia time (Sumatra, Java, West and Central Kalimantan) is seven hours ahead of GMT, central Indonesia time (Bali, South and East Kalimantan, Sulawesi and Nusa Tenggara) is eight hours ahead, and east Indonesia time (Maluku and Irian Jaya) is nine hours ahead.

TOILETS

Public toilets are extremely rare except in bus and train stations. Expect to have to dive into restaurants and hotels frequently.

INDONESIA

Indonesian toilets are basically holes in the ground with footrests on either side, although Western-style toilets are becoming more common. To flush the toilet, reach for that plastic scooper, take water from the tank and flush it away.

TOURIST INFORMATION

The usefulness of tourist offices varies greatly from place to place. Those in places that attract lots of tourists, like Bali or Yogyakarta, provide good maps and information, while offices in the less-visited areas may have nothing to offer at all. Wherever you are, signs are not always in English; look for *dinas pariwisata* (tourist office).

The Indonesian **Directorate General of Tourism** (Map p170; ☎ 021-383 8000; www.tourismindonesia.com; Jl Merdeka Barat 16-19, Jakarta) has its headquarters in Jakarta, but it is really more of a coordinating body than a helpful source of information.

Often a really clued-up guesthouse owner or travel agent is the best source of tourist information.

TRAVELLERS WITH DISABILITIES

Laws covering the disabled date back to 1989, but Indonesia has very few dedicated programmes, and is a difficult destination for those with limited mobility. Bali, with its wide range of tourist facilities, and Java are the easiest destinations to navigate.

VISAS

Most Western nationalities (including those from Australia, Canada, Japan, New Zealand, South Africa, the UK, the US and most European countries, plus China and India) qualify for a 30-day Visa on Arrival (US$25) at the main points of entry; for a full list of these consult www.indonesianembassy.org.uk.

At the time of research getting a 60-day visa could be extremely problematic. From a Western nation this required a bank statement, proof of exit, sufficient funds (at least US$1500) and even a letter from an employer stating that you were planning to return to your home country, and other – frankly absurd – official requirements.

On the other hand, those seeking a 60-day visa in some Asian countries, including Malaysia and Singapore, were not being asked for all these, usually just proof of funds and an onward ticket.

Mercifully, at the time of writing the Indonesian vice president had signalled a change of policy and announced a four-month visa was to be introduced. But, being Indonesia, this may or may not happen; you should check one of the embassy websites (see p336) for the latest.

Tourist passes are not extendable. If you do overstay you may be lucky and get charged the official US$20 per day, but then again an immigration official may decide not to let you board your flight. The maximum penalty for an overstay of 60 days is a five-year prison sentence!

Indonesia requires that your passport is valid for six months following your date of arrival.

Travel Permits

Technically, if you're heading to Aceh, Papua or parts of Maluku, you should obtain a *surat jalan* (special permit) from the Indonesian Immigration Office. It rarely translates to necessity though, but checking with your nearest Indonesian embassy before you go is wise.

VOLUNTEERING

Volunteering opportunities are pretty thin on the ground unless you prebook through one of the large NGOs or gap-year organisations.

Yudi Sujana's excellent homestay programme (see p182), based in the west Javan town of Cianjur, offers travellers the opportunity to help out with English teaching in schools, and has contacts with local development projects.

The **Orangutan Foundation** (www.orangutan.co.uk) offers six-week programmes for volunteers (£600 per person) in Kalimantan. In Sumatra, **Orangutan Health** (www.orangutan-health.org) also welcomes volunteers (two-week programme US$1289). Neither programme offers direct contact with the apes themselves – volunteers help out with field work and construction.

WOMEN TRAVELLERS

Indonesia is predominantly a Muslim society and though it is male oriented, the sexes are not as divided here compared with many other Islamic nations. It's easy to strike up conversations with Indonesian women, and you'll see women on the streets and working in offices.

Travelling alone is considered an oddity – women travelling alone, even more of an oddity – and it is certainly tougher-going for a woman travelling alone in isolated regions.

Some women invent a husband, who they are 'meeting soon'. A wedding ring can also be a good idea, while a photo of you and your 'partner' also works well.

Plenty of Western women travel in Indonesia either alone or in pairs – most seem to enjoy the country and its people, and get through the place without any problems. Dressing modestly can help you avoid being harassed.

Be prepared for plenty of male attention in places like Kuta, the Gili islands and parts of Sumatra, where local self-styled gigolos are renowned for their charm and flattery (and thirst for your cash).

As ever the Lonely Planet Thorn Tree forum is a superb resource for female travellers (even if we do say so ourselves); if you've any questions or concerns check out http://thorntree.lonelyplanet.com.

Laos

HIGHLIGHTS

- **Luang Prabang** – enchanted mystical city of treasured wats, French cuisine and Indochinese villas overlooking the Mekong River (p368)
- **Luang Nam Tha and Muang Sing** – taking eco-conscious treks into the feral jungle of Nam Ha National Protected Area and ethnic Akha villages (p385, p387)
- **Si Phan Don** – a lazy maze of shady islands and rocky islets, home to the rare Irrawaddy dolphin (p400)
- **Wat Phu Champasak** – Khmer-era ruins perfectly placed beneath a mountain facing the peaceful riverside village of Champasak (p399)
- **Bolaven Plateau** – home to the best coffee in Laos and dotted with ice-cold waterfalls to relieve the heat of the south (p398)
- **Off the beaten track** – visiting Vieng Xai caves, the remote and forbidding home of Pathet Lao revolutionaries and the prison of the last king of Laos (p382)

FAST FACTS

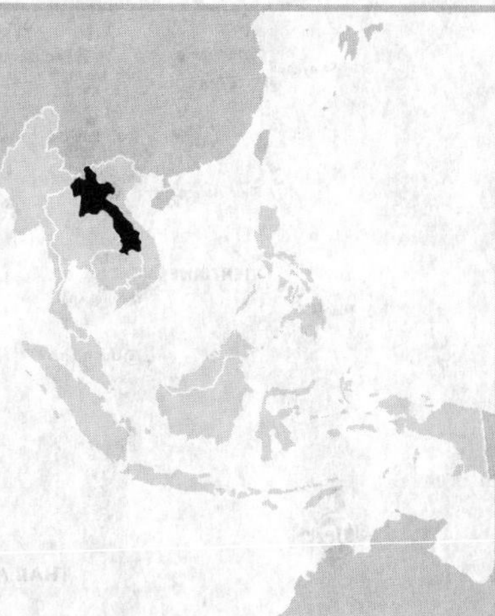

- **ATMs** two in Vientiane, one in Luang Prabang, Vang Vieng and Pakse, all with international facilities
- **Budget** US$15 to US$20 a day
- **Capital** Vientiane
- **Costs** city guesthouse US$4-10, four-hour bus ride US$1.50, Beer Lao US$0.80
- **Country code** ☎ 856
- **Languages** Lao, ethnic dialects
- **Money** US$1 = 9627 kip
- **Phrases** *sábąai-dii* (hello), *sábąai-dii* (goodbye), *khàwp jąi* (thank you)
- **Population** 6.5 million
- **Time** GMT + seven hours
- **Visas** Thirty-day tourist visas are available in advance in Thailand, China, Vietnam or Cambodia. On-the-spot 30-day visas are available for US$30 with two photos on arrival in Vientiane, Luang Prabang and Pakse international airports, and when crossing the border from Thailand, China and Vietnam.

TRAVEL HINT

Flat tyres, breakdowns and unexpected detours are a feature of Laos bus travel; take plenty of provisions and share them round. iPods and inflatable neck cushions may turn out to be your best friends.

OVERLAND ROUTES

Landlocked Laos has multiple entry points from Thailand and Vietnam, one from China, and an unofficial crossing from Cambodia.

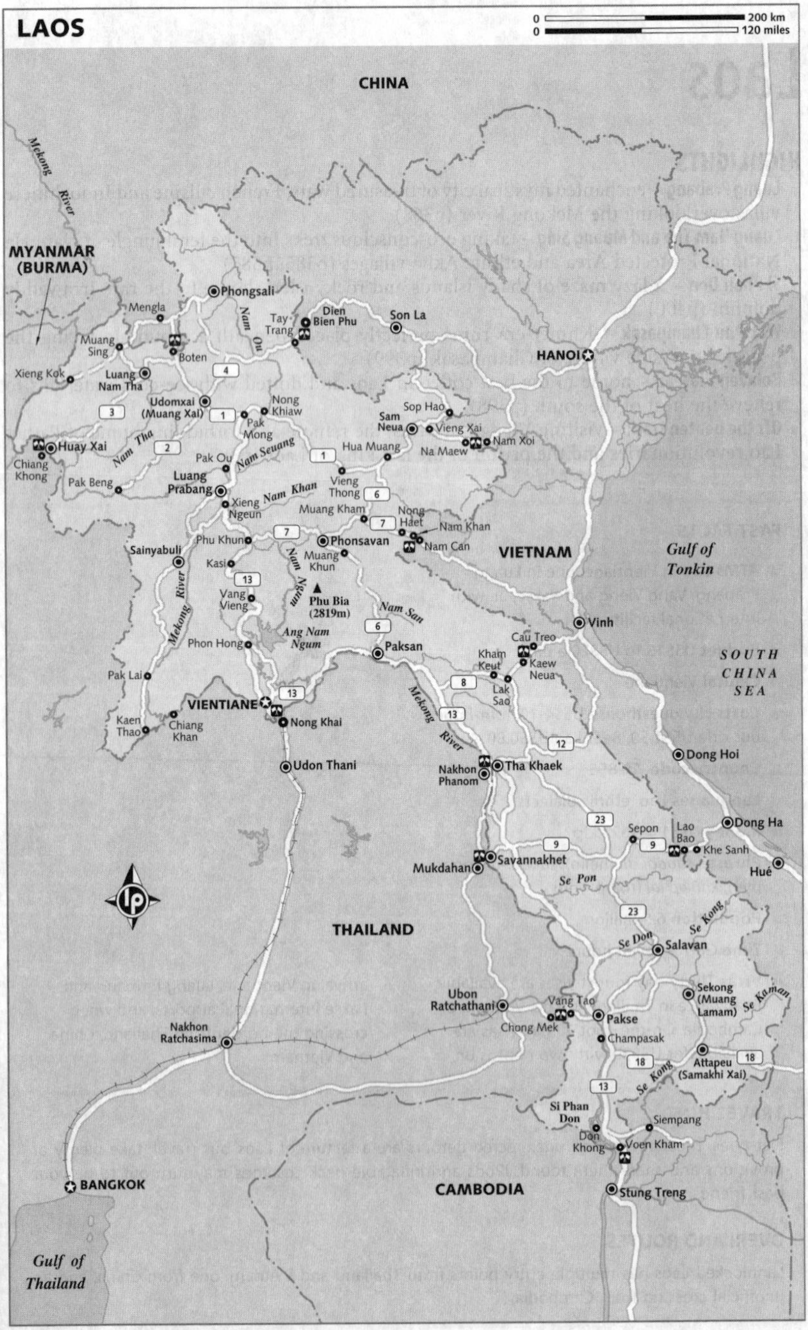

LAOS

0 — 200 km
0 — 120 miles

CHINA
Mekong River
MYANMAR (BURMA)
Phongsali
Mengla
Nam Ou
Dien Bien Phu
Tay Trang
Son La
Muang Sing
Boten
HANOI
Xieng Kok
Luang Nam Tha
4
Udomxai (Muang Xai)
3
1
Nong Khiaw
Pak Mong
Sam Neua
Sop Hao
Vieng Xai
Huay Xai
Nam Tha
2
Chiang Khong
Nam Seuang
Hua Muang
Na Maew
Nam Xoi
Pak Ou
1
Vieng Thong
Pak Beng
Luang Prabang
Nam Khan
6
Xieng Ngeun
Muang Kham
Nong Haet
7
Nam Khan
Phu Khun
7
Phonsavan
Nam Can
Sainyabuli
Kasi
Muang Khun
VIETNAM
Gulf of Tonkin
13
Nam Ngum
Phu Bia (2819m)
Vang Vieng
Mekong River
Nam San
6
Vinh
Ang Nam Ngum
Phon Hong
Paksan
Cau Treo
Kham Keut
Kaew Neua
SOUTH CHINA SEA
Pak Lai
8
Lak Sao
13
VIENTIANE
Mekong River
13
Kaen Thao
Chiang Khan
Nong Khai
12
Dong Hoi
Udon Thani
Nakhon Phanom
Tha Khaek
23
Sepon
Lao Bao
Dong Ha
9
9
Khe Sanh
Mukdahan
Savannakhet
Hué
Se Pon
23
Se Kong
THAILAND
Se Don
Salavan
Sekong (Muang Lamam)
Se Kaman
Ubon Ratchathani
Vang Tao
Pakse
Chong Mek
Champasak
Nakhon Ratchasima
18
Attapeu (Samakhi Xai)
18
13
Se Kong
Si Phan Don
Siempang
Don Khong
Voen Kham
BANGKOK
CAMBODIA
Stung Treng
Gulf of Thailand

Were Laos, Thailand and Vietnam túk-túk drivers, the Thai driver would take you to your destination via a silk shop, the Vietnamese would almost run you over for your custom, while you'd probably have to go find the Lao driver, wake him up and *then* persuade him to do some work. No teeming, smoggy metropolis, no aggressive entrepreneurialism, this is Southeast Asia's most relaxing country to travel in.

In the north, a rugged terrain of emerald mountains and dramatic limestone peaks, criss-crossed with rivers, makes travel impossibly slow. Flat as a pancake and sprinkled with palm trees, the languid south is the quasi market garden of Laos; separated from the economic powerhouse of Thailand by the massive Mekong River.

After 30 years of communist inertia, Laos is hurrying to play catch-up with its neighbours. And while economic reforms have spawned a new urban elite, for the rest of the country subsistence village life remains virtually unchanged since the French sidled in more than a hundred years ago.

CURRENT EVENTS

Eschewing the international arena since its take-over in 1975, the Communist regime learnt by the late 80s that further isolation would be its downfall and gingerly opened its doors to foreign investment. As such Laos has reinvented itself as the crossroads state. Major highways are being built between China, Thailand and Vietnam, transforming the country from being landlocked to land-linked.

And while the government concerns itself over the falling standards of morality with so much Thai TV invading the airwaves, the world's environmentalists are more anxious as to what's happening to the country's wildlife, disrupted by the building of 11 lucrative hydroelectric dams and the continued logging of huge swathes of forest. It's a difficult balance, the preservation of one of the world's richest ecosystems resources versus Laos' need to financially support itself and keep up with other members of Asean.

Rural poverty – and the skyrocketing scrap-metal trade in China – has also seen a rise in unexploded ordnance (UXO) fatalities. A lasting legacy of the US-led Secret War, UXOs are another factor in Laos' slow development as land is virtually unusable until it's cleared – an expensive and time-consuming process.

Government-forced resettlement of Hmong villages, in an attempt to rein in more than three decades of minor insurrection, is having mixed results; security alerts are frequent – though often unpublicised – around Xieng Khouang and Xaisamboun Provinces (Special Zone). Don't be surprised to see the odd gun-toting guard knocking around on bus journeys to Phonsavan and around.

Finally, the problem of *swidden* (slash and burn) farming practiced for centuries by ethnic farmers in the cultivation of coffee, rice and rubber, has led to extensive deforestation of original growth forest. Environmentalists are working in earnest to approach change through re-education, but reversing tradition and convincing sceptical tribes is not an overnight process.

On the plus side, literacy has risen considerably; inter-country communication is improving; more hospitals are being built and life expectancy has risen incrementally.

HISTORY

The Kingdom of Lan Xang

Before the French, British, Chinese and Siamese drew a line around it, Laos was a collection of disparate principalities subject to an ever-revolving cycle of war, invasion, prosperity and decay.

Laos' earliest brush with nationhood was in the 14th century, when Khmer-backed Lao warlord Fa Ngum conquered Wieng Chan (Vientiane).

It was Fa Ngum who gave his kingdom the title still favoured by travel romantics and businesses – Lan Xang, or (Land of a) Million Elephants. He also made Theravada Buddhism the state religion and adopted the symbol of Lao sovereignty that remains in use today, the Pha Bang buddha image, after which Luang Prabang is named.

Lan Xang reached its peak in the 17th century, when it was the dominant force in Southeast Asia.

French Rule

By the 18th century, the nation had crumbled, falling under the control of the Siamese, who coveted much of modern-day

Laos as a buffer zone against the expansionist French. It was to no effect. Soon after taking over Annam and Tonkin (modern-day Vietnam), the French negotiated with Siam into relinquishing her territory east of the Mekong, and Laos was born.

The country's diverse ethnic make-up and short history as a nation-state meant nationalism was slow to form. The first nationalist movement, the Lao Issara (Free Lao), was created to prevent the country's return to French rule after the invading Japanese left at the end of WWII. In 1953 France granted full sovereignty, but 20 years of chaos followed as Laos became a stage on which the clash of communist ambition and USA anxiety over the perceived Southeast Asian 'domino effect' played itself out.

A period of shifting alliances and political mayhem saw multiple parties with multiple agendas settle into two factions: the Pathet Lao supported by the North Vietnamese, Chinese and Soviets, and the right-wing elite backed by the US government.

The Secret War

From 1965 to 1973, the US devastated eastern and northeastern Laos with nonstop carpet-bombing to counter the presence of the North Vietnamese in the country. The campaign intensified the war between the Pathet Lao and the Royal Lao armies and if anything, increased domestic support for the communists. The US withdrawal in 1973 saw Laos divided up between Pathet Lao and non-Pathet Lao, but within two years the communists had taken over and the Lao People's Democratic Republic (PDR) was created under the leadership of Vietnamese protégé Kaysone Phomvihan.

Around 10% of Laos' population fled, mostly into Thailand. The remaining opponents of the government – notably tribes of Hmong (highland dwellers) in Xieng Khuang and Luang Prabang – were suppressed, often brutally.

A New Beginning

The Lao government quickly recognised the shortcomings of the socialist experiment and since the 1980s socialism has been softened to allow for private enterprise and foreign investment (but not political dissent of course). Laos entered the political family of Southeast Asian countries known as Asean in 1997, two years after Vietnam.

In 2004 the USA promoted Laos to Normal Trade Relations, cementing the end to a trade embargo in place since the communists took power in 1975. The Lao government has set its goal to haul Laos out of the Least Developed Country bracket by 2020. While still heavily reliant on foreign aid, Laos has committed to income-generating projects in recent years in a bid to increase its prosperity.

THE CULTURE

National Psyche

Lao people are generally very laid-back and unassuming, and appreciate others being the same. They love a celebration (and a dirty joke), and at festival time you'll see the characteristic Lao diffidence dissolve as if by magic (or by *lào-láo* aka rice whisky) into bawdy boisterousness. Many are also very superstitious and belief in spirits and ghosts is almost universal; the Hmong still believe in werewolves.

Lifestyle

Laos' strongest cultural and linguistic links are with Thailand, reasserted in a distinctly modern way, with Thai music and TV an almost ubiquitous presence in the country. Similarly, touching another person's head is taboo, as is pointing your feet at another person or at a buddha image. Strong displays of emotion are also discouraged. As in Thailand, the traditional greeting gesture is the *nop* or *wâi,* a prayer-like placing together of the palms in front of the face or chest, although in urban areas the handshake is becoming more commonplace.

Socially, Laos is very conservative and regular waves of prohibition sweep the land in response to the perceived menace of bourgeois liberalism seeping over the border from Thailand and the West.

For all temple visits, dress neatly and take your shoes off when entering religious buildings. You should also take off your shoes when entering people's homes, guesthouses and shops. In general you won't see many shirtless Lao; to their credit, visiting *falang* (foreigners) are generally respectful of this rule (it gets harder to maintain in the boiling islands of Si Phan Don). A free booklet, *Do's & Don'ts in Laos,* produced by the Lao National Tourism Authority (p354) comically describes how to dress and behave in a way that will not offend or encourage irresponsible behaviour among the young and impressionable.

Population

The government has been at pains to encourage national pride and a 'Lao' identity, despite the fact that more than 30% of the country is made up of non-Lao-speaking non-Buddhist hill tribes with little connection to traditional Lao culture. Government education also ensured that knowledge of the outside world was very limited, though Thai TV and the growing accessibility of the internet are changing that.

RELIGION

Most lowland Lao are Theravada Buddhists and many Lao males choose to be ordained temporarily as monks, typically spending anywhere from a month to three years at a wat. Indeed, a young man is not considered 'ripe' until he has completed his spiritual term. After the 1975 communist victory, Buddhism was suppressed, but by 1992 the government had relented and it was back in full swing, with a few alterations. Monks are still forbidden to promote *phî* (spirit) worship, which has been officially banned in Laos along with *sâiyasaat* (folk magic).

Despite the ban, *phî* worship remains the dominant non-Buddhist belief system. Even in Vientiane, Lao citizens openly perform the ceremony called *sukhwăn* or *bąsi*, in which the 32 *khwăn* (guardian spirits of the body) are bound to the guest of honour by white strings tied around the wrists (you'll see many Lao people wearing these).

Outside the Mekong River valley, the *phî* cult is particularly strong among tribal Thai, especially the Thai Dam. *Mâw* (priests) who are trained to appease and exorcise troublesome spirits preside at important Thai Dam festivals and other ceremonies. The Khamu and Hmong-Mien tribes also practise animism; the latter group also adds ancestral worship.

SPACE INVADERS

Don't be surprised if an old man puts his hand on your leg in a friendly gesture, or the kid next to you on a long bus journey falls asleep and drools on your shoulder. In Laos they haven't acquired the hang of spatial awareness; what seems like an invasion of privacy to Westerners is perfectly normal in a crammed bus where there's no room (quite literally) for Western reserve.

ARTS

Lao art and architecture can be unique and expressive, and mostly religious in nature. Distinctively Lao is the Calling for Rain Buddha, a standing image with a rocket-like shape. Wats in Luang Prabang feature *sĭm* (chapels), with steep, low roofs.

Traditional Lao art has a more limited range than its Southeast Asian neighbours, partly because Laos has a more modest history as a nation-state and partly because successive colonists from China, Vietnam, Thailand, Myanmar and France have run off with it.

Upland crafts include gold- and silversmithing among the Hmong and Mien tribes, and tribal Thai weaving (especially among the Thai Dam and Thai Lü peoples). Classical music and dance have been all but lost in Laos, although performances are occasionally held in Luang Prabang at the Royal Palace (p374) and in Vientiane.

Foot-tapping traditional folk music, usually featuring the *khaen* (Lao panpipe), is still quite popular and inspires many modern Lao tunes. Increasingly, though, soppy heartbreak Thai pop and its Lao imitations are the music of choice.

ENVIRONMENT

The Land

Laos' small population and 236,800 sq km of rugged geography mean this is the least altered environment in Southeast Asia. Unmanaged vegetation covers an estimated 85% of the country, and 10% of Laos is original growth forest. A hundred years ago this statistic was nearer 75%, which provides a clear idea of the detrimental effects of relentless logging and slash and burn farming.

Nonetheless, most Lao still live at or just above subsistence level, consuming far fewer of their own natural resources than the people of any developed country.

Wildlife

Laos' forest cover means it has a greater concentration of wild animals than neighbouring Thailand. Its pristine forests, mountains and rivers harbour a rich variety of creatures, including an estimated 437 kinds of bird and, in southern Laos alone, an incredible 320 different fish species.

There are also wild elephants, jackals, bears, leopards, tigers and the rare Irrawaddy dolphin. Its habitat is concentrated in the southern Mekong particularly around Si Phan Don, where you have the best chance of sighting them in the dry season (we saw three of the 10-strong pod within minutes, so it's worth the journey).

National Parks

In 1993 the government set up 18 National Protected Areas (NPAs), comprising a total of 24,600 sq km, just over 10% of the land. An additional two were added in 1995 (taking the total coverage to 14% of Laos). International consulting agencies have also recommended another nine sites, but these have yet to materialise. Despite these conservation efforts, illegal timber felling and the smuggling of exotic wildlife are still significant threats to Laos's natural resources; the former, sadly, facilitated by the government's granting lucrative logging licenses to China.

Most conservation areas are in southern Laos. However, for the majority of foreign travellers Nam Ha NPA in the northern province of Luang Nam Tha is the most accessible and popular wilderness area to visit (see p385).

TRANSPORT

GETTING THERE & AWAY

Air

There are currently no intercontinental flights to Laos. You can enter or exit Laos by air at Vientiane (from or to Cambodia, China, Thailand and Vietnam), Luang Prabang (Cambodia, Thailand and Vietnam) or Pakse (Cambodia).

Lao Airlines, Thai Airways International (THAI), Bangkok Airways and Vietnam Airlines all operate flights into the country. All fares listed in this chapter are one-way.

Bangkok Airways (code PG; ☎ 071-253334; www.bangkokair.com)
Lao Airlines (code QV; ☎ 021-212051; www.laos-airlines.com)
Thai Airways International (THAI, code TG; ☎ 021-216143; www.thaiairways.com)
Vietnam Airlines (code VN; ☎ 021-217562; www.vietnamairlines.com)

DEPARTURE TAX

Departure tax is US$10, payable in US dollars, baht or kip (cash only) at the airport. At overland crossings, the exit fee should be 5000 kip. Domestic airport tax is also 5000 kip.

CAMBODIA

Lao Airlines flies regularly from Vientiane to Siem Reap (US$150) and Phnom Penh (US$150). Tourist visas are available on arrival at airports in Cambodia for US$20 (plus one passport photo) for most nationalities.

CHINA

Lao Airlines and China Yunnan Airlines fly between Vientiane and Kunming (US$140).

THAILAND

Lao Airlines and Thai Airways International fly from Bangkok to Vientiane (US$100, daily). Bangkok Airways flies to Luang Prabang (US$220, daily), sometimes stopping en route at Sukhothai in Thailand. Lao Airlines also flies to Chiang Mai (US$90, Tuesday, Friday and Sunday) from Luang Prabang.

VIETNAM

Lao Airlines and Vietnam Airlines fly between Vientiane and Hanoi (US$120, daily) and Ho Chi Minh City (HCMC; US$180, daily).

Land

Laos has open land borders with Cambodia, China, Thailand and Vietnam, but the situation at all of them is prone to change without warning. Under current rules, a 30-day tourist visa is available on arrival at all international checkpoints (except at the Cambodian border), but this can change rapidly, so check the situation before leaving. See p929 for a list of border crossings.

GETTING AROUND

Air

Lao Airlines (code QV; ☎ 021-212051; www.laos-airlines.com) handles all domestic flights in Laos. Pur-

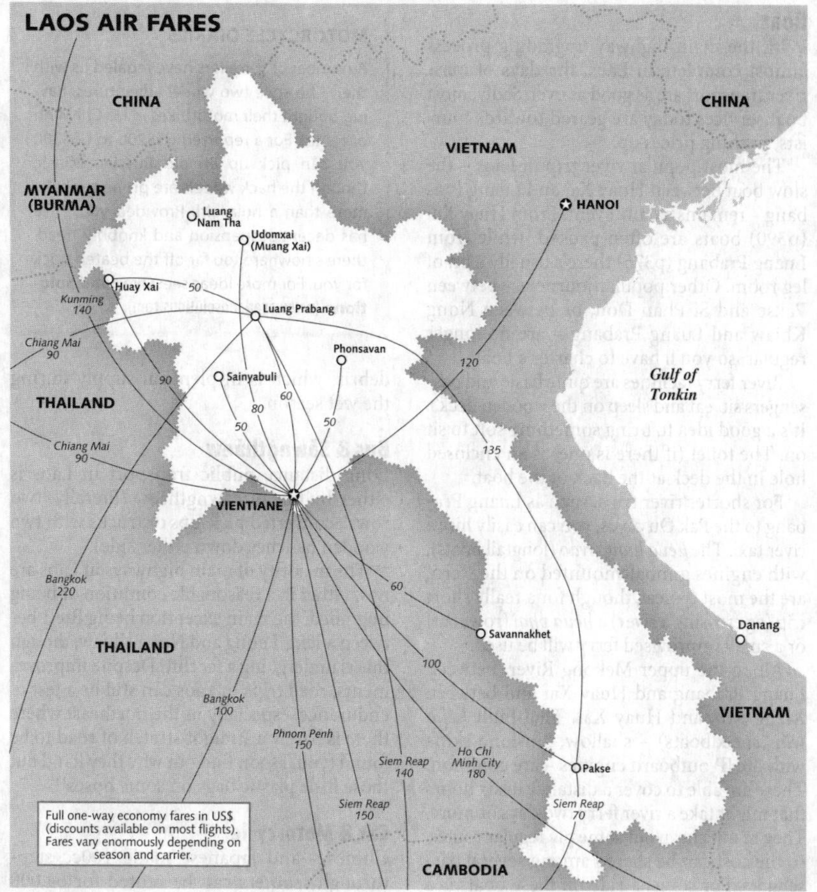

chasing tickets using credit cards carries an additional surcharge. Schedules are unreliable and during holiday seasons it can be very difficult to get a seat to some destinations, so book ahead.

Safety records for Lao Airlines aren't made public, and many international organisations and Western embassies advise staff not to use this airline. That said a new range of MA60 Chinese-made planes are gradually phasing out the old accident-prone M12s, improving the company's reputation. The international flights and busy domestic routes are as safe as any but flying into Sam Neua, where the descent is tricky and conditions unpredictable, is not for timid air travellers.

Always reconfirm your flights a day or two before departing as undersubscribed flights may be cancelled, or you could get bumped off the passenger list.

Bicycle

The light and relatively slow traffic in most Lao towns makes for favourable cycling conditions and you'll see many hardy cyclists scaling mountains. Bicycles are available for rent in major tourist destinations, costing around 10,000 kip per day for a cheap Thai or Chinese model. For long-distance cyclists, bicycles can be brought into the country usually without any hassle, and if the mountainous north proves too challenging, a bus will always pick you up along the road.

Boat

With the main highway upgrading process almost complete in Laos, the days of mass river transport are as good as over. Sadly, most boat services today are geared towards tourists, pushing prices up.

The most popular river trip in Laos – the slow boat between Huay Xai and Luang Prabang – remains a daily event. From Huay Xai (p390) boats are often packed, while from Luang Prabang (p375) there's usually a bit of leg room. Other popular journeys – between Pakse and Si Phan Don, or between Nong Khiaw and Luang Prabang – are no longer regular, so you'll have to charter a boat.

River ferry facilities are quite basic and passengers sit, eat and sleep on the wooden decks. It's a good idea to bring something soft to sit on. The toilet (if there is one) is an enclosed hole in the deck at the back of the boat.

For shorter river trips, such as Luang Prabang to the Pak Ou caves, you can easily hire a river taxi. The *héua hang nyáo* (longtail boats), with engines gimbal-mounted on the stern, are the most typical, though for a really short trip (eg crossing a river) a *héua phai* (rowboat) or a small improvised ferry will be used.

Along the upper Mekong River, between Luang Prabang and Huay Xai and between Xieng Kok and Huay Xai, Thai-built *héua wái* (speedboats) – shallow, 5m-long skiffs with 40HP outboard engines – are common. These are able to cover a distance in six hours that might take a river ferry two days or more. They're not cheap but some ply regular routes, so the cost can be shared among several passengers. For some, a ride on these boats is a major thrill. For others, it's like riding on a giant runaway chainsaw, a nightmare that can't end soon enough. Speedboats, as well as being deafeningly loud, kill and injure people every year. They tend to flip and disintegrate on contact with any solid floating debris, which is in plentiful supply during the wet season.

WHEEL POWER

Thanks to a much improved road-system, travelling by bike has really taken off; mountain-bikers are reaching dizzying altitudes, pushing further into frontiers and mountain villages previously considered inaccessible. Our only advice is to take plenty of fruit and water on untravelled roads, and a healthy stock of inner-tubes.

MOTORCYCLE DIARIES

A number of travellers have regaled us with their Che-style two wheel adventures, having bought their motorbikes in Ho Chi Minh or Hanoi. For a reported US$200 to US$300 you can pick up an old Russian Minsk, though the back wheels are prone to shake more than a hula girl. Provided your bike has decent suspension and knobbly tread, there's nowhere too far off the beaten track for you. For more ideas see: **Overland Solutions** (www.overlandsolutions.com).

Bus & Săwngthăew

Long-distance public transport in Laos is either by bus or săwngthăew (literally 'two rows'; converted pick-ups or trucks with two wooden benches down either side).

The majority of main highways in Laos are now either in a reasonable condition or being upgraded; the main exception being Rte 1 between Vieng Thong and Nong Khiaw, though this is undergoing a facelift. Despite improvements, road trips in Laos can still be a test of endurance, especially in the northeast where there is barely a straight stretch of road to be found (you'll soon find out why they hand out those little plastic bags on some buses!).

Car & Motorcycle

Chinese- and Japanese-made 100cc step-through scooters can be rented for 64,000 kip to 80,000 kip per day in Vientiane, Vang Vieng, Savannakhet, Pakse and Luang Nam Tha. A driving licence is increasingly required in larger places like Vientiane where it's also possible to rent dirt bikes for around US$20 per day. You'll be expected to leave your passport as a deposit, but it's unlikely you'll be covered by the rental company's insurance in the event of an accident. Motorcycle tours of Laos are offered by **Asian Motorcycling Adventures** (www.asianbiketour.com). If you're caught without a helmet, expect to be fined US$5 by vigilant policemen eager to pocket a little extra cash. Try to get a Japanese bike if you're travelling any distance out of town. Motorcyclists planning to ride through Laos should check out the wealth of information at www.gt-rider.com.

MUST READ

Laos: Culture & Society, edited by Dr Grant Evans, contains a series of academic essays that will deepen your understanding of the history, culture and politics of Laos.

Car rental in Laos is expensive, but it's a great way of reaching remote places. In Vientiane, **Asia Vehicle Rental** (AVR; Map p356; ☎ 021-17493; avr@loxinfo.co.th; Th Samsenthai) has sedans, minibuses, 4WDs and station wagons, with or without drivers, from around US$70 per day, not including fuel. If you have your own car or motorcycle, you are allowed to import it for the length of your visa after filling in a few forms at the border. Temporary import extensions are possible for up to two weeks, sometimes more.

Hitching

Hitching is possible in Laos, but it's never entirely safe and definitely not recommended for women as the act of standing beside a road and waving at cars might be misinterpreted! In any case, public transport is inexpensive and will pick you up almost anywhere. Otherwise long-distance cargo trucks or cars with red-on-yellow number plates (private vehicles) are also a good bet.

VIENTIANE

☎ 021 / pop 203,000

This delightfully friendly capital, studded with crumbling French mansions, bougainvillea-blooming streets and steaming noodle stalls, is somewhere between a big town and a diminutive city; the kind of place you might find a Graham Greene protagonist. Its conveniently compact travellers' enclave is based around Nam Phu, the Mekong riverside and Setthariat and Samsenthai streets. Full of things to see, from Buddha Park to the Morning market and an impossibly rich selection of international cuisine – most pointedly French – you'll find yourself slowly won over by the easy charms of this evolving backwater. The city may reveal its beauty less readily than Luang Prabang, but spend a few days visiting its unusual sights, sampling its excellent food and enjoying a Beer Lao at sunset by the river, and you'll soon feel at home here.

HISTORY

Vientiane's peaceful demeanour belies a turbulent history. Over the 1000 or so years of its history, it's been variously abused by successive Vietnamese, Burmese, Siamese, Khmer and French conquerors. The French cemented Vientiane's status as a capital city when they took over the protectorship of Laos in the late 19th and early 20th centuries; it was further inhabited by CIA 'spooks' and the charismatic Ravens (the screw-loose CIA-funded pilots of Air America) in the 60s and early 70s. After their victory in 1973 the Pathet Lao briefly considered moving the capital to Vieng Xai but then relented and stuck with Vientiane, and the city began a rapid transformation from notorious den of vice to austere socialist outpost. Since opening up to international investment, Vientiane has slowly been shedding its parochial skin. In 2004, it enjoyed the honour of hosting the Asean Summit, placing it firmly on Southeast Asia's diplomatic map. In 2009 Vientiane will host the Asean Games, litmus proof this once backward-looking country has its sights firmly set on the future.

ORIENTATION

The three main streets parallel to the Mekong – Th Fa Ngum, Th Setthathirat and Th Samsenthai – form the central inner city of Vientiane and are where most of the budget guesthouses, bars and restaurants are located. Nam Phu is the best inner-city landmark if you're catching a taxi or túk-túk into town. Heading northeast at a 90-degree angle to Th Setthathirat is the wide tree-lined boulevard of Th Lan Xang, where you'll find the

GETTING INTO TOWN

Most buses coming in and out of Vientiane arrive at the northern bus station. If you're coming in by the more comfortable KVT and Laody buses, you'll be arriving at the Si Muang bus station, while buses from within Vientiane Prefecture arrive at the Talat Sao bus station. All are a short ride from the centre of the city.

Arriving by air at the now impressive Wattay International Airport, you can expect to pay US$5 to get into town in a licensed taxi. To save money, lug your bag onto the main road and wait for a passing túk-túk.

VIENTIANE

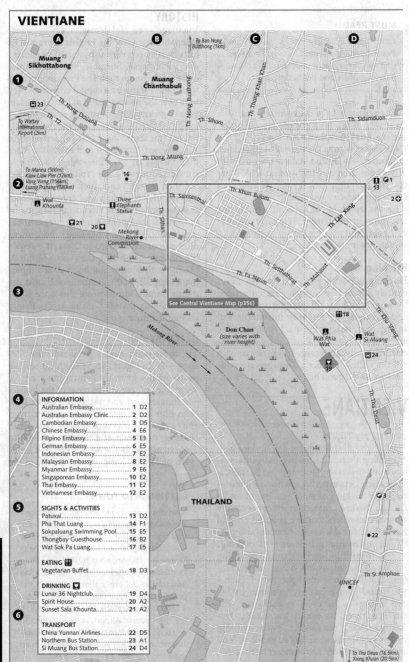

INFORMATION		
Australian Embassy	1	D2
Australian Embassy Clinic	2	D2
Cambodian Embassy	3	D5
Chinese Embassy	4	E6
Filipino Embassy	5	E3
German Embassy	6	E5
Indonesian Embassy	7	E2
Malaysian Embassy	8	E2
Myanmar Embassy	9	E6
Singaporean Embassy	10	E2
Thai Embassy	11	E2
Vietnamese Embassy	12	E2
SIGHTS & ACTIVITIES		
Patuxai	13	D2
Pha That Luang	14	F1
Sokpaluang Swimming Pool	15	E5
Thongbay Guesthouse	16	B2
Wat Sok Pa Luang	17	E5
EATING		
Vegetarian Buffet	18	D3
DRINKING		
Lunar 36 Nightclub	19	D4
Spirit House	20	A2
Sunset Sala Khounta	21	A2
TRANSPORT		
China Yunnan Airlines	22	D5
Northern Bus Station	23	A1
Si Muang Bus Station	24	D4

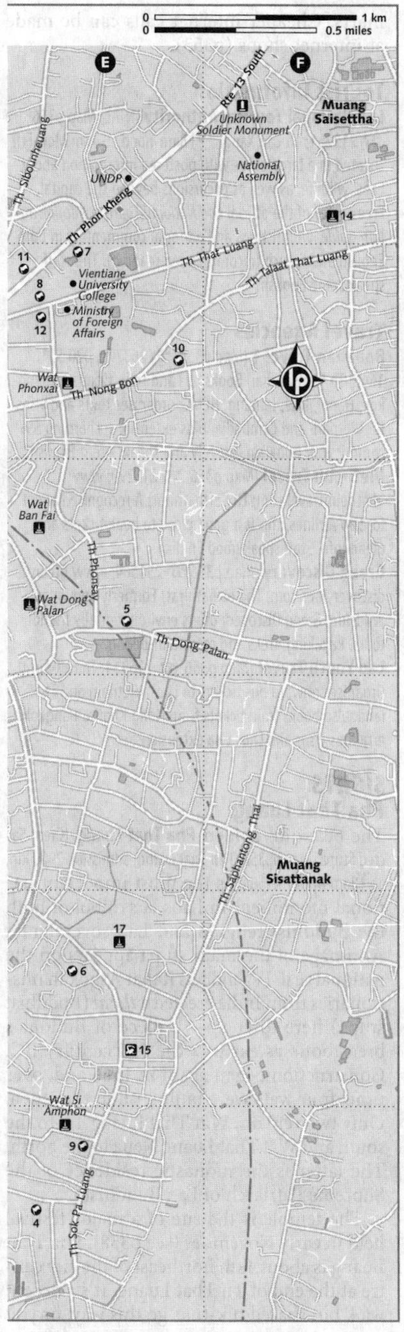

Talat Sao (Morning Market) and the Patuxai monument. Heading further northeast from Patuxai is Th That Luang, home to a number of foreign embassies and crowned by the magnificent golden Pha That Luang, Laos' most distinctive structure.

INFORMATION

Bookshops

Kosila Bookshop 1 (Map p356; ☎ 241352; Th Chanta Khumman; 🕑 9am-5pm Mon-Fri) Shelves are stocked with secondhand fiction and old travel guides selling for around 80,000 kip.

Monument Books (Map p356; ☎ 243708; Th Nokeo Khumman; 🕑 9am-5pm Mon-Fri) A great range of English, French and German books on offer, ranging from thrillers and nonfiction to coffee table pictorials.

Vientiane Book Centre (Map p356; ☎ 213031; Th Pangkham; 🕑 8.30am-5.30pm Mon-Fri, 8.30am-4pm Sat) As well as secondhand and antique books, it sells international news magazines, academic texts and old NGO reports.

Cultural Centres

Centre Culturel et de Coopération Linguistique (French Cultural Centre; Map p356; ☎ 215764; www.ambafrance-laos.org in French; Th Lan Xang; 🕑 9.30am-6.30pm Mon-Fri, 9.30am-noon Sat) The centre has a library, a large selection of newspapers and magazines from around the Francophone world, French and Lao language lessons, and a popular lunchtime café. French films are shown at 7pm Thursdays.

Emergency

Ambulance (☎ 195)
Fire (☎ 190)
Police (☎ 191)
Tourist Police (Map p356; ☎ 251128; Th Lan Xang)

Internet Access

Internet access in Vientiane is generally pretty quick and decent value (100 kip per minute). Below are some of the quickest we tried.

A1 Internet (Map p356; Th Setthathirat; per min 100 kip; 🕑 8am-11.30pm) Has Skype and broadband connection with a private glass booth for international calls (1000 kip per min).

Fastnet Internet (Map p356; ☎ 020 549 2677; Th Samsenthai; per min 100 kip; 🕑 8am-11p) As the name suggests, good internet access. Overseas internet calls available too.

PlaNet Online (Map p356; ☎ 241251; Th Setthathirat; per min 100 kip; 🕑 8am-11.30pm) Also has a large-screen TV often tuned to the BBC. You can burn photo cards onto CD for 20,000 kip.

Laundry
Most guesthouses offer same-day laundry service for 10,000 kip per kilo.

House of Fruit Shakes (Map p356; Th Samsenthai; per item 500-4000 kip; 7am-9pm) Do your laundry at this delightful family-run fruit-drink bar that delivers a vitamin punch.

Media
Laos' only English-language newspaper, published five times a week, is the government-run *Vientiane Times*, so don't expect too many truthful exposés. More informative is the *Bangkok Post*. International news magazines such as the *Economist*, *Newsweek* and *Time* are sold at minimarts and the Vientiane Book Centre (p353).

Medical Services
Aek Udon International Hospital (0066 4234 2555; 24hr). If you're seriously ill seek an emergency evacuation to this hospital in Thailand.

Australian Embassy Clinic (Map pp352-3 413603; Th Mahasot; 8.30am-12.30pm & 2-5pm Mon-Fri) Citizens of Commonwealth countries can access treatment here.

Mahasot Hospital (Map p356 214023; Th Mahasot) Come here for treatment of minor ailments.

Money
Several banks in Vientiane change cash and travellers cheques and do cash advances against credit cards for a commission. There are also a number of 24-hour ATMs.

Banque pour le Commerce Extérieur Lao (BCL; Map p356 213200; cnr Th Pangkham & Th Fa Ngum; 8.30am-5pm Mon-Fri) Good rates for travellers cheques.

Joint Development Bank (Map p356 213535; Th Lan Xang; 8.30am-4pm Mon-Fri) Charges lower commission on cash advances against credit cards.

Lao Development Bank (Map p356; 213300; Th Setthathirat; 8.30-11.30am & 2-4pm Mon-Fri)

Lao-Viet Bank (Map p356; 215418; Th Lan Xang; 8.30am-4pm Mon-Fri)

Post
Post, Telephone & Telegraph (PTT; Map p356; cnr Th Lan Xang & Th Khu Vieng; 8am-noon & 1-5pm Mon-Fri, 8am-noon Sat) Stamps, poste restante and (slow) internet services available here.

Telephone
International call phonecards can be purchased from the PTT (above) and minimarts. Cheaper internet calls can be made at internet shops (p353).

Tourist Information
Lao National Tourism Authority (NTAL; Map p356 212251; Th Lan Xang; 8am-noon, 1-4pm Mon-Fri) Located in a large office with postered information about Laos' wildlife, as well as excursions beyond the capital. Free copies of the official *Lao National Tourism Administration Guide*, with listings and editorial commentary in both English and French (recommended reading). The staff speak some English.

Travel Agencies
Boualian Travel 1 (Map p356 263772, 020 551 1646; Th Samsenthai) Books bus and train tickets to Bangkok, Hanoi, Hué, Danang, HCMC; organises tours and visas for Vietnam and Cambodia, plus extensions, charging 5% commission. Boualian is lovely and speaks great English.

Diethelm Travel (Map p356 215290; www.diethelmtravel.com; Th Setthathirat) A recognised agent for Lao Airlines, this is a good place to book tickets and glean info. Staff speak good English.

Green Discovery (Map p356 251564; www.greendiscoverylaos.com; Th Setthathirat) Formerly known as Wildside, Green Discovery offers environmentally friendly tours, kayaking, treks and mountain-biking.

Lao Youth Travel (Map p356 216314; Th Fa Gnum) Organises onward bus tickets to Laos, Vietnam and Thailand; also books train tickets from Nong Khai to Bangkok; arranges visas and Laos visa extensions.

SIGHTS
Pha That Luang
The beautiful golden **Pha That Luang** (Great Sacred Stupa; Map pp352-3 Th That Luang; admission 2000 kip; 8am-4pm Tue-Sun) is the most important national monument in Laos, a symbol of both the Buddhist religion and Lao sovereignty. An image of the main stupa appears on the national seal. Legend has it that Ashokan missionaries from India erected a *thâat* (Buddhist stupa) here to enclose a piece of Buddha's breastbone as early as the 3rd century BC. Construction began again in 1566 and, over time, four wats were built around the stupa. Only two remain, Wat That Luang Tai to the south and Wat That Luang Neua to the north. The latter is the monastic residence of the Supreme Patriarch of Lao Buddhism.

The temple is the site of a major festival held in early November (see p358). Pha That Luang is about 4km northeast of the city centre at the end of Th That Luang. It's a decent walk but shared túk-túks go this way, or you can hire a bike. The best time to visit is late afternoon to catch the reflected setting sun.

Wat Si Saket

Built in 1818 by King Anouvong (Chao Anou), **Wat Si Saket** (Map p356 cnr Th Lan Xang & Th Setthathirat; admission 2000 kip; 8am-noon & 1-4pm, closed public holidays) is the oldest temple in Vientiane and well worth a visit even if you've overdosed on temples. Wat Si Saket has several unique features. The interior walls of the cloister are riddled with small niches that contain more than 2000 silver and ceramic buddha images. More than 300 seated and standing buddhas of varying age, size and material (wood, stone and bronze) rest on long shelves below the niches. Most of the images are from 16th- to 19th-century Vientiane, but a few hail from 15th- to 16th-century Luang Prabang. A Khmer-style Naga Buddha is also on display, brought from a Khmer site at nearby Hat Sai Fong.

Patuxai

Vientiane's haughty Arc de Triomphe replica is an imposing if slightly incongruous sight, dominating the commercial district around Th Lan Xang. Officially called **Patuxai** (Victory Monument; Map pp352-3 Th Lan Xang; admission 2000 kip; 8am-5pm), but more commonly known by locals as *anusawali*, it commemorates the Lao who died in pre-revolutionary wars. It was built in 1969 with cement donated by the USA for the construction of a new airport, hence expats refer to it as 'the vertical runway'. The entrance fee allows you to climb the stairway interior to the top of the monument, with views over Vientiane.

Lao National History Museum

Housed in a well-worn classical mansion originally built in 1925 as the French governor's residence, the **Lao National History Museum** (Map p356 ☎ 212462; Th Samsenthai; admission 3000 kip; 8am-noon & 1-4pm) was formerly known as the Lao Revolutionary Museum. Rooms near the entrance feature cultural and geographical exhibits. Inner rooms are dedicated to the 1893–1945 French colonial period, the 1945–54 struggle for independence, the 1954–63 resistance to American imperialism, the 1964–69 provisional government, and the 1975 communist victory. Many of the displays are now in English as well as Lao. If you get museum-fatigue, you can keep your ticket and come back later the same day.

> **WARNING**
>
> Always check your government's travel advisories for up-to-date security information before travelling.

Xieng Khuan (Buddha Park)

In a grassy field by the Mekong River, 25km southeast of Vientiane, **Xieng Khuan** (Buddha Park; off Map pp352-3; off Th Tha Deua; admission 5000 kip, camera 2000 kip; 8am-sunset) is a park full of Buddhist and Hindu sculptures, a monument to one eccentric man's bizarre ambition. Xieng Khuan was designed and built in 1958 by Luang Pu (Venerable Grandfather) Bunleua Sulilat, a yogi-priest-shaman who merged Hindu and Buddhist philosophy, mythology and iconography into a cryptic whole. The concrete sculptures at Xieng Khuan (which means Spirit City) include statues of Shiva, Vishnu, Arjuna, Avalokiteshvara, Buddha and just about every other Hindu or Buddhist deity imaginable.

Buses passing here (3000 kip, 45 minutes) leave the Talat Sao terminal every 30 minutes during the day. You could charter a săwngthăew for 50,000 kip return.

ACTIVITIES

Bowling

Bright lights and the high-pitched clatter of wooden pins await you at the **Lao Bowling Centre** (Map p356; ☎ 218661; Th Khun Bulom; per game with shoe hire 20,000 kip; 9am-midnight). Even before its 'official' closing time, it may look deserted, but entry is on the right side of the building. As well as good old-fashioned bowling, you'll find pool tables, beer, and refreshments are available.

Gym & Aerobics

If all that Beer Lao is taking its toll, get thyself to the conveniently located, small, street-level gym at the **Tai-Pan Hotel** (Map p356; ☎ 216906; Th François Nginn; per visit 40,000 kip).

Massage & Herbal Saunas

For a traditional massage experience, head to **Wat Sok Pa Luang** (Map pp352-3; Th Sok Pa Luang; 1-7pm). Located in a semirural setting (*wat pàa* means 'forest temple') the wat is famous

LAOS

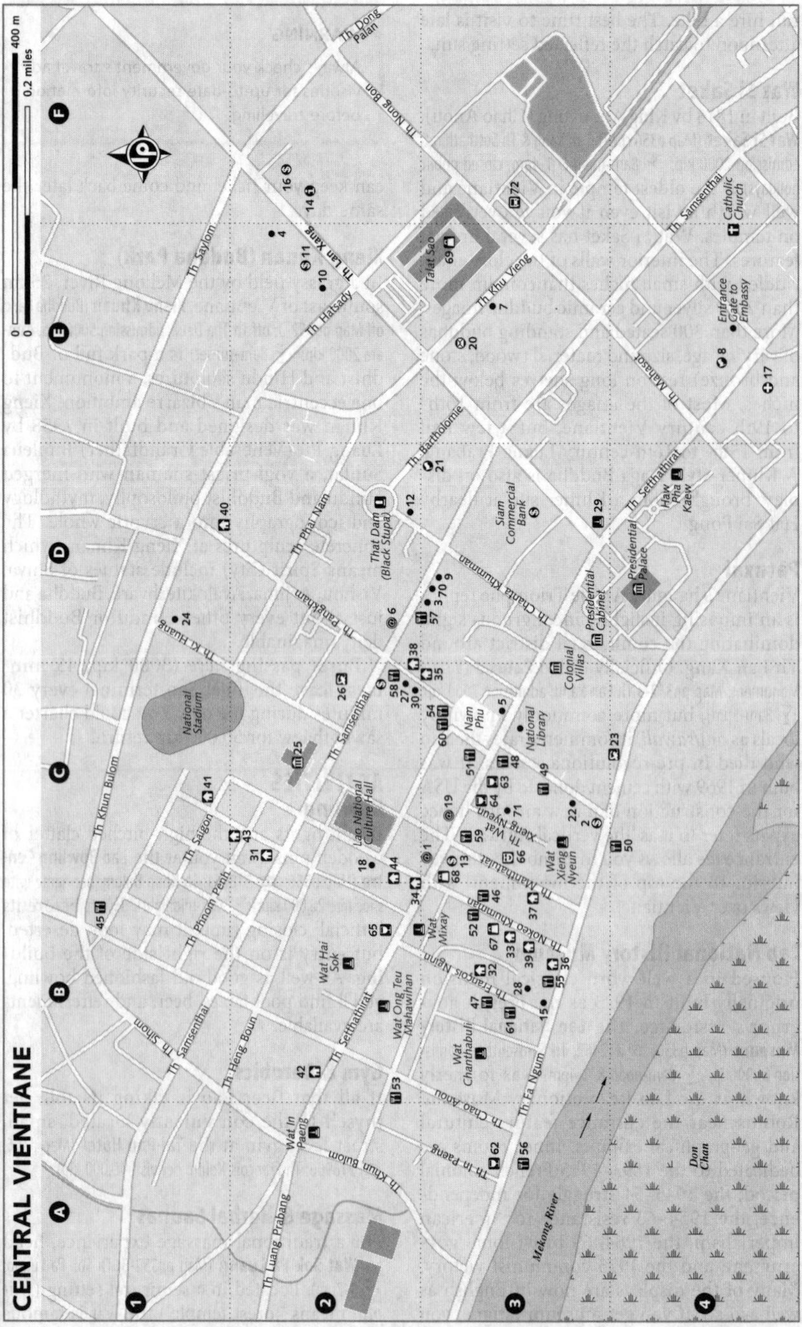

CENTRAL VIENTIANE

0 400 m
0 0.2 miles

Th Khun Bulom
Th Saylom
Th Hatsady
Th Lan Xang
Th Nong Bon
Th Dong Palan
Th Saigon
Th Phnom Penh
Th Samsenthai
Th Heng Boun
Th Setthathirat
Th Sihom
Th Luang Prabang
Th Chao Anou
Th Fa Ngum
Th In Paeng
Th François Ngin
Th Nokeo Khumman
Th Manthathurat
Th Wat Xieng Nyeun
Th Pangkham
Th Phai Nam
Th Ki Huang
Th Bartholomie
Th Chanta Khumman
Th Khu Vieng
Th Mahasot

National Stadium
Lao National Culture Hall
That Dam (Black Stupa)
Talat Sao
Siam Commercial Bank
Nam Phu
National Library
Colonial Villas
Presidential Cabinet
Presidential Palace
Haw Pha Kaew
Entrance Gate to Embassy
Catholic Church
Wat In Paeng
Wat Hai Sok
Wat Ong Teu Mahawihan
Wat Mixay
Wat Chanthabuli
Wat Xieng Nyeun
Mekong River
Don Chan

INFORMATION
- A1 Internet 1 C3
- Banque pour le Commerce Extérieur Lao 2 C3
- Boualian Travel 1 .... 3 D3
- Centre Culturel et de Coopération Linguistique 4 E2
- Diethelm Travel 5 C3
- Fastnet Internet 6 D2
- Federal Express 7 E3
- French Embassy 8 E4
- Green Discovery .... (see 51)
- House of Fruit Shakes 9 D3
- Immigration Office 10 E2
- Joint Development Bank 11 E2
- Kosila Bookshop 1 .... 12 D2
- Lao Development Bank 13 C3
- Lao National Tourism Authority 14 F2
- Lao Youth Travel 15 B3
- Lao-Viet Bank 16 F2
- Mahasot Hospital 17 E4
- Monument Books 18 C2
- PlaNet Online 19 C3
- Post, Telephone & Telegraph 20 E3
- Tourist Police .... (see 16)
- US Embassy 21 D3
- Vientiane Book Centre 22 C3

SIGHTS & ACTIVITIES
- Green Discovery .... (see 51)
- Lane Xang Hotel 23 C4
- Lao Bowling Centre 24 D1
- Lao National History Museum 25 C2
- Lao Plaza Hotel 26 C2
- Mandarina Massage 27 C2
- Tai-Pan Hotel 28 B3
- Wat Si Saket 29 D3
- White Lotus Massage & Beauty 30 C2

SLEEPING
- Dragon Lodge 31 C2
- Lao Sakonh Guest House 32 B3
- Mixay Guest House 33 B3
- Mixok Guest House 34 B2
- Nali Namphu Guest House 35 C3
- Orchid Guest House 36 B3
- Phatoumphone Guest House 37 B3
- Phonepaseuth Guest House 38 C2
- RD Guest House 39 B3
- Soukxana Guest House 40 D1
- Syri 1 Guest House 41 C1
- Syri 2 Guest House 42 B2
- Thawee Guest House 43 C2
- Vayakorn Guest House 44 C2

EATING
- Ban Anou Night Market 45 B1
- Croissant D'Or 46 B3
- Full Moon Café 47 B3
- JoMa Bakery Café 48 C3
- Just for Fun 49 C3
- Katusha Restaurant 50 C4
- Khop Chai Deu 51 C3
- La Terrasse 52 B3
- La Vendome 53 B2
- Le Provencal 54 C3
- Nazim 55 B3
- Open-air Riverside Food Vendors 56 A3
- PVO 57 D3
- Rashmi's Indian Fusion 58 C2
- Sabaidee Restaurant 59 C3
- Scandinavian Bakery 60 C3
- Sticky Fingers Café & Bar 61 B3

DRINKING
- Borpennyang 62 A3
- Dao Fa Bistro 63 C3
- Full Moon Café .... (see 47)
- Jazzy Brick 64 C3
- Khop Chai Deu .... (see 51)
- Samlo 65 B2
- Sticky Fingers Café & Bar .... (see 61)

ENTERTAINMENT
- Centre Culturel et de Coopération Linguistique .... (see 4)
- Lao Traditional Show 66 C3

SHOPPING
- Camacrafts 67 B3
- Satri Lao 68 C3
- Talat Sao 69 E3

TRANSPORT
- Asia Vehicle Rental 70 D3
- Boualian Travel 1 .... (see 3)
- KT Shop 71 C3
- PVO .... (see 57)
- Talat Sao Bus Station 72 F3

for herbal saunas (10,000 kip) and massages (30,000 kip). It's about 3km from the city centre, but túk-túk drivers all know how to get there.

In the centre of town, **White Lotus Massage & Beauty** (Map p356; ☎ 217492; Th Pangkham; 🕑 10am-10pm) is a day spa offering oil massage and traditional Lao-style massages (US$4 to US$5 per hour).

Mandarina Massage (Map p356; ☎ 218703; Th Pangkham; 🕑 10am-10pm) is next door and with its soothing interior and scented air, may be the superior of the two. Massages cost US$4 to US$5 per hour.

Meditation

Foreigners are welcome at a regular Saturday afternoon sitting at Wat Sok Pa Luang (p355). The session runs from 4pm until 5.30pm with an opportunity to ask questions afterwards.

Rafting

Green Discovery (Map p356; ☎ 251564; www.greendiscoverylaos.com; Th Setthathirat) Reliable, well-trained guides with Laos' most successful low impact ecotourism specialists.

Swimming

For serious lap swimming, there's the 25m-long **Sokpaluang Swimming Pool** (Map pp352-3; ☎ 350491; Th Sok Pa Luang; admission 6000 kip; 🕑 9am-8pm Tue-Sun), which also has a children's paddling pool and change rooms and is best visited at the weekend. Alternatively, for a more relaxed swim try the kidney-shaped pool at the **Lane Xang Hotel** (Map p356; ☎ 214102; Th Fa Gnum; admission US$2) or the slick **Lao Plaza Hotel** (Map p356; Th Samsenthai; admission US$5)

COURSES

Cooking

Courses at the **Thongbay Guesthouse** (Map pp352-3; ☎ 242292; www.thongbay-guesthouses.com; Ban Nong Douange; US$10) are organised on demand and start at 10am or 3pm. A half-day class includes a trip to the market before you cook up a storm, then feast on your culinary creations for lunch or dinner.

Yoga

To regain your balance look for signposted information on yoga classes in shop windows around Nam Phu (try the Scandinavian Bakery).

FESTIVALS & EVENTS

The **That Luang Festival** (Bun Pha That Luang), held in early November, is the largest temple fair in Laos. The full moon festival peaks with a colourful procession of thousands between Pha That Luang (p354) and Wat Si Muang. One traveller from London described it as Wembley Stadium on a cup final day, with everyone on happy drugs!

Another huge annual event is **Bun Nam** (River Festival) at the end of Buddhist Lent in October, when boat races are held on the Mekong River. Rowing teams from all over the country, as well as from Thailand, China and Myanmar compete, and the riverbank is lined with food stalls, temporary discos, carnival games and beer gardens for three nights.

The riverbank is the focus of yet more celebrations on 31 December for the **International New Year**, and again for **Vietnamese Tet-Chinese New Year**, usually in February, then once more in mid-April for the mass water-fight of **Pii Mai** (Lao New Year).

SLEEPING

The old flophouses, once complacent in offering the bare minimum, are slowly being edged out in favour of better, more sanitary accommodation. Anywhere that's cheap and clean fills up very quickly, but there are still some great bargains listed below. Remember also that you can eat for very little in Vientiane and move into a less expensive place once you've had a chance to find your bearings.

Mixay Guest House (Map p356; ☎ 020 526 0558; Th Nokeo Khumman; r 20,000-50,000 kip) Very basic rooms in this spooky old house; with fan and outside toilet, redeemed by amazing sunset views from the vertiginous roof terrace.

Mixok Guest House (Map p356; ☎ 251606; Th Setthathirat; r 40,000-60,000 kip) Rooms in reasonable condition. Blankets available for cooler nights. Fills up by midday during the high season, mostly due to its very convenient location.

Lao Sakonh Guest House (Map p356; Th François Nginn; ☎ 216571; r 40,000-70,000 kip) With its thin partitioned walls and grubby atmosphere this is like something out of *The Beach*. On a plus it's cheap and you can hire bikes for US$1.

Syri 2 Guest House (Map p356; Th Setthathirat; r with shared/private bathroom 60,000/80,000 kip) Rooms are basic and clean with a choice of attached and outside toilets. Also offers laundry service and bicycles for rent. A nice area to read upstairs. It's run by lovely people.

Soukxana Guest House (Map p356; 13 Th Pangkham; r 60,000-80,000 kip; ❄) This impeccably house-proud accommodation has spotless rooms with a pleasant family-run atmosphere. Fresh as a daisy.

our pick **Syri 1 Guest House** (Map p356; ☎ 212682; Th Saigon; r 60,000-100,000 kip) In a relatively quiet location, Syri is welcoming to newcomers and home to a little tribe of artists who paint out the back. The owner, Air, also offers special bike rides promising another side of Vientiane. A great place to chill, watch a wide range of films and meet other travellers, rooms are large and cool, décor is old style with a palpable sense of atmosphere.

Thawee Guest House (Map p356; Th Phnom Penh; ☎ 217903; r with/without air-con 60,000/120,000 kip; ❄) Adequate digs if a little murky, with attached bathrooms and fan. Make sure you ask for a room with a window, though. Also, be warned, the owner plays guitar. Badly.

Phatoumphone Guest House (Map p356; ☎ 212318; Th Manthatulat; r with shared bathroom 80,000 kip) This friendly old stalwart, with paint-thirsty walls, is showing her age. Set in a peaceful courtyard it's a fun place to meet other travellers or try and make sense of the freaky mural after a large Beer Lao.

Phonepaseuth Guest House (Map p356; Th Pangkham; ☎ 212263; www.phonepaseuth-gh.com; r 100,000 kip; ❄) Just north of Nam Phu (and the delights of the Scandinavian Bakery!) rooms are spotless and elegant with attached bathrooms. For an extra 30,000 kip you can have a balcony.

Nali Namphu Guest House (Map p356; Th Pangkham; ☎ 263298; www.malinamphu.com; r incl breakfast 100,000 kip) Recently opened with pristine rooms, bamboo furnishings, fresh white linen and tiled floors. This is great value if there are two of you. Ask for a room with a view.

RD Guest House (Map p356; Th Nokeo Khumman; ☎ 262112; r 120,000 kip) Spotlessly clean thanks to a recent refurbishment, this is quality accommodation with a hint of luxury. Has fans, laundry service and a very cool lobby. Plush.

Vayakorn Guest House (Map p356; ☎ 241911; Th Nokeo Khumman; r 120,000-170,000 kip) Luxurious accommodation in a salubrious setting, and so it should be given the price. Vayakorn's rooms have hot water, satellite TV – and, wait for it – a telephone! Newspapers and magazines available downstairs.

Dragon Lodge (Map p356; ☎ 250112; dragonlodge2002@yahoo.com; Th Samsenthai; r 120,000-230,000 kip; ❄) Ambient music, a relaxed atmosphere in the downstairs bar and good service (the information boards are packed with useful tips if you've just arrived). Also runs air-con minibuses to Vang Vieng (US$5) and organises onwards visas – all good news if you're feeling lazy.

Orchid Guest House (Map p356; ☎ 252825; Th Fa Ngum; r 130,000-140,000 kip; ❄) Opposite the Mekong with a tiled rooftop to watch the sunset over Vientiane, this place has generously sized rooms with small TVs and BBC. Bikes also available to hire. We found staff a little unapproachable on our visit.

EATING

The dining options here are so varied you'll be reeling with the angst of choice, especially if you've been in the middle of nowhere. Close to Nam Phu are some popular eating spots for homesick *falang* with plenty of pizza and pasta plus Indian, Chinese, Japanese – even Russian. Vegetarians won't be disappointed either. And of course there's the night market – for those on a strict budget you've probably already shelled out too much for a room already, so it's time to take to the streets.

Breakfast

PVO (Map p356; ☎ 020 551 5655; Th Samsenthai; meals 5000-20,000 kip; 🕑 breakfast & lunch) Crunchy baguettes with juicy fresh salad, cheese and pâté. The *bo bûn* (cold Vietnamese noodle dish) is delicious. A top choice for lunch and to takeaway.

Scandinavian Bakery (Map p356; ☎ 215199; Nam Phu; meals 10,000-30,000 kip; 🕑 7am-7pm; ❄) Despite close competition this original wellspring of delicious coffee and pastries is still the best bakery in town. Since its expansion a couple of years ago there's more room to read and sip coffee.

> **NIGHTCRAWLERS**
>
> As you walk along Th Seththathirat, shapes may take form in darkened doorways, followed by an echo of footfalls behind you. These 'ladies', with five o'clock shadows, impossibly long stilettos and croaky voices have chosen this street as their after-dark calling card. Smile and keep walking but in no event laugh; last year a man was admitted to hospital after being attacked with a handbag.

Croissant D'Or Bakery (Map p356; Th Nokeo Khumman; meals 10,000-30,000 kip) Cosy little eatery specialising in delicious pastries. Not as refrigerated as Scandinavian.

JoMa Bakery Café (Map p356; ☎ 215265; Th Setthathirat; meals 20,000-30,000 kip; 🕑 breakfast, lunch & dinner Mon-Sat; ❄) This sanctuary of cool next to Dao Fa Bistro caters to a wide palate with pastries, salads and fresh bespoke-filled baguettes. The yoghurt and muesli is a welcome alternative to the heat outside. Wi-fi available.

French

Where else but Vientiane could you enjoy steak au poivre for less than US$5? Forget your waistline, by the time you're in the back of beyond you'll wish you had tried the whole menu.

La Terrasse (Map p356; ☎ 218550; Th Nokeo Khumman; meals 30,000-50,000 kip; 🕑 5-11pm) Delightful rustic setting with wood-fired pizzas and delicious French menu; one of the distinguished oldies.

Le Provencal (Map p356; ☎ 216248; Nam Phu; meals 30,000-50,000 kip; 🕑 5-11pm) Piping out jazz across the square by day, glowing invitingly by night, Le Provencal has a charming Franco-rustic feel. The steaks are superb, as are the wood-fired pizzas. A romantic place to score some credit with the other half.

Le Vendome (Map p356; ☎ 216402; Th Inpeng; meals 40,000-50,000 kip; 🕑 5-11pm) This literally hidden gem (fight your way through the ivy) is a slice of Gallic heaven. Staff is friendly, the ambience atmospheric, and curiously, the walls are decked with Spanish bull-fighting posters. Principally French cuisine plus terrific pizzas.

Vegetarian

Vegetarian Buffet (Map pp352-3; ☎ 020 566 6488; Th Saysetha; lunch buffet 15,000 kip, meals 5000-15,000 kip; 🕑 lunch & dinner Mon-Sat) One of several venues doing an excellent all-you-can-eat vegetarian buffet. Head east along Th Setthathirat to Th Saysetha (a Honda store on the left side marks the street). Turn left and the restaurant is a few doors along with a wooden front.

Just For Fun (Map p356; ☎ 213642; Th Pangkham; meals 20,000-30,000 kip; 🕑 5-10pm) Still the most popular veggie haunt with a varied menu and great shakes. Also sells fair-trade honey, a selection of teas and delicious homemade cheesecake. Yum!

Lao & Asian

Ban Anou night market (Map p356; off Th Chao Anou; meals 5000-20,000 kip; 5-10pm) Up Th Chao Anou, Vientiane's Chinatown district, turn right before the T-junction and behold a short street lined with food vendors selling *ping kai* (barbecue chicken on a stick), *làap* (spicy salad), curries, noodles and other delights.

Open-air riverside food vendors (Map p356; Th Fa Ngum; meals 10,000-30,000 kip; 5-11pm) Numerous stands serve up fresh Lao- and Chinese-influenced dishes. If it's popular with locals, it's probably good. Take your pick.

Sabaidee Restaurant (Map p356; ☎ 214278; Th Setthathirat; meals 15,000-40,000 kip; breakfast, lunch & dinner) Also popular, and just down the road from Khop Chai Deu, the mixed menu includes Thai dishes. At night, the beer-garden setting is illuminated with red and yellow fairy lights.

Indian

Nazim (Map p356; ☎ 223480; Th Fa Ngum; meals 10,000-30,000 kip; lunch & dinner) Great riverside location, dining alfresco with excellent breakfast and lunchtime options. Consistent as ever.

Rashmi's Indian Fusion (Map p356; ☎ 252789; Th Samsenthai; meals 30,000-50,000 kip; 5-11pm) Impressive double-floored restaurant opposite Lao Plaza Hotel with a smattering of neon and awhiff of art deco. Varied menu, lavish ambience; the cooler side of Vientiane's nightlife.

International

Katusha Restaurant (Map p356; Th Samsenthai; fruit shakes 4000-7000 kip; 7am-9pm) The premium fruit-shake shop in Vientiane. Seasonal highlights include anything with strawberry from December to February or anything with passionfruit from May to July.

Full Moon Café (Map p356; ☎ 243373; Th François Nginn; meals 20,000-40,000; 5-11pm) Mellow tunes and style converge in this sumptuously comfy haunt, with an upstairs bar and quiet veranda to read. Asian fusion menu, featuring a combo of Lao/Thai and Vietnamese dishes.

Khop Chai Deu (Map p356; ☎ 223022; Th Setthathirat; meals 30,000-50,000 kip; lunch & dinner;) The most popular *falang* hang-out in town. You can dine out on modern Lao, Chinese, Indian or Western, followed by lashings of over-priced Beer Lao.

Sticky Fingers Café & Bar (Map p356; ☎ 215972; Th François Nginn; meals 40,000-60,000 kip; breakfast, lunch & dinner Sun-Sat;) Owned and operated by Aussie expats; the staff is friendly, newspapers and magazines make a thankful diversion for solo diners, and the food is delicious.

DRINKING

Sunset Sala Khounta (Map pp352-3; ☎ 251079; 1-11pm) Shipwrecked on the river bank, this charming bar is, as the name would suggest, the best place in Vientiane for a sunset beer. Rustic in style, overflowing with secluded calm, it's worth every calorie expended in the long walk here.

Khop Chai Deu (Map p356; ☎ 223022; Th Setthathirat; noon-midnight;) This place takes up two floors in a beautifully restored French mansion next to Nam Phu; one of the busiest and most convivial places to drink. Beware the older ladies eating beetles at the bar who all claim to be hairdressers! See left for more.

Borpennyang (Map p356; ☎ 261373; Th Fa Ngum; lunch & dinner) This is a kicking rooftop bar with widescreen TV (generally showing sports) and pool tables. There's a great view of the Mekong and urban roof-scape. It also serves meals (10,000 to 30,000 kip).

Jazzy Brick (Map p356; ☎ 212489; Nam Phu; lunch & dinner) Combining club-lux sophistication with the flickering ambience of old Indochina; great place to sit in the scented darkness and savour an alchemized Bloody Mary. Better make it just the one at US$4!

Full Moon Café (Map p356; ☎ 243373; Th François Nginn; 5-11pm) Relax in the upstairs bar or grab a book and head for the veranda. The Asian fusion menu features Lao, Thai and Vietnamese dishes.

Spirit House (Map pp352-3; ☎ 243795; 1-11pm) By far the most modish joint on the river, this is a place to drink and betray your shoestringer genes for a few hours. Dim-lit Manhattan ambience and a list of cocktails that would make your liver glow.

Samlo (Map p356; Th Setthatharit; 9am-11pm) Atmospheric seedy barfly joint; if there was a Laotian Tom Waits you'd find him in the corner. More call girls than punters.

Sticky Fingers Café & Bar (Map p356; ☎ 215972; Th François Nginn; 9am-11pm Sun-Sat) During happy hour, on Wednesday and Friday nights, 'Stickies' heaves with NGO workers letting off steam.

CLUBBING

Don Chan Palace – described by expat Jamie Davis as a 'Lego monster' – hosts the **Lunar 36 Nightclub** (Map pp352-3; ☎ 244288; www.donchanpalacelaopdr.com; Don Chan Palace, Piawat village; 🕒 6pm-4am; admission US$3), Vientiane's official late-night altar of hedonism. It's the only uncensored joint open seven nights a week, and with a heaving dance floor and outside lounging area it's vaguely reminiscent of *Lost in Translation*.

ENTERTAINMENT

Lao Traditional Show (Map p356; ☎ 242978; Th Manthatulat; admission 70,000 kip; 🕒 shows 8pm) For those looking for a cultural experience, there are performances of traditional dance, love songs and music nightly to an entirely foreign audience.

Centre Culturel et de Coopération Linguistique (French Cultural Centre; Map p356; ☎ 215764; www.ambafrance-laos.org; Th Lan Xang; 🕒 9.30am-6.30pm Mon-Fri, 9.30am-noon Sat) The centre runs a year-round programme of events such as musical performances and English-subtitled films and documentaries (Thursdays, 7pm). Details are published on fliers out the front and in the *Vientiane Times*.

SHOPPING

Talat Sao (Morning Market; Map p356; Th Lan Xang; 🕒 7am-5pm) This labyrinthine market, with its recently expanded concrete market next door, is a bustling weave-world of stalls selling everything from Lao silks and jewellery, to white goods, electronics and bedding. A bit fetid under the food canopies out back but an authentic place to grab a barbecued lunch.

Camacrafts (Mulberries; Map p356; ☎ 241217; www.mulberries.org; Th Nokeo Khumman; 🕒 10am-6pm Mon-Sat) This is a not-for-profit company that contributes to villages through training and resource preservation practices. It sells naturally dyed clothing, weavings, bed spreads and cushion covers.

Satri Lao (Map p356; ☎ 216592; Th Setthatharit; 🕒 9am-8pm) This three-storeyed boutique is a treasure trove of choice clothes, jewellery, silk pashminas and lacquered paintings of images from *Tintin* books. If you're desperate to do your presents shopping in one fell swoop this may be the place to come, though it's not cheap.

GETTING THERE & AWAY

Air

Lao Airlines (code QV; ☎ 212051; www.laos-airlines.com), **Thai Airways International** (THAI, code TG; ☎ 251041; www.thaiair.com) and also **Vietnam Airlines** (code VN; ☎ 217562; www.vietnamairlines.com) are the main carriers for Vientiane. From here you can fly to Siem Reap (US$140), Phnom Penh (US$50), Pakse (US$100), Savannakhet (US$60), HCMC (US$180), Bangkok (US$100), Chiang Mai (US$90), Kunming (US$140), Huay Xai (US$90), Luang Prabang (US$60), Phonsavan (US$50) and Hanoi (US$120).

Boat

It's possible to take a slow cargo boat to Luang Prabang (US$26, upstream four days to one week). Ferries leave from Kiaw Liaw Pier, 3.5km west of the fork in the road where Rte 13 heads north in Ban Kao Liaw. Go to the Kiaw Liaw Pier to reserve a spot the day before. Boats make several stops and passengers typically sleep on board.

Bus & Săwngthăew

The **northern bus station** (Map p356; ☎ 260255; Th T2), a 5000-kip túk-túk ride from the centre of town, is the main departure point for domestic and international buses. Buses leave here for everywhere from Phongsali in the far north to Attapeu in the south, and HCMC.

Buses for Luang Prabang (US$10, 10 hours, four daily at 6.30am, 7.30am, 9am, 7pm; VIP US$16, eight hours, one daily at 8am); Phonsavan (60,000 kip, 12 hours, three daily at 6.30am, 9.30am and 4pm; VIP 80,000 kip, 10 hours, one daily at 7am); Udomxai (85,000 kip, 16 hours, two daily at 6.30am and 2pm) depart from the northern bus station. The long haul to Hanoi is a gruelling 20 hours on an air-con bus (US$18) versus a swift ride by plane ($120, Lao Airlines) and leaves at 7pm from the same location.

From Talat Sao, regular buses head to Vang Vieng (15,000 kip, three to four hours) until 3pm. After that, săwngthăew leave from a truck station 7km west of Vientiane. Seats on air-con minibuses to Vang Vieng (US$7, three hours) can be purchased from guesthouses and travel agents around town.

Si Muang bus station (Map pp352-3; Th Tha Deua) is where the more expensive **KVT** (☎ 242101) and **Laody** (☎ 242102) buses head south to Pakse, via Tha Khaek and Savannakhet.

GETTING TO THAILAND & VIETNAM

To Thailand

The Thai-Lao Friendship Bridge is 20km southeast of Vientiane. The Vientiane–Nong Khai border is open daily between 6am and 10pm and the easiest way to cross is on the comfortable Thai-Lao International Bus (10,000 kip, 90 minutes), which leaves Vientiane's Talat Sao bus station at 7.30am, 10.30am, 3.30pm and 6pm. Buses, túk-túk and tourist minibuses run from the capital to the bridge almost every hour. From Nong Khai there are regular buses and trains to Bangkok. The border crossing is easy, with visas issued on arrival in both countries. Alternative means of transport between Vientiane and the bridge include túk-túk (50,000 kip), or the regular public bus 14 from Talat Sao (5000 kip) between 6.30am and 5pm. At the bridge, shuttle buses ferry passengers between immigration posts every 20 minutes or so. On the Thai side you can take a túk-túk between the bridge and the bus or train station.

See p758 for information on travelling in the opposite direction.

To Vietnam

The border crossing between Kaew Neua in Laos and Cau Treo in Vietnam can be accessed from Vientiane.

Buses run to Lak Sao in the early morning from Vientiane's northern bus station; from there buses head across the border to Vinh, in Vietnam. It is also possible to organise transport to Hanoi with traders in Lak Sao, but don't relinquish any money until you're physically in the city – horror stories of people being left in the middle of nowhere abound.

Vietnamese guards at the border are rigorous in their checks, and it's vital to organise a visa before you attempt to enter here. The border is open from 8am to 5pm.

See p838 for details on doing the trip in reverse.

The other key departure point is the **Talat Sao bus station** (Map p356; ☎ 216507; Th Mahasot) from where buses run to destinations within Vientiane province and south. This is also where the Thai-Lao International Bus begins its trip across the Thai-Lao Friendship Bridge to Nong Khai (see the boxed text, above).

Local buses leave Talat Sao for Savannakhet (US$6, eight hours), departing at 7am and every two hours thereafter until 3pm, and for Pakse (US$12, 14 hours, nine daily from 10am to 4pm), stopping for a break in Tha Khaek on the way through. VIP buses to Pakse (US$18, 11 hours), including an overnighter, leave Si Muang Air Bus Station at 8pm. Tickets can be purchased from travel agents in Vientiane.

Up-to-date bus-fare information is published in the *Vientiane Times* or pop into Boualian Travel (p354) for information.

GETTING AROUND

Bicycle & Motorcycle

Bicycles can be rented for 15,000 kip per day from tour agencies and guesthouses in the city centre. Scooters cost around US$6 to US$8 per day. Shop around for one in good condition (your safety depends on it). Without insurance, most hirers expect you to pay to replace the bike if it is seriously damaged or stolen. Read the fine print before signing any contracts and ask your guesthouse to lock your bike inside overnight.

Boualian Travel 1 Map p356; ☎ 263772; Th Samsenthai; bicycle per day 15,000 kip; 🕒 8am-6pm)

KT Shop (Map p356; ☎ 020 561 4201; ktbikerental@yahoo.com; Th Wat Xieng Nyeun; scooters/motorcycles per day US$8/20)

PVO (Map p356; ☎ 020 551 5655; Th Samsenthai; scooters per day US$7) Hire scooters at this eatery.

Túk-Túk

Standard trip costs are posted inside túk-túks, which makes haggling difficult though not impossible. Túk-túks standing in a queue on a street corner won't leave the stand for less than the price already agreed with the other drivers (ie approximately 5000 kip for 1km to 2km; 10,000 kip for 2km to 4km). You're better off trying a free-roaming túk-túk (one driving along the street) where a bit of fare negotiation is possible. You can also flag down a shared túk-túk (one with passengers already in it) that is heading in the direction you want to go. A journey in a shared túk-túk will cost you around 2000 to 5000 kip depending on your destination.

NORTHERN LAOS

Mist-laced mountains carpeted in thick forest, diverse ethnic hill-tribe villages and a wealth of trekking adventures await the intrepid. Over the last ten years, Northern Laos has blossomed beyond the beautiful destination of Luang Prabang, the karst-graced resort of Vang Vieng and Phonsavan's Plain of Jars; improved roads, though still sinuously slow, are seeing more and more travellers push further toward the Chinese border and remote regions like Muang Sing and Phongsali.

VIENTIANE PROVINCE

Heading through Vientiane province (a different area from Vientiane Prefecture, which holds the capital) you may wish to take in the serenity of the Ang Nam Ngum Reservoir, or if it's been declared safe, the mountainous Special Zone. The roads are poor but navigable by motor-cross bike, the landscape pristine and rarely seen due to the government's historical problems in the area with Hmong guerrillas.

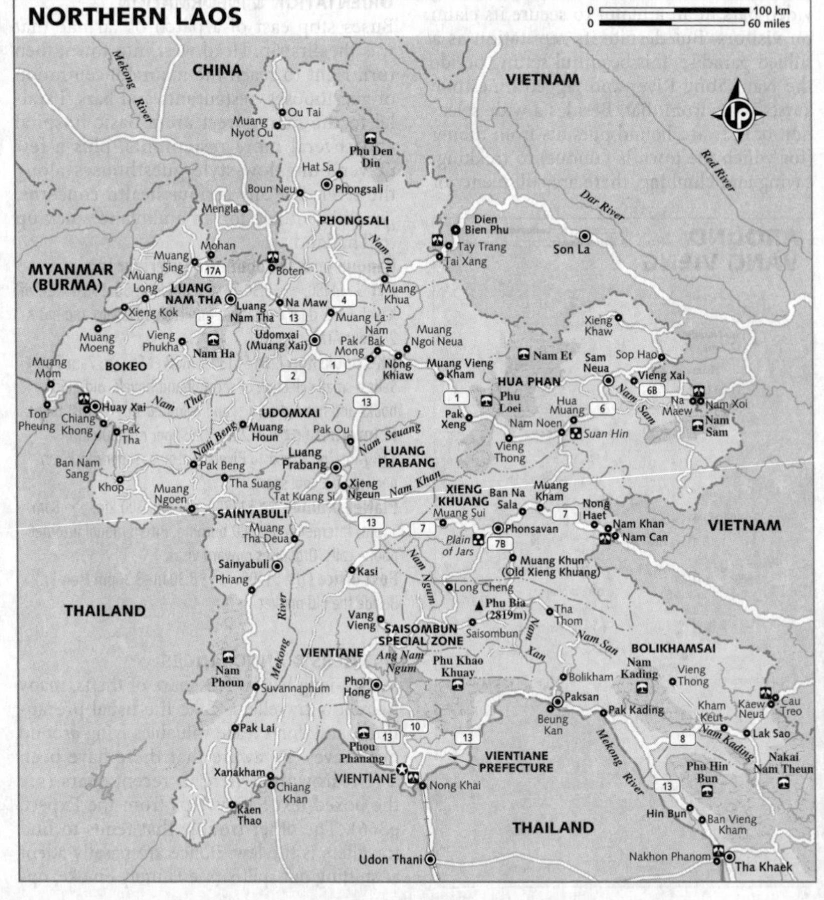

> **UNHOLY SMOKE**
>
> Travellers passing through Vang Vieng told us of the latest brazen hustle – people pretending to be plain-clothes coppers. Sven, a traveller from Finland said, 'They're like bloodhounds on the scent of reefer. If they catch you with a joint, the on the spot fine is from US$500 to US$700. The impersonators are quite credible, so try and remain calm and ask for ID. If it fails to materialise suggest you take a trip with them to the police station. I heard some girls did this and ended up paying US$30 to get rid of them.'
>
> Quasi police aside, if you bump into the real article (they're all plain-clothed in Vang Vieng) you have no choice but to pay the fine or be deported/jailed.

Vang Vieng

☎ 023 / pop 25,000

As if a section of Bangkok's Khao San Rd has been transplanted to this once sleepy retreat, Vang Vieng offers a plethora of western comforts and comatose-inducing video bars in an attempt to secure its claim on visitors. But despite its reputation as a sullied paradise, this beautiful setting beside the Nam Song River and jagged limestone karsts is far from that. Besides a wide selection of outward bound pursuits from tubing (for which the town is famous) to trekking, caving and climbing, there are still plenty of authentic spots to savour a slice of old Vang Vieng. It grew up around the river, and this is where you should spend your time if you want to enjoy the best of it.

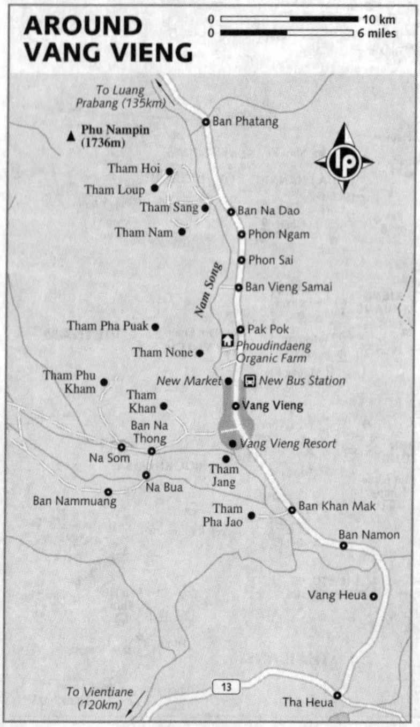

ORIENTATION & INFORMATION

Buses stop east of a patch of tarmac that was the airstrip. Head west into town, then turn right to reach the main concentration of guesthouses, restaurants and bars. Parallel to the main street are a basic hospital and several more restaurants, plus a few newer bungalow-style guesthouses along the river. For any serious health concerns, get to Vientiane for an ambulance pick-up to Thailand.

Banque pour le Commerce Extérieur Lao (☎ 5114480; 8.30am-3.30pm Mon-Sun) Just west of Xayoh Café, does exchanges and cash advances and has a 24-hour ATM.

BKC Bookshop (☎ 511303; Market St; 7am-7pm) Sells a small selection of secondhand novels, old guidebooks and hand-drawn – and coloured-in – tourist maps.

IT Internet (☎ 020 2244 7755; per min 300 kip; 7am-7pm) Next to Riverside Tours, super quick connection in a cool space.

PlaNet Online (☎ 511209; per min 300 kip; 8am-11pm) Internet access, CD burning, international internet phone calls. Organises onward visas.

Post office (☎ 511009; 8.30am-3.30pm Mon-Fri) Beside the old market.

DANGERS & ANNOYANCES

Vang Vieng has its fair share of thefts, many by fellow travellers. Take the usual precautions, and don't leave valuables lying around near caves. Be aware that there have been a few drownings here in recent years (see the boxed text Safety Tips from the Expert, p366). The other trouble that tends to find travellers is the law. Police are nasally adept at sniffing out spliffs (see Unholy Smoke, op-

AROUND VANG VIENG

0 10 km
0 6 miles

To Luang Prabang (135km)
Ban Phatang
Phu Nampin (1736m)
Tham Hoi
Tham Loup
Tham Sang
Ban Na Dao
Tham Nam
Phon Ngam
Phon Sai
Nam Song
Ban Vieng Samai
Tham Pha Puak
Pak Pok
Phoudindaeng Organic Farm
Tham None
Tham Phu Kham
New Market
New Bus Station
Tham Khan
Vang Vieng
Ban Na Thong
Vang Vieng Resort
Na Som
Tham Jang
Na Bua
Ban Nammuang
Tham Pha Jao
Ban Khan Mak
Ban Namon
Vang Heua
13
To Vientiane (120km)
Tha Heua

posite). Three months in jail without appeal or US$500 to US$700 on-the-spot fine.

SIGHTS & ACTIVITIES

There are two outfits running trekking, cycling, caving and tubing options. The best known is **Green Discovery** (☎ 511230; www.greendiscoverylaos.com; Th Luang Prabang; 🕑 7am-7pm) while **Riverside Tours** (☎ 020 2244 7755; www.riversidetourslaos.com; Th Luang Prabang; 🕑 7am-7pm) also offers a similar range at competitive prices and can assist with booking onward air and bus tickets.

Caves

The caves around Vang Vieng are generally open from dawn to dusk and with the addition of signs in English there are now entrance charges and, although not strictly compulsory, guide fees. Guides lead you by torchlight, but it's wise to bring your own for back-up. You can buy a local map from BKC Bookshop (opposite) and at several guesthouses. There's someone trying to make a quid at every turn around Vang Vieng, so take plenty of small notes and a sense of humour.

The most famous cave, **Tham Jang** (admission 9000 kip) south of town, was used as a hide-out from marauding Yunnanese Chinese in the early 19th century. A set of stairs leads up to the main cavern entrance. There's also a cool spring at the foot of the cave. Follow the signs from the Vang Vieng Resort.

Another popular cave is **Tham Phu Kham** (admission 4000 kip). To reach it, cross the **bamboo footbridge** (toll 2000 kip) near the Hotel Nam Song, then walk or pedal 6km along a scenic, unsealed road to Ban Na Thong, from where you have to walk 1km to a hill on the northern side of the village: follow the signs. It's a tough final 200m climb but worth it for a dip in the blue stream afterward. Climb the tree and take a jump into the pool far below. Can you get to level three?

Kayaking

Kayaking is another popular pursuit. All-day trips (US$8 to US$12 per person) typically take you down a few rapids and include visits to caves and villages. Kayaking trips to Vientiane, advertised around town for about US$15, involve paddling for half a day then going the rest of the way by road. Though all guides are supposed to be trained, many are not. Before using a cheap operator, check the guides' credentials.

> **VOLUNTEERING IN VANG VIENG**
>
> *Jamie Thomas, Herefordshire, Uk*
>
> Mr Thi at the **Phoudindaeng Organic Farm** (☎ 511220; www.laofarm.org) welcomes those who wish to stay for a week or more and are keen to lend a hand. The days of WWOOF-ing have gone, but there's still plenty of work for anyone who has the initiative and patience to hang around and to muck in wherever they're needed. Mr Thi's enthusiasm for community development has seen the building of a community centre, a library and the establishment of a free school bus for local children. Teaching at the local school is perhaps the most valuable contribution visitors can make. Teaching local children offers a great opportunity to interact with Lao youngsters and hand something back to the community.

Rock Climbing

Green Discovery (☎ 511230; www.greendiscoverylaos.com; Th Luang Prabang) operates guided rock-climbing courses for novices (around US$30 per day) up Vang Vieng's dramatic limestone cliffs. If you're a climber you can DIY, but permits (US$5 per day for a group) must be obtained from the Green Discovery office in Vang Vieng.

Tubing

Tubing down the Nam Song is one of Vang Vieng's biggest attractions and there are dozens of tube rental places in shops and guesthouses around town. Prices are fixed at 30,000 kip, which includes the túk-túk ride to the launch point 3km north of town. The trip can take two or more hours depending on river conditions and how many of the makeshift bars you stop at en route! Of course it's pretty stupid and dangerous to tackle the rapids intoxicated.

SLEEPING

There are so many guesthouses in Vang Vieng they're doing each other out of business. The best options, if you're in search of tranquillity, are by the river.

SAFETY TIPS FROM THE EXPERT *Mick O'Shea*

Professionally managed kayaking and rafting trips are a great way to experience the wonderful environments of Laos yet it is important to ensure you go with outfitters who are equipped and prepared should something go wrong. The following questions will help you identify who to trust.

- Do your tours have all of the relevant safety equipment such as life jackets, throw ropes, a first-aid kit and helmets?
- Can I see your first-aid kit, boats and throw bag?
- How long is the pretrip safety briefing and practice session?
- Are your guides trained in basic first aid (discuss CPR) and river rescue? By whom?
- Is the lead guide fluent in English? How long has he or she been leading paddle tours?

Several tourists have drowned while tubing in Vang Vieng during the rainy season. Even if you're a confident swimmer wear a lifejacket. Look well ahead for obstructions such as trees or branches in the river; water flows through such obstructions, tubers don't. Stay together so that you can help your friends if they have trouble.

The caves of Vang Vieng are fascinating and delicate ecosystems that should be enjoyed yet treated with respect and caution. It is strongly recommended to go caving with guides; this is relatively cheap and will ensure that you go directly to the most interesting caves. Cave exploration without a guide is not recommended, tourists have been lost in Vang Vieng caves for days on end and several have perished when search parties could not locate them.

Finally, please promote sustainable ecotourism by paying the signposted fees to cave minders; encouraging locals to use flashlights (torches) rather than candles; not smoking or urinating in caves; and not touching formations, which soon become degraded due to the chemical reactions with human sweat.

Mick O'Shea is a certified white-water kayaking expert and the expedition leader of the first descent of the Mekong River from source to sea in 2004.

Paradise Island Bungalows (r 20,000-40,000 kip) Perfectly positioned to the west of the bamboo footbridge, this peaceful new venue has lovely cabanas with some of the best river views in town. Its alfresco bar throws off candy light reflections into the water by night. Deserves to become one of the most popular places in town.

our pick **Maylyn Guest House** (☎ 511083; r 30,000-40,000 kip) West of the bamboo footbridge across the Nam Song, this secluded paradise is set in lush vegetation and landscaped gardens. The views of the nearby karsts and river are divine. Its 15 cabanas are basic with fan and en suite. Maylyn now has a herbal steam sauna, and the only place in town to hire a powerful set of Baja motorbikes.

Phoubane Guest House (☎ 511037; r 30,000-40,000 kip) Head south from the market taking the river road before taking your first left. Bungalows are clean and simple with a fan included. Perhaps a little nondescript, but who cares with such a fantastic view of the river.

Thavisouk Guest House (☎ 511124; r 30,000-40,000 kip) opposite The Rising Sun off Khao San Rd, this charming wood-fronted house has decent rooms and friendly staff who also offer free rides to the bus station. Fans are included.

Nana Guest House & Restaurant (☎ 511036; Khao San Rd; r 30,000-50,000 kip;) Close to the night market (ear plugs may be an option) this recently spruced-up accommodation is great value with slick modern rooms and fans. The bouncy beds will swallow you up.

Phoudindaeng Organic Farm (☎ 511220; www.laofarm.org; r 30,000-60,000 kip) Around 3km north of town on the banks of the Nam Song, this farm, which grows mulberry trees and organic fruits and vegetables, offers accommodation in dorms or small private rooms with shared bathroom. The attached restaurant (meals 10,000 to 15,000 kip), open for lunch and dinner, makes delicious organic dishes. See the website for directions. You can also organise volunteer work through the farm; see p365 for details.

LAOS

Dok Khoun 1 Guest House (☎ 511032; r 30,000-70,000 kip; ❄) Right in the centre of town between the old market and Th Luang Prabang, Dok Khoun is an oldie but goodie, with some rooms fresher than others. Fan is a standard inclusion.

Vang Vieng Orchid (☎ 020 220 2259; r 60,000-100,000 kip; ❄) Fresh three-storey venue on the banks of the Nam Song, Orchid has 20 spacious rooms, 12 with views over to Don Khang and the karst peaks beyond. Walk down through the old market and turn right (north), then it's another 50m on the left.

Riverside Bungalows (☎ 511035, 020 352 3426; r 60,000-120,000 kip; ❄) Situated just north of town where the river bends to the west. The basic bamboo bungalows all have balconies and shared bathrooms, or you can move upmarket and take a room with private bathroom and air-con. The view is truly like something out of *Crouching Tiger, Hidden Dragon*.

EATING

You won't have any problem finding something to suit your tastes among a range of Lao, Thai, Chinese and Western cuisine. Following are a few restaurants that have so far been uninfected by Vang Vieng's *Friends* phenomenon. Please also note: in most of Southeast Asia, including Vang Vieng, the word 'happy' before 'pizza' does not mean, as one traveller discovered, extra pineapple.

Nokeo (meals 6000-20,000 kip; 🕑 lunch & dinner) Nokeo serves consistently good Lao dishes at prices even locals can afford. It's on the corner opposite the old market.

Restaurant Luang Prabang Bakery (☎ 511145; meals 7000-30,000 kip; 🕑 breakfast, lunch & dinner) Offering cakes, brownies, pastries and bespoke sandwiches, plus a great view of the karsts whilst having your alfresco latte.

Organic Farm Café (☎ 511174; meals 10,000-25,000 kip; 🕑 breakfast, lunch & dinner) Innovative dishes, an alliterative menu and Laos-famous mulberry shakes make this an excellent choice. The best veggie food on the strip. See opposite for more about the farm.

Sisavang Restaurant (Khao San Rd; meals 20,000-30,000 kip) A feeding hole on the video-chain gauntlet of Khao San offering a rich selection of Western fare, and for those who might have forgotten where they are, Lao food.

Xayoh Café (☎ 511088; meals 20,000-40,000 kip; 🕑 breakfast, lunch & dinner) A typically Western menu of pizza, pasta, burgers and chips – similar to what's on offer at the Vientiane branch.

Sunset Restaurant (☎ 511096; meals 20,000-50,000 kip; 🕑 breakfast, lunch & dinner) On the river, this is an ideal spot for breakfast, lunch and sundowners. The menu ranges from Western breakfasts to Lao cuisine.

Nazim Indian Restaurant (☎ 511214; Khao San Rd; meals 30,000 kip; 🕑 breakfast, lunch & dinner) Generic but ever tasty Indian food from the Nazim franchise.

DRINKING

With its corner location, pool table, both indoor and outdoor seating, and an easy atmosphere, Xayoh Café (above) is a popular drinking spot.

Babylon Bar (Khao San Rd) Down the south end of the street, Babylon Bar is a welcoming joint where you can recline on comfy cushions and soak up the low-tempo atmosphere. Playstation 2 is also available.

Jaidee's Bar (☎ 606339; Khao San Rd) Psychedelic walls, flickering interior and reclined cushions make this is a good place to regain your equilibrium. Slightly 'too cool for school' staff.

GETTING THERE & AWAY

From the airstrip bus stop buses leave for Luang Prabang (55,000 kip, six to seven hours, five daily), Vientiane (25,000 kip, four to five hours, almost every hour until dark) and Phonsavan (75,000 kip, eight to nine hours, one daily at 9am – a tortuous, winding journey so try and sit near a window).

Tickets for minibuses and VIP buses with air-con, travelling direct to Vientiane (US$5, three hours) or Luang Prabang (US$7, six to seven hours) are sold at guesthouses, tour agencies and internet cafés in town.

GETTING AROUND

The township is small enough to walk around with ease. Bicycles can be rented for around US$2 per day, mountain bikes cost US$5. A few places hire out scooters for US$5 per day. A túk-túk up to the organic farm or the Tham Sang Triangle costs around 10,000 kip per person.

LUANG PRABANG PROVINCE

Luang Prabang

☎ 071 / pop 52,466

Nestled on the sacred confluence of the Nam Khan and Mekong Rivers, this Unesco-protected World Heritage city is both enchanting and diverse in what it has to offer the traveller. From the fascinating history of the Royal Family to its myriad stunning wats, glittering in emerald and gold, this once sleepy capital is perhaps the most sophisticated, photogenic city in the whole of Southeast Asia. With its orange-robed monks, and fantastic food at the many bistros, cafés and night-market, Luang Prabang is a wonderful place to kick back for a few days. Be it wandering through the old city streets peppered with shuttered French mansions or enjoying sybaritic evenings in ubertrendy bars such as the Hive Bar, you may find yourself staying longer than planned.

ORIENTATION

Most of Luang Prabang's tourist attractions are in the old quarter, on the peninsula bounded by the Mekong and Nam Khan Rivers. Dominating the centre of town, Phu Si is an unmissably good landmark. The majority of restaurants, tour companies and internet cafés line Th Sisavangvong, while more accommodation options and eateries can be found in the streets running from Th Sisavangvong to the Mekong and Nam Khan Rivers. The old quarter is easily covered on foot, but hiring a bicycle is an excellent way to explore the city and its attractions.

INFORMATION

Bookshops

L'Étranger Books & Tea (☎ 537 7826; booksinlaos@yahoo.com; Th Kingkitsarat; 7am-10pm Mon-Sat, 10am-10pm Sun; books per hr/day 20,000/50,000 kip) The city's best bookshop-cum Indie cinema; with a café outside and upstairs lizard lounge. Titles, fiction and non-fiction, are generally French, English and German. Pedigree films shown nightly at 7pm. Trade your old books for vouchers or take half the equivalent in cash.

Internet Access

You won't have any trouble getting online here. Internet shops are dotted along Th Sisavangvong and charge between 150 and 200 kip per minute. The best place is **All Lao Travel Co** (☎ 253522; Th Sisavangvong; per hr 10,000 kip; 8am-11pm) – it's easily the coolest and most spacious place to catch up on your email.

Medical Services

Lao-China Friendship Hospital (☎ 252049; Th Setthathirat) All-new and eerily deserted. About 5km south off Th Naviengkham, after the stadium (a 10,000 kip túk-túk trip). A large white tower signals the spot. Serious cases need to be flown to Thailand.

Pharmacie (Th Sakkarin; 8.30am-8pm) Stocks basic medicines. Open daily, although closes sometimes for a few hours on weekends.

Money

Banque pour le Commerce Extérieur Lao (☎ 252983; Th Sisavangvong; 8.30am-5pm Mon-Fri, 8.30am-3.30pm Sat & Sun) Now has ATM (MasterCard symbol only) Will change travellers cheques and cash including Thai baht; US, Australian and Canadian dollars; euros; and UK pounds. Open weekends, cash advances available weekdays only.

Lao Development Bank (Th Sisavangvong; 8.30am-noon & 2-3.30pm) Good exchange rates.

Post

Post office (cnr Th Chao Fa Ngum & Th Kitsarat; 8.30am-3.30pm Mon-Fri, 8.30am-noon Sat & Sun)

Telephone

Internet shops along Th Sisavangvong offer long-distance internet calls. You can make regular international calls from the post office with a phonecard or from the **Telephone Office** (Th Phothisalat; 8am-noon & 1-5pm).

Tourist Information

Unesco World Heritage office (www.unesco.org; Th Sakkarin; 8.30am-4.30pm Mon-Fri) An anteroom in an old French customs house at the northeastern tip of the peninsula contains posted public information on the Unesco project in Luang Prabang.

Travel Agencies

Diethelm Travel (☎ 212277; ditralpt@laotel.com; Th Xieng Thong) Books air tickets, organises cars with guides.

All Lao Travel Co (☎ 253522; Th Sisavangvong; 8am-6pm) The best travel centre on the peninsula. Authorized agents for Thai Airways International, and Bangkok and Vietnam Airways, can also sort bus and boat tickets. Most staff speak good English and can advise on trips to Pak Ou caves and other attractions in the surrounding area.

SIGHTS

Royal Palace Museum

To get a foothold on the city's history visit the **Royal Palace Museum** (☎ 212470; Th Sisavangvong; admission 20,000 kip; ⌚ 8-11.30am & 1.30-4pm, last entry 3.30pm, closed Tue). The palace was originally constructed beside the Mekong River in 1904 as a residence for King Sisavangvong and his family. When the king died in 1959 his son Savang Vattana inherited the throne, but shortly after the 1975 revolution he and his family were exiled to northern Laos and imprisoned in the caves of Vieng Xai, following which the palace was converted into a museum. Various royal religious objects are on display in the large entry hall, as well as rare Buddhist sculptures from India, Cambodia and Laos. The right front corner room of the palace, which opens to the outside, contains the museum's most prized art, including the Pha Bang, the gold standing buddha after which the town is named. The murals on the walls in the king's former reception room, painted in 1930 by French artist Alix de Fautereau, depict scenes from traditional Lao life. Each wall is meant to be viewed at a different time of day, according to the changing light. Footwear can't be worn inside the museum, no photography is permitted and you must leave bags with the attendants. A dress code declares that foreigners must not wear shorts, T-shirts or sundresses.

Markets

Luang Prabang's main market, the newly built **Phousy Market** (Th Phothisarat; ⌚ 6am-5pm), which is located just a few kilometres south of the town centre, is heaving with vendors selling an impressive array of hardware, cookware and mountains of fresh produce. To get there follow Th Chao Fa Ngum south towards Tat Kuang Si. You'll see the market on the left at a major intersection.

At sundown, Th Sisavangvong is closed to traffic between the Royal Palace and Th Kitsalat for the candle-lit gauntlet of the **Hmong Night Market** (⌚ 5.30-10pm). Lao textiles, handicrafts, jewellery, traditional medicine and antique weavings, mulberry-paper lanterns, mass-produced T-shirts and other souvenirs are all sold here.

Phu Si

The temples on the slopes of **Phu Si** (admission 10,000 kip; ⌚ 8am-6pm) are all of relatively recent construction, but the magnolia-laced climb to the temples is well worth it for the superb views – especially near sunset. An admission fee is collected at the northern entrance near Wat Pa Huak. At the summit is That Chomsi, the starting point for a colourful Pii Mai (Lao New Year) procession. Behind the stupa is a small cave-shrine sometimes referred to as Wat Tham Phu Si. Around the northeast flank are the ruins of Wat Pha Phutthabaht, which was originally constructed in 1395 during the reign of Phaya Samsenthai on the site of a Buddha footprint.

Wat Xieng Thong

Near the northern tip of the peninsula formed by the Mekong and Nam Khan rivers, **Wat Xieng Thong** (off Th Sakkarin; admission 10,000 kip; ⌚ 8am-5pm) is Luang Prabang's most magnificent temple. Built by King Setthathirat in 1560, it remained under royal patronage until 1975. Like the royal palace, Wat Xieng Thong was placed within easy reach of the Mekong River. The *sĭm* (main sanctuary) represents classic Luang Prabang temple architecture, and its rear wall features an impressive tree-of-life mosaic. Inside, richly decorated wooden columns support a ceiling that's vested with *dhammacakka* (dharma wheels). Near the compound's eastern gate stands the royal funeral chapel. Inside are an impressive 12m-high funeral chariot and various funeral urns for each member of the royal family. The exterior of the chapel features gilt panels depicting erotic episodes from the Ramayana.

Wat Wisunalat (Wat Visoun)

To the east of the town centre and originally constructed in 1513 (which makes it the oldest continually operating temple of Luang Prabang) is **Wat Wisunalat** (Th Wisunalat; admission 5000 kip; ⌚ 8am-5pm). It was rebuilt in 1898 following an 1887 fire started by a marauding gang of Yunnanese robbers known as the Black Flag Haw. Inside the high-ceilinged *sĭm* is a collection of wooden Calling for Rain buddhas and 15th- to 16th-century Luang Prabang *sima* (ordination stones). In front of the *sĭm* is That Pathum (Lotus Stupa), which was built in 1514.

Other Temples

In the old quarter, the ceiling of **Wat Xieng Maen** (admission free; ⌚ 8am-5pm) is painted with gold *naga* (mythical serpent-beings) and the elaborate

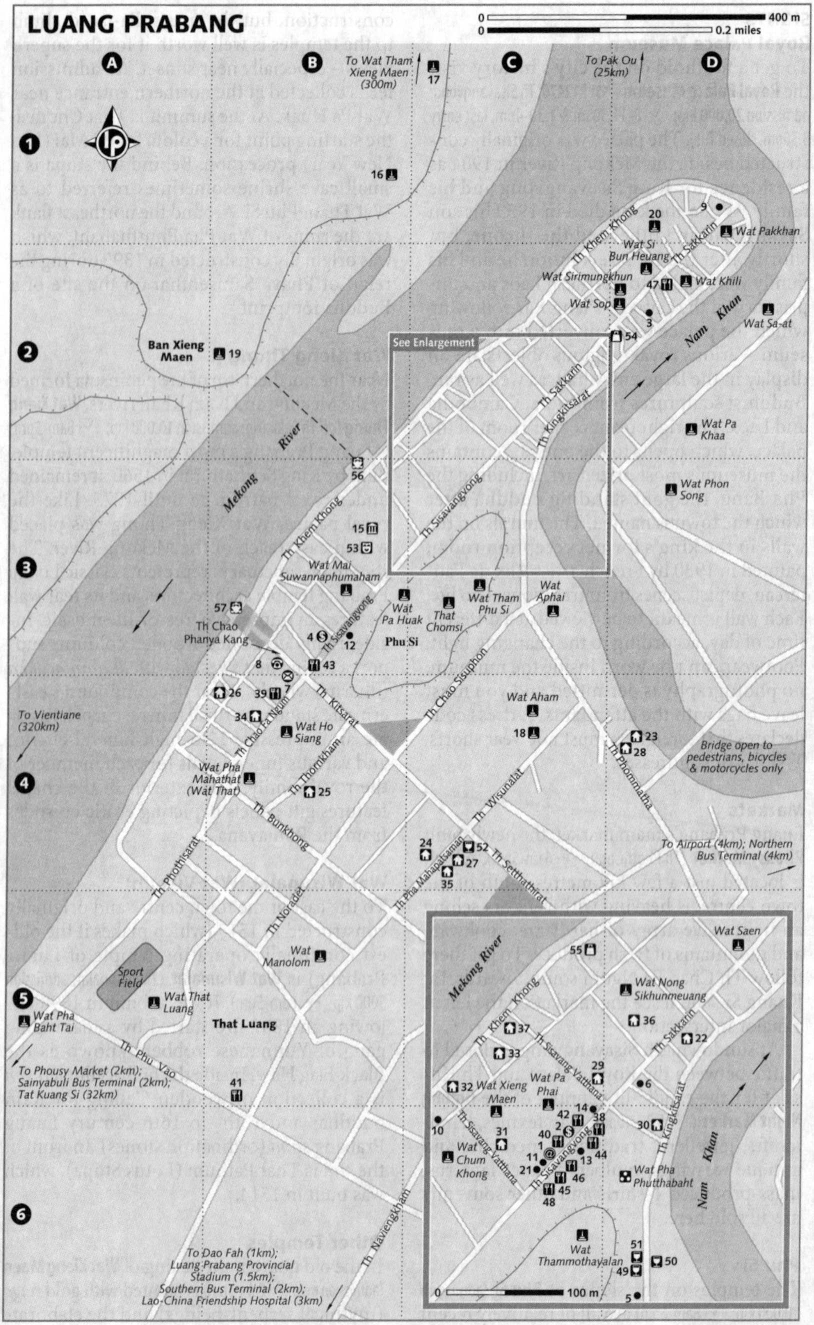

LUANG PRABANG

0 400 m
0 0.2 miles

A B C D
1 2 3 4 5 6

To Wat Tham Xieng Maen (300m)
17
To Pak Ou (25km)
16
20
9
Th Khem Khong
Wat Si Bun Heuang
Th Sakkarin
Wat Pakkhan
Wat Sirimungkhun
47
Wat Khili
Wat Sop
3
Nam Khan
Wat Sa-at
See Enlargement
54
Ban Xieng Maen
19
Th Sakkarin
Th Kingkitsarat
Mekong River
Wat Pa Khaa
56
Wat Phon Song
Th Sisavangvong
Th Khem Khong
15
53
Wat Mai Suwannaphumaham
Wat Pa Huak
That Chomsi
Wat Tham Phu Si
Wat Aphai
57
Th Chao Phanya Kang
4
12
Th Sisavangvong
Phu Si
8
43
7
Th Chao Sisuphon
26
39
Th Kitsarat
Wat Aham
To Vientiane (320km)
34
Th Chao Pa Ngum
Wat Ho Siang
18
23
28
Th Thornkham
Wat Pha Mahathat (Wat That)
25
Bridge open to pedestrians, bicycles & motorcycles only
Th Phommatha
Th Wisunalat
Th Bunkhong
24
52
27
35
Th Pha Mahapatsaman
Th Setthathirat
To Airport (4km); Northern Bus Terminal (4km)
Th Phothisarat
Th Noradet
Wat Manolom
Sport Field
Wat That Luang
Wat Pha Baht Tai
That Luang
Th Phu Vao
To Phousy Market (2km); Sainyabuli Bus Terminal (2km); Tat Kuang Si (32km)
41
Th Naviengkham
To Dao Fah (1km); Luang Prabang Provincial Stadium (1.5km); Southern Bus Terminal (2km); Lao-China Friendship Hospital (3km)

Wat Saen
55
Mekong River
Wat Nong Sikhunmeuang
Th Khem Khong
36
37
Th Sakkarin
22
33
Th Sisavang Vatthana
29
6
32
Wat Xieng Maen
Wat Pa Phai
14
42
38
30
10
31
2
Th Sisavang Vatthana
40
Wat Chum Khong
1
44
11
13
21
Th Sisavangvong
46
Wat Pha Phutthabaht
45
48
Th Kingkitsarat
Nam Khan
Wat Thammothayalan
51
50
49
0 100 m
5

LAOS

INFORMATION	
All Lao Travel Co	1 C6
Banque pour le Commerce Extérieur Lao	2 C6
Diethelm Travel	3 D2
Lao Development Bank	4 B3
L'Étranger Books & Tea	5 D6
Pharmacie	6 D5
Post Office	7 B4
Telephone Office	8 B3
Unesco World Heritage Office	9 D1
SIGHTS & ACTIVITIES	
Action Max Laos	10 C6
Green Discovery	11 C6
Hmong Night Market	12 B3
Khmu Massage	13 C6
Lotus Du Lao Herbal Spa & Massage	14 C6
Royal Palace Museum	15 B3
Wat Chom Phet	16 B1
Wat Long Khun	17 C1
Wat Wisunalat	18 C4
Wat Xieng Maen	19 B2
Wat Xieng Thong	20 D1
White Elephant	21 C6
SLEEPING	
Chittana Guest House	22 D5
Cold River	23 D4
Jaliya Guest House	24 C4
Khounsavanh Guest House	25 B4
Maethao Khao Guest House	26 B4
Mano Guest House & Restaurant	27 C4
Merry Guest House 1 & 2	28 D4
Paphai Guest House	29 C5
Pathoumphone Guest House	30 D6
Phousi Guest House	31 C6
Phousi Guest House II	32 C5
Silichit Guest House	33 C5
Suankeo Guest House No 2	34 B4
Thavisouk Guest House	35 C4
Vatthanaluck Guest House	36 D5
View Khem Khong	37 C5
EATING	
Dao Fa Bistro	38 C6
JoMa Bakery Café	39 B4
Lasi Cuisine	40 C6
Maly Lao Food	41 B5
Nazim	42 C6
Night Food Market	43 B3
Pizza Luang Prabang	44 C6
Samsara	45 C6
Scandinavian Bakery	46 C6
Tum Tum Cheung Restaurant & Cooking School	47 D2
Yongkhoune Restaurant	48 C6
DRINKING	
Hive Bar	49 D6
Khob Chai & Ban Aphay	50 D6
Lao Lao Garden	51 D6
L'Étranger Books & Tea	(see 5)
Maylek Pub	52 C4
ENTERTAINMENT	
Royal Ballet Theatre	53 B3
SHOPPING	
Baan Khily Gallery	54 D2
OckPopTok	55 C5
TRANSPORT	
Boats to Pak Ou	(see 56)
Ferry Boat Pier	56 B3
Long-Distance Ferries	57 B3

háang thíen (candle rail) has *naga* at either end. With backing from Unesco and New Zealand, young novices and monks have been trained in the artistic skills needed to maintain and preserve Luang Prabang's temples.

Across the Mekong from central Luang Prabang are several notable temples, including **Wat Long Khun** (admission 5000 kip; 8am-5pm). **Wat Tham Xieng Maen** (admission 5000 kip; 8am-5pm) is in a 100m-deep limestone cave where decayed buddha statues come to rest. At the top of the hill peaceful **Wat Chom Phet** (admission free; 8am-5pm) offers undisturbed views of the Mekong.

ACTIVITIES

Cycling

Cycling is one of the best ways to enjoy Luang Prabang. Bicycles can be rented from numerous guesthouses and shops around Th Phothisalat (US$2-3 per day). The old quarter's temples can easily be covered in half a day, it doesn't take much effort to get out of town either: head south past Phousy Market and into the hills. The road to Kuang Si Waterfalls is a gently undulating 35km through rice paddy.

Massage

The city, with its ever growing sophistication, has upped its game to cater for those in search of refined pampering, at affordable prices. There are a couple of heavenly (legit) massage parlours and beauty spas on Th Phothisalat. Go on, after that two-day trip from Huay Xai you deserve it.

Khmu Massage (☎ 5672888; Th Phothisalat; per hr US$3) Irresistible oeuvre of herbal steams, foot, body and neck massages brought to you with flair and style. Who said shoestringers can't have a little comfort now and again?

Lotus Du Lao Herbal Spa & Massage (253448; Th Sisavangvong; per hr US$3-7) Beneath the wood blade fans, suspended in Indochinese luxury, you'll listen to the cheesy sounds and think you've gone to nirvana.

COURSES

Attend a half-day cooking course at **Tum Tum Cheung Restaurant & Cooking School** (☎ 252019; Th Sakkarin). You can choose which meal you want to learn, then you're taken to the Phousy Market to buy ingredients, before returning to prepare authentic Luang Prabang cuisine under supervision. Classes are US$10 per person. If you prefer to leave the cooking to the experts, Tum Tum Cheung (p373) also has its own restaurant.

TOURS

Overnight stays in villages, trekking in the forest, kayaking on the river and mountain biking tours are all available. Below are the most established tour operators.

White Elephant (☎ 254481; white_elephant_adventures@yahoo.ca; Th Sisavangvong; trips per day from US$20) offers excursions combining rafting, kayaking, trekking and cycling with an overnight stay in a nearby village. Tours are set at a maximum of six people with two guides.

Geared towards low-impact tourism and a popular outfit with good reports from travellers, **Action Max Laos** (☎ 253489; www.actionmaxasia.com; Ban Xieng Mouan; guided trek 1-/3-day US$25/65) offers combination trips as well as elephant riding. French and English guides available.

Green Discovery (☎ 212093; www.greendiscoverylaos.com; Th Sisavangvong; per day US$35) specialises in all-inclusive guided white-water rafting on the Nam Seuang, plus treks from one- to four-days through the forests and villages around Luang Prabang.

If you're not keen on outdoor pursuits, Action Max Laos hosts historical tours of the town with Unesco support.

FESTIVALS & EVENTS

The two most important annual events in Luang Prabang are **Pii Mai** (Lao or Lunar New Year) in April, when Luang Prabang gets soaked in a giant water-fight in an incantation to the coming monsoon (book accommodation well in advance), and the boat races during **Bun Awk Phansa** (End of the Rains Retreat) in October. See p407 for more.

SLEEPING

Post-tsunami depression in Thailand saw an added migration of travellers to Luang Prabang and consequently prices have risen sharply. Also, thanks to improved transport links it's no longer an inaccessible oasis but something of an intrepid package destination. Locals have been quick to push for as much as they can get, though you may be able to haggle a bit in the low season. There are a multitude of guesthouses to choose from in and around the old city. Below we've listed the pick of a very varied bunch.

Luang Prabang

Pathoumphone Guest House (☎ 212946; Th Kingkitsarat; r 50,000-60,000 kip) Just off the corner of Savang Vatthana St, this sweet little guesthouse is a well-kept secret with serene views, a sense of calm and simple little rooms with fan. The best value for money on the peninsula.

Paphai Guest House (☎ 212752; Th Sisavang Vatthana; r with shared bathroom 50,000-100,000 kip) With its giggly employees, central location and eccentric garden, this wilting house offers very basic but colourful rooms. The upstairs ones have a communal veranda.

Maethao Khao Guest House (☎ 252061; off Th Khem Khong; r 60,000 kip) One street north of Rattana, this peaceful blue and white timbered house near the river offers clean and simple accommodation with fans and separate bathroom.

Thavisouk Guest House (☎ 252022; Th Pha Mahapatsaman; r 60,000 kip) Thavisouk has massage, hairdressing, internet, laundry and ticket-booking services. Great value with clean rooms and fan.

Phousi Guest House (☎ 212973; Th Kitsalat; r 60,000-80,000 kip) On the north side of the Royal Palace heading toward the Mekong, this charming old colonial mansion offers a sense of peace and escape (provided new construction's finished by the time you read this). Eight spacious rooms, with fan and wooden floors.

Phousi Guest House II (☎ 253717; Th Khem Khong; r 60,000-80,000 kip) Set in a typical wood-frame building overlooking the Mekong, rooms have fans, modern bathrooms and if you've chosen one on the riverside, excellent views. The lobby is impressive with a nice restaurant for breakfast and a few computers with medium speed internet.

Khounsavanh Guest House (☎ 5670989; Th Thornkham; r with shared bathroom 60,000-90,000 kip) In a quiet location with a nice garden view of Phu Si, this is one of the better budget options in Luang Prabang. Beds are in the main building with timber walls, or across the street in the new house where facilities are more upmarket.

Silichit Guest House (☎ 212758; Th Sisavang Vatthana; r 60,000-150,000 kip) Beautiful rooms with fan in a newly renovated house yards from the Mekong. Wooden floors, comfy mattresses, relaxing lobby…the list goes on. Prices above reflect the maximum you can expect to pay in high season. Off season expect to pay 80,000 kip for two of you.

View Khen Khong (☎ 213032; Th Khem Khong; r 80,000-100,000 kip) A spit from the Mekong, this neat little guesthouse is run by a friendly family. All rooms come with private hot-water bathrooms and are cleaned daily. Nice riverside restaurant over the road.

Mano Guest House & Restaurant (☎ 253112; manosotsay@hotmail.com; Th Pha Mahapatsaman; r 80,000-120,000 kip; air-con) Rooms, though a little small, are clean, have fans and there's a sumptuous Lao-style lobby to relax in.

Suankeo Guest House No 2 (☎ 254740; Ban Ho Xiang; r 80,000-150,000 kip; air-con) Impeccably clean accommodation near the Mekong. Run by a kindly gentleman, this is a sanctuary of calm. Cheaper rooms include a fan and more expensive rooms have air-con.

Jaliya Guest House (☎ 202150; Th Pha Mahapatsaman; r with shared/private bathroom 90,000/150,000 kip; air-con) Tidy new guesthouse in an authentic part of the city. Behind the main building a row of small motel-style rooms open onto a sunny garden area. Bicycles are available to hire.

Old Quarter

In and around the old quarter budget options are also limited, but at the following you will get what you pay for.

Chittana Guest House (☎ 020 567 2243; off Th Sakkarin; r with shared bathroom 40,000-80,000 kip) Opposite Villa Santi, this old-fashioned part-timbered guesthouse offers simple but characterful accommodation with fans. Near the Nam Khan River.

Vatthanaluck Guest House (☎ 212838; off Th Sakkarin; r 60,000-80,000 kip) Family-owned guesthouse deliciously sandwiched between nearby Wat Nong Sikhunmeuang and Villa Santi. Rooms are pristine, fragrant with cool, tiled floors and fans.

East of Phu Si

More budget options are found 300m east of Phu Si down a rocky lane running to the Nam Khan.

our pick Cold River (☎ 252810; off Th Phommatha; r 40,000-70,000 kip) With its exquisite views of the Nam Khan River, family-run Cold River offers the tired traveller comfort and ambience. Rooms are house proud with fans (some with verandas). The shared outside area buzzes with family and friends teaching backpackers to speak Lao.

Merry Guest House 1 & 2 (☎ 252325; off Th Phommatha; r 60,000-80,000 kip) Just over the way from Cold River, Merry has attractive rooms with wooden floors (recently refurbished), fans and regularly fresh linen. The views of the Nam Khan River are also spectacular.

EATING

Luang Prabang has its own unique cuisine – consider trying one of the local specialities, no matter how unnerving they sound. A local favourite, *jąew bąwng* is a thick condiment made with chillies and dried buffalo skin. Another is *Áw lám*, a soup made with dried meat, mushrooms, eggplant and a bitter-spicy root (roots and herbs with bitter-hot effects are a force in Luang Prabang cuisine).

For dining on a strict budget, Th Chao Phanya Kang between Th Kitsalat and the river closes to vehicles at night and transforms into a bustling **night food market** (meals 10,000 kip; dinner) with a large array of food stalls. Sample some Luang Prabang specialities at one of the open-air wooden bench tables.

Lining the Mekong are numerous **riverside restaurants** (meals 20,000-40,000 kip; breakfast, lunch & dinner), often with kitchens in a namesake guesthouse across the street, serving delicious Lao fare at good prices, with excellent sunset views and a lanterns-and-fairy-lights festive atmosphere.

Cafés

The ghost of French occupation leaves an aromatic trail of freshly baked baguettes and redolent, ground coffee at every turn.

JoMa Bakery Café (☎ 252292; Th Chao Fa Ngum; meals 12,000-25,000 kip; breakfast, lunch & dinner, closed Sun;) Everything about JoMa shows considerable thought and care: breakfast-sets include coffee (cappuccinos come with cinnamon sprinkles) or juice. The lunch menu includes quiche, muffins, pizza, pasta, sandwiches and salads.

Scandinavian Bakery (Th Sisavangvong; mains 15,000 kip; breakfast, lunch & dinner) This haven of chocolate cake, pastries and deliciously fresh breakfasts will soon put back the pounds you lost trekking in Muang Sing. The oldest bakery in town, it's perfect for people-watching and pretending to be interested in the contents of the *Bangkok Post*.

Restaurants

Restaurants competing for the western dollar are concentrated on Th Sisavangvong, with more upmarket options as you head down the peninsula.

Nazim (Th Sisavangvong; meals 10,000-25,000 kip; breakfast, lunch & dinner) For a taste of southern India, both veggies and carnivores will find Nazim's to be the healthy equivalent of McDonalds – ubiquitous, but without the plastic toy giveaways.

Tum Tum Cheung Restaurant & Cooking School (☎ 252019; Th Sakkarin; meals 10,000-30,000 kip; lunch & dinner) Renowned for its excellent cooking classes (p371), this place has top-notch Lao food. It's a short walk north from the centre, in a quieter area next to Wat Khili.

Maly Lao Food (☎ 252013; Th Phu Vao; meals 10,000-30,000 kip; lunch & dinner) If you're tiring of pizzas, this restaurant is worth the trek from town, specialising in *làap* made with buffalo, deer or fish, *tôm jąew pąa* (spicy fish and eggplant soup) and *sáa* (minced fish or chicken salad with lemon grass and ginger).

Yongkhoune Restaurant (☎ 212342; Th Sisavangvong; meals 15,000-30,000 kip; ⏰ breakfast, lunch & dinner) Alfresco dining near the top of the main drag (superb people-watching location), this endearing old place was established in 1960. Thanks to a generic Western and Lao menu, plus consistently good fare, it's often packed with *falang*.

Samsara (☎ 254678; Th Sisavangvong; meals 15,000-40,000 kip; ⏰ lunch & dinner) A chichi interior and table settings – even the menu is an object of beauty. But the modern Indochinese dishes, although a happy change from the standard Lao fare, do not match up to the expectations raised by the 'look' – or the prices.

Pizza Luang Prabang (☎ 253858; Th Sisavangvong; meals 20,000-30,000 kip; ⏰ breakfast, lunch & dinner) Typical Western fare, from the eponymous pizzas to burgers and Italian dishes. Lavish setting and a good place to stock up on carbs before heading north.

Lasi Cuisine (212342; Th Sisavangvong; meals 20,000-40,000 kip; ⏰ breakfast, lunch & dinner) Romantic candle-flickering venue (dark enough to go home with the wrong person) serving up tasty Lao and Thai food.

Dao Fa Bistro (☎ 252656; Th Sisavangvong; meals 20,000-40,000 kip; ⏰ breakfast, lunch & dinner) Run by a French expat, this chic establishment offers a sophisticated menu and tasteful ambience. Cool tunes and Franco-Italian menu. Carbonara recommended.

DRINKING

L'Étranger Books & Tea (☎ 537 7826; booksinlaos@yahoo.com; Th Kingkitsarat; ⏰ 7am-10pm Mon-Sat, 10am-10pm Sun) Twenty-five different teas are available in the upstairs café of this funky little bookstore, gallery and minicinema.

Lao Lao Garden (Th Kingkitsarat; ⏰ 5pm-late) With its tiered garden, the centre-piece of which is a nightly lit bonfire, the Garden's an easy-on-the-eye venue to chill out in and listen to Western sounds. Also serves Lao and Western food.

Khob Chai & Ban Aphay (☎ 020 997 0106; Th Kingkitsarat; ☎ noon-late) Nestled in a curve in the road, this bar serves mainly Western burgers-and-chips-style meals, but the upbeat atmosphere and occasional live music draws locals here.

Hive Bar (hive_bar@yahoo.com; Th Kingkitsarat; ⏰ 5pm-1am) Also on the northeast side of Phu Si, this ubertrendy, moody-lit watering hole is a magnet for *falang* seeking a slice of sophistication. Trip-hop and trance tunes, two-for-one spirits from 5pm to 9pm. Check out the illuminated bottle sculpture.

Maylek Pub (cnr Th Pha Mahapatsaman & Th Setthathirat; ⏰ 5-11pm) Stylishly decorated with modern furniture, Maylek Pub has a fully stocked bar that includes hard-to-find-in-Laos drinks such as Bailey's Irish Cream, making it a popular choice for travellers staying in the area. Snacks are available if you're feeling peckish.

ENTERTAINMENT

Royal Ballet Theatre (☎ 253705; Royal Palace Museum, Th Sisavangvong; admission US$6-15; ⏰ shows 6pm Mon, Wed & Sat) Here you can attend performances of different episodes of the 600-year-old Ramayana ballet, plus traditional dances of Lao ethnic minorities such as the Phoo Noi and Hmong people.

SHOPPING

Luang Prabang has become a shopping mecca. Dozens of handicraft and souvenir stores line Th Sisavangvong, while the Hmong Night Market (p369) on Th Sisavangvong has stalls selling similar goods as shops, but without the additional overheads and middlemen, so they're cheaper.

While you're in town, also check out **Ock-PopTok** (☎ 253219, 020 570148; www.ockpoptok.com; Ban Vat Nong; ⏰ 8.30am-9pm), a quality handicrafts gallery and workshop selling naturally dyed Lao silk and cotton in modern and traditional styles, as well as clothes and other decorative items. **Baan Khily Gallery** (☎ 212622; Th Sakkarin; ⏰ till 7pm) sells hand-crafted lamps, stationery and cards made from mulberry bark. The gallery building and the charming owner are worth a visit alone.

GETTING THERE & AWAY

Air

Lao Airlines (code QV; ☎ 212172; www.laos-airlines.com) flies from Luang Prabang to Vientiane (US$60, daily), Huay Xai (US$50), and to Chiang Mai in Thailand (US$90; Tuesday, Friday, Sunday). Flights to Phonsavan, Luang Nam Tha and Udomxai were still cut from schedules at the time of research.

Bangkok Airways (code PG; ☎ 253334; www.bangkokair.com) flies from Luang Prabang to Bangkok

(US$225). **Siem Reap Airways** (code FT; ☎ 380330; www.siemreapairways.com) goes direct from Luang Prabang to Siem Reap (US$140); bookings through travel agents.

Boat

Slow boats northwest to Huay Xai (US$24) depart at 8am. The long-distance ferries stand by the Mekong from the day before departure; you can buy tickets there or from a travel agent in town. The trip takes two days with an overnight stop in Pak Beng, a tiny village roughly halfway between Huay Xai and Luang Prabang. From Pak Beng (US$12, 10 to 12 hours) it's also possible to take the bus northeast to Udomxai.

White-knuckle speedboats up the Mekong leave from Ban Don, a 7km 10,000-kip shared túk-túk ride from the centre, to Pak Beng (US$32, three hours) and Huay Xai (US$26, six hours), but it's a trip you take at your own risk. In the dry season boatmen shouldn't take you, but there's always someone keen to make a buck.

Although it is quicker by road, many travellers charter a boat for the beautiful seven-hour karst-rich trip up the Nam Ou to Nong Khiaw for around US$100 for up to 10 people. You can inquire about these trips at the Navigation Office in Luang Prabang or with the travel agents in town, who will post a list of names outside their office where you can join a trip.

Cargo boats to Vientiane have become less frequent since Rte 13 was sealed, but it's still possible to hop on a ferry for the three-day downstream trip for around US$24. Check the chalkboard outside the Navigation Office for departures.

CAN I CARRY YOUR LUGGAGE PLEASE?

Two Pak Beng scams to be mindful of: firstly your bag will be grabbed from the boat by porters before you've had a chance to disembark. Stories have circulated about rucksacks occasionally disappearing. One traveller put out a reward for his lost luggage and said bag turned up very quickly! Secondly, stow your bag away from your guesthouse window if it doesn't lock – unusual in Laos, but some rooms have been burgled while travellers were asleep.

Bus

Turn up early at the bus station and buy a ticket on the spot for less than you'll pay in town; contrary to popular wisdom – there are no reserved seats!

There are three main bus terminals in Luang Prabang. The northern bus terminal is 6km from town (a 15,000-kip túk-túk ride), while the southern terminal is 3km south of the town centre (10,000 kip by túk-túk). A third terminal, on the road to Tat Kuang Si, serves buses going to Sainyabuli Province.

Buses leave the southern terminal for Vientiane (90,000 kip, 11 hours, six daily starting at 6.30am) stopping in Vang Vieng (US$5, eight hours) en route. Travel agents also sell tickets for VIP express buses to Vientiane (US$12, nine hours).

Buses and sǎwngthǎew leave the northern bus terminal for Udomxai (40,000 kip, five hours, three daily at 8am, 9am and 10am), Luang Nam Tha (70,000 kip, nine hours, one daily at 6pm) and Nong Khiaw (45,000 kip, four to five hours, three daily at 8am, 9am and 10am). Alternatively catch a morning sǎwngthǎew to Pak Mong (20,000 kip, two to three hours) and catch another sǎwngthǎew to these destinations from there.

There is one direct bus to Phonsavan (70,000 kip, eight hours, daily at 8am). Buses going on to Sam Neua from Vientiane pass through Luang Prabang once a day at around 1pm going the long route north on Rte 13, then east on Rte 1 through Nong Khiaw.

GETTING AROUND

From the airport a túk-túk ride will cost around 15,000 kip, though túk-túk drivers have become accustomed to charging foreigners special tourist prices. Bicycles (10,000 kip per day) are available from many guesthouses and rental shops around town. Motorbike rental is still banned due to rather accident-prone *falang*.

Around Luang Prabang

PAK OU

About 25km by boat from Luang Prabang up the Mekong River, at the mouth of the Nam Ou, are the famous caves at Pak Ou. The two caves in the lower part of a limestone cliff are crammed with a variety of buddha images, a kind of graveyard where unwanted images are placed. If you go by boat, most trips will involve a stop at small villages along the way. Quite popular is a stop at Ban Xang Hai, or what boatmen call the 'Whisky Village', a now-tourist-dominated village that specialises in producing large jars of *lào-láo* (rice whisky). An enthusiastic collection of boatmen congregates below the Royal Palace Museum touting for Pak Ou passengers. A six- to seven-hour trip including stops at the Whisky Village costs around US$5 per person. Trips can also be arranged through guesthouses and tour operators.

TAT KUANG SI

This beautiful spot 32km south of Luang Prabang features a wide, multi-tiered waterfall tumbling over limestone formations into a series of cool, turquoise-green pools. The lower level of the falls has been turned into a public park with shelters, picnic tables and food vendors. A trail ascends through the forest along the left side of the falls to an idyllic second tier, which is usually very private except for thousands of butterflies, and has a pristine swimming hole. Entry to the falls site is 15,000 kip. Pak Ou boatmen do the return trip to Tat Kuang Si for around US$5 per person, plus US$2 for the túk-túk ride to reach the falls at the other end. Exercise junkies can also get to Tat Kuang Si by road by bicycle. Túk-túks can be chartered for about US$10 return.

Nong Khiaw

If you've suffered the sinuous highland journey from Udomxai, you'll feel more than rewarded by the sight that greets you here. Nestled on the banks of the Nam Ou river and positively towered over by limestone karsts, Nong Khiaw is magical. By night you can eat at a clutch of tasty restaurants, listen to the cicadas and watch the lights of the fishermen on the water. By day it's a friendly little town with happy locals and blossom-bursting river banks.

SIGHTS & ACTIVITIES

If it's trekking you're after, go to Sunrise Guest House; they can organise up to three-day excursions to neighbouring Hmong and Khamu villages. Trips cost around 80,000 kip per day. Alternatively walk yourself to Tham Pha Tok, a cave where villagers hid during heavy shelling during the second Indochina War. It's about 2.5km out of town as you head over the bridge past Phanoy Guest House. Near the cave is a waterfall.

SLEEPING & EATING

Phanoy Guest House (r 20,000-30,000 kip) Just over the bridge on the east side, Phanoy's seven bungalows are fresh and cosy with not only fans, wooden floors and mossie nets, but a great adjoining restaurant and bakery. The food is mainly Western (breakfasts recommended) plus there's a good place to lounge in the café and read from a wide selection of books (Q: Why do you always find Ron Hubbard books and romance novels in the middle of nowhere?).

Sunset Guest House & Restaurant (☎ 253933; r 20,000-30,000 kip) First on your right after the Phanoy Guest House, Sunset's hidden down a U-bend lane. The town's oldest guesthouse, rooms here are available with outside toilets at affordable prices; however, cabanas are top end. Rates can vary according to season. The views from the sun deck and chill lounge are terrific, as is the service.

Sunrise Guest House (r 30,000-40,000 kip) Over the bridge opposite Phanoy, this delightful guesthouse hugs the mountainside, boasting the best views in town and a clutch of beautifully finished bungalows with fan, attached showers, mosquito nets and flowered verandas. Dip and pour showers due for an upgrade in 2008.

Chittavong Guest House (r 30,000-70,000 kip) Next to the bridge with fine views of the river, Chittavong has nine lovingly furnished wooden bungalows. Rooms have balcony, fan and hot water. There's a nice spot to read under the blossom tree in the large garden; by night the candlelit restaurant looks alluring.

Nong Kiau Restaurant (mains 10,000-30,000 kip) Built from recovered timber and perched on the side of the opposite river bank, Nong Kiau is a journey into taste and vista, with an amazing view to match a seafood-dominated menu. Banana pancake to die for!

GETTING THERE & AWAY

If you're heading upriver to Muang Ngoi Neua (15,000 kip; one hour) boats leave at 11am and 1.30pm. Expect to stop off at various villages en route. Tickets are bought at a small office near the boat landing 100m south of the bridge. The journey by boat to Luang Prabang is one of the most dramatic in Laos;

that said you need a few of you to cut the cost as the boatman charges US$75 per boat (up to 10 people).

The bus for Luang Prabang (32,000 kip) leaves at 11am (if you're returning from Muang Ngoi Neua to catch it the driver usually waits for the boat). A public bus leaves Nong Khiaw for Luang Prabang at 8am from outside the post office on the west side of the bridge. Săwngthăew for Pak Mong leave regularly when full. For Udomxai, the bus leaves at 11am (31,000 kip, four hours), or catch a săwngthăew back to Pak Mong to pick up a bus there. The bus heading for Sam Neua passes through Nong Khiaw about 6pm.

If you're heading east, you can catch a săwngthăew as far as Muang Vieng Kham (15,000 kip, three hours), where you change vehicles for Sam Neua (30,000 kip, six hours), Nam Noen (15,000 kip, three hours), or Phonsavan (75,000 kip, 12 hours). These leave when full – arrive early.

Muang Ngoi Neua

Watching the sun set between the jagged karsts you'll feel as if you've stepped into a silkscreen painting. So peaceful is this secluded riverside village it's become something of a traveller's gem; you can either relax supine in your hammock or undertake a more-active trek. Accommodation has over-mushroomed during the last few years making the guesthouse-dollar a competitively sought commodity.

INFORMATION

Generators provide electricity to guesthouses and restaurants from 6pm to 10pm. There's no internet but you can make international calls at the Restaurant Nangphonekeo. You can exchange US dollars at Lattanavongsa on the main road, behind the guesthouse of the same name, for unexceptional rates. A couple of pharmacies sell basic medicines; for anything serious get yourself back to Luang Prabang.

SIGHTS & ACTIVITIES

Trekking is one of Muang Ngoi Neua's main attractions. From the main street turn east at Kaikeo Restaurant, then follow the path through the large schoolyard and into an area of secondary forest. An admission fee, by donation, will be collected here by a volunteer from town (between dawn and dusk). After a 5km walk along a path passing rice fields you come to a stream running into **Tham Kang**, a popular spot for spear-fishing. After another five minutes on the same trail you arrive at another cave, **Tham Pha Kaew**. Beyond the caves you can continue on to the villages of **Huay Bo** (one hour, 3km), **Huay Sen** (1½ hours) and **Ban Na** (another 20 minutes, 1km). It's also possible to organise a **village stay** if you want to experience something less touristy, although this is also popular so be prepared to walk back again if there's no room at the inn.

Run by a former teacher, Mr Kongkeo, **Muang Ngoi Tour Office** (7-8am & 6-7pm) is located behind the main street, 300m south of the boat landing – look for the signs directing you. Mr Kongkeo takes treks to the caves and local villages (US$15), and he'll be happy to organise canoeing and fishing trips (US$10). The only noise you're likely to hear is the puttering of pirogues and kids playing in the Nam Ou river.

To the left of the boat landing is **Lao Youth Travel** (7.30-10.30am & 1.30-6pm), which organises overnight treks (from US$10 per day) or will take you up the river with a tube (from 15,000 kip) from where you can amble back.

SLEEPING & EATING

There's little to differentiate between many of the riverfront guesthouses in terms of price or standard; most feature bungalows with shared cold-water bathrooms, squat toilets and small restaurants. That said there are a few luxurious exceptions.

Ning Ning Restaurant & Guest House (r 20,000 kip) With its fine panoramic view, alfresco dining on a lovely decked area, the Ning Ning is a favourite. The menu is an amalgam of Thai, Lao and Western (mains 15,000 kip). Its three rustic-style bungalows are superior and spacious.

Phetdavanh Guest House (r 20,000-30,000 kip) West at the top of the boat landing steps, this venue definitely competes with Lattanavongsa as the most tasteful accommodation on the street. Spacious rooms in this attractive old wooden house have comfy sprung mattresses and a fairy-lit decked area conducive for chilling. They also serve food (mains 15,000 kip).

Nixsa's Place (r 20,000 kip) Decent wooden bungalows, outside toilet, no fan. Good restaurant here with a decent view of the mountain.

Banana Café & Restaurant (r 20,000 kip; breakfast, lunch & dinner) Simple balconied bungalows with outside toilet and pour-and-scrub showers. Ideal for pondering the river. The family-run restaurant is nondescript but fresh. Watch out for the lovely old guy out back who skins rat for his dinner!

Say Lom Guest House (r 20,000 kip) Generic riverfront digs next to the boat landing, with outside toilet and shower, this is good shoestring value – you may even get a faded Leo DiCaprio poster on your wall.

Lattanavongsa Guest House (r 50,000-60,000 kip) Definitely edging out the competition with its immaculate wooden bungalows offering fine views over the river. Rooms have balconies with a beautiful garden of flame trees and flowers. The restaurant is also good (mains 15,000 kip), offering a varied Western and Thai/Lao menu. Opposite the steps at the Boat Landing.

Kaikeo Restaurant (mains 5000-15,000 kip; breakfast, lunch & dinner) A couple of doors east of the main intersection this is a great breakfast spot (where you can watch local kids hurrying off to school, ball of sticky rice in hand). There's a mix of tables and cushioned seating.

Sengala Bakery (mains 15,000 kip; breakfast, lunch & dinner) Specialises in mouth-watering pancakes and fresh bread (baked at 7am and 4pm), with an interesting variation on steak (buffalo?) sandwich.

Restaurant Nangphonekeo (mains 30,000 kip; breakfast, lunch & dinner) This friendly café does a good turn in Lao food and Western fare. You can also make international calls here.

GETTING THERE & AWAY

Boats to Nong Khiaw leave at 8.30am, 9.30am and 1pm (15,000 kip, one hour).

XIENG KHUANG PROVINCE

Virtually every town and village in Xieng Khuang Province was bombed between 1964 and 1973. Today the awesome beauty of the mountains and valleys is overshadowed by the denuded hills and valleys pockmarked with bomb craters, where little or no vegetation grows. This remains the province most heavily contaminated with UXO in Laos; walking off paths is extremely inadvisable.

Most visitors come to Xieng Khuang to visit the mysterious Plain of Jars, but there are also several fascinating sites relating to the war open to tourists. Rte 7 from Phu Khun (intersecting with Rte 13 between Luang Prabang and Vang Vieng) is now sealed, making travel to Phonsavan by road a lot quicker.

Phonsavan

☎ 061 / pop 57,000

A sprawling collection of wide streets and austere concrete shophouses, Phonsavan has little aesthetic appeal except for the ubiquitous collections of war scrap that decorate guesthouses and restaurants. Essentially the place merits a visit for its involvement in The Secret War, or to see the enigmatic Plain of Jars; an eerie conundrum of large stone jars randomly positioned over three sites.

INFORMATION

Diethelm Travel Laos (☎ 213200; chansmon@laotel.com; Rte 7) Opposite the old bus station; books plane tickets back to Vientiane, and organises tours of the province if you want to create your own sightseeing itinerary. You'll need a few people to make the costs manageable.

Hot Net (Rte 7; per min 300 kip; 8am-10pm) A few doors along from the post office; has slow internet connections.

Indochina Travel (☎ 312409; Rte 7) offers Visa advances (6% commission) as well as organising onward

BONES & BOONIES

American MIA (Missing In Action) recovery missions have long given up hope of finding bearded waifs limping around bamboo jungle compounds (sorry Rambo). Instead, the MIA programme visits Laos for three months a year to try and recover the interred bones of their soldiers, but not without considerable expense (US$30 million per year). Considering Laos is carpeted in dense 'boonies' forest (more than 10% of its total land mass), this makes for slow and difficult work.

In contrast, the money the US donates to Laos to help with the UXO problem it created is a paltry sum rumoured to be less than US$5 million per year. Whilst this might enrage the reader, historically, attempts to financially salve the wound were rejected by the ever dogmatic Lao Government – there was also the possibility the money would never find its way to the right places. Instead, the US sends mine detection apparatus – lots of it. As one anonymous mine-clearance NGO said, 'there are rooms full of metal detectors just sitting there. We've got more than we need.'

travel and trips to the Jars (US$15 per person, including lunch and English speaking guide). Speak to Mr Thong.

Lao-Mongolian Friendship Hospital (☎ 312166) 500m west of the Maly Hotel. Medical emergencies will need to be taken to Vientiane for possible transfer to Thailand.

Post office (Rte 7; 8am-4pm Mon-Fri) On the eastern corner of the town triangle.

SLEEPING

Accommodation here has barely improved, but there are a few gems in an otherwise drizzly crown.

Vinh Thong Guest House (☎ 212622; Rte 7; r 30,000-40,000 kip) On a street corner located just past Nisha Guest House, this is basic accommodation. Rooms have rattan walls plus there is a very atmospheric lobby with recovered UXO and Secret War paraphernalia.

Phoukham Guest House (Rte 7; r 50,000 kip) Opposite the old bus station, the modern two-storey Phoukham Guest House has reasonably soft beds. You can also get onward visas and make internet phone calls or download digital photos to disk.

Dok Khoun Guest House (☎ 312189, 020 563 4792; Rte 7; r 50,000 kip) A well-run guesthouse on the main road, with hot water in some rooms and tiled floors. Laundry service is available for 10,000 kip per kilo and onward visas can be arranged. You'll need your own sleeping bag and earplugs (it's next to Phonsavan Nightclub).

Vanealoun Guest House (☎ 312070; Rte 7; r 50,000 kip) Despite the cell-like rooms, this is another good option for its cleanliness and electric hot-water showers. It even has shampoo satchels in each bathroom: very swish! The tiled floors are cool, and rooms come with fan. Doors close at 11pm.

Kong Keo Guest House (☎ 211354; www.kongkeojar.com; r 60,000-80,000 kip) Still the only interesting option in town, King Kong prevails with his delightful cabanas featuring hot water and en suites. Rooms in the house are cheaper. The garden is peaceful, as is the little lounge-café where you can request to watch *Bombies*, a documentary about UXO. This is a much needed exposé which will enrich your stay here. It's 150m off Rte 7, across the old air field.

Nice Guest House (☎ 312454; Rte 7; r 80,000 kip) A favourite with NGOs, this new venue is both modern and immaculate with fresh tiled floors and friendly staff. After Kong Keo, probably the best place to stay if you don't mind forking out the extra cash.

> **MUST SEE**
>
> To get a greater handle on not only the history of Laos but also its continuing curse, keep an eye out for the critically acclaimed documentary, *Bombies* (2001). Filmmaker Jack Silberman examines the legacy of the US-led Secret War in Laos through the experiences of those people dealing with the unexploded ordnance (UXOs) scattered throughout the country today. While the foreign policies of old administrations are relegated to the archives, *Bombies* is a powerful reminder of the open and still smarting wounds left behind on innocent people. More than 10,000 people have been killed by UXO, with the figure rising all the time. The surest place to see this uncompromising doc is Kong Keo Guest House (see left for details).

EATING

Cuisine in town is somewhat two dimensional – aren't you missing Luang Prabang now? There are a couple of tasty places that will keep you vertical, most of them along Rte 7.

Kong Keo Guest House (☎ 020 551 6365; www.kongkeojar.com; dishes 8000-20,000 kip) Even if you're not staying, this is a great place to eat if you want to meet fellow travellers. The service can be errr…a little forgetful, but you're in Laos: sip a beer by the fire – in a former bomb casing – while sitting cross-legged on cushions soaking up the convivial atmosphere. Try the excellent rice-paper rolls.

Nisha (☎ 020 569 8140; Rte 7; mains 10,000-30,000 kip) For vegetarians, who haven't many options in these more remote parts of the country, Indian curries are a gift from Ganesh. It's on the left as you head east.

China Restaurant (☎ 312220; Rte 7; meals 10,000-20,000 kip) Chinese dumplings, spicy eel slices… an excellent option if your tastebuds desperately desire something Chinese. A popular *falang* haunt with a little more life than some places. Near the *dead* centre of town.

Craters Restaurant (☎ 7805775; Rte 7; mains 20,000-40,000 kip) The nearest you'll get to brasserie sophistication, this little eatery, west of Diethelm Travel, serves up western food. Omelettes are tasty and the chicken soup, if it's a cold rainy

AN ENDURING LEGACY

Between 1964 and 1973, the USA conducted one of the largest sustained aerial bombardments in history, flying 580,344 missions over Laos and dropping two million tons of bombs, costing US$2.2 million a day. Around 30% of the bombs dropped on Laos failed to detonate, leaving the country littered with unexploded ordnance (UXO).

For people all over eastern Laos (the most contaminated provinces are Xieng Khuang, Salavan and Savannakhet), living with this appalling legacy has become an intrinsic part of daily life. Since the British Mines Advisory Group (MAG) began clearance work in 1994, only a tiny percentage of the quarter of a million pieces in Xieng Khuang and Salavan has been removed. At the current rate of clearance it will take more than 100 years to make the country safe. The **Mines Advisory Group Office** (☎ 312459; www.magclearsmines.org; Rte 7; 🕑 8am-4pm Mon-Fri) has information on UXO-clearing projects in Laos including the Plain of Jars. Donations are greatly appreciated.

day, warms the soul. Also the only place in town to get a proper coffee.

Located one block south of Rte 7, the **fresh food market** (🕑 6am-5pm) has an undercover section with numerous noodle stands, ideal for a delicious and inexpensive meal. Fresh fruit and vegetables, deep-fried bananas, sticky rice-balls, slippery noodle spring rolls and other culinary treasures also await. The old dry market beside the bus station has moved south a few blocks on Rte 7, to a more sturdy concrete building. It's about 10 minutes' walk.

GETTING THERE & AWAY

Lao Airlines (code QV; ☎ 312027; www.laos-airlines.com) flies to Vientiane from Phonsavan (US$50, daily).

The old bus and săwngthăew station is above the main triangle intersection. At the time of research, buses departed from here then did a pick-up at the new bus station, situated 13km west along Rte 7. There are regular direct buses to Vientiane (90,000 kip), via Vang Vieng (70,000 kip, 12 to 13 hours, 7am, 9.30am and 4pm), plus buses to Luang Prabang (85,000 kip, eight hours), with an optional VIP bus (95,000 kip) leaving at 7pm.

For Sam Neua (60,000 kip, eight hours) the bus leaves at 6pm. There's a daily bus to Udomxai (90,000 kip, 13 hours). A bus for Thavieng (30,000 kip) departs at 10am.

The roads on these routes are in good condition but because of continuing Hmong insurrection in this area you may see the presence of a gun-toting guard on board. Don't be alarmed, recent attacks have been minimal.

GETTING TO VIETNAM

The Nam Can–Nam Khan border east of Phonsavan is not as convenient as it may appear; even though you're a long way north of the Kaew Neua Pass crossing, the road on the Vietnam side runs so far south (almost to Vinh) before joining north–south Hwy 1 that this border is totally inconvenient. Public transport from Nam Can (on the Vietnamese side) to Hanoi or to Vinh is a little scarce; be prepared to wait.

The border is open from 8am to 5pm daily; make sure you have your Vietnamese visa before attempting to cross.

See p838 on doing the trip in the opposite direction.

Plain of Jars

The Plain of Jars is a large area extending around Phonsavan from the southwest to the northwest where huge jars of unknown origin are scattered about in dozens of groupings. There are three main sites for visitors to wander around, which have been largely cleared of UXO.

Site 1 is 10km southwest of Phonsavan and is the largest, featuring 250 jars mostly between 1m and 3m tall and weighing between 600kg and one tonne. There's an undercover rest area at this site, where you can buy snacks and drinks – plus read comprehensive information boards provided by Unesco, on the jars and the UXO-clearing project here.

Two other jar sites are accessible by an unsealed road from Phonsavan and have fewer jars, but much better views. **Site 2**, about 25km south of town, features 90 jars spread across two adjacent hillsides. Vehicles can reach the base of the hills, then it's a short, steep walk to the jars.

More impressive is 150-jar **Site 3**, which is also known as Hai Hin Lat Khai, located about 10km south of Site 2. This site is on a scenic hilltop near the charming village of Ban Sieng Di, where there's also a small monastery containing the remains of Buddha images damaged in the war. The site is a stiff 2km walk across rice paddies and up a hill.

TOURS

Officially, vehicles must be 'registered' to visit the sites, meaning you have to go on a tour. It seems inconvenient, but there are a number of tours available. Tours can be arranged in Phonsavan, which is notable for its excellent English-speaking guides.

Organised tours to the jars are often extended to include other interesting sites, including a crashed US Thunder Chief 105 plane, a Russian tank, Viet Cong bunkers, the US Lima S 108 airstrip supposedly used for drug running, and hot springs. Trips can also be arranged to the Tham Piu cave, about 60km east, where 400 local people were killed in a US bombing raid.

Speak to Mr Sawat at **Lao Youth Travel** (☎ 312409; Rte 7) for info on their tours. Prices including entrance fee to the sites and lunch cost US$15. Alternatively, tours from **Kong Keo Guest House** (☎ 020 551 6365; www.kongkeojar.com; off Rte 7) have received glowing reports. A car with driver and guide costs around US$8 per person, depending on the size of the group. The first stop is the fresh food market where you're expected to buy your own provisions for the day.

GETTING THERE & AWAY

It is possible to charter a săwngthăew from Phonsavan to Site 1, 10km from the centre, for 50,000 kip return, including waiting time, for up to six people.

HUA PHAN PROVINCE

Rugged and beautiful, Hua Phan province is unlike any other province in Laos. Although it is home to 22 different ethnic groups including Yao, Hmong, Khamu, Thai Khao and Thai Neua, the province clearly shows the influence of the Vietnamese. The province's high altitude means the climate can be cool – even in the hot season – and its forested mountains are shrouded in mist. Road journeys to Hua Phan are memorably scenic; it was described by one local as 'a journey of a million turns'. Now that the border here to Vietnam is open to foreigners, you no longer have to turn around and go all the way back along that twisting road again. With improved public transport across the border to Hanoi, this remote corner of Laos will hopefully see visitor numbers increase over the coming years.

Sam Neua

☎ 064 / pop 46,800

There is an unmistakable 'frontier' feeling to the town of Sam Neua. Men in military caps and jackets nurse coffees and cigarettes, wrapped up against the morning chill; and pick-up trucks piled high with local villagers, crates of chilli sauce or striped bags stuffed with goods pass through. It's one of the least touristy provincial centres in Laos. While the town offers little in terms of sights, the riverside market is fascinating – all manner of freshly slaughtered or harvested delicacies, as well as textiles, jewellery and consumer goods are sold here. In mid-December, local ethnic groups take part in all-important courtship games and festivities during a **Hmong Lai Festival**.

JARS OF THE STONE AGE

The purpose of these possibly 2000-year-old jars remains a mystery and without any organic material – such as bones or food remains – there is no reliable way to date them. Archaeological theories and local myth suggest the enigmatic jars were used for burial purposes – as stone coffins or urns – or maybe for storing *lào-láo* (rice whisky) or rice.

In the 1930s, pioneering French archaeologist Madeline Colani documented the jars in a 600-page monograph, *Mégalithes du Haut Laos (Megaliths of Highland Laos)*, concluding that they were funerary urns carved by a vanished people. Colani found a human-shaped bronze figure in one of the jars at Site 1, as well as tiny stone beads in the area. Today the whereabouts of these cultural artefacts is unknown.

INFORMATION

Hua Phanh Tourist Office (☎ 312567; 🕑 8am-3.30pm Mon-Fri) Located 200m north of the bus station. The staff, who speak a little English, have a few dusty pamphlets on hand and can arrange vehicles around the province to more remote sites such as Suan Hin (Sao Hin Tang), a stone garden often likened to Britain's Stonehenge.

Lao Development Bank (☎ 312171; 🕑 8am-4pm Mon-Fri) On the main road 400m north of the bus station on the left; exchanges cash and travellers cheques.

Post office (🕑 8am-4pm Mon-Fri) In a large building directly opposite the bus station. A telephone office at its rear offers international calls using a phonecard and is open the same hours.

SLEEPING & EATING

The block between the bus station and the Nam Xam is where the reputable guesthouses and a few restaurants can be found, all within a short walking distance. Accommodation is of a similar standard: multistorey buildings with a sitting area and a pot of tea on each floor, rooms with or without an attached bathroom, and reasonably clean although hard beds to kip in.

Shuliyo Guest House (☎ 312462; r with shared bathroom 30,000-50,000 kip) Turning right from the bus station, this is the first place you come to. The family owners speak almost no English, so this is your chance to practise your Lao (or signing skills). The rooms on the top floor come with shared bathroom – on the ground floor. The electric hot-water tanks in each bathroom provide only five minutes of water at a moderate pressure, so be kind to your roommate and have a quick shower.

Khaem Xam (☎ 312111; r with shared bathroom 30,000-60,000 kip) Located on the corner next to the bridge and opposite the river, the tiled fan-cooled rooms here have long been a popular choice for foreign travellers and travelling businesspeople. The attached restaurant does simple Lao dishes that are hearty and filling.

Bounhome Guest House (☎ 312223, 020 234 8125; r 35,000-40,000 kip) The distinguishing feature of this multistorey guesthouse directly opposite Phatphousay is the balcony on each floor. Otherwise the standards are similar to the rest and the price differences are a little inexplicable.

Phatphousay Guest House (☎ 312943; r with shared bathroom 40,000-50,000 kip) On a dark laneway running parallel to the river, this is another family-run guesthouse with clean rooms, twin or double beds.

Chittavanh Restaurant (☎ 312265; meals 8000-20,000 kip) On the river road between the bridge and the market is another good option, with a short menu of fried meat and fish, soups and fried rice. It's popular for breakfast or dinner and warming glasses of *lào-láo*.

Dan Nao Muang Xam Restaurant (☎ 314126; meals 10,000-20,000 kip) At the end of the laneway and a few doors west of Khaem Xam, this is the best eatery in a town that's not winning any gourmet awards. The basic Lao menu also includes Western-style breakfasts, excellent fried rice, fresh baguettes and tender beef salad.

Mitsampanh Restaurant (☎ 312151; meals 10,000-30,000 kip) In the laneway, a few doors north of Phatphousay Guest House, this restaurant does reasonable Lao food for good prices, but unfortunately it doesn't have much on offer for vegetarians.

At lunchtime, the market is a source of all sorts of delights including bamboo-leaf-wrapped curry with rice, noodle soups, and creepy-crawlies plucked straight from the river, for the adventurous diner!

GETTING THERE & AWAY

Lao Airlines (code QV; www.laos-airlines.com) flies to and from Sam Neua from Vientiane (US$70, twice a week). The descent through the Nam Xam valley is tricky; the mountains are frequently shrouded in mist.

There are three main bus departures daily all heading for Vientiane (120,000 kip, 24 hours). The first leaves at 7.30am and arrives in Vientiane at 6am the next day, going via the southern route through Phonsavan (50,000 kip, eight hours), on a good but very winding sealed road. The second leaves at 8am via Rte 1 through Muang Vieng Thong (30,000 kip), Nong Khiaw (60,000 kip) and down through Luang Prabang (70,000 kip, 15 hours), arriving in Vientiane around midnight. If you're heading for Udomxai, take this bus and change to a săwngthăew at Pak Mong. This is a slow, uncomfortable trip, especially in the wet season. The third option is the VIP express bus (130,000 kip) leaving Sam Neua at midday and arriving in Vientiane around 5am.

Vieng Xai (Pathet Lao Caves)

In a narrow valley of limestone peaks are caves that served as the elaborate homes and shelters of the Pathet Lao leaders and their followers for more than a decade before their victory in 1975. The caverns are virtually unassailable by land or air, but the area was still heavily pounded by American bombs. Today, the most historically significant caves, named after the leaders who lived in them, are open to tourists.

This is a fascinating and peaceful town to spend a day or two in. A wooden board in front of the market features a map of Vieng Xai.

You must report to the **Kaysone Phom Vihan Memorial Tour Cave Office** (☎ 064-314321; ⏰ 8am-noon & 1.30-4pm), a 2km walk from the bus station, to pay the caves entrance fee of 10,000 kip, plus 10,000 kip for a guide who will take you to the caves and let you in. It's another 2000 kip to take a camera.

At the time of writing two guides spoke English. A dozen caves at three different sites are open for visitors and tours take two to three hours. The leaders' caves feature multiple entrances, bedrooms, offices, and emergency rooms fitted with steel doors and equipped with large Russian oxygen machines in case of a chemical attack. Many of the caves are now fringed by magnificent gardens, making them look more like holiday grottoes than scenes of war and hardship.

Tham Than Souphanouvong, named after the Red Prince, has a crater from a 500lb bomb near the entrance that has been concreted as a war relic. **Tham Than Kaysone**, named after a former president and Pathet Lao leader, has the most to look at, with original beds, clothing, office equipment, books, a portrait of Che Guevara and a politburo meeting room. **Tham Than Khamtay** is the most spectacular of the caves, where up to 3000 Pathet Lao rank and file would hide out.

SLEEPING & EATING

Naxay Guesthouse (☎ 064-314336, 020 576 4729; r with shared bathroom 10,000-20,000 kip) Clean rooms in a rickety wooden house with lino floors. The cold-water bathrooms are in a nearby building. Hot water is provided in a thermos.

Government Hotel (☎ 064-314356; r with shared bathroom 10,000-30,000 kip) The best location in town by a small lake. The shared bathrooms come with small electric hot-water tanks. Rooms with up to three beds have mosquito nets. Leather armchairs line up

> **GETTING TO VIETNAM**
>
> Buses to Na Maew on the Vietnam border depart from Sam Neua at 7am (20,000 kip, three hours), passing through Vieng Xai on the way. The crossing here is open from 8am to 5pm; make sure you've organised your Vietnamese visa in advance as they can't be granted at the border.
>
> At the time of research transport on the Vietnamese side was scarce, but with more travellers making the journey this will pick up. It's a long winding journey from Nam Xoi in Vietnam to Hanoi.
>
> See p839 for information on making the journey in the reverse direction.

on the red-tiled veranda and a small restaurant serving simple meals, with notice, is downstairs.

Next to the Naxay, a small **restaurant** (☎ 064-314336; meals 10,000 kip) does Korean-style steamboat, heating coals in an empty bombshell out the front.

GETTING THERE & AWAY

A bus leaves Sam Neua for Vieng Xai at 6am (7000 kip, 40 minutes), or săwngthăew leave almost every hour when full until mid-afternoon. From Vieng Xai, săwngthăew for Sam Neua leave the market almost hourly until 5pm.

UDOMXAI PROVINCE

This rugged province is wedged between Luang Prabang, Phongsali, Luang Nam Tha, Bokeo and Sainyabuli, with a small section that shares a border with China's Yunnan Province. It is home to 23 ethnic minorities, mostly Hmong, Akha, Mien, Phu Thai, Thai Dam, Thai Khao, Thai Lü and Thai Neua. The Yunnanese presence continues to intensify with the influx of Chinese skilled labourers working in construction, as well as tradespeople from Kunming, the capital of Yunnan.

Udomxai

☎ 081 / pop 80,000

During the Second Indochina War the regional capital became the centre for Chinese troops supportive of the Pathet Lao.

GETTING TO VIETNAM

The border at Tay Trang (Laos) and Dien Bien Phu (Vietnam) started operating in April 2007 after years of rumours of its impending opening.

To cross the border, catch a bus from Udomxai to the town of Muang Khua (US$4, four hours, two daily), set on the banks of the Nam Ou. (Two daily buses also travel from Luang Prabang to Muang Khua; the trip costs US$6 and takes eight hours.) From Muang Khua, a bus leaves for Dien Bien Phu (40,000 kip) three times a week at 7am. There is transport to Hanoi from Dien Bien Phu.

The border is open from 8am to 5pm daily, but does not issue Vietnamese visas; you'll need to organise one in advance in Luang Prabang or Vientiane.

See p839 for information on travelling from Vietnam to Laos.

Today, if Northern Laos were to host a beauty contest for all its towns, Udomxai wouldn't be allowed in the building. A dusty amalgam of randomly erected Chinese- and Thai-style buildings, there is little that is Lao here; indeed many of the inhabitants of this important trading town are Chinese lorry drivers who use the town as a transport hub. Try and get here early in order to catch a connecting bus out. If the inevitable happens, here are a few decent places to seek solace.

INFORMATION

Banque pour le Commerce Extérieur Lao (☎ 211260; Rte 1; ⌚ 8.30am-4pm) Changes US dollars, Thai baht or Chinese yuan into kip.

Lao Development Bank (☎ 312059; Rte 4; ⌚ 8.30am-3.30pm) Also changes US dollars, Thai baht or Chinese yuan into kip.

Oudomsay Provincial Tourism Office (☎ 211797; ⌚ 8am-4.30pm Mon-Fri, 8am-noon Sat) Located just up the hill from the bridge; can help you plan your forward escape.

Post office (⌚ 8am-4pm Mon-Fri, 8am-noon Sat) You can make international calls at the post office with a phonecard.

Udomxai Travel (☎ 212020; travel_kenchan@yahoo.com; Rte 1) For tours to local attractions such as the Houay Nam Kat Reserve find Mr Kenchan O'Phetsan at this travel agency, located next to the bus station.

SIGHTS & ACTIVITES

Besides checking out the **Chinese market**, a vast sprawl of stalls beside the **Kaysone Monument**, there's little to do apart from taking a Swedish-style massage at the **Lao Red Cross** (☎ 312269; massage per hour US$1-3). Alternatively you can take a sunset trip up to **Wat Santiphap** to chat with the monks, who are usually keen to brush up on their English.

SLEEPING & EATING

Saylomyen Guest House (☎ 211377; off Rte 1; r with shared/private bathroom 30,000/50,000 kip) Turn right at the main intersection about 800m north of the bus station; Saylomyen is well signposted. The main building has clean rooms with shared bathroom. In a newer construction next door, rooms have attached bathrooms – all with hot water. Great views can be enjoyed from the top floor of the main building.

Saensabay Guest House (off Rte 1; r 40,000 kip) Six undistinguished yet peaceful rooms on a road 27m back from Saylomyen Guesthouse, with a pleasant view of the mountains.

Linda Guest House (☎ 312147; Rte 1; r 40,000-50,000 kip) Has 14 pongy rooms in a three-storey, ornate building on the main street opposite the petrol station. If full, there's another branch, Linda 2, on Rte 4, behind the Kaysone Monument, with the same prices and amenities.

Vivanh Guest House (Rte 1; r 50,000 kip; ❄) Pristine, cool accommodation with fresh linen daily. Located beside the bridge. Friendly owner.

Lithavixay Guest House (☎ 212175; Rte 1; r 60,000 kip) Offering a pleasant internet-enabled communal area plus enormous rooms with armoire and TV. About 90m on the left up from Linda Guest House, heading toward the bus station.

Pholay (☎ 312324; Rte 1; meals 10,000-30,000 kip) Located next to a petrol station, Pholay is another reliable place to eat, with an extensive menu of Chinese and Lao food.

Keomongkoun Restaurant (Rte 1; mains 20,000 kip) Located on Rte 1 opposite Linda Guest House, this unpretentious little restaurant is garnering plenty of praise from passing *falang* with its delectable Chinese and Western fare.

GETTING THERE & AWAY

Lao Airlines runs an irregular flight from Udomxai over to Vientiane (US$80). The Chinese-built bitumen roads that radiate from Udomxai are in fair condition (except for the road to Pak Beng) and the city is the largest land-transport hub in the north. The bus terminal at the southwestern edge of town has buses to and from Luang Prabang (30,000 kip, five hours, three daily), Nong Khiaw (24,500 kip, three hours, one daily), Pak Beng (26,500 kip, four hours, two daily), Luang Nam Tha (26,000 kip, three to five hours, three daily), Boten (23,000 kip, four hours, two daily), Phongsali (50,000 kip, eight hours, one daily) and Vientiane (ordinary 90,000 kip, 15 hours; VIP 100,000 kip, 14 hours).

LUANG NAM THA PROVINCE

Luang Nam Tha

☎ 086 / pop 35,400

Razed to the ground during the Indochina War, Luang Nam Tha is essentially two towns; the new town, in which you'll find the bulk of restaurants and guesthouses, and the old village near the airport and boat landing (for river trips to Huay Xai), some 7km away. Give it a day and the place will grow on you; be it its excellent coffee houses, diverse cuisine, or the amicable charm of the locals – and not forgetting its deserved status as a mecca for ecotourism.

With its proximity to the beguiling wilds of the Nam Ha NPA, Luang Nam Tha is the perfect base. Hire a bike and explore the nearby waterfall or Thai Lue, Thai Dam and Khamu villages; take a trek or kayak in some of the most virginal forests in northern Laos.

INFORMATION

BCL Bank (🕑 8.30am-3.30pm Mon-Fri) Opposite the telecom office on the main road, this place charges 2% commission for cashing travellers cheques into US dollars and 4% for Visa cash advances (kip) and 5% (US dollars). There's also a BCL exchange booth at the bus station.

Green Mountain Internet (☎ 020 519 7999; per min 500 kip; 🕑 8am-8pm) Near Many Chan Guest House, the place has Skype and a super-speedy broadband connection.

KNT Internet (☎ 211066; per min 500 kip; 🕑 8am-11pm). Opposite Green Discovery, KNT has slow internet connection. Downloading of digital photos and international phone calls also available. KNT sells an informative not-to-scale local map for 3000 kip.

Lao Development Bank (☎ 312232; 🕑 8.30am-noon & 2-3.30pm Mon-Fri) Next to KNT.com; exchanges cash and travellers cheques.

Lao Telecom office (🕑 8am-noon & 1-5pm) Next door to Saikhonglongsack Guest House.

Nam Ha Ecotourism Project (☎ 312047; namha guides@hotmail.com; 🕑 8am-noon & 2-5pm) Treks range from one to three days, costing around US$10 per day. The provincial tourism office has information on trips as well as excellent brochures on responsible tourism. To find it, turn left after the post office on the corner then take the first right.

Planet Online (☎ 312435; per min 650 kip) This solar-powered internet café on the main road has broadband connection and offers decent maps of the town detailing neighbouring hill tribe villages.

Post office (☎ 312007; 🕑 8am-noon & 1-4pm Mon-Fri) A little further north of the Many Chan Guest House on the opposite side of the road.

SIGHTS & ACTIVITIES

Most people are drawn here for the hiking and trekking possibilities in the **Nam Ha NPA**. Within the Eden-like jungle lurk 37 species of large mammals including clouded leopard, elephant, gaur and tiger. Rumours of tigers entering tribes-people's villages are denied for obvious reasons, but still linger.

Tours to the park are organised by **Nam Ha Ecotourism Project** (☎ 312150; namhaguides@yahoo.com). One to 3 day treks cost 80,000 kip per day. Your best bet, however, is the excellent **Green Discovery** (☎ 211484; www.greendiscoverylaos.com;

BROTHER CAN YOU LEND YOUR TIME

If you want to get involved in improving local literacy, seek out **Big Brother Mouse**, a home-grown initiative that aims to bring the delights of the written word to infants who, for lack of materials, rarely get the chance to read. Buy a few books and carry them with you to donate to children. Or better still, hang out at your local BBM for a couple of hours and read to the kids who attend; the more *falang* drop in, the more children will come to listen. They have a range of colourful self-published books, plus great stories such as *Where the Wild Things Are*, currently being translated into Lao. Look out for them in Luang Nam Tha, Luang Prabang and Vientiane (www.bigbrothermouse.com).

THE GREEN CRUSADE

Nam Ha NPA (National Protected Area) was the first of 18 eco parks set up in '93 by the Lao government to protect its wildlife and forests from slash-and-burn farming, hunting and logging. Unlike Thailand which seems to have learned too late, Laos is flourishing as an eco-conscious nation – if you forget about the destructive HE power dams and logging licenses granted to the Chinese, who are munching their way through ancient teak and rosewood forests (in return for aiding with road-building and the odd stadium in Vientiane for the Asean Games 2009). To be fair, Laos is still one of the poorest nations on earth, trying desperately to become self-sufficient; the fact the government has welcomed international eco-advice is encouraging in itself.

The environmental blueprint, designed to benefit both travellers and ethnic peoples in a sustainable controlled way, has improved hygiene, education and commerce. A number of villages receiving organised visits from trekkers have seen a reduction in opium addiction and a renewed zeal to preserve their natural heritage. Your visit counts.

main road). Besides offering a range of easy to difficult one- to four-day treks with experienced local guides, Green Discovery has been careful to limit the numbers of travellers in its groups and the frequency with which tribes are visited. So far the low-impact blueprint is working; 32% of the money you pay goes directly to the village visited. If possible, try and remember to take some spare toothpaste, soap and biros to give away.

For **mountain biking** tours contact the **Boat Landing Guest House** (☎ 312398; www.theboatlanding.com), which runs one- to four-day tours of the dramatic Nam Tha valley for around US$30 a day. Places of interest within easy cycling distance include two 50-year-old wats, **Wat Ban Vieng Tai** and **Wat Ban Luang Khon**, near the airfield; a hill-top stupa, **That Phum Phuk**, about 4km west of the airfield; a small **waterfall** about 3km northeast of town past **Ban Nam Dee**; plus a host of **Khmu, Lenten, Thai Dam** and **Thai Lü** villages dotted along dirt roads through rice fields.

SLEEPING

Thanks to a growing number of local entrepreneurs eager for a slice of the *falang* eco-rush, fresh and reasonably priced accommodation is popping up all over town. Cuisine here is equally diverse and Western-friendly. If you want to get off the beaten path there are a couple of cafés opposite the bus station.

Many Chan Guest House (☎ 312209; r 20,000-40,000 kip) Family run, consistently friendly accommodation. Rooms are generous with fan and hot water and an atmospheric balconied café serving up Thai, Lao and Western fare.

Luang Kham Guest House (☎ 211888; r 40,000 kip) If you're catching an early morning ride down the river from the boat landing, this is a good place to stay. Accommodation here is clean and roomy, with hot water and TVs in the heart of old town Luang Namtha.

Bounthavong Guest House (☎ 312256; r 40,000 kip) Peaceful accommodation set off a side road near the Coffee House, Bounthavong sports 10 fresh rooms that are generous on size, and cool thanks to the tiled floors. Hot water and fan are included in the price.

Bus Station Guest House (☎ 211090 r 40,000-50,000 kip) Positioned near the market and bus station, these secluded bungalows offer hot water, and some have TV. That said they're screaming for a lick of paint (someone with muddy shoes has been playing Spiderman on the walls).

Khamking Guest House (r 50,000 kip) Situated next to Many Chan, this new and pristine accommodation, comprising 15 rooms with fan and tiled floors, really does deliver. Immaculate bathrooms with hot water and a great laundry service next door.

Dalsavath Guest House (☎ 211299; r with shared bathroom 50,000 kip) Beside Lao Airlines at the southern edge of the strip, this place has seven bungalows with hot water.

Tipphavanh Guest House (r 50,000 kip) This is a good place to stay if you want the peace of the old town and consider the steep prices of the Boat Landing beyond your range. Tipphavanh is situated a few kilometres past the latter toward Huay Xai. If your driver is confused, mention the Teacher Training College; you'll find the guesthouse a further two klicks from here.

Saikhonglongsack Guest House (☎ 312257; r 50,000 kip) Next to Lao Telecom and a little threadbare, this last resort is being edged off the map by superior upstarts. Rooms are basic and functional.

our pick Zuela Guest House (☎ 312183; r 60,000 kip) Tucked down a quiet lane beside Many Chan, this handsomely built guesthouse of wood and brick offers large rooms with wooden floors, hot water and fan. Within its tranquil, landscaped courtyard is a great restaurant. It's easily the best bet in Luang Nam Tha.

Palanh Guest House (☎ 312439; r 60,000 kip) Next to the Yamuna Restaurant and a little noisy thanks to its proximity to the main road, the 11 rooms in this modern-style house are clean with hot water and internet services in the lobby.

EATING

Panda Restaurant (mains 10,000-20,000 kip) Two blocks east of the bus station, Panda has moved more times than Liz Taylor's had husbands (and is due for another relocation). Great fruit shakes and a generally Oriental and Western menu. Sweet and sour chicken is mouth-watering.

Coffee House (mains 10,000-20,000 kip) An open eatery with a comprehensive Western and Thai menu, this new *falang* magnet serves fantastic lattes and cappuccinos. Great fruit shakes, plus a friendly atmosphere will have you coming back for more. Nithat, the owner, is also an ecologist and worth a chat if you're interested in finding out more about environmental matters.

our pick Yamuna Restaurant (☎ 211529; meals 10,000-20,000 kip) Delicious Indian food to rival the omnipresent Nazim. Generous portions, excellent service and low-lit ambience all make this one of the best places to eat after a long day's trek.

Baytong Restaurant (mains 20,000 kip) Just north of Palanh Guest House this is an authentic eatery offering Lao and Chinese food. Noodles are cooked up in a bubbling cauldron before your eyes.

Over the road from the Baytong Restaurant are food stalls which spring to life after twilight. Eating barbequed grub by candlelight is a nice way to meet local people and save a little money.

GETTING THERE & AWAY

Air

Currently Luang Nam Tha airport is closed for refurbishment until 2008. Given Lao time that may well mean 2009, so if you're pushed for time and want to trek here, take the daily flight from Vientiane to Udomxai (US$80) and catch the bus headed for Luang Nam Tha (four hours).

Boat

Charter boats headed for Pak Tha (US$100) or Huay Xai (US$110) can be caught at the Boat Landing Guest House in the old town. Boats run all year except sometimes in the dry season (March to May) when river levels become dangerously low. The figures above can be split between up to 10 people, but make sure you bring shade or shelter with you as the boats are open-topped. Also ensure the price agreed at dock is written down to avoid any later misunderstandings.

Bus

The bus station is next to the morning market and about 400m west of the main road. Buses for Luang Prabang leave each morning at 9.30am (70,000 kip, nine hours) and Vientiane at 8.30am (90,000 kip, 20 hours).

GETTING AROUND

Bicycles (10,000 kip per day), mountain bikes (15,000 kip per day) and not-in- exemplary-condition scooters (80,000 kip per day) are for rent at **Yook Mai** (☎ 312183; 🕑 7am-6pm), north of the Many Chan Guest House. Other guesthouses and shops hire bicycles for 10,000 kip.

Muang Sing

☎ 081

Within whispering distance of China, this mountainous border town offers an authentic

> **GETTING TO CHINA**
>
> Crossing the Chinese border at Boten is easy provided you have your visa already. There are regular buses to Boten from Luang Nam Tha (one hour) and Udomxai (four hours). From Mohan, on the Chinese side, it's a two- to three-hour ride to Mengla, the nearest large town and a good stopover point on the way north.

atmosphere of wilting shop-fronts (punctuated occasionally by the broken form of an opium addict) and an extremely rich diversity of ethnic hill tribes, including Hmong, Akha, Thai Lu, Lolo and Thai Deu; many of whom you're likely to see at the colourful local market. The town's main draw however, is its reputation as a trekker's paradise, ideally situated for visits to the jungle of the nearby Nam Ha Protected Area or local hill tribes. If you're keen to visit ethnic minorities on a socially and environmentally responsible tour, this is possibly your best bet in Southeast Asia.

Muang Sing follows a quadratic grid pattern. A map of the old city is on display in the Visitor Information & Trekking Guide Services Office, just north of the post office.

INFORMATION

Muang Sing has two banks, a **BCL** branch and the **Lane Xang Bank** opposite the market, changing US dollars, baht and yuan. The post office is opposite the market.

The **Visitor Information & Trekking Guide Services** (☎ 020 570 80318; 8-11.30am & 2-5.30pm) is just north of the post office. Bicycles are available for rent around town for between 5000 and 10,000 kip per day.

SIGHTS & ACTIVITIES

Most people come to Muang Sing for the trekking. Unlike Thailand, Laos has gone to considerable trouble to ensure its ethnic culture is viewed with minimal invasion.Thanks to an ethnically friendly blueprint developed by the **Visitor Information & Trekking Guide Services** (☎ 020 570 80318; 8-11.30am & 2-5.30pm), a little wooden building that's signposted off the main street, you can visit without too much of the 'human zoo' guilt clouding your experience. A minimum of five people is required (costs US$15 per person). After the guide has been paid, the money goes directly to the tribe. Drug use is banned on these treks. Guides include former farmers, teachers, police and agricultural workers.

The **Nam Ha National Protected Area (NPA)** is nearby and offers the intrepid an adventure into pristine, triple-canopied jungle; a few minutes into the feral cathedral and you'll be looking for Col Kurtz, your daydream *possibly* broken by the roar of a local tiger – it happens!

In a beautiful Lao-French wooden building further north on the main street is the **Muang Sing Exhibitions Museum** (admission 5000 kip; 8.30am-4.30pm Mon-Fri, 8.30-11.30am Sat). A photographic exhibition, 'The Last Guardians of the Mountains', is dedicated to the hill tribes of the area, represented in honest up-close black-and-white portraits.

Next to Sing Charean Hotel, a small family-run **traditional massage & sauna** (sauna/massage 10,000/30,000 kip) has been set up in a bamboo thatched building, with the herbal sauna located out the back.

SLEEPING & EATING

Thanks to a raft of new accommodation, you no longer have to worry about your guesthouse falling over. Here are a few gems and slightly more vertical flophouses.

Thai Lu Guest House (r 20,000-30,000 kip) Ageing rooms in a wooden building near the BCL bank on the main street. Offering hot water and mossie nets. Rooms out front are best, with a friendly restaurant – the town's main *falang* nucleus – downstairs. Try the sticky rice pancake.

Muang Sing Guest House (r 20,000-30,000) Flophouse ambience, offering a great rooftop in the main house from where to ponder the sunset mountains and crumbling nearby wat. The owner is a delightful multilingual lady who will make you feel welcome, even if the room won't.

Adima Guest House (☎ 212372; s/d with shared/private bathroom 40,000/60,000 kip) Comfortable accommodation 8km north of Muang Sing, this tranquil guesthouse is favoured among travellers wishing to do their own trek from here to neighbouring Akha and Yao villages – hand-drawn maps available from reception. Rooms vary from wooden to brick bungalow accommodation.

Anousone Guest House (r 50,000 kip) Next to Muang Sing hospital, Anousone is fresh, new and well worth the five-minute walk out of town. Rooms are spacious and cool with tiled floors.

Sangduane Guest House (☎ 212376; r 50,000 kip) With nine large rooms, each with fan, plus two more intimate bungalows out the back, this is tranquil accommodation 100m north of the main street. Also has a restaurant with a karaoke machine to relive those Dean Martin fantasies.

our pick **Phouiou Guest House** (r 60,000 kip) Set off the south end of the main drag, Phouiou boasts nine lovingly crafted rattan cabanas

LAOS

placed in a flowered, landscaped garden. With spotlessly clean rooms, hot water, fan and friendly management, this accommodation is worth every dollar compared to the sloppy competition.

Chieng Theung Guest House (☎ 312085; r 70,000 kip) This hidden gem is situated 5km south of Muang Sing on a hillside overlooking the rice paddy. The wooden bungalows are comfortable, tastefully-finished with hot water, and most importantly, a sense of peace barely equalled in town with exception to Phouiou.

Many of the guesthouses, as is normal in Laos, double as restaurants; however, beyond the friendly, reasonably comprehensive menu at Thai Lu, there's only the **Hasina Indian Restaurant** (mains 7000-25,000 kip) worth a visit. You'll find it at the northern end of town after the bridge.

Fresh fruit and vegetables as well as local delicacies can be bought at the **morning market** (🕑 6-8am). To get here, turn left (west) at the exhibitions building and then right (north) two blocks up. *Fŏe* (rice noodle) stands are bustling early in the morning, and Laos' ubiquitous roaming baguette vendors sell fresh rolls with condensed milk for breakfast.

GETTING THERE & AROUND

Săwngthăew leave from the bus station in front of the morning market for Luang Nam Tha at 8am, 9.30am and 11am (20,000 kip, one to two hours). Heading west, săwngthăew bound for Muang Long leave four times a day between 8am and 1pm (15,000 kip, two hours). Heading southwest, for Xieng Kok on the Burmese border, săwngthăew (19,000 kip, three to four hours) depart at 9.30am, 11am, 1pm and 2pm. From Xieng Kok it's possible to charter a boat down the Mekong to Huay Xai (outside of the dry season).

Bicycles are available to rent (5000 kip per day) from several shops on the main road, for journeys to local villages.

BOKEO PROVINCE

Laos' smallest province, wedged between the Mekong River border with Thailand and Luang Nam Tha Province, is a popular entry point for travellers from Thailand. Despite Bokeo's small size and tiny population, the province is home to 34 different ethnic groups, second only to Luang Nam Tha for ethnic diversity.

Huay Xai

☎ 084 / pop 17,500

Hugging the banks of the Mekong, overlooking Thailand's Chiang Khong, Huay Xai is a major border-entry point, as well as being the HQ of the much talked about **Gibbon Experience** (www.gibbonx.org), a three-day gibbon watch in tree-houses perched high above the Bokeo Nature Reserve. Travellers freshly arrived from Thailand needn't concern themselves Huay Xai is the shape of Laos to come; just two days south on a slow boat will take you to the majesty of Luang Prabang (six hours on a speedboat if you're a masochist) or five hours north to sleepy Luang Namtha. That said, the locals are friendly and by night the dusty street is aglow with burning braziers and fairy lights.

INFORMATION

The **Lao Development Bank** (🕑 8.30am-3.30pm Mon-Fri), opposite Arimid Guest House, is 200m up the hill from the slow-boat landing.

The **post office** (🕑 8am-4pm Mon-Fri) also contains a telephone office.

Phoudoi Travel (☎ 020 598 5732) offers one-day tours to Thai Du ethnic villages combined with visits to the waterfalls. Speak to Saytha.

SLEEPING & EATING

A recent boom in Thai-Roman-style guest houses has seen a slight improvement in what you can expect for your money, plus a number of stalwart traveller favourites are still turning a good trade.

Friendship Guest House (☎ 211219; Th Saykhong; r 40,000-60,000 kip) With its breezy rooftop views, communal satellite TV and clean, spacious rooms, the Friendship Guest House is a good place to hang your hat. The owner's a genuine individual, his English is solid and he can arrange your bus and boat tickets. All rooms have a fan.

BAP Guest House (☎ 211083; Th Saykhong; r 40,000-70,000) This old trusty offers immaculate, wood-veneered rooms, communal places to chat and an adequate restaurant. The owner can organise onward travel and day trips. Rooms overlooking the Mekong are the best but expect to pay more.

Sabaydee (☎ 020 548 4075; Th Saykhong; r incl breakfast 60,000-70,000 kip) Well-situated Thai-style villa offering 14 clean rooms with fan. It's 100m north of BAP Guest House.

Armid Guest House (☎ 211040; Ban Huay Xai Neua; r 60,000-150,000) Located 200m from the slow-boat landing, this secluded complex is a peaceful place to stay if you want to get out of town. The wooden bungalows are well constructed, there's a decent restaurant and multilingual owner who's happy to dispense advice – just don't try and haggle on price!

Oudomphone Guest House (r 70,000-80,000 kip) Set slightly off the main drag, Oudomphone is fresh and new with fans in all its rooms. There's also a restaurant downstairs.

Riverview Restaurant (mains 20,000 kip) Atmospheric diner featuring reindeer ornamented rattan walls; you may feel like you've stepped into an old colonial living room. Wood-fired pizzas and local staple are fresh, as are the fruit shakes – electricity allowing. Perhaps the best place to meet other *falang*, absorb their stories and plan your route accordingly. It's a few doors down from BAP.

Deen Restaurant (mains 30,000 kip) Just down the road from the Friendship, Deen offers crisp, no-nonsense Indian cuisine. The chicken tikka masala is particularly delicious as is the wood-fired nan bread.

GETTING THERE & AWAY

Lao Airlines (code QV; www.laos-airlines.com) flies Monday, Wednesday and Friday from Huay Xai to Vientiane (US$90) and Luang Prabang (US$50).

The ferry ride to Chiang Khong costs 20B. The border to Thailand is open from 8.30am to 5pm; the same opening hours apply to arriving in Laos. At weekends and after 4pm it's normal for Lao border guards to charge 15B surcharge. On crossing the border you'll automatically be granted a 30-day visa (US$35).

Thanks to the all but finished Highway 3, the bus journey to Luang Namtha is no longer a tortuous experience; minibuses (which can be organised at BAP, Phoudoi and Friendship guesthouses and cost 400B) leave at 11am and take an easy five hours.

Boats for Luang Prabang leave at around 11.30am from the boat landing at the north end of town, costing US$13 per person. Get there the afternoon before to buy a ticket or purchase one through your guesthouse. The trip takes two days by slow boat (US$25), with an overnight stop in Pak Beng, and is a great way to take in the increasingly dramatic scenery toward Luang Prabang, but check whether your boat offers views and if you're allowed on deck. In high heat it can be unbearable if you're stowed away in the bowels of your charter. If asked to pay for insurance, refuse point blank; it's a scam.

Speedboats for Luang Prabang (US$40) leave from the landing 2km south of town at 11am. The trip takes six hours and unless you love white-knuckle experiences, don't mind being cramped and narrowly avoiding pillars of underwater rocks, this may not be your idea of fun. Helmets and life-jackets are provided. In the dry season it's advised not to travel; officially sanctioned boats are forbidden; however, there's always someone prepared to take the risk. Considering someone dies in these flimsy boats almost yearly it's worth asking yourself if you're really in that much of a hurry.

One of the most talked about boat journeys is the route upriver to Luang Nam Tha (impossible in the dry season), terminating at the now famous Boat Landing Eco lodge (ww.theboatlanding.laopdr.com). Boats take up to 10 people with a typical charter costing US$110.

GETTING TO THAILAND

Heading to northern Thailand, cross the border at Huay Xai to Chiang Khong, where there are connecting buses or săwngthăew (small pick-up truck with two benches in the back) to Chiang Rai and Chiang Saen. Huay Xai is accessible by boat from Luang Prabang, Luang Nam Tha and Xieng Kok or by bus from Luang Nam Tha. The ferry ride to Chiang Khong costs 10,000 kip and the Thai border is open from 8.30am to 5pm. Thirty-day visas are issued on arrival on either side. At weekends or during their lunch hour, Lao immigration officers charge an additional 10,000 kip 'overtime' fee. Boats from Pak Beng almost always arrive just a little too late to make the border crossing to Thailand as do buses from Luang Nam Tha. So make sure you're not on the last day of your Laos visa, or you'll be charged for overstaying.

See p744 for information on travelling in the reverse direction.

SOUTHERN LAOS

The tourist industry is much less developed in southern Laos than in the north, with only a handful of areas visited by travellers heading to and from Vietnam and Cambodia. Most travellers make time to visit the Unesco World Heritage–listed Khmer ruins at Wat Phu Champasak and otherworldly Si Phan Don (Four Thousand Islands). However, the lush fertile highlands of the Bolaven Plateau, with its coffee plantations and dramatic, plunging waterfalls, and the faded charms of Savannakhet are also must-sees on your travels around the south.

SAVANNAKHET PROVINCE

Savannakhet

☎ 041 / pop 120,000

Laos' third-largest city is a confection of beautifully faded Indochinese mansions and flat-topped Soviet-style houses. Indeed, the crumbling colonial buildings, some sheltering food vendors, others overgrown with weeds, have a ghostly charm that has been lost in the gentrification of Luang Prabang. The streets are abloom with bougainvillea, and the locals are still curious about visitors. Thanks to the recent opening of the Mekong Bridge, further connecting Laos with Thailand, the city's status as an important trade hub has been resuscitated.

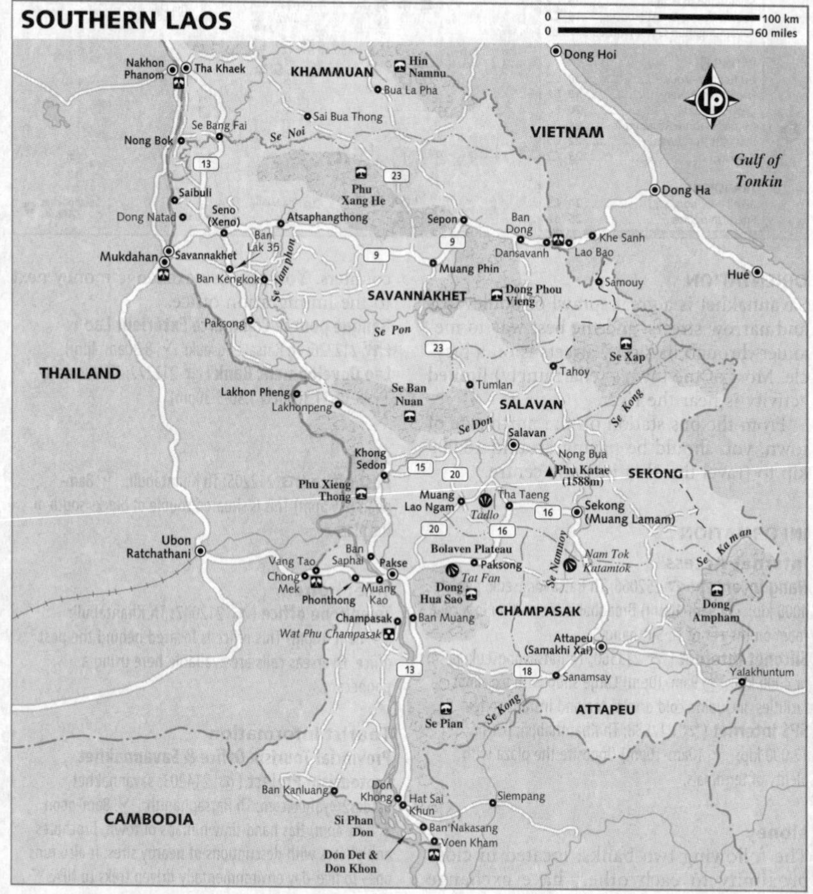

ORIENTATION

Savannakhet is a great sprawl of boulevards and narrow streets, and the best way to meander through its sleepy streets is on a bicycle. Most of the town's (charmingly) limited activity is near the river.

From the bus station on the north side of town, you should be paying around 10,000 kip to travel the 2km into the centre.

INFORMATION

Internet Access

Nang Internet (☎ 252066; Th Ratsavongseuk; per hr 4000 kip; 9am-10pm) Broadband connection in a cool room on the cnr of Th Sutthanu.

Silconet Internet (☎ 213560; Th Ratsavongseuk; per hr 4000 kip; 9am-10pm) Large shop with excellent facilities, including cold drinks, tea and instant coffee.

SPS Internet (☎ 212888; Th Khanthabuli; per hr 12,000 kip; 10am-10pm) Opposite the plaza with plenty of terminals.

Money

The following two banks, located in close proximity to each other, have exchange counters. You can also exchange money next to the immigration office.

Banque pour le Commerce Extérieur Lao (☎ 212226; Th Ratsavongseuk; 8.30am-4pm)

Lao Development Bank (☎ 212272; Th Udomsin; 8.30-11.30am & 1.30-3.30pm)

Post

Post office (☎ 212205; Th Khantabuli; 8am-noon & 1-5pm) This is situated couple of blocks south of the plaza.

Telephone

Telephone office (☎ 212047; Th Khantabuli; 8am-10pm) This office is located behind the post office. Overseas calls are available here using a phonecard.

Tourist Information

Provincial Tourism Office & Savannakhet Ecotourism Project (☎ 214203; savannakhetguides2@yahoo.com; Th Ratsaphanith; 8am-noon & 1.30-4pm) Has hand-drawn maps of town, brochures and photos with descriptions of nearby sites. It also runs one- to five-day environmentally driven treks to NPAs

BEER SHOPS

If an establishment looks like a restaurant, but inside there are only men sitting around drinking beer and there's no sign of a kitchen or menu, you have probably stumbled on one of Laos' 'special' beer shops, where a bottle of draught is sometimes followed by an appointment with a friendly lady whose affections come at a price.

in the region, which leave on different days of the week with a minimum number of participants. Nang, a lovely lady, works here both as a guide and info officer and her English is solid.

SIGHTS & ACTIVITIES

The **Savannakhet Provincial Museum** (Th Khantabuli; admission 5000 kip; 8-11.30am & 1-4pm Mon-Sat) is a good place to see war relics, artillery pieces and inactive examples of the deadly UXO that has claimed the lives of over 10,000 Lao (one third of them children) over the last 30 years. There's also a display dedicated to political leader Kaysone Phomvihane, who was born only 1km away from Savannakhet. To gain access to the collection try the curator's house – a wooden building in the southwest corner of the School of Medicine compound.

The nostalgia-evoking exhibits at the **Dinosaur Museum** (212597; Th Khantabuli; admission 1000 kip; 8am-noon & 1-4pm Mon-Fri) inspire a certain childlike wonderment at prehistoric times. Savannakhet Province is home to five dinosaur sites. This is a well-presented little museum with an enthusiastic curator.

The oldest and largest monastery in southern Laos, **Wat Sainyaphum** (Th Tha He) was originally built in 1542, although most of what stands today is from the last century. The grounds are large and include a couple of centuries-old trees; the one by the northern gate is colourfully decorated with a small shrine at its base.

Lao Red Cross (214670; Th Phetsalat; 10am-9pm) offers traditional herbal sauna (15,000 kip) plus vigorous Lao-style massages (25,000 kip). Money raised, coupled with donations from the government, Médecins Sans Frontières and Unicef, helps fund AIDS-prevention workshops and care for those in the province infected with HIV.

SLEEPING

our pick **Saisouk Guest House** (212207; Th Phetsalat; r 30,000-50,000 kip) A few blocks south of the centre, this large wooden house is spotlessly clean and the owner welcoming. There's also a communal area with a large TV to catch up on the news (satellite). One room comes with air-con and private bathroom. Showers are cold-water only. The guesthouse's gates are locked at 11pm.

Savan Phatthana Guest House (214242; Th Saenna; r 30,000-50,000 kip) An OK option if Souannavong Guest House is full, or you're on a tighter budget. The rooms, off a wide corridor, are a little musty and resident geckos are complimentary. All have fans and attached cold-water bathrooms without sinks.

Xayamungkhun Guest House (212426; Th Ratsavongseuk; r 35,000-80,000 kip;) In one of the last colonial-era buildings still being used as a guesthouse, Xayamungkhun has clean wood-floored rooms with an inviting atmosphere. The downstairs sitting area has a shelf full of second-hand books to peruse.

Savanbanhao Hotel (212202; Th Saenna; r 45,000-90,000 kip;) Plenty of rooms, all with electric hot water, though a little shabby and nondescript. Also hires scooters for US$8 per day, more if you want to leave the city. The restaurant is now closed as is the tour agency which used to operate here.

Leena Guest House (212404; Th Chao Kim; r 50,000-60,000 kip;) One of the better guesthouses, rooms here are quiet and shaded with air-con and fan. There's a sense of pride and sanitary obsessiveness (extending as far as free contraceptives).

Souannavong Guest House (Th Semma; 212600; r 60,000-80,000 kip) Fresh accommodation offering shady spots to read with very clean rooms with fan and hot water. It is located down a peaceful bougainvillea-bordered street.

EATING

With only a few restaurants catering for the Western palate, Savannakhet has a more authentic feel to its gastronomy than some of the major places you'll visit. Besides the places highlighted here, there are also dozens of street-side vendors (especially by the river in the evening) serving up local food and atmosphere to go with it.

Starlight Restaurant (213026; Th Sainyamungkhun; mains 2000 kip; breakfast, lunch & dinner) Situated in

GETTING TO THAILAND

To Mukdahan

With the bridge at the Savannakhet–Mukdahan border now built, you no longer have to catch the ferry to Thailand. Buses leave Savannakhet's Public Bus Station to Mukdahan every hour from 8.15am till 7pm. The border is open from 9am to 4.30pm; travellers are automatically granted a free 30-day visa on arrival in Thailand. It's a long way south to Ubon, where you can catch a night sleeper train or VIP bus to Bangkok.

See p756 for information on doing the journey in the reverse direction.

To Nakhon Phanom

Another river border crossing further south takes you from Tha Khaek in Laos to Nakhon Phanom in Thailand, although it is rarely used by *falang* (foreigners).

There are frequent sǎwngthǎew (small pick-up truck with two benches in the back) and buses to Tha Khaek from Savannakhet (see opposite for details), and boats between Tha Khaek and Nakhon Phanom run half a dozen times a day.

The border is open from 8.30am to 3.30pm daily, and free 30-day Thai visas are granted to most nationalities on entry.

See p757 for information on doing the trip from Thailand to Laos.

an attractive colonial building, Starlight has a dazzlingly comprehensive menu ranging from steamboat barbeque to Western, noodles and a handsome selection of Mekong seafood. Try the fried squid…umm!

Mama's Home Restaurant (☎ 231592; off Th Mak Haveha; meals 5000-15,000 kip) A few blocks from the centre but well worth the trek. Follow the signs from the canal and bring a torch (flashlight) if it's after dark. Literally in Mama's home replete with photos of her kids on the walls. You can catch up on some cable TV news, or watch a film – you just have to ask.

Lao-Paris Cafe (☎ 212792; Th Si Muang; meals 8000-25,000 kip; 🕑 lunch & dinner) Located across the road from the old ferry terminal, this *falang* haunt is a low-ceilinged affair decorated with red lanterns and stone floors. The menu covers both Lao and French food. The service is indifferent but who cares – the food is good and the place has atmosphere.

Friendship Bakery (Th Tha Dan; ☎ 213026; meals 10,000-20,000kip; 🕑 breakfast & lunch) Next to the now derelict Santyphab Hotel, this fresh, new café has a fine array of alchemized chocolate fudge brownies, cakes and pastries.

Au Rendez-Vous (☎ 213181; Th Ratsavongseuk; meals 10,000-30,000 kip; 🕑 breakfast, lunch & dinner) Open, ventilated restaurant on the busiest road in town, serving a range of Chinese, Vietnamese and international dishes. Sadly the service is lacking due to the Thai music channel blaring from the TV a few yards away.

Xokxay (☎ 213122; Th Si Muang; mains 20,000 kip; 🕑 breakfast, lunch & dinner) Tucked at the side of the square down from the Catholic church, this authentic little diner delivers with chiefly Chinese and Lao food, and Western breakfasts.

For a Lao-style dinner on a budget try the riverside vendors that are situated both north and south of the ferry pier, plus the restaurants on the plaza.

GETTING TO VIETNAM

If you're heading through Laos in a hurry to get to Vietnam, Rte 9 takes you from Savannakhet to the Dansavanh–Lao Bao border; this is the most popular land crossing into Vietnam. It takes 3½ hours to travel from Savannakhet to Dansavanh; bus times and tickets are available from the Provincial Tourist Office (p392). From the border, you're near Hué, but a long way south of Hanoi if you wanted to visit Vietnam's north. Buses go to Dong Ha in Vietnam (nine hours), from where there are connecting buses to Hué (three hours), Danang (six hours) and Hanoi (15 hours). A tourist bus also does the trip every other day.

See p858 for information on doing the journey in the opposite direction.

GETTING THERE & AWAY

Lao Airlines (code QV; ☎ 212140; www.laos-airlines.com) flies twice weekly to Savannakhet from Vientiane (US$60).

Buses to Vientiane (55,000 kip, eight to 10 hours) leave from the bus terminal at the north end of town from 6am until 6pm. A VIP express bus leaves the private bus station (70,000 kip, six to seven hours) at 9.30am. For Tha Khaek, frequent sǎwngthǎew (20,000 kip, two to three hours) depart all morning, enabling you to stop for a few hours to break up the journey to Vientiane. All public buses heading north go via the bus station on the outskirts of Tha Khaek.

Heading south, regular buses (US$12, five hours) depart all morning for Pakse. A tourist bus to Dong Ha in Vietnam leaves from the Savanbanhao Hotel (US$12, nine hours) at 7.30am.

GETTING AROUND

A túk-túk to the bus station or just about any location around Savannakhet costs 5000 kip per person. Bicycles can be rented from the **Friendship Shop** (☎ 213026; Th Si Muang; per day 10,000 kip; 8am-7pm) or a **bike hire shop** (☎ 213149, 020 565 8379; Th Ratsavongseuk; per day 10,000 kip; 8am-6pm), two doors north of Xayamungkhun Guest House.

Pakse

☎ 031 / pop 70,000

Pakse is very much the transport hub of the south thanks to its location beside the Mekong and the country's main highway, Rte 13. It's generally viewed as a stepping-stone by travellers en route to Si Phan Don further south or fresh out of Cambodia heading north. Perhaps not the most photogenic place, it has an easy charm and is a great base for day trips to ancient Wat Phu, sleepy Don Kho, and waterfalls Tad Lo and Tad Fan, high up in the coffee-growing region of the Bolaven Plateau. Thanks to the opening of a **Green Discovery branch** (☎ 252908; www.greendiscoverylaos.com; Rte 13), white-water rafting trips and three-day paddles to Si Phan Don are taking form.

ORIENTATION

Central Pakse is bound by the Mekong to the south and by the Se Don to the north and west. Rte 13 cuts through the northern edge of town. On and below Rte 13 towards the Mekong are most of Pakse's guesthouses, shops and restaurants. Heading west across Se Don takes you to the northern bus terminal. The southern bus station and market are 8km in the opposite direction.

INFORMATION

Emergency

Hospital (☎ 212018; cnr Th 10 & Th 46)

Police (☎ 212145; Th 10)

Internet Access

@d@m's Internet (☎ 251445; Rte 13; per hr 5000 kip) Fast connections, but the extra expense per minute – even if time is calculated more accurately than elsewhere – was sending customers to other outlets.

Lankham Internet (☎ 213314; Rte 13; per hr 6000 kip) Broadband connection in a cool room annexed to the Lankham Hotel, drinks available.

Vandersa Internet Service (☎ 212982; Rte 13; per min 200 kip; 8am-11pm) Internet plus fruit shakes, the perfect combination!

Money

There is one **ATM** in town, at the **Banque pour le Commerce Exterieur Lao** (☎ 212770; Th 11; 8.30am-3.30pm Mon-Fri), which also offers good rates and does cash advances from Monday to Friday. The ATM however, only accepts cards with a MasterCard symbol and often runs out of cash at the weekend. If the latter happens your only option for exchanging cash and travellers cheques or getting a cash advance, all for a hefty commission, is at **Champa Residence Hotel** (☎ 212120; Rte 13), 2km east of the centre. If you have no joy here and your time is short, you'll have to head over to Thailand and have your driver wait while you cross the border (with an explanation to Thai passport control you can leave your passport with them without getting stamped, while you pop to the ATM).

Lao Development Bank (☎ 212168; Rte 13; 8.30am-3.30pm) Exchanges travellers cheques and cash.

Post

Post office (☎ 212293; cnr Th 1 & Th 8; 8am-noon & 1-5pm)

Travel Agencies

Diethelm Travel (☎ 212596; dtlpkz@laotel.com; Th 21) Around the corner from Sabaidy 2 Guesthouse. Organises tours to the Bolaven Plateau and Wat Phu Champasak.

Green Discovery (☎ 252908; Rte 13; www.greendiscoverylaos.com) Still finding its feet here, offering white-water rafting, treks to the Bolaven Plateau and three-day canoeing trips down to Four Thousand Islands. It can also

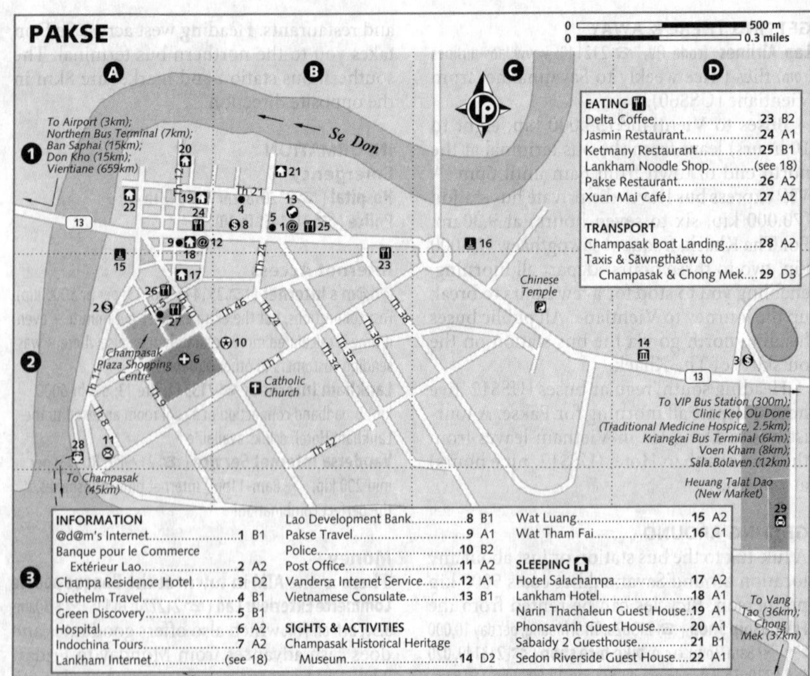

provide minibus transport to Four Throusand Islands for a competitive US$6, leaving at 8.30am and 11.30am (2½hr).

Indochina Tours (☎ 212620) At the northern entrance to the market off Rte 5, Indochina is a good place to head for advice; organises visas, trips to Wat Phu, travel tickets. Some of the staff speak good English.

Pakse Travel (☎ 277277; Rte 13) Next to the Lankham Hotel, this little outfit can organise visas, forward travel tickets north and south and a range of treks.

SIGHTS & ACTIVITIES

There are 20 wats in town, the largest are **Wat Luang**, featuring ornate concrete pillars and carved wooden doors and murals, and **Wat Tham Fai**, which has a small Buddha footprint shrine in its grounds.

The Champasak Historical Heritage Museum (Rte 13; admission 3000 kip; 8-11.30am & 1-4pm) documents the history of the province, with historical photos and ethnological displays. Some exhibits have captions in English, for others you'll have to let the pictures tell the story.

For a vigorous Lao massage (albeit slightly distracted by pressing mobile-phone calls) **Clinic Keo Ou Done** (Traditional Medicine Hospice; ☎ 251895; 4-9pm Mon-Fri & 10am-9pm Sat) can be found down a road off to the right, 100m before the Km 3 marker east along Rte 13.

For the languid fishing island of **Don Kho**, an easy 30km drive south of Pakse, head north out of town following signs for Savannakhet, and take the Ban Xaphai turn on your left. A pleasant ride past buffalo-dotted emerald paddy takes you to the port where you can catch a longtail for US$2. The island itself has a couple of wats, a handicraft market and motley gang of toddlers who may extort money from you on the northern tip of the island.

For something different, **Sala Bolaven** (☎ 020 580 0787; Km 12 Rte 16; 9am-4pm) offers free tastings and sells produce exported to Europe through the Fair Trade network. Try jams, iced tea, Lao Bia (palm beer), local wine and coffee. To get here take Rte 13 to the southern bus station and follow the road to the left towards Paksong. It's a 12km slightly uphill (downhill on the way home!) bike ride, or a 10,000-kip túk-túk ride. The newish shop has outdoor seating and at the time of research there was talk of opening a small kitchen down the track.

SLEEPING

our pick Sabaidy 2 Guesthouse (☎ 212992; Th 24; dm 20,000 kip, r 40,000-50,000 kip) This old-timbered French building is a traveller's rest. The owner, Mr Vong, extends a warmth and hospitality unrivalled elsewhere in town. Free maps are available should you decide to rent one of their mopeds (US$8 per day) and explore the Bolaven Plateau. There's a pleasant arbour to chill and meet others. Rooms are basic, all with fan. Beds could be comfier and less itchy but it's the atmosphere you pay for here.

Sedon Riverside Guest House (☎ 212735; Th 10; r from 40,000 kip) A tranquil setting with great views of the river from a secluded communal area. Rooms are large with fan but nothing to shout about. What it lacks in finesse, Sedon compensates with the friendliness of its staff; the owner may offer you a free coconut with a straw in it on your arrival.

Phonsavanh Guest House (☎ 212482; Th 12; r 50,000-70,000 kip) Tucked down a dirt road, this is an adequate prospect with simple fan rooms, some with en suites and hot showers. Management is a little surly though.

Lankham Hotel (☎ 213314; latchan@laotel.com; Rte 13; r 50,000-80,000 kip; ❄) This four-storey behemoth is an old favourite, rooms are clean, some with en suite and TV. Try for one at the back as you get a dramatic view of the mountain. Downstairs is one of Pakse's best noodle shops. Also rents bikes (25,000 kip per day) and Baja motorbikes (US$18 per day).

Narin Thachaleun Guest House (☎ 212927; Th 21; r 60,000-80,000 kip; ❄) This place has 12 rooms, all of them cool with high ceilings in a modern Thai-style house. Nondescript accommodation except for the room in the garage, which offers fine views of a souped-up Morris Minor – seriously!

Hotel Salachampa (☎ 212273; Th 10; r 120,000-170,000; ❄) One of the prettiest remnant French villas in town, Salachampa has sumptuous outside bungalows with air-con or more expensive rooms in the main house. There's also a lovely lounge to sit and read in. Fresh linen every day.

EATING

Ketmany Restaurant (☎ 212615; Rte 13; meals 10,000-30,000 kip; 🕑 lunch & dinner) Lit up like Christmas, Ketmany serves decent Chinese and international dishes. Coconut ice cream recommended. Does the owner remind you of a Lao Basil Fawlty?

Delta Coffee (☎ 212488; Rte 13; meals 15,000-30,000 kip; 🕑 breakfast, lunch & dinner) Offering decent Western breakfasts, Italian and Thai food, this popular spot is a five-minute walk from Sabaidy 2. The best cappuccino in Pakse.

Jasmin Restaurant (☎ 251002; Rte 13; meals 20,000 kip; 🕑 breakfast, lunch & dinner) Beside Nazim's, this no-frills backpacker haunt is consistently on form with its tasty southern Indian fare. The wood-fired, envelope-thin nan bread is delicious and the owner, Deen, so welcoming you may be coming back a few times.

Xuan Mai Cafe (Rte 10; meals 20,000-30,000 kip; 🕑 breakfast, lunch & dinner) On the corner of Rtes 5 and 10, this is an authentic pavement joint cooking up sizzling Lao and Vietnamese dishes before your eyes. Street alchemy.

Pakse Restaurant (☎ 212131; Th 5; meals 20,000-40,000 kip) Seven floors up, this new roof-terraced restaurant is both relaxing and dramatic. From this lavish vantage you can see the Mekong rolling by and soak up the sunset with a cool Beer Lao. The menu is keen to please with Lao and Western food on offer. The *lap moo* is pretty tasty.

GETTING THERE & AWAY

Air

Lao Airlines (code QV; ☎ 212252; www.laos-airlines.com; Th 11; 🕑 8am-4pm Mon-Fri) flies to Pakse daily to and from Vientiane (US$100 one way). Flights from Pakse to Siem Reap on Wednesday, Friday and Sunday (US$70) are a good option if you've come this far without a Cambodian visa.

Boat

Regular local boat services run from Pakse to Don Khong via Champasak (US$3 going south, US$5 coming north, six to 10 hours), leaving at 8am from near the junction of the Se Don and the Mekong. You'll be dropped in Ban Hua Khong, a small village near the north tip of Don Khong. From there a túk-túk (1000 kip per person, 12km) or motorcycle taxi (1500 kip) will take you around to Muang Khong where plenty of guesthouses are located. Boats heading back to Pakse usually leave Ban Hua Khong between 6.30am and 8am and take about 11 hours.

Bus & Săwngthăew

There are four different bus stations in Pakse and as such it can be a little confusing. Pakse has several bus and *săwngthăew* terminals.

VIP buses leave the **VIP Bus Station** (Km 2 Bus Station; ☎ 212228), off Rte 13, for Vientiane (US$13, eight to 10 hours, 677km) every evening, though they usually also stop in town.

At the **northern bus terminal** (☎ 251508; Rte 13), agonisingly slow normal buses (without air-con) rattle north every hour or so between 6.30am and 4.30pm for Savannakhet (US$3, four to five hours, 277km), Tha Khaek (US$5.50, eight to nine hours) and, for those with a masochistic streak, Vientiane (US$8.50, 16 to 18 hours).

For transport south and east, go to the Kriangkai bus terminal (aka southern terminal), 8km south of town on Rte 13 and a 5000 kip túk-túk ride away. To Champasak buses (US$1.30, two hours, two daily) depart at 10am and noon. Other departures include Don Khong (US$3, three hours) at 8am and 10am; Tat Lo (US$1.20, two hours) at 9am; and Ban Nakasang for Don Det and Don Khon (US$2, three to four hours) at 7am, 8.30am, 10am and 11.30am. Săwngthăew and pick-up trucks also leave the southern bus station regularly between about 7am and 3pm for Champasak (US$1, two hours), Don Khong (US$3, three hours), Ban Nakasang (US$2, three to four hours) and Voen Kham (US$2.50, three to five hours).

KVT (☎ 212228), which operates out of Kriangkai bus terminal, runs a well-oiled service to Ubon (US$3, 2.30pm, 3.30pm), for those headed over the border to Thailand. Take the earlier bus if you want to ensure getting to Ubon train station to catch the night-sleeper to Bangkok (7pm), or book a through ticket to Bangkok's main bus terminal with KVT (US$18).

Regular săwngthăew and pick-ups leave Talat Dao Heuang (New Market) for the Thai border (see the boxed text, below).

GETTING AROUND

Pakse's main attractions are accessible on foot. Bicycles (10,000 kip per day) and scooters (US$8 to US$10 per day) can be hired from **Sabaidy 2 Guesthouse** (☎ 212992; Th 24) and **Lankham Hotel** (☎ 213314; latchan@laotel.com; Rte 13).

Bolaven Plateau

The fertile Bolaven Plateau (Phu Phieng Bolaven in Lao) rises 1500m above the Mekong valley – a beautiful claw-shaped highland fortress of forests, rivers, waterfalls and plantations. The plateau is a centre for several Mon-Khmer ethnic groups, including the Alak, Laven, Ta-oy, Suay and Katu. The Alak and Katu arrange their palm-and-thatch houses in a circle. They are well known in Laos for a water buffalo sacrifice, which they perform yearly, usually on a full moon in March (see also opposite). The area wasn't farmed intensively until the French planted coffee, rubber and bananas here. Today the Laven, Alak and Katu tribes have revived cultivation and it's here that the distinctive Lao coffee is grown.

TADLO

Cool and peaceful, the broad 10m-high Tadlo falls and Seset River are surrounded by forests and villages inhabited by the Katu and Alak. This is a popular spot for day treks, elephant riding and of course swimming. Although the recent guesthouse boom gives the area a

GETTING TO THAILAND

The crossing at Vang Tao (Laos) and Chong Mek (Thailand) is the busiest in southern Laos and is open from 6am to 5pm daily. From Pakse, săwngthăew (8000 kip, 75 minutes) and taxis run between Talat Dao Heuang and Vang Tao regularly. When you arrive walk up the hill to the building with the green roof, where you'll be stamped in and can buy or sell kip at the exchange office.

Walk through the border to Thai immigration, who'll issue you with a visa; it's free for most nationalities. Continue about 500m to the end of the stall-lined street to the bus station and find a săwngthăew to Phibun (B30, one hour). It will drop you at Chong Mek, a small lively market town where another săwngthăew will soon pick you up for the trip to Ubon Ratchathani (B30, 1½ hours). Buses leave Ubon regularly (including overnight) for Bangkok, and there are several trains as well, including overnight sleepers at 5.55pm (1st class available) and 7.15pm (2nd and 3rd class only); ensure you book ahead to guarantee a berth.

See p755 for information on making the trip in the reverse direction.

resort-like feel, the nearby local village is still distinctly Lao.

Activities

Most travellers spend their time **swimming** around Tadlo and Tadhang, reading, walking in the surrounding forest, and generally relaxing with the sounds of constantly tumbling waterfalls. Tadhang, a few hundred metres along, has a deep swimming hole and is also a popular local fishing spot.

Other activities include **trekking** in the forest either on your own (stick to the track) or with a guide from Tim's Guest House & Restaurant to surrounding villages and waterfalls. Guided treks start at 30,000 kip per person. For more information and maps ask at Tim's. Both Tadlo Lodge and Tim's Guest House & Restaurant organise **elephant rides** through the forest and streams, costing 50,000 kip for 1½ hours. Tim's also hires out bikes for 8000 kip per hour to cycle to local villages.

Sleeping & Eating

Tim's Guest House & Restaurant (☎ 214176; r with shared bathroom 25,000 kip) This is by far the best set-up in Tadlo, with comfortable bungalows, ceiling fans, shared hot-water bathrooms and internet facilities. The restaurant serves breakfast, lunch and dinner (meals 6000 to 15,000 kip). Tim's also offers water-bottle refills (1000 kip), transport to the main road (3000 kip) and a book exchange. The English- and French-speaking owner has travel information in a neighbouring hut.

Sephaseuth Guest House & Restaurant (☎ 214185; r 40,000-60,000 kip) There are five clean – although a little gloomy – rooms here, in a wooden building by the river. The attached restaurant, serving breakfast, lunch and dinner (15,000 to 30,000 kip for a meal), is a popular spot in the afternoon.

Saylomyen Guest House (020 227 5542; r with shared bathroom 30,000 kip) This guesthouse offers the cheapest river views from simple huts with fans.

Getting There & Away

From Pakse, buses heading for Salavan drop you at the Tadlo turn-off (just ask for Tadlo). They leave at 7am, 9am, 10am, 11am and 1pm (12,000 kip, 1½ hours). From the turn-off just after the bridge, it's a 2km walk (or a 3000 kip túk-túk ride) to Tadlo. Leaving Tadlo, get to the bridge early to catch a Pakse bus.

Champasak

☎ 031

Once the capital of a Lao kingdom, Champasak is now a lazy one-street town. The main road runs parallel to the river then turns inland and makes its way to the dramatic mountainside location of Wat Phu Champasak. Most visitors use the town as a base for visiting the ruins, although some choose to see the ruins on a day trip from Pakse. Champasak boasts great views of the Mekong's riverside beaches and a serene atmosphere. Activity centres on the ferry wharf and, at the other end of town, Wat Phu Champasak. Guesthouses are mainly found near the fountain.

This town cranks it up every year when pilgrims from near and far amass for **Bun Wat Phu Champasak**. During this three-day Buddhist festival (usually February) worshippers wind their way up and around Wat Phu Champasak, praying and leaving offerings; bands play traditional and modern music; young and old dance together; and Thai boxing, comedy shows and cockfights all add to the entertainment.

If you've got time, visit the nearby fishing island of **Don Daeng**; secluded, sleepy and utterly unblemished by the tourist trail. There's neither guesthouse nor restaurant to be found, which is what makes the short ferry trip here (3000 kip return) so rewarding. Ask your boatman to pick you up after two hours and take your bike for a blissful trip around the happy-faced island of paddy fields and horizontal locals. There's a beach for swimming in the cool green water, but mind the currents; the wider the river the stronger it gets.

SIGHTS

Overlooking the Mekong valley, **Wat Phu Champasak** (admission 30,000 kip; 8am-4.30pm), while not being in the same league as Angkor Wat, is one of the most impressive archaeological sites in Laos and well worth visiting. It's divided into lower and upper parts and is joined by a steep stone stairway, which will stretch your calves a bit so take a break halfway and take in the valley below. The whole site is earmarked for restoration, but progress appears to be very slow.

The lower part consists of two ruined palace buildings at the edge of a large square pond, itself split in two by a causeway, used for ritual ablutions. The upper section is the temple sanctuary itself, which once enclosed a large Shiva phallus. Some time later the sanctuary was converted into a Buddhist temple, but original Hindu sculpture remains in the lintels. Just north of the Shiva-lingam sanctuary you'll find the elephant stone and the enigmatic crocodile stone (if you can locate it!). The *naga* stairway leading to the sanctuary is lined with *dok jampa* (jacaranda) trees. The upper platform affords spectacular views of the Mekong valley below.

As well as Bun Wat Phu Chamapasak, in February each year a ritual water buffalo sacrifice to the ruling earth spirit for Champasak, Chao Tengkham, is performed each year. The blood of the buffalo is offered to a local shaman who serves as a medium for the appearance of this spirit.

SLEEPING & EATING

Champasak has a number of good guesthouses strung along its main road, most of which have bedrooms with fans.

Vong Phaseud Guest House (☎ 920038; r 15,000 kip) A popular and friendly place on the river with plain rooms and a small but social restaurant area serving up good Lao food with fantastic views over the Mekong. Crack a Beer Lao and watch the river slide through a dozen colour changes before nightfall.

Dokchampa Guest House & Restaurant (☎ 020 206 248; r 15,000 kip) On the southwest corner of the fountain. Gloomy and could-be-cleaner rooms, but cheap and popular, with good food.

Khampoui Guest House (r with shared bathroom 20,000 kip) It's not on the river, but this new place, just south of the roundabout, has the cleanest, most modern budget rooms in town. Rooms in the main house have shared bathrooms.

GETTING THERE & AWAY

From Pakse, regular buses and săwngthăew leave between 7am and 3pm (10,000 kip, two hours).

To get south to Ban Nakasang (for Don Det) or Muang Khong (on Don Khong) by road, catch a morning ferry from Ban Phaphin (2km north of Champasak) over the Mekong to Ban Muang (2000 kip). On the other side hop on a săwngthăew or motorcycle taxi (3000 kip) to Ban Lak 30 (an intersection on the main road where a couple of small road-side stalls sell food and drink). There, you can flag down one of the regular buses or pick-up trucks heading south.

For Pakse (15,000 kip, two hours), several buses and săwngthăew depart between 6.30am and 8am.

GETTING AROUND

Bicycles can be rented from guesthouses for 10,000 kip per day for the 8km ride to Wat Phu Champasak. A túk-túk will take you there and back for around 30,000 kip.

Si Phan Don (Four Thousand Islands)

☎ 031

Si Phan Don, an archipelago of sandbars and rocky islets, amidst the teal-green expanse of the Mekong River, is a rewarding destination if you've made it this far south. At night the river's dotted with the lights of fishing boats, while during the wet season the lush, palm-studded islands are alight with fireflies. In the morning women wash their clothes and children in the river, and a steady flow of longtails from the mainland glide to and fro past bathing water buffalo. Si Phan Don is also home to the rare Irrawaddy dolphins, which can sometimes be seen at the southern tip of Don Khon, plus two impressive waterfalls.

DON KHONG

Eighteen kilometres long, 8km wide, Don Khong is a friendly, easy-going place to spend a couple of days. A little more switched on than its neighbouring islands, thanks to 10 years of electricity, you'll find some beautiful, aged Indochinese villas here, as well as a strip lit by fairy lights by night from which to gaze at the river and eat some very decent food. While inland there are paddy fields and a few temples to cycle past (one traveller said she'd even seen ostriches), there's little to do here but relax.

Information

One road back from the river, 400m south of the Muang Khong town square the **Agricultural Promotion Bank** (🕑 8.30am-3.30pm Mon-Fri) exchanges travellers cheques and cash (dollars, kip and baht – no sterling) for a high commission and poor rates. Better to come prepared with kip from Pakse as there are no credit card advances available on the island. For medical problems, the hospital is a little further south of the bank (Dr Bounthavy and Dr Soubanh speak good English and French). The **telephone office** (🕑 8am-noon

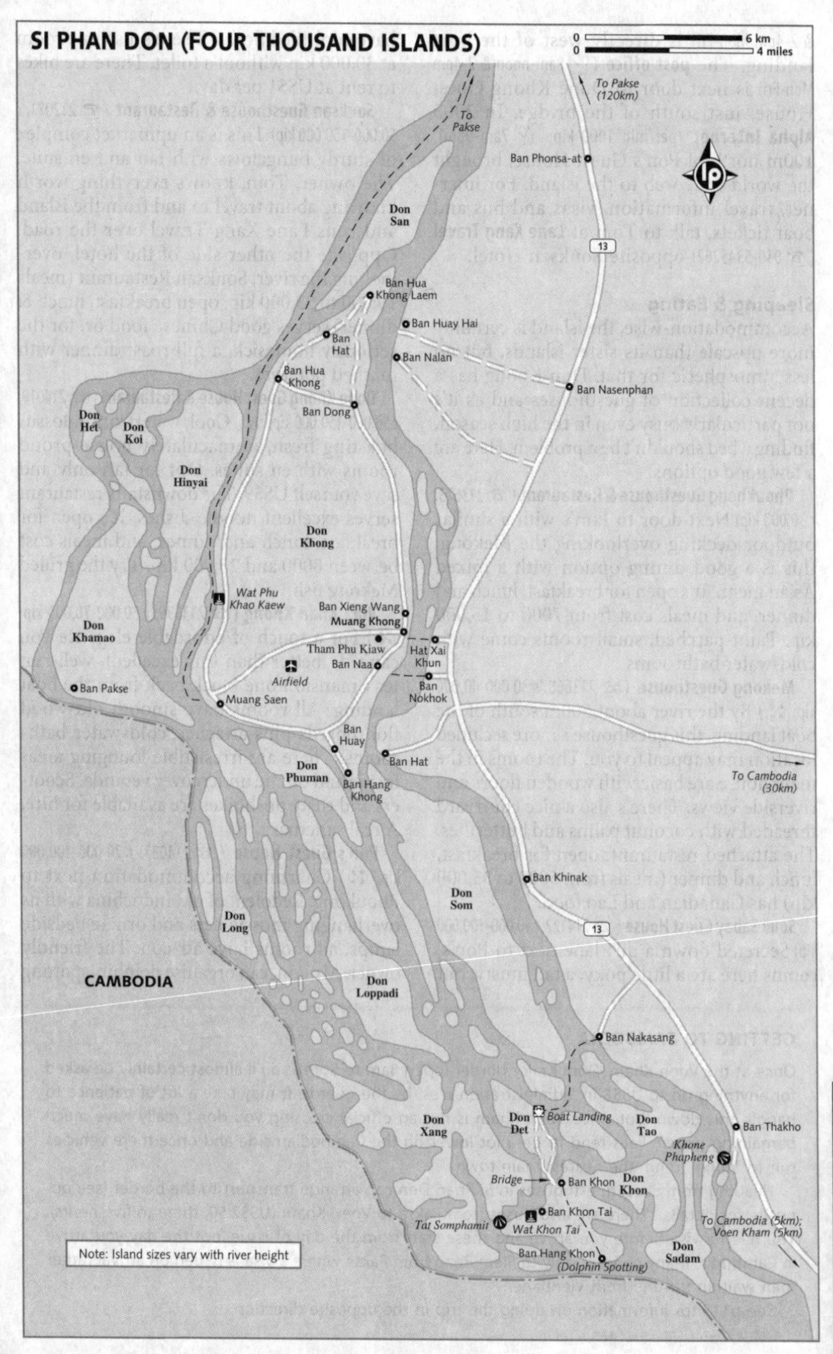
SI PHAN DON (FOUR THOUSAND ISLANDS)
0 6 km
0 4 miles
To Pakse (120km)
To Pakse
Ban Phonsa-at
Don San
13
Ban Hua Khong Laem
Ban Huay Hai
Ban Hat
Ban Nalan
Ban Hua Khong
Ban Nasenphan
Ban Dong
Don Het
Don Koi
Don Hinyai
Don Khong
Wat Phu Khao Kaew
Ban Xieng Wang
Muang Khong
Don Khamao
Tham Phu Kiaw
Hat Xai Khun
Ban Naa
Airfield
Ban Nokhok
Ban Pakse
Muang Saen
Ban Huay
Ban Hat
Don Phuman
Ban Hang Khong
To Cambodia (30km)
Ban Khinak
Don Som
Don Long
13
CAMBODIA
Don Loppadi
Ban Nakasang
Don Xang
Don Det
Boat Landing
Don Tao
Ban Thakho
Khone Phapheng
Bridge
Ban Khon
Don Khon
Ban Khon Tai
Tat Somphamit
Wat Khon Tai
To Cambodia (5km); Voen Kham (5km)
Ban Hang Khon
(Dolphin Spotting)
Don Sadam
Note: Island sizes vary with river height
LAOS

& 2-4pm Mon-Fri) is directly west of the boat landing. The **post office** (8am-noon & 2-4pm Mon-Fri) is next door to Done Khong Guest House, just south of the bridge. In 2005 **Alpha Internet** (per min 1000 kip; 7am-9pm), 100m north of Pon's Guest House, brought the world wide web to the island. For internet, travel information, visas and bus and boat tickets, talk to Tom at **Lane Xang Travel** (030-5345262) opposite Souksan Hotel.

Sleeping & Eating

Accommodation-wise, the island is certainly more upscale than its sister islands, but no less atmospheric for that. Don Khong has a decent collection of guesthouses and as it's not particularly busy even in the high season, finding a bed shouldn't be a problem. Here are a few good options.

Phoukhong Guesthouse & Restaurant (213673; r 30,000 kip) Next door to Pon's with a similar outdoor decking overlooking the Mekong, this is a good dining option with a mixed Asian menu. It's open for breakfast, lunch and dinner, and meals cost from 7000 to 15,000 kip. Paint-parched, small rooms come with cold-water bathrooms.

Mekong Guesthouse (213668; r 30,000-40,000 kip;) By the river about 500m south of the boat landing, this guesthouse's more secluded location may appeal to you. The rooms in the main house are basic with wooden floors and riverside views. There's also a nice courtyard threaded with coconut palms and butterflies. The attached restaurant, open for breakfast, lunch and dinner (meals from 5000 to 35,000 kip) has Canadian and Lao food.

Souk Sabay Guest House (214122; r 50,000-100,000 kip) Secreted down a dirt lane next to Pon's, rooms here are a little poky, a tad musty, but have cool-tiled floors. There's also one room at 30,000 kip without a toilet. There are bikes to rent at US$1 per day.

Souksan Guesthouse & Restaurant (212071; r 50,000-150,000 kip) This is an upmarket complex of sturdy bungalows with fan and en suite. The owner, Tom, knows everything worth knowing about travel to and from the island and runs Lane Xang Travel over the road. Opposite the other side of the hotel, overlooking the river, Souksan Restaurant (meals 19,000 to 53,000 kip; open breakfast, lunch & dinner) serves good Chinese food or, for the seriously homesick, a full roast dinner with mashed potatoes.

Done Khong Guest House & Restaurant (214010; r 50,000-150,000 kip;) Cool, waterfront colossus boasting fresh, immaculately house-proud rooms with en suites. Opt for fan only and save yourself US$9. The downstairs restaurant serves excellent noodle dishes. It's open for breakfast, lunch and dinner, and meals cost between 8000 and 25,000 kip. Try the grilled Mekong fish.

Villa Khan Khong (213539; r 60,000-70,000 kip;) For a touch of affordable elegance you can't do better than this excellent, well-run teak mansion one block back from the boat landing. All rooms have smooth old-wood floorboards plus attached cold-water bathrooms. There are irresistible lounging areas inside and on the undercover veranda. Scooters and rusty pushbikes are available for hire. A real sanctuary.

Pon's Guest House (214037; r 70,000-100,000 kip;) Charming accommodation next to Phoukong. Redolent of old Indochina with its overhanging mossie nets and ornate bedside lamps, all rooms have air-con. The friendly owner, Mr Pon, can organise dolphin-spotting

GETTING TO CAMBODIA

Once at the Voen Kham–Dom Kralor border (open 8am to 5pm), you'll almost certainly be asked for anything up to US$5 in 'administration fees' by the guards. It may take a lot of patience to haggle this down, but since Voen Kham is not an official crossing you don't really have much bargaining power. Fees tend to be a lot lower on the Cambodian side and once there vehicles run to Stung Treng, the nearest main town.

Heading from Laos, guesthouses in Si Phan Don can arrange transport to the border (see opposite for details). There are also buses from Pakse to Voen Kham (US$2.50, three to five hours). You need a visa before you arrive and these start from the day of issue, not the day you arrive in Cambodia. Many choose to fly to Siem Reap from Pakse where a visa is issued on arrival rather than waiting for one from Vientiane.

See p115 for information on doing the trip in the opposite direction.

day trips to Don Khon. The restaurant, which serves breakfast lunch and dinner (meals 8000 to 20,000 kip), is on decking overlooking the Mekong and the fish specialities are a highlight. Order ahead for the mouthwatering *mak pai* (steamed fish).

Getting There & Away

Lane Xang Travel, Pon's and Done Khong Guest House can organise your return from the island to wherever you need to go, catching a boat first to Hat Xai Khun to pick up your minibus. To Pakse, the bus leaves Hat Xai Khun at around 11.45am (70,000 kip, three hours), stopping en route at Champasak (50,000 kip). For Ubon catch the 11.45am bus (180,000 kip), while for Stung Treng, in Cambodia, the bus leaves at 10am (180,000 kip). Alternatively, Pon's Guest House arranges transport to the border for 50,000 kip.

For Don Det, organise a ride on a boat taking people on a day trip to see the Irrawaddy dolphins (try Pon's Guest House, 40,000 kip one way) or negotiate with the boat drivers near the bridge (you'll need to employ your Lao language skills).

Getting Around

Bicycles can be rented for 15,000 kip per day from guesthouses along the river road or from Alpha Internet. Villa Khan Khong has motorcycles for US$10 per day. Buses, motorcycle taxis or túk-túks run irregularly from Ban Hua Khong to Muang Khong and Ban Huay, from where the car ferry departs.

DON DET & DON KHON

Despite a major tourism boom resulting in an oversaturation of guesthouses, these steamy islands 16km south of Don Khong have managed to retain their beauty and charm, as sarong-clad villagers ply their trade on the iridescent waterways. The two islands are connected by a railway bridge (the only line the French ever laid in Laos) and are traversed by narrow shady paths, which make them ideal for walking and cycling. Don Det has the bigger backpacker scene (avoid the main bungalows strip if you want an early night). Don Khon is better value for money in terms of quality accommodation options, it's also the better island for exploring by day.

Electricity is supposed to arrive on the islands in 2008 which will unavoidably impact on the escapist, candlelit evenings you enjoy at present; however, you can help protect the islands from becoming the south's answer to Vang Vieng by voting with your feet if anyone thinks a TV bar is a great business idea.

Information

It's possible to change US dollars cash at several guesthouses on the island. **Bungalow Souksan** (☎ 020 227 0414) also exchanges travellers cheques with passport ID for a poor rate and high commission (in other words come here with enough money to see you through your stay if you can). **Khieo Internet** (☎ 020 584 1290) offers quick connection for 600 kip per min and can be found near Souksan Bungalows. **Happy Island Internet** (☎ 5494928), around 100m south down the main path, offers the same rate plus travel information, tubing, kayaking, white-water rafting (in the wet season) and tours to see the dolphins. Speak to Mr Boun.

Sights & Activities

If you like dolphin-watching in natural environments you've come to the right place. The best chance of seeing these unusual beak-nosed cetaceans is in the dry season, either early or late in the day. Some people get lucky and view them up-close; we saw them appear within minutes.

The easiest way to get to the sand bar viewing area is to join an organised half-day trip (for around 50,000 kip); sign-up on one of the whiteboards along Sunrise Blvd. Others charter a boat from the pier at Kong Ngay (around 25,000 kip per person). Alternatively, walk or ride to the beach at Ban Hang Khon and ask the boatman to take you from there see the boxed text, p404).

Another must-do-if-you're-motivated, is to **walk** or hire a **bicycle** for the day and explore the dirt pathways circumnavigating and crisscrossing Don Det and Don Khon. The defunct **railway line** (a little rocky on a bike: don't be shocked if you get a puncture and have to walk home) takes you to a French loading pier at the southern end of Don Khon. You can also visit the French-built **concrete channels** on the eastern edge of the Don Khon (head northwest from the railway bridge then turn south about 1km along), or the dramatic **Tat Somphamit** waterfalls (go under the railway bridge then follow the road southwest for

DIY DOLPHIN

While you can pay to be taken to see the Irrawaddy dolphins by a tour operator it's cheaper to do it yourself. Hire a bike at Souksan Hotel (US$1), meander down the path over the old French bridge to Don Khon (admission US$1), then follow the road to the little beach of Ban Hang Khon and you'll find a few boatmen. Try and haggle the price down to US$4 per person if there's two of you. The longtail trip through the unearthly, rocky waterway is worth the money alone. Should you be lucky enough to see these shy creatures consider it a privilege; there's less than a dozen left in these waters. Local fishermen and the WWF are making efforts to ensure gill-net fishing is practiced away from their habitat as much as possible. Fortunately the Khmer Rouge, their other nemesis, is no longer around to throw grenades in the water.

around 2km). There's a charge of 10,000 kip per day to cross the bridge.

Admirers of waterfalls will like **Khone Phapheng**. Although less dramatic than Tat Somphamit, it is considered the largest (by volume) in Southeast Asia and is therefore a boast-worthy sight to visit. Entry is 10,000 kip and the falls are often included on the itinerary of dolphin-viewing day trips.

Tubing and **kayaking** are both possible around the islands, either organised for you, or do-it-yourself. Tubes are available for hire at a number of guesthouses. Lazing in a tube by the small beach at the northern tip of Don Det is another popular way to pass the day.

Sleeping & Eating

The myriad sleeping opportunities on the two islands vary considerably in quality and price. Near the boat landing on Don Dhet, there's an alley with a dozen cabana guesthouses and self-styled restaurants, which are much of a muchness; however, by heading south you'll find some superior places. Over the bridge on Don Khon, new and fresh accommodation, many featuring fans and en suites as standard, are looking to oust the ultra basic resorts.

If you do opt for a stilted thatched bungalow, make sure it has a mosquito net and hammock (paramount for chilling). Also, try and get one with two windows so you can rely on natural ventilation to keep cool.

River Garden Guest House (☎ 030-5274785; Don Det; r 10,000-20,000 kip) Recent sunrise-facing addition offering spruce and comfortable accommodation. The owner's very friendly and keen to extend a welcome to any gay people looking for a relaxed environment. There's also a nice sundeck festooned in flags, to eat dinner on.

Mamas & Papas Guest House (☎ 020 227 4293; Don Det; r 10,000-20,000 kip) Has cabanas without attached toilet and fan but it catches the river breeze nicely. Losing ground now to the new competition but still good value.

Santiphab Guest House & Mekong Restaurant (☎ 030 5346233; Don Det; r with shared/private bathroom 20,000/50,000 kip) Overlooking the old French bridge this idyllic spot features eight cabanas – Rooms 3 and 4 are new with attached bathroom.

Mr Tho's Bungalows & Restaurant (☎ 020 656 7502; Don Det; r 22,000-25,000 kip) This popular riverside digs has sturdier cabanas than Mamas & Papas. Rooms are basic with two windows for decent ventilation, plus hammocks on verandas. Nice restaurant facing the river, plus a decent stock of old books.

Bounphan Guest House (Don Det; r 40,000 kip) Has sturdy (vertical!) bungalows with hammock-strung verandas. All set in a pretty little garden to watch river-life go by.

our pick **Pan's Guest House** (☎ 030-5346939; pkounnavong@yahoo.co.uk; Don Khon; r 50,000 kip) These new riverside bungalows, with their tastefully finished bathrooms and south-facing rooms (avoiding the morning microwave effect) have fans and lovely clean verandas. Definitely head and shoulders over the competition. The restaurant offers a mixed Thai and Western menu with great shakes to boot.

Bungalow Souksan (☎ 030-5345154; Don Det; s/d with shared bathroom 60,000-120,000 kip) On the northern tip of the island, Souksan offers pristine, minimalist bungalows without attached bathrooms in its flower-proud garden. The owner, once she decides she likes you, is very nice and speaks English. The attached restaurant serves Chinese food and a range of cocktails and uses purified water.

Miss Noy's Guesthouse & Restaurant (☎ 020 233 7112; Don Det) The still dazzling Miss Noy is building new accommodation so her guesthouse is currently closed. By the time you read this her delightful garden should have blossomed with eight new, well-appointed rooms, all enjoying westerly views.

Seng Ahloune Restaurant (☎ 5345807; Don Khon; mains 10,000-30,000 kip) Ambient spot for a Beer Lao moment as the sun sets over the mossy river islets and the night fishermen set to work. Decent authentic Lao menu with an array of fruit shakes.

Chanthounma's Restaurant (Don Khon; mains 15,000 kip) A shaded little café north of the bridge Don Khon side. Specialities include local grilled fish with garlic in an atmospheric setting.

Bamboo Restaurant (Don Khon; mains 20,000-30,000 kip) A little further along past Pan's Guest House, you'll find Bamboo leaning into the river. By night it's decked in lights and has a dash of élan combined with an earthy local menu. Enjoy the local catch whilst watching fishermen drift by in pirogues. Bring some mossie repellent!

Getting There & Around

From Pakse, buses and săwngthăew leave the southern market to Ban Nakasang, the jumping off point for Don Det and Don Khon, every hour until 1.30pm (40,000 kip, four to five hours). From the boat landing it's a 15,000 kip trip to Don Det (slightly more if it's late in the day or if you have fewer passengers). When the river is low and fewer trips are being made, it's harder to get a boat to go further around to Don Khon, so prepare to negotiate.

For buses and săwngthăew back to Pakse, get across to Ban Nakasang early to be sure of a seat and some legroom.

LAOS DIRECTORY

ACCOMMODATION

There's no shortage of accommodation in Laos, where even the smallest town will have a guesthouse or a village homestay option. The standard of guesthouses has risen in the last few years, as have prices. Guesthouses usually advertise rates in either US dollars or kip and many also accept payment in Thai baht.

Accommodation is cheapest in the rural north and far south, where it's still possible to find a US$2 bungalow in backpacker spots like Muang Ngoi Neua and Si Phan Don. In larger towns like Vientiane, Luang Prabang, Savannakhet, Pakse and Luang Nam Tha, expect to pay 50,000 kip for a budget room with shared bathroom and around 80,000 kip for a room with a bathroom or air-con. Unless otherwise noted, prices are for rooms with private bathroom.

ACTIVITIES

Cycling

Laos' relatively peaceful roads are a haven for cyclists. It's easy to bring your own bicycle into Laos if you're on a long-distance trip, and if cycling up mountains in the north gets too much, you can flag down a bus. Laos' main towns all have bicycle-rental shops. Note that it is wise to tie your bag in your basket when riding in town. While theft isn't a particular problem in Laos, if the opportunity presents itself you could lose your day-pack to a passing motorcyclist. Mountain-bike tours are run from Luang Nam Tha see p386) and Luang Prabang (see p371).

Kayaking & Rafting

Kayaking and white-water rafting have taken off here and Laos has several world-class rapids, as well as lots of beautiful, although less challenging, waterways. Unfortunately, the industry remains dangerously unregulated and you should not go out on rapids during the wet season unless you are completely confident in your guides and equipment. **Green Discovery** (www.greendiscoverylaos.com) is the most professional kayaking and rafting outfit in the country and should be your first stop for advice.

Rock Climbing

Currently there is only one organised rock-climbing operation in Laos, also run by **Green Discovery** (☎ 023-511440; www.greendiscoverylaos.com) in the karst cliffs around Vang Vieng. Experienced rock climbers also organise climbing expeditions in Southeast Asia. Contact clubs in your home country to find out more.

Trekking

Laos' endless areas of wilderness are a trekker's dream. Fortunately, responsible travel has taken root in Laos and some of the country's adventure tour companies are keen to avoid repeating the damage wreaked on Thailand's hill tribes by the tourism industry there. The most popular areas for trekking are Luang Nam Tha, Nong Khiaw, Luang Prabang and the Bolaven Plateau.

Tubing

Something of a Lao phenomenon, 'tubing' simply involves inserting yourself into an enormous tractor tube inner and floating down a river. Vang Vieng is the tubing capital of the country, with Muang Ngoi Neua and Si Phan Don popular runners-up.

BOOKS

Lonely Planet's *Laos* has all the information you'll need for extended travel in Laos. Lonely Planet also publishes the *Lao Phrasebook*, an introduction to the Lao language.

For some light predeparture reading have a look at *Another Quiet American*, where Brett Dakin shares his sometimes very funny experiences and insights into Laos from an outsider's perspective. *Stalking the Elephant Kings: In Search of Laos*, by Christopher Kremmer, presents a fascinating insight into the last days of King Savang Vatthana before he was removed from the royal palace by the Pathet Lao, and takes up the challenge of solving the mystery of his demise. Harder to track down though often available in Bangkok's airports, *The Ravens: Pilots of the Secret War of Laos*, by Christopher Robbins, is a compelling journey into the lives of the brave, some say lunatic CIA-hired pilots who flew jungle sorties over Laos during the Secret War.

BUSINESS HOURS

Government offices are typically open from 8am to noon and 1pm to 4pm, Monday to Friday. Banking hours are generally 8.30am to 4pm Monday to Friday. Shops have longer hours and are often open on weekends. Restaurants typically close by 10pm and bars stay open until around midnight.

CLIMATE

Laos has two distinct seasons: May to October is wet and November to April is dry. The coolest time of year is November to January and the hottest is March to May, when Southern Laos becomes almost too hot for the locals. The lowlands of the Mekong River valley are the hottest, peaking at around 38°C in March and April and dropping to a minimum of around 15°C in the cool season. Up in the mountains of Xieng Khuang and Sam Neua, cool season night-time temperatures can drop to freezing and even in the hot season it can be pleasant.

The wettest area of the country is southern Laos, where the Annamite mountain peaks get more than 3000mm of rain a year. Luang Prabang and Xieng Khuang receive less than half that amount of rain and Vientiane and Savannakhet get from 1500mm to 2000mm.

See the climate charts, charts, p916.

CUSTOMS

Customs inspections at ports of entry are very lax as long as you're not bringing in more than a moderate amount of luggage. You're not supposed to enter the country with more than 500 cigarettes or 1L of distilled spirits. Of course, all the usual prohibitions on drugs, weapons and pornography apply.

DANGERS & ANNOYANCES

Urban Laos is generally safe. You should still exercise ordinary precautions at night, but your chances of being robbed, mugged, harassed or assaulted are much lower than in most Western countries. There are significant dangers around the country, however. For the latest travel warnings for Laos, check government travel advisories on the internet.

Shootings have plagued Rte 13 between Vang Vieng and Luang Prabang since the '75 revolution, though it seems pacific at the moment. Rte 7, between Phu Khun and Phonsavan, is rumoured to be smarting with a little Hmong activity and guns are again being carried by some bus drivers.

In 2003 the security situation deteriorated. Ambushes in and around Sam Neua in Hua Phan province, bombings in Vientiane and attacks on public transport in southern Laos caused considerable anxiety for travellers and locals alike. While there have been no recent incidents of serious civil unrest that have affected tourists, the population of Laos is not exactly happily and peacefully governed by the current administration, so be sure to stay abreast of the political situation before – and while – travelling in Laos.

In the eastern provinces, particularly Xieng Khuang, Salavan and Savannakhet, UXO is a hazard. Never walk off well-used paths.

EMBASSIES & CONSULATES

Embassies & Consulates in Laos

Visas can be obtained in your home country through the Lao embassy or consulate. See p411 for more details.

Australia (Map pp352-3; ☎ 021-413610; Th Nehru, Ban Phonxay, Vientiane)
Cambodia (Map pp352-3; ☎ 021-314952; Th Tha Deua Km 2, Ban Phonxay, Vientiane)
China (Map pp352-3; ☎ 021-315105; Th Wat Nak, Ban Wat Nak, Vientiane)
France (Map p356; ☎ 021-215253; Th Setthathirat, Ban Sisaket, Vientiane)
Germany (Map pp352-3; ☎ 021-312111; Th Sok Pa Luang, Vientiane)
Indonesia (Map pp352-3; ☎ 021-413900; Th Phon Kheng, Ban Phonsaat, Vientiane)
Malaysia (Map pp352-3; ☎ 021-414203; Th That Luang, Vientiane)
Myanmar (Map pp352-3; ☎ 021-314991; Th Sok Pa Luang, Vientiane)
Philippines (Map pp352-3; ☎ 021-315179; Th Salakokthan, Vientiane)
Singapore (Map pp352-3; ☎ 021-412477; Th Nong Bon, Vientiane)
Thailand (Map pp352-3; ☎ 021-214582; Th Phon Kheng, Vientiane)
UK (☎ 021-413610; Th Nehru, Ban Phonxay, Vientiane)
USA (Map pp352-3; ☎ 021-212581; Th Bartholomie, Vientiane)
Vietnam Pakse (Map p396; ☎ 031-212058; Th 24); Vientiane (Map pp352-3; ☎ 413400; Th That Luang)

Lao Embassies & Consulates Abroad

Australia (☎ 02-6286 4595; 1 Dalman Cres, O'Malley, ACT 2606)
China Beijing (☎ 01-532 1224; 11 Sanlitun Dongsie Jie, Beijing 100600); Kunming (☎ 0871-317 6623; Room 3226, Camelia Hotel, 154 East Dong Feng Rd, 650041)
France (☎ 01-45 53 02 98; 74 av Raymond Poincaré, 75116 Paris)
Germany (☎ 030-890 60647; hong@laos/botschaft.de; Bismarckallee 2A, 14193 Berlin)
Japan (☎ 03-5411 2291; 3-3-21 Nishi Azabu, Minato-ku, Tokyo)
Sweden (☎ 08-668 5122; Hornsgaten 82-B1 TR 11721, Stockholm)
USA (☎ 202-332 6416; 2222 S St NW, Washington, DC 20008)

FESTIVALS & EVENTS

The Lao Buddhist Era (BE) calendar calculates year one as 638 BC, so AD 2006 is 2644 BE according to the Lao Buddhist calendar. Festivals are mostly linked to agricultural seasons or historic Buddhist holidays.

February

Magha Puja (Makkha Busaa; Full Moon) This is held on the full moon of the third lunar month. It commemorates a speech given by Buddha to 1250 enlightened monks who came to hear him without prior summons. Chanting and offerings mark the festival, culminating in the candlelit circumambulation of wats throughout the country.

Vietnamese Tet-Chinese New Year This is celebrated in Vientiane, Pakse and Savannakhet with parties, deafening nonstop fireworks and visits to Vietnamese and Chinese temples. Chinese- and Vietnamese-run businesses usually close for three days.

April

Pii Mai (Lunar New Year) This festival begins in mid-April (the 15th, 16th and 17th are official public holidays) and practically the entire country comes to a halt and celebrates. Houses are cleaned, people put on new clothes and buddha images are washed with specially purified water. Later the citizens, their hair dyed red, their faces whitened with talcum powder, take to the streets, drink lots of beer and dowse one another with water. Expect to get very, very wet.

May

International Labour Day 1 May is a public holiday.

Visakha Puja (Visakha Busaa; Full Moon) Falling on the 15th day of the sixth lunar month (usually in May), this is considered the day of the Buddha's birth, enlightenment and *parinibbana* (passing into nirvana).

Bun Bang Fai (Rocket Festival) One of the wildest festivals in Laos, a pre-Buddhist rain ceremony celebrated alongside Visakha Puja, involving huge home-made rockets, music, dance, drunkenness, cross-dressing, large wooden penises and sometimes a few incinerated houses.

July

Khao Phansaa (Khao Watsa; Full Moon) Late July is the beginning of the traditional three-month rains retreat, when Buddhist monks are expected to station themselves in a single monastery.

September/October

Awk Phansaa (Awk Watsa; Full Moon) Celebrating the end of the three-month rains retreat.

Bun Nam (Water Festival) Held in association with Awk Phansaa. Boat races are commonly held in towns on the Mekong, such as Vientiane, Luang Prabang and Savannakhet.

November

That Luang Festival (Bun That Luang; Full Moon) Takes place at Pha That Luang in Vientiane in early November. Hundreds of monks assemble to receive alms and floral votives early in the morning on the first day of the festival. There is a colourful procession between Pha That Luang and Wat Si Muang.

December

Lao National Day Held on 2 December, this public holiday celebrates the 1975 victory of the proletariat over the Royal Lao with parades and speeches.

FOOD & DRINK

Food

Lao cuisine lacks the variety of Thai food and foreigners often limit themselves to a diet of noodles, fried rice and the ubiquitous 'travellers' fare' that has swept Southeast Asia (fruit pancakes, muesli, fruit shakes…) But there are some excellent Lao dishes to try.

The standard Lao breakfast is *fõe* (rice noodles), which are usually served floating in a bland broth with some vegetables and a meat of your choice. The trick is in the seasoning, and Lao people will stir in some fish sauce, lime juice, dried chillies, mint leaves, basil, or one of the wonderful speciality hot chilli sauces that many noodle shops make, testing it along the way, before slurping it down with chopsticks in one hand and a spoon in the other.

Làap is the most distinctively Lao dish, a delicious spicy salad made from minced beef, pork, duck, fish or chicken, mixed with fish sauce, small shallots, mint leaves, lime juice, roasted ground rice and lots of chillies. Another famous Lao speciality is *tạm màak hung* (known as *som tam* in Thailand), a salad of shredded green papaya mixed with garlic, lime juice, fish sauce, sometimes tomatoes, palm sugar, land crab or dried shrimp and, of course, chillies by the handful.

Most Lao food is eaten with *khào nio* (sticky rice), which is served up in a small wicker container. Take a small amount of rice and, using one hand, work it into a walnut-sized ball before dipping it into the food. When you've finished eating, replace the lid on the container. Less often, food is eaten with *khào jâo* (plain white rice), which is eaten with a fork and spoon.

In rural areas, where hunting is more common than raising animals for food, you're likely to encounter some exotic meats. Apparently these are delicious: wild boar, wild fowl, wild dog and wild squirrel. Monitor lizard and bush rat might take some getting used to.

In main centres, French baguettes are a popular breakfast food. Sometimes they're eaten with condensed milk or with *khai* (eggs) in a sandwich that contains Lao-style pâté and vegetables. When they're fresh, they're superb.

Drink

The Lao Brewery Co produces the ubiquitous and excellent Beer Lao. Imported beers are also available in cans. Lao Bia – a dark, sweetish palm beer made in Savannakhet – is an interesting brew and is sold mostly around southern and central Laos in small bottles with a distinctly antique-looking label.

Lào-láo (Lao liquor, or rice whisky) is a popular drink among lowland Lao. Strictly speaking, *lào-láo* is not legal but no-one seems to care. The government distils its own brand, Sticky Rice, which is of course legal. *Lào-láo* is usually taken neat, sometimes with a plain water chaser.

In a Lao home the pouring and drinking of *lào-láo* takes on ritual characteristics – it is first offered to the house spirits, and guests must take at least one offered drink or risk offending the spirits.

In rural provinces, a weaker version of *lào-láo* known as *lào hái* (jar liquor) is fermented by households or villages. *Lào hái* is usually drunk from a communal jar using long reed straws. It's not always safe to drink, however, since unboiled water is often added to it during and after fermentation.

Water purified for drinking purposes is simply called *nâam deum* (drinking water), whether it's boiled or filtered. All water offered to customers in restaurants or hotels will be purified and bottles of purified water are sold everywhere.

Lao coffee is usually served very strong and sweet enough to make your teeth clench. If you don't want sugar or sweetened condensed milk, ask for *kạa-fáe dạm* (black coffee).

Chinese-style green or semicured tea is the usual ingredient in *nâam sáa* or *sáa láo* – the weak, refreshing tea traditionally served free in restaurants. The black tea familiar to Westerners is usually found in the same places as Lao coffee and is usually referred to as *sáa hâwn* (hot tea).

GAY & LESBIAN TRAVELLERS

Like Thailand, Laos has a very liberal attitude towards homosexuality, but a very conservative attitude to public displays of affection. Gay couples are unlikely to be given frosty treatment anywhere. Unlike Thailand, Laos does not have an obvious gay scene, but in Vientiane's late-night clubs you'll see plenty of young gay Lao whooping it up with everyone else. Luang Prabang boasts Laos' first openly gay bar, with the rainbow-coloured gay pride flag flying in a few places around town. See right for information on relations with Lao nationals.

HOLIDAYS

Aside from government offices, banks and post offices, many Lao businesses do not trouble themselves with weekends and public holidays. Most Chinese- and Vietnamese-run businesses close for three days during Vietnamese Tet and Chinese New Year in February.

Most businesses are closed for the following holidays.

Pii Mai (Lunar New Year) 15, 16 and 17 April
Labour Day 1 May
Lao National Day 2 December

INTERNET ACCESS

In Vientiane, there are dozens of internet places with rates at a standard 100 kip per minute. The further you get from Vientiane, the slower and more expensive connections become. At press time, reasonably priced internet was available in most tourism centres outside Vientiane, including Vang Vieng, Luang Prabang, Savannakhet, Pakse and Luang Nam Tha; plus Phonsavan, Udomxai, Don Khong and most recently on Don Det (where internet can be slow and expensive).

INTERNET RESOURCES

Central Intelligence Agency – The World Factbook (https://www.cia.gov/library/publications/the-world-factbook/geos/la.html) An encyclopaedic overview of the country.

Laos Globe (www.laosguide.com) This well-organised site compiles news stories about Lao PDR and the overseas Lao community from many online news services.

Laos National Unexploded Ordnance Program (www.uxolao.org) Information regarding ongoing mine-clearing work in Laos.

Laos-Travel.net (www.laos-travel.net) Travel information and news, with a slick design.

Laos WWW Virtual Library (www.global.lao.net/laovl.html) Comprehensive site with features on Lao culture, art, government and political issues.

Vientiane Times (www.vientianetimes.com) Not affiliated with the newspaper of the same name. Its tag-line, the Gateway to Democracy, says it all.

Visit Laos (www.visit-laos.com) Not the official tourist authority site, but more helpful than many of its offices!

LEGAL MATTERS

There is virtually nothing in the way of legal services in Laos. If you get yourself in legal strife, contact your embassy in Vientiane, though the assistance it can provide may be limited.

It's against the law for foreigners and Lao to have sexual relations unless they're married. Travellers should be aware that a holiday romance could result in being arrested and deported.

MAPS

An excellent road map of Laos, with city maps of Vientiane, Luang Prabang, Vang Vieng, Muang Sing and Luang Nam Tha, is produced by motorcycle tour company **Golden Triangle Rider Ltd** (www.gt-rider.com).

MEDIA

Laos' proximity to Thailand means Thai satellite TV, which also runs BBC and CNN, is the main source of uncensored world news for many Lao. Two official foreign-language newspapers, the English *Vientiane Times* and the French *Le Rénovateur,* are available at minimarts in Vientiane. Thailand's English-language dailies, the *Bangkok Post* and the *Nation,* are also found in guesthouses and cafés frequented by foreigners.

Lao Airline's *Laos Magazine* looks like it was put together by a high-school student in the 1960s, but has some useful listings and sometimes runs interesting cultural features.

MONEY

The only legal currency is the Lao kip, but three currencies are in everyday use: the kip, US dollar and Thai baht. Prices in this chapter are quoted in kip or US dollars, but pretty much anywhere in Laos will accept any of kip, US dollars or Thai baht, or combinations of all three, as payment. Kip come in denominations of 500, 1000, 2000, 5000, 10,000 and new 20,000 kip notes.

ATMs
There are a growing number of 24-hour ATMs in Vientiane, Vang Vieng, Luang Prabang and Pakse. Some (as is the case in Pakse) are only partial to credit cards with a MasterCard symbol.

Bargaining
Almost everything for sale in Laos can be bargained over and although more upmarket shops have fixed prices it never hurts to suggest an alternative. Lao people are not usually aggressive hagglers and a quiet, gentle bargaining technique works much better than arm-waving melodramatics.

There is a two-tier price system in Laos and foreigners often pay more for goods and services than locals (foreign residents are charged up to 10 times more for utilities, so it's not just tourists being asked for more!). In more heavily touristed areas the concept of overcharging tourists has caught on, particularly among túk-túk drivers; but generally in Laos price differences are not worth getting angry about, unless you are being dramatically ripped off.

Black Market
The days of favourable black market moneychanging are over and the best exchange rates are usually available in banks, though most guesthouses and many travel agents will change dollars and baht cash at bank rates.

Credit Cards
Visa cards are becoming more widely accepted these days and many travel agents, upmarket guesthouses, restaurants and shops in tourist areas accept them. MasterCard and Amex are much less common. Cash advances on Visa cards are available in some regional centres but not all so plan ahead.

Exchanging Money
US dollars and Thai baht can be exchanged all over the country. US-dollar travellers cheques can be exchanged in most provincial capitals and attract a better rate than cash. Banks in Vientiane and Luang Prabang change UK pounds, euro, Thai baht, Japanese yen, and Canadian, US and Australian dollars.

The best overall exchange rate is usually offered by Banque pour le Commerce Extérieur Lao. The only advantage of licensed moneychangers is longer opening hours. Exchange rates are as follows:

Country	Unit	Kip
Australia	A$1	8117
Cambodia	1000r	2389
Canada	C$1	9348
Euro zone	€1	13,360
Japan	¥100	8,358
New Zealand	NZ$1	6871
Thailand	10B	3008
UK	UK£1	19,335
USA	US$1	9627
Vietnam	10,000d	5932

Travellers Cheques
Banks in all provincial centres will exchange US-dollar travellers cheques. If you are changing cheques into kip there is usually no commission, but changing into dollars attracts a minimum 2% charge.

POST
Postal services from Vientiane are painfully slow but generally reliable, the provinces less so. If you have valuable items or presents to post home, there is a **Federal Express** (Map p356; ☎ 021-223278; 🕒 8am-noon & 1-5pm Mon-Fri, 9am-noon Sat) office inside the main post office compound in Vientiane.

RESPONSIBLE TRAVEL
In terms of tourism, Laos is very young and the rapid growth in the country's popularity has taken Lao society a little by surprise. Travellers and locals both raise two main tourism concerns over and over again.

The first is drugs. As Laos opened up to tourism, it gained a reputation as a free-for-all drug haven. It isn't. While opium use has traditionally been sanctioned only for the elderly, attitudes to drugs like marijuana are not very liberal. There is a strong feeling that widespread opium and marijuana use by travellers, who are often seen as wealthy and cool by young Lao, is having a negative influence and drawing them into trouble from which they have little means of escape. If caught smoking opium in the far north you can expect three months in jail. In Vang Vieng possession of a joint may cost you US$500 in fines. Exercise a little respect and caution before you light up.

Many are also concerned that the exploitative and intrusive Thai-style hill-tribe trekking business is spilling over into Laos. There seems to be a simple solution: the Nam Ha Ecotourism Project Map p356, run from Luang Nam Tha town and Muang Sing, has set up treks with strict guidelines to limit the impact and maximise the economic benefits of trekking to villages, as has Green Discovery. So far the signs are good; it's a project worth supporting. A similar experiment is being conducted by the Provincial Tourism Office & Savannakhet Ecotourism Project (p392).

STUDYING

There are no formal opportunities to study in Laos, but if you are passionately keen to learn more about this country, consider setting up your own study exchange, or develop a research topic, through your home university. Short courses in cooking are available in the capital and informal Lao language lessons are advertised in Vientiane.

TELEPHONE

Laos' country code is ☎ 856. To dial out of the country press ☎ 00 first.

Mobile Phones

If you bring an overseas mobile phone to Laos you can buy a sim card from GMS providers such as Tango for around US$5 and then purchase credits. But at the time of research coverage was limited to Vientiane province, Luang Prabang, Savannakhet and Pakse, where international SMSing is possible.

Mobile phone numbers in Laos have the prefix 020 followed by seven digits.

Phonecards

Phonecards for domestic calls can be bought at telephone offices and minimarts for use at the increasing number of public phones in provincial towns. International calls can be made from fixed landlines using an international phonecard.

TOILETS

Unlike Thailand, the hole-in-the-floor toilet is not common. The exception is if you're visiting out-of-the-way destinations such as hill-tribe villages.

TOURIST INFORMATION

The Lao National Tourism Authority maintains offices throughout Laos. Travel agencies and tour companies like Green Discovery, Diethelm and Lane Xang Travel are also excellent sources of information, often staffed by English speakers.

TRAVELLERS WITH DISABILITIES

Laos has virtually no facilities to meet the needs of disabled travellers. Urban pavements are full of hazards and public transport is often cramped. Any trip to Laos will require considerable forward planning. Many international organisations, such as **Mobility International USA** (☎ 541 343 1284; www.miusa.org; PO Box 10767, Eugene OR, USA), have resources, information and tips on travelling with disabilities.

VISAS

On-the-spot 30-day (recently upgraded from 14 days) tourist visas (US$30 to US$35 with two passport photos) are available at Vientiane's Wattay International Airport, Luang Prabang International Airport and Pakse International Airport, as well as at the Thai-Lao Friendship Bridge at Nong Khai, the Thai border at Huay Xai, Savannakhet, Pakse and the Boten border with China in Luang Nam Tha.

However, the Lao government can be very fickle about its visa regulations and prices. It has cancelled all automatic visas without warning in the past so check the current situation before trying to enter the country. Lao consulates and travel agents in Vietnam, China, Cambodia and Thailand all issue visas and will be able to advise on the latest border crossing situation.

Once in Laos it is easy to obtain a visa extension costing US$1 per day (from the immigration office in Vientiane; Map p356), up to a maximum of 30 days. Elsewhere, guesthouses and travel agents in provincial centres offer visa extension services for around US$2 to US$3 per day. Your passport will be sent to Vientiane, so it can take up to five days depending on how far from the capital you are. If you overstay your visa, you must pay a fine at the immigration checkpoint upon departure. The fine is US$10 for each day over the visa's expiry date.

VOLUNTEERING

It's not easy to find short-term volunteer work in Laos; however, one place you can walk in off the street is the Phoudindaeng Organic Farm (p365) in Vang Vieng. Occasionally groups seeking assistance from foreigners, such as the teachers' college in Luang Prabang or the orphanage in Phonsavan, will advertise at *falang* hang-outs like restaurants, tourist offices or guesthouses. If you're keen to contribute to the country in any small way, ask around for ideas or projects you can join. If you're passing through Luang Prabang, Luang Nam Tha or Vientiane try and spend some time at Big Brother Mouse (see box p385).

WOMEN TRAVELLERS

Women travellers rarely get hassled in Laos, but it does occur. In fact, you are more likely to be troubled by aggressive Western 'guru' male travellers (you know, the ones who have unravelled the spiritual mysteries of existence and are willing to share them with you in exchange for an invitation to your room) than you are by Lao men. Apart from wandering darkened streets alone at night of course, the main potential danger areas are guesthouses and long-distance buses. Picking a guesthouse run by women will dramatically reduce your chances of trouble. Some women have also been hassled on overnight bus trips, particularly the bus to Vietnam from Vientiane. The best way to combat this threat is to travel in a group and stay alert.

WORKING

Compared to other countries in the region, finding work in Laos is relatively simple. There are an inordinate number of development organisations in Laos (160 at last count), where foreigners with skills can find employment; see www.directoryofngos.org for info. The old standby of teaching English is always an option and schools in Vientiane are often hiring. Ask around.

Malaysia

HIGHLIGHTS

- **Taman Negara** – exploring the steamy, ancient jungle by riverboat and on foot (p472)
- **Pulau Perhentian** – hiking along coastal trails to dreamy, Crusoe-esque beaches to snorkel with psychedelically hued fish (p466)
- **Mt Kinabalu** – climbing the 4095m summit to watch the sunrise over northern Borneo (p484)
- **Pulau Penang** – gorging on Indian curries, laksa, rojak, spicy Chinese dishes, and more (p444)
- **Gunung Mulu** – plunging into caves then climbing Gunung Api to see the bizarre Pinnacles formations (p506)
- **Off the beaten track** – trekking from longhouse to longhouse in Bario and the Kelabit Highlands, where the only way in or out is by small plane (p507)

FAST FACTS

- **Budget** US$15 a day
- **Capital** Kuala Lumpur (KL)
- **Costs** dorm bed RM10, three basic meals RM20, two beers RM18, four-hour bus ride RM24
- **Country code** ☎ 60
- **Languages** Bahasa Melayu (official), Chinese (Hakka and Hokkien dialects), Tamil, English
- **Money** US$1 = RM3.50 (ringgit)
- **Phrases** *selamat pagi* (good morning), *terima kasih* (thank you)
- **Population** 24,821,300
- **Time** GMT + eight hours
- **Visas** people of most nationalities visiting Malaysia are presented with a 30- to 90-day visa on arrival

TRAVEL HINT

Malaysia is a Muslim country. Both men and women should dress appropriately by covering (at least) everything to the knees and over the shoulders; never bring alcohol or non-halal food to a guesthouse without the owner's permission.

OVERLAND ROUTES

From Peninsular Malaysia, you can head into Thailand and Singapore. From Sarawak, you can enter Indonesia (Kalimantan) and Brunei. Brunei can also be entered from Sabah.

Malaysia's reputation as a benign country makes some people think that it's going to be boring. It's true, pushy touts are rare, natural disasters only seem to happen across the border and the multi-ethnic population gets along well. What to do without the hassles? Why not stroll around Penang where wafts of Chinese incense mingle with sour durian while Bollywood tunes blast from an Indian shop. Next head to the Cameron Highlands where you can visit tea plantations in the cool air; or, on the east coast islands, snorkel through coral gardens and lounge on a mind-poppingly perfect beach. Put on your leech-proof boots to track elephants in Taman Negara, and how about delving into the depths of Sarawak and Sabah on mythical Borneo where you can see wild orang-utans and climb massive Mt Kinabalu? Unexciting? We think not.

CURRENT EVENTS

Speculators predict that Malaysia's Prime Minister Abdullah bin Ahmad Badawi will call an election in 2008 instead of waiting for the scheduled election in 2009. While the country's economy is strong, Abdullah has not been able to keep his pre-election promises to curb official corruption and cronyism or to increase freedom of the press. Critics hail that Islamic conservatism and racial tension has increased under Abdullah's leadership. Nevertheless, he remains very popular.

Abdullah's most outspoken critic is former deputy prime minister Anwar Ibrahim who was controversially jailed in 1998 by then prime minister Dr Mahathir Mohamad on sodomy and corruption charges. Anwar was released in September 2004, the sodomy charges overturned, and he has now announced that he will run for parliament in 2008. While most people don't believe that Anwar's party, the People's Justice Party, has much chance of gaining seats from the current majority party, his bold statements on multiracism are bringing up issues that are often glazed over in the current arena of leadership.

HISTORY

Early Influences

The earliest evidence of human life in the region is a 40,000-year-old skull found in Sarawak's Niah Caves. But it was only around 10,000 years ago that the aboriginal Malays, the Orang Asli (see p416), began moving down the peninsula from a probable starting point in southwestern China.

By the 2nd century AD, Europeans were familiar with Malaya, and Indian traders had made regular visits in their search for gold, tin and jungle woods. Within the next century Malaya was ruled by the Funan empire, centred in what's now Cambodia, but more significant was the domination of the Sumatra-based Srivijayan empire between the 7th and 13th centuries.

In 1405 the Chinese admiral Cheng Ho arrived in Melaka with promises to the locals of protection from the Siamese encroaching from the north. With Chinese support, the power of Melaka extended to include most of the Malay Peninsula. Islam arrived in Melaka around this time and soon spread through Malaya.

European Influence

Melaka's wealth and prosperity attracted European interest and it was taken over by the Portuguese in 1511, then the Dutch in 1641 and the British in 1795.

In 1838 James Brooke, a British adventurer, arrived to find the Brunei sultanate fending off rebellion from inland tribes. Brooke quashed the rebellion and in reward was granted power over part of Sarawak. Appointing himself Raja Brooke, he founded a dynasty that lasted 100 years. By 1881 Sabah was controlled by the British government, which eventually acquired Sarawak after WWII when the third Raja Brooke realised he couldn't afford the area's up-keep. In the early 20th century the British brought in Chinese and Indians, which radically changed the country's racial make-up.

Independence to the Current Day

Malaya achieved *merdeka* (independence) in 1957, but it was followed by a period of instability due to an internal Communist uprising and an external confrontation with neighbouring Indonesia. In 1963 the north Borneo states of Sabah and Sarawak, along with Singapore, joined Malaya to create Malaysia. In 1969 violent interracial riots broke out, particularly in Kuala Lumpur, and hundreds of people were killed. The government moved to dissipate the tensions, which existed mainly between the Malays and the Chinese. Present-day Malaysian society is relatively peaceful and cooperative.

Led from 1981 by outspoken Prime Minister Dr Mahathir Mohamad, Malaysia's economy grew at a rate of over 8% per year until mid-1997, when a currency crisis in neighbouring

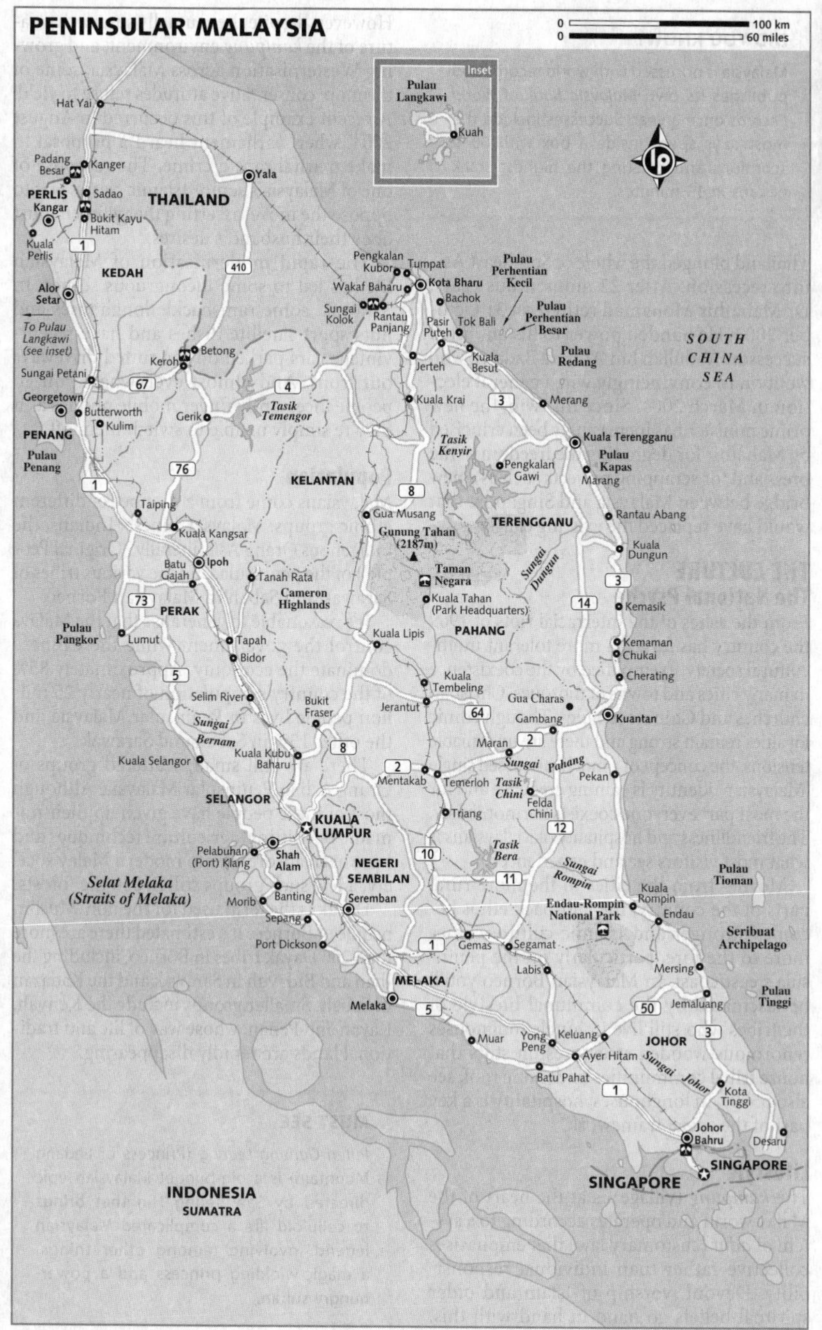
PENINSULAR MALAYSIA
0 100 km
0 60 miles
Inset
Pulau Langkawi
Kuah
THAILAND
Hat Yai
Yala
Padang Besar
Kanger
PERLIS
Sadao
Kangar
Bukit Kayu Hitam
Kuala Perlis
KEDAH
Alor Setar
To Pulau Langkawi (see inset)
Betong
Keroh
Sungai Petani
Georgetown
Butterworth
Kulim
PENANG
Pulau Penang
Gerik
Tasik Temengor
KELANTAN
Pengkalan Kubor
Tumpat
Wakaf Baharu
Kota Bharu
Bachok
Sungai Kolok
Rantau Panjang
Pasir Puteh
Tok Bali
Jerteh
Kuala Besut
Kuala Krai
Pulau Perhentian Kecil
Pulau Perhentian Besar
Pulau Redang
SOUTH CHINA SEA
Merang
Kuala Terengganu
Pulau Kapas
Marang
Tasik Kenyir
Pengkalan Gawi
TERENGGANU
Rantau Abang
Kuala Dungun
Sungai Dungun
Kemasik
Kemaman
Chukai
Cherating
Kuantan
Taiping
Kuala Kangsar
Batu Gajah
Ipoh
Tanah Rata
Cameron Highlands
PERAK
Pulau Pangkor
Lumut
Tapah
Bidor
Gua Musang
Gunung Tahan (2187m)
Taman Negara
Kuala Tahan (Park Headquarters)
PAHANG
Kuala Lipis
Kuala Tembeling
Jerantut
Gua Charas
Gambang
Selim River
Bukit Fraser
Sungai Bernam
Kuala Kubu Baharu
Kuala Selangor
SELANGOR
Maran
Sungai Pahang
Pekan
Mentakab
Temerloh
Tasik Chini
Felda Chini
Triang
KUALA LUMPUR
Pelabuhan (Port) Klang
Shah Alam
NEGERI SEMBILAN
Tasik Bera
Sungai Rompin
Selat Melaka (Straits of Melaka)
Morib
Banting
Seremban
Sepang
Port Dickson
Gemas
Segamat
Endau-Rompin National Park
Kuala Rompin
Endau
Pulau Tioman
Seribuat Archipelago
Pulau Tinggi
Labis
Mersing
MELAKA
Melaka
Jemaluang
Muar
Yong Peng
Keluang
Ayer Hitam
JOHOR
Sungai Johor
Batu Pahat
Kota Tinggi
Johor Bahru
Desaru
SINGAPORE
INDONESIA
SUMATRA
1
410
67
4
3
76
8
73
14
5
64
2
12
10
11
50

DID YOU KNOW?

Malaysia is obsessed with world records and publishes its own *Malaysia Book of World Records* once a year. Successes include the most days spent inside a box with 6069 scorpions and creating the highest stack of cans in 15 minutes.

Thailand plunged the whole of Southeast Asia into recession. After 22 momentous years, Dr Mahathir Mohamad retired on 31 October 2003. He handed power to his anointed successor, Abdullah bin Ahmad Badawi, who went on to convincingly win a general election in March 2004. Since this win, the new prime minister has increasingly been criticised by Mahathir for degrading the freedom of the press and for scrapping projects such as a new bridge between Malaysia and Singapore that would have replaced the existing causeway.

THE CULTURE

The National Psyche

From the ashes of the interracial riots of 1969 the country has forged a more tolerant multicultural society, exemplified by the coexistence in many cities and towns of mosques, Christian churches and Chinese temples. Though ethnic loyalties remain strong and there are undeniable tensions, the concept of a much-discussed single 'Malaysian' identity is gaining credence and for the most part everyone coexists harmoniously. The friendliness and hospitality of Malaysians is what most visitors see and experience.

Moving from the cities to the more rural parts of the country, the laid-back ethos becomes stronger and Islamic culture comes more to the fore, particularly on the peninsula's east coast. In Malaysian Borneo you'll be fascinated by the communal lifestyle of the tribes who still live in jungle longhouses (enormous wooden structures on stilts that house tribal communities under one roof; see also p500). In longhouses, hospitality is a key part of the social framework.

Lifestyle

The *kampung* (village) is at the heart of the Malay world and operates according to a system of *adat* (customary law) that emphasises collective rather than individual responsibility. Devout worship of Islam and older spiritual beliefs go hand in hand with this. However, despite the mutually supportive nature of the *kampung* environment, and growing Westernisation across Malaysia, some of the more conservative attitudes refuse to yield. A recent example of this occurred in August 2004, when parliament heard a proposal to make marital rape a crime. The response of one of Malaysia's senior Islamic clerics was to oppose the move, asserting that women must obey their husband's desires.

The rapid modernisation of Malaysian life has led to some incongruous scenes. In Sarawak, some ramshackle longhouses and huts sport satellite dishes and have recent-vintage cars parked on the rutted driveways out front. And almost everywhere you go people incessantly finger mobile phones as if they're simply unable to switch them off.

Population

Malaysians come from a number of different ethnic groups: Malays, Chinese, Indians, the indigenous Orang Asli (literally, 'Original People') of the peninsula, and the various tribes of Sarawak and Sabah in Malaysian Borneo.

It's reasonable to generalise that the Malays control the government while the Chinese dominate the economy. Approximately 85% of the country's population of nearly 25 million people lives in Peninsular Malaysia and the other 15% in Sabah and Sarawak.

There are still small, scattered groups of Orang Asli in Peninsular Malaysia. Although most of these people have given up their nomadic or shifting-agriculture techniques and have been absorbed into modern Malay society, a few such groups still live in the forests.

Dayak is the term used for the non-Muslim people of Borneo. It's estimated there are more than 200 Dayak tribes in Borneo, including the Iban and Bidayuh in Sarawak and the Kadazan in Sabah. Smaller groups include the Kenyah, Kayan and Penan, whose way of life and traditional lands are rapidly disappearing.

MUST SEE

Puteri Gunung Ledang (Princess of Ledang Mountain) is a big-budget Malaysian epic directed by Saw Teong Hin that brings to celluloid life a complicated Malaysian legend involving (among other things) a magic-wielding princess and a power-hungry sultan.

RELIGION

The Malays are almost all Muslims. But despite Islam being the state religion, freedom of religion is guaranteed. The Chinese are predominantly followers of Taoism and Buddhism, though some are Christians. The majority of the region's Indian population comes from the south of India and are Hindu and Christian, although a sizable percentage are Muslim.

While Christianity has made no great inroads into Peninsular Malaysia, it has had a much greater impact in Malaysian Borneo, where many indigenous people have been converted and carry Christian as well as traditional names. Others still follow animist traditions.

ARTS

It's along the predominantly Malay east coast of Peninsular Malaysia that you'll find Malay arts and crafts, culture and games at their liveliest. Malaysian Borneo is replete with the arts and crafts of the country's indigenous peoples.

Arts & Crafts

A famous Malaysian Bornean art is *pua kumbu*, a colourful weaving technique used to produce both everyday and ceremonial items.

The most skilled woodcarvers are generally held to be the Kenyah and Kayan peoples, who used to carve enormous, finely detailed *kelirieng* (burial columns) from tree trunks.

Originally an Indonesian craft, the production of batik cloth is popular in Malaysia and has its home in Kelantan. A speciality of Kelantan and Terengganu, *kain songket* is a handwoven fabric with gold and silver threads through the material. *Mengkuang* is a far more prosaic form of weaving using pandanus leaves and strips of bamboo to make baskets, bags and mats.

Dance

Menora is a dance-drama of Thai origin performed by an all-male cast dressed in grotesque masks; *mak yong* is the female version. The upbeat *joget* (better known around Melaka as *chakuncha*) is Malaysia's most popular traditional dance, often performed at Malay weddings by professional dancers.

Rebana kercing is a dance performed by young men to the accompaniment of tambourines. The *rodat* is a dance from Terengganu and is accompanied by the *tar* drum.

MUST READ

Into the Heart of Borneo by Redmond O'Hanlon is the account of this cheerfully ill-prepared naturalist's journey into the remote interior of the island, accompanied by several idiosyncratic guides and a perpetually bewildered British poet.

ARTS WEB TIP

The best source of information on what's currently going on in the Malaysian arts scene is www.kakiseni.com.

Music

Traditional Malay music is based largely on the *gendang* (drum), of which there are more than a dozen types. Other percussion instruments include the *gong*, *cerucap* (made of shells), *raurau* (coconut shells), *kertuk* and *pertuang* (both made from bamboo), and the wooden *celampang*.

Wind instruments include a number of types of flute (such as the *seruling* and *serunai*) and the trumpet-like *nafiri*, while stringed instruments include the *biola*, *gambus* and *sundatang*.

The *gamelan*, a traditional Indonesian gong-orchestra, is also found in the state of Kelantan, where a typical ensemble will comprise four different gongs, two xylophones and a large drum.

ENVIRONMENT

The Land

Malaysia covers 329,758 sq km and consists of two distinct regions. Peninsular Malaysia is the long finger of land extending south from Asia and is mostly covered by dense jungle, particularly the mountainous northern half. The peninsula's western side has a large fertile plain running to the sea, while the eastern side is fringed with sandy beaches. Malaysian Borneo consists of Sarawak and Sabah; both states are covered in thick jungle and have extensive river systems. Sabah is crowned by Mt Kinabalu (4095m), the highest mountain between the Himalayas and New Guinea.

Wildlife

Malaysia's ancient rainforests are endowed with a cornucopia of life forms. In Peninsular Malaysia alone there are over 8000 species of flowering plants, including the world's tallest tropical tree species, the *tualang*. In Malaysian

Borneo, where hundreds of new species have been discovered since the 1990s, you'll find the world's largest flower, the rafflesia, measuring up to 1m across, as well as the world's biggest cockroach. Mammals include elephants, rhinos (extremely rare), tapirs, tigers, leopards, honey bears, *tempadau* (forest cattle), gibbons and monkeys (including, in Borneo, the bizarre proboscis monkey), orang-utans and scaly anteaters *(pangolins)*. Bird species include spectacular pheasants, sacred hornbills and many groups of colourful birds such as kingfishers, sunbirds, woodpeckers and barbets. Snakes include cobras, vipers and pythons. Once a favourite nesting ground for leatherback turtles, recorded landings now hover around 10 per year.

National Parks

Malaysia's 19 national parks cover barely 5% of the country's landmass. The country's major national park is Taman Negara, on the peninsula, while Gunung Mulu and Kinabalu are the two main parks in Sarawak and Sabah respectively. Especially on Borneo, the rarity and uniqueness of local flora and fauna is such that scientists – from dragonfly experts to palm-tree specialists – are regular visitors and vocal proponents of new parks and reserves both on land and in the surrounding waters. There are also 13 marine parks in Malaysia, notably around Pulau Perhentian, Tioman and Sipadan, although enforcement of protection measures is very loose.

Environmental Issues

When it comes to environmental faux pas, Malaysia has done it all. Logging is believed to have destroyed more than 60% of the country's rainforests and generates some US$4.5 billion per year for big business. Another growing phenomenon, particularly in Sabah, is the palm-tree plantation, where vast swathes of land are razed and planted with trees that yield lucrative palm oil. But the crown of eco and social irresponsibility goes to the construction of the controversial Bakun Dam in Sarawak, scheduled to become Southeast Asia's biggest dam in late 2007. The dam will drown approximately 700 sq km of virgin rainforest and will have forced up to 10,000 indigenous people from their homes. In equally bad environmental news, much of the power generated at Bakun looks likely to go to a giant aluminium smelter in Sarawak.

Responsible ecotourism is the traveller's best weapon in a country where cold cash is fiercer than tigers. See p515 for more information.

TRANSPORT

GETTING THERE & AWAY

Air

The gateway to Peninsular Malaysia is the city of Kuala Lumpur, although Pulau Penang and Johor Bahru (JB) also have international connections. Singapore is a handy arrival/departure point, since it's just a short trip across the Causeway from JB and has more international connections. Malaysia Airlines is the country's main airline carrier although Air Asia flights are much cheaper. At the time of writing Air Asia was planning services to Europe, India and China.

There are weekly flights between Kuching and Pontianak in Kalimantan (Indonesia), and between Tawau in Sabah and Tarakan in Kalimantan.

The following are some airlines servicing Malaysia; numbers beginning with ☎ 03 are for Kuala Lumpur.

Aeroflot (code SU; ☎ 03-2161 0231; www.aeroflot.ru/eng)
Air Asia (code AK; ☎ 03-8775 4000; www.airasia.com)
Air India (code AI; ☎ 03-2142 0166; www.airindia.com)
British Airways (code BA; ☎ 1800 881 260; www.britishairways.com)
Cathay Pacific Airways (code CX; ☎ 03-2035 2788; www.cathaypacific.com)
China Airlines (code CI; ☎ 03-2142 7344; www.china-airlines.com)
Garuda Indonesian Airlines (code GA; ☎ 03-2162 2811; www.garuda-indonesia.com)
Japan Airlines (code JL; ☎ 03-2161 1722; www.jal.com)
Lufthansa (code LH; ☎ 03-2161 4666; www.lufthansa.com)
Malaysia Airlines (code MH; ☎ 1300 883 000, 03-2161 0555; www.malaysiaairlines.com)
Qantas (code QF; ☎ 1800 881 260; www.qantas.com)
Royal Brunei Airlines (code BI; ☎ 03-2070 7166; www.bruneiair.com)
Singapore Airlines (code SQ; ☎ 03-2692 3122; www.singaporeair.com)
Thai Airways International (THAI, code TG; ☎ 03-2031 2900; www.thaiairways.com)
Vietnam Airlines (code VN; www.vietnamairlines.com)
Virgin Atlantic (code VS; ☎ 03-2143 0322; www.virgin-atlantic.com)

DEPARTURE TAX

The RM40 airport departure tax is always included in the ticket price.

BRUNEI

You can fly from KL and Kota Kinabalu to Bandar Seri Begawan. Because of the difference in exchange rates, it's cheaper to fly to Brunei from Malaysia than vice versa.

CAMBODIA

Flights between KL and Phnom Penh are available with Malaysia Airlines, Air Asia and Royal Phnom Penh Airways. Air Asia also flies from KL to Siem Reap.

INDONESIA

It's a short hop from Pulau Penang to Medan in Sumatra. To Java, the cheapest connections are from Singapore. There are also weekly flights between Kuching and Pontianak in Kalimantan (Indonesia), and between Tawau in Sabah and Tarakan in Kalimantan.

PHILIPPINES

You can fly with Malaysia Airlines or Air Asia from KL to Cebu/Manila. Air Asia also has flights to Manila from Kota Kinabalu.

SINGAPORE

Malaysia Airlines and Singapore Airlines have frequent services to KL. Malaysia Airlines also connects Singapore to Langkawi and Penang.

THAILAND

There are flights between Bangkok and KL or Kota Kinabalu, and between Phuket and Koh Samui with Penang.

VIETNAM

Malaysia Airlines and Vietnam Airlines operate flights from KL to Ho Chi Minh City and Hanoi. Air Asia runs flights from KL to Hanoi.

Land

BRUNEI

You can catch buses and taxis between Miri in Sarawak and Kuala Belait in Brunei (see p506). Kuala Belait has easy bus connections with Bandar Seri Begawan; you can also cross from Lawas to Bangar (in Brunei), and then head on to Limbang (see p509).

INDONESIA

In Borneo, regular buses run between Kuching and the Indonesian city of Pontianak via the Tebedu–Entikong crossing (see p498).

SINGAPORE

At the southern tip of Peninsular Malaysia you can cross into Singapore via Johor Bahru by bus (see p456). Taking the train from JB is less convenient.

THAILAND

On the western side of Peninsular Malaysia, you can travel by bus from Alor Setar to the border crossing at Bukit Kayu Hitam (p453). There are also two trains passing through Alor Setar to Padang Besar and then continuing north into Thailand (see p453); the first stops at Hat Yai, while the second terminates in Bangkok. Some visitors may not feel safe travelling through Hat Yai, which has been a hot spot for Muslim and Buddhist clashes in Thailand.

On the peninsula's eastern side you can bus it from Kota Bharu to the border town of Rantau Panjang but at the time of writing this was not a safe place to cross due to violence in this area of southern Thailand; if the situation changes, see p470 for border-crossing information.

There is also a border crossing between Keroh (Malaysia) and Betong (Thailand), but at the time of writing it was extremely inadvisable to travel here due to the violence in Yala Provinc, Thailand.

Sea

There are no services connecting the peninsula with Malaysian Borneo.

BRUNEI

You can travel by sea between Bandar Seri Begawan (Muara Port), Brunei, and Pulau Labuan, Sabah (see p484). You can also travel by boat between Limbang in Sarawak and Brunei (see p508).

INDONESIA

The main ferry routes between Peninsular Malaysia and Sumatra are Georgetown–Medan and Melaka–Dumai.

The popular crossing between Georgetown (on Pulau Penang) and Medan has services most days of the week. The boats actually land in Belawan in Sumatra, and the journey to Medan is completed by bus (included in the price). See p451 for full details of this route.

Twice-daily high-speed ferries run between Melaka and Dumai in Sumatra. Dumai is now a visa-free entry port into Indonesia for citizens of most countries. See p438 for details.

You can also take a boat from the Bebas Cukai ferry terminal in JB direct to Pulau Batam and Pulau Bintan, both in the Riau Islands (see p456).

Boats head between Tawau in Sabah and Tarakan in Kalimantan daily except Sunday. There are also daily boats between Tawau and Nunukan in Kalimantan, most of which continue on to Tarakan (see p492).

PHILIPPINES

Passenger ferries run twice weekly between Sandakan in Sabah and Zamboanga in the Philippines (see p488).

THAILAND

Regular daily boats run between Pulau Langkawi and Satun in Thailand; see p455. There are customs and immigration posts here, but it's an expensive entry/exit point.

GETTING AROUND

Air

With all airlines, it pays to check websites for specials.

Malaysia Airlines (code MH; ☎ 1300 883 000; www.malaysiaairlines.com.my) is the country's main domestic operator, linking major regional centres on the peninsula and on Pulau Langkawi and a network of Bornean flights, including a rural air service. Economical, five-city Discover Malaysia air passes are valid for 28 days but can only be purchased with an international Malaysia Airlines ticket.

Firefly (code FY; ☎ 03-7845 4543; www.fireflyz.com), a subsidiary of Malaysia Airlines that began services in April 2007, has budget flights from Pulau Penang to Pulau Langkawi, Kuala Terengganu, Kuantan and Kota Bharu, and to Phuket and Koh Samui in Thailand. Services are expected to expand.

Air Asia (code AK; ☎ 03-8775 4000; www.airasia.com) is a no-frills airline offering super-cheap flights. Air Asia flies to/from KL, Johor Bahru, Penang, Kota Kinabalu and Kuching as well as a handful of smaller Malaysian cities.

Tiny **Berjaya Air** (code J8; ☎ 03-2145 2828; www.berjaya-air.com) has flights between KL, Pulau Tioman and Pulau Pangkor.

Boat

Boats and ferries sail between the peninsula and offshore islands. If a boat looks overloaded or otherwise unsafe, do not board it. There are no ferry services between Malaysian Borneo and the peninsula. Travel on the larger rivers, such as the Rejang and Baram in Borneo, is accomplished in fast passenger launches known by the generic term *ekspres*, which carry around 100 people. Travel on smaller, squeezier Bornean waterways is mainly by costly motorised longboat. It's best to organise a group to share costs.

Bus

Peninsular Malaysia has an excellent bus system. Public buses do local runs and a variety of privately operated buses generally handle the longer trips. In larger towns there may be several bus stations. Local and regional buses often operate from one station and long-distance buses from another; in other cases, KL for example, bus stations are differentiated by the destinations they serve.

Buses are an economical form of transport, reasonably comfortable and on major runs you can often just turn up and get on the next bus. On many routes there are air-conditioned buses, which usually cost just a few ringgit more than regular buses.

Ekspres, in the Malaysian context, often means indeterminate stops. To make up this time many long-distance bus drivers tend to think of the *lebuhraya* (highway) as their personal Formula One track.

The main highway routes in both Sabah and Sarawak are well served by buses. The main road in Sarawak winds from Kuching to the Brunei border and, although sealed, can be rough in parts. Roads in Sabah are better, but have unmarked hazards.

The main destinations in Sabah are linked by a reasonable system of roads. You can travel between Sabah and Sarawak by road via Brunei, but there are several immigration stops and no public transport on some sections – we recommend travelling by boat

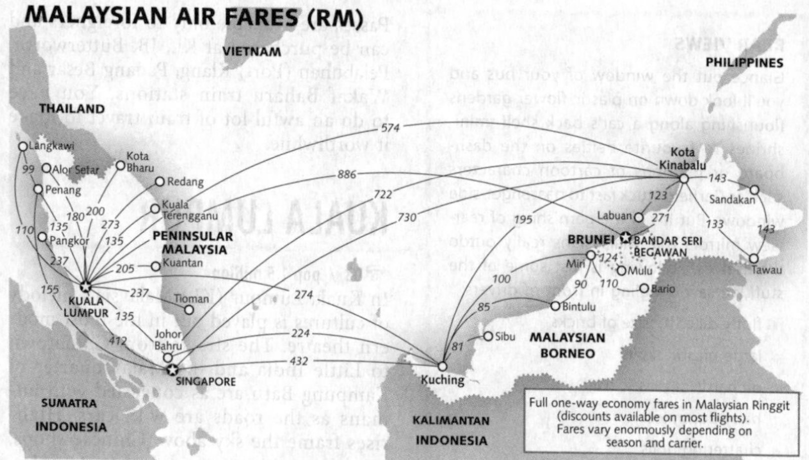

between Kota Kinabalu and Bandar Seri Begawan via Pulau Labuan for this section (see p482).

Car & Motorcycle

Driving in Peninsular Malaysia is a breeze compared to most other Asian countries; the roads are generally high quality, there are plenty of new cars available and driving standards aren't too hair-raising. Road rules are basically the same as in Britain and Australia. Cars are right-hand drive and you drive on the left side of the road. However, you should be constantly aware of the hazards posed by stray animals and numerous motorcyclists.

Unlimited-distance car-rental rates cost from around RM145/920 per day/week, including insurance and collision-damage waiver.

Be aware that insurance companies will most likely wash their hands of you if you injure yourself driving a motorcycle without a licence.

Hitching

Hitching is never entirely safe in any country and we don't recommend it. True, Malaysia has long had a reputation for being an excellent place to hitchhike but, with the ease of bus travel, most travellers don't bother. On the west coast, hitching is quite easy but it's not possible on the main *lebuhraya*. On the east coast, traffic is lighter and there may be long waits between rides.

Local Transport

Local transport varies but almost always includes local buses and taxis. In many Peninsular Malaysian towns there are also bicycle rickshaws. While these are dying out in KL, they are still a viable form of transport in a few towns. Indeed, in places such as Georgetown, with its convoluted and narrow streets, a bicycle rickshaw is the best way of getting around.

Taxi

Good luck finding a taxi with an operational meter in Malaysia. Except where prepurchased coupons are involved or where drivers have agreed on a standard route fare, you will inevitably have to negotiate with the driver about fares. On their worst days, taxi drivers will charge extortionate amounts. Don't be afraid to turn down a fare you think is too high and walk over to the next taxi to negotiate a fairer price. Even better, ask at your hotel or a visitors centre about reasonable fares.

Compared to buses, long-distance (or share) taxis are an expensive way to travel around Malaysia. The taxis work on fixed fares for the entire car and will only head off when a full complement of passengers (usually four people) turns up. Between major towns you will have a reasonable chance of finding other passengers without having to wait around too long; otherwise, you'll probably have to charter a whole taxi at four times the single fare.

REAR VIEWS

Glance out the window of your bus and you'll look down on plastic flower gardens flourishing along a car's back shelf, mini-shrines to favourite deities on the dashboard or platoons of cartoon characters such as Garfield stuck fast to passenger-side windows. But it's in the garnishing of rear-view mirrors that Malaysians really outdo themselves. Following is just some of the stuff we saw dangling in front of drivers:

- fluffy dice the size of bricks
- large plastic skulls
- orchards of plastic fruit
- baby dummies
- chattering dolls
- CDs
- old sunglasses

Train

Peninsular Malaysia has a modern, comfortable and economical railway service that has basically two lines. One runs from Singapore to KL, then to Butterworth and on into Thailand. The other line, known as the Jungle Railway, cuts through the interior of Malaysia linking Gemas, Taman Negara with Kota Bharu, a transit town for Pulau Perhentian.

In Sabah on Borneo there's a narrow-gauge railway line that runs from Kota Kinabalu south to Beaufort and then through Sungai Pegas gorge to Tenom.

Peninsular Malaysia has three main types of rail services: express, limited express and local trains. Express trains are air-conditioned and generally 1st and 2nd class only, and on night trains there's a choice of berths or seats. Limited express trains may have 2nd and 3rd class only but some have 1st, 2nd and 3rd class with overnight sleepers. Local trains are usually 3rd class only, but some have 2nd class.

The privatised national railway company, **Keretapi Tanah Melayu** (KTM; ☎ 03-2267 1200, 2773 1430; www.ktmb.com.my), offers a tourist Rail Pass for five days (adult US$35), 10 days (adult US$55) and 15 days (adult US$70). This pass entitles the holder to unlimited travel on any class of train, although it does not include sleeping-berth charges. Rail Passes are available only to foreigners and can be purchased at KL, JB, Butterworth, Pelabuhan (Port) Klang, Padang Besar and Wakaf Baharu train stations. You have to do an awful lot of train travel to make it worthwhile.

KUALA LUMPUR

☎ 03 / pop 1.5 million

In Kuala Lumpur (KL) Malaysia's melody of cultures is played out in the most modern theatre. The streets from Chinatown to Little India and the Malay quarter of Kampung Baru are as congested with humans as the roads are with cars. Highrises frame the sky above Chinese shops, towering mosques and Indian temples. Around the sparkling twin Petronas Towers the city spreads into manicured parks, air-conditioned deluxe megamalls and fine restaurants.

From being only a tiny tin town some 150 years ago, KL has advanced at lightning pace – a feat that's best shown through its cutting-edge international airport and rail system. Yet even with all the crowds and technology, KL remains undeniably humane, culturally fascinating and an easy landing pad for anyone not yet ready to tackle Southeast Asia's harsher capitals.

ORIENTATION

Merdeka Sq is the traditional heart of KL. Southeast across the river, the banking district merges into Chinatown, popular with travellers for its budget accommodation and lively night market.

East of Merdeka Sq is Masjid Jamek, at the intersection of the Star and Putra Light Rail Transit (LRT) lines. Jl Tun Perak, a major trunk road, leads east to the long-distance transport hub of the country, the Puduraya bus station.

To the east of Puduraya bus station, around Jl Sultan Ismail, the Golden Triangle is the modern, upmarket heart of the new KL.

The transport-hub KL Sentral station (which holds the KL City Air Terminal, from where you catch the KLIA Ekspres to the international airport) is in the Brickfields area, southeast of the centre.

INFORMATION

Bookshops

Kinokuniya (Map p429; ☎ 2164 8133; 4th fl, Suria KLCC Shopping Complex)

MPH Bookstores (Map p429; ☎ 2142 8231; Ground fl, BB Plaza, Jl Bukit Bintang) Also a branch at Mid Valley Megamall (off Map pp424-5).

Emergency

Fire (☎ 994)

Police & ambulance (☎ 999)

Immigration Offices

Immigration office – city centre branch (Map pp424-5; ☎ 2698 0377; Kompleks Wilayah, cnr Jl Dang Wangi & Jl TAR)

Main immigration office (off Map pp424-5; ☎ 2095 5077; Block I, Pusat Bandar Damansara) For visa extensions; it's 1km west of Lake Gardens.

Internet Access

Internet cafés turn over frequently but are usually replaced by another nearby. Try Jl Sultan or the streets surrounding Kota Raya shopping centre in Chinatown (both on Map p426). Rates per hour start at RM2.

Libraries

National Library of Malaysia (Map pp424-5; ☎ 2687 1700; www.pnm.my; 232 Jl Tun Razak)

Medical Services

Kuala Lumpur General Hospital (Map pp424-5; ☎ 2615 5555; Jl Pahang)

Twin Towers Medical Centre (Map pp424-5; ☎ 2382 3500; Lot 401 F&G, 4th fl, Suria KLCC Shopping Complex)

Money

Banks and ATMs are concentrated around Jl Silang at the northern edge of Chinatown. Moneychangers are located in shopping malls, along Lebuh Ampang and near Klang bus station on Jl Sultan (see Map p426).

Post

Main post office (Map p426; JL Raja Laut; 8.30am-6pm Mon-Sat) The office is closed on the first Saturday of the month.

Telephone

Phonecards are widely available in KL but finding a compatible public phone is a challenge, especially if you leave KL. Shops in Chinatown and on Jl Bukit Bintang, in the Golden Triangle, have pay-per-call IDD-STD phones. Call ☎ 103 for local directory inquiries and ☎ 108 for the international operator.

Telekom Malaysia (Map p426; Jl Raja Chulan; 8.30am-4.30pm Mon-Fri, 8.30am-12.30pm Sat) Calls can be made here.

Tourist Information

Malaysian Tourist Information Complex (Matic; Map p429; ☎ 2164 3929; 109 Jl Ampang; 9am-midnight) KL's largest and most useful tourist office; it also holds regular cultural performances.

Tourism Malaysia (Map pp424-5; ☎ 03-2615 8188; www.tourism.gov.my; 17th fl, Putra World Trade Centre, 45 Jl Tun Ismail) Has good maps of Malaysia.

Travel Agencies

For discount airline tickets, long-running and reliable student-travel agencies include the following:

GETTING INTO TOWN

The efficient KLIA Ekspres (adult one way/return RM35/65, 28 minutes, every 15 to 20 minutes from 5am to midnight) spirits you to/from the international airport (KLIA) to the KL City Air Terminal, located in KL Sentral train station. This is without doubt the easiest way to travel to/from the airport.

If you have more time than money, catch the express bus (RM14, 45 minutes, hourly from 7am to 9pm) from the KLIA bus terminal (ground level, Block C of the covered car park) to Chan Sow Lin station on the Star Light Rail Transit (LRT) line, which will deliver you to various central KL destinations. Build in a lot of time for traffic.

For transport die-hards, airport coaches (RM20) also connect KLIA to Chan Sow Lin station on the Star LRT (about one hour). These buses depart for the airport every 30 minutes from 5am to 10.30pm and 6.15am to 12.30pm in the opposite direction.

Taxis from KLIA operate on a fixed-fare coupon system. Purchase a coupon from a counter at the arrival hall and use it to pay the driver. Standard taxis cost RM60 to RM70.

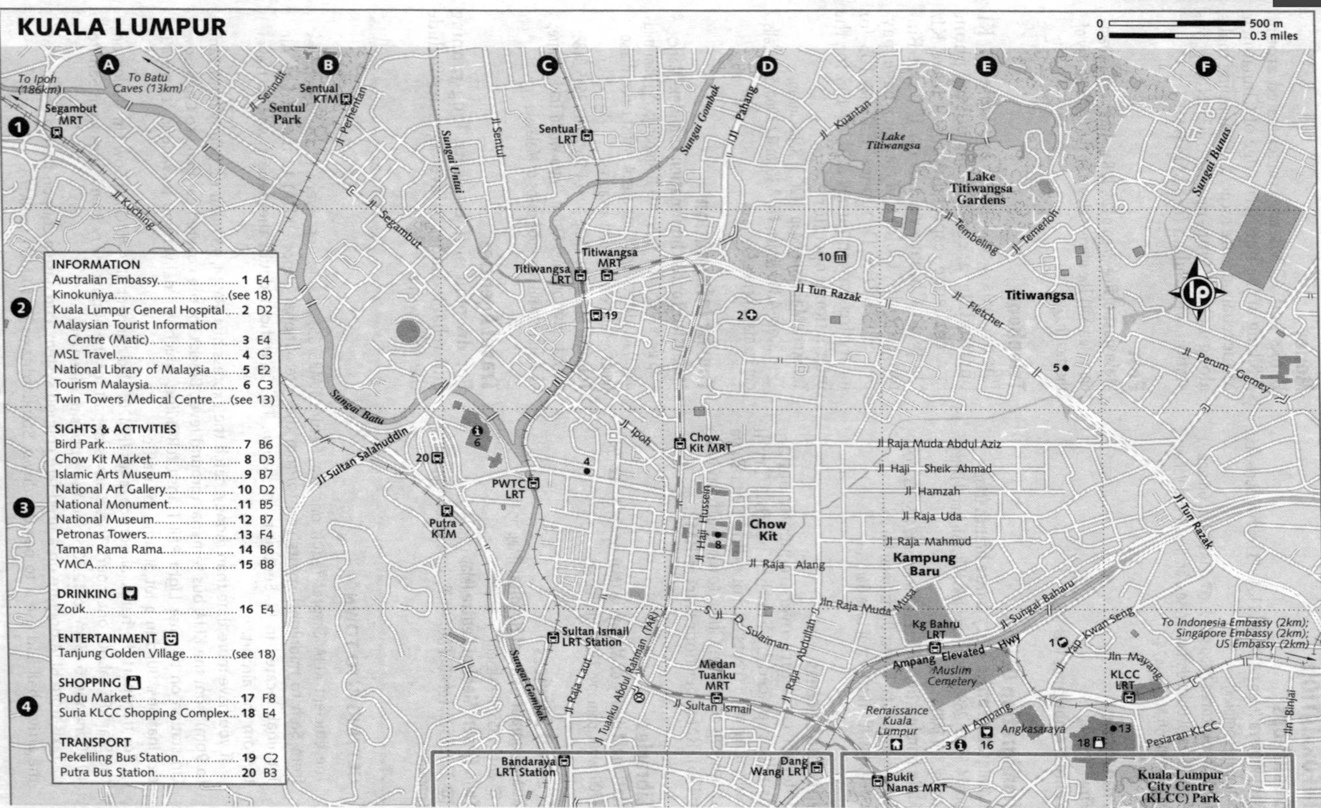

KUALA LUMPUR
INFORMATION
Australian Embassy 1 E4
Kinokuniya (see 18)
Kuala Lumpur General Hospital 2 D2
Malaysian Tourist Information Centre (Matic) 3 E4
MSL Travel 4 C3
National Library of Malaysia 5 E2
Tourism Malaysia 6 C3
Twin Towers Medical Centre (see 13)
SIGHTS & ACTIVITIES
Bird Park 7 B6
Chow Kit Market 8 D3
Islamic Arts Museum 9 B7
National Art Gallery 10 D2
National Monument 11 B5
National Museum 12 B7
Petronas Towers 13 F4
Taman Rama Rama 14 B6
YMCA 15 B8
DRINKING
Zouk 16 E4
ENTERTAINMENT
Tanjung Golden Village (see 18)
SHOPPING
Pudu Market 17 F8
Suria KLCC Shopping Complex 18 E4
TRANSPORT
Pekeliling Bus Station 19 C2
Putra Bus Station 20 B3
500 m
0.3 miles
To Ipoh (186km)
To Batu Caves (13km)
Segambut MRT
Sentul KTM
Sentul Park
Sentul LRT
Jl Sentul
Sungai Untui
Jl Segambut
Jl Kuching
Jl Perhentian
Jl Serindit
Titiwangsa LRT
Titiwangsa MRT
PWTC LRT
Putra KTM
Sungai Batu
Jl Sultan Salahuddin
Sungai Gombak
Jl Pahang
Jl Tun Razak
Lake Titiwangsa
Lake Titiwangsa Gardens
Titiwangsa
Jl Kuantan
Jl Tembeling
Jl Temerloh
Jl Fletcher
Jl Perum Gerney
Sungai Bunus
Chow Kit MRT
Chow Kit
Jl Ipoh
Jl Haji Hussein
Jl Raja Alang
Jl Raja Muda Abdul Aziz
Jl Haji Sheik Ahmad
Jl Hamzah
Jl Raja Uda
Jl Raja Mahmud
Kampung Baru
Kg Bahru LRT
Jln Raja Muda Musa
Jl Raja Abdullah
Jl S D Sulaiman
Jl Sultan Ismail
Medan Tuanku MRT
Jl Tuanku Abdul Rahman (TAR)
Jl Raja Laut
Sultan Ismail LRT Station
Bandaraya LRT Station
Dang Wangi LRT
Bukit Nanas MRT
Renaissance Kuala Lumpur
Ampang Elevated Hwy
Muslim Cemetery
Jl Ampang
Angkasaraya
KLCC LRT
Jln Mayang
Jl Yap Kwan Seng
Jl Sungai Baharu
Pesiaran KLCC
Kuala Lumpur City Centre (KLCC) Park
Jln Binjai
To Indonesia Embassy (2km); Singapore Embassy (2km); US Embassy (2km)

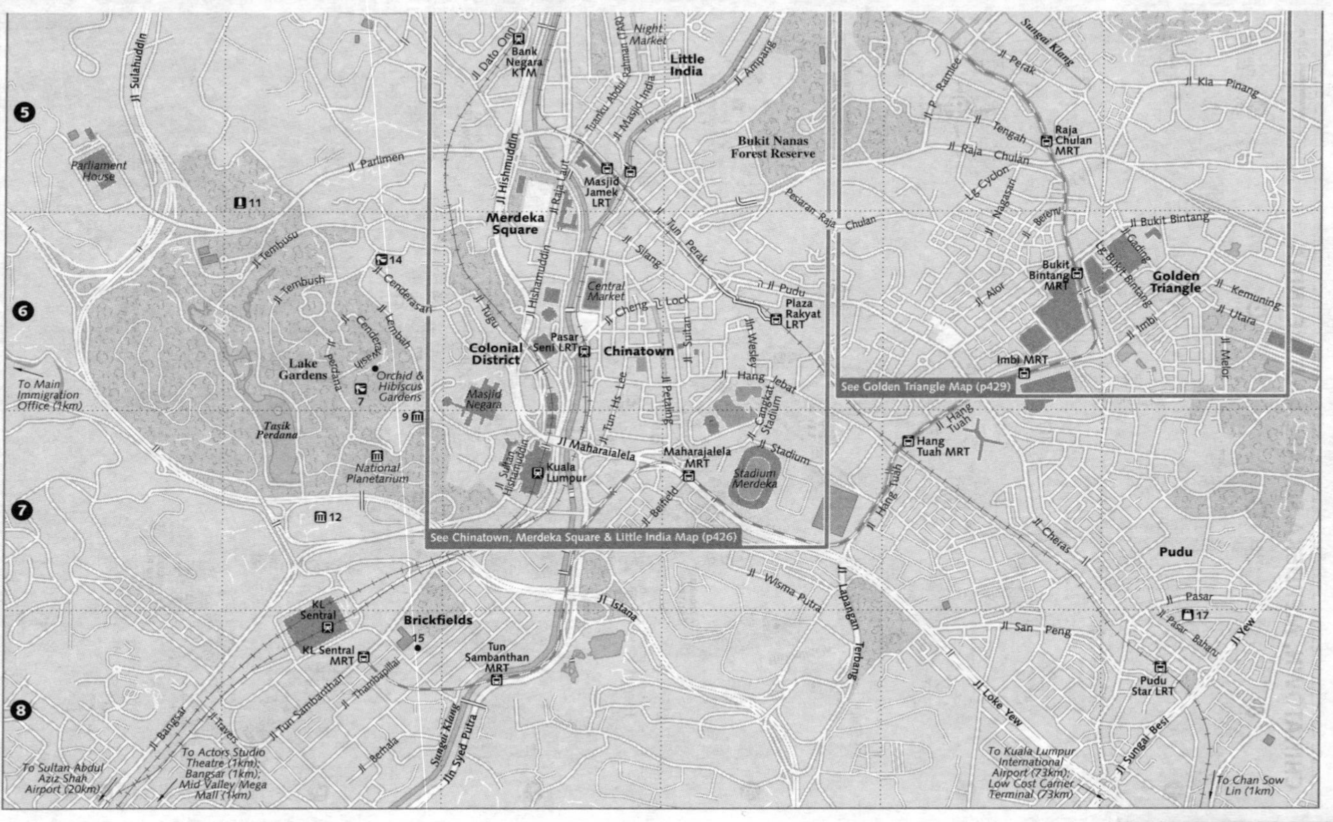
See Golden Triangle Map (p429)
See Chinatown, Merdeka Square & Little India Map (p426)
Golden Triangle
Bukit Bintang MRT
Raja Chulan MRT
Imbi MRT
Hang Tuah MRT
Pudu
Pudu Star LRT
Bukit Nanas Forest Reserve
Little India
Night Market
Masjid Jamek LRT
Merdeka Square
Bank Negara KTM
Plaza Rakyat LRT
Central Market
Chinatown
Pasar Seni LRT
Colonial District
Masjid Negara
Kuala Lumpur
Maharajalela MRT
Stadium Merdeka
Orchid & Hibiscus Gardens
National Planetarium
Lake Gardens
Tasik Perdana
Parliament House
Brickfields
Tun Sambanthan MRT
KL Sentral
KL Sentral MRT
Sungai Klang
Jl Sultan Hishamuddin
Jl Hishamuddin
Jl Tun Perak
Jl Petaling
Jl Tun HS Lee
Jl Maharajalela
Jl Hang Tuah
Jl Hang Jebat
Jl Loke Yew
Jl Cheras
Jl Sungai Besi
Jl Lapangan Terbang
Jl Wisma Putra
Jl Istana
Jln Syed Putra
Jl Tun Sambanthan
Jl Travers
Jl Bangsar
Jl Parlimen
Jl Sulahuddin
Jl Tembusu
Jl Perdana
Jl Cenderasari
Jl Tugu
Jl Ampang
Jl Raja Chulan
Jl P Ramlee
Jl Bukit Bintang
Jl Imbi
Jl Pudu
Jl Tuanku Abdul Rahman (TAR)
Jl Masjid India
Pesiaran Raja Chulan
Jl Kia Pinang
Jl Pasar
Jl Yew
Jl San Peng
To Kuala Lumpur International Airport (73km); Low Cost Carrier Terminal (73km)
To Chan Sow Lin (1km)
To Actors Studio Theatre (1km); Bangsar (1km); Mid Valley Mega Mall (1km)
To Sultan Abdul Aziz Shah Airport (20km)
To Main Immigration Office (1km)
5
6
7
8

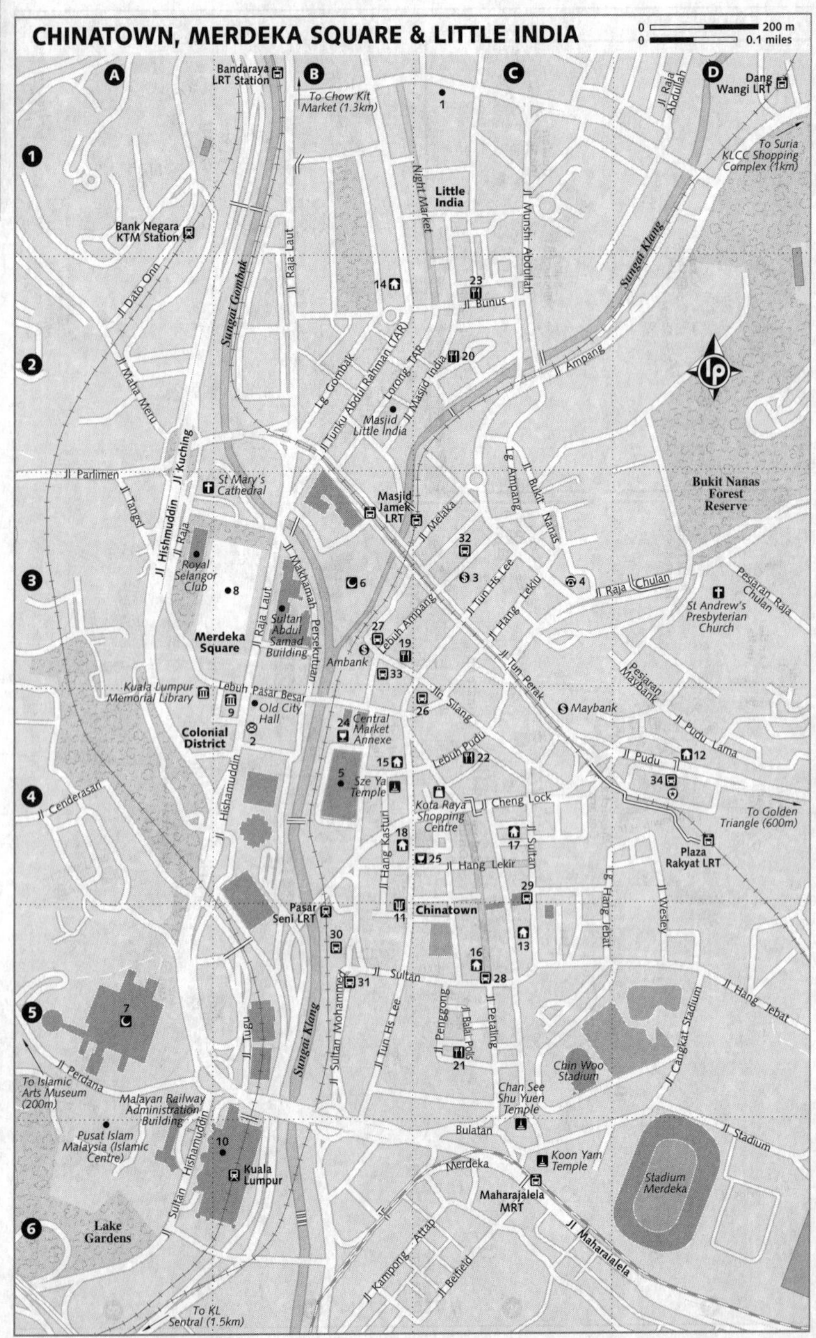

CHINATOWN, MERDEKA SQUARE & LITTLE INDIA
0 200 m
0 0.1 miles
Bandaraya LRT Station
To Chow Kit Market (1.3km)
Dang Wangi LRT
To Suria KLCC Shopping Complex (1km)
Little India
Bank Negara KTM Station
Jl Dato Onn
Sungai Gombak
Jl Raja Laut
Night Market
Jl Munshi Abdullah
Sungai Klang
Jl Raja Abdullah
Jl Bunus
Jl Ampang
Jl Maha Meru
Lg Gombak
Jl Tunku Abdul Rahman (TAR)
Lorong TAR
Jl Masjid India
Masjid Little India
Jl Parlimen
Jl Kuching
St Mary's Cathedral
Jl Tangsi
Masjid Jamek LRT
Jl Melaka
Lg Ampang
Jl Bukit Nanas
Bukit Nanas Forest Reserve
Jl Hishmuddin
Jl Raja
Royal Selangor Club
Jl Mahkamah Persekutuan
Jl Raja Laut
Sultan Abdul Samad Building
Merdeka Square
Lebuh Ampang
Ambank
Jl Tun Hs Lee
Jl Hang Lekiu
Jl Raja Chulan
Pesiaran Raja Chulan
St Andrew's Presbyterian Church
Jl Tun Perak
Pesiaran Maybank
Maybank
Kuala Lumpur Memorial Library
Lebuh Pasar Besar
Old City Hall
Colonial District
Central Market Annexe
Jln Silang
Lebuh Pudu
Jl Pudu
Jl Pudu Lama
Jl Cenderasari
Hishamuddin
Sze Ya Temple
Kota Raya Shopping Centre
Jl Cheng Lock
To Golden Triangle (600m)
Plaza Rakyat LRT
Jl Hang Kasturi
Jl Hang Lekir
Jl Sultan
Pasar Seni LRT
Chinatown
Lg Hang Jebat
Jl Wesley
Jl Sultan
Jl Hang Jebat
Jl Tugu
Sungai Klang
Jl Sultan Mohammed
Jl Tun Hs Lee
Jl Penggong
Jl Balai Polis
Jl Petaling
Chin Woo Stadium
Jl Cangkat Stadium
Jl Perdana
To Islamic Arts Museum (200m)
Malayan Railway Administration Building
Pusat Islam Malaysia (Islamic Centre)
Jl Sultan Hishamuddin
Kuala Lumpur
Chan See Shu Yuen Temple
Bulatan
Jl Stadium
Merdeka
Koon Yam Temple
Maharajalela MRT
Stadium Merdeka
Jl Maharajalela
Lake Gardens
Jl Kampong Attap
Jl Belfield
To KL Sentral (1.5km)

INFORMATION

Immigration Office	1 C1
Main Post Office	2 B4
Moneychangers	3 C3
Telekom Malaysia	4 C3

SIGHTS & ACTIVITIES

Actors Studio Academy	(see 8)
Central Market	5 B4
Masjid Jamek	6 B3
Masjid Negara	7 A5
Merdeka Square	8 B3
National History Museum	9 B4
Old Railway Station	10 B6
Sri Mahamariamman Temple	11 B5

SLEEPING

Anuja Backpackers Inn	12 D4
Backpackers Travellers Inn	13 C5
Coliseum Hotel	14 B2
Le Village	15 B4
Lee Mun Guest House	16 C5
Red Dragon Backpacker's Hostel	17 C4
Wheelers Guesthouse	18 B4

EATING

Fatt Yan Vegetarian Restaurant	19 B3
Food Court	20 C2
Old China Café	21 C5
Restoran Wilayah Baru	22 C4
Restoran Yasin	23 C2

DRINKING

Liquid	24 B4
Reggae Bar	25 C4

TRANSPORT

Buses for Batu Caves	26 C4
Buses for Batu Caves	27 B3
Buses to Kuala Tembeling (Hotel Mandarin Pacific)	28 C5
Buses to Kuala Tembeling (Swiss Inn)	29 C4
Jl Sultan Mohammed Bus Stop	30 B5
Klang Bus Station	31 B5
Lebuh Ampang Bus Stop	32 C3
Long-distance taxis	(see 34)
Medan Pasar Bus Stop	33 B3
Puduraya Bus Station	34 D4

MSL Travel (Map pp424-5; ☎ 4042 4722; msl@po.jaring.my; 66 Jl Putra)
STA Travel (Map p429; ☎ 2143 9800; stakul@po.jaring.my; Lot 506, 5th fl, Plaza Magnum, 128 Jl Pudu)

SIGHTS

Colonial District

Hugging Sungai Klang (Sungai River) between Jl Tun Perak and Jl Kinabalu is Kuala Lumpur's colonial district (Map p426). The symbolic heart is **Merdeka Square** (Jl Raja Laut), a formal parade ground around which dutifully pose the architectural legacies of Malaysia's successive conquerors, both Islamic and European. Fittingly, the nation's independence was proclaimed here in 1957.

Further south is the **old railroad station** (Jl Hishamuddin), a fanciful castle of Islamic arches and spires.

The **National History Museum** (☎ 2694 4590; 29 Jl Raja Laut; admission free; 🕒 9am-6pm) will instil a sense of Malaysian pride in a new arrival, plus the 2nd-floor view of Merdeka Sq is stunning.

Masjid Jamek (Jl Tun Perak; admission free; 🕒 8.30am-12.30pm & 2.30-4pm) is a tranquil creation built in 1907 and set in a grove of palm trees; headscarves and robes are provided at the gate. It's closed during Friday prayers (11am to 2.30pm).

Masjid Negara (National Mosque; Jl Perdana; admission free; 🕒 9am-12.30pm, 2-3.30pm & 5-6.30pm) is one of Southeast Asia's largest mosques. The main dome is an 18-pointed star, symbolising the 13 states of Malaysia and the five pillars of Islam. You should dress conservatively and remove your shoes.

The colonial district is served by the Pasar Seni LRT station to the south and the Masjid Jamek station to the north.

Chinatown

Circuitous streets and cramped chaos create a pressure-cooker of sights and sounds in Chinatown (Map p426). **Jl Petaling** is a bustling street market selling souvenirs, such as 'authentic' Paul Frank and cheap Birkenstocks and Levis; it opens around 10am and shuts late at night. Chinatown is accessed on the Putra LRT to Pasar Seni station or on the KL Monorail to Maharajalela station.

Chinese **coffee shops** are along Jl Penggong and Jl Balai Polis. You'll spot temples and shophouses in the side streets – check out KL's principal Hindu temple, **Sri Mahamariamman Temple** (Jl HS Lee).

Near the city's original market and gambling sheds is **Central Market** (Jl Cheng Lock; 🕒 10am-10pm), a refurbished Art Deco building that sells Malay crafts and art.

Little India

Little India (Map p426) has all the feel of a bazaar. The sari shops and the women shopping along **Jl Masjid India**, the district's main street, are swathed in vibrant sherbets, turquoise and vermilions. Meanwhile Indian pop blasts through tinny speakers, and musky incense and delicious spices flavour the air. The district swings into full spectacle during the Saturday *pasar malam* (night market). Little

India is best reached on the Star or Putra LRT to Masjid Jamek station.

Golden Triangle

A forest of high-rises, the Golden Triangle is central KL's business, shopping and entertainment district. Several nightspots hang out along Jl Sultan Ismail and Jl Ramlee.

Sitting on a forested hill, **Menara Kuala Lumpur** (Kuala Lumpur Tower; Map p429; ☎ 2020 5448; Jl Punchak; adult/child RM20/10; 9am-10pm, last tickets 9.30pm) is the fourth-highest telecommunications tower in the world. Visitors can ride the lift right up to the viewing deck (276m) for superb panoramic views, superior to those from the Petronas Towers. Take the KL Monorail to Bukit Nanas station.

Formerly the world's tallest skyscrapers (until Taipei 101 took the title in 2004), the twin **Petronas Towers** (Map pp424-5; www.petronas.com.my/petronas; Jl Ampang; admission free; 9am-1pm & 2.30-4.45pm Tue-Sun) serve as the elegant headquarters of the national petroleum company. This steel-and-glass monument weaves together traditional Islamic symbolism with modern sophistication. First-come, first-serve tickets are available for visiting the 41st-floor Skybridge that connects the two towers; tickets are issued from 8.30am and 15-minute visits start at 10am. Arrive around 8am to start queuing if you're particular about the time you want to go up, but tickets are often available until around 11am. To get here, take the Putra LRT to KLCC station.

Lake Gardens & Around

Escape from the heat and concrete to this inner-city garden district (Map pp424–5) at the western edge of central KL. From Chinatown, Intrakota bus 21C from the Jl Sultan Mohammed bus stop, or buses 21B, 22, 48C and F3, will take you there. It is also a 20-minute walk from Masjid Jamek.

The gardens contain a host of attractions such as the **Bird Park** (☎ 2273 5423; adult RM28; 9am-7.30pm) and **Taman Rama Rama** (Butterfly Park; adult RM15; 9am-6pm). You can take a leisurely stroll around them, or catch the shuttle bus (adult RM1; operating 9am to 6pm Thursday to Saturday and noon to 3pm Friday) that does a loop of the area.

At the edge of the Lake Gardens, the **National Museum** (Muzium Negara; ☎ 2282 6255; Jl Damansara; adult RM2; 9am-6pm) boasts colourful displays on Malaysia's history, economy, arts, crafts and culture.

Near Lake Gardens, the **Islamic Arts Museum** (Muzium Kesenian Islam Malaysia; ☎ 2274 2020; Jl Lembah Perdana; adult RM12; 10am-6pm Tue-Sun) has scale models of the world's most famous mosques and a full-scale interior reproduction of a typical Muslim room of the Ottoman Empire.

Northern KL

In the characterless expanse of Chow Kit is the claustrophobic, covered **Chow Kit Market** (Map pp424-5; Jl TAR; 8am-8pm) for sundries by day and food by night. Take the KL Monorail to Chow Kit station for this place. See p432 for more details

Further north near Lake Titiwangsa, the **National Art Gallery** (Map pp424-5; Balai Seni Lukis Negara; ☎ 4025 4990; Jl Temerloh, off Jl TAR; admission free; 10am-6pm) displays works by contemporary Malaysian and international artists. Take any Len Seng bus from Lebuh Ampang (north of Central Market) in Chinatown or from along Jl Raja Laut; get off at the hospital stop.

ACTIVITIES

There's a concentration of **Chinese massage** and reflexology places along Jl Bukit Bintang,

BATU CAVES

Get closer to KL's Indian culture by visiting the **Batu Caves** (admission free; 8am-8pm), a system of three caves 13km northwest of the capital. The most famous is Temple Cave, because it contains a Hindu shrine reached by a straight flight of 272 steps, guarded by a 43m-high Murga statue, the highest in the world. About a million pilgrims come here every year during Thaipusam (January/February) to engage in or watch the spectacularly masochistic feats of the devotees.

From Chinatown, take Intrakota bus 11D (RM1.20, 30 minutes) from the stop in front of the Bangkok Bank (next to Le Village) on Jl Tun HS Lee, or Cityliner bus 69 (RM1.20) from Medan Pasar, near the HSBC bank. Bus 11D also stops along Jl Raja Laut in the Chow Kit area. During Thaipusam special trains and buses run to the caves.

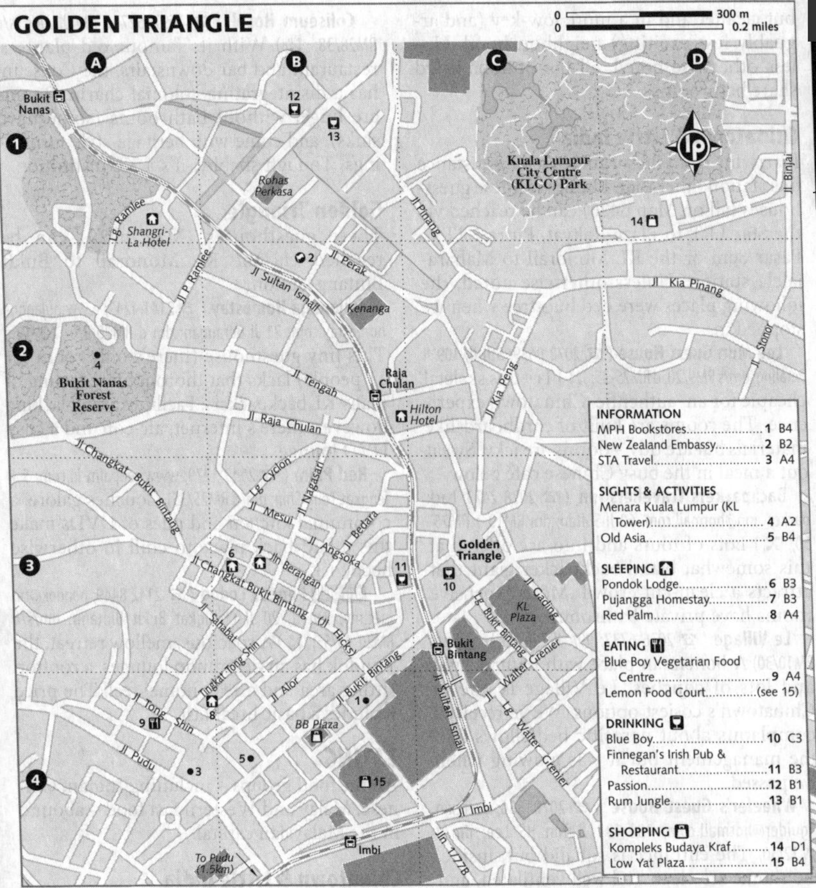

south of BB Plaza. The going price is usually RM65 for a one-hour full-body massage, but try bargaining for RM50. Expect to pay about RM25 for 30 minutes of foot reflexology. **Old Asia** (Map p429; ☎ 2143 9888; 14 Jl Bukit Bintang; 🕙 10am-10pm), one of the more reliable and pleasantly designed places, offers a 20% discount between noon and 7pm.

If you'd rather be the one pounding your hands, you can join the **Tugu Drum Circle** at the National Monument (Map pp424–5) in the Lake Gardens from 5.30pm to 8.30pm every Sunday.

COURSES

Actors Studio Academy (Map p426; ☎ 2697 2797; www.theactorsstudio.com.my; Lot 19, Plaza Putra) This academy in the underground Plaza Putra at Merdeka Sq has workshops on everything from modern choreography and classical Indian dance to Chinese orchestral music.

YMCA (Map pp424-5; ☎ 2274 1439; 95 Jl Padang Belia) This Brickfield hostel and community centre offers a variety of short- and long-term language classes in Bahasa Malaysia, Hindi, Thai, Mandarin, Cantonese and Japanese, as well as courses in martial arts.

SLEEPING

Vibrant Chinatown is your best hunting ground for rock-bottom crash pads and is an easy walk from the Puduraya bus station. Unfortunately, at the time of writing it was swarming with bed bugs. The Golden Triangle area's budget options are pricier but cleaner and in a more low-key (and arguably less exciting) neighbourhood. Unless otherwise noted, all the options listed share bathrooms.

Chinatown & Little India

If arriving from the airport or a long-distance bus station other than Puduraya, these guesthouses (all on Map p426) can be reached via the Star LRT to Plaza Rakyat, Putra LRT to Pasar Seni or the KL Monorail to Maharajalela station. Unless otherwise noted, the following places were bed bug-free when we stopped in.

Lee Mun Guest House (☎ 2078 0639; 5th fl, 109 Jl Petaling; dm/s RM9/20, d RM25-35;) Try this skeletal cheapie for an 'authentic' Chinatown experience. The rooms are built of cardboard-like materials but are tidy – dorms are icky. Sweat out a meal in the busy Chinese café below.

Backpackers Travellers Inn (☎ 2078 2473; backpacker_inn@hotmail.com; 60 Jl Sultan; dm RM10, r RM25-50;) Lots of tours and info are offered at this somewhat bland backpacker giant that attracts a clean-cut crowd. More expensive rooms have private bathrooms.

Le Village (☎ 2026 6737; 99A Jl Tun HS Lee; dm/r RM10/30) A bohemian place with natural light and lots of couches, Le Village is one of Chinatown's cosiest options. We've received complaints about parasitic bedfellows and the management but it was glowing when we passed.

Wheeler's Guest House (☎ 20701386; szerzxin_guider@hotmail.com; 131-133 Jl Tun HS Lee; dm/d RM12/30) The entrance is squalid but, inside, the rooms are clean and well ventilated, and the staff are friendly. Character comes from potted plants, fish and murals and there's even a rooftop garden.

Red Dragon Backpacker's Hostel (☎ 2078 9366; 83 Jl Sultan; dm RM12, r RM40-60;) Everything from the cavernous entrance to the internet station is supersized at this megalith – except the rooms and the welcome. Some rooms have private bathrooms. Try the 3rd floor if you want a window. Grab a cheap beer and catch a movie on one of the common area TVs.

Anuja Backpackers Inn (☎ 2026 6479; anuja@sgsmc.com; 1st-3rd fl, 28 Jl Pudu; r RM25-40;) There's hardly room to change your mind, but this reliably clean and friendly place is convenient for early departures or late arrivals from the Puduraya bus station.

Coliseum Hotel (☎ 2692 6270; 100 Jl TAR; s/d RM28/38;) With its famous old planters' restaurant and bar downstairs, the Coliseum has a disintegrating colonial charm. Rooms are huge, without bathrooms (some have sinks), and come with heritage-style furnishings. Though shabby, it's a KL institution.

Golden Triangle

These guesthouses (Map p429) can be reached via the KL Monorail to Bukit Bintang station.

Pujannga Homestay (☎ 2141 4243; www.pujanggahomestay.com; 21 Jl Berangan; dm/d RM20/35;) This tiny guesthouse (there's only room for 11 people) lacks that thoroughfare feeling of many KL backpackers. Facilities aren't lacking however: there's internet, air-con and a cosy DVD lounge.

Red Palm (☎ 2143 1279; www.redpalm-kl.com; 5 Jl Tengkat Tong Shin; dm/d RM25/35) Couches galore, a communal kitchen and piles of DVDs make this a laid-back place to chill in otherwise hectic KL.

our pick **Pondok Lodge** (☎ 2142 8449; pondok@tm.net.my; 3rd fl, 20 Jl Changkat Bukit Bintang; dm/s/d RM20/45/55;) A spacious, mellow retreat, the Pondok has airy common lounges, a rooftop sitting area and a real 'home' feel. The price includes a basic breakfast.

EATING

All the food groups – including Indian, Chinese, Malay and Western fast food – abound in the Malaysian capital.

Chinatown & Little India

In the morning, grab a marble-topped table in one of the neighbourhood's *kedai kopi* (coffee shops) for a jolt of joe spiked with condensed milk. The midday meal can be slurped down at the stalls that line Jl Sultan serving all the you-name-it noodles, from prawn or *won ton mee* (Chinese-style egg noodles served with stuffed wontons) to *laksa lemak* (white rounded noodles served with coconut milk, also called curry laksa). Jl Petaling market is closed to traffic in the evenings and Chinese restaurants set up tables beside all the action.

Little India is your best hunting ground for a slap-up Indian curry sopped up with flaky *roti canai* (Indian-style flaky flat bread, also known as 'flying dough'). All places are on Map p426.

GAY & LESBIAN KUALA LUMPUR

Check out Prince World KL at www.princeworldkl.com for upcoming dance parties around KL.

Liquid (Map p426; ☎ 2078 5909; Central Market Annexe; admission RM10; 5pm-3am Wed-Sun) This relaxed riverside bar heats up Saturday nights when the 2nd-floor disco opens up. It attracts a mixed, sophisticated crowd and lots of couples.

Blue Boy (Map p429; ☎ 2142 1067; 54 Jl Sultan Ismail; 5pm-3am) Malaysia's oldest gay club is a gritty pick-up joint with karaoke-singing lady boys and grimy toilets.

Restoran Wilayah Baru (29 Lebuh Pudu; meals RM2-5; breakfast, lunch & dinner) An excellent eatery with cheap Indian-Malay food.

Restoran Yasin (☎ 2698 2710; 141 Jl Bunus; meals RM3.50-7; breakfast, lunch & dinner) A locals' institution serving incredibly tasty South and North Indian fare.

Fatt Yan Vegetarian Restaurant (☎ 2070 6561; cnr Jl Tun HS Lee & Jl Silang; meals RM18; lunch & dinner) Herbivores will approve of this Buddhist Chinese restaurant that eschews meat but cooks up some awfully good substitutes.

Old China Café (☎ 20725915; 11 Jl Balai Polis; meals RM25-40; dinner) Granted it's a tourist spot, but one that nails the 1920s Sino fantasy of shadow-casting ceiling fans, time-worn antiques and a soundtrack of sparrow sopranos. Spicy dishes of the Baba Nonya (descendants of Chinese Straits settlers who intermarried with Malays) are a speciality.

A busy **food court** (Jl Masjid India) gobbles up a big block. Little India's Saturday night market, at the north end of Lorong TAR, has sensational tucker and a great atmosphere.

Golden Triangle & KLCC

Jl Nagsari, off Jl Changkat Bukit Bintang (Map p429), is lined with Malay food stalls and open-air restaurants. Jl Alor, two streets northwest of Jl Bukit Bintang, has a carnival-like night market of Chinese hawker stalls. When it's hot outside, head to central KL's air-con shopping centres for international and local food. Take the KL Monorail to Bukit Bintang to reach these.

Lemon Food Court (Map p429; Low Yat Plaza; meals RM4-8; lunch & dinner) Lemon Food Court has sizzling hot plates, mouth-watering aromas and a more proletarian ambience than hoity-toity KLCC. It's in the basement of Low Yat Plaza (see p432).

Blue Boy Vegetarian Food Centre (Map p429; ☎ 2144 9011; Jl Tong Shin; meals RM5-10; 7.30am-9.30pm) Get all your meat and fish substitutes prepared local style at this spotless, backstreet eatery.

Suria KLCC Shopping Complex (Map pp424-5; ☎ 2382 2828; Jl Ampang; meals RM10-20; lunch & dinner) This upscale shopping centre has a modern 2nd-floor food court with everything from sushi and pizza to Malaysian cuisine.

DRINKING

Drinking in Malaysia is no budget activity (around RM10 per bottle of beer) and drinks at 'proper' bars are nearly double in price. The cheapest places to imbibe are Chinese eateries or open-air hawker stalls.

The intersection of Jl Sultan Ismail and Jl P Ramlee forms a Texas-sized watering-hole complex with lots of freshly pressed patrons.

Reggae Bar (Map p426; ☎ 2272 2158; 158 Jl Tun HS Lee) Here you'll find Bob Marley tunes, drink promotions and a lot of backpackers.

Finnegan's Irish Pub & Restaurant (Map p429; ☎ 2284 9024; 6 Jl Telawi Lima) This is a first-rate place for a knees up with live ESPN sports coverage, enthusiastic staff, stout and a decent menu.

Rum Jungle (Map p429; ☎ 2148 0282; cnr Jl P Ramlee & Jl Pinang) Take a trip on the wild side with the other party animals who roam this sprawling complex of thatched huts.

CLUBBING

Check out the latest club news in **KLue** (www.klue.com.my; RM5) or **Juice** (www.juiceonline.com; free). Clubs usually open Wednesday to Sunday and charge a RM20 to RM30 cover charge Thursday to Saturday. The whole scene is very premillennium.

Zouk (Map pp424-5; ☎ 2171 1997; www.zoukclub.com.my; 113 Jl Ampang) There's a theme for everyone here from the small and edgy Loft Bar, to a plastic palm-fringed main venue and sophisticated Velvet Underground (including entry to Zouk RM45).

Passion (Map p429; ☎ 2141 8888; www.poppy-collection.com; 18-1 Jl P Ramlee; cover RM25) R&B and house music literally have the floors shaking at this very popular club right in the epicentre of the Golden Triangle party zone.

ENTERTAINMENT

Tanjung Golden Village (Map pp424-5; ☎ 7492 2929; www.tgv.com.my; 3rd fl, Suria KLCC Shopping Complex) The latest Bollywood and Hollywood blockbusters can be viewed in the arctic atmosphere of KL's most convenient multiscreen cinema.

Actors Studio Theatre (off Map pp424-5; ☎ 2694 5400; www.theactorsstudio.com.my; 3rd fl, New Wing, Bangsar Shopping Centre, 285 Jl Maarof; tickets RM25-45) This well-regarded company hosts contemporary Malaysian plays and adaptations of classic theatre performances. Workshops are also offered – see p429.

Regular cultural performances and shows are held at the **Malaysian Tourist Information Complex** (Matic; Map pp424-5; ☎ 2164 3929, 2163 3667; 109 Jl Ampang; adult RM5; 🕑 2-2.30pm Tue, Thu, Sat & Sun) and the **Central Market** (Map p426; ☎ 2274 6542; admission free; 🕑 available from information desk).

SHOPPING

Jl Petaling in the heart of Chinatown is a noisy, writhing mass of people and outdoor stalls selling cheap clothes, fruit, pirated CDs and a smattering of crafts; bargain very, very hard. More everyday items can be found at the tightly jammed **Chow Kit Market** (Map pp424-5; Jl TAR; 🕑 8am-8pm); also see p428 for details. For produce and weird meats from stingray to pig's penises, go to KL's largest wet market, the frenetic **Pudu Market** (Map pp424-5; 🕑 6am-2pm). The best *pasar melam* are on Saturday nights along Lorong TAR in Little India (Map p426) and Jl Raja Muda in Kampung Baru (Map pp424–5), southeast of Chow Kit. The Jl Masjid India in Little India is the place to shop for saris, Indian silks, carpets and other textiles.

Low Yat Plaza (Map p429; ☎ 2148 3651; 7 Jl 1/77 off Bukit Bintang) Go here for all your digital and electronic needs.

Kompleks Budaya Kraf (Map p429; ☎ 2162 7459; Jl Conlay; 🕑 10am-6pm) This place has a large selection of handicrafts.

> **STREET FASHION**
>
> The diversity of Malaysian fashion makes Western wardrobes look like government-issued uniforms. Walking the streets, you might pass a Muslim woman framed by a tropically coloured headscarf and a flowing full-length skirt and blouse *(baju kurung)*. Turn a corner and you pass a Chinese woman wearing a catwalk miniskirt and a tank top. Following close behind is an older Indian woman wrapped tight in a sari. She and her daughter, in jeans and flip-flops, both wear *bindis* (the Hindu forehead dot). In just one block, the street fashions have spanned continents and no one has given another a disapproving look.

GETTING THERE & AWAY

Kuala Lumpur is Malaysia's principal international arrival gateway and it forms the crossroads for domestic bus, train and taxi travel.

Air

For details of international airlines, see p418.

Kuala Lumpur International Airport (KLIA; off Map pp424-5; ☎ 8777 8888; www.klia.com.my; Pengrus Besar) is a flamboyant structure, located 75km south of the city centre at Sepang. Many airlines service this airport, but the country's international airline, **Malaysia Airlines** (☎ 1300 883 000; www.malaysiaairlines.com.my), is the major carrier. **Air Asia** (code AK; ☎ 8775 4000; www.airasia.com) flights arrive and depart from the nearby **Low Cost Carrier Terminal** (LCCT; off Map pp424-5; ☎ 1300 889 933) while **Berjaya Air** (code J8; ☎ 2145 2828; www.berjaya-air.com) flights use **Sultan Abdul Aziz Shah Airport** (off Map pp424-5; ☎ 7845 8382) in Subang, about 20km west of the city centre. See p421 for information on domestic routes and costs.

Bus

Most long-distance buses operate from the **Puduraya bus station** (Map p426; Jl Pudu), situated just east of Chinatown. A few travellers have reported being robbed late at night, so stay alert while in the area. The tourist police and information counters are right inside the main entrance. The left-luggage office is at the back. From Puduraya, buses go all over Peninsular Malaysia, Singapore and Thailand. The only long-distance destinations that Puduraya doesn't handle are Kuala Lipis and Jerantut, which leave only from Pekeliling bus station.

Pekeliling (Map pp424-5; ☎ 4042 7256; Jl Tun Razak) and **Putra** (Map pp424-5; ☎ 4042 9530; Jl Putra) bus stations in the north of the city handle a greater number of services to the east coast than Puduraya. Buses at these stations often have seats available when Puduraya buses are fully booked.

Typical fares and journey times travelling from KL:

Destination	Fare (RM)	Duration (hr)
Cameron Highlands	20	3½
Georgetown (Penang)	24	5
Ipoh	14	3
Johor Bahru	24	4
Kota Bharu	30	10
Kuala Terengganu	30	7
Kuantan	17	4½
Lumut	19	4
Melaka	10	2½
Mersing	20	5½
Singapore	30	5½

Taxi

The long-distance taxi stand is on the 2nd floor of the **Puduraya bus station** (Map p426; Jl Pudu). Fixed whole-taxi fares include: Cameron Highlands (RM200), Melaka (RM150) and Penang (RM360). Do your homework on prices before dealing with taxi drivers who are unscrupulous about ripping-off tourists.

Train

KL is the hub of the **KTM** (☎ 2267 1200; www.ktmb.com.my) national railway system. The long-distance trains depart from KL Sentral (Map pp424–5). The **KTM information office** (🕑 10am-7pm) in the main hall can advise on schedules. There are departures for Butterworth, Alor Setar, Wakaf Baharu, Johor Bahru, Singapore and Thailand. Express-train seats can be booked up to 60 days in advance.

Not to be confused with the intercity long-distance line is the KTM Komuter, which runs from KL Sentral, linking central KL with the Klang Valley and Seremban.

GETTING AROUND

KL has an extensive public transport system. See p423 for details of getting to the city centre from KLIA airport. The only transport option to Sultan Abdul Aziz Shah Airport is a taxi; expect to pay RM50 to RM80.

Bus

Of the many local bus companies, **Intrakota** (☎ 7727 2727) and **Cityliner** (☎ 7982 7060) are the largest. Local buses leave from many of the bus terminals around the city, including **Puduraya bus station** (Map p426; Jl Pudu), near Plaza Rakyat LRT station, and Klang bus station (Map p426), near Pasar Seni LRT station. The maximum fare is usually RM1 for destinations within the city limits; try to have the correct change ready when you board.

Taxi

Taxis in KL have meters but drivers refuse to use them so you have to bargain. Ask at your hotel about approximate fares before heading to a taxi stand, since the price skyrockets when a tourist approaches. Watch out for drivers who use the meter only when traffic is heavy – in this case the fare might be double (or more) the bargained rate. Trips around town are about RM5 to RM10.

Train

KL's pride and joy is the user-friendly **Light Rail Transit** (LRT; ☎ 1800 388 288; www.rapidkl.com.my) system, which is composed of the Ampang/Sentul Timur, Sri Petaling/Sentul Timur and Kelana Jaya/Terminal Putra lines. Fares range from RM1 to RM2.80 and trains run every six to 10 minutes from 6am to 11.50pm (11.30pm Sunday and holidays).

The **KL Monorail** (☎ 2273 1888) is a 16km elevated single-track train convenient for hops between Chinatown and the northern areas of Bukit Bintang and Chow Kit. Fares are RM1.20 to RM2.50 and trains run every 15 minutes from 6am to midnight.

KTM Komuter (☎ 2272 2828), not to be confused with the long-distance KTM service (see left), links Kuala Lumpur with outlying suburbs and the historic railway station.

KL Sentral station (Map pp424–5), in the Brickfields area, is the central transit station for all train travel in KL. Other interchange stations include Masjid Jamek (Map p426), for transfer between Star and Putra LRT; Hang Tuah and Titiwangsa (Map pp424–5), for transfer between KL Monorail and Star LRT; Bukit Nanas (Map p429), transfer between KL Monorail and Putra LRT; and Tasik Selatan, for transfer between KTM Komuter and Star LRT.

PENINSULAR MALAYSIA – WEST COAST

Malaysia's multiculturalism is best viewed along the west coast. Nestled against the Straits of Melaka, protected, for the most part, against swells and tsunamis, this part of the peninsula has entertained foreign visitors since the days of early traders. Such a convenient shipping route has, over the centuries, created a cosmopolitan populace, well-schooled in English. The beaches and islands of this coast don't compare to those in the east or in other areas of Southeast Asia, but offer a laid-back opportunity to experience an authentic Malay way of life.

MELAKA

☎ 06 / pop 648,500

Lovers of beauty and food will become instantly intoxicated by the sultry charms of Melaka. The narrow streets of Chinatown exude small-town calm yet every cosmopolitan necessity is here, from funky cafés and eclectic art galleries to a diverse collection of restaurants and a congenial drinking scene. Beyond Chinatown, Melaka loses its soul to traffic, cement and over-sized shopping malls.

Historically Melaka has been one of the most sought-after havens in the region. In the 14th century Parameswara, a Hindu prince from Sumatra, chose Melaka as a favoured port for resupplying trading ships. From this time, Melaka became protected by the Chinese in 1405, then dominated by the Portuguese in 1511, then the Dutch in 1641 and then finally ceded to the British in 1795. The intermingling of peoples created the Peranakan people (also called Baba Nonya) who are descended from Chinese settlers who intermarried with Malays, the Chitties who are of mixed Indian and Malay heritage and Eurasians born of Malay and Portuguese love affairs.

Orientation

Chinatown is undoubtedly Melaka's most interesting and scenic area. Town Sq, also known as Dutch Sq, is the centre of a well-preserved museum district. Further to the northeast is Melaka's tiny Little India. Most of the backpacker guesthouses are in the newer, less charming part of town off Jl Melaka Raya.

Information

BOOKSHOPS

MPH (Ground fl, Mahkota Parade Shopping Complex; Jl Merdeka)

EMERGENCY

Tourist Police (☎ 285 4114; Jl Kota)

IMMIGRATION OFFICES

Immigration office (☎ 282 4958; 2nd fl, Wisma Persekutuan, Jl Hang Tuah)

INTERNET ACCESS

Internet Centre (Jl Bunga Raya)

MEDICAL SERVICES

Southern Hospital (☎ 283 588; 169 Jl Bendahara)

MONEY

Moneychangers are scattered about town, especially near the guesthouses off Jl TMR and Chinatown.

HSBC (Jl Hang Tuah) With 24-hour ATMs that accept international cards.

OCBC Bank (Lorong Hang Jebat) Has a 24-hour ATM at a branch just over the bridge in Chinatown.

POST & TELEPHONE

Post office (Jl Laksamana) A small post office can be found off Town Sq.

Telekom Malaysia (🕑 8am-5pm) East of Bukit St Paul.

TOURIST INFORMATION

Tourist office (☎ 281 4803; www.melaka.gov.my; Jl Kota; 🕑 8.45am-5pm, closed 12.15-2.45pm Fri) West of Town Sq.

Sights

TOWN SQUARE & BUKIT ST PAUL

The most imposing relic of the Dutch period in Melaka is **Stadthuys** (Town Sq; adult RM5; 🕑 9am-5.30pm Sat-Thu, 9am-12.15pm & 2.45-5.30pm Fri), the massive red town hall and governors' residence. Believed to be the oldest Dutch building in the East, it now houses the **Historical, Ethnographic & Literature Museums**, which is included in the price of admission and exhaustively recounts Malaysian history and literary development. Facing the square is the bright-red **Christ Church** (1753), completing the geographic and cultural fantasy that this is just another Dutch village beside a tamed river.

From Stadthuys, steps lead up Bukit St Paul, which is a hill topped by the ruins of **St Paul's Church**, built in 1521 by a Portuguese sea captain, and overlooking the famous Straits of Melaka.

It took the Portuguese a month to divide and conquer Melaka's sultan rulers. After the siege ended, the Portuguese ousted the city's Muslim traders, tore down the primary mosque and replaced it with a fort named A Famosa ('The Famous'). Later, Dutch and

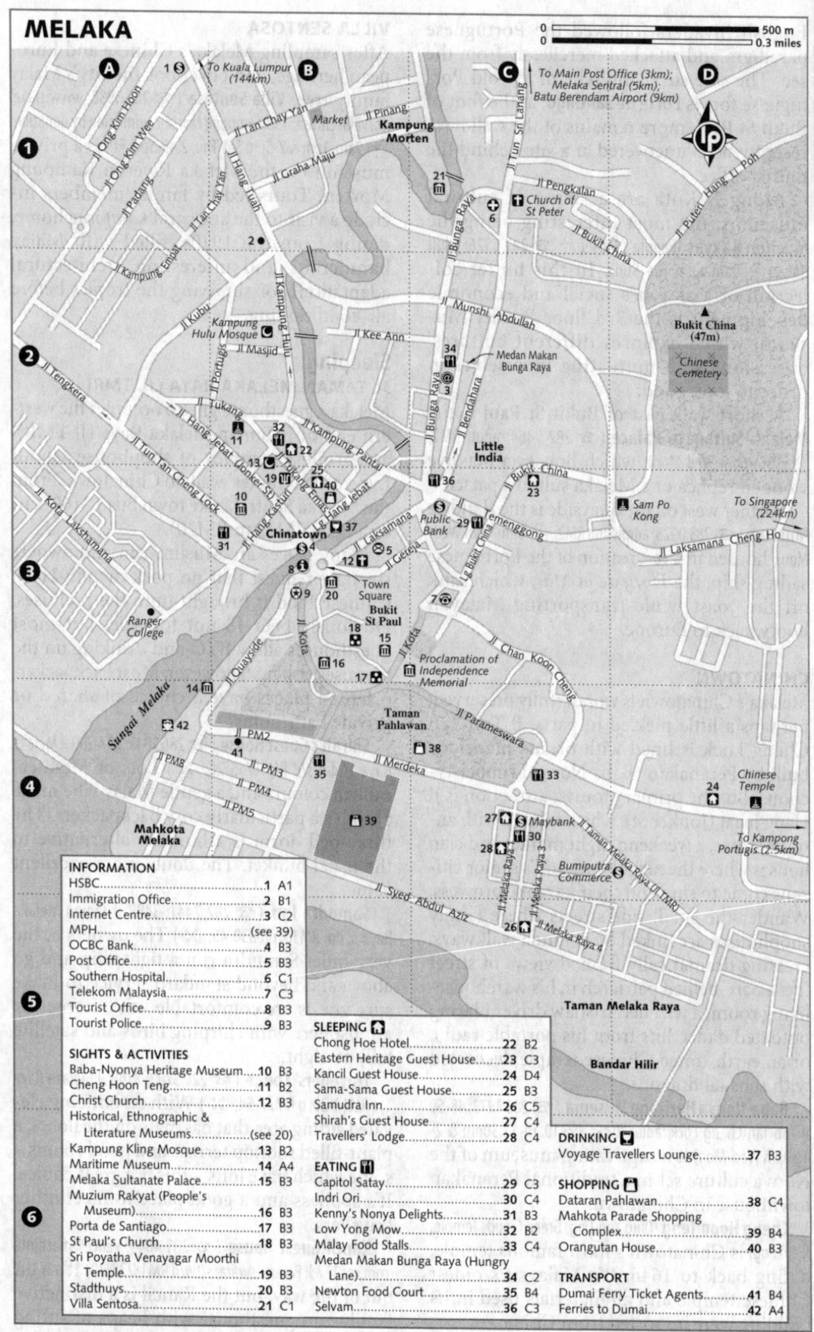
MELAKA
0 500 m
0 0.3 miles
To Kuala Lumpur (144km)
To Main Post Office (3km); Melaka Sentral (5km); Batu Berendam Airport (9km)
To Singapore (224km)
To Kampong Portugis (2.5km)
Kampung Morten
Market
Jl Tan Chay Yan
Jl Pinang
Jl Ong Kim Hoon
Jl Ong Kim Wee
Jl Graha Maju
Jl Hang Tuah
Jl Padang
Jl Kampung Empat
Jl Tun Sri Lanang
Jl Pengkalan
Church of St Peter
Jl Bukit China
Jl Puteri Hang Li Poh
Jl Bunga Raya
Jl Kampung Hulu
Jl Kubu
Kampung Hulu Mosque
Jl Kee Ann
Jl Masjid
Jl Munshi Abdullah
Bukit China (47m)
Chinese Cemetery
Medan Makan Bunga Raya
Jl Bendahara
Jl Tengkera
Jl Portugis
Jl Tukang
Jl Hang Jebat (Jonker St)
Jl Kampung Pantai
Little India
Jl Tun Tan Cheng Lock
Jl Tukang Emas
Lg Hang Jebat
Jl Bukit China
Sam Po Kong
Jl Kota Lakshamana
Jl Hang Kasturi
Chinatown
Public Bank
Jl Temenggong
Jl Laksamana
Jl Gereja
Lg Bukit China
Jl Laksamana Cheng Ho
Town Square
Bukit St Paul
Ranger College
Jl Kota
Jl Chan Koon Cheng
Jl Quayside
Proclamation of Independence Memorial
Sungai Melaka
Taman Pahlawan
Jl Parameswara
Jl PM2
Jl PM8
Jl PM3
Jl PM4
Jl PM5
Jl Merdeka
Chinese Temple
Mahkota Melaka
Maybank
Jl Taman Melaka Raya (Jl TMR)
Jl Melaka Raya 1
Jl Melaka Raya 3
Jl Melaka Raya 4
Bumiputra Commerce
Jl Syed Abdul Aziz
Taman Melaka Raya
Bandar Hilir
INFORMATION
HSBC 1 A1
Immigration Office 2 B1
Internet Centre 3 C2
MPH (see 39)
OCBC Bank 4 B3
Post Office 5 B3
Southern Hospital 6 C1
Telekom Malaysia 7 C3
Tourist Office 8 B3
Tourist Police 9 B3
SIGHTS & ACTIVITIES
Baba-Nyonya Heritage Museum 10 B3
Cheng Hoon Teng 11 B2
Christ Church 12 B3
Historical, Ethnographic & Literature Museums (see 20)
Kampung Kling Mosque 13 B2
Maritime Museum 14 A4
Melaka Sultanate Palace 15 B3
Muzium Rakyat (People's Museum) 16 B3
Porta de Santiago 17 B3
St Paul's Church 18 B3
Sri Poyatha Venayagar Moorthi Temple 19 B3
Stadthuys 20 B3
Villa Sentosa 21 C1
SLEEPING
Chong Hoe Hotel 22 B2
Eastern Heritage Guest House 23 C3
Kancil Guest House 24 D4
Sama-Sama Guest House 25 B3
Samudra Inn 26 C5
Shirah's Guest House 27 C4
Travellers' Lodge 28 C4
EATING
Capitol Satay 29 C3
Indri Ori 30 C4
Kenny's Nonya Delights 31 B3
Low Yong Mow 32 B2
Malay Food Stalls 33 C4
Medan Makan Bunga Raya (Hungry Lane) 34 C2
Newton Food Court 35 B4
Selvam 36 C3
DRINKING
Voyage Travellers Lounge 37 B3
SHOPPING
Dataran Pahlawan 38 C4
Mahkota Parade Shopping Complex 39 B4
Orangutan House 40 B3
TRANSPORT
Dumai Ferry Ticket Agents 41 B4
Ferries to Dumai 42 A4

English invaders followed the Portuguese paradigm and attacked mercilessly from the sea. The sole surviving relic of the old Portuguese fort is **Porta de Santiago**, at the foot of Bukit St Paul; more remains of the wall have recently been uncovered at a site behind the tourist office.

Along Jl Kota are a string of cultural museums, the most interesting being the **Muzium Rakyat** (People's Museum; ☎ 282 6526; adult RM2; 🕑 9am-6pm Tue-Sun). In this buffet collection of Malaysia's social and economic development is the 3rd-floor Beauty Museum, which explores different cultures' obsessions with mutilating themselves in order to look good.

A short walk east of Bukit St Paul is the **Melaka Sultanate Palace** (☎ 282 7464; adult RM2; 🕑 9am-6pm Wed-Mon), which houses a massive wooden replica of a Melaka sultan's palace.

Further west on the quayside is the **Maritime Museum** (☎ 283 0926; admission RM2; 🕑 9am-6pm Wed-Mon), housed in a re-creation of the Portuguese sailing ship, the *Flora de la Mar*, which sank off the coast while transporting Malayan booty back to Europe.

CHINATOWN

Melaka's Chinatown is wonderfully preserved; perhaps a little pickled in parts. Jl Tun Tan Cheng Lock is lined with ornate mansions built by Peranakan (Baba Nonya) rubber tycoons. But the primary tourist attraction is Jl Hang Jebat (Jonker St), which is lined with antique stores, a weekend night market and clan houses where the neighbourhood's senior citizens come to show off their karaoke prowess. Wander the small side streets where family shophouses are linked by veranda walkways, creating dramatically framed views of street life: a bare-bellied patriarch in his warehouse-living room, a wizened trishaw driver blaring outdated dance hits from his portable radio, or an earth-toned Chinese temple decorated with sensual dragons.

Baba-Nonya Heritage Museum (☎ 283 1273; 48-50 Jl Tun Tan Cheng Lock; adult RM8; 🕑 10am-12.30pm & 2-4.30pm Wed-Mon) is a captivating museum of the Nonya culture set in a traditional Peranakan townhouse in Chinatown.

Cheng Hoon Teng (Qing Yun Ting, Green Clouds Temple; Jl Tukang) is Chinatown's most famous temple, dating back to 1646. It's Malaysia's oldest Chinese temple and all materials used in its building were imported from China.

VILLA SENTOSA

After sampling Melaka's Chinese and European heritage, don't overlook the city's Malay family tree. **Villa Sentosa** (☎ 282 3988; www.travel.to/villasentosa; 138 Kampong Morten; admission by donation; 🕑 9am-1pm & 2-5pm Sat-Thu, 2.45-5pm Fri) is a private museum on the Melaka River in Kampung Morten. Tours led by family members include a visit to the ancestral *kampung* home, dating from the 1920s, filled with Malay handicrafts and interesting architectural adaptations for surviving the tropics before air-conditioning.

Sleeping

JL TAMAN MELAKA RAYA (JL TMR)

Melaka's guesthouse ghetto occupies the western end of Jl Taman Melaka Raya (Jl TMR), a charmless complex of shophouses about five- to 10-minutes' walk to Chinatown. From the Melaka Sentral, take town bus 17 (60 sen) or a taxi (RM15 to RM20).

Many places are Muslim-run and owners strongly request that no pork or non-Halal Chinese food is brought onto the premises. Obviously beer IS not for sale, but most guesthouses allow BYO and drinking on the premises; ask first, however. Most backpacker-oriented places have a choice of shared or private bathrooms.

Shirah's Guest House (☎ 286 1041; 207-209 Jl Melaka Raya 1; dm/s/d RM10/15/20; ❄) Lots of Mediterranean colours and a gentle Malay vibe make Shirah's a particularly cosy backpackers. The three-bed dorm is a humane alternative to the usual bunker. The doubles are excellent value.

Samudra Inn (☎ 282 7441; 348B Jl Taman Melaka Raya 3; dm RM10, r RM30-45; ❄) The owners at the very quiet Samudra run a tight ship and go above and beyond standard service to make sure guests are comfortable. It's a homestay atmosphere with chirping birds and satellite telly at night.

Travellers' Lodge (☎ 226 5709; 214B Jl Melaka Raya 1; s RM14-20, d RM27-54; ❄) With an enticing elevated sitting area that has mats on the floors, a plant-filled rooftop terrace and good rooms – some which have lofts – this is a great choice. It's spotless and a good place to meet other travellers.

Kancil Guest House (☎ 281 4044; kancil@machinta.com.sg; 177 Jl Parameswara; s/tw/d RM18/28/30) It's a bit out of the way, but the Kancil is a distinctive family-run guesthouse with heaps of sitting

THE CULINARY PROWESS OF BABA NONYA

Fusion cuisine isn't a new phenomenon. In Melaka, Chinese-Malay cooking is called Nonya food, after the Peranakan women, known as Nonya, who did most of the cooking (men are Baba); the two cuisines merged back in the days when most people still believed the Earth was flat. Dishes here favour sweet flavours of coconut, coriander and dill due to an Indonesian influence. Penang also has Nonya food but the flavours tend to have more Thai-inspired sour and spicy notes. A few must-tries are:

Chicken Kapitan Chicken curry with tamarind juice, candlenut, turmeric and shrimp paste.
Popiah Spring rolls with meat, tofu, chilli, garlic and shallots.
Kankung Belacan Water spinach stir-fried in a blend of chilli and shrimp paste.

areas and a lush garden at the back. Over its 15 years, travellers from far-flung destinations have painted murals on the walls. Laundry services and bike hire are available.

CHINATOWN

Melaka's most scenic section of town is a truly delightful place to stay. Because of preservation restrictions, however, the following places only have shared bathrooms. Take town bus 17 from Melaka Sentral to Town Sq (70 sen). A taxi should cost RM15 to RM20.

Eastern Heritage Guest House (☎ 283 3026; 8 Jl Bukit China; dm RM8, s/d/tr RM22/26/33;) In a 1918 building, Eastern Heritage has polished wood floors, ancient tiles and an antique look from lots of eroding paint. The dorm is airless but the rooms are brightened up with murals – it's an all-round social place. Take a dip in the plunge pool on a hot day.

Sama-Sama Guest House (☎ 012 305 1980; www.sama-sama-guesthouse.com; 26 Jl Tukang Besi; r RM15-35) Scatterbrained Sama-Sama has big, creaky rooms arranged around an interior courtyard of water lilies and cool breezes. Downstairs lazy cats and the odd human snooze to a soundtrack of reggae; the neighbourhood characters assemble here after sunset.

Chong Hoe Hotel (☎ 282 6102; 26 Jl Tukang Emas; r RM25-45;) This Chinese-run hotel is straight-up basic but you can't beat the location.

Eating

Melaka's most famous cuisine is Nonya food (see boxed text, above). In Melaka the Portuguese might have wreaked havoc on civic order, but they built up a tradition for cakes and seafood, most obvious in the Eurasian dish of devil's curry. Then there are the immigrant contributions of Indian curries and the versatile Chinese noodle dishes.

Hawker stalls around the lively Jl TMR roundabout are a good bet for the regional version of laksa.

Low Yong Mow (32 Jl Tukang Emas; dim sum RM1-3; 5am-noon Wed-Mon) A bustling Chinese favourite for a traditional dim sum breakfast and famed for its giant *pao* (pork buns).

Indi Ori (☎ 282 4777; 236 & 237 Jl Melaka Raya 1; dishes RM1-15; breakfast, lunch & dinner) Get delicious Indonesian Padang food here – it's just like the real thing but without the flies. Order plates of food from the counter and enjoy them family style with rice. Other favourites include avocado juice with chocolate sauce (RM4.50), and Sekotang (hot ginger with egg yolk, sweet cream and peanut dumplings; RM5.80).

Kenny's Nonya Delights (Jl Tun Tan Cheng Lock; meals RM1.50-5; breakfast & lunch Tue-Sun) The best place for Nonya food on a budget, Kenny's whips up an excellent *nasi lamak* (RM1.50) at breakfast and *popiah* (spring rolls; RM4) and laksa (RM3) at lunch. The owners bottle some of their sauces, which are a great, if heavy, souvenir.

Medan Makan Bunga Raya (btwn Jl Bunga Raya & Jl Bendahara; dishes RM2-6; breakfast, lunch & dinner) When you hear the sound of the meat cleaver, you've reached 'Hungry Lane', known for Indian-style curry-pork rice and *gula melaka* (palm sugar) during the day. At night more stalls pop up.

Newton Food Court (Jl Merdeka; meals RM3-15; lunch & dinner) Get Chinese in the main hall and halal food at the back of this new food court under an elegant Malay-style roof and bordered by palms.

our pick Capitol Satay (☎ 283 5508; 41 Lorong Bukit China; meals RM5-10; Tue-Sun) Capitol is enough to make you move to Melaka. It's famous for satay *celup* (a Melaka adaptation of satay steamboat). Stainless-steel tables have a bubbling vat of satay sauce in the middle, which is regularly replenished. You dunk skewers of okra (ladies' finger) stuffed with fish, tofu, Chinese sausage, chicken, pork, prawns, bok choy, and side dishes of pickled egg with pickled ginger.

Selvam (☎ 281 9223; 3 Jl Temenggong; meals RM7; breakfast, lunch & dinner) Melakans love this Little India banana-leaf smorgasbord. There's a choice range of tasty and cheap curries and roti, plus a Friday afternoon vegetarian special with 10 tasty dishes for only RM6.

Kampong Portugis (dinner) In the eastern part of the city, 3km from Town Sq, is a small community claiming mixed Portuguese-Indian ancestry. Often hyped as a mini-Lisbon, this otherwise nondescript neighbourhood caters to the curious tourists with food stalls and a few clunky Eurasian restaurants. On weekend evenings, Restoran de Lisbon (meals RM30) is known for its chilli crabs and devil curry. At any other time of the week, Medan Portugis has food stalls, serving many of the same dishes at seaside tables. Take town bus 17 to Kampong Portugis and walk towards the sea; coming back to town, hop off the bus at Mahkota Parade Shopping Complex before it speeds onto the flyover.

Drinking

During the weekend night market on Jonker St, the happening bar strip on Jl Hang Lekir turns into a street party closed off to traffic. Medan Portugis, in Kampong Portugis (see above), has cheap beers and sunset views. The alleys in the backpacker ghetto off Jl TMR have lots of watering troughs.

Voyage Travellers Lounge (40 Lorong Hang Jebat;) Melt into a wicker chair with a snack and a beer and chat with the friendly regulars. Movie night is 9.30pm Wednesday and patrons can use the internet for half an hour for free.

Shopping

A wander through Chinatown will have you wishing for more room in your pack with its quality assortment of clothing, trinket and antique shops. **Dataran Pahlawan** (Jl Merdeka) and **Mahkota Parade Shopping Complex** (Jl Merdeka) are Melaka's two megamalls, the former being the larger, more fashion-conscious and the latter being better for practical needs such as a pharmacy or camera shop.

Orangutan House (☎ 282 6872; www.charlescham.com; 59 Lorong Hang Jebat) Doubling as an art gallery, this place sells colourful works by very hip local artist Charles Cham.

GETTING TO INDONESIA

High-speed ferries make the trip from Melaka to Dumai, in Sumatra, twice daily at around 9.30am and 3pm (one way/return RM80/129, 1¾ hours). **Madai Shipping** (☎ 06-284 0671; Jl PM2) and **Tunas Rumpat Express** (☎ 06-283 2506; Jl PM2) have ticket offices near the jetty (which is on Jl Quayside). Travellers will need a visa to enter Dumai (for more information, see p341).

See p267 for information on doing the trip in reverse.

Getting There & Away

Melaka is 144km southeast of KL.

Melaka's local bus station, express bus station and taxi station are all combined into the massive **Melaka Sentral** (Jl Panglima Awang), roughly 5km north of Town Sq. Because Melaka is a popular weekend destination, make advance bus reservations for Singapore and Kuala Lumpur.

The following long-distance destinations can be reached from Melaka: KL (RM10, two hours, hourly from 8am to 7.30pm), Georgetown (RM35, eight hours, two daily), Ipoh (RM25, five hours, two daily), Jerantut (RM16.50, five hours, one daily), Johor Bahru (RM15, three hours, hourly 8am to 11am and 1pm to 6pm), Kota Bharu (RM32, 10 hours, five daily), Kuala Terengganu (RM34, nine hours, five daily), Kuantan (RM19, five hours, two daily), Mersing (RM14.80, 4½ hours, two daily) and Singapore (RM16, 4½ hours, hourly 8am to 6pm).

If you're hustling back to KL International Airport, you can bypass KL by taking a Seremban-bound bus (RM5, 1½ hours, every 30 minutes) and then catch a local bus (RM6) to KLIA; give yourself plenty of time, though.

Getting Around

Bus 17 runs frequently from the Melaka Sentral bus station to Town Sq, Mahkota Parade Shopping Complex, Taman Melaka Raya (50 sen) and Medan Portugis (80 sen).

Melaka is a walking city. Bicycles can be hired at some guesthouses for around RM10 per day; there are also a few bike-hire outfits around town.

A trishaw should cost around RM10 for any one-way trip within town, but you'll have to bargain. Taxis charge around RM8 to RM10 within a 5km radius with a 50% surcharge between 1am and 6am.

CAMERON HIGHLANDS

☎ 05

A winding road east of Hwy 1 leads into the cool mountains of forest-clad Cameron Highlands, which demurely blankets an area 1300m to 1829m above sea level. In a suspended state of British colonial calm, altitude-loving tea fields dress the undulating hills in an emerald-coloured corduroy scattered with strawberry and honeybee farms. All this is in the middle of a biodiverse jungle where trail-eating tree roots get you clambering on all fours and carnivorous flowers swig insects.

Overdevelopment has been an ongoing problem and deforestation is held responsible in a marked rise in temperature recently. Moreover, there have been severe water shortages and contamination problems. Use water sparingly while in the highlands and take care to create as little waste as possible (in the form of drink cans, plastic packaging etc). A new water booster system in Kuala Terlah began operating in March 2007 but water shortages still remain. To help with projects including trash removal and recycling go to www.reach.org.my.

Orientation & Information

The Cameron Highlands stretches along the road from the town of Ringlet, through to the main highland towns of Tanah Rata, Brinchang and beyond to smaller villages in the northeast.

Tanah Rata is the main highland town for budget accommodation and other essentials. Most guesthouses offer internet access for around RM3 an hour.

Maybank (Jl Mentigi) The only bank/moneychanger in Tanah Rata.

Tourist Information Centre (☎ 519 7246; mctic@tm.net.my; off Jl Dayang Endah; 🕑 8.30am-1pm & 2-5pm) Very helpful with maps and trail information.

Sights & Activities

Taking in a jungle stroll is often the best way to reach some of the area's other tourist attractions. Most walks and sights can be accessed by the local bus, a rattler that chugs up and down the main highway.

Visiting one of the tea plantations is another must. The rolling hills are carpeted with hectares of green and occasionally speckled with tea pickers wading between the rows snipping the tender green tips. **Sungai Palas Boh Tea Estate** (Gunung Brinchang Rd, Brinchang; admission free; 🕑 8.30am-4.30pm Tue-Sun) is the easiest plantation to visit on your own. Tours are free and the tea rooms out the back offer grand vistas. Take the local bus north from Tanah Rata bus station past Brinchang towards Kampung Raja. In between is a tourist strip of strawberry and butterfly farms; hop off at the roadside vegetable stalls and follow the intersecting road.

Boh Tea Estate (Boh Rd Habu, Ringlet; admission free; 🕑 8.30am-4.30pm) below Tanah Rata, 8km from the main road, is also open to the public. It's only a 45-minute walk from the end of jungle Trail 9A, which you can pick up outside of Tanah Rata.

Sam Poh Temple (Brinchang; admission by donation; 🕑 8.30am-6pm) is a typically Chinese kaleidoscope of Buddha statues, stone lions and incense burners. It's accessible from Tanah Rata – take Trail 3, near the golf course, and then connect to Trail 2.

When you head out on a trail, go in pairs, take lots of drinking water and rain gear. Check with the Tourist Information Centre about the state of the trails and recommended walks. Guesthouses in Tanah Rata often employ informal guides who lead daily walks. Inexperienced walkers are advised to employ a guide on the longer trails; in recent years, several people have become lost. Single women have also been attacked in remote areas. At the time of writing there was an 'exhibitionist' showing his goods near and around Robinson's Falls.

Tour operators in Tanah Rata offer a variety of day trips that include a visit to a tea plantation, strawberry farm, flower and cactus nursery, honey farm and butterfly farm for around RM25 per person. Tours operating out of Father's Guest House include a good jungle-flora trip perfect for plant nerds.

Sleeping

Book early during peak holiday periods (April, August and December). Most guesthouses have a mix of rooms with shared and private bathrooms, and all have hot water. Many also have libraries, video lounges, laundry, internet access and trekking information.

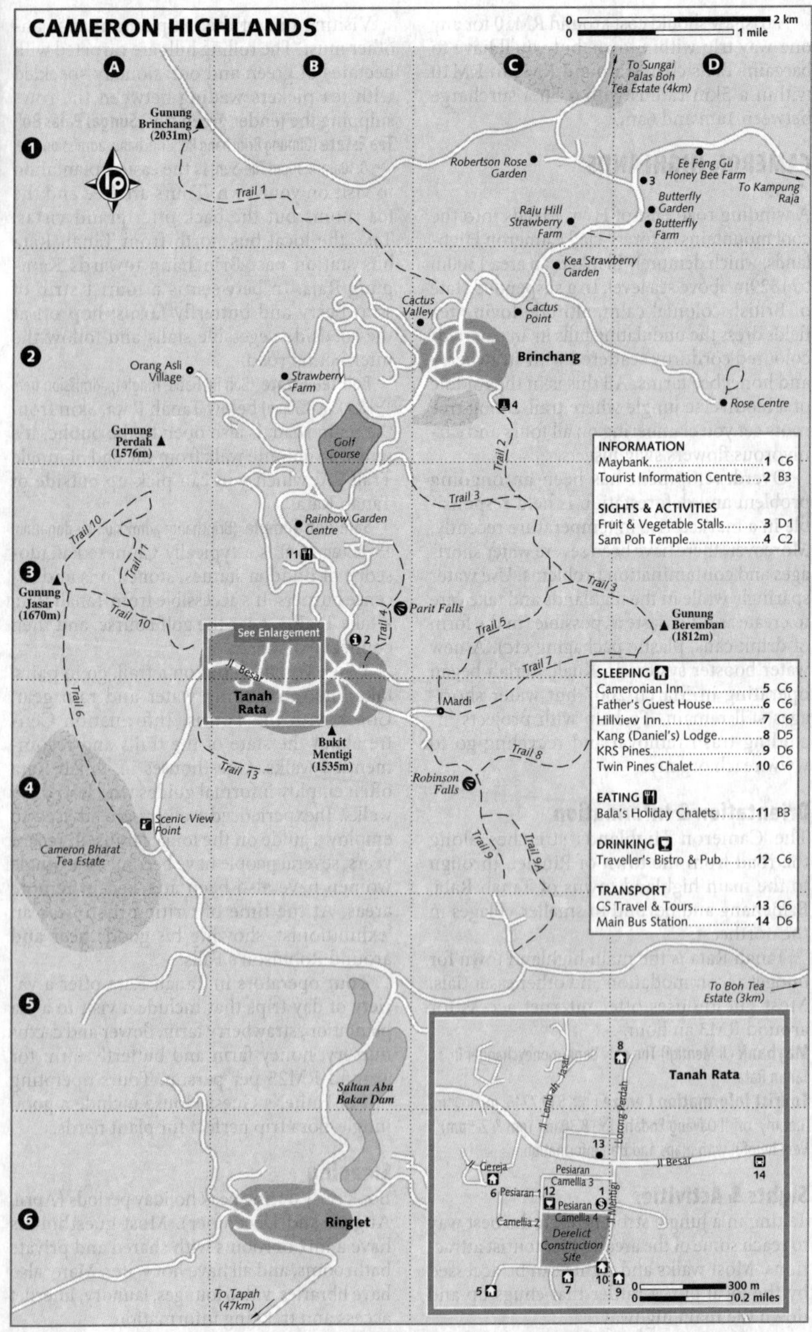
CAMERON HIGHLANDS
0 2 km
0 1 mile
To Sungai Palas Boh Tea Estate (4km)
Gunung Brinchang (2031m)
Trail 1
Robertson Rose Garden
Ee Feng Gu Honey Bee Farm
To Kampung Raja
Butterfly Garden
Butterfly Farm
Raju Hill Strawberry Farm
Kea Strawberry Garden
Cactus Valley
Cactus Point
Brinchang
Orang Asli Village
Strawberry Farm
Rose Centre
Gunung Perdah (1576m)
Golf Course
Trail 2
Trail 3
Rainbow Garden Centre
Trail 10
Trail 11
Gunung Jasar (1670m)
Parit Falls
Trail 4
Gunung Beremban (1812m)
Trail 5
Trail 7
See Enlargement
Jl Besar
Tanah Rata
Trail 6
Mardi
Bukit Mentigi (1535m)
Trail 13
Trail 8
Robinson Falls
Scenic View Point
Cameron Bharat Tea Estate
Trail 9
Trail 9A
To Boh Tea Estate (3km)
Sultan Abu Bakar Dam
Ringlet
To Tapah (47km)
INFORMATION
Maybank.....1 C6
Tourist Information Centre.....2 B3
SIGHTS & ACTIVITIES
Fruit & Vegetable Stalls.....3 D1
Sam Poh Temple.....4 C2
SLEEPING
Cameronian Inn.....5 C6
Father's Guest House.....6 C6
Hillview Inn.....7 C6
Kang (Daniel's) Lodge.....8 D5
KRS Pines.....9 D6
Twin Pines Chalet.....10 C6
EATING
Bala's Holiday Chalets.....11 B3
DRINKING
Traveller's Bistro & Pub.....12 C6
TRANSPORT
CS Travel & Tours.....13 C6
Main Bus Station.....14 D6
Tanah Rata
Jl Lembah Jasar
Lorong Perdah
Jl Besar
Gereja
Pesiaran Camellia 3
Pesiaran 1
Pesiaran Camellia 4
Camellia 2
Jl Mentigi
Derelict Construction Site
0 300 m
0 0.2 miles

Kang (Daniel's) Lodge (☎ 491 5823; danielslodge@hotmail.com; 9 Lorong Perdah; dm/s/d/tr/q RM8/30/40/50/60) Home to the bamboo-clad Jungle Bar, Daniel's is set up for partying. The cosy front terrace doubles as a sociable lounge area good for chilling out after a night at the bar. Concrete rooms are clean and tiled but dark and dank. The 'F**k the Lonely Planet' sign at the reception desk enhances the lodge's rowdy attitude.

Twin Pines Chalet (☎ 491 2169; www.twinpines.cameronhighlands.com; 2 Jl Mentigi; dm/d/tr/q RM8/25/35/45) Another social place where nights are spent around a bonfire, watching films in the lounge or sipping tea with other travellers on the patio. Room walls actually seem to enhance the sounds from the exterior but it's a clean and well-cared for place.

Cameronian Inn (☎ 491 1327; 16 Jl Mentigi; dm/s/d/f RM8/20/40/60) Take tea and scones on the Tudor-style patio of this place, which is nestled among English gardens. The rooms aren't as appealing as the exterior and are mostly the standard, windowless variety. Paying more ups the standards.

our pick **Father's Guest House** (☎ 491 2484; www.fathers.cameronhighlands.com; PO Box 15, Tanah Rata; dm/s/d RM9/20/45) Perched on a flower bedecked butte, Father's excellent reputation is earned from its tip-top management and cheerful setting. Garden-side rooms have doors that open onto a flower-filled patio, the old bunker-style Nissen huts are surprisingly comfortable and the dorm has a summer-camp camaraderie. It's a family-run business and is a couple of minutes' walk from Jl Besar.

KRS Pines (☎ 491 2777; 7 Jl Mentigi; dm/d/tr RM30/50/80) Run by the Twin Pines gang, this brand-new blocklike cement structure has spotless rooms reminiscent of a college dorm. Rooms without private bathroom are windowless and essentially closets – sliding doors and all – while the dorm is bright and cheerful.

Hillview Inn (☎ 491 2915; hillview_inn@hotmail.com; 17 Jl Mentigi; d RM55-88) Carpeted, spacious rooms, all with attached bathroom go above and beyond backpacker standards. Most rooms have their own terrace looking out over the hills; there's a very relaxed vibe and a prevalent sense of brightness and space.

Eating & Drinking

Eating in Tanah Rata is a no-brainer. There are three blocks' worth of options – Malay, Indian and Chinese. The cheapest food in town is found at a row of Malay stalls along Jl Besar, near the bus station. Keep an eye out for locally produced strawberry ice cream.

Bala's Holiday Chalet (☎ 491 1660; ⏰ lunch & dinner) A local highlands tradition is taking tea with the requisite scones and jam; many guesthouse in town offer this midday meal but this place, between Tanah Rata and Brinchang, is worth checking out because of its historic and wooded setting.

Traveller's Bistro & Pub (68A Prsn Camelia 3; ⏰ 4pm-2am) The only bar in Tanah Rata besides the Jungle Bar at Kang Lodge (see left) pumps cheesy jazz over its sidewalk-side terrace and serves cocktails as well as beer. It ain't Vegas but it's not a bad place for a drink.

Getting There & Around

From Tanah Rata, buses go to/from KL (RM20, four hours, six daily between 8am and 4.30pm). Another bus leaves Tanah Rata bound for Ipoh (RM7.90, two hours, five daily) and Georgetown (RM23). Buses also go to Singapore (RM95, six hours, one daily). Book tickets at the bus station. For east coast destinations, connect through Ipoh.

CS Travel & Tours (☎ 491 1200; 47 Jl Besar) sells tickets for daily minibuses to Kuala Besut (RM60, six hours) to catch a boat to Pulau Perhentian (see p467 for details) or Kuala Tahan (Taman Negara; RM85, eight hours). You can also take these minibuses partway and get off at Gua Musang to catch the Jungle Railway (see p471).

Local buses run from Tanah Rata to Brinchang (RM1, every 1½ hours from 6.30am to 6.30pm) and less frequently on to Kampung Raja (RM2.40), passing butterfly attractions and the turn-off to Sungai Palas Boh.

Taxi services from Tanah Rata include Ringlet (RM15), Brinchang (RM6), Sungai Palas Boh Tea Estate (RM20) and Boh Tea Estate (RM25). For touring around, a taxi costs RM25 per hour, or you can go up to Gunung Brinchang and back for RM80.

IPOH

☎ 05 / pop 710,800

Ipoh (ee-po) is a convenient transit link to the Cameron Highlands, Pulau Pangkor and beyond that does little else to entice a longer stay. It's dubbed the 'Bougainvillea City', and although it's blessed with a spacious *padang* (town square) and some decent architecture, it's not exactly exploding with flowers. If you do hang around, stick to the 'Old Town' area at night since the 'New Town' has a reputation for prostitution.

Orientation & Information

Many of Ipoh's streets have been renamed, but some may still be known by their old names. These include Jl CM Yussuf (formerly Jl Chamberlain), Jl Bandar Timah (formerly Jl Leech), Jl Dato Maharajah Lela (formerly Jl Station), Jl Sultan Idris Shah (Jl Clarke) and Jl Panglima Bukit Gantang Wahab (Jl Kelab). Ipoh's 'Old Town' is west of Sungai Kinta, New Town is east.

The two banks listed here are near the clock tower.

HSBC (Jl Dato Maharajah Lela)
Perak Tourist Information Centre (☎ 241 2957; Jl Tun Sambanthan; 8am-1pm & 2-4.30pm Mon-Thu, 8am-12.15pm & 2.45-4.30pm Fri, 8am-1pm Sat)
Standard Chartered Bank (Jl Dato Maharajah Lela)

Sights

Ipoh's **Old Town** showcases elegant colonial architecture and the **train station** (known locally as the 'Taj Mahal') is magnificent.

There are spiritual Buddhist cave-temples on the outskirts of the city, including **Perak Tong** (8am-6pm), 6km north on the road to Kuala Kangsar, and **Sam Poh Tong** (8am-4.30pm), a few kilometres to the south. Both are easily accessible by local bus.

Sleeping & Eating

Ipoh's culinary specialities include *kway teow* (rice-noodle soup) and a regional variation of curry laksa merging Chinese barbecue pork with an Indian-style curry.

Decent budget places are in short supply in Ipoh.

Sun Golden Inn (☎ 243 6255; 17 Jl Che Tak; r RM50;) This simple spot has a fashion-fearless owner who will be eager to bargain over rates.

New Caspian (☎ 255 1221; Jl Ali Pritchay; r RM55) One of the town's better options, the New Caspian is run by a nice couple and rooms have TV and mould-free bathrooms. Don't confuse it with its less appealing namesake on Jl Jubilee.

Grand View Hotel (☎ 243 1488; 36 Jl Horley; r RM70-80;) One of the smarter midrange places, with clean, brightly furnished rooms in a quiet area near the city centre; the hotel is aptly named.

FMS Bar & Restaurant (☎ 253 7678; 2 Jl Sultan Idris Shah; dishes from RM7; lunch & dinner) It's an excellent Chinese restaurant in a beautifully restored colonial building on the edge of the *padang*. Seafood and bean-curd dishes are winners and there's a small saloon-style bar downstairs.

Medan Selera Dato Tawhil Azar (Jl Raja Musa Aziz; dinner) This large open-air food stall around a small square is a good spot for a Malay meal in the evening.

Getting There & Away

Ipoh is 205km north of KL and 164km south of Butterworth. The **long-distance bus station** (Medan Gopeng) is south of the train station and the city centre; a taxi ride from the main hotel area should be around RM10.

Destinations and standard fares: Alor Setar (RM17, four hours, two daily), Butterworth (RM10.70, three hours, five daily), Hat Yai in Thailand (RM35, nine hours, one daily), Johor Bahru (RM37, eight hours, two daily), Kota Bharu (RM25.40, seven hours, one daily), KL (RM14, three hours, hourly), Lumut (RM6.50, two hours, frequent), Melaka (RM22.70, five hours, three daily) and Tanah Rata (RM7.90, two hours, frequent). There is also an Ipoh–KLIA (KL International Airport) express service (RM48, three hours, four daily). From the airport, the Ipoh-bound bus makes four trips from 7.30am to 6.30pm.

The local bus station is northwest of the long-distance station on the other side of the roundabout. Local buses depart from here for outlying regions close to Ipoh, such as Kuala Kangsar (RM4.70) and Lumut (RM6.50).

Ipoh's **train station** (☎ 254 7987) is on the main Singapore–Butterworth line. The train to KL (*ekonomi*/2nd class RM10/18) leaves after midnight, arriving early morning; in the opposite direction, a daily train heads to Butterworth (*ekonomi*/2nd class RM9/17) after midnight, arriving early morning, before continuing to Hat Yai in Thailand.

LUMUT

☎ 05

Lumut is the departure point for Pulau Pangkor. **Tourism Malaysia** (☎ 683 4057; Jl Sultan Idris Shah; 9am-5pm Mon-Fri, 9am-1.45pm Sat) is midway between the jetty and the bus station. Next door you'll find a moneychanger offering better rates than on Pulau Pangkor, and Maybank further down the street.

If you get marooned in town, head straight to **Era Backpackers Hotel** (7-9 Jl Raja Muda Musa; dm RM15, r RM25-60) directly across from the bus station, which was being remodelled when we passed and has a helpful and knowledgeable owner. Some rooms have private bathrooms.

Direct buses run to/from KL (RM16, four hours, eight daily), Butterworth (RM15, five hours, three daily), JB (RM48, 10 hours, two daily), Kota Bharu (RM30.90, eight hours, four daily) and Melaka (RM31, eight hours, two daily). There are no direct buses from Lumut to the Cameron Highlands; take a bus to Ipoh (RM7.50, two hours, hourly), then transfer to Tanah Rata. Try to get on a bus going to the Medan Gopeng bus station in Ipoh or you'll have to hop on a shuttle bus from the city bus station (1RM, frequent) to connect with Tanah Rata buses.

The Pulau Pangkor pier is an easy walk from the bus station. Boats run every 30 minutes and cost RM10.

PULAU PANGKOR

☎ 05 / pop 25,000

Pulau Pankor is more of a girl-next-door island as opposed to the supermodels of the east coast and Langkawi. That said, it feels good to get away from the glitz and settle into an honest *kampung* with a lazy island atmosphere. The jungle is swarming with monkeys and hornbills and you can dine nightly on fresh fish while watching the sunset. Only a half-day from KL, it's a great place to burn up a few days before a flight.

Pangkor's piece of history, the foundations of a **Dutch fort** dating from 1670, is 3km south of Pangkor Town at Teluk Gedong.

Ferries from Lumut first stop on the eastern side of the island at Sungai Pinang Kecil (SPK) and then go to Pangkor Town, where you'll find banks, restaurants and shops.

Sights & Activities

The main beaches are on the west coast. Travellers, especially women, should take care on empty stretches at the island's northeastern side and south of Pangkor Town.

Five minutes' walk north of Teluk Nipah, **Coral Bay** is the best beach on this side of the island, with clear, emerald-green water, due to the presence of limestone.

Pasir Bogak is a swimming beach favoured by holidaying Malaysians, and gets crowded during holidays when it also gets trashed. It's narrow, with white sand and mostly midrange accommodation.

A popular backpacker haven, **Teluk Nipah** is north of Pasir Bogak. This is a scenic beach with offshore islands, a variety of budget accommodation and a lively atmosphere.

Sleeping

TELUK NIPAH

Most accommodation is set on access roads between the beachfront road and the jungle – a blessing in disguise when the local kids start racing their motorcycles along the main drag. Inexpensive A-frame huts have shared bathrooms.

Nazri Nipah Camp (☎ 685 2014; rozie1982@hotmail.com; dm RM10, r RM30-45) Hugging the jungle, this reggae-vibed, bamboo-clad, back-to-nature spot gets two thumbs up for ambience and will get your feet up for some serious chilling. Chess sets and a garden common area inspire social get togethers.

D'Lima Chalets (☎ 567 6923; r RM30) Clean, basic rooms with fan and TV are similar to a slew of other places except the price is lower and the welcome more friendly. Go figure.

Ombak Inn (☎ 685 5223; r RM40-70; ❄) Get an exceptionally warm Malay welcome at this collection of A-frame ovens and cheery air-conditioned rooms set in a cat-filled garden. The price includes a generous breakfast.

Sunset View Chalet (☎ 685 5448; sunsetvu@tm.net.my; r RM50-70; ❄) Rows of tidy wooden bungalows are linked by a bright bougainvillea archway. At around 6.45pm the owner attracts local hornbills by feeding them bread. Anyone can come by and try tossing crumbs in the air to be caught by the swooping birds.

PASIR BOGAK

The atmosphere here is lacking compared to Teluk Nipah; the place tends to be strewn with litter – fewer overseas travellers stay here. If you choose to get away from the 'scene', try **Pankor Village Beach Resort** (☎ 685 2163; dm/r from RM25/145; ❄) at the cleaner western end of the beach. Besides the dorm and comfortable rooms, you can also rent tents (RM14).

Eating & Drinking

Several of Teluk Nipah's guesthouses have restaurants, though outside the high season

November to March), these often close down. Most restaurants serve alcohol. There are also some basic food stalls at the beach.

Ashraff Tom Yam Thai Corner (Teluk Nipah; whole fish RM35; lunch & dinner) Everyone in Pangkor will tell you to go here for fresh fish – listen to 'em! A whole fish prepared to your liking feeds two people and accompaniments cost extra. Tables are right on the beach and perfectly situated for sunsets. There's also cheaper Malay fare such as fried rice and noodles (RM4).

Nipa' Nipa' Beach Cafe (Teluk Nipah; lunch & dinner) Open till 'silly hours', this stylish, outdoor pub-café at the southern end of the beach has cool (as in from this decade) music, a pool table, beer (10RM), cocktails (from RM12) and quality Western food.

Getting There & Away

Berjaya Air (code J8; ☎ 685 5828; www.berjaya-air.com) flies to/from KL's Sultan Abdul Aziz Shah Airport (RM237), daily except on Tuesday and Thursday.

In the high season, ferries (return RM10, 45 minutes, every 30 minutes from 7am to 8pm) run to and from Lumut and Pangkor Town.

Getting Around

There are no public buses but pink minibus taxis operate between 6.30am and 9pm. Fares are set for the entire vehicle to/from the jetty in Pangkor Town and go to Pasir Bogak (RM4), Teluk Nipah (RM10) and around the island (RM35 to RM45).

Motorcycles (RM30) and bicycles (RM15) can be rented in Pangkor town and at main beaches.

BUTTERWORTH

This mainland town is the jumping-off point for Pulau Penang. The Butterworth–Penang ferry jetty (RM1.20, every 20 minutes from 5.30am to 12.30pm) is conveniently located next to the train and bus stations. Fares for the ferry are charged only for the journey from Butterworth to Georgetown (on Penang); returning to Butterworth is free.

Buses depart from Butterworth to the following destinations: Johor Bahru (RM49, 12 hours, six daily), KL (RM26, five hours, hourly), Kota Bharu (RM27.90, seven hours, two daily), Kuala Terengganu (RM40, 10 hours, two daily), Kuantan (RM43, 12 hours, six daily), Melaka (RM36, 12 hours, two daily) and Singapore (RM53, nine hours, two daily).

There is a nightly train to KL (economy/2nd class/berth RM17/38/48) from the **train station** (☎ 323 7962) that arrives the next morning. Heading north, there are two daily trains to Hat Yai, Thailand (economy/2nd class/berth RM19/27/68); one leaves early morning and arrives mid-morning Thai time (one hour behind), and the other leaves early afternoon and arriving in Hat Yai in the evening. The latter service continues to Bangkok arriving at around noon the next day. Times and fares vary.

PULAU PENANG

Back when the distinction between governments, armies and companies was less precise, the British-based East India Company sailed into Penang harbour and took over the 28-sq-km island as its first settlement on the Malay peninsula, a move intended to break Dutch Melaka's monopoly of the spice trade.

What evolved on the formerly unpopulated 'Betel Nut Island' was a bustling port. Entrepreneurs of every imaginable ethnicity, most notably Chinese, flocked to this new land, creating wealth and cultural hybrids. Like many company settlements, Penang wilted after the collapse of the British Empire. Today it's become the 'Silicon Valley' of Malaysia although this high-tech world is scarcely noticeable to the casual traveller.

Beyond Georgetown's heat and decay are beach resorts, such as Batu Ferringhi, and the sleepy Malay fishing village of Teluk Bahang.

Georgetown

☎ 04

It's full of car exhaust and has a marked lack of sidewalks, but Georgetown is able to woo even the most acute cityphobe with its never-ending cultural surprises. Dodge traffic while strolling past Chinese shophouses where folks might be roasting coffee over a fire or artistically sculpting giant forms of incense for a ceremony. Little India is like a street party at night with its twinkling lights and blaring Bollywood music while the serious white buildings of the Colonial District sit mutely along the waterfront. It's a grazing city, showcasing the culinary offspring of the island's unique cultural intermingling. Off the island, Georgetown is often referred to as Penang (Pinang).

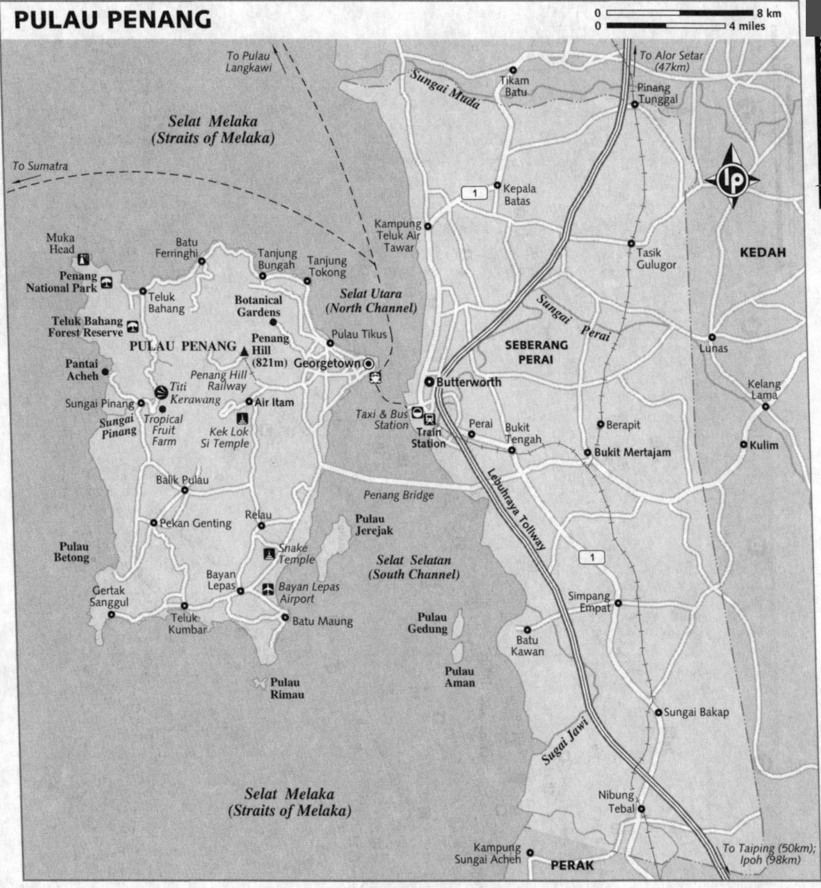

ORIENTATION

Georgetown is at the northeastern corner of Pulau Penang. Central Georgetown is compact and easily navigated on foot. Many of the town's oldest mosques, temples and churches can be found at, and around, Lebuh Pitt (also called Jl Masjid Kapitan Keling). Following Jl Penang southwest, you'll reach Kompleks Komtar (Kompleks Tun Abdul Razak), the island's transport hub and shopping centre.

INFORMATION

Branches of major banks and 24-hour ATMs are concentrated around Kompleks Komtar and around Lebuh Pantai and Lebuh Downing, near the main post and Telekom offices. Internet access is widely available on Lebuh Chulia (rates start at RM1 per minute). You can stock up on reading supplies at the host of secondhand bookshops.

General Hospital (☎ 229 3333; Jl Residensi) About 2km west of Kompleks Komtar.

HS Sam Book Store (☎ 262 2705; 473 Lebuh Chulia)

Immigration Office (☎ 261 5122; 29A Lebuh Pantai)

Loh Guan Lye Specialist Centre (☎ 228 8501; 19 Jl Logan) Medical services, 1km west of Kompleks Komtar.

Penang Tourist Guides Association (☎ 261 4461; 3rd fl, Kompleks Komtar, Jl Penang; 🕑 10am-6pm Mon-Sat) Excellent tourist office, but hard to find; look for signs near the McDonald's on the 3rd floor.

Popular Bookshop (☎ 263 6122; Kompleks Komtar)

Tourism Malaysia (☎ 262 0066; 10 Jl Tun Syed Sheh Barakbah; 🕑 8am-5pm Mon-Fri)

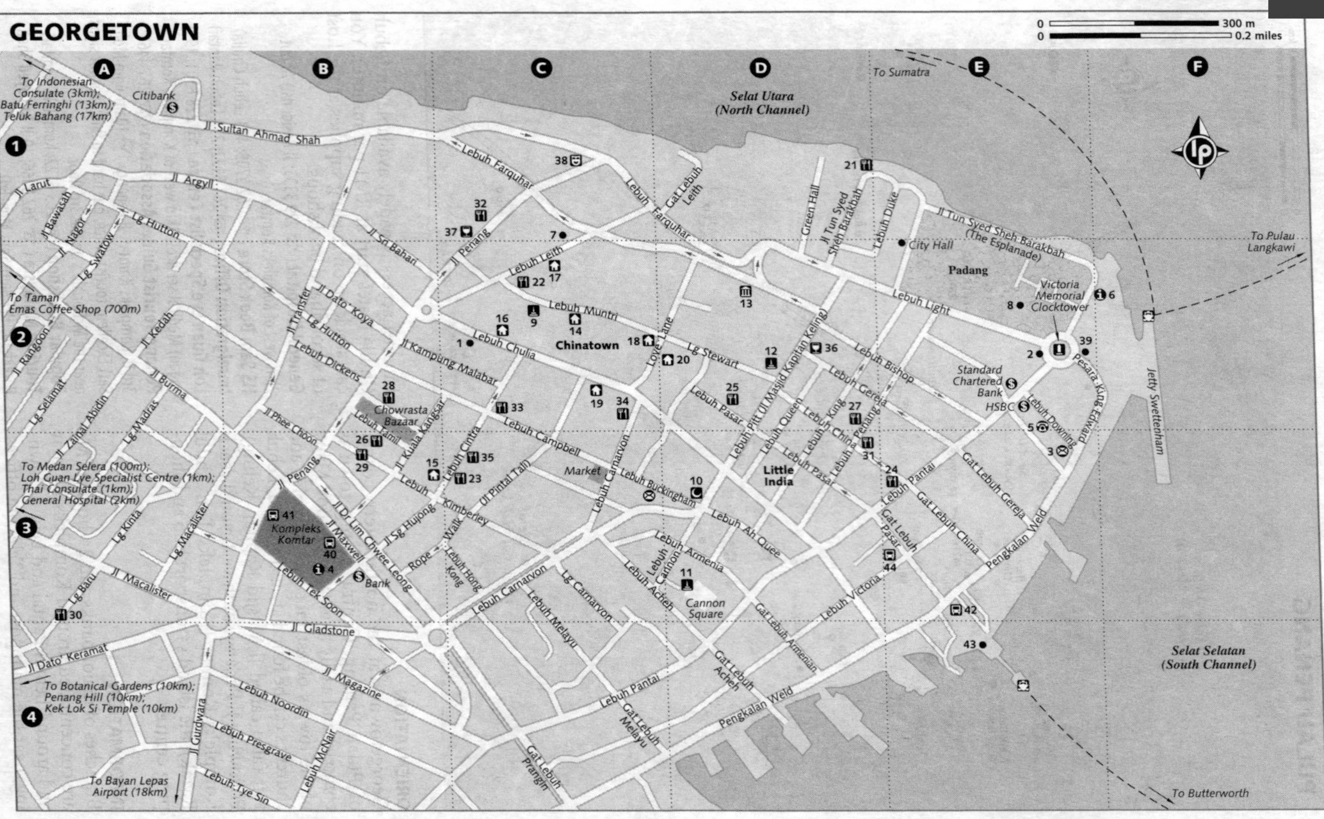
GEORGETOWN
0 300 m
0 0.2 miles
Selat Utara (North Channel)
Selat Selatan (South Channel)
To Pulau Langkawi
To Sumatra
To Butterworth
Jetty Swettenham
Victoria Memorial Clocktower
Padang
City Hall
Jl Tun Syed Sheh Barakbah (The Esplanade)
Lebuh Light
Lebuh Duke
Jl Tun Syed Sheh Barakbah
Green Hall
Lebuh Farquhar
Gat Lebuh Leith
Standard Chartered Bank
HSBC
Lebuh Downing
Pesara King Edward
Pengkalan Weld
Gat Lebuh Gereja
Gat Lebuh China
Gat Lebuh Pasar
Lebuh Bishop
Lebuh Gereja
Lebuh Penang
Lebuh King
Lebuh China
Lebuh Pantai
Lebuh Pasar
Lebuh Queen
Lebuh Pitt (Jl Masjid Kapitan Keling)
Little India
Lebuh Victoria
Lebuh Ah Quee
Gat Lebuh Armenian
Lebuh Armenia
Lebuh Cannon
Cannon Square
Gat Lebuh Acheh
Lebuh Acheh
Lebuh Buckingham
Lg Stewart
Love Lane
Lebuh Muntri
Chinatown
Lebuh Chulia
Lebuh Carnarvon
Market
Lebuh Campbell
Lg Carnarvon
Lebuh Melayu
Lebuh Pantai
Gat Lebuh Melayu
Gat Lebuh Prangin
Lebuh Leith
Jl Penang
Jl Pintal Tali
Lebuh Cintra
Lebuh Kimberley
Rope Walk
Lebuh Hong Kong
Jl Kampung Malabar
Lebuh Kuala Kangsar
Chowrasta Bazaar
Lebuh Tamil
Jl Sg Hujong
Jl Dr Lim Chwee Leong
Jl Maxwell
Bank
Kompleks Komtar
Lebuh Tek Soon
Jl Gladstone
Jl Magazine
Lebuh McNair
Lebuh Noordin
Lebuh Presgrave
Lebuh Tye Sin
Jl Gurdwara
Jl Sultan Ahmad Shah
Jl Sri Bahari
Jl Dato Koya
Lg Hutton
Jl Transfer
Lebuh Dickens
Jl Phee Choon
Jl Argyll
Citibank
Lg Hutton
Lg Swatow
Jl Nagor
Jl Bawasah
Jl Larut
Jl Burma
Jl Kedah
Lg Madras
Jl Zainal Abidin
Lg Selamat
Jl Rangoon
Lg Macalister
Lg Kinta
Jl Macalister
Lg Baru
Jl Dato' Keramat
To Indonesian Consulate (3km); Batu Ferringhi (13km); Teluk Bahang (17km)
To Taman Emas Coffee Shop (700m)
To Medan Selera (100m); Loh Guan Lye Specialist Centre (1km); Thai Consulate (1km); General Hospital (2km)
To Botanical Gardens (10km); Penang Hill (10km); Kek Lok Si Temple (10km)
To Bayan Lepas Airport (18km)

DANGERS & ANNOYANCES

While generally a safe place to wander around, Georgetown has its seamy side. Travellers have been mugged at Love Lane and other dimly lit side streets, so take care around this area if you're out late, and take a taxi or trishaw to your accommodation. Motorcycle snatch thieves are also a problem, so take care of shoulder bags and purses. Women get hassled a lot here; dressing conservatively eases, but doesn't erase, the problem.

SIGHTS & ACTIVITIES

Cheong Fatt Tze Mansion

A magnificent periwinkle-blue mansion, **Cheong Fatt Tze Mansion** (☎ 262 5289; Lebuh Leith; adult RM10; ⏰ tours 11am & 3pm Mon-Fri, 11am Sat & Sun) was built in the 1880s by Cheong Fatt Tze, a local Hakka merchant-trader who left China penniless and eventually established a vast financial empire, earning himself the sobriquet 'Rockefeller of the East'.

The 38-room mansion blends Eastern and Western influences and promotes good feng shui by sitting on a 'dragon's throne' – a mountain (Penang Hill) behind, and water (the Channel) in front. The mansion doubles as a luxurious **bed and breakfast** (www.cheongfatttzemansion.com; r from RM250).

Heritage Trail

You can follow the Heritage Trail walking tours that take in Georgetown's historic colonial architecture and some temples and mosques in Chinatown – pick up a pamphlet showing the routes at the tourist offices.

There's also a free **shuttle bus** (⏰ 7am-7pm Mon-Fri, 7am-2pm Sat) that runs between the jetty and Kompleks Komtar, winding its way through Georgetown's colonial core. Pick up a copy of the route at the **Penang Tourist Guides Association** (☎ 261 4461; 3rd fl, Kompleks Komtar, Jl Penang; ⏰ 10am-6pm Mon-Sat).

Temples & Mosques

In honour of the goddess of mercy, good fortune, peace and fertility, the **Kuan Yin Teng** (Lebuh Pitt; admission by donation; ⏰ 9am-5pm) was built in the early 19th century by the first Hokkien and Cantonese settlers in Penang. It's usually buzzing with worshippers burning paper money.

Dedicated to Mar Chor, the patron saint of seafarers, **Hainan Temple** (Lebuh Muntri; admission by donation; ⏰ 9am-5pm) was completed in 1895. Remodelling in 1995 has refreshed its distinctive swirling dragon pillars and brightened the ornate carvings.

Built by Penang's first Indian-Muslim settlers, the yellow **Kapitan Keling Mosque** (Lebuh Pitt) has a single minaret in an Indian-influenced Islamic style. This building is best appreciated from the street.

Khoo Kongsi (Lebuh Cannon; adult RM5; ⏰ 9am-5pm) is Penang's finest *kongsi* (clan house), and is decorated with a colourful mix of dragons, other statues, paintings, lamps, coloured tiles and carvings. A *kongsi* is a building that's used partly as a temple and partly as a meeting hall for Chinese people of the same clan or surname. This building dates from 1906.

INFORMATION
- HS Sam Book Store 1 C2
- Immigration Office 2 E2
- Main Post Office 3 E3
- Penang Tourist Guides Association 4 B3
- Popular Bookshop (see 4)
- Telekom Malaysia 5 E2
- Tourism Malaysia 6 F2

SIGHTS & ACTIVITIES
- Cheong Fatt Tze Mansion 7 C1
- Fort Cornwallis 8 E2
- Hainan Temple 9 C2
- Kapitan Keling Mosque 10 D3
- Khoo Kongsi 11 D3
- Kuan Yin Teng 12 D2
- Penang Museum 13 D2

SLEEPING
- 75 Travellers' Lodge 15 C2
- 100 Cintra Street 14 B3
- Blue Diamond Hotel 16 C2
- Cathay Hotel 17 C2
- Love Lane Inn 18 C2
- New Banana 19 C2
- SD Guesthouse 20 D2

EATING
- Esplanade Food Centre 21 D1
- Green Hut 22 C2
- Hsiang Yang Fast Food 23 C3
- Hui Sin Vegetarian Restaurant 24 E3
- Krsna Restaurant 25 D2
- Lebuh Tamil Hawker Stalls 26 B3
- Madras New Woodlands Restaurant 27 D2
- Morning Chinese Hawker Stalls 28 B2
- Night Chinese Hawker Stalls 29 B3
- Night Malay & Baba Nonya Hawker Stalls 30 A3
- Sri Ananda Bahwan 31 D3
- Sup Hameed 32 C1
- Tho Yuen Restaurant 33 C2
- Tiek Sen 34 C2
- Wen Chang 35 C3

DRINKING
- Pitt Street Corner 36 D2
- Soho Free House 37 C1

ENTERTAINMENT
- Lush 38 C1
- Slippery Senoritas (see 38)

TRANSPORT
- Ferry Ticket Offices 39 E2
- Local Bus Station 40 B3
- Long-Distance Bus Offices 41 B3
- Pengkalan Weld Bus Stop 42 E3
- Railway Booking Office 43 E4
- TransitLink City Bus Station 44 E3

GETTING INTO TOWN

Penang's Bayan Lepas International Airport is 18km south of Georgetown. The U307 and U401 buses run to/from the airport (RM3, one hour) every half-hour from 6am to 11pm. Buses stop at Komtar and terminate at Weld Quay.

If arriving via the Butterworth–Penang ferry, exit towards Pengkalan Weld and catch any Kompleks Komtar–bound bus (RM1.50, 15 minutes) to reach accommodation in Chinatown.

Other Sights

Fort Cornwallis (Lebuh Light; adult RM3; 9am-7pm) was built on Georgetown's cape, the historic landing of the city's founder Captain Francis Light in 1786. A visit involves lots of panel reading.

Penang Museum (☎ 261 3144; Lebuh Farquhar; adult RM1; 9am-5pm Sat-Thu) is one of the best-presented museums in Malaysia. In front is a bronze statue of Captain Light, and excellent exhibits on the ground floor illustrate the customs and traditions of Penang's various ethnic groups with impressive appreciation for diversity. Upstairs is the history gallery.

SLEEPING

Georgetown has plenty of cheap accommodation, mainly clustered in Chinatown along bustling Lebuh Chulia and quieter Love Lane. During holidays, most notably Chinese New Year (January/February), hotels fill up very quickly and prices soar. Cheaper rooms have shared bathrooms.

75 Travellers' Lodge (☎ 262 3378; 75 Lebuh Muntri; dm RM7, s RM15-18, d RM18-40;) Mr Low is an exceptionally friendly and helpful owner and it's easy to be social over a beer or coffee on the balcony. It was spic and span when we passed but we've received the odd grumble about this place.

Blue Diamond Hotel (☎ 261 1089; 422 Lebuh Chulia; dm/s/d RM8/20/30;) Barflies apply here; even staff have stiff drinks in hand by 11am and the place is dominated by its sidewalk-side beer garden. The Chinese clunker of a building is graced with natural light, some lovely old carvings and high ceilings but the rust-stained tubs and grotty staircase take away from the charm. Still, the large rooms are enticingly old world.

our pick **100 Cintra Street** (☎ 264 3581; 100 Lebuh Cintra; dm/s/d RM10/25/38) Housed in a sometimes-operating museum in a semirestored Peranakan mansion, this is by far and away Penang's most atmospheric budget option. You get a (very thin) mattress on a wooden platform with a fan and a mosquito net for that Eastern colonial experience. Dorm beds are on an open landing and have absolutely zero privacy.

Love Lane Inn (☎ 412 9002; 54 Love Lane; s/d/tr RM16/30/40;) Pastel colours brighten this otherwise basic, but well-serviced hostel. While owner Jimmy gets rave reviews from travellers we've heard complaints about his staff. There's a little on-site café.

SD Guesthouse (☎ 264 3763; 16 Love Lane; www.sdguesthouse.com.my; s/d RM18/25) Clean, modern, windowless rooms line bright corridors and a sweet little garden. Baths get all the proper scrubbing. This would be one of the quietest places in town were it not for the 'bird hotel' (for collecting nests for bird's-nest soup) next door. Luckily the squawkers slumber around 9pm.

New Banana (☎ 262 6171; 355 Lebuh Chulia; d without/with air-con RM25/30;) It's not just an appellation, this place actually really is new – which makes it stand out against the paint-chipped competition. No windows as usual but carpeting makes a change and bathrooms are sparkling. There's a big café-bar downstairs that promises to become a traveller favourite.

Cathay Hotel (☎ 262 6271/6272; 22 Lebuh Leith; r RM50-70;) Recapture the romance of the colonial era in this ageing diva of a hotel. Once grand, high-ceilinged rooms now have one too many mould stains but with a touch of imagination you could feel quite sophisticated staying here. You may remember seeing the hotel in the 1995 film *Beyond Rangoon*.

EATING

Penang cuisine is legendary: Indian, Chinese and Malay purveyors jostle with one another for affection from a constantly snacking populace. Along with Melaka, Penang boasts the indigenous fusion of Baba Nonya cuisine (see p437). If you'd rather rest the tastebuds with a sandwich or shepherd's pie, head to **Green Hut** (102 Lebuh Muntri; breakfast & lunch Wed-Sun), which is also a great place for travellers' information.

Chinese

In the morning an umbrella village of food stalls sets up across from Chowrasta Bazaar near the market along Jl Kuala Kangsar (from 6am to noon daily). Here you'll find vendors dexterously folding and stuffing slippery *chee cheong fun* (broad rice noodles filled with prawns or meat). Wander this lush market to dine or snack on fruit and Chinese baked goods.

Lebuh Cintra is lined with bustling Chinese noodle and dim sum joints.

Tho Yuen Restaurant (92 Lebuh Campbell; RM1-5; breakfast & lunch Wed-Mon) The best of the dim sum joints around Lebuh Cintra with a staff who speak enough English to explain what's what to clueless Westerners. Beyond dumplings, try the meat and mushroom sticky rice (RM2.20) or fresh savoury baked goods with a chaser of Chinese tea.

Wen Chang (63 Lebuh Cintra; meals RM2-5; breakfast & lunch) This is an extremely popular chicken-and-rice spot with enthusiastic staff. Steamed white rice and tender chicken cooked and flavoured in Hainanese style is served with a herbal broth.

Hsaing Yang Fast Food (97 Lebuh Cintra; meals RM2-6; breakfast & lunch) Point and choose from the array of seafood, meat and vegetarian fare tantalisingly displayed in stainless steel trays. It's best to arrive noon-ish when the dishes are fresh.

Hui Sin Vegetarian Restaurant (11 Lebuh China; meals RM3-6; breakfast & lunch Mon-Sat) Pick from an excellent buffet of veggie and tofu dishes at great prices.

our pick **Teik Sen** (Lebuh Carnavon; meals RM8-24; lunch & dinner Wed-Mon) It looks like just another hole in the wall Chinese place so why is everyone so dressed up? After trying the food here such as crispy chicken with plum sauce (RM12) or curry prawns (RM6), you'll understand. Come early if you don't want to wrestle the locals for a table.

Malay & Nonya

You'll have to venture outside of Chinatown to Jl Nagor to sample Penang's Baba Nonya cuisine. Lorong Baru, just off Jl Macalister, has a row of food stalls whipping up satay; however, things don't start sizzling until nightfall.

Taman Emas Coffee Shop (1W Jl Gottlieb; laksa RM2.50; breakfast & lunch) You might need a taxi or a helpful local to be able to find this place off Jl Burma, but this is hands down the most phenomenal laksa you'll ever taste.

Esplanade Food Centre (Jl Tun Syed Sheh Barakbah; meals RM3-6; dinner) This is Penang's best hawker centre, as much for the delightful sea breezes as the Malay stalls serving *laksa asam*, *rojak* (a fruit and veggie salad topped with a sweet and spicy gravy) and radioactive-coloured bowls of ABC and cendol. The more restaurant-like Chinese section features seafood and icy-cold cheap beer.

Sup Hameed (Jl Penang; meals RM4-6; lunch & dinner) Sprawling well beyond the actual restaurant

PENANG MUST EATS

Penang is known as the hawker capital of Malaysia and most of the city's specialities – claiming mixed Malay and Chinese extraction – are best fetched from a portable cart or food centre.

Cendol Garishly coloured green strands (made from sweetened pea flour) are layered with crushed ice, coconut milk and brown-sugar syrup. The related dessert of ABC is the shepherd's pie of sweets, with shaved ice, ice cream, flavoured sugar water, beans and tapioca balls.

Char kway teow Medium-width rice noodles are stir-fried with egg, vegetables, shrimp and Chinese sausage in a dark soy sauce.

Chee cheong fun A popular dim sum dish, these are broad, paper-thin rice noodles that are steamed and rolled around a filling of prawns served with an oily, chilli dipping sauce.

Curry mee Curly egg noodles *(mee)* are served in a spicy coconut-curry soup, garnished with bean sprouts, prawn, cuttlefish, cockles, bean curd and mint.

Hokkien mee A busy and spicy pork-broth soup crowded with egg noodles, prawns, bean sprouts, *kangkong*, egg and pork.

Laksa asam Also known as Penang laksa, this is a fish-broth soup spiked with a sour tang from tamarind paste *(asam)* and a mint garnish; it's served with thick, white rice noodles (laksa).

Rojak A fruit and vegetable salad tossed in a sweet-tamarind-and-palm-sugar sauce and garnished with crushed peanuts, sesame seeds and chillies.

like a trail of busy ants down the sidewalk, diners at this ultrapopular smorgasbord at the north end of Jl Penang sample everything from spicy *sup* (soup!), *nasi kandar* (mixed dishes to go with rice) and *roti canai* (flaky pancakes).

Indian

Georgetown's Little India is along Lebuh Pasar, Lebuh China and the side streets between Lebuh Penang and Lebuh Pitt. Lebuh Tamil, off Jl Penang by Chowrasta Bazaar, is an easy-going alley for a shady respite of Indian and Malay dishes or a cup of *teh tarik* ('pulled tea'; tea with frothy milk).

Madras New Woodlands Restaurant (60 Lebuh Penang; meals RM2.50-6; breakfast, lunch & dinner) The street-side glass display case of traditional Indian sweets tempts you into this fabulous vegetarian eatery. Here you can have your pudding without eating your meat, but don't pass up the delicious *thosai masala* (spicy potatoes wrapped in a crepe) and the mango lassi.

Sri Ananda Bhawan (☎ 264 4204; 55 Lebuh Penang; meals RM3-6; breakfast & dinner) A neighbourhood favourite for banana-leaf meals. You can be cheap and vegetarian with the basic fare or add a few side dishes such as pepper chicken. Chase away the fire in your belly with a lassi and call yourself a lucky eater.

Krsna Restaurant (☎ 264 3601; 75 Lebuh Pasar; meals RM5-10; breakfast & dinner) Sweaty and busy, this vegetarian South Indian spot does a great *oothaban*, which is like a veggie-filled pizza you eat with your hands (your right hand, that is).

DRINKING

Jl Penang is a renovated string of ancient shophouses where nouveau bars and bistros show off their multilingual sophistication. The cheapest beer can be found at Esplanade Food Centre (see p449) while Lebuh Chulia has plenty of waterholes that cater specifically to Westerners, and locals looking for lonely foreign friends.

Pitt Street Corner (94 Lebuh Pitt) Sit back with a beer to the sounds of Bollywood at this very friendly Wild West–style saloon in Little India.

Soho Free House (50A Jl Penang) This place starts rocking out early (80s music anyone?) with a mostly Chinese clientele who nosh bangers and mash (RM13.50) and swill pints like good Brits.

CLUBBING

Lush (The Garage, 2 Jl Penang) This is a contemporary nightclub with slick minimalist design in stark tones of red, grey and black. DJs and nightly promotions are a fun diversion to the usual backpacker night sweats.

Slippery Senoritas (SS; The Garage, 2 Jl Penang) In the same complex as the Lush, Slippery Senoritas is brasher but is still good for a laugh, and the Tom Cruise *Cocktail*esque show put on by the bar staff is mesmerising.

GETTING THERE & AWAY

See Butterworth (p444) for information about reaching Penang from the mainland, and for long-distance train and bus travel from the mainland.

Advance bookings on long-distance trains can be made at the **Railway Booking Office** (Pengkalan Weld), near the Butterworth–Penang ferry jetty.

Air

Airlines with services to Pulau Penang:

Air Asia (code AK; ☎ 644 8701; www.airasia.com) Flies to and from KL one way/return RM56/112.

Firefly (code FY; ☎ 03-7845 4543; www.fireflyz.com.my) To Phuket or Koh Samui, Thailand one way RM70.

Malaysia Airlines (code MH; ☎ 262 0011; www.malaysiaairlines.com) To KL one way RM135.

Singapore Airlines (code SQ; ☎ 226 6211; www.singaporeair.com) To Singapore one way RM255.

Thai Airways International (THAI, code TG; ☎ 226 6000; www.thaiair.com) To/from Bangkok RM937.

Boat

All the offices for the ferry service between Pulau Langkawi or Belawan (Sumatra, Indonesia) and Penang are clustered together near the tourist office, and all put you on the same boats.

For information about ferries to Belawan see opposite. There are daily ferries from Georgetown to Langkawi (one way/return RM50/90, 2½ hours). Boats leave at 8.15am (direct) and 8.30am (one stop at Pulau Paya), returning from Langkawi at 2.30pm and 5.30pm. Check the times the day before, as schedules vary. Note that Langkawi ferries depart the jetty off Pesara King Edward near the clock tower.

Bus

Buses to all major towns on the peninsula leave from both Georgetown and Butterworth. Several long-distance bus services leave from

GETTING TO INDONESIA

Travellers can skip over to the Indonesian island of Sumatra from Pulau Penang via ferry. There are several ferries each way in the morning, and times can change, but generally ferries depart Georgetown at 8.30am and return at 10.30am (one way/return RM150/250); the trip takes 4½ to five hours. The boats leave from Georgetown's Swettenham jetty and land in Belawan where the remaining journey to Medan is completed by bus (included in the price). Buy tickets the day before to verify departure times. Upon arriving at Belawan port, most nationalities will need to pay a US$25 per person fee for a 30-day Indonesian visa.

See p262 for information on doing the trip in reverse.

Kompleks Komtar; some leave from the long-distance bus offices, while others leave from the local bus stop. Buy tickets direct from the bus companies as we've received letters and talked to travellers whose agent-bought tickets from Georgetown only got them partway to where they were going.

There are daily buses to Ipoh (RM14, three hours, hourly), Tanah Rata in the Cameron Highlands (RM25, six hours, five daily), KL (RM27, five hours, hourly), Kuantan (RM42, eight hours, one daily), Melaka (RM35, seven hours, two daily), and Singapore (RM50, nine hours, two daily).

There are also bus and minibus services to Thailand: Hat Yai (RM22), Phuket (RM60) and Ko Samui (RM55). The minibuses usually don't go directly to some destinations so there are significant waiting times. The train from Butterworth is usually quicker.

GETTING AROUND

Penang has a good public transport system that connects Georgetown with the rest of the island.

Bus

There are several local bus stops in Georgetown. Kompleks Komtar and Pengkalan Weld, in front of the Butterworth-Penang jetty, are two of the largest stops. Most of the buses also have stops along Lebuh Chulia. Fares within Georgetown are RM1.50 to RM3, points beyond are RM1 to RM3 depending on the destination (exact change required). See boxed text, below, for destinations.

For around RM6 you can do a circuit of the island by public transport.

Motorcycle & Bicycle

You can hire bicycles from shops at Lebuh Chulia, Batu Ferringhi (13km northwest of Georgetown) and some guesthouses. Bicycles cost RM10, and motorcycles start at RM30 per day. Remember that if you don't have a motorcycle licence, your travel insurance probably won't cover you in the case of an accident.

Taxi

You'll need to bargain for a reasonable fare. Typical taxi rates around town are RM5 to RM10. Other fares include Batu Ferringhi (RM30), Penang Hill/Kek Lok Si Temple (RM20) and Bayan Lepas airport (RM38).

Trishaw

Bicycle rickshaws are an ideal way to negotiate Georgetown's backstreets and cost around RM1 per kilometre but, as with taxis, agree on the fare before departure. For touring around, the rate is about RM35 per hour.

Penang Hill

Once a fashionable retreat for the city's elite, Penang Hill (800m) provides cool temperatures and spectacular views. There are pretty gardens, an old-fashioned kiosk, a restaurant and a hotel, as well as a lavishly decorated Hindu temple and a mosque at the top. Penang Hill is particularly wonderful at dusk as Georgetown, far below, starts to light up.

From Kompleks Komtar, or at Lebuh Chulia in Georgetown, you can catch one

USEFUL BUSES ON PULAU PENANG

Penang has streamlined its bus system to be very simple. Destinations include the following:

Air Itam U201, U202 or U203
Batu Ferringhi U105 or U101
Bayan Lepas International Airport U307 or U401
Penang Hill U204
Snake Temple U302
Teluk Bahang U101

of the frequent local buses (U201, U202 or U203) to Air Itam. From Air Itam, walk five minutes to the funicular railway (adult/child RM4/3, 30 minutes, every 15 to 30 minutes from 6.30am to 9.30pm) where long queues may await. The energetic can get to the top by an interesting three-hour trek, starting from the Moon Gate at the Botanical Gardens.

Kek Lok Si Temple, the largest Buddhist temple in Malaysia, stands on a hilltop at Air Itam. Construction started in 1890, took more than 20 years and was largely funded by donations. To reach the entrance, walk through the souvenir stalls until you reach the seven-tier, 30m-high **Ban Po Thar** (Ten Thousand Buddhas Pagoda; admission RM2). The design is said to be Burmese at the top, Chinese at the bottom and Thai in between.

Batu Ferringhi

☎ 04

Following the coastal road east will lead you to Batu Ferringhi, Penang's best beach area, which is lined with resorts at one end and guesthouses at the other. While it doesn't compare with Malaysia's east coast beaches or those on Langkawi, the sleepy village ambience at the eastern end of the beach is a lovely respite. The 2004 tsunami grazed this portion of Penang, causing minimal property damage and flooding. Locals say the beach sands got a much-needed polish from the hungry waves.

SLEEPING

Low-key guesthouses are clustered together opposite the beach, and most will give discounts for multiday stays.

ET Budget Guest House (☎ 881 1553; 47 Batu Ferringhi; s/d RM25/30; ❄) A laid-back double-storey Chinese house with basic rooms, most with a common bathroom. The pricier rooms come with air-con, TV and shower.

Baba Guest House (☎ 881 1686; 52 Batu Ferringhi; r RM35-55; ❄) This big Chinese family home with plain rooms (most with shared bathrooms) is a hive of activity with sister at reception, grandma doing laundry, dad fixing the plumbing and so on. They can help organise tours and transport around and beyond Penang.

Ali's Guest House (☎ 881 1316; alisferringhiguesthouse@cnetmyne.com; 53 Batu Ferringhi; s/d/f RM50/60/130; ❄) With the antique-style balcony, comfy sitting area and lots of leafy accompaniments, this place has more style than the competition and is priced accordingly.

GETTING THERE & AWAY

Bus U101 or U105 from Kompleks Komtar takes around 40 minutes to reach Batu Ferringhi and costs RM2.50.

Teluk Bahang

☎ 04

If you're looking to get off the beaten path, head east of Batu Ferringhi to Teluk Bahang, a sleepy Malay fishing village that has faded away from the backpacker radar. There isn't a lot to do in Teluk Bahang and that's the point.

The road ends at blissfully deserted Penang National Park where you can hike to white, sparkling beaches that are devoid of humans but popular with monkeys. Start at the **Penang National Park Office** (☎ 881 3500; end of Jl Hassan Abbas; 🕑 8am-4.30pm Mon-Fri, 8am-noon & 2-4pm Sat & Sun) for maps and suggestions. Guides cost RM100 per day but might be hard to rustle up.

If you want to stay the night, stop at **Miss Loh's Guest House** (☎ 885 1227; 159 Jl Teluk Bahang; dm/s/d with shared bathroom from RM8/15/30; ❄), which is set amid a fruit orchard. This is the kind of place where you can put down roots, as some travellers do, and stay on for months.

Bus U101 runs from Georgetown every half-hour all the way along the north coast of the island to just beyond the roundabout in Teluk Bahang.

ALOR SETAR

☎ 04

For transport reasons, if you're in Kedah state you'll pass through its capital. Alor Setar (allo-*star*) is north of Butterworth on the main road to the Thai border and is the transfer point to Kuala Kedah, the main port town for ferries to Pulau Langkawi. This region is conservative and not accustomed to seeing shockingly white foreigners. To better fit in with Islamic dress norms, wear clothes that cover your elbows and knees.

Flora Inn (☎ 732 2376; 8 Kompleks Medan Raja; s/f RM20/65; ❄) is a well-maintained place that overlooks the river and is above a small food court.

To reach Langkawi, take a local Kuala Kedah bus (RM1, 15 minutes, frequent) to the ferry jetty. A shuttle bus (90 sen) connects the town centre with the bus station; a taxi will

GETTING TO THAILAND

There are several options for crossing the Malay–Thai border on the west coast; see also p455.

To Sadao

Frequent buses go from Alor Setar to the Bukit Kayu Hitam–Sadao border crossing (RM4), which is open from 7am to 7pm daily. You'll have to take a minibus on the Thai side of the border to the transport hub of Hat Yai.

See p784 for information on doing the trip in reverse.

To Kanger

Trains travelling south and north pass through the border towns of Padang Besar and Kanger, linking the towns along the train line (including Penang-Butterworth) to the border. Trains leave Alor Setar in the morning and arrive in the currently dodgy transport hub town of Hat Yai (2nd class/berth RM27/45) three hours later; travellers can also catch an international express that leaves Alor Setar in the late afternoon, arrives in Hat Yai in the evening and continues on to Bangkok, arriving around midday the next day. The border is open 7am to 10pm daily.

See p784 for details on travelling from Thailand to Malaysia.

cost RM8. From about 7am to 7pm, regular ferries operate roughly every hour in either direction between Kuala Kedah and Kuah on Langkawi (RM18, one hour).

The bus station is 3.5km outside the town centre. Buses serve the following destinations: Ipoh (RM19.70, three daily, four hours), Johor Bahru (RM55, 10 hours, one daily), Kota Bharu (RM28.60, two daily, six hours), Kuala Lumpur (RM30, hourly, six hours), Kuala Terengganu (RM38, 10 hours, one daily), Kuantan (RM42, 10 hours, one daily) and Melaka (RM38.70, eight hours, two daily).

The **train station** (☎ 731 4045; Jl Stesyen) is a 15-minute walk southeast of town. There are two daily northbound trains that head across the Thailand–Malaysia border; see above for details. Heading south, the train to KL (economy/2nd class/berth RM20/35/43) departs in the evening, reaching the capital 12 hours later. The express train leaves Alor Setar around midday and terminates in Butterworth two hours later (economy/2nd class RM31/45). Times are variable so check the schedule.

KUALA PERLIS

☎ 04

This small port town in the extreme northwest of the peninsula is a departure point for ferries to Pulau Langkawi. Your least-grotty sleeping option if you stop to sample the region's special laksa is **Pens Hotel** (☎ 985 4122; Jl Kuala Perlis; r RM75; ❄).

Ferries depart for Kuah, on Pulau Langkawi (RM15, every hour between 8am and 6pm).

The bus and taxi stations are behind the row of shophouses across from the jetty. A limited number of destinations are served from Kuala Perlis' bus station; these include Butterworth (RM9, four daily), Kuala Lumpur (RM20, frequent) and Kuantan (RM32, one daily). For other destinations, take a taxi (RM12) to the larger bus station in Kangar, which has buses bound for Alor Setar (RM3) and the border town of Padang Besar (RM2.50).

PULAU LANGKAWI

☎ 04

Visiting Langkawi is almost like taking a vacation from the rest of Southeast Asia. While you can still grab some *nasi lemak* (rice boiled in coconut milk and served with sides of beef and a hard-boiled egg) for breakfast, the wide roads, cleaned-up beaches and duty-free shopping complexes give the island a Western resort feel; exploring beyond the main tourist areas, though, will bring you back to Malaysia. The island itself is out of a daydream, with knife-edged peaks that float in dark vegetation and beaches so bright you've gotta wear shades. Besides the tax-free beer, everything else here will cost you.

Vacationing Malaysians are Langkawi's primary fan base and former prime minister Dr Mahathir even lobbied to move the state capital from Alor Setar to Langkawi.

Orientation

The Langkawi archipelago comprises 99 islands, of which Pulau Langkawi is the largest and most visited. It sits 30km off the coast from Kuala Perlis and 45km from the Thai border town of Satun. In the southeast corner of Langkawi is Kuah, the major town and the arrival point for ferries. On the west coast are Pantai Cenang (cha-*nang*), a lively beach strip with shops and restaurants, and also adjacent Pantai Tengah, which is a bit quieter and a short walk to Pantai Cenang. During the monsoons (May to October) and sometimes beyond, jellyfish make swimming a problem.

Information

The only banks are at Kuah, and are open Monday to Friday. Moneychangers are tucked in and around the duty-free shops at Kuah.

Tourism Malaysia (☎ 966 7789; Jl Persiaran Putra, Kuah; 🕑 9am-1pm & 2-6pm) offers comprehensive information and advice about the island.

Sleeping

Rates drop considerably in the off season between March and October. Upon arriving in Langkawi, touts swarm the disembarking ferry passengers; their commission, if you choose to follow them, will be built into your nightly rate.

PANTAI CENANG

The following places are grouped on either side of the main road and are listed here in north-to-south order. Most budget options are across the road from the beach.

Gecko Guesthouse (☎ 019 428 3801; dm RM10, r with shared bathroom RM25-50; ❄) Travellers love the friendly vibe and island-bamboo style of this place so it books up fast. Friday and Saturday nights hop with barbecues and live music.

Shirin Guesthouse (☎ 955 5991; s/d/tr RM25/40/36; ❄) The Japanese and Iranian owners have built a rainbow of tidy bungalows in a little garden across from the beach.

our pick **Malati Tanjung** (☎ 955 1099; r RM40-100) It has ultracomfy doubles with beach views (RM70) that are worth the splurge. Sheets are hospital-clean, all rooms have attached bathrooms and the Malay owners are lovely.

AB Motel (☎ 955 1300; abmotel@hotmail.com; r RM60-120; 💻) A buzzing complex with a restaurant, internet café and motorbike rental. The cheapest of the bland rooms look over the main road.

PANTAI TENGAH

Pantai Tengah is less built-up and popular with Malay families.

Zackry Guesthouse (☎ 019 447 0490; zackryghouse@gmail.com; s/d/tr RM25/35/50) Off the main tourist drag towards Kuah, this funky and social Chinese-style backpackers is about 150m from the beach. It's close to the best of Langkawi's duty-free watering holes.

Tanjung Malie (☎ 955 1891; r RM40-60) Near Pantai Cenang, this cluster of little beach huts is within sunstroke-stumbling distance of the beach. Only the priciest rooms have private bathrooms.

Eating

Pantai Cenang has the most eating options. Langkawi's proximity to Thailand means that the Thai penchant for fiery chillies has found its way into local dishes.

Tomato Nasi Kandar (meals RM1-6; 🕑 lunch & dinner) Actually a group of restaurants, you'll find cheap and tasty *tosei* (pancake with a curried potato filling; from RM1.20) and other Indian food in the open-air area by the road, halal food in the air-conditioned restaurant and pricier Western food just behind the building in a little makeshift on-the-beach café.

Warung Tenggek (meals RM3-5; 🕑 breakfast & lunch) Snag a plastic table for the best and cheapest breakfast in town. *Roti canai* and *nasi lamak* (coconut rice wrapped in banana leaf) are the locals' favourites, but there are also pancakes, and American egg breakfasts (RM5).

Warung Kita (meals RM3.50-4; 🕑 dinner) Swarming with locals, Kita's whips up *roti canai* (60 sen to RM1.80) and standard Malay noodle and rice dishes. It's just north of Underwater World across from the beach.

Artisans Pizza Shop (☎ 955-1231; pizzas from RM12; 🕑 lunch & dinner) Rest the tastebuds with a generously topped pie at this roadside eatery.

Champor-Champor (meals RM15-25; 🕑 lunch & dinner) With an emphasis on Thai food, this splurge-worthy option serves Asian-Western cuisine, including vegetarian options, in a Bali-style garden setting with twinkling fairy lights.

Drinking

Nearly all the hotels have bars and most restaurants serve alcohol.

Big Joe's Bar (Pantai Tengah) In front of Zackry Guesthouse, quirky Joe's serves the cheapest beer we found in Malaysia (RM2) and is set up for live music.

Reggae Café (Pantai Tengah) A free shuttle (hourly from 9.30pm to 11.30pm) that stops just south of AB Motel whisks Pantai Cenang residents to bum-shaking action.

Getting There & Away

AIR

Malaysia Airlines (code MH; ☎ 966 6622; www.malaysiaairlines.com.my), to/from KL RM275, and **Air Asia** (code AK; ☎ 955 7751), to/from KL RM110, have 10 flights every day. **Firefly** (code FY; www.fireflyz.com.my) also flies to/from Pulau Penang (RM99, daily).

SilkAir (code MI; ☎ 955 9771; www.silkair.com) flies to/from Singapore (RM453, four times a week).

BOAT

All passenger ferries to/from Langkawi operate out of Kuah. Coupon-fare taxis run to/from Kuah jetty to Pantai Cenang (RM20).

From about 7am to 7pm, regular ferries operate roughly every hour in either direction between Kuah and the mainland ports of Kuala Perlis (RM15, 45 minutes) and Kuala Kedah (RM18, one hour).

Daily ferries also run between Kuah and Georgetown on Pulau Penang (one way/return RM50/90, 2½ hours), departing from Georgetown at 8am and 8.30am and departing Kuah at 2.30pm and 5.30pm. Check at the jetty as times do vary.

Getting Around

There is no public transport. Car hire is excellent value starting at RM50 per day for a Kancil or RM20 for a motorbike. A few places also rent mountain bikes for RM15 per day.

Otherwise, taxis are the main way of getting around. Fixed fares for the entire vehicle (which can be split between passengers) cost the following from the Kuah jetty: Kuah town (RM6), Pantai Cenang (RM20) and Pantai Tengah (RM22).

PENINSULAR MALAYSIA – EAST COAST

Less wrapped up in history, less multicultural but still refreshingly Malay, the peninsula's east coast is an entirely different experience from the mobile-phone obsessed, traffic-clogged west coast. Headscarves, skullcaps and the hauntingly melodious call to prayer are as ubiquitous here as the white-sand beaches that fringe the sunrise-drenched coasts and jewel-like islands. Wooden *kampung* houses squat amid coconut groves and rubber plantations and everyone seems to be smiling about how wholesome life can be.

> **GETTING TO THAILAND**
>
> **Langkawi Ferry Services** (LFS; ☎ 04-966 1125) has ferries from Kuah on Pulau Langkawi to Satun (one way/return RM27/54, 1¼ hours) four times daily.
>
> See p803 for information on doing the border crossing in the opposite direction.

JOHOR BAHRU

☎ 07

You'll pass through the state capital of Johor Bahru (known as JB) if you're travelling to/from peninsular Malaysia and Singapore. Most Malaysian buses only service Johor Bahru, where you'll need to transfer to a local Singapore-bound bus, stopping for border formalities en route. Johor Bahru is connected to Singapore by the 1038m-long Causeway.

There is little reason to hang around, unless you are a fan of dodgy transport-hub towns. The immigration office is across from Merlin Tower, which is surrounded by a walkable downtown of midrange hotels, food shops and banks.

Tourism Malaysia (☎ 222 3590; www.johortourism.com.my; 5th fl, Jotic Bldg, 2 Jl Air Molek; 🕓 8am-4.30pm Mon-Thu, 8am-12.15pm & 2.45-4.30pm Fri, 8am-12.45pm Sat) is walking distance from Merlin Tower; ask for directions to the Jotic Building.

The finest museum of its kind in Malaysia, **Muzium Diraja Abu Bakar** (☎ 223 0555; adult US$7; 🕓 9am-5pm Sat-Thu) conveys the wealth and privilege of the sultans. Tickets are payable in ringgit at a bad exchange rate; the ticket counter closes at 4pm.

Sleeping & Eating

There's little reason to stay in JB since hopping on any bus would bring you somewhere with better sleeping options.

JB Hotel (☎ 223 4989; 80-A Jl Wong Ah Fook; d RM40-50; ❄) It's central and clean which is about the best you can hope for around here.

Gateway Hotel (☎ 223 5029; 61 Jl Meldrum; r RM70; ❄) Probably the best-value place in this price bracket in the city centre. All rooms have attached bathrooms.

Make the best of your time in JB by eating at the excellent hawker venues, including the daily **Pasar Malam** (Night Market; Jl Wong Ah Fook) outside the Hindu temple. The **Tepian Tebrau food centre** (Jl Abu Bakar) is famous for its *ikan bakar* (grilled fish).

Getting There & Away

AIR

JB is well served by Malaysia Airlines and flights to other places in Malaysia are much cheaper than from Singapore. But most domestic flights connect through KL, a four-hour bus ride away. **Malaysia Airlines** (☎ 334 1011; www.malaysiaairlines.com.my) is 2.5km north of the city centre.

JB's airport is 32km northwest of town at Senai.

BOAT

Ferries leave Johor Bahru for Singapore and Indonesia; see below for more information on the service.

BUS & TAXI

Most people travel from Johor Bahru to Singapore by bus; see below for further information on the trip.

Johor Bahru's long-distance bus station is Larkin station, located 5km north of the centre. Buses run to and from Larkin to all parts of the country, including Melaka (RM14, three hours, hourly), Kuala Lumpur (RM24, four hours, hourly), Ipoh (RM45, seven hours, one daily), Butterworth (RM49, 12 hours, one daily), Mersing (RM8.80, three hours, four daily), Kuantan (RM20.40, five hours, four daily), Kuala Terengganu (RM32, nine hours, two daily) and Kota Bharu (RM49, 10 hours, two daily). Long-distance taxis also leave from Larkin (there's a price list at the stand).

A taxi across the Causeway to the Queen St terminal in Singapore should cost about RM30. A taxi from central JB to the bus station should cost RM8.

TRAIN

Daily trains depart Johor Bahru (2nd class/berth RM33/37) four times per day for Kuala Lumpur. It is also possible to change

GETTING TO SINGAPORE & INDONESIA

To Singapore

There are frequent buses between JB's Larkin bus station, 5km north of the city, and Singapore's Queen St bus station. Most convenient is the air-conditioned Singapore–Johor Bahru Express (RM2.40, one hour, every 10 minutes from 6.30am to midnight). Alternatively, there's the slower city bus 170 (RM1.70). Both buses stop at the Malaysian and Singapore immigration checkpoints; disembark from the bus with your luggage, go through immigration and reboard on the other side (keep your ticket). There's also a bridge that connects Tanjung Kupang in Malaysia with the suburb of Tuas in Singapore, but it's a minor entry point and most traffic will use the Causeway.

There are also trains to Singapore, but it's more convenient to take a bus or taxi. You can also walk across the Causeway; the trip takes 25 minutes.

See p654 for details on doing the trip in the opposite direction.

To Indonesia

The Johor Bahru International Ferry Terminal at Kompleks Bebas Cukai, about 2km east of the Causeway, has services heading to Indonesia. The easiest way to get to the jetty is by taxi (RM8) or take city bus 170 from Larkin to the city centre and then transfer to a Stulang/Duty Free Zone bus. At the duty-free complex, **Sriwani Tours and Travel** (☎ 07-221 1677; Kompleks Bebas Cukai, 88 Jl Ibrahim Sultan, Stulang Laut) handles tickets to most destinations. There are departures to Batam Centre (adult one way RM57, hourly from 7.50am to 6.40pm) and Sekupang (RM57, 8.30am and 12.20pm departures), both port towns on the Indonesian island of Batam. Boats also go to Tanjung Pinang (adult one way RM82, hourly from 8.15am to 5.30pm), a port town on the Indonesian island of Bintan. Both Indonesian arrival ports have connecting services to mainland towns on other islands.

See p267 for information on doing the trip in reverse.

at Gemas (RM21 to RM38) and hop aboard the 'jungle train' for connections to Jerantut (for Taman Negara) and Kota Bharu. See p471 for further information on the Jungle Railway.

MERSING

☎ 07

Fishing boats are everywhere in Mersing, while stray cats seem to have been drawn into town from far and away by tasty smells fresh from the sea. Mersing is a kick-back place with some good cheap eats but is most renowned as the main port for boats to Pulau Tioman.

The **Mersing Tourist Information Centre** (☎ 799 5212; Jl Abu Bakar; 🕑 8am-1pm & 2-4.30pm Mon-Thu, 8am-noon & 2.45-4.30pm Fri, 8am-12.45pm Sat) provides information about both Mersing and Pulau Tioman.

Sleeping & Eating

East Coast Hotel (☎ 799 3546; rockyanwar2002@hotmail.com; 43A Jl Abu Bakar; dm/s/d with shared bathroom RM10/15/25) If you're looking for a friendly welcome in Mersing, this efficient and backpacker-oriented hotel gets the thumbs up – cheap beds, informative and helpful staff and a relaxed ambience.

Omar's Backpackers' Hostel (☎ 799 5096, 019 774 4268; Jl Abu Bakar; dm/d with shared bathroom RM10/20) This is a cheap and popular travellers' den. Doubles with fan and four-bed dorms are clean, there's a balcony and the owners can offer local knowledge. Phone ahead in peak season (June to September).

Restoran Al-Arif (44 Jl Ismail; meals RM7) This place serves tasty Indian food, but you should expect very slow service.

There are several places around town for *roti canai* and *kopi* (coffee).

Getting There & Away

Long-distance buses depart from Plaza R&R (where there are ticket booths), located near the jetty. Destinations include Kuala Lumpur (RM23, six hours, five daily), Johor Bahru (RM8.80, three hours, two daily), Butterworth (RM52.30, 11 hours, one daily), Kuantan (RM12.60, five hours, two daily), Kuala Terengganu (RM26.20, nine hours, two daily) and Ipoh (RM39.40, nine hours, one daily).

See p459 for information on ferries to/from Pulau Tioman.

PULAU TIOMAN

☎ 09

Pulau Tioman is a scattering of cheery Malaysian villages dripping in a decidedly Polynesian lushness. The beaches aren't as voluptuous as those on Langkawi or the Perhentians, but it's not a hardship to saunter past crystalline rivers and rows of hibiscus to find a patch of sand between the rocky stretches. The proximity to Singapore and the availability of upscale digs has made Tioman relatively touristy but somehow the locals don't seem affected. Diving through the coral gardens to find turtles, sharks and some billions of fish are what most people come here for although there's plenty of jungle trekking for land-lubbers.

During the east-coast monsoon, from about November to March, boat services to the island are infrequent or suspended. If you plan to visit Tioman during this time, call the tourist office in Mersing for weather conditions and ferry schedules as the monsoon season often varies.

Orientation & Information

Most budget accommodation is clustered on Air Batang (ABC) and Salang on the northern end of the west coast. Salang has wider stretches of sand and the mood is decidedly 'spring break' with oiled up bodies and all-day beer swilling. In sharp contrast, ABC is like a charming Malay village with one narrow, flower-bedecked footpath linking family businesses to each other.

Connected to ABC by a footpath over a rocky headland, Tekek is the island's main village, where you'll find a bank, telephones and a post office. The duty-free shop at the airport in town sells beer cheaper than water.

On the east coast of the island, Juara has a stunning beach and affordable accommodation, but is difficult to reach on the cheap.

Sights & Activities

According to one guesthouse operator, you come to Tioman for what's under the water, not above – since the land is jaw-dropping gorgeous, this says a lot for the diving. Most places rent snorkelling gear and you can join day trips to Pulau Tulai, better known as Coral Island, where you can swim with nibbling fish and aloof sharks.

Open-water dive courses cost around RM820, and two dives with equipment rental

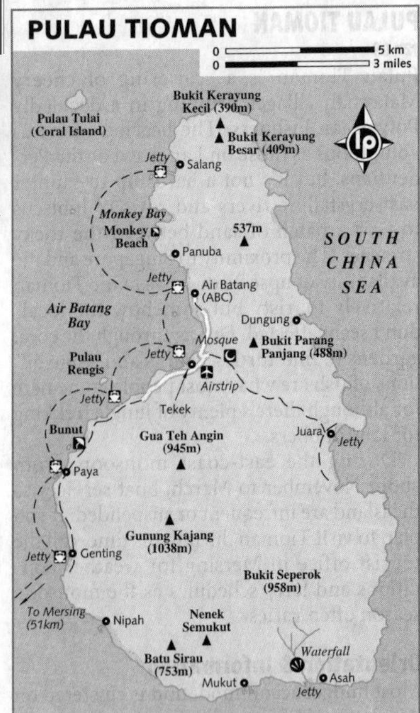

around RM180. There are nearly more dive shops than accommodation options so shop around for the best deal.

There's a fantastic 7km hike that crosses the island's waist from Tekek to Juara (carry plenty of water). It takes around 2½ hours, is steep in parts and starts about 1km north of the jetty in Tekek. Near the top of the hill, you pass a small waterfall and the jungle is awesome.

Power Batik (www.welcome.to/rikkipower; ABC), a tiny batik workshop, is run by Rikki Power, a Malaysian artist with a fine-art background. Sarongs cost from RM65.

Sleeping & Eating

From June to August, when the island swarms with visitors, accommodation becomes tight. Either side of these months it's a buyer's market.

Most restaurants, with similar menus, are attached to chalet operations. ABC, Tekek and Salang all have small convenience stores.

AIR BATANG (ABC)

The far north and southern ends of the beach here have the best sand while some in-between areas are rocky and marshy. Places here are listed from north to south.

ABC Bungalows (☎ 419 1154; chalet RM35-120; ❄) With gardens that look like something out of a Balinese landscaping book, the tidy bungalows here nab the best location in north ABC.

Nazri's II (☎ 419 1375; s RM25-30, d RM50-80; ❄) Nazri's seems to be trying to get the best garden award from ABC Bungalows and it almost has it. Hillside chalets have sea views and the beachfront café is sublime for watching sunsets.

Johan's Resort (☎ 419 1359; dm RM10, r RM25-120; ❄) Well-maintained bungalows grace a rocky beach while shabbier ones hide in the background. The two five-bed dorms are great value.

South Pacific (☎ 419 1176; chalets RM20-35) Just north of the jetty, this bright and friendly place sprawls along to a frangipani-scented Malay graveyard.

My Friend's Place (☎ 419 1150; r from RM25) Busy and social, the basic bungalows are well looked after.

Mokhtar's Place (RM25-50; ❄) Mokhtar's has funky but passable rooms and a particularly

TIOMAN SCAMS

Oh those tenacious entrepreneurs have cooked up a good one for Tioman-bound travellers arriving in the port town of Mersing. The Mersing-bound bus is supposed to stop at the bus station near the jetty, but instead foreigners are 'advised' to get off at a travel agent office in town. The agent sells standard boat tickets (no loss to the traveller here), but accommodation rates can often be doubled, turning what would otherwise be a great budget hut into an overpriced disappointment. If you're worried about finding accommodation, call the guesthouse yourself to reserve a room.

If you don't want to get off at the travel agency, simply tell the bus driver that you want to go to the bus station. Depending on the driver, you might get resistance so just say you are visiting Mersing for the day.

good on-site restaurant that might be the only place in Malaysia serving Canadian poutine (cheesy chips with gravy).

SALANG

The small bay at the south of Salang has a beautiful beach and swimming area backed by a murky river that's teeming with giant monitor lizards. At night everyone who slept on the beach all day is keen to indulge in duty-free beer till the wee hours of the morn. Ugly it might be, but the Medan Selera food court serves the best cheap eats in town. Accommodation is listed here from north to south.

Salang Hut (chalets RM30) At the very quiet north end of the beach, these new huts are a steal with attached bathroom, fan and mosquito net.

our pick Ella's Place (☎ 419 5005; chalets RM25-60; ❄) Ella's has all the attributes of Salang Hut but is directly on a sublime white beach, has a small café, an air-con option and a lovely family-run ambiance.

Salang Indah Resort (☎ 419 5015; r RM25, chalets RM50-150; ❄) Sprawling north of the jetty, this mosquelike resort is the biggest of the bunch, with a huge restaurant, a bar, a shop and a wide variety of mediocre accommodation options.

Salang Pusaka (☎ 419 5317; salangpusaka@yahoo.com; chalets RM45-100; ❄) Formerly Khalid's Place, this complex is tucked behind the lagoon. The garden is attractive, but the rooms are showing some age.

JUARA

For now, Juara's divine beach is practically deserted during the shoulder seasons. There's little to do except swim and snooze under the coconut trees or take a gander into the jungle. If the interior road is ever finished (and this is questionable), town criers say that Juara is destined for high-rolling resort life.

Rainbow Chalets (☎ 419 3109; r RM30) Traveller-recommended Rainbow Chalets lives up to its name with multicoloured bungalows brightly fronting a turquoise sea. The affiliated Bushman Café is a great place to grab a meal after hiking through the jungle and to meet up with the other three or four travellers who might be staying in Juara.

Mizani's Place (chalets RM30) Dilapidated huts make you feel like a bona fide beach bum.

Getting There & Away

Berjaya Air (code J8; ☎ 419 1303; www.berjaya-air.com), with offices at Berjaya Tioman Beach Resort (about halfway up the west cost) and at the airstrip, has daily flights to/from KL (one-way/return RM237/474) and Singapore (RM305/610).

Mersing is the ferry port for Tioman. Several companies run boat services to the island; tickets can be bought around Mersing town or at the jetty near R&R Plaza. There are usually five to six departures throughout the day between 7am and 5pm, but specific departure times vary with the tides. Regular ferries (RM35, two to three hours) leave from the Mersing jetty and drop off passengers in south to north order on the island. Speedboats (RM45, 1½ hours) make a white-knuckled ride from the same jetty. Many green-faced arrivals swear they'll never set foot on another speedboat and promptly book a return trip on the regular boat.

Getting Around

Getting around the island is, for the moment, problematic. You can walk from ABC to Tekek in about 20 minutes. But you'll need to charter a boat through a guesthouse or restaurant to travel between ABC and Salang (RM20).

Boats from Mersing don't travel to Juara; you'll have to get off at Tekek and then hire a 4WD (RM100 for four people). From Juara it's possible to hire a motorbike up the hill (RM30) then you can hike downhill pack-on-back to Tekek (about one hour).

KUANTAN

☎ **09**

Many travellers find themselves on an overnight stopover in Kuantan, the pious and functional state capital, as it's the main transit point between Taman Negara and Pulau Tioman. Kuantan's star attraction is **Masjid Negeri**, the east coast's most impressive mosque, which presides regally over the *padang*. At night it's a magical sight with its spires and lit turrets.

Information

Banks are clustered at Jl Bank and there are plenty of ATMs around Jl Haji Abdul Aziz (the continuation of Jl Mahkota). Internet can be found along Jl Haji Abdul Rahman.

Hamid Bros Books (☎ 516 2119; 23 Jl Mahkota) Licensed moneychanger and English-language bookseller.

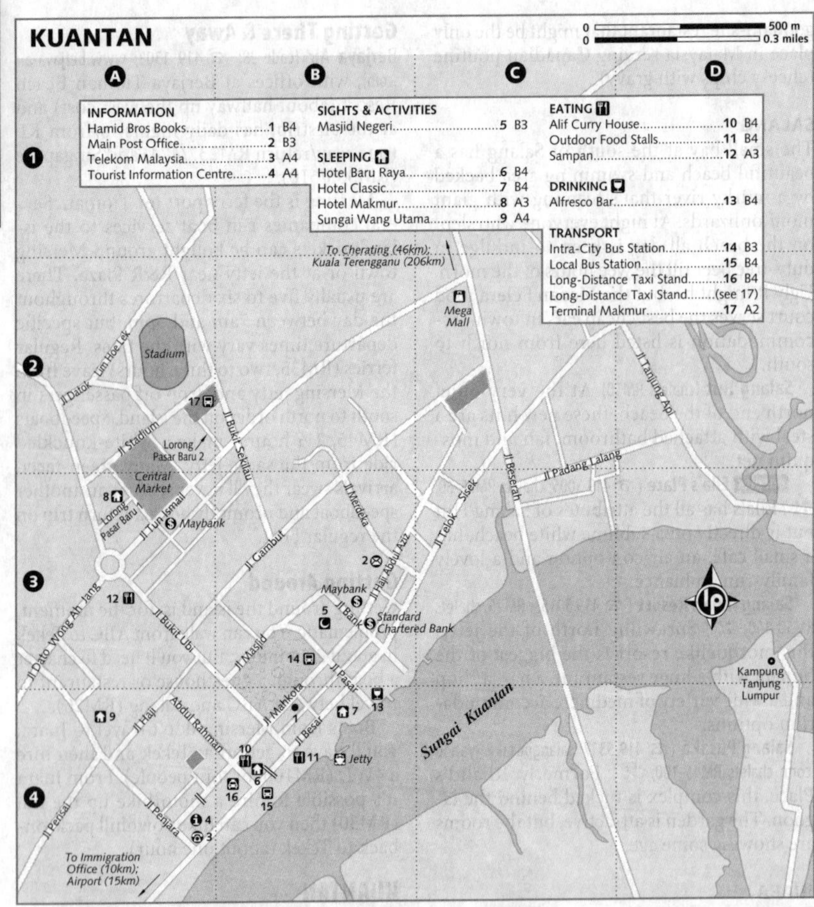

Immigration office (☎ 573 220; Kompleks Khedm, Bandar Indera Mahkota) About 10km south of town.

Main post office (Jl Haji Abdul Aziz) Near the soaring Masjid Negeri.

Telekom Malaysia (☎ 513 9191; 168 Jl Besar)

Tourist information centre (☎ 516 1007; Jl Mahkota; 9am-10pm Mon-Thu, 2.45-5pm Fri, 9am-1pm & 2-5pm Sat) One of Malaysia's most helpful.

Sleeping

Kuantan would be an OK place for a stopover if it had any good budget options. It doesn't.

Sungai Wang Utama (☎ 514 8273; 16 Jl Penjara; r RM15-35;) The vibe is a little sleazy but the windowless, cleanish rooms here are the best value around.

Hotel Makmur (☎ 514 1363; 1st & 2nd fl, B14 & 16, Lorong Pasar Baru 1; r RM28-68;) It's got an institutional feel but, in this town, hospital cleanliness is a godsend. There's a friendly reception and it's an easy pack-haul from the long-distance bus station.

Hotel Baru Raya (☎ 513 9746; 134-136 Jl Besar; r RM35-60) You could spend hours here just contemplating the origins of the astounding variety of stains on the walls. It's friendly and near the local bus station.

Hotel Classic (☎ 516 4599; 7 Jl Besar; r RM75-85;) A true class act, the Classic offers a punch of elegance for relatively few ringgit. There are terrific views of Masjid Negeri from the balcony, freshly painted walls and crisp sheets. Rates include breakfast.

Eating & Drinking

our pick **Alif Curry House** (☎ 514 1415; 19 Jl Mahkota; meals RM1.20-6; 24hr) Dine on amazingly cheap curries in air-conditioned bliss. There's an exceptional variety of *roti canai* on offer including ones stuffed with pineapple or durian (1RM).

Sampan (Jl Bukit Ubi; meals RM2-4; lunch) A group of Chinese food stalls serving restorative herbal drinks plus all-day Chinese breakfast treats such as chicken or century egg porridge (RM2.50).

Food stalls can be found along the riverbank across from Hotel Baru Raya, and at the **central market** (Jl Bukit Ubi).

Kuantan is a very Muslim town, so drinking venues close down more often than they open up. Your best bet for a beer is the **Alfresco Bar** (Mega View Hotel, Lot 567, Jl Besar) on the riverfront.

Getting There & Away

AIR

Malaysia Airlines (code MH; ☎ 531 2123; www.malaysiaairlines.com.my) has direct flights to KL (RM205, three daily). **Kuantan airport** (Lapangan Terbang Sultan Ahmad Shah; ☎ 538 2923) is 15km from the city centre; take a taxi (RM25).

BUS & TAXI

There are three bus stations in Kuantan. Long-distance buses operate from **Terminal Makmur** (Jl Stadium). Services include KL (RM16.90, 4½ hours, hourly), Mersing (RM12.60, 3½ hours, three daily), JB (RM20.40, five hours, frequent), Kuala Terengganu (RM13.50, three hours, frequent), Kota Bharu (RM24.20, seven hours, frequent), Jerantut (RM12.30, 3½ hours, five daily), Melaka (RM19, five hours, three daily) and Butterworth (RM39, eight hours, four daily).

Northbound local buses operate out of a **local bus station** (Jl Besar) near the river, including services between Cherating (RM3) and Marang (RM8). There is also an **intra-city bus station** (cnr Jl Pasar & Jl Mahkota) for destinations within Kuantan town.

There are two long-distance taxi stands – one on Jl Stadium in front of the long-distance bus station, and the other on Jl Mahkota near the local bus station. Destinations and costs (per car) include Mersing (RM160), Cherating (RM50) and Jerantut (RM150).

TASIK CHINI

☎ 09

Delve into one of Peninsular Malaysia's most legend-enshrouded regions, Tasik Chini, where you can find out about Malaysia's own version of the Loch Ness Monster. A series of 12 linked lakes surrounded by thick jungle and fringed with pink lotus blossoms (blooming from June to September), the lake is home to the Jakun people, an Orang Asli (indigenous) tribe. Located inland from Kuantan, it's not that easy to reach scenic Taski Chini; however, it is a popular domestic attraction, so to avoid the crowds try to arrive during the week. You can also visit the lakes as part of a group tour from Cherating for around RM70 per person.

Across the lake at Kampung Gumum, **Rajan Jones Guest House** (r incl 3 meals RM22.50) is about 10 minutes' walk up the main road and offers extremely basic accommodation. Rajan speaks excellent English, is knowledgeable about the Orang Asli and can arrange a spectrum of activities. Grab a brochure with directions to the guesthouse from the Kuantan tourist information centre (opposite).

The best way to get to Tasik Chini is to take a bus from Kuantan's **local bus station** (Jl Mahkota) to Felda Chini (Chini Village; RM5, two hours, six daily from 8.30am to 5.30pm) or Pekan (RM3.60, four daily from 11am to 5.45pm). From Felda Chini, hire a private car or motorcycle (around RM5, 10 minutes).

A taxi direct from Kuantan is around RM70 to Kampung Gumum.

CHERATING

☎ 09

At first glance Cherating looks like it's dying. Shops, restaurants and guesthouses line the main road, monkeys have taken over an old shack or two, but where are the people? Cherating's faded past as a travellers' pick-up scene gives the village a sense of melancholy but there's still a huge draw here: the effortless mingling of the locals and foreigners. Cherating invites you in, makes you feel like an old friend then pampers you with its lazy beach and fresh seafood.

During the monsoon season (November to March), storms kick up surfable waves, especially good for beginners as there are no underwater head-splitters. There's a friendly collection of Malay surfers who hang out year-round.

Batik workshops are enormously popular, and part of the Cherating experience. **Matahari Chalets** (☎ 581 9835) has the largest artists' studios, but other workshops have sprung up along the same road. A batik sarong starts at around RM40.

There are also myriad adventures on the river – kayaking, spotting monkeys and river otters, fishing trips etc.

Information

There are no banks in Cherating; **Travelpost** (☎ 581 9796; 9am-11pm) arranges bus and air ticketing, bicycle and vehicle hire, internet, tourist information, nature tours and will change travellers cheques and cash at a poor rate.

Sleeping

Cherating has a 'strip' where most of the restaurants and guesthouses congregate.

Maznah's Guest House (☎ 581 9072; chalets RM15-30) Some of Maznah's large bungalows were under renovation at the time of writing but even the older ones still look good. Little English is spoken, half-naked kids run laughing through the garden with a few stray chickens and *nasi lemak* (RM1.50) is served for breakfast.

Shadow of the Moon at Half-Past Four (☎ 581 9186; dm 18, r RM35-50) This dark place has resident characters who suspiciously seem like escapees from the pages of a well-worn novel. Rickety, moulding chalets and dorms hide amid the trees, with nocturnal monkeys and wild boars. Most people spend their time here in the central bar–common area of the Deadly Nightshade Bar, drinking and listening to tales of the owner's adventures.

Matahari Chalets (☎ 581 9835; chalets RM20-25) On the road between the beachfront and the main highway, the Matahari has fan-only weathered wood chalets with a balcony, fridge and mosquito net.

our pick **Mimi's Guest House** (☎ 019 904 5251; r RM30-50) If the village of Cherating doesn't inspire you to extend your stay, this place might. Impromptu barbecues and a regular crowd of surfing locals and travellers who never went home make you feel like you joined up with long lost friends. The bungalows and garden are tiny but bursting with artistic flair and all have attached bathrooms and TVs.

Payung Guest House (☎ 019 917 1934; r RM45-70) Absurdly popular Payung stands out for its tip-top management. Solid bungalows with attached bathrooms line up to salute a standard regulation garden; some of the best tours originate from here.

Eating & Drinking

At the western tail-end of the strip are a row of concrete food stalls, serving *roti canai* and Malay specialities. Most of the Chinese-run restaurants serve beer and there are a handful of bars in town.

Restoran Duyong (☎ 581 9578; dishes RM3-10; lunch & dinner) Although this spot looks like a family-style place, there's enough beer swilling going on to give it a frat-boy edge. Dine on Western, Thai or Malay food, including adventurous dishes such as chicken-feet salad (RM10), while gazing out over Cherating's famous surf.

Matahari Restaurant (meals RM5-6; breakfast, lunch & dinner) Directly across from the Malay food stalls, this is where the region's best seafood comes in fresh and is then barbecued in front. Pick your fish (priced by the kilo at market rates) and watch it sizzle. Breakfasts are Western.

Rhana Pippins Bar (dinner) A local expat hang-out right on the beach, this is a lively spot to make friends.

Deadly Nightshade Bar (lunch & dinner) This is the restaurant and bar portion of the Shadow of the Moon guesthouse where all the guests converge at a communal table to feast over devil curry (a Eurasian speciality) made of wild boar and drink whisky.

Getting There & Away

Cherating doesn't have a bus station, but any Kuantan–Terengganu bus will drop off passengers at the turn-off to the village road, which will involve a short stroll. To go south from Cherating you'll need to wave down the local bus bound for Kuantan that runs every 30 minutes (RM3, 1¼ hours); for Kuala Terengganu book long-distance bus tickets (RM13, three hours, frequent) through **Travelpost** (☎ 581 9796; 9am-11pm).

MARANG

☎ 09

Marang, a fishing village at the mouth of Sungai Marang, was once a favourite stopover for travellers making their way along the east coast. Unfortunately, because of poor development strategy, all that you'll find nowadays is a dingy strip of ramshackle houses and roadside stalls up against a deserted beach. The main reason to come to Marang is to catch a ferry to Pulau Kapas, located 6km offshore. Both Marang and Pulau Kapas can be explored as day trips from Kuala Terengganu.

If you're around on Sunday, check out the excellent **Sunday Market**, which starts at 3pm near the town's jetties.

Directly across the jetty to Pulau Kapas is **Nusantara Hostel** (☎ 013 980 7385; dm RM20, r RM35-45), a colourful backpackers with a friendly owner and plenty of travel info.

There are regular local buses to/from Kuala Terengganu (RM1.80). For long-distance buses, there's a **ticket office** (☎ 618 2799; Jl Tanjung Sulong Musa) near the town's main intersection. There are buses to/from Kuala Lumpur (RM30.40, two daily), Johor Bahru (RM34, two daily), and Kuantan (RM13.90, two daily) via Cherating.

PULAU KAPAS

☎ 09

Kapas is the kind of place you could melt into and forget to leave. Not that there's much going on, but that's the beauty of the place – it's a beach without the scene. Outside July, August and a few holiday weekends expect to have the scorching white beaches, and aquamarine waters to yourself. All accommodation and the few restaurants are clustered together on two small beaches on the west coast, but you can walk around the headlands to quieter beaches.

Note that accommodation on the island shuts down during monsoon season (November to March).

There is only one budget-accommodation option on Kapas, **Lighthouse** (☎ 019 215 3558; dm/d with shared bathroom RM20/50), an elevated jungle longhouse with Che posters, hammocks and Nora Jones tunes.

It is also possible to camp on some of the isolated beaches at the northern and southern ends of the island, but bring your own food and water.

Six kilometres offshore from Marang, Kapas is reached by boats in mere minutes from Marang's main jetty. Tickets (slow boat RM20, speedboat RM30) can be purchased from any of the agents nearby. Boats depart when four or more people show up. Be sure to arrange a pick-up time when you purchase your ticket. You can usually count on morning departures from 8.30am.

KUALA TERENGGANU

☎ 09

As the capital of Malaysia's oil producing region, Kuala Terengganu has money and has used it to tastefully redecorate. Large brick sidewalks and elegant mosque-like shopping complexes have gussied the place up yet the soul of the former fishing village has been maintained.

Kuala Terengganu is a convenient staging post to nearby attractions such as Tasik Kenyir, Pulau Kapas and Pulau Redang. Note that official business in Terengganu is closed on Friday and Saturday in observance of the Islamic faith.

Information

Jl Sultan Ismail is the commercial hub of the town and home to most of the banks. Internet shops are along Jl Tok Lam.

Hospital Terengganu (☎ 623 3333; Jl Sultan Mahamud)

Immigration office (☎ 622 1424; Wisma Persekutuan, Jl Sultan Ismail)

Mr Dobi Laundry (☎ 622 1671; Jl Masjid Abidin) Around RM3.50 per kilogram.

Ping Anchorage (☎ 626 5020; www.pinganchorage.com; 77A Jl Sultan Sulaiman) Organises accommodation to nearby resort islands (see p465) and sightseeing tours.

State Tourist Office (☎ 622 1553; Jl Sultan Zainal Abidin; 🕘 9am-5pm Sat-Thu)

Tourism Malaysia (☎ 622 1433; Menara Yayasan Islam Terengganu, Jl Sultan Omar; 🕘 9am-5pm Sat-Thu)

Sights

Kuala Terengganu's compact **Chinatown** is situated along Jl Kampung Cina (also called Jl Bandar). It's a colourful array of hole-in-the-wall Chinese shops, hairdressing salons and restaurants, as well as a sleepy **Chinese temple** and some narrow alleys leading to jetties on the waterfront.

The **central market** (cnr Jl Kg Cina & Jl Banggol; 🕘 8am-5pm Sat-Thu) is a lively place to graze on exotic snacks, and the floor above the fish section has a wide collection of batik and *kain songket* (handwoven fabric). Across from the market is a flight of stairs leading up to **Bukit Puteri** (Princess Hill), a 200m hill with city vistas and the remains of a fort. **Istana Maziah** (Sultan's Palace; Jl Masjid Abidin) and **Zainal Abidin Mosque** (Jl Masjid Abidin) are not camera shy.

Kompleks Muzium Negeri Terengganu (Terengganu State Museum; ☎ 622 1444; adult RM5, 🕑 9am-5pm) claims to be the largest museum in the region, and it attractively sprawls over landscaped gardens along the banks of the Sungai Terengganu. Traditional architecture, fishing boats and textiles comprise the bulk of the collection. The museum is 5km south of Terengganu; to get there take minibus 10 (RM1).

In the middle of Sungai Terengganu, **Pulau Duyung Besar** carries on the ancient boat-building tradition handed down for generations; the village is good for a day of wandering and snacking. Take the local ferry (60 sen) from the jetty near the Immigration Office across Bukit Puteri.

Sleeping

Awi's Yellow House (☎ 624 5046; dm/d with shared bathroom RM6/15) This is a unique guesthouse built on stilts over Sungai Terengganu, on Pulau Duyung Besar, a 10-minute ferry ride across the river from Terengganu. It may be a little rustic for some, but it's a friendly and relaxed place.

Travellers Inn (☎ 626 2020; 77A Jl Sultan Sulaiman; dm RM8, r with shared bathroom RM18-36; ❄) This is the only budget option in town, affiliated with the attached Ping Anchorage; it's clean and secure but distinctly unhelpful. You can also grab a mediocre Western-style breakfast or beer from its Travellers Cafe.

Hotel Grand Paradise (☎ 622 8888; 28 Jl Tok Lam; r RM60-80; ❄) It's a far cry from Paradise but

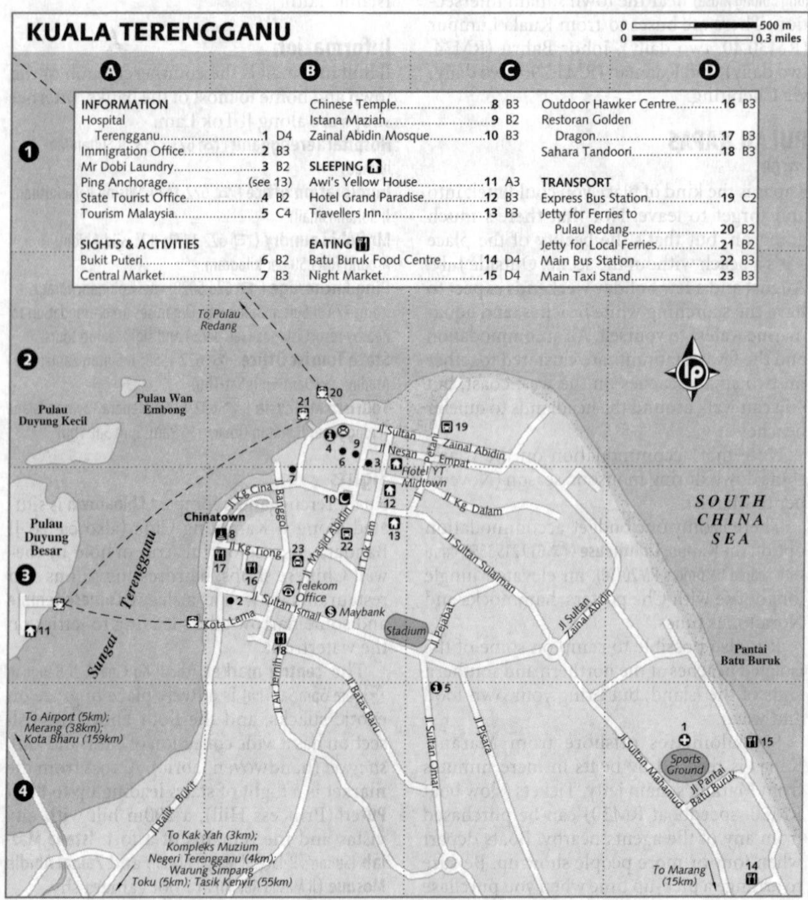

this worn, friendly spot is good value for the price.

Eating & Drinking

Terengganu has several regional specialities, such as *nasi dagang* (glutinous rice cooked with coconut milk and served with fish curry) and *keropok lekor* (deep-fried fish crackers), that draw food enthusiasts from across the country.

Batu Buruk Food Centre (Jl Pantai Batu Buruk; ⌚ lunch & dinner) This is a great outdoor food centre near the beach; don't leave without trying its famous *ais-krim goreng* (fried ice cream).

Restoran Golden Dragon (☎ 622 3034; 198 Jl Kg Cina; dishes RM3-6; ⌚ lunch) Point and choose from delicious green-bean and chilli salad, roast pork, spinach salad and tofu dishes. This place serves beer and the staff are tickled by foreign clients.

Sahara Tandoori (☎ 623 7777; Jl Air Jernih; dishes RM3-7; ⌚ lunch) Tasty snacks such as banana fritters and *roti canai* are served at the popular Sahara. Be sure to try *abok abok*, a glutinous rice treat sweetened with coconut sap and wrapped in a banana leaf.

There's a night market at the beachfront every Friday evening, and Chinatown's outdoor hawker centre, divided into Chinese and Malay sections, is also worth a graze.

Getting There & Away

For details on getting to/from Pulau Redang, see right.

AIR

Malaysia Airlines (code MH; ☎ 622 1415; www.malaysiaairlines.com.my) has direct daily flights to/from Kuala Lumpur (RM135). **Air Asia** (code AK; ☎ 631 3122; www.airasia.com) also has flights to KL (from RM50, two daily). A taxi to/from the **airport** (☎ 666 3666), located 13km northeast of the town centre, costs around RM30.

BUS & TAXI

The **main bus station** (Jl Masjid Abidin) serves as a terminus for all local buses. Some long-distance buses depart from here as well, but most use the **express bus station** (Jl Sultan Zainal Abidin), in the north of town.

At the main bus station, there are services to/from Marang (RM2, 30 minutes, every half-hour from 6.30am to 6.30pm) and Kuala Besut (RM10, 2½ hours, hourly).

From the express bus station, there are regular services running to/from Johor Bahru (RM34, nine hours, two daily), Ipoh (RM37, 10 hours, two daily), Kuala Lumpur (RM30, seven hours, frequent), Melaka (RM33.20, nine hours, one daily), Mersing (RM26.20, seven hours, two daily) and Kota Bharu (RM11, three hours, seven daily).

The main taxi stand is at Jl Masjid Abidin across from the main bus station.

MERANG

☎ 09

The main gateway to Pulau Redang, the sleepy little fishing village of Merang (*mer*-ang; not to be confused with Marang, further south) is one of the few remaining villages to have escaped development. There is little of interest to do in the village other than to descend into the slowness of harvesting coconuts, repairing fishing nets and gossiping about neighbours.

The best place to stay is friendly **Kembara Resort** (☎ 653 1770; kembararesort@hotmail.com; dm/d/chalets from RM10/30/60; ❄ 💻), about 500m south of the village (follow the signs from the main road).

There are daily buses from the main bus station in Kuala Terengganu to Merang (RM2). There are no regular public ferries between Merang and Pulau Redang; rather, the island's resorts have boats that make the trip. See below for details.

PULAU REDANG

Pulau Redang is one of nine islands that form a protected marine park, and it is considered one of the best dive spots in the world thanks to its ancient coral gardens and good visibility. Hawksbill and green turtles nest on parts of the island and leatherbacks are occasionally spotted feasting on jellyfish. Accommodation options range from international-class hotels to air-conditioned chalets and are nearly exclusively booked on all-inclusive package tours.

Luckily **Ping Anchorage** (☎ 626 5020; www.pinganchorage.com) in Kuala Terengganu acts as a clearinghouse for unsold rooms, offering three-day, two-night packages (including transfer to/from the island, all meals and an activity or two) from RM320 to RM500 per person. Prices are lowest off season and mid-week and go down even lower if you book four people to a room. While you could go to

Redang on your own by hopping on one of the resort's boats, you'll end up paying considerably more for room and board.

KUALA BESUT

The primary jetty town for boats to Pulau Perhentian is Kuala Besut (bee-su), south of Kota Bharu. It is a sleepy fishing village with a handful of collaborating boat companies and a small bus station.

Some taxi drivers get paid commission to take travellers to the upstart jetty of **Tok Bali**, just across the river. The Symphony boat company operates out of Tok Bali. Ferries here aren't quite – but are nearly as frequent – as Kuala Besut based boats; unless you are set on a certain departure time, this shouldn't pose a problem. For more details see opposite.

Most Kota Bharu guesthouses arrange shared taxis to Kuala Besut (RM35) or Tok Bali (RM30); the fare can be split between four people. There is also local bus 639 (RM4.50, 2½ hours, two daily) and taxis pick up passengers at the Wakaf Baharu train station (RM40).

From Kuala Besut's small bus station, you can travel to Kuala Lumpur (RM30, eight hours, two daily) and to the transport hubs of Jerteh (RM2, every 20 minutes) and Pasir Puteh (RM2, every 20 minutes). For Kuala Terengganu (RM7, 2½ hours, hourly) buses wait at **Restaurant Petani Jaya** (☎ 697 4517; 779 Jl Semarak), a short walk away from the jetty.

The agent at Kuala Besut's jetty also sells minibus tickets to the Cameron Highlands (RM60, six hours) and Taman Negara (RM85, eight hours), which leave at 10am daily.

PULAU PERHENTIAN

☎ 09

Long Beach on Pulau Kecil of the Perhentian Islands is one of Malaysia's most popular backpacker congregation spots. The near-perfect crescent of white sand is clogged with guesthouses (but no cars!) and has a burgeoning litter problem but the jungle setting and fiesta vibe are hypnotically soothing, the turquoise water utterly sublime. Coral Beach, also on Kecil, is a touch classier than Long Beach, while the digs on Pulau Besar verge on the resortlike.

The best time to visit is from March to mid-November. The Perhentians close for the monsoon season, but usually reopen around Chinese New Year in February. Dates vary depending on the whim of the monsoons.

There are no banks on the Perhentians. Generators are the source of power and are run during limited hours. There are no public phones but mobile phones work. If you're desperate you can make international calls from one of the little internet-café-cum-shacks on Long Beach for a heart-stopping RM15 per minute.

Activities

Dive operators on the island contend that the Perhentians offer all the underwater delights of the east coast of Thailand without the 'dive-factory' feel. Classes are smaller and more relaxed than the dive diva of Ko Tao. A four-day open-water course starts at RM850 and is pro-rated for various initiation steps. For the surface skimmers, guesthouses arrange snorkelling trips around the island (RM30 to RM50).

Sleeping & Eating

On Pulau Kecil (Small Island), Long Beach has the biggest range of budget chalets and 'nightlife' (that means two beachfront bars). In the high season (usually from late May to early September), finding accommodation here can be tough, so book ahead or arrive early. Accommodation on Pulau Besar (Big Island) is more upmarket and usually includes air-con and an attached bathroom; but the beaches aren't as pretty as on Kecil.

Alcohol is available in a few bars and hotel restaurants on both islands, though it's not openly displayed and you will have to ask for it. The best hunting grounds for a beer are the more popular Long Beach cafés and Watercolours Resort on Pulau Perhentian Besar.

PULAU PERHENTIAN KECIL

A trail over the narrow waist of the island leads from Long Beach to smaller Coral Bay (sometimes known as Aur Bay) on the western side of the island. It's a 15-minute walk along a footpath through the jungle interior (watch for monitor lizards). Coral Bay has a more chilled ambience and gear rentals and excursions are slightly cheaper; it also faces the west for an uninterrupted view of the brilliant sunsets and has calm swimming. The surf can get rather big on Long Beach and several places along the beach rent boogie boards (RM15 per hour) and old clunky surfboards (RM30 per hour) but bargain for better rates.

There are a number of small bays around the island, each with one set of chalets, and often only accessible by boat.

Rock Garden (Long Beach; r with shared bathroom RM15) Slap-up shacks on the rocky headland above Lemon Grass Chalet have a bed, a mosquito net and a view.

Chempaka Chalets (☎ 010 985 7329; Long Beach; r RM20-30) Yet another group of bungalows in a bland but tidy garden, Chempaka gets extra points for cleanliness and its beach-bum vibe.

Panorama Chalets & Restaurant (☎ 010 934 0123; Long Beach; r RM25-150) This is a social place with a jungle-groovy atmosphere, a good café and nightly movies. Rooms are a little flimsy for the price and the shared bathrooms are less than luxurious.

Matahari Chalets (☎ 019 956 5756; Long Beach; chalets RM35-65) The spacious longhouse rooms and A-frame huts are in much better condition than those of the competition. They ramble around a well-kept but shadeless garden off the beach.

Butterfly Chalets (Coral Bay; r RM30-40) Ageing huts look out over uninterrupted sea views and are tucked in by hibiscus flowers. To get here, clamber up the hill at the far end of the beach beyond Suria Beach Resort.

Aur Bay Chalets (☎ 010 985 8584; Coral Bay; r RM30-40) This well-groomed but fading place feels like a mini *kampong* with its sweet Malay owners and kids jump-roping in the sand.

Maya Beach Resort (☎ 019 937 9136; Coral Bay; r RM35-45) British-run Maya is neat, trim and a good place for friendly advice.

our pick **Petani Beach** (Pasir Petani; r RM30-50) On a secluded south coast beach, the driftwood naturalistic décor here is set off by bows of magenta bougainvillea. We've had very enthusiastic traveller recommendations for the quality of the bungalows, the service and the food.

D' Lagoon Chalets (☎ 019 985 7089; Teluk Kerma; r RM25-50) This place fronts a gorgeous but often agitated bay on the northeastern side of the island. There are longhouse rooms and chalets, as well as a more unusual tree house (RM25) for a more Tarzan experience.

Mira Chalets (☎ 010 964 0582; r RM30-50) Mira, on the west coast, was scheduled to reopen when we passed. Sea-weathered, rustic huts with mosquito nets are perched over a beach so deserted and perfect, you'll think you're hallucinating. There's one rather adventurous jungle toilet for everyone to share.

PULAU PERHENTIAN BESAR

Of the three main beaches, the sand surrounding the Perhentian Island Resort is the rockiest, heading south the sand is less cluttered, and finally Teluk Dalam, a secluded bay with a long stretch of shallow beach, is just silken. An easily missed track leads from behind the second jetty over the hill to Teluk Dalam.

It's possible to camp on the beach south of the Government Resthouse; this area is busy at long weekends.

The options here are listed from north to south.

Watercolours Resort (☎ 010 911 3852; www.watercoloursworld.com; r RM60-80; ❄) It's a bit of a factory here with lots of comings and goings, staff everywhere and divers heading to the water like lemmings. The bungalows are musty but the restaurant is the best in the islands.

ABC Guesthouse (☎ 019 906 4823; r RM30; 💻) Over the headland from Watercolours there's another stretch of beach that's also the main ferry stop so there's lots of boat activity. Elevated above the smooth sands is this big, bright, Wild West–looking longhouse. Rooms are basic, but a bargain.

Abdul's (☎ 010 983 7303; r RM40-80) Clambering over the next headland brings you to a quiet beach where you'll find this popular place with fan chalets and attached bathrooms. Unfortunately, a giant government pier was under construction here at the time of writing so the calm may not last.

Everfresh Beach Resort (☎ 697 7620; Teluk Dalam; r RM20-40) Rooms here are tatty and dark but who cares when you've got a beach like this one out front.

Flora Bay Resort (☎ 697 7266; www.florabayresort.com; Teluk Dalam; r RM50-150; ❄ 💻) A huge range of rooms, a restaurant, movies at night and super helpful staff make this a good choice although the rooms could use some sprucing up.

Getting There & Around

Pulau Perhentian is 21km off the coast. Both speedboats (RM70 return, 30 minutes) and slow boats (RM50 return, 1½ hours) run several times a day from Kuala Besut to the Perhentians, from 8am to 3pm. In the other direction, speedboats depart from the islands daily at around 8am, noon and 4pm; slow boats leave hourly from 8am to noon. Note that you can board a speedboat going in either direction with a slow-boat ticket if you pay the RM10 fare difference. See p466 for more information about the competing jetty of Tok Bali.

When the waves are high on Long Beach, you'll be dropped off or picked up on the other side of the island at Coral Bay. Also, guesthouse operators on Kecil now charge RM2 per person for ferry pick-ups and drop-offs.

The easiest way to island (or beach) hop is by boat. Posted fares and boat operators usually camp out under a shady coconut tree. From island to island, the trip costs RM12.

KOTA BHARU

☎ 09

Just because it's a state capital doesn't mean it's a sprawling metropolis. Kota Bharu is a shy, manageable town and a convenient base to explore Malay and Islamic culture. While some visitors just pass through en route to Pulau Perhentian, the cultural centre demonstrations and lip-smacking night market should not be missed by the culturally inclined.

Information

Banks and ATMs are scattered around town; the Maybank moneychanger (near the corner of Jl Padang Garong and Jl Mahmud), near the central market, is usually open till 7pm. Internet shops can be found in the alleys between Jl Doktor and Jl Kebun Sultan.

General Hospital (☎ 748 5533; Jl Hospital)
Immigration office (☎ 748 212; Jl Temenggong)
Tourist Information Centre (☎ 748 5534; Jl Sultan Ibrahim; 🕑 8am-1pm & 2-4.30pm Sun-Thu)

Sights & Activities

Kota Bharu's main attraction is its **central market** (Jl Padang Garong), housed in a modern octagonal building where traders sell fresh produce, spices, basketware and other goods. You might come to observe the locals, but the locals are more than happy to look at you.

For a dose of Malay tradition, don't miss the cultural centre, **Gelanggang Seni** (☎ 744 3124; Jl Mahmud; admission free; 🕑 3.30-5.30pm Mon, Wed & Sat, 9pm-midnight Wed & Sat), for top spinning, *seni silat* (martial arts), shadow puppetry, kite making etc. Check with the tourist information centre, as opening and performance times vary.

Exhibits at the **Muzium Negeri Kelantan** (☎ 748 2266; Jl Hospital; adult RM2; 🕑 8.30am-4.45pm Sun-Thu) combine an eclectic array of artefacts, including traditional instruments, kites and shadow puppets.

Other museums are clustered around Padang Merdeka (Independence Sq). **Istana Jahar** (Royal Customs Museum; ☎ 748 2266; Jl Hilir Kota; adult RM3; 🕑 8.30am-4.45pm Sun-Thu) exhibits royal rites of passage and traditional ceremonies, such as circumcision and engagement, from birth to death; this may not sound that engaging, but wandering around the scenic building gives a glimpse into Malay Muslim architecture. **Muzium Islam** (☎ 744 0102; Jl Sultan; admission free; 🕑 8.30am-4.45pm Sun-Thu) is also worth a look and **Istana Batu** (☎ 748 7737; Jl Hilir Kota; adult RM2; 🕑 8.30am-4.45pm Sun-Thu) has displays on royal history.

Sleeping

Central city crash-pads are convenient for late central bus station drop-offs, but wandering just minutes away brings you to more charming options. The backpacker places listed here have shared-bathroom and private-bathroom (read: pricier) options.

Zeck's Travellers' Inn (☎ 743 1613; www.zeck-traveller.com; 7088G Jl Sri Cemerlang; dm/s/d RM7/15/20; ❄ 💻) An oasis just 10 minutes' walk from the city, Zeck's is relaxed, clean (it was being painted when we passed) and over-the-top hospitable. Many travellers on a short stop stay on longer just because of this place. The turn-off from Jl Sri Cemerlang is easy to miss; keep an eye out for the roadside shack selling fresh fritters.

Ideal Travellers' Guest House (☎ 744 2246; www.ugoideal.com; 3954F Jl Kebun Sultan; dm/s/d/q RM7/15/25/35; 💻) Down an alley off Jl Pintu Pong, the Ideal is a deservedly popular place of happy, mingling backpackers. Spacious rooms are airy and have lots of natural light. Bathrooms get a regular scrub down and there's a shady backyard reading area.

KB Backpackers Lodge (☎ 747 0125; 1872A Jl Padang Garong; dm/s/d/q RM7/15/22/40; 💻) This is a good choice for a dark and dormy night on a good mattress. It's right in the heart of town.

Bunga Raya Backpackers Lodge (☎ 748 9866; 2981B Jl Padang Garong; dm/s/d RM8/15/28; ❄ 💻) Central and spanning three floors of an apartment complex, this is a social, city-feeling place with a good common area and bright basic rooms. Dorms are cramped and the communal bathrooms have seen better days.

Menora Guest House (☎ 748 1669; 3338D Jl Sultanah Zainab; r RM15-38; ❄) Menora's prime attraction is its rooftop garden with views of the city, Sungai Kelantan and beyond. There's one room on the rooftop that has its own open-air shower. Inside, there are a variety of clean rooms. Note that the gate is locked at 11.30pm.

Eating & Drinking

Kota Bharu is a conservative Muslim city so alcohol is not widely available; head to Chinese restaurants if you're hankering for a beer.

our pick **Night Market** (cnr Jl Datok Pati & Jl Pintu Pong; 🕑 dinner) For a bonanza of regional Malay and Indian specialities at hawker prices, head to this vibrant market. Here you will find *ayam*

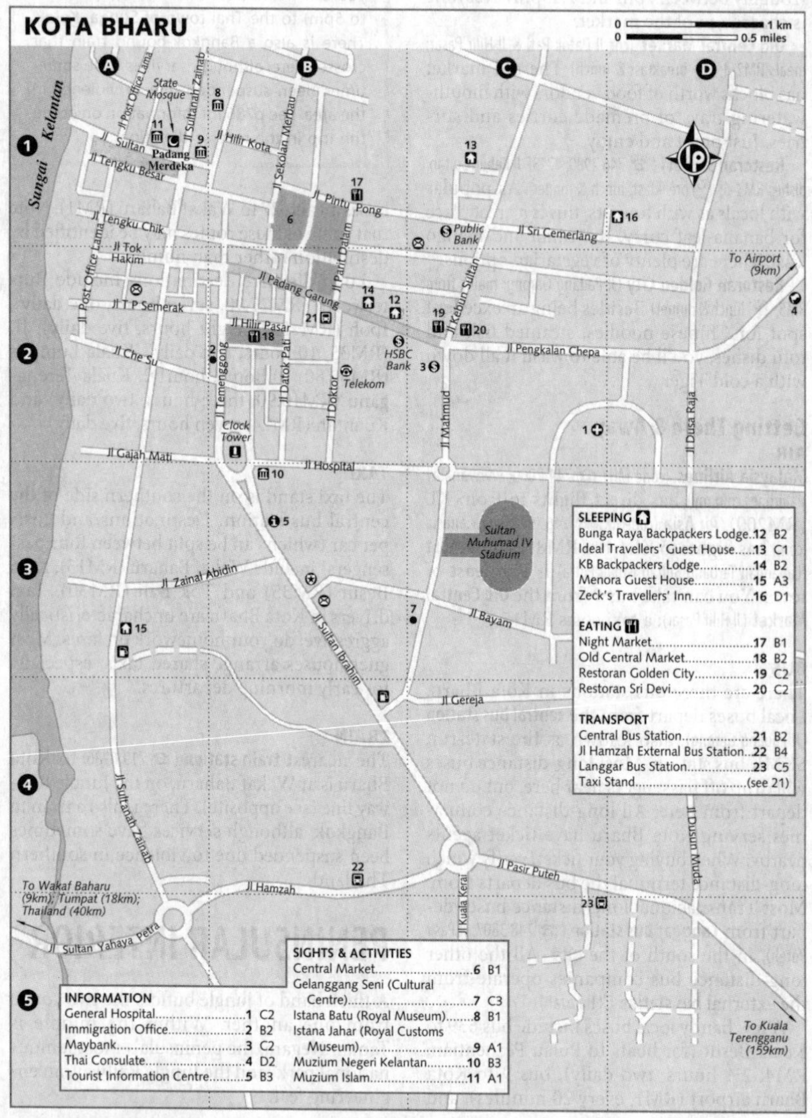

percik (marinated chicken on bamboo skewers), *nasi kerabu* (rice tinted blue with herbs, mixed with coconut, fish, vegetables and spices), squid-on-a-stick, sweet banana and savoury *murtabak* (thick Indian pancake stuffed with onion, egg, chicken, mutton or vegetables), and a bewildering array of cakes. Prayer always pulls rank over food and at prayer time (roughly between 7pm and 7.45pm) everyone is chased out of the market.

Old Central Market (cnr Jl Datok Pati & Jl Hilir Pasar; meals RM2-4; breakfast & lunch) The old market has blocks worth of food vendors with mouth-watering trays of premade curries and stir-fries. Just point and enjoy.

Restoran Sri Devi (☎ 746 2980; 4213F Jl Kebun Sultan; dishes RM3-6; breakfast, lunch & dinner) As popular with locals as with tourists, this is a great place for banana-leaf curry, *roti canai* and mango lassi. There are plenty of vegetarian options.

Restoran Golden City (Jl Padang Garong; mains from RM5; lunch & dinner) Besides being an excellent spot for Chinese noodles, steamed fish and tofu dishes, you'll be able to wash it all down with a cold Tiger.

Getting There & Away

AIR

Malaysia Airlines (code MH; ☎ 744 7000; www.malaysiaairlines.com.my) has direct flights to/from KL (RM200). **Air Asia** (code AK; ☎ 746 1671; www.airasia.com) has flights to KL from RM81. The **airport** (Lapangan Terbang Sultan Ismail Petra) is 9km east of town. You can take bus 9 from the **Old Central Market** (Jl Hilir Pasar); a taxi costs RM15.

BUS

There are three bus stations in Kota Bharu. Local buses depart from the **central bus station** (Jl Padang Garong), also known as the state-run SKMK bus station. Most long-distance buses will drop off passengers near here, but do not depart from here. All long-distance companies serving Kota Bharu have ticket agents nearby. When buying your ticket, verify which long-distance terminal the bus departs from. Most Transnacional long-distance buses depart from **Langgar bus station** (☎ 748 3807; Jl Pasir Puteh), in the south of the city. All the other long-distance bus companies operate from the external **bus station** (Jl Hamzah).

A few handy local buses include bus 639 to Kuala Besut (for boats to Pulau Perhentian; RM4, 2½ hours, two daily), bus 9 to Kota Bharu airport (RM1, every 20 minutes), and buses 19 and 27 to Wakaf Baharu (RM1). Note that some of these routes may be identified by destination rather than number.

Long-distance destinations include Butterworth (RM27.90, seven hours, one daily), Ipoh (RM25.40, eight hours, five daily), JB (RM35, 10 hours, five daily), Kuala Lumpur (RM30.80, 10 hours, hourly), Kuala Terengganu (RM10.90, three hours, two daily) and Kuantan (RM24, seven hours, five daily).

GETTING TO THAILAND

It's not advised to cross the border here due to violence and instability on this coast of southern Thailand. If you must risk it, take local bus 29 from Kota Bharu (RM3, one hour, every 30 minutes) to the Malaysian border town of Rantau Panjang. From here, you can walk across the border (open 6am to 5pm) to the Thai town of Sungai Kolok. There is also a Bangkok-bound train that crosses here, although services have sometimes been suspended due to violence in the area. See p786 for information on doing the trip in the reverse direction.

TAXI

The taxi stand is on the southern side of the central bus station. Destinations and costs per car (which can be split between four passengers) include Wakaf Baharu (RM15), Kota Besut (RM35) and Tok Bali (RM30). Taxi drivers in Kota Bharu are uncharacteristically aggressive; do your homework on fares. Most guesthouses arrange shared taxis, especially for early morning departures.

TRAIN

The nearest **train station** (☎ 719 6986) to Kota Bharu is at Wakaf Baharu, on the Jungle Railway line (see opposite). There is also a train to Bangkok, although services have sometimes been suspended due to violence in southern Thailand.

PENINSULAR INTERIOR

A thick band of jungle buffers the two coasts from one another. Within the middle is Taman Negara, the peninsula's most famous national park, and the Jungle Railway, an engineering feat.

JUNGLE RAILWAY

This line trundles into the mountainous, jungle-clad interior, stopping at every ramshackle *kampung*, packing in chattering school children and headscarfed women lugging oversized bundles. Travellers' reports range from sheer awe of the natural splendour and amusement with the local camaraderie to boredom and irritation with faulty air-conditioning in the carriages and dirty windows. If you're in good company and have a lot of time, then there are worse ways to travel between Pulau Perhentian and Taman Negara.

The northern terminus is Tumpat, but most travellers start/end at Wakaf Baharu, the closest station to the transport hub of Kota Bharu. The train departs from Wakaf Baharu on its southbound journey around 6am. It reaches Jerantut, the jumping-off point for Taman Negara, anywhere from eight to 11 hours later (RM14.60). The train continues south to Gemas (RM21.20), meeting the Singapore–KL train line.

There are also express trains that travel at night, but that would defeat the purpose of seeing the jungle. There is a daily express train that leaves Wakaf Baharu at 6pm and arrives in KL at 7.25am the following day. There is also a daily express train to Singapore (RM35) leaving at 7pm and arriving at 9am the following day.

Northbound trains leave Gemas at 7.45am, reaching Jerantut at noon and arriving at Wakaf Baharu at 9.30pm.

Note that the KTM railway company changes its schedule every six months, so it pays to double-check departure times.

JERANTUT

☎ 09

Jerantut is the first of several stepping stones to Taman Negara. It's a friendly, easy town, where you can pick up supplies, change money or stay overnight to break up your trip. Most guesthouses are affiliated with travel agencies that offer transfers to Kuala Tembeling jetty (where boats leave for Taman Negara national park), ferry services to Kuala Tahan (the base-camp village for the national park) and park tours.

Sleeping & Eating

Hotel Sri Emas (☎ 266 4499; www.taman-negara.com; Jl Besar; dm RM8, r RM15-64; ❄) This place is backpacker central, and it can make full arrangements for your trip to Taman Negara (although just organising transport should generally be enough). Rooms are average and the use of some cleaning products wouldn't go astray.

Greenleaf Guesthouse (1st fl, Jl Diwangsa; dm RM10, r with shared bathroom RM20-30; ❄) Another backpacker favourite, the Greenleaf is open 24 hours, and has free pick-up and drop-off to the train and bus stations, luggage storage etc. It is across from the bus station near the AM Finance bank.

Hotel Chet Fatt (☎ 266 5805; 177 Jl Diwangsa; dm/d with shared bathroom RM10/20; 💻) This is near the bus station and has spacious, window-lit rooms, free filtered water and friendly service.

The food stalls situated between the market and Jerantut's train station are excellent. Cheap *kedai kopi* can be found along Jl Besar and in the buildings across from the bus station.

Getting There & Away

BOAT

Motor-run canoes make the scenic journey between Kuala Tembeling, 16km north of Jerantut, and Kuala Tahan. Several ferry companies sell tickets at the jetty, if you arrive independent of arranged transport from Jerantut. In most cases, though, travel agents sell combination tickets that include transfer from Jerantut to the jetty and ferry to Kuala Tahan.

For more information on ferries to Kuala Tahan, see p475.

BUS & TAXI

The bus station and taxi stand are in the centre of town.

Most people arriving in Jerantut want to head directly to the Kuala Tembeling jetty (where boats leave for Taman Negara). The easiest way to do this is to follow the representative from Hotel Sri Emas, who meets arriving buses and trains and organises minibus transfers (RM5) from Jerantut to Kuala Tembeling.

If you want to resist the herding, there is a local bus between Kuala Tembeling and Jerantut bus station (signed as 'Kerambit'; RM1.50, 45 minutes, with 8.15am, 11.15am, 1.45pm and 5.15pm departures), but the times are not pegged to boat departures or arrivals (see p475 for ferry times); the return bus leaves Kuala Tembeling at 10am, 1pm and 3.30pm.

You can also skip the boat journey and hop on a Kuala Tahan–bound bus (signed as 'Latif'; RM6, one to two hours, four daily); Kuala Tahan is the base-camp village for Taman Negara.

Alternatively, you can hire a taxi to Kuala Tembeling (RM16 for the entire car) or to Kuala Tahan (RM60).

Beware of touts at the train and bus stations who tell you there are no boats running from Tembeling to the park; they're only trying to get you to take their very expensive alternatives.

When you are ready to get the hell out of Jerantut, there are six daily buses to/from KL's Pekeliling bus station (RM12.80, 3½ hours, four daily) via Temerloh. If you miss the bus to KL, buses go every hour to Temerloh (RM5, one hour), from where there are more connections to KL and other destinations; the last bus to Temerloh leaves at 6pm. If you're itching to get to Pulau Tioman, you'll have to catch a bus to Kuantan (RM12.40, 3½ hours, three daily) and then a bus to Mersing.

You can also take a bus from Jerantut to Melaka (RM16.70, five hours, one daily). Long-distance taxis go to Temerloh (RM30), KL (RM120) and Kuantan (RM100).

TRAIN

Jerantut is on the Jungle Railway (Tumpat–Gemas line; see p471). The train station is off Jl Besar, just behind Hotel Sri Emas. For the famed jungle view, catch the northbound local train at 12.10pm (RM15). If you opt to skip the view, a daily northbound express train leaves Jerantut at 2am (RM17 to RM22, four hours).

For southbound trips, there is a midnight express train leaving Jerantut for Sentral KL (RM20 to RM24, seven hours), a 1am express train for Singapore (RM16 to RM22, seven hours) and an 8.40am local train for Singapore (RM11 to RM18, nine hours). Another local southbound train leaves at 3.30pm terminating at Gemas (RM9 to RM12, four hours), where you can catch an inconvenient 2am Singapore (RM28 to RM33) or KL train.

TAMAN NEGARA

☎ 09

A buzzing, leech-infested mass of primary forest over 130 million years old, Taman Negara sprawls across 4343 sq km. Trudge along muggy trails in search of (very) elusive wildlife, explore bat caves, balance on the creaky canopy walk or spend the night in a 'hide' where jungle sounds make you feel like you've gone back to the caveman days. Although you probably won't get to see any large beasts such as tigers or elephants, sightings of smaller critters such as snakes, 'small' big cats, flying squirrels and slow loris are frequent. The most action is at night so either spend the night at a salt lick or take a night tour.

The best time to visit the park is in the dry season between February and September. During the wet season, or even after one good rainfall, leeches come out in force.

Orientation & Information

Kuala Tahan is the base camp for Taman Negara and has accommodation, minimarkets and floating-barge restaurants. Directly opposite Kuala Tahan, across Sungai Tembeling, is the entrance to the national park, Mutiara Taman Negara Resort and the park headquarters located at the Wildlife Department, behind the resort's restaurant.

You must pay a RM1 entrance fee and an optional RM5 camera permit at the **Wildlife Department** (☎ 266 1122; 🕑 8am-10pm Sat-Thu, 8am-noon & 3-10pm Fri). The reception desk also provides basic maps, guide services and advice.

Internet access is painfully slow and expensive (per hour RM6). There are a handful of terminals at Tembling Riverview Hostel and a few more at an unnamed shop across from Teresek View Motel. There are no banks in Taman Negara.

Activities

HIDES & SALT LICKS

Animal-observation hides *(bumbun)* are built overlooking salt licks and grassy clearings, which attract feeding nocturnal animals. You'll need to spend the night in order to see any real action. There are several hides close to Kuala Tahan (Tabing and Kumbang hides being the most popular) and Kuala Trenggan that are a little too close to human habitation to attract the shy animals. Even if you don't see any wildlife, the jungle sounds are well worth it – the 'symphony' is best at dusk and dawn.

Hides (per person per night RM5) need to be reserved at the Wildlife Department and they are very rustic with pit toilets. Some travellers

PLANNING FOR TAMAN NEGARA

Stock up on essentials in Jerantut. If it's been raining, leeches will be unavoidable. Mosquito repellent, tobacco, salt, toothpaste and soap can be used to deter them, with varying degrees of success. A liberal coating of insect spray over shoes and socks works best. Tuck pant legs into socks.

Wear long sleeves and long pants when hitting the trails to protect you from insects and brambles. Take plenty of water, even on short walks, and on longer walks take water-purifying tablets to sterilise stream water.

Sturdy boots are essential; lightweight, high-lacing canvas jungle boots that keep out leeches can be hired from the camping-ground office. Camping gear can also be hired at Kuala Tahan jetty or Mutiara Taman Negara resort.

Taman Negara: Malaysia's Premier National Park, by David Bowden (available in the bigger bookshops of Kuala Lumpur or online), is an excellent resource, with detailed route maps and valuable background information.

hike independently in the day to the hides, then camp overnight and return the next day, while others go to more far-flung hides that require some form of transport and a guide; the Wildlife Department can steer you in the right direction. For overnight trips you'll need food, water and a sleeping bag. Rats on the hunt for tucker are problematic, so hang food high out of reach.

Some of the following hides can be reached by popular treks (see right):

Bumbun Blau & Bumbun Yong On Sungai Yong. From the park headquarters, it's roughly 1½ hours' walk to Bumbun Blau (3.1km), which sleeps 12 people and has water nearby, and two hours to Bumbun Yong (4km). You can visit Gua Telinga along the way. Both hides can also be reached by the riverbus service (see p475).

Bumbun Cegar Anjing Once an airstrip, this is now an artificial salt lick, established to attract wild cattle and deer. A clear river runs a few metres from the hide. It's 1½ hours' walk from Kuala Tahan; after rain Bumbun Cegar Anjing may only be accessible by boat (per four-person boat RM40). The hide sleeps eight people.

Bumbun Kumbang From the park headquarters, it's roughly five hours' walk to Bumbun Kumbang. Alternatively, take the riverboat service from Kuala Tahan up Sungai Tembeling to Kuala Trenggan (per four-person boat RM90, 35 minutes), then walk 45 minutes to the hide. Animals most commonly seen here are tapirs, rats, monkeys and gibbons, and – rarely – elephants. The hide has bunks for 12 people.

Bumbun Tahan Roughly five minutes' walk from the park headquarters. There's little chance of seeing any animals, apart from monkeys and deer at this artificial salt lick.

Tabing Hide About 1½ hours' walk (3.1km) from park headquarters, this hide is near the river so it's also accessible by the riverbus service (p475). The best animal-watching (mostly rats, tapir and squirrels) here is at nightfall and daybreak.

TREKKING

There are treks to suit all levels of motivation, from a half-hour jaunt to a steep nine-day tussle up and down Gunung Tahan (2187m). It's unanimous that the guides are excellent.

Popular do-it-yourself treks, from one to five hours, include the following:

Bukit Teresik From behind the Canopy Walkway a trail leads to the top of this hill from which there are fine views across the forest. It's steep and slippery in parts. The return trip is about one hour.

Canopy Walkway (admission RM5; 11am-2.45pm Sat-Thu, 9am-noon Fri) Anyone who says walking isn't an adrenalin sport has never been suspended on a hanging rope bridge constructed of wooden planks and ladders elevated 45m above the ground; come early to avoid long waits in line.

Gua Telinga From the park headquarters, it's roughly a 1½-hour walk (2.6km). Think wet: a stream runs through this cave (with sleeping bats) and a rope guides you for the strenuous 80m half-hour trek – and crawl – through the cave. Return to the main path through the cave or take the path round the rocky outcrop at its far end. From the main path, it's 15 minutes' walk to Bumbun Blau hide or you can walk directly back to Kuala Tahan.

Kuala Trenggan The well-marked main trail along the bank of Sungai Tembeling leads 9km to Kuala Trenggan. This is a popular trail for those heading to Bumbun Kumbang.

Lubok Simpon This is a popular swimming hole. Near the Canopy Walkway, take the branch trail that leads across to a swimming area on Sungai Tahan.

Longer treks, which require a guide, include the following:

Gunung Tahan For the gung-ho, Gunung Tahan, 55km from the park headquarters, is Peninsular Malaysia's highest peak (2187m). The return trek takes nine days at a steady pace, although it can be done in seven. Guides are compulsory (RM550 per person for nine days if there are four people; prices vary depending on how many are in the group). Try to organise this trek in advance through the Wildlife Department (p472).

Rentis Tenor (Tenor Trail) From Kuala Tahan, this trek takes roughly three days. Day one: take the trail to Gua Telinga, and beyond, for about seven hours, to Yong camp site. Day two: a six-hour walk to the Renuis camp site. Day three: cross Sungai Tahan (up to waist deep) to get back to Kuala Tahan, roughly six hours' walk, or you can stop over at the Lameh camp site, about halfway.

OTHER ACTIVITIES

Catch-and-release fishing is allowed along Sungai Keniam. The sport fish known locally as *ikan kelah* (Malaysian mahseer) is a cousin of India's king of the Himalayan rivers and is a prized catch. You'll need a fishing licence, transport and a guide to fish along the river; head to the **Wildlife Department** (☎ 266 1122; 🕗 8am-10pm Sat-Thu, 8am-noon & 3pm-10pm Fri) for more information. If that sounds too hard, you can fish along Sungai Tembling without a permit.

Tours

Guides who are licensed by the Wildlife Department have completed coursework in forest flora, fauna and safety and are registered with the department. But often the Kuala Tahan tour operators offer cheaper prices than the Wildlife Department, although there is no guarantee that the guide is licensed. Guides cost RM150 per day (one guide can lead up to 12 people), plus there is a RM100 fee for each night spent out on the trail.

There are popular night tours (RM25), which are on foot or by 4WD. You're more likely to see animals (such as slow loris, snakes, civets and flying squirrels) on the drives, which go through palm-oil plantations outside the park.

Many travellers sign up for tours to an Orang Asli settlement. Tribal elders give a general overview and you'll learn how to use a long blowpipe and start a fire. While local guides insist that these tours provide essential income for the Orang Asli, most of your tour money will go to the tour company. A small handicraft purchase in the village will help spread the wealth.

Consider booking tours *after* you arrive in Kuala Tahan. Talk to fellow travellers about which tour operators are doing a good job since a recommendation by a certain guidebook can cause quality to deteriorate. Readers have also complained that certain tour operators will promise a particular tour, but may only be able to fulfil a portion of the planned itinerary upon arrival.

Sleeping & Eating

Guesthouses are listed here in south-to-north order. Malay food (dishes for around RM3 to RM10) is available from barge restaurants and at a couple of places attached to guesthouses. The barge restaurant furthest north serves delicious Indian banana-leaf meals (RM6). Kuala Tahan is dry, so if you're after a beer you'll have to cross over to **Mutiara Taman Negara Resort** (☎ 266 3500; beers RM8) where you can also dine on overpriced Western food (RM17 to RM55).

For details on staying at a hide, see p472.

KUALA TAHAN

Dakili Hostel (dm RM10) The Dakili is an immaculate block of white cement dorms that promise quiet nights and no bites. It's up the steps from the NKS restaurant and to the right.

Ekoton Chalets (☎ 266 9897; tamannegara@hotmail.com; dm RM13-20, r RM90; ❄) Rather pricey because of the air-con, this place is run by the same mob as Sri Emas (in Jerantut). Both rooms and dorms are in good condition and the gardens are soothing.

Tembeling River Hostel & Chalets (☎ 266 6766; dm RM10, chalets RM35-50; 💻) Straddling the thoroughfare footpath, folks stay here to be close to the action, not for privacy. Everything from laundry to internet is right at your fingertips. Rooms are barrack basic.

Agoh (☎ 019 928 0414; d RM40) This place looks completely unenticing until you step past reception and into the shade of the garden. New flooring adds a clean spark to the standard chalets and the staff make the place even more peaceful.

Teresek View Motel (☎ 266 9177; dm RM10, r RM35-90; ❄) The small bungalows across from this motel's eye-sore of a main building are where you'll find the budget accommodation. Floors give way underfoot and beds are lumpy, but the place is spotless and is one of the better-value places in town. It's in the 'centre' of Kuala Tahan.

our pick **Tahan Guesthouse** (☎ 266 7752; dm RM10, r RM50) It feels like a happy preschool here with giant murals of insects and flowers all over the place along with catchy, feel-good phrases like 'why 1+1=2 not 11?' The airy concrete rooms are unsurpassed in comfort for Kuala Tahan and the four-bed dorms all have their own bathroom.

Durian Chalet (☎ 266 8940; r RM25-50) Go past Tahan Guesthouse, then past the rubber-tapping farm, and veer left just as you smell this chalet's namesake fruit. It is far enough from town that the silvery stars and moon bid you goodnight, and jungle noises rouse you from sleep. There's a restaurant with a simple Malay menu.

NUSA CAMP

Nusa Holiday Village (☎ 266 3043/2369; www.tamannegara-nusaholiday.com.my; camp sites RM5, 2-person tent rental RM15, dm RM15, r RM55-110) Fifteen minutes by boat up Sungai Tembeling from Kuala Tahan, this 'jungle camp' has a range of deteriorating accommodation. Though much quieter than the main village, the same activities are available here but cost more because of the extra ferry trips. The staff's lack of English skills makes everything from eating at the restaurant to trying to go anywhere quite taxing.

Getting There & Away

Getting to Taman Negara involves a lot of transfers: taking a bus or train to Jerantut, then minibus to Kuala Tembeling, and river boat to Kuala Tahan. It is an all-day affair, but the languid boat ride up the undeveloped river will soothe any sweaty bus frustration. If you're pressed for time in either direction, you can also take a taxi or a minibus between Jerantut and Kuala Tahan; for more details, see p472.

BOAT

The river jetty for Taman Negara–bound boats is in Kuala Tembeling, 18km north of Jerantut.

Boats (one way RM25) depart Kuala Tembeling daily at 9am and 2pm (and an additional 2.30pm departure on Friday). On the return journey, boats leave Kuala Tahan at 9am and 2pm (and 2.30pm on Friday). The journey takes three hours upstream and two hours downstream. Note that the boat service is irregular during the November-to-February wet season.

BUS & TAXI

See p471 for details on buses and taxis from Jerantut to Kuala Tembeling.

There are several daily minibus shuttles direct from Kuala Lumpur to Kuala Tembeling jetty (RM35). NKS leaves from **Hotel Mandarin Pacific** (Jl Petaling, Chinatown, KL), and Nusa Camp leaves from **Swiss Inn** (Jl Sultan, Chinatown, KL). You can also book bus transfers from Kuala Tahan to the Cameron Highlands (RM55, eight hours) and to Tok Bali jetty for Pulau Perhentian (RM55, 10 hours) that leave at 8am daily.

A local bus travels from Kuala Tahan to Jerantut (RM6, one to two hours, four times daily). The bus stop is on the access road to the main highway, around the corner from the row of sundry stalls.

Getting Around

There is a frequent cross-river ferry (RM3) that shuttles passengers across the river from Kuala Tahan to the park and Mutiara Taman Negara Resort. It will also pick up and drop off people at the trailhead for Gua Telinga, across a small tributary from the resort.

Nusa Camp's floating information centre in Kuala Tahan runs scheduled riverboat (also called riverbus) services upriver to Bumbun Blau/Bumbun Yong (one way/return RM10/20, two daily) and Kuala Terengganu (RM20, two daily). Check with the information desk for times and prices, as they vary considerably by season. Keep in mind that these regularly scheduled riverboat services run pretty much on time during the peak season, but may be dropped entirely during the wet season.

In addition to the riverbus, you can also charter a boat for considerably more – Bumbun Blau (RM60) and Kuala Trenggan (RM90). You can arrange private boat trips at the Wildlife Department (p472), at the resort or at the restaurants in Kuala Tahan (the latter are usually 10% cheaper).

MALAYSIAN BORNEO – SABAH

The mere mention of the word Borneo conjures up a host of vivid images: thick jungle teeming with wildlife; wild rivers flowing through tunnels of overhanging trees;

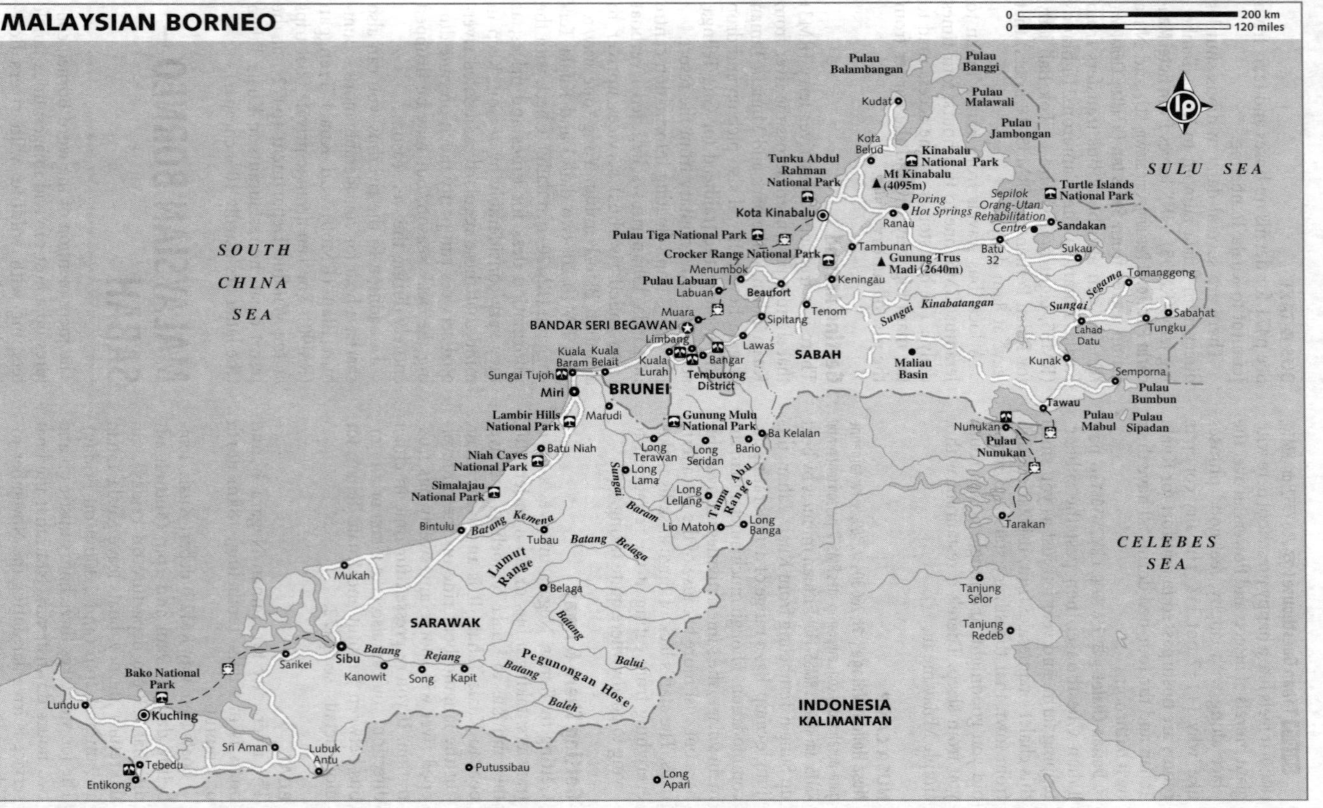
MALAYSIAN BORNEO
0 200 km
0 120 miles
SULU SEA
SOUTH CHINA SEA
CELEBES SEA
SABAH
SARAWAK
BRUNEI
INDONESIA
KALIMANTAN
BANDAR SERI BEGAWAN
Kota Kinabalu
Kuching
Pulau Balambangan
Pulau Banggi
Pulau Malawali
Pulau Jambongan
Kudat
Kota Belud
Kinabalu National Park
Mt Kinabalu (4095m)
Tunku Abdul Rahman National Park
Poring Hot Springs
Ranau
Sepilok Orang-Utan Rehabilitation Centre
Turtle Islands National Park
Sandakan
Pulau Tiga National Park
Crocker Range National Park
Tambunan
Gunung Trus Madi (2640m)
Batu 32
Sukau
Menumbok
Pulau Labuan
Labuan
Beaufort
Keningau
Tenom
Sungai Kinabatangan
Sungai Segama
Tomanggong
Sabahat
Tungku
Lahad Datu
Muara
Sipitang
Limbang
Lawas
Bangar
Temburong District
Kuala Baram
Kuala Belait
Kuala Lurah
Sungai Tujoh
Miri
Maliau Basin
Kunak
Semporna
Pulau Bumbun
Tawau
Pulau Mabul
Pulau Sipadan
Nunukan
Pulau Nunukan
Lambir Hills National Park
Marudi
Gunung Mulu National Park
Ba Kelalan
Bario
Long Terawan
Long Seridan
Niah Caves National Park
Batu Niah
Long Lama
Sungai Baram
Long Lellang
Tama Abu Range
Simalajau National Park
Lio Matoh
Long Banga
Tarakan
Bintulu
Batang Kemena
Tubau
Batang Belaga
Lumut Range
Mukah
Belaga
Tanjung Selor
Tanjung Redeb
Batang Balui
Sibu
Batang Rejang
Sarikei
Kanowit
Song
Kapit
Pegunungan Hose
Batang Baleh
Bako National Park
Lundu
Sri Aman
Lubuk Antu
Tebedu
Entikong
Putussibau
Long Apari

orang-utans swinging through forest canopy; craggy mountains soaring above the steaming lowlands; remote longhouses inhabited by the descendents of head-hunters.

Incredibly, all of these images are accurate – you'll find all this and more in Malaysian Borneo – but you'll also find some things that may surprise you: prosperous cities with international restaurants; first-class resorts complete with spas and golf courses; efficient public transport and an increasingly extensive network of paved roads – even suburban sprawl and traffic jams to go with it.

The two states of Malaysian Borneo, Sabah and Sarawak, have their own distinct personalities and attractions. Sabah is a nature-lover's paradise, the place to see some of Borneo's famed wildlife: orang-utans in Sepilok, proboscis monkeys along the Kinabatangan, and hornbills just about anywhere there's jungle. It's also home to one of the world's best dive sites: Pulau Sipadan, the coral-fringed summit of an oceanic pinnacle in the South China Sea. And then there's Mt Kinabalu, that 4095m freak of a mountain that dominates northern Borneo with its peculiar crown of granite towers.

Sarawak, in contrast, offers boat trips up winding jungle rivers; visits to the longhouses of Borneo's indigenous peoples; vast cave chambers inside limestone mountains; and the historical and cultural attractions of Kuching, Sarawak's capital city. For more on Sarawak, see p492.

KOTA KINABALU

☎ 088 / pop 270,000

Sabah's prosperous capital city lies sandwiched between the green peaks of the Crocker Range and the waves of the South China Sea. It's a bustling boom town with a pleasantly varied ethnic mix: Chinese, Malays, Filipinos, Asian holidaymakers, and an increasing population of Western expats. This eclectic mix is almost as colourful as some of the coral reefs that lie right offshore in Tunku Abdul Rahman National Park.

Above all, KK (as it's universally known) is remarkable for its sunsets: the city faces straight west across the sea and each night the low clouds of the tropics come alive with brilliant reds, oranges and purples. If these don't get you, the relentless smiles of the city's inhabitants surely will. And when you factor in the great seafood and thriving markets of the place, you'll see why KK is a great place to start your Borneo adventure.

Information

BOOKSHOPS

Borneo Books I (ground fl, Phase 1, Wisma Merdeka; ☎ 538077; www.borneobooks.com; 10am-7pm)

Borneo Books II (ground fl, Phase 1, Wisma Merdeka; ☎ 538077; 10am-7pm) A brilliant selection of Borneo books, maps and a small used book section. There's free internet.

Iwase Books (ground fl, Phase 1, Wisma Merdeka; ☎ 233757; 10am-7pm) Iwase has a great selection of new titles as well as lots of Borneo titles.

EMERGENCY

Ambulance (☎ 999, 218166)

Fire (☎ 994, 214822)

Police (☎ 999, 212092; Jl Dewan)

INTERNET ACCESS

Borneo Net (Jl Haji Saman; per hr RM3; 9am-midnight) This popular spot has around 20 terminals with fast connections. Just ignore the earsplitting heavy-metal music.

IT Point (2nd fl, Centre Point Jl Pasar Baru; per hr RM3; 9.30am-9.30pm) If you need access while in Centre Point, this is a convenient spot.

Net Access (Jl Pantai; per hr RM3; 9am-2am) Plenty of connections and less noise than other net places in KK. LAN connections are available for use of your own laptop.

IMMIGRATION

Immigration office (☎ 488700; Kompleks Persekutuan Pentadbiran Kerajaan, Jl UMS; 8am-1pm & 2-5pm Mon-Thu, 8-11.30am & 2-5pm Fri)

GETTING INTO TOWN

Kota Kinabalu International Airport (KKIA) is 7km southwest of the centre. Minivans leaving from the main terminal charge RM2, while minivans or local buses that pass the airport bus stop (turn right as you leave the terminal and walk for 10 minutes) charge RM1. Taxis heading from the terminal into town operate on a system of vouchers (RM20), sold at a taxi desk on the terminal's ground floor. In practice, you can usually just board a taxi and pay RM20 in cash.

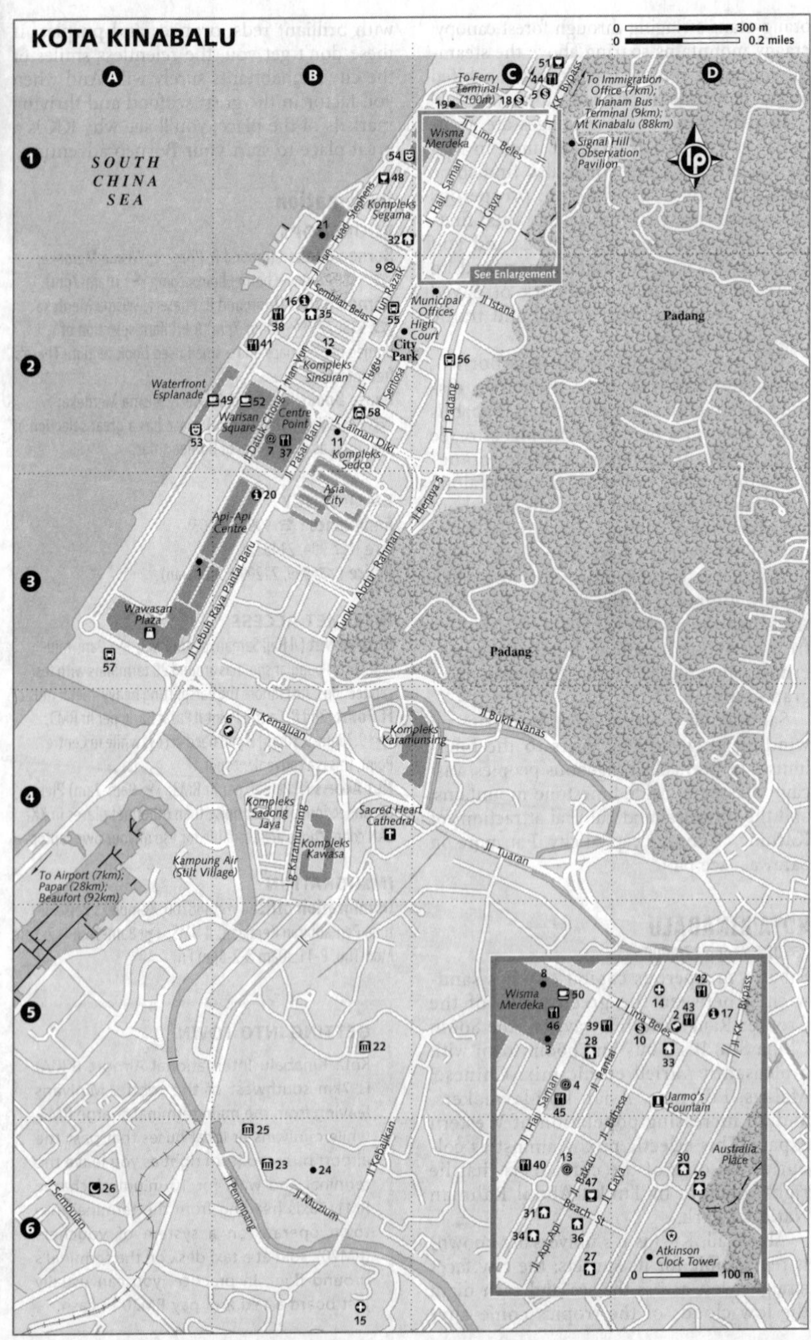
KOTA KINABALU
0 300 m
0 0.2 miles
SOUTH CHINA SEA
To Ferry Terminal (100m)
To Immigration Office (7km); Inanam Bus Terminal (9km); Mt Kinabalu (88km)
Signal Hill Observation Pavilion
Wisma Merdeka
Jl Lima Beles
KK Bypass
Jl Haji Saman
Jl Gaya
Kompleks Segama
Jl Tun Fuad Stephens
Jl Sembilan Belas
Jl Tun Razak
See Enlargement
Municipal Offices
High Court
City Park
Jl Istana
Padang
Kompleks Sinsuran
Jl Tugu
Jl Sentosa
Jl Padang
Waterfront Esplanade
Warisan Square
Centre Point
Jl Datuk Chong Thian Vun
Jl Pasar Baru
Jl Laiman Diki
Kompleks Sedco
Asia City
Jl Berjaya 5
Api-Api Centre
Jl Tunku Abdul Rahman
Jl Lebuh Raya Pantai Baru
Wawasan Plaza
Jl Kemajuan
Kompleks Karamunsing
Jl Bukit Nanas
Kompleks Sadong Jaya
Sacred Heart Cathedral
Kompleks Kawasa
Lg Karamunsing
Kampung Air (Stilt Village)
Jl Tuaran
To Airport (7km); Papar (28km); Beaufort (92km)
Jl Kebajikan
Jl Penampang
Jl Muzium
Jl Sembulan
Jl Pantai
Jl Bahasa
Jarmo's Fountain
Australia Place
Jl Bakau
Beach St
Jl Api-Api
Atkinson Clock Tower
0 100 m

INFORMATION
Airworld Travel & Tours 1 A3
Australian Consulate 2 D5
Borneo Books I 3 C5
Borneo Books II (see 3)
Borneo Net 4 C5
HSBC 5 C1
Indonesian Consulate 6 B4
IT Point 7 B2
Iwase Books 8 C5
Main Post Office 9 B2
Maybank 10 D5
Mega Laundry (Kampung Air) 11 B2
Mega Laundry (Kompleks Sinsuran) 12 B2
Net Access 13 C6
Permai Polyclinic 14 D5
Queen Elizabeth Hospital 15 B6
Sabah Parks Office 16 B2
Sabah Tourism Board 17 D5
Standard Chartered Bank 18 C1
Sutera Sanctuary Ledges 19 C1
Tourism Malaysia 20 B3

SIGHTS & ACTIVITIES
Central Market 21 B1
Food Market (see 38)
Handicrafts Centre (see 21)
Museum of Islamic Civilisation 22 B5
Sabah Art Gallery (see 25)
Sabah Museum 23 B6
Sabah Museum's Heritage Village 24 B6
Science & Education Centre 25 B6
State Mosque 26 A6

SLEEPING
Akinabalu Youth Hostel 27 C6
Ang's Hotel 28 C5
Backpackers Lodge/Lucy's Homestay 29 D6
Borneo Backpackers 30 D6
City Park Lodge 31 C6
Hotel Holiday 32 B1
North Borneo Cabin 33 D5
Pantai Inn 34 C6
Step-In Lodge 35 B2
Summer Lodge 36 C6

EATING
7-11 (see 45)
Centre Point Basement Food Court 37 B2
Filipino Market 38 B2
Kedai Kopi Fatt Kee (see 28)
Little Italy 39 C5
Milimewa Superstore 40 C6
Night Market Food Stalls 41 B2
Nishiki 42 D5
Snack 43 D5
Tong Hing Supermarket 44 C1
Viet Café 45 C5
Wisma Merdeka Food Court 46 C5

DRINKING
BB Café 47 C6
Cocoon 48 B1
Coffee Bean & Tea Leaf 49 B2
Coffee Bean & Tea Leaf 50 C5
Q Bar 51 C1
Starbucks 52 B2

ENTERTAINMENT
Bed 53 A2
Shenanigan's 54 B1

TRANSPORT
Local Bus Stand (Buses to Airport & Train Station) 55 B2
Merdeka Field Bus Station (Old Bus Station) 56 C2
Minibus & Minivan Stand 57 A3
Taxis 58 B2

LAUNDRY

Mega Laundry (RM6 per kilo; ⏲ 8am-8pm) Kompleks Sinsuran (☎ 238970; Ruang Sinsuran 2); Kampung Air (☎ 231970; Chinese Chamber of Commerce Bldg, Jl Laiman Diki) This fast laundry is one of the few open on Sunday. Ask staff not to write your name on your laundry.

MEDICAL SERVICES

Permai Polyclinic (☎ 232100; 4 Jl Pantai) A private outpatient clinic.

Queen Elizabeth Hospital (☎ 218166; Jl Penampang) Past the Sabah Museum.

MONEY

You'll find numerous moneychangers on the ground floors of Centre Point and Wisma Merdeka.

HSBC (☎ 212622; 56 Jl Gaya; ⏲ 9am-4.30pm Mon-Thu, 9am-4pm Fri) Also has a 24-hour ATM.

Maybank (☎ 254295; 9 Jl Pantai; ⏲ 9am-4.30pm Mon-Thu, 9am-4pm Fri) Has a 24-hour ATM.

Standard Chartered Bank (☎ 298111; 20 Jl Haji Saman; ⏲ 9.15am-3.45pm Mon-Fri) Has a 24-hour ATM.

POST

Main post office (☎ 210855; Jl Tun Razak; ⏲ 8am-5pm Mon-Fri) Western Union cheques and money orders can be cashed here.

TOURIST INFORMATION

Sabah Parks Office (☎ 211881; Lot 1-3, ground fl, Block K, Kompleks Sinsuran, Jl Tun Fuad Stephens; ⏲ 8am-1pm & 2-4.30pm Mon-Thu, 8-11.30am & 2-4.30pm Fri, 8am-12.50pm Sat) Good source of information on the state's parks.

Sabah Tourism Board (☎ 212121; www.sabahtourism.com; 51 Jl Gaya; ⏲ 8am-5pm Mon-Fri, 8am-4pm Sat, 9am-4pm Sun) An excellent source of information on all aspects of Sabah.

Sutera Sanctuary Lodges (☎ 243629; www.suterasanctuarylodges.com; Lot G15, ground fl, Wisma Sabah, Jl Haji Saman; ⏲ 9am-6.30pm Mon-Fri, 9am-4.30pm Sat, 9am-3pm Sun) Books accommodation in Kinabalu National Park (including Poring Hot Springs and Mesilau) and on Manukan Island in Tunku Abdul Rahman National Park.

Tourism Malaysia (☎ 248698; www.tourism.gov.my; ground fl, 1 Chester St; ⏲ 8am-4.30pm Mon-Thu, 8am-noon & 1.30-4.30pm Fri) It's geared towards travel throughout Malaysia. The office is also open 8am to 2.45pm on the second and fourth Saturday of every month.

TRAVEL AGENCIES

Airworld Travel & Tours (☎ 242996; airworld@tm.net.my; ground fl, block 2, Api-Api Complex, Jl Pasar Baru) This efficient travel agency is the place to go for domestic and international air tickets.

Sights

The main building of the **Sabah Museum** (☎ 253199; Jl Muzium; admission RM15; ⏲ 9am-5pm Sat-Thu) is modelled on a Rungus longhouse and is a true ethnographic treat, exhibiting traditional items such as ceramics and colourful wedding costumes from many of Sabah's 30 indigenous groups. In a separate building a little further along is the **Sabah Art Gallery**, which shows works by local artists, including oil paintings and sculptural works. Down the hill from the car park (opposite the main hall) is the museum's fascinating **Heritage Village**, with re-creations of longhouses. A road connects the main complex to the small but interesting **Museum of Islamic Civilization** (a 10-minute walk from the main hall). Bus 13 can drop you on Jl Penampang, where there's a footbridge and a path leading uphill to the museum, saving you a long walk around the corner – the footbridge gate is often locked for some reason, but it's easy to climb around.

Southwest of here is the **State Mosque**, which is a fine example of contemporary Islamic architecture.

The **Central Market** (Jl Tun Fuad Stephens; 8.30am-6pm) is in two sections: the waterfront area sells fish and the area bordering Jl Tun Fuad Stephens sells fruit and vegetables. Next door is the **Handicraft Centre** (Jl Tun Fuad Stephens; 8.30am-6pm), jammed with craft, textile and jewellery stalls. At the small adjacent **fruit market**, drain a coconut for RM2.50. A section of Jl Gaya is closed to traffic on Sunday morning to accommodate the stalls of KK's popular **Gaya St Fair** (7am-1pm Sun).

Sleeping

North Borneo Cabin (272800; www.northborneocabin.com; 74 Jl Gaya; dm with fan/air-con RM18/20, r with fan/air-con RM50/56) Right downtown, the Cabin offers large, well-lit rooms, clean showers and toilets and a spacious common area. It also offers free internet and luggage storage for while you're away in the jungle.

Backpacker's Lodge/Lucy's Homestay (261495; backpackerkk@yahoo.com; Lot 25, Lorong Dewan; dm RM18, r from RM42) The eponymous Lucy runs a friendly and homey backpacker joint that is fairly unique in offering cooking facilities. It's a little lived in, but clean enough and has a veranda for chilling out in the evening.

Summer Lodge (244499; www.summerlodge.com.my; Lot 120, Jl Gaya; dm RM18, r from RM55) The Summer is a large new hostel right on one of the main pedestrian malls of KK. It has a spacious and pleasant common area and free internet. You can't miss the bright yellow façade as you approach.

Borneo Backpackers (234009; www.borneobackpackers.com; 24 Lorong Dewan, Australia Pl; dm with fan/air-con RM20/25) This long-running backpackers is a little cramped but still popular. There's free internet but no cooking facilities. It's fairly clean and the location is good.

Akinabalu Youth Hostel (272188; akinabaluyh@yahoo.com; Lot 133, Jl Gaya; dm with fan/air-con RM20/23, r from RM50) With a big common area, clean showers and a friendly staff, the Akinabalu Youth Hostel (it's actually a backpackers) is another decent choice for budget travellers, although there are no cooking facilities.

our pick **Step-In Lodge** (233519; www.stepinlodge.com; Block L, Sinsuran Complex; dm with fan/air-con from RM25/35, r with fan/air-con from RM60/80) The best backpackers in town, the Step-In has a large and airy common area, clean rooms and bathrooms and very informative staff. It's a great place to meet other travellers and exchange information.

Ang's Hotel (234999; 28 Jl Bakau; s/d from RM60/65) We've got a fondness for clean, well-maintained simple Chinese hotels and Ang's is a perfect example. The deluxe rooms are light and spacious, if a little sparse. The standard windowless rooms are similar but not as appealing. This is a good-value choice.

City Park Lodge (257752; cplodge@streamyx.com; 49 Jl Pantai; d from RM60) The brand-new City Park Lodge tries hard to please and it does a good job. It's clean and well taken care of. The deluxe doubles (actually twins) are good value, and if you don't mind being up on the 4th floor or not having a window, you'll get the same type of room for RM5 less.

Pantai Inn (217095; 57 Jl Pantai; s/tw/f from RM67/73/88) There's a lot of competition in this price bracket in KK, but the Pantai still manages to rank near the top. With hot-water showers, neat and sunny rooms, it's great value and in a convenient spot.

Hotel Holiday (213116; www.hotelholiday.com.my; Block F, Kompleks Segama; s/d from RM70/80) The Holiday is a very friendly spot right downtown in the Segama Complex. It's showing its age, and hot water here is an on-again-off-again affair, but the folks at the front desk will make you feel at home.

Eating

Night Market Food Stalls (meals from RM2; dinner) Located off Jl Tun Fuad Stephens, the night market is the best, cheapest and most interesting place in KK for dinner. You can choose between Malay *nasi campur* (buffet with rice), grilled chicken wings and fish, and the usual *mee goreng* (fried noodles) and *nasi goreng* (fried rice), among others. At the north end of the market, behind the Filipino Market, you'll find the excellent Filipino barbecued seafood section, which is the place for incredibly fresh grilled tuna, shrimp, crab and so on. Highly recommended.

Centre Point Basement Food Court (Basement, Centre Point Shopping Centre, Jl Pasar Baru; meals RM2-10; lunch & dinner) Your ringgit will go a long way at this popular and varied food court at Centre Point mall. There are Malay, Chinese and Indian places, as well as drink and dessert specialists.

Wisma Merdeka Food Court (6th fl, Jl Haji Saman; meals RM3; lunch & dinner) Not as large as the one in Centre Point mall, this simple food court is still a good option for a cheap meal up at the northern end of town.

Snack (Jl Gaya; drinks from RM3, sandwiches RM4; 8am-6.30pm Mon-Fri, 8am-3pm Sat) This hole-in-the-wall joint offers a tempting line-up of real espresso, fresh fruit juice and simple sandwiches – perfect for a break while exploring this part of KK.

Viet Café (Jl Haji Saman; meals RM5; lunch & dinner) This clean and bright Vietnamese place serves decent *pho* (noodles in soup), good fresh fruit juices, and tasty fresh and fried spring rolls.

Kedai Kopi Fatt Kee (28 Jl Bakau; dinner from RM15; lunch & dinner Mon-Sat) The woks are always busy at this popular semi-outdoor Chinese place next to Ang's Hotel. Unless you show up early or late for mealtimes, you may have to wait for a table, and even after you order, you may wind up waiting a while for your food – but the wait is always worth it. *Midin* (jungle fern) cooked in *belacan* (partially fermented shrimp paste) is a Borneo classic, and the salt and pepper prawns are great.

our pick Nishiki (☎ 230582; 59 Jl Gaya; set meals RM16; lunch & dinner) Operated by a Japanese expat, this authentic Japanese restaurant takes advantage of the good seafood available in this city. The atmosphere is pleasantly traditional, right down to the sushi counter. There are good-value set meals, sushi sets and plenty of à la carte choices.

Little Italy (☎ 232231; Jl Haji Saman; dinner from RM20; lunch & dinner) After an ascent of Kinabalu or a long jungle trek, why not reward yourself with a feed at this popular, casual Italian specialist? It has good salads (RM10), pizzas (small/large RM18/24) and pasta from RM12.

Self-catering choices include:

7-11 (Jl Haji Saman; 24hr)

Millimewa Superstore (Jl Haji Saman)

Tong Hing Supermarket (Jl Gaya)

Drinking & Entertainment

While KK is filled with the usual Chinese, Malay and Indian *kedai kopi,* which always serve good coffee and tea, you'll have to hit one of the big foreign chains if you hanker for a latte or similar.

CAFÉS

Coffee Bean & Tea Leaf (ground fl, Wisma Merdeka, Jl Haji Saman; coffee from RM3; breakfast, lunch & dinner;) Free wi-fi and proper coffee are the draws at this popular chain. In addition to this branch, there's another in the Waterfront Esplanade complex off Jl Tun Fuad Stephens.

Starbucks (Jl Tun Fuad Stephens; drinks from RM3; breakfast, lunch & dinner) We assume you've heard of this place – you know, the one with the green sign.

BARS

KK has a surprisingly lively nightlife scene. There are two main centres for nightlife: the somewhat upscale Waterfront Esplanade complex, which has a variety of good restaurants and Western-style pubs, and the more backpacker-oriented Beach St, which has at least one good bar with indoor/outdoor seating. The following are some of the more reliable venues.

BB Café (Beach St) Pool tables, outdoor seating and a convenient location near many of KK's backpacker lodges make this an obvious place to start your evening.

Cocoon (Jl Tun Fuad Stephens) Three separate zones, all of them quite stylish, make this an interesting, if somewhat pricey, spot for a drink or three.

Q Bar (Jl KK Bypass) We like the style and the tunes at this gay-friendly bar at the north end of town.

Shenanigan's (Waterfront Esplande, Jl Tun Fuad Stephens) This is one of several Western-style pubs in this complex. It's got sports on the tube, imported draught beer and occasional live music. If it doesn't suit, just walk to the next one.

Bed (Jl Tun Fuad Stephens) This cavernous club has live music most nights of the week. It can be pretty dead early in the evening.

Getting There & Away

AIR

Malaysia Airlines (code MH; ☎ 1-300-883000, 515555; www.malaysiaairlines.com) has regular flights to/from Kuching (RM195), Pulau Labuan (RM123), Lahad Datu (RM125), Sandakan (RM143) and Tawau (RM133). Standard Malaysia Airlines fares from Johor Bahru/KL are around RM722/574, but cheaper advance-purchase fares are usually available. The regular KK–Singapore fare is about double this, so it's usually better to fly from Johor Bahru.

FAX (Fly Asian Xpress, code D7; ☎ 03-877 4000; www.flyasianxpress.com) has cheap flights between KK and Pulau Labuan, Limbang, Lawas, Sandakan, Lahad Datu, Bintulu and Sibu.

Air Asia (code AK; ☎ within Malaysia 03-8775-4000, outside Malaysia 60-3-8660-4343; www.airasia.com) has cheap fares to/from KL and Bangkok. The Air Asia counter at Terminal 2 of KKIA handles all bookings less than 24 hours prior to departure. It's open 8am to 7pm.

BOAT

Passenger ferries (RM31, three hours) depart KK for Pulau Labuan Monday to Saturday at 8am and 1.30pm. On Sunday they sail at 8am and 3pm. In the opposite direction, they depart Labuan for KK Monday to Saturday at 8am and 1pm, while on Sunday they depart at 10.30am and 3pm. From Labuan there are onward services to Brunei (see p484).

For information on boats to Tunku Abdul Rahman National Park, see opposite.

BUS & MINIVAN

Buses serving eastern Sabah destinations operate from the Inanam bus terminal, north of the town. Destinations, fares, durations and times include: Sandakan (RM35, six hours, departures at 7am, 8am, 10am, 12.30pm, 2pm and 8pm), Tawau (RM40, nine hours, 7am and 8am), Lahad Datu (RM50, 6½ hours, 7am, 9am and 8pm) and Semporna (RM50, 10 hours, 7.30am and 7.30pm). Fares include a meal.

Buses and minivans serving destinations on the west coast and northern Sabah operate from Merdeka Field bus station on Jl Padang. Destinations served from this terminal include Ranau (bus/minibus RM10/12, bus at 8am and minibuses 7am to 5pm on demand), Tenom (minibus RM16) and Keningau (minibus RM13). Buses and minibuses to Ranau will drop passengers at Kinabalu National Park. If you're going to Poring Hot Springs, take a minibus to Ranau and switch to a Poring-bound minibus.

TAXI

Shared and private taxis operate from a terminal at Merdeka Field bus station on Jl Padang. Several shared taxis do a daily run between KK and Ranau, passing the entrance road to the Kinabalu National Park office. The fare to Ranau or Kinabalu National Park is RM20 or you can charter a taxi for RM80 per car (note that a normal city taxi will charge RM150 for a charter).

TRAIN

The North Borneo Railway between KK and Papar was closed for repairs at the time of writing, and it is unclear if or when it is going to reopen.

Getting Around

Minibuses marked 'Putatan' run regularly to the airport (RM2) from the minibus station (bay 17) opposite Wawasan Plaza; alternatively, the minibuses can drop you off at the airport access road (RM1.50), from where it's a five-minute walk to the airport. Local buses departing the local bus stand can also drop you off at the access road (RM1). Taxis head to the airport for RM20.

For more information on getting to/from the airport, see boxed text, p477.

Some members of KK's large taxi population are metered but most are not, in which case negotiate a fare before heading off. There are several hubs where taxis congregate, including outside the Milimewa Superstore on Jl Lintas. Most trips around town cost RM5 to RM8.

TUNKU ABDUL RAHMAN NATIONAL PARK

Just a few kilometres off the KK waterfront is **Tunku Abdul Rahman National Park** (admission RM10). The park comprises five beautiful offshore islands: Gaya, Mamutik, Manukan, Sapi and Sulug, all of which can easily be visited as day trips from KK. These islands have some of Borneo's best beaches, crystal-clear water and some fairly healthy coral and tropical fish.

The three most interesting islands for travellers are Manukan, Mamutik and Sapi. **Mamutik** has the best snorkelling, with a healthy coral garden off its west side (accessible by a trail that starts just past the toilet block at the south end of the beach). It's also got a nice stretch of beach and some camp sites. **Manukan** has good beaches and some decent snorkelling off its southwest end. There is a resort here, which means things are a little busier. Tiny **Sapi** also has good beaches and decent snorkelling, and you can swim over to Gaya if you feel like a little adventure.

Note that all three islands are very popular with day-trippers on weekends. At other times, you'll find the islands very quiet and peaceful. You can rent snorkels on Sapi, Manukan and Mamutik or at the KK ferry terminal, but you'll want to bring your own equipment if you're a serious snorkeller.

The admission fee covers all the islands, so if you plan to visit more than one, save your receipt.

Sleeping & Eating

You can **camp** (camp sites per person RM5) on Sapi, Mamutik and at Teluk Malohom on Gaya. Park permits and camping fees are paid on arrival at each island. There are small, simple stores on these islands, but you'll want to bring your own food for cooking.

On Manukan, **Manukan Island Resort** (☎ 088 256637; www.suterasanctuarylodges.com.my; 4-person units from RM320) has pleasant huts and semi-detached chalets and rooms, as well as a proper restaurant.

Getting There & Away

Boats to the islands are arranged inside the waiting room at KK's ferry terminal (commonly known as 'the jetty' by locals and taxi drivers). Inquire at the counter for the next available boat. Sign up for your chosen destination and then take a seat until there are enough passengers (usually eight) to depart. Services run from 7am to 6pm daily but it's best to catch a boat in the morning, as it's much harder to make up boat numbers in the afternoon.

Return fares to Mamutik, Manukan and Sapi are RM17 to RM25, depending on which boat company you go with. You can also buy two-/three-island passes for RM33/43. The set fee for boat charter to one island is RM204, but you can negotiate a lower price. Try to deal directly with a boatman if you do this – don't deal with the touts who prowl the area. And don't consider paying until you return to the dock for your trip. Note that there is an RM3 terminal fee added to all boat journeys.

PULAU LABUAN

☎ 087 / pop 76,000

About 115km southwest of KK and only 50km northeast of Bandar Seri Begawan (Brunei) is the small island of Labuan, which serves as the main transit point between Brunei and Sabah. This is the best route to travel between Sabah and Brunei and onward to Sarawak, as the overland journey is time-consuming and arduous. There's not much to detain you on Labuan, but if you get stuck between ferry sailings, you'll find it a pleasant spot to spend an evening.

Most of the island's most interesting sites are on the northwest coast, including a couple of decent shallow **beaches** and a **peace park** marking the spot where the Japanese surrendered to the Allies in WWII. Closer to town, you'll find a **WWII Memorial** commemorating the Australian soldiers who died in Borneo. Information on these is available at the **Tourism Malaysia office** (☎ 423445; cnr Jl Dewan & Jl Berjaya; 9am-5pm), off Jl Merdeka, near Labuan Sq.

Sleeping & Eating

Budget accommodation in Labuan is of poor quality. Midrange hotels are a better option.

Melati Inn (☎ 416307; Jl Perpaduan; s/d RM45/50;) This is a peach-coloured place with rooms that are a little the worse for wear, but it's the only acceptable budget option. Jl Perpaduan runs inland from the waterfront, close to the wharf.

Ambassador Hotel (☎ 423233; Lot 0142, Jl Bunga Mawar; r from RM79;) The well-run Ambassador is easily the best-value hotel in town, with clean rooms, comfortable beds, wi-fi and nice bathrooms. Jl Bunga Mawar is in the middle of town – follow Jl Bunga Raya inland from the ferry terminal and turn right at Hotel Pulau Labuan.

Kedai Kopi Fah Fah (cnr Jl Bunga Raya & Jl Bunga Melati; meals RM3-10; breakfast, lunch & dinner) With indoor and outdoor seating, an English menu, tasty fresh juice and cheap beer, this simple Chinese restaurant is a good choice. We particularly liked the *kway teow goreng* (fried *kway teow* noodles).

Getting There & Away

Malaysia Airlines (code MH; ☎ 1-300-883-000; www.malaysiaairlines.com.my) has flights to KK (RM123).

GETTING TO BRUNEI

Eight express boats (RM35, one hour) go daily from Pulau Labuan to the Serasa Ferry Terminal in Muara Port, Brunei, the main port for Bandar Seri Begawan, some 25km away. There are departures between 9am and 4.30pm. For information on doing this route in the other direction, see p49.

Passenger ferries (RM31, three hours) depart KK for Labuan at 8am and 1.30pm. On Sunday they sail at 8am and 3pm Monday to Saturday. In the opposite direction, they depart Labuan for KK at 8am and 1pm Monday to Saturday, while on Sunday they depart at 10.30am and 3pm. There are also daily speedboats from Labuan to Limbang in Sarawak (RM28, 2.30pm) and Lawas, also in Sarawak (RM33, 12.30pm).

KINABALU NATIONAL PARK

Sabah's main attraction is the highest mountain between the mighty Himalaya and New Guinea: **Mt Kinabalu**, which towers 4095m above northern Borneo. The mountain is quite unlike any other on Earth, rising almost twice as high as its Crocker Range neighbours and sporting a crown of granite towers that demand your attention.

Thousands of people of all ages climb Mt Kinabalu every year, but an ascent of the mountain is not to be taken lightly. The climb is like spending eight hours climbing steep flights of steps, in gradually thinning air (altitude sickness can strike as low as 3000m or even lower for some people), followed by an equally taxing descent. And it can be close to freezing near the summit.

If the weather is clear on your summit day, you'll be rewarded with an incredible view that starts with the otherworldly summit plateau and extends across all of northern Borneo and as far as the islands of southern Palawan, in the Philippines.

Even if you don't climb to the summit, a trip to the park is highly recommended, as there are some great trails around the park headquarters area, including the fine Liwagu River trail.

Information

The Kinabalu park headquarters is located 88km east of KK, on the KK–Ranau road. The **Sabah Parks office** (⌚ 7am-7pm), which handles permits and guides, and the **Sutera Sanctuary Lodges office** (⌚ 7am-7pm), which handles accommodation at the base and on the mountain, are both to your immediate right as you enter.

PERMITS & GUIDES

Park entry costs RM15 for adults. A climbing permit (RM100) and insurance (RM7) are compulsory if you intend to climb Mt Kinabalu. Guides are also compulsory for the summit trek (RM70/74/80 per group for one to three/four to six/seven to eight climbers). Porters can be hired to carry a maximum load of 10kg; for one to three/four to six/seven to eight climbers the cost is RM60/80/90.

Pay all fees at the park headquarters before you climb and don't consider an 'unofficial' climb as permits are scrupulously checked at several points along the climb.

EQUIPMENT & CLOTHING

Temperatures can dip close to freezing at the summit and it's usually windy and occasionally rainy. You will need good walking shoes, light gloves, a wool or fleece hat, a fleece top, windproof pants, a shell jacket and a knapsack to carry all this. You will also need a headlamp for the predawn summit climb (don't bring a hand-held torch because you'll need your hands free to climb the ropes on the summit massif). A water bottle is also recommended, and you can fill this from tanks en route.

Sights & Activities

Climbing Mt Kinabalu is a two-day exercise for most people. The summit trail works upward through gradually thinning stands of coniferous and montane oak forests, into a subalpine zone populated by low shrubs and gnarled trees before traversing the granite slabs of the mountain's barren summit massif.

On the first day of the hike, take a minibus (RM15 per minibus, 10 minutes) from the park headquarters to Timpohon Gate (1866m), the official trailhead. Leave no later than 11am to cover the 6km to Laban Rata (3273m), the first day's stopping point. This section will take between 3½ and six hours depending on your fitness level.

The next morning, hit the trail at around 3.30am and spend the next 2½ to four hours scaling the 2.7km trail to the summit at Low's

Peak, ideally in time for sunrise, which happens around 6am in these parts. Then you pick your way back down to the park headquarters the same day.

The climb is uphill 99% of the way – an unrelentingly steep path up large dirt steps and over piled rocks. A couple of sections on the summit massif require that you haul yourself up using thick ropes. Every step can be a struggle as you suck oxygen from the thin air, and it is not unusual for people to give up within sight of the summit.

Your best chance of finding clear weather at the summit is if you get there around dawn, but there are plenty of mornings that see the summit wrapped in clouds. If it's raining when you wake at Laban Rata, you should consider abandoning your summit attempt, as the chance of it clearing that day is slim indeed and you'll freeze in the cold, wet weather.

Sleeping & Eating

Advance bookings through **Sutera Sanctuary Lodges** (☎ 088-243629; www.suterasanctuarylodges.com.my; Lot G15, ground fl, Wisma Sabah, Jl Haji Saman) in KK or online are essential for the huts at Laban Rata, and you won't be permitted to climb without a spot in one of the huts. Sutera handles bookings for all accommodation around park headquarters and at Laban Rata, Mesilau Nature Resort and Poring Hot Springs.

PARK HEADQUARTERS

Grace Hostel (dm RM46) and **Rock Hostel** (dm RM40) have dorm accommodation. Both are clean, comfortable and have drink-making facilities and a fireplace-warmed sitting area. Grace Hostel is the more appealing of the two, while Rock Hostel is somewhat institutional. In addition, there are a variety of cabins and private rooms available, the cheapest of which are the semidetached units of **Hill Lodge** (2-person unit RM135).

The canteen-style **Balsam Restaurant** (meals RM3-12; breakfast, lunch & dinner) offers basic but decent fare and a nice outside deck with occasional views of the mountain.

LABAN RATA

Laban Rata Resthouse (dm RM69) has four- and six-bunk rooms equipped with heaters, and sporadic hot-water showers in shared bathrooms. You can also stay near the resthouse in unheated huts with basic cooking facilities. The resthouse has a simple restaurant that serves meals and drinks starting at 2.30am.

Getting There & Away

Express buses and minivans travelling between KK and Ranau and Sandakan pass the park turn-off, from where it's 100m uphill to the park. Air-conditioned express buses (RM15, three hours) leave from KK's Inanam long-distance bus terminal six times daily, starting at 7am.

Shared taxis operate from the terminal at Merdeka Field on Jl Padang in Kota Kinabalu. Several shared taxis do a daily run between KK and Ranau, passing the entrance road to the Kinabalu National Park office. The fare to Ranau or Kinabalu National Park is RM20 or you can charter a taxi for RM80 per car (note that a normal city taxi will charge RM150 for a charter). Minivans (RM15) depart from the same station.

If you're heading back to KK from the park, minivans pass the park headquarters until mid-afternoon (stopping on the main road), but the best time to catch one is between 8am and noon. The park also operates three minibuses daily to KK (RM40) and one daily to Poring Hot Springs (RM25).

RANAU

☎ 088 / pop 49,800

Ranau is a collection of concrete shop blocks on the road between KK and Sandakan, or Kinabalu National Park and Poring Hot Springs. There's a busy Saturday **tamu** (night market). Otherwise, it's of interest mainly as a transport junction.

Bank Simpanan Nasional (Jl Kibarambang) has an ATM.

Sleeping & Eating

Rafflesia Inn (☎ 879359; 1st fl, Block E, Sedco Bldg; r from RM35;) If you (or your wallet) prefer a budget place, this is a spartan but well-kept place. It's in the centre of town, above Koktas Restaurant.

Kinabalu View Lodge (☎ 879111; 1st fl, Tokogaya Bldg, Jl Lorong Kibarambang; r RM64-79;) This is the best of an uninspiring lot in Ranau and is run by the same owners as the Rafflesia. It's a bit threadbare, but the rooms are clean and there are hot-water showers. If you stand on the back railing, you can catch views of Kinabalu. It's near the top of town – aim for the radio tower.

Restaurant Double Luck (☎ 879246; Jl Kibarambang; meals RM6-10; ⏰ breakfast, lunch & dinner) This is not the cheapest eatery in town but has the best food, friendly staff and ice-cold beer. Ask for a filled omelette for breakfast or try the tofu claypot for a veggie treat.

Restoran Tanjung Putri (Jl Lorong Kibarambang; meals from RM3; ⏰ breakfast, lunch & dinner) Diagonally opposite Kinabalu View Lodge, this simple Malay place does a great *sup ayam* (chicken soup), which really hits the spot after a climb up the mountain.

Getting There & Away

Minibuses operate from the blue-roofed shelter at the bottom of town, 100m in from the main roundabout on the main road. Destinations include KK (RM15), Kinabalu National Park (RM5) and Poring Hot Springs (RM5). You can charter a whole minibus or taxi to the park or Poring for RM30 if you negotiate.

Express buses to Sandakan (RM20, four hours, departures hourly between 9am and 1pm) stop on the main road in front of the church (roughly opposite the Shell station), 100m uphill from the main roundabout.

PORING HOT SPRINGS

These **hot springs** (admission RM15; ⏰ visitors centre 9am-4.30pm) lie within Kinabalu National Park some 43km from the park headquarters and 19km north of Ranau. If you arrive here directly after climbing Mt Kinabalu, you can use your national-park entry ticket to gain admission to Poring (and vice versa).

Steaming, sulphurous water is channelled into pools and tubs in which visitors relax their tired muscles after summiting Mt Kinabalu. The outdoor tubs are free but are often either occupied or painfully slow to fill (test the taps before choosing one). Consider renting an indoor tub (per hour RM15); these fill quickly and give you private soaking time.

Note that the place is somewhat poorly maintained and there are no proper changing rooms, coin lockers or towel rental. Bring a bathing suit and towel and a bag to carry your wet things when you're done.

The other features here include **walking trails**, a **tropical garden** (admission RM3; ⏰ 9am-4pm), a **butterfly farm** (admission RM4; ⏰ 9am-4pm) and a 41m-high **canopy walkway** (admission RM5; ⏰ 9am-4pm). The canopy walk was partially closed at the time of writing and it seems likely to remain so.

Rafflesia flowers sometimes bloom in the vicinity of the hot springs. Ask at the shops opposite the hot-springs entrance. If any are in bloom, villagers will lead you to them for RM20.

Sleeping & Eating

Reserve accommodation in advance through **Sutera Sanctuary Lodges** (☎ 088-243629; www.suterasanctuarylodges.com.my; Lot G15, ground fl, Wisma Sabah, Jl Haji Saman) in KK. The reception at Poring is on the right as you pass through the building above the parking lot.

Serindit Hostel (dm RM12) is clean enough, with six- and eight-person dorms and cooking facilities for rent (RM100). Otherwise, **Kelicap Lodge** (tw with shared bathroom RM150) has decent private rooms. A **camping ground** (camp sites RM6) is available for tent-equipped visitors.

The **Rainforest Restaurant** (meals RM6-20; ⏰ breakfast, lunch & dinner) is a proper sit-down restaurant near the hot springs. There are also inexpensive eating places located opposite the springs' entrance.

Getting There & Away

Kinabalu National Park has a minivan that departs the park headquarters at noon for Poring (RM25). In the opposite direction, the minivan departs Poring for the park headquarters at 2pm (and continues to KK).

From outside Poring Hot Springs visitors centre, minivans can be chartered for around RM30 to transport you to Ranau, where you can catch minivans onward to Kinabalu National Park or KK. Otherwise, nonscheduled minivans go to/from Ranau for RM5.

SANDAKAN

☎ 089 / pop 223,000

Once boasting the world's greatest concentration of millionaires, Sandakan is still a fairly prosperous place thanks to bird's nests, fish and palm oil. For travellers, Sandakan serves as the gateway to East Sabah's natural treasures and boasts some interesting attractions of its own between its green hills and picturesque bay.

Downtown Sandakan was once dominated by busy docks during the day and shuttered shops at night. But the wharves have moved to the outskirts of town, paving the way for waterfront redevelopment, including a new market and a nascent nightlife hub. Of course, most travellers still use Sandakan primarily as a base for trips to the Sepilok Orangutan Rehabilitation Centre and up Sungai Kinabatangan.

Information

EMERGENCY

Emergency (☎ 999)
Police (☎ 212222; Lebuh Empat)

INTERNET ACCESS

JazzCyber (1st fl, Centre Point, Jl Pelabuhan Lama; per hr RM4; 9am-8pm Mon-Sat, 9am-7pm Sun)
Sandakan Cyber Café (3rd fl, Wisma Sandakan, Lebuh Empat; per hr RM3; 9am-9pm)

MONEY

HSBC (Lebuh Tiga)
Maybank (Lebuh Tiga) In addition to being a full-service bank with ATM, a sidewalk currency-exchange window is open 9am to 5pm daily for cash and travellers cheques.
Wang Liau Chun Mii Moneychanger (Tung Seng Huat, 23 Lebuh Tiga; 8.30am-4.30pm) Changes cash only.

POST

Main post office (☎ 210594; Jl Leila)

TOURIST INFORMATION

Tourist Information Centre (☎ 229751; pempt.j.mps@sabah.gov.my; Wisma Warisan; 8am-12.30pm & 1.30-4.30pm Mon-Thu, 8-11.30am & 2-4.30pm Fri) Opposite the municipal offices (known as MPS) and up the stairs from Lebuh Tiga. The garrulous staff are extremely helpful, dispensing advice on everything from regional attractions to local restaurants, and can also hook you up with fellow travellers for group excursions.

TRAVEL AGENCIES

Jetliner (☎ 222737; Lebuh Dua) Official Air Asia agent.
Sandakan Travel Service (☎ 218112; skantrvl@steamyx.com; Lebuh Tiga) Opposite Standard Chartered Bank, it offers accommodating, English-speaking help for domestic and overseas flights.

Sights

Sandakan Memorial Park (Taman Peringatan; admission free; 9am-5pm) marks the former site of an infamous WWII Japanese prisoner of war camp and the starting point of the 'death marches' to Ranau. These three marches took place early in 1945 when, in the face of the imminent arrival of the Allies, the Japanese forced their prisoners to walk 250km through jungle to Ranau. Out of the 1577 prisoners subjected to the 'death marches', over half died on the walks and the rest – with the exception of a half-dozen Australians who escaped – were dead of disease, starvation or violence within six months. To get there, take any Batu 8 or higher-number bus (RM1.50); get off at the turn-off signposted 'Taman Rimba' and walk down Jl Rimba to reach the park. A taxi will cost about RM15.

On the hill above town overlooking Sandakan Bay, **Agnes Keith House** (Jl Istana; admission RM15; 9am-5pm) is a trip back to Sandakan's colonial heyday. Keith was an American who came to Sandakan in the 1930s and wrote several books about her experiences, most famously *The Land Below the Wind*. The two-storey wooden villa was destroyed during WWII and rebuilt identically when the Keiths returned. To reach the museum, follow Jl Singapura and turn right up the hill, or head up the shady Tangga Seribu (translated as 100 Steps, even though *seribu* means 1000) to Jl Residensi Dr and turn left.

Tours

Sandakan has many local and regional tour operators offering packages to Sungai Kinabatangan, Sepilok Orangutan Rehabilitation Centre and other eastern Sabah attractions. Keep in mind that it's possible to visit many attractions independently, and in some cases, such as the Orangutan Rehabilitation Centre, this is probably preferable. Also note that tour prices differ massively, sometimes due to dorm versus room-accommodation occupants, sometimes for no good reason at all, so shop around.

Discovery Tours (☎ 274106; www.discoverytours.com.my; 9th fl, Wisma Khoo Siak Chiew, Lebuh Empat)
MB Permai Tours (☎/fax 671535; 1st fl, Sandakan Airport) Tours and car rental from RM100 per day (4WD from RM350).
Sepilok Tropical Wildlife Adventure (☎ 271077; www.stwadventure.com; 13 Lebuh Tiga) Mid-priced tour specialist. Owners of Sepilok Jungle Resort and Bilit Adventure Lodge on Sungai Kinabatangan.
SI Tours (☎ 213502; www.sitoursborneo.com; 10th fl, Wisma Khoo Siak Chiew, Lebuh Empat) This full-service agency opened Abai Jungle resort in December 2006 as a base for Kinabatangan tours. Also has an airport branch.
Wildlife Expeditions (☎ 219616; www.wildlife-expeditions.com; 9th fl, Wisma Khoo Siak Chiew, Lebuh Empat) Tour options include its Sukau River Lodge on the Kinabatangan.

Sleeping

May Fair Hotel (☎ 219855; 24 Jl Pryer; s/d RM40/50;) This budget classic's large, tidy rooms come fully equipped, including its own big TV and DVD player with a massive library of movies available free in the lobby. Gruff but helpful owner Mr Lum knows where to find and how to get virtually anything done around town. Call ahead for bookings to avoid getting shut out.

Selingan Hotel (☎ 227733; fax 221001; 14 Lebuh Dua; s/d/f RM50/60/80;) Best of the budget choices honeycombed around downtown, this has fresh, completely furnished rooms with attractive bedding and hot-water showers. A good alternative if the May Fair is full.

Hotel London (☎ 219855; www.hlondon.com.my; 10 Lebuh Empat; s/d/tr incl breakfast RM55/65/75;) Renovated up from its shoestring roots, rooms are bright and comfortable. Guests love the rooftop sitting area overlooking the harbour where breakfast is served.

Eating

For no-frills food, try one of the stalls in the waterfront market next to the local bus station. A night market sets up outside the post office each evening and there are more Malay food stalls at the western end of Jl Coastal.

King Cheong (34 Lebuh Dua; dishes RM2-12; breakfast & lunch) The clatter of dim sum carts and chatter of local merchant diners will make you think it's Hong Kong. The menus on the wall are in Chinese, but feel free to point at what you see on other plates.

Fat Cat V (☎ 216867; 21 Lebuh Tiga; dishes RM3-10; lunch & dinner) This branch of a local chain has an air-con dining room with a broad menu of Malay, Chinese and Western food. Stop in at its bakery to take home something for breakfast or a late snack. Fat Cat is surrounded by fast-food places open past 9pm, a pocket of the nightlife downtown.

Getting There & Away

AIR

Malaysia Airlines (code MH; ☎ 1-300-883000; www.malaysiaairlines.com.my) flies direct to KK (RM143) and Tawau (RM143).

FAX (Fly Asian Xpress, code D7; www.flyasianxpress.com; ☎ 03-877-4000) has direct flights to KK.

Air Asia (code AK; ☎ 1-300-889933; www.airasia.com) has several direct flights daily between KL and Sandakan (RM100).

BUS

Buses to Kota Kinabalu, Lahad Datu, Semporna and Tawau leave from the long-distance bus station in a large parking lot at Batu 2½, 4km north of town, which is not a particularly convenient location. Most buses, and all minivans, leave in the morning. Get the latest schedule from hotels or the tourist office. To reach the bus station, catch a local bus (RM1) from the stand at the waterfront. A taxi from the station to town is around RM10.

Bus companies have booths at the bus station and touts abound. Most express buses to Kota Kinabalu (RM45, six hours) leave between 7.30am and 2pm, with a couple of evening services. All pass the turn-off to Kinabalu National Park headquarters (RM30).

Buses depart regularly for Lahad Datu (RM20, 2½ hours) and Tawau (RM30, 5½ hours). There's also a bus to Semporna (RM30, 5½ hours) at 8am. If you miss it, head to Lahad Datu, then catch a frequent minivan to Semporna.

Minibuses depart frequently throughout the morning from the bus station for Ranau (RM24, four hours) and Lahad Datu, some continuing to Tawau. Minibuses for Sukau (RM15) leave from a lot behind Centre Point Mall in town.

Getting Around

The airport is about 11km from downtown. The Batu 7 Airport bus (RM1.50) stops on the main road about 500m from the terminal. A coupon taxi from the airport to the town

GETTING TO THE PHILIPPINES

The boats operated by **Weesam Express** (☎ 089-212872; www.weesamexpress.com) from Sandakan take 13 hours to sail to Zamboanga in the Philippines, departing 7am Wednesday and Friday. Operating bigger, more comfortable boats on this route, but taking 16 hours, is **Timmarine** (☎ 089-224009), which sails at 5pm Tuesday and Friday. Both operators leave from Karamunting jetty, 4km west of town, where all the immigration formalities take place. Economy fares start around RM210.

For information on boats going the other way, see p635.

centre costs RM22; going the other way, a cab should cost around RM20.

The local bus terminal is on Jl Pryer, in front of Gentingmas Mall. Buses run on the main road to the north, Jl Utara, and are marked by how far from town they go, ie Batu 8, and run from 6am to about 6pm. Fares range from RM1 to RM4.

Local minibuses depart from behind Centre Point Mall; the fares are from RM2. Use them for getting to the Pasir Putih seafood restaurants and the harbour area.

Taxis cruise the town centre, and wait near the main hotels. Many hotels will steer you towards a preferred driver, which isn't a bad thing. Short journeys around the town centre should cost RM5, and a trip out to Sepilok is RM35.

SEPILOK ORANGUTAN REHABILITATION CENTRE

☎ 089

Sepilok (SORC) is one of only four orang-utan sanctuaries in the world and is one of Sabah's major tourist attractions. The apes are brought here to be rehabilitated into forest life and at feeding times (usually 10am and 3pm) some of these fascinating animals usually swing into view along suspended ropes and clamber onto a feeding platform. The surrounding reserve has **nature trails** varying in length from 250m to 5km.

The **Rainforest Discovery Centre** (RDC; ☎ 533780; admission MR5; 🕑 8.30am-4.30pm Mon-Fri, ticket window closed 12.30-2pm Mon-Thu, 11.30am-2pm Fri), about 1.5km away, offers an easy to swallow graduate level education in tropical flora and fauna. Outside the exhibit hall, a botanical garden presents samples of every tropical plant you've heard of and dozens more you haven't, with descriptions as vibrant as the foliage alongside them.

Information

Morning and afternoon programmes are posted at the **visitor centre** (☎ 531180; soutan@po.jaring.my; admission RM30; 🕑 9am-noon & 2-4pm). The centre tries to charge an extra RM10 for use of cameras, which is annoying when you've already paid a hefty admission fee. However, this is practically impossible to enforce.

Informative videos are screened five times daily. There are free lockers for your valuables; orang-utans have been known to make off with tourists' belongings.

Sleeping & Eating

Unless you're planning to go the centre in the morning, there's little reason to stay in Sepilok. Budget lodging isn't great value and nightlife is nonexistent. All places below have restaurants on site, rates include breakfast (unless noted otherwise) and you're unlikely to venture elsewhere for dinner.

Sepilok Jungle Resort (☎ 533031; www.sepilokjungleresort.com; dm RM20, r RM50-130; ❄ 💻) Everyone seems to stay here but it's awfully hard to see why; rooms in 1970s style are musty, and staff are indifferent, except in steering guests to better-kept, higher-priced digs.

Sepilok Resthouse (☎ 534900; sephse@tm.net.my; dm RM20, r RM50-130; ❄ 💻) Mainly for volunteers and staff, this house is ideally situated right outside the centre. It's usually full, and staff lack enthusiasm for walk-in visitors. If you can get in, you'll get the inside scoop on the centre.

Sepilok B&B (☎ 534050; www.sepilokbednbreakfast.com; Jl Arboretum; dm RM22, r RM40-85; ❄) The dorms and budget rooms are recently renovated with pastel décor and bamboo accents at this welcoming inn. The deluxe rooms accommodate up to four people. The drawback here is the location, about 1km from SORC, but you can rent a bike to pedal around.

SORC Cafeteria (meals from RM4; 🕑 7am-4pm) Serves breakfast, sandwiches, noodle and rice dishes, snacks and drinks, though it's prone to run out of food.

Getting There & Away

To get directly to the rehabilitation centre from Sandakan, look for the blue bus marked 'Sepilok Batu 14' from the local bus stand next to the market on the waterfront (RM3.50, 30 minutes). Minivans also make the trip every hour or so. Returning, the last bus leaves for Sandakan at 4.30pm.

Regular buses (Batu 14 or a higher number) can drop you at the turn-off to Jl Sepilok, 2.5km from the orang-utan centre. Taxis wait to take you to a hotel or SORC (or both) for RM2.

Most of the B&Bs and guesthouses can organise transport to/from the bus station and the airport. A taxi should cost around RM30 one way.

SUNGAI KINABATANGAN

The wide, muddy Sungai Kinabatangan is Sabah's longest river. Some stretches of the river, particularly the upper reaches, have been devastated by logging or the clearing of jungle for plantations. But elsewhere, its shallow depths and shores are teeming with wildlife.

Short of trekking into Borneo's interior, a visit to the Kinabatangan is one of the best ways to observe the island's wild animals close up. Visitors usually get to see orang-utans and elusive proboscis monkeys, crocodiles, bearded pigs, pythons, bats that sleep during the day in funnel-shaped leaves, monitor lizards, frogs, myriad bird species including kingfishers and hornbills, and of course the ubiquitous macaque. If you're very lucky, you may even encounter pygmy elephants.

You need experienced guides to show you around and point out the animals hiding in trees, bushes, on riverbanks, above your head and under your feet. A couple of Sandakan-based outfits transport you to jungle camps and lodges and from there take you on boat rides and hikes to meet the locals; see p487.

Sleeping

There are several accommodation and tour possibilities in Sukau, located on the Kinabatangan, 135km southeast of Sandakan.

Sukau B&B (☎ 230269; r per person RM20) This friendly family guesthouse provides meals, boat hire and transfers on request. It's 1km east of the village.

Uncle Tan's B&B (☎ 531639; www.uncletan.com; Mile 16, Jl Gum Gum; dm 3 days & 2 nights RM320) This famed Kinabatangan jungle camp operator's simple bed and breakfast is fairly convenient to both Sepilok and the Kinabatangan. Uncle Tan's family lives there: some visitors relish the homey atmosphere while others find it lacks privacy. The price includes three meals a day plus transport to and from the SORC feeding platforms.

Getting There & Away

Minivans go to Sukau from Sandakan (RM15, two hours), or you can take a minivan to Lahad Datu and get out at the Sukau turn-off. Expect to wait a while for a minivan from here to Sukau (RM10, one to 1½ hours). If you're on a package tour, transport will be provided. The last 45km to Sukau are along a gravel road that becomes a mud track after rain. Public transport is often suspended when it's wet; 4WD transport is available from Sandakan or Lahad Datu, or perhaps through your accommodation.

If you're heading south from Sukau, ask to be dropped at the highway, where you can catch a minivan to Lahad Datu or possibly a bus to Semporna or Tawau to save repeating the long drive from Sandakan.

SEMPORNA & PULAU SIPADAN

☎ 089 / pop 91,900

Though not a particularly appealing town, Semporna does have a lively waterfront market and a mosque attractively framed against the waters of the Celebes Sea.

Most of Semporna's visitors are en route to/from Pulau Sipadan, a small island 36km offshore that's regarded as one of the world's best dive sites. Divers take exhilarating plunges off a 600m limestone wall, while snorkellers can expect to have sea turtles and other marine creatures glide under them.

Since the beginning of 2005, Sipadan has been under Parks & Wildlife management and there's no longer any accommodation or dive operators on the island. The number of divers allowed at Sipadan is limited to 120 per day and there have been some complaints that this isn't transparently or fairly enforced.

There's an ATM-equipped branch of Maybank opposite the mosque.

Activities

Most of the Semporna-based operators conducting diving and snorkelling tours to Sipadan, Mabul and nearby islands have offices located beside the entrance to Dragon Inn. Day trips involving three dives (usually two at Sipadan and one at Mabul) cost around RM300 (RM260 if you have your own equipment). All trips include lunch and can normally be arranged the day before, though sometimes groups book out available slots. Operators include:

Borneo Jungle River Island Tours (aka Uncle Chang; ☎ 781789; unclechang99@hotmail.com; SOTC; r incl meals & transport to island per person RM50) Budget lodge on Mabul island built on stilts, with good snorkelling off the pier, and diving options. The friendly staff get raves from travellers. Dive packages to Sipadan are RM300 from Semporna or Mabul, or RM210 to Mabul sites from the lodge.

North Borneo Dive (☎ 781788, 919128; www.northborneo.net; Jl Causeway) Reliable dive operator that also has a Tawau office. It offers transport from that airport. Dive packages are RM300 per day.

Scuba Junkie (☎ 785372; www.scuba-junkie.com; 36 Semporna Seafront; dm/r incl breakfast for diving customers from RM15/40;) This dive operator offers accommodation at good rates if you dive with it. The rooms are basic but adequate. Dive packages are RM300 per day including equipment. The restaurant (meals from RM7) downstairs serves a full English breakfast, and pizza at night.

Sleeping

Many dive operators also have their own accommodation (see opposite). If there is space, nondivers are usually welcome.

Dragon Inn (☎ 781088; www.dragoninnfloating.com.my; 1 Jl Kastam; dm/r from RM15/66;) A popular place with crowded dorms and somewhat overpriced rooms.

Damai Travellers Lodge (☎ 782011; Jl Masjid; s/d from RM30/45;) A clean budget hotel that's less than 10 minutes' walk from the seafront. The cheap 'economy' rooms are fan-cooled with an attached bathroom.

Eating

There are several good *kedai kopi* serving tasty fish and seafood dishes, and cold beer between Jl Shop Block and the main road. The food stalls at the market are great for breakfast.

Anjung Paghalian Cafe (Jl Kastam; meals RM3-5; dinner) Beside the Tun Sarakan Marine Park entrance sign, this indoor-outdoor place on a pier features fish, prawn, chicken, squid, venison sold by portion (for two or more people) and cooked in your choice of up to 12 different ways. It also serves Malay standards and even burgers.

Mabul Steak House (Semporna Seafront; meals from RM4.90; lunch & dinner) This place is renowned for ice-blended juices, a great aprés-boat thirst quencher; the servings are large and glacial. Set meals for RM4.90 and RM7.90 include soup, a main and fruit. The restaurant also serves seafood by weight, as well as steaks and chops.

Getting There & Away

Buses and minibuses leave from the town centre. Dayana Express runs air-conditioned buses to Kota Kinabalu (RM58.50, nine to 10 hours) at 7.30am and 7.30pm daily with stops in Kunak, Lahad Datu, Sandakan and Ranau. The ticket office on Jl Hospital is open all day. Other bus companies do this trip but Dayana is the only guaranteed departure.

Minibuses to Tawau (RM10, 2½ hours) leave from the town centre near the main road. Minibuses to Lahad Datu (RM10, 2½ hours) depart when full from the corner of Jl PG Jaji and Jl Masjid.

TAWAU

☎ 089 / pop 245,000

Tawau is the port for the boat trip to/from the Indonesian province of Kalimantan; see p492 for more details. The road trip to Tawau from either Lahad Datu or Semporna reveals how palm-tree plantations, harvested for palm-tree oil, are choking the landscape of eastern Sabah.

There's internet access at **City Internet Zone** (☎ 760016; 37 Kompleks Fajar, Jl Perbandaran; per hr RM2-3; 9am-midnight).

Sleeping & Eating

Hotel Soon Yee (☎ 772447; 1362 Jl Stephen Tan; r RM25-40;) This is an excellent budget hotel, and a much better bet than the lodging houses (mostly brothels) around the local bus station. There is no hot water in some of the upper rooms. Opt for a quieter back room.

Loong Hotel (☎ 778100; 3868 Jl Abaca; r RM45-60;) Situated alongside wooden houses in a quiet street in the town's northwest. Standard rooms are nothing special but the family room (RM70) has four single beds and is ideal for a group. There's a decent *kedai kopi* downstairs with dim sum.

Tawau is famed for its fine, inexpensive Chinese seafood restaurants on Jl Chen Fook. Good View and Kam Ling are the most popular. Everything's sold by weight. It's best to go with a group and you should plan on around RM40 per head. Around the block, closer to the waterfront, there's a Malay seafood place with grilled fish meals for RM15.

Restoran Aul Bismillah (☎ 764675; Jl Bunga Tan Jung; meals RM2-6; breakfast, lunch & dinner) The Aul Bismilla is a cheerful, no-fuss restaurant that's good for catching the breeze coming in off the ocean. It serves good meals, such as tofu curry.

Getting There & Away

Malaysia Airlines (code MH; ☎ 761293, 1-300-883000; www.malaysiaairlines.com.my) has flights between Tawau and both KK (RM133) and Sandakan (RM143).

FAX (code D7; ☎ 761946, 749162) has four flights a week to Johor Baru and daily flights to Sandakan. The sales office opposite Heritage Hotel is a good alternative to hunting down an internet café or phoning.

GETTING TO INDONESIA

Boats leave the customs wharf (next to the fish market) for the Indonesian province of Kalimantan. Tickets can be purchased from a half-dozen booths and shops near the wharf entrance. There are several departures daily for Pulau Nunukan (RM25, 1½ hours), from where you can continue to the mainland Kalimantan town of Tarakan (150,000Rp, 2½ hours).

You must get your visa prior to crossing the border as Indonesia doesn't issue visas on arrival; there's an **Indonesian consulate** (☎ 089-752969; Jl Tanjong Batu; 🕒 8am-1pm Mon-Fri) in Tawau.

See p304 for information on doing the trip in the reverse direction.

Air-conditioned express buses to Kota Kinabalu (RM 45 to RM55, 10 hours) leave from lot on Jl Chen Fook. Most buses leave from 6.30am to 8am, with a handful of night buses. Land Cruisers also operate from this station.

Buses to Kunak (RM10, one hour), Lahad Datu (RM15, two hours) and Sandakan (RM32, six hours) leave from inside the block of Sabindo Sq diagonally east of the KK bus terminal, behind the big purple sign for Yassin Curry House. Minibuses also leave from there for Kunak (RM10) and Lahad Datu (RM17) from 6am to 1pm; and Semporna (RM10, 2½ hours) from 7am to 4pm.

MALAYSIAN BORNEO – SARAWAK

Rajah Brooke's former kingdom of Sarawak sprawls along the northwest coast of Borneo – a vast expanse of secondary forest and palm-oil plantations that gives rise to jungle-clad mountains along the border with Indonesian Kalimantan.

The main attractions of Sarawak include some of the world's most incredible caves: the huge chambers of Niah National Park would be the state's most impressive natural highlight if they weren't overshadowed by those of Gunung Mulu National Park. The mighty Batang Rejang is rightly called the Amazon of Borneo, and a trip upriver is the quintessential Borneo experience. Then there's the Kelabit Highlands – Borneo's very own Shangri La – where you can trek from longhouse to longhouse through thick jungle. Finally, there's Kuching, a surprisingly cosmopolitan city with intriguing reminders of the White Rajahs and some excellent Chinese, Malay and Indian food.

All told, Sarawak has enough varied and interesting charms to keep anyone interested for a couple of weeks.

KUCHING

☎ 082 / pop 496,000

Sarawak's state capital is almost sure to surprise you, for who would expect to find a stylish, hip and progressive city perched on this corner of Borneo? It's easy to see why Rajah Brooke chose this city as his base of operations: overlooking the languid Sungai Sarawak, it seems the perfect gateway to both jungle and sea.

The most attractive part of the city is the old Chinatown area that merges into a neighbouring Little India area. The main artery of this area is Jl Carpenter, which runs between Jl Wayang and Jl Tun Abang Haji Openg. The area is punctuated by excellent little restaurants, craft shops and bustling wet and dry markets. The east side of the city is more modern, but not without its charms, including Jl Padungan, a strip of cool restaurants that you might expect to find in Melbourne, London or San Francisco. Additional attractions include a brilliant weekend market, some fine museums and a couple of well-preserved relics from the time of Brooke. All told, Kuching is one of the more character-filled cities in Southeast Asia.

Information

BOOKSHOPS

Mohamed Yahia & Sons (☎ 416928; Basement, Sarawak Plaza, Jl Tunku Abdul Rahman; 🕒 9am-5pm) Has English-language fiction and books on Borneo, plus Sarawak maps.

Popular Book Co (☎ 411378; Level 3, Tun Jugah Centre, 18 Jl Tunku Abdul Rahman; 🕒 9am-7pm) This is a more modern and spacious bookshop with a good selection of international titles. There are fewer books of local interest, however.

EMERGENCY

Ambulance (☎ 999)
Fire (☎ 994)
Police (☎ 999)

IMMIGRATION

Immigration office (☎ 245661; 2nd fl, Sultan Iskandar Bldg, Jl Simpang Tiga) For visa extensions. It's located 3km south of the town centre.

INTERNET ACCESS

Cyber City (☎ 243680; per hr RM4; 🕑 10am-11pm Mon-Sat, 11am-11pm Sun) Easily the best internet café in town. It's off Jl Borneo.

LAUNDRY

City Laundry (per 2kg RM20; 🕑 7.45am-5pm Mon-Fri, 7.45am-12.30pm Sat) Overpriced compared to Mr Clean. It's off Jl Borneo.

Mr Clean (Jl Green Hill; per kilo RM6; 🕑 8am-6pm Mon-Sat, 8am-4pm Sun) Next to the Mandarin Hotel, it's reliable and economical.

MEDICAL SERVICES

Sarawak General Hospital (☎ 257555; Jl Ong Kee) For emergencies and major ailments only; it's 1km south of town.

Timberland Medical Centre (☎ 234991; Mile 3, Jl Rock) Private hospital with highly qualified staff.

MONEY

Everrise Money Changer (☎ 233200; 199 Jl Padungan; 🕑 9am-5pm) Has English-language fiction and books on Borneo, plus Sarawak maps.

Majid & Sons (☎ 422402; 45 Jl India) A licensed moneychanger dealing in cash only.

Maybank (☎ 416889; Jl Tunku Abdul Rahman; 🕑 9.15am-4.30pm Mon-Thu, 9.15am-4pm Fri, ATM 6am-midnight daily)

Mohamed Yahia & Sons (☎ 416928; Basement, Sarawak Plaza, Jl Tunku Abdul Rahman; 🕑 9am-5pm) Inside the bookshop.

Standard Chartered Bank (☎ 252233; Jl Padungan; 🕑 9.15am-4.30pm Mon-Thu, 9.15am-4pm Fri)

POST

Main post office (Jl Tun Abang Haji Openg; 🕑 8am-4.30pm Mon-Sat)

TOURIST INFORMATION

Visitors Information Centre (☎ 410944; www.sarawaktourism.com; Sarawak Tourism Complex, Jl Tun Abang Haji Openg; 🕑 8am-6pm Mon-Fri, 9am-3pm Sat, Sun & holidays) Located in the old courthouse and with extremely helpful staff. Pick up the free *Kuching Tourist Map*.

Sights

WATERFRONT

Kuching's lovely paved waterfront makes for a fine stroll, especially when a cool evening breeze blows off the river. At night the promenade is ablaze with colourful lights and is busy with people buying cheap dinners or snacks from the permanent riverside food stalls (the best of which can be found in front of the Hilton Hotel). While you're strolling the waterfront, be sure to have a look at the **Brooke Memorial**, in front of the Visitor Information Centre.

MUSEUMS

The **Sarawak Museum** (☎ 244232; www.museum.sarawak.gov.my/main.htm; Jl Tun Abang Haji Openg; admission free; 🕑 9am-6pm) has a fascinating collection of cultural artefacts and is a must for anyone wanting to learn more about the region's indigenous peoples. It consists of two buildings connected by an ornate footbridge. The Old Wing houses the main ethnology exhibits and is filled with tribal masks, totem poles, fetishes, explanations of tattooing and body art, and a walk-in longhouse. The New Wing (Tun Abdul Razak Hall) has temporary exhibits and is of less interest.

While you're at the Sarawak Museum, be sure to have a look at the museum's **Art Museum** and **Natural Science Museum**, both of which are just down the hill from the museum's Old Wing. The former houses both permanent and temporary exhibits, some of which are very good. The latter was not open at the time of writing, but was expected to open soon.

Over the hill from the Sarawak Museum is the **Islamic Museum** (☎ 244232; Jl P Ramlee;

VISAS & PERMITS

Sarawak is semiautonomous and treated in some ways like a separate country. If you travel from Peninsular Malaysia or Sabah into Sarawak, your passport will be checked on arrival in Sarawak and a new stay-permit issued, either for 30 days or for the same period as your original Malaysia entry visa. If you are travelling directly to Sarawak, you will usually be given a 30-day entry stamp on arrival. When you leave Sarawak, your passport will be checked and a departure stamp put in your passport. When you travel from Sarawak to Peninsular Malaysia or into Sabah, you do not start a new entry period, so your 30-day (or longer) permit from Sarawak remains valid.

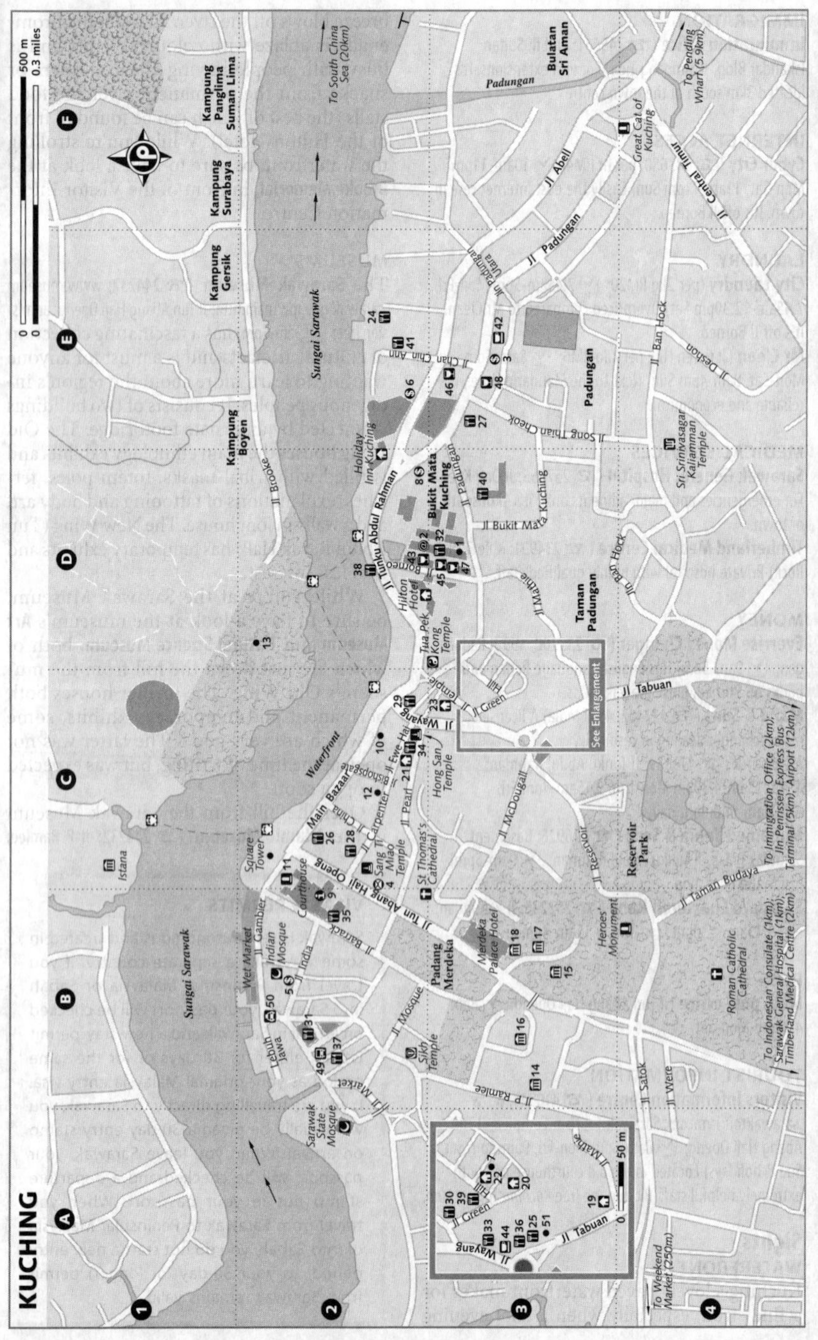
KUCHING
0 500 m
0 0.3 miles
Sungai Sarawak
Waterfront
Main Bazaar
Jl Tunku Abdul Rahman
Jl Tun Abang Haji Openg
Jl Padungan
Jl Abell
Jl Tabuan
Jl Ban Hock
Jl Central Timur
Jl Song Thian Cheok
Jl Bukit Mata Kuching
Jl Mathie
Jl McDougall
Jl Reservoir
Jl Taman Budaya
Jl P Ramlee
Jl Satok
Jl Were
Jl Market
Jl Mosque
Jl India
Jl Gambier
Jl Barrack
Jl Carpenter
Jl China
Jl Bishopsgate
Jl Ewe Hai
Jl Wayang
Jl Temple
Jl Green Hill
Jl Pearl
Jl Brooke
Jl Chan Chin Ann
Jl Borneo
Lebuh Jawa
Kampung Boyen
Kampung Gersik
Kampung Surabaya
Kampung Panglima Seman Lima
Bulatan Sri Aman
Padungan
Taman Padungan
Bukit Mata Kuching
Holiday Inn Kuching
Hilton Hotel
Tua Pek Kong Temple
Hong San Temple
St Thomas's Cathedral
Sang Ti Miao Temple
Courthouse
Square Tower
Istana
Wet Market
Indian Mosque
Sarawak State Mosque
Sikh Temple
Padang Merdeka
Merdeka Palace Hotel
Heroes' Monument
Reservoir Park
Roman Catholic Cathedral
Sri Srinivasagar Kaliamman Temple
Great Cat of Kuching
See Enlargement
0 50 m
To South China Sea (20km)
To Pending Wharf (5.9km)
To Weekend Market (250m)
To Indonesian Consulate (2km); Sarawak General Hospital (1km); Timberland Medical Centre (2km)
Jln Penrissen Express Bus Terminal (5km); Airport (12km)

INFORMATION
City Laundry....1 D3
Cyber City....2 D2
Everrise Moneychanger....3 E3
Main Post Office....4 C2
Majid & Sons....5 B2
Maybank....6 E2
Mohamed Yahia & Sons....(see 52)
Mr Clean....7 A3
Popular Book Co....(see 53)
Standard Chartered Bank....8 D2
Visitors' Information Centre....9 B2

SIGHTS & ACTIVITIES
Borneo Interland Travel....10 C2
Brooke Memorial....11 C2
Bumbu Cooking School....12 C2
Fort Margherita....13 D2
Islamic Museum....14 B3
Sarawak Museum (Old Wing)....15 B3
Sarawak Museum (Tun Abdul Razak Hall)....16 B3
Sarawak Museum Art Museum....17 B3
Sarawak Museum Natural Science Museum....18 B3

SLEEPING
B&B Inn....19 A3
Borneo B&B....20 A3
Carpenter Guesthouse....21 C2
Mandarin Hotel....22 A3
Singgahsana Lodge....23 C3

EATING
Benson's Seafood....24 E2
Bla Bla Bla....25 A3
Briyani Café....26 C2
Chin Sa Barbeque Specialist....27 E3
Chinese Food Stalls....28 C2
Deli Café....(see 50)
Gallery Café....29 C2
Green Hill Corner....30 A3
Hawker Centre....31 B2
Hawker Centre....32 D3
Junk....33 A3
Life Café....34 C2
Little Lebanon....35 B2
Living Room....36 A3
Oriental Park....37 B2
Riverside Food & Drink Stalls....38 D2
Sin Mei Café....39 A3
Top Spot Food Court....40 D3
Zhun San Yen Vegetarian Food Centre....41 E2

DRINKING
Bing....42 E3
Cat City....43 D2
Coffee Bean & Tea Leaf....(see 52)
Havana Café....44 A3
Miami....45 D3
Mojo....46 E3
Rainforest....47 D3
Soho....48 E3

TRANSPORT
Biaramas Express....(see 49)
Matang Transport Co....(see 49)
Petra Jaya Bus Station....49 B2
Taxi Stand....50 B2
Teck Hua Motor....51 A3

admission free; 9am-6pm), with magnificent examples of Islamic interior decoration and architecture, including an intricate model of Jerusalem's Dome of the Rock inlaid with mother-of-pearl.

MARKET

Kuching has a wonderfully chaotic **weekend market** (Jl Satok; late afternoon Sat, 5am-noon Sun) held in the labyrinth of side streets along the southern edge of Jl Satok. The smells of fresh herbs, fruits and meats compete with the scent of delicious fried foods such as pancakes to pull you every which way. Saturday afternoon is the best time to visit, when throngs of locals snap up the freshest goods.

FORT MARGHERITA

Built by Charles Brooke in 1879, **Fort Margherita** (admission free; dawn-dusk) guarded the approach to Kuching against pirates. Now, the impressive whitewashed building has been left to rot under the Borneo sun. It seems the city fathers have decided that there's no point in maintaining the place, which is a shame, considering its historical significance. Now, all you can do is wander the weed-strewn grounds and look at the building from the outside. To get there, take a *tambang* (small passenger ferry; 80 sen) from the pier on the waterfront, opposite the Hilton, walk up through the *kampong*, bearing left, past the school, through the parking lot and into the grounds.

GETTING INTO TOWN

Kuching International Airport is 12km south of the city centre. Sarawak Transport Co's (STC) green-and-cream bus 12A does a circuit that takes in the airport (RM1.60), while Chin Lian Long's (CLL) blue-and-white bus 8A does a direct airport to city run (RM1.40). In Kuching, these buses stop on Jl Tun Abang Haji Openg, near the Padang Merdeka. To catch the bus from the airport, exit the terminal and turn right. Minivans also swing by the stop and can transport you to town for about RM3. A coupon-fare taxi between Kuching airport and the city centre costs RM17. Buy coupons at the counter outside the terminal entrance.

The express-boat wharf is 6.5km east of town in the suburb of Pending. CLL bus 1 (RM1.50, 40 minutes) connects the wharf with Kuching (the Kuching stop is on Jl Tunku Abdul Rahman just west of the Holiday Inn). Taxis cost RM20.

The express bus terminal is 5km southeast of the city centre. Numerous STC buses run between the terminal and city for 90 sen. A taxi costs RM15.

Courses

Bumbu Cooking School (☎ 256050; bumbucookingclass@hotmail.com; 57 Jl Carpenter; class per person RM70) is a great way to learn how to cook some of the dishes you've enjoyed in local restaurants. You start with a shopping trip to a local market, then you cook four dishes and sit down to enjoy them.

Tours

Travel agents and tour operators in Kuching can arrange trips to nearby attractions such as Bako National Park and the Batang Rejang. Tour operators include **Borneo Interland Travel** (☎ 413595; www.bitravel.com.my; 1st fl, 63 Main Bazaar).

Festivals & Events

The three-day **Rainforest World Music Festival** (www.rainforestmusic-borneo.com) unites Borneo's indigenous tribes with international artists for a musical extravaganza in the Sarawak Cultural Village outside Kuching. It's held annually in the middle of July.

Sleeping

B & B Inn (☎ 237366; bnbswk@streamyx.com; Jl Tabuan; dm RM16, s/d RM25/35; ❄ 💻) Simple but clean rooms, a rooftop patio and a fairly convenient location make this a very good choice in the budget bracket.

Borneo B&B (☎ 231200; borneobedbreakfast@yahoo.com; 3 Jl Green Hill; dm RM17, s RM28-32, d RM34-36; ❄ 💻) This homey place is popular with backpackers, although it's a little run-down and can be hot.

our pick **Mandarin Hotel** (☎ 418269; 6 Jl Green Hill; r from RM50; ❄) This fine budget hotel is head and shoulders above the similarly priced joints located nearby. It's simple, clean and good value.

Carpenter Guesthouse (☎ 256050; www.carpenterguesthouse.com; 94 Jl Carpenter; dm RM28, r from RM60; ❄) In an old Chinese shophouse, this brand-spanking-new guesthouse has a great atmosphere and helpful owners. Rooms are on the small side and quite spartan, but the hotel is clean, well run and has wi-fi. It's also in a great location.

Singgahsana Lodge (☎ 429277; www.singgahsana.com; 1 Jl Temple; dm RM30, r from RM80; ❄ 💻) This stylish and well-run guesthouse has an unbeatable location and nice common areas. It's a touch overpriced, but very popular with Western backpackers.

Eating

Oriental Park (noodles RM2.40; 🕒 5am-11.30am) Many Kuching Chinese start their day with a bowl of *kolo mee* (*ramen*-style egg noodles in soup). This friendly little place off Jl Mosque does a brilliant version of this dish, complete with savoury bits of pork and a wonderfully rich soup.

our pick **Chinese Food Stalls** (Jl Carpenter; meals from RM3; 🕒 breakfast, lunch & dinner) There are some brilliant Chinese hawker stalls in the small covered courtyard across from Sang Ti Miao Temple. At the front on the right side there is a stall that does a sublime bowl of laksa (RM4; morning until lunchtime only). At the back on the left there is a stall that does a great ginger chicken in the evenings.

Hawker Centre (Jl Khoo Hun Yeang; meals from RM3; 🕒 breakfast, lunch & dinner) There's a good hawker centre with Malay and Chinese sections at the west end of town near the state mosque. It's a good place for a cheap meal when exploring the markets of the area. There's another, less interesting hawker centre (off Jl Borneo; meals from RM3; open breakfast, lunch and dinner) in the shopping complex opposite the Hilton.

Top Spot Seafood Centre (Jl Padungan; meals RM4-35; 🕒 breakfast, lunch & dinner) An excellent rooftop plaza with acres of tables and a good variety of stalls. Order anything from abalone to banana prawns or numerous varieties of fish, and chase it down with a cold bottle of Tiger. To get here, climb the stairs leading from Jl Padungan to Tapanga restaurant, and keep heading upstairs from there.

Deli Café (☎ 232788; 88 Main Bazaar; drinks from RM4, sandwiches RM5; 🕒 9am-6pm Tue-Sun; 💻) What's not to like about a place that serves proper coffee in cool air-conditioned surroundings, along with simple sandwiches and a good selection of desserts, with free wi-fi thrown in for good measure?

Briyani Café (16 Main Bazaar; meals from RM5; 🕒 8am-7pm) The oddly spelled Briyani Café is a good place for a morning roti or a hot cup of tea; just stay out of the bathroom – we rank it as Borneo's worst.

Life Café (Jl Carpenter; drinks from RM2, meals from RM5; 🕒 lunch & dinner) This atmospheric little tea house–Chinese eatery offers a wide range of mostly Chinese dishes, including several good vegetarian choices.

Junk (☎ 259450; 80 Jl Wayang; mains RM18-40; 🕒 dinner Wed-Mon) Bla Bla Bla's sister restaurant, Junk is like a funky antique store that happens to serve whopping portions of Western comfort food. If you're ready for a break from *mee goreng*, this is a fascinating choice.

Bla Bla Bla (☎ 233944; 27 Jl Tabuan; main dishes from RM25; ⌚ dinner) Borneo's most stylish restaurant serves tasty fusion food in a cool indoor dining area that you access by traversing stepping stones across a carp pool under the watchful eye of a Buddha.

Living Room (☎ 233944; Jl Wayang; main dishes from RM25; ⌚ dinner) The same management also runs the impossibly cool Living Room, where you can drink and dine in outdoor *salas* while soaking up the soothing ambience. You will no doubt find yourself wondering where you are: is this Borneo, Bali or Barcelona?

Benson Seafood (Jl Chan Chin Ann; meals from RM30; ⌚ dinner) Ignore the aircraft-hangar ambience and concentrate on the wonderful fresh Chinese seafood at this giant riverside eatery. The oyster omelettes are enough to make us want to hop on the next plane back to Kuching and the *midin* (jungle fern) stir-fried with *belacan* (shrimp paste) is a Sarawak classic.

Some other options:

Green Hill Corner (Jl Temple; meals RM2-4; ⌚ breakfast, lunch & dinner) Several hawker stalls here crank out a variety of noodle and rice dishes, including a brilliant plate of *kway teow goreng* (fried *kway teow* noodles). Problem is, the creator of this dish only shows up when he damn well feels like it.

Chin Sa Barbeque Specialist (Jl Padungan; chicken & rice from RM3; ⌚ breakfast, lunch & dinner) Eat in or take away at this popular Jl Padungan barbie joint, where savoury chicken or pork slices over rice are the speciality of the house.

Sin Mei Café (Jl Green Hill; meals from RM5; ⌚ breakfast & lunch) If you're staying in one of the Chinese cheapies nearby, you'll find this friendly little *kedai kopi* to be a great spot for your morning congee, noodles or toast and eggs.

Riverside Food & Drink Stalls (Waterfront Promenade; meals from RM5; ⌚ dinner) What could be better than an evening constitutional along the river followed by a fresh fruit juice and a few sticks of satay? It's opposite the Hilton Hotel.

Little Lebanon (☎ 247523; Sarawak Tourism Complex; mains from RM8; ⌚ lunch & dinner Tue-Sun) This simple restaurant is a pleasant spot for a drink or a snack while exploring the Chinatown/Little India area.

Zhun San Yen Vegetarian Food Centre (Jl Chan Chin Ann; meals from RM10; ⌚ lunch & dinner) If you find yourself in the east end of town in need of simple vegetarian food, this buffet-style restaurant is a decent choice.

Drinking

Coffee Bean & Tea Leaf (ground fl, Sarawak Plaza; drinks from RM3; ⌚ breakfast, lunch & dinner; 💻) This popular chain coffee shop offers wi-fi and air-con.

Bing (☎ 421880; 84 Jl Padungan; drinks from RM4; ⌚ breakfast, lunch & dinner; 💻) Bing is a stylish, dimly lit café in the heart of the Jl Padungan nightlife zone. It's equally good for an afternoon cuppa or an evening tipple.

The shopping complex across from the Hilton Hotel on Jl Borneo has a collection of bars and nightclubs that make for an easy pub crawl – if one isn't happening, just head next door. Bar-clubs are pretty casual and can get a little rowdy at times. The main players here are Cat City, Miami and Rainforest.

Jl Padungan is a more upscale and civilised affair, with a selection of cool nightspots that would be equally at home in New York. Two spots to check are Mojo and Soho.

Finally, there is an intriguing collection of restaurant-bars on Jl Tabuan, just south of the roundabout, including Bla, Bla, Bla, Living Room and Junk (see left). You'll also find Havana Café here, which is more of a straight -up bar.

Getting There & Away

AIR

Malaysia Airlines (code MH; ☎ 1-300-883000; www.malaysiaairlines.com.my) flies between Kuching and KL (RM274). There are also several flights daily from Kuching to Johor Bahru (RM224) and Singapore (RM432).

Within Malaysian Borneo, from Kuching there are regular flights to Sibu (RM81), Bintulu (RM85), Miri (RM100), Kota Kinabalu (RM195) and Labuan (RM120).

Air Asia (code AK; ☎ 1-300-889933; www.airasia.com) has numerous daily flights to KL at bargain-basement prices (from RM80).

BOAT

Express Bahagia (☎ 410076) boats run to and from Sibu (RM36, 4½ hours), departing from the express boat wharf in Pending at 8.30am daily. Note that this is an easier and faster trip to Sibu than the bus, which takes eight hours.

BUS

Long-distance buses depart the **express bus station** (Jl Penrissen), situated 5km southeast of the centre. There are regular services

GETTING TO INDONESIA

From the express bus terminal in Kuching, there are services to Pontianak (RM45, nine hours, four departures daily between 7am and noon) in Kalimantan. Buses cross at the Tebedu–Entikong crossing. Travellers making land crossings into Kalimantan are required to obtain a visa beforehand from the **Indonesian consulate** (☎ 082-241734; 6th fl, Bangunan Binamas, Jl Padungan, Kuching; 9am-1pm Mon-Thu, 9am-noon Fri), as the officials at border posts on the Kalimantan border do not issue visas on arrival. Fees and requirements differ from country to country; contact the consulate for more information.

See p310 for information on doing the trip in the opposite direction.

to Sibu (RM40, eight hours, 10 departures daily between 6.30am and 10pm), Bintulu (RM60, 10 hours, nine departures daily between 6.30am and 10pm), and Miri (RM80, 14 hours, eight departures daily between 6.30am and 10pm).

Petra Jaya bus 6 leaves from the open-air market to Bako National Park.

Getting Around

For information on travelling into Kuching from the airport, express boat wharf or express bus station, see boxed text, p495.

Tambang (80 sen) will ferry you across the Sungai Sarawak.

There are taxi ranks at the market and express bus terminal. Most short trips around town cost between RM6 and RM10.

AROUND KUCHING

Bako National Park

Lying between the mouths of the Sarawak and Batang rivers is the unspoilt promontory of **Bako National Park** (☎ 011-225049; admission RM10; park office 8am-5pm), an exceptionally beautiful spot where rocky headlands are indented with picturesque beaches.

Bako is famous for its wildlife, including long-tailed macaques, bearded pigs and the unusual proboscis monkey. The **Lintang Trail** (5.3km, three to four hours) is an undulating loop of the promontory's interior that links up with other trails – combine it with the side trail to **Telok Paku** (45 minutes return), which offers your best chance of seeing the elusive proboscis.

In the evening, park rangers offer a guided night trek if there is enough interest from guests. This is an opportunity not to be missed, as the wildlife present at night is entirely different from that seen during the day. The rangers are also particularly good at spotting things that an ordinary traveller would miss. Inquire at the welcome desk to see if there is a trek on that night. The trek lasts between 1½ to two hours and costs about RM10 per person.

Register for the park (adult/child RM10/5) upon arrival at the boat dock in Bako Bazaar. From here it's a choppy 30-minute boat ride to the **park headquarters** (☎ 011-225049; Telok Assam), where you'll find accommodation, a cafeteria and the park office. The office is about 400m along a wooden boardwalk from the boat dock. Staff will show you to your quarters and can answer any questions about trails. There's a large trail map hanging outside the office; ask for a free copy. Storage lockers are available for RM5 per day.

SLEEPING & EATING

Book accommodation through the **Visitors Information Centre** (☎ 082-410944; www.sarawaktourism.com) in Kuching. There are hostels, chalets and a camping ground.

The **hostel** (dm/r RM15/40) has four beds with shared kitchen and bathroom. Variously sized **chalets** (r RM50-100) are also available. Bookings are essential for the chalets and advisable for the hostel rooms, though you should be able to get a bed if you arrive on a weekday.

Camp sites (per person RM5) are available but the camping ground is a swamp for much of the year. There's a shower block, and lockers can be hired for RM5 per day. Bring your own utensils, sheets and sleeping bags.

The cafeteria at the park headquarters is open from 8am to 9pm. It sells cheap buffet noodle and rice meals. The adjoining shop sells a good variety of reasonably priced tinned and dried food, chocolate, biscuits, film and toiletries, although fresh bread and vegetables are not always available.

GETTING THERE & AWAY

To get to Bako from Kuching, first take a bus to Bako Bazaar in Kampung Bako, then charter a boat to the park. Petra Jaya bus 6 leaves from the open-air market in Kuching every hour (approximately) from 7.20am to 6pm (RM2.50, 45 minutes). The last bus back to Kuching leaves Kampung Bako at 5pm.

A boat from Bako Bazaar to the park headquarters costs RM40 each way for up to five people, or RM8 per person for larger groups. The chances are that someone on the bus will be looking to share a boat, especially on a weekend; tourists sometimes wait at the boat dock for the same reason.

Take note of the boat's number and be sincere when you agree to a pick-up time. If you do want to share a different boat back, tell the staff at park headquarters your boat number – they are happy to call and cancel your original boat.

BATANG REJANG

The Batang Rejang has been called the Amazon of Borneo. Until the advent of 4WD roads and jungle airstrips, the river served as the main 'highway' into the interior of Sarawak. Even now, it sees a daily parade of express boats and barges moving people and goods along its muddy length. Though it's not the jungle-lined wilderness that many travellers imagine, it still retains some of its wild and romantic nature – and a journey up the river into the interior is a classic Borneo adventure.

Many of the indigenous people of the Batang Rejang area still live in communal dwellings known as longhouses. These are large structures raised above the ground on stilts that provide shelter for villagers under their long rooflines. For more on longhouses, see boxed text, p500.

The best time for a trip up the Rejang is in late May/early June. This is the time of **Gawai**, the indigenous Dayak harvest festival, when longhouses are busy with feasts and traditional dancing, and visitors are welcomed.

SIBU

☎ 084 / pop 201,000

Sibu is the gateway to the Batang Rejang, making it a major transit point for travellers and the nexus of trade between the coast and the upriver hinterland. It's a somewhat chaotic jumble of concrete buildings, with several large markets and a bustling Chinatown on the banks of the Rejang. While it's no rival for Kuching in terms of charm, it's certainly not a bad spot to spend a day before or after a trip upriver.

Information

Emergency (☎ 999)

Golden Horse Travel & Tours (☎ 323288; 62 Jl Kampung Nyabor; 🕒 8am-5pm Mon-Sat, 8am-noon Sun) This competent travel agency near Premier Hotel is the place to go for plane tickets etc.

Hospital (☎ 343333)

Police (☎ 336144)

Visitor centre (☎ 340980; www.sibu.com.my; 32 Jl Tukang Besi; 🕒 8am-5pm Mon-Fri, 8am-12.50pm Sat, closed 1st & 3rd Sat of every month) This office provides information about upriver trips out of Song, Kapit and Belaga.

Wisma Sanyan (Jl Sanyan) There are several internet cafés on the 4th floor here.

Sights

Tua Pek Kong Temple (Jl Temple; admission free; 🕒 dawn-dusk) is an interesting riverside Chinese temple where, if you're lucky, you'll find Mr Tan Teck Chiang in attendance. Mr Tan will give you a tour of the temple and explain (in lavish detail) his interpretation of Taoism and Buddhism. You can also scale the seven-storey pagoda to get a brilliant view over the town and the muddy Batang Rejang as it slowly makes its way towards the sea.

Sleeping

Most of the budget lodging in Sibu is of a very low standard. If you don't stay in the Hoover Lodging House, you should consider dropping a little extra cash to stay in a midrange place.

Hoover Lodging House (☎ 334490; Jl Pulau; dm/s/tw RM20/30/45; ❄) The accommodation offered in the administration building of the Methodist Church is excellent value for money. Most rooms have high ceilings and attached bathrooms. You can also safely store gear here while travelling upriver. It's about 200m north (inland) from Tua Pek Kong Temple.

Li Hua Hotel (☎ 324000; 1 Lorong Lanang; r RM45-80; ❄) On the riverfront, about 100m south (upriver) of the Swan Statue, you will find Sibu's best-value hotel, with spotless tile-floor rooms and good views from the upper floors.

Victoria Inn (☎ 320055; 80 Jl Market; r RM50-85; ❄) If the Hoover and the Li Hua are full, this centrally located budget hotel is a good choice. It's a tightly packed warren of rooms located about a block away from the high-rise Tamhamas Hotel.

THE BORNEO LONGHOUSE

Longhouses are the traditional dwellings of the indigenous peoples of Borneo. These communal dwellings are raised above the ground and may contain up to 100 individual family 'apartments' under one long roof. The most important area of a longhouse is the common veranda, which serves as a social area and sometimes as sleeping space.

It's fair to say that there are two types of longhouse: 'tourist longhouses' and 'residential longhouses'. The former, as you can guess, are set up for tourists and are often built using traditional materials and construction techniques. They look like you might imagine (or hope) a longhouse should look, but they're pretty much just for display purposes.

In contrast, residential longhouses are where people actually live. If you're expecting these longhouses to look like something out of the Rajah Brooke era, you might be disappointed: most residential longhouses these days are quite modern in construction, with electronic appliances in all the apartments, TV aerials, and parking lots out front. Still, this is where real life happens, and if you want to see how Borneo's modern-day indigenous peoples live, a visit to a longhouse is a must.

When visiting a longhouse, it is polite to wait outside until someone from the longhouse invites you in. Bringing a few gifts is always appreciated. Usually, if you are travelling upriver with a guide, your guide will take you to a longhouse where he or she has relatives or friends.

Eating

In the late afternoon a host of food stalls set up near the concrete **SMC Market** (Jl Channel). Some of the waterfront Chinese *kedai kopi* open around dawn, handy if you're catching an early boat.

Victorious Cafe (Jl Maju; meals RM3-8; 🕑 breakfast, lunch & early dinner) Dine under the gaze of the Sibu swan at this popular, mostly Chinese, *kedai kopi* across the street from the Li Hua Hotel. There's a stall here that makes a smoky and wonderful plate of *kway teow*, which you can wash down with a nice iced lemon tea.

SCR (meals from RM3; 🕑 breakfast, lunch & dinner) The name stands for Singapore Chicken Rice, and that's what packs 'em in here at this popular chain. Not much on ambiance, but it's tasty and cheap. It's off Jl Kampong Nyabor.

New Capital Restaurant (☎ 326066; meals around RM25; 🕑 lunch & dinner) If you feel like a splurge, this brilliant Chinese eatery off Jl Kampong Nyabor is sure to satisfy, with excellent fish, meat and vegetable dishes. We recommend the butter prawns and stir-fried *midin* (jungle fern) washed down with a fresh fruit juice.

Getting There & Around

AIR

Malaysia Airlines (code MH; ☎ 1-300-883000; www.malaysiaairlines.com.my) has several flights daily from Sibu to Kuching (RM81), Miri (RM130), Kota Kinabalu (RM200) and KL (RM274). **Air Asia** (code AK; ☎ 1-300-889933; www.airasia.com) has dirt-cheap flights between Sibu and both KL and Johor Bahru.

BOAT

Boats leave from the River Express Terminal at the western end of Jl Bengkel (which is at the southwestern end of town). At least two companies run express boats to Kuching (RM40, 4½ hours, departures at 7.30am and 12.45pm daily). Ticket booths are inside the terminal.

Getting to Kapit is the first leg of the journey up the Batang Rejang. Several boats motor the 140km from Sibu to Kapit (RM17 to RM30, three hours, departures between 5.30am and 1pm). Some boats continue up to Belaga, but most terminate in Kapit. All boat companies have booths at the terminal and they display their next departure times with large clocks outside their booths, making choosing your boat a snap.

BUS

Bus companies have ticket stalls at the **long-distance bus station** (Sungai Antu) and around the local bus station on the waterfront. Starting from 7am, local buses run regularly from the long-distance station into town (80 sen). A taxi between town and the bus station should cost RM10.

Long-distance buses travel between Sibu and Kuching (RM40, eight hours, regular departures between 6.30am and 10pm), Miri (RM40, 7½ hours, departures roughly hourly from 6am to 10pm) and Bintulu (RM20, 3½ hours, departures roughly hourly from 5.30am to 6pm).

KAPIT

☎ 084 / pop 8200

The main upriver settlement on the Rejang, Kapit is a bustling trading and transport centre that dates back to the days of the white rajas. The main activity here is wandering around the docks and market stalls to see what upriver people are buying and selling. Apart from this, you can visit **Fort Sylvia** (Jl Kubu; admission free; ⏰ 10am-noon & 2-5pm Tue-Sun), which dates back to 1880. Although Belaga is further upstream and seems to promise more authentic longhouse experiences, Kapit is in some ways better for this – it offers a wider choice of river systems and several interesting longhouses within easy reach by river or road.

Information

Good Time Cyber Centre (☎ 746303; 354 Jl Yong Moh Chai; per hr RM3) Internet access.

Hua Chiong Travel Service (☎ 796681; Jl Temenggong Koh) Airline tickets and local travel services.

Hyper Link Cyber Station (17 Jl Tan Sit; per hr RM3) Internet access.

KL Ling Moneychanger (☎ 796488; Jl Penghulu Gerinang) Changes cash and travellers cheques.

Lee Cyber Centre (Jl Tan Sit; per hr RM3) Internet access.

Maybank (☎ 790122; 73C Jl Penghulu Atan)

Sleeping & Eating

Ark Hill Inn (☎ 796168; 451 Jl Penghulu Gerinang; r RM35-70; ❄) This is about as close as you can get to riverfront accommodation in Kapit, although unfortunately the rooms don't have any riverfront views. It can be a bit noisy here, but it's usually bearable.

Kapit River View Inn (☎ 796310; krvinn@tm.net.my; 10 Jl Tan Sit Leong; r RM55-60; ❄) Small windowless but clean rooms, located directly on the town square and near the boat pier.

New Rejang Inn (☎ 796600; 104 Jl Teo Chow Beng; r RM60-75; ❄) Clean, tiled rooms with TV, phone and fridge, and a location a mere stone's throw away from the boat wharf make this the best-value accommodation option in town. The in-room cable TV is nice, as long as you're happy watching the same programme as the hotel staff in the lobby!

Kong Hua Café (1 Jl Wharf; meals RM2-5; ⏰ breakfast, lunch & dinner) A fine example of the type of old-school Chinese coffee shop that Malaysia does so well. Breakfast here is not much more than sugary snacks though.

Syarikat Morshidi (Restaurant and Coffee Shop) (cnr Jl Teo Chow Beng & Jl Putena Jaya; dishes RM2-6; ⏰ breakfast) If the thought of yet another breakfast of coffee and a sweet snack in a Chinese café makes your teeth hurt, stop by this tiny roadside café that serves a variety of Muslim breakfast specialities, including *nasi lemak* and milky tea.

Madam Ma's Kitchen (☎ 796119; Hotel Meligai, 334 Jl Airport; mains RM5-15; ⏰ breakfast, lunch & dinner) Ma's is one of the only places in town with air-con, making it a refuge on a hot day (which is every day). The staff are friendly and speak some English and the chicken curry is pretty tasty. It has changing menus and special offers.

Kapit is packed with small restaurants and *kedai kopi*, but the best place to eat in the evening has to be the busy **night market** (dishes RM0.50-3.50), which is near the centre of town, roughly behind Ing Hing Cold Storage. In contrast to the rest of Kapit's dining scene, which is overwhelmingly Chinese, this market is almost exclusively Malay-Muslim. As such, the emphasis is on *satay* and other halal dishes.

Food stalls set up in the evening by the wet market at the western end of town. A triangular covered hall off Jl Penghulu Nyanggau has also food stalls.

Getting There & Away

Express boats leave for Sibu between 6.30am and 2.30pm. The trip takes 2½ to three hours and tickets are RM17 to RM20 for economy, or RM25 to RM30 for 1st class.

Boats depart for Belaga (RM30, 4½ hours) at 9am. When the river is low, express boats can't get past the Pelagus Rapids, and smaller speedboats are used instead. Fares for these boats start at RM50. If you want to do a day trip to Pelagus, ask around the wharf or at your hotel, as the express boats don't stop there.

Express boats bound for the Batang Baleh depart before noon and go as far as Rumah Penghilu Jambi (RM30, four to five hours), an Iban longhouse community. The last boat back to Kapit departs Rumah Penghilu Jambi at 12.30pm.

BELAGA

☎ 084 / pop 2500

Belaga is a small bazaar town and administrative centre located where the Rejang divides into the Belaga and Balui rivers. Its friendly population makes it an excellent base from which to explore the interior, and there are many Kayan and Kenyah **longhouses** along the rivers nearby. If you speak with a local on the way upriver, you may end up being invited to stay at their longhouse. Otherwise, it shouldn't take long to find someone in Belaga with a suggestion of a longhouse to visit or an offer to guide you.

Boats will drop you at the bottom of a steep set of concrete steps leading up to the small town centre; all the town's facilities are found here, in the handful of blocks across from the small park. There's no bank here, but the Teck Hua Chan supermarket will change cash.

Tours

Longhouse visits typically last three days and two nights, and start at RM200 (minimum two people). The most prominent guide operating out of Belaga these days is Daniel Levoh; he can be found at **Daniel's Corner** (☎ 461997, 013-848 6351; daniellevoh@hotmail.com; Jl Teh Ah Kiong). A Kayah and former teacher, Daniel is friendly and knowledgeable, and gets good reviews from travellers. Mark, a licensed guide based out of Hasbee Enterprises, can also arrange longhouse visits, as can Belaga's District Office.

Sleeping & Eating

Belaga's accommodation is of the cheap and cheerful variety, but if you're doing the longhouse circuit you shouldn't really need to sleep here for more than a night or two.

Hotel Belaga (☎ 461244; 14 Main Bazaar; r RM20-35;) A convenient location makes up for less-than-perfect standards at Belaga's principal dosshouse. The cheap beds here are on the verge of collapse, but the place is clean and the fellow running the place is helpful enough. There's a decent Chinese coffee shop downstairs that serves mediocre but filling food.

Jea Corner (meals from RM3; dinner) This tiny stall off Jl Ului Lian is literally the only place in Belaga still serving food after 6pm, and it serves up a small variety of decent Malaysian rice-based dishes. The friendly proprietor, Albert, will probably find you before you find him. He has a wealth of information about the surrounding area and its people and culture – just don't get him started on politics! It's near the District Office.

Kafetaria Mesra Murni (Jl Temengong Mat; dishes RM3-5; breakfast, lunch & dinner) This family-run Muslim restaurant can lay claim to having the only real riverfront dining in Belaga. Try the decent *mee goreng* or the exceptionally refreshing *limau ais* (iced lime juice). It's past the park-playground.

Getting There & Away

Belaga's tiny airstrip is 20 minutes downriver of town by longboat (RM10). There are twice-weekly flights (Wednesday and Saturday) between Belaga and Bintulu (RM50, one hour). Contact **Malaysia Airlines** (code MH; ☎ 461512; www.malaysiaairlines.com.my).

Boats leave Kapit for Belaga (RM30, 4½ hours) at 9am. When the river is low you'll need to take a speedboat instead; fares start at RM50. Returning to Kapit from Belaga, express boats leave Belaga early (between 6am and 6.30am), from where you can catch onward boats downriver to Sibu.

Boats go upriver from Belaga as far as the Bakun Dam area near Rumah Apan (RM10, one hour), from where you can explore the resettled river country north of the Rejang. It's possible to do a loop back to Bintulu this way along a recently paved road.

BINTULU

☎ 086 / pop 102,800

Bintulu is a busy little river town roughly midway between Sibu and Miri. In the centre of town overlooking the river, you'll find the interesting **Pasar Utama Market** (Jl Main Bazaar; dawn-late afternoon), as well as **Tua Pek Kong** (Jl Main Bazaar; admission free; dawn-dusk), a colourful Chinese temple, about a block away. If you want a break from the city, hire a taxi (about RM10) for the 10km trip to **Tanjung Batu Beach**.

Information

Bintulu Hospital (☎ 331455) Off Lebuh Raya Abang Galau.

HSBC (☎ 315928; 25 Jl Law Gek Soon; 9am-3pm Mon-Fri) The best bank in Bintulu; it has an ATM.

Star Internet (Jl Law Gek Soon; per hr RM3; 9am-11pm) Internet access; it's noisy, with slow machines.

Sleeping & Eating

Bakun Inn (☎ 311111; 7 Jl Law Gek Soon; r RM45-60;) This simple hotel on the corner of Jl Law Gek Soon and Jl Keppel is arguably the best budget deal in town. The entrance is out back, near the parking lot.

Sunlight Inn (☎ 332577; 7 Jl Pedada; r RM68-78;) Free wi-fi and a fairly central location make this clean and well-run hotel a good second choice after the Bakun Inn. It's opposite City Point Shopping Centre.

Kintown Inn (☎ 333666; 93 Jl Keppel; r RM69-80.50; ❄ 💻) If you can spare a little bit of extra cash, this is a great choice. Rooms are clean and well appointed, with nice hot showers and good views from the upper floors. There's an also internet terminal in the lobby. The inn is situated on the corner of Jl Law Gek Soon and Jl Keppel.

Restoran PJ Corner (Jl Abang Galau; meals from RM3; 🕑 breakfast, lunch & dinner) This friendly Malay place serves good fresh fruit juice, rotis, *nasi campur* and a nice plate of *mee goreng*. It's on the eastern end of Jl Abang Galau, roughly opposite the Regency Plaza Hotel.

Ban Kee Café (meals from RM10; 🕑 lunch & dinner) Run, don't walk, to this brilliant indoor/outdoor Chinese seafood specialist. It doesn't look like much, but the food here is enough to make us want to head back to Bintulu as soon as possible. Try the butter prawns or the baby *kalian* (a Chinese vegetable similar to baby bok choy). It's located off Jl Abang Galau.

Finally, on the upper floor of the Pasar Utama, you'll find several **food stalls** (meals RM2-5; 🕑 breakfast, lunch & early dinner).

Getting There & Around

AIR

Bintulu airport is 24km west of the centre. A taxi there costs RM25.

Malaysia Airlines (code MH; ☎ 1-300-883000; www.malaysiaairlines.com.my) flies between Bintulu and Kota Kinabalu (RM271), Kuching (RM85), Miri (RM90) and Sibu (RM85). Malaysia Airlines Twin Otters fly twice weekly to Belaga (RM50).

BUS

The long-distance bus station is 5km north of town. Travel between the two by local bus or taxi (RM8).

There are frequent daily services between Bintulu and Kuching (RM60, 10 hours), Miri (RM20, 4½ hours) and Sibu (RM20, 3½ hours).

NIAH CAVES NATIONAL PARK

☎ 085

The vast caverns of **Niah Caves National Park** (☎ 737454; admission RM10; 🕑 park office 8am-5pm) are among Borneo's most incredible natural attractions. Located in the limestone hills about 3km north of Batu Niah town, the caves contain some of the oldest evidence of human habitation in Southeast Asia; rock art and small canoe-like coffins (death ships) within the greenish walls of the **Painted Cave** indicate that it was once a burial ground, and carbon dating puts the oldest relics back 40,000 years ago.

The caves are 3.5km away from the park headquarters via a wonderful plankwalk through old-growth rainforest. First, you walk from the headquarters to the jetty on the Sungai Niah, then cross the river in a small boat (RM1, departs on demand), before climbing to a small **visitors centre** (admission free; 🕑 9am-5pm) where you can rent a torch for RM5 (check it works before setting out – you'll need it if you want to go any distance into the caves). The plankwalk is not well marked – when you reach the place where local villagers sell souvenirs, pass through the gate and climb up to the caves.

You'll pass under a limestone overhang before entering the aptly named **Great Cave**. Ascend up to your left here and make your way to the back of the cave. The trail disappears down into the castellated gloom at the back of the cave, and you may find yourself thinking of Jules Verne's *Journey to the Centre of the Earth* or the city of Zion in the *Matrix* films. You then make your way through a dark passage known as the **Gan Kira**, or Moon Cave. It's not narrow enough to induce claustrophobia (unless you're severely affected), but it will certainly make you wonder what would happen if your torch suddenly died. You then emerge into the forest and traverse another section of boardwalk before arriving at the **Painted Cave**. To return, retrace your steps (taking the steps up to your left to close the loop in the Great Cave).

Sleeping & Eating

Niah Caves can be visited as a day trip from Miri or Bintulu, especially if you go by hire car all the way. If you would like to stay at or near the caves, the best choice is the park accommodation. Otherwise, there are a few simple hotels in Batu Niah town.

Niah Caves National Park (☎ 737454; camp sites RM5, r from RM45) There are simple and clean dorm rooms and private rooms at the park headquarters, along with a basic canteen. Camping is another option.

Niah Cave Hotel (☎ 737726; 155 Batu Niah Bazaar; r RM30; ❄) Set over a café, the simple rooms here with common bathroom are just barely acceptable.

Niah Cave Inn (☎ 737333; 621 Batu Niah Bazaar; r economy/standard from RM64/75; ❄) Despite the unfortunate connotations of its name, this is the best hotel in town. The economy rooms aren't worth the price, but the standard rooms are decent.

There are several *kedai kopi* in town, including the **Friendly Café** (Batu Niah Bazaar; meals from RM3; ⏰ breakfast, lunch & dinner), which serves the usual coffee shop fare. It's opposite the Niah Cave Inn.

Getting There & Away

Batu Niah, the gateway to the park, is 11km west of Niah Junction on the Miri-Bintulu highway. Some express buses travelling between Miri and Bintulu stop at Niah Junction (RM11, two hours to/from Bintulu; RM10, 1¾ hours to/from Miri). When you buy your ticket in Miri or Bintulu, check that the bus stops in Niah Junction, as there are two highways between these two towns, and some buses do not go via Niah Junction.

From Niah Junction, you will have to hire a private car to Batu Niah town (RM10) or direct to the park (RM15). The latter is the better option unless you intend to spend the night at Batu Niah. From Batu Niah, you can walk to park headquarters by taking the path that starts behind the town near the Chinese temple and following the river. If you are not staying at the park, make prior arrangements with a car to pick you up and return you to Batu Niah or Niah Junction when you finish visiting the caves.

LAMBIR HILLS NATIONAL PARK

Although **Lambir Hills National Park** (☎ 085-491030; admission RM10; ⏰ park office 8am-5pm) doesn't have the spectacular scenery of Niah and Mulu, it is the most easily accessed primary rainforest in the Miri area. Activities include jungle walks and swimming.

The main trail here follows a small river past two attractive waterfalls to **Latuk Waterfall**, which has a picnic area and is suitable for swimming. It takes no more than 25 minutes to walk the 835m from the park headquarters to Latuk Waterfall. A path branches off just before the second falls and runs to **Tengkorong Waterfall**, which is a somewhat strenuous 2.6km walk (one way) from the park headquarters.

Although the national park is best visited as a day trip from Miri, there is comfortable accommodation here for those travellers who want to stay the night. The park's fan-cooled **chalets** (r RM75) have two bedrooms, each with two beds. Air-conditioned **chalets** (r RM100) also have two bedrooms, which are equipped with either three single beds or one single and one double bed. There is also **camping** (RM5 per person). There is a simple canteen here as well.

The park office, canteen and accommodation are situated beside the highway 30km south of Miri. From Miri, any bus (RM3, 35 minutes) bound for Bekenu or Niah Junction can drop you here. A taxi from Miri costs RM40.

MIRI

☎ 085 / pop 177,800

An oil-rich boom town situated at the northern end of Sarawak, Miri is a major transport hub for travellers heading to/from Brunei, the Kelabit Highlands and three of Sarawak's national parks: Mulu, Niah Caves and Lambir Hills. The town itself is a somewhat poorly laid out jumble of big hotels, shops, restaurants and a surprising number of bars. While it's not the most prepossessing town in Borneo, it's still not a bad place to lay over for a day or two en route to or from the jungle.

Information

Cyber Corner (1st fl, Wisma Pelita, Jl Padang; per hr RM3)

Main post office (☎ 441222; Jl Post)

Maybank Bureau de Change (☎ 438467; 1271 Centre Point Commercial Centre; ⏰ 9am-5pm) Dedicated exchange and cash advance facilities.

Miri City Medical Centre (☎ 426622; 918 Jl Hockien) Private medical centre.

Miri General Hospital (☎ 420033; Jl Cayaha) South of town, off the Miri bypass.

Planet Café (1st fl, Bintang Plaza, 1264 Jl Miri Pujut; per hr RM4)

Popular Book Store (☎ 439052; 2nd fl, Bintang Plaza, 1264 Jl Miri Pujut)

Standard Chartered Bank (☎ 434944; Jl Calliandra) Changes travellers cheques.

Tally Laundry Services (☎ 430322; Jl Merbau; per kilo RM7; ⏰ 8am-6pm)

Unique Moneychanger (☎ 425757; 1328 Centre Point Commercial Centre; ⏰ 7am-9pm) Cash only.

Visitors Information Centre (☎ 434181; 452 Jl Melayu; ⏰ 8am-6pm Mon-Fri, 9am-3pm Sat & Sun) At the southern end of the town centre.

Sights & Activities

The atmospheric old part of town begins around the southern end of Jl Brooke; this is the area most worth exploring. There's plenty of lively commerce around the Chinese shophouse blocks, the **central market** and the **Tamu Muhibbah**, where local Dayak come to sell their vegetables. The wide courtyard of the **Tua Pek Kong temple**, near the fish market, is a good spot to watch the river traffic float by. During Chinese New Year, virtually the whole of this area is taken over by a lively street fair, which crams the crowds in under red lanterns and gold foil.

About 3km south of town, Miri has a passable beach and recreation park at **Brighton Beach**, where the open-air **Taman Selera** (food centre) juts out into the sea for perfect sunset dining. Further on, **Hawaii Beach** is a clean, palm-lined stretch of sand about 15 minutes outside town by bus. To get to either of the beaches, take bus 11 or 13 (RM1.50) from the local bus station.

Sleeping

Highlands (☎ 422327; www.borneojungles.com; 1271 Jl Sri Dagang; dm RM25, r from RM40; ❄ 💻) The only proper backpacker-style option for miles around, Highlands is a clean and popular place with dorms and private rooms. This is a great place to meet other travellers and the staff are informative about travel in Sarawak. It's on the top floor of a block of shops on the west side of town beside the Sungai Miri, above Wheels Café/Bar. Look for the five-storey car park.

Brooke Inn (☎ 412881; brookeinn@hotmail.com; 14 Jl Brooke; s/d/tr RM43/48/53; ❄) While it stops short of midrange quality, the Brooke Inn is better than most of its competitors. It's a little noisy, but is decent value. It's on Jl Brooke, smack dab in the middle of town.

Palace Inn (☎ 421999; siewpoh@pc.jaring.my; Lot 192 Jl Kwangtung; s/d from RM70/75; ❄ 💻) The Palace is significantly more comfortable and better run than most others in this price range and free wi-fi sweetens the deal. The tiled floors are a good move in this swampy Borneo climate. It's roughly in the centre of town, opposite the much larger Somerset Hotel.

Eating

Central Market (Jl Brooke; meals from RM2; 🕑 breakfast, lunch & dinner) The lively Central Market has a large hawker centre that covers all the bases of Malay, Indian and Chinese food. This is easily the cheapest and best place to eat in Miri. Across the street, you'll find still more choices at the similar Unity Food Centre. It's not far from Yu Lan Plaza, the high building in the centre of town.

Khan's Bilal Restaurant (229 Jl Maju; meals from RM3; 🕑 breakfast, lunch & dinner) This simple canteen is one of Miri's better Indian eateries, whipping up tasty treats such as tandoori chicken and *aloo gobi* (Indian potato-and-cauliflower dish), as well as the usual *roti canai* and a good biryani (rice baked with spices and meat, seafood or vegetables). The market is opposite Mega Hotel.

Apollo Seafood Centre (4 Jl South Yu Seng; meals from RM30; 🕑 lunch & dinner) This deservedly popular Chinese seafood restaurant is the best place for a splurge in Miri. Just about anything you order will be delicious, and we recommend the crabs and the fried *midin* with *belacan*. If you are a big spender, you could always go for some lobsters straight from the tank.

Drinking

Pelita Commercial Centre (cnr Jl Miri Pujut & Sehati) Those keen on a pub crawl might consider catching a taxi (about RM8) to this warren of small bar-lined streets 3km north of the centre. Anyone with an aversion to disco glitter balls, karaoke and expats need not apply for the experience.

Getting There & Away

AIR

Miri is well served by **Malaysia Airlines** (code MH; ☎ 1-300-883000; www.malaysiaairlines.com.my), which has Twin Otter services to Bario (RM110), Lawas (RM70), Limbang (RM65), Marudi (RM50) and Gunung Mulu (RM90). Larger aircraft fly direct to Bintulu (RM90), Sibu (RM130), Kuching (RM100), Pulau Labuan (RM50) and Kota Kinabalu (RM70). Book flights to/from Bario (one flight daily) or Mulu (two flights daily) as far in advance as possible.

Air Asia (code AK; ☎ 1-300-889933; www.airasia.com) does cheap flights between Miri and both KL and Johor Bahru.

BUS

Buses run from the long-distance bus terminal to Bintulu (RM20, 4½ hours), Sibu (RM40, 7½ hours) and Kuching (RM80, 14 hours).

GETTING TO BRUNEI

The ticket office at the local bus station sells a combined ticket (RM13) for travel on bus 2 (departs 7am, 10am, 1pm and 3.30pm) from Miri to the border crossing at Sungai Tujoh, and then on another bus to Kuala Belait. Including the drudgerous immigration formalities, the Miri–Kuala Belait trip takes about 2½ hours.

For information on crossing the border in the other direction, see p50.

From the local bus station, beside the visitors centre, bus 1A (RM4, 45 minutes) takes you to the wharf in Kuala Baram for Marudi-bound boats.

Getting Around

At the time of writing, a new long-distance bus terminal was under construction and it's not certain which local bus will make the run between the city and the new terminal. Ask on arrival.

Taxis from the airport to the city centre run on a coupon system (RM14).

GUNUNG MULU NATIONAL PARK

Gunung Mulu National Park (☎ 085-433561; www.mulupark.com; admission RM10; ⏲ park office 8am-5pm) may well be the single most impressive destination in all of Borneo. There are few parks in the world that pack so many natural marvels into such a small space. From some of the world's most incredible (and accessible) caves, to brilliant old-growth tropical rainforest, and some out and out natural oddities such as the Pinnacles formation on Mt Api, Mulu National Park is truly one of the world's great wonders.

Note that Mulu is only accessible by plane or an all-day river journey. Bring plenty of cash as there are no ATMs or credit card facilities.

Sights & Activities

Mulu's caves are its most popular attraction, and for good reason: they are awesome. The star of the lot is **Deer Cave**, which contains what's claimed to be the world's largest cave passage – over 2km in length and 174m in height. The cave is reached from the park headquarters by a fascinating 3km plankwalk. In an unfortunate bit of bureaucratic overkill, the park requires that you join a guided tour to the cave (RM10 per person, tours depart the park headquarters at 1.45pm and 2.30pm). After visiting Deer Cave, your guide will take you to the adjoining **Lang's Cave**, which is smaller but has some fascinating limestone formations.

After visiting Deer and Lang's Caves, your guide may take you to a viewing area where you can observe the giant mouth of Deer Cave, from which millions of bats issue forth in the late afternoon to feed on jungle insects. Problem is, this is not a daily occurrence and, more likely than not, you'll find yourself spending an hour or more peering hopefully at the cave entrance only for the sun to go down and your guide to have to lead you back to headquarters along the plankwalk in near total darkness (actually, we kind of liked that part).

Next on the Mulu menu are two more so-called 'show caves': **Wind Cave** and **Clearwater Cave**. Like Deer and Lang's Caves, the park requires that you join a guided tour to visit these caves (RM10 per person, tours depart park headquarters at 9.45am and 10.30am). However, in this case, it's worth it, and the fee includes a great boat trip up the Sungai Melinau. Wind Cave, first on the tour, contains several chambers filled with phantasmagorical forests of stalactites and stalagmites.

Clearwater Cave, another 400m away by river or plankwalk, is said to be the longest cave in Southeast Asia (the tour only visits a tiny segment of the cave near one of its mouths). The real highlight of Clearwater Cave is the underground river that runs through the chambers – it's straight out of *King Solomon's Mines*. Bring a swimsuit, because there's a wonderful swimming hole outside the entrance to Clearwater Cave.

If you like, you can walk back from these caves to the park headquarters via a concrete path and plankwalk that winds through the narrow passage of **Moonmilk Cave**. This is a highly recommended variation, but be warned that there is a steep climb en route, and you'll need a headlamp for the cave.

The next highlight of the park is its brilliant new **Mulu Canopy Skywalk**, easily the best in Southeast Asia. Once again, the park requires that you traverse it as part of a guided walk (RM30 per person, walks depart at 7am, 8.30am, 10.30am, 1pm, 2pm and 2.15pm). Despite the relatively steep cost, we urge you not to skip this attraction – every step of the 480m length is unforgettable. Climbing to the canopy is really the only way to see what a tropical rainforest is all about, since most of the action happens in the canopy, not on the ground.

Finally, if you've got more time, energy and money, you can climb to the 2376m summit of **Gunung Mulu**, a four-day excursion that will test anyone's stamina (guides are required and cost RM1000 for up to five people). Lesser mortals should consider the three-day trek to **the Pinnacles**, an incredibly bizarre collection of arrowhead-shaped limestone pinnacles that jut 50m out of the forest floor on the flank of Mt Api. Once again, a guide is needed for this strenuous climb (RM400 for up to five people).

Sleeping & Eating

Due to the park's popularity, it's best to book your accommodation in advance with **Mulu Park** (☎ 085-792300; enquiries@mulupark.com). You can also make bookings through the Visitors Information Centres in Kuching (p493) or Miri (p504).

Accommodation in the national park is in the form of a 21-bed **hostel** (dm RM20) and private **longhouse rooms** (r without/with air-con from RM50/80; ❄).

There are no cooking facilities. Simple but tasty meals are served at **Café Mulu** (meals RM4-9; 🕒 breakfast, lunch & dinner). There's also a pair of café-bars across the suspension bridge from the park headquarters.

Getting There & Around

Malaysia Airlines (code MH; ☎ 1-300-883000; www.malaysiaairlines.com.my) flies in direct from Miri (one way/return RM100/200) and Kota Kinabalu (one-way/return from RM200/390). The park office is a half-hour walk from the airstrip, or minivans can shuttle you to/from the terminal for RM3/5.

It's also possible to travel to Mulu from Miri by river, but it's a long, long journey and it actually costs more than flying. First, you must take a taxi from Miri to the pier at Kuala Beram to catch the 8am river express to Marudi (RM30, 2½ hours). From Marudi, take the noon boat upriver to Long Terawan (destination plate reads 'Tutoh'; RM20, six hours). Once there, you must charter a boat for the final three-hour journey upriver to the park (RM250). It's best to call ahead to the park to make sure that a boat will be available take you from Long Terawan to the park.

BARIO & THE KELABIT HIGHLANDS

☎ 085

A lovely hanging valley in eastern Sarawak, the Kelabit Highlands are tucked up against the Indonesian state of Kalimantan and ringed by jungle-covered mountains on all sides. The main population centre is the languid village of Bario, home to about 800 souls, mostly members of Borneo's indigenous Kelabit people. The main activity here, other than merely enjoying the clean, cool air, is trekking from longhouse to longhouse on mountain trails. The natural hospitality of the Kelabit people and the relatively unspoiled flora and fauna of the high jungle make any trip to the highlands a memorable experience, and we highly recommend it for those who have the time and energy.

There are no banks or credit-card facilities in the highlands so bring plenty of cash.

Activities

Guided treks range from overnight excursions to five-day slogs as far as distant villages such as Ba Kelalan. Every guesthouse and longhouse in Bario can arrange guides and accommodation, as well as transport to trailheads, if necessary. It's certainly possible to just turn up and make arrangements after you arrive, especially if you don't mind waiting a day or two in Bario before the start of your trek. If you're in a hurry, it makes sense to make arrangements by email or phone before you arrive.

The most popular trip is a two-night, three-day trek around the longhouses south of Bario, including Pa Dalih, Pa Ramadu and Pa Mada. This is sometimes called the Bario Loop, although it's less a loop than an out-and-back trek with a small loop at one end. Portions of this can be done by 4WD or riverboat. All three longhouses en route are welcoming, friendly places where you'll get a good glimpse into Kelabit life.

If you do intend to do some trekking, be sure to bring leech-resistant socks and proper footwear (light hikers or running shoes are better than heavy leather hiking boots). And be aware that the treks are fairly strenuous – you'll enjoy them a lot more if you get in shape before you arrive.

Going rates for guides (and porters if you need them) start at RM80 per day. To stay overnight in a longhouse, expect to pay RM40 per person (including food). Some treks involve either river trips (highly recommended if the water is high enough) or 4WD trips, which, naturally, significantly increase the cost of the trek.

Sleeping & Eating

All Bario accommodation options give you a choice between a bed-only price and a package deal that includes all meals (utilising Bario's famous long-grain rice) and transport.

Bariew Backpackers Lodge (☎ 791038; bariewlodge@yahoo.com; r per person RM15-20, incl meals RM45-55) Perfectly placed in Bario town, a short walk from the shops past the old airstrip, this is an excellent family-run guesthouse frequented by sociable locals as well as visitors. The proprietor, Reddish, knows everyone in town and has close ties with the longhouses on the treks around the highlands. As well as basic fan rooms, tasty meals and evening barbecues, the lodge can arrange guides and activities.

De Plateau Lodge (deplateau@gmail.com; r per person RM20, full-board package RM60) This is another good choice, with comfortable rooms and nice common areas. The owner here can arrange treks, bird-watching and other activities. It's located in a white-timber house surrounded by a lovely garden, 2km east of Bario; stick left when the road forks.

Getting There & Away

The only practical way to Bario is by air and it's easily one of the most exciting flights in Southeast Asia. After crossing the lowlands of western Sarawak, you sweep by the dense rainforest of Brunei, followed by the brilliant peaks of Gunung Mulu National Park (you can peer right into the yawning maw of Deer Cave) before flying by the fantastic spire of 2046m Batu Lawii (all of these sights are only visible from the left side of the aircraft as you fly from Miri to Bario).

Malaysia Airlines (code MH; ☎ 1-300-883000; www.malaysiaairlines.com.my) has at least one flight daily between Miri and Bario (return flight RM145, 50 minutes). Communication between the Malaysian Airlines office in Bario and other offices elsewhere is haphazard, so reconfirm your flight out of Bario as soon as you arrive. Flights are often booked out well in advance and are dependent on the weather; cancellations aren't uncommon.

It takes 25 minutes to walk into Bario from the airport. You should turn left at the T-junction.

If the planes are grounded and you really need to get back to Miri from Bario, guesthouse operators can arrange 4WD transport on logging roads down to Miri, but you'll have to pay around RM500 (and your butt cheeks will pay even more dearly as you bounce your way down the hellish roads).

GETTING TO BRUNEI

To Bandar Seri Begawan

Boats between Limbang and Bandar Seri Begawan (BSB) in Brunei (RM20 or B$10, 30 minutes) are infrequent in either direction and may not run after early afternoon; they leave from the jetty outside the immigration hall, upstream from the market.

From outside the riverfront immigration post, a minivan departs when it has enough passengers for Kuala Lurah (RM5, 45 minutes) on the Bruneian border; from here you catch a local bus to BSB (B$1, 30 minutes). The minivan driver isn't always in attendance but stay near the vehicle and eventually he'll turn up. If you're the only passenger and you want to leave for the border immediately, the driver won't budge for less than RM20. This service is far preferable to using local taxis, which can charge upwards of RM40 for the trip to Kuala Lurah, and to the local Limbang–Kuala Lurah bus service, which runs infrequently.

For details on coming in from Brunei, see boxed text, p49.

To Bangar

It is possible to travel from Limbang to Bangar in Brunei, but the trip is fiddly and we don't recommend it. There's no public transport, so you'll have to hire a private taxi, which is both expensive and difficult. If you do decide to make the journey, border posts are open daily from 6am to 9pm.

See p51 for information on doing the trip in reverse.

LIMBANG

☎ 085 / pop 3700

Limbang is the centre of the section of Sarawak that divides Brunei into two parts. It's of limited interest to travellers, but you may find yourself passing through here en route between Brunei and Sabah. Those expecting to find a sleepy backwater will be surprised to discover a bustling and relatively prosperous town on the banks of the Sungai Limbang.

Sleeping & Eating

Being a port town, most of Limbang's cheaper places are a little sleazy, with hourly rates and grotty rooms. You'll escape the sleaze by paying a bit more for midrange accommodation.

Metro Hotel (☎ 211133; Lot 781, Jl Bangkita; r from RM50;) If you can't be bothered to walk up to the Royal Park, the Metro is a just barely acceptable option in the middle of town. It's a little smoky and threadbare, but it's within easy walking distance of the jetty and the bus station.

Royal Park Hotel (☎ 212155; Lot 1089, Jl Buagsiol; r from RM60;) Much better value than the budget fleabags in the centre of town, it's worth the walk to get to this clean, well-run hotel. From the town centre, walk north (downstream) along the river. It's about 400m north of Limbang town centre, just in from the river.

There are food stalls on the 1st floor of the waterfront market, at the bus station and along the river. Basic Malay and Chinese food is served in *kedai kopi* in the town centre.

Getting There & Around

AIR

Malaysia Airlines (code MH; ☎ 1-300-883000; www.malaysiaairlines.com.my) has flights to Miri (RM65) and Kota Kinabalu (RM75). The airport is situated 4km south of the town centre, a RM10 taxi ride.

BOAT

The express boat to Pulau Labuan in Sabah leaves at 8.30am daily (RM25, two hours). When sufficient passengers turn up (you may find yourself waiting quite a while) speedboats go to Lawas in Sarawak (RM25, one hour) and to Bandar Seri Begawan in Brunei; see opposite for more details. Boats leave from the jetty outside the immigration hall on the river, just upstream from the large pink building housing the market (Bengunan Tamu Limbang).

> **GETTING TO BRUNEI**
>
> The road trip from Lawas to Bangar in Brunei's remote Temburong district will likely entail an expensive taxi ride. If you do decide to take this route, the border posts are open 6am to 9pm daily. From Bangar, it's a 45-minute boat trip to Bandar Seri Begawan.
>
> For information on crossing the Malaysia–Brunei border in the other direction, see p51.

LAWAS

☎ 085 / pop 1080

Lawas is a transit point in the sliver of Sarawak pinched between Sabah and the Temburong district of Brunei. There is little of interest to travellers, but you might find yourself here while en route between Sabah and Brunei. There is a branch of Maybank in the centre of town.

Hotel Perdana (☎ 285888; Lot 365 Jl Punang; r from RM46;) is the best economy hotel in town, although it's a little frayed round the edges. To get there, start with your back to the main market (Pasar Baru Lawas) and go left, following the main road out of town. The hotel will be on your right after about 300m.

There are several **Malaysia Airlines** (code MH; www.malaysiaairlines.com.my) flights each week to/from Miri (RM70). The airport is 2km from town.

A boat to Limbang (RM28, one hour) leaves at 9am daily but Thursday. A boat to Pulau Labuan (RM33, two hours) leaves at 7.30am every day except Tuesday and Thursday. Boats leave from the jetty on the west side of town, just downstream from the Shell station.

Buses head to Kota Kinabalu in Sabah (RM20) at 7am and 1pm daily.

MALAYSIA DIRECTORY

ACCOMMODATION

Accommodation in Malaysia costs slightly more than elsewhere in Southeast Asia. Be aware that you'll pay more for a place to stay in Malaysian Borneo than in Peninsular Malaysia, and that beach and island accommodation is generally more expensive than other mainland digs.

The cheapest accommodation is found at hostels and guesthouses (or backpackers) that cluster around tourist hot spots. These places often book tours and offer laundry services and transport.

A dorm bed costs anywhere from RM7 to RM30, fan-only rooms with a shared bathroom RM17 to RM40, and rooms with air-con and attached bathroom RM40 to RM60. Bathrooms are often a hand-held shower above a toilet with cold water.

In cities, most backpackers are on the top floors of multistorey buildings where lifts are about as conspicuous as a Bornean rhino. At beaches and smaller towns, accommodation ranges from A-frame chalets with a fan and attached bathroom to rooms in a private house.

For hotels, Chinese-run places are the cheapest, offering spartan rooms. The showers and toilets (sometimes Asian squat-style) may be down the corridor but are usually clean. Ultrabudget options will only have a *mandi* (dip shower, ie bucket and water).

Budget hotels can sometimes be terribly noisy as they're often on main streets and the walls rarely reach the ceiling – the top is simply meshed or barred in, which is great for ventilation but terrible for privacy.

Note that in Malaysia, 'single' often means one bed, as opposed to one person, and 'double' means two beds, or what we would call a twin. If you're after a double bed, just say 'one big bed'.

Check-out times are usually 11am or noon for hostels and guesthouses and from around noon until 3pm for hotels. See opposite for a warning about theft in guesthouses.

Many of Malaysia's national parks have camping grounds, and will also permit camping at nondesignated sites once you are into the back country. There are also many lonely stretches of beach through Malaysia, particularly on the peninsula's east coast, which are ideal for camping. Likewise, it is possible to camp on uninhabited bays on many of Malaysia's islands.

In Malaysia there's a 5% government tax (+; plus) that applies to hotel rooms. Additionally, there's a 10% service charge (++; plus plus) in more expensive places. Cheap Malaysian hotels generally quote a net price inclusive of the government tax, but double-check the total price before checking in.

Longhouses are the traditional dwellings of the indigenous peoples of Borneo, though some have been built just for tourists. The most important area of a longhouse is the common veranda, which serves as a social area and sometimes as sleeping space. If you want to see how Borneo's modern-day indigenous peoples live, a visit to a longhouse is a must. See p500 for more information on longhouses.

ACTIVITIES

Caving

Malaysia's limestone hills are riddled with caves. Some are easily accessible and can be visited without any special equipment or preparation, while others are strictly for experienced spelunkers. There are caves on the peninsula and dotted around Malaysian Borneo, including one of the world's premier caving destinations: Gunung Mulu.

Climbing

Sabah's Mt Kinabalu is an obvious choice for those interested in mountain climbing, but it isn't the only Malaysian mountain worth climbing. Sarawak's Gunung Mulu is a challenging four-day climb and, on the peninsula, there are overnight climbs in Taman Negara National Park.

Cycling

Peninsular Malaysia is one of the better places in Southeast Asia for bike touring but there is little in the way of organised tours. The most popular route heads up the east coast via relatively quiet, flat roads – Malaysian Borneo and the peninsular interior are more hilly while the west coast of the peninsula has more traffic. Wherever you go expect little road shoulder, fast and careless buses, high temperatures and rain. Carry lots of water. Rental bikes aren't usually of high standard so it's best to bring your own.

Diving & Snorkelling

Malaysia has many beautiful dive sites, decorated with shipwrecks, intricate coral formations and gloriously colourful marine life. It's also one of the cheapest places in the world to learn how to dive, with a four-day open-water course costing around RM850. Including boat and equipment hire, snorkelling costs from RM180 and three dives cost from RM280. Prime spots include Pulau Perhentian, Pulau

Redang and Pulau Tioman, but the best site of all is the spectacular limestone abyss off Pulau Sipadan.

Trekking

Despite intense logging, Malaysia is still home to some of the world's most impressive stands of virgin tropical jungle. Almost all of Malaysia's national parks offer excellent jungle trekking, including Taman Negara and the Cameron Highlands on the peninsula, and Gunung Mulu National Park in Sarawak.

BOOKS

Lonely Planet's *Malaysia, Singapore & Brunei* has all the information you'll need for extended travel to these countries. Lonely Planet also publishes the *Malay Phrasebook*, an introduction to the Malay language.

Although *Lord Jim* is based on the exploits of absconding seaman AP Williams, Joseph Conrad's tale of derring-do on the South China Seas also recalls the real-life story of Raja Brooke of Sarawak. Wallow in tales of life in Malaysia (and Singapore) during colonial times by reading *Malaysian Stories*, penned by short-story master Somerset Maugham.

For glimpses of traditional village life, try to track down the translations of fine Malaysian writers offered in the paperback series, Oxford in Asia: Modern Authors.

A work of contemporary Malaysian fiction (in English) that's wholeheartedly recommended is KS Maniam's *The Return*. Maniam shines a light on the Indian Malaysian experience through his character's search for a home on returning from being educated abroad. For more modern Malaysian fiction, including plays and poetry, keep an eye out for books published by KL-based **Silverfish Books** (www.silverfishbooks.com).

Budding explorers should read *Stranger in the Forest*, Eric Hansen's account of a remarkable half-year journey across Borneo on foot, and Redmond O'Hanlon's marvellous *Into the Heart of Borneo*. Essential reading for anyone intending to do a lot of local mountain walking is *Mountains of Malaysia – A Practical Guide and Manual*, by John Briggs.

BUSINESS HOURS

Usual business hours in Malaysia:

Banks 10am to 3pm Monday to Friday, 9.30am to 11.30am Saturday
Department stores 10am to 8pm
Government offices 8am to 12.45pm and 2pm to 4.15pm Monday to Thursday, 8am to 12.15pm and 2.45pm to 4.15pm Friday, 8am to 12.45pm Saturday
Shopping malls 10am to 8pm
Shops 9am to 6pm Monday to Saturday

In the more Islamic-minded states of Kedah, Perlis, Kelantan and Terengganu, government offices, banks and many shops close on Friday and on Saturday afternoon.

Exceptions to these hours are noted in individual reviews.

CLIMATE

Malaysia is hot and humid year-round. The temperature rarely drops below 20°C, even at night, and usually climbs to 30°C or higher during the day.

It rains throughout the year. Peninsular Malaysia gets heavier rainfall from September to March, with the east coast bearing the full brunt of the monsoon rains from November to February. Rainfall on the west coast peaks slightly during the May to October monsoon. Malaysian Borneo also gets the northeast and southwest monsoons, but they are less pronounced and rain tends to be variable.

See p916 for more information.

CUSTOMS

When arriving in Malaysia, note that you are legally entitled to carry 1L of alcohol and 200 cigarettes. Other restrictions limit you to only one pair of shoes and three items of clothing, but this is unlikely to be enforced. Trafficking of illegal substances can result in the death penalty – don't do it.

DANGERS & ANNOYANCES

In general Malaysia is very safe, with violent attacks being uncommon. However, the usual travel precautions apply, such as restraining your urge to go wandering around seedy areas alone late at night. Credit-card fraud is a growing problem so only use your cards at established businesses and guard your credit-card numbers. The snatching of bags by thieves on motorcycles is a recurring crime in KL and Penang's Georgetown, so keep bags away from the roadside in these areas. In seedy areas such as Ipoh and KL's Golden Triangle, male travellers may be harassed to buy pirated porn DVDs, drugs or the services of prostitutes.

A disturbingly high incidence of theft occurs in guesthouse dorms. Sometimes this involves an outsider sneaking in and other times it involves fellow travellers. Don't leave valuables or important documents unattended, and carry a small padlock.

See p516 for issues specific to women travellers.

Rabies is an ever present problem in Malaysia – you should treat any animal bite very seriously. Leeches can be a nuisance after heavy rain on jungle walks; see p473 for tips on discouraging them.

DRIVING LICENCE

A valid overseas driving licence is required for vehicle rental.

EMBASSIES & CONSULATES

Embassies & Consulates in Malaysia

Embassies and consulates are in Kuala Lumpur unless otherwise indicated. Most embassies are located east of the city, along Jl Ampang (off Map pp424–5). For information on visas see p516.

Australia Kuala Lumpur (Map pp424-5; ☎ 03-2146 5555; 6 Jl Yap Kwan Seng); Kota Kinabalu (☎ 088-267151; Suite 10.1, 10th fl, Wisma Great Eastern Life, 65 Jl Gaya)
Brunei (off Map pp424-5; ☎ 03-2161 2800; 19-01 Tingkat 19, Menara Tan & Tan, Embassy Row)
Canada (☎ 03-2718 3333; 7th fl, Plaza OSK, 172 Jl Ampang)
France (☎ 03-2162 0671; Pesuruhjaya Tinggi Perancis, Jl Ampang)
Germany (off Map pp424-5; ☎ 03-2175 1666; Menara Tan & Tan, Jl Tun Razak, Embassy Row)
Indonesia Kuala Lumpur (off Map pp424-5; ☎ 03-2142 1151; 233 Jl Tun Razak); Georgetown (☎ 04-227 4686; 467 Jl Burma); Kuching (☎ 082-241734; 111 Jl Tun Abang Haji Openg); Kota Kinabalu (☎ 088-218600; Jl Kemajuan); Tawau (☎ 089-752969; Jl Tanjong Batu)
Ireland (☎ 03-2161 2963; 5th fl, The Ampwalk, 218 Jl Ampang)
Japan (☎ 03-2142 7044; 11 Persiaran Stonor)
Netherlands (☎ 03-2161 0148; 7th fl, The Ampwalk, 218 Jl Ampang)
New Zealand (Map p429; ☎ 03-2078 2533; 21st fl, Menara IMC, 8 Jl Sultan Ismail)
Philippines (☎ 03-2148 9989; Jl Changkat Kia Peng)
Singapore (off Map pp424-5; ☎ 03-2161 6277; 209 Jl Tun Razak)
Thailand Kuala Lumpur (☎ 03-2148 8222; Jl Ampang); Kota Bharu (☎ 09-744 0867; Jl Pengkalan Chepa); Georgetown (☎ 04-226 8029; 1 Jl Tunku Abdul Rahman)
UK (☎ 03-2148 2122; 185 Jl Ampang)
USA (off Map pp424-5; ☎ 03-2168 5000; 376 Jl Tun Razak)

Malaysian Embassies & Consulates Abroad

For a full list of Malaysian embassies and consulates abroad, check out www.tourism.gov.my.

Australia (☎ 02-6273 1543; mwcnbera@aucom.com.au; 7 Perth Ave, Yarralumla, ACT 2600)
Brunei (☎ 238 1095; mwbrunei@brunet.bn; 61 Simpang 336, Jl Kebangsaan, Bandar Seri Begawan BS 4115)
Canada (☎ 613-241 5182; mwottawa@istar.ca; 60 Boteler St, Ottawa, Ontario K1N 8Y7)
France (☎ 01 45 53 11 85; mwparis@wanadoo.fr; 2 bis, rue Benouville, 75116 Paris)
Germany (☎ 030-885 7490; mwberlin@compuserve.com; Klingelhofer Strasse 6, 10785 Berlin)
Indonesia (☎ 21-522 4947; mwjakarta@indosat.net.id; 1-3 Jl HR Rasuna Said, Jakarta 12950)
Japan (☎ 03-3476 3840; mwtokyo@malaysia.or.jp; 20-16, Nanpeidai-cho, Shibuya-ku, Tokyo 150 0036)
Netherlands (☎ 070-350 6506; mwthehague@euronet.nl; Rustenburgweg 2, 2517 KE, The Hague)
New Zealand (☎ 04-385 2439; mwwelton@xtra.co.nz; 10 Washington Ave, Brooklyn, PO Box 9422, Wellington)
Singapore (☎ 6235 0111; 30 Hill St 02-01)
Thailand (☎ 02-679 2190; mwbangkok@samart.co.th; 35 Sth Sathorn Rd, Tungmahamek Sathorn, Bangkok 10120)
UK (☎ 020-7235 8033; mwlondon@btlnternet.com; 45-46 Belgrave Sq, London SW1X 8QT)
USA (☎ 202-572 9700; malwash@kln.gov.my; 3516 International Court NW, Washington, DC 20008)

FESTIVALS & EVENTS

There are many cultures and religions coexisting in Malaysia, which means there are many occasions for celebration throughout the year. Some holidays (see opposite) also involve festivities.

A few of the major events:

January/February

Thaipusam (January/February) One of the most dramatic Hindu festivals, in which devotees honour Lord Subramaniam with acts of amazing physical resilience. Self-mutilating worshippers make the procession to the Batu Caves outside KL.

May–August

Gawai Dayak (late May/early June) Festival of the Dayaks in Sarawak, marking the end of the rice season. War dances, cock fights and blowpipe events take place.
Dragon Boat Festival (June to August) Celebrated in Penang.

September

Moon Cake Festival (September) Chinese festival celebrating the overthrow of Mongol warlords in ancient China with the eating of moon cakes and the lighting of colourful paper lanterns.

October/November

Festival of the Nine Emperor Gods (October) Involves nine days of Chinese operas, processions and other events honouring the nine emperor gods.

Fire-walking Ceremonies (October/November) Held in KL and Penang.

Deepavali (November) The Festival of Lights, in which tiny oil lamps are lit outside Hindu homes, celebrates Rama's victory over the demon King Ravana.

Ramadan is the major annual Muslim event, connected with the 30 days during which Muslims cannot eat, drink, smoke or have sex from sunrise to sunset. The dates of Ramadan change every year; in 2008 it begins on 1 September, and in 2009 it begins on 21 August.

FOOD & DRINK

Food

Mealtime in Malaysia is a highly social event and the food strongly reflects the country's Malay, Chinese and Indian influences. You can feast at hawker stalls for RM1 to RM3. A meal in a restaurant costs around RM4 to RM15.

There are less culinary choices outside the cities, where staple meals of *mee goreng* (fried noodles) and *nasi goreng* (fried rice) predominate. Vegetarian dishes are usually available at both Malay and Indian cafés, but are hardly sighted at *kedai kopi* (coffee shops). You can also find an excellent selection of fruits and vegetables at markets.

Roti canai (flaky flat bread dipped in a small amount of dhal and potato curry) is probably the cheapest meal (from 80 sen) in Malaysia but don't let price completely limit your diet. Try a bit of everything, from seafood laksa to the freshly caught and cooked wild cat or mouse deer you may be offered at a longhouse. Speaking of sweets, halfway between a drink and a dessert is *ais kacang*, something like an old-fashioned snow-cone; however, the shaved ice is topped with syrups and condensed milk, and it's all piled on top of a foundation of beans and jellies (sometimes corn kernels). It sounds and looks gross but tastes terrific.

Drink

Tap water is safe to drink in many cities but check with locals if you're unsure.

With the aid of a blender and crushed ice, delicious juice concoctions are whipped up in seconds. Lurid soybean drinks are sold at street stalls and soybean milk is also available in soft-drink bottles. Medicinal teas are a big hit with the health-minded Chinese.

Alcohol isn't popular with the Muslim population and incurs incredibly high taxes. A mug of beer at a *kedai kopi* will cost around RM6, and around RM12 to RM15 at bars and clubs. Anchor and Tiger beers are popular, as are locally brewed Carlsberg and Guinness. Indigenous people have a soft spot for *tuak* (rice wine), which tends to revolt first-timers but is apparently an acquired taste. Another rural favourite is the dark-coloured spirit *arak*, which is smooth and potent.

GAY & LESBIAN TRAVELLERS

Conservative political parties and religious groups make a regular habit of denouncing gays and lesbians in Malaysia, a country where Muslim homosexuality is punishable by imprisonment and caning. Fortunately, these groups remain on the fringe and outright persecution of gays and lesbians is rare. Nonetheless, while in Malaysia, gay and lesbian travellers (particularly the former) should avoid behaviour that attracts unwanted attention. Personal accounts from gays and lesbians living in Malaysia are provided on www.utopia-asia.com/tipsmala.htm and www.utopia-asia.com/wommala.htm.

HOLIDAYS

Although some public holidays have a fixed annual date, Hindus, Muslims and Chinese follow a lunar calendar, which means the dates for many events vary each year. Chinese New Year is the year's most important celebration for the Chinese community and is marked with dragon dances and street parades. Families have an open house, unmarried relatives (especially children) receive *ang pow* (money in red packets), businesses traditionally clear their debts and everybody wishes you a *kong hee fatt choy* (a happy and prosperous new year).

The major holiday of the Muslim calendar, Hari Raya Puasa marks the end of the month-long fast of Ramadan with three days of joyful celebration; in 2008 and 2009, this will fall in September or October.

During Hari Raya Puasa and Chinese New Year, accommodation may be difficult to obtain. At these times, many businesses may also be closed and transport can be fully booked.

National holidays:

New Year's Day 1 January
Chinese New Year January/February
Birth of the Prophet March
Wesak Day April/May
Labour Day 1 May
Agong's (King's) Birthday 1st Saturday in June
National Day 31 August
Hari Raya Puasa September/October
Deepavali November
Hari Raya Haji December
Awal Muharam December
Christmas Day 25 December

INTERNET ACCESS

Internet access is widespread and available at numerous internet cafés, backpacker hang-outs and shopping malls, generally on fast broadband connections. In cities, rates range from RM2 to RM4 per hour; on islands and in remote areas, rates skyrocket (and speed plummets) to around RM6 to RM10 per hour.

INTERNET RESOURCES

Lonely Planet (www.lonelyplanet.com) Succinct summaries on travelling to Southeast Asia, and the Thorn Tree bulletin board; including the Travel Links site for other useful travel resources.
Malaysiakini (www.malaysiakini.com) Practically Malaysia's only independent daily news source, with uncensored features and commentaries.
Tourism Malaysia (www.tourism.gov.my) The official government site for tourist information, with events calendars, regional links, background information and listings of domestic and international tourist offices.

LEGAL MATTERS

In any of your dealings with the local police, it pays to be deferential. Minor misdemeanours may be overlooked, but don't count on it and don't offer anyone a bribe.

It's simply not worth having anything to do with drugs in Malaysia: drug trafficking carries a mandatory death penalty, and even possession of tiny amounts of drugs for personal use can bring about a lengthy jail sentence and a beating with the *rotan* (cane).

MAPS

The best map for Peninsular Malaysia is the 1:650,000 *West Malaysia* map produced by Nelles Verlag. Nelles also produces *Malaysia*, which shows both Peninsular Malaysia and Malaysian Borneo. Periplus produces an excellent series of Malaysia city and state maps, including *Johor*, *Kuala Lumpur*, *Melaka*, *Penang*, *Sabah* and *Sarawak*.

Tourism Malaysia's *The Map of Malaysia* has useful distance charts and inset maps of many major cities.

MEDIA

The government tightly controls the main media outlets, and will often pursue its critics through the courts. The main newspapers tend to parrot the official line and the less said about news on Malaysian TV channels, the better.

Newspapers

Malaysia has newspapers in English, Malay, Chinese and Tamil. The *New Straits Times* is the main English-language publication, while *Borneo Post* focuses more on issues relevant to Sabah and Sarawak. Foreign magazines are widely available.

Radio

There's a variety of radio stations in Malaysia broadcasting in Bahasa Malaysia, English and various Chinese and Indian languages and dialects. The number of English stations is highest around KL, while radio-wave pickings are scarce in Malaysian Borneo.

TV

Malaysia has two government TV channels (RTM 1 and 2) and two commercial stations. Programmes range from local productions in various languages to Western imports.

MONEY

For information on basic costs, see Fast Facts (p413).

The Malaysian ringgit (RM) consists of 100 sen. Coins in use are one, five, 10, 20 and 50 sen, and RM1; notes come in RM1, RM2, RM5, RM10, RM50 and RM100. Locals sometimes refer to the ringgit as a 'dollar'.

The ringgit, pegged to the US dollar until 2005, now floats against an undisclosed basket of currencies. At the time of writing, US$1 was RM3.50.

Bargaining & Tipping

Bargaining is not usually required for everyday goods in Malaysia, but feel free to bargain when purchasing souvenirs, antiques and other tourist items, even when the prices are displayed. Transport prices are generally fixed, but negotiation is required for trishaws and taxis around town or for charter.

Tipping is not common in Malaysia.

Exchanging Money

The US dollar is the most convenient currency to take to Malaysia, but you'll have no problems changing other major currencies either.

Banks are efficient and there are plenty of moneychangers in the main centres. Credit cards are widely accepted and many ATMs accept international key cards, Visa and MasterCard. Some banks are also connected to networks such as Cirrus, Maestro and Plus.

Exchange rates at the time of press:

Country	Unit	Ringgit (RM)
Australia	A$1	2.90
Brunei	B$1	2.35
Canada	C$1	3.35
Euro zone	€1	4.85
Indonesia	10,000Rp	3.75
Japan	¥100	3.10
New Zealand	NZ$1	2.45
Philippines	P100	7.55
Singapore	S$1	2.30
Thailand	100B	10.90
UK	UK£1	7.15
USA	US$1	3.50

POST

There are poste restante services at all major post offices, which are open from 8am to 5pm daily except Sunday and public holidays (also closed on Friday in Kedah, Kelantan and Terengganu districts).

Aerograms and postcards cost 50 sen to send to any destination. Letters weighing 10g or less cost 90 sen to Asia, RM1.40 to Australia or New Zealand, RM1.50 to the UK and Europe, and RM1.80 to North America.

You can send parcels from any major post office, although the rates are fairly high (from RM20 to RM60 for a 1kg parcel, depending on the destination).

RESPONSIBLE TRAVEL

Malaysia has a serious rubbish problem, so try to create as little waste as possible by drinking tea or fresh juice instead of packaged drinks and eating locally grown food; if possible, bring your own water filter to avoid buying water in plastic bottles. When diving and snorkelling never touch or walk on coral and avoid tour operators who practise poor ecological habits such as dropping anchor on coral. Try to buy local handicrafts and souvenirs in preference to mass-produced items, so that the money goes back to local communities. It might seem obvious, but never buy butterflies or any products made from endangered species.

STUDYING

Several of Malaysia's cultural centres offer classes in traditional Malaysian handicrafts. Kota Bharu and Cherating are the best places to get a hands-on feel for batik, puppet making and kite making, while Kuala Lumpur is the place to study Bahasa Malaysia. Cooking courses are occasionally offered in Kuala Lumpur and Penang.

See p429 for some options in KL, or ask at local tourist offices to see what's on offer when you're in town.

TELEPHONE

International direct dial (IDD) phone calls and operator-assisted calls can be made from any private phone. The access code for making international calls to most countries is ☎ 00. For information on international calls, dial ☎ 103. For operator-assisted calls, dial ☎ 108. Phone calls to Singapore are STD (long-distance) rather than international.

To make an IDD call from a pay phone, look for a Telekom pay phone marked 'international' (with which you can use coins or Telekom phonecards; dial the international access code and then the number). However, these phones are often in disrepair and frustratingly difficult to find.

Alternatively, you can buy the phonecards of other companies (such as Uniphone and Cityphone) and look for the corresponding pay phone. But there's no guarantee you'll find phones belonging to the same company in the next town you visit and your card may then be useless. The best option is to make a pay-per-minute call from a shop with an IDD-STD phone or at the Telekom office.

The card phones mentioned above all allow STD calls. Local calls cost 10 sen for three minutes.

If you have arranged 'global roaming' facilities with your home provider, your GSM digital phone will automatically tune into one of the region's digital networks. If not, and you are carrying your phone with you, the simplest way to go mobile is to buy a prepaid SIM card on arrival in the country.

TOILETS

Western-style toilets are slowly replacing the Asian squat-style toilet in many towns, hence the doors of some newly installed sit-down toilets carry a poster with a diagram instructing locals not to squat on top of the toilet seat. A hose to be used as a bidet is in most toilets; cheaper places have a bucket of water and a tap. Toilet paper (and soap) are rarely provided.

Public toilets in shopping malls and at transport depots are usually staffed by attendants and cost 10 sen to 30 sen to use; an extra 10 sen often gets you a dozen sheets of toilet paper.

TOURIST INFORMATION

Domestic tourist offices are usually helpful and can often (but not always) provide specific information on accommodation, attractions and transport. Within Malaysia there are also various state tourist-promotion organisations, which often have more information about specific areas.

Tourism Malaysia (Map pp424-5; ☎ 03-2615 8188; www.tourism.gov.my; 17th fl, Putra World Trade Centre, 45 Jl Tun Ismail, Kuala Lumpur) has overseas offices, which are useful for predeparture planning.

TRAVELLERS WITH DISABILITIES

For the mobility impaired, Malaysia can be a nightmare. In most cities and towns there are often no footpaths, kerbs are very high and pedestrian crossings are few and far between. Budget hotels almost never have lifts. On the upside, KL's modern urban railway lines are reasonably wheelchair-accessible.

Malaysia Airlines and Keretapi Tanah Melayu (the national railway service) offer 50% discounts for disabled travellers.

VISAS

Visitors must have a passport valid for at least six months beyond the date of entry into Malaysia. Nationals of most countries are given a 30- to 90-day visa on arrival.

Commonwealth citizens (except those from India, Bangladesh, Sri Lanka and Pakistan) and citizens of Austria, Belgium, the Czech Republic, Denmark, Finland, France, Germany, Hungary, Iceland, Ireland, Italy, Japan, Luxembourg, the Netherlands, Norway, Slovakia, South Africa, South Korea, Sweden, the USA and most Arab countries should not require a visa for a visit of less than three months.

Citizens of many South American and African countries do not require a visa for a visit not exceeding one month. Most other nationalities are given a shorter stay period or require a visa. Citizens of Israel cannot enter Malaysia.

Sarawak is semi-autonomous. If you travel from Peninsular Malaysia or Sabah into Sarawak, your passport will be checked on arrival and a new stay-permit issued, either for 30 days or for the same period as your original Malaysia entry visa. See p493 for more details.

For more information (albeit scant), see the website of the **Malaysian Ministry of Foreign Affairs** (www.kln.gov.my). For listings of embassies and consulates in Malaysia, and of Malaysian embassies and consulates abroad, see p512.

VOLUNTEERING

For volunteering opportunities, check out online directories such as **Volunteer Abroad** (www.volunteerabroad.com), which detail conservation and community programmes, or charity organisations such as **Raleigh International** (www.raleigh.org.uk/volunteer/nonuk.html). Check www.mycen.com.my/malaysia/ngo.html for a list of NGOs.

WOMEN TRAVELLERS

Foreign women travelling in Malaysia can expect some attention, though a lot of it will just involve stares from locals unfamiliar with (or curious about) Westerners. It helps if you dress conservatively by wearing long pants or skirts and loose tops. Western women are not expected to cover their heads with scarves (outside of mosques, that is).

Malaysia's islands are fairly easy-going, but while travelling on the mainland, especially on the peninsula's east coast and in Malaysian Borneo, women should cover themselves from shoulders to knees. It isn't appropriate to sunbathe topless on beaches.

Tampons and pads are widely available, especially in big cities, and over-the-counter medications are also fairly easy to find.

Myanmar (Burma)

HIGHLIGHTS

- **Bagan** – witness the beauty of a misty dawn breaking over 4000 Buddhist temples on the shores of the Ayeyarwady (p562)
- **Inle Lake** – take to the water at this pristine lake (p547), a mythical landscape of floating villages, stilted monasteries and aquatic gardens
- **Around Mandalay** – Burma's former capital (p559) is the gateway to the intriguing old cities of Amarapura with its famed teak bridge, and some stupa-pendous views from Sagaing
- **Yangon** – forget Naypyidaw, Yangon (p528) is the social, economic and cultural capital of the country, home to the dazzling Shwedagon Paya where all that glitters *is* gold
- **Kalaw** – something of a backpacker scene, Myanmar's trekking HQ (p550) is the spot to view pretty scenery and visit friendly minority villages
- **Off the beaten track** – make a pilgrimage to the gravity-defying golden rock of Kyaiktiyo (p544), a sacred and surreal sight

FAST FACTS

- **Budget** US$15 to US$25 a day
- **Capital** Naypyidaw is the new one, but it's still Yangon to you and me
- **Costs** guesthouse US$3 to US$8, four-hour bus ride US$2 to US$3, big bottle of beer US$1.50
- **Country code** ☎ 95
- **Languages** Burmese, English
- **Money** US$1 = about K1250 (kyat)
- **Phrases** *min gala ba* (hello), *thwa-ba-oun-meh* (goodbye), *chè zù bèh* (thanks)
- **Population** about 52 million
- **Time** GMT + 6½ hours
- **Visas** around US$20 for 28 days, issued by Myanmar embassies and consulates abroad

TRAVEL HINT

Many visitors use up a 28-day visa travelling in and around the 'big four' – Yangon, Inle Lake, Mandalay and Bagan. Don't try to pack too much in, as overland travel takes time. If you're flying out, you can easily overstay your visa by a week or more, at a penalty of US$3 per day (see p582).

OVERLAND ROUTES

It is possible to enter Myanmar from Ruili in China, and from Mae Sai and Ranong in Thailand.

'This is Burma', wrote Kipling. 'It is quite unlike any place you know about.' How right he was, and more than a century later Myanmar remains a world apart. Contemplate 4000 sacred stupas scattered across the plains of Bagan. Stare in disbelief at the golden rock teetering impossibly on the edge of a chasm. Encounter men wearing skirt-like *longyi*, women smothered in *thanaka* (traditional make-up) and betel-chewing grannies with blood red juices dripping from their mouths – and that's just the airport! Meet the multitalented monks who have taught their cats to jump. Ride a Wild West stagecoach past grand British mansions. Trade jokes about the rulers who move capitals on the whim of a fortune teller. Indeed, this is Burma.

Turn back the clock with a trip to this time-warped country where the adventure travel of old lives on. This is the authentic Asia with creaking buses, potholed roads, locals who greet you like long lost family and not a 7-Eleven in sight. Forget the internet for a moment and connect with a culture where holy men are more revered than rock stars and golden buddhas are bathed every day at first light. Drift down the Ayeyarwady in an old river steamer, stake out a slice of beach on the blissful Bay of Bengal, trek through pine forests to minority villages around Kalaw – there are so many experiences awaiting in Myanmar that one trip is simply never enough. It's a country that fuels your emotions, stimulates your senses and stays in your soul.

Isolated and ostracised by the international community, the country is in the grip of tyrants. Most travellers avoid a visit, backing the boycott, but the long-suffering people are everything the regime is not. Gentle, humorous, engaging, considerate and inquisitive, they want to play a part in the world. They are some of the sweetest people on earth and deserve a brighter future.

CURRENT EVENTS

Events took a surreal turn in November 2005 with the relocation of the capital to remote Naypyidaw, about 400km northeast of Yangon (Rangoon). The name means 'Royal City' or 'Abode of the Kings', suggesting the generals have delusions of grandeur. Foreigners are not officially allowed to visit and embassies are staying put in Yangon. Many government staff were forced to relocate under the threat of arrest and imprisonment.

Changing capitals aside, it has been business as usual. Democracy leader Aung San Suu Kyi remains under house arrest, which was extended for another year in May 2006. Sanctions remain in place, although they don't seem to be hurting the leadership, only the average person in the street. Asean continues to duck the subject of Burmese democracy in the interest of 'noninterference', although this seems to be creating a split in the organisation, with 'southern' members such as Malaysia, Indonesia and Singapore being more critical of the regime and 'northern' members such as Cambodia, Laos and Vietnam almost apologetic. EU pressure at least saw several important regional meets in Myanmar cancelled.

Hardline General Than Shwe continues to wield power. A secret video of his daughter's lavish wedding made its way on to YouTube in 2006, and further outraged the international community with its excess. It is in stark contrast to the way 'the lady' is forced to live under house arrest, denied basic communication.

Systematic abuse of ethnic minorities, verging on ethnic cleansing in the case of the Rohingya and others, continues in remote border regions of the country. Opium poppies and the 'Big H' (heroin) provide money and arms to forces on both sides of the conflict. Meanwhile the country's assets such as timber and minerals continue to be sold off at a pinch in return for political legitimacy in Beijing.

In August 2007, the military regime suspended fuel subsidies, sending the price of petrol skyrocketing. Monks took to the streets in an outpouring of popular protest and when the army opened fire on demonstrators, anger spread nationwide. For a moment, it looked like Myanmar might enjoy its own saffron revolution, but the army cracked down hard.

The international reaction was swift and strong, but its impact was muted by the silence of China and India, two of the regime's biggest backers. However, the government has lost any lingering legitimacy with its brutal treatment of the monks, and have been forced to accept the return of UN envoys. There is a glimmer of hope that a compromise can be reached, but it may simply be yet another smokescreen put in place by the generals.

HISTORY

Myanmar was ruled with an iron fist long before the current regime came to power. From the early 19th century until WWII, the insatiable machine that was the British Empire held sway over Burma. Before the

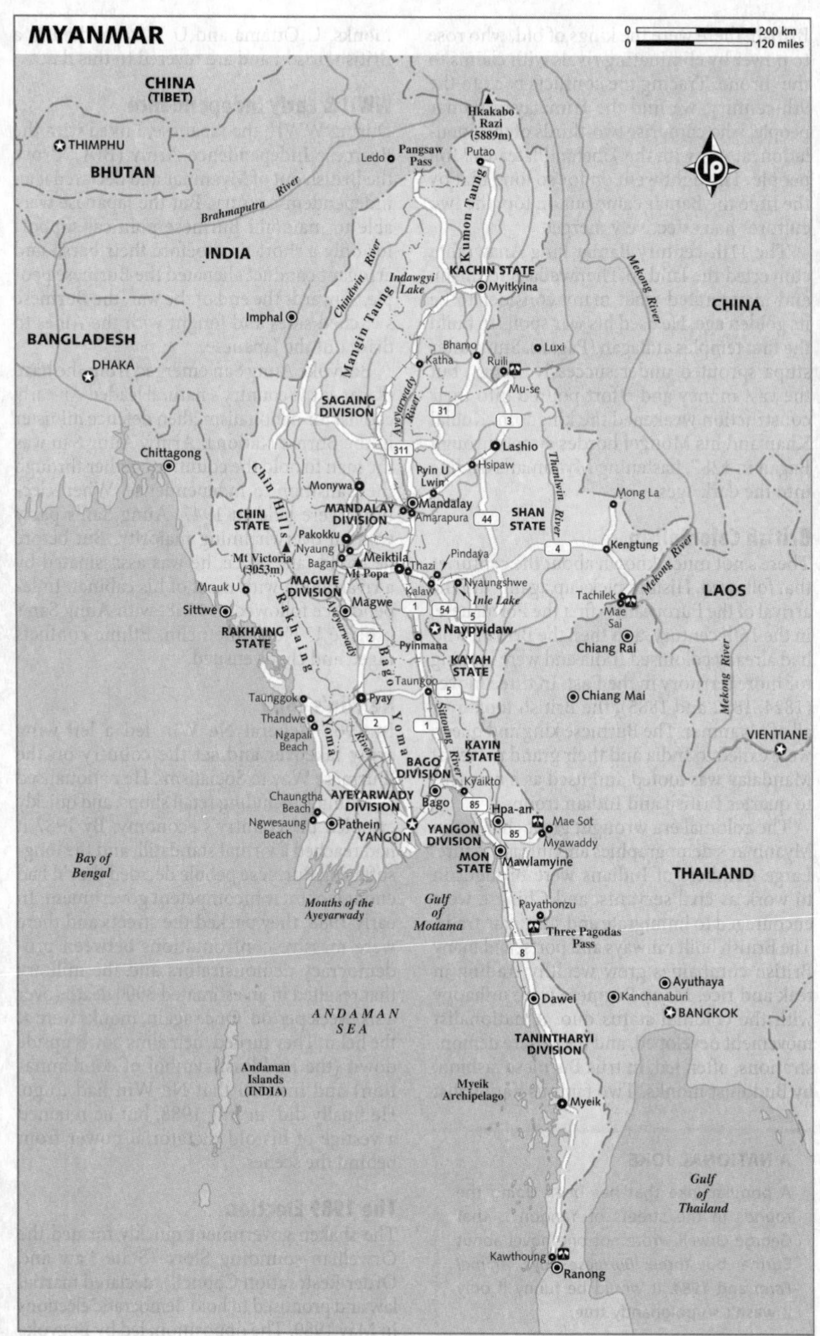
MYANMAR
0 200 km
0 120 miles
CHINA (TIBET)
THIMPHU
BHUTAN
Brahmaputra River
INDIA
BANGLADESH
DHAKA
Chittagong
Ledo
Pangsaw Pass
Hkakabo Razi (5889m)
Putao
Kumon Taung
Chindwin River
Indawgyi Lake
Mangin Taung
KACHIN STATE
Myitkyina
Imphal
Mekong River
CHINA
Bhamo
Luxi
Katha
Ruili
Mu-se
SAGAING DIVISION
Ayeyarwady River
31
3
311
Lashio
Hsipaw
Pyin U Lwin
Thanlwin River
Monywa
Chin Hills
Mandalay
MANDALAY DIVISION
Amarapura
44
SHAN STATE
Mong La
CHIN STATE
Pakokku
Nyaung U
Bagan
Mt Victoria (3053m)
Meiktila
Mt Popa
Thazi
Pindaya
Nyaungshwe
Inle Lake
Kalaw
4
Kengtung
Mekong River
Mrauk U
MAGWE DIVISION
Magwe
Tachilek
Mae Sai
LAOS
Sittwe
RAKHAING STATE
Rakhaing
Ayeyarwady
1
54
5
Naypyidaw
Chiang Rai
2
Pyinmana
Bago
KAYAH STATE
Taungoo
5
Chiang Mai
Mekong River
Taunggok
Pyay
Thandwe
Ngapali Beach
Yoma
River
2
Yoma
1
Sittoung River
KAYIN STATE
VIENTIANE
BAGO DIVISION
Kyaikto
Chaungtha Beach
AYEYARWADY DIVISION
Bago
85
Hpa-an
Mae Sot
Ngwesaung Beach
Pathein
YANGON
YANGON DIVISION
85
Myawaddy
MON STATE
Mawlamyine
THAILAND
Bay of Bengal
Mouths of the Ayeyarwady
Gulf of Mottama
Payathonzu
Three Pagodas Pass
8
Ayuthaya
Dawei
Kanchanaburi
BANGKOK
ANDAMAN SEA
TANINTHARYI DIVISION
Andaman Islands (INDIA)
Myeik Archipelago
Myeik
Gulf of Thailand
Kawthoung
Ranong

British, there were the kings of old, who rose to power by eliminating rivals with claims to the throne. Tracing the conflicts back to the 9th century, we find the Himalayan Bamar people, who comprise two-thirds of the population, at war with the Tibetan Plateau's Mon people. The fight went on for so long that by the time the Bamar came out on top, the two cultures had effectively merged.

The 11th-century Bamar king Anawrahta converted the land to Theravada Buddhism, and inaugurated what many consider to be its golden age. He used his war spoils to build the first temples at Bagan (Pagan). Stupa after stupa sprouted under successive kings, but the vast money and effort poured into their construction weakened the kingdom. Kublai Khan and his Mongol hordes swept through Bagan in 1287, hastening Myanmar's decline into the dark ages.

British Colonialism

There's not much known about the centuries that followed. History picks up again with the arrival of the Europeans – first the Portuguese, in the 16th century, and then the British, who had already colonised India and were looking for more territory in the East. In three moves (1824, 1852 and 1885), the British took over all of Myanmar. The Burmese king and queen were exiled to India and their grand palace at Mandalay was looted and used as a barracks to quarter British and Indian troops.

The colonial era wrought great changes in Myanmar's demographics and infrastructure. Large numbers of Indians were brought in to work as civil servants, and Chinese were encouraged to immigrate and stimulate trade. The British built railways and ports, and many British companies grew wealthy trading in teak and rice. Many Burmese were unhappy with the colonial status quo. A nationalist movement developed, and there were demonstrations, often led, in true Burmese fashion, by Buddhist monks. Two famous nationalist monks, U Ottama and U Wizaya, died in a British prison and are revered to this day.

A NATIONAL JOKE

A popular joke that has been doing the rounds in the streets of Yangon is that George Orwell wrote not one novel about Burma, but three: *Burmese Days, Animal Farm* and *1984*. It would be funny if only it wasn't so poignantly true.

WWII & Early Independence

During WWII, the Japanese, linked with the Burmese Independence Army (BIA), drove the British out of Myanmar and declared it an independent country. But the Japanese were able to maintain Burmese political support for only a short time before their harsh and arrogant conduct alienated the Burmese people. Towards the end of the war, the Burmese switched sides and fought with the Allies to drive out the Japanese.

Bogyoke Aung San emerged from the haze of war as the country's natural leader. An early activist for nationalism, then defence minister in the Burma National Army, Aung San was the man to hold the country together through the transition to independence. When elections were held in 1947, Aung San's party won an overwhelming majority. But before he could take office, he was assassinated by a rival, along with most of his cabinet. Independence followed in 1948, with Aung San's protégé U Nu at the helm. Ethnic conflicts raged and chaos ensued.

Ne Win's Coup

In 1962 General Ne Win led a left-wing army takeover and set the country on the 'Burmese Way to Socialism'. He nationalised everything, including retail shops, and quickly crippled the country's economy. By 1987 it had reached a virtual standstill, and the long-suffering Burmese people decided they'd had enough of their incompetent government. In early 1988, they packed the streets and there were massive confrontations between pro-democracy demonstrators and the military that resulted in an estimated 3000 deaths over a six-week period. Once again, monks were at the helm. They turned their alms bowls upside down (the Buddhist symbol of condemnation) and insisted that Ne Win had to go. He finally did, in July 1988, but he retained a vestige of his old dictatorial power from behind the scenes.

The 1989 Election

The shaken government quickly formed the Orwellian-sounding Slorc (State Law and Order Restoration Council), declared martial law and promised to hold democratic elections in May 1989. The opposition, led by Bogyoke

SHOULD YOU GO?

Lonely Planet believes anyone thinking of going to Myanmar must consider this complicated question before undertaking a trip.

Myanmar is ruled by an oppressive military regime. Some refugee and human-rights groups urge foreigners not to visit Myanmar, believing that tourism legitimises the government and contributes to its coffers. Others have reversed their stance in recent years. National League for Democracy (NLD) general secretary Aung San Suu Kyi urged outsiders to boycott Myanmar during the government's 'Visit Myanmar Year 1996' campaign, in which the forced labour of tens of thousands (maybe more) of Burmese was used to rebuild infrastructure and some sites such as Mandalay Palace. Suu Kyi asked visitors to 'visit us later', saying that visiting at the time was 'tantamount to condoning the regime'.

Much of the international criticism is directed towards package tourists, who spend the most money and stay in expensive joint-venture hotels that are often in cahoots with the government. Thai, Chinese and Japanese tourists are the main visitors, with Germans, French and Americans leading the way in the West. Tourism in all its forms brought in US$164 million in 2006, possibly 12% of which went to the government. (This compares with US$2.16 billion in natural-gas exports that year.) Obviously the less you spend, the less that 12% figure will be. A pro-NLD, pro-tourism Yangon resident told us, 'Don't come in with your camera and only take pictures. We don't need that kind of tourist. Talk to those who want to talk. Let them know of the conditions of your life.'

Tourism remains one of the few industries to which ordinary locals have access in terms of income and communication; the vast majority of locals seem to want you here. And there are plenty of other reasons to consider visiting. Human-rights abuses are less likely to occur in areas where the international community is present; keeping the people isolated from international witnesses to internal oppression may only cement the government's ability to rule. The government has stopped forcing foreigners to change US$200 into government notes upon arrival, so the majority (possibly over 80%) of a careful independent traveller's expenses can now go into the private sector.

The boycott debate will rumble on, but right now, with oil and gas, minerals, heroin, timber and other resources to draw on, and with sanctions-busters such as China and India as close allies, tourism is pretty much loose change to the generals, but not to the people trying their hardest to survive.

If You Go

Here are a few ways to minimise the money that goes to the government:

- Avoid government-run hotels (often named after the city, eg Mrauk U Hotel) and stay in cheap family-run guesthouses. See p574 for more.
- Try to avoid government-run services: Myanmar Travel & Tours (MTT) is the government-operated travel agency and Myanma Airways is the government airline. Nearly all buses are independent, while IWT ferries and trains are government-controlled. See p525 for more.
- Spread the wealth – don't take care of all your needs (food, beer, guides, taxi, toilet paper) at one source (eg a guesthouse).
- Buy handicrafts directly from artisans.
- Try to get off the beaten track a bit, including towns not covered in this book.
- Read about Myanmar – see p574 for some book suggestions. It's important to know about Ne Win's coup, the events of 1988 and Aung San Suu Kyi before coming.

About this Chapter

We believe travellers to Myanmar should support private tourist facilities wherever possible. We've not reviewed any restaurants, hotels or shops known to be government-run. We flag any government-run services (such as trains or MTT).

Read Lonely Planet's expanded 'Should You Go?' coverage in the Myanmar guidebook or get the free download at www.lonelyplanet.com/worldguide/destinations/asia/myanmar.

Aung San's charismatic daughter, Aung San Suu Kyi, organised an opposition party, the National League for Democracy (NLD). Around the same time, Slorc changed the country's official name from the Union of Burma to the Union of Myanmar, claiming 'Burma' was a vestige of European colonialism.

While the Burmese population rallied around the NLD, the Slorc grew increasingly nervous. It placed Aung San Suu Kyi under house arrest and postponed the election. In spite of this and other dirty tactics, the NLD won more than 85% of the vote. Sore losers, Slorc refused to allow the NLD to assume its parliamentary seats and arrested most of the party leadership.

The Plight of Aung San Suu Kyi

Aung San Suu Kyi was awarded the Nobel Peace Prize in 1991 and was finally released from house arrest in July 1995. She was arrested again in 2000 and held in her home until the UN brokered her unconditional release in May 2002. She was rearrested in May 2003 and remains under house arrest. Aung San Suu Kyi continually refuses offers of freedom in exchange for exile from the country and, despite an ongoing debate in the pro-democracy movement over future strategy, her stature throughout Myanmar is as great as ever.

For more on recent developments in Myanmar, see p518.

THE CULTURE

The National Psyche

Although isolated, subjugated and poor, the Myanmar people are as proud of their country and culture as any nationality on earth. Locals gush over ancient kings, *pwe* (festivals), *mohinga* (noodles with chicken or fish) breakfasts, great temples and their religion. For the majority, Buddhism is the guiding principle and life centres on the monastery. A typical Burmese values meditation, gives alms freely and sees his or her lot as the consequence of sin or merit in a past life. The social ideal for most Burmese citizens is a standard of behaviour commonly termed *bamahsan chin* (or 'Burmese-ness'). The hallmarks of *bamahsan chin* include showing respect for elders, acquaintance with Buddhist scriptures and discretion in behaviour towards the opposite sex. Most importantly, *bamahsan chin* values the quiet, subtle and indirect over the loud, obvious and direct. Burmese also love a good laugh, and puns are considered a very high form of humour.

> **MUST READ**
>
> *The River of Lost Footsteps: Histories of Burma* (2006), by UN diplomat Thant Myint U, is a beautifully crafted assessment of the country's current plight in the context of its long and complex history.

> **MUST READ**
>
> *Living Silence: Burma under Military Rule* (2001), by Christina Fink, is a very readable account of Myanmar's military years, and offers humanising glimpses into both sides of the conflict.

Lifestyle

Families are generally big and several generations may share one roof. Electricity remains in short supply and even running water is uncommon in the countryside, where farming is the backbone of life. Visitors find it easy to engage with city folk, particularly the older generation, who often have good English.

Life is one long struggle for survival for many in Myanmar, thanks in no small part to a government that governs in the interests of a small military elite and not the wider nation. Higher education is disrupted every time there's a hint of unrest in the country, as the government shuts down the universities. The banks are under government control, so savings can be (and have been) wiped out at the whim of the rulers. Nominally, Burmese people have relative economic freedom, but just about any business opportunity requires bribes or connections. The small elite has modern conveniences, good medical treatment, fancy, well-fortified homes and speedy cars. Peaceful political assembly is banned and citizens are forbidden to discuss politics with foreigners, although many relish doing so as long as they're sure potential informers aren't listening.

Population

The population is made up of around 135 ethnic groups indigenous to Myanmar, including the Bamar (or Burman, around 68%), Shan

(9%), Kayin (or Karen, 7%), Rakhaing (4%), Mon (less than 3%), Kachin (less than 3%), Chin (less than 3%) and Kayah (1%). There are still large numbers of Indians and Chinese in Myanmar, but only a sprinkling of other foreigners and immigrants.

RELIGION

About 87% of Myanmar's citizens are Theravada Buddhists, but this is blended with a strong belief in *nat* (guardian spirit beings). Many of the hill tribes are Christian, and smaller Hindu and Muslim communities are dotted throughout the country.

For the average Burmese Buddhist everything revolves around the merit (*kutho,* from the Pali *kusala,* meaning 'wholesome') one is able to accumulate through rituals and good deeds. One of the more common rituals performed by individuals visiting a stupa is to pour water over the Buddha image at their astrological post (determined by the day of the week they were born) – one glassful for every year of their current age plus one extra to ensure a long life.

Every Burmese male is expected to take up temporary monastic residence twice in his life: once as a *samanera* (novice monk), between the ages of five and 15, and again as a *pongyi* (fully ordained monk), some time after the age of 20. Almost all men or boys under 20 years of age participate in the *shinpyu* (initiation ceremony), through which their family earns great merit.

While there is little social expectation that they should do so, a number of women live monastic lives as *dasasila* ('ten-precept' nuns). Burmese nuns shave their heads, wear pink robes and take vows in an ordination procedure similar to that undertaken by monks.

Buddhism in Myanmar has overtaken, but never entirely replaced, the pre-Buddhist practice of *nat* worship. The 37 *nat* figures are often found side by side with Buddhist images. The Burmese *nats* are spirits that can inhabit natural features, trees or even people. They can be mischievous or beneficent.

The *nat* cult is strong. Mt Popa (p569) is an important centre. The Burmese divide their devotions and offerings according to the sphere of influence: Buddha for future lives, and the *nat* – both Hindu and Bamar – for problems in this life. A misdeed might be redressed with offerings to the *nat* Thagyamin, who annually records the names of those who perform good deeds in a book made of gold leaves. Those who commit evil are recorded in a book made of dog skin.

DOS & DON'TS

- Don't touch anyone's head, as it's considered the spiritual pinnacle of the body.
- Don't point feet at people if you can help it, and avoid stepping over people.
- Burmese women don't ride atop pick-ups as it can be insulting to men beneath them.
- Hand things – food, gifts, money – with your right hand, tucking your left under your right elbow.
- Dress modestly when visiting religious sites – no shorts, tight clothes or sleeveless shirts.
- Take off your shoes when entering temple precincts, usually including the long steps up to a hilltop pagoda.

MUST SEE

Burmese Harp (1956) by Japanese director Kon Ichikawa is a classic anti-war film told from the perspective of a Japanese soldier disguised as a Buddhist monk.

ARTS

Burmese fine art, at the court level, has not had an easy time since the forced exile of the last king, Thibaw Min. Architecture and art were both royal activities, which have floundered and faded without royal support. On the other hand, Burmese culture at the street level is vibrant and thriving.

Marionette Theatre

Yok-thei pwe, or Burmese marionette theatre, was the forerunner of Burmese classical dance. Marionette theatre declined following WWII and is now mostly confined to tourist venues in Mandalay and Bagan.

Music

Traditional Burmese music relies heavily on rhythm and is short on harmony, at least to the Western ear. Younger Burmese listen to heavily Western-influenced sounds – you're likely to hear Burmese-language covers of your favourite oldies. A few Burmese rock musicians, such as Lay Phyu of the band Iron Cross, produce serious tunes of their own. **Myanmar Future Generations** (www.mm-fg.net) is an anonymous rap collective that posts politically charged songs online.

Pwe

The *pwe* (show) is everyday Burmese theatre. A religious festival, wedding, funeral, celebration, fair, sporting event – almost anything can be a good excuse for a *pwe*. Once under way, a *pwe* traditionally goes on all night. If an audience member is flaking at some point during the performance, they simply fall asleep. Ask a trishaw driver if one is on nearby.

Myanmar's truly indigenous dance forms are those that pay homage to the *nat*. In a special *nat pwe*, one or more *nat* are invited to possess the body and mind of a medium; sometimes members of the audience seem to be possessed instead, an event that is greatly feared by most Burmese.

ENVIRONMENT

Myanmar covers an area of 671,000 sq km, which is roughly the size of Texas or France. From the snow-capped Himalaya in the north to the coral-fringed Myeik (Mergui) Archipelago in the south, Myanmar's 2000km length crosses three distinct ecological regions: the Indian subregion, along the Bangladesh and India borders; the Indochinese subregion in the north, bordering Laos and China; and the Sundaic subregion, bordering peninsular Thailand. Together, these regions produce what is quite likely the richest biodiversity in Southeast Asia.

At the moment, deforestation by the timber industry poses the greatest threat to wildlife habitats, with Chinese demand for hardwoods fuelling the destruction. Optimistically, about 7% of the country is protected by national parks and other protected areas, but most of these are just lines on maps. Wildlife laws are seldom enforced, partly due to corruption. While many animals are hunted for food, tigers and rhinos are killed for the lucrative overseas Chinese pharmaceutical market.

BURMA OR MYANMAR?

The government changed most of the country's geographical names after 1988's uprising, in an attempt to purge the country of the vestiges of colonialism, and to avoid exclusive identification with the Bamar ethnic majority. ('Burma' is actually an English corruption of 'Bamar', and never has been the name of the country locally, at least since Marco Polo dropped by in the 13th century.) So Rangoon switched to Yangon, Pagan to Bagan, Irrawaddy River to Ayeyarwady River and so on.

In this book, 'Myanmar' is used in text to describe the country's history and people. 'Burmese' refers to the language, the food and the Bamar people.

TRANSPORT

GETTING THERE & AWAY

Air

All international flights arrive at sleepy Yangon airport (RGN), except direct flights from Chiang Mai to palatial Mandalay airport (MDL). The most common route is via Bangkok, a good place to pick up cheap tickets to Myanmar. From there a one-way ticket to Yangon starts at US$90, cheaper still with an Air Asia budget fare. Flights also connect Yangon with Kolkata, Delhi, Dhaka, Hong Kong, Kuala Lumpur, Kunming and Singapore.

It is important to reconfirm outgoing flights from Myanmar for all airlines other than Thai International Airways (THAI) and SilkAir. You do not need to show onward tickets to enter Myanmar.

The following airlines have regular links to (and offices in) Yangon.

Air Asia (code AK; ☎ 01-722299; www.airasia.com) Budget airline serving Bangkok.

Air China (code CA; ☎ 01-505024; www.airchina.com) Flight connections to Kunming.

Air Mandalay (code 6T; ☎ 01-525488; www.airmandalay.com) Connects Mandalay with Chiang Mai.

Bangkok Airways (code PG; ☎ 01-255122; www.bangkokair.com) Connects Yangon and Bangkok.

Biman Bangladesh Airlines (code BG; ☎ 01-240922; www.bimanair.com) Has connections with Bangkok and Dhaka.

> **DEPARTURE TAX**
>
> The official departure tax is US$10, payable in US dollars only, not kyat.

Indian Airlines Limited (code IC; ☎ 01-253598; http://indian-airlines.nic.in) Flights to Bangkok and Kolkata.
Malaysia Airlines (code MH; ☎ 01-241001; www.malaysiaairlines.com) Connects Yangon and Kuala Lumpur.
Myanmar Airways International (MAI, code 8M; ☎ 01-255180; www.maiair.com) National carrier offering connections with Bangkok, Kuala Lumpur and Singapore.
SilkAir (code MI; ☎ 01-255287; www.silkair.com) Daily connections with Singapore.
Thai Airways International (code TG; ☎ 01-255499; www.thaiair.com) Connects Yangon with Bangkok and Chiang Mai.

Land

Most of Myanmar's borders are closed. The following sections outline when and how to cross into Myanmar by land. It is not possible to reach Myanmar by sea or from Bangladesh, India or Laos.

CHINA

You can enter Myanmar from China, but it is not possible to exit Myanmar this way. To enter from China requires a 28-day tourist visa – get one at Kunming's **Myanmar consulate** (☎ 0871-360 3477; www.mcg-kunming.com; Room A504, 5th fl, Longyuan Haozhai, 166 Weiyuan Jie; 8.30am-noon & 1-4.30pm Mon-Fri) for Y185 to Y285.

To cross from the Chinese town of Ruili (20 hours from Kunming), it is necessary to book a multiday 'package trip' to go from Mu-se, Myanmar (at the border), and on to Lashio (northeast of Hsipaw). This will end up costing a hefty US$175 to US$225.

THAILAND

It is possible to cross from the northern Thai town of Mae Sai to dreary Tachilek. See the boxed text on p552 for more. It is also possible to cross from the Thai town of Ranong to the southern tip of Myanmar at Kawthoung. See p546 for more details. Visitors from Thailand can enter Myanmar for the day at the Mae Sot–Myawaddy border and Three Pagodas Pass, but tourists in Myanmar can't enter Thailand at these points; see p726 and p716 for information on these crossings.

GETTING AROUND

Unless you fly, all travel in Myanmar takes time. Lots of time. Much of the country, unfortunately, is off limits, including places not covered here, such as Chin State and much of Shan State. However, there is no law against stopping in villages between places listed in this chapter and having a look around.

Air

Four airlines, including three private companies and the government-run Myanma Airways, ply Myanmar's skyways (and 66 airstrips). Bear in mind that some of the private airlines are pretty closely connected to the government, otherwise they wouldn't be allowed to operate.

The following are the domestic airlines operating in Myanmar:
Air Bagan (code W9; ☎ 01-513322; www.airbagan.com) Privately run domestic carrier. However, the company has close links to senior generals.
Air Mandalay (code 6T; ☎ 01-525488; www.airmandalay.com) Singapore-Malaysia joint venture.
Myanma Airways (MA, code UB; ☎ 01-374874) The government's airline.
Yangon Airways (code HK; ☎ 01-383106; www.yangonair.com) Thai joint venture.

One-way tickets are half the return fare and should be bought at least a day in advance. You'll need to have your passport and US

> **GOVERNMENT-OWNED TRANSPORT**
>
> Be aware that the government profits from the use of transport services that it owns and/or operates. Try to avoid the following government companies:
>
> - Inland Water Transport (IWT) – Foreigner pricing means the government is profiteering.
> - Myanma Airways (domestic) – We do not recommend this airline, as much for its safety record as its ownership.
> - Myanma Five Star Line (MFSL; ships) – Few travellers use its services, as schedules are so hard to come by.
> - Myanmar Railways – Try to avoid its overpriced sleeper services between Yangon and Mandalay. Foreigner pricing exists on all services.

dollars handy to pay for the ticket. Travel agencies tend to sell tickets for slightly less than airline offices. All prices should include the US$3 insurance fee. There's no domestic departure tax.

MA's fleet is a bunch of old Fokkers and the airline has a hit-and-miss safety record. Schedules are approximate at best, although prices are often US$10 or US$20 less than the private carriers.

Boat

There is 8000km of navigable river in Myanmar. Even in the dry season, boats can travel on the Ayeyarwady (Irrawaddy) from the delta to Bhamo, and in the wet they can reach Myitkyina. Other important rivers include the Twante Canal, which links the Ayeyarwady to Yangon, and the Chindwin, which joins the Ayeyarwady a little north of Bagan. The main drawback is speed: boats typically take three to four times as long as road travel, with the exception of some speedboats. Most ferries are operated by the government's Inland Water Transport (IWT).

The Mandalay–Bagan service is popular among travellers. A ferry runs daily, but better still is the **Malikha speedboat** (www.malikhatravels.com). If you take the slower local boats, this trip can be extended to Pyay (Prome) or even all the way to Yangon. Arguably the best long-haul river trip – in season – is drifting south from Bhamo or Myitkyina. The most rewarding short trip is between Mawlamyine (Moulmein) and Hpa-an.

The government's Myanma Five Star Line (MFSL) travels very infrequently and irregularly from Yangon's MFSL Passenger Jetty (south of Strand Rd), heading north to Sittwe (Akyab) and south to Kawthoung. Ask at Myanmar Travel & Tours (MTT; p531) or call the **MFSL office** (Map p530; ☎ 01-295279; 132-136 Thein Byu Rd) in Yangon.

Bus

A handful of the long-distance buses are new and comfortable. More common are the older ones that are packed to the ceiling with people and goods and are often hours late. They break down often, too, and the roads are so bad in most places that two vehicles travelling in opposite directions can't pass without pulling off the road. On the other hand, bus travel is cheap and frequent, and it's easy to meet local people. Long-haul buses make a rest stop every few hours. Buy your ticket as far as possible in advance so as not to get stuck sitting on a sack in the aisle. On minibuses, beware of the back seat – on Myanmar's rough roads, you'll be bouncing around like popcorn. Have a blanket handy for air-con or trips through mountains.

Bus tickets are priced in kyat. There are usually different prices for foreigners and citizens, particularly on popular tourist routes. Bear in mind that prices have risen dramatically in recent years, due to the ending of government subsidies and high oil prices. Guesthouse staff can save you a trip to an often remote bus station to buy tickets.

Car & Motorcycle

The cost of hiring a car and driver is tied to the black-market price of petrol, which can fluctuate. Older cars without air-con cost about US$50 to US$70 per day (including driver and petrol) from Yangon.

Many locals remain reluctant to rent motorcycles to foreigners, but it is possible in some places, such as Mandalay.

Local Transport

In most places, bicycle rickshaws or trishaws (*sai-kaa* – that's pidgin for sidecar), horse carts *(myint hlei)*, vintage taxis *(taxi)*, tiny four-wheeled Mazdas (*lei bein*, or 'four wheels') and modern Japanese pick-up trucks (also called *kaa*) double as public transport. Rates are negotiable. There are some sample rates in this chapter, but prices can and do change.

Bigger cities – including Yangon, Mandalay, Pathein (Bassein) and Mawlamyine – have public buses plying the main streets, from K20 to K200 per ride.

It's possible to rent a bicycle almost anywhere in Myanmar. Rates range from K500 to K2500 per day.

Pick-Up

You can get almost anywhere in Myanmar on the ubiquitous trucks with bench seats known variously as pick-ups, *lain-ka* (linecar) or *hilux*. They leave when full and make frequent stops. They're a bit cheaper than buses. Usually you can pay 50% more to sit up front with the driver. Journey times are wildly elastic.

Train

We do not recommend travelling by train as Myanmar Railways is government owned and

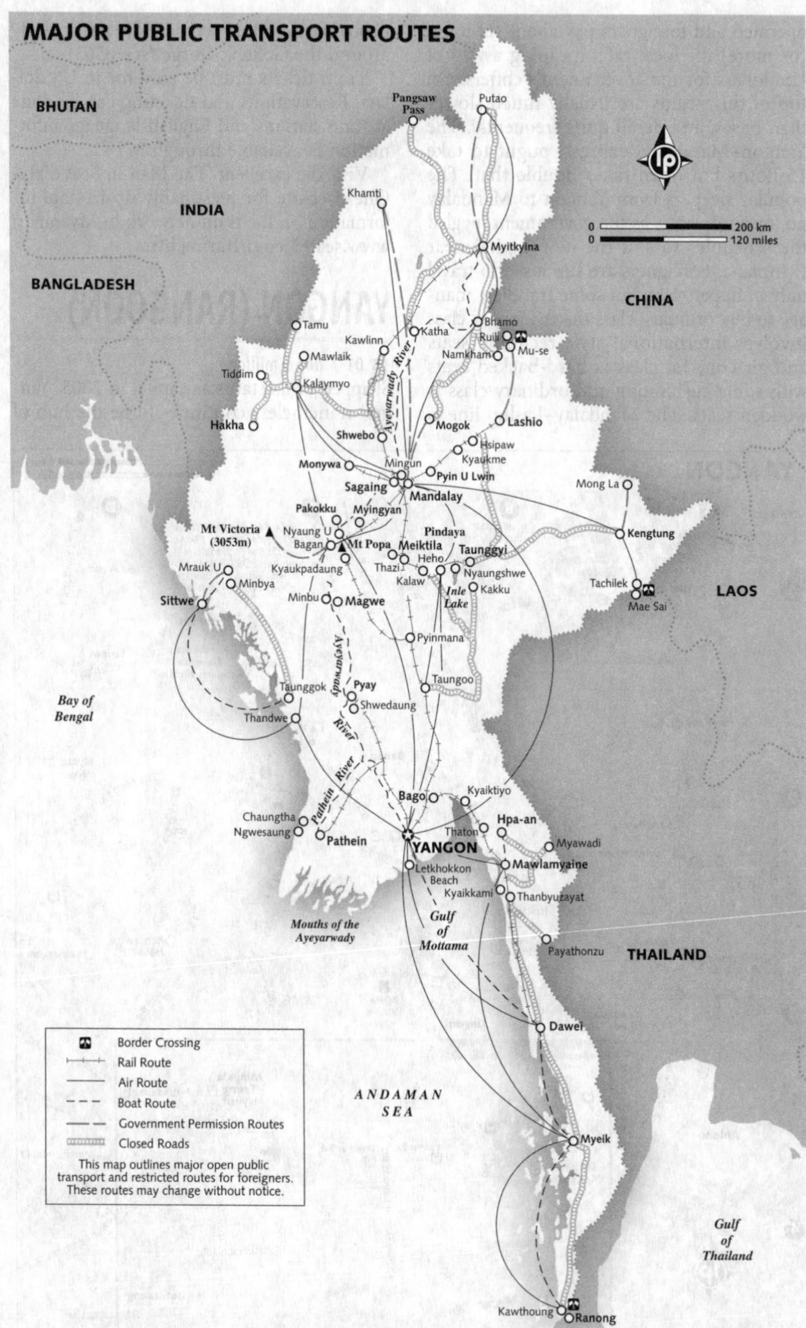

MAJOR PUBLIC TRANSPORT ROUTES
BHUTAN
INDIA
BANGLADESH
CHINA
LAOS
THAILAND
Bay of Bengal
ANDAMAN SEA
Gulf of Thailand
Gulf of Mottama
Mouths of the Ayeyarwady
Ayeyarwady River
Pathein River
Inle Lake
0 200 km
0 120 miles
Pangsaw Pass
Putao
Khamti
Myitkyina
Tamu
Kawlinn
Katha
Bhamo
Ruili
Mu-se
Namkham
Mawlaik
Tiddim
Kalaymyo
Hakha
Mogok
Lashio
Shwebo
Hsipaw
Kyaukme
Monywa
Mingun
Pyin U Lwin
Sagaing
Mandalay
Mong La
Pakokku
Myingyan
Mt Victoria (3053m)
Nyaung U
Bagan
Mt Popa
Meiktila
Pindaya
Taunggyi
Kengtung
Heho
Thazi
Kalaw
Nyaungshwe
Kakku
Kyaukpadaung
Mrauk U
Minbya
Sittwe
Minbu
Magwe
Tachilek
Mae Sai
Pyinmana
Taungoo
Taunggok
Pyay
Shwedaung
Thandwe
Bago
Kyaiktiyo
Chaungtha
Ngwesaung
Pathein
Thaton
Hpa-an
YANGON
Myawadi
Letkhokkon Beach
Mawlamyaine
Kyaikkami
Thanbyuzayat
Payathonzu
Dawei
Myeik
Kawthoung
Ranong
Border Crossing
Rail Route
Air Route
Boat Route
Government Permission Routes
Closed Roads
This map outlines major open public transport and restricted routes for foreigners. These routes may change without notice.

operated and foreigners pay about six times (or more) the local rate, meaning a wad of US dollars for the government's coffers. On top of this, trains are usually much slower than buses, and derail quite frequently. The Yangon–Mandalay 'express' ought to take 15 hours but often takes double that. The popular sleepers from Yangon to Mandalay no longer operate, as the government juggled the schedules to suit the new capital near Pyinmana. Foreigners are supposed to travel only in upper class, but some travellers manage to buy ordinary-class tickets. Upper class involves international-style reclining seats and air-con, 1st class is hard-backed seats with some cushioning and ordinary class is wooden seats. The Mandalay–Lashio line is probably the most scenic ride, particularly around the Gokteik Gorge (see p562).

Train tickets must be paid for in US dollars. Reservations and ticketing can be done at train stations and English-language information is available through MTT.

Visit the excellent 'The Man in Seat Sixty-One' website for reasonably up-to-date information on the train network in Myanmar: www.seat61.com/Burma.htm.

YANGON (RANGOON)

☎ 01 / pop 5 million

Stripped of its status as capital in 2005, Yangon nonetheless continues to be the hub of

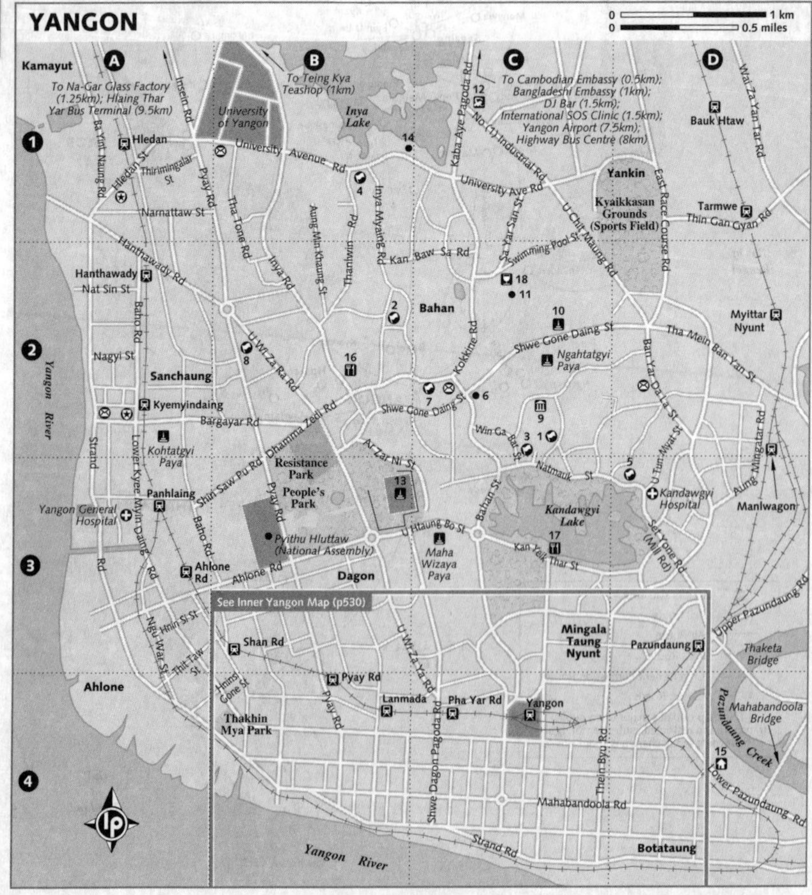

economic activity, a hive of underground intellectual debate and the gateway for most international visitors. The stunning Shwedagon Paya is the centrepiece of the city, a gleaming golden stupa visible from all over town. Closer to the waterfront, downtown Yangon is a warren of historic streets concealing some of the best British colonial-era architecture in the region. Forget the cosmetic renovations in Singapore: this is the real deal. A walk along the Strand or Pansodan St is like strolling down Pall Mall, albeit without the paint job.

Vibrant and dynamic, sweaty and steamy, reaching for the future but trapped in the past, Yangon is a fascinating introduction to Myanmar. It's diverse too – home to Burmese, Shan, Mon, Chinese, Indians and Western expats. Aung San Suu Kyi remains under house arrest here in her home on University Ave. General Than Shwe is rumoured to return on weekends, perhaps unable to survive the boredom of sterile Naypyidaw, the new 'capital'.

ORIENTATION

The city is bounded to the south and west by the Yangon River (also known as the Hlaing River) and to the east by Pazundaung Creek, which flows into the Yangon River. The whole city is divided into townships, and street addresses are often suffixed with these (eg 52nd St, Botataung Township).

INFORMATION		
German Embassy	1	C2
Italian Embassy	2	B2
Japanese Embassy	3	C2
Korean Embassy	4	B1
Nepali Embassy	5	D3
New Horizons Travels & Tours	6	C2
Singapore Embassy	7	C2
Vietnamese Embassy	8	B2
SIGHTS & ACTIVITIES		
Bogyoke Aung San Museum	9	C2
Chaukhtatgyi Paya	10	C2
Mahasi Meditation Centre	11	C2
Sedona Hotel	12	C1
Shwedagon Paya	13	B3
Suu Kyi's House	14	B1
SLEEPING		
Motherland Inn II	15	D4
EATING		
Café Dibar	16	B2
Sandy's Myanmar Cuisine	17	C3
DRINKING		
Lake View	(see 17)	
Mr Guitar Café	18	C2
Patty O'Malleys	(see 12)	

GETTING INTO TOWN

Walk past the taxi stands in the airport terminal (about 15km north of the centre) and negotiate with drivers outside. It's about US$5 to the centre of Yangon and it is best to have small bills handy. Most buses arrive at the Highway Bus Centre (Aung Mingalar Bus Terminal), a few kilometres northeast of the airport; a taxi to town will cost about the same as the airport run.

Most travellers stick with downtown Yangon, which has a grid-style layout and is easy enough to explore on foot.

The *Yangon Tourist Map*, produced by Design Printing Services, is pocket-sized. Some places give it away free, others charge up to K1000.

INFORMATION

Bookshops

There are lots of bookstalls (Map p532) across from Bogyoke Aung San Market and along 37th St near the corner of Merchant St, selling pulpy Buddhist comics, maps and old books, some in English.

Bagan Bookshop (Map p532; ☎ 377227; 100 37th St; 🕒 9am-5.30pm Tue-Sun) A favourite for its eclectic selection of English-language books. The friendly owner has reprints of lots of old English-language books on Burma.

Inwa Bookstore (Map p532; 232 Sule Paya Rd) Stocks some maps, coffee-table books and general English titles, plus has recent news magazines.

Cultural Centres

Alliance Francaise (Map p530; ☎ 282122; Pyidaungsu Yeiktha Rd; 🕒 Tue & Fri) Check the *Myanmar Times* for film and concert listings.

American Center (Map p530; ☎ 223140; 14 Taw Win Rd; 🕒 9am-4pm Mon-Fri) English-language magazines and books.

British Council Library (Map p532; ☎ 295300; 80 Strand Rd; 🕒 8.30am-8pm Mon-Fri, to 4.30pm Sat) Excellent collection of English-language Burmese-history books located in the UK embassy.

Emergency

Your embassy may also be able to assist in an emergency.

Ambulance (☎ 192)

Fire (☎ 191)

Police (☎ 199)

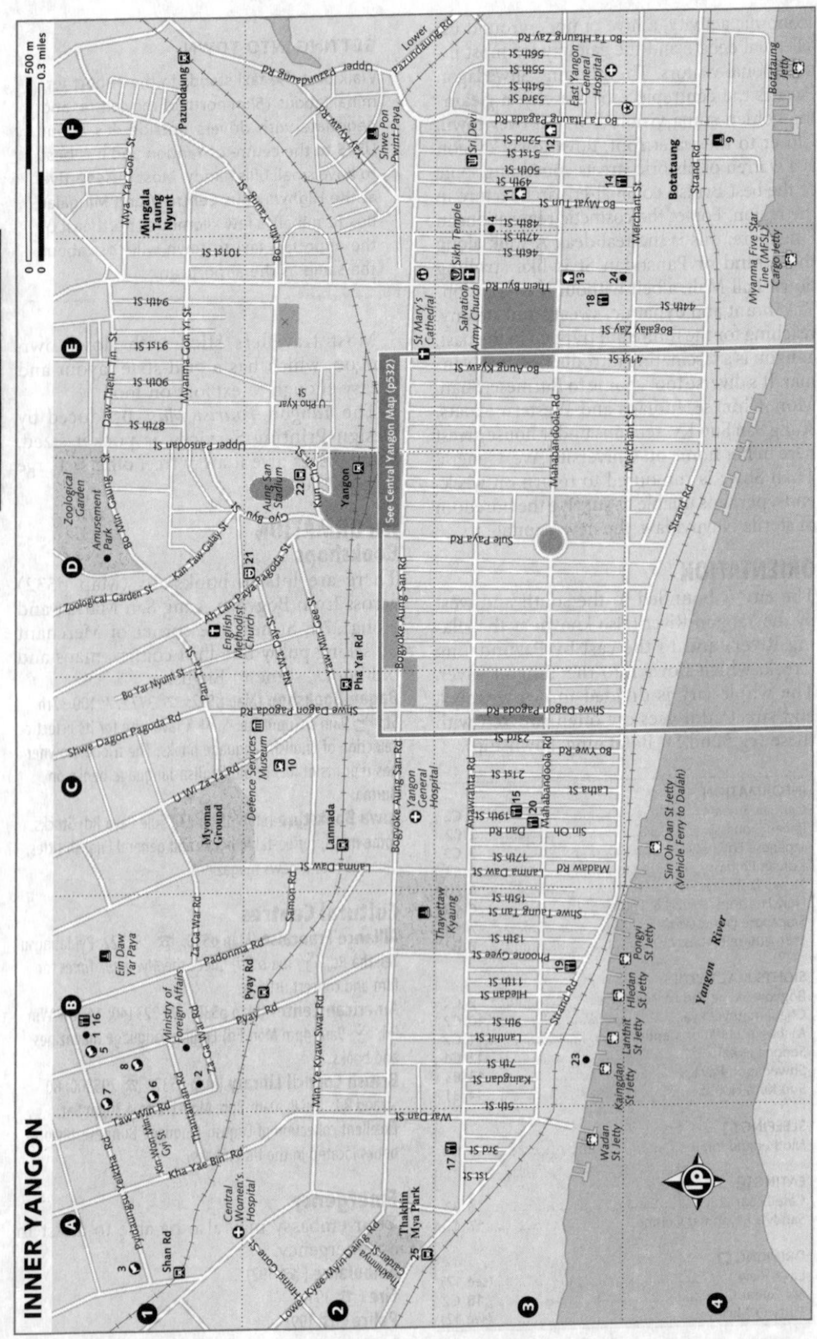
INNER YANGON
0 500 m
0 0.3 miles
Yangon River
Botataung
Mingala Taung Nyunt
Myoma Ground
Thakhin Mya Park
Zoological Garden
Amusement Park
Aung San Stadium
Yangon
Lanmada
Pazundaung
Pha Yar Rd
Pyay Rd
Shan Rd
See Central Yangon Map (p532)
St Mary's Cathedral
Salvation Army Church
Sikh Temple
Sri Devi
English Methodist Church
Defence Services Museum
Ministry of Foreign Affairs
Central Women's Hospital
Yangon General Hospital
East Yangon General Hospital
Ein Daw Yar Paya
Shwe Pon Pwint Paya
Thayettaw Kyaung
Sin Oh Dan St Jetty (Vehicle Ferry to Dalah)
Myanma Five Star Line (MFSL) Cargo Jetty
Botataung Jetty
Pongyi St Jetty
Hledan St Jetty
Lanthit St Jetty
Kaingdan St Jetty
Wadan St Jetty
Strand Rd
Merchant St
Mahabandoola Rd
Anawrahta Rd
Bogyoke Aung San Rd
Sule Paya Rd
Shwe Dagon Pagoda Rd
U Wi Za Ya Rd
Kaba Aye Pagoda Rd
Ah Lan Paya Pagoda St
Bo Min Gaung St
Upper Pansodan St
Bo Aung Kyaw St
Thein Byu Rd
Bo Myat Tun St
Bo Ta Htaung Pagoda Rd
Bo Ta Htaung Zay Rd
Upper Pazundaung Rd
Lower Pazundaung Rd
Yay Kyaw Rd
Lower Kyee Myin Daing Rd
Hninsi Gone St
Min Ye Kyaw Swar Rd
Padonma Rd
Lanma Daw St
Za Ga War Rd
Kha Yae Bin Rd
Taw Win Rd
Thantaman Rd
Pyidaungsu Yeiktha Rd
Kan Taw Galay St
Zoological Garden St
Bo Yar Nyunt St
Pan Tra St
Yaw Min Gee St
Na Wa Day St
Kun Chan St
Gyo Byu St
U Pho Kyar St
Myanma Gon Yi St
Daw Thein Tin St
Mya Yar Gon St
101st St
94th St
91st St
90th St
87th St
War Dan St
Bo Ywe Rd
Latha St
Sin Oh Dan Rd
Madaw Rd
Lanma Daw St
Shwe Taung Tan St
Phoone Gyee St
Hledan St
Lanthit St
Kaingdan St
1st St
3rd St
5th St
7th St
9th St
11th St
13th St
15th St
17th St
19th St
21st St
23rd St
41st St
44th St
46th St
47th St
48th St
49th St
50th St
51st St
52nd St
53rd St
54th St
55th St
56th St
Bogalay Zay St
A B C D E F
1 2 3 4

Internet Access

Many guesthouses offer internet connections, but it's usually cheaper to go to a dedicated internet café.

Cyber World (Map p532; 246-248 Sule Paya Rd; per hr K1000) Central location with a reasonably fast connection.

Medical Services

City Mart Supermarket (Map p530; cnr Anawrahta Rd & 47th St) Well-stocked shop that includes a pharmacy.

International SOS Clinic (off Map p528; ☎ 24hr alarm centre 667879; 37 Kaba Aye Paya Rd) On the ground floor of the Dusit Inya Lake Hotel on the east bank of the lake, this is an international-standard option in Yangon when it comes to emergencies.

Money

Yangon generally offers the best exchange rate in the country. Touts around Sule Paya or the northern end of the adjacent Mahabandoola Garden offer the best rates, but you shouldn't make the exchange before counting all the kyat. Hotels and guesthouses are the safer option.

At a pinch, a couple of top-end hotels (such as the Sedona Hotel; p533) accept credit cards.

Post

DHL office (Map p532; Traders Hotel, 223 Sule Paya Rd; 8am-6pm Mon-Fri) To send or receive anything valuable, head here.

Main post office (Map p532; Strand Rd; 7.30am-6pm Mon-Fri) Grand old building for all postal services, but not phone calls.

Telephone

Central Telephone & Telegraph office (CTT; Map p532; cnr Pansodan St & Mahabandoola Rd) Can set you up (literally) with overseas calls at US$3 to US$6 per minute.

Tourist Information

Myanmar Travel & Tours (MTT; Map p532; ☎ 275328; 77/91 Sule Paya Rd; 8.30am-5pm) Government-run travel agency. Partake of its free maps, but not its services. A useful stop to get the latest story on off-limits areas of the country.

Travel Agencies

Privately run travel agencies are a good option for hiring a car or guide, checking on travel permits to off-limits areas, or extending a visa.

Columbus Travel & Tours (Map p532; ☎ 255123; www.travelmyanmar.com; Sakura Tower, 339 Bogyoke Aung San Rd) Convenient location to buy competitively priced air tickets.

Good News Travel (Map p532; ☎ 501904; goodnews@mptmail.net.mm; 4th fl, FMI Centre, 380 Bogyoke Aung San Rd) Very well-run agency, though usually geared to high-end travellers.

New Horizons Travels & Tours (Map p528; ☎ 542949; tun@mptmail.net.mm; 64 B2R Shwe Gone Plaza) Some way out of town, this place books trips for overseas groups and is quite responsible.

DANGERS & ANNOYANCES

Many travellers report being overcharged when buying bus tickets from the kiosks around Aung San Stadium. Moneychangers on the street are unlikely to do a runner, but they might slip in a few torn (therefore unusable) bills.

SIGHTS

Shwedagon Paya

The glorious golden spire of the gilded **Shwedagon** (Map p528; admission US$5; 5am-10pm), located a couple of kilometres north of the centre, is the defining image of Yangon and a symbol of Burmese identity. Rising 98m from its base, it positively glistens on a sunny day. Dating back 2500 years – if legend is to be believed –

MYANMAR (BURMA)

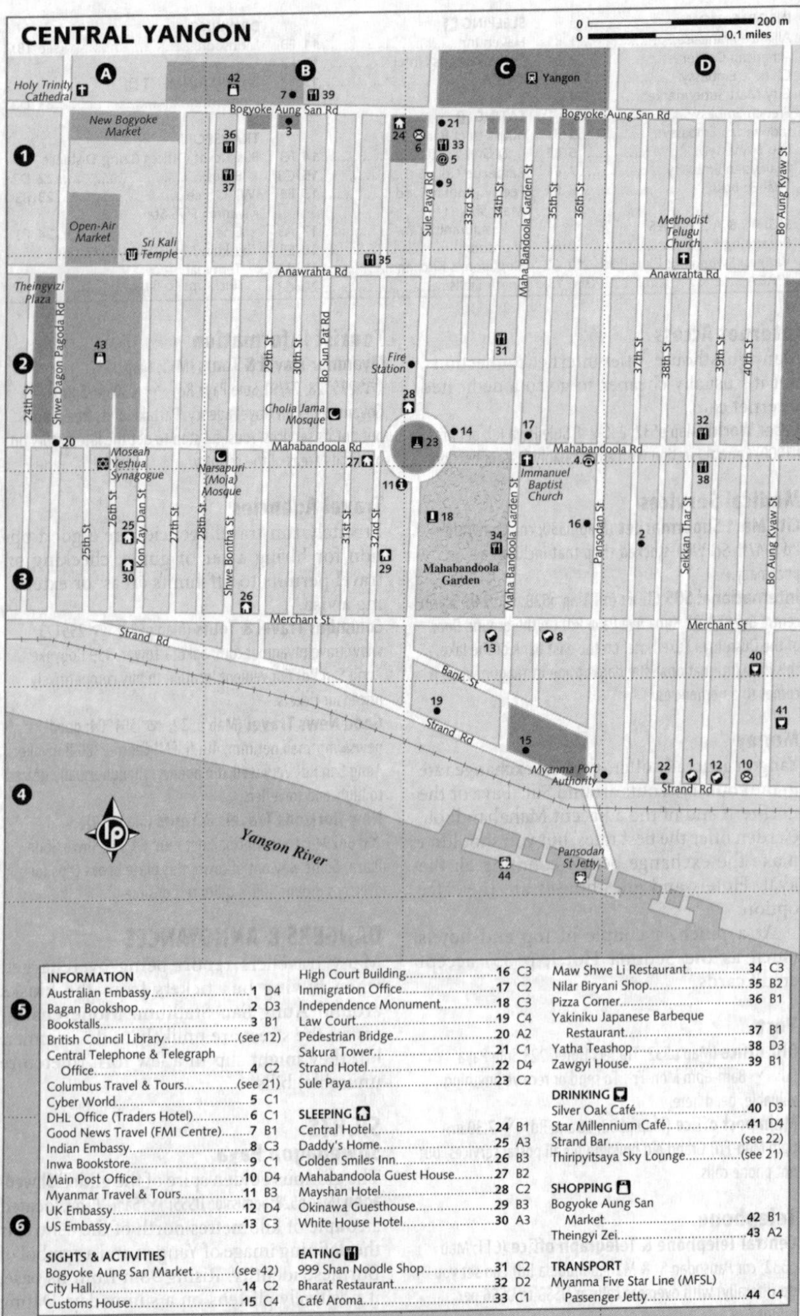
CENTRAL YANGON
0 200 m
0 0.1 miles
A
B
C
D
1
2
3
4
5
6
Holy Trinity Cathedral
New Bogyoke Market
Open-Air Market
Sri Kali Temple
Yangon
Bogyoke Aung San Rd
Sule Paya Rd
33rd St
34th St
Maha Bandoola Garden St
35th St
36th St
Methodist Telugu Church
Bo Aung Kyaw St
Anawrahta Rd
Theingyizi Plaza
Shwe Dagon Pagoda Rd
24th St
29th St
30th St
Bo Sun Pat Rd
Fire Station
Cholia Jama Mosque
37th St
38th St
39th St
40th St
Mahabandoola Rd
Moseah Yeshua Synagogue
Narsapuri (Moja) Mosque
Immanuel Baptist Church
25th St
26th St
Kon Zay Dan St
27th St
28th St
Shwe Bontha St
31st St
32nd St
Mahabandoola Garden
Pansodan St
Seikkan Thar St
Merchant St
Strand Rd
Bank St
Myanma Port Authority
Yangon River
Pansodan St Jetty
INFORMATION
Australian Embassy.....1 D4
Bagan Bookshop.....2 D3
Bookstalls.....3 B1
British Council Library.....(see 12)
Central Telephone & Telegraph Office.....4 C2
Columbus Travel & Tours.....(see 21)
Cyber World.....5 C1
DHL Office (Traders Hotel).....6 C1
Good News Travel (FMI Centre).....7 B1
Indian Embassy.....8 C3
Inwa Bookstore.....9 C1
Main Post Office.....10 D4
Myanmar Travel & Tours.....11 B3
UK Embassy.....12 D4
US Embassy.....13 C3
SIGHTS & ACTIVITIES
Bogyoke Aung San Market.....(see 42)
City Hall.....14 C2
Customs House.....15 C4
High Court Building.....16 C3
Immigration Office.....17 C2
Independence Monument.....18 C3
Law Court.....19 C4
Pedestrian Bridge.....20 A2
Sakura Tower.....21 C1
Strand Hotel.....22 D4
Sule Paya.....23 C2
SLEEPING
Central Hotel.....24 B1
Daddy's Home.....25 A3
Golden Smiles Inn.....26 B3
Mahabandoola Guest House.....27 B2
Mayshan Hotel.....28 C2
Okinawa Guesthouse.....29 B3
White House Hotel.....30 A3
EATING
999 Shan Noodle Shop.....31 C2
Bharat Restaurant.....32 D2
Café Aroma.....33 C1
Maw Shwe Li Restaurant.....34 C3
Nilar Biryani Shop.....35 B2
Pizza Corner.....36 B1
Yakiniku Japanese Barbeque Restaurant.....37 B1
Yatha Teashop.....38 D3
Zawgyi House.....39 B1
DRINKING
Silver Oak Café.....40 D3
Star Millennium Café.....41 D4
Strand Bar.....(see 22)
Thiripyitsaya Sky Lounge.....(see 21)
SHOPPING
Bogyoke Aung San Market.....42 B1
Theingyi Zei.....43 A2
TRANSPORT
Myanma Five Star Line (MFSL) Passenger Jetty.....44 C4

Shwedagon is an absolute must. Every good Buddhist in Myanmar tries to make at least one pilgrimage here in their lifetime; many come for the **Shwedagon festival** held on the full moon in February/March. Any national festival quickens the pulse here.

The compound, with its main stupa and 82 other buildings, is astounding any time of day, but evening and sunrise – when slanting light illuminates the gilding – are the most magical times to visit.

The *paya* ('holy one', a religious monument) is said to be built upon the hill where Buddha relics have been enshrined, including eight hairs of the Buddha. In the 15th century, Queen Shinsawbu gilded it with her own weight in gold, beaten to gold leaf. Her son-in-law offered four times his own weight and that of his wife's. The *zedi* (stupa) has reportedly accumulated more than 53 metric tonnes of gold leaf. The top of the spire is encrusted with more than 5000 diamonds and 2000 other stones.

In the compound's northwestern corner is a huge bell that the British managed to drop into the Yangon River while trying to carry it off. Unable to recover it, they gave the bell back to the Burmese, who refloated it using low-tech lengths of bamboo.

The entrance fee supposedly goes to pagoda upkeep. There is a lift large enough to accommodate a wheelchair, an impressive rarity when it comes to ancient sites in Southeast Asia. To get here, either take packed bus 37 from the east side of Mahabandoola Park, or grab a taxi (about K2000 one way).

Other Attractions

One of Yangon's top *paya*, the slightly kitsch riverside **Botataung Paya** (Map p530; Strand Rd; admission US$2) is named for the 1000 military leaders who escorted Buddha relics from India 2000 years ago. Its *zedi* is, unusually, hollow, so you can walk through it. There are good river views nearby.

If you don't make it to Bago (Pegu), the reclining Buddha at **Chaukhtatgyi Paya** (Map p528; Shwe Gone Daing St) is nearly as impressive.

Although it may not be possible to visit Aung San Suu Kyi's present home, you can see where she grew up at the **Bogyoke Aung San Museum** (Map p528; ☎ 541359; Bogyoke Aung San Museum St, Bahan Township; admission US$3; 🕒 10am-3.30pm Tue-Sun). Dedicated to her father, an independence leader who was assassinated in 1947, the museum is just north of Kandawgyi Lake.

The **Na-Gar Glass Factory** (off Map p528; ☎ 526053; 152 Yawgi Kyaung St, Hlaing Township; admission free; 🕒 9.30-11am & 12.30-3.30pm) is a fun place to explore. Glassblowers here made the mesmerising eyes for a reclining Buddha in Yangon's Chaukhtatgyi Paya, and the owner is a genial host. Some drivers aren't familiar with the factory, so getting there requires some patience.

For the best 360-degree views of Yangon, including the Shwedagon Paya, take the (free) lift to the top of the **Sakura Tower** (Map p532; cnr Bogyoke Aung San & Sule Paya Rds).

For more Yangon sights, see the walking tour (p534).

ACTIVITIES

Good strolling grounds can be found at **Kandawgyi Lake** (Map p528), north of the city centre. About 3km north, **Inya Lake** (Map p528) offers little chance for shade, but is five times larger, and not far from **Suu Kyi's home** (Map p528; 54 University Ave).

The **YMCA** (Map p530; ☎ 294128; Mahabandoola Rd; 🕒 beginners 7-9am Tue, Thu & Sat, experienced 3-5pm Mon, Wed & Fri) offers first-rate kickboxing instruction.

If you feel the need to take the plunge and do some **swimming**, most top-end hotels allow dips for a few dollars; one of the nicest pools is at the **Sedona Hotel** (Map p528; ☎ 666900; 1 Kaba Aye Pagoda Rd, Inya Lake; admission US$5). Or try the **Yangon Swimming Club Pool** (Map p530; U Wi Za Ya Rd).

COURSES

Yangon is a popular centre for *satipatthana vipassana*, or insight-awareness meditation. Meditation centres around town:

Chanmyay Yeiktha Meditation Centre (☎ 661479; www.chanmyay.org; 55A Kaba Aye Rd) There's also a second location outside town.

International Meditation Centre (☎ 535549; 31A Inya Myaing Rd)

Mahasi Meditation Centre (Map p528; ☎ 541971; http://web.ukonline.co.uk/buddhism/mahasi.htm; 16 Thathana Yeiktha Rd, Bahan Township) Myanmar's most famous meditation centre.

Panditarama Meditation Centre (☎ 535448; http://web.ukonline.co.uk/buddhism/pandita.htm; 80A Than Lwin Rd, Bahan Township) There's also a second branch outside town.

DOWNTOWN WALKING TOUR

The streets of downtown Yangon (Map p532) are bursting with majestic government buildings from the British era. Tucked away down the narrow side streets are row upon row of grand apartment buildings from the 1920s and 1930s. There is nowhere else quite like it in Southeast Asia and the best way to soak it up is to wander about on foot. Try starting at 2200-year-old **Sule Paya**, a big-time Buddhist traffic circle with an unusual octagonal shape. Just east is golden **City Hall** and, further east, the **Immigration Office** (Mahabandoola Rd), once a mammoth department store.

Continuing east, the **High Court Building** (Pansodan St) is on the right. Heading south on Pansodan St is a real joy, passing monumental old buildings that wouldn't look out of place around Trafalgar Sq, before hitting Strand Rd. To the left is the colonial stand-out **Strand Hotel**, with an air-conditioned (expensive) bar if you want a break, and the **British Council Library** (p529).

West on the Strand is the 1915 **Customs House** and the colonnaded **Law Court**. Head north to the popular **Mahabandoola Garden** (admission K50), a slightly faded park that is home to the **Independence Monument** (and some shade). Just north is the Sule Paya. Walking west, through the chaotic Indian and Chinese quarters, there's a great **pedestrian bridge** for photos of Yangon traffic. Then wander north to **Bogyoke Aung San Market**.

FESTIVALS & EVENTS

Several festivals and events centre on Yangon, although some of the more political ones may shift to Naypyidaw in time. Independence Day on 4 January includes a fair at Kandawgyi Lake; Buddha's birthday in April or May is a big event at Shwedagon Paya; Martyr's Day commemorates the assassination of Bogyoke Aung San on 19 July; and Tazaungdaing sees speed-weaving competitions at Shwedagon Paya in October or November. For more details, see p576.

SLEEPING

The best bargains are found in the downtown area, by far the liveliest part of the city. Not only is this the heart of Yangon, but staying here will save you a small fortune in taxi fares. All prices include a free breakfast.

Okinawa Guesthouse (Map p532; ☎ 374318; 64 32nd St; dm US$5, s US$9-13, d US$13-17; ❄) Hidden away down a side street, but just a stroll from Sule Paya, this is a lovingly furnished, warm and welcoming home. Rooms with bathroom cost are at the higher end of the price range. The dorms are a good budget option.

Golden Smiles Inn (Map p532; ☎ 373589; myathiri@mptmail.net.mm; 644 Merchant St; s US$5-8, d US$8-12; ❄) Tucked away down near the waterfront, this guesthouse is housed upstairs in a rambling old building. As the name suggests, the welcome is warm, but the rooms are quite basic.

White House Hotel (Map p532; ☎ 240780; whitehouse@mptmail.net.mm; 69/71 Kon Zay Dan St; s US$6-14, d US$10-18; ❄ 💻) Rooftop hammocks, cold beer and expansive views reward those willing to tackle the steep climb here. One of the longest-running budget hotels in town, its rooms are clean, although some are strangely shaped. Pricier rooms include a private bathroom. There is a useful travel desk downstairs for onward travels.

Motherland Inn 2 (Map p528; ☎ 291343; www.myanmarmotherlandinn.com; 433 Lower Pazundaung Rd; s US$7-10, d US$10-15; ❄ 💻) A little way from the action, the Motherland has long been popular with travellers. Rooms come in a variety of combinations involving bathrooms, fans or air-con. All are clean and well furnished. There is a free airport shuttle running twice daily.

Haven Inn (Map p530; ☎ 295500; phyuaung@mptmail.net.mm; 216 Bo Myat Tun St; s/d US$10/15; ❄) Small, but, according to some, perfectly formed, Dr Htun's five well-furnished rooms are often fully booked in the high season. No rooms have windows, but they're finished with a wood trim and have private bathroom and air-con.

Three Seasons Hotel (Map p530; ☎ 293304; phyuaung@mptmail.net.mm; 83/85 52nd St; s/d US$15/20; ❄) Same email, same family as Haven Inn, this is another little haven. The polished wood floors sparkle so brightly you can skate across the room. Higher prices reflect a slightly smarter finish than the Haven.

our pick **Mayshan Hotel** (Map p532; ☎ 252986; www.mayshan.com; 115 Sule Paya Rd; s/d from US$15/20; ❄ 💻) When it comes to location, this place is hard to beat, looking on to Sule Paya as it does. Run by a friendly family, the rooms are smart and comfortable, including satellite TV and hot water bathtubs. The lift is a bonus, as is the fast access to internet email.

Central Hotel (Map p532; ☎ 241001; www.myanmars.net/central; 355-357 Bogyoke Aung San Rd; s/d from US$30/35;) Hidden under the shadow of the giant Traders Hotel, this is the closest you're going to get to the major league for this kind of money. The rooms are large and clean, and include everything you might crave after an adventure upcountry, such as international news 24/7 and hot water.

Other recommended places in the centre:

Mahabandoola Guest House (Map p532; ☎ 248104; 93 32nd St; s/d with shared bathroom US$3/5) Housed in a decaying old colonial relic, this place has oodles of potential, but the interior is almost as decrepit as the building itself.

Daddy's Home (Map p532; ☎ 252169; 107 Kon Zay Dan St; s US$5-8, d US$6-10;) Reliable stand-by choice if the nearby White House is full.

YMCA (Map p530; ☎ 294128; 263 Mahabandoola Rd; s US$8-10, d US$16-19;) The old wing has large, spartan rooms, while the new wing has smarter rooms with reliable hot water.

EATING

Yangon has Myanmar's best range of restaurants. There are lots of inexpensive Bamar, Shan, Chinese and Indian restaurants in the downtown area. Slightly smarter restaurants are tucked away to the north of the centre on various embassy rows or around the pretty lakes. Footpath stalls are the cheapest eats in town. Remember that many places close early, by 9pm.

Bamar & Shan

For a lively local night out, head to the open-air **barbecue grills** (Map p530; 19th St; after 5pm) in Chinatown, located between Mahabandoola and Anawrahta Rds. The area is wall to wall with smoking grills. Pick some skewers from the meat, fish and vegetable selection (from K200 each) and down a chilled Myanmar Beer while your dinner's cooking. If you're game, pick up some 'mouth-watering snacks' (crickets and the like) at the **snack stalls** (Mahabandoola Rd) around the corner to accompany the beer.

999 Shan Noodle Shop (Map p532; 130B 34th St; noodles from K500) This blink-and-you'll-miss-it tiny place behind City Hall has an English-language menu for sampling Shan meals such as *hkauq sweh* (thin rice noodles in spiced chicken broth).

our pick **Feel Myanmar Food** (Map p530; ☎ 725736; 124 Pyidaungsu Yeiktha Rd; mains from K1500) Want to get a feel for Myanmar cuisine? This is the place to do it, with dozens of traditional dishes available each day. Just point and eat. Staff speak enough English to help with selections.

Sandy's Myanmar Cuisine (Map p528; ☎ 249255; 290 U Weizara Rd; mains K1500-5000) In a peaceful setting overlooking Kandawgyi Lake, Sandy's Myanmar Cuisine is one of the more stylish addresses to get to grips with Bamar cuisine. The prices aren't bad for such a top spot, and the menu includes some authentic curries.

Maw Shwe Li Restaurant (Map p530; ☎ 221103; 316 Anawrahta Rd, Lanmadaw Township; mains K2000) This popular Shan eatery lies west of the city centre. Specialities include a tasty fried dried eel with chilli. There is now a more central branch on Mahabandoola Garden St (Map p532).

'MOUTH-WATERING SNACKS'

Tha yei za (literally 'mouth-watering snack' in Burmese) come in a mind-boggling array of sizes and shapes and are a real bargain. Seek them out at 'night markets' in Yangon and at street stalls around the country. Makeshift desserts come in the form of multicoloured sticky-rice sweets, poppyseed cakes, banana puddings and the like. Others test local claims that 'anything that walks on the ground can be eaten' and are definitely in the unidentified frying object category:

- *wek thaa douk htoe* (barbecue stands) – footpath stools selling graphic, sliced-up pig parts; about K50 a hit
- *pa-yit kyaw* (fried cricket) – sold on skewers or in a 10-pack for about K300
- *bi-laar* (beetle) – prepared like crickets; locals suggest 'suck the stomach out, then chew the head part'
- *thin baun poe* (larva) – insect larva, culled from bamboo, are lightly grilled and served still wriggling

MYANMAR (BURMA)

Other Asian

There is a huge number of Indian restaurants in the city. Along Anawrahta Rd, west of Sule Paya Rd, there are many super-cheap Indian biryani shops (*keyettha dan bauk* in Burmese) and roti-and-dosa makers set up at night. All-you-can-eat thali meals or biryani cost K500 or so. **Nilar Biryani Shop** (Map p532; Anawrahta Rd) is a reliable spot.

Bharat Restaurant (Map p532; ☎ 281519; 356 Mahabandoola Rd; veg mains K700) Specialising in southern Indian food, Bharat offers cheap dosas and a range of thalis with vegetable, mutton, chicken or fish.

Yakiniku Japanese Barbeque Restaurant (Map p532; ☎ 374738; 357 Shwe Bontha St; barbecue dishes from K1500; ⏲ lunch & dinner) Yakiniku has anything you can think of to barbecue and some you can't. Cook things up on your very own gas-fired grill or go wild and sample the sushi.

Singapore's Kitchen (Map p530; ☎ 226297; 524 Strand Rd; mains from K2000; ⏲ lunch & dinner) Chinese restaurants are another fixture in Yangon and this is one of the best. Tables spill onto the footpath on a breezy night and the duck is delicious. It's between 12th and Phoone Gyee Sts.

International

Pizza Corner (Map p532; ☎ 254730; Shwe Bontha St; pizzas K2000-2800) New arrivals might be thinking 'Pizza? Why would I want pizza?'. Wait until you've spent a month upcountry and all will be revealed. The décor is bad burger joint to the hilt, but the pizzas are tasty.

Monsoon (Map p530; ☎ 295224; 85 Thein Byu Rd; mains K2500-7500) More like East meets West, this place has an eclectic menu of regional favourites from Myanmar, Cambodia, Laos and beyond, plus plenty of home comfort food. Set in a grand old colonial-era building, the menu is very reasonably priced given the elegant surrounds.

Café Dibar (Map p528; ☎ 006143; 14 Than Lwin Rd; mains from K3000) A little way out, but in striking distance of Shwedagon Paya, Café Dibar is a homely Italian bistro with authentic pizzas and pastas.

Cafés & Teashops

Café Aroma (Map p532; Sule Paya Rd; ⏲ 8am-11pm) Caffeine cravers should head here for a morning fix. It also has an extensive menu of Asian and international food and is popular with well-heeled young Burmese.

Zawgyi House (Map p532; ☎ 380398; 372 Bogyoke Aung San Rd) Take a pew on the porch for some top people watching in front of this grand old wooden house. Teas, coffees, shakes and snacks, plus an expensive handicraft showroom inside.

Sei Taing Kya Teashop (off Map p528; ⏲ 7am-5pm) This is the Burmese teashop answer to Starbucks, with several branches around the city. The liveliest branch is near the Israeli embassy and serves tea by the gallon and plenty of snacks.

Yatha Teashop (Map p532; 352 Mahabandoola Rd) A traditional Indian-style teashop between Seikkan Thar and 39th Sts.

DRINKING

After one night in Bangkok, you would be forgiven for thinking Yangon is a sleepy backwater. However, dig a little deeper and there is some action. For those on a strict budget, the cheapest options are downtown beer gardens serving Dagon or Myanmar draught beer. Expat-oriented places – mostly north of the centre – are comparatively pricey. Check out the *Myanmar Times* for more extensive listings.

Thiripyitsaya Sky Lounge (Map p532; ☎ 255255; 20th fl, Sakura Tower, 339 Bogyoke Aung San Rd) *The* place to come for big views of Yangon; come for a sundowner and see the sky change colour. Pricey drinks, but short of chartering a chopper you won't get a better view of the Shwedagon.

Lake View (Map p528; ☎ 382917; 290 U Weizara Rd) For a ground-level view of attractive Kandawgyi Lake, this place has draught Myanmar beer for less than US$1. Check out the impressive replica of the royal barge Karaweik across the water, but don't venture in as it is government-owned.

50th Street Bar & Grill (Map p530; ☎ 298096; 9-13 50th St) Long one of the only bars in town, this place feels a little lost and lonely in the backstreets, but it's worth a drink or two during the extensive happy hours. There are cheap drinks from 5pm to 8pm daily and Sunday is an all-day happy hour, the perfect way to overcome a hangover.

Monsoon (Map p530; ☎ 295224; 85 Thein Byu Rd) It's more of a restaurant, but the extensive drinks menu here includes happy hour cocktails from 5.30pm to 7.30pm.

Star Millennium Café (Map p532; ☎ 380346; 70 Bo Aung Kyaw St) 'The place where the stars hang out' or at least the place where they hang pictures

GAY & LESBIAN YANGON

After Bangkok, expect a subdued scene here in conservative Yangon. **Silver Oak Café** (Map p532; ☎ 299993; 83/91 Bo Aung Kyaw St) is one of the few centres of gay nightlife in the city with live music almost every night. **Patty O'Malleys** (Map p528; ☎ 666900; 1 Kaba Aye Pagoda Rd, Inya Lake) is an underground Irish bar at the Sedona Hotel with a gay-friendly vibe.

of the stars. From Beckham to Bruce Lee, they are all here. Affordable drinks and an international menu make this a good spot to stop by.

Mr Guitar Café (Map p528; ☎ 550105; 22 Sa Yar San St; 6pm-midnight) Burmese music legends often swing by this café-bar, founded by popular singer Nay Myo Say. There is live music nightly from 7pm to midnight. Drinks are expensive compared with downtown bars.

Strand Bar (Map p532; Strand Rd; 11am-11pm) The most expensive digs in town has introduced 'Stranded' happy hours from 5pm to 11pm on Friday. A lot of expats come out of the woodwork for this one and draught beer is just US$1.

CLUBBING

Yangon nightclubs can be an interesting cultural experience for the uninitiated. Most seem to include lots of amateur model shows and little dancing.

Pioneer (Map p530; Yuzuna Garden Hotel, 44 Ah Lan Paya Pagoda St; admission around K4000) This is one of the most popular clubs in town. More a conventional nightclub, it's packed with young, wealthy Burmese. Prices sometimes include a free drink.

DJ Bar (off Map p528; Dusit Inya Lake Hotel, 37 Kaba Aye Paya Rd) The *in* place at the time of writing, this late-night bar with a dance floor rumbles on until 4am on weekends. Way out on Inya Lake.

SHOPPING

Theingyi Zei (Map p532) is the local market for everyday homewares and textiles. It extends four blocks east to west from Kon Zay Dan St to 24th St, and north to south from Anawrahta Rd to Mahabandoola Rd. Theingyi Zei is also renowned for its traditional Burmese herbs and medicines.

Bogyoke Aung San Market (Scott Market; Map p532; Bogyoke Aung San Rd; 8am-6pm Tue-Sun) This grand old labyrinthine market has the largest selection of Burmese handicrafts in Yangon, as well as jewellery, *longyi* (wraparound garment worn by women and men), shoes, bags and pretty much anything else.

GETTING THERE & AWAY

Air

See p524 for information on international air services. For details on domestic flights, which leave from the same airport, see p525.

Boat

There are four main passenger jetties on the Yangon River waterfront, which wraps itself around southern Yangon. Long-distance ferries head up the delta towards Pathein or travel north along the Ayeyarwady River to Pyay, Bagan and Mandalay.

When purchasing a ticket for a particular ferry from the government-run **IWT** (Map p530; ☎ 284055) at the back of Lanthit St jetty, be sure to check from which jetty the boat departs.

Bus

Yangon has two main bus stations. The Highway Bus Centre (Aung Mingalar Bus Terminal; off Map p528) serves the most destinations, while the **Hlaing Thar Yar Bus Terminal** (off Map p528; Hwy No 5, Yangon-Pathein Rd) serves the Delta.

The Highway Bus Centre is a confusing array of competing bus companies in a dusty lot, just southwest of Yangon Airport.

The Hlaing Thar Yar Bus Terminal is a good 45 minutes west of the centre on the other side of the Hlaing River.

Guesthouses can assist with purchasing tickets, which will certainly save time, if not money. Bigger companies with bus-ticket offices (Map p530) opposite the Central Train Station include **Kyaw Express** (☎ 242473), **Sun Moon Express** (☎ 642903) and **Transnational Express** (☎ 249671).

Several buses to Pathein (K3000, three to four hours), Chaungtha Beach (K5000 to K6000, six to seven hours) and Ngwesaung Beach (K5000 to K6000, five hours) leave from the Hlaing Thar Yar Terminal from early morning until about 1pm. The comfiest ones leave early.

BUSES FROM YANGON

The following are some sample fares and trip durations for buses leaving the Highway Bus Centre.

Destination	Fare	Duration
Bagan	K15,000	14hr
Bago	K1000	2hr
Hpa-an	K4500	8hr
Kyaikto	K3000	4½hr
Mandalay	K15,000	12hr
Mawlamyine	K9000	6hr
Taunggyi (for Kalaw & Inle Lake)	K15,000	20hr
Thandwe (for Ngapali)	K12,000	20hr

Train

The 716km-long trip from Yangon to Mandalay is the only train trip most visitors consider, but the government profits handsomely from the overpriced tickets, so we don't recommend it. The express trains are much more comfortable than the average Burmese train. Reserve sleepers (ie anything that contains sleeping berths, including some day trains) several days in advance. There is currently no conventional night sleeper to Mandalay, just a 12.45pm departure that arrives at the absurd hour of 3am. Book advance tickets at the **Yangon train station** (Map p530; ☎ 274027; 🕒 6am-4pm).

GETTING AROUND

Bus

More than 40 numbered city bus routes – on dodgy old pick-ups and newer Japanese or Korean buses with air-con – connect the townships of Yangon. Some can be quite crowded, but midday hops across the centre (for example) beat a taxi. Tickets cost from K20 to K200 depending on the type of bus.

Useful routes:

- Bogyoke Aung San Market to Mingala Zei (near Kandawgyi Lake) – pick-up 1
- Sule Paya to Pyay Rd (University of Yangon; near Inya Lake) to airport – blue bus 51, 52 and air-con bus 51
- Sule Paya to Highway Bus Centre – bus 43, 45, 51
- Sule Paya to Hlaing Thar Yar Bus Station – bus 54, 59, 96
- Sule Paya to Shwedagon Paya – bus 37, 43, 46

Taxi

Licensed taxis carry red licence plates, though there is often little else to distinguish a taxi from any other vehicle in Yangon. The most expensive are the *car-taxis,* beaten-up old Japanese cars. Breakdowns are not exactly unknown. Fares are highly negotiable; trips around the central area cost about K1000 to K1500. Sule Paya to Shwedagon Paya runs at about K2000. Late at night, expect to pay more. A taxi for the day is US$20 to US$30.

Trishaw

There are far fewer trishaws, bicycles or motorcycles in Yangon than anywhere else in Myanmar. Trishaws are useful for getting around downtown, but Yangon is too spread out to use them for sightseeing. Trishaws aren't permitted on the main streets from midnight to 10am. Rides cost about K300 to K1000, depending on the distance covered.

WEST COAST BEACHES & THE DELTA

Thailand may be the beach capital of Southeast Asia, but it's no secret and you'll have to share the sand with everybody else. Myanmar's curvaceous coastline has some tasty slices of sand itself and there are few tourists during the week. Remote Ngapali Beach is the finest, but is rapidly pricing itself out of the backpacker market. Chaungtha Beach and Ngwesaung Beach are easier to reach from Yangon, both via the sleepy delta town of Pathein.

TRAINS FROM YANGON

Destination	Ordinary class	Upper class	Sleeper	Duration
Bagan	US$11	US$31	US$34	19hr
Kyaikto	US$3	US$8	n/a	7hr
Mandalay	US$15	US$30-35	US$40-50	14hr
Thazi	US$9	US$25	US$33	12hr

During the monsoon season (mid-May to mid-September) heavy rains blanket the coast and chase away most travellers.

PATHEIN (BASSEIN)

☎ 042 / pop 300,000

A good staging post on the way to Chaungtha or Ngwesaung Beaches, Pathein is, believe it or not, Myanmar's fourth-largest city. Located in the heart of the Ayeyarwady delta, Pathein is a good place to check the pulse of real local life. It's home to a flourishing parasol industry and is a good place to pick one up during the blasting heat. The wide, scenic Pathein River curves through town, delivering constant action.

Sights

Pathein is famous throughout the country for its 'umbrella' industry – actually parasols for the sun, not rain. These are made in parasol workshops scattered across the northern part of the city, particularly around the Twenty-Eight Paya, off Mahabandoola Rd. Saffron-coloured ones are waterproof. Prices start from just a few thousand kyat. The **Shwe Sar Umbrella Workshop** (☎ 25127; 653 Tawya Kyaung Rd; 🕑 8am-5pm) is a good place to see them being made.

Shwemokhtaw Paya, in the centre of Pathein near the riverfront, is a huge, golden, bell-shaped stupa. The *hti* (decorated top of a pagoda) consists of a top tier made from 6.3kg of solid gold, a middle tier of pure silver and a bottom tier of bronze – the Olympic pagoda perhaps? The seated Buddha in the southern shrine apparently floated here on a raft from Sri Lanka.

Settayaw Paya is the most charming of the several lesser-known *paya* in Pathein. The *paya* compound wraps around a couple of green hillocks dotted with a number of well-constructed *tazaung* (shrine buildings).

Sleeping & Eating

Electricity ebbs and flows in Pathein, but mostly ebbs.

Taan Taan Ta Guest House (☎ 22290; 7 Merchant St; s US$5-7, d US$6-10; ❄) One of the taller hotels in town, top-floor rooms here are brighter, but all rooms are clean and include a bathroom.

Paradise Guest House (☎ 25055; 14 Zegyaung Rd; r US$10; ❄) It may not be paradise, but it delivers the best bang for your buck. Fronting a canal, a short walk from the central market, the rooms are clean and include satellite TV.

Golden Land Restaurant (Merchant St; mains K2000; 🕑 lunch & dinner) North of the clock tower, this place has a leafy garden for alfresco dining and a relaxed atmosphere away from the street action. The menu includes Burmese and Chinese cuisine.

Night market (Strand Rd) After dark, this riverside market draws the young-uns for a spot of flirting. It offers a veritable smorgasbord of treats, including coconut crepes with syrup, fritters, fresh fruit and peanuts steamed in bamboo.

Getting There & Away

Pathein is about 120km west of Yangon.

BOAT

Chinese triple-deckers sail between Yangon and Pathein (ordinary class/cabin US$7/42, 17 hours), leaving at 5pm in either direction. In Yangon, boats depart from the Lanthit St jetty.

BUS

Many buses go to Pathein from Yangon's Hlaing Thar Yar Bus Terminal, most leaving before noon. Tickets range from K2500 to K5000 for the three- to four-hour trip.

Overloaded minibuses leave for Chaungtha Beach (K3000, 2½ hours) around 7am, 11am and 1pm from Pathein's **bus station** (Yadayagone St). It is more comfortable to get a direct bus from Yangon.

Shwe Min Than buses go to Ngwesaung (K3000, 1½ hours) every other hour from 7am to 3pm.

CHAUNGTHA BEACH

☎ 042

This beach is incredibly popular on weekends and holidays, with locals having fun in the sun and sea – fully clothed. Come during the week for some solitude. The best stretch of sand is a 15-minute walk north of town. Chaungtha is a bumpy 40km west of Pathein.

Boats head out to **Whitesand Island** (one way K4000, one hour) at 8am, returning at 5pm. It's a good place for swimming and snorkelling, although there are only three trees for shade. The **market** (🕑 6-9am) is a lively vestige of a time before tourism; it comes to life when the catch comes in.

Sleeping & Eating

Of Myanmar's beach towns, Chaungtha has the cheapest places to stay, though most places are moving up to midrange. Some places close during the wet season.

Shwe Hin Tha Hotel (☎ 24098, in Yangon 01-650588; r US$12-25; ❄) The only affordable hotel facing the beach, the cheaper rooms here are small bungalows with private porches facing the courtyard.

There are several budget places located away from the beach. **Win Villa** (s/d US$3/6) is a wooden home with a balcony and very simple rooms.

Food is available at all guesthouses and hotels, plus there are some point-and-eat restaurants along the village's main street.

Getting There & Away

Guesthouses can arrange boats to Ngwesaung Beach (from K30,000, 1½ hours). Seriously overcrowded minibuses leave for Pathein (K3000, 2½ hours) at 7am, 11am and 1pm from the bus station in the village. Better air-con buses go to Yangon (K5000 to K6000, six to seven hours) at 7am.

NGWESAUNG BEACH

☎ 042

Long touted as the new Ngapali, this is both good news and bad news. The good news is that the beach is a gorgeous 15km stretch of white sand. The bad news is that almost all the resorts and hotels are swanky places geared towards high-spending visitors. The water is deeper and clearer than at Chaungtha, plus there is space to spread out.

Sleeping

Golden Sea Resort (☎ in Yangon 01-241747; s/d US$7/15) This place is one of the only affordable options in Ngwesaung – but it's anyone's guess how long it will hold out. Rooms are in small wooden bungalows with attached bathroom.

Yuzana Resort (☎ 40323; r US$25-45; ❄) This was the first of the mega-resorts built in Ngwesaung. It has a whopping 133 rooms, all equipped with satellite TV, minibar and bathroom. The terrace restaurant here is popular with locals.

Getting There & Away

Shwe Min Than buses go to Pathein (K3000, 1½ hours) every other hour from 7am to 3pm. There are several direct buses to Yangon (K5000 to K6000, five hours).

There are no roads to Chaungtha. Boats can be chartered (from K30,000, 1½ hours) or you can travel by bus via Pathein.

NGAPALI BEACH

☎ 043

The premier beach destination in Myanmar, it's one hell of a ride for those planning on travelling overland. Given its name, some say, by a homesick Italian, Ngapali boasts 3km of palm-fringed sands on the beautiful Bay of Bengal. The turquoise waters deliver a bounty from the sea and this town serves up some of the country's best food. It has moved steadily upmarket in recent years, so there are slim pickings for budget travellers. It is only really worth the trip for those planning to continue on to Sittwe and the temples of Mrauk U (Myohaung).

Sights & Activities

Half-day **snorkel trips** (incl boat, mask & snorkel for up to 5 people US$12-15) are widely promoted. The coral's not spectacular compared with parts of Thailand, but there are plenty of brightly coloured fish to follow.

Jade Taw is a fishing village south of the beach, easily reached on foot, where fish lie drying in the sun on bamboo mats (providing a timely reminder to use sunscreen in this hot place!). Further south by road is **Lontha**, home to a hilltop stupa with superb views. Turn left at the market crossroads and follow the water.

Sleeping & Eating

Grand Resort (s/d US$6/10) Grand and resort aren't the first two words that come to mind when you see this simple place, but it has Ngapali's only surviving budget rooms. Just north of the main strip, the bare-bones rooms have a mattress on the floor and attached bathrooms over the water.

Royal Beach Hotel (☎ 42411, in Yangon 01-243880; royalngapali@myanmar.com.mm; r US$20-50) This atmospheric little hotel, hidden away amid a small forest of palms, has five categories of room available. Rooms have wooden floors, mosquito nets and private bathrooms. Power is sporadic unless you opt for the top-rate rooms with 24-hour generator power.

Linn Thar Oo Lodge (☎ 42333, in Yangon 01-229928; www.linntharoo-ngapali.com; s US$25-40, d US$30-45)

Prices keep on rising at Linn Thar Oo Lodge, but it's one of the cheaper deals in Ngapali. There are 42 bungalows and some of them offer sea views. The more expensive rooms are wood-panelled and include satellite TV and hot water.

The only places serving food or drink for a sunset over the sea are the hotels. Head to the parallel road behind the beach and you'll find some superb open-air, family-run restaurants. Squid with garlic and ginger sauce is a local speciality here. Crab, squid or barracuda is about K3000, tiger prawns K5000. Moonlight, 200m north of Royal Beach, is one of the old favourites here.

Getting There & Around

Visitors reach Ngapali via the **Thandwe Airport** (☎ 42611), 5km north of the beach, or the Thandwe bus station, 9.5km northeast. Flights to Yangon start at US$56, and to Sittwe at US$46.

Long-distance bus services to and from Yangon take about 20 hours, leaving Ngapali around 2pm, and cost K11,000. **Ye Aung Lan** (☎ 43500) sends buses along the smoother route (via Gwa). **Aung Thit Sar** (☎ 43499) goes via Pyay on a stomach-churning trip over the mountains, the bus stuffed with bags of dried fish. Buses will pick you up from your guesthouse. Alternatively, a pick-up from Ngapali leads to Thandwe (K500, 45 minutes), from where it is a trishaw ride to the bus station.

Overland travel to Sittwe is currently not allowed, but it is possible to take a boat from Taunggok, reached by pick-up or the Pyay bus from Thandwe. See p571 for more information.

Guesthouses around Ngapali rent bicycles for about K2000 per day.

CENTRAL MYANMAR

The central plains of Myanmar may lack the iconic sights of places such as Bagan and Inle Lake, but the towns in this area are a rewarding way to escape the tourist trail. The region is primarily an agricultural heartland, but there are some historic towns to break up the long cross-country journeys, and you'll meet incredibly friendly locals along the way.

BAGO (PEGU)

☎ 052 / pop 220,000

Welcome to Buddha World! Bago has carved a niche for itself – and many thousands of niches for its sacred Buddhas – as home to some monumental religious sites. The town lies 80km north of Yangon (en route to Inle Lake or Mandalay), but sees just a handful of travellers, most of whom are on day trips or on their way to the Golden Rock. Founded in AD 573 by the Mon, Bago's days as a major river-port town declined as the river changed course, and the final nail in the coffin came when marauding Burmese king Alaungpaya destroyed it in 1757.

Sights

A US$10 ticket covers entrance to Shwethalyaung, Shwemawdaw Paya, Mahazedi Paya, Kyaik Pun Paya and the Kanbawzathadi Palace. Some of this money may go to site maintenance, but the bulk goes to the government. Ticket checkers finish work at about 4.30pm for those wanting to avoid the fee. All other sights listed have free admission.

SHWETHALYAUNG & AROUND

The Shwethalyaung is a 55m reclining Buddha image that's 9m longer than the famous one at Wat Pho in Bangkok and has a sweet, lifelike face. The jewelled soles of the feet are particularly beautiful. A mural tells the temple's melodramatic story, which began in AD 994.

Just before the Shwethalyaung is the reconstructed **Maha Kalyani Sima** (Hall of Ordination) and a curious quartet of standing Buddha figures.

Carry on beyond the Shwethalyaung and you reach the **Mahazedi Paya**, where men (only) can climb to the top for fine views. Just beyond is **Shwegugale Paya**, including a tunnel lined with 64 seated Buddha images.

SHWEMAWDAW PAYA & AROUND

Rebuilt after an earthquake in 1930, the Shwemawdaw Paya is 14m higher than Shwedagon Paya in Yangon. Look out for the large chunk of the *zedi*'s spire, toppled by an earthquake in 1917, resting at the northeastern corner of the *paya*. The stupa, reached by a covered walkway lined with stalls, draws plenty of

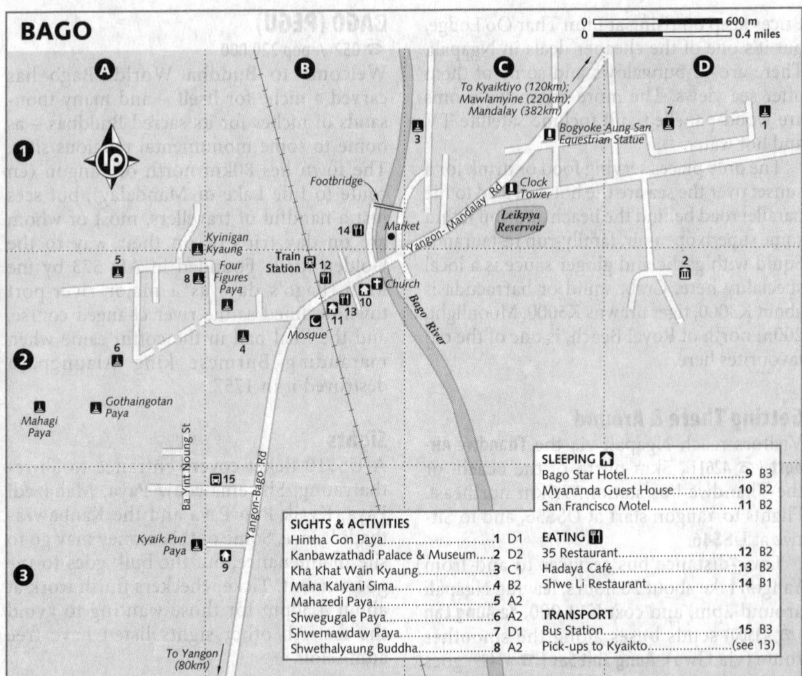

pilgrims during the **full-moon festival** at Tagu (March/April).

Beyond the Shwemawdaw Paya is **Hintha Gon Paya**, a hilltop shrine guarded by mythical swans. This is the place for Bago views without the US$10 charge.

KHA KHAT WAIN KYAUNG

One of the top three biggest *kyaung* (Buddhist monasteries) in Myanmar, this is a bustling hive of 1200 monks, and a welcoming place. Tourists come to watch the 10.30am lunch, but it's more relaxed at other times of the day.

KANBAWZATHADI PALACE & MUSEUM

This Mon-style palace, just south of Shwemawdaw Paya, was the home of a 16th-century Taungoo king. The excavated walls are the only authentic 16th-century artefacts. Everything else is a reproduction, similar to the palace in Mandalay.

Sleeping

Bago has plenty of good-value rooms, but few travellers spend the night here.

San Francisco Motel (☎ 22265; 14 Yangon-Mandalay Rd; s/d from US$5/8; ❄) In the same area as the Myananda, the SF has small but spotless rooms, some offering a balcony.

Myananda Guest House (☎ 22275; 10 Yangon-Mandalay Rd; s US$5-10, d US$8-12; ❄) This is a friendly place located on the busy main road; the cheaper rooms here only have a fan and access to a shared bathroom. Longtime local guide Mr Han hangs out here.

Bago Star Hotel (☎ 23766; 11-13 Kyaikpon Pagoda Rd; s/d US$24/30; ❄ 🏊) The star of the Bago hotel scene, rooms here are set in well-appointed bungalows with satellite TV, hot water and 24-hour air-con. On the same road as Kyaik Pun Paya, the pool is popular after tramping around the temples.

Eating & Drinking

For cheap eats, there are a number of food stalls, including some good Indian biryani sellers, in the centre of town near the market. Beer stations are clustered near the bridge on Main Rd.

Shwe Li Restaurant (194 Strand St; dishes from K1500) For the best all-rounder in town, head to this clean and tidy place with Shan and Indian curries.

35 Restaurant (Yangon-Mandalay Rd; dishes K1500) It's a touch tatty, but this restaurant turns out good-value Bamar, Chinese and even European dishes. Famous for its 'goat fighting balls', that's a load of bollocks, as the British might say.

Hadaya Café (Yangon-Mandalay Rd; 24hr) One of the better teashops in town, Hadaya has a good selection of pastries.

Getting There & Away

BUS & PICK-UP

Buses from Yangon (K2000, two hours) depart approximately hourly from 6am from Yangon's Highway Bus Centre. Pick-ups to Bago (K1500, front seat K2500, up to four hours) depart frequently from Yangon's **Tha-khin Mya Pan-gyan Gate terminal** (Map p530; Strand Rd).

Hadaya Café can help with boarding a Yangon bus heading north. To Mandalay, buses arrive around 7pm; you'll have to pay the full fare (from K9000) for the 12-hour ride.

Air-con buses to Nyaungshwe (Yaunghwe), for Inle Lake, leave around 1.30pm (from K9000, 15 hours), arriving at 4.30am.

To reach Bagan, take a Mandalay-bound bus to Meiktila and catch a ride the next morning to Nyaung U.

Pick-ups east to Kyaikto (for Golden Rock) leave from Hadaya Café (K2500, three hours). Buses go from near the Emperor Hotel (K3000).

TAXI

Some travellers make a day trip out of Bago with a hired car from Yangon, starting from about US$40. One-way rides should cost US$20.

TRAIN

There are several trains daily to Mandalay (ordinary/upper class US$11/29, 14 hours), stopping in Taungoo (US$4/8, four hours), though it can be tricky getting a seat. There are also trains for Yangon (US$2/5, two hours).

Getting Around

Trishaw is the main form of local transport in Bago. A trip in the central area should cost no more than K500. A wise idea is getting one for the day, which should cost about K4000 to K6000.

TAUNGOO

☎054 / pop 90,000

It's hard to imagine this was once the nerve centre of a powerful kingdom. Today's Taungoo is a sleepy place that most people see from a bus or train window. However, it gets the 'real-deal experience' thumbs up from those who do stop and is home to one of Myanmar's more memorable guesthouses. Taungoo is just under halfway from Yangon to Mandalay.

Shwesandaw Paya (1597) is the main pilgrimage site. Several other Buddhist sites are on and around the 'royal lake'. The old moat is on the town's west side.

Up in the Karen mountains, **Seinyay Forest Camp** is a popular elephant camp that some tour groups pop by. The guesthouse following arranges trips for about US$50 per person, which is actually less than half the Yangon rate.

Owned by a wonderfully hospitable pair of doctors, **Myanmar Beauty Guest House II, III & IV** (☎23270; fourdoctors@mptmail.net.mm; Pauk Hla Gyi St; r US$8-25;) are three teak houses with poster beds, hot showers and wide-open views of the rice paddies. Rates include a large breakfast and lively conversation. It's just north of the bridge, to the south of town.

Heading north or south on air-con buses you'll pay the full fare. Most stop at Golden Myanmar Restaurant, in the centre. Rattletrap local buses go to Yangon (K4000) and Mandalay (K5000) around 6pm.

PYAY (PROME)

☎053 / pop 95,000

All roads lead to Pyay, at least some important ones from Yangon, Bagan and Ngapali Beach do, not forgetting the mighty Ayeyarwady River. But the trouble is most visitors just keep on going. It's laid-back enough, with river views and nearby ruins older than Bagan's.

The central statue of Aung San on horseback is 2km west of the bus station, just south of the main market, and a block east of the Ayeyarwady.

Sights

Perched atop a central hill, the attractive **Shwesandaw Paya** is actually 1m taller than Shwedagon Paya in Yangon, and apparently dates from 589 BC. The double golden *hti* atop the *zedi* represent peace between the Mon and Burmese; the second was put up when Burmese leader Alaungpaya captured the city in 1755. Facing the *paya* from the east is **Sehtatgyi Paya** (Big Ten Storey), a giant seated Buddha.

Sleeping & Eating

Aung Gabar Guesthouse (☎ 21400; 1462 Bogyoke Rd; s/d US$3/6) Under friendly management, this is the bargain basement in town. Rooms are small, bathrooms are shared, but at least it's clean.

Myat Lodging House (☎ 21361; 222 Bazaar St; s US$8-10, d US$10-12, tr US$16-18; ❄) Just a block away from the centre of the action, this family-run guesthouse has simple carpeted rooms. Fork out an extra US$2 for a private bathroom, hot water and satellite TV. Pyay maps are available.

Pyay Star Restaurant (cnr Bogyoke & Pyay-Yangon Rds; dishes from K1500) Overlooking the Aung San statue, Pyay Star Restaurant is a lively little beer hall with an upstairs balcony to escape the dusty streets.

Getting There & Away

BOAT

Ferry routes on the Ayeyarwady centre on Pyay. A couple of weekly ferries go to Yangon (ordinary/upper class US$10/20, two or three days) and Mandalay (US$12/25, six or seven days). The **IWT office** (☎ 24503; The Strand; 🕑 9am-5pm Mon-Fri) can help with tickets and times.

BUS

The highway bus station, 2km east of the centre, sends frequent buses to Yangon (K5000, six hours). No direct buses go to Bagan, so it is necessary to change in Magwe for Nyaung U. To reach Thandwe (near Ngapali Beach), catch a bus to Taunggok (K7000 to K9000, nine hours) around at 6pm, from where you can catch a bus or pick-up to Thandwe (four or five hours).

TRAIN

Trains connect Pyay with Yangon (ordinary/upper class US$6/15, 12 hours).

AROUND PYAY

About 8km east of Pyay, **Thayekhittaya** (Sri Ksetra; admission US$4; 🕑 8am-5pm) is a sprawling oval-shaped walled city of the enigmatic Pyu, who ruled here as far back as 1500 years ago. The only real way around the site is by ox cart (K5000), which makes a 12km loop in three hours. Few sites are still standing, but the trip is slow-paced and there are unlikely to be any other tourists. The 46m cylindrical Bawbawgyi Paya is the finest of the temples. From the centre of Pyay, pick-ups go to the bus station, from where eastbound buses go within 2km of the site. A return taxi to the site is about K10,000, including waiting time. It is possible to cycle to the site, but not around it.

West of the road to Yangon, about 14km south of Pyay, **Shwemyetman Paya** (Paya of the Golden Spectacles) is home to a large, white-faced, seated Buddha – sporting a pair of giant gold-plated glasses! Hop on a local Yangon-bound bus or south-bound pick-up, and get off in Shwedaung town.

SOUTHEASTERN MYANMAR

Teetering on the brink, the Golden Rock of Kyaiktiyo draws a few visitors off the main trail, but there is more to the southeast than this sacred and surreal stone. Mawlamyine offers glimpses of old Burma and is the launching pad for the beautiful boat ride upriver to Hpa-an. Some travellers enter Myanmar from Ranong, Thailand, to Kawthoung and the nearby Myeik Archipelago, a flight or boat ride from the rest of Myanmar.

KYAIKTIYO (GOLDEN ROCK)

☎ 035

The gravity-defying golden rock Kyaiktiyo is one of the most enigmatic and intriguing sights among many in Myanmar. Perched on the very edge of a cliff on Mt Kyaikto, this giant, gold-leafed boulder marks the spot of a Buddha hair donated by a hermit in the 11th century. Apparently, the king salvaged it from the bottom of the sea and brought it to this spot by a boat that subsequently turned to stone, visible a few hundred metres away. The place has a mystical and magical aura; it's a place of miracles, not least of which is how the boulder has managed to hang on all these years. Golden Rock draws pilgrims in their thousands during the cooler months between October and March.

Some travellers make a gruelling day trip from Yangon. This is madness, as it warrants more time and is especially beautiful illuminated at night. Plan on spending a night here or in Bago.

Orientation

The town of Kyaikto is 9km away from the foot of Mt Kyaikto. The village of **Kinpun**, sometimes referred to as 'base camp', is a collection of restaurants and guesthouses right at the foot of Mt Kyaikto, and the most common starting point for an ascent.

Sights

There are two ways to see the rock: hiking 11km from Kinpun (four to six hours one way), or trucking and then walking. Most do the latter. Packed trucks from Kinpun (K1000, front seat K2000) ply upwards from 6am to 7pm, stopping for a fascinating 45-minute walk to the stupa. The steep, paved path throngs with pilgrims and monks.

If you want to feel like an extra in *Burmese Days,* locals may offer to carry you up in a sedan-chair for K7000 to K10,000. Only men are permitted to walk along a short chasm-spanning bridge to the boulder itself.

There is a US$6 entrance fee collected at the **MTT office** (6am-6pm).

Sleeping & Eating

Only a few guesthouses in Kinpun accept foreigners; all rates include breakfast.

Pann Myo Thu Inn (s US$4-8, d US$7-15;) The small rooms here could be mistaken for prison cells, but stepping up in price brings wooden floors, furnishings and air-con.

Sea Sar Guest House (s US$4-10, d US$8-20;) The best of a basic bunch in Kinpun, Sea Sar Guest House is popular with the local touts. It's set in shady grounds; splash the cash on the more expensive bungalow-style rooms with private bathroom.

Spend the sunset or sunrise contemplating the Golden Rock by staying up top. **Golden Rock Hotel** (in Yangon 01-502479; grtt@goldenrock.com.mm; s/d US$40/60, bungalows US$50/80;) has the smarter rooms set amid lush vegetation, but it's a 40-minute walk to the balancing boulder. Rooms at **Mountain Top Inn & Restaurant** (in Yangon 01-502479; grtt@goldenrock.com.mm; s/d US$50/60) are surprisingly basic for the buck, but then you're paying for the views from its perfect position on the mountaintop.

Pilgrims aplenty mean that plenty of Chinese and Bamar restaurants line the main street of Kinpun. All are pretty similar, so just look out for places with a crowd. The hotels 'at the top' both have credible restaurants with incredible views.

Getting There & Away

Buses en route from Yangon to points further south stop in Kyaikto. There are buses between Yangon and Kyaikto (K3000, 4½ hours) leaving from Yangon's Highway Bus Centre. The bus stop in Kyaikto is across from Sea Sar Guest House, where you can get a bus to Bago (K2500, three hours) or pick-up (K2000, three hours).

Pick-ups head south to Hpa-an and Mawlamyine (K2500, front seat K4000, four hours) from 6am to 1pm.

There are three trains a day from Yangon (ordinary/1st/upper class US$3/6/8, six hours), two leaving at convenient times in the morning.

MAWLAMYINE (MOULMEIN)

057 / pop 300,000

Moulmein to George Orwell during his time as a policeman here, Myanmar's third-largest city feels more like an overgrown provincial town. Much of the colonial architecture has gone in recent years, replaced by bland Chinese blocks overlooking the Thanlwin (Salween) River. The 3km bridge, the longest in the country, offers long-overdue connections with the north. The real reason to come to Mawlamyine is the beautiful boat ride up to Hpa-an.

The **Mon Cultural Museum** (cnr Baho & Dawei Jetty Rds; admission US$2) has a modest selection of Mon pieces. For a cityscape, climb the tallest stupa, **Kyaikthanlan Paya**, or other nearby pagodas. The mosques in town are the best-kept buildings, particularly the green-and-turquoise **Kaladan Mosque**. The central **zeigyo** (market; South Bogyoke Rd), on the west side of the road, features a few 'off the back of a boat' black-market items.

Pa-Auk-Taw-Ya Kyaung (032-22132; www.paauk.org; c/o Major Kan Saing, 653 Lower Main Rd) is one of the largest meditation centres in Myanmar, about 14km south of town.

A picturesque isle off the city's northwestern end is **Shampoo Island** (Guangse Kyun), reached by boat for K2000.

The best budget place to stay in Mawlamyine is **Breeze Rest House** (Lay Hnyin Tha; 21450; 6 Strand Rd; s US$4-10, d US$8-15;). Set in an old villa, rooms upstairs include a balcony. The friendly owner is a wealth of information on the area.

Attran Hotel (25764; North Bogyoke Rd; s/d US$25/35;) is the most comfortable hotel in town; its riverside setting is an advantage and rooms include satellite TV.

Double-decker ferries from the Hpa-an jetty in Mawlamyine leave on a gorgeous trip amid limestone mountains and sugarcane fields for Hpa-an (US$2, five hours) between noon and 2pm Monday and Friday.

Several overnight buses connect Mawlamyine with Yangon (K9000, seven or eight hours). Pick-ups to Hpa-an (K2000, two hours) leave from the *zeigyo* hourly from 8am to 3pm.

The train station is north of the river in Mottama (Martaban). Three daily express trains connect Mottama with Yangon (ordinary/1st/upper class US$7/13/18, nine hours), stopping in Bago.

HPA-AN

☎ 058

Hpa-an is not so much about the destination as the journey: by riverboat from Mawlamyine. That said, Hpa-an is verdant and villagelike, hemmed in by higgledy-piggledy hills that rise abruptly from the fields. The best activity is to climb the steps up **Mt Zwegabin** (722m), 11km south of town. The views are pretty impressive. Arrive at 11am for the monkey feeding and the monastery offers a free lunch (rice, orange, tea). Watch your rice!

There isn't a huge amount of choice when it comes to staying in Hpa-an. Rooms at **Soe Brothers Guest House** (☎ 21372; 46 Thitsa Rd; s US$4-7, d US$8-10) have windows, but no mosquito nets and shared bathrooms only. However, the owners are helpful and offer information on boats and buses if you ring ahead. Around the corner, **Parami Hotel** (r with shared bathroom per person US$5, r with private bathroom US$22) has mozzie nets, even in the cheapies, but the US$22 rooms are ambitiously priced just for the joy of a private bathroom.

The boat to Mawlamyine leaves on Tuesday and Saturday around 7am. The bus to Yangon's Highway Bus Centre (K5000, 10 to 11 hours) leaves at 6pm. Pick-ups to Kyaikto (K3000) leave from the central green mosque.

KAWTHOUNG

Crossing the Pagyan River from Ranong, Thailand to Myanmar's southernmost tip is like stepping back in time. The waterfront is lined with teashops and moneychangers, plus touts offering boat trips to Thailand. At **Cape Bayinnaung** (Victoria Point), look for the statue of King Bayinnaung, who invaded Siam in the 16th century, pointing a sword towards Thailand.

The offshore **Myeik (Mergui) Archipelago** is one of Myanmar's most beautiful places and the thousands of islands here are almost completely unexplored. The archipelago is home to 'sea gypsies', as the nomadic Salon people are known. Phuket-based tour groups offer high-priced diving and kayaking trips, or try **Moby Dick Tours** (☎ in Yangon 01-202110; www.moby-dick-adventures.com) for overnight trips to islands.

Accommodation pickings are slim in this part of Myanmar. **Kawthoung Motel** (☎ 51046; Bogyoke Rd; r 800B; ❄), 500m up from the jetty, has simple rooms with cold-water private bathrooms. Cheaper, and even more basic, is **Tanintharyi Guest House** (☎ 51748; Garden St; r 400B).

Foreigners can't go from here into Myanmar's 'mainland' by road. **Air Bagan** (code W9; ☎ 01-513322; www.airbagan.com) flies to Yangon (US$135), stopping in Dawei (Tavoy) and Myeik.

GETTING TO THAILAND

It is possible to enter Thailand at Kawthoung; most travellers don't need a visa to enter the country (see p812).

Boats shuttle between Kawthoung and Ranong (Thailand), 10km away, regularly from about 6am to 4.30pm (40 minutes); you can charter a whole boat for 300B. The **immigration office** (🕑 8am-5.30pm) in Kawthoung is at the jetty, while the Thai **immigration office** (☎ 0 7782 2016; Th Ruangrat; 🕑 8.30am-6pm) is 700m north of Saphan Pla (Pla Bridge) pier, where the boats dock. The pier is 4.5km from the centre of Ranong, but you should be able to catch a săwngthăew (small pick-up truck with two benches in the back) into town (7B). Bear in mind that Myanmar is half an hour behind Thailand.

When leaving here, some foreigners have been charged a US$25 'fee' by MTT. Problems may arise for anyone travelling on an expired visa.

See p787 for information on doing the trip in the opposite direction.

Boats from Ranong cost 300B, but prices start much higher – you'll need to haggle. There are daily fast boats to Myeik (US$25, 6½ hours). MFSL ferries to Yangon run to a random timetable and officials may not be willing to sell tickets to foreigners.

INLE LAKE & SHAN STATE

Shan State is vast, untamed and – with rebel groups, warlords and drug dealers living in its mysterious mountains – largely unexplored. Inle Lake is the main attraction, a beautiful body of water hemmed in by mountains and populated by floating communities. Trekking is a popular activity and Kalaw is an affordable base for adventure. This is one of the few parts of Myanmar where homestays are possible and the Shan are some of the friendliest folk in the country. However, ask around locally for the latest situation before making plans to venture into rural areas.

INLE LAKE

☎ 081 / pop 150,000

A wonderful watery world of floating gardens, stilted villages and crumbling stupas, Inle Lake is an absolute must. Mountains tumble down towards the lakeshore, blurring the distinction between heaven and earth. For many travellers, Inle is heaven on earth, a place to while away the days canoeing, cycling and walking through the lush countryside. The Intha people are famous for their leg rowing, although these days many just turn it on for the tourists. There is even a monastery where meditating monks have taught the cats to jump – that's enlightenment for you. Inle deserves to be savoured, not rushed, and many travellers end up staying for longer than they expected.

In September and October, the **Phaung Daw U festival** runs for nearly three weeks and is followed by the **Thadingyut festival**, one of Myanmar's best-known events (see p577).

Always cooler, Inle gets downright chilly at night in January and February.

Orientation & Information

There are many villages in and around Inle Lake, but Nyaungshwe (Yaunghwe) is the biggest and best thanks to a good range of budget accommodation. The transport hub at Shwenyaung is 13km away. Taunggyi is the main town in the area, east of Nyaungshwe, but there is no compelling reason to visit.

To enter the Inle Lake zone, tourists are required to pay a US$3 entry fee at the MTT booth on the main road into Nyaungshwe from Shwenyaung.

There are several internet places in Nyaungshwe. **Freak Internet** (Yone Gyi Rd; per hr K3000) can connect to Hotmail and Yahoo.

Sights & Activities

THE LAKE

The best way to experience the lake is to play the tourist and take a full-day **motorboat tour**. Any guesthouse – or anyone with a boat near the waterfront – can arrange one for K15,000 to K20,000 a day, depending on the places to be visited. Half-day trips cost about K10,000. Popular stops include the **floating gardens of Kela**, the 'jumping cat' monastery of **Nga Phe Kyaung**, the wooded stupas of **Indein**, and whichever village market is on that day. They'll also take you to artisans' shops, where weaving, blacksmithing and jewellery-making go on. The workshops are interesting, but there's no obligation to buy anything. Cloth is one of the better buys around Inle Lake.

Another option that avoids the buzzing motors of the longtail boats is a self-guided **canoe trip** through the villages on the lesser-seen north end of the lake. Check out the *nat* shrine opposite Nanthe village, south of Nyaungshwe. Rates start at K1000 per hour. Ask at guesthouses or try the local boatmen.

IN NYAUNGSHWE

The **Museum of Shan Chiefs** (Third St; admission US$2; 🕑 9.30am-3.30pm Tue-Sun), housed in a stately teak-and-brick mansion, was once the palace of the last Shan *sao pha* (chieftain). There are many Shan furnishings and costumes on display, plus a teak-floored audience hall in the north wing.

There are plenty of Buddhist sites around town (see Map p548); the oldest is **Yadana Man Aung Paya**, with a step-spired stupa.

OTHER ACTIVITIES

Turn up the heat at the **hot spring** (public/private bathing US$1/3; 🕑 7am-5pm), close to the Intha village of Kaungdaing. Rent a *longyi* for bathing for K200. A boat comes here from Nyaungshwe (K1000 each way), or it is possible to cycle on a bumpy, hour-long ride.

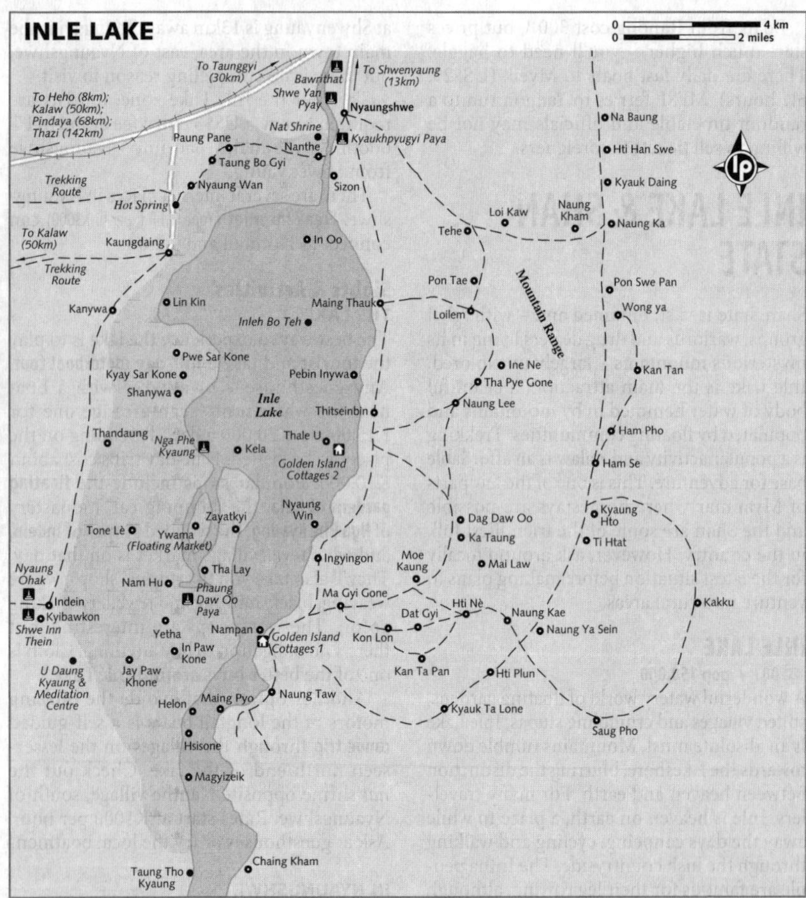

Guided **day treks** can usually be arranged through guesthouses for approximately US$7 to US$8 per day. There is a good, but fairly rugged, all-day trip that leads to the monastery of **Koun Soun Taungbo** and to a nearby cave, heading past two Pa-O villages along the way.

Sleeping

Nyaungshwe is teeming with good budget rooms. All include breakfast and rent bicycles unless otherwise noted.

Queen Inn (☎ 29544; s/d from US$5/7) The Queen has a selection of little bungalows set on the banks of the river opposite town. The friendly family can't do enough for guests and offers tasty home cooking.

Remember Inn (☎ 29257; remember@myanmar.com.mm; Haw St; s US$5-10, d US$8-15; 💻) Friendly and informative, Remember is just as popular with taxi drivers as with travellers (commission and all that). The cheaper bamboo rooms are fine, or invest more for a bathtub.

Aquarius Inn (☎ 29352; 2 Phaung Daw Pyan Rd; s/d US$7/12) Large, cosy, all-wooden rooms make this a traveller favourite. There is a large garden with table tennis, plus a small library.

Four Sisters Inn (☎ 29190; 105 Nan Pan Qtr; s/d US$7/12) Run by, you guessed it, four sisters, this is a friendly, family guesthouse in the south of town. Rooms include hot water and are set around a small garden.

Teakwood Hotel (☎ 29250; teakwoodhtl@myanmar.com.mm; r old wing US$12-15, new wing US$15-30) One of the classier places in town, Teakwood has some cheap rooms in the original house and some smarter rooms in a new 'boutique' wing with some decorative flourish. The family is very welcoming, including matriarch Mrs Tin.

Viewpoint Hotel (☎ 29062; Jetty Rd; s/d US$15/20) The canalside location of this hotel is wonderfully atmospheric, but the morning boats wake guests at the crack of dawn. The bungalows are large with breezy balconies, but are starting to show signs of age.

Golden Island Cottages 1 & 2 (☎ in Taunggyi 081-23136, in Yangon 01-549019; www.gicmyanmar.com; s US$40-80, d US$45-100; 💻) This is the place to sleep over the water in Inle. Boasting two locations in Nampan and Thale U, the main lodge is connected to smart, stilted cottages via elevated walkways. Nampan offers better lake views, but Thale U is more peaceful. Both places are run as a Pa-O collective, benefiting the local community.

Other budget options:

Joy Hotel (☎ 29083; Jetty Rd; s US$4-8, d US$6-12) Quiet escape from the main drag overlooking a small canal to the west of the market.

Nawng Kham (Little Inn; ☎ 29195; Phaung Daw Pyan Rd; s/d US$5/10) Just seven rooms, it's little, but has good views of the nearby *zedi*.

Eating & Drinking

Aroma Restaurant (Chaung Rd; dishes from K1500; 🕑 lunch & dinner) This tiny restaurant is the hole-in-the-wall relation of Aroma in Bagan and turns out the best Indian curries in town.

Golden Kite Restaurant (Yone Gyi Rd; dishes K2000-4000; 🕑 breakfast, lunch & dinner) The name sounds Chinese, but the menu is Italian, including homegrown herbs, homemade pasta, imported cheese, pizzas and gnocchi.

Unique Superb Food House (3 Myawady Rd; mains K2000-4000) So modesty is not its strong point, but it's a modest-looking set-up with an extensive menu of international favourites.

Viewpoint (☎ 29250; Talk Nan Bridge; mains K2500-5000) Set in a colonial-style baroque building that beckons you in, this is the smartest restaurant in town. It promises 'Shan nouvelle cuisine' and blends European presentation with local flavours. The decoration is opulent, the drinks list extensive, but tax and service charge are an extra hit.

MYANMAR (BURMA)

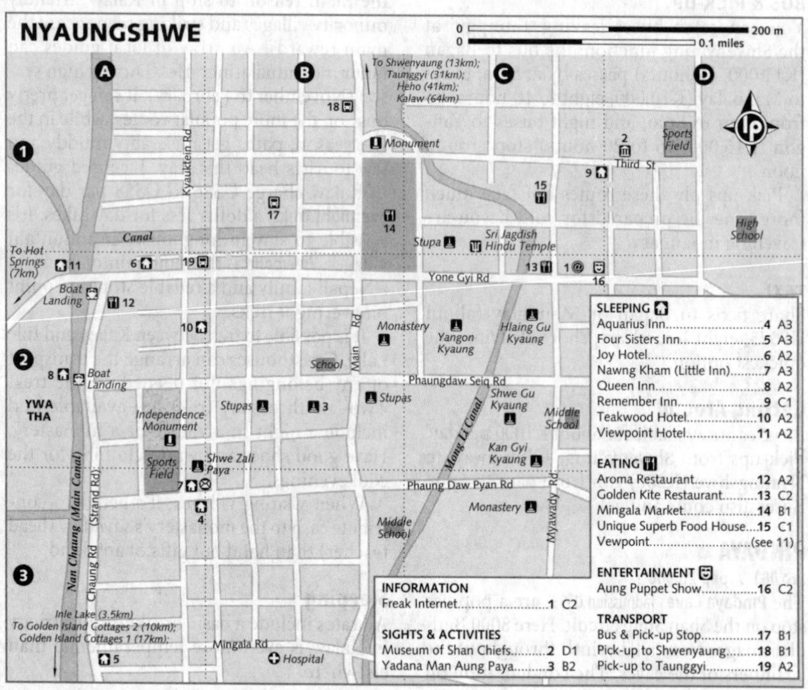

If you are no longer egg-cited by the hotel breakfast, head to Nyaungshwe's **Mingala market** (Main Rd) for a Shan *hkauq-sweh* (noodle soup) in the morning. Later in the day, there is a range of exotic-looking snacks available, plus luscious fresh fruits.

Entertainment

Aung Traditional Puppet Show (Yone Gyi Rd; admission K2000; 7pm & 8.30pm) This house is home to a local puppet troupe that performs nightly. It's a good deal compared with US$8 in Mandalay.

Getting There & Away

AIR

Air Bagan (code W9; ☎ 01-513322; www.airbagan.com), **Air Mandalay** (code 6T; ☎ 01-525488; www.airmandalay.com) and **Yangon Airways** (code HK; ☎ 01-383106; www.yangonair.com) fly to Heho, 41km northwest. Guesthouses can help you arrange tickets. Flights to Yangon start at US$75, Mandalay at US$35. A taxi from Heho is hard to get for under US$18. Going to the airport it should be possible to arrange something cheaper.

BUS & PICK-UP

You can catch buses leaving Taunggyi at the Shwenyaung junction: the bus to Bagan (K11,000, 12 hours) passes by at 5am; buses to Mandalay (K10,000, eight to 10 hours) go from 6pm to 8pm; and night buses to Yangon (K15,000, 16 to 20 hours) stop around noon.

Pick-ups ply these routes but take much more time. Be prepared for cold if you are travelling in January.

TAXI

Share taxis to Bagan or Mandalay (about US$75, eight hours) are, short of flying, the quickest option.

Getting Around

Bicycles are available for about K1000 per day. Pick-ups from Shwenyaung, 13km away, to Nyaungshwe (K300) run from 6am to 6pm. Buses also come and go.

PINDAYA

☎ 081 / pop 20,000

The **Pindaya Caves** (admission US$3) are a popular stop on the Shan State circuit. Here 8000 Buddha images form a labyrinth throughout the chambers of the caves. The condensation on the 'perspiring Buddhas' is rubbed on the face for good luck.

Golden Cave Hotel (☎ 40227; s US$15-25, d US$20-30; ❄) is the best place to stay in town, with wooden rooms, some with balcony views of the cave entrance.

From Kalaw, take a local bus to Aungban (K300) and catch another to Pindaya (K1000) – leave early and allow a full day. It's more convenient to hire a taxi from Kalaw for US$20 to US$25.

KALAW

☎ 081 / pop 12,000

Kalaw is earning a cool reputation among budget travellers, and it's not just due to its chilly winter weather. Located at 1320m on the rolling, pine-clad hills of the Shan Plateau, this is Myanmar's budget trekking heartland. Located to the west of beautiful Inle Lake, some travellers enjoy hiking between the two (about 45km), on mountains dotted with Palaung, Pa-O, Intha and Shan villages.

Activities

Exploring the pretty countryside on foot is the main reason to stop in Kalaw; friendly minority villages and striking scenery are the main rewards. An array of local guides can tailor individual itineraries. During high season (November to February), it can get pretty busy on the more popular routes, while in the wet season, paths get miserably muddy and few tourists head this way. Licensed guides in Kalaw charge US$6 to US$8 per day for **overnight treks**, a dollar less for day hikes. It's possible to stay in longhouses in mountain villages; **Viewpoint** is the mountaintop home of a Nepali family and a reliable stopping point on overnight treks.

It is possible to trek between Kalaw and Inle Lake. Guesthouses can arrange the transport of any belongings not needed on the trek. Two- or three-day treks are available and include a night in a village or a monastery. Have good shoes and warm clothing for the cool evenings.

When visiting villages, it's better to contribute cash to the monastery's *sayadaw* (head teacher) than hand out gifts of any kind.

Sleeping

All rates include a basic breakfast. Electricity in Kalaw is even more temperamental than elsewhere.

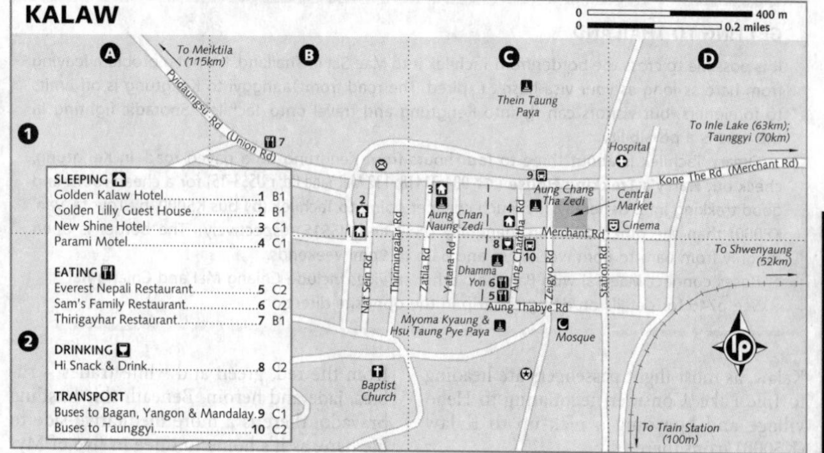

Golden Lilly Guest House (☎ 50108; goldenlilly@myanmar.com.mm; 5/88 Nat Sein Rd; s/d US$3/6) A popular family-run place, the Golden Lilly has large, threadbare rooms with a front porch and an attached bathroom at the rear. Robin is a reliable trekking guide based here. Email is available but, like the rest of Kalaw, there's no internet.

Golden Kalaw Hotel (☎ 50311; 66 Nat Sein Rd; s/d US$3/6, with bathroom US$6/8) Right next door to Lilly, this old house is a rambling place with large rooms and a communal area for hanging out downstairs.

Parami Motel (☎ 50027; Merchant Rd; s US$5-7, d US$10-12) A large hotel near the market, the Parami Motel has cheapies with shared bathrooms, as well as some more expensive rooms (with private bathrooms) that have just been upgraded.

New Shine Hotel (☎ 50028; newshine@myanmar.com.mm; 21 Union Rd; s US$15-20, d US$25-30) Part of the local chain Golden Express, this is a possibility for those seeking a step up in comfort. Superior rooms are bigger with a bath, but all have satellite TV.

Eating & Drinking

Everest Nepali Restaurant (Aung Chantha Rd; dishes from K1500; breakfast, lunch & dinner) Recently relocated over the road, this is an old favourite for chapatis and curry, washed down with freshly squeezed juices.

Sam's Family Restaurant (Aung Chantha Rd; dishes from K1500) Love is in the air... The white tablecloths and candlelight here are unexpected finds in the Kalaw backstreets. This is a reliable stop for Chinese and Bamar meals.

Thirigayhar Restaurant (Union Rd; mains from K2500; breakfast, lunch & dinner) This place sometimes draws the tour groups for Shan, Indian or Western cuisine, thanks to a homely set-up that is the most appealing in town.

Hi Snack & Drink (Aung Chantha Rd) For a dose of local nightlife, try this wooden bar that churns out beer and hosts occasional impromptu guitar concerts.

Getting There & Away

Many buses pass through Kalaw (heading towards Bagan, Yangon, Mandalay and Taunggyi), so it may be easier to stop here first, then leave the region from Inle Lake or Taunggyi to the east. Guesthouses can help with bus tickets, as can the general store next to the main bus stop in town.

Yangon-bound buses from Taunggyi pass by in the evening (K11,000, about 15 hours). It's also possible to board a bus to Bagan (K9000) or Mandalay (K8000). A bus to Shwenyaung (the Inle Lake junction) costs K4000 and takes three hours. A taxi to Meiktila is about US$35.

There are also slow train services to Thazi (ordinary/upper class US$3/5), Heho (US$2/3) and Shwenyaung (US$2/3).

Kalaw is about the same distance from Heho Airport as Nyaungshwe, so it is possible to get in or out by air. (See opposite for more on flights and taxis.) However, it is harder to find people to share with for

GETTING TO THAILAND

It is possible to cross the border from Tachilek into Mae Sai in Thailand. It's not a problem leaving from here as long as your visa hasn't expired. The road from Taunggyi to Kengtung is off limits to foreigners, but visitors can fly into Kengtung and travel onto Tachilek. Sporadic fighting in the area is a possibility.

Dreary Tachilek is about three to four hours from Kengtung on a paved road. In Kengtung, check out **Harry's Trekking House** (☎ 084-21418; 132 Mai Yang Rd; r US$3-15) for a cheap room and good trekking info. Generally, it's much cheaper going to Tachilek (by bus K5000, by Toyota 'van' K8000) than the other direction (generally US$7 and US$15 respectively). The border is open roughly from 6am to 6pm weekdays, and 6am to 9pm weekends.

Buses connect Mae Sai with Bangkok; other services include Chiang Mai and Chiang Rai.

See p746 for details on doing the trip in the opposite direction.

Kalaw, as most flight passengers are heading to Inle Lake. Consider negotiating to Heho village and boarding a pick-up to Kalaw (K5000) from there.

MANDALAY

☎ 02 / pop 950,000

Compared with the ancient treasures surrounding the city, Mandalay is a veritable whippersnapper at just 150 years old. Founded as capital of the Burmese empire in 1861, Mandalay saw the swansong of the last kings of Burma. The British stormed in and took over in 1885 in a one-sided conflict.

Poetic though the name may be, Mandalay is a thoroughly modern city, the second largest in the country. The dusty streets sprawl east of the Ayeyarwady and south of Mandalay Hill, a stupa-studded hill looming over the flat cityscape. It's impossible not to be impressed by the golden Buddha of Mahamuni Paya, but the real attractions lie beyond town in the nearby ancient cities.

The town continues to boom thanks to Chinese investment and, so the story goes, from the red, green and white trades – rubies, jade and heroin. Beneath this bustling bravado, there is a more meditative side to life here, as it's home to three in five of Myanmar's Buddhist monks.

GETTING INTO TOWN

Most visitors arrive at the ramshackle Highway Bus Station, 7km south of the centre. A share taxi to town is about K4000. The train station is downtown, south of the Mandalay Palace; trishaws cannot linger at the entry/exit ramps, but are nearby. The airport is a staggering 45km from the centre. A taxi to town is about US$15, more like US$10 if going *to* the airport.

ORIENTATION

Lower numbered streets run east–west, starting from north to south. The north–south-running streets are numbered 60 and above, higher streets to the west. The main arteries include 35th and 80th Sts. The city centre, called 'downtown' by English-speaking locals, runs roughly from 21st to 35th Sts, and 80th to 88th Sts. Street addresses usually include cross streets; in Mandalay, '66th St, 26/27' means '66th St between 26th and 27th Sts'.

Look out for the free foldout Mandalay map, produced by Delta Media.

INFORMATION

Internet Access

Many guesthouses have a lone computer offering internet access for K1000 or so per hour. Other reliable places for that online fix:

Fuji Cyber Coffee House (Map p555; 78th St, 37/38; 8am-11pm) On the top floor of 78 Shopping Centre, an air-con retreat with fast terminals.

Micro-Electronics Email Service (Map p555; 83rd St, 23/24; 9am-8.30pm) Near the backpacker heartland.

PAC Internet (Map p553; 83rd St, 35/36; 8am-8pm) Switched-on place with access to all websites and cheap internet calls.

Medical Services

Main Hospital (Map p553; 30th St, 74/77)

Money

Exchange rates in Mandalay are slightly lower than in Yangon, but better than elsewhere.

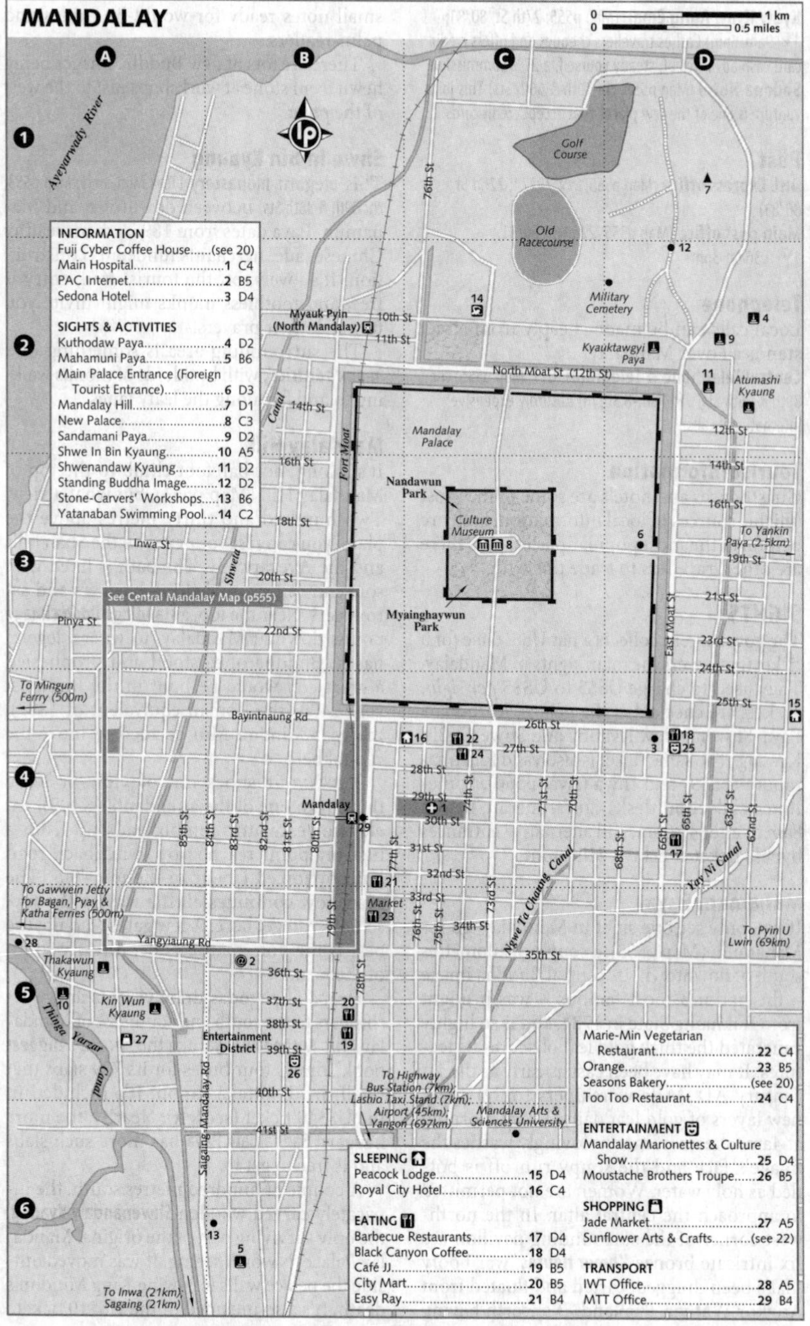
MANDALAY
INFORMATION
Fuji Cyber Coffee House......(see 20)
Main Hospital.......1 C4
PAC Internet.......2 B5
Sedona Hotel.......3 D4
SIGHTS & ACTIVITIES
Kuthodaw Paya.......4 D2
Mahamuni Paya.......5 B6
Main Palace Entrance (Foreign Tourist Entrance).......6 D3
Mandalay Hill.......7 D1
New Palace.......8 C3
Sandamani Paya.......9 D2
Shwe In Bin Kyaung.......10 A5
Shwenandaw Kyaung.......11 D2
Standing Buddha Image.......12 D2
Stone-Carvers' Workshops.......13 B6
Yatanaban Swimming Pool.......14 C2
SLEEPING
Peacock Lodge.......15 D4
Royal City Hotel.......16 C4
EATING
Barbecue Restaurants.......17 D4
Black Canyon Coffee.......18 D4
Café JJ.......19 B5
City Mart.......20 B5
Easy Ray.......21 B4
Marie-Min Vegetarian Restaurant.......22 C4
Orange.......23 B5
Seasons Bakery.......(see 20)
Too Too Restaurant.......24 C4
ENTERTAINMENT
Mandalay Marionettes & Culture Show.......25 D4
Moustache Brothers Troupe.......26 B5
SHOPPING
Jade Market.......27 A5
Sunflower Arts & Crafts.......(see 22)
TRANSPORT
IWT Office.......28 A5
MTT Office.......29 B4
Ayeyarwady River
Golf Course
Old Racecourse
Military Cemetery
Myauk Pyin (North Mandalay)
Kyauktawgyi Paya
Atumashi Kyaung
North Moat St (12th St)
Mandalay Palace
Nandawun Park
Culture Museum
Myainghaywun Park
Fort Moat
East Moat St
Shweta Canal
See Central Mandalay Map (p555)
To Mingun Ferry (500m)
To Yankin Paya (2.5km)
To Gawwein Jetty for Bagan, Pyay & Katha Ferries (500m)
To Pyin U Lwin (69km)
Thakawun Kyaung
Kin Wun Kyaung
Thinga Yarzar Canal
Entertainment District
To Highway Bus Station (7km); Lashio Taxi Stand (7km); Airport (45km); Yangon (697km)
Mandalay Arts & Sciences University
To Inwa (21km); Sagaing (21km)
Saigaing-Mandalay Rd
Nyawe Ta Chaung Canal
Yay Ni Canal
Market
Mandalay
Inwa St
Pinya St
Bayintnaung Rd
Yangyiaung Rd
0 1 km
0 0.5 miles

MYANMAR (BURMA)

Kyaw Kyaw Aung Email (Map p555; 27th St, 80/81; 9am-6pm) Cashes travellers cheques and offers credit card cash advances at, steady yourself, a 27% commission.
Sedona Hotel (Map p553; cnr 26th & 66th Sts) This joint venture is one of the few places that accept credit cards.

Post

DHL Express office (Map p555; ☎ 39274; 22nd St, 80/81)
Main post office (Map p555; 22nd St, 80/81; 9.30am-3pm)

Telephone

Local calls can be made cheaply from street stands all over Mandalay.
Central Telephone & Telegraph (CTT; Map p555; cnr 80th & 26th Sts; 7am-8.30pm) Absurdly expensive international calls.

Tourist Information

Guesthouses and hotels are some of the most reliable sources of local information. Staff are helpful at the most popular places, plus there are other travellers to trade tips with.

SIGHTS

The government collects a flat US$10 fee for a ticket that covers the main sights in Mandalay. They used to charge US$3 to US$5 *per sight.* Tickets are checked at the palace, Kuthodaw Paya, Shwenandaw Kyaung and Shwe Ta Bin Kyaung. The same ticket is also valid for Amarapura (p559) and Inwa (Ava; p560). Sometimes collection desks don't operate before 8am or after 4.30pm, and alternative entrances bypass ticket checkers. Hint hint.

Mahamuni Paya

If you only see one sight in Mandalay, go for Mahamuni (Map p553), a couple of kilometres south of downtown. Its central Buddha image – the nation's most famous – was brought from Rakhaing State in 1784, and is so highly venerated the thick gold leaf obscures its features. It may have been cast as early as the 1st century AD. Male worshipers (only) apply new layers of gold leaf daily. Every morning at 4am, a team of monks lovingly washes the image's face and the soupy run-off is bottled as holy water. Women are not permitted to approach the central altar. In the northwest corner of the surrounding pavilion are six intricate bronze **Khmer figures**, war booty that's been dragged, carted and floated from Angkor Wat via Thailand. It's worth having small notes ready for would-be guides and palm-readers.

There are lots of new Buddha images being hewn from stone at workshops just to the west of the *paya.*

Shwe In Bin Kyaung

This elegant **monastery** (Teak Monastery; Map p553; cnr 89th & 38th Sts) between downtown and Mahamuni Paya dates from 1895, when wealthy Chinese jade merchants funded its construction. It's lovely, off the tourist trail, entry is free, and toothless monks might invite you to watch their prayers.

The surrounding area is something of a **'monk's district'**, with hundreds of monks walking to and fro along the leafy lanes.

Mandalay Hill

It's a long, hot barefoot climb to the top of Mandalay Hill (Map p553), but what a view. Two hundred and thirty metres above the plain, you can rest your eyes on the Shan hills and the Ayeyarwady. The path is lined with souvenir sellers, cold-drink hawkers and astrologers. Near the top, a **standing Buddha image** points down at Mandalay, to where, legend has it, Buddha once stood and prophesied a great city would be built in the Buddhist year 2400 (the Roman equivalent of 1857), the year Mindon Min decided to move the capital here.

Tuck your shoes out of view or leave them with one of the attendants (K100). An elevator/escalator combo leads up from a halfway point reached by switchback road built by forced labour in the mid-'90s. The road now continues all the way to the top, so taxis can get here. A few gates lead up; the best is the lion-guarded one, directly south of the peak.

Heaps of pagodas draw visitors and worshippers to the south and southeast of Mandalay Hill. **Kuthodaw Paya**, aka the 'world's biggest book', draws tour buses for its 729 slabs that retell the Tripitaka canon. It's included in the US$10 ticket (see left). Nearby, the more haggard **Sandamani Paya** has more such slabs and is free to get in.

A couple of hundred metres south, the intricately carved wooden **Shwenandaw Kyaung**, the only surviving part of the original Mandalay Palace, is worth seeing. It was moved outside the palace walls following King Mindon's death. It's also included in the US$10 ticket.

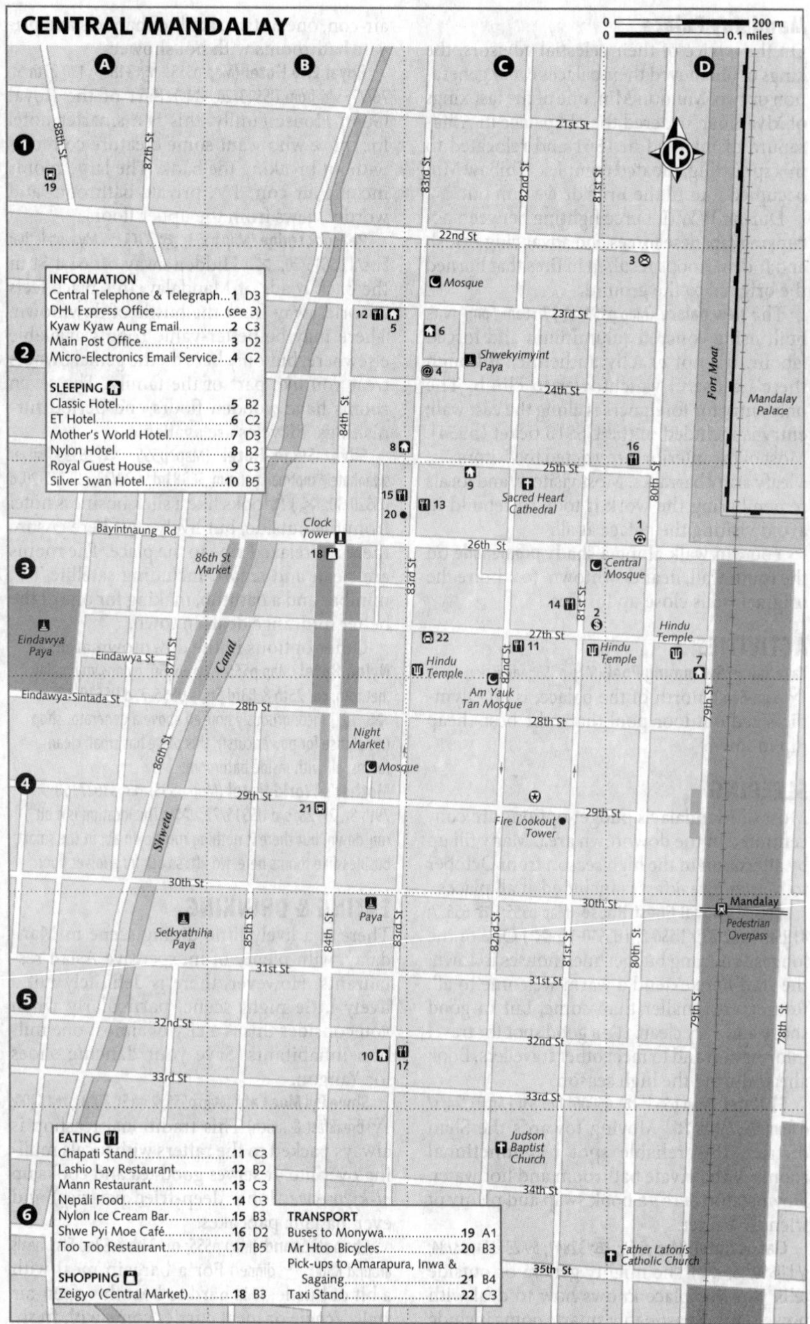
CENTRAL MANDALAY
0 200 m
0 0.1 miles
A
B
C
D
1
2
3
4
5
6
INFORMATION
Central Telephone & Telegraph....1 D3
DHL Express Office....(see 3)
Kyaw Kyaw Aung Email....2 C3
Main Post Office....3 D2
Micro-Electronics Email Service....4 C2
SLEEPING
Classic Hotel....5 B2
ET Hotel....6 C2
Mother's World Hotel....7 D3
Nylon Hotel....8 B2
Royal Guest House....9 C3
Silver Swan Hotel....10 B5
EATING
Chapati Stand....11 C3
Lashio Lay Restaurant....12 B2
Mann Restaurant....13 C3
Nepali Food....14 C3
Nylon Ice Cream Bar....15 B3
Shwe Pyi Moe Café....16 D2
Too Too Restaurant....17 B5
SHOPPING
Zeigyo (Central Market)....18 B3
TRANSPORT
Buses to Monywa....19 A1
Mr Htoo Bicycles....20 B3
Pick-ups to Amarapura, Inwa & Sagaing....21 B4
Taxi Stand....22 C3
88th St
87th St
86th St
85th St
84th St
83rd St
82nd St
81st St
80th St
79th St
78th St
21st St
22nd St
23rd St
24th St
25th St
26th St
27th St
28th St
29th St
30th St
31st St
32nd St
33rd St
34th St
35th St
Bayintnaung Rd
Eindawya St
Eindawya-Sintada St
Mosque
Shwekyimyint Paya
Fort Moat
Mandalay Palace
Sacred Heart Cathedral
Clock Tower
86th St Market
Central Mosque
Eindawya Paya
Canal
Hindu Temple
Am Yauk Tan Mosque
Night Market
Shweta
Fire Lookout Tower
Mandalay
Pedestrian Overpass
Setkyathiha Paya
Paya
Judson Baptist Church
Father Lafonis Catholic Church

MYANMAR (BURMA)

Mandalay Palace

On the advice of their celestial advisors, the kings of old moved their palaces every generation or two. Mindon Min, one of the last kings of Myanmar, ordered the old palace in Amarapura dismantled in 1861 and relocated to this sprawling, moated complex. Thibaw Min occupied it until the Brits drove him out.

During WWII, fierce fighting between occupying Japanese forces and advancing British and Indian troops resulted in fires that burned the original to the ground.

The **new palace** (Map p553; 7.30am-5pm) was built using concrete, aluminium and forced labour. It's not exactly authentic, although there's a useful watchtower to climb. The only entry for foreigners is along the east wall; entry is included in the US$10 ticket (p554). Most of the interior – restricted to visitors – is a leafy army barracks. Most visitors, and locals remembering the work it took to rebuild it, avoid visiting the palace at all.

You can walk along a shady **promenade** on the south wall, near downtown, to admire the original walls close up for free.

ACTIVITIES

Yatanaban Swimming Pool (Map p553; admission K200; 5am-6pm), north of the palace, is an Olympic-sized outdoor pool that's the best cheap dip in town.

SLEEPING

Most of Mandalay's budget options are concentrated in the downtown area. Many fill up by afternoon in the high season from October to March. Breakfast is included at all places.

our pick **Royal Guest House** (Map p555; 65697; 41 25th St, 82/83; s US$6-8, d US$10-15;) One of the longest-running budget guesthouses in town, the staff here extend a warm welcome to all. Rooms are smaller than some, but in good shape and very clean. It's a good spot for travel information and to meet other travellers. Book ahead during the high season.

ET Hotel (Map p555; 65006; 129 83rd St, 23/24; s/d from US$7/10;) Moving towards the Shan district, this reliable spot has functional rooms with private bathroom and hot water. Downstairs there's a book swap and plenty of friendly banter.

Classic Hotel (Map p555; 32841; 59 23rd St, 83/84; s/d US$8/15;) The mighty generator outside tells you this place knows how to deal with power cuts. Reasonably smart rooms include air-con, one or two satellite channels and private bathrooms with hot showers.

Royal City Hotel (Map p553; 31805; 130 27th St, 76/77; s/d from US$13/20;) Part of the Royal Guest House family, this is a smarter hotel for those who want some creature comforts without breaking the bank. The large rooms include air-con, TV, private bathroom and worthy views from the upper floors.

Peacock Lodge (Map p553; 33411; 5 Myaypadethar St; s/d US$15/20;) Hidden away off 61st St in the back roads of Mandalay, this place feels a world away from the bustle of downtown. There may be better-value rooms available elsewhere, but only here do the genial owners treat you like part of the family. The seven rooms have wooden floors and period furnishings. Bicycles are available.

Silver Swan Hotel (Map p555; 36333; silverswanhotel@mptmail.net.mm; 568 83rd St, 32/33; s US$15-20, d US$20-30;) It looks like a slick business hotel from the outside, but lively staff here ensure there is a relaxed vibe to the place. The rooms are clean and smart, including satellite TV, minibar and a bathtub, making for one of the better midrange deals in town.

Other options in the downtown area:

Nylon Hotel (Map p555; 66550; nylon@mandalay.net.mm; cnr 25th & 83rd Sts; s US$5-7, d US$10-15;) Incongruously housed above a generator shop (no excuse for power cuts!), this place has small clean rooms, all with inside bathroom.

Mother's World Hotel (Map p555; 33627; 58 79th St, 27/28; s/d US$15/22;) The location is a bit run-down, but there is nothing run-down about the smart, businesslike rooms here. No lift, so ask for a lower floor.

EATING & DRINKING

There is a lively little dining scene in Mandalay, with plenty of inexpensive Asian restaurants. However, there is definitely not a lively little night scene, particularly when you consider this is a city of almost one million inhabitants. Save your dancing shoes for Yangon.

Shwe Pyi Moe Café (Map p555; 25th St, 80/81; tea K100; breakfast & lunch) This traditional teashop is always packed to the rafters with locals mulling over life. It serves good tea and cooks up *ei-kyar-kwe* (long, deep-fried pastries) and even banana pancakes.

Chapati Stand (Map p555; cnr 27th & 82nd Sts; meals around K500; dinner) For a bargain meal with a bit of bustle, it is hard to beat this open-air stall. Veggie or meat curries come with fresh, steaming chapatis. There's a mixed crowd: *longyi*, skullcaps, turbans and Kathmandu backpacks.

Easy Ray (Map p553; ☎ 60396; 78th St, 32/33; drinks from K500; breakfast, lunch & dinner) Spread over three floors, this is where young, cool couples come to hang out. Yes, sorry, this is as cool as it gets in Mandalay and that's only thanks to the air-con.

Marie-Min Vegetarian Restaurant (Map p553; 27th St, 74/75; dishes K600-1400; breakfast, lunch & dinner, closed May) Long a budget favourite, this Indian restaurant offers a wholesome range of vegetarian dishes. Chapatis are a major feature, with a range of dips and curries on the side. The delicious lassis are made with purified water. It's down a lane just off the main drag.

Too Too Restaurant (Map p553; 27th St, 74/75; meals K800; lunch & dinner) Burma's greatest culinary hits are all available here, bubbling away in saucepans each day. Catfish, prawn, chicken, veggie, the curries come in many flavours. Locals swear it's best at lunch. There's a second larger branch (Map p555; 83rd St, 32/33) opposite the Silver Swan Hotel.

our pick **Lashio Lay Restaurant** (Map p555; 65 23rd St, 83/84; dishes around K1000; breakfast, lunch & dinner) This no-frills Shan restaurant has some of the best food in town. If you don't believe us, just look at the queue of locals coming for lunchtime takeaway. Choose from about 25 or more dishes daily, all with soup, salad and rice.

Nepali Food (Map p555; 81st St, 26/27; dishes K1000; breakfast, lunch & dinner) Can't wait until Kathmandu for that curry fix, Nepal style? This place serves no meat, no alcohol and no eggs, just bargain thalis with three curries, chapati, rice and dhal.

Mann Restaurant (Map p555; 83rd St, 25/26; dishes K1000-2000; breakfast, lunch & dinner) This creaky Chinese place is showing its age, but the middle kingdom meals remain a good deal. There are usually a few travellers swilling beers; the local girls promoting Dagon Beer also serve a fair share of boozy locals.

Black Canyon Coffee (Map p553; ☎ 68123; 66th St, 26/27; coffees from K2000, meals K2000-7000; breakfast, lunch & dinner) This Thai exile is a fine spot for creative coffee kicks by day and authentic Thai dining by night. It's opposite the Sedona in a stylish town house.

Café JJ (Map p553; ☎ 66511; cnr 78th & 38th Sts; mains K2500-5000; lunch & dinner) A most unexpected oasis, this designer restaurant includes lavish Burmese décor, subtle lighting and soft seating. The menu is mainly international, and there's a well-stocked bar and live music on the weekend.

Nylon Ice Cream Bar (Map p555; 173 83rd St, 25/26; breakfast, lunch & dinner) This timeless ice-cream parlour is a popular meeting place for locals on a sunny afternoon to cool off over some ice cream. Most travellers prefer to cool off with a chilled Myanmar Beer.

Barbecue Restaurants (Map p553; 30th St, 65/66; lunch & dinner) For a barbecue fix hit 30th St, where there is a strip of open-air barbecue restaurants cooking up skewers of pork, chicken, fish, veggies, spiced bean curd and lady fingers. Beer flows and the locals are friendly. A full meal with a drink costs about K5000.

Anyone planning a long boat or train journey or some trekking around Hsipaw should head to one of the better-stocked supermarkets in town for some treats. **City Mart** (Map p553; 78 Shopping Centre, 78th St, 37/38) is one of the best with lots of imported temptations. **Seasons Bakery** (Map p553; 78 Shopping Centre, 78th St, 37/38), in the same complex, offers fresh breads, cakes and savouries. Or try **Orange** (Map p553; Skywalk Shopping Centre, 78th St, 33/34), another reliable supermarket. Purchase fresh fruit from locals along the way.

ENTERTAINMENT

Mandalay Marionettes & Culture Show (Map p553; ☎ 34446; 66th St, 26/27; admission US$8; 8.30pm) This traditional puppet show, with live musical accompaniment, includes episodes of *zat pwe* (re-creation of Buddhist tales) and *yama pwe* (tales from the Indian epic Ramayana). The show has more than doubled in price in recent years; cheaper shows (some free) are available in Bagan and Inle Lake.

SHOPPING

Crafts are a popular purchase in Mandalay. It is possible to pick up marionettes (new and old) for a few dollars, as well as *kalaga* (a traditional tapestry) and other antiques.

Sunflower Arts & Crafts (Map p553; 27th St, 74/75) Part of Marie-Min Vegetarian Restaurant includes two showrooms of old wood and bronze pieces and some anatomically correct (read dangling genitalia) puppets. Mandalay Marionettes (above) also sells puppets.

Zeigyo (Central Market; Map p555; 84th St, 26/28) Spread over two large modern buildings, this market is packed with plenty of Myanmar-made items (including handicrafts) that spill onto the surrounding footpaths.

Jade market (Map p553; admission US$1; 7am-5pm) Amid the 'monk district', this market features dozens of stalls and tables where locals get serious about green rocks. Beware of fakes.

GETTING THERE & AWAY

See p560 for details on pick-ups and other transport to Amarapura, Inwa, Sagaing and Mingun.

Air

Mandalay sees daily services to and from Yangon (from US$75), Nyaung U (for Bagan; from US$35) and Heho (for Inle Lake; from US$35), as well as flights to Kengtung, Bhamo and Myitkyina. **Air Bagan** (code AB; ☎ 61791; www.airbagan.com), **Air Mandalay** (code 6T; ☎ 31548; www.airmandalay.com) and **Yangon Airways** (code HK; ☎ 31799; www.yangonair.com) all serve Mandalay. Domestic fares are usually slightly cheaper at travel agents.

Boat

The **IWT office** (Map p553; ☎ 36035; 35th St; 10am-2pm) has information on boats on the Ayeyarwady, including trips to Bagan (lower deck/upper deck US$10/20, 15 hours, 5.30am Wednesday and Sunday) on the slow boat, and to Bhamo (lower deck/upper deck/cabin US$9/24/54, two to three days, 6am Monday, Thursday and Sunday). Gawwein Jetty is a little further to the west and is the place to buy tickets. IWT boats are government-owned and operated. Express boats to Bagan had been suspended at the time of writing. However, private operator **Malikha** (☎ 72279, 09511 8357; www.malikhatravels.com) has high-speed boats to Bagan. The schedule isn't yet fixed, but it is likely to depart three times a week and will cost US$23, double the price of upstream due to demand.

Bus

Mandalay's dusty Highway Bus Station (off Map p553) sees a mind-numbing array of daily options for transport. You can arrange

THE MOUSTACHE BROTHERS ARE UNDER SURVEILLANCE

Comprising Myanmar's best-known dissident comedians, the **Moustache Brothers Troupe** (Map p553; 39th St, 80/81; donation US$5; 8.30pm) performs nightly in the brothers' simple home in Mandalay's backstreets. Officially banned from outdoor performances, the three brothers and their family have celebrated traditional Burmese folk opera for three decades. It has to be one of the smallest 'theatres' in the world and the action is an in-yer-face blend of slapstick, political satire, Myanmar history, traditional dance and music. Lu Maw's English is pretty good, but he is a wealth of idioms and slang, which can make it hard for non-native English speakers to follow. He jokes about traditional *a-nyeint pwes* (folk operas) being all-night affairs: 'Now just one hour, we rip you off, you are sitting ducks'.

The three brothers, Par Par Lay, Lu Zaw and Lu Maw have won international acclaim for their bravery in facing up to the military regime in Myanmar. Invited to perform at Aung San Suu Kyi's house in 1996, Par Par Lay and Lu Zaw were arrested by police for telling political jokes and sentenced to seven year's hard labour. Lu Maw was in Mandalay 'holding the fort' at the time. Soon the imprisoned brothers became a cause célèbre and celebrities such as Rob Reiner were petitioning for their release. Par Par Lay even got a mention in the Hugh Grant film *About a Boy*.

The brothers were released in 2002 and celebrated with some signature performances. They were then told they could no longer perform, so began to 'demonstrate' performances without costume. So the show went on, every night, deriding the government for everything from corruption to stupidity. Somehow the government seemed to leave them alone, although Lu Maw would tell the audience that the KGB is watching, as the Moustache Brothers are under surveillance. 'If they come, father gives a whistle. The performers run away and they arrest the tourists,' he laughed. Guests would look nervous, but he'd give them a reassuring wink. However, in September 2007 Par Par Lay was arrested again.

Lu Maw's wife once featured on the cover of an Italian edition of the Lonely Planet guide to Myanmar. The whole family is friendly and welcomes visitors for a chat before the show, which continues despite Par Par Lay's disappearance. We urge our readers to support their performance, as they are one of the few dissenting voices in a nation silenced by oppression.

MANDALAY BUSES & FARES

Destination	Fare	Duration	Departures	Type of Bus
Bagan	K6500	8hr	9am, 2pm & 9pm	local
Meiktila	K3000	3hr	frequent	local
Taunggyi (to Inle Lake)	K11,000	10-12hr	6pm	air-con
Yangon	K15,000	12-15hr	5.30pm	air-con

tickets to Yangon at small stands downtown or check with your guesthouse on the latest, greatest company.

Buses for Monywa (K5000, four hours) leave from a small downtown station (Map p555) off 88th St. Some Monywa-bound drivers refuse to take foreigners.

Taxi

The easiest way to Pyin U Lwin (Maymyo) is via share taxi (per person about K4000, 1½ hours). Check at your guesthouse or at the **taxi stand** (Map p555; cnr 27th & 83rd Sts). The Highway Bus Station has a **Lashio taxi stand** (off Map p553; ☎ 80765) for vehicles to Hsipaw (K8000, five hours) or Lashio (K10,000, seven hours).

Train

Mandalay's enormous train station includes a government-run **MTT office** (Map p555; ☎ 22541; ⏲ 9.30am-6pm), just inside the main (east) entrance. Come here for English-language information on train times, but aim to buy your tickets upstairs to avoid the MTT commission. Better still don't use the train, as it is a government operation.

At the time of research, just four trains a day were heading to Yangon (via Thazi, Taungoo and Bago). Three are inconveniently bunched together on the half-hour between 5am and 6am, while one night train departs at 10.30pm. Ordinary tickets cost US$12 to US$16, 1st class US$33 to US$38 and sleepers US$36 to US$44.

Trains also leave for Nyaung U (Bagan; 1st class US$10, 10 hours) at 9pm. Three daily trains go to Myitkyina (ordinary/upper class from US$11/30, 24 hours). One morning train goes northeast to Pyin U Lwin (US$3/5, three hours) and Hsipaw (US$4/7, 10 hours).

GETTING AROUND

Try not to shop with a driver, as you'll end up paying over the odds thanks to commission deals drivers work out with shop owners.

Bicycle & Motorcycle

There are several central places to rent bicycles, including **Mr Htoo Bicycles** (Map p555; 83rd St, 25/26; per day K2000; ⏲ 8am-7pm). Marie-Min Vegetarian Restaurant (p557) can usually help to arrange a motorbike.

Bus

Mandalay's city buses are very crowded, particularly during the 7am to 9am and 4pm to 5pm rush hours.

Taxi

White taxis and 'blue taxis' (which are ancient Mazda pick-ups) whisk folks around Mandalay most hours. Prices are negotiable. A ride from downtown to the Bagan jetty is about K2000 or so. A full-day trip by blue taxi to nearby attractions is about K20,000.

Trishaw

Trishaws are the usual around-town transport. Count on K300 to K500 for a short ride, and K1000 for a longer one, such as Mandalay Hill to downtown. Always bargain. At night, expect rates to rise.

AROUND MANDALAY

For most visitors, the real draw of Mandalay is day-tripping to the four old cities nearby. Lesser-seen Monywa is on an interesting less-travelled route from Mandalay to Bagan via Pakokku.

AMARAPURA

The 'City of Immortality', a short-lived capital 11km south of Mandalay, is famed for **U Bein's Bridge**, the world's longest teak bridge at 1.2km. At 200 years old, the bridge sees lots of life along its 1060 teak posts, with monks and fishers commuting to and fro. It leads to **Kyauktawgyi Paya** and small **Taungthaman** village, with tea and toddy shops. A popular sunset activity is renting a **boat** (about K2000) to drift by as the skies turn orange, or watching life go by from a waterside beer station.

Just west is the **Ganayon Kyaung**, where hundreds, if not thousands of monks breakfast at 11am. Resist the temptation to thrust a camera in their faces, as some travellers do.

The highway is about 1km west of the bridge; ask the pick-up driver for directions. It's possible to cycle from Mandalay in about 45 minutes.

Amarapura is included in the Mandalay US$10 ticket (see p554) and checks were in place during our last visit.

INWA (AVA)

Cut off by rivers and canals, Inwa (called Ava by the British) served as the Burmese capital for nearly four centuries. **Horse carts** (2 people K5000) lead a three-hour loop around Inwa's handful of sights. Beside the road, villagers till soil or bathe in ponds in an area picturesquely dotted with abandoned temples. Admission is included in the US$10 Mandalay ticket (see p554).

The finest sight is the atmospheric and unrenovated **Bagaya Kyaung**, a teak monastery supported by 267 posts. The 27m **Nanmyin** watchtower leans precariously. Look for the breast-shaped Kaunghmudaw Paya in the distance, across the river about 10km west of Sagaing. **Maha Aungmye Bonzan** (aka Ok Kyaung) is a brick-and-stucco monastery dating from 1822.

Take a pick-up to the Inwa junction. From here it's 1km south to the water, where there are boats to Inwa.

SAGAING

Across the Ava Bridge from the Inwa junction, the stupa-studded hilltops of Sagaing loom over the Ayeyarwady. With 500 stupas and monasteries galore, Sagaing is where Burmese Buddhists come to relax and meditate – friendly monks have been known to invite visitors to stay. Travellers wanting to practise *satipatthana vipassana* like this spot too. Try the meditation centre **Kyaswa Kyaung** (☎ 072-21541; ulkyaswa@myanmar.com.mm). Sagaing is also known for **silver shops** and **guitars**.

Sagaing Hill (admission US$3) is the big attraction. Trees hang over stone steps leading past monasteries to the top. **Tilawkaguru** (donation K500), near the southwest base, is a mural-filled cave temple dating from 1672. There are great views above, and pathways lead all the way to the water for the adventurer. The hill is 1km north of the market. Some locals know free ways up, but the admission fee also includes Mingun.

Pick-ups leave from near the market. Sagaing is spread out. A trishaw driver can take the strain for about K4000 for half a day.

SEEING THE ANCIENT CITIES 101

Frequent **pick-ups** (Map p555; cnr 29th & 84th Sts) leave when full from Mandalay, stopping at Amarapura (30 minutes) and the Inwa junction (40 minutes) before reaching Sagaing (45 minutes). It's K200 during the day, K400 after dark. Some shoestringers pool kyat for a 'blue taxi', which costs from K20,000 to K25,000 for a full day. Seeing the three in one day is a real rush, but can be done. Mingun is only accessible by boat (see below).

MINGUN

Up and across the Ayeyarwady from Mandalay, **Mingun** (admission US$3) is an adventurous visit. The boat drifts peacefully for 11km, and a half dozen sights face the water, all peppered with ample opportunities for noodles, art and postcards. The **Mingun Paya** is actually the remains of a planned 150m stupa, surely a candidate for the world's largest pile of bricks. It is still possible to climb up. Just north is the **Mingun Bell**, the world's largest uncracked bell. It's worth pressing on 200m north to the white, wavy-terraced **Hsinbyume Paya**. Admission to Mingun includes Sagaing.

Negotiate with private boats for a return ride for about K10,000, including some stops along the way. There is also a government-run boat (K1500, 1½ hours) that departs daily at 9am and returns at 1pm.

MONYWA

☎ 071 / pop 140,000

This scrappy trade town, 136km west of Mandalay, is missed by most visitors, but has some superb sights nearby. About 20km south, **Thanboddhay Paya** (admission US$3; 6am-5pm) bursts with carnival shades of pink, orange, yellow and blue. Inside are over half a million Buddhas filling nooks and crannies. About 4km east of the *paya* is a Buddha frenzy in the foothills, including a 90m **reclining Buddha** and the world's second-tallest standing Buddha. The easiest way to visit is by taxi.

Across the Chindwin River and 25km west, the 492 **Hpo Win Daung Caves** (admission US$2) occupy a mountain shaped like a reclining Buddha. There are many carved Buddhas, with streams of light beaming through holes in the walls, plus whole temples carved into the rock, giving the feeling of a mini Petra. It's best to go with a guide. To get here, catch a boat from the Monywa jetty (each way K1500), then a jeep from a jeep stand (five people one way K8000, charter return about K20,000).

The rooms at the rear of **Shwe Taung Tarn Hotel & Restaurant** (☎ 21478; 70 Station Rd; r/bungalows US$5/8; ❄) are a pretty good deal, with wooden floors, air-con and TV. There is also a good range of Burmese food available in the restaurant.

Hourly buses leave for Mandalay (K5000, four hours) from the station, 1.5km south of the centre. For information on going the other way, see p558. Four daily buses go to Pakokku (K4000, 4½ hours) en route to Bagan. There are no passenger ferries.

PYIN U LWIN (MAYMYO)

☎ 085 / pop 80,000

This is little Britain, colonial stylée, with cooler weather than in Mandalay and wide boulevards lined with stately homes from a bygone era. Set in the foothills of northern Shan State, this former British hill town was known as Maymyo during the British era. It is easy to while away some time biking along shady avenues or sipping tea with the friendly locals. Local transport includes cute pony-led miniature wagons, straight out of the Wells Fargo days of the American West.

Domestic tourists gravitate here during the hottest months (from March to May).

Orientation & Information

For a small town, Pyin U Lwin is very spread out. The highway between Mandalay and Hsipaw doubles as the main road.

Get online opposite the bus stand at **Shwe Htay Internet** (Main Rd; ⏲ 8am-9pm).

Sights

Modelled on the famous Kew Gardens of London, the **National Kandawgyi Gardens** (☎ 22130; admission K2000, camera/video K200/K1000; ⏲ 8am-5pm) is a 176-hectare little Eden, with an inviting pool facing a small lake. It's a few kilometres to the west of the town centre.

In town, the **Purcell Tower**, a gift from Queen Victoria, still chimes to the tune of Big Ben. The **market** is filled with local strawberry jam and wine, plus pullover-makers leaning over old sewing machines.

The most enjoyable day trip is to the attractive **Anisakan Falls** (admission free), a 45-minute hilly trek from the village of Anisakan, itself 8km south of Pyin U Lwin. It may be easiest to go with a guide (including taxi about K20,000). Pick-ups run to Anisakan (around K500) from the main road in Pyin U Lwin.

Sleeping & Eating

The most appealing hotels are located to the south and southwest of town. All rates include breakfast. For reliable Chinese food, try the restaurants lining the side streets to the north and south of the main road.

Golden Dream Hotel (☎ 21302; 42/43 Main Rd; s US$3-5, d US$6-10) If you want to be in the thick of the (limited) action, this old stand-by is run by a friendly Indian family. Cheap rooms have a balcony but no bathroom.

Grace Hotel 1 (☎ 21230; 114A Nann Myaing Rd; s & d per person US$7) The Grace is set in spacious gardens just a stroll away from the centre of town. The rooms are basic but include a bathroom.

Dahlia Motel (☎ 22255, 09-204 4153; s US$8-15, d US$15-25) There's a traveller vibe here thanks to the outgoing owner, a self-confessed 'rock and roll Muslim' (translation: drinks beer, eats pork sometimes). All rooms have private bathrooms and satellite TV.

Golden Triangle Café & Bakery (☎ 24288; Mandalay-Lashio Rd; sandwiches & pizzas K2000-4000; ⏲ breakfast, lunch & dinner) Housed in a grand old building, this is a good bet for a snack, pastry or freshly brewed local coffee.

Getting There & Away

Pyin U Lwin has limited bus services. By far the easiest way to or from Mandalay or Hsipaw is by share taxi. A small share-taxi stand on the main road, 200m east of the clock tower, arranges taxis to Mandalay (K4000, two hours) and Hsipaw (K5500, three hours). Most go from 7am to 2pm or 3pm.

Pick-up trucks, lingering near Purcell Tower, head to Mandalay (K2000) and, less frequently, Hsipaw (K3500).

The train station is north of the main road, 1km east of the taxi stand. See p562 for more information about this famous stretch of railway.

HSIPAW

☎ 082 / pop 15,000

Hsipaw has its own time zone where the clocks tick more slowly. Travellers come to this laid-back highland town for a couple of days and before they know it a week has passed. Hsipaw is a popular base for trekking and hosts a bustling riverside market each morning.

Bawgyo Paya Pwe is held here in February/March (see p576). Technically in Shan State, the usual gateways are Pyin U Lwin and Mandalay.

Sights & Activities

The **Shan Palace** (suggested donation US$2; 4pm-sunset), built in 1924, is home to the nephew of the last prince of Hsipaw and his wife. The gracious couple shows guests the mansion's memorabilia and tells its story, which is intertwined with that of Shan State. For more, read *Twilight over Burma: My Life as a Shan Princess*, by Austrian-American Inge Sargent. The palace is in the north part of town.

For a great sunset, walk to either **Five Buddha Hill** or **Nine Buddha Hill**. Cross the bridge on the Lashio road, walk 200m and look for a path leading to both hills.

Boat trips along the Dokhtawady can be arranged through the Mr Charles or Nam Khae Mao Guest Houses from about US$5 per person.

Talk to **Mr Book**, who runs a bookshop on the main road and gives out hand-drawn maps of outlying-area treks. He also organises river tubing in the summer.

Sleeping & Eating

Nam Khae Mao Guest House (☎ 80088; nkmao@myanmar.com.mm; 134 Bogyoke Rd; s/d with shared bathroom US$3/6, with private bathroom US$6/10) Next to the clock tower, this friendly place is pretty rundown, but a fallback if Mr C is full.

Mr Charles Guest House (☎ 80105; 105 Auba St; s US$3-6, d US$6-15) This is one of the best-known budget places in Myanmar, and the veranda here has seen many a late-night beer session over the years. Smarter rooms are in a new annexe, which is also a bit quieter.

The market stalls offer Hsipaw's best cheap eats. **Mr Food** (Law Chun; Namtu Rd), on the main road, pulls the travellers thanks to its English-language menu and satellite TV. Across from Mr Food, **Burmese Cuisine** (Namtu Rd; curry K500) has a row of pots filled with tasty curries, including pumpkin for vegetarians.

Getting There & Away

Bus services often involve unscheduled stops, known as breakdowns. Buses leave Hsipaw at 6am for Mandalay (K5000), stopping in Pyin U Lwin. Buses also head to Lashio (K2000, two hours), 72km northeast.

Most people go by share taxi to or from Mandalay (per person K8000, four hours). Taxis to Lashio cost K3500.

The train to Pyin U Lwin crosses the Gokteik Gorge and is revered as one of Myanmar's most beautiful rides, though the carriages can rock like a horse. It's supposed to leave Hsipaw at 9.30am daily but is often late.

BAGAN (PAGAN) REGION

BAGAN

☎ 02 & 061

Gather all of Europe's medieval cathedrals onto Manhattan island and throw in a whole lot more for good measure, and you'll start to get a sense of the ambition of the temple-filled plain of Bagan. Rivalling the temples of Angkor for the crown of Southeast Asia's most memorable sight, the 4400 temples here date from around the same period more than 800 years ago. Angkor's individual temples may be more spectacular, but Bagan's brilliance is in the wonderful collective views of stupa upon stupa dotting the plain. High season can get very busy, while low season allows some silence and solitude, although the vendors will usually track you down eventually.

History

Bagan was born when King Anawrahta took the throne by force in 1044. He unified the country, introduced Theravada Buddhism and began building Bagan's first temple, the grand Shwezigon. The hubristic Anawrahta coveted the sacred Buddhist scriptures (the Tripitaka) held by the very Mons who enlightened him. When they refused to hand them over, he took them by force. Anawrahta was eventually killed by a wild buffalo, but his dynasty ruled for 200 years. This was Bagan's golden age, a period of manic temple building. Things began to go bad under

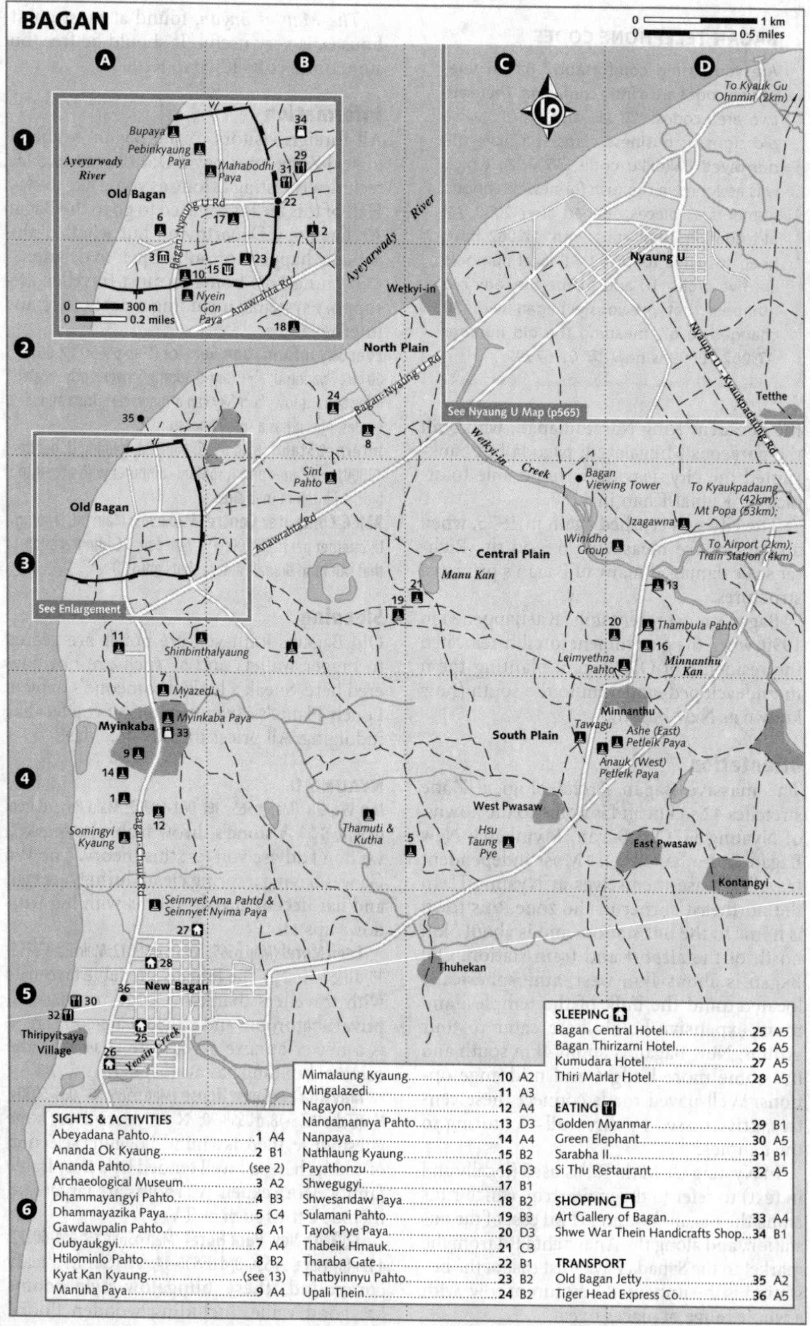
BAGAN
0 1 km
0 0.5 miles
A
B
C
D
1
2
3
4
5
6
Bupaya
Pebinkyaung Paya
Mahabodhi Paya
Ayeyarwady River
Old Bagan
Bagan-Nyaung U Rd
Anawrahta Rd
Nyein Gon Paya
0 300 m
0 0.2 miles
Ayeyarwady River
Wetkyi-in
North Plain
Bagan-Nyaung U Rd
Sint Pahto
Old Bagan
See Enlargement
Central Plain
Manu Kan
Shinbinthalyaung
Myazedi
Myinkaba
Myinkaba Paya
Somingyi Kyaung
Bagan-Chauk Rd
Seinnyet Ama Pahto & Seinnyet Nyima Paya
New Bagan
Thiripyitsaya Village
Yeosin Creek
Thamuti & Kutha
Thuhekan
To Kyauk Gu Ohnmin (2km)
Nyaung U
Nyaung U - Kyaukpadaung Rd
Tetthe
See Nyaung U Map (p565)
Wetkyi-in Creek
Bagan Viewing Tower
To Kyaukpadaung (42km); Mt Popa (53km);
Izagawna
To Airport (2km); Train Station (4km)
Winidho Group
Thambula Pahto
Leimyethna Pahto
Minnanthu Kan
Minnanthu
South Plain
Tawagu
Ashe (East) Petleik Paya
Anauk (West) Petleik Paya
West Pwasaw
Hsu Taung Pye
East Pwasaw
Kontangyi
SIGHTS & ACTIVITIES
Abeyadana Pahto 1 A4
Ananda Ok Kyaung 2 B1
Ananda Pahto (see 2)
Archaeological Museum 3 A2
Dhammayangyi Pahto 4 B3
Dhammayazika Paya 5 C4
Gawdawpalin Pahto 6 A1
Gubyaukgyi 7 A4
Htilominlo Pahto 8 B2
Kyat Kan Kyaung (see 13)
Manuha Paya 9 A4
Mimalaung Kyaung 10 A2
Mingalazedi 11 A3
Nagayon 12 A4
Nandamannya Pahto 13 D3
Nanpaya 14 A4
Nathlaung Kyaung 15 B2
Payathonzu 16 D3
Shwegugyi 17 B1
Shwesandaw Paya 18 B2
Sulamani Pahto 19 B3
Tayok Pye Paya 20 D3
Thabeik Hmauk 21 C3
Tharaba Gate 22 B1
Thatbyinnyu Pahto 23 B2
Upali Thein 24 B2
SLEEPING
Bagan Central Hotel 25 A5
Bagan Thirizarni Hotel 26 A5
Kumudara Hotel 27 A5
Thiri Marlar Hotel 28 A5
EATING
Golden Myanmar 29 B1
Green Elephant 30 A5
Sarabha II 31 B1
Si Thu Restaurant 32 A5
SHOPPING
Art Gallery of Bagan 33 A4
Shwe War Thein Handicrafts Shop 34 B1
TRANSPORT
Old Bagan Jetty 35 A2
Tiger Head Express Co 36 A5

BAGAN TELEPHONE CODES

Are you sitting comfortably? Bagan telephone codes are a little confusing. There are two area codes: ☎ 061 and ☎ 02. Some old signs or business cards still have the borrowed Pakokku code (☎ 062), which was assigned in the rush for new telephone numbers as places opened after 2000. All old numbers that start with ☎ 062 have been switched to ☎ 02. All local numbers are five digits. To add to the fun, any old numbers that previously began with 70 changed to 67, meaning the old number ☎ 062-70999 is now ☎ 02-67999.

the decadent King Narathihapati, who built the gorgeous Mingalazedi pagoda but bankrupted the city, leaving it vulnerable to attack by Kublai Khan in 1287.

The city was crushed again in 1975, when an earthquake measuring 6.5 on the Richter scale damaged many of Bagan's principal structures.

Bagan's most recent upheaval happened in 1990, when the government forcibly relocated the residents of Old Bagan, planting them in undeveloped land 4km to the south (now known as New Bagan).

Orientation

The massive Bagan Archaeological Zone stretches 42 sq km and is home to the 'towns' of Nyaung U, Old Bagan, Myinkaba, New Bagan and a few others. Most independent travellers base themselves at Nyaung U. In the northeast corner of the zone, this town is home to the bus station, and is about 5km north of the airport and train station. Old Bagan is about 4km west, atmospherically located amid the bulk of the temples, and more expensive hotels here cater to tour groups. New Bagan is about 4km south and has some more budget and midrange options. Well-paved roads connect these centres, crisscrossed by dirt trails venturing to the temples.

In Nyaung U, 'Main Rd' is used (locally and in text) to refer to the main strip, which runs along the Bagan–Nyaung U Rd east of the bus station, and along the Anawrahta Rd from the market to the Sapada Paya. Just east of the bus station is the unnamed 'restaurant row' with a whole range of places to eat.

The Map of Bagan, found at most guesthouses, is very useful. It should be free, but sometimes costs K500 to K1000.

Information

All foreign visitors to the Bagan Archaeological Zone must pay a US$10 entrance fee, technically lasting as long as you'd like to stay. Half of this fee is supposed to go to the Bagan Archaeology Department, but whether this actually happens or not is open to debate.

Nyaung U is home to most traveller life-support systems, including a post office and internet access.

Ever Sky Information Service (Map p565; ☎ 061-60146; Nyaung U; 7am-9.30pm) Conveniently located in restaurant row, Ever Sky can arrange cars, trips and guides, plus it has a small bookstore.

Internet Stand (Map p565; Main Rd, Nyaung U; per hr K2000; 8am-8pm) A solitary computer with access to blocked internet mail sites.

RMCG Computer Centre (Map p565; Main Rd, Nyaung U; internet per hr K2500; 7am-9pm) Computer shop that can burn digital camera shots onto CD.

Sleeping

Old Bagan's joint-venture hotels are geared to bigger wallets and as such are not covered here. Sneak a look at someone's copy of Lonely Planet's *Myanmar* guide if you feel like indulging. All prices include breakfast.

NYAUNG U

Inn Wa Ga (Map p565; ☎ 061-60902; Main Rd; s/d from US$4/8;) A stone's throw from the market, we don't advise you test this theory. The Wa Ga was having a spring clean during our visit and has decent air-con rooms with big windows upstairs.

Eden Motel (Map p565; ☎ 061-60812; Main Rd; s US$5-10, d US$7-15;) The Eden is a reliable favourite with travellers thanks to large rooms with private bathroom and efficient air-con. There is a newer annexe across the road, but the original building has atmosphere.

May Kha Lar Guest House (Map p565; ☎ 061-60304; Main Rd; s US$5-18, d US$8-20;) A deceptively large guesthouse, there is a mind-boggling selection of rooms here, all well tended by a hospitable family. More expensive rooms are larger and include extras such as TV.

our pick **New Park Hotel** (Map p565; ☎ 061-60322; 4 Thiripyitsaya; s US$6-8, d US$10-14;) Set in a leafy compound, these bungalow-style rooms are good value, including wooden floors, attached bathrooms and porches. The owners are friendly and informed, plus it's just a stroll to 'restaurant row'.

Golden Express Hotel (Map p565; ☎ 02-67101; geh@myanmar.com.mm; Main Rd; s US$15-25, d US$18-30;) The cheaper rooms here are a cheap ticket to the swimming pool (US$3 for non-guests), which is a real draw after a hot day exploring the temples. Rooms are well-equipped with bathrooms and satellite TV. It is a couple of kilometres west of town.

Thante Hotel (Map p565; ☎ 02-67317; nyaungu thante@mptmail.net.mm; Main Rd; s/d US$30/35;) The Thante is a fair deal for those wanting some extra creature comforts and access to a pool. The extensive gardens are home to roomy bungalows with satellite TV, minibar and deck chairs on a small porch. Nonguests can use the pool for US$3.

Other cheap deals:

Pann Cherry Guest House (Map p565; ☎ 061-60075; Main Rd; s US$3-4, d US$6-8) The rooms are small and simple, but the price is right. Close to the bus station.

Shwe Na Di (Map p565; ☎ 061-60409; Main Rd; s/d US$4/6;) Basic rooms with a capital B; shared bathroom only.

BAGAN SKYSCRAPER

Is that really what it looks like? A concrete skyscraper looming over ancient Bagan? Surely not? Unfortunately it is. Conceived by the generals and flouting all Unesco guidelines for historic sites, the **Bagan Viewing Tower** is open for business. We are sure the views are impressive from up top, but it's a real blight on the landscape and costs a hefty US$10 to experience, so give it a miss.

NEW BAGAN

Bagan Thirizarni Hotel (Map p563; ☎ 061-60309; Main Rd; s/d from US$10/15;) The most southerly hotel in town, this bungalow complex is great value, as all the rooms include satellite TV, fridge, telephone and bathroom.

Bagan Central Hotel (Map p563; ☎ 02-67141; Main Rd; s/d US$15/20;) This friendly place is pretty central as far as New Bagan goes. Rooms include satellite TV, hot water and wooden floors, set around a leafy courtyard with tables for open-air breakfast.

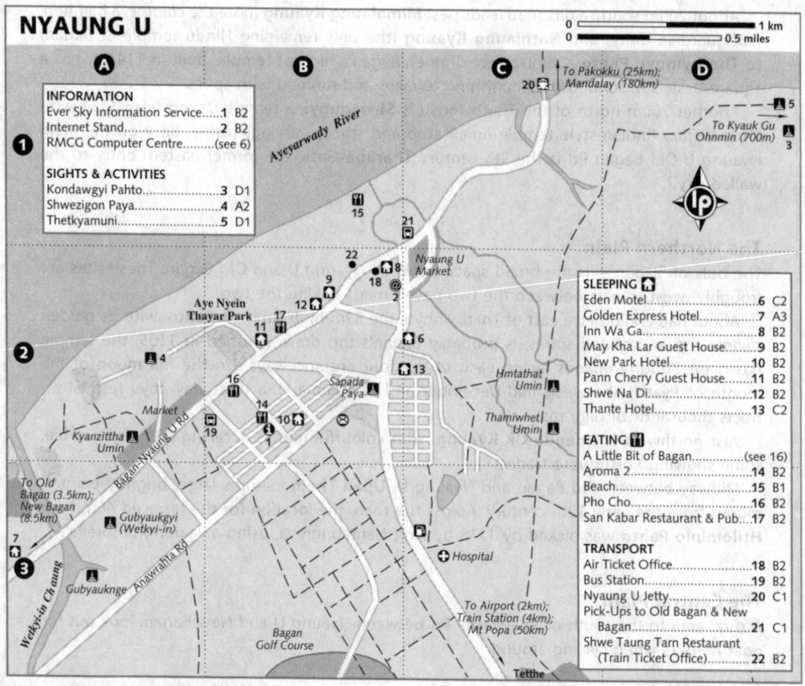

THE TEMPLES OF BAGAN

Ancient Bagan may be one of the most spectacular sights in Southeast Asia, but with so many temples to choose from it is easy to find a solitary stupa or decaying mural to take in alone. This section groups some of the more popular (and impressive) temples in Bagan (all on Map p563, unless otherwise noted). See p569 for info on getting around.

Top Temples

With more than 4000 temples to choose from, it pays to work out in advance which are the biggest and best.

- Ananda Pahto – one of the finest, best-preserved and most revered of all the Bagan temples.
- Dhammayangyi Pahto – an absolute colossus, this red brick temple is visible from all over Bagan.
- Gawdawpalin Pahto – considered the crowning achievement of the late period.
- Shwezigon Paya (Map p565) – the original golden stupa, prototype for the Shwedagon in Yangon.
- Thatbyinnyu Pahto – the tallest temple at Bagan, topped with a golden spire.

Old Bagan

This 2km anticlockwise circuit takes in sites within the old city walls. It's manageable on foot or by bicycle.

North of the unsubtle **Archaeological Museum** (Nyaung U-Old Bagan Rd), the 60m-high **Gawdawpalin Pahto**, one of the finest late-period temples, was rocked by the 1975 earthquake but has been restored.

About 200m south, a dirt road leads past **Mimalaung Kyaung** (note the *chinthe*, a half-lion, half-guardian deity) and **Nathlaung Kyaung** (the only remaining Hindu temple at Bagan) to **Thatbyinnyu Pahto** (Omniscience Shrine). Bagan's highest temple, built in 1144, it has a square base, surrounded by diminishing terraces and rimmed with spires.

Another 200m north of the Thatbyinnyu is **Shwegugyi**, a temple dating from 1131 with lotus *sikhara* (Indian-style temple finial) atop and stucco carvings inside. Back on the main Nyaung U-Old Bagan Rd is the 9th-century **Tharaba Gate**, the former eastern entry to the walled city.

The Northern Plain

The bulk of 'Bagan' fills the broad space between Nyaung U and Old Bagan. These sites are (roughly) west to east between the two paved roads linking the two.

About half a kilometre east of Thatbyinnyu, the 52m-high **Ananda Pahto**, with its golden *sikhara* top and gilded spires, is probably Bagan's top draw. Finished in 1105, the temple has giant Buddha images facing each of the four entranceways. On the full moon of the month of Pyatho (between mid-December and mid-January), a three-day *paya* festival attracts thousands of pilgrims.

Just northwest is **Ananda Ok Kyaung**, with colourful murals detailing 18th-century life, some showing Portuguese traders.

Midway between Old Bagan and Nyaung U, **Upali Thein** features large, brightly painted murals from the early 18th century. Across the road, the location for the terraced 46m-high **Htilominlo Pahto** was picked by 1218 by King Nantaungmya, using a 'leaning umbrella'.

The Central Plain

A rural area to the south of Anawrahta Rd between Nyaung U and New Bagan, look out for goat herders when cycling around.

South of Thatbyinnyu, the 11th-century five-terraced **Shwesandaw Paya** (1057) is a graceful white pyramid-style pagoda with 360-degree views of Bagan's temples. It is packed for sunset, but it's otherwise empty during the day. Note the original *hti* lying to the south – it was toppled by the quake. Half a kilometre south, the ever-visible, walled **Dhammayangyi Pahto** has two encircling passageways, the inner one of which has been intentionally filled. It's said that King Narathu was such a bastard that the workers ruined it after his assassination in 1170. Bat calls echo down from the dark ceilings.

One kilometre to the east, the broad two-storeyed **Sulamani Pahto** (1181) is one of the Bagan region's prettiest temples, with lush grounds and carved stucco. Just 150m east, **Thabeik Hmauk** looks like a mini Sulamani, but without the hawkers – *and* it is possible to climb to the top.

Around Myinkaba

The area around Myinkaba village, located between Old Bagan and New Bagan, is brimming with sites. One of the most popular is **Mingalazedi** (1274), with three receding terraces lined with 561 glazed tiles and tasty views of the nearby river and surrounding temples.

Just north of town, **Gubyaukgyi** (1113) sees a lot of visitors thanks to its richly coloured interior paintings. You should bring a torch (flashlight). In the village, the modern-looking **Manuha Paya** (1059) was built by the captive Mon king. Note the four giant Buddha images that are seemingly too large for the enclosure, symbolic of Manuha's discontent with his prison life. Stairs at the rear lead above the reclining Buddha. Just south, **Nanpaya**, from the same era, is a cave-style shrine; it was possibly once Hindu as suggested by the three-faced Brahma on the pillars.

About 400m south of town, the Sinhalese-style stupa of the 11th century, **Abeyadana Pahto**, was likely built by King Kyanzittha's Bengali wife and features original frescoes. Across the road, **Nagayon** has some tight stairs leading up to the roof. Its lotus-shaped *sikhara* was possibly a prototype for Ananda.

South Plain

This rural stretch is accessed via the road from New Bagan to the airport, or by dirt roads from the Central Plain. About 3.5km east of New Bagan, **Dhammayazika Paya** (1196) is unusual for its five-sided design. It's very well tended with lush grounds and lavish attention from worshippers. A dirt road leads 2km to Dhammayangyi.

An excellent cluster of sites is about 3km east. North of the road, **Tayok Pye Paya** has good westward views of Bagan. To the south, 13th-century **Payathonzu**, a small complex of three interconnected shrines, draws visitors to its murals.

About 200m north, **Nandamannya Pahto**, from the same period, features the 'temptation of Mura' murals – in the form of topless women reaping no response from a meditating Buddha. It's often locked; ask at Payathonzu for the 'key master'. Just behind, the **Kyat Kan Kyaung** has been a cave-style monastery for nearly one thousand years.

Around Nyaung U

In town, the gilded bell of **Shwezigon Paya** (1102; Map p565) is considered by many to be the prototype for many Burmese pagodas. The 37 pre-Buddhist *nat* were endorsed by the Bamar monarchy here. A yellow compound located on the east side (called '37 Nats' in English) features figures of each.

From the Nyaung U jetty, it is possible to arrange a fun boat trip (about K5000 or so) to see temples just off the Ayeyarwady: **Thetkyamuni** and **Kondawgyi Pahto** are about 1km east. **Kyauk Gu Ohnmin** cave temple, dating back a thousand years, was supposedly the start of a tunnel intended to go 18km – only 50m is accessible nowadays.

Thiri Marlar Hotel (Map p563; ☎ 02-67370; thirimarlar@mptmail.net.mm; s/d US$20/25; ❄) Worth the extra dollars, this quiet retreat has 21 smart rooms facing a leafy courtyard. Book ahead in the high season, as it fills up fast. There is a bar and breakfast area up top.

Kumudara Hotel (Map p563; ☎ 02-67080; www.kumudara-bagan.com; s/d US$36/45; ❄ 💻 🏊) Head here for the best views in Bagan. Rooms at the Kumudara have balconies offering an unobscured panorama of the soaring temples, and include satellite TV, minibar, IDD phone and a big bathroom. As well as the pool with a view, guests enjoy free internet access.

Eating

NYAUNG U

This is the dining capital of Bagan and there are plenty of restaurants along the main street and the famous 'restaurant row'. Italianesque food is popular at most places, but there's also an Asian assortment of Burmese, Chinese, Thai and Indian available.

Pho Cho (Map p565; restaurant row; mains from K1500; 🕑 breakfast, lunch & dinner) Also confusingly known as Puppet, this place has some pretty tasty Thai food, although Bangkok regulars won't find it 100% authentic.

our pick **Aroma 2** (Map p565; restaurant row; dishes K2000-4000; 🕑 lunch & dinner) This is the best Indian restaurant in town offering a spicy selection of classics that will keep even curry-craving Brits happy. There is a large garden area that overflows with candelit tables in the dry season.

San Kabar Restaurant & Pub (Map p565; Main Rd; pastas K2000-4000, pizzas K3000-4000; 🕑 breakfast, lunch & dinner) The birthplace of Bagan pizza, the San Kabar remains a popular stop for its Italian-inspired creations. Like Aroma, the candlelit courtyard is a major draw in the dry season.

A Little Bit of Bagan (Map p565; restaurant row; dishes K2000-5000; 🕑 breakfast, lunch & dinner) Another fixture in restaurant row, this place is slightly pricier, but more atmospheric than most. The menu includes Burmese, Indian and Italian, plus there is internet access available.

Beach (Map p565; ☎ 02-67370; dishes K3000-7000; 🕑 7am-11pm) An impressive new restaurant overlooking the Ayeyarwady, the Beach is set in a striking pavilion surrounded by lush gardens. The menu includes flavours from Europe and the East, plus there is a happy hour from 4pm to 6pm, the perfect excuse for a sundowner.

OLD BAGAN

By day, Old Bagan's eateries are the closest spots to the heart of the temples.

Sarabha II (Map p563; dishes K1200-6000; 🕑 lunch & dinner) The quieter of the two Sarabha restaurants, this has a leafy garden and plenty of tables. The prices reflect the target audience of tour groups, but the menu includes something from every corner of the globe.

Golden Myanmar (Map p563; buffet K2000; 🕑 lunch & dinner) Come here hungry, as the 'personal buffet', delivered to your table, is enough to feed a family. Four curries come with 10 or more bowls of local condiments. Invite your horse cart driver along to help.

NEW BAGAN

The cheapest eats are the hole-in-the-wall Burmese places along the main drag. There are several large riverside restaurants in New Bagan, with fine views, nightly puppet shows and busloads of tourists in peak season.

Green Elephant (Map p563; mains K3000-6000; 🕑 lunch & dinner) Part of a countrywide empire, this has a delightful garden for intimate dining.

Si Thu Restaurant (Map p563; mains K3000-6000; 🕑 lunch & dinner) Puppet show at 7.30pm every night.

Shopping

Shwe War Thein Handicrafts Shop (Map p563; ☎ 061-67032; dsavariau@mptmail.net.mm; 🕑 7am-9pm) This shop, just east of Tharabar Gate in Old Bagan, is a treasure trove of Myanmar trinkets.

The town of Myinkaba is the lacquerware epicentre of Myanmar. Several family-run workshops sell traditional pieces, which are better quality than offerings from hawkers around temples. One reliable place is **Art Gallery of Bagan** (Map p563; ☎ 061-60307).

Getting There & Away

Most travel services operate out of Nyaung U. Ask at Ever Sky (p564) or your guesthouse about hiring a share taxi. A charter to Inle is about US$90 or so, Mandalay US$60.

AIR

Regular services connect Bagan with Yangon (from US$75), Mandalay (from US$35) and Heho (from US$55). There is an **air ticket office** (Map p565; ☎ 02-67406; 🕑 9am-5pm) on the main road in Nyaung U that sells domestic tickets.

Air Bagan (code AB; ☎ 061-60588; www.airbagan.com), **Yangon Airways** (code HK; ☎ 061-60476; www.yangonair

.com) and **Air Mandalay** (code 6T; ☎ 061-60240; www.airmandalay.com) fly into Bagan.

BOAT

The Shwe Keinnery Express ferry leaves from Bagan for Mandalay at 5.30am (US$16, 12 hours, five times weekly), but it wasn't operating at the time of writing. More visitors opt to drift downriver from Mandalay. The slow boat to Mandalay (ordinary/upper class US$10/20) departs on Monday and Thursday at 5.30am. There are also services to Pyay (US$10, two nights). Bear in mind that all these options are government owned and operated. **Malikha Express** (www.malikhatravels.com) was launching services to Mandalay (upstream US$12, seven hours). The schedule isn't yet fixed, but it's likely to run three days a week. Most boats leave from the Nyaung U jetty (Map p565), a kilometre northeast of the market; some operate from Old Bagan (Map p563), depending on the tide and time of year.

From the Nyaung U jetty local ferries go to Pakokku (K1500, 2½ hours), where there are buses to Monywa.

BUS

Local buses to Mandalay (K6500, eight hours), via Meiktila, leave at 7am and 9am from the bus station in Nyaung U (Map p565). Here you can catch a 3pm air-con bus to Yangon (K7500 to K12,000, 12 to 15 hours) or a 5am bus to Taunggyi (K11,000, about 12 hours). Book tickets well in advance in peak season.

PICK-UP

Tiger Head Express Co (Map p563) sends daily pick-ups from New Bagan to Taunggyi (inside/outside K10,000/8000, 10 hours) via Kalaw at 3am. Pick-ups to Mt Popa leave from the Nyaung U bus station.

TRAIN

There is one morning train to Mandalay (ordinary/1st class US$4/9, nine hours) at 7am. Services to Yangon were not operating at the time of writing, but it is possible to take a train to Pyinmana (US$5/10, 10 hours) and connect from there. The train station is 4km southeast of Nyaung U. More convenient for buying tickets is the train station office in Nyaung U, part of the **Shwe Taung Tarn Restaurant** (Map p565; Main Rd).

Getting Around

Bicycles are a leisurely way to see Bagan. The going rate is K1000 per day in Nyaung U, double that in New Bagan. Carry water though, as some temples don't have vendors.

A horse cart isn't a bad way to get to grips with Bagan on day one. It's K10,000 for the whole day, but there is only really sufficient space for two people. Try and arrange one with a foam cushion, as it can get pretty uncomfortable after a few hours.

A pick-up runs between Nyaung U and New Bagan, stopping in Old Bagan and Myinkaba. A ride costs K300. A taxi for the day costs about US$20 to US$25.

A taxi from the airport costs K5000/6000/7000 to Nyaung U/Old Bagan/New Bagan.

AROUND BAGAN

Mt Popa

The Mt Olympus of Myanmar, Mt Popa is the stupa-studded centre of *nat* worship in the country. This 1520m-high monastery-topped hill is visible from Bagan on a clear day – look to the right end of the mountains to the west – and offers breathtaking views of the plain. The 30-minute climb up goes past monkeys and many pilgrims, including the slow-stepping nonordained hermit monks called *yeti*. The **Mahagiri shrine**, at the foot of the mountain, features a display of the 37 *nat*. Festivals include the full moon of **Nayon** (May/June) and **Nadaw** (November/December). It's possible to swim at the summit at the upmarket **Popa Mountain Resort** (☎ 02-69168; s/d from US$70/80; ❄) for US$5.

The Popa trip up is only worth it if you have at least two full days for Bagan itself. It's possible to visit by pick-up from Nyaung U (about K1000), often with a change in Kyaukpadaung. Far easier is getting a slot in a share taxi for US$7 per person. Ask the driver to point out remnants of the petrified forest along the way.

Meiktila & Thazi

If you find yourself in Meiktila while travelling the Bagan-to-Inle corridor, the **Honey Hotel** (☎ 064-21588; Pan Chan St; s US$5-10, d US$8-15; ❄) is a converted mansion on the shores of Lake Meiktila.

Thazi, the rail junction, is home to the basic **Moon-Light Rest House** (r from US$3; ❄).

MUST READ

Finding George Orwell in Burma (2006) sees US journalist Emma Larkin following in the footsteps of the famous novelist. A great read, but sadly what she discovers is more *Animal Farm* than *Burmese Days*.

Pakokku

An alternative route between Bagan and Monywa goes by this slow-paced authentic town on the west bank of the Ayeyarwady. Stay at **Mya Yatanar Inn** (☎ 062-21457; 75 Lanmataw St; r per person K4000), a downtown mansion on the water run by a priceless old couple who have been taking travellers in for more than 20 years. Bicycles and motorbikes are available for rent.

UPPER AYEYARWADY

Drifting down the Ayeyarwady, through jungle-clad gorges and past friendly villagers for whom the river and its traffic are a lifeline to the outside world, is one of the most memorable experiences in Myanmar. The best of the action is way north of Mandalay in Kachin State. Most travellers fly north or take the train to Myitkyina or Bhamo before going with the flow and enjoying life in the slow lane.

Much of the area away from the river is closed to foreigners.

MYITKYINA

☎ 074 / pop 140,000

This is the end of the line as far as overland travel in the north goes. The Kachin capital of Myitkyina is a popular embarkation point for a river trip south. It is also a low-key trekking centre for visits to nearby Kachin villages. Rice grown here is considered Myanmar's best.

Snowland Tours (☎ 23498; snowland@mptmail.com.mm; closed Sun) has a local office in town and can help with trekking tours to Kachin villages.

Several Buddhist sites are in the area, though many locals are Christian. The modest **Kachin State Culture Museum** (Youngyi Rd; admission US$2; 10am-3pm Tue-Sun) is 3km from the centre.

The **YMCA** (☎ 23010; mka-ymca@myanmar.com.mm; 12 Myothit Rd; s US$6-10, d US$10-14;) is the most traveller-friendly place in town. The Y has basic rooms, but staff are pretty switched on when it comes to the local area. Internet access is, like the pace of life, slow.

Air Bagan (code W9; ☎ 01-513322; www.airbagan.com) and government-run **Myanma Airways** (MA, code UB; ☎ 01-374874) connect Myitkyina and Mandalay (US$70).

Foreigners are not supposed to travel on the fast boats to Bhamo (US$10, seven hours), but it's worth checking the latest. Pick-ups on the 188km road between Bhamo and Myitkyina leave from near the Y at 8.30am. Have passport copies ready for checkpoints.

A blanket is mandatory for nights on the train to and from Mandalay (1st-class/sleeper from US$31/36, 25 to 50 hours).

A shop behind the Y can rent motorcycles for K7000 per day.

BHAMO

☎ 074 / pop 20,000

More of a charmer than Myitkyina, the riverside town of Bhamo has a bustling daily market, drawing Lisu, Kachin and Shan folk from surrounding villages. The ruinous old Shan city walls of **Sampanago** are located 3km north of town. Interesting **Kachin villages** lie within reach.

Check out the **homemade helicopter**, made by Sein Win, who was inspired by James Bond movies. Ask about it at the **Friendship Hotel** (☎ 50095; yonekyi@baganmail.net.mm; per person with shared bathroom US$7, s/d with private bathroom US$20/25;), one of the better provincial pads, with satellite TV and minibar in the top rooms.

Deck/cabin on the ferry to Mandalay costs US$9/54. The trip takes 1½ days. Fast boats to Katha (ordinary/1st class K5000/15,000, six to seven hours) are exceptional value.

KATHA

Fans of George Orwell's *Burmese Days* will enjoy foraging around this sleepy town. Eric Blair (his real name) was stationed here in 1926–27 and based his novel on this setting. The old **British Club**, around which much of the novel revolves, is now an agricultural co-op. The tennis court mentioned in the novel is still used.

Ask for a front-facing room upstairs to catch some river views at the basic **Ayeyarwady Guest House** (Strand Rd; r K3000-5000).

The ferry south to Mandalay (deck/cabin US$7/42, around 24 hours) goes three times weekly. It's also possible to take a bus to Mandalay (K8000, 12 hours). The nearest train station is 25km west at Naba (US$1, one hour).

WESTERN MYANMAR

Western Myanmar, home to the proud Rakhaing people, is a land unto itself. Isolated and inaccessible from the rest of the country, this enigmatic region is in many ways closer to Bangladesh than Burma. Sittwe is only accessible by air or water and 'baby Bagan', the atmospheric temple city of Mrauk U, is reached by a boat ride inland.

The Rakhaing people, dubbed 'Burmese' by the government, love their own language and culture. The Mahumuni Buddha remains a sensitive subject and locals love to tell the story of how it was stolen by the Burmese and moved to Mandalay in 1784.

The Muslim population, known as the Rohingya, is frequently in conflict with the Buddhist majority, as the Rohingya have been heavily persecuted by the government. The government doesn't recognise them as citizens, and many have escaped across the border to Bangladesh as refugees.

See p540 for information on Ngapali Beach, which is in southern Rakhaing State.

SITTWE (AYKAB)

☎ 043 / pop 200,000

Used as a hub for visiting the temples of Mrauk U, Sittwe has a striking waterfront location. The population is about 30% Muslim, with the central Jama Mosque the most historic and impressive religious site in town.

Information

Internet stand (Main Rd; per hr K3000; 8am-9pm) One of the few internet places in town; it's slow.

Sights

A busy port town for generations, Sittwe's main attractions are found where the wide Kaladan River kisses the Bay of Bengal. The morning **fish market** kicks off at 6am, with thousands of fish splashed on the stone pier. About 2km south, via the Strand, is the **Point**, a peninsula boasting big sunset views.

Back in the centre, the **Rakhaing State Cultural Museum** (Main Rd; admission US$2; 10am-4pm Tue-Sat) features a Mrauk U model, many artefacts of the era, and watercolours of traditional wrestling moves.

A couple of hundred metres north of the centre, the **Maka Kuthala Kyaungdawgyi** (Large Monastery of Great Merit; Main Rd; admission free) features an interesting collection of relics in an old British colonial-era mansion.

Sleeping & Eating

Electricity is erratic at best. Try some Rakhaing specialities, which involve seafood and spice, for the best dining.

Sittwe Prince Hotel (☎ 24075; www.mraukuprincehotel.com; 27 Main Rd; s US$10-25, d US$15-30) The most traveller-friendly hotel, cheaper rooms here are small and have shared bathrooms. Air-con is available in the more expensive rooms.

Noble Hotel (☎ 23558; 45 Main Rd; noble@myanmar.com.mm; s/d with breakfast US$25/35) These smart rooms are reasonable value, including 24-hour air-con and satellite TV.

Mondi stand (bowls K300; breakfast & lunch) *Mondi* is the tasty local variant of Burmese *mohinga*, with chillies instead of peanuts. Locals swear this place has the best in town. It's opposite City Hall on the airport road.

Nyein Chan (Set Yone Su St; dishes K1500-3000; breakfast, lunch & dinner) Near City Hall lies a good strip of family-style Burmese/Chinese restaurants, including this place with a steaming, prawn-filled Rakhaing curry soup.

City Point Music Restaurant (The Strand; dishes K2000-4000; breakfast, lunch & dinner) The best of the riverfront restaurants, there is a one-man band here by night.

Getting There & Away

Foreigners cannot travel by road to Sittwe.

AIR

Air Mandalay (code 6T; ☎ 21638; www.airmandalay.com) and **Yangon Airways** (code HK; ☎ 24102; www.yangonair.com) fly to Yangon (from US$82) via Thandwe (from US$46) most days, although there are just two flights a week in the low season. The airport is 2.5km southwest of the centre; head outside the gate to get a cheap ride into town.

BOAT

Malikha Express (☎ 23441; www.malikhatravels.com; Main Rd; ⏰ 9am-5pm) has connections from Sittwe to Mrauk U and Taunggok, from where you can reach Ngapali or Yangon. Fast boats head between Taunggok and Sittwe (US$40, eight hours) on Monday, Wednesday, Friday and Saturday, connecting with fast boats to/from Mrauk U. From Taunggok, buses or pick-ups go to Pyay or Thandwe (Ngapali). Buy tickets in advance.

See opposite for information on boat services to and from Mrauk U.

MRAUK U (MYOHAUNG)

☎ 043 / pop 25,000

Like Bagan to the east, the Rakhaing kings of Mrauk U (mrau-oo) went on a merry old building spree in this ancient capital, home to more than 150 temples. Accessible via a pretty 65km boat ride northeast from Sittwe, Mrauk U is smaller than Bagan but more alive. Shepherds lead their flocks past curvy hillocks dotted with temples, and smouldering fires add a mysterious haze to the timeless setting. A huge **pagoda festival** is held in mid-May.

Mrauk U served as the Rakhaing capital from 1430 to 1784, when the Brits relocated it to Sittwe. It was a fine time, with the kings hiring Japanese samurais as bodyguards and the naval fleet of 10,000 boats terrorising neighbouring countries from the Bay of Bengal.

It's worth reading up. Tun Shwe Khine's *A Guide to Mrauk U* or U Shwe Zan's *The Golden Mrauk U: An Ancient Capital of Rakhine* are only available in Yangon.

Sights

The more than 150 temples blend into the small town over a 7-sq-km area. Foreigners pay US$10 to visit, plus a K1000 'donation' for tacky fluorescent lights in some temples. Payment can be made at the Shittaung temple.

PALACE SITE & AROUND

Apart from crumbling walls, little is left of the central palace, located just east of the market. Apparently astrologers advised King Minbun to move his home here in 1429 to shun 'evil birds' at his Launggret palace. Inside the

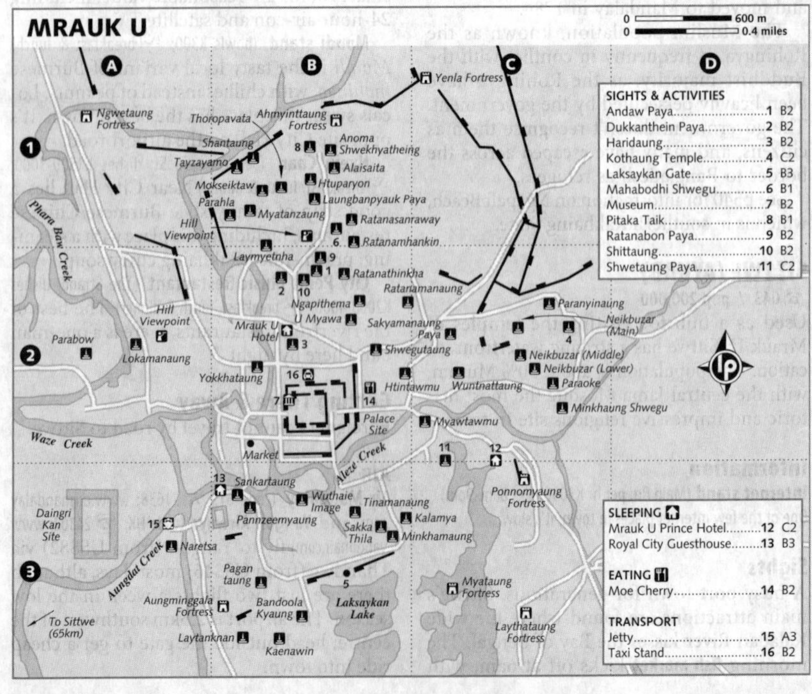

CHIN STATE EXCURSIONS

Excursions to inland Chin State from Mrauk U have been on and off in the last few years. Currently, day trips are once again possible, but not overnight trips, although the situation will no doubt change again during the lifetime of this book. The cost is about US$85 including boat, vehicle, lunch and visit and this can be shared by three people. Working out at less than US$30 per person, this is a bargain compared with the US$550-and-up tours run by MTT out of Bagan. The trips take in a traditional Chin village where older women still have weblike tattoos on their faces.

western walls, the Department of Archaeology's **museum** (admission free; 11am-3pm Mon-Fri) has prerestoration photos, a site model and a replica of the Shittaung pillar.

On a hill just north, the 18th-century **Haridaung** pagoda has nice westward views.

NORTH GROUP

The main sites of Mrauk U are clustered beyond the **Shittaung** (Shrine of the 80,000 Images), the most intricate of the surviving temples. Built in 1535, the pagoda has a maze-like floor plan. An outer chamber, accessible via the far left door at the entry hall to the east side, passes 1000 sculptures; the inner chamber coils to a dead end, passing a 'Buddha footprint' on the way. On the outer walls, there are some rather pornographic renderings of local figures.

Just north is the 16th-century **Andaw Paya**, and beyond is the **Ratanabon Paya**, a stupa dating from 1612 that survived a WWII bomb.

Across the road west from Shittaung, the bunkerlike **Dukkanthein Paya** (1571), set amid a green field, is the most impressive of the batch: look for Mrauk U's 64 traditional hairstyles on sculptures on the coiling path leading to a sun-drenched Buddha in the inner chamber.

Further north of Ratanabon, hilltop **Mahabodhi Shwegu** (1448) features 280 *jakata* (stories of the Buddha's past lives) on its narrow entry walls. About 200m north, the compact and ornate **Pitaka Taik** (1591) is the last remaining library at Mrauk U.

EAST GROUP

East of the palace walls, the temples are spaced further apart and some temples stand on hilltops with good vantage points. One of Mrauk U's highlights is located 2km east. The massive **Kothaung Temple** (Shrine of the 90,000 Images) was named by King Minbun's son to beat daddy's 80,000 images at Shittaung. The outer passageway is lined with thousands of evocative bas-reliefs of Buddha images.

SOUTH GROUP

Tucked away in the lively village back lanes, this area has a number of pagodas. Mrauk U's best view is at the **Shwetaung Paya** (Golden Hill Pagoda; 1553), which is southeast of the palace. Trails disappear into vegetation at times, so it is best to return before dark. A guide might be useful. Views of the Chin Hills and the river to the west justify the scrapes.

To the south, **Laksaykan Gate** leads to the eponymous lake, a water source.

Sleeping & Eating

Royal City Guesthouse (☎ 23808-19; d US$8-12, bungalows US$15) The closest accommodation to the jetty, this amiable riverside guesthouse has small rooms with mozzie nets. Shared bathrooms are open air – that's basic rather than Balinese-style.

Mrauk U Prince Hotel (☎ 24200; www.mraukuprincehotel.com; s US$10-25, d US$15-30) Rooms here are finished in bamboo and include a private bathroom with hot water on request. Helpful staff give away free maps of the temples.

Moe Cherry (dishes K1500-3000; lunch & dinner) The most popular place in town with travellers, the Moe Cherry has a range of local Rakhaing-style curries and some good veggie options. The restaurant is also a good place to ask about car rental or boat information.

Getting There & Around

The only way to Mrauk U is by boat. The two-tier government-run IWT runs to Mrauk U from Sittwe (US$4, six to seven hours), leaving three mornings a week from a jetty 1km north of Sittwe's centre. Other days you can catch a small 'private boat' (US$10 to US$15, four to five hours) at 7am or 2.30pm. Private boat charter is possible for small groups and starts from about US$80 to US$100, including waiting in Mrauk U. **Malikha** (☎ 23159; www.malikhatravels.com) runs enclosed 'fast boats' (US$20, three hours), leaving at 2.30pm. In the other direction, boats usually leave Mrauk U at 8am from the jetty, 1km south of the market, but double-check with your guesthouse or hotel.

In late 2004, seven people, including five Italian tourists, were killed when an unexpected storm overturned a fast boat after dark.

A horse cart around the temples is about K10,000 per day. Bicycle rental is about K2000 per day. The taxi stand (for jeeps) is on the north side of the palace.

MYANMAR DIRECTORY

ACCOMMODATION

Hotels and guesthouses are a touch more expensive in Myanmar than in neighbouring countries. In places with choice, it is possible to find a plain room for a fistful of dollars (US$4 to US$6 per person). Don't expect much more than concrete floors, squashed mosquitoes on the walls and a shared bathroom down the hall, but a basic breakfast might be included. For a few dollars more, extras will include aircon, hot water and even TV. Unless stated otherwise, prices in this chapter include private bathroom.

Nearly all hotels and guesthouses quote prices in US dollars. Most accept kyat at a slightly disadvantageous rate. Prices listed in this chapter are for peak season, roughly October to March. Small discounts may be available in the low season; don't be afraid to haggle gently if planning a longer stay.

GOVERNMENT HOTELS

The big question many travellers ask themselves in Myanmar is how to avoid government-run hotels? Government officials have their fingers in the pockets of top-end and joint-venture hotels, but rarely bother with small-time guesthouses. Full-on government hotels are often named after the destination (eg Mrauk U Hotel in Mrauk U) and fly the national flag outside. Generally 10% of what you spend at any guesthouse goes to the government. The less your room costs, the less the government gets its hands on.

All accommodation supposedly must be licensed to accept foreign guests. Passport and visa details are required at check-in, but hotels don't need to hold onto your passport. Sometimes unlicensed guesthouses will say they're 'full' rather than explain the full story. In out-of-the-way towns, some local guesthouses will accept weary travellers. Prices are about US$2 (in kyat) and conditions are basic.

ACTIVITIES

Barefoot pilgrimages up pagoda-topped hills (such as Mandalay Hill) or biking around town are the most common activities, but there are some other options for the adventurous traveller.

Cycling

With your own bike and spare parts, Myanmar's highways are there to be conquered. Popular stretches include Mandalay to Bagan, via Myingyan, or the hilly terrain from Mandalay to Hsipaw. Roads are actually smoother than in some other Southeast Asian countries. The brutal hot season may deflate even the most committed pedal pusher.

Diving & Snorkelling

Unfortunately, there's not much underwater action available in Myanmar for the budget traveller. You can snorkel past colourful fish and some coral off Ngapali Beach or Chaungtha Beach. The more spectacular Myeik Archipelago, near Kawthoung, is generally only accessible via expensive liveaboard cruises operating out of Thailand (see p787).

Trekking

Treks between Kalaw and Inle Lake (see p550) take in an overnight stay in a longhouse. Other inspiring hikes are available around Hsipaw. Winter nights can get chilly so bring some warm clothes. Avoid the wet season, as heavy rain makes for slippery trails.

BOOKS

Even more than with most countries, it's wise to read up before arriving in Myanmar. Pick up Lonely Planet's *Myanmar* for more comprehensive coverage, or the helpful *Burmese Phrasebook*.

Other top books:

- *From the Land of Green Ghosts: A Burmese Odyssey* (2002) by Pascal Khoo Thwe. The literary memoir of a Karenni tribesman escaping the post-1988 chaos to study literature at Cambridge.
- *Trouser People* (2002) by Andrew Marshall. The author follows the footsteps of a colonial-era Scot who introduced football to hill tribes in the late 19th century.
- *Burmese Days* (1934) by George Orwell. The definitive novel of the last lonely days of Britain's colonial experience, this is a must on any trip to old Burma.
- *The Glass Palace* (2001) by Amitav Ghosh. This modern classic interweaves a motley crew of locals (Indians, Chinese, Burmese) amid lushly recounted historical events.
- *Freedom from Fear & Other Writings* (1995) by Aung San Suu Kyi. A collection of essays from the country's leading lady.

BUSINESS HOURS

Usual business hours in Myanmar:

Government offices 8am to 4.30pm, Monday to Friday
Post offices 9.30am to 3.30pm, Monday to Friday
Restaurants 7am to 9pm
Shops 9.30am to 6pm or later

CLIMATE

November through to February is the best time to visit. Temperatures can get quite cold in the hills, and close to freezing in places such as Kalaw. From mid-February, it gets increasingly hot – April being the 'cruellest month', to quote TS Eliot, until rains bless the land from mid-May through to mid-October. See the climate charts (p916) for average temperatures and rainfall.

CUSTOMS

Immigration officers at Yangon airport are friendlier than some of their stone-faced contemporaries around the region. Even customs officers appear relatively cheerful. Officially, visitors must declare foreign currency in excess of US$2000, as well as electronic goods such as laptops, iPods, radios and cameras. However, we found checks to be pretty lax on our last visit.

Technically, antiques cannot be taken out of the country, although this is not often enforced.

DANGERS & ANNOYANCES

Usually the only time a local will be running with your money or belongings is if they're chasing you down the road with something you've dropped. For now theft remains quite rare, but don't tempt fate in this poor country by flashing valuables or leaving them unguarded.

The only real scams are dodgy moneychangers slipping in torn notes, and drivers or guides getting a commission for purchases at any shops you visit.

A few bomb incidents have occurred in Yangon in recent years, but these seem to have halted of late. Areas around the Myanmar–Thai border, home to the country's notorious drug trade, can be dangerous (and off limits) to explore.

Talking politics with locals can potentially endanger them, so be discreet. A taxi driver taking foreigners to see the area around Aung San Suu Kyi's house might get into trouble. Generally let a local dictate the conversation. In private places, and some teashops, some will be quite frank. Don't force political issues.

Power outages are pretty common, even in Yangon, but many businesses have their own generators. Check with guesthouses whether the power will be on all night, especially in the hot season.

DRIVING LICENCE

Licences aren't usually required when renting a motorbike. Would-be drivers need an International Driving Permit from the Road Transport Administration Department in Yangon, but this is not that easy to arrange.

EMBASSIES & CONSULATES

For visa information, see p581.

Embassies & Consulates in Myanmar

Myanmar is usually a good place to get visas for other countries, as the embassies don't see a lot of business. Sometimes you can pay with kyat. Countries with diplomatic representation in Yangon:

Australia (Map p532; ☎ 01-251810; 88 Strand Rd)
Bangladesh (off Map p528; ☎ 01-549557; 56 Kabe Aye Pagoda Rd)

MYANMAR (BURMA)

Cambodia (off Map p528; ☎ 01-546156; 34 Kabe Aye Pagoda Rd)
Canada Represented by the Australian embassy.
China (Map p530; ☎ 01-221280; 1 Pyidaungsu Yeiktha Rd)
France (Map p530; ☎ 01-212520; 102 Pyidaungsu Yeiktha Rd)
Germany (Map p528; ☎ 01-548951; 32 Natmauk St)
India (Map p532; ☎ 01-243972; 545-547 Merchant St)
Indonesia (Map p530; ☎ 01-254465; 100 Pyidaungsu Yeiktha Rd)
Japan (Map p528; ☎ 01-549644; 100 Natmauk St)
Laos (Map p530; ☎ 01-222482; A1 Diplomatic Quarters, Taw Win Rd)
Malaysia (Map p530; ☎ 01-220249; 82 Pyidaungsu Yeiktha Rd)
New Zealand Represented by the UK embassy.
Singapore (Map p528; ☎ 01-559001; 238 Dhamma Zedi Rd, Bahan Township)
Thailand (Map p530; ☎ 01-226721; 45 Pyay Rd)
UK (Map p532; ☎ 01-281700; 80 Strand Rd)
USA (Map p532; ☎ 01-282055; 581 Merchant St) This embassy will move to Inya Lake during the lifetime of this book.
Vietnam (Map p528; ☎ 01-548905; 36 Wingaba Rd, Bahan Township)

Myanmar Embassies & Consulates Abroad

For Myanmar diplomatic offices in Southeast Asia, see the relevant country chapter.

Australia (☎ 02-6273 3811; 22 Arkana St, Yarralumla, ACT 2600)
Bangladesh (☎ 02-60 1915; 89B Rd No 4, Banani, Dhaka)
Canada (☎ 613-232 6434; Apt 902-903, The Sandringham, 85 Range Rd, Ottawa, Ontario K1N 8J6)
China (☎ 010-6532 1584; 6 Dong Zhi Men Wai St, Chaoyang District, Beijing 100600)
France (☎ 01 42 25 56 95; 60 rue de Courcelles, 75008 Paris)
Germany (☎ 30-206 1570; Zimmerstrasse 56, 10117 Berlin)
India (☎ 11-688 9007; 3/50F Nyaya Marg, Chanakyapuri, New Delhi 110021)
Israel (☎ 03-517 0760; 26 Hayarkon St, Tel Aviv 68011)
Italy (☎ 06-854 9374; 1st fl, Int 2, Viale Gioacchino Rossini, 18, 00198 Rome)
Japan (☎ 03-3441 9291; 8-26, 4-chome, Kita-Shinagawa, Shinagawa-ku, Tokyo 140-0001)
South Korea (☎ 02-792 3341; 723-1/724-1 Hannam-Dong Yongsam-ku, Seoul 140-210)
UK (☎ 020-7499 8841; 19A Charles St, London W1X 5DX)
USA (☎ 202-332 9044; 2300 S St NW, Washington, DC 20008)

FESTIVALS & EVENTS

Traditionally Myanmar follows a 12-month lunar calendar, so most festival dates cannot be fixed on the Gregorian calendar. Most festivals in Myanmar are on the full moon of the Burmese month in which they occur, but the build-up can go for days. Besides Buddhist holy days, some Hindu, Muslim and Christian holidays and festivals are also observed.

January

Independence Day 4 January. A major public holiday marked by a seven-day fair at Kandawgyi Lake in Yangon, and countrywide celebrations.

February/March

Union Day 12 February. Marks Bogyoke Aung San's short-lived achievement of unifying Myanmar's disparate ethnic groups.
Bawgyo Paya Pwe Held the day after the Tabaung full moon, this is one of the oldest and largest Shan festivals.
Shwedagon Festival This is the largest *paya* festival in Myanmar and takes place on the full moon.
Armed Forces Day 27 March. This event is celebrated with parades and fireworks. Since 1989, the government has pardoned prisoners on this day.

March/April

Full-Moon Festival The Tagu full moon is the biggest event of the year at Shwemawdaw Paya in Bago.

April/May

Buddha's Birthday The full moon also marks the day of the Buddha's enlightenment and the day he entered nirvana. One of the best places to observe this ceremony is at Yangon's Shwedagon Paya.
Thingyan (Water Festival) The Burmese New Year is celebrated with a raucous nationwide water fight. Traditional Burmese restraint goes out the window. It is impossible to go outside without getting drenched so just join the fun. Businesses close and some transport grinds to a halt. It's a favourite with youngsters but many adults check into meditation centres until the insanity is over.
Workers' Day 1 May.

June/July

Buddhist Lent Start of the Buddhist Rains Retreat (aka 'Buddhist Lent'). Laypeople present monasteries with new robes, because during the three-month Lent period monks are restricted to their monasteries.

July/August

Martyr's Day 19 July. Commemorates the assassination of Bogyoke Aung San and his comrades on 19 July 1947.

Wreaths are laid at his mausoleum, north of Shwedagon Paya in Yangon.
Wagaung Festival Lots are drawn to see who will have to provide monks with their alms.

September/October

Boat Races This is the height of the wet season, so boat races are held in rivers, lakes and even ponds all over Myanmar. The best place to be is Inle Lake.
Festival of Lights (Thadingyut) Celebrates Buddha's return from a period of preaching. For the three days of the festival, all Myanmar is lit by oil lamps, fire balloons, candles and even mundane electric lamps.

October/November

Tazaungdaing Another 'festival of lights', particularly celebrated in the Shan State. In Taunggyi there are fire-balloon competitions. In some areas there are also speed-weaving competitions during the night. The biggest weaving competitions occur at Shwedagon Paya in Yangon.
Kathein A one-month period at the end of Buddhist Lent during which new monastic robes and requisites are offered to the monastic community.

December

Christmas Day 25 December. Christmas Day is a public holiday in deference to the many Christian Kayin (Karen).
Kayin New Year December/January. Considered a national holiday, when Karen communities throughout Myanmar celebrate by wearing their traditional dress and by hosting folk dancing and singing performances. The largest celebrations are held in the Karen suburb of Insein, just north of Yangon, and in Hpa-an.
Ananda Festival December/January. Held at the Ananda Pahto in Bagan at the full moon.

FOOD & DRINK

Food

Mainstream Burmese cuisine represents a blend of Bamar, Mon, Indian and Chinese influences. If you're arriving from Thailand, Vietnam or Malaysia, it may not instantly inspire, but there are some cracking dishes out there.

A typical meal has *htamin* (rice) as its core, eaten with a choice of *hin* (curry dishes), most commonly fish, chicken, prawns or mutton. Beef and pork are less popular, as they are considered offensive to most Hindus and Buddhists. Soup is always served, along with a table full of condiments (including pickled veggies as dipping sauces). Most meals include free refills, so come hungry.

Outside of Rakhaing State (near Bangladesh), most Burmese food is pretty mild on the chilli front. Most cooks opt for a simple masala of turmeric, ginger, garlic, salt and onions, plus plenty of peanut oil and shrimp paste. *Balachaung* (chillies, tamarind and dried shrimp pounded together) or the pungent *ngapi kyaw* (spicy shrimp paste with garlic) is always nearby to add some kick. Almost everything in Burmese cooking is flavoured with *ngapi* (a salty paste concocted from dried and fermented shrimp or fish).

Noodle dishes are often eaten for breakfast or as light snacks between meals. By far the most popular is *mohinga* (moun-hinga), rice noodles served with fish soup and as many other ingredients as there are cooks.

Shan khauk-swe (Shan-style noodle soup; thin wheat noodles in a light broth with meat or tofu) is a favourite all over Myanmar, but is most common in Mandalay and the Shan State. Another Shan dish worth seeking out is *htamin chin,* literally sour rice, a turmeric-coloured rice salad.

See p535 for examples of snacks found in street markets around Myanmar.

The seafood served along the coasts, particularly grilled squid in Ngapali Beach, is delicious.

Drink

Only drink purified water. Be wary of ice in remote areas, but it is usually factory produced in towns and cities. Bottled water costs just K150 or K200 from stalls and shops.

Burmese tea, brewed Indian-style with lots of condensed milk and sugar, is the national drink. Most restaurants will provide as much free Chinese tea as you can handle. Teashops, a national institution, are good places to sample the tea experience and munch on inexpensive snacks such as *nam-bya* and *palata* (flat breads) or Chinese pastries. Ordering isn't as easy as in restaurants. Ask for *lahpeq ye* (tea with a dollop of condensed milk); *cho bouk* is less sweet, and *kyauk padaung* is very sweet.

Locally produced soft drinks (such as Fantasy, Max and Star) are just K150 per bottle, compared with the (rare) bottle of Coke for nearer K1000. Sugarcane juice is a very popular streetside drink.

Let's not forget the beer, which is almost as popular as tea. Myanmar Beer (about US$1.50 for a big bottle) is the best local brew. It's available in draught, as is the newer Dagon Beer. Mandalay Beer is considered the weakest link. Yangon is one of the only places to find out-and-out bars. Elsewhere open-air barbecue restaurants and 'beer stations' embrace a steady crew of red-faced local drinkers. It's fine to buy a bottle to take to your guesthouse, or sit at a restaurant and get plastered.

International wines are available in some hotels and restaurants, as are a selection of stronger tipples. Local wine, Aythaya, is now produced near Inle Lake and is very palatable. Local firewaters are not, but sampling them is a great way to earn your stripes with the local boozers.

GAY & LESBIAN TRAVELLERS

Lesbians and gays are generally accepted in Burmese culture. In fact local women walking with foreign men raise more eyebrows. Yangon has the most active gay 'scene'. It's OK to share rooms, but public displays of affection – for anyone – are frowned upon.

HOLIDAYS

Apart from the big festivals such as New Year, other major public holidays include:

Independence Day 4 January
Peasants Day 2 March
Armed Forces Day 27 March
Workers' Day 1 May
National Day late November/early December
Christmas Day 25 December

INTERNET ACCESS

Myanmar only joined the cyberworld in 2001, but access to the internet is on the rise. It's about K500 to K1000 per hour in Yangon, though at places such as Bagan, Ngapali Beach and Inle Lake it costs more like K2000. The government tries to restrict web-based email sites such as Hotmail and Yahoo, but most places have software to beat the censors. Sites such as www.bbc.co.uk or www.nytimes.com were accessible during the time of research.

Bear in mind that all local email ending in '.mm' is subject to government censorship in both directions. This can result in emails being delayed by hours, sometimes days. Worse, when a backlog develops, it's not unknown for them to hit the delete button! If trying to book a room via email, resend if you don't hear anything after a few days.

There are two ISPs – a government-run dial-up and a military-run broadband service.

INTERNET RESOURCES

Irrawaddy (www.irrawaddy.org) The website of a Bangkok-based publication, it focuses on political issues, but covers many cultural news topics.
Mizzima (www.mizzima.com) A nonprofit news service organised in 1998 by Burmese journalists in exile.
Myanmar Home Page (www.myanmar.com) Provides a funny government dictum, and two local English-language papers, including the useful *Myanmar Times* (for entertainment listings, flight schedules).
Myanmar Travel Information (www.myanmartravelinformation.com) Includes train and airline schedules (though these date quickly).
Online Burma/Myanmar Library (www.burmalibrary.org) Comprehensive database of books on Myanmar.

LEGAL MATTERS

Myanmar does not have an independent judiciary. If you engage in political activism (eg handing out pro-democracy leaflets as some Westerners have), illegally cross the border into the country, or get caught with drugs, you have no legal recourse. We've heard of a French traveller bribing his way out of a heroin-possession arrest. Political activists are less likely to be able to cut a deal.

MAPS

The best map found outside Myanmar is Periplus Editions' 1:2,000,000 *Myanmar Travel Map;* find it at **MapLink** (www.maplink.com). In Myanmar, Design Print Services (DPS) produces handy foldout maps, including the *Tourist Map of Myanmar* and local maps for Yangon, Mandalay and Bagan.

MEDIA

Magazines

Reasonably up-to-date copies of *The Economist, Newsweek* and *Time* are available at upmarket hotel shops or at **Inwa Bookstore** (Map p532; 232 Sule Paya Rd, Yangon).

Newspapers

For the official line, the *New Light of Myanmar* is hilarious, overflowing with Orwellian propaganda and clunky English. Look out for the anti-Western poems. Far more useful is the *Myanmar Times,* with a schedule of international flights and entertainment listings. Both are scarce beyond Yangon.

Radio

All legal radio and TV broadcasts are state controlled. Radio Myanmar broadcasts news in Burmese, English and eight other national languages three times a day. Only music with Burmese-language lyrics goes out on the airwaves.

Many Burmese listen to Burmese-language broadcasts from the Voice of America and the BBC for news from the outside world.

TV

TV Myanmar (MRTV) operates from 5pm to midnight, although it's at the mercy of the local power supply. Check out the 9.15pm national news, when a newscaster coldly reads the censored news before a mural of a power plant. English Premiership games are often broadcast.

Many hotels have satellite TV, if only in the lobby. CNN and the BBC are available on these sets and there seems to be no censorship by the government.

MONEY

Kyat, dollars, even the dreaded FECs (see p580): money comes in many shapes and sizes here. Kyat covers the little things (bottles of water, renting a bike, some rice), while dollars (or vanishing FEC notes) are usually requested for ferries, air tickets, hotels and museums. While inflation has skyrocketed in recent years, costs in US dollars don't fluctuate much. Be sure to carry all the US dollars you need and more. Crisp, new US$100 bills attract the best exchange rates. Small bills are useful for guesthouses, most of which price rooms in dollars rather than kyat. The euro is also increasingly being accepted.

ATMs

Myanmar has no ATMs (cash points).

Bargaining, Bribes & Tipping

Essentially almost any price is open to negotiation. Exceptions are transport (other than taxis) and entrance fees. Handicrafts can often be purchased for half the first offer. Guesthouses and hotels may drop prices during quiet periods, or if you're planning a longer stay.

Minor bribes – called 'presents' or 'tea money' in Burmese English – are part of everyday life in Myanmar. Extra compensation is expected for the efficient completion of many standard bureaucratic services, such as a visa extension.

Tipping, as it is known in the West, is not the rule in any but the fanciest hotels and restaurants. Rounding up a restaurant bill is certainly appreciated.

Cash

Myanmar's everyday currency, the kyat (pronounced chat, and abbreviated K) is divided into the following banknotes: K1, K5, K10, K15, K20, K45 (seriously), K50, K90 (no joke), K100, K200, K500, K666 (all right, we're being devilish, sorry) and K1000.

Credit Cards

Need a credit card bailout? Fly to Bangkok! Very, very few upmarket hotels accept credit cards here and no one else does. Before the banking crisis in 2003, most credit cards were accepted.

Exchanging Money

Offers to 'change money' nearly outnumber *longyi* in this country. Essentially the only sensible way to get kyat is via the 'black market', through guesthouses, shops, travel agencies or less reliable blokes on the street. Some won't accept US dollar bills starting with the serial numbers 'CB'. The airport exchange counter at research time offered K450 for the dollar, while in Yangon rates were about K1250. The official exchange rate is a hilarious K6 to the US dollar!

Only US dollars and euros can be exchanged in Myanmar. Baht can be exchanged only at the border with Thailand. The exchange rates here are based on those used in the streets of Myanmar; other sources differ considerably from this.

Many travellers do the bulk of their changing in Yangon, where rates are a little better than elsewhere. Count the cash before handing over dollars, and don't change in the street. Honest exchangers won't mind you counting. Generally kyat are banded in stacks of 100 K1000 bills. If you want to be well and

DOLLARS VS KYAT

Prices in this book follow local usage: dollars when locals ask for them, kyat otherwise. Note some strict museum staff and boat operators will insist on dollars.

truly stitched up, then by all means change at a government bank or airport.

Foreign Exchange Certificates (FECs)

In 2003, the government stopped requiring visitors to change US$200 worth of Foreign Exchange Certificates (FEC) upon arrival. The FEC, pegged at 1:1 to the US dollar, is still accepted at hotels and for tourism-related services such as ferries or air tickets, but it's increasingly rare.

Travellers Cheques

In Yangon, you can cash travellers cheques at some upscale hotels for a 3% to 10% commission.

PHOTOGRAPHY & VIDEO

Most internet cafés can burn digital photos onto a CD for about K1000, but you should have your own adapter. Colour print film is widely available in most towns. Some sights, including some pagodas, charge small camera fees. Avoid taking photos of military facilities, uniformed individuals, road blocks, bridges, NLD offices and Aung San Suu Kyi's house.

POST

Myanmar is the place to get retro with postcards at just K50 to anywhere in the world. That's US$0.05! The government has to be losing money on this, so send as many as you can. For bigger (or more valuable) packages, **DHL** (Yangon Map p532; ☎ 01-664423; Traders Hotel, 223 Sule Paya Rd; Mandalay Map p555; ☎ 02-39274; 22nd St, 80/81) sends packages to anywhere but the USA (restricted due to sanctions). A 0.5kg package to Europe or Canada is about US$65, to Australia, US$50.

RESPONSIBLE TRAVEL

See 'Should You Go?' (p521) for more on the pros and cons of visiting Myanmar.

Much of Myanmar remains mired in poverty. Support local businesses by buying locally made products. Eat in local restaurants when possible and dine in villages rather than taking picnics from town. Use local guides for remote regions, including indigenous minority peoples where available.

When bargaining for goods or transport, remember the aim is not to get the lowest possible price, but one that's acceptable to both you and the seller. Coming on too strong or arguing over a few cents does nothing to foster positive feelings towards foreign visitors.

Begging is quite a common sight in Myanmar these days. Remember that the military government doesn't give a damn about the people and there is little in the way of a social security net to catch the fallen. Avoid giving money to children, as it is most likely going straight to a 'begging pimp' or family member. Food is one option, but better still is to make a donation to one of the many local organisations trying to assist in the battle against poverty.

STUDYING

Most foreign students in Myanmar are getting busy with *satipatthana vipassana*, or insight-awareness meditation. Yangon is meditation HQ, with several centres. Sagaing is another good place to find opportunities. Often food and lodging are provided at no charge, but meditators must follow eight precepts, including no food after noon, as well as no music, dancing, jewellery or perfume. It's for the experienced only. Daily schedules are rigorous – sometimes nonstop practice from 3am to 11pm.

For practice sessions of less than one month, a tourist visa suffices. For longer terms, it's necessary to apply for a 'special-entry visa', which you cannot apply for while in Myanmar on a tourist visa. Applicants must receive a letter of invitation from a centre. The process takes eight to 10 weeks.

For individual meditation centres, see entries under Yangon (p533) and Sagaing (p560).

SAVE THE INTERNATIONAL CALLS FOR THAILAND!

Try to avoid making international calls in Myanmar, as they're ludicrously expensive by regional standards and the money from them goes directly into the government's pocket. If you need to stay in touch with family and friends, switch to email or consider signing up for an instant messaging service such as Google Talk, which isn't blocked by the government censors. Look out for (the few) internet cafés that have cheaper internet telephone services using MediaRing Talk or other software that isn't blocked.

There is useful information on meditation centres at www.rainbow2.com/burma and http://web.ukonline.co.uk/buddhism/meditate.htm.

TELEPHONE

Local calls can be made cheaply or for free from guesthouses. Domestic long distance is cheap from a Central Telephone & Telegraph (CTT) office or from phone stalls on the street. International calls – made at a CTT office or from guesthouses – are a whopping US$4 or US$5 per minute to Australia or Europe, an extra dollar to North America. Some smaller towns still use manual switchboards, which can be a hoot to see in action.

Mobile Phones

Myanmar has mobile phones, but at a whopping US$2500 for a number they are few and far between. Roaming is not possible anywhere in Myanmar, save for a couple of border towns where you can tap into Thailand. If you're carrying a mobile, it is supposed to be declared on arrival.

Phone Codes

To call Myanmar from abroad, dial your country's international access code, then ☎ 95 (Myanmar's country code), the area code (less the 0) and the five- or six-digit number. To dial long distance within Myanmar, dial the area code (including 0) and the number. Bear in mind that it can be very difficult to contact some regions of the country – patience and perseverance are required.

TOILETS

In many backwater places, toilets are often squat jobs, generally in a cobweb-filled outhouse reached by a dirt path behind a restaurant. In guesthouses and hotels, you'll find Western-style sit-down flush toilets. Toilet paper is widely available, but should not be flushed.

TOURIST INFORMATION

Myanmar Travel & Tours (MTT; www.myanmars.net/mtt) is part of the Ministry of Hotels & Tourism (MHT), the official government tourism organ in Myanmar. Its main office is in Yangon (p531) and there are also offices in Mandalay, Bagan and Inle Lake. We certainly don't recommend using its services, but the staff can be useful in terms of gauging prices and getting info on travel restrictions.

TRAVELLERS WITH DISABILITIES

Myanmar is a tricky country for mobility-impaired travellers. Wheelchair ramps are virtually unheard of and transport is crowded and difficult even for the fully ambulatory.

VISAS

Passport holders from Asean countries, China, Bangladesh and Russia do not need to apply for visas to visit Myanmar. All other nationalities do. A tourist visa's validity expires 90 days after issue and only allows a 28-day, single-entry visit. It costs US$20. You'll need three passport-sized photos for the process.

There are also 28-day business visas (US$30) and 28-day special visas (US$30) for former Myanmar citizens (which can be extended for three to six months once in Yangon for US$36). A multiple-entry business visa is US$150. There are also meditation visas (US$30) for those travelling for this purpose.

Travel agencies along Bangkok's Khao San Rd specialise in getting quick tourist visas for Myanmar. Rates depend on turnaround times, which always aren't met: visa in one day 1800B, two days 1600B and three days 1100B. The process at the Bangkok embassy can take a couple of days. It may be easier to plan ahead and arrange the visa in a 'quieter' capital, such as Phnom Penh or Vientiane.

Visitors from Thailand can get very short-term 'visas' that allow minimal travel in border regions of Myanmar.

Applications

Myanmar's embassies and consulates abroad are scrupulous in checking out the backgrounds of visa applicants. Consider declaring another profession if you're a journalist, photographer, editor, publisher, motion-picture director or producer, cameraperson or writer. Otherwise you're likely to be rejected.

Extensions

At the time of research, it was possible to extend a tourist visa by an additional 14 days (only) beyond its original 28-day validity in Yangon only. The process costs US$36 and usually takes about two to five days. A travel agent can help navigate the bureaucracy for a total of US$50. You'll need two copies of your passport and visa, two passport-sized photographs and a recommendation letter from MTT. The process cannot be started in advance or from elsewhere in Myanmar.

Overstaying Your Visa

Another option, if you want just a few more days, is overstaying your visa. Check with a Yangon agent before your visa's up, but at research time there was generally little hassle to overstay *if* you were leaving from the Yangon or Mandalay airports. Be prepared to spend at least 20 minutes with some paperwork, and to pay US$3 per day overstayed, plus a US$3 'registration fee'. Try to have correct change handy. Apparently, it's possible to overstay by up to six weeks without major incident; many travellers have reported overstaying a week or more.

When departing overland to Thailand on an expired visa, it's best to enlist help from a travel agency before popping up at the border. In one case, an extra US$35 fee was lopped onto the US$3-per-day penalty to cross to Ranong, Thailand.

VOLUNTEERING

You'll have plenty of chances to help locals with English over tea. Some foreigners have been able to volunteer as English teachers at monasteries. In November 2004, seven foreigners doing so at Mandalay's Phaungdaw Kyaung were deported, though this was likely a repercussion of the monastery's connection with ousted prime minister Khin Nyunt.

WOMEN TRAVELLERS

Women travelling alone are more likely to be helped than harassed. In some areas, you'll be regarded with friendly curiosity – and asked, with sad-eyed sympathy, 'Are you only one?' – because Burmese women tend to prefer to travel en masse. At the more remote religious sites, a single foreign woman is likely to be 'adopted' by a young Burmese woman, who will take you by the hand to show you the highlights. At some sites, such as Mandalay's Mahamuni Paya (p554), 'ladies' are not permitted to the central altar; signs will indicate this if it is the case.

You can get tampons at upmarket shops in Yangon and Mandalay.

WORKING

Work permits in Myanmar are not totally impossible to get these days. The first step is to arrange sponsorship from a local company and have a persuasive reason to be here – an English teacher at one of the international schools, for example. Seek out expats in Yangon for more information.

Philippines

HIGHLIGHTS

- **Cordillera region** – trekking through immense rice terraces around Banaue (p609) and Bontoc (p609) in Luzon's rugged north
- **Isolated beaches** – doing the Robinson Crusoe thing in remote Siquijor (p623), Sipalay (p621), Port Barton (p638) and Camiguin (p635)
- **Party beaches** – diving in Puerto Galera (p614), kite-surfing in Boracay (p618) and drinking all night in both places
- **Biggest fish** – snorkelling with the whale sharks of Donsol (p613) and Southern Leyte (p632)
- **Ride the wave** – surfing the Philippines' gnarliest break – classic Cloud Nine – and imbibing surfer-dude culture on laid-back Siargao Island (p634)
- **Off the beaten track** – exploring sunken WWII wrecks and hidden lagoons in the bays and islands around Coron (p639)

FAST FACTS

- **Budget** US$20 to US$25 a day
- **Capital** Manila
- **Costs** island cottage US$5 to US$15, four-hour bus ride US$2 to US$3, beer US$0.40
- **Country code** ☎ 63
- **Languages** Filipino (Tagalog), English, 11 regional languages and 87 dialects
- **Money** US$1 = P46.28 (peso)
- **Phrases** *paálam* (goodbye), *salámat* (thanks), *iskyus* (sorry); raise eyebrows while tilting head upwards (nonverbal hello)
- **Population** 89 million, including up to 10 million Filipinos working overseas
- **Time** GMT + eight hours
- **Visas** free 21-day visa given on arrival; extensions for up to 59 days are US$42, and are available in major cities

TRAVEL HINTS

Try to fly into Manila and out of Cebu, or vice versa, to save yourself lots of backtracking. Bring earplugs for those long, loud *bangka* (pumpboat) rides, and to muffle ubiquitous early morning distractions such as roosters, tricycles and over-caffeinated courtyard sweepers.

WARNING

The situation in some parts of Mindanao and the Sulu Archipelago is volatile. Travel in these regions should be considered dangerous and only undertaken with careful, independent research on the ground.

Just when you thought you had Asia figured out, you get to the Philippines. Instead of monks you have priests; instead of túk-túks you have tricycles; instead of *pho* you have *adobo*. At first glance the Philippines will disarm you more than charm you, but peel under the country's skin and there are treasures to be found – aplenty. For starters, you can swim with whale sharks, scale volcanoes, explore desert islands, gawk at ancient rice terraces, submerge at world-class dive sites and venture into rainforests to visit remote hill tribes.

Beyond its obvious physical assets, the Philippines possesses a quirky streak that takes a bit longer to appreciate. There are secret potions and healing lotions, guys named Bong and girls named Bing, grinning hustlers, deafening cock farms, wheezing *bangkas* (pumpboats), crooked politicians, fuzzy *caribao* (water buffalo), graffiti-splashed jeepneys and – best of all – cheap beer to enjoy as you take it all in.

Transport connections are extensive, but in remote areas may require intestinal fortitude and an affinity for the Filipino maxim *bahala na:* go with the flow. Gregarious locals everywhere dispense smiles like they're going out of style. Be sure not to leave before seeing one of the country's spirited festivals and sampling the Filipino zeal for living *la vida loca*.

CURRENT EVENTS

In some ways not much has changed in the political and economic structure of the Philippines in decades – the same clannish circle of politicians runs the show, the population boom continues and corruption cuts the potential for growth. Despite this, the economy has been growing by around 5% since President Gloria Macapagal-Arroyo replaced disgraced Joseph Estrada in 2001. Arroyo is far from popular: her allies won only three of the 12 influential Senate seats up for grabs in the 2007 elections, and she barely survived coup attempts and street protests in 2005 and 2006. But 'GMA', as the president is known, has at least given the country a semblance of stability, something it has lacked since the 'People Power' revolution deposed President Ferdinand Marcos in 1986.

Meanwhile, a Muslim insurgency in this predominantly Christian country continues to affect the Philippines' south. The country's largest Muslim rebel group is the 12,000-strong Moro Islamic Liberation Front (MILF), but the group that grabs all the headlines is Abu Sayyaf, which was responsible for a highly publicised kidnapping in 2001 and is accused of a 2004 ferry bombing that killed more than 100 people near Manila. In recent years the killing of several top leaders has weakened Abu Sayyaf substantially, while the government has been extending the olive branch to the MILF. Despite that, fighting in parts of Mindanao remains common, and few are predicting that peace will break out in the south any time soon.

The government's other bugbear is the communist New People's Army (NPA), which has been fighting the government for years from remote bases in Luzon, Mindanao, Samar and elsewhere. In 2006 there were dozens of unsolved 'extrajudicial' killings of left-leaning activists, journalists and priests with alleged links to the NPA; human rights groups have assailed the Arroyo administration for the killings, but little had been done to address the problem as of this writing. It's worth noting that the NPA is not considered a threat to tourists.

HISTORY

First Filipinos

Negrito tribes may have started migrating here over land bridges up to 30,000 years ago. Later migrants arrived by outrigger canoes. The Philippines was one of the earliest centres of the Austronesian migration wave, which started in China, skipped to Taiwan and the Philippines and swept out as far as New Zealand, Hawaii and Madagascar. Outrigger canoes safely carried new crops and animals such as pigs, and you can bet that a protocockfighting fanatic on board was tenderly holding his prize rooster.

Spanish Colonialists

In 1519 Ferdinand Magellan set off from Europe with instructions to sail around the world, claim anything worth claiming and extend Spain's spice empire into the Pacific region. Reaching the Islamic Sultanate of Cebu in 1521, Magellan managed to convert a number of people to Christianity before he was killed by Chief Lapu-Lapu on Mactan Island.

In 1565 the Spanish returned. Miguel de Legazpi stormed the island of Cebu and established the first permanent Spanish settlement.

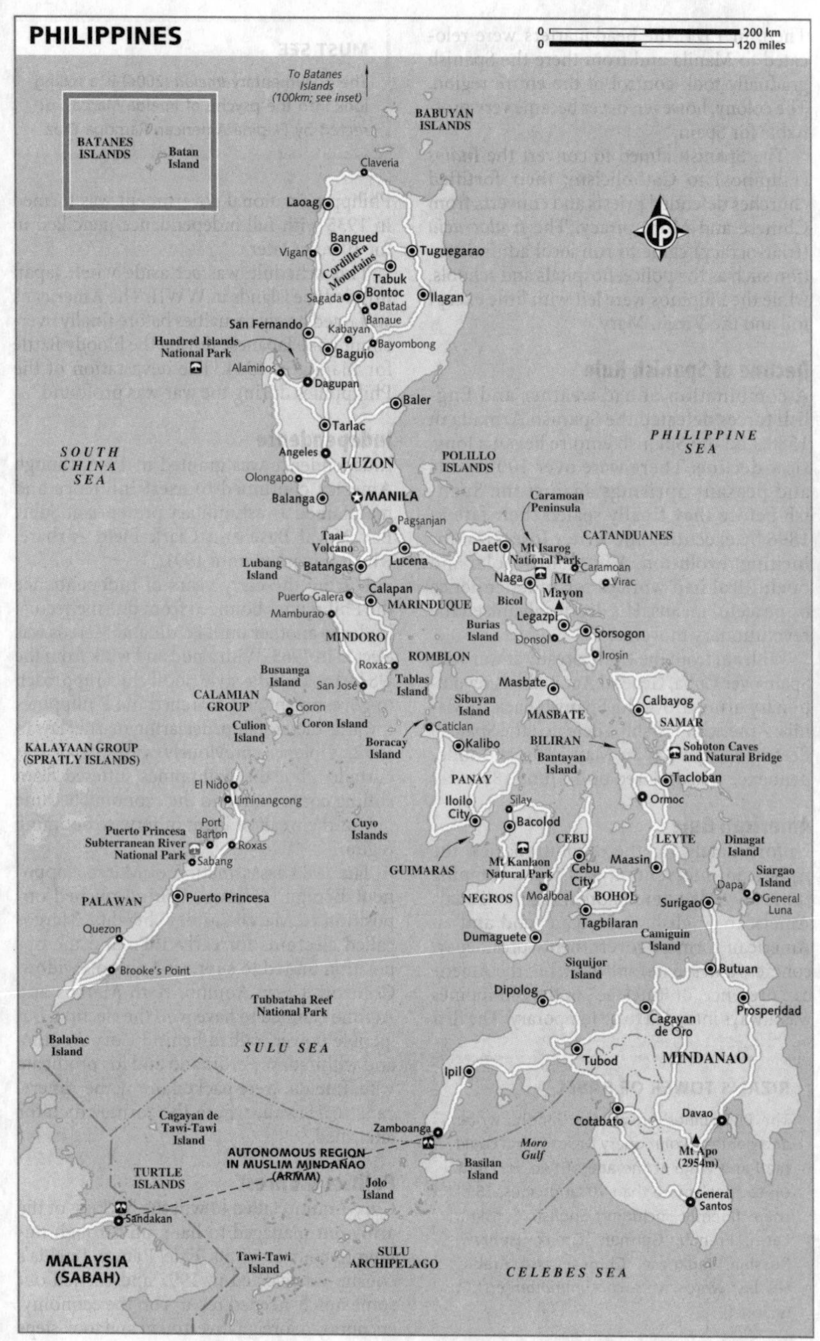

PHILIPPINES

Then, in 1571, the headquarters were relocated to Manila and from there the Spanish gradually took control of the entire region. The colony, however, never became very profitable for Spain.

The Spanish aimed to convert the *Indios* (Filipinos) to Catholicism; their fortified churches defended priests and converts from Chinese and Moro piracy. The *frialocracia* (friar-ocracy) came to run local administration such as the police, hospitals and schools, while the Filipinos were left with little except toil and the Virgin Mary.

Decline of Spanish Rule

A combination of bad weather and English forces defeated the Spanish Armada in 1588, and the Spanish empire began a long, slow decline. There were over 100 revolts and peasant uprisings against the Spanish before they finally sealed their fate in 1896 by executing the writer José Rizal for inciting revolution. A brilliant scholar and poet, Rizal had worked for independence by peaceful means. His death galvanised the revolutionary movement.

With aid from the USA, already at war with Spain over Cuba, General Aguinaldo's revolutionary army drove the Spanish back to Manila. American warships defeated the Spanish fleet in Manila Bay in May 1898, and independence was declared on 12 June 1898.

American Rule

Unfortunately for the revolutionaries, the American intervention was just a stepping stone towards a new colonial regime. Today, American English, American food and an American form of government (presidency, congress and senate) still exist, but the American presence, or 'tutelage', in the Philippines was always intended to be temporary. The first Philippine national government was formed in 1935 with full independence pencilled in for 10 years later.

This schedule was set aside when Japan invaded the islands in WWII. The Americans sustained heavy casualties before finally overcoming the Japanese during the bloody Battle for Manila in 1944. The devastation of the Philippines during the war was profound.

> **RIZAL'S TOWER OF BABEL**
>
> The Philippines' answer to Gandhi, writer and gentle revolutionary Dr José Rizal could read and write at the age of two. He grew up to speak more than 20 languages, 18 of them fluently, including English, Sanskrit, Latin, French, German, Greek, Hebrew, Russian, Japanese, Chinese and Arabic. His last words were *consummatum est!* (it is done!).

> **MUST SEE**
>
> The documentary *Imelda* (2004) is a telling look into the psyche of Imelda Marcos, directed by Filipina American Ramona Diaz.

Independence

Independence was granted in 1946, though America continued to exert influence and maintained a vast military presence at Subic Bay Naval Base and Clark Field Airbase, which remained until 1991.

During the early years of independence the Philippines bounced from one ineffectual leader to another until Ferdinand Marcos was elected in 1965. With a nod and wink from the US he took a *datu*-style (local chief) approach to government and marched the Philippines towards dictatorship, declaring martial law in 1972. Violence, previously widespread, was curtailed, but the Philippines suffered from stifling corruption and the economy became one of the weakest in an otherwise booming region.

The 1983 assassination of Marcos' opponent Benigno 'Ninoy' Aquino pushed opposition to Marcos to new heights. Marcos called elections for early 1986 and the opposition united to support Aquino's widow, Corazon 'Cory' Aquino. Both Marcos and Aquino claimed to have won the election, but 'people power' rallied behind Cory Aquino, and within days Ferdinand and his profligate wife, Imelda, were packed off by the Americans to Hawaii, where the former dictator later died.

Politics & Unrest

Cory Aquino failed to win the backing of the army but managed to hang on through numerous coup attempts. Fidel Ramos, Imelda's cousin, was elected in 1992 and carried out some much-needed repairs on the economy, encouraged foreign investment and took steps to end the guerrilla war with the NPA and Muslim rebels in the south. In 1996 the government signed a peace agreement with the main Muslim rebel group, the Moro National Liberation Front (MNLF), and the Autonomous Region in Muslim Mindanao (ARMM) was created. A faction calling itself the Moro Islamic Liberation Front (MILF) split from the MNLF and continued the fight.

In 1998 Ramos was replaced by B-grade movie actor Joseph 'Erap' Estrada, who promised to redirect government funding towards rural and poor Filipinos. Unfortunately, Erap spent most of his time redirecting government funding towards his own coffers and was impeached two years later. What followed was a kind of middle-class revolt, which was called EDSA 2 (EDSA was the Manila ring road where the demonstrators gathered and EDSA 1 had been the overthrow of Marcos). Replacing Estrada was his diminutive vice-president, Arroyo. For more information, see Current Events on p584.

THE CULTURE

The National Psyche

Probably the first thing you'll notice about the people of the Philippines is their calm demeanour. Filipinos greet adversity with all the fuss that a *caribao* greets a fly on its back – they shrug their shoulders, smile and move on. This whatever-will-be-will-be attitude has a name: *bahala na*. It expresses the idea that all things shall pass and that in the meantime life is to be lived. *Bahala na* also helps explain one of the Filipinos' more appealing traits: they tolerate just about everybody, regardless of nationality, skin colour or sexual orientation.

Another force that shapes the Filipino psyche is *hiya*, which means, roughly, 'sense of shame'. Showing a lack of *hiya* in front of others is similar to 'losing face' and for the Filipino there are few worse fates. Expressing strong or negative emotions in public are sure ways to show you are *walang-hiya* – without shame. Most problems that travellers run into result from a lack of respect for the Filipino

GEMS OF THE PHILIPPINES

This is our completely subjective list of the best and strangest in this incredible country.

Favourite Small Mercies

- The widespread distribution of what is probably the cheapest beer in the world
- The availability of tricycles to take you anywhere, any time, for less than US$5
- All-you-can-eat buffets after 18-hour boat trips

Most Tragically Popular Karaoke Songs

- *Glory of Love*, Peter Cetera
- *Even the Nights Are Better*, Air Supply
- *My Heart Will Go On*, Celine Dion

Most Challenging Moments

- Roosters with dysfunctional circadian rhythms crowing at 3am
- When your bus loses its breaks on a single-lane road with a truck coming the other way – and you're riding shotgun
- Being stuck on the tarmac with a Tanduay hangover in a sweltering plane running on 'Filipino time'

Best Perches

- On the deck at Rita's or Simon's, gazing at the rice terrace amphitheatre in Batad (p610)
- On top of Mt Kanlaon, Negros Occidental (p621)
- In an over-water *nipa* hut (traditional hut made of palm leaves) at Guiwanon Spring Park Resort (p623), Siquijor, watching a seaside sunset

> **MUST READ**
>
> *Ghosts of Manila* (1994) by James Hamilton-Paterson is a chilling 'docu-fiction' of life, death and the corrupt chains binding Filipinos in the city's slums.

codes of *hiya* and *amor propio*, or self-esteem. The golden rule when travelling in the Philippines is to treat problems with the same graciousness as the average Filipino. A smile and a joke go a long way, while anger just makes things worse.

Filipinos are a superstitious lot. In the hinterland, a villager might be possessed by a wandering spirit, causing them to commit strange acts. In urban areas, faith healers, psychics, fortune-tellers, tribal shamans, self-help books and evangelical crusaders can all help cast away ill-fortune.

Lifestyle

First-time visitors to Manila are often lulled into thinking the Philippines is Westernised. They soon realise that the chain restaurants, malls and American R&B music disguise a unique Asian culture still very much rooted in an ancient values system.

For centuries the two most important influences on the lives of Filipinos have been family and religion. The Filipino family unit, or 'kinship group', extends to distant cousins, multiple godparents and one's *barkada* (gang of friends). With few exceptions, all members of one's kinship group are afforded loyalty and respect. Filipino families, especially poor ones, tend to be large. It's not uncommon for a dozen family members to live together in a tiny apartment, shanty or *nipa* hut (traditional hut made of palm leaves).

Another vital thread in the fabric of Filipino society is the overseas worker. Nearly one in 10 Filipinos works abroad. Combined they sent a record US$12 billion back home in 2006, or about 10% of the GDP. The true figure is probably much higher than that. The Overseas Filipino Worker (OFW) – the nurse in Canada, the construction worker in Qatar, the entertainer in Japan, the cleaner in Singapore – has become a national hero. When OFWs retire, they return to their home provinces as *balikbayan* (literally 'returnees to the home country') and build gaudy concrete homes.

Population

A journey from the northern tip of Luzon to the southern tip of the Sulu islands reveals a range of ethnic groups speaking almost 100 different dialects. Filipinos are mainly of the Malay race, although there's a sizable and economically dominant Chinese minority and a fair number of *mestizos* (Filipinos of mixed descent).

The country's population is thought to be between 80 million and 90 million (the 2005 census was cancelled for budgetary reasons). Partially because of the Catholic church's hard line on 'artificial' birth control, the population is growing at one of the fastest rates in Asia. It's also becoming younger and more urban: the median age is only 22.5 and almost a quarter of the population lives in or around metro Manila.

RELIGION

The Philippines is one of the only predominantly Christian country in Asia – almost 90% of the population claims to be Christian and over 80% are Roman Catholic. The largest religious minority is Muslim (5%), although Islam is actually an older presence than Christianity. Filipino Muslims live chiefly in the ARMM and belong to the mainstream Sunni sect. Popular Christian sects include the Jehovah's Witnesses, Mormons (Church of Jesus Christ of Latter-Day Saints) and various brands of southern Baptists.

While the separation of church and state is formalised in the Filipino constitution, a subtle hint from the church can swing a mayoral race and mean millions of votes for presidential or senatorial candidates.

ARTS

Cinema

The Philippines has historically been Southeast Asia's most prolific film-making nation.

> **THE SEARCH FOR SPOILS**
>
> Legends of buried treasure flourish in the Philippines. The most famous urban myth talks of Yamashita's Horde, a cache of bullion sunk on a WWII Japanese ship, which Ferdinand Marcos claimed to have found. Modern-day Indiana Jones types, including ex-Japanese soldiers and CIA operatives, supposedly still scour the country's remote regions in search of plunder.

MUST SEE

Kubrador, about the life of a *juetang* bet collector, won awards in several international film festivals in 2006. *Juetang* is an illegal lottery-style numbers game popular throughout the country.

The movie industry's 'golden age' was the 1950s, when Filipino films won countless awards. In the 1980s and 1990s the industry surged again thanks to a genre called 'bold' – think sex, violence and dudes with great hair in romantic roles. Today the mainstream studios are in decline, but the flip side is that the quality of films is getting better with the proliferation of independent films such as *Kubrador* (see boxed text, p586). Over the years, the Philippines has also served as a backdrop for many big foreign films, most notably *Apocalypse Now* and *Platoon*.

Dance
Among the most beautiful traditional dances in the Philippines are *tinikling* (bamboo or heron dance) and *pandanggo sa ilaw* (dance of lights); the best-known Filipino-Muslim dance is *singkil* (court dance). You will also often see performances of the Filipino variations of the Hispanic dances *habanera, jota* and *paypay* (the fan dance).

Music
Filipino rock music is known as 'OPM' (Original Pinoy Music – 'Pinoy' is what Filipinos call themselves). It actually encompasses a wide spectrum of rock, folk and new age genres – plus a subset that includes all three. Embodying the latter subset is the band Pinikpikan, which performs a sometimes frantic fusion of tribal styles and modern jamband rock. The 11-piece band uses bamboo reed pipes, flutes and percussion instruments and sings in languages as diverse as Visayan, French and Bicol.

The Philippines' best-loved form of traditional music is the *kundiman*, a bittersweet combination of words and music. Traditional instruments include the *kulintang gong*, or chime, found in North Luzon, and the *kutyapi*, an extremely demanding, but hauntingly melodic, two-stringed lute, commonly found in Mindanao.

DID YOU KNOW?

The traditional welcome dance, the *kuratsa*, is based on the courtship dances of chickens!

ENVIRONMENT
The Land
An assemblage of 7107 tropical isles scattered about like pieces of a giant jigsaw puzzle, the Philippines stubbornly defies geographic generalisation. The typical island boasts a jungle-clad, critter-infested interior and a sandy coastline flanked by aquamarine waters and the requisite coral reef. More populated islands have less jungle and more farmland.

Wildlife
The country's flora includes well over 10,000 species of trees, bushes and ferns, including 900 types of orchid. About 10% of the Philippines is still covered by tropical rainforest.

Endangered animal species include the mouse deer (see boxed text, p631), the tamaráw (a species of dwarf buffalo) of Mindoro, the Philippine crocodile of Northeast Luzon, the Palawan bearcat and the flying lemur. As for the national bird, there are thought to be about 500 pairs of haribons, or Philippine eagles, remaining in the rainforests of Mindanao, Luzon, Samar and Leyte.

There's an unbelievable array of fish, seashells and corals, as well as dwindling numbers of the *duyong* (dugong, or sea cow). If your timing's just right you can spot *butanding* (whale sharks) in Donsol and Southern Leyte.

National Parks
The Philippines' numerous national parks, natural parks and other protected areas comprise about 10% of the country's total area, but most lack services such as park offices, huts, trail maps and sometimes even trails. The most popular national park, at least amongst foreigners, is surely Palawan's Subterranean River National Park (p638).

Environmental Issues
As with many of the government departments, the budget of the Department of Environment & Natural Resources (DENR) is never quite what it seems. The Philippines has strict environmental laws on its books,

DID YOU KNOW?

The Philippine eagle was known as the 'monkey eating eagle' until the government officially changed the name in 1978.

but they just aren't enforced. Only 3% of the reefs are in a pristine state, and 60% have been severely damaged.

The biggest culprit of reef damage is silt, washed down from hills and valleys indiscriminately – and often illegally – cleared of their original forest cover. Illegal logging also exacerbates floods and causes landslides, such as the one in February 2006 that killed more than 1000 people in St Bernard, Southern Leyte. Lip service is given to the issue by the government, but little is done.

Incredibly short-sighted techniques for making a few extra bucks include dynamite and cyanide fishing. The uncontrolled harvesting of seashells for export, particularly in the Visayas, is another problem. Don't go buying souvenirs made from shell or coral (souvenirs made from farmed oyster shells are an exception).

PHILIPPINES

TRANSPORT

GETTING THERE & AWAY

Air

The three main points of entry are Manila, Cebu and Clark Special Economic Zone. In addition, domestic carrier Asian Spirit runs a thrice-weekly flight between Zamboanga (Mindanao) and Sandakan, Malaysia. Indonesian carrier Sriwijaya Airlines has two weekly flights from Manado, Indonesia, to Davao (Mindanao).

MANILA

Unless you fly in with Philippine Airlines (PAL), which uses the tidy new Centennial Terminal II, you'll have to fight your way through Terminal I of Ninoy Aquino International Airport (NAIA). Expect disorganisation, long queues at immigration and diabolical transport connections to the city.

A brand new international terminal was completed in 2002, but as of this writing its opening remained on hold.

The two budget airlines flying to/from NAIA are domestic carrier Cebu Pacific and Singapore's Jetstar. Tickets for both airlines can be bought online.

Manila is well connected to Europe, the US, Australia and Asia. The following are the main airlines serving Manila nonstop from Southeast Asia, China and the South Pacific.

Asian Spirit (code 6K; ☎ 02-855 3333; www.asianspirit.com) From Palau.

Cathay Pacific (code CX; ☎ 02-757 0888; www.cathaypacific.com) From Hong Kong.

Cebu Pacific (code 5J; ☎ 02-702 0888; www.cebupacificair.com) From Bangkok, Hong Kong, Jakarta, Singapore and Taipei.

China Southern Airlines (code CZ; www.cs-air.com) From Beijing and Guangzhou.

Continental Airlines (code CO; ☎ 02-818 8701, 02-817 9666; www.continental.com) From Palau.

Jetstar Asia (code 3K; www.jetstar.com) From Singapore.

Malaysia Airlines (code MH; www.malaysiaairlines.com) From Kuala Lumpur.

Philippine Airlines (code PR; ☎ 02-855 8888; www.philippineairlines.com) From Bangkok, Beijing, Kuala Lumpur, Shanghai and Singapore.

Thai Airways International (THAI, code TG; ☎ 02-834 0366; www.thaiairways.com) From Bangkok.

CEBU

If you're heading to the Visayas, a much better option is to fly into Cebu City's **Mactan International Airport** (☎ 032-340 2486; www.mactan-cebuairport.com.ph). The Philippines' budget airline, Cebu Pacific, flies direct to Cebu from Hong Kong and Singapore. Cathay Pacific has direct flights to/from Hong Kong, Malaysia Airlines has twice weekly flights to Kuala Lumpur, and Asian Spirit flies direct to Palau.

CLARK SPECIAL ECONOMIC ZONE

Macapagal International Airport (DMIA, Clark Airport; www.clarkairport.com) in the Clark Special Economic Zone (near Angeles, about a two-hour bus ride north of Manila) is becoming a hot destination for Asian low-cost airlines. **Tiger Airways** (code TGW; ☎ 02-884 1524; www.tigerairways.com) now flies to Clark from Singapore and Macau, and **Air Asia** (code AXM; www.airasia

DEPARTURE TAX

International departure tax is P700 at NAIA, P550 at Cebu and P500 at Clark.

ONWARD TICKETS

The Philippines requires all tourists to show an onward ticket before entering the country. While this rule is rarely enforced at Philippine immigration, most airlines adamantly refuse to let passengers board Philippine-bound planes without an original onward ticket (photocopies will not work, although e-tickets will).

.com) flies to Clark from Kuala Lumpur and Kota Kinabalu, all for well under US$100 return. The airport's website has instructions on transport from the airport to Manila or Angeles. Also see p603 for information on catching a bus from Manila to the airport.

Sea

Although there are plenty of shipping routes within the Philippines, international services are scarce. The only route open to foreigners, as of this writing, was Zamboanga to Sandakan in the Malaysian state of Sabah. See p635 for further details.

GETTING AROUND

Air

The Philippines now has two budget domestic carriers – Cebu Pacific and Air Philippines (a subsidiary of PAL). Domestic flights on either of these airlines do not usually exceed P1800 one-way (including all surcharges) provided you book in advance.

Cebu Pacific and PAL have the most modern fleets and serve the most cities, although almost all flights originate in Manila or Cebu. PAL tends to be much pricier than Cebu Pacific, although it's worth checking out its 'promo' fares. Air Philippines serves only a handful of cities from Cebu and Manila.

Two smaller carriers, Asian Spirit and Southeast Asian Airlines (Seair), have fleets of small planes serving minor towns such as El Nido, Palawan and Caticlan (the jump-off point for Boracay) from Manila. These airlines are more expensive than their larger rivals. One-way prices (including all surcharges) range from P3200 for Caticlan to P6200 for El Nido.

In Manila, all PAL flights leave from Terminal II of NAIA, while all other domestic services leave from the domestic airport, about a five-minute taxi ride from NAIA.

Flight times range from 45 minutes for short hops such as Manila–Caticlan to 1½ hours for flights from Manila to southern Mindanao.

Airline details:

Air Philippines (code 2P; ☎ 02-855 9000; www.airphils.com)
Asian Spirit (code 6K; ☎ 02-855 3333; www.asianspirit.com)
Cebu Pacific (code 5J; ☎ 02-702 0888; www.cebupacificair.com)
Philippine Airlines (code PR; ☎ 02-855 8888; www.philippineairlines.com)
Seair (code DG; ☎ 02-849 0100; www.flyseair.com)

Boat

If boats are your thing, this is the place for you. The islands of the Philippines are linked by an incredible network of ferry routes and services are extremely cheap. The vessels used range from tiny, narrow outrigger canoes (known locally as *bangka*, or pumpboats) to luxury 'fastcraft' vessels and, for long-haul journeys, vast multidecked ships such as the SuperFerry.

The jeepney of the sea, the *bangka*, comes sometimes with a roof, sometimes without. *Bangkas* ply regular routes between islands and are also available for hire for diving, sightseeing or just getting around. The engines on these boats can be deafeningly loud, and they aren't the most stable in rough seas, but on islands such as Palawan the *bangka* can be preferable to travelling overland.

For the most part, ferries are an easy, enjoyable way to hop between islands, but accidents are not unknown. Follow your instincts – if the boat looks crowded, it is, and if sailing conditions seem wrong, they are. Pumpboats during stormy weather are especially scary.

'Fastcraft' services are becoming increasingly popular on shorter routes. They can cut travel times by half but usually cost twice as much as slower 'roll-on, roll-off' (RORO) car ferries. Some shipping lines give 20% to 30% off for students.

Booking ahead is essential for long-haul liners and can be done at ticket offices or travel agents in most cities. For fastcraft and *bangka* ferries, tickets can usually be bought at the pier before departure.

Buses & Vans

Philippine buses come in all shapes and sizes, from rusty boxes on wheels to luxury air-con coaches. Bus depots are dotted throughout towns and the countryside, and most buses will stop if you wave them down. Terminals are usually on the outskirts of town, but tricycle drivers should know where they are.

Generally, more services run in the morning – buses on unsealed roads may run only in the morning, especially in remote areas. Most buses follow a fixed schedule but may leave early if they're full. Night services – including deluxe 27-seaters – are common between Manila and major provincial hubs in Luzon but should be booked a few days in advance.

Air-con minivans shadow bus routes in many parts of the Philippines (especially Bicol, Leyte and Cebu) and in some cases have replaced buses altogether (such as on the Legazpi–Donsol route). However, you may have to play a waiting game until the vehicles are full. Minivans are quicker than buses, but they are also more expensive and more cramped.

Local Transport

HABAL-HABAL

Common in many Visayan islands and northern Mindanao, these are simply motorcycle taxis with extended seats (literally translated as 'pigs copulating', after the level of intimacy attained when sharing a seat with four people). *Habal-habal* function like tricycles, only they are a little bit cheaper. Outside of the Visayas they're known as 'motorcycle taxis'.

JEEPNEY

The first jeepneys were modified army jeeps left behind by the Americans after WWII. They have been customised with Filipino touches such as chrome horses, banks of coloured headlights, radio antennae, paintings of the Virgin Mary and neon-coloured scenes from action comic books. Modern jeepneys are built locally from durable aluminium and stainless steel but are faithful to the original design.

Jeepneys form the main urban transport in most cities and complement the bus services between regional centres. Within towns, the starting fare is usually P6 to P7.50, rising modestly for trips outside of town. Routes are usually clearly written on the side of the jeepney.

KALESA

Kalesa are two-wheeled horse carriages found in Manila's Chinatown, Vigan (North Luzon) and Cebu City (where they're known as *tartanillas*). In Manila they seem to exist solely to help tourists part with large sums of money, so be careful to agree on a fare before clambering aboard. You shouldn't pay more than P200 for a 20-minute ride.

TAXI

Taxis exist only in Manila and major provincial hubs. Most taxi drivers will turn on the meter; if they don't, politely request that they do. If the meter is 'broken' or your taxi driver says the fare is 'up to you', the best strategy is to get out and find another cab.

Taxi drivers at many regional airports charge a fixed price – usually P150 to P250 – to get into the town centre. An exception is Manila domestic airport, where metered cabs are readily available.

The taxi flag fall is P35 in Manila, P30 in Cebu and Bacolod, and P25 in Baguio. After that it's about P0.60 per 300m.

TRICYCLE

Found in most cities and towns, the tricycle is the Philippine rickshaw – a little, roofed sidecar bolted to a motorcycle. The standard fare for local trips in most provincial towns is P6. Tricycles that wait around in front of malls, restaurants and hotels in tourist centres will attempt to charge five to 10 times that for a 'special trip'. Avoid these by standing roadside and flagging down a passing P6 tricycle. You can also charter tricycles for about P200 per hour or P120 per 10km if you're heading out of town.

Many towns also have nonmotorised push tricycles, alternatively known as *put-put* or *podyak*, for shorter trips.

MANILA

☎ 02 / pop 11.2 million

Manila's moniker, the 'Pearl of the Orient', couldn't be more apt – its cantankerous shell reveals its jewel only to those resolute enough to pry. No stranger to hardship, the city has endured every disaster both man and nature could throw at it, and yet today the chaotic 600-sq-km metropolis thrives as a true Asian megacity. Gleaming skyscrapers pierce the hazy sky, mushrooming from the grinding poverty of expansive shantytowns. The congested roads snarl with traffic, but like the overworked arteries of a sweating giant, they are what keep this modern metropolis alive. The tourist belt of Ermita and Malate flaunts an uninhibited nightlife that would make Bangkok's go-go bars blush, and the gleaming malls of Makati foreshadow Manila's brave new air-conditioned world. The determined will discover Manila's tender soul, perhaps among the leafy courtyards and cobbled streets of serene Intramuros, where little has changed since the Spanish left. Or it may be in the eddy of repose arising from the generosity of one of the city's 11 million residents.

HISTORY

The Spanish brushed aside a Muslim fort here in 1571 and founded the modern city as the capital of their realm. They named it Isigne y Siempre Leal Ciudad (Distinguished and Ever Loyal City), but the name Manila (from Maynilad, derived from a local term for a mangrove plant) soon became established. Spanish residents were concentrated around the walled city of Intramuros until 1898, when the Spanish governor surrendered to the Filipinos at San Agustin Church. After being razed to the ground during WWII, the city grew exponentially during the post-war era as migrants left the countryside for new opportunities. Marcos consolidated 17 towns and villages into Metro Manila in 1976.

ORIENTATION

Metro Manila's traditional tourist belt is located in the relatively compact 'downtown' area just south of the mouth of the Pasig River. The old walled city of Intramuros (Map p600) lies just south of the river; south of that are Rizal Park and the districts of Ermita and Malate (Map pp598–9), where most budget accommodation and dining options are located.

On the northern side of the Pasig (Map pp596–7) you'll find Binondo (Manila's old Chinatown), Quiapo and North Harbor, the departure point for many interisland ferries.

In recent years many of Manila's best restaurants and bars have moved uptown (east) to the relatively posh business district of Makati (Map pp596–7). While many tourists have followed, budget accommodation remains practically nonexistent in Makati.

North of Makati is the smaller business and shopping district of Ortigas, followed by Quezon City, site of the University of the Philippines' flagship Diliman campus.

Epifanio de los Santos Ave (EDSA; Map pp596–7) is the main artery linking downtown Manila with Makati, Ortigas and Quezon City. The MRT conveniently runs right along EDSA, linking with the LRT at Taft Ave.

The main downtown bus depots are along EDSA near the LRT–MRT interchange in Pasay City; the uptown bus hub is at the other end of EDSA in Cubao, a district of Quezon City.

The airport is about 6km south of Malate, in Parañaque (Map pp596–7).

INFORMATION

Bookshops

Most big malls have several good bookshops.

Powerbooks (Map pp598-9; ☎ 523 5167; Robinsons Place) In Ermita.

Solidaridad Book Shop (Map pp598-9; 531 Padre Faura St, Ermita; 9am-6pm) This famous leftie bookshop is particularly good for titles on local history and politics.

Tradewinds Books (Map p600; 3rd fl, Silahis Arts & Artifacts Centre, 744 General Luna St, Intramuros) Small bookstore with great collection of books on Filipino culture, arts, history and other subjects.

Emergency

Ambulance (☎ 117)

Fire brigade (☎ 160)

Police (☎ 166)

Tourist Security Division (Map pp598-9; ☎ 524 1728, 524 1660) Based at the Department of Tourism, this unit is available 24 hours and is more reliable than regular police.

Internet Access

There are internet cafés all over the place; malls such as Robinsons Place (Map pp598–9) often have several. Rates vary from P30 to P60 per hour.

Medical Services

Makati Medical Center (Map pp596-7; ☎ 815 9911; 2 Amorsolo St, Makati)

Manila Doctors Hospital (Map pp598-9; ☎ 524 3011; 677 United Nations Ave, Ermita)

Money

Malate, Ermita and Makati are littered with ATM machines. For cash transactions, there are numerous moneychangers along Mabini and Adriatico Sts but, as always, be careful when using these services. Cashing travellers

GETTING INTO TOWN

Domestic and international flights share the same runways, but use three separate terminals: Ninoy Aquino International Airport (NAIA); Centennial Terminal II (for all domestic and international PAL flights); and the domestic terminal (for all other domestic flights).

A line of booths around each departure hall sells taxi coupons; it costs P350 to get to Malate or Makati. At NAIA and Centennial Terminal II you'll save money by walking upstairs to arrivals and flagging down a metered taxi, which only costs about P120 to Malate or Makati. The domestic terminal has a designated queue for metered taxis.

Since there are no direct public transport routes to the tourist belt in Malate, you're better off biting the bullet and taking a taxi. If you arrive in Manila by boat, you're also better off catching a taxi into town, as the harbour is a pretty rough area and public transport routes are complicated.

With the number of different bus stations in Manila, if you arrive by bus you could end up pretty much anywhere. Luckily, most terminals are located on or near Manila's major artery, Epifanio de los Santos Ave (EDSA). To get to Malate, take a bus or the Metro Rail Transit (MRT) west along EDSA to Pasay City, and continue to Malate by Light Rail Transport (LRT; see p604 for tips on using Manila's metro).

If you're flying into Clark, see the bus information on p603.

cheques is difficult (see p645) and is best done through the office of the issuing company.

The following places are particularly useful for travellers:

Amex (Map pp598-9; ☎ 524 8681/2; 513 Remedios St, Malate; 8.30am-4pm Mon-Fri, 9am-noon Sat)

HSBC (Map pp598-9; 648 Remedios St, Malate) Its ATM agrees with most Western bank cards and allows withdrawals of more than P20,000.

Thomas Cook (Map pp596-7; ☎ 816 3701; cnr Sen Gil Puyat Ave & Tindabo St, Makati; 8.30am-5.30pm Mon-Fri, to 12.30pm Sat)

Post

Ermita Post Office (Map pp598-9; Pilar Hidalgo Lim St) Contrary to what the name implies, it's actually in Malate.

Manila Central Post Office (Map p600; ☎ 527 0085/79; 8am-noon & 1-5pm Mon-Fri, 8am-noon Sat) This imposing, neoclassical building north of Intramuros handles most postal transactions, including poste restante.

Telephone

Phone calls can be made from the numerous offices of PLDT, BayanTel, Smart Telecom and Globe Telecom (for rates see p646).

Tourist Information

Department of Tourism Information Centre (DOT; Map pp598-9; ☎ 524 2384; www.wowphilippines.ph; TM Kalaw St; 7am-6pm) This large, friendly office is in a beautiful pre-WWII building at the Taft Ave end of Rizal Park. There are also smaller DOT offices at Manila's Ninoy Aquino International Airport and the Centennial Terminal II.

Intramuros Visitors Center (Map p600; ☎ 527 2961; Santa Clara St; 8am-5pm Mon-Sat) Hands out simple maps and information.

Travel Agencies

Malate and Ermita are filled with travel agencies. Shop around for international air tickets, as prices vary. The following cater specifically to foreign tourists:

Filipino Travel Center (Map pp598-9; ☎ 528 4504, 528 4507; www.filipinotravel.com.ph; 1555 Adriatico St, Ermita) No commission on Seair and Asian Spirit flights. Books Autobus tickets to Banaue.

Swagman Travel (Map pp598-9; ☎ 523 8541; www.swaggy.com; 411 A Flores St, Ermita) Books Cebu Pacific and Asian Spirit flights commission free.

DANGERS & ANNOYANCES

Manila can be a pretty dodgy place, particularly after dark. The tourist areas of Ermita, Malate and Makati are considered some of the safer areas, but even here it pays to be careful after dark. See also the Scams boxed text on p642.

SIGHTS

Intramuros

A spacious borough of wide streets, leafy plazas and lovely colonial houses, the old walled city of Intramuros (Map p600) was the centrepiece of Spanish Manila. At least it was until WWII, when the Americans and Japanese levelled the whole lot. Only a handful of buildings survived the firestorm; over 100,000 Filipino civilians were not so lucky.

The Spanish replaced the original wooden fort with stone in 1590, and these walls stand much as they were 400 years ago. They're still studded with bastions and pierced with gates *(puertas)*. At the mouth of the Pasig River you'll find Manila's premier tourist attraction, **Fort Santiago** (Map p600; admission P40; 8am-6pm), fronted by a pretty lily pond and the Intramuros Visitors Center. During WWII the fort was used as a prisoner-of-war camp by the Japanese. Within the fort grounds you'll find the **Rizal Shrine** in the building where national hero José Rizal was incarcerated as he awaited execution. It contains Rizal's personal effects and an original copy of his last poem, 'Mi Ultimo Adios' (My Last Farewell).

The most interesting building to survive the Battle of Manila is the church and monastery of **San Agustin** (Map p600; General Luna St). The interior is truly opulent and the ceiling, painted in three-dimensional relief, will make you question your vision. The former Augustinian monastery next door is now an excellent **religious museum** (Map p600; General Luna St; admission P75; 9am-noon & 1-6pm). **Casa Manila** (Map p600; 527 4088; cnr Real & General Luna Sts; admission P40; 9am-6pm Tue-Sun) is a beautifully restored, three-storey Spanish colonial mansion filled with priceless antiques. Nearby, the flashy **Bahay Tsinoy Museum** (Map p600; cnr Anda & Cabildo Sts; admission P100; 1-5pm Tue-Sun) uses vivid dioramas and photographs to tell the story of the Chinese in Manila.

Also of interest is the grand Romanesque **Manila Cathedral** (Map p600; cnr Postigo & General Luna Sts; 6.30am-5.30pm), which is a Vatican-funded reconstruction of the cathedral destroyed in WWII, and the sixth church on this site. The gilded altar and stained-glass windows are spectacular, and there's an enormous organ.

Rizal Park

One of the precious few bits of green in Manila, the 60-hectare Rizal Park (also known as Luneta; Map pp598–9) offers urbanites a place to decelerate among ornamental gardens and a whole pantheon of Filipino heroes. On Sunday afternoon you can watch martial arts displays here, including the Filipino school of *arnis*, a style of stick-fighting.

Located at the bay end of the park are the **Rizal Memorial** (Map pp598–9) and the moving **site of Rizal's execution** (Map pp598-9; admission P10; 7am-8.30pm Wed-Sun). The planetarium is flanked by a **Japanese garden** (Map pp598-9; admission P10) and a **Chinese garden** (Map pp598-9; admission P10), which are favourite meeting spots for young couples. At the Taft Ave end of the park the gigantic three-dimensional **relief map** (Map pp598–9) of the Philippines is worth a look – see if you can spot 'perfect' Mt Mayon.

The splendid **National Museum of the Filipino People** (Map pp598-9; T Valencia Circle, Rizal Park; admission P100, free Sun; 10am-4.30pm Wed-Sun) has interesting displays on the wreck of the *San Diego*, a Spanish galleon from 1600, plus plenty of artefacts and comprehensive exhibits on the various Filipino ethnic groups.

Museums

As well as the offerings in Intramuros and Rizal Park, Manila has plenty of other interesting museums. The best is probably the **Ayala Museum** (Map pp596-7; Makati Ave, Makati; admission P350; 9am-6pm Tue-Fri, 10am-7pm Sat & Sun), where dioramas tell the story of the Filipino quest for independence. It also houses the Philippines' best contemporary art collection. The **Metropolitan Museum of Manila** (Map pp596-7; 521 1517; BSP Complex, Roxas Blvd; admission P80; 10am-6pm Mon-Sat) is in the Central Bank Complex and features an avarice-inducing collection of pre-Hispanic gold.

Chinese Cemetery

Boldly challenging the idea that you can't take it with you, the mausoleums of wealthy Chinese in the **Chinese Cemetery** (Map pp596-7; Rizal Ave Extension or Aurora Blvd; admission free; 7.30am-7pm), north of Santa Cruz, are fitted with flushing toilets and crystal chandeliers. Hire a guide (P300 to P400) for access to the best tombs. To get here take a 'Monumento' jeepney to Aurora Blvd (where Rizal Ave becomes Rizal Ave Extension) and walk east to F Heurtes St, which leads to the south gate. Abad Santos is the closest LRT station.

TOURS

If you're in Manila over a weekend don't miss out on the flamboyant tours of Chinatown, Intramuros and other destinations hosted by **Carlos Celdran** (0906 304 9598; www.celdrantours.blogspot.com; tours per person P500). Carlos' 'Living La Vida Imelda!' tour is fast attaining legend status.

SLEEPING

Manila's budget accommodation centres around Ermita and Malate, with a couple of good deals near the airport as well.

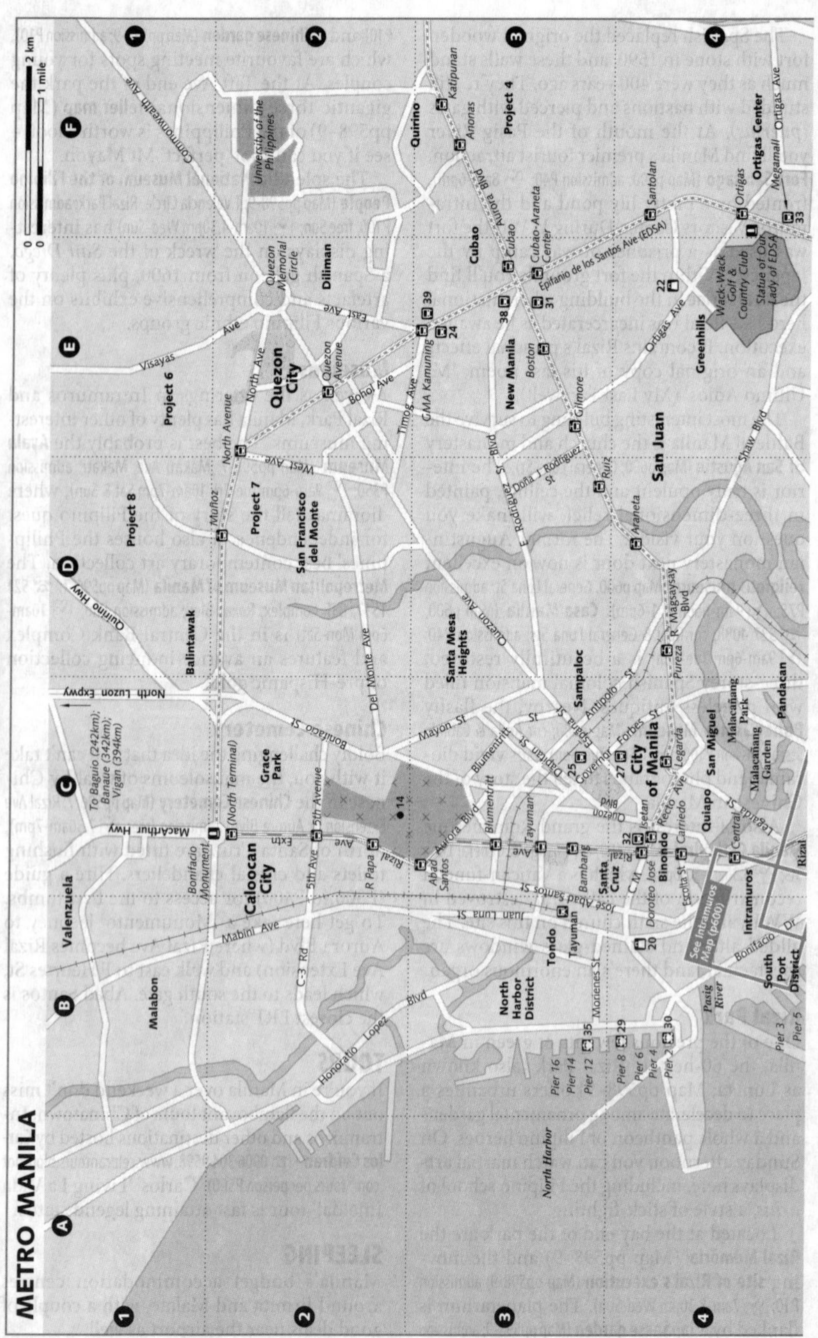
METRO MANILA
0 2 km
0 1 mile
To Baguio (242km); Banaue (342km); Vigan (394km)
North Luzon Expwy
Valenzuela
Malabon
Caloocan City
Bonifacio Monument
(North Terminal)
Grace Park
Balintawak
Project 8
Project 7
Project 6
San Francisco del Monte
Quezon City
Quezon Memorial Circle
Diliman
University of the Philippines
Commonwealth Ave
Visayas Ave
Quirino Hwy
Quirino
Project 4
Katipunan
Anonas
Cubao
Aurora Blvd
Cubao-Araneta Center
Santolan
Epifanio de los Santos Ave (EDSA)
Ortigas Center
Ortigas
Megamall
Ortigas Ave
Wack-Wack Golf & Country Club
Statue of Our Lady of EDSA
Greenhills
New Manila
Boston
Gilmore
San Juan
Shaw Blvd
Santa Mesa Heights
Quezon Ave
Sampaloc
City of Manila
Malacañang Park
Malacañang Garden
Pandacan
San Miguel
Quiapo
Binondo
Santa Cruz
Tondo
North Harbor District
North Harbor
Intramuros
See Intramuros Map (p600)
South Port District
Pasig River
Bonifacio Dr
Rizal
Honoratio Lopez Blvd
Mabini Ave
C-3 Rd
5th Ave
5th Avenue
R Papa
Abad Santos
Blumentritt
Tayuman
Bambang
Doroteo José
Carriedo
Central
Legarda
Pureza
R Magsaysay Blvd
Araneta
Ruiz
E Rodriguez Sr Blvd
Doña J Rodriguez St
Muñoz
North Avenue
North Ave
West Ave
East Ave
Quezon Avenue
Bohol Ave
Timog Ave
GMA Kamuning
Del Monte Ave
Bonifacio St
Mayon St
Juan Luna St
José Abad Santos St
Moriones St
Pier 16
Pier 14
Pier 12
Pier 8
Pier 6
Pier 4
Pier 2
Pier 3
Pier 5
Macarthur Hwy
Espana St
Antipolo St
Dapitan St
Governor Forbes St
Recto Ave
Quezon Blvd
Escolta St
Isetan

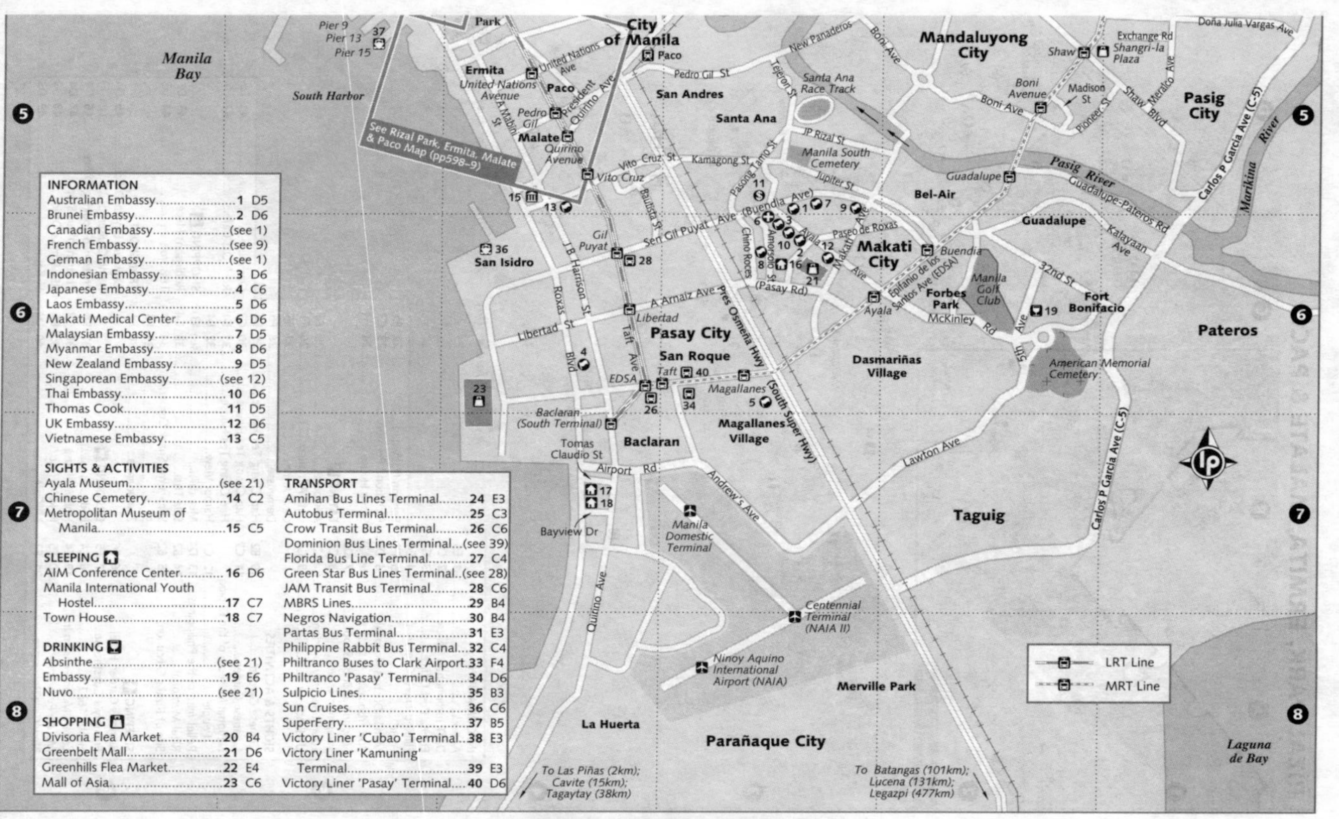
INFORMATION
Australian Embassy 1 D5
Brunei Embassy 2 D6
Canadian Embassy (see 1)
French Embassy (see 9)
German Embassy (see 1)
Indonesian Embassy 3 D6
Japanese Embassy 4 C6
Laos Embassy 5 D6
Makati Medical Center 6 D6
Malaysian Embassy 7 D5
Myanmar Embassy 8 D6
New Zealand Embassy 9 D5
Singaporean Embassy (see 12)
Thai Embassy 10 D6
Thomas Cook 11 D5
UK Embassy 12 D6
Vietnamese Embassy 13 C5
SIGHTS & ACTIVITIES
Ayala Museum (see 21)
Chinese Cemetery 14 C2
Metropolitan Museum of Manila 15 C5
SLEEPING
AIM Conference Center 16 D6
Manila International Youth Hostel 17 C7
Town House 18 C7
DRINKING
Absinthe (see 21)
Embassy 19 E6
Nuvo (see 21)
SHOPPING
Divisoria Flea Market 20 B4
Greenbelt Mall 21 D6
Greenhills Flea Market 22 E4
Mall of Asia 23 C6
TRANSPORT
Amihan Bus Lines Terminal 24 E3
Autobus Terminal 25 C3
Crow Transit Bus Terminal 26 C6
Dominion Bus Lines Terminal (see 39)
Florida Bus Line Terminal 27 C4
Green Star Bus Lines Terminal (see 28)
JAM Transit Bus Terminal 28 C6
MBRS Lines 29 B4
Negros Navigation 30 B4
Partas Bus Terminal 31 E3
Philippine Rabbit Bus Terminal 32 C4
Philtranco Buses to Clark Airport 33 F4
Philtranco 'Pasay' Terminal 34 D6
Sulpicio Lines 35 B3
Sun Cruises 36 C6
SuperFerry 37 B5
Victory Liner 'Cubao' Terminal 38 E3
Victory Liner 'Kamuning' Terminal 39 E3
Victory Liner 'Pasay' Terminal 40 D6
LRT Line
MRT Line
See Rizal Park, Ermita, Malate & Paco Map (pp598-9)
Manila Bay
South Harbor
Pier 9
Pier 13
Pier 15
City of Manila
Ermita
Paco
Malate
Mandaluyong City
Pasig City
San Andres
Santa Ana
Santa Ana Race Track
Manila South Cemetery
Bel-Air
Guadalupe
Makati City
Forbes Park
Manila Golf Club
Fort Bonifacio
Pateros
American Memorial Cemetery
Dasmariñas Village
San Isidro
Pasay City
San Roque
Magallanes Village
Baclaran
Taguig
Manila Domestic Terminal
Centennial Terminal (NAIA II)
Ninoy Aquino International Airport (NAIA)
Merville Park
La Huerta
Parañaque City
Laguna de Bay
Pasig River
Marikina River
To Las Piñas (2km); Cavite (15km); Tagaytay (38km)
To Batangas (101km); Lucena (131km); Legazpi (477km)
PHILIPPINES

RIZAL PARK, ERMITA, MALATE & PACO

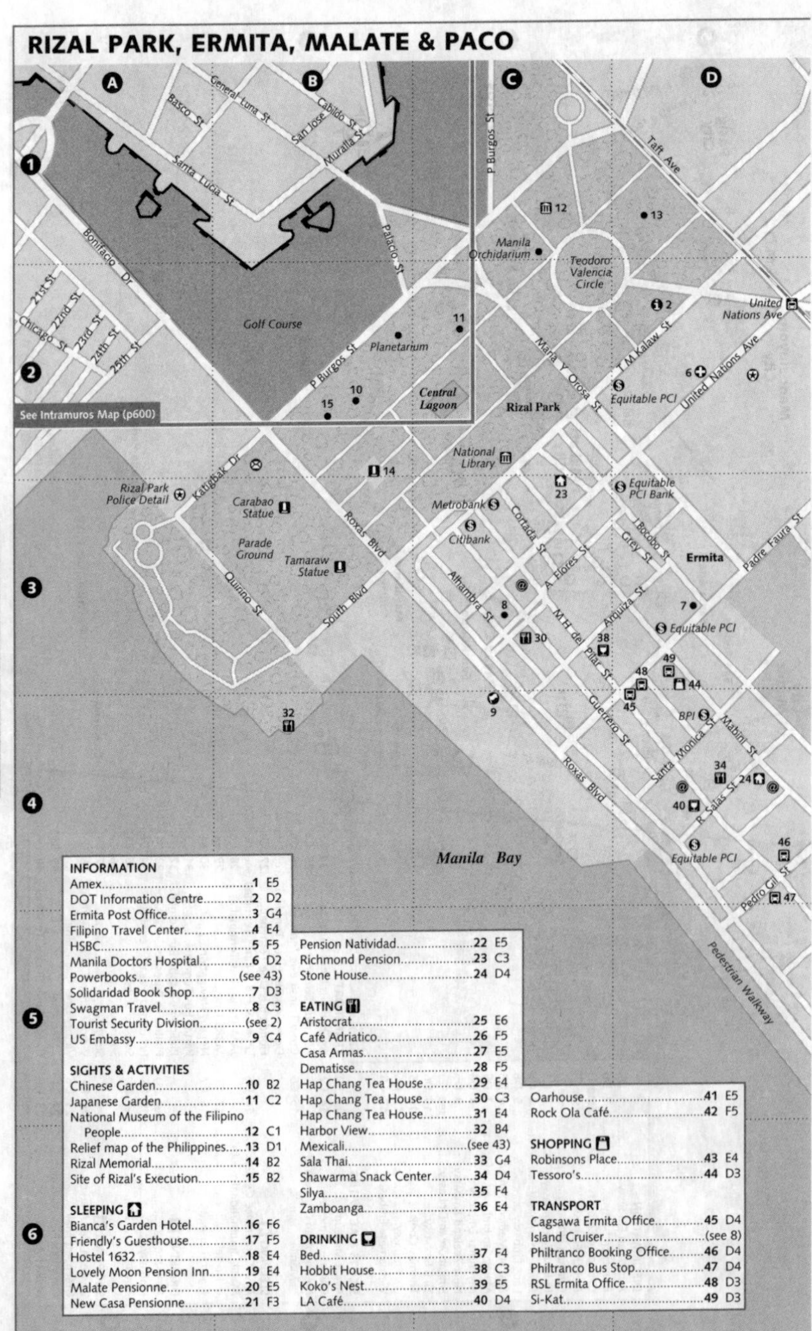

INFORMATION
Amex..........1 E5
DOT Information Centre..........2 D2
Ermita Post Office..........3 G4
Filipino Travel Center..........4 E4
HSBC..........5 F5
Manila Doctors Hospital..........6 D2
Powerbooks..........(see 43)
Solidaridad Book Shop..........7 D3
Swagman Travel..........8 C3
Tourist Security Division..........(see 2)
US Embassy..........9 C4

SIGHTS & ACTIVITIES
Chinese Garden..........10 B2
Japanese Garden..........11 C2
National Museum of the Filipino People..........12 C1
Relief map of the Philippines..........13 D1
Rizal Memorial..........14 B2
Site of Rizal's Execution..........15 B2

SLEEPING
Bianca's Garden Hotel..........16 F6
Friendly's Guesthouse..........17 F5
Hostel 1632..........18 E4
Lovely Moon Pension Inn..........19 E4
Malate Pensionne..........20 E5
New Casa Pensionne..........21 F3
Pension Natividad..........22 E5
Richmond Pension..........23 C3
Stone House..........24 D4

EATING
Aristocrat..........25 E6
Café Adriatico..........26 F5
Casa Armas..........27 E5
Dematisse..........28 F5
Hap Chang Tea House..........29 E4
Hap Chang Tea House..........30 C3
Hap Chang Tea House..........31 E4
Harbor View..........32 B4
Mexicali..........(see 43)
Sala Thai..........33 G4
Shawarma Snack Center..........34 D4
Silya..........35 F4
Zamboanga..........36 E4

DRINKING
Bed..........37 F4
Hobbit House..........38 C3
Koko's Nest..........39 E5
LA Café..........40 D4
Oarhouse..........41 E5
Rock Ola Café..........42 F5

SHOPPING
Robinsons Place..........43 E4
Tessoro's..........44 D3

TRANSPORT
Cagsawa Ermita Office..........45 D4
Island Cruiser..........(see 8)
Philtranco Booking Office..........46 D4
Philtranco Bus Stop..........47 D4
RSL Ermita Office..........48 D3
Si-Kat..........49 D3

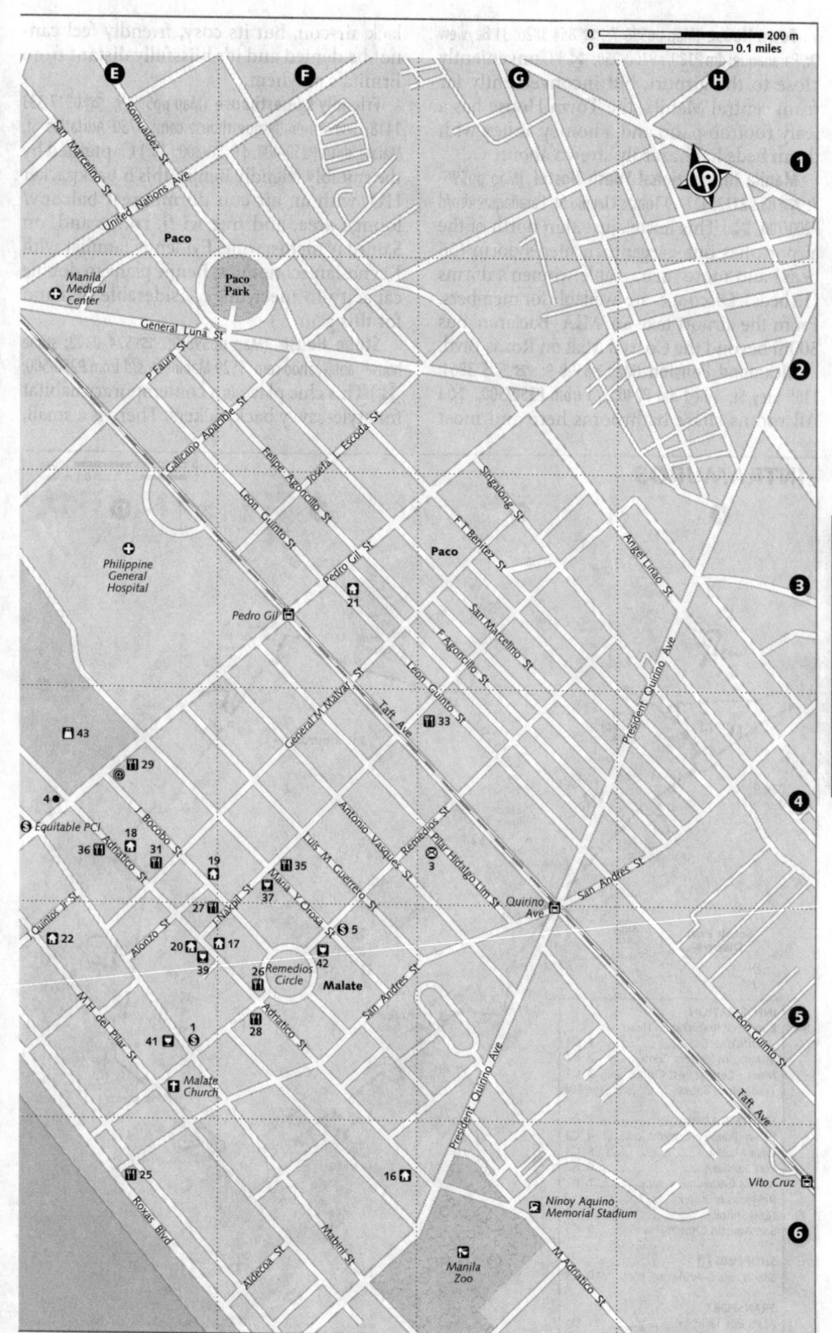

PHILIPPINES

Town House (Map pp596-7; 854 3826; 31 Bayview Dr, Parañaque; dm P180, r P300-950;) Conveniently close to the airport, but inconveniently far from central Manila, the Town House has a leafy rooftop patio and a homey annex with dorm beds haphazardly strewn about.

Manila International Youth Hostel (Map pp596-7; 832 2112; 4227-9 Tomas Claudio St, Parañaque; dm/d P200/700;) This hostel, just 3km north of the airport, has one gargantuan men's dorm (36 beds) and more manageable women's dorms (12 beds). Discounts are available for members. From the airport take an 'MIA–Baclaran' bus 500m beyond the Coastal Mall on Roxas Blvd.

Richmond Pension (Map pp598-9; 525 3864; 1165 Grey St; 3-bed dm P240, s/d from P350/500;) All rooms share bathrooms here and most lack air-con, but its cosy, friendly feel cannot be denied and it's blissfully distant from Ermita's mayhem.

Friendly's Guesthouse (Map pp598-9; 0917 333 1418; www.friendlysguesthouse.com; 1750 Adriatico St, Malate; dm/s P250/400, d P450-800;) Captained by the suitably friendly Benjie, this is backpacker HQ, with an air-con dorm, great balcony/lounge area, and free wi-fi, coffee and, on Saturday nights, wine. Evidently familiar with Keynesian economics, Benjie plans to double capacity to meet the considerable demand for this gem.

Stone House (Map pp598-9; 524 0302; stonehouse_apt@yahoo.com; 1529 Mabini St; s/d from P250/500;) This chic place is a contemporary habitat for style-savvy backpackers. There is a small,

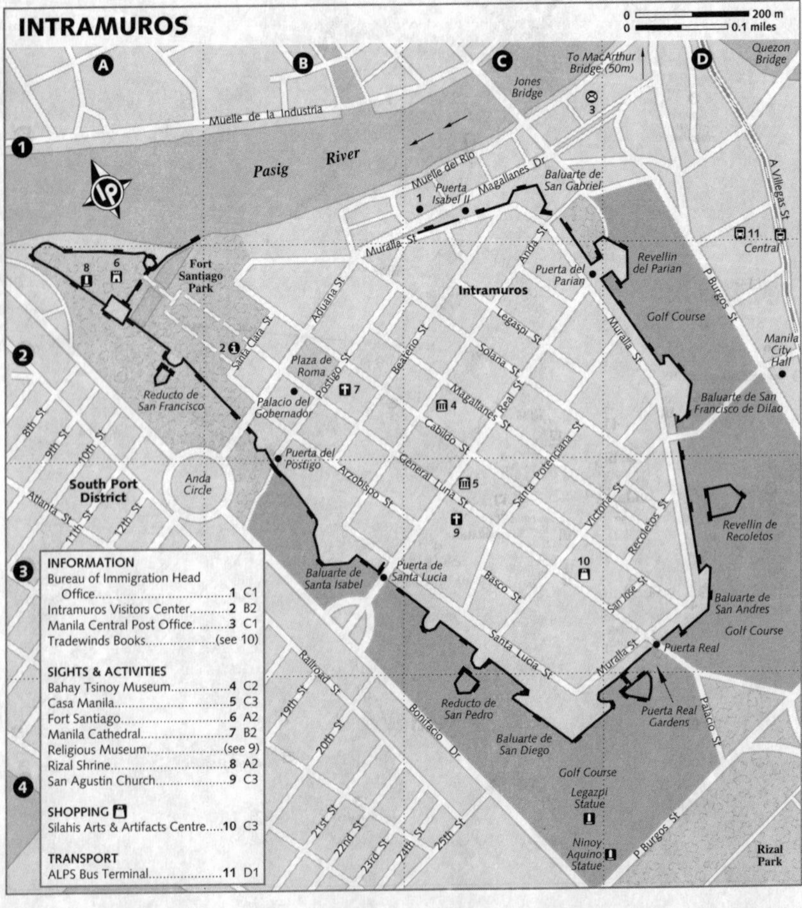

elegant bar downstairs and, while the budget singles are shoeboxes, the better doubles are great value.

our pick **Malate Pensionne** (Map pp598-9; ☎ 523 8304; 1771 Adriatico St, Malate; dm P300, d P600-1300; ❄) This homey, woodsy old mansion shares a quiet courtyard with Starbucks and has a useful traveller message board. The rooms, while small, are much better appointed than anything else in this price range, with rustic wooden furniture, large wardrobes and above-average bathrooms. The dorms are simple three-bed affairs so you won't have to arm wrestle 10 neighbours for fan rights.

Pension Natividad (Map pp598-9; ☎ 521 0524; 1690 MH del Pilar St, Malate; dm with fan P350, d P800-1200; ❄) Set around a private courtyard, this popular Peace Corps volunteer roost features low-priced munchies and large single-sex dorms. However, the P800 fan rooms aren't great value.

Bianca's Garden Hotel (Map pp598-9; ☎ 526 0351; 2139 Adriatico St, Malate; r P1000-1800; ❄ 🏊) Set back from the street in a quieter part of Malate, this Spanish-style boutique is a real charmer. The 11 rooms feature traditional Filipino furniture, art and numerous antiques.

AIM Conference Center (Map pp596-7; ☎ 867 4033; www.accm.aim.edu.ph; Benavidez St; r from P1800; ❄ 💻 🏊) There are no true budget places in central Makati but this is stupendous value. Free broadband internet, squeaky clean bathrooms and a prime location opposite Greenbelt are all part of the equation.

Also recommended:

New Casa Pensionne (Map pp598-9; ☎ 522 1375; cove@skyinet.net; Leon Guinto St, Paco; s/d from P380/490; ❄) Tidy rooms in mercifully quiet neighbourhood north of Taft Ave.

Lovely Moon Pension Inn (Map pp598-9; ☎ 536 2627; 1718 Bocobo St, Malate; d P400-850; ❄) Quirkiness begins and ends with the psychedelic mural in the lobby, but still serviceable.

Hostel 1632 (Map pp598-9; ☎ 526 1000; www.hostel1632.com; 1632 Adriatico St, Malate; s/d P1600/1800; ❄ 💻) New midrange offering has curiously designed rooms and free breakfast.

EATING

Manila should get more kudos as a dining city – every style of Asian food is well represented and there are some solid French, German and Middle Eastern restaurants as well. The city's upscale restaurants have mostly moved uptown to Makati's Greenbelt area and Fort Bonifacio (Map pp596–7), where a large chunk of Manila's expat community lives. These recommendations cover only the main backpacker haunts of Ermita and Malate.

For vegetarian food try the dozens of Korean and Chinese restaurants in Malate. If you care for street fare, try the boardwalk along Roxas Blvd or Santa Monica St in Ermita (Map pp598–9). Mall food courts are always a good bet for affordable sustenance. **Robinsons Place** (Map pp598-9; Pedro Gil St, Ermita) has dozens of options, including the always reliable **Mexicali** (burritos P125) on the 1st floor near the Padre Faura entrance.

Filipino

Silya (Map pp598-9; 642 J Nakpil St, Malate; breakfast P75, mains P110-160) Besides serving affordable Filipino classics such as *adobo* (chicken, pork or fish in a dark tangy sauce), Silya is also a great place to warm up your karaoke skills before hitting the provinces.

Aristocrat (Map pp598-9; ☎ 524 7671; cnr Roxas Blvd & San Andres St; mains P150-250; 🕑 24hr) This multi-chambered Malate institution has been serving up Filipino classics such as grilled *bangus* (milkfish) and pork knuckles for over 60 years.

Harbor View (Map pp598-9; ☎ 524 1532; South Blvd, Rizal Park; mains P170-300) This is the best of a clutch of fresh seafood *inahaw* (grill) restaurants jutting into Manila Bay (hope for an offshore breeze). The fish is best enjoyed with the golden sunset and some amber refreshments.

Zamboanga (Map pp598-9; ☎ 521 7345; 1619 Adriatico St; mains P265-500) The prices here aren't bad considering the nightly entertainment consists of a one-hour Filipino cultural program, complete with colourful costumes and indigenous dances such as *tinikling* (see Dance, p589). The food is best described as gourmet Filipino.

Asian

our pick **Shawarma Snack Center** (Map pp598-9; ☎ 525 4541; 485 R Salas St; pita sandwiches P45-65, mains P150-250; 🕑 24hr) With freshly grilled kebabs and delectable appetizers such as falafel, *muttabal* (purée of aubergine mixed with tahini, yogurt and olive oil) and hummus, this streetside Middle Eastern eatery is a gastronomic delight. Hookah pipes round out the effect. We'd gladly eat here every day.

Hap Chang Tea House (Map pp598-9; cnr General Malvar & Adriatico Sts; mains P120-250; 🕑 24hr) Delicious, steaming platters of Hong Kong specialities are the name of the game here. It's popular for a reason. Additional branches on Pedro Gil and A Flores Sts.

Sala Thai (Map pp598-9; ☎ 522 4694; 866 J Nakpil St, Paco; mains P120-250; lunch & dinner Mon-Sat) The granddaddy of Manila's Thai restaurants, the dishes here are authentically prepared by a Thai chef, the prices are sensible and the ambience is pure Old Manila.

Western

Dematisse (Map pp598-9; 548 Remedios St, Malate; pasta dishes P120-160; 5pm-7am) While their pasta's pretty good, the icing on the cake is the P25 San Miguel.

Café Adriatico (Map pp598-9; 1790 Adriatico St, Malate; appetizers P140-200, mains P200-400) Long-time Malate residents call this their 'Cheers'. The menu is Spanish with English, American and Italian effects, but you come here for the people-watching as much as the food.

Casa Armas (Map pp598-9; ☎ 523 0189; 573 J Nakpil St, Malate; mains P250-500; lunch & dinner) You'll usually encounter several groups of Manila expats pounding sangria and throwing back tapas here. One of Manila's best restaurants.

DRINKING

Whether you're into Whitney Houston, Pearl Jam or gay bars, there's a good chance you'll find it in Malate. The area also draws its share of party-going university students, driven here by the low beer prices. You'll find many of them chugging cheap suds curbside just west of Remedios Circle on Remedios St – dubbed the 'Monoblock Republic' because of the preponderance of brittle plastic furniture. Male travellers in this area – especially on Mabini St – will get insistent offers to various types of nightclubs to meet girls euphemistically called GROs – 'guest relations officers'.

Oarhouse (Map pp598-9; 1803 Mabini St; beer P30) This snug little haunt, a favourite among Peace Corps volunteers, is one oar house you won't mind getting caught in late at night.

our pick **Rock Ola Café** (Map pp598-9; ☎ 0920 853 2128; 604 Remedios St; 6pm-2am Tue-Sat) On Wednesday and Saturday this tiny bar-cum-gallery (formerly Penguin Café) squeezes in some of the finest musical talent in town, including, on occasion, Pinikpikan (see p589). Bonus points if you can count the geckos on the wall.

KARAOKE & COVERS

You haven't *really* travelled in the Philippines until you've spent an inebriated evening around a karaoke machine paying homage to Celine Dion and Chicago. Filipinos pursue karaoke without a hint of irony, so whatever you do don't insult the guy who sounds like a chicken getting strangled. Live music is also popular; most towns have live-music bars with local talent belting out flawless cover versions of classic rock and recent hits. Adriatico St in Malate has several such venues.

Koko's Nest (Map pp598-9; Adriatico St) Cheap snacks and P23(!!) San Miguel in a small streetside nook sheltered by a bamboo awning. Need we say more?

Bed (Map pp598-9; cnr J Nakpil & Maria Y Orosa Sts) This place is known for its wild gay and straight crowds, who will dance with abandon till dawn.

LA Café (Map pp598-9; 1429 MH del Pilar St; 24hr) A notorious dive, this place features live music, billiards, fairly priced food and drinks, a rowdy expat crowd and round-the-clock GROs. If you want to get a glimpse of the raunchy side of Manila, look no further.

Hobbit House (Map pp598-9; ☎ 521 7604; 1212 MH del Pilar St; admission P100-200; to 3am) Often forgotten amid the vertically challenged waiters is that Hobbit House consistently draws Manila's best live blues acts. It recently moved after 34 years on Mabini St.

For some uberhip bar and club action, take the MRT or grab a cab (P120) uptown to Makati, where you'll find the likes of **Absinthe** (Map pp596-7; Greenbelt 3; admission Fri & Sat P100-200; 8pm-late Mon-Sat), **Nuvo** (Map pp596-7; Greenbelt 2; 11am-3am) and **Embassy** (Map pp596-7; The Fort Entertainment Centre, Fort Bonifacio; admission P100-200; 10pm-6am Wed-Sat).

ENTERTAINMENT

Check fliers around Malate and weekend entertainment supplements in the newspapers for big club events and concerts. Manila sadly lacks a *Time Out*–style weekly entertainment guide, but the website www.clickthecity.com fills the gap, with entertainment as well as extensive shopping and eating listings. Also try www.myph.com.ph and, for big club events, www.superfly.com.ph.

For free entertainment, don't miss the boardwalk along Roxas Blvd (Map pp598–9) as it turns into a veritable 'battle of the bands' after sunset. There's an abundance of street-side restaurants, hip live bands and throngs of ambling Filipinos in their element.

Manila's 200 movie screens are dominated by imported blockbusters. All the shopping centres have multiscreen, air-con cinemas – there are seven screens in Robinsons Place Ermita. Check www.clickthecity.com for listings. Admission is P75 to P150.

SHOPPING

With a hulking shopping centre seemingly around every corner, Manila is a mall rat's fantasy. The closest to the tourist belt is Robinsons Place (Map pp598–9), which is currently being expanded to include an outdoor shopping and eating courtyard, à la **Greenbelt Mall** (Map pp596-7; Makati Ave) in Makati. The city's best mall is the newish **Mall of Asia** (Map pp596-7; Pasay City), with an Olympic-sized ice rink and an Imax theatre.

If you're after DVDs and brand-name clothing of questionable legitimacy, the flea market Greenhills (Map pp596–7) in Ortigas and Divisoria Flea Market (Map pp596–7) in Binondo are your best bets.

Popular souvenir items include wood-carved Ifugao *bulol* (rice guards) and textiles from North Luzon and Mindanao. Try the following:

Silahis Arts & Artifacts Centre (Map p600; 744 General Luna St, Intramuros; 🕐 10am-7pm) Has a textile museum on the top floor.

Tessoro's (Map pp598-9; 1325 Mabini St, Ermita; 🕐 9am-7.30pm) Likewise houses a small textile and crafts museum.

GETTING THERE & AWAY

Air

Most international airlines have offices at the NAIA terminal, as well as satellite offices in Makati. PAL is based at Centennial Terminal II. Domestic airlines have offices at the domestic terminal and booking agents dotted around town. See p590 for details on airlines and domestic flights.

Boat

Manila's port is divided into two sections: South Harbor and North Harbor. Two of the three main shipping lines serving Manila use the hardscrabble, hard-to-reach North Harbor. It's best to take a taxi to North Harbor (about P75 from Malate), as the area is no place to be wandering around.

The following are the main lines operating long-haul ferries out of Manila to most major cities in the Visayas, Mindanao and Palawan. Full schedules are on their websites.

Negros Navigation (Map pp596-7; ☎ 245 5588; www.negrosnavigation.ph; Pier 2, North Harbor)

Sulpicio Lines (Map pp596-7; ☎ 245 0616; www.sulpiciolines.com; Pier 12, North Harbor)

SuperFerry (Map pp596-7; ☎ 528 7000; www.superferry.com.ph; Pier 15, South Harbor) Also has a ticket office on the 3rd floor of Robinsons Place in Ermita.

Bus

Confusingly there's no single long-distance bus station in Manila. The terminals are mainly strung along EDSA, with a cluster near the intersection of Taft Ave in Pasay City to the south, and in Cubao (part of Quezon City) to the north. Another cluster is north of Quiapo in Sampaloc. If you're confused just tell a taxi driver which station you want in which city (eg 'the Victory Liner terminal in Cubao'), and they should know where it is. Heading into Manila, most buses will just have 'Cubao', 'Pasay' or 'Sampaloc' on the signboard.

Philtranco runs a convenient shuttle service to Clark Airport, with three trips daily from its Pasay station (P350, 1¾ hours) and four trips daily from Megamall in Ortigas (Map pp596–7; P300, 1½ hours). Philtranco also makes a masochists-only haul to Davao in southern Mindanao (P2200, two days) via Samar, Leyte and Cagayan de Oro.

RSL, Philtranco and Cagsawa have overnight buses straight from Ermita to Naga and Legazpi.

Several bus lines run 27-seat 'deluxe' overnight express buses to Legazpi via Naga in Southeast Luzon, and to Vigan in North Luzon. It's essential to book these several days ahead. Advance reservations are also highly recommended for the few direct buses to Banaue.

The following is a list of useful bus companies:

Northbound

Autobus (Map pp596-7; ☎ 735 8098; cnr Tolentino St & España St, Sampaloc) Buses to Banaue (P450 to P650, eight hours) and Vigan (P480, nine hours).

Dominion Bus Lines (Map pp596-7; ☎ 741 4146; cnr EDSA & East Ave, Kamuning) Buses to Vigan (P450, nine hours).

PHILIPPINES

Florida Bus Line (Map pp596-7; ☎ 731 5358; cnr Extremadura & Earnshaw Sts, Sampaloc) Buses to Banaue (P450, eight hours).
Partas (Map pp596-7; ☎ 725 1740; Aurora Blvd, Cubao) Partas has buses to Vigan (air-con/deluxe P585/705, nine hours) and Baguio (P365, six hours).
Philippine Rabbit (Map pp596-7; ☎ 734 9836; 819 Orokueta St, Santa Cruz) Buses to Baguio (P340, six hours).
Victory Liner (Map pp596-7); Cubao (☎ 727 4688; cnr EDSA & New York Ave); Kamuning (☎ 921 3296; cnr EDSA & East Ave); Pasay (☎ 833 4019; cnr EDSA & Taft Ave) Buses to Baguio (P380, six hours) leave from the Cubao and Pasay terminals; Banaue buses (P400 to P650, eight hours) leave from Kamuning.

Southbound

ALPS Transit (Map p600; A Villegas St, Intramuros) ALPS has buses to Batangas (P150, three hours).
Amihan Bus Lines (Map pp596-7; ☎ 925 1758; JAM main terminal, cnr EDSA & Timog Ave, Quezon City) Buses to Naga (P575, nine hours) and Legazpi (P700, 11 hours).
Cagsawa (Map pp598-9; ☎ 524 8704; Padre Faura Centre, Ermita) Buses to Naga (air-con/deluxe P600/750, nine hours) and Legazpi (air-con/deluxe P700/900, 11 hours).
Crow Transit (Map pp596-7; cnr EDSA & Taft Ave, Pasay City) Crow has buses to Tagaytay (P80, two hours).
JAM Transit (Map pp596-7; ☎ 831 0465; 'Buendia' LRT stop, Taft Ave) Buses to Batangas (P147, three hours).
Philtranco Ermita booking office (Map pp598-9; Food Haus, cnr Pedro Gil & MH del Pilar Sts); Pasay Terminal (Map pp596-7; ☎ 851 5420; cnr EDSA & Apelo Cruz St) Buses to Naga (P650, nine hours) and Legazpi (P800, 11 hours). Buses from Ermita leave from in front of DHL office on Pedro Gil St (Map pp598–9).
RSL (Map pp598-9; ☎ 525 7077; Padre Faura St) RSL has buses to Naga (air-con/deluxe P560/760, nine hours) and Legazpi (air-con/deluxe P760/900, 11 hours).

For Puerto Galera on Mindoro, several companies run combination bus/boat services, leaving around 8am from Ermita. These take about 4½ hours and cost roughly P250 more than fending for yourself. Companies include the following:
Island Cruiser (Map pp598-9; Swagman Travel, 411A Flores St, Ermita) Tickets P600.
Si-Kat (Map pp598-9; ☎ 521 3344; Citystate Tower Hotel, 1315 Mabini St, Ermita) Tickets P600.

GETTING AROUND

Bus

The most useful routes for travellers are the buses that run along EDSA. These pass through Makati and Cubao, where you'll find many of the major shopping centres and bus terminals. There are also buses to Makati from Malate via Gil Puyat Ave (Buendia). Destinations are displayed in the bus window. Fares are from P10 on regular buses, and P12 on air-con services.

Jeepney

Heading south from Ermita/Malate along M H del Pilar St, 'Baclaran' jeepneys end up on EDSA just west of the Pasay bus terminals and just east of the Mall of Asia. Going north from Ermita/Malate along Mabini St, jeepneys go to Rizal Park before heading off in various directions: 'Divisoria' jeepneys skirt the east edge of Intramuros before taking the Jones Bridge to Divisoria Market; 'Santa Cruz' and 'Monumento' jeepneys take the MacArthur Bridge, passing the main post office; and 'Cubao' jeepneys go to the Cubao bus terminals via Quezon Bridge and Quiapo church.

FX vans follow similar routes to jeepneys, with fares around P12 for a few blocks to P20 for longer hauls.

Taxi

Metered taxis, a few of which even have working air conditioners, are the easiest way to get anywhere and are dirt cheap by world standards. Short trips cost only about P50, and even the longest hauls rarely cost more than P200.

Train

There are three elevated railway lines in Manila. The most useful if you're staying in the Malate/Ermita tourist belt is the LRT-1, which runs south along Taft Ave to the MRT interchange at EDSA near the Pasay bus terminals. From the EDSA interchange, the MRT runs north to Makati and Cubao. The Metro Manila map on pp596–7 shows all metro routes. During rush hour these trains can get mosh-pit crowded and pickpockets can be a problem, but for the rest of the day they are a great way to avoid traffic. Rides start at P11. Multiple-trip tickets do exist but they are hard to find. Trains run from 5.30am to 10.30pm.

AROUND MANILA

There are several worthy excursions that offer opportunities to escape the oppressive heat and traffic of Manila. Taal volcano is the country's terrestrial femme fatale, as dangerous as it is beautiful, while the spirits of fallen WWII soldiers supposedly haunt

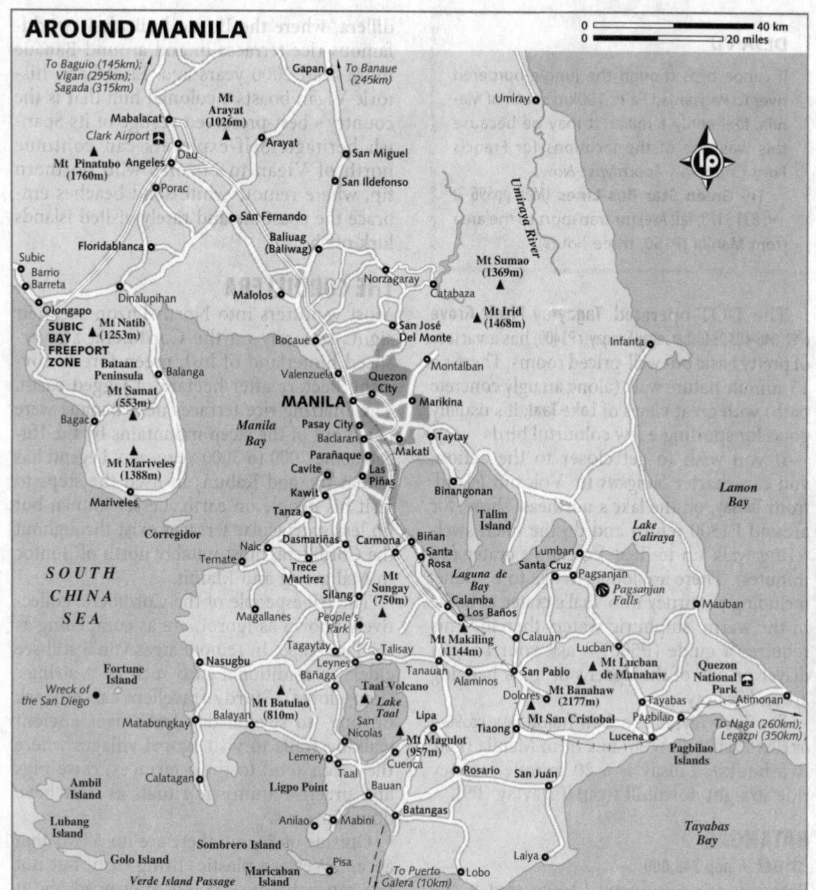

historic Corregidor island. Weekenders from the capital can overwhelm Manila's nearby destinations – especially Tagaytay – so it's best to visit during the week.

CORREGIDOR

Jealously guarding the mouth of Manila Bay, this tiny island is where General MacArthur is said to have uttered 'I shall return' as he fled the invading Japanese. He was eventually true to his word, and day-tripping Filipinos have also been heeding his call: Corregidor's rusty WWII relics are now a big tourist draw. The **Malinta tunnels**, which once housed an arsenal and a hospital, penetrate the island's rocky heart and there's a small museum displaying leftover uniforms and weapons.

Sun Cruises (Map pp596-7; ☎ 02-831 8140; www.corregidorphilippines.com; excursions P1300) has the market for trips to Corregidor pretty much cornered. It loads up 100 to 200 passengers every morning at 8am; you'll return to Manila by 2.30pm. The price includes two meals and a comprehensive tour of the island.

TAAL VOLCANO & TAGAYTAY

Don't be fooled by the small size of this bubbling volcano-within-a-lake. Taal's sudden and violent eruptions have claimed more than its fair share of lives. Meandering along the rim of an ancient 30km caldera, the noticeably cool town of **Tagaytay** (640m) has a bird's-eye view of the volcano and is an easy day trip from Manila.

DEJA VU

If canoe trips though the jungle-bordered river to Pagsanjan Falls, 100km south of Manila, feel eerily familiar, it may be because this was one of the locations for Francis Ford Coppola's *Apocalypse Now*.

Try **Green Star Bus Lines** (Map pp596-7; ☎ 831 3178; Taft Ave) for transport to the area from Manila (P150, three hours).

The DOT-operated **Tagaytay Picnic Grove** (☎ 046-483 0346; barangay Sungay; r P1400) has a variety of pretty basic but well-priced rooms. There's a 15-minute nature walk (along an ugly concrete path) with great views of **Lake Taal**; it's usually good for spotting a few colourful birds.

If you wish to get closer to the action, you can charter *bangkas* to 'Volcano Island' from **Talisay**, on the lake's northeast shore, for around P1500 return and do the often sweltering walk up to Taal Volcano's crater (45 minutes). There are longer walks to be done, including a journey into Taal's crater to bathe in the warm, sulphuric waters therein. This requires a guide (P500) – ask your *bangka* driver or one of the dozens of touts hanging around Talisay.

For Tagaytay, take a **Crow Transit** (Map pp596-7; cnr EDSA & Taft Ave, Pasay City) bus from Manila (P80, two hours). Talisay is a 20-minute jeepney ride straight downhill from Tagaytay (P9).

PHILIPPINES

BATANGAS

☎ 043 / pop 248,000

Batangas is an industrial town that is the jumping off point to Puerto Galera on Mindoro (see p614 for information on boats to Puerto Galera). A short jeepney ride west of Batangas are several **dive resorts** at Anilao, while the well-preserved historical town of **Taal**, birthplace of several Filipino heroes and patriots, lies a little further up the coast.

ALPS Transit and JAM Transit have buses every 30 minutes or so to Batangas pier from Manila (see p604).

NORTH LUZON

Luzon's north is a vast expanse of misty mountains, sprawling plains and endless coastline. The region's trophy piece is the central mountainous area known as the Cordillera, where the Ifugao built their world-famous rice terraces in and around Banaue more than 2000 years ago. Elsewhere, historic Vigan boasts a colonial hub that is the country's best-preserved vestige of its Spanish heritage. Self-explorers can continue north of Vigan to Luzon's wild northern tip, where remote white-sand beaches embrace the coastline and rarely visited islands lurk offshore.

THE CORDILLERA

Most venturers into North Luzon set their sights squarely on the Cordillera, a river-sliced hinterland of lush green forests covering hectare after hectare of jagged earth. The amazing rice terraces near Banaue were hewn out of the steep mountains by the Ifugao some 2000 to 3000 years ago. Legend has it that the god Kabunyan used the steps to visit his people on earth. Lesser known but no less spectacular terraces exist throughout the Cordillera, most notably north of Bontoc in Maligcong and Mainit.

The tribespeople of the Cordillera, collectively known as Igorot, are as compelling as the landscape. In remote areas you'll still see elders in traditional garb such as 'g-strings' (loin cloths). Sturdy travellers can embark on one- to several-day treks over ancient walking trails to visit Igorot villages where the locals tend to their terraces, raise pigs and practise animistic rituals as they have done for eons.

Outside of Baguio there are no ATMs that accept Western plastic. Bring cash, but not too much because you'll only need about $10 (in any currency!) a day. Throw a poncho in your bag too, as the Cordillera can get chilly at night.

GETTING THERE & AROUND

Travel in the Cordillera is exhilarating but requires patience, and ideally a pillow to sit on. The twisting roads are rough, dusty affairs that are subject to landslides in the June to September wet season. Baguio is the traditional launching pad for forays north to Sagada and Banaue, although Banaue can be reached via sealed roads from Manila (eight to nine hours). The trip from Baguio to Sagada is six hours in good weather, mostly over the winding, perilous Halsema Hwy. Sagada to Banaue is three hours, with a jeepney change in Bontoc.

The Halsema Hwy – about two-thirds of which is now sealed – has to be one of the world's most scenic drives. A real engineering feat when it was built in the 1920s, the road snakes along a narrow ridge, usually at well above 2000m (the high point is 2255m). It offers up astonishing, often petrifying views of precipitous valleys, bright green rice terraces and the Philippines' second-highest peak, Mt Pulag (2922m).

Baguio

☎ 074 / pop 275,500 / elev 1450m

Vibrant, woodsy and cool by Philippine standards, Baguio (*bah*-gee-oh) is the Cordillera's nerve centre. For Filipinos, it's the escape of choice from the stifling heat of the lowlands. For foreigners, it's the primary gateway to backpacker bliss up north in Sagada and Banaue.

Baguio's character is shaped by the quarter of a million college students who double Baguio's population for much of the year. Acoustic music wafts out of windows on every street; walking around with a guitar strapped to your back is decidedly *de rigueur*.

Unfortunately, even without tricycles (which can't make it up the hills), Baguio has a traffic problem. If you don't stray far from the main drag of Session Rd, you can be forgiven for disliking this city. Baguio's charm lies well outside the centre, in pine-forested parks such as Camp John Hay.

INFORMATION

Session Rd hosts several internet cafés, banks and telephone offices. The **tourist office** (☎ 446 3434; Lake Dr, Burnham Park; 🕑 8am-5pm) sells maps and can arrange private transport to points north of Baguio.

SIGHTS

The **city market** near the west end of Session Rd shouldn't be missed – it's an infinite warren of stalls selling everything from soap to fresh-grilled chicken foetus. You can also pick up all manner of mass-produced handicrafts, including basketwork, textiles, Ifugao woodcarvings and jewellery (silver is a local speciality).

Eight traditional Ifugao homes and two rare Kalinga huts were taken apart and then reassembled on the side of a hill at the artists' colony **Tam-awan Village** (☎ 446 2949; tamawan@skyinet.net; Long-Long Rd, Pinsao; s/d P500/900). Spending the night in one of these huts is a rare treat. You can learn indigenous dance, music and the martial art *arnis* at the colony, and on a clear day there are wonderful views of the South China Sea, hence the name Tam-awan, which literally means 'Vantage Point'. To get here, take a Quezon Hill–Tam-awan or Tam-awan–Long-Long jeepney (P7.50) from the corner of Kayang and Abano Sts.

SLEEPING

The most unique choice is Tam-awan Village, but note it's at least a 15-minute ride from the centre. Beyond that, Baguio's budget options are perfectly grim. Book well ahead on weekends in the Philippine 'summer' months (March to May).

Baguio Harrison Inn (☎ 442 7803; 37 Harrison Rd; d P400-700) In the YWCA building, the cheapest rooms here are tiny and share a common bathroom, but are good value for Baguio.

Mile Hi-Inn (☎ 446 6141; Mile Hi Center; dm P450) Located in a bizarre duty-free shopping centre within Camp John Hay, this place offers a woodsy escape from the mayhem of Session Rd. It has four single-sex dorm rooms with four beds each. It's a 10-minute FX van ride to Session Rd.

our pick **Burnham Hotel** (☎ 442 2331; 21 Calderon St; d from P985) Beautifully adorned with local handicrafts and staffed by a lively, informative family, this graceful place is well worth a couple of extra pesos.

Also recommended:

Benguet Pine Tourist Inn (☎ 442 7325; 82 Shanum St; dm/d P300/800) Quiet option near buses to Banaue.

OFF THE BEATEN TRACK

A beaten 4WD track heading north out of Baguio for 50 bone-rattling kilometres leads to picturesque **Kabayan**, the site of several caves containing eerie mummies entombed centuries ago by the Ibaloi people. Some of these caves can be visited, while others are known only to Ibaloi elders. After exploring Kabayan for a day or two you can walk back to the Halsema Hwy (six hours) via the **Timbac Caves**, the spot where the best-preserved mummies lurk. You'll need to bring along a guide with a key to unlock the gates protecting the caves.

PHILIPPINES

Red Lion Pub/Inn (☎ 304 3078; 92 Upper General Luna Rd; d P800) Has a few basement rooms if you don't mind the noise overhead.

EATING

In the evenings, Perfecto St (near Burnham Park) turns into a freeway of street stalls barbecuing pretty much everything under the sun.

our pick **Bliss** (www.blissnbaguio.com; 21 Leonard Wood Rd; mains P100-150; closed Mon) Owner/chef Shanti home-cooks delectable vegetarian pasta and a few Indian dishes. She and husband Jim hold regular art shows and events – Sunday is art-house flick night. It shares space with the Munsayac Inn.

Cafe by the Ruins (25 Chuntug St; mains P100-150) The 'ruins' in this case are merely the former residence of an ex-governor, but the effect is still sublime, and the organic food as original as the ambience.

Don Henrico's (Session Rd btwn Carlo & Assumption Sts) Don Henrico's sturdy pizza wraps (P120) have no rival when it comes to slaying the late-night munchies.

DRINKING

Red Lion Pub/Inn (92 Upper General Luna Rd) Red Lion is Baguio's preferred expat watering hole. It's also renowned for its steaks and ribs (P350 to P450).

Nevada Square (Loakan Rd off Military Circle) This innocuous-looking collection of bars and clubs turns into one giant fraternity party on weekends, complete with shooters, bar sports and inebriated Filipino students dancing on tabletops.

Rumours (56 Session Rd) For something a little more sophisticated try this long-time traveller fave.

GETTING THERE & AWAY

Victory Liner, which has its own flashy terminal off Upper Session Rd, has buses to/from Manila every 30 minutes (P380, six hours). Several other bus companies serve Manila from Governor Pack Rd, just south of the intersection with Session Rd; for details, see p603.

GL Lizardo has hourly buses until 1pm to Sagada (P220, 6½ hours) from the **Dangwa Terminal** (Magsaysay Ave), a five-minute walk north of Session Rd. D'Rising Sun buses to Bontoc (P212, six hours) leave hourly from the **Slaughterhouse Terminal** (Magsaysay Ave), five minutes by jeepney beyond the Dangwa Terminal. Both routes follow the Halsema Hwy.

KMS and Ohayami have several buses to Banaue (P400, nine hours) each day along the sealed, southern route via Solano. The terminal is on Shanum St, west of Burnham Park.

Sagada

pop 3000

Sagada (1477m) is a delightfully laid-back village where you can fall asleep to the sound of chickens and cicadas rather than cars and karaoke. It's home to hearty Kankanay mountain folk and is set amid jagged limestone rock formations that slice through Sagada's rich fir forests. Adventurers will find loads to explore in the area, including spooky **burial caves** and **hanging coffins**, an underground river system and several waterfalls. Most hotels sell maps (P10) that list the main attractions.

Take a guide for pretty much any trekking or caving you do around here or you'll almost surely get lost; grab one (per day P800 to P1200) at the tourist information centre, where you can also hire a private jeepney if need be. If you only have time for one excursion, our pick would be the half-day **cave connection** (per person with guide P400).

SLEEPING

Sagada's basic but charming guesthouses, featuring cosy linen and buckets of hot water (P25), are a delight. Prices listed are for rooms with common bathrooms; most places also have rooms with private bathrooms in the P800 to P1200 range.

Sagada Guesthouse (☎ 0919 300 2763; edaoas@yahoo.com; d per person P200) The rustic, cheerful doubles here, overlooking the central square, are perhaps the town's best value.

St Joseph's Resthouse (☎ 0918 559 5934; s/d/tr per person P200;) Set on a hill overlooking town, this is probably the best all-around choice, with a wide variety of rooms to choose from, good food and excellent views. The cheaper rooms are shoeboxes.

Olahbinan Resthouse (☎ 0928 406 7646; d per person P250) It's wood from floor to ceiling inside this immaculately kept, rambling house, located behind the Sagada Igorot Inn.

EATING

Sagada has a few surprisingly good eating options.

Masferré (sandwiches P60, mains P90-600) Sagada's most popular restaurant is run by the family of the late Sagada-born photographer Eduardo Masferré. Ask the proprietor for a tour of the Masferré Gallery, in a private house just outside of town.

Yoghurt House (pastas P110-130) A local gallery and craft museum as much as a restaurant, Yoghurt House has a lip-smacking menu offering spicy Indian curries, filling pastas and its trademark yoghurt muesli breakfasts (P60 to P80).

our pick **Log Cabin** (☎ 0920 520 0463; meals from P300; dinner) The fireplace dining here hits the spot on those chilly evenings. On Saturday there's a buffet (P250; prepaid reservations only) prepared by a French chef.

GETTING THERE & AWAY

There are jeepneys to Bontoc every hour until noon (P35, one hour). The last bus to Baguio leaves at 1pm (see opposite for details).

Bontoc

☎ 074 / pop 3600

This Wild West frontier town is the central Cordillera's transport and market hub. You can still see tribal elders with full body tattoos and g-strings strolling the streets, especially on Sunday when people descend from the surrounding villages to sell their wares at Bontoc's bustling market. Don't even think about leaving Bontoc without visiting the **Bontoc Museum** (admission P50; 8am-noon & 1-5pm), which has fascinating exhibits on each of the region's main tribes. Check out the grisly photos of head-hunters and their booty.

There's some mint trekking to be done around Bontoc, most notably to the stone-walled **rice terraces of Maligcong**, which rival those in Batad. To really get off the beaten track, head even further north into Kalinga Province, where you can hike to remote villages and meet aged former head-hunters. Ask around the hotels for Kinad (for treks around Bontoc) or Francis Pa-In (for Kalinga treks).

If you are staying a night, **Churya-a Hotel & Restaurant** (☎ 0906 430 0853; darwin_churyaa@yahoo.com; dm/d/tr P100/350/600) has clean if unspectacular rooms, and a pleasant balcony overlooking Bontoc's main street.

Cable Tours has the only direct bus to/from Manila, leaving Bontoc daily at 3pm (P600, 12 hours) and leaving Manila nightly at 8.30pm. It goes via Banaue (P150, two hours). To Banaue, there are also two jeepneys around noon (P130, two hours) and four morning buses. Jeepneys to Sagada (P35, one hour) leave hourly until 5pm from near the Eastern Star Hotel. For buses to Baguio, see opposite.

Banaue & the Rice Terraces

☎ 074 / pop 2700

Banaue is synonymous with Luzon's most famous icon, the Unesco World Heritage–listed Ifugao rice terraces, etched out of the hillsides using primitive tools and an ingenious irrigation system over 2000 years ago. The Ifugao by no means had a monopoly on rice terraces in the Cordillera, but they were arguably the best sculptors, as the mesmerizing display overlooking Banaue suggests.

Banaue itself – a ragged collection of tin-roofed edifices along a ridge – often spoils things for those looking for a perfect first ooh-and-ahh moment. But you can't argue with Banaue's setting, and accommodation remains of stellar value compared with most tourist hot spots in the Philippines. Meanwhile, that perfect ooh-and-ahh is not far away, in Batad.

The Ifugao are almost as famous for carving wood as they are for carving earth into green, fuzzy, rice-bearing steps. You'll find myriad locally made carvings and other crafts in the shops surrounding the main plaza. Two kilometres north of town you can ogle rice terraces to your heart's content at the **viewpoint**; a tricycle there and back costs P200. If your heart's still not content, there are similarly impressive specimens lurking in nearby Hapao and Kiangan, as well as around Bontoc and in Kalinga Province to the north.

INFORMATION

The **tourist office** (☎ 386 4010; 7am-6pm) adjacent to the plaza arranges accredited guides (P1000 to P1500) and private transport according to a remarkably transparent list of set prices. Good little maps of the main hiking routes are widely available for P10. You can change money and access the internet at the upscale Banaue Hotel or in the plaza area.

SLEEPING & EATING

People's Lodge (☎ 386 4014; s/d from P150/300) Service couldn't be friendlier at this sweet value spot, which has one of the more popular restaurants in town.

Sanafe Lodge & Restaurant (☎ 386 4085; dm/s/d P150/600/750) Wood panelling is the theme in the small rooms here. The rice terrace-facing barstools precariously perched over the Banaue valley are perfect for a posthike frosty one.

Banaue View Inn (☎ 386 4078; 3-bed dm P200, d/tr P700/900) This inn off the main road above town boasts a bird's-eye view of the rice terraces and has shipshape rooms. Karen, the owners' daughter, is a great source of information.

Restaurants in Banaue close annoyingly early, except for **Las Vegas** (☎ 0918 440 9932), which also has cheap rooms.

GETTING THERE & AWAY

There are now three bus companies making the direct trip nightly to Manila (see p603). If you miss those take a jeepney to Solano (P100, two hours) and pick up a Manila-bound bus there.

For bus companies serving Baguio, see p608. Most buses to Baguio ply the lowland route via Solano. To take the scenic but perilous highland route (ie via Bontoc and the Halsema Hwy), you must transfer in Bontoc. There are two early morning jeepneys to Bontoc, and a handful of Bontoc-bound buses pass through Banaue throughout the day (about P150, two hours).

Batad

pop 1150

To really see the **Ifugao rice terraces** in all their glory, you'll need to trek to Batad (900m), nestled halfway up an imposing amphitheatre of rice fields. Most of the inhabitants still practise traditional tribal customs in what must be one of the most serene, picture-perfect villages to grace the earth. A slippery 45-minute walk beyond the village itself is the gorgeous 25m-high **Tappiya Waterfall** and swimming hole.

SLEEPING

Although electricity is now common in Batad, accommodation remains decidedly rustic. Rather than being a disadvantage, this, and the distinct absence of any kind of engine, is a big part of the town's appeal. Most guesthouses overlook the amphitheatre from a ridge above Batad, and provide blankets to take the edge off the chilly nights.

Hillside Inn, Rita's Mount View Inn and Simon's Inn all have restaurants and rooms for P150 per head. They're all simple, clean and homey, but Rita's wins our hearts with its all-round charm.

GETTING THERE & AWAY

From Banaue, it's 12km over a rocky road to Batad Junction, where a 4WD track leads three bone-jarring kilometres up to the 'saddle' high above Batad. From the saddle it's a 45-minute hike to Batad.

A few morning jeepneys go from Banaue to Batad Junction (P60); one afternoon jeepney goes to the saddle (P100). You can also take a tricycle to the junction (one-way P350, return P700 including waiting time). Sturdier tricycles can make it to the saddle. You can also team up with other travellers in Banaue and hire a private jeepney to the saddle (one-way/return P1500/2000).

If you are overnighting in Batad, get out to the saddle by 9am (or to the junction by 10am) the next morning to catch the last jeepney back to Banaue.

VIGAN

☎ 077 / pop 46,500

Spanish-era mansions, cobblestone streets and *kalesa* (horse-drawn carriages) are the hallmarks of Unesco World Heritage site Vigan. Miraculously spared bombing in WWII, the city is considered the finest surviving example of a Spanish colonial town. One of Vigan's finer mansions is now the **Crisologo Museum** (Liberation Blvd; admission free; 8.30-11.30am & 1.30-4.30pm Tue-Sat).

After being razed several times by earthquakes, **St Paul Cathedral** (Plaza Salcedo) was rebuilt in 1641, bigger and better, in a style known as 'earthquake baroque'. It was a successful technique, and the church is now one of the oldest and biggest in the Philippines.

The **Vigan Town Fiesta** is in the third week of January, while the **Viva Vigan Festival of the Arts** takes place in early May.

Sleeping

It's worth paying a little extra to stay in one of Vigan's charismatic colonial homes. Prices go way down from June to October.

Vigan Hotel (☎ 722 1906; Burgos St; s/d from P395/495;) The once popular Vigan Hotel today suffers from a decided lack of TLC. It's still cheap though.

Gordian Inn (☎ 722 2562; www.gordianinn.netfirms.com; cnr V de los Reyes & Salcedo Sts; d P600-1500;) This old mansion has a new wing with some budget-friendly rooms.

Villa Angela (☎ 722 2914; 26 Quirino Blvd; d from P1200;) This magnificent place has a giant

PHILIPPINES

JULIA CAMPBELL (1967–2007)

The murder of Peace Corps volunteer Julia Campbell at the hands of a local man on the main trail to Batad in April 2007 shocked the country. Her blog – www.juliainthephilippines.blogspot.com – quickly turned into a poignant shrine where Filipinos issued their condolences and expressed their shame. While the country's justice minister despicably blamed Campbell for hiking alone, the truth is that the incident was extremely uncharacteristic of the hospitable Ifugao people, who were so upset by the murder that they donated a 40-hectare forest plot as a memorial. The murder was a random act of violence, not a terrorist act or hate crime, and the killer was swiftly caught and brought to justice. Nonetheless, in the wake of the murder local authorities strongly advise all tourists to hire a guide for any hikes around Banaue, Bontoc and Sagada, and to register with the local tourist office upon arrival.

sala (living room) festooned with antiques and four bedrooms looking much as they would have in the 18th century.

Eating

Café Leona (Mena Crisologo St; snacks P50-75, mains P200-300) Just off Plaza Burgos, popular Café Leona serves terrific Ilocano food and passable Japanese specials on the cobbled street. Around the corner is the more economical Plaza Sanitary (Florentino St; mains P60 to P100).

Evening **street stalls** (Plaza Burgos) serve snacks such as *empanadas* (deep-fried tortillas with shrimp, cabbage and egg) and *okoy* (shrimp omelettes).

Getting There & Away

There are plenty of companies serving Manila (see p603), but the trip is most comfortable on the 'deluxe' 27-seater overnight buses run by Partas (☎ 722 3369; Alcantara St). Partas also has 10 daily trips to Baguio (P300, five hours).

SOUTHEAST LUZON

Fiery food, fierce typhoons and furious volcanoes characterise the adventure wonderland known as Bicol. The region's most famous peak, Mt Mayon, may just be the world's most perfect volcano. And it's no sleeping beauty, either. A steady stream of noxious fumes leaks out of its maw, and minor eruptions are frequent. You can climb most of the way up Mayon, but there is better hiking to be had in Mt Isarog National Park and on the remote Caramoan Peninsula. Below water, Bicol is famous for one of the Philippines' most famous attractions: the gentle, graceful *butanding* (whale sharks) of Donsol.

You'll want to pay extra attention to the news before heading to Bicol, lest you waltz into one of the region's patented typhoons. The Pan-Philippine or Maharlika Hwy runs right through Bicol down to Matnog, where ferries cross to Samar (P100, one hour).

NAGA

☎ 062 / pop 161,000

Naga is relatively cosmopolitan by Philippine standards, with a young, vibrant student population. The city centres on a pleasant double plaza that often hosts large concerts or festivals after sundown. In September don't miss the famous **Peñafrancia Festival**, held in honour of Naga's patron, the Virgin of Peñafrancia. Be sure to sample the spicy local Bicol cuisine, as well as pili nuts (a local favourite).

Activities

Hiking is the big activity around here, especially in two areas: the **Caramoan Peninsula** and **Mt Isarog National Park**. The former is actually more renowned for its coastal jewels – untouched beaches and jagged limestone cliffs similar to those found in Palawan. But you can explore the area on foot, stopping along the way to go island hopping in boats hired from local fishermen. There are several places to stay in Caramoan town or you can camp on white-sand **Gota Beach**. Talk to the helpful caretaker there, Tiyo, for advice. The town tourist office rents out tents. To get there go to Sabang (see p612), then take a scenic *bangka* ride to Guijalo (P130, two hours, last trip 1pm), which is 10 minutes by tricycle from Caramoan town.

Looming over Naga, craggy **Mt Isarog** (1966m) is easier to get to. You can launch an assault on its summit or there are several shorter hikes through the jungle lower down.

Access to the national park is from the town of Panicuason, where you can find guides.

The **Kadlagan Outdoor Shop & Climbing Wall** (☎ 472 3305; kadlagan@yahoo.com; 16 Dimasalang St, Naga) hires out tents and other camping gear, and guides excursions to Mt Isarog and the Caramoan Peninsula. Jojo Villareal knows all the local rocks and routes and is usually here in the evenings. Guides cost roughly P1000 per day, not including meals, equipment, island-hopping boats, porters etc.

Sleeping

Sampaguita Tourist Inn (☎ 473 8896; Panganiban Dr; s/d from P150/350) The cookie-cutter rooms here won't excite you, but they won't give you any major problems either. Choose between windowless or loud.

Golden Leaf Hotel (☎ 471 6507; Misericordia St; s/d from P300/400; ❄) Positively gleaming new rooms are a welcome change to Naga's usual musty offerings. Cross the Panganiban Dr bridge, then take the second left.

Eating & Drinking

San Francisco food court (Peñafrancia Ave; portions P10-20) This lane of food stalls next to San Francisco Church is a great place to get down with the locals and sample fiery Bicol dishes, such as *pinangat* (taro leaves wrapped around minced fish or pork) and *ginataang pusit* (squid cooked in coconut milk).

'Magsaysay' jeepneys along Peñafrancia Ave lead to a new food mall, **Avenue Square** (Magsaysay Ave). Beyond this mall is a huddle of popular bars and restaurants, the best of which is **Coco Leaf** (Magsaysay Ave; mains P75-50), with Filipino and Asian-fusion dishes. **Molino Bar & Grill** (Magsaysay Ave; 6-beer bucket P150) was the party nexus for the cool university crowd when we visited.

Getting There & Away

Air Philippines has a daily flight to Manila.

The bus station is just over Panganiban Bridge. Cagsawa and RSL bus lines go directly to Ermita in Manila, while several others go to Cubao (see p603). The night buses to Manila fill up fast so book a few days ahead.

Minivans are the preferred method of local travel. They go to Panicuason (P30, 30 minutes), Sabang (P75, one hour) and Legazpi (P120, two hours). Air-con buses to Legazpi take longer and cost the same, while ordinary (non–air-con) buses sometimes take six hours!

LEGAZPI

☎ 052 / pop 184,000

Charm is in short supply in the city of Legazpi, but with the towering cone of Mt Mayon hogging the horizon no-one seems to really notice. The city is divided into Albay District, where the provincial government offices and airport are located, and commercial Legazpi City. A steady stream of jeepneys connects the two districts (P7.50) along the national highway. You can pick up a great map of the city at the **Provincial Tourism Office** (☎ 820 6315; http://tourism.albay.gov.ph; Astrodome Complex, Aquende Dr, Albay District).

Sleeping

Dreams Inn & Cafe (☎ 480 0885; F Imperial St, Legazpi City; s/d from P150/575; ❄) This extra-value special across from Pacific Mall has well-maintained cookie-cutter rooms. Don't plan on throwing a party in the singles.

Catalina's Lodging House (☎ 481 1634; 96 Peñaranda St, Legazpi City; s P180-240, d P240-550; ❄) The small rooms here have fragrant old wooden floors and range from very cheap and basic to less cheap and basic.

Legazpi Tourist Inn (☎ 480 6147; V&O Bldg, Quezon Ave, Legazpi City; s/d from P500/560; ❄) The best midrange option is this modern place, with clean and well-kept rooms, quality TVs and lots of mirrors.

Eating & Drinking

The nightly street stalls along Quezon Ave near the Trylon Monument in Legazpi City dish out fried chicken, noodles and fiery, coconut milk–cooked Bicol specialities for P10 to P30 per portion.

Waway's Restaurant (Peñaranda St, Legazpi City; dishes P60-100) On the northern side of town, this is the best place in the country to try Bicol food. A surprisingly palatable choice for the adventurous eater is *candingga* (diced pig liver and carrots sweetened and cooked in vinegar).

our pick **Small Talk** (Doña Aurora St & National Hwy, Albay District; mains P75-125) This delightful little eatery adds Bicol touches to its Italian fare. Try the pasta *pinangat* or 'Bicol express' pasta.

Buckets of beer (P150) and live music are the themes at the bars on the 3rd floor of the **Silver Screens Entertainment Centre** (cnr Magallanes & Ramon Santos Sts, Legazpi City). This is also the place to catch big-budget Hollywood movies.

PHILIPPINES

Getting There & Away

Cebu Pacific flies twice daily and PAL once daily to/from Legazpi. Sit on the left side flying out of Legazpi for prime views of Mt Mayon.

The main bus terminal is at the Satellite Market, just west of Pacific Mall in Legazpi City. Cagsawa and RSL bus lines have popular deluxe night buses that go directly to Ermita in Manila, while several others go to Cubao (see p603).

For options to Naga, see opposite. The only direct trip to Donsol is by air-con minivan (P60, 1¼ hours).

AROUND LEGAZPI

Mt Mayon

Bicolanos hit the nail on the head when they named this monolith – *magayon* is the local word for 'beautiful'. The impossibly perfect slopes of the volcano's cone rise to 2462m above sea level, emitting a constant plume of smoke over the flat plains and surrounding coconut plantations.

The spirit of the mountain is an old king whose beloved niece ran away with a young buck. The grumpy old man's pride still erupts frequently. In February 1993, 77 people died and a further 50,000 were evacuated. This was followed by an ash eruption in 1999, streaming lava in 2000, and more lava in 2001, 2004 and 2006. Shortly after the lava flows of 2006 subsided, a biblical typhoon triggered mudslides on Mt Mayon that killed more than 1000 people.

Despite that, the mountain's 'knife edge' – the highest point to which you can climb, at about 2200m – was reopened in 2007 after being off-limits for three years. For most people it's a 1½-day climb, but extremely fit climbers may be able to do it in a day with an early start. The best time to climb is February to April. From May to August it's unbearably hot; from September to January it's unbearably wet.

Guides are mandatory and can be secured through the **Region V Department of Tourism** (DOT; ☎ 482 0712; National Hwy, Rawis), 2.5km north of Legazpi City, or through **Bicol Adventure & Tours** (☎ 480 2266; bicoladventure@digitelone.com; V&O Bldg, Quezon Ave, Legazpi City). Organised treks cost about US$100/110/145 for one/two/three persons and include transport from Legazpi, camping equipment, porters, food etc. Figure on P2000 per day for just a guide.

Donsol

pop 4200

Every year, between December and early June, a large number of whale sharks, or *butanding*, frolic in the waters off this sleepy fishing village about 50km from Legazpi. It's truly an exhilarating experience swimming along with these silver-spotted marine leviathans, which can reach 18m in length. In the peak months of February to May, the question isn't whether you will see a shark, but how many you will see. Call Salvador Adrao at the **Donsol Visitors Center** (☎ 0927 233 0364; 7.30am-5pm) to make sure they're around before you visit.

When you arrive in town head to the visitors centre to pay your registration fee (P300) and arrange a boat and spotter (P3500, good for seven people), plus a *Butanding* Interaction Officer (BIO; P700). There is a limited supply of snorkelling equipment available for hire, so bring your own just in case. Scuba diving is prohibited.

SLEEPING & EATING

Santiago Lodging House (tr P300) Located across from the town hall, this is basically a homestay with three good, clean rooms in a beat-up wooden house.

Amor Farm Beach Resort (d from P500;) Right next to the visitors centre, Amor Farm is a peaceful place, albeit not quite as well kept as Woodland.

Woodland Farm Beach Resort (cottages from P800;) This is a stylish place with tidy, comfortable duplex cottages, a restaurant and a narrow brown-sand beach. It's just north of the visitors centre.

GETTING THERE & AWAY

Air-con minivans leave to/from Legazpi every hour until about 4pm (P60, 1¼ hours).

MINDORO

This large and attractive island just south of Luzon has something of a split personality. The beach centre of Puerto Galera in the north is all dive schools and skin tone culture. Further south, sons of peasants are fighting for the communist NPA (see p584), and in the forested mountains in the middle the Mangyan tribal people live as slash-and-burn farmers.

Puerto Galera's first-rate scuba-diving opportunities in the surrounding Unesco-protected marine reserve are the big tourist draw. Sabang is diving HQ. For something off this well-beaten path, make a beeline for the west coast's Apo Reef, where the world-class underwater action involves plenty of sharks and stingrays.

Getting There & Away

Asian Spirit flies to San José in southern Mindoro daily, but the way to Puerto Galera is by boat from Batangas (see Getting There & Around, below).

There are also hourly SuperCat fastcraft ferries from Batangas to Calapan in northern Mindoro (P230, one hour) as well as slower car ferries (P160, 2½ hours). Montenegro Shipping has three ferries per week from Batangas to San José (P582, 12 hours). Regular ferries to Boracay depart from Roxas (see p616).

PHILIPPINES

PUERTO GALERA

☎ 043 / pop 25,700

It lacks the beautiful beach, classy resorts and edgy nightlife of Boracay, but this diving hot spot on the northern tip of Mindoro is conveniently located just a hop, skip and a *bangka* ride from Manila. That alone easily qualifies it as the country's second most popular tourist destination after Boracay.

The name Puerto Galera typically refers to the town of Puerto Galera and the resort areas surrounding it – namely Sabang, 7km to the east, and White Beach, 7km to the west. The town proper has a breathtakingly beautiful harbour, but otherwise is of little interest. Indeed, most travellers take ferries directly to Sabang or White Beach and never step foot in Puerto Galera town.

Many internet cafés dot Sabang and White Beach, but there are no ATMs in the area so bring cash. The privately owned **Tourist Center** (☎ 287 3108; ⌚ 9am-9pm Mon-Sat), on the main road in Sabang, has information on transport and hotels and also exchanges currency.

GETTING THERE & AROUND

Speedy *bangka* ferries to Puerto Galera, Sabang Beach and White Beach leave regularly throughout the day from Batangas pier until about 4.30pm (P180, one hour). The last trip back to Batangas from Sabang leaves at 1.45pm, from White Beach at 3.30pm, and from Puerto Galera it's the 5.30pm car ferry (P190, 2½ hours). This crossing can be rough, but the boats usually sail unless there's a tropical storm brewing.

To Calapan, frequent jeepneys leave from the petrol station 500m south of Puerto Galera proper (P60, two hours). Transfer in Calapan for Roxas, where ferries depart to Boracay.

Jeepneys ply the routes between Sabang and Puerto Galera town, and White Beach and Puerto Galera town, leaving every 30 minutes or so until 6pm; both rides cost P15 and take 20 minutes. A tricycle from Sabang to Puerto Galera costs a steep P150; from Puerto Galera to White Beach it is P100. You'll save some money by taking a motorcycle taxi.

Off-road motorcycles can be rented for around P800 a day.

> **DID YOU KNOW?**
>
> Whale shark–watching in Donsol is the Philippines' highest profile – and probably most successful – community-based ecotourism project. Many *Butanding* Interaction Officers (BIOs) and spotters are former fishermen who once hunted whale sharks and dynamite-fished on the local reefs.

Sabang Beach

Drinking and underwater pursuits are the activities of choice in Sabang, with plenty of establishments offering variations on this theme. The local divers' association keeps dive prices uniform at about US$30 for a one-tank dive if you lack your own equipment. An open-water course will set you back US$350 to US$400. Snorkel and fin hire is P3 to P5 per day. By night Sabang serves up plenty of action, much of it less than wholesome.

Just around the headland and a stone's throw from Sabang, the cleaner and more laid-back **Small La Laguna Beach** has several resorts fronting a brown strip of sand. Beyond that is **Big La Laguna Beach**.

SLEEPING

Expect big discounts off these prices in the June to October low season.

VIP Dive Resort (☎ 0917 795 9062; d P400-1000) Sabang's cheapest rooms are a bit worn but

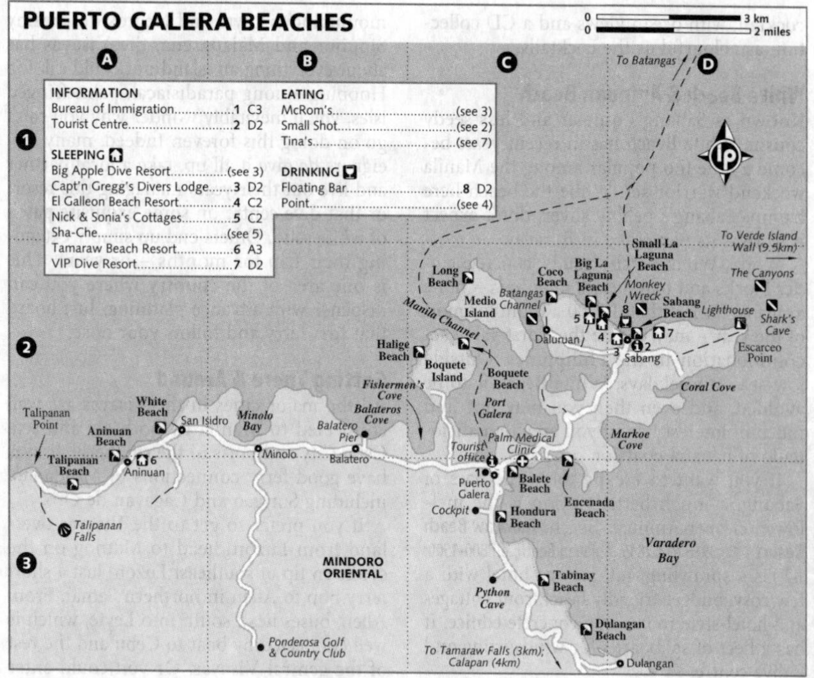

still have verandas, hot water and small kitchens. It's at the quieter east side of the beach.

Big Apple Dive Resort (☎ 0919 852 3442; www.dive-bigapple.com; s/d P750/850;) Professionally run Big Apple has a popular beachfront bar and reasonably large rooms set around a garden out the back. There's free wi-fi.

Capt'n Gregg's Divers Lodge (☎ 287 3070; www.captngreggs.com; d P800-1400;) This Sabang institution is great value. The wood-lined rooms, right over the water, earn the best-view plaudit. All rooms have TV, minibar and free wi-fi.

El Galleon Beach Resort (☎ 0917 814 5170; www.elgalleon.com; Small La Laguna Beach; d from US$40;) Elegant hut-style rooms with wicker furniture and verandas creep up a beachfront cliff and slink around the pool. Yes it's a splurge, but completely worth it.

Right next to each other on Small La Laguna Beach are two similarly good-value places: **Nick & Sonia's Cottages** (☎ 0917 803 8156; r P800-1500) and **Sha-Che** (☎ 0917 641 0112; r P1000-2500). Both offer what are essentially small studio apartments, complete with kitchens and TVs, in concrete rows just off the beach.

EATING

The restaurants in Sabang are, in a word, expensive.

Tina's (mains P75-200) Way down at the east end of Sabang Beach, Tina's has the best-priced food on the beachfront. Do try Tina's schnitzel.

McRom's (Sabang Beach; mains P120-350) Popular with expats in the know, McRom's serves up sizzling local and Western dishes.

There are several simple Filipino eateries down the main road leading away from the beachfront. **Small Shot** (noodle dishes from P50) is the pick of the lot.

DRINKING

Floating Bar (9am-7pm) This popular bar, moored off Sabang, is the place to go if you really want to drink like a fish. Remember to apply plenty of sun protection while you're still sober. Free shuttle boats leave from in front of Capt'n Gregg's Divers Lodge.

Point (10am-midnight) El Galleon's enviably placed bar is the best spot for a sundowner cocktail, with ocean views and a CD collection as colourful as the cocktails.

White Beach & Aninuan Beach

Known as Sabang's quieter and less seedy cousin, White Beach has in recent years become a little too popular among the Manila weekend warrior set. While the beach here trumps Sabang's pebbly sliver, don't expect it to rival its namesake in Boracay.

Worse, White Beach's gaudy, concrete cinder blocks and bare-bones *nipa* huts – none available for less than P1500 a room for most of the year – may just be the worst-value accommodation in the Philippines. Outside low-season weekdays, White Beach is to be avoided, and even then you may not find much of interest here if you aren't an aficionado of banana boats or karaoke.

If you want to escape the girlie bars of Sabang, a much better option is the mellower, cleaner Aninuan Beach. **Tamaraw Beach Resort** (☎ 0916 613 2845; Aninuan Beach; d P800-1500; 💻) is a sprawling, full-service hotel with a few cosy, budget-friendly beachfront cottages and hotel-style rooms in a concrete edifice. It has a fleet of sailboards for windsurfing and a dive centre.

PHILIPPINES

ROXAS

☎ 043 / pop 10,000

Roxas is a dusty little spot with ferry connections to Caticlan (the jumping-off point for Boracay). The anthropologically inclined can take a day trip and walk to the villages of nearby Mangyan. Talk to Boy Villaluna, owner of the Roxas Villa Hotel & Restaurant.

If you need to stay the night, the **Roxas Villa Hotel & Restaurant** (☎ 289 2026; Administration St; s/d P350/450; ❄ 💻) is in the town centre.

There are about six daily ferries to Caticlan (P330, four hours) from Dangay, a P6 jeepney ride from town. Vans to the pier in Calapan (P180, 2½ hours) leave from Dangay pier and from Morente St near the town plaza. From Calapan there are jeepneys to Puerto Galera and ferries to Batangas see p614.

THE VISAYAS

If it's white sand, rum and coconuts you're after, look no further than the jigsaw puzzle of central islands known as the Visayas. From party-mad Boracay and Cebu, to mountainous Leyte and Negros, to dreamy Siquijor and Malapascua, the Visayas has about everything an island nut could ask for. Hopping among paradisiacal, palm-fringed isles, you'll inevitably wonder why you can't go on doing this forever. Indeed, many foreigners *do* give it all up, take a local partner and live out their years managing this resort or that dive centre on some exquisite patch of white sand. Others end up simply extending their trip for months – or years. This is one area of the country where you can dispense with advance planning. Just board that first ferry and follow your nose.

Getting There & Around

All the major cities in the Visayas are well connected to Manila by both air and sea. Cebu City and ports in the southern Visayas have good ferry connections to Mindanao, including Surigao and Cagayan de Oro.

If you prefer to get to the Visayas overland from Luzon, head to Matnog on the southern tip of southeast Luzon, just a short ferry hop to Allen in northern Samar. From Allen, buses head south into Leyte, which is well connected by boat to Cebu and the rest of the central Visayas. Or you could enter the region via Roxas on Mindoro, which is connected by boat to Caticlan (see left).

The six main islands of the Visayas – Panay, Negros, Cebu, Bohol, Leyte and Samar – are linked to each other by a veritable armada of so-called 'fastcraft' ferries, with plenty of 'roll-on, roll-off' car ferries (ROROs) following in their wake. Cebu City is the Visayas' main hub, with frequent ferry connections to all major and minor Visayan ports.

PANAY

The large, triangular island of Panay is where you'll enter the Visayas if taking the ferry from Mindoro. To most travellers, mainland Panay is just a giant, clumsy planet around which orbits diminutive party satellite Boracay island. Yet Panay has plenty to offer plucky independent travellers willing to part with their guidebooks for a few days, including decaying forts, Spanish churches, remote thatch-hut fishing villages and the mother of all Philippine fiestas, Kalibo's Mardi Gras–like **Ati-Atihan**, which peaks in the third week of January. Panay's capital and gateway to the rest of the Visayas is Iloilo, a five-hour bus ride south of Boracay.

THE VISAYAS

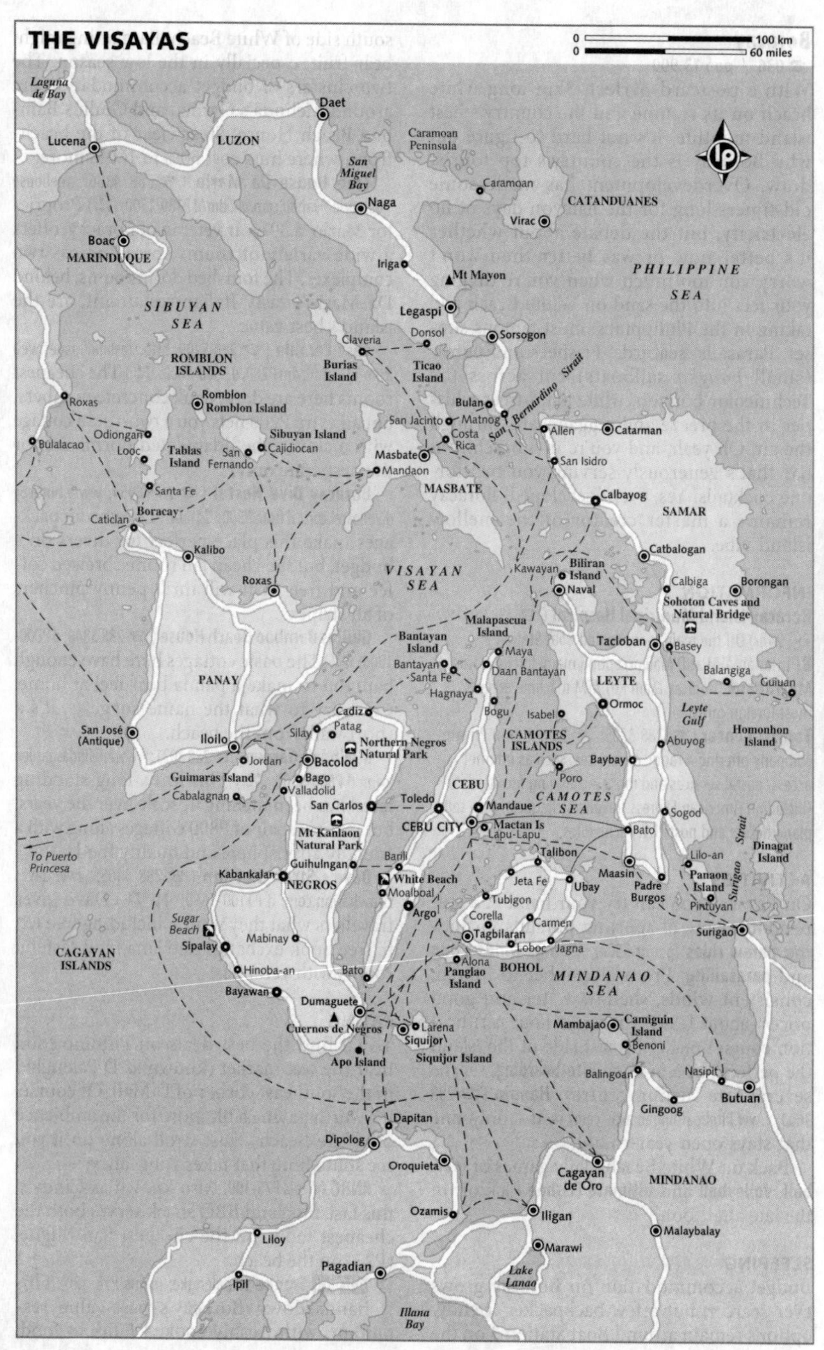
0 100 km
0 60 miles
Laguna de Bay
Daet
Lucena
LUZON
Caramoan Peninsula
San Miguel Bay
Caramoan
Naga
CATANDUANES
Virac
Boac
MARINDUQUE
Iriga
Mt Mayon
PHILIPPINE SEA
SIBUYAN SEA
Legaspi
Sorsogon
Donsol
Claveria
ROMBLON ISLANDS
Burias Island
Ticao Island
San Bernardino Strait
Roxas
Romblon
Romblon Island
Bulan
San Jacinto
Matnog
Odiongan
Sibuyan Island
Allen
Catarman
Costa Rica
Bulalacao
Looc
Tablas Island
San Fernando
Cajidiocan
Masbate
San Isidro
Mandaon
Santa Fe
MASBATE
Calbayog
Boracay
SAMAR
Caticlan
Kalibo
Catbalogan
Kawayan
Biliran Island
VISAYAN SEA
Roxas
Naval
Calbiga
Borongan
Sohoton Caves and Natural Bridge
Malapascua Island
Bantayan Island
Tacloban
Basey
Maya
Bantayan
Daan Bantayan
Santa Fe
PANAY
LEYTE
Balangiga
Guiuan
Hagnaya
Ormoc
Bogu
Isabel
Leyte Gulf
Cadiz
CAMOTES ISLANDS
Homonhon Island
San José (Antique)
Silay
Patag
Northern Negros Natural Park
Iloilo
Abuyog
Jordan
Bacolod
Baybay
Poro
Guimaras Island
Bago
CEBU
Cabalagnan
Valladolid
CAMOTES SEA
Toledo
San Carlos
Mandaue
Sogod
Mt Kanlaon Natural Park
CEBU CITY
Mactan Is
Lapu-Lapu
Bato
Surigao Strait
To Puerto Princesa
Talibon
Dinagat Island
Barili
Lilo-an
Guihulngan
Maasin
Kabankalan
NEGROS
White Beach
Jeta Fe
Ubay
Panaon Island
Padre Burgos
Moalboal
Tubigon
Pintuyan
Argo
Corella
Sugar Beach
Carmen
Surigao
Sipalay
Tagbilaran
Mabinay
Loboc
Jagna
CAGAYAN ISLANDS
Alona
Panglao Island
BOHOL
Hinoba-an
Bato
MINDANAO SEA
Bayawan
Dumaguete
Camiguin Island
Mambajao
Cuernos de Negros
Larena
Siquijor
Benoni
Apo Island
Siquijor Island
Balingoan
Nasipit
Butuan
Gingoog
Dapitan
Dipolog
Oroquieta
Cagayan de Oro
MINDANAO
Ozamis
Iligan
Liloy
Malaybalay
Marawi
Pagadian
Lake Lanao
Ipil
Illana Bay
PHILIPPINES

Boracay

☎ 036 / pop 13,900

With a postcard-perfect, 3km-long white beach on its résumé and the country's best island nightlife, it's not hard to figure out why Boracay is the country's top tourist draw. Overdevelopment has made some old-timers long for the halcyon days of no electricity, but the debate about whether it's better now or was better then won't worry you too much when you're digging your feet into the sand on White Beach and taking in the Philippines' most famous sunset. Parasails, seabirds, Frisbees and *paraw* (small *bangka* sailboats) cut across the Technicolor horizon, while palm trees whisper in the breeze and reggae wafts through the air. Oh yeah, and you're in a beachfront bar that's generously serving you two-for-one cocktails. Yes, even 'developed' Boracay remains a master creator of the mellow island vibe.

INFORMATION

Boracay Island Municipal Hospital (☎ 288 3041; 24hr) Off the main road, behind Boat Station 2.

BPI Has an ATM at D'Mall accepting many foreign cards.

Metrobank (Boracay Main Rd) ATM machine accepts most foreign cards.

Tourist Center (☎ 288 3705; 9am-11pm) Private company offering a range of services, such as internet access, postal services and money-changing facilities (including American Express travellers cheques). Also sells plane tickets and posts ferry schedules.

ACTIVITIES

On Boracay you can try your hand at a stupendous array of sporting pursuits, including **paraw rides** (per hr P500), **diving**, **windsurfing** and **parasailing**. From December to March, consistent winds, shallow water and good prices (about US$350 for a 14-hour certification course) make the east side of the island the perfect place to learn **kite-boarding**. Of the several kite-surfing centres, **Hangin** (☎ 288 3663; www.kiteboardingboracay.com) is the only one that stays open year-round.

Back on White Beach, daily games of **football**, **volleyball** and **ultimate Frisbee** kick off in the late afternoon.

SLEEPING

Budget accommodation on Boracay grows ever scarcer, but a few backpacker-friendly options remain around Boat Station 3 on the south side of White Beach. Bargaining might bear fruit, especially in the low season. The two clusters of budget accommodation are around Melinda's Garden and Giulius Bamboo Beach House. Steer clear of the beachfront, where huts cost 50% to 100% more.

Tree House Da Mario (☎ 288 4386; treehouse_damario@yahoo.com.ph; dm/d P180/1500;) Proprietor Mario, a 30-year veteran of Boracay, offers a wide variety of rooms spread across two complexes. The four-bed dorm rooms, behind Da Mario's tasty Italian restaurant, are the island's best value.

Casa Camilla (☎ 288 5209; http://asiabill.pages.web.com/id1.html; dm P250, d P600-1800;) The cheapest rooms here are dark, dank concrete numbers, but an extra P200 nets you a two-room cottage with a stove. The dilapidated dorms are for the desperate only.

Boracay Dive Hostel (☎ 288 6954; www.boracaydivehostel.com; d from P500;) Dive/room packages make this place perfect for divers on a budget, but the cheap fan rooms, brewed coffee and free wi-fi will thrill penny pinchers of all stripes.

Giulius Bamboo Beach House (☎ 288 5840; d P800-1000;) The basic cottages here have enough bamboo to make a panda bear feel at home. Contrary to what the name suggests, it's a short walk from the beach.

Melinda's Garden (☎ 288 3021; www.melindasgarden.com; d P800-1500;) This leafy, long-standing jewel has been inching upscale over the years, but retains a pair of P800 cottages along with a friendly atmosphere and quality food.

Dave's Straw Hat Inn (☎ 288 5465; www.davesstrawhatinn.com; d P1100-1650;) Dave gives travellers what they want – including free wi-fi, free book exchange and small but tasteful rooms with verandas.

EATING

You'll find the best deals on Filipino food near the wet market (known as D'Palengke) in the southeast corner of D'Mall. Of course, it's worth paying a bit more for the ambience of White Beach – just stroll along until you see something that takes your fancy.

RNRC (meals P75-100) Also known as Cindy's, this fast-food and BBQ shack serves both the cheapest food and the cheapest San Miguel (P25) on the beach.

our pick **Smoke** (d'palengke; mains P75-120) This is hands down Boracay's best-value restaurant, with freshly cooked Filipino food,

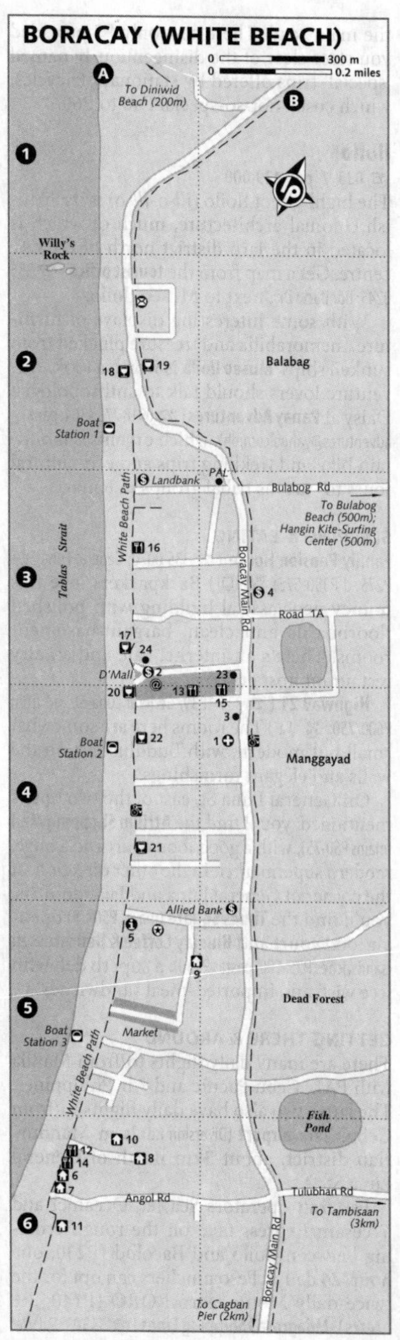

appetizing coconut-milk curries and a P60 Filipino breakfast.

bei Kurt und Madz (mains P115-250) Has a blissfully long happy hour (2pm to 8pm) featuring P25 San Miguel and a diverse, affordable menu to satisfy both noodle lovers and meat-and-potatoes types.

Cyma (☎ 288 4283; D'Mall; mains P140-300) This Greek restaurant is a little more upscale but has affordable gyros, appetizers such as flaming *saganaki* (fried salty cheese) and outstanding salads.

Steak House (steaks P350) A bit of a splurge but its juicy steaks are actually a bargain in the grand scheme of things.

DRINKING

Boracay has no shortage of bars, from peaceful, beachfront cocktail affairs, where you can sip a mai tai while you watch the sunset, to throbbing discos that run late into the night.

ourpick Nigi Nigi Nu Noos (happy hour 5-7pm) Its legendary, quart-sized Long Island iced teas – like all drinks here, they're two-for-one during happy hour – more than capably kick-start any evening.

Bom Bom (5pm-2am) With nightly bongo-infused live music, Bom Bom practically

INFORMATION
- Boracay Island Municipal Hospital....1 B4
- BPI....2 A3
- Bureau of Immigration....3 B4
- Metrobank....4 B3
- Tourist Center....5 A5

SLEEPING
- Boracay Dive Hostel....6 A6
- Casa Camilla....7 A6
- Dave's Straw Hat Inn....8 A6
- Giulius Bamboo Beach House....9 A5
- Melinda's Garden....10 A6
- Tree House Da Mario....11 A6

EATING
- bei Kurt und Madz....12 A6
- Cyma....13 A4
- RNRC....14 A6
- Smoke....15 B4
- Steak House....16 A3

DRINKING
- Bom Bom....17 A3
- Cocamangas Beach Bar....18 A2
- Cocamangas Nightclub....19 A2
- Hey Jude....20 A4
- Nigi Nigi Nu Noos....21 A4
- Summer Place....22 A4

TRANSPORT
- Asian Spirit....23 B3
- Seair....24 A3

PHILIPPINES

defines cool and is the best spot to kill time between dinner and late-night dancing.

The same three open-air bars have been dominating the late-night scene for years: **Hey Jude** (9am-late) is the swankiest of the lot and has the best DJs; **Summer Place** (11am-late) begins the evening as a Mongolian BBQ and ends it as White Beach's rowdiest disco; and **Cocamangas** (11am-late) has a shooters-crazy beach bar and a notoriously sleazy dance club across the main road.

GETTING THERE & AWAY

To get to Boracay you must first travel to Caticlan. From Caticlan small *bangka* ferries leave every 10 minutes or so throughout the day to Boracay's Cagban pier (P90 including terminal and environmental fee, 10 minutes). Tricycles from Cagban pier cost an extortionate P100 regardless of your destination.

Air

Asian Spirit (D'Mall) and **Seair** (D'Mall) each have flights roughly every half-hour throughout the day from Manila to Caticlan for about P3500. Asian Spirit has one daily flight between Cebu and Caticlan. From the airport to the pier in Caticlan it's a five-minute walk or a one-minute tricycle ride (P40).

Cebu Pacific has much cheaper flights from both Manila and Cebu to Kalibo in northern Panay, where air-con vans meet the flights and run to Caticlan pier (P100, 1½ hours). PAL also flies the Manila–Kalibo route.

Boat

MBRS Lines (Map pp596-7; ☎ 02-241 8497; Pier 8, North Harbor, Manila) has twice-weekly ferries between Manila and Caticlan (from P840, 12 hours).

From Caticlan there are six RORO ferries per day to Roxas, Mindoro (P330, four hours). From March to May, Negros Navigation runs a ferry along the Manila–Caticlan–Puerto Princesa route.

Bus

Ceres Lines has five daily buses to Iloilo from Caticlan, the last one departing at 2pm (ordinary/air-con P190/240, five hours), or take a van to Kalibo and grab a bus from there to Iloilo.

GETTING AROUND

To get from one end of White Beach to the other, either walk or flag down a tricycle along the main road. These cost only P7 provided you steer clear of the disingenuously named 'special' trips offered by stationary tricycles, which cost a not-so-special P40 to P60.

Iloilo

☎ 033 / pop 429,000

The highlight of Iloilo (*ill-o-ill-o*) is its Spanish colonial architecture, much of which is located in the Jaro district north of the city centre. Get a map from the **tourist office** (☎ 335 0245; Bonifacio Dr), next to Museo Iloilo.

With some interesting displays of furniture, memorabilia and treasure plucked from sunken ships, **Museo Iloilo** is worth a look. Adventure lovers should talk to anthropologist Daisy at **Panay Adventures** (☎ 0918 778 4364; panay_adventures@yahoo.com.ph), which organises mountain bike and trekking trips and eco-cultural tours to various tribal groups in Panay.

SLEEPING & EATING

Family Pension House (☎ 335 0070; General Luna St; s P275, d P350-575;) Backpackers love this homey neoclassical building with polished floorboards and clean, bargain-basement rooms. There's an internet café and an airy restaurant upstairs.

Highway 21 (☎ 335 1839; General Luna St; s/d from P600/750;) The rooms here are somewhat small but modern, with Buddhist art on the walls and elegant furnishings.

On General Luna St, east of the two hotels mentioned, you'll find the **Atrium Shopping Mall** (mains P50-75), with a good food court and a huge, modern supermarket. In the other direction, at the corner of General Luna and Jalandoni Sts, you'll find the **Times Square** (mains P50-75) open-air food court and **Bluejay Coffee & Delicatessen** (sandwiches P75-100, pastas P130), a superb deli with free wi-fi and imported-meat sandwiches.

GETTING THERE & AROUND

There are many daily flights to/from Manila with PAL, Cebu Pacific and Air Philippines. The latter two also have daily flights to/from Cebu. The **airport** (Diversion Rd) is in Mandurriao district, about 3km north of General Luna St.

Fastcraft operators Sea Jet, Oceanjet and Weesam Express take on the rough crossing between Iloilo and Bacolod (P230, one hour, 24 daily). Peso pinchers can opt for the twice-daily Montenegro RORO (P140, 2½ hours). **Milagrosa J Shipping Lines** (☎ 335 0955; Jarfel

Bldg, La Puz Norte) offers a twice-weekly service between Iloilo and Puerto Princesa (P1150, 30 hours). Negros Navigation sails weekly to/from Cagayan de Oro (P2000, 21 hours) via Bacolod. There are also many ferries to both Manila and Cebu. Iloilo has several piers – your tricycle driver should know which one you need.

Ceres buses to Caticlan (P233, five hours) leave every hour until 3pm from the brand-new **Tagbac Bus Terminal** (☎ 320 3163), about 7km north of the centre. Alternatively, you can take a bus to Kalibo and grab an air-con van there.

NEGROS

Negros is the sweet tooth of the Philippines, heart of the country's sugar production. Split in two by intimidating mountains, its unspoilt coastline and natural finery earn it plenty of traveller kudos. The Kanlaon volcano is being touted as the next big thing in volcano scrambling, while lovely, laid-back Dumaguete is a fine base for exploring the central Visayas – better than Cebu, in many ways. If you like to get away from it all, look no further than Sipalay.

Bacolod

☎ 034 / pop 500,000

Bacolod is a little too large and intractable to be of much appeal to travellers. The city boomed in the 19th century when Iloilo's clothing industry collapsed and the textile barons migrated across the Panay Gulf to try their luck at sugar. Most people in Bacolod still speak Ilongo, the language of Iloilo. Locals masquerade in grinning masks for October's **MassKara Festival**.

ACTIVITIES

The main reason to stay in Bacolod is to get permits for climbing in **Mt Kanlaon Natural Park** (admission P300), site of the highest peak in the Visayas (2645m). These can be obtained through Angelo Bivar at the **Park Superintendent Office** (☎ weekdays 433 3813, weekends 0917 301 1410 or 0919 836 1905; Penro compound, South Capitol Rd). In an effort to preserve the park's fragile ecosystem, access is tightly controlled and guides are mandatory, so call ahead to reserve a spot. There are three routes to the top, one of which can be done by fit climbers in a day. The climbing season is March to May and October to November.

The trekking is at least as good in bird-infested **Northern Negros Natural Park**, accessible from Patag, a small town due east of Silay. The park office in Silay can help you get a guide, or just ask around in Patag. The **Biodiversity Conservation Center** (☎ 433 9234; South Capitol Rd; 9am-5pm Mon-Sat) has information on the natural park and also runs a small zoo.

SLEEPING & EATING

Pension Bacolod (☎ 433 3377; 27 11th St; s P100-370, d P165-460;) Look no further than this professionally run bargain, with a diverse array of rooms on a quiet side street near the Ceres north bus terminal. Mice reportedly like this place too.

Around 21st St and Lacson you'll find a bunch of restaurants and bars popular with students, including **Bob's** (sandwiches P70-125), a clean, bright, coffee shop/deli/pizzeria/ice cream parlour with free wi-fi. There's another cluster of restaurants around Mayfair Plaza at 13th St and Lacson, or try the new SM Mall near the pier.

GETTING THERE & AWAY

Air Philippines and Cebu Pacific each fly at least daily to/from Manila and Cebu.

Fastcraft operators Sea Jet, Oceanjet and Weesam Express each run eight trips per day to Iloilo (P230, one hour). SuperFerry and Negros Navigation have several trips weekly to/from Manila (P1850, 23 hours), and also service Cagayan de Oro (P1650, 21 hours, weekly).

From the **Ceres north bus terminal** (cnr Lopez Jaena St & IV Ferrer Ave) there are several buses every morning to Cebu City (P550, including San Carlos–Toledo ferry; seven hours). Any bus heading north passes through Silay.

From the **Ceres south bus terminal** (cnr Lopez Jaena & San Sebastian Sts), buses run regularly until mid-afternoon to Dumaguete via Kabankalan (P230, 5½ hours), and until mid-evening to Sipalay (P180, 4½ hours).

To get to the Ceres terminals, take a 'Shopping' jeepney from city plaza for P7; after hours take a taxi (P60).

Sipalay

☎ 034 / pop 11,400

You could get stuck for days – make that months – in this remote fishing town on Negros' southwest edge. At delicious Sugar Beach a small outcrop of resorts caters to those looking to achieve the full Robinson Crusoe effect. The town proper has an endless beach where every morning fishermen unload their catches, which can include several-hundred-pound tuna. Divers should head 6km south of Sipalay to the pricier resorts of *barangay* (village) Punto Ballo.

SLEEPING

The following are two of the five resorts on Sugar Beach.

our pick **Driftwood Village** (☎ 0920 252 9472; www.driftwood-village.com; cottages P400-1100;) Hosts Daisy and Peter (he's Swiss) are a lot of fun, and so is their resort, which features 11 cosy *nipa* huts, good Thai food and a range of bar sports, including table football.

Takatuka Lodge & Dive Resort (☎ 0920 230 9174; www.takatuka-lodge.com; cottages P650-1450;) Awash in funky furniture, psychedelic colours and kitsch, this eclectic boutique place offers five rooms done up in different themes. The owner has an extensive collection of heavy metal music and makes a mean mango milk shake (P85).

If you're really on a tight budget and/or prefer to live among locals, stay opposite the City Park in Sipalay proper at the quaint **Langub Pension House** (☎ 0910 289 4393; cnr Lacson & Alvarez Sts; r P200-650;).

GETTING THERE & AWAY

Ceres buses to/from Bacolod leave every half-hour until evening (P180, 4½ hours). For Dumaguete, see opposite.

Sugar Beach is about 5km north of Sipalay proper, across two rivers. To get there arrange a boat transfer from your resort (per boat P250 to P400, 15 minutes), or take a tricycle via Montilla to *barangay* Nauhung (P150, 20 minutes), where small paddle boats will bring you across the river to Sugar Beach for P5.

Dumaguete

☎ 035 / pop 119,000

There are only a few Philippine provincial cities worth more than a day of your time, and Dumaguete (doo-ma-*get*-ay) is one of them. A huge college campus engulfs much of its centre, saturating the city with youthful energy and attitude. The location – in the shadow of twin-peaked Cuernos de Negros (1903m) and just a few clicks from some marvellous hiking, beaches and diving – takes care of the rest.

The city's main commercial drag is Perdices St, which runs from central Rizal Park up to Silliman University. However, most dining, drinking and strolling happens on and around the waterfront promenade flanking Rizal Blvd. The **city tourist office** (☎ 225 0549; City Hall, Santa Catalina St), east of Rizal Park, has maps.

ACTIVITIES

Budget-conscious divers looking to dive **Apo Island** – one of the top dive sites in the Philippines – can base themselves in Dumaguete, where accommodation costs much less than in Dauin, the principal jumping-off point for Apo Island. Snoopy Montenegro, owner of **Scuba Ventures** (☎ 0917 304 3033; Hibbard Ave), is the authority on Apo Island.

Back on terra firma there's **caving**, **rock climbing** and **trekking** around Cuernos de Negros and Mt Kanlaon in northern Negros. Michelle at **Dumaguete Outdoors** (☎ 226 2110; www.dumagueteoutdoors.com; 3 Noblefranca St) arranges tours and dispenses advice.

SLEEPING

Vintage Inn (☎ 225 1076; Legazpi St; s/d from P242/352;) Centrally located opposite the market, this place has some of the cheapest rooms in the Philippines. Rooms are hardly luxurious, but are bigger than expected, with wardrobes.

Harold's Mansion Tourist Inn (☎ 225 8000/1; www.haroldsmansion.com; 205 Hibbard Ave; dm/s/d from P275/330/415;) Besides offering free wi-fi and a roomy six-bed dorm room complete with balcony, Harold is a goldmine of information on the region.

Bethel Guest House (☎ 225 2000; www.bethelguesthouse.com; Rizal Blvd; s/d from P850/1000;) This big, bright, sea-facing property with spacious rooms, giant TVs and all the mod-cons is a worthwhile splurge.

EATING & DRINKING

Qyosko (cnr Santa Rosa & Perdices Sts; mains P50-75; 24hr) A budget traveller's dream, this spot serves up hot Filipino dishes, sandwiches and breakfast for under P50.

Persian Palate (San Juan St; dishes P50-100) Vegetarians will find much to praise on the menu here, including hummus and *baba ganoush* (eggplant purée). Outside they sell gyro-like pitta sandwiches for P25.

Why Not (☎ 225 4488; Rizal Blvd; mains P150-200; to 2am) The continental and Thai food here is wildly popular among foreigners, but Why

Not is most famous for its always-happening nightclub.

For live music there is a cluster of lively student bars on the waterfront about 2km north of Why Not. The best is **Hayahay** (Flores St), known for its reggae Wednesdays.

GETTING THERE & AWAY

Cebu Pacific, Air Philippines and PAL all fly daily to/from Manila.

OceanJet fastcraft go to/from Cebu (P800, four hours, daily) via Tagbilaran (P520, two hours) on Bohol. There are also RORO ferries to Cebu (see p627). For Siquijor, see right. SuperFerry and Sulpicio Lines have weekly trips to Manila (P2000, 25 hours).

From the nearby port of Tampi there are frequent fastcraft to Bato on Cebu island (P50, 20 minutes), from where there are buses to Cebu City and Moalboal.

Ceres Bus Lines (Perdices St) connects Dumaguete and Bacolod (P230, 5½ hours). Buses depart hourly until about 2.30pm, or you can get a bus to Kabankalan and transfer to Bacolod.

Getting to Sipalay requires three separate Ceres buses: Dumaguete–Bayawan (two hours), Bayawan–Hinoba-an (1½ hours) and Hinoba-an–Sipalay (45 minutes). The entire trip costs P150 and takes 4½ to 5½ hours, depending on waiting time in Bayawan.

SIQUIJOR

☎ 035 / pop 96,000

Spooky little Siquijor is renowned for its witches and healers, but don't be scared away. This is backpacker paradise, with breathtaking scenery and some of the best-value accommodation in the Philippines. With your own transport you can travel around the island in a day and explore beaches, colonial relics, waterfalls, caves and charming villages.

> **COCKSURE GAMBLERS**
>
> Heavy male drinking and bonding occur over gambling – on anything from *sabong* (cockfights) to horse racing. But *sabong* are what Filipino men get most excited about. All over the country, every Sunday and public holiday, irritable and expensive fighting birds are let loose on one another. The cockpits are full to bursting and the audience is high with excitement – as much as P100,000 may be wagered on a big fight. All this plus cheap booze, lots of guns, pimps, players and prostitutes make for an interesting life for police.

A good strategy is to arrange for motorbike hire (per day P500) at the pier in Siquijor town when you arrive and investigate accommodation options on your own. The best budget places are in **Sandugan**, 15km northeast of Siquijor town. The best beaches and a few good midrange lodging options are along the west coast at **Solangon**, 9km southwest of Siquijor town. The marine reserve near Sandugan gets many divers' tails wagging.

Sleeping

Guiwanon Spring Park Resort (☎ 0926 978 6012; cottages P250-300) The three cottages here are essentially stilted, over-water tree houses in the middle of a mangrove forest. They are very basic, but two of them directly face the ocean. It's certainly one of the quirkiest lodging experiences you'll ever have, but check it out first to see if it's for you. It's about 5km east of Siquijor town.

Coral Cay Resort (☎ 0919 269 1269; www.coralcayresort.com; d P750-2500; ✣ 🏊) This resort has lavish rooms on a perfect stretch of white-sand beach at Solangon. There's an infinity pool, mountain-bike rental, sea kayaks, windsurfing, plenty of palm trees and the only thatch-hut gym we've ever seen.

In Sandugan the two best options are neighbouring **Kiwi Dive Resort** (☎ 424 0534; www.kiwidiveresort.com; dm P200, d P450-790; ✣) and **Islander's Paradise** (☎ 0918 332 0906; www.islandersparadisebeach.com; d P300-850). The latter's cottages are all beachfront.

Getting There & Around

The vast majority of visitors arrive at the pier in Siquijor town via diminutive fastcraft from Dumaguete. There are at least four trips per day each way (P190, one hour). Montenegro Lines has two daily RORO ferries from Dumaguete to Larena, 9km northeast of Siquijor town (P180, two hours). Palacio Shipping has five weekly boats from Larena to Cebu (P360, eight hours) via Tagbilaran (P274, two hours).

Jeepneys meet ferries at the pier and run to all points on the perimeter of the island.

CEBU

Surrounded on all sides by the Philippine isles and dotted with tranquil fishing villages, Cebu is the island heart of the Visayas. Cebuanos are proud of their heritage – it is here that Magellan sowed the seed of Christianity and was pruned for his efforts at the hands of the mighty chief Lapu-Lapu. The island's booming metropolis, Cebu City, is a transport hub to pretty much anywhere you may wish to go. Pescador Island, near the laid-back town of Moalboal, placed Philippine diving on the world map, while the Malapascua marine scene boasts close encounters of the thresher-shark kind.

Cebu City

☎ 032 / pop 843,000

The island capital is much more laid-back than Manila as a place to arrive in or leave the Philippines. One of the first stops on Spain's conquest agenda, Cebu lays claim to everything old – including the oldest street (Colon St), the oldest university and the oldest fort. By night Cebu turns decidedly hedonistic. However, the excellent transport links to the rest of the Philippines are the city's biggest attraction.

Cebu's downtown district (Map p625) is its mercantile nucleus. Most of the sights are here, but you must wade through exhaust fumes, beggars, prostitutes and block after block of downmarket retail madness to get to them. Uptown (Map p626) is much more pleasant and has better accommodation.

PHILIPPINES

INFORMATION

There are plenty of internet cafés and ATMs around.

Cebu Doctors Hospital (Map p626; ☎ 253 7511; Pres Osmeña Blvd) Near the Capitol Building.

Central post office (Map p625; Quezon Blvd)

Department of Tourism Downtown (Map p625; ☎ 254 2811; LDM Bldg, Legazpi St; ⌚ 7.30am-5.30pm Mon-Fri); Mactan International Airport (off Map p625; ☎ 340 8229; ⌚ 6am-8pm) The downtown office is near Fort San Pedro.

HSBC Bank (off Map p626; Ayala Center, Lahug district) Allows P20,000 withdrawals.

National Bookstore (Map p626; General Maxilom Ave) Good range of maps but threadbare book collection.

Visayas Community Hospital (off Map p626; ☎ 253 3025; Osmeña Blvd)

SIGHTS

Fort San Pedro (Map p625; Legazpi St; admission P20; ⌚ 8am-6pm) was built by Miguel Legazpi in 1565 as a defence against marauding pirates. This gently crumbling ruin with gardens is the oldest Spanish fort in the country. The Santo Niño statuette is the main attraction in the **Basilica Minore del Santo Niño** (Map p625; Juan Luna St), built in 1740. This image of Jesus as a child is said to have been given to Queen Juana of Cebu by Magellan on the queen's baptism in 1521. It's the oldest religious relic in the country.

In the central Parian district, the **Casa Gorordo Museum** (Map p625; ☎ 255 5630; 35 L Jaena St; admission P70; ⌚ 10am-6pm) is in an astonishingly beautiful mid-19th-century house that was restored in 2006.

Mactan Island, where Magellan came a distant second in a fight with Chief Lapu-Lapu, is now the site of Cebu's airport and is joined to the city by a bridge. There are several **guitar factories** on Pajac-Maribago Rd, southwest of the airport. The most tourist friendly is **Alegre** (☎ 340 4492; ⌚ 8am-6pm Mon-Sat), with hundreds of beautiful guitars (P2000 to P60,000) on display.

SLEEPING

While good super-budget rooms are hard to find in Cebu, there are some terrific deals in the P800 to P1000 range. If the following are full, there's a cluster of cheap pension houses in the vicinity of Jasmine Pension on DG Garcia St.

our pick **Kukuk's Nest Pension House** (Map p626; ☎ 231 5180; www.geocities.com/kukuksnestcebu; 157 Gorordo Ave; s P315, d P450-700; ❄ 🖳) This colourful old house defines 'quirky', with contemporary art hanging about, a resident armless charcoal sketcher and a 24-hour resto-bar that draws all types. Booking ahead is essential.

Jasmine Pension (Map p626; ☎ 254 2686; cnr Jasmine & DG Garcia Sts; s/d from P480/580; ❄) Located in a pretty yellow building with a North Asian feel, Jasmine has a few spacious, wood-lined rooms – some with fab retro black-tile bathrooms.

> **GETTING INTO TOWN**
>
> Metered taxis between Cebu City and Mactan International Airport cost around P150. A cheaper option is to take a tricycle (if you can find one) to Lapu-Lapu city and then take a 'Lahug' jeepney into town from there (P6).
>
> To get uptown from the ports, catch one of the jeepneys that pass by the piers to Pres Osmeña Blvd, then transfer to a jeepney going uptown.

Mayflower Pension House (Map p626; ☎ 255 2800; www.mayflowerpensionhouse.com; Villalon Dr; s/d P650/900;) The rooms are spacious, the soundproofing is tight and the earthy-toned paint is meticulously applied at this clean and modern gem.

Casa Rosario (Map p626; ☎ 255 0535; R Aboitiz St; s/d P900/1000;) Cebu's best midrange option, this is a warm, welcoming place in an ideal location. The rooms are airy and some have balconies facing the northern hills.

Also recommended:

Hotel de Mercedes (Map p625; ☎ 253 1105; 7 Pelaez St; s/d from 600/820;) Good option if you need to stay downtown.

C'est La Vie Pension (Map p626; ☎ 253 5266; 13 J Osmeña St; d from P650;) Fantastic value near Casa Rosario.

Pensionne La Florentina (Map p626; ☎ 231 3318; 18 Acacia St; s/d P650/750;) Quiet digs in a stately wooden house.

EATING

Pete's Kitchen (Map p625; Pelaez St; mains P75-100) A local favourite, this Filipino-style eatery is actually two restaurants – walk south to the more ambient outdoor version across from Metrobank.

Sideline Garden Restaurant (Map p626; J Osmeña St; mains P75-150) The smell of fresh seafood being grilled under a large pagoda heralds the presence of this charming streetside eatery. Equally pleasant for eating or drinking.

Indian Ocean (Map p626; N Escario St; mains P100-150; 4pm-4am) This late-night hangout near

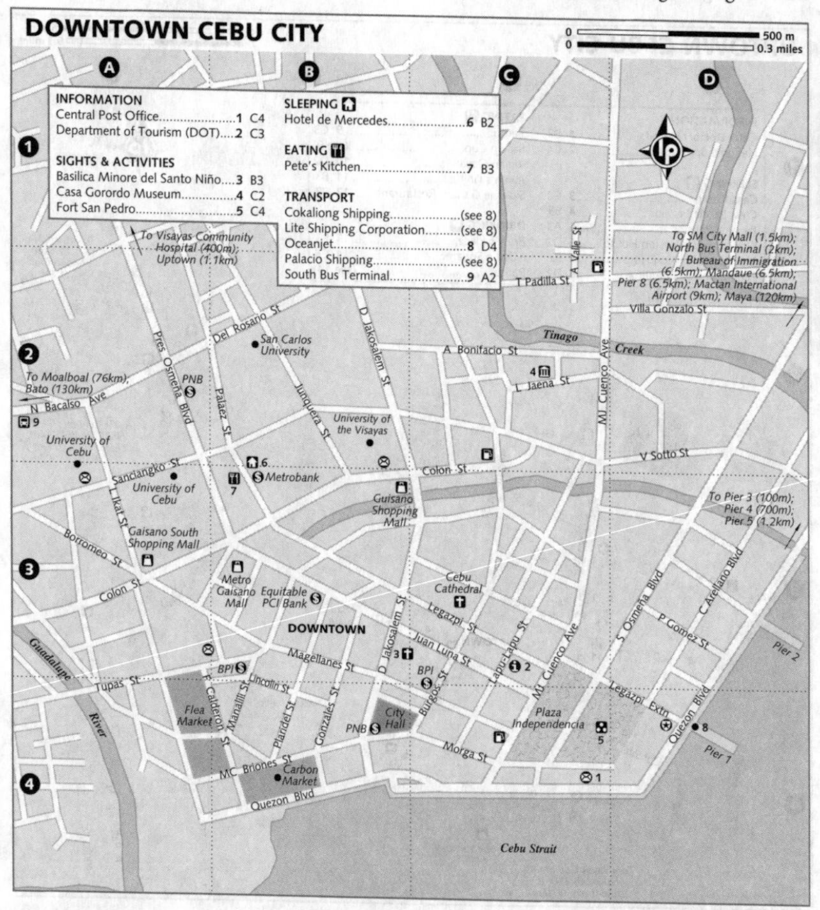

PHILIPPINES

Kukuk's Nest has great curries and other specialities of the subcontinent. It also serves mediocre Middle Eastern food.

Joven's Grill (Map p626; cnr Pres Osmeña Blvd & Jasmine St; all-you-can-eat buffet P145; lunch & dinner) The best place to gorge after an extended boat journey.

As in Manila, many of the best restaurants are in the malls, particularly the **Ayala Center** (off Map p626; Lahug district). On the ground floor you'll find good Thai cuisine at **Lemongrass** (Pad Thai P155), while Mexican food and Margarita lovers should head to **Tequila Joe's** (mains P150-250). There's a food court on the 3rd floor for budget meals.

St Patrick's Sq (Map p626) near Casa Rosario has a great little coffee shop, **Brown Cup** (breakfast P100), and a few cheap restaurants, including affordable Japanese eatery **Bento** (sushi platters P100).

DRINKING

Brew's Place (Map p626; J Osmeña St) Near Sideline Garden Restaurant, this is another fantastic place to perch for a few hours while hoisting cold ones. Inoffensive live acoustic music plays until at least 2am nightly.

Ratsky (off Map p626; Ayala Center; 11am-3am) This live-music club has all-you-can-consume pizza *and* beer for just P150 from 2pm to 6pm daily. After that you'll be so oiled that it won't matter whether the music is any good.

Mango Square (Map p626; cnr Gen Maxilom Ave & J Osmeña St) There are a couple of rowdy bars

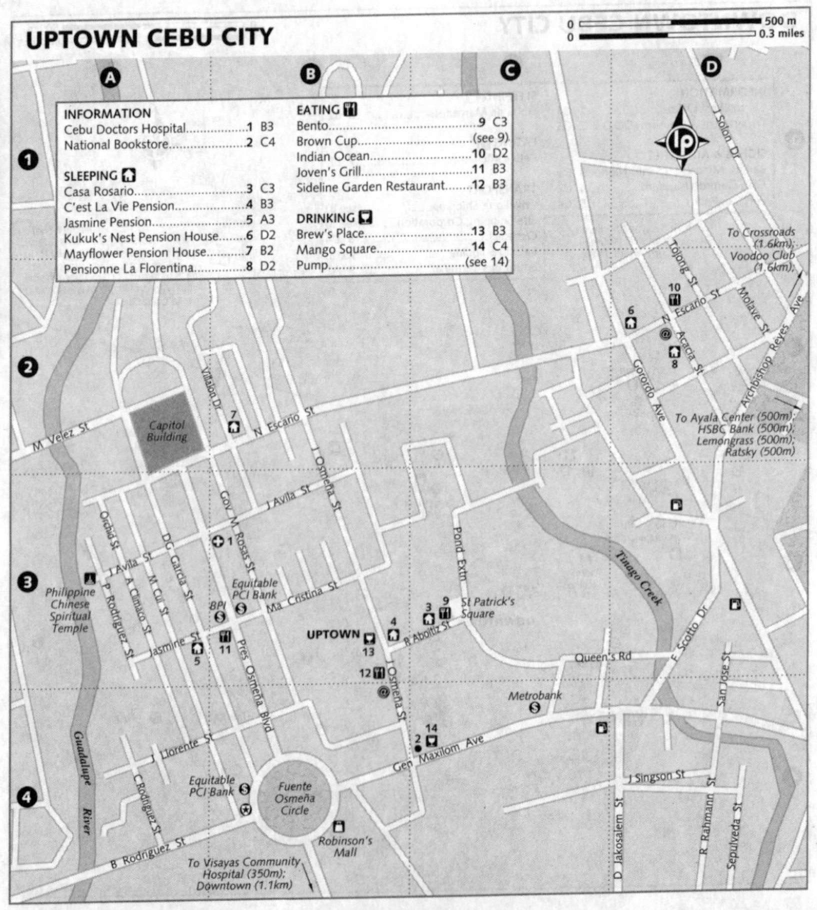

upstairs at this complex, as well as the more upscale club Pump (admission P100).

Serious clubbers will want to head north to the Crossroads strip mall in Lahug and try to breach the velvet rope at swanky **Voodoo Club** (off Map p626; admission P150). It's a five-minute cab ride (P50) northeast of the Ayala Center.

GETTING THERE & AWAY

Air

For international flights into Cebu's Mactan International Airport, see p590. Cebu Pacific, Air Philippines and PAL all have regular connections to Manila. Cebu Pacific also has nonstop flights from Cebu to a number of regional centres, including Puerto Princesa, Kalibo, Bacolod and Iloilo.

Boat

Many of the long-haul ferries from Manila to ports in the southern islands stop in Cebu City, including SuperFerry and Sulpicio Lines. Fastcraft such as SuperCat, Oceanjet and Weesam Express have speedy connections to Bohol, Leyte and Negros. Check the weekly schedules in the *Sun Star* and *Cebu Daily News* for updates.

Useful shipping companies in Cebu City include the following:

Cokaliong Shipping (Map p625; ☎ 232 7211-18; www.cokaliongshipping.com; Pier 1) Boats to Surigao (P850, 13½ hours, daily except Monday); Maasin, Leyte (P390, five hours, five weekly); Dumaguete (P393, six hours, daily); Tagbilaran (P150, four hours, six weekly); and Iloilo (P778, 12 hours, three weekly).

Kinswell (off Map p625; ☎ 416 6516; Pier 3) Boats to Bato, Leyte (P350, three hours, daily); and Tubigon, Bohol (P168, 1½ hours, two daily).

Lite Shipping Corporation (Map p625; ☎ 255 1721; Pier 1) Ferries to Tagbilaran (P300, four hours, two daily); and Ormoc, Leyte (P450, 4½ hours, six weekly).

Oceanjet (Map p625; ☎ 255 7560; www.oceanjet.net; Pier 1) Oceanjet has boats to Tagbilaran (P300, two hours, four daily) and Dumaguete (P800, four hours, daily).

Palacio Shipping (Map p625; ☎ 255 4538; Pier 1) Has ferries to Larena, Siquijor (P360, eight hours, five weekly) via Tagbilaran (P95, four hours).

Roly Shipping Lines (off Map p625; ☎ 234 0827; Pier 3) Boats to Tubigon, Bohol (P158, two hours, two daily).

Sulpicio Lines (off Map p625; ☎ 232 5361; www.sulpiciolines.com; Pier 5) Ferries to Manila (P1800, 22 hours, five weekly), Cagayan de Oro (P728, 11 hours, four weekly) and Surigao (P504, eight hours, weekly).

SuperCat (off Map p625; ☎ 234 9630-34; www.supercat.com.ph; Pier 4) Supercat has boats to Ormoc (P672, 2¾ hours, four daily) and Tagbilaran (P350, two hours, three daily).

SuperFerry (off Map p625; ☎ 233 7000; www.superferry.com.ph; Pier 4) Four boats weekly to Manila (P1900, 23 hours) and two boats weekly to Cagayan de Oro (P800, eight hours).

Super Shuttle Ferry (off Map p625; ☎ 233 5733; Pier 8) Ferries to Ormoc (P336, seven hours, six weekly) and Camiguin (P616, eight hours, weekly).

Trans-Asia Shipping Lines (off Map p625; ☎ 254 6491; www.transasiashipping.com; Pier 5) Ferries to Cagayan de Oro (P950, 12½ hours, daily) and Iloilo (P1150, 14 hours, daily).

Weesam Express (off Map p625; ☎ 412 9562; www.weesamexpress.com; Pier 4) Boats to Tagbilaran (P300, two hours, four daily) and Ormoc (P550, 2½ hours, two daily).

You can buy tickets for all ferries at the handy **Travellers Lounge** (☎ 232 0291; 🕑 8am-8pm) just outside SM City Mall. You can also buy tickets at the piers.

Bus

There are two bus stations in Cebu. **Ceres Bus Lines** (☎ 345 8650) services southern and central destinations, such as Bato (P150, 3¼ hours) via Moalboal (P90, 2½ hours), from the **South bus terminal** (Map p625; Bacalso Ave). Air-con vans ('V-hires') leave for Moalboal from the Citilink station near the South bus terminal (P80, two hours).

The **North bus terminal** (Wireless St) is beyond SM City Mall. From here Ceres has frequent buses to Hagnaya (P70, three hours) for Bantayan Island, and Maya (P90, four to five hours) for Malapascua Island.

Moalboal

☎ 032 / pop 26,400

The Philippines' original dive hotbed, Moalboal remains a throwback to the days when diving came cheap and minus the attitude. **Panagsama Beach**, where the resorts are, meanders lazily along a sea wall within rock-skipping distance of a stunning diving wall (also snorkellable). While the beach itself is hardly worthy of the name, Moalboal's mellow vibe and quirky, mischievous nightlife attract divers and nondivers alike.

ACTIVITIES

Divers can paddle out to the coral-studded wall or take a 10-minute *bangka* ride to **Pescador Island**, which swarms with marine life. A single-tank dive shouldn't exceed US$25.

PHILIPPINES

Beach lovers can take a *habal-habal* (P20) 3km north to lovely **White Beach**. For adrenalin junkies, **Planet Action** (☎ 0916 624 8253; www.action-philippines.com), run by the wry and affable Jochen, runs mountain biking, canyoning and other mountain tours, including a trip across the Tañon Strait to climb Mt Kanlaon on Negros (see p621).

SLEEPING

Mollie's Place (☎ 0917 254 7060; d P500-1500) Mollie's has a few cute concrete cottages with a shared bathroom, along with much roomier but TV-less air-con abodes.

Sunshine Pension House (☎ 474 0049; sunshinepension@yahoo.com; d from P600;) It's on the wrong side of the beach path but this place is great value, with a clear pool, a Swiss restaurant and sizeable fan rooms.

Coral's Palm Court (☎ 0906 210 3876; r P700-1200;) Earthy owner Philip has been running this character-laden backpacker haunt near the bar strip on Panagsama Beach since 1984. He offers discounts to like-minded souls.

Quo Vadis (☎ 474 0018; www.visayadivers.info; d P750-2000;) This place is pure money, with spectacular views and gigantic rooms littered with bamboo furniture. Its nearby sister resort, Nido's Garden, has rooms for P500 to P750.

EATING & DRINKING

Drinking is the national sport of the Moalboal Republic, and there are dozens of eateries where you can secure food to soak up the deluge of beer.

Chilli Bar (mains P150-200) A tried-and-true recipe of bar sports, shooters and comely waiters ensures a solid crowd every night at this place.

Last Filling Station (Thai dishes P165) On an isolated perch south of the bar strip, this is an ideal spot to watch the sunset.

Sunset View & Restaurant (mains P175) More great views and P25 San Miguel.

Lloyd's Music Lounge takes over when others shut down, while the Saturday-night discos at Pacita's Resort are famous – or infamous, depending on your point of view.

GETTING THERE & AROUND

Ceres buses pass through town heading south to Bato (P60, two hours) and north to Cebu's South bus terminal (P89, 2½ hours) regularly until about 5.30pm. To Cebu, there are also air-con vans driven by notoriously sadistic drivers (P80, two hours).

Tricycles to Panagsama Beach from Moalboal cost P35.

Malapascua Island

Blessed with a long ribbon of pearly white sand, this little island off the northern tip of Cebu has long been touted as 'the next Boracay'. Truth be told, this sleepy little dive mecca remains light years away from that goal, although gradually rising prices are starting to turn backpackers away.

ACTIVITIES

Thresher sharks are the big attraction here. Divers head out at 5.30am to **Monad Shoal**, where they park on the seabed at 35m hoping to catch a glimpse of these critters. The chances are pretty good – about 75%. By day Monad Shoal attracts manta rays. More terrestrial sorts can lounge on Malapascua's signature **Bounty Beach**, or hike the walking path leading up to the **lighthouse** on the northern tip.

SLEEPING

Malapascua's electricity grid functions only from 6pm to midnight, so make sure your resort has a generator to avoid sweltering to death.

BB's (☎ 0916 756 6018; r from P300) The fan rooms here are serviceable and friendly on the wallet but get hot when the power cuts out at midnight. It's off the beach, next to Ging-Ging's restaurant.

White Sands Bungalows (☎ 0927 318 7471; s/d P600/700) These simple raised, thatched, beachfront cottages facing less touristy Poblacion Beach are the best value in Malapascua. Danish owner Kurt is useful for tips and sets a perfect vibe.

Cocobana Beach Resort (☎ 437 1001; www.cocobana.ch; s/d from P800/1100;) This is Malapascua's first resort; the 24-hour generator, speedy internet connection and good restaurant here make it worth the splurge.

EATING & DRINKING

Expect anything on Bounty Beach to cost more than you want to pay.

Ging-Ging's Flower Garden (mains P35-77) Inland from the beach, Ging-Ging's serves tasty, cheap, filling vegetarian food and curries and P30 San Miguel.

La Isla Bonita Restaurant (pizzas from P120, mains about P180) Next to Ging-Ging's, this is still the best restaurant on the island even after the recent passing of its founder, Uwe. It concocts an array of Greek, Thai and Indian dishes.

Sunsplash (⏰ 7am-late) Despite the floating bar, pool tables and 'drink for your country' shooter-drinking competitions, this open-air resto-bar stays mellow *most* of the time.

GETTING THERE & AWAY

The scheduled boat from Maya (P50, 20 to 40 minutes) to Malapascua leaves when full. Get to Maya before 5pm or you may miss the last trip and have to charter a boat for P800.

For information on getting to Maya from Cebu City see p627. The last bus heading back to Cebu City leaves around 6pm.

BOHOL

Bohol is a short hop from Cebu. It's difficult to reconcile its bloody history with the relaxed isle of today. It's here that Francisco Dagohoy led the longest revolt in the country against the Spaniards, from 1744 to 1829. The Chocolate Hills, rounded mounds resembling chocolate drops, are the big tourist magnet. Bohol also has endearing little primates, coral cathedrals off Panglao Island and lush jungle, ripe for exploration, around the town of Loboc.

GETTING THERE & AWAY

Tagbilaran is the main gateway, but there are also many ferries between Cebu and Tubigon in northwest Bohol (see the shipping companies under Boat, p627), and twice-daily RORO ferries between Bato, Leyte, and Ubay in northeast Bohol (P180, 2½ hours).

Tagbilaran

☎ 038 / pop 91,000

There's no reason to waste much time in traffic-snarled Tagbilaran. Your first port of call should be the newly opened **tourist office** (⏰ 8am-6pm) at the ferry dock, which can help with transport arrangements.

If you do need to stay the night, your best bet is **Nisa Travelers Inn** (☎ 411 3731; CP Garcia Ave; s/d from P250/750; ❄), with a nice range of rooms in an attractive wooden townhouse. Eat, cool off and escape the tricycle madness across the street in the food court in BQ Mall.

Cebu Pacific and PAL each fly from Tagbilaran to Manila twice daily.

There are various fastcraft and slow craft heading to Cebu every day (see the shipping companies under Boat, p627). OceanJet operates a daily fastcraft to/from Dumaguete (P520, two hours). SuperFerry has two weekly trips to/from Manila (P2100, 26 hours). Trans Asia has three trips weekly and SuperFerry one trip weekly to/from Cagayan de Oro.

The main bus terminal is in Dao, a few kilometres north of the centre; 'multicabs' (small jeepneys) run here from the city market on Carlos P Garcia St (P6).

To avoid expensive van rides and tricky public transport connections on Bohol, consider hiring your own motorbike at Tagbilaran pier for about P350 per day.

Around Tagbilaran

It's just a short drive north of Tagbilaran to two of the Philippines' signature attractions – the **Chocolate Hills** and that lovable palm-sized primate, the **tarsier**.

You can visit both in a single day on an excursion from Tagbilaran, but you're much better off basing yourself in Loboc at **Nuts Huts** (☎ 0920 846 1559; www.nutshuts.com; dm P200-250, d P450-650), a backpacker Shangri-la in the middle of the jungle. With a sublime location overlooking the emerald-tinged Loboc River, Nuts Huts provides at least as much reason to visit inland Bohol as brown loam lumps or miniature monkeys. The Belgian hosts can tell you everything you need to know about exploring the area, and you can hike and mountain bike on a network of trails in the immediate vicinity.

To get to Nuts Huts from Tagbilaran, catch a Carmen-bound bus and get off at the Nuts Huts sign (P25, one hour). It's a 15-minute walk from the road. Alternatively, take a bus to Loboc and then a *habal-habal* (P50) or shuttle boat up the river from the Sarimanok landing (P130/160/240 for one/two/three passengers).

You are unlikely to spot the nocturnal tarsier in the wild, so head to the **Tarsier Visitors Center** (requested donation P20; ⏰ 9am-4pm) in *barangay* Canapnapan, between the towns of Corella and Sikatuna. About 10 saucer-eyed tarsiers hang out in the immediate vicinity of the centre – the guides will bring you right to them. This is a much more humane and eco-friendly way to appreciate the tarsier, better than visiting the animals kept in cages by tourist operators in Loboc.

From Nuts Huts the Tarsier Center is a 30- to 45-minute motorbike ride, or take a jeepney from Loboc (P15, 45 minutes). From Tagbilaran catch a bus or jeepney to Sikatuna (P25, one hour) from the Dao terminal and ask to be dropped off at the centre.

An interesting quirk of nature, the **Chocolate Hills** consist of over 1200 conical hills, up to 120m high. They were supposedly formed over time by the uplift of coral deposits and the effects of rainwater and erosion. Since this explanation cannot be confirmed, the local belief that they are the remnants of a battle between two giants may one day prove to be correct. In the dry season, when the vegetation turns brown, the hills are at their most chocolate-y.

From Nuts Huts, the Chocolate Hills are a 45-minute motorbike ride; alternatively, flag down a bus bound for Carmen (4km north of the Chocolate Hills). From Tagbilaran there are regular buses from the Dao terminal to Carmen (P60, two hours). From Carmen, *habal-habal* whisk tourists up to the main Chocolate Hills viewing point (P30). A more fun method is to take a *habal-habal* in and around the hills; a 1½-hour ride costs P250.

PHILIPPINES

Panglao Island

☎ 038

Linked by two bridges to Bohol, Panglao is where divers head to take advantage of the spectacular coral formations and teeming marine life on the nearby islands of Balicasag, Cabilao and Pamilacan. Ground zero for divers is **Alona Beach**, which is sort of like a mini Boracay minus the stunning beach and nightlife. As Alona Beach has gone upscale in recent years, its appeal to budget travellers has waned. Even the diving is more expensive than elsewhere – at least US$30 per dive with equipment.

ACTIVITIES

Most resorts offer early morning dolphin watching tours near Pamilacan Island, but the best group to go with is the community-based **Pamilacan Island Dolphin & Whale Watching Tours** (☎ 540 9279; per person P850-1900 depending on group size), which uses old converted whaling boats and local crews. Spotting whales is rare, but you almost always see dolphins. It's based in Baclayan, 6km east of Tagbilaran, but they do pick-ups on Alona Beach. Smaller groups are better off with Alona Beach dive outfit **Baywatch** (☎ 502 9028; 4-person boat P1500).

SLEEPING & EATING

Citadel Alona Inn (☎ 502 9424; www.citadelalona.com; d P500-700;) Inland from the beach is this appealing, artsy house where all rooms share squeaky-clean bathrooms. There's a big kitchen for self-caterers.

Bohol Divers Resort (☎ 502 9047; s P500, d P800-6000;) This sprawling complex is one of the few places on the beach still offering budget rooms. Accommodation runs the gamut from basic fan rooms to upscale villas.

Beachfront dining opportunities on Alona Beach are ample but come at a price. The one notable exception is **Trudi's Place** (mains P65-95, beer P30). Other affordable eateries and bars are located north of the beach, on the way to Citadel Alona. The **Powder Keg** (mains P100-150) has meaty mains, P30 San Miguel, darts and a crusty expat clientele.

GETTING THERE & AROUND

From Tagbilaran, minibuses to Panglao town leave when full from the corner of Dagahoy and F Rocha Sts (P18, 50 minutes). Get off in Tawala and walk 15 minutes or take a tricycle (P40) to Alona Beach. An easier option is to hire a *habal-habal* (P150) or tricycle (P200, 25 to 45 minutes).

SAMAR & LEYTE

'Rugged' is usually the word you hear associated with these two eastern Visayan provinces, separated from each other by the narrowest of straits near Leyte's capital, Tacloban. It's an apt tag. The interior of both islands is consumed by virtually impenetrable forest. This naturally creates opportunities for adventure, although you either have to learn advanced backcountry navigation or scrounge up one of the region's few qualified guides to take advantage of it.

The coastlines of both islands serve up a few gems of their own, most notably tourist-free whale shark viewing in southern Leyte. For fanatical surfers, the eastern seashore of Samar offers a coastline of unexplored breaks facing the onslaught of Pacific currents – getting there is the only problem. There's history here too – in 1521 Magellan first stepped ashore on what would become Philippine soil on the island of Homonhon, off Samar. In October 1944, General MacArthur fulfilled his pledge to return to the Philippines on Red Beach south of Tacloban. And who can forget the notorious Balangiga Massacre (see boxed text, p632)?

ALL CREATURES SMALL & GREAT

Contrary to popular belief, the loveable tarsier is *not* the world's smallest primate. That distinction belongs to the pygmy mouse lemur of Madagascar. However, the Philippines can still proudly lay claim to the world's smallest hoofed mammal – the rare Philippine mouse deer of Palawan. Meanwhile, the Philippines' 24mm *Hippocampus bargibanti* recently lost the title of world's smallest seahorse to a newly discovered rival in Indonesia: the 16mm *Hippocampus denise*.

Catbalogan

☎ 055 / pop 98,000

Catbalogan is the preferred base for exploring the interior of Samar. A ban on motorized tricycles in the city centre also makes it a pleasant stopover on the road from Allen to Tacloban. From the pier you can spot about 30 different islands offshore, plus some giant peaks in northern Leyte.

Spelunking, climbing, scrambling, birdwatching, mountain biking – you name it, Samar's got it. **Trexplore** (☎ 251 2301; www.bonifaciojoni.blogspot.com; Allen Ave), run by North Face–clad Joni Bonifacio, is the only one doing tours around here, and yes, you will need a guide. Check out his website for some ecotourism ideas. Joni specialises in tours of the **Langub-Gobingob Cave** near Calbiga, 50km south of Catbalogan. It is one of the longest caves in the world and hosts rare blind crabs.

SLEEPING & EATING

Casa Cristina (☎ 543 9237; r from P200; ⊠) This budget option has decent fan-cooled rooms decorated with brightly coloured walls. The shared bathrooms are clean.

Rolet Hotel (☎ 251 5512; s/d P750/950; ⊠) The well-kept rooms here (some windowless) are somewhat small, but you could bounce a 25 centavo coin on the expertly made beds. Unbelievable value.

For American-style snacks and pizza try **Ernie's Pizza** (pizzas P65-135) by the town square. **Fortune Restaurant** (555 Del Rosario St; mains P75-225) has yummy Chinese food.

GETTING THERE & AWAY

Asian Spirit flies thrice weekly from Manila to Calbayog, a two-hour bus ride north of Catbalogan. Palacio Shipping has three weekly ferries between Catbalogan and Cebu (P531, eight hours).

Eagle Star buses plod north to Allen (P122, five hours), where you catch the ferry to Matnog in southeast Luzon (P74, one hour). Heading south to Tacloban there are buses (P100, three hours) and air-con vans. The brutal road to Tacloban is gradually being repaired, which should trim travel times.

Sohoton Caves & Natural Bridge

Named for a magnificent stone bridge connecting two mountain ridges, this **national park** (admission P150) has an expansive cave system, subterranean rivers, waterfalls and limestone formations. Day trips include a one- to two-hour cave tour (per group without/with guide P300/500; fees include kerosene lanterns), or you can just walk to the natural bridge. You can sleep inside the park at the simple **DENR Guest House** (☎ 053-327 9528; per person P150).

To get to the park you need to take a *bangka* (per boat P700, two hours) from the pier in Basey, which is in southwest Samar just over the San Juanico bridge from Tacloban, Leyte. In Basey go to the **Municipal Tourism Office** (☎ 055-276 1471) near the pier to pay the park entry and boat fees. Regular jeepneys (P20, 45 minutes) and swifter vans head to Basey from the bus terminal in Tacloban. The last trip back from Basey is around 5pm. Trina at the regional tourism office in Tacloban (see below) is an excellent source of information on the park.

Tacloban

☎ 053 / pop 209,000

The birthplace of Imelda Marcos – the 'Rose of Tacloban' – is a busy commercial centre and transport hub. It's hardly chic, but it does have a strip of decent restaurants where you can escape the rat race and cool off with an iced latte and air-con. Travellers between Cebu and southern Leyte won't pass through here, as most ships from Cebu pull into Ormoc.

The **regional tourism office** (☎ 321 2048; F Mendoza Commercial Complex, 141 Santo Niño St) has maps, brochures and information about both Leyte and Samar.

There's a unique **memorial** of Macarthur's Red Beach landing in Palo, 6km south of Tacloban. Grab a 'Palo' jeepney to get there. Northwest of Tacloban, volcanic **Biliran Island** has some splendid beaches and waterfalls. For how to get there, see Getting There & Away, p632.

PHILIPPINES

SLEEPING & EATING

Steer clear of the noisy, congested city centre and stay closer to the internet cafés, restaurants and bars around Burgos St.

Welcome House Pension (☎ 321 2739; 161 Santo Niño St; s/d from P350/500; ❄) This quiet place set off the street has an assortment of bright, immaculate rooms. It's especially good value for groups of three or four. TVs cost extra.

Rosvenil Pensione (☎ 321 2676; Burgos St; s/d from P410/500; ❄) Located in a great rambling house with a pleasant garden out the front, Rosvenil offers an enticing mix of rooms, including some truly swanky digs in its new wing.

Restaurant row is Veteranos Ave near the corner of MH del Pilar St. Near there you can scratch your Mexican food itch at **Hugo's American & Mexican Cuisine** (cnr Burgos & MH del Pilar Sts; burritos from P120).

GETTING THERE & AWAY

Cebu Pacific and PAL each have three daily flights to Tacloban from Manila. Long-haul ferries run to Manila from the **pier** (Bonifacio St).

Most land transport now uses the new bus terminal, about 3km west of the old waterfront bus terminal. You'll find plenty of transport to Catbalogan (bus/van P100/120, three/2½ hours) and other points on Samar; Ormoc (bus/van P100/120, three/two hours); Naval on Biliran Island (bus/van P120/150, three/two hours); and Sogod (bus P100, 2½ hours), where there are connections to Padre Burgos and Pintuyan.

Ormoc

☎ 053 / pop 181,000

Ormoc is mainly a springboard for boats to Cebu. If you arrive late, stay in the hulking **Don Felipe Hotel** (☎ 255 2460; cnr Bonifacio St & Imelda Blvd; s/d from P360/580; ❄) on the waterfront opposite the pier. Pricier rooms have wonderful views.

SuperCat runs four efficient but pricey fastcraft per day to Cebu (P672, 2¾ hours). For slower, cheaper options see Boat on p627. Conveniently, the bus terminal is just over the road from the port, with connections to Tacloban and all points south.

Southern Leyte

☎ 053

Leyte's bowlegged rump straddles Sogod Bay, where **whale sharks** frolic from about mid-October to late April. The sharks here are fewer and more elusive than their more famous cousins in Donsol (see p613), but for many this just makes the thrill of spotting one that much greater. For now the village of Pintuyan, where the whale sharks congregate, is a far cry from the *butanding*-chasing frenzy of Donsol. That's largely because whale sharks only recently started coming to Pintuyan. They were once further north, near Lilo-an, but have gradually moved south – some say because of increased boat traffic around Lilo-an. The hope is that Pintuyan is too remote to draw Donsol's hordes. If you go, tread softly around these beasts and go only with sanctioned operators, who are collectively working to control the number of visitors.

THE BALANGIGA MASSACRE

On 28 September 1901, Filipino guerrillas masquerading as women massacred 59 members of the US garrison stationed at Balangiga in Eastern Samar. For the Americans it was the bloodiest day of the Filipino–American War, and it triggered a massive retribution campaign led by General Jacob 'Howling Mad' Smith, who killed scores of innocent civilians while fulfilling his vow to turn Samar into a 'howling wilderness'. There is an annual re-enactment and commemoration on that date.

PADRE BURGOS

If you have the money, an organised boat trip from this friendly little dive colony (simply called 'Burgos') is the easiest way to see the whale sharks. The dive resorts listed here run one or two excursions per week across Sogod Bay to snorkel with the sharks. Unlike in Donsol, they'll even let you scuba dive with the sharks here, although that may change. An excursion takes most of the day and costs roughly US$80 for scuba divers and US$24 for snorkellers. Whale sharks aside, the reef diving on both sides of Sogod Bay is first-rate all year.

Sleeping

Peter's Dive Resort (☎ 573 0015; www.whaleofadive.com; s P336, d P480-1200; ❄ 💻) Peter's has a colourful, turtle-laden house reef and rooms that cater to all budgets. The rooms have verandas with superb sea views. A few cottages are practically lapped by waves.

PHILIPPINES

Southern Leyte Dive Resort (☎ 572 4011; www.leyte-divers.com; r P600-1300; ❄) This charming resort sports imaginative circular duplex cottages. It's 1km northeast of Burgos, which makes whale shark excursions a bit longer. On the other hand, there's an actual beach and sunset views here.

Getting There & Away

From Cebu you can take a Kinswell or Cokaliong ferry to Bato (see Boat, p627), which is a two-hour bus ride to Burgos; or take a ferry to Ormoc (opposite), which is a four-hour bus ride to Burgos. There are also RORO ferries between Ubay, on Bohol, and Bato (P180, 2½ hours, two daily).

From Tacloban, take a bus to Sogod (P100, 2½ hours) and transfer to Burgos (P40, one hour). From Lilo-an, bus it to Sogod (P50, one hour) and transfer.

LILO-AN

This scenic town is where the ferries from Surigao disembark. Sightings of whale sharks feeding in the raging current under the bridge, once common, are now rare. The only place to stay in town is the eminently affordable and better-than-passable **Ofelia's Lodge** (r P150-300) near the pier.

There are four ferries per day plying the route between Surigao and Lilo-an (from P165, three to 4½ hours). Vans make the trip to/from Tacloban (P250, three hours) via Sogod.

PINTUYAN

Few people make the overland journey down to Pintuyan, so here's your chance to be ahead of the pack. A small tourism office near the pier organises community-based snorkelling trips to see the whale sharks in three-passenger *bangka* owned by the local fishermen's association. Tours cost P1300/2100/2900 for one/two/three people, including boat, guide and spotters. **Moncher Bardos** (☎ 0916 952 3354) in Pintuyan has the details and can arrange homestays with local families for P500, including three square meals a day. You may even spot a few whale sharks from land around here, as these sharks swim closer to the shoreline than their friends in Donsol.

Buses to Pintuyan from Sogod (P80, six daily) take 2½ hours over a smooth sealed road and go via Lilo-an. From Tacloban take a bus to Sogod or Lilo-an and transfer. A *habal-habal* to/from Lilo-an costs P250.

MINDANAO

Sprawling Mindanao, the world's 19th-largest island, is known for dazzling scenery, primitive hill tribes and an almost complete lack of tourists because of political unrest and occasional fighting between the government and Muslim separatists. What most tourists don't realise is that the lovely coastal stretch of northern Mindanao between Cagayan de Oro and Siargao Island is Catholic, Cebuano (Visayan) speaking – and quite safe. The area is known for first-rate surfing on Siargao and a peaceful island-life existence on Camiguin. Elsewhere, Mindanao offers up plenty of cherries for the intrepid traveller, including the Philippines' highest mountain, Mt Apo (2954m), accessible from Davao in southern Mindanao. Exercise caution if you are heading south or west of Cagayan de Oro (see boxed text, p634).

Getting There & Away

The four Philippine domestic airlines together service most major cities in Mindanao, including Cagayan de Oro and Surigao. There are also plenty of ferries from Manila and from all the major Visayan cities, including Cebu, Dumaguete and Tagbilaran.

SURIGAO

☎ 086

Unless you fly directly from Cebu to Siargao, you'll need to travel through Surigao, the capital of Surigao del Norte province.

If you need to stay the night in Surigao, **Dexter Pension House** (☎ 232 7526; cnr San Nicolas & Magallanes Sts; s P150, d P300-600; ❄) has a central location and small but passable rooms – many windowless.

From Surigao, ferries head to the town of Dapa on Siargao. The schedule changes frequently, but you can bank on at least one fastcraft (P380, two hours) and one or two RORO car ferries (from P120, 3¼ hours) per day.

There are various ways to get to Surigao. Asian Spirit has five weekly flights to/from Manila, or you can fly Cebu Pacific or Philippine Airlines to Butuan and take a bus from there. Several ferries sail to Lilo-an in Leyte every day from the port of Lipata, 10km northwest of Surigao (P175 to P300, 2½ to four hours). Take a tricycle (P150) to Lipata. For services to Cebu, see p627. SuperFerry has a weekly trip to Manila (from P2000, 32 hours) via Bacolod, and Sulpicio Lines has twice-weekly ferries to Manila.

Bachelor buses run regularly from Surigao to Butuan (ordinary/air-con P130/160, two hours) and Davao (air-con P650, 10 hours) from the Integrated Bus & Jeepney Terminal near the airport, 5km west of the city centre. You must transfer in Butuan for Cagayan de Oro.

SIARGAO

☎ 086

It's best known for having one of the world's great surf breaks, but Siargao (75km east of Surigao in northeast Mindanao) is no one-trick pony. Surrounded by idyllic islands and sprinkled with coves and quaint fishing villages, it's an island hopper's dream. The legendary **Cloud Nine break** off Tuazon Point is what put Siargao on the map. After years of being an inside secret for the mostly Australian veterans of the area, the break is now jokingly referred to by some locals as Crowd Nine. That's probably an exaggeration, although the sleepy village of Cloud Nine does get overrun for the **Siargao International Surfing Cup**, held every October. The breaks around here are reef breaks, but it's a soft, spongy reef and there are some moderate swells around for beginners. Lessons cost about P500 per hour including board rental – ask one of the surf bums hanging out around Laida's Restaurant in Cloud Nine.

Most of the resorts are in the village of Cloud Nine, which is a bumpy 15-minute *habal-habal* ride north of the town of General Luna ('GL'). All resorts can organise island-hopping trips. GL is a sleepy village where you'll find cheap eateries and a couple of bars frequented by local surfer dudes and chicks. From GL or the port town of Dapa you can take a boat (30 minutes) or rent a motorbike (P500, 1½ hours) and ride up to stilt house–studded Pilar, where the surf-sprayed **Magpoponco Beach** turns into a moonscape of natural pools at low tide. Continuing around the island you'll discover waterfalls and isolated beaches.

Sleeping & Eating

Prices mushroom and rooms fill up fast in the high surfing season (July to November). Some resorts shut down during the low, rainy season (December to March).

> **WARNING**
>
> Most embassies strongly warn tourists against travelling to potential conflict zones such as Maguindanao province (and its notoriously violent capital, Cotabato), Zamboanga and the entire Sulu Archipelago. While embassies tend to be a bit alarmist, it pays to exercise considerable caution when travelling to these areas. Check local news sources to make sure your destination and travel route are safe. See p584 for more on the Muslim separatist movement in Mindanao.

Cloud Nine (☎ 0918 564 5981; Cloud Nine; cottages P500-3500;) Its location right by the surfers' boardwalk is ideal, although management was in flux when we visited. Pricier *nipa* huts have kitchens, DVD players and bathrooms.

Ocean 101 Beach Resort (☎ 0919 826 8837; Cloud Nine; r from P660;) This is the most popular hangout among foreign surfers, featuring big beachfront rooms in two ugly blue concrete edifices. It has a great common area with a restaurant, pool table and satellite TV.

Also recommended:

Drop In (☎ 0919 652 0961; Cloud Nine; d P400) Across the road from Ocean 101.

Jadestar Lodge (☎ 0919 234 4367; General Luna; cottages from P400) Basic option just south of GL centre.

Getting There & Away

Seair's on-again, off-again direct flights from Cebu to Siargao's small airport were on again at the time of writing; flights are on Monday and Friday. Otherwise you'll need to catch a ferry from Surigao to get to the island; see p633 for more information.

Getting Around

On Siargao, jeepneys meet the ferries and run from Dapa to GL (P20) and Pilar (P30), or you can take a *habal-habal* to GL (P100) or Cloud Nine (P150).

CAGAYAN DE ORO

☎ 088 / pop 542,000

It may not be the most cosmopolitan city in the world, but every Friday and Saturday of the year the good people of this city descend on the central boulevard and engage in a giant, boozy street party. Take that, Rio! If you're too cool for the masses, 'CDO' also has some great

PHILIPPINES

clubs. This pleasant city, enviably placed on the banks of the swimmable Cagayan River, is the one place in the Philippines that does organised rafting trips year-round. Contact **Cagayan de Oro Whitewater Rafting Adventure** (☎ 857 1270; per person from P900). The **tourist office** (☎ 856 4048; Velez St) is south of the city centre.

Sleeping

Park View Hotel (☎ 857 1197; cnr T Neri & General Capistrano Sts; r from P285) An organised place that has economical rooms – check out a few, as many are windowless.

Ramon's Hotel (☎ 857 4804; cnr Burgos & Tirso Neri Sts; r from P550; ❄) Rooms here are nothing special, but the quiet, riverside location is. Alas, river-view rooms lack balconies, although the restaurant has one.

Nature's Pensionne (☎ 857 2274; T Chavez St; d from P635; ❄) This hotel located in the concrete jungle of downtown CDO is the best midrange option. Its clean, tastefully decorated rooms have cable TV and hot water.

Eating & Drinking

Gazebo Home Store Café (cnr Apolinar Velez & Gaerlan Sts; sandwiches P90) This clean, cool deli doubles as a souvenir store and has real coffee and free wi-fi.

Reina del Rey (cnr Burgos & Chavez Sts; mains P120-200) This floating restaurant in the Cagayan River is a great place to enjoy a beer and cheap snacks and sandwiches.

Karachi (Hayes St; mains P150-200) Feels like a hole in the wall, but has scrumptious Pakistani food, hookah pipes and a smattering of halal Middle Eastern dishes.

The bar and club action is centred on Tiano Brothers St between Hayes and Gaerlan. **Pulse** (Tiano Brothers St), **Ralf's** (Tiano Brothers St) and swanky Manila-style club **Eleven Fifty** (Gaerlan St; admission P100) were hot when we were there.

Getting There & Around

Between Cebu Pacific, Air Philippines and PAL, there are several flights per day to both Manila and Cebu. The airport is about 10km west of town (P120 by taxi).

At Macabalan Pier, 5km north of the city centre, various ferry companies serve Cebu (see Boat, p627) and Tagbilaran (P560, 12 hours). SuperFerry, Negros Navigation and Sulpicio Lines have a few trips per week to/from Manila (from P2500, 32 hours); many of these go via Bacolod and Iloilo.

> **GETTING TO MALAYSIA**
>
> At the time of writing, the only route open to foreigners was Zamboanga to Sandakan, Sabah. **Weesam Express** (www.weesamexpress.com) has a fast ferry that covers this route twice a week (P2800, 13 hours) and there are slower ferries that make this trip too. However, travel in the Zamboanga region is considered risky (see opposite). The boats to Sabah from Palawan are off limits to foreigners.
>
> See p488 for information on the crossing from Malaysia.

Bachelor Tours buses head up the coast to Butuan (air-con P280, four hours) via Balingoan (P120, 1½ hours). Change in Butuan for Surigao.

The main bus terminal is on the edge of town, beside the Agora Market (take a 'Gusa' or 'Cugman' jeepney from town).

CAMIGUIN

☎ 088 / pop 87,000

With seven volcanoes, various waterfalls, hot springs, cold springs and underwater diversions aplenty, Camiguin is developing a reputation as a top adventure-tourism destination. Its undulating landscape, with cloud-tipped volcanoes as a continuous backdrop, makes it a great place to strike out on your own and explore, preferably by motorbike (per day P500) and on foot.

Adventure lovers should seek out Barbie at Camiguin Action Geckos (see p636) or Johnny at **Johnny's Fun N' Dive** (☎ 0920 953 6680; www.johnnysdive.com; Secret Cove Beach Resort). Not only do they both offer a range of trekking, rappelling, mountain biking and diving tours, but they are also happy to dispense advice to do-it-yourselfers.

GETTING THERE & AROUND

Seair flies to Camiguin airport, located in Mambajao, three times a week from Cebu. Alternatively, you can catch regular boats from Balingoan on mainland Mindanao to Benoni or Guinsiliban (P100, about one hour) on Camiguin. Frequent buses and vans run to Balingoan from Cagayan de Oro (see Getting There & Around, left).

Jeepneys circle the island in both directions, passing any given point roughly every half-hour until about 5pm. The jeepney fare from Benoni pier to Mambajao is P30 (35 minutes).

Mambajao

In this shady capital of Camiguin, life rarely gets out of first gear. The Camiguin **tourist office** (☎ 387 1097; Provincial Capitol Bldg) has free maps of the island. Mambajao is a good place to observe ornate *okkil* architecture. The best example is the Landbank building along the National Hwy in the city centre. Notice the intricate patterns cut into the wooden awning.

Penny-pinchers can bunk in the town centre at tidy **GV Tower Hotel** (☎ 387 1041; Burgos St; d P300-500) or the bare-bones **Travel Lodge** (☎ 0928 214 7729; Reyes St; s/d P100/200) opposite the market.

our pick **Enigmata** (☎ 387 0273; r from P500;) is a memorable, hippyesque artist hangout that's more a way of life than a resort. Most rooms are in a fantastic tree house built around a towering hardwood tree and swathed in wooden furniture, murals and artwork. Head honcho Ros does much to promote Camiguin arts and is a fine artist in her own right. The dirt road here turns off the highway at the Tarzan statue about 2km east of Mambajao.

There are a couple of Filipino eateries on the waterfront, or try **Green Tropical Pub** (mains P100-150; Tue-Sun), an open-air restaurant with pizzas and Thai and Filipino dishes just west of Mambajao.

Around Mambajao

Most of Camiguin's resorts are on the black-sand beaches in *barangay* Bug-Ong, about 4km west of Mambajao. You can take a jeepney or hire a tricycle for a negotiable P75 to P100 to get to any of the resorts.

Everything is cut-rate at **Jasmine by the Sea** (☎ 387 9015; Bug-Ong; d P500), including food, island hopping, motorbike rental and – perhaps worryingly? – diving. Run by an eccentric German, it has cosy garden cottages with sea-view balconies.

Camiguin Action Geckos (☎ 387 1266; www.camiguinaction.com; Bug-Ong; r/cottages P600/1500) has some cosy budget rooms above the restaurant, as well as some truly exceptional beachfront fan cottages.

Right next to Jasmine, **Seascape** (☎ 0906 256 4384; Bug-Ong; d without/with air-con from P700/1200) has big, austere bungalows on a quiet stretch of beach.

PALAWAN

Palawan is fast becoming a haven for nature buffs and intrepid adventurers. Drifting on the Philippines' western edge, this long sliver of jungle is one of the country's last ecological frontiers. The Amazonian interior is barely connected by a few snaking roads that will make your fillings jingle, and the convoluted coast is comprised of one breathtaking bay after another. Puerto Princesa is the energetic capital from where you can explore nearby Sabang, with its famous underground river, and laid-back Port Barton. Towering limestone cliffs shelter the northern community of El Nido, while the Calamian group of islands offers beaches, unbeatable wreck diving and a few El Nido-esque cliffs of their own.

Only the road between Puerto Princesa and Roxas is sealed, and the infrequency of transport can test a Zen master's patience – seafaring *bangkas* are a popular way of avoiding dusty inland routes.

Getting There & Around

Cebu Pacific has daily flights to Puerto Princesa from both Manila and Cebu, while PAL and Air Philippines fly from Manila only. Seair and Asian Spirit both service Coron from Manila. Seair has a very useful 'hopping' route between Manila, Coron, El Nido and Puerto Princesa. Sample fares are P4000 for Manila–Coron, P3100 for Coron–El Nido, and P3200 for El Nido–Puerto Princesa.

SuperFerry (☎ 048-434 5736; Rizal Ave, Puerto Princesa) and **Negros Navigation** (Puerto Princesa Pier) both have weekly vessels to Puerto Princesa from Manila (from P1800, 26 hours) via Coron (P1450, 12 hours). Slower craft make the haul from Manila to El Nido via Coron (see p639). **Milagrosa J Shipping** (☎ 048-433 4806) sails between Puerto Princesa and Iloilo (P1150, 30 hours, two weekly) via the Cuyo Islands. From March to May, Negros Navigation runs a weekly ferry to Caticlan.

PUERTO PRINCESA

☎ 048 / pop 190,000

If only all Philippine cities could be a little more like earthy Puerto Princesa. Strictly enforced fines for littering (P200) keep the streets clean (we're not kidding!), while the municipal government actively promotes the city as an eco- and adventure-tourism hub. Scattered around town is a handful of funky restaurants and guesthouses, where the design motif is part native Filipino, part tripped-out '60s hippy. Yes, there's the usual stream of tricycles down the main commercial drag, Rizal Ave. But even the tricycles seem a bit quieter and less dense than in most other provincial centres. In short, 'Puerto' makes a great launching pad for checking out the myriad natural attractions in the surrounding area. The big one is the Subterranean River, while overnight hikes to tribal villages in the south are also gaining traction. If you're in town, give the small **Palawan Museum** (City Plaza, Rizal Ave; admission P20; 8.30am-noon & 1.30-5pm Mon-Sat) a gander.

Information

Most internet cafés are clustered near the intersection of Rizal Ave and the National Hwy.

Equitable PCI Bank (Rizal Ave) Has the only working ATM in Palawan.

Provincial Tourism Office (433 2968; Provincial Capitol Compound, Rizal Ave; 8.30am-5pm Mon-Fri) Distributes information-packed brochure on Palawan, including map of Puerto Princesa.

Tourist Information & Assistance Counter (434 4211; airport arrivals hall; 8am-5pm) Run by City Tourism Office, which has an office next door.

Underground River Booking Office (433 2409; 7 Plates Bldg, National Hwy, north of Rizal Ave; 8am-noon & 1-5pm Mon-Sat) Issues Subterranean River permits (see p638).

Sleeping

Ancieto's Pension (0917 789 4664; cnr Mabini & Roxas Sts; s/d from P150/250) If Banwa is full – and it often is – walk three minutes down Roxas St to this family-run bargain. Rooms are basic and susceptible to some street noise, but there's a cosy sitting area with a TV.

our pick **Banwa Art House** (434 8963; www.banwa.com; Liwanag St; dm P225, s/d from P300/350) This backpacker oasis oozes charm from every artisan craft adorning its walls. There's a groovy bamboo lounge, surrounded by a waterfall of vines, that has cool tunes wafting from the house CD player.

Casa Linda Tourist Inn (433 2606; casalind@mozcom.com; Trinidad Rd; s/d P750/850) Slightly upmarket, this splendid place off Rizal Ave is wall-to-wall bamboo and has a big, tranquil garden courtyard with a bamboo reading gazebo. It has one coveted fan room (P600).

WARNING

Malaria is an issue in rural areas. Use the mosquito nets provided by most guesthouses and coat yourself with insect repellent at dusk. Minuscule, stinging sandflies (aptly named *nik-niks*) delight in biting exposed skin and can be a curse on some western beaches.

Eating & Drinking

Vegetarian House (cnr Burgos & Manalo Sts; dishes P30-50) Serves up incredibly cheap and tasty faux-meat dishes in decidedly austere surrounds.

Neva's Place (Taft St; mains P75-160) Great budget Filipino and Thai food, as well as pizzas, all served in a blissful garden.

Kinabuch Grill & Bar (Rizal Ave; mains P100-150) Sprawling 'KGB' has two pool tables and is the watering hole of choice for the thirsty masses. It's Russian owned. Really.

our pick **Ka Lui Restaurant** (369 Rizal Ave; meal P150-175; dinner Mon-Sat) This seafood specialist in a funky *nipa* complex thoroughly deserves its reputation as one of the finest restaurants in the country.

Getting There & Around

The main bus terminal is at the San Jose market 6km north of town; to get there grab a multi-cab (mini-jeepney) from anywhere along Rizal Ave (P10).

From Puerto Princesa there are frequent buses south to Quezon (P150, 3½ hours) and north to Roxas (P130, three hours). There are three morning buses to El Nido (P300, eight hours). Buses also run to Sabang and Port Barton.

OFF THE BEATEN TRACK

To really see Palawan in all her jungle-clad glory, take the 'coast-to-coast' walk from Tanabag, an hour's drive north of Puerto Princesa, to Sabang. The three-day trek brings you up close and personal with Batak tribespeople, tropical birds, monkeys and possibly snakes. Local guides for this trek cost P800 per day; inquire at the Provincial or City Tourism Offices in Puerto Princesa.

The set tricycle rate into town from the airport is P40, but if you flag down a ride from the road out front it's only P6.

SABANG

☎ 048

Tiny Sabang has a long expanse of beach and is famed for the navigable **Puerto Princesa Subterranean River National Park** (admission P200), which winds through a spectacular cave before emptying into the sea. Tourist paddle boats are allowed to go 1.5km upstream into the cave (45 minutes return); in the June to November low season you can proceed 4.3km upstream (three hours return), but only with a separate permit (P400) from the Underground River Booking Office in Puerto Princesa (see p637). From the beach in Sabang it's a thrilling 5km walk through the jungle to the mouth of the river, or you can book a boat (P700 for up to six people, 15 minutes) through the Tourist Information & Assistance Center at the pier.

Sleeping & Eating

Most places shut off their generators at 10pm. That may change with the impending additions of two new resorts – native style Puerto Pension Resort and the Sheradon Hotel & Convention Centre.

Mary's Cottages (☎ 0919 757 7582; s P250, d P350-450) This is a half-decent budget option. Expect simplicity and you will not be let down. It's out past Taraw Lodge at the east end of the beach.

Taraw Lodge & Restaurant (☎ 0919 601 1227; cottages P450-600) A 10-minute walk east of the pier, this was our favourite, with five comfortable beachfront cottages, a lush garden, good food and plenty of hammocks. It's popular with Puerto Princesa travel agencies so book ahead.

Getting There & Away

The road out to Sabang is now about half sealed. Jumbo jeepneys between Sabang and Puerto Princesa leave at 7am, 9am and 2pm in either direction (P110, 2½ hours). Foreigners with luggage will be asked to pay P200. For Port Barton and El Nido backtrack by road to Salvacion and flag down a northbound bus from the highway.

High season *bangkas* chug up to Port Barton (P800, 2½ hours) and El Nido (P1500, seven hours) about thrice weekly.

PORT BARTON

☎ 048 / pop 4800

People find themselves unable to leave Port Barton, and only partly because of the town's poor transport links. Set on a small, attractive cove, the area has some fine islands in the bay and good snorkelling, but most people spend their days reading and hammock-hopping. **Island-hopping excursions** (P1000) and **mangrove tours** (P600) are easily arranged. Port Barton shuts down in the low season.

Sleeping & Eating

our pick Greenviews Resort (☎ 0921 699 4339; www.palawandg.clara.net; s/d from P350/400) The last place on the east end of the beach is probably the best all-round choice. It certainly has the finest restaurant – try the shrimp omelette (P150). The basic rooms with shared bathrooms are more than acceptable, and the more luxurious cottages are set around a garden.

Elsa's Beach Cottages (☎ 0919 424 6975; d P350-650) The friendly family who runs this place recently gave the native-style beachfront cottages a much-needed facelift.

Ysobelle's Beach Resort (☎ 0928 503 0388; ysobellepalawan@yahoo.com.ph; d P700-800) The resort formerly known as Swissippini has a new owner. So far, so good. The newly renovated beachfront A-frames and garden cottages are Port Barton's classiest abodes.

Getting There & Away

In the high season (December to April), *bangkas* leave roughly every other day to Sabang (P800, 2½ hours) and El Nido (P1000, four hours). In the low season you'll have to hire a private *bangka*, although it's often possible to share with other travellers.

One excruciatingly slow bus per day departs at around 9.30am to Puerto Princesa (P200, four hours). The Puerto–Port Barton jeepney leaves around 7.30am. From Puerto, you can always take a more frequent Roxas-bound jeepney as far as San Jose and transfer to a motorcycle taxi (P600, 45 minutes).

To get to El Nido, make your way to Roxas, about 3km north of San Jose, and pick up a northbound jeepney.

EL NIDO

☎ 048 / pop 5100

Concealed in a cove on Palawan's northwest tip and punctured by immense limestone

PHILIPPINES

cliffs, El Nido is the island's Aladdin's Cave. The friendly town clings to the bay's small brown beach and graciously integrates the swelling number of backpackers who find their way here. The edible nests of the tiny swiftlets that inhabit the cliffs give the town its name. There's some good snorkelling and limitless possibilities for exploring the islands, lagoons and perfect beaches of the **Bacuit Archipelago**.

Information

Run like Swiss clockwork by Judy, the **El Nido Boutique & Art Café** (☎ 0920 902 6317), near the wharf, is a repository for all things informative about El Nido. You can buy plane tickets here, check boat and bus schedules, get cash advances on Visa cards (with a hefty 12% surcharge), browse the library, buy art, eat good food and drink real coffee. It's also as good a place as any to arrange boat or sea kayaking excursions into stunning Bacuit Bay.

Activities

All-day island-hopping trips cost P600 to P700 per person, including lunch. Miniloc Island's **Big Lagoon** and **Small Lagoon** are not to be missed; for full effect get there at dawn when you'll have them to yourself. There are several dive operators in town. Art Café has a list of short hiking expeditions you can do on your own.

Sleeping & Eating

There's a dearth of rooms in El Nido. If the following are full, a stroll down the main beach should turn something up. For cheap eats try the *turo-turo* (literally 'point-point'; restaurants that display their food in glass cases so you simply point-point to your order) restaurants near the corner of Real and Del Pilar Sts.

OG's Pensionne (☎ 0916 707 0393; Hama St; d P300-500, tr P700) Has enough rooms (15) that there's a good chance of something being available. The rooms are good value to boot – especially the luscious triples.

Ralf's Lodge & Restaurant (☎ 0920 584 4193; Serona Rd; s/d P350/400) The four rooms here are dead basic, but the views are great and the price is right.

El Nido Cliffside Cottages (☎ 0919 785 6625; Rizal St; s/d/tr P350/500/600) This tranquil place has simple courtyard bungalows under the eerie cliffs just south of town.

our pick **Alternative Centre** (☎ 0917 896 3506; Serona Rd; r from P500; 💻) The beach-facing rooms here are beyond creative. Enter through garage-style front doors into a tangle of intricately carved wooden furniture, cascading streamers and vinelike plants. The cheaper rooms upstairs, with octagonal mattresses among other design liberties, adjoin an equally funky restaurant (it's 65% vegan, and 100% scrumptious; mains P160 to P260) and spa/wellness centre.

Seaslug's (Hama St; mains P90-180) Right in the middle of the beach, newcomer Seaslug's has quickly earned a loyal following among fans of grilled seafood and suds in the sand.

Getting There & Around

Seair flies from El Nido to Manila, Coron and Puerto Princesa (see Getting There & Around, p636). The only way to the airport is by tricycle for a non-negotiable P150 (we smell tricycle mafia).

San Nicolas Shipping (☎ in Manila 02-243 4595) and **Atienza Shipping Lines** (☎ 0918 566 6786) have weekly trips in small, fully loaded cargo boats to/from Manila (P1100, 32 hours). All passenger 'seating' is in cramped economy bunks. It's arguably worse than prison. Meals are included. Both of these companies also go weekly to Coron (P850, nine hours). The pricier option to Coron is a twice-weekly, 40-passenger *bangka* ferry (P2000, eight hours).

High-season *bangkas* wade down to Port Barton (P1200, four hours) and Sabang (P1500, seven hours) roughly every other day.

Three morning buses make the journey to Puerto Princesa (P300, eight hours).

CORON

pop 38,000

Divers know it as a wreck-diving hot spot, but the area known as Coron also has untouched beaches, crystal-clear lagoons and brooding limestone cliffs to tempt nondivers. Coron itself is actually just the sleepy main town of Busuanga Island – not to be confused with Coron Island to the south. Both Busuanga Island and Coron Island are part of the Calamian Group, located about halfway between Mindoro and Palawan.

Activities

Fifteen Japanese ships sunk by US fighter planes roost on the floor of Coron Bay just south of Busuanga. Getting to the wrecks from Coron town involves a two- to four-hour boat ride, but diving is still affordable, averaging about US$40 for a two-tank dive. Most of the wrecks are for advanced divers only, although there are a few in less than 25m that are suitable for beginners.

Coron town lacks a beach, but you can hire a motorbike (P500) or boat (per day about P1250 for three people) and bounce around the seemingly infinite supply of untouched beaches on the west coast of Busuanga and surrounding islands. **Coron Island**, with its towering spires of stratified limestone, is the star attraction. There's an incredible dive in Coron Island's **Barracuda Lake** (admission P75), where the clear water gets scorching hot as you descend through its swirling, volcanic thermals. You can also paddle around on a bamboo raft and swim in unspoiled **Lake Cayangan** (admission incl raft P200).

Sleeping & Eating

Apart from Sangat Island Reserve, all of the following places are in Coron town. All hotels listed have dive shops and hire out boats for island hopping.

Sea Dive Resort (☎ 0918 400 0448; www.seadiveresort.com.ph; d P400-800; ⌘) A three-storey monolith on the sea accessed by a long walkway, this place has it all – decent rooms, restaurant, bar, internet and a busy dive shop.

Krystal Lodge (d P600-1000) Like much of Coron, this sprawling bamboo complex is built on stilts over the water. It's a maze of shady walkways ending in rooms that range from passable boxes to simple 'apartments'.

Sangat Island Reserve (☎ 0920 954 4328; www.sangat.com.ph; cottages per person from US$65) If you really want to treat yourself – and be close to the wrecks – this jewel of a resort is on its own island, about a one-hour boat ride from Coron (free transfer for guests). Prices include all meals.

our pick **Bistro Coron** (meals P150-500) A mouth-watering French bistro on one of the Philippines' most isolated islands? It works for us. Consider splurging for the jumbo prawns, one of the best meals we've had in the Philippines. Hopefully proprietor/chef Bruno won't move back to his former home in southern Palawan any time soon.

Getting There & Away

For air connections, see p636. Coron's YKR Airport is a bumpy one-hour ride north of Coron town; jeepneys (P150, one hour) meet the flights.

The weekly Negros Navigation and SuperFerry vessels between Manila and Puerto Princesa pass through Coron town (see p636). To/from Manila takes about 13 hours and costs from P1500; Puerto Princesa takes about 12 hours and costs from P1200. For boats to El Nido see Getting There & Around, p639.

PHILIPPINES DIRECTORY

ACCOMMODATION

Accommodation in the Philippines ranges from plush beachside bungalows to stuffy hotel shoeboxes, and everything in between. Many budget hotels offer a mix of fan-cooled and air-con rooms. In this book, unless otherwise noted, rooms in the P150 to P300 range are generally fan-cooled with a shared bathroom, and rooms in the P350 to P500 range usually have fans and private bathrooms. Anything higher should have air-conditioning. Prices are approximately double in Manila and in trendy resort areas such as Boracay and Alona Beach, although reasonable dorm beds can be had in Manila for about P350.

As the Philippines becomes more popular, it's becoming more difficult to just walk in and find a room in smaller resort areas and touristy towns such as Vigan. Booking ahead is a good idea, at least in the high season (roughly December to May, with some regional variations).

Prices listed in this chapter are high season rates. Room rates in tourist hot spots go down by up to 50% in the low season, but may triple or even quadruple during Holy Week (Easter) and around New Year's.

ACTIVITIES

Scuba diving is the most popular adventure activity in the Philippines, but there is also a small surf scene, kite-surfing and windsurfing on Boracay, and trekking just about everywhere. Other popular adventure sports covered in less detail in this book include cycling and mountain biking (see www.bugoybikers

DID YOU KNOW?

In the early 1900s, the Americans turned the Calamian Group island of Culion into what would eventually become the world's largest leper colony.

.com), spelunking (see www.bonifaciojoni.blogspot.com) and rock climbing (see www.geocities.com/powerupgyms).

Diving

Despite the destruction wrought by widespread dynamite fishing, the Philippines still boasts some top-notch dive sites. The WWII shipwrecks at Coron (Busuanga Island) offer outstanding wreck dives, while the impressive reefs around Puerto Galera (Mindoro), Apo Island (Negros), Panglao Island (Bohol), Padre Burgos (Leyte), and Moalboal and Malapascua Island (Cebu) offer a more traditional fish-and-coral environment. Beginners should head for the dozens of competitive scuba schools in Puerto Galera or Boracay. Generally, it costs certified divers about US$25 to US$30 for a single-tank dive with all equipment. Open-water diving courses go for about US$350 to US$400. See www.divephil.com for more diving tips.

Kite-Surfing & Windsurfing

The island of Boracay is the Philippine mecca for windsurfers and kite-surfers. The east side of Boracay has a huge, shallow lagoon that gets steady winds from November to March. That and cheap prices (US$300 to US$350 for a 14-hour certification course, equipment included) make Boracay one of the best places in the world to learn kite-surfing.

Surfing

The top surfing destination in the Philippines is Siargao Island, off the northeast coast of Mindanao. In the right weather conditions, the waves here can be Hawaiian in scale. Cloud Nine, the best surfing spot on the island, is the setting for the annual Siargao International Surfing Cup held in October. Other good breaks can be found all along the Philippines' eastern border, although many of the best breaks are virtually inaccessible and must be reached by boat. The season on the east coast generally coincides with typhoon season, roughly August to November. There is smaller surf to be had from December to March in San Juan, near San Fernando (La Union) on the west coast of Luzon.

Trekking

The entire archipelago is crisscrossed with paths and trails. They are not always clearly marked, so bring a guide unless you have extensive experience in backcountry navigation. Some of the best trekking areas are in the Cordilleras of North Luzon, the rainforests of Palawan and the rugged interior of Samar and Leyte. Volcano climbing is a Philippine speciality – the big names are Mt Mayon in southeast Luzon and Mt Kanlaon on Negros.

BOOKS

Lonely Planet publishes *Philippines* and the pint-sized *Filipino (Tagalog) Phrasebook*. If you want to brush up on some recent history, Stanley Karnow's Pulitzer Prize–winning effort *In Our Image* takes an intriguing look at the US relationship with its biggest colony. *Ants for Breakfast – Archaeological Adventures among the Kalinga,* by James M Skibo, is a tasty work of asides and insights gleaned from fieldwork among the Kalinga people of the Cordilleras.

BUSINESS HOURS

Unless otherwise noted, restaurants are open for breakfast, lunch and dinner.

The following are other usual business hours in the Philippines:

Airline offices 8am to 6pm (airport branches stay open until the last flight).
Banks 9am to 3pm
Government offices generally 8am to noon and 1pm to 5pm Monday to Friday
Shopping malls 10am to around 9pm
Tourist offices generally 8am to noon and 1pm to 5pm Monday to Friday

THE PERFECT BEACH

There's a rumour that the island described in Alex Garland's backpacker classic *The Beach* was somewhere in the Calamian island group. Garland set the book in Thailand, but admits that the real island was somewhere in the Philippines. He lived in the Philippines for a spell and set his second novel, *The Tesseract*, in Manila.

PHILIPPINES

CLIMATE

The Philippines is hot and humid throughout the year, with brief respites possible in January and February. For most of the country, the dry season is roughly November to May. Rains start in June, peak in July through to September, and start tapering off in October. Typhoons are common from June to early December.

However, in parts of the country the seasons are flipped. Eastern Mindanao, southern Leyte, eastern Samar and parts of southeast Luzon are rainy from December to March and fairly dry when the rest of the country is sopping.

The central Visayas – including Bohol, Negros and Cebu – are sheltered from the monsoon rains and thus have less pronounced seasons. These areas are liable to have rain at any time of the year, but it usually won't be too serious unless there's a typhoon stirring up trouble on the eastern seaboard.

See also p916 for climate charts.

CUSTOMS

You can bring up to 2L of alcohol and up to 400 cigarettes into the country without paying duty.

DANGERS & ANNOYANCES

Mindanao (the central and southwest regions in particular) and the Sulu Archipelago are the scenes of clashes between the army and US 'advisers' on one side and separatist groups on the other (see p584 and p633).

Bus companies and shipping lines in the Philippines are legendary for their cavalier attitude to safety. There have been a number of high-profile shipping disasters in recent years, and bus accidents are common (as the author of this chapter found out first hand when the bus he was riding on lost its breaks and collided awkwardly, but not seriously, with an oncoming truck). By contrast, the record of Philippine aviation companies in recent years has been fairly good.

As for annoyances, you'll probably find you don't share the Filipino enthusiasm for roosters, particularly when the little beasts wake you for the 15th time in one night. Just as inescapable are the wail of karaoke and the whine of tricycles, which seem to start their engines in unison at 6am. Heavy air pollution is a serious annoyance in cities such as Manila and Cebu.

DRIVING LICENCE

Tourists are free to use their home-country driving licence in the Philippines.

EMBASSIES & CONSULATES

Embassies & Consulates in the Philippines

The following are located in Manila:

Australia (Map pp596-7; ☎ 02-757 8100; 23rd fl, Tower 2, RCBC Plaza, 6819 Ayala Ave, Makati)

Brunei (Map pp596-7; ☎ 02-816 2836; 11th fl, BPI Bldg, cnr Ayala Ave & Paseo de Roxas, Makati)

Canada (Map pp596-7; ☎ 02-857 9000; 6th fl, Tower 2, RCBC Plaza, 6819 Ayala Ave, Makati)

France (Map pp596-7; ☎ 02-857 6900; 16th fl, Pacific Star Bldg, cnr Gil Puyat & Makati Aves, Makati)

Germany (Map pp596-7; ☎ 02-702 3000; 25th fl, Tower 2, RCBC Plaza, 6819 Ayala Ave, Makati)

Indonesia (Map pp596-7; ☎ 02-892 5061; 185 Salcedo St, Makati)

Japan (Map pp596-7; ☎ 02-551 5710; 2627 Roxas Blvd, Pasay City)

SCAMS

Manila, in particular, has a fine tradition of con artists, rip-off merchants and pickpockets. Thankfully, most rely on guile, so violent crime isn't so common.

Beware of people who claim to have met you before or claim to be staying in your hotel, particularly in Ermita. Confidence tricksters prey on solo travellers, particularly new arrivals, and invite them home. The situation ends with the traveller being drugged and robbed. If you feel that a stranger is acting overly friendly to you, walk away.

People who approach you on the street to change money at kiosks on Mabini St can nail you with really good amateur-magician card tricks – turning P1000 into P100 with sleight of hand. If an exchange kiosk asks to recount the wad of pesos they've just handed you, don't let them.

Several of the *kalesa* (two-wheeled horse-drawn cart) drivers around Ermita and Intramuros can be hard work as well – prices can change suddenly. Just make sure you agree on the price before setting off.

Laos (Map pp596-7; ☎ 02-852 5759; 34 Lapu-Lapu Ave, Magallanes, Makati)
Malaysia (Map pp596-7; ☎ 02-817 4581; 107 Tordesillas St, Makati)
Myanmar (Map pp596-7; ☎ 02-893 1944; Gervasia Bldg, 152 Amorsolo St, Makati)
New Zealand (Map pp596-7; ☎ 02-891 5358; 23rd fl, BPI Buendia Center, Gil Puyat Ave, Makati)
Singapore (Map pp596-7; ☎ 02-751 2345; 35th fl, Tower 1, Enterprise Center, 6766 Ayala Ave, Makati)
Thailand (Map pp596-7; ☎ 02-815 4220; 107 Rada St, Makati)
UK (Map pp596-7; ☎ 02-580 8700; 15th fl, LV Locsin Bldg, 6752 Ayala Ave, Makati)
USA (Map pp598-9; ☎ 02-528 6300; 1201 Roxas Blvd, Ermita)
Vietnam (Map pp596-7; ☎ 02-524 0364; 554 Vito Cruz St, Malate)

Philippine Embassies & Consulates Abroad

For Philippine diplomatic offices in Southeast Asia, see the relevant country chapter.
Australia (☎ 02-6273 2535; www.philembassy.org.au; 1 Moonah Place, Yarralumla, ACT 2600)
Canada (☎ 613-233 1121; www.philcongen-toronto.com/; Suite 606, 130 Albert St, Ottawa, ON KIP5G4)
France (☎ 01 44 14 57 00; ambaphilparis@wanadoo.fr; 4 Hameau de Boulainvilliers, 75016 Paris)
Germany (☎ 030-864 9500; www.philippine-embassy.de; Uhlandstrasse 97, 10715 Berlin)
Japan (☎ 03-5562 1600; www.tokyope.org; 5-15-5 Roppongi, Minato-ku, Tokyo 106-8537)
New Zealand (☎ 04-472 9848; wellingtonpe@dfa.gov.ph; 50 Hobson St, Thorndon, Wellington)
UK (☎ 020-7937 1600; www.philemb.org.uk; 9A Palace Green, Kensington, London W8 4QE)
USA (☎ 202-467 9300; www.philippineembassy-usa.org; 1600 Massachusetts Ave NW, Washington, DC, 20036)

FOOD & DRINK

Food

The native cuisine blends a number of influences, particularly from China and Spain, with the main flavours being ginger, tamarind, onion, vinegar, soy sauce and herbs such as bay leaves rather than Asian spices. *Turo-turo* (literally 'point-point') restaurants are everywhere – they display their food in cafeteria-style glass cases and you simply point-point to your order.

Favourite Filipino snacks and dishes:
Adobo Chicken, pork or fish in a dark tangy sauce.
Arroz caldo Thick rice soup with chicken, garlic, ginger and onions.
Balut Half-developed duck embryo, boiled in the shell.
Halo-halo A tall, cold glass of milky crushed ice with fresh fruit and ice cream.
Kare-kare Meat (usually intestines) in coconut sauce.
Lechon Spit-roast baby pig with liver sauce.
Lumpia Spring rolls filled with meat or vegetables.
Mami Noodle soup, like *mee* soup in Malaysia or Indonesia.
Menudo Stew with vegetables, liver or pork.
Pancit Stir-fried *bihon* (white) or *canton* (yellow) noodles with meat and vegetables.
Pinakbet Vegetables with shrimp paste, garlic, onions and ginger.
Sisig Crispy fried pork ears and jowl.

TOP FIVE FESTIVALS

Every Filipino town manages to squeeze in at least one fiesta a year, accompanied by frenzied eating, drinking and merry-making. These are our top five festivals, in descending order:

- **Ati-Atihan** (p616) Kalibo, Panay; mid-January
- **Moriones Festival** Marinduque; Holy Week
- **Peñafrancia Festival** (p611) Naga, southeast Luzon; third week of September
- **MassKara** (p621) Bacolod, Negros; around October 19
- **Crucifixion Ceremony** Many locations, but the most famous is in San Fernando, Pampanga, central Luzon; Good Friday

Drink

The national brew, San Miguel, is very palatable and despite being a monopolist is affordable at around P20 (P25 to P35 in bars). San Miguel also brews a beer called Red Horse; it's ludicrously strong so make sure you are close to home when you order your 1L bottle. Tanduay rum is the national drink, and amazingly cheap at around P75 per litre. It's usually served with coke. Popular nonalcoholic drinks include *buko* juice (young coconut juice with floating pieces of jelly-like flesh) and sweetened *calamansi* juice (*calamansi* are small local limes).

GAY & LESBIAN TRAVELLERS

Bakla (gay men) and *binalaki* (lesbians) are almost universally accepted in the Philippines. There are well-established gay centres

PHILIPPINES

DID YOU KNOW?

One of the first major email viruses was invented and unleashed by a Filipino IT student in 1999. It seems very Filipino that it was called the 'I love you' virus.

in major cities, but foreigners should be wary of hustlers and police harassment. Remedios Circle in Malate, Manila, is the site of a June gay-pride parade and the centre for nightlife. For up-to-date information on gay life in the Philippines, you can check out **Utopia Asian Gay & Lesbian Resources** (www.utopia-asia.com) and the **Asian Gay Guide** (www.dragoncastle.net).

HOLIDAYS

Offices and banks are closed on public holidays, although shops and department stores stay open. Maundy Thursday and Good Friday are the only days when the entire country closes down – even most public transport stops running, and Asian Spirit even grounds its planes. The public holidays are:

New Year's Day 1 January
Maundy Thursday, Good Friday & Easter Sunday March/April
Araw ng Kagitingan (Bataan Day) 9 April
Labour Day 1 May
Independence Day 12 June
Ninoy Aquino Day 21 August
National Heroes Day Last Sunday in August
All Saints' Day 1 November
Bonifacio Day (National Heroes Day) 30 November
Christmas Day 25 December
Rizal Day 30 December
New Year's Eve 31 December

INTERNET ACCESS

Internet cafés are all over the Philippines. Speedy connections are readily available in all cities for P15 to P25 per hour, and even some remote areas with limited electricity, such as Port Barton in Palawan, have slow connections available for no more than P60 per hour.

INTERNET RESOURCES

Department of Foreign Affairs (www.dfa.gov.ph) The Department of Foreign Affairs site has updated embassy listings and visa regulations.
Lakbay.net (www.lakbay.net) This site has lots of useful Philippines links, as well as some shipping and bus schedules, and an online air-ticket booking service.
National Commission for Culture & the Arts (www.ncca.gov.ph) This outstanding website contains primers on the arts and background on the Philippines' various ethnic groups and tribes.
Philippine Newslink (www.philnews.com) This has a fantastically thorough pile of local news and views, and includes links to all the main daily newspapers.
Tanikalang Ginto (www.filipinolinks.com) This vast directory has an extensive set of links relating to all aspects of the country.
US Department of State (www.travel.state.gov) Mildly paranoid but useful travel information and advisories. The US is said to have the best Western intelligence-gathering network in the Philippines.
WOW Philippines (www.tourism.gov.ph) This official tourism site is a good place to start, but is weak on adventure sports and ecotourism.

LEGAL MATTERS

Drugs are risky; even being caught with marijuana for personal use can mean jail, while traffickers could face life in prison. Should you find yourself in trouble, your first recourse is your embassy, so make a point of writing down the phone number. If you are arrested your embassy may not be able to do anything more than provide you with a list of local lawyers and keep an eye on how you're being treated. Another good number to know is the Department of Tourism's **Tourist Security Division** (☎ 524 1728, 524 1660). This unit is available 24 hours and is more reliable than regular police.

MAPS

The Nelles Verlag *Philippines* map is a good map of the islands at a scale of 1:1,500,000. More useful to the traveller are the excellent locally produced *E-Z* maps of each region, which cost P99 per map.

MEDIA

Magazines & Newspapers

There are about 20 major national and regional English-language newspapers, ranging from the staid *Manila Bulletin* to the American big city daily–style *Philippine Daily Inquirer*

LEGAL AGE

- you can begin driving at 16
- voting age is 18
- drinking is allowed from 18
- sex is legal at 18

PHILIPPINES

and *Philippine Star*. One of the better newspapers is *Business World*, which has national news and a good weekend guide in addition to business news. These national papers can be found in newspaper stands all over the country, although they have a heavily Manila-centric world view. *Newsbreak* and *Graphic* are weekly news magazines in the mould of *Newsweek*. International publications such as the *International Herald Tribune* and *The Economist* are readily available at airports and top-end hotels in major cities.

TV

There are about seven major channels broadcast from Manila, sometimes in English, sometimes in Tagalog. Most midrange hotels have cable TV with access to between 20 and 120 channels, including some obscure regional channels, a couple of Filipino and international movie channels, the big global news and sports channels such as BBC and ESPN, and the country's own 24-hour English-language news channel, ANC. The latter is owned by ABS-CBN, which competes with the GMA network for national supremacy, providing Tagalog-language programming aimed at the lowest common denominator. Think racy Latin American–style variety shows, cheap local soaps and Filipino action movies.

MONEY

The unit of currency is the peso, divided into 100 centavos. Banknotes come in denominations of 20, 50, 100, 500 and 1000 pesos. The most common coins are one, five and 10 pesos.

ATMs

ATMs are located in all major cities and towns throughout the country. Where a region covered in this chapter does not have ATMs (such as most of Palawan), it is noted in that chapter. The Maestro/Cirrus network is most readily accepted, followed by Visa/Plus cards, then by American Express (Amex). The most prevalent ATMs that accept most Western bank cards belong to Equitable PCI Bank (PCI), Bank of the Philippine Islands (BPI) and Metrobank. Most ATMs have a P6000 per-transaction withdrawal limit; the HSBC and Citibank ATMs in Manila and Cebu let you take out P15,000 to P20,000 per transaction.

Cash

Emergency cash in US dollars is a good thing to have in case you get stuck in an area with no working ATM. Other currencies, such as the euro or UK pound, are more difficult to change outside of the bigger cities.

'Sorry, no change' becomes a very familiar line. Stock up on notes smaller than P500 at every opportunity.

Credit Cards

Major credit cards are accepted by many hotels, restaurants and businesses. Outside of Manila, businesses tend to charge from 5% to 12% extra for credit card transactions. Most Philippine banks will let you take a cash advance on your card.

Exchanging Money

Moneychangers are much faster than the banks and give a better rate for cash, but can be dodgy, particularly in Manila. They prefer US dollars. Ask your hotel front desk to recommend a local moneychanger. In the provinces, hotels will often change money for you.

Exchange rates at the time of writing were as follows:

Country	Unit	Pesos (P)
Australia	A$1	39.02
Canada	C$1	44.95
Euro zone	€1	64.24
Indonesia	10,000Rp	49.42
Japan	¥100	40.16
Malaysia	RM1	13.28
New Zealand	NZ$1	33.04
UK	UK£1	92.92
US	US$1	46.28

Travellers Cheques

We don't recommend bringing travellers cheques as banks in the Philippines seem to have a vendetta against them. Without exception you will need your passport and the original receipts and you may find that banks and moneychangers will only change cheques between 9am and 10am, or only at limited branches. You stand the best chance with Amex US-dollar cheques – other companies and denominations may not be changeable. The best places to cash Amex and Thomas Cook travellers cheques are at their respective branches in Manila (see p593).

POST

The postal system is generally quite efficient, but mail from the provinces can take weeks to reach Manila, let alone the outside world. Wait until you get back to the capital if you're sending anything internationally.

RESPONSIBLE TRAVEL

As in other Asian countries, always allow locals a way of extracting themselves from an awkward situation. Publicly dressing down a Filipino is a sure-fire way to stir up trouble. Most Filipinos love having their photo taken, but tribespeople in rural areas in particular might resent it if you snap away without asking.

The Philippines is home to 100 or so cultural groups, and while visiting tribal villages is extremely rewarding, you should consider that your presence can have a destabilising and corrosive influence on their culture. Obvious displays of wealth are a no-no. Gifts are warmly received but should be kept modest; matches and small bottles of *ginebra* (local gin) work well. Ask to meet the village headman before staying overnight, and always respect the wishes of the locals. Ask permission to photograph, and don't insist if permission is denied.

The Philippines has an abominable environmental record, and visitors are often put off by the way Filipinos throw their garbage everywhere and urinate in public. This is one situation where the 'When in Rome…' maxim does not apply. Set an example by using garbage bins (when you can find them) and politely refusing the 7-Eleven clerk's offer to put your tiny pack of chewing gum in a big plastic bag. As with anywhere, tread particularly softly in environmentally sensitive areas such as coral reefs, rice terraces, rainforests and whale shark zones.

TELEPHONE

Mobile phones are the biggest thing here since watches, and half the country spends much of the time furiously texting the other half. Many remote provincial villages lack landlines but are connected to one or both of the Philippines' two mobile networks – Globe Telecom and Smart Telecom. For travellers, a mobile phone can be a good thing to have in the event of an emergency. They are also useful for booking rooms (often accomplished by text message) and texting newly made Filipino friends.

The best strategy is to bring your own GSM phone and purchase a local prepaid SIM card (P100) to avoid hefty overseas roaming charges. Text messages cost only P1 per message, and calls to other mobile phones or land lines P7.50 per minute. International text messages cost P15 per message and international calls cost US$0.40 per minute. Philippine mobile phone numbers all begin with 09.

If you don't have a mobile phone, international calls can be made from many hotels (for a hefty price) or from any PLDT or BayanTel office. PLDT and BayanTel offer flat rates of US$0.40 per minute for international calls.

The country code for the Philippines is ☎63. The international dialling code is ☎00. For local area codes, dial the first zero when calling from within the Philippines. For the PLDT directory, call ☎187 nationwide. For the international operator, dial ☎108.

TOILETS

Toilets are commonly called a 'CR', an abbreviation of the delightfully euphemistic

PROSTITUTION IN THE PHILIPPINES

One social issue related to travel in the Philippines is prostitution and its most insidious form, child prostitution. In some European and Japanese magazines, the Philippines is actively promoted as a prime sex-tourism destination. Among the major sex-tour operators is the Japanese organised-crime group Yakuza.

Although prostitution is officially illegal in the Philippines, the 'red light' districts of most big cities operate openly and freely, with karaoke bars, 'discos', go-go bars and strip clubs all acting as fronts. The call girls are euphemistically called 'GROs' – guest relations officers.

The Asia-Pacific office of the **Coalition Against Trafficking in Women** (☎02-426 9873; www.catw-ap.org) is based in Quezon City. Its website has information about prostitution in the Philippines and several useful links. Travellers can also contact the Quezon City office of **End Child Prostitution in Asian Tourism** (ECPAT; ☎02-925 2803; www.ecpat.net), a global network of organisations that works to stop child prostitution, child pornography and the trafficking of children for sexual purposes.

'comfort room'. Public toilets are virtually nonexistent, so aim for one of the ubiquitous fast-food restaurants should you need a room of comfort.

TOURIST INFORMATION

The Philippines' tourism authority is run out of the **Department of Tourism Information Centre** (DOT; Map pp598-9; ☎ 02-524 2384; www.wowphilippines.ph; TM Kalaw St; 7am-6pm) in Manila. The DOT's website has contact information for DOT representatives in the US, UK, Australia and other countries.

TRAVELLERS WITH DISABILITIES

Steps up to hotels, tiny cramped toilets and narrow doors are the norm outside of four-star hotels in Manila, Cebu and a handful of larger provincial cities. Lifts are often out of order, and boarding any form of rural transport is likely to be fraught with difficulty. On the other hand, most Filipinos are more than willing to lend a helping hand, and the cost of hiring a taxi for a day and possibly an assistant as well is not excessive.

VISAS

Visa regulations vary with your intended length of stay. Whey you arrive you'll receive a 21-day visa free of charge. As usual, your passport must be valid for at least six months beyond the period you intend to stay.

To extend a 21-day visa to 59 days costs US$42 at any immigration office. It takes less than an hour to extend your visa at most provincial bureau of immigration offices (see following). The process is infinitely more painful at the **Bureau of Immigration head office** (Map p600; ☎ 02-527 3248; Magallanes Dr, Intramuros, Manila; 8am-noon & 1-5pm Mon-Fri) – consider paying a travel agent about P500 to do it for you.

For a full list of provincial immigration offices, see http://immigration.gov.ph. Useful offices include the following:

Boracay (Map p619; ☎ 036-288 5267; Nirvana Beach Resort; 2-5.30pm Mon, 8am-noon & 1-5.30pm Tue & Wed)

Cebu City (off Map p625; ☎ 032-345 6442; cnr Burgos St & Mandaue Ave) Relatively hassle-free visa extensions. It's behind the Mandaue Fire Station, opposite the Mandaue Sports Complex, 6.5km northeast of town.

Puerto Galera (Map p615; Puerto Galera municipal compound; Mon-Wed)

Puerto Princesa (☎ 048-433 2248; Rizal Ave; 8am-noon & 1-5pm Mon-Fri) Upstairs in a white building next to the Palawan Hotel.

LENDING A HELPING HAND

Andrea Gillespie, Volunteer

Volunteering in the Philippines, I learned that a coconut shell works better than a shovel sometimes and that a smile (and a lift of the eyebrows) can go a long way. This was my third time volunteering with Hands On Disaster Response and my first visit to the Philippines. It was amazing to be welcomed with such warmth and to have an opportunity to learn, work and activate change together.

If you just can't be bothered extending your visa, don't sweat it. You can extend it retroactively at the airport upon departure, paying all relevant fees plus a modest P1000 fine. Using this method will not adversely affect your chances of entering the country in the future.

VOLUNTEERING

Hands On Manila (☎ 02-843 5231; www.handsonmanila.org) is a wonderful organisation that is always looking for eager volunteers to help with disaster assistance and other projects. You might also inquire at the **Springboard Foundation** (☎ 02-821 5440; www.springboard-foundation.org), which has ties to various charity organisations that do volunteer work in the Philippines.

To get involved with biodiversity and species conservation projects contact the **Haribon Foundation** (www.haribon.org.ph) or **WWF Philippines** (www.wwf.org.ph).

WOMEN TRAVELLERS

Many male Filipinos think of themselves as irresistible macho types, but can also be surprisingly considerate, and especially keen to show their best side to foreign women. They will address you as 'Ma'am', shower you with compliments and engage you in polite conversation. Note that in Filipino dating culture, striking up a private conversation may be seen as a step towards something more intimate.

Filipinas rarely miss the chance to ask personal questions out of curiosity – about your home country, family, marital status and so on. It's worth packing a few stock answers to these questions in your luggage for cheerful distribution.

Tampons are fairly widely available but it's a good idea to stock up.

Singapore

HIGHLIGHTS

- **Little India** – a jumble of gold, textiles and cheap eats minutes from Orchard Rd, this could be another country entirely (p660)
- **Singapore Zoo** – tucked into the forest, this outstanding open concept zoo is notable for its primates, particularly its free-ranging orang-utans (p660)
- **Clarke Quay** – despite its garish riverfront design, resurgent Clarke Quay is the place to go for nightlife, boasting some of the city's best bars and clubs (p667)
- **Asian Civilisations Museum** – a sumptuous tour of the region's cultures housed in a 150-year-old building, this is one of Singapore's gems (p659)
- **Sentosa** – yes, we know it's a little tacky, but after flying down the luge track a few times, you'll no longer care (p663)
- **Off the beaten track** – take a hike through one of the world's only patches of primary urban rainforest at Bukit Timah (p663)

FAST FACTS

- **Budget** US$40 a day
- **Costs** hostel dorm bed S$18 to S$20, four-hour bus ride S$2 to S$3, beer S$5 to S$15
- **Country code** ☎ 65
- **Languages** English, Mandarin, Malay, Tamil
- **Money** US$1 = S$1.51 (Singaporean dollar)
- **Phrases** *ni hao ma?* (how are you?), *zai jian* (goodbye), *xie xie* (thanks), *dui bu qi* (sorry)
- **Population** 4.6 million
- **Time** GMT + seven hours
- **Visas** most travellers get a 30-day tourist visa on arrival

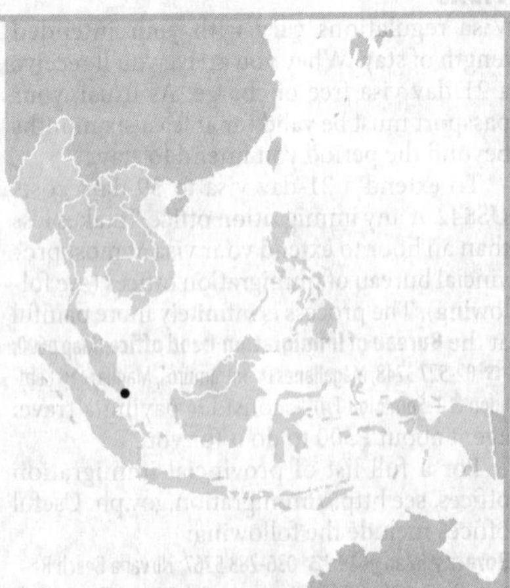

TRAVEL HINT

Museums are free after 6pm (Singapore Art Museum and National Museum of Singapore) or discounted after 7pm (Asian Civilisations Museum).

OVERLAND ROUTES

Take the Causeway across to Johor Bahru in Malaysia, or cross the bridge at Tuas to Tanjung Kupang in Malaysia, but avoid crossing into Singapore on Sunday evenings.

One of Southeast Asia's most remarkable success stories, immaculate Singapore confirms and undermines popular stereotypes in equal measure. Yes, it's modern, clean and organised. No, it's not stifling, strait-laced and dull. What you have here is a dynamic 21st-century metropolis with a culture, history and cuisine that's remarkably rich for a place so small.

Board the ultra-efficient Mass Rapid Transit (MRT) train system and, within a few short stops, you can surface among the glitter of the Orchard Rd retail mecca, the Palladian columns of the Colonial District, the pungent ramshackle lanes of Little India, or the besuited bustle of the central business district (CBD). It's affluent, hi-tech and occasionally a little snobbish, but the great leveller is the hawker centre, the ubiquitous and raucous food markets where everyone mucks in together to indulge the local mania for cheap eating.

Singapore might only warrant a few days on most itineraries, but there's an awful lot to pack in.

CURRENT EVENTS

The People's Action Party, which has held power since independence, surprised no-one by retaining power in the 2006 general election, winning 66.6% of the vote but still taking all but two of the seats up for grabs. The untold story of this election, one that never appeared in the local press, was the huge crowds that turned up for opposition rallies. Whether this was a sign of an upsurge in discontent with a government that has presided over an ever widening income gap, or merely due to the novelty of seeing an opposition denied anything except negative coverage remains to be seen.

Singapore is undergoing a fresh development boom, gearing up to boost its population to 6.5 million and reposition itself as a centre for everything from biomedical research to tourism. Two huge casino resorts are being built on Sentosa Island and at Marina South, while the entire Marina Bay area around the futuristic Esplanade theatre is being turned into an upmarket commercial-residential-leisure centre.

HISTORY

Lion City

According to Malay legend, a Sumatran prince spotted a lion while visiting the island of Temasek, and based on this good omen he founded a city there called Singapura (Lion City). Records of Singapore's early history are patchy; originally it was a tiny sea town squeezed between powerful neighbours Sumatra and Melaka.

Raffles

Sir Thomas Stamford Raffles arrived in 1819 on a mission to secure a strategic base for the British Empire in the Malacca Strait (Strait of Melaka). He decided to transform the sparsely populated, swampy island into a free-trade port. The layout of central Singapore is still as Raffles drew it.

World War II

The glory days of the Empire came to an abrupt end on 15 February 1942, when the Japanese invaded Singapore. For the rest of WWII the Japanese ruled the island harshly, jailing Allied prisoners of war (POWs) at Changi Prison and killing thousands of locals. Although the British were welcomed back after the war, the Empire's days in the region were numbered.

Foundation for the Future

The socialist People's Action Party (PAP) was founded in 1954, with Lee Kuan Yew as its secretary general. Lee led the PAP to victory in elections held in 1959, and hung onto power for over 30 years. Singapore was kicked out of the Malay Federation in 1965, but Lee made the most of one-party rule and pushed through an ambitious industrialisation programme and a strict regulation of social behaviour.

His successor in 1990 was Goh Chok Tong, who loosened things up a little, but maintained Singapore on the path Lee had forged. In 2004 Goh stepped down to make way for Lee's son, Lee Hsien Loong.

Lee the Younger faces the huge challenge of positioning Singapore to succeed in the modern, globalised economy. As manufacturing bleeds away to cheaper competitors, the government knows it must boost its population, attract more so-called 'foreign talent' and develop industries like tourism, financial services, digital media and biomedical research if its success story is to continue into the future.

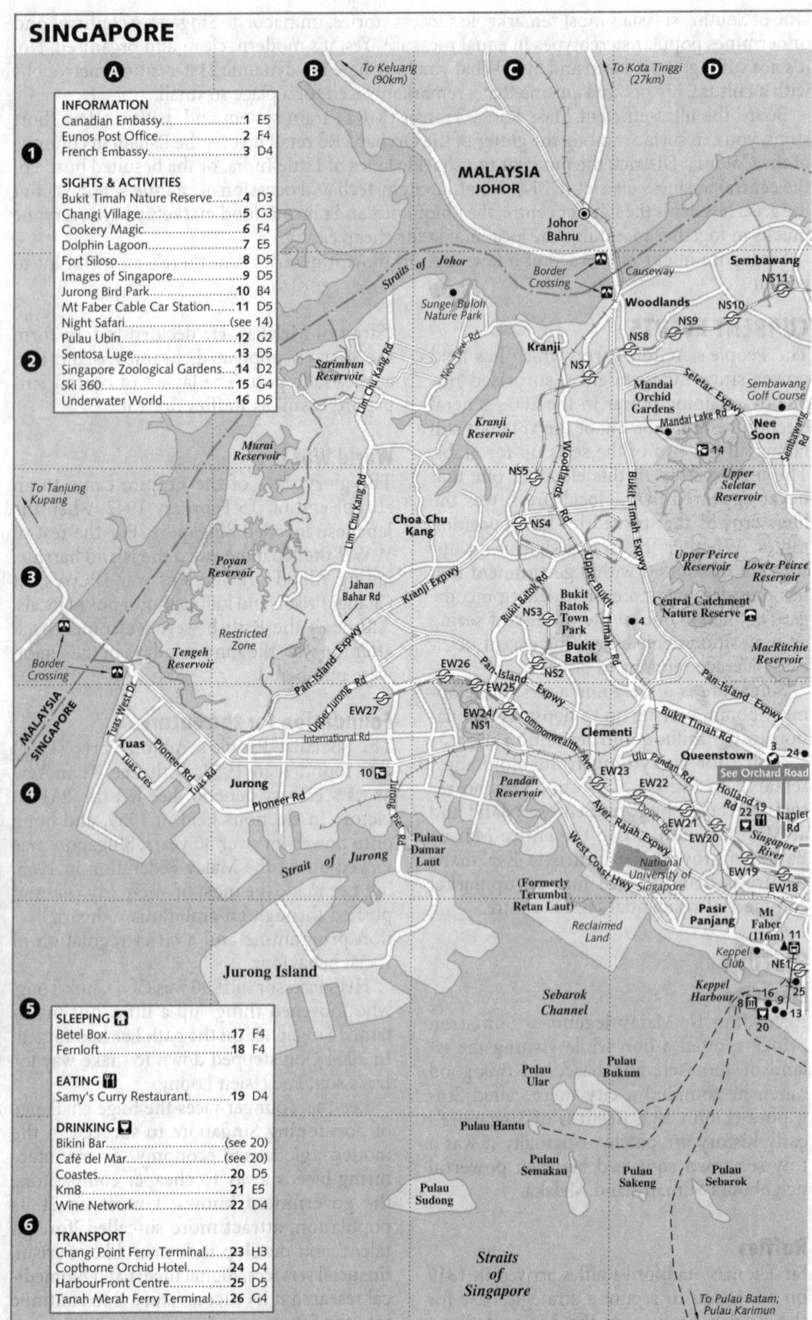
SINGAPORE
A
B
C
D
1
2
3
4
5
6
INFORMATION
Canadian Embassy....1 E5
Eunos Post Office....2 F4
French Embassy....3 D4
SIGHTS & ACTIVITIES
Bukit Timah Nature Reserve....4 D3
Changi Village....5 G3
Cookery Magic....6 F4
Dolphin Lagoon....7 E5
Fort Siloso....8 D5
Images of Singapore....9 D5
Jurong Bird Park....10 B4
Mt Faber Cable Car Station....11 D5
Night Safari....(see 14)
Pulau Ubin....12 G2
Sentosa Luge....13 D5
Singapore Zoological Gardens....14 D2
Ski 360....15 G4
Underwater World....16 D5
SLEEPING
Betel Box....17 F4
Fernloft....18 F4
EATING
Samy's Curry Restaurant....19 D4
DRINKING
Bikini Bar....(see 20)
Café del Mar....(see 20)
Coastes....20 D5
Km8....21 E5
Wine Network....22 D4
TRANSPORT
Changi Point Ferry Terminal....23 H3
Copthorne Orchid Hotel....24 D4
HarbourFront Centre....25 D5
Tanah Merah Ferry Terminal....26 G4
To Keluang (90km)
To Kota Tinggi (27km)
MALAYSIA
JOHOR
Johor Bahru
Straits of Johor
Border Crossing
Causeway
Sembawang
Woodlands
Kranji
Sungei Buloh Nature Park
Sarimbun Reservoir
Lim Chu Kang Rd
Neo Tiew Rd
Mandai Orchid Gardens
Mandai Lake Rd
Seletar Expwy
Sembawang Golf Course
Nee Soon
Sembawang Rd
Kranji Reservoir
Murai Reservoir
Woodlands Rd
Bukit Timah Expwy
Upper Seletar Reservoir
To Tanjung Kupang
Choa Chu Kang
Upper Bukit Timah Rd
Upper Peirce Reservoir
Lower Peirce Reservoir
Poyan Reservoir
Jahan Bahar Rd
Kranji Expwy
Bukit Batok Rd
Bukit Batok Town Park
Central Catchment Nature Reserve
Restricted Zone
Tengeh Reservoir
Bukit Batok
MacRitchie Reservoir
Pan-Island Expwy
Upper Jurong Rd
Commonwealth Ave
Clementi
Bukit Timah Rd
MALAYSIA
SINGAPORE
Tuas West Dr
Tuas
Pioneer Rd
Tuas Cres
Tuas Rd
International Rd
Queenstown
Ulu Pandan Rd
See Orchard Road
Jurong
Jurong Pier Rd
Pandan Reservoir
Holland Rd
Napier Rd
Dover Rd
Ayer Rajah Expwy
Singapore River
Strait of Jurong
Pulau Damar Laut
West Coast Hwy
National University of Singapore
(Formerly Terumbu Retan Laut)
Reclaimed Land
Pasir Panjang
Mt Faber (116m)
Keppel Club
Jurong Island
Sebarok Channel
Keppel Harbour
Pulau Ular
Pulau Bukum
Pulau Hantu
Pulau Semakau
Pulau Sakeng
Pulau Sebarok
Pulau Sudong
Straits of Singapore
To Pulau Batam; Pulau Karimun
NS11
NS10
NS9
NS8
NS7
NS5
NS4
NS3
NS2
EW26
EW25
EW24/NS1
EW27
EW23
EW22
EW21
EW20
EW19
EW18
NE1

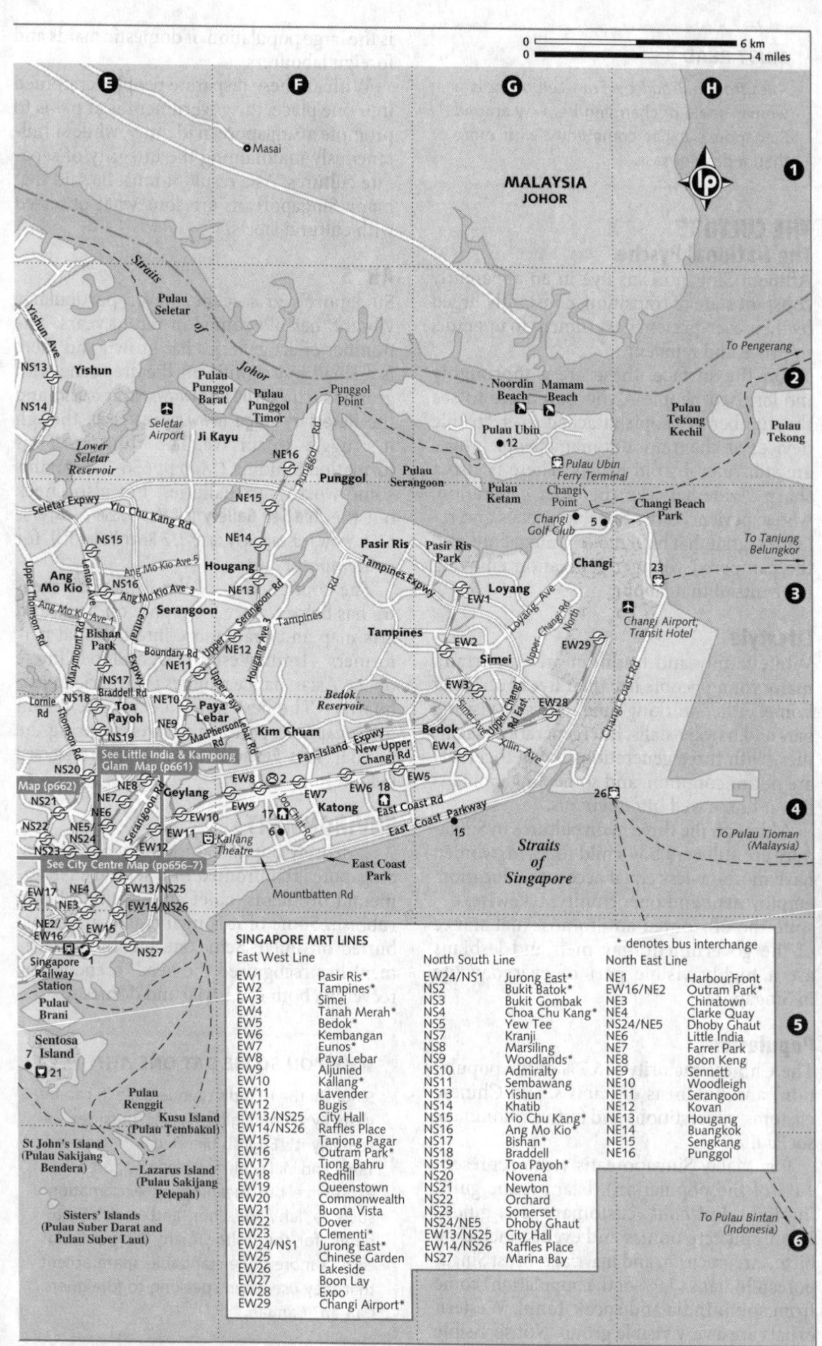
0 6 km
0 4 miles
E
F
G
H
1
2
3
4
5
6
Masai
MALAYSIA
JOHOR
Straits of Johor
Pulau Seletar
Yishun Ave
Yishun
NS13
NS14
Pulau Punggol Barat
Pulau Punggol Timor
Punggol Point
Seletar Airport
Ji Kayu
Lower Seletar Reservoir
NE16
Punggol Rd
Punggol
Pulau Serangoon
Noordin Beach
Mamam Beach
Pulau Ubin
12
Pulau Ubin Ferry Terminal
To Pengerang
Pulau Tekong Kechil
Pulau Tekong
Pulau Ketam
Changi Point
Changi Golf Club
5
Changi Beach Park
Seletar Expwy
Yio Chu Kang Rd
NE15
NE14
NS15
Hougang
Pasir Ris
Pasir Ris Park
To Tanjung Belungkor
Changi
23
Ang Mo Kio Ave 5
Ang Mo Kio Ave 3
Ang Mo Kio Ave 1
Ang Mo Kio
NS16
Upper Thomson Rd
Lentor Ave
Central Expwy
NE13
Serangoon
Upper Serangoon Rd
Tampines Expwy
Tampines Rd
Tampines
EW1
Loyang
Loyang Ave
Upper Changi Rd North
Changi Airport; Transit Hotel
EW29
Bishan Park
Marymount Rd
Boundary Rd
NE12
NE11
Hougang Ave 3
EW2
Simei
Changi Coast Rd
NS17
Braddell Rd
Upper Paya Lebar Rd
Bedok Reservoir
EW3
Simei Ave
Upper Changi Rd East
EW28
Lornie Rd
NS18
Toa Payoh
NE10
Paya Lebar
Thomson Rd
NS19
NE9
MacPherson Rd
Kim Chuan
Bedok
Pan-Island Expwy
New Upper Changi Rd
Xilin Ave
EW4
See Little India & Kampong Glam Map (p661)
NS20
Map (p662)
NE8
Serangoon Rd
Geylang
EW8
2
EW5
NS21
NE7
EW6
18
EW9
EW7
Katong
East Coast Rd
26
NE6
Joo Chiat Rd
17
NS22
NE5/NS24
EW10
6
East Coast Parkway
15
EW11
Kallang Theatre
NS23
EW12
East Coast Park
Straits of Singapore
To Pulau Tioman (Malaysia)
See City Centre Map (pp656–7)
Mountbatten Rd
EW17
NE4
EW13/NS25
NE3
EW14/NS26
NE2/EW16
EW15
NS27
1
Singapore Railway Station
Pulau Brani
Sentosa Island
7
21
Pulau Renggit
Kusu Island (Pulau Tembakul)
St John's Island (Pulau Sakijang Bendera)
Lazarus Island (Pulau Sakijang Pelepah)
Sisters' Islands (Pulau Suber Darat and Pulau Suber Laut)
To Pulau Bintan (Indonesia)
SINGAPORE MRT LINES
* denotes bus interchange
East West Line
EW1 Pasir Ris*
EW2 Tampines*
EW3 Simei
EW4 Tanah Merah*
EW5 Bedok*
EW6 Kembangan
EW7 Eunos*
EW8 Paya Lebar
EW9 Aljunied
EW10 Kallang*
EW11 Lavender
EW12 Bugis
EW13/NS25 City Hall
EW14/NS26 Raffles Place
EW15 Tanjong Pagar
EW16 Outram Park*
EW17 Tiong Bahru
EW18 Redhill
EW19 Queenstown
EW20 Commonwealth
EW21 Buona Vista
EW22 Dover
EW23 Clementi*
EW24/NS1 Jurong East*
EW25 Chinese Garden
EW26 Lakeside
EW27 Boon Lay
EW28 Expo
EW29 Changi Airport*
North South Line
EW24/NS1 Jurong East*
NS2 Bukit Batok*
NS3 Bukit Gombak
NS4 Choa Chu Kang*
NS5 Yew Tee
NS7 Kranji
NS8 Marsiling
NS9 Woodlands*
NS10 Admiralty
NS11 Sembawang
NS13 Yishun*
NS14 Khatib
NS15 Yio Chu Kang*
NS16 Ang Mo Kio*
NS17 Bishan*
NS18 Braddell
NS19 Toa Payoh*
NS20 Novena
NS21 Newton
NS22 Orchard
NS23 Somerset
NS24/NE5 Dhoby Ghaut
EW13/NS25 City Hall
EW14/NS26 Raffles Place
NS27 Marina Bay
North East Line
NE1 HarbourFront
EW16/NE2 Outram Park*
NE3 Chinatown
NE4 Clarke Quay
NS24/NE5 Dhoby Ghaut
NE6 Little India
NE7 Farrer Park
NE8 Boon Keng
NE9 Sennett
NE10 Woodleigh
NE11 Serangoon
NE12 Kovan
NE13 Hougang
NE14 Buangkok
NE15 Sengkang
NE16 Punggol

SINGAPORE

MUST READ

Tales from a Broad by Fran Leibowitz is a woman's tale of charming her way around Singapore's expat community with more than a dash of sass.

THE CULTURE

The National Pysche

Affluent Singaporeans live in an apparently constant state of transition, constantly urged by their ever-present government to upgrade, improve and reinvent.

On the surface, these are a thoroughly modernised people – you only have to see the number of people attached to electronic devices on the train. But many people's lives are still ruled by old beliefs. There is also a sharp divide between the older generation, who experienced the huge upheavals and relentless graft that built modern Singapore, and the pampered younger generation enjoying the fruits of that labour.

Lifestyle

While family and tradition are important, many young people live their lives outside of home, either working long hours or visiting bars and hawker stalls. Intergenerational families (with three generations living together) are not uncommon, and some Singaporeans live at home well into their 30s.

Although the three main cultures in Singapore are still very boy-child focused, women have more-or-less equal access to education, employment and opportunity. Likewise, despite the oft-touted antihomosexual stance of the government, gay men and lesbians are a highly visible part of everyday life in Singapore.

Population

The Chinese majority (76.7% of the population) are Buddhists or Taoists, and Chinese customs, superstitions and festivals dominate social life.

For Malay Singaporeans (who represent 14% of the population), Islam is the guiding light, but *adat* (customary law) guides important ceremonies and events, including birth, circumcision and marriage. Most Singaporean Indians (7.9% of the population) come from south India and speak Tamil. Western expats are a very visible group. Not so visible is the large population of domestic maids and foreign labourers.

With all these disparate peoples crammed into one place, the government is at pains to promote a Singaporean identity, while simultaneously maintaining the integrity of separate cultures. As a result, it must be said that many Singaporeans are somewhat obsessed with cultural labels.

ARTS

Singapore's arts scene, never particularly vibrant, has blossomed in recent years. The number of art galleries has grown and there is a small but significant theatre scene with groups such as **Wild Rice** (www.wildrice.com.sg) and the **Necessary Stage** (www.necessary.org), though it struggles to survive. The Ministry of Information building (Map pp656–7) contains some worthy art galleries, but also check out the **Red Sea Gallery** (off Map pp656-7; ☎ 6732 6711; www.redseagallery.com; 232 River Valley Rd) for contemporary art.

The construction of the Esplanade theatre has helped place Singapore on the world arts map and draw more international performers – from Western classical to Chinese opera, Asian dance troupes to American jazz quartets. The best time to catch the cream of Singapore's performing arts is during the annual **Arts Festival** (www.singaporeartsfest.com) held in June.

ENVIRONMENT

As a densely populated island of 604 sq km, Singapore is confronted with several environmental problems, chief among them being rubbish. Some of it is incinerated and some buried on Pulau Semakau, but the government has recognised the need to encourage recycling, both industrial and domestic.

WHY YOU SO LIE DAT ONE AH?

Singlish, the island's unique dialect, can be virtually unintelligible to the outsider. Essentially it's English blended with Hokkien, Tamil and Malay phrases and peppered with expressive but meaningless exclamations such as 'lah', 'lor', 'hor' and 'meh'. Fortunately for the visitor, many Singaporeans carry a more understandable spare accent that they use when speaking to foreigners. Can ah? Can lah.

Air quality is generally much better than most large Southeast Asian metropolises, but the annual haze that descends on the island around September and October, generated by slash-and-burn fires in Indonesia, is a serious concern.

Keeping 4.6 million people supplied with fresh water is another headache. Much of it is imported from Malaysia, but with large reservoirs, desalination plants and a huge waste-water recycling project called Newater, Singapore hopes to become self-sufficient within the next few decades. Tap water is safe.

Singapore has a proud and well-deserved reputation as a garden city. Parks, often beautifully landscaped, are abundant and the entire centre of the island is a green oasis. Outside of the zoo and bird park, wildlife sightings are largely limited to long-tailed macaques, squirrels and the prehistoric monitor lizard, but it's still possible to spot flying lemurs and pythons in more remote spots. There are even crocodiles in the mangroves of the island's northwest.

TRANSPORT

GETTING THERE & AWAY

Air

Singapore is an ideal point to begin any Southeast Asian journey. The city's budget air travel boom is good news for shoestring travellers, connecting Changi Airport cheaply with dozens of regional destinations.

Budget airlines operating out of Changi include the following:

Air Sahara (code S2; ☎ 6557 4550; www.airsahara.net) Flies to 15 cities in India, as well as Kathmandu.

Cebu Pacific Air (code 5J; ☎ 6735 7155; www.cebupacificair.com) Flies to Cebu, Manila and Davao in the Philippines.

Jetstar Asia (code 3K; ☎ 6822 2288; www.jetstarasia.com) Flies to Australia, Cambodia, Hong Kong, Indonesia, Myanmar, Philippines, Taiwan, Thailand and Vietnam.

Tiger Airways (code TR; ☎ 1800-388 8888; www.tigerairways.com) Flies to Australia, China, Indonesia, Macau, Philippines, Thailand and Vietnam.

> **DEPARTURE TAX**
>
> A departure tax of S$21 is automatically added to air tickets.

The bigger airlines:

Lufthansa (code LH; ☎ 6835 5933; www.lufthansa.com)

Malaysia Airlines (code MH; ☎ 6336 6777; www.sg.malaysiaairlines.com)

Qantas (code QF; ☎ 6589 7000; www.qantas.com.sg)

Singapore Airlines (code SQ; ☎ 6223 8888; www.singaporeair.com)

If you plan to fly to Malaysia, including Borneo, head to Johor Bahru. Flights on **Air Asia** (code AK; ☎ 6733 9933; www.airasia.com) and Malaysia Airlines are considerably cheaper from there. Malaysia Airlines passengers can take a connecting bus service (S$12) from Singapore's **Copthorne Orchid Hotel** (Map pp650-1; ☎ 6250 3333; 214 Dunearn Rd), leaving at 9am, 12.20pm and 3.50pm every day. Advance bookings are necessary.

Land

BUS

For Johor Bahru, the quickest method is to go to Kranji MRT station and take bus 160 from there. Share taxis to many places in Malaysia leave from the Queen St bus terminal (Map p661).

Coming from Johor Bahru, take a bus from Larkin station, or a shared taxi (RM8, four people) from the taxi terminal opposite the Puteri Pan Pacific Hotel.

The buses stop at the Singapore checkpoint; keep your ticket and hop on the next bus that comes along after you've cleared immigration. You'll go through the same process at Malaysian immigration and customs across the Causeway. The bus continues to the Larkin bus terminal on the edge of town.

If you are travelling beyond Johor Bahru, it is easier to catch a long-distance bus from Singapore. Cheap luxury coaches, with huge seats, lots of legroom and TVs, make the journey pretty pleasant.

Agents at the **Golden Mile Complex** (off Map p661; Beach Rd) and **Golden Mile Tower** (off Map p661; Beach Rd) sell tickets for Melaka, Kuala Lumpur, Penang, Cameron Highlands and many other destinations. **Grassland Express** (☎ 6293 1166; www.grassland.com.sg; 01-26 Golden Mile Complex) and **Konsortium** (☎ 6392 3911; www.konsortium.com.sg; 01-52 Golden Mile Tower) both run excellent coaches.

Arriving from Malaysia by coach, you'll be dropped either at the **Lavender St bus terminal** (Map p661; cnr Lavender St & Kallang Bahru), a 500m walk north from Lavender MRT station, or outside the Golden Mile Complex.

TRAIN

Malaysian company **Keretapi Tanah Melayu Berhad** (☎ 6222 5165; www.ktmb.com.my) operates three air-con express trains daily for the six-hour run from Singapore to Kuala Lumpur at 8.10am, 3.05pm and 10.10pm (3rd/2nd class S$19/34), with connections on to Thailand.

Sea

Ferries connect Singapore to Indonesia's Riau archipelago. There are two departure points: the HarbourFront Centre (Map pp650–1), next to HarbourFront MRT station, and **Tanah Merah ferry terminal** (Map pp650-1; ☎ 6542 7102).

From HarbourFront, boats leave for Pulau Batam, Tanjung Balai and Tanjung Batu. The Tanah Merah terminal handles boats to Pulau Bintan and Nongsapara on Batam, as well as Desaru in Malaysia. To get here, take the MRT to Bedok and then bus 35. A taxi from the city is around S$15.

Ferry operators are **Penguin** (☎ 6271 4866; www.penguin.com.sg) for Batam, Bintan and Tanjung Balai; **Batam Fast** (☎ 6270 0311; www.batamfast.com), **Berlian** (☎ 6546 8830) and **Dino Shipping** (☎ 6276 9722) for Batam only; **Indo Falcon** (☎ 6275 7393; www.indofalcon.com.sg) for all four Riau destinations, plus Malaysia; and **Bintan Resort Ferries** (6542 4369; www.brf.com.sg). Expect to pay around S$16 for a one-way ticket to Batam, S$24 to S$36 to Bintan, Balai or Batu.

GETTING AROUND

Bicycle

Singapore has few hills, but the city's aggressive drivers make life on two wheels unpleasant. Happily, there is an ever expanding network of bike paths connecting Singapore's many parks that will eventually stretch 300km around the island. The 12km bike path along East Coast Park makes a decent ride, but avoid weekends when it's extremely crowded. See the website of the **National Parks Board** (www.nparks.gov.sg/imgs/parkconnectors/sporemap.pdf) for a map of the bike paths.

Hire a decent mountain bike for S$6 to S$8 at one of the numerous hiring booths at East Coast Park. You can also get Rollerblade here too.

Boat

A tour of the Singapore River in a bumboat (small motorised boat) strung with Chinese lanterns is a popular way to spend an hour and is especially romantic at night. **Singapore River Cruises** (☎ 6336 6111; www.rivercruise.com.sg) and **Singapore Explorer** (☎ 6339 6833; www.singaporeexplorer.com.sg) both charge S$12/6 per adult/child for a half-hour tour, or S$15/8 for a 45-minute tour, complete with a syrupy commentary pointing out the many historical landmarks. **Watertours** (☎ 6533 9811; www.watertours.com.sg) runs 2½-hour cruises around the coastline on a replica Chinese junk. Departing from HarbourFront Centre (Map pp650–1), there are day cruises at 10.30am and 3pm (adult/child S$25/12) and a dinner cruise at 6.30pm (S$53/27).

Bumboats also leave the Changi Point ferry terminal (Map pp650–1) for Pulau Ubin.

Bus

Public buses run between 6am and midnight. Each bus stop has information on bus

GETTING TO INDONESIA & MALAYSIA

To Indonesia

Ferries and speedboats run between Singapore and the Riau Archipelago in Indonesia; see above for details. Immigration is straightforward, though expect to pay for an Indonesian visa (US$20 for three days) at the other end.

For travel in the reverse direction, see p267.

To Malaysia

A 1km-long Causeway in the north, at Woodlands, connects Singapore with Johor Bahru in Malaysia. To the west a bridge connects the suburb of Tuas with Tanjung Kupang in Malaysia. Immigration procedures on both sides of the bridges are straightforward. See p653 for details of buses and trains heading across the border.

When travelling into Malaysia by train, passports are checked by Malaysian immigration at the Singapore train station (officially part of Malaysia) but *not* stamped. This should not be a problem when you leave Malaysia if you keep your train ticket and immigration card.

For travel in the reverse direction, see p456

numbers and routes, or check the bus company journey planners (www.sbstransit.com.sg; www.smrt.com.sg). Fares start from 80c and rise to a maximum of S$1.70. When you board the bus, tell the driver where you're going, drop the exact money into the fare box (no change is given) and collect your ticket from the machine.

Ez-link cards (see Mass Rapid Transit, below) can be used on all buses and trains. You'll need to flash the card in front of the card reader when boarding the bus and again when leaving.

The **SIA Hop-On** (☎ 9457 2896; http://siahopon.asiaone.com.sg/; 1-day ticket for Singapore Airlines passengers S$3, nonpassengers adult/child S$12/6) tourist bus does 19 loops of the city between 9am and 7.30pm, stopping at 21 points of interest.

Car

Hiring a car in Singapore is easy, but with efficient public transport and parking a nightmare, it's completely pointless unless you plan to explore the outer reaches of the island. Expensive surcharges make it pricey to take a hire car into Malaysia, where rental cars are much cheaper anyway.

Mass Rapid Transit

The ultramodern MRT subway system is the easiest, quickest and most comfortable way to get around. The system operates from 6am to midnight, with trains at peak times running every three minutes, and off-peak every six minutes.

Single-trip tickets cost from 90c to S$1.90, but you have to pay a S$1 deposit for every ticket, then redeem it at the end of the trip by feeding it back into the machine. If you're going to be using the MRT a lot, it's cheaper and more convenient to buy a S$15 ez-link card from any MRT station (which includes a S$5 deposit and S$10 credit). This electronic card can be used on all public buses and trains. Fares using an ez-link card range from 66c to S$1.75.

Taxi

The major cab companies are **City Cab** (☎ 6552 2222), **Comfort** (☎ 6552 1111), **SMRT** (☎ 6555 8888) and **TransCab** (☎ 6553 3333).

Fares for most companies start from S$2.40 for the first kilometre, then 10c for each additional 220m. There are various surcharges, eg for late-night services, airport pick-ups and bookings, but they are still pretty cheap. You can flag down a taxi any time or use a taxi rank (there are signs in English) outside hotels and malls.

STRANDED IN SINGAPORE

Despite the large number of cabs in Singapore, finding one in the city centre at peak hour, or when it's raining, or late at night, can be maddening. If you need an early-morning cab, book it the night before. In the city at night, the most reliable spots are:

- Circular Rd
- next to the Elgin Bridge at Boat Quay (before 1am)
- the bottom of Emerald Hill on Orchard Rd
- Clarke Quay
- outside major hotels (as a last resort)

If you're around the Bugis area, Chinatown, Little India or Suntec City at night, start praying.

TRISHAW

Bicycle trishaws congregate at popular tourist places, such as Raffles Hotel, the pedestrian mall at Waterloo and Albert Sts, Clarke Quay and the end of Sago Lane. Always agree on the fare beforehand, and expect to pay around S$50 for half an hour.

SINGAPORE

Grab a plastic chair, throw some supersweet coffee and *kaya* (coconut jam) toast down your gullet, and set out to explore the social phenomenon that is modern Singapore. Beneath the veneer of sameness and respectability are some surprising discoveries waiting to be made.

ORIENTATION

The Singapore River cuts the city in two: south is the CBD and Chinatown, and to the north of the river is the Colonial District. The trendy Clarke and Robertson Quays, and the popular Boat Quay dining areas hug the riverbanks.

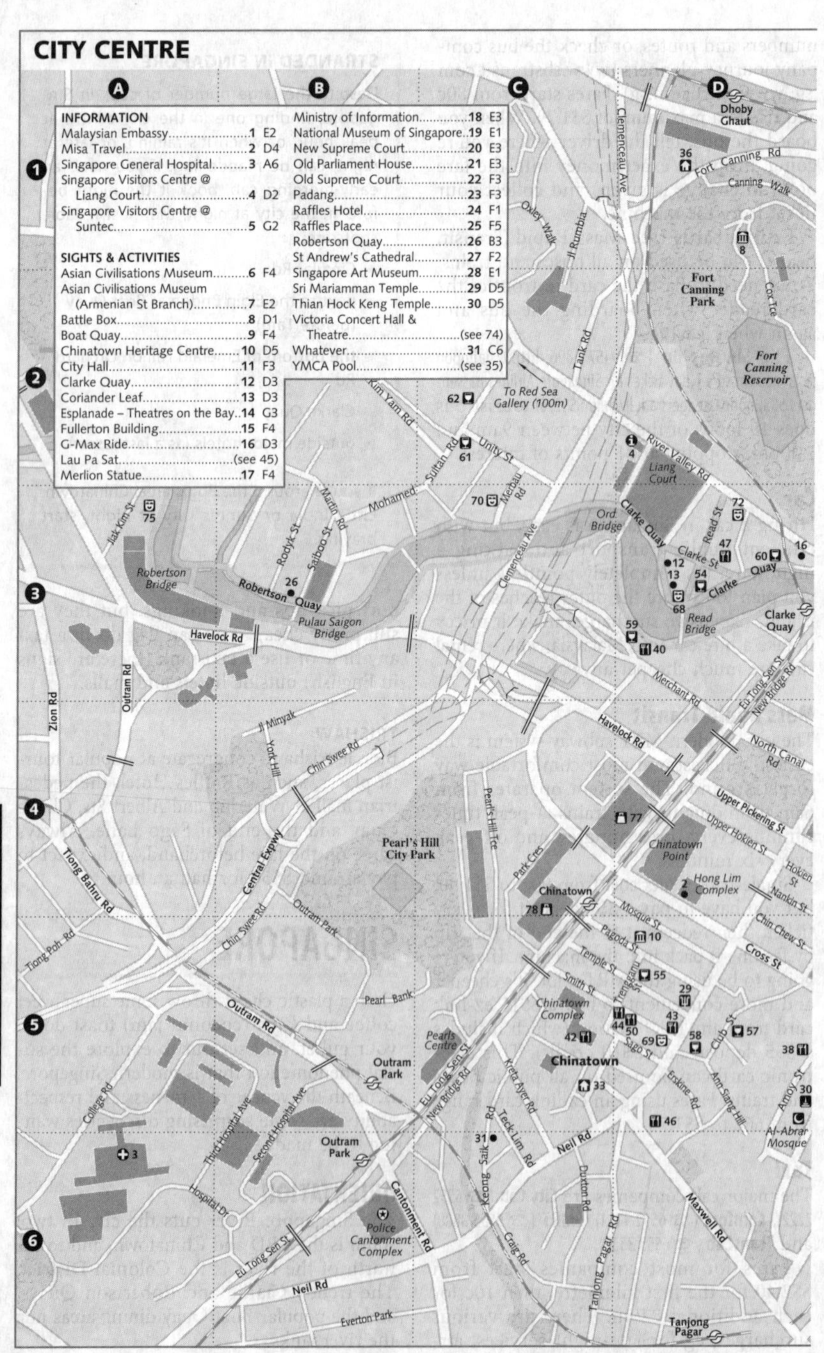
CITY CENTRE
A
B
C
D
1
2
3
4
5
6
INFORMATION
Malaysian Embassy....1 E2
Misa Travel....2 D4
Singapore General Hospital....3 A6
Singapore Visitors Centre @ Liang Court....4 D2
Singapore Visitors Centre @ Suntec....5 G2
SIGHTS & ACTIVITIES
Asian Civilisations Museum....6 F4
Asian Civilisations Museum (Armenian St Branch)....7 E2
Battle Box....8 D1
Boat Quay....9 F4
Chinatown Heritage Centre....10 D5
City Hall....11 F3
Clarke Quay....12 D3
Coriander Leaf....13 D3
Esplanade – Theatres on the Bay....14 G3
Fullerton Building....15 F4
G-Max Ride....16 D3
Lau Pa Sat....(see 45)
Merlion Statue....17 F4
Ministry of Information....18 E3
National Museum of Singapore....19 E1
New Supreme Court....20 E3
Old Parliament House....21 E3
Old Supreme Court....22 F3
Padang....23 F3
Raffles Hotel....24 F1
Raffles Place....25 F5
Robertson Quay....26 B3
St Andrew's Cathedral....27 F2
Singapore Art Museum....28 E1
Sri Mariamman Temple....29 D5
Thian Hock Keng Temple....30 D5
Victoria Concert Hall & Theatre....(see 74)
Whatever....31 C6
YMCA Pool....(see 35)
Dhoby Ghaut
Fort Canning Rd
Canning Walk
Clemenceau Ave
Oxley Walk
Jl Rumbia
Tank Rd
Fort Canning Park
Fort Canning Reservoir
Cox Tce
To Red Sea Gallery (100m)
Kim Yam Rd
Sultan Rd
Unity St
Mohamed
Martin Rd
Merbau Rd
River Valley Rd
Liang Court
Read St
Ord Bridge
Clarke Quay
Clarke St
Clarke Quay
Read Bridge
Jiak Kim St
Rodyk St
Saiboo St
Robertson Bridge
Robertson Quay
Pulau Saigon Bridge
Havelock Rd
Outram Rd
Zion Rd
Jl Minyak
York Hill
Chin Swee Rd
Merchant Rd
Eu Tong Sen St
New Bridge Rd
Havelock Rd
North Canal Rd
Upper Pickering St
Upper Hokien St
Hokien St
Nankin St
Chin Chew St
Cross St
Central Expwy
Pearl's Hill Tce
Pearl's Hill City Park
Park Cres
Chinatown Point
Hong Lim Complex
Chinatown
Mosque St
Pagoda St
Temple St
Smith St
Trengganu St
Sago St
Tiong Bahru Rd
Tiong Poh Rd
Chin Swee Rd
Outram Park
Pearl Bank
Outram Rd
Chinatown Complex
Chinatown
Club St
Ann Siang Hill
Erskine Rd
Amoy St
Al-Abrar Mosque
Pearls Centre
Outram Park
College Rd
Third Hospital Ave
Second Hospital Ave
Kreta Ayer Rd
Teck Lim Rd
Keong Saik Rd
Neil Rd
Outram Park
Hospital Dr
Cantonment Rd
Police Cantonment Complex
Duxton Rd
Maxwell Rd
Craig Rd
Eu Tong Sen St
Neil Rd
Everton Park
Tanjong Pagar Rd
Tanjong Pagar

SINGAPORE

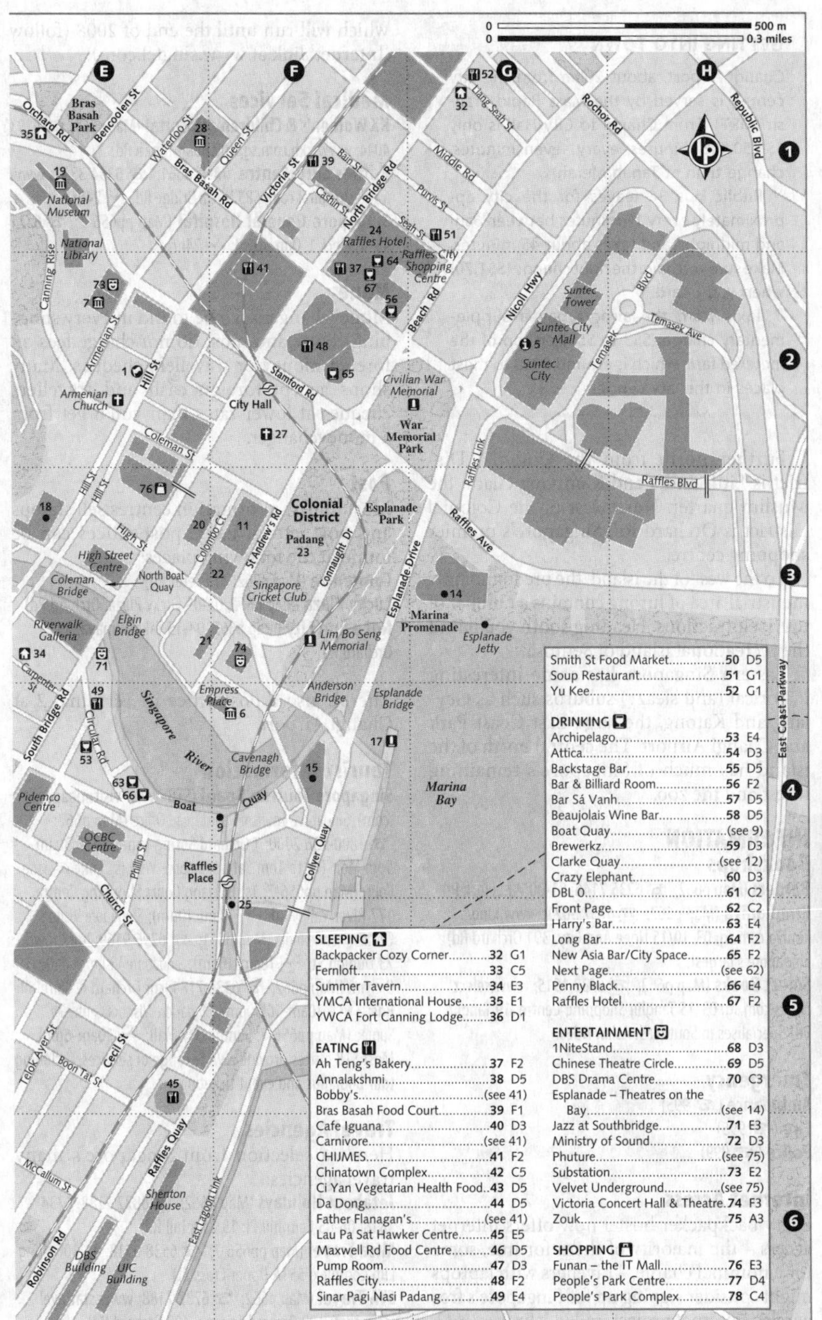
0 500 m
0 0.3 miles
E
F
G
H
1
2
3
4
5
6
Bras Basah Park
Orchard Rd
Bencoolen St
Waterloo St
Queen St
Bras Basah Rd
Victoria St
Bain St
Cashin St
North Bridge Rd
Liang Seah St
Middle Rd
Purvis St
Seah St
Rochor Rd
Republic Blvd
National Museum
National Library
Canning Rise
Armenian St
Hill St
Armenian Church
City Hall
Stamford Rd
24 Raffles Hotel
Raffles City Shopping Centre
Beach Rd
Nicoll Hwy
Suntec Tower
Suntec City Mall
Suntec City
Temasek Blvd
Temasek Ave
Civilian War Memorial
War Memorial Park
Raffles Link
Raffles Blvd
Coleman St
High St
Colombo Ct
St Andrew's Rd
Colonial District
Padang
Connaught Dr
Esplanade Park
Esplanade Drive
Raffles Ave
High Street Centre
North Boat Quay
Coleman Bridge
Singapore Cricket Club
Marina Promenade
Esplanade Jetty
Riverwalk Galleria
Elgin Bridge
Lim Bo Seng Memorial
Carpenter St
South Bridge Rd
Circular Rd
Singapore River
Empress Place
Anderson Bridge
Esplanade Bridge
Cavenagh Bridge
Marina Bay
Boat Quay
Pidemco Centre
OCBC Centre
Phillip St
Raffles Place
Collyer Quay
Church St
East Coast Parkway
Telok Ayer St
Cecil St
Boon Tat St
Raffles Quay
McCallum St
Shenton House
East Lagoon Link
Robinson Rd
DBS Building
UIC Building
SLEEPING
Backpacker Cozy Corner.......32 G1
Fernloft.......33 C5
Summer Tavern.......34 E3
YMCA International House.......35 E1
YWCA Fort Canning Lodge.......36 D1
EATING
Ah Teng's Bakery.......37 F2
Annalakshmi.......38 D5
Bobby's.......(see 41)
Bras Basah Food Court.......39 F1
Cafe Iguana.......40 D3
Carnivore.......(see 41)
CHIJMES.......41 F2
Chinatown Complex.......42 C5
Ci Yan Vegetarian Health Food.......43 D5
Da Dong.......44 D5
Father Flanagan's.......(see 41)
Lau Pa Sat Hawker Centre.......45 E5
Maxwell Rd Food Centre.......46 D5
Pump Room.......47 D3
Raffles City.......48 F2
Sinar Pagi Nasi Padang.......49 E4
Smith St Food Market.......50 D5
Soup Restaurant.......51 G1
Yu Kee.......52 G1
DRINKING
Archipelago.......53 E4
Attica.......54 D3
Backstage Bar.......55 D5
Bar & Billiard Room.......56 F2
Bar Sá Vanh.......57 D5
Beaujolais Wine Bar.......58 D5
Boat Quay.......(see 9)
Brewerkz.......59 D3
Clarke Quay.......(see 12)
Crazy Elephant.......60 D3
DBL O.......61 C2
Front Page.......62 C2
Harry's Bar.......63 E4
Long Bar.......64 F2
New Asia Bar/City Space.......65 F2
Next Page.......(see 62)
Penny Black.......66 E4
Raffles Hotel.......67 F2
ENTERTAINMENT
1NiteStand.......68 D3
Chinese Theatre Circle.......69 D5
DBS Drama Centre.......70 C3
Esplanade – Theatres on the Bay.......(see 14)
Jazz at Southbridge.......71 E3
Ministry of Sound.......72 D3
Phuture.......(see 75)
Substation.......73 E2
Velvet Underground.......(see 75)
Victoria Concert Hall & Theatre.......74 F3
Zouk.......75 A3
SHOPPING
Funan – the IT Mall.......76 E3
People's Park Centre.......77 D4
People's Park Complex.......78 C4

SINGAPORE

GETTING INTO TOWN

Changi Airport, about 20km from the city centre, is served by the Mass Rapid Transit (MRT). From Changi to City Hall is only S$1.50 (28 minutes, every seven minutes, change train at Tanah Merah).

Public bus 36 leaves for the city approximately every 10 minutes between 6am and midnight, and takes about 45 minutes. Make sure you have the right change (S$1.70) when you board.

Taxis from the airport pay a supplementary charge (S$3 to S$5) on top of the metered fare, which is around S$18 to most places in the city centre.

Further north from the Colonial District is Little India and Kampong Glam, the Muslim quarter. Northwest of the Colonial District is Orchard Rd, Singapore's premier shopping centre.

To the west of the island, the predominantly industrial area of Jurong contains a number of tourist attractions. Heading south you'll find the recreational island of Sentosa.

Eastern Singapore has some interesting historical (and sleazy) suburbs such as Geylang and Katong, the large East Coast Park and Changi Airport. The central north of the island has much of Singapore's remaining forest and the zoo.

INFORMATION

Bookshops

Borders (Map p662; ☎ 6235 7146; 01-00 Wheelock Pl)
Kinokuniya (Map p662; ☎ 6737 5021; www.kinokuniya.com.sg; 03-10/15 Ngee Ann City, 391 Orchard Rd) Singapore's largest.
Select Books (Map p662; ☎ 6732 1515; www.selectbooks.com.sg; 03-15 Tanglin Shopping Centre, 19 Tanglin Rd) Specialises in Southeast Asian titles.

Emergency

Ambulance (☎ 995)
Fire (☎ 995)
Police (☎ 999)

Internet Access

Every backpacker hostel now offers internet access – the majority of them for free, some for a nominal charge. Travellers with laptops might consider signing up for Singapore's free wireless internet project, called Wireless@SG, which will run until the end of 2008 (follow 'Internet' link at www.singtel.com).

Medical Services

KK Women's & Children's Hospital (Map p661; ☎ 6293 4044; www.kkh.com.sg; 100 Bukit Timah Rd)
Raffles SurgiCentre (Map p661; ☎ 6334 3337; www.raffleshospital.com; 585 North Bridge Rd; 🕐 24hr)
Singapore General Hospital (Map pp656-7; ☎ 6321 4311; Block 1, Outram Rd; 🕐 24hr)

Money

Moneychangers can be found in every shopping centre and most do not charge fees on foreign money or travellers cheques. Many shops accept foreign cash and travellers cheques at lower rates than you'd get from a moneychanger.

Post

Most tourist information centres sell stamps and post letters. Large post offices can be found at the following places:

Comcentre (Map p662; 31 Exeter Rd)
Lucky Plaza (Map p662; 02-09 Lucky Plaza, Orchard Rd)
Ngee Ann City (Map p662; 04-15 Takashimaya, 391 Orchard Rd)

There's also a post office in Terminal 2 at Changi Airport.

Tourist Information

Singapore Tourism Board (STB; www.visitsingapore.com); Singapore Tourism Board Head Office (Map p662; ☎ 1800-736 2000; 1 Orchard Spring Lane; 🕐 8.30am-5pm Mon-Fri, to 1pm Sat); Singapore Visitors Centre @ Liang Court (Map pp656-7; 1st fl, Liang Court Shopping Centre, 177 River Valley Rd; 🕐 10am-10pm); Singapore Visitors Centre @ Little India (Map p661; ☎ 6296 9169; Inn Crowd, 73 Dunlop St; 🕐 10am-10pm); Singapore Visitors Centre @ Orchard (Map p662; ☎ 6336 7184; cnr Orchard & Cairnhill Rds; 🕐 9.30am-10.30pm); Singapore Visitors Centre @ Suntec (Map pp656-7; Suntec City Mall; 🕐 10am-6pm) Most STB offices provide a wide range of services, including tour bookings and event ticketing.

Travel Agencies

Here's a selection from Singapore's many travel agencies:

Jetabout Holidays (Map p662; ☎ 6822 2288, 6734 1818; 06-05 Cairnhill Pl; 15 Cairnhill Rd)
Misa Travel (Map pp656-7; ☎ 6538 0318; 03-106 Hong Lim Complex, 531A Upper Cross St)
STA Travel (Map p662; ☎ 6737 7188; www.statravel.com.sg; 07-02 Orchard Towers, 400 Orchard Rd)

SIGHTS

Colonial District

To the north of Singapore River is the Colonial District (Map pp656–7), where you'll find many imposing remnants of British rule, including **Victoria Concert Hall & Theatre**, **Old Parliament House** (now an arts centre), **St Andrew's Cathedral**, **City Hall**, and the **old Supreme Court**, which are arranged around the **Padang**, an old cricket pitch. Rising above them is the spaceship of the new Norman Foster–designed **Supreme Court** building.

Nearby, the state-of-the-art **Asian Civilisations Museum** (Map pp656-7; ☎ 6332 7789; www.acm.org.sg; 1 Empress Pl; adult/child & concession S$5/2.50; 1-7pm Mon, 9am-7pm Tue-Thu, Sat & Sun, 9am-9pm Fri) has 10 thematic galleries that explore different aspects of Asian culture, from the Islamic world to Japanese *anime*. At the **Armenian St branch** (Map pp656-7; ☎ 6332 3015; 39 Armenian St; adult/child & concession S$3/1.50; 1-7pm Mon, 9am-7pm Tue-Thu, Sat & Sun, 9am-9pm Fri) permanent displays include Peranakan culture, Chinese ceramics and Buddhist artefacts. A combined ticket for both branches costs S$6/$3 per adult/child and concession, while there is discounted admission between 7pm and 9pm on Fridays.

The sparkling white Victorian splendour of the **National Museum of Singapore** (Map pp656-7; ☎ 6332 3659; www.nationalmuseum.sg; 93 Stamford Rd; adult/child S$10/5; 10am-9pm), with its architecturally brilliant modern annex, is well worth a look, too. The Singapore History Gallery could easily consume a day, while the four Living Galleries are equally fascinating – particularly the Food room. Between 6pm and 9pm you can visit the Living Galleries for free. Entry to the building itself is also free.

The spiky metallic roof of **Esplanade – Theatres on the Bay** (Map pp656-7; ☎ 6828 8222; www.esplanade.com; 1 Esplanade Dr) has earned it the nickname of the 'big durians'. It attracts Singaporeans for its performing-arts spaces, arts library and shops, but mostly for its restaurants.

Raffles Hotel (Map pp656-7; ☎ 6337 1886; www.raffles.com; 1 Beach Rd) is a Singaporean icon that should not be missed. Most tourists head to the famous Long Bar (p667) to sit under the ceiling fans and chuck peanut shells on the floor, but if you want a quieter, more authentic atmosphere, go the **Bar & Billiard Room**. The hotel is open to nonguests, though tie-dye shirts and flip-flops will make you unwelcome.

Three blocks west of Raffles Hotel, the **Singapore Art Museum** (Map pp656-7; ☎ 6332 3222; www.museum.org.sg/sam; 71 Bras Basah Rd; adult/child S$3/1.50; noon-6pm Mon, 9am-6pm Tue-Thu, Sat & Sun, 9am-9pm Fri) is in St Joseph's Institution, a former Catholic boys' school, and hosts world-class exhibitions.

Fort Canning Park (Map pp656–7) offers a wonderfully peaceful, leafy retreat from the broiling masses below. The **Battle Box** (Map pp656-7; ☎ 6333 0510; 51 Canning Rise; adult/child S$8/5; 10am-6pm Tue-Sun) is a warren of 26 underground rooms and tunnels that once served as a British base during WWII. A lengthy audiovisual exhibition tells the story of the fall of Singapore in 1942.

CBD & the Quays

South of the river is the CBD, the financial pulse of Singapore. Once the city's vibrant heart, **Raffles Place** (Map pp656–7) is now a rare patch of grass surrounded by the gleaming towers of commerce. At the river mouth is the freakish **Merlion statue** (Map pp656–7), a bizarre hybrid lion/fish creature cooked up in the 1960s as a tourism icon for the Singapore Tourism Board. And you thought they'd banned drugs.

Along the quays are several kiosks offering river and harbour cruises taking you past Empress Place and the **Fullerton Building** (Map pp656–7), the former general post office now reborn as one of the city's top hotels. Further south along the waterfront is **Lau Pa Sat** (Map pp656-7; 18 Raffles Quay) hawker centre, an impressive rotunda of Victorian ironwork.

The latest darling among Singapore's fickle night-trippers is **Clarke Quay** (Map pp656–7), a strip of former warehouses dating back to the river's days as a trading hub and now home to popular bars, restaurants and clubs. Once out of favour, it's been startlingly redeveloped, with horrible Dr Seuss–like lily pad riverside decks and imposing futuristic canopies designed to keep the area cool. **Boat Quay** (Map pp656–7) and **Robertson Quay** (Map pp656–7) are known for their nightspots and eateries.

Chinatown

Bustling Chinatown is crammed with small shops, eateries and tradition, though the tradition is gradually disappearing under a wave of renovation and regeneration. Some of it is good (the restored shophouses), some

TOP FIVE WAYS TO VISIT SINGAPORE CHEAPLY

- Always eat at hawker centres or food courts.
- Visit the museums after 6pm, and catch free concerts at the Esplanade.
- Pack a picnic and spend a day at the beach in East Coast Park or Sentosa.
- Only drink at hawker centres, or during bar happy hours.
- Take a hike on Bukit Timah.

of it is not (the overkill of the Pagoda St tourist market). One highlight is the **Thian Hock Keng Temple** (Map pp656-7; ☎ 6423 4626; 158 Telok Ayer St; 🕑 7.30am-5.30pm), Singapore's oldest Hokkien building. Chinatown's most recognised and photographed icon, oddly, is the colourful **Sri Mariamman Temple** (Map pp656-7; ☎ 6223 4064; 244 South Bridge Rd; 🕑 7.30-11.30am & 5.30-8.30pm), Singapore's oldest Hindu house of worship.

For a peek into the past, the excellent **Chinatown Heritage Centre** (Map pp656-7; ☎ 6325 2878; www.chinatownheritage.com.sg; 48 Pagoda St; adult/child S$8/4.80; 🕑 10am-7pm) is crammed with interactive, imaginative displays.

Little India & Kampong Glam

Disorderly and pungent, Little India is a world away from the rest of Singapore. The area is a sight in itself and one of its pleasures is wandering the little side streets and soaking it all in. For temple hounds there is the **Sri Veeramakaliamman Temple** (Map p661; ☎ 6293 4634; 141 Serangoon Rd; 🕑 8am-12.30pm & 4-8.30pm), dedicated to the goddess Kali.

Further out is the Thai Buddhist **Sakaya Muni Buddha Gaya Temple** (Map p661; ☎ 6294 0714; 366 Race Course Rd; 🕑 8am-4.45pm), popularly known as the Temple of 1000 Lights. It houses a 15m-high seated Buddha. Across the road is the **Taoist Leong San See temple** (Map p661; ☎ 6298 9371; 371 Race Course Rd; 🕑 6am-6pm), built in 1917 and beautifully decorated with carved timber beams.

Southeast of Little India is Kampong Glam, Singapore's Muslim quarter. Here you'll find Malaysian and Indonesian shops and the golden-domed **Sultan Mosque** (Map p661; ☎ 6293 4405; 3 Muscat St; 🕑 5am-8.30pm), the biggest mosque in Singapore.

Istana Kampong Glam is the former palace of the last Sultan of Singapore, recently restored and turned into the **Malay Heritage Centre** (Map p661; ☎ 6391 0450; www.malayheritage.org.sg; 85 Sultan Gate; admission adult/child S$3/2, cultural show S$10/5; 🕑 10am-6pm Tue-Sun, 1-6pm Mon). The museum contains a moderately interesting exhibition on Malay culture.

Orchard Road Area

No-one visits Orchard Rd for the sights, though the Christmas light displays are breathtaking. The only major historical site is the **Istana** (President's Palace; Map p662; ☎ 6737 5522; Orchard Rd) but it's only open on selected public holidays.

When you're about to lose your mind from retail overload, the expansive, serene **Singapore Botanic Gardens** (Map p662; ☎ 6471 7361; www.sbg.org.sg; 1 Cluny Rd; admission free; 🕑 5am-midnight) is a beautiful spot to rest and revive.

East Coast & Changi

Changi Village (Map pp650–1) is the jumping-off point for the rural retreat of **Pulau Ubin** (Map pp650–1). Boats (one way S$2, 15 minutes) run 24/7 and depart for the island whenever there are 12 people to fill one. Once at the island's sleepy village you can hire a bicycle (S$5 to S$10, depending on condition) to explore this last undeveloped pocket of Singapore. Take the MRT to Tanah Merah and get bus 2 or 29 to Changi Village.

Northern & Central Singapore

Nestled among the forests of central Singapore, the superb **Singapore Zoological Gardens** (Map pp650-1; ☎ 6269 3411; www.zoo.com.sg; 80 Mandai Lake Rd; adult/child S$15/7.50; 🕑 8.30am-6pm) has an open concept. The baboon enclosure and free-ranging orang-utans are a highlight, as is the Fragile Forest, a large netted section of forest where you can have close encounters with free-ranging lemurs. Next door is the **Night Safari** (Map pp650-1; ☎ 6269 3411; www.nightsafari.com.sg; adult/child S$15.45/10.30; 🕑 7.30pm-midnight), a 40-hectare forested park where you view nocturnal animals, including tigers, lions and leopards.

Southern & Western Singapore

For a beautiful view, walk up 116m **Mt Faber** (Map pp650–1), then catch the **cable car** (☎ 6270 8855; www.cablecar.com.sg; adult/child S$8.50/3.90; 🕑 8.30am-9pm) to the HarbourFront Centre or across to Sentosa Island.

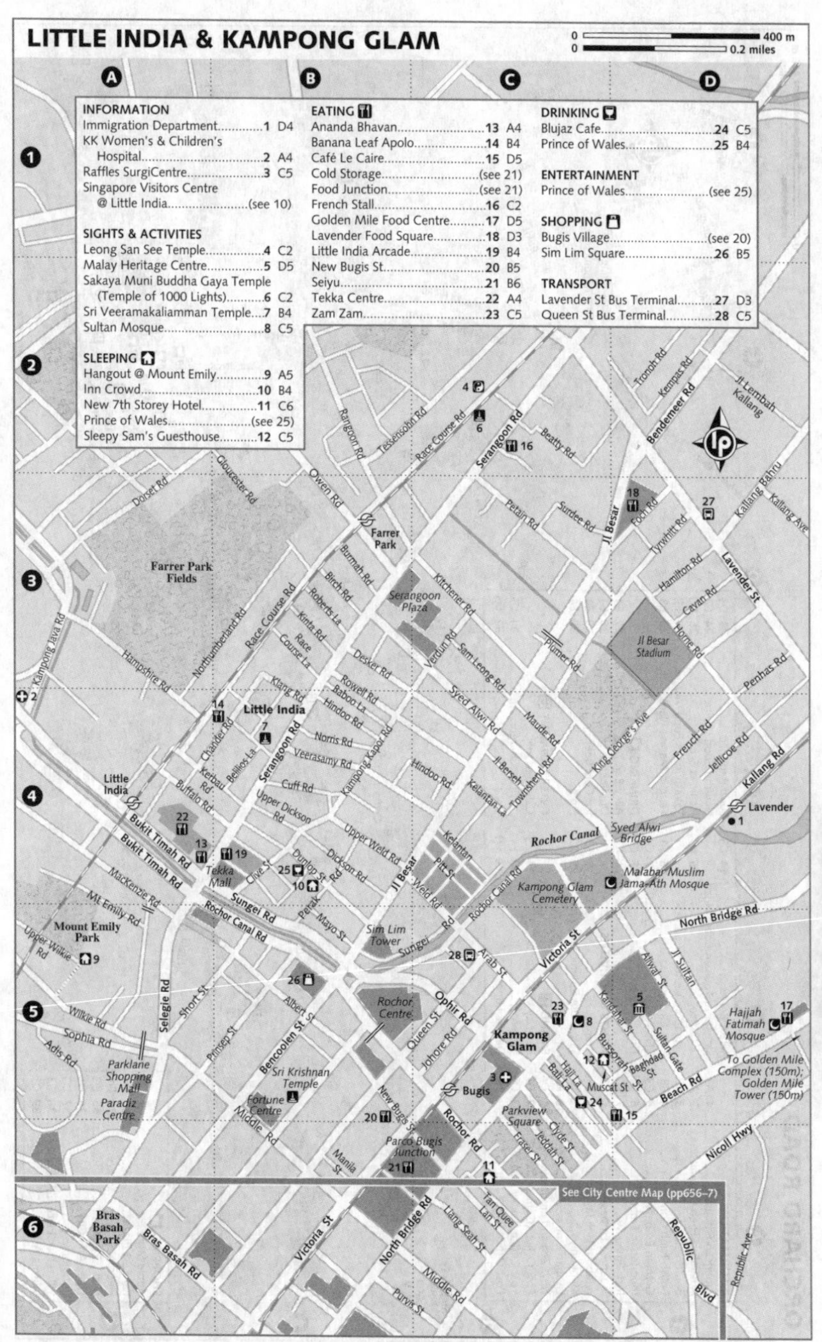
LITTLE INDIA & KAMPONG GLAM
0 400 m
0 0.2 miles
A
B
C
D
1
2
3
4
5
6
INFORMATION
Immigration Department.............1 D4
KK Women's & Children's Hospital.............2 A4
Raffles SurgiCentre.............3 C5
Singapore Visitors Centre @ Little India.............(see 10)
SIGHTS & ACTIVITIES
Leong San See Temple.............4 C2
Malay Heritage Centre.............5 D5
Sakaya Muni Buddha Gaya Temple (Temple of 1000 Lights).............6 C2
Sri Veeramakaliamman Temple.............7 B4
Sultan Mosque.............8 C5
SLEEPING
Hangout @ Mount Emily.............9 A5
Inn Crowd.............10 B4
New 7th Storey Hotel.............11 C6
Prince of Wales.............(see 25)
Sleepy Sam's Guesthouse.............12 C5
EATING
Ananda Bhavan.............13 A4
Banana Leaf Apolo.............14 B4
Café Le Caire.............15 D5
Cold Storage.............(see 21)
Food Junction.............(see 21)
French Stall.............16 C2
Golden Mile Food Centre.............17 D5
Lavender Food Square.............18 D3
Little India Arcade.............19 B4
New Bugis St.............20 B5
Seiyu.............21 B6
Tekka Centre.............22 A4
Zam Zam.............23 C5
DRINKING
Blujaz Cafe.............24 C5
Prince of Wales.............25 B4
ENTERTAINMENT
Prince of Wales.............(see 25)
SHOPPING
Bugis Village.............(see 20)
Sim Lim Square.............26 B5
TRANSPORT
Lavender St Bus Terminal.............27 D3
Queen St Bus Terminal.............28 C5
Farrer Park Fields
Farrer Park
Serangoon Plaza
Jl Besar Stadium
Little India
Tekka Mall
Mount Emily Park
Sim Lim Tower
Rochor Centre
Kampong Glam
Kampong Glam Cemetery
Malabar Muslim Jama-Ath Mosque
Hajjah Fatimah Mosque
Rochor Canal
Syed Alwi Bridge
Lavender
Bugis
Sri Krishnan Temple
Fortune Centre
Parklane Shopping Mall
Paradiz Centre
Parco Bugis Junction
Parkview Square
Bras Basah Park
To Golden Mile Complex (150m); Golden Mile Tower (150m)
See City Centre Map (pp656–7)
Serangoon Rd
Race Course Rd
Rangoon Rd
Tessensohn Rd
Owen Rd
Beatty Rd
Petain Rd
Surdee Rd
Jl Besar
Foch Rd
Tronoh Rd
Kempas Rd
Bendemeer Rd
Jl Lembah Kallang
Kallang Bahru
Kallang Ave
Tyrwhitt Rd
Hamilton Rd
Cavan Rd
Horne Rd
Lavender St
Penhas Rd
French Rd
Jellicoe Rd
Kallang Rd
King George's Ave
Plumer Rd
Kitchener Rd
Verdun Rd
Sam Leong Rd
Syed Alwi Rd
Maude Rd
Jl Berseh
Townshend Rd
Kelantan La
Hindoo Rd
Desker Rd
Burmah Rd
Birch Rd
Roberts La
Kinta Rd
Race Course La
Dorset Rd
Gloucester Rd
Northumberland Rd
Hampshire Rd
Kampong Java Rd
Klang Rd
Rowell Rd
Baboo La
Norris Rd
Veerasamy Rd
Kampong Kapor Rd
Cuff Rd
Upper Dickson Rd
Upper Weld Rd
Dickson Rd
Dunlop St
Clive St
Chander Rd
Belilios La
Kerbau Rd
Buffalo Rd
Bukit Timah Rd
MacKenzie Rd
Mt Emily Rd
Upper Wilkie Rd
Sungei Rd
Rochor Canal Rd
Perak Rd
Mayo St
Weld Rd
Kelantan
Pitt St
Victoria St
North Bridge Rd
Arab St
Jl Sultan
Aliwal St
Kandahar St
Sultan Gate
Baghdad St
Bussorah St
Muscat St
Haji La
Bali La
Beach Rd
Nicoll Hwy
Ophir Rd
Queen St
Johore Rd
New Bugis St
Rochor Rd
Clyde St
Jeddah St
Fraser St
Albert St
Bencoolen St
Prinsep St
Short St
Selegie Rd
Wilkie Rd
Sophia Rd
Adis Rd
Middle Rd
Manila St
Tan Quee Lan St
Liang Seah St
Purvis St
Bras Basah Rd
Republic Blvd
Republic Ave
SINGAPORE

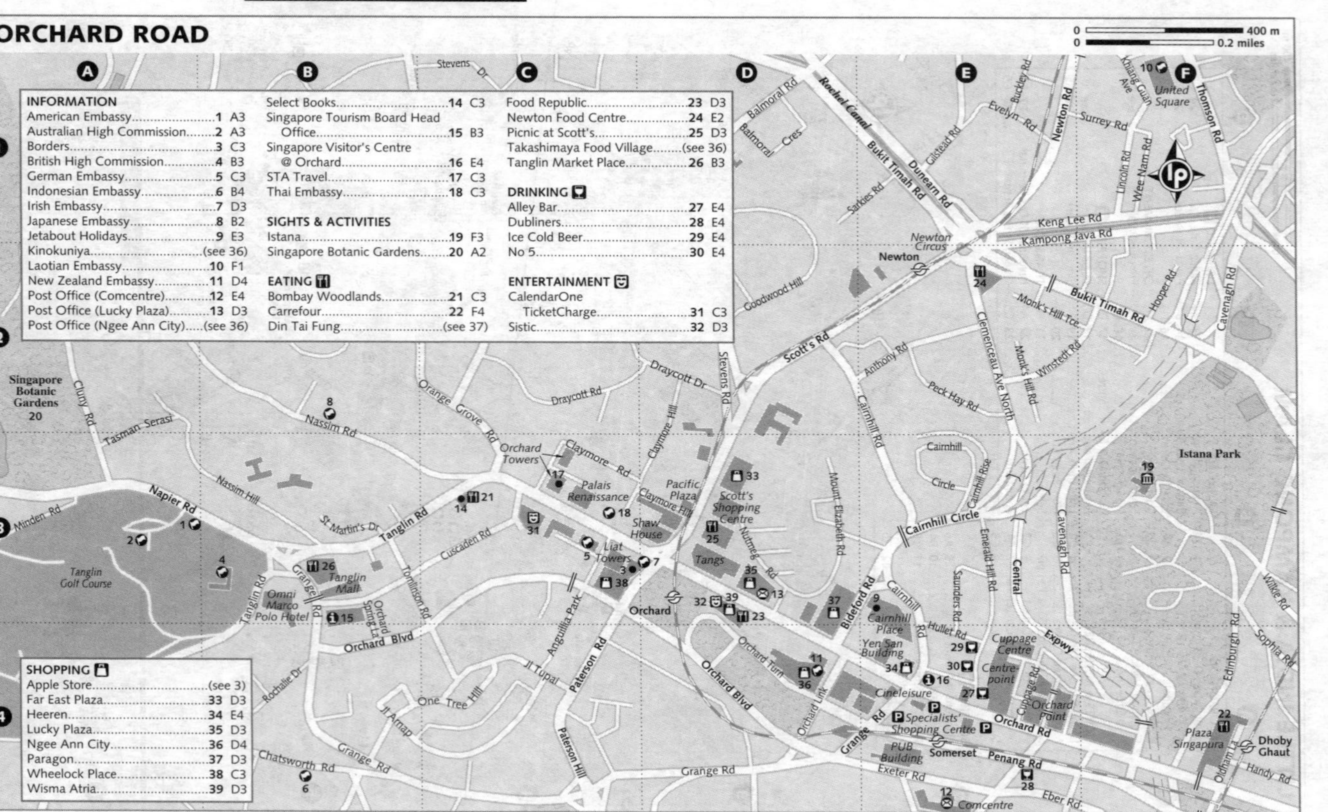
ORCHARD ROAD
0 400 m
0 0.2 miles
A
B
C
D
E
F
1
2
3
4
INFORMATION
American Embassy....1 A3
Australian High Commission....2 A3
Borders....3 C3
British High Commission....4 B3
German Embassy....5 C3
Indonesian Embassy....6 B4
Irish Embassy....7 D3
Japanese Embassy....8 B2
Jetabout Holidays....9 E3
Kinokuniya....(see 36)
Laotian Embassy....10 F1
New Zealand Embassy....11 D4
Post Office (Comcentre)....12 E4
Post Office (Lucky Plaza)....13 D3
Post Office (Ngee Ann City)....(see 36)
Select Books....14 C3
Singapore Tourism Board Head Office....15 B3
Singapore Visitor's Centre @ Orchard....16 E4
STA Travel....17 C3
Thai Embassy....18 C3
SIGHTS & ACTIVITIES
Istana....19 F3
Singapore Botanic Gardens....20 A2
EATING
Bombay Woodlands....21 C3
Carrefour....22 F4
Din Tai Fung....(see 37)
Food Republic....23 D3
Newton Food Centre....24 E2
Picnic at Scott's....25 D3
Takashimaya Food Village....(see 36)
Tanglin Market Place....26 B3
DRINKING
Alley Bar....27 E4
Dubliners....28 E4
Ice Cold Beer....29 E4
No 5....30 E4
ENTERTAINMENT
CalendarOne TicketCharge....31 C3
Sistic....32 D3
SHOPPING
Apple Store....(see 3)
Far East Plaza....33 D3
Heeren....34 E4
Lucky Plaza....35 D3
Ngee Ann City....36 D4
Paragon....37 D3
Wheelock Place....38 C3
Wisma Atria....39 D3
Singapore Botanic Gardens
Tanglin Golf Course
Istana Park
Orchard Rd
Orchard Blvd
Scott's Rd
Tanglin Rd
Bukit Timah Rd
Newton Circus
Newton
Orchard
Somerset
Dhoby Ghaut
Central Expwy
Cairnhill Circle
Paterson Rd
Grange Rd
Napier Rd
Nassim Rd
Stevens Rd
Clemenceau Ave North
Cavenagh Rd
Thomson Rd
Newton Rd
Dunearn Rd
Rochol Canal
Keng Lee Rd
Kampong Java Rd
Orchard Towers
Palais Renaissance
Liat Towers
Shaw House
Pacific Plaza
Scott's Shopping Centre
Tangs
Cairnhill Place
Yen San Building
Cineleisure
Specialists' Shopping Centre
PUB Building
Cuppage Centre
Centrepoint
Orchard Point
Plaza Singapura
Comcentre
Tanglin Mall
Omni Marco Polo Hotel
United Square

Jurong Bird Park (Map pp650-1; ☎ 6265 0022; www.birdpark.com.sg; 2 Jurong Hill; adult/child S$14/7; ⏲ 8am-6pm) offers impressive enclosures and beautifully landscaped gardens for over 8000 birds. Get here on bus 194 or 251 from Boon Lay MRT station.

Sentosa Island

Once a dismal flop, the island of **Sentosa** (Map pp650-1; ☎ 1800-736 8672; www.sentosa.com.sg; admission S$3; ⏲ 7am-midnight) was resurrected under the guidance of an American and is now a roaring success. By 2010 it will host one of Singapore's two casino resorts and a Universal Studios theme park.

Lazing on the imported-sand beaches is the cheapest option, but if you want to experience the attractions, our favourite is racing on the **Sentosa Luge** (Map pp650-1; luge & chairlift $9, or 3 rides for $16; ⏲ 10am-9.30pm), which allows you to hurtle recklessly down a winding track from the cable-car station to the beach, and go back up again on a chairlift affording fantastic views. Other worthwhile attractions include the **Underwater World** (Map pp650-1; ☎ 6275 0030; www.underwaterworld.com.sg; adult/child S$19.50/12.50; ⏲ 9am-9pm) aquarium, though it is often unbearably crowded. The ticket also includes a pass to see the performing pink dolphins at **Dolphin Lagoon** (Map pp650-1; ⏲ shows 11.30am, 1.30pm, 3.30pm & 5.30pm). The former military base **Fort Siloso** (Map pp650-1; adult/child S$8/5; ⏲ 10am-6pm) re-creates the Japanese invasion and occupation. History buffs might also enjoy the visual displays of Singapore's past at the **Images of Singapore** (Map pp650-1; adult/child S$10/7; ⏲ 9am-7pm), while kids will prefer the visuals at **Sentosa 4D Magix** (adult/child $16/9.50; ⏲ 10am-9pm).

A free shuttle coach leaves for Sentosa regularly from behind HarbourFront MRT station (follow the signs), but the best bet is the new Sentosa Express light rail, which runs between 7am and 11.45pm and takes you from the VivoCity shopping centre next to the MRT station to the beach. For a more spectacular ride, take the cable car (adult/child S$10.90/5.50 return) from the World Trade Centre, also signposted from the MRT station.

ACTIVITIES

Though the national pastimes are probably shopping and eating, there are opportunities for athletic, outdoorsy types. To find out more about sports and activities in Singapore check out www.ssc.gov.sg.

Trekking & Cycling

There are good trails in **Bukit Timah Nature Reserve** (Map pp650-1; ☎ 1800-468 5736; www.nparks.gov.sg; ⏲ 8.30am-6pm), the only large area of primary rainforest left in Singapore. Pulau Ubin also has a few good trails. Or try MacRitchie Nature Reserve. The best spot for cycling is definitely East Coast Park, though it's packed at weekends. For off-road action, **Detour Outdoors** (☎ 6243 1174; www.detouroutdoors.com; 1-/2-day tours S$75/130) runs bike tours to Pulau Bintan, in Indonesia.

Water Sports

Sea-sports-lovers can head to one of the **PA Sea Sports Clubs** (www.water-venture.org.sg) to rent sailing boats, windsurfers and kayaks – though you'll need to show some certification. Wakeboarders and water-skiers should check out the **Ski360** (Map pp650-1; www.ski360degree.com; per hr S$30) circuit at East Coast Park Lagoon.

For **swimming** there are reasonable beaches on Sentosa and East Coast Park. The latter holds regular **triathlons** (www.triathlonsingapore.org). Or you can do a few laps at the **YMCA pool** (Map pp656-7; ☎ 6336 6000; www.ymca.org.sg; 1 Orchard Rd).

Other Activities

The eatery **Whatever** (Map pp656-7; ☎ 6221 0300; www.whatever.com.sg; 31 Keong Saik Rd; 2hr class S$25) offers drop-in Ashtanga and Hatha yoga classes.

For a real adrenaline rush, strap yourself into the reverse bungee **G-Max Ride** (Map pp656-7; ☎ 9385 0697; River Valley Rd; adult/student S$30/25; ⏲ 5-9pm).

COURSES

There are a few short-term options for the casual cooking enthusiast.

Cookery Magic (Map pp650-1; ☎ 6348 9667; www.cookerymagic.com; Jl Tembusu,Katong; classes from S$60) Try this excellent place, which offers a large range of Asian cooking classes.

Coriander Leaf (Map pp656-7; ☎ 6732 3354; www.corianderleaf.com; 02-03 3A River Valley Rd; 1-day courses from S$110) Another cookery course is run by this Asian fusion restaurant, which teaches various cuisines in batches of eight recipes per class.

TOURS

If you only have a few days, some worthwhile tours offer a peek underneath the city's modern veneer. Best of all are the **Original Singapore Walks** (☎ 6325 1631; www.singaporewalks.com; half-day

SCARE YOUR PANTS OFF

For the last few years, **Singapore Paranormal Investigators** (www.spi.com.sg/news/tours/index.htm) have been supplementing their work by taking groups of people around Singapore's 'haunted' sites and generally frightening the wits out of them. This is no theme park haunted-house thrill trip though – these guys are serious. Email ghoulish@spi.org.sg for upcoming trips.

adult/child from S$25/15), which offer insightful tours of Chinatown, Little India, Kampong Glam, the Colonial District and even Singapore's battlefields.

FESTIVALS & EVENTS

Singapore's multicultural population celebrates an amazing number of festivals and events. For details on public holidays in Singapore, see p672.

Chinese New Year The major festival, held in January/February. Look out for parades throughout Chinatown and festive foods in shops.

Singapore Food Festival (www.singaporefoodfestival.com) This month-long festival in March and April celebrates eating, and is held at hawker centres and gourmet restaurants.

Great Singapore Sale During this sale, held around July, merchants drop prices to boost Singapore's image as a shopping destination.

SLEEPING

Once, budget room hunters in Singapore were limited to flea-bitten flophouses, but thankfully these days there are excellent hostels and guesthouses even in the more expensive parts of the city. Unless otherwise stated, prices are for shared bathrooms.

Colonial District

Backpacker Cozy Corner (Map pp656-7; ☎ 6338 8826, 6224 6859; www.cozycornerguest.com; 490 North Bridge Rd; dm/s S$8/28; ❄ 💻) It's not exactly homy, but the owners are generally friendly and at these prices you can hardly be fussy. Add S$4/17 if you want an air-con dorm/private room and watch out for hidden surcharges on the 'facilities'.

YMCA International House (Map pp656-7; ☎ 6336 6000; www.ymca.org.sg; 1 Orchard Rd; dm incl breakfast S$30; ❄ 💻 🏊) Even after you add on the S$3.15 temporary membership, the Y's spacious dorms are a steal, coming with a pool and a perfect central location. There are also hotel-quality rooms, at hotel-quality prices.

YWCA Fort Canning Lodge (Map pp656-7; ☎ 6338 4222; reservations@ywcafclodge.org.sg; 6 Fort Canning Rd; dm S$57.75; ❄ 💻) With facilities similar to YMCA International House, and an equally fine location, this is a decent option. The five-bed dorms are girls-only and come with air-con, TV and attached bathrooms.

CBD & the Quays

Summer Tavern (Map pp656-7; ☎ 6535 6601; www.summertavern.com; 31 Carpenter St; dm/d incl breakfast S$30/60; ❄ 💻) The dorms are a little too cramped, but the location, close to the river, Chinatown and the Colonial District, is tough to beat. The price, with free internet and local calls, is decent too. The downstairs bar, done out like an olde taverne, is cheap and popular.

Chinatown

Fernloft (Map pp656-7; ☎ 6323 3221; www.fernloft.com; 02-92, Block 5, Banda St; dm/d S$18/45) A pleasant hostel smack in the middle of 'old' Chinatown (the part not yet hit by the redevelopment craze). Dorms are standard and functional, but the double rooms are particularly good value.

Little India & Kampong Glam

New 7th Storey Hotel (Map p661; ☎ 6337 0251; www.nsshotel.com; 229 Rochor Rd; dm S$17, d S$53-80; ❄ 💻) This well-run hotel has four-bed dorms, some with access out onto scenic balconies. Doubles (shared or private bathroom) are spacious and clean and have individual TVs. A panoramic rooftop garden and bike rental (from S$2.50 per hour) are bonuses.

Prince of Wales (Map p661; ☎ 6299 0130; www.pow.com.sg; cnr Dunlop & Madras Sts; dm/d S$18/42) Functional, good-value rooms above a friendly Australian pub, with a free beer thrown in. Stay here only if you're willing to listen to live bands every night.

Inn Crowd (Map p661; ☎ 6296 9169; www.the-inncrowd.com; 73 Dunlop St; dm/d incl breakfast S$18/48; ❄ 💻) Extremely popular for its Little India location, friendly atmosphere and very cheap dorm, The Inn Crowd bills itself as the backpacker party spot – and does pretty well at it. Rates include use of a locker and free internet access, and it has a wealth of travel information on hand.

Sleepy Sam's Guesthouse (Map p661; ☎ 9277 4988; www.sleepysams.com; 55 Bussorah Rd; dm/s/d incl breakfast

S$25/45/69; 💻) By far the most peaceful of the area's hostels, Sam's dorms and rooms are a bit cramped, but the location on this pedestrianised strip of restored heritage shophouses in the Muslim quarter more than makes up for it. It's blissfully quiet at night. Includes free internet.

our pick **Hangout@Mount Emily** (Map p661; ☎ 6438 5588; www.hangouthotels.com; 10A Upper Wilkie Rd; dm S$35, d with private bathroom S$88, all incl breakfast; ❄ 💻) For state-of-the-art hostelling you can't beat the Hangout. Clean, ultramodern rooms with dorm beds (not bunks) are a treat, plus there's free internet and gym. The only downside is the hike up the steps – not too easy with a hefty bag, or after a long, hot day in the city. Book online and the dorm/double rate is S$25/76.

East Coast

Fernloft (Map pp650-1; ☎ 6449 9066; www.fernloft.com; 693A East Coast Rd; dm/d S$18/45) Bright orange, very friendly and a short walk from the beach at East Coast, this is an excellent alternative to staying in the city, with the added appeal of a cheap pub on the ground floor.

Betel Box (Map pp650-1; ☎ 6247 7340; www.betelbox.com; 200 Joo Chiat Rd; dm/d S$18/50) Not far from the city, this top-notch hostel occupies an old shophouse in the historic Katong district. The dorms are a little stark, but the communal area is warm and welcoming, and its food and drinking tours of the area are recommended.

EATING

Eating probably ranks above shopping as Singapore's national obsession – and nowhere is that obsession more apparent than in the city's ubiquitous hawker centres and food courts. For budget travellers, these places are a blessing. Dishes rarely cost more than S$5 (unless you're eating seafood) and each centre has a huge variety of cuisines, including Malay, South Indian, Cantonese, Hokkien, Teochew and Indonesian. The choice is endless. There are also countless excellent restaurants, though your costs are going to spiral up to at least S$12 per plate.

Colonial District

Ah Teng's Bakery (Map pp656-7; ☎ 6337 1886; Raffles Complex, 1 Beach Rd; tea & pastries S$12; 🕑 7.30am-5.30pm) One of the Raffles Hotel eateries, this splendid genteel café, serving up scones, pastries and even dim sum, looks like the sort of place your grandmother used to frequent before the war. For shoestringers, it's about the only opportunity to experience Raffles without busting your wallet.

Soup Restaurant (Map pp656-7; ☎ 6333 9388; 39 Seah St; meals S$15; 🕑 lunch & dinner Mon-Sat, lunch Sun) Specialises in MSG-free, double-boiled herbal soups (all under S$12) and luscious Samsui ginger chicken (entrée/main S$13/24).

CHIJMES (Map pp656-7; 30 Victoria St) is, bizarrely, a former convent beautifully converted into a den of worldly pleasure housing more than 20 bars, restaurants and clubs set around a Gothic chapel. Try well-known rib joint **Bobby's** (☎ 6337 5477; mains S$20-30; 🕑 noon-2.30pm & 5.30-11pm), popular Irish pub-cum-eatery **Father Flanagan's** (☎ 6333 1418; mains S$15-25; 🕑 11am-1am Sun-Thu, to 2am Fri & Sat) and Brazilian meat-fest **Carnivore** (☎ 6334 9332; mains S$14-30; 🕑 noon-10.30pm).

Also try the following food centres:

Bras Basah Food Court (Map pp656-7; 232 Victoria St; 🕑 7am-9pm)
Food Junction (Map p661; 200 Victoria St) In the basement of Seiyu.
New Bugis St (Map p661; New Bugis St)
Raffles City (Map pp656-7; 3rd fl, 252 North Bridge Rd)

The supermarket **Cold Storage** (Map p661; www.coldstorage.com.sg; Seiyu Department Store, 200 Victoria St) has several branches across the city.

CBD & the Quays

Yu Kee (Map pp656-7; ☎ 6337 7525; cnr Liang Seah St & North Bridge Rd; mains S$3-7; 🕑 7am-11pm Sun-Thu, to 2pm Fri & Sat) Hugely popular and usually packed, Yu Kee does great duck rice (S$3). Friday and Saturday nights see a devoted crowd of cab drivers and clubbers slurping down the Katong *laksa* (noodles served in a rich, spicy coconut broth with prawns, cockles, fried bean curd and bean sprouts; S$3).

Sinar Pagi Nasi Padang (Map pp656-7; ☎ 6536 5302; 13 Circular Rd; meals S$4-6; 🕑 9am-1am Mon-Fri, noon-4am Sat) For spicy, simple Indonesian with red-hot *sambal* (relish) and plenty of fish, you can't go past this down-to-earth place. Perfect for a cheap late-night feed.

Pump Room (Map pp656-7; ☎ 6334 2628; 01-09 Clarke Quay; mains from S$12; 🕑 11.30am-3am) This microbrewery has an excellent Australian-style menu to accompany its very drinkable beers and live music. A good night out.

Cafe Iguana (Map pp656-7; ☎ 6236 1275; 01-03 Riverside Point; mains S$13-27; 🕑 6pm-1am Mon-Thu,

6pm-3am Fri, noon-3am Sat, noon-1am Sun) Unpromisingly large, Iguana manages to dish up the best Mexican food in Singapore, made all the better for the riverside location and the 100-plus varieties of tequila, which are half price before 9pm.

Famous for its renovated Victorian market building, **Lau Pa Sat** (Map pp656-7; 18 Raffles Quay; 24hr) hawker centre can be so bewildering it even has street numbers.

Chinatown

Da Dong (Map pp656-7; ☎ 6221 3822; 39 Smith St; yum cha S$2.80-4.80, mains S$12-20; 7am-11pm) Grab a serve of the celebrated dim sum from the steamer trolleys that are wheeled to your table in old-school Chinese style. Quick service and excellent food have made this a local legend.

Ci Yan Vegetarian Health Food (Map pp656-7; ☎ 6225 9026; 2 Smith St; mains S$4-6; noon-10.30pm) Delicious concoctions of tofu and steamed veggies pour out of this place, all served on hearty brown rice for the fibre-conscious.

Annalakshmi (Map pp656-7; ☎ 6223 0809; 104 Amoy St; 11am-7pm) A real gem, serving up Indian vegetarian buffets on an 'eat as you like, pay as you feel' basis (S$5 per head is acceptable). It's run by volunteers and profits help support various charities.

Explore the overwhelming options at the following food centres:

Chinatown Complex (Map pp656-7; cnr Sago & Trengganu Sts; 24hr)

Maxwell Rd Food Centre (Map pp656-7; cnr South Bridge & Maxwell Rds; 24hr) Famous for the Tian Tian chicken rice at stall 10.

Smith St Food Market (Map pp656-7; Smith St; 6pm-midnight) The seafood stall near the South Bridge Rd end is excellent.

Little India & Kampong Glam

Ananda Bhavan (Map p661; ☎ 6297 9522; 58 Serangoon Rd; mains from S$3; 7.30am-10pm) There are several branches of this superlative South Indian vegetarian eatery, which serves up excellent *idli* (rice dumplings), thali (traditional 'all-you-can-eat' meals) and dosa (paper-thin lentil-flour pancakes) and lots of Indian sweets. Order at the counter, present your ticket to the chefs, then wait for your number to come up.

Zam Zam (Map p661; ☎ 6298 7011; 699 North Bridge Rd; murtabak S$4; 7am-11pm) Around a century old, Zam Zam has been churning out *murtabak* (flaky flat bread stuffed with mutton, chicken or vegetables, with spicy sauce) forever – and it's pretty good at it.

Banana Leaf Apolo (Map p661; ☎ 6293 8682; 54-58 Race Course Rd; meals from S$6; 10am-10pm) The runaway winner among Singapore's many fish-head curry joints. If the dish sounds terrible, this place will make you change your mind. You can either order à la carte (fish-head curry costs from S$18) or wait for the waiters to bring around buckets of various curries, all served onto banana leaves.

Cafe Le Caire (Map p661; ☎ 6292 0979; 39 Arab St; mains S$6-12, shisha S$12; lunch & dinner) Not the swankiest of the Middle Eastern eateries around Kampong Glam, but the best for food. For a filling budget meal, you can't go past the mezze platter, washed down with an iced mint tea and a relaxing puff on a water pipe.

French Stall (Map p661; ☎ 6299 3544; 544 Serangoon Rd; mains from S$10; lunch & dinner Tue-Sun) A small shop, set up by a two-star Michelin chef who decided to bring superb French food to Singapore at the kind of prices that might buy you a starter in the city's other French restaurants.

Food centres:

Golden Mile Complex (off Map p661; 10am-10pm) Has many Thai food stalls.

Golden Mile Food Centre (Map p661; 505 Beach Rd; 10am-10pm) Offers a wide range of local specialities.

Lavender Food Square (Map p661; Jl Besar; 24hr)

Little India Arcade (Map p661; Serangoon Rd; 7am-late)

Tekka Centre (Map p661; cnr Serangoon & Buffalo Rds; 10am-10pm)

Orchard Road Area

our pick Samy's Curry Restaurant (Map pp650-1; ☎ 6472 2080; Civil Service Clubhouse, Dempsey Rd; dishes from S$3; noon-10pm) A Singaporean institution and well worth the effort to get here. Housed in an old wooden army mess hall, this banana-leaf curry joint is magnificent. Grab a table and the waiters will come round with silver buckets of curry (they always bring the most expensive stuff first). A veggie meal will cost around S$3 to S$4, meat a fair bit more.

Bombay Woodlands (Map p662; ☎ 6235 2712; B01/02, Tanglin Shopping Centre, Tanglin Rd; mains from S$6; 9.30am-10;m) Boasting a charm not often found in shopping centres, this gem serves up S$14 thalis big enough to feed a family.

SINGAPORE

Din Tai Fung (Map p662; ☎ 6836 8336; B1-03/06 Paragon Bldg, 290 Orchard Rd; mains S$8-17; ⏰ 10am-10pm) Originally from Taiwan, Din Tai Fung is famous for its dumplings, but its *wonton* noodle soups are also excellent.

Most malls have food courts, usually in the basement. Try the following:

Picnic at Scott's (Map p662; Scott's Shopping Centre, 6 Scott's Rd; ⏰ 10am-10pm) The city's first air-con hawker centre and still among the best.

Food Republic (Map p662; Wisma Atria; 435 Orchard Rd; ⏰ 10am-10pm) Slightly upmarket food court, with views along Orchard Rd.

Newton Food Centre (Map p662; Scott's Rd; ⏰ 24hr) Outdoor dining and excellent chilli stingray.

Takashimaya Food Village (Map p662; Takashimaya, Ngee Ann City, 391 Orchard Rd; ⏰ 10am-10pm)

Self-catering? **Tanglin Market Place** (Map p662; Tanglin Mall, 163 Tanglin Rd; ⏰ 10am-10pm) is popular with expats. **Carrefour** (Map p662; Plaza Singapura, 68 Orchard Rd) is a outlet of the French hypermarket chain.

DRINKING

Drinking is an expensive pastime. The cheapest way to drink is to park yourself in a hawker centre, where beers cost S$5 to $6 for a large bottle. If you're hitting the bars and clubs, start early: happy hours generally finish at 9pm, with some bars adding a late-night happy hour after midnight or 1am. Many bars offer additional cheap deals, including 'house pours' (their choice of wines/spirits) and Ladies' Nights (cheap drinks for women, which attracts lots of men). The main party places include Mohamed Sultan Rd, Clarke and Boat Quays, and Emerald Hill Rd off Orchard Rd. Most bars open from 5pm daily until at least midnight Sunday to Thursday, and 2am on Friday and Saturday.

Colonial District

Raffles Hotel (Map pp656-7; ☎ 6337 1886; raffles@raffles.com; 1 Beach Rd) It's a compulsory cliché to sink a Singapore sling (S$16, or S$25 with a souvenir glass) in the Long Bar (open 11am to 12.30am), but for a less touristy experience head for the century-old snooker tables at the Bar & Billiard Room (open 11.30am to 12.30am), where you can almost hear Somerset Maugham clacking away on his typewriter in the courtyard.

New Asia Bar/City Space (Map pp656-7; ⏰ 6431 5672; Swissôtel the Stamford, 2 Stamford Rd) The breathtaking views from this noisy, fashionable bar on the 70th floor of the Swissôtel make the drink prices worthwhile, but be warned there are strict dress codes and a S$25 cover charge on Fridays and Saturdays. Alternatively, go to City Space next door for armchairs, Cuban cigars, port and piano music. Very civilised.

CBD & the Quays

Falling into disrepair a few years ago, Clarke Quay has been breathtakingly revamped, and is now far and away the most popular nightspot in Singapore, along with Riverside Point across the river. As much as we loathe the gaudy lily pads along the riverfront – and the dubious space-age canopy designed to give the area 'outdoor air conditioning' – we have to admit it's done a good job in luring the punters back.

Brewerkz (Map pp656-7; ☎ 6438 7438; www.brewerkz.com; 01-05 Riverside Point Centre, 30 Merchant Rd) Don't be put off by the size of this sprawling riverside microbrewery; it's the perfect spot to settle in for a night's drinking and some very good food. Unusually for a place this big in Singapore, the service is excellent too. Check out the lunchtime happy hours, when pints go for S$3.

Archipelago (Map pp656-7; ☎ 6327 8408; www.archipelagobrewery.com; 79 Circular Rd) Another fine microbrewery, serving up refreshing beers with an Asian accent that incorporate ingredients like lemongrass and *gulu melaka* (palm sugar).

Crazy Elephant (Map pp656-7; ☎ 6337 1990; 01-07 Clarke Quay) One of Clarke Quay's oldest and best bars, the grungy Elephant has been bashing out live blues and rock forever.

Boat Quay is a popular haunt for expat city workers. The British-style **Penny Black** (Map pp656-7; ☎ 6538 2300; 26/27 Boat Quay) gets very busy, as does **Harry's Bar** (Map pp656-7; ☎ 6538 3029; 28 Boat Quay) next door, a relaxed jazz pub that has been a longtime favourite and now has branches all over the city.

The Mohamed Sultan Rd area is a popular spot for a bar crawl, though bars have a cover charge (around S$10) after 9pm on Fridays and Saturdays. Longtime haunts include **Front Page** (Map pp656-7; ☎ 6238 7826; 17/18 Mohamed Sultan Rd), and the adjoining **Next Page** (Map pp656-7; Mohamed Sultan Rd), which is good for serious drinking in big comfy chairs. **DBLO** (Map pp656-7; ☎ 6735 2008; 01-24, 11 Unity St) is a raucous club well known for its cheap drinks.

Chinatown

Tanjong Pagar Rd has an active gay and lesbian bar scene and welcomes drinkers regardless of their sexuality.

The sophisticated bars of Club St are housed in attractive, restored shophouses (many are closed Sunday).

Backstage Bar (Map pp656-7; ☎ 6227 1712; 13A Trengganu St; 🕑 7pm-2am Sun-Thu, to 3am Fri & Sat) This gay and lesbian hang-out has a breezy balcony with great views of the street below.

Bar Sá Vanh (Map pp656-7; ☎ 6323 0503; 49A Club St) Ultratrendy, dim-lit bar with a water wall, koi pond and lots of Buddhas.

Beaujolais Wine Bar (Map pp656-7; ☎ 6224 2227; 1 Ann Siang Hill) A tiny, friendly little shophouse bar that feels like it was plucked out of a small French town.

Little India & Kampong Glam

Prince of Wales (Map p661; ☎ 6299 0130; www.pow.com.sg; cnr Dunlop & Madras Sts) The drinking scene in Little India is quiet, but the Australian-style Prince of Wales has drink specials and regular live bands.

Blujaz Cafe (Map p661; ☎ 6292 3800; 1 Bali Lane) One of the few places to get alcohol in Kampong Glam – a relaxed, friendly bar next door to an artists' commune, with occasional live jazz.

Orchard Road Area

Dubliners (Map p662; ☎ 6735 2220; 165 Penang Rd) Housed in a colonial plantation mansion, this spit and sawdust pub is a warm and welcoming retreat from the Orchard bustle.

Emerald Hill has a collection of bars in the renovated shophouses just off Orchard Rd, including the cool **Alley Bar** (Map p662; ☎ 6738 8818; 2 Emerald Hill Rd) and even cooler **No 5** (Map p662; ☎ 6732 0818; 5 Emerald Hill Rd). At the end of the strip, **Ice Cold Beer** (Map p662; ☎ 6735 9929; 9 Emerald Hill Rd) is a noisy spot with indie/rock music at high decibels and a range of chilled brews.

For a night out with a difference, combine a meal at Samy's Curry Restaurant (p666) with a few bottles of wine at the rustic **Wine Network** (Map pp650-1; ☎ 6479 5739; Block 13 Dempsey Rd), nestled among the trees and old army barracks of Dempsey Rd.

Sentosa Island

Sentosa has recently shaken off its tacky image and become something of a fashionable hang-out, especially at weekends, when its beach bars are busy day and night with the tanned and scantily clad. Beach parties are held fairly regularly. **Km8** (Map pp650-1; ☎ 6274 2288; Tanjong Beach), **Coastes** (Map pp650-1; ☎ 6274 9668; Siloso Beach) and **Bikini Bar** (Map pp650-1; ☎ 6274 9668; Siloso Beach), and **Cafe del Mar** (Map pp650-1; ☎ 6235 1296; Siloso Beach) are all Ibiza-inspired restaurant-bars. The latter is open 24 hours a day between Friday and Sunday.

CLUBBING

Singapore's club scene, like its bar scene, is extremely fickle, with clubs opening and closing regularly. Cover charges range from S$15 to S$25, and this includes at least one drink.

Zouk (Map pp656-7; ☎ 6738 2988; www.zoukclub.com.sg; 17 Jiak Kim St) This stayer of the Singaporean club scene still nabs top-name DJs. It's actually three clubs in one, plus a wine bar, so go the whole hog and pay the full entrance (men/women including two drinks S$45/38; before 10pm S$25). Zouk (admission S$25; open 7pm to 3am Wednesday, Friday and Saturday) is a multilevel party throbbing to techno and House beats. Spacey Phuture (admission S$25; open 7pm to 3am Wednesday, Friday and Saturday) has hip-hop, grooves and big beats. Plushly decorated Velvet Underground (admission S$35; open 9pm to 3am Tuesday to Saturday) draws a more artsy crowd.

Ministry of Sound (Map pp656-7; ☎ 6235 2292; www.ministryofsound.com.sg; 01-02 Clarke Quay; cover charge from S$15-25) Its international credentials made it an instant success, attracting big-name DJs and huge weekend crowds. Expect state-of-the-art audiovisuals, beamed onto a large water wall, and plenty of drunk youngsters.

Attica (Map pp656-7; ☎ 6333 9973; 3A River Valley Rd) Modelled after the hip New York clubs, Attica quickly established itself as one of the more popular venues, with an energetic dance floor and an outdoor area for the more noise-sensitive.

ENTERTAINMENT

The *Straits Times*, *I-S Magazine* and *Time Out* have listings for movies, theatre and music. Tickets for most events can be bought either through **Sistic** (Map p662; ☎ 6348 5555; www.sistic.com.sg; Wisma Atria, 435 Orchard Rd) or **CalendarOne TicketCharge** (Map p662; ☎ 6296 2929; www.ticketcharge.com.sg; Orchard Rd). Sistic also has agencies at Parco Bugis Junction, Raffles City, the Singapore Visitors Centre located on Orchard Rd,

Suntec City, and Esplanade – Theatres on the Bay; TicketCharge has other agencies at the Substation and Funan Centre.

Chinese Opera, Comedy & Theatre

Chinese Theatre Circle (Map pp656-7; ☎ 6323 4862; www.ctcopera.com.sg; 5 Smith St; tickets through Sistic; 1-/2-hr show S$20/35) Get into Chinese opera at a teahouse session organised by this nonprofit company. Friday and Saturday shows start at 7pm and 8pm with a brief talk (in English) on Chinese opera, followed by an excerpt from a Cantonese opera.

National Arts Council (☎ 6746 4622; www.nac.gov.sg) This council organises the occasional free concert in the Botanical Gardens – the stage, at the centre of a lake, is magical.

1NiteStand (Map pp656-7; ☎ 6334 1954; www.the1nitestand.com; 01-04 3A River Valley Rd; gigs from S$40) A little pricey, but the acts that perform here are usually worth the money. Also has live music and a restaurant.

Other big venues that feature various comedy, theatre and musical acts:

DBS Drama Centre (Map pp656-7; ☎ 6733 8166; 20 Merbau Rd)

Esplanade – Theatres on the Bay (Map pp656-7; ☎ 6828 8222; www.esplanade.com; 1 Esplanade Dr)

Victoria Concert Hall & Theatre (Map pp656-7; ☎ 6345 8488; Empress Pl)

Live Music

Jazz at Southbridge (Map pp656-7; ☎ 6327 4671; www.southbridgejazz.com.sg; 82B Boat Quay) A classy two-level bar, this is the best place in town for live jazz.

Substation (Map pp656-7; ☎ 6337 7800; www.substation.org; 45 Armenian St; box office 4-8.30pm Mon-Fri) Walk around the back of this alternative arts venue and there's a large, alfresco pub with a big stage, where you can see local bands at weekends.

Local bands play every night at the knockabout **Prince of Wales** (Map p661; ☎ 6299 0130; www.pow.com.sg; cnr Dunlop & Madras Sts). The **Esplanade – Theatres on the Bay** (Map pp656-7; ☎ 6828 8222; www.esplanade.com; 1 Esplanade Dr) has free outdoor gigs on Fridays, Saturdays and Sundays that kick off around 7pm; check the website for details.

SHOPPING

Once renowned as a bargain paradise, Singapore has been overtaken by other cities in the region, but there are still bargains to be had on items such as clothing, electronics, IT gear and books.

Orchard Rd (Map p662) is so overwhelming it would take a week to explore thoroughly. Starting at the Scott's Rd end, there is **Wheelock Place** (Map p662; ☎ 6738 8660; 501 Orchard Rd) for the Apple store and a huge Borders bookshop. Up Scott's Rd is **Far East Plaza** (Map p662; ☎ 6235 2411; 14 Scott's Rd), the best spot for cheap clothes and shoes, including some funky Japanese street fashions. Next to Orchard MRT is **Wisma Atria** (Map p662; ☎ 6235 8177; 435 Orchard Rd), for more expensive mainstream clothes. Next door is the huge chocolate-coloured **Ngee Ann City** (Map p662; ☎ 6733 0337; 391 Orchard Rd), packed with high-end brands and Kinokuniya, the best bookshop in the city. Next is **Lucky Plaza** (Map p662; ☎ 6235 3294; Orchard Rd), which is good for cheap electronics (but you must shop around and bargain). **Paragon** (Map p662; ☎ 6738 5535; 290 Orchard Rd) is only for those who enjoy receiving red-coloured credit card bills. Then comes **Heeren** (Map p662; ☎ 6733 4725; www.heeren.com.sg/; 260 Orchard Rd), which specialises in hip clothing and accessories for the young, and also has a large HMV outlet. There's a lot more, so explore away.

In Chinatown, **People's Park Complex** (Map pp656-7; 1 Park Cres) and **People's Park Centre** (Map pp656-7; 110 Upper Cross St) sell almost everything (watch out for tourist prices), and house lots of travel agents. Bugis Village (Map p661), not far from Raffles Hotel, is a good hunting ground for cheap clothes and is one of the few places you'll encounter knock-offs of famous brands.

Sim Lim Square (Map p661; ☎ 6332 5839; 1 Rochor Canal Rd) is geek paradise, overflowing with cheap IT gear and electronics. It's a cutthroat world in there and we'd only advise going if you know your stuff, because novices will be creamed. IT greenhorns should instead try **Funan – the IT Mall** (Map pp656-7; ☎ 6337 4235; 109 North Bridge Rd), where computers, software, camera gear and MP3 players are more expensive, but at least they're priced and labelled.

For handicrafts, wandering Bussorah St in Kampong Glam and Chinatown's Pagoda, Smith and Temple Sts is worthwhile, though Chinatown has several touts keen to tailor you a suit (see boxed text, p670). Little India bursts with handicrafts, gold, saris, incense and Bollywood music and DVDs.

SINGAPORE DIRECTORY

ACCOMMODATION

Hostels are booming in Singapore, so expect competitive prices (S$18 to S$20 for a dorm bed) and facilities like free internet, breakfast and laundry use. Cheaper hotel rooms (S$50 to S$70) are cramped, often windowless, with shared facilities. Most places offer air-con rooms, with cheaper fan rooms. Most establishments will quote net prices, which include all taxes. If you see +++ after a price it means you'll need to add on 10% service charge, 7% GST and 1% government tax. All room prices quoted in this chapter include all taxes.

BOOKS

For almost every visitor, Lonely Planet publishes a guidebook: for foodies there's *World Food: Malaysia & Singapore;* for quick visits there's *Best of Singapore;* for longer visits it may be worth investing in *Malaysia, Singapore & Brunei* or the *Singapore* city guide; and for budget trips, the book in your hands is the last word.

For a deeper insight into the two men who 'made' Singapore, look for *Raffles* by Maurice Collis and the ubiquitous *The Singapore Story* and *From Third World To First* by Lee Kuan Yew.

For contemporary fiction by Singaporeans, try *Foreign Bodies* and *Mammon Inc.* by Hwe Hwe Tan and *Tigers in Paradise* by Philip Jeyaretnam.

TOP FIVE TOUTS' CALLS

Sure they may be annoying, but touts can also be very witty in their attempts to lure you. The five best we've heard:

- 'I'll make you long pants for short price.'
- 'Here's my business card so you can send me Christmas cards.'
- 'You have beautiful English skin, like fish and chips.'
- 'Why pay so much, lah? My brand also the same for less!'
- 'Would you like a ride in my air-conditioned helicopter?' (from a rickshaw driver).

BUSINESS HOURS

Government offices are usually open from Monday to Friday and on Saturday morning. Hours vary, starting at around 7.30am to 9.30am and closing between 4pm and 6pm. On Saturday, closing time is between 11.30am and 1pm.

Shopping malls are open from 10am to 10pm daily; and though many small shops in Chinatown close Sundays, it is the busiest shopping day in Little India. Banks are open from 9.30am to 3pm weekdays (and until 11.30am on Saturday).

Singapore's food centres and hawker stalls open various hours (some 24 hours), but regular restaurants open for lunch from noon to 2.30pm and then for dinner from 6pm to 10.45pm.

Most bars are open from 5pm until at least midnight Sunday to Thursday, and from 5pm to 2am on Friday and Saturday.

CLIMATE

There are virtually no seasons in Singapore – the weather is uniformly hot, humid and wet all year round. November to January are considered slightly wetter months, though you should always be prepared for a soaking, no matter how clear the skies appear when you go out. See p915 for climate charts.

CUSTOMS

You can bring in 1L of wine, beer or spirits duty-free, but no unopened packets of cigarettes. Electronic goods, cosmetics, watches, cameras, jewellery (but not imitation jewellery), footwear, toys, arts and crafts are not dutiable; the usual duty-free concession for personal effects, such as clothes, applies. Duty-free concessions are not available if you are arriving from Malaysia or if you leave Singapore for less than 48 hours.

Toy currency and coins, obscene or seditious material, gun-shaped cigarette lighters, pirated recordings and publications, and retail quantities of chewing gum are prohibited. If you bring in prescription drugs you should have a doctor's letter or a prescription.

Restrictions on liquids and gels apply to air passengers' carry-on baggage.

DANGERS & ANNOYANCES

Short-term visitors are unlikely to be troubled by Singapore's notoriously tough laws, which have turned the city into one of the safest in

Asia. Street crime is minimal, though pickpockets have been known to operate in Chinatown, Little India and other tourist areas. Taxi drivers routinely try to cheat new arrivals from Malaysia at the Tanjong Pagar railway station, so have a rough route worked out and insist the driver uses the meter. See also Legal Matters, p672.

DRIVING LICENCE

To drive in Singapore you'll need your home driver's licence and an international permit from a motoring association in your country.

EMBASSIES & CONSULATES

Embassies & Consulates in Singapore

The following embassies, consulates and high commissions are in Singapore:

Australia (Map p662; ☎ 836 4100; www.australia.org.sg; 25 Napier Rd)
Canada (Map pp650-1; ☎ 6325 3200; www.cic.gc.ca; IBM Towers, 80 Anson Rd)
France (Map pp650-1; ☎ 6880 7800; www.france.org.sg; 101-103 Cluny Park Rd)
Germany (Map p662; ☎ 6737 1355; 14-01 Far East Shopping Centre, 545 Orchard Rd)
Indonesia (Map p662; ☎ 6737 7422; 7 Chatsworth Rd)
Ireland (Map p662; ☎ 6238 7616; www.ireland.org.sg; 08-00 Liat Towers, 541 Orchard Rd)
Japan (Map p662; ☎ 6235 8855; www.sg.emb-japan.go.jp; 16 Nassim Rd)
Laos (Map p662; ☎ 6250 6044; 10-01 United Sq, 101 Thomson Rd)
Malaysia (Map pp656-7; ☎ 6235 0111; 30 Hill St 02-01)
New Zealand (Map p662; ☎ 6235 9966; www.nzembassy.com/home.cfm?c=28; 15-06/10 Ngee Ann City, 391 Orchard Rd)
Thailand (Map p662; ☎ 6737 2644; www.thaiembsingapore.org; 370 Orchard Rd)
UK (Map p662; ☎ 6424 4200; www.britain.org.sg; 100 Tanglin Rd)
USA (Map p662; ☎ 6476 9100; http://singapore.usembassy.gov/index.shtml; 27 Napier Rd)

Singaporean Embassies & Consulates Abroad

For a list of Singaporean missions abroad see www.visitsingapore.com, and click on the Travellers Essentials link (listed under About Singapore). It also has a full list of foreign embassies and consulates in Singapore.

Australia (☎ 02-6273 3944; 17 Forster Cres, Yarralumla, ACT 2600)
France (☎ 01 45 00 33 61; 12 Square de l'Ave Foch, Paris 75116)
Germany (☎ 030-226 34 30; Friedrichstrasse 200, 10117 Berlin)
Indonesia (☎ 021-520 1489; Blk X/4 Kav 2, Jl Rasuna Said, Kuningan, Jakarta 12950)
Malaysia (☎ 03-2161 6277; 209 Jl Tun Razak, Kuala Lumpur 50400)
New Zealand (☎ 04-470 0850; 17 Kabul St, Khandallah, PO Box 13-140, Wellington)
Thailand (☎ 02-286 2111; 9th & 18th fls, Rajanakam Bldg, 183 South Sathorn Rd, Bangkok)
UK (☎ 020-7235 8315; 9 Wilton Cres, Belgravia, London)
US (☎ 202-537 3100; 3501 International Pl, NW, Washington DC 20008)

For information on visas, see p673.

FESTIVALS & EVENTS

See p664 for information on festivals and events in Singapore.

FOOD & DRINK

Singapore's rich cultural brew has spawned one of Asia's great eating cities. Food is often cheap and since English is nearly universal you'll rarely have trouble ordering. There is not really such a thing as Singaporean cuisine, though. Most of the island's specialities are imported: Hainanese chicken rice, Chinese *char kway teow* (stir-fried flat noodles with soy sauce, prawns, cockles, egg and Chinese sausage), the Indo-Malay breakfast favourite *roti pratha* (flaky, flat bread served with curry sauce) and the famous *laksa* (noodles served in a rich, spicy coconut broth with prawns, cockles, fried bean curd and bean sprouts). Unmissable local innovations include chilli crab and fish-head curry, which is far, far tastier than it sounds.

GAY & LESBIAN TRAVELLERS

Male homosexuality is still technically illegal, but the city is slowly opening up and the laws have not prevented the emergence of a thriving gay scene. In 2007, Lee Kuan Yew made a public statement opposing the repression of homosexuals – and when Mr Lee speaks, government policy is never far behind.

Ministers are still reluctant to endorse what they see as a promiscuous, antifamily lifestyle. There's also no official recognition of gay and lesbian groups, such as **People Like Us** (www.plu.sg). A good web resource is the Asia-wide **Fridae** (www.fridae.com), which has a guide to Singapore's hot spots. Also see p668 for some gay-friendly drinking spots.

SINGAPORE

HOLIDAYS

The following days are public holidays. Many are based on the lunar calendar, and their dates are variable.

New Year's Day 1 January
Chinese New Year January/February (two days)
Thaipusam January/February
Good Friday March/April
Vesak Day May
Labour Day 1 May
National Day 9 August
Hari Raya Puasa September
Deepavali October/November
Hari Raya Haji December
Christmas Day 25 December

INTERNET ACCESS

You'll have no problem finding places to get online, and many hostels offer free internet – some even have zippy broadband connections – and much of the city is covered by a wireless access zone. Expect to pay S$5 per hour in internet cafés.

INTERNET RESOURCES

SINGOV Government Information (www.gov.sg) With seemingly endless information and services.
TalkingCock.com (www.talkingcock.com) Singapore's favourite satirical website, offering a biting but affectionate look at the city's life, politics and people.
Uniquely Singapore (www.visitsingapore.com) Singapore Tourism's site, with plenty of links to things to see and do.

LEGAL MATTERS

The law is extremely tough in Singapore, but also relatively free from corruption. Possession of drugs means a long jail term and a beating, with trafficking punishable by death. Smoking in all public places, including bars and restaurants and hawker centres, is banned.

MAPS

The Official Map of Singapore, available free from the STB and hotels, is excellent. Periplus and Lonely Planet also produce maps.

MEDIA

Magazines

Free publications with events information, such as *Where Singapore, I-S Magazine, Banter* and *Juice*, are available at tourist offices, most major hotels and several restaurants, cafés and bars. The international listings magazine *Time Out* now has a Singapore edition, too.

Newspapers

English dailies include the parochial progovernment spin sheet *Straits Times* (which includes the *Sunday Times*), the *Business Times* and the tabloid-style *New Paper*. *Straits Times* has decent coverage of Asia, if you want to get the latest on your future destinations. *New Paper* is best for a flavour of 'real life' Singapore. Many Singaporeans and foreigners prefer the more free-speaking *Today* newspaper, a freebie tabloid (50c at weekends) you can pick up at MRT stations in the mornings.

MONEY

The unit of currency is the Singaporean dollar, which is made up of 100 cents. Singapore uses 5c, 10c, 20c, 50c and S$1 coins, while notes come in denominations of S$2, S$5, S$10, S$50, S$100, S$500 and S$1000.

Banks and ATMs are everywhere. Exchange rates vary from bank to bank and some charge a service fee on each exchange transaction – usually S$2 to S$3, but it can be more, so ask first.

Exchange rates at time of press:

Country	Unit	Singaporean dollars (S$)
Australia	A$1	1.28
Canada	C$1	1.47
Euro zone	€1	2.10
Indonesia	10,000Rp	1.62
Japan	¥100	1.32
Malaysia	RM10	4.35
New Zealand	NZ$1	1.08
Philippines	100P	3.27
Thailand	100B	4.73
UK	UK£1	3.04
USA	US$1	1.51

Contact details for credit-card companies in Singapore:

American Express (☎ 6299 8133)
Diners Card (☎ 6294 4222)
JCB (☎ 6734 0096)
MasterCard & Visa (☎ 1800-345 1345)

POST

Post in Singapore is among the most reliable in Southeast Asia. Postcards cost 50c to anywhere in the world, but letters start at 70c to Australia, New Zealand and Japan, or S$1 to Europe or the USA. Post offices are open from 8am to 6pm Monday to Friday, and 8am to 2pm Saturday. Call ☎ 1605 to find the nearest post office branch, or check www.singpost.com.sg. Letters addressed to 'Poste Restante' are held at the **Eunos Post Office** (Map pp650-1; ☎ 6741 8857; 10 Eunos Rd), next to the Paya Lebar MRT.

RESPONSIBLE TRAVEL

Modern and cosmopolitan though it appears, Singapore is a little sensitive when it comes to the behaviour of foreigners. In common with much of the region, Singaporeans do not like to stand out in public and look askance at people who do – quiet, polite behaviour will win you more respect.

The government is alive to environmental issues, so it's usually no problem to find a recycling bin, use public transport, or even order a hybrid fuel taxi.

STUDYING

See p663 for details of short cooking courses.

TELEPHONE

Mobile Phones

Mobile phone numbers in Singapore start with 9. If you have 'global roaming', your GSM digital phone will tune into one of Singapore's two networks, MI-GSM or ST-GSM. There is complete coverage over the whole island and rates are reasonable.

You can buy a SIM card (usually S$20) or a 'disposable' mobile from most post offices and 7-Eleven stores, though due to 'security concerns' you can't get one without showing your passport.

Phonecards

Local phonecards are widely available from 7-Eleven stores, post offices, Telecom centres, stationers and bookshops, and come in denominations of S$5, S$10, S$20 and S$50. Most phone booths take phonecards, and some take credit cards, with only a few booths around that still take coins. For more details see www.singtel.com.

From public phones, local calls cost S$0.10 for three minutes.

Phone Codes

To call Singapore from overseas, dial your country's international access number and then dial ☎ 65 (Singapore's country code), before entering the eight-digit telephone number.

Calls to Malaysia are considered to be STD (trunk or long-distance) calls. Dial the access code 020, followed by the area code of the town in Malaysia that you wish to call (minus the leading zero) and then your party's number.

There are no area codes in Singapore; telephone numbers are eight digits unless you are calling toll-free (☎ 1800).

TOILETS

Generally toilets in Singapore are clean and well maintained, though they might vary between the sit-down and squatting types. In some hawker centres you may have to pay a small fee (between S$0.10 and S$0.50).

TOURIST INFORMATION

See p658 for branches of the Singapore Tourist Board (STB).

TRAVELLERS WITH DISABILITIES

Wheelchair travellers can find Singapore difficult, though a massive accessibility project to improve life for the elderly and disabled has seen things improve. Check out *Access Singapore,* a useful guidebook for the disabled, which is available from STB offices, or contact the **National Council of Social Services** (☎ 6336 1544; www.ncss.org.sg).

The **Disabled People's Association** (☎ 6899 1220; www.dpa.org.sg/access/contents.htm) has an online accessibility guide to the country.

VISAS

Citizens of British Commonwealth countries (except India) and citizens of the Republic of Ireland, Liechtenstein, Monaco, Netherlands, San Marino, Switzerland and the USA do not require visas to visit Singapore. Citizens of Austria, Belgium, Denmark, Finland, France, Germany, Iceland, Italy, Japan, Korea, Luxembourg, Norway, Spain and Sweden do not require visas for stays up to 90 days for social purposes.

You will be given a 30-day visitor's visa if you arrive by air, and a 14-day visa if you are arriving by land or sea. Extensions can be applied for at the **Immigration Department** (Map p661; ☎ 6391 6100; 10 Kallang Rd), one block southwest of Lavender MRT station.

For details of embassies and consulates, see p671.

VOLUNTEERING

Singapore serves as a base for many NGOs, but most recruit skilled volunteers from their home countries. In Singapore itself the **National Volunteer & Philanthropy Centre** (www.nvpc.org.sg) co-ordinates a number of community groups, including grassroots projects such as education, environment and multiculturalism.

WOMEN TRAVELLERS

There are few problems for women travelling in Singapore. In Kampong Glam and Little India skimpy clothing may attract unwanted stares, so consider wearing long pants or skirts and loose tops. Tampons and pads are widely available across the island, as are over-the-counter medications.

SINGAPORE

Thailand

HIGHLIGHTS

- **Southern islands** – diving into underwater worlds on Ko Tao (p771), contemplating life on the beaches of Ko Samui (p772), and letting it all hang out in Ko Pha-Ngan (p777)
- **Krabi Province** – kayaking to the islands near Ao Nang (p799) and rising to new heights while rock climbing at Hat Rai Leh (p800)
- **Chiang Mai** – soaking up the intellectual atmosphere of Thailand's northern capital of culture (p727), a sophisticated base to study Thai cooking, massage or meditation
- **Ko Chang** – tuning out in a postcard-perfect beach bungalow, exploring a fishing village and losing yourself in the dense rainforest (p765)
- **Khao Yai National Park** – bird-watching, waterfall hunting and endless trekking through the evergreen forests and grasslands of this Unesco World Heritage site (p751)
- **Off the beaten track** – braving the bumpy, six-hour sǎwngthǎew trip from Mae Sot to Mae Sariang along the Myanmar border (p725)

FAST FACTS

- **Budget** US$11 to US$15 (500B to 650B) a day
- **Capital** Bangkok
- **Costs** guesthouse in Bangkok US$5 to US$10, four-hour bus ride US$2.50 to US$5, rice and curry US$0.75
- **Country code** ☎ 66
- **Language** Thai
- **Money** US$1 = 41B (baht)
- **Phrases** *sà wàt dii* (hello), *kà rú naa* (please), *khàwp khun* (thank you)
- **Population** 62 million
- **Time** GMT + seven hours
- **Visas** 30-day visa-free entry for most nationalities

TRAVEL HINT

Throughout most of Thailand, internet connections are frustratingly slow. The solution? Skip the cafés filled with web-surfing foreign travellers, and instead look for the online video game outposts that seem to be packed at all hours with locals kids and teens; their broadband speeds are usually lightning fast. Keep your eyes peeled for the huge window posters advertising Asian video games.

OVERLAND ROUTES

Thailand shares land borders with Cambodia, Laos, Malaysia and Myanmar. Buses are best for Cambodia, crossing the Mekong by boat or bridge is more common for Laos, while comfortable trains and sleeper buses run to Malaysia. There are two day-trip points on the Myanmar–Thailand border, as well as two 'regular' crossings.

Thailand. Close your eyes, let the word roll over your tongue, and almost instantly the pictures begin to form in your mind. Maybe you're seeing a stark white beach, with piles of softly pillowing sand stretching on forever. There isn't another person in sight, and a mammoth coconut tree with a curved trunk stretches out over the startlingly blue ocean. Or maybe Thailand to you is the chaos and confusion of big-city Bangkok, with bodies moving in every direction at once, and stinging neon lights beckoning you to drink liquor with bikini-clad bargirls.

Perhaps your Thailand is an open field and an ancient stone Buddha so large its feet are longer than your body. Tourists have captured his image on film thousands of times, but he continues to sit still, eyes closed and peaceful, seemingly keeping a secret.

And that's the thing about Thailand: it is fast and stressful and frightening, and it's quiet and meditative and kind. And yes, it holds secrets, but very few of them will come to you easily.

There's a perfectly good reason why this country is one of the most popular destinations in all of Asia. When you see something here you've never seen before – the wrinkled face of a hill tribe villager, or the come-hither glance of a ladyboy – you start to think hard about what else you don't know, and where else you've not been. Thailand is like that. If you're lucky, it will seep into your pores, and settle heavily on your soul.

Many of you starting your journeys in Thailand have weeks, or months, or even years of Asian exploration ahead, and the good news is that you couldn't possibly have picked a more appropriate place to begin your education. But here's a fair warning: surrender yourself deeply enough to this Land of Smiles, and to its people, and you may find that the person you once were has changed forever. Is that a good thing? The decision, of course, is all yours. Why not just close your eyes and let the pictures begin to form in your mind?

CURRENT EVENTS

The year 2006 did not turn out to be a happy one for former Prime Minister Thaksin Shinawatra, a populist billionaire who was elected by a landslide in 2001, and during the following fours years had managed to greatly raise the public profile of his Thai Rak Thai (Thais Love Thais) party among even the country's poorest citizens.

It all started on the evening of 19 September. Led by General Sonthi Boonyaratglin, the Royal Thai Army overthrew the elected government in what would become a soft coup; the event was bloodless, and there were no resulting casualties.

The coup had hardly taken the country by surprise, however. Rumours about a possible overthrow had been growing in the media and among the public for months. And while Sonthi offered a number of major issues as an explanation for the revolt – government corruption, human rights abuses, worsening social divisions – the military-installed government hasn't exactly had an easy time turning things around.

Thaksin, for instance, has yet to be tried for corruption. And after nearly a year in power, the junta had still done nothing to prove its claim that Thaksin had disrespected the king – a very serious allegation in Thailand.

Random bomb attacks in Bangkok have also created confusion. Prior to the coup, anonymous bombings were nearly always assumed to be the work of Muslim insurgent groups from the south. But many are now guessing that pro-Thaksin supporters, still furious about the ousting of their leader, have become the country's most recent terrorist threat. Still talked about in hushed tones are the multiple bombings that took place on 31 December 2006. Three people were killed and dozens injured when two waves of explosions hit six different targets in the city. The city's New Year's Eve celebrations were promptly cancelled. Soon after, the interim government made the subtle suggestion that Thaksin's people were behind it all.

Regardless of the Thaksin situation, the separatist war in the south continues to rage on. Some elements of the minority Muslim community want more autonomy, and even a separate state. Once nothing more than a simmering cauldron of tension, the southern provinces of Pattani, Yala and Narathiwat have deteriorated into literal war zones, where Buddhist men, monks and even schoolchildren are killed daily. The papers in Bangkok are filled with stories of beheadings, bodies charred beyond recognition and execution-style murders. This is particularly bad news for the new government, now led by the former Army Chief Surayud Chulanont, who many assumed would succeed in quelling the southern violence.

Disease has been a big topic of discussion over the past few years. First came SARS and an attempted cover-up, which damaged the country's image. More recently, avian influenza (bird flu) has been breaking out at regular intervals and has claimed some lives.

HISTORY

Rise of Thai Kingdoms

It is believed that the first Thais migrated southwest from modern-day Yunnan and Guangxi, China, to what is today known as Thailand. They settled along river valleys and formed small farming communities that eventually fell under the dominion of the expansionist Khmer Empire of present-day Cambodia. What is now southern Thailand, along the Malay peninsula, was under the sway of the Srivijaya empire in Sumatra.

By the 13th and 14th centuries, what is considered to be the first Thai kingdom – Sukhothai (meaning 'Rising Happiness') – emerged and began to chip away at the crumbling empire of Angkor. The third Sukhothai king, Ramkhamhaeng, is credited for developing a Thai writing system as well as building Angkor-inspired temples that defined early Thai art. The kingdom sprawled from Nakhon Si Thammarat in the south to the upper Mekong River and even into Myanmar (Burma), and is regarded as the cultural and artistic kernel of the modern state.

Sukhothai's intense flame was soon snuffed out by another emerging Thai power, Ayuthaya, established by Prince U Thong in 1350. This new centre developed into a cosmopolitan port on the Asian trade route, courted by various European nations attracted to the region by plenty of commodities and potential colonies. The small nation managed to thwart foreign takeovers, including one orchestrated by a Thai court official, a Greek man named Constantine Phaulkon, to advance French interests. For 400 years and 34 successive reigns, Ayuthaya dominated Thailand until the Burmese led a successful invasion in 1765, ousting the monarch and destroying the capital.

The Thais eventually rebuilt their capital in present-day Bangkok, established by the Chakri dynasty, which continues to occupy the throne today. As Western imperialism marched across the globe, King Mongkut (Rama IV, r 1851–68) and his son and successor King Chulalongkorn (Rama V, r 1868–1910) successfully steered the country into the modern age without becoming a colonial vassal. Their progressive measures included adopting Western-style education systems, forging trade agreements and introducing Western-style dress. In return for the country's continued independence, King Chulalongkorn returned huge tracts of Laos and Cambodia to French-controlled Indochina – an unprecedented territorial loss in Thai history.

A Struggling Democracy

In 1932 a peaceful coup converted the country into a constitutional monarchy, loosely based on the British model. Nearly half a century of chaos followed in its wake. During the mid-20th century, a series of anticommunist military dictators wrestled each other for power, managing little more than the suppression of democratic representation and civil rights. In 1973, student activists staged demonstrations calling for a real constitution and the release of political dissidents. A brief respite came, with reinstated voting rights and relaxed censorship. But in October 1976, a demonstration on the campus of Thammasat University in Bangkok was brutally quashed by the military, resulting in hundreds of casualties and the reinstatement of authoritarian rule. Many activists went underground to join armed communist insurgency groups hiding in the northeast.

In the 1980s, as the regional threat of communism subsided, the military-backed Prime Minister Prem Tinsulanonda stabilised the country and moved towards a representative democracy. Not content to step out of the political theatre, the military overthrew the democratically elected government in February 1991. This was Thailand's 19th coup attempt and the 10th successful one since 1932. In May 1992, huge demonstrations led by Bangkok's charismatic governor Chamlong Srimuang erupted throughout the city and the larger provincial capitals. The bloodiest confrontation occurred at Bangkok's Democracy Monument, resulting in nearly 50 deaths, but it eventually led to the reinstatement of a civilian government.

Thailand's 16th constitution was enacted in October 1997 by parliamentary vote. Because it was the first charter in the nation's history not written under military order, it is commonly called the 'people's constitution'. Among other changes, the new charter

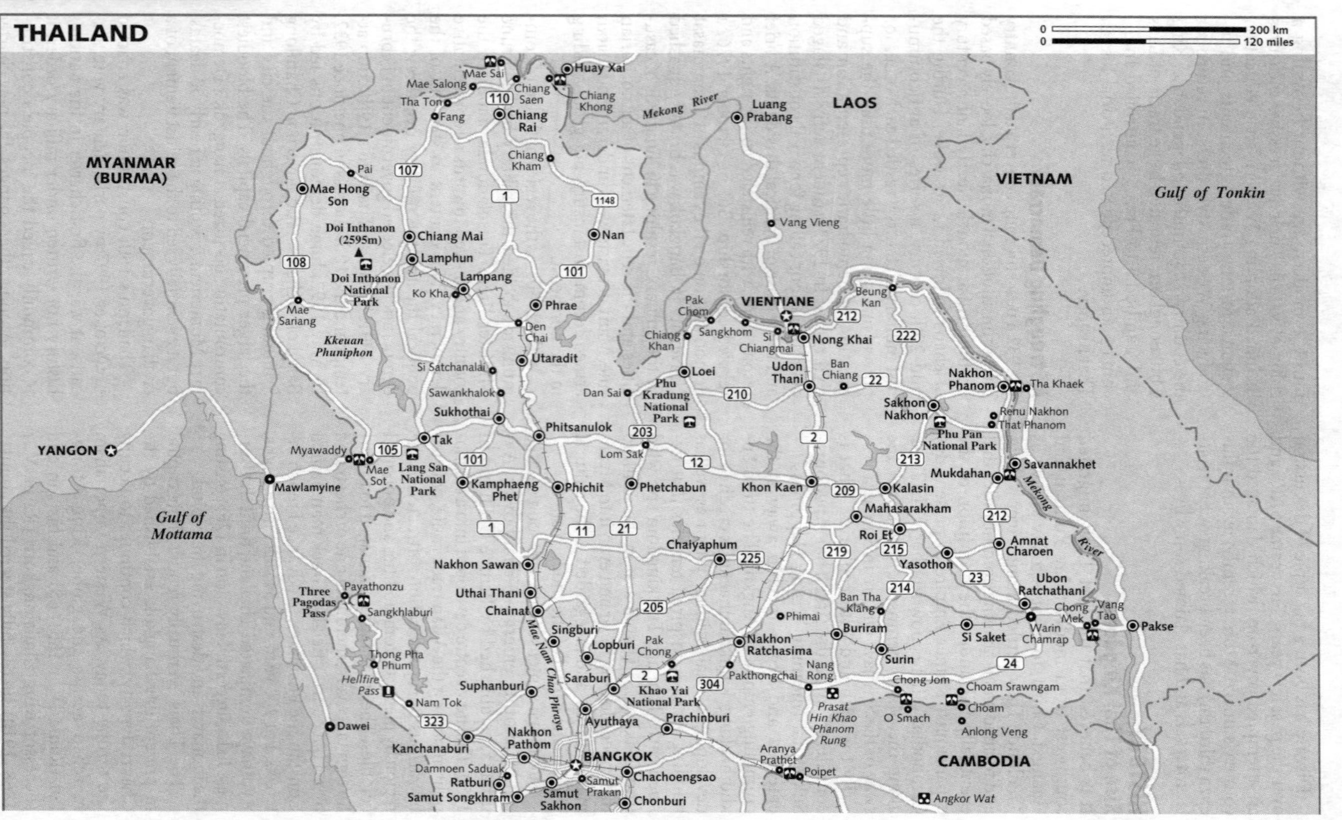
THAILAND
0 200 km
0 120 miles
MYANMAR (BURMA)
LAOS
VIETNAM
CAMBODIA
Gulf of Tonkin
Gulf of Mottama
YANGON
VIENTIANE
BANGKOK
Mekong River
Mae Nam Chao Phraya
Mae Sai
Mae Salong
Tha Ton
Fang
Chiang Saen
Chiang Rai
Huay Xai
Chiang Khong
Luang Prabang
Vang Vieng
Chiang Kham
Pai
Mae Hong Son
Doi Inthanon (2595m)
Doi Inthanon National Park
Chiang Mai
Lamphun
Lampang
Ko Kha
Nan
Phrae
Den Chai
Mae Sariang
Kkeuan Phuniphon
Utaradit
Si Satchanalai
Sawankhalok
Sukhothai
Tak
Myawaddy
Mae Sot
Lang San National Park
Mawlamyine
Kamphaeng Phet
Phitsanulok
Phichit
Dan Sai
Lom Sak
Phetchabun
Loei
Phu Kradung National Park
Pak Chom
Chiang Khan
Sangkhom
Si Chiangmai
Nong Khai
Beung Kan
Udon Thani
Ban Chiang
Nakhon Phanom
Tha Khaek
Sakhon Nakhon
Renu Nakhon
That Phanom
Phu Pan National Park
Savannakhet
Mukdahan
Khon Kaen
Kalasin
Mahasarakham
Roi Et
Yasothon
Amnat Charoen
Ubon Ratchathani
Chong Mek
Vang Tao
Pakse
Warin Chamrap
Si Saket
Chaiyaphum
Nakhon Sawan
Uthai Thani
Chainat
Singburi
Lopburi
Pak Chong
Saraburi
Khao Yai National Park
Nakhon Ratchasima
Pakthongchai
Phimai
Buriram
Ban Tha Klang
Surin
Nang Rong
Prasat Hin Khao Phanom Rung
Chong Jom
O Smach
Choam Srawngam
Choam
Anlong Veng
Angkor Wat
Three Pagodas Pass
Payathonzu
Sangkhlaburi
Thong Pha Phum
Hellfire Pass
Nam Tok
Dawei
Suphanburi
Kanchanaburi
Nakhon Pathom
Ayuthaya
Prachinburi
Aranya Prathet
Poipet
Damnoen Saduak
Ratburi
Samut Songkhram
Samut Sakhon
Samut Prakan
Chachoengsao
Chonburi
1
2
11
12
21
22
23
24
101
105
107
108
110
203
205
209
210
212
213
214
215
219
222
225
304
323
1148

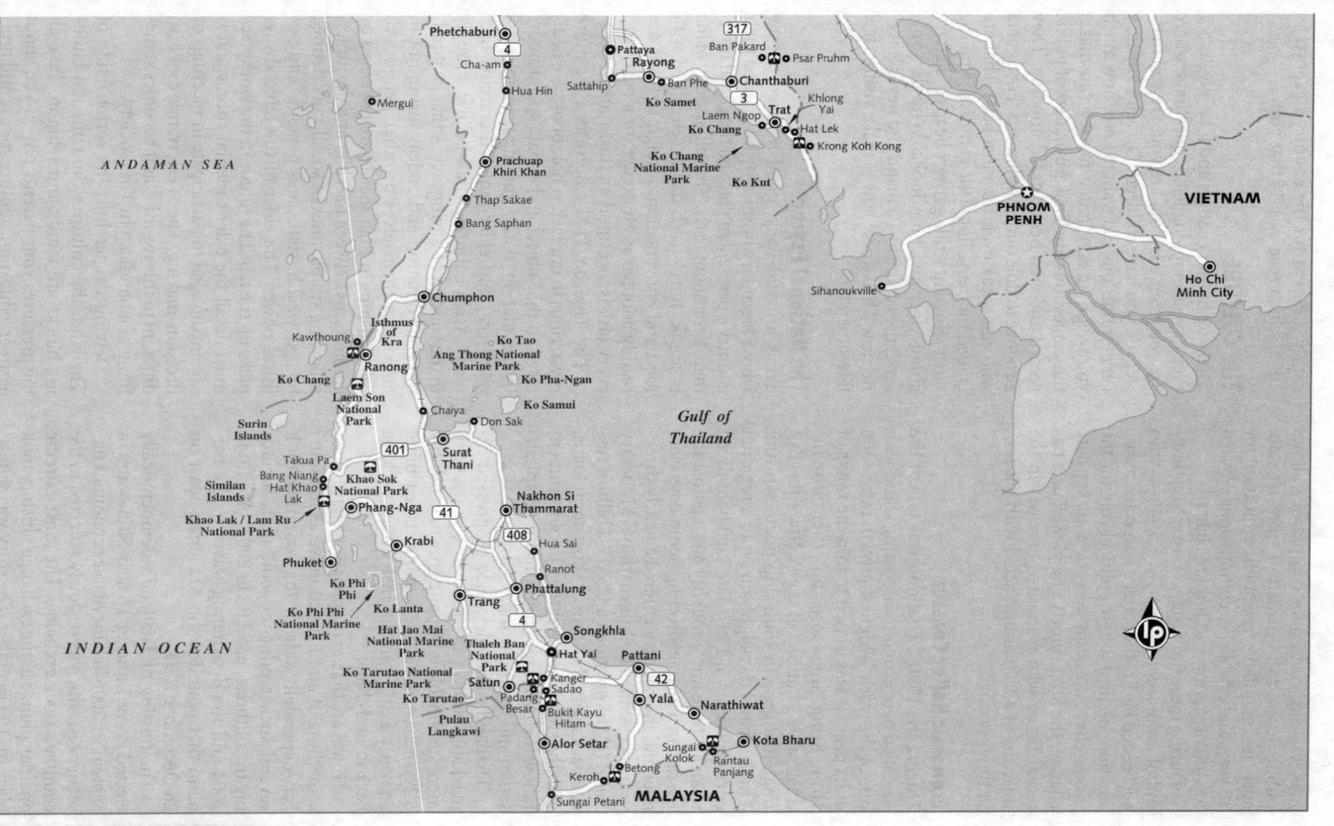
Phetchaburi
4
Cha-am
Hua Hin
Mergui
Pattaya
Rayong
Sattahip
Ban Phe
317
Ban Pakard
Psar Pruhm
Chanthaburi
3
Ko Samet
Laem Ngop
Trat
Khlong Yai
Ko Chang
Hat Lek
Krong Koh Kong
Ko Chang National Marine Park
Ko Kut
ANDAMAN SEA
Prachuap Khiri Khan
Thap Sakae
Bang Saphan
PHNOM PENH
VIETNAM
Sihanoukville
Ho Chi Minh City
Chumphon
Isthmus of Kra
Kawthoung
Ranong
Ko Tao
Ang Thong National Marine Park
Ko Pha-Ngan
Ko Chang
Laem Son National Park
Ko Samui
Chaiya
Don Sak
Surin Islands
Gulf of Thailand
401
Surat Thani
Takua Pa
Bang Niang
Hat Khao Lak
Khao Sok National Park
Similan Islands
Nakhon Si Thammarat
Phang-Nga
41
Khao Lak / Lam Ru National Park
408
Hua Sai
Krabi
Phuket
Ranot
Ko Phi Phi
Phattalung
Trang
Ko Phi Phi National Marine Park
Ko Lanta
4
Hat Jao Mai National Marine Park
Songkhla
INDIAN OCEAN
Thaleh Ban National Park
Hat Yai
Pattani
Ko Tarutao National Marine Park
Satun
Kanger
42
Sadao
Ko Tarutao
Padang Besar
Yala
Narathiwat
Bukit Kayu Hitam
Pulau Langkawi
Alor Setar
Sungai Kolok
Kota Bharu
Rantau Panjang
Betong
Keroh
Sungai Petani
MALAYSIA

THAILAND

makes voting in elections compulsory, allows public access to information from all state agencies, mandates free public education for 12 years and establishes commissions devoted to anticorruption and human rights.

During these tumultuous times, King Bhumibol Adulyadej (Rama IX, r 1946–), who succeeded his brother after a suspected assassination, defined a new political role for the monarchy. Although powerless to legislate change, the king came to be viewed as a paternal figure who restrained excesses in the interests of all Thais and acted with wisdom in times of crisis.

Economic Roller Coaster

During the 1990s, Thailand was one of the so-called tiger economies, roaring ahead with one of the world's highest growth rates – 9% at its peak. It was poised to join the ranks of Hong Kong, Singapore and other more industrialised nations of the Pacific Rim. But unabated growth soon imploded, sending Thailand and its neighbours into a regional currency crisis in 1997. The Thai baht dived to an all-time low – roughly 40% against the US dollar. The freewheeling boom days were over and the country entered a nearly three-year recession. The International Monetary Fund (IMF) provided a US$17.2 billion rescue package in the form of short-term loans, with the stipulation that the Thai government follow the IMF's prescriptions for recapitalisation and restructuring.

Thailand's convalescence progressed remarkably well in the following years, with more sustainable economic growth (a healthy 6.3% in 2004, so say the economists) enabling an 'early exit' from the IMF's loan package back in mid-2003.

However, that exit appears to have been something of an ill-timed move as the tourism-dependent side of the economy took several sucker punches soon after, including the outbreak of SARS in 2003, bird flu in 2004 and the devastating waves of the tsunami that pounded the Andaman coast on 26 December 2004.

The ousting of Thailand's democratically elected Prime Minister Thaksin Shinawatra in September 2006 had inevitable economic consequences, which were slowly reflected in the country's stock exchange. The most extreme one-day plunge in the exchange's history took place on 19 December. The story was significantly different for the country's exports in 2006, which rose by 17% that year.

THE CULTURE

Thais are master chatters and for a Westerner they have a shopping list of questions: where are you from, how old are you, are you married, do you have children? Occasionally they get more curious and want to know how much you weigh or how much money you make; these questions to a Thai are matters of public record and aren't considered impolite. They also love to dole out compliments. Foreigners who can speak even the most basic Thai are lauded for being linguistic geniuses. And the most reluctant smile garners heaps of flattery about your ravishing looks. Why do some foreigners come to Thailand and never leave? Because Thais know how to make visitors feel like superstars.

The National Psyche

Thais are laid-back, good-natured people whose legendary hospitality has earned their country a permanent place on the global travel map. Paramount to the Thai philosophy of life is *sànùk* (fun) – each day is celebrated with food and conversation, foreign festivals are readily adopted as an excuse for a party and every task is measured on the *sànùk* meter.

The Thai-on-Thai culture is a lot more mysterious to unravel. Whole books are dedicated to the subject and expats spend hours in speculation. A few guiding principles are *nâa* (face) and elder-junior hierarchy. Like many Asian cultures, Thais believe strongly in the concept of 'saving face' – that is, avoiding confrontation and endeavouring not to embarrass themselves or other people. All relationships in Thai society are governed by connections between the elder and the junior, following simple lines of social rank defined by age, wealth, status and personal and political power. The elder of the table always picks up the tab. The junior in the workplace must do all the elder's menial chores and is not encouraged to participate in meetings or decision-making. The Western mindset is so different in this regard that it becomes something of a handicap in Thai society.

Delving deeper into the serious side of Thailand, the culture's fundamental building blocks are family and religion. Take all the pressures your parents put on you about a career, education, a future spouse and mul-

DID YOU KNOW?

- His Majesty Bhumibol Adulyadej, on the throne for more than 60 years, is the longest-reigning king in Thai history, as well as the longest-reigning current monarch worldwide.
- It is illegal to step on money in Thailand, as the king's image is on all coins and notes.
- The minimum daily wage in Bangkok and surrounding provinces is 175B (US$4.50).
- Traditional Thai tattoos are believed to have mystical powers, protecting those bearing them from illness, and bringing them good luck.
- Thailand is 543 years ahead of the West, at least according to the Thai calendar that measures from the beginning of the Buddhist Era (in 543 BC).

tiply that by 10 – now you are approaching the environment of your Thai peer. Young Thais from poor families are also expected to support the family financially. Many do so with side jobs; they sell sweets from their front porch, run small internet cafés or sell orange juice to tourists. For a culture that values having a good time, they work unimaginably long hours, usually wearing a beaming smile.

Religion and the monarchy, which is still regarded by many as divine, are the culture's sacred cows. You can turn your nose up at fish sauce or dress like a retro-hippy, but don't insult the king and always behave respectfully in the temples. One of Thailand's leading intellectuals, Sulak Sivarak, was once arrested for describing the king as 'the skipper' – a passing reference to his fondness for sailing. Pictures of the king, including Thai currency and stamps, are treated with deference as well.

Lifestyle

Thailand has a split personality – the highly Westernised urban Thais in major cities, and the rural farming communities more in tune with the ancient rhythms of life. But regardless of this divide, several persisting customs offer us a rough snapshot of daily life. Thais wake up early, thanks in part to the roosters that start crowing sometime after sunset. The first events of the day are to make rice and to sweep the floor and common spaces – very distinct smells and sounds. In the grey stillness of early morning, barefoot monks carrying large round bowls travel through the town to collect their daily meals from the faithful. Several hours later, business is in full swing: the vendors have arrived at their favourite corner to sell everything imaginable, and some things that are not, and the civil servants and students clad in their respective uniforms swoop in and out of the stalls like birds of prey.

A neat and clean appearance complements Thais' persistent regard for beauty. Despite the hot and humid weather, Thais rarely seem to sweat and never stink. Soap-shy backpackers take note: if you don't honour the weather with regular bathing you will be the sole source of stench on the bus. Thais bathe three or four times a day, more as a natural air-conditioner than as compulsive cleaning. They also use talcum powder throughout the day to absorb sweat, and as one Thai explained, 'for freshy'.

Superficially, eating makes up the rest of the day. Notice the shop girls, ticket vendors or even the office workers: they can be found in a tight circle swapping gossip and snacking (or *gin lên,* literally 'eat for fun'). Then there is dinner and after-dinner and the whole seemingly chaotic, yet highly ordered affair starts over again.

Population

About 75% of citizens are ethnic Thais, further divided by geography (north, central, south and northeast). Each group speaks its own Thai dialect and to a certain extent practises customs unique to its region or influenced by

WHY WÂI?

Traditionally, Thais greet each other not with a handshake but with a prayerlike palms-together gesture, known as a *wâi.* If someone *wâis* you, you should *wâi* back (unless *wâi*-ed by a child or a serviceperson). The placement of the fingertips in relation to the facial features varies with the recipient's social rank and age. The safest, least offensive spot is to place the tips of your fingers to nose level and slightly bow your head.

neighbouring countries. Politically and economically the central Thais are the dominant group. People of Chinese ancestry make up roughly 14% of the population, many of whom have been in Thailand for generations. Ethnic Chinese probably enjoy better relations with the majority population here than in any other country in Southeast Asia. Other large minority groups include the Malays in the far south, the Khmers in the northeast and the Lao, spread throughout the north and east. Smaller non-Thai-speaking groups include the colourful hill tribes living in the northern mountains.

SPORT

Muay Thai (Thai Boxing)

The wild musical accompaniment, the ceremonial beginning of each match and the frenzied betting around the stadium – almost anything goes in this martial sport, both in the ring and in the stands.

Bouts are limited to five three-minute rounds separated by two-minute breaks. Contestants wear international-style gloves and trunks (always either red or blue) and their feet are taped. All surfaces of the body are considered fair targets and any part of the body except the head may be used to strike an opponent. Common blows include high kicks to the neck, elbow thrusts to the face and head, knee hooks to the ribs and low crescent kicks to the calf. A contestant may even grasp an opponent's head between his hands and pull it down to meet an upward knee thrust. Punching is considered the weakest of all blows and kicking merely a way to 'soften up' one's opponent; knee and elbow strikes are decisive in most matches.

Matches are held every day of the year at the major stadiums in Bangkok (see p707) and the provinces. There are about 60,000 full-time boxers in Thailand.

Tàkrâw

The most popular variation of *tàkrâw*, sometimes called Siamese football, is best described as volleyball for the feet. Using a *lûuk tàkrâw* (rattan ball), players assemble on either side of the net, using similar rules to volleyball except that only the feet and head are permitted to touch the ball. Like gymnasts the players perform aerial pirouettes, spiking the ball over the net with their feet. Another variation has players kicking the ball into a hoop 4.5m above the ground – basketball with feet, but without a backboard!

The traditional way to play *tàkrâw* is for players to stand in a circle and simply try to keep the ball airborne by kicking it, like hacky sack. Points are scored for style, difficulty and variety of kicking manoeuvres.

RELIGION

Alongside the Thai national flag flies the yellow flag of Buddhism – Theravada Buddhism

ARE YOU A DEEP-FRIED FARÀNG?

Faràng is the word that Thais use for foreigners. It is derived from the word for French *(faràngsèht)* and can be merely descriptive, mildly derogatory or openly insulting, depending on the situation. When kids yell it as they pass by on bikes, it is usually the first, as if they were pointing out a big truck. You can graduate to the last category by being clueless or disrespectful towards the culture. Here are some tips on how to avoid the label:

- Before every movie and in bus and train stations, when the national anthem is played you are expected to stand with your arms by your side.
- Don't lick stamps, which usually bear an image of the king, or your fingers – to the Thais only animals lick things.
- Don't get angry, yell or get physically violent; keep your cool and things will usually work out in your favour.
- Feet are the lowest and 'dirtiest' part of the body in Thailand. Keep your feet on the floor, not on a chair; never touch anyone or point with your foot; never step over someone (or something) sitting on the ground. Take your shoes off when you enter a home or temple.
- Dress modestly and don't sunbathe topless.
- Woman aren't allowed to touch or sit next to a monk or his belongings. The very back seat of the bus and the last row on public boats are reserved for monks.

(as opposed to the Mahayana schools found in East Asia and the Himalayas). Country, family and daily life are all married to religion. Every Thai male is expected to become a monk for a short period in his life, since a family earns great merit when a son 'takes robe and bowl'. Traditionally, the length of time spent in a wat is three months, during the Buddhist lent *(phansăa),* which begins around July and coincides with the wet season, or when an elder in the family dies.

More evident than the philosophical aspects of Buddhism is the everyday fusion with animist rituals. Monks are consulted to determine an auspicious date for a wedding or the likelihood of success for a business. Spirit houses *(phrá phuum)* are constructed outside buildings and homes to encourage the spirits to live independently from the family, but to remain comfortable so as to bring good fortune to the site. The spirit houses are typically ornate wat-like structures set on a pedestal in a prominent section of the yard. Food, drink and furniture are all offered to the spirits to smooth daily life. Even in commerce-crazy Bangkok, ornate spirit houses eat up valuable real estate and become revered shrines to local people.

Roughly 95% of the population practises Buddhism, but in southern Thailand there is a significant Muslim minority community.

ARTS

Music

TRADITIONAL

Classical central Thai music features an incredible array of textures and subtleties, hair-raising tempos and pastoral melodies. Among the more common instruments is the *pìi,* a woodwind instrument with a reed mouthpiece; it is heard prominently at Thai boxing matches. A bowed instrument, similar to examples played in China and Japan, is aptly called the *saw*. The *ránâat èhk* is a bamboo-keyed percussion instrument resembling the Western xylophone, while the *khlùi* is a wooden flute. This traditional orchestra was originally developed as an accompaniment to classical dance-drama and shadow theatre, but these days it can be heard at temple fairs and concerts.

In the north and northeast there are several popular wind instruments with multiple reed pipes, which function basically like a mouth organ. Chief among these is the *khaen,* which originated in Laos; when played by an adept musician it sounds like a rhythmic, churning calliope organ. It is used chiefly in *măw lam* music. The *lûuk thûng,* or 'country' (literally, 'children of the fields') style, which originated in the northeast, has become a favourite throughout Thailand.

MUST SEE

Based on a true Thai festival known as the Illuminated Boat Procession, the 2002 film *Mekong Full Moon Party* takes a close look at how the spiritual faith of Thailand is being challenged by the technological scepticism of today. International audiences praised the film for its wonderfully insightful characterisation of modern Thai culture.

MODERN

Popular Thai music has borrowed much from the West, particularly its instruments, but retains a distinct flavour. The best example of this is the famous rock group Carabao. Recording and performing for more than 20 years now, Carabao has crafted an exciting fusion of Thai classical and *lûuk thûng* forms with heavy metal.

Another major influence on Thai pop was a 1970s group called Caravan.It created a modern Thai folk style known as *phleng phêua chii-wít* (songs for life), which features political and environmental topics rather than the usual moonstruck love themes.

Sculpture & Architecture

On an international scale, Thailand has probably distinguished itself more in traditional religious sculpture than in any other art form. Thailand's most famous sculptural output has been its bronze Buddha images, coveted the world over for their originality and grace.

Architecture, however, is considered the highest art form in traditional Thai society. Ancient Thai homes consist of a single-room teak structure raised on stilts, since most Thais once lived along river banks or canals. The space underneath also serves as the living room, kitchen, garage and barn. Rooflines in Thailand are steeply pitched and often decorated at the corners or along the gables with motifs related to the *naga* (mythical sea serpent), long believed to be a spiritual protector.

Temple architecture symbolises elements of the religion. A steeply pitched roof system tiled in green, gold and red, and often constructed in tiered series of three levels, represents the Buddha (the Teacher), the Dhamma (Dharma in Sanskrit; the Teaching) and the Sangha (the fellowship of followers of the Teaching).

Theatre & Dance

Traditional Thai theatre consists of six dramatic forms: *khŏhn,* formal masked dance-drama depicting scenes from the Ramakian (the Thai version of India's Ramayana) and originally performed only for the royal court; *lákhon,* a general term covering several types of dance-dramas (usually for nonroyal occasions), as well as Western theatre; *lí-keh,* a partly improvised, often bawdy folk play featuring dancing, comedy, melodrama and music; *mánohraa,* the southern-Thai equivalent of *lí-keh,* but based on a 2000-year-old Indian story; *năng,* or shadow plays, limited to southern Thailand; and *hùn lŭang* or *lákhon lék* puppet theatre.

ENVIRONMENT

Thailand's shape on the map has been likened to the head of an elephant, with its trunk extending down the Malay peninsula. The country covers 517,000 sq km, which is slightly smaller than the US state of Texas. The centre of the country, Bangkok, sits at about 14° north latitude – level with Madras, Manila, Guatemala and Khartoum. Because the north–south reach spans roughly 16 latitudinal degrees, Thailand has perhaps the most diverse climate in Southeast Asia.

The Land

The country stretches from dense mountain jungles in the north to the flat central plains to the southern tropical rainforests. Covering the majority of the country, monsoon forests are filled with a sparse canopy of deciduous trees that shed their leaves during the dry season to conserve water. The landscape becomes dusty and brown until the rains (from July to November) transform everything into a fecund green. Typically, monsoon rains are brief afternoon thunderstorms that wet the parched earth and add more steam to a humid day. As the rains cease, Thailand enters its 'winter', a period of cooler temperatures, virtually unnoticeable by a recent arrival except in the north where night-time temperatures can drop to 13°C. By March, the hot season begins with little fanfare and the mercury climbs to 40°C or more at its highest, plus humidity.

In the south, the wet season lasts until January, with months of unrelenting showers and floods. Thanks to the rains, the south supports the dense rainforests more indicative of a 'tropical' region. Along the coastline, mangrove forests anchor themselves wherever water dominates.

Thailand's national flower, the orchid, is one of the world's most beloved parasites, producing such exotic flowers that even its host is charmed.

> **MUST READ**
>
> Like a ripe mangosteen, you won't put down Alex Garland's 1997 novel *The Beach* until you've devoured it. A tale of island-hopping backpackers trying to carve out their own private paradise, this is essential reading for any Thailand trip beginning in a Th Khao San fleapit. A glossy Hollywood film based on the novel and starring Leonardo DiCaprio was released in 2000.

Wildlife

Thailand is particularly rich in bird life: more than 1000 resident and migrating species have been recorded and approximately 10% of all world bird species dwell here. Thailand's most revered indigenous mammal, the elephant, once ran wild in the country's dense virgin forests. Since ancient times, annual parties led by the king would round up young elephants from the wild to train them as workers and fighters. Integral to Thai culture, the elephant symbolises wisdom, strength and good fortune. White elephants are even more auspicious and by tradition are donated to the king. Sadly, elephants are now endangered, having lost their traditional role in society and much of their habitat.

National Parks

Despite Thailand's rich natural diversity, it's only in recent decades that most of the 96 national parks and 100 wildlife sanctuaries have been established. Together these cover 13% of the country's land and sea area, one of the highest ratios of protected to unprotected areas of any nation in the world.

The majority of the preserved areas remain untouched thanks to the **Royal Forest Department** (www.forest.go.th/default_e.asp), but a few – notably Ko Phi Phi, Ko Samet and Ko Chang – have allowed rampant tourism to threaten the natural environment. Ironically, the devastating tsunami had one positive effect in Ko Phi Phi, washing away the worst of the developments and allowing the island to be reborn. Poaching, illegal logging and shifting cultivation have also taken their toll on protected lands.

Environmental Issues

Like all countries with a high population density, there is enormous pressure on Thailand's ecosystems: 50 years ago about 70% of the countryside was forest; by 2000 an estimated 20% of the natural forest cover remained. In response to environmental degradation, the Thai government has created a large number of protected areas since the 1970s. It is now illegal to sell timber felled in Thailand, and the government hopes to raise total forest cover to 40% by the middle of this century.

Air and water pollution are problems in urban areas. The passing of the 1992 Environmental Act was an encouraging move by the government, but standards still lag centuries behind Western nations.

Thailand is a signatory to the UN Convention on International Trade in Endangered Species (CITES). Forty of Thailand's 300 mammal species are on the International Union for Conservation of Nature (IUCN) list of endangered species. As elsewhere in the region, the tiger is one of the most endangered of large mammals. Tiger hunting or trapping is illegal, but poachers continue to kill the cats for the lucrative overseas Chinese pharmaceutical market. Around 200 wild tigers are thought to be hanging on in the national parks of Khao Yai, Kaeng Krachan, Thap Lan, Mae Wong and Khao Sok.

Corruption continues to impede the government's attempts to shelter species coveted by the illicit global wildlife trade. The Royal Forest Department is currently under pressure to take immediate action in those areas where preservation laws have not been enforced, including coastal zones where illegal tourist accommodation has flourished.

TRANSPORT

GETTING THERE & AWAY

Air

Thailand has six international airports: Bangkok, Chiang Mai, Phuket, Ko Samui, Sukhothai and Hat Yai. Most international flights arrive at Bangkok.

Airlines operating out of Thailand:

Air Asia (code AK; ☎ 0 2515 9999; www.airasia.com)
Bangkok Airways (code PG; ☎ 0 2265 5678; www.bangkokair.com)
Cathay Pacific Airways (code CX; ☎ 0 2263 0606; www.cathaypacific.com)
Garuda Indonesia (code GA; ☎ 0 2679 7371; www.garuda-indonesia.com)
Lao Airlines (code QV; ☎ 0 2236 9822; www.lao-airlines.com)
Malaysia Airlines (code MH; ☎ 0 2263 0520; www.malaysiaairlines.com)
Myanmar Airways International (code 8M; ☎ 0 2261 5060; www.maiair.com)
Singapore Airlines (code SQ; ☎ 0 2236 0440; www.singaporeair.com)
Thai Airways International (THAI, code TG; ☎ 0 2280 0060; www.thaiair.com)
Vietnam Airlines (code VN; ☎ 0 2280 0060; www.vietnamair.com)

It is possible to fly return from Bangkok to the US, Europe and Australia for less than US$1000. Cheaper indirect options are available, particularly via Hong Kong, Taiwan and Japan to the US, or via the Middle East to Europe.

Land

Thailand enjoys open and relatively safe border relations with Cambodia, Laos and Malaysia. Myanmar's internal conflicts require a restricted border that is subject to frequent closings and shifting regulations.

DEPARTURE TAX

After staying steady for ages at 500B, the departure tax on international flights was recently raised to 700B, which is paid before passing through immigration. Rumours have been spreading, however, that the departure tax will soon be folded into the price of the plane ticket. This is standard practice at most international airports.

CAMBODIA

Along the Thailand–Cambodia border, there are small border crossings that have opened up recently, but they see little traffic due to roller-coaster roads on the Cambodian side. The Chong Jom–O Smach border (p753) connects Surin Province with Siem Reap, but it is very remote on the Cambodian side. There is also another remote crossing that links Choam Srawngam in Si Saket Province with Choam, in the former Khmer Rouge stronghold of Anlong Veng, but access is tough on both sides of the border (see p753). More popular border crossings include Aranya Prathet–Poipet (p709), Hat Lek–Krong Koh Kong (p765) and Ban Pakard–Psar Pruhm (p765).

LAOS

Nong Khai (p758) is the most popular land border crossing between Thailand and Laos. Other crossings include Chiang Khong–Huay Xai (p744), Chong Mek–Vang Tao (p755), Mukdahan–Savannakhet (p756) and Nakhon Phanom–Tha Khaek (p757).

MALAYSIA

The main border crossing into Malaysia is Kanger–Padang Besar (p784), although you can also cross at nearby Sadao (p784). There is also a crossing at Satun–Pulau Langkawi (p803), and you can access Malaysia's east coast at the Sungai Kolok–Rantau Panjang crossing (p786). There has been unrest, however, in the Muslim-majority southern provinces of Thailand, and until the safety situation improves we advise avoiding the journey between Sungai Kolok and this area. There is also a border crossing to Malaysia between Betong and Keroh, but at the time of writing using the border was extremely inadvisable due to violence in the area.

Anyone planning on crossing from Thailand to Malaysia, and then returning to Thailand should ensure they get stamped out as not doing so has caused difficulties for some travellers.

MYANMAR

In peaceful times, foreigners may cross from Mae Sai into Tachilek, Myanmar (p746); there is another crossing at Ranong–Kawthoung (p787). You can also sometimes make day trips into Myanmar at Three Pagodas Pass (p716) and Mae Sot (p726).

GETTING AROUND

Air

Thailand's major domestic carrier is Thai Airways International (THAI), with Bangkok Airways running a close second, but there has been an explosion of no-frills budget airlines serving popular routes in recent years, making for some dirt-cheap deals for the vigilant traveller. The most useful routes for shoestringers are Mae Hong Son–Chiang Mai, Ko Samui–Bangkok and Phuket–Bangkok – in each case a bus ride of eight to 15 hours is condensed to a one-hour hop. But there are also some amazing deals available on the Bangkok–Chiang Mai route, because competition is fierce. Book your tickets several days in advance for all domestic air travel.

Leading airlines for domestic routes:

Air Andaman (code ADW; ☎ 0 2229 9555)
Air Asia (code AK; ☎ 0 2515 9999; www.airasia.com)
Bangkok Airways (code PG; ☎ 0 2265 5678; www.bangkokair.com)
Nok Air (code DD; ☎ 1318; www.nokair.com)
Orient Thai (code OX; ☎ 0 2267 3210; www.orient-thai.com)
Thai Airways International (code TG; ☎ 0 2280 0060; www.thaiair.com)

Thai Airways is currently offering a countrywide air pass to travellers living outside Thailand. The first three coupons in economy class are US$169; each additional coupon is US$59. The pass must be purchased outside Thailand.

Bicycle

Bicycles are available for rent in many areas; guesthouses often have a few for rent at only 30B to 50B per day. Just about anywhere outside Bangkok, bikes are the ideal form of local transport because they're cheap, nonpolluting and keep you moving slowly enough to see everything. Carefully note the condition of the bike before hiring; if it breaks down, you are responsible and parts can be expensive.

See p804 for information on bicycle touring in Thailand.

Boat

Being a riverine people, Thais have colourful boats of traditional design. With a long graceful breast that barely skims the water and a tail-like propeller, longtail boats are used as island-hoppers, canal coasters and river ferries.

Small wooden fishing boats, brilliantly painted, sometimes shuttle tourists out to nearby islands. Longer trips to the islands of Ko Pha-Ngan and Ko Tao are undertaken by slow yet determined cargo boats through the dark of night. Boat schedules are subject to change depending on weather conditions and demand.

Bus

The Thai bus service is widespread, convenient and phenomenally fast – nail-bitingly so. While private companies usually bag unsuspecting travellers, you're better off with companies operating out of the government bus station. These buses cater to the Thai community, making them more culturally engaging and safer for your belongings. Starting at the top, VIP buses are the closest you will come to being pampered like a rock star. The seats recline, the air-con is frosty and your very own 'air hostess' dispenses refreshments and snacks. Various diminishing classes of air-con buses begin to strip away the extras until you're left with a fairly beat-up bus with an asthmatic cooling system.

Incredibly punishing but undeniably entertaining are the 'ordinary' buses. These rattletraps have fans that don't work when the bus has come to a stop, school-bus sized seats and a tinny sound system that blares the driver's favourite music. The trip is sweaty, loud and usually involves as many animals and babies as adult passengers. At stops along the way, vendors walk the aisles selling food, everyone throws their rubbish out the window and the driver honks at every passer-by hoping to pick up another fare. It's a real trip!

For long-distance trips, check out schedules and/or purchase tickets the day before. Visit www.transport.co.th for bus routes and timetables in English.

ALWAYS LOOK ON THE BRIGHT SIDE...

...unless you happen to be on a Thai bus. If you get on board and everyone has clustered to one side, don't celebrate that you've scored a whole row. Thais instinctively know where the sun will be at all times of the day. The deserted side of the bus will be the side that gets bleached by the sun for the entire trip. Banish the urge to populate virgin territory and join the dark side for the day.

Car & Motorcycle

Cars, 4WDs or vans can be rented in Bangkok and large provincial capitals. Check with travel agencies or hotels for rental locations. Always verify that the vehicle is insured for liability before signing a rental contract, and ask to see the dated insurance documents. If you have an accident while driving an uninsured vehicle, you're in for some major hassles.

Thais drive on the left-hand side of the road – most of the time. Like many places in Asia, every two-lane road has an invisible third lane in the middle that all drivers feel free to use at any time. Passing on hills and curves is common – as long as you've got the proper Buddhist altar on the dashboard, what could happen? The main rule to be aware of is that 'might makes right' and smaller vehicles always yield to bigger ones.

Motorcycle travel is a popular way to get around Thailand. Dozens of places along the guesthouse circuit rent motorbikes for 150B to 300B a day. It is also possible to buy a new or used motorbike and sell it before you leave the country – a good used 125cc bike costs around 40,000B. If you've never ridden a motorcycle before, stick to the smaller 100cc step-through bikes with automatic clutches. Motorcycle rental usually requires that you leave your passport.

Hitching

It is uncommon to see people hitching alongside the highway, since bus travel between towns is fairly inexpensive and reliable. Hitching becomes a better option in the country where public transport isn't available. If you get dropped off by a bus outside a national park or historical site, you can catch a ride along the remainder of the road with an incoming vehicle. Just remember to use the Asian style of beckoning: hold your arm out towards the road, palm-side down and wave towards the ground.

That said, hitching is never entirely safe, and travellers who do so should understand that they are taking a small but potentially serious risk.

Local Transport

Rarely does anyone get stuck anywhere in Thailand, but it is also impossible to escape the hungry drivers who have mastered the most irritating phrase in the English language, 'Hey you, where you go?' A literal translation from the typical Thai inquiry, this phrase will drive you to the edge of insanity, but keep in mind that most don't intend offence, they only want to make a living.

SĂAMLÁW & TÚK-TÚK

Săamláw (also written samlor), meaning 'three wheels', are pedal rickshaws, and you'll see them in a few towns in the northeast and in Chiang Mai. These are good for relatively short distances, but expect to pay a little more if you take one further afield, as it is all human powered. Then there are the motorised săamláw, called túk-túk because of the throaty cough their two-stroke engines make. In Bangkok especially, túk-túk drivers give all local transporters a bad name. The worst are unscrupulously greedy – exorbitantly inflating the fares or diverting passengers to places that pay commissions.

You must bargain and agree on a fare before accepting a ride, but in many towns there is a more-or-less fixed fare anywhere in town.

SĂWNGTHĂEW

Săwngthăew (literally, 'two benches') are small pick-ups with a row of seats down each side. In some towns, săwngthăew serve as public buses running regular routes for fixed fares. But in tourist towns, you'll also find săwngthăew performing the same function as túk-túk, transporting people to and from the bus station or to popular attractions for a bargained fare.

Train

All rail travel originates in Bangkok and radiates out, forming the following four spurs: Ayuthaya–Phitsanulok–Chiang Mai; Nakhon Ratchasima (Khorat)–Surin–Ubon Ratchathani; Nakhon Ratchasima–Khon Kaen–Nong Khai; and Hua Hin–Surat Thani–Hat Yai. The government-operated trains (www.railway.co.th) in Thailand are comfortable and moderately priced, but rather slow. On comparable routes, the buses can often be twice as fast, but the relatively low speed of the train means you can often leave at a convenient hour in the evening and arrive at your destination at a pleasant hour in the morning. Very useful condensed railway timetables are available in English at the Hualamphong train station in Bangkok. These contain schedules and fares for all rapid and express trains, as well as a few ordinary trains.

First-, 2nd- and 3rd-class cabins are available on most trains, but each class may vary considerably depending on the type of train (rapid, express or ordinary). First class is typically a private cabin. Second class has individually reclining seats or padded bench seating; depending on the train some cabins have air-con. Non-air-conditioned, 3rd class is spartan and cheap with shared wooden-bench seating.

Ordinary trains only have the most basic version of 3rd class and stop at every itsy bitsy station. Express and rapid are, well, faster and make fewer stops, but there is a 60B surcharge for express trains and 40B for rapid trains. Some 2nd- and 3rd-class services are air-con, in which case there is a 70B surcharge. For the special-express trains that run between Bangkok and Padang Besar (Malaysia) and between Bangkok and Chiang Mai, there is an 80B to 100B surcharge (or 120B if a meal is included).

Overnight trains have sleeping berths in 1st and 2nd class. The charge for 2nd-class sleeping berths is 100B for an upper berth and 150B for a lower berth (or 130B and 200B, respectively, on a special express). For 2nd-class sleepers with air-con add 250/320B for upper/lower. No sleepers are available in 3rd class.

All 1st-class cabins come with individually controlled air-con. For a two-bed cabin the surcharge is 520B per person.

Trains are often heavily booked, so it's wise to reserve your place well ahead, especially for long-distance trips. At **Hualamphong Station** (☎ 0 2220 4334) in Bangkok, you can book trains on any route in Thailand. The advance booking office is open from 8.30am to 4pm daily. Seats, berths or cabins may be booked up to 60 days in advance. Visit www.railway.co.th for train timetables in English.

BANGKOK

pop 6 million

Ladies and gentlemen, fasten your seatbelts. You are now entering Bangkok, a city that is always on the move. Ancient temples in the shadow of space-age shopping malls, soaring skyscrapers towering over tumbledown hov-

DON'T MISS...

- catching cool breezes on the Chao Phraya River Express
- shopping for items you never knew existed at the weekend Chatuchak Market
- gawking at sex-tourists along Soi Cowboy and inside Nana Plaza
- taking a ride on the Skytrain

els, ubercool cafés and restaurants surrounded by simple street stalls: Bangkok is an interchange of the past, present and future, and a superb subject for any urban connoisseur. It's your decompression chamber, softening the landing in another world, familiar enough to feel like a hot version of home, exotic enough to point the way to adventures ahead. Delve beneath the elevated highways and skyways and you'll find a small village napping in the narrow *soi* (lanes) with an unmistakable *khwaam pen thai* (Thai-ness).

The capital of Thailand was established at Bangkok in 1782. But the name Bangkok, baptised by foreigners, actually refers to a small village within the larger beast. The Thais call their capital Krung Thep, or City of Angels, a much shortened version of the very official and very long tongue-twister of *Krungthep mahanakhon amonratanakosin mahintara ayuthaya mahadilok popnopparat ratchathani burirom udomratchaniwet mahasathan amonpiman avatansathit sakkathattiya witsanukamprasit*.

ORIENTATION

The Mae Nam Chao Phraya divides Bangkok from the older city of Thonburi, where the Southern Bus Terminal and the Thonburi (Bangkok Noi) train station are located.

Bangkok can be further divided into east and west by the main railway line, which feeds in and out of Hualamphong station. Sandwiched between the western side of the tracks and the river is the older part of the city, crowded with historical temples, bustling Chinatown and the popular travellers' centre of Banglamphu. This section of town is less urban, relatively speaking, with low-slung residential homes and shops built along the *khlong* (canals).

East of the railway line is the new city, devoted to commerce and its attendant temples of skyscrapers and shopping centres. Th Phra Ram I feeds into Siam Sq, a popular shopping district, and eventually turns into Th Sukhumvit, a busy commercial centre. Between Siam Sq and Sukhumvit, Th Withayu shelters many of the cities foreign embassies. South of these districts, Th Silom is another concentration of high-rise hotels and multinational offices.

This simple sketch of Bangkok's layout does a real injustice to the chaos that the city has effortlessly acquired through years of unplanned and rapacious development. Street names are unpronounceable, compounded by the inconsistency of romanised Thai spellings. Street addresses are virtually irrelevant as the jumble of numbers divided by slashes and dashes are a record of lot distribution rather than sequential order along a block. *Soi* can't be trusted as they change course more frequently than unfettered rivers.

In short, you will need a good map and a lot of patience. If you plan to use Bangkok's very economical bus system, you should buy the *Tour 'n' Guide Map to Bangkok Thailand*. *Nancy Chandler's Map of Bangkok* is a colourful schematic map of the usual attractions, popular restaurants and other tips from Nancy Chandler, a longtime Bangkok resident. Another contender on the market, *Groovy Map's Bangkok by Day Map 'n' Guide*, combines an up-to-date bus map, sightseeing features and a short selection of restaurant and bar reviews.

INFORMATION

Bookshops

The bookshops in Bangkok are among the best in Southeast Asia. Options include the following places:

Aporia Books (Map p698; 131 Th Tanao, Banglamphu) Used books.

Asia Books Th Sukhumvit (Map pp694-5; Soi 15); Th Ploenchit (Map pp694-5; 3rd fl, Central World Plaza); Th Silom (Map pp694-5; 3rd fl, Thaniya Plaza); Th Ratchadamri (Map pp694-5; Peninsula Plaza); Th Phra Ram I (Map pp694-5; Siam Discovery Center) Books on anything and everything.

Shaman Books (Map p698; 71 Th Khao San, Banglamphu) Huge selection of used books.

Emergency

Bangkok does not have an emergency phone system staffed by English-speaking operators.

Tourist Assistance Centre (☎ 0 2281 1348; 🕑 8am-midnight) A division of the Tourism Authority of Thailand (TAT) dealing with tourist safety.

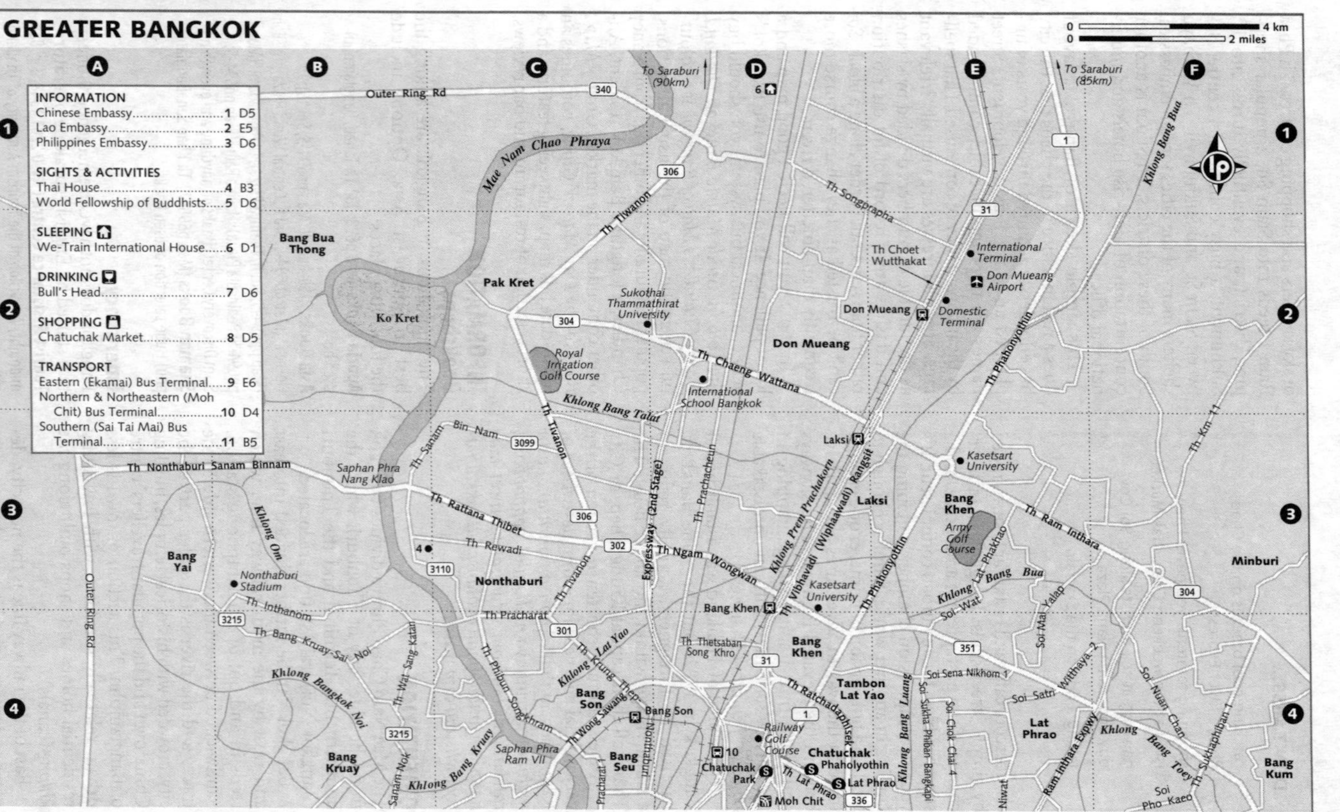
GREATER BANGKOK
0 4 km
0 2 miles
INFORMATION
Chinese Embassy 1 D5
Lao Embassy 2 E5
Philippines Embassy 3 D6
SIGHTS & ACTIVITIES
Thai House 4 B3
World Fellowship of Buddhists 5 D6
SLEEPING
We-Train International House 6 D1
DRINKING
Bull's Head 7 D6
SHOPPING
Chatuchak Market 8 D5
TRANSPORT
Eastern (Ekamai) Bus Terminal 9 E6
Northern & Northeastern (Moh Chit) Bus Terminal 10 D4
Southern (Sai Tai Mai) Bus Terminal 11 B5
To Saraburi (90km)
To Saraburi (85km)
Outer Ring Rd
Mae Nam Chao Phraya
Bang Bua Thong
Ko Kret
Pak Kret
Th Tiwanon
Th Songprapha
Th Choet Wutthakat
International Terminal
Don Mueang Airport
Domestic Terminal
Don Mueang
Khlong Bang Bua
Sukhothai Thammathirat University
Royal Irrigation Golf Course
Th Chaeng Wattana
International School Bangkok
Khlong Bang Talat
Th Phahonyothin
Th Km 11
Bin Nam
Th Sanam
Laksi
Kasetsart University
Th Nonthaburi Sanam Binnam
Saphan Phra Nang Klao
Th Rattana Thibet
Expressway (2nd Stage)
Th Prachacheun
Khlong Prem Prachakorn
Th Vibhavadi (Wiphawadi) Rangsit
Bang Khen
Army Golf Course
Th Ram Inthara
Khlong Om
Bang Yai
Th Rewadi
Th Ngam Wongwan
Minburi
Nonthaburi Stadium
Nonthaburi
Khlong Lat Phakhao
Bang Bua
Soi Wat
Soi Mai Yalap
Th Inthanom
Th Pracharat
Th Thetsaban Song Khro
Th Bang Kruay-Sai Noi
Th Wat Sang Katan
Khlong Lat Yao
Th Krung Thep
Th Ratchadaphisek
Tambon Lat Yao
Soi Sena Nikhom 1
Soi Satri
Witthaya 2
Khlong Bangkok Noi
Th Phibun Songkhram
Bang Son
Th Wong Sawang
Nonthaburi
Railway Golf Course
Chatuchak
Phaholyothin
Khlong Bang Luang
Soi Sukha Phiban Bangkapi
Soi Chok Chai 4
Lat Phrao
Ram Inthara Expwy
Khlong Bang Toey
Soi Nuan Chan
Th Sukhaphiban 1
Bang Kruay
Khlong Bang Kruay
Saphan Phra Ram VII
Sanam Nok
Pracharat 1
Bang Seu
Chatuchak Park
Th Lat Phrao
Moh Chit
Niwat
Soi Pho Kaeo
Bang Kum

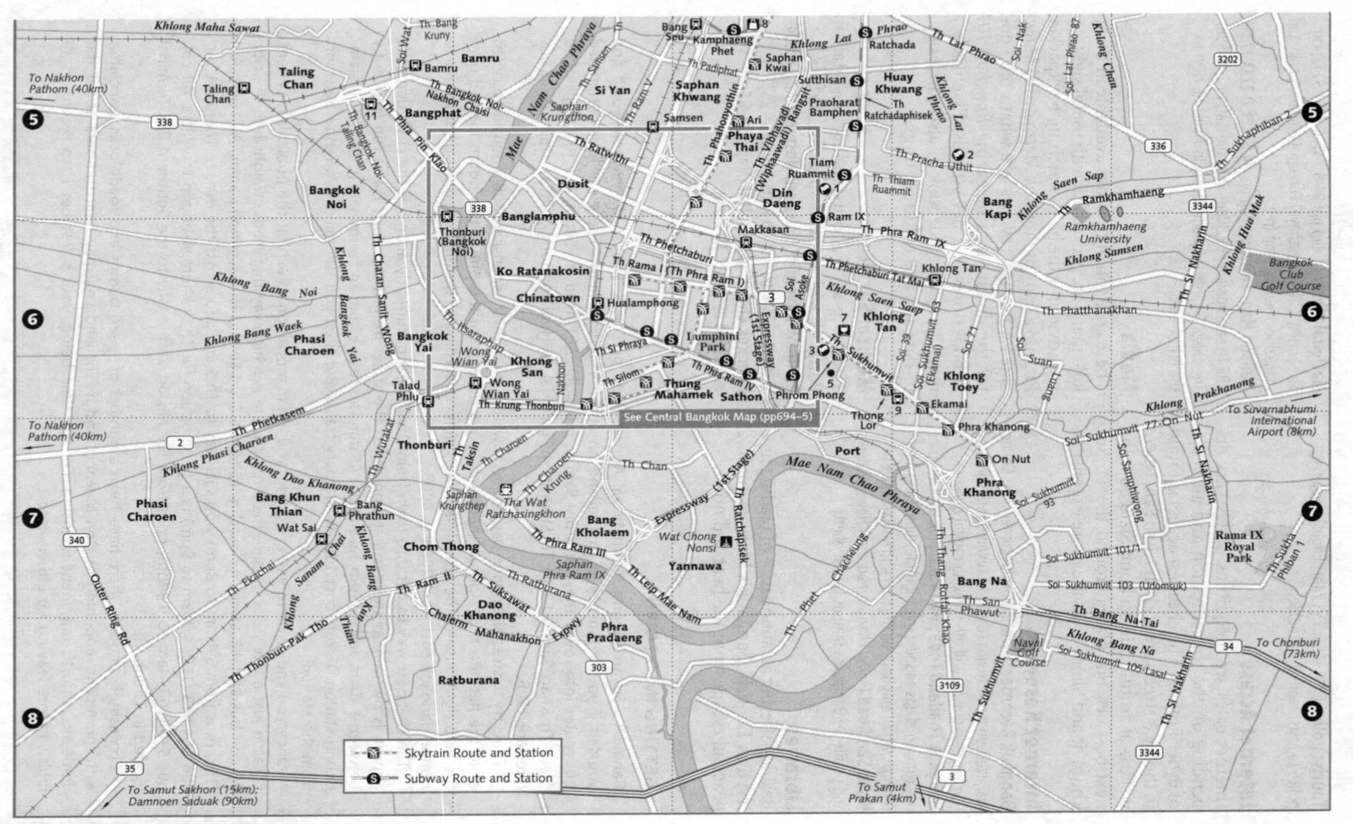
Skytrain Route and Station
Subway Route and Station
See Central Bangkok Map (pp694–5)
Mae Nam Chao Phraya
Dusit
Banglamphu
Ko Ratanakosin
Chinatown
Thonburi
Bangkok Noi
Bangkok Yai
Khlong San
Lumphini Park
Din Daeng
Bang Kapi
Khlong Toey
Khlong Tan
Phra Khanong
Bang Na
On Nut
Port
Yannawa
Bang Kholaem
Phra Pradaeng
Ratburana
Dao Khanong
Chom Thong
Bang Khun Thian
Phasi Charoen
Taling Chan
Bamru
Bangphat
Si Yan
Saphan Khwang
Huay Khwang
Ratchada
Rama IX Royal Park
Naval Golf Course
Bangkok Club Golf Course
Ramkhamhaeng University
Outer Ring Rd
Th Sukhumvit
Th Si Nakharin
Th Ratchapisek
Th Charan Sanit Wong
Th Phra Pin Klao
Th Phetkasem
Th Thang Rotfai Khao
Expressway (1st Stage)
Wat Chong Nonsi
To Suvarnabhumi International Airport (8km)
To Chonburi (73km)
To Samut Prakan (4km)
To Samut Sakhon (15km); Damnoen Saduak (90km)
To Nakhon Pathom (40km)

Tourist police (☎ 1155; 🕒 24hr) English-speaking police to assist tourists in trouble.

Internet Access

Internet cafés are ubiquitous. Rates vary depending on the concentration and affluence of cyber junkies. The cheapest access is found in the back streets around Th Khao San, where it starts at around 30B an hour. Siam Sq is the next best bet, but places around the Th Sukhumvit and Silom areas are more expensive.

Internet Resources

Bangkok Recorder (www.bangkokrecorder.com) Online magazine on music trends (the indie revolution), nightlife (curfew crackdowns) and other vexing capital questions.
Bangkok Thailand Today (www.bangkok.thailandtoday.com) Solid tips on shopping, nightlife, dining and sightseeing, with an emphasis on the river and Ko Ratanakosin.
Khao San Road (www.khaosanroad.com) News, reviews and profiles of Bangkok's famous tourist ghetto.

Libraries

Besides offering an abundance of reading material in English, Bangkok's libraries make a peaceful escape from the heat and noise.

National Library (Map pp694-5; ☎ 0 2281 5212; cnr Th Samsen & Th Si Ayuthaya) Foreign-language books and magazines; membership free.
Neilson Hays Library (Map pp694-5; ☎ 0 2233 1731; 195 Th Surawong; 🕒 9.30am-4pm Tue-Sat, to 2pm Sun) The oldest English-language library in Thailand. Next to the British Club.

Media

There are a ton of free rags available in Bangkok; many are packed full with useful sightseeing advice for the baht-watching backpacker. Pick up a copy of *Bangkok Metro* or *BK Magazine* for listings, reviews and what's on. Look for the digest-sized magazine *Bangkok 101* at bookstores and newsstands. Essentially a mini-Bangkok guidebook, it also carries up-to-date arts and culture listings.

Medical Services

There are several outstanding hospitals in Bangkok with English-speaking staff.

Bangkok Adventist (Mission) Hospital (Map pp694-5; ☎ 0 2281 1100; 430 Th Phitsanulok)
Bangkok Christian Hospital (Map pp694-5; ☎ 0 2634 0560; 124 Th Silom)

GETTING INTO TOWN

Bangkok's Suvarnabhumi International Airport (Map pp690–1) is most likely where you'll find yourself if you've journeyed to Thailand on an international flight. There are four designated bus routes into town; they run from 5am to midnight. AE1 heads to Silom, AE2 to Banglamphu (near Th Khao San), AE3 to Th Sukhumvit and AE4 to Hualamphong railway station. All bus fares are 150B.

Touts try to steer all arriving passengers towards one of their expensive 650B limousine services or to the flat-rate taxis; ignore them and buy a ticket from the public taxi booth located near the kerb right outside the arrival hall. Fares differ according to destination; most destinations in central Bangkok cost from 200B to 400B.

The cheapest way to get into town from Don Mueang, currently acting as the city's domestic airport, is by train, as there is a station across the street from the airport. Trains run frequently between 4.40am and 9.45pm, take about 45 minutes to one hour and terminate in central Hualamphong station. Tickets cost 10B for ordinary trains. But then you still need to arrange transport from the station!

Once you know where you are going, you are in a position to exploit the public bus system. Located just a few steps outside the airport there is a highway that leads straight into the city. Air-con bus 29 (16B, runs 24 hours) goes to the Siam Sq and Hualamphong areas. Air-con bus 4 (16B, runs from 5.45am to 8pm) works its way to Th Silom and across the river to Thonburi. Air-con bus 513 (16B, 4.30am to 9pm) is a good option for Th Sukhumvit-bound travellers. Air-con bus 510 (16B, 4am to 9.30pm) goes from the airport all the way to the Southern Bus Terminal located in Thonburi.

Confusingly enough, there have been a number of speed bumps and roadblocks associated with the recent reopening of Don Mueang, and in Thailand you may hear rumours about the domestic airport's imminent reclosing. For the time being, your safest bet is to reconfirm all flights before leaving for either airport.

Bumrungrad Hospital (Map pp694-5; ☎ 0 2253 0250; 33 Soi 3, Th Sukhumvit)

Money

Thai banks have currency exchange kiosks in many parts of Bangkok, although a large number of exchange kiosks are concentrated in the Th Sukhumvit, Th Khao San, Siam Sq and Th Silom areas. Hours sometimes vary, but most kiosks are open from 8am to 8pm daily. Regular bank hours in Bangkok are 10am to 4pm. ATMs are located everywhere.

Post

Main post office (Map pp694-5; Th Charoen Krung; 8am-8pm Mon-Fri, to 1pm Sat & Sun) Poste restante and a packing service for sending parcels home. Branch post offices also offer poste restante and parcel services.

Telephone

Communications Authority of Thailand (CAT; Map pp694-5; Th Charoen Krung; 24hr) Next to the main post office.

Telephone Organisation of Thailand (TOT; Map pp694-5; Th Ploenchit) International faxes and calls.

Tourist Information

Bangkok Tourist Division (Map p698; ☎ 0 2225 7612; www.bangkoktourist.com; 17/1 Th Phra Athit; 9am-7pm)

Tourism Authority of Thailand (TAT; www.tourismthailand.org) main office (Map pp694-5; ☎ 0 2250 5500; 4th fl, 1606 Th Phetburi Tat Mai; 8.30am-4.30pm); airport information desk (☎ 0 2504 2701; Arrival Hall, Terminal 1, Bangkok International Airport; 8am-midnight) To get to the main office, take air-con bus 512, microbus 10 and ordinary buses 11, 38, 58, 60, 72, 99 and 113 or walk from Asoke Skytrain station.

Travel Agencies

There is no shortage of travel agents in Bangkok, but not all of them are legitimate or trustworthy, especially when it comes to cheap airline tickets. Whenever possible, try to see the tickets before you hand over the money. Try the following established agencies:

IBS Travel (Map p698; ☎ 0 2810 1219; 108/11 Th Khao San) One of the most reliable options in backpackersville, just off Th Khao San near Susie Pub.

STA Travel (Map pp694-5; ☎ 0 2236 0262; www.statravel.com; 14th fl, Wall St Tower, 33/70 Th Surawong) Bangkok branch of an international institution.

DANGERS & ANNOYANCES

Bangkok's most heavily touristed areas – Wat Phra Kaew, Th Khao San, Jim Thompson's House – are favourite hunting grounds for professional con artists. Smartly dressed and slick talking, not all are Thai, but all will speak your native language fluently. Their usual spiel is that the attraction you want to visit is closed for the day and they can arrange a bargain tour for you elsewhere. This is the bait for the infamous gem scam (see p806).

More obvious are the túk-túk drivers who are out to make a commission by dragging you to a local silk or jewellery shop, even though you've requested an entirely different destination. In either case, if you accept an invitation for 'free' sightseeing or shopping, you're quite likely to end up wasting an afternoon or – as happens all too often – losing a lot of money.

SIGHTS

The cultural gems of Bangkok are found in Ko Ratanakosin, the oldest and holiest part of town. For good old-fashioned wandering, sample the commercial chaos of Chinatown; to escape the heat and congestion, explore the Mae Nam Chao Phraya.

Ko Ratanakosin Area

Bordering the eastern bank of the Mae Nam Chao Phraya, this area is a veritable Vatican City of Thai Buddhism, filled with some of the country's most honoured and holy sites: Wat Phra Kaew, the Grand Palace and Wat Pho. These are also the most spectacular tourist attractions the city has to offer and a must for even the most unmotivated students of culture and history. Many Thais make religious pilgrimages here, so remember to dress modestly (clothes to elbows and knees) and behave respectfully (remove shoes when instructed). And for walking in the grounds, wear shoes with closed toes and heels, not sandals.

Wat Phra Kaew (Map pp694-5; ☎ 0 2623 5500; Th Na Phra Lan; admission 200B; 8.30am-3.30pm), also known as the Temple of the Emerald Buddha,

THÀNŎN & SOI

Throughout this book, *Thànŏn* (meaning 'street') is abbreviated as 'Th'. A *soi* is a small street or lane that runs off a larger street. The address of a site located on a *soi* will be written as 48/3-5 Soi 1, Th Sukhumvit, meaning off Th Sukhumvit on Soi 1.

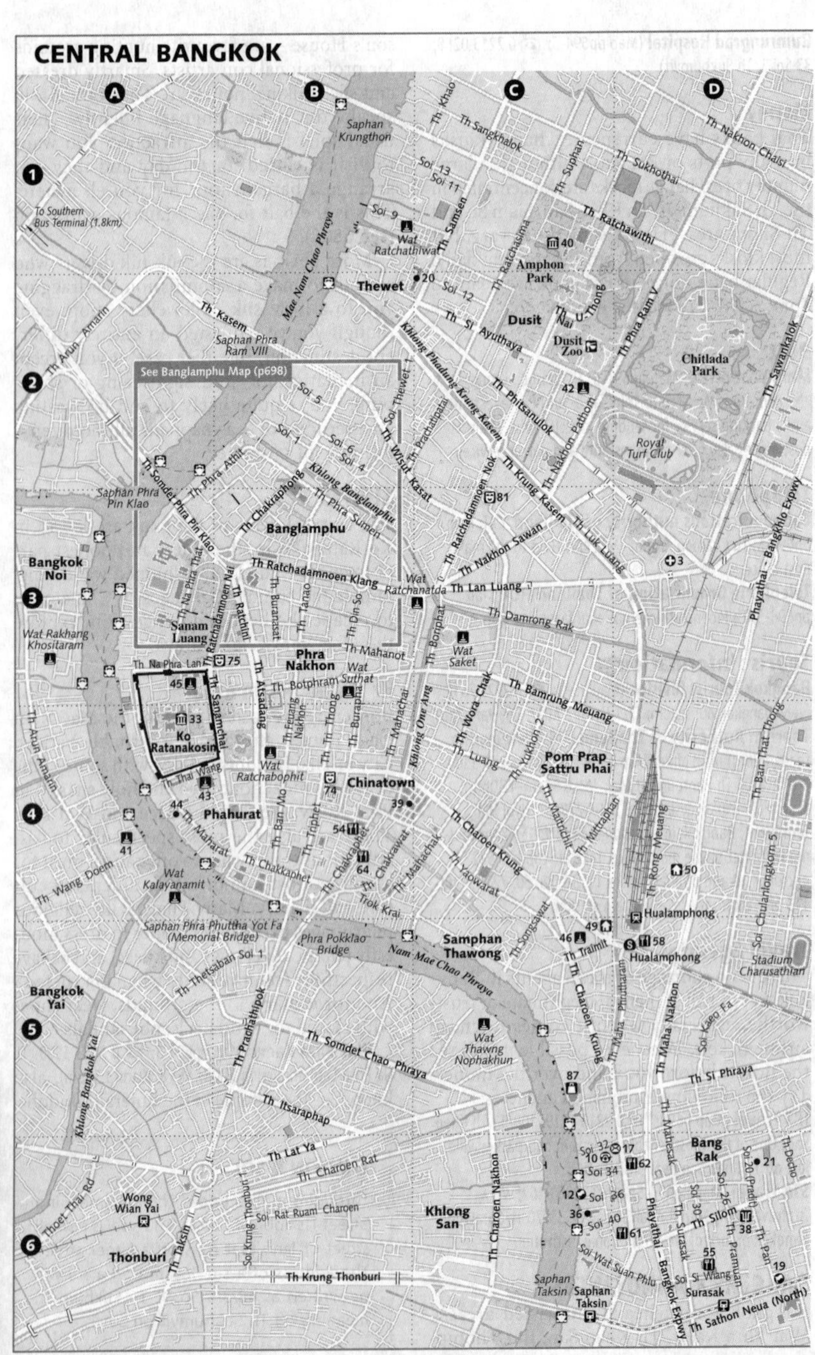
CENTRAL BANGKOK
See Banglamphu Map (p698)
To Southern Bus Terminal (1.8km)
Saphan Krungthon
Mae Nam Chao Phraya
Thewet
Wat Ratchathiwat
Amphon Park
Dusit
Dusit Zoo
Chitlada Park
Royal Turf Club
Saphan Phra Ram VIII
Saphan Phra Pin Klao
Banglamphu
Bangkok Noi
Wat Rakhang Khositaram
Sanam Luang
Phra Nakhon
Wat Suthat
Wat Saket
Wat Ratchanatda
Ko Ratanakosin
Wat Ratchabophit
Chinatown
Phahurat
Pom Prap Sattru Phai
Wat Kalayanamit
Saphan Phra Phuttha Yot Fa (Memorial Bridge)
Phra Pokklao Bridge
Samphan Thawong
Nam Mae Chao Phraya
Hualamphong
Stadium Charusathian
Bangkok Yai
Wat Thawng Nophakhun
Bang Rak
Wong Wian Yai
Klhong San
Thonburi
Saphan Taksin
Surasak
Th Kasem
Th Arun Amarin
Th Sangkhalok
Th Sukhothai
Th Ratchawithi
Th Nakhon Chaisi
Th Si Ayuthaya
Th Phitsanulok
Th Krung Kasem
Th Ratchadamnoen Klang
Th Lan Luang
Th Nakhon Sawan
Th Damrong Rak
Th Bamrung Meuang
Th Charoen Krung
Th Yaowarat
Th Chakkraphet
Th Wang Doem
Th Somdet Chao Phraya
Th Itsaraphap
Th Lat Ya
Th Charoen Rat
Th Krung Thonburi
Th Si Phraya
Th Silom
Th Sathon Neua (North)
Th Prachathipok
Th Taksin
Th Charoen Nakhon
Phayathai - Bangkhlo Expwy
Phayathai – Bangkok Expwy
Khlong Bangkok Yai
Khlong Phadung Krung Kasem
Khlong Banglamphu
Khlong Ong Ang
THAILAND

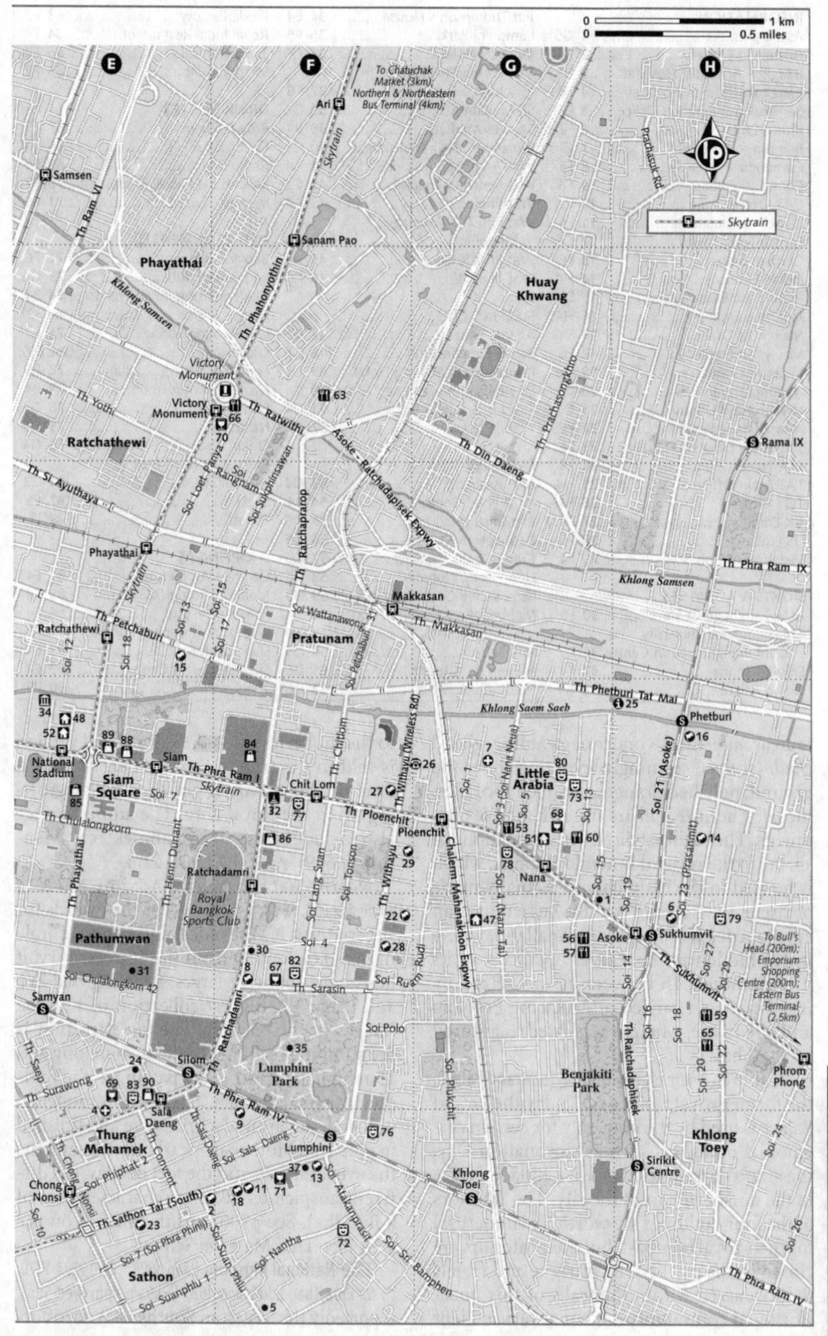
E
F
G
H
To Chatuchak Market (3km); Northern & Northeastern Bus Terminal (4km)
Ari
Samsen
Sanam Pao
Skytrain
Phayathai
Huay Khwang
Khlong Samsen
Th Phahonyothin
Victory Monument
Th Yothi
Th Ratwithi
Ratchathewi
Th Din Daeng
Th Prachasongkhro
Rama IX
Th Si Ayuthaya
Asoke - Ratchadapisek Expwy
Soi Rangnam
Soi Sukphimsawan
Soi Loet Panya
Th Ratchaprarop
Th Phra Ram IX
Makkasan
Th Makkasan
Soi Wattanawong
Th Petchaburi
Pratunam
Soi Petchaburi 31
Th Phetburi Tat Mai
Khlong Saem Saeb
Phetburi
National Stadium
Siam
Siam Square
Th Phra Ram I
Chit Lom
Th Chitlom
Th Withayu (Wireless Rd)
Little Arabia
Soi 21 (Asoke)
Th Ploenchit
Ploenchit
Th Chulalongkorn
Th Henri Dunant
Ratchadamri
Royal Bangkok Sports Club
Nana
Soi 3 (Soi Nana Neua)
Soi 4 (Nana Tai)
Soi 23 (Prasanmit)
Pathumwan
Soi Chulalongkorn 42
Asoke
Sukhumvit
Th Sukhumvit
To Bull's Head (200m); Emporium Shopping Centre (200m); Eastern Bus Terminal (2.5km)
Samyan
Th Sarasin
Soi Ruam Rudi
Soi Polo
Soi Lang Suan
Soi Tonson
Chalerm Mahanakhon Expwy
Th Ratchadamri
Lumphini Park
Silom
Benjakiti Park
Th Ratchadaphisek
Phrom Phong
Th Surawong
Sala Daeng
Th Phra Ram IV
Th Sala Daeng
Soi Sala Daeng 1
Lumphini
Soi Plukchit
Thung Mahamek
Th Convent
Khlong Toei
Khlong Toey
Sirikit Centre
Chong Nonsi
Soi Phiphat 2
Th Sathon Tai (South)
Soi Atakanprasit
Soi Suan Phlu
Soi 7 (Soi Phra Phinit)
Soi Nantha
Soi Sri Bamphen
Sathon
Soi Suanphlu 1
Th Saep
Th Phayathai
Th Chong Nonsi
0 1 km
0 0.5 miles

INFORMATION
Asia Books 1 G5
Australian Embassy 2 E6
Bangkok Adventist Hospital 3 D3
Bangkok Christian Hospital 4 E6
Bangkok Immigration Office 5 F6
Brunei Embassy 6 H5
Bumrungrad Hospital 7 G4
Cambodian Embassy 8 F5
Canadian Embassy 9 F6
CAT Office 10 C6
French Consulate 11 F6
French Embassy 12 C6
German Embassy 13 F6
Indian Embassy 14 H4
Indonesian Embassy 15 E3
Japanese Embassy 16 H4
Main Post Office 17 D6
Malaysian Embassy 18 F6
Myanmar Embassy 19 D6
National Library 20 C2
Neilson Hays Library 21 D6
New Zealand Embassy 22 F5
Singapore Embassy 23 E6
STA Travel 24 E5
TAT Main Office 25 H4
TOT Office 26 F4
UK Embassy 27 F4
US Embassy 28 F5
Vietnamese Embassy 29 F4

SIGHTS & ACTIVITIES
AUA Language Center 30 F5
Chulalongkorn University Continuing Eduction Centre 31 E5
Erawan Shrine 32 F4
Grand Palace 33 A4
Jim Thompson's House 34 E4
Lumphini Park 35 F5
Oriental Hotel 36 C6
Siri Pattana Thai Language School 37 F6
Sri Mariamman 38 D6
Thieves Market 39 B4
Vimanmek Teak Mansion 40 C1
Wat Arun 41 A4
Wat Benchamabophit 42 C2
Wat Pho 43 A4
Wat Pho Thai Massage School 44 A4
Wat Phra Kaew 45 A3
Wat Traimit 46 C5

SLEEPING
Atlanta Hotel 47 G5
Bed & Breakfast Inn 48 E4
Krung Kasem Srikung Hotel 49 C5
Sri Hualamphong Hotel 50 D4
Suk 11 51 G4
Wendy House 52 E4

EATING
Al Hussain 53 G4
ATM Food Centre 54 B4
Ban Chiang 55 D6
Cabbages & Condoms 56 G5
Crepes & Co 57 G5
Hong Kong Noodles 58 D5
Larry's Dive Center, Bar & Grill 59 H5
Mahboonkrong (MBK) Food Centre (see 85)
Mrs Balbir's 60 G4
Muslim Restaurant 61 D6
Naaz 62 D6
Pickle Factory 63 F2
Royal India Restaurant 64 B4
Tamarind Café 65 H5
Victory Point 66 F2

DRINKING
Brown Sugar 67 F5
Cheap Charlie's 68 G4
Radio City 69 E5
Saxophone Pub & Restaurant 70 F2
Vertigo 71 F6

ENTERTAINMENT
Babylon Bangkok 72 F6
Bed Supperclub 73 G4
Chalermkrung Royal Theatre 74 B4
Erawan Shrine (see 32)
Lak Meuang Shrine 75 B3
Lucifer (see 69)
Lumphini Boxing Stadium 76 F6
Maneeya Lotus Room 77 F4
Nana Plaza 78 G4
Narcissus 79 H5
Q Bar 80 G4
Ratchadamnoen Boxing Stadium 81 C3
Shela 82 F5
Tapas 83 E5

SHOPPING
Central World Plaza 84 F4
Mahboonkrong (MBK) 85 E4
Peninsula Plaza 86 F4
River City Shopping Complex 87 C5
Siam Center 88 E4
Siam Discovery Center 89 E4
Thaniya Plaza 90 E5

is an architectural wonder of gleaming, gilded *chedi* (stupas) seemingly levitating above the ground, polished orange and green roof tiles, mosaic-encrusted pillars and rich marble pediments. The highly stylised ornamentation is a shrine to the revered Emerald Buddha, which is housed in the main chapel. Actually made of jasper, the Emerald Buddha has endured an epic journey from northern Thailand, where it was hidden inside a layer of stucco, to its present home. In between it was seized by Lao forces and carried off to Luang Prabang and Vientiane, where it was later recaptured by the Thais.

Within the same grounds is the **Grand Palace**, the former royal residence. Today the Grand Palace is used by the king only for certain ceremonial occasions such as Coronation Day; the king's current residence is Chitlada Palace in the northern part of the city. The exteriors of the four buildings are worth a swift perusal for their royal bombast, but their interiors are closed to the public. The intrigue and rituals that occurred within the walls of this once-cloistered community are not always evident to the modern visitor. A fictionalised version is told in the trilogy *Four Reigns,* by Kukrit Pramoj, about a young girl named Ploi, growing up in the Royal City. The admission fee also includes entry to Vimanmek Teak Mansion (p699), near the Dusit Zoo.

Nearby **Wat Pho** (Map pp694-5; ☎ 0 2221 9911; admission 20B; 8am-5pm) sweeps the awards for superlatives: it's the oldest and largest temple in Bangkok, dating from the 16th century; it houses the country's largest reclining Buddha; and it has the biggest collection of Buddha images in the country. The *big* attraction is the stunning reclining Buddha, 46m long and 15m high, illustrating the passing of the Buddha into final nirvana. The figure is modelled out of plaster around a brick core and finished in gold leaf. Mother-of-pearl inlay ornaments the eyes and feet, and the feet display 108 different auspicious *láksànà* (characteristics of a Buddha). See p700 for information on the Wat Pho Thai Massage School.

The **National Museum** (Map p698; ☎ 0 2224 1370; Th Na Phra That; admission 40B; 9am-4pm Wed-Sun), reportedly the largest in Southeast Asia, offers visitors an overview of Thai art and culture, a useful stepping stone to exploring the ancient capitals of Ayuthaya and Sukhothai. On the downside, the labelling isn't exactly illuminating and there is no air-conditioning to help you keep your cool on a hot day. Try the free guided tour (on Wednesdays at 9.30am in English, French and German) to gain some perspective on the collection.

Wat Arun (Map pp694-5; ☎ 0 2466 3167; Th Arun Amarin; admission 20B; 9am-5pm) is a striking temple, named after the Indian god of dawn, Aruna. It looms large on the Thonburi side of the Mae Nam Chao Phraya, looking as if it were carved from granite; a closer inspection reveals a mosaic of porcelain tiles covering the imposing 82m Khmer-style *praang* (spire). The tiles were left behind by Chinese merchant ships no longer needing them as ballast.

Chinatown & Phahurat

Gleaming gold shops, towering neon signs in Chinese characters, shopfronts spilling out onto the footpath – welcome to Chinatown (Map pp694–5), the epicentre of Bangkok's bustling commercial cult. The neighbourhood's energy is at once exhilarating and exhausting. Slicing through the centre of the district, the famous **Sampeng Lane** (Map pp694-5; Soi Wanit) runs roughly parallel to Th Yaowarat and is jam-packed with the useful and the useless, but all at bargain prices. On the corner of Th Yaowarat and Th Chakrawat is **Thieves**

PUBLIC TRANSPORT

Want to save money and get around town like a local? Then ignore those pesky túk-túk drivers and flag down a bus, or better yet catch a river taxi. Here is an at-a-glance guide to a few popular spots.

Neighbourhoods

Banglamphu & Th Khao San Air-con buses 511 and 512; ordinary buses 3, 15, 30, 32 and 53; Chao Phraya River Express boat to Tha Phra Athit.

Chinatown Air-con bus 507 or ordinary bus 53; Chao Phraya River Express boat to Tha Ratchawong; Metro to Hualamphong.

Siam Sq Air-con buses 508, 515 and 529; ordinary buses 15, 16, 25 and 40; Skytrain to Siam or National Stadium.

Th Silom Air-con buses 502 and 505; Skytrain stations Sala Daeng, Chong Nonsi and Surasak; Metro to Silom.

Th Sukhumvit Air-con buses 501, 508, 511 and 513; ordinary buses 2, 25, 38 and 40; Nana, Asoke and Phrom Phong Skytrain stations; Metro to Sukhumvit.

Thewet Air-con buses 505 and 506; ordinary buses 3, 16, 30, 32, 33 and 53; Chao Phraya River Express boat to Tha Thewet.

Bus & Train Terminals

Eastern (Ekamai) Bus Terminal Air-con buses 508, 511 and 513; ordinary buses 25 and 40; Skytrain to Ekamai.

Hualamphong train station Air-con buses 501, 507 and 529; ordinary buses 25, 40 and 53; Metro to Hualamphong.

Northern & Northeastern (Moh Chit) Bus Terminal Air-con buses 510, 512 and 513; ordinary bus 3; Skytrain to Moh Chit.

Southern Bus Terminal (Thonburi) Air-con buses 507 and 511; ordinary buses 30 and 40.

Sights

Lumphini Park Air-con bus 507; ordinary bus 15; Skytrain to Ratchadamri; Metro to Lumphini.

National Museum Across the street, Sanam Luang is a hub for several bus lines, including ordinary buses 30, 32 and 53.

Wat Arun Cross-river ferry from Tha Tien, near Wat Pho.

Wat Pho Air-con buses 508 and 512; ordinary bus 32; Chao Phraya River Express boat to Tha Tien.

Wat Phra Kaew & the Grand Palace Air-con buses 508, 512 and 515; ordinary buses 25 and 32; Chao Phraya River Express boat to Tha Chang.

Vimanmek Teak Mansion Ordinary buses 18, 70 and 72.

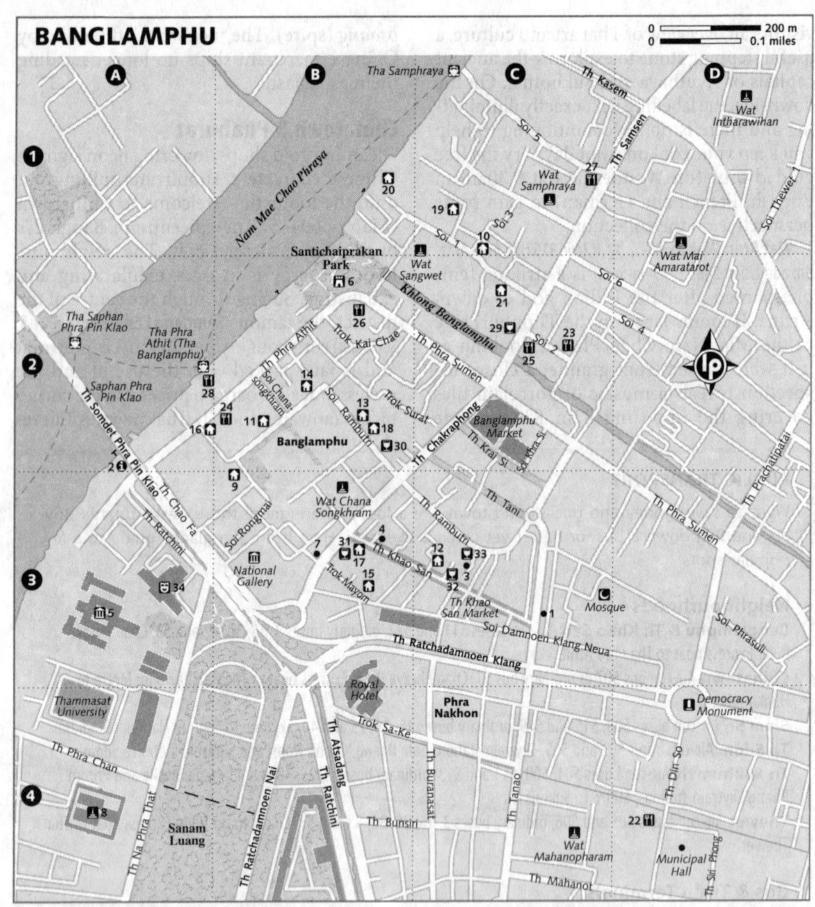

Market (Nakhon Kasem; Map pp694–5), so named for the 'hot' items once sold here. The neighbourhood is fun to explore at night when it is lit up like a Christmas tree.

On the western side of Chinatown is a small Indian district, known as Phahurat. Th Chakraphet is popular for its Indian restaurants and shops selling Indian sweets.

Wat Traimit (Map pp694-5; ☎ 0 2623 1226; cnr Th Yaowarat & Th Charoen Krung; admission 20B; 🕓 9am-5pm) shelters a 3m-tall, 5.5-tonne, solid-gold Buddha image – an impressive sight, even in the land of a million Buddhas. This gleaming figure was once covered in stucco, but during efforts to move it in the 1960s, the figure fell, cracking the stucco and revealing the treasure inside. The covering was probably intended to hide it during one of the many invasions by Burma. Located near Hualamphong station, this temple's English name is, surprise surprise, Temple of the Golden Buddha.

Mae Nam Chao Phraya

Once upon a time, Bangkok was called the 'Venice of the East'. Canals, not roads, transported goods and people, and the mighty Mae Nam Chao Phraya (Chao Phraya River) was the superhighway leading to the interior of the country. All life centred on these vast canal networks and Thais considered themselves *jâo náam* (water lords). Times have changed, but you can observe remnants of urban river life by boarding a Chao Phraya River Express

INFORMATION		SLEEPING		DRINKING	
Aporia Books	1 C3	Bella Bella House	11 B2	Hemlock	24 B2
Bangkok Tourist Division	2 A2	Khao San Palace Inn	12 C3	Je Hoy	25 C2
IBS Travel	3 C3	Lamphu House	13 B2	Roti-Mataba	26 B2
Shaman Books	4 B3	My House	14 B2	Sabah Café & Cinema	27 C1
		New Joe Guesthouse	15 B3	Ton Pho	28 A2
SIGHTS & ACTIVITIES		New Merry V Guest House	16 A2		
National Museum	5 A3	Prakorb's House	17 B3	DRINKING	
Santichaiprakan Park	6 B2	Rambuttri Village Inn	18 B2	Ad Here the 13th	29 C2
Sor Vorapin Thai Boxing Gym	7 B3	River Guest House	19 C1	Bangkok Bar	30 B2
Wat Mahathat	8 A4	Riverline Guesthouse	20 B1	Gullivers Traveller's Tavern	31 B3
		Villa Guest House	21 C2	Sunset Street	32 C3
SLEEPING				Susie Pub	33 C3
Baan Sabai	9 B3	EATING			
Bamboo Guest House	10 C1	Arawy	22 D4	ENTERTAINMENT	
		Café Corner	23 C2	National Theatre	34 A3

boat at any *thâa* (pier). This is also one of the more pleasant commuting options in Bangkok and is used by a healthy cross-section of the populace, from uniformed schoolchildren to saffron-robed monks.

Just across the river in the area known as Thonburi, **Khlong Bangkok Noi** train station provides a quick escape from Bangkok's modern madness. The further into the *khlong* you venture, the better the rewards, with teak houses on stilts and plenty of greenery.

Foreigners also had a presence on the river during the bygone shipping era. Two Dutch sea captains built the majestic **Oriental Hotel** (Map pp694-5; ☎ 0 2659 9000; www.mandarinoriental.com; 48 Soi Oriental, Th Charoen Krung), an attraction in its own right. Somerset Maugham and Joseph Conrad were among the Oriental's famous guests. You can toast those literary giants in the hotel's Author Wing café or the riverside bar; dress smartly.

Other Attractions

Jim Thompson's House (Map pp694-5; ☎ 0 2216 7368; Soi Kasem San 2, Th Phra Ram I; adult/child 100/50B; 9am-5pm) is the beautiful house of the American entrepreneur Jim Thompson, who successfully promoted Thai silk to Western markets. After a long career in Thailand, he mysteriously disappeared in 1967 in Malaysia's Cameron Highlands; the reason remains unknown and many suspect foul play. Atmospherically sited on a small *khlong*, his house was built from salvaged components of traditional Thai houses. In addition to remarkable architecture, his collection of Thai art and furnishings is superb. Admission proceeds go to Bangkok's School for the Blind.

Vimanmek Teak Mansion (Map pp694-5; ☎ 0 2628 6300; foreigner/Thai 100/50B, free with Grand Palace ticket; 9.30am-4pm), in the serene Dusit Palace grounds, is reputedly the world's largest golden teak building. In the early 20th century Rama V lived in this mansion of graceful staircases, octagonal rooms and lattice walls. The interior contains various personal effects of the king, and a treasure-trove of early Ratanakosin art objects and antiques.

Lumphini Park (Map pp694-5; cnr Th Phra Ram IV & Th Ratchadamri; 5am-8pm) offers a shady respite from the city's noise and traffic; the afternoon drop-in aerobics class is great free entertainment whether or not you join the synchronised crowd.

Although religion and commerce may seem diametrically opposed, Thai Buddhism is a flexible faith, as witnessed by the numerous and popular shrines built in front of huge shopping centres and hotels throughout Bangkok. Outside the Grand Hyatt Erawan hotel, the **Erawan shrine** (San Phra Phrom; Map pp694-5; cnr Th Ratchadamri & Th Ploenchit) is dedicated to the Hindu deity of creation and is credited for bringing good fortune and lottery winnings to many of the faithful. If a wish is granted, the wishmaker repays the favour by hiring musicians and dancers to perform in front of the shrine.

Wat Benchamabophit (Map pp694-5; cnr Th Si Ayuthaya & Th Phra Ram V; admission 20B; 8am-5.30pm), built under the reign of Rama V in 1899, is made of white Carrara marble and is a stunning example of modern temple architecture. The real treasure here is a rear courtyard containing a large collection of Buddha images from all periods of Thai Buddhist art. Wat Ben is diagonally opposite Chitlada Palace. Buses 503 (air-con) and 72 stop nearby.

A small Hindu Shiva temple, **Sri Mariamman** (Maha Umi Devi, Wat Phra Si Maha Umathewi; Map pp694-5; 5am-8pm) sits on the corner of Th Pan and Th Silom.

FREE STUFF

Despite Bangkok's consumer frenzy, you can soak up city life without spending a baht. In the evenings, break dancers practise their moves on the elevated walkway between the Siam Sq Skytrain station and the various shopping malls. This walkway has become an urban park with cuddling couples, as well as an unsanctioned bazaar with sellers displaying their wares and keeping an eye out for the police.

The narrow lanes of **Little Arabia** (Map pp694-5; Soi 3, Th Sukhumvit), a Middle Eastern transplant that feels like a modern medina, come complete with lively cafés and smoky *sheesha* (water pipe) bars.

More spectacular and synchronised are the evening aerobics classes that occur in **Lumphini Park** (Map pp694–5) and also in **Santichaiprakan Park** (Map p698; Th Phra Sumen, Banglamphu). The combination of the techno beat, setting sun and crowd of bouncing bodies attracts almost as many onlookers as participants.

COURSES

Cooking

One of the best ways to crack Thailand's lengthy menu is to take a cooking course.

Thai House (Map pp690-1; ☎ 0 2903 9611; www.thaihouse.co.th; 32/4 Moo 8, Bang Yai, Nonthaburi; programme 3550-16,650B) Set in a homely traditional teak house about 40 minutes north of Bangkok by boat. Choose from a one- to three-day programme, which includes preparing Thai standards (*tôm yam,* pad thai and various curries). There are also cooking and lodging packages available.

Language & Culture

AUA Language Centre (Map pp694-5; ☎ 0 2252 8170; www.auathai.com; 179 Th Ratchadamri) One of the most popular places to study Thai, the American University Alumni school is also one of the largest private language institutions in the world.

Chulalongkorn University Continuing Education Centre (Map pp694-5; ☎ 0 2218 3908; www.cec.chula.ac.th; 5th fl, Vidhyabhathan Bldg, 12 Soi Chulalongkorn, Chulalongkorn University; course US$950) The most prestigious university in Thailand offers a two-week intensive Thai studies course called Perspectives on Thailand. The 60-hour programme includes classes in Thai culture, history, politics, art and language.

Siri Pattana Thai Language School (Map pp694-5; ☎ 0 2286 1936; YWCA, 13 Th Sathon Tai) This place offers Thai language courses and preparation for the *paw hòk* exam, required for teaching in Thai public schools.

Massage

Wat Pho Thai Massage School (Map pp694-5; ☎ 0 2221 3686; watpottm@netscape.net; 392/25-28 Soi Phenphat 1, Th Maharat; course 7000B) Affiliated with Wat Pho, this massage school offers two 30-hour courses – one on general Thai massage, the other on massage therapy – that you attend for three hours per day for 10 days, or two hours per day for 15 days. Other coursework includes a 15-hour foot massage course (3600B) and longer one- to three-year programmes that combine Thai herbal medicine with massage for a full curriculum in Thai traditional medicine. Some knowledge of Thai will ease the communication barrier for all of these courses.

Meditation

Contact the Buddhist Meditation Centre (☎ 0 2623 5881), affiliated to Wat Mahathat, for information on meditation centres or English-speaking teachers.

Wat Mahathat (Map p698; ☎ 0 2222 6011; Th Maharat) This 18th-century wat opposite Sanam Luang provides meditation instruction daily at Section 5, a meditation hall near the monks' residences. Some of the Thai monks here speak English, and there are often Western monks or long-term residents available to interpret.

World Fellowship of Buddhists (Map pp690-1; ☎ 0 2661 1284; www.wfb-hq.org; Soi 24, Th Sukhumvit) At the back of Benjasiri Park, next to the Emporium, this is a centre for information on Theravada Buddhism. It also sells a handy booklet listing meditation centres throughout Thailand.

Muay Thai (Thai Boxing)

Sor Vorapin Thai Boxing Gym (Sor Vorapin; Map p698; ☎ 0 2282 3551; www.thaiboxings.com; 13 Soi Krasab, Th Chakraphong; courses per day/week/month 400/2500/8000B) In Banglamphu near Th Khao San, this school specialises in training foreign students (women and men). Especially serious boxers should enquire about Sor Vorapin Gym 2, a nearby live-in training facility.

TOURS

ABC Amazing Bangkok Cyclists (☎ 0 2665 6364; www.realasia.net; tour 1000B; 🕑 1-6pm) Discover another side to Bangkok on a cycling tour through Thonburi. The trip starts with a longtail boat ride across the river and includes a slice of village life in the city.

FESTIVALS & EVENTS

Chinese New Year Thai-Chinese celebrate the lunar new year in February or March, with a week of house-cleaning, lion dances and fireworks. Festivities centre on Chinatown.

Kite-Flying Season In March, during the windy season, colourful kites battle it out over the skies of Sanam Luang and Lumphini Park.

Songkran Held from 13 to 15 April, the celebration of the Thai new year has morphed into water warfare with high-powered pistols and lots of talc being launched at suspecting and unsuspecting participants around Th Khao San. Prepare to be soaked or stay away.

Royal Ploughing Ceremony His Majesty the King commences rice-planting season with a royal-religious ceremony at Sanam Luang, in early May.

Loi Krathong A beautiful festival where on the night of the full moon in early November, small lotus-shaped boats made of banana leaf containing a lit candle are set adrift on the river.

King's Birthday On 5 December locals celebrate their monarch's birthday with lots of parades and fireworks.

SLEEPING

Bangkok possesses arguably the best variety and quality of budget places to spend the night of any Asian capital city, which is one of the reasons it's become such a popular destination for roving world travellers. Due to the geographic spread of places, narrow the options by working out where you want to base yourself.

Where there are backpackers, there you will find Th Khao San wannabes. The guesthouse rooms come in every shape and size from cheap cells to fancy frills; the late-night bars are loud and the constant pedestrian traffic is an attraction in itself. Banglamphu, the neighbourhood surrounding Th Khao San, is a sedate residential area with better-value guesthouse options. The drawback is that Banglamphu is far removed from central Bangkok, so trips to other parts of town take some time.

The Siam Sq area is centrally located and on both Skytrain lines. Accommodation in Siam Sq is more expensive than Banglamphu, but then so is the real estate in this popular shopping district.

Th Sukhumvit is a major business area with only a handful of budget hotels. Many hotels attract sex tourists visiting the nearby go-go bars. The Skytrain and Metro have made this otherwise congested area much easier to traverse, but taxi travel is still a nightmare.

Other options include hotels near Hualamphong train station or somewhere near the airport if you have an early flight.

In Bangkok, budget accommodation includes places with rooms ranging from about 100B to 750B per night.

Thànŏn Khao San & Banglamphu

If you are on a tight budget, head straight to the *soi* around Th Khao San, the main travellers' centre. It is getting a little gentrified of late, and there are some superb options with swimming pools along Soi Rambutri. Along Khao San itself room rates tend to be higher than smarter places just a few blocks beyond. At the budget end, rooms are quite small and the dividing walls are thin. Bathrooms are usually down the hall. Stepping up the price scale, rooms are a smidgen bigger with real walls; another leap forward brings a bathroom, a hot shower and air-con. Some of these guesthouses have small attached cafés with limited menus.

Delving deeper into Banglamphu brings more bang for your baht. The places off Th Samsen are close to Tha Saphan Ram VIII, where you can catch the river taxi.

River Guest House (Map p698; ☎ 0 2280 0876; Soi 3/Soi Wat Samphraya, Th Samsen; r 140-380B) Popular with couples, this place is tucked away down a mazelike *soi*. Bathrooms are shared and breakfast is included.

My House (Map p698; ☎ 0 2629 5861; 37 Soi Chanasongkran; s 150-190B, d 250-500B; ❄ 💻) One of the most consistently popular old-timers on this continuation of Soi Rambutri, My House packs in the lounging shoestringer set with nightly videos and cheap food. Rooms are a bit rough around the edges.

Prakorb's House (Map p698; ☎ 0 2281 1345; 52 Th Khao San; s/d/tr 160/250/360B) Small but heavy on atmosphere, the nine rooms here – all with shared bathrooms – are inside a gorgeous old house with teakwood floors. If you're looking for intimacy with flavour, Prakorb's could be a good fit.

our pick **Lamphu House** (Map p698; ☎ 0 2629 5861; www.lamphuhouse.com; 75-77 Soi Rambutri; s 190-360B, d 350-890B; ❄ 💻) The cheapest rooms here are tiny Khao San standards, but the higher-end digs here have a modern, boutique-hotel feel. The large and serene courtyard café is one of the area's nicest retreats, where even nonguests congregate for wireless access (per hour 40B).

Bella Bella House (Map p698; ☎ 0 2629 3090; 74 Soi Chanasongkran; s 200-250B, d 270-520B; ❄) Rooms are nondescript at this big, modern guesthouse, although some have wonderful neighbourhood views. Satellite TV can be found in the café, making this a decent alternative if the more popular places nearby are full.

New Joe Guesthouse (Map p698; ☎ 0 2281 2948; www.newjoe.com; 81 Trok Mayom; s 280B, d 300-450B, tr 400-550B; ❄ 💻) Tucked away in an alley just off Th Khao San and consistently packed, amenities here include a garden restaurant, a large lobby complete with pool table, and young and friendly staff.

Khao San Palace Inn (Map p698; ☎ 0 2282 0578; 139 Th Khao San; s 290-450B, d 400-750B; ❄ 🏊) New, comfortable, clean and much more Westernised than your average Khao San fleapit. Ascend to the top floor for swimming pool bliss and a knockout city view.

Rambuttri Village Inn (Map p698; ☎ 0 2282 9162; www.khaosan-hotels.com; 95 Soi Rambutri; s 290-580B, d 580-950B; ❄ 💻 🏊) This sprawling budget guesthouse is awash in cleanliness and comfort, although there's not much atmosphere to speak of. The massive rooftop swimming pool offers unspeakable luxury during those boiling-hot Bangkok afternoons.

Villa Guest House (Map p698; ☎ 0 2281 7009; 230 Soi 1, Th Samsen; s 300B, d 400-600B) If you're dying to spend the night in a traditional teak house, head to this place. Rooms are furnished with battered antiques, and there's a decent travel library in the living room. Bathrooms are shared.

Other places worth considering:

New Merry V Guest House (Map p698; ☎ 0 2280 3315; 18-20 Th Phra Athit; s 140-350B, d 200-500B; ❄ 💻) Conveniently located opposite the Phra Athit pier, this is one of the better cheapies around here.

Riverline Guest House (Map p698; ☎ 0 2282 7464; 59/1 Soi 1, Th Samsen; r 150-470B; ❄) Around the corner from River Guest House, each room has its own bathroom here, and the rooftop lounge boasts an impressive river view.

Baan Sabai (Map p698; ☎ 0 2629 1599; 12 Soi Rongmai; s 170B, tw 270-550B; ❄) Quiet and relaxing, with a shaded sitting garden.

Bamboo Guest House (Map p698; ☎ 0 2282 3412; 67 Soi 1, Th Samsen; s/d 200/260B; ❄) This large, traditional Thai house appeals to long-stay travellers. A great choice if you need to escape the crowds and Khao San mayhem for a while.

Hualamphong

Hotels near the train station are cheap, but the area is so noisy that the traffic along Th Phra Ram IV has to be heard to be believed. Exercise a lot of street smarts around the station, which is crawling with razor artists, scammers and lowlifes.

Sri Hualamphong Hotel (Map pp694-5; 44 Th Rong Meuang; d 250B) Along the eastern side of Hualamphong station, this Chinese-run hotel is a creaky old spot with a grand staircase and terrace seating. Share bathrooms only.

Krung Kasem Srikung Hotel (Map pp694-5; ☎ 0 2225 0132; 1860 Th Krung Kasem; d 600B; ❄) West of the station, Krung Kasem is worth the extra investment, as it is a well-managed business hotel. Large, clean rooms have TV, air-con and hot water.

Siam Square

Siam Sq is a microcosm of this megacity: supermodern shopping centres, nonstop traffic jams and a simple village with traveller-friendly facilities hidden in the small *soi* off Th Phra Ram 1.

Bed & Breakfast Inn (Map pp694-5; ☎ 0 2215 3004; Soi Kasem San 1; s/d 500/600B; ❄) The décor doesn't seem to have been updated since the 1970s, and the two poodles living in the lobby look like they could use a serious dose of Wellbutrin. But every room comes with air-con, and – surprise! – breakfast is included.

Wendy House (Map pp694-5; ☎ 0 2216 2436; www.wendyguesthouse.com; Soi Kasem San 1; s/d from 800/900B; ❄ 💻) Easily the slickest and most modern digs on the street, with wireless access in the lobby. The staff are especially eager to please.

Thànŏn Sukhumvit

North of Th Phra Ram IV and east of the railway line, Th Sukhumvit is a major commercial artery, with several enclaves of long-term expats. Most hotels are out of the budget traveller's price range, but it provides a change of scene after an overdose of Banglamphu.

Suk 11 (Map pp694-5; ☎ 0 2253 5927; www.suk11.com; 1/33 Sukhumvit 11, Sukhumvit Rd; dm/s/d 250/480/650B; ❄) Once a well-kept secret, this Robinson Crusoe–style guesthouse is popular with seasoned backpackers who've graduated from the Khao San scene. All rooms have air-con, and free breakfast is served in the leafy courtyard. Advance reservations required.

Atlanta (Map pp694-5; ☎ 0 2252 1650; www.theatlantahotelbangkok.com; 78 Soi 2, Th Sukhumvit; r 353-590B; ❄ 💻 🏊) A Bangkok institution, a conceptual art project, a chic refuge from the fast-paced, postmodern world outside – the Atlanta is all of these things and more. The timeless 1950s lobby, which is filled with an astonishing collection of literary accoutrements and a checkerboard floor, often doubles as a film set. Check out the brilliant guidebook filled with tips on Bangkok travel and Thai culture, and have at least one meal in the retro coffee shop. Sex tourists are not permitted.

Airport

Finding decent, moderately priced accommodation in the airport area is difficult. Most of the hotels charge nearly twice as much as comparable hotels in the city. The following option is convenient only to those travellers flying into or out of Don Mueang Airport, which handles domestic flights.

We-Train International House (Map pp690-1; ☎ 0 2967 8550; www.we-train.co.th; 501/1 Mu 3, Th Dechatungkha, Sikan, Don Mueang; dm 280B, r from 400B;) Run by a nonprofit women's group, We-Train offers a free pick-up from Don Mueang Airport. Download a map and directions from the hotel's website if making your own way. An especially large pool and a gym are open to guests.

EATING

No matter where you go in Bangkok, food is never far away. The variety of places to eat is simply astonishing and defeats all but the most dogged food samplers in their quest to say they've tried everything. Street surfing the stalls may be the cheapest option, but don't neglect to explore the city's food courts in the shopping centres, as these are the indoor versions (pollution free and air-conditioned) of the city's outdoor markets.

While Thai food may be sufficiently exotic, Bangkok offers an incredible international menu thanks to its many immigrant communities. Chinatown is naturally a good area for Chinese food and the Phahurat quarter around Th Silom is Little India, where cubicle-sized Indian restaurants turn out the best of the subcontinent. In the crowded bazaarlike area of Little Arabia, just off Th Sukhumvit, there is Muslim cuisine from every far-flung corner of the region. Western cuisine, ranging from Italian to Mexican, is prepared in the latest, greatest way for power diners or as pub grub to keep the homesickness at bay.

Vegetarians are onto a good thing in Bangkok. In addition to all of the veggie-speciality spots, Indian and Muslim restaurants frequently have veggie options, as do most Thai and Chinese restaurants. During the vegetarian festival in October, the whole city goes mad for tofu, and stalls and restaurants indicate their nonmeat menu with yellow flags.

Thànŏn Khao San & Banglamphu

Th Khao San is lined with restaurants, but the prices tend to be higher and the quality somewhat lower than in the surrounding streets of Banglamphu. Serial snackers can survive by surfing up and down the many street vendors here. For a cheap and authentic meal, leave Khao San behind and head to the stalls along Soi Rambutri or Th Chakraphong. Fresh seafood barbecues are now a big hit on Soi Rambutri, washed down with dirt-cheap Beer Chang at 50B a go.

Arawy (Map p698; 152 Th Din So; dishes 35B; breakfast, lunch & dinner) When it comes to genuine vegetarian delights, Arawy is one of the best Thai restaurants in the city. Pre-prepared point-and-eat dishes keep it simple. The restaurant was inspired by ex-Bangkok governor Chamlong Srimuang's strict vegetarianism. The roman-script sign reads 'Alloy' and it is opposite the Municipal Hall.

our pick **Café Corner** (Map p698; ☎ 0 1342 4755; www.cafe-corner.tk; 106/13 Soi 2, Th Samsen; dishes 40-120B; breakfast, lunch & dinner) Part organic-vegetarian restaurant and part ambient chill-out lounge, the menu here is a mix of standard Thai soups, salads and entrées, all of them inventively prepared. Don't miss the fruit shakes.

Je Hoy (Map p698; Soi 2, Th Samsen; dishes 50-100B; dinner) Don't be fooled by its rough-and-ready atmosphere; the dishes at this open-air Chinese-Thai restaurant are considered by many to be some of the finest in all of Banglamphu. Open until 4am nightly.

Hemlock (Map p698; ☎ 0 2282 7507; 56 Th Phra Athit; dishes 80-200B; lunch & dinner) On the small stretch of Phra Athit where trend-setting Thais congregate nightly for dinner and drinks, Hemlock is a current favourite. The kitchen prepares Thai dishes you're not likely to spot on other menus, and the atmosphere is both artsy and intimate.

Also worth seeking out:

Roti-Mataba (Map p698; ☎ 0 2282 2119; 136 Th Phra Athit; dishes 50-80B; breakfast, lunch & dinner) Fried Indian flat breads are what you'll find here, in practically every possible form. And because rotis are small snack foods, you'll want to order a bunch.

Ton Pho (Map p698; ☎ 0 2280 0452; Th Phra Athit; dishes 60-100B; ⏲ breakfast, lunch & dinner) Overlooking the Mae Nam Chao Phraya, this is a great spot for authentic Thai standards. No roman-script sign.

Sabah Café & Cinema (Map p698; ☎ 0 1552 4439; 131 Th Samsen; dishes 100-450B; ⏲ breakfast, lunch & dinner) Should you find yourself consistently disappointed by the Western breakfasts on and around Khao San, head straight to Sabah, where you'll find heaping portions with real sausage, bacon, coffee and homemade bread. Films are screened in a tiny upstairs cinema (80B).

Hualamphong, Chinatown & Phahurat

Hualamphong Food Centre (Map pp694-5; Hualamphong station; dishes 30-60B; ⏲ breakfast, lunch & dinner) In most countries, station food is the blandest of the bland, but in Thailand the vendors know the importance of fulfilling their customers' needs before a long journey. Stop here for a top selection of Thai, Chinese and Indian dishes.

Royal India Restaurant (Map pp694-5; 392/1 Th Chakraphet; dishes under 80B; ⏲ breakfast, lunch & dinner) Hidden away down a dark alley across from the ATM Shopping Centre, Royal India has long been considered one of the best North Indian restaurants in town. Staying in Khao San and feeling lazy? Check out Royal India's smart sister restaurant on Soi Rambutri (open for breakfast, lunch and dinner), set around a pond in the grounds of Rambuttri Village Inn (p702).

Other options:

ATM Food Centre (Map pp694-5; Th Chakraphet, Phahurat; ⏲ breakfast, lunch & dinner) Indian food centre on the top floor, plus Indian food stalls in the nearby alley.

Hong Kong Noodles (Map pp694-5; Th Phra Ram IV; dishes 30-80B; ⏲ breakfast, lunch & dinner) Just outside Hualamphong Metro station, this air-conditioned place has slick Chinese food.

Siam Square

Food vendors on Soi Kasem San 1 do a brisk business of feeding hungry clockwatchers and lounging *faràng*; they are masters at communicating with hand gestures.

Mahboonkrong Food Centre (MBK; Map pp694-5; cnr Th Phra Ram I & Th Phayathai; ⏲ breakfast, lunch & dinner) The 7th-floor food court in this shopping centre is one of the busiest in the city, thanks to an assortment of tasty dishes that competes with the best on offer in the streets below.

Thànŏn Sukhumvit

Larry's Dive Center, Bar & Grill (Map pp694-5; ☎ 0 2663 4563; www.larrysdive.com; 8 Soi 22, Th Sukhumvit; dishes 95-175B; ⏲ breakfast, lunch & dinner) A Tex-Mex restaurant with a surf-and-sand beach theme. There's also a sports bar and, yes, an attached dive shop. Seriously. Diners can work up an appetite at the pool table or pinball machines before digging into *quesadillas*, burritos, chilli con carne or even a good ol' American steak. Free wireless internet access.

Cabbages & Condoms (Map pp694-5; ☎ 0 2229 4610; Soi 12, Th Sukhumvit; dishes 100-200B; ⏲ lunch & dinner) Founded by a Thai philanthropist with a soft spot for birth control, diners at this eatery are offered condoms instead of after-meal mints. But this is no novelty theme restaurant – all proceeds go to a nonprofit population control organisation, which spends the money on sex education and AIDS prevention programmes. Most of the standard Thai dishes have been thoughtfully tweaked to accommodate sensitive *faràng* palates.

Tamarind Café (Map pp694-5; ☎ 0 2663 7421; 27 Soi 20, Th Sukhumvit; dishes 100-250B; ⏲ breakfast, lunch & dinner) Try the Tamarind for divine desserts and one of the most creative vegetarian menus in town. This artistic space, home to the F-Stop photographic gallery, includes a sweeping bar, making for hard choices: should you take the innovative fruit shake or the ice-cold beer?

Al-Hussain (Map pp694-5; 1/4 Soi 3/5, Th Sukhumvit; dishes 100-300B; ⏲ breakfast, lunch & dinner) Just off Th Sukhumvit and Soi 3 (Soi Nana Neua), there is a winding maze of cramped sub-*soi* known as 'Little Arabia', where the number of Middle Eastern and African residents makes Thais seem like the foreigners. This open-air café has a colourful table of subtly spiced curries and dhal. Air-con inside, street action outside.

Also recommended:

Crepes & Co (Map pp694-5; ☎ 0 2653 3990; 18/1 Soi 12, Th Sukhumvit; dishes 140-280B; ⏲ breakfast, lunch & dinner) Crepes of all kinds, European-style breakfasts and a nice selection of Mediterranean dishes.

Mrs Balbir's (Map pp694-5; ☎ 0 2651 0498; 13/2 Soi 11/1, Th Sukhumvit; dishes 150-250B, buffet lunches 150B; ⏲ breakfast, lunch & dinner) Mrs Balbir has been teaching Indian and Thai cooking for many years.

Thànŏn Silom & Thànŏn Surawong

The small *soi* on the western end of Th Silom and parallel Th Surawong are home to an active Muslim and Indian community, which provides visiting business folk with a taste of home. Also well worth a diversion south towards the river are the food vendors on Soi 20 (Soi Pradit), off Th Silom near the mosque. The street throngs with office workers at lunchtime and the smells are divine.

Muslim Restaurant (Map pp694-5; 1356 Th Charoen Krung; dishes under 40B; breakfast, lunch & dinner) This faded old restaurant may not look all that great, but it has been feeding various Lonely Planet authors for more than 20 years. Near the intersection of Th Charoen Krung and Th Silom, the assortment of curries and roti is displayed in a clean glass case for easy pointing and eye-catching allure.

Naaz (Map pp694-5; Soi 43, Saphan Yao; dishes 50-70B; breakfast, lunch & dinner) Pronounced 'Naat' in Thai, this neighbourhood café is often cited as having the richest *khâo mòk kài* (chicken biryani) in the city. Dabble with a dessert, as the house speciality is *firni*, a Middle Eastern pudding spiced with coconut, almonds, cardamom and saffron.

Ban Chiang (Map pp694-5; ☎ 0 2236 7045; 14 Soi Si Wiang, Th Surasak; dishes 90-150B; lunch & dinner) Ban Chiang pays homage to the fiery cuisine of the northeast. Occupying a restored wooden house with simple décor, get acquainted with the tastes of Isan by trying *yam plaa duk foo* (fried shredded catfish salad).

Greater Bangkok

Both of the following places are easily accessible by riding the Skytrain to Victory Monument.

Victory Point (Map pp694-5; cnr Th Phayathai & Th Ratwithi; dishes 25-50B; dinner) Lining the busy roundabout is a squatters' village of stalls known collectively as 'Victory Point'. Near the fairy lights is a beer-and-food garden with live music. Order a pitcher and a few plates of the zesty Thai classics for a thoroughly satisfying meal.

Pickle Factory (Map pp694-5; ☎ 0 2246 3036; 55 Soi 21, Th Ratwithi; dishes 150-200B; dinner) Occupying a 1970s-vintage Thai house, the Pickle Factory creates a dinner-party mood with indoor sofa seating and outdoor tables around a swimming pool – the perfect place to chill out for an evening. The menu includes creatively topped pizzas such as Chiang Mai sausage and holy basil paste with wing beans.

DRINKING

Officially Bangkok has a curfew of 1am for bars and 2am for clubs, and this is quite strictly enforced at most establishments. The Khao San area is the exception, where guesthouses and restaurants let the drinks flow, but disguise them in plastic cups. Most short-term travellers passing through stick around Khao San, where the carnival atmosphere keeps drinkers entertained till dawn. There are also some great bars in the surrounding *soi*, as this area is now attracting as many Thais as tourists. If you can rouse yourself from a Beer Chang stupor, brave a pub crawl in such nightspots as Th Silom-Patpong or Th Sukhumvit.

GAY & LESBIAN BANGKOK

Bangkok's gay community is loud, proud and knows how to party. A newcomer might want to visit the website of **Utopia** (www.utopia-asia.com), a great resource for news and happenings in Thailand and Southeast Asia. **Anjaree** (☎ 0 2477 1776) is a lesbian group that organises social events and community outreach programmes. The **Lesbian Guide to Bangkok** (www.bangkoklesbian.com) is one of the only English-language trackers of the scene.

A four-storey gay sauna, **Babylon Bangkok** (Map pp694-5; ☎ 0 2213 2108; 50 Soi Atakanprasit, Th Sathon Tai; 5am-11pm) has been described as one of the top 10 gay men's saunas in the world. Facilities include a bar, roof garden, gym, massage room, steam and dry saunas, and spa baths. The spacious, well-hidden complex also has accommodation.

Conveniently located near Lumphini Park, **Shela** (Map pp694-5; ☎ 0 2254 6463; 106 Soi Lang Suan, Th Ploenchit) is one of Bangkok's very few must-visit lesbian nightclubs. A live band bangs out Thai and Western covers nightly.

Patpong Soi 2 and Soi 4 have the highest concentration of gay dance clubs in the city. DJ Station and JJ Park are just two of many clubs that pack narrow Soi 2 with late-night energy. DJ Station also boasts *kàthoey* (transvestite) cabaret. Chill out at Expresso, beside the waterfall wall, for a bird's-eye view of the pretty boys. On Soi 4, Telephone, Bangkok's oldest gay bar, has a 'telephone' by which patrons can get to know one another. Across the street, Balcony has prime people-watching tables.

The Khao San area is a cheap place to warm up for a night out, thanks to the proliferation of street bars. Sometimes they are stalls, sometimes VW camper vans with the roof hacked off, but all of them offer dirt-cheap beer and 'very strong' cocktails. Throw in the informal draught beer stands and you are never more than a few metres from an alcoholic drink.

Bars

Sunset Street (Map p698; Th Khao San) Essentially a small assortment of bars and cafés, the establishments along this mini-*soi* represent the polar opposite of your average Banglamphu beer hall. In other words, they're slightly sophisticated and upscale, with a price point to match.

Gullivers Traveller's Tavern (Map p698; Th Khao San) This place pulls the punters as the night wears on. Downstairs is mayhem most nights, but upstairs is usually quieter with a couple of pool tables. Four free internet terminals encourage drunk emailing.

Bangkok Bar (Map p698; 149 Soi Rambutri) One of the very few clubs in backpacker-land where the thump of dance music won't drown out all attempts at conversation. The slick interior design wins extra points as well, although do beware that weekend nights often find this place predictably packed.

Susie Pub (Map p698; Soi 11, Th Khao San) In a covered *soi* off the northern side of Khao San, this longstanding favourite pumps out a nightly dance marathon with the volume cranked to 11. It's especially popular with Thai university students.

Bull's Head (Map pp690-1; Soi 33/1, Th Sukhumvit) One of many British pubs in the Sukhumvit area, the Bull's Head is a beautiful galleried bar that looks like it has been shipped in from London. This is a popular stop for stand-up comedians touring Asia, plus there are quiz nights.

Cheap Charlie's (Map pp694-5; Soi 11, Th Sukhumvit; closed Sun) Owned and operated for more than 25 years by a truly legendary Bangkok character, this outdoor beer stall is decorated with hundreds of novelty gewgaws and other curious *objets d'art*. As the name suggests, drinks are easy on the wallet, so it figures that expats flock here in big numbers. On a sub-*soi* off Soi 11, look for the 'Sabai Sabai Massage' sign.

Vertigo (Map pp694-5; ☎ 0 2679 1200; Banyan Tree Hotel, 21/100 Th Sathon Tai) Definitely not for Cheap Charlies, this sky-high, open-air bar will quite literally take your breath away. From ground level, the elevator delivers you to the 59th floor where you emerge above the roar of Bangkok traffic far below. Expensive, but the view is priceless.

Live Music

Saxophone Pub & Restaurant (Map pp694-5; ☎ 0 2246 5472; 3/8 Th Phayathai) A popular live-band jazz and blues venue for more than 20 years now, Saxophone is also a perennial favourite with fans of reggae and rock. Appetising Thai and Western dishes are on offer, as are more than 100 cocktail varieties. Accessible via Skytrain to Victory Monument station.

Ad Here the 13th (Map p698; 13 Th Samsen) Just over the Khlong Banglamphu bridge, elbow space is at a premium in this lively hole-in-the-wall bar. A blues band bangs out crowd favourites six nights a week from 9.30pm (no music on Sundays), which is also when the international Khao San crowd filters in.

Brown Sugar (Map pp694-5; ☎ 0 2250 0103; 231/20 Th Sarasin) Jazz up your life by dropping in on this popular club near Lumphini Park; live blues is occasionally on the menu as well. On Sunday nights, the serious musicians touring the luxury hotels come here to jam. Skytrain to Ratchadamri.

Radio City (Map pp694-5; ☎ 0 2266 4567; Soi Patpong 1) A refreshing slice of slickness in an otherwise seedy locale, this club is next door to Lucifer in the infamous Patpong night market. A live rock band cranks out sing-along cover songs nightly. And make sure you don't miss the Thai Elvis, a longtime Patpong legend who performs at 11pm nightly, except Sundays.

CLUBBING

High-powered cocktails and high heels are the name of the game in the dance and lounge clubs in the City of Angels. The fickle beautiful people are constantly on the move, leaving behind the stylish carcasses to tourists and working girls. Cover charges range from 500B to 700B and usually include a drink or two. Don't even think about showing up before 11pm.

Bed Supperclub (Map pp694-5; ☎ 0 2651 3537; 26 Soi 11, Th Sukhumvit) One of Bangkok's most terminally trendy see-and-be-seen spots, clubbers here lounge about on mattresses while downing overpriced cocktails or noshing on four-

BANGKOK A GO-GO

'We don't come to Thailand for the ruins', was an overheard insult delivered by a veteran sex tourist to an unsuspecting backpacker. True enough, many male visitors come solely for the women or, in some cases, the men. The shopping venues for potential partners occupy a whole subset of Bangkok's nightlife, from massage parlours and go-go clubs to pick-up bars.

Patpong (Soi Patpong 1 & 2, Th Silom), Bangkok's most famous red-light district, has mellowed a lot over the years and now draws more sightseers than flesh-seekers. The open-air tourist market on Patpong 1 has drawn much of the attention away from erotica. There is still a handful of go-go bars that have morphed into a circus of ping-pong shows for tourists and couples. Avoid bars touting 'free' sex shows, as there are usually hidden charges and when you try to ditch the outrageous bill the doors are suddenly blocked by muscled bouncers.

The gay men's equivalent can be found on nearby Soi Thaniya, Soi Pratuchai and Soi Anuman Ratchathon. Along with male go-go dancers and 'bar boys', several bars feature live sex shows, which are generally much better choreographed than the hetero equivalents on Patpong.

Soi Cowboy (btwn Soi 21 & Soi 23, Th Sukhumvit), a single-lane strip of 25 to 30 bars, claims direct lineage to the post-Vietnam War '70s, when a black American ex-GI nicknamed 'Cowboy' was among the first to open a self-named go-go bar off Th Sukhumvit.

Nana Plaza (Soi 4/Soi Nana Tai, Th Sukhumvit) is a three-storey place that's quite literally a strip-mall, complete with its own guesthouses and used almost exclusively by female bar workers for illicit assignations. The 'female' staff at Casanova consists entirely of Thai transvestites and transsexuals – this is a favourite stop for foreigners visiting Bangkok for sex-reassignment surgery.

course meals. Both resident and international DJs create the minimalist mood.

Q Bar (Map pp694-5; ☎ 0 2252 3274; 34 Soi 11, Th Sukhumvit) Supposedly home to the city's largest cocktail selection, the Q Bar experience is meant to mirror that of an exclusive New York lounge. Touring international DJs of the house, hip-hop and drum-and-bass varieties perform here often. To find it, take Soi 11 all the way to the end and hang a left. No sandals and no shorts.

Narcissus (Map pp694-5; ☎ 0 2258 2549; 112 Soi 23, Th Sukhumvit) A typically over-the-top European-style disco, the opulent Narcissus offers all the stereotypical club trappings: multiple bars and dance floors, techno and trance on the sound system, and split levels all around. The building's Romanesque architecture must be seen to be believed.

Tapas (Map pp694-5; Soi 4, Th Silom) Mix it up Moroccan style at this Th Silom dance club. The drapes and décor are straight out of Marrakesh, but the tunes are jazz, Latin and other world grooves.

Lucifer (Map pp694-5; 76/1-3 Patpong Soi 1, Th Silom) Trance- and techno-heavy Lucifer, with its amusing cave and flaming torch décor, is inside the Patpong night market.

Also check out the string of dance clubs near Lucifer on Soi 2 and Soi 4 (Soi Jaruwan), both parallel to Soi Patpong 1 and 2, off Th Silom, which attract a mixed clubbing crowd.

ENTERTAINMENT

Muay Thai (Thai Boxing)

Lumphini Boxing Stadium (Map pp694-5; Th Phra Ram IV; 🕑 bouts 6pm Tue & Fri, 5pm & 6pm Sat), near Lumphini Park, and **Ratchadamnoen Boxing Stadium** (Map pp694-5; Th Ratchadamnoen Nok; 🕑 bouts 5pm Mon, Wed & Thu, 6pm Sun), near the Democracy Monument, both host popular *muay thai* fights. The cheapest seats are 500B for the outer circle, 800B for the middle circle and 1500B for ringside. This is for eight to 10 fights of five rounds each; the last three are the headliner events when the stadiums fill up. Aficionados say the best-matched bouts are reserved for Tuesday night at Lumphini and Thursday night at Ratchadamnoen. Always buy tickets from the ticket window, not from a hawker hanging around outside the stadium.

Ratchadamnoen Stadium can be reached via air-con bus 503 and ordinary bus 70. Lumphini Stadium can be reached via ordinary bus 47.

Thai Classical Dance

Chalermkrung Royal Theatre (Sala Chaloem Krung; Map pp694-5; ☎ 0 2222 0434; cnr Th Charoen Krung & Th Triphet) In this Thai Art Deco building at the edge of the Chinatown-Phahurat district, Chalermkrung provides a striking venue for *khŏhn* performances (see p684). When it opened in 1933, the royally funded Chalermkrung was the largest and most modern theatre in Asia, with state-of-the-art film-projection technology and the first chilled-water air-con system in the region.

National Theatre (Map p698; ☎ 0 2224 1342; Th Na Phra That; admission 20-200B) Near Saphan Phra Pin Klao, the National Theatre hosts performances of the traditional *khŏhn*. The theatre holds performances on the last Friday and Saturday of each month, but call ahead for confirmation.

Maneeya Lotus Room (Map pp694-5; ☎ 0 2282 6312; 518/5 Th Ploenchit) Sponsors dinner-theatre performances of Thai classical dance; the food is nothing special, but the prices are reasonable (200B to 500B).

To see some examples of Thai classical dancing for free, hang out at Lak Muang Shrine (Map pp694–5), near Sanam Luang, or Erawan Shrine (Map pp694–5), next to Grand Hyatt Erawan. Dancers are hired in thanks for the shrines' mystical assistance in picking winning lottery numbers.

SHOPPING

Bangkok is not the place for recovering shopaholics, as the temptation to stray from the path is overwhelming. From mesmerising markets to state-of-the-art shopping centres, shopping in Bangkok sets the pulse racing in even the most ardent of antishoppers.

Markets

Phenomenal bargains are on offer at the city's informal markets. Most are an odd assortment of plastic toys, household goods, copy clothing and some knock-off designer watches and bags. Even more interesting are the food markets where food-savvy Thais forage for brightly coloured tapioca desserts, spicy curries and fruits that look like medieval torture devices.

Chatuchak Market (Map pp690-1; Th Phahonyothin; ⌚ 8am-6pm Sat & Sun) Chatuchak is the mother of all markets. It sprawls over a huge area with 15,000 stalls and an estimated 200,000 visitors a day. Deep in the bowels of the market, you'll forget that it is daylight. Everything is sold here, from live chickens and snakes to handicrafts and antiques to aisles and aisles of clothes. Everyone leaves thoroughly exhausted with empty wallets and armfuls of plastic bags – it's great fun. To navigate the market like a local, pick up a copy of *Nancy Chandler's Map of Bangkok*, which comes with a detailed Chatuchak section. North of central Bangkok off Th Phahonyothin, air-con buses 502, 503, 509, 510, 512 and 513, ordinary bus 77 and a dozen others serve the market. The Skytrain runs direct to Moh Chit station, which looks over the market.

> **WARNING: THE GEM SCAM**
>
> Unless you really know your stones, Bangkok is no place to seek out 'the big score'. Never accept an invitation from a friendly stranger to visit a gem shop, as you will end up with an empty wallet and a nice collection of coloured glass. See p806 for more on this.

Other recommendations:

Banglamphu Day Market (Th Chakraphong, Th Tanao & Th Tani) Clothes, foodstuffs and household goods.

Patpong Soi 2 Night Market More popular than the ping-pong shows these days.

Th Khao San Night Market T-shirts, artwork, souvenirs and traveller ghetto gear.

Shopping Centres

All of the following places are shown on Map pp694–5.

Central World Plaza (cnr Th Ploenchit & Th Ratchadamri) Formerly known as World Trade Center, Central World is Bangkok's glass-panelled embodiment of consumer excess, complete with eight floors of restaurants, beer gardens, cinemas – even an ice-skating rink. The plaza's lifeblood is the Zen department store, which is dotted with high-end fashion brands. Skytrain to Chit Lom.

Siam Center (cnr Th Phayathai & Th Phra Ram I) Thailand's first shopping centre, Siam Center opened its doors in 1976. And while it has aged well, there's even more fun to be had at Siam Paragon and Siam Discovery Center, both of which are attached by pedestrian walkways to Siam Center. The Paragon is probably the most bizarre of the three. In its basement, for instance, you'll find a rather impressive aquarium known as Siam Ocean World, and on the 2nd floor there are actual showrooms for Maseratis, Lamborghinis and Ferraris. Culture vultures should head directly to the large Kinokuniya bookstore on the 3rd floor, or to the cinema or IMAX theatre on the upper levels. Skytrain to Siam Sq.

Mahboonkrong (MBK; cnr Th Phayathai & Th Phra Ram I) Thai teenagers worship this shopping centre, which is just across the road from Siam Sq. Small, inexpensive stalls and shops sell mobile phone accessories, cheap T-shirts, wallets and handbags, plus there is the midrange Tokyu department store.

River City Shopping Complex (Th Charoen Krung) Almost worshipped as a museum, River City contains a number of high-quality art and antique shops on its 3rd and 4th floors. Acala (shop 312) is a gallery of unusual Tibetan and Chinese artefacts. Old Maps & Prints (☎ 0 2237 0077, ext 432; shop 432), owned by two German expats, stocks an impressively wide selection of one-of-a-kind rare and antique maps of Asia. You'll also find pre-20th-century books, prints and engravings.

GETTING THERE & AWAY

Air

Bangkok acts as the air travel hub for Thailand and mainland Southeast Asia. For airlines with representation in Bangkok, see p685. For a list of mainly domestic airlines, see p686. Most domestic flights currently use Bangkok's Don Mueang Airport, 25km outside the city. The city's new Suvarnabhumi International Airport, which opened in September 2006, now handles some domestic and all international flights. Find more information at www.suvarnabhumiairport.com.

Bus

Buses departing from the government bus station are recommended over those departing from Th Khao San and other tourist areas, due to a lower incidence of theft and greater reliability. The Bangkok bus terminals (all with left-luggage facilities) are as follows:

Eastern Bus Terminal (Ekamai; Map pp690-1; ☎ 0 2391 2504; Soi 40/Soi Ekamai, Th Sukhumvit) Pattaya, Rayong, Chanthaburi and Trat (mainland departure points for boats to Ko Samet and Ko Chang).

Northern & Northeastern Bus Terminal (Moh Chit; Map pp690-1; ☎ northern routes 0 2936 3659, northeastern routes 0 2936 2841; Th Kamphaeng Phet) All northern and northeastern cities including Chiang Mai, Nakhon Ratchasima, as well as central destinations such as Ayuthaya, Lopburi and Aranya Prathet (near the Cambodian border). The terminal's near Chatuchak Park.

Southern Bus Terminal (Sai Tai Mai; Map pp690-1; ☎ 0 2435 7192; cnr Hwy 338 & Th Phra Pin Klao, Thonburi) Nakhon Pathom, Damnoen Saduak, Kanchanaburi, Hua Hin, Surat Thani, Phuket, Hat Yai and all points south.

Train

There are two main train stations in Bangkok. **Hualamphong station** (Map pp694-5; ☎ general information 0 2220 4334, advance booking 0 2220 4444; Th Phra Ram IV) handles services to the north, northeast and most of the services to the south. **Thonburi station** (Bangkok Noi; Map pp690-1) handles Kanchanaburi and some services to the south. If you're heading south, check which station you need.

GETTING AROUND

The main obstacle to getting around Bangkok is the troubling traffic, which adds a half-hour to an hour delay to daytime outings, depending on the route. See p697 for handy routes to popular destinations.

Boat

Slow barges being pulled by determined tug boats, kids splashing around the river banks, majestic Wat Arun rising in the distance like a giant lingam – all these sights are courtesy of the inexpensive river taxis, which ply a regular route along the Mae Nam Chao Phraya. The **Chao Phraya River Express** (☎ 0 2623 6001-3)

GETTING TO CAMBODIA

Anyone undertaking the Angkor pilgrimage into Cambodia will want to cross over the Thai–Cambodian border at Aranya Prathet–Poipet. Most people start this run from Bangkok, which makes for an epic journey: start out early, bring a lot of snacks and practise Buddhist calm.

Frequent daytime buses (four hours) and two trains per day (six hours) connect Bangkok with Aranya Prathet, and from Poipet buses go to Siem Reap (three to six hours). To travel between the two border towns, you must take a túk-túk (motorised rickshaw) or săwngthăew (small pick-up). The immigration post is open from 7.30am to 5pm. If the ticket offered to you on Th Khao San sounds too good to be true, it is; they are setting you up for a ride on the Bangkok to Siem Reap Bus Scam (see p89 for more details on avoiding this).

See p97 for information on crossing from Cambodia into Thailand.

operates between Tha Wat Ratchasingkhon in south central Bangkok northwards to Nonthaburi Province. There are four boat lines: two express lines (indicated by yellow or orange flags), the local line (without a flag) and the tourist line. Express boats stop at certain piers during morning and evening hours (usually 6am to 9am and 3pm to 7pm) and cost 10B to 25B, depending on the destination. Local boats stop at all piers from 6am to 7.40pm, and fares range from 6B to 10B, plus small boats ply the width of the river for 2B.

See p697 for the closest *thâa* to your destination.

Bangkok Metropolitan Authority operates two **Khlong Taxi** (ticket 5-8B; 6am-7pm) routes along the canals: Khlong Saen Saep (Banglamphu to Bang Kapi) and Khlong Phasi Charoen in Thonburi (Kaset Bang Khae port to Saphan Phra Ram I). The Khlong Saen Saep canal service is the most useful one for short-term visitors as it provides a traffic-free trip between Siam Sq and Banglamphu. In Siam Sq, the pier (Tha Ratchathewi) is by the bridge next to the Asia Hotel; in Banglamphu (the last stop on the line) the pier is near Wat Saket and Phra Samen Fort. If travelling from Banglamphu to Siam Sq, it is really easy to miss the stop, so let the person sitting next to you know that you want '*See*-yahm *Sa*-quare'. The canals make the Chao Phraya river look like a mountain spring, so try not to get splashed.

Bus

The Bangkok bus service is frequent and frantic, so a bus map *(Tour 'n' Guide Map to Bangkok Thailand)* is an absolute necessity. Don't expect it to be 100% correct though, as routes change regularly.

Fares for ordinary buses vary according to the type of bus: from 3.50/4B (red/green buses) to 5B (white-and-blue buses) for any journey under 10km. There are also the cream-and-blue air-con buses that start at 8B but jump to 20B on longer trips. Orange Euro 2 air-con buses are 12B for any distance, while white-and-pink air-con buses cost 25B to 30B. The least crowded are the red microbuses, which stop taking passengers once every seat is filled, and cost a 25B flat fare (have exact change ready).

Metro

The first line of Bangkok's subway or underground (depending on your nationality!) opened in 2004 and is operated by the **Metropolitan Rapid Transit Authority** (MRTA; www.mrta.co.th). Thais call it the Metro, which no doubt pleases the French. The line connects the train station of Bang Sue with Chatuchak (Skytrain interchange to Moh Chit), Sukhumvit (Skytrain interchange to Asoke), Lumphini Park and Silom (Skytrain interchange to Sala Daeng), and terminates at Hualamphong station.

Trains operate from 5am to midnight and cost 14B to 36B, depending on distance. Future extensions will connect Hualamphong to Chinatown and Thonburi.

Motorcycle Taxi

Motorcycle taxis typically camp out at the beginning of a residential *soi* to transport people the last few kilometres home. Since the corners are always overstaffed, drivers will gladly take you anywhere for the right price. Fares for a motorcycle taxi are about the same as túk-túk fares except during heavy traffic, when they may cost more. Riding on the back of a speeding motorcycle taxi in Bangkok traffic is a close approximation to an extreme sport.

Skytrain

The ultramodern elevated **Bangkok Mass Transit System Skytrain** (BTS; ☎ 0 2617 7300; www.bts.co.th) arrived at just the right time to rescue Bangkok from choking traffic jams. OK, the jams are still there, but everyone smart enough to use the Skytrain can consider themselves rescued. The Skytrain offers a new perspective on the city from on high, plus you get to sit in air-conditioned comfort.

Trains run frequently from 6am to midnight along two lines. The trains are labelled with their final destination and handy maps in the stations explain the layout. Free maps also outline the system, and friendly English-speaking ticket vendors are old-hands at helping confused *farang*.

The Sukhumvit line starts at Moh Chit station, near Chatuchak Market and the Northern & Northeastern Bus Terminal and eventually swings east along Th Sukhumvit with plenty of stations along this popular strip. The Silom line runs from the National Stadium station, near Siam Sq, through the popular Th Silom area to Saphan Taksin on the banks of the Mae Nam Chao Phraya. The two lines share an interchange at Siam station and there are Skytrain interchanges with the newer Metro at Silom (called Sala Daeng by the Metro) and Asoke.

Fares vary from 10B to 40B, and machines only accept coins (get change from the ticket windows). There is a variety of stored-value tickets for one-day and multiday unlimited trips; inquire at the stations.

Taxi

Fares for metered taxis are always lower than those for nonmetered taxis; look for ones with signs on top reading 'Taxi Meter'. Don't be shy about asking the driver to use the meter; sometimes they 'forget'. In tourist haunts they may refuse to use the meter; just find another taxi. Fares should generally run from 50B to 100B. In most large cities, the taxi drivers are seasoned navigators familiar with every out-of-the-way neighbourhood or street. However, this is not the case in Bangkok where, if you succeed in correctly pronouncing your destination, the taxi driver might still stare vacantly at your map. To ensure that you'll be able to return home, grab your hotel's business card, which will have directions in Thai.

Túk-Túk

You must fix fares in advance for túk-túks and they are only really sensible for shorter trips, if at all. Many have seemingly graduated from the Evel Knievel school of driving and that doesn't always work with three wheels on a sharp bend! Some travellers swear by túk-túk, others have a hard time bargaining a fair price – it all depends on your patience and a winning smile. Beware of túk-túk drivers who offer to take you on a sightseeing tour for 10B or 20B – it's a touting scheme designed to pressure you into purchasing overpriced goods.

AROUND BANGKOK

If you're tied to Bangkok for several days but feel the urge for some fresh air, take a day trip to some of the nearby attractions.

DAMNOEN SADUAK FLOATING MARKET

The image is iconic: wooden canoes laden with multicoloured fruits and vegetables, paddled by Thai women wearing indigo-hued clothes and wide-brimmed straw hats. This is the realm of postcards. The reality reveals a scene of commercial chaos, more souvenir stalls than market vendors, more tourists than locals. But like all jamborees, it can still be fun. The action takes place on the water and the key is to get here early before the big buses arrive.

The smart money says arrive in Damnoen Saduak the night before, crash at the conveniently located **Noknoi Hotel** (Little Bird; ☎ 0 3225 4382; s/d 220/350B) and get up at 7am to see the market while the light is good, the sun forgiving and the tourists absent. By 9am the hordes from Bangkok arrive and the atmosphere drains away.

You can hire a boat from any pier that lines Th Sukhaphiban 1, which is the land route to the floating market area. The going rate is 150B to 200B per person, per hour. If the boat operator wants to charge you more, keep shopping.

Damnoen Saduak is 105km southwest of Bangkok. Air-con buses 78 and 996 (65B, two hours, every 20 minutes from 6.30am to 9pm) go direct from Bangkok's Southern Bus Terminal to Damnoen Saduak.

NAKHON PATHOM

Nakhon Pathom, 56km west of Bangkok, claims to be the oldest city in Thailand, but the only clue to its longevity is the **Phra Pathom Chedi**, originally erected in the early 6th century by the Theravada Buddhists of Dvaravati. The contemporary bell-shaped structure was built over the original in the early 11th century by the Khmer king, Suryavarman I of Angkor. This alteration created the world's tallest Buddhist monument, 127m high. Sitting in the middle of town, Phra Pathom Chedi makes for a pleasant stroll or interesting sketching subject. Opposite the *bòht* (central sanctuary) is a **museum** (admission 20B; ⌚ 9am-4pm Wed-Sun), which contains some Dvaravati sculpture. In November, there's the **Phra Pathom Chedi Fair**, which packs in everyone from fruit vendors to fortune-tellers.

Air-con buses 997 and 83 (35B, one hour, frequent) leave from Bangkok's Southern Bus Terminal to Nakhon Pathom. To return to Bangkok, catch one of the idling buses from Th Phayaphan on the canal side of the road, a block from the train station. Bus 78 to Damnoen Saduak Floating Market (left) leaves from the same stop.

Two trains daily (7.45am and 1.45pm) depart Thonburi (Bangkok Noi) station for

Nakhon Pathom (3rd class 14B, about 1¼ hours). Returning to Thonburi there are also two departures (8.55am and 4.20pm). There are also connections with Hualamphong, but the journey takes longer.

SAMUT PRAKAN'S ANCIENT CITY

Samut Prakan's claim to fame is the **Ancient City** (Muang Boran; ☎ 0 2323 9253; www.ancientcity.com; adult/child 300/200B; ⏰ 8am-5pm), alleged to be the world's largest outdoor museum. Around 12km south of the city centre, it is home to 109 scaled-down replicas of Thailand's most famous historic sites, including some that no longer survive. Visions of Las Vegas and tiny tacky treasures may spring to mind, but the Ancient City is architecturally sophisticated and a preservation site for classical buildings and art forms. For students of Thai architecture or even for those who want an introduction to the subject, it is definitely worth the trip. It is also a good place for leisurely walks or bicycle rides (50B rental), as it's rarely crowded.

Ordinary bus 25 (3.50B) and air-con buses 507, 508 and 511 (16B) ply regular routes between central Bangkok and Samut Prakan. The trip can take up to two hours depending on traffic. Ancient City is 33km from Bangkok along the Old Sukhumvit Hwy. From Samut Prakan take a green minibus 36 (6B), which passes the entrance to Ancient City; sit on the left-hand side of the bus to spot the 'Muang Boran' sign. To return to town, cross the main highway and catch white sǎwngthǎew 36 (5B).

CENTRAL THAILAND

The fertile plains of central Thailand are the geographic and cultural heart of the country. Along the banks of life-giving Mae Nam Chao Phraya, the cultural and military identity of the early Thai nation is known to have evolved in the ancient capitals of Sukhothai and Ayuthaya. Once known as the Siamese language, today the region's dialect is considered standard Thai. Featuring history, superb scenery and easy adventures, central Thailand is fast becoming a must for travellers.

KANCHANABURI

pop 61,800

West of Bangkok, Kanchanaburi is blessed with an idyllic location, nestled in between rugged limestone peaks and the pretty Mae Nam Khwae (Kwai River). The peaceful atmosphere belies the town's tragic past as the site of a WWII prisoner-of-war camp and the infamous bridge over the River Kwai. Today visitors come to pay their respects to fallen Allied soldiers or to discover for themselves more about the town's dark past. But Kan, as locals call it, is also a great place to relax at riverside guesthouses or venture to nearby natural attractions.

Information

Check out www.kanchanaburi-info.com for general information on the town and around. Several major Thai banks can be found around Th Saengchuto near the market and bus terminal. There are plenty of places to get online along Th Mae Nam Khwae.

Post office (Th Saengchuto)

TAT office (☎ 0 3451 1200; Th Saengchuto; ⏰ 8.30am-4.30pm) Near the bus terminal, it provides information on trips beyond Kanchanaburi, as well as bus and train schedules.

Thanakarn Hospital (☎ 0 3462 2358) Best-equipped place for foreigners.

Tourist police (☎ 0 3451 2668) Several locations around town.

Sights

THAILAND-BURMA RAILWAY CENTRE

Before you head out to the Kwai River Bridge, get a little history under your belt at this **museum** (☎ 0 3451 0067; 73 Th Jaokannun; adult/child 60/30B; ⏰ 9am-5pm). Professional exhibits outline Japan's aggression in Southeast Asia during WWII and its plan to connect Yangon (in Burma) with Bangkok via rail for transport of military supplies. Captured Allied soldiers as well as Burmese and Malay captives were transported to the jungles of Kanchanaburi to build 415km of rail – known today as the Death Railway because of the many lives (more than 100,000 men) the project claimed.

KANCHANABURI ALLIED WAR CEMETERY

Across the street from the Thailand-Burma Railway Centre, the **Kanchanaburi Allied War Cemetery** (Th Saengchuto; admission free; ⏰ 7am-6pm) is a touching gift from the Thai people to remember the POWs, mainly from Britain and Holland, who died on their soil.

KWAI RIVER BRIDGE (DEATH RAILWAY BRIDGE)

While the story made famous by the film *The Bridge on the River Kwai* is one of endurance,

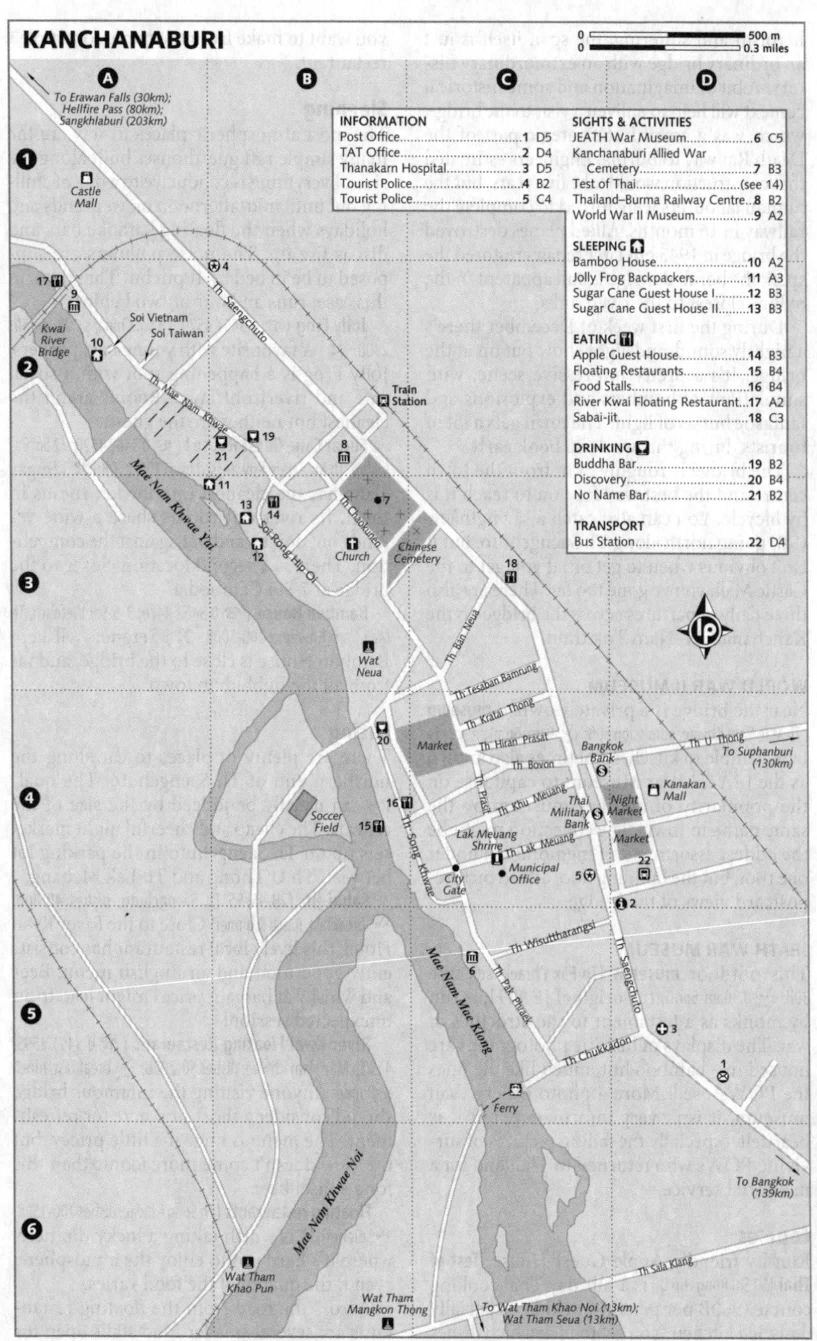
KANCHANABURI
0 500 m
0 0.3 miles
To Erawan Falls (30km); Hellfire Pass (80km); Sangkhlaburi (203km)
INFORMATION
Post Office 1 D5
TAT Office 2 D4
Thanakarn Hospital 3 D5
Tourist Police 4 B2
Tourist Police 5 C4
SIGHTS & ACTIVITIES
JEATH War Museum 6 C5
Kanchanaburi Allied War Cemetery 7 B3
Test of Thai (see 14)
Thailand–Burma Railway Centre 8 B2
World War II Museum 9 A2
SLEEPING
Bamboo House 10 A2
Jolly Frog Backpackers 11 A3
Sugar Cane Guest House I 12 B3
Sugar Cane Guest House II 13 B3
EATING
Apple Guest House 14 B3
Floating Restaurants 15 B4
Food Stalls 16 B4
River Kwai Floating Restaurant 17 A2
Sabai-jit 18 C3
DRINKING
Buddha Bar 19 B2
Discovery 20 B4
No Name Bar 21 B2
TRANSPORT
Bus Station 22 D4
Castle Mall
Kwai River Bridge
Soi Vietnam
Soi Taiwan
Th Saengchuto
Th Mae Nam Khwae
Train Station
Mae Nam Khwae Yai
Soi Rong Hip Oi
Th Chaokunen
Church
Chinese Cemetery
Th Ban Neua
Wat Neua
Th Tesaban Bamrung
Th Kratai Thong
Th Hiran Prasat
Th Bovon
Th U Thong
To Suphanburi (130km)
Bangkok Bank
Kanakan Mall
Market
Th Prasit
Th Khu Meuang
Thai Military Bank
Night Market
Soccer Field
Lak Meuang Shrine
Th Lak Meuang
Th Song Khwae
City Gate
Municipal Office
Th Wisuttharangsi
Mae Nam Mae Klong
Th Pak Phraek
Th Saengchuto
Th Chukkadon
Ferry
Mae Nam Khwae Noi
To Bangkok (139km)
Th Sala Klang
Wat Tham Khao Pun
Wat Tham Mangkon Thong
To Wat Tham Khao Noi (13km); Wat Tham Seua (13km)

heroism and suffering, the span itself is just an ordinary bridge with an extraordinary history. A bit of imagination and some historical context will help to enliven a visit to the bridge, which was a small but strategic part of the Death Railway to Burma. Engineers estimated that construction would take five years, but the human labourers were forced to complete the railway in 16 months. Allied planes destroyed the bridge in 1945 but later repairs restored the span; the bomb damage is still apparent in the pylons closest to the riverbanks.

During the first week of December there's a nightly sound-and-light show put on at the bridge. It's a pretty impressive scene, with simulations of bombers and explosions and fantastic bursts of light. The town gets a lot of tourists during this week, so book early.

The bridge is roughly 3km from the town centre and the best way for you to reach it is by bicycle. You can also catch a sǎwngthǎew (5B) going north along Th Saengchuto, but it isn't obvious when to get off; if you get to the Castle Mall, you've gone too far. There are also three daily departures across the bridge on the Kanchanaburi–Nam Tok train.

WORLD WAR II MUSEUM

Near the bridge is a privately owned **museum** (Th Mae Nam Khwae; admission 30B; 9am-6pm), a veritable temple to kitsch, sometimes also known as the JEATH War Museum to capitalise on the popularity of another museum by the same name in town. The collection might be the oddest assortment of memorabilia under one roof, but the building does afford picture-postcard views of the bridge.

JEATH WAR MUSEUM

This outdoor **museum** (Th Pak Phraek; admission 30B; 8.30am-6pm), the original JEATH, is run by monks as a testament to the atrocities of war. The displays of historic photographs are housed in a bamboo hut, much like the ones the POWs used. More a photo gallery than museum, it isn't very informative, but it is heartfelt, especially the fading pictures of surviving POWs who returned to Thailand for a memorial service.

Courses

Run by friendly Apple Guest House, **Test of Thai** (52 Soi Rong Hip Oi) is a full-day Thai cooking course (900B per person), held in a specially designed kitchen. You get to pick which dishes you want to make from the menu for Apple's restaurant.

Sleeping

The most atmospheric places to stay are the many simple raft guesthouses built along the river. Everything is conducive to a day of chilling out until mid-afternoon on weekends and holidays when the floating karaoke bars and discos fire up. The noise polluters are supposed to be in bed by 10pm but Thai time, in this case, runs an hour or two behind.

Jolly Frog (☎ 0 3451 4579; 28 Soi China; s 70B, d 150-290B;) A favourite with young backpackers, Jolly Frog is a happening spot with a social café and riverfront lawn. Rooms aren't the cleanest but neither are the guests.

Sugar Cane Guest House I (☎ 0 3462 4520; 22 Soi Pakistan, Th Mae Nam Khwae; s/d from 150/250B;) Sugar Cane has the cleanest interior fan rooms in town. Its river-raft rooms share a wide veranda but don't stand out against the competition. There is a second location closer to the bridge at 7 Soi Cambodia.

Bamboo House (☎ 0 3462 4470; 3-5 Soi Vietnam, Th Mae Nam Khwae; r 200-500B;) Serene, well-kept Bamboo House is close to the bridge, and far from all the hubbub in town.

Eating

There are plenty of places to eat along the northern end of Th Saengchuto. The quality can usually be judged by the size of the crowds. The cheap and cheerful night market sets up on Th Saengchuto in the parking lot between Th U Thong and Th Lak Meuang.

Sabai-jit (28-45/55 Th Saengchuto; dishes 40-80B; breakfast, lunch & dinner) Close to the River Kwai Hotel, this lively local restaurant has consistently good food and an English menu. Beer and whisky at bargain prices might lead to an unexpected session!

River Kwai Floating Restaurant (☎ 0 3451 2595; 415 Th Mae Nam Khwae; dishes 50-200B; breakfast, lunch & dinner) Anyone visiting the infamous bridge should consider a short stop here for refreshment. The menu is huge if a little pricey, but the view doesn't come more iconic than this for a sunset beer.

Floating restaurants (Th Song Khwae; dishes 100-150B; dinner) It is worth taking a lucky dip here, where it's hard not to enjoy the atmosphere, even if the quality of the food varies.

Across the road from the floating restaurants are several smaller food stalls open for breakfast, lunch and dinner; perfect for the thrifty drifter, with dishes from 50B.

Most of the popular guesthouses have restaurants churning out the greatest hits from banana pancakes to *tôm yam* (spicy and sour soup). The food at **Apple Guest House** (☎ 0 3451 2017; 52 Soi Rong Hip Oi; 🕑 breakfast, lunch & dinner) is a cut above the rest, but it lacks a river view.

Drinking

Buddha Bar (Th Mae Nam Khwae) There is a whole strip of small bars opposite the 7-Eleven, but most are about pink lights and pretty girls. Buddha Bar is the not-so-Zen exception – it's more of a biker's haunt, rocker's bar and hard-drinking club.

No Name Bar (Th Mae Nam Khwae) With the slogan 'Get shitfaced on a shoestring', who could resist this brash backpacker hang-out? Besides coming here for suds, there's a range of Western snacks, and satellite TV for football games and the BBC.

Discovery (Th Song Khwae) Loud and flashy, this riverside disco fills to the gills on weekends with locals and Bangkok Thais who don't need karaoke to have a good time.

Getting There & Away

Kanchanaburi's bus station is located on Th Saengchuto, near Th Lak Meuang and the TAT office.

Bus trips go to Bangkok's Southern Bus Terminal (air-con 62B to 79B, three hours, every 15 minutes until 7pm), Nakhon Pathom (ordinary 28B, 1½ hours), Ratburi (36B, 2½ hours), Sangkhlaburi (90B, five hours) and Suphanburi (35B, 2½ hours) for connections to Ayuthaya.

Kanchanaburi is on the Thonburi (Bangkok Noi)–Nam Tok train line. The **train station** (Th Saengchuto) is 500m from the river. There are only two trains a day originating from Thonburi (25B). West of Kanchanaburi to Nam Tok, the train travels a portion of the Death Railway (17B, two hours, three daily).

Getting Around

Săamláw within the city cost 30B a trip. Regular săwngthăew in town are 5B to 10B and ply Th Saengchuto, but be careful you don't accidentally 'charter' one – these are a rip-off at 500B an hour.

There are plenty of places hiring motorbikes along Th Mae Nam Khwae. The going rate is 150B to 250B per day and it's a good way of getting to the rather scattered attractions around Kanchanaburi.

Bicycles can be rented from most guesthouses for around 50B a day.

AROUND KANCHANABURI

Most of the popular guesthouses in town offer tours that take in the main attractions around Kanchanaburi. Shop around for the best deal.

Erawan National Park (☎ 0 3457 4222; admission per person 200B; 🕑 8am-4pm) is the home of the seven-tiered **Erawan Falls**, which makes for a refreshing day trip; bring along a swimsuit for a plunge in some of the enticing pools. To get yourself to the park take an early morning bus (26B, 1½ hours, hourly from 8am) from Kanchanaburi to the end of the line, from where you will have to walk a couple of kilometres to the waterfall trail. The last bus back to Kanchanaburi leaves at 4pm.

Carved out of unforgiving mountain terrain, the section of the Death Railway called **Hellfire Pass** (suggested donation 30-100B; 🕑 9am-4pm) was so named for the unearthly apparitions cast by the nightly fires of the labouring POWs. Today a 4km-long trail follows the old route with some remnants of the rail line still intact. Located near Km Marker 66 on the Sai Yok–Thong Pha Phum road, Hellfire Pass can be reached by a Sangkhlaburi-bound or Thong Pha Phum–bound bus (27B, 1½ hours, last bus back at 4pm); use the Thai script for 'Hellfire Pass' that is printed on the TAT-distributed map to inform the attendant of your destination.

SANGKHLABURI & THREE PAGODAS PASS

Northwest of Kanchanaburi is a legal day-trip crossing into Myanmar at Three Pagodas Pass (Chedi Sam Ong). The village on the Myanmar side has been the scene of fire fights between minority insurgents and the Burmese government; both parties want to control the collection of 'taxes' levied on smuggling. In 1990, the Burmese government regained control of the area, rebuilt the bamboo village in wood and concrete and renamed it Payathonzu. A row of souvenir shops and the three pagodas, which are rather inconspicuous, are all the town offers. The trip is more for bragging rights of being in Myanmar than a rewarding excursion. At the time of writing the border was open to foreigners.

Sleeping

Burmese Inn (☎ 0 3459 5146; www.sangkhlaburi.com; 52/3 Mu 3; r 80-500B; ❄) It isn't the cleanest in town, but it is the cheapest. The flimsy huts are hammered into a hillside overlooking the wooden bridge, and the Austrian co-owner is knowledgeable about the area.

P Guest House (☎ 0 3459 5061; www.pguesthouse.com; 8/1 Mu 1; r 200-700B) Well worth the 1.2km walk from the bus stop, P Guest House has spacious, stone bungalows with verandas along a slope overlooking the lake. Cheaper rooms share a remarkably clean bathroom. P also organises elephant treks and rents canoes and kayaks.

Getting There & Away

To travel from Kanchanaburi to Sangkhlaburi, take ordinary bus 8203 (90B, five hours, 6am, 8.40am, 10.20am and noon) or the air-con bus (151B, four hours, 9am and 1.30pm).

A minivan service to Kanchanaburi via Thong Pha Phum (118B, three hours, six daily from 7.30am to 4.30pm) leaves Sangkhlaburi from near the market.

If you go by motorcycle or car, you can count on about three to four hours to cover the 203km from Kanchanaburi to Sangkhlaburi. Alternatively, you can make it an all-day trip and stop off in Ban Kao (a museum displaying Neolithic artefacts), Meuang Singh (the remains of a 13th-century shrine of the Khmer empire) and Hellfire Pass. Be warned, however, that this is not a trip for inexperienced motorcycle riders. The Thong Pha Phum to Sangkhlaburi section of the journey (74km) requires sharp reflexes and previous experience on mountain roads. This is also not a motorcycle trip to do alone, as stretches of the highway are practically deserted.

From Sangkhlaburi, there are hourly săwngthăew (30B, 40 minutes) to Three Pagodas Pass all day.

AYUTHAYA

pop 81,400

In their race to reach the Gulf of Thailand, three rivers (Mae Nam Lopburi, Chao Phraya and Pa Sak) converge to form the island of Ayuthaya, the former Thai capital, named after the home of Rama in the Indian epic Ramayana.

The rivers formed both a natural barrier to invasion and an invitation to trade. From 1350 to 1767, Ayuthaya was the cultural centre of the emerging Thai nation. Throughout Ayuthaya's domination of central Thailand, Asian and Western foreign powers eyed up this strategic city and successive Thai kings had to foil coups and play foreign powers off against one another. But the river defences were unable to repulse persistent attacks by the Burmese. After two years of war, the capital fell; the royal family fled to Thonburi, near present-day Bangkok, and the Burmese looted the city's architectural and religious treasures.

Today a modern city has sprung up around the holy ruins. Life revolves around the river, which acts as transport, bath and kitchen sink for its residents. The holiday of **Loi Krathong** – held on the proper full-moon night, when tiny votive boats are floated on rivers as a tribute to the River Goddess – is celebrated with great fanfare in Ayuthaya.

GETTING TO MYANMAR

Foreigners are allowed to enter Myanmar for a day trip at Three Pagodas Pass, and all immigration formalities can be arranged at the border. This crossing does not issue extensions for Thai visas. You will need to temporarily surrender your passport, along with a passport photo, to the Thai immigration office before crossing the border. At the Myanmar immigration office, you must submit a copy of the photo page of your passport and a passport photo, in addition to 500B or US$10. Upon your return into Thailand, you will receive your passport back. There is a small photocopy shop near the Thai immigration office where you can arrange border documentation.

Occasionally this border is closed, especially during conflicts between ethnic armies and the central Myanmar government, but these incidents are now less frequent than in years past.

Săwngthăew (small pick-up trucks with two benches in the back) leave Sangkhlaburi's bus station (30B) every half-hour from 6am to 4pm. Along the way you'll pass little bamboo-hut villages inhabited by Mon or Karen people. The border is only a short walk from the săwngthăew stop in Three Pagodas Pass.

Information

ATMs are abundant, especially along Th Naresuan near Amporn Shopping Centre. The internet shops on and around Soi 1, Th Naresuan, offer the cheapest deals.

Main post office (Th U Thong)
Nakorn Sri Ayutthaya Hospital (☎ 0 3524 1027)
TAT office (☎ 0 3524 6076; 108/22 Th Si Sanphet; 9am-5pm) Distributes an Ayuthaya tourist map and bus schedule.
Tourist police (☎ 0 3524 1446, emergency 1155; Th Si Sanphet)

Sights

A Unesco World Heritage site, Ayuthaya's historic temples are scattered throughout this once magnificent city, and along the encircling rivers. The ruins are divided into two geographical areas: ruins 'on the island', in the central part of town between Th Chee Kun and the western end of Th U Thong, which are best visited by bicycle; and those 'off the island' on the other side of the river, which are best visited on an evening boat tour (from 250B; book through guesthouses) or by bicycle. Getting a handle on the religious and historical importance of the temples is difficult to do without some preliminary tutoring. **Ayuthaya Historical Study Centre** (☎ 0 3524 5124; Th Rotchana; adult/student 100/50B; 9am-4.30pm Mon-Fri, to 5pm Sat & Sun) has informative, professional displays that paint an indispensable picture for viewing the ancient city. Also purchase the *Ayuthaya* pamphlet (15B) for sale at Wat Phra Si Sanphet's admission kiosk.

There are also two national museums in town. The building that houses the **Chantharakasem National Museum** (admission 30B; 9am-4pm Wed-Sun) is a museum in itself. King Rama IV had this palace rebuilt and established as a museum in 1936. The less charming but larger **Chao Sam Phraya National Museum** (cnr Th Rotchana & Th Si Sanphet; admission 30B; 9am-4pm Wed-Sun) has a first-class collection of gold artefacts in a secure room upstairs.

Most of the temples are open from 8am or 9am until 5pm or 6pm daily.

ON THE ISLAND

The most distinctive example of Ayuthaya architecture is **Wat Phra Si Sanphet** (admission 30B) thanks to its three bell-shaped *chedi* that taper off into descending rings. This site served as the royal palace from the city's founding until the mid-15th century, when it was converted into a temple. Although the grounds are now well tended, these efforts cannot hide the ravages of war and time. The surrounding buildings are worn through to their orange bricks, leaning to one side as gravity takes its toll. The complex once contained a 16m-high standing Buddha covered with 250kg of gold, which was melted down by the Burmese conquerors.

The adjacent **Wihaan Phra Mongkhon Bophit** houses a huge bronze seated Buddha, the largest in Thailand.

Wat Phra Mahathat (admission 30B) has one of the first Khmer-style *praang* built in the capital. One of the most iconic images in Ayuthaya is the Buddha head engulfed by tentacle-like tree roots.

OFF THE ISLAND

The main *wíhăan* (large hall in a Thai temple) of **Wat Phanan Choeng** (admission 30B) contains a 19m-high sitting Buddha image, which reportedly wept when the Burmese sacked Ayuthaya. The temple is dedicated to Chinese seafarers and on weekends is crowded with Buddhist pilgrims from Bangkok who pay for saffron-coloured cloth to be ritually draped over the image.

Wat Chai Wattanaram used to be one of Ayuthaya's most overgrown lost-city ruins, with stately rows of disintegrating Buddhas. Today, some harsh restoration work (and the wonders of cement) has produced a row of brand-new Buddhas. It is still a lovely temple and a photogenic subject for sunset photo shoots.

The **Golden Mountain Chedi** (Phu Khao Thong) lies to the northwest of the city and has a wide view over the flat country. Also to the north is the **elephant kraal**, a restored version of the wooden stockade once used for the annual roundup of wild elephants. To the southeast, **Wat Yai Chai Mongkon** has a massive ruined *chedi*, which contrasts with the surrounding contemporary Buddha statues.

Sleeping

Baan Lotus Guest House (☎ 0 3525 1988; 20 Th Pamaphrao; s 200-250B, d 350B) The university lecturer who operates this old and somewhat secluded wooden house was also born and raised inside it. Staying here will likely remind you more of staying with a kindly relative than a stranger.

Tony's Place (☎ 0 3525 2578; 12/18 Soi 1, Th Naresuan; r 200-700B;) Tony's Place is an Ayuthaya old-timer, and continues to be the town's top choice among the backpacking

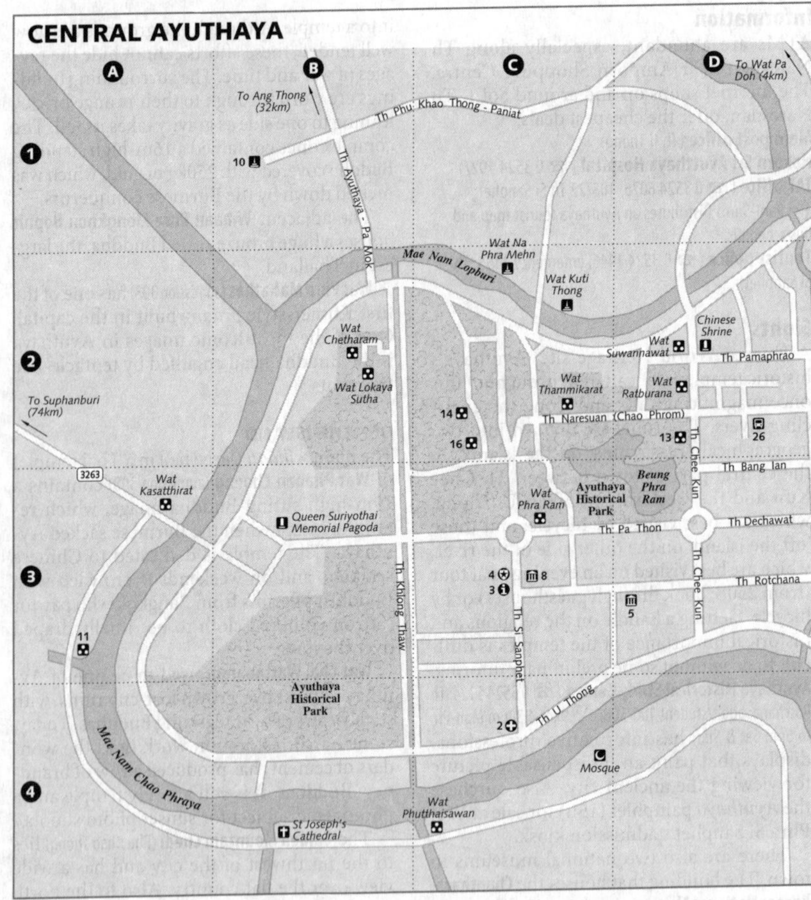

crowd. The always busy restaurant offers free wireless access.

our pick Bann Kun Pra (☎ 0 3524 1978; www.bannkunpra.com; 48/2 Th U Thong; dm/s 250/300B, d 400-600B) A stunning and stylish old teak house, this is the top choice in Ayuthaya for those who prefer to stay alongside the river. Dining and late-night lounging take place on an outdoor patio that overlooks the water. The recently renovated rooms are beautifully outfitted in the traditional Thai style; some even come with antiques and four-poster beds.

PU Guest House (☎ 0 3525 1213; www.puguesthouse.com; 20/1 Soi Thaw Kaw Saw; s 250-350B, d 350-700B) Just up the road from Tony's, PU is set in a smart, modern villa with scrubbed-clean rooms. The friendly family know their stuff: tourist information on tap, bikes for rent and boat tours are all available.

HI-Ayutthaya (☎ 0 3521 0941; www.tyha.org; 7 Moo 2, Th Rotchana; r 350-450B;) This quiet and relaxing teakwood house has friendly staff and free breakfast. Ask for the fan room with satellite TV!

Eating

The range of restaurants in Ayuthaya can come as a disappointment after living it up in Bangkok. Eating in at the guesthouse is normally a dull option, but the riverside terrace restaurant at Bann Kun Pra is worth a visit, even for those staying elsewhere. Tony's Place has the best general menu, with a reliable mix of Thai and Western dishes, and is the

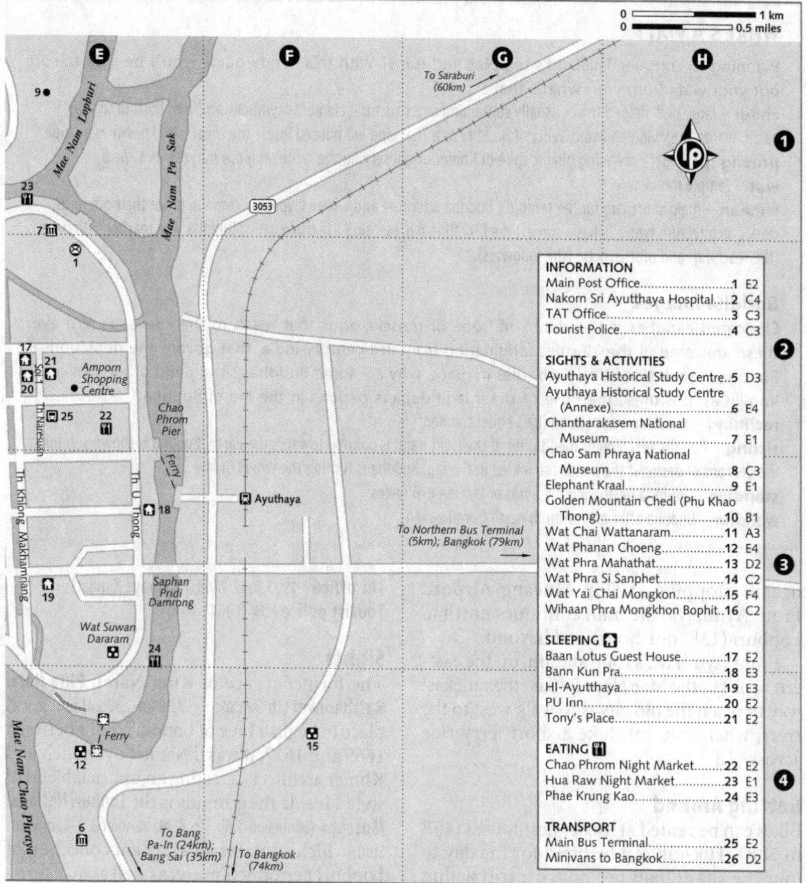

closest thing to a backpacker bar, complete with pool table.

The Hua Raw and Chao Phrom night markets, both on Th U Thong, have Muslim-style roti as well as popular Thai wok-wonders. Strike for here if you are in the market for a bargain dinner.

Phae Krung Kao (Th U Thong; dishes 60-120B; lunch & dinner) Floating restaurants are a popular fixture in Ayuthaya and Phae Krung Kao, on the southern side of the bridge, is good enough to draw a local crowd in droves.

Getting There & Away

BUS

Ayuthaya has two bus terminals. Buses from the south, west and east stop at the **main bus terminal** (Th Naresuan). Long-distance northern buses stop at the northern terminal, 5km east of the centre.

Frequent buses run to Bangkok's Don Meuang airport (40B, 1½ hours) and Bangkok's Northern & Northeastern Bus Terminal (45B, two hours) from the main bus terminal from about 5am to 7pm. Minivans to Bangkok (60B, two hours) leave from Th Naresuan, just near the main bus terminal, every 20 minutes between 5am and 5pm. Passengers are dropped off at Bangkok's Victory Monument.

TRAIN

Trains to Ayuthaya leave Hualamphong station in Bangkok (3rd class 15B to 20B, 1½ hours) almost hourly between 6am and 10pm,

WHAT'S A WAT?

Planning to conquer Thailand's temples and ruins? With this handy guide, you'll be able to sort out your wats from your what's that:

chedi – large bell-shaped tower usually containing five structural elements symbolising (from bottom to top) earth, water, fire, wind and void; relics of Buddha or a Thai king are housed inside the *chedi;* also known as a stupa

praang (prang) – towering phallic spire of Khmer origin serving the same religious purpose as a *chedi*

wat – temple monastery

wíhaan – main sanctuary for the temple's Buddha sculpture and where laypeople come to make their offerings; classic architecture typically has a three-tiered roofline representing the triple gems: Buddha (the teacher), Dharma (the teaching) and Brotherhood (the followers)

Buddha Images

Elongated earlobes, no evidence of bone or muscle, arms that reach to the knees, a third eye: these are some of the 32 rules, originating from 3rd-century India, that govern the depiction of Buddha in sculpture. With such rules in place, why are some Buddhas sitting and others walking? Known as 'postures', the pose of the image depicts periods in the life of Buddha:

reclining – exact moment of Buddha's enlightenment

sitting – Buddha teaching or meditating: if the right hand is pointed towards the earth, Buddha is shown subduing the demons of desire; if the hands are folded in the lap, Buddha is turning the wheel of law

standing – Buddha bestowing blessings or taming evil forces

walking – Buddha after his return to earth from heaven

usually stopping at Don Mueang Airport. From Ayuthaya, the train continues north to Lopburi (13B, one hour) and beyond.

From Ayuthaya's train station, on the eastern banks of the Mae Nam Pa Sak, the quickest way to reach the old city is to walk west to the river, where you can take a short ferry ride across (3B).

Getting Around

Bikes can be rented at most guesthouses (40B to 50B). Túk-túk can be hired for the day to tour the sites (200B per hour); a trip within the city should be about 20B or about 30B to the train station.

LOPBURI

pop 57,600

An ancient town even by Thai standards, Lopburi has been inhabited since at least the Dvaravati period (6th to 11th centuries AD). Yet while the city is abundant in picturesque stone ruins and statuary, Lopburi actually owes the majority of its tourism-generated income to a renegade gang of trouble-making monkeys who reside in and around Prang Sam Yot, the area's principal shrine.

Information

Hospital (☎ 0 3641 1250)

Post office (Th Phra Narai Maharat)

TAT office (☎ 0 3642 2768; Th Phraya Kamjat)

Tourist police (☎ 0 3641 1013)

Sights

The former palace of King Narai, **Phra Narai Ratchaniwet** (Th Sorasak; 7.30am-5.30pm) is a good place to begin a tour of Lopburi. Built between 1665 and 1677, it was designed by French and Khmer architects, creating an unusual blend of styles. Inside the grounds is the **Lopburi National Museum** (admission 30B; 8.30am-noon & 1-4pm Wed-Sun), which contains an excellent collection of Lopburi period sculpture, as well as an assortment of Khmer, Dvaravati, U Thong and Ayuthaya art, plus traditional farm implements.

Opposite the San Phra Kan, near the Muang Thong Hotel, **Prang Sam Yot** (Sacred Three Spires; admission 30B; 8am-6pm) represents classic Khmer-Lopburi style and is a Hindu-turned-Buddhist temple. Originally, the three towers symbolised the Hindu trinity of Shiva, Vishnu and Brahma. Now two of them contain ruined Lopburi-style Buddha images.

Directly across from the train station, **Wat Phra Si Ratana Mahathat** (admission 30B; 7am-5pm Wed-Sun) is a large 12th-century Khmer temple that's worth a look.

Sleeping & Eating

Noom Guest House (☎ 0 3642 7693; 15-17 Th Phraya Kamjat; r 150-250B) A tiny little dive attached to the

Come On Bar, this budget-backpacker place has a handful of fan rooms with mattress-only beds and shared bathrooms.

Lopburi City Hotel (☎ 0 3641 1245; 1/1-1/5 Th Naprakan; r 300B; ❄) If you've come to Lopburi for the monkeys, this is where you'll want to stay. The creatures have turned the window bars here into their own personal jungle gym. This is otherwise a standard business hotel with air-con and clean showers in every room.

Come On Bar (15-17 Th Phraya Kamjat; dishes 30-120B; 🕑 breakfast & dinner) Attached to Noom Guest House, this open-air bar offers affordable Western breakfasts from 8am to 11am, as well as traditional Thai and Western dishes for dinner. Come nightfall, it's a decent place to mix with backpackers.

Central market (Th Ratchadamnoen & Th Surasongkhram) Just north of the palace, this is a great place to pick up *kài thâwt* or *kài yâang* (fried or grilled chicken) with sticky rice for a long trip further north.

In the evenings a night market sets up along Th Na Phra Kan, with some great little treats for compulsive snackers.

Getting There & Away

Ordinary buses leave from Ayuthaya (47B, 1½ hours, every 10 minutes) or from Bangkok's Northern & Northeastern Bus Terminal (130B, three hours, every 20 minutes). For Kanchanaburi, take a bus to Suphanburi (55B, 2½ hours) and change. The scenery is beautiful along this route.

You can also reach Lopburi by local train from Ayuthaya (3rd class 13B, one hour) or by express train from Bangkok (170B, 1½ hours). One way of visiting Lopburi on the way north is to take the train from Ayuthaya (or Bangkok) early in the morning, leave your gear at the station while you look around, then continue north on the night train.

Getting Around

Săamláw go anywhere in old Lopburi for 30B. Săwngthăew run a regular route between the old and new towns for 8B per person.

PHITSANULOK

pop 100,300

Partly because of its convenient location on an important train route, many travellers use vibrant Phitsanulok as a base for visiting the ancient city of Sukhothai, as well as other parts of the lower north. The town's own attractions include **Wat Phra Si Ratana Mahathat** (known locally as Wat Yai), which contains Phra Phuttha Chinnarat, one of the most beautiful and revered Buddha images in Thailand. Phitsanulok is often abbreviated as 'Philok'.

Information

Internet shops dot the streets around the railway station and on the western bank of the river.

Bangkok Bank (35 Th Naresuan) ATM, plus after-hours exchange window.
Post office (Th Phuttha Bucha)
Pra Buddha Chinnaraj Hospital (☎ 0 5371 1303)
TAT office (☎ 0 5525 2742; 209/7-8 Th Borom Trailokanat; 🕑 8.30am-4.30pm)

Sleeping

London Hotel (☎ 0 5522 5145; 21-22 Soi 1, Th Sailuthai; d 100-150B; 💻) Near Th Phuttha Bucha, this rickety old wooden house resembles a Chinese junk shop; nostalgia buffs will eat this place up. To walk here from the train station, turn left on the main road, then take the first right on to Th Sailuthai.

Phitsanulok Youth Hostel (☎ 0 5524 2060; phitsanulok@tyha.org; 38 Th Sanam Bin; dm/s/d/tr 120/200/300/450B) Philok's youth hostel has something of a lost-in-the-jungle feel to it, complete with swinging hammocks and a large outdoor dining area overflowing with knick-knacks. There is a friendly café here and breakfast is included in the rates. The hostel is 1.5km east of the city centre; take a săamláw (30B).

Lithai Guest House (☎ 0 5521 9626; 73/1-5 Th Phayalithai; r 220-460B; ❄) The 60 rooms here are plain and a touch depressing, although there is a wide variety of options. The priciest choices have air-con, TV and hot showers. Breakfast is included. For something cosier, try the slightly more expensive Bon-Bon Guesthouse next door.

Eating

Phitsanulok is a market crossroads for the country's vegetable industry and gets the pick of the harvest. A good sampler dish is *phàt phàk ruam* (stir-fried vegetables). Sniff out this and other veggie dishes at the **food stalls** (dishes 20-40B), just west of London Hotel near the cinema.

At the night market along the river, a couple of **street vendors** (dishes 40-80B; 🕑 dinner) specialise in preparing *phàk bûng lawy fáa,* which translates as 'flying vegetable' – referring to the 'air' the dish catches as it's tossed in the wok. It's all about the preparation, like watching a cocktail waiter in full flow, as the dish is a fairly standard water spinach stir-fried in soya bean sauce and garlic.

Pa Lai (Th Phuttha Bucha; dishes 20-30B) This noodle shop has become a local legend thanks to its famous *kŭaytĭaw hâwy khàa* (literally, 'legs-hanging rice noodles'). The name comes from the way customers sit on a bench facing the river, with their legs dangling below.

Phae Fa Thai (Th Wangchan; dishes 30-80B) Floating restaurants on the Mae Nam Nan are a hit at night. This old favourite fulfils the senses as much as the stomach with its dinner river cruise; pay a small fee to board the boat and order away from the menu – there is no minimum charge.

Drinking

Along Th Borom Trailokanat near the Pailyn Hotel is a string of popular, rockin' Thai pubs. **Jao Samran** (Th Borom Trailokanat) features live Thai-folk and pop with food from 6pm and music from 8pm.

The most happening nightspot in town is the **Phitsanulok Bazaar** (Th Naresuan), where several pubs and dance clubs are clustered in a hedonist's mall. It doesn't get started until at least 9pm, but it is heaving by midnight.

Getting There & Away

Thai Airways International (☎ 0 5525 8020; www.thaiair.com; 209/26-28 Th Borom Trailokanat) offers daily connections between Phitsanulok and Bangkok.

Phitsanulok is a major junction between the north and northeast. Most buses stop at the government bus station on Hwy 12 about 1.5km from the town centre. Buses for Bangkok depart from private bus company offices in the town centre on Th Ekathotsarot, south of the train station.

Available bus trips include Bangkok (air-con 185B to 250B, six hours), Chiang Mai (ordinary/air-con 140/196B, five hours), Sukhothai (ordinary/air-con 24/33B, one hour, every 30 minutes from 6am to 6pm), Kamphaeng Phet (ordinary/air-con 43/60B, two hours) and Khon Kaen (ordinary 130B, air-con 153B to 203B, five hours).

The train station is located in the centre of town on Th Ekathotsarot and Th Naresuan. Trains to Bangkok (1st/2nd/3rd class 324/159/69B, ordinary eight to nine hours, rapid seven hours) are a more convenient option, since Bangkok's train station is in the centre of the city.

Trains north to Chiang Mai (1st/2nd/3rd class 269/122/52B, five hours) usually depart in the afternoon.

Getting Around

Buses run between the town centre and the airport (bus 4) or bus terminal (bus 1) for 4B. The TAT office distributes a local bus route hand-out. The terminal for city buses is south of the train station on Th Ekathotsarot. Săamláw rides within the town centre should cost you around 20B to 30B per person.

Run by TAT, the Phitsanulok Tour Tramway (PTT) lets you see all the sights in one day. The tram leaves from Wat Yai at 9am, costs 20B and stops at 15 sights before returning to Wat Yai at 3pm.

Motorcycles can be rented at **PN Motorbike** (☎ 0 5524 2424; Th Borom Trailokanat). Rates are 200B per day for a 125cc motorbike.

SUKHOTHAI

pop 39,800

Established in the 13th century and subsequently going on to be the centre of rule for more than 150 years, Sukhothai (Rising Happiness) was the first independent kingdom of Siam. Before its rise, the Khmer empire had extended its own influence deep into modern-day Thailand. But thanks to Sukhothai's formidable sway, the emerging Thai nation managed to flourish in massive leaps and bounds – artistically, and especially architecturally – before it was eventually superseded by Ayuthaya to the south. If you can only digest one 'ancient city', Sukhothai should top the list; the ruins here are better preserved and less urban than those at Ayuthaya.

The modern town of Sukhothai (12km from the ruins) doesn't quite live up to its ancestor. It is a standard provincial town, and many travellers opt for Sukhothai as a day trip from nearby Phitsanulok.

Information

There are banks with ATMs scattered around the central part of New Sukhothai, plus one in Old Sukhothai. Internet is common in New Sukhothai and some guesthouses offer access. The tourist police maintain an office in the Sukhothai Historical Park, opposite the Ramkhamhaeng National Museum.

Post office (Th Nikhon Kasem, New Sukhothai; 8.30am-noon Mon-Fri, 1-4.30pm Sat & Sun) Has an attached international phone office.

TAT office (Th Prawet Nakhon; 9am-5pm Mon-Fri) North of the River View Hotel in New Sukhothai.

Sights

The original capital of the first Thai kingdom was surrounded by three concentric ramparts and two moats bridged by four gateways. Today the area is known as the Sukhothai Historical Park, and the remains of 21 historical sites can be seen within the old walls, plus there are 70 sites within a 5km radius. The ruins are divided into five zones and there is a 30B admission fee for each zone; the central zone is 40B, plus 10B if you ride in on a bicycle. Invest in the 150B ticket that includes entrance to all sites and associated museums.

A lot of the religious symbolism here is lost on a Westerner; see What's a Wat? (p720) for a beginner's dip into this complicated realm.

The historical park (or *meuang kào* – 'old city') is best reached from town by sǎwngthǎew (10B, every half-hour from 6am to 6pm) leaving from Th Jarot Withithong near the Mae Yom, across the street from the 7-Eleven. Bicycles (20B) are essential for getting around the park and can be rented at the gate.

CENTRAL ZONE

Ramkhamhaeng National Museum (admission 30B; 9am-4pm) provides an introduction to Sukhothai history and culture and is a good place to begin exploring. If it were air-conditioned there would be a lot more 30B scholars.

The crown jewel of the old city, **Wat Mahathat** is one of the best examples of Sukhothai architecture, typified by the classic lotus-bud stupa that features a conical spire topping a square-sided structure on a three-tiered base. This vast assemblage, the largest in the city, once contained 198 *chedi*, as well as various chapels and sanctuaries. Some of the original Buddha images remain, including a 9m standing Buddha among the broken columns.

Wat Si Sawai, just south of Wat Mahathat, has three Khmer-style *praang* and a moat. From images found in the *chedi*, this was originally a Hindu temple, later retrofitted for Buddhism.

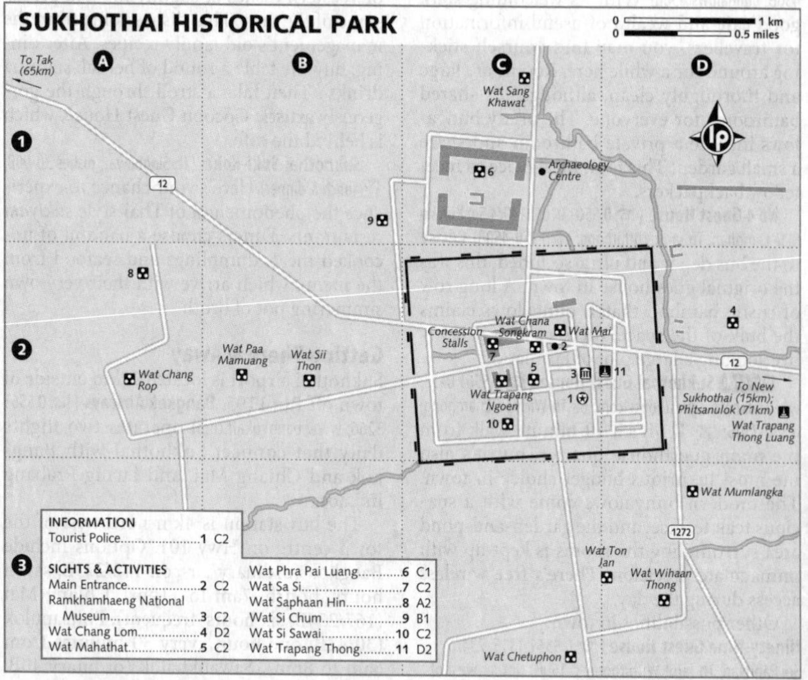

THAILAND

Wat Sa Si is a classically simple Sukhothai-style temple set on an island. **Wat Trapang Thong**, next to the museum, is reached by the footbridge crossing the large, lotus-filled pond that surrounds it. It remains in use today.

OTHER ZONES

In the northwestern corner, **Wat Si Chum** contains a massive seated Buddha tightly squeezed into this open, walled building. Somewhat isolated to the north of the city, **Wat Phra Pai Luang** is similar in style to Wat Si Sawai. **Wat Chang Lom**, to the east, is surrounded by 36 elephants. **Wat Saphaan Hin** is a couple of kilometres west of the old city walls on a hillside and features a large Buddha looking back to Sukhothai.

Sleeping

At the bus station a small sǎwngthǎew mafia has emerged to promote guesthouses that pay commissions. If you're set on a particular guesthouse, don't believe them when they say the place is closed or dirty – always check for yourself.

Ban Thai (☎ 0 5561 0163; guesthouse_banthai@yahoo.com; Th Prawet Nakhon; d with shared bathroom 150-450B, bungalows 450B) With its welcoming staff, good café and wealth of useful information for travellers, you may find yourself sticking around for a while here. Rooms are large and thoroughly clean, although it's shared bathrooms for everyone. The pretty bungalows include a private bathroom and share a small garden. This is an ideal place to meet fellow backpackers.

No 4 Guest House (☎ 0 5561 0165; 140/4 Soi Khlong Mae Lamphan, Th Jarot Withithong; s & d 150-450B) Close to the bus depot and ultra-secluded, this was the original guesthouse in town. A long row of rustic bamboo-thatch bungalows claims the bulk of the space; there's also a balcony overlooking a large plot of farmland.

our pick Sukhothai Guest House (☎ 0 5561 0453; www.sukhothaiguesthouse.com; 68 Th Wichien Chamhong; d 350-750B;) It's a 10-minute walk from the main guesthouse quarter, but it's also the most luxurious budget choice in town. The modern bungalows come with a spacious teak terrace, and the garden-and-pond area surrounding the rooms is kept up with immaculate precision. There's free wireless access during the day.

Other possibilities in town:

Ninety-Nine Guest House (☎ 0 5561 1315; 234/6 Soi Panitsan, Th Jarot Withithong; d 150B) Not far west of No 4, this teak family house has cheap, clean rooms with shared bathroom.

JJ Guest House (jjguesthouse@hotmail.com; Soi Khlong Mae Ramphan; r 300-600B;) Large and modern bungalows, friendly staff and a kitchen famous for its fresh breads and pastries.

Eating

Thai towns love to claim a signature dish as their own and Sukhothai weighs in with its own version of *kǔaytǐaw* (noodle soup). In addition to the basic recipe, cutting-edge cooks add pickled cabbage, pork skins and peanuts for a local twist. Only *kǔaytǐaw* purists will notice the difference. The **night market** (Th Jarot Withithong & Th Rat Uthit), near the Mae Nam Yom bridge, and the **municipal market** (btwn Th Rat Uthit & Th Ratchathani) are purveyors of this and other quick eats.

Evening meals centre on the series of open-air restaurants south of Chinnawat Hotel just off Th Nikhon Kasem.

Dream Cafe (86/1 Th Singhawat; dishes 80-150B) Decorated with the owner's own 19th-century Thai antique collection, this restaurant is truly a feast for the eyes. The menu features a bevy of Western dishes at slightly inflated prices; some of the tasty Thai dishes come from the management's old family recipes. After dining, buy the table a round of herbal 'stamina drinks'. Then take a stroll through the gorgeously artistic Cocoon Guest House, which is behind the café.

Sukhothai Suki-Koka (Th Singhawat; dishes 30-90B; lunch & dinner) Here's your chance to experience the phenomenon of Thai-style *sukiyaki* restaurants. Diners choose a handful of uncooked meat, dumplings and seafood from the menu, which arrive with their very own simmering pot of broth.

Getting There & Away

Sukhothai airport is located 27km outside of town off Rte 1195. **Bangkok Airways** (☎ 0 5563 3266; www.bangkokair.com) operates two flights daily that connect Sukhothai with Bangkok and Chiang Mai, and Luang Prabang in Laos.

The bus station is 4km northwest of the town centre on Hwy 101. Options include Bangkok (ordinary/air-con 142/273B, seven hours, hourly 7am to 11pm), Chiang Mai (167/234B, six hours, frequent), Phitsanulok (30/42B, one hour, every 30 minutes from 6am to 8pm), Sawankhalok (ordinary 40B, hourly), Si Satchanalai (27/38B, one hour, hourly) and Tak (40/56B, 1½ hours, hourly).

Getting Around

From the bus station a chartered săwngthăew should cost 40B to any guesthouse. When returning to the bus station, catch a public săwngthăew (6B) in front of the 7-Eleven on Th Jarot Withithong. Across the road is the stop for buses to the old city (15B).

SI SATCHANALAI-CHALIANG HISTORICAL PARK

Set amid rolling mountains, Si Satchanalai and Chaliang were a later extension of the Sukhothai empire. The **park** (admission 40B, plus per car/bicycle/motorcycle 50/10/30B; 8.30am-5pm) encompasses ruins of the old cities of Si Satchanalai and Chaliang, 56km north of Sukhothai.

Climb to the top of the hill supporting **Wat Khao Phanom Phloeng** for a view over the town and river. **Wat Chedi Jet Thaew** has a group of stupas in classic Sukhothai style. **Wat Chang Lom** has a *chedi* surrounded by Buddha statues set in niches and guarded by the fine remains of some elephant buttresses. Walk along the riverside for 2km or go back down the main road and cross the river to **Wat Phra Si Ratana Mahathat**, a very impressive temple that has a well-preserved *praang* and a variety of seated and standing Buddhas.

The Si Satchanalai-Chaliang area was traditionally famous for its beautiful **pottery**, much of which was exported. The Indonesians were once keen collectors, and some fine specimens can still be seen in the National Museum in Jakarta. Much of the pottery was made in Si Satchanalai. Rejects, buried in the fields, are still being discovered. Several of the old kilns have been carefully excavated and can be viewed along with original pottery samples at the **Si Satchanalai Centre for Study & Preservation of Sangkhalok Kilns** (admission 30B). So far the centre has opened two phases of its construction to the public: a site in Chaliang with excavated pottery samples and one kiln; and a larger outdoor site, 2km northwest of the Si Satchanalai ruins. The exhibits are very well presented despite the lack of English labels.

Si Satchanalai-Chaliang Historical Park is off Rte 101 between Sawankhalok and new Si Satchanalai. From Sukhothai, take a Si Satchanalai bus (ordinary/air-con 27/38B, one hour) and ask to get off at *meuang kào* (old city). The last bus back leaves around 4pm.

KAMPHAENG PHET

pop 27,500

Kamphaeng Phet (Diamond Wall) previously played a role as an important front line of defence for the Sukhothai kingdom. It's a nice place to spend a day or so wandering around the ruins and experiencing a small northern provincial capital that sees few tourists.

The **Kamphaeng Phet Historical Park** (☎ 0 5571 1921; admission 40B, plus per bicycle/motorcycle 10/20B; 8am-5pm) contains a number of temple ruins, as well as the very fine remains of a long city wall. Wat Phra Sri Iriyabot features the shattered remains of standing, sitting, walking and reclining Buddha images. Wat Chang Rop (Temple Surrounded by Elephants) is just that – a temple that has an elephant-buttressed wall.

Sleeping & Eating

Teak Tree Guest House (☎ 0 1675 6471; Soi 1 Th Chakungrao; s/d 170/250B) Next to the old city wall, the Teak Tree Guest House is the original guesthouse in town – just three fan rooms set in a tidy wooden house on stilts with shared hot-water bathroom. Open high season only.

Three J Guest House (☎ 0 5571 3129; threejguest@hotmail.com; 79 Th Rachavitee; r 200-400B;) Mr Charin, the congenial host of this backpackers' bungalow set-up, is happy to pick up guests from the bus terminal. Each of the bungalows is different, and the cheaper ones share a clean bathroom. Bicycles and motorbikes are available for rent.

A small night market sets up every evening in front of the provincial offices, near the old city walls, and there are some cheap restaurants near the roundabout.

Getting There & Away

The government bus station is located across the river from town and is served by the following destinations: Bangkok (ordinary/air-con 125/165B), Sukhothai (45B, 1½ hours), Phitsanulok (ordinary/air-con 43/60B, two hours) and Tak (35B).

MAE SOT

Like many border towns, Mae Sot is a hotbed of illicit activities. Gems, drugs and even the Burmese people themselves are smuggled here from neighbouring Myanmar, although the chances are quite low that an average tourist will bear witness to any of these questionable goings-on. What visitors will see, however, is nearly as unique: due to its strategic border location and its proximity to hill-tribe regions, Mae Sot is a colourful and curious mix of Indo-Burmese, Chinese, Karen, Hmong and Thai. The town also hosts a relatively large population of Western doctors and NGO aid workers, whose presence attests to the human cost of an unstable border.

Săwngthăew can take you right to the Mae Nam Moei border for 10B.

Route 1085 runs north from Mae Sot to Mae Hong Son Province and makes an interesting trip.

GETTING TO MYANMAR

Frequent săwngthăew (10B) go to the Burmese border across the Mae Nam Moei, 6km from Mae Sot, to Myawaddy. This border periodically closes due to fighting, but currently foreigners are allowed to do a day crossing into Myawaddy, a fairly typical Burmese town, for a fee of US$10. The Pan-Asian Hwy (Asia Rte 1) continues from here west to Mawlamyine (Moulmein) and Yangon – and eventually Istanbul – but that adventure still sits in the 'some day' category. The border is open from 6am to 6pm.

Information

There are several banks with ATMs in the town centre.

DK Book House (Th Intharakhiri) Attached to the DK Mae Sot Square Hotel, it has good maps.

River Book Exchange (☎ 0 5553 4700; Th Intharakhiri; 🕑 10am-6pm Mon-Fri) Good for tourist information, plus free maps and lots of information about local volunteer opportunities and Thai language lessons. Ask for Prasong.

Southeast Asia Tours (Th Intharakhiri) Internet access and international calls.

Tourist police (☎ 0 5553 3523, 0 5553 4341; Th Asia) One block east of the bus terminal.

Sleeping

Green Guest House (☎ 0 5553 3207; www.greenguesthouse.th.gs; 460/9 Th Intharakhiri; dm/s/d from 100/150/200-250B; 💻) Run by an English-teaching husband-and-wife team, this friendly place is close to the main săwngthăew departure terminal. At the time of research, a new dorm building was being constructed. Wi-fi access available for 10B an hour.

our pick Ban Thai Guest House (☎ 0 5553 1590; www.mountain-designs.com/accom/banthai.html; 740 Th Intharakhiri; s/d from 250/450B; ❄ 💻) The guesthouse of choice among volunteers, this is Mae Sot's best budget accommodation. Five converted Thai houses sit atop a well-manicured lawn, and the common area, where you're practically guaranteed to meet someone interesting, has free wi-fi access. Ask about long-term discounts.

Eating

The day market intersects with Th Prasat Withi near Siam Hotel and extends for several winding blocks to a covered area surrounded by simple Burmese food counters. A favourite local snack is *krabawng jaw* (Burmese for 'fried crispy'), a sort of vegetable tempura. While you tuck into your curry, other customers might stop in for a nip of the under-the-counter hooch.

Food stalls set up at night along Th Prasat Withi. Several Burmese-Indian shops, opposite the mosque, serve curries, *khâo sawy* (chicken curry with noodles) and tasty samosas (in the morning).

Aiya Restaurant (533 Th Intharakhiri; dishes 30-160B; ☎ lunch & dinner) Directly across the street from the popular Bai Fern restaurant, this (definitely superior) eatery offers a unique menu of Thai and Burmese dishes along with some Western standards and vegetarian dishes. There's a small art gallery upstairs and live music on Friday and Saturday at 8pm; inquire here about Burmese language conversation courses.

Drinking

For a night on the town Mae Sot style, head to the bars at the western end of Th Intharakhiri. A current favourite is **Thaime's** (Th Intharakhiri), featuring an extensive selection of mixed drinks, live music and many drunken travellers and volunteers. It's between No 4 Guest House and Bai Fern.

Getting There & Away

The Mae Sot airport was not operating at the time of research. For updates, contact **Phuket Air** (code 9R; ☎ 0 5553 1440; www.phuketairlines.com).

The government bus station, which is located just off Th Asia, handles transport to Bangkok (air-con/VIP 365/565B, nine hours).

For travel to any other destination, it is best to change in Tak (ordinary/air-con 53/74B), which offers smooth connections to points in the north such as Lampang and Chiang Mai. You can also travel the western rim of Thailand by catching a bus or săwngthăew to Mae Sariang (160B, six hours) for transport to Mae Hong Son.

NORTHERN THAILAND

The peaks and valleys of northern Thailand are the guardians of an abundance of natural and cultural attractions that make it a must for most travellers traversing the kingdom. These ancient mountains cascade across northern Thailand, Myanmar and south-western China, where Yunnanese trading caravans of mule-driven carts once followed the mountain ridges all the way to the sea. Centuries before, another group, considered to be the original Thais, followed a similar route into the lush river valleys of what is modern-day Thailand. Eventually the independent state known as Lanna Thai (Million Thai Rice Fields) emerged here; its modern descendants maintain a distinct northern culture that is not easily diluted by the passage of time. Other wanderers, such as the autonomous hill-tribe peoples, traversed the range, limited only by altitude rather than political boundaries.

Travellers trek through the wilderness towards hill-tribe villages hoping to find out what they lost when life became as easy as the flick of a switch. Along twisting mountain roads, small towns awaken to a thick morning fog, offering the simple pleasures of reflective walks and breathtaking vistas.

CHIANG MAI

pop 1.6 million

To Thais, Chiang Mai is a national treasure – a cultured symbol of nationhood. For visitors, it's a cool place to kick back and soak up some of the Thai-ness that may have been missed on the beaches of the south coast. The climate is forgiving, bookshops outmuscle synthetic shopping centres, and the region's unique cultural heritage is worn as proudly as its vibrant hand-woven textiles. For culture vultures, Chiang Mai forms a playground, with classes in Thai language, cooking, meditation and massage.

The old city of Chiang Mai is a neat square bounded by moats and remnants of a medieval-style wall built 700 years ago to defend against Burmese invaders. A furious stream of traffic flows around the old city, but inside narrow *soi* branch off the clogged arteries into a quiet world of charming guesthouses, leafy gardens and friendly smiles.

Orientation

Th Moon Muang, along the east moat, is the main traveller centre. Intersecting with Th Moon Muang, Th Tha Phae runs east from the exterior of the moat towards the Mae Nam Ping. Once it crosses the river, the road is renamed Th Charoen Muang and eventually arrives at the main post office and train station.

Finding your way around Chiang Mai is fairly simple. A copy of Nancy Chandler's *Map Guide to Chiang Mai* is a good investment if you plan extensive exploration of the city. Pick up a copy at bookshops or guesthouses.

Information

BOOKSHOPS

By the Book (42 Th Ratwithi; 🕓 10am-1am) Booze, billiards and used books – what a concept!

DK Book House (Th Kotchasan) New books on history, culture and travel in the region.

Gecko Books (☎ 0 5387 4066; Th Chiang Moi Kao) Largest choice of used books in the city.

Suriwong Book Centre (☎ 0 5328 1052; 54 Th Si Donchai) Best selection of new books in town.

EMERGENCY

Tourist police (☎ 0 5327 8798, 24hr emergency 1155; Th Chiang Mai-Lamphun; 🕓 6am-midnight) Near the TAT office, Chiang Mai's tourist police enjoys a good reputation.

INTERNET ACCESS

Internet cafés are everywhere.

Chiang Mai Disabled Center (☎ 0 5321 3941; www.infothai.com/disabled; 133/1 Th Ratchaphakhinai; per hr 20B) A nonprofit organisation funding services for the disabled. Provides internet access, bicycle rental and massages.

INTERNET RESOURCES

Chiang Mai Online (www.chiangmai-online.com) Basic background on Chiang Mai, along with comprehensive accommodation listings.

City Life (www.chiangmainews.com) Articles on local events, culture and art, plus current news.

Yellow Chiang Mai (www.yellowthailand.com/chiangmai) A searchable citywide phonebook complete with user-generated content.

MEDIA

Chiangmai Mail Weekly newspaper, good for local news.
City Life Popular with residents and tourists; articles on local culture and politics, and events listings.

MEDICAL SERVICES

Chiang Mai Ram Hospital (☎ 0 5322 4861; Th Bunreuangrit) The most sophisticated hospital in town.
Malaria Centre (☎ 0 5322 1529; 18 Th Bunreuangrit) Does free blood checks for malaria.
McCormick Hospital (☎ 0 5324 1311; Th Kaew Nawarat) The best-value place for minor treatment.

MONEY

All major Thai banks have several branches throughout Chiang Mai, many of them along Th Tha Phae, and there is no shortage of ATMs around town.

POST

Main post office (Th Charoen Muang) East of town; there's also a handy branch at the airport.

TELEPHONE

Overseas calls can also be made from one of the private offices along Th Tha Phae.
CAT office (Th Charoen Muang; 7am-10pm) Behind the main post office.

TOURIST INFORMATION

TAT office (☎ 0 5324 8604; 105/1 Th Chiang Mai-Lamphun; 8am-4.30pm) Has a list of registered trekking guides, plus maps and brochures.

Dangers & Annoyances

Many travellers have reported that their belongings (particularly credit cards) stored at Chiang Mai guesthouses have gone walkabout while they are trekking. Most guesthouses recommend you take such sensitive items with you, but be sure that you are travelling in safe areas as there are occasional incidents of whole trekking groups being robbed in the jungle. You can't win on this one, so before you stow your bags, make an itemised list of all belongings, including travellers cheques, and note your credit card balance.

Guesthouses in Chiang Mai have recently reported a rise in bag snatchings; local men on motorbikes are the usual perpetrators, and women carrying conspicuous purses seem to be the most common victims. See p732 for more crafty scams.

Sights

TEMPLES

Chiang Mai has more than 300 temples – almost as many as Bangkok, which is a far larger city. The temple architecture here is markedly different from other parts of Thailand. Notice the intricate woodcarvings and colourful murals; these are hallmarks of the Lanna period (13th and 14th centuries). Three-tiered umbrellas adorning the tops of the temples, Singha lions guarding the entrances and high-base *chedi* are all Burmese influences imported into the city by wealthy teak merchants when they migrated to this important trade centre.

Wat Phra Singh (☎ 0 5381 4164; Th Singharat; 6am-6pm) is the real star amid the inner city's soaring stupas, and a perfect example of Lanna architecture. Established in 1345, this wat contains murals depicting Lanna customs and dress, as well as a scripture repository. It is also the focal point for Songkran (Water Festival) festivities in mid-April.

Wat Chiang Man (☎ 0 5337 5368; Th Ratchaphakhinai; 6am-6pm) is the oldest wat within the city walls and was erected by King Mengrai, Chiang Mai's founder, in 1296. Two famous Buddha images (Buddha Sila and the Crystal Buddha) are kept here in the *wíhăan* to the right of the main *bòht*. The Crystal Buddha is believed to have the power to bring seasonal rains.

Wat Chedi Luang (☎ 0 5327 8595; Th Phra Pokklao; 6am-6pm) contains the ruins of a huge *chedi* that collapsed during an earthquake in 1545. A partial restoration has preserved the 'ruined' look while ensuring the *chedi* doesn't crumble further. The venerable Emerald Buddha, now housed in Bangkok's Wat Phra Kaew, occupied the eastern niche here in 1475.

Wat Jet Yot (☎ 0 5321 9483; Superhighway; 6am-6pm) is modelled somewhat imperfectly on the Mahabodhi Temple in Bodhgaya, India. The seven spires represent the seven weeks Buddha was supposed to have spent in Bodhgaya after his enlightenment. Find it near the National Museum, 1.5km northwest of town.

Wat Suan Dok (☎ 0 5327 8967; Th Suthep; 6am-6pm) contains a 500-year-old bronze Buddha image and colourful jataka murals showing scenes from Buddha's past lives. Scenic sunsets are the temple's biggest attraction, especially for shutterbugs. A 'monk chat' from

5pm to 7pm Monday, Wednesday and Friday is hosted, free of charge, on the grounds, for foreigners to meet and chat with novice monks studying at the monastic university. It's 1km west of town.

Wat U Mong (☎ 0 5327 3990; Soi Wat U Mong; ⏰ 6am-6pm) is a forest temple dating from Mengrai's rule and has a fine image of the fasting Buddha. Brick-lined tunnels in an unusual-looking large, flat-topped hill were supposedly fashioned around 1380 for a clairvoyant monk; some are still open for exploration. Resident foreign monks give talks in English on Sunday afternoon at 3pm by the lake. It's 4km west of town.

CHIANG MAI NATIONAL MUSEUM

Lanna history and artworks are documented at the **Chiang Mai National Museum** (☎ 0 5322 1308; Hwy 11/Superhighway northern loop; admission 30B; ⏰ 9am-4pm Wed-Sun), 500m past Wat Jet Yot, northwest of town. Buddha images, northern Thai handicrafts and pottery fill the halls.

TRIBAL MUSEUM

If you decide against trekking through the hill-tribe villages, check out the worthwhile **Tribal Museum** (☎ 0 5321 0872; Th Chotana; admission free; ⏰ 9am-4pm Mon-Fri, slide & video shows 10am-2pm) at Ratchamangkhla Park north of the city. This renovated museum houses a large collection of artefacts and other displays on the various cultural nuances and ethnic backgrounds of the hill tribes in Thailand.

CHIANG MAI NIGHT BAZAAR

Chiang Mai's leading tourist attraction is in fact the legacy of the original Yunnanese trading caravans that stopped here along the ancient trade route between Simao (in China) and Mawlamyine (on Myanmar's Indian Ocean coast). Today commerce is alive and well, sprawling over several blocks on Th Chang Khlan from Th Tha Phae to Th Si Donchai, towards the river. Made up of several different covered areas, ordinary glass-fronted shops and dozens of street vendors, the market offers a huge variety of Thai and northern Thai goods. Some good buys include Phrae-style *sêua mâw hâwm* (blue cotton farmer's shirt), northern and northeastern Thai hand-woven fabrics, *yâam* (woven shoulder bags) and hill-tribe crafts – many tribespeople set up their own stalls here, while the Akha wander around on foot.

Activities

ROCK CLIMBING

Chiang Mai Rock Climbing Adventures (☎ 0 6911 1470; www.thailandclimbing.com; 55/3 Th Ratchaphakhinai; day trips per person 1500-2000B, multiday intensives 5500-9500B) organises climbs of the limestone cliffs called Crazy Horse Buttress, behind Tham Meuang On, about 20km east of Chiang Mai.

TREKKING

Chiang Mai is one of the most popular places in Thailand to arrange a trek. Many guesthouses and lots of travel agents are looking for a slice of the action in this 'competitive' (read cut-throat) business, so it pays to shop around before signing up. Most treks include visits to minority villages, some jungle action, plus the option of rafting or elephant rides. See p740 for more on trekking in northern Thailand.

Courses

BUDDHIST MEDITATION

Northern Insight Meditation Centre (☎ 0 5327 8620; watrampoeng@hotmail.com; Wat Ram Poeng; admission free) Ten- to 26-day individual intensive courses in *vipassana* (insight meditation) are taught by a Thai monk or nun, with Western students or bilingual Thais acting as interpreters.

Wat Suan Dok (☎ 0 5327 3105/20/49; Th Suthep; admission free) An English-language introduction to Buddhist meditation from Sunday afternoon to Monday morning, with an overnight stay at the monastery, 4km west of town.

COOKING

Cooking classes are a big hit in Chiang Mai and typically include an introduction to Thai herbs and spices, a local market tour, cooking instructions and a recipe booklet. Plus you get to eat the delicious Thai food you cook – everything from Chiang Mai–style chicken curry to steamed banana cake. Cooking classes usually cost 700B to 1000B a day.

We've heard consistently good things about the following places:

Baan Thai (☎ 0 5335 7339; www.cookinthai.com; 11 Soi 5, Th Ratchadamnoen) Lunch and dinner courses.

Chiang Mai Thai Cookery School (☎ 0 5320 6388; www.thaicookeryschool.com; 1-3 Th Moon Muang) Owned by a famous Thai TV chef.

Gap's Thai Culinary Art School (☎ 0 5327 8140; gap_house@hotmail.com; Gap's House, 3 Soi 4, Th Ratchadamnoen)

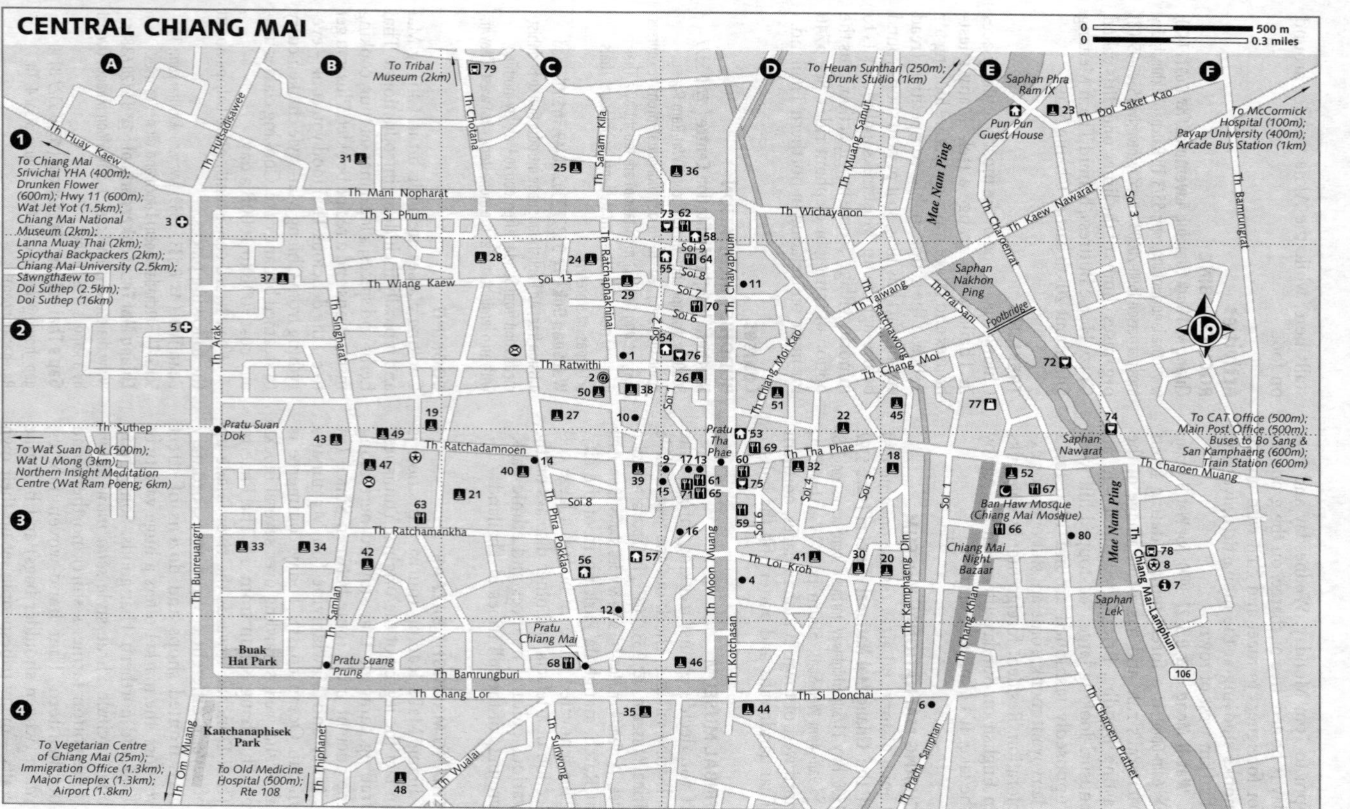

CENTRAL CHIANG MAI
0 500 m
0 0.3 miles
To Chiang Mai Srivichai YHA (400m); Drunken Flower (600m); Hwy 11 (600m); Wat Jet Yot (1.5km); Chiang Mai National Museum (2km); Lanna Muay Thai (2km); Spicythai Backpackers (2km); Chiang Mai University (2.5km); Sawngthaew to Doi Suthep (2.5km); Doi Suthep (16km)
To Tribal Museum (2km)
To Heuan Sunthari (250m); Drunk Studio (1km)
To McCormick Hospital (100m); Payap University (400m); Arcade Bus Station (1km)
To CAT Office (500m); Main Post Office (500m); Buses to Bo Sang & San Kamphaeng (600m); Train Station (600m)
To Wat Suan Dok (500m); Wat U Mong (3km); Northern Insight Meditation Centre (Wat Ram Poeng; 6km)
To Vegetarian Centre of Chiang Mai (25m); Immigration Office (1.3km); Major Cineplex (1.3km); Airport (1.8km)
To Old Medicine Hospital (500m); Rte 108
Th Huay Kaew
Th Hutsadisawee
Th Arak
Th Suthep
Th Bunreuangrit
Th Om Muang
Th Thiphanet
Th Wualai
Th Mani Nopharat
Th Si Phum
Th Singharat
Th Wiang Kaew
Th Chotana
Th Sanam Kila
Th Ratchaphakhinai
Th Ratwithi
Th Ratchadamnoen
Th Ratchamankha
Th Phra Pokklao
Th Samlan
Th Bamrungburi
Th Chang Lor
Th Suriwong
Th Moon Muang
Th Kotchasan
Th Chaiyaphum
Th Chiang Moi Kao
Th Tha Phae
Th Loi Kroh
Th Si Donchai
Th Kamphaeng Din
Th Chang Moi
Th Ratchawong
Th Tawang
Th Wichayanon
Th Muang Samut
Th Prai Sani
Th Chang Khlan
Th Pracha Samphan
Th Charoen Prathet
Th Charoen Muang
Th Chiang Mai-Lamphun
Th Charoenrat
Th Kaew Nawarat
Th Doi Saket Kao
Th Bamrungrat
Soi 1
Soi 2
Soi 3
Soi 4
Soi 6
Soi 7
Soi 8
Soi 9
Soi 13
Pratu Suan Dok
Pratu Suang Prung
Pratu Chiang Mai
Pratu Tha Phae
Buak Hat Park
Kanchanaphisek Park
Mae Nam Ping
Saphan Phra Ram IX
Pun Pun Guest House
Saphan Nakhon Ping
Footbridge
Saphan Nawarat
Saphan Lek
Ban Haw Mosque (Chiang Mai Mosque)
Chiang Mai Night Bazaar
106
A B C D E F
1 2 3 4

INFORMATION
By the Book......1 C2
Chiang Mai Disabled Center......2 C2
Chiang Mai Ram Hospital......3 A1
DK Book House......4 D3
Gecko Books......(see 69)
Malaria Centre......5 A2
Suriwong Book Centre......6 E4
TAT Office......7 F3
Tourist Police......8 F3

SIGHTS & ACTIVITIES
American University Alumni......9 D3
Baan Thai......10 C2
Ban Nit......11 D2
Chiang Mai Rock Climbing Adventures......12 C3
Chiang Mai Thai Cookery School......13 D3
Chiang Mai Thai Language Center......14 C3
Gap's Thai Culinary Art School......15 D3
Jungle Survival Cooking Course......16 D3
Lek Chaiya......17 D3
Wat Bupparam......18 E3
Wat Chai Kiat......19 B2
Wat Chang Khong......20 E3
Wat Chedi Luang......21 C3
Wat Chetawan......22 D2
Wat Chetuphon......23 E1
Wat Chiang Man......24 C2
Wat Chiang Yuen......25 C1
Wat Dok Euang......26 D2
Wat Duang Di......27 C2
Wat Hua Khwang......28 C2
Wat Lam Chang......29 C2
Wat Loi Kroh......30 D3
Wat Lokmoli......31 B1
Wat Mahawan......32 D3
Wat Meh Thang......33 B3
Wat Meun Ngoen Kong......34 B3
Wat Muang Mang......35 C4
Wat Pa Pao......36 D1
Wat Pa Phrao Nai......37 B2
Wat Pan Ping......38 C2
Wat Phan An......39 C3
Wat Phan Tao......40 C3
Wat Phan Thong......41 D3
Wat Phra Jao Mengrai......42 B3
Wat Phra Singh......43 B3
Wat Pugchang......44 D4
Wat Saen Fang......45 E2
Wat Sai Mun Myanmar......46 D4
Wat Si Koet......47 B3
Wat Sisupan......48 B4
Wat Thung Yu......49 B3
Wat U Mong Klang Wiang......50 C2
Wat U Sai Kham......51 D2
Wat Upakhut......52 E3

SLEEPING
Daret's House......53 D3
Eagle House 2......54 D2
Grace House......55 D2
Julie Guesthouse......56 C3
Same-Same Guesthouse......57 C3
SK House......58 D1

EATING
Aroon (Rai) Restaurant......59 D3
Art Café......60 D3
AUM Vegetarian Restaurant......61 D3
Biaporn......62 D1
Heuan Phen......63 B3
Indian Restaurant......64 D2
Jerusalem Falafel......65 D3
Kalare Food Centre......66 E3
Khao Soi Islam......67 E3
Pratu Chiang Mai Night Market......68 C4
Pulcinella da Stefano......69 D3
Somphet Market......70 D2
Zest......71 D3

DRINKING
Brasserie......72 E2
Rasta Art Bar & Restaurant......73 D1
Riverside Bar & Restaurant......74 F2
THC......75 D3
UN Irish Pub......76 D2

SHOPPING
Warorot Market......77 E2

TRANSPORT
Buses to Lampang......78 F3
Chang Pheuak Bus Station......79 C1
Chiang Mai Disabled Center......(see 2)
Contact Travel......80 E3

Jungle Survival Cooking Course (☎ 0 5320 8661; www.smilehousechiangmai.com; Smile House, 5 Th Ratchamankha) Learn how to live in the wild using only your wits.

LANGUAGE

American University Alumni (AUA; ☎ 0 5327 8407; aualanna@loxinfo.co.th; 73 Th Ratchadamnoen; 30/60hr course 2700/3500B) The basic AUA Thai course consists of three levels with 60 hours of instruction. There are also 30-hour courses in 'small talk', reading and writing, and northern Thai dialect.

Chiang Mai Thai Language Center (☎ 0 5327 7810; cmat@loxinfo.co.th; 131 Th Ratchadamnoen; 30hr course 2200B) Thai language courses from beginners to advanced.

Payap University (☎ 0 5330 4805, ext 250-1; intpros@payap.ac.th; Th Kaew Nawarat; 60/120hr course 6000/12,000B) Intensive Thai language courses at beginning, intermediate and advanced levels. Conversational skills, reading and writing, and Thai culture.

MUAY THAI (THAI BOXING)

Lanna Muay Thai (Kiatbusaba; ☎ 0 5389 2102; www.lannamuaythai.com; 64/1 Soi Chiang Khian; day/month courses 250/7000B) A boxing camp northwest of town that offers authentic *muay thai* instruction to foreigners as well as Thais. Lanna-trained *kàthoey* boxer Parinya Kiatbusaba triumphed at Lumphini stadium in Bangkok in 1998. Part of his opening routine, when the boxers pay homage to their trainers, included a flamboyant show of putting on make-up.

TRADITIONAL MASSAGE

More visitors learn the art of Thai massage in Chiang Mai than anywhere else in Thailand. Tuition starts at around 3500B for 10 days. The following places are recommended for their massage classes:

Ban Nit (☎ 0 1180 9769; Soi 2, Th Chaiyaphum; day/week courses from 1000/3500B; 🕒 10am-4.30pm) A unique, one-on-one course in deep-tissue, nerve and herbal massages. Most students live in and eat meals with Nit and her family.

Lek Chaiya (☎ 0 5327 8325; www.nervetouch.com; 25 Th Ratchadamnoen; 5-day course 4000B) Khun Lek, a Thai woman who has been massaging and teaching for more than 40 years, specialises in *jàp sên* (similar to acupressure) and the use of medicinal herbs.

Old Medicine Hospital (OMH; ☎ 0 5327 5085; 78/1 Soi Siwaka Komarat, Th Wualai; courses 3500B) Just south of town, the OMH curriculum is very traditional, with a northern-Thai slant. There are two 11-day courses a month year-round, except for the first two weeks of April. Classes tend to be large during the months of December to February, but smaller the rest of the year.

Festivals & Events

Flower Festival The mother of Chiang Mai festivals, including parades, the Queen of the Flower Festival beauty contest and plenty of flower-draped floats. It's held in the first week of February.

Songkran (Water Festival) Think you can handle a water pistol? Chiang Mai is the place to find out, as it is waterworld here in mid-April.

Winter Fair Held from late December to early January, this is a big event in the Chiang Mai calendar, with all sorts of activities and interesting visitors from the hills.

Sleeping

Most of the leading guesthouses are clustered on either side of the east moat. If you're having problems finding a room during peak periods (December to March and July to August), stop by the TAT office and pick up a free copy of *Accommodation in Chiang Mai*.

Most guesthouses make their 'rice and curry' from running trekking tours and reserve rooms for those customers. Usually a guesthouse will inform you in advance how many days (usually two to three) the room is available for nontrekkies, but to avoid surprises, check first.

The most atmospheric places are tucked away into narrow *soi* where pedestrians outnumber vehicles, and most will arrange free transport from the bus station with advance warning.

Julie Guesthouse (☎ 0 5327 4355; www.juliequesthouse.com; 7/1 Soi 5, Th Phra Pokklao; dm 70B, r 100-350B) The raging popularity of nearby Banana Guest House seems to have transferred here, and for good reason: the common area is huge, and packed at all hours with friendly backpackers. There's a pool table and relaxing down tempo on the stereo. The rooms could use a good scrubbing, but they're passable for the price. Don't miss the rooftop chill-out area.

Daret's House (☎ 0 5323 5440; darets-house@yahoo.com; 7/1 Soi 5, Th Chaiyaphum; r 100-350B) One of CM's old-school backpacker spots, Daret's is best known for the great-food-and-low-prices combo at its open-air café. Rooms are clean enough but not exactly desirable; stay here if you're dying to re-create the Khao San experience.

Chiang Mai Srivichai YHA (☎ 0 5389 2192; www.yhathailand.com; 72/9 Moo 1, Th Huay Kaew; dm 150B, r 300-500B; ❄ 💻) Quite possibly the hippest Hostelling International location in Thailand, the rooms here seem to have come straight from an IKEA catalogue. There are also dorms, a wheelchair accessible room, and One Red Dog, a fashion-forward café and bar. The hostel organises city tours.

Same-Same Guesthouse (☎ 0 5320 8056; www.samesameguesthouse.net; 104 Th Ratchaphakhinai; r 250-450B; ❄ 💻) Not yet as popular as the affiliated Same-Same location on Ko Pha-Ngan, this new spot is nevertheless catching on quickly. Graffiti covering the walls sings its praises, and there's a great crash-pad vibe.

Spicythai Backpackers (☎ 0 5340 0444; www.spicythaibackpackers.com; 4/80 Nanthawan Village, Th Nimmanhaemin; dm 250B, r 360-700B; ❄ 💻) Aside from its slightly inconvenient location outside of the old city, Spicythai is easily one of the most comfortable and unique places to stay in CM. Guests enjoy free breakfast, high-speed internet and cable TV. Choose from a mixed dorm, a female-only dorm or one of the two private rooms.

SK House (☎ 0 5321 0690; www.sk-riverview.com; 30 Soi 9, Th Moon Muang; r 400-800B; ❄ 💻 🏊) More of a hotel than a guesthouse, this is the place to stay if you're looking for modern comfort and are willing to spend just a bit more than you'd shell out at the surrounding dives.

Also recommended out of the hundreds of other options:

Eagle House 2 (☎ 0 5341 8494; www.eaglehouse.com; 26 Soi 2, Th Ratwithi; dm 80B, r 200-360B) Fairly standard rooms, but the lush garden is perfect for killing a day or three with a good book. This place has a good reputation for treks, and its cooking school, the Chilli Club Cooking Academy, has received top marks from readers.

Grace House (☎ 0 5341 8161; 27 Soi 9, Th Moon Muang; s/d 150/250B) One of the cheapest sleeps in the backpacker ghetto; rooms are sufficiently clean.

> **MORE CRAFTY SCAMS**
>
> Bus or minivan services from Th Khao San in Bangkok often advertise a free night's accommodation in Chiang Mai if you buy a Bangkok–Chiang Mai ticket. What usually happens on arrival is that the 'free' guesthouse demands you sign up for one of the hill treks immediately; if you don't, the guesthouse is suddenly 'full'. Sometimes they levy a charge for electricity or hot water. The better guesthouses don't play this game.

Eating

Indulge your intestines in Chiang Mai as the food here is top drawer. You can become a disciple of northern cuisine at one of the age-old institutions, or chase up some comfort food from home.

THAI

Chiang Mai is famed for its fine *khâo sawy*. The oldest area for this dish is the Jin Haw (Yunnanese Muslim) area around the Ban Haw Mosque on Soi 1, Th Charoen Prathet, not far from the night market.

Khao Soi Islam (Soi 1, Th Charoen Prathet; dishes 20-40B; breakfast, lunch & dinner) A reliable choice for *khâo sawy*, this place also serves Muslim curries and a good goat biryani. There is no roman-script sign out the front.

Aroon (Rai) Restaurant (0 5327 6947; 45 Th Kotchasan; dishes 30-80B; breakfast, lunch & dinner) To watch all of CM drive by while you eat, grab a plastic chair near the front entrance at this open-air dining hall. On the menu is a solid selection of traditional northern Thai dishes at very agreeable prices, along with standard Thai and Chinese plates. It's situated on the eastern side of the moat, south of Th Tha Phae.

Heuan Phen (0 5327 7103; 112 Th Ratchamankha; dishes 30-120B; breakfast, lunch & dinner) This famous local eatery suffers from a split personality. The outdoor eating area out front is just like any other local canteen, but the northern and northeastern menu is one of the strongest in town. Well worth the detour.

Heuan Sunthari (0 5325 2445; 46/2 Th Wan Singkham; dishes 40-90B; lunch & dinner) Northeast of the old town, the menu of northern, central and Isan cuisine draws a crowd here, and so does the rustic riverfront setting. But the real pulling power is the owner, famous northern Thai singer Soontaree Vechanont, who performs nightly. No roman-script sign.

Also recommended is the busy **Somphet market** (Th Moon Muang), north of Th Ratwithi, which sells cheap takeaway Thai food and northern-style sausages. **Pratu Chiang Mai night market** (Th Bamrungburi) has plenty of tables where people make an evening of eating and drinking. **Kalare Food Centre** (dishes 20-50B; breakfast, lunch & dinner), opposite the main night market building, is a food court with lots of Thai dishes and free Thai classical dancing.

INTERNATIONAL

Indian Restaurant (0 5322 3396; Soi 9, Th Moon Muang; dishes 20-60B; breakfast, lunch & dinner) You'll find this family-run place directly underneath Grace House. Vegetarians are especially well cared for here, and a very popular Indian cooking class is run out of the restaurant.

Jerusalem Falafel (0 5327 0208; 35/3 Th Moon Muang; dishes 40-80B; breakfast, lunch & dinner, closed Fri) The falafel is fast becoming Thailand's most popular adopted dish and this hole-in-the-wall place does a good range of Middle Eastern favourites.

Art Café (0 5320 6365; cnr Th Tha Phae & Th Kotchasan; dishes 50-120B; breakfast, lunch & dinner;) Has a massive menu with everything from Italian entrées to Mexican food to standard Thai dishes and banana splits.

Zest (0 5321 3088; Th Moon Muang; dishes 50-150B; breakfast, lunch & dinner) Serving Thai, Chinese, Western and even macrobiotic food, this is a

NORTHERN CUISINE

Thanks to northern Thailand's cooler climate, your dreaded or beloved vegetables from home – such as broccoli and cauliflower – might make an appearance in a stir-fry or bowl of noodles. Untranslatable herbs and leaves from the dense forests are also incorporated into more regional dishes, imparting a distinct flavour of mist-shrouded hills. Even coffee grows here, and with a little luck you can find a chewy cup of arabica, although somewhere in that mythical handbook on foreigners that all Thais read, Nescafé is the *faràng* prescription. Day-market vendors sell blue sticky rice, which is dyed by a morning-glory-like flower and topped with a sweetened egg custard that will rot a whole row of teeth.

Showing its Burmese, Chinese and Shan influences, the north prefers curries that are more stewlike than the coconut-milk curries of southern and central Thailand. Sour notes are enhanced with the addition of pickled cabbage and lime, rather than the tear-inducing spiciness favoured in most Thai dishes. The most famous example of northern cuisine is *khâo sawy*, a mild chicken curry with flat egg noodles, which is comforting on a cool foggy morning. A Burmese expat, *kaeng hang-leh*, is another example of a northern-style curry and is accompanied by sticky rice, which is eaten with the hands.

spacious and roomy garden restaurant where breakfast is served from morning till night. Rock bands and folk musicians occasionally set up on the small stage.

Pulcinella da Stefano (☎ 0 5387 4189; 2/1-2 Th Chang Moi Kao; dishes 100-200B; ⌚ lunch & dinner) This romantic little trattoria is the perfect place to bring a date, and you won't need to max out the credit card in the process. Great seafood pastas, professional antipasto and one of the better wine lists in town.

VEGETARIAN

Chiang Mai has a huge choice of vegetarian food thanks to its reputation for all things healthy and holistic.

Vegetarian Centre of Chiang Mai (☎ 0 5327 1262; 14 Th Mahidon; dishes 10-15B; ⌚ breakfast, lunch & dinner) Sponsored by the Asoke Foundation, this cafeteria offers the cheapest Thai vegetarian food this side of the street vendors. The restaurant is south of the southwestern corner of the city wall.

Biaporn (Soi 1, Th Si Phum; dishes 20-40B; ⌚ breakfast, lunch & dinner) Right in the heart of the guesthouse ghetto, this tiny café sells healthy vegetarian classics. Chlorophyll drinks are 20B each.

our pick **AUM Vegetarian Restaurant** (☎ 0 5327 8315; 65 Th Moon Muang; dishes 30-70B; ⌚ breakfast, lunch & dinner) Popular with Chiang Mai expats and visitors alike. The traditional northern Thai dishes are astounding, but so is the restaurant's massive collection of used paperbacks (AUM doubles as a bookstore). Sit upstairs, where you'll find low tables and floor seating.

Drinking

The ale flows fast and furiously at the strip of bars along Th Moon Muang near the Pratu Tha Phae. It's a familiar sight: lots of sweaty *faràng*, cheap beer and lots of neon. Some of the best bar-restaurants with live music are on the east bank of the Mae Nam Ping.

Riverside Bar & Restaurant (☎ 0 5321 1035; Th Charoenrat; dishes 60-200B) Chiang Mai's version of the Hard Rock Café, Riverside has been serving fantastic meals on the banks of the Mae Nam Ping for almost 25 years. Two live bands set up on either side of the building, making for a roaring party atmosphere most nights.

Brasserie (☎ 0 5324 1665; 37 Th Charoenrat) This intimate little café plays host to the clinking of knives and forks until around 10pm when the drinkers drift in. The famous guitarist Khun Took is the house musician here; he plays superb blues guitar, but entertains the crowd most nights with classic rock covers.

THC (19/4-5 Th Kotchasan) The marijuana motif says it all. This place is so chilled out it's horizontal. Occupying a rooftop overlooking the old city, there is a rave up here every Sunday and beers daily.

Rasta Art Bar & Restaurant (☎ 0 1690 1577; Th Si Phum) Formerly the most popular place to party on the always hoppin' Music St, the Rasta Bar has a new location just a stone's throw from the northeast corner of the moat. Old-school regulars will no doubt be pleased to experience the more-than-ample elbow room here – ideal for the spontaneous dance parties that materialise with startling frequency. Expect reggae cover versions of 'My Girl' and 'Under the Boardwalk'.

UN Irish Pub (24/1 Th Ratwithi) Originally known as the Crusty Loaf, this place still runs a popular bakery. Come early and grab one of the coveted window seats upstairs, where you can watch the night unfold below while pounding back pints.

Drunken Flower (end of Soi 1, Th Nimanhaemin) The posh end of town, this is where you will find well-heeled Thais and the local expat crowd of NGO workers. Lonely Planet's own Joe Cummings performs here often with his band, The Tonic Rays.

Drunk Studio (☎ 0 9997 7037; 32/3 Th Atsadathon) An alternative, industrial bar near the flower market, this is Chiang Mai's unofficial headquarters for live alternative music. Thai bands play grunge, hardcore, nu-metal and *phêua chîiwít* (Thai 'songs for life') nightly.

Near Eagle House 2, in what at first glance is just a dusty car park, there is a cluster of low-key garden bars turning out cheap beers and cool tunes. This strip is referred to as Music St or Reggae St; much of the live music here is in fact of the reggae variety.

Entertainment

Major Cineplex (☎ 0 5328 3939; Central Airport Plaza, 2 Th Mahidon) is the best cinema spot in town. Every Sunday at 3pm, **Chiang Mai University** (☎ 0 5322 1699; Th Huay Kaew; admission free), 1.5km northwest of the old town, presents a different foreign film in the main auditorium of the Art & Culture Centre.

Shopping

Long before tourists began visiting the region, Chiang Mai was an important centre for handcrafted pottery, weaving, umbrellas, silverwork and woodcarvings, and today it's still the country's number-one source of handicrafts. The **Pratu Chiang Mai night market** (Th Bamrungburi), on the southern edge of town, is a great place to bargain like a local. A former royal cremation grounds, Warorot Market (also locally called Kat Luang, or Great Market) is the oldest market in Chiang Mai. It's a good spot for Thai fabrics, cooking implements and prepared foods (especially northern Thai foods).

Getting There & Away

AIR

Regularly scheduled international flights arrive at **Chiang Mai International Airport** (☎ 0 5327 0222) from the following cities: Kunming (China), Singapore, Taipei (Taiwan), Vientiane and Luang Prabang (Laos), and Yangon and Mandalay (Myanmar).

Domestic routes include Bangkok, Chiang Rai, Mae Hong Son, Mae Sot, Nan, Phitsanulok, Phrae, Phuket and Sukhothai. Worthwhile options include the short hop to Mae Hong Son with Thai Airways International and the discount flights to Bangkok with Air Asia and Nok Air, almost as cheap as a VIP bus.

Airlines operating out of Chiang Mai:

Air Asia (code AK; ☎ 0 2515 9999; www.airasia.com)
Air Mandalay (code 6T; ☎ 0 5381 8049; www.air-mandalay.com)
Bangkok Airways (code PG; ☎ 0 5321 0043; www.bangkokair.com)
Lao Airlines (code QV; ☎ 0 5322 3401; www.lao-airlines.com)
Mandarin Airlines (code AE; ☎ 0 5320 1268; www.mandarin-airlines.com)
Nok Air (code DD; ☎ 1318; www.nokair.com.th)
Orient Thai (code OX; ☎ 0 5392 2159; www.orient-thai.com)
SilkAir (code MI; ☎ 0 5327 6459; www.silkair.com)
Thai Airways International (THAI, code TG; ☎ 0 5321 1044; www.thaiair.com)

BUS

There are two bus stations in Chiang Mai: **Arcade bus station** (Th Kaew Nawarat), northeast of town, handles Bangkok and most of the long-distance cities, while **Chang Pheuak bus station** (Th Chang Pheuak), north of the town centre, handles buses to Fang, Tha Ton, Lamphun and destinations within Chiang Mai Province. From the town centre, a túk-túk or chartered sǎwngthǎew to the Arcade bus station should cost about 40B; to the Chang Pheuak bus station get a sǎwngthǎew at the normal 10B-per-person rate.

TRAIN

The **train station** (☎ 0 5324 5363; Th Charoen Muang) is on the eastern edge of town. There are four express trains and two rapid trains per day between Chiang Mai and Bangkok

BUSES FROM CHIANG MAI

Destination	Class	Fare (B)	Duration (hr)	Frequency
Bangkok	VIP	558-863	10	several daily
Chiang Rai	ordinary	100	3	frequent daily
	air-con	140		
Khon Kaen	ordinary	267	12	regular daily
	air-con	421-469		
Mae Hong Son	ordinary	187	8	regular daily
	air-con	337	5	
Mae Sai	ordinary	126	4	regular daily
	air-con	176		
Mae Sariang	ordinary	100	5	7 daily
	air-con	180		
Mae Sot	ordinary	253	6	2 daily
	air-con	326		
Nan	ordinary	158	6	5 daily
	air-con	221		
Pai	ordinary	80	4	5 daily
	air-con	142		
Phitsanulok	ordinary	227	6	hourly 7am-3pm
	air-con	292		

BORDER PATROLS

In an effort to stop the smuggling of drugs and other contraband, staffed patrol posts search all vehicles headed towards the Burmese border. Police usually board public buses, sniff around a bit, give the evil eye to boys wearing make-up and perfunctorily check everyone's ID or passport. *Faràng* are usually ignored, but if you don't want trouble, don't look for it. And stuff that souvenir opium pipe deep inside your bag.

(1st/2nd class 593/281B, fare without surcharges). Advance booking is advised. Transport to the station via sǎwngthǎew should cost 20B.

Getting Around

Airport taxis cost 100B. Pick up a ticket at the taxi kiosk just outside the baggage-claim area, then present the ticket to the taxi drivers outside arrivals. The airport is only 3km from the city centre. You can charter a túk-túk or red sǎwngthǎew from the centre of Chiang Mai to the airport for 50B or 60B.

Plenty of red sǎwngthǎew circulate around the city with standard fares of 10B per person, but drivers often try to get you to charter (60B or less). If you're travelling alone, they typically ask for 20B. The sǎwngthǎew don't have set routes; you simply flag them down and tell them where you want to go. Túk-túk only do charters at 30B for short trips and 40B to 60B for longer ones. Chiang Mai still has loads of sǎamláw, especially in the old city around Talat Warorot. Sǎamláw cost around 20B to 30B for most trips.

You can rent bicycles (30B to 50B a day) or 100cc motorcycles (from 100B to 200B) to explore Chiang Mai. Bicycles are a great way to get around the city.

Chiang Mai Disabled Center (☎ 0 5321 3941; www.infothai.com/disabled; 133/1 Th Ratchaphakhinai) Bicycle rental to assist Chiang Mai's disabled community.

Contact Travel (☎ 0 5327 7178; www.activethailand.com; 73/7 Th Charoen Prathet; per day 200B) Topnotch 21-speed mountain bikes.

AROUND CHIANG MAI

Doi Suthep

Perched on a panoramic hilltop, **Wat Phra That Doi Suthep** (admission 30B) is one of the north's most sacred temples. The site was 'chosen' by an honoured Buddha relic mounted on the back of a white elephant; the animal wandered until it stopped (and died) on Doi Suthep, making this the relic's new home. A snaking road ascends the hill to a long flight of steps, lined by ceramic-tailed *naga*, that leads up to the temple and the expansive views of the valley below. Watching the sunset from up here is an institution.

About 4km beyond Wat Phra That Doi Suthep are the palace gardens of **Phra Tamnak Phu** (admission free; 8.30am-12.30pm & 1-4pm Sat, Sun & holidays), a winter residence for the royal family. The road that passes the palace splits off to the left, stopping at the peak of Doi Pui. From there, a dirt road proceeds for a couple of kilometres to a nearby **Hmong village**, which is well touristed and sells handicrafts.

Sǎwngthǎew to Doi Suthep leave from Th Huay Kaew, near the main gate of Chiang Mai University, for the 16km trip (40B up, 30B down); for another 10B, you can take a bicycle up with you and zoom back downhill.

Bo Sang & San Kamphaeng

The 'umbrella village' of Bo Sang (Baw Sang) is 9km east of Chiang Mai. It's a picturesque though touristy spot where the townspeople engage in just about every type of northern Thai handicraft, including making beautiful paper umbrellas.

About 5km further down Rte 1006 is San Kamphaeng, which specialises in cotton and silk weaving.

Frequent buses to Bo Sang (6B) and San Kamphaeng (8B) leave from Chiang Mai near the main post office on the northern side of Th Charoen Muang. White sǎwngthǎew (6B) leave from the Chang Pheuak bus station and make the trip to either destination.

Doi Inthanon

The highest peak in the country, Doi Inthanon (2595m), and the surrounding **national park** (admission 200B), can be visited as a day trip from Chiang Mai. There are some impressive waterfalls and popular picnic spots on the road to the summit. Between Chiang Mai and Doi Inthanon, the small town of Chom Thong has a fine Burmese-style temple, **Wat Phra That Si Chom Thong**, where 26-day *vipassana* meditation courses are available.

Buses to Chom Thong (23B) leave from inside Pratu Chiang Mai at the south moat, as well as from the Chang Pheuak bus station in Chiang Mai. From Chom Thong there are regular sǎwngthǎew to Mae Klang (15B), about 8km north. Sǎwngthǎew from Mae Klang to Doi Inthanon leave almost hourly until late afternoon and cost 30B per person.

Lampang & Around

Lampang is like a low-key, laid-back little Chiang Mai. Like its larger sibling, Lampang was constructed as a walled rectangle and boasts magnificent temples, many of which were built from teak by Burmese and Shan artisans. Lampang is also known throughout Thailand as Meuang Rot Mah (Horse Cart City) because it's the only town in Thailand where horse-drawn carriages are still used as transport.

SIGHTS & ACTIVITIES

Temples

The old town's fine structures include **Wat Si Rong Meuang**, **Wat Si Chum** and **Wat Phra Kaew Don Tao** (one of the many former homes of the Emerald Buddha, now residing in Bangkok's Wat Phra Kaew) on the bank of the Mae Nam Wang, north of town.

In the village of Ko Kha, about 18km to the southwest of Lampang, lies **Wat Phra That Lampang Luang**, arguably the most beautiful wooden Lanna temple in northern Thailand. It is an amazing structure with walls like a huge medieval castle. To get there, catch a blue sǎwngthǎew south on Th Praisani to the market in Ko Kha (10B), then take a Hang Chat–bound sǎwngthǎew (5B) 3km north to the entrance of Wat Phra That Lampang Luang. A motorcycle taxi from Ko Kha to the temple costs approximately 30B.

Thai Elephant Conservation Center

At one time in Thai society, elephants were war machines, logging trucks and work companions. The automobile has rendered the elephant jobless and orphaned in the modern world. The **Thai Elephant Conservation Center** (☎ 0 5422 9042; www.changthai.com; admission 50B; ⏲ public shows 10am & 11am daily, 1.30pm Fri, Sat & holidays Jun-Feb) attempts to remedy this by promoting ecotourism, providing medical care and training young elephants.

The centre offers elephant rides (from 200B for 15 minutes) and elephant bathing shows. The animals appreciate a few pieces of fruit – 'feels like a vacuum cleaner with a wet nozzle', reported one visitor. Travellers can sign on for a one-day mahout course (1500B) or a three-day programme (4000B).

To reach the elephant camp, take a bus or sǎwngthǎew bound for Chiang Mai from Lampang's main bus station and get off at the Km 37 marker. Free vans shuttle visitors the 2km distance between the highway and the centre.

Pasang

Only a short sǎwngthǎew (10B) ride south of Lamphun, Pasang is a centre for **cotton weaving**. Near the wat is a cotton-products store called Wimon (no roman-script sign), where you can watch people weaving on looms or buy floor coverings, cotton tablecloths and other utilitarian household items. You'll also find a few **shops** (opposite Wat Pasang Ngam) near the main market in town.

SLEEPING & EATING

Boonma Guest House (☎ 0 5432 2653; 256 Th Talat Kao; r 250-300B) This family-run place features a couple of rooms in a gorgeous teak home, and cement rooms behind. Some have shared bathrooms. It lacks a comfortable place to hang out.

Kim Hotel (☎ 0 5421 7721; fax 0 5422 6929; 168 Th Boonyawat; r 250-350B; ❄) On the other side of the road to Kelangnakorn Hotel, the rooms in this three-storey place have tiled walls, making the bedrooms feel like bathrooms; however, they are clean, comfortable and have cable TV.

Kelangnakorn Hotel (☎ 0 5421 6137; Th Boonyawat; r 260-340B; ❄) Popular with travelling salesmen, this hotel has modernish rooms with wooden furniture and cable TV, and a friendly reception.

GETTING THERE & AWAY

From Chiang Mai, buses to Lampang (ordinary 25B, air-con 50B to 65B, two hours, every half-hour) leave from the Arcade bus station and also from near the TAT office in the direction of Lamphun. Buses also depart for Lamphun (29B).

You can also travel to Lampang from Chiang Mai by train (2nd/3rd class 37/15B, two hours).

PAI

pop 3000

The hippy trail is alive and well in Pai, a flashback to stories from the '70s and counterculture colonies in Kabul and Kathmandu. Pai emerged from nowhere in a cool, moist corner of a mountain-fortressed valley along a rambling river. Foreigners stumbled through here on their way to somewhere else and realised Pai was a mountain paradise of easy living. A steady scene has since settled in with the town's more permanent population of Shan, Thai and Muslim Chinese. The town itself can be explored in a matter of minutes, but the real adventure lies along the paths in the hills beyond.

Information

Pick up a copy of the *Pai, Soppong, Mae Hong Son Tourist Map* (20B) for extensive listings. Several places around town offer internet services and they all charge around 40B per hour.

Krung Thai Bank (Th Rangsiyanon) Has an ATM and foreign-exchange service.

Siam Used Books (Th Rangsiyanon) Best place for second-hand books in town.

Activities

All the guesthouses in town can provide heaps of information on local trekking and a few offer guided treks for as little as 600B per day if there are no rafts or elephants involved.

Thai Adventure Rafting (TAR; ☎ 0 5369 9111; www.activethailand.com; Th Rangsiyanon; per person 2000B) has two-day, white-water rafting trips on the Mae Nam Pai from Pai to Mae Hong Son. The main rafting season runs from July to December. Cheaper river activities include tubing; tubes can be hired for 50B around town.

Thom's Pai Elephant Camp Tours (☎ 0 5369 9286; www.geocities.com/pai_tours; 4 Th Rangsiyanon; 1hr/3hr rides per person 400/800B) offers jungle rides year-round from Thom's camp near the hot springs, which include a soak in the camp's hot-spring-fed tubs afterwards.

Pai Traditional Massage (☎ 0 5369 9121; Th Sukhapiban 1; massages per hr 150B, saunas 60B; 4.30am-8.30pm Mon-Fri, 8.30am-8.30pm Sat & Sun) has very good northern Thai massage, as well as a sauna where you can steam yourself in *sàmǔn phrai* (medicinal herbs).

Need to cool off and chill out? Sun yourself on the deck, sip a drink and take a dip at **Fluid** (admission 50B; 9am-8.30pm), a 25m swimming pool. To find it, head over the bridge towards the waterfall, then walk up the steep hill on your left.

Sleeping

From December to March it can be difficult to find a room. The most atmospheric guesthouses are spread along the banks of the Mae Nam Pai and they number in the dozens.

Baan Pai Riverside (☎ 0 5369 8152; r 150-250B) This rambling village of creaky bungalow huts sits right on the banks of the Mae Nam Pai, on the opposite side of town. The more expensive huts come with attached bathrooms and hot-water showers. The carpet-covered platform restaurant is perfect for lounging.

Golden Hut (☎ 0 5369 9949; 107 Moo 3; r 150-400B) The rooms and bungalows here encircle a decent-sized lawn, and the main common area looks directly out over the Pai river. If it's empty (and if you're a steady climber), give the tree house a try.

Pai River Lodge (☎ 0 9520 2898; s/d 200/250B) The lengthy lawn is a draw here, ringed by typical A-frame huts (with share bathrooms) and a couple of smarter options. It's south of Th Ratchadamnoen.

Sun Hut (☎ 0 5369 9730; www.thesunhut.com; 28/1 Mae Yen; s/d from 250/350B) You'll need a motorbike to reach this destination, a psychedelic collection of zodiac-inspired bungalows that seems to have come straight out of the hippie-era cliché encyclopaedia. The turn-off is signposted about 3km from town on the road to the hot springs.

Eating & Drinking

There is an incredible number of places to get a good feed in Pai. Many of the riverfront guesthouses are capitalising on their location with rustic restaurants built on stilts near the water.

All About Coffee (☎ 0 5369 9429; Th Chaisongkhram; dishes 35-65B; breakfast, lunch & dinner) The espresso here isn't cheap, but if you're having trouble waking up, look no further. Like most everything in Pai, the décor is creative and inviting. The sandwiches are fantastic here too. It closes at 6pm.

Phu Pai Art Café (Th Rangsiyanon; dishes 40-100B; 6pm-midnight) One of Pai's more sophisticated on-the-town destinations, Phu Pai is a beautifully decorated room with local art on the walls and a small beer and wine bar in the corner. The live music is a world away from the bad cover bands you've grown accustomed to in Thailand; you might hear acoustic guitarists, violinists or genuine gypsy bands.

Bebop Restaurant & Music (Th Rangsiyanon; 6pm-1am) If you want to become a card-carrying member of the Pai nightlife patrol, simply show up at Bebop around midnight, when half the town seems to arrive. Live rock and cover bands perform nightly, and when it's time to close, do like the locals and head to one of the late-night places across the bridge.

Getting There & Away

The **bus stop** (Th Chaisongkhram) is in a dirt lot in the centre of town. All buses that stop here follow the Chiang Mai–Pai–Mae Hong Son–Mae Sariang loop in either direction. Buses to Chiang Mai (air-con/ordinary 142/80B, four hours) and Mae Hong Son (97/62B, four hours) leave five times daily. The road is savagely steep and snaking; grab a window seat and ride on an empty stomach if motion sickness is a problem.

MAE HONG SON

pop 8300

Hemmed in by mountains on all sides, Mae Hong Son feels like the end of the road, but sees its fair share of foreigners thanks to the daily flights from Chiang Mai. Many travellers skip the sales pitch in Chiang Mai in favour of the localised trekking scene in Mae Hong Son, Thailand's far northwestern provincial capital. The town's population is predominantly Shan, but the feel is more a Thai town than minority mountain getaway. Head down to the shores of Nong Jong Kham (Jong Kham Lake) to escape the bustle of the busy streets.

Information

Most of the banks on Th Khunlum Praphat have ATMs. Internet access is widely available in the town centre but connections can be slow.

Post office (Th Khunlum Praphat)

Sri Sangwarn Hospital (0 5361 1378; Th Singhanat Bamrung)

TAT office (0 5361 2982; Th Khunlum Praphat; 8.30am-4.30pm Mon-Fri) Across from the post office.

Thai Airways International (0 5361 1297; www.thaiair.com; 71 Th Singhanat Bamrung)

Tourist police (0 5361 1812, emergencies 1155; Th Singhanat Bamrung; 8.30am-9.30pm) To report thefts or lodge complaints against trekking companies or guesthouses.

Sights & Activities

Wat Jong Klang and **Wat Jong Kham** (south of Nong Jong Kham) are the focal point of the **Poi Sang Long Festival** in March, when young Shan boys are ordained as novice monks. The boys are carried on the shoulders of friends and paraded round the wat under festive parasols.

Guesthouses in town arrange **treks** to nearby hill-tribe villages, as well as **white-water rafting** on the Mae Nam Pai. Reliable operators:

Nam Rim Tours (0 5361 3925; Th Khunlum Praphat) Funny, professional and knowledgeable.

PA Tours (Th Pradit Jong Kham) Across the street from Friend House; recommended by locals.

Sunflower Café (Th Udom Chaonithet) Consistently good feedback.

Sleeping & Eating

Johnnie House (Th Pradit Jong Kham; d 100-200B) An established crash pad near Nong Jong Kham, this place is a bit rustic and has only a few rooms. The 200B rooms come with a hot-water shower.

Friend House (0 5362 0119; 20 Th Pradit Jong Kham; r 100-400B) Clean, efficient and deservedly popular. The management here is, in fact, quite friendly, and the affiliated trekking company (PA Tours, across the street) is said to be good. Shared hot-water showers.

Palm House Guest House (0 5361 4022; 22/1 Th Chamnansthit; r from 300B;) It's not exactly exploding with character, although everything here is scrubbed clean and even the fan rooms have satellite TV and little balconies. Popular with families.

Salween River Restaurant (0 5361 2050; dishes 35-80B; breakfast, lunch & dinner) Salween is the place to come for hill-tribe coffee and hearty Western breakfasts. The owners are a rich source of information and it's a popular hang-out for volunteers. Thai, Shan and Burmese food is available.

Lakeside Bar & Restaurant (Th Pradit Jong Kham; buffets 59B; lunch & dinner) With a sharp setting on the shores of the lake, this open-air restaurant and bar has a popular daily buffet. By night, it livens up and slowly but surely the drinkers outnumber the diners. There's live music until midnight most nights.

Getting There & Away

Mae Hong Son is 368km from Chiang Mai, but the terrain is so rugged (and beautiful) that the trip takes at least eight long, sweaty hours. For this reason, many people fly to or from Chiang Mai with **Thai Airways International** (THAI, code TG; 0 5361 2220; www.thaiair.com; Th Singhanat Bamrung), which has four flights daily.

TREKKING TO THE CORNERS

One of the most popular activities from Chiang Mai, Chiang Rai or Mae Hong Son is to take a trek through the mountains to observe the region's traditional hill-tribe villages. The term 'hill tribe' refers to ethnic minorities living in mountainous northern and western Thailand. The Thais refer to them as *chao khao,* literally meaning 'mountain people'. Each hill tribe has its own language, customs, mode of dress and spiritual beliefs. Most are of seminomadic origin, having migrated to Thailand from Tibet, Myanmar, China and Laos during the past 200 years or so, although some groups may have been in Thailand for much longer. The Tribal Research Institute in Chiang Mai recognises 10 different hill tribes, but there may be up to 20 in Thailand. The institute estimates the total hill-tribe population to be around 550,000. Lonely Planet's *Hill Tribes Phrasebook* gives a handy, basic introduction to the culture and languages of a number of the tribes.

BE AN INFORMED TREKKER

For the hill-tribe groups of Southeast Asia, tourism is a mixed blessing. It has helped to protect these cultures from widespread dismantling by majority governments, but has also contributed to the erosion of traditional customs through continued exposure to outside influences. Because trekking is big business, some villages have become veritable theme parks with a steady supply of visitors filtering in and out, creating exactly the opposite environment to the one trekkers hope to find, and eroding the fabric of the village.

Do your homework before you sign up for a trek. Find out if the tour group will be small, if the guide speaks the hill-tribe language and can explain the culture, and how many other groups will visit the village on the same day. Also find out if the village has a voice in its use as an attraction and whether it shares in the profits.

Remember that these villages are typically the poorest in the region, and what you consider to be your 'modest' belongings might be viewed as unthinkable luxuries to your hosts. While it is impossible to leave the community unaffected by your visit, at least respect its culture by observing local taboos:

- Dress modestly no matter how hot and sweaty you are.
- Don't take photographs unless permission is granted. Because of traditional belief systems, many individuals and even whole tribes may object strongly to being photographed. Always ask first, even if you think no-one is looking.
- Show respect for the community's religious symbols and rituals. Don't touch totems at village entrances, or any other object of obvious symbolic value, without asking permission. Unless you're asked to participate, keep your distance from ceremonies.
- Don't use drugs; set a good example to hill-tribe youngsters by not smoking opium or using other drugs.
- Don't litter while trekking or staying in villages; rather, take your rubbish away with you.
- Don't hand out sweets and refrain from giving out other forms of charity (such as pens and money) to children, as this encourages begging and undermines the parents' ability to be breadwinners for their families. Talk to your guide beforehand about materials the local school or health centre may need in order to benefit the community as a whole.

HILL-TRIBE COMMUNITIES

Akha (Thai: I-kaw)

Population 48,500
Origin: Tibet
Present Locations: Thailand, Laos, Myanmar, Yunnan (China)
Economy: rice, corn, opium
Belief Systems: animism, with an emphasis on ancestor worship
Distinctive Characteristics: The Akha wear headdresses of beads, feathers and dangling silver ornaments. Villages are set along mountain ridges or on steep slopes 1000m to 1400m in altitude. They are among the poorest of Thailand's ethnic minorities and tend to resist assimilation into the Thai mainstream. Like the Lahu, the Akha often cultivate opium for their own consumption.

Hmong (Thai: Meo or Maew)

Population: 124,000
Origin: southern China

Present Locations: southern China, Thailand, Laos, Vietnam
Economy: rice, corn, opium
Belief Systems: animism
Distinctive Characteristics: Hmong tribespeople wear simple black jackets and indigo trousers with striped borders, or indigo skirts, and silver jewellery. Most women wear their hair in a large bun. They usually live on mountain peaks or plateaus. Kinship is patrilineal and polygamy is permitted. They are Thailand's second-largest hill-tribe group and are numerous in Chiang Mai Province.

Karen (Thai: Yang or Kariang)

Population: 322,000
Origin: Myanmar
Present Locations: Thailand, Myanmar
Economy: rice, vegetables, livestock
Belief Systems: animism, Buddhism or Christianity, depending on the group
Distinctive Characteristics: The Karen have thickly woven V-neck tunics of various colours (unmarried women wear white). They tend to live in lowland valleys and practise crop rotation rather than swidden (slash and burn) agriculture. Kinship is matrilineal and marriage is endogamous (ie only within the tribe). There are four distinct Karen groups: White Karen (Skaw Karen), Pwo Karen, Black Karen (Pa-o) and Kayah. These groups combined comprise the largest hill tribe in Thailand, numbering well over a quarter of a million people, or about half of all hill-tribe people. Many Karen continue to migrate into Thailand from Myanmar, fleeing Burmese government persecution.

Lahu (Thai: Musoe)

Population: 73,000
Origin: Tibet
Present Locations: southern China, Thailand, Myanmar
Economy: rice, corn, opium
Belief Systems: theistic animism (supreme deity is Geusha), Christianity
Distinctive Characteristics: Lahu wear black-and-red jackets, with narrow skirts for women. They live in mountainous areas at about 1000m. Their intricately woven *yâam* (shoulder bags) are prized by collectors. There are four main groups: Red Lahu, Black Lahu, Yellow Lahu and Lahu Sheleh.

Lisu (Thai: Lisaw)

Population: 28,000
Origin: Tibet
Present Locations: Thailand, Yunnan (China)
Economy: rice, opium, corn, livestock
Belief Systems: animism with ancestor worship and spirit possession
Distinctive Characteristics: The Lisu women wear long multicoloured tunics over trousers and sometimes wear black turbans with tassels. Men wear baggy green or blue pants that are pegged in at the ankles. They also often wear lots of bright colours. Lisu villages are usually in the mountains, located at about 1000m. Premarital sex is said to be common in the villages, along with freedom in choosing marital partners. Patrilineal clans have pan-tribal jurisdiction, which makes the Lisu unique among the hill-tribe communities (most hill tribes have power centred at the village level with either the shaman or a village headman as leader).

Mien (Thai: Yao)

Population: 40,000
Origin: central China
Present Locations: Thailand, southern China, Laos, Myanmar, Vietnam
Economy: rice, corn, opium
Belief Systems: animism with ancestor worship and Taoism
Distinctive Characteristics: Women wear black jackets with red furlike collars and trousers decorated with intricately embroidered patches, along with large dark-blue or black turbans. They tend to settle near mountain springs at between 1000m and 1200m. They have been heavily influenced by Chinese traditions and use Chinese characters to write the Mien language. Kinship is patrilineal and marriage is polygamous.

The **airport** (☎ 0 5361 2057; Th Nivit Pisan) is near the centre of town.

The **bus station** (Th Khunlum Praphat) is near the Siam Hotel. There are two routes from Mae Hong Son: the northern route is faster by about an hour, but the southern route includes more bathroom stops. Buses travelling south from Mae Hong Son stop at Mae Sariang (ordinary 80B, four hours, five daily), while buses heading north stop at Pai (ordinary

105B, four hours, seven to eight daily). Both eventually reach Chiang Mai (ordinary/air-con 200/261B).

THA TON & AROUND

In the far northern corner of Chiang Mai Province, Tha Ton is the launching point for river trips to Chiang Rai. The ride down Mae Nam Kok is a big hit with tourists and the villages along the way are geared to groups, but it remains a relaxing route to avoid the bone-rattling buses for a day. Tha Ton is little more than a boat dock with a few guesthouses and souvenir stands, so come equipped with money and other sundries.

Guesthouses line the main road into town on either side of the river. **Chan Kasem Guest House** (☎ 0 5345 9313; d 90-300B) is the nearest spot to the boat dock, and has simple rooms with shared bathroom in the old house and smarter rooms in a brick block. There's also an atmospheric restaurant on the river.

Buses from Chiang Mai (70B, four hours, six departures daily) leave Chang Pheuak starting at 6am, which is the only departure that will arrive in time for the 12.30pm boat to Chiang Rai. From Tha Ton, yellow sǎwngthǎew run north to Mae Salong (50B, 1½ hours, departures every 30 minutes) and south to Fang (12B, 40 minutes).

Chiang Rai–bound boats taking up to 12 passengers leave from the pier in Tha Ton at 12.30pm only (250B, three to five hours). Six-person charters are available for 1700B between 7am and 3pm. Many travellers like to do the trip in stages, stopping in minority villages along the way. Guesthouses in Tha Ton can arrange combination rafting and trekking trips ending in Chiang Rai.

CHIANG RAI

pop 40,000

Leafy and well groomed, Chiang Rai is more liveable than visitable, lacking any major tourist attractions except being a gateway to the Golden Triangle and an alternative spot for arranging hill-tribe treks. Of late, Chiang Rai has become more popular with well-heeled international conventioneers than with those lacking an expense account.

Information

Chiang Rai has a good number of banks, especially along Th Thanalai and along Th Utarakit. Internet access is readily available.

CAT office (cnr Th Ratchadat Damrong & Th Ngam Meuang; 🕑 7am-11pm Mon-Fri)

Chiang Rai Prachanukroh Hospital (☎ 0 5371 1303)

Garé Garon (869/18 Th Phahonyothin; 🕑 10am-10pm) New and used English books, plus coffee, tea and handicrafts in an artsy environment.

Orn's Bookshop (1051/61 Soi 1, Th Jet Yot; 🕑 8am-8pm) By far the city's best selection of second-hand English books, and with lower prices than Garé Garon. A separate room is devoted to various European-language titles.

Post office (Th Utarakit) South of Wat Phra Singh.

TAT office (☎ 0 5371 7433; 448/16 Th Singkhlai; 🕑 8.30am-4.30pm)

Tourist police (☎ 0 5371 1779)

Sights & Activities

In the mid-14th century, lightning struck open the *chedi* at **Wat Phra Kaew** (cnr Th Trairat & Th Reuang Nakhon), thus revealing the much honoured Emerald Buddha hiding inside.

Hilltribe Museum & Handicrafts Center (☎ 0 5374 0088; www.pda.or.th/chiangrai; 620/1 Th Thanalai; admission 50B; 🕑 9am-6pm Mon-Fri, 10am-6pm Sat & Sun), run by the nonprofit PDA, displays clothing and the history of major hill tribes. PDA also organises hill-tribe treks.

In excess of 20 travel agencies, guesthouses and hotels offer trekking, typically in the Doi Tung, Doi Mae Salong and Chiang Khong areas. **Fat Free Mountain Bikes** (☎ 0 5375 2532; contact@fatfreebike.com; 542/2 Th Banphaprakan) has imported mountain bikes for sale or rent, does bike repairs and organises mountain biking trips. Three agencies in Chiang Rai operate treks and cultural tours where profits from the treks go directly to community development projects:

Natural Focus (☎ 0 5371 5696; natfocus@loxinfo.co.th) Specialises in nature tours.

PDA Tours & Travel (☎ 0 5374 0088; Hilltribe Museum & Handicrafts Center, 620/1 Th Thanalai) Culturally sensitive tours led by PDA-trained hill-tribe members.

Sleeping

Chat House (☎ 0 5371 1481; chathouse32@hotmail.com; 3/2 Soi Saengkaew, Th Trairat; dm/s 70/80B, d 150-250B; 🖧) Rooms here are small and somewhat plain, but the sprawling common area makes up for it. The young Thai employees are fun and eager to speak English. Bicycles and motorcycles for rent, plus guided treks offered.

Garden House (☎ 0 5371 7090; 163/1 Th Banphaprakan; r 100-200B) Aesthetically speaking, this is the most creative guesthouse in town.

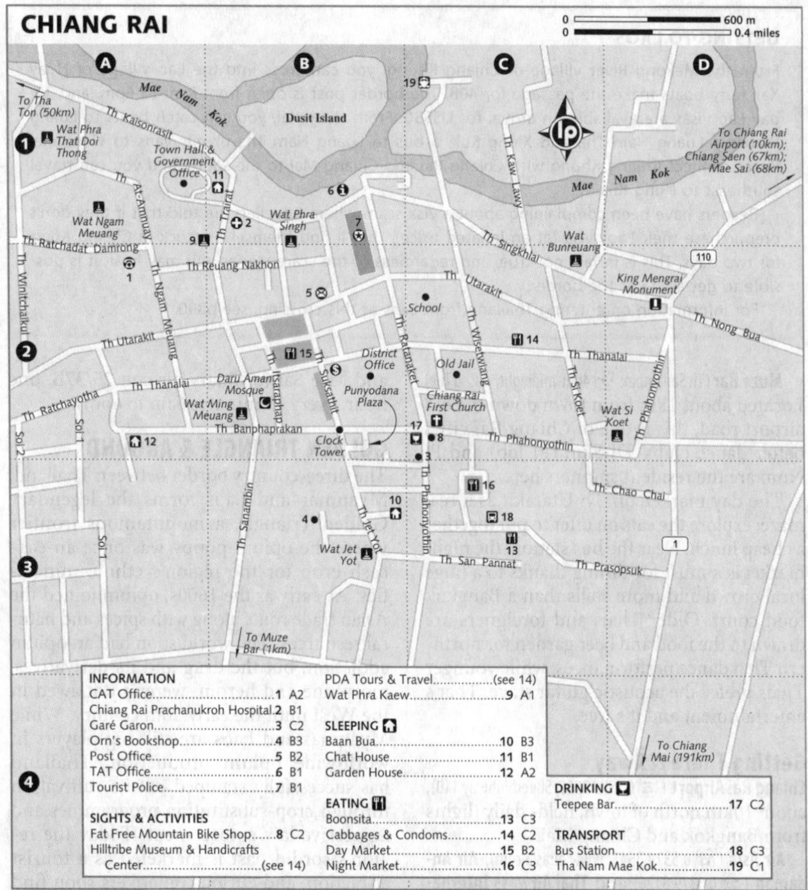

Traditional A-frame bungalows, lots of teak and a lovingly cared-for garden complete the picture. Stay here if it's comfort and quiet you're craving.

Baan Bua (☎ 0 5371 8880; baanbua@yahoo.com; 879/2 Th Jet Yot; s/d from 180/200B;) Currently the pearl of Chiang Rai, this place boasts a large garden area that's perfect for breakfast in the morning. All rooms have private bathrooms with hot showers. This place always seems to be full, so book ahead.

Eating & Drinking

our pick Boonsita (☎ 0 5375 5055; Th Prasopsuk; dishes 25B; breakfast, lunch & dinner) A cafeteria-style vegetarian restaurant, this is one of the very few restaurants in Thailand serving unbleached brown rice. The food is absolutely perfect, and in it you'll find no dairy, poultry or MSG. It's across Th San Pannat from the bus station.

Cabbages & Condoms (☎ 0 5374 0784; 620/1 Th Thanalai; dishes 35-90B; breakfast, lunch & dinner) Right next door to the Hilltribe Museum, profits from this restaurant are used to distribute condoms and fund sex-education initiatives throughout Thailand. Especially toothsome northern Thai dishes are on the menu.

Teepee Bar (Th Phahonyothin) This hole-in-the-wall hang-out is dark, dank and in serious need of a good dusting. But it's also seriously fun, and you'll find a mixture of backpackers, volunteers and expats stuffed onto the 2nd floor nearly every night. (Good luck finding the staircase.)

GETTING TO LAOS

From the Mekong River village of Chiang Khong, you can cross into the Lao village of Huay Xai; ferry boats make the passage for 40B. The border post is open from 8am to 6pm, and 30-day Lao visas are available on arrival for US$30. From Huay Xai, you can catch boats to Luang Prabang, Luang Nam Tha and Xieng Kok, a bus to Luang Nam Tha or minivans to Vientiane. Buses connect Chiang Khong with Chiang Rai and Chiang Mai to the south, and you can travel southeast to Nong Khai.

Readers have been complaining about a visa scam where travellers are told that if they don't prepurchase their Laos visa (at an inflated price), they'll find themselves stuck in Chiang Kong for two days. This is in fact not true, and regardless of the scare stories you may hear, it is possible to get a visa at the border.

For information on entering Thailand from Laos at this crossing, see p390.

Muze Bar (Th Sanambin; 4pm-midnight, closed Tue) Located about 1km from town down the old airport road, this is one of Chiang Rai city's better dance clubs. DJ Skin (Pi Job) and Pi Num are the resident spinners here.

The day market, off Th Utarakit, is a real maze; explore the eats on offer to put together a cheap lunch. Near the bus station, the night market is a must for dining thanks to a huge local crowd and more stalls than a Bangkok food court. Older Thais and foreigners are drawn to the food and beer garden for northern Thai dance performances, while younger Thais prefer the acoustic guitar stage. That's entertainment and it's free.

Getting There & Away

Chiang Rai Airport (☎ 0 5379 3555; Superhighway 110), about 10km north of town, fields daily flights from Bangkok and Chiang Mai.

Air Asia (☎ 0 5379 3545; www.airasia.com), **Air Andaman** (☎ 0 5379 3726) and **Thai Airways International** (☎ 0 5477 1179; www.thaiair.com) all offer daily flights between Bangkok and Chiang Rai.

Chiang Rai is also accessible by a popular boat journey from Tha Ton (see p742 for details). For boats heading upriver, go to the pier in the north corner of town at Tha Nam Mae Kok. Boats embark daily at 10.30am. You can charter a boat to Tha Ton for 1600B. Call **Chiang Rai Boat Tour** (☎ 0 5375 0009) for further information.

Chiang Rai's **bus station** (Th Prasopsuk) is in the heart of town. Bus services connect Chiang Rai with Bangkok (air-con 370B to 452B, VIP 700B, 10 hours), Chiang Mai (ordinary/air-con 77/139B, four hours, hourly 6am to 5pm), Chiang Khong (ordinary 42B, three hours, hourly 7am to 5pm), Chiang Saen (ordinary 25B, 1½ hours, every 15 minutes 6am to 6pm) and Mae Sai (ordinary/air-con 25/37B, one hour, every 15 minutes 6am to 6pm).

GOLDEN TRIANGLE & AROUND

The three-country border between Thailand, Myanmar and Laos forms the legendary Golden Triangle, a mountainous frontier where the opium poppy was once an easy cash crop for the region's ethnic minorities. As early as the 1600s, opium joined the Asian trade route along with spices and natural resources. The world soon had an opium addiction, but the drug and its derivatives, morphine and heroin, weren't outlawed in the West until the early 20th century. While Myanmar and Laos are still big players in worldwide opium production, Thailand has successfully stamped out its cultivation through crop-substitution programmes and aggressive law enforcement. Today the region's sordid past is marketed as a tourist attraction, and curious onlookers soon find that souvenirs of opium pipes and Golden Triangle T-shirts are the main success story of the substitution programme.

Chiang Khong

pop 9000

Chiang Khong is an important market town for local hill tribes and for trade with northern Laos. It is quite a lively little community and a lot of travellers pass this way between Thailand and Laos. Nearby are several villages inhabited by Mien and White Hmong.

Si Ayuthaya, Kasikornbank and Siam Commercial Bank all have branches in town with ATMs and foreign-exchange services.

Bamboo Riverside Guest House (☎ 0 5379 1621/9; sweepatts@hotmail.com; 71 Mu 1 Hua Wiang; dm 70B, r 150-250B) is a great introduction to Thailand or somewhere to leave for Laos on a high. It has bamboo-thatched dorm rooms as well as private rooms, all with fan and attached hot shower. The owner ensures a bohemian atmosphere and the restaurant has views of Laos and good food.

Buses depart hourly for Chiang Rai (42B, three hours, 4am to 5pm) and Chiang Saen (50B, two hours). Daily buses to Bangkok (ordinary/air-con/VIP 382/491/573B, nine hours) leave in the evening.

Boats taking up to 10 passengers can be chartered up the Mekong River from Chiang Khong to Chiang Saen for 1800B. Boat crews can be contacted near the customs pier behind Wat Luang, or further north at the pier for ferries to Laos.

Chiang Saen

pop 55,000

Since it isn't in the officially marketed 'Golden Triangle', Chiang Saen is still a sedate little town on the Mekong River. You can while away a day exploring ruins of the long-extinct Chiang Saen kingdom, visiting the small national museum or watching the boat traffic.

Gin's Guest House (☎ 0 5365 1023; 71 Mu 8; bungalows 200-250B, r 300-700B), on the north side of town (about 1.5km north of the bus terminal), is a friendly and secluded place with solid rooms. The upper terrace is a good place to watch the Mekong flow by. Mountain-bike and motorcycle rentals are available.

Cheap noodle and rice dishes are available at food stalls in and near the market on the river road, and along the main road through town from the highway, near the bus stop. A small night market sets up each evening at the latter location and stays open until around midnight.

Chiang Saen is most easily reached via Chiang Rai (ordinary 25B, 1½ hours, frequent departures). Săwngthăew go to Mae Sai (30B, one hour) and Chiang Khong (50B, two hours).

Six-passenger speedboats go to Sop Ruak (one way/return 400/700B, 30 minutes) or Chiang Khong (one way 1500B, 1½ hours), but be ready to bargain.

Sop Ruak

Busloads of package tourists converge on Sop Ruak's 'Welcome to the Golden Triangle' sign

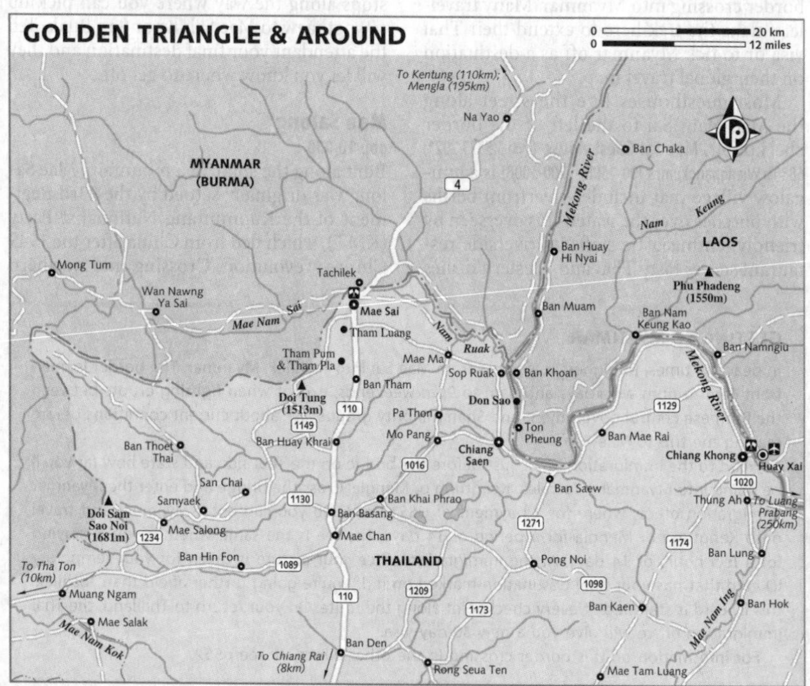

THAILAND

to pose proudly for photos. It is an all-out tourist trap, lacking the romance people might hope to find in such an infamous place.

House of Opium (admission 30B; 7am-7pm), in the centre of town, is worth a peek. It's a small museum telling the story of opium culture, and is the cheaper alternative to the **Opium Exhibition Hall** (0 5378 4444; www.goldentrianglepark.com; admission 300B), an ultraflash exhibition hall on the history and production of opium, as well as the debilitating effects of the drug. It is located about 1km beyond Sop Ruak on the road to Mae Sai.

Sop Ruak is 9km from Chiang Saen, and sǎwngthǎew and share taxis cost around 10B; these leave every 20 minutes. It's an easy bicycle ride from Chiang Saen to Sop Ruak; guesthouses in Chiang Saen can arrange rentals.

Mae Sai

pop 25,800

Thailand's northernmost town, Mae Sai, is a handy launching pad for exploring the Golden Triangle and Mae Salong. The frontier town is a busy trading post for gems, jewellery, cashews and lacquerware, and also forms a legal border crossing into Myanmar. Many travellers make the trek here to extend their Thai visa or to tick Myanmar off as a destination on their global travel map.

Most guesthouses line the street along the Mae Nam Sai to the left of the border checkpoint. **Mae Sai Guest House** (0 5373 2021; 688 Th Wiengpangkam; s 100-150B, d 200-500B) is a bungalow village that includes riverfront berths with porches over the water. It is overseen by friendly, enthusiastic staff. Its riverside restaurant serves tasty Thai and Western dishes and you can keep one eye on Myanmar while you dine. It's about 150m beyond what seems like the end of Th Sailomjoi.

Northern Guest House (0 5373 1537; 402 Th Tham Pha Jum; r 120-350B;) is on the banks of the Nam Ruak – the sign has about a dozen names for this popular guesthouse set in spacious gardens. Choose from rustic huts to modern air-con rooms in a two-storey building by the river.

Mae Sai has a **night market** (Th Phahonyothin) with an enticing mix of Thai, Burmese, Chinese and Indian dishes.

The **bus station** (0 5364 6437), off Th Phahonyothin, is 3km from the border or 1km from the immigration office. For information on crossing into Myanmar, see below.

Buses connect Mae Sai with Bangkok (air-con 374B to 481B, VIP 685B, 12 hours, regular departures). Other services include Chiang Mai (ordinary/air-con 95/171B, four to five hours, regular departures) and Chiang Rai (ordinary/air-con 25/37B, one hour, frequent departures). The bus to Tha Ton (36B) and Fang (45B) leaves at 7am and takes two hours.

The Chiang Rai–bound bus makes stops along the way where you can pick up sǎwngthǎew to Mae Salong or Sop Ruak. Tell the attendant your final destination and they will let you know where to get off.

Mae Salong

pop 10,000

Built along the spine of a mountain, Mae Salong was originally settled by the 93rd Regiment of the Kuomintang Nationalist Party (KMT), which fled from China after the 1949 Chinese revolution. Crossing into northern

GETTING TO MYANMAR

In peaceful times, foreigners may cross from Mae Sai into Tachilek, Myanmar. The border is open from 6am to 6pm weekdays and 6am to 9pm weekends, except when fighting erupts between the Burmese central government and Shan minority groups; ask about current conditions before making the trip to Mae Sai.

Head to the immigration office just before the bridge on the Thai side and state how far you'll be going into Myanmar – Tachilek, Kengtung or Mengla. Cross the bridge and enter the Myanmar immigration office, where for a payment of US$10 or 500B you can enter Myanmar and travel onto Kengtung or Mengla for a period of 14 days. The fee is the same whether you're staying for a few hours or 14 days. At the immigration office your picture is taken for your temporary ID card that has your final destination marked on it. If you're going further afield than Tachilek, this ID card is stamped at every checkpoint along the route. On your return to Thailand, the Thai immigration office will give you a new 30-day visa.

For information on this border crossing in the other direction, see p552.

Thailand with their pony caravans, the ex-soldiers and their families re-created a society that was much like the one they had left behind in Yunnan. Chinese rather than Thai is more frequently spoken here, and the land's severe inclines boast tidy terraces of tea and coffee plantations.

An interesting **morning market** (5-7am) convenes at the T-junction near Shin Sane Guest House. The market attracts town residents and many tribespeople from the surrounding districts. Most of the guesthouses in town can arrange **horseback treks** around the area.

Shin Sane Guest House (Sin Sae; 0 5376 5026; r 50-300B) is Mae Salong's original guesthouse, and the cheapies are as cell-like as you'd expect for such few baht. It has reliable information on trekking and a small restaurant. Next door to Shin Sane, **Akha Mae Salong Guest House** (0 5376 5103; Th Mae Salong; dm/s/d 50/100/150B) is run by a friendly Akha family. Handicrafts are made and sold in the reception area.

To get to Mae Salong, take a Chiang Rai–Mae Sai bus and get off at Ban Basang (ordinary 15B, 1½ hours). From there, săwngthăew climb the mountain to Mae Salong (50B per person, one hour). Yellow săwngthăew follow the scenic road west of the village to Tha Ton (50B).

NAN

pop 24,300

Nan was a semiautonomous kingdom until 1931 and it still retains something of its former isolation and individuality. Surveying the town's distinctive **temples** and visiting the **National Museum** (0 5477 2777, 0 5471 0561; Th Pha Kong; admission 30B; 9am-4pm Mon-Sat) help to pass an unhurried day. Many visitors stop in Nan only long enough to arrange a trek into mountainous **Doi Phu Kha National Park** and the adjacent hill-tribe villages of the Thai Lü, Htin, Khamu and Mien people.

Information

There are several banks with ATMs on Th Sumonthewarat. Internet services are available around town for 40B per hour.

Post office (Th Mahawong) In the centre of town.

Tourist information centre (8am-5pm) Opposite Wat Phumin.

Activities

Fhu Travel Service (0 5471 0636, 0 1287 7209; www.fhutravel.com; 453/4 Th Sumonthewarat) offers treks to minority villages. It has been leading tours for almost two decades, and is a professional, honest and reliable organisation. Trekking tours start from 700B for a day. Fhu also offers white-water rafting trips, kayaking trips and elephant tours.

Sleeping

Doi Phukha Guest House (0 5475 1517; 94/5 Soi 1, Th Aranyawat; s/d 100/150B) This rambling old house in a residential neighbourhood is awkward to get to but offers basic sleep space with clean cold-water bathrooms. To find it, follow Th Mayayot north through town, take a right on Soi Aranyawat and, after passing Wat Aranyaway on your left-hand side, take a left on Soi 1.

Amazing Guest House (0 5471 0893; 23/7 Th Rat Amnuay; s/d 120/350B;) In a tidy, two-storey wooden house on a quiet lane off Th Rat Amnuay, this intimate place is a bit like staying with your long-lost Thai grandparents. All rooms have wooden floors, clean beds and hot shared showers. Bicycles and motorbikes can be rented here, and free pick-up from the bus station is available.

Nan Guest House (0 5477 1849; www.nan-guesthouse.com; 57/16 Th Mahaphrom; r 230-350B;) This well-maintained place has spotless spacious rooms, most with attached hot-water bathrooms. For a clean, comfortable place to sleep, it's an excellent choice.

Eating

You can buy Nan's famous golden-skinned oranges from the **day market** (cnr Th Khao Luang & Th Jettabut), as well as takeaway food such as *sôm-tam* (papaya salad). At night, vendors set up along the banks of the Mae Nam Nan to bring nourishment to the masses.

Yota Vegetarian Restaurant (Th Mahawaong; dishes 10-30B; breakfast & lunch) This is one of the best deals in town, and *the* best if you're vegetarian. Once the food runs out, it's all over red rover.

Da Dario (0 5475 0258; 37/4 Th Rat Amnuay; dishes 60-100B; dinner Tue-Fri, lunch & dinner Sat & Sun) Next to Amazing Guest House, Da Dario is an Italian-Thai restaurant that makes delicious pizza, minestrone and other treats. Prices are reasonable and the service impressive.

Getting There & Away

Air Andaman (0 5471 1222) offers services that connect Nan with Chiang Mai (four flights weekly) or Bangkok (daily). The airline offers free transport between Fahthanin Hotel and the airport. **PB Air** (www.pbair.com) also has flights from Bangkok (four flights weekly).

The government bus station is located roughly 500m southwest of town on the highway to Phrae. Buses travel between Nan and Bangkok (air-con 300B to 387B, VIP 600B, 10 to 12 hours). There are also services available to Chiang Mai (ordinary 128B, air-con 179B to 230B, six to seven hours, four daily), Chiang Rai (air-con 110B, six to seven hours, 9.30am) and Phrae (ordinary/air-con 44/62B, 2½ hours, frequent departures).

NORTHEASTERN THAILAND

Kiss goodbye to the tourist trail, as the northeast is a trip back in time to old Thailand. Rice fields stretch as far as the eye can see in every direction, haphazardly divided by earthen paths and punctuated by tired, sun-beaten trees and lonely water buffaloes submerged in muddy ponds. During the wet season the land is so vivid with tender rice shoots that your eyes ache, but in the dry season the land withers to the texture of a desert. Traditional culture is the rich lifeblood of the Lao, Thai and Khmer people, coursing as deliberately as the mighty Mekong River.

Also referred to as Isan, the northeast is Thailand's least-visited region, as it lacks a well-developed tourist infrastructure. Few towns boast a backpacker scene and fewer have mastered English as a second language. On the wide arc of the Mekong River between the Laos gateways of Nong Khai and Mukdahan there's an inviting array of small towns, best visited during a local festival when music, dancing and food are out in force. Elsewhere, the ancient Angkor kings left behind magnificent temples on their far-flung frontier, part of a holy road connecting Angkor Wat with present-day Thailand.

NAKHON RATCHASIMA (KHORAT)

pop 2 million

Thailand's second-largest city, Nakhon Ratchasima (Map pp750–1), which goes by the nickname 'Khorat', is a slow burner with little evident charm for the whistle-stop visitor. Development has buried much of its history, but unlike other Thai metropolises, Nakhon Ratchasima has a genuine core. This is the gateway to Isan, and a real city where tourism takes a backseat to real life. It is also a handy base for exploring the nearby Khmer ruins of Phimai or Khao Yai National Park.

Information

There are banks galore in Nakhon Ratchasima, all with ATMs and exchange services.

Post office (Th Jomsurangyat; 8am-5pm Mon-Fri, to noon Sat)

Ratchasima Hospital (0 4426 2000; Th Mittaphap)

TAT office (0 4421 3666; Th Mittaphap; 8.30am-4.30pm) On the western edge of town, beyond the train station.

T-Net (1st fl, The Mall, Th Mittaphap; per hr 20B; 10am-10pm) Internet access.

Tourist police (1155) Opposite bus station No 2, north of the city centre.

Sights

In the city centre is the defiant statue of **Khun Ying Mo** (Thao Suranari Memorial), a local heroine who led the inhabitants against Lao invaders during the reign of Rama III (r 1824–51). A holy shrine, the statue receives visitors offering gifts and prayers or hiring singers to perform Khorat folk songs. The steady activities of the devotees make for a lively cultural display.

For a dose of Khmer and Ayuthaya art, visit **Mahawirawong National Museum** (0 4424 2958; Th Ratchadamnoen; admission 10B; 9am-4pm), housed in the grounds of Wat Sutchinda.

Sleeping

Sakol Hotel Korat (0 4424 1260; Th Atsadang; r 150B;) This hotel shows a little more attention to detail than most of the cheapies. The bright rooms are good value, given they include a bathroom, and you can upgrade to air-con for 400B.

Doctor's House (0 4425 5846; 78 Soi 4, Th Seup Siri; r with shared bathroom 180B) One of the few cheapies where guests bearing backpacks are the norm, this homestay has three spacious rooms with shared bathroom in an old wooden house. It is not for party animals as the owner locks the gate at 10pm.

Tokyo Hotel Mansion (0 4424 2873; 331 Th Suranari; r 240-366B;) A lick of paint, a brace of ornamental gold lions and some new signs out the front have revamped this old-school contender. It's a little less fresh on the inside, but the rooms are clean and the price is right.

THAILAND

Eating & Drinking

Nakhon Ratchasima is overflowing with tasty Thai and Chinese restaurants, particularly along Th Ratchadamnoen near the Thao Suranari Memorial and western gate to central Nakhon Ratchasima.

Kai Yang Seup Siri (Th Seup Siri; dishes 30-40B; lunch) This spartan spot is famous for its grilled chicken, and reportedly has the best *sôm-tam* in town. There's no roman-script sign, but just look for the roasting chickens.

Thai Phochana Restaurant (142 Th Jomsurangyat; dishes 40-120B; breakfast & lunch;) A slice of old Khorat, this atmospheric wooden house is popular for its mixture of Thai and local specialities, including *mìi khoràat* (Khorat-style noodles) and *yam kòp yâang* (roast frog salad). The *kaeng phèt pèt* (duck curry) is a winner.

Kai Yang Wang Fa (Th Ratchadamnoen; whole chickens 75B; lunch & dinner) Another famed roast chicken spot, this is takeaway only. No roman-script sign.

Hua Rot Fai Market (Th Mukkhamontri; 6-10pm), located near the Nakhon Ratchasima train station, is a lively place to head after dark. Slower paced are the **night food stalls** (Th Phoklang) that set up beside the Chinese temple and offer a good range of Thai and Isan cuisine.

Try your hand at street surfing along the open-air bars that are dotted about the **night bazaar** (Th Manat). Local drinkers are pretty friendly here and you might end up on a pub crawl you didn't expect.

Shopping

Light up your life with a wander through the Th Manat night bazaar, which is so well lit you'll need shades. Anything and everything is available on this strip and you don't have to bargain as hard as in Bangkok. Several Khorat-style **silk shops** (Th Ratchadamnoen) can be found close to the Thao Suranari Memorial.

Getting There & Away

Nakhon Ratchasima has two bus stations: **No 1** (Th Burin) serves Bangkok's Northern & Northeastern Bus Terminal and provincial destinations; **No 2** (Th Chang Pheuak) serves all other destinations.

Buses travel from Nakhon Ratchasima to Bangkok (ordinary/air-con 96/157B, four to five hours, frequent departures daily), Nong Khai (ordinary/air-con 110/220B, six hours, several departures daily), Phimai (40B, one hour, frequent departures between 5.30am and 10pm) and also to Ubon Ratchathani (ordinary/air-con 149/260B, six hours, regular departures daily).

The **train station** (Th Mukkhamontri) is on the western side of the city. Destinations such as Bangkok, Surin and Buriram are all more conveniently reached by train than bus. Up to seven trains a day connect Nakhon Ratchasima with Bangkok's Hualamphong train station (2nd/3rd class 110/50B), plus there are six services on to Ubon Ratchathani (2nd/3rd class 213/138B).

Getting Around

Local buses and sǎwngthǎew ply fixed routes through Nakhon Ratchasima. Get onto sǎwngthǎew 1 (Th Phoklang–Th Mukkhamontri) or 2 (Th Jomsurangyat–Th Mukkhamontri) to reach the train station or the TAT office from the town centre. Local bus 15 hits both bus stations and can be picked up on Th Ratchadamnoen. Túk-túk and motorbike taxis are also available if you feel the need for speed.

ISAN CUISINE

The food of hard-working farmers who have honed their tolerance for peppers as well as their sinewy muscles against exhaustion, Isan cuisine is true grit. The holy trinity of the cuisine – *kài yâang* (grilled chicken), *sôm-tam* (papaya salad) and *khâo niaw* (sticky rice) – are integral to the culture and reminisced like lost lovers by displaced Isan taxi drivers in Bangkok. Early in the morning a veritable chicken massacre is laid out on an open grill, sending wafts of smoke into the dry air as free advertising. Beside the grill is a huge earthenware *khrók* (mortar) and wooden *sàak* (pestle) beating out the ancient rhythm of *sôm-tam* preparation: in go grated papaya, sliced limes, peppers, sugar and a host of preferential ingredients. People taste the contents and call out adjustments: more *náam plaa* (fish sauce) or *plaa ráa* (fermented fish sauce, which looks like rotten mud). Everything is eaten with the hands, using sticky rice to help offset the chilli burn. Isan food is almost flammable, with a fistful of potent peppers finding their way into every dish, especially *láap*, a super-spicy salad originating from Laos.

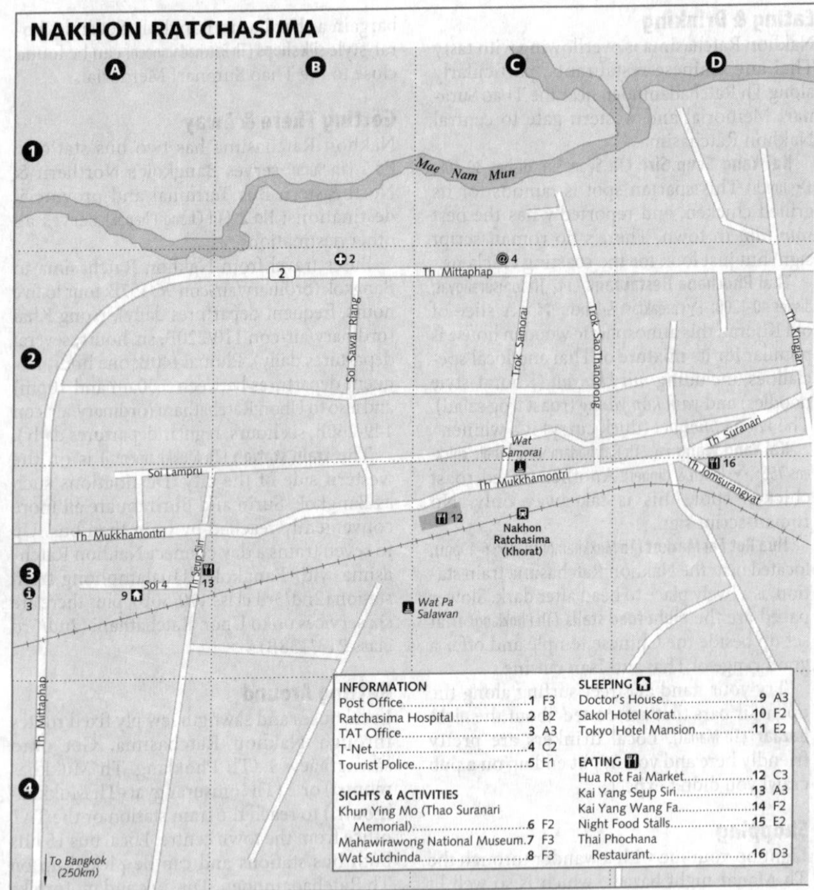

PRASAT HIN PHIMAI

When the Khmer empire was at the height of its vast power, present-day northeastern Thailand was an important regional centre for the Khmer rulers. An ancient laterite highway, lined with temples, linked Prasat Hin Phimai with the heart of the empire at Angkor in Cambodia. The Phimai temple, along with the other Khmer monuments in this part of Thailand, predates the Angkor Wat complex.

Originally started by Khmer King Jayavarman V in the late 10th century and finished by King Suryavarman I (r 1002–49), **Prasat Hin Phimai** (admission 40B; 6am-6pm), 60km northeast of Nakhon Ratchasima, projects a majesty that transcends its size.

The 28m-tall main shrine, of cruciform design, is made of white sandstone, while the adjunct shrines are of pink sandstone and laterite. The sculptures over the doorways to the main shrine depict Hindu gods and scenes from the Ramayana. Extensive restoration work is also evident.

Phimai National Museum (admission 30B; 9am-4pm), outside the main complex, has a fine collection of Khmer sculpture, including a serene bust of Jayavarman VII, Angkor's most powerful king.

Sleeping & Eating

It is easy enough to visit Phimai as a day trip from Nakhon Ratchasima, but some prefer the easy pace of this little town.

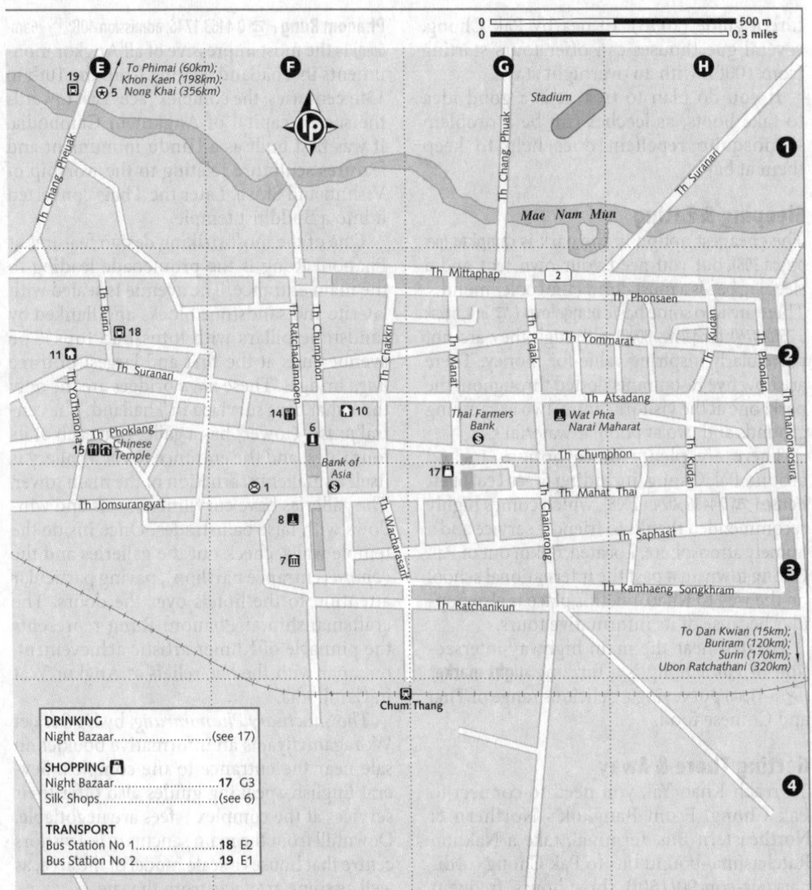

Old Phimai Guest House (☎ 0 4447 1918; dm/s/d 80/130/150B;) This homey place down a *soi* is a little scruffy, but the backpacker vibe prevails and there's a welcoming atmosphere.

Baiteiy Restaurant (☎ 0 4447 1725; dishes 30-40B; breakfast, lunch & dinner) Offers a lively little menu of Thai and Chinese food, and also rents out bicycles.

It's cheaper to eat on the street and there are sizzling woks aplenty at the night market, just north of the regular day market.

Getting There & Away

Buses going to Phimai (ordinary 40B, one hour or so, every half-hour) leave from Nakhon Ratchasima's bus station No 1. Catching the 8am bus to Phimai leaves ample time to explore the ruins; the last bus back to Nakhon Ratchasima is at 6pm.

KHAO YAI NATIONAL PARK

Up there with the world's finest national parks, **Khao Yai** (☎ 0 3731 9002; adult/child 200/100B) includes one of the largest intact monsoon forests in mainland Asia. The park has more than 50km of trekking trails, many of them formed by the movement of wildlife. Elevations range from 100m to 1400m, where the western edge of Cambodia's Dangrek mountain range collides with the southern edge of the Khorat Plateau.

Somewhat inaccurate trail maps are available from the park headquarters. It's easy to get lost on the longer trails, so it's wise to hire a guide (200B). In nearby Pak Chong, several guesthouses can offer tours starting from 1000B with an overnight stay.

If you do plan to trek, it is a good idea to take boots, as leeches can be a problem – mosquito repellent does help to keep them at bay.

Sleeping & Eating

The cheapest option in the park is **camping** (per person 30B), but you need your own tent and a sleeping bag is a must during the cooler months. There are also some basic **bungalows** (☎ in Bangkok 0 2562 0760; bungalows 800B), although they are not particularly inspiring value for money. There are now five restaurants dotted throughout the park: one at the visitors centre, two at camping grounds and two at popular waterfalls.

There are plenty more options in and around Pak Chong, including **Green Leaf Guest House** (☎ 0 4436 5024; r 200B), which comes highly recommended thanks to friendly service and a homely atmosphere. Located 7.5km out of Pak Chong town, just past the international school on the way to Khao Yai, this place is also popular because of its informative tours.

Located near the main highway intersection in Pak Chong is a buzzing **night market** (⏰ 5-11pm) purveying a delicious range of Thai and Chinese food.

Getting There & Away

To reach Khao Yai, you need to connect to Pak Chong. From Bangkok's Northern & Northeastern Bus Terminal, take a Nakhon Ratchasima–bound bus to Pak Chong (ordinary/air-con 90/150B, three hours, frequent departures from 5am to 10pm). From Nakhon Ratchasima take a Bangkok-bound bus and get off in Pak Chong (ordinary/air-con 28/65B, one hour).

From in front of the 7-Eleven store in Pak Chong, you can catch a sǎwngthǎew to the park gates for 10B. You may also be able to take a direct bus from Bangkok at certain times of the year – inquire at the Northern & Northeastern Bus Terminal.

You can also easily access Pak Chong by train from Ayuthaya (2nd/3rd class 58/26B, three hours) and Nakhon Ratchasima (2nd/3rd class 50/20B, 1½ hours).

PHANOM RUNG HISTORICAL PARK

Spectacularly located atop an extinct volcano, the elegantly restored temple of **Prasat Hin Khao Phanom Rung** (☎ 0 4463 1746; admission 40B; ⏰ 6am-6pm) is the most impressive of all Angkor monuments in Thailand. Dating from the 10th to 13th centuries, the complex faces east towards the sacred capital of Angkor in Cambodia. It was first built as a Hindu monument and features sculpture relating to the worship of Vishnu and Shiva. Later the Thais converted it into a Buddhist temple.

One of the most striking design features at Phanom Rung is the promenade leading to the main entrance. The avenue is sealed with laterite and sandstone blocks and flanked by sandstone pillars with lotus-bud tops. The avenue ends at the first and largest of three *naga* bridges. These *naga* bridges are the only three that have survived in Thailand. The central *prasat* (tower) has a gallery on each of its four sides, and the entrance to each gallery is itself a smaller incarnation of the main tower. The galleries have curvilinear roofs and windows with false balustrades. Once inside the temple walls, check out the galleries and the *gopura* (entrance pavilion), paying particular attention to the lintels over the doors. The craftsmanship at Phanom Rung represents the pinnacle of Khmer artistic achievement, on a par with the bas-reliefs at Angkor Wat in Cambodia.

The Sanctuary Phanomrung, by Dr Sorajet Woragamvijya, is an informative booklet on sale near the entrance to the complex. Several English-speaking guides also offer their services at the complex – fees are negotiable. Downhill from the main sanctuary is a visitors centre that houses a scale model of the area, as well as some artefacts from the site.

Sleeping

Phanom Rung can be undertaken as a day trip from Nakhon Ratchasima, Buriram, Nang Rong or Surin. Although Buriram is the closest large base, the selection of accommodation is miserable, making other towns more attractive options. The pick of a poor pack in Buriram is the **Thai Hotel** (☎ 0 4461 1112; 38/1 Th Romburi; r 250-400B; ❄), but that's hardly a glowing endorsement. In the small village of Nang Rong, **Honey Inn** (☎ 0 4462 2825; 8/1 Soi Ri Kun; s/d 200/250B) is a homestay run by a local school teacher who speaks English. Bathrooms are shared and motorbikes are available for rent, which is handy for Phanom Rung. See p748 and opposite for other options.

Getting There & Away

From Nakhon Ratchasima, take a Surin-bound bus and get off at Ban Ta-Ko (ordinary/air-con 35/60B), which is well marked as the turn-off for Phanom Rung. Likewise, from Surin take a Nakhon Ratchasima-bound bus to Ban Ta-Ko.

Once in Ban Ta-Ko, it is time for multiple choice. At the Ban Ta-Ko intersection you can wait for a săwngthăew that's going as far as the foot of Phanom Rung (20B), 12km away, or one that's headed south to Lahan Sai. If you take a Lahan Sai truck, get off at the Ban Ta Pek intersection (10B). From Ban Ta Pek, take a motorcycle taxi (50B) the rest of the way or book a return trip with waiting time for about 150B.

It's easier from Buriram. From here, Chanthaburi-bound buses stop at Ban Ta Pek (ordinary 30B, one hour); you can then continue by motorcycle taxi as suggested.

From Nang Rong, catch a săwngthăew to Ban Ta-Ko and continue from there. Or for more freedom, rent a motorcycle from the Honey Inn for 250B.

SURIN

pop 41,200

Sleepy Surin goes wild in November during its annual **Elephant Roundup**, drawing huge numbers of foreign visitors. Elephant races, tug-of-war and a spot of soccer – these tuskers sure have a diverse repertoire.

Culturally, the town of Surin is a melting pot of Lao, Khmer and Suay (a minority elephant-herding tribe) cultures, resulting in an interesting mix of dialects and customs. Surin silk is renowned; it's worn by the college-educated professional and the illiterate vegetable-seller alike.

Sights

Surin is best enjoyed as a base for day trips to nearby attractions. To see Surin's elephants during the low season, visit **Ban Tha Klang** (☎ 0 1966 5284) in Tha Tum District, about 60km north of Surin. Many of the performers at the annual festival are trained here and there are two-hour shows (admission 200B) every Saturday at 9am. Silk weaving can be observed at local villages including **Khwaosinarin** and **Ban Janrom**. You can also visit **Phanom Rung**, and other minor Angkor temples.

As an evening reward, Surin's main attraction is a pedestrian-only **night market** (Th Krung Si Nai) that delivers healthy doses of eating and people-watching.

Sleeping & Eating

During the elephant roundup, accommodation vacancies shrink and rates triple; book well in advance.

Pirom's House (☎ 0 4451 5140; 242 Th Krung Si Nai; s/d 100/150B) At Surin's one and only guesthouse, host Pirom offers a warm welcome at his atmospheric (read: basic, with shared bathrooms) teak home. Pirom is a mine of information on the surrounding area. The guesthouse may move during the lifetime of this book – call Pirom's mobile (☎ 08 9355 4140) to check.

New Hotel (☎ 0 4451 1341; 6-8 Th Thanasan; r 200B; ❄) Just across from the train station, this pad has clean rooms of varying sizes and shapes. Air-con rooms are 350B a pop.

Petmanee 1 (dishes 50-80B; 🕒 breakfast, lunch & dinner) Down a small *soi* across from Wat Salaloi, Th Thesaban 4, this famous *sôm-tam* shop has won national competitions for its local variation of the papaya salad, using a native herb. Don't speak Thai? No problem, tick the 14th item on the menu.

Also recommended are the **municipal market** (Th Krung Si Nai), near Pirom's House, for *khâo phàt* (fried rice) and the **night market** (Th Krung Si Nai) for *khanŏm jiin* (curry noodles served with a huge tray of veggies) and *hăwy thâwt* (batter-fried mussels).

Getting There & Away

The **bus terminal** (Th Chit Bam Rung) is one block from the train station. Destinations include Bangkok (air-con/VIP 250/385B, eight hours,

> **GETTING TO CAMBODIA**
>
> Foreigners are able to cross the border from Chong Jom in Thailand to O Smach in Cambodia. Several săwngthăew (small pick-up trucks with two benches in the back; 40B, 3½ hours) and minibuses (60B, two hours) run daily from Surin to Chong Jom. Once on the Cambodian side, there are shared taxis to Siem Reap. This is not the easiest border crossing to access, but because so few foreigners cross here it's relatively hassle free.
>
> See p89 for information on doing the trip in the opposite direction.

regular departures), Ubon (air-con 188B, four hours, frequent departures) and Nakhon Ratchasima (air-con 115B, four hours, frequent departures).

These destinations, however, are more convenient by train (Bangkok 2nd/3rd class 210/80B). The train station is centrally located at the intersection of Th Nong Toom and Th Thawasan.

UBON RATCHATHANI

pop 115,300

Although it is one of the bigger cities in the region, Ubon still retains a small-town feel and is easily traversed by foot. Through something as simple as workday attire, Ubon stays true to its values, with middle-class professionals donning traditional silks from local weavers rather than the latest foreign imports.

With the Thai–Lao border crossing at nearby Chong Mek open to foreigners, Ubon (not to be confused with Udon Thani) has been receiving many more travellers who are finding it a good place to decompress after the relatively rustic conditions of southern Laos.

Information

Bangkok Bank (Th Suriyat) One of many banks in town.

MD.Com (221 Th Kheuan Thani; 11am-10pm) Internet access near the post office.

Post office (Th Si Narong)

Saphasit Prasong hospital (0 4526 3043; Th Saphasit)

TAT office (0 4524 3770; 264/1 Th Kheuan Thani; 8.30am-4.30pm) Helpful place opposite Sri Kamol Hotel; provides maps and advice on outlying attractions.

Tourist police (0 4524 5505, emergency 1155; Th Suriyat) Behind the police station.

Sights

Housed in a former palace of the Rama VI era, west of the TAT office, **Ubon National Museum** (0 4525 5071; Th Kheuan Thani; admission 30B; 9am-4pm Wed-Sun) is a good place to delve into Ubon's history and culture before exploring the city or province.

Across the Mae Nam Mun in the Warin Chamrap District is **Wat Pa Nanachat Bung Wai** (Ban Bung Wai, Amphoe Warin, Ubon Ratchathani 34310), which is directed by an Australian abbot and populated by European, American and Japanese monks. Write in advance for information about overnight stays and meditation classes.

Pastel-coloured silks displaying Lao influences are unpacked like contraband along the streets near Ubon's hotel districts; the making of these and other handicrafts can be observed in the nearby villages of **Ban Khawn Sai**, **Ban Pa-Ao** and **Khong Jiam**.

Festivals & Events

Ubon's **Candle Festival**, usually held in July, is a grand parade of gigantic, elaborately carved wax sculptures that are a celebration of Khao Phansa, a Buddhist holiday marking the start of the monks' retreat during the wet season.

Sleeping

Rates shoot up and availability goes down during the Candle Festival.

River Moon Guesthouse (0 4528 6093; Th Si Saket; s/d 120/150B) Travellers arriving from Laos will appreciate the calm and tranquillity at River Moon, a flashback to island life in Si Phan Don. The rustic bungalows have more function than flair, and bathrooms are shared, but the atmosphere is laid-back. Find it across the river from central Ubon in the Warin Chamrap District, near the train station.

New Nakornluang Hotel (0 4525 4768; 84-88 Th Yutthaphan; r 150-200B) The heart of old Ubon is blessed with some attractive Indo-Chinese architecture that the French left behind from Hanoi to Phnom Penh. The New Nakornluang is not that new, but it's a comfortable option near some classic buildings.

Tokyo Hotel (0 4524 1739; 178 Th Uparat; old bldg r 250B, new bldg d 500B;) The best of the budget deals in the centre of town, the Tokyo has some old cheapies that are starting to show their age. Flash the cash and opt for the swish newer rooms with TV and textbook trim.

Eating & Drinking

It's worth sniffing out Ubon's two night markets: one by the river near the main bridge, and the other near the bus station on Th Chayangkun.

Kai Yang Wat Jaeng (0 1709 9393; Th Suriyat; dishes 20-50B; breakfast, lunch & dinner) Spit and sawdust Thai-style. It may be a simple shack, but it is considered by those in the know to do the best *kài yâang* (grilled Lao-style chicken). The chicken is sold from 9am to 2pm only, after which it's curries only. Seek it out one block north of Wat Jaeng.

Chiokee (0 4525 4017; Th Kheuan Thani; dishes 20-60B; breakfast, lunch & dinner) East meets West at this popular spot, with Chinese-Thai décor and bright white tablecloths. Professional

THAILAND

GETTING TO CAMBODIA & LAOS

Getting to Cambodia

A remote crossing links Choam Srawngam with Choam, in the former Khmer Rouge stronghold of Anlong Veng, but access is tough on both sides of the border.

From Ubon Ratchathani you can catch a bus (ordinary/air-con 40/59B, 1¼ hours) or a train (2nd/3rd class from 139/13B, one hour) to the town of Si Saket, from where you can get a taxi to the border. It is also possible to travel from Surin to Si Saket by bus (ordinary/air-con 50/80B, 2½ hours).

See p101 for details on travelling from Cambodia to Thailand.

Getting to Laos

Chong Mek is the only place in Thailand where you don't have to cross the Mekong to get into Laos. The southern Lao city of Pakse is about 45 minutes away by road from Vang Tao, the village on the Lao side of the border, where you can now buy a 30-day visa on the spot. Buses crossing here wait for passengers to complete the paperwork. The border is open from 6am until 6pm, but Lao border officials charge a 40B 'overtime' levy if you arrive before 8am or after 4pm, or any time on a weekend. They also try to extract a 50B 'stamping fee', no matter what the hour.

Air-con buses leave Ubon for Pakse (200B, three hours) four times daily; they wait for passengers to get their visas. Otherwise, you can catch a Phibun bus (25B, 1½ hours) from Ubon's bus terminal and change to a săwngthăew bound for Chong Mek (35B, one hour, every 20 minutes). To get to Pakse, catch a bus (50B) on the Lao side.

For information on crossing this border in the opposite direction, see p398.

breakfasts, including Thai, Chinese and Western, plus coffee with a kick to start the day.

Indochine (☎ 0 4524 5584; Th Saphasit; dishes 50-150B; ⏲ lunch & dinner) Near Wat Jaeng, this old teak house has been swallowed by vines and creepers. Downstairs you'll find excellent Vietnamese food until 6pm when the action moves upstairs to the Intro Pub until midnight. Live music joins the nightshift.

U-Bar (☎ 0 4526 5141; 97/8-10 Th Phichit Rangsan; ⏲ 6pm-2am) This is as hip as it gets in Isan, a full-on bar-club to see and be seen in, for young Thais at least. Upstairs is a slow-paced terrace balcony, where there is often live music; it heaves at the hinges from 10pm most nights.

Getting There & Away

Thai Airways International (☎ 0 4531 3340-4; www.thaiair.com; 364 Th Chayangkun) has three daily flights from Bangkok to Ubon. **Air Asia** (☎ 0 2515 9999; www.airasia.com) has a cheaper daily flight between Ubon and Bangkok.

Ubon's **bus terminal** (☎ 0 4531 2773; Th Chayangkun) is located at the far northern end of town, 3km from the centre. Local buses 2 and 3 can drop you off near the TAT office (20B). Chartered transport is more like 100B into town.

Buses link Ubon with Bangkok's Northern & Northeastern Bus Terminal (ordinary/air-con 200/300B, nine hours, hourly from 6am to midnight), and with Buriram (65/150B, four to five hours), Nakhon Ratchasima (149/260B, six hours), Mukdahan (80/144B, 3½ hours) and Surin (75/88B, three hours).

The **train station** (☎ 0 4532 1004; Th Sathani) is located in Warin Chamrap, south of central Ubon. Use local bus 2 to cross the Mae Nam Mun into Ubon (5B). There are a couple of night trains in either direction connecting Ubon and Bangkok (express 2nd/3rd class 301/175B, express 2nd-class sleeper 401B). Express trains also stop in Surin and Nakhon Ratchasima, but not necessarily at convenient times!

MUKDAHAN

pop 34,300

Looking across to the Lao city of Savannakhet, Mukdahan is a well-oiled revolving door between the two countries. A popular Thai-Lao market, nicknamed **Talat Indojin** (Indochina Market), sets up along the river near the border checkpoint. The town experienced something of a sea change in late 2006, when construction on the second Thai-Lao Friendship Bridge was finally completed. As a small but pivotal link in the massive Trans-Asia Highway project, the bridge has not only connected Thai traders with the Vietnamese port town of Danang,

GETTING TO LAOS

With the second Thai-Lao Friendship Bridge now linking Mukdahan and Savannakhet, travellers no longer have to cross the Mekong by ferry, although that option is still available. Crossing by bus seems to be the more popular choice, and there are now 12 daily buses making the journey between Mukdahan and Savannakhet (45B, 40 minutes) between 7am and 5.30pm. Should you choose a ferry crossing (50B, 20 to 30 minutes), your departure point will be the pier in the heart of town. At our last visit, boat departures were six times daily between 9.10am and 4pm on weekdays, less often on weekends. Lao immigration is very efficient, making solo border crossings a relatively simple matter.

Travellers can apply for a 30-day Lao visa on arrival at the Savannakhet checkpoint, but will need two passport-sized photos and US$30.

For information on crossing from Laos into Thailand, see p394.

it has also delivered much needed economic relief to the surrounding region.

There are a few cheap if cheerless sleeping options near the pier. **Mukdahan Hotel** (☎ 0 4261 1619; 8 Th Samut Sakdarak; r 150-250B; ❄) is home to the cheapest digs in town; rooms are pleasantly large, although the staff speak almost no English. **Huanam Hotel** (☎ 0 4261 1137; 36 Th Samut Sakdarak; r 150-320B; ❄ 💻) has been to self-improvement classes in recent years and offers good-value rooms, which are nonetheless not quite as slick as the lobby. Mountain-bike rentals are 100B per day. **Hong Kong Hotel** (☎ 0 4261 1143; 161/1-2 Th Phitak Santirat; d 200B) remains lower in the pecking order, as the large rooms are sagging at the seams and could stand for a scrubbing.

Wine Wild Why? (☎ 0 4263 3122; 11 Th Samron Chaikhongthi; mains 40-130B; 🕑 lunch & dinner) is an atmospheric eatery housed in a wooden building right on the river. It's a rather romantic little spot serving delicious Thai food, though the wine list is history.

Mukdahan's main bus terminal is on Rte 212, north of town. Take a yellow sǎwngthǎew (8B) from the fountain near the 7-Eleven on Th Samut Sakdarak for a cheap connection to the centre.

There are frequent buses to Nakhon Phanom (ordinary/air-con 52/93B, two hours) via That Phanom (ordinary/air-con 28/50B, one hour); Khon Kaen (air-con 155B, 4½ hours); Ubon Ratchathani (ordinary/air-con 80/144B, 3½ hours) and Bangkok's Northern & Northeastern Terminal (air-con/VIP 364/760B, 11 hours).

THAT PHANOM

This place might have been forgotten to the world were it not for the looming spire of **Wat Phra That Phanom** (🕑 5am-8pm). It's a badge of Isan identity and an icon in the region. A lively Lao **market** gathers by the river from 8.30am to noon on Monday and Thursday.

The original backpacker pad, **Niyana Guest House** (☎ 0 4254 0880; 65/14 Soi 33; r with shared bathroom 140B), northeast of the Lao Arch of Victory, is a tad chaotic, but smiles and advice flow freely from the friendly owner. A bit further north, **Kritsada Rimkhong Resort** (☎ 0 4254 0088; www.kritsadaresort.com; 90-93 Th Rimkhong; r 400-600B; ❄) isn't fancy – but it's as fancy as it gets in That Phanom.

There is a small **night market** (🕑 3-9pm) and a clutch of **riverside eateries** (Th Rimkhong).

Buses depart from the south side of town regularly for Nakhon Phanom (ordinary/air-con 27/49B, one hour, five daily), and for Ubon Ratchathani (ordinary/air-con 102/178B, 4½ hours) via Mukdahan (ordinary/air-con 28/50B, one hour). There are also sǎwngthǎew to Nakhon Phanom (36B, 1½ hours, every 10 minutes).

NAKHON PHANOM

pop 31,700

In Sanskrit-Khmer, Nakhon Phanom means 'City of Hills', but they're talking about the ones across the Mekong River in Laos. The fabulous views across the Mekong adorn this somnolent town, as does a scattering of graceful French colonial buildings. The **TAT** (☎ 4251 3490; Th Sunthon Wijit; 🕑 8.30am-4.30pm) office has a map pointing out several of them.

Ho Chi Minh lived and planned his resistance movement here in 1928–29, and **Uncle Ho's House** (donations appreciated; 🕑 daylight) and the **Friendship Village** (donations appreciated; 🕑 8am-5pm) community centre have displays about his time here. They are about 4km west of town in Ban Na Chok.

GETTING TO LAOS

Foreigners are permitted to cross by ferry from Nakhon Phanom to Tha Khaek, a two-hour bus ride from Savannakhet; Mukdahan (see opposite), however, is a more convenient border crossing for Savannakhet. If you do want to make the crossing at Nakhon Phanom, stop by the **immigration office** (☎ 0 4251 1235; Th Sunthon Wijit; 8.30am-4.30pm Mon-Fri), across the street from the Indochine souvenir market, for an exit stamp before boarding the ferry (60B) across the river. Once in Laos, you'll need to pay an entry tax of 50B. The border is open from 9am to 4pm.

See p394 for information on doing the trip in the reverse direction.

Sleeping & Eating

Rarely is a 'Grand' hotel that grand in provincial Thailand, and Nakhon Phanom's **Grand Hotel** (☎ 0 4251 1526; 210 Th Si Thep; d 190-390B) is no exception – but it's better than average for the price. The view at **Mae Nam Khong Grand View Hotel** (☎ 0 4251 3564; www.mgvhotel.com; 527 Sunthon Wijit; r 700-2600B), on the other hand, lives up to its name.

There are restaurants along the river, but most of the better eateries are back in the centre of town. **O-Hi-O** (☎ 4252 1300; 24 Th Fuang Nakhon; mains 30-220B; dinner) is an airy bar-eatery with the usual Thai, Isan and Chinese menu, plus movies on the big screen. The outdoor terrace at the **Indochina Market** (Th Sunthon Wijit; breakfast, lunch & dinner) food court has choice seats that frame the mountain views.

Getting There & Away

PB Air (code 9Q; ☎ 0 2261 0222; www.pbair.com) flies daily from Bangkok (2905B).

The **bus terminal** (Th Fuang Nakhon) is east of the town centre. From here, buses head to Nong Khai (ordinary/air-con 160/205B, five hours, nine daily until 11.30am), Sakhon Nakhon (ordinary/air-con 47/85B, 1½ hours) and Mukdahan (ordinary/air-con 52/94B, two hours) via That Phanom (27/49B, one hour). VIP buses to Bangkok (13 hours) cost 664B to 820B.

NONG KHAI

pop 61,500

Time ticks past slowly in charming Nong Khai and many travellers find themselves staying here longer than expected. Nestled on the banks of the Mekong River, Nong Khai is the perfect preparation for understanding the unhurried pace of Laos, the town's neighbour and cultural parent. The soaring Thai-Lao Friendship Bridge connects Nong Khai with the Lao capital, Vientiane, creating one of the busiest border points between the two countries and ensuring the town is a hot stop on the travellers' map of Thailand.

Information

There is no shortage of banks with ATMs in town, while cash machines remain a rarity in Laos. For a wealth of information on Nong Khai and the surrounding area, visit www.mutmee.net.

Hornbill Bookshop (☎ 0 4246 0272; Th Kaew Worawut; 10am-7pm) On the *soi* leading to Mut Mee Guest House, it has new and used English-language books, plus internet access.

Nong Khai Hospital (☎ 1669; Th Meechai) For medical emergencies.

Post office (Th Meechai)

TAT office (☎ 0 4246 7164; 8.30am-4.30pm) In a row of shops next to the Thai-Lao Friendship Bridge checkpoint.

Tourist police (☎ 0 4224 0616, emergency 1155; Th Meechai)

Sights

Sala Kaewkoo (admission 10B; 7.30am-5.30pm) is a surreal spiritual and sculptural journey into the mind of a mystic Shaman of Lao descent. This park offers a potpourri of the Hindu and Buddhist pantheon of deities, and the immense statues offer some freaky photo opportunities. While the motivations for its 20-year construction were undoubtedly spiritual, the end result is a masterpiece of mysterious modern art for the casual browser. The gardens are in the grounds of Wat Khaek, 5km southeast of town. It is easily reached by bicycle from Nong Khai; Mut Mee Guest House distributes handy maps.

Talat Tha Sadet (Th Rimkhong) follows the river, obscuring the view with stalls selling crusty French baguettes, silks, souvenirs, kitchen utensils and, if you look really hard, possibly the kitchen sink.

In an effort to preserve an ancient art and stem the migration of young women to the bright lights of the big city, **Village Weaver Handicrafts** (☎ 0 4242 2651; Soi Jittapunya, Th Prajak), a nonprofit organisation, established a village weaving cooperative. It sells high-quality fabrics and ready-made clothes. The *mát-mìi* (cloth made of tie-dyed silk or cotton thread) is particularly fine here. Visitors are welcome to watch the weaving process.

Sleeping

Mut Mee Guest House (☎ 0 4246 0717; www.mutmee.net; 111/4 Th Kaew Worawut; dm 90B, r 120-600B;) Overlooking the mighty Mekong, the Mut Mee is one of those rare guesthouses that has become a destination in itself. The dorms are bare bones, but the rooms are good value (especially those with shared bathrooms for 120B to 280B) and there is even one air-con indulgence in the owner's house. Retreat here for some reflection before or after an adventure in Laos. The pedestrian *soi* verges on a traveller ghetto, with bookshops, internet access and yoga available. Mut Mee is a reliable spot for traveller info.

Chongkohn Guesthouse (☎ 0 4246 0548; 649 Th Rimkhong; s/d 100/160B) The sleepy riverfront road is lined with small guesthouses, among them the go-slow Chongkohn, a converted home with 2nd-floor rooms and shared bathrooms. Try to bag a room at the back for views of Laos.

Sawasdee Guest House (☎ 0 4241 2502; Th Meeihai; s/d from 100/140B;) A little slice of history, the Sawasdee is housed in a classic Indochine-era shophouse. The rooms don't quite match the romantic exterior, but fan rooms with shared bathroom are keenly priced at 100/140B for singles/doubles, and the air-con room is a steal at 300B.

Eating

The riverside restaurants are the most atmospheric in town and there is a whole cluster of them on Th Rimkhong. For a bargain bite, check out the evening vendors on Th Prajak, who stoke up their woks each night between Soi Cheunjit and Th Hai Sok.

Daeng Namnuang (☎ 0 4241 1961; Th Banthoengjit; mains 30-60B; breakfast, lunch & dinner;) The house speciality at this little eatery is *nǎem neuang* – spicy pork sausages that are rolled up in rice wrappers with lettuce leaves, star fruit and veggies, and then dipped in various condiments. A hive of buzzing activity, the air-con sure helps on a hot day. It closes at 7pm.

Udom Rod Restaurant (☎ 0 4241 3555; Th Rimkhong; mains 30-80B; lunch & dinner) An authentic eatery on the popular riverfront strip, Udom Rod draws a crowd around sundown to soak up the views. It's a rambling, creaky old place, but the food is temptingly priced.

Nong Naen Pla Phao (Th Rimkhong; dishes 50-150B; breakfast, lunch & dinner) This lively little Lao-style restaurant turns out delicious salt-baked *plaa châwn* (river fish) stuffed with herbs, plus *kài yâang, kaeng lao* (Lao-style bamboo-shoot soup), grilled sausages and grilled prawns. The dining area includes free river views.

Also recommended:

Mut Mee Guest House (dishes 40-100B; breakfast, lunch & dinner) Best guesthouse food in town, including a healthy vegetarian selection and lots of company.

Thai Thai (cnr Th Prajak & Soi Vietnam; dishes 50-150B; breakfast, lunch & dinner) Thai and Chinese standards, but at least it's open all night.

Drinking

Crawling along Th Rimkhong, the riverfront road, there is no shortage of *faràng*-style pubs with cocktail specials. For something a little

GETTING TO LAOS

Nong Khai is the most popular land border crossing between Thailand and Laos. Take a túk-túk to the border crossing, where you get stamped out of Thailand. From there, regular minibuses ferry passengers across the bridge (15B) to the Lao checkpoint between 6am and 9.30pm. It's then 22km to Vientiane – there will be plenty of buses, túk-túk and taxis waiting for you. If you already have a visa for Laos, there are also six direct buses a day to Vientiane from Nong Khai's bus terminal (55B, one hour).

Despite what travel agents in Bangkok might tell you, the Lao government issues 30-day tourist visas on arrival at Nong Khai's Thai-Lao Friendship Bridge and the other border crossings open to those who are not Thai or Lao citizens. Most *faràng* pay either US$30 or US$35, though Canadians get socked with a US$42 fee. You are also allowed to pay in baht, but the price works out much higher. Besides the fee, you'll need a passport photo and the name of a hotel you will be staying at in Laos.

For information on making this crossing in the opposite direction, see p362.

more Thai, follow the road past Talat Tha Sadet (keep going, don't give up) until it delivers full views of the Mekong River. This is the domain of neon-lit restaurant-bars churning out dinner and drinks to a Thai crowd of all ages.

Mittraphaap Bar (Th Kaew Worawut) Welcome to the Wild East. This is a good introduction to Thai country bars if you have just arrived from Laos. Thais can't get enough of the cowboy thang and this bar offers live music, hard drinking and occasional wobbly dancing. On a full tank, you could wander over to the Thai-Lao Riverside Hotel disco to cut some moves on the dance floor.

Getting There & Away

Nong Khai's main **bus terminal** (☎ 0 4241 1612) is just off Th Prajak, by the Pho Chai market, about 1km from the riverfront guesthouses. Services link Nong Khai to Bangkok (air-con/VIP/Super VIP 273/351/545B, 11 hours, eight daily); Udon Thani's No 2 bus terminal (40B, one hour, hourly), a transfer point to other destinations; Khon Kaen (140B, four hours, regular departures); Si Chiangmai (22B, 1½ hours); and Loei (84B, six hours, frequent departures).

The **train station** (☎ 0 4246 4513; Hwy 212) is 1.5km from town, near the bus stop for transport to Laos. Nong Khai is at the end of the railway line that runs from Bangkok through Nakhon Ratchasima, Khon Kaen and Udon Thani. When making the long trip to or from Bangkok, most people opt for a sleeper train. There are two night trains out of Bangkok and one departing Nong Khai daily. Fares range from 318/183B for a 2nd-/3rd-class seat to 1117B for a 1st-class sleeper cabin.

NONG KHAI TO LOEI

You've hit all the highlights, now it is time to enjoy the easy life. Cradled by the meandering Mekong River, little villages slumber in the shade of Laos' voluptuous hills. With a visit to **Si Chiangmai**, **Sangkhom**, **Pak Chom** or **Chiang Khan**, the day's most pressing business is to stroll the riverside road with no particular destination in mind. The crowds usually hurry on to more famous spots, leaving the family guesthouses quiet, friendly and cheap (around 100B).

LOEI & AROUND

Loei is little more than a brief base to prepare your adventures into the more remote pockets of the country beyond. **Phu Kradung National Park** (☎ 0 4287 1333; reserve@dnp.go.th; admission 200B; 🕒 8.30am-4.30pm Oct-Jun), about 75km to the south, encloses a bell-shaped mountain blessed with unhindered sunrise and sunset views. The climb to the summit takes about four hours if you're in shape. Being the northeast's version of a 'spring break' destination, the park fills up with guitar-toting college students during school holidays and weekends.

Dan Sai's three-day **Spirit Festival**, usually in June, is a curious cross between the drunken revelry of Carnival and the spooky imagery of Halloween. On the second day of the festival, villagers don elaborate masks to transform themselves into ghosts, and down shots of *lâo khǎo* (rice whisky) to get themselves drunk. The colourful and rowdy group then parades through town to the local temple for more processing until they stagger home to sleep it off. Dan Sai is 80km west of Loei.

Sleeping & Eating

LOEI

Friendship Guest House (☎ 0 4283 2408; Th Charoenrat; d 150B) The only real guesthouse in town, Friendship has the cheapest digs around, but the rooms are basic with a capital 'B' and bathrooms are shared.

Sun Palace Hotel (☎ 0 4281 5714; Th Charoenrat; d 330-400B; ❄) It is worth shelling out some shekels for the Sun Palace, which offers meticulously clean rooms, hot water and satellite TV. Near the main post office, the hotel is midway between town and the bus station.

Charcoal Restaurant (☎ 0 4281 5675; Th Nok Kaew; mains 30-90B; 🕒 lunch & dinner) Locals flock here in droves after dark and the beers go down well amid a whirlwind of eager servers. The spicy Thai dishes come in generous portions and there's a limited English-language menu.

Also worth seeking out are the **night market** (cnr Th Ruamjai & Th Charoenrat), for cheap eats and local specialities such as *khài pîng* (toasted eggs), and the morning vendors, selling *khanǒm pang mǔu* (mini-baguette pork sandwiches).

PHU KRADUNG NATIONAL PARK

A **visitors centre** (☎ 0 2562 0760; 🕒 7am-3pm) at the base of the mountain distributes detailed maps and rents tents (100B) and A-frame huts (200B). Amazing but true, after walking for hours you will find a friendly vendor at the top of the mountain eager to flog you food;

life at the top is pricey, but it beats hauling it up the mountain yourself.

DAN SAI

Few people stop in Dan Sai outside the festival season, so the accommodation options available are extremely limited within the town itself. The **information centre** (☎ 0 4289 1094; Th Kaew Asa; 8am-5pm Mon-Fri) can arrange basic homestay accommodation from 100B per person.

Getting There & Around

Loei **bus station** (Hwy 201) is roughly 500m west of the town centre; hired transport to get you into town costs about 5B per person or 30B for a charter. Routes include Bangkok's Northern & Northeastern Bus Terminal (air-con 250B to 350B, 10 hours), Udon Thani (ordinary/air-con 60/110B, four hours, five daily) and Nong Khai (ordinary 84B, six hours, four daily).

To get yourself to Phu Kradung National Park from the Loei bus station, take a Khon Kaen–bound bus (35B, 1½ hours, every half-hour from 6am to 6.30pm) to the town of Phu Kradung. From there, hop on a *săwngthăew* (10B) to the visitors centre at the base of the mountain, 7km away. There is no admission after 3pm. The last bus back to Loei leaves around 6pm.

Buses between Loei and Dan Sai (45B, two hours) depart almost hourly during the day.

UDON THANI & AROUND

pop 227,200

Udon Thani is never going to draw visitors in big numbers, with the charms of Nong Khai to the north and the student-driven sophistication of Khon Kaen to the south. Sprawling Udon Thani is too big to be charming and too conservative to be cultured. It boomed on the back of the Vietnam War, exploding into life as US air bases opened nearby. These days, with the bases closed, it feels a little like the city is still searching for something to fill the vacuum.

Why make the trip? For skeletons of the past. Fifty kilometres east, **Ban Chiang** is one of the earliest prehistoric cultures known in Southeast Asia, and the site's **excavation pit** (admission 30B; 8.30am-5pm) at Wat Pho Si Nai displays 52 human skeletons, in whole or in part. More artefacts can be viewed at Ban Chiang's **national museum** (admission 30B; 9am-4.30pm).

Information

Banks are spread liberally across town.

Aek Udon International Hospital (☎ 0 4234 2555; www.aekudon.com; 555/5 Th Pho Si)

Post office (Th Wattananuwong)

T & A Net Corner (☎ 0 4232 9123; 124/8-9 Th Sri Suk; 11am-10pm) Internet access.

TAT office (☎ 0 4232 5406; Th Thesa; 8.30am-4.30pm)

Tourist police (☎ 0 4224 0616, emergency 1155; Th Thesa) Next to the TAT office.

Sleeping & Eating

Accommodation in Udon Thani is entirely in high-rise hotels of varying quality. The best of the bunch includes **Chai Porn** (☎ 0 4222 1913; 209-211 Th Mak Khaeng; d 180-250B;), a friendly spot with spartan rooms, and **King's Hotel** (☎ 0 4222 1634; Th Pho Si; r 190-200B), a Vietnam War–era hangover that offers cheap fan rooms.

Clinging to the banks of the Nong Prajak reservoir, **Rabiang Phatchani** (Th Suphakit Janya; mains 30-80B; lunch & dinner) whips up a selection of local dishes in simple surrounds. Head here for sundown when the views look best.

The big draw at **Steve's Bar** (☎ 0 4224 4523; www.stevesbarudon.com; 234/25 Th Prajak Silpakorn; lunch & dinner) is the big Sunday roast, best served in front of English premiership football shown on a very impressive 50-inch screen.

Getting There & Away

Thai Airways International (www.thaiair.com) and **Nok Air** (www.nokair.co.th) have several daily flights to Bangkok. **Air Asia** (☎ 0 2515 9999; www.airasia.com) connects Udon twice daily with Bangkok.

Udon has two bus stations. Bus Terminal No 1, near the Charoen Hotel in the southeastern part of town, serves Bangkok (air-con/VIP 251/500B, 10 hours, hourly), Khon Kaen (air-con 110B, 2½ hours, hourly) and Nakhon Ratchasima (air-con 142B, 4½ hours).

Bus Terminal No 2 is on the northwestern outskirts of the city next to the highway and serves Loei (ordinary/air-con 60/110B, four hours, five daily) and Nong Khai (40B, one hour, hourly).

To reach Ban Chiang, take a *săwngthăew* from the morning market on Th Pho Si to Ban Chiang (25B, 40 minutes); they run from late morning until around 3.45pm. Returning to Udon Thani from Ban Chiang, *săwngthăew* stop running at 10.30am! Instead, take a *túk-túk* (50B) to the highway at Ban Pulu, and flag a bus on the Sakhon Nakhon–Udon Thani route.

Trains from Udon Thani's train station, at the east end of Th Prajak Silpakorn, travel to Bangkok (1st/2nd/3rd class 459/220/95B, plus applicable sleeper chargers), taking nine or so hours. Take a sleeper for this long trip. Nong Khai (3rd class 11B, one hour) is also accessible by train.

KHON KAEN

pop 145,300

It's not the big cities that draw visitors to Isan, but Khon Kaen might just be the exception thanks to a vibrant energy that is shifting the skyline and diversifying the dining scene. Home to the northeast's largest university, the city is youthful, educated and on the move. It also makes a sensible base for exploring nearby silk-weaving villages and scattered Khmer ruins, and is a gateway to the northeast from Phitsanulok and Sukhothai.

The town's only tourist attraction is the well-curated **Khon Kaen National Museum** (☎ 0 4324 2129; Th Lang Sunratchakan; admission 30B; ⏲ 9am-noon & 1-5pm Wed-Sun), which features ancient art and artefacts.

Information

It's hard to walk around Khon Kaen without bumping into an ATM or bank.

Internet (Th Si Chan; per hr 15B; ⏲ 10am-midnight) Near the Sofitel Hotel.

Khon Kaen Ram Hospital (☎ 0 4333 3900; Th Si Chan)

Post office (cnr Th Si Chan & Th Klang Meuang)

TAT office (☎ 0 4324 4498; 15/5 Th Prachasamoson; ⏲ 8.30am-4.30pm)

Tourist police (☎ 0 4323 6937, emergency 1155; Th Prachasamoson) Next door to TAT.

STRING-TYING CEREMONY

To occupy yourself on those long, boring bus rides, do a survey of Thais wearing thin yellow or white strings round their wrists. In rural villages in Isan, elders and family members assemble to tie *bai sii* (sacred thread) as a bon voyage measure. The strings act as leashes for important guardian spirits and ensure safety during a trip. Some people believe that the strings must fall off naturally rather than be cut off, but this can take weeks, turning sacred thread into stinky thread.

Festivals & Events

Khon Kaen's biggest annual event is the **silk and phùuk sìaw festival**, which runs over a period of 12 days and nights from late November to early December. Centred on Ratchadanuson Park and the Provincial Hall, the festival celebrates the planting of the mulberry tree, which is an essential step in the production of silk. Also considered particularly important is *phùuk sìaw* (friend-bonding), a reference to the *bai sǐi* ceremony in which sacred threads are tied round one's wrists to give spiritual protection; see boxed text, left. Music, folk dancing and food, and all things Isan, are major highlights.

Sleeping & Eating

Si Monkon (☎ 0 4323 7939; 61-67 Th Klang Meuang; r 120-200B; ❄) This wooden pad has some ramshackle charm, but the walls are thin for light sleepers. Air-con is available for 300B.

Saen Samran Hotel (☎ 0 4323 9611; 55-59 Th Klang Meuang; s/d 150/200B; ❄) Reputedly Khon Kaen's oldest hotel (not always a good claim to fame), Saen Samran is an ageing wooden building with a certain charm and character. Fan rooms are clean and air-con kicks in at 350B.

First Choice (☎ 0 4333 3352; 18/8 Th Phimphaseut; r 150-200B; ❄) On its way to becoming the town's first backpacker hostel, the rooms here are spartan but certainly cheap. Downstairs is a traveller-friendly eatery, serving the usual selection of shakes and snacks.

Em Oht (Th Klang Meuang; dishes 30-50B; ⏲ breakfast, lunch & dinner) Em Oht is a popular place to sample some Isan fare, including the signature breakfast *khài kàthá* (eggs served in a pan with local sausages), with a cup of real coffee to wash it down.

Heuan Lao (☎ 0 4324 7202; 39 Th Phimphaseut; mains 40-140B; ⏲ lunch & dinner; ❄) Housed in an elegant old wooden villa, this restaurant is piled with antique bric-a-brac and serves mouthwatering Thai and Isan dishes. There's a verdant garden for alfresco dining or a dose of air-con to hide away in. It's open till midnight. No roman-script sign.

Well worth a visit is Khon Kaen's lively **night market** (Th Reun Rom), the heart and soul of budget dining in town. Find it next to the air-con bus station, between Th Klang Meuang and Th Na Meuang.

Shopping

Khon Kaen is a good place to buy handcrafted goods such as *mát-mìi* and silk, silverwork and basketry. **PK Prathamakhan Local Goods Center** (☎ 0 4322 4080; 79/2-3 Th Reun Rom), just west of Th Na Meuang, is a local handicraft centre with a small museum. Also good are **Rin Mai Thai** (☎ 0 4322 1042; 412 Th Na Meuang) and **Klum Phrae Phan** (☎ 0 4333 7216; 131/193 Th Chatapadung), the latter run by the Handicraft Centre for Northeastern Women's Development.

Getting There & Away

The **airport** (☎ 0 4323 6523/8835) is a few kilometres west of the city centre. **Thai Airways International** (code TG; ☎ 0 4322 7701; www.thaiair.com) flies three times daily between Bangkok and Khon Kaen. **Air Asia** (code AK; ☎ 0 2515 9999; www.airasia.com) flies daily to and from Bangkok.

Khon Kaen has two bus stations: the **ordinary bus terminal** (Th Prachasamoson) is a five-minute walk northwest of Th Klang Meuang, while the **air-con bus terminal** (Th Klang Meuang) is in the town centre near the night market.

Buses travel to and from Bangkok (air-con 259B, seven hours, every half-hour from 7am to 11pm), Chiang Mai (air-con 394B, 12 hours, 8pm and 9pm), Nakhon Ratchasima (ordinary 70B, three hours) and Nong Khai (air-con 140B, four hours, six daily).

Khon Kaen is on the Bangkok–Nakhon Ratchasima–Udon Thani railway line, but buses are much faster along this section. Track down information from Khon Kaen **railway station** (☎ 0 4322 1112).

EASTERN GULF COAST

The ideal jaunt from jostling Bangkok, Thailand's east coast is a popular and increasingly upmarket stretch favoured for its convenience to the capital. For pure escapism, the more stunning and affordable southern destinations win out, but the east coast's charms (candlelit beach dining, healthy strips of sand and smooth transfers) mean it's always busy.

RAYONG

pop 49,000

For the traveller, the dusty strip of banks, markets and motorcycle dealerships that makes up Rayong holds few surprises. You're most likely to be here taking advantage of its location as a major transport interchange, but if you do arrive too late to secure an onward connection for a boat to Ko Samet, there are a couple of OK hotels.

Information

Krung Thai Bank (144/53-55 Th Sukhumvit) One of several banks along Rayong's main drag, Th Sukhumvit, with exchange services and ATMs.

Rayong President Hotel (☎ 0 3861 1307; Th Sukhumvit; per 10 min 5B) For internet access.

TAT office (☎ 0 3865 5420; tatyong@tat.or.th; 153/4 Th Sukhumvit; 🕑 8.30am-4.30pm) Located 7km east of Rayong on Hwy 3; a worthwhile stop if you have your own transport.

Sleeping & Eating

Rayong President Hotel (☎ 0 3861 1307; Th Sukhumvit; r incl breakfast 700B; ❄ 💻) There's not much English spoken here, but the welcome is friendly and it's quiet at night. From the bus station, cross to the other side of Th Sukhumvit, turn right and after about 500m you'll see a sign pointing down a side street.

Star Hotel Rayong (☎ 0 3861 4901; www.starhotel.th.com; 109 Th Rayong Trade Center; r incl breakfast 1500B; ❄ 🏊) Rayong's ritziest spot is a favourite with business and government honchos who demand swanky four-star hotels. The rooms are huge and there is a bowling alley and two swimming pools. From the bus station, walk away from Th Sukhumvit, turn left at the top of the square and the hotel is on your right.

For cheap food, check out the market near the Thetsabanteung cinema, or the string of restaurants and noodle shops along Th Taksin Maharat, just south of Wat Lum Mahachaichumphon. There are food stalls around the bus station.

Getting There & Away

See p764 for information on getting to Ko Samet.

KO SAMET

Every thriving metropolis should have a Ko Samet nearby – somewhere close enough for a quick escape, yet worlds enough away for the urbanite to hang loose. A favourite weekend getaway for young Thais, Ko Samet is equally popular with travellers getting their last sun and sand before being whisked home. While there's no comparison with its southern counterparts, or even nearby Ko Chang, low-key Ko Samet is perfect for a couple of days of cheery abandonment, and enjoys better weather during the wet season than many islands. It's been a **national park** (admission 400B) since 1981, and there are walking trails all the way to the southern tip of the island, as well

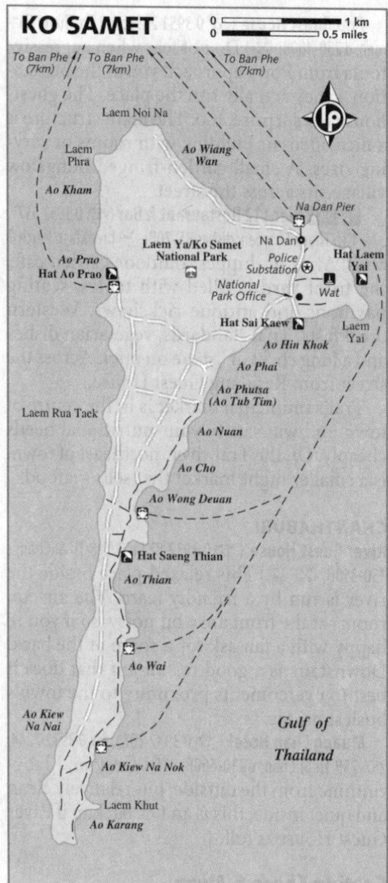

as a few cross-island trails, but it does have problems with litter and overcrowding.

Information

Internet access is relatively plentiful considering the island's small size. Naga Bungalows has fast connections (per minute 2B) and powerful air-con.

Ko Samet Health Centre (☎ 0 3864 4123; 2/2 Moo 4, Phe Mang Rayong; 8.30am-4.30pm) For minor medical problems.

Siam City Bank (Th Nadaan) There are no banks on Ko Samet, but this ATM is located at the 7-Eleven near the national park entrance. There's another ATM at the 7-Eleven near the ferry.

Tourist information (☎ 0 3864 4240; 7am-midnight) Conveniently located near the pier.

Sleeping & Eating

NORTHEASTERN BEACHES

In the northeast part of the island, Ao Hin Khok and Ao Phai (*ao* means 'bay') are the main places for seafood-eating, novel-reading and email-sending. The further south you go, the more Thai and isolated it becomes.

our pick **Naga Bungalows** (Ao Hin Khok; d 300-700B;) A sprawling combo of bamboo and concrete bungalows climbs the hill here, and the common area, complete with billiards table and internet café, is a good place to meet travellers. Ask about *muay thai* lessons, which take place across the dirt path.

Jep's Bungalows (☎ 0 3864 4112; www.jepbungalow.com; Ao Hin Khok; r 300-1200B;) One of the cleanest and smartest bungalow operations on this stretch of sand. The waterfront restaurant is quite popular – look for the star paper lanterns.

Tub Tim Resort (☎ 0 3864 4025; www.tubtimresort.com; 13/15 Moo 4, Tumbol Phe, Ao Phutsa; d from 500B;) Just over the rocks from Ao Phai, Tub Tim may only be a five-minute walk from the action, but it's a world away when it comes to peace and quiet.

Nuan Bungalows (Ao Nuan; d from 500B) The only occupant of private Nuan beach, this place has creatively built bungalows, some with little wrap-around balconies.

AO WIANG WAN

Get away from the tourist ghetto and consider quiet and pretty Ao Wiang Wan in the island's north as a base.

Baan Praguy Kaew (☎ 0 9603 2609; s 300B, d 400-500B) Located right next door to Lung Ritt Bungalow, this much nicer German-owned guesthouse is on stilts over the water. Stay in a clean waterfront room, or choose one of the bungalows that sit across the street.

Lung Ritt Bungalow (☎ 0 3864 4032; d 1000B) Walk to the right (as you face the island) from Na Dan Pier past some derelict buildings and you'll find this place on your right. The only real amenity is the nearby water, which you can almost reach out and touch.

Most bungalows have restaurants offering mixed menus of Thai and traveller food. Eat locally at the cheap noodle bars and seafood joints or pick up supplies such as water and snacks in Na Dan, the small village next to the pier. For alcohol and camaraderie, try Papa Roger's, a homey little Finnish pub in Na Dan.

Getting There & Around

Ko Samet is reached by boat from the mainland town of Ban Phe (one way/return 50/100B, 45 minutes, departures 6am to 6pm). Ban Phe has a small bus station beyond the boat piers. Regular direct buses go to Bangkok's Eastern (Ekamai) Bus Terminal (140B, three hours, hourly from 5am to 8.30pm). Blue săwngthăew to Rayong (15B, 45 minutes) ply the main road near the pier. For a few extra baht (200B, depending on the number of people) private boat charters can drop you elsewhere on the island.

Săwngthăew on the island cost from 10B to 100B per person, depending on how far you're going and the number of passengers. From the pier, reaching some locations furthest south can cost 300B to 500B if there are only one to two people travelling.

CHANTHABURI & TRAT

There's an earthiness about these two provincial towns, which are enveloped by palm trees and plantations. While travellers use them mostly for swift connections to Ko Chang or the Cambodian border, if you stop to catch your breath in sleepy Trat, you'll get a feel for small-town living. East of Trat, as Thailand merges with Cambodia, a number of little-known beaches, including **Hat Sai Si Ngoen**, **Hat Sai Kaew**, **Hat Thap Thim** and **Hat Ban Cheun**, are worth a look.

Information

Tle & Tin Internet (☎ 0 3952 4567; 35 Th Sukhumvit, Trat; per hr 30B; 10am-10pm) Your Facebook-checking headquarters.

Tratosphere Bookshop (23 Rimklong Soi, Trat; 8am-10pm) Run by a friendly Frenchman, this is a handy place to pick up your next read (books 50B to 200B) or get travel tips on the area.

Sleeping & Eating

TRAT

Windy Guesthouse (69 Th Thana Charoen; s 100B, d 120-140B) This tiny wooden house sits on stilts right in the river. There's no air-con, only six rooms and it's all shared bathrooms, but this is one of Trat's most intimate and uncommon spots to stay.

Ban Jaidee Guesthouse (☎ 0 3952 0678; 67-69 Th Chaimongkol; d 120-150B) A traditional Thai place, this is the best pad in town with glossy polished floors, a lounge area, clean shared bathrooms with hot water, and welcoming staff. Breakfast is available.

Pop Guest House (☎ 0 3951 2392; 1/1 Th Thana Charoen; d 250-400B) Do not fear when aggressive touts from Pop's approach you at the bus station – they actually run the place. The guesthouse is a surprise, too. The main structure is a nice open-air building with rooms of varying sizes. A small garden-fringed bungalow village sits across the street.

our pick **Pier 112 Restaurant & Bar** (☎ 0 3952 5577; 274/1 Th Thana Charoen; dishes 35-70B; breakfast, lunch & dinner) At Trat's hippest outdoor garden café, the front yard is filled with tables, seating pavilions and antique rickshaws. Western breakfasts, Thai standards, vegetarian dishes and a long cocktail list are on offer. Across the street from Residang Guest House.

Trat's municipal market is in the centre of town and will satisfy your nutritional needs cheaply. On the Trat river, northeast of town, is a smaller night market that sells seafood.

CHANTHABURI

River Guest House (☎ 0 3932 8211; 3/5-8 Th Si Chan; r 150-350B) This relaxed place beside the river is run by a friendly team. The air-con rooms at the front are a bit noisy, so if you're happy with a fan ask for a room at the back. Downstairs is a good restaurant that does it best to overcome its proximity to the town's busiest bridge.

Muang Chan Hotel (☎ 0 3932 1073; fax 0 3932 7244; 257-259 Th Si Chan; r 230-600B) Grey and labyrinthine from the outside, but relatively clean and quiet inside, this is an OK backup if River Guest House is full.

Getting There & Away

Bangkok Airways (☎ in Bangkok 0 2265 5555; www.bangkokair.com) has two daily flights to Trat (around 1800B, 50 minutes). The airport is 40km from town and a taxi to or from the airport will cost around 300B (depending on how many people are catching a ride).

Chanthaburi has the larger **bus station** (Th Saritidet), with connections to Nakhon Ratchasima (air-con 260B, seven hours), Aranya Prathet (air-con 200B, eight hours) and east coast towns. Buses going to Bangkok's Eastern (Ekamai) Bus Terminal stop in Chanthaburi en route to Trat (ordinary/air-con 250/331B, five to six hours, six departures daily from 6.30am to 5.30pm). Between Chanthaburi and Trat, ordinary buses (60B, 1½ hours) and share taxis (100B) are also happy to have you.

GETTING TO CAMBODIA

To Krong Koh Kong

To get to the border at Hat Lek–Krong Koh Kong, take an air-con minibus from Trat to Hat Lek (110B, one hour, departures every 45 minutes from 6am to 6pm); these leave from Trat's Th Sukhumvit in front of the municipal market. An alternative way to reach the border is to take a sǎwngthǎew (small pick-up with two benches in the back; 50B), which also leave from Trat's municipal market. Motorcycles and taxis are available from Hat Lek across the border to Krong Koh Kong (50B to 80B). From Krong Koh Kong, there is only one boat per day to Sihanoukville (600B, four to five hours, departing at 8am). If you want to get from Trat to Sihanoukville in one day, you should be on the 6am minibus from Trat to Hat Lek and at the border with passport in hand as soon as it opens at 7am. This border crossing closes at 5pm.

Cambodian tourist visas (1200B) are available at the border (bring a passport photo), but you should check with the Cambodian embassy in Bangkok before heading out there. Although Cambodian tourist visas cost US$20 at other borders, payment is only accepted in baht here. If you want to debate the issue, be prepared for a frustrating time.

For information on making this crossing in the other direction, see p113.

To Psar Pruhm

Foreigners can cross the border from Ban Pakard in Thailand to Psar Pruhm in Cambodia, and then on to Pailin. To travel this way independently, first take a minibus from Chanthaburi to Ban Pakard (100B, one to two hours). Cross the border to Psar Pruhm and then arrange a share taxi into Pailin (100B). From Pailin it is possible to connect with Battambang (200B, four hours) by share taxi on a real joker of a road.

See p101 for information on crossing in the other direction.

To get to Ko Chang from Trat, take a sǎwngthǎew (30B) to the pier in the village of Laem Ngop (10 to 20 minutes). Scores of sǎwngthǎew line Trat's main road, fishing for customers; keep shopping if you're quoted 'charter' prices (150B).

See above for info on crossing over the border into Cambodia.

KO CHANG

Just a few years back, Ko Chang was an outpost near 'war-torn' Cambodia where hippies revelled in some of Southeast Asia's best untamed forests and isolated coast. Then the world caught up.

Ko Chang has lost its virginity – its virgin forest, that is. This **national park** was once undeveloped and lacking modern amenities such as 24-hour electricity, souvenir stands and ATMs. Under the government's new plan for the island, backpackers are *out* and luxury tourists are *in*. Spiffy air-con set-ups are swiftly replacing cheap bungalows, although Hat Tha Nam (Lonely Beach) has managed to retain its backpacker street cred. And if you fancy spending your time in Ko Chang trekking to mountainous waterfalls or catching dazzling views while whizzing by on a motorbike, don't despair: this sprawling island still fits the bill.

Information

Internet cafés are plentiful on the island and access charges average 2B per minute.

Ko Chang Hospital (☎ 0 3958 6131; Ban Dan Mai) Near the police headquarters.

Police (☎ 0 3958 6191; Ban Dan Mai) There are also police based near KC Grande Resort.

Post office (🕑 9am-4.30pm Mon-Fri) Near the ferry terminal at Ban Khlong Son.

Siam Commercial Bank (Hat Sai Khao; 🕑 8.30am-3.30pm) Also has an exchange window that stays open until 8pm.

Sleeping & Eating

Tree House Lodge (www.treehouse-kohchang.de; Hat Tha Nam; d 150-250B) If you're after a lazy, village-like atmosphere, the Tree House Lodge will please with its seclusion and simple stilt bungalows. There's a fantastic, rambling deck area with a sea view where you can feast on Indian dhal – meals here cost from 45B to 70B – or kick back with a book. It's often full.

KC Grande Resort (☎ 0 3955 1199; www.kckohchang.com; Hat Sai Khao; d 300-500B) At the northern end of the island at pretty Hat Sai Khao (White Sand Beach), KC is one of the island's originals. Affordable beachfront bungalows can still be had, although KC seems to be following Ko Chang's general lead with its 'superior' rooms and overpriced restaurants.

our pick **Magic Garden** (☎ 0 3955 8135; www.magicgardenthailand.com; Hat Tha Nam; d incl breakfast 500-1000B; 💻) With an architectural design based on an owner's experience at Burning Man Festival, it's no surprise this place resembles a cross between a Rainbow Gathering and an Ewok village. DJ parties happen a few times weekly, cosy chill-out areas are scattered about and fire shows take place in a cement-filled pit dubbed 'The Volcano'. Even better, the bungalows are clean and tastefully decorated, and all come with hot showers and a free breakfast. There's free wireless access here as well.

Menus at all the bungalows on Ko Chang are pretty similar. There are several small eateries (dishes 40B) along the eastern side of the main road in Hat Sai Khao.

Also worth trying out are the seafood restaurants located on the pier at Ban Bang Bao, including **The Bay Bar & Restaurant** (☎ 0 3955 8079; seafood priced by weight; 🕒 lunch & dinner). Get ice cream at **Little Havana** (☎ 0 6842 8568; dishes 30-120B), a groovy little thatched-roof hut turning out tapas, burritos, pasta and cocktails. The nearby **Bangbao Delight Bakery Café** (☎ 0 3955 8073; takeaways 15-25B; 🕒 breakfast, lunch & dinner) puts together a mean pastry treat and also serves breakfast. Try a doughnut while you wait.

Getting There & Around

From the pier in Laem Ngop, boats go to Ko Chang (100B return, one hour, departures hourly) from 7am to 5pm. The schedule is reduced to about every two hours in the low season.

From Ko Chang's pier (either Tha Dan Kao or Ao Sapparot), săwngthăew will be waiting to take you to any of the various beaches along the west coast (30B to 80B).

SOUTHERN GULF COAST

Beach lovers unite! Any fully fledged itinerary through Southeast Asia will surely feature the dreamy beaches, renowned islands and world-class dive sites of Thailand's southern Gulf Coast. On this legendary stretch of the Asian trail, you're not a Londoner or Swede but that universal species: a sunworshipper.

Although the varied geography of the southern Gulf allows for a wide variety of travel experiences, the truth is that most visitors to the region arrive for three reasons only: Ko Tao, Ko Pha-Ngan and Ko Samui. And while each island has successfully managed to maintain its own unique attitude and energy, the similarities are such that no matter which bungalow or which stretch of sand you end up with, certain consistencies remain. A reassuring sense of calm, for instance. A significantly reduced blood pressure. And the possibly life-altering knowledge that after a few months of hard work back home, an eternity of beachfront Thai massage could be yours.

Need even more good news? The best time to visit Thailand's southern reaches is from March to May, when the rest of the country is practically melting from the angry sun. If the earth is burning in the city, in other words, it might be time to sample the many surprises of the Gulf.

Deeper south the geography is flanked by glossy palm trees and rubber plantations. It's pure cultural exchange here: Thai-ness fuses with Malay, Indian and Chinese influences in an intoxicating stir-fry of colour, culture and tradition. Southern Thais speak a dialect that confounds even visitors from other Thai regions. Diction is short and fast and the clipped tones fly into the outer regions of intelligibility.

Beware: you're dealing with a potential lifelong addiction once you delve into the south.

CHA-AM

pop 48,600

A low-key seaside town located 40km south of Phetburi, Cha-am specialises in good old-fashioned Thai fun: jet-skis pull banana boats with teams of laughing Thai students behind, shop vendors sport tropical shirts, fully clothed locals float on inner tubes, and families scoot around on tricycles. Whereas Hua Hin, 26km further south, could be described as a pseudo-sophisticated elder sibling, Cha-am is more like the coy teenager.

Sleeping & Eating

Cha-am is a big weekend destination, so from Friday to Sunday expect a 20% to 50% increase on most prices listed here. Accommodation on Th Ruamjit is opposite the casuarina-lined waterfront promenade. There are no grass huts in sight.

Nirundorn Resort (☎ 0 3247 1038; 247/7 Th Ruamjit; d 250-300B; ❄) Housed in a modern building, the clean monotone rooms here have cable TV and fridge, while cheaper rooms (200B) share bathrooms. Breakfast is served downstairs (70B); caffeine addicts will be chuffed to find cappuccino.

Memory House (☎ 0 3247 2100; cha_am memory@yahoo.com; 200 Th Ruamjit; d from 300B; ❄) In the same vein as Nirundorn, this guesthouse has comfortable rooms with hot water, cable TV and fridge. Free maps of the town are available here.

Poom Restaurant (☎ 0 3247 1036; 274/1 Th Ruamjit; dishes 40-350B) Poom has a large outdoor patio and specialises in seafood; it's very popular among visiting Thais.

Getting There & Away

Most ordinary and air-con buses stop in the town centre on Phetkasem Hwy. Some private air-con buses to and from Bangkok conveniently go all the way to the beach, stopping at a small bus station a few hundred metres south of the Th Narathip intersection.

The frequent bus services going to and from Cha-am include Bangkok (ordinary/air-con 95/113B, three hours), Phetburi (ordinary 25B, 40 minutes) and Hua Hin (ordinary 20B, 30 minutes).

The **train station** (Th Narathip) is inland, west of Phetkasem Hwy and a 20B motorcycle ride from the beach. There are daily services to Cha-am from three stations in Bangkok: Hualamphong (3.50pm), Sam Sen (9.27am) and Thonburi (7.15am, 1.30pm and 7.05pm). Tickets cost from 80B to 193B. Cha-am isn't listed on the English-language train schedule.

HUA HIN

pop 48,700

A sanitised version of Thailand for the masses, and the longtime retreat of Thai royalty, it seems as though Hua Hin, 230km from Bangkok, is on constant alert for the King himself. Chock-a-block with modern restaurants, tailors, masseurs and souvenir shops, it's probably the easiest and safest southern Thai coastal retreat, favoured by families and oldies who frequent the colossal beachfront resorts hogging the nicest stretches of sand. Nonetheless, this quiet spot possesses steady weather and a certain finesse – just like Thai cuisine minus the spice.

Sleeping

Accommodation in Hua Hin tends to be a bit on the expensive side due to its proximity to Bangkok.

All Nations Guest House (☎ 0 3251 2747; www.geocities.com/allnationsguesthouse; 10-10/1 Th Dechanuchit; s/d from 150/450B; ❄) Owned by a friendly Canadian-Thai couple, this place is often packed with backpackers. The small open-air café has a billiards table and a bar. Climb to the top floor and exit onto the roof for a great city view.

our pick **Pattana Guest House** (☎ 0 3251 3393; www.observergroup.net/pattana.htm; 52 Th Naresdamri; d 200-525B; ❄) This is the absolute picture of peace and serenity – just walking into the plant-filled lobby causes your stress level to drop three points. Rooms have loads of character, and quiet is the name of the game here; when we visited, everyone was silently reading.

SOUTHERN CUISINE

The dishes of southern Thailand are as flamboyant and seductive as its award-winning beaches. Blessed by the bounty of the sea and the region's abundant rainfall, southern cuisine is effortlessly delicious and morbidly spicy. Dishes such as *khâo mòk kài* (chicken biryani) and other standard curries are a brilliant yellow colour (thanks to the liberal use of turmeric), and represent a geographic map of the region's Chinese, Malay and Indian influences. Of Chinese-Malay heritage, *khanŏm jiin náam yaa* is a dish of thin rice noodles doused in a fish curry sauce. A large tray of green vegetables to accompany the dish is prominently displayed at the communal table – a helpful signal to the illiterate traveller.

Malay-style *rotii kaeng* is a fluffy flat bread served with a curry dip; order another if you like to watch the hooded Muslim women slap the dough into a gossamer circle, then toss it into a spitting wok.

Fulay (☎ 0 3251 3145; www.fulay-huahin.com; 110/1 Th Naresdamri; s/d from 350/450B; ❄) With the walls and floors covered in linoleum, the cheapest rooms here feel a bit, well, cheap. But no matter – the real reason to check in is the sprawling pier that reaches out over the beach. If you're looking to splurge, get a load of the private suite (1750B) facing the ocean.

Eating & Drinking

Hua Hin is noted for seafood, especially *plaa mèuk* (squid), *puu* (crab) and *hăwy* (clams). In the centre of town, the colourful **Chatchai Market** (Th Phetkasem & Th Dechanuchit) feeds hordes of hungry visitors night and day. At the **night market** (cnr Th Dechanuchit & Th Phetkasem), there's a smorgasbord of food stalls equipped with well-seasoned woks and display cases packed with fruits of the sea. It's barely possible to break 100B for a bellyful of feasting.

El Murphy's Mexican Restaurant (☎ 0 3251 1525; 25 Soi Selakam; dishes 70-400B; 🕑 lunch & dinner) At this Tex-Mex place run by an Irish expat, prices aren't exactly budget, but you get what you pay for: massive burritos, huge nacho plates, even chicken fajitas! Cricket and footy fans gather here to watch matches projected onto an outdoor wall.

For more serious drinkers, check out the gaudy bars on Soi Bintaban, off Th Naresdamri.

Getting There & Around

Buses to Bangkok (air-con 171B, three hours, departures hourly) leave from next to the Siripetchkasem Hotel.

All other buses leave from Hua Hin's regular **bus station** (Th Liap Thang Rot Fai), located 400m from the train station. Buses travel to/from Prachuap Khiri Khan (ordinary 80B, two hours, frequent departures daily between 6.30am and 4pm), Chumphon (air-con 160B, four hours, hourly from 7am to 2am), Surat Thani (air-con 270B, seven hours, 13 daily between 8am and 1.30am) and Phuket (air-con 378B, 11½ hours, 12 daily between 9am and 1.30am).

The impressive train station, at the end of Th Damnoen Kasem, services Bangkok (2nd class 292B to 383B, 3rd class 104B).

Săamláw from the train station to the beach cost 50B to 70B; from the bus station to Th Naresdamri, 50B to 70B; and from Chatchai Market to the fishing pier, 20B.

PRACHUAP KHIRI KHAN

pop 27,700

Roughly 80km south of Hua Hin, this small town retains an unhurried pace. Consider mellow Prachuap (pra-*juap*) if you're looking for somewhere to break up the long trip to the island beaches or are desperate to escape your Khao San compatriots.

The bus dumps you off in the centre of town – not a pushy motorcycle taxi or foreigner in sight. If you arrive in the heat of the day, it might even feel like a ghost town. At the base of Prachuap is a sparkling blue bay sprinkled with brightly coloured fishing boats. To the north is **Khao Chong Krajok** (Mirror Tunnel Mountain), topped by a wat with spectacular views; the hill is claimed by a clan of monkeys who supposedly hitched a ride into town on a bus from Bangkok to pick up some mangoes. There isn't much else to do except walk along the waterfront promenade or explore nearby **Ao Manao** (Lime Bay) and **Ao Noi** (Little Bay).

Sleeping & Eating

Yuttichai Hotel (☎ 0 3261 1055; 115 Th Kong Kiat; d from 160B) Run by a smiley family, this place is close to the bus station and night market. There's some beautiful timber flooring throughout, and old-style rooms are big enough to stretch your legs.

Suk Sant Hotel (☎ 0 3261 1145; 11 Th Suseuk; s/d from 300/350B; ❄) You'll have to forsake all architectural taste at this monstrous pink building near the waterfront promenade (Th Chai Thaleh), but you'll be rewarded with lovely views (in the fan rooms only). Very basic but clean rooms.

Vegetarian café (☎ 0 3261 1672; dishes around 23B) Noncarnivores might want to shuffle on down to this blink-and-you'll-miss-it café on the same street as Suk Sant Hotel (no roman-scipt sign). There's no menu but the friendly women running the kitchen will happily wok up something.

Pan Phochana Restaurant (☎ 0 3261 1195; 40 Th Chai Thaleh; dishes 40-120B; 🕑 breakfast, lunch & dinner) Near Suk Sant Hotel, this place is famous for its *hàw mòk hăwy* (ground fish curry steamed in mussels on the half-shell).

At the foot of Th Thetsaban Bamrung is a small **night market** (Th Chai Thaleh) that's good for seafood.

Getting There & Away

Buses to and from Bangkok, Hua Hin, Cha-am and Phetburi stop on Th Phitak Chat, near

Yuttichai Hotel. Regular buses stop a block away near Inthira Hotel.

Services run to Bangkok (air-con 230B, five hours), Hua Hin (ordinary 65B, two hours, frequent departures between 6.30am and 4pm) and Chumphon (ordinary 160B, four hours), the transfer point for Surat Thani buses and boats to the Samui islands.

The train station is at the end of Th Kong Kiat, a block from Th Phitak Chat. There are several afternoon departures to Bangkok (2nd class 220B to 357B, 3rd class 128B), Hua Hin (19B to 79B) and also to Chumphon (2nd-class air-con 34B to 278B).

CHUMPHON

pop 480,000

Roughly 500km from Bangkok, Chumphon marks out where southern Thailand really begins in terms of dialect and religion. Chumphon is a revolving door for travellers going to or coming from Ko Tao. The transition from arriving in Chumphon to getting a boat ticket to Ko Tao is painless. Travel agencies are within spitting distance of the bus station and provide all sorts of free amenities (such as luggage storage, shower and toilet).

Suda Guest House (☎ 0 7750 4366; 8 Soi Bangkok Bank; s/d 180/400B; 💻) is currently clobbering its competitor Farang Bar in the popularity department, and that's probably because prices are low, management is helpful (with Ko Tao travel arrangements and more) and most everything in sight is perfectly clean.

You can stock up on food supplies for the slow boat at the small **night market** (Th Krom Luang Chumphon).

There are three daily boats to Ko Tao from Chumphon pier. Speed and express boats (400B, 1½ to two hours) leave in the morning around 7am (leave Chumphon town at 6am) to Ko Tao, catamarans (500B to 550B, 1½ hours) leave at 1pm and the ferry (300B, six hours) departs at 11pm. Transport to the pier, 14km from Chumphon, is included in the fare.

Buses arrive at and depart from Chumphon's **bus station** (Th Paramin-mankar). Destinations include Bangkok (air-con 211B to 320B, seven hours, nine daily), Ranong (air-con 90B, three hours, hourly) and Surat Thani (air-con 130B, three hours, hourly).

The **train station** (Th Krom Luang Chumphon) is within walking distance of the centre of town. Destinations include Bangkok (2nd class 310B to 390B, 3rd class 202B to 252B, 7½ to nine hours, 11 daily), Surat Thani (35B, two to 3½ hours, 11 daily) and Hat Yai (80B, six to 8½ hours, five daily). Northern- and southern-bound trains have several afternoon departures.

SURAT THANI

pop 125,500

This busy port is of interest to most travellers only as a jumping-off point for the islands off the coast. If you arrive in Surat by train or bus in the morning you'll have no problem making a connection with one of the day express boats.

Sleeping & Eating

If you need a place to stay, check out **Ban Don Hotel** (☎ 0 7727 2167; 268/2 Th Na Meuang; d from 200B; ❄), the best budget value in Surat, with small yet extremely clean rooms. The entrance is through a Chinese restaurant – quite good for inexpensive rice and noodle dishes. **Thai Tani** (☎ 0 7727 2977; Th Talat Mai; s/d 240/300B) is across the street from the local bus station. If you get stuck at the train station, which is in nearby Phun Phin, try **Queen** (☎ 0 7731 1003; 916/10-13 Th Mahasawat; s/d 180/260B; ❄). It is round the corner from the train station on the road to Surat Thani. Look at a couple of rooms as quality varies.

The market near the bus station has cheap provisions. Stalls near the bus station specialise in hearty *khâo kài òp* (marinated baked chicken on rice). The **night market** (Th Ton Pho) is the place for fried, steamed, grilled or sautéed delicacies.

Getting There & Away

Be wary of dirt-cheap combo tickets to the islands sold on Th Khao San in Bangkok – they often have extra surcharges, invalid legs or dubious security. For the Bangkok–Surat Thani trip, it is recommended that you use buses departing from government bus stations or ask an island survivor to advise of a reliable travel agent.

AIR

There is a twice-daily service to Bangkok on **Thai Airways International** (☎ 0 7727 2610; www.thaiair.com; 3/27-28 Th Karunarat).

BOAT

There are three piers located in and around Surat Thani: Ban Don, in the centre of town,

MEDITATION WITH THE MONKS

About 60km north of Surat Thani, Chaiya is one of the oldest cities in Thailand, dating back to the Srivijaya empire, and home to Wat Suanmok (Wat Suan Mokkhaphalaram), a forest wat founded by Ajahn Buddhadasa Bhikkhu, arguably Thailand's most famous monk. At the affiliated International Dharma Hermitage (IDH), across the highway 1.5km from Wat Suanmok, resident monks hold English-language guided meditation retreats in the first 10 days of every month. Anyone is welcome to participate; the cost is 1500B (150B per day for 10 days; non-refundable), which includes meals. Advance registration is not possible; simply arrive in time to register on the morning of the final day of the month preceding the retreat. Be prepared for deep, meditative silence that lasts for 10 days.

To get to Wat Suanmok from Surat, catch one of the frequent 3rd-class trains from Phun Phin (10B, one hour) or take a sǎwngthǎew (small pick-up with two benches in the back; 50B, 45 minutes) from Talat Kaset bus station to Chaiya. Until late afternoon sǎwngthǎew from Chaiya's train station travel the 7km to Wat Suanmok for 15B per passenger; if these aren't running you can hire a motorcycle taxi for 50B from anywhere along the main street.

receives the night ferries; Tha Pak Nam (Tha Thong pier), 5km from Surat Thani, receives **Songserm's** (☎ 0 7728 6340) express boats; and Don Sak, 60km from central Surat Thani, receives the car-passenger ferries and **Seatran** (☎ 0 7727 5060; www.seatranferry.com; 136 Th Na Meuang) express boats.

For travellers heading to Ko Samui, there are various options. Seatran offers bus-ferry combinations (150B, 3½ hours, departures every hour between 5.30am and 5.30pm) leaving from the bus station in Surat Thani and boarding a car ferry at Don Sak pier. Seatran's bus–express boat combinations (250B) also leave from the bus station in Surat Thani and board at Don Sak pier at 8.30am and 2.30pm. **Raja Ferry** (☎ 0 7747 1151) also leaves from Don Sak (84B, 1½ hours, departures every hour between 6am and 6pm). A night ferry (150B, six hours, departing at 11pm) leaves from Ban Don pier.

To Ko Pha-Ngan, Raja Ferry (160B, 2½ hours, four departures daily) leaves from Don Sak. Songserm's express boat (250B, 3½ hours, departing once daily at 8am) leaves from Tha Pak Nam. The night ferries (200B, seven hours, departing at 11pm) leave from Ban Don pier. **Pha-Ngan Tour** (☎ 0 7720 5799) does a bus-ferry combination for this service (240B).

To Ko Tao, night ferries (500B, seven to eight hours, departing at 11pm) and express boats (500B, five hours, one morning departure) leave from Ban Don pier.

BUS & MINIVAN

There are three bus stations in Surat Thani: Talat Kaset 1, off Th Talat Mai and Th Na Meuang, for local and provincial destinations, including Chumphon and the Surat Thani train station; **Talat Kaset 2** (btwn Th Talat Mai & Th That Thong) for air-con minivans and towns outside the province; and a station outside town for Bangkok-bound buses. The travel agencies also run cramped minivan services to popular tourist destinations; these are usually faster, but have unreliable departure times and tickets tend to cost 50B to 100B more.

Buses travel to and from Bangkok (air-con 350B to 590B, 10 to 11 hours), Chumphon (ordinary 80B, three hours), Hat Yai (air-con 295B, four to five hours), Krabi (ordinary 80B, three to four hours, hourly) and Phuket (ordinary/air-con 200/240B, seven hours). Minivans also run to Hat Yai (210B) and Krabi (170B).

TRAIN

The train station is in Phun Phin, 14km from Surat Thani. Destinations include Bangkok (2nd-class sleeper 498B to 748B, 2nd class 368B to 478B, 3rd class 227B to 297B, 12 hours), and there are several afternoon and evening departures for northern-bound trains. For destinations south of Surat Thani, there are several early morning departures, but seats tend to sell quickly.

Getting Around

Orange buses (10B, departures every 15 minutes) depart from Talat Kaset 1 local bus station, which is within walking distance of the Ban Don pier, for the train station. Orange sǎwngthǎew (30B, departures every 15 minutes) leave from Talat Kaset 1 to Don Sak pier, but most island tickets include transport to the pier. Taxis from the train station in Phun Phin to town cost about 100B.

KO TAO

pop 5000

Mountainous Ko Tao perches on a ledge of coral reefs like a sunbathing turtle (*tao* means 'turtle'). The island is famous as a diving and snorkelling mecca thanks to the water's high visibility, abundant coral and diverse marine life. The absence of traditional package tourists keeps prices low, but in the popularity contest with the other Gulf Coast islands, Ko Tao is catching up.

Whether you're an aspiring diver on a cheap certification mission, a new-age spa junkie or just an all-round sun lover, everyone finds a little of what they want on Ko Tao.

Orientation & Information

Only 21 sq km in area, Ko Tao lies 45km north of Ko Pha-Ngan. Boats dock at the Mae Hat pier, on the west coast. Mae Hat has a small collection of travel services, internet cafés and post and money-exchange facilities, but no presence of a Thai community unaffiliated with the tourist trade. North of Mae Hat is the diver headquarters of Hat Sai Ri. The nondiving crowd generally scatters to the other beaches and coves on the south and east coasts. These are reached along treacherous unsealed roads that cut through the interior of the island. Hat Sai Ri also has traveller facilities and services.

Activities

Ko Tao's best **diving and snorkelling** sites are offshore islands or pinnacles, including White Rock, Shark Island, Chumphon Pinnacle, Green Rock, Sail Rock and Southwest Pinnacles. About 40 dive operators eagerly offer their services to travellers. The larger dive operators aren't necessarily better than the smaller ones, and will often take out bigger groups of divers. These operators usually have more than one office around the island (such as at Mae Hat and Hat Sai Ri).

Rates are similar everywhere, and typically cost 800B per dive to 5400B for a 10-dive package. An all-inclusive introductory dive lesson costs 1600B, while a four-day, open-water PADI certificate course costs around 8000B – these rates include gear, boat, instructor, food and beverages. Any bungalow or dive shop can arrange snorkelling day trips around the island for 400B. If you just want to rent a snorkel, mask and fins it will cost you about 100B for the day.

Sleeping & Eating

Food can be expensive on Ko Tao as there are no community markets or non-tourist-related vendors. Except for Hat Sai Ri, which has an assortment of restaurants, you are captive to the guesthouse kitchens. If you're not on the mango-shake-and-banana-pancake train, now is the time to get on board or go hungry.

HAT SAI RI

This is the island's longest stretch of beach, and the most populated, with a string of busy cafés, restaurants and simple (largely overpriced) accommodation. Some guesthouses are affiliated with a dive company and don't accept customers who aren't enrolled in a course.

Mr J's (☎ 0 7745 6066; r from 250B) Rooms here are plain but the owner is a wildly eccentric Ko Tao legend. Free chocolate, Pepsi, beer or banana, depending on how long you stay. Seriously.

Sai Ree Cottages (☎ 0 7745 6374; nitsairee@hotmail.com; d 250-700B; ❄) You'll find roomy and modern concrete cottages in the front here, less exciting options further back and postcard-perfect bamboo huts right on the beach.

In-Touch Bungalow (☎ 0 7745 6514; d 300-500B) A 15-minute walk from the pier, this place is popular with divers and nondivers alike. The round hobbitlike huts near the main path have huge bathrooms, but even the bungalows at the back are fairly large. And you could easily spend a day doing nothing in the ultra-chilled-out restaurant and bar, which is one of this beach's most consistently crowded.

Simple Life Villa (☎ 0 7745 6142; r 400-600B, d 600B) Simple Life is right – this is a small village of low-slung concrete bungalows shaded by massive coconut trees. It's popular with divers, as Simple Life runs a nearby dive school and the students stay here.

CHALOK BAAN KAO BAY

A crowded but good-looking bay favoured by the young and carefree, this might just be your version of paradise.

Freedom Beach (☎ 0 7745 6539; bungalows 100-250B) On its own secluded beach at the eastern end of Ao Chalok, these little huts are as basic as they come – wooden boxes with mattresses on the floor. However, if you crave solitude with great views for your pennies, then Freedom could be for you. The bungalows are a 10-minute walk from the action on the main beach.

HAT TAA TOH

The Thai-run **Freedom Beach** (☎ 0 7745 6596; Haad Taa Toh Klaang; d 300B) is a little slice of heaven. There's a small selection of old-school bungalows positioned on a ridge. The casual restaurant has stellar views (dishes from 45B to 60B). Pale-skinned travellers will delight in the shady protection offered by small trees on the tiny beach below, not to mention the translucent water.

AO LAEM THIAN & AO TANOT

Through the dense jungle canopy along roads better suited for water drainage, you reach the northeast cape of Laem Thian and its small rocky cove. Further south, Ao Tanot is a pretty cove surrounded by huge limestone rock formations and a sandy beach. Here you have a handful of guesthouses making an amenable compromise between isolation and socialisation.

Bamboo Hut (☎ 0 7745 6531; Ao Tanot; bungalows 150-500B) Surrounded by trees, there are 20 decked bungalows here, but the older they are, the smaller they are. The restaurant is very laid-back and the kitchen specialises in spicy southern Thai-style food.

Laem Thian Bungalows (☎ 0 7745 6477; pingpong_laemthian@hotmail.com; Laem Thian; d 350-1000B) Having done a trekking trip before you try negotiating the steep steps here will serve you well. The lone occupier of this cove has ultrabasic huts and dim shared bathrooms. The reception/dining area is crying out for a makeover, but you'll probably spend your days snorkelling and hardly notice. Ring ahead for pick-up from Ban Mae Hat pier.

Diamond Beach (☎ 0 7745 6591/2; Ao Tanot; bungalows 400-500B) These bungalows are relatively new, modern and comfortable. They have interesting designs with windows placed on the huts' corners. It's a good spot, with upbeat music playing and an appealing restaurant near the beach.

Black Tip Dive Resort (☎ 0 7745 6488; www.blacktip-kohtao.com; Ao Tanot; bungalows 800-1700B; ❄) Part of a dive shop and water-sports centre, Black Tip has a handful of lovely bungalows. If you fun dive with them you get 25% off the room rates and if you do a course it's 50% off. The dive centre has a wacky, white adobe design with strange geometrical configurations.

HAT SAI DAENG

New Heaven Nature Huts (d 400-500B) Run by a quirky crew, this rustic ensemble blends nicely into the hilltop. Dishes in the restaurant average 50B to 110B.

Coral View Resort (☎ 0 7745 6482; www.coralview.net; d 500-900B) On the southern coast in stunning Hat Sai Daeng, Coral View has comfortable 'grown-up' bungalows, plus original bamboo ones, sea views and one of the best two-tier restaurants on the island. Coral View is run by a friendly Australian-Thai couple, and if you call in advance and make a reservation, they will pick you up at the Ban Mae Hat pier.

Drinking

At night, the action centres on Hat Sai Ri's bars, a mix of diving and suntanning afterglow. The crowds bulk up during some of the weekly parties, advertised on fliers posted throughout the village. Because travel between beaches is difficult, people staying on the east or south coast tend to hang out in their guesthouses recounting the day's adventures.

Getting There & Away

There is only one pier in Ko Tao. To reach Surat Thani, take an express boat (500B, five hours, one morning departure) or night ferry (500B, seven to eight hours, one departure nightly). An additional express boat service does the island jump to Thong Sala on Ko Pha-Ngan (180B to 250B, one to two hours, six departures daily from 9.30am to 3.30pm) and on to Na Thon on Ko Samui (280B to 550B).

Chumphon is another mainland option, reached by express boats (400B, 1½ to two hours, departing from 10.30am to 3pm) and a slow boat (250B, six hours, departing at 10am).

KO SAMUI

pop 39,000

Possibly no island in all of Thailand provokes such a wide range of differing opinions as does Ko Samui. Because of the heavy Western influence and its chain restaurants, holier-than-thou backpackers have been turning up their noses at the mere mention of the place for years. But families, honeymooners and vacationing romantics see the island differently: as a place where the conveniences of home are just a stone's throw away from tropical beach paradise.

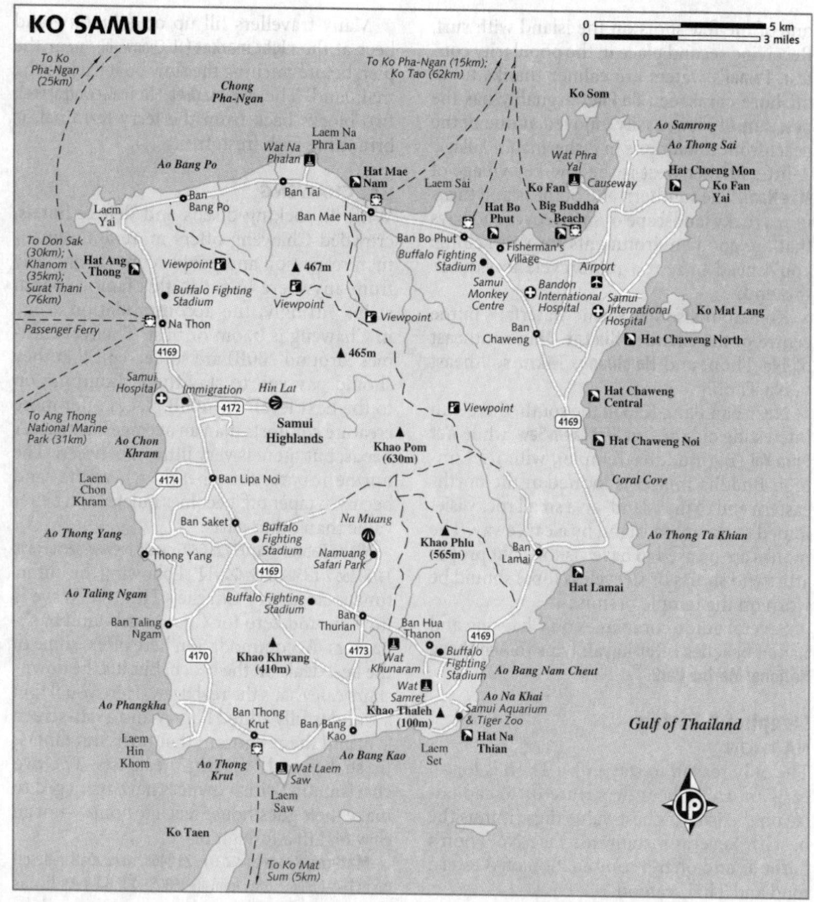

Probably the best way to approach an island this beautiful and this complex, however, is without preconceived notions. If you've come to eat and drink with the crowds, you'll soon find yourself in the heart of glittery Hat Chaweng. But don't forget – Samui is still a very large island. If you'd like to escape the crowds, it shouldn't be too tough to make that happen.

Information

Bank of Ayudha (☎ 0 7742 0176; Na Thon; 🕒 8.30am-3.30pm) Head about 200m from the ferry towards the police station and then 50m left. Also has branches at Hat Chaweng and Hat Mae Nam.

Post office (Th Chenwithee, Na Thon; 🕒 8.30am-4.30pm Mon-Fri, 9am-noon Sat, Sun & public holidays) Go on, mail those postcards! Overseas calls can be made here (from 8am to 8pm).

Samui International Hospital (Chaweng Hospital; ☎ 0 7742 2272) For medical or dental needs.

Tourist information (☎ 0 7420 7202; tatsamui@tat.or.th; Th Malitra Vanitchroen, Na Thon; 🕒 8.30am-noon & 1-4.30pm)

Tourist police (☎ 0 7742 1281, 24hr emergencies 1155)

Sights & Activities

The beaches are beautiful and, naturally, the main attraction. If you tire of the same pitch of land outside your guesthouse, be sure to set your sights a bit further afield and explore some other stretches of sand. **Chaweng** is famous for a reason – the water is crystal clear and the beach is 6km long; it is also one of the few spots on the island with surf. Receiving second place in the popularity contest, **Lamai**'s waters are calmer thanks to an offshore coral reef. **Bo Phut** arguably has the best sunset view, easily enjoyed at one of the beachfront restaurants in Fisherman's Village. A little further west is the low-key village of **Mae Nam**. The southern end of the island turns into a rocky landscape of small coves and bays that are good environments for snorkelling; you'll need to rent a motorcycle to explore this end.

Ko Samui also has scenic waterfalls in the centre of the island – **Hin Lat**, 3km southeast of Na Thon, and **Na Muang**, 14km southeast of Na Thon.

Near Ban Bang Kao in the south, there's an interesting old *chedi* at **Wat Laem Saw**, while **Wat Phra Yai** (Big Buddha Temple), with its 12m-high Buddha image, is located at the north-eastern end of the island, on a small rocky islet joined to the main island by a causeway. The monks are pleased to have visitors, but proper attire (no shorts or sleeveless tops) should be worn on the temple premises.

Several guide companies on Chaweng and Lamai beaches offer kayak trips to **Ang Thong National Marine Park**.

Sleeping & Eating

NA THON

The only reason to stay in Na Thon is for an early morning boat departure or to capitalise on the island's best-value digs (minus the beach). Several restaurants face Na Thon's harbour and offer a combination of Western food and Thai seafood.

Wang Bua Home Guesthouse (☎ 0 7742 0317; 212/7 Th Chonwithi; d from 350B; ❄) Opposite the Thai Farmers Bank, this place is popular with Thais and astute travellers.

Nathon Residence (☎ 0 7723 6058; Th Thawi Ratchaphakdi; r 500B; ❄) Most places in this town are on the drab side, but this is your best bet. There are big, sparkling tiled rooms here as well as a downstairs café and great staff. The rooms all come with satellite TV.

About Art & Craft (☎ 0 6789 1190; 90/3 Th Chonwithi; dishes 40-240B) This is actually a café serving a healthy line-up: try the pumpkin and tofu salad (100B).

Coffee Island (dishes 50-180B; 🕑 6.30am-10pm) Opposite the new pier, Coffee Island has a good selection of its namesake as well as bakery goodies.

Many travellers fill up on *kŭaytĭaw* and beer at the **night market** (Th Chonwithi), near the pier, before catching the slow boat back to the mainland. The **day market** (Th Thaweeratpakdee), two blocks back from the ferry terminal, is brimming with fresh fruit.

HAT CHAWENG

With its rocking discos and deluxe hotels, crowded Chaweng offers more amusement than relaxation and people come a long way from anywhere to get to this famous beach strip. Fittingly, the accommodation scene in Chaweng is boom or bust. The real cheapies (around 200B) are so decrepit that they should pay you to stay there. Bumping up to the next level, the 400B places offer more creature comforts than an average backpacker needs, but there is very little in between. The northern part of the beach, where the sand begins to taper off, becomes quieter and better value than other parts.

Wave Samui (☎ 0 7723 0803; www.thewavesamui.com; 11/5 Moo 2; r 350-850B; ❄ 💻) Following the unfortunate closure of Charlie's Hut, the Wave is now ground zero for Chaweng-bound backpackers. Accommodation here offers some of the best deals on the beach, but it's the downstairs café that's the real draw. Here you'll find a wonderfully edited library and a flat-screen TV, and the restaurant that turns out fantastic shakes and Western breakfasts. The two charismatic British owners have managed to make their guesthouse feel like home – not an easy feat in a foreign place.

Matlang Resort (☎ 0 7723 0468; www.matlangresort.com; 154/1 Moo 2; d/tw from 400/600B; ❄ 💻) As far as picture-perfect beauty goes, this place can't be beaten. Dozens of bungalows are dotted along a winding red-brick path in a lush garden setting, and the entire operation is smack bang on the prettiest stretch of the beach.

Baan Chaweng Guest House (☎ 0 7422 2153; 45/10 Moo 3; d 400-600B; ❄) This semihidden guesthouse couldn't possibly have less character. But for pure value, it may be this beach's top draw. Rooms are spacious and each one comes with satellite TV and freezing cold air-con – even the 400B rooms. Unfortunately, it's all shared bathrooms, but the water is hot and the tiles are scrubbed clean daily.

Green Guest House (☎ 0 7742 2611; 156/7 Moo 2; d 450-1000B) On the same *soi* as Lucky Mother (which is across the street from Khun Chaweng Shopping Center), this tidy place has a small row of rooms tucked into a pleasant garden setting. Everything here is clean and comfortable, so it's a smart choice if the ruggedness of bungalow life has you beaten. It's just seconds from the beach.

Also recommended:

Chaweng Pearl Cabana (☎ 0 7741 3109; d 350B) This collection of tin-roofed bungalows is popular with the fresh-faced set.

Dew Drop Hut Bungalow (☎ 0 7723 0551; 14/1 Moo 2; d 400B) Wooden bungalows in a little sliver of forest.

At night, restaurants set up romantic candlelit tables on the beach. You pick your meal from the iced tray of seafood, which is priced by the kilo, and then it hits the barbecue grill. Salty folklore says to pick a fish with unclouded eyes (a sign of freshness) and a fairly small body (a sign of tenderness).

There is also a series of cheap food stalls near the nightclub *soi*, just off the main drag in central Chaweng. As daylight disappears, *kàthoey* fuel up here for a night of female impersonation.

HAT LAMAI

Samui's second-most popular beach is just as busy as Chaweng – yes, McDonald's has arrived – but the crowd is younger and less well groomed. Behind the beach, a shopping, eating and low-key girly-bar strip caters to all your needs. A shoestringer could rent a spot right in the midst of the party, but for quieter times head to the northern end of the beach.

Jah Peace (www.jahpeace.com; s/d 150/200B) Formerly a much-loved beach tavern known as the Chill Out Bar, Jah Peace is a series of 12 A-frame backpacker bungalows with nary a mod con in sight; it's fan rooms and shared bathrooms for everyone. But as the owner proudly proclaims, 'this is the cheapest place on Lamai'. It's also a great place to hunker down and stay awhile – DVDs screen often in the common area, and beach parties here are said to be good. Fair warning: the shared bathrooms are a thing of pure terror.

Sea Breeze Bungalows (☎ 0 7742 4258; seabreeze_bungalow@yahoo.com; 124/3 Moo 3, Th Maret; d 250-400B; ❄) At the busy southern end, Sea Breeze has fan-cooled wooden bungalows in shady grounds.

Beer's House Beach Bungalows (☎ 0 7723 0467, 0 1958 4494; 161/4 Moo 4, Th Maret; d 450-500B) Run by a pleasant Thai couple, the chunky bungalows here are small but clean and cosy. Best feature? They all come complete with rather large front decks, perfect for daydreaming while the waves crash just a stone's throw away, or maybe for entertaining your next-door neighbour as the sun sets. Air-con and TV rooms on the other side of the road (and thus further from the beach) are 700B.

Utopia Bungalow (☎ 0 7723 3113; www.utopia-samui.com; 124/105 Moo 3, Th Maret; d incl breakfast from 500B; ❄ 💻) Beautiful grounds with dozens and dozens of bungalows – some of them rugged and some quite luxurious – and a large beachfront restaurant (dishes 60B to 140B).

Spa Samui Resort (☎ 0 7723 0855; www.spasamui.com; r 500-1000B; ❄ 🏊) This American-owned spa is considered to be one of Asia's finer health resorts. And assuming you're up for an internal adventure, you won't be bored – the menu includes seven-day fasts, colonics, meditation, yoga, massage, raw food classes and more. (Prior to your visit, check the website to see what's on.) The basic bungalows are perfectly well manicured and the vegetarian food (dishes from 30B to 280B) is said to be of the highest quality.

HAT BO PHUT & BIG BUDDHA BEACH

Many visitors to Ko Samui are prepared to sacrifice the picture-perfect contours of crowded Hat Chaweng for the slower pace of bohemian Bo Phut. It's particularly popular with European sun-seekers who don't seem to mind the shallow waters that sometimes verge on the muddy side.

You're better off looking in the 500B range in and around compact Fisherman's Village, at Bo Phut, which has several charming restaurants serving Thai and Western food.

Big Buddha Beach is the preferred spot for many independent travellers.

Rasta Baby II (☎ 0 1082 0339, 0 9475 7656; 176 Moo 1, Bo Phut; d from 200B) If you're adamant about hunting down a bargain, try your luck here. If this place was a hairstyle, it would be a set of dreadlocks. Get comfortable in unpretentious bungalows. Dishes in the restaurant average 40B to 120B.

Chalee Bungalows (☎ 0 7724 5035; freddy_raymond@hotmail.com; 58/1 Moo 4, Big Buddha Beach; d 800B; ❄) This is a lovely nook with well-maintained bungalows boasting personable interiors. The attached Shabash Restaurant & Bar dishes out Indonesian, Indian and Middle Eastern fare.

HAT MAE NAM

If you find yourself lying on the beach wondering what country you're in, it is time to pack up and move to Mae Nam. Although the beach isn't jaw-droppingly beautiful, the surrounding village is a much-needed dose of Thailand. The foreign crowd tends to be calmer, complementing the laid-back Thai community. Finding a Thai meal in Mae Nam is much easier than at other beaches. Grab an iced Thai coffee at the morning market, or a bowl of *khànŏm jiin* (thin wheat noodles) at the food stalls in the village of Mae Nam.

Mae Nam Village Bungalows (☎ 0 7742 5151; 129/2 Moo 1, Th Maenam; d 300-400B;) This end of Mae Nam is a good starting point for budget digs. You'll find basic white concrete bungalows here; the ones around 350B to 400B are the best bet.

Café Talay Bar Restaurant (dishes 100B; lunch & dinner) Savour spicy meals at this bohemian spot, positioned near where the beach meets Th Maenam. It's a fitting place to soak up the low-key beachside mood; try the zesty and light *yam kûng* (spicy shrimp salad).

Drinking

Ko Samui's nightlife can be summed up with one word: Chaweng. Back behind the main drag, opposite the ocean, is a maze of *soi* lined with open-air bars with competing stereo systems and gyrating Thai women. An odd mix of depravity and innocence imbues these alleyways. Lonely hearts and content crowds of friends play dominoes with the young garland sellers, while the female bartenders do raunchy pole dances. Although the scene is probably better appreciated by men, women shouldn't feel uncomfortable.

Green Mango (☎ 0 7742 2148; Soi Green Mango; admission free; from 10pm) This huge open-air meat-market dance club has been throbbing on Samui for 20 years straight. Considering it's on the same small *soi* as a group of girlie bars with names such as Club 69 and Snatch, you can probably deduce it's located in one of Samui's many red-light districts. Hard house on the hi-fi gets the place popping around midnight.

Reggae Pub (☎ 0 7742 2331; 3/3 Moo 2; 6pm-2am) You'll have to brave a small *soi* filled with aggressive bar girls to reach this open-air warehouse, where Asian reggae groups crank out Bob Marley covers by the dozen. This is also a great spot for dancing – everyone's doing it! To find the place, just look for the big neon Rasta guys on the opposite side of the lake.

Getting There & Away

Be cautious when booking mainland train and bus tickets with agents; the bookings don't always get made or are not for the class you paid for.

Bangkok Airways (code PG; ☎ in Chaweng 0 7742 2512-9) flies about 20 times daily between Ko Samui and Bangkok (one way 2400B to 3800B). Other destinations include Phuket and Singapore (about twice a day). The **Samui airport** (☎ 0 7742 2512; btwn Hat Chaweng & Hat Bang Rak) departure tax is 400B for domestic flights and 500B for international flights.

Na Thon is Ko Samui's main pier for passenger and car ferries to Surat Thani; at other areas such as Hat Bang Rak (Big Buddha Beach), Hat Bo Phut and Hat Mae Nam, there is a seasonal service to Ko Pha-Ngan and Ko Tao. Ferry schedules are subject to change and services decrease during the low season.

Songserm (☎ 0 7742 0157; Na Thon pier) runs an express boat (150B, 2½ hours, one daily) to Surat Thani's Tha Thong pier (Tha Pak Nam). **Seatran** (☎ 0 7742 6000) runs an express boat (250B, two hours, two departures daily) to Surat Thani's Don Sak pier and a car ferry (150B, 2½ hours, hourly from 5.30am to 6pm) also to Surat Thani's Don Sak pier, and then a bus to central Surat Thani. The night ferry (150B, six hours, departing at 9pm) arrives at the Ban Don pier in Surat Thani.

To get to Ko Pha-Ngan (Thong Sala) there are regular departures from Na Thon pier (four daily), Hat Mae Nam pier (three daily) and Phra Yai pier (four daily); see p781 for more information.

To reach Ko Tao, take Songserm's speedboat (550B, 1½ hours, two departures daily) from Hat Bo Phut and Hat Mae Nam piers. A slower ferry (380B, 3½ hours, one morning departure) leaves from Hat Mae Nam pier.

For more information contact the **Thai Ferry Centre** (☎ 0 7747 1151/2) in Surat Thani.

Getting Around

The island's roads are well sealed, making transportation easy and affordable. Săwngthăew can be flagged down on the island's main road or at the Na Thon pier as the drivers do their loops round the island; from Na Thon to the beaches expect to pay 30B to 50B. It's always a good idea to establish the price beforehand so that you aren't socked with a surprise 'charter'.

You can rent motorcycles on Ko Samui for about 150B to 200B a day; there are numerous outlets. Take it easy on the bikes; every year several *faràng* die or are seriously injured in motorcycle accidents on Samui, and a helmet law is enforced. To deter snatch thieves, don't put valuables in the bike's basket.

KO PHA-NGAN

pop 10,300

Wedged between Ko Tao and Ko Samui, Ko Pha-Ngan is part of backpacking folklore, a place custom-made for hammock swinging and navel gazing. Swaying coconut trees, brooding mountains, ribbons of turquoise water – Ko Pha-Ngan is everything a tropical island paradise should be. While the island is devoid of an airport and the roads remain unruly, it will be spared from full-throttle development; however, the days of 100B beachfront bungalows are rarer with each passing year.

Every sunburnt face you meet in Khao San's bars will tell you of the best beach to head to, and the truth is you're spoilt for choice here and it ain't such a bad idea to move from one beach to the next depending on how much time you have up your cheesecloth sleeve.

Orientation

The island of Ko Pha-Ngan is 100km from Surat Thani and 15km north of Ko Samui. Most boats arrive in the southwestern corner of the island at Thong Sala, a dusty port town of shops and tourist services. In the far southeastern corner is the famed party beach quarter of Hat Rin, divided into Hat Rin Nai (to the west) and Hat Rin Nok (to the east). On the west coast are the quieter outposts of Hat Yao (Long Beach) and Ao Mae Hat. On the northern side is Ao Chalok Lam and its thriving fishing village, as well as Hat Khuat (Bottle Beach), reachable only by boat. Transport around the island is expensive because of rugged terrain and unsealed roads.

Information

Ko Pha-Ngan Hospital (☎ 0 7737 7034) Around 2.5km north of Thong Sala; 24-hour emergency service.

PJ Home (☎ 0 7737 5403; 95/15 Moo 6, Hat Rin; per min 2B) Internet access at this travel agency near Hat Rin's pier.

Police (☎ 0 7737 7114, emergency 191)

Siam City Bank (☎ 0 7737 5476; 9/60 Moo 6, Hat Rin; 🕑 8.30am-3.30pm Mon-Fri) ATM and currency exchange bureau. There are also several banks in Thong Sala.

Sights & Activities

In the eastern part of the island, **Nam Tok Than Sadet** (Than Sadet Falls) has attracted three generations of Thai kings as well as countless *faràng*. Take a longtail boat from Hat Rin to Hat Sadet and walk into the island along the river for 2.5km. The east coast, especially **Hat Thian** and **Ao Thong Nai Pan**, is lauded as having the best snorkelling and swimming.

At **Wat Khao Tham**, on a hilltop on the southwestern side of the island, 10-day Buddhist meditation retreats are conducted by an American-Australian couple during the latter half of most months. The cost is 4000B. Contact the **wat** (www.watkowtahm.org; PO Box 18, Ko Pha-Ngan, Surat Thani 84280) for information, or preregister in person from 1pm to 2pm the day before the retreat is due to begin. A different preregistration process exists for people under 26; check the website for more details.

Sleeping

As you get off the ferry in Ko Pha-Ngan, consider this question: do you want to party like a rock star or sleep like a baby? If your answer is the former, head straight to Hat Rin; if it's the latter, pick any beach *except* Hat Rin.

HAT RIN & AROUND

Ground zero for the monthly full moon parties, Hat Rin is a thriving offspring of Bangkok's Th Khao San. The village is a rabbit warren of shops to keep your baht rolling over, movies on constant rotation, scruffy dogs nipping flees and second-hand bookstores to peruse. This long cape is divided into two beaches: Hat Rin Nok (Sunrise Beach), along the eastern shore, and Hat Rin Nai (Sunset Beach), along the western shore. Hat Rin Nok is a touch Rio de Janeiro, with everyone comparing tans. Hat Rin Nai is a little quieter. Accommodation tends to be both expensive (jumping by around 200B a night when everyone is full-mooning) and average, because there's a long queue of backpackers drooling to get in.

Sea View Haad Rin Resort (☎ 0 7737 5160; Hat Rin Nok; d 300-800B; ❄) Located within stumbling distance of the cliffside Mellow Mountain Bar, bungalows here range wildly in quality. The wooden beachfront digs are sublime, but be prepared to pay!

Paradise Bungalows (☎ 0 7737 5242; Hat Rin Nok; d & tw from 350B; ❄) One of the oldest guesthouses on the beach, Paradise started the full moon

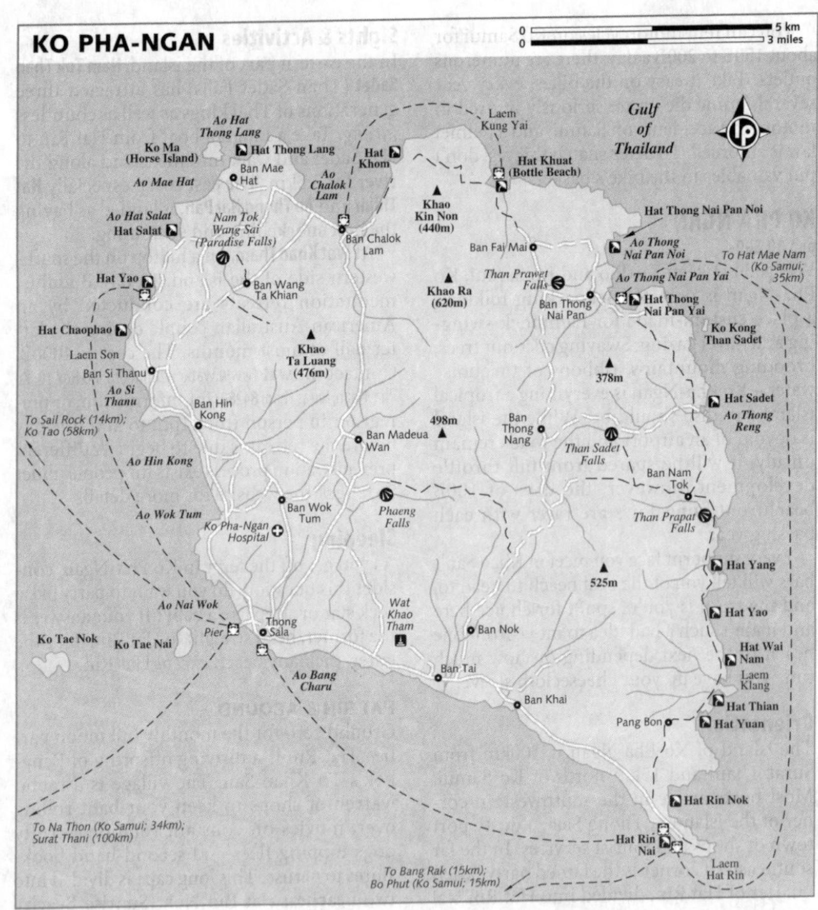

parties more than a decade ago (see opposite). Simple cottages line the beach and crawl up the cliff for sea views. Frankly, things here are looking a little worse for wear these days, but what do you expect at a place that parties as hard as Paradise does?

Neptune's Villa (☎ 0 7737 5251; neptune1@thaimail.com; Hat Rin Nai; d from 400B; ❄) Within shouting distance of the Hat Rin pier, the stone and concrete bungalows here are absolutely immaculate. The larger, air-con units exude most of the charm, but solo travellers can still snag a tiny tin-roofed hut that sits just metres from the sea. The 2nd floor has a Moroccan and Israeli restaurant with stunning sunset views.

Same Same Lodge & Restaurant (☎ 0 7904 3923; www.same-same.com; 139/19 Th Ban Tai, Hat Rin Nok; r 400-700B) Mighty popular with some readers, Same Same is Party Central and caters to shoestringers, with 22 rooms, billiards, island trips (500B), cooking classes (800B) and 'warm-up' full moon preludes. It's a short walk to Hat Rin village and the beach from this pink base. The restaurant here serves dishes from 35B to 160B.

Phangan Bay Shore Resort (☎ 0 7737 5224; 141 Moo 6, Hat Rin Nok; s/d from 500/600B; ❄) Towards the far end of Sunrise Beach, this is one of the nicer options – both the grounds and concrete bungalows are well maintained. At the time of research, another collection of bungalows was being constructed in front of the restaurant, and it's tough to say what effect this will have on the view, not to mention the vibe. The resort was also building a hotel-like structure next door.

WEST OF HAT RIN

If Hat Rin is a flashy pair of trainers, then the area between Ban Khai and Ban Tai, about 4km west, is a happily weathered sandal. Although the area isn't ideal for swimming, it is within attack-and-retreat range of Hat Rin and you have a better chance of securing beachfront real estate.

Liberty Guesthouse (☎ 0 7723 8171; libertybantai@hotmail.com; Ban Tai; d 250-400B) Another traveller's haven, with a great pavilion eating area (dishes 40B to 250B). Lino-floored bungalows are simple but homely.

Mac Bay Resort (☎ 0 7723 8443; www.macbayresort.com; btwn Ban Tai & Ban Khai; d from 350B; ❄) Decent hardwood and concrete bungalows and a welcoming vibe. Meals here cost from 25B to 60B.

SOUTHWESTERN KO PHA-NGAN

Cookie Bungalows (☎ 0 7737 7499; cookies_bungalows@hotmail.com; Woktum Bay; d 250-400B; 🅿) North of Thong Sala pier, this is a real find if the happy snaps of past punters are anything to go by. Lush gardens and mango trees envelop nicely spaced bamboo huts. If the *faràng*-friendly restaurant or rocky cove don't titillate, take a dip in the above-ground pool.

Stone Hill Resort (☎ 0 7723 8654; d from 400B; ❄) Nearby, this place boasts modern, clean villas with awesome views, and its high-altitude Amsterdam Bar & Restaurant is unique. Try to get the taxi to take you up here, as it's one hell of a steep driveway.

WESTERN KO PHA-NGAN

On the western side of the island, the sealed road extends as far as Hat Yao, a long curve of beach round a shallow bay popular with families and couples.

Further north on a rutted road, Ao Mae Hat is scenic in its own way and the anchored fishermen in their longtail boats break up the monotony of sun, sand and sea. A sandbar connects the beach to a nearby island during low tide and there's wonderful snorkelling in these parts. Stay at well-positioned

GET YOUR MOON ON

As the moon reaches its monthly climax, it seems that every other traveller you meet is making the migration to Ko Pha-Ngan and its famous full moon rave party. Under the cover of darkness Hat Rin becomes charged with drug-induced euphoria, and excited glow-torch dancers become hypnotised by the DJs' electro-charged turntables.

As is the case with most infamous legends, the story of the full moon party's founding comes in a number of differing versions. One fact most full mooners can agree on is that the family operating Paradise Bungalows – one of the oldest guesthouses at Hat Rin – is responsible for starting the tradition. The occasion was probably a birthday party, although some claim it was a going-away party for a longtime Paradise guest. Whatever the original purpose, it's clear that most backpackers who make the monthly pilgrimage to Hat Rin do so for one reason only: pure unadulterated fun, with very few rules attached.

And now a word from your mother... Even in paradise you should practise common sense. Readers have reported having valuables stolen from rooms, or being drugged and then robbed. Returning home alone at night is also an invitation for trouble, especially for women. Lonely Planet has received reports of alleged assaults by people 'posing' as longtail boat drivers.

Be careful about going on midnight swims, as Hat Rin has dangerous and unpredictable riptides; drownings have occurred. And don't hop on that handy motorcycle for a little cruising mayhem. Accidents happen.

In January 2005, a speedboat leaving Ko Pha-Ngan's full moon party en route to Ko Samui was overloaded with party-goers and tragically capsized leaving 15 foreigners dead. Don't get on packed boats – or crammed pick-up trucks for that matter.

Even though it seems like the entire island is a drug buffet, narcotics are illegal in Thailand and police enforcement is stepped up during full moon parties. Thai police take this *very* seriously.

Accommodation is slim nearing the actual event, when crowds numbering between 5000 and 8000 people arrive; to secure a pad show up several days early.

Now be safe and have a good time.

and quiet **Mae Hat Bay Resort** (☎ 0 7737 4171; Ao Mae Hat; d/tw from 350/400B; ❄) or **Island View Cabana** (☎ 0 7737 4172; Ao Mae Hat; d 200-300B), which has lots of older-style white bungalows and a busy restaurant (dishes from 45B to 120B). Apart from the sound of wind ruffling the palm trees you'll have few nightly disturbances around here. The **Village Green** (81/7 Moo 8, Hat Chaophao) is a favourite among shoestringers for its tasty Euro-Asian food and Pirate Bar.

NORTHERN KO PHA-NGAN

Travelling the winding road towards Ao Chalok Lam you descend into a verdant valley below mountains the colour of bruised storm clouds. Camped out by the water is the small fishing village of Ban Chalok Lam, where residents have seen their island change like a growing child. The road officially stops at Ban Chalok Lam, and to continue on to beautiful and remote Hat Khuat (Bottle Beach) – the current darling of the self-respecting backpacker posse – you have to catch a longtail boat (50B, dawn to dusk). The thick sandy beach and its glassy water are the main attractions at Bottle Beach – you'll never want to leave, unless you're chasing a cranking nightlife.

Fanta Bungalows (☎ 0 7737 4132; fantaphangan@yahoo.com; Ao Chalok Lam; d from 150B; ❄ 💻) Sleeping quarters here are nothing special, although they are solidly built and each balcony sports its own hammocks. Fanta's restaurant serves dishes from 35B to 100B.

Sai Thong Resort (☎ 0 7737 4115; Ao Chalok Lam; tw & d 300-600B; ❄ 💻) Bungalows here are a bit rough around the edges but they are likeable nonetheless. The real drawcard is the restaurant's views over the sea and its estuary.

Smile Bungalows (☎ 0 1780 2881; Hat Khuat; d 350-500B) You'll find this supremely orderly set-up at the end of the beach. Expect 28 very clean and neighbourly bungalows and a garden straight out of a Disney film.

Bottle Beach Three (☎ 0 7744 5154; Hat Khuat; s/d 350/550B, 2-storey bungalows 850B) Thai pop drawls from the spic-and-span restaurant (dishes from 40B to 210B), and timber bungalows on the beach strike a good-looking pose. Rendered *Truman Show*–style 'homes' are found at the back of the property. Opting for one of the spiffy two-storey pads is a good choice if there are two couples together (two double beds; one in the attic).

Also recommended:

Bottle Beach Two (☎ 0 7744 5156; Hat Khuat; d 300-350B) About 22 blue crash pads have prime beach frontage. There's a shady eating space – shell chimes mix it with a set of imposing speakers. Run by distracted young staff. Dishes in the restaurant cost from 40B to 180B.

Bottle Beach One (☎ 0 7744 5125; Hat Khuat; d 300-850B; 💻) Bottle Beach's original cluster of bungalows to suit low, high and in-between budgets. Spotless restaurant: chip sandwich anyone (60B)? Other dishes range from 40B to 220B.

EASTERN KO PHA-NGAN

In the northeastern corner, Ao Thong Nai Pan Yai and Ao Thong Nai Pan Noi have well-regarded swimming beaches. The two bays are separated by a steep 20-minute walk over a headland, or a longtail boat ride.

Sanctuary (☎ 0 1271 3614; www.thesanctuary-kpg.com; Hat Thian; dm 100B, d 450-1200B) At Hat Thian, way down the east coast near Hat Rin, health and nature are emphasised with a great community feeling at Sanctuary. Also on offer: daily yoga, meditation and full spa treatments (*including* colonic cleansing). Assuming you've got a big enough group (usually eight people), boats from Hat Rin cost 50B; alternatively it's a one-hour walk along a rough trail.

Ta Pong (☎ 0 7744 5079; Ao Thong Nai Pan Noi; d from 150B) Rustic, unshaven-looking bungalows with wooden balconies overlook the beach (number eight has stellar views) and tend to attract an alternative crowd. There's a great bar-cum-meeting-place – *the* spot to head for sundowners. Restaurant dishes cost from 40B to 80B.

Star Hut Bungalow (☎ 0 7744 5085; star_hut@hotmail.com; Ao Thong Nai Pan Noi; d from 220B; ❄) Choose from basic thatched huts with zero creature comforts or more upscale digs with wonderfully designed decks. There's a decent restaurant offering some traveller services.

Baan Panburi (☎ 0 7723 8599; www.baanpanburi.bigstep.com; Ao Thong Nai Pan Noi; d from 370B; ❄) If you can afford to stay here, do it! Oodles of character and friendly staff. Bamboo bungalows, set among tropical gardens, average around 570B per night. The restaurant is a classy affair – relish nightly barbecues under romantic fairy lights.

White Sand (☎ 0 7744 5123; Ao Thong Nai Pan Yai; d/tw 500/700B) At the east end of Thong Nai Pan Yai, it has neat bungalows with wooden floors.

Eating & Drinking

For all its strong points, Ko Pha-Ngan isn't known for fabulous cuisine. Virtually all beach accommodation has a simple café with typical *faràng* versions of Thai food, plus the usual muesli/yogurt/banana pancake concoctions. Some safe Thai dishes to order are *khâo phàt* and *kài phàt kà-phrao* (chicken stir-fried with basil). In Thong Sala, you can find *kŭaytĭaw* vendors and food stalls. Waiting for a ferry? The **Yellow Cafe** (dishes 60-90B), opposite the pier, feeds the hungry and idle with baked potatoes, sandwiches and teas.

As the moon begins to wane, Hat Rin's beachside bars are cocktail-in-a-bucket heaven for ragers. Hat Rin's **Backyard** (from 11am) is a popular day club following the full-moon assault. **Outback Bar** (94/25 Moo 6, Hat Rin Village; dishes 40-200B; 8am-midnight) is a typical pub with boppy tunes and no fewer than 10 TVs. Get your Sunday roast fix here (199B).

After 10pm taxi prices explode, making it cheaper for solos or couples to find a room in Hat Rin for the night rather than make the return trip to a distant beach.

Getting There & Around

Most ferries arrive and depart from the pier in Thong Sala, but during the high season there are endless combinations of services between Ko Pha-Ngan's Hat Rin and several beaches on Ko Samui's north coast. Schedules and frequency vary according to the season.

To Surat Thani, there are express boats via Ko Samui (250B, four hours, four departures daily) and night ferries (230B, seven hours, departing at 10pm). These boats leave from Thong Sala on Ko Pha-Ngan and arrive in Ban Don, Surat Thani.

There are 10 to 11 daily ferry departures between Ko Pha-Ngan and Ko Samui. These boats leave throughout the day from 7am to 4.30pm, take from 30 minutes to an hour and cost 180B to 250B. All leave from either Thong Sala or Hat Rin on Ko Pha-Ngan and arrive either in Na Thon, Mae Nam, Hat Bo Phut or Hat Bang Rak on Ko Samui. If you have a preference, clearly state it when buying a ticket.

Boats to Ko Tao (180B to 350B, one to three hours, six departures from 8.30am to 12.30pm daily) leave from Thong Sala.

Săwngthăew do daytime routes from Thong Sala to Hat Yao, Ban Chalok Lam or Hat Rin for 50B to 100B; travelling solo you'll pay around 250B to get to most places on the island. On the northwestern and northeastern coasts, roads are unsealed and the terrain is difficult. Taxis moving around the island are expensive, especially at night, ranging from 500B to 1000B. Longtail boats also service Thong Sala, Hat Yao, Hat Rin and other beaches for 50B to 100B.

NAKHON SI THAMMARAT

pop 122,400

Off the tourist trail, Nakhon Si Thammarat is a quintessential southern town. During early Thai history, it functioned as a major hub for trade within Thailand as well as between the western and eastern hemispheres. Clergy from Hindu, Islamic, Christian and Buddhist denominations established missions here over the centuries, and many of their houses of worship are still active today.

Information

Bovorn Bazaar (Th Ratchadamnoen) A small *faràng*-oriented centre with a few restaurants and internet cafés.
Main post office (Th Ratchadamnoen; 8.30am-4.30pm Mon-Fri)
TAT office (0 7534 6515; tatnakon@nrt.cscoms.com; Th Ratchadamnoen; 8.30am-4.30pm)
Telephone office (8am-11pm) International service; upstairs in the post office.

Sights

The city boasts the oldest and biggest wat in the south, **Wat Phra Mahathat** (Th Ratchadamnoen), reputed to be over 1500 years old and comparable in size to Wat Pho in Bangkok. The temple is 2km south of town; any săwngthăew chugging south will take you there for a bargain 6B.

To atone for all that mindless sunbathing you did on the islands, pay a visit to the **National Museum** (0 7534 1075, 0 7534 0419; Th Ratchadamnoen; admission 30B; 9am-4pm Wed-Sun), 1km south of Wat Phra Mahathat, for its interesting 'Art of Southern Thailand' exhibition.

Thai *năng tàlung* (shadow theatre) was developed in Nakhon Si Thammarat. The acknowledged master of shadow puppets is Suchart Subsin, and you can view a performance at his **workshop** (0 7534 6394; Soi 3, 110/18 Th Si Thammasok; admission 50B, minimum 2 people; shows 8.30am & 5pm). Puppets can also be purchased at reasonable prices.

Sleeping

You're not going to fall in love with the city's budget hotels, but at least you're out of the gutter.

Phetpailin Hotel (☎ 0 7534 1896; 1835/38-39 Th Yommarat; d from 180B; ❄) Simply a place to crash, with dim corridors and spaciously dreary rooms.

Thai Hotel (☎ 0 7534 1509; 1375 Th Rajdamnoen; d from 220B; ❄) Convenient to the night market and Bovorn Bazaar eats, this place offers secure old-fashioned rooms with TV.

Nakron Garden Inn (☎ 0 7531 3333; 1/4 Th Pak Nakhon; d 445B; ❄) The other choices are rather bleak, so you would be wise to expand your budget and shoot for a tidy room at this hotel.

Eating

At night the entire block running south of Th Neramit is lined with cheap food vendors preparing *rotii klûay* (banana pancakes), *khâo mòk kài* (chicken biryani) and *mátàbà* (pancakes stuffed with chicken or vegetables).

Hao Coffee (☎ 0 7534 6563; Bovorn Bazaar; dishes 20-100B; 🕑 breakfast, lunch & dinner) Select one of 18 international or southern Thai-style coffees ('Hao coffee' on the menu) and sit at a table encasing old collectables such as watches and currency.

Getting There & Away

Ordinary, VIP and air-con buses to Bangkok and Phuket depart from the bus station, 1km west of the TAT office. Minivans to Krabi, Phuket and Surat Thani leave from the City Hall area between Th Jamroenwithi and Th Ratchadamnoen, while minivans to Hat Yai depart from the Mae Somjit market area on Th Yommarat.

Buses head to Bangkok (VIP/air-con/ordinary 705/454/350B, 10 to 12 hours, 8am, 9am and hourly from 5pm to 7pm), Hat Yai (air-con 73B to 102B, three to four hours, hourly), Krabi (air-con/ordinary 120/65B, three hours), Phuket (air-con/ordinary 200/125B, eight hours) and Surat Thani (air-con/ordinary 95/55B, two hours).

HAT YAI

pop 191,200

If you've just crossed into Thailand from Malaysia, welcome to the Land of Smiles. Hat Yai is southern Thailand's commercial centre where the east and west coast roads and the railway line all meet. It is a steaming pot of ethnicities – made up of Chinese, Muslim and Thai faces – with a dash of debauchery for visitors from Thailand's puritanical southern neighbour. The city, perhaps with the highest concentration of hairdressers and beauticians this side of Bangkok, is one big shopping spree, with customers eyeing gold jewellery and ladies dressed like orchids encased behind glass doors. Like every good border town, Hat Yai knows how to party, especially during its signature holiday of the Chinese New Year in February.

Information

Bangkok Bank (cnr Th Prachathipat & Th Niphat Uthit 3) Currency exchange between 8.30am and 5pm, plus ATM.

Hat Yai Hospital (☎ 0 7423 0800; Th Rattakan)

Owen Tour (☎ 0 7423 4173; 49 Thamnoonvithi; per hr 40B; 🕑 8.30am-10pm) Internet access, just round the corner from Cathay Guest House.

TAT office (☎ 0 7424 3747; 1/1 Soi 2, Th Niphat Uthit 3; 🕑 8.30am-4.30pm)

Tourist police (☎ 0 7424 6733, emergency 1155) Near the TAT office.

Sleeping

Hat Yai has dozens of hotels within walking distance of the train station.

Cathay Guest House (☎ 0 7424 3815; 93/1 Th Niphat Uthit 2; dm 100B, r 250B) Even though it has seen better days, this has become the travellers' headquarters in Hat Yai because of its good location, helpful staff and plentiful information about onward travel. It's a great place to meet other travellers, leaf through mountains of brochures and catch up on overdue laundry. Inexpensive breakfasts and lunches are served in an on-site café and there's a reliable travel agency downstairs.

Louise Guest House (☎ 0 7422 0966; 21-23 Th Thamnoonvithi; r 300-400B; ❄) This place is conveniently located and has more appealing rooms than the Cathay Guest House, but lacks its buzz. With more of an apartment-style layout, the rooms here aren't very big but are well maintained and you have the option of air-con.

Eating & Drinking

You can eat your way through three superb ethnic cuisines in a six-block radius. Many Hat Yai restaurants, particularly the Chinese ones, close in the afternoon between 2pm and 6pm. The extensive **night market** (Th Montri 1), across from the Songkhla bus station, specialises in fresh seafood and *khànŏm jiin*.

Vegetable Food (☎ 0 7423 5369; 138/4 Th Thamnoonvithi; dishes 25B) Vegetarians on the hunt will be able to feast themselves silly on Chinese-influenced dishes at this very local haunt, opposite the Prince Hotel. There's a small roman-script sign out the front.

Muslim Ocha (Th Niphat Uthit 1; dishes 25-120B; breakfast, lunch & dinner) *Rotii kaeng* (flat bread with curry dip) every-which-way, plus daytime rice and curry, soups and vegetarian selections. Opposite King's Hotel.

Dao Thiam (0 7424 3268; 79/3 Th Thamnoonvithi; dishes 40-80B; breakfast, lunch & dinner;) Opposite Odean Department Store, this diner is something of a local institution serving reliable Thai-Chinese meals (including meat-free options). Currency from around the world adorns the walls, but don't even think about funding the next leg of your trip – it's all framed behind glass.

Post Laser Disc Pub (0 7423 2027; 82-83 Th Thamnoonvithi; dishes 40-120B; lunch & dinner) Whether a farewell or maiden night in Thailand, raise a frothy glass to the house band mumbling its way through English tunes, or join the *kàthoey* headbanging to Guns n' Roses – now that's postmodern.

Brass Monkey (0 7424 5886; 94 Th Thamnoonvithi) This club/billiards hang-out looks like it's ready to party, even though it was deserted when we called in.

Getting There & Around

For information on travelling to Malaysia from Hat Yai, see p784.

Flights to Bangkok with **Thai Airways International** (0 7423 3433; www.thaiair.com; 182 Th Niphat

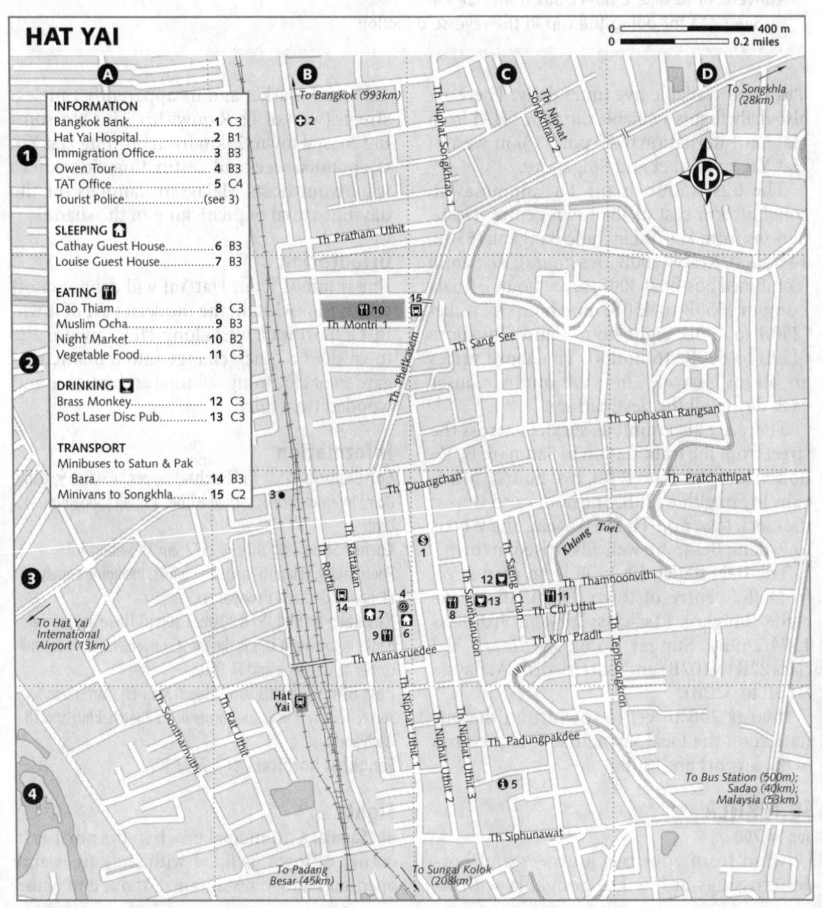

THAILAND

GETTING TO MALAYSIA

Hat Yai is the gatekeeper for passage into Malaysia. To hit targets on Malaysia's west coast, you can plough straight through, with the appropriate border formalities, from Hat Yai to Alor Setar, Butterworth and Kuala Lumpur by either bus or train. A bus to Butterworth costs 250B and takes four hours, while a train costs 180B to 322B and is slower and less frequent.

To Padang Besar

The Malaysian border is about 50km south of Hat Yai at Kanger–Padang Besar, and many travellers pass through town just to extend their Thai visas. Private taxis cost 600B return (one hour), share taxis are 150B (one hour), minivans 80B (1½ hours, hourly) and buses 40B (1½ hours, every 25 minutes). It's also possible to take the train, but this option is not very fast or frequent.

See p453 for information on doing the trip in reverse.

To Bukit Kayu Hitam

The Sadao–Bukit Kayu Hitam border is also accessible via minivan from Hat Yai. Once through the border (open 7am to 7pm), you can take a bus to Alor Setar (RM 4). However, it's much more convenient to take a direct bus from Hat Yai.

See p453 for doing the trip in the reverse direction.

Uthit 1) are available five times daily. There are also daily flights available through THAI from Hat Yai International Airport, 13km west of Hat Yai, to Phuket and Singapore.

The bus station is off Th Siphunawat, roughly 2km east of the town centre. Destinations from Hat Yai include Bangkok (550B, 14 hours), Krabi (200B, five hours), Ko Samui (combined bus-boat 300B, seven hours), Kuala Lumpur (350B to 450B, nine hours), Phuket (250B to 450B, eight hours) and Singapore (450B to 600B, 16 hours). The above prices are all for air-con. There are multiple buses each day to all the destinations.

There are also minibus services across the street from the train station to Satun (65B, 1½ hours) and Pak Bara (70B, two hours). Minivans to Songkhla (20B, one hour) also stop at the clock tower on Th Phetkasem. Share taxis to Padang Besar are well advertised in town.

The **train station** (Th Rotfai) is an easy stroll from the centre of town. Destinations include Bangkok (1st-class air-con/3rd class 1394/269B), Sungai Kolok (ordinary 3rd class 82B to 102B) and Butterworth, Malaysia (180B to 322B).

It costs 20B to get to town from the bus station on the local sǎwngthǎew. Share taxis to the airport are 180B.

SONGKHLA

pop 86,700

Unwind from your bus journeys and border crossings at low-key Songkhla with its colourful market and its apparently timeless streets (west of Th Ramwithi). This blossoming coastal town, 25km from bustling Hat Yai, is a popular weekend destination. Songkhla's waterfront hosts Malaysian families for the daytime ritual of picnicking in the shade.

Orientation

The minibus from Hat Yai will drop you off on Th Ramwithi in the modern part of town. Just a short walk west along Th Ramwithi, the town does a quick change into a manicured garden of charming colonial architecture and wooded twin hills.

Information

Coffeebucks (25/1 Th Phetchakhiri; per hr 30B; 🕑 8am-8pm) Internet access, tucked within a small shopping centre.

Corner Shop (☎ 0 7431 2577; cnr Th Saiburi & Th Phetchakhiri) English-language books, including Lonely Planet guides, and newspapers.

Kasikorn Bank (🕑 8.30am-3.30pm) There are several banks in town but this is the most convenient; it's near the corner of Th Chana and Th Platha.

Post office (🕑 8.30am-4.30pm Mon-Fri, 9am-noon Sat, Sun & holidays) Near the corner of Th Phetchakhiri and Th Wichianchom

Songkhla Hospital (☎ 0 7432 1072)

Sights

Hat Samila, a municipal beach in the northeast corner of town, is lined with leafy trees and open-air seafood restaurants. At one end of the beach a sculptured mermaid squeezes water from her hair (similar to the image of Mae Thorani, the Hindu-Buddhist earth goddess). The local people regard the mermaid statue as a shrine, tying the waist with coloured cloth and rubbing the breasts for good luck.

Wander through the breezy halls of polished teak at the **National Museum** (☎ 0 7431 1728; cnr Th Rong Meuang & Th Saiburi; admission 30B; 9am-4pm Wed-Sun), housed in a 100-year-old Sino-Portuguese palace. Other rambles in town include a climb up **Khao Tang Kuan**, or a stroll through **Wat Matchimawat** (Th Phattalung), southwest of the town centre, which has frescoes, an old marble Buddha image and a small museum.

Sleeping

Amsterdam Guest House (☎ 0 7431 4890; 15/3 Th Rong Meuang; r 150-200B) This homey, quirky Dutch-run place is popular and clean, with plenty of cushions, wandering pet dogs and cats, and a caged macaque that is said to bite the unwary. All rooms share bathrooms.

Guest House Romantic (☎ 0 7430 7170; 10/1-3 Th Platha; r 250-390B;) Substantial, airy abodes here smell fresh and come with TVs. Even the air-con rooms are cheap, and the bamboo wood beds are impressive for this price range. Overall a good budget choice if you're willing to pay more than 200B.

Green World Palace Hotel (☎ 0 7443 7900-8; 99 Th Samakisukson; r 750-900B;) Green World Palace is not only the best value in town, it's also classy, boasting chandeliers, a spiralling staircase in the lobby and a 5th-floor swimming pool with views. Rooms are immaculate and filled with enough amenities to keep you comfortable and entertained. The hotel is immensely popular so book ahead. Look for it a few hundred metres south of town.

Rajamangala Pavilion Beach Resort (☎ 0 7448 7222; www.pavilionhotels.com; 1 Th Rajdamnoen Nok; r 1400B;) This miniresort is actually owned by the local university and looks over the road to Songkhla's eastern beach. The enormous lobby is filled with water features and Thai artefacts and the rooms are elementary but stylish. This place is often booked so you may want to call ahead.

Eating & Drinking

For cheap food, try the seafood places on Th Ratchadamnoen. Curried crab claws or fried squid are always a hit. At the tip of Songkhla's

SOUTHERN UNREST

Four of Thailand's southernmost and predominantly Muslim provinces (Songkhla, Yala, Pattani and Narathiwat) go through hot and cold periods that involve the Pattani United Liberation Organization (PULO), a small armed group that, since its formation in 1959, has been dedicated to making a separate Muslim state.

Between 2002 and early 2005 a series of arson attacks, bombings and assaults took place in Pattani, Yala and Narathiwat Provinces. Most attacks were on military posts or police posts; at that time, the PULO had an avowed policy not to target civilians or tourists.

Unfortunately the Thai government's heavy-handed military and police response to the 40-year-old Muslim nationalist movement (including the 2004 massacre of 108 machete-armed youths in a Pattani mosque and the suffocation deaths of 78 in brutal arrests in Narathiwat that same year) seems destined to provoke further trouble. And in 2006–07, trouble exploded into pure terror throughout Yala, Pattani and Narathiwat. (Songkhla has lately avoided the worst violence.)

At the time of research, the former policy of not injuring innocent civilians seemed to have been abandoned, and although PULO has assumed a small degree of responsibility for the violence, and was even rumoured to have had secret talks with the Thai government, no-one is entirely sure which terrorist groups the various insurgents represent.

In January 2007, a group known as the Pattani Fighters beheaded a Buddhist man in Yala; near him was a note declaring 'we will kill all Thai Buddhists'. Since 2004, more than 2000 deaths have occurred in the south, including Muslim and Buddhist schoolchildren and Buddhist monks.

We urge travellers to exercise extreme caution when travelling in Yala, Pattani and Narathiwat. Avoid military or police installations and avoid road travel at night.

As for crossing the Thai–Malaysian border at Sungai Kolok via train, we advise careful monitoring of the situation. Trains are still running and foreign travellers are still making the crossing, but this train station has been bombed in the past and is still considered a target.

GETTING TO MALAYSIA

On the east coast, Sungai Kolok–Rantau Panjang is the handiest border crossing for trips onward to Kota Bharu. The border is open from 5am to 5pm, but on slow days officials may close the border as early as 4.30pm.

The border is about 1km from the centre of Sungai Kolok or the train station. Transport to the border is by motorcycle taxi – the going rate is 20B. The Harmony Bridge connects Sungai Kolok with the Malaysian town of Rantau Panjang. The Malaysian immigration checkpoint is just across the bridge and can be easily reached by walking. Once in Malaysia you can either catch a bus or taxi to Kota Bharu or Pasir Mas, from where you can catch trains to Kuala Lumpur or Singapore.

However, as is the case in all of southern Thailand's Muslim regions, tourism in Sungai Kolok has drastically fallen off over the past few years. In 2005, several bombs exploded here, and Muslim separatists are assumed to be responsible. We suggest exercising extreme caution when travelling through this region, and until the fighting clears up we don't recommend train travel at all.

For information on crossing this border in the opposite direction, see p470.

northern finger are food carts that set out mats in the waterfront park. There's also a seriously good roti vendor on Th Sisuda in the evenings. For relief from the heat, see if you can squeeze in between the tables of teenagers at one of the air-con fast-food restaurants on the corner of Th Sisuda and Th Platha.

Khao Noi Phochana (Th Wichianchom; dishes 30-50B) has a good lunchtime smorgasbord of Thai and Chinese rice dishes on display. No roman-script sign.

A string of bars just east of the Indonesian consulate is jokingly referred to among local expats as 'The Dark Side'. Not as ominous as it sounds, this strip caters mainly to oil company employees and other Westerners living in Songkhla. Near the Pavilion Songkhla Hotel, on Th Platha, are a few other casual bars worth checking out. As the sun begins to set, **Corner Bier** (Th Sisuda) and **Timber Hut** (Th Sisuda) swell with the town's expat Canadian community.

Getting There & Away

The **bus station** (Th Tao It) is 2km from the town centre. For more options or to travel by train, you must connect to Hat Yai. Destinations include Bangkok (air-con 600B, 14 hours, three departures daily), with stops in Nakhon Si Thammarat and Surat Thani.

Hat Yai minibuses (20B, every 30 minutes from 10am to 10pm) can be picked up in town from in front of Wat Jaeng, on Th Ramwithi, or at the bus station.

SUNGAI KOLOK

pop 39,000

Thailand's Wild West border town is a dusty spot that's more than a little rough around the edges. As the main eastern coastal gateway between Malaysia and Thailand, Sungai Kolok oozes seediness, and the main industries around here revolve around catering to a weekend crowd of Malaysian men looking for sex.

The town's **TAT office** (☎ 0 7361 2126; 18 Th Asia; 8.30am-4.30pm), tourist police and immigration are all at the border. There's another **Thai immigration office** (9am-4pm Mon-Fri) in town, near the Merlin Hotel.

The town centre is just a 15B sǎamláw ride from the border or a five-minute walk south of the train station.

When you cross the border from Rantau Panjang in Malaysia, the train station is about 50m straight ahead on the right-hand side, or 20B by motorcycle taxi.

The bus station is another 1km beyond the train station. From here, Bangkok buses (VIP 1090B, air-con 546B to 702B, 17 to 18 hours, three daily) go through Surat Thani (air-con 280B, nine to 10 hours).

Minivans to Hat Yai (150B, three to four hours, hourly from 6am to 5pm) leave from near the train station.

Trains from Sungai Kolok to Bangkok include the 11.55am rapid and 2.05pm special express trains (260B to 1493B). Trains to Hat Yai (82B to 126B, four hours) have two morning departures.

ANDAMAN COAST

Spend enough time hopping from island to island in the tropical dream world of Thailand's south, and you may run the risk of suffering from a nasty case of a classic backpacker's malaise. In some equatorial regions of the world, it's known as beach burnout. The symptoms? Every last piece of paradise begins to look the same. Postcard-perfect sunsets that once caused your jaw to drop are no longer provoking a reaction. But not to worry. In the Land of Smiles, there happens to be a fail-safe cure. Its name? The Andaman Sea coast.

Many come only for Phuket, the country's largest and most visited island, where both amusements and package tourists abound. Yet it's on the beaches and in the forests of the otherworldly Krabi and Phang-Nga Provinces, with their massive limestone cliffs and luscious greenery, that the Andaman truly begins to shine.

But the discoveries don't end there. This is also the place where the majestic Ko Phi Phi exists, where a nomadic sea-gypsy community travels, and where you, intrepid traveller, will likely regain a newfound appreciation of the unique art of world travel.

RANONG

pop 24,500

This small and friendly provincial capital has a bustling fishing port and is separated from Myanmar only by Pak Chan, the estuary of Mae Nam Chan (Chan River). Burmese residents from nearby Kawthoung (Ko Song; also known as Victoria Point) easily hop across the border. The city is also a gateway to Kawthoung and Thahtay Island, and many expats (and a growing number of switched-on travellers) pass through on quick trips across the border to renew their visas.

Information

Most of Ranong's banks are on Th Tha Meuang (the road to the fishing pier), near the intersection with Th Ruangrat. Many have ATMs. The main post office is on Th Chonrau near the intersection of Th Dap Khadi. The CAT telephone office is south on Th Phoem Phon.

Chonakukson Bookstore (Th Ruangrat) Sells English-language books and Phuket Air tickets to Bangkok.

Sights & Activities

Although there is nothing of great cultural interest in town, Ranong's **hot springs** (Wat Tapotaram; admission free), just outside town, attract Thai and foreign visitors alike.

Because of its close proximity to southern Myanmar, Ranong is a base for **dive trips** to the Burma Banks, within the Mergui (Myeik) Archipelago, as well as the world-class Surin and Similan Islands. Because of the distances involved, dive trips are mostly live-aboard and not cheap. Expect to pay more than US$200 for a two-day/two-night deal.

A couple of dive shops in Ranong can get you started. Try **Aladdin Dive Cruise** (☎ 0 7781 2967; www.aladdindivecruise.de) or **A-One-Diving** (☎ 0 7783 2984; www.a-one-diving.com; 77 Saphan Pla).

Sleeping & Eating

Kiwi House (☎ 0 7783 2812; www.kiwiorchid.com; d 250B; 💻) Conveniently located near the bus

GETTING TO MYANMAR

It is now legal to travel from Ranong, Thailand, to Kawthoung, Myanmar, and from there into the interior of Myanmar – eg Dawei or Yangon – by plane and boat. Road travel north of Kawthoung, however, is forbidden. When the Thai–Myanmar border is open, boats to Kawthoung leave the Saphan Pla (Pla Bridge) pier, about 4.5km from the centre of Ranong. Departures are frequent from around 8.30am until 6pm, and cost 60B to 100B per person. To reach the pier, take săwngthăew 2 from Ranong (7B) and get off at the **immigration office** (☎ 0 7782 2016; Th Ruangrat; ⏲ 8.30am-6pm), 700m north of the pier, to get your passport stamped.

Upon arrival at the Kawthoung jetty, there's a stop at Myanmar immigration. At this point you must inform the authorities if you're a day visitor – in which case you must pay a fee of US$5 for a day permit, which actually allows a two-night stay. Travel agents in Ranong should be able to arrange 28-day Myanmar visas. Bear in mind when you are returning to Thailand that Myanmar time is half an hour behind Thailand's. Though Thai immigration seems to have changed its hours in order to avoid return hassles, you should double-check when leaving the country.

For an effortless visa run, **Kiwi House** (☎ 0 7783 2812; www.kiwiorchid.com) in Ranong organises a 2½ hour door-to-door service (300B plus your day permit) with departures at 9am, 11am, 1.30pm and 3.30pm daily.

See p546 for making this crossing in the opposite direction.

station is this bright yellow travellers' pad run by a Thai-New Zealand couple. You'll find clean rooms and bed-bug-free beds, although bathrooms are shared. The restaurant serves dishes from 45B to 70B. Pick up a free map of the town here. Information and bookings for trips around Ranong are also available.

Also recommended:

Banggan Bar (☎ 0 9727 4334; Th Ruangrat; d 90B) Near the 7-Eleven, this kooky place does cheap drinks, trippy wallpaper and old TVs as tables. Rooms have mattresses on lino flooring and bathrooms are shared.

Asia Hotel (☎ 0 7781 1113; 39/9 Th Ruangrat; d from 200B; ❄) An institutional place near the market.

For inexpensive Thai and Burmese breakfasts, try the **morning market** (Th Ruangrat) or nearby traditional Hokkien coffee shops with marble-topped tables.

Getting There & Away

There are daily flights between Ranong and Bangkok with **Phuket Air** (code 9R; ☎ 0 7782 4590; www.phuketairlines.com).

The Ranong bus station is on Hwy 4 towards the south end of town, near Kiwi House, although some buses stop in town before going on to the bus station. You can reach Ranong from Bangkok (VIP 520B, air-con 260B to 330B, 10 hours, 8.30am and 8pm), Chumphon (air-con/ordinary 70/50B, three to five hours, hourly departures) and Phuket (ordinary 130B, five to six hours). From town, blue sǎwngthǎew 2 passes the bus station.

SURIN ISLANDS MARINE NATIONAL PARK (MU KO SURIN NATIONAL PARK)

The five gorgeous islands that make up **Surin Islands Marine National Park** (www.dnp.go.th; admission 400B; ⏲ mid-Nov–mid-May) are situated 60km offshore, just 5km from the Thailand–Myanmar marine border. Healthy rainforest, pockets of white-sand beach in sheltered bays and rocky headlands that jut out into the ocean characterise these granite-outcrop islands. The clearest of water makes for great diving, with underwater visibility often up to 20m. The islands' sheltered waters also attract *chao náam* – sea gypsies – who live in a village onshore during the May to November monsoon season. Here they are known as Moken, from the local word *oken* meaning 'salt water'.

Ko Surin Nuea (north) and Ko Surin Tai (south) are the two largest islands. Park headquarters and all visitor facilities are at Ao Chong Khad on Ko Surin Nuea, near the jetty.

Khuraburi is the jumping-off point for the park. The pier is about 9km north of town, as is the mainland **national park office** (☎ 0 7649 1378; ⏲ 8am-5pm) with good information, maps and helpful staff.

Sights & Activities

DIVING & SNORKELLING

Dive sites in the park include **Ko Surin Tai**, and **HQ Channel** between the two main islands. In the vicinity is **Richelieu Rock** (a seamount 14km southeast) where whale sharks are often spotted during March and April. Sixty kilometres northwest of the Surins – but often combined with dive trips to the park – are the famed **Burma Banks**, a system of submerged seamounts. The three major banks, **Silvertip**, **Roe** and **Rainbow**, provide five-star diving experiences, with coral gardens laid over flat plateaus, and large oceanic and smaller reef marine species. There's presently no dive facility in the park itself, so dive trips (four-day live-aboards around 20,000B) must be booked from the mainland; see opposite for more information.

Snorkelling is excellent due to relatively shallow reef depths of 5m to 6m, and most coral survived the tsunami intact. Two two-hour snorkelling trips by boat (per person 70B, gear per day 150B) leave island headquarters daily.

WILDLIFE & WALKS

Around the park headquarters you can explore the forest fringes, looking out for the crab-eating macaques (cheeky monkeys!) and some of the 57 resident bird species, which include the fabulous Nicobar pigeon, endemic to the islands of the Andaman Sea. Along the coast you're likely to see the chestnut Brahminy kite soaring, and reef herons on the rocks. Twelve species of bat live here, most noticeably tree-dwelling fruit bats, also known as flying foxes.

A rough-and-ready **walking trail** – not for the unsteady – winds 2km along the coast and through forest to the beach at **Ao Mai Ngam**, where there's good snorkelling. At low tide it's easy to walk between the bays near the headquarters.

OTHER ACTIVITIES

On Ko Surin Tai, the **Moken village** at Ao Bon welcomes visitors; take a longtail boat from park headquarters (80B). Post-tsunami, Moken have settled in this one sheltered bay where a major ancestral worship ceremony (Loi Reua) takes place in April. Painted *law bong* – protective **totem poles** – stand at the park entrance.

Sleeping & Eating

Accommodation is simple and fine, but – because of the island's short, narrow beaches – it's *very* close together and can feel seriously crowded when full (around 300 people). For park accommodation, book online at www.dnp.go.th or with the mainland national park office in Khuraburi.

Bungalows (incl fan, bathroom & balcony 2000B) and **on-site tents** (1-/2-person tents 300/450B) are available at Ao Chong Khad; tents should also now be available at Ao Mai Ngam. You can pitch your own **tent** (per night 80B). There's generator power until about 10pm.

A park **restaurant** (dishes from 60B) serves Thai food.

If you need to stay overnight in Khuraburi, try the new **Country Hut Riverside** (☎ 08 6272 0588; r 300-500B; ❄) or long-standing **Tararin Resort** (☎ 0 7649 1789; r 300-500B; ❄). On either side of the bridge at the north end of town, each has clean, basic, tiny fan/air-con rooms. A more luxurious option, **Kuraburi Greenview Resort** (☎ 0 7640 1400; www.kuraburigreenview.co.th; d from 1900B; ❄ 💻 🏊) is 15km south of town, set among forest and river, with curious but comfortable wood and slate-and-cobblestone bungalows.

Getting There & Away

A 'big boat' (return 1200B, 2½ hours one way) leaves the Khuraburi pier at 9am daily, returning at 1pm. Tour operators use speedboats (return 1600B, one hour one way) and will transfer independent travellers on their daily runs.

Several tour operators, all located near the pier, run day/overnight tours (around 2600/3500B) to the park; agencies in Khao Lak and Phuket can make bookings for these and for dive trips. In Khuraburi town, try the affable **Tom & Am Tour** (☎ 08 6272 0588; www.surinislandtour.com) for on-spec bookings. Tour operators include transfers from Khao Lak in their prices.

Buses run three times daily between Phuket and Khuraburi (160B, 3½ hours) and between Khuraburi and Ranong (60B, 1½ hours).

KHAO SOK NATIONAL PARK

When your head starts to sizzle from endless sunbathing, head to the refreshing jungles of Khao Sok National Park. Conveniently wedged between Surat Thani to the east and Phang-Nga to the west, it's littered with clear streams and swimming holes sitting by limestone cliffs. Adding to its credentials, the Khao Sok rainforest is a remnant of a 160-million-year-old forest ecosystem that is believed to be much older and richer than the forests of the Amazon and central Africa – at least according to Thom Henley, author of *Waterfalls and Gibbon Calls*.

The best time of year to visit Khao Sok is in the dry season (December to May), when there are fewer blood-sucking leeches. In January and February, a wild lotus *(Rafflesia kerri meyer)*, the largest flower in the world, bursts into bloom emitting a rotten-meat stench that attracts pollinating insects.

The **park headquarters and visitors centre** (☎ 0 7739 5139; www.dnp.go.th; admission per day 200B) are 1.8km off Rte 401, near the 109km marker.

Sleeping & Eating

Near the visitors centre you can pitch your own **tent** (camp site for 2 people 60B, tent & bedding hire 225-405B) or rent **bungalows** (1-4 people 800B, 5-8 people 1000B). At picturesque Chiaw Lan Lake, park-managed substations have **floating raft houses** (☎ 0 7739 5139; 2/4/6 people 400/800/1200B).

Off the main road are several private guesthouses that can organise day and overnight trips in the area.

Morning Mist Resort (☎ 0 9971 8794; www.morningmistresort.com; d 350-700B) Family-run Morning Mist has clean river bungalows and cheaper mountainside ones too. A restaurant filled with hanging lanterns and romantic fairy lights serves terrific food for breakfast, lunch and dinner (dishes 45B to 60B); try the *matsaman* curry or slurp down a sapodilla shake. The cocktails look wickedly good.

Art's River Lodge (☎ 0 7276 3933; d 450-1200B) A peaceful place with a tasteful selection of old- and new-style bungalows. A traditional Thai building perched by the river houses the idyllic restaurant (dishes 55B to 95B); come here around 5pm to feed the monkeys.

Our Jungle House (☎ 0 9909 6814; ourjunglehouse 2005@yahoo.de; d 600-800B) Catering for small groups and independent travellers, this place has some super tree-house bungalows by the river and serves good food priced from 50B to 120B, making it deservedly popular.

Also recommended:

Freedom Resort (☎ 0 7739 5157; freedomresort@yahoo.com; 200 Moo 6; tent hire 50B, d 200B;) Australian-run with barbecues and a relaxed vibe. For 500B you get air-con. Dishes in the restaurant range from 45B to 70B.

Khao Sok Rainforest Resort (☎ 0 7739 5136; d 400-600B) A tranquil spot with tiled bungalows reminiscent of the cartoon show, *The Flintstones*. You'll pay 45B to 85B for a feed in the restaurant.

Getting There & Away

To get to the national park, take a Takua Pa–Surat Thani bus; tell the driver 'Khao Sok'. Khao Sok (50B, one hour, nine daily) is 40km from Takua Pa (on the west coast) and almost 100km from Surat Thani (on the east coast).

SIMILAN ISLANDS MARINE NATIONAL PARK (MU KO SIMILAN NATIONAL PARK)

Renowned by divers the world over, the beautiful **Similan Islands Marine National Park** (www.dnp.go.th; admission 400B; Nov-May) is located 70km offshore. Its smooth granite islands are as impressive above water as below, topped with rainforest, edged with white-sand beaches and fringed with coral reef.

Two of the nine islands, Ko Miang (Island Four) and Ko Similan (Island Eight), have ranger stations and accommodation; park headquarters and most visitor activity centres on Ko Miang. 'Similan' comes from the Malay word *sembilan*, meaning 'nine', and while each island is named they're just as commonly known by their numbers.

Khao Lak is the jumping-off point for the park. The pier is at Thap Lamu,10km south of town, where you'll find a cluster of tour operators. The **mainland park office** (☎ 0 7659 5045; 8am-4pm) is about 500m before the pier, but there's no information in English available.

Sights & Activities

DIVING & SNORKELLING

The Similans offer exceptional diving for all levels of experience, at depths from 2m to 30m. There are seamounts (at **Fantasy Rocks**), rock reefs (at **Ko Payu**) and dive-throughs (at **Hin Pousar** or 'Elephant-head'), with marine life ranging from tiny plume worms and soft corals to schooling fish and whale sharks. There are dive sites at each of the six islands north of Ko Miang; the southern part of the park is off limits to divers. No facilities for divers exist in the national park itself, so you'll need to take a dive tour. Agencies in Khao Lak and Phuket book dive trips (see opposite).

Snorkelling is good at several points around **Ko Miang**, especially in the main channel; you can hire snorkel gear from the park (per day 100B). Day-tour operators usually visit three or four different snorkelling sites. **Poseidon Bungalows** (☎ 0 7644 3258; www.similantour.com) at Khao Lak offers snorkelling-only trips (three-day live-aboard trips around 6500B).

WILDLIFE & WALKS

The forest around the park headquarters on Ko Miang has a couple of walking trails and some great wildlife. The fabulous Nicobar pigeon, with its wild mane of grey-green feathers, is common here; it's one of some 39 bird species in the park. Hairy-legged land crabs and flying foxes (or fruit bats) are relatively easily seen in the forest, as are flying squirrels.

Small Beach Track, with information panels, leads 400m to a tiny, pretty snorkelling bay. Detouring from it, the **Viewpoint Trail** – 500m or so of steep scrambling – has panoramic vistas from the top. A 500m walk to **Sunset Point** takes you through forest to a smooth granite platform facing – obviously – west.

On Ko Similan there's a 2.5km forest hike to a **viewpoint**, and a shorter, steep scramble off the main beach to the top of **Sail Rock**.

Sleeping & Eating

Accommodation in the national park is available for all budgets. Book online at www.dnp.go.th or with the mainland park office at Khao Lak.

On Ko Miang there are sea-view **bungalows** (r 2000B;) with balconies; two dark five-room wood-and-bamboo **longhouses** (r 1000B) with fans; and crowded on-site **tents** (2-person 570B). There's electricity from 6pm to 6am.

On-site tents are also available on Ko Similan. You can pitch your own **tent** (per night 80B) on either island.

A **restaurant** (dishes 100B) near the park headquarters serves simple Thai food.

Getting There & Away

There's no public transport to the park, but independent travellers can book a speedboat transfer (return 1700B, 1½ hours one way) with a day-tour operator. They will collect you from Phuket or Khao Lak, but if you book through the national park (which uses the same tour operators' boats anyway) be aware that you'll have to find your own way to the park office, and then wait for a transfer to the pier.

Agencies in Khao Lak and Phuket book day/overnight tours (from around 2500/3500B) and dive trips (three-day liveaboards from around 11,000B).

Public buses run regularly between Phuket and Khao Lak (60B, 1½ hours), and Khao Lak and Ranong (100B, three hours).

PHANG-NGA

pop 9700

Fringed by limestone cliffs and the luscious Andaman Sea, you'll go gaga over little Phang-Nga, a scenic day trip or overnighter from Phuket. The biggest attraction is a longtail boat tour through **Ao Phang-Nga**, a widely promoted bay of mangrove forests, 120 mountainous islands and caves virtually melting with waxlike stalactites.

Tours usually include a stop at a **Muslim fishing village** and **James Bond Island** (the island rock in *The Man with the Golden Gun*) within Ao Phang-Nga National Marine Park. The tours cost around 950B for two to three hours and can be arranged through tour agencies at the Phang-Nga bus station.

Sleeping & Eating

Thawisuk Hotel (☎ 0 7641 2100; 77-79 Th Phetkasem; r 150-200B) A rambling, pastel-blue building in the middle of town, this place is friendly and offers bright simple rooms. There's a rooftop with good views.

Phang-Nga Guest House (☎ 0 7641 1358; Th Phetkasem; r 220-1000B; ❄) The best-value budget digs in town, with 12 clean, neat and pleasant rooms that come in a variety of sizes and prices. Sayan Tours takes its clients here.

Phang-Nga Inn (☎ 0 7641 1963; phang-ngainn@png.co.th; 2/2 Soi Lohakit; r 500-1400B; ❄) The most pleasant hotel in town. A converted family mansion, it has 12 homey quiet rooms. All are comfortably modern and well furnished; there's an eating area in the front. It's on a side street off the main road near the centre of town.

Several food stalls on the main street sell delicious *khànŏm jiin* with chicken curry, *náam yaa* (spicy ground-fish curry) or *náam phrík* (sweet and spicy peanut sauce).

Phang-Nga Satay (184 Th Phetkasem; dishes 20-60B) A tiny shack that specialises in Malay-style satay – try the shrimp version.

Cha-Leang (☎ 0 7641 3831; dishes 40-90B) This is one of the best and most popular restaurants in town, cooking up well-priced seafood dishes – try the 'clams with basil leaf and chilli' or the 'edible inflorescence of banana plant salad'. There's a simple but pleasant back patio.

Getting There & Away

Frequent Phuket-bound buses (36B to 65B) run until 8pm and take 1½ to 2½ hours depending on who's at the wheel. Buses depart from the **bus station** (Th Phetkasem) in Phang-Nga.

PHUKET

pop 82,800

Phuket (poo-get) reigns supreme as southern Thailand's undisputed tourism king – it's Thailand's rock and roll and it's either your gig or not. And Phuket's popularity isn't just hype. The beaches are wide and luxurious with squeaky-clean sand and jade-coloured water. This large teardrop island is largely the domain of package tourists fortressed in minicity resorts that claim huge portions of waterfront property, but backpackers can still enjoy Phuket's vocabulary of seafood, swimming and shopping.

Here is an unorthodox suggestion: don't stay at the beach. Most beach communities are cluttered with lame strip malls and overpriced accommodation. Instead, consider staying in underrated Phuket town, a stylish city of Sino-Portuguese architecture and culinary diversity from the its bygone days as a stop on the India–China trade route. From Phuket town, public transport radiates out to a buffet of silky sand beaches.

Also note that Phuket's beaches are subject to strong seasonal undercurrents. During the monsoon season from May to the end of October, drowning is the leading cause of death for tourists visiting Phuket. Some, but not all, beaches have warning flags (red flag – dangerous for swimming; yellow flag – rough, swim with caution; green flag – stable).

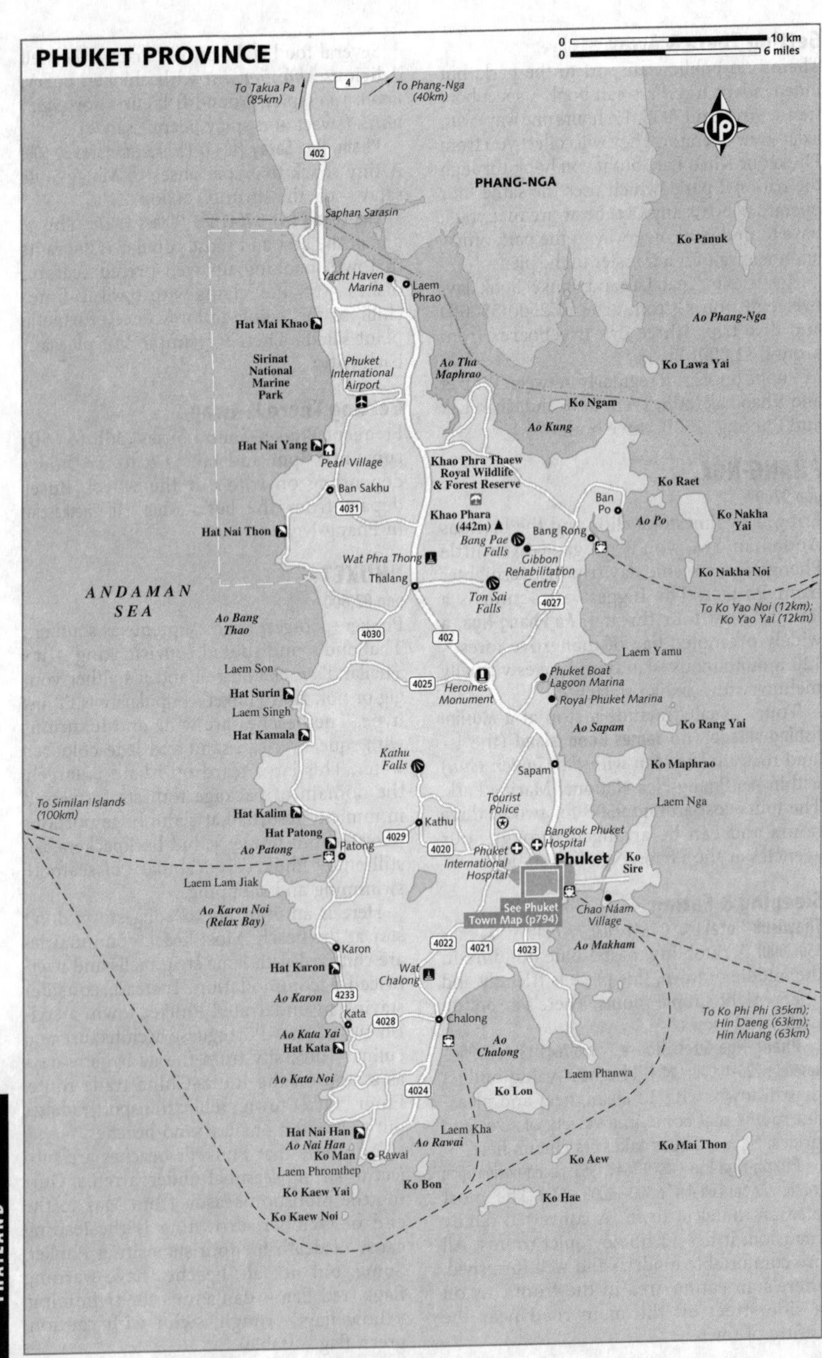
PHUKET PROVINCE
0 10 km
0 6 miles
To Takua Pa (85km)
4
To Phang-Nga (40km)
402
PHANG-NGA
Saphan Sarasin
Ko Panuk
Yacht Haven Marina
Laem Phrao
Ao Phang-Nga
Hat Mai Khao
Sirinat National Marine Park
Phuket International Airport
Ao Tha Maphrao
Ko Lawa Yai
Ko Ngam
Ao Kung
Hat Nai Yang
Pearl Village
Khao Phra Thaew Royal Wildlife & Forest Reserve
Ko Raet
Ban Sakhu
Ban Po
Ao Po
Ko Nakha Yai
4031
Khao Phara (442m)
Hat Nai Thon
Bang Pae Falls
Bang Rong
Gibbon Rehabilitation Centre
Wat Phra Thong
Ko Nakha Noi
Thalang
Ton Sai Falls
ANDAMAN SEA
4027
To Ko Yao Noi (12km); Ko Yao Yai (12km)
Ao Bang Thao
4030
402
Laem Yamu
Laem Son
Phuket Boat Lagoon Marina
4025
Heroines Monument
Hat Surin
Royal Phuket Marina
Laem Singh
Ao Sapam
Ko Rang Yai
Hat Kamala
Kathu Falls
Sapam
Ko Maphrao
Tourist Police
Laem Nga
To Similan Islands (100km)
Hat Kalim
Kathu
Bangkok Phuket Hospital
Hat Patong
4029
Ao Patong
Patong
4020
Phuket International Hospital
Phuket
Ko Sire
Laem Lam Jiak
See Phuket Town Map (p794)
Chao Nâam Village
Ao Karon Noi (Relax Bay)
4022
4021
4023
Ao Makham
Karon
Hat Karon
Wat Chalong
Ao Karon
4233
Kata
4028
Chalong
To Ko Phi Phi (35km); Hin Daeng (63km); Hin Muang (63km)
Ao Kata Yai
Hat Kata
Ao Chalong
Laem Phanwa
Ao Kata Noi
4024
Ko Lon
Hat Nai Han
Laem Kha
Ao Nai Han
Ao Rawai
Ko Mai Thon
Ko Man
Rawai
Ko Aew
Laem Phromthep
Ko Bon
Ko Kaew Yai
Ko Hae
Ko Kaew Noi
THAILAND

THE PRICE OF PARADISE

Southern Thailand is at a crossroads. In 2006, Thailand received around 13 million visitors, with the majority visiting the south – and this immensely popular area is paying the price for unsustainable levels of development.

Thailand's islands and beaches face myriad environmental woes: uncontrolled developments and laissez-faire building controls; declining forests; irresponsible boating and scuba diving; water pollution; waste dumping by hotels and restaurants; and fresh water shortages.

The current cash-cow mentality ('a company is a country, a country is a company', according to former Thai prime minister, Thaksin Shinawatra) isn't helping. And while Ko Samui has been a pilot for 'green tourism' projects, it is becoming a case of too little, too late.

So, when travelling in southern Thailand, think about how you're impacting on the environment. Try to deposit nonbiodegrable rubbish on the mainland rather than on the islands: on Ko Samui alone, visitors and inhabitants produce more than 50 tonnes of rubbish a day, much of it plastic. Shorten showers. Request glass water bottles and minimise consumption of plastic bottles. If you don't need a bag for a purchase at a shop, say so. Support genuine ecotourism outfits and suss out the credentials of dive operators.

Information

Bank of Asia (Map p794; Th Phuket) ATM and currency exchange from 8.30am to 6pm. There are several other banks near On On Hotel.

Juice Internet Cafe (Map p794; 49 Th Phuket; per hr 50B; 8am-midnight) Supposedly the fastest connections on the island. A café serves snacks and sandwiches.

Phuket International Hospital (Map p792; ☎ 0 7624 9400, emergency 0 7621 0935; Th Charlerm Pra Kiat)

Post office (Map p794; ☎ 0 7621 1020; Th Montri; 8.30am-4.30pm Mon-Fri, 9am-noon Sat, Sun & public holidays)

South Wind Books (Map p794; ☎ 0 7625 8302; 9 Th Phang-Nga; 9am-7pm Mon-Sat) Second-hand reads in seven languages; cheap used magazines too.

TAT office (Map p794; ☎ 0 7621 2213; 73-75 Th Phuket; 8.30am-4.30pm) Distributes a handy guide to local transport fares.

Sights & Activities

BEACHES

Set along the jagged western coast of this 810-sq-km island are the beach communities of **Patong**, **Karon** and **Kata**. All were affected to some extent by the tsunami, but remain majestic sweeps of sand. Their interior villages are a dizzying dose of neon and concrete, good for night-time prowling, but a drag in the noon-time sun. Manicured **Hat Nai Han**, at the southern tip of the island, is strictly beach without the diversions of T-shirt shops and pub grub. Rounding the tip towards the east, **Hat Rawai** is a good place to charter boats to nearby islands. Absurdly beautiful **Laem Singh**, north of Patong on the west coast, may be that elusive piece of paradise. On the northwestern coast, **Hat Mai Khao** is part of the Sirinat National Marine Park and the nesting grounds for sea turtles from late October to February.

DIVING & SNORKELLING

Although there are many, many places to dive around Thailand, Phuket is to-dive-for; it's indisputably the primary centre for the Thai scuba-diving industry and one of the world's top 10 dive destinations. The island is ringed by good to excellent dive sites, including several small islands to the south. Live-aboard excursions (you'll never be content with a dive day trip again) to the fantastic Surin and Similan Islands, or to the Burma Banks, in the Mergui (Myeik) Archipelago off the southern coast of Myanmar, are also possible from Phuket (though these destinations are far away). Snorkelling is best along Phuket's west coast, particularly at the rocky headlands between beaches. As with scuba diving, you'll find better snorkelling, with greater visibility and variety of marine life, along the shores of small outlying islands such as Ko Hae, Ko Yao Noi and Ko Yao Yai and Ko Raya.

Dive shops with supplies:

Dive Supply (☎ 0 7634 2513; www.divesupply.com; 189 Th Rat Uthit, Patong) Lots of diving equipment and good service in several languages.

Phuket Wetsuits (☎ 0 7638 1818; Th Chao Fa west, Ao Chalong) Offers both custom- and ready-made wet suits. This place is 2km north of Ao Chalong.

Festivals & Events

Phuket's most important festival is the **Vegetarian Festival** (www.phuketvegetarian.com), which is

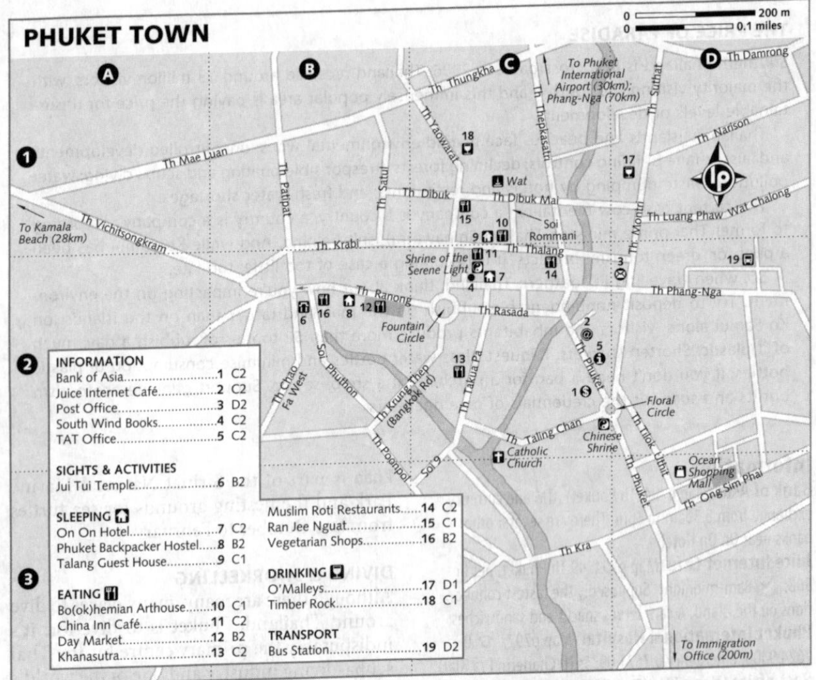

centred on five Chinese temples, including Jui Tui on Th Ranong in Phuket town, and Bang Niaw and Sui Boon Tong temples. The TAT office in Phuket prints a helpful schedule of events for the Vegetarian Festival each year.

Sleeping & Eating

PHUKET TOWN

Phuket Backpacker Hostel (Map p794; ☎ 0 7625 6680; www.phuketbackpacker.com; 167 Th Ranong; dm 200B, d from 350B; 💻) Quite possibly the newest building in all of Phuket town, this sparkling-clean boutique hostel has brand-new bunk beds, free internet, a great backyard garden and a large-screen TV.

On On Hotel (Map p794; ☎ 0 7621 1154; 19 Th Phang-Nga; s/d from 200/280B; ❄ 💻) Phuket's first hotel has a white yesteryear façade. In the common areas are signs of faded glamour, none of which is retained in the rooms that posed as the Khao San flophouse in the filming of *The Beach* (room 38, in fact).

Talang Guest House (Map p794; ☎ 0 7621 4225; 37 Th Thalang; s from 300B, d 350-450B, tr 450-500B, all incl breakfast; ❄) Architecture buffs will fall in love with this crumbling old place. Rooms have high ceilings and 1960s furniture, and a few rooms open out to breezy balconies; one balcony room overlooks the street below. A continental breakfast of coffee, toast and a token banana is included.

Phuket cuisine is a mix of Thai, Malay and Chinese with some exceptional twists on the country's standard dishes. The **day market** (Th Ranong), just off Fountain Circle, sells fresh fruit. At night the area is just as crammed with vendors selling grilled skewers of meat and seafood. When you pick out your order, hand it to the vendor so it can be heated up; point to the vats of sauce on the counter if you like spicy dipping sauces.

Ran Jee Nguat (Map p794; Th Yaowarat; dishes 20B; 🕑 breakfast & lunch) Four doors down from the corner of Th Dibuk, this long-running institution serves up Phuket's most famous dish: *khànǒm jiin náam yaa phuukèt* (Chinese noodles in a puréed fish and curry sauce). It might be helpful to come armed with your Thai phrasebook and to know that there is no roman-script sign out the front.

Khanasutra (Map p794; ☎ 0 1894 0794; 18-20 Th Takua Pa; dishes 60-120B; 🕑 lunch & dinner Mon-Sat, dinner Sun)

Enjoy some of the best Indian tucker this side of Delhi. You almost expect Bollywood dancers to shimmy out from the 'tent' area. Spicy? You bet!

China Inn Café (Map p794; ☎ 0 7635 6239; 20 Th Thalang; mains 150-280B; ⏰ breakfast, lunch & dinner Tue-Sun) This stylish café, fashioned from the pages of an interiors magazine, rolls out delicious Thai, Chinese and Western food in a cute courtyard. The café is located in a building that was renovated by a local artist (it's practically an antique gallery) – it was even designed to feng shui principles.

Bo(ok)hemian Arthouse (Map p794; ☎ 0 9652 4223; 61 Th Thalang; ⏰ lunch & dinner) Coffee, tea, beer, independent films and cool Thai magazines you wish you could read. Indie films can be screened in the little cinema upstairs; prices are 80B if you're alone, 120B for two people, or 150B for three or more.

A few vegetarian shops (Map p794) line Th Ranong east of the garish Jui Tui Chinese temple. **Muslim roti restaurants** (Map p794; Th Thalang) huddle near Th Thepkasatri.

HAT PATONG

Going cheap in popular Patong is like slumming in Beverly Hills – you're sure to have hotel envy.

Crown Hostel (☎ 0 7634 2297; 169/3-4 Th Rat Uthit; dm 200B, r from 500B; ❄ 💻) Friendly and central, this place attracts a hard-partying backpacker crowd. There are air-conditioned single-sex dormitories, plus a communal fridge. Rooms resemble Khao San shoe boxes.

Touch Villa (☎ 0 7634 4011; touchvilla@hotmail.com; 151/4 Th Rat Uthit; d from 350B; ❄) Two small strips of pastel pink concrete rooms separated by a pretty garden.

C&N Hotel (☎ 0 7634 1892; www.cnhotelpatong.com; 151 Th Rat Uthit; r 800-1500B; ❄ 💻) This place is fresh and sparkling clean, with a decidedly modern edge. Some rooms come with balconies, and all come with TVs.

Got a hankering for some seafood but are intimidated by the restaurants packed with platinum-card users? Head on down to Soi Eric, a claustrophobic alley just off Th Bang-La. With barely space to loiter, the cheap **seafood stalls** (dishes 80-100B) feed a rotating crowd of expectant diners, who are rarely disappointed.

HAT KARON & HAT KATA

South of Hat Patong is a string of three beaches: the long golden sweep of Hat Karon; the smaller but equally beautiful Hat Kata Yai (Big Kata); and Kata Noi (Little Kata), where you'll find good snorkelling. If you're beach-bound, Karon and classy Kata are better bets than saturated Patong.

Bazoom Hostel (☎ 0 7639 6913; www.bazoomhostel.com; Karon Plaza, 269/2-3 Th Patak East, Hat Karon; dm 80-120B, d from 240B; ❄ 💻) Colourful and happening, with mixed dorms and double rooms with share bathrooms (but you're literally *in* the dorm). Better rooms have funky window seats, cool bed heads and air-con. Dishes in the Bazoom restaurant (open for breakfast, lunch and dinner) will set you back 50B to 120B.

Kata on Sea (☎ 0 7633 0594; 96/6 Th Thai Na, Hat Kata Yai; d from 250B; ❄) This collection of simple bungalows (with fans) provides great views of Phuket's voluptuous hills. Getting to the beach is a bit of a trek, but Th Thai Na is filled with affordable backpacker traps to make the walk entertaining.

Lucky Guest House (☎ 0 7633 0572; 110/44-45 Th Thai Na, Hat Kata Yai; d from 300B; ❄) On the southern side of Th Thai Na, Lucky is well run and spotlessly clean. Bungalows are also available.

Ann Guesthouse (☎ 0 7639 8288; berniesbistrobar@hotmail.com; Hat Karon; d from 450B; ❄) At the northern end of Karon, about 500m from the roundabout, this Australian-owned guesthouse has clean rooms in concrete blocks plopped down in a fairly deserted strip between several major resort complexes. The restaurant serves dishes from 50B to 275B.

HAT MAI KHAO

Phuket Campground (☎ 0 1370 1579; www.phuketcampground.com; Ao Mai Khao; tent 150-300B, d 600B) This

PHUKET GIBBON REHABILITATION CENTRE

Near Nam Tok Bang Pae (Bang Pae Falls) is the **Phuket Gibbon Rehabilitation Centre** (Map p792; ☎ 0 7626 0492; www.warthai.org; admission by donation; ⏰ 8am-6pm). What's a gibbon you ask? A too-cute monkey with a white-rimmed face that looks like it's covered with shag-carpet. Financed by donations and run by volunteers, the centre cares for gibbons that have been kept in captivity and reintroduces them into the wild. Visitors who wish to help may 'adopt' a gibbon for 1800B, which will pay for one animal's care for a year.

privately operated camping ground rents large, 4-sq-metre tents near the beach, each with rice mats, pillows, blankets and a torch; it also has two-person cabins and a small restaurant. The camping ground is 2km south of the police kiosk in Ban Mai Khao.

Drinking

PHUKET TOWN

The major hotels have discos and/or karaoke clubs.

Timber Rock (Map p794; ☎ 0 7621 1839; Th Yaowarat) A Western-style rock pub with rustic décor, this is one of the most popular live-music venues in town. Arrive after 9pm, although by 10pm it's usually standing room only.

O'Malleys (Map p794; ☎ 0 7622 0170; 2/20-21 Th Montri) This chain Irish pub is good fun and has innovative promotions, such as 'Bring in a Party Photo and Get a Free Beer'. Mexican buffets are sometimes held.

HAT PATONG

Throngs of people graze at watering holes along Th Bang-La, which is a neon-lit zoo after dark. If you think 'Patong' sounds like Bangkok's 'Patpong', you're on to something – it looks like it too. In addition to foamy drinks, the bars serve gyrating girls, gay boys and lady boys.

Molly Malone's (☎ 0 7629 2771; Th Thawiwong) This pub rocks with Irish gigs every night at 9.45pm. There's a good atmosphere, lots of pub food and some great tables out the front from which to admire the ocean and legions of tourist passers-by.

Two Black Sheep (Th Rat Uthit) In the thick of the inland action, next to K Hotel, this place has mostly an intimate bar atmosphere, with good live rock music nightly in a trendy, dark space.

Gonzo Bar (Th Bangla) This large bar attracts hordes of *faràng,* who come in partly for the bar games. Grab a stool and watch others humiliate themselves while sipping cheap drinks, or lose your inhibitions and join in the fun.

Banana Disco (☎ 0 1271 2469; 96 Th Thawiwong; admission 200B) An Aztec-like theme prevails at this club. It's on the main beach strip and the cover charge includes two drinks.

Getting There & Away

AIR

Phuket international airport (Map p792; ☎ 0 7632 7230) is 30km to the north of the city centre, just off Hwy 402. Thai Airways International, Phuket Air and Air Andaman operate a heap of daily flights from Bangkok. There are also regular flights to Hat Yai, as well as to international destinations such as Penang, Langkawi, Kuala Lumpur, Singapore, Hong Kong, Taipei and Tokyo.

Taxis ask 340B for the trip from the airport to the city, or 500B to 600B to the beaches.

Airlines servicing Phuket:

Air Asia (code AK; ☎ 0 7635 1428; www.airasia.com)
Bangkok Airways (code PG; ☎ 0 7622 5033; www.bangkokair.com)
Dragonair (code HDA; ☎ 0 7621 5734; www.dragonair.com)
Malaysia Airlines (code MH; ☎ 0 7621 3749; www.malaysiaairlines.com)
Phuket Air (code 9R; ☎ in Bangkok 0 2679 8999; www.phuketairlines.com)
SilkAir (code MI; ☎ 0 7621 3891; www.silkair.com)
Singapore Airlines (code SQ; ☎ 0 7621 3891; www.singaporeair.com)
Thai Airways International (THAI, code TG; ☎ 0 7621 1195; www.thaiair.com)

BOAT

There are a couple of major boat and ferry operators providing services out of Phuket, including **Phuket Boat Lagoon Marina** (Map p792; ☎ 0 7623 9055; www.phuketboatlagoon.com/marina/marina.php; 22/1 Moo 2, Th Thepkasattri, T Kohkaew A Muang) and **Yacht Haven Marina** (Map p792; ☎ 0 7620 6704-5; www.yacht-haven-phuket.com; 141/2 Moo 2, Tumbol Maikhao Thalang).

BUS

Phuket's **bus station** (Map p794) is off Th Phang-Nga, right in the centre of Phuket town and a comfortable walk to the nearby guesthouses. From Phuket, buses go to Bangkok (VIP 486B to 755B, air-con 378B to 567B, 12 to 15 hours, morning and several evening departures daily), Hat Yai (air-con 210B to 270B, six to eight hours, several morning departures daily), Krabi (air-con/ordinary 117/65B, three to four hours, departures regularly from 7am to 6.30pm), Phang-Nga (ordinary 36B, 2½ hours, five departures from 10am to 4.30pm), Surat Thani (air-con/ordinary 170/105B, five to six hours, several daily) and Trang (air-con/ordinary 189/105B, five to six hours, hourly from 5am to 6.30pm).

Getting Around

When you first arrive in Phuket, beware of the rip-off artists who claim that the tourist office is 5km away, that the only way to get to the beaches is to take a taxi, or that a săwngthăew from the bus station to the town centre will cost you a small fortune.

Săwngthăew depart from Th Ranong, near the market, to different spots on the island between 6am and 6pm. To go around town, the standard fare is 10B, to Hat Patong it's 15B, and to Hat Kata, Hat Karon and Hat Rawai it's 20B. These prices are only for trips originating or terminating in Phuket town; between the beaches you have to haggle.

You can also hire motorcycles almost anywhere for 150B to 200B. Exercise extreme caution as Phuket's roads are winding and accidents claim close to 200 lives every year on Phuket alone.

KO PHI PHI

Despite the tragic tsunami that swept through Ko Phi Phi in December 2004, if there was to be a contest for one of the planet's most jaw-dropping beauties, Ko Phi Phi would be a frontrunner. Stunning limestone cliffs, translucent water, fine white arcs of sand – Ko Phi Phi is so beautiful it will evoke tears. Shed a few more when you realise that you have to share it with every Speedo on the planet.

The crowds and development belie the fact that Ko Phi Phi (officially named Ko Phi Phi Don) is part of a national marine park. Ko Phi Phi Leh, a satellite island, remains uninhabited thanks in part to a more profitable business than tourism – harvesting nests of swiftlets for medicinal purposes. Visiting the island is expensive, but just to behold it for a day is worthwhile. Ko Phi Phi was hit particularly hard by the tsunami – virtually every standing structure on the twin bays of Ao Ton Sai and Ao Lo Dalam was destroyed, although much has now been rebuilt.

Activities

The **diving** on Ko Phi Phi is world-class and some think it's even better than Ko Tao. The best months for visibility are December to April, though certain other months (such as June and July) see fewer divers and can be less hectic. Where there is diving, there is **snorkelling** too. Shop around for competitive prices and ask for recommendations from other travellers.

Sleeping

Budget accommodation on Ko Phi Phi? Don't kid yourself: there isn't any, although there are a few pockets of relative affordability, especially in the interior of the island. Things get tight during the high season from December to March.

Rock (Ao Ton Sai; dm 300B, d 350-1000B; ❄) An easy walk from Ton Sai village and located right next to Maprao Resort (look for the life-sized

TSUNAMI: SORROW & SURVIVAL IN SOUTHERN THAILAND

tsuna'mi *n. a series of long, high sea waves caused by disturbance of ocean floor or seismic movement*

The wave that shook the world on 26 December 2004 and left more than 220,000 people dead did not spare parts of southern Thailand. Sumatra's monster 9.0-magnitude quake travelled up to 1000km per hour, hitting the shores of the Andaman Sea just 60 minutes later, swallowing resorts around Khao Lak and Phuket and pummelling parts of Ko Phi Phi. But the real cost was human life: 5395 dead, 8457 injured and 2932 missing in Thailand alone.

After this monumental tsunami, which struck 12 countries, it's not surprising that holidaymakers were fearful of returning to the region, causing an enormous drop in tourist numbers and revenue. Thankfully, the picture has improved since then. It's perhaps not surprising that in areas where tourism is the leading income generator, redevelopment efforts kicked into high gear almost as soon as the water receded. If travellers who hadn't heard of the tsunami visited even the most popular Andaman coast beaches today, they'd never know of the tragedy that took place there. There has even been good news from Phuket's Patong Beach, which was among the hardest hit: authorities there were keen to take advantage of the clean slate to curb the number of businesses and vendors operating on the prime beach strip.

By travelling in southern Thailand, you're part of a bigger picture. The killer waves may have struck more than once on that fateful day, but an economic crisis sustained by tourists cancelling or postponing trips would be yet another unfair blow for the locals.

Thanks for coming.

pirate ship), the Rock is home to Phi Phi's only dorm beds; they go for as low as 150B during the slow season. Many longtime Phi Phi expats live here.

Phi Phi Paradise Pearl Resort (☎ 0 7562 2100; www.ppparadise.com; Hat Yao; d 500-1500B; ❄) Choose from plain but clean rooms with bathrooms, or surprisingly large bamboo huts with a simple mattress-on-the-floor setup. Rates soar if you want air-con. The restaurant (dishes 40B to 95B) is open for breakfast, lunch and dinner.

Phi Phi Long Beach (☎ 0 7561 2217; Hat Yao; d 600-1000B) This village of bamboo and concrete bungalows is right on the beach, but is quite rough around the edges. Splash out for your own bathroom if you can afford it – the cold-water-only shared showers are a nightmare.

Eating & Drinking

Most of the hotels and bungalows around the island have their own restaurants. Cheaper and often better food can be found in the restaurants and cafés in Ton Sai village. Some of the most popular eateries are relative newcomers, having been built – along with the rest of the village – after the tsunami. Others are old favourites that were lovingly reconstructed.

Papaya (meals 50-70B; ⏲ breakfast, lunch & dinner) The most authentic Thai restaurant on the island, this place has toothsome dishes that are served in almost ridiculously large portions. (Save your leftovers for a *soi* dog.) Papaya is often packed, so prepare for a long wait if you've come for dinner.

Cosmic (pizza & pasta 120B; ⏲ breakfast, lunch & dinner) Specialising in wood-fired pizza, this place seems to be consistently packed. Can't get a table? Ask for directions to Cosmic 1.

Getting There & Away

Ko Phi Phi is equidistant from Phuket and Krabi, but Krabi is the more economical point of departure. Boats run regularly from November to May, but schedules depend on the weather during the monsoon.

From Ton Sai pier in Ko Phi Phi, boats depart for Krabi (200B, 1½ hours, three daily), Phuket (one way 300B to 500B, return 700B to 900B, 1½ hours, five daily) and Ao Nang (250B to 400B, two hours, three daily).

KRABI

pop 89,980

For many, a stop-off in Krabi is part of a well-balanced diet after a rendezvous on the Gulf of Thailand coast or vice versa. In fact, the path from Surat Thani on the Gulf coast to Krabi (gra-*bee*) on the Andaman coast is so well oiled that you will find yourself being herded off the ferry into cramped cattle cars for delivery across the peninsula before you can even deliberate.

Krabi Town

Often referred to as if it were a beach destination, Krabi is a jumping-off point for the epically beautiful island of Ko Phi Phi, as well as the popular mainland beaches of Ao Nang, Ton Sai and Rai Leh.

INFORMATION

Almost all of Krabi's budget travel agencies and restaurants offer internet access for 40B to 60B per hour.

Bangkok Bank (Th Utarakit) ATM and money exchange.

Krabi Hospital (☎ 0 7561 1210) One kilometre north of town.

Main post office (Th Utarakit; ⏲ 8.30am-4.30pm Mon-Fri, 9am-noon Sat & Sun) A telephone office is attached.

SLEEPING & EATING

Good Dream Guesthouse (☎ 0 7562 2993; 83 Th Utarakit; r 100-400B; ❄ 💻) Owned and managed by an American divemaster, Good Dream isn't quite as slick as the nearby Chan-Cha-Lay, but it does have some of the cheapest rooms in Krabi town. There's free wireless in the restaurant, and even nonguests can check email on a free terminal if they purchase food or beer. Add to that a real espresso machine, good videos shown nightly and helpful management, and you've got one of the better guesthouses around.

Chan-Cha-Lay Guesthouse (☎ 0 7562 0952, 0 1817 3387; chanchalay_krabi@hotmail.com; 55 Th Utarakit; r 200-600B; ❄ 💻) Very friendly and with clean, modern rooms, this is an excellent place to stay. If you've been staying in fleabags for a while, you'll be amazed at how clean and comfortable the sheets are. The restaurant is decked out in a great baby blue beach motif, and is open for breakfast and lunch. It's no surprise this place is popular.

K Guesthouse (☎ 0 7562 3166; 15-25 Th Chao Fah; d from 250B) This family-run place with wooden exterior is heavy on the atmosphere. Rooms are fairly plain; ask for one with a balcony overlooking Chao Fah. There's a small café (dishes 40B to 60B).

KR Mansion Hotel (☎ 0 7561 2761; www.kr-mansion.com; 52/1 Th Chao Fah; r 300-600B;) A reliable old favourite with basic, run-of-the-mill rooms. The café is pleasantly spacious, and the rooftop Moon Bar is the place to unwind with a drink in hand.

Pizzeria Firenze (☎ 0 7562 1453; 10 Th Khong Ka; dishes 100-200B) For those spaghetti napolitano and gelati cravings.

For cheap food, pull up a pew at the waterfront night market. The **morning market** (Th Si Sawat & Th Pruksauthit), near the Vieng Thong Hotel in the centre of town, has delicious takeaway dishes such as *phàt thai* (stir-fried noodles), *khâo màk kài* (chicken biryani) and *khâo kà-pì* (rice with red shrimp paste).

DRINKING

Old West Bar (Th Chao Fah; 1pm-2am) Don't expect to find a whole lot of locals in Krabi town's one and only cowboy-themed tavern. But no matter – with its tastefully rustic décor, overpriced draughts and hordes of shamelessly flirting *faràng*, you'll feel right at home.

Beaches

Dramatic karst formations soaring from emerald waters like a surreal dreamscape surround the crescent-shaped coves, creating the illusion of islands rather than a peninsula disconnected from Krabi town by road. These beaches tend to attract a more active crowd of travellers who earn their nightly beers after a day of walking, paddling or other sweaty pursuits. **Rock climbing** has become a major activity on Hat Ton Sai and Hat Rai Leh. In the low season, from May to October, prices are slashed by nearly half. During the high season, arrive early as competition for rooms is fierce.

AO NANG

The furthest western beach, Ao Nang is connected to Krabi town via Hwy 4203, which parades traffic within arm's length of the shore. On the paved inland side of the road, a string of tourist shops is more reminiscent of beach towns back home than castaway tropical paradises. Favoured by families and the well heeled, Ao Nang emits a comfortable air.

KRABI FOR CLIMBERS *Melanie Mills & Scott Welch*

Rock climbers from the world over congregate at this climbing mecca to test their strength and endurance on some of the world's most picturesque climbs. But this place isn't just for hard-core rock jocks – there are hundreds of climbs for all abilities. The local guides are only too happy to rope you up, get the adrenaline pumping and scare you silly. The euphoria of reaching the top is complemented by postcard views of 100m-high cliffs, dense jungle and perfect beaches. An excellent guide for the area is King Climbers' *Route Guide Book,* which you can pick up at most of the climbing shops.

The climbing ranges from steep pocketed walls to muscle-bursting overhanging horrors. The limestone rises directly out of the Andaman Sea and has huge stalactites hanging down, requiring interesting acrobatic moves.

If you're after a climbing guide or want to do a course, head for Railay (officially Laem Phra Nang), south of Ao Nang. There are numerous climbing schools that provide all the necessary equipment, and from what we have seen the guides are very friendly, patient and professional. A half-day climb with guide, equipment and insurance costs around 800B, while one-day/three-day climbs cost 1600/5000B.

If you have your own gear, it's useful to bring a 60m rope and a rope bag to keep the sand off. Krabi is a sport-climbers' paradise, so just bring your quickdraws and follow the bolts. Alternatively, you can rent sport-climbing equipment for two people (half/full day 600/1000B), which includes harnesses, shoes, a rope, 12 quickdraws, a belay device, a locking karabiner, chalk and a guidebook.

Hat Ton Sai, part of the jagged Railay peninsula, is where the more advanced climbers tend to strut their stuff; however, the 'groove tube' climb is a real favourite with beginners and advanced climbers alike.

If you're after a bit of an adventure, pack a torch and head to Tum Choee cave, which you can see at the northern end of Hat Tham Phra Nang. Bats eventually emerge halfway up the huge monolith of Thaiwand Wall. A 25m abseil into the jungle and a 10-minute scramble will bring you to West Hat Rai Leh for a well-deserved Beer Chang.

Melanie Mills and Scott Welch are go-anywhere rock climbers from Melbourne, Australia.

There's a cluster of guesthouses about a block from the beach where Hwy 4203 turns inland.

Just down the *soi* from PK and J Mansions, you'll find **Bream Guesthouse** (Moo 2; r with shared bathroom 200B;) next to the giant pint of Guinness. These seem to be the cheapest rooms in town – all are fan-cooled and share bathrooms. Management seems a bit surly, but when we visited this was the only no-vacancy spot around.

Found next to a popular Irish bar at the end of a laneway, **PK Mansion** (0 7563 7431; pkmansion@hotmail.com; 247/12-15 Moo 2; d from 300B;) has big, tiled ('hygienic') rooms and feels secure. Dishes in the PK restaurant cost 50B to 80B.

Aside from its fantastic plant-filled lobby, **J Mansion** (0 7563 7878; 302 Moo 2; d from 400B;) appears to be a virtual reproduction of the neighbouring PK Mansion. The pressure's on, backpacker: which one will you choose?

The waterside **Lavinia Restaurant & Bakery** (0 7569 5404; dishes 50-440B; breakfast, lunch & dinner) claims to be Ao Nang's 'trendsetter'. It offers all manner of homemade pastas, while the meats and the stone oven are both imported from Europe. The bakery is said to be topnotch.

Somkiat Buri Restaurant (0 7563 7574; dishes 60-250B) cooks up great Thai food, but the best reason to come here is the lush open-sided pavilion where you sit.

Climb up to the Sunset Balcony at **75 Million Years Pub** (0 7563 7130; regular cocktails 130B), a faux-Flintstones beach bar, and drink among the trees. Can't find the place? It's inside the creatively designed Phra Nang Inn.

HAT TON SAI

Not to be confused with the Hat Ton Sai on Ko Phi Phi, this beach is the type of place rock climbers in distant lands dream about because it's surrounded by climbing cliffs (with bolts) on all sides. It isn't as spectacular as neighbouring Hat Rai Leh, but remains the cheapest and least-developed beach on Krabi's mainland. Its relative isolation and popularity with a cool young crowd hasvefuelled an alternative full moon party. No-one is in a hurry here.

Andaman Nature Resort (0 7562 2585; d 200-500B) is a climbers' hang-out that offers a variety of bamboo, wood or concrete bungalows – some are crying out for a revamp, but the grungy and sporty don't seem to mind.

Choose from bamboo, wooden or concrete bungalows at **Dream Valley** (0 7562 2583; www.dreamvalleyresortkrabi.com; d from 300B;) – all sit among myriad trees. The air-con choices are presentable.

Near the beach, the sprawling **Tonsai Bay Bungalows** (0 7562 2584; d from 600B;) is a mixture of upmarket (and overpriced) bungalows and older ones with grotty share bathrooms (for 200B to 350B). The restaurant doubles as a common area – the bronzed and barely clothed climbers lounging on pillows and shooting pool make for a rather titillating pre- or postmeal show.

HAT RAI LEH

On the very tip of the peninsula, hypnotic Hat Rai Leh is divided into the superior West Rai Leh and the affordable East Rai Leh. The epitome of a honeymoon destination, West Rai Leh has only dream-on resort bungalows that monopolise the stunning scenery. Shoestring accommodation is off a public path in East Rai Leh, whose beach is a muddy mangrove forest unsuitable for swimming. Don't fret, though: the postcard-perfect beaches at West Rai Leh and Tham Phra Nang (south of East Rai Leh) are both open to the public (you just pay less to use them).

Popular with climbers and backpackers alike, **Ya-Ya** (0 7562 2593; East Rai Leh; r from 380B) sits right on the beach; longtail boats from Krabi will practically deposit you at the registration desk. Room size here doesn't seem to have anything to do with cost, so take care to see a few before deciding – and try for a balcony room while you're at it. The restaurant here (dishes 70B to 190B) is popular, and seems like a good place to make new friends.

Up 48 steps, **Rapala** (0 7562 2586; rapala@loxinfo.co.th; East Rai Leh; d 400-800B) has a smashing view of the surrounding limestone cliffs, but the log cabin bungalows are set pretty far back from the beach. The restaurant serves Indian fare.

Getting There & Around

Krabi's airport is 17km northeast of town on Hwy 4. Several airlines service Krabi. **Thai Airways International** (code TG; 0 7562 2439; www.thaiair.com) has three daily flights to and from Bangkok (2560B, 1¼ hours). PB Air and Phuket Air also fly to Bangkok, although these flights are more sporadic and depend on demand.

The bus station is 4km north of Krabi town at Talat Kao. Red săwngthăew (20B) deliver passengers from the bus station to town, in front of the 7-Eleven on Th Maharat. Buses travel between Krabi and Bangkok (air-con 357B to 710B, 12 hours, seven daily); Hat Yai (air-con/ordinary 173/96B, four to five hours, hourly; note only the 1pm departure is for the non-air-con service); Phuket (air-con/ordinary 117/65B, three to four hours, hourly); and Surat Thani (air-con/ordinary 140/80B, two to three hours, regular daily departures until 4pm).

White săwngthăew (20B during the day, 50B after 6pm) to Krabi from Ao Nang take about 45 minutes. Longtail boats bounce between Krabi and Hat Rai Leh (70B) and Hat Ton Sai (110B), when enough passengers have accumulated.

KO LANTA

pop 20,000

Slip into a beachy existence on Ko Lanta. Don't be put off by the dusty unsealed road slithering down its coastline: you'll soon be greeted with great, flat beaches. The resident Muslim and Thai community don't want to see their island become someone else's to exploit, so there are strict building and development restrictions in place to fend off the big end of town (for the time being anyway). Things are quickly moving upmarket nonetheless.

Pick-up share taxis (30B to 120B) and motorbike hires (200B to 250B per day) are available from Ban Sala Dan, near the 7-Eleven in Saladan Village. Saladan's main street is lined with internet cafés and travel agencies selling onward and upward tickets.

Information

Ko Lanta Hospital (☎ 0 7569 7017)

Post office (🕑 8.30am-3.30pm) In the street southeast of the pier.

Siam Commercial Bank (☎ 0 7568 4577) Opposite the 7-Eleven in Saladan village, it has currency exchange from 8.30am to 9.30pm, plus an ATM.

Sleeping & Eating

HAT PHRA AE

Many shoestringers head over to Hat Phra Ae (Long Beach) where the beach is long (surprise, surprise). There's a convenience store, ATM and internet access in close proximity to the accommodation mentioned following.

Reggae House Pub & Restaurant (☎ 0 1091 1201; d 80-150B) A little piece of Jamaica in southern Thailand. Brick tepee-style huts are as cheap as they look. There's nightly bongo drumming and 'jam sessions' in the rambling driftwood bar and restaurant, which is open for breakfast, lunch and dinner (dishes 40B to 80B). Swing by on Bob Marley's birthday (6 February) or from 22 to 26 December for annual music festivals.

Sanctuary (☎ 0 1891 3055; sanctuary_93@yahoo.com; d 300-500B) Put some 'om' back into your life at this traveller's utopia. Beachfront bungalows capture sea breezes and there are cheaper cuties. Join a stretchy yoga class in the beachside pavilion from Monday to Saturday (per class 300B, or 1000B for four classes). The restaurant (open for breakfast, lunch and dinner) dishes out to-die-for banana fried rice, roti and breakfast burritos for 60B to 200B…mmm.

Nautilus Bungalows (☎ 0 6996 5567; 147 Moo 2; d from 600B; ❄) Next door to Reggae House, by a rocky cove, this place is run by a helpful family. You'll find tastefully decorated bungalows with outdoor bathrooms, high wooden beds and roomy decks.

Earth Bar (☎ 0 7265 9662; drinks 50-380B; 🕑 nightly) Behind the Sanctuary, Earth Bar projects a cool ambience and dazzling lighting made for after-dusk raging.

HAT KHLONG KHONG

Where Else? (☎ 0 1536 4870; d 200-500B) Backpacker-friendly bungalows. Decent Thai, Indian and vegetarian meals are served in the guesthouse restaurant.

AO KANTIANG

A fine sprinkling of sand on which to rest your travel-weary bones awaits you on Ao Kantiang. There are several nearby tour offices providing internet access and motorcycle hire.

Kantiang Bay View Resort (☎ 0 1787 5192; reekantiang@hotmail.com; d 400-1200B; ❄) Bamboo and pricier modern bungalows with fan or air-con to suit your budget and personal thermostat.

Getting There & Away

Ko Lanta is accessible by bus from Trang (ordinary 90B, two hours, two morning and two afternoon departures) or by minivan from

Trang (180B) or Krabi (150B, 1½ hours, three daily). Passenger boats between Ko Lanta's Ban Sala Dan and Krabi's Kong Ka (Chao Fa) pier run from October to April (200B, two hours, two departures daily).

TRANG

pop 69,100

Midway between Krabi and Hat Yai, bustling Trang is a cheerful and pleasant Thai town. We love the lolly-coloured Vespas and vintage túk-túk whizzing around the place.

The city's **Vegetarian Festival**, taking place in September/October, is a frenzied fiesta complete with acts of self-mortification that would be struggling to attract even the most committed of Western activists.

Information

Should you need to top up your baht, there's a Bangkok Bank opposite the post office on Th Phra Ram VI, the main strip running east of the train station. Staff at **Chao Mai Tour** (☎ 0 7521 6380; 15 Th Phra Ram VI; per min 1B) travel agency are very helpful and you can jump on the internet here.

Sleeping & Eating

Ko Teng Hotel (☎ 0 7521 8622; 77-79 Th Phra Ram VI; d from 180B) 'Yes, I have room for you!' is Ko Teng's catch phrase. It feels like a massive school boarding house from the 1950s and offers clean rooms with sparse furnishings.

Yamawa (☎ 0 7521 6617; yamawa@cscoms.com; 94 Th Visetkul; d 200B) This budget haven has clean, pleasantly decorated rooms with bamboo interiors.

Look for Trang's speciality, *khànŏm jiin,* at the night market, just east of the provincial offices. Trang is also famous for its *ráan kaa-fae* or *ráan ko-píi* (coffee shops), which are usually run by Hokkien Chinese. These shops serve real filtered coffee. When you order coffee here, be sure to use the Hokkien word *ko-píi* rather than the Thai *kaa-fae,* otherwise you may end up with Nescafé or instant Khao Chong coffee – the proprietors often think this is what *faràng* want. Check out **Yuchiang** (Th Phra Ram VI; dishes 25-50B) opposite Khao Tom Phui.

Sin Ocha Bakery (Th Sathani; dishes 25-50B; 🕑 breakfast, lunch & dinner) Near the train station, popular Sin Ocha is the most convenient *ráan ko-píi* around. Simple Thai dishes and breakfast are served (try the oversized muesli with fruit and yogurt), along with huge coffee drinks (10B to 40B) and teas. Takeaway cakes and biscuits are tempting glucose hits.

Khao Tom Phui (☎ 0 7521 0127; Th Phra Ram VI; dishes 30-50B; 🕑 dinner) Run by a gaggle of Thai teenage girls, this simple Thai eatery occupies a corner and has English menus on hand. It's open late.

Wang Boa Restaurant (dishes 30-80B; 🕑 breakfast, lunch & dinner) Right next door to the train station, this casual place is popular with locals and serves Thai and Western dishes. Go on: try the 'Like a Virgin' salad.

Getting There & Away

The **bus station** (Th Huay Yot) is 400m from the centre. Buses travel to Bangkok (VIP 580B to 750B, air-con 490B, 12 to 13 hours, five daily), Hat Yai (ordinary 60B), Satun (air-con/ordinary 100/55B, two hours), Krabi (air-con/ordinary 90/55B, three hours) and Phuket (air-con 189B, five hours).

Share taxis and minibuses also service many of the popular destinations. Most leave from the train station. Minibuses to the nearby beaches (50B) leave from different spots around town.

The **train station** (Th Phra Ram VI) serves only two trains travelling all the way from Trang to Bangkok (175B to 1240B, 16 hours, evening departures).

KO TARUTAO NATIONAL MARINE PARK

Isolated, serene and full of rugged gorgeousness, Ko Tarutao National Marine Park – a little-known archipelago of 51 islands in the furthest southwestern reaches of Thai territory – is one of those rare places in Thailand that's far from the madding crowds and devoid of beachfront bars and maxed-out stereo systems. Let's just hope it manages to stay that way.

Admission to the park is 200B for foreigners, and the park is only 'officially' open from around November to May, depending on the weather patterns during the monsoon period.

Sleeping & Eating

Of the five accessible islands, park accommodation is available on mountainous Ko Tarutao and Ko Adang. Looking to do a little tourist activism? Think twice before you sign up for Ko Lipe, the only island in the park open to private development. Please excuse the soapboxing, but consider this: once building restrictions have been removed, development will meet demand and before long Ko Lipe will be just as touristed as other 'national parks', such as Ko Phi Phi, Ko Samet and Ko Chang. If Ko Lipe is a successful moneymaker, then how long will other islands in the park be protected?

Park-managed **accommodation options** (☎ in Pak Bara 0 7478 3485, 0 7472 9002, in Bangkok 0 2562 0760; camp sites 30B, 4-person longhouse 500B, 2-/4-person bungalows 600/1200B) on Ko Tarutao should be booked ahead in peak times, but can also be arranged at the park office in Pak Bara. Tents are available to rent (150B) and can be pitched right on the beach.

On Ko Adang, you'll find longhouse accommodation similar to that on Ko Tarutao for 400B (sleeps four).

Before leaving the mainland, load up on food and water supplies as the park shop is limited and the food at **Tarutao Café** (breakfast & lunch) is average.

Getting There & Away

From Pak Bara pier, boats go to Ko Tarutao (one way/return 180/300B, one hour, 10.30am, 3pm, 4.30pm plus another afternoon departure depending on demand), Ko Adang (one way/return 500/900B, 1½ hours, 1.30pm) and Ko Lipe (one way/return 500/900B, 1.30pm). For up-to-date fast-ferry times call the **Tarutao Speed Boat Ferry Team & Tour** (☎ 0 7478 3055) and for regular-ferry times call **Andrew Tours** (☎ 0 7478 3459), **Adang Sea Tour** (☎ 0 7478 3368) or **Wasana Tour** (☎ 0 7471 1782).

Minibuses (60B to 70B) and vans (80B) to Hat Yai park near the pier, and share taxis will take you to the moon for the right price.

SATUN

pop 33,400

Travelling to the deepest western corner of Thailand, you pass woven bamboo huts and harvested fields where villagers stage football games, plus men dressed in the traditional Muslim garb, headscarved women and onion-domed mosques. With a large Muslim population speaking Yawi, Satun is barely Thailand – it didn't join the country as a province until 1932 and still clamours, along with other southern provinces, for independence.

The town boasts one major attraction: the **Satun National Museum** (☎ 0 7472 3140; Soi 5, Th Satun Thani; admission 30B; 9am-4pm Wed-Sun), which gives its visitors a surprisingly thorough introduction to the traditions and folk ways of the Thai-Muslim southern provinces.

GETTING TO MALAYSIA

You can travel by boat between Satun and Pulau Langkawi in Malaysia. Boats leave from Tha Tammalang daily at 8am, 9am, 1.30pm and 4pm (250B, 1½ hours). Tha Tammalang is 9km from Satun; to get there, take an orange săwngthăew (small pick-up with two benches in the back; 20B) across the street from Wat Chanathip on Th Buriwanit. You can buy ferry tickets in Satun at the **Thai Ferry Centre** (☎ 0 7473 0511; Th Sulakanukoon), near Wat Chanathipchaloeem.

Remember there is a one-hour time difference between Thailand and Malaysia.

See p455 for information on doing the trip in the reverse direction.

Sleeping & Eating

There is just a handful of large dormlike hotels in Satun, including **Rian Thong Hotel** (Rain Tong; ☎ 0 7472 2518; Th Samanta Prasit; s/d from 250/300B) and **Udomsuk** (☎ 0 7471 1006; Th Hatthakam Seuksa; s/d from 150/250B). Rooms facing the street at both hotels suck in noise like a vacuum cleaner.

Near the gold-domed Bambang Mosque in the centre of town, there are several inexpensive Muslim shops. Morning coffee can be shared with chatty vegetable sellers at the **day market** (Khlong Bambang), south of town. The **night market** (btwn Th Buriwanit & Th Satun Thani), north of the mosque, provides the pleasurable evening entertainment of eating fluffy roti and watching the communal TV.

Getting There & Away

Minibuses to Hat Yai (65B, 1½ hours) stop at the bus shelter on Th Buriwanit, across from Bangkok Bank.

To get to Pak Bara pier (for boats to Ko Tarutao National Marine Park), take a săwngthăew (20B) from this same bus shelter to the nearby village of La-Ngu, where you can pick up a motorcycle taxi (30B) for the remainder of the trip to Pak Bara. Getting yourself onto the right săwngthăew is a little tricky, so let a Thai waiting at the bus station know where you're headed. The Satun–Pak Bara trip takes 1¾ hours.

See p803 for information on ferries to Pulau Langkawi.

THAILAND DIRECTORY

ACCOMMODATION

There is a healthy range of budget accommodation in Thailand, kicking off at around US$2 (80B) for a dorm bed or a cheap single with fan and share bathroom. Make the leap to US$6 (250B) and you get an attached bathroom, while US$10 (400B) will see you enter the air-con league. The cheapest rooms include four walls of varying cleanliness, a bed of varying comfort and a creaking fan. Check out the sanitary standards of the shared bathroom before you make a decision. Although basic, the most comfortable lodging is at 'guesthouses'. Some long-running establishments will make a destination, while others can make you suspicious of all Thai motivations. More impersonal but sometimes the only choice in nontouristy places are the Chinese-run hotels that cater to Thai clientele. The rates run a little higher than budget guesthouses (200B to 350B) and include a private bathroom, TV and sometimes a view. However, communication with the staff will require a lot of hand gestures.

During Thailand's high season (December to February), prices increase and availability decreases. Reservations at most of the small family-run hotels are not recommended as bookings are rarely honoured. Advance payment to secure a reservation is also discouraged as this tends to disappear on arrival.

Practising Buddhists may be able to stay overnight in some temples for a small donation. Facilities are very basic, and early rising is expected. Temple lodgings are usually for men only. Neat, clean dress and a basic knowledge of Thai etiquette are mandatory.

In this chapter, assume that the prices listed are for rooms with a fan and en suite bathroom unless otherwise indicated.

ACTIVITIES

Despite the hot and humid weather, Thailand offers all sorts of athletic escapes. The most popular pursuits include diving, snorkelling and jungle trekking, but cycling, kayaking and rock climbing aren't far behind.

Cycling

Many visitors bring their own bicycles to Thailand. In general, drivers are courteous, and most roads are sealed with roomy shoulders. Grades in most parts of the country are moderate; exceptions include the far north, especially Mae Hong Son and Nan Provinces, where you'll need iron legs. Favoured touring routes include the two-lane roads along the Mekong River in the north and northeast – the terrain is mostly flat and the river scenery is inspiring. The 2500-member **Thailand Cycling Club** (☎ 0 2612 5510; www.thaicycling.com/index_en.html) serves as an information clearing house on bicycle tours and cycle clubs around the country.

Diving & Snorkelling

Thailand's two coastlines and countless islands are popular among divers for warm waters and colourful marine life. The biggest diving centre is still Pattaya, simply because it's less than two hours' drive from Bangkok. Phuket is the second-biggest jumping-off point and has the advantage of offering the largest variety of places to choose from. Reef dives off the coast of Phuket are particularly rewarding – some 210 hard corals and 108 reef fish have so far been catalogued in this understudied marine zone.

Dive operations have multiplied on the palmy islands of Ko Samui, Ko Pha-Ngan and Ko Tao, all in the Gulf of Thailand. Newer frontiers include the so-called Burma Banks (in the Mergui Archipelago northwest of Ko Surin) and islands off the coasts of Krabi and Trang Provinces.

Most of these places have areas that are suitable for snorkelling as well as scuba diving, since many reefs are covered by water no deeper than 2m.

Masks, fins and snorkels are readily available for hire, but quality is often second-rate. Most dive shops can offer basic instruction and NAUI or PADI qualification for first-timers. An average four-day, full-certification course costs around 10,000B, including instruction, equipment and several open-water dives. Shorter, less expensive 'resort' courses are also available.

Kayaking

Exploring the islands and limestone karsts around Phuket and Ao Phang-Nga by inflatable kayak is a whole lot of fun. Typical trips seek out half-submerged caves, which can be accessed at low tide for a bit of on-the-water underground adventure.

Trekking

Trekking is one of northern Thailand's biggest attractions. Typical trekking programmes run for four or five days and feature daily walks through forested mountain areas, coupled with overnight stays in hill-tribe villages to satisfy both ethnotourism and ecotourism urges.

Other trekking opportunities are available in Thailand's larger national parks, including Khao Sok and Khao Yai, where park rangers may be hired as guides and cooks for a few days at a time. Rates are reasonable.

BOOKS

Lonely Planet titles include *Thailand*, *Thailand's Islands & Beaches* and *Bangkok*. *Diving & Snorkelling Thailand* is chock-a-block full of colour photos and essential diving information. *Bangkok Encounter* is a compact guide that's ideal for short-stay visitors. *World Food Thailand* is a unique culinary guide that takes you to the heart of the kingdom's culture.

Everyone in the City of Angels has a story and author James Eckardt tells it through a series of short stories and interviews with motorcycle drivers, noodle vendors, go-go dancers and heavy hitters in *Bangkok People*.

Meet a prepubescent Thai 12-year-old who lives in Bangkok, lusts after girls and meets the adult world, in the semiautobiographical *Jasmine Nights* by wunderkind SP Somtow. Born in Bangkok, educated at Eton and Cambridge, and now a commuter between two 'cities of angels' (Los Angeles and Bangkok), Somtow's prodigious output includes a string of well-reviewed science fiction/fantasy/horror stories.

What can a 1950s housewife teach you about Thailand? A lot! Author Carol Hollinger writes of her romance with Thai culture in *Mai Pen Rai Means Never Mind* as the atypical wife of an American businessman living in Bangkok.

Celebrated writer Pira Sudham was born into a poor family in northeastern Thailand, and brilliantly captures the region's struggles against nature and nurture. *Monsoon Country* is one of several titles Sudham wrote originally in English.

BUSINESS HOURS

Most government offices are open from 8.30am to 4.30pm weekdays, but often close from noon to 1pm for lunch. Businesses usually operate between 8.30am and 5pm weekdays and sometimes on Saturday morning. Larger shops usually open from 10am to 6.30pm or 7pm, but smaller shops may open earlier and close later. Restaurants keep erratic hours, but most are open from mid-morning to late at night.

Any exceptions to these hours are noted in specific listings. Note that all government offices and banks are closed on public holidays.

CLIMATE

Tropical Thailand is warm year-round. The three seasons are: hot (from March to May), wet (from June to October) and cool (from November to February). Towards the end of the hot season the northeast can get even hotter than Bangkok, although it's a drier heat. In the cool season, night-time temperatures in the north can drop as low as 4°C. Brrrrr!

The wet season is no reason to put off a visit to Thailand, even though Bangkok is often flooded come September – the whole place is sinking, just like Venice.

See the climate charts on p916 for more.

CUSTOMS

A reasonable amount of clothing for personal use, toiletries and professional instruments are allowed in duty free. Up to 200 cigarettes and 1L of wine or spirits can be brought into the country duty free. The **customs department** (www.customs.go.th) maintains a helpful website with more specific information.

DANGERS & ANNOYANCES

Although Thailand is not a dangerous country, it's wise to be cautious, particularly if travelling alone. Theft in Thailand is still usually a matter of stealth rather than strength; travellers are more likely to have pockets picked than to be mugged. Take care of valuables, don't carry too much cash around and watch out for razor artists who ingeniously slit bags open in crowded quarters.

All travellers should ensure their rooms are securely locked and bolted at night. Inspect cheap rooms with thin walls in case there are strategic peepholes. We receive regular reports of thefts frequently occurring from guesthouses in Bangkok's Th Khao San and on the island of Ko Pha-Ngan.

Take caution when leaving valuables in hotel 'safes', usually a filing cabinet or desk drawer. Many travellers have reported problems with leaving valuables in Chiang Mai guesthouses while trekking, particularly credit cards taking themselves out on shopping sprees. Make sure you obtain an itemised receipt for property left with hotels or guesthouses – note the exact quantity of travellers cheques and all other valuables.

When you're on the road, keep zippered luggage secured with small locks, especially while travelling on buses and trains. Several readers letters have recounted tales of thefts from their bags or backpacks during long overnight bus trips, particularly on routes between Bangkok and Chiang Mai or Ko Samui.

Thais are friendly and their friendliness is usually genuine. Nevertheless, on trains and buses, particularly in the south, beware of strangers offering cigarettes, drinks or chocolates. Several travellers have reported waking up with a headache to find their valuables have disappeared. Travellers have also encountered drugged food or drink offered by friendly strangers in bars and by prostitutes in their own hotel rooms.

Armed robbery does occur in some remote areas of Thailand, but the risk is fairly low. Avoid going out alone at night in remote areas and, if trekking in northern Thailand, always travel in groups.

There has been widespread unrest in the four southernmost provinces of Thailand during the last few years. Muslim separatists have been clashing with government forces in Songkhla, Yala, Pattani and Narathiwat, and civilians have been targeted and killed, including children and monks. The government's response has been pretty heavy-handed and the violence shows no signs of dying down. See the boxed text on p785 for more details.

Penalties for drug offences are stiff these days in Thailand: if you are caught using marijuana, mushrooms or LSD, you face a fine of 10,000B plus one year in prison; for heroin or amphetamines, the penalty can be anywhere from a 5000B to 10,000B fine and six months' to 10 years' imprisonment, or worse. Remember that it is illegal to buy, sell or possess opium, heroin, amphetamines, LSD, mushrooms or marijuana in any quantity.

DRIVING LICENCE

An International Driving Permit is necessary to drive vehicles in Thailand, but this is rarely enforced for motorcycle hire.

SCAMS

As old as the hippy trail, the gem scam is still alive and well. Over the years, Lonely Planet has received dozens of letters from victims who've been cheated of large sums of money by buying colourful pieces of glass masquerading as rare gems. Every report Lonely Planet receives follows the same scenario: you, the traveller, are headed to a popular attraction, when a friendly local approaches you speaking your native language fluently and tells you that the attraction is closed. You curse Lonely Planet for not telling you and then look imploringly at your new friend who says that there are other interesting attractions nearby and they will arrange a ride for you. Now you are being taken for the proverbial 'ride'. What comes next is a one-day only, super bargain opportunity to learn an expensive lesson. If the price is too good to be true, then a scam is afoot.

The scam has also morphed into deals on clothing and card games. If you happen to become involved in one of these scams, the police (including the tourist police) are usually of little help: it's not illegal to sell gems at outrageously high prices and everyone's usually gone by the time you come back with the police.

Any túk-túk (three-wheeled motorcycle taxi) driver who offers you a ride for only 10B or 20B is a tout who will undoubtedly drag you somewhere else for a commission.

When you land in a bus station, a crowd of touts, as tactful as celebrity paparazzi, jockey for your business. Often these guys are harmless and even helpful, but some are crafty and will steer you to hotels that pay higher commissions rather than long-established places that don't 'tip' the driver. Hence, don't believe them if they tell you the hotel or guesthouse you're looking for is closed, full, dirty or bad – this is all 'tout speak' for no commission.

EMBASSIES & CONSULATES

For information on Thai visas, see p812.

Embassies & Consulates in Thailand

Unless otherwise stated, the following embassies are found in Bangkok:

Australia (Map pp694-5; ☎ 0 2287 2680; 37 Th Sathon Tai)
Brunei (Map pp694-5; ☎ 0 2204 1476-9; 132 Soi 23, Th Sukhumvit)
Cambodia (Map pp694-5; ☎ 0 2254 6630; 185 Th Ratchadamri)
Canada (Map pp694-5; ☎ 0 2636 0540; 15th fl, Abdulrahim Bldg, 990 Th Phra Ram IV)
China Bangkok (Map pp690-1; ☎ 0 2245 7043; 57 Th Ratchadaphisek); Songkhla (☎ 0 7431 1494; Th Sadao)
France Embassy (Map pp694-5; ☎ 0 2266 8250; 35 Soi 36, Th Charoen Krung); Consulate (Map pp694-5; ☎ 0 2287 1592; 29 Th Sathon Tai)
Germany (Map pp694-5; ☎ 0 2287 9000; 9 Th Sathon Tai)
India (Map pp694-5; ☎ 0 2258 0300; 46 Soi 23, Th Sukhumvit)
Indonesia Bangkok (Map pp694-5; ☎ 0 2252 3135; 600-602 Th Petchaburi); Songkhla (☎ 0 7431 1544; Th Sadao)
Japan (Map pp694-5; ☎ 0 2207 8500, 0 2696 3000; 177 Th Withayu)
Laos Bangkok (Map pp690-1; ☎ 0 2539 6679; 520/1-3 Th Pracha Uthit, end of Soi 39, Th Ramkhamhaeng); Khon Kaen (☎ 0 4324 2856; 191/102-3 Th Prachasamoson)
Malaysia Bangkok (Map pp694-5; ☎ 0 2679 2190; 35 Th Sathon Tai); Songkhla (☎ 0 7431 1062; 4 Th Sukhum)
Myanmar (Map pp694-5; ☎ 0 2233 2237; 132 Th Sathon Neua)
New Zealand (Map pp694-5; ☎ 0 2254 2530; 19th fl, M Thai Tower, All Seasons Pl, 87 Th Withayu)
Philippines (Map pp690-1; ☎ 0 2259 0139; 760 Th Sukhumvit)
Singapore (Map pp694-5; ☎ 0 2286 2111; 9th & 18th fl, Rajanakam Bldg, 183 Th Sathon Tai)
UK (Map pp694-5; ☎ 0 2305 8333; 1031 Th Withayu)
USA (Map pp694-5; ☎ 0 2205 4000; 120-122 Th Withayu)
Vietnam Bangkok (Map pp694-5; ☎ 0 2251 5836; 83/1 Th Withayu); Khon Kaen (☎ 0 4324 2190; 65/6 Th Chatapadung)

Thai Embassies & Consulates Abroad

Thai diplomatic offices abroad:

Australia (☎ 02-6273 1149; 111 Empire Circuit, Yarralumla, ACT 2600)
Canada (☎ 613-722 4444; 180 Island Park Dr, Ottawa, Ontario K1Y 0A2)
France (☎ 01 56 26 50 50; 8 rue Greuze, 75116 Paris)
Germany (☎ 030-794 810; Lepsiusstrasse 64-66, 12163 Berlin)
Israel (☎ 972-3 695 8980; 21 Shaul Hamelech Blvd, Tel Aviv)
New Zealand (☎ 04-476 8618; 2 Cook St, Karori, PO Box 17226, Wellington)
UK (☎ 020-7589 0173; 29-30 Queen's Gate, London SW7 5JB)
USA (☎ 202-944 3608; 1024 Wisconsin Ave NW, Washington, DC 20007)

FESTIVALS & EVENTS

Many Thai festivals are linked to Buddhist rituals and follow the lunar calendar. Thus they fall on different dates each year, depending on the phases of the moon. Many provinces hold annual festivals or fairs to promote their specialities. A complete, up-to-date schedule of events around the country is available from TAT offices in each region or from the central Bangkok TAT office. See p809 for public holiday listings.

Businesses typically close and transportation becomes difficult during the following festivals:

Chakri Memorial Day Held on 6 April to celebrate the founder of the current royal dynasty.
Songkran Festival From 12 to 14 April, Buddha images are 'bathed', monks and elders have their hands respectfully sprinkled with water by younger Thais, and a lot of water is generously tossed about for fun. Songkran generally gives everyone a chance to release their frustrations and literally cool off during the peak of the hot season. Hide out in your room or expect to be soaked; the latter is a lot more fun.
Queen's Birthday (Mother's Day) Held on 12 August; festivities occur mainly in Bangkok.

Lunar festivals include the following:

Magha Puja (Maakhá Buuchaa) Held on the full moon of the third lunar month to commemorate Buddha preaching to 1250 enlightened monks who came to hear him 'without prior summons'. It culminates with a candlelit walk around the *wian tian* (main chapel) at every wat.
Visakha Puja (Wísăakhà Buuchaa) This event falls on the 15th day of the waxing moon in the sixth lunar month and commemorates the date of the Buddha's birth, enlightenment and passing away. Activities are centred on the wat.
Khao Phansa (Khâo Phansăa) This marks the beginning of Buddhist 'lent', the traditional time of year for young men to enter the monkhood for the wet season. It's a good time to observe a Buddhist ordination.
Loi Krathong On the night of the full moon, small lotus-shaped baskets or boats made of banana leaves containing

flowers, incense, candles and a coin are floated on Thai rivers, lakes and canals.

FOOD & DRINK

Food

Thai food is a complex balance of spicy, salty, sweet and sour. The ingredients are fresh and light with lots of lemon grass, basil, coriander and mint. The chilli peppers pack a slow, nose-running burn. And pungent *náam plaa* (fish sauce; generally made from anchovies) adds a touch of the salty sea. Throw in a little zest of lime and a pinch of sugar and the ingredients make a symphony of flavours that becomes more interesting with each bite. A relationship with Thai food has a long courtship phase – at first the flavours are too assertive and foreign, the hot too hot, the fish sauce too fishy. But with practice you'll smell rice cooking in the morning and crave a fiery curry instead of dull toast and jam. Now you are 'eating', which in Thai literally means to 'eat rice', or *kin khâo*.

Thailand is a country where it is cheaper and tastier to eat out than to cook at home. Day and night markets, pushcart vendors, makeshift stalls, open-air restaurants – prices stay low because of few or no overheads, and cooks become famous in all walks of life for a particular dish. It is possible to eat well and cheaply without ever stepping foot into a formal restaurant. No self-respecting shoestringer would shy away from the pushcarts in Thailand for fear of stomach troubles. The hygiene standards are some of the best in the region, and sitting next to the wok you can see all the action, unlike some of the guesthouses where food is assembled in a darkened hovel.

Take a walk through the day markets and you will see mounds of clay-coloured pastes all lined up like art supplies. These are the finely ground herbs and seasonings that create the backbone for Thai *kaeng* (curries). The paste is thinned with coconut milk and decorated with vegetables and meat. Although it is the consistency of a watery soup, *kaeng* is not eaten like Western-style soup, but is ladled onto a plate of rice.

For breakfast and late-night snacks, Thais nosh on *kŭaytĭaw*, a noodle soup with chicken or pork and vegetables. There are two major types of noodles you can choose from: *sên lek* (thin) and *sên yài* (wide and flat). Before you dig into your steaming bowl, first use the chopsticks (or a spoon) to cut the noodles into smaller segments so they are easier to pick up. Then add to taste a few teaspoonfuls of the provided spices: dried red chilli, sugar, fish sauce and vinegar. Now you have the true taste of Thailand in front of you. The weapons of choice when eating noodles (either *kŭaytĭaw* or *phàt thai*) are chopsticks, a rounded soup spoon or a fork.

Not sure what to order at some of the popular dinner restaurants? Reliable favourites are *yam plaa mèuk* (spicy squid salad with mint leaves, coriander and Chinese celery), *tôm yam kûng* (coconut soup with prawns, often translated as 'hot and sour soup') or its sister dish *tôm khàa kài* (coconut soup with chicken and galangal).

At the simple open-air restaurants there is a standard range of dishes that every cook worth their fish sauce can make. These are the greatest hits of the culinary menu and include the following:

kài phàt bai kà-phrao – fiery stir-fry of chopped chicken, chillies, garlic and fresh basil
khâo phàt – fried rice
phàt phrík thai krà-thiam – stir-fried chicken or pork with black pepper and garlic
phàt thai – fried rice noodles, bean sprouts, peanuts, eggs, chillies and often prawns
phàt phàk khanáa – stir-fried Chinese greens, simple but delicious

Thais are social eaters: meals are rarely taken alone and dishes are meant to be shared. Usually a small army of plates will be placed in the centre of the table, with individual servings of rice in front of each diner. The protocol goes like this – ladle a spoonful of food at a time on to your plate of rice. Dishes aren't passed in Thailand; instead you reach across the table to the different items. Using the spoon like a fork and your fork like a knife, steer the food (with the fork) onto your spoon, which enters your mouth. To the Thais placing a fork in the mouth is just plain weird. When you are full, leave a little rice on your plate (an empty plate is a silent request for more rice) and place your fork so that it is cradled by the spoon in the centre of the plate.

Even when eating with a gang of *faràng*, it is still wise to order 'family style', as dishes are rarely synchronised. Ordering individually will leave one person staring politely at a piping hot plate, and another staring wistfully at the kitchen.

Drink

Water purified for drinking is simply called *náam dèum* (drinking water), whether boiled or filtered. All water offered in restaurants, offices or homes will be purified. Ice is generally safe in Thailand. *Chaa* (tea) and *kaa-fae* (coffee) are prepared strong, milky and sweet – an instant morning buzz.

Thanks to the tropical bounty, exotic fruit juices are sold on every corner. Thais prefer a little salt to cut the sweetness of the juice; the salt also has some mystical power to make a hot day tolerable. Most drinks are available in a clear plastic bag designed especially for takeaway customers; in time you'll come to prefer the bag to a conventional glass.

Cheap beer appears hand-in-hand with backpacker ghettos. Beer Chang and Beer Singha (pronounced 'sing', not 'sing-ha') are a couple of local brands you'll learn to love, although they pack a punch. Thais have created yet another innovative method for beating the heat; they drink their beer with ice to keep the beverage cool and crisp.

More of a ritual than a beverage, Thai whisky (Mekong and Sang Thip brands) usually runs with a distinct crowd – soda water, Coke and ice. Fill the short glass with ice cubes, two-thirds whisky, one-third soda and a splash of Coke. Thai tradition dictates the youngest in the crowd is responsible for filling the other drinkers' glasses. Many travellers prefer to go straight to the ice bucket with shared straws, not forgetting a dash of Red Bull for a cocktail to keep them going.

GAY & LESBIAN TRAVELLERS

Gays won't have a problem travelling in Thailand as the country has a long history of homosexuality. Prominent gay communities exist in large cities such as Bangkok and Chiang Mai, and gay pride events are celebrated in Bangkok, Pattaya and Phuket. While public displays of affection are common (and usually platonic) between members of the same sex, you should refrain from anything beyond friendly handholding for the sake of social etiquette.

Gay, lesbian and transsexual Thais are generally tolerated, living peaceably in even the most conservative Thai towns. All is not love and understanding, though. Labelled 'sexual deviants', suspected gays are barred from studying to become teachers or from joining the military.

Utopia (www.utopia-asia.com) is a good starting point for more information on Thailand for the gay traveller. **Anjaree Group** (☎ 0 2668 2185; PO Box 322, Th Ratchadamnoen, Bangkok 10200) is Thailand's premier (and only) lesbian society.

HOLIDAYS

Businesses typically close and transportation becomes difficult during the following public holidays:

New Year's Day 1 January
National Labour Day 1 May
Coronation Day 5 May
Chulalongkorn Day King Chulalongkorn is honoured on 23 October.
King's Birthday (Father's Day) 5 December
Constitution Day 10 December
New Year's Eve 31 December

Also see p807 for details on festivals and events.

INTERNET ACCESS

You can't walk far without tripping over an internet café in Thailand. Connections tend to be slow and unreliable, but rates are usually cheap (20B to 50B per hour).

INTERNET RESOURCES

Bangkok Post (www.bangkokpost.com) This English-language newspaper posts its entire newspaper content online; check out Bernard Trink's 'Night Owl' column for this dirty old man's unabashed coverage of the go-go bar scene, as well as wit and wisdom.
Elephant Guide (www.elephantguide.com) Find news and reviews of Bangkok restaurants, clubs and events.
Nation (www.nationmultimedia.com) Another English-language newspaper that also posts content on the web.
Thaifootball.com (www.thaifootball.com) The online headquarters of the Thai national football team profiles players and posts news and scores. Great prereading for conversations with taxi drivers.
TourismThailand.org (www.tourismthailand.org) Thailand's official tourism website covers major tourist spots and lists operators.
Virtual Hilltribe Museum (www.hilltribe.org) This virtual hill-tribe museum is a good way to learn about the hill tribes of northern Thailand and etiquette in minority villages.

LEGAL MATTERS

In general, Thai police don't hassle foreigners, especially tourists. One major exception is in regard to drugs (see p805).

If you are arrested for any offence, the police will allow you the opportunity to make a phone call to your embassy or consulate in

Thailand, if you have one, or to a friend or relative if not. Thai law does not presume an indicted detainee to be either 'guilty' or 'innocent' but rather a 'suspect', whose guilt or innocence will be decided in court. Trials are usually speedy.

MAPS

The Roads Association of Thailand produces a useful bilingual road atlas, *Thailand Highway Map*. Updated every year, it has city maps, distance charts and an index.

MEDIA

Newspapers

Thailand is considered to have the freest print media in Southeast Asia, although there is self-censorship in matters relating to the monarchy, and the Royal Police Department reserves the power to suspend publishing licences for national security reasons. The *Bangkok Post* in the morning and the *Nation* in the afternoon are the country's two English-language newspapers.

Radio

Thailand has more than 400 radio stations, almost all of them government owned and operated. English-language broadcasts of the international news services can be picked up over short-wave radio. The frequencies and schedules appear in the *Post* and *Nation*.

TV

Thailand possesses five VHF TV networks based in Bangkok, all but one of which are government operated. The single private network, ITV, was taken over by the government's public relations department in 2007 and is now called Thai Independent Television (TITV).

MONEY

The baht (B) is divided into 100 satang, although 25 and 50 satang are the smallest coins that you're likely to see. Coins come in 1B, 5B and 10B denominations. Notes are in 20B (green), 50B (blue), 100B (red), 500B (purple) and 1000B (beige) denominations of varying shades and sizes.

ATMs

All major Thai banks, which are well distributed throughout the country, offer ATM services; most of the machines will accept international credit and debit cards. ATMs typically dispense 1000B notes that should be broken at 7-Elevens or guesthouses rather than in the market.

Bargaining

Bargaining is mandatory in markets and small family-run stores, and with túk-túk and taxi drivers (unless the cab is metered). By and large bargaining is not appropriate in hotels or guesthouses unless staff initiate it, but you can ask politely if there's anything cheaper. Always smile and never become frustrated.

Credit Cards

Credit cards are widely accepted at upmarket hotels, restaurants and other business establishments. Visa and MasterCard are the most commonly accepted, followed by American Express (Amex) and Diners Club. Cash advances are available on Visa and MasterCard at many banks and exchange booths.

Exchanging Money

Banks give the best exchange rates and hotels give the worst. In the larger towns and tourist destinations, there are also foreign-exchange kiosks that open longer hours, usually from 8am to 8pm. Since banks charge commission and duty for each travellers cheque cashed, use larger cheque denominations to save on commission. British pounds and euros are second to the US dollar in general acceptability.

Exchange rates at the time this book went to press were as follows:

Country	Unit	Baht (B)
Australia	A$1	26.68
Cambodia	1000r	7.94
Canada	C$1	31.14
Euro zone	€1	44.39
Japan	¥100	27.81
Laos	1000 kip	3.34
Malaysia	RM1	9.18
New Zealand	NZ$1	22.60
Singapore	S$1	21.08
UK	£1	63.80
USA	US$1	32.00

LEGAL AGE

- voting starts at 18
- you can begin driving at 18
- sex is legal at 15

THAILAND

POST

The Thai postal system is relatively efficient and few travellers complain about undelivered mail or lost parcels. Never send cash or small valuable objects through the postal system, even if the items are insured. Poste restante can be received at any town that has a post office.

RESPONSIBLE TRAVEL

Be aware about having a negative impact on the environment or the local culture. Read p680 for guidance on observing social mores. See p4 for suggestions on treading lightly through Thailand's environment and through tribal peoples' villages.

Despite Thailand's reputation among sex tourists, prostitution was declared illegal in the 1950s. Many of the sex workers are uneducated women or girls from villages who are struggling to support children or who have been sold into the business by their parents. The government does little to enforce anti-prostitution laws in cases of consenting adults; however, a jail term of four to 20 years and/or a fine up to 40,000B can be imposed on anyone caught having sex with a person under 15 years of age. If the child is under 13, the sentence can amount to life imprisonment. Many Western countries have also instituted extraterritorial legislation where citizens can be charged for child prostitution offences committed abroad.

The Thai government encourages people to help eradicate child prostitution by reporting child sexual abuse. You can contact **End Child Prostitution & Traffic International** (Ecpat; ☎ 0 2215 3388; www.ecpat.org; 328 Th Phayathai, Bangkok 10400), a global network of organisations that works to stop child prostitution, child pornography and the traffic of children for sexual purposes.

STUDYING

Thai cooking, traditional medicine, language, *muay thai* (Thai boxing): the possibilities of studying in Thailand are endless and range from formal lectures to week-long retreats.

Especially popular are meditation courses for Western students of Buddhism. Unique to Buddhism is the system of meditation known as *vipassana*, a Pali word that roughly translates as 'insight'. Foreigners who come to study *vipassana* can choose from dozens of temples and meditation centres. Thai language is usually the medium of instruction but several places provide instruction in English. Contact details for some popular meditation-oriented centres are given in the city, town and province sections of this chapter. Instruction and accommodation are free at temples, but donations are expected.

Described by some as a 'brutally pleasant experience', Thai massage does not directly seek to relax the body, but instead uses the hands, thumbs, fingers, elbows, forearms, knees and feet to work the traditional pressure points. The client's body is also pulled, twisted and manipulated in ways that have been described as 'passive yoga'. The objective is to distribute energies evenly throughout the nervous system to create a harmony of physical energy flows. The muscular-skeletal system is also manipulated in ways that can be compared to modern physiotherapy. Thailand offers ample opportunities to study its unique tradition of massage therapy. Wat Pho (p700) in Bangkok is considered the master source for all Thai massage pedagogy, although Chiang Mai (p731) boasts a 'softer' version.

Training in *muay thai* takes place at dozens of boxing camps around the country. Be forewarned, however: training is gruelling and features full-contact sparring. Many centres are reluctant to take on foreign trainees. Rates vary from US$50 to US$250 per week, including food and accommodation. The website www.muaythai.com contains loads of information including the addresses of training camps. Also see the Bangkok (p700) and Chiang Mai (p731) sections for information on *muay thai* training programmes in these two cities.

Several language schools in Bangkok and Chiang Mai offer courses in Thai language. Tuition fees average around 250B per hour. See the Courses sections in this chapter for further detail.

TELEPHONE

The telephone system in Thailand, operated by the government-subsidised Telephone Organization of Thailand (TOT) under the Communications Authority of Thailand (CAT), is quite efficient and offers International Direct Dial (IDD) universally. In smaller towns these services are available at the main post office. You can make international calls from public telephone booths with a prepaid phonecard available from 7-Eleven stores. Rates tend to be about the same as the government phone offices. Guesthouses also offer phone services that are considerably more expensive.

Roaming charges are quite reasonable in Thailand for those with mobile phones. There are several cheap international call carriers that offer significant savings on international calls from a mobile: dial out using ☎ 008 or ☎ 009 for a bargain.

The telephone country code for Thailand is ☎ 66. All Thai phone numbers listed in this book are preceded by ☎ 0, but you only need to include the zero when dialling numbers within Thailand. City prefixes were recently integrated into the phone numbers for all calls regardless of their origin.

TOILETS

As in many other Asian countries, the 'squat toilet' is the norm except in hotels and guesthouses geared towards tourists and international business travellers. These sit more-or-less flush with the surface of the floor, with two footpads on either side. For travellers who have never used a squat toilet, it takes a bit of getting used to.

Even in places where sit-down toilets are installed, the plumbing may not be designed to take toilet paper. In such cases the usual washing bucket will be standing nearby or there will be a waste basket where you're supposed to place used toilet paper.

TOURIST INFORMATION

The **Tourist Authority of Thailand** (TAT; www.tat.or.th) has offices throughout the country, which are helpful for bus schedules, local maps and finding accommodation. Contact information for regional offices is listed under each town.

TRAVELLERS WITH DISABILITIES

Thailand presents one large, ongoing obstacle course for the mobility-impaired. With its high kerbs, uneven pavements and nonstop traffic, Bangkok can be particularly difficult. Rarely are there ramps or other access points for wheelchairs.

For wheelchair travellers, any trip to Thailand will require advance planning. The book *Exotic Destinations for Wheelchair Travelers* by Ed Hansen and Bruce Gordon contains a useful chapter on seven locations in Thailand. See p923 for organisations promoting travel for special-needs travellers.

VISAS

Citizens of 39 countries (including most European countries, Australia, New Zealand and the USA) can enter Thailand visa-free for 30 days at no charge. See the website of Thailand's **Ministry of Foreign Affairs** (www.mfa.go.th) for the full story. For a longer stay, just leave and re-enter the country at any border point: upon re-entry you get another 30 days, thank you very much. You can also extend the 30-day visa for seven to 10 days at any Thai immigration office for 500B.

With advance planning, a 60-day tourist visa is available from Thai embassies or consulates worldwide (see p807). Application fees are usually US$30 and take up to a week. Contact the embassy for an application form and additional instructions.

The Non-Immigrant Visa is good for 90 days, must be applied for in your home country, costs US$60 and is not difficult to obtain if you are travelling for business, study, retirement or an extended family visit. For anyone planning on staying longer than three months, this is the one to go for.

If you overstay your visa, the usual penalty is a fine of 200B for each extra day, with a 20,000B limit; fines can be paid at any official exit point or in advance at the **Bangkok Immigration Office** (Map pp694-5; ☎ 0 2287 3101; Soi Suan Phlu, Th Sathon Tai; 🕑 9am-noon & 1-4.30pm Mon-Fri, 9am-noon Sat); go to the Investigation Unit on the 4th floor.

Cambodian and Lao visas are now available at most land-border crossings with Thailand and all international airports. For trips to Myanmar, short-visit visas are available for day crossings, but get a visa in advance if you are flying into Yangon. Most visitors to Malaysia do not require a visa.

Immigration offices in major centres:

Chiang Mai (off Map p730; ☎ 0 5320 1755; ☎ 9am-noon & 1-4.30pm Mon-Fri, 9am-noon Sat) Located near the airport, off Rte 1141.

Hat Yai (Map p783; ☎ 0 7425 7019; Th Phetkasem) Near the railway bridge, in the same complex as the tourist police station.

Nakhon Phanom (☎ 0 4251 1235; Th Sunthon Wijit; 🕑 8.30am-4.30pm Mon-Fri)

Nong Khai (☎ 0 4241 2089; 🕑 8.30am-4.30pm Mon-Fri) On the road leading to the Thai-Lao Friendship Bridge, south of the bus stop.

Phuket Town (off Map p794; ☎ 0 7621 2108) South of town, almost at the end of Th Phuket near Saphan Hin park.

Ranong (☎ 0 7782 2016; Th Ruangrat; 🕑 8.30am-6pm Mon-Fri) Seven hundred metres north of Saphan Pla pier, 4.5km from Ranong centre. Border check for travellers crossing to Myanmar by boat.

Satun (☎ 0 7271 1080; 🕑 8.30am-4.30pm Mon-Fri) Processes visa extensions for 500B. There's also an immigration office at Tha Tammalang, but it doesn't extend visas.

Songkhla (☎ 0 7430 1011; Th Lang Prarum; 🕑 8.30am-4.30pm Mon-Fri)

VOLUNTEERING

Voluntary and paid positions with charitable organisations can be found in the education, development or public health sectors.

Mon, Karen and Burmese refugee camps along the Thailand–Myanmar border often need volunteers. Since none of the camps are officially sanctioned by the Thai government, few of the big NGOs or multilateral organisations are involved here. If this interests you, travel to Mae Sot and ask around for the 'unofficial' camp locations, or contact **Burma Volunteer Programme** (www.geocities.com/maesotesl), which offers three-month volunteer jobs teaching English or working on human rights issues.

Other volunteer organisations:

Ecovolunteer Programme (www.ecovolunteer.org; per person US$600-800) A network of NGOs working on environmental issues; in Thailand volunteers collect data on mangrove forests, study sea turtles or help run an animal rescue sanctuary. Minimum stay is around three weeks, but longer stays are encouraged; an average stay is around two to three months.

Habitat for Humanity (www.habitat.org; per person US$2000-3000) One- to three-week house-building trips in northeast Thailand with a charitable organisation founded by former US president Jimmy Carter.

Human Development Foundation (www.fatherjoe.org) A community outreach centre in the Bangkok slum of Khlong Toei; volunteers work on basic medical care, HIV/AIDS education and drug prevention.

WOMEN TRAVELLERS

By and large women are safe travelling in groups or solo through Thailand. Extra caution needs to be exercised at night, especially when returning home from a bar or arriving in a new town late at night. Thais, both men and women, are chatty and will extend the hand of friendship, give you a ride or take you to the disco. Often accepting these invitations is a fun experience, but women should be aware that Thai men don't adhere to their own culture's rules when dealing with foreign women. While hand-holding, hugging or any other public contact between members of the opposite sex is a huge no-no in Thai society, Thai men think it is appropriate to touch (however innocently) foreign women even if the advances aren't encouraged.

Despite Thailand's peaceful nature, rape is a concern. Over the past decade, several foreign women have been attacked while travelling alone in remote areas and there have been several high-profile murders. Still, given the huge tourist numbers visiting Thailand, there is no need to be paranoid.

WORKING

Teaching English is one of the easiest ways to immerse yourself into a Thai community. Those with academic credentials, such as teaching certificates or degrees in English as a second language (ESL) or English as a foreign language (EFL), get first crack at the better-paying jobs at universities and international schools. But there are hundreds of language schools for every variety of native English speaker.

Maintained by an EFL teacher in Bangkok, www.ajarn.com has tips on where to find teaching jobs and how to deal with Thai classrooms, as well as current job listings.

Rajabhat Institute (☎ 0 2628 5281, ext 2906; teerawat23@hotmail.com; Teerawat Wangmanee, Office of Rajabhat Institute, Ministry of Education, Th Ratchadamnoen Nok, Bangkok 10300) has one-year English-teaching positions available in 41 teachers colleges right across the country. These positions pay well by Thai standards, and most students are preparing to be the country's next generation of primary- and secondary-school English teachers.

Vietnam

HIGHLIGHTS

- **Northern mountains** – hill-tribe women hawking handmade tapestries in Sapa, and a base for visiting tribal villages set in lush terraced valleys as well as Fansipan, Vietnam's highest peak (p849)
- **Hanoi** – frenetic scenes of modern Hanoi play out in a labyrinth of French colonial buildings (p823)
- **Ho Chi Minh City** – visiting remnants of the American War by day and living it up by night in the backpacker area that never sleeps (p881)
- **Hoi An** – roaming Cham ruins at dawn, then sunbathing and sampling local culinary specialities dressed in custom-made clothes (p862)
- **Nha Trang** – beaches, diving and a thriving nightlife lets you choose your own adventure (p867)
- **Off the beaten track** – heading to Phu Quoc Island for the ultimate in chill, with long stretches of untouched nature and pristine coral reefs (p901)

FAST FACTS

- **Budget** US$25 a day
- **Capital** Hanoi
- **Costs** guesthouse in Hanoi US$8 to US$15, four-hour bus ride US$4 to US$6, beer US$0.65
- **Country code** ☎ 84
- **Languages** Vietnamese, ethnic dialects
- **Money** US$1 = approx 16,000d (dong)
- **Phrases** *xin chao* (hello), *tam biet* (goodbye), *cam on* (thanks), *xin loi* (sorry), *khong cam on, di bo* (no thanks, I'll walk)
- **Population** 85.2 million
- **Time** GMT + seven hours
- **Visas** arrange in advance, with fixed arrival and departure dates; US$30-60 for 30 days

TRAVEL HINT

To avoid unwanted attention from touts, say no politely and keep moving; take breaks from big cities to enjoy the country's natural beauty and warm people.

OVERLAND ROUTES

Take a boat to Phnom Penh in Cambodia from Chau Do, or a high-speed ferry to the Chinese border from Halong City or Haiphong. Those who prefer terra firma can travel via bus to Cambodia and Laos, or by bus or rail to China.

Vietnam is a country in overdrive that's a wonder to watch and sometimes overwhelming. Nearly mythical in the Western imagination thanks to a slew of American War movies, this is the place everyone will be asking about back home and you'll have more than a few good stories to share.

The big cities feel like Wild West towns where the horses have been replaced by a stampede of motorbikes and everyone's gunning to make a buck. Make no mistake, though, there's plenty of peace and quiet here but unlike other places you have to seek it out.

The national parks are lightly visited, but are often only a few hours off the main tourist trail. Bach Ma National Park is a pristine mountain getaway near Hué, at the midpoint of many a traveller's itinerary – in the words of the old Coca-Cola slogan, it's the pause that refreshes. Think of the calm spots here as the sweetened condensed milk in an ice coffee so strong it would be illegal in other countries. Both are good by themselves, but together they're even better.

CURRENT EVENTS

The Communist Party is alive, but not well. Only a very small percentage of the population are party members and government officials are struggling to keep their hands on the steering wheel of the zooming economy.

There is only one political party and people who speak out are often jailed for long periods without a trial. In 2004 a protest by hill-tribe people against government restrictions on religious practices and confiscation of ancestral lands saw 10 people dead in clashes with police (the government claims only two people died). Three protestors received long prison sentences.

The country has a nascent prodemocracy movement with the rather stark name of Bloc 8406 (named for 8 April 2006, when it issued a prodemocracy manifesto), but a number of its founding members have been harassed and arrested. The movement's leader, Catholic priest Father Ly, was sentenced to eight years in prison and five years of house arrest in March 2007. If a picture is worth a thousand words there is not much that's good to say about the authorities involved: a televised image from his trial shows a dour prison guard with a hand clamped over the priest's mouth.

Nevertheless, foreign investors are setting up joint ventures with Vietnamese companies, cultural exchange is exerting international influence over fashion, technology and a new generation, and Vietnam is speeding towards the future.

HISTORY

Early Vietnam

The sophisticated Indian-influenced kingdom of Funan flourished from the 1st to the 6th centuries AD in the Mekong Delta area. Archaeological evidence reveals that Funan's busy trading port of Oc-Eo in the Mekong area had contact with China, India, Persia and even the Mediterranean.

Around the late 2nd century AD when the Cham empire was putting down roots in the Danang area, the Chinese had conquered the Red River Delta near Hanoi. So began a 1000-year pattern of the Vietnamese resisting the yoke of Chinese rule, while at the same time adopting many Chinese innovations. The most famous act of resistance during this period (ending in AD 938) was the rebellion of the two Trung sisters (Hai Ba Trung), who drowned themselves rather than surrender to the Chinese.

By the 10th century, Vietnam had declared independence from China and begun almost 1000 years of a dynastic tradition. During this era, the Vietnamese successfully repulsed attacks by the Khmers, Chams, Mongols and Chinese, eventually assimilating the Cham civilisation into Vietnamese society.

Vietnam & the West

As far back as AD 166, Vietnam had contact with Europeans from the Rome of Marcus Aurelius. In the early 16th century European merchants and missionaries trickled into the country, among them the brilliant Alexandre de Rhodes who developed the *quoc ngu* script still used for written Vietnamese.

In 1858 a joint military force from France and the Spanish colony of the Philippines stormed Danang after several missionaries were killed. Early the following year, it seized Saigon. By 1883 the French had imposed a Treaty of Protectorate on Vietnam; French colonial rule often proved cruel and arbitrary. Ultimately, the most successful resistance came from the communists. The Vietnam Revolutionary Youth League was founded by Ho Chi Minh in 1925.

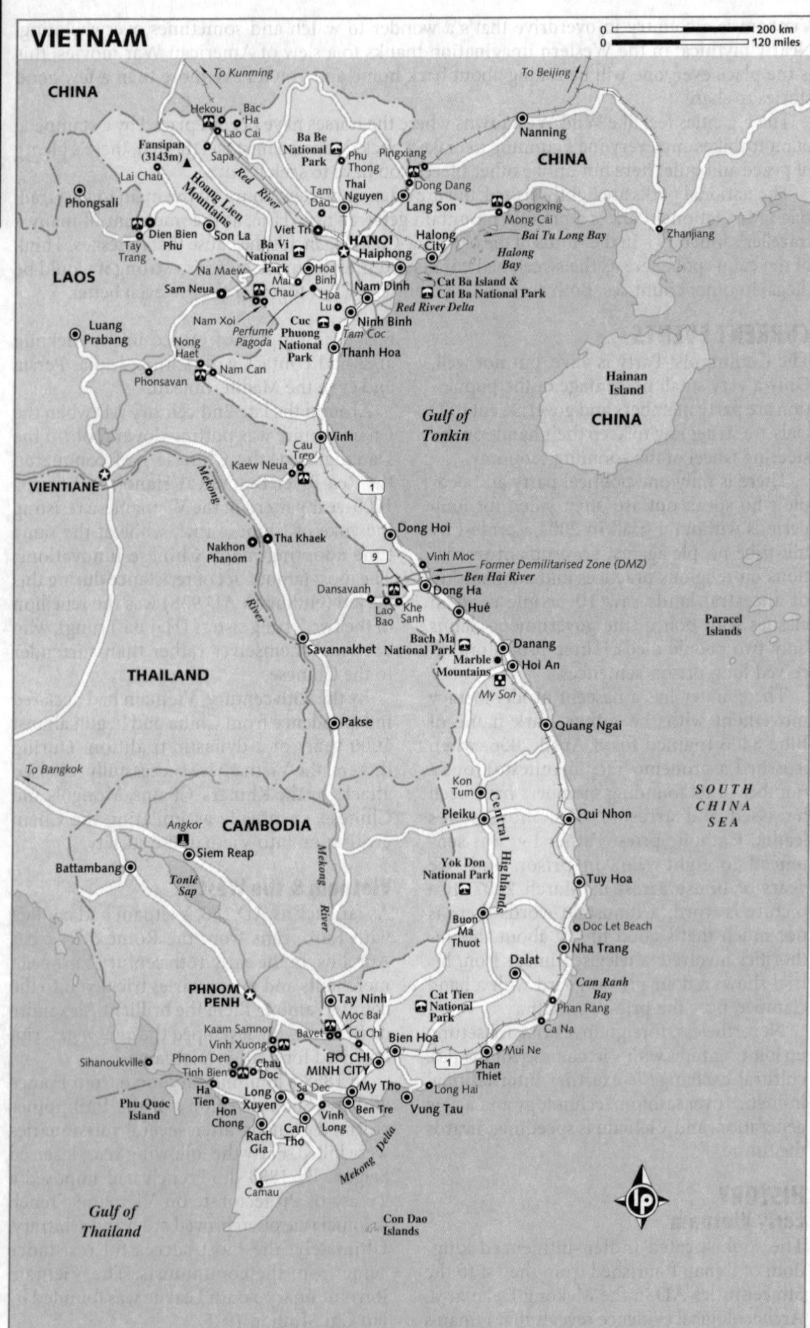
VIETNAM
0 200 km
0 120 miles
To Kunming
To Beijing
CHINA
Hekou
Bac Ha
Lao Cai
Sapa
Fansipan (3143m)
Hoang Lien Mountains
Red River
Lai Chau
Phongsali
Dien Bien Phu
Tay Trang
Son La
Ba Be National Park
Phu Thong
Tam Dao
Thai Nguyen
Viet Tri
Ba Vi National Park
HANOI
Haiphong
Pingxiang
Dong Dang
Lang Son
Nanning
CHINA
Dongxing
Mong Cai
Bai Tu Long Bay
Halong City
Halong Bay
Zhanjiang
Cat Ba Island & Cat Ba National Park
Red River Delta
LAOS
Na Maew
Sam Neua
Mai Chau
Hoa Binh
Hoa Lu
Nam Dinh
Ninh Binh
Nam Xoi
Perfume Pagoda
Cuc Phuong National Park
Tam Coc
Thanh Hoa
Luang Prabang
Nong Haet
Nam Can
Phonsavan
Hainan Island
CHINA
Gulf of Tonkin
Vinh
Cau Treo
Kaew Neua
VIENTIANE
Mekong
1
Dong Hoi
Nakhon Phanom
Tha Khaek
9
Vinh Moc
Former Demilitarised Zone (DMZ)
Ben Hai River
Dansavanh
Lao Bao
Khe Sanh
Dong Ha
Hué
River
Savannakhet
Bach Ma National Park
Danang
Marble Mountains
Hoi An
My Son
Paracel Islands
THAILAND
Pakse
Quang Ngai
To Bangkok
Kon Tum
Pleiku
Central Highlands
Qui Nhon
SOUTH CHINA SEA
Angkor
CAMBODIA
Siem Reap
Battambang
Tonlé Sap
Mekong River
Yok Don National Park
Tuy Hoa
Buon Ma Thuot
Doc Let Beach
Nha Trang
Dalat
Cam Ranh Bay
PHNOM PENH
Tay Ninh
Moc Bai
Cat Tien National Park
Phan Rang
Ca Na
Kaam Samnor
Bavet
Cu Chi
Vinh Xuong
Bien Hoa
Mui Ne
Sihanoukville
Phnom Den
Chau Doc
Tinh Bien
HO CHI MINH CITY
1
Phan Thiet
Ha Tien
Sa Dec
My Tho
Long Hai
Phu Quoc Island
Hon Chong
Long Xuyen
Vinh Long
Ben Tre
Vung Tau
Rach Gia
Can Tho
Mekong Delta
Camau
Gulf of Thailand
Con Dao Islands
lp

During WWII, the only group that significantly resisted the Japanese occupation was the communist-dominated Viet Minh. When WWII ended, Ho Chi Minh – whose Viet Minh forces already controlled large parts of the country – declared Vietnam independent. French efforts to reassert control soon led to violent confrontations and full-scale war. In May 1954, Viet Minh forces overran the French garrison at Dien Bien Phu.

The Geneva Accords of mid-1954 provided for a temporary division of Vietnam at the Ben Hai River. When Ngo Dinh Diem, the anticommunist, Catholic leader of the southern zone, refused to hold the scheduled 1956 elections, the Ben Hai line became the border between North and South Vietnam.

Around 1960 the Hanoi government changed its policy of opposition to the Diem regime from one of 'political struggle' to one of 'armed struggle'. The communist guerrilla group popularly known as the Viet Cong (VC) was founded.

A brutal ruler, Diem was assassinated in 1963 by his own troops. After Hanoi ordered units of the North Vietnamese Army (NVA) to infiltrate the South in 1964, the situation for the Saigon regime became desperate. In 1965 the USA committed its first combat troops, soon joined by soldiers from South Korea, Australia, Thailand and New Zealand.

As Vietnam celebrated the Lunar New Year in 1968, the VC launched a deadly surprise attack (the Tet Offensive), marking the beginning of the end of American involvement. The Paris Agreements, signed in 1973, provided for a cease-fire, the total withdrawal of US combat forces and the release of American prisoners of war.

Reunification

Saigon surrendered to the NVA on 30 April 1975. Vietnam's reunification by the communists meant liberation from more than a century of colonial repression, but it was soon followed by large-scale internal repression. Hundreds of thousands of southern Vietnamese fled the country, creating a flood of refugees for the next 15 years.

Vietnam's campaign of repression against the ethnic-Chinese, plus its invasion of Cambodia at the end of 1978, prompted China to attack Vietnam in 1979. The war lasted only 17 days, but Chinese-Vietnamese mistrust lasted well over a decade.

Transition & Globalisation

With the end of the Cold War and the collapse of the Soviet Union in 1991, Vietnam and Western nations sought *rapprochement*. The 1990s brought foreign investment and Asean (Association of South-East Asian Nations) membership. The USA established diplomatic relations with Vietnam in 1995, and in 2000, Bill Clinton became the first US president to visit northern Vietnam.

Vietnam is a country that's been dealing with a rapid transition since the mid 1990s, and the pace of social and economic change should quicken now that it has been accepted into the World Trade Organization (WTO).

COPY CULTURE

Even people who understand that pirating hurts legitimate businesses will have a hard time finding the real thing in Vietnam. A US-based software group estimates that 90% of the software for the Windows operating systems in Vietnam is pirated. The country's recent admission into the World Trade Organization (WTO), though, means that the pirating party may be coming to an end.

Vietnam has had antipiracy laws on the books for some time, but one of the conditions of WTO membership – and by extension, the international business ties needed to grow the economy – is that officials have to start cracking down on counterfeiting. Local newspapers have been reporting more police visits to the fake DVD shops in Hanoi, and international companies have been hosting seminars galore for customs officials on how to stop counterfeit goods from leaving the country.

The Vietnamese people have said they're afraid they won't be able to afford the technological basics, such as computer software, that they need to run a business or go to school. Nevertheless, some business people are accepting of the change, and in a few years there just might be one less hassle for travellers; the heads of reputable tour companies say they're looking forward to a future where it won't be so easy for others to steal their good name.

THE CULTURE

The National Psyche

It's been a long hard road to become an independent, unified country – and by long we mean thousands of years – and the Vietnamese have the art of getting ahead under the worst of conditions seemingly ingrained in their DNA.

The north-south divide lingers on. Southerners think people in the north are uptight and northerners think southerners aren't serious enough and obsessed with business.

Finally, keep in mind 'face' – or more importantly the art of not making the locals lose face. Face is all in much of Asia, and in Vietnam it is above all. This is why foreigners should never lose their tempers with the Vietnamese; this will bring unacceptable 'loss of face' to the individual involved and end any chance of a sensible solution to the dispute.

Lifestyle

Family, work, working with family, then more work. It's no surprise that the country has an unemployment rate of only 2% (guys lounging on their motorbike calling out to tourists are considered to be on the job), because people of all ages work from sunrise to late at night seven days per week on a regular basis.

Between working, people socialise over small meals throughout the day with friends and family and then return to back-breaking labour without a moment's hesitation.

Population

Vietnam's population hovers at around 84 million, making it the 13th most populous country in the world, and with its population growth rate it might soon hit the top 10. Vietnam is a young country, with an incredible 65% of the people under the age of 30. Traditionally a rural agrarian society, the race is on for the move to the cities to be a part of the economic surge.

RELIGION

Over the centuries, Confucianism, Taoism and Buddhism have fused with popular Chinese beliefs and ancient Vietnamese animism to form what's collectively known as the Triple Religion (Tam Giao). Most Vietnamese people identify with this belief system, but if asked, they'll usually say they're Buddhist. Vietnam also has a significant percentage of Catholics (7% of the population).

The unique and colourful Vietnamese sect called Caodaism was founded in the 1920s. It combines secular and religious philosophies of the East and West, and was based on séance messages revealed to the group's founder.

ARTS

Water Puppetry

Vietnam's ancient art of *roi nuoc* (water puppetry) originated in northern Vietnam at least 1000 years ago. Developed by rice farmers, the wooden puppets were manipulated by puppeteers using water-flooded rice paddies as their stage. Hanoi is the best place to see water-puppetry performances, which are accompanied by music played on traditional instruments.

Architecture

Most early Vietnamese buildings were made of wood and other materials that proved temporary in the tropical climate. The grand exception is the stunning towers built by Vietnam's ancient Cham culture. These are most numerous in central Vietnam. The Cham ruins at My Son (p867) are a major tourist draw.

Plenty of pagodas and temples founded hundreds of years ago are still functioning, but they have usually been rebuilt many times with little concern for the original.

Sculpture

Vietnamese sculpture has traditionally centred on religious themes and has functioned as an adjunct to architecture, especially that of pagodas, temples and tombs.

The Cham civilisation produced exquisite carved sandstone figures for its Hindu and Buddhist sanctuaries. Cham sculpture was profoundly influenced by Indian art but over the centuries it managed to also incorporate Indonesian and Vietnamese elements. The largest single collection of Cham sculpture is at the Museum of Cham Sculpture (p860) in Danang.

MUST READ

The Girl in the Picture by Denise Chong (2000), tells the fascinating story of how one picture – of a terrified, naked child running from a bombing attack – changed many lives.

MUST SEE

The Daughter from Danang (2002) is a gut-wrenching documentary about a woman sent to the US for adoption as a child and her return to Vietnam.

Cinema

Vietnamese cinema is the most exported of the contemporary arts. Tran Anh Hung, who fled to France, is the most famous Vietnam-born *auteur;* he wrote and directed *The Scent of Green Papaya, Cyclo* and *Vertical Rays of the Sun*. The lyrical, sombre *Buffalo Boy*, by Minh Nguyen-Vo, was Vietnam's submission to the Academy Awards in 2005.

Music

Like the rest of Southeast Asia, Vietnam has a thriving domestic pop scene. The most celebrated artist is Khanh Ly, who left Vietnam in 1975 for the USA.

Painting & Photography

The work of contemporary painters and photographers covers a wide swathe of styles and gives a glimpse into the modern Vietnamese psyche. The work of one of the country's most acclaimed photographers, Long Thanh, is on display in Nha Trang (see p869).

Theatre & Dance

It's sometimes possible to catch modern dance, classical ballet and stage plays in Hanoi and Ho Chi Minh City (HCMC; Saigon). Check the *Guide* or *Time Out* for current theatre or dance listings in Hanoi and HCMC.

ENVIRONMENT

The Land

Vietnam stretches more than 1600km along the eastern coast of the Indochinese peninsula. The country's area is 326,797 sq km, making it a bit bigger than Italy and slightly smaller than Japan. Vietnam has 3451km of mostly gorgeous coastline and 3818km of land borders.

The most striking geological features are the karst formations (limestone regions with caves and underground streams), particularly in the north around Halong Bay and Tam Coc.

Wildlife

With a wide range of habitats – from equatorial lowlands to high, temperate plateaus and

DOING YOUR BIT

- Vietnam has a low level of environmental awareness and responsibility, and many people remain unaware of the implications of littering. Try and raise awareness of these issues by example, and dispose of litter as responsibly as possible.
- Money talks; spending it at environmentally aware businesses sends a clear message to others. For example, proprietors of some beachfront accommodations make it a point to keep the beach and swimming area litter free.
- Plastic water bottles wreak havoc on the environment; kudos goes to the small but growing number of travellers who have been refilling their bottles from the large jugs at bars and restaurants.
- Vietnam's fauna and flora are under considerable threat from domestic consumption and the illegal international trade in animal and plant products. Though it may be 'exotic' to try wild meat such as muntjac, bats, deer, sea horses, shark fins and so on – or to buy products made from endangered plants and animals – doing so will add to the demand for them.
- When visiting coral reefs and snorkelling or diving, or simply boating, be careful not to touch live coral or anchor boats on it, as this damages the coral. If it's possible to anchor in a sandy area, try to convince the operator to do so and indicate your willingness to swim to the coral. Don't buy coral souvenirs.
- When visiting limestone caves, be aware that touching the formations hinders growth and turns the limestone black. Don't break off the stalactites or stalagmites as they take lifetimes to regrow. Don't carve graffiti onto limestone formations, cave walls or other rock.
- Do not remove or buy 'souvenirs' that have been taken from historical sites and natural areas.

even alpine peaks – the wildlife of Vietnam is enormously diverse. It is home to 275 species of mammal, more than 800 species of bird, 180 species of reptile, 80 species of amphibian, hundreds of species of fish and thousands of species of invertebrates.

Officially, the government has recognised 54 species of mammal and 60 species of bird as endangered. In a positive sign, some wildlife populations are re-establishing themselves in reforested areas. Birds, fish and crustaceans have reappeared in replanted mangrove forests.

National Parks

There are now almost 30 national parks in Vietnam. The most interesting and accessible national parks are Cat Ba, Ba Be and Cuc Phuong in the north; Bach Ma in the centre; and Cat Tien and Yok Don in the south.

Environmental Issues

The country is facing a slew of environmental problems. Logging and slash-and-burn agricultural practices contribute to deforestation and soil degradation, pollution and overfishing threaten marine life, groundwater contamination limits potable water supply, growing urban industrialisation and population migration are rapidly degrading the environment.

The government passed environmental protection laws in 1993 but changing the decades-long habits of farmers and loggers is easier said than done and even industrial-waste enforcement has been patchy. The exhaust fumes from motorbikes are so bad in the cities that a face mask to breathe easier is standard motorbike gear.

To its credit, the government has been proactive about expanding the boundaries of national parks and adding new protected areas, and has made the planting and taking care of trees part of the school curriculum.

TRANSPORT

GETTING THERE & AWAY

Air

Hanoi has fewer international flights than HCMC, but with a change of aircraft in Hong Kong or Bangkok you can get to either city. Danang international airport offers connections to Bangkok, Hong Kong and Singapore.

Maximise your time and minimise cost and hassle by booking an open-jaw ticket – then you can fly into HCMC and out of Hanoi (or vice versa). These tickets save you from backtracking and are easily arranged in hubs such as Bangkok and Hong Kong.

Keep in mind that international flights purchased in Vietnam are always more expensive than the same tickets purchased outside. For more information about flights from outside Southeast Asia, see p925; from within the region, see p927.

Airlines flying to and from Vietnam within the region often operate code-share flights with Vietnam Airlines. The following phone numbers are for Hanoi; when ringing from outside the city, add ☎ 04 as the area code.

Air Asia (code AK; www.airasia.com) Flights between Kuala Lumpur and Hanoi.

Air France (code AF; www.airfrance.com) Flights between Bangkok and HCMC, Hanoi.

Bangkok Airways (code PG; www.bangkokair.com) Flights between HCMC, Siem Reap and Hong Kong.

Cathay Pacific (code CX; ☎ 826 7298; www.cathaypacific.com) Flights between Hong Kong and HCMC, Hanoi. It occasionally has All Asia Pass specials.

Lao Airlines (code QV; www.laoairlines.com) Flights between Vientiane and Hanoi.

Malaysia Airlines (code MH; ☎ 826 8819; www.malaysiaairlines.com) Flies from Kuala Lumpur to HCMC, Hanoi.

Singapore Airlines (code SQ; ☎ 826 8888; www.singaporeair.com) Flights between Singapore and HCMC, Hanoi.

Thai Airways International (THAI, code TG; ☎ 826 7921; www.thaiair.com) Flights between Bangkok and HCMC, Hanoi.

Tiger Airways (code TR; www.tigerairways.com) Flights between Singapore and Hanoi.

Vietnam Airlines (code VN; ☎ 943 9660; www.vietnamairlines.com) Operates daily flights throughout the region.

Land

There are land-border crossing points from Vietnam into China (p837, p843 and p848), Laos and Cambodia; see p932 for a full list of border crossings for Laos and Cambodia. At the time of writing there was also word that a new border crossing between Vietnam and

> **DEPARTURE TAX**
>
> There is an international departure tax of US$14 from the main airports at Hanoi, HCMC and Danang. Dollars or dong will do, but take small change if paying in dollars.

Cambodia had opened up at Xa Xia (Vietnam) and Prek Chek (Cambodia).

GETTING AROUND

Air

Air travel within Vietnam is dominated by **Vietnam Airlines** (code VN; ☎ in Hanoi 04-943 9660, in Ho Chi Minh City 08-832 0320; www.vietnamairlines.com). Its competitor **Pacific Airlines** (code BL; ☎ in Hanoi 04-851 5350, in Ho Chi Minh City 08-823 1285; www.pacificairlines .com.vn) offers limited routes between Ho Chi Minh City, Danang and Hanoi. The reasonably priced domestic flights can trim precious travel time off a busy itinerary.

A domestic departure tax of 25,000d is included in the ticket price.

Bicycle

Long-distance cycling is becoming a popular way to tour Vietnam, most of which is flat or moderately hilly. With the loosening of borders in Southeast Asia, more and more people are planning overland trips by bicycle. All you need to know about bicycle travel in Vietnam, Laos and Cambodia is contained in Lonely planet's *Cycling Vietnam, Laos & Cambodia*.

The main hazard for bicycle riders is the traffic, and it's wise to avoid certain areas (notably National Hwy 1). The best cycling is in the northern mountains and the Central Highlands, though you'll have to cope with some big hills.

Purchasing a good bicycle in Vietnam is hit or miss. It's recommended that you bring one from abroad, along with a good helmet and spare parts.

Hotels and some travel agencies rent bicycles for about US$1 to US$3 per day and it is a great way to explore some of the smaller cities. Be sure to check the condition of the bicycle before pedalling into the sunset.

Boat

Commercial hydrofoils connect HCMC with the beach resort of Vung Tau, as well as points in the Mekong Delta. The extensive network of canals in the Mekong Delta makes getting around by boat feasible in the far south. Travellers to Phu Quoc Island can catch ferries from Rach Gia.

In the northeast, fast and slow boats connect Haiphong with Cat Ba Island in Halong Bay. Day cruises on Halong Bay are extremely popular.

Bus

Bus drivers rely on the horn as a defensive driving technique. Motorists use the highway like a speedway; accidents, unsurprisingly, are common. On bus journeys, keep a close eye on your bags, never accept drinks from strangers, and consider bringing earplugs. Try to sit away from little kids; they have the bad habit of getting sick.

LOCAL BUS & MINIBUS

On the highways you'll often see big public buses packed to the gills. It's the cheapest means of getting around and these buses cover the entire country. They can sometimes be crowded and experience breakdowns, but overall they're not a bad way to go for shorter trips.

A step up – in speed at least – are the express minibuses that go everywhere the public buses go. Run by private companies, they're a bit more expensive. They'll pick up passengers along the way until full – minibuses can sometimes get overcrowded as well and unfortunately often have video screens that play Vietnamese music videos on the loud side. Private minibuses almost always have a stop in the middle of nowhere for food – open-tour bus travellers (see p822) can rest easy knowing that the Vietnamese get the same abuse.

It's a good idea to try to buy tickets at the station the day before; while not always possible, this reduces your chances of having to bargain with the driver immediately before departure.

The only time we recommend avoiding these private minibuses (and the public ones) is around Tet when drivers are working overtime and routes are dangerously overcrowded.

Generally, buses of all types leave very early in the morning, but shorter, more

> **THINGS CHANGE...**
>
> The information in this section is particularly vulnerable to change. Check directly with the airline or a travel agent to make sure you understand how a fare (and ticket you may buy) works and be aware of the security requirements for international travel. The details given in this chapter should be regarded as pointers and are not a substitute for your own careful, up-to-date research.

popular routes will often leave at intervals throughout the day, and usually until about mid-afternoon.

OPEN-TOUR BUS

For the cost of around US$23, the sold-everywhere open ticket can get you from HCMC to Hanoi at your own pace, sometimes even in air-conditioned comfort. Open-tour tickets entitle you to exit or board the bus at any city along its route without holding you to a fixed schedule. Confirm your seat the day before departure.

These tickets are inexpensive because they're subsidised by an extensive commission culture. You're never obligated to stay at the hotel you've been dropped at; if you don't like it, find another.

Once you buy the ticket, you're stuck with it and the company you've bought it from ('guaranteed' refunds are not always honoured).

An alternative to the open-tour ticket is to buy individual, point-to-point tickets along the way. This will give you more flexibility to try different companies or modes of travel.

All companies offering open-tour tickets have received both glowing commendations and bitter complaints from travellers. Your best bet is to ask your fellow travellers about specific routes. Look for open tickets at traveller cafés throughout Vietnam.

Car & Motorcycle

Except for legal foreign residents, buying a motorbike for touring Vietnam is technically illegal. However, so far the authorities seem to be turning a blind eye to the practice. The big issue is what to do with the motorbike at trip's end. Some sell it back to the shop they bought it from (for less than they paid, of course). Others sell it to another shop or to a foreigner travelling in the opposite direction. But, since buying a motorbike is illegal a crackdown could come at any time.

Motorbikes can be hired from US$5 per day, depending on the make of the cycle and what region you're in; with someone driving for you, the cost can go up to US$12 per day. Hiring a car with a driver costs around US$40 per day. In smaller towns and cities, you should be fine on your own if you first watch how people ride and go with the flow. In HCMC or Hanoi, consider hiring a driver unless you're used to driving in Southeast Asia. Fifteen minutes on a bus travelling National Hwy 1 should convince you to leave the long-distance driving to a local.

Some of the most memorable experiences come from hiring a motorbike guide. If guides don't come to you, traveller cafés can often recommend one. Hiring a motorbike guide leaves you free to gawk at daily life and scenery, and guides are experts on their own turf.

For the long haul, drivers usually charge around US$45 per day. You should also expect to pay for their meals.

The road rule to remember: small yields to big (always). Traffic cops may (or may not) be looking to be paid off. Vehicles drive on the right-hand side of the road (usually). Spectacular accidents are frequent. There were almost 13,000 traffic fatalities in 2006, a 10% increase from the year before.

When driving on Vietnam's highways, helmets are required by law only for motorbikes (and a necessary accessory if you're fond of your skull).

Never leave a motorbike unattended – if you can't park it where you can keep it in constant view, park it with a motorbike valet (2000d) and don't lose your claim ticket.

MOTORCYCLING VIETNAM

David and Sarah Zimmerman motorcycled through Vietnam and have some tips for would-be two-wheeled adventurers. Read more about their 14-country odyssey at sarahetdavid.top-depart.com (in French, but with more than 1000 photos).

According to the pair: 'Have some motorcycling experience and wear motorcycle clothes and a helmet. Be careful. Have enough time – don't expect to have a higher average speed than 30-40km/h. If you have to choose one region, do only the north by motorbike, as Hwy 1 is not very fun to drive. If you do only the north consider renting a bike in Hanoi. Minsks are not easy to sell in Ho Chi Minh City. Nobody wants them there, so be prepared to sell it for very cheap unless you're lucky enough to find a foreigner that wants to do the same trip. Vietnamese people won't pay more than US$100.'

Hitching

As in any country, hitching is never entirely safe in Vietnam, and it is not recommended. If you do decide to hitch, keep in mind that drivers will usually expect to be paid for picking you up, so negotiate the fare before getting in. Never hitch alone, especially if you're female.

Local Transport

You'll never have to walk in Vietnam if you don't want to; drivers will practically chase you down the street.

At least once during your visit, take a whirl on a *xich lo (cyclo)*, a bicycle rickshaw with the chair at the front, the bicycle at the back. They're a pleasant, nonpolluting way to see a city but are being phased out by authorities. Generally, short *cyclo* rides should cost 10,000d, and an hourly rate equivalent to US$1 to US$2 is the norm. Be sure to negotiate up front and make sure the final price is crystal clear; bring a map if possible and stick to bargaining in dong. Don't take *cyclo*s at night; travellers have been mugged by their drivers.

Xe om or *Honda om* (literally, 'Honda hug'; motorcycle taxi) are faster – made up of a motorbike, a driver and you. Prices are roughly the same as with *cyclo*s.

Metered taxis are abundant, but check the meter before you get in and make sure the driver uses it. Better yet, negotiate a fixed price.

Hiring a bicycle is arguably the most fun way to see any city, and an adventure in itself. Hotels and traveller cafés usually hire them out for about US$1 to US$3 per day.

Train

Vietnam Railways (Duong Sat Viet Nam; ☎ 04-747 0308; www.vr.com.vn) operates the 2600km-long Vietnamese train system that runs along the coast between HCMC and Hanoi, and links the capital with Haiphong and northerly points all the way into China. Odd-numbered trains travel south; even-numbered trains go north.

There are five classes of train travel in Vietnam: hard seat, soft seat, hard sleeper, soft sleeper (normal) and soft sleeper (air-con). Conditions in hard seat and soft seat can be rough – it can be even less comfortable than the bus.

A relatively new upscale train service called **5-Star Express** (☎ 08-920 6868 HCMC main office; www.5starexpress.com.vn; one-way 220,000d-450,000d) runs a private, comfy train that goes between Nha Trang and HCMC.

Theft can be a problem. In sleeper cars, the bottom bunk is best because you can stow your pack underneath the berth; otherwise, secure it to something for the duration of the trip. Though trains are sometimes slower than the bus they are more comfortable and a terrific way to meet local people.

HANOI

☎ 04 / pop 3.5 million

The capital of the Socialist Republic of Vietnam (SRV), Hanoi is the place for the country's best sights, cheap *bia hoi* (draught beer), and shopping on its speciality streets for everything from shoes to traditional lanterns. The trappings of a country on the rise punctuate scenes of traditional beauty – there's an ATM in the Temple of Literature and pavements on the oldest streets are filled with motorbikes. These odd juxtapositions are everywhere, but instead of ruining the city, add to its charm.

Stroll around Hoan Kiem Lake, take in a museum or two and end the day by diving into the flourishing café culture and lively bar scene.

ORIENTATION

Rambling along the banks of the Red River (Song Hong), Hanoi's centre extends out from the edges of Hoan Kiem Lake. Just to the north of this lake is the Old Quarter, with narrow streets whose names change every block or two. Travellers mostly like to base themselves in this part of town.

About 1.5km west of the Old Quarter is Ho Chi Minh's mausoleum, in the neighbourhood where most foreign embassies are found, many housed in classical architectural masterpieces from the French colonial era. Hanoi's largest lake, Ho Tay (West Lake), lies north of the mausoleum.

Street designations in Hanoi are shortened to P for *Pho* or Đ for *duong* (both meaning street).

There are decent city maps for sale at bookshops in Hanoi for around US$2.

INFORMATION

Bookshops

Bookworm (Map pp826-7; ☎ 943 7226; bookworm@fpt.vn; 15A P Ngo Van So; 🕙 10am-7pm Tue-Sun) Hanoi's best selection of new and used English-language books including travel guides, a Vietnam section, and fiction.

Love planet (Map p830; ☎ 828 4864; 25 P Hang Bac) Trade in used books for other second-hand reads – lots of books in English and several other languages.

Map and photo Shop (Map p830; ☎ 926 0564; www.mapandphoto.com; 5 P Hang Be) A cartophile's dream: Hanoi and special-interest Vietnam maps of Hanoi bus lines, ecotourism, and Halong Bay drawn by hand.

Cultural Centres

American Club (Map p830; ☎ 824 1850; americanclubhanoi.com; 19-21 P Hai Ba Trung) Regular volleyball games and other activities – the first visit is free but after that membership is US$225 per year.

British Council (Map pp826-7; ☎ 843 6780; www.britishcouncil.org/vietnam; 40 P Cat Linh) Next to the Hanoi Horison Hotel.

Centre Culturel Française de Hanoi (Map p830; ☎ 936 2164; alli@hn.vnn.vn; 24 P Trang Tien) Has regular art and film (in French or Vietnamese) showings.

Emergency

Ambulance (☎ 115)

Fire (☎ 114)

Information (☎ 1080)

Police (☎ 113)

Internet Access

It's hard to go more than a few hundred metres anywhere in the city without stumbling across an internet café, in particular those at backpacker cafés and travel agencies along P Hang Bac and P Hang Be in the Old Quarter. Many places do not display prices, so check. Many budget hotels offer free internet access in the lobby.

Wi-fi has come to Hanoi with a vengeance and lots of hotels, cafés and bars offer free access. In the claustrophobic Old Quarter, it's not uncommon to have a choice of several networks. Try and sign into a secure network.

Internet Resources

There are several good websites to help get the most out of Hanoi.

New Hanoian (www.newhanoian.com) Places to see, dining out, special events, even jobs.

Sticky Rice (http://stickyrice.typepad.com) The lowdown on dozens of places to dine and drink.

Medical Services

Dental Clinic (Map pp826-7; ☎ 846 2864, 0903 401 919; Van Phuc Diplomatic Compound, 298 P Kim Ma, Ba Dinh District) Take your aching teeth here.

Institute of Acupuncture (Map pp826-7; ☎ 853 4253; 49 P Thai Thinh, Dong Da District) US$10 gets you needles in whatever part of your body ails you with electric pulses, and for most people, a feeling of better health afterwards. The lobby is on the 2nd level.

Institute of Traditional Medicine (Map pp826-7; ☎ 826 2850; 26-29 P Nguyen Binh Khiem) Worth a visit for the display of jars of plants used to make medicine – labelled with Vietnamese and scientific names – in the courtyard.

International SOS (Map p830; ☎ 934 0555; Central Bldg, 31 P Hai Ba Trung; initial consultations US$55-65) Has a 24-hour emergency clinic with international physicians speaking English, French and Japanese; house calls available.

GETTING INTO TOWN

From Noi Bai airport, Vietnam Airlines' airport minibus (US$2, 45 minutes, 35km) is cheap and easy. It drops you on P Quang Trung in the Old Quarter. Catch the airport bus at the concrete island across the road as you exit the terminal.

Official airport taxis charge US$10 for a ride door-to-door to or from Noi Bai airport. Drivers do *not* require that you pay the toll for the bridge you cross en route. Some other taxi drivers require that you pay the toll, though, so ask first. The official taxi rank is outside the concourse and you buy tickets from the seller at the head of the taxi line.

The cheapest option is the Hanoi public bus company's service from the airport (3500d). Lines 7 and 17 go to Kim Ma bus station and Long Bien bus station (Map pp826–7) respectively, every 15 minutes from 5am to 9pm.

From the city's three central train stations, you can walk the 15 to 20 minutes to the Old Quarter to find budget accommodation. However, it's worth the 10,000d for a *xe om* (motorcycle taxi) if you have a big pack to haul around. The same goes for Long Bien bus station (Map pp826–7), which is across the street from Long Bien train station.

From other bus stations, a motorbike taxi to the Old Quarter should cost 15,000d to 25,000d, depending which station you're coming from.

A DAY IN HANOI

Travellers with one day in Hanoi can spend the morning roaming the **Vietnam Museum of Ethnology** (p828), then grab some lunch before checking out the **Temple of Literature** (p828). Stroll by French colonial embassy buildings on P Hoang Dieu, and cycle or catch a *xe om* to the **Ho Chi Minh Mausoleum Complex** (p828). Finish with some *bia hoi* in the Old Quarter. Simple, cheap, satisfying.

Vietnam-Korea Friendship Clinic (Map pp826-7; ☎ 843 7231; 12 Chu Van An) Probably the least-expensive medical facility in Hanoi; maintains a high international standard.

Money

Citibank (Map p830; ☎ 825 1950; 17 P Ngo Quyen) Cashes travellers cheques and has a 24-hour ATM that lets you take out three million dong instead of the usual two million maximum; eases the pain of flat bank fees just a little.
Incombank (Temple of Literature; Map pp826-7; P Quoc Tu Giam; 🕑 8am-5pm) Confucius must be rolling in his grave; the Temple of Literature has an ATM, near the gift shop.
Vietcombank P Hang Bai (Map p830; ☎ 826 8031; 2 P Hang Bai); P Tran Quang Khai (Map p830; ☎ 826 8045; 198 P Tran Quang Khai; 🕑 7.30-11.30am & 1-3.30pm Mon-Fri, 7.30-11.30am Sat) The main branch on P Tran Quang Khai is the best bet for all currency exchange services. ATMs are scattered around the Old Quarter.

Post

Postal kiosks are all over the city, for picking up stamps or dropping off letters.
Domestic post office (Map p830; ☎ 825 7036; 85 P Dinh Tien Hoang; 🕑 7am-8.30pm)
International post office (Map p830; ☎ 825 2030; cnr P Dinh Tien Hoang & P Dinh Le; 🕑 7.30-11.30am & 1-4.30pm Mon-Fri) Only international parcels can be shipped from here.

International courier services in Hanoi:
DHL (Map pp826-7; ☎ 733 2086; 49 P Nguyen Thai Hoc)
Federal Express (Map p830; ☎ 824 9054; 6C P Dinh Le)
UPS (Map p830; ☎ 824 6483; 4C P Dinh Le)

Telephone

To make domestic or international calls, the domestic post office is a reliable bet, but internet cafés, guesthouses and traveller cafés will let you use their phone for a small fee, and many internet cafés also have internet telephoning. Calls outside the local area or to mobile phones will levy a higher rate.

Tourist Information

The new **Tourist Information Center** (Map p830; ☎ 926 3366; www.vntourists.com; 4G Đ Le Loi) is an air-conditioned haven for information and plenty of handouts on hotels, restaurants and activities. It's privately run and sells tours.

The best source of tourist information in Hanoi, as in the rest of Vietnam, is asking around at guesthouses, travel agencies and bars, and talking to fellow travellers.

Travel Agencies

Tourist-style minibuses that often transport locals can be booked through most hotels and cafés. However, tour companies and traveller cafés are your best bet for buying other types of tickets and tours. See p831 for a list of some recommended ones.

DANGERS & ANNOYANCES

One of the most scenic cities in Vietnam is unfortunately also the most prone to scams. Taxis and motorbikes have the annoying habit of taking travellers to hotels that give a commission. We've even heard stories of travellers who took a legitimate Vietnam Airlines bus from the airport into the Old Quarter only to see a fake representative of Vietnam Airlines board the bus and try to tout people into hotels. There are several substantiated reports of verbal aggression and physical violence towards tourists when deciding against a hotel

SAFE CROSSING

Wherever you roam, you'll have to cross the street eventually, so go armed with this survival tip: wait for a break in traffic and slowly make your way across. It used to be that a slow and confident walk into the constant stream of motorbikes was like parting the Red Sea, but now with the occasional and oft-ignored cross walks and pedestrian signals in many cities, motorists are downright resentful.

Keep in mind that might makes right (of way). Buses and lorries yield to no-one, scooters yield to buses, and pedestrians yield to everyone. If you lack the nerve, look for locals crossing the street and creep behind.

CENTRAL HANOI

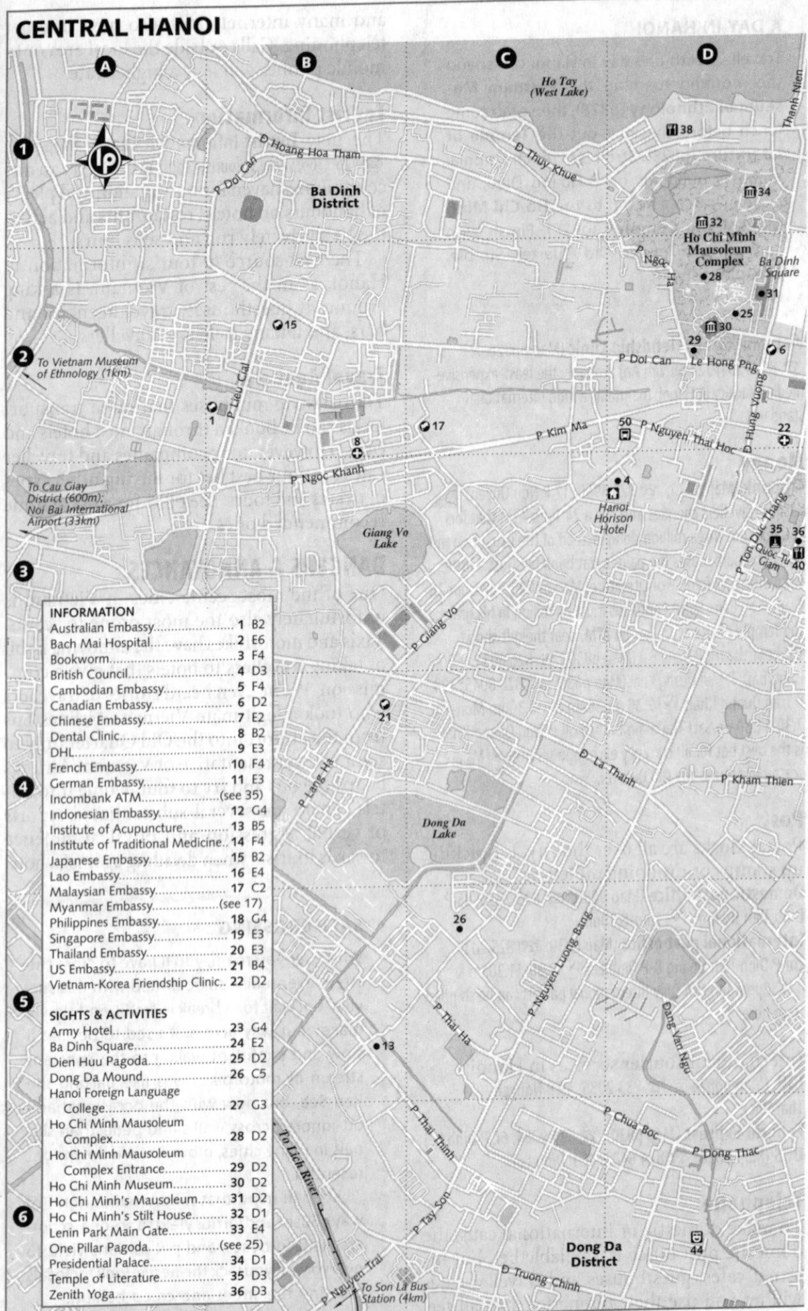

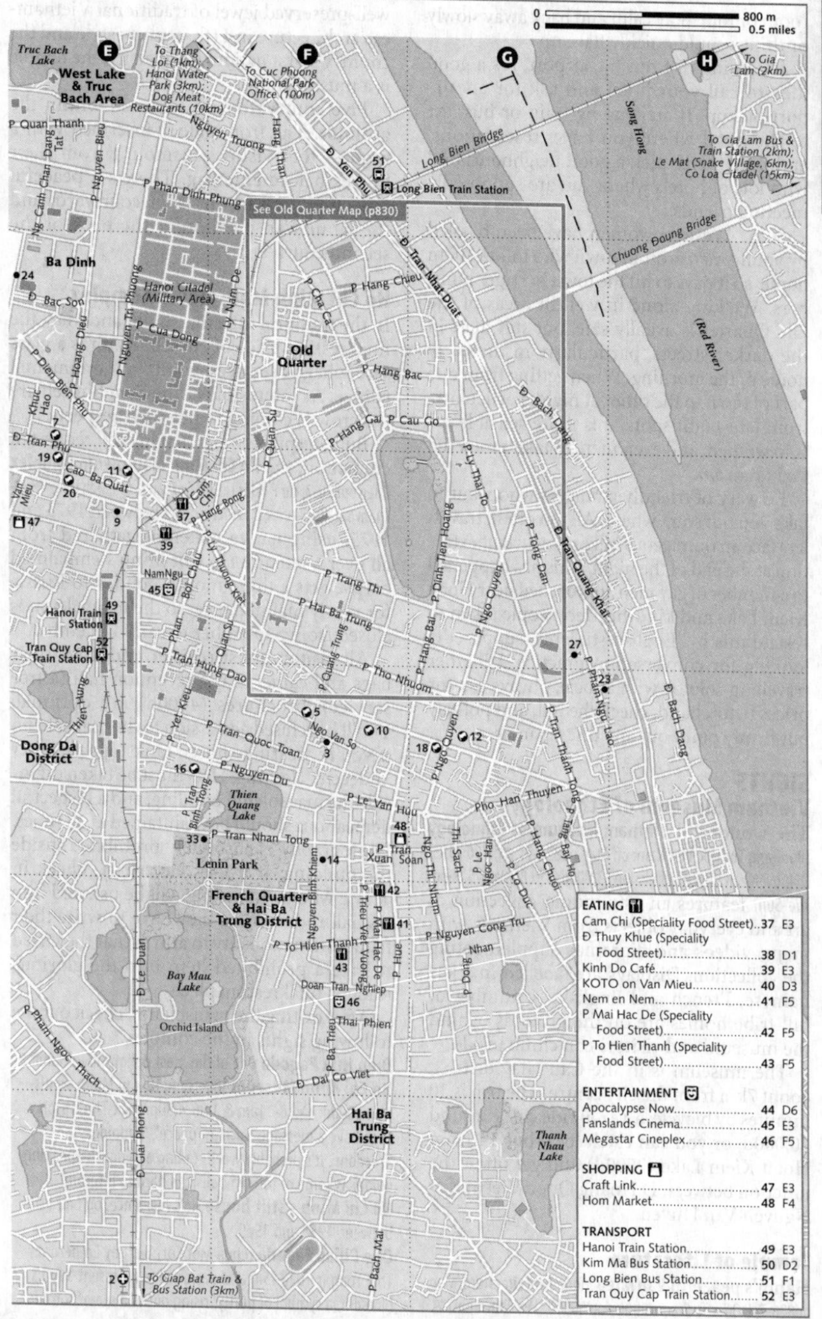
0 800 m
0 0.5 miles
E
F
G
H
Truc Bach Lake
West Lake & Truc Bach Area
To Thang Loi (1km); Hanoi Water Park (3km); Dog Meat Restaurants (10km)
To Cuc Phuong National Park Office (100m)
To Gia Lam (2km)
Song Hong
To Gia Lam Bus & Train Station (2km); Le Mat (Snake Village, 6km); Co Loa Citadel (15km)
Long Bien Bridge
Long Bien Train Station
Chuong Đuong Bridge
(Red River)
See Old Quarter Map (p830)
P Quan Thanh
Nguyen Truong
Hang Than
Đ Yen Phu
Ng Canh Chan
Dang Tat
P Nguyen Bieu
P Phan Dinh Phung
Ba Dinh
Đ Bac Son
Hanoi Citadel (Military Area)
P Nguyen Tri Phuong
P Cua Dong
Ly Nam De
P Hoang Dieu
P Dien Bien Phu
Khuc Hao
Đ Tran Phu
Cao Ba Quat
Van Mieu
Cam Chi
P Hang Bong
P Cha Ca
P Hang Chieu
Đ Tran Nhat Duat
Old Quarter
P Hang Bac
P Hang Gai
P Cau Go
P Quan Su
Đ Bach Dang
P Ly Thai To
P Dinh Tien Hoang
P Tong Dan
Đ Tran Quang Khai
P Trang Thi
P Hai Ba Trung
P Ngo Quyen
P Hang Bai
P Quang Trung
P Tho Nhuom
NamNgu
P Ly Thuong Kiet
Phan Boi Chau
Quan Su
Hanoi Train Station
Tran Quy Cap Train Station
P Tran Hung Dao
Thien Hung
P Yet Kieu
P Tran Quoc Toan
Ngo Van So
P Ngo Quyen
P Pham Ngu Lao
P Tran Thanh Tong
Đ Bach Dang
Dong Da District
P Nguyen Du
P Tran Binh Trong
Thien Quang Lake
P Le Van Huu
Pho Han Thuyen
P Tang Bat Ho
P Tran Nhan Tong
P Tran Xuan Soan
Lenin Park
Nguyen Binh Khiem
Ngo Thi Nham
Thi Sach
P Le Ngoc Han
P Hang Chuoi
P Lo Duc
French Quarter & Hai Ba Trung District
P Trieu Viet Vuong
P Mai Hac De
P Hue
P To Hien Thanh
P Nguyen Cong Tru
Doan Tran Nghiep
Đong Nhan
Đ Le Duan
Bay Mau Lake
Orchid Island
Thai Phien
P Ba Trieu
P Pham Ngoc Thach
Đ Dai Co Viet
Hai Ba Trung District
Thanh Nhau Lake
Đ Giai Phong
P Bach Mai
To Giap Bat Train & Bus Station (3km)
EATING
Cam Chi (Speciality Food Street) 37 E3
Đ Thuy Khue (Speciality Food Street) 38 D1
Kinh Do Café 39 E3
KOTO on Van Mieu 40 D3
Nem en Nem 41 F5
P Mai Hac De (Speciality Food Street) 42 F5
P To Hien Thanh (Speciality Food Street) 43 F5
ENTERTAINMENT
Apocalypse Now 44 D6
Fanslands Cinema 45 E3
Megastar Cineplex 46 F5
SHOPPING
Craft Link 47 E3
Hom Market 48 F4
TRANSPORT
Hanoi Train Station 49 E3
Kim Ma Bus Station 50 D2
Long Bien Bus Station 51 F1
Tran Quy Cap Train Station 52 E3

room or tour. Stay calm and back away slowly or things could quickly flare up.

If coming in from the airport, it's a good idea to call your hotel and ask for an airport pickup. If arriving by train or bus, get to the hotel where you have 'reservations' and if that fails, pick a good neighbourhood with lots of hotels where you are supposedly meeting friends.

Some Western women have been hassled by young men around town who follow them home, so it pays to hit the town in larger numbers. Walking alone in well-lit areas of the Old Quarter is usually safe, but stay alert in the darker streets, particularly in the early hours of the morning. When getting from one part of town to the other at night, particularly from late-night spots, it is more sensible for solo women, and even men, to take a metered taxi or *xe om*.

Be wary of friendly strangers who want to take you out somewhere. All too often, travellers face an outrageous bill or downright extortion at the end of the night. This has happened to a number of gay men approached near Hoan Kiem Lake and kind-hearted people taken to restaurants by 'English students' supposedly looking for conversation practice. Whether travelling solo or with a local, always ask for prices beforehand, check the bill, and politely but firmly point out any discrepancies.

SIGHTS

Vietnam Museum of Ethnology

The wonderful **Vietnam Museum of Ethnology** (Bao Tang Toc Hoc Viet Nam; off Map pp826-7; ☎ 756 2193; Đ Nguyen Van Huyen; admission 33,000d; 🕒 8.30am-5.30pm Tue-Sun) features an astounding collection of art and everyday objects from Vietnam, with maps, videos and dioramas supplementing the collection. Displays are labelled in Vietnamese, French and English. A number of hill-tribe homes are on the grounds behind the museum and visitors can climb inside.

The museum is in the Cau Giay district, about 7km from the city centre. The trip is 30 minutes by bicycle; a *xe om* ride costs around 20,000d, or you can catch local bus 14 from Hoan Kiem Lake (2500d) and get off at the junction between Đ Hoang Quoc Viet and Đ Nguyen Van Huyen.

Temple of Literature

Hanoi's peaceful **Van Mieu** (Temple of Literature; Map pp826-7; P Quoc Tu Giam; admission 5000d; 🕒 8am-5pm) A well-preserved jewel of traditional Vietnamese architecture in 11th-century style and the country's first national university, the temple is a must-visit.

Five courtyards are enclosed within the grounds. The front gate is inscribed with a request that visitors dismount from their horses before entering. There's a peaceful reflecting pool in the front courtyard, and the Khue Van pavilion at the back of the second courtyard.

Ho Chi Minh Mausoleum Complex

In the tradition of Lenin, Stalin and Mao, the final resting place of Ho Chi Minh is a glass sarcophagus set deep within a monumental edifice. As interesting as the man himself are the crowds coming to pay their respects.

Built despite the fact that his will requested cremation, the **Ho Chi Minh Mausoleum Complex** (Map pp826-7; cnr P Ngoc Ha & P Doi Can; admission free; 🕒 8-11am Sat-Thu) was constructed between 1973 and 1975, using native materials gathered from all over Vietnam. Ho Chi Minh's embalmed corpse gets a three-month holiday to Russia for yearly maintenance, so the mausoleum is closed from September to early December.

All visitors must register and leave their bags and cameras at a reception hall (a free service); brochures (4000d) are optional. You'll be refused admission to the mausoleum if you're wearing shorts, tank tops or other 'indecent' clothing. Hats must be taken off inside the mausoleum building, and a respectful demeanour should be maintained at all times. Photography is absolutely prohibited inside the building. If it uses electricity, check it. Those who guess wrong will be ushered into a small room where they have to write their name and nationality to affirm that they tried to take a prohibited item into the glorious leader's final resting place.

After exiting the mausoleum, check out the following sights in the complex.

Dien Huu Pagoda One of the most delightful in Hanoi.

Ho Chi Minh Museum (Bao Tang Ho Chi Minh; admission 5000d; 🕒 8-11am & 1.30-4.30pm Sat-Thu) Displays each have a message, such as 'peace', 'happiness' or 'freedom'. It's probably worth taking an English-speaking guide, as some of the symbolism is hard to interpret.

Ho Chi Minh's stilt house Ho's residence, on and off, between 1958 and 1969.

One Pillar Pagoda (Chua Mot Cot) Built by Emperor Ly Thai Tong (r 1028–54) and designed to represent a lotus blossom, a symbol of purity, rising out of a sea of sorrow.

Presidential Palace (admission 5000d; 8-11am & 2-4pm Sat-Thu) Constructed in 1906 as the palace of the governor general of Indochina.

Old Quarter

The following are all on the Old Quarter map (p830).

Hoan Kiem Lake is the liquid heart of the Old Quarter, and a good orientation landmark. Legend has it that, in the mid-15th century, Heaven sent Emperor Ly Thai To a magical sword, which he used to drive the Chinese out of Vietnam. One day after the war he happened upon a giant golden tortoise swimming on the surface of the water; the creature grabbed the sword and disappeared into the depths of the lake. Since that time, the lake has been known as Ho Hoan Kiem (Lake of the Restored Sword) because the tortoise restored the sword to its divine owners. A respected Vietnamese scientist has been crusading since 1991 for the protection of the very few real giant turtles that live in the lake, but the most recent turtle sighting was in 2006. There's a monument to Ly Thai To on the west side of Hoan Kiem.

Ngoc Son Temple (Jade Mountain Temple; admission 2000d; 8am-5pm), which was founded in the 18th century, is on an island in the northern part of Hoan Kiem Lake. It's a meditative spot to relax, but also worth checking out for the embalmed remains of a gigantic tortoise supposedly from the lake itself.

Tiny **Thap Rua** (Tortoise Tower), on an islet in the southern part of the lake, is often used as an emblem of Hanoi.

Memorial House (87 P Ma May; admission 5000d; 9-11.30am & 1-5pm) is worth a visit. Thoughtfully restored, this traditional Chinese-style dwelling gives you an excellent idea of how local merchants used to live in the Old Quarter. Unusual souvenirs, such as compasses made from ox bones (48,000d), are for sale.

Bach Ma Temple (cnr P Hang Buom & P Hang Giay; 8-11.30am & 2.30-5.30pm) is the oldest temple in Hanoi and resides in a shred of Chinatown. Legend has it that Emperor Ly Thai To prayed at this temple for assistance in building the city walls because they continually collapsed, no matter how many times he rebuilt them. His prayers were finally answered when a white horse appeared out of the temple and guided him to the site where he eventually built his walls. Inside the Pagoda is a statue of the honoured white horse. Admission is free, but you might drop a few thousand dong in the box for maintenance and preservation.

Stepping inside **St Joseph Cathedral** (P Nha Tho; 5-7am & 5-7pm) is like being transported to medieval Europe. Around Christian holidays there is quite the scene in front of the church – Easter sees a re-enactment of the crucifixion with actors speaking their lines into microphones.

Other Attractions

The **Women's Museum** (Bao Tang Phu Nu; Map p830; 36 P Ly Thuong Kiet; admission 10,000d; 8am-4pm Tue-Sun) was under renovation with only one exhibit open at the time of research. The museum usually includes the predictable tribute to women soldiers, balanced by some wonderful exhibits from the international women's movement protesting the American War. Exhibits have Vietnamese, French and English explanations.

Hoa Lo Prison Museum (Map p830; ☎ 934 2253; 1 P Hoa Lo; admission 33,000d; 8-11.30am & 1.30-4.30pm Tue-Sun) is all that remains of the former Hoa Lo prison, ironically nicknamed the 'Hanoi Hilton' by US POWs during the American War. Famous prisoners included Pete Peterson, who later became the first US ambassador to a unified Vietnam in 1995, and Senator John McCain, who cannot raise his arms above his head because of his torture here and tried to commit suicide twice while imprisoned. Some exhibits have explanations in English and French.

ACTIVITIES

Feel like a dip? There are several places for swimming in Hanoi. Some of the nicer hotels charge a US$10 day-use fee.

MAKE THAT COMPLAINT COUNT...

We get a lot of letters complaining about hotels, guesthouses, travel companies and more. We're not complaining – it's great to get your feedback about all these things, as it helps us work out which businesses care about their customers and which don't. However, as well as telling us, make sure you tell the **Vietnam National Administration of Tourism** (Map p830; ☎ 824 7652; 3 P Le Lai); its Hanoi office is reasonably helpful and needs to know about the problems before it can do anything about them. In time your effort might well pressure the cowboys into cleaning up their act.

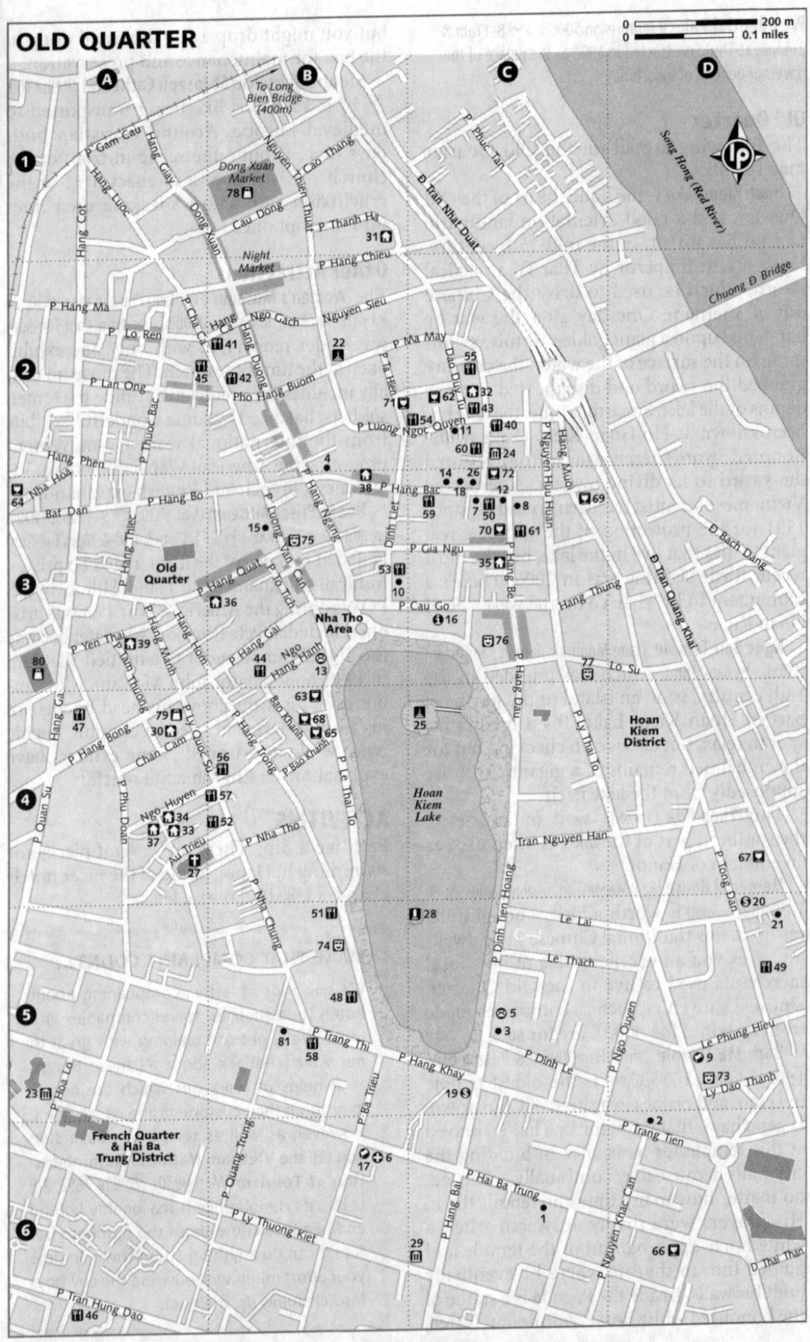
OLD QUARTER
0 200 m
0 0.1 miles
To Long Bien Bridge (400m)
Dong Xuan Market
Night Market
Old Quarter
Nha Tho Area
Hoan Kiem Lake
Hoan Kiem District
French Quarter & Hai Ba Trung District
Song Hong (Red River)
Chuong Đ Bridge
P Gam Cau
Hang Giay
Hang Luoc
Hang Cot
Dong Xuan
Cau Dong
Nguyen Thien Thuat
Cao Thang
P Thanh Ha
P Hang Chieu
P Phuc Tan
Đ Tran Nhat Duat
P Hang Ma
P Lo Ren
P Cha Ca
Hang Ca
Ngo Gach
Nguyen Sieu
P Ma May
P Lan Ong
Pho Hang Buom
Hang Duong
P Ta Hien
Dao Duy Tu
P Luong Ngoc Quyen
P Thuoc Bac
Hang Phen
Nha Hoa
Bat Dan
P Hang Bo
P Hang Bac
P Hang Ngang
P Luong Van Can
Dinh Liet
P Nguyen Huu Huan
Hang Muoi
Đ Bach Dang
P Gia Ngu
P Hang Be
P Hang Thiec
P Hang Quat
P To Tich
P Cau Go
Hang Thung
Đ Tran Quang Khai
P Yen Thai
P Hang Manh
Hang Hom
P Hang Gai
Ngo Hang Hanh
P Tam Thuong
P Hang Dau
Lo Su
Hang Ga
P Ly Quoc Su
Bao Khanh
P Bao Khanh
P Hang Trong
P Ly Thai To
P Hang Bong
Chan Cam
P Le Thai To
P Quan Su
P Phu Doan
Ngo Huyen
P Nha Tho
Au Trieu
Tran Nguyen Han
P Nha Chung
P Dinh Tien Hoang
P Tong Dan
Le Lai
Le Thach
P Ngo Quyen
Le Phung Hieu
P Trang Thi
P Hang Khay
P Dinh Le
Ly Dao Thanh
P Hoa Lo
P Ba Trieu
P Trang Tien
P Quang Trung
P Hai Ba Trung
P Hang Bai
P Nguyen Khac Can
P Ly Thuong Kiet
Đ Thai Than
P Tran Hung Dao

Army Hotel (Khach San Quan Doi; Map pp826-7; ☎ 825 2896; 33C P Pham Ngu Lao; day use US$3.50) Big enough to do laps, the pool is open all year.

Hanoi Water Park (off Map pp826-7; ☎ 753 2757; 🕑 9am-9pm Wed-Mon Apr 15-Nov) About 5km from the city centre, it features a variety of pools and slides.

Thang Loi Hotel (Cuban Hotel; off Map pp826-7; ☎ 829 4211; thangloihtl@hn.vnn.vn; Đ Yen Phu; day use 30,000d; 🕑 May-Oct) Near Ho Tay (West Lake).

COURSES

Cooking

Highway 4 (Map p830; ☎ 926 0639; 5 P Hang Tre) is a popular restaurant and bar that also has cooking classes. Prices range from US$19 to US$32 per class.

Old Hanoi (Map p830; ☎ 824 5251; www.hanoicooking.com; 106 P Ma May,) has half-day classes for US$19 that include a trip to the market. Students can usually share their culinary creation with a guest if they ask in advance.

Language

Hanoi Foreign Language College (Map pp826-7; ☎ 826 2468; 1 P Pham Ngu Lao) is a branch of Hanoi National University housed in the History Museum compound. Vietnamese-language tuition varies with class size, but shouldn't cost more than US$7 per lesson.

Yoga

Zenith Yoga (Map pp826-7; ☎ 464 1171; 31A P Van Mieu), upstairs from Maison des Arts Spa, charges 100,000d for a drop-in class.

TOURS

Not many travellers are happy after taking a budget tour. Those willing to spend extra for quality or get around on their own usually rave about their trips. It's easy enough to do Halong Bay solo by using Cat Ba Island as a starting point and booking excursions from there. The same goes for Sapa.

It is not advisable to book trips or tickets through guesthouses and hotels. Dealing directly with tour operators gives you a much better idea of what you'll get for your money. Seek out tour operators that stick to small groups and use their own vehicles and guides.

INFORMATION
American Club....1 C6
Centre Culturel Française de Hanoi....2 D6
Citibank....(see 16)
Domestic Post Office....(see 5)
Federal Express....3 C5
Footprint Travel....4 B2
Handspan Adventure Travel....(see 60)
International Post Office....5 C5
International SOS....6 B6
Love Planet....7 C3
Map & Photo Shop....8 C3
New Zealand Embassy....9 D5
Ocean Tours....10 B3
ODC Travel....11 C2
Onbike Tours....12 C3
Post Office....13 B3
Sinh Café 1....14 C3
Sinh Café 2....15 B3
Tourist Information Center....16 C3
UK Embassy....17 B6
UPS....(see 3)
Vega Travel....18 C3
Vietcombank....19 C5
Vietcombank....20 D5
Vietnam National Administration of Tourism....21 D5

SIGHTS & ACTIVITIES
Bach Ma Temple....22 B2
Highway 4....(see 69)
Hoa Lo Prison Museum....23 A5
Memorial House....24 C2
Ngoc Son (Jade Mountain) Temple....25 C4
Old Hanoi....26 C3
St Joseph Cathedral....27 A4
Thap Rua (Tortoise Tower)....28 C5
Women's Museum....29 C6

SLEEPING
Camellia Hotel 12....30 A4
City Gate Hotel....31 B1
Dong A Hotel....32 C2
Especen....33 A4
Hanoi Backpacker's Hostel....34 A4
Hanoi Spirit House....35 C3
Real Darling Café....36 B3
Rose Hotel....37 A4
Sports Hotel....38 B3
Tam Thuong Guesthouse....39 A3
Thu Giang Guesthouse....(see 39)
Viet Fun Hotel....(see 32)

EATING
69 Bar-Restaurant....40 C2
Baan Thai Restaurant....41 B2
Baguette & Chocolat....42 B2
Bay Restaurant and Café....43 C2
Bodha Café....44 B3
Cha Ca La Vong....45 B2
Com Chay Nang Tam....46 A6
Cyclo Bar & Restaurant....47 A4
Dong Xuan Market....(see 78)
Fanny....48 B5
Fivimart....49 D5
H Silk Restaurant....50 C3
Highway 4....(see 69)
Intimex....51 B5
La Place....52 B4
Linh Phung....53 B3
Little Hanoi 1....54 C2
New Day Restaurant....55 C2
Pepperoni's Pizza & Café....56 B4
Pho....57 B4
Saigon Sakura....58 B5
San Xuan....59 C3
Tamarind Café....60 C2
Tandoor....61 C3

DRINKING
1/2 Man, 1/2 Noodle....62 C2
Balcony Bar and Café....63 B4
Bia Hoi Ha Noi....64 A3
Bia Hoi Hanoi....65 B4
Camellia Café & Bar....66 D6
Gambrinus....67 D4
GC Pub....68 B4
Highway 4....69 C3
Le Pub....70 C3
Mao's Red Lounge....71 B2
Red Beer....72 C3

ENTERTAINMENT
Club Opera....73 D5
I-Box....74 B5
Jazz Club by Quyen Van Minh....75 B3
Municipal Water Puppet Theatre....76 C3
R&R Tavern....77 C3

SHOPPING
Dong Xuan Market....78 B1
Hai Van....79 A4
Hang Da Market....80 A3

TRANSPORT
Airport Minibus....81 B5

Successful tour operators often have their names cloned by others looking to trade on their reputations, so check addresses and websites carefully. Consider the following places in the Old Quarter (Map p830):

Footprint Travel (☎ 826 0879; www.footprintsvietnam.com; 16 P Hang Bac) Highly capable Vietnamese management and guides arrange trips that emphasise doing over seeing: Halong Bay outings, bicycle trips and 18-day eco-adventure tours.

Handspan Adventure Travel (☎ 926 0581; www.handspan.com; 80 P Ma May) At the Tamarind Café. Offers kayaking and sleep-aboard boat tours on a refurbished junk in Halong Bay. We've heard nothing but good reports.

Ocean Tours (☎ 926 0463; www.oceantours.com.vn; 16 P Hang Bac) This operator, specialising in Halong Bay, has been earning a good name for itself.

ODC Travel (☎ 824 3024; www.camellia-hotels.com; Camellia Hotel, 13 P Luong Ngoc Quyen) Formerly Old Darling Café, this is one of the most established names in the business for budget tours.

Onbike Tours (☎ 914 1539; www.onbikevietnam.com; 16 P Hang Bac) Bicycle tours to the craft villages outside of Hanoi and further for one or more days.

Sinh Café 1 & 2 (☎ 828 7552; 18 P Luong Van Can & 52 P Hang Bac) At two locations, and with every service a traveller could need, ranging from visa extensions to travel arrangements to tours.

Vega Travel (☎ 926 2092; www.vega-travel.com; 24A P Hang Bac) Formerly known as Fansipan Tours, the company decided to change its name after as many as 10 copycats sprung up. Despite the address, enter on P Ma May. Specialises in Halong Bay and Sapa trips, but also has a good selection of sporty and cultural adventures through the north.

FESTIVALS & EVENTS

Tet (Tet Nguyen Dan/Vietnamese Lunar New Year) A flower market is held on P Hang Luoc during the week preceding Tet, in late January or early February. In addition, there's a colourful two-week flower exhibition and competition, beginning on the first day of the Lunar New Year, which takes place in Lenin park (Cong Vien Le Nin; Map pp826–7) north of Bay Mau Lake.

Quang Trung Festival On the 15th day of the first lunar month (February or March) wrestling matches, lion dances and chess games are played at Dong Da Mound (Map pp826–7) in west Hanoi – Dong Da is the site of the uprising against Chinese invaders led by Emperor Quang Trung (Nguyen Hué) in 1788.

Vietnam's National Day Celebrated at Ba Dinh Sq (Map pp826-7) – in front of the Ho Chi Minh Mausoleum Complex – with a rally and fireworks on 2 September; boat races are also held on Hoan Kiem Lake in the Old Quarter.

SLEEPING

Head to the Old Quarter once you land in Hanoi; the majority of Hanoi's budget accommodation lies within 1km of Hoan Kiem Lake. Most of the budget hotels are near P Hang Bac or St Joseph Cathedral. The following places are all on the Old Quarter map (p830).

Dong A Hotel (☎ 828 2249; www.dongahotels.com; 50 P Ma May, dm US$3; ❄ 💻) It offers nice dorm beds. A long thin room with a line of bamboo bunks, the layout of the place means that yes, the bunks are close, but since travellers can't see each other they'll *finally* stop staring at you while you sleep.

Hanoi Backpackers' Hostel (☎ 828 5372; www.hanoibackpackershostel.com; 48 P Ngo Huyen; dm US$7, r US$25; ❄ 💻) This Aussie-style backpackers' pad offers smart and secure dorms and a couple of expensive dedicated rooms. The rooftop bar is a sort of country club for the backpack set and has unusually expensive beers, but it's the best spot in Hanoi to get good travel advice from fellow travellers.

Tam Thuong Guesthouse (☎ 828 6296; three_men_on_business@yahoo.com; 10A1 P Yen Thai; r US$7-8; ❄ 💻) Run by warm and friendly people, visitors leave feeling good about their stay. This guesthouse is in the narrow alley between P Yen Thai and P Hang Gai, near Hong Da Market.

Real Darling Café (☎ 826 9386; darling_café@hotmail.com; 33 P Hang Quat; r US$8-10) An old standby that's cheap and centrally located, it advertises dorm rooms in Japanese but only wanted to give us prices for regular rooms. Inquire within.

Viet Fun Hotel (☎ 926 2353; vietfunhotels@yahoo.com; 48 P Ma May; r US$8-15; ❄ 💻) This place should appeal to those for whom size matters almost as much as money. Enthusiastic service and helpful advice ensure a fun stay.

City Gate Hotel (☎ 828 0817; www.citygatehotel.com.vn; 10 P Thanh Ha; r US$8-18; ❄ 💻) Hidden down a small lane near the old East Gate, this smart minihotel offers a warm welcome and friendly service. Rooms are super clean.

Hanoi Spirit House (☎ 826 7356; hanoispirithouse@yahoo.com; 50 P Hang Be; r US$10-14 ❄ 💻) With a restaurant, massive internet café that charges US$1 per hour, cheap Tiger beer on draft (10,000d), and small but clean rooms, spirits and bank balances fly high here.

Thu Giang Guesthouse (☎ 828 5734; thugiangn@hotmail.com; 5A P Tam Thuong; r US$10-15; ❄ 💻) Spitting distance from Tam Thuong Guesthouse, it's another friendly place that gets good reviews.

Rose Hotel (☎ 26 0471; bonghonghotel.@fPt.vn; 56 P Ngo Huyen; d US$12;) A good place to get some peace and quiet. The hot water doesn't last forever but the staff are pleasant and the rooms are comfy, if a little retro.

our pick **Especen** (☎ 824 4401; www.especen.net; 28 P Tho Xuong St; d US$13-15;) Free wi-fi and nice big rooms that look brand new even though the owners say this is one of the first minihotels in the area. The hotel is often full; there's an Especen 2 right next door.

Sports Hotel (☎ 926 0154; carmellia12cc@yahoo.co.uk; 96 P Hang Bac; d US$13-17;) One of the few places where quiet, windowless rooms away from the street don't have that musty smell that soon turns tired travellers into bloodhounds when sniffing around for a good night's sleep.

Camellia Hotel 12 (☎ 828 5936; carmellia12cc@yahoo.co.uk; 12 P Chan Cam; d US$15-20;) One of the many Camellia incarnations that are fairly similar, this one is decent value on a quieter street.

EATING

What's on the menu in Hanoi? Everything, ranging from the famous local speciality of *cha ca* (filleted fish slices grilled over charcoal) to the less appealing option of Fido over an open fire. In between, if it comes from a Vietnamese kitchen, it's here. And, there's a wide choice of international cuisine.

Finding good budget eats at a sit-down restaurant can be a tad more challenging here than in other cities, but street vendors and tiny sidewalk eateries are cheaper than cheap.

A number of speciality food streets dot the city like so many sprinkles on a cup cake (see Map pp826–7). Cam Chi, 500m northeast of Hanoi train station, is an alley crammed full of street stalls serving delicious budget-priced food. P Mai Hac De, in the south-central area east of Bay Mau Lake, has several blocks of restaurants running south from the northern terminus at P Tran Nhan Tong. Đ Thuy Khue, on the south bank of West Lake, features a strip of 30-odd outdoor seafood restaurants with pleasant lakeside seating. P To Hien Thanh, east of Bay Mau Lake, also specialises in small seafood restaurants. P Nghi Tam, 10km north of central Hanoi, has 1km of dog-meat restaurants.

It's also easy to self-cater thanks to the supermarkets and outdoor markets inside the usual backpacker neighbourhoods.

Vietnamese

The following listings are all on the Old Quarter map (p830) unless otherwise noted.

Pho (10 P Ly Quoc Su; pho 15,000d; breakfast, lunch & dinner) When a restaurant does one thing very well there's really no need for a fancy name.

Little Hanoi 1 (☎ 926 0168; 9 P Ta Hien; mains 25,000d; breakfast, lunch & dinner) A big sign declaring its move up the street and a pointed warning about impostors is all that's left at the old location. The new spot does not disappoint with authentic fare that draws a lively crowd of travellers most nights of the week.

New Day Restaurant (☎ 828 0315; 72 P Ma May; mains from 15,000d; breakfast, lunch & dinner) This place is packed with foreigners and locals alike for good reason; the setting is cafeteria but the Hanoi specialities are first-class. If you can't get enough of this goodness, next door is a buffet with take-away boxes.

Linh Phung (☎ 926 0592, 7 P Dinh Liet; seafood 25,000d; breakfast, lunch & dinner) Great prices on seafood and two small fish in a pond near the counter give diners a cheap taste of nature in the big city. Open until midnight or so depending on business.

Nem en Nem (House of Nem; Map pp826-7; ☎ 943 3152; 43 P Mai Hac De; mains 25,000d; breakfast, lunch & dinner) A spring-roll lover's dream, *nem* variations here include sweet corn and shrimp rolls, Singapore-style rolls, preserved pork rolls, and crab rolls; they're all guaranteed to melt in your mouth, not in your hand.

69 Bar-Restaurant (☎ 926 0452; 69 P Ma May; meals from 40,000d; lunch & dinner) Set in a restored Vietnamese house built in the 19th century, this is one of the most charming spots in the Old Quarter for a meal or to watch life go by.

Highway 4 (☎ 926 0639; www.highway4.com; 5 P Hang Tre; lunch & dinner; mains 50,000-150,000d) Highway 4 is good at explaining a particular dish and its place in Vietnamese culture. It also has sampler sets of their signature Son Tinh rice wine and it's perfectly fine to just sit with a drink and appetisers.

Cha Ca La Vong (☎ 825 3929; 14 P Cha Ca; cha ca 70,000d; lunch & dinner) The *cha ca* capital of the Old Quarter has been family-run for five generations. The succulent fish is all that's on the menu.

Cyclo Bar & Restaurant (☎ 828 6844; 38 P Duong Thanh; set lunch 80,000d; lunch & dinner) Sipping a Singapore Sling in the seat of a converted *cyclo* while nibbling on French and Vietnamese food – here is where *Indochine* day dreams come to life. Good for drinks or a meal.

Other Asian

Asian cuisine, especially Japanese, can be pricey in Hanoi but these offer some decent deals. All are on the Old Quarter map (p830).

Baan Thai Restaurant (☎ 828 1120; 3B P Cha Ca; mains from 30,000d; ⏰ lunch & dinner) One of the longer-running, central Thai restaurants in the Old Quarter, Baan Thai is popular with the growing Thai community in Hanoi. There's also a photo-illustrated menu.

Tandoor (☎ 824 5359; 24 P Hang Be; mains around 50,000d; ⏰ lunch & dinner) The reasonably priced *thali* (set meal) is a good deal, and it's a cosy place in the Old Quarter.

Saigon Sakura (☎ 825 7565; 17 P Trang Thi; mains around 60,000d; ⏰ lunch & dinner) More than just sushi, the extensive menu features noodle soups, grilled fish and seaweed salads.

International

These are all on the Old Quarter map (p830).

our pick **H Silk Restaurant** (☎ 825 0804, 17 P Hang Bac; mains from 25,000d; ⏰ breakfast, lunch & dinner) To find this place look for a silk shop, not a restaurant; the food is upstairs. At night, balcony tables have candles but the real love affair will be with the food, especially the fish.

Bodha Café (38 Cafe; ☎ 828 6052; 36-38 P Hang Hanh; mains from 25,000d; ⏰ breakfast, lunch & dinner) A little smoky because of all the Vietnamese guys (and only guys, it seemed) eating and drinking here, this dimly lit hot spot has good Western fare and above-average Vietnamese food for the price.

Bay Restaurant and Café (☎ 928 0736; 36 P Ma May; mains from 30,000d; ⏰ breakfast, lunch & dinner) It serves some of the best pizza and pasta around and good Italian coffee to wash it down. Northern Vietnamese specialities are also on the menu.

La Place (☎ 928 5859; 4 P Au Trieu; mains from 30,000d; ⏰ breakfast, lunch & dinner) There is no shortage of hip little places near St Joseph Cathedral but this is a traveller favourite with iced shakes, savoury crepes and big windows with a perfect view of the cathedral.

Pepperoni's Pizza & Cafe (☎ 928 5246; 29 P Ly Quoc Su; pizzas from 40,000d; ⏰ lunch & dinner) A US$2 all-you-can-eat weekday lunchtime pasta and salad bar – that's *amore*. It also has authentic pizza and takeaway.

Vegetarian

Com Chay Nang Tam (Map p830; ☎ 942 4140; 79A P Tran Hung Dao; mains 10,000d) Famed for veggie creations named for, and remarkably resembling, meat dishes; try the 'fried snow balls'. It can be hard to find this place but it really is on the microscopic alley off P Tran Hung Dao – ask a local if need be.

Tamarind Café (Map p830; ☎ 926 0580; tama rind_café@yahoo.com; 80 P Ma May; mains from 60,000d; ⏰ breakfast, lunch & dinner) The cushion-laden chill atmosphere helps take the sting out of the prices. Dishing out Asian-style vegetarian dishes and rejuvenating fresh-fruit smoothies. Handspan Adventure Travel (p832) is set in the rear of the restaurant.

Cafés

For a much-needed respite from pounding the pavement or simply to get up to speed with the Vietnamese via caffeine, check the following.

Kinh Do Café (Map pp826-7; ☎ 825 0216; 252 P Hang Bong; pastries 7000d; ⏰ breakfast & lunch) This is where Catherine Deneuve took her morning coffee during the filming of *Indochine*; unlike the movie this place is unassuming and good.

Fanny (Map p830; ☎ 828 5656; 48 P Le Thai To; ice cream from 10,000d; ⏰ lunch & dinner) Serves delicious French ice cream across from Hoan Kiem's lakefront. It has unusual seasonal flavours such as *com* (sticky rice), *khoai mon* (taro) or *mang cau* (custard apple).

KOTO on Van Mieu (Map pp826-7; ☎ 747 0338; www.streetvoices.com.au; 59 P Van Mieu; mains 30,000-50,000d; ⏰ breakfast, lunch & dinner; 💻) This spot offers local specialities, home comforts, delicious sandwiches and cakes, and free wi-fi. Standing for 'Know One, Teach One', KOTO is a nonprofit grassroots project providing opportunities for former street kids.

Baguette & Chocolat (Map p830; ☎ 923 1500; 11 P Cha Ca; quiche 40,000d; ⏰ breakfast, lunch & dinner) From the same people behind KOTO; just like a café in Paris, there are French newspapers on the tables and the tastiest quiche sell out quickly.

Self-Catering

The following listings are all on the Old Quarter map (p830).

Dong Xuan Market (P Dong Xuan) Swing by for fresh fruits and veggies and baguettes.

San Xuan (71 P Hang Bac) A 24-hour bakery with sweets, sandwiches and beer.

Fivimart (☎ 826 0167; P Tong Dan) East of Hoan Kiem Lake, it's a very well stocked supermarket.

Intimex (☎ 825 6148; 22-32 P Le Thai To) Enter at the narrow driveway next to the Clinique shop, on the western side of the lake. It sells everything you need to make sandwiches or a full meal, and the 1st level has Vietnamese take-away dishes that are a little less expensive than at a restaurant. The 2nd level has the cheapest rain ponchos in town.

DRINKING

There's a good selection of pubs for everyone, but beer drinkers will especially like Hanoi. Not only are there *bia hoi* places scattered everywhere, there are also a number of microbreweries and beer bars in town. Thirsty travellers will find these drinking places within stumbling distance of each other in the Old Quarter (Map, p830).

Mao's Red Lounge (☎ 926 3104; 7 P Ta Hien) This funky two-level bar is standing room only on weekend nights when local expats come to get their groove on and backpackers join the impromptu booty-shaking.

GC Pub (☎ 825 0499; 7 Bao Khanh) Bars come in and out of fashion in Hanoi, and GC has swung right back into favour with Hanoi residents. There's a popular pool table and very friendly staff.

Bia Hoi Hanoi (☎ 824 6754, 1 P Bao Khanh) Cheap *bia hoi* and an eccentric selection of fish, ostrich eel and frog. On a street full of nightlife, it's a good place to start or end the evening.

Red Beer (☎ 826 0247; 97 P Ma May) One of the first microbreweries in town and still one of the best, its signature brew is red but there are a few others on tap.

Gambrinus (☎ 935 1114; 198 P Tran Quang Khai) Czech yourself before you wreck yourself; Gambrinus is a mellow Czech beer that goes down easier with each fresh mug. It's a vast, impressive *brauhaus* with shiny vats of freshly brewed Czech beer that's very popular with the Vietnamese.

½ Man, ½ Noodle (☎ 926 1943; 52 P Dao Duy Tu) Staff often play '70s and '80s rock classics and their motto is 'Drink here or we shoot the puppy'. The only evidence of canines we saw was hair of the dog the next morning, but, it's probably best to follow orders just in case.

Balcony Bar and Cafe (☎ 928-8608; 4 P Le Thai To) On the loungey side, the balcony overlooking Hoan Kiem Lake is full most nights of the week. Share a hookah pipe (80,000d) with friends or groove out to DJ Zcool's House and hip hop.

Le Pub (☎ 926 2104; 25 P Hang Be) A good place to drink anything you could imagine from back home, and there is a special US$1 beverage all day long most days of the week. It's like happy hour, all the time.

CLUBBING

The shelf life of Hanoi's discos is short, so ask around about what's hot or not during your visit. Unlike other cities, there's really not a backpacker mainstay since Apocalypse Now changed locations.

Apocalypse Now (Map pp826-7; P Dong Thac; Dong Da District; 8pm-late) Dropping its old digs and downscale demeanour, Apocalypse continues to pack in the pretty people. There's no cover but the drinks and taxi ride will cost you, and the taxi drivers outside are wily. Loud, thumping and open late, it's worth the trek if you want to dance the night away.

I-Box (Map p830; ☎ 828 8820; 32 P Le Thai Tho;) Café-bar by day, with luxurious drapes and free wi-fi, at night it feels like a whole new place as it turns club with decent DJs and an ear-throbbing sound system.

ENTERTAINMENT

Water Puppetry

Municipal Water Puppet Theatre (Roi Nuoc Thang Long; Map p830; ☎ 825 5450; 57B P Dinh Tien Hoang; admission 20,000-40,000d; performances 4pm, 5.15pm, 6.30pm, 8pm & 9.15pm) The higher admission buys better seats and a cassette of the music; you must pay extra fees to take photos and video. Programmes are multilingual, making it easier to follow the action.

GAY & LESBIAN HANOI

There's a thriving gay scene in Hanoi, with cruising areas such as the cafés on P Bao Khanh and around Hoan Kiem Lake. Gay guys should take care not to fall victim to the organised extortion scam going on around the lake (see p825).

Gay and lesbian venues tend to maintain a low profile; Mao's Red Lounge (left) is a gay-friendly place with good Friday and Saturday night parties. There's a healthy gay presence at Apocalypse Now (above), but watch out for hustlers.

Live Music

There is traditional live music performed daily at the Temple of Literature (p828).

Jazz Club By Quyen Van Minh (Cau Lac Bo; Map p830; ☎ 825 7655; 31-33 P Luong Van Can; ⏰ performances 9-11.30pm) *The* place in Hanoi to catch live jazz.

R&R Tavern (Map p830; ☎ 934 4109; 47 P Lo Su) A reliable little venue for live music, the Vietnamese band here knows all the counter-culture '60s classics. Drinks are very reasonably priced given the free soundtrack.

Club Opera (Map p830; ☎ 824 6950; 59 P Ly Thai To) Splash out for good food and traditional tunes, in the same building as the Terrace Bar.

Cinemas

Megastar Cineplex (Map pp826-7; ☎ 974 3333; 6th fl, Vincom Tower, 191 Ba Trieu) This is a serious place, complete with the latest international films.

Centre Culturel Français de Hanoi (Map p830; ☎ 936 2164; alli@hn.vnn.vn; 24 P Trang Tien) For French flicks.

Fanslands Cinema (Map pp826-7; ☎ 825 7484; 84 P Ly Thuong Kiet) It shows mainstream Western movies but be sure to make sure they're subtitled, not dubbed.

SHOPPING

Your first shopping encounter will likely be with the kids selling postcards and books. They're notorious overchargers (asking about triple the going price), so a reasonable amount of bargaining is called for. The Old Quarter (Map p830) is crammed with appealing loot; price tags signal set prices.

Handicrafts & Souvenirs

If you don't make it up to Sapa, you can find a wide selection of ethnic-minority garb and handicrafts in Hanoi; a stroll along P Hang Bac or P To Tich will turn up a dozen places.

Local artists display their paintings at private art galleries, the highest concentration of which is on P Trang Tien, between Hoan Kiem Lake and the Opera House. The galleries are worth a browse even if you're not buying.

Craft Link (Map pp826-7; ☎ 843 7710; www.craftlink-vietnam.com; 43 P Van Mieu) Make socially conscious purchases at Craft Link, near the Temple of Literature. It is a nonprofit organisation that buys tribal handicrafts at fair-trade prices.

Hai Van (Map p830 ☎ 826 0028; 2C P Ly Quoc Su) It specialises in made-to-order T-shirts, and let's just say the custom-made 'Hello, motorbike?' apparel went over well.

Markets

Dong Xuan Market (Map p830; P Dong Xuan) With hundreds of stalls that sell everything under the sun, this three-storey market is 600m north of Hoan Kiem Lake.

Hom Market (Map pp826-7; P Hué) On the northeastern corner of P Hué and P Tran Xuan Soan, this is a good general-purpose market with lots of imported food items.

Hang Da Market (Map p830; Yen Thai) West of Hoan Kiem Lake, Hang Da is relatively small, but good for imported food and drink. The 2nd floor is good for fabric and ready-made clothing.

Silk Products & Clothing

P Hang Gai, about 100m northwest of Hoan Kiem Lake, and its continuation, P Hang Bong, is a good place to look for embroidery such as tablecloths, T-shirts and wall hangings. This is also the modern-day silk strip, with pricey boutiques offering tailoring services and selling ready-to-wear clothing. It's a good place to look for silk ties, scarves and other threads.

Other fashionable streets are near St Joseph Cathedral, west of the lake.

GETTING THERE & AWAY

Air

For details of international flights to Hanoi, see p820. For domestic flights, see p821.

Bus

Hanoi has several bus stations, each with services to a particular area. It's a good idea to arrange travel a day or two before you want to leave. The stations are well organised with ticket offices, printed schedules and prices.

Gia Lam bus station (☎ 827 1529; Đ Ngoc Lam), 2km northeast of the city centre, is the place for buses to points north and northeast of Hanoi. These include Halong Bay (40,000d, 3½ hours), Haiphong (35,000d, two hours), and Lang Son (50,000d, three hours) and Lao Cai (53,000d, nine hours), both near the Chinese border. To get to the bus station, cross the Song Hong (Red River). *Cyclos* can't cross the bridge, so take a taxi (around 30,000d) or motorbike.

Kim Ma bus station (Ben Xe Kim Ma; Map pp826-7; ☎ 845 2846; cnr P Nguyen Thai Hoc & P Giang Vo) has buses to the west of Hanoi, including Hoa Binh (25,000d, two hours) and Dien Bien Phu (120,000d, 16 hours).

Son La bus station (Ben Xe Son La; off Map pp826-7; Km 8, P Nguyen Trai) destinations include Son La (63,000d, 12 to 14 hours), Dien Bien Phu (100,000d, 16 hours) and Lai Chau. It's southwest of Hanoi, near Hanoi University.

Giap Bat bus station (Ben Xe Giap Bat; ☎ 864 1467; Đ Giai Phong) serves points south of Hanoi, including Ninh Binh (28,000d, two hours), Hué (80,000d, 12 hours) and further. It is 7km south of the Hanoi train station.

Tourist-style minibuses can be booked through most hotels and cafés. Popular destinations include Halong Bay and Sapa.

Many open-ticket tours through Vietnam start or finish in Hanoi – for more details see p822.

Car & Motorcycle

To hire a car or minibus with driver, contact a traveller café or travel agency (see p831). The main roads in the northeast are generally OK, but in parts of the northwest they're awful (you'll need a high-clearance vehicle or 4WD).

A six-day trip in a 4WD can cost US$200 to US$400 (including 4WD, driver and petrol). You should inquire about who is responsible for the driver's room and board – most hotels have a room set aside for drivers, but work out ahead of time what costs are included.

Train

For trains to Lao Cai, gateway to Sapa, buy tickets as early as possible, especially if travelling over the weekend or if you're set on a soft sleeper. For short-distance trains, though, sometimes it's only possible to purchase tickets 30 minutes to one hour before departure, and room for baggage is severely limited.

Hanoi train station (Gad Hang Co; Map pp826-7; ☎ 825 3949; 120 Đ Le Duan; ⏲ ticket office 7.30-11.30am & 1.30-7.30pm) is the terminus for most trains and is at the western end of P Tran Hung Dao. Trains from here go to destinations south. It's best to buy tickets at least one day before departure to ensure a seat or sleeper. Look for the sign for foreign travellers – this agent, and the person at the information booth in the next room, usually speak some English.

If arriving early in the morning from Sapa, know that a line of coffee and food stalls across from the station will be open.

The place you purchase your ticket is not necessarily where the train departs, so be sure to ask exactly *where* you need to catch your train.

Tran Quy Cap station (B station; Map pp826-7; ☎ 825 2628; P Tran Qui Cap) is just two blocks south of the main station on Đ Le Duan. Northbound trains leave from here. It's considered a substation of the main Hanoi station.

Gia Lam station (Nguyen Van Cu, Gia Lam District), east of the Red River, has some northbound (Yen Bai, Lao Cai, Lang Son) and eastbound (Haiphong) trains.

To make things complicated, some of the same destinations served by Gia Lam can also be reached from **Long Bien station** (Map pp826-7; ☎ 826 8280).

GETTING AROUND

Bicycle

Pedalling around the city is invigorating, to say the least. Some hotels and cafés offer cycles to rent for US$1 to US$3 per day.

If you want to purchase your own set of wheels for a big trip, P Ba Trieu and P Hué are the best places to look for bicycle shops.

Bus

Public buses are clean and comfortable, and the fare is just 3500d. Pick up a copy of the *Xe Buyt Hanoi* (Hanoi Bus Map; 5000d)

GETTING TO CHINA

The busiest border crossing to China is near Dong Dang (open 7am to 5pm), 20km north of Lang Son in northeastern Vietnam. The border post itself is at Huu Nghi Quan (Friendship Gate), 3km north of Dong Dang. You need to organise your Chinese visa before reaching the border; Hanoi is the easiest place to do this.

Catch a bus from Hanoi to Lang Son (50,000d, 2½ hours), a small minibus (5000d) to Dong Dang and a *xe om* (20,000d) to the border. On the Chinese side, it's 20 minutes from the border to Pingxiang by bus or a shared taxi. Pingxiang is connected by train and bus to Nanning.

Trains from Hanoi to Beijing (US$125) via the Friendship Gate depart the capital at 6.30pm on Tuesday and Friday, a 48-hour journey that involves a three-hour stop for border formalities.

GETTING TO LAOS

Be aware that unscrupulous travel agencies sell bus tickets purportedly going to various destinations in Laos, when in fact they drop travellers at the Lao border without onward transport. Talk to other travellers before booking through an agency.

To Kaew Neua

The Cau Treo–Kaew Neua border (open 7am to 6pm) is 96km west of Vinh. While it's one of the most travelled routes, especially by tour buses making the Hanoi–Vientiane run (US$25, 24 hours), there are still many horror stories arising from the trip.

If you're eschewing the Vientiane-bound bus (available from guesthouses and traveller cafés in Hanoi), the *Reunification Express* train is a good way to get to Vinh (124,000d, five to seven hours, six daily) from Hanoi. Buses from Vinh to Tay Son (formerly Trung Tam; 10,000d) leave 10 times a day between 6am and 2pm; a lot of travellers have reported bad experiences on this bus, including chronic overcharging and being kicked off in the middle of nowhere. From Tay Son it's a further 25km to the border through some spectacular forested country. Take a minibus or hire a motorbike to cover this last stretch; both cost 50,000d. There is absolutely nothing at the border except the border post itself, so stock up on water and snacks in Tay Son.

The Vietnamese border guards have been known to close the country for lunch any time from 11.30am to 1.30pm. It's also quite common for them to ask for a US$1 to stamp your visa.

From the Vietnamese side it's a short walk to the Laos border, where 30-day Lao visas (US$30) are available. Once in the country there's a decent amount of transport options.

See p362 for information on travelling from Laos to Vietnam.

To Nam Khan

The Nam Can–Nam Khan border crossing (open 7am to 6pm) to Phonsavan in Laos can be a marathon trip – and you must have your visa arranged beforehand. From Hanoi, the first order of business is to get to Vinh. The *Reunification Express* train (124,000d, five to seven hours, six daily) is the most reliable method. On Tuesday, Thursday and Sunday it's possible to catch a bus at 6am from Vinh to Phonosavan (US$12, 11 hours); book through **Mr Lam** (☎ 038-383 5783). Otherwise catch a morning bus from Vinh to Muang Xen (29,000d, seven hours), which departs when full.

from almost any bookshop with a decent map selection.

Cyclo

Around the city centre, most *cyclo* rides should cost around 10,000d. Realize that the asking price can be two or thee times higher than the final, and fair, price. If it sounds like too much, start walking. Longer rides – from the Old Quarter to the Ho Chi Minh Mausoleum Complex – are in the 20,000d to 30,000d range.

The *cyclo* drivers in Hanoi are less likely to speak English than the ones in HCMC, so take a map, paper and pencil.

Motorcycle

Walk 5m down any major street and you'll be bombarded by offers for *xe om*. They should cost about the same as a *cyclo* and are infinitely quicker. Insist on getting to your final destination, as occasionally to save time drivers like to drop people off a few blocks early.

If you fervently desire to ride by yourself in Hanoi, make absolutely sure to closely observe driving patterns before revving up.

Taxi

Flag fall is around 10,000d to 15,000d, which takes you 1km to 2km; every kilometre thereafter costs about 8000d. Bear in mind that there are dodgy operators with high-speed meters. Try to use the more reliable companies:

Airport Taxi (☎ 873 3333)
Hanoi Taxi (☎ 853 5353)
Mai Linh Taxi (☎ 822 2666)
Taxi CP (☎ 824 1999)

AROUND HANOI

It takes only a short journey before the city soon falls away and is replaced with a scenic countryside filled with handicraft villages and ancient pagodas. The area also has two stand-

Grab a motorbike for the spectacular 25km uphill run to the border (50,000d) and get ready to wait around for infrequent public transport on the Laos side.

See p380 for information on doing the trip in the opposite direction.

To Na Maew

The crossing at Nam Xoi–Na Maew (open 7am to 6pm) in Thanh Hoa province is the most remote crossing into Laos, set in a mountainous area 175km northwest of Thanh Hoa city and 70km east of Sam Neua in Laos.

Trains between Hanoi and Thanh Hoa city (67,000d, three to four hours, six daily) are quick and reliable, but we've heard reports of minibus drivers demanding 300,000d for the long, bumpy journey from Thanh Hoa to Na Maew – over six times the going rate. The best thing to do is to buy a ticket at Thanh Hoa bus station (40,000d), but last we heard this bus ran irregularly, sometimes only once a week. Needless to say, travellers are advised to consider a different crossing into Laos.

See p383 for information on doing the trip in the opposite direction.

To Tay Trang

The Lao border at Tay Trang, gateway to Phongsali province, is only 34km from Dien Bien Phu. It opened in April 2007, and there was a collective cheer from travellers who had been hearing for years that this crossing was on the verge of opening.

At the time of writing it was possible to get Laos visas on arrival, but double-check with the Laos embassy before making the trek. **Vietnam Airlines** (code VN; ☎ in Hanoi 04-943 9660; www.vietnamairlines.com) operates a daily service between Hanoi and Dien Bien Phu; otherwise, take a bus to Dien Bien Phu from Hanoi's Kim Ma or Son La bus stations (100,000d to 120,000d, 16 hours). It's also possible – but not easy – to piece together bus rides to Dien Bien Phu from Lao Cai if you're prepared to sleep a night or two in small towns so you can catch public transport in the early morning.

From Dien Bien Phu, there's a bus at 5.30am on Monday, Wednesday and Friday to the transit hub (relatively speaking) of Muang Khua, 75km inside Laos (60,000d). Travellers say there's no other public transport on the Laos side of the border, so unless you're travelling under your own steam – the crossing is already much loved by cyclists and motorcyclists – this bus is the only option.

See p384 for details on crossing the border in the reverse direction.

out national parks – including one of Ho Chi Minh's personal favourites – and the karst formations that seemingly dropped from the sky into Tam Coc are a must-see.

HANDICRAFT VILLAGES

There are numerous villages surrounding Hanoi that specialise in particular cottage industries. Visiting these villages can make a rewarding day trip, though you'll need a good guide to make the journey worthwhile. Traveller cafés in Hanoi (p832) offer day tours covering several handicraft villages.

Bat Trang is known as the ceramic village. You can watch artisans create superb ceramic vases and other masterpieces in their kilns. Bat Trang is located 13km southeast of Hanoi.

You can see silk cloth being produced on a loom in **Van Phuc**, a silk village that is 8km southwest of Hanoi in Ha Tay province. There's also a small produce market every morning.

So, known for its delicate noodles, is where the yam and cassava flour for noodles are milled. It is in Ha Tay province, about 25km southwest of Hanoi.

The locals in **Le Mat** raise snakes for the upmarket restaurants in Hanoi, and for producing medicinal spirits. Le Mat is 7km northeast of central Hanoi.

Dong Ky survives by producing beautiful, traditional furniture inlaid with mother-of-pearl. It is 15km northeast of Hanoi.

Other handicraft villages in the region produce conical hats, delicate wooden bird cages and herbs.

PERFUME PAGODA

The **perfume Pagoda** (Chua Huong; boat journey & admission 35,000d), about 60km southwest of Hanoi by road, is a complex of pagodas and Buddhist shrines built into the limestone cliffs of **Huong Tich Mountain** (Mountain of the Fragrant Traces). The pagoda is a highlight of the area; the scenery resembles that of Halong Bay, though you're on a river rather than by the sea.

Vast numbers of Buddhist pilgrims come here during a festival that begins in the middle of the second lunar month and lasts until the last week of the third lunar month. These dates usually end up corresponding to March and April. Also keep in mind that weekends tend to draw large crowds, with the attendant litter, vendors and noise.

If you want to do the highly recommended scenic river trip, you need to travel from Hanoi by tour or car to My Duc (two hours), then take a small boat rowed by two women to the foot of the mountain (1½ hours).

The main pagoda area is about a 4km walk up from where the boat lets you off. Two bits of advice: be in decent shape, and bring good walking shoes. The path on this two-hour-plus climb to the top is very steep in places, and when wet, the ground can get very slippery. Shorts are considered disrespectful at the pagoda; wear long pants and long-sleeved shirts.

Hanoi's travel agencies and traveller cafés (see p832) offer day tours to the pagoda for as little as US$9, inclusive of transport, guide and lunch (drinks excluded). If you're going with a group tour, prices start at around US$15. Private small group tours start at around US$80 per person. You can also rent a motorbike to get there on your own; it takes around two to three hours to drive.

BA VI NATIONAL PARK

☎ 034 / elev 1276m

Centred on scenic Ba Vi Mountain (Nui Ba Vi), **Ba Vi National park** (☎ 881 205; admission per person/motorbike 10,000/5000d) boasts more than 2000 flowering plants. There are trekking opportunities through the forested slopes of the mountain, and those who climb up to the summit will be rewarded with a spectacular view of the Red River valley – at least between April and December, when the mist doesn't hide the landscape.

Ba Vi Guesthouse (☎ 881 197; r 120,000-150,000d;) spreads over several blocks in the heart of the park. Prices are an extra 50,000d per room on weekends and there's a big swimming pool that is chaos in the summer months. Go for one of the less-noisy guesthouses away from the pool and restaurant area if you're here on a weekend. You *must* have your passport with you to check into the guesthouse here.

The park restaurant serves good, cheap, fresh-cooked food; a tasty meal for two costs around 50,000d, so make this your lunch stop if you're on a day trip. The toilets are terrible – pee behind a tree.

Ba Vi National park is about 65km west of Hanoi, and is not served by public transport. Make sure your driver knows you want to go to the park rather than Ba Vi town.

NINH BINH

☎ 030 / pop 53,000

Although it started as a travel hub due to its proximity to Tam Coc (9km away; opposite), Hoa Lu (12km; opposite) and Cuc Phuong National Park (45km; opposite), it has evolved into a slow-paced destination in its own right – a welcome respite if you've just escaped the bustle of Hanoi.

The surrounding countryside is gorgeous, with water buffalos, golden-green rice paddies, majestic limestone formations and more. There are plenty of sights in the vicinity to justify a stay of several days. While not a difficult place to visit, Ninh Binh seems to attract interesting travellers with a zest for new experiences. It's a great place to make travel buddies.

Sleeping & Eating

Folks who run guesthouses in Ninh Binh have a reputation for honest, friendly service, although we've had reports of a tout at the train station (claiming to be a guesthouse owner) becoming abusive if travellers chose to ignore his offer. All the places listed here can arrange tours and hire motorbikes and bicycles. And in case you're headed that way, tours to Sapa (p849) can be booked more cheaply here than in Hanoi.

Queen Mini-Hotel (☎ 871 874; 21 Đ Hoang Hoa Tham; dm US$3, r US$5-15;) Though only 30m from Ninh Binh train station, it's a quiet place to stay with a good restaurant.

our pick **Xuan Hoa Hotel** (☎ 880 970; 31D P Minh Khai; dm US$3, r US$8-15;) Mr Xuan has received great reports from readers for his fatherly manner and the cooking from his wife has thrilled some people so much they swear it's the best food in Vietnam. Find the hotel 350m south of the main bridge intersecting Hwy 1, on the other side of a small reservoir.

Thanh Binh Hotel (☎ 872 439; thaibinhhotel@yahoo.com; 31 Đ Luong Van Tuy; r US$6-18; ❄) Very friendly, nice and new, the lower floors have larger rooms but there are some cheapies upstairs. Breakfast is included in the price.

Thuy Anh Hotel (☎ 871 602; 55A P Truong Han Sieu; r US$15-40; ❄ 💻) A long-time family-run backpacker favourite, this place has grown into a busy, clean hotel that pulls in the tour groups. It has a large restaurant, rooftop bar and diversions including a dart board and pool table.

Getting There & Away

The bus station in Ninh Binh is located near the Lim Bridge, just below the overpass to Phat Diem. Regular public buses leave almost hourly for the Giap Bat bus station in Hanoi (28,000d, 2½ hours, 93km). Ninh Binh is also a stop for open-tour buses between Hanoi (US$4, two hours) and Hué (US$6, 10 hours), which drop off and pick up passengers at some of the hotels. If it's not a scheduled stop, friendly pleading usually works on drivers.

Ninh Binh's **train station** (☎ 673 619; 1 Đ Hoang Hoa Tham) is a scheduled stop for the *Reunification Express* trains, with destinations including Hanoi (40,000d, two to 2½ hours, three daily), Thanh Hoa (20,000d, one to 1½ hours, two daily, 60km) and Hué (205,000d, 12½ to 13½ hours, two daily).

AROUND NINH BINH

Tam Coc

Known as 'Halong Bay on the Rice Paddies' for its huge rock formations jutting out of vibrant green rice paddies, Tam Coc definitely gives Halong Bay a run for its money.

Tam Coc (admission 30,000d, boat trip 40,000d) is named after the low caves through which the Ngo Dong River flows. The essential Tam Coc experience is to sit back and be rowed through the caves – a serene and scenic trip, which turns into a surreal dance towards the end.

The boat trip takes about two hours and tickets are sold at the small booking office by the car park. Even on cloudy days, bring sunscreen and a hat or umbrella, as there's no shade in the boats. It pays to arrive early in the morning or around mid-afternoon to avoid the day-tripping crowds from Hanoi.

Restaurants are plentiful at Tam Coc, and if you want to see where all the embroidery comes from, you can visit **Van Lan village**, famous for its embroidery. Here local artisans make napkins, tablecloths, pillowcases and T-shirts.

About 2km past Tam Coc is **Bich Dong**, a cave with a built-in temple. Getting there is easy enough by river or road.

Tam Coc is 9km southwest of Ninh Binh. Follow Hwy 1A south and turn west at the Tam Coc turn-off. Ninh Binh hotels run day tours, but it is more fun to make your own way by bicycle or motorbike; there is a 2000d parking fee. Hotel staff can also advise you on some beautiful back roads that link Tam Coc with Hoa Lu. Traveller cafés in Hanoi book day trips to Tam Coc and Hoa Lu; the fast-food version goes for about US$15, but it's closer to US$20 with a smaller group, comfortable vehicle and professional guide.

Hoa Lu

The scenery here resembles nearby Tam Coc, though Hoa Lu has an interesting historical twist. Hoa Lu was the capital of Vietnam under the Dinh dynasty (968–80) and the Le dynasties (980–1009). The site was a suitable choice for a capital city due to its proximity to China and the natural protection afforded by the region's bizarre landscape.

The **ancient citadel** (admission 10,000d) of Hoa Lu, most of which, sadly, has been destroyed, once covered an area of about 3 sq km. The outer ramparts encompassed temples, shrines and the palace where the king held court. The royal family lived in the inner citadel.

There is no public transport to Hoa Lu, which is 12km northwest of Ninh Binh. Most travellers get here by bicycle, motorbike or car; guesthouses in Ninh Binh can provide basic maps for guidance. Hanoi's traveller cafés (p832) organise day tours combining visits to Hoa Lu and Tam Coc.

CUC PHUONG NATIONAL PARK

Ho Chi Minh personally took time off from the war in 1963 to dedicate **Cuc Phuong National Park** (☎ 848 006; www.cucphuongtourism.com; adult/child 40,000/20,000d), one of Vietnam's first and most important reserves. The hills are laced with grottos and the climate is subtropical at the park's lower elevations.

Excellent trekking opportunities abound in the park, including a trek (8km return) to an enormous **1000-year-old tree** (*Tetrameles nudiflora,* for botany geeks), and to a **Muong village** where you can also go rafting. A guide is not essential for short walks, but is recommended for long trips and mandatory for longer treks.

During the wet season (July to September) leeches are common in the park; the best time to visit is between December and April. Try to visit during the week, as weekends and Vietnamese school holidays get hectic.

One marvellous organisation based in the park is the **Endangered Primate Rescue Center** (☎ 848 002; www.primatecenter.org; admission free; 9-11am & 1-4pm), run by German biologists. The centre is home to around 120 rare monkeys bred in captivity or confiscated from illegal traders. These gibbons, langurs and lorises are rehabilitated, studied and, whenever possible, released back into their native environments or into semiwild protected areas.

Guided tours of the primate centre are free but must be arranged from the main park office. Consider making a donation, or buying some postcards or a poster to support this critical conservation project.

Sleeping & Eating

The best place to stay, if you want to wake up and trek, is in the centre of the park at the **Bong Substation** (18km from the gate). Besides a restaurant and snack shop, there are rooms in a concrete, cold-water **stilt house** (s/d with shared bathroom US$6/12) and a few rooms with hot water in the **bungalows** (r US$25); electricity is an evening-only affair. Nearby is a huge river-fed swimming pool.

There's another **stilt house** (r US$5) near the park headquarters. **Camp sites** (US$2) are also offered here, but you need to bring your own gear. Rooms in the park's **guesthouse** (d US$10-25;) or detached **bungalows** (r US$20;) can be reserved by contacting **Cuc Phuong National Park** (☎ 848 006; www.cucphuongtourism.com; Nho Quan District, Ninh Binh province), or its **Hanoi office** (off Map pp826-7; ☎ 04-829 2604; 1 P Doc Tan AP, Hanoi). All the accommodation here has hot water. There's a stilt house dorm exclusively for large groups and detached bungalows 2km from the park headquarters on **Mac Lake** with similar pricing.

Getting There & Away

Cuc Phuong National park is 45km from Ninh Binh. The turn-off from Hwy 1A is north of Ninh Binh and follows the road that goes to Kenh Gad and Van Long Nature Reserve. There is no public transport all the way to the park so it's best to arrange a motorbike or car in Ninh Binh.

NORTHERN VIETNAM

This is where the magic happens. Here in the head of this dragon-shaped country are many of Vietnam's best sights; limestone cliffs looming in Halong Bay like so many ancient guardians, terraced rice paddies stepping up the side of mountains and colourful gangs of hill-tribe women jogging towards you with warm hellos.

A highly recommended journey from Hanoi is the 'northwest loop'. Head first for Mai Chau, followed by Son La and Dien Bien Phu, then north to Lai Chau, Sapa, Lao Cai, Bac Ha and back to Hanoi. This loop route requires a 4WD or motorbike on many sections, and you should allow at least a week for the trip.

HALONG BAY

With more than 3000 islands rising from the emerald waters of the Gulf of Tonkin, Halong Bay is a Unesco World Heritage site and one of the country's natural marvels. The vegetation-covered islands are dotted with innumerable grottos created by the wind and the waves, and visits to the caves – which ones depends on the weather – are a part of almost every visit here.

From February to April, the weather is often cold and rainy, and the ensuing fog can cause low visibility, although the temperature rarely falls below 10°C. Tropical storms are frequent during the summer months.

To see the islands and grottos, a boat trip is mandatory. Travellers can either book a two- or three-day Halong Bay tour at a traveller café in Hanoi (p832), or can head to Haiphong or Halong City themselves and book a day tour, or head to Cat Ba Island (p845) and explore the bay at their leisure.

Organised trips are reasonably priced, starting as low as US$15 per person on a jam-packed 45-seat bus, and rising to US$40 or more for small-group tours where you can sleep on a junk (recommended!). Most tours include transport, meals, accommodation and boat tours.

If you book a tour package, there is always a small chance that the boat trip may be cancelled due to bad weather. This may entitle you to a partial refund, but remember that the boat trip is only a small portion of the cost of the journey.

Halong City

☎ 033 / pop 149,900

This is one of those travel hubs that stays a travel hub because it doesn't have a whole lot to offer besides access to Halong Bay. It does have a flourishing Thai massage and karaoke scene (read: prostitution).

ORIENTATION & INFORMATION

The town is bisected by a bay – the western side is called Bai Chay and in official schedules is usually treated as a separate city. It's just a short ferry ride (5000d) from the eastern side, known as Hon Gai. Accommodation can be found on both sides but Bai Chay has the bus and boat stations (300m south of the ferry pier), and has a better choice of hotels and restaurants.

Industrial & Commercial Bank (Đ Le Thanh Tong) Useful ATM for those staying in Hon Gai.

Main post office (Đ Halong) Along with the usual postal services, there's cheap and fast internet access with plenty of webcams.

Vietcombank (Đ Halong) A new and more convenient branch in Bai Chay with the usual exchange facilities and ATM.

TOURS

You can wrangle a tour the day you arrive in Halong City, at the marina. If you catch a morning bus to Bai Chay from Hanoi, you can easily grab some lunch before heading to the docks to hire a boat (100,000d). You'll find a lot of Vietnamese and foreign travellers milling around the harbour trying to arrange afternoon tours around the bay.

The **booking office** (🕑 8.30am-5.30pm; 3-4hr tour 30,000d) at the marina (1.5km west of Bai Chay), offers a range of tours at fixed prices. Tickets usually include admission to several caves and grottos on the bay. Day tours are fine, but staying overnight on a boat is recommended.

GETTING TO CHINA

In the far northeast, the Mong Cai border crossing (open 7.30am to 4.30pm) is just opposite the Chinese city of Dongxing. To use this border, your Chinese visa *must* be issued in Hanoi. Hydrofoils (US$12, three hours) to Mong Cai leave Bai Chay in Halong City at 8am and 1pm. Haiphong has a fast boat (200,000d, four hours) and an economical slower boat (70,000d); see p846 for details.

SLEEPING

In Bai Chay, the heaviest concentration of hotels is in the 'hotel alley'. Expect to pay US$10 to US$15 for a double room with private bathroom and air-con. Up the hillside from Đ Halong, a couple of hotels with views of the bay provide an interesting alternative.

Bong Lai Hotel (☎ 845 658; d US$10; ❄) Clean, cheap and friendly.

Thanh Hué Hotel (☎ 847 612; 17 Đ Vuon Dao; r US$10-12; ❄) On the same hill as the Hoang Lan, the climb up is worth it.

OUR PICK Hoang Lan Hotel (☎ 846 504; 17 Đ Vuon Dao; r US$10-18; ❄) Friendly hosts and the usual amenities: hot water, satellite TV and fridge, with the added bonus of a free breakfast.

Hai Long Hotel (☎ 846 378; d US$12; ❄) Of a slightly higher standard, this place is a bit bigger with more great views from the rooftop.

EATING

The area just west of central Bai Chay contains a solid row of cheap restaurants. Over in Hon Gai, check out the string of local eateries along P Ben Doan. If you're on a tour, meals should be included in the price.

GETTING THERE & AWAY

Buses from Hanoi leave the Gia Lam station for Bai Chay (35,000d, three hours). From Bai Chay to Hanoi, buses leave from Mien Tay bus station until 2.30pm. Buses to Haiphong (18,000d, two hours) leave from across the road of Mien Tay station. Buses bound for Mong Cai (35,000d, six hours) on the Chinese border leave from Hon Gai bus station.

Slow boats connecting Hon Gai with Haiphong (30,000d, three hours) leave at 6.30am, 11am and 4pm daily. Schedules are prone to change, so always check the times beforehand.

A slow boat connects Hon Gai to Cat Hai Island (30,000d, two hours) but departure times vary. At Cat Hai you can hop on another small ferry to get to Cat Ba Island (30,000d, two hours).

For China-bound travellers, there are hydrofoils to Mong Cai; see left for details.

Cat Ba Island

☎ 031 / pop 7000

Laid-back and oddly endearing, the only populated island in Halong Bay is a nice destination on its own but the location makes it a must-visit. Half of the island was declared a national park in 1986 in order to protect the diverse ecosystems and wildlife here. There are long beaches, lakes, waterfalls and grottos set in the spectacular limestone hills.

The most famous native here is the endangered Cat Ba langur; a golden-haired little monkey that has a punk-rock hairdo. The island's human population is concentrated in the southern part of the island, around the town of Cat Ba.

INFORMATION

There are no banks in Cat Ba town, but there are a few jewellery stores north of the harbour that exchange dollars.

Pacific Internet Café (Per min 200d; 8am-7pm) Has a roomful of terminals.

Post office (7.30am-9pm Mon-Fri) Near the ferry landing on the main drag; international calls can be made from here.

Tourism Information & Development Centre (688 215; D 1-4) The staff here can bring you up to speed on transport options on and around Cat Ba, plus they have *Cat Ba Biosphere Reserve* maps.

SIGHTS & ACTIVITIES

Home to 32 species of monkey, wild boar and hedgehog, **Cat Ba National Park** (216 350; admission 15,000d, guide per day US$5; dawn-dusk) has a myriad trekking opportunities. Even though a guide is not mandatory, it's recommended.

There's a very challenging 18km trek (five to six hours) through the park that many enjoy. You need a guide, transport to the trailhead and a boat to return, all of which can be arranged in Cat Ba town.

To reach the national-park headquarters at Trung Trang, take a minibus from one of the hotels in Cat Ba town (15,000d, 30 minutes). Another option is to hire a motorbike (one way 30,000d).

Hospital Cave (Admission 30,000d) was used as a secret hospital during the American War – an amazing example of Vietnamese engineering born of necessity. It's best to ask the hotel or motorbike driver to call ahead to the colourful guardian of the cave, Vu Dinh Khoi, who served here during the American War.

The white-sand **Cat Co beaches** (called simply Cat Co 1, Cat Co 2 and Cat Co 3) are perfect places to lounge around for the day; however,

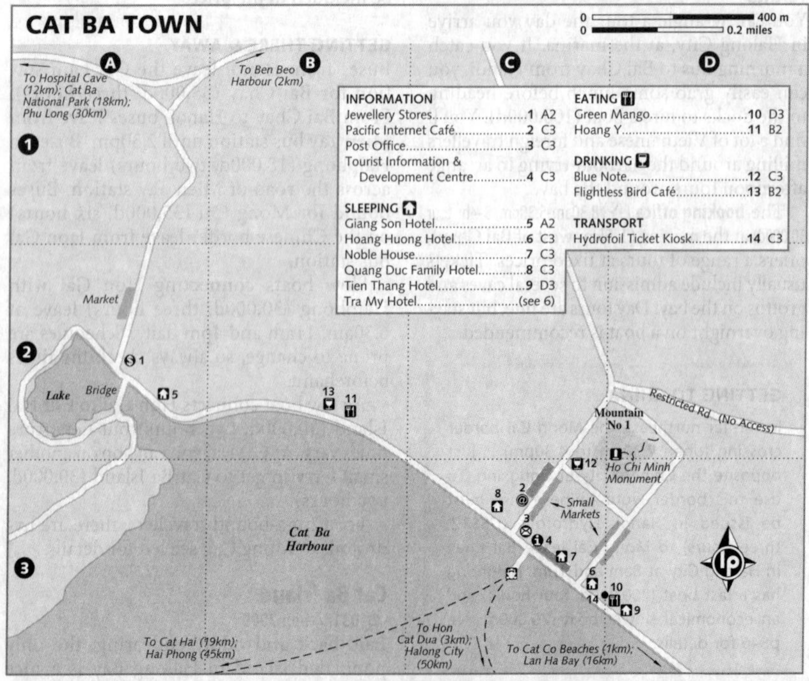

Cat Co 1 and 3 are being transformed into big resorts. Cat Co 2 is the least busy and the most attractive beach, also offering simple accommodation and camping (see right). To get there, take the wooden cliffside walkway connecting it to Cat Co 1.

The beaches are about 1km from Cat Ba town and can be reached on foot or by motorbike for about 10,000d.

TOURS

Tours of the island and national park, boat trips around Halong Bay and fishing trips are Peddled by nearly every hotel and restaurant in Cat Ba town. Typical prices are US$10 per person for day trips and US$20 for a two-day/one-night trip.

SLEEPING

Most of the island's hotels are concentrated along the bayfront in Cat Ba town. Room rates fluctuate greatly between high-season summer months (May to September) and the slower winter months (October to April). Listed here are winter prices, which you can often bargain down; high season rates are anywhere from two to six times as much as the low season rates.

Giang Son Hotel (☎ 888 214; d US$4-15; ❄) On the western side of town, some rooms have great views of the rocky outcrop across the harbour and there's a decent restaurant downstairs.

our pick **Hoang Huong Hotel** (☎ 888 274; d US$6-12; ❄) The front rooms of this family-run place have enormous windows looking out on the water.

Tra My Hotel (☎ 888 650; d US$6-12) Right next to the Hoang Huong Hotel, the rooms look sparkling new and there are some rather oddly decorated tiles in some of the bathrooms – there was a topless woman in blue jeans above our tub.

Quang Duc Family Hotel (☎ 888 231; d US$8; ❄) Cat Ba's original family-run hotel keeps quacking away, with rooms equipped with satellite TV.

Tien Thang Hotel (☎ 888 568; tienthanghotel@yahoo.com; r US$10; ❄) It offers midrange standards at budget prices with satellite TV, big bathrooms and private sea-view balconies.

Noble House (☎ 888 363; www.hihostels.com, do a country search; Đ 1-4; r US$10-30; ❄) Small in size, big in character, it has a 2nd-floor bar and a good restaurant downstairs that spills into the street.

If the town gets too busy, try a night in the rustic **guesthouse** (r 120,000d) over on Cat Co 2. The national park also has a **guesthouse** (r US$10) offshore on Hon Cat Dua (Pineapple Island). If you want to camp here, you'll have to bring your own gear and plan on being self-sufficient for the night. Private boats (90,000d) and accommodation on the island can be arranged at Quang Duc Family Hotel.

EATING & DRINKING

There are a number of small markets along the two small streets that intersect the main drag. A cheap beer stall opens up in the evening on the western side of the strip.

Hoang Y (mains 35,000d; 🕑 lunch & dinner) Serves a variety of fantastic seafood and vegetarian dishes.

Phuong Phuong (☎ 888 254; meals 45,000d; 💻) Dinner is swimming in large tanks near the tables and sometimes the staff put up a large screen for sporting events.

Green Mango (☎ 887 151; Đ 1-4; mains 50,000-100,000d) The birth of cool in Cat Ba; if you don't want to cough up the price of dinner here, the outdoor patio is good for a drink and a long hour of smoking tobacco in hookahs (60,000d).

Flightless Bird Cafe (☎ 888 517; 🕑 from 6.30pm) A hip waterfront spot that has darts, movies, music, books and Australian wine (20,000d a glass). The Kiwi owner is a good source of local information, and he'll even make you a packed lunch if you order ahead.

Blue Note (Đ Nui Ngoc) The place to rock the Cat Ba; besides a bar that stays open late it has a stage for karaoke and a big selection of English-language hits.

GETTING THERE & AROUND

Cat Ba Island is 45km east of Haiphong, and 20km south of Halong City. Hydrofoils (70,000/90,000d, 45/75 minutes) travel daily between Cat Ba town and Haiphong; the longer boat trips provide lots of sightseeing on the way. Ask locally about departure times, which change frequently, and show up early if travelling during the high season. On Cat Ba there's a hydrofoil ticket kiosk about 100m east of the ferry landing, but you can also buy tickets at the landing a few hours before departure.

Another way to get from Halong City to Cat Ba is to hop on one of the tourist boats (100,000d, five hours) that leave several times a day. This is less organised going in the other direction to Halong City but hotels can help.

Most hotels can find you a cheap Chinese bicycle; inquire at Flightless Bird Cafe (p845) about mountain-bike rentals.

Motorbike rentals (with or without driver) are available from most of the hotels. If you're heading to the beaches or national park, pay the 2000d parking fee to ensure your vehicle isn't stolen or vandalised.

Haiphong

☎ 031 / pop 1.67 million

Vietnam's third-most populous city retains a relaxed feel with its tall colonial-style buildings and tree-lined avenues. An important seaport and a major industrial centre, Haiphong is mostly used as a stepping-stone by travellers on their way to Cat Ba Island and Halong Bay. But, people who sit a spell find that it's a charming place to spend a day.

INFORMATION

A number of ATMs and internet cafés line P Dien Bien Phu near the main tourist highlights.

Main post office (3 P Nguyen Tri Phuong) It's easy to spot, standing on a corner in dignified yellow.

Vietcombank (11 P Hoang Dieu; closed Sat) Cashes travellers cheques, does cash advances and has an ATM.

Vietnam-Czech Friendship Hospital (P Nha Thuong) In emergencies, get medical help here; otherwise head for Hanoi.

SIGHTS & ACTIVITIES

The slow-paced appeal is enhanced by the **French colonial architecture** along the streets between the ferry landing and the Tam Bac bus station. The tree-shaded avenues in this neighbourhood make for a nice stroll if you've got time to kill.

Du Hang Pagoda (Chua Du Hang; 121 P Chua Hang; 7-11am & 1.30-5.50pm), founded three centuries ago and rebuilt several times since, has architectural elements that look Khmer-influenced. Just as cool is meandering along the narrow alley it's on, **P Chua Hang**, which is bustling with Haiphong street life.

SLEEPING

Hotel du Commerce (☎ 384 2706; 62 P Dien Bien Phu; r US$10-18;) Housed in an old French Colonial building, basics include satellite TV, fridge and hot water.

Duyen Hai Hotel (☎ 384 2134; 6 Đ Nguyen Tri Phuong; r 200,000-300,000d;) This is a good deal with a central location. The cheaper rooms are small but clean. All rooms come with TV and bathtubs.

Khach San Thang Nam (☎ 374 7216; vntourism.hp@bdvn.vnmail.vnd.net; 55 P Dien Bien Phu; r US$15-18;) This is one of the best all-rounders in town, with bright, clean rooms and modern conveniences.

EATING

P Minh Khai offers a good selection of cheap eateries; and most hotel restaurants dish up variations on the fresh seafood available in Haiphong. Also check out P Quang Trung with its many cafés and *bia hoi*.

Galaxy Cafe (☎ 382 3530; 91 Dien Bien Phu; mains from 15,000d; breakfast, lunch & dinner) A friendly little place, the red wine *pho* with succulent chunks of beef (18,000d) is a winner.

Com Vietnam (☎ 384 1698; 4 P Hoang Van Thu; mains from 20,000d; lunch & dinner) It's consistently popular with locals thanks to affordable local seafood and Vietnamese specialities. It sometimes waits for the dinner crowd before it opens.

GETTING THERE & AWAY

Be careful of the touts near the Haiphong ferry pier. They've been known to give misinformation on transport options to try to make a commission.

Vietnam Airlines (code VN; ☎ 9381 0890; www.vietnamair.com.vn; 30 P Hoang Van Thu) serves the Haiphong–Ho Chi Minh City (HCMC) and the Haiphong–Danang routes.

Transtour (☎ 384 1009) runs the *Mekong Express* (100,000d), which is the safest and most comfortable boat to Cat Ba; it also has a daily fast boat to Mong Cai (200,000d, four hours). **Tahaco** (☎ 374 7055) has smaller hydrofoils, which are cheaper at 70,000d. There are no longer hydrofoils operating to Halong City, as the road journey is faster. All boats leave from the **ferry Pier** (Đ Ben Binh), 10 minutes' walk from the centre of town.

Haiphong has three long-distance bus stations. Buses to Hanoi (35,000d, two hours) leave from **Tam Bac bus station** (P Tam Bac) about every 10 minutes throughout the day. Buses to points south such as Ninh Binh leave from **Niem Nghia bus station** (Đ Tran Nguyen Han).

Lac Long bus station (P Cu Chinh Lan) has buses to Bai Chay (Halong City; 25,000d, 1½ hours), and to/from Hanoi.

The express local train (22,000d, two hours) goes to Hanoi from the **Haiphong train station** (cnr Đ Luong Khanh Thien & Đ Pham Ngu Lao) at 6.25pm daily. There is also a train at 8.55pm (22,000d, 2½ hours). From Hanoi, trains leave **Tran Quy Cap station** (B station; ☎ 04-825 2628; P Tran Qui Cap) at 5.50am; other trains leave from Long Bien train station several times daily.

BA BE NATIONAL PARK

☎ 0281 / elev 145m

Boasting waterfalls, rivers, deep valleys, lakes and caves, **Ba Be National park** (Ba Be Lakes; ☎ 894 014; fax 894 026; admission per person/car 10,000/20,000d) is surrounded by steep mountains that reach up to 1554m high. In other words, this place has it all.

The surrounding area is home to members of the Tay minority, who live in stilt homes. The park is a tropical rainforest area with more than 400 named plant species. The 300 wildlife species in the forest include bears, monkeys, bats and butterflies.

Ba Be (Three Bays) is in fact three linked lakes, the largest freshwater lake system in the country. The Nang River is navigable for 23km between a point 4km above Cho Ra and the **Dau Dang Waterfall** (Thac Dau Dang), which is a series of spectacular cascades between sheer walls of rock. The interesting **Puong Cave** (Hang Puong) is about 30m high and 300m long, and passes completely through a mountain. A navigable river flows through the cave.

The park staff can organise several tours. Costs depend on the number of people, but expect to pay at least US$25 per day if you're travelling alone. There's the option of a one-day tour by boat, or a one-day tour combining motorboat, a 3km or 4km walk, and a trip by dugout canoe; longer treks can also be arranged.

Sleeping & Eating

Not far from the park headquarters are two accommodation options. Rooms in the newer **guesthouse** (r 165,000d) are fine, if a bit pricey. There are also comfortable two-room **cottages** (r 275,000d) with air-con. There's a reasonable **restaurant** (mains 10,000-30,000d) – note that you'll need to place your order an hour or so before you want to eat.

Homestays at the **stilt houses** (per person 60,000d) in Pac Ngoi village, on the lakeshore, are becoming quite popular. The park office can help organise this onsite or call ahead. Food is available at the homestays, which can include fresh fish from the lake, and prices are reasonable.

Take enough cash for your visit – there are no money-exchange facilities, although there are banks in Bac Kan, the provincial capital en route from Hanoi.

Getting There & Away

The lakes are 240km north of Hanoi. Most visitors to the national park get here by chartered vehicle from Hanoi and since the 2000 opening of a new road into the park, 4WD is no longer necessary. The one-way journey from Hanoi takes about six hours; most travellers allow three days and two nights for the trip. Some traveller cafés in Hanoi (see p832) offer tours to Ba Be starting at US$60 per day. The longer the tour the lower the price per day, usually.

It's possible to get here solo. Take a bus from Hanoi to Phu Thong (50,000d, five hours) via Thai Nguyen and/or Bac Kan, and from there take another bus to Cho Ra (15,000d, one hour). In Cho Ra arrange a motorbike (about 40,000d) to cover the last 18km.

MAI CHAU

Mai Chau is one of the closest places to Hanoi where you can visit a hill-tribe village. The modern village is an unappealing sprawl, but as you emerge on the rice fields and scenes of rural life it is transformed into a real paradise. Most people here are ethnic White Thai, distantly related to tribes in Thailand, Laos and China. Although most locals no longer wear traditional dress, the Thai women are masterful weavers. Polite bargaining is the norm rather than endless haggling.

Information

Guides can be hired for around US$5 for a 7km to 8km walk. There is a popular 18km trek from **Lac village** (Ban Lac) in Mai Chau to **Xa Linh village**, near a mountain pass (elevation 1000m) on Hwy 6. Lac village is home to the White Thai people, while the inhabitants of Xa Linh are Hmong. The trek is quite strenuous to undertake in a day, so most people spend the night in a village along the way. Arrange a local guide and a car to meet you at the mountain pass for the journey back to Mai Chau.

Staying overnight in White Thai stilt houses and trekking to minority villages further afield can also be arranged. Ask around the Mai Chau villages of Lac or Pom Coong. Be aware that Mai Chau sees a lot of tourists and has all the modern comforts: TVs, toilets and all.

Tourists must pay an admission fee of 5000d to enter Mai Chau, but the booth where the fee is collected in rarely staffed.

Sleeping & Eating

Most backpackers prefer to stay a few hundred metres back from the main road in **White Thai stilt houses** (per person 50,000d) in Lac or Pom Coong villages. Most of these homes serve meals for about 20,000d and travellers are usually very pleased with their stay and the food. Reservations are not necessary, but it's advisable to arrive before dark.

Villagers will sometimes organise traditional song-and-dance performances in the evenings and anyone is free to join in the fun. A mild word of warning about the showers: the doors may have fairly large gaps between the walls; use your towel to good effect.

Getting There & Away

Mai Chau is 135km southwest of Hanoi and just 5km south of Tong Dau junction on Hwy 6. There's no direct public transport to Mai Chau from Hanoi; however, buses to nearby Hoa Binh (25,000d, two hours) are plentiful. From Hoa Binh there are several scheduled buses to Mai Chau (20,000d, two hours) daily. Usually these stop at Tong Dau junction; a *xe om* from there to Mai Chau proper will cost about 15,000d.

Many traveller cafés and travel agencies in Hanoi (p832) run inexpensive trips to Mai Chau.

LAO CAI

☎ 020 / pop 100,000

Travellers can raise their arms on the back of a motorbike here à la *Titanic* and truthfully exclaim, 'I'm on top of Vietnam!' One could almost bump into China by accident – that giant looms just 3km from the train station. Lao Cai is now the main hub for travellers journeying between Hanoi, Sapa and Kunming.

Information

There is internet access across from the train station.

BIDV bank (Đ Thuy Hoa) Does currency exchange and has an ATM; it's on the west side of the river, near Lao Cai's bus station.

Post office (⏰ 7am-7pm) If you're facing the train station, the post office stands directly to the left.

Sleeping & Eating

Binh Minh Hotel (☎ 830 085; 39 P Nguyen Hué; d US$7-10; ❄) It has very friendly staff, and clean rooms with all the basics.

Gia Nga (☎ 830 459; P Moi; s & d US$8-10, shower & soap 20,000d; ❄) Very clean, and closest to the train station, this is good value. There's also a shower and luggage room for groggy arrival and departure clean-ups.

Friendly Cafe (☎ 832 759; 322 Đ Nguyen Hué; meals 15,000d, ⏰ breakfast, lunch & dinner) This is a popular café located near the entrance of the train station.

our pick **Hoang Hai** (☎ 835 437; 339 322 Đ Nguyen Hué; meals 15,000d; ⏰ breakfast, lunch & dinner) Good food and very friendly staff who will let you leave bags here.

Getting There & Away

Lao Cai is 340km northwest of Hanoi. Minibuses to Sapa (25,000d, 1½ hours) leave regularly until late afternoon. Minibuses to Bac Ha (28,000d, two hours) leave several times daily; the last at 1pm. Sometimes there's a table-top ticket booth right before the station exit. This is where the Vietnamese buy bus tickets; it's the usual price but the buses fill up and leave right away. Train tickets to Hanoi (10 hours) start at 79,000d for a hard seat to 223,000d for an air-conditioned soft sleeper, and rise by about 10% at weekends. A motorbike taxi to the Chinese border will cost about 10,000d.

GETTING TO CHINA

The Lao Cai–Hekou crossing (open 7am to 5pm), northwest of Hanoi, is popular with travellers making their way between northern Vietnam and China's Yunnan province. China is separated from Vietnam by a bridge over the Red River that pedestrians pay a 3000d toll to cross. The border is about 3km from Lao Cai train station; the short motorbike journey costs 15,000d. To get to Kunming, take a train to Lao Cai (see above), cross the border into China, and catch a midmorning or overnight sleeper bus (US$11, 12 hours) or train (US$10, 16 hours) from the Chinese border town of Hekou.

CHINA GUIDEBOOKS CONFISCATED

Travellers entering China by road or rail from Vietnam report that Lonely Planet *China* guidebooks have been confiscated by border officials. This is due to sensitivity regarding maps of China that do not include Taiwan. Travellers should consider putting a cover on the book to make it less recognisable or copying crucial details.

SAPA

☎ 020 / pop 36,200

Sapa is the most heavily touristed place in northwestern Vietnam for good reason. Originally a hill station built by the French in 1922 it still feels like a mountain town, albeit a busy one during weekend markets. Hill-tribe women with colourful head gear, and some with retro-looking leggings, dye and sell their fabrics on the sidewalk while their children chase tourists. Hill-tribe men have an out-of-this-world look as they run errands on motorbikes wearing black petticoats with high collars, leather tunics, silver chain-link necklaces and bubble-visor helmets. This city in the clouds is nestled in spectacular scenery and makes a great base for day trips or overnights in the many hill-tribe villages nearby. Don't forget your warm clothes – Sapa is known for its cold, foggy winters.

Information

A minute on the internet will cost you about 100d at guesthouses and travel agencies around town. Most hotels will exchange dollars for dong (at worse exchange rates than in Hanoi). Tour agencies can arrange a visa to China here, but it's much less expensive and quicker in Hanoi.

There is an official **Railway Booking Office** (☎ 871 480; 7.30-11am & 1.30-4pm) on P Cau May, which charges a 7000d service booking fee for seats, and 10,000d for a sleeper. It's probably best to buy train tickets to Hanoi here. Travellers have reported bad experiences buying tickets through hotels.

Sapa Tourism Information & Promotion Centre (☎ 871 975; 2 Đ Phan Xi Pang; 8.30-11.30am & 1.30-5.30pm) is a ground-floor kiosk in a French Colonial house set back from the street that can arrange local tour guides, provide information on lodging and has information for short-term volunteer work at nearby villages.

BIDV (☎ 872 569; Đ Ngu Chi Son; 7-11.30 & 1.30-4.30pm) is currently the best all-rounder in town, with an ATM, plus it changes travellers cheques and cash. It is by the lake in the new part of town.

Sights & Activities

Surrounding Sapa are the Hoang Lien Mountains, including **Fansipan**, which at 3143m is Vietnam's highest peak. The trek from Sapa to the summit and back usually takes two nights and three days, with an overnight in a base camp both nights. Treks can be arranged at guesthouses and travel agencies around town. Check these:

Auberge Hotel (☎ 871 243; auberge@sapadiscovery.com; P Cau May)

Mountain View Hotel (Ninh Hong Guesthouse; ☎ 871 334; ninhhong@hn.vnn.vn; 54A P Cau May)

Topas Travel (☎ 871 331; www.topas-adventure-vietnam.com; 28 P Cau May) Also offers half-day mountain-bike tours (US$28) that are an absolute must for maniacs who love flying down big hills.

Some of the better-known sights around Sapa include **Tram Ton Pass**, **Thac Bac** (Silver Falls) and **Cau May** (Cloud Bridge), which spans the Muong Hoa River.

Ham Rong Mountain (P Ham Rong; admission 30,000d; 7am-7pm, open later for cultural events) is perfect for those who are eager to see a bit of nature but are too tired after the night train to commit to a full-day trek; this is more a manicured light-trekking area than a national park.

Sleeping

our pick **Queen Hotel** (☎ 871 301; sapaqueenhotel@yahoo.com; Đ Muong Hoa; r US$5-10) Has fun and friendly staff and all rooms have hot water and TV. Aim high for views.

Sapa Green Valley (☎ 872 164; sapawelcomes@vnn.vn; 45 29 Đ Muong Hoa; r USUS$6-8) The rooms are less fresh than at other places but it doesn't get much cheaper than this.

Mountain View Hotel (☎ 871 334; hong64@yahoo.com; 54A P Cau May; s & d US$6-15) The hotel has a great location in the centre of everything and lives up to its name with stunning views.

Tulip Hotel (☎ 871 914; 29 Đ Muong Hoa; r US$7-8) The Tulip has small, simple, clean rooms and some have terrific views. One could do wind sprints on its huge terrace to train for hard-core trekking and it serves French and Vietnamese food in its restaurant.

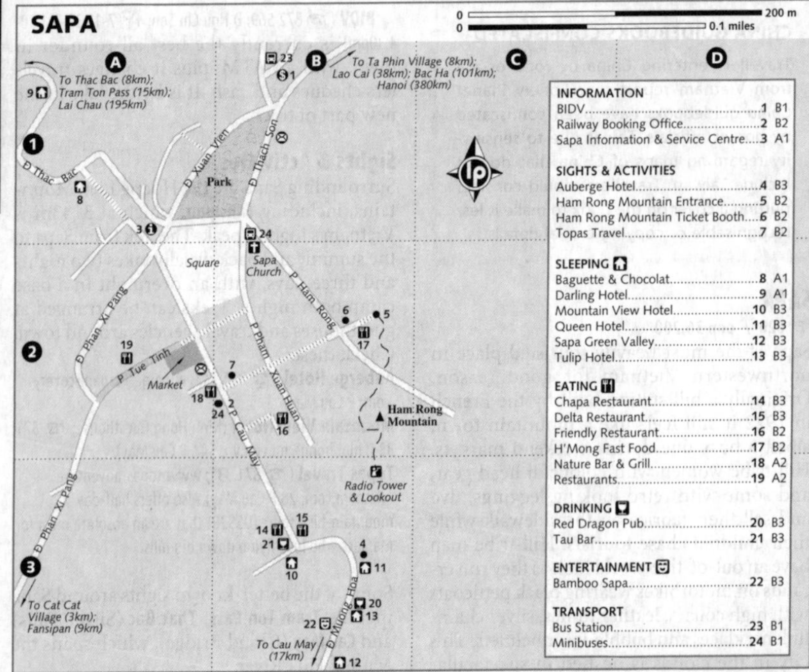

Darling Hotel (☎ 835 463; Đ Thac Bac; r US$10-12) A good deal considering that even the cheapest rooms are huge and have a working fireplace. There's satellite TV and real bathtubs, and shared balconies that have great views.

Baguette & Chocolat (☎ 871 766; Đ Thac Bac; r US$18) Rents out four cosy rooms with names such as 'Cookies', but book well in advance. A favourite for couples and families, it has a pleasant restaurant, and your bill goes toward providing valuable career training for disadvantaged local kids.

Eating

If none of the suggestions below work there are also several small family-run restaurants serving inexpensive Vietnamese food on P Tue Tinh in the market area.

H'Mong Fast Food (Ban H'Mohng; ☎ 216 651; P Ham Rong; mains 15,000d; breakfast, lunch & dinner) The menu is outside and nothing is in English but it's easy to point to the simmering Hmong goodies on display. The soup with floating dumplings is very good.

our pick **Nature Bar & Grill** (☎ 872 094; 24 P Cau May; meals 15,000-50,000d; breakfast, lunch & dinner) Offers an extensive menu of Vietnamese food and a few Western dishes set in what feels like a mountain lodge.

Friendly Restaurant (P Cau May; mains 20,000d; breakfast, lunch & dinner) Up some stairs off P Cau May and set between two other good and cheap eateries, what sets this place apart is the tastiness of the food.

Chapa Restaurant (☎ 871 045; 40 P Cau May; mains from 25,000d; breakfast, lunch & dinner) The nicest of the traveller cafés that line P Cau May, it has the usual suspects on the menu and some slightly pricier Vietnamese specialities.

Delta Restaurant (☎ 871 799; P Cau May; mains US$5; lunch & dinner) The taste of Italy in Sapa, Delta turns out the most authentic pizzas in town. It also boasts a good selection of wines and offers take-away and delivery.

Drinking & Entertainment

Depending on the night of the week and season you may have the undivided attention of the barman; trekking seems to put a damper on late-night carousing. A number of new places are springing up but these two are your best bets for signs of life.

Red Dragon Pub (☎ 872 085; 21 Đ Muong Hoa) A veritable wee Britain, upstairs is the go-to place for backpackers of all ages to have a drink, a meal, or make a friend.

Tau Bar (☎ 871 322; 42 P Cau May) Claiming to be 'slightly lounge', Tau brings a different kind of cool to the mountains of the north. There is a DIY jukebox on the computer, the cocktails are mixed by a pro and there is a good pool table.

Bamboo Sapa (☎ 871 076; bamboosapa@hn.vnn.vn; P Cau May) Hosts a free traditional hill-tribe music-and-dance show from 8.30pm Friday and Saturday.

Getting There & Away

The gateway to Sapa is Lao Cai, 38km away on the Chinese border. Buses to points west, such as Dien Bien Phu, pass through a few times a day from Lao Cai. Sapa's bus station (for minibuses in this case) is in the north of town.

Minibuses make the trip from the Lao Cai train station regularly between 5am and 5pm (25,000d, 1½ hours). In Sapa, minibuses wait in front of the church but do not run to any particular schedule. The advertised rate of hotel minibus services to Bac Ha (110km) for the Sunday market is around US$10 per person.

For excursions out of Sapa, you can hire a self-drive motorbike for about US$6 per day or take one with a driver for about US$10. Renting a jeep with a driver is a fun way to tool around, and costs about US$12 for a half-day for up to four people. Driving a motorbike from Hanoi to Sapa is feasible, but the distance is 380km. The last 38km are straight uphill – not advised on a bicycle unless you are a very serious and in-shape cyclist.

Getting Around

Downtown Sapa can be walked in 20 minutes. Cat Cat village (3km) is an easy downhill walk through green fields and small houses along a winding path.

BAC HA

☎ 020 / pop 70,200

A quieter and slightly less scenic alternative to Sapa, Bac Ha is a small highland town that becomes downright hectic during the Sunday market. Unless travellers are looking for a souvenir water buffalo or horse, the most interesting thing for sale here is moonshine – rice wine, cassava wine and corn liquor. There's an entire area devoted to Bac Ha's famous hooch at the Sunday market.

Arriving midweek makes for a relaxing visit and good base to explore the surrounding highlands. Around 900m above sea level, it is noticeably warmer than Sapa. There are 10 Montagnard ethnic groups that live around Bac Ha and many of them sell their handicraft wares: the colourful Flower Hmong are the most visible.

Sights & Activities

BAN PHO VILLAGE

The Hmong villagers in Ban Pho are some of the kindest people you'll meet in Vietnam. Ban Pho is a 7km return trip from Bac Ha. You can take a loop route to get there and back.

Other nearby villages include **Trieu Cai** (8km return), **Na Ang** (6km return) and **Na Hoi** (4km return). Ask at your hotel for directions.

MONTAGNARD MARKETS

Other than the colourful Sunday **Bac Ha market** in town, there are several interesting markets nearby, all within about 20km of each other.

Can Cau market, one of Vietnam's most exotic open-air markets, is 20km north of Bac Ha and just 9km south of the Chinese border. The market runs on Saturday.

Coc Ly market takes place on Tuesday, about 35km from Bac Ha. There's a pretty good road, or you can go by road and river; ask at hotels in Bac Ha to organise trips.

Lung Phin market is between Can Cau market and Bac Ha town, about 12km from the town. It's less busy, and runs on Sunday.

Sleeping & Eating

There are quite a lot of hotels in Bac Ha but very few stand out from the pack. Room rates tend to increase on weekends when tourists flock to town for the Sunday market; it can be hard to find a room at these times.

Dai Thanh Hotel (☎ 880 448; r 60,000d) Rooms include hot water, TV, mosquito net and ceiling fan – a real steal.

Toan Thang Hotel (☎ 880 444; r 80,000d) Set in a sweet but solid wooden house, the rooms here are very good value. All include a fan, local TV and a hot-water bathroom.

Minh Quan Hotel (☎ 880 222; r 120,000-150,000d) Enjoy a bird's-eye view of the Sunday market from this comfortable hotel. Rooms include smart bathrooms and some have immense views of the mountains beyond.

Cong Phu Restaurant (☎ 880 254; mains 15,000-30,000d) No, the waiters don't look like extras out of a Bruce Lee movie, but they do offer wholesome meals. Just tick the boxes on the photocopy menus and food will arrive.

Getting There & Away

Minibuses depart from Lao Cai for Bac Ha (28,000d, two hours) around 6.30am and 1pm daily. Buses from Bac Ha leave for Lao Cai between 5.30am and 1pm. The road is well maintained and the rural scenery sublime.

Locals on motorbikes will do the Lao Cai–Bac Ha run for about US$10, or even Sapa–Bac Ha (110km) for US$15, but it's a long way to be on the back of a bike. Sunday minibus tours from Sapa to Bac Ha start at US$10, including transport, guide and trekking to a minority village. On the way back to Sapa you can bail out in Lao Cai and catch the night train back to Hanoi.

Bac Ha is about 330km (10 hours) from Hanoi. Some cafés in Hanoi (see p832) offer four-day bus trips to Sapa, with a visit to Bac Ha included.

CENTRAL COAST

Stretching from the former capital of Vietnam down to the ancient trading Port of Hoi An, the coast is sprinkled with the country's most cultured cities and sites that include Cham ruins and storeyed pagodas. The area also saw the fiercest fighting in the American War; battlegrounds where blood and sacrifice changed the course of a nation now lie desolate.

HUÉ

Big enough to have plenty to see and do but not so big that it's overwhelming, Hué is one of Vietnam's cultural, religious and educational centres. Hué served as the political capital from 1802 to 1945 under the 13 emperors of the Nguyen dynasty. Today, Hué's decaying, opulent tombs of the Nguyen emperors and grand, crumbling Citadel comprise a Unesco World Heritage site. Most of these architectural attractions lie along the northern side of the Song Huong (Perfume River).

For rest, refreshment and recreation, the river's south side is where the action's at.

Information

INTERNET ACCESS

There are plenty of internet cafés along the northern end of Đ Hung Vuong and around the intersection of Đ Nguyen Tri Phuong. Many hotels and traveller cafés also offer internet access for 6000d to 10,000d per hour.

MEDICAL SERVICES

Hué Central Hospital (Benh Vien Trung Uong Hué; ☎ 822 325; 16 Đ Le Loi) Close to Phu Xuan Bridge.

MONEY

It would take an effort miss the many ATMs here. Some safe bets for travellers cheques and money exchange:

Industrial & Development Bank (☎ 823 361; 41 Đ Hung Vuong) Same services as Vietcombank, sans ATM.

Vietcombank (54 Đ Hung Vuong) Exchanges travellers cheques, processes cash advances and has an ATM. Another convenient branch with a 24-hour ATM is on Đ Hung Vuong in front of Hotel Saigon Morin.

POST

Branch post office (18 Đ Le Loi) Near the river.

Main post office (8 Đ Hoang Hon Thiem; 6.30am-9.30pm) In an imposing building that's hard to miss, this post office offers international calling, phone cards, and processes domestic and international packages.

TRAVEL AGENCIES

See opposite for more travel-agency options.

Mandarin Cafe (☎ 821 281; mandarin@dng.vnn.vn; 3 Đ Hung Vuong) Watched over by the eagle eyes of photographer Mr Cu, this place is great for information, transport and tours. You can also eat here (see p857).

Sinh Café (☎ 823 309; www.sinhcafevn.com; 7 Đ Nguyen Tri Phuong) Books open-tour buses and buses to Laos.

Sights & Activities

CITADEL

Give yourself plenty of time to explore one of Vietnam's disintegrating treasures, Hué's **Citadel** (Kinh Thanh). A former imperial city on the northern bank of the Song Huong, and later heavily bombed by the Americans, much of it is now used for agriculture but its scope and beauty still impress.

Construction of the moated Citadel, by Emperor Gia Long, began in 1804. The emperor's official functions were carried out in the **Imperial Enclosure** (Dai Noi, or Hoang Thanh; admission 55,000d; 6.30am-5.30pm), a 'citadel within the Citadel'. Inside the 6m-high, 2.5km-long wall is a surreal world of deserted gardens and ceremonial halls.

Within the Imperial Enclosure is the **Forbidden Purple City** (Tu Cam Thanh), which was reserved for the private life of the emperor. The only servants allowed inside were eunuchs, who posed no threat to the royal concubines. Nowadays, all are welcome.

ROYAL TOMBS

Set like gems on the banks of the Song Huong, the **Tombs of the Nguyen Dynasty** (8-11.30am & 1.30-5.30pm) are 7km to 16km south of Hué. Visiting several tombs can be expensive, with *xe om* (motorbike taxi) shuttles and individual admission – if you visit only one, make it Tu Duc or Minh Mang.

Tomb of Tu Duc (admission 55,000d), Emperor Tu Duc's tomb complex, is a majestic site, laced with frangipani and pine trees and set alongside a small lake. The buildings are beautifully designed. Near the entrance, the pavilion where the concubines used to lounge is a peaceful spot on the water.

Perhaps the most majestic of the Royal Tombs is the **Tomb of Minh Mang** (admission 55,000d), who ruled from 1820 to 1840. This tomb is renowned for its architecture, which blends into the natural surroundings.

The best way to visit the tombs is on a river cruise (see p856).

PLACES OF WORSHIP

Thien Mu Pagoda (Đ Le Duan; 7.30-11.30am & 1.30-5.30pm), an octagonal pagoda, is one of the most famous structures in Vietnam. Founded in 1601, it was the home pagoda of Thich Quang Duc, who publicly burned himself to death in 1963 to protest the policies of president Ngo Dinh Diem. Thien Mu is on the banks of the Song Huong, 4km southwest of the Citadel.

Monks and students gather to study in the peaceful orchid-lined courtyard behind the sanctuary of **Bao Quoc Pagoda** (Ham Long Hill, Phuong Duc District; 7.30-11.30am & 1.30-4.30pm). To get here, head south from Đ Le Loi on Đ Dien Bien Phu and turn right immediately after crossing the railway tracks.

Surrounded by trees and with a big koi pond in the middle, one doesn't have to be a Buddhist to sense something special at **Tu Hieu Pagoda**. Occasionally Zen master Thich Nhat Hanh – nominated by American civil rights icon Martin Luther King Jr for a Nobel Peace price – comes to give lectures. The pagoda is located at Duong Xuan Thuong III hamlet, in Thuy Xuan village, 4km southwest of Hué. Motorbike driver **Tran Van Thinh** (☎ 522 637, 0905 731 537; tranvanthinhcyclo@yahoo.com) studied Buddhism here and makes an excellent guide; he can often be found near the entrance to the Citadel.

Notre Dame Cathedral (Dong Chua Cuu The; 80 Đ Nguyen Hué; mass 5am & 5pm, Sun 7pm) is a blend of European and Asian architectural elements; this modern cathedral was built between 1959 and 1962.

Tours

Motorbike day tours of the city and environs start at around US$6. If you have a specific agenda in mind, motorbike guides from local traveller cafés can do customised day tours of the Royal Tombs, the Citadel, the Demilitarised Zone (DMZ) and surrounding countryside. Try:

PEACE TREES

A nonprofit organisation in the war-torn Quang Tri province, the mission of PeaceTrees Vietnam is to remove landmines and unexploded ordinance (UXO) and then reforest the land with the help of former American soldiers and 'citizen diplomats' who volunteer from around the world.

Started in 1995 by the family of Daniel Cheney, a helicopter pilot who died in Vietnam in 1969, the first UXO-clearing and reforestation project was spearheaded by the late Danaan Parry, who co-founded the Earthstewards Network in 1980, and by his wife, Jerilyn Brusseau.

Brusseau, an American, recounts how Quang Tri province was devastated by war. For every resident of the province, there was 6.6 tonnes of ordinance dropped, and only three out of the 30 villages remained by war's end. Much of the area still have UXOs, which are still dangerous.

PeaceTrees Vietnam runs the Danaan Parry Landmines Education Center in Dong Ha (see boxed text, p858, for transport information to Dong Ha) and visitors are welcome; Brusseau notes that it's the only landmine education centre currently operating in Vietnam. Learn more at www.peacetreesvietnam.org.

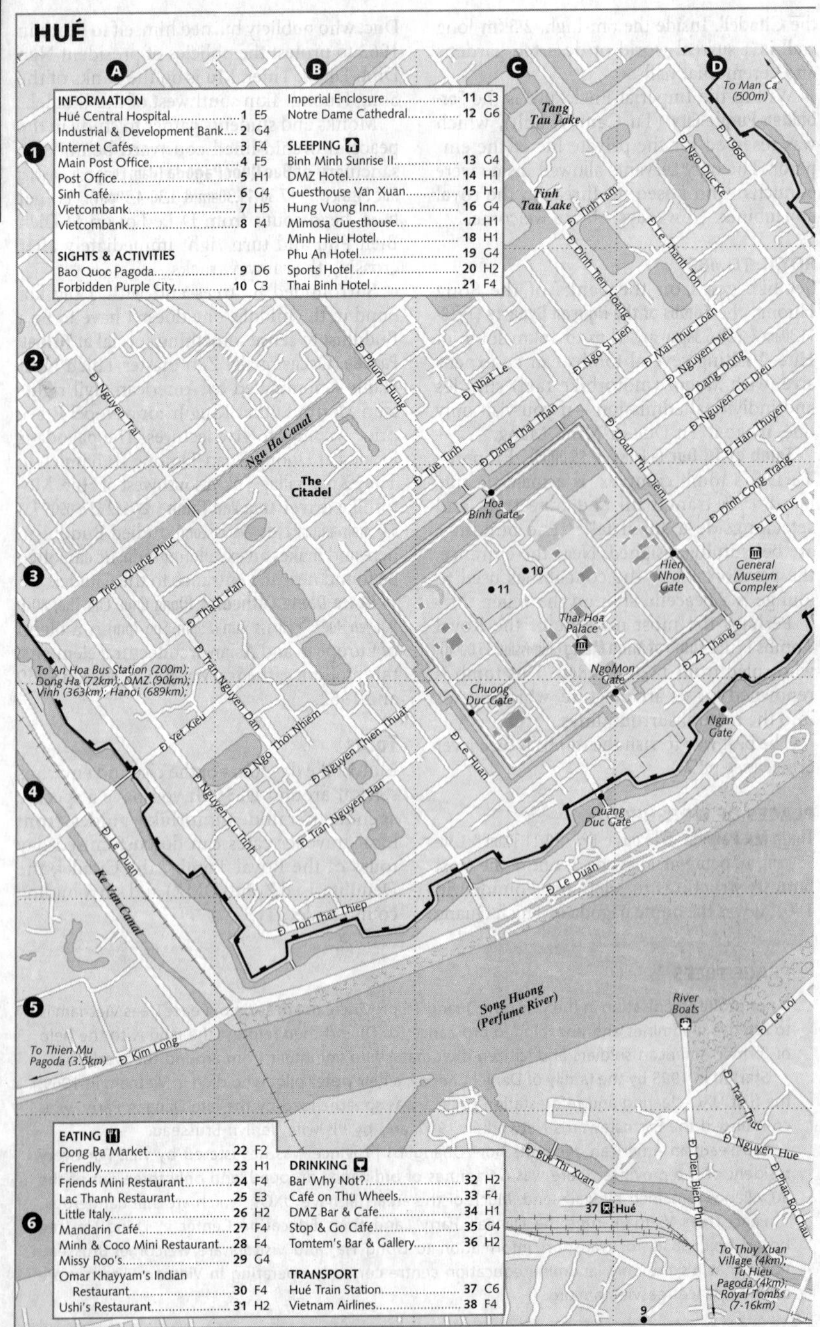
HUÉ
A
B
C
D
1
2
3
4
5
6
INFORMATION
Hué Central Hospital 1 E5
Industrial & Development Bank 2 G4
Internet Cafés 3 F4
Main Post Office 4 F5
Post Office 5 H1
Sinh Café 6 G4
Vietcombank 7 H5
Vietcombank 8 F4
SIGHTS & ACTIVITIES
Bao Quoc Pagoda 9 D6
Forbidden Purple City 10 C3
Imperial Enclosure 11 C3
Notre Dame Cathedral 12 G6
SLEEPING
Binh Minh Sunrise II 13 G4
DMZ Hotel 14 H1
Guesthouse Van Xuan 15 H1
Hung Vuong Inn 16 G4
Mimosa Guesthouse 17 H1
Minh Hieu Hotel 18 H1
Phu An Hotel 19 G4
Sports Hotel 20 H2
Thai Binh Hotel 21 F4
To Man Ca (500m)
Tang Tau Lake
Tinh Tau Lake
Đ 1968
Đ Ngo Duc Ke
Đ Tinh Tam
Đ Dinh Tien Hoang
Đ Le Thanh Ton
Đ Ngo Si Lien
Đ Mai Thuc Loan
Đ Nguyen Dieu
Đ Dang Dung
Đ Nguyen Chi Dieu
Đ Han Thuyen
Đ Dinh Cong Trang
Đ Le Truc
Đ Phung Hung
Đ Nhat Le
Đ Dang Thai Than
Đ Doan Thi Diem
Đ Nguyen Trai
Ngu Ha Canal
The Citadel
Đ Tue Tinh
Hoa Binh Gate
Hien Nhon Gate
General Museum Complex
10
11
Thai Hoa Palace
Đ 23 Thang 8
NgoMon Gate
Chuong Duc Gate
Ngan Gate
Đ Trieu Quang Phuc
Đ Thach Han
Đ Tran Nguyen Dan
To An Hoa Bus Station (200m); Dong Ha (72km); DMZ (90km); Vinh (363km); Hanoi (689km);
Đ Yet Kieu
Đ Ngo Thoi Nhiem
Đ Nguyen Thien Thuat
Đ Le Huan
Đ Nguyen Cu Trinh
Đ Tran Nguyen Han
Quang Duc Gate
Đ Le Duan
Ke Van Canal
Đ Ton That Thiep
Song Huong (Perfume River)
River Boats
Đ Le Loi
To Thien Mu Pagoda (3.5km)
Đ Kim Long
Đ Tran Thuc
Đ Nguyen Hue
Đ Bui Thi Xuan
Đ Dien Bien Phu
Đ Phan Boi Chau
37 Hué
To Thuy Xuan Village (4km); Tu Hieu Pagoda (4km); Royal Tombs (7-16km)
9
EATING
Dong Ba Market 22 F2
Friendly 23 H1
Friends Mini Restaurant 24 F4
Lac Thanh Restaurant 25 E3
Little Italy 26 H2
Mandarin Café 27 F4
Minh & Coco Mini Restaurant 28 F4
Missy Roo's 29 G4
Omar Khayyam's Indian Restaurant 30 F4
Ushi's Restaurant 31 H2
DRINKING
Bar Why Not? 32 H2
Café on Thu Wheels 33 F4
DMZ Bar & Cafe 34 H1
Stop & Go Café 35 G4
Tomtem's Bar & Gallery 36 H2
TRANSPORT
Hué Train Station 37 C6
Vietnam Airlines 38 F4

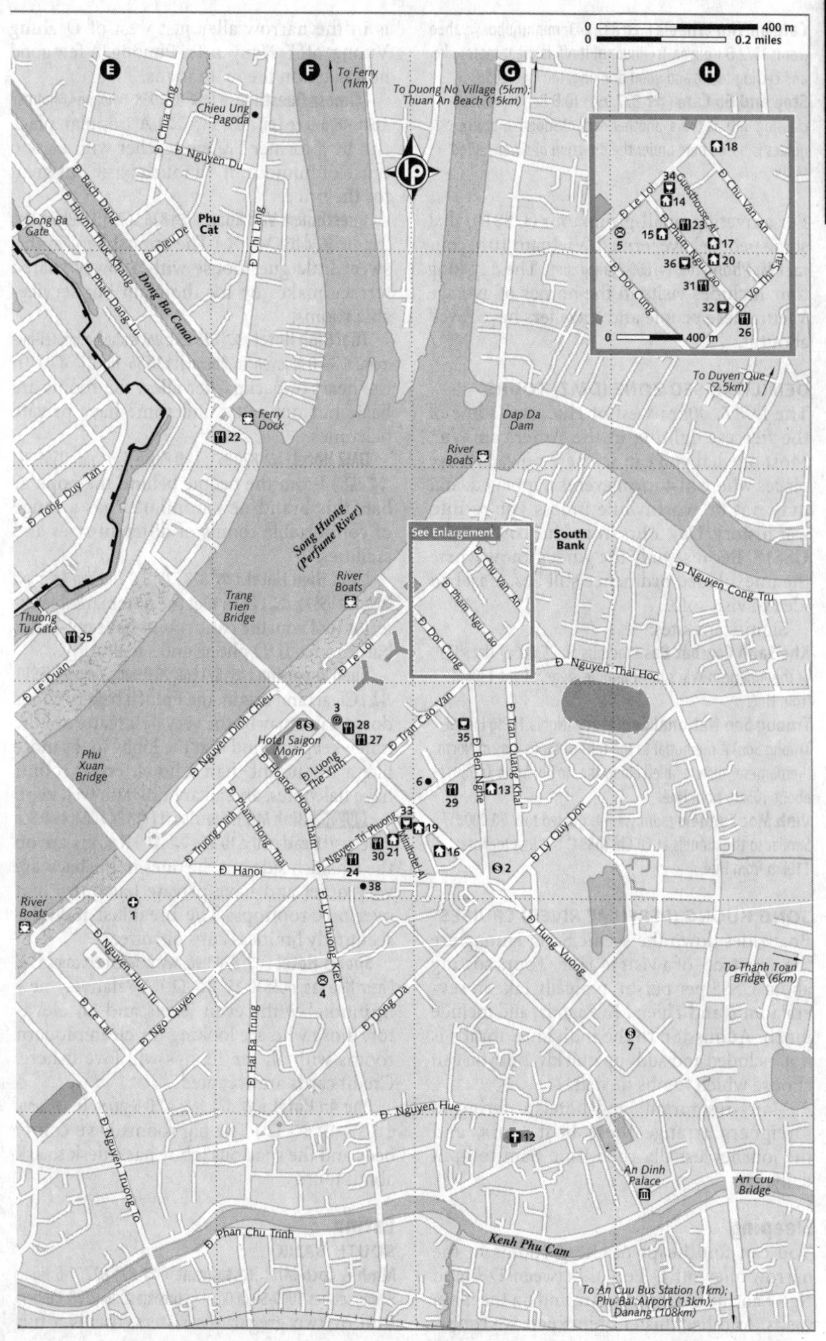
0 400 m
0 0.2 miles
E
F
G
H
To Ferry (1km)
To Duong No Village (5km); Thuan An Beach (15km)
Chieu Ung Pagoda
Đ Chua Ong
Đ Nguyen Du
Đ Bach Dang
Đ Huynh Thuc Khang
Đ Phan Dang Lu
Đ Dieu De
Đ Chi Lang
Phu Cat
Dong Ba Canal
Dong Ba Gate
Ferry Dock
22
Đ Tong Duy Tan
Song Huong (Perfume River)
River Boats
Dap Da Dam
Trang Tien Bridge
Thuong Tu Gate
25
Đ Le Duan
Đ Le Loi
See Enlargement
Đ Chu Van An
Đ Pham Ngu Lao
Đ Doi Cung
South Bank
Đ Nguyen Cong Tru
Đ Nguyen Thai Hoc
To Duyen Que (2.5km)
18
34
Guesthouse Al
14
Đ Le Loi
15
23
17
20
5
36
31
32
26
Đ Vo Thi Sau
0 400 m
Phu Xuan Bridge
Đ Nguyen Dinh Chieu
3
8
28
27
Hotel Saigon Morin
Đ Tran Cao Van
35
Đ Ben Nghe
Đ Tran Quang Khai
Đ Hoang Hoa Tham
Đ Luong The Vinh
Đ Pham Hong Thai
Đ Truong Dinh
6
29
13
33
19
Đ Nguyen Tri Phuong
Minihotel Al
30
21
16
24
Đ Ly Quy Don
Đ Hanoi
2
38
River Boats
1
Đ Ly Thuong Kiet
Đ Hung Vuong
Đ Nguyen Huy Tu
4
To Thanh Toan Bridge (6km)
Đ Le Lai
Đ Ngo Quyen
Đ Dong Da
7
Đ Hai Ba Trung
Đ Nguyen Truong To
Đ Nguyen Hue
12
An Dinh Palace
An Cuu Bridge
Đ Phan Chu Trinh
Kenh Phu Cam
To An Cuu Bus Station (1km); Phu Bai Airport (13km); Danang (108km)

Cafe on Thu Wheels (☎ 832 241; minhthuhue@yahoo.com; 10/2 Đ Nguyen Tri Phuong) It offers great motorbike and cycling tours, and good drinking, too (see p858).

Stop and Go Cafe (☎ 827 051; 10 Đ Ben Nghe) Specialising in DMZ tours, another pack of superb motorbike guides is based here under the direction of silver-haired Mr Do.

For a riveting small-group tour (US$10) that some people have termed 'Vietnam 101,' contact **Mr Phong** (tho147860@yahoo.com). The day-long tour includes visits to the homes of average Vietnamese people and travellers have raved about it.

DEMILITARISED ZONE (DMZ) TOURS

The DMZ, 90km west of Hué, saw some of the fiercest fighting in the American War. Most of what you can see here nowadays are places where historical events happened, and may not be worthwhile unless you're into war history. Day tours from Hué cost around US$18. Because only the guides know where the unexploded ordinance still lies, it's a bad idea to visit solo.

Significant sites:

Khe Sanh Combat Base (admission 25,000d) The site of the American War's most famous siege, about 130km from Hué.

Truong Son National Cemetery (Nghia Trang Liet Si Truong Son) A memorial to the tens of thousands of North Vietnamese soldiers killed along the Ho Chi Minh Trail; about 105km from Hué.

Vinh Moc Tunnels (admission & guided tour 20,000d) Similar to the tunnels at Cu Chi (p894) but less touristy; 110km from Hué.

SONG HUONG (PERFUME RIVER) CRUISES

Boat rides down the scenic Song Huong are the 'must-do' of a visit to Hué. Tours costing about US$5 per person typically take in several tombs and Thien Mu Pagoda, and include lunch. Admission to the individual tombs is not included and adds up quickly, but you can choose which tombs to visit.

Many restaurants and hotels catering to foreigners arrange these boat tours, and the journey usually runs from 8am to 4pm daily.

Sleeping

You can find heaps of cheap rooms in the narrow alley off Đ Le Loi between Đ Pham Ngu Lao and Đ Chu Van An, and on the main roads. Another cluster of inexpensive rooms is in the narrow alley just west of Đ Hung Vuong, off Đ Nguyen Tri Phuong. A few good hotels are on the main roads.

Mimosa Guesthouse (☎ 828 068; tvhoang4@hotmail.com; 46/6 Đ Le Loi; r US$5-7; ❄) A popular place run by a former French teacher with a good sense of humour, it's a touch basic but great for the price.

Guesthouse Van Xuan (☎ 826 567; 10 Đ Pham Ngu Lao; s US$6, d US$7-8; ❄) The atmosphere in this sweet little guesthouse with a lovely shared terrace makes up for the plain but serviceable rooms.

Thai Binh Hotel (☎ 828 058; www.thaibinhhotel-hue.com; 6/34 Đ Nguyen Tri Phuong; r US$6-18; ❄ 💻) In the heart of backpacker alley, the rooms are basic but not ratty, and some have private balconies.

DMZ Hotel (☎ 826 831; 1A Đ Pham Ngu Lao; r US$9-14; ❄ 💻) From the people behind the popular bar, this brand-new minihotel has a range of comfortable rooms of different sizes and facilities.

Minh Hieu Hotel (☎ 828 725; 3 Đ Chu Van An; r incl breakfast US$10; ❄) Don't let the unremarkable exterior fool you; the basic rooms have hot-water bathrooms, IDD phone and satellite TV.

Hung Vuong Inn (☎ 821 068; 20 Đ Hung Vuong; r US$10; ❄) Clean and bright, the French bakery goods downstairs may be the very best feature of the hotel; keep in mind that the lobby looks more like a restaurant than a hotel. Front rooms have balconies, and all are tidy and well kept.

our pick **Binh Minh Sunrise II** (☎ 849 007; 45 Đ Ben Nghe; r incl breakfast US$10-15; ❄ 💻) Rooms are on the smallish side but the ones in the back are very quiet and have private balconies that overlook rooftops. The breakfast includes seemingly limitless cups of coffee.

Sports Hotel (☎ 828 096; www.huestays.com; 15 Đ Pham Ngu Lao; r US$10-15; ❄ 💻) A relatively new minihotel with seven levels and an elevator, those who are looking for clean modern rooms with all the fixings will love it here. Credit cards are accepted.

Phu An Hotel (☎ 821 168; 42 Đ Nguyen Tri Phuong; d US$12-15; ❄ 💻) The big rooms have comfy beds and the spacious lobby has a desk to ask about tours.

Eating

SOUTH BANK

Minh & Coco Mini Restaurant (☎ 821 822; 1 Đ Hung Vuong; dishes 5000-50,000d; 🕑 breakfast, lunch & dinner) Run by two gregarious sisters, this is a fun

AN 'AMERICAN WAR' VETERAN RETURNS *As told to Josh Krist*

Rod lives in Northern California with his wife, Jean. The couple have travelled all over the world but in 2007 Rod decided to revisit the country where he fought as a young man.

When did you first go to Vietnam? I first knew I was off to 'Nam' as a 20-year-old kid back in '66. I last left the war in 1971.

What was your experience there during the war? As an army infantryman, officer and aviator I got to see a lot of the warring country, including the Central Highlands, the central coast, and too much of the DMZ. I was lucky enough to spend some time with nonmilitary Vietnamese and tribal people – in their space and on their terms. I also spent thousands of hours flying 'slow and low' over what even then was a beautiful piece of the world. I tried to keep my memories of the people and the country separate from the stain of the war.

You've visited countries all over Asia, why not Vietnam until now? I think I was avoiding it. Vietnam made me a different person, for sure. There's the pain of physical wounds, mental pain of losing friends – and memories of pants-peeing fear and gleefully inflicting death. The thought of returning to the sites of these memories brought up new fears. Would I face hatred or guilt, open old wounds, or even sink back into the depression I felt when I left Vietnam and was greeted by an indifferent country?

What was your experience this time? I sought out and found former enemies – they often work for the government. They are now older too. We traded stories, drinks and handshakes with lots of people who seem positive, prospering, and devoid of any ill-will. They were happy to meet me and we were happy to be there; good vibes.

Would you recommend Vietnam to other veterans? Well, it sure is a great tourist destination and it satisfied all the needs of my personal history lessons – and therapy sessions. People there look forward to a future that is far better than their past – a past that for them, and now me, is old history. Yeah, go for it.

place to eat a cheap lunch and watch life go by on busy Đ Hung Vuong.

Mandarin Cafe (☎ 821 281; mandarin@dng.vnn.vn; 3 Đ Hung Vuong; breakfast 10,000d; breakfast, lunch & dinner) The owner, Mr Cu, is helpful and cheery – and has consistently improved his services since the first LP mention, a rarity worth noting. The Mandarin also provides good information about tours. The BLTs, potato salad and banana pancakes are all good.

Friends Mini Restaurant (☎ 825 248, 30 Đ Nguyen Tri Phuong; mains from 15,000d; breakfast, lunch & dinner) A definite backpacker haunt with graffiti-filled walls with messages from travellers in all languages.

Ushi Restaurant (☎ 821 143; 42 Đ Pham Ngu Lao; mains from 15,000d; breakfast, lunch & dinner) Formerly known as Hien's Canteen, this place is popular with French travellers and has cheap food, a pool table, cold beer, local information and internet access.

Missy Roo's (☎ 284 945; 63 Đ Nguyen Tri Phuong; shakes 20,000d; breakfast & lunch) This takeaway-salad and juice bar serves some of the coolest, most refreshing concoctions in Hué.

our pick **Friendly** (☎ 851 548; 7 Đ Pham Ngu Lao; mains 20,000-25,000d; breakfast, lunch & dinner) The snappy menu has a sampler plate of Hué specialities that's a good start to culinary adventures here. There's funky art on the walls and the place fills up quickly in the evenings.

Omar Khayyam's Indian Restaurant (☎ 821 616; 10 Đ Nguyen Tri Phuong; curries 30,000-60,000d; lunch & dinner) A vegetarian-friendly curry house that looks plain but the food is very good.

Little Italy (☎ 826 928; littleitalyhue@gmail.com; 2A Đ Vo Thi Sau; mains around 40,000d; lunch & dinner) Where else do you think you'll find Hué's best Italian food? The pizzas are respectable, while pastas are perfectly *al dente*.

NORTH BANK

Lac Thanhn Restaurant (6A Đ Dinh Tien Hoang; mains from 17,000d; lunch & dinner) This restaurant owned by the deaf-mute Mr Lac is a great place to fuel up on Hué specialities before a day of sightseeing. Mr Lac truly cares about his customers; on hot days he'll make sure people drink a lot of water and wear a hat when venturing out.

Dong Ba market (Đ Tran Hung Dao; 6.30am-8pm) Although the dining conditions aren't ideal, the market is a good place to put together cheap meals and do some shopping.

Duyen Que (☎ 890 589; QL 49, Thon Ngoc Anh, Phu Thuong, Phu Vang; main 80,000d; ⏰ dinner) At this delightful place, tables surround a small pond and diners can try to catch their own fish. To get here, head northeast on Pham Van Dong for 3km, look to the right for the restaurant sign and follow a dark little road for about 200m. Or, ask the staff at Missy Roo's (p857) – it's one of their favourite spots.

Drinking

In the evenings, backpackers gather over Huda beers in the cafés along Đ Hung Vuong. If you're looking to party, try these spots.

Tomtem's Bar & Gallery (Đ Pham Ngu Lao) Vietnamese cocktails that pack a punch (15,000d), cool modern art on the walls, mellow tunes and a pool table make this place a winner.

DMZ Bar & Cafe (44 Đ Le Loi) The DMZ is a long-running pool-shooting and dance spot for expats and travellers. It stays open late and keeps the party going.

Bar Why Not? (☎ 824 793; 21 Đ Vo Thi Sau) This corner place mixes respectably potent cocktails and has outdoor seating to contemplate life over a drink. It also serves good bar food and has a pool table.

Stop & Go Cafe (☎ 889 106; 4 Đ Ben Nghe) Stop for a cold beer and a warm conversation with the tour guides and go for a ride – it's an excellent place to arrange motorbike tours (p856); it also has rooms for rent.

Cafe on Thu Wheels (☎ 832 241; 10/2 Đ Nguyen Tri Phuong) This is the most popular café to swap stories and throw back a few. Miss Thu can smell out new arrivals so be ready to hear about her good motorbike tours (p856).

Shopping

Hué is known for producing the finest conical hats in Vietnam. The city is famous for its 'poem hats', which, when held up to the light, reveal black cut-out scenes sandwiched between the layers of translucent Palm leaves.

Hué is also a prime place to look for rice-paper and silk paintings, but the prices that are initially quoted are usually about four times the actual price. Walking away from a souvenir stall will often bring the bargaining down.

Dong Ba market (Đ Tran Hung Dao; ⏰ 6.30am-8pm) Apart from its eateries (see earlier) you can buy everything from machetes to pyjamas at this market, a few metres north of Trang Tien Bridge on the northern bank of the river.

Getting There & Away

AIR

The main office of **Vietnam Airlines** (code VN; ☎ 824 709; www.vietnamairlines.com; 23 Đ Nguyen Van Cu; ⏰ 7.15-11.15am & 1.30-4.30pm Mon-Sat) handles reservations. Several flights a day connect Hué to both Hanoi and HCMC.

GETTING TO LAOS

The Lao Bao border is the most popular and least problematic crossing between Laos and Vietnam. You can get a 30-day Lao visa (US$30) on arrival in Dansavanh, but Vietnamese visas still need to be arranged in advance; drop in on the Vietnamese consulate in Savannakhet. The border is open from 7am to 6pm.

The junction town for Lao Bao is Dong Ha, which has regular bus services to/from An Hoa bus station in Hué (25,000d, 1½ hours). The *Reunification Express* also links Hué to Dong Ha (25,000d, 1½ to 2½ hours, six daily). From Dong Ha, there are regular buses to Lao Bao town (20,000d, two hours). From the Lao Bao town bus station, the price for a *xe om* (motorbike taxi) to the border is 10,000d, or walk it in about 20 minutes. Between the Vietnam and Laos border posts is a short walk of a few hundred metres.

Sepon Travel (☎ 53-855 289; 1 Đ Phan Boi Chau) in Dong Ha has buses to Savannakhet (US$12, 7½ hours), continuing on to Vientiane (13 hours); they leave Dong Ha at 8am every second day and return the next day. These buses also continue on to Hué (US$14 to US$15, add 1½ hours), and can be booked from the Mandarin and Sinh Cafés there (see p852).

If you're travelling across the border by tourist bus, expect a wait while documents are checked. When booking a tourist bus, make sure to confirm (preferably in writing) that the same bus carries on through the border. We've heard plenty of stories of tourists on this route being bundled off nice buses on the Vietnamese side and on to overcrowded local buses once they reach Laos.

See p394 for details on doing the trip in the opposite direction.

Phu Bai airport is 13km south of the city centre and takes about 25 minutes by car. Taxi fares are typically around US$8, although share taxis cost as little as US$2 – inquire at hotels. Vietnam Airlines runs its own shuttle (20,000d) from its office to the airport, a couple of hours before flight times.

BUS

The Au Cuu bus station is 4km to the southeast on the continuation of Đ Hung Vuong (it becomes Đ An Duong Vuong and Đ An Thuy Vuong). The first main stop south is Danang (40,000d, three hours, six daily). **An Hoa bus station** (Hwy 1A), 200m northwest of the Citadel, serves northern destinations, including Dong Ha (25,000d, 1½ hours).

Hué is also a regular stop on the open-tour bus routes. Traveller cafés (see p852 and p856) can arrange bookings.

TRAIN

Hué train station (Ga Hué; ☎ 822 175; 2 Đ Bui Thi Xuan; ⏲ ticket office 7.30am-5pm) is on the south bank of the river, at the southwestern end of Đ Le Loi. Many local services and some long-distance services operate both north and south from here daily.

Getting Around

Bicycles (US$1), motorbikes (US$5) and cars (US$30 per day, with driver) can be hired from hotels all over town. Both **Co Do Taxi** (☎ 830 830) and **Mai Linh** (☎ 898 989) have air-con vehicles with meters. *Cyclos* and *xe om* will find you when you need them, prices start at (10,000d) for rides in the central area and double or more for trips to the Citadel.

BACH MA NATIONAL PARK

☎ 054 / elev 1450m

Forty-five kilometres southeast of Hué, **Bach Ma National park** (Vuon Quoc Gia Bach Ma; ☎ 871 330; www.bachma.vnn.vn; admission 10,500d) is a French-era hill station known for its cool weather. Although relatively close to a major city, the steep road up to the park entrance feels like it is heading to a different world. Sometimes the mist is so thick it's hard to see more than 10m ahead, and on the many trekking trails scenes of raging waterfalls or lazy brooks suddenly materialize out of nowhere. From the peak of the summit trail there are sweeping 360-degree views across the stone remains of villas dotted around the nearby hills.

The national park is rich in flora and fauna and is a bird-watcher's paradise. The best time to visit is between March and June. It's a good idea to bring decent rain gear as they only sell very thin ponchos at the snack shop. If hiring an English- or French-speaking guide for the day (150,000d), they can sometimes loan out proper waterproof pants and jackets. Guides can also point out the many medicinal plants in the park. People walking around here with their pants tucked into their socks are not making a fashion statement, but are trying to avoid the many freeloading leeches.

Trails are marked on the national-park map, which you receive with your ticket. Further information is found in the *Bach Ma National Park* booklet, available for 12,000d at the park entrance.

Sleeping & Eating

National Park Guesthouse (☎ 871 330; camp site per person 3000d, 6-person tents 80,000d, r 100,000-300,000d) The park authority has a small camping ground and four guesthouses near the summit and two more guesthouses near the entrance. One of the summit guesthouses has a 12-person dorm with a shared bathroom. The more expensive twin-bed rooms are a better bet for views and facilities. This is a prime spot, rebuilt from the ruins of Emperor Bao Dai's summer retreat. Bookings should be made at the visitor centre.

The snack shop and restaurant is rebuilt from one of the old French ruins and sits in the middle of the park. Because meals are prepared to order and require a trip to the market, give at least four hours advance notice.

There's a canteen near the visitors centre, and those wishing to dine at the summit can make advance orders to eat here.

Getting There & Around

The entrance and visitors centre is at Km 3 on the summit road, which starts at the town of Cau Hai on National Hwy 1. It's another meandering 16km from the gate to the summit, and unless you are willing to walk it (three to four hours; bring lots of water and wear a hat), you'll need to hire private transport from the park.

Four-passenger jeeps/eight-passenger vans are available to hire (350,000/400,000d) from the park entrance for same-day return, with an additional 50,000d fee for next-day return.

There are buses from Danang (US$3, two hours) and Hué (US$2, one hour) that will drop travellers on the main road near the entrance of the park, but arrange a pick-up from the guesthouse beforehand – or be ready for a half-day uphill hike. Numerous local buses stop at Cau Hai, where *xe om* drivers can ferry you to the entrance. Cau Hai also has a **train station** (☎ 871 362; Loc Dien village), but the one daily service in either direction is slow and departs in the middle of the night.

Hotels and traveller cafés in Hué can arrange all-inclusive one-night trips to Bach Ma starting at US$55 per person.

DANANG

☎ **0511 / pop 1.1 million**

Danang is Vietnam's fourth-largest city and where the first US Marines landed for the American War; it forms a mere transit stop for most travellers who wish to visit the Museum of Cham Sculpture. Tour groups and their big buses are a common sight but there are very few independent travellers – whether or not people like Danang depends on whether they like to give a warm hello every few steps.

Information

INTERNET ACCESS

Internet cafés around town are plentiful; you can find several around Đ Tran Quoc Toan, between Đ Yen Bai and Đ Nguyen Chi Thanh. Most charge around 6000d per hour.

MEDICAL SERVICES

Danang Family Medical practice (☎ 582 700, 24-hr emergency 917 303; www.vietnammedicalpractice.com; 50-52 Đ Nguyen Van Linh) One of Vietnam's most trusted foreign-owned clinics comes to Danang.

Hospital C (Benh Vien C; ☎ 822 480; 35 Đ Hai Phong) The most advanced medical facility in Danang.

MONEY

VID Public Bank (2 Đ Tran Phu)

Vietcombank (140 Đ Le Loi) The only place in town to cash travellers cheques, and it has an ATM.

POST

Danang domestic & international post offices (Đ Bach Dang) On opposite sides of the road.

TRAVEL AGENCIES

Dana Tours (☎ 825 653; danamarle@dng.vnn.vn; 76 Đ Hung Vuong) With an enlightened attitude compared with other state-run agencies, this is a great option.

Trekking Travel (☎ 843 122; trekking-travel@hn.vnn.vn; 4 Đ Tran Quoc Toan) Worth checking out for bus tickets and local tours.

Sights & Activities

Danang's high point is the famed **Museum of Cham Sculpture** (Bao Tang Cham; cnr Đ Trung Nu Vuong & Đ Bach Dang; admission 30,000d; 🕒 7am-5pm). This small, breezy museum with architecture that echoes a Cham structure houses the finest collection of Cham sculpture to be found anywhere. For a dose of kitsch see the cloth portraits – one is of Fidel Castro – at the gift shop outside.

Guides sometimes hang out at the museum's entrance but there's enough signage in French and English to get a good experience without one. Should you hire a guide, agree on a fee beforehand.

Sleeping

While the budget options have been slow in coming, things are looking up for Danang lodging.

Minh Travel Hotel (☎ 812 661; mtjraymond@yahoo.ca; 105 Đ Tran Phu; r US$3-9; ❄) This tiny place is developing a reputation among superbudget travellers for the friendliness and honesty of its owners and its rock-bottom prices.

Hoa's Place (☎ 969 216; hoasplace@hotmail.com; r US$4-6) If you'd like easy access to the beach, consider this laid-back little gem. This famously cosy spot is near China Beach.

Tan Minh Hotel (☎ 827 456; tanminhhotel@dng.vnn.vn; 142 Đ Bach Dang; d US$10-12; ❄) The best of the budget bunch, this small family-run place has clean good-sized rooms. Rooms with balconies look onto the river, and all rooms have air-con, satellite TV and hot water.

Phuong Tam (☎ 824 288; 174 Đ Bach Dang, r US$16-25; ❄) Not too far from the Cham Sculpture Museum, this nice new minihotel faces the river and has all the basics.

Eating & Drinking

Com Chay Chua Tinh Hoi (574 Đ Ong Ich Khiem; dishes from 3000d) Known for the best vegetarian food in town, it's just inside the entrance gate to the Phap Lam Pagoda. In the streets near the pagoda, there are several other cheap vegetarian shops.

Bread Of Life (☎ 893 456; 215 Đ Tran Phu; cakes 10,000d, breakfast 20,000d; 🕒 breakfast & lunch Mon-Sat) A great spot for a Western-style breakfast or a coffee and cake, this little café employs deaf staff and

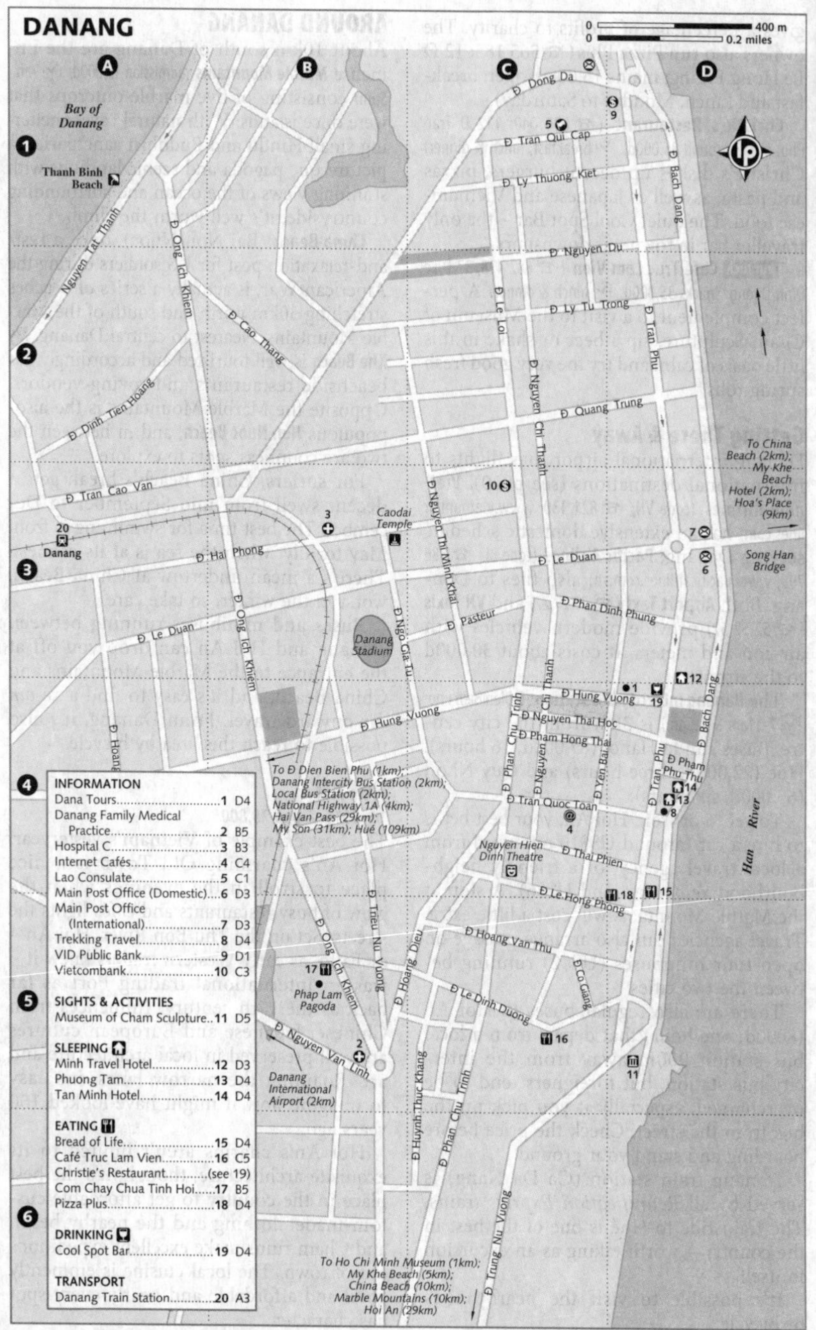

INFORMATION

Dana Tours	1	D4
Danang Family Medical Practice	2	B5
Hospital C	3	B3
Internet Cafés	4	C4
Lao Consulate	5	C1
Main Post Office (Domestic)	6	D3
Main Post Office (International)	7	D3
Trekking Travel	8	D4
VID Public Bank	9	D1
Vietcombank	10	C3

SIGHTS & ACTIVITIES

Museum of Cham Sculpture	11	D5

SLEEPING

Minh Travel Hotel	12	D3
Phuong Tam	13	D4
Tan Minh Hotel	14	D4

EATING

Bread of Life	15	D4
Café Truc Lam Vien	16	C5
Christie's Restaurant	(see 19)	
Com Chay Chua Tinh Hoi	17	B5
Pizza Plus	18	D4

DRINKING

Cool Spot Bar	19	D4

TRANSPORT

Danang Train Station	20	A3

gives a percentage of profits to charity. The owners also run Pizza Plus (☎ 565 185; 12 Đ Le Hong Phong; mains 15,000d; open breakfast and lunch, Monday to Saturday).

Christie's Restaurant (☎ 824 040; 112 Đ Tran Phu; meals around 35,000d; breakfast, lunch & dinner) Christie's dishes up decent burgers, pizzas and pasta, as well as Japanese and Vietnamese food. The quiet Cool Spot Bar – the only traveller bar in town – is downstairs.

our pick **Cafe Truc Lam Vien** (☎ 582 428; 37 Đ Le Dinh Duong; snacks 35,000d; lunch & dinner) A perfect complement to a visit to the Museum of Cham Sculpture, sip a beer or shake in this little oasis of calm and try the very good fresh spring rolls.

Getting There & Away

Danang international airport has flights to international destinations (see p820). **Vietnam Airlines** (code VN; ☎ 821 130; www.vietnamairlines.com) has an extensive domestic schedule serving Danang; **Pacific Airlines** (code BL; ☎ 886 799; www.pacificairlines.com.vn) also flies to Danang. Both **Airport Taxi** (☎ 27 27 27) and **VN Taxis** (☎ 52 52 52) provide modern vehicles with air-con and meters. It costs about 30,000d to the airport.

The **Danang intercity bus station** (Đ Dien Bien Phu; 7-11am & 1-5pm) is 3km from the city centre. Buses run to Hanoi (87,000d, 16 hours), Hué (22,000d, three hours) and Quy Nhon (65,000d, six hours).

To get to or from Hoi An, your best bet is to hire a car (around US$10 one-way) from a local travel agency, or a friendly neighbourhood *xe om* (around US$6). A stop at the Marble Mountains will cost a little extra. Travel agencies can also arrange passage on open-tour minibuses (US$2) running between the two cities.

There are also regular buses to Hoi An (8000d, one hour) that depart from a local bus station 200m away from the intercity bus station, but foreigners tend to be overcharged, especially if you pick up the bus from the street. Check the price before boarding and stand your ground.

Danang train station (Ga Da Nang) is served by all *Reunification Express* trains. The train ride to Hué is one of the best in the country – worth taking as an excursion in itself.

It's possible to visit the nearby sites by bicycle.

AROUND DANANG

About 10km south of Danang are the immense **Marble Mountains** (admission 15,000d; 7am-5pm) consisting of five marble outcrops that were once islands. With natural caves sheltering small Hindu and Buddhist sanctuaries, a picturesque pagoda and scenic landings with stunning views of the ocean and surrounding countryside, it's well worth the climb.

China Beach (Bai Non Nuoc), once a rest-and-relaxation post for US soldiers during the American War, is actually a series of beaches stretching 30km north and south of the Marble Mountains. Nearest to central Danang, **My Khe Beach** is well touristed and accordingly has beachside restaurants and roving vendors. Opposite the Marble Mountains is the also-populous **Non Nuoc Beach**, and in between the two are countless spots to explore.

For surfers, China Beach's break gets a decent swell from mid-September to December. The best time for swimming is from May to July, when the sea is at its calmest. There's a mean undertow at China Beach, worst in the winter, so take care.

Buses and minibuses running between Danang and Hoi An can drop you off at the entrance to the Marble Mountains and China Beach, and it's easy to find a *xe om* for onward travel. From Danang, it's also possible to reach this area by bicycle.

HOI AN

☎ 0510 / pop 75,800

The best example of Vietnam's yesteryear, Hoi An's charming Old Town is a nice place to stroll in the evenings when the glow of busy restaurants and cafés lights the streets. Set on the Thu Bon River, Hoi An – or Faifo, as early Western traders knew it – was an international trading Port as far back as the 17th century. Influences from Chinese, Japanese and European cultures are well preserved in local architecture and art. Roaming the narrow lanes, it's easy to imagine how it might have looked 150 years ago.

Hoi An's charms aren't limited to its exquisite architecture, though; it's the best place in the country to get affordable custom-made clothing and the nearby beach and Cham ruins make excellent expeditions out of town. The local cuisine is eminently good and affordable and nearly every spot has character.

Information

EMERGENCY

Hoi An Hospital (☎ 861 364; 10 Đ Tran Hung Dao) Serious problems should be taken to Danang.

Hoi An Police station (☎ 861 204; 84 Đ Hoang Dieu)

INTERNET ACCESS

Internet cafés are hard to miss in Hoi An. Popular places to check email over a cool drink include the following:

Banana Split Café (☎ 861 136; 53 Đ Hoang Dieu)

Hai's Scout Café (☎ 863 210; 98 Đ Nguyen Thai Hoc)

MONEY

There is a good number of ATMs in Hoi An, but they tend to be temperamental. Use the ATMs in front of a bank during business hours so that you can talk to a human being if there's a problem.

Many travel agencies will exchange cash and/or cash travellers cheques; count your money before leaving.

Incombank (☎ 861 261; 4 Đ Hoang Dieu, also 9 Đ Le Loi) These branches change cash and travellers cheques, give cash advances and have ATMs.

POST

Post office (48 Đ Tran Hung Dao) Staff are used to travellers sending back a new wardrobe and can supply boxes and large envelopes for a fee.

TRAVEL AGENCIES

Travel agencies are scattered throughout town with a concentration of places along Đ Tran Hung Dao. Since most agencies offer the same services and tours for similar costs, one cannot be recommended over the other. Competition is fierce, so if you want to book something expensive or complicated, check out a few options and then negotiate. One popular tour is to My Son (p867).

Dangers & Annoyances

For the most part, Hoi An is very safe at any hour. However, late-night bag-snatchings in the isolated, unlit market are on the rise. Avoid walking around this area alone when the market day is over.

There have also been (extremely rare) reports of women being followed to their hotels and assaulted. Lone women should have a friend walk home with them at night (and don't underestimate the results of yelling your lungs out).

At the My Son ruins, there's a running scam involving motorbike vandalism and extortionist 'repairs' made by the vandals themselves. It's recommended that you hire a driver if you visit independently.

Sights

HOI AN OLD TOWN

Having been named a Unesco World Heritage site, **Hoi An Old Town** (admission 75,000d) ostensibly charges an admission fee, which goes towards funding the preservation of the town's historic architecture. But, this fee is not always enforced. Buying the ticket gives you a choice of heritage sites to visit, including an 'intangible culture' option, like a traditional musical concert or stage play.

Our list of sites is by no means comprehensive; buying a ticket at the Hoi An Old Town booths will also get you a tourist guide for all the sites.

Tan Ky House (☎ 861 474; 101 Đ Nguyen Thai Hoc; 🕑 8am-noon & 2-4.30pm) is a lovingly preserved 19th-century house that once belonged to a Vietnamese merchant. Japanese and Chinese influences are visible throughout the architecture. The house is a private home, and the owner – whose family has lived here for seven generations – speaks French and English.

The **Japanese Covered Bridge** (Cau Nhat Ban/Lai Vien Kieu; Đ Tran Phu & Đ Nguyen Thi Minh Khai) was constructed in 1593. The bridge has a roof for shelter and a small temple built into its northern side. According to one story, the bridge's construction began in the year of the monkey and finished in the year of the dog; thus one entrance is guarded by monkeys, the other by dogs (neither side is willing to talk).

Showcasing a collection of blue-and-white ceramics of the Dai Viet period, the **Museum of Trading Ceramics** (80 Đ Tran Phu; 🕑 8am-noon & 2-4.30pm) is in a simply restored house. It's delightful. In particular, notice the great ceramic mosaic that's set above the pond in the inner courtyard.

The **Old House at 103 Tran Phu** (103 Đ Tran Phu; 🕑 8am-noon & 2-4.30pm) is picturesque with its wooden front and shutters; inside is an eclectic shop where women make silk lanterns. There are also ornamental aquarium fish for sale, *and* you can buy shampoo.

ARTS & CRAFTS VILLAGES

All those neat fake antiques sold in Hoi An's shops are manufactured in nearby villages.

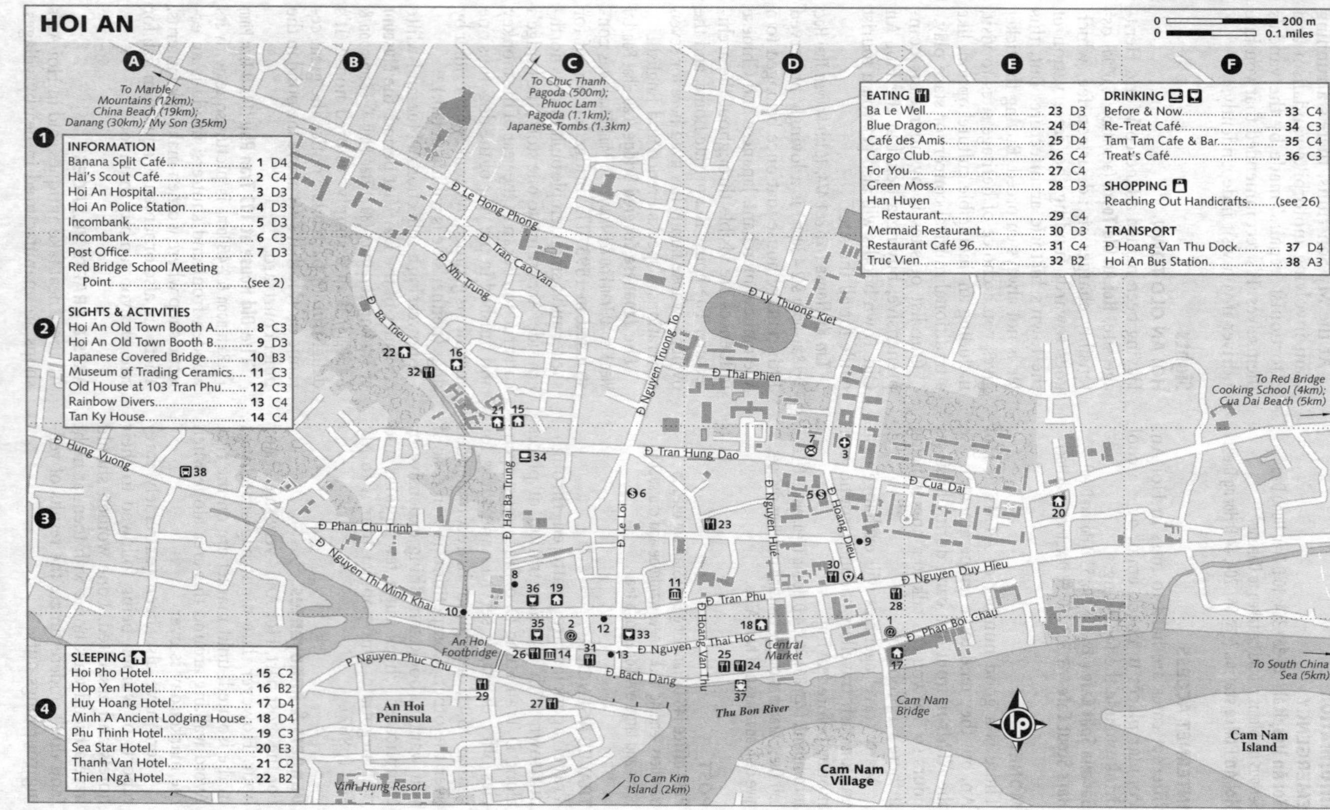
HOI AN
0 200 m
0 0.1 miles
A B C D E F
1 2 3 4
To Marble Mountains (12km); China Beach (19km); Danang (30km); My Son (35km)
To Chuc Thanh Pagoda (500m); Phuoc Lam Pagoda (1.1km); Japanese Tombs (1.3km)
INFORMATION
Banana Split Café 1 D4
Hai's Scout Café 2 C4
Hoi An Hospital 3 D3
Hoi An Police Station 4 D3
Incombank 5 D3
Incombank 6 C3
Post Office 7 D3
Red Bridge School Meeting Point (see 2)
SIGHTS & ACTIVITIES
Hoi An Old Town Booth A 8 C3
Hoi An Old Town Booth B 9 D3
Japanese Covered Bridge 10 B3
Museum of Trading Ceramics 11 C3
Old House at 103 Tran Phu 12 C3
Rainbow Divers 13 C4
Tan Ky House 14 C4
SLEEPING
Hoi Pho Hotel 15 C2
Hop Yen Hotel 16 B2
Huy Hoang Hotel 17 D4
Minh A Ancient Lodging House 18 D4
Phu Thinh Hotel 19 C3
Sea Star Hotel 20 E3
Thanh Van Hotel 21 C2
Thien Nga Hotel 22 B2
EATING
Ba Le Well 23 D3
Blue Dragon 24 D4
Café des Amis 25 D4
Cargo Club 26 C4
For You 27 C4
Green Moss 28 D3
Han Huyen Restaurant 29 C4
Mermaid Restaurant 30 D3
Restaurant Café 96 31 C4
Truc Vien 32 B2
DRINKING
Before & Now 33 C4
Re-Treat Café 34 C3
Tam Tam Cafe & Bar 35 C4
Treat's Café 36 C3
SHOPPING
Reaching Out Handicrafts (see 26)
TRANSPORT
Đ Hoang Van Thu Dock 37 D4
Hoi An Bus Station 38 A3
Đ Le Hong Phong
Đ Tran Cao Van
Đ Nhi Trung
Đ Ba Trieu
Đ Ly Thuong Kiet
Đ Nguyen Truong To
Đ Thai Phien
Đ Tran Hung Dao
Đ Hung Vuong
Đ Hai Ba Trung
Đ Le Loi
Đ Cua Dai
Đ Phan Chu Trinh
Đ Nguyen Thi Minh Khai
Đ Nguyen Hue
Đ Hoang Dieu
Đ Nguyen Duy Hieu
Đ Tran Phu
Đ Phan Boi Chau
Đ Nguyen Thai Hoc
Đ Hoang Van Thu
Đ Bach Dang
P Nguyen Phuc Chu
An Hoi Footbridge
Central Market
An Hoi Peninsula
Thu Bon River
Cam Nam Bridge
Cam Nam Village
Cam Nam Island
Vinh Hung Resort
To Cam Kim Island (2km)
To Red Bridge Cooking School (4km); Cua Dai Beach (5km)
To South China Sea (5km)

Cross the An Hoi footbridge to reach the **An Hoi Peninsula**, noted for its boat factory and mat-weaving factories. South of the Peninsula is **Cam Kim Island**, where you see many people engaged in the woodcarving and boatbuilding industries (take a boat from the Đ Hoang Van Thu dock). Back in town, cross the Cam Nam bridge to **Cam Nam village**, a lovely spot also noted for arts and crafts.

Activities

Rainbow Divers (☎ 911 123; www.divevietnam.com; 98 Đ Le Loi) has an office in the Old Town, where you can book dives at Cu Lao Cham Marine Park.

Courses

Restaurants all over town advertise cooking courses where attendees learn how to make several dishes and then sit down to enjoy the meal they've made.

Red Bridge (☎ 933 222; www.visithoian.com) offers a reasonably priced half-day course (US$16) that covers it all, beginning with a trip to the local market and including a boat trip down the river to the cooking class.

Festivals & Events

The **Hoi An Legendary Night** takes place on the 14th day (full moon) of every lunar month from 5.30pm to 10pm. These festive evenings feature traditional food, song and dance, and games along the lantern-lit streets in the town centre.

Sleeping

For a small place Hoi An has a big selection of accommodation options and with so many rooms to fill sometimes hoteliers are willing to make sweet deals.

Hop Yen Hotel (☎ 863 153; hopyenhotel@yahoo.com; Đ Ba Trieu; r US$6-12;) This is a humble hostel that has helpful staff. The cheapest rate will get you a small room with no air-con up four flights of stairs.

Sea Star Hotel (Sao Bien Hotel; ☎ 861 589; saobien_hotel@yahoo.com; 15 Đ Cua Dai; r US$7;) On the road leading to Cau Dai Beach, this is as basic as it gets – no air-con – but the rooms are a nice surprise given the hotel's dowdy exterior.

Hoi Pho Hotel (☎ 916 382; hoiphohotel@yahoo.com; 627 Đ Hai Ba Trung; r US$7-10;) This modest family-owned minihotel offers straightforward value for money, with clean rooms and attentive service.

Minh A Ancient Lodging House (☎ 861 368; 2 Đ Nguyen Thai Hoc; r US$10-15;) Staying in this family-owned historic home is like sleeping in a museum; for good reason its three rooms fill up fast.

Huy Hoang Hotel (☎ 861 453; kshuyhoang1@dng.vnn.vn; 73 Đ Phan Boi Chau; r incl breakfast US$10-15;) With an airy riverside restaurant that just begs for leisurely lounging, the rooms are comfortable and the location is prime.

our pick **Thien Nga Hotel** (☎ 916 330; thienngahotel@gmail.com; 52 Đ Ba Trieu; r incl breakfast US$10-20;) An old favourite that keeps getting better, this great little place is terrific value, offering clean, comfortable rooms and free breakfast.

Phu Thinh I Hotel (☎ 861 297; www.phuthinhhotels.com; 144 Đ Tran Phu; r US$10-20;) Set back from a quiet but central block of Đ Tran Phu, this Chinese-style place has comfortable rooms, though some are windowless and on the small side. Still, this is one of the best value places in the historic heart of Hoi An.

Thanh Van Hotel (☎ 916 916; www.thanhvanhotel.com; 78 Đ Tran Hung Dao; r US$15-20;) With clean newish rooms and modern amenities, the owners will knock off a few dollars for guests who opt out of breakfast.

Eating

There are three local specialities here but most famous is *cao lau*, doughy flat noodles mixed with croutons, bean sprouts and greens, topped with pork slices and served in a savoury broth. The real thing can only be had in Hoi An, as the water for *cao lau* noodles must come from Ba Le well. The other two culinary specialities are fried wonton, and 'white rose', a petite steamed dumpling stuffed with shrimp.

Han Huyen Restaurant (☎ 861 462; 35 Đ Nguyen Phuc Chu; mains 7000-20,000d; breakfast, lunch & dinner) The view and ambiance here are nice and the sampler plate of Hoi An cuisine is worth the trip.

For You (☎ 081 460; 33 Đ Nguyen Phuc Chu; mains 7000-20,000d; breakfast, lunch & dinner) Besides some of the most affordable set menus in town the balcony is a nice place to enjoy the 5pm to 8pm happy hour with cheap (15,000d) cocktails.

Green Moss (☎ 863 728; 341 Đ Nguyen Duy Hieu; mains 10,000-30,000d) Housed in a lovely French colonial-era house, Green Moss serves a tasty mix of Asian dishes with plenty of vegetarian options cooked by the friendly Ms The Lee.

It has informal cooking classes; for the price of the dish you like plus US$2.

Ba Le Well (☎ 864 443; 45/51 Đ Tran Hung Dao; mains 12,000d; ⏲ lunch & dinner) Near the famous well is this modest family restaurant of the same name. The house specialities include *thit nuong* (spiced, grilled rolls of pork) and *banh xeo* (stuffed rice crepe that you wrap in lettuce and herbs and dip in fish sauce).

our pick **Truc Vien** (☎ 917 310; 88 Đ Ba Trieu, mains 14,000d; ⏲ breakfast, lunch & dinner) Good for *pho* or *cao lau*. The grandmotherly cook is so sure of her food she responds to every order of her delicious soups with 'number one!'

Blue Dragon (☎ 910 742; www.bdcf.org; 46 Đ Bach Dang; mains 15,000 ⏲ breakfast, lunch & dinner) The usual local specialities are done right here and it's a good place to spy on the frantic riverside market stalls. A portion of the profits here go to the Blue Dragon Foundation to help disadvantaged kids stay in school.

Restaurant Café 96 (☎ 910 441; 96 Đ Bach Dang; mains 15,000d; ⏲ breakfast, lunch & dinner) The food is sublime and the place has a certain tattered decadence – try the grilled fish in banana leaf.

Mermaid Restaurant (☎ 861 527; 2 Đ Tran Phu; mains 18,000d; ⏲ breakfast, lunch & dinner) A long-running favourite in a prime people-watching location, the Mermaid serves fabulous 'white rose' and has a nice atmosphere.

Cargo Club (☎ 910 489; 107 Đ Nguyen Thai Hoc; mains 18,000-70,000d; ⏲ breakfast, lunch & dinner) If you're chasing an omelette for breakfast or a baguette for lunch, this is your place. After dark it morphs into a groovy bar.

Café des Amis (☎ 861 616; 52 Đ Bach Dang; 5-course set menu 90,000d; ⏲ dinner) A tribute to Georges Brassens, the late French singer's posters and music fill this riverside spot where dinner is whatever the chef, Mr Kim, says it is. There's always a vegetarian option.

Drinking

There are a few *bia hoi* places scattered around Hoi An that serve ice cold brew for as cheap as 3000d. Look for the signs; a good bet is to look along Đ Bach Dang.

Tam Tam Cafe & Bar (☎ 862 212; 110 Đ Nguyen Thai Hoc) The mainstay of nightlife in Hoi An is this thoughtfully restored tea warehouse. If the crowd on the balcony isn't a clue to where the action is, enter the ground floor restaurant and take the stairs.

Before & Now (☎ 910 599; 51 Đ Le Loi) The pool table, foosball and two-for-one drinks from 6pm to 9pm draw a healthy crowd. The walls are plastered in pop-art portraits of everyone from Marx to Gandhi.

Treat's Café (☎ 861 125; 158 Đ Tran Phu) The backpacker bar of old Hoi An, this place is regularly full to bursting. The oh-so-happy happy hours between 4pm and 9pm include two-for-one spirits and bargain beer.

Re-Treat Café (31 Đ Phan Dinh Phung) There are a few places on this street with similar and confusing names. This is the one closest to the budget lodging on Đ Ba Trieu, but all the incarnations have nice patio seating, a pool table, good drinks, and, well, tasty treats.

Shopping

Yes, those backpackers from two cities ago are suddenly wearing collared shirts and looking quite spiffy. Tailor-made clothing is one of Hoi An's best trades, and there are more than 200 tailor shops in town that can whip up a custom-tailored *ao dai* (traditional Vietnamese tunic and trousers) or formal wear for the weddings and graduation ceremonies waiting back home. Bring your favourite clothes for cloning, or, just bring a picture from a magazine. Custom shoes are also popular, and those who want ready-to-wear duds will find a huge selection.

Bargaining has a place here, but basically you get what you pay for. The better tailors and better fabrics are more expensive. One of the hundreds of tailors will probably knock out a men's suit for US$20, but a good quality, lined woollen suit is more likely to cost US$40 to US$70. Shirts, skirts and casual trousers hover around the US$10 mark.

Hoi An also boasts a growing array of interesting art galleries, especially on the west side of the Japanese Covered Bridge, and does a thriving business in wood carvings, fake antiques, and reproductions of famous paintings.

Reaching Out Handicrafts (Hoa Nhap Handicrafts; ☎ 910 168; hoanhap@yahoo.com; 103 Đ Nguyen Thai Hoc; ⏲ 7.30am-7.30pm) sells handicrafts made by disabled craftspeople from all over Vietnam and profits support community programmes for disabled people locally and throughout Vietnam.

Getting There & Away

All hotels in Hoi An book minibuses to Nha Trang (US$8), Danang (US$2) and Hué (US$4). Buses to Danang via the Marble Mountains depart from the **Hoi An bus station** (Ben Quoc Doanh Xe

Khach; 74 Đ Huynh Thuc Khang), 1km west of the town centre. A taxi to the beach should cost around US$2 and to Danang US$10.

Getting Around

It's extremely easy to get around on foot here but motorbike drivers wait to solicit business outside all the tourist hotels. Many hotels also offer bicycles for hire for around US$1 to US$2 per day.

AROUND HOI AN

My Son

Set within the jungle 35km from Hoi An are the enigmatic ruins of **My Son** (☎ 731 309; admission 60,000d; 🕑 6.30am-4.00pm), the most important remains of the ancient Cham empire and a Unesco World Heritage site. Although Vietnam has better preserved Cham sites, none are as extensive and few have such beautiful surroundings – clear streams run between the structures and past nearby coffee plantations.

Day tours to My Son can be arranged in Hoi An for about US$3, not including admission. Some agencies offer the option of returning to Hoi An by boat, which adds an extra couple of hours to the trip. A hire car with driver from Hoi An to My Son costs around US$15 to US$20; a little expensive for sure but wandering around alone often seems to be the difference between disappointment and enchantment here.

Cua Dai Beach

You can sometimes find this white-sand beach deserted on weekdays, though weekends tend to be a little crowded. Swimming is best between April and October. To get there, take Đ Cua Dai east out of Hoi An about 5km. As is the national standard, motorbike parking should cost 2000d.

SOUTH-CENTRAL COAST

The 'fun zone' of Vietnam, this is the place for parties, adrenaline-junkies and sun worshippers – and that's just on land. Underwater, the diving is outstanding, with bright coral gardens galore.

NHA TRANG

☎ 058 / pop 315,200

Anything a person wants in Vietnam is here; partying like a disco star around the clock, snorkelling or diving reefs full of colourful fish, checking out Cham ruins and Buddhist pagodas with fabulous views, or sweating away bad juju in hot mineral mud. Roving vendors offer massage and lunch on the beaches where travellers frolic and soak up the sun, and boat trips range from booze cruises to mellow tours of nearby islands.

Information

BOOKSHOPS

Shorty's Bar (☎ 524 057; 1E Đ Biet Thu) Books in English, food, drink, a pool table and a happening atmosphere; the place to live out librarian fantasies.

INTERNET ACCESS

Heaps of hotels, traveller cafés and internet cafés offer web access all over town.

Hugo.net ADSL (☎ 521 339; 41 Đ Hung Vuong; per min 50d; 🕑 9am-11pm) Beside fast connections, it offers internet phone service and burns photo CDs (10,000d).

MEDICAL SERVICES

Hon Chong Hospital (☎ 831 103; Đ Hon Chong) About 1.5km northeast of the centre, it has a few English-speaking doctors.

Pasteur Institute Center for preventative Medicine (☎ 822 355; 10 Đ Tran Phu) Offers medical consultations and vaccinations.

MONEY

Nha Trang is full of ATMs so finding one should be no problem.

Vietcombank (🕑 Mon-Fri); Đ Quang Trung (☎ 822 720; 17 Đ Quang Trung); Đ Hung Vuong (☎ 524 500; 5 Đ Hung Vuong) Both branches exchange travellers cheques and have ATMs. The Đ Quang Trung branch processes cash advances; and the Đ Hung Vuong branch exchanges cash.

POST

Main post office (☎ 823 866; 4 Đ Le Loi; 🕑 6.30am-10pm)

Post office branch (☎ 652 070; 50 Đ Le Thanh Ton; 🕑 7am-11pm)

TRAVEL AGENCIES

Hanh Cafe (☎ 814 227; hanhcafe@dng.vnn.vn; 26 Đ Tran Hung Dao) Sells open-tour bus tickets, and for a fee can arrange train and air tickets.

Khanh Hoa Tours (☎ 526 753; www.nhatrangtourist.com.vn; 1 Đ Tran Hung Dao) Extensive offerings include maps, visas, tours, vehicle rental and guides.

Sinh Café (☎ 524 329; www.sinhcafevn.com; 10 Đ Biet Thu) Offers bargain-basement local tours as well as open-tour buses.

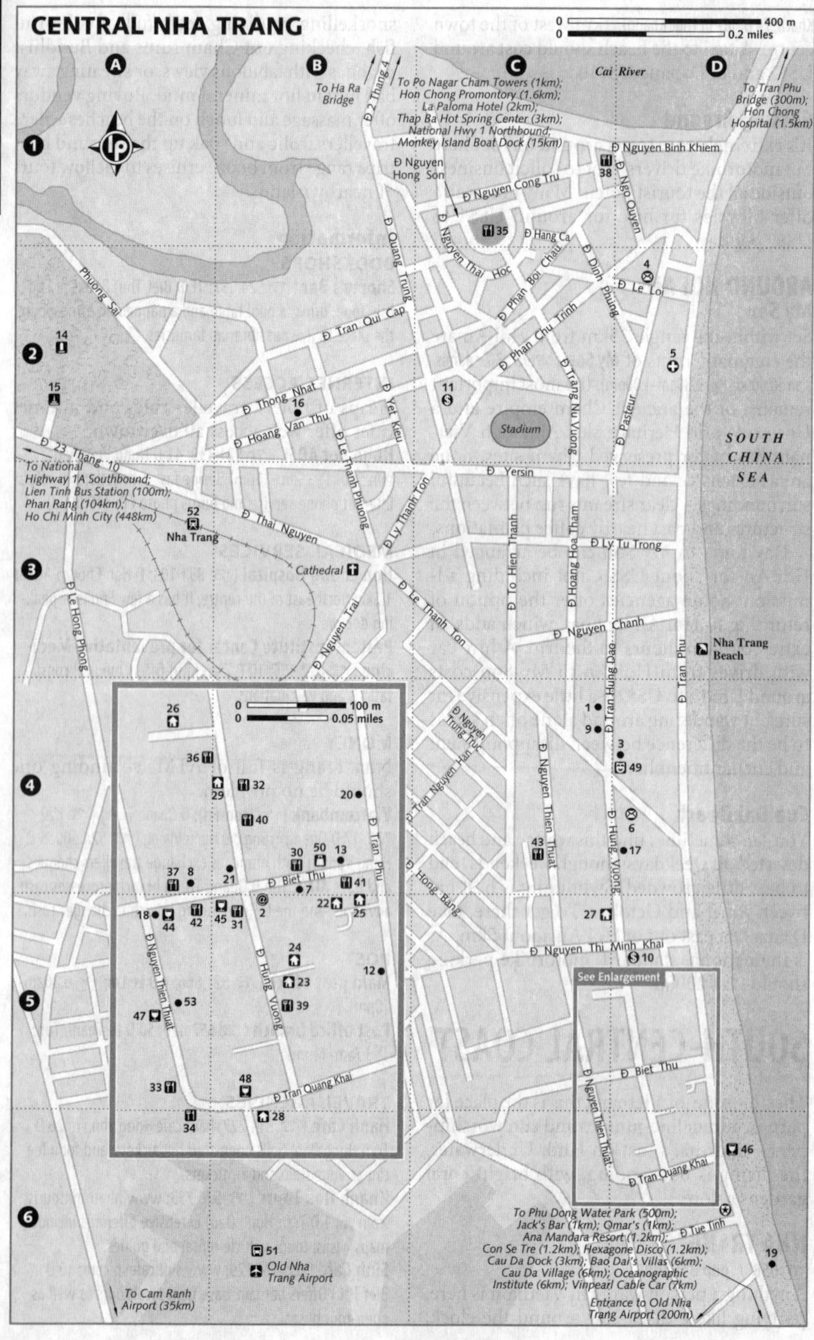
CENTRAL NHA TRANG
400 m
0.2 miles
Cai River
To Ha Ra Bridge
To Po Nagar Cham Towers (1km); Hon Chong Promontory (1.6km); La Paloma Hotel (2km); Thap Ba Hot Spring Center (3km); National Hwy 1 Northbound; Monkey Island Boat Dock (15km)
To Tran Phu Bridge (300m); Hon Chong Hospital (1.5km)
Đ Nguyen Binh Khiem
Đ Nguyen Hong Son
Đ Nguyen Cong Tru
Đ Ngo Quyen
Đ 2 Thang 4
Đ Quang Trung
Đ Nguyen Thai Hoc
Đ Hang Ca
Đ Phan Boi Chau
Đ Dinh Phung
Đ Le Loi
Phuong Sai
Đ Tran Qui Cap
Đ Phan Chu Trinh
Đ Thong Nhat
Đ Hoang Van Thu
Đ Yet Kieu
Đ Trang Nu Vuong
Đ Pasteur
Stadium
SOUTH CHINA SEA
Đ 23 Thang 10
To National Highway 1A Southbound; Lien Tinh Bus Station (100m); Phan Rang (104km); Ho Chi Minh City (448km)
Đ Le Thanh Phuong
Đ Ly Thanh Ton
Đ Yersin
Nha Trang
Đ Thai Nguyen
Đ To Hien Thanh
Đ Hoang Hoa Tham
Đ Ly Tu Trong
Cathedral
Đ Le Thanh Ton
Đ Le Hong Phong
Đ Nguyen Trai
Đ Nguyen Chanh
Nha Trang Beach
Đ Tran Hung Dao
Đ Tran Phu
Đ Nguyen Trung Truc
Đ Tran Nguyen Han
Đ Nguyen Thien Thuat
Đ Hung Vuong
Đ Biet Thu
Đ Hong Bang
Đ Nguyen Thi Minh Khai
See Enlargement
100 m
0.05 miles
Đ Tran Quang Khai
To Phu Dong Water Park (500m); Jack's Bar (1km); Omar's (1km); Ana Mandara Resort (1.2km); Con Se Tre (1.2km); Hexagone Disco (1.2km); Cau Da Dock (3km); Bao Dai's Villas (6km); Cau Da Village (6km); Oceanographic Institute (6km); Vinpearl Cable Car (7km)
Đ Tue Tinh
Old Nha Trang Airport
To Cam Ranh Airport (35km)
Entrance to Old Nha Trang Airport (200m)

INFORMATION
Hanh Cafe....1 C4
Hugo net DSL....2 B5
Khanh Hoa Tours....3 D4
Main Post Office....4 D2
Pasteur Institute for Preventative Medicine....5 D2
Post Office....6 D4
Shorty's Bar....7 B4
Sinh Cafe....8 A4
TM Brothers Cafe....9 C4
Vietcombank....10 D5
Vietcombank....11 C2

SIGHTS & ACTIVITIES
Blue Diving Club....12 B5
Coco Dive Center....13 B4
Giant Seated Buddha....14 A2
Long Son Pagoda....15 A2
Long Thanh Gallery....16 B2
Lucky Foot Massage....17 D4
Mama Linh's Boat Tours....18 A5
Mana Mana Beach Club....19 D6
Octopus Diving Club....20 B4
Rainbow Divers....21 B4
Sailing Club Diving....(see 46)

SLEEPING
Hotel An Hoa....22 B5
Mai Huy....23 B5
Nice Hotel....24 B5
Pho Bien....25 B5
Phong Lan Hotel....26 A4
Phu Quy Hotel....27 C5
Sakura Hotel....28 B6
Thien Tan Hotel....29 B4

EATING
A-Mart....(see 45)
Café des Amis....30 B4
Checkpoint Charlie's....31 B5
Cheers Café....32 B4
Cool Kangaroo....33 A5
Cyclo Café....34 A6
Dam Market....35 C1
El Coyote....36 A4
Hai Phong Restaurant....37 A4
Lac Canh Restaurant....38 C1
Pho Cali....39 B5
Red Star....40 B4
Romy's Homemade Ice Cream....41 B4
Truc Linh 1....42 A5
Turkish Cuisine Kebab Restaurant....43 C4

DRINKING
Crazy Kim Bar....44 A5
Guava....45 B5
Nha Trang Sailing Club....46 D6
Shamrock Irish Pub....47 A5
Tiny Bar Nghia....(see 39)
Why Not Bar....48 B5

ENTERTAINMENT
Vien Dong Hotel....49 D4

SHOPPING
Andy's....50 B4
Kim Quang....(see 46)

TRANSPORT
Buses to Cam Ranh Airport....51 B6
Nha Trang Train Station....52 A3
Vietnam Airlines....53 A5

TM Brothers Cafe (☎ 523 556; hoanhaont@dng.vnn.vn; 22B Đ Tran Hung Dao) Another open-tour mainstay.

Dangers & Annoyances

Though not all the rip-offs here are alcohol-related, most are. Getting too drunk, especially by yourself, at a bar or club late at night is like spraying on 'rob me' perfume. We've also heard reports of thefts on the beach (don't hug strangers), during massages (don't fall asleep), and from hotel rooms (none of the ones listed in this book, but stay cautious). Consider leaving surplus cash at the hotel reception; count it in front of the clerk and put it in an envelope that you both sign.

A persistent scam exists at the Long Son Pagoda, where you will be approached by children with preprinted name badges (and occasionally older people) claiming to work for the monks. After a tour, extortion 'for the monks' ensues. Tell them straight off the only money you're leaving is going into the donation box.

Sights

Built between the 7th and 12th centuries on a site used by Hindus for worship, the **Po Nagar Cham Towers** (Đ 2 Thang 4; admission 4500d; ⌚ 6am-6pm) are 2km north of central Nha Trang on the left bank of the Cai River. From the hill are blue views of the harbour below.

The impressively adorned **Long Son Pagoda** (Chua Tinh Hoi Khanh Hoa; Đ 23 Thang 10; admission free; ⌚ 7.30-11.30am & 1.30-8pm) is decorated with mosaic dragons covered with glass and ceramic tile. Founded in the late 19th century, the pagoda still has resident monks. At the top of the hill, behind the pagoda, is the **Giant Seated Buddha** visible from town. From where the Buddha sits, you too can contemplate the view of Nha Trang. The pagoda is about 500m west of the train station.

The work of Nha Trang's most acclaimed photographer, Long Thanh, is shown at **Long Thanh Gallery** (☎ 824 875; lvntrang50@hotmail.com; 126 Đ Hoang Van Thu; ⌚ 8.30-11.30am & 1-6pm Mon-Sat). The entrance is hidden behind ferns and near a row of aquarium shops, and even if it looks closed the staff will usually turn on the lights for visitors.

Swimming around in the **Oceanographic Institute** (Vien Nghiem Cuu Bien; ☎ 590 037; 15,000d; ⌚ 7.30am-noon & 1-4.30pm), a French colonial building 6km south of the town centre, are colourful representatives of squirming sea life. Sometimes feeling more like an amateur home aquarium than a true museum, the shark pool, however in need of cleaning, is impressive. A hall in the back has thousands of pickled specimens of marine life; sunlight passing through the jars gives the place an eerie beauty.

Vinpearl Cable Car (☎ 598 123; www.vinpearlland.com; round-trip 100,000d; ⌚ 9.30am-10pm) About 7km south of downtown Nha Trang is a cable car that stretches from Phu Quy Tourism pier on the mainland to Vinpearl Land Resort & Amusement park on Hon Tre Island. The park is an exercise in kitsch and kids, but the 15-minute,

3320m-long cable-car ride is a great way to see Nha Trang and the surrounding islands from a bird's-eye view. A ride from Nha Trang proper to the '*capo*,' as locals call it, should cost 10,000d to 20,000d on a motorbike.

BEACHES

Coconut palms provide shelter for sunbathers and strollers along most of Nha Trang's 6km of beachfront; beach chairs are available for hire.

Hon Chong promontory, 1.8km north of central Nha Trang, is a scenic collection of granite rocks jutting into the South China Sea. The beach here has a more local flavour than Nha Trang Beach, but the accompanying refuse makes it a less attractive option for swimming or sunbathing.

ISLANDS

The nine outlying islands of Nha Trang beckon offshore; hop on one of the boat tours sold all over town. For as little as US$5, you can join a day tour visiting four islands (see opposite). Or, cobble together your own trips to various islands.

There's a working fish farm on **Hon Mieu** (Mieu Island) that's also a beautiful outdoor **aquarium** (Ho Ca Tri Nguyen). From there, you can rent canoes, or hire someone to paddle you out to **Hon Mun** (Ebony Island) or **Hon Yen** (Swallow Island). Rustic bungalows on the island rent for about 90,000d. Ferries to Hon Mieu (5000d) leave regularly throughout the day from Cau Da dock at the southern end of Nha Trang. Catch ferries back to Nha Trang at Tri Nguyen village on Hon Mieu.

Idyllic **Hon Tre** (Bamboo Island) is the largest island in the area. You can get boats to **Bai Tru** (Tru Beach) at the northern end of the island, but it's also recommended to take the day or overnight trips here offered by **Con Se Tre** (☎ 811 163; 1006 Đ Tran Phu), south of town. There's great snorkelling and diving off **Hon Mun**, **Hon Tam** and **Hon Mot**.

The cheapest way to get out on the water is to take the regular local ferry to Vinpearl on Hon Tre (adult/child 40,000/15,000d each way), leaving from Phu Quy harbour. Or, more expensive but more scenic, take the cable car across (see p869)

THAP BA HOT SPRING CENTER

A good place for dirty fun is **Thap Ba Hot Spring Center** (☎ 834 939; 25 Ngoc Son; ⌚ 8am-8pm). For 180,000d you can sit in a wooden bathtub full of hot thermal mud, or for 60,000d per person wallow in the mud with friends in a larger pool. To get here, follow the signpost on the second road to the left past the Po Nagar Cham Towers and take the twisting, bumpy road for 2.5km.

Activities

DIVING

Nha Trang is still Vietnam's premier diving locale, with around 25 dive sites in the area. Visibility averages 15m, but can be as much as 30m, depending on the season (late October to early January is the worst time of year).

A full-day outing, including two dives and sometimes a lunch, costs between US$60 and US$75. Dive operators also offer a range of courses, including a 'Discover Diving' programme for uncertified, first-time divers. Consider the following outfits, but shop around:

Blue Diving Club (☎ 527 034; www.vietnam-diving.com; 66 Đ Tran Phu) Owned and operated by French and British divers.

Coco Dive Center (☎ 812 900; www.cocodivecenter.com; 2E Đ Biet Thu) A friendly outfit where you can book directly with the dive masters to get your own read on them; has the nicest boat of the lot.

Octopus Diving (☎ 521 629; 62 Đ Tran Phu) See Sailing Club Diving.

Rainbow Divers (☎ 524 351; www.divevietnam.com; 90A Hung Vuong) Run by Briton Jeremy Stein, Rainbow Divers is the standard setter for diving in Vietnam, operating out of five centres nationwide. This, its head office, also includes a restaurant and bar.

Sailing Club Diving (☎ 522 788; www.sailingclubvietnam.com; 72-74 Đ Tran Phu) This and Octopus Diving are two names for the same operation that have separate locations on the same street. Get it?

SWIMMING & WATER SPORTS

Mana Mana Beach Club (☎ 524 362; www.manamana.com; Louisiane Brewhouse, 29 Đ Tran Phu) offers windsurfing, sea kayaking, wakeboarding and sailing lessons. Mana Mana uses good equipment and has access to some great surfing spots in Cam Ranh Bay.

MASSAGE

Despite what the name might imply to some people, **Lucky Foot Massage** (☎ 521 417; 1 Đ Hung Vuong; ⌚ 9am-9pm) offers first-class massages. Find paradise in a 45-minute foot, leg and hand massage (US$6).

Tours

Mama Linh's Boat Tours (☎ 522 844; mamalihnvn@yahoo.com; 23C Đ Biet Thu) runs daily island-hopping party boats, stopping at Hon Mun, Hon Mot, Hon Tam and Hon Mieu (see opposite). Tickets (US$6) are sold from the home office, but you can book almost anywhere around town for an additional commission.

Con Se Tre (☎/fax 527 522; 100/16 Đ Tran Phu) offers tours to Hon Tre that include a visit to Vinpearl, a look around the village and lunch (US$15), and snorkelling trips to Hon Mun (two people US$44, group per person US$12). It also charters speed boats (US$35 to US$50) and wooden boats (US$30 to US$45), including snorkels and a guide.

Travel agencies in town also offer various tours (see p867).

Sleeping

The place is full of guesthouses and hotels that offer some of the best value for money in the county.

Mai Huy (☎ 527 553; 7H Đ Hung Vuong; r US$5-7; ❄) Pronounced 'may we' (or 'mais oui!' if you're French), it's worth searching out this new family-run minihotel, hidden down a small laneway. The cost of a simple clean room with a fan, fridge, satellite TV and private bathroom with hot water, is unbelievable value.

our pick **Phong Lan Hotel** (Orchid Hotel; ☎ 522 647; orchidhotel2000@yahoo.com; 24/44 Đ Hung Vuong; r US$5-10; ❄) This family-run place is in a quiet alley off Hung Vuong, with small clean rooms with TV and fridge. The owners speak French and English and seem to take personal responsibility for the happiness of guests.

Hotel An Hoa (☎ 524 029; anhoahotel@yahoo.com; 64B/6 Đ Tran Phu; r US$6-11; ❄) One of the better options in the new, fabulously located, budget alley, rooms range from cheapies without windows or air-con, to larger pads with bathtubs and decks.

Phu Quy Hotel (☎ 521 609; Phuquyhotel@dng.vnn.vn; 54 Đ Hung Vuong; r US$6-20; ❄ 💻) The highlight of this minihotel is its rooftop terrace – all the rooms are comfortable, and for US$10 expect a balcony, bathtub and sea view.

Nice Hotel (☎ 527 379; nicehotel@vnn.vn; Đ Hung Vuong; r US$7-10; ❄ 💻) Awesome views from the higher levels of this big new minihotel are only marred by the constant dinging of the elevator. But, with some ear plugs you'll sleep easy knowing that the rooms are truly nice for the price. Rooms may be cooled by either fan or air-con.

Sakura Hotel (☎ 524 669; 1/32 Đ Tran Quang Khai; r US$7-12; ❄ 💻) A comfy minihotel, the Sakura has rooms equipped with satellite TV, IDD phone and fridge. As an added bonus, it offers free transport to and from train or bus station.

Thien Tan Hotel (New Sky Hotel; ☎ 521 304; thientanhhotel@hotmail.com; 78 Đ Hung Vuong; r US$7-18; ❄) This clean minihotel has comfortable, bright rooms with satellite TV and phone.

Pho Bien (☎ 524 858; phobienhotelint@yahoo.com; 64/1 Đ Tran Phu; r US$8-12; ❄) The best of the budget alley minihotels, some of the cheapest rooms have views and large balconies, if you can handle the stairs.

Eating

Central Nha Trang teems with dining choices. As always, taking a meal in the market is a cheap adventure, and **Dam market** (Đ Nguyen Hong Son) in the north end of town has lots of local food stalls, including *com chay* (vegetarian food). **A-Mart** (☎ 523 035; 17A Đ Biet Thu; 🕑 6am-10pm) has a food court outside with lots of Western treats and the ingredients to make snacks or a real meal should you have access to a kitchen.

Frozen treats don't get much better than at **Romy's Homemade Ice Cream** (☎ 527 677; 1C Đ Biet Thu; dessert 25,000d). The waffles laden with ice cream or fruit are a sweet way to start the day.

VIETNAMESE

Café des Amis (☎ 521 009; 2D Đ Biet Thu; dishes 7000-40,000d) A popular cheapie focusing on seafood and vegetarian fare, the walls are covered with interesting works by Vietnamese painters.

Lac Canh Restaurant (☎ 821 391; 44 Đ Nguyen Binh Khiem; mains 10,000-85,000d; 🕑 lunch & dinner) A Nha Trang institution; beef, squid, giant prawns, lobsters and the like are grilled at your table.

Pho Cali (☎ 525 885; 7G Đ Hung Vuong; mains 15,000-25,000d; 🕑 breakfast, lunch & dinner) The meals are delicious, and the set menu – comprising soup, rice and a hotpot – is outrageously good value at 20,000d.

Hai Phong Restaurant (☎ 521 771; 12B Đ Biet Thu; mains 15,000-30,000d; 🕑 lunch & dinner) It looks like an average travellers café but the Vietnamese and seafood dishes are a very tasty surprise. It also has plenty of backpacker favourites on the menu.

our pick **Red Star** (☎ 524-980; 27A Đ Hung Vuong; mains from 16,000d; breakfast, lunch & dinner) All of their food is good, but the seafood *ben xeo* stands out as the best way to sample the sea's bounty on the cheap.

Truc Linh 1 (☎ 526-742; 11 Đ Biet Thu; 30,000-80,000d; lunch & dinner) With two other nearby locations, the Truc Linh restaurants nearly take over a city block with crates of fresh seafood on ice. Good presentation and service are just the warm-up to great food.

Cyclo Café (☎ 524 208; 130 Đ Nguyen Thien Thuat; mains about 30,000d; breakfast, lunch & dinner) Run by a local couple with many years of experience in Nha Trang's restaurant business; it serves real Vietnamese food at local prices.

INTERNATIONAL

Cheers Café (☎ 524 840; Đ Hung Vuong; mains from 7000-45,000d; breakfast, lunch & dinner) Serving good French, Italian, and Vietnamese fare, this is the place (there's one in every city in Southeast Asia) that always has at least one table full of beer bottles surrounded by older guys.

Checkpoint Charlie's (☎ 527 829; 1L Đ Hung Vuong; mains from 15,000d; lunch & dinner) The owner, Charlie, is a German who serves great sauerkraut and other Teutonic favourites such as meatballs and black bread.

Cool Kangaroo (☎ 527 307; 116 Đ Nguyen Thien Thuat; mains from 16,000d; breakfast, lunch & dinner) Come here for Vietnamese and Russian food in addition to the usual traveller favourites. The staff are friendly but the place has odd décor; plush toy kangaroos hang next to portraits of Russian Orthodox saints.

El Coyote (☎ 526 320; 76 Đ Hung Vuong; mains from 30,000d; lunch & dinner) Great food. Guests are often treated to a shot of banana rum and the happy hour set menu runs from 5pm to 9pm; choose a burrito, nachos, or tacos as a main dish for 40,000d with a soft drink or 50,000d with a beer.

Turkish Cuisine Kebab Restaurant (☎ 525 328; 24B Đ Hung Vuong; mains 40,000-100,000d; breakfast, lunch & dinner) It serves kebabs, pizza and pasta. Hookah pipes add to the atmosphere.

Drinking

Shamrock Irish Pub (☎ 527 548; www.raftingvietnam.com; 56A Đ Nguyen Thien Thuat) This is an ultrafriendly pub favoured by local expats.

Tiny Bar Nghia (☎ 527 011, 7G3 Đ Hung Vuong) 'Very good, very cheap, very Vietnam' is the motto at this *bia hoi* bar, and its definitely right. Get there early because by the time the sun sets it's packed.

Crazy Kim Bar (☎ 523 072; www.crazykimbar.com; 19 Đ Biet Thu) A fun party spot run by the ebullient Kimmy Le, there's a permanent classroom for vulnerable street kids in an upstairs corner of the bar. Part of the proceeds from the food, booze and T-shirt sales go towards the cause. Sign up at the bar if you're interested in volunteering to teach English.

Guava (☎ 524 140; www.clubnhatrang.com; 17 Đ Biet Thu) A little lounge, a little sports bar, a lot of fun. The crowd is a hip mix of locals and tourists.

Why Not Bar (☎ 522 652; 24 Đ Tran Quang Khai; until 4am) Try the wicked 'Why not?' bucket of booze (30,000d), available all night long. Dancing in the big airy space and whatever else on the plush couches are sure to follow.

Nha Trang Sailing Club (☎ 826 528; www.sailingclubvietnam.com; 72-74 Đ Tran Phu; until 4am) This Aussie-run, open-air beach bar is where most of the party crowd ends up at some point in the evening; usually the latter half. It has thumping music, wild dancing, flowing shots, pool and general mayhem.

Entertainment

Vien Dong Hotel (☎ 821 606; 1 Đ Tran Hung Dao; admission free; performances 7.30pm) Hosts nightly ethnic-minority song and dance performances.

Shopping

Many restaurants and bars around town display the works of local photographers and artists, which are usually for sale. You'll find a lot of seashells and coral for sale, but their harvesting destroys the beauty and ecology of Nha Trang's reefs.

Check out the hand-painted T-shirts done by a friendly local painter named **Kim Quang** (☎ 0983 884 5397), who you can find between 2pm and 9pm working from his wheelchair at the Sailing Club (above).

Andy's (4 Đ Biet Thu) sells beach wear, maps, books and one-of-a-kind clothing. The best part of the shop is the chance to watch traditional fabric weaving on a small loom.

Getting There & Away

AIR

Vietnam Airlines (code VN; ☎ 826 768; www.vietnamairlines.com; 91 Đ Nguyen Thien Thuat) has flights connecting Cam Ranh airport (35km south of Nha Trang) with HCMC, Hanoi and Danang. To get to the airport, catch a shuttle bus (45,000d) from the old Nha Trang airport terminal (near 86 Đ Tran Phu), two hours before your flight. Taking a taxi to catch your flight should cost around US$10, and it's a fairly scenic drive.

BUS

About 500m west of the train station, **Lien Tinh bus station** (Ben Xe Lien Tinh; ☎ 822 192; Đ 23 Thang 10) is Nha Trang's main intercity bus terminal. Buses from here head to Danang (120,000d, seven hours), HCMC (110,000d, 11 hours), and Dalat (60,000d, seven hours).

Nha Trang is a major stopping point on all of the tourist open-bus tours. These are the best option for accessing Mui Ne, which is not served by local buses. Open-tour buses also run to Dalat (six hours) and Hoi An (11 hours). The only buses to Hoi An are night buses, however. Prepare for a long night as this leg of a trip is usually described as 'prison' or 'hell.'

CAR & MOTORCYCLE

A series of roughly parallel roads head inland from near Nha Trang, linking Vietnam's deltas and coastal regions with the Central Highlands.

TRAIN

The **Nha Trang train station** (Ga Nha Trang; ☎ 822 113; Đ Thai Nguyen; ticket office 7-11.30am, 1.30-5pm & 6-10pm) is down the hill west of the cathedral. Destinations include Danang (203,000d, 8½ to 12½ hours, seven daily) and other points north, Thap Cham (35,000d, 1½ to 2½ hours, eight daily) and HCMC (160,000d, seven to 12½ hours, nine daily).

A relatively new upscale train service called **5-Star Express** (☎ 08-920 6868 HCMC main office; www.5starexpress.com.vn; one way 220,000d-450,000d) runs a private, comfy train that travels between Nha Trang and HCMC.

Getting Around

There is no shortage of motorbikes, taxis and *cyclo* drivers looking for passengers. The old Nha Trang airport, from which buses shuttle passengers to Cam Ranh airport, is on the southern side of town. *Cyclos* go to both the old airport and the train station for about US$1.

Nha Trang Taxi (☎ 824 000) and **Khanh Hoa Taxi** (☎ 810 810) have cars with air-con and meters.

Many hotels have bicycle rentals for around US$1 per day.

MUI NE

☎ 062

This 11km-stretch of beach outside the fishing village of Mui Ne is only three hours away from HCMC and is *the* place to ease into slow-motion beachside Zen. Or, take the other extreme and tear up the waves with wind and kite-surfing. There are a number of luxury resorts here but some budget deals are still available. Mui Ne is a long stretch of restaurants and hotels but not a proper town, so, wherever you sleep will probably become the centre or your universe.

Orientation & Information

Local addresses are designated by a kilometre mark measuring the distance along Rte 706 from Hwy 1 in Phan Thiet. To mix things up a bit, Rte 706 is also known in town as Đ Nguyen Dinh Chieu. Small restaurants along the road offer internet access; the going rate is about 300d per minute.

Hanh Cafe/Ha Phuong Tourist (☎ 847 347; Km 13) Travel arrangements, backpacker grub and internet access can be found at this travellers café.

Incombank (68 Đ Nguyen Dinh Chieu; Sun-Fri) At Tropico Resort, this branch can exchange currency and travellers cheques.

Mui Ne Sailing Club (☎ 847 440; www.sailingclubvietnam.com; 24 Đ Nguyen Dinh Chieu) Has a registered nurse. For serious medical problems, head to HCMC.

TM Brothers Cafe (☎ 847 359; Km 13) About 200m from Hanh Cafe, with similar services.

Sights

Mui Ne is most famous for its fish sauce but the enormous **sand dunes** smell better and are a lot more fun. To get to the **red dunes** (sometimes called yellow) head east out of town and follow the signs to Pandasa Resort. Pass the resort and soon you'll see the dunes filled with little kids selling rides on plastic sheets down the sandy slopes. The **white dunes** are another 20km after that – definitely more impressive and worth a look. Wear real shoes because even in sandals the dunes are sizzling. Riding the dunes is an art, so try to rent a sheet of plastic from the kids rather than paying for each slide.

It's possible to cycle to the first dunes but start in a cool part of the day and bring plenty of sunscreen. A motorbike-taxi trip to both dunes (50,000d to 80,000d) is a better deal than a jeep tour (US$10) because you get dropped off at the same place no matter how you get there.

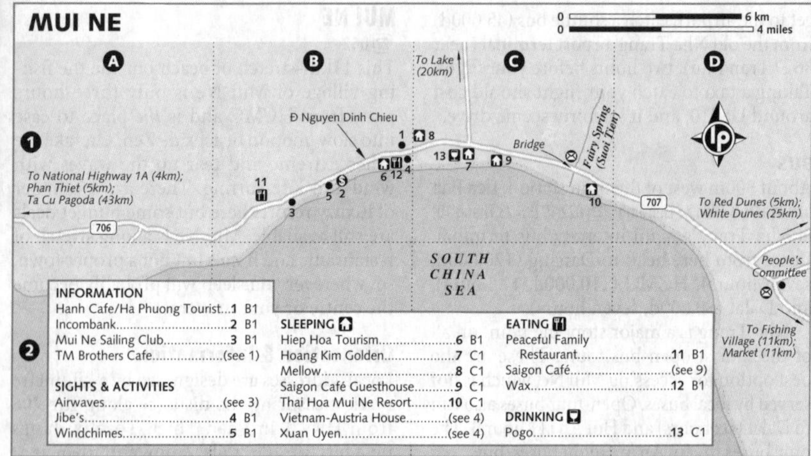

If taking a jeep be careful to agree on an itinerary for the tour, preferably in writing. We've heard complaints, particularly about 'sunset tours' that cut short with the sun high in the sky and the drivers getting aggressive when challenged.

The **Fairy Spring** (Suoi Tien) is a stream that flows through a patch of the dunes and rock formations east of town. Also nearby are a **red stream, market** and **fishing village**.

Activities

The season for windsurfers is from late October to late April. Ask at **Jibe's** (☎ 847 405; www.windsurf-vietnam.com; Km 13, 90 Đ Nguyen Dinh Chieu) for information. It rents state-of-the-art boards of all sorts, by the hour or day. It also offers kite-surfing and windsurfing lessons overseen by head instructor Armando, a friendly Lisbon native who is the utmost professional on the job and a barrel of fun once the sun goes down.

Airwaves (☎ 847 440; www.airwaveskitesurfing.com), based at Mui Ne Sailing Club, is another outfit offering lessons and equipment rentals.

Windchimes (☎ 0909 720 017; www.windsurfing-vietnam.com) is another watersports option, operating out of **Saigon Mui Ne Resort** (56 Đ Nguyen Dinh Chieu) and **Swiss Village** (44 Đ Nguyen Dinh Chieu).

Sleeping

Mui Ne has two main clusters of hotels; at the 13km mark where some nice budget places loom in the shadow of resorts, and at the cheaper end of town around the 18km mark. Most open-tour buses stop at the first location. Hop on a motorbike taxi to sniff around the other side if nothing suits your fancy.

Saigon Café Guesthouse (☎ 847 091; 168-170 Đ Nguyen Dinh Chieu; r US$5; 💻) These bamboo and thatched-roof bungalows are as cheap and humble as it comes.

Mellow (☎ 743 086; 117C Đ Nguyen Dinh Chieu; r US$6-12) The cheaper rooms share bathrooms and toilets. A favourite hangout of kite-surfers, the rooms fill up quick and there's a nice crowd at the bar-restaurant.

Hoang Kim Golden (☎ 847 689; www.hoangkim-golden.com; 140 Đ Nguyen Dinh Chieu; r US$6-25; ❄ 💻) The cheapie rooms here are very basic – shared bathrooms and no air-con. The rest cover a range of prices from good, clean budget options to newer rooms with bathtubs and minibars. There are two restaurants.

our pick **Thai Hoa Mui Ne Resort** (☎ 847 320; dtP@hcm.vnn.vn; Km 18; US$8-15; ❄ 💻) The clean beachfront has chairs and umbrellas and there's a nice restaurant at this great spot. The least expensive rooms don't have hot water or air-con.

Vietnam-Austria House (☎ 847 047; ngothikimhong@hotmail.com; km13.5; r US$8-20; ❄ 🍽) This established place has wooden bungalows and a block of simple rooms (the cheapest without hot water or air-con).

Hiep Hoa Tourism (☎ 847 262; hiephoatourism@yahoo.com; 80 Đ Nguyen Dinh Chieu; r US$10-15; ❄) Hiep Hoa is sandwiched between big resorts but manages to retain its laid-back vibe. It has a beautiful clean beach and tiny café. It's often full, so call ahead.

Xuan Uyen (☎ 847 476; 78 Nguyen Dinh Chieu; r US$10-15; 🖳) Entering through a leafy walkway you'll soon see travellers lolling on the beach or hanging in hammocks at this cool little place. The basic bungalow rooms have hot water.

Eating & Drinking

If you tire of your home café, Rte 706 is lined with small family restaurants serving similar dishes at comparable prices. Try the *com* shops for a plate of rice and fish for 6000d.

Saigon Café (☎ 847 091; 168-170 Đ Nguyen Dinh Chieu; dishes 12,000-45,000d) Great Vietnamese BBQ food is served in a basic setting, with profundities written on the walls in beautiful calligraphy.

Wax (☎ 847 001; 68 Đ Nguyen Dinh Chieu; mains from 20,000d; ⏲ breakfast, lunch & dinner) Wax is an airy beachside restaurant during the day but transforms into the most happening spot in Mui Ne at night with lots of pick-up lines and the spontaneous wiggling of hips. Try the tasty seafood macaroni (35,000d).

Peaceful Family Restaurant (Yen Gia Quan; ☎ 741 019; 53 Đ Nguyen Dinh Chieu; dishes 30,000-70,000d; ⏲ lunch & dinner) This friendly family eatery serves wonderful Vietnamese cuisine in a lovely open setting.

Pogo (☎ 0909 479 346; 138 Đ Nguyen Dinh Chieu) A fun, open-air bar decorated with colourful infantile paintings – it has a pool table, big sound system and bean bags.

Getting There & Around

From HCMC, the 200km drive to Mui Ne takes three hours – in theory. Depending on traffic in HCMC it can take up to seven. Traveller cafés in HCMC and Mui Ne sell tickets on open-tour buses for about US$5.

It's best to cruise around Mui Ne on bicycle, which most guesthouses rent for US$1 to US$3 a day. A motorbike should cost from US$5 to US$8 a day; almost all places to stay rent these, too. The roads are fairly quiet, but a German tourist on a motorbike was killed by a bus on this stretch in 2006, so be careful. There are plenty of *xe om* drivers to take you up and down the strip; no trip should cost more than 10,000d.

CENTRAL HIGHLANDS

The Central Highlands covers the southern part of the Truong Son Mountain Range. This geographical region, home to many Montagnard ethnic groups, is renowned for its cool climate, beautiful mountain scenery and innumerable streams, lakes and waterfalls. For those who can't make it to the far north of the country, this is the place for outdoor frolicking.

DALAT

☎ 063 / pop 130,000

Kitschy sights, honeymooning Vietnamese and cool weather are the main attractions that visitors find in Dalat, but just outside the city limits is a mecca for outdoor activities that should not be overlooked. Dotted with lakes and waterfalls and surrounded by evergreen forests, Dalat is nicknamed the City of Eternal Spring. The days are fine and nights frosty at 1475m, and wool hats and scarves abound in the market if you're caught unprepared. Still, the cool temperatures make trekking or cycling easier.

Orientation

Dalat's sights are spread out and the terrain in and around the city is hilly. The central market, set in a hollow, marks the middle of the town. To the southeast the 'Eiffel Tower' of the main post office is a useful landmark, rising above the southern shore of Xuan Huong Lake. Finding your way around can be frustrating in Dalat because of well-hidden street signs, roads that look like alleys at first glance, and sharp turns up and down hills that make navigation difficult.

Information

INTERNET ACCESS

There are several internet cafés along either side of Đ Nguyen Chi Thanh (Map p878). Rates for internet use are around 150d per minute.

MEDICAL SERVICES

Lam Dong Hospital (Map p878; ☎ 822 369; 4 Đ Pham Ngoc Thach)

MONEY

Though ATMs aren't as plentiful here as in other Vietnamese cities, getting more money is no problem. These downtown banks exchange cash and travellers cheques and do credit card-cash advances.

Agribank (Ngan Hang Nong Nghiep Viet Nam; Map p878; ☎ 827 740; 36 Hoa Binh Sq)

Incombank (Map p878; ☎ 822 586; 1 Đ Le Dai Hanh) No ATM, but this big branch exchanges travellers cheques and foreign currencies.

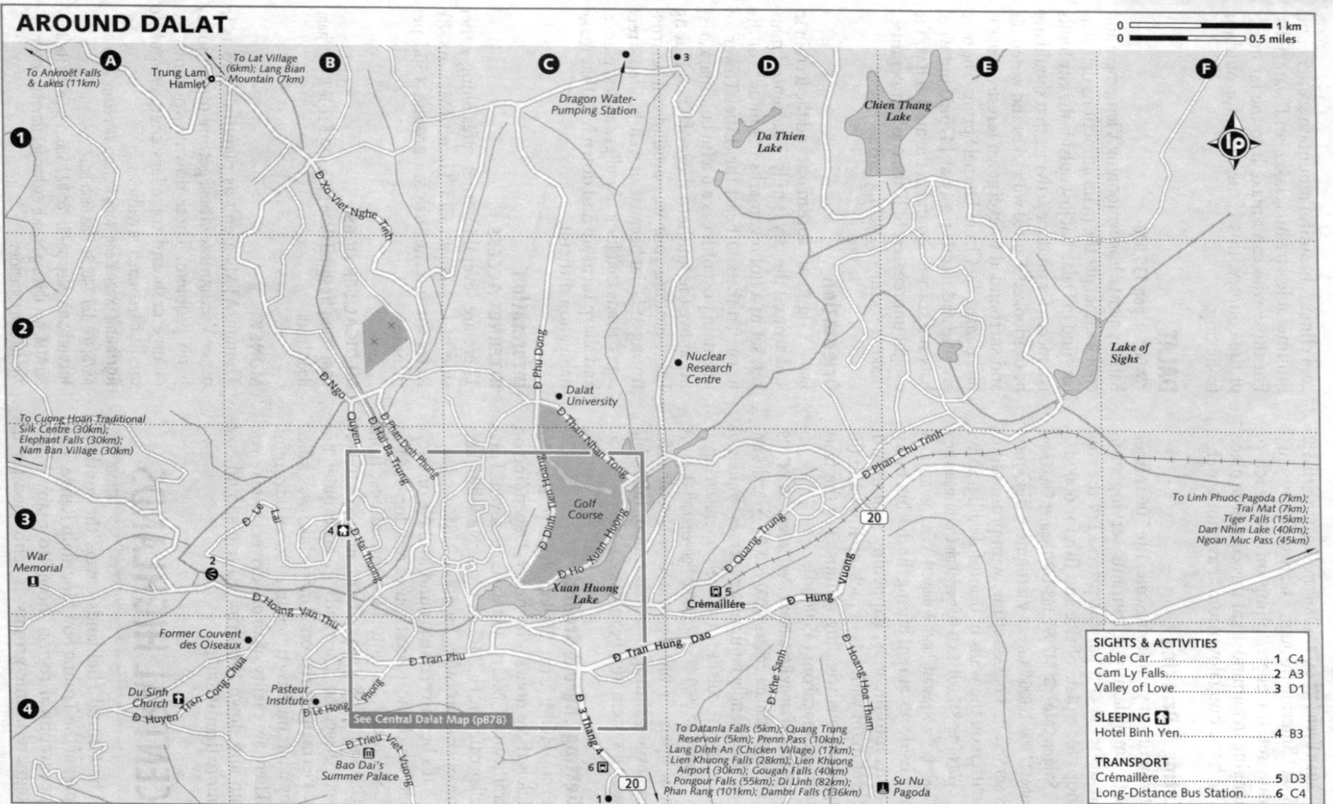
AROUND DALAT
SIGHTS & ACTIVITIES
Cable Car 1 C4
Cam Ly Falls 2 A3
Valley of Love 3 D1
SLEEPING
Hotel Binh Yen 4 B3
TRANSPORT
Crémaillère 5 D3
Long-Distance Bus Station 6 C4
To Ankroët Falls & Lakes (11km)
To Lat Village (6km); Lang Bian Mountain (7km)
Trung Lam Hamlet
Dragon Water-Pumping Station
Nuclear Research Centre
Dalat University
Chien Thang Lake
Da Thien Lake
Lake of Sighs
To Linh Phuoc Pagoda (7km); Trai Mat (7km); Tiger Falls (15km); Dan Nhim Lake (40km); Ngoan Muc Pass (45km)
To Cuong Hoan Traditional Silk Centre (30km); Elephant Falls (30km); Nam Ban Village (30km)
To Datanla Falls (5km); Quang Trung Reservoir (5km); Prenn Pass (10km); Lang Dinh An (Chicken Village) (17km); Lien Khuong Falls (28km); Lien Khuong Airport (30km); Gougah Falls (40km); Pongour Falls (55km); Di Linh (82km); Phan Rang (101km); Dambri Falls (136km)
Golf Course
Xuan Huong Lake
See Central Dalat Map (p878)
War Memorial
Former Couvent des Oiseaux
Du Sinh Church
Pasteur Institute
Bao Dai's Summer Palace
Su Nu Pagoda
Crémaillère
Đ Xo Viet Nghe Tinh
Đ Ngo Quyen
Đ Hai Ba Trung
Đ Phan Dinh Phung
Đ Phu Dong
Đ Than Nhan Tong
Đ Phan Chu Trinh
Đ Quang Trung
Đ Hung Vuong
Đ Hoang Hoa Tham
Đ Khe Sanh
Đ Tran Hung Dao
Đ 3 Thang 4
Đ Ho Xuan Huong
Đ Dinh Tien Hoang
Đ Tran Phu
Đ Hai Thuong
Đ Le Lai
Đ Hoang Van Thu
Đ Trieu Viet Vuong
Đ Le Hong Phong
Đ Tran Cong Chua
Đ Huyen
0 1 km
0 0.5 miles

POST

Main post office (Map p878; ☎ 836 638; 14 Đ Tran Phu; ⏲ 6.30am-9pm) International phone calls and internet access are available here.

TRAVEL AGENCIES

The tour companies listed (see right) act as travel agents. Most hotels, especially the Peace Hotels (p878), also double as travel agents.

Sights

Dalat has attractions you won't find elsewhere in Vietnam – and this may be a good thing. Tour companies (right) offer a range of activities.

The **Crémaillère** (Map p876; ☎ 834 409; Đ Quang Trung; return 70,000d; departures 8am, 9.30am, 2pm & 3.30pm) is a cog railway, about 500m east of Xuan Huong Lak. The return trip to Trai Mat village, where you can visit the ornate **Linh Phuoc Pagoda**, is 17km.

Southwest of central Dalat, **Hang Nga Crazy House** (Hang Nga Guesthouse & Art Gallery; Map p876; ☎ 822 070; fax 831 480; 3 Đ Huynh Thuc Khang; admission 8000d) is a funky place that's earned the Crazy House moniker from local residents. It's notable for its *Alice in Wonderland* architecture, where you can perch inside a giraffe or get lost in a giant spider web. You can also stay in one of these kooky, slightly spooky rooms (US$19 to US$84), but book well in advance.

At **Xuan Huong Lake** (Map p878) you can rent a paddleboat shaped like a giant swan. About 5km north of the lake is the **Valley of Love** (Thung Lung Tinh Yeu; Map p876; Đ Phu Dong Thien Vuong; adult/child 6000/3000d; ⏲ 8am-8pm) where you can pose for photos on a pony accompanied by a Vietnamese dude dressed as a cowboy.

Dalat's newest attraction, a **cable car** (Cap Treo; Map p876; ☎ 837 938; off Đ 3 Thang 4; adult/child return 50,000/25,000d; ⏲ 7-11.30am & 1.30-5pm), dangles along a 2.3km wire to Quang Trung Reservoir. The views are stunning but not for the faint-hearted.

WATERFALLS

Dalat's waterfalls are obviously at their gushing best in the wet season but still run during the dry season.

Datanla Falls (admission 5000d) is 5km southeast of Dalat off Hwy 20, about 200m past the turn-off to Quang Trung Reservoir. It's a nice walk through the rainforest and a steep hike downhill to the falls. Butterflies and birds are abundant.

If you feel that you must have Vietnamese cowboys and stuffed jungle animals in your holiday photos, look no further than **Cam Ly Falls** (Map p876; admission 5000d; ⏲ 8am-6pm).

LAT & LANG BIAN MOUNTAIN

The nine hamlets of **Lat village**, whose inhabitants are ethnic minority groups, are about 12km northwest of Dalat at the base of Lang Bian Mountain.

With five volcanic peaks ranging in altitude from 2100m to 2400m, **Lang Bian Mountain** (Nui Lam Vien; admission 5000d) makes for a scenic trek (it's three to four hours from Lat village). You might spot some semiwild horses grazing on the side of the mountain, where rhinoceros and tigers lived only half a century ago. The views from the top are tremendous.

Dalat Travel Service (below) offers guided tours that combine the mountain with Lat village.

CHICKEN VILLAGE

Known locally as Lang Dinh An, Chicken Village is a minority village 17km south of Dalat. It gets its name from an enormous concrete **chicken statue** in the middle of the huts.

Tours

The Easy Riders are an informal crew of local motorbike guides who can whirl you around Dalat and the vicinity on their vintage motorbikes. It's highly recommended that you test-drive with a day tour before committing to a longer trip. Most speak great English and/or French. The going rate for long trips is around US$45 a day. City tours, from the Easy Riders or others, cost US$8 to US$12. Success attracts imitators so don't rest easy because of the reputation.

Other tour companies:

Dalat Travel Service (Map p878; ☎ 822 125; ttdhhd@hcm.vnn.vn; 7 Đ 3 Thang 2) Vehicle rentals and local tours with knowledgeable guides.

Groovy Gecko Tour (Map p878; ☎ 836 521; ggtour@yahoo.com; 65 Đ Truong Cong Dinh; ⏲ 7.30am-8.30pm) Offers tours, trekking and mountain biking, including single-day descents to Mui Ne or Nha Trang for US$60.

Hardy Dalat (Map p878; ☎ 836 840; hardydl@hcm.vnn.vn; 66 Đ Phan Dinh Phung) An experienced team of French- and English-speaking tour guides, offering abseiling trips to local waterfalls, trekking, rock climbing, swimming and bird-watching tours.

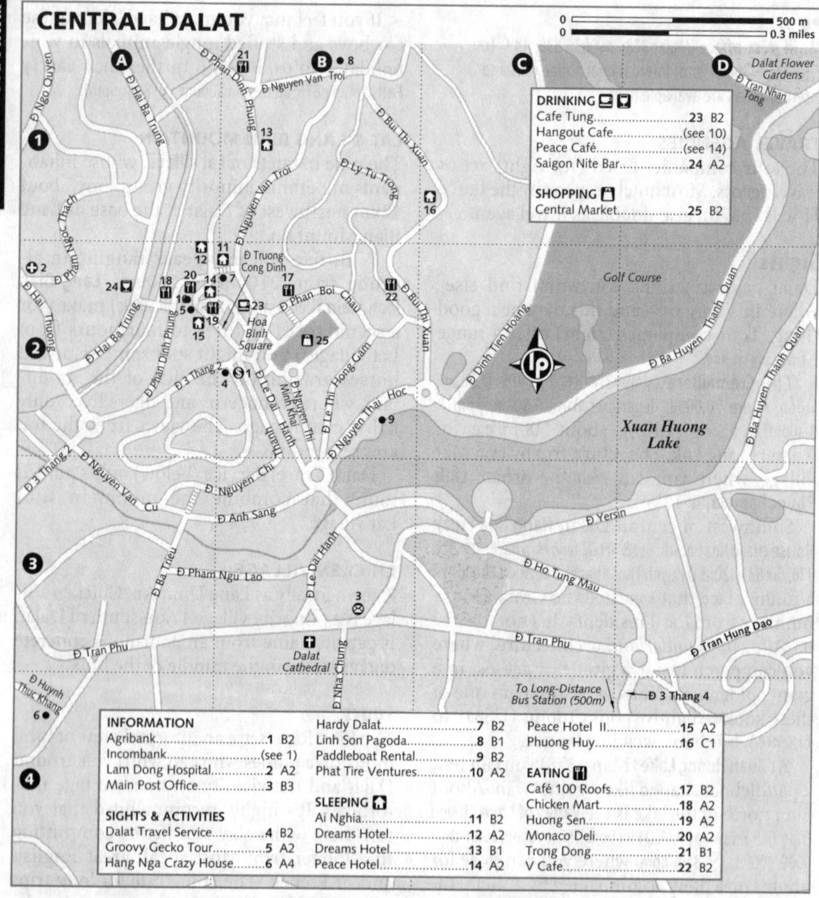

Phat Tire Ventures (Map p878; ☎ 829 422; www.phattireventures.com; 73 Đ Truong Cong Dinh) Does mountain-biking tours around Dalat but it has the full range of adventure sports. It offers a few mainly downhill bicycle rides to the coast – the ride to Nha Trang (US$67) sure beats the bus.

Sleeping

Phuong Huy (Map p878; ☎ 520 243; 5 Đ Bui Thi Xuan; r US$5-8) This clean, new minihotel has good facilities and a wonderfully kitsch *Last Supper* reproduction and mirrored crucifix in reception.

our pick **Ai Nghia** (Map p878; ☎ 520 529, 80 Đ Dinh Phung; r US$5-8) Another sparkling new minihotel, which has quiet rooms towards the back and satellite TV.

Hotel Binh Yen (Map p876; ☎ 823 631; hotelbinhyen@yahoo.com; 7 Đ Hai Thuong; r incl breakfast US$6-10; 💻) A real gem, the rooms at this well-priced hotel are comfortable and spacious and guests can use the free internet in the lobby.

Peace Hotel (Map p878; ☎ 822 787; peace12@hcm.vnn.vn; 64 Đ Truong Cong Dinh; r US$7-15) Exuding well-worn charm, the Peace Hotel is a longtime favourite and the café downstairs is a popular gathering place. There's another villa-style branch across the street known as Peace Hotel II (Map p878; 67 Đ Truong Cong Dinh). The rooms at this second location are big and a touch nicer than at the original.

Dreams Hotel (Map p878; ☎ 833 748; dreams@hcm.vnn.vn; 151 Đ Phan Dinh Phung; r incl breakfast US$10-15; ❄ 💻) Highly recommended by travellers, this is one of the best deals in Dalat. A welcoming place, it has tidy, comfortable rooms, some with balconies. There's free internet access in the lobby. You can pay with a credit card and, best of all, there is no pressure for taking tours. There's a slightly more upscale twin sister further north on the same street; it's also called Dreams Hotel (Map p878; ☎ 833 748; dreams@hcm.vnn.vn; 164B Đ Phan Dinh Phung; rooms US$15 to US$20).

Eating

Along Đ Phan Dinh Phung (Map p878), across from the original Dreams Hotel are several good restaurants serving inexpensive Vietnamese, Chinese and Western food. At night, when the market area becomes festive, check out the food stalls on Đ Nguyen Thi Minh Khai and the steps leading to the market. The stalls, and the other eateries listed following are on the Map p878.

our pick **Huong Sen** (☎ 510 236, 46 Đ Truong Cong Dinh; mains from 10,000d; breakfast & lunch & dinner) Huong Sen does good vegetarian and fake-meat dishes at great prices. Late-night diners are out of luck; it closes around 8pm.

Café 100 Roofs (Way to the Moon; ☎ 822 880; puppy@hcm.vnn.vn; 57 Đ Phan Boi Chau; ice creams 24,000d) More of Dalat's wacky sculptural architecture. Have some ice cream inside this labyrinthine café created by a friend and colleague of the Crazy House architect.

Trong Dong (☎ 821 889; 220 Đ Phan Dinh Phung; mains 24,000-55,000d; lunch & dinner) This is a good place to sample superb Vietnamese food; house specialities include grilled shrimp paste on sugar cane and fish hotpot. It's is a bit outside the centre, but well worth the walk.

Monaco Deli (☎ 510 820; 62 Đ Phan Ding Phung; mains 40,000d; breakfast, lunch & dinner) Sometimes there's no taste like home; Monaco Deli has a long menu of Western treats. The daily specials such as grilled fish or fancy pizza are always good.

V Cafe (☎ 837 576; 1 Đ Bui Thi Xuan; mains 40,000d; breakfast, lunch & dinner) East meets West in a casual but refined setting. The friendly atmosphere has made it a longtime favourite rendezvous point for travellers.

Chicken Mart (☎ 521 153; 97 Đ Phan Ding Phuong; breakfast & lunch) What is the Dalat fascination with the humble flightless bird? True to its name, Chicken Mart is a small cafeteria-style place that prepares chicken in nearly 20 different ways.

Drinking

All these places are on Map p878.

Cafe Tung (6 Khu Hoa Binh Sq) This famous hangout of Saigonese intellectuals during the 1950s now has a less lively atmosphere, but it's a good place to have a jolt of coffee on a cold Dalat evening.

Peace Café (☎ 822 787; 64 Đ Truong Cong Dinh) The de facto backpacker hangout in Dalat, it also serves food. Depending on the amount of customers, it sometimes closes on the early side (10pm).

Saigon Nite Bar (☎ 820 007; 11A Đ Hai Ba Trung) Open later than many places in Dalat, this is the place to go to shoot pool with expats.

Hangout Cafe (☎ 510 822; 71 Đ Troung Cong Dinh) We didn't see anyone hanging out, but with a pool table, movie nights and a full bar the place has promise.

Shopping

If you can't make it further into the Central Highlands, this is the place to buy tasty Vietnamese coffee. Hoa Binh Sq (Map p878) and the market building adjacent to it are the places to go for purchasing ethnic handicrafts from the nearby Montagnard villages and kitschy knick-knacks.

Getting There & Around

Vietnam Airlines (code VN; Map p878; ☎ 833 499; www.vietnamairlines.com) runs daily flights connecting Dalat with HCMC and Hanoi. Dalat's Lien Khuong Airport is located 30km south of the city.

Long-distance bus services leave from the **bus station** (Map p876; Đ 3 Thang 2), about 1km south of the city centre. Buses here travel to most of the country, including to HCMC (60,000d, six to seven hours), Nha Trang (60,000d, seven hours) and Buon Ma Thuot (65,000d, four hours).

Open-tour minibuses between Dalat and HCMC, Mui Ne and Nha Trang are plentiful. Any travellers café or hotel can arrange a ticket.

Mountain roads connect Dalat with other Central Highlands towns. Dalat Travel Service (see p877) can arrange daily car rentals (with a driver) for around US$25.

Full-day tours with local motorbike guides (p877) are a great way to see the area, as many of the sights lie outside Dalat's centre. Expect to pay between US$10 and US$12 for a day tour.

Many hotels offer bicycle and motorbike hire.

BUON MA THUOT

☎ 050 / pop 186,600

The biggest town in the Central Highlands, Buon Ma Thuot is surrounded by coffee plantations and sells superb coffee at lower prices than in Hanoi or HCMC.

Dam San Tourist (☎ 851 234; damsantour@dng.vnn.vn; 212-214 Đ Nguyen Cong Tru), attached to the Damsan Hotel, and **Daklak Tourist** (☎ 852 108; www.daklaktourist.com.vn; 3 Đ Phan Chau Trinh), can arrange tours and your travel permits for the Ede, M'nong and Bahnar villages nearby.

Other sights of interest include the **Ethnographic Museum** (☎ 850 426; 4 Đ Nguyen Du; admission 10,000d; 7.30-11am & 2-5pm), which has exhibits covering some of the 31 ethnic groups from Dac Lac province. For amazing views from the hills head to **Lak Lake**, near a M'nong village. Nearby **Yok Don National park** (Vuon Quoc Gia Yok Don; ☎ 783 049; yokdon@dng.vnn.vn) is home to 38 endangered mammal species.

Sleeping

In town, good budget choices include the following three places, all of which are clean and central. The more expensive rooms have air-con and private toilet.

Thanh Binh Hotel (☎ 853 812; 24 Đ Ly Thuong Kiet; r US$8-10;) Probably the best deal in town.

Duy Hoang Hotel (☎ 858 020; 30 Đ Ly Thuong Kiet; r US$10;) The rooms here vary in size and quality, so choose carefully.

Cao Nguyen Hotel (☎ 851 913; www.daklaktourist.com/english/hotels/info.html; 65 Đ Phan Chu Trinh; r US$15-45;) Faded grandeur and on-site karaoke and dancing – a beautiful combination.

At the national park headquarters, **Yok Don Guesthouse** (☎ 853 110; r 150,000d;) has four basic rooms (cold water only), each with two beds.

Eating

Thanh Loan (☎ 818 464; 14-16 Đ Ly Thuong Kiet; meals 12,000d) Roll your own stuffed rice paper here. Delicious.

Dac Biet Bun Bo (☎ 810 135; 10 Đ Le Hong Phong; meals 12,000d) Big hunks of meat are served in a spicy broth over white noodles, served with a plate of fresh herbs.

Getting There & Away

Vietnam Airlines (code VN; ☎ 955 055; www.vietnamairlines.com; 65-67 Đ Nguyen Chi Thanh) connects Buon Ma Thuot with HCMC and Danang. The airport is about 8km west of town. A taxi should cost less than 20,000d.

Buon Ma Thuot is served by buses from HCMC, Nha Trang, Dalat, Pleiku, Kon Tum and Danang. National Hwy 27 from Dalat is best travelled by motorbike or 4WD.

PLEIKU

☎ 059 / pop 141,700

Most travellers prefer to skip the market town of Pleiku in favour of Kon Tum, 49km to the north. Authorities are worried about further unrest among the local ethnic minorities (see p815); you need a permit to visit villages in the area and you'll also be required to hire a guide.

Gia Lai Tourist (☎ 874 571; www.gialaitourist.com; 215 Đ Hung Vuong) Located beside the Hung Vuong Hotel, staff can arrange a permit and guide as part of one of its packages.

Incombank (☎ 871 054; 12 Đ Tran Hung Dao) Branch offering foreign currency and travellers cheque exchanges, and credit-card advances.

Sleeping & Eating

Thanh Lich Hotel (☎ 824 674; 86 Đ Nguyen Van Troi; r US$6-15;) Backpackers tend to gravitate towards this centrally located, but ageing, hotel. Some rooms have small terraces and some of the staff speak OK English.

Ialy Hotel (☎ 824 843; 89 Đ Hung Vuong; r 220,000-400,000d;) Also on the shabby side, but the Ialy still remains a solid choice. The more expensive rooms are large and suitelike, fitted with new furniture including a desk and lounge area.

Tamba (☎ 826 774; 5-7 Đ Tran Phu) is a cross between a bakery and a supermarket, while **Nem Ninh Hoa** (80 Đ Nguyen Van Troi; mains 15,000d) turns out Pleiku's best spring rolls.

Getting There & Away

Vietnam Airlines (code VN; ☎ 824 680; www.vietnamairlines.com; 55 Đ Quang Trung; 7.30-11am & 1.30-4.30pm) has flights between Pleiku and HCMC and Danang.

Buses run from HCMC, Buon Ma Thuot and most coastal towns between, and including, Nha Trang and Danang.

KON TUM

☎ 060 / pop 89,800

Kon Tum seems to hold the most thrall for travellers in the area, especially for cyclists, as motorised traffic is light, the scenery fine and the climate pleasant. No matter how you get around here, the people are among the warmest in Vietnam.

Around the edges of town are a couple of **Bahnar villages** within walking distance. Along Đ Nguyen Hué, there's a ceremonial *rong* house – a community hall on stilts – and a **Catholic seminary** with a **hill-tribe museum** on the 2nd floor.

A short walk from the town centre, the **Vinh Son 1** and **Vinh Son 2** orphanages welcome visitors who come to share some time with the adorable multiethnic resident children. Donations, canned food, clothing or toys for the kids are much appreciated.

Exchange dollars for dong at **BIDV** (☎ 862 340; 1 Đ Tran Phu; ⏲ closed Sat). The terrific **Kon Tum Tourist** (☎ 861 626; www.kontumtourist.com.vn; 2 Đ Phan Dinh Phung; ⏲ 8-11am & 1-4.30pm) has its booking office in Dakbla Hotel.

Sleeping

Viet Tram (☎ 869 269; fax 869 334; 162 Đ Nguyen Hué; r US$8-10; ❄ 💻) A friendly minihotel with basic but clean and comfortable rooms.

Dakbla Hotel (☎ 863 333; 2 Đ Phan Dinh Phung; r incl breakfast US$15-24; ❄) The plushest of the bunch, the Dakbla is near the river. You have to ask for the cheapest room or staff quote US$20 as the lowest rate.

Quang Trung Hotel (☎ 862 249; 168 Đ Ba Trieu; r US$15-30; ❄) The cheapest rooms are Spartan, fan-only cells.

Eating & Drinking

Nghia II (72 Đ Le Loi; mains 10,000d) There's good vegetarian food here.

Dakbla's (☎ 826 584; 168 Đ Nguyen Hué; mains from 25,000d) If you're after local fare, try this popular place.

Eva Cafe (☎ 862 944; 1 Đ Phan Chu Trinh) For hot coffee or cold beer, stop by Eva's atmospheric garden. There's a fantastic sculpture of a soldier fashioned from a large bomb, wearing a peace sign around its neck.

Getting There & Away

Buses from Ho Chi Minh City take 12 hours along scenic National Hwy 14. Kon Tum's bus station is 13km north of town, but buses often drive through Kon Tum, where they can drop you instead. Kon Tum buses connect with Pleiku, Buon Ma Thuot and Danang.

HO CHI MINH CITY (SAIGON)

☎ 08 / pop 5.38 million

Ho Chi Minh City (HCMC) – still Saigon to everyone who lives here – is a city on constant fast-forward with the volume cranked all the way up. Everything is quick here; people are quick to make a deal, quick to laugh and quick to let you know that this is the best place in Vietnam. Although it may appear like absolute chaos at first, Saigon works a slow magic on visitors that is in marked contrast to the pace of life. With all the comforts of home in a setting where just watching the street is more fascinating than any film, it's easy to fall in love with the city.

ORIENTATION

A sprawl of 16 urban and five rural *quan* (districts) make up the vast geography of HCMC, though most travellers stick to the centre around the Dong Khoi and Pham Ngu Lao neighbourhoods. Cholon, the city's Chinatown, lies southwest of the centre, and the Saigon River snakes down the eastern side.

The heart of central HCMC beats in Districts 1 and 3, where stately tamarind trees shade fading French colonial buildings and narrow Vietnamese shophouses. High-rise hotels jostle with towers of commerce near the Saigon River.

Street labels are shortened to Đ for *duong* (street), and ĐL for *dai lo* (boulevard).

INFORMATION

Bookshops

To find a good read for the bus or beach, just sit down at any traveller hangout and wait for what looks like an escaped library shelf gone vertical to lumber towards you. For reference, Vietnamese literature or how-to books in French or English consider **Fahasa Bookshop** Đ Dong Khoi (Map p890; ☎ 822 4670; 185 Đ Dong Khoi); ĐL Nguyen Hué (Map p890; ☎ 822 5446; 40 ĐL Nguyen Hué; ⏲ 8am-5pm).

Cultural Centres

British Council (Map p886; ☎ 823 2862; www.britishcouncil.org/vietnam; 25 ĐL Le Duan)

Institute of Cultural Exchange with France (Idecaf; Map p890; ☎ 829 5451; 31 Đ Thai Van Lung) Has French-language films and videos (see p892).

Emergency

Ambulance (☎ 115)
Fire (☎ 114)
Police (☎ 113)

Internet Access

Hundreds of internet cafés thrive in HCMC – in Pham Ngu Lao (Map p892) you can't swing a dead cat without hitting one. Rates are generally a cheap 100d per minute with a minimum charge of 2000d.

Media

Hotels, bars and restaurants around HCMC carry the free entertainment magazines the *Guide* and *Time Out* (see p907).

Especially in the morning there are vendors who visit traveller cafés to sell newspapers and magazines. Give the papers a close look before buying; often the original price is bleached out and replaced with highway robbery.

Medical Services

Cho Ray Hospital (Benh Vien Cho Ray; Map pp884-5; ☎ 855 4137; fax 855 7267; 201 ĐL Nguyen Chi Thanh, District 5; consultations from US$4; 24hr) The largest medical facility in Vietnam, with 24-hour emergency services and excellent, inexpensive care. About one-third of the physicians speak English.

International Medical Center (Map p890; ☎ 827 2366, 24hr emergency 865 4025; fac@hcm.vnn.vn; 1 Đ Han Thuyen; consultations US$40-80; 24hr) This nonprofit organisation may be the least expensive Western health-care centre in the city.

Maple Dental Clinic (Map p886; ☎ 820 1999; 72 Đ Vo Thi Sau; 8am-8pm Mon-Fri, 9am-5pm Sat) Dental care by experienced English-speaking dentists.

Money

Finding an ATM to get money from is the easy part; keeping the cash in this free-spending city is another issue. The following all exchange money and most exchange travellers cheques.

Sacombank (Map p892; ☎ 836 4231; 211 Đ Nguyen Thai Hoc) In backpacker central, it also has an ATM.

Sasco (Map pp884-5; ☎ 848 7142) Just inside the airport exit, gives the official exchange rate but keeps irregular hours. In case it's closed, have sufficient US dollars in small denominations to get into the city centre.

Vietcombank (Map p886; ☎ 829 7245; 29 Đ Ben Chuong; closed Sun & last day of the month) The eastern building is for foreign exchange only, but is also worth a visit just to see the stunningly ornate interior.

Post

Main post office (Buu Dien Thanh Pho Ho Chi Minh; Map p890; ☎ 829 6555; 2 Cong Xa Paris; 7am-9.30pm) Saigon's French-era post office is next to the Notre Dame Cathedral and offers long-distance and domestic calls in addition to the usual post and parcel services. It's an impressive structure that merits a peek.

Tourist Information

Tourist Information Center (Map p890; ☎ 822 6033; www.vntourists.com; 4G Le Loi; 8am-8pm) It has free city maps and brochures and can give limited advice about goings-on in Saigon. There are a few computers for free internet access and there's also currency exchange.

Travel Agencies

You will find the following budget agencies in the backpacker area of Pham Ngu Lao (Map p892).

GETTING INTO TOWN

Tan Son Nhat international airport (Map pp884–5) is 7km northwest of the city centre. The going rate for taxis between central Ho Chi Minh and the airport is US$5. In theory you could ask for a metered ride but the trip is magically faster when there's a flat fee. There are literally hundreds of taxi drivers waiting outside the airport so be prepared.

Most economical is the air-conditioned airport bus 152 (1000d). Buses leave the airport about every 15 minutes, stopping briefly at both the international and domestic terminals before heading to the city centre. They then make regular stops along Đ De Tham (Pham Ngu Lao area) and international hotels along Đ Dong Khoi, such as the Caravelle and the Majestic. Buses are labelled in English, but you might also look for the words 'Xe Buyt San Bay'.

From the Saigon train station (Ga Sai Gon; Map pp884–5), a *xe om* (motorcycle taxi) to Pham Ngu Lao should cost around 15,000d.

From Saigon's intercity bus stations, most fares on a *xe om* should be between 15,000d and 25,000d. Public buses (3000d) from the stations stop near Ben Thanh Market, but these cease midafternoon.

A DAY IN SAIGON

Downtown HCMC can be walked in a day, making a loop from **Pham Ngu Lao** (Map p886) going via **Ben Thanh Market** (p893), and then walking to the **Reunification Palace** (right) and the nearby **War Remnants Museum** (right). Head back to pulsing **Pham Ngu Lao** to enjoy the nightlife.

A day tour on a *xe om* to points further afield such as **Cholon** (p886) should cost US$5 to US$10.

Unless otherwise noted, the following places all offer train, plane and bus bookings for Vietnam and beyond; visa assistance; city and Cu Chi Tunnel tours; and open-tour bus tickets.

Delta Adventure Tours (☎ 836 8542; www.deltaadventuretours.com;187A Đ Pham Ngu Lao) Great Mekong Delta tours, many of which can take travellers by boat all the way to Phnom Penh.

Kim Travel (☎ 920 5552; www.kimtravel.com; 270 Đ De Tham)

Linh Cafe (☎ 836 0643; www.linhtravelvn.com; 291 Đ Pham Ngu Lao)

Sinh Cafe (☎ 836 7338; www.sinhcafevn.com; 246 Đ De Tham)

Sinhbalo Adventures (☎ 837 6766, 836 7682; www.sinhbalo.com; 283/20 Đ Pham Ngu Lao) More upmarket, long-running and eminently reliable operator for custom tours, especially in the Mekong Delta and Central Highlands.

STA Travel (Orient Star Travel; 920-6951; www.statravel.com.vn; 230 Đ De Tham) A franchise of the well-known student travel company.

TM Brothers (☎ 837 8394; huuhanhnguyen@yahoo.com; 288 Đ De Tham)

TNK Travel (☎ 920 4766; www.tnktravelvietnam.com; 216 Đ De Tham)

DANGERS & ANNOYANCES

Although travellers very rarely face any physical danger in HCMC (besides the traffic), the city has the most determined thieves in the country. Drive-by crooks on motorbikes – especially along the riverfront – can steal bags off your arm and pickpockets work all crowds. Some of the worst perpetrators are the cute children crowding around you, wanting to sell postcards and newspapers with one hand and helping themselves to your valuables with the other. Tourist police in bright green uniforms are increasingly patrolling the streets and are a source of help if anything goes wrong.

While it's generally safe to take *cyclos* during the day, it is not always safe at night – take a metered taxi or motorbike taxi instead.

Sometimes *cyclo* and motorbike drivers will demand more than the agreed price after a trip. Be sure to be crystal clear beforehand about whether the fee is per person or the total.

SIGHTS

Reunification Palace

Built in 1966 to serve as South Vietnam's presidential palace is the **Reunification Palace** (Hoi Truong Thong Nhat; Map p886; ☎ 829 4117; 106 Đ Nguyen Du; admission 15,000d; 🕑 7.30-11am & 1-4pm). This is where the communist tank crashed the gate on 30 April 1975, the day Saigon surrendered. Apart from a repaired front entrance, the building has been left just as it looked on that momentous day.

Enter on Đ Nam Ky Khoi Nghia, where English- and French-speaking guides are on duty.

War Remnants Museum

Documenting the atrocities of war, the **War Remnants Museum** (Bao Tang Chung Tich Chien Tranh; Map p886; ☎ 930 5587; 28 Đ Vo Van Tan; admission 15,000d; 🕑 7.30-noon & 1.30-5pm) is the kind of place that even the museum-adverse will appreciate; but it's not for the faint of heart. The museum displays the relics of war and a heartbreaking array of photographs of the victims of war. Exhibits are labelled in Vietnamese, English and Chinese.

Pagodas, Temples & Churches

Whether the traffic has inspired a new religious streak or travellers are just seeking some relative peace, places of worship here tend towards the colourful and architecturally impressive.

CENTRAL HCMC

Notre Dame Cathedral (Map p890; Đ Han Thuyen; 🕑 mass 9.30am Sun), built between 1877 and 1883, stands regally in the heart of the government quarter. Its red-brick neo-Romanesque form and two 40m-high square towers tipped with iron spires dominate the skyline. Inside, there are neon lights around some of the religious statues.

A splash of southern India's colour in Saigon, **Mariamman Hindu Temple** (Chua Ba Mariamman;

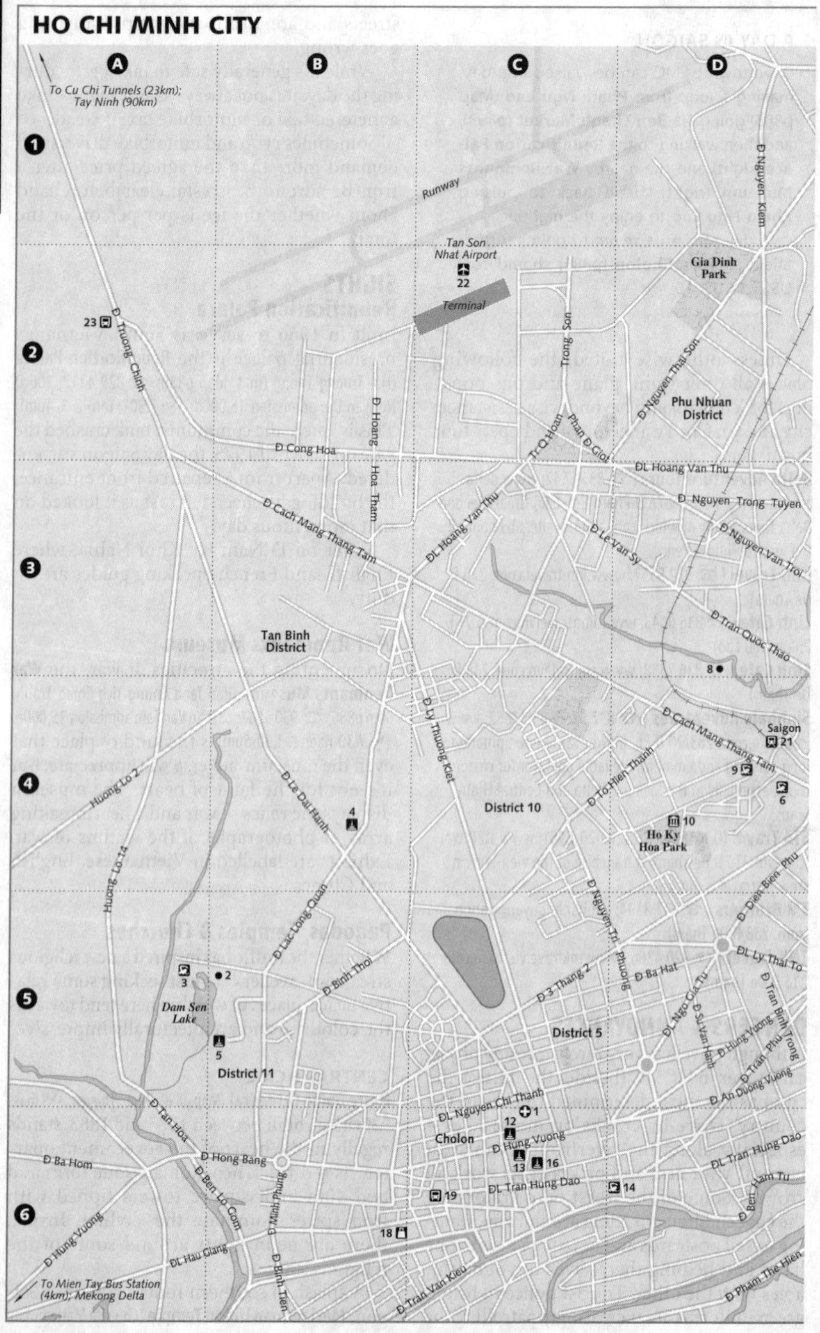
HO CHI MINH CITY
To Cu Chi Tunnels (23km); Tay Ninh (90km)
Runway
Tan Son Nhat Airport
22
Terminal
Gia Dinh Park
Phu Nhuan District
Tan Binh District
District 10
Ho Ky Hoa Park
Dam Sen Lake
District 11
District 5
Cholon
Saigon
To Mien Tay Bus Station (4km); Mekong Delta
Đ Truong Chinh
Đ Cong Hoa
Đ Hoang Hoa Tham
Đ Cach Mang Thang Tam
ĐL Hoang Van Thu
Trong Son
Tr O Hoan
Phan Đ Giot
Đ Nguyen Thai Son
Đ Nguyen Kiem
ĐL Hoang Van Thu
Đ Nguyen Trong Tuyen
Đ Le Van Sy
Đ Nguyen Van Troi
Đ Tran Quoc Thao
Đ Ly Thuong Kiet
Đ To Hien Thanh
Đ Le Dai Hanh
Huong Lo 2
Huong Lo 14
Đ Lac Long Quan
Đ Binh Thoi
Đ Nguyen Tri Phuong
Đ Dien Bien Phu
ĐL Ly Thai To
Đ Ba Hat
Đ 3 Thang 2
Đ Ngo Gia Tu
Đ Su Van Hanh
Đ Tran Binh Trong
Đ Hung Vuong
Đ Tran Phu
Đ An Duong Vuong
Đ Tan Hoa
ĐL Nguyen Chi Thanh
Đ Hung Vuong
ĐL Tran Hung Dao
Đ Ba Hom
Đ Hong Bang
Đ Ben Lo Gom
Đ Minh Phung
ĐL Tran Hung Dao
Đ Ben Ham Tu
Đ Hung Vuong
ĐL Hau Giang
Đ Binh Tien
Đ Tran Van Kieu
Đ Pham The Hien
A
B
C
D
1
2
3
4
5
6

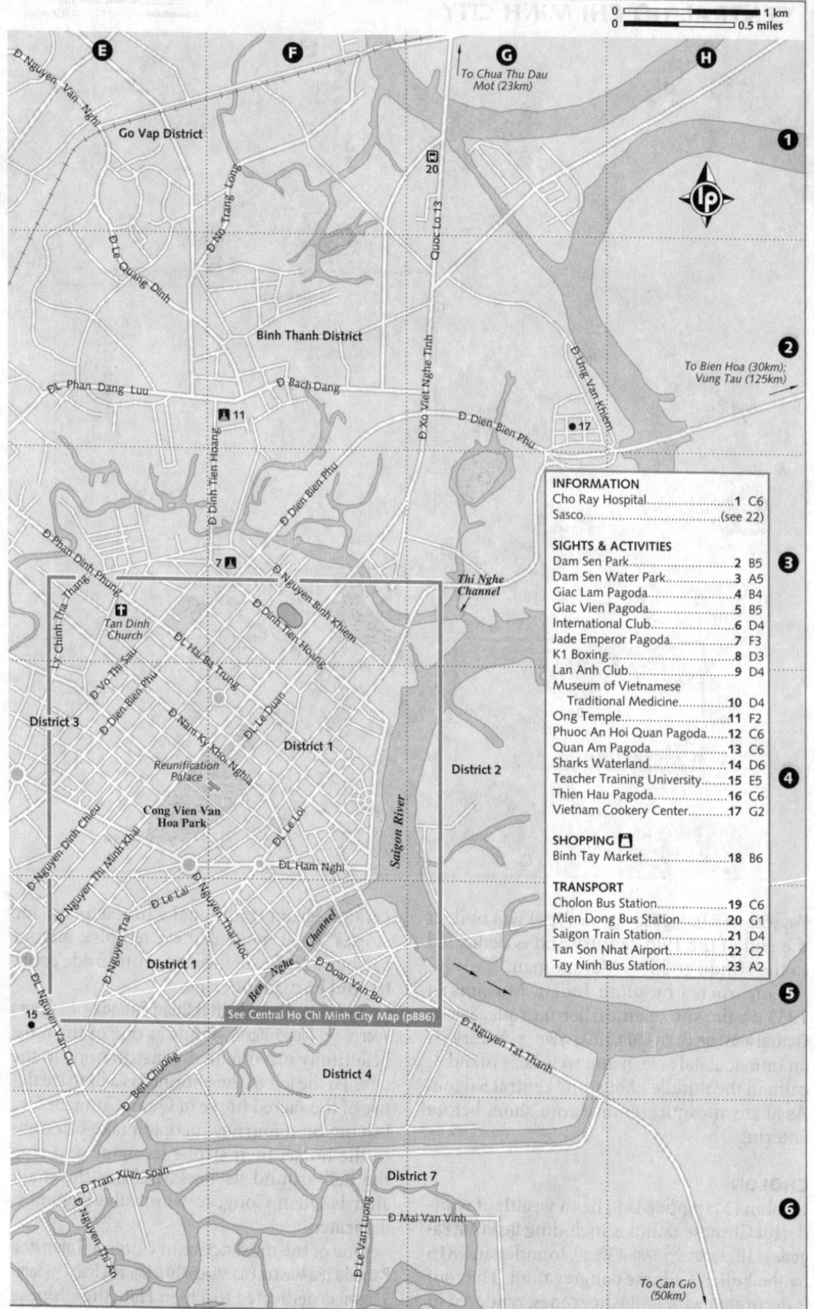
0 1 km
0 0.5 miles
E
F
G
H
1
2
3
4
5
6
To Chua Thu Dau Mot (23km)
To Bien Hoa (30km); Vung Tau (125km)
To Can Gio (50km)
Go Vap District
Binh Thanh District
District 1
District 2
District 3
District 4
District 7
Đ Nguyen Van Nghi
Đ No Trang Long
Đ Le Quang Dinh
Quoc Lo 13
Đ Xo Viet Nghe Tinh
Đ Ung Van Khiem
ĐL Phan Dang Luu
Đ Bach Dang
Đ Dien Bien Phu
Đ Dinh Tien Hoang
Đ Phan Dinh Phung
Đ Nguyen Binh Khiem
Ly Chinh Tha Thang
Tan Dinh Church
Đ Vo Thi Sau
ĐL Hai Ba Trung
Đ Le Duan
Đ Nam Ky Khoi Nghia
Reunification Palace
Cong Vien Van Hoa Park
Đ Nguyen Dinh Chieu
Đ Nguyen Thi Minh Khai
ĐL Le Loi
ĐL Ham Nghi
Đ Le Lai
Đ Nguyen Thai Hoc
Đ Nguyen Trai
Ben Nghe Channel
Đ Doan Van Bo
Saigon River
Thi Nghe Channel
ĐL Nguyen Van Cu
Đ Ben Chuong
Đ Nguyen Tat Thanh
Đ Tran Xuan Soan
Đ Nguyen Thi An
Đ Le Van Luong
Đ Mai Van Vinh
See Central Ho Chi Minh City Map (p886)
INFORMATION
Cho Ray Hospital....1 C6
Sasco....(see 22)
SIGHTS & ACTIVITIES
Dam Sen Park....2 B5
Dam Sen Water Park....3 A5
Giac Lam Pagoda....4 B4
Giac Vien Pagoda....5 B5
International Club....6 D4
Jade Emperor Pagoda....7 F3
K1 Boxing....8 D3
Lan Anh Club....9 D4
Museum of Vietnamese Traditional Medicine....10 D4
Ong Temple....11 F2
Phuoc An Hoi Quan Pagoda....12 C6
Quan Am Pagoda....13 C6
Sharks Waterland....14 D6
Teacher Training University....15 E5
Thien Hau Pagoda....16 C6
Vietnam Cookery Center....17 G2
SHOPPING
Binh Tay Market....18 B6
TRANSPORT
Cholon Bus Station....19 C6
Mien Dong Bus Station....20 G1
Saigon Train Station....21 D4
Tan Son Nhat Airport....22 C2
Tay Ninh Bus Station....23 A2

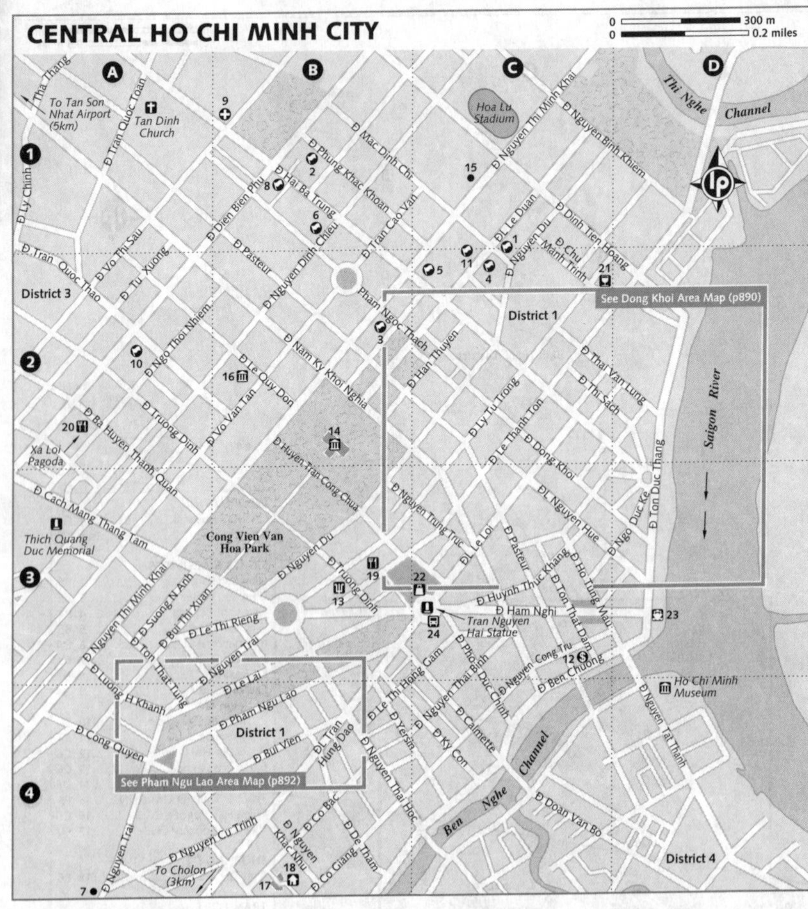

Map p886; 45 Đ Truong Dinh; 7am-7pm) was built at the end of the 19th century and is dedicated to the Hindu goddess Mariamman.

Constructed by south Indian Muslims in 1935 on the site of an earlier mosque, **Saigon Central Mosque** (Map p890; 66 Đ Dong Du; 9am-5pm) is an immaculately clean and well-kept island of calm in the middle of bustling central Saigon. As at any mosque, remove your shoes before entering.

CHOLON

Cholon (Map pp884–5) has a wealth of wonderful Chinese temples including **Quan Am Pagoda** (12 Đ Lao Tu; 8am-4.30pm), founded in 1816 by the Fujian Chinese congregation. The roof is decorated with fantastic scenes, rendered in ceramic, from traditional Chinese plays and stories. As at most Chinese temples, anyone can buy a packet of incense at the inside counter and burn an offering.

Nearby, **Phuoc An Hoi Quan Pagoda** (184 Đ Hung Vuong; 7am-5.30pm) stands as one of the most beautifully ornamented constructions in the city. To the left of the entrance is a life-size figure of the sacred horse of Quan Cong. Before leaving on a journey, people make offerings to the horse, then stroke its mane and ring the bell around its neck. Behind the main altar is Quan Cong, to whom the pagoda is dedicated.

One of the most active in Cholon, **Thien Hau Pagoda** (Ba Mieu or Pho Mieu; 710 Đ Nguyen Trai; 6am-5.30pm) is dedicated to Thien Hau, the Chinese

INFORMATION	
British Consulate	(see 1)
British Council	1 C1
Cambodian Consulate	2 B1
Chinese Consulate	3 B2
Dutch Consulate	4 C2
French Consulate	5 C2
German Consulate	6 B1
Immigration Police Office	7 A4
Lao Consulate	8 B1
Maple Dental Clinic	9 B1
New Zealand Consulate	(see 3)
Thai Consulate	10 A2
US Consulate	11 C2
Vietcombank	12 C3
SIGHTS & ACTIVITIES	
Mariamman Hindu Temple	13 B3
Reunification Palace	14 B2
Saigon Yoga	15 C1
War Remnants Museum	16 B2
SLEEPING	
Guest House California	(see 18)
Guesthouses	17 B4
Miss Loi's Guesthouse	18 B4
Ngoc Son	(see 18)
EATING	
banh cuon LA	19 B3
Ben Thanh Market Eateries	(see 22)
Vegetarian Food Stalls	20 A2
DRINKING	
Lush	21 C2
SHOPPING	
Ben Thanh Market	22 C3
TRANSPORT	
Bach Dang Jetty	23 D3
Bus Station	24 C3
Hydrofoils to Vung Tau	(see 23)
Local Boats for Hire	(see 23)

goddess of the sea. As she protects fisherfolk, sailors, merchants and any other maritime travellers, you might stop by to ask for a blessing for your next boat journey.

GREATER HCMC

The towering **Giac Lam Pagoda** (Map pp884-5; 118 Đ Lac Long Quan; 6am-9pm) dates from 1744 and is believed to be the oldest in the city. The architecture and ornamentation have not changed since 1900, and the compound is a very meditative place to explore; strains of classic Vietnamese music waft over the adjacent park where old men stroll slowly in walking meditation.

In a semirural setting next to Dam Sen Lake, serene **Giac Vien Pagoda** (Map pp884-5; 247 Đ Lac Long Quan; 7am-7pm) was founded by Hai Tinh Giac Vien about 200 years ago and there are literally hundreds if not thousands of Buddha statues inside the well-shaded main building.

Jade Emperor Pagoda (Phuoc Hai Tu or Chua Ngoc Hoang; Map pp884-5; 73 Đ Mai Thi Luu; 7.30am-6pm) is a gem of a Chinese temple, filled with colourful statues of phantasmal divinities and grotesque heroes. Built in 1909 by the Cantonese congregation, it is one of HCMC's most spectacular pagodas.

Other Attractions

Housed in a beautiful grey neoclassical structure, the **Museum of Ho Chi Minh City** (Bao Tang Thanh Pho Ho Chi Minh; Map p890; ☎ 829 9741; 65 Đ Ly Tu Trong; admission 15,000d; 8am-4pm) was built in 1885 and has displays of artefacts from the various periods of the communist struggle for power in Vietnam. Some of the French-language communist newspapers on display saw Ho Chi Minh as a contributor when he was going under the name of Nguyen Ai Quoc during his days in Paris.

The beautiful **Museum of Vietnamese Traditional Medicine** (Fito Museum; Map pp884-5; ☎ 846 2430; www.fitomuseum.com.vn; 41 Đ Hoang Du Khong St, District 10; admission 32,000d; 8.30am-5.30pm) traces the history of Vietnamese natural remedies from the 2nd century to now. English-speaking guides come with the admission price and the inside of the building is stunning with massive wood tableaux of scenes from medicinal history. There's a re-creation of a traditional medicine shop and visitors can try their hand (or foot) at the tools used to pulverize healing plants. A short film is the only time the corporate sponsorship of the museum becomes apparent.

Boat tours around the Mekong Delta are offered by many travel agencies (see p882).

ACTIVITIES

Massage

Most upmarket hotels offer massage service (some more legitimate than others); the cheapest option is the **Vietnamese Traditional Medicine Institute** (Map p892; ☎ 839 6697; 185 Đ Cong Quynh; per hr 40,000d, sauna 20,000d; 9am-9pm). It offers no-nonsense, muscle-melting massages performed by blind masseurs.

If you're so sore you can't even make it to a real massage place, in the evenings listen for the metallic clacking sound that signals roving masseurs. They'll massage you right in your chair after dinner (30,000d to 40,000d) for 20 minutes or so. Add another 10,000d for 'cupping,' the art of applying heated glass cups to the skin that form a seal to supposedly suck out disease. The circular marks last for a long time.

Swimming & Exercise

Nonguests can pay an admission fee of US$5 to US$13 per day to use the swimming pools at plush hotels. Local clubs with lower fees:

International Club (Map pp884-5; ☎ 865 7695; 285B Đ Cach Mang Thang Tam; admission 25,000d; ⏲ 9am-midnight) pool, sauna, steam rooms and gym. It also offers massage.

K1 Boxing Centre (Map pp884-5; ☎ 0918 337 111; www.teamminetti.com; 11th fl, 159/52/21B Đ Tran Van Dang; per class 200,000d; ⏲ 9am-9.30pm Mon-Fri) It offers a full range of martial-arts and fitness classes including lessons in Viet Vo Dao, the martial art of Vietnam.

Lan Anh Club (Map pp884-5; ☎ 862 7144; 291 Đ Cach Mang Thang Tam; admission gym/pool 40,000/25,000d; ⏲ 6am-9pm) There's also a good gym here.

Saigon Yoga (Map p886; ☎ 910 5181; www.saigonyoga.com; 10F Đ Nguyen Thi Minh Khai; price per class/month US$12/90; ⏲ 8am-7pm) A small yoga studio (tucked down a narrow alley) where short-term visitors can take advantage of seven days of unlimited yoga for US$20.

Water Parks

Dam Sen Water Park (Map pp884-5; ☎ 858 8418; www.damsenwaterpark.com.vn; 3 Đ Hoa Binh; adult/child 45,000/30,000d; ⏲ 9am-6pm) It has water slides, rivers with rapids (or slow currents) and what is advertised as a new sunbathing area 'for foreigners'.

Sharks Waterland (Map pp884-5; ☎ 853 7867; 600 Đ Ham Tu, District 5; admission 20,000-45,000d; ⏲ 8am-9pm Mon-Fri, 10am-9pm Sat & Sun) It may sound like a shark aquarium but it's a waterpark.

COURSES

Cooking

Bi Saigon (Map p892; ☎ 836 0678; www.bisaigon.com; 185/26 Đ Pham Ngu Lao, District 1; per person per dish US$15) Organises private cooking classes on request.

Vietnam Cookery Center (☎ 512 2764; www.vietnamcookery.com; 362/8 Đ Ung Van Khiem, Binh Thanh District 1; 2½hr class per person US$30; ⏲ 9.30am & 4.30pm Mon-Fri) offers two sessions daily where students learn to prepare a five-course meal.

Language

Teacher Training University (Dai Hoc Su Pham; Map pp884-5; ☎ 835 5100; ciecer@hcm.vnn.vn; 280 Đ An Duong Vuong; private/group class US$4/2.50)

Utopia Café (Map p890; ☎ 824 2487; shop@utopia-café.com; 17/6A Đ Le Thanh Ton, District 1; private lessons per 60/90 min 70,000/90,000d; ⏲ 8.30am-9pm) A less formal option with one-on-one instruction. Utopia can also arrange visa extensions.

FESTIVALS & EVENTS

Saigon Cyclo Race In mid-March, professional *cyclo* drivers find out who's fastest; the money raised is donated to local charities.

Festival at Lang Ong On the 30th day of the 7th lunar month, people pray for happiness and the health of the country at the Ong Temple (Map pp884–5) in HCMC's Binh Thanh district; plays and musical performances are staged.

SLEEPING

Saigon's backpacker central is known as Pham Ngu Lao. Good deals abound, but some of the sweetest places are on the many little alleys off the main roads.

Pham Ngu Lao

The following hotels are all on the Pham Ngu Lao map (p892).

Yellow House (☎ 836 8830; yellowhousehotel@yahoo.com; 31 Đ Bui Vien; dm/s/d US$5/9/12; ❄ 💻) Yellow House has two dorms (a mixed seven-bed and a three-bed for men or women – whoever arrives first) as well as private rooms. Rooms are basic but acceptable, and breakfast is included.

Ngoc Minh (☎ 837 6407; ngocminhhotel@vnn.vn; 283/11 Đ Pham Ngu Lao; r US$10-15; ❄ 💻) The airy lobby here feels like a living room decorated with dark lacquered wood. The clean rooms come with all the amenities.

Quyen Thanh Hotel (☎ 836 8570; quyenthanhhotel@hcm.vnn.vn; 212 Đ De Tham; r US$10-15; ❄) The big bright rooms with vaulted ceilings look down on the all-night bars on Đ De Tham. For those about to rock, it doesn't get more central than this. There's a souvenir shop downstairs.

Faifo Guesthouse (Hoai Pho; ☎ 920 3268; hoaiphohotel@yahoo.com; 28/9 Đ Bui Vien; r US$12-15; ❄ 💻) The basic rooms with satellite TV are a good bargain.

Peace Hotel (☎ 837 2025; 272 Đ De Tham; d US$10-12; ❄) Another good well-established place; the least expensive rooms are fan-only.

Hotel 127 (☎ 836 8761; madamecuc@hcm.vnn.vn; 127 Đ Cong Quynh; r US$12-20; ❄) Madam Cuc and her staff consistently give a warm and welcoming reception and constantly get raves from readers; her places are clean and outfitted with satellite TV, bathrooms and fridges. Madam Cuc's happy dominion also includes Hotel 64 (☎ 836 5073; 64 Đ Bui Vien) and MC Hotel (☎ 836 1679; 184 Đ Cong Quyen); both offer the same facilities and same prices as the original.

Hong Hoa Hotel (☎ 836 1915; www.honghoavn.com; 185/28 Đ Pham Ngu Lao; r US$13-20;) The Hong Hoa has it all: clean rooms, shuttles to and from the airport, free internet, a convenience store and amiable, helpful staff.

Hotel Anh Phuong (☎ 836 9248; 295 Đ Pham Ngu Lao; r US$15-20;) Prominently advertising its double-glazed windows, this hotel delivers peace and quiet in its range of tidy rooms; the best are spacious, with heavy wooden furniture and Eastern décor.

Saigon Comfort Hotel (☎ 837 6516; www.saigoncomfort.com; 175/21 Đ Pham Ngu Lao; r US$17-25;) Attracting more flashpackers (older backpackers with decent-paying jobs on short trips) than backpackers, this quiet and classy place has free but weak in-room wi-fi, free internet stations, a small book library and friendly staff. Cedit cards are accepted.

Co Giang

About 10 minutes on foot from the Pham Ngu Lao area is a string of guesthouses on a quiet alley connecting Đ Co Giang and Đ Co Bac. To reach the guesthouses, walk southeast on Đ Co Bac and turn left after you pass the *nuoc mam* (fish sauce) shops. The following are on the Central Ho Chi Minh City map (p886).

Ngoc Son (☎ 836 4717; ngocsonguesthouse@yahoo.com; 178/32 Đ Co Giang; r US$7-11;) A quiet, eight-room guesthouse, Ngoc Son is a family-style place that rents motorbikes and offers breakfast for US$1 extra.

Miss Loi's Guesthouse (☎ 837 9589; missloi@hcm.fPt.vn; 178/20 Đ Co Giang; r incl breakfast US$10-20;) Miss Loi cultivates a family atmosphere with her warm staff and homy set-up. The breakfasts in the open lobby are a great way to start the day.

our pick Guest House California (☎ 837 8885; guesthousecalifornia-saigon@yahoo.com; 171A Đ Co Bac; r US$13-16;) Boasting modern rooms, it's low-key, neat and clean and also rents out reliable bicycles and motorbikes.

EATING

Ranging from dirt-cheap but tasty meals from street stalls and markets to upscale dining dreams come true, this city has it all.

Markets always have a vast dining area, often on the ground floor or in the basement. Clusters of food stalls can be found in Ben Thanh (Map p886) and Thai Binh (Map p892) Markets. A large bowl of beef noodles costs 10,000d to 16,000d. Just look for the signs with the words *pho* or *hu tieu*. Don't eat meat? Look for the magic word *chay* (vegetarian) tacked on the end of the sign.

Đ Pham Ngu Lao and Đ De Tham form the axis of Saigon's budget eatery haven, where traveller cafés dish out cuisine that ranges from acceptable to exceptional and book tours on the side.

Vietnamese

Quan An Ngon (Map p890; ☎ 825 7179; 138 Đ Nam Ky Khoi Nghia; mains 17,000-60,000d; lunch & dinner) Poke around the outside edge of the garden-style patio first, where cooks at individual stations make traditional dishes. It's a dining experience you won't soon forget.

banh cuon LA (Map p886; ☎ 822 8213; 221 Đ Ly Tu Trong; mains 20,000d; breakfast, lunch & dinner) This new, hip spot specialises in steamed rice-flour rolls. The menu is made for à la carte sampling.

Pho 24 (Map p892; 271 Đ Pham Ngu Lao; mains 24,000d; breakfast, lunch & dinner) Part of an ever expanding chain, this polished noodle shop serves fantastic bowls of high-quality *pho* – along with fresh juices and spring rolls.

Bunta (Map p890; ☎ 822 9913; 136 Đ Nam Ky Khoi Nghia; mains 30,000d; breakfast, lunch & dinner) Fuel up Vietnam's tastiest take on vermicelli salad in this classic house that's been converted into a restaurant.

Black Cat Cafe 13 (Banh Mi 13; Map p890; ☎ 829 2055; 13 Đ Phan Van Quan; mains from 30,000d; breakfast, lunch & dinner) Thanks in part to an on-site bakery the Vietnamese sandwiches here are mind-blowingly good.

Café Zoom (Map p892; 169A Đ De Tham; mains 32,000d; breakfast, lunch & dinner) This busy little place has lots of Vespa-type style and serves Vietnamese and foreign fare to an equally eclectic crowd.

Other Asian

our pick Asian Kitchen (Map p892; ☎ 836 7397; 185/22 Đ Pham Ngu Lao; mains 18,000d; breakfast, lunch & dinner) Offers budget-priced Indian, Japanese and vegetarian, in Minihotel Alley. There's a great bar upstairs called the Hideaway that was closed during research.

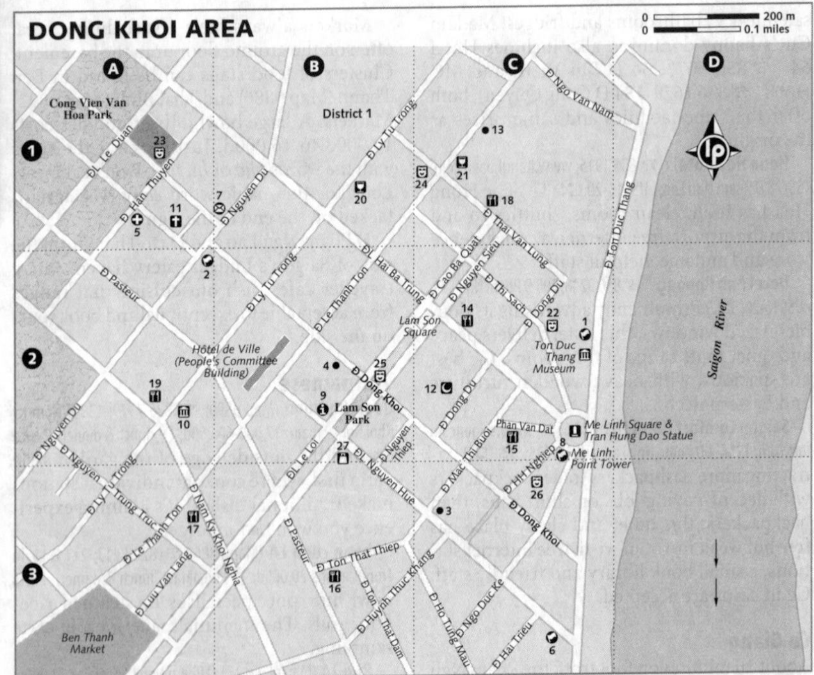

Noodles Japan Number One (Map p890; ☎ 822 8835; 8A/5D2 Thai Van Lung; mains 35,000d; 🕐 lunch & dinner) Open until 2am and down the street from Apocalypse Now (p892), discover why *ramen* is the preferred food of the Japanese after a late night out. The sign is mainly in Japanese but there are pictures of *ramen* in the front window.

Akbar Ali (Map p892; ☎ 836 4205; 240 Đ Bui Vien; mains 55,000d; 🕐 lunch & dinner) Popular with the Indian expat community, Akbar Ali serves up authentic Indian cuisine to the backdrop of a Bollywood video playing discreetly overhead.

Akatombo (Map p890; ☎ 824 4928; 36-38 Đ Hai Ba Trung; meals 60,000d; 🕐 lunch & dinner) Delicious *ramen*, sashimi and traditional Japanese food at affordable prices.

International

Minh Minh Café (Map p892; ☎ 837 3789; 201 Đ Pham Ngu Lao; 20,000-30,000d; 🕐 breakfast, lunch & dinner) The American and European food is better than the Vietnamese dishes here; a rarity. The top 40 music playing here and the busy street scene outside make for a festive meal.

Margherita Pizza (Map p892; ☎ 837 0760; 175/1 Đ Pham Ngu Lao; pizza from 25,000d; 🕐 breakfast, lunch & dinner) The place to go for takeaway pizza or to eat in; it's a favourite hangout of expats because of the casual but classy atmosphere and good prices.

La Cantina (Map p892; ☎ 886 0369; 175/3 Đ Pham Ngu Lao; mains 30,000-40,000d; 🕐 breakfast, lunch & dinner) La Cantina offers a delicious mish-mash of Mexican, European and Asian dishes. The margaritas (35,000d) pack a punch and it does BBQ ribs and chicken every Sunday.

Le Jardin (Map p890; ☎ 825 8465; 31 Đ Thai Van Lung; mains 35,000-55,000d; 🕐 lunch & dinner) The charming little bistro has a shaded terrace café in the front garden – it's a popular hangout for French people.

Vegetarian

Remember that on the 1st and 15th of every month many food stalls go veggie for the day.

Dinh Y (Map p892; ☎ 836 7715; 171B Đ Cong Quynh; mains 7000d; 🕐 breakfast, lunch & dinner) Across the road from Thai Binh Market, Dinh Y is run by a friendly Caodai family. The food, especially

INFORMATION	
Australian Consulate	1 C2
Canadian Consulate	2 A2
Fahasa Bookshop	3 C3
Fahasa Bookshop	4 B2
International Medical Center	5 A1
Japanese Embassy	6 C3
Main Post Office	7 B1
Malaysian Embassy	8 C2
Tourist Information Center	9 B2
SIGHTS & ACTIVITIES	
Museum of Ho Chi Minh City	10 A2
Notre Dame Cathedral	11 A1
Saigon Central Mosque	12 C2
Utopia Café	13 C1
EATING	
Akatombo	14 C2
Black Cat Café	15 C2
Bunta	(see 19)
Fanny	16 B3
La Fenetre Soleil	17 A3
Le Jardin	(see 24)
Noodles Japan Number One	18 C1
Quan An Ngon	19 A2
DRINKING	
Blue Gecko Bar	20 B1
Heart of Darkness	(see 21)
Sheridan's Irish House	21 C1
ENTERTAINMENT	
Apocalypse Now	22 C2
Diamond Plaza Cinema	23 A1
Institute of Cultural Exchange with France	24 C1
Municipal Theatre	25 B2
Tropical Rainforest Disco	26 C3
SHOPPING	
Tax Department Store (Russian Market)	27 B2

the noodle soups, make it worthwhile to seek out this little gem.

Original Bodhi Tree (Map p892; ☎ 836 9545; 175/6 Đ Pham Ngu Lao; mains 12,000d; breakfast, lunch & dinner). The food here – ranging from Vietnamese to Japanese to Western – is excellent and very cheap.

Zen (Map p892; ☎ 837 3713; 185/30 Đ Pham Ngu Lao; mains 15,000-30,000d; breakfast, lunch & dinner) Good cheap veggie food in a mellow family atmosphere in Minihotel Alley.

Cafés

There are a number of cafés, especially around Notre Dame Cathedral.

Sinh Cafe (Map p892; ☎ 838 5068; 246 Đ De Tham; pastries from 16,000d) It has a bakery with scrumptious cakes and croissants, in addition to a full food menu.

Fanny (Map p890; ☎ 821 1633; 29-31 Đ Ton That Thiep; per ice-cream scoop 6000-15,000d;) Set in a French villa, Fanny creates excellent Franco-Vietnamese ice cream of many sublime tropical-fruit flavours (try the durian or litchi). It has wi-fi access.

La Fenetre Soleil (Map p890; 135 Đ Le Thanh Ton; health drinks 40,000k) Up some stairs that one would find in a deserted building, this café looks like a large comfy living room. On Wednesday evening there are free swing dance parties (www.saigonswing.com); beginners get a free lesson at 8pm.

Bobby Brewers (Map p892; ☎ 610 2220; www.bobbybrewers.com; 45 Đ Bui Vien; coffee US$1-2.30) This multilevel café shows free movies each day of the week; check their website for the line-up. The menu features coffees, fresh juices, sandwiches, burgers and salads. There's free delivery in District 1 (US$3 minimum).

Self-Catering

Simple, dirt-cheap meals can be cobbled together from street stalls and markets.

Hanoi Mart (Map p892) and **Co-op Mart** (Map p892; Đ Cong Quynh; 8am-8pm) are just down the street from each other, west of the traffic circle near Thai Binh Market. They are the biggest supermarkets near backpacker central and offer everything from Western junk food to frozen Vietnamese food.

DRINKING

Saigon's normally happening nightlife is sometimes shut down – when officials are in a tizzy about 'social evils' everything closes by midnight. Often enough though, many of the places below stay open until people stop drinking, which is next to never here.

Pham Ngu Lao Area

All these are on the map, p892.

Eden Bar (☎ 836 8154; 185/22 Đ Tham) This multilevel spot has red lanterns over the bar, a cosy, inviting vibe and staff dressed in red *ao dai*. Their 6pm to 9pm happy hour has small but stiff drinks for 25,000d and free garlic bread.

Long Phi (☎ 920 3805; 325 Đ Pham Ngu Lao) This Frenchie hangout doesn't open until late afternoon, but the 5pm to 9pm happy hour with good pours of Ricard pastis (30,000d) make up for the wait. They also serve a limited menu of French bistro favourites.

Santa Café (cnr Đ Bui Vien & Đ Do Quang Dau) Divey little place with outdoor seating that's a favourite of the backpacker crowd.

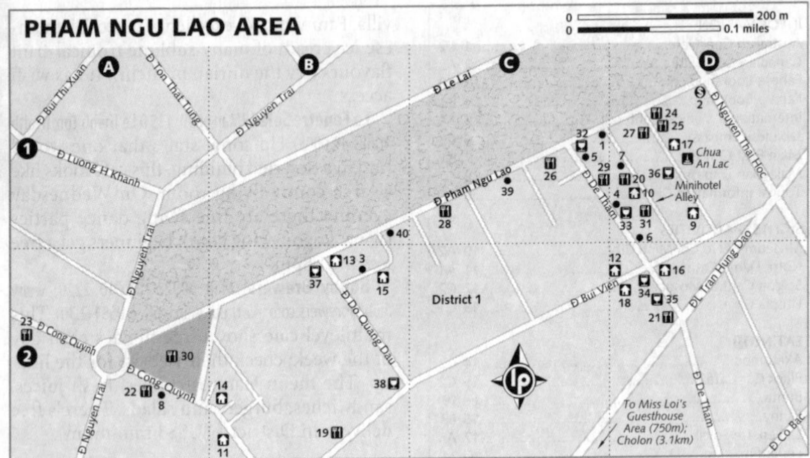

Go2 Bar (☎ 836 9575; 187 Đ De Tham; 🕑 8am-late) The music and flashing lights make this place on the corner of Đ Bui Vien and Đ De Tham impossible to miss. There's an upstairs club to dance the night away.

Allez Boo Bar (☎ 837 2505; 187 Đ Pham Ngu Lao; 🕑 noon-late) There's a definite tiki thing going on at this busy backpacker hangout.

Ice Blue (183 Đ De Tham) One of many little bars on this part of the street, the Ice Blue is a good place to meet expats and drink for relatively cheap on the main strip.

Le Pub (☎ 837 7679; www.lepub.org; 175/22 Đ Pham Ngu Lao) This spiffy place feels like a party at a friend of a friend's house in the evenings. It has a full bar – including champagne – and a different drink on sale for US$1 every day, all day.

Dong Khoi Area

Apart from Lush, find these on the map, p890. They are all fairly friendly, but you may at least want to put on a clean shirt.

Blue Gecko Bar (☎ 824 3483; 31 Đ Ly Tu Trong; 🕑 5pm-late) The 'non-members only' sign outside the door is a clue to the friendliness inside. It's got a mainly Aussie crowd, and you can shoot some pool or watch sports on TV. It also posts a sport schedule so you can be sure to save the date for your favourite team.

Sheridan's Irish House (☎ 823 0973; 17/13 Đ Le Thanh Ton; 🕑 11am-midnight) A traditional Irish pub that's been beamed straight from the backstreets of Dublin, Sheridan's showcases live music most nights and good times every night.

Heart of Darkness (☎ 823 1080; 17B Đ Le Thanh Ton; drinks 25,000-60,000d) This dark, moody bar is a mostly expat affair. There's a DJ presiding over a small dance floor in the back room.

Lush (Map p886; ☎ 0903 155 461; 2 Đ Ly Tu Trong; drinks 40,000-80,000d) This is an *anime*-themed bar that gathers an attractive, mixed crowd. Pool tables and a 2nd-floor bar are hidden out the back.

CLUBBING

The following (on the Dong Khoi map, p890) have shown staying power, but ask around to find the latest and greatest.

Apocalypse Now (☎ 824 1463; 2C Đ Thi Sach) For a study in the seamier side of international relations, Apocalypse Now is a late-night stand-by for dancing the night away. All orientations are welcome.

Tropical Rainforest Disco (Mua Rung; ☎ 825 7783; 5-15 Đ Ho Huan Nghiep; cover US$4) A popular spot for young Vietnamese and travellers, the cover charge entitles you to one free drink.

ENTERTAINMENT

Municipal Theatre (☎ 829 9976; Lam Son Sq) has plays and musical performances.

Cinemas around the Dong Khoi area (p890) include the following:

Diamond Plaza Cinema (☎ 825 7751; 34 Đ Le Duan) Sometimes screens films in English; call ahead for details.

Institute of Cultural Exchange with France (Idecaf; ☎ 829 5451; 31 Đ Thai Van Lung) Screens French-language films; videos also available to rent.

INFORMATION
Delta Adventure Tours....1 C1
Kim Travel....(see 5)
Linh Cafe....(see 13)
Sacombank....2 D1
Sinh Cafe....(see 29)
Sinhbalo Adventures....3 B2
STA Travel....4 D1
TM Brothers....5 C1
TNK Travel....6 D1

SIGHTS & ACTIVITIES
Bi Saigon....7 D1
Vietnamese Traditional Medicine Institute....8 A2

SLEEPING
Faifo Guesthouse....9 D1
Hong Hoa Hotel....10 D1
Hotel 127....11 B2
Hotel 64....12 D2
Hotel Anh Phuong....13 B2
MC Hotel....14 B2
Ngoc Minh....15 B2
Peace Hotel....(see 5)
Quyen Thanh....16 D2
Saigon Comfort Hotel....17 D1
Yellow House....18 D2

EATING
Akbar Ali....19 B2
Asian Kitchen....20 D1
Bobby Brewers....(see 18)
Café Zoom....21 D2
Co-op Mart....(see 23)
Dinh Y....22 A2
Hanoi Mart....23 A2
La Cantina....24 D1
Margherita Pizza....25 D1
Minh Minh Café....26 C1
Original Bodhi Tree....27 D1
Pho 24....28 C1
Sinh Cafe....29 C1
Thai Binh Market....30 A2
Zen....31 D1

DRINKING
Allez Boo Bar....32 C1
Eden Bar....33 D1
Go2 Bar....34 D2
Ice Blue....35 D2
Le Pub....36 D1
Long Phi....37 B2
Santa Café....38 B2

TRANSPORT
5-Star Express....39 C1
Saigon Railways Tourist Services....40 B1

SHOPPING

Boutiques along Đ Le Thanh Ton and Đ Pasteur sell handmade ready-to-wear fashion cheaper than you'll find in Hanoi. In Pham Ngu Lao, shops sell fabrics woven by ethnic minorities, as well as handicrafts and T-shirts, while roving salesmen push 'designer' sunglasses and lighters made to look like they once belonged to soldiers. As elsewhere in Vietnam, stores selling communist propaganda are springing up all over. See www.dogmavietnam.com for an idea of what's out there.

Đ Dong Khoi (Map p890) is one big arts-and-crafts tourist shopping haven but the large amount of well-heeled shoppers means prices are high – negotiate if no prices are posted.

Ben Thanh Market (Cho Ben Thanh; Map p886) If you need to stock up on necessities such as soap or to find souvenirs, this is a great place to start and an easy walk from the Pham Ngu Lao area. When night falls the market moves outside and even more food and T-shirt stands sprout up. The large number of tourists here attract pickpockets.

Tax Department Store (Russian Market; Map p890; cnr Đ Le Loi & Đ Nguyen Hué) An upscale shopping haven that sometimes has live music in the lobby, there are still a few bargains to be found. Look for a place called tim! that sells souvenir T-shirts that are hip, not cheesy (80,000d).

GETTING THERE & AWAY

Air

For details on international flights to HCMC, see p820; for domestic flights, see p821.

Boat

Cargo ferries serving the Mekong Delta depart from the **Bach Dang jetty** (Map p886; Đ Ton Duc Thang). Costs for these slow ferries are negotiable; after asking how long it will take to your desired destination, ask yourself how much you're willing to pay for such a trip. Also departing from here are hydrofoils to Vung Tau (US$10, 80 minutes) throughout the day.

Bus

Intercity buses depart from and arrive at several stations around HCMC. Local buses (around 3000d) to the intercity bus stations leave from the bus station opposite Ben Thanh Market (Map p886). There are four useful bus stations around the city:

Cholon bus station (Ben Xe Cho Lon; Map pp884-5; Đ Le Quang Trung) Convenient buses to My Tho and other Mekong Delta towns; one street north of Binh Tay Market.

GETTING TO CAMBODIA

Crossing at the Moc Bai–Bavet border is easily done on buses going from Ho Chi Minh City (HCMC) to Phnom Penh (US$8, six hours); tickets are sold at most traveller cafés and agencies in HCMC. One-month visas are issued on arrival (US$20, although minor overcharging is common), but bring a passport-sized photo. This is the only border that accepts Cambodian e-visas; see http://evisa.mfaic.gov.kh for details. Border formalities can take a few hours, but it's the quickest way into Cambodia.

See p79 for info on doing the trip in the reverse direction.

Mien Dong bus station (Ben Xe Mien Dong; Map pp884-5; ☎ 829 4056) Buses from here go as far as Hanoi (320,000d, 49 hours); it's in Binh Thanh district, about 5km north of central Saigon on National Hwy 13.

Mien Tay bus station (Ben Xe Mien Tay; ☎ 825 5955) Even more buses to points south of HCMC, but located about 10km southwest of Saigon in An Lac.

Tay Ninh bus station (Ben Xe Tay Ninh; Map pp884-5; ☎ 849 5935) Buses to Tay Ninh, Cu Chi and points northeast of HCMC, located in Tan Binh district.

Car & Motorcycle

Traveller cafés can arrange car rentals (US$45 per day with driver) or motorbike rentals (US$7 to US$10 per day); those in the Pham Ngu Lao area generally offer the lowest prices. For long-haul motorcycle treks, it is probably best to buy one. Look for posters at traveller and internet cafés from foreign motorcyclists who want to unload their machine.

Train

5-Star Express (Map p892; ☎ 920 6868; www.5starexpress.com.vn; 296 Đ Pham Ngu Lao; one-way 220,000d-450,000d) Comfy train between HCMC and Nha Trang.

Saigon Railways Tourist Services (Map p892; ☎ 836 7640; 275C Đ Pham Ngu Lao) A convenient place to purchase tickets.

Saigon train station (Ga Sai Gon; Map pp884-5; ☎ 824 5585; 1 Đ Nguyen Thong; 🕒 7.15-11am & 1-3pm) Has trains that chug north along the coast to Hanoi.

GETTING AROUND

Bicycle

Bicycles are available for hire from many budget hotels and cafés, especially around Pham Ngu Lao. To deal with HCMC's traffic, glide along the edge of the action and steer clear of big trucks and buses.

Cyclo

Cyclos are the most interesting way of getting around town, but avoid them at night and always agree on fares beforehand. In the eyes of the authorities they slow down traffic – probably true, but a good thing overall – and are being phased out completely.

Motorcycle & Motorbike Taxi

Motorbikes are available for hire around Pham Ngu Lao for US$7 to US$10 per day. Make sure to do a test drive before plunking down your cash; you'll usually be asked to leave your passport or yellow customs slip as collateral. We'd advise having good health insurance as well.

There are more than enough motorbike drivers at all times ready to give a ride if you're not ready to take a few years off your life. Trips in the city centre start at around 10,000d and a trip between the sites in Dong Khoi and Pham Ngu Lao is usually around 15,000d.

Taxi

On the street simply hail a taxi. If you don't find one straight away, ring one up and your ride will be there in no time. Companies include the following:

Ben Thanh Taxi (☎ 842 2422)

Mai Linh Taxi (☎ 822 2666)

Red Taxi (☎ 844 6677)

Saigon Taxi (☎ 842 4242)

Vina Taxi (☎ 811 1111)

AROUND HO CHI MINH CITY

This area is home to Vietnam's most popular tourist attraction related to the American War and the most popular beach resort – for the Vietnamese, at least – and there are more peaceful sites as well. For a dose of calm visit the birthplace of the country's homegrown religion or soak up the charm of Long Hai.

CU CHI TUNNELS

The ground around the **tunnel network** (admission 70,000d) is marked by shallow craters – some have become small ponds – made by American bombs in a futile attempt to dislodge the Viet Cong from the tunnel network here. This subterranean web of hospitals, kitchens and armouries once stretched from Saigon to the Cambodian border. In the district of Cu Chi alone, there were more than 200km of tunnels.

Even though some parts have been enlarged for Westerners, it's a hot, claustrophobic experience to duck walk for 40m underground. For an extra charge travellers can fire real machine guns at a shooting range.

Day tours operated by traveller cafés charge around US$5 per person (transport only); most include a stop at the Caodai Great Temple in Tay Ninh. Public buses going to Tay Ninh can drop you in Cu Chi; however, since the tunnel complex is about 15km outside town, you'll have to hire a motorbike to get to the tunnels.

TAY NINH

☎ 066 / pop 41,300

Tay Ninh town, capital of Tay Ninh province, is 96km northwest of HCMC and serves as the headquarters of one of Vietnam's most interesting indigenous religions, Caodaism (see p818). The **Caodai Great Temple** was built between 1933 and 1955. Victor Hugo is among the Westerners especially revered by the Caodai; look for his likeness in the Great Temple.

The Caodai Holy See complex is situated 4km east of Tay Ninh. One-day tours from Saigon, including Tay Ninh and the Cu Chi Tunnels, cost around US$5. Public buses to Tay Ninh leave from the Mien Tay station in HCMC.

VUNG TAU

☎ 064 / pop 161,300

A resort town since the French holidayed here, this quick getaway from HCMC is full of bass-thumping action on the weekends as Saigonese visitors pour into town. Weekdays are much quieter and there are long stretches of lonely beach. Oil-drilling is big here and there's the expat population to prove it. It's a commercialised beach resort – with a few mega-developments in the works including a theme park – but it's easy enough to escape the seedy karaoke scene.

Information

International SOS (☎ 858 776; Đ Le Ngoc Han; consultations US$55-65; ⏲ 24hr) A Babel of foreign languages are spoken here, including English.

Main post office (8 Đ Hoang Dieu) This is located on the ground level of the Petrovietnam Towers building.

OSC Vietnam Travel (☎ 852 008; www.oscvn.com; 9 Đ Le Loi) Vung Tau's biggest travel agency sells a decent city map (20,000d) and offers a host of unique tours, including an old battlefield tour (US$49 per person).

Vietcombank (☎ 852 024; 27-29 Đ Tran Hung Dao) Exchanges cash, travellers cheques and gives credit-card advances. You'll also find an ATM at the Rex Hotel at 1 Đ Le Quy Don.

Sights & Activities

Atop Nui Nho (Small Mountain), a **giant Jesus** (admission free, parking 2000d; ⏲ 7.30-11.30am & 1.30-5pm) waits with arms outstretched to embrace the South China Sea – showing off the swallows' nests in his armpits. At his foot is a sad collection of monkeys and snakes in small cages.

The nearby **lighthouse** (admission 2000d; ⏲ 7am-5pm) boasts a spectacular 360-degree view. From the ferry dock on Đ Ha Long, take a sharp right on the alley north of the Hai Au Hotel, then roll on up the hill.

Pagodas dot the length of Đ Ha Long, but prim **Hon Ba Pagoda** sits offshore on an islet accessible only at low tide.

Sleeping & Eating

There's a guesthouse strip at Back Beach. On weekends, lodging gets very pricey – rates can be two or three times those charged on weekdays. Below are the weekday rates.

Thien Nhien (☎ 853 481; 145A Đ Thuy Van; d 100,000-200,000d; ❄) On the main drag, this airy place has clean rooms, some with balconies, air-con and ocean views.

Song Bien (☎ 523 311; 131A Đ Thuy Van; d 120,000-150,000d; ❄) The Chinese-style décor brightens this fairly comfortable place; although there are no ocean views, there's a shared terrace on the top floor.

our pick **My Tho Guesthouse** (☎ 832 035; 47 Đ Tran Phu; r US$8-14) With simple rooms, this is the sweetest little guesthouse on the Peninsula, about 2km north of central Vung Tau in a quiet area called Mulberry Beach (Bai Dau). The warm couple running the guesthouse serve delicious, cheap home-cooked meals on the cosy terrace. From the centre, take Đ Quang Trung going north, which turns into Đ Tran Phu.

The road along Back Beach, Đ Thuy Van, is crammed with *com* shops and seafood restaurants. A good bet on Back Beach is **Dai Loc** (☎ 858 124; 170 Đ Hoang Hoa Tham; mains 15,000d; ⏲ lunch & dinner), which serves both Vietnamese and Western food in a friendly atmosphere.

Mulberry Beach's main road has several good seafood places down on the water. Go to local favourite **Cay Bang** (☎ 838 522; 69 Đ Tran Phu; mains 45,000d; ⏲ 11am-10pm) for fresh seafood and a happening weekend atmosphere. For nightlife and good Western food, local expats head to **BB Bar/Whispers Restaurant** (☎ 856 028; 13-15 Nguyen Trai; ⏲ until midnight).

Getting There & Away

From Mien Dong bus station in HCMC, air-conditioned minibuses (25,000d, two hours, 128km) leave for Vung Tau throughout the day until around 4.30pm.

Should convenience outweigh cost, catch a **Petro Express hydrofoil** (☎ HCMC 08-821 0650, Vung Tau

816 308) or **Vina Express hydrofoil** (☎ in HCMC 08-829 7892, Vung Tau ☎ 856 530) to Vung Tau (US$10, 80 minutes) at Bach Dang jetty in HCMC. Boats leave every two hours starting at 6.30am, but check in HCMC for the latest schedule. In Vung Tau, the boat leaves from Cau Da Pier, across from the Hai Au Hotel.

Getting Around

Vung Tau is easily traversed on two wheels. Guesthouses can arrange bicycle hire (per day US$2); motorbikes cost US$5 to US$10 per day. Or, just make eye contact with that *cyclo* or motorbike driver on the corner.

A *xe om* from the **Vung Tau bus station** (192A Đ Nam Ky Khoi Nghia) to Mulberry Beach or Back Beach should cost around 10,000d.

LONG HAI

☎ 064

A rustic beach and a quick getaway from HCMC are the two main draws for the fishing village of Long Hai. If you want social interaction with fellow travellers head to Mui Ne (p873) instead. Although it has more character than Vung Tau, Long Hai is also mobbed on weekends.

Outside Long Hai are a few interesting sights, although you'll likely need to hire a guide from Vung Tau to find them. **Chua Phap Hoa**, a peaceful pagoda set in a forest with lots of wild monkeys, has some good trails nearby for short treks.

At Minh Dam, 5km from Long Hai, there are **caves** with historical connections to the Franco-Viet Minh and American Wars. Nearby there's a **mountaintop temple** with great panoramic views of the coastline.

Sleeping & Eating

Huong Bien Hotel (☎ 868 356; bungalows 120,000-180,000d; ❄) Down a signposted dirt driveway off Rte 19, the Huong Bien has simple concrete bungalows among palms and casuarinas. Most have private bathroom and fan, some have air-con, and all nestle right on the beach.

Military Guesthouse 298 (Doan an Dieu Duong 298; ☎ 868 316; Rte 19; r 150,000-200,000d; ❄) At the dead end of Rte 19, this guesthouse is run by the navy, which may help explain its prime beachfront location. Rooms here are clean and comfortable, with tile floors and hot water; the cheapest rooms are fan only.

There's a cluster of beachside restaurants called **Can Tin 1**, **2**, **3** and **4** (mains around 15,000-70,000d; 🕑 7am-7pm) located near Military Guesthouse 298. These serve decent Vietnamese meals – including good, simple seafood dishes. Apart from these relaxed places, there aren't many other eating options in Long Hai.

Getting There & Around

Long Hai is 124km southeast of HCMC and takes about two hours to reach by car. To get here by public transport, get to Vung Tau and take a 30km *xe om* for about 50,000d.

Motorbike-taxi drivers hang around all the likely tourist spots in the area.

MEKONG DELTA

The Mekong Delta is where the countryside comes alive. Tilling the ground with buffalo-drawn ploughs, planting rice, harvesting by hand and waiting for the murky Mekong to flood and renew the soil is the wheel of life that has been rolling here for centuries. There are too many shades of electric green to count and the hellos are rarely followed by invitations to buy something.

After winding its way from its source in Tibet, the Mekong River meets the sea in southernmost Vietnam. Once part of the Khmer kingdom, the Mekong Delta was the last part of modern-day Vietnam to be annexed and settled by the Vietnamese.

MY THO

☎ 074 / pop 169, 300

My Tho is an easy day trip from Saigon and acts as the gateway to the Mekong Delta for most visitors. Everything moves a little slower and the warmth of southern Vietnam – in the people and in the temperature – is readily apparent.

In My Tho, river-boat tours can be booked at the main riverfront office of **Tien Giang Tourist** (Cong Ty Du Lich Tien Giang; ☎ 873 184; 8 Đ 30 Thang 4; 🕑 7am-5pm). Depending on what you book, destinations usually include a coconut-candy workshop, a honey-bee farm and an orchid garden. Also of interest are several islands in the area.

Hiring a boat with a big group makes these local-government tours economical; on your own, they're expensive at US$25 for two to three hours, though it is possible to bargain down to US$20 in slower (read hot or wet) seasons. Significantly cheaper independent guides may approach you on the riverfront near **Cuu Long Restaurant** (☎ 870 779; Đ 30 Thang 4; mains 25,000d). Keep in mind that these guys operate illegally and, though enforcement is erratic and unlikely, there's a small risk that you or they may be fined by zealous river cops.

Sleeping & Eating

Huong Duong (☎ 872 011; huongduonghotel2005@yahoo.com; 33 Đ Thien Ho Duong; 100,000-200,000d; ❄) Huong Duong has decent, large rooms near the channel and cheap breakfasts at the rooftop Galaxy Coffee Bar.

Rang Dong Hotel (☎ 874 400; 25 Đ 30 Thang 4; r 130,000-150,000d; ❄) Rang Dong is centrally located along the waterfront, with sidewalk cafés and *xe om* galore. The original is becoming a little rundown but it recently birthed a nicer sister hotel (see below).

Song Tien Hotel (☎ 872 009; 101 Đ Trung Trac; r US$10-20 ❄) The Song Tien has clean, comfortable rooms with TV, fridge and shared balconies overlooking both town and channel. It has an onsite restaurant.

our pick Rang Dong (II) (☎ 970 085; www.rangdonghotel.net; 4 Đ Duong Le Thi Hong Gam; r 200,000-300,000d; ❄) The rooms are sparkling clean, spacious and many have river views. There's a (seemingly legitimate) karaoke bar and riverside restaurant. The caterwauling is sometimes accompanied by live traditional music and usually stops at 11pm.

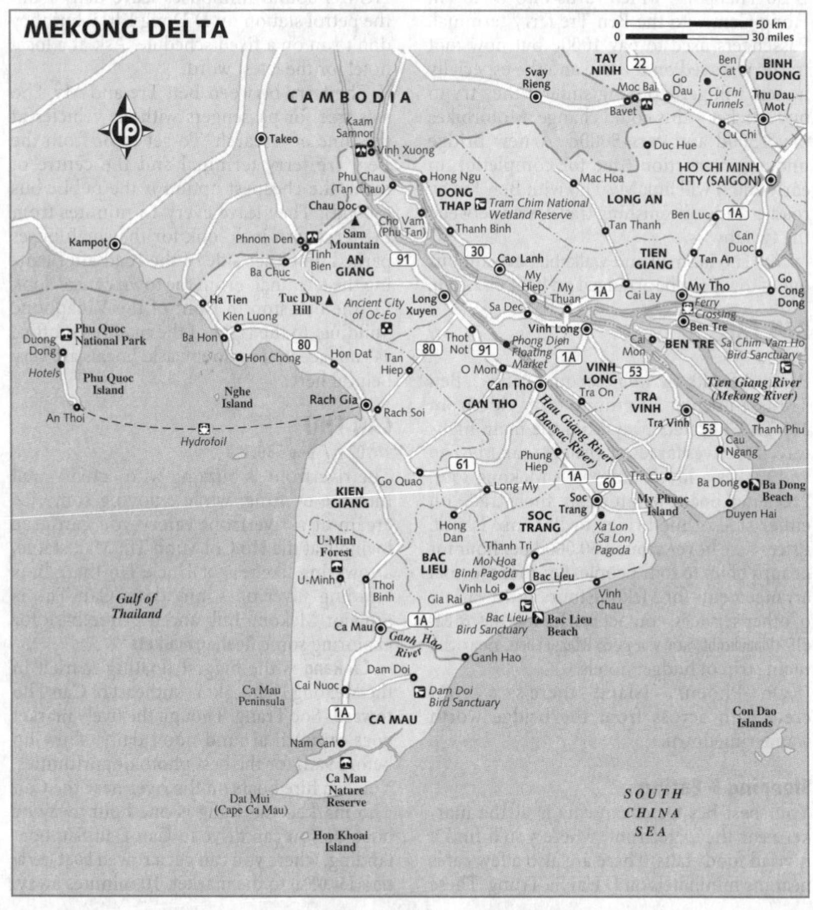

Try My Tho's speciality, *hu tieu my tho,* a rice-noodle soup full of fresh vegetables, pork, chicken and dried seafood in a rich broth.

Hu Tieu Chay 24 (24 Đ Nam Ky Khoi Nghia; soups 3000d; breakfast & lunch) Happily, there's a delicious vegetarian version, too.

Hu Tieu 44 (44 Đ Nam Ky Khoi Nghia; soups 6000d; breakfast & lunch)

Getting There & Around

Buses leaving from the Cholon bus station in HCMC (19,000d, two hours) drop you at the My Tho bus station (Ben Xe Khach Tien Giang), several kilometres west of town. From My Tho's centre, take Đ Ap Bac westward and continue on to National Hwy 1.

To get to Ben Tre, head west for 1km on Đ 30 Thang 4 – which turns into Đ Le Thi Hong Gam – to the Ben Tre ferry terminal. Passengers used to pay 1000d but now foot traffic is waved on for free and the especially honest will get a pitying smile if they try to buy a ticket – this could change. Motorbikes pay 1500d and cars 5000d. A new bridge under construction (due for completion in early 2009) will link My Tho with Ben Tre by road, greatly diminishing travel time between the two towns.

My Tho is small and walkable; expeditions out of town can be arranged on boat or *xe om.*

BEN TRE

☎ 075

Famous for its *keo dua* (coconut candy), Ben Tre is a bucolic 20-minute ferry ride from My Tho. Located away from the main highway, it receives far fewer visitors than My Tho and makes a lovely stop on a Mekong tour. Freelance boat operators ply their trade on either side of the bridge to Phoenix Island. Prices here hover around 60,000d per hour for groups of up to four people. For more formal arrangements for Mekong tours and a variety of other services, contact **Ben Tre Tourist** (☎ 829 618; ttdhbulichbt@hcm.vnn.vn; 65 Đ Dong Khoi), near the main strip of budget hotels.

On Phoenix Island there's a concrete path across from the bridge worth wandering down.

Sleeping & Eating

Your best bet for cheap eats is at the market near the waterfront, where you'll find a myriad food stalls. There are also a few cafés near the minihotels on Đ Hai Ba Trung. These hotels and family-run restaurants face the tiny Truc Giang Lake:

Cong Doan Hotel (☎ 852 083; 36 Đ Hai Ba Trung; d 100,000-170,000d;) Cong Doan is a no-frills but clean place to lay your weary head.

Dong Khoi Hotel (☎ 822 501; dongkhoihotelbtre@vnn.vn; 16 Đ Hai Ba Trung; r 150,000-200,000d;) The Dong Khoi is as good as it gets in Ben Tre; it has spotless rooms with bathrooms, and offers boat and canoe rentals in addition to the standard Mekong tours. Credit cards are accepted.

Phuong Hoang Hotel (☎ 821 385; 28 Đ Hai Ba Trung; r US$10;) This 10-room minihotel is decent value.

Getting There & Around

HCMC-bound minibuses leave daily from the petrol station on Đ Dong Khoi, but they don't run on a fixed schedule. Ask at a local hotel for the latest word.

The ferry between Ben Tre and My Tho was free for passengers without vehicles at the time of research. To get to or from the Ben Tre ferry terminal and the centre of town, the cheapest option is the public bus (5000d). They leave every 15 minutes from the ferry terminal; look for the small buses parked on either side of the road after exiting the terminal. From the town centre, look for the bus stop in front of the Vinaphone building, to the right of the main post office as you face it. If in doubt, ask. Locals are very helpful here.

CAN THO

☎ 071 / pop 330,100

The riverfront is buzzing with activity well into the evening; while enjoying some ice cream at a riverfront eatery you can gaze lovingly at the Ho Chi Minh Tin Man statue, a towering likeness of Uncle Ho that glints blinding silver on sunny days. Can Tho is a major Mekong hub and a prime base for exploring some **floating markets**.

Cai Rang is the biggest floating market in the Mekong Delta, 6km southeast of Can Tho towards Soc Trang. Though the lively market goes on until around noon daily, show up before 9am for the best photo opportunities. You can hire boats on the river near the Can Tho market. Cai Rang is one hour away by boat, or you can drive to Cau Dau Sau boat landing, where you can get a rowed **boat** (per hr around 50,000d) to the market, 10 minutes away.

Less crowded and less motorised is the **Phong Dien** market, with more stand-up rowboats. It's best between 6am and 8am. Twenty kilometres northwest of Can Tho, it's easy to reach by road and you can hire a boat on arrival. There will be plenty of offers for US$3 tours that hit both markets and stop at a local orchard for good measure.

The **Muniransyaram Pagoda** (36 ĐL Hoa Binh) is the one must-see in the city for the impressive Khmer-style architecture.

Tours of the markets and canals in the area can be arranged by the friendly staff at **Cantho Tourist** (☎ 821 852; canthotour@hcm.vnn.vn; 20 Đ Hai Ba Trung). It also has bicycle tours (360,000d) to the markets and staff will help you to book transport.

There are a few ATMs on the riverfront.

Sleeping & Eating

Phuong Hang Hotel (☎ 814 978; 41 Đ Ngo Duc Ke; d 70,000-120,000d; ❄) The rooms aren't brand new but they are clean and big; the bathrooms are so large a small regiment of soldiers could tidy up inside.

Hien Guesthouse (☎ 812 718; hien_gh@yahoo.com; 118/10 Đ Phan Dinh Phung; r US$8-9; ❄) Tucked down a narrow and quiet alley a few minutes' walk from the city centre, some rooms in the new wing (down the alley, though reception is at the original location) have private balconies but pick a room on the top floor for views. The friendly owner is an excellent source of local travel information and rents out dependable motorbikes.

Tan Phuoc Hotel (☎ 816 822; 9 Đ Ngo Quyen; r 150,000-200,000d; ❄) The staff doesn't speak a word of English but this new minihotel near the riverfront has big new rooms with satellite TV and a minibar. You can pay by credit card.

our pick **Tay Ho Hotel** (☎ 823 392; kstayho-ct@hcm.vnn.vn; 42 Đ Hai Ba Trung; r US$12-16; ❄) The only budget hotel on the riverfront, this bargain is across from the Tin Man statue has a friendly staff, clean modern rooms and satellite TV.

If self-catering, head to **Co-op Mart** (☎ 763 585; 1 ĐL Dai Hoa Binh), a multilevel supermarket and department store.

There are a dozen local restaurants on both sides of **Restaurant alley** (Đ Nam Ky Khoi Nghia), situated in an alley between Đ Dien Bien Phu and Đ Phan Dinh Phung.

You'll find several other popular eateries along the riverfront strip, across from the huge silver Uncle Ho statue.

Mekong (☎ 821 646; 38 Đ Hai Ba Trung; mains 20,000d; 🕑 breakfast, lunch & dinner) One of the main traveller hangouts, the Mekong is always packed and stays open late.

Nam Bo (☎ 823 908; 50 Đ Hai Ba Trung; mains 25,000-50,000d; 🕑 lunch & dinner) Housed in a restored French villa, it serves excellent European and Vietnamese food, desserts and drinks. The upstairs balcony is prime people-watching territory.

Getting There & Around

Buses and minibuses from HCMC leave from the Mien Tay station (65,000d, five hours). The Can Tho bus station is at Đ Nguyen Trai and Đ Tran Phu, about 1km north of town. Buses and private minibuses between other Mekong Delta destinations are cheap and plentiful; ask at restaurants or hotels.

Xe loi (motorbikes with two-seater carriages on the back) cost 3000d for rides around town. Most guesthouses also hire out bicycles. **International Hotel** (☎ 822 080; ksquocte-ct@hcm.vnn.vn, 12 ĐL Hai Ba Trung) rents good mountain bikes (10,000/40,000d per hour/day).

CHAU DOC

☎ 076 / pop 100,000

A major transit point for Cambodia because of the popular river-crossing here (p893), shyly charming Chau Doc houses mosques, pagodas and temples, including the cave temples at **Sam Mountain**.

War remnants near Chau Doc include **Ba Chuc**, the site of a Khmer Rouge massacre with a bone pagoda similar to that of Cambodia's Choeung Ek memorial; and **Tuc Dup Hill**, where an expensive American bombing campaign in 1963 earned it the nickname Two Million Dollar Hill. It's also possible to visit fish farms set up underneath floating houses on the river.

Get cash or exchange foreign currency at **Incombank** (☎ 866 497; 68-70 Đ Nguyen Huu Canh). A good place to start for local travel information is the tourist desk at the Vinh Phuoc Hotel.

Sleeping & Eating

Vinh Phuoc Hotel (☎ 866 242; 12 Đ Quang Trung; r US$6-15; ❄) A good budget deal, this place is run by an amiable Brit who is an excellent source of local travel information. There's a good in-house restaurant serving Vietnamese and Western food (mains around 30,000d).

Thuan Loi Hotel (☎ 866 134; hotelthuanloi@hcm.vnn.vn; 18 Đ Tran Hung Dao; r 100,000-190,000d; ❄)

GETTING TO CAMBODIA

Numerous agencies in Chau Doc sell boat tickets taking you from Chau Doc to Phnom Penh via the Vinh Xuong–Kaam Samnor border. One-month visas are issued on arrival (US$20, although some overcharging is common), but bring a passport photo.

Slow boats for the trip cost around US$8 to US$10 (leaving around 8am and arriving in Phnom Penh at 4pm). There are also several companies offering faster boats between the two cities; **Hang Chau** (☎ in Phnom Penh 012-883 542) departs Chau Doc at 7am and costs US$15. It takes about four hours, including a slow border check.

See p79 for details on doing the trip in reverse.

Overlooking the riverside, this pleasant place with a communal terrace has friendly staff and a relaxed atmosphere. The fan rooms are very basic, with cold-water bathrooms, while the air-conditioned rooms are bright and airy.

Delta Adventure Inn (Nha Khach Long Chau; ☎ 861 249; deltaadventureinn@hotmail.com; r 120,000-240,000d;) This cosy terracotta-tiled compound sits amid the rice paddies about 4km from Chau Doc. The views of Sam Mountain are lovely from the island café-restaurant on the grounds.

Good local eateries include **Mi Vach Tuong**, (Đ Thu Khoa Nghia; noodles 7000d; breakfast & dinner) and **Thanh Tinh** (☎ 865 064; 13 Đ Quang Trung; mains 15,000d; breakfast, lunch & dinner).

Getting There & Around

Cargo boats run twice weekly between Chau Doc and Ha Tien on the coast via the Vinh Te Canal (150,000d, eight to 12 hours), which straddles the Cambodian border; it's an interesting trip. Departures are at 5am from a tiny pier (near 60 Đ Trung Hung Dao). Cargo boats also travel to/from Vinh Long, to the east.

The buses from HCMC to Chau Doc leave from the Mien Tay bus station; the express bus can make the run in six hours and costs around 84,000d.

Xe loi can be hired for a few thousand dong to get around town.

RACH GIA

☎ 077 / pop 172,400

The place to catch a high-speed ferry for Phu Quoc Island, Rach Gia is the prosperous capital of Kien Giang province and a prime smuggling hub due to its proximity to Cambodia, Thailand and the great wide ocean. The centre of town sits on an islet embraced by the two arms of the Cai Lon River; the north side has your getaway options out of town.

Information

Kien Giang Tourist (Du Lich Lu Hanh Kien Giang; ☎ 862 081; dlluhanhkg@hcm.vnn.vn; 5 Đ Le Loi; 7am-5pm) The provincial tourism authority.

Rach Gia Internet Cafe (152 Đ Nguyen Trung Truc) Has a pretty fast connection.

Vietcombank (☎ 863 178; 2 Đ Mac Cuu) Has a 24-hour ATM.

Sleeping & Eating

Phuong Hong Hotel (☎ 866 138; 5 Đ Tu Do; r 80,000-180,000d;) Near the port, this friendly place offers clean, small rooms. Some bathrooms are cold-water only.

Kim Co Hotel (☎ 879 610; 141 Đ Nguyen Hung Son; r 150,000-200,000d;) Kim Co is the best deal for budget travellers in Rach Gia and it comes with a prime location in the centre of town. The rooms are spacious, colourful and look brand new.

Hong Nam Hotel (☎ 873 090; fax 873 424; Đ Ly Thai To; r 150,000-250,000d;) It's a nice minihotel across from the Rach Gia Trade Centre – a market with food stalls – the staff are friendly and the clean rooms have all the modern conveniences.

Cheap, tasty Vietnamese food is sold from food stalls along Đ Hung Vuong between Đ Bach Dang and Đ Le Hong Phong and there are also food stalls outside the Rach Gia Trade Centre.

Other places to try, all with English menus:

Ao Dai Moi (☎ 866 295; 26 Đ Ly Tu Trong; soups 8000d; breakfast) *Ao dai* is the traditional Vietnamese tunic and trousers, and *moi* means new – this place is run, fittingly, by a tailor. It serves very good morning *pho* and won ton soup.

Ao Dai Moi (II) (☎ 866 272; 18 Đ Nguyen Hung Son; soups 8000d; dinner) The latest from the friendly family that runs the original Ao Doi Moi, around the corner.

Hung Phat (☎ 867 599; 7 Đ Nguyen Du; meals 25,000d; breakfast, lunch & dinner) It does excellent sweet-and-sour soups and a good vegetarian fried rice.

Getting There & Away

Vietnam Airlines (code VN; www.vietnamairlines.com) flies once daily between HCMC and Rach Gia; reserve well ahead. There's also a daily morning flight from Rach Gia to Phu Quoc Island. You'll have to catch a *xe om* or *xe loi* from the airport to Rach Gia.

Hydrofoils (180,000d, 3½ hours), leaving at 8am and 1.30pm, zip from Rach Gia to An Thoi on Phu Quoc Island. Stop by the Rach Gia office of **Duong Dong** (☎ 879 765) or **Bien Xanh** (☏ 254 234), both at the ferry terminal, to buy tickets at least a day beforehand. In the slow season it may be possible to book same-day tickets.

Buses from HCMC to Rach Gia leave from the Mien Tay bus station; the express bus takes six to seven hours (around 90,000d). Night buses leave Rach Gia for HCMC between 7pm and 11pm.

The **central bus station** (Đ Nguyen Binh Khiem) is in town, near the Rach Gia New Trade Center, and has daily express services to other cities in the region. There's also a bigger **Rach Gia bus station** (Ben Xe Rach Soi; 78 Đ Nguyen Trung Truc), 7km south of the city (towards Long Xuyen and Can Tho). Buses here link Rach Gia with Can Tho, Dong Thap, Ha Tien, Long Xuyen and HCMC.

PHU QUOC ISLAND

☎ 077 / pop 52,700

Phu Quoc is the place to take a vacation from your vacation. Deserted white-sand beaches wrap around the island and just offshore the untouched reefs will have divers and snorkellers thinking that they have the ocean to themselves. Renting a motorbike and exploring long stretches of empty dirt road through the untouched forest is another way to lose yet one more day to the beauty of this place. However, mass tourism is just ramping up here, with big plans or megaresorts and maybe even an international airport on the horizon. Get here before they pave paradise.

Addresses outside of Duong Dong's centre are designated by the kilometre mark south of town. Bring a torch (flash light or burning stick) to navigate the road and beach at night.

The most famous English-speaking guide in Phu Quoc is **Tony Anh** (☎ 0913 197 334), who speaks with a Brooklyn accent thanks to growing up with American GIs in Hué.

Because almost everything is shipped from the mainland and the island supports very little agriculture, this is one of the pricier destinations in Vietnam but deals can be found; sun bathing is free.

Sights & Activities

About 90% of Phu Quoc Island is protected forest. The mountainous northern half of the island, where the trees are most dense, has been declared a **national park** (Khu Rung Nguyen Sinh). You'll need a motorbike to get into the reserve and there are no real trekking trails.

The **An Thoi Islands** – 15 islands and islets at the southern tip of Phu Quoc – can be visited by chartered boat (US$40 per day), and it's a fine area for swimming, snorkelling and fishing.

Diving and snorkelling in Phu Quoc are just taking off, with few people and a more pristine marine environment than along the mainland coast. A two-tank dive costs around US$65; snorkelling trips cost US$25. The following shops usually close from late April to September, when the water off the western shore is too murky. There is talk of opening up new sites on the eastern shore for year-round diving.

Rainbow Divers (☎ 0913 400 964; www.divevietnam.com) has a desk at the Rainbow Bar (see p902)

GETTING TO CAMBODIA

The Tinh Bien–Phnom Den border (open 8am to 4pm) is remote but, because the roads are in better shape than they used to be, this crossing may appeal to cyclists. It's necessary to arrange a Cambodian visa before showing up here – Ho Chi Minh City travel agencies can easily arrange one.

There are a few daily buses to Ha Tien from the Rach Gia bus station. From Ha Tien, take a local bus or haggle with a motorbike driver to make the 50km trip to Tinh Bien; it'll cost somewhere in the order of US$7 to US$10.

Another way to get to Ha Tien is to take a slow boat from Chau Doc (150,000d, eight to 12 hours). The twice-weekly boats leave at 5am from a tiny pier near 60 Đ Trung Hung Dao.

See p79 for information on making the journey from Cambodia to Vietnam.

on the beach and an office near the Saigon-Phu Quoc Resort, just after the road becomes paved.

Coco Dive Center (☎ 982 100; cocodive@dng.vnn.vn; 58 Đ Tran Hung Dao) has friendly dive masters.

Sleeping

All of these places are on the western shore and have great views of the sunset.

Mai Phuong Beach Resort (☎ 0918 288 647; maiphuongmanager@maiphuongbeachresort.com; Vung Au Beach; bungalow US$10) An hour-and-a-half motorbike ride from An Thoi, Mai Phuong Beach Resort capitalises on its remoteness with plenty of space to lounge beside the tranquil bay and the bungalows are set far apart. The resort also offers canoe snorkelling and fishing trips. It has an on-site restaurant.

Phu Quoc Resort Thang Loi (☎ 985 002; www.phu-quoc.de; bungalows US$10-30) On Ong Lang Beach, north of Duong Dong, the Thang Loi is a secluded enclave of 12 basic bungalows overlooking a stretch of pristine beach. The staff are friendly and the restaurant is good.

Lam Ha Eco Resort (☎ 847 369; r/bungalow US$12/15;) This friendly, family-run place on Long Beach is excellent value for money, with trim and tidy rooms and bungalows (some with verandas) scattered around a lush setting.

our pick **Beach Club** (☎ 980 998; www.beachclubvietnam.com; Km 2.7; r US$15-20) Towards the southern end of the strip of hotels on Long Beach, the place lives up to its name with bungalows and a restaurant that are literally on the beach. It's one of the best places to stay on the island.

Tropicana Resort (☎ 847 127; reservation@tropicanavietnam.com; d US$15, bungalows US$35-70;) Travellers who are trying to avoid big resorts might be surprised how much they like this beautiful, unpretentious place on Long Beach. Rates include breakfast.

Eating & Drinking

Most guesthouses have their own lively cafés or restaurants in-house; wander along Long Beach until you find somewhere appealing. There are cheap food stalls near the Duong Dong market.

Rainbow Bar (☎ 0903 177 923; mains from 20,000d; breakfast, lunch & dinner) An established party spot, this is also the place to book trips with Rainbow Divers after the main office closes. It's near the Tropicana Resort.

Eden (☎ 994 208; 118/10 Đ Tran Hung Dao; mains 20,000-60,000d; breakfast, lunch & dinner) An open-air restaurant-bar on the beach plus a live DJ equals a new traveller favourite. The menu is like a small phone book and the cooks here actually wear white hats. The Eden also rents rooms for US$10.

Buddy Info Cafe (☎ 994 181; 26 Đ Nguyen Trai; desserts 30,000d; breakfast, lunch & dinner;) Sweet treats with New Zealand ice cream and free internet for patrons.

German Biergarten (50 Đ Tran Hung Dao; mains 30,000-80,000d; lunch & dinner) A favourite meeting spot of expats, there's all the German food and beer the name implies. There's bench-style seating and Johnny Cash singing overhead. In possible tribute to the sorrowful singer, there are some good deals on mixed drinks (25,000d).

Getting There & Around

Phu Quoc is often a last stop on a Delta visit and travellers can fly back to HCMC to avoid back-tracking. **Vietnam Airlines** (code VN; www.vietnamairlines.com) has five daily flights between Ho Chi Minh City and Phu Quoc; reserve early. A *xe om* from the airport to guesthouses south of town should be around 15,000d.

Hydrofoils (see p901) shuttle between Rach Gia and Phu Quoc twice per day. Hydrofoil companies include **Super Dong** (☎ in Rach Gia 077-878 475, Phu Quoc 980 111), **Duong Dong** (☎ in Rach Gia 077-879 765, Phu Quoc 990 747; www.duongdongexpress.com.vn) and **Hai Au** (☎ in Rach Gia 077-879 455, Phu Quoc 990 555). All have offices by the dock in Rach Gia, and in Phu Quoc there are many offices near the An Thoi dock and in Duong Dong. Most travel agents can book tickets as well.

Some hydrofoil companies have cheap (15,000d) buses from their Duong Dong offices to An Thoi for passengers. In Duong Dong, arrange transport at the hydrofoil office; in An Thoi ask on the boat before disembarking or just look for the small minibuses waiting near the dock. Be ready for a swarm of motorbike touts.

Slow boats between Phu Quoc and mainland Ha Tien are very risky; don't take them if you value your life.

Xe om rides from An Thoi ferry port on the southern tip of the island to Duong Dong cost about 40,000d. Almost all places to stay rent motorbikes for 100,000d per day. Most of the roads are dirt, so cover up for potential spills and to keep the fine red sand off your skin.

VIETNAM DIRECTORY

ACCOMMODATION

Accommodation is at a premium during Tet (late January or early February), when the country is on the move and overseas Vietnamese flood back into the country. Prices at this time can rise by 25%. Christmas and New Year represent another high season, but to a lesser extent than Tet.

Family-run guesthouses are usually the cheapest option, ranging from around US$6 to US$15 per person with private bathroom. Some places offer dorm beds for US$3 to US$4 per person, with shared bathroom. Guesthouse accommodation is generally plentiful, and discounts are negotiable if you plan to stay for a few days or are travelling alone.

A step up from the guesthouses, minihotels typically come with more amenities: satellite TV, minifridges and IDD phones. Rates sometimes include breakfast, and as with smaller guesthouses, some discounts can be negotiated. Although minihotel rates can be as high as US$20 to US$25, it's still fairly easy to find rooms for around US$12. Rates often go down the more steps you have to climb. Many places now offer free internet for guests in the lobby.

Unless otherwise noted, prices in this chapter include private bathrooms.

ACTIVITIES

Vietnam's roads and rivers, sea and mountains provide ample opportunity for active adventures. Travel agencies and traveller cafés all over the country can arrange local trips, from kayaking on Halong Bay to trekking up Fansipan to kite-surfing in Mui Ne.

Cycling

The flatlands and back roads of the Mekong Delta are wonderful to cycle through and observe the vibrant workaday agricultural life. Another spot well away from the insane traffic of National Hwy 1 is Hwy 14, winding through the Central Highlands. Arrange mountain-biking tours in the northern mountains at **Handspan Adventure Travel** (Map p830; ☎ 04-926 0581; www.handspan.com; 80 P Ma May, Hanoi); or stop by **Sinhbalo Adventures** (Map p892; ☎ 08-837 6766, 08-836 7682; www.sinhbalo.com; 283/20 Đ Pham Ngu Lao) in HCMC if you wish to meander the Mekong Delta or further afield.

Diving & Snorkelling

Vietnam has several great dive destinations. Long established, with many dive sites, is the beachside town of Nha Trang. A notable emerging dive destination is Phu Quoc Island, with fewer visitors and a more pristine environment, and even Hoi An has got in on the underwater action.

Kayaking

For an even closer look at those limestone crags, it's possible to paddle yourself around Halong Bay. Inquire at travel agencies in Hanoi (p832) for more details.

Trekking

The most popular region for trekking is the northwest – notably around Sapa, which includes Vietnam's tallest mountain, Fansipan. There's also good trekking in the jungle of Cuc Phuong National Park, and the trekking trails in Bach Ma National Park are very nice. The trek up Lang Bian Mountain (p877) near Dalat also gets good reviews.

Water Sports

Mui Ne has Vietnam's best shoreline for kitesurfing and windsurfing fiends. Nha Trang is another good locale for windsurfing, sailing or wakeboarding. The area around China Beach (p862), south of Danang, also gets passable surf between September and December.

BOOKS

Lonely Planet's *Vietnam* guide provides the full scoop on the country. If you're interested in cuisine and the culture behind it, sink your teeth into *World Food Vietnam*. The *Vietnamese Phrasebook* is practical and helps pass the time on long bus rides. If you prefer cycling it, put *Cycling Vietnam, Laos & Cambodia* into your panniers.

For insight into the country's history and juicy stories about political leaders, Robert Templer's *Shadows and Wind* (1999) is a compelling read. *Catfish & Mandala* (1999), by Andrew X Pham, is the author's bicycle journey that wheels from HCMC (Saigon) to Hanoi and far beyond. It's exquisitely intimate but broadly illuminating.

One of the finest books about the American War written by a Vietnamese is *The Sorrow of War: A Novel of North Vietnam* (1996) by Bao Ninh.

BUSINESS HOURS

Many small, privately owned shops, restaurants and street stalls stay open seven days a week, often until late at night. Restaurants tend to open very early and serve food all day long.

We only specify business hours in this chapter if they differ from the hours given below; keep in mind the hours given below may vary an hour or so each way.

Banks 8am to 11am and 2pm to 4pm Monday to Friday, 8am to 11.30am Saturday
Government offices 7.30am to 4.30pm Monday to Friday (with a long lunch from noon), 7.30am to noon Saturday
Museums 8am to 11am and 2pm to 4pm; closed Monday
Offices and public buildings 8am to 11am and 2pm to 4pm
Post offices 6.30am to 9pm
Temples All day, every day

CLIMATE

Vietnam's south is tropical but the north can experience chilly winters – in Hanoi, an overcoat can be necessary in January.

The southwestern monsoon blows from April or May to October, bringing warm, damp weather to the whole country, except those areas sheltered by mountains, namely the central part of the coastal strip and the Red River Delta.

Typhoons can strike the central coast especially hard between August and November, and can cause flooding that closes roads for a day or two and delays flights.

Also see the climate charts (p916).

CUSTOMS

Though you're probably not travelling on a shoestring in order to support your antique-collection mania, keep in mind that customs may seize suspected antiques or other 'cultural treasures', which cannot legally be taken out of Vietnam. If you do purchase authentic or reproduction antiques, be sure to get a receipt and a customs clearance form from the seller.

DANGERS & ANNOYANCES

Since 1975 many thousands of Vietnamese have been maimed or killed by unexploded rockets, artillery shells, mortars, mines and other ordnance left over from the war. *Never* touch any war relics you come across – such objects can remain lethal for decades, and one bomb can ruin your whole day.

SCAMS

Most of the scams in Vietnam are based in a particular town or area, from train-ticket cheats in Sapa to 'English students' in Hanoi. But they all involve either surprise costs, or charging for one thing and delivering another. The best thing to do is to buy directly from the source (especially for transport and tours) and to make sure everything is negotiated upfront. The best approach is to stay firm, fair and friendly when doing business.

Violent crime is still relatively rare in Vietnam, but petty theft is definitely not. Drive-by bag snatchers on motorbikes are not uncommon, and thieves on buses, trains and boats stealthily rifle through bags or haul them off altogether. Skilled pickpockets work the crowds.

One important suggestion, in particular for HCMC, is to not have anything dangling off your body that you are not ready to part with. This includes cameras and any jewellery. When riding a *xe om,* sling shoulder bags across the front of your body. On public buses, try to stow your bag where you're sitting; on trains, secure it to something if you have to leave it.

DRIVING LICENCE

International driving licences are not valid in Vietnam. If you have a motorcycle licence, you must have the document translated into a Vietnamese equivalent in order for it to be officially recognised. In practice, most foreigners drive without a licence.

EMBASSIES & CONSULATES

Visas can be obtained in your home country through the Vietnamese embassy or consulate. See p923 for more information.

Embassies & Consulates in Vietnam

Australia Hanoi (Map pp826-7; ☎ 04-831 7755; 8 Duong Dao Tan, Ba Dinh District); HCMC (Map p890; ☎ 08-829 6035; 5th fl, 5B Đ Ton Duc Thang)
Cambodia Hanoi (Map pp826-7; ☎ 04-942 4789; arch@fpt.vn; 71A P Tran Hung Dao); HCMC (Map p886; ☎ 08-829 2751; cambocg@hcm.vnn.vn; 41 Đ Phung Khac Khoan)
Canada (www.dfait-maeci.gc.ca/vietnam) Hanoi (Map pp826-7; ☎ 04-734 5000; 31 P Hung Vuong); HCMC (Map p890; ☎ 08-827 9899; 10th fl, 235 Đ Dong Khoi)

China Hanoi (Map pp826-7; ☎ 04-845 3736; eossc@hn.vnn.vn; 46 P Hoang Dieu); HCMC (Map p886; ☎ 08-829 2457; 39 Đ Nguyen Thi Minh Khai)
France Hanoi (Map pp826-7; ☎ 04-943 7719; www.ambafrance-vn.org; 57 P Tran Hung Dao); HCMC (Map p886; ☎ 08-829 7231; www.consulfrance-hcm.org; 27 Đ Nguyen Thi Minh Khai)
Germany Hanoi (Map pp826-7; ☎ 04-845 3836; www.hanoi.diplo.de; 29 P Tran Phu); HCMC (Map p886; ☎ 08-829 1967; 126 Đ Nguyen Dinh Chieu)
Indonesia (Map pp826-7; ☎ 04-825 3353; komhan@hn.vnn.vn; 50 P Ngo Quyen, Hanoi)
Japan Hanoi (☎ 04-846 3000; www.vn.emb-japan.go.jp; 27 P Lieu Giai, Ba Dinh District); HCMC (Map p890; ☎ 08-822 5314; 13-17 ĐL Nguyen Hué)
Laos Hanoi (Map pp826-7; ☎ 04-825 4576; 22 P Tran Binh Trong); HCMC (Map p886; ☎ 08-829 7667; 181 Đ Hai Ba Trung); Danang (☎ 0511-821 208; 12 Đ Tran Quy Cap
Malaysia Hanoi (Map pp826-7; ☎ 04-831 3400; mwhanoi@hn.vnn.vn; 16th fl, 6B P Lang Ha, Ba Dinh District); HCMC (Map p890; ☎ 08-829 9023; Ste 1208, Me Linh Point Tower, 2 Đ Ngo Duc Ke)
Myanmar (Map pp826-7; ☎ 04-845 3369; Bldg A3, Van Phuc Diplomatic Quarter, P Kim Ma, Ba Dinh District, Hanoi)
Netherlands (Map p886; ☎ 08-823-5932; 29 ĐL Le Duan, HCMC)
New Zealand Hanoi (Map p830; ☎ 04-824 1481; nzembhan@fpt.vn; 5th fl, 63 P Ly Thai To); HCMC (Map p886; ☎ 08-822 6907; 5th fl, 41 Đ Nguyen Thi Minh Khai)
Philippines (Map pp826-7; ☎ 04-943 7873; hanoipe@dfa.gov.ph; 27B P Tran Hung Dao, Hanoi)
Singapore (Map pp826-7; ☎ 04-823 3965; www.mfa.gov.sg; 41-43 P Tran Phu, Hanoi)
Thailand Hanoi (Map pp826-7; ☎ 04-823 5092; thaconho@hcm.vnn.vn; 63-65 P Hoang Dieu); HCMC (Map p886; ☎ 08-932 7637; 77 Đ Tran Quoc Thao)
UK (www.uk-vietnam.org) Hanoi (Map p830; ☎ 04-936 0500; 4th fl, 31 P Hai Ba Trung); HCMC (Map p886; ☎ 08-829 8433; 25 ĐL Le Duan)
USA (http://usembassy.state.gov/vietnam) Hanoi (☎ 04-772 1500; 7 P Lang Ha, Ba Dinh District); HCMC (Map p886; ☎ 08-822 9433; 4 ĐL Le Duan)

Vietnamese Embassies & Consulates Abroad

Australia Canberra (☎ 02-6286 6059; vembassy@webone.com.au; 6 Timbarra Cres, O'Malley, ACT 2606); Sydney (☎ 02-9327 2539; tlssyd@auco.net.au; 489 New South Head Rd, Double Bay, NSW 2028)
Canada (☎ 613-236 0772; www.vietnamembassy-canada.ca; 470 Wilbrod St, Ottawa, ON K1N 6M8)
China Beijing (☎ 010-6532 1125; vnaemba@mailhost.cinet.co.cn; 32 Guanghua Lu, 100600); Guangzhou (☎ 020-8652 7908; Jin Yanf Hotel, 92 Huanshi Western Rd)
France (☎ 01 44 14 64 00; 62-66 rue Boileau, 75016 Paris)
Germany (☎ 228-357 021; Konstantinstrasse 37, 5300 Bonn 2)
Hong Kong (☎ 22-591 4510; 15th fl, Great Smart Tower, 230 Wan Chai Rd, Wan Chai)
Japan Tokyo (☎ 03-3466 3311; 50-11 Moto Yoyogi-Cho, Shibuya-ku, 151); Osaka (☎ 06-263 1600; 10th fl, Estate Bakurocho Bldg, 1-4-10 Bakurocho, Chuo-ku)
UK (☎ 020-7937 1912; 12 Victoria Rd, London W8 5RD)
USA Washington (☎ 202-861 0737; www.vietnamembassy-usa.org; Ste 400, 1233 20th St NW, DC 20036); San Francisco (☎ 415-922 1707; www.vietnamconsulate-sf.org; Ste 430, 1700 California St, CA 94109)

FESTIVALS & EVENTS

Vietnam's major festival is Tet – see p906 for details.

Ngay Mot & Ngay Ram Pagodas are packed with Buddhist worshippers on the 1st and 15th days of the lunar month; and tasty, cheap vegetarian meals are served around them.
Tiet Doan Ngo (Summer Solstice) Human effigies are burnt to satisfy the need for souls to serve in the God of Death's army, on the 5th day of 5th lunar month.
Trung Nguyen (Wandering Souls Day) On the 15th day of the 7th lunar month, offerings are presented to the ghosts of the forgotten dead.
Mid-Autumn Festival On the night of 15 August, children walk the streets carrying glowing lanterns, and people exchange gifts of mooncakes.

FOOD & DRINK

Food

One of the delights of visiting Vietnam is the cuisine; there are said to be nearly 500 traditional Vietnamese dishes. Generally, food is superbly prepared and very cheap…and you never have to go very far to find it.

Aside from the usual delightful Southeast Asian fruits, Vietnam has its own unique *trai thanh long* (green dragon fruit), a bright fuchsia-coloured fruit with green scales. Grown mainly along the coastal region near Nha Trang, it has white flesh flecked with edible black seeds, and tastes something like a mild kiwifruit.

Pho is the Vietnamese name for the noodle soup that is eaten at all hours of the day, but especially for breakfast. *Com* are rice dishes. You'll see signs saying *pho* and *com* everywhere. Other noodle soups to try are *bun bo Hué* and *hu tieu*.

Spring rolls (*nem* in the north, *cha gio* in the south) are a speciality. These are normally dipped in *nuoc mam* (fish sauce), though many foreigners prefer soy sauce (*xi dau* in the north, *nuoc tuong* in the south).

Because Buddhist monks of the Mahayana tradition are strict vegetarians, *an chay* (vegetarian cooking) is an integral part of Vietnamese cuisine.

Street stalls or roaming vendors are everywhere, selling steamed sweet potatoes, rice porridge and ice-cream bars even in the wee hours. There are many other Vietnamese nibbles to try:

Bap xao Fresh, stir-fried corn, chillies and tiny shrimp.
Bo bia Nearly microscopic shrimp, fresh lettuce and thin slices of Vietnamese sausage rolled up in rice paper and dipped in a spicy-sweet peanut sauce.
Hot vit lon For the brave. Steamed, fertilised duck egg in varying stages of development (all the way up to recognisable duckling), eaten with coarse salt and bitter herb.
Sinh to Shakes made with milk and sugar or yogurt, and fresh tropical fruit.

Vietnamese people don't usually end meals with dessert, which isn't to say they don't have a sweet tooth. Many sticky confections are made from sticky rice, such as *banh it nhan dau,* made with sugar and bean paste and sold wrapped in banana leaf.

Try *che,* a cold, refreshing sweet soup made with sweetened black bean, green bean or corn. It's served in a glass with ice and sweet coconut cream on top.

Drink

Memorise the words *bia hoi,* which mean 'draught beer'. Similar to this is *bia tuoi,* or 'fresh beer'. Quality varies but it's generally OK and supercheap (3000d per litre!). Places that serve *bia hoi* usually also have cheap food.

Several foreign labels brewed in Vietnam under licence include BGI, Tiger, Fosters, Carlsberg and Heineken. National and regional brands – cheaper, and typically lighter than light – include Halida, Huda, Saigon and Bia 333 *(ba ba ba).*

Whatever you drink, make sure that it's been boiled or bottled. Ice is generally safe on the tourist trail, but not guaranteed elsewhere.

Vietnamese *ca phe* (coffee) is fine stuff and there is no shortage of cafés in which to sample it. Try seeking out the fairy-lit garden cafés where young couples stake out dark corners for smooch sessions.

Foreign soft drinks are widely available. An excellent local treat is *soda chanh* (carbonated mineral water with lemon and sugar) or *nuoc chanh nong* (hot, sweetened lemon juice).

GAY & LESBIAN TRAVELLERS

Vietnam is pretty hassle-free for gay travellers. There's not much in the way of harassment, nor are there official laws on same-sex relationships (although the government considers homosexuality a 'social evil'). Vietnamese same-sex friends often walk with arms around each other or holding hands, and guesthouse proprietors are unlikely to question the relationship of same-sex travel companions. But be discreet – public displays of affection are not socially acceptable whatever your sexual orientation.

Check out **Utopia** (www.utopia-asia.com) to obtain contacts and useful travel information.

HOLIDAYS

The Lunar New Year (Tet) is Vietnam's most important annual festival. The Tet holiday officially lasts three days, but many Vietnamese take the following week off work, so hotels, trains and buses are booked solid – and most everything else shuts down. If visiting Vietnam during Tet, memorise this phrase: *Chuc mung nam moi!* (Happy New Year!). Smiles in response are guaranteed. Vietnamese public holidays:

Tet (Tet Nguyen Dan) 7 February 2008 (Year of the Rat), 26 January 2009 (Year of the Buffalo)
Liberation Day 30 April; in 1975 Saigon surrendered to the Hanoi-backed forces on this date.
International Workers' Day 1 May
Ho Chi Minh's Birthday 19 May
National Day 2 September; commemorates the proclamation of the Declaration of Independence of the Democratic Republic of Vietnam by Ho Chi Minh in 1945.

INTERNET ACCESS

Internet access is available throughout Vietnam, sometimes in the most surprising backwaters. Faster ADSL connections are becoming more widespread and wi-fi is becoming common in the bigger cities. USB drives are often available at photography shops and most computers have USB inputs in Vietnam. Travellers can put portable web browsers on their USB drives with all their saved passwords to bypass potential spyware at internet cafés.

The cost for internet access ranges from about 100d to 500d per minute.

INTERNET RESOURCES

Economist.com (www.economist.com/countries/Vietnam/index.cfm) A great news source with an in-depth country profile.

Travelfish.org (www.travelfish.org) Well-written and in-depth articles and reviews on the region.

Vietnam Adventures (www.vietnamadventures.com) Full of practical travel information, and features monthly adventures and specials.

LEGAL MATTERS

Most Vietnamese never call the police, preferring to settle legal disputes on the spot (either with cash or fists). If you lose something really valuable such as your passport or visa, you'll need to contact the police. For incidents on the street, seek out the tourist police that patrol the main tourism (and theft) spots in the biggest cities.

The Vietnamese government is seriously cracking down on the burgeoning drug trade. You may face imprisonment and/or large fines for drug offences, and drug trafficking can be punishable by death.

MAPS

Basic road maps of Vietnam and major cities such as Hanoi, HCMC (Saigon), Hué and Nha Trang are readily available. Vietnam Tourism publishes a handy travel atlas (*ban do du lich*), available at bigger bookshops.

MEDIA

Magazines & Newspapers

The English-language *Vietnam News* is published daily and will do at a pinch.

Of more interest are the monthly *Vietnam Economic Times* (VET) and the weekly *Vietnam Investment Review* (VIR). VET's free insert, the *Guide*, is an excellent source of leisure information and can be picked up in hotels, bars and restaurants in larger cities. VIR's free supplement, *Time Out*, is another good rag for finding what's on in Ho Chi Minh City and Hanoi.

Radio & TV

Foreign radio services such as the BBC World Service, Radio Australia and Voice of America can be picked up on short-wave frequencies.

Vietnamese TV broadcasts little of interest to foreigners, but satellite dishes are everywhere, and many hotels now offer Hong Kong's Star TV, BBC, CNN and other channels.

MONEY

Vietnam's official currency is the dong (d). Banknotes come in denominations of 200, 500, 1000, 2000, 5000, 10,000, 20,000, 50,000, 100,000 and 500,000. Plastic banknotes are now in circulation, so in addition to the new 500,000 notes, there are two different types each of 50,000 and 100,000 notes. Adding even more confusion, the government has also begun minting small-denomination coins (from 200 to 5000).

US dollars and euros are the easiest currencies to exchange.

Needless to say, for your own security try to avoid carrying large wads of cash.

ATMs

ATMs are almost everywhere now. All ATMs dispense cash in dong only.

Bargaining & Tipping

For *xe om* and *cyclo* trips, as well as anywhere that prices aren't posted, you'll be expected by the locals to bargain. In high-tourist areas, you may be quoted as much as five times the going price, but not everyone is trying to rip you off. In less-travelled areas, foreigners are often quoted the Vietnamese price (you'll still want to bargain a little bit).

Bargaining politely usually invites reciprocal good-faith negotiation; getting belligerent gets you nowhere. If you can't agree on a price, thanking the vendor and walking away sometimes brings about a change of heart. When it's a matter of just a few thousand dong, don't drive too hard a bargain.

Tipping isn't expected in Vietnam, but it's enormously appreciated. Many travellers take up a collection (each contributing a few dollars) for their tour guides and drivers, after multiday tours or for outstanding service. For someone making under US$50 per month, the cost of your drink can equal half a day's wages.

Cash

The US dollar acts as a second local currency. Hotels, airlines and travel agencies all normally quote their prices in dollars, due in part to unwieldy Vietnamese prices (US$100 is around 1,600,000d). For this reason, we quote some prices in US dollars. For the best exchange rate, you should pay in dong.

Credit Cards

Visa, MasterCard and American Express (Amex) credit cards are accepted in most cities at a growing number of hotels, restaurants and shops. Getting cash advances on credit cards is also possible, but you'll be charged between 1% and 5% commission.

Exchanging Money

If you need to exchange money after hours, jewellery shops will exchange US dollars at rates comparable to, or even slightly better than, the banks.

Exchange rates at the time of press were as follows:

Country	Unit	Dong (d)
Australia	A$1	13,482
Cambodia	1000r	4012
Canada	C$1	15,735
Euro zone	€1	22, 425
Japan	¥100	14,072
Laos	1000 kip	1690
New Zealand	NZ$1	11,417
Thailand	10B	5,054
UK	UK£1	32,245
USA	US$1	16,177

Travellers Cheques

Travellers cheques in US dollars can be exchanged for local dong at certain banks; Vietcombank is usually a safe bet, although staff will charge a commission of 1% if you exchange cheques for dong. Most hotels and airline offices will not accept travellers cheques.

POST

International postal service from Vietnam is not unreasonably priced when compared with most countries, though parcels mailed from smaller cities and towns may take longer to arrive at their destinations. Be aware that customs will inspect the contents before you ship anything other than documents, so don't show up at the post office with a carefully wrapped parcel ready to go. It will get eviscerated on the table.

Take your letters to the post office yourself and make sure that the clerk franks them while you watch so that someone for whom the stamps are worth a day's salary does not soak them off and throw your letters away.

Poste restante works in the larger cities but don't count on it elsewhere. There is a small surcharge for picking up poste restante letters. All post offices are marked with the words *buu dien*.

RESPONSIBLE TRAVEL

The tourism industry in Vietnam is very responsive to the desires of travellers; if you make it clear that you'll vote with your dong for businesses and tour operators who do what they can to pick up trash, not harm wildlife, treat animals humanely and act in a generally responsible manner then hopefully 'ecotourism' and 'responsible travel' will become more than marketing buzz words.

Buying coral, limestone or dried sea life encourages such harvesting to meet the demand, meanwhile destroying or killing the living ecosystems that travellers visit to enjoy. In the same vein, sampling 'exotic' meats such as muntjac, seahorse or bat may seem culinarily adventurous, but many of these species are endangered. Help preserve vulnerable species by not eating them.

Beggars, especially young ones, are often part of an organised operation run by shady characters. Giving money only perpetuates the exploitation. If nothing else, giving handouts encourages a reliance on begging. Donating to a country-specific development organisation or patronising businesses that provide job training to those in need is a better use of good intentions.

A growing crisis in Vietnam is the accelerating spread of HIV/AIDS. For the protection of others and yourself, please practise safe sex.

STUDYING

To qualify for a student visa, you need to study at a bona fide university (as opposed to a private language centre or with a tutor). Universities require that you study 10 hours per week. Lessons usually last for two hours per day, for which you pay tuition of around US$5.

Decide whether you want to study in northern or southern Vietnam, because the regional dialects are very different. See Courses in Hanoi (p831) or HCMC (p888) for school listings.

TELEPHONE

The cheapest and simplest way to make an International Direct Dial (IDD) call is to dial ☎ 17100 plus the country code and phone number. These calls cost about 20,000d per minute to most countries. Vietnam's country code is ☎ 84.

In HCMC and Hanoi, it's possible to make reverse-charge calls at the main post offices. The telephone booking desk has a list of toll-free numbers you can call for a nominal fee, to connect with an international operator or long-distance service.

Useful numbers:

Directory assistance (☎ 116)
General information (☎ 1080)
International operator (☎ 110)
International prefix (☎ 00)
Time (☎ 117)

For mobile phones, Vietnam uses GSM 900/1800, which is compatible with most of Southeast Asia, Europe and Australia but not with North America. If you have a compatible phone, you can buy a SIM card with a local number in Vietnam. Mobile-phone service providers such as Vinaphone and MobiFone sell prepaid phonecards in denominations of 30,000d and up.

Calls to mobile phones cost more than those to local numbers. Mobile-phone numbers start with the digits ☎ 0903, ☎ 0913 or ☎ 0908.

TOILETS

Most hotels have the familiar Western-style sit-down toilets, but squat toilets in varying states of refinement exist in some cheap hotels and public places such as restaurants and bus stations. Hotels usually supply a roll, but you'd be wise to keep a stash of toilet paper with you while travelling.

As public toilets are scarce, ask and ye shall usually receive the blessing to use the toilet at a nearby hotel, restaurant or shop – again, BYOTP (bring your own toilet paper).

TOURIST INFORMATION

Tourist offices in Vietnam have a different philosophy from the majority of tourist offices worldwide. These government-owned enterprises are really travel agencies whose primary interest is turning a profit.

Though traveller cafés have a similar agenda, they're generally a better source of information and offer cheaper ways of getting to where you're going. Hitting up your fellow travellers for information is an excellent way to get the latest, greatest scoop on the where and how.

TRAVELLERS WITH DISABILITIES

Vietnam poses many technical challenges for the disabled traveller, some of which include the lack of lifts; a steeplechase of kerbs, steps and uneven pavements, where they exist; plus problematic squat toilets in narrow stalls.

Nonambulatory Vietnamese people get around in hand-pumped vehicles or tricked-out motorbikes, while the poorest of the poor are simply hand-pulled or self-propelled on boards outfitted with wheels. Foreigners can get around in a hired car with driver and/or guide, which is not prohibitively expensive.

Travellers with crutches or canes should do OK, and can usually find ground-floor rooms. Those who have vision, hearing or speech impairments might want to hire a guide or travel with a companion in order to get around.

Check out Lonely Planet's **Thorn Tree** (http://thorntree.lonelyPlanet.com) to connect with other travellers; search under the Southeast Asia branch.

Vietnam-veteran groups that organise tours to Vietnam might also have some good travel tips, or seek advice from the organisations listed in the Southeast Asia Directory (p923).

VISAS

People of all nationalities require a visa to enter the country, and while Vietnamese bureaucracy is legendary, completing the visa application is pretty painless. You'll need at least one passport-sized photo to accompany the visa application. Travellers shouldn't arrive at a Vietnamese border or airport without a visa; it's necessary to get one in advance from a Vietnamese embassy or consulate abroad.

Tourist visas are valid for a single 30-day stay and enable you to enter and exit the country via any international border (make sure to specify this when arranging your visa). Depending on where you acquire it, prices for single-entry tourist visas vary from US$30 to US$60. Cambodia, where your visa application can be processed on the same day, is the most convenient place in Southeast Asia to get a Vietnamese visa. Bangkok is another popular place, as many travel agents offer cheap packages including both an air ticket and a visa.

If you plan to spend more than a month in Vietnam or travel overland between Laos, Vietnam and Cambodia, it's possible to get a three-month multiple-entry visa. These are not available from all Vietnamese embassies but can be picked up for US$70 in Cambodia and for US$85 in the USA.

Business Visas

There are several advantages in having a business visa: such visas are usually valid for three or six months; they can be issued for multiple-entry journeys; you are permitted to work in Vietnam; and the visas can be extended with relative ease. The notable disadvantage is cost, which is about four times as much as a tourist visa.

Getting a business visa tends to be easier once you've arrived in Vietnam; most travel agencies can arrange one for you, sponsor and all.

Visa Extensions

If you've got the dollars, they've got the rubber stamp. Visa extensions cost around US$30, but go to a travel agency to get this taken care of – turning up at the immigration police yourself usually doesn't work. The procedure takes one or two days (your passport is needed) and is readily accomplished in major cities such as Hanoi, HCMC, Danang and Hué.

Official policy is that you are permitted one visa extension only, for a maximum of 30 days. Be on the lookout for sudden changes to these regulations.

VOLUNTEERING

Some good options:

15 May School (☎ 08-837 7591; www.15mayschool.org; 245 Đ Nguyen Trai) A school in HCMC for disadvantaged children, which provides free education and vocational training.

Idealist.org (www.idealist.org) Look up volunteer opportunities with nonprofit organisations worldwide.

Street Voices (www.streetvoices.com.au) Donate your skills, time or money to help give street children career opportunities. Street Voices' primary project is KOTO on Van Mieu restaurant (see p834); check its website to see what you can do to help in Vietnam or Australia.

United Nation's Development programme (www.undp.org.vn) Information on development issues in Vietnam and a limited selection of volunteer and internship opportunities.

WOMEN TRAVELLERS

While it always pays to be prudent (avoid dark lonely alleys at night), foreign women have rarely reported problems in Vietnam. Most Vietnamese women do not frequent bars on their own; be aware that you may receive unwanted – though usually harmless – advances if drinking or travelling alone. When travelling on overnight trains it's a good idea to travel with a companion to keep an eye on your bags when you use the toilet, and on each other if you have any overly friendly strangers sharing your compartment.

Some Asian women travelling with Western men have occasionally reported verbal abuse from Vietnamese people who stereotype them as prostitutes. However, with the increase of foreign tourists visiting the country, locals are becoming more accustomed to seeing couples of mixed ethnicity.

Southeast Asia Directory

CONTENTS

This chapter includes general information about Southeast Asia. Specific information for each country is listed in the individual country directories.

ACCOMMODATION

The accommodation listed in this guidebook occupies the low end of the price and amenities scale. 'Bare bones', 'basic' and 'simple' typically mean that the room has four walls, a bed and a fan (handy for keeping mosquitoes at bay). In the cheapest instances, the bathroom is usually shared. Most places geared to foreigners have Western-style toilets, but multistorey hotels that cater to locals usually have Asian squat toilets. Air-con, private bathrooms and well-sealed rooms are treated as 'splurges' in this guidebook. Camping is not a widespread option. Accommodation in this book is listed by price and, unless stated otherwise, includes private bathrooms.

Be a smart shopper when looking for a room. Always ask for the price first, then ask to see a room for cleanliness, comfort and quiet. Don't feel obligated to take a room just because the place is mentioned in Lonely Planet. Sometimes the quality of a guesthouse plummets after gaining a mention in Lonely Planet, but this can be corrected by diligent travellers who exercise their own judgment.

If the price is too high, ask if they have anything cheaper. Don't use the price listed in Lonely Planet as a bargaining chip. We list independent businesses that can raise or lower their prices at will without notifying us. Unless it is the low season, most lodgings don't bargain over their rates. Once you've paid for a room there is no chance of a refund, regardless of the size of the rat that scurried across the floor. It is recommended to pay per day rather than in bulk, but be courteous and pay first thing in the morning to keep staff from resorting to pushiness. Settle your bill the night before if you are catching an early bus out of town; most hotels and guesthouses do not staff their desks from midnight to 6am.

Advance reservations (especially with advance deposits) are generally not necessary. If you do make a booking, don't rely on an agent; the price will mysteriously double to pay the extra outstretched hand.

ACTIVITIES

Ocean sports and jungle trips are the major outdoor activities in Southeast Asia. For ocean sports, operators are plentiful and many beach resorts rent out gear. If you're not a beginner, consider bringing required gear from home as equipment here can be substandard.

Diving & Snorkelling

Southeast Asia is a diving and snorkelling paradise. If you've never seen Southeast Asia's jewel-hued waters before, just about anywhere will seem amazing. But there are many diving and snorkelling hot spots in Thailand, Malaysia, Indonesia and the Philippines.

In Indonesia, Bali is the diving superstar, but there are countless small islands and reefs between Flores, Timor, Komodo, Maluku and Sulawesi. Pulau Weh, off the coast of Sumatra, has a stunning underwater landscape to explore.

There's some diving on the west coast of Malaysia, but it's better on the east coast, where Pulau Tioman, Pulau Redang and Pulau Perhentian are just some of the possibilities. There are also sites in Malaysian Borneo.

In Thailand, well-heeled divers from across the globe travel to Phuket and its nearby islands, including Phang-Nga and the world-famous Similan and Surin Islands. However, some of the inland reefs on Thailand's west coast bear scars from the 2004 tsunami. In the Gulf of Thailand, off the east coast, Ko Samui, Ko Pha-Ngan and Ko Tao all have dive outfits that tend to be in the backpacker price range.

In the Philippines, head to diving hot spot Puerto Galera, or to Palawan for wreck dives.

A few noteworthy spots for snorkelling include Lovina in Bali and the Gili Islands, both in Indonesia; Pulau Tioman and Pulau Perhentian on Malaysia's east coast; and Ko Pha-Ngan and Ko Tao in Thailand.

Before scuba diving or snorkelling, obtain reliable information about physical and environmental concerns at the diving or snorkelling site (eg from a reputable local dive operation). If you're diving, make sure you're healthy and that you're only diving at sites within your realm of experience; if available, engage the services of a competent, professionally trained dive instructor.

Opinions vary about whether Southeast Asia is a reputable spot to gain diving certificates; the island of Ko Tao in Thailand is regarded as one of the cheapest places to do so, but dive operators in other locations complain that Ko Tao is a dive factory, simply passing people through the machine.

Surfing

Indonesia is the biggest surfing destination in Asia. For years surfers have been carting their boards to isolated outposts in search of long, deserted breaks. Kuta in Bali is a famous spot, but there's surf right along the south coast of the inner islands – from Sumatra

RESPONSIBLE DIVING

Please consider the following tips when diving and help preserve Southeast Asia's reefs:

- Never use anchors on the reef and take care not to ground boats on coral.
- Avoid touching or standing on living marine organisms or dragging equipment across the reef. Polyps can be damaged by even the gentlest contact. If you must hold on to the reef, only touch exposed rock or dead coral.
- Be conscious of your fins. Even without contact, the surge from fin strokes near the reef can damage delicate organisms. Take care not to kick up clouds of sand, which can smother organisms.
- Practise and maintain proper buoyancy control. Major damage can be done by divers descending too fast and colliding with the reef.
- Take great care in underwater caves. Spend as little time within them as possible as your air bubbles may be caught within the roof and thereby leave organisms high and dry. Take turns to inspect the interior of a small cave.
- Resist the temptation to collect or buy coral or shells or to loot marine archaeological sites (mainly shipwrecks).
- Ensure that you take home all your rubbish and any litter you may find as well. Plastics in particular are a serious threat to marine life.
- Do not feed fish.
- Minimise your disturbance of marine animals. Never ride on the backs of turtles.

RESPONSIBLE TREKKING

To help preserve the ecology and beauty of Southeast Asia, consider the following tips when trekking.

Rubbish

- Carry out all your rubbish. Don't overlook easily forgotten items, such as silver paper, orange peel, cigarette butts and plastic wrappers. Empty packaging should be stored in a dedicated rubbish bag. Make an effort to carry out rubbish left by others.
- Never bury your rubbish: digging disturbs soil and ground cover, and encourages erosion. Buried rubbish is likely to be dug up by animals, who may be injured or poisoned by it. It may also take years to decompose.
- Minimise waste by taking minimal packaging and no more food than you will need. Take reusable containers or stuff sacks.
- Sanitary napkins, tampons, condoms and toilet paper should be carried out, despite the inconvenience. They burn and decompose poorly.

Human Waste Disposal

- Contamination of water sources by human faeces can lead to the transmission of all sorts of nasties. Where there is a toilet, please use it. Where there is none, bury your waste. Dig a small hole 15cm (6in) deep and at least 100m (320ft) from any watercourse. Cover the waste with soil and a rock.
- Ensure that these guidelines are applied to a portable toilet tent if one is being used by a large trekking party. Encourage all party members, including porters, to use the site.

Washing

- Don't use detergents or toothpaste in or near watercourses, even if they are biodegradable.
- For personal washing, use biodegradable soap and a water container (or even a lightweight, portable basin) at least 50m (160ft) away from the watercourse. Disperse the waste water widely to allow the soil to filter it fully.
- Wash cooking utensils 50m (160ft) from watercourses using a scourer, sand or snow instead of detergent.

Erosion

- Hillsides and mountain slopes, especially at high altitudes, are prone to erosion. Stick to existing tracks and avoid short cuts.
- If a well-used track passes through a mud patch, walk through the mud so as not to increase the size of the patch.
- Avoid removing the plant life that keeps topsoils in place.

Fires & Low-Impact Cooking

- Don't depend on open fires for cooking. The cutting of wood for fires in popular trekking areas can cause rapid deforestation. Cook on a light-weight kerosene, alcohol or Shellite (white gas) stove and avoid those powered by disposable butane gas canisters.
- Fires may be acceptable below the tree line in areas that get very few visitors. If you light a fire, use an existing fireplace. Don't surround fires with rocks. Use only dead, fallen wood. Remember the adage 'the bigger the fool, the bigger the fire'. Use minimal wood, just what you need for cooking. In huts, leave wood for the next person.
- Ensure that you fully extinguish a fire after use. Spread the embers and flood them with water.

through to Sumbawa, and Sumba across to Papua. Pulau Nias, off the coast of Sumatra, is another beloved spot.

Siargao in the Philippines is another surf spot.

Trekking

Trekking in Southeast Asia isn't on the same mountain scale as in Nepal, but the more demure peaks are home to many minority hill-tribe villages, which host overnight trekking parties. The northern Thai cities of Chiang Mai, Mae Hong Son and Chiang Rai are very popular with prospective trekkers, turning Dr Livingstone fantasies into organised-tour realities.

Muang Sing in Laos has developed an award-winning ecotourism project for visits to local ethnic minority villages. The treks to Gunung Rinjani in Indonesia have earned similar praise for preserving the environment and local culture. The mountain village of Sapa in Vietnam is another base for organised hill-tribe journeys.

Malaysia has some excellent national parks, including Taman Negara, Gunung Mulu National Park and Kinabalu National Park, which holds the summit of 4101m-high Mt Kinabalu, one of the region's highest peaks.

Once you've climbed a volcano, sucked in a lungful of sulphur gas and peered into the forbidding caldera, you may never again be satisfied by the rewards of an ordinary mountain trek. In Indonesia, it's easy to organise treks through Sumatra's volcanic peaks in Berastagi. Java's volcanic peaks, such as Gunung Merapi, can be a taxing climb, while spectacular Gunung Bromo is more of a stroll. Gunung Batur and Gunung Agung volcanoes in Bali are popular day trips. But volcanoes aren't the only trekking options in Indonesia: Bukit Lawang has orang-utan-filled jungle, and outer regions such as Papua and Sulawesi, offer more adventurous, deep-immersion trekking.

In the Philippines, the volcanic Mt Mayon, Mt Kanlaon and Mt Isarog are interesting climbs. There are also some stunning trips in the Cordillera region of North Luzon, including treks around the rice terraces of Banaue and Bontoc.

Before embarking on a trek, make sure you are healthy and feel comfortable walking for a sustained period. Ask before you set out about the environmental characteristics that can affect your walk, and ensure you walk only in tracks within your realm of experience. You should also be aware of local laws, regulations and etiquette about wildlife and the environment.

BATHING

Most hotels and guesthouses do not have hot-water showers, though places in the larger cities or in colder regions may have hot-water options for an extra charge.

At basic hotels in rural towns the bathrooms usually have a large jar or cement trough filled with water for bathing purposes. A plastic or metal bowl is used to sluice water from the jar or trough over the body – don't jump in the trough!

Many rural people bathe in rivers or streams. If you choose to do the same, be aware that public nudity is not acceptable. Do as the locals do and bathe with some clothing on.

BOOKS

See the country chapters for recommended reading about each country (fiction and non-fiction), and the Snapshots chapter (p29) for books covering the whole region's history and culture.

For more detailed information on a country, region or city, refer to the large range of travel guidebooks produced by Lonely Planet; see the individual country directories for area-specific titles.

If you're looking to indulge a passion for underwater exploration, you might like to check out *Diving & Snorkeling Thailand*. If, on the other hand, you have a passion for simply indulging, you can't do better than *World Food Thailand, World Food Indonesia, World Food Malaysia & Singapore* or *World Food Vietnam*.

Also of interest to travellers who like to get chatty is Lonely Planet's *Southeast Asia Phrasebook*; country-specific phrasebooks include the *Burmese Phrasebook, East Timor Phrasebook, Filipino (Tagalog) Phrasebook, Hill Tribes Phrasebook, Indonesian Phrasebook, Lao Phrasebook, Malay Phrasebook, Thai Phrasebook* and *Vietnamese Phrasebook*.

BUSINESS HOURS

In the Buddhist countries of Southeast Asia businesses are typically open seven days a week. In the Muslim countries some businesses close during Friday afternoon prayers. Refer to Business Hours in the individual country directories for more details; in each chapter, opening hours will only be listed when they diverge from those in Business Hours.

CLIMATE

With the exception of northern Myanmar (Burma), all of Southeast Asia lies within the tropics. This means that regardless of when you visit, the weather is likely to be warm or even downright hot. High humidity is also common, with few areas far enough inland to enjoy thoroughly dry weather. Of course, temperatures are much cooler in the mountains.

Broadly speaking, there are two main weather patterns in the region: that of mainland Southeast Asia and that of oceanic Southeast Asia. A brief description of these patterns is provided in this section, but be sure to check the country chapters of this book, as there are significant regional variations within these patterns.

Countries located in mainland Southeast Asia generally have a relatively cool dry season from November to February, a hot dry season from March to May, and then a hot rainy season that starts sometime in June and peters out during September or October. In drier parts of the region, it might only rain in the afternoons for an hour or so during the rainy season. However, do note the Malay peninsula (ie Thailand and Malaysia) is much wetter than the rest of the subregion and that the rainy season there can bring storms that last anywhere from an hour to a week. Near the end of the monsoon season, flooding is common.

The climates of countries located in oceanic Southeast Asia are governed by two monsoons: one from the northeast, which usually falls between the months of October and April; and one from the southwest, which usually falls between the months of May and September. What this means is that it basically rains every day throughout the year, even in the so-called dry season, when afternoon showers last for about an hour. Only during the peak of the rainy season can travel be adversely affected.

See p916 for climate charts, and check out individual country directories for further information.

CUSTOMS

Customs regulations vary little around the region. Drugs and arms are strictly prohibited – death or a lengthy stay in prison are common sentences. Pornography is also a no no. Check the Customs sections in the directories of the country chapters for further details.

DANGERS & ANNOYANCES

Drugs

The risks associated with recreational drug use and distribution have grown to the point where all travellers should exercise extreme caution even in places with illicit reputations; just down the road from Kuta Beach in easy-going Bali is a jail where a number of travellers are enjoying the tropical climate for much longer than they had intended. Indeed, in Indonesia you can actually end up behind bars because your travel companions had dope and you didn't report them. A spell in a Thai prison is true Third World torture; in Malaysia and Singapore, possession of certain quantities of dope can lead to hanging.

The death penalty, prison sentences and huge fines are given as liberally to foreigners as to locals; no-one has evaded punishment because of ignorance of local laws. And don't think that your government can save you – it can't.

With heightened airline security after the 9/11 attacks in the USA, customs officials are zealous in their screening of both luggage and passengers.

Prostitution & Sex Tourism

Prostitution, including child prostitution, is unfortunately common in parts of Southeast Asia. Many are forced into the industry by conditions of poverty; others, including most child prostitutes, are sold into the business by relatives. These sex slaves are either trafficked overseas or forced to cater to domestic demand and local sex-tourism operators.

Fear of contracting HIV/AIDS from mature sex workers has led to increasing exploitation of (supposedly uninfected) children. Those who aren't put off by the stark realities of child prostitution in Southeast Asia should keep in mind that penalties in the region for paedophiles are severe, and other countries around the world – including Australia, New Zealand, the USA and a number of European countries – now prosecute and punish citizens for paedophile offences committed abroad.

For more information about groups working to end this exploitation, visit the website of **End Child Prostitution & Trafficking** (Ecpat; www.ecpat.net). This is a global network that works to stop child prostitution, child pornography and the trafficking of children for sexual purposes.

Scams

Every year we get hundreds of letters and emails from hapless travellers reporting that they've been scammed in Southeast Asia. In almost all cases there are two culprits: a shrewd scam artist and the traveller's own greed.

Almost all scams revolve around the unlikely scenario of a local presenting you with an opportunity to save or make lots of money. The perennial favourites include card games and gemstones. If someone asks you to join a card game be extremely wary. If the game involves money, walk away – it's rigged.

As for gemstones, if there really were vast amounts of money to be made by selling gems back home, savvy businesspeople would have a monopoly on the market already. Don't believe the people who say that they support their global wanderings by reselling gemstones; in reality they support themselves by tricking unsuspecting backpackers.

See Dangers & Annoyances in the country chapters for local scams.

Theft

Theft in Southeast Asia is usually by stealth rather than by force. Keep your money and valuables in a money belt worn underneath your clothes. Be alert to the possible presence of snatch thieves, who will whisk a camera or a bag off your shoulder. Don't store valuables in easily accessible places such as backpack pockets or packs that are stored in the luggage compartment of buses. Be especially careful about belongings when sleeping in dorm rooms.

Violent theft is very rare but occurs from time to time – usually late at night and after the victim has been drinking. Be careful walking alone at night and don't fall asleep in taxis.

Always be diplomatically suspicious of overfriendly locals.

However, don't let paranoia ruin your trip. With just a few sensible precautions, most travellers make their way across the region without incident.

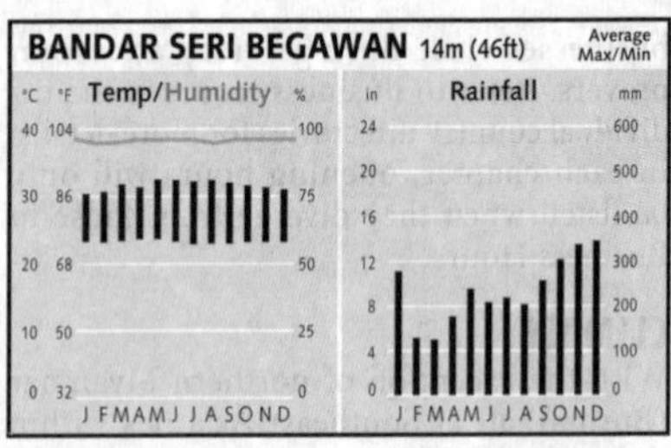

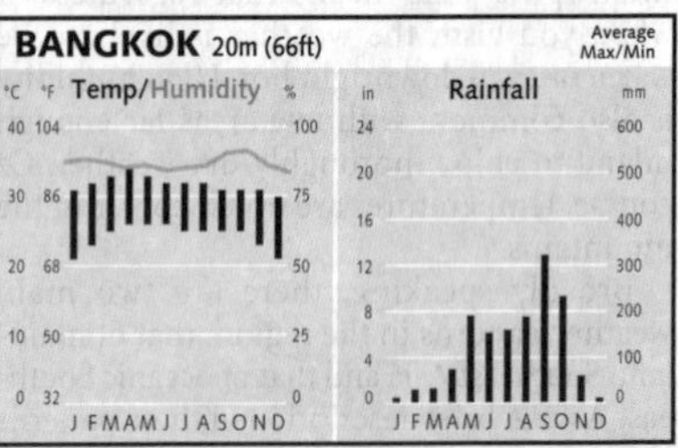

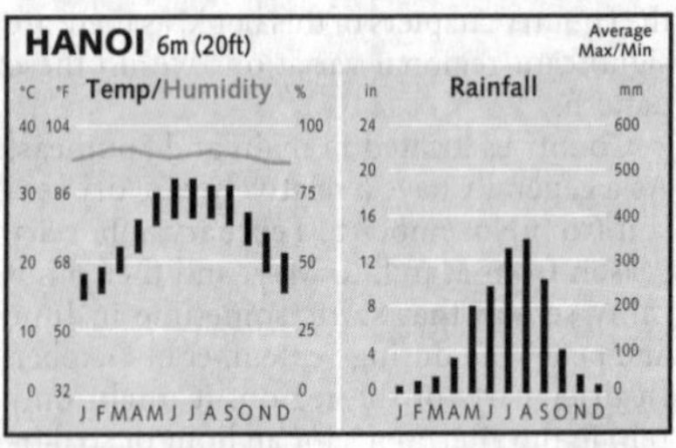

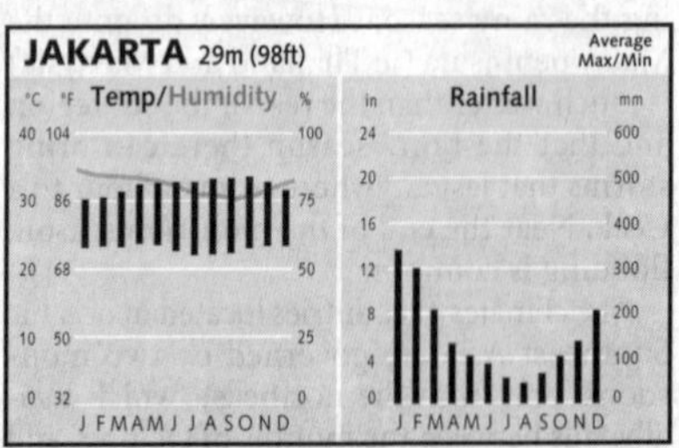

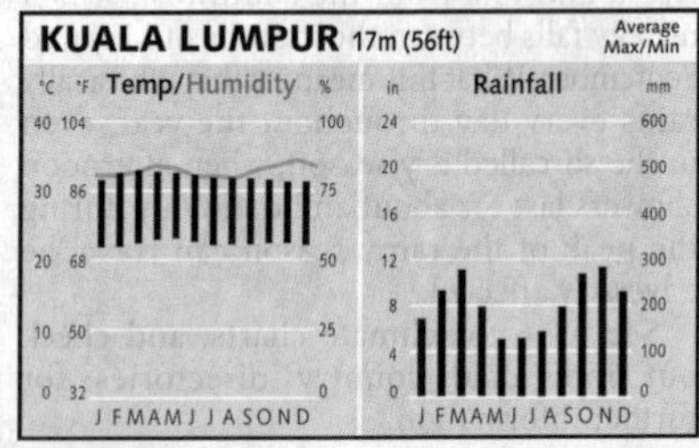

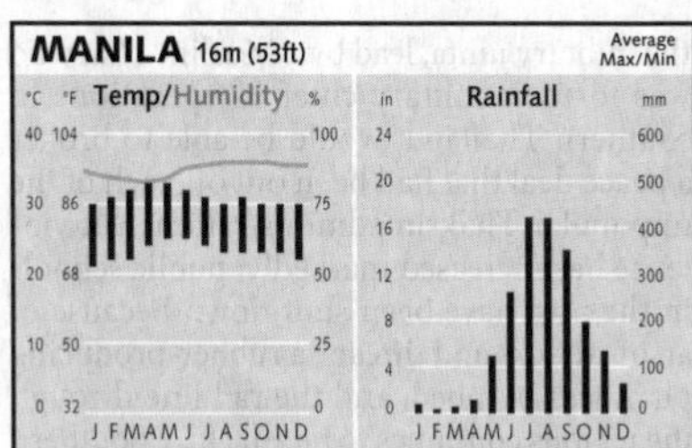

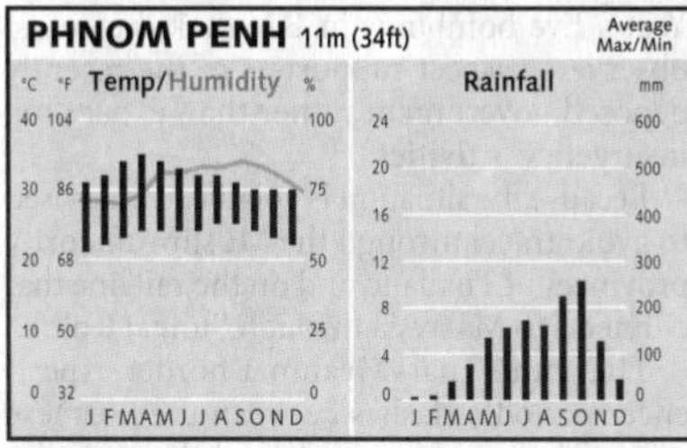

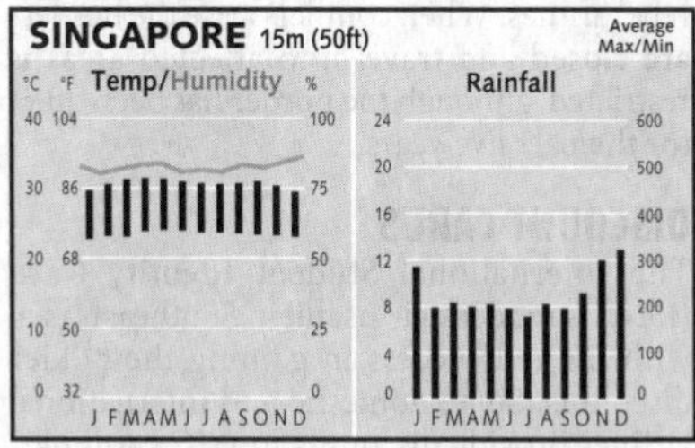

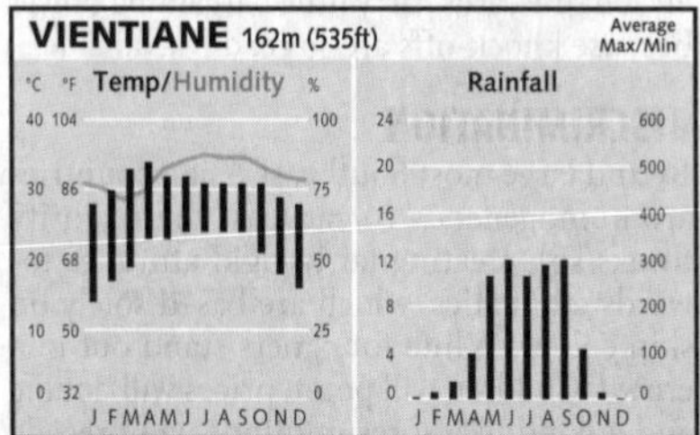

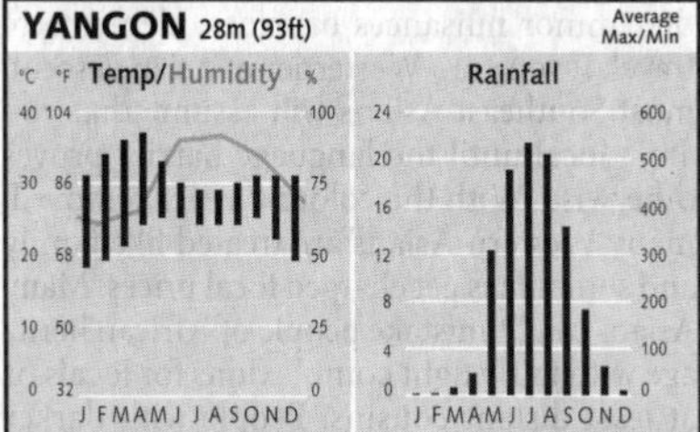

Trouble Spots

Civilian terrorism is a threat in Southeast Asia, although high-profile incidents such as the 2002 and 2005 Bali bombings have not been repeated in recent years. Indonesia, Thailand and the Philippines have fairly isolated areas where separatist groups are active. Though the violence is usually self-contained, there is always the concern that more densely populated areas or international communities will be targeted to draw attention to an insurgency's cause. Make sure you get the most up-to-date information on local conditions before setting off (and even while you're on the road). The governments of most countries issue travel warnings for their citizens, and the local English-language newspapers available in most parts of Southeast Asia are also good sources of information. At the time of writing, the following areas were considered trouble spots.

EAST TIMOR

Despite warnings and media reports, East Timor is usually fairly safe; the reported violence has been mostly political and has not been aimed at visitors. Dili is fairly safe by day but the streets are deserted at night – more due to perceived threats than actual ones. The best way to avoid trouble is to simply avoid it; if you encounter a political rally, it's best to give it a wide berth.

INDONESIA

Indonesia has several active cells of Jemaah Islamiyah (JI), a militant Islamic group with links to Al-Qaeda. This group is believed to have orchestrated the 2002 Bali nightclub bombings, in which 202 people, mainly foreign tourists, were killed. Other attacks with possible links to JI include the 2004 bombing of the Australian embassy, the 2003 bombing of the Marriott Hotel in Jakarta and the 2005 Bali bombing. However, at the time of writing, there had been a lengthy hiatus in attacks on high-profile Western targets.

Previously the site of an armed independence struggle, Sumatra's northern province of Aceh is a rare success story. After the 2004 tsunami, the Free Aceh Movement (GAM) reached a so-far lasting peace deal with Jakarta that opened up the province to international aid organisations in an effort to rebuild tsunami-destroyed communities. More recently, independent travellers have been visiting the province without incident.

Central Sulawesi is still experiencing sectarian violence, and travellers should pay careful attention to current events before visiting the region. Kota Ambon in Maluku has experienced sectarian violence in the past but there have not been any recent outbreaks.

PHILIPPINES

Insurgency groups active in the Philippines include the Moro Islamic Liberation Front (MILF) and Abu Sayyaf Group (ASG), both of which are Islamic separatist groups operating in Mindanao and the Sulu archipelago. Having orchestrated bombings and kidnappings throughout the region, ASG is the more militant and dangerous of the two. It allegedly has ties to other global Islamic terror networks and espouses a goal of a pan-Islamic state. With help from the US government, the Philippine army has weakened ASG by killing the group's reported leader, Khadaffy Janjalani, in 2006. An independence movement in the Moro (Islamic) southern region, MILF broke with its parent organisation, the Moro National Liberation Front, in the 1990s after rejecting an offer from Manila for semiautonomy. Several cease fires have been brokered and broken in the past.

Avoid travel in the Sulu archipelago and Mindanao, except for the city of Davao and the areas of northern Mindanao covered in this book. Travellers to the region should also monitor events and watch for flare-ups in violence.

The New People's Army (NPA) is the military arm of the outlawed communist party and is active throughout the country, but it is not considered a major threat to tourists.

THAILAND

The predominately Muslim southern provinces of Narathiwat, Yala, Pattani and Songkhla have long experienced periods of unrest between Islamic separatist groups and the central Thai government. Since 2002 violence has re-emerged in the region, and what was a low-wattage war on government targets has steadily escalated into the civilian sector. There are now concerns that the insurgency will morph into a purging of non-Muslim residents from the region.

In 2006, coordinated bombings on 22 commercial banks in Yala Province signalled a maturation point for terrorist activities. After the 2006 coup, observers hoped that the military junta, lead by a Muslim Thai who was former military chief of operations in southern Thailand, would be able to broker a peace deal that had been out of reach of the unpopular Thaksin administration. But violence has increased markedly: public schools in the area have been shut down because of arson attacks and threats, a rubber-producing plant was bombed, and the rail line through the regions continues to be attacked. Southern insurgents were also blamed for the 2006 New Year's Eve bombings in Bangkok, but most observers suspect supporters of the recently deposed government rather than expanding insurgency activities.

Because the situation is volatile, it is advised to avoid travel through the Muslim-majority provinces of Thailand and on the rail line that connects to Malaysia through Sungai Kolok.

The entire Thai–Myanmar border experiences periodic clashes between the Burmese army, Thai border patrols and the minority rebel armies. When conflicts arise the borders are closed and travel into affected areas is restricted, although the border has been quiet for the past five years.

DISCOUNT CARDS

The International Student Identity Card (ISIC) is moderately useful in Southeast Asia, with limited success in gaining the holder discounts. Some domestic and international airlines provide discounts to ISIC cardholders, but the cards carry little bargaining power because knock-offs are so readily available.

DISCRIMINATION

By and large most Southeast Asian countries are homogeneous (or at least the majority thinks so), creating fairly rigid attitudes towards ethnicities, which are based solely on skin colour. White foreigners stand out in a crowd. Children will point, prices will double and a handful of presumptions will precede your arrival. In general, these will seem either minor nuisances or exotic elements of travel. If you are a Westerner of Asian descent, most Southeast Asians will assume that you are a local until the language barrier proves otherwise. With the colour barrier removed, many Western Asians are treated like family and sometimes get charged local prices. Many Asians might mistake people of African heritage with fairly light complexions for locals or at least distant cousins. People with darker complexions will be regarded as foreign as white visitors, but will also be saddled with the extra baggage of Africa's inferior status in the global hierarchy. Mixed Asian and foreign couples will attract some disapproval, especially in Thailand where the existence of a large sex-tourism industry suggests that the Asian partner is a prostitute. See also right for information for gay and lesbian travellers, and p923 for tips for female travellers.

DRIVING LICENCE

Parts of Southeast Asia, including Malaysia, Indonesia and Thailand, are good spots for exploring by car and motorcycle. If you are planning to do any driving, get an International Driving Permit (IDP) from your local automobile association before you leave your home country; IDPs are inexpensive and valid for one year. In some countries (eg Malaysia) your home driving licence is sufficient, but elsewhere (eg Indonesia and Thailand) an IDP is required.

ELECTRICITY

Most countries work on a voltage of 220V to 240V at 50Hz (cycles); note that 240V appliances will happily run on 220V. You should be able to pick up adaptors in electrical shops in most Southeast Asian cities.

EMBASSIES & CONSULATES

It's important to realise what your own embassy – the embassy of the country of which you are a citizen – can and can't do to help you if you get into trouble.

Generally speaking, it won't be much help in emergencies if the trouble you're in is remotely your own fault. Remember that you are bound by the laws of the country you are in. Your embassy will not be sympathetic if you end up in jail after committing a crime locally, even if such actions are legal in your own country.

In genuine emergencies you might get some assistance, but only if other channels have been exhausted. For example, if you need to get home urgently, a free ticket home is exceedingly unlikely – the embassy would expect you to have insurance. If you have all your money and documents stolen, it might assist with getting a new passport, but a loan for onward travel is out of the question.

Most travellers should have no need to contact their embassy while in Southeast Asia, although if you're travelling in unstable regions or really going off the beaten track, it may be worth letting your embassy know – be sure to let them know when you return. In this way valuable time, effort and money won't be wasted looking for you while you're relaxing on the beach somewhere in a different country.

For details of embassies in Southeast Asia – and of Southeast Asian embassies in other countries – see Embassies & Consulates in the individual country directories.

FESTIVALS & EVENTS

Most Southeast Asian holidays revolve around religious events and provide an excellent display of the country's culture, food and music. Businesses are usually closed and travelling is difficult, so plan ahead. See also Festivals & Events in country chapters for country-specific festivals.

February

Vietnamese Tet & Chinese New Year Probably one of the loudest festivals on the planet, this is celebrated countrywide in Vietnam and in Chinese communities throughout the region with fireworks, temple visits and all-night drumming. It occurs in February.

March/April

Easter Week In March or April, the Christian holiday of Easter is observed in the Philippines, Indonesia and East Timor.

Thai, Lao & Cambodian New Year The lunar New Year begins in mid-April and, in addition to displaying religious devotion, the citizens take to the streets to dowse one another with water.

June/July

Buddhist Lent At the start of the monsoonal rains in June or July, the Buddhist monks retreat into monasteries in Myanmar, Laos and Thailand. This is the traditional time for young men to visit the monasteries.

October/November/December

Ramadan Observed in Malaysia, Indonesia, Brunei and southern Thailand during August or September, the Muslim fasting month requires that Muslims abstain from food, drink, cigarettes and sex between sunrise and sunset.

Christmas In December, various local celebrations occur in the Philippines, East Timor and Indonesia.

GAY & LESBIAN TRAVELLERS

The Philippines, Thailand and Laos have the most progressive attitudes in the region towards homosexuality; the Philippines even has legislation against gay discrimination. Singapore has a thriving gay scene, despite its antiquated antisodomy laws. Even in countries such as Malaysia, where religious law forbids homosexuality, and Vietnam, where the country's institutional attitudes are discriminatory, police arrests have been either on the decline (in the case of Vietnam), or only enforced on Muslims (in the case of Malaysia). Most urban centres have gay communities and are fairly relaxed in their attitude towards gay men and lesbians, while the countryside is more conservative.

While same-sex displays of affection are part of most Asian cultures, be discreet and respectful of the local culture. **Utopia Asian Gay & Lesbian Resources** (www.utopia-asia.com) has an excellent profile of each country's record on acceptance, as well as short reviews on gay nightspots.

INSURANCE

A travel insurance policy to cover theft, loss and medical problems is a necessity. There's a wide variety of policies available, so check the small print. For more information about the ins and outs of travel insurance, contact a travel agent or travel insurer.

Some policies specifically exclude 'dangerous activities', which can include scuba diving, motorcycling and even trekking. A locally acquired motorcycle licence is also not valid under some policies. Check that the policy covers ambulance rides, emergency flights home and, in the case of death, repatriation of a body.

Also see p934 for further information on health insurance. For info on car and motorcycle insurance, see p933.

INTERNET ACCESS

You can access email and internet services in all countries of the region, and you'll find high-speed connections in major urban areas. Good internet connections are usually commensurate with a destination's road system: well-sealed highways usually mean speedy travel through the information highway as well. Access points in Southeast Asia vary from internet cafés to post offices to guesthouses, and the cost is generally low (see Internet Access in the country directories for further details). Wireless connections are available in the bigger cities but, in general, wi-fi is still priced to suit business travellers' expense accounts.

Censorship of some sites is in effect to varying degrees across the region. In Myanmar, the government tries to restrict access to web-based email and other direct communication applications.

LEGAL MATTERS

Be sure to know the national laws so you don't unwittingly commit a crime. In all of the Southeast Asian countries, using or trafficking drugs carries stiff punishments that are enforced even if you're a foreigner.

If you are a victim of a crime, contact the tourist police, if available; they are usually better trained to deal with foreigners and foreign languages than the regular police force.

MAPS

Country-specific maps are usually sold in English bookstores in capital cities. Local tourist offices and guesthouses can also provide maps of smaller cities and towns.

MONEY

Most experienced travellers will carry their money in a combination of travellers cheques, cash, credit cards and bank cards. You'll always find situations in which one of these cannot be used, so it pays to carry them all.

ATMs

In fairly large cities ATMs are widespread and most networks talk to overseas banks, so you can withdraw cash (in the local currency) directly from your home account. But before banking on this option review the Money section in the country directories for specifics: Cambodia and Laos are virtually ATM-free.

Use your bank card only when you are dealing with cash machines, not for point-of-sale purchases. Having your card number stolen is a concern, and you will have more consumer protection with a credit card (which is paid after the purchase) than an ATM card (which deducts the cost at the time of purchase). Talk to your bank before heading off about compatibility with foreign ATMs and surcharges.

Bargaining & Tipping

Most Southeast Asian countries practise the art of bargaining. Remember that it is an art, not a test of wills, and the trick is to find a price that makes everyone happy. Bargaining is acceptable in markets and in souvenir shops where fixed prices aren't displayed. As a beginner, tread lightly by asking the price and then asking if the seller can offer a discount. The price may creep lower if you take your time and survey the object. If the discounted price isn't acceptable give a counter offer but be willing to accept something in the middle. Once you counter you can't name a lower price. Don't start haggling unless you're interested in actually buying it. If you become angry or visibly frustrated then you've lost the game.

Tipping is not standard practice but is greatly appreciated. In some international restaurants in big cities, a service charge or gratuity will be added automatically to the bill.

Cash

Having some cash (preferably US dollars) is handy, but is risky too; if you lose it, it's gone.

Credit Cards

For a splurge at a nice hotel or a crazed shopping spree in Singapore, a credit card is your best friend; however, keep careful tabs on purchases as fraud is a concern.

Exchanging Money

Currency exchange is generally straightforward throughout the region. Most banks have exchange counters that usually offer the market rate; guesthouses and businesses that deal with tourists will exchange currencies, often as a courtesy rather than an advertised endeavour, but the rates tend to be lower than businesses dealing in greater volumes of exchanges. See the individual country chapters for more details.

Other major currencies, such as the euro and the Australian dollar, are easy to change in the main centres; it's when you start getting away from regularly visited areas that your currency options become more limited.

Travellers Cheques

Travelling with a stash of travellers cheques can help if you hit an ATM desert. Get your cheques in US dollars and in large denominations, say US$100 or US$50, to avoid heavy per-cheque commission fees. Keep careful records of which cheques you've cashed, and keep this information separate from your money so you can file a claim if any cheques are lost or stolen.

PASSPORT

To enter most countries your passport must be valid for at least six months from your date of entry, even if you're only staying for a few days. It's probably best to have at least a year left on your passport if you are heading off on a trip around Southeast Asia.

Testy border guards may refuse entry if your passport doesn't have enough blank pages available. Before leaving get more pages added to a valid passport (if this is a service offered by your home country). Once on the road, you can apply for a new passport in most major Southeast Asian cities.

PHOTOGRAPHY

Airport Security

X-ray machines that claim to be film safe generally are, but you are advised to have very sensitive film (1000 ISO and above) checked by hand. *Never* put your film in your checked baggage – the X-ray machines used to check this luggage will fog your film.

Film & Equipment

For those travelling with a digital camera, most internet cafés in well-developed countries allow customers to transfer their images to an online email account or storage site and, in some cases, burn a CD. Before leaving home, find out if your battery charger will require a power adapter by visiting the website of the **World Electric Guide** (www.kropla.com/electric.htm).

Print film is readily available in cities and larger towns across Southeast Asia.

The best places to buy camera equipment or have repairs done are Singapore, Bangkok or Kuala Lumpur. Be aware that the more equipment you travel with, the more vulnerable you are to theft.

If you're after some tips, check out Lonely Planet's *Travel Photography: A Guide to Taking Better Pictures,* written by internationally renowned travel photographer, Richard I'Anson. Other books in the Lonely Planet Travel Photography series include *Landscape Travel Photography, People Travel Photography, Urban Travel Photography* and *Wildlife Travel Photography.*

Photographing People

You should always ask permission before taking a person's photograph. Many hill-tribe villagers seriously object to being photographed, or they may ask for money in exchange; if you want the photo, you should honour the price.

POST

Postal services are generally reliable across the region. Of course, it's always better to leave important mail and parcels for the big Asian centres such as Bangkok, Singapore, Kuala Lumpur and Jakarta.

There's always an element of risk in sending parcels home by sea, though as a rule they eventually reach their destination. If it's something of value, you're better off mailing home your dirty clothes to make room in your luggage for precious keepsakes. Don't send cash or valuables through government-run postal systems.

Poste restante is widely available throughout the region and is the best way of receiving mail. When getting people to write to you, ask them to leave plenty of time for mail to arrive and to print your name very clearly. Underlining the surname also helps.

SOCIAL PROBLEMS

The disparity between rich and poor is one of Southeast Asia's most pressing social concerns. Few of the region's countries have established social nets to catch people left homeless or jobless by debt mismanagement or larger problems associated with rapid industrialisation. Most destitute people migrate to the cities, doing menial labour for barely subsistence wages, or selling their bodies for more handsome profits. The attendant problems of displaced citizens include drug abuse, HIV/AIDs, and unsanitary and dangerous living conditions. Because of the Buddhist belief in reincarnation, the prevailing political wisdom is that the poor are fated to suffer because of wrongdoings committed in previous lives.

STUDYING

There is a variety of courses available throughout the region, from language, meditation and massage to *muay thai* (Thai boxing) and cooking, and from formal programmes sponsored by international agencies to informal classrooms run in homes.

Council on International Educational Exchange (www.ciee.org/study) arranges study-abroad programmes in language, art and culture in Thailand and Vietnam, hosted in local universities. The University of Texas at Austin maintains a useful website, **Study Abroad Asia** (http://asnic.utexas.edu/asnic/stdyabrd/StdyabrdAsia.html), which lists universities that sponsor overseas study programmes in Southeast Asia. Also visit Lonely Planet's **Travel Links** (www.lonelyplanet.com/travel_links), and see Studying the individual country directories for more information.

TELEPHONE

Phone systems vary widely across Southeast Asia. For international calls, most countries have calling centres (usually in post offices) or public phone booths that accept international phonecards. Each country's system is different, so it's a good idea to check under Telephone in the country directories before making a call.

You can take your mobile phone on the road with you and get respectable coverage in major population centres. However, not all mobile phones are outfitted for international use; this is especially the case for mobile phones from the USA. Check with your service provider for global-roaming fees and other particulars.

Fax services are available in most countries across the region.

TOILETS

Across the region, squat toilets are the norm, except in hotels and guesthouses geared towards tourists and international business travellers.

Next to the typical squat toilet is a bucket or cement reservoir filled with water. A plastic bowl usually floats on the water's surface or sits nearby. This water supply has a two-fold function: toiletgoers scoop water from the reservoir with the plastic bowl and use it to clean their nether regions while still squatting over the toilet; and a bowl full of water poured down the toilet takes the place of the automatic flush. More rustic toilets in rural areas may simply consist of a few planks over a hole in the ground.

Even in places where sit-down toilets are installed, the plumbing may not be designed to take toilet paper. In such cases, the usual washing bucket will be standing nearby and there will be a waste basket in which you place used toilet paper.

Public toilets are common in department stores, bus and railway stations, and large hotels. Elsewhere you'll have to make do. Of course, in land-mine-affected countries such as Laos and Cambodia, stay on the roadside and do the deed, or grin and bear it until the next town.

TOURIST INFORMATION

Most of the Southeast Asian countries have government-funded tourist offices with varying capacities of usefulness. Better information is sometimes available through guesthouses and fellow travellers. See Tourist Information in the individual country chapters for contact information.

TRAVELLERS WITH DISABILITIES

Travellers with serious disabilities will likely find Southeast Asia to be a challenging place to travel. Even the more modern cities are very difficult to navigate for mobility- or vision-impaired people. In general, care of a person with a disability is left to close family members throughout the region, and it's unrealistic to expect much in the way of public amenities.

International organisations that can provide information on mobility-impaired travel include the following:

Mobility International USA (☎ 541-343 -1284; www.miusa.org; 132 E Broadway, Suite 343; Eugene, Oregon 97401, USA)

Royal Association for Disability & Rehabilitation (Radar; ☎ 020-7250 3222; www.radar.org.uk; 12 City Forum, 250 City Rd, London EC1V 8AF, UK)

Society for Accessible Travel & Hospitality (SATH; ☎ 212-447-7284; www.sath.org; 347 Fifth Ave, Suite 610, New York, NY 10016, USA)

VISAS

Visas are available to people of most nationalities on arrival in most Southeast Asian countries, but rules vary depending on the point of entry. See Visas in the individual country directories.

Get your visas as you go rather than getting them all before you leave home; they are often easier and cheaper to get in neighbouring countries. Visas are also only valid within a certain period, which could interfere with an extended trip.

Procedures for extending a visa vary from country to country. In some cases, extensions are nearly impossible, in others they're a mere formality. And remember: look smart when you're visiting embassies, consulates and borders.

In some Southeast Asian countries you are required to have an onward ticket out of the country before you can obtain a visa to enter.

VOLUNTEERING

For long-term commitments in health, agriculture or education, contact **Voluntary Service Overseas** (VSO; www.vso.org.uk), **Australian Volunteers International** (AVI; ☎ in Australia 03-9279 1788; www.australianvolunteers.com) or the **US Peace Corps** (☎ in the USA 800-424-8580; www.peacecorps.gov) for placement in one of the Southeast Asian countries. See also Volunteering in the individual chapters for country-specific organisations.

WOMEN TRAVELLERS

While travel in Southeast Asia for women is generally safe, solo women travelling in Muslim areas have reported some negative reception. In conservative Muslim areas, local women rarely go out unaccompanied and are usually modestly dressed (including headscarves). Foreign women who enter these areas without observing local customs infrequently incur a sexual or anti-Western backlash.

Keep in mind that modesty in dress is culturally important across all Southeast Asia. Covering past the shoulders and above the knees helps define you as off limits. The ever popular spaghetti-strap singlets inadvertently send the message that you're a prostitute; likewise, save the topless sunbathing for home or the nude-magazine spread.

In conservative Muslim areas, you can sometimes cut your hassles in half just by tying a bandanna over your hair (a minimal approximation of the headscarf worn by most Muslim women).

Solo women should also be on guard when returning home late at night or arriving in a new town at night. While physical assault is rare, local men often consider foreign women as being exempt from their own society's rules of conduct regarding members of the opposite sex.

Treat overly friendly strangers, both male and female, with a good deal of caution.

Many travellers have reported small peepholes in the walls and doors of cheap hotels, some of which operate as boarding houses or brothels (often identified by the advertisement of 'day use' rates). If you can afford it, move to another hotel or guesthouse.

Use common sense about venturing into dangerous-looking areas, particularly at night or if you're alone. If you do find yourself in a tricky situation, try to extricate yourself as quickly as possible – hopping into a taxi or entering a business establishment and asking them to call a cab are often the best solutions.

Finally, you can reduce hassles by travelling with other backpackers. This doesn't necessarily mean bringing a friend from home; you can often pair up with other travellers you meet on the way.

WORKING

Teaching English is the easiest way to support yourself in Southeast Asia. For short-term gigs, Bangkok, Ho Chi Minh City (Saigon) and Jakarta have a lot of language schools and a high turnover. In Malaysia, expat families sometimes need English-speaking au pairs and, in the Philippines, English speakers are often needed as language trainers for the call centres. In Indonesia and Thailand there is some dive-school work. There is also limited opportunity for bar work in some of the beach resorts, but often these jobs are reserved for locals.

Payaway (www.payaway.co.uk) provides a handy online list of language schools and volunteer groups looking for recruits for its Southeast Asian programmes.

Transitions Abroad (www.transitionsabroad.com) and its namesake magazine cover all aspects of overseas life, including landing a job in a variety of fields. The website also provides links to other useful sites and publications.

Transport

CONTENTS

This chapter gives an overview of the transport options for getting to Southeast Asia, and getting around the region once you're there. For more specific information about getting to (and around) each country, see Transport in the country chapters.

GETTING THERE & AWAY

Step one is to get to Southeast Asia, and flying is the easiest option. The only overland possibilities from outside the region are from Papua New Guinea into Indonesia, and China into Myanmar (Burma), Vietnam or Laos.

AIR

Tickets

The major Asian gateways for cheap flights are Bangkok, Kuala Lumpur, Singapore and Denpasar (Bali). The boom of Asian budget carriers has brought about cheap fares between Chinese cities and Southeast Asia. Compare the cost of flying to an East Asian city from your home country and then connecting to a budget carrier into Southeast Asia. Some of the budget carriers based in Asia are starting to offer long-distance routes to smaller European hub cities. These low-cost fares are sometimes only available on the company's website rather than online fare search engines, so it is worth perusing the internet for budget carriers.

Also be flexible with your travel dates and know when to buy a ticket. Trips that last longer than two weeks tend to be more expensive. Buying a ticket too early or too late before your departure will affect the price as well. The ticket-purchasing sweet spot is 21 to 15 days before departure. When researching airline fares, be sure to dump your computer's cookies, which track your online activity and can sometimes result in a higher fare upon subsequent searches.

The following online resources can help in researching bargain airfares:

Attitude Travel (www.attitudetravel.com) Offers a guide to low-cost carriers in Asia, including a list of airlines and destinations.

Lonely Planet (www.lonelyplanet.com) Click on Booking & Services to research multidestination trips.

COURIER FLIGHTS

Courier flights – in which you get a bargain fare by acting as a passenger agent for a company's parcel shipment on a commercial flight – are available for trips to Asia, but they don't always represent the best deal. Travel is usually last-minute and luggage is limited to a carry-on bag. You'll need to join the Air Courier Association or the International Association of Air Travel Couriers to obtain flight listings.

ROUND-THE-WORLD & CIRCLE ASIA TICKETS

If Asia is one of many stops on a worldwide tour, consider a round-the-world (RTW) ticket, which allows a certain number of stops within a set time period as long as you don't backtrack; for more information, talk to a travel agent.

> **THINGS CHANGE…**
>
> The information in this chapter is particularly vulnerable to change. Check directly with the airline or a travel agent to make sure you understand how a fare (and ticket you may buy) works and be aware of the security requirements for international travel. Shop carefully. The details given in this chapter should be regarded as pointers and not as a substitute for your own careful, up-to-date research.

Circle Asia fares (sometimes called All Asia Passes or Discovery Pass) are offered by various airline alliances for a circular route originating in the USA, Europe or Australia and travelling to certain destinations in Asia, including Southeast and East Asia. Before committing, check out the fares offered by the budget regional carriers to see if the circle pass provides enough of a saving. Contact the individual airlines or a travel agent for more information.

From Asia

India and China are fused to major Southeast Asian cities through several low-cost airlines. Some budget carriers making the hop include **Pacific Airlines** (code BL; http://pacificairlines.com.vn), **One-Two-Go** (code OTG; www.fly12go.com), **Jetstar Asia** (code 3K; www.jetstar.com), **Air Asia** (code AK; www.airasia.com) and **Tiger Airways** (code TR; www.tigerairways.com). In most large cities with a tourist industry, there are also bucket shops that can sell cheap tickets to any destination you can dream of.

From Australia

Jetstar (code JQ; www.jetstar.com) flies into several Southeast Asian cities from Australia. Also look for cheap fares is in the travel sections of weekend newspapers such as the *Age* and the *Sydney Morning Herald*. Also try searching **Travel.com** (www.travel.com.au).

Two well-known agencies for cheap fares:

Flight Centre (☎ 133 133; www.flightcentre.com.au) Has dozens of offices throughout Australia.

STA Travel (☎ 134 782; www.statravel.com.au) Has offices in all major cities and on many university campuses.

From Canada

Canadian air fares tend to be higher than those sold in the USA, and it is more expensive to fly from the east coast than the west. The *Globe & Mail*, the *Toronto Star*, the *Montreal Gazette* and the *Vancouver Sun* are good places to look for cheap fares. **Travel CUTS** (www.travelcuts.com) is Canada's national student travel agency and has offices in all major cities.

From Continental Europe

France has a network of student travel agencies, including **OTU Voyages** (www.otu.fr), which can supply discount tickets to travellers of all ages. General travel agencies in Paris include **Nouvelles Frontières** (☎ 08 25 00 07 47; www.nouvelles-frontieres.com; 21 ave des Gobelins) or **Voyageurs du Monde** (☎ 08 92 68 83 63; www.vdm.com; 55 rue Sainte Anne).

In Switzerland, **STA Travel** (☎ 058 450 4020; www.statravel.ch; Ankerstrasse 12, Zurich) specialises in student, youth and budget fares; there are also branches in other major Swiss cities.

In the Netherlands, **NBBS Reizen** (☎ 0900 1020 300; www.nbbs.nl; Kleinpolderlaan 4, 2911 PA, Nieuwerkerk a/d IJssel) is the official student travel agency.

In Germany, **STA Travel** (☎ 01805 456 422; www.statravel.de) caters for travellers under 26.

From New Zealand

The *New Zealand Herald* has a helpful travel section. **Flight Centre** (☎ 0800 243 544; www.flight centre.co.nz) has a large central office in Auckland and many branches throughout the country, while **STA Travel** (☎ 0800 474 400; www.statravel.co.nz) has offices in Auckland, Hamilton, Palmerston North, Wellington, Christchurch and Dunedin.

From the UK

Budget carriers such as **Oasis** (code O8; www.oasishongkong.com) and **Mahan Air** (code W5; www.mahan.aero) have begun long-haul flights to Southeast Asia. Advertisements for many travel agencies appear in the travel pages of the weekend broadsheets, such as the *Independent* and the *Sunday Times*.

For students or travellers under 26, the following are popular travel agencies:

STA Travel (☎ 0871 2300 040; www.statravel.co.uk) Has offices throughout the UK.

Trailfinders (☎ 0845 058 5858; www.trailfinders.co.uk)

From the USA

Ticket promotions frequently connect Asia to Los Angeles, New York and other big cities. The *New York Times*, the *Los Angeles Times*, the *Chicago Tribune* and the *San Francisco Examiner* all produce weekly travel sections in which you will find a number of travel-agency ads and fare promos.

Students and travellers aged under 26 should try the US offices of **STA Travel** (☎ 800 781 4040; www.statravel.com).

LAND

The land borders between Southeast Asia and the rest of Asia include the frontier that Myanmar shares with India and Bangladesh, and the Chinese border with Myanmar, Laos and Vietnam. Of these, it is possible to travel overland from China into Myanmar (but not vice versa) and in either direction between China and Laos, and China

CLIMATE CHANGE & TRAVEL

Climate change is a serious threat to the ecosystems that humans rely upon, and air travel is the fastest-growing contributor to the problem. Lonely Planet regards travel, overall, as a global benefit, but believes we all have a responsibility to limit our personal impact on global warming.

Flying & Climate Change

Pretty much every form of motor travel generates CO2 (the main cause of human-induced climate change) but planes are far and away the worst offenders, not just because of the sheer distances they allow us to travel, but because they release greenhouse gases high into the atmosphere. The statistics are frightening: two people taking a return flight between Europe and the US will contribute as much to climate change as an average household's gas and electricity consumption over a whole year.

Carbon Offset Schemes

Climatecare.org and other websites use 'carbon calculators' that allow jetsetters to offset the level of greenhouse gases they are responsible for with financial contributions to sustainable travel schemes that reduce global warming – including projects in India, Honduras, Kazakhstan and Uganda.

Lonely Planet, together with Rough Guides and other concerned partners in the travel industry, supports the carbon offset scheme run by climatecare.org. Lonely Planet offsets all of its staff and author travel.

For more information check out our website: lonelyplanet.com.

and Vietnam. See p525 for information on the Myanmar–China border crossing; p387 for the Laos–China border crossing; and p837, p843 and p848 for Vietnam–China border crossings.

Another international crossing is between Indonesia and Papua New Guinea; see p330 for more information.

SEA

Ocean approaches to Southeast Asia from your home continent can be made aboard cargo ships plying various routes around the world. Ridiculously expensive and hopelessly romantic, a trip aboard a cargo ship is the perfect opportunity to write that novel that never writes itself. Ships usually have space for two to eight non-crew members, who have their own rooms but eat meals with the crew. Prices vary widely depending on the departure point, but start at around US$5000.

Charter boats can transport you from Papua New Guinea to Papua (formerly Irian Jaya) in Indonesia.

GETTING AROUND

AIR

Air travel can be a bargain within the region, especially from transit hubs such as Bangkok, Singapore and Kuala Lumpur. No-frills regional carriers such as **Air Asia** (code AK; www.airasia.com) have made travelling between capital cities cheaper than taking land transport in some cases. Air routes between Southeast Asian countries are listed in the Transport sections of each country chapter.

A little caution is necessary when buying tickets from travel agents. Carefully check the tickets to make sure that the dates meet your specifications and confirm with the airline as soon as possible. Favourite tricks include tickets with limited validity (when you've been told the tickets are valid for one year). Get recommendations from fellow travellers or ask for a list of licensed agents from the country's tourist office.

Most airports in Southeast Asia charge a departure tax, so make sure you have a bit of local currency left.

Approximate intra-Asia fares are shown on the Southeast Asian Air Fares map (p928).

Air Passes

National airlines of Southeast Asian countries frequently run promotional deals from select Western cities or for regional travel. **Airtimetable.com** (www.airtimetable.com) posts seasonal passes and promotions.

An ongoing deal is the Asean Air Pass, offered through cooperating airlines for travel in

Southeast Asia. Visit **Thai Airways International** (THAI, code THA; www.thaiair.com) for more details.

BICYCLE

Touring Southeast Asia on a bicycle has been gaining more and more supporters. Many long-distance cyclists start in Thailand and head south through Malaysia to Singapore. Road conditions are good enough for touring bicycles in most places, but mountain bikes are recommended for forays off the beaten track.

Vietnam is a great place to travel by bicycle – you can take bikes on buses, and the entire coastal route is feasible. If flat-land cycling is not your style, then Indonesia might be the challenge you're looking for. Road conditions are bad and inclines steep, but the Sumatran jungle is still deep and dark. In Laos and Cambodia, road conditions can impede two wheeling, but light traffic, especially in Laos, makes pedalling more pleasant than elsewhere. **Mr Pumpy** (www.mrpumpy.net) provides all the inside information to get your wheels spinning.

Top-quality bicycles and components can be bought in major cities such as Bangkok but, generally, fittings are hard to find. Bicycles can travel by air; check with the airline about extra charges and shipment specifications.

BOAT

Ferries and boats make trips between Singapore and Indonesia, Malaysia and Indonesia, and Thailand and Malaysia.

Typically, guesthouses or travel agents sell tickets and can provide updated departure times. Be sure to check the visa regulations at port cities.

BORDER CROSSINGS

Going through the region overland is getting easier as potholed ditches become major highways. The border crossings for the region are listed here by country; the following abbreviations are used for convenience: B (Brunei), ET (East Timor), C (Cambodia), I (Indonesia), L (Laos), M (Malaysia), My (Myanmar), P (Philippines), T (Thailand) and V (Vietnam).

Be aware of border closing times, visa regulations and any transport scams by asking your fellow travellers before making a long-distance trip or by referring to the relevant country chapters.

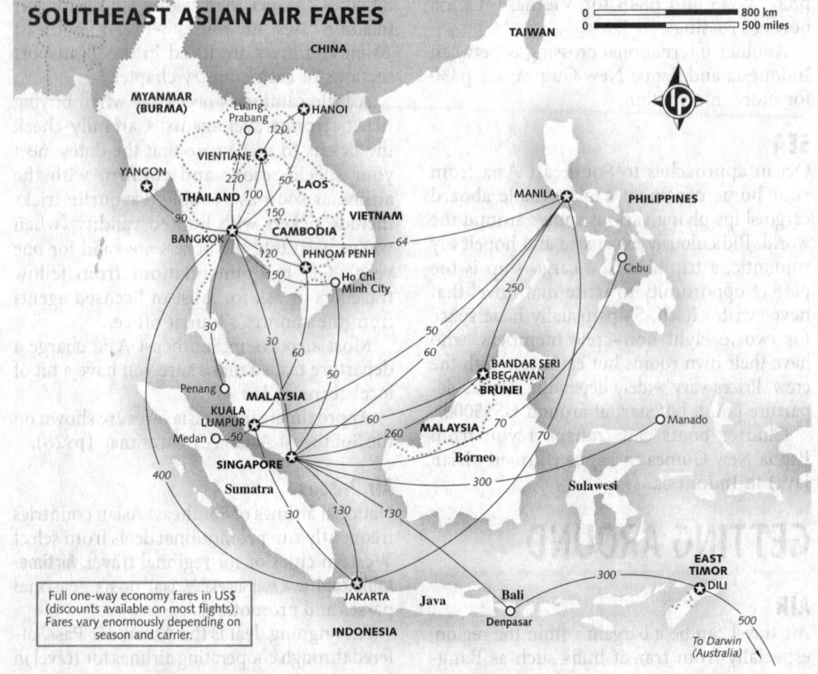

Full one-way economy fares in US$ (discounts available on most flights). Fares vary enormously depending on season and carrier.

Brunei

The Malaysian states of Sarawak and Sabah form a C clamp around Brunei. All border crossings feed into the Brunei capital of Bandar Seri Begawan.

The first four of the following crossings are from Sarawak, while the fifth is from Sabah:

- Kuala Baram (M) to Kuala Belait (B), from Miri (M); see p50, p506
- Limbang (M) to Kuala Lurah (B); see p49, p508
- Limbang (M) to Bangar (B); see p51, p508
- Lawas (M) to Bangar (B); see p51, p509
- Pulau Labuan (M) to Muara Port (B); see p49, p484

Cambodia

FROM LAOS

The only border passage to Cambodia is south of Si Phan Don (Four Thousand Islands) through Voen Kham (L) to Dom Kralor (C); see p115, p402. The main town on the Cambodian side is Stung Teng.

FROM THAILAND

There are five border crossings between Thailand and Cambodia:

- Aranya Prathet (T) to Poipet (C), which links Bangkok (T) to Siem Reap (C); see p97, p709
- Hat Lek (T) to Krong Koh Kong (C), which runs along the coast; see p113, p765

There are also three crossings in remote areas:

- Chong Jom (T) to O Smach (C); see p89, p753
- Choam Srawngam (T) to Choam (C); see p101, p755
- Ban Pakard (T) to Psar Pruhm (C); see p101, p765

FROM VIETNAM

There are three border-crossing options and word of a fourth:

- Moc Bai (V) to Bavet (C), for quick passage between Ho Chi Minh City (V) and Phnom Penh (C); see p79, see p893
- Vinh Xuong (V) to Kaam Samnor (C), linking Chau Doc (V) in the Mekong Delta to Phnom Penh (C); see p79, p900
- Tinh Bien (V) to Phnom Den (C), a remote crossing; see p81, p901
- Prek Chek (C) to Xa Xia (V), a possible new border crossing

East Timor

The Motoain (I) to Batugade (ET) border crossing (between East Timor and Indonesian West Timor) is open and serviced by bus; see p141, p297.

Indonesia

FROM EAST TIMOR

See the entry under East Timor.

FROM MALAYSIA

High-speed ferries run between Malaysia and the Indonesian island of Sumatra:

- Pulau Penang (M) and Belawan (I), which links to Medan (I); see p262, p451
- Melaka (M) and Dumai (I), which links to Bukittinggi (I); see p267, p438
- Johor Bahru (M) to Pulau Bintan and Pulau Batam in the Riau Islands (I); see p267, p456

On the island of Borneo, the Indonesia–Malaysia border can be crossed at the following spots:

- Tawau (M) to Nunukan (I), linking to Tarakan (I); see p304, p492
- Tebedu (M) and Entikong (I), which links to Kuching (M); see p310, p498

FROM SINGAPORE

Ferries run from Singapore to Pulau Bintan and Pulau Batam in the Riau Islands (I); see p267, p654.

Laos

FROM CAMBODIA

See the entry under Cambodia.

FROM THAILAND

There are five border crossings into Laos:

- Chiang Khong (T) to Huay Xai (L), which links northern Thailand to Luang Prabang (L) via boat; see p390, p744
- Nong Khai (T) to Vientiane (L); see p362, p758
- Mukdahan (T) to Savannakhet (L), a popular route between southern Laos and northeast Thailand; see p394, p756
- Chong Mek (T) to Vang Tao (L), which links Ubon Ratchathani (T) to Pakse (L); see p398, p755

TRANSPORT

- Nakhon Phanom (T) to Tha Khaek (L), a far-flung river crossing in the northeast of Thailand; see p394, p757

FROM VIETNAM

There are five land crossings from Vietnam, but only three are easily accessible:

- Lao Bao (V) to Dansavanh (L), an easy border crossing linking to Savannakhet (L); see p394, p858
- Dien Bien Phu (V) to Tay Trang (L), gateway to Phongsali province (L); see p384, p839

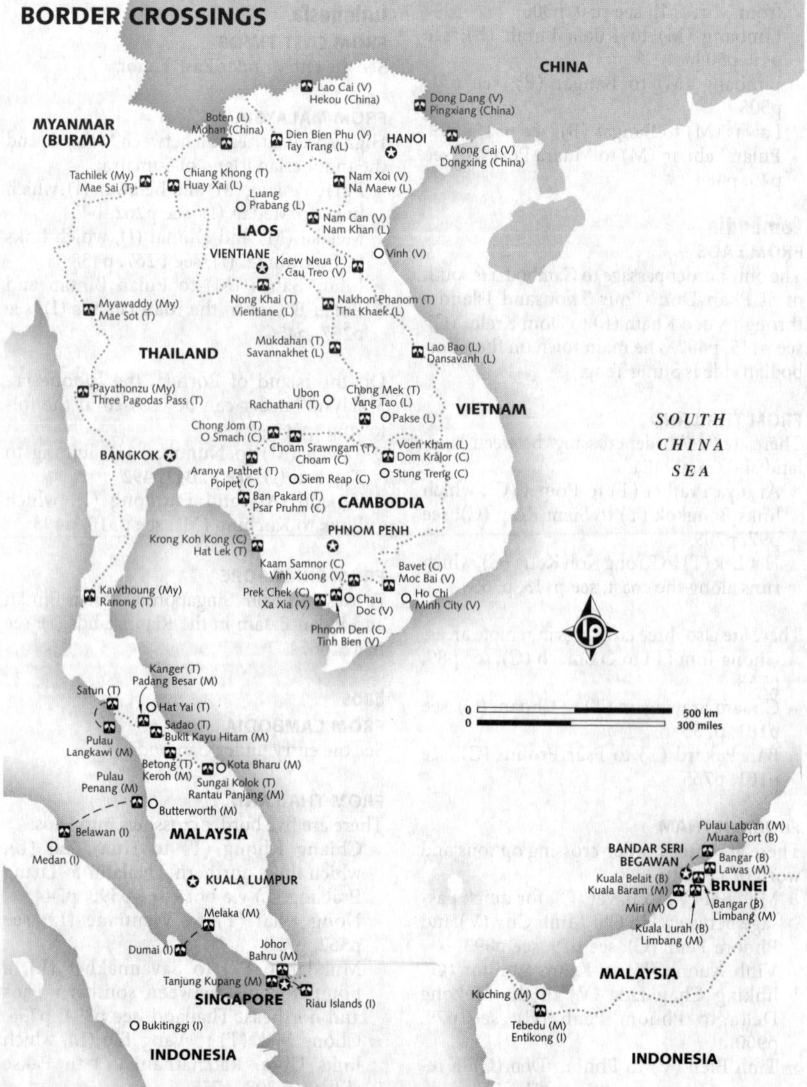

- Cau Treo (V) to Kaew Neua (L), linking to Vinh (V); see p362, p838
- Nam Can (V) to Nam Khan (L), a remote crossing; see p380, p838
- Nam Xoi (V) to Na Maew (L), another remote crossing; see p383, p839

Malaysia

FROM BRUNEI

See the entry under Brunei.

FROM INDONESIA

See the entry under Indonesia

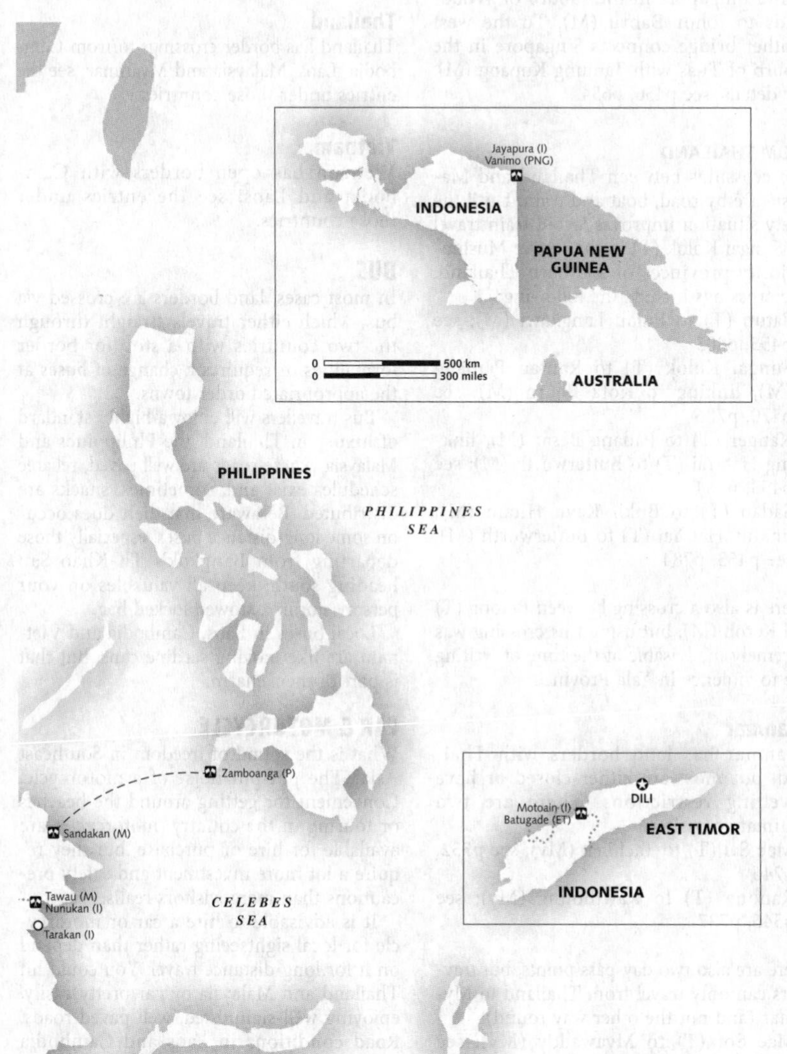

FROM THE PHILIPPINES

There are infrequent passenger ferries from Zamboanga (P) on Mindanao to Sandakan (M) in Sabah; see p488, p635.

FROM SINGAPORE

A 1km-long causeway connects the northern end of Singapore in the suburb of Woodlands to Johor Bahru (M). To the west another bridge connects Singapore in the suburb of Tuas with Tanjung Kupang (M). For details, see p456, p654.

FROM THAILAND

The crossings between Thailand and Malaysia are by road, boat and train. Until the safety situation improves, avoid train travel via Sungai Kolok (T) in the restive Muslim-majority provinces of southern Thailand. The crossings include the following:

- Satun (T) to Pulau Langkawi (M); see p455, p803
- Sungai Kolok (T) to Rantau Panjang (M), linking to Kota Bharu (M); see p470, p786
- Kanger (T) to Padang Besar (M), linking Hat Yai (T) to Butterworth (M); see p453, p784
- Sadao (T) to Bukit Kayu Hitam (M), linking Hat Yai (T) to Butterworth (M); see p453, p784

There is also a crossing between Betong (T) and Keroh (M), but using this crossing was extremely inadvisable at the time of writing due to violence in Yala Province.

Myanmar

Myanmar has land borders with Thailand, but most are either closed or have travelling restrictions. There are two legitimate crossings:

- Mae Sai (T) to Tachilek (My); see p552, p746
- Ranong (T) to Kawthoung (My); see p546, p787

There are also two day-pass points, but travellers can only travel from Thailand to Myanmar (and not the other way round):

- Mae Sot (T) to Myawaddy (My); see p726
- Three Pagodas Pass (T) to Payathonzu (My); see p716

Philippines

See the entry under Malaysia.

Singapore

Singapore has land crossings into Malaysia and sea crossings into Indonesia; see the entries under those countries.

Thailand

Thailand has border crossings to/from Cambodia, Laos, Malaysia and Myanmar; see the entries under those countries.

Vietnam

Vietnam has open borders with Cambodia and Laos; see the entries under those countries.

BUS

In most cases, land borders are crossed via bus, which either travels straight through the two countries with a stop for border formalities or requires a change of buses at the appropriate border towns.

Bus travellers will enjoy a higher standard of luxury in Thailand, the Philippines and Malaysia, where roads are well paved, reliable schedules exist and, sometimes, snacks are distributed. Be aware that theft does occur on some long-distance buses, especially those departing from Bangkok's Th Khao San heading south; keep all valuables on your person, not in a stowed locked bag.

Local buses in Laos, Cambodia and Vietnam are like moving sardine cans, but that is part of their charm.

CAR & MOTORCYCLE

What is the sound of freedom in Southeast Asia? The put-put noise of a motorcycle. Convenient for getting around the beaches or touring in the country, motorcycles are available for hire or purchase, but they require a lot more investment and safety precautions than many visitors realise.

It is advisable to hire a car or motorcycle for local sightseeing rather than depend on it for long-distance travel. You could hit Thailand and Malaysia by car pretty easily, enjoying well-signposted, well-paved roads. Road conditions in Laos and Cambodia vary, although sealed roads are becoming the norm. Indonesia and the Philippines have roads that vary between islands but most are in need of repair. Vietnam's major highways are in relatively good health.

See p919 for driving licence laws.

Hire

There are Western car-hire chains camped out at Southeast Asian airports, capital cities and major tourist destinations. On many tourist islands, guesthouses and locals will hire motorcycles and cars for an affordable rate.

Insurance

Get insurance with a motorcycle if at all possible. The more reputable motorcycle-hire places insure all their motorcycles; some will do it for an extra charge. Without insurance you're responsible for anything that happens to the bike. To be absolutely clear about your liability, ask for a written estimate of the replacement cost for a similar bike – take photos as a guarantee. Some agencies will only accept the replacement cost of a new motorcycle.

Insurance for a hired car is also necessary. Be sure to ask the car-hire agent about liability and damage coverage.

Road Rules

Drive carefully and defensively; lives are lost at astounding rates on Southeast Asian highways. Remember too that smaller vehicles yield to bigger vehicles regardless of circumstances – on the road, might is right. The middle of the road is typically used as a passing lane, even if there is oncoming traffic, and your horn is used to notify other vehicles that you intend to pass them.

Safety

Always check a machine thoroughly before you take it out. Look at the tyres for treads, check for oil leaks, test the brakes. You may be held liable for any problems that weren't duly noted before your departure.

When riding a motorcycle, wear protective clothing and a helmet; long pants, long-sleeved shirts and shoes are highly recommended as sunburn protection and as a second skin if you fall. If your helmet doesn't have a visor, wear goggles, glasses or sunglasses to keep bugs, dust and other debris out of your eyes.

HITCHING

Hitching is never entirely safe in any country in the world, and is not recommended. Travellers who decide to hitch should understand that they are taking a small but potentially serious risk. People who do choose to hitch will be safer if they travel in pairs and let someone know where they are planning to go.

> **MOTORCYCLE TIP**
>
> Most Asians are so adept at driving and riding on motorcycles that they can balance the whole family on the front bumper or even take a quick nap as a passenger. Foreigners unaccustomed to motorcycles are not as graceful. If you're riding on the back of a motorcycle remember to relax. For balance hold on to the back bar, not the driver's waist. Tall people should keep their long legs tucked in as most drivers are used to shorter passengers. Women wearing skirts should collect loose material so that it doesn't catch in the wheel or drive chain. Now enjoy the ride.

LOCAL TRANSPORT

Because personal ownership of cars in Southeast Asia is limited, local transport within a town is a roaring business. For the right price, drivers will haul you from the bus station to town, around town, around the corner, or around in circles. The bicycle rickshaw still survives in the region, assuming such aliases as sǎamláw in Thailand and cyclo in Vietnam. Anything motorised is often modified to carry passengers – from Thailand's obnoxious three-wheeled chariots known as túk-túk to the Philippines' altered US Army jeeps. In large cities, extensive public bus systems either travel on fixed routes or do informal loops around the city, picking up passengers along the way. Bangkok, Kuala Lumpur and Singapore also boast state-of-the-art light-rail systems that make zipping around town feel like time travel.

TRAIN

For intercountry travel, the *International Express* train travels from Thailand all the way through the Malay peninsula, ending its journey in Singapore. Trains also serve Nong Khai, on the Thailand–Cambodia border, and Aranya Prathet, on the Thailand–Laos border.

You'll find that Thailand and then Malaysia have the most extensive intracountry rail systems, although trains rarely run on time.

Health

Dr Trish Batchelor

CONTENTS

Health issues and the quality of medical facilities vary enormously depending on where you travel in Southeast Asia. Many of the major cities are now very well developed, although travel to rural areas can expose you to a variety of health risks and inadequate medical care.

Travellers tend to worry about contracting infectious diseases when in the tropics, but infections are a rare cause of serious illness or death in travellers. Pre-existing medical conditions, such as heart disease, and accidental injury (especially traffic accidents) account for most life-threatening problems. Becoming ill in some way, however, is relatively common. Fortunately, most common illnesses can be either prevented with some common-sense behaviour or treated easily with a well-stocked traveller's medical kit.

The following advice is a general guide and does not replace the advice of a doctor trained in travel medicine.

BEFORE YOU GO

Pack medications in their original, clearly labelled containers. A signed, dated letter from your physician describing your medical conditions and medications, including generic names, is a good idea. If carrying syringes or needles, have a physician's letter stating their medical necessity. If you have a heart condition, bring a copy of your ECG.

If you take any regular medication, bring a double supply in case of loss or theft. In most Southeast Asian countries, excluding Singapore, you can buy many medications over the counter, but it can be difficult to find some of the newer drugs, particularly the latest antidepressants, blood-pressure medications and contraceptive pills.

INSURANCE

Even if you are fit and healthy, don't travel without health insurance – accidents do happen. Declare any existing medical conditions you have – the insurance company *will* check if your problem is pre-existing and will not cover you if it is undeclared. You may require extra cover for adventure activities such as rock climbing. If your health insurance doesn't cover you for medical expenses abroad, consider getting extra insurance. If you're uninsured, emergency evacuation is expensive – bills of more than US$100,000 are not uncommon.

Find out in advance if your insurance plan will make payments directly to providers or reimburse you later for overseas health expenditures. (In many countries doctors expect payment in cash.) You may prefer a policy that pays doctors or hospitals directly rather than you having to pay on the spot and claim later. If you have to claim later, make sure you keep all documentation. Some policies ask you to call (reverse charges) a centre in your home country, where an immediate assessment of your problem is made. Some policies offer a range of medical-expense options; the higher ones are chiefly for countries that have extremely high medical costs, such as the USA.

VACCINATIONS

Specialised travel-medicine clinics are your best source of information; they stock all available vaccines and will be able to give recommendations specifically for you and your trip. The doctors will take into account factors such as past vaccination history, the length of your trip, activities you may be undertaking and underlying medical conditions, such as pregnancy.

Most vaccines don't produce immunity until at least two weeks after they're given, so visit a doctor four to eight weeks before departure. Ask your doctor for an International Certificate of Vaccination (otherwise known as the yellow booklet), which will list all the vaccinations you've received.

Recommended Vaccinations

The World Health Organization (WHO) recommends the following vaccinations for travellers to Southeast Asia:

Adult diphtheria and tetanus Single booster recommended if you haven't had one in the previous 10 years. Side effects include a sore arm and fever.

Hepatitis A Provides almost 100% protection for up to a year; a booster after 12 months provides at least another 20 years' protection. Mild side effects such as a headache and a sore arm occur in 5% to 10% of people.

Hepatitis B Now considered routine for most travellers. Given as three shots over six months. A rapid schedule is also available, as is a combined vaccination with Hepatitis A. Side effects are mild and uncommon, usually a headache and a sore arm. Lifetime protection occurs in 95% of people.

Measles, mumps and rubella (MMR) Two doses of MMR are required unless you have had the diseases. Occasionally a rash and a flulike illness can develop a week after receiving the vaccine. Many young adults require a booster.

Polio Only one booster is required as an adult for lifetime protection. Inactivated polio vaccine is safe during pregnancy.

Typhoid Recommended unless your trip is less than a week long and is only to developed cities. The vaccine offers around 70% protection, lasts for two to three years and comes as a single shot. Tablets are also available. However, the injection is usually recommended as it has fewer side effects. A sore arm and fever may occur.

Varicella If you haven't had chickenpox, discuss this vaccination with your doctor.

The following immunisations are recommended for long-term travellers (more than one month) or those at special risk:

Japanese B Encephalitis Three injections in all. A booster is recommended after two years. A sore arm and headache are the most common side effects, although a rare allergic reaction comprising hives and swelling can occur up to 10 days after any of the three doses.

Meningitis Single injection. There are two types of vaccination: the quadrivalent vaccine gives two to three years' protection, while the meningitis group C vaccine gives around 10 years' protection. Recommended for long-term backpackers aged under 25.

Rabies Three injections in all. A booster after one year will then provide 10 years' protection. Side effects are rare – occasionally a headache and a sore arm.

Tuberculosis (TB) A complex issue. It is usually recommended that long-term adult travellers have a TB skin test before and after travel, rather than vaccination. Only one vaccine is given in a lifetime.

Required Vaccinations

The only vaccine required by international regulations is for yellow fever. Proof of vaccination will only be required if you have visited a country in the yellow-fever zone within the six days before entering Southeast Asia. If you are travelling to Southeast Asia from Africa or South America you should check to see if you require proof of vaccination.

MEDICAL CHECKLIST

Recommended items for a personal medical kit:

- antibacterial cream, eg mupirocin
- antibiotic for skin infections, eg amoxicillin/clavulanate or cephalexin
- antibiotics for diarrhoea, such as norfloxacin or ciprofloxacin; azithromycinfor bacterial diarrhoea; tinidazole for giardiasis or amoebic dysentery
- antifungal cream, eg clotrimazole
- antihistamine, such as cetirizine for daytime and promethazine for night
- anti-inflammatory such as ibuprofen
- antiseptic, eg Betadine
- antispasmodic for stomach cramps, eg Buscopan
- contraceptives
- decongestant, eg pseudoephedrine
- DEET-based insect repellent
- diarrhoea treatment; consider bringing an oral rehydration solution (eg Gastrolyte), diarrhoea 'stopper' (eg loperamide) and antinausea medication (eg prochlorperazine)
- first-aid items such as scissors, plasters, bandages, gauze, thermometer (but not one with mercury), sterile needles and syringes, safety pins and tweezers
- indigestion medication, eg Quick Eze or Mylanta
- iodine tablets (unless you are pregnant or have a thyroid problem) to purify water
- laxative, eg Coloxyl

- migraine medication; sufferers should take their personal medicine
- paracetamol
- permethrin to impregnate clothing and mosquito nets
- steroid cream for allergic or itchy rashes, eg 1% to 2% hydrocortisone
- sunscreen and hat
- throat lozenges
- thrush (vaginal yeast infection) treatment, eg Clotrimazole pessaries or Diflucan tablet
- Ural or equivalent if you're prone to urine infections

ONLINE RESOURCES

There is a wealth of travel health advice on the internet. For further information, **Lonely Planet** (www.lonelyplanet.com) is a good place to start. The **World Health Organization** (www.who.int/ith) publishes a superb book called *International Travel & Health,* which is revised annually and is available online at no cost. Another website of general interest is **MD Travel Health** (www.mdtravelhealth.com), which provides complete travel health recommendations for every country and is updated daily. The **Centers for Disease Control and Prevention** (CDC; www.cdc.gov) website also has good general information.

FURTHER READING

Lonely Planet's *Healthy Travel – Asia & India* is a handy pocket-size book that is packed with useful information, including pretrip planning, emergency first aid, immunisation and disease information, and what to do if you get sick on the road. Other recommended references include *Traveller's Health* by Dr Richard Dawood and *Travelling Well* by Dr Deborah Mills – check out www.travellingwell.com.au.

IN TRANSIT

DEEP VEIN THROMBOSIS (DVT)

Deep vein thrombosis (DVT) occurs when blood clots form in the legs during plane flights, chiefly because of prolonged immobility. The longer the flight, the greater the risk. Although most blood clots are reabsorbed uneventfully, some may break off and travel through the blood vessels to the lungs, where they may cause life-threatening complications.

The chief symptom of DVT is swelling of or pain in the foot, ankle or calf, usually but not always on just one side. When a blood clot travels to the lungs, it may cause chest pain and difficulty in breathing. Travellers with any of these symptoms should immediately seek medical attention.

To prevent the development of DVT on long flights you should walk about the cabin, perform isometric compressions of the leg muscles (ie contract the leg muscles while sitting), drink plenty of fluids and avoid alcohol.

JET LAG & MOTION SICKNESS

Jet lag is common when crossing more than five time zones; it causes symptoms including insomnia, fatigue, malaise or nausea. To avoid jet lag, try drinking plenty of (nonalcoholic) fluids and eating light meals. Upon arrival seek exposure to natural sunlight and readjust your schedule (for meals, sleep etc) as soon as possible.

Antihistamines such as dimenhydrinate (Dramamine) and meclizine (Antivert or Bonine) are usually the first choice for treating motion sickness. Their main side effect is drowsiness. A herbal alternative is ginger, which works like a charm for some people.

IN SOUTHEAST ASIA

AVAILABILITY OF HEALTH CARE

Most capital cities in Southeast Asia now have clinics that cater specifically to travellers and expats. These clinics are usually more expensive than local medical facilities, but are worth utilising as they will offer a superior standard of care. Additionally, they understand the local system and are aware of the safest local hospitals and best specialists. They can also liaise with insurance companies should you require evacuation. Recommended clinics are listed under Information in the capital city sections of country chapters in this book.

It is difficult to find reliable medical care in rural areas. Your embassy and insurance company are good contacts.

Self-treatment may be appropriate if your problem is minor (eg traveller's diarrhoea), you are carrying the appropriate medication and you cannot attend a recommended clinic. If you think you may have a serious disease, especially malaria, do not waste time – travel to the nearest quality facility to receive attention. It is always better to be assessed by a doctor than to rely on self-treatment.

Buying medication over the counter is not recommended, as fake medications and poorly stored or out-of-date drugs are common.

The standard of care in Southeast Asia varies from country to country:

Brunei General care is reasonable. There is no local medical university, so expats and foreign-trained locals run the health-care system. Serious or complex cases are better managed in Singapore, but adequate primary health care and stabilisation is available.

Cambodia There are a couple of international clinics in Phnom Penh, and one in Siem Reap, that provide primary care and emergency stabilisation.

East Timor No private clinics. The government hospital is basic and should be avoided. Contact your embassy or insurance company for advice.

Indonesia Local medical care in general is not yet up to international standards. Foreign doctors are not allowed to work in Indonesia, but some clinics catering to foreigners have 'international advisers'. Almost all Indonesian doctors work at government hospitals during the day and in private practices at night. This means that private hospitals often don't have their best staff available during the day. Serious cases are evacuated to Australia or Singapore.

Laos There are no good facilities in Laos; the nearest acceptable facilities are in northern Thailand. The Australian Embassy Clinic in Vientiane treats citizens of Commonwealth countries.

Malaysia Medical care in the major centres is good, and most problems can be adequately dealt with in Kuala Lumpur.

Myanmar (Burma) Local medical care is dismal and local hospitals should only be used in desperation. There is an international medical clinic in Yangon (Rangoon). Contact your embassy for advice.

Philippines Good medical care is available in most major cities.

Singapore Has excellent medical facilities, and it acts as the referral centre for most of Southeast Asia.

Thailand There are some very good facilities in Thailand, particularly in Bangkok. After Singapore this is the city of choice for expats living in Southeast Asia who require specialised care.

Vietnam Government hospitals are overcrowded and basic. In order to treat foreigners, the facility needs to obtain a special licence, and so far only a few have been provided. The private clinics in Hanoi and Ho Chi Minh City should be your first port of call. They are familiar with the local resources and can organise evacuations if necessary.

INFECTIOUS DISEASES

Cutaneous Larva Migrans

Risk areas All countries except Singapore.

This disease, caused by dog hookworm, is particularly common on the beaches of Thailand. The rash starts as a small lump, then

AVIAN INFLUENZA (BIRD FLU)

Six Southeast Asian countries (Cambodia, Indonesia, Laos, Thailand, Vietnam and Myanmar), plus China, Japan and South Korea, reported an outbreak of avian influenza (bird flu). The strain in question, known as 'Influenza A H5N1' or simply 'the H5N1 virus', is a highly contagious form of avian influenza that has since spread as far as Europe to the west. Throughout the region, government officials are scrambling to contain the spread of the disease, which wreaks havoc with domesticated bird populations.

While the avian influenza virus usually poses little risk to humans, there have been several recorded cases of the H5N1 virus spreading from birds to humans. Human cases of avian influenza in the region have been reported from Indonesia and Thailand. At the time of writing, Thailand had reported 25 cases of humans contracting the virus since 2003, with 17 deaths. In Indonesia, there had been more than 100 cases, with more than 80 deaths, since July 2005. The main risk is to people who directly handle infected birds, or come into contact with contaminated bird faeces or carcasses. Because heat kills the virus, there is no risk of infection from cooked poultry.

There is no clear evidence that the H5N1 virus can be transmitted between humans. However, the main fear is that this highly adaptable virus may mutate and be passed between humans, perhaps leading to a worldwide influenza pandemic.

Thus far, however, infection rates are limited and the risk to travellers is low. Travellers to the region should avoid contact with any birds and should ensure that any poultry is thoroughly cooked before consumption.

slowly spreads in a linear fashion. It is intensely itchy, especially at night. It is easily treated with medications and should not be cut out or frozen.

Dengue

Risk areas All countries.

This mosquito-borne disease is becoming increasingly problematic throughout Southeast Asia, especially in the cities. As there is no vaccine available it can only be prevented by avoiding mosquito bites. The mosquito that carries dengue bites day and night, so use insect-avoidance measures at all times. Symptoms include high fever, severe headache and body ache (dengue used to be known as breakbone fever). Some people develop a rash and experience diarrhoea. Thailand's southern islands are particularly high risk. There is no specific treatment, just rest and paracetamol – do not take aspirin as it increases the likelihood of haemorrhaging. See a doctor to be diagnosed and monitored.

Filariasis

Risk areas All countries except Singapore.

This mosquito-borne disease is very common in the local population, yet very rare in travellers. Mosquito-avoidance measures are the best way to prevent this disease.

Hepatitis A

Risk areas All countries.

A problem throughout the region, this food- and water-borne virus infects the liver, causing jaundice (yellow skin and eyes), nausea and lethargy. There is no specific treatment for hepatitis A; you just need to allow time for the liver to heal. All travellers to Southeast Asia should be vaccinated against hepatitis A.

Hepatitis B

Risk areas All countries.

The only sexually transmitted disease that can be prevented by vaccination, hepatitis B is spread by body fluids. In some parts of Southeast Asia, up to 20% of the population carry hepatitis B, and usually are unaware of this. The long-term consequences can include liver cancer and cirrhosis.

Hepatitis E

Risk areas All countries.

Hepatitis E is transmitted through contaminated food and water, and has similar symptoms to hepatitis A but is far less common. It is a severe problem in pregnant women, and can result in the death of both mother and baby. There is currently no vaccine, and prevention is by following safe eating and drinking guidelines.

HIV

Risk areas All countries.

HIV is now one of the most common causes of death in people under the age of 50 in Thailand. The Southeast Asian countries with the worst and most rapidly increasing HIV problem are Cambodia, Myanmar, Thailand and Vietnam. Heterosexual sex is now the main method of transmission in these countries.

Influenza

Risk areas All countries.

Present year-round in the tropics, influenza (flu) symptoms include high fever, muscle aches, runny nose, cough and sore throat. It can be very severe in people over the age of 65, and in those with underlying medical conditions such as heart disease or diabetes; vaccination is recommended for these individuals. There is no specific treatment, just rest and paracetamol.

Japanese B Encephalitis

Risk areas All countries except Singapore.

While rare in travellers, this viral disease, transmitted by mosquitoes, infects at least 50,000 locals each year. Most cases of the disease occur in rural areas and vaccination is recommended for travellers spending more than one month outside of cities. There is no treatment – a third of infected people will die while another third will suffer permanent brain damage. Highest-risk areas in the region include Vietnam, Thailand and Indonesia.

Leptospirosis

Risk areas Thailand and Malaysia.

Leptospirosis is most commonly contracted after river rafting or canyoning. Early symptoms are very similar to the flu, and include headache and fever. The disease can vary from very mild to fatal. Diagnosis is through blood tests and it is easily treated with doxycycline.

Malaria

Risk areas All countries except Singapore and Brunei.

For such a serious and potentially deadly disease, there is an enormous amount of misinformation concerning malaria. You must get expert advice about whether your trip actually puts you at risk. Many parts of Southeast Asia, particularly city and resort areas, have minimal to no risk of malaria, and the risk of side effects from the prevention tablets may outweigh the risk of getting the disease. For most rural areas, however, the risk of contracting the disease far outweighs the risk of any side effects. Remember that malaria can be fatal. Before you travel, seek medical advice on the right medication and dosage for you.

Malaria is caused by a parasite transmitted by the bite of an infected mosquito. The most important symptom of malaria is fever, but general symptoms such as headache, diarrhoea, cough or chills may also occur. Diagnosis can only be made by taking a blood sample.

Two strategies should be combined to prevent malaria – mosquito avoidance and antimalarial medications. Most people who catch malaria are taking inadequate or no antimalarial medication.

Travellers are advised to prevent mosquito bites by taking the following steps:

- Use an insect repellent containing DEET on exposed skin. Wash this off at night, as long as you are sleeping under a mosquito net. Natural repellents such as citronella can be effective, but must be applied more frequently than products containing DEET.
- Sleep under a mosquito net that is impregnated with permethrin.
- Choose accommodation with screens and fans (if not air-conditioned).
- Impregnate clothing with permethrin when in high-risk areas.
- Wear long sleeves and trousers in light colours.
- Use mosquito coils.
- Spray your room with insect repellent before going out for your evening meal.

There are a variety of medications available. Derivatives of artesunate are not suitable as a preventive medication, although they are useful treatments under medical supervision.

The effectiveness of the chloroquine and paludrine combination is now limited in most of Southeast Asia. Common side effects include nausea (40% of people) and mouth ulcers. The combination is generally not recommended.

The daily doxycycline tablet is a broad-spectrum antibiotic that has the added benefit of helping to prevent a variety of tropical diseases, including leptospirosis, tick-borne disease, typhus and meliodosis. The potential side effects include photosensitivity (a tendency to sunburn), thrush in women, indigestion, heartburn, nausea and interference with the contraceptive pill. More serious side effects include ulceration of the oesophagus – you can help prevent this by taking your tablet with a meal and a large glass of water, and by never lying down within half an hour of taking it. It must be taken for four weeks after leaving the risk area.

Lariam (mefloquine) has received much bad press, some of it justified, some not. This weekly tablet suits many people. Serious side effects are rare but include depression, anxiety, psychosis and seizures. Anyone with a history of depression, anxiety, other psychological disorders or epilepsy should not take Lariam. It is considered safe in the second and third trimesters of pregnancy. It is around 90% effective in most parts of Southeast Asia, but there is significant resistance in parts of northern Thailand, Laos and Cambodia. Tablets must be taken for four weeks after leaving the risk area.

Malarone is a combination of atovaquone and proguanil. Side effects are uncommon and mild, most commonly nausea and headache. It is the best tablet for scuba divers and for those on short trips to high-risk areas. It must be taken for one week after leaving the risk area.

A final option is to take no preventive medication but to have a supply of emergency medication should you develop the symptoms of malaria. This is less than ideal, and you'll need to get to a good medical facility within 24 hours of developing a fever. If you choose this option, the most effective and safest treatment is Malarone (four tablets once daily for three days). Other options include mefloquine and quinine, but the side effects of these drugs at treatment doses make them less desirable. Fansidar is no longer recommended.

Measles

Risk areas All countries except Singapore and Brunei.

Measles remains a problem in some parts of Southeast Asia. This highly contagious bacterial infection is spread via coughing and sneezing. Most people born before 1966 are immune as they had the disease during childhood. Measles starts with a high fever and rash, and can be complicated by pneumonia and brain disease. There is no specific treatment.

Meliodosis

Risk areas Thailand only.

This infection is contracted by skin contact with soil. It is rare in travellers, but in some parts of northeast Thailand up to 30% of the local population is infected. The symptoms are very similar to those experienced by tuberculosis sufferers. There is no vaccine but it can be treated with medications.

Rabies

Risk areas All countries except Singapore and Brunei.

Still a common problem in most parts of Southeast Asia, this uniformly fatal disease is spread by the bite or lick of an infected animal, most commonly a dog or monkey. You should seek medical advice immediately after any animal bite and commence postexposure treatment. Having a pretravel vaccination means the postbite treatment is greatly simplified. If an animal bites you, gently wash the wound with soap and water, and apply iodine-based antiseptic. If you are not prevaccinated you will need to receive rabies immunoglobulin as soon as possible.

Schistosomiasis

Risk areas Philippines, Vietnam and Sulawesi (Indonesia).

Schistosomiasis is a tiny parasite that enters your skin after you've been swimming in contaminated water travellers usually only get a light infection and hence have no symptoms. If you are concerned, you can be tested three months after exposure. On rare occasions, travellers may develop 'Katayama fever'. This occurs some weeks after exposure, as the parasite passes through the lungs and causes an allergic reaction; symptoms are coughing and fever. Schistosomiasis is easily treated with medications.

STDs

Risk areas All countries.

Sexually transmitted diseases most commonly found in Southeast Asia include herpes, warts, syphilis, gonorrhoea and chlamydia. People carrying these diseases often have no signs of infection. Condoms will prevent gonorrhoea and chlamydia but not warts or herpes. If after a sexual encounter you develop any rash, lumps, discharge or pain when passing urine, seek immediate medical attention. If you have been sexually active during your travels, have an STD check on your return home.

Strongyloides

Risk areas Cambodia, Myanmar and Thailand.

This parasite, transmitted by skin contact with soil, is common in travellers but rarely affects them. It is characterised by an unusual skin rash called *larva currens* – a linear rash on the trunk that comes and goes. Most people don't have other symptoms until their immune system becomes severely suppressed, when the parasite can cause an overwhelming infection. It can be treated with medications.

Tuberculosis

Risk areas All countries.

While TB is rare in travellers, any medical and aid workers and long-term travellers who have significant contact with the local population should take precautions. Vaccination is usually only given to children under five, but it is recommended that adults at risk have pre- and posttravel testing. The main symptoms are fever, cough, weight loss and tiredness.

Typhoid

Risk areas All countries except Singapore.

This serious bacterial infection is spread via food and water. It gives a high and slowly progressive fever, a headache and may be accompanied by a dry cough and stomach pain. It is diagnosed by blood tests and treated with antibiotics. Vaccination is recommended for all travellers spending more than a week in Southeast Asia, or travelling outside of the major cities. Be aware that vaccination is not 100% effective so you must still be careful with what you eat and drink.

Typhus

Risk areas All countries except Singapore.

Murine typhus is spread by the bite of a flea, whereas scrub typhus is spread via a mite.

These diseases are rare in travellers. Symptoms include fever, muscle pains and a rash. You can avoid these diseases by following general insect-avoidance measures. Doxycycline will also prevent them.

TRAVELLER'S DIARRHOEA

Traveller's diarrhoea is by far the most common problem that affects travellers – between 30% and 50% of people will suffer from it within two weeks of starting their trip. In over 80% of cases, traveller's diarrhoea is caused by bacteria (there are numerous potential culprits), and therefore responds promptly to treatment with antibiotics. Treatment will depend on your situation – how sick you are, how quickly you need to get better, where you are etc.

Traveller's diarrhoea is defined as the passage of more than three watery bowel actions within 24 hours, plus at least one other symptom such as fever, cramps, nausea, vomiting or feeling generally unwell.

Treatment consists of staying well hydrated; rehydration solutions such as Gastrolyte are the best for this. Antibiotics such as norfloxacin, ciprofloxacin or azithromycin will kill the bacteria quickly.

Loperamide is just a 'stopper' and doesn't get to the cause of the problem. It can be helpful, for example, if you have to go on a long bus ride. Don't take loperamide if you have a fever, or blood in your stools. Seek medical attention quickly if you do not respond to an appropriate antibiotic.

Amoebic Dysentery

Amoebic dysentery is very rare in travellers but is often misdiagnosed by poor-quality labs in Southeast Asia. Symptoms are similar to bacterial diarrhoea, ie fever, bloody diarrhoea and generally feeling unwell. You should always seek reliable medical care if you have blood in your diarrhoea. Treatment involves two drugs: tinidazole or metronidazole to kill the parasite in your gut, and then a second drug to kill the cysts. If left untreated, complications such as liver or gut abscesses can occur.

Giardiasis

Giardia lamblia is a relatively common parasite in travellers. Symptoms include nausea, bloating, excess gas, fatigue and intermittent diarrhoea. 'Eggy' burps are often attributed solely to giardiasis, but work in Nepal has shown that they are not specific to this infection. The parasite will eventually go away if left untreated but this can take months. The treatment of choice is tinidazole, with metronidazole being a second option.

ENVIRONMENTAL HAZARDS

Air Pollution

Air pollution, particularly vehicle pollution, is an increasing problem in most of Southeast Asia's major cities. If you have severe respiratory problems, speak with your doctor before travelling to any heavily polluted urban centres. This pollution also causes minor respiratory problems such as sinusitis, dry throat and irritated eyes. If troubled by the pollution, leave the city for a few days and get some fresh air.

Diving

Divers and surfers should seek specialised advice before they travel to ensure their medical kit contains treatment for coral cuts and tropical ear infections, as well as the standard problems. Divers should ensure their insurance covers them for decompression illness – get specialised dive insurance through an organisation such as **Divers Alert Network** (DAN; www.danseap.org). Have a dive medical before you leave your home country; there are certain medical conditions that are incompatible with diving, and economic considerations may override health considerations for some dive operators in Southeast Asia.

Food

Eating in restaurants is the biggest risk factor for contracting traveller's diarrhoea. Ways to avoid diarrhoea include eating only freshly cooked food, and avoiding shellfish and food that has been sitting around in buffets. Peel all fruit, cook vegetables, and soak salads in iodine water for at least 20 minutes. Eat in busy restaurants with a high turnover of customers.

Heat

Many parts of Southeast Asia are hot and humid throughout the year. For most people it takes at least two weeks to adapt to the hot climate. Swelling of the feet and ankles is common, as are muscle cramps caused by excessive sweating. You can prevent these by avoiding dehydration and excessive activity in the heat; you should also take it easy when you first arrive. Don't eat salt tablets (they aggravate the gut), but drinking rehydration solution or eating salty food helps. Treat cramps by stopping activity, resting, rehydrating with double-strength rehydration solution and gently stretching.

Dehydration is the main contributor to heat exhaustion. Symptoms include weakness, headache, irritability, nausea or vomiting, sweaty skin, a fast pulse, and a normal or slightly elevated body temperature. Treatment involves getting out of the heat, fanning the person and applying cool wet cloths to the skin, laying the person flat with their legs raised, and rehydrating them with water containing a quarter of a teaspoon of salt per litre. Recovery is usually rapid, though it is common to feel weak afterwards.

Heat stroke is a serious medical emergency. Symptoms come on suddenly and include weakness, nausea, a hot dry body with a body temperature of over 41°C, dizziness, confusion, loss of coordination, seizures, and eventually collapse and loss of consciousness. Seek medical help and commence cooling by getting the person out of the heat, removing their clothes, fanning them and applying cool wet cloths or ice to their body, especially to the groin and armpits.

Prickly heat is a common skin rash in the tropics caused by sweat being trapped under the skin. The result is an itchy rash of tiny lumps. Treat by moving out of the heat and into an air-conditioned area for a few hours and by having cool showers. Creams and ointments clog the skin so they should be avoided. Locally bought prickly heat powder can be helpful.

Tropical fatigue is common in long-term expats based in the tropics. It's rarely due to disease and is caused by the climate, inadequate mental rest, excessive alcohol intake and the demands of daily work in a different culture.

Insect Bites & Stings

Bedbugs don't carry disease but their bites are very itchy. They live in the cracks of furniture and walls, and then migrate to the bed at night to feed on you. You can treat the itch with an antihistamine.

Lice inhabit various parts of your body, but most commonly your head and pubic area. Transmission is via close contact with an infected person. Lice can be difficult to treat and you may need numerous applications of an antilice shampoo. Pubic lice are usually contracted from sexual contact.

Ticks are contracted after walking in rural areas. They are commonly found behind the ears, on the belly and in armpits. If you have had a tick bite and experience symptoms such as a rash at the site of the bite or elsewhere, or fever or muscle aches, you should see a doctor. Doxycycline prevents tick-borne diseases.

Leeches are found in humid rainforest areas. They do not transmit any disease but their bites are often intensely itchy for weeks afterwards and can easily become infected. Apply an iodine-based antiseptic to any leech bite to help prevent infection.

Bee and wasp stings mainly cause problems for people who are allergic to them. Anyone with a serious bee or wasp allergy should carry an injection of adrenaline (eg an Epipen) for emergency treatment. For others, pain is the main problem – apply ice to the sting and take painkillers.

Most jellyfish in Southeast Asian waters are not dangerous, just irritating. First aid for jellyfish stings involves pouring vinegar onto the affected area to neutralise the poison. Do not rub sand or water onto the stings. Take painkillers, and if you feel ill in any way after being stung seek medical advice. Take local advice if there are dangerous jellyfish around and keep out of the water.

DRINKING WATER

- Never drink tap water.
- Bottled water is generally safe – check the seal is intact at purchase.
- Avoid ice.
- Avoid fresh juices – they may have been watered down.
- Boiling water is the most efficient method of purifying it.
- The best chemical purifier is iodine. It should not be used by pregnant women or those with thyroid problems.
- Water filters should also filter out viruses. Ensure your filter has a chemical barrier such as iodine and a small pore size, eg less than four microns.

Parasites

Numerous parasites are common in local populations in Southeast Asia; however, most of these are rare in travellers. The two rules for avoiding parasitic infections are to wear shoes and to avoid eating raw food, especially fish, pork and vegetables. A number of parasites are transmitted via the skin by walking barefoot, including strongyloides, hookworm and cutaneous *larva migrans*.

Skin Problems

Fungal rashes are common in humid climates. There are two common fungal rashes that tend to affect travellers. The first occurs in moist areas that get less air, such as the groin, armpits and between the toes. It starts as a red patch that slowly spreads and is usually itchy. Treatment involves keeping the skin dry, avoiding chafing and using an antifungal cream such as clotrimazole or Lamisil. *Tinea versicolor* is also common – this fungus causes small, light-coloured patches, most commonly on the back, chest and shoulders. Consult a doctor.

Cuts and scratches become easily infected in humid climates. Take meticulous care of any cuts and scratches to prevent complications such as abscesses. Immediately wash all wounds in clean water and apply antiseptic. If you develop signs of infection (increasing pain and redness), see a doctor. Divers and surfers should be particularly careful with coral cuts as they can be easily infected.

Snakes

Southeast Asia is home to many species of both poisonous and harmless snakes. Assume that all snakes are poisonous and never try to catch one. Always wear boots and long pants if walking in an area that may have snakes. First aid in the event of a snakebite involves pressure immobilisation using an elastic bandage firmly wrapped around the affected limb, starting at the bite site and working up towards the chest. The bandage should not be so tight that the circulation is cut off, and the fingers or toes should be kept free so the circulation can be checked. Immobilise the limb with a splint and carry the victim to medical attention. Do not use tourniquets or try to suck the venom out. Antivenin is available for most species.

Sunburn

Even on a cloudy day sunburn can occur rapidly. Always use a strong sunscreen (at least factor 30), making sure to reapply after a swim, and always wear a wide-brimmed hat and sunglasses outdoors. Avoid lying in the sun during the hottest part of the day (10am to 2pm). If you become sunburnt, stay out of the sun until you have recovered, apply cool compresses and take painkillers for the discomfort. One percent hydrocortisone cream applied twice daily is also helpful.

WOMEN'S HEALTH

Pregnant women should receive specialised advice before travelling. The ideal time to travel is in the second trimester (between 16 and 28 weeks), when the risk of pregnancy-related problems is at its lowest and women generally feel at their best. During the first trimester there is a risk of miscarriage and in the third trimester complications such as premature labour and high blood pressure are possible. It's wise to travel with a companion. Always carry a list of quality medical facilities available at your destination and ensure you continue your standard antenatal care at these facilities. Avoid rural travel in areas with poor transport and medical facilities. Most of all, ensure travel insurance covers all pregnancy-related possibilities.

Malaria is a high-risk disease during pregnancy. WHO recommends that pregnant women do *not* travel to areas with chloroquine-resistant malaria. None of the more effective antimalarial drugs are completely safe in pregnancy.

Traveller's diarrhoea can quickly lead to dehydration and result in inadequate blood flow to the placenta. Many of the drugs used to treat various diarrhoea bugs are not recommended in pregnancy. Azithromycin is considered safe.

In the urban areas of Southeast Asia, supplies of sanitary products are readily available. Birth-control options may be limited so bring adequate supplies of your own form of contraception. Heat, humidity and antibiotics can all contribute to thrush. Treatment is with antifungal creams and pessaries such as clotrimazole. A practical alternative is a single tablet of fluconazole (Diflucan). Urinary tract infections can be precipitated by dehydration or long bus journeys without toilet stops; bring suitable antibiotics.

TRADITIONAL MEDICINE

Throughout Southeast Asia, traditional medical systems are widely practised. There is a big difference between these traditional healing systems and 'folk' medicine. Folk remedies should be avoided, as they often involve rather dubious procedures with potential complications. In comparison, healing systems such as traditional Chinese medicine are well respected, and aspects of them are being increasingly utilised by Western medical practitioners.

All traditional Asian medical systems identify a vital life force, and see blockage or imbalance of this force as causing disease. Techniques such as herbal medicines, massage and acupuncture are used to bring this vital force back into balance, or to maintain balance. These therapies are best used for treating chronic disease such as chronic fatigue, arthritis, irritable bowel syndrome and some chronic skin conditions. Traditional medicines should be avoided for treating serious acute infections such as malaria.

Be aware that 'natural' doesn't always mean 'safe', and there can be drug interactions between herbal medicines and Western medicines. If you are using both systems, ensure you inform each practitioner of what the other has prescribed.

Language

CONTENTS

This language guide offers useful words and phrases for basic communication in the nine main languages spoken in the regions covered by this book. For more comprehensive coverage of these languages we recommend Lonely Planet phrasebooks: the *Southeast Asia Phrasebook* for Burmese, Khmer, Lao, Thai and Vietnamese, and the *East Timor, Filipino, Indonesian* and *Malay Phrasebooks* for the other languages.

BAHASA INDONESIA

ACCOMMODATION

guesthouse	*losmen*
bathroom	*kamar mandi*
bed	*tempat tidur*
toilet	*WC (way say)/kamar kecil*
Is there a room available?	*Adakah kamar kosong?*
May I see the room?	*Boleh saya melihat kamar?*
one night	*satu malam*
two nights	*dua malam*

CONVERSATION & ESSENTIALS

Good morning.	*Selamat pagi.*
Good day.	*Selamat siang.*
Good afternoon.	*Selamat sore.*
Good evening/night.	*Selamat malam.*
Goodbye. (to person staying)	*Selamat tinggal.*
Goodbye. (to person going)	*Selamat jalan.*
How are you?	*Apa kabar?*
I'm fine.	*Kabar baik.*
Please.	*Tolong.*
Thank you (very much).	*Terima kasih (banyak).*
Yes.	*Ya.*
No.	*Tidak/Bukan.*
Excuse me.	*Maaf/Permisi.*
I don't understand.	*Saya tidak mengerti.*
Do you speak English?	*Bisa berbicara bahasa Inggris?*

EMERGENCIES

Help!	*Tolong!*
Call a doctor!	*Panggil dokter!*
Call the police!	*Panggil polisi!*
I'm lost.	*Saya kesasar.*
Go away!	*Pergi!*

FOOD & DRINK

I'm a vegetarian/ I eat only vegetables.	*Saya hanya makan sayuran.*
beef	*daging*
chicken	*ayam*
crab	*kepiting*
egg	*telur*
fish	*ikan*
food	*makanan*
fried noodles	*mie goreng*
pork	*babi*
potato	*kentang*
prawns	*udang-udang*
rice with odds & ends	*nasi campur*
fried rice	*nasi goreng*
white rice	*nasi putih*
soup	*soto*
mixed vegetables	*sayur-sayuran*
fried vegetables	*cap cai*
beer	*bir*
coffee	*kopi*
drinking water	*air minum/air putih*
milk	*susu*
orange juice	*air jeruk*
tea with sugar	*teh manis/teh gula*
tea without sugar	*teh pahit*

NUMBERS

1	*satu*
2	*dua*
3	*tiga*
4	*empat*

5	*lima*
6	*enam*
7	*tujuh*
8	*delapan*
9	*sembilan*
10	*sepuluh*
11	*sebelas*
20	*duapuluh*
21	*duapuluh satu*
30	*tigapuluh*
50	*limapuluh*
100	*seratus*
1000	*seribu*
2000	*duaribu*

SHOPPING & SERVICES

Where is a/the ...? *Dimana ...?*
- **bank** *bank*
- **post office** *kantor pos*
- **public telephone** *telepon umum*
- **public toilet** *WC umum*
- **tourist office** *dinas pariwisata*

How much is it? *Berapa harganya ini?*
expensive *mahal*
open/close *buka/tutup*

TIME & DAYS

When? *Kapan?*
At what time ...? *Pada jam berapa ...?*
today *hari ini*
tonight *malam ini*
tomorrow *besok*
yesterday *kemarin*

Monday *hari Senin*
Tuesday *hari Selasa*
Wednesday *hari Rabu*
Thursday *hari Kamis*
Friday *hari Jumat*
Saturday *hari Sabtu*
Sunday *hari Minggu*

TRANSPORT

What time does the ... leave/arrive? *Jam berapa ... berangkat/tiba?*
- **bus** *bis/bus*
- **boat** *kapal*
- **train** *kereta api*

bus station *setasiun bis/terminal*
ticket *karcis/tiket*

Directions

I want to go to ... *Saya mau pergi ke ...*
How far? *Berapa jauh?*
near/far *dekat/jauh*
straight ahead *terus*
left/right *kiri/kanan*

BAHASA MALAYSIA

ACCOMMODATION

hotel *hotel*
guesthouse *losmen*
room *bilik*
bed *tempat tidur*
expensive *mahal*

Is there a room available? *Ada bilik kosong?*
How much is it per night/person? *Berapa harga satu malam/orang?*
May I see the room? *Boleh saya lihat biliknya?*

CONVERSATION & ESSENTIALS

Good morning. *Selamat pagi.*
Good day. (around midday) *Selamat tengah hari.*
Good evening. *Selamat petang.*
Good night. *Selamat malam.*
Goodbye. (to person staying) *Selamat tinggal.*
Goodbye. (to person leaving) *Selamat jalan.*
Yes. *Ya.*
No. *Tidak.*
Please. *Tolong/Silakan.*
Thank you (very much). *Terima kasih (banyak).*
You're welcome. *Kembali.*
Sorry/Pardon. *Maaf.*
Excuse me. *Maafkan saya.*
Do you speak English? *Bolehkah anda berbicara bahasa Inggeris?*
I don't understand. *Saya tidak faham.*

EMERGENCIES

Help! *Tolong!*
Call a doctor! *Panggil doktor!*
Call the police! *Panggil polis!*
I'm lost. *Saya sesat.*
Go away! *Pegi/Belah!*

FOOD & DRINK

I'm a vegetarian/eat only vegetables. *Saya hanya makan sayuran.*

vegetables only	*sayur saja*
fish	*ikan*
chicken	*ayam*
egg	*telur*
pork	*babi*
crab	*ketam*
beef	*daging lembu*
prawns	*udang*
fried rice	*nasi goreng*
boiled rice	*nasi putih*
rice with odds & ends	*nasi campur*
fried noodles	*mee goreng*
soup	*sup*
fried vegetables	*cap cai*
potatoes	*kentang*
vegetables	*sayur-sayuran*
drinking water	*air minum*
orange juice	*air jeruk/air oren*
coffee	*kopi*
tea	*teh*
milk	*susu*
sugar	*gula*

NUMBERS

1	*satu*
2	*dua*
3	*tiga*
4	*empat*
5	*lima*
6	*enam*
7	*tujuh*
8	*delapan*
9	*sembilan*
10	*sepuluh*
11	*sebelas*
12	*dua belas*
13	*tiga belas*
20	*dua puluh*
21	*dua puluh satu*
30	*tiga puluh*
100	*seratus*
1000	*seribu*
2000	*dua ribu*

SHOPPING & SERVICES

Where is a/the ...?	*Di mana ada ...?*
bank	*bank*
hospital	*hospital*
post office	*pejabat pos*
public toilet	*tandas awam*
tourist office	*pejabat pelancong*
What time does it open/close?	*Pukul berapa buka/tutup?*
How much is it?	*Berapa harganya ini?*

TIME & DAYS

When?	*Bila?*
How long?	*Berapa lama?*
today	*hari ini*
tomorrow	*besok*
yesterday	*kelmarin*
Monday	*hari Isnin*
Tuesday	*hari Selasa*
Wednesday	*hari Rabu*
Thursday	*hari Kamis*
Friday	*hari Jumaat*
Saturday	*hari Sabtu*
Sunday	*hari minggu*

TRANSPORT

What time does the ... leave?	*Pukul berapakah ... berangkat?*
bus	*bas*
train	*keretapi*
ship	*kapal*
boat	*bot*

Directions

How can I get to ...?	*Bagaimana saya pergi ke ...?*
Go straight ahead.	*Jalan terus.*
Turn left/right.	*Belok kiri/kanan.*
near/far	*dekat/jauh*
here/there	*di sini/di sana*

BURMESE (MYANMAR)

TONES & PRONUNCIATION

Like Thai, Lao and Vietnamese, Burmese is a tonal language, where changes in the relative pitch of the speaker's voice can affect meaning. There are three basic tones in Burmese:

high tone – produced with the voice tense and high-pitched; indicated by an acute accent, eg *ká* (dance)

high falling tone – starts with the voice high, then falling; indicated by a grave accent, eg *kà* (car)

low tone – the voice is relaxed and remains low; indicated by no accent, eg *ka* (shield)

Three other features important to Burmese pronunciation:

a stopped syllable – with a high pitch, the voice is cut off suddenly to produce a glottal stop (similar to the 'non' sound in the middle of the exclamation 'oh-oh'); it's indicated in this guide by a 'q' after the vowel, eg *kaq* (join)

a weak syllable – only occurs on the vowel a, and is pronounced like the 'a' in 'ago'; indicated by a 'v' accent, eg *ălouk* (work)

aspirated consonants – pronounced with an audible puff of breath; indicated by a following apostrophe, eg *s'i* (cooking oil)

ACCOMMODATION

hotel	*ho·the*
guesthouse	*tèh·k'o·gàn*
May I see the room?	*ăk'àn cí·bayá·ze?*
How much is ...?	*... beh·lauq·lèh?*
one night	*tăyeq*
two nights	*hnăyeq*
a single room	*tăyauq·k'an*
a double room	*hnăyauq·k'an*

CONVERSATION & ESSENTIALS

Hello.	*min·găla·ba*
How are you?	*k'ămyà* (m)/*shin* (f) *ne·kaùn·yéh·là?*
I'm well.	*ne·kaùn·ba·deh*
Have you eaten?	*t'ămìn sà·pì·bi·là?*
I have eaten.	*sà·pì·ba·bi*
Thanks.	*cè·zù·bèh*
Thank you.	*cè·zù tin·ba·deh*
You're welcome.	*keiq·sá măshí·ba·bù*
Yes.	*houq·kéh*
No.	*măhouq·p'ù*
Do you speak English?	*k'ămyà* (m)/*shin* (f) *ìn·găleiq·zăgà lo pyàw·daq·thălà?*
I don't understand.	*nà·măleh·ba·bù*

EMERGENCIES

Help!	*keh·ba!*
Call a doctor!	*s'ăya·wun·go k'aw·pè·ba!*
Call an ambulance!	*lu·na·din·gà k'aw·pè·ba!*
I'm lost.	*làn pyauq·thwà·bi*
Go away!	*thwà·zàn!*

FOOD & DRINK

Is there a ... near here?	*di·nà·hma shí·dhălà?*
Chinese restaurant	*tăyouq·s'ain*
food stall	*sà·thauq·s'ain*
restaurant	*sà·daw·s'eq*
Shan noodle stall	*shàn·k'auk·swèh·zain*
breakfast	*măneq·sa*
lunch	*né·leh·za*
dinner	*nyá·za*
snack/small meal	*móun/thăye·za*
I can't eat meat.	*ăthà măsà·nain·bù.*
beef	*ămèh*
bread	*paun·móun*
butter	*t'àw·baq*
chicken	*ceq·thà*
coffee	*kaw·fi*
egg (boiled)	*ceq·ú·byouq*
egg (fried)	*ceq·ú·jaw*
fish	*ngà*
hot (spicy)	*saq·deh*
pork	*weq·thà*
noodles	*k'auq·s'wèh*
rice (cooked)	*t'ămìn*
soup	*hìn·jo*
sugar	*thăjà*
plain green tea	*lăp'eq·yeh·jàn*
toast	*paun·móun·gin*
vegetables	*hìn·dhì·hìn·yweq*
vegetarian	*theq·thaq·luq*
water	*ye*
water (boiled, cold)	*ye·jeq·è*
water (bottled)	*thán·ye*

NUMBERS

1	*tiq/tă*
2	*hniq/hnă*
3	*thòun*
4	*lè*
5	*ngà*
6	*c'auq*
7	*k'ú·hniq/k'ú·hnă*
8	*shiq*
9	*kò*
10	*(tă)s'eh*
11	*s'éh·tiq*
12	*s'éh·hniq*
20	*hnăs'eh*
35	*thòun·zéh·ngà*
100	*tăya*
1000	*(tă)t'aun*
10,000	*(tă)thàun*
100,000	*(tă)thèin/lakh*

SHOPPING & SERVICES

Where is a/the ...?	*... beh·hma·lèh?*
bank	*ban·daiq*
hospital	*s'è·youn*
market	*zè*
pharmacy	*s'è·zain*
post office	*sa·daiq*
Where can I buy ...?	*... beh·hma weh·yá·măleh?*
Do you have ...?	*... shí·là*
How much is ...?	*... beh·lauq·lèh?*
expensive	*zè·ci·deh*
cheap	*zè·pàw·deh*

LANGUAGE

TIME & DAYS

today	*di·né*
tomorrow	*măneq·p'yan*
yesterday	*măné·gá*
Monday	*tănìn·la·né*
Tuesday	*in·ga·né*
Wednesday	*bouq·dăhù·né*
Thursday	*ca·dhăbădè·né*
Friday	*thauq·ca·né*
Saturday	*săne·né*
Sunday	*tănìn·gănwe·né*

TRANSPORT

Where is the ...?	*... beh·hma·lèh?*
bus station	*baq·săkà·geiq*
railway station	*bu·da·youn*
riverboat jetty	*thìn·bàw·zeiq*
When will the ... leave?	*... beh·ăc'ein t'weq·mălèh?*
bus	*baq·săkà*
train	*mì·yăt'à*
riverboat	*thìn·bàw*
taxi	*ăhngà·kà*
rickshaw/sidecar	*s'aiq·kà*
bicycle	*seq·bèin*
motorcycle	*mo·ta s'ain·keh*

Directions

How do I get to ...?	*... ko beh·lo thwà·yá·dhălèh?*
Is it nearby?	*di·nà·hma·là?*
Is it far?	*wè·dhălà?*
straight (ahead)	*téh·déh*
left/right	*beh·beq/nya·beq*

FILIPINO

ACCOMMODATION

camping ground	*kampingan*
guesthouse	*báhay pára sa nga turist*
cheap hotel	*múrang hotél*
price	*halagá*
Do you have any rooms available?	*May bakánte hó ba kayo?*
How much for one night?	*Magkáno hó ba ang báyad pára sa isang gabi?*

CONVERSATION & ESSENTIALS

Hello.	*Haló.*
Good morning.	*Magandáng umága.*
Good evening.	*Magandáng gabí.*
Welcome/Farewell.	*Mabúhay.*
Goodbye.	*Paálam.*
Thank you.	*Salámat hô.*
Excuse me.	*Mawaláng-galang nga hô.*
Yes.	*Oó.*
No.	*Hindí.*
Do you speak English?	*Marunong ba kayóng mag-Inglés?*
I don't understand.	*Hindí ko hô náiintindihán.*

EMERGENCIES

Help!	*Saklolo!*
Where are the toilets?	*Násaán hô ang CR?*
Go away!	*Umalís ka!*
Call ...!	*Tumawag ka ng ...!*
a doctor	*doktór*
the police	*pulís*

FOOD & DRINK

breakfast	*almusal/agahan*
lunch	*tanghalian*
dinner	*hapunan*
snack	*meryenda*
I'm a vegetarian.	*Gulay lamang ang kinákain ko.*
(cup of) tea	*(isang tásang) tsaá*
beer	*serbésa*
boiled water	*pinakuluáng túbig*
coffee	*kapé*
food	*pagkaín*
milk	*gátas*
restaurant	*restorán*
salt	*ásin*
sugar	*asúkal*
vegetables	*gulay*
water	*túbig*

NUMBERS

English numbers are often used for prices.

1	*isá*
2	*dalawá*
3	*tatló*
4	*apát*
5	*limá*
6	*ánim*
7	*pitó*
8	*waló*
9	*siyám*
10	*sampú*

11	*labíng-isá*
12	*labíndalawá*
20	*dalawampû*
30	*tatlumpû*
100	*sandaán*
1000	*isáng libo/sanlíbo*

SHOPPING & SERVICES

Where is a/the ...?	*Saán hô may ...?*
bank	*bangko*
market	*palengle*
post office	*pos opis*
public telephone	*telépono*
public toilet	*CR/pálikuran*
How much?	*Magkáno?*
too expensive	*mahál*

TIME & DAYS

What time is it?	*Anong óras na?*
today	*ngayon*
tomorrow	*búkas*
yesterday	*kahápon*
Monday	*Lunes*
Tuesday	*Martes*
Wednesday	*Miyérkolés*
Thursday	*Huwebes*
Friday	*Biyernes*
Saturday	*Sábado*
Sunday	*Linggó*

TRANSPORT

Where is the ...?	*Násaan ang ...?*
bus station	*terminal ng bus*
train station	*terminal ng tren*
road to ...	*daan papuntang ...*
What time does the bus leave/arrive?	*Anong óras áalis/ dárating ang bus?*

Directions

Is it far from/near here?	*Maláyó/malápit ba díto?*
straight ahead	*dirétso lámang*
to the right	*papakánan*
to the left	*papakaliwá*

KHMER (CAMBODIA)

PRONUNCIATION

The pronunciation guide below covers the trickier parts of the transliteration system used in this chapter. It uses the Roman alphabet to give the closest equivalent to the sounds of the Khmer language. The best way to improve your pronunciation is to listen carefully to native speakers.

Vowels

Vowels and diphthongs with an **h** at the end should be pronounced hard and aspirated (with a puff of air).

uh	as the 'u' in 'but'
eu	like saying 'oo' while keeping the lips spread flat rather than rounded
euh	as **eu** above; pronounced short and hard
oh	as the 'o' in 'hose'; pronounced short and hard
ow	as in 'glow'
ua	as the 'ou' in 'tour'
uah	as **ua** above; pronounced short and hard
aa-œ	a tricky one that has no English equivalent; like a combination of **aa** and **œ**
œ	as 'er' in 'her', but more open
eua	combination of **eu** and **a**
ai	as in 'aisle'
ae	as the 'a' in 'cat'
ao	as the 'ow' in 'cow'
av	no English equivalent; sounds like a very nasal **ao**; the final 'v' is not pronounced
euv	no English equivalent; sounds like a very nasal **eu**; the final 'v' is not pronounced
ohm	as the 'ome' in 'home'
am	as the 'um' in 'glum'
oam	a combination of 'o' and 'am'
eah	combination of 'e' and 'ah'; pronounced short and hard
awh	as the 'aw' in 'jaw'; pronounced short and hard
aw	as the 'aw' in 'jaw'

Consonants

Khmer uses some consonant combinations that may sound rather bizarre to Western ears and be equally difficult for Western tongues, eg 'j-r' in *j'rook* (pig), or 'ch-ng' in *ch'ngain* (delicious). In this guide these types of consonants are separated with an apostrophe to make pronunciation easier.

k	as the 'g' in 'go'
kh	as the 'k' in 'kind'
ng	as the 'ng' in 'sing'; a difficult sound for Westerners to emulate; practise by repeating 'singing-nging-nging-nging' until you can say 'nging' clearly
ny	as in 'canyon'
t	a hard, unaspirated 't' sound with no direct equivalent in English; similar to the 't' in 'stand'
th	as the 't' in 'two', never as the 'th' in 'thanks'

LANGUAGE

p a hard, unaspirated 'p', as the final 'p' in 'puppy'
ph as the 'p' in 'pond', never as 'f'
r as in 'rum', but hard and rolling, with the tongue flapping against the palate; in rapid conversation it is often omitted entirely
w as in 'would'; contrary to the common transliteration system, there is no equivalent to the English 'v' sound in Khmer

ACCOMMODATION

Where is a (cheap) hotel?	*sahnthaakia/ohtail (thaok) neuv ai naa?*
Do you have a room?	*niak mian bantohp tohmne te?*
How much is it per day?	*damlay muy th'ngay pohnmaan?*
I'd like a room ...	*kh'nyohm sohm bantohp ...*
for one person	*samruhp muy niak*
for two people	*samruhp pii niak*
with a bathroom	*dail mian bantohp tuhk*
with a fan	*dail mian dawnghahl*
with a window	*dail mian bawng-uit*

CONVERSATION & ESSENTIALS

Forms of Address

The Khmer language reflects the social standing of the speaker and subject through various personal pronouns and 'politeness words'. These range from the simple *baat* for men and *jaa* for women, placed at the end of a sentence, meaning 'yes' or 'I agree', to the very formal and archaic *Reachasahp* or 'Royal Language', a separate vocabulary reserved for addressing the king and very high officials. Many of the pronouns are determined on the basis of the subject's age and sex in relation to the speaker. Foreigners are not expected to know all of these forms. The easiest and most general personal pronoun is *niak* (you), which may be used in most situations and with either sex. Men of your age or older may be called *lowk* (mister). Women of your age or older can be called *bawng srei* (older sister) or for more formal situations, *lowk srei* (madam). *Bawng* is a good informal, neutral pronoun for men or women who are (or appear to be) older than you. For third person, male or female, singular or plural, the respectful form is *koat* and the common form is *ke.*

Hello.	*johm riab sua/sua s'dei*
Goodbye.	*lia suhn hao-y*
See you later.	*juab kh'nia th'ngay krao-y*
Yes.	*baat* (used by men)
	jaa (used by women)
No.	*te*
Please.	*sohm*
Thank you.	*aw kohn*
Excuse me/I'm sorry.	*sohm toh*
Hi. How are you?	*niak sohk sabaay te?*
I'm fine.	*kh'nyohm sohk sabaay*
Where are you going?	*niak teuv naa?* (a very common question used when meeting people, even strangers; an exact answer isn't necessary)
Does any one here speak English?	*tii nih mian niak jeh phiasaa awngle te?*
I don't understand.	*kh'nyohm muhn yuhl te/ kh'nyohm s'dap muhn baan te*

EMERGENCIES

Help!	*juay kh'nyohm phawng!*
Call a doctor!	*juay hav kruu paet mao!*
Call the police!	*juay hav polih mao!*
Where are the toilets?	*bawngkohn neuv ai naa?*

FOOD & DRINK

restaurant	*resturaan/phowjuhniiyathaan*
food stall	*kuhnlaing luak m'howp*
market	*p'saa*
I'm a vegetarian.	*kh'nyohm tawm sait*
beef	*sait kow*
chicken	*sait moan*
fish	*trei*
coffee	*kaafe*
boiled water	*tuhk ch'uhn*
milk	*tuhk dawh kow*
tea	*tai*
sugar	*skaw*

NUMBERS & AMOUNTS

Khmers count in increments of five. Thus, after reaching the number five *(bram)*, the cycle begins again with the addition of one, ie 'five-one' *(bram muy)*, 'five-two' *(bram pii)* and so on to 10, which begins a new cycle. This system is a bit awkward at first (for example, 18, which has three parts: 10, five and three) but with practice it can be mastered.

You may be confused by a colloquial form of counting that reverses the word order for numbers between 10 and 20 and

LANGUAGE

separates the two words with *duhn: pii duhn dawp* for 12, *bei duhn dawp* for 13, *bram buan duhn dawp* for 19 and so on. This form is often used in markets, so listen keenly.

1	*muy*
2	*pii*
3	*bei*
4	*buan*
5	*bram*
6	*bram muy*
7	*bram pii/puhl*
8	*bram bei*
9	*bram buan*
10	*dawp*
11	*dawp muy*
12	*dawp pii*
16	*dawp bram muy*
20	*m'phei*
21	*m'phei muy*
30	*saamsuhp*
40	*saisuhp*
100	*muy roy*
1000	*muy poan*
1,000,000	*muy lian*

SHOPPING & SERVICES

I'm looking for the ...	*kh'nyohm rohk ...*
Where is a/the ...	*... neuv ai naa?*
bank	*th'niakia*
hospital	*mohntii paet*
market	*p'saa*
police station	*poh polih/ s'thaanii nohkohbaal*
post office	*praisuhnii*
public telephone	*turasahp saathiaranah*
public toilet	*bawngkohn saathiaranah*

How much is it?	*nih th'lay pohnmaan?*
That's too much.	*th'lay pek*

TIME & DAYS

What time is it?	*eileuv nih maong pohnmaan?*
today	*th'ngay nih*
tomorrow	*th'ngay s'aik*

Monday	*th'ngay jahn*
Tuesday	*th'ngay ahngkia*
Wednesday	*th'ngay poht*
Thursday	*th'ngay prohoah*
Friday	*th'ngay sohk*
Saturday	*th'ngay sav*
Sunday	*th'ngay aatuht*

TRANSPORT

What time does the ... leave?	*... jein maong pohnmaan?*
boat	*duk*
bus	*laan ch'nual*
train	*roht plœng*
plane	*yohn hawh/k'pal hawh*

airport	*wial yohn hawh*
bus station	*kuhnlaing laan ch'nual*
bus stop	*jamnawt laan ch'nual*
train station	*s'thaanii roht plœng*

Directions

How can I get to ...?	*phleuv naa teuv ...?*
Is it far?	*wia neuv ch'ngaay te?*
Is it near here?	*wia neuv juht nih te?*
Go straight ahead.	*teuv trawng*
Turn left.	*bawt ch'weng*
Turn right.	*bawt s'dam*

LAO

PRONUNCIATION

Vowels

ae	as the 'a' in 'bad' or 'tab'
eh	as the 'a' in 'hate'
oe	as the 'u' in 'fur'
eu	as the 'i' in 'sir'
u	as in 'flute'
aai	as the 'a' in 'father' plus the 'i' in 'pipe'
ao	as in 'now' or 'cow'
aw	as in 'jaw'
eua	diphthong of 'eu' and 'a'
uay	'u-ay-ee'
iu	'i-oo' (as in 'yew')
iaw	a triphthong of 'ee-a-oo'
aew	as the 'a' in 'bad' plus 'w'
ehw	as the 'a' in 'care' plus 'w'
ew	same as **ehw** above, but shorter (not as in 'yew')
oei	'oe-i'
awy	as the 'oy' in 'boy'
ohy	'oh-i'

Consonants

Transliterated consonants are mostly pronounced as per their English counterparts (the exceptions are listed below). An 'aspirated' consonant is produced with no audible puff of air. An 'unvoiced' or 'voiceless' consonant is produced with no vibration in the vocal chords.

k	as the 'k' in 'skin'; similar to the 'g' in 'good', but unaspirated and unvoiced
kh	as the 'k' in 'kite'
ng	as in 'sing'; used as an initial consonant in Lao
j	similar to 'j' in 'join' or, more closely, the second 't' in 'stature' or 'literature' (unaspirated and unvoiced)
ny	as in 'canyon'; used as an initial consonant in Lao
t	a hard 't', unaspirated and unvoiced – a bit like 'd'
th	as in 'tip'
p	a hard 'p' (unaspirated and unvoiced)
ph	'p' as in 'put', never as 'f'

Tones

Lao is a tonal language, whereby many identical phonemes are differentiated only by tone (changes in the pitch of a speaker's voice). The word *sao*, for example, can mean 'girl', 'morning', 'pillar' or 'twenty', depending on the tone. Pitch variations are relative to the speaker's natural vocal range, so that one person's low tone isn't necessarily the same pitch as another person's.

low tone – produced at the relative bottom of your conversational tonal range, usually flat level, eg *dji* (good)
mid tone – flat like the low tone, but spoken at the relative middle of the speaker's vocal range. No tone mark is used, eg *het* (do)
high tone – flat again, but at the relative top of your vocal range, eg *heúa* (boat)
rising tone – begins a bit below the mid tone and rises to just at or above the high tone, eg *săam* (three)
high falling tone – begins at or above the high tone and falls to the mid level, eg *sâo* (morning)
low falling tone – begins at about the mid level and falls to the level of the low tone, eg *khào* (rice)

ACCOMMODATION

Where's a ...? *... yùu săi?*
camping ground *born dâng kêm*
guesthouse *héu-an pak*
hotel *hóhng háem*

Do you have a ...? *jôw míi ... wâhng baw?*
double room *hàwng náwn tĭang khuu*
single room *hàwng náwn tĭang diaw*

How much is it per ...? *... thao dạ?*
night *khéun-la*
person *khón-la*

bathroom *hàwng nâm*
toilet *sùam*

CONVERSATION & ESSENTIALS

Greetings/Hello. *sábạai-dĭi*
Goodbye. (general farewell) *sábạai-dĭi*
Goodbye. (person leaving) *láa kawn pại kawn*
Goodbye. (person staying) *sŏhk dĭi* (lit: good luck)
See you later. *phop kạn mai*
Thank you. *khàwp jại*
Thank you very much. *khàwp jại lăi lăi*
Excuse me. *khăw thŏht*
How are you? *sábạai-dĭi baw?*
I'm fine. *sábạai-dĭi*
And you? *jâo dêh?*
Can you speak English? *jâo pàak pháasăa ạngkít dâi baw?*
I don't understand. *baw khào jại*

EMERGENCIES

Help! *suay dae!*
Go away! *pại dôe!*
I'm lost. *khàwy lŏng tháang*
Where are the toilets? *hàwng sùam yuu săi?*
Call a doctor! *suay tạam hăa măw hài dae!*
Call the police! *suay ôen tam-lùat dae!*

FOOD & DRINK

I eat only vegetables. *khàwy kịn tae phák*
chicken *kai*
crab *pŭ*
fish *pạa*
pork *mŭu*
shrimp/prawns *kûngy*
fried rice with ... *khào (phát/khùa) ...*
steamed white rice *khào nèung*
sticky rice *khào nío*
fried egg *khai dạo*
plain omelette *jẹun khai*
fried potatoes *mán falang jẹun*
fried spring rolls *yáw jẹun*
plain bread (usually French-style) *khào jii*
boiled water *nâam tọm*
cold water *nâam yén*
hot water *nâam hâwn*
soda water *nâam sah·dạa*
ice *nâam kâwn*
weak Chinese tea *nâam sáa*
hot Lao tea *sáa hâwn*
no sugar (a request) *baw sai nâam·tạan*
coffee *kạa·féh*
orange juice/soda *nâam màak kîang*
plain milk *nâam nóm*
yoghurt *nóm sòm*

beer	*bịa*
rice whisky	*lào-láo*

NUMBERS

0	*sŭun*
1	*neung*
2	*săwng*
3	*săam*
4	*sii*
5	*hàa*
6	*hók*
7	*jét*
8	*pàet*
9	*kâo*
10	*síp*
11	*síp-ét*
12	*síp-săwng*
20	*sáo*
21	*sáo-ét*
22	*sáo-săwng*
30	*săam-síp*
100	*hâwy*
200	*săwng hâwy*
1000	*phán*
10,000	*meun (síp-phán)*
100,000	*săen (hâwy phán)*

SHOPPING & SERVICES

Where is the ...?	*... yùu săi?*
I'm looking for (the) ...	*khàwy sâwk hăa ...*
bank	*thanáakháan*
hospital	*hóhng măw*
pharmacy	*hâan khăai yạa*
post office	*pại-sá-nii (hóhng săai)*
public toilet	*hòrng nâm să-ta-là-nà*
telephone	*thóhlasáp*

How much (for) ...?	*... thao dại?*
The price is very high.	*láakháa pháeng lăai*

TIME & DATES

What time is it?	*wáir-láh ják móhng*
At what time?	*dorn ják móhng*
At ...	*dorn ...*
today	*mêu nîi*
tomorrow	*mêu eun*

Monday	*wán jạn*
Tuesday	*wán ạngkháan*
Wednesday	*wán phut*
Thursday	*wán phahát*
Friday	*wán súk*
Saturday	*wán săo*
Sunday	*wán ạthit*

TRANSPORT

What time will the ... leave?	*... já àwk ják móhng?*
boat	*héua*
bus	*lot*
minivan	*lot tûu*
plane	*héua bĭn*
What time (does it) arrive there?	*já pai hâwt phûn ják móhng?*

Where is the ...?	*... yùu săi?*
airport	*doen bĭn*
bus station	*sathăanii lot pájạm tháang*
bus stop	*bawn jàwt lot pájạm tháang*

Directions

I want to go to ...	*khàwy yàak pại ...*
Turn left/right.	*lîaw sâai/khwăa*
Go straight ahead.	*pại seu-seu*
How far?	*kại thao dại?*
near/not near	*kâi/baw kâi*
far/not far	*kại/baw kại*

TETUN (EAST TIMOR)

Tetun is the most widely spoken lingua franca in East Timor. Originally spoken on the south coast of Timor, a form of Tetun was brought to Dili by the Portuguese in the late 18th century. Although Portuguese was nominated East Timor's official language after East Timor gained independence, Tetun became the national language with the intention of making it co-official with Portuguese.

PRONUNCIATION

j	as the 's' in 'pleasure' (sometimes as the 'z' in 'zoo')
r	trilled
x	as the 'sh' in 'ship' (the Portuguese-style spelling is **ch**); sometimes pronounced as the 's' in 'summer'

ACCOMMODATION

I'm looking for a ...	*Hau buka hela ...*
guesthouse	*losmen/pensaun*
hotel	*otél*

Do you have any rooms available?	*Ita iha kuartu ruma mamuk?*

I'd like ...	*Hau hakarak ...*
a single room	*kuartu mesak ida*
to share a room	*fahe kuartu ida*

CONVERSATION & ESSENTIALS

Hello.	*Haló.* (pol)/*Olá.* (inf)
Goodbye.	*Adeus.*
Yes.	*Sin/Diak/Los.*
No.	*Lae.*
Please.	*Favór ida/Halo favór/ Faz favór/Por favór.*
Thank you (very much).	*Obrigadu/a (barak).*
You're welcome.	*La (iha) buat ida./(De) nada.*
Excuse me.	*Kolisensa.*
What's your name?	*Ita-nia naran sa/saida?*
My name is ...	*Hau-nia naran ...*
Do you speak English?	*Ita koalia Inglés?*
I don't understand.	*Hau la kompriende.*

EMERGENCIES

Help!	*Ajuda!*
Call a doctor!	*Bolu dotór!*
Call the police!	*Bolu polísia!*
I'm lost.	*Hau lakon tiha.*
Where are the toilets?	*Sintina iha nebé?*

FOOD & DRINK

breakfast	*matebixu; han dadér*
lunch	*han meudia*
dinner	*jantár*
I'm a vegetarian.	*Hau (ema) vejetarianu.*
bread	*paun*
butter	*manteiga*
chicken	*nan manu*
eggs	*manutolun*
fish	*ikan*
fruit	*aifuan*
milk	*susubén*
pepper	*pimenta*
salt	*masin*
sugar	*masin midar* (lit: sweet salt)
vegetables	*modo tahan*
water	*be*
mineral water	*be minerál*
boiled water	*be tasak/nono*
bottled water	*ákua; be botir*
tea	*xa*
(Timorese) coffee	*kafé (Timór)*
beer	*serveja*

NUMBERS

Larger numbers are given in Tetun, Portuguese or Indonesian.

	Tetun	Portuguese
0	*nol*	*zero*
1	*ida*	*um/uma*
2	*rua*	*dois/duas*
3	*tolu*	*três*
4	*hat*	*quatro*
5	*lima*	*cinco*
6	*nen*	*seis*
7	*hitu*	*sete*
8	*ualu*	*oito*
9	*sia*	*nove*
10	*sanulu*	*dez*
11	*sanulu-resin-ida*	*onze*
12	*sanulu-resin-rua*	*doze*
20	*ruanulu*	*vinte*
100	*atus ida*	*cem*
1000	*rihun ida*	*mil*

SHOPPING & SERVICES

Where is a/the ...?	*... iha nebé?*
bank	*banku*
general store	*loja*
market	*basar/merkadu*
post office	*koreiu; kantor pos*
public telephone	*telefone públiku; wartel*
toilet	*sintina/WC*
What time does ... open/close?	*Tuku hira maka ... loke/taka?*
How much is it?	*Folin hira?*

TIME & DAYS

What time is it?	*Tuku hira (ona)?*
(It's) one o'clock.	*Tuku ida.*
today	*ohin*
tonight	*ohin kalan*
tomorrow	*aban*
Monday	*segunda*
Tuesday	*tersa*
Wednesday	*kuarta*
Thursday	*kinta*
Friday	*sesta*
Saturday	*sábadu*
Sunday	*dumingu*

TRANSPORT

When does the ... leave/arrive?	*Tuku hira maka ... ba/to?*
bus	*bis/biskota*
minibus	*mikrolet*
plane	*aviaun*
bus station	*terminál bis nian*
road to (Aileu)	*dalan ba (Aileu)*

Directions

Go straight ahead.	*Los deit.*
To the left.	*Fila ba liman karuk.*

To the right.	*Fila ba liman los.*
near	*besik*
far	*dok*

THAI

PRONUNCIATION

The 'ph' in a Thai word is always pronounced like an English 'p', not as an 'f'. The letter **đ** represents a hard 't' sound, like a sharp 'd'.

Tones

Thai is a tonal language, where changes in pitch can affect meaning. The range of all five tones is relative to each speaker's vocal range, so there's no fixed 'pitch' intrinsic to the language. The five tones of Thai:

low tone – 'flat' like the mid tone, but pronounced at the relative bottom of one's vocal range. It is low, level and has no inflection, eg *bàht* (baht – the Thai currency)
mid tone – pronounced 'flat', at the relative middle of the speaker's vocal range, eg *dee* (good); no tone mark is used
falling tone – starting high and falling sharply; this tone is similar to the change in pitch in English when you are emphasising a word, or calling someone's name from afar, eg *mâi* (no/not)
high tone – usually the most difficult for Westerners. It is pronounced near the relative top of the vocal range, as level as possible, eg *máh* (horse)
rising tone – starting low and gradually rising; sounds like the inflection used by English speakers to imply a question ('Yes?'), eg *săhm* (three)

ACCOMMODATION

I'm looking for a ...	*pŏm/dì·chăn gam·lang hăh ...*
guesthouse	*bâhn pák/ gèt hów* ('guest house')
hotel	*rohng raam*
youth hostel	*bâhn yow·wá·chon*

Do you have any rooms available?	*mee hôrng wâhng măi?*

I'd like (a) ...	*đôrng gahn ...*
bed	*đee·ang norn*
single room	*hôrng dèe·o*
double room	*hôrng kôo*
room with two beds	*hôrng têe mee đee·ang sŏrng đoo·a*
ordinary room (with fan)	*hôrng tam·-má·dah (mee pát lom)*
to share a dorm	*pák nai hŏr pák*

How much is it ...?	*...tôw rai?*
per night	*keun lá*
per person	*kon lá*

CONVERSATION & ESSENTIALS

When being polite, the speaker ends his or her sentence with *kráp* (for men) or *kâ* (for women). It is the gender of the speaker that is being expressed here; it is also the common way to answer 'yes' to a question or show agreement.

Hello.	*sà·wàt·dee (kráp/kâ)*
Goodbye.	*lah gòrn*
Yes.	*châi*
No.	*mâi châi*
Please.	*gà·rú·nah*
Thank you.	*kòrp kun*
Excuse me.	*kŏr à·pai*
Sorry. (Forgive me)	*kŏr tôht*
How are you?	*sà·bai dee rĕu?*
I'm fine, thanks.	*sà·bai dee*
Do you speak English?	*kun pôot pah·săh ang·grìt dâi măi?*

EMERGENCIES

Help!	*chôo·ay dôo·ay!*
I'm lost.	*chăn lŏng tahng*
Go away!	*ɓai sí!*
Stop!	*yùt!*

Call ...!	*rêe·ak ... nòy!*
a doctor	*mŏr*
the police	*đam·ròo·at*

FOOD & DRINK

I'd like ...	*kŏr ...*
I'm allergic to ...	*pŏm/dì·chăn páa ...*
I don't eat ...	*pŏm/dì·chăn gin ... mâi dâi*
chicken	*gài*
fish	*ɓlah*
meat	*néu·a sàt*
pork	*mŏo*
seafood	*ah·hăhn tá·lair*

rice	*kôw*
rice noodles	*gŏo·ay đĕe·o*
beer	*bee·a*
coffee	*gah·faa*
tea	*chah*
milk	*nom jèut*
water	*nám*
ice	*nám kăang*

NUMBERS

0	*sŏon*
1	*nèung*
2	*sŏrng*
3	*săhm*
4	*sèe*
5	*hâh*
6	*hòk*
7	*jèt*
8	*ɓàat*
9	*gôw*
10	*sìp*
11	*sìp·èt*
12	*sìp·sŏrng*
13	*sìp·săhm*
20	*yêe·sìp*
21	*yêe·sìp·èt*
22	*yêe·sìp·sŏrng*
30	*săhm·sìp*
40	*sèe·sìp*
100	*nèung róy*
200	*sŏrng róy*
1000	*nèung pan*
2000	*sŏrng pan*
10,000	*nèung mèun*
100,000	*nèung sáan*

SHOPPING & SERVICES

I'm looking for ...	*pŏm/dì·chăn gam·lang hăh ...*
a bank	*tá·nah·kahn*
the market	*đà·làht*
the post office	*ɓrai·sà·nee*
a public toilet	*hôrng nám săh·tah·rá·ná*
the telephone centre	*sŏon toh·rá·sàp*
the tourist office	*săm·nák ngahn tôrng têe·o*

I'd like to buy ...	*yàhk jà séu ...*
How much?	*tôw rai?*
It's too expensive.	*paang geun ɓai*

TIME & DAYS

What time is it?	*gèe mohng láa·ou?*
It's (8 o'clock).	*ɓàat mohng láa·ou*
When?	*mêu·a·rai?*
today	*wan née*
tomorrow	*prûng née*

Monday	*wan jan*
Tuesday	*wan ang·kahn*
Wednesday	*wan pút*
Thursday	*wan pá·réu·hàt*
Friday	*wan sùk*
Saturday	*wan sŏw*
Sunday	*wan ah·tít*

TRANSPORT

What time does the ... leave?
... jà òrk gèe mohng?
What time does the ... arrive?
... jà tĕung gèe mohng?

boat	*reu·a*
bus (city)	*rót mair*
bus (intercity)	*rót too·a*
plane	*krêu·ang bin*
train	*rót fai*

airport	*sa·năhm bin*
bus station	*sa·tăh·nee kŏn sòng*
bus stop	*ɓâi rót mair*
train station	*sa·tăh·nee rót fai*

Directions

Where is (the) ...?	*... yòo têe năi?*
(Go) Straight ahead.	*đrong ɓai*
Turn left.	*lée·o sái*
Turn right.	*lée·o kwăh*
far	*glai*
near	*glâi*
not far	*mâi glai*

VIETNAMESE

There are differences between the Vietnamese of the north and the Vietnamese of the south; where different forms are used in this guide, they are indicated by 'N' for the north and 'S' for the south.

TONES & PRONUNCIATION

To help you make sense of what is (for non-Vietnamese) a very tricky writing system, the words and phrases in this language guide include pronunciations that use a written form more familiar to English speakers. The symbols used for marking the tones are the same as those used in standard written Vietnamese.

	SYMBOL	PRONUNCIATION
c, k	ğ	an unaspirated 'k'
đ	đ	(with crossbar) as in 'do'
d	z/y	(without crossbar) as the 'z' in 'zoo' (N); as the 'y' in 'yes' (S)
gi-	z/y	as a 'z' (N); as a 'y' (S)
kh-	ch	as the 'ch' in German *buch*
ng-	ng	as the '-nga-' sound in 'long ago'
nh-	ny	as the 'ny' in 'canyon'
ph-	f	as in 'farm'

r	**z/r**	as 'z' (N); as 'r' (S)
s	**s/sh**	as 's' (N); as 'sh' (S)
tr-	**ch/tr**	as 'ch' (N); as 'tr' (S)
th-	**t**	a strongly aspirated 't'
x	**s**	like an 's'
-ch	**k**	like a 'k'
-ng	**ng**	as the 'ng' in 'long' but with the lips closed; sounds like English 'm'
-nh	**ng**	as in 'singing'

Vietnamese has six tones, so that a single syllable can have as many as six different meanings. The word *ma*, for example, can be read to mean 'phantom', 'but', 'mother', 'rice seedling', 'tomb' or 'horse'. The six tones are represented by five diacritical marks in the written language (the first tone is left unmarked).

ma (ghost) – middle of the vocal range
mà (which) – begins low and falls lower
mả (tomb) – begins low, dips and then rises to higher pitch
mã (horse) – begins high, dips slightly, then rises sharply
mạ (rice seedling) – begins low, falls to a lower level, then stops
má (mother) – begins high and rises sharply

ACCOMMODATION

Where is there a (cheap) ...?
Đâu có ... (rẻ tiền)? — đoh ğó ... (zả đee·ùhn)?
camping ground
nơi cắm trại — ner·ee ğúhm chại
guesthouse
nhà khách — nyaà kaák
hotel
khách sạn — kaák sạn

air-conditioning
máy lạnh — máy laạng
bathroom
phòng tắm — fòm dúhm
hot water
nước nóng — nuhr·érk nóm
toilet
nhà vệ sinh — nyaà vẹ sing

I'd like (a) ...
Tôi muốn ... — doy moo·úhn ...
single room
phòng đơn — fòm dern
double-bed
giường đôi — zuhr·èrng đoy
room with two beds
phòng gồm hai giường ngủ — fòm gàwm hai zuhr·èrng ngoỏ

EMERGENCIES

Help!
Cứu tôi! — ğuhr·oó doy!
I'm lost.
Tôi bị lạc đường. — doi beẹ laạk đuhr·èrng
Leave me alone!
Thôi! — toy!
Where's the toilet?
Nhà vệ sinh ở đâu? — nyaà vẹ sing ẻr doh?

Please call ...
Làm ơn gọi ... — laàm ern gọy ...
a doctor
bác sĩ — baák seẽ
the police
công an — ğawm aan

How much is it ...?
Giá bao nhiêu ...? — zaá bow nyee·oo ...?
per night
một đêm — mạwt đem
per person
một người — mạwt nguhr·eè

CONVERSATION & ESSENTIALS

There are many different forms of address in Vietnamese. The safest way to address people is *ông* (to a man of any status), *anh* (to a young man), *bà* (to a middle-aged or older woman), *cô* (to a young woman) and *em* (to a child).

Hello.
Xin chào. — sin jòw
Goodbye.
Tạm biệt. — dụm bee·ẹt
Please.
Làm ơn. — làm ern
Thank you.
Cảm ơn. — kảm ern
Excuse me.
Xin lỗi. — sin lõ·ee
Yes.
Vâng. (N) — vang
Dạ. (S) — yạ
No.
Không. — kom
How are you?
Có khỏe không? — káw kwẻir kom?
Fine, thank you.
Khỏe, cám ơn. — kwẻir kảm ern
Do you speak English?
Bạn có nói được tiếng anh không? — Baạn ğó nóy đuhr·ẹrk díng aang kawm?

LANGUAGE

I (don't) understand.
Tôi (không) hiểu. doy (kawm) heẻ·oo

FOOD & DRINK

I'm a vegetarian.
Tôi ăn chay. doy uhn jay

bread	
bánh mì	baáng mèe
steamed rice	
cơm trắng	ğerm chúhng
vegetables	
rau sống	zoh sáwm
noodles	
mì	meè
beef	
thịt bò	tịt bò
chicken	
thịt gà	tịt gaà
fish	
cá	ğaá
pork	
thịt heo	tịt hay-oo
mineral water	
nước khoáng/ nước suối (N/S)	nuhr-érk kwaáng/ nuhr-érk soo-eé
tea	
chè/trà (N/S)	jà/chaà
coffee	
cà phê	ğaà fe
milk	
sữa	sũhr·uh
beer	
bia	bi·uh
ice	
đá	đaá

NUMBERS

1	*một*	mạwt
2	*hai*	hai
3	*ba*	baa
4	*bốn*	báwn
5	*năm*	nuhm
6	*sáu*	sóh
7	*bảy*	bảy
8	*tám*	dúhm
9	*chín*	jín
10	*mười*	muhr·eè
11	*mười một*	muhr·eè mọt
19	*mười chín*	muhr·eè jín
20	*hai mươi*	hai muhr·ee
21	*hai mươi mốt*	hai muhr·ee máwt
22	*hai mươi hai*	hai muhr·ee hai
30	*ba mươi*	ba muhr·ee
90	*chín mươi*	jín muhr·ee
100	*một trăm*	mạwt chuhm
200	*hai trăm*	hai chuhm
900	*chín trăm*	jín chuhm
1000	*một nghìn* (N)	mạwt ngyìn
	một ngàn (S)	mọt ngaàn
10,000	*mười nghìn* (N)	muhr·eè ngyìn
	mười ngàn (S)	muhr·eè ngaàn

SHOPPING & SERVICES

I'm looking for ...
Tôi tìm ... doy dìm ...

a bank	
ngân hàng	nguhn haàng
the hospital	
nhà thương	nyaà tuhr·erng
the market	
chợ	jẹr
the post office	
bưu điện	buhr·oo đee·ụhn
a public phone	
phòng điện thoại	fòm đee·ụhn twaị
a public toilet	
phòng vệ sinh	fòm vẹ sing
tourist office	
văn phòng hướng dẫn du lịch	vuhn fòm huhr·érng zũhn zoo lịk

How much is this?
Cái này giá bao nhiêu? ğaí này zaá bow nyee·oo?

It's too expensive.
Cái này quá mắc. ğaí này gwaá múhk

TIME & DAYS

What time is it?
Mấy giờ rồi? máy zèr zòy?

It's ... o'clock.
Bây giờ là ... giờ. bay zèr laà ... zèr

now	*bây giờ*	bay zèr
today	*hôm nay*	hawm nay
tomorrow	*ngày mai*	ngày mai
Monday	*thứ hai*	túhr hai
Tuesday	*thứ ba*	túhr baa
Wednesday	*thứ tư*	túhr duhr
Thursday	*thứ năm*	túhr nuhm
Friday	*thứ sáu*	túhr sóh
Saturday	*thứ bảy*	túhr bảy
Sunday	*chủ nhật*	jỏo nhụht

TRANSPORT

What time does the (first)... leave/arrive?
Chuyến ... (sớm nhất) chạy lúc mấy giờ?
jwee·úhn ... (sérm nyúht) jay lúp máy zèr?

boat	
tàu/thuyền	dòw/twee·ùhn

bus	
xe buýt	sa beét
plane	
máy bay	máy bay
train	
xe lửa	sa lủhr·uh

Directions

Where is ...?	
ở đâu ...?	ẻr đoh ...?
I want to go to ...	
Tôi muốn đi ...	doy moo·úhn đee ...
Go straight ahead.	
Thẳng tới trước.	tủhng der·eé chuhr·érk
Can you show me (on the map)?	
Xin chỉ giùm (trên bản đồ này)?	sin jeẻ zùm (chen baản đàw này)?
Turn left.	
Sang trái.	saang chaí
Turn right.	
Sang phải.	saang faỉ
at the corner	
ở góc đường	ẻr góp đuhr·èrng
at the traffic lights	
tại đèn giao tawm	dại đèn zow *thông*
far	
xa	saa
near (to)	
gần	gùhn

LANGUAGE

Glossary

ABBREVIATIONS
B – Brunei
C – Cambodia
ET – East Timor
I – Indonesia
L – Laos
M – Malaysia
My – Myanmar (Burma)
P – Philippines
S – Singapore
T – Thailand
V – Vietnam

ABC (M) – Air Batang
adat (B, I, M, S) – customary law
alun alun (I) – main public square of a town
andong (I) – four-wheeled horse-drawn cart
angguna (ET) – tray truck where passengers (including the odd buffalo or goat) all pile into the back
angkot (I) – see *bemo*
ao (T) – bay, gulf
ao dai (V) – traditional Vietnamese tunic and trousers
apsara (C) – dancing girl, celestial nymph
argo (I) – taxi meter; 'luxury' class on trains
Asean – Association of Southeast Asian Nations
asura (C) – demon

bâan (T) – house, village; also written as *ban*
Baba Nonya (M) – descendents of Chinese settlers in the Straits Settlements (Melaka, Singapore and Penang) who intermarried with Malays and adopted many Malay customs; also written as 'Baba Nyonya'
bajaj (I) – motorised three-wheeled taxi
Bamar (My) – Burmese ethnic group
bangka (P) – local outrigger, pumpboat
barangay (P) – village
batik (I, M) – cloth coloured by a waxing and dyeing process
BE (L) – Buddhist Era
becak (I) – bicycle rickshaw
bemo (I) – three-wheeled pick-up truck, often with two rows of seats down the side
bendi (I) – two-person horse-drawn cart
benteng (I) – fort
bis kota (I) – city bus
bisnis (I) – business class on buses, trains etc
boeng (C) – lake
BSB (B) – Bandar Seri Begawan
bukit (B, I, M, S) – hill
bumboat (S) – motorised *sampan*
bun (L) – festival
butanding (P) – whale shark
buu dien (V) – post office

Caodaism (V) – Vietnamese religion
CAT (T) – Communications Authority of Thailand
Cham (C,V) – ethnic minority descended from the people of Champa, a Hindu kingdom dating from the 2nd century BC
chedi (T) – see *stupa*
chunchiet (C) – ethnolinguistic minorities
cidomo (I) – horse-drawn cart
colt (I) – see *opelet*
CPP (C) – Cambodian People's Party
CTT (My) – Central Telephone & Telegraph
cyclo (C, V) – pedicab

Đ (V) – abbreviation of *duong*
ĐL (V) – abbreviation of *dai lo*
dai lo (V) – boulevard; abbreviated as 'ĐL'
dangdut (I) – Indonesian dance music with strong Arabic and Hindi influences (I)
datu (P) – traditional local chief, head of village
DENR (P) – Department of Environment & Natural Resources
deva (C) – god
devaraja (C) – god-king
DMZ (V) – Demilitarised Zone
dokar (I) – two-wheeled horse-drawn cart
DOT (P) – Department of Tourism
duong (V) – road, street; abbreviated as 'Đ'

Ecpat – End Child Prostitution & Trafficking
ekonomi (I, M) – economy class on buses, trains and other transport
eksekutif (I, M) – executive (ie 1st) class on buses, trains and other transport

falang (L) – Western, Westerner; foreigner
faràng (T) – Western, Westerner; foreigner
FEC (My) – Foreign Exchange Certificate

gamelan (I, M) – traditional Javanese and Balinese orchestra with large xylophones and gongs
gang (I) – alley, lane
gua (I, M) – cave
gunung (I, M) – mountain

hàat (T) – beach; also written as *hat*
habal-habal (P) – motorcycle taxi
HCMC (V) – Ho Chi Minh City
héua hang nyáo (L) – longtail boat
héua phai (L) – rowboat
héua wái (L) – speedboat
Honda om (V) – see *xe om*
hti (My) – decorated top of a *stupa*

ikat (I) – cloth in which a pattern is produced by dyeing individual threads before the weaving process
istana (B, I, M, S) – palace

jalan (B, ET, I, M, S) – road, street; abbreviated as 'Jl'
jataka (T) – stories of the Buddha's past lives, often enacted in dance-drama
JB (M) – Johor Bahru
jeepney (P) – wildly ornamented public transport, originally based on WWII US Army Jeeps
Jl (B, ET, I, M, S) – abbreviation of *jalan*

kaa (My) – city bus
kain songket (M) – fabric woven with gold and/or silver thread
kaki lima (I) – mobile food stall; food court
kalaga (My) – tapestry embroidered with silver threads and sequins
kalesa (P) – two-wheeled horse-drawn cart
kampung (B, I, M, S) – village; also written as *kampong*
kantor pos (I) – post office
kapal biasa (I) – river ferry
karst – limestone region with caves, underground streams, potholes etc
kàthoey (T) – transvestite, transsexual
kedai kopi (M) – coffee shop
khăo (T) – hill, mountain; also written as *khao*
khlong (T) – canal; also written as *khlawng*
khwăn (L) – guardian spirits of the body
KK (M) – Kota Kinabalu
KL (M) – Kuala Lumpur
KLIA (M) – Kuala Lumpur International Airport
klotok (I) – motorised canoe
ko (T) – island
koh (C) – island
kongsi (M) – Chinese clan organisations, also known as ritual brotherhoods, heaven-man-earth societies, triads or secret societies; meeting house for Chinese of the same clan
kota (ET, I, M) – fort, city
krama (C) – checked scarf
kraton (I) – palace
kris (I) – traditional dagger
KTM (M) – Keretapi Tanah Melayu; national rail service
kyaung (My) – Buddhist monastery

labuan (M) – port
lákhon (T) – dance drama
lí-keh (T) – popular form of folk dance-drama; also written as *likay*
longhouse (I, M, My) – enormous wooden structure on stilts that houses a tribal community under one roof
longyi (My) – wraparound garment worn by women and men
losmen (I) – basic accommodation
LRT (M) – Light Rail Transit

macet (I) – gridlock
mae nam (T) – river
mandi (ET, I, M) – large concrete basin from which you scoop water to rinse your body and flush the toilet
masjid (M) – mosque
mát-mìi (T) – cloth made of tie-dyed silk or cotton thread; also written as *mat-mii*
merdeka (I, M) – independence
mesjid (I) – mosque
mestizo (ET, P) – person of mixed descent
meuang (T) – city
mikrolet (ET, I) – see *opelet*
MILF (P) – Moro Islamic Liberation Front
Montagnards (V) – highlanders, mountain people; specifically the ethnic minorities inhabiting remote areas of Vietnam
moto (C) – motorcycle taxi
MRT (S) – Mass Rapid Transit; metro system
MTT (My) – Myanmar Travel & Tours
muay thai (T) – Thai boxing
myint hlei (My) – horse cart

nâam (L, T) – water, river
naga (C, L, T) – mythical serpent-being
nákhon (T) – city
năng (T) – shadow play
nat (My) – spirit-being with the power to either protect or harm humans; Myanmar's syncretic Buddhism
Negrito (P) – ancient Asian race distinguished by their black skin, curly hair and short size
NLD (My) – National League for Democracy
nop (L) – see *wâi*
NPA (L) – National Protected Area
NPA (P) – New People's Army

ojek (I) – motorcycle taxi
opelet (I) – small minibus
Orang Asli (M) – Original People; Malaysian aboriginal people

P (V) – abbreviation of *pho*
padang (M, S) – open grassy area; town square
pantai (B, ET, I, M) – beach
pasar (I, M) – market

pasar malam (I, M) – night market
paya (My) – holy one; often applied to Buddha figures, *zedi* and other religious monuments
Pelni (I) – national shipping line
pendopo (I) – open-sided pavilion
penginapan (I) – simple lodging house
Peranakan (S) – combination of Malay and Chinese cultures of pre-colonial Singapore
Ph (C) – abbreviation of *phlauv*
phlauv (C) – road, street; abbreviated as 'Ph'
phleng phêua chii-wít (T) – songs for life; modern Thai folk songs
pho (V) – street; abbreviated as P; also rice-noodle soup
PHPA (I) – Perlindungan Hutan dan Pelestarian Alam; Directorate General of Forest Protection & Nature Conservation
pinisi (I) – fishing boat
polres (I) – local police station
pongyi (My) – Buddhist monk
pousada (ET) – traditional Portuguese lodging
praang (T) – Khmer-style tower structure found on temples; serves the same purpose as a *stupa*
prasat (C, T) – tower, temple
psar (C) – market
pulau (I, M) – island
pwe (My) – show, festival

quan (V) – urban district
quoc ngu (V) – Vietnamese alphabet

raja (B, I, M) – king
Ramakian (T) – Thai version of the *Ramayana*
Ramayana (I, L, M, T) – Indian epic story of Rama's battle with demons
remorque-kang (C) – bicycle-pulled trailer
remorque-moto (C) – motorcycle-pulled trailer
roi nuoc (V) – water puppetry
rumah makan (I) – restaurant, food stall

săamláw (T) – three-wheeled pedicab; also written as *samlor*
sai-kaa (My) – bicycle rickshaw
sampan (I, M, S) – small boat
săwngthăew (L, T) – small pick-up truck with two benches in the back; also written as *songthaew*
sima (L) – ordination-precinct marker
Slorc (My) – State Law & Order Restoration Council
soi (T) – lane, small street
STB (S) – Singapore Tourism Board
stung (C) – river
stupa (C, I, L, M, T) – religious monument, often containing Buddha relics
sungai (B, I, M) – river; also written as *sungei*
surat jalan (I) – visitor permit

taman (B, I, M) – park
taman nasional (I) – national park
tambang (M) – double-oared river ferry; small river boat
tamu (B, M) – weekly market
tasik (M) – lake
TAT (T) – Tourism Authority of Thailand
teluk (I, M, S) – bay; also written as *telok*
Tet (V) – lunar New Year
Th (L, T) – abbreviation of *thànŏn*
thâa (T) – ferry, boat pier; also written as *tha*
thâat (L) – Buddhist *stupa*; also written as *that*
thànŏn (L, T) – road, street, avenue; abbreviated as 'Th'
tongkonan (I) – traditional house with roof eaves shaped like buffalo horns
tonlé (C) – river, lake
travel (I) – door-to-door air-con minibus
túk-túk (L, T) – motorised *săamláw*

UXO (L, V) – unexploded ordnance

vipassana (My, T) – insight-awareness meditation

wâi (L, T) – palms-together greeting
wartel (I) – telephone office
warung (I, M) – food stall
wat (C, L, T) – Buddhist temple-monastery
wayang golek (I) – wooden puppet
wayang kulit (I) – shadow-puppet play enacting tales from the *Ramayana*
wayang orang (I) – dance-drama enacted by masked performers, recounting scenes from the *Ramayana*
wíhăan (T) – any large hall in a Thai temple, except for the central sanctuary used for official business
wisma (B, I, M, S) – guesthouse, lodge; office block, shopping centre

xe om (V) – motorbike taxi

yâam (T) – woven shoulder bag

zedi (My) – see *stupa*

Behind the Scenes

THIS BOOK

This is the 14th edition of *Southeast Asia on a Shoestring*. The 1st edition was written by Tony and Maureen Wheeler in 1975, funded by the cult success of their first guidebook, *Across Asia on the Cheap*, a compilation of journey notes put together in 1973. As the scope of the book grew, so did the need to share the load: this edition is the work of 13 authors. Coordinating author extraordinaire China Williams led a stellar team: Greg Bloom, Celeste Brash, Muhammad Cohen, Dan Eldridge, Josh Krist, Mat Oakley, Nick Ray, Chris Rowthorn, Adam Skolnick, Iain Stewart, Ryan Ver Berkmoes and Richard Waters.

This guidebook was commissioned in Lonely Planet's Melbourne office, and produced by the following:

Commissioning Editors Carolyn Boicos, Kalya Ryan
Coordinating Editor Laura Stansfeld
Coordinating Cartographer Ross Butler
Coordinating Layout Designer Barry Cooke
Managing Editor Imogen Bannister
Managing Cartographer David Connolly
Managing Layout Designer Adam McCrow
Assisting Editors Brigitte Barta, Michelle Bennett, Kate Daly, Evan Jones, Anne Mulvaney, Charlotte Orr, Susan Paterson, Averil Robertson, Diana Saad, Louisa Syme, Jeanette Wall
Assisting Cartographers Alissa Baker, Fatima Basic, Mick Garrett, Erin McManus, Sam Sayer
Assisting Layout Designers David Kemp, Jacqui Saunders, Wibowo Rusli
Cover Designer Yukiyoshi Kamimura
Project Manager Chris Love
Language Content Coordinator Quentin Frayne
Thanks to Dave Burnett, Eoin Dunlevy, Mark Germanchis, Emma Gilmour, Nicole Hansen, Laura Jane, Lisa Knights, John Mazzocchi, Corie Waddell, Tashi Wheeler, Celia Wood

THANKS

CHINA WILLIAMS

Thanks to my husband for taking care of all the crises that arise as soon as I step on the plane, and for picking me up from the airport with a heavy coat if the weather insists. Heaps to Felix who occupied himself during work time by chewing on my desk, hand and sometimes his toys. And a nod to Kalya Ryan for another go on the Shoestring and congratulations to the assisting authors for their work on this legendary title.

GREG BLOOM

No laundry list of helpers to acknowledge this time around, so I can at last properly thank my wife for her support and for holding down the family fort during my frequent absences. Thanks to baby Anna for her language advice ('goo' is apparently a great way to endear oneself to Filipinos) and for accompanying me on my rounds in Boracay. Temporary sidekick Johnny Weekend demonstrated an eye for architectural details and a nose for Middle Eastern cuisine in Mindanao, while Glen Carberry selflessly spent a Tuesday evening guiding a bar crawl of Malate. As usual my *barkada* in Manila lent moral and inebriatory support. Tourist offices across the country were a big help; a special nod to Trina in Tacloban and Salvador in Donsol.

CELESTE BRASH

Thanks to my mom Jan for taking time off to explore the west coast with me and to my husband, Josh, and kids, Jasmine and Tevai, for braving leech-infested forests with me on the east coast. Jeremy Tan doesn't have a big head as far as I can tell but was a great and helpful guy to meet; Joann Khaw is my hero history buff and Peck Choo is one wild and crazy woman. The folks at Samudra Inn, Melaka, saved my gut and a lot of work hours by getting me to a good doctor on a Sunday.

MUHAMMAD COHEN

Aside from the dozens of people who chased me down when I forgot hat or pen, cheerfully offered directions, bought me meals, offered *ojek*, and let me have the window seat, special thanks to my extended Indonesia family: Adelaide Worcester, Rapinah Worcester, Heri, Dan and friends in Tarakan; the staff and family of YK RASI that sent my pants from Samarinda to Tarakan to me; Marinda in Bamjarmasin; Ika in Pontianak; Borneo Bob Kendall in Bali and his brother-in-law Pak Husni in Banjarmasin; and Sari of Tirian. Most all, thanks to my wife, who held the arrival of our first-born until after I finished the research.

DAN ELDRIDGE

A big thanks to Kalya Ryan for helping a long-held dream come to fruition; to Daniel Cooper and Cameron Cooper of *Untamed Travel* for the camaraderie and hot tips; to Col Dan Eldridge, USAF (Retired), for the intel; to Carrie, whose email accounts from home kept me sane; to Carolyn for injecting a healthy dose of fun back into the project when I was on the verge of burnout; to Cynthia 'Wander Woman' Barnes for seeing me off in style on my final night in Bangkok; and to Annick and Ulrike for the much needed conversation and laughs.

JOSH KRIST

To my wife and eagle-eyed travel partner, Helene Goupil. A double thanks to Didier Bruneel. Thanks to Jesse and Kerri Krist, Bill Krist, Rose and Jacob Whitt, Jacqui Cerullo, Jeff Ficker, Greg Greunke, Brant Herman, Lisa Lynham, Hans and Kurt Opsahl, Carl and Olga Pezold, David Proffitt, Alex Robinson, Mayte Saras, Wipawee Somsakul, Christine Zender. Great friendship and tips on the road: Alan Coleman, Tressa Gibbard, Christa Lund, Sandy Moos, Kristen Smith. A special thanks to Mark Markand, Dan Eldridge, Julie Jares, Nikki Goth Itoi, Leif Pettersen and Andy Symington.

MAT OAKLEY

As usual, huge thanks to Shiwani for help and suggestions and to Mae for acting as my surrogate memory. Thanks also to Rishad, Shefali and Mr Lobin for various tips. Special thanks must be reserved for Yin Pheng for her undisputed talents, Alan J for his invaluable guidance and Arti for her impressive range of 'contacts' and her calm, sober analysis.

NICK RAY

First thanks to my wonderful wife Kulikar Sotho who has joined me on many a trip, sharing boats and bikes the length and breadth of the region. Thanks also to our young son Mr J (aka Julian) for joining in the softer adventures along the way. It's a hideous cliché, but there really are too many people to thank when so many people have assisted over the years. To those of you that have helped, my heartfelt thanks and I extend an invitation for a sunset drink somewhere in Southeast Asia.

CHRIS ROWTHORN

Chris would like to thank Dr Stephen Sutton, Mike and Judy Steel, Ah Ming, Lawrence Lee, Julie and Steve Wickham, Nobutaka Iwase, Gavin Sham, George Hong Kok Khiong, Asran from the Holiday, Karen Chin, Jeremy Tan, AB, George and Rosalyn, Frankie See, Brian and Sue Clark, Bian, Robert Grani, Peter and Fiona Ninnes, Sanna Raisanen, Junaidi Payne and Cathy Day.

ADAM SKOLNICK

There were countless helpful hands and warm smiles on my life-affirming outer-island tour, but I'm most grateful for Tom at Boraspati Express; Chris, Christine, Sherlie and Johan at Batang Arau; Huntje and her Togean Island brood; Martin and Paulus in Toraja; Anti and Wick in Sorong; the brilliant Max Ammer; 'the man' Sami in Sentani; the beautiful Dayu sisters and cool Kadek in Penastanan; Jakko and Living Colours in Bunaken; Wayan Widi Astra; and put your hands together…for Mr Brett Black and Ms Sasha Moon.

IAIN STEWART

Thanks to Yudi, Adang and Kumis for revealing the charms of Cianjur; Eno in Yogya for everything; Bill Quinlan in Bali; Alwi in Bogor; Simon Grigg of the Opinionated Diner blog for some great tips and his contribution to the Indo Punk feature; and to LP's own Neal Bedford for all his Java advice. Atik and Wildan, Guy, Nadine, Simon and the Gili T massive also helped considerably. And thanks to Fee, Dave and Simone for very good times in Bali.

RYAN VER BERKMOES

Who do I start with in a place where I could never pay for a beer? Wayne Lovell and Ann Turner gave me a warm welcome that never cooled off (despite trying with many cold ones). Tracey Morgan is an oracle, a delight and a leader of the fun-filled Dili expat crowd (a delightful bunch who make you sorry to leave). Miguel Lobato greased the wheels that got me to obscure corners of the country and Manny Napoleão shared his encyclopedic knowledge as well as an adventurous voyage to Atauro. Gino Favaro was a fine host and Cindy Mendonca guided me straight. And thanks to the scores of folks around Timor-Leste who disproved every bad thing you've heard about the place.

RICHARD WATERS

My special thanks to my long-suffering girlfriend Ali and son Finn, who held the fort with worrying ease in my absence. In Laos I'd like to thank Bill Tuffin of the Boat Landing Guest House who enlightened my understanding of ecotourism. Similar thanks to Oliver Bandman, who always makes a good cup of tea and matches wit with wisdom. To Khet, my forest guide who withstood hidden tiger snarls and was nice enough to lie and say it was a bird. To Louis, the smoothest cat this side of Savannakhet, who fixed my motorbike and set me back on the road to meet my deadline and night sleeper train. To Mr Vong who was a source of information and welcome. To Paddy, who spouted Nietzsche and

Kant, and nightly drank my Beer Lao. To Rachel, who kept me company in 4k islands, and likewise the roguish leprechaun, Jamie. And finally to the people of Laos, who, despite constant adversity, remain one of the most gentle, generous people I have been lucky enough to meet.

OUR READERS

Many thanks to the travellers who used the last edition and wrote to us with helpful hints, useful advice and interesting anecdotes:

A Lachlan Abbott, Matt Ambrey, Peter Ansted, Roni Askey-Doran, David Atkinson **B** Katharina Balgavy, Graham Banks, Victoria Baroek, Martin Batty, Julia Baumhoegger, Joan Beets, Pepijn Ten Berge, Tina Bernhardt, Michael Bihr, Richard Bisset, Jaap Boer, Eef Bos, Leo Bourne, Tara Bowden, David Boyall, Alison Brown, Louise Brown, Sarah Brown, Dan Buijs, Arjen Buschman, Katrina Busick, Ianthe Butt **C** Alexandra Candet, Jawad Cantin, Jack Carey, Gemma Casey, Nick Chalupa, Luc Chapdelaine, Sherryn Ciavaglia, Becci Collacott, Matt Collins, Grace Connell, Helen Cooley, Wendy Cove, Russ Croker, Margaret Cruz **D** Clarke Davis, Emily Day, Joanna Dean, Gian Defilla, Sven Deger, Carlo Dionisio, Matthew Donaldson, Christina Doyle, Goga Drews **E** Kathrin Ecker, Martin Engeset **F** Tim Farnsworth, Nicola Ferris, Stephanie Follebouckt, Steve Foster, Karl Johan Froh, Simon Fry **G** Jesus Garcia, Mark Given, Cathy Goeldner, Gina Grubbe, Coralyn Gunton **H** J Hale, Brita Hannestrand, Susanna Hansson, Chevonne Hassan, Joanna He, Mark Heald, Francois Henrard, Alejandro Hernandez, Warren Hill, Julie Holden, Sarah Horgan **I** Gavin Imhof **J** Tom Jackson, Menoud Jean-Philippe, Dorothy Jekill, John Jenks, Howard Johnson, Martyn Johnson, Chris Jones, Paul Jones, Fernando Jucá, Rachel Judd **K** Iris Kaidar, Barry Kaiser, Farah Kanberagha, Alexandra Keith, Colter Kinner, Igo Kirchlechner, Dave Krafchik, Dale Kruger, Arja Kugele, Sebastiaan Kuijper **L** Nick Lauw, Gloria Lee, Lenore Lee, Louis Lehenaff, Rhainnon Lewis, Jena Lichtenstein, Trevor Lightbody, Courtney Lilly, Rebecca Lubarsky, Kai Luethi **M** Marja De Man, Rebecca Mann, Beachie Manzanilla, Shahaf Margalit, Fabrice Marnier, Immo Martin, Laura Mason, Mats Mats, Rosemary Mccully, Suzanne Mcelhinney, Ailish Mckenna, Joanne Mcwhinney, Anna Midgley, Harley Mitchell, Bjarke Moller, Keren Moskal, Dirk Mueller, Michael Mueller, Patricio Musalem **N** Alex Nicholas, Geoff Nicholls, Dennis Nizzero, Sally Nobbs, Thongchai Nonthleeruk **O** Rebecca Oakes, Roy Oltmans, Stacy Orr, Sven Osten **P** Katie Parkin, Sailesh Patel, Vera Pawlowski, Katy Peak, Alice Pearson, Sara Penellum, Patrick Perkes, Omar Pestoni, Therese Picado, Gemma Pilgrim, Fleur Powell, Marieke Prommenschenckel **R** Kamera Raharaha, Phil Rawlings, Nigel Rees, Paul Reikie, Ricardo Renido, Tom Reynolds, Michael Richardson, Amy Rickit, Anton Rijsdijk, Sharon Roberts, Tom Rooke **S** Tim Sanders, Sandra Sandra, Daniel Saunders, Leonardo Savino, Thomas Schaefer, Susan Schlieve, Marianne Schmid, Britta Schmidjoerg, Bernd Schober, Rene Schueler, Christian Schulz, Denise Schwerin, Mette Selchau, Karen Sheehan, Roey Skifr, Jez Quin Smith, Kathryn Smith, Charles Lim Wei Song, Alex Starey, Shannon Stark, Holly Stevens, Matthew Stonebridge, Valentin Straessle, Roman Stutz, Ramona Suhr **T** Elizabete Tavares, Kelly Taylor, Laura Tempest, Lior Tepper, Robin Thompson, Louisa Thornton, Daniel Tinsley, Ik Ly Tjoeng, Eka Tresnawan, Marni Triggs, Anders Tvegard **V** Donald van Gilder, Rosemary der van Meer, Guido van Spellen, Andrew Venables, Andrea Vera, Paula Verheijen, Katleen Verloo, Daan Vermeer, Mike Verrelli, Pamela Villasenor, Jasper Vogelaar **W** Simon Waddell, Vallry Waldman, Julie Walls, Howard Watkinson, Jeannette Werner, Alan Wightman, Adam Wilby, Sam Winterson, Jonathan Wojcik, Lucy Wooding, Lee Wyatt **Y** Shaun Yap

ACKNOWLEDGMENTS

Many thanks to the following for the use of their content:

Globe on title page ©Mountain High Maps 1993 Digital Wisdom, Inc.

Index

000 Map pages
000 Location of colour photographs

000 Map pages
000 Location of colour photographs

INDEX

R

000 Map pages
000 Location of colour photographs

000 Map pages
000 Location of colour photographs

000 Map pages
000 Location of colour photographs

INDEX

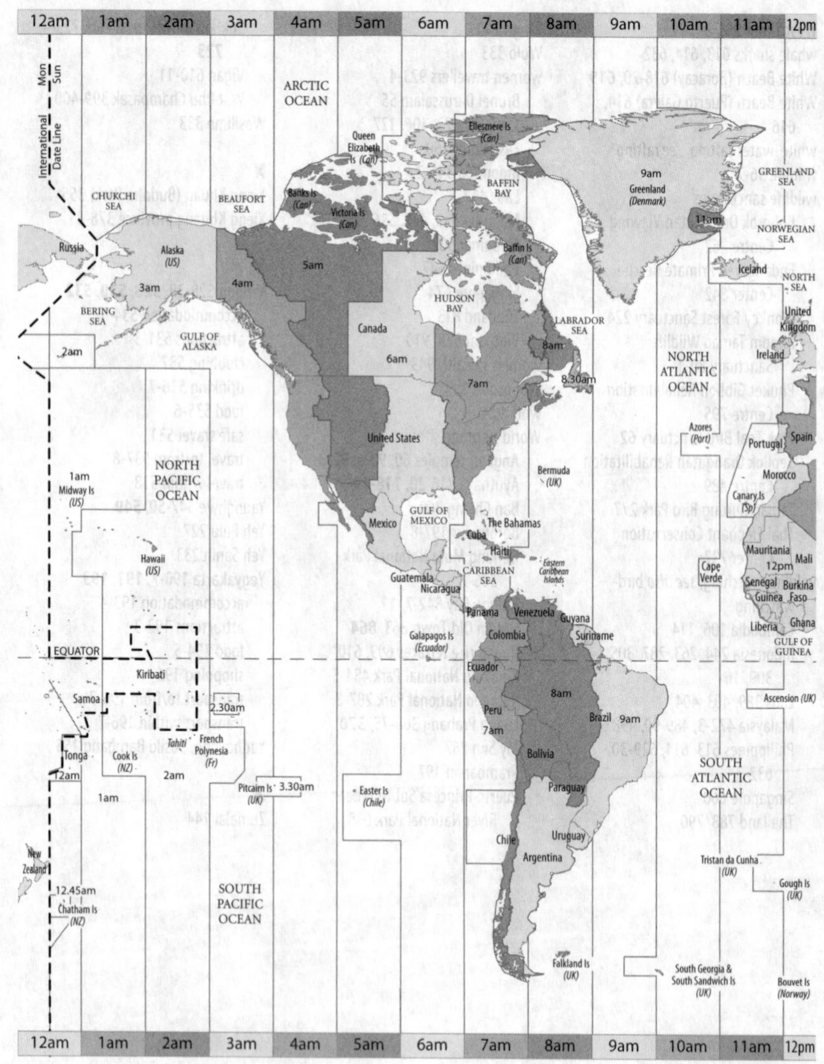
12am
1am
2am
3am
4am
5am
6am
7am
8am
9am
10am
11am
12pm
International Date Line
Mon
Sun
ARCTIC OCEAN
Queen Elizabeth Is (Can)
Ellesmere Is (Can)
BAFFIN BAY
9am
Greenland (Denmark)
GREENLAND SEA
11am
NORWEGIAN SEA
CHUKCHI SEA
BEAUFORT SEA
Banks Is (Can)
Victoria Is (Can)
Russia
Alaska (US)
5am
4am
3am
Baffin Is (Can)
Iceland
NORTH SEA
BERING SEA
GULF OF ALASKA
HUDSON BAY
Canada
LABRADOR SEA
United Kingdom
Ireland
2am
6am
8am
8.30am
NORTH ATLANTIC OCEAN
7am
United States
Azores (Port)
Portugal
Spain
1am
Midway Is (US)
NORTH PACIFIC OCEAN
Bermuda (UK)
Morocco
Canary Is (Sp)
Mexico
GULF OF MEXICO
The Bahamas
Cuba
Haiti
Hawaii (US)
Eastern Caribbean Islands
CARIBBEAN SEA
Mauritania
Mali
12pm
Cape Verde
Guatemala
Nicaragua
Senegal
Burkina Faso
Guinea
Panama
Venezuela
Guyana
Suriname
Colombia
Liberia
Ghana
Galapagos Is (Ecuador)
GULF OF GUINEA
EQUATOR
Ecuador
Kiribati
Samoa
2.30am
8am
Brazil
9am
Ascension (UK)
Peru
7am
Tahiti
French Polynesia (Fr)
Tonga
Cook Is (NZ)
Bolivia
12am
2am
SOUTH ATLANTIC OCEAN
1am
Pitcairn Is (UK)
3.30am
Easter Is (Chile)
Paraguay
Chile
Uruguay
Argentina
New Zealand
Tristan da Cunha (UK)
12.45am
Chatham Is (NZ)
SOUTH PACIFIC OCEAN
Gough Is (UK)
Falkland Is (UK)
South Georgia & South Sandwich Is (UK)
Bouvet Is (Norway)

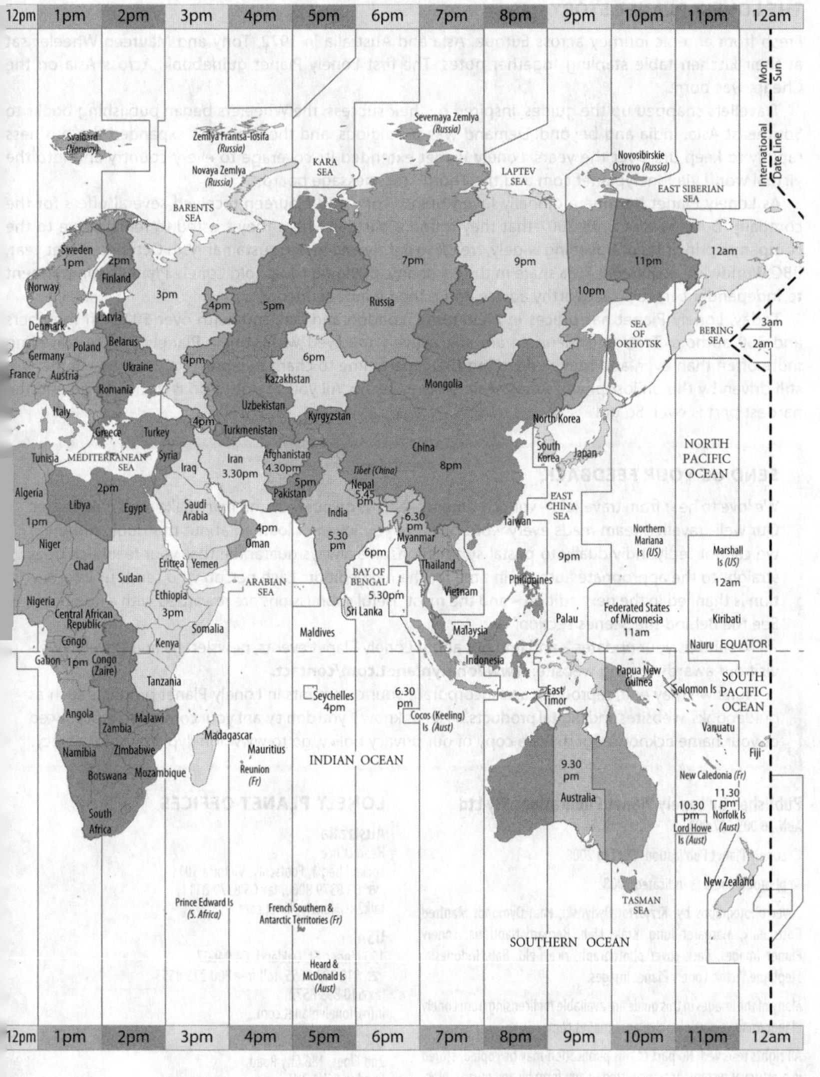
12pm 1pm 2pm 3pm 4pm 5pm 6pm 7pm 8pm 9pm 10pm 11pm 12am
Mon
Sun
International Date Line
Svalbard (Norway)
Zemlya Frantsa-Iosifa (Russia)
Novaya Zemlya (Russia)
Severnaya Zemlya (Russia)
Novosibirskie Ostrovo (Russia)
BARENTS SEA
KARA SEA
LAPTEV SEA
EAST SIBERIAN SEA
Sweden 1pm
2pm
Finland
Norway
3pm
4pm
5pm
7pm
9pm
12am
11pm
10pm
Russia
Latvia
Denmark
Belarus
Poland
Germany
Ukraine
France
Austria
4pm
6pm
Kazakhstan
Mongolia
SEA OF OKHOTSK
BERING SEA
3am
2am
Romania
Italy
Uzbekistan
Kyrgyzstan
Greece
Turkey
4pm
Turkmenistan
North Korea
China
8pm
South Korea
Japan
NORTH PACIFIC OCEAN
Tunisia
MEDITERRANEAN SEA
Syria
Iraq
Iran 3.30pm
Afghanistan 4.30pm
5pm
Pakistan
Tibet (China)
Nepal 5.45 pm
Algeria
2pm
Libya
Egypt
Saudi Arabia
India 5.30 pm
EAST CHINA SEA
Taiwan
1pm
4pm
Oman
6.30 pm
Myanmar
Northern Mariana Is (US)
Marshall Is (US)
Niger
Chad
Sudan
Eritrea
Yemen
6pm
Thailand
9pm
12am
ARABIAN SEA
BAY OF BENGAL
5.30pm
Philippines
Vietnam
Nigeria
Ethiopia 3pm
Sri Lanka
Palau
Federated States of Micronesia 11am
Kiribati
Central African Republic
Somalia
Maldives
Malaysia
Congo
Kenya
Nauru
EQUATOR
Gabon
1pm
Congo (Zaire)
Indonesia
Tanzania
Papua New Guinea
SOUTH PACIFIC OCEAN
Solomon Is
Seychelles 4pm
6.30 pm
East Timor
Angola
Malawi
Cocos (Keeling) Is (Aust)
Zambia
Madagascar
Vanuatu
Fiji
Namibia
Zimbabwe
Mauritius
INDIAN OCEAN
9.30 pm
Reunion (Fr)
Botswana
Mozambique
Australia
New Caledonia (Fr)
11.30 pm
Norfolk Is (Aust)
10.30 pm
Lord Howe Is (Aust)
South Africa
New Zealand
Prince Edward Is (S. Africa)
French Southern & Antarctic Territories (Fr)
TASMAN SEA
SOUTHERN OCEAN
Heard & McDonald Is (Aust)
12pm 1pm 2pm 3pm 4pm 5pm 6pm 7pm 8pm 9pm 10pm 11pm 12am

THE LONELY PLANET STORY

Fresh from an epic journey across Europe, Asia and Australia in 1972, Tony and Maureen Wheeler sat at their kitchen table stapling together notes. The first Lonely Planet guidebook, Across Asia on the Cheap, was born.

Travellers snapped up the guides. Inspired by their success, the Wheelers began publishing books to Southeast Asia, India and beyond. Demand was prodigious, and the Wheelers expanded the business rapidly to keep up. Over the years, Lonely Planet extended its coverage to every country and into the virtual world via lonelyplanet.com and the Thorn Tree message board.

As Lonely Planet became a globally loved brand, Tony and Maureen received several offers for the company. But it wasn't until 2007 that they found a partner whom they trusted to remain true to the company's principles of travelling widely, treading lightly and giving sustainably. In October of that year, BBC Worldwide acquired a 75% share in the company, pledging to uphold Lonely Planet's commitment to independent travel, trustworthy advice and editorial independence.

Today, Lonely Planet has offices in Melbourne, London and Oakland, with over 500 staff members and 300 authors. Tony and Maureen are still actively involved with Lonely Planet. They're travelling more often than ever, and they're devoting their spare time to charitable projects. And the company is still driven by the philosophy of Across Asia on the Cheap: 'All you've got to do is decide to go and the hardest part is over. So go!'

SEND US YOUR FEEDBACK

We love to hear from travellers – your comments keep us on our toes and help make our books better. Our well-travelled team reads every word on what you loved or loathed about this book. Although we cannot reply individually to postal submissions, we always guarantee that your feedback goes straight to the appropriate authors, in time for the next edition. Each person who sends us information is thanked in the next edition – and the most useful submissions are rewarded with a free book. See the Behind the Scenes section.

To send us your updates – and find out about Lonely Planet events, newsletters and travel news – visit our award-winning website: **www.lonelyplanet.com/contact.**

Note: we may edit, reproduce and incorporate your comments in Lonely Planet products such as guidebooks, websites and digital products, so let us know if you don't want your comments reproduced or your name acknowledged. For a copy of our privacy policy, go to www.lonelyplanet.com/privacy.

Published by Lonely Planet Publications Pty Ltd
ABN 36 005 607 983

Cover photographs by: Krzysztof Dydynski, Paul Dymond, Manfred Gottschalk, Margaret Jung, Kraig Lieb, Bernard Napthine; Lonely Planet Images. Back cover photograph: rice field, Bali, Indonesia, Stephane Victor; Lonely Planet Images.

Many of the images in this guide are available for licensing from Lonely Planet Images: www.lonelyplanetimages.com.

Printed through Colorcraft Ltd, Hong Kong. Printed in China

LONELY PLANET OFFICES

Australia
Head Office
Locked Bag 1, Footscray, Victoria 3011
☎ 03 8379 8000, fax 03 8379 8111
talk2us@lonelyplanet.com.au

USA
150 Linden St, Oakland, CA 94607
☎ 510 893 8555, toll free 800 275 8555
fax 510 893 8572
info@lonelyplanet.com

UK
2nd Floor, 186 City Road,
London ECV1 2NT
☎ 020 7106 2100, fax 020 7106 2101
go@lonelyplanet.co.uk